Schroeder's
ANTIQUES
Price Guide

MOXIE

"I like it"

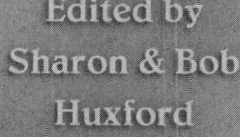

Edited by
Sharon & Bob
Huxford

COLLECTOR BOOKS
A Division of Schroeder Publishing Co., Inc.

COLLECTOR BOOKS
P.O. Box 3009
Paducah, Kentucky 42002-3009
www.collectorbooks.com

The current values in this book should be used only as a guide. They are not intended to set prices, which vary from one section of the country to another. Auction prices as well as dealer prices vary greatly and are affected by condition as well as demand. Neither the editors nor the publisher assumes responsibility for any losses that might be incurred as a result of consulting this guide.

Searching For A Publisher?

We are always looking for people knowledgeable within their fields. If you feel that there is a real need for a book on your collectible subject and have a large comprehensive collection, contact Collector Books.

Introduction

As the editors and staff of *Schroeder's*, our goal is to compile the most useful, comprehensive, and accurate background and pricing information possible. Our guide encompasses nearly five hundred categories, many of which you will not find in other price guides. Our sources are varied; we use auction results and dealer lists, and we consult with national collectors' clubs, recognized authorities, researchers, and appraisers. We have by far the largest Advisory Board of any similar publication on the market. Each year we add several new advisors and now have over 450 who cover almost all our categories. They go over our computer print-outs line by line, deleting listings that are misleading or too vague to be of merit; they often send background information and photos. We appreciate their assistance very much. Only through their expertise and experience in their special fields are we able to offer with confidence what we feel are useful, accurate evaluations that provide a sound understanding of the dealings in the marketplace today. Correspondence with so large an advisory panel adds months of extra work to an already monumental task, but we feel that to a very large extent this is the foundation that makes *Schroeder's* the success that it has become.

Our Directory, which you will find in the back of the book, lists each contributor by state. These are people who have allowed us to photograph various examples of merchandise from their show booths, sent us pricing information, or in any way have contributed to this year's book. If you happen to be traveling, consult the Directory for shops along your way. We also list clubs who have worked with us and auction houses who have agreed to permit us the use of photographs from their catalogs.

Our Advisory Board lists only names and home states, so check the Directory for addresses and telephone numbers should you want to correspond with one of our experts. Remember, when you do, **always** enclose a self-addressed, stamped envelope (SASE). Thousands of people buy our guide, and hundreds contact our advisors. The only agreement we have with our advisors is that they edit their categories. They are in no way obligated to answer mail. Some are dealers who do many shows a month. The time they spend at home may be very limited, and they may not be open to contacts. There's no doubt that the reason behind the success of our book is their assistance. We regret seeing them becoming more and more burdened by phone and mail inquiries. We have lost some of our good advisors for this reason, and when we do, the book suffers and consequently, so do our readers. Many of our listed reference sources report that they constantly receive long distance calls (at all hours) that are really valuation requests. If they are registered appraisers, they make their living at providing such information and expect a fee for their service and expertise.

If you find you need more information than *Schroeder's* provides, there are other sources available to you. Go to your local library; check their section on reference books. Museums are public facilities that are willing and able help you establish the origin and possibly even the value of your particular treasure. In today's world of e-commerce, there are many websites you may visit that are full of pertinent, up-to-date information. Check the yellow pages of your phone book. Other cities' phone books are available from either your library or from the telephone company office. Look under the heading *Antique Dealers*. Those who are qualified appraisers will mention this credit in their advertisement. But remember that if you sell to a dealer, he will expect to buy your merchandise at a price low enough that he will be able to make an appreciable profit when he sells it. Once you decide to contact one of these appraisers, unless you intend to see them directly, you'll need to take photographs. Don't send photos that are under or over exposed, out of focus, or shot against a background that detracts from important details you want to emphasize. It is almost impossible for them to give you a value judgement on items they've not seen when your photos are of poor quality. Shoot the front, top, and the bottom; describe any marks and numbers (or send a pencil rubbing), explain how and when you acquired the article, and give accurate measurements and any further background information that may be helpful.

The auction houses listed in the Directory nearly all have a staff of appraisal experts. If the item you're attempting to research is of the caliber of material they deal with, they can offer extremely accurate evaluations. Of course, most have a fee. Be sure to send them only professional-quality photographs. Tell them if you expect to consign your item to their auction. If you disagree with the value they suggest, you are under no obligation to do so.

Nearly 500 categories are included in our book. We have organized our topics alphabetically, following the most simple logic, usually either by manufacturer or by type of product. If you have difficulty in locating your subject, consult the index. Our guide is unique in that much more space has been allotted to background information than in any other publication of this type. Our readers tell us that these are features they enjoy. To be able to do this, we have adopted a format of one-line listings wherein we describe the items to the fullest extent possible by using several common-sense abbreviations; they will be easy to read and understand if you will first take the time to quickly scan through them.

The Editors

Editorial Staff

Editors
Sharon and Bob Huxford

Research and Editorial Assistants
Loretta Suiters, Michael Drollinger, Donna Newnum, Norma Klinger

Layout
Beth Ray and Donna Ballard

Cover Design
Beth Summers

On the front cover: Wayne Precision Wobbler fishing lure, jointed body and front metal lip, $25.00; Sioux beaded hide moccasins, $1,035.00; Moxie tip tray, 6", $300.00 (photo courtesy Gary Metz); Eastlake desk, walnut, $3,000.00; Tiffany blue iridescent compote, flared rim, 4¾", $1,000.00; Glass eye Lenci Spanish doll, 19", $1,500.00 (photo courtesy McMasters Doll Auctions); Roseville Falline vase, 6½", $1,100.00.

On the back cover: Roseville green Baneda jardiniere and pedestal, $3,250.00.

Listing of Standard Abbreviations

The following is a list of abbreviations that have been used throughout this book in order to provide you with the most detailed descriptions possible in the limited space available. No periods are used after initials or abbreviations. When two dimensions are given, height is noted first. If only one dimension is listed, it will be height, except in the case of bowls, dishes, plates, or platters, when it will be diameter. The standard two-letter state abbreviations apply.

For glassware, if no color is noted, the glass is clear. Hyphenated colors, for example blue-green, olive-amber, etc., describe a single color tone; colors divided by a slash mark indicate two or more colors, i.e. blue/white. Teapots, sugar bowls, and butter dishes are assumed to be 'with cover.' Condition is extremely important in determining market value. Common sense suggests that art pottery, china, and glassware values would be given for examples in pristine, mint condition, while suggested prices for utility wares such as Redware, Mocha, and Blue and White Stoneware, for example, reflect the probability that since such items were subjected to everyday use in the home they may show minor wear (which is acceptable) but no notable damage. Values for other categories reflect the best average condition in which the particular collectible is apt to be offered for sale without the dealer feeling it necessary to mention wear or damage. For instance, advertising items are assumed to be in excellent condition since mint items are scarce enough that when one is offered for sale the dealer will most likely make mention of that fact. The same holds true for toys, banks, coin-operated machines, and the like. A basic rule of thumb is that an item listed as VG (very good) will bring 40% to 60% of its mint price — a first-hand, personal evaluation will enable you to make the final judgement; EX (excellent) is a condition midway between mint and very good, and values would correspond.

AD......after dinner	dtd......dated	litho......lithograph	rfn......refinished
Am......American	dvtl......dovetail	lt......light	rnd......round
appl......applied	emb......embossed, embossing	M......mint	rpl......replaced
att......attributed to	embr......embroidered	mahog......mahogany	rpr......repaired
bbl......barrel	Emp......Empire	mc......multicolor	rpt......repainted
bk......back	eng......engraved, engraving	MIB......mint in box	rstr......restored
bl......blue	EPNS...electroplated nickel silver	MIG......Made in Germany	rtcl......reticulated
blk......black	EX......excellent	MIP......mint in package	rvpt......reverse painted
brn......brown	Fed......Federal	mk......mark	s&p......salt and pepper
bulb......bulbous	fr......frame, framed	MOC......mint on card	sgn......signed
bsk......bisque	Fr......French	MOP......mother-of-pearl	SP......silverplated
b3m......blown 3-mold	ft, ftd......foot, feet, footed	mt, mtd......mount, mounted	sq......square
C......century	G......good	NE......New England	std......standard
c......copyright	gr......green	NM......near mint	str......straight
ca......circa	grad......graduated	NRFB...never removed from box	sz......size
cb......cardboard	grpt......grain painted	NP......nickel plated	trn......turned, turning
Chpndl......Chippendale	H......high, height	opal......opalescent	turq......turquoise
CI......cast iron	Hplwht......Hepplewhite	orig......original	uphl......upholstered
compo......composition	hdl, hdld......handle, handled	o/l......overlay	VG......very good
cr/sug......creamer and sugar	HP......hand painted	o/w......otherwise	Vict......Victorian
c/s......cup and saucer	illus..illustration, illustrated by	Pat......patented	W......width
cvd......carved	imp......impressed	pc......piece	wht......white
cvg......carving	ind......individual	ped......pedestal	w/......with
dbl......double	int......interior	pk......pink	w/o......without
decor......decoration	Invt T'print..Inverted Thumbprint	pnt......paint	X, Xd......cross, crossed
demi......demitasse	irid......iridescent	porc......porcelain	yel......yellow
dk......dark	L......length, long	prof......professional	(+)......has been reproduced
Dmn Quilt...Diamond Quilted	lav......lavender	QA......Queen Anne	
drw......drawer	ldgl......leaded glass	re......regarding	

A B C Plates

Children's plates featuring the alphabet as part of the design were popular from as early as 1820 until after the turn of the century. The earliest English creamware plates were decorated with embossed letters and prim moralistic verses, but the later Staffordshire products were conducive to a more relaxed mealtime atmosphere, often depicting playful animals and riddles or scenes of pleasant leisure-time activities. They were made around the turn of the century by American potters as well. All featured transfer prints, but color was sometimes brushed on by hand to add interest to the design.

Be sure to inspect these plates carefully for damage, since condition is a key price-assessing factor, and aside from obvious chips and hairlines, even wear can substantially reduce their values. Another problem for collectors is the fact that there are current reproductions of glass and tin plates, particulary the glass plate referred to as Emma (child's face in center) and a tin plate showing children with hoops. These plates are so common as to be worthless as a collectible.

For further information we recommend *A B C Plates & Mugs, Identification and Value Guide*, by Irene and Ralph Lindsay (Collector Books). Our advisor for this category is Dr. Joan George; she is listed in the Directory under New Jersey.

Ceramic

Aesop's Fables, man & boy riding donkey, brn transfer, unmk, 7" ..**135.00**
At the Seaside, 2 girls, blk transfer, HC Edmiston, England, 7¼" ..**130.00**
Blood Relations, 2 pups in a basket, brn transfer, unmk, England, 7" ...**140.00**
Canary, Bullfinch & Goldfinch, mc transfer, unmk, 6¾" **150.00**
Cat playing w/mouse, mc transfer, unmk, England, 7" **180.00**
Cavalier fighting foot soldier, mc transfer, CA Sons, England, 6½" ..**250.00**
Christmas Day, blk transfer, F&B Godwin, 7" **340.00**
Elephants on parade w/patriotic symbols, mc transfer, Germany, 6" ..**130.00**
Experience Keeps a Dear School..., mc transfer, unmk, England, 5" ..**150.00**
First Nibble, kids fishing, mc transfer, unmk, England, 6¼" **145.00**
For My Nephew, boys at play, pk transfer, Staffordshire, 5½" **175.00**
Franklin's Proverb, Keep Thy Shop..., blk transfer/mc, 6", NM ..**150.00**
Garden Flower, mc transfer, unmk, England, 8" **145.00**
Girls (2) & ducks, mc transfer, Elsmore & Son, England, 7" **140.00**
Harvest-Home, mc transfer, J&G Meakin, England, 6" **140.00**
He That Hath a Trade..., brn transfer, unmk, England, 6¼" **140.00**
Hunter & 2 dogs, bl transfer, unmk, England, 6¾" **125.00**
Little Boys at Marbles..., blk transfer/mc, Elsmore Forster, 5½" ..**170.00**
Lost, sm girl w/doll crying, mc transfer, unmk, England, 8¼" **145.00**
Maj Gen Geo G Meade, blk transfer, unmk, England, 5" **225.00**
Man w/Alpine horn & dog, blk transfer, lettering, unmk, England, 6" .**125.00**
Man w/Alpine horn & dog, mc transfer, unmk, England, 6" **140.00**
Merry Christmas, sleigh scene, mc transfer, unmk, Germany, 7" .**130.00**
Mug, ship at dock, gr transfer, England, 2¾" **170.00**
New Pony, blk transfer/mc, Staffordshire, 5", VG **130.00**
New Pony, 3 around pony in stable, blk transfer, unmk, England, 8" ..**130.00**
Nursery Rhymes, Goosey Goosey Gander, mc transfer w/bl, unmk, 8½" ...**200.00**
Nursery Tales, Cinderella, mc transfer w/brn, #75,500, England, 7¼" ...**200.00**
Pig, Pigeon, Pins, lg letter P, brn transfer, unmk, England, 6¼" ..**140.00**
Punch & Judy, brn transfer, unmk, England, 7½" **140.00**
Rupert & Spot, boy & dog, mc transfer, BP & Co, England, 7¼" ..**140.00**
Scottish hunters/dogs/deer in distance, brn transfer, Staffordshre, 6" ...**95.00**
Simple Simon, mc transfer, unmk, England, 6½" **200.00**
Sly Fox, sepia transfer, unmk, England, 7" **150.00**
Snuffing, portrait, mc transfer, unmk, England, 5" **250.00**
The Dog, mc transfer, unmk, England, 7¼" **180.00**
The Walk, rider on horse, mc transfer, unmk, England, 7" **145.00**
Three girls w/fans, mc transfer, gold trim, unmk, Germany, 7" ...**130.00**

Trap Bat & Ball, GHI, pk transfer, Allerton & Sons, 6", NM.....**130.00**
Walk, rider on horse, blk transfer/mc, Staffordshire, 6", NM **170.00**
Who Are You, monkey & dog, blk transfer, unmk, England, 6¼" ..**140.00**
Wild Animals (Bear w/Cubs), mc transfer, BP Co, England, 7½"...**225.00**
Young Charioteer, girls in carriage, mc transfer, unmk, 5½" **145.00**

Glass

Child's face (Emma), any color, unmk, 8", ea................................**30.00**
Christmas Eve, unmk, 6", from $175 to...**200.00**
Clock face, ABCs & numerals, scalloped rim, unmk, 7", from $50 to ..**60.00**
Clock face, months, days, ABCs, unmk, 7", from $50 to..............**60.00**
Diamond center (resembling snowflake), ABC rim, unmk, 6¼", $50 to ..**60.00**
Ducks, deep yel, unmk, 6", from $60 to..**70.00**

Elephant with howdah on back, ABC rim, Ripley & Co., 6", $110.00.

Fan center, scalloped rim, unmk, 6", from $65 to..........................**75.00**
Milk glass w/brn enameling on raised letters & beads at rim, unmk, 7"...**60.00**
Numbers around center/ABCs around rim, carnival glass, unmk, 7½"..**120.00**
Rooster, smooth rim, unmk, 6", from $65 to **75.00**
Sancho Panza & Dapple, smooth rim, unmk, 6", from $60 to **70.00**

Tin

ABCs around rim, deep dish, unmk, 6", from $15 to.....................**25.00**
After Supper Run a Mile, mc litho, Kemp Mfg, 6", from $150 to...**200.00**
Cats (2) w/yarn basket, litho, Ohio Art Co, 4¼", from $65 to ...**110.00**
General Tom Thumb, mc enamel, unmk, 3", from $200 to.........**300.00**
Her Majesty Queen Victory, unmk, 8" **300.00**
Jack & Jill, gr & blk litho, Lava, 6" **100.00**
Jumbo, unmk, 5½", from $100 to **160.00**
Kittens, Ohio Art Co, 6¼" **110.00**
Liberty, unmk, 5½", from $110 to **150.00**
Lion, unmk, 2⅞" **250.00**
Numbers around center/ABCs around rim, mc litho, unmk, 6", fr..**125.00**
Peter Rabbit, mc litho, unmk, 7¾", from $200 to **350.00**
Simple Simon Met a Pieman..., Tudor Plate Oneida Community, 6", up to...**95.00**
Washington bust & stars, ABC rim, unmk, 6" **185.00**
Who Killed Cock Robin, unmk, 7¾", from $130 to...................**150.00**

Abingdon

From 1934 until 1950, the Abingdon Pottery Co. of Abingdon, Illinois, made a line of art pottery with a white vitrified body decorated with various types of glazes in many lovely colors. Novelties, cookie jars, utility ware, and lamps were made in addition to several lines of simple yet striking art ware. Fern Leaf, introduced in 1937, featured molded vertical feathering. La Fleur, in 1939, consisted of flowerpots and flower-arranger bowls with rows of vertical ribbing. Classic, 1939 – 40, was a line of vases, many with evidence of Chinese influence. Several marks were used, most of which employed the company name. In 1950 the company reverted to the manufacture of sanitary ware that had been their mainstay before the art ware division was formed.

Highly decorated examples and those with black, bronze, or red glaze usually command at least 25% higher prices.

For further information we recommend *Abingdon Pottery Artware 1934 – 1950, Stepchild of the Great Depression*, by Joe Paradis (Schiffer).

#30, vase, Chang, bronze..200.00
#101, vase, Alpha, 10"...25.00
#103, vase, Gamma, 10"...36.00
#105, vase, Alpha, 8"...25.00
#112, vase, Delta, 6"..38.00
#113, water jug...95.00
#118, vase, Classic, 10"...32.00
#119, vase, Classic, 10"...30.00
#120, planter w/bow, bl...20.00
#125, bowl, Classic, 6½x11"..35.00
#133, vase, Classic, 8"...25.00
#149, flowerpot, Le Fleur, 3"...16.00
#150, flowerpot, La Fleur, 4"...15.00
#152, vase, yel, 8¾"..22.00
#153, vase, Classic, 9"...30.00
#155, vase, Classic, 9"...20.00
#158, candle holder, La Fleur, 2x3½"..................................14.00
#170, Vase, Classic, 7"...20.00
#181, vase, Floral, 10"..20.00
#258, lamp base, fluted shaft, 23".......................................95.00
#301, jar, Ming, 7¼"...120.00
#305, bookends, Sea Gull, 6", pr.......................................155.00
#307, ashtray, Abingdon, 3x8"..40.00
#309, vase, Neo Classic, 12½"..120.00
#314, vase, Swedish, 8¼"..72.00
#315, vase, Athenian, 1947, 9"...35.00
#321, bookends, Cossack/Russian, blk, 6½" or 8½", pr.................95.00
#327, vase, Modern #2, 6"...70.00
#337, dessert dish, Square, 5x5"...22.00
#348, cigarette box, Trix, 3¾x4¾".......................................48.00
#370, bookends, Cactus, 6", pr...50.00
#377, wall pocket, Morning Glory, ivory, 9x6¼"......................40.00
#383, bowl, Daisy, 9½"..35.00
#3906, figurine, Shepherdess & Faun, blk, 11½"................200.00
#401, vase, Box, 5½"...50.00
#403, bowl, Chain, 2½x8½"..50.00
#411, vase, Volute, 10½"...65.00
#415, plate, Apple Blossom, 1½"..40.00
#421, vase, Fern Leaf, 8¾"...50.00
#427, candle holders, Fern Leaf, 5½", pr..............................35.00
#432, fruit boat, Fern Leaf, 6½x15"......................................50.00
#438, vase, Han Square, 6½" sq...15.00
#442, vase, Laurel, 5½"..50.00
#445, Vase, Laced Cuff, 8"...35.00
#449, cornucopia, Shell, 4½"..35.00
#450, bowl, Asters, flared rim, oval, 11½" L...........................35.00
#454, bowl, Asters, 6½"...55.00
#455, vase, Asters, 11½"...35.00
#456, ashtray, New Mode, 5¾"..30.00
#459, vase, Lattice, 10¼"...40.00
#463, vase, Star, 7½"...25.00
#467, vase, Wreath, 8"..67.50
#473, bowl/candle holder, Combination, 7x12"..................100.00
#481, bowl, Ivy, 7x12"...48.00
#483, vase, Petite Bud, 8"...30.00
#486, vase, Acanthus, silver o/l birds on peach, 11"...........125.00
#493, wall pocket, dbl; horn shaped, 8½"............................75.00

#504, vase, Shell, 7½"...25.00
#511, vase, Ionic, 8"...35.00
#513, vase, Swirl, 9"...25.00
#514, vase, Swirl, chartreuse, 11", from $25 to..................35.00
#520, vase, gr, 9"..25.00
#529, bowl, Ti Leaf, 5x16"..40.00
#534, vase, Boyne, 9"..32.00
#536, bowl, Regency, gr, 7x9x5"..35.00
#538, urn, Wreath, 9"...22.00
#540, bowl, Flare, 8x11½"..35.00
#543, bowl, Bulb, 5½"...12.50
#544, bowl, Streamliner, 6x9"..20.00
#548, bowl, Round, 14""..25.00
#549, wall bracket, Acanthus, 8¾".......................................60.00
#555, ashtray, 8" dia...18.00
#559, planter, Donkey, 7½"..75.00
#560, cache pot, 6½"...20.00
#563, urn, Coral, wht decor, 9"..35.00
#564, bowl, Scallop, 11"...20.00
#568, mint compote, pk, ftd, 1942-47, 6" dia......................25.00
#570D, window box, 10"...20.00
#573, figurine, Penguin, decor, 5½".....................................30.00
#574, figurine, Heron, 5¼"...30.00
#581, vase, dbl cornucopia; bl, 8½"......................................40.00
#584, vase, Boot, 8"..40.00
#594, vase, Hour Glass, 9"..32.00
#595, bookends, Quill Pen, 8½", pr....................................100.00
#597, vase, Trumpet, 9"...40.00
#599, vase, Quilted, 9"...50.00
#600, vase, Laurel, 12", from $45 to....................................50.00
#604D, vase, Tulip, 6"...50.00

**#609D, Pelican jar, rare, 6½",
from $150.00 to $175.00.**

#629, vase, Poppy, 6½"...30.00
#634, vase, Heirloom, 6½"...45.00
#647, urn, 13½"..50.00
#657, figurine, Swordfish, 4½"...50.00
#670, planter, Pooch, 4"...35.00
#675D, wall pocket, Matchbox, 5½".....................................50.00
#683, teapot, Daisy, 6¼"...50.00
#685, bowl, Ribbed, 13¾"...20.00
#698, vase, Chinese Terrace, 6"..40.00
#699, wall vase, Apron, 6"...65.00
#705, vase, Modern, 8"..35.00
#710, planter, Drape, 7"...25.00
#711, wall vase, Carriage Lamp, 10".....................................35.00
Cookie jar, #471, Old Lady, decor, minimum value...........300.00
Cookie jar, #495, Fat Boy..250.00
Cookie jar, #549, Hippo, decor, 1942..................................325.00
Cookie jar, #588, Money Bag...75.00
Cookie jar, #602, Hobby Horse..185.00
Cookie jar, #611, Jack-in-Box..275.00
Cookie jar, #622, Miss Muffet...205.00

Cookie jar, #651, Choo Choo (Locomotive) 150.00
Cookie jar, #653, Clock, 1949 ....100.00
Cookie jar, #663, Humpty Dumpty, decor..............................250.00
Cookie jar, #664, Pineapple 95.00
Cookie jar, #665, Wigwam..............................250.00
Cookie jar, #674, Pumpkin, 1949, minimum value.....................325.00
Cookie jar, #677, Daisy, 1949..............................50.00
Cookie jar, #678, Windmill, from $200 to 225.00
Cookie jar, #693, Little Girl, from $60 to..............................75.00
Cookie jar, #694, Bo Peep, from $250 to..............................275.00
Cookie jar, #695, Mother Goose, from $295 to 295.00
Cookie jar, #696, Three Bears, from $90 to 100.00

Adams

William Adams, whose potting skills were developed under the tutelage of Josiah Wedgwood, founded the Greengates Pottery at Tunstall, England, in 1769. Many types of wares including basalt, ironstone, parian, and jasper were produced; and various impressed or printed marks were employed. Until 1800 'Adams Co.' or 'Adams' impressed in block letters identified the company's earthenwares and a fine type of jasper similar in color and decoration to Wedgwood's. The latter mark was used again from 1845 to 1864 on parian figures. Most examples of their product found on today's market are transfer-printed dinnerwares with ornate backstamps which often include the pattern name and the initials 'W.A. & S.' This type of product was made from 1820 until about 1920. After 1890 the word 'England' was included in the mark; 'Tunstall' was added after 1896. From 1914 through 1940, a printed crown with 'Adams, Estbd 1657, England,' identified their products. From 1900 to 1965, they produced souvenir plates with transfers of American scenes, many of which were marketed in this country by Roth Importers of Peoria, Illinois. In 1965 the company affiliated with Wedgwood. Although there were other Adams potteries in Staffordshire, their marks incorporate either the first name initial or a partner's name and so are easily distinguished from those of this company.

See also Adams Rose; Flow Blue; Spatter; Staffordshire; Tea Leaf.

Bowl, covered vegetable; foreign courtyard, brn transfer, 13"......300.00
Bowl, vegetable; Columbus Discovering Am, gr transfer, 11" L..195.00
Candlesticks, Cries of London, pr.....................................90.00
Cup & saucer, Sower, pk transfer, scalloped 75.00
Jug, 4 Seasons, bl/wht Jasper w/metal lid, 10" 475.00
Plate, Bologna, lt bl transfer, 10¾"..............................70.00
Plate, Caledonia, purple transfer, 8½", 3 for 200.00
Plate, Currier & Ives, 10" 30.00
Plate, Dr Syntax Bound to a Tree, pearlized rim, 9½" 60.00
Platter, Sea, red transfer, 15" 375.00
Teapot, Oriental scenic view, dk bl transfer, 7¼"..................400.00
Urn, coat of arms, wht on cobalt, mini, 2½"..............................85.00

Adams, Matthew

In the 1950s a trading post in Alaska contacted Sascha Brastoff to design a line of porcelain with scenes of Eskimos, Alaskan motifs, and animals indigenous to that country. These items were to be sold in Alaska to the tourist trade.

Brastoff selected Matthew Adams, born in April, 1915, to design the Alaska series. Pieces from the line he produced have the Sascha B mark on the front; some have a pattern number on the reverse. They did not have the rooster backstamp. (See the Sascha Brastoff category for information on this mark.)

After the Alaska series was introduced and proved to be successful,

Matthew Adams left the employment of Sascha Brastoff (working three years there in all) and opened his own studio. Pieces made in his studio are signed Matthew Adams in script and may have the word Alaska on the front. Mr. Adams's studio is now located in Los Angeles, but at this time, due to his age, he has ceased production. Our advisor for this category is Marty Webster; he is listed in the Directory under Michigan. Feel free to contact Mr. Webster if you have any further information.

**Vase, Eskimo hunter, #115a, 10",
from $80.00 to $90.00.** (Photo courtesy
Lisa Pigg)

Ashtray, Eskimo face, hollow star shape, 13"..............................75.00
Ashtray, Eskimo family, 8½" 40.00
Ashtray, Husky, 13x10" 65.00
Ashtray, walrus, boomerang on gr, 6x11"..............................65.00
Ashtray, walrus, star shape, walrus, 10x12"..............................95.00
Bowl, console; glacier on bl, 12x20"..............................165.00
Bowl, Eskimo leaving igloo, #111, 6"..............................50.00
Bowl, grizzly bear on brn, free-form, 6½" L 55.00
Bowl, Husky, 6"..............................40.00
Bowl, igloo & dog, #138 boat shape, 9½" 50.00
Bowl, polar bear on gr, free-form, 7½" L..............................50.00
Bowl, ram on gr, free-form, 7" 55.00
Bowl, seal, oval, 9"..............................50.00
Bowl, seal on blk, free-form, w/lid, #145, 7½" L 75.00
Bowl, walrus, yel, w/lid, 7"..............................75.00
Bowl, walrus & glacier on brn, free-form, 8" 65.00
Bowl, walrus on blk, free-form, #104, 6½" L..............................50.00
Box, glacier on bl, w/lid, 12"..............................95.00
Box, seal, wht, 2¼x6"..............................50.00
Charger, caribou on dk bl, 18"..............................150.00
Charger, Eskimo w/harpoon, 16" 135.00
Charger, walrus on dk bl, 17"..............................150.00
Cigarette lighter, cabin on stilts, 5x5" 50.00
Cigarette, lighter, glacier, 6"..............................40.00
Coffeepot, ram on gr, 11½", +6 4½" mugs..............................180.00
Compote, grizzly bear on brn, tall, 8½" dia 70.00
Cracker jar, Eskimo mother & child on brn, 7" 75.00
Creamer, polar bear on blk, 4¾"..............................43.00
Cup & saucer, sled on bl 25.00
Dish, Eskimo lady on gr, elbow shape, 12"..............................50.00
Humidor, seal on gr, #025, 5¾"..............................85.00
Jar, Eskimo on ice bl, 6"..............................30.00
Jar, Eskimo woman on brn, w/lid, 7½"..............................50.00
Jar, ginger; seal on brn/wht, #095, 6½"..............................45.00
Jar, polar bear on gr, w/lid, 7½'..............................65.00
Jar, walrus on lt bl, w/lid, #1492, 7½"..............................50.00
Mug, Husky, #112A, 4½x4¾"..............................45.00
Pitcher, Eskimo, 13"..............................90.00
Pitcher, Eskimo mother & child, 13", +6 5½" mugs.....................195.00
Pitcher, grizzly bear, 11", +6 4" tumblers 200.00
Pitcher, Husky, wht on teal, bulbous, 5"..............................65.00

Plate, Eskimo girl, #162, 7½" 50.00
Plate, igloo & Northern Lights, #162, 7½" 36.00
Platter, house, 12" 45.00
Pot, walrus, w/lid, 12" 55.00
Shakers, rams on gr, 4", pr 50.00
Tankard, man on brn, 12', +6 mugs 250.00
Tankard, polar bear on blk, w/lid, 13" 200.00
Teapot, walrus on ice bl, 6½" 75.00
Tile, Eskimo mother & child, 12¾x10½" 125.00
Tile, mountains & glacier on blk, 10x8½" 75.00
Tile, walrus on bl, 10x8½" 75.00
Tumbler, cabin..20.00
Vase, glacier on gray, #143, 5½" 50.00
Vase, house on yel, 11½' 100.00
Vase, iceberg on gray, 7" 50.00
Vase, mother & child on teal, cylindrical, 17" 165.00
Vase, mountain & glacier on blk, #114, 12" 80.00
Vase, polar bear on gr, 10" 100.00
Vase, reindeer, 4½" 45.00
Vase, sea lion & seaweed, oval, #128, 8" 95.00
Vase, seal & glacier on brn, free-form, #911, 11" 125.00
Vase, walrus on Ice on bl, 10" 110.00
Water set, walrus, 11½" pitcher, + 6 4½" mugs 255.00

Adams Rose, Early and Late

In the second quarter of the nineteenth century, the Adams and Son Pottery produced a line of hand-painted dinnerware decorated in large, red brush-stroke roses with green leaves on whiteware, which collectors call Adams Rose. Later, G. Jones and Son (and possibly others) made a similar ware with less brilliant colors on a gray-white surface.

Note: Early English dinnerware values have softened considerably due to the influence of the Internet which makes good examples that once were hard to find much more accessible. Unless otherwise noted, our values are for items in mint condition or nearly so; be sure to discount prices for damage.

Bowl, early, rare sz, 9" 825.00
Bowl, late, mk Imperial Royal, Belgium, 3x5½" 35.00
Bowl, late, 3x6¼" 70.00
Bowl, vegetable; late, oval, 1⅝x8x6" 170.00
Coffeepot, early, scroll hdl, dome lid, mk Adams, 12", EX 575.00
Creamer, late, scalloped rim, 4⅝' 210.00
Pitcher, late, 7" 325.00
Pitcher, water; late, scalloped rim, 8½" 500.00
Plate, early, mk Adams, 10½" 175.00
Plate, early, scalloped rim, Adams, 7" 60.00
Plate, late, England, 9" 90.00
Plate, toddy; early, plain rim, mk Adams, 5", EX 120.00
Platter, early, mk Adams, 13½" 385.00
Platter, late, 12", EX 135.00

Sugar bowl, late, 6¾", from $225.00 to $250.00. (Photo courtesy Ken and Jan Silveri)

Sugar bowl, late, w/lid, 6"..340.00
Tea bowl & saucer, early 330.00
Tea bowl & saucer, red spatter rim 440.00
Teapot, early, dolphin hdl, 8x11", VG...............................475.00
Wash bowl, late, emb floral vine at rim, 14½"..................175.00

Advertising

The advertising world has always been a fiercely competitive field. In an effort to present their product to the customer, every imaginable gimmick was put into play. Colorful and artfully decorated signs and posters, thermometers, tape measures, fans, hand mirrors, and attractive tin containers (all with catchy slogans, familiar logos, and often-bogus claims) are only a few of the many examples of early advertising memorabilia that are of interest to today's collectors.

Porcelain signs were made as early as 1890 and are highly prized for their artistic portrayal of life as it was then . . . often allowing amusing insights into the tastes, humor, and way of life of a bygone era. As a general rule, older signs are made from a heavier gauge metal. Those with three or more fired-on colors are especially desirable.

Tin containers were used to package consumer goods ranging from crackers and coffee to tobacco and talcum. After 1880 can companies began to decorate their containers by the method of lithography. Though colors were still subdued, intricate designs were used to attract the eye of the consumer. False labeling and unfounded claims were curtailed by the Pure Food and Drug Administration in 1906, and the name of the manufacturer as well as the brand name of the product had to be printed on the label. By 1910 color was rampant with more than a dozen hues printed on the tin or on paper labels. The tins themselves were often designed with a second use in mind, such as canisters, lunch boxes, even toy trains. As a general rule, tobacco-related tins are the most desirable, though personal preference may direct the interest of the collector to peanut butter pails with illustrations of children, or talcum tins with irresistible babies or beautiful ladies. Coffee tins are popular, as are those made to contain a particularly successful or well-known product.

Perhaps the most visual of the early advertising gimmicks were the character logos, the Fairbank Company's Gold Dust Twins, the goose trademark of the Red Goose Shoe Company, Nabisco's ZuZu Clown and Uneeda Kid, the Campbell Kids, the RCA dog Nipper, and Mr. Peanut, to name only a few. Many early examples of these bring high prices on the market today.

Our listings are alphabetized by product name or, in lieu of that information, by word content or other pertinent description. When no condition is indicated, the items listed below are assumed to be in excellent condition, except glass and ceramic items, which are assumed mint. Remember that condition greatly affects value (especially true for tin items). For instance, a sign in excellent or mint condition may bring twice as much as the same one in only very good condition, sometimes even more. On today's market, items in good to very good condition are slow to sell, unless they are extremely rare. Mint (or near-mint) examples are high.

We have several advertising advisors; see specific subheadings. For further information we recommend *General Store Collectibles, Vols. I* and *II*, by David L. Wilson; *Hake's Price Guide to Character Toys, 3rd Edition*, by Ted Hake; *Advertising Thermometers* by Curtis Merritt; *Advertising Character Collectibles* by Warren Dotz; *Value Guide to Advertising Memorabilia. Second Edition*, and *Antique & Contemporary Advertising Memorabilia* by B.J. Summers; *Encyclopedia of Advertising Tins, Vol. II*, by David Zimmerman, and *Advertising Paperweights* by Richard Holiner and Stuart Kammerman. *Huxford's Collectible Advertising* and *Garage Sale and Flea Market Annual* by Sharon and Bob Huxford are other good references. All of these books are available at your local bookstore or from Collector Books. See also Advertising Dolls; Advertising Cards; Automobilia;

Coca-Cola; Banks; Calendars; Cookbooks; Paperweights; Posters; Sewing Items.

Key:
cb — cardboard	sf — self-framed
dc — diecut	tc — tin container
fs — flange sign	ts — tin sign
ps — porcelain sign	

Adams' Pepsin-Tutti Frutti, pocket mirror, girl on gr, oval, EX ...**475.00**
Admiration Cigars, plaque sign, molded plaster, moon-faced man, EX+..**1,400.00**
Allen & Ginter's Straight Cut No 1, paper litho, girl, fr, 22x16", EX+ **365.00**
Alphabet Candy, tc/bank, mc graphics, oval, 3x4½", EX+ **135.00**
American Beauty Talcum Powder, tc, before/after baby, 4¾", EX+..**550.00**
Anheuser-Busch, litho, girl in red dress, 1907, fr, 39x24", VG...**575.00**
Arbuckles' Ariosa Coffee, paper litho, girl/store lady, 1900, 16", EX+ **275.00**
Arbuckles' Ground Coffee, emb ts, Dad/girl, 1920s-30s, 11x26", EX...**1,600.00**
Argo Corn Starch, product box display, 1930s-40s, 18", EX+ **200.00**
Arrow Coffee, tc, slip lid, Indian graphics, 1-lb, EX+ **1,125.00**
Aunt Jemima Pancake Four, string climber, dc emb cb figure, 1905, 13" .**3,050.00**
Baby Ruth Gum, change receiver, rvpt glass dish, 2x4x6", EX......**80.00**
Bagdad Tobacco, humidor, ceramic, name/portrait on bl, 6½", NM .**120.00**
Baker's Cocoa, tray, chocolate lady/home scene on gold, 6", EX+.....**160.00**
Banquet Hall Little Cigars/Ponies, cigar holder, tin litho, 4", NM....**325.00**
Bay State Liquid Paints, string holder, dc tin, HD Beach litho, EX...**700.00**
Bee No 2 Club Special Playing Cards, 2 lg display boxes, 12x6x8", NM ...**300.00**
Bell Brand Chocolates & Bon Bons, sf ts, cherubs/bell, oblong, VG+ ..**350.00**
Big Ben Roll Cut Smoking Tobacco, pocket tin, vertical, EX+ ..**950.00**
Black Cat Shoe/Stove Dressing, match holder, tin litho, EX+ ...**1,600.00**
Black Rose Tea, emb dc cb sign, girl holding sign, 16", EX+.......**155.00**
Bliss Native Herbs, match holder, tin, Capitol building, 1910s, 6", VG ...**275.00**
Blue Jay Corn Plasters, display, 3-D, dc tin Grandpa, 14", EX+ .**1,200.00**
Bluhill Coffee, milk pail, bl & wht, 5-lb, EX+ **200.00**
Bob White Granulated Smoking Tobacco, pouch, 1910 tax stamp, 4", EX+...**400.00**
Bohemian tobacco, tc, sq w/rnd slip lid, graphics, 4", EX+ **3,600.00**
Borden, egg beater, glass jar w/wire works, screw lid, NM **100.00**
Bright Globe Range, tip tray, Am Art Works, 1907 stock image, EX+...**175.00**
Broadway Brewing Co Pure Beers, tip tray, Niagara Litho, EX+ .**200.00**
Buffalo Brewing Co, sf tin litho, bottles on table/window, 23x29", NM..**1,450.00**
Bull Dog Cut Plug, flange sign, Won't Bite, image on yel, 14x9", VG+..**1,250.00**
Bull Durham, cb stringer, bull's head, New Size/5¢, 2-sided, 13", EX+........**625.00**
Bunny Bread, dc tin bunny's head, yel & bl, 1965, 36x26", NM..**350.00**
Bunte Marshmallows, tc, graphics on lt bl/wht, 12½x10", EX **200.00**

Buster Brown

Buster Brown was the creation of cartoonist Richard Felton; his comic strip first appeared in the *New York Herald* on May 4, 1902. Since then Buster and his dog Tige (short for Tiger) have adorned sundry commercial products but are probably best known as the trademark for the Brown Shoe Company established early in this century. Today hundreds of Buster Brown premiums, store articles, and advertising items bring substantial prices from many serious collectors.

Balloon, inflatable head, w/cape & pants, EX **750.00**
Book, Buster Brown Goes Fishing, muslin, Saalfield, EX...............**75.00**
Camera, box type, EX..**100.00**
Cigar tin, ...Cigar/2 for 5¢, strong graphics, 5x5" dia, EX **4,000.00**
Clock, glass face & front w/metal fr, light-up, Pam, 15" dia, EX.**925.00**
Display, Shoes, tin dc, Tige jumping for cracker, 2-pc, 40", G .**2,000.00**
Match holder, tin litho, Buster Brown Bread, mc graphics, 7", EX+.**1,800.00**
Painting box, paper on cb, Milton Bradley, 1910, 10½x7x¾", EX....**50.00**
Sign, cb hanger, Bread, Buster Brown writes on chalkbrd, 11x8", EX.**200.00**
Sign, flange, dc image of Buster winking & holding up shoe, 24x15", G+....**1,000.00**

Sign, 2-pc dc image of Buster pointing & Tige upright, G+........**950.00**
Whistle, Buster Brown & Tige, tin, rectangular, EX+...................**32.00**

Butter Krust, paper litho, young girl, Haskell Coffin art, 33", EX+ **800.00**
Cabin Still Bourbon, alto-plaster cabin scene w/wood fr, 13x17", NM...**120.00**
Campus Mixture, tc, sq corners, Leavitt & Pierce, 4x3x2", VG+....**640.00**
Carnation Condensed Milk, tip tray, HD Beach litho, oval, EX+......**325.00**
Cascade Beer, tray, We Never Disagree..., Uncle Sam, 13x17", EX+..**500.00**
CD Kenney, tip tray, Thanksgiving Greetings, Kaufmann & Strauss, NM.**130.00**
Ceylon Tea, store bin, tin, red w/gold detail, 28x18x18", VG........**75.00**
Chase & Sanborn's Choice Quality Coffee, milk pail, red/gold, 11", EX....**465.00**
Cherry Smash, bottle topper, dc cb, 10", EX................................**150.00**
Chicklets, ts, Spearmint/Peppermint Flavor, red, 11x24", EX.....**235.00**
Clark's ONT, paper litho, The Cat Congress, fr, 16x23", VG.....**600.00**
College Town Coffee, tc, 1-lb, VG...**1,100.00**
Colonial Electric Co, yard-long litho, Yard of Puppies, EX.........**175.00**
Continental Cubes, tc, red w/pocket-tin graphics, 5x5x5", EX.....**1,650.00**
Continental Insurance Co, sf ts, Revolutionary soldier, 30x20", NM..**1,125.00**
Cottolene Shortening, tip tray, cotton field w/pickers, 4" dia, EX ...**70.00**
Coulee Coffee, cb container w/paper label, pry lid, 1-lb, EX+ **200.00**
Cow-Ease/Carpenter-Morton Co, pocket mirror, bl & wht, oval, EX...**275.00**
CPF Meerschaum Pipes, sf ts, man reads news, 16x19", VG **345.00**
Cressman's Counsellor Cigars, textured paper sign, lady, 25x20", VG...**375.00**
Crusader Tobacco, cb litho, crusader w/banner, 14x8", VG............**55.00**
Cudahy's Diamond C Hams, dc fs, lady serving, Shonk litho, EX..**2,800.00**
CWS Soaps, cb sign, boy w/fishing pole, girl crying, 23x19", VG.....**435.00**
Cy Young Mild Havana Blend, tc, slip lid, graphics on wht, 5" dia, EX+.**6,100.00**
Dad's Root Beer, ts, dc bottle cap w/name panel below, 28x20", EX....**200.00**
Daddy's Choice Coffee, tc, girl's head/Sterling Grocery, 1-lb, VG......**235.00**
Dairyland Milk/Ice Cream, clock, red & wht emblem on yel, 14" dia, EX..**200.00**
De Laval, match holder, machine replica, EXIB..........................**550.00**
De Laval, porc fs, Authorized Agency, machine on bl, 27", EX+..**1,300.00**
De Laval, sf ts, mother/child, 26" dia, VG.................................**1,700.00**
De Laval, wood cabinet w/tin litho front, 25", G........................**250.00**

Dauntless Coffee, cloth banner, 5x36", NM, $200.00. (Photo courtesy Buffalo Bay Auction Co.)

Delaware Punch, bottle display, lady golfer, 1910s-20s, 14", M...**550.00**
Dennis-Shields Ice Cream, sign, light-up, boy w/cone, 14x11", EX.............**275.00**
Dentyne/Beeman's, display, tin, 3-tier flanked by dc ladies, 1920s, EX....**4,000.00**
Dewar's White Label Whisky, dc tin Colonial butler, 21", EX+ **250.00**
Diamond Dyes, cabinet, balloon/children, rfn, 24x15", G **1,000.00**
Diamond Dyes, cabinet, children/steps/mansion 24x15", EX...**1,500.00**
Diamond Dyes, cabinet, fairies, 24x18", EX+ **2,000.00**
Diamond Dyes, cabinet, governess/children, 30x22", G...........**1,200.00**
Diamond Dyes, cabinet, lady dying clothes, 30x22", EX..........**1,450.00**
Diamond Inks, cabinet, wood w/glass front, 1910-20, 22", VG+....**1,250.00**
Dixie Kid Cut Plug, lunch box, Kid sitting on product box, EX+ ..**1,600.00**
Dixie Queen Plug Cut Smoking Tobacco, lunch pail, red/bl on wht, EX ..**200.00**
Double Cola, dc cb stand-up, photo image of girl w/glass, 15x11", VG.....**100.00**

Dr Daniels' Veterinary Medicines, cabinet, wood/tin front, 29", VG.....**1,425.00**
Dr Lesure's Warrented Remedies, dc cb horse head sign, 18x8", EX+....**1,300.00**
Dr Moore's Root Pills, dc cb stand-up, Indian family on horse, 25", EX....**150.00**

Dr. Pepper

A young pharmacist, Charles C. Alderton, was hired by W.B. Morrison, owner of Morrison's Old Corner Drug Store in Waco, Texas, around 1884. Alderton, an observant sort, noticed that the drugstore's patrons could never quite make up their minds as to which flavor of extract to order. He concocted a formula that combined many flavors, and Dr. Pepper was born. The name was chosen by Morrison in honor of a beautiful young girl with whom he had once been in love. The girl's father, a Virginia doctor by the name of Pepper, had discouraged the relationship due to their youth, but Morrison had never forgotten her. On December 1, 1885, a U.S. patent was issued to the creators of Dr. Pepper. Our advisor for Dr. Pepper is Craig Stifter; he is listed in the Directory under Illinois. See also Soda Fountain Collectibles.

Calendar, girl in fur-lined parka, 1947, NM, $275.00.
(Photo courtesy Craig Stifter)

Clock, grid logo w/10-2-4 highlighted in red, red fr, 11½" dia, EX......**175.00**
Clock, wht plastic bottle cap, Dr Pepper on red band, 10" dia, VG **55.00**
Cooler, wht metal airline type w/Red Dr Pepper, aluminum hdl, VG ...**70.00**
Door push bar, porc, 10-2-4 grid logo on wrought-iron bar, VG .**750.00**
Game, Tin Can Alley, shooting game w/gun & accessories, EXIB...**50.00**
Menu board, tin, oval-&-V logo on wht, gr board, 28x20", EX ..**150.00**
Sign, cb, A Lift for Life, cheerleader/cap logo, 2-sided, orig fr, VG ...**275.00**
Sign, cb, Dick Clark's...ABC-TV, photo head shot, 1960s, 15x25", NM...**75.00**
Sign, cb, Onward Garden Soldiers, woman/girl/garden, 1940s, G.**85.00**
Sign, celluloid disk, Drink.../grid logo/10-2-4 clock, 1930s, 9", EX....**1,050.00**
Sign, neon, Dr above Pepper, 13x21", NM **130.00**
Sign, tin dc hanger w/bracket, 2-sided, 1940s, 24x36", EX+ **950.00**
Thermometer, dial, Hot or Cold, wht & yel, Pam, 1963, 12" dia, EX..**135.00**
Thermometer, tin, 10-2-4 bottle & grid logo on yel, 26x10", VG....**200.00**
Tray, girl w/2 bottle, red rim w/logos, yel border, VG **150.00**

Dr White's Cough Drops, pocket tin, flat, red on wht, EX+ **550.00**
Dukes Mixture, porc door push, The Roll of Fame, 8x5", NM....**975.00**
Duluth Imperial Flour, ts, Black chef, beveled, 25x18", EX+ **800.00**
Dunlop, ps, blk diagonal name on yel/man in wheel 'car,' 38x12", NM ...**675.00**
Dutch Boy Paints, dc tin fs, famous logo, 1949, 28x18", EX **600.00**
Ebbert Wagons, sf ts, In the Shade of the Old Apple Tree, 26x38", EX+...**1,600.00**
Egg-O-See, sf ts, Dere Ain't Gon'er Be No Leavies, 1915, 10x16", VG+...**1,100.00**
Elkay's Straw Hat Dye, cb sign, '20s ladies dyeing hats, 33x20", EX..**200.00**
Ell-Ell Whiskey, sf ts, dock scene, Lemle Levy Co, 22x28", EX ...**1,450.00**
Ensign Perfection Cut Tobacco, pocket tin, vertical, 4½", EX+ .**900.00**

Everhart Confectionary, sf ts, girl/flowers, oval, 19x13", EX+ **350.00**
Fairbank's Gold Dust, banner, dc twins/lettering atop boxes, 1912, EX...**2,600.00**
Fairbank's Gold Dust, dc stand-up, twins/box, 15", EX **1,050.00**
Fairbank's Gold Dust, sf ts, Cleans Everything, twins, 1901, 38", VG...**2,600.00**
Fairy Soap, trolley card, sm girl atop bar of soap, 10½x20½", EX........**175.00**
Fast Mail Chewing Tobacco, pocket tin, flat, train graphics, EX+...**1,000.00**
Fatima Cigarettes, cb sign, 20 for 15¢, pack/city, 34x21", VG.......**65.00**
Ferry's Seeds, dc sign, girl waters flowers, 1915, 27x15", VG **345.00**
Folger's, mirror, JA Folger & Co/Pioneer.., wood fr, 9x13", NM....**50.00**
Foltz Maid, tc, 1-lb, screw lid, image of girl, EX+ **500.00**
Frictionless Metal Co, sf ts, nude boy, Meek & Beach litho, 1903, EX...**1,400.00**
G Wiedemann Brewing, dc tin stand-up, man w/paper, 2 look on, 14", EX...**1,450.00**
Ghirardelli's Flicks Chocolate, cb stand-up, Dutch kids, 12x9", EX..**40.00**
Good Luck Baking Powder, printer's proof poster, 27x31", G......**250.00**
Grant's Cheery Whiskey, tin litho, 2 gents outside pub, 13x10", EX+ ..**240.00**
Grape Nuts, sf ts, girl/St Bernard, 30x20", VG **1,380.00**
Grape Smash, ts, 5¢ Drink 5¢/graphics, cb bk, beveled rim, 9x7", VG+....**925.00**
Grapette, ts, lg bottle on yel w/red raised rim, 1930s-40s, 39x13", EX.....**1,300.00**
Green Turtle Selects, tc, sq, hinged lid, graphics, 4½x6x4", EX+ ..**1,000.00**
Green-Wheeler Shoes, emb ts on cb, lady in profile, 1911, 14", EX+ **600.00**
Greenback Smoking Tobacco, dc cb frog sign, 7x11", VG+ **200.00**
Gulf Supreme Motor Oil, ps, touring car graphics, 1920s, 61x28", VG ..**1,600.00**
Hartford Fire Insurance Co, rvpt sign, stag image, fr, 21x15", EX .**85.00**
Harvard Beer, tin litho, lady in Turkish-style room, fr, 45x36", EX...**1,500.00**
Hazard Smokeless Gun Powder, tc, sq, hunting graphics, 1890s, 6", EX+ .**1,000.00**
Heinz Pineapple Preserves, crock, 1901 on lid, Keystone label, 7½"...**275.00**
Heinz Pure Malt Vinegar, bottle, salesman's sample, 4½", EX+ ..**130.00**
Heinz Strawberry Preserves, crock, 1883 pure food label, w/lid, G...**115.00**
Helmar Turkish Cigarettes, paper sign, lady in hat, 21x17", EX+..**200.00**
Henalfa Hair Restorer, tc, girl w/long hair, 4", VG+ **400.00**

Hires

Charles E. Hires, a drugstore owner in Philadelphia, became interested in natural teas. He began experimenting with roots and herbs and soon developed his own special formula. Hires introduced his product to his own patrons and began selling concentrated syrup to other soda fountains and grocery stores. Samples of his 'root beer' were offered for the public's approval at the 1876 Philadelphia Centennial. Today's collectors are often able to date their advertising items by observing the Hires boy on the logo. From 1891 to 1906, he wore a dress. From 1906 until 1914, he was shown in a bathrobe; and from 1915 until 1926, he was depicted in a dinner jacket. The apostrophe may or may not appear in the Hires name; this seems to have no bearing on dating an item. Our advisor for Hires is Craig Stifter; he is listed in the Directory under Illinois. See also Soda Fountain Collectibles.

Bottle topper, cb, Enjoy Hires, couple, 1930s-40s, 7x9", EX+ **155.00**
Bottle topper, cb, Hires to You/A Toast to Good Taste, couple, 11", NM ...**100.00**
Clock, light-up, wood-grain logo on wht plastic, 16" sq, EX **100.00**
Festoon, girl in shuttered window/R-J logo/flowers, 5-pc, 1930s, EX..**1,465.00**
Festoon, girl/R-J logo/4 food-&-drink disks, 5-pc, 1930s, NM .**1,200.00**
Menu board, tin chalkbaord, It's High Time For..., 27x18", EX.....**75.00**
Mug, wht ceramic barrel, Hires boy, Villeroy & Boch, 4", EX........**75.00**
Sign, cb cutout, Say, Drink..., Hires boy, 1905-15, 15", VG+ **400.00**
Sign, cb dc stand-up, lady in bl gown next to display, 1940s, 14", EX..**100.00**
Sign, flange, tin, ...So Refreshing/check mk logo on bl, 12x14", EX **175.00**
Sign, sf tin oval w/2 ladies drinking from straws, 20x24", VG+ ..**675.00**
Sign, tin, And It's Always Pure/...In Bottles, '20s lady, 14x20", EX **575.00**
Sign, tin, dc oval, Drink Hires/bottle, wht/bl stripes, 20x29", EX **175.00**
Sign, tin, emb dc oval, bottle on bl/wht stripes, Drink..., 16x24", VG...**200.00**
Sign, tin hanger/bracket, Fountain Service/R-J logo, 2-sided, 16", VG..**475.00**
Thermometer, tin bottle form, bl dot logo, 18", EX...................**120.00**
Thermometer, tin bottle form, 1876 logo, 28", EX **150.00**

Tray, Josh Slinger, Just What the Dr Ordered, ca 1914, rnd, EX+ ..**1,750.00**

Home Run Stogie, tc, 3 for 5¢, dk gr variation, rnd, 5¾", EX .**1,850.00**
Honest Scrap, paper litho, classic cat/dog image, fr, 23x30", EX+ ..**1,800.00**
Honest Scrap, store bin, tin, slant top, image, 18x14x12", EX+ **4,000.00**
Hood's Ice Cream, rnd flange, cow, 2-sided, 1930s, 22", NM ...**3,100.00**
Imperial Egg Food, paper litho, workers gather/package/load, 35", EX+ ...**930.00**
Imperial Shaving Stick, tin litho, man shaving, rnd, 3⅜x1½", EX+ **325.00**
Indiana Mfg, paper litho, Wind Stackers Reign …, 1900, 12x18" ..**220.00**
Indianapolis Brewing Co, litho, allegory/brewery, fr, vertical, VG **700.00**
International Tailoring, clock, mantel; ornate bronze finish, 16", EX .**1,000.00**
Iten Biscuit Co Animal Cookies, tc, oblong w/swing hdl, mc, EX+ **200.00**
J&P Coats, litho cb sign, Gulliver & Liliputians, 21x24", VG ...**345.00**
Jack Frost Baking Powder, tc w/paper label, emb lid, 5½", EX+ ..**350.00**
Jack Sprat Peanut Butter, tc, pry lid, yel, 10x10½" dia, VG+ ..**1,665.00**
Jersey Creme, tray, lady in profile, Shonk litho, 12" dia, VG+ ...**180.00**
Jesse Welden 10¢ Cigar, corner ts, curved, yel on dk bl, 20x14", EX+ ..**750.00**
Johnson's Peacemaker Coffee, store bin, tin cabin shape, VG .**1,700.00**
Juicy Fruit Gum, match holder, tin, The Man...Made Famous, 5", EX ...**140.00**
Jumbo Peanut Butter, pail, 1-lb, elephant on gold w/wht stripes, VG+ ..**775.00**
Kellogg's Corn Flakes, dc ts, baby in wicker chair, 19x14", VG ...**2,500.00**
Kenmore Aero Craft Motor Oil, tc, plane/racer graphics, 1-qt, VG ..**1,050.00**
Kenny Tobacco, fan, dc cb w/wood handle, girl's face/bouquet, 9", NM ...**35.00**
Kentucky Wagon MFG Co, ts, factory, Shonk litho, fr, 12x31", VG **475.00**
Kimball Sweet Lavender, poster, 6 Black images, 1880s, 36x25", EX .**1,550.00**
King Cole Tea & Coffee, porc door push, blk/red on yel, 11", NM **225.00**
Knox's Gelatin, paper sign, nanny/child, 1901, 17x25", VG **450.00**
Knox Sparkling Gelatin, dc cb litho display, 16x14x10", VG+ ...**750.00**
Kool Cigarettes, dc cb penguin waiter w/pack on tray, 48", G ...**800.00**
Korbel Champagne, sign, lady w/grapes, bottle, 13x19", NM **190.00**
Leisy Brewing Co, tray, factory street scene, ornate trim, oval, EX+ ...**1,700.00**
Lifesavers, store case, tin w/emb lift-lid, Shonk, 9x9x16", VG ...**1,600.00**
Log Cabin Syrup, display, The Syrup Camp/The Syrup Can, 22x32", EX .**1,500.00**
Log Cabin Syrup, tc, Blacksmith, 2-lb 1-oz, EX **130.00**
Log Cabin Syrup, tc, boy (bl) in door, 1918, 1-pt 11-oz, EX **110.00**
Log Cabin Syrup, tc, Stockade School, 2-lb 1-oz, no cap, EX **60.00**
Long's Ox-Heart Chocolates, 2-sided cb disk, We Sell..., 11", VG+ ..**65.00**
Lucky Strike, cb stand-up sign, girl/lg pack on leaf, 18x12", VG ...**100.00**
Lucky Strike Cigarettes, cb stand-up, Lucky Girls-Lucky Boy, 32", VG ...**300.00**
Magic Yeast, litho, fortune teller, You'll Marry Money..., 15x19", VG **500.00**
Mail Pouch Tobacco, cb sign, girl in straw hat, ca 1906, G **1,050.00**
Mammy Salted Peanuts, tc, pry lid, 10-lb, VG **700.00**
Mandeville & King Co, paper litho, girl on rock/flowers, 26x17", EX ...**2,100.00**
Mansfield's Choice Pepsin Gum, case, glass/metal/wood base, VG+ **700.00**
Maxwell House Coffee, cup & saucer, red & bl on wht, gold trim, EX **110.00**
Maxwell House Coffee, dc flange, lg cup, 2-sided, 1940s-50s, 27", NM ..**1,400.00**
Mayo's Tobacco, roly poly, Inspector, EX+ **1,450.00**
Mayo's Tobacco, roly poly, Mammy, EX+ **825.00**
Mentholatum, dc cb standup, boy/girl carpenters, he crying, 14" ..**250.00**
Metz Beer, clock, The Old Reliable/bottle, sf tin, 15" sq, EX **175.00**
Michelin, ps, red shield w/Mr Bib on motorbike, 18x15", NM ...**1,000.00**
Milwaukee Harvesting Machines, match holder, tin litho, 5½", VG+ ...**550.00**
MK Goetz Brewing Co, sf tin litho oval, Jerry's Smile, 28", EX+ **4,400.00**
Mobiloil, ps, dc/CI fr, Pegasus on wht circle atop nameplate, 37", VG ...**400.00**
Mobiloil Marine, oil can, Pegasus/speedboat graphics, 1-qt, VG **1,050.00**
Mogul Egyptian Cigarettes, sf tin oval, image of Mogul, 24x20", EX+ **2,200.00**
Morgan & Wright Tires, paper sign, boy in coat & cap, 20x15", EX **150.00**
Mother Goose Baby Powder, tc, graphics on bl, 6⅜", EX+ **1,150.00**

Moxie

The Moxie Company was organized in 1884 by George Archer of Boston, Massachusetts. It was at first touted as a 'nerve food' to improve the appetite, promote restful sleep, and in general to make one 'feel better'! Emphasis was soon shifted, however, to the good taste of the brew, and extensive advertising campaigns rivaling those of such giant competitors as Coca-Cola and Hires resulted in successful marketing through the 1930s. Today the term Moxie has become synonymous with courage and audacity, traits displayed by the company who dared compete with such well-established rivals. Our advisor for Moxie is Craig Stifter; he is listed in the Directory under Illinois.

Ashtray, ceramic, Moxie man in center, 5½" dia, EX.................**175.00**
Coin token, Good for One Drink at Moxie Wagon, 1¼", EX.......**40.00**
Fan, celluloid foldout w/cut-out logos, EX+ **100.00**
Fan, Muriel Ostriche in red cap, Moxie man on bk, 1919, EX......**50.00**
Fan, Muriel Ostriche on top half, Moxie man below, 12x10", EX ..**145.00**
Glass, flared, hdl, frosted band w/logo, NM **100.00**
Glass, str-sided, frosted logo, NM+ **165.00**
Pin, dc tin bust image of Moxie girl w/bottle & glass, EX+.........**150.00**
Pitcher, wht ceramic w/rnd Moxie girl & decorative band, EX....**160.00**
Platter, wht ceramic w/Moxie girl in center, decorative rim, 11", G+ ...**85.00**
Purse, mesh featuring Moxie kid & dog, chain hdl, NM+ **1,320.00**
Sign, cb cutout, man/lady w/parasol/Moxie crates, 1910-15, 37", EX+ ..**1,300.00**
Sign, rvpt hanger w/canted corners, Moxie girl & logo, 8x10", G ...**75.00**
Sign, tin, Drink Moxie, Old/New bottle caps on red, 19x27", VG ..**75.00**
Sign, tin, Drink...Distinctly Different, fr, 1930s-40s, 20x28", NM ..**300.00**
Sign, tin, hand holding bottle, 1950-60, 9½x28", VG **100.00**
Sign, tin, Of Course You'll..., lady pouring, fr, 1890s, 28", EX...**2,860.00**
Sign, tin, red oval logo on navy, 19x27", EX................................**450.00**
Sign, tin, Try Our Soda Syrups, lists flavors, ornate border, 19", G ..**665.00**

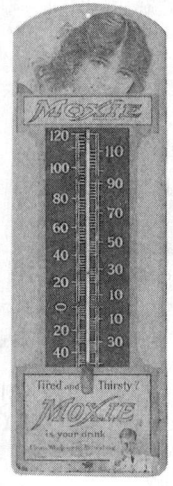

Thermometer, tin, girl at top and man at bottom corner, H.D. Beach Co., Coshocton, O, ca 1918, VG, 26½x9", $225.00.

Tip tray, lady against lilacs, I Just Love Moxie..., 6" dia, EX........**200.00**
Tip tray, lady w/glass, I Just Love Moxie...., 1907, 6" dia, EX **230.00**
Toy top, celluloid, featuring horsemobile, NM+ **135.00**
Walking stick, 'Hitchy Koo' head w/logo, EX+ **585.00**

Munsing Wear, dc ts, boy/girl on seesaw pendulum, rare, 21", EX **3,400.00**
Napoleon Flour, paper sign w/oval image of Napoleon, 35x18", EX+ ..**500.00**
National Bisquit Co, display rack, wood, 5 shelves, 60x47x10", EX **375.00**
Nehi, book, Nehi Advertising 1928, cb cover, 16 pgs, 15x11", EX.......**575.00**
Nesbitt's, ts, text & bottle on blk, wht border, 32x56", EX **300.00**
New Process Blue Flue Oil Stove, match holder, tin, curved front, EX+ ..**275.00**
Niagara Fire Ins Co, rvpt sign, orig fr, 25x33", EX+ **340.00**
NuGrape Soda, ts, bottle cap form, More Fun With..., 36" dia, EX...**165.00**
Ojibwa Fine Cut Tobacco, bin, yel w/graphics, rnd, 11", EX.......**800.00**

Old Crow

Old Crow Whiskey items have become popular with collectors primarily because of the dapper crow dressed in a tuxedo, top hat, etc.. that was used by the company for promotional purposes during the 1940s through the 1960s. However, there is a vast variety of Old Crow collectibles, some of which carry only the whiskey's name. In the 1970s ceramic decanters shaped like chess pieces were available; these carried nothing more than a paper label and a presentation box to identify them. In 1985, the 150th anniversary of Old Crow, the realistic crow that had been extensively used prior to 1950 re-emerged.

Very little Old Crow memorabilia has been issued since National Distillers Products Corporations, the parent company since 1933, was purchased by Jim Beam Brands in 1987. No reproductions have surfaced, although a few fantasies have been found where the character crow was borrowed for private use. Note that with the increased popularity of Old Crow memorabilia, many items have surfaced, especially the more common ones, thus their values have decreased. Our advisors for Old Crow collectibles are Judith and Robert Walthall; they are listed in the Directory under Alabama.

Ashtray, Bakelite, 3½" dia, NM......................................25.00
Ashtray, ceramic, blk w/'Old Crow,' etc, 5" dia.....................35.00
Back-bar display, ceramic 'Broken Leg' mug holds bottle, 5¼", NM...200.00
Bank, wooden bbl, 1985, 6", EX......................................15.00
Bingo card, 100 proof, late 1940s, 7½x8¼".............................45.00
Bottle display, glass cylinder w/gold plastic crow...................50.00
Bottle opener, metal bottle shape, 2⅝", NM..........................25.00
Bottle pourer, plastic figure, sm....................................5.00
Chess set (32 decanters), ltd ed, empty w/orig boxes & rug.........200.00
Cocktail glass, crow stem, Libbey, safety edge, 1970s, from $10 to...15.00
Decanter, figural, Old Crow Distillery Co of Frankfort KY, 13½"....50.00
Decanter, figural, orange vest, Royal Doulton, w/box, 12½".......125.00
Dice, I Buy, You Buy, crow on 1, ½", set of 2.......................45.00
Dice cup, Bakelite, blk w/yel lettering, felt-lined, NM.............100.00
Doorstop, cut-out wood crow, 21", EX................................125.00
Figure, brass, on rnd ftd base, 11".................................85.00
Figure, compo, name emb on base, 1940s, 27½", VG..................450.00
Figure, plastic, Advertising Novelty & Sign Co, 32", EX............200.00
Figure, plastic, in birdcage, 9"...................................125.00
Jigger, blk lettering on clear glass, no crown, NM...................5.00
Key chain, 2-D figural Old Crow, from $3 to..........................5.00
Label, paper, gold, shows Hermitage Distillery bbls, ca 1903, 4+x4+"...25.00
Lighter, 14k gold-plated, Florentine, from $25 to...................30.00
Lipstick tissue booklet, Cub Products, 1⅞x3", M....................25.00
Money clip, chromed metal, emb disc w/crow on 2" clip, EX...........35.00
Phone dialer, figural hard plastic crow, 'Call For' emb on bk, EX....5.00
Pitcher, ceramic, 'Broken Leg' decor, NM...........................100.00
Pitcher, ceramic, olive gr w/emb crow in reserve, McCoy, 7".........35.00
Pitcher, glass w/metal ring & hdl, 5"...............................25.00
Plaque, ceramic plate w/applied 4¾" crow, 8", NM...................125.00
Pocketknife, pearlized hdls, 2 blades................................30.00
Roly-poly, plastic, 9"..95.00
Shot glass, Old Crow & crow fired on in blk.........................20.00
Stirrer, plastic, full-figure crow on end, from $1 to................3.00
Thermometer, rnd dial, 1950s, 9x13", EX............................150.00
Thermometer, Taste the Greatness, 1960, 5¾x13½", from $75 to..100.00

Old Reliable Coffee, ps, Cossack-style gent on yel, vertical, EX.200.00
Old Style Lager, thermometer, tin dc Falstaff figure on box, 13", EX......725.00
Old Virginia Cheroot, paper signs (Uncle Sam, etc), 1900, 23", 5 for.1,000.00
Oliver Chilled Plows, sf ts, cowboy/merchant, 1890s, 37x27", G+......1,000.00

Orange-Crush, bottle, dk amber w/paper label, EX......................60.00
Orange-Crush, clock, 5¢ disc logo, metal w/wood case, 15" sq, G..275.00
Orange-Crush, match striker/door push, porc, 6x4", VG.............400.00
Orange-Crush, sign, cb foldout, girl/beach/bottle/oranges, 1930s, EX+.2,300.00
Orange-Crush, sign, paper on cb, girl w/dog, sf, 19x14", NM+...150.00
Orange-Crush, thermometer, dc tin bottle, 28½", NM...............325.00
Oriental Toilet Water, paper litho, exotic girl, orig fr, 26x32", VG..300.00
P Lorillard Tin Tag Tobacco, cabinet, wood/etched glass, 32x32x17", EX..2,100.00
Pal-O-Mine, tc, 1-lb, slip lid, gold, NM.........................675.00
Pan-Handle Scrap, litho, cops/dice game, Currier & Ives, 1890, VG+..490.00
Paragon Cut Plug Mixture, pocket tin, vertical oval, 3¾", EX+..1,300.00

Pepsi-Cola

Pepsi-Cola was first served in the early 1890s to customers of Caleb D. Bradham, a young pharmacist who touted his concoction to be medicinal as well as delicious. It was first called 'Brad's Drink' but was renamed Pepsi-Cola in 1898. Various logos have been registered over the years. The familiar oval was first used in the early 1940s. At about the same time, the two 'dots' (indicated in our listings by '=') between the words Pepsi and Cola became one, though more recent items may carry the double-dot logo as well, especially when they're designed to be reminiscent of the old ones. The bottle cap logo came along in 1943 and with variations was used through the early 1960s. Our advisor for Pepsi is Craig Stifter; he is listed in the Directory under Illinois. See also Soda Fountain Collectibles.

Sign, cardboard, beach pinup girl, 1941, 21x17", trimmed, EX, $400.00. (Original size, 17x25", NM, $750.00.) (Photo courtesy Autopia, Inc.)

Bottle, str-sided emb glass, P=C logo, Durham NC, 8½", NM......75.00
Bottle carrier, 4-carton, aluminum w/stamped-out letters, 12x18", EX...40.00
Bottle topper, dc cb, P=C Double Size 5¢, 1930s, 13x6", EX+....275.00
Calendar, 1911, complete, VG.....................................3,200.00
Clock, Be Sociable/Have a Pepsi, light-up, 15¾" sq, EX...............50.00
Clock, modern Pepsi logo at bottom, 12-3-6-9, sf, electric, 40x36", VG.50.00
Clock, More Bounce to the Ounce, Deco stepped shape, electric, EX..700.00
Clock, Say Pepsi Please/P-C cap on yel, dbl bubble, 15" dia, EX...600.00
Clock, Time for Cloverdale Beverages/P=C, wood fr, 15" sq, EX...525.00
Display, chalkware girl in red gown/bottle/cap on base, 1940s, EX+...3,400.00
Display rack, wire w/metal bottle cap sign, holds 6 packs, 36", EX+.......100.00
Door push, tin, Come In.../5¢ P=C/On the Lips of Millions!, 10", NM.350.00
Door push, tin, Pick a Pepsi w/P=C caps at curved top/bottom, NM.....400.00
Door push, tin, 5¢ P=C logo, wht on bl, 10⅛x2¾", NM............300.00
Fan, dc cb w/wood hdl, girl w/hands to face, Drink PC, 1912-13, VG..475.00
Fan, paper w/rattan hdl, boy drinking/lg bottle, 1910-15, VG+.1,100.00
Lighter, Scripto, plastic w/metal flip top, cap logo, 1950s, EX+....75.00
Napkin holder, P=C bottle cap logo on wht w/bl trim, 5x7x4", EX..200.00
Poster, paper, dapper couple on yel, he in straw hat, 68x41", EX..30.00
Poster, paper, Stay Young & Fair, unused, 2-sheet, 82x41", EX...125.00
Rack sign, fiberboard, dc, Drink P-C oval on bl/wht stripe, 18x23", EX.45.00
Rack sign, tin, Take Home a Carton/P=C/Double Size, 6x8", VG...185.00

Sign, cb, Drink P=C A Nickel Drink Worth a Dime/bottle, fr, 15", EX .145.00
Sign, cb standup, high-stepping Santa w/bottle, N Rockwell, 20", NM ...25.00
Sign, celluloid oval hanger, Black couple, 12x8", NM 125.00
Sign, metal over cb, Say Pepsi Please/cap/bottle on yel, sf, 9x11", NM .50.00
Sign, plastic bottle cap light-up, Drink P-C Ice-Cold, 1950s, 16", EX .250.00
Sign, plastic P=C bottle cap w/easel bk, VG.................................100.00
Sign, tin, Drink upper left of emb slanted P-C cap, sf, 30x26", EX 100.00
Sign, tin, Drink 5¢ P=C 5¢, emb, rnd corners, 1930s, 10x30", EX+ ...500.00
Sign, tin, Say Pepsi Please/bottle/modern cap logo, yel, 46x17", NM .200.00
Sign, tin/cb hanger, P=C on gr w/red border, 5x9", G 500.00
Sign, wood arrow, P=C Sold Here/Beverage Dept, 15x15", VG ..400.00
Syrup barrel, red/wht/bl metal w/P-C cap logo, EX......................150.00
Syrup dispenser, ceramic, bl w/ornate decor, 1970s repro, NM+ ..2,600.00
Tap knob, bottle cap encased in chrome on wood base, musical, NM .150.00
Tap knob, chrome bottle on wood base, P=C oval logo, 11½", VG 400.00
Thermometer, tin, Bigger/Better, P=C bottle w/oval label, 16x6", EX .325.00
Thermometer, tin, Have a Pepsi/bottle cap on yel, 27", EX 100.00
Thermometer, tin, The Light Refreshment, emb cap, yel, 27x7", EX ..125.00
Toy dispenser bank, P=C logo, Linemar, EXIB 385.00

Peter Rabbit Peanut Butter, tc, 3½x3½", G...................................290.00
Phillips 66, ps, 2-sided dc shield, orange & blk, 30", VG+..........300.00
Pickwick Ale, tin litho, horse-drawn cart w/barrels, fr, 6x23", NM..250.00
Piedmont Cigarettes, ts, Mt Vernon interior, 1911, 20x26", VG ..1,000.00

Planters Peanuts

The Planters Peanut Co. was founded in 1906. Mr. Peanut, the dashing peanut man with top hat, spats, monocle, and cane, has represented Planters since 1916. He took on his modern-day appearance after the company was purchased by Standard Brands in November 1960. He remains perhaps the most highly recognized logo of any company in the world. Mr. Peanut has promoted the company's products by appearing in ads; on product packaging; on or as store displays, novelties, and premiums; and even in character at promotional events (thanks to a special Mr. Peanut costume).

Among the favorite items of collectors today are the glass display jars which were sent to retailers nationwide to stimulate 'point-of-sale' trade. They come in a variety of shapes and styles. The first, distributed in the early 1920s, was a large universal candy jar (round covered bowl on a pedestal) with only a narrow paper label affixed at the neck to identify it as 'Planters.' In 1924 an octagonal jar was produced, all eight sides embossed, with Mr. Peanut on the narrow corner panels. On a second octagon jar, only seven sides were embossed, leaving one of the large panels blank to accommodate a paper label.

In late 1929 a fishbowl jar was introduced, and in 1932 a beautiful jar with a blown-out peanut on each of the four corners was issued. The football shape was also made in the 1930s, as were the square jar, the large barrel jar, and the hexagon jar with yellow fired-on designs alternating on each of the six sides. All of these early jars had glass lids which after 1930 had peanut finials.

In 1937 jars with lithographed tin lids were introduced. The first of these was the slant-front streamline jar, which is also found with screened yellow lettering. Next was a squat version, the clipper jar, then the upright rectangular 1940 Leap Year jar, and last, another upright rectangular jar with a screened, fired-on design similar to the red, white, and blue design on the cellophane 5¢ bags of peanuts of the period. This last jar was issued again after WWII with a plain red tin lid.

In 1959 Planters first used a stock Anchor Hocking one-gallon round jar with a 'customer-special' decoration in red. As the design was not plainly evident when the jar was full, the decoration was modified with a white under-panel. The two jars we've just described are perhaps the rarest of them all due to their limited production. After Standard Brands purchased Planters, they changed the red-on-white panel to show their more modern Mr. Peanut and in 1963 introduced this most plentiful, thus very common, Planters jar. In 1966 the last counter display jar was distributed: the Anchor Hocking jar with a fired-on large four-color design such as that which appeared on peanut bags of the period. Prior to this, a plain jar with a transfer decal in an almost identical but smaller design was used.

Some Planters jars have been reproduced: the octagon jar (with only six of the sides embossed), a small version of the barrel jar, and the four peanut corner jar. Some of the first were made in clear glass with 'Made in Italy' embossed on the bottom, but most have been made in Asia, many in various colors of glass (a dead giveaway) as well as clear, and carrying only small paper stickers, easily removed, identifying the country of origin. At least two reproductions of the Anchor Hocking jar with a four-color design have been made, one circa 1978, the other in 1989. Both, using the stock jar, are difficult to detect, but there are small differences between them and the original that will enable you to make an accurate identification. With the exception of several of the earliest and the Anchor Hocking, all authentic Planters jars have 'Made in USA' embossed on the bottom, and all, without exception, are clear glass. Unfortunately, several paper labels have also been reproduced, no doubt due to the fact that an original label or decal will greatly increase the value of an original jar. Jar prices continue to remain stable in today's market.

In the late 1920s, the first premiums were introduced in the form of story and paint books. Late in the 1930s, the tin nut set (which was still available into the 1960s) was distributed. A wood jointed doll was available from Planters Peanuts Stores at that time. Many post-WWII items were made of plastic: banks, salt and pepper shakers, cups, cookie cutters, small cars and trucks, charms, whistles, various pens and mechanical pencils, and almost any other item imaginable. In recent years the company, now a division of Nabisco, has continued to distribute a wide variety of novelties.

Note that there are many unauthorized Planters/Mr. Peanut items. Although several are reproductions or 'copycats,' most are fantasies and fakes. Our advisors for Planters Planters are Judith and Robert Walthall; they are in the Directory under Alabama.

Key:
al — aluminum   pfl — peanut finial lid
cc — common colors   pl — plastic
 (green, light blue, red, tan)   pm — papier-mache
MrP — Mr. Peanut   pnut — peanut
okl — octagon knob lid   shp — shipping

Ashtray, gold-plated metal w/MrP figure, 50th Anniversary, 6x5", MIB.130.00
Bank, figural, pl, cc, 9", from $15 to 20.00
Charm, figural, pl, cc, 2", from $3 to 4.00
Cookie cutter, MrP figure bowing or tipping hat, red pl, EX 15.00
Cookie jar, MrP head, ceramic, Nabisco Classics Collection, 10½" ...50.00
Costume, compo MrP figure, 1950s, 48", EX+ 2,000.00
Display box, Salted Peanuts, yel w/multi MrP images, 1930s-40s, EX..350.00
Doll, MrP, cloth, Chase Bag Co, 1967, 21", EX 40.00
Doll, MrP, wood-jointed, 1930s, 9", EX..200.00
Figure, MrP, pot metal, blk & gold w/name on base, 1930s, 7", EX+ ..700.00
Jar, Anchor Hocking, rnd w/wht frosted & red label, 1960, 7½", NM..50.00
Jar, Clipper, PLANTERS emb across front, tin lid, 5x10x7½", EX 100.00
Jar, Fishbowl, pfl, 11", EX...60.00
Jar, Four Peanut Corner, pfl, 1932, 14" (+) 225.00
Jar, Hexagon, 6 sides w/yel screened design, pfl, 7¼", EX 125.00
Jar, Octagon, 7 sides emb, pfl, 10", EX, from $85 to 100.00
Lapel pin, figural, pl, 1", from $1 to 2.00
Mask, cb MrP face w/monocle & wraparound hat, 15½x11½", EX 375.00
Nodder, MrP figure, compo, 6½", MIB 150.00

Nut spoon, pl, MrP finial, cc, from $3 to...**4.00**

Peanut butter pail, allover MrP graphics, pry lid, 1-lb, EX **925.00**

Peanut butter pail, High Grade, red w/red MrP on wht label, 5-lb, VG+ .**2,800.00**

Peanut butter tin, Homogenized, key-wind lid, MrP/peanuts, 2-lb, EX...**230.00**

Puppet, hand; MrP figure, rubber, tan w/blk hat/monocle, early, 6", EX.**750.00**

Race car, plastic peanut shape w/MrP driver, 1960s, 5¼" L, EX .**500.00**

Shakers, figural, pl, 3¼", pr from $10 to..**15.00**

Trolley card, Delicious w/Cocktails, waiter w/tray, 1950, 11x21", EX...**400.00**

Trolley card, When Guests Drop In, maid serving, 1950, 11x21", EX..**400.00**

Umbrella, yel/bl. single image of MrP, 1982, M **40.00**

Whistle, figural, pl, 2½", from $3 to **4.00**

Whistle, siren, figural, pl, loop at base, 3½" **35.00**

Poehler Quick Cooking Rolled Oats, container, 1-lb 4-oz, EX+ .**450.00**

Prestone Anti-Freeze, thermometer, porc, 36x9", EX **325.00**

Prexy Plug Cut Tobacco, pocket tin, vertical, red, 4½", EX+ ..**2,700.00**

Providence Washington Ins Co, ts, image of Washington, 24x18", NM....**300.00**

Pulver Chewing Gum, dispenser, bl, Traffic Cop, 1920s, 21", EX .**1,200.00**

Pulver Chewing Gum, dispenser, red porc, Yellow Kid, 20½", VG+ ..**675.00**

Pulver's Chocolate Cocoa Gum, dispenser, Foxy Grandpa, 24", VG..**4,400.00**

Pulver's Yellow Kid Chewing Gum, wrapper, blk on yel, EX **160.00**

Quaker Oats, cb sign, silhouette/sunset/text, wood fr, 11x21", VG..**50.00**

Quaker Oats, dc cb platform skirt w/images of Dionne Quints, 30x60"..**120.00**

Quick Meal Ranges, tip tray, chicks, Shonk litho, oval, EX+........**80.00**

R Brand & Co Whiskies & Fine Wines, ts, lady, fr, 1880s, 23x17", EX+.**3,700.00**

Rahr Beer, Vitrolite corner sign, curved, brass fr, 23x15", EX ..**1,450.00**

RCA Victor

Nipper, the RCA Victor trademark, was the creation of Francis Barraud, an English artist. His pet's intense fascination with the music of the phonograph seemed to him a worthy subject for his canvas. Although he failed to find a publishing house who would buy his work, the Gramophone Co. in England saw its potential and adopted Nipper to advertise their product. The painting was later acquired and trademarked in the United States by the Victor Talking Machine Co., which was purchased by RCA in 1929. The trademark is owned today by EMI in England and by General Electric in the U.S. Nipper's image appeared on packages, accessories, ads, brochures, and in three-dimensional form. You may find a life-size statue of him, but all are not old. They have been manufactured for the owner throughout RCA history and are marketed currently by licensees, BMG Inc. and Thomson Consumer Electronics (dba RCA). Except for the years between 1968 and 1976, Nipper has seen active duty, and with his image spruced up only a bit for the present day, the ageless symbol for RCA still listens intently to 'His Master's Voice.' Many of the items have been reproduced in recent years. Exercise care before you buy.

The recent phenomenon of Internet auctions has played havoc with prices paid for Victor and RCA Victor collectibles. Often prices paid for online sales bear little resemblance to the true value of the item. Reproductions are often sold as old on the Internet and bring prices accordingly. It is common knowledge that auction prices, more often than not, are inflated over sales made through traditional sales outlets. The Internet has exacerbated the situation by focusing a very large number of buyers and sellers through the narrow portal of a modem. The prices here are intended to reflect what one might expect to pay through traditional sales. Our advisor for RCA Victor is Roger R. Scott; he is listed in the Directory under Oklahoma.

Bank, flocked metal, 9" **125.00**

Buckle, His Master's Voice, brass, Nash Tiffany London.................**25.00**

Chair, NP pipe fr w/armrest, plastic bk/seat, logo on bk, M **100.00**

Clock, RCA Victor Records, w/Nipper **400.00**

Curtains, RCA...**40.00**

Figure, Nipper, chalkware, Victor, 4" **40.00**

Figure, Nipper, chalkware, 8", EX **60.00**

Figure, Nipper, crystal, Fenton, 4"...**50.00**

Figure, Nipper, papier-mache, 11"...**50.00**

Figure, Nipper, papier-mache, 18"...**350.00**

Figure, Nipper, papier-mache, 36"...**600.00**

Figure, Nipper, papier-mache, rpt, 32"..**525.00**

Figure, Nipper, plaster, 14½x7½x5", VG..**200.00**

Figure, Nipper, plastic, 36", EX...**235.00**

Figure, Radio Man, jtd wood, Maxfield Parrish, M.......................**900.00**

Needle tin, Nipper, 3-color, NM, from $25 to...................................**50.00**

Pin-bk button, I Support Nipper, 1930s...**45.00**

Plate, Nipper, collector's edition **50.00**

Puzzle record, Victor, MIP...**100.00**

Record brush, Lucite hdl, in faux leather snap case **30.00**

Record display, dog & phonograph, chalkware **150.00**

Shakers, dog & RCA phonograph, plastic, pr **45.00**

Shakers, Nipper, Lenox, pr **50.00**

Sign, canvas, His Master's Voice, 26x19".......................................**1,500.00**

Sign, neon, letters on metal fr, 14x40" **125.00**

Sign, plastic/metal, ...Radio, light-up, 1940s, 15x37", EX............**180.00**

Sign, porc. record shape w/trademark image on red label, 24", VG .**300.00**

Smoker's set, Nipper, old...**500.00**

Snow globe...**50.00**

Watch fob, EX **30.00**

Water glass, etched Nipper, set of 6...**100.00**

Red Goose Shoes

Realizing that his last name was difficult to pronounce, Herman Giesceke, a shoe company owner resolved to give the public a modified, shortened version that would be better suited to the business world. The results suggested the use of the goose trademark with the last two letters, 'ke,' represented by the key that this early goose held in his mouth. Upon observing an employee casually coloring in the goose trademark with a red pencil, Giesceke saw new advertising potential and renamed the company Red Goose Shoes. Although the company has changed hands down through the years, the Red Goose emblem has remained. Collectors of this desirable fowl increase in number yearly, as do prices. Beware of reproductions; new chalkware figures are prevalent.

Display, nodding goose, paper on composition, electric, 1930s, 27x11x20", EX original on wooden box, $1,475.00. (Photo courtesy Buffalo Bay Auction Co.)

Card game, Cities, incomplete, w/box, VG **18.00**

Dispenser, Golden Egg, cb & papier-mache goose, kid prizes, EX..**325.00**

Rug, Half the Fun of Having Feet, gold/gray, rare, 27x59", EX ...**325.00**

Sign, neon, Red Goose form w/wht name, 12x24", EX **2,100.00**
Sign, wood, Red Goose Boots, stenciled, zigzag ends, 5½x24", EX ..**35.00**
Welcome mat, rubber, VG **50.00**
World globe, metal, w/stand, 9x6" dia, EX **165.00**

Red Jacket Smoking Tobacco, pocket tin, vertical, red, 4½", EX .**1,000.00**
Red Raven, tip tray, woman & bird, Shonk litho, rectangular, EX+ ..**90.00**
Red Raven, tray, nude child reaches for bottle, 12" dia, G **290.00**
Red Raven Splits, tip tray, little girl, Shonk litho, VG+ **110.00**
Red Raven Splits, tip tray, World's Fair 1904, birds, VG+ **55.00**
Red Rock Ginger Ale, paper sign w/chain fr & hanger, girl, 8x6", EX.**185.00**
Red Wolf Coffee, tc, 1-lb, key-wind lid, red on yel, EX **575.00**
Rex Tobacco, porc door push, It's in the Blend, gr/wht, 6½", EX ...**350.00**
Royal Crown Cola, bottle carrier w/6 bottles, aluminum, EX **85.00**
Royal Crown Cola, dc tin hanger, 25¢ 6-pack on emblem, 16x24", VG+ ..**525.00**
Royal Crown Cola, sign, sf cb, mom & kids shopping, 1940s, 11x28", NM....**80.00**
Royal Crown Cola, ts, dc hanger w/bracket, 2-sided, 1940, 16x24", EX...**800.00**
Sander's Candy, pail, pry lid, 1950s, 5½", NM **110.00**
Sanford's Inks, sf ts, product graphics, Kaufmann/Strauss, 14x20", EX ..**900.00**
Santa-Bana 5¢ Cigar, paper litho, lady, fr, VG+ **850.00**
Sauer's Extract, clock, New Haven regulator, 42", VG............**1,495.00**
Sauer's Flavoring Extracts, clock, Gilbert regulator, VG **550.00**
Savage Rifles, watch fob, emb metal w/Indian motif, enamel trim, NM..**325.00**
Schlitz Beer, sf ts, gent w/globe body, Shonk litho, 19x14", EX+...........**2,030.00**
Sea Island Sugar, product sack w/uncut cloth Uncle Sam doll, 14", EX **35.00**
Sealy Mattress, sf cb sign of cotton pickers w/3 stand-up figures, EX.....**1,550.00**

Seven-Up

The Howdy Company of St. Louis, Missouri, was founded in 1920 by Charles L. Grigg. His first creation was an orange drink called Howdy. In the late 1920s Howdy's popularity began to wane, so in 1929 Grigg invented a lemon-lime soda called Seven-Up as an alternative to colas. Grigg's Seven-Up became a widely accepted favorite. Our advisor for this category is Craig Stifter; he is listed in the Directory under Illinois. See also Soda Fountain Collectibles.

Bottle carrier, wood w/triangular ends, cut-out hdl, 6-pack, NM .**200.00**
Clip board, Diet 7-Up, Side Stack Attack, red w/football detail, G+ ..**20.00**
Cooler, wht metal airline type w/bail hdl, red/wht logo, 18x12x9", VG..**50.00**
Door push, aluminum, Come In/7-Up (red oval)/Likes You, 1940s, 9", EX..**175.00**
Door push, aluminum, In Case of an Emergency, 8x4", NM **45.00**
Game, Mysto Card Trick, w/card, instructions & envelope, EX....**35.00**
Menu board, rvpt w/orig fr, 8 slots, 1930s-40s, 17x10", VG+ **120.00**
Sign, bottle, dc tin, 1962, 45x13", EX+ **90.00**
Sign, cb hanger, Santa in wreath, 'Tis the Uncola Season, 10", EX ..**35.00**
Sign, cb hanger, 3-D flower basket w/rnd logo, 1940s, 20", EX+ ...**300.00**
Sign, flange, rnd, red, ...Sold Here, Canadian, 1940s, 13", EX....**425.00**
Sign, flange, spinner w/different slogans on both sides, 1961, EX+ ..**450.00**
Sign, flange, sq w/rnd corners, red, ...Sold Here, 1930s-40s, 12", VG...**200.00**
Sign, neon, 7-Up cup w/bubble & straw, 3-color, 28x13", NM ...**200.00**
Sign, rvpt, grocer holding 'on duty' sign, sq logo/phrase, 6x11", EX+...**480.00**
Sign, steel, wht & blk on red logo form, 1950s, 13x11", EX+ **120.00**
Sign, tin, emb oval w/fan detail at bottom, Fresh Up, 1963, 41", VG...**350.00**
Sign, tin, octagonal, Fresh Up!..., red w/gr rim, 1940s, 14", NM ...**300.00**
Sign, tin, sq logo in silver scalloped fr on gr, 1947, 18x14", NM ...**200.00**
Sign, tin, sq logo/bottle neck on wht, gr trim, 1950s, 36x60", NM..**325.00**
Sign, tin, sq logo/Fresh Up... on wht, gr trim, 1956, 13x7", EX ..**120.00**
Sign, tin, sq logo/hand-held bottle/Your Fresh Up, 1947, 11x31", EX..**325.00**
Sign, tin, sq logo/Nothing Does It, wht/gr rim, 1956, 19x13", EX ..**240.00**
Sign, tin, sq logo/phrase above on wht, gr fr, 1955, 13x7", EX....**120.00**
Sign, tin, sq logo/phrase/scroll detail on gr, 1946, 18x54", NM+ ...**500.00**

Sign, tin, sq logo/7-Up Your Thirst Away on wht/gr, 15x33", VG ...**60.00**

Sharples, stone litho, maiden in cow pasture, ca 1890, fr, 20x13", NM+ .**400.00**
Sharples Tubular Cream Separators, dc ts, father/girl, 2-sided, 27", G ...**400.00**
Sherwin Williams Paints, ps, Cover the Earth logo, 36x24", EX.**300.00**
Sickle Plug Smoking, cloth banner, sickle/product on wht, 18x36", VG..**275.00**
Skinner's Satins, sf ts, Indian chief, Shonk litho, oval, 20x16", EX+..**3,375.00**
Smith Bros Chewing Gum, display box, w/17 orig packs, early, 6x4", EX..**5,500.00**
Snow, emb brass sign, For Men's Wear/Stylish & Serviceable, 7x14", VG....**250.00**
Snow King Baking Powder, dc cb stand-up, Santa in sleigh, 17x29", VG+..**750.00**
Socony Mobil, dc porc Pegasus, red w/wht trim, 45x64", EX...**1,050.00**
Sparrow's Empress Chocolates, sf ts, empress, 23x17", EX **1,000.00**
Squirrel Brand Salted Peanuts, jar, emb glass w/knob lid, 13", NM........**325.00**
Squirrel Brand 5¢ Salted Jumbo Peanuts, dc ts, squirrel, 10x9", EX **600.00**
Squirt, menu board, emb tin chalkboard, swirl bottle/boy, 1960s, NM ..**250.00**
St Bruno Flake, 3-D dc cb stand-up, field hands, fr, 15x20", EX+...........**850.00**
Star Brand Shoes, dc tin racer w/driver, 8½" L, unused, M **1,400.00**
Stoneware Food Containers, ts, boy/dog at table, beveled, 19x13", EX+...**1,750.00**
Strawbridge Clothier, pocket mirror, Santa graphics, 2" dia, EX.**850.00**
Success Manure Spreader, ash/tip tray, Kemp & Burpee litho, 3x5", EX+ .**190.00**
Sunbeam Bread, cb display, Miss Sunbeam holds loaf in lap, 1950s, EX **775.00**
Sunbeam Bread, thermometer, dial, tin/glass, Pam, 1957, 12" dia, EX+ **575.00**
Sunlight Soap, dc ts of soap box w/cord hanger, EX+ **400.00**
Sweet Girl Peanut Butter, pail, 1-lb, bl, EX+ **1,200.00**
Sweet Girl Peanut Butter, tc, sand castle on bk, Rasmussen, 3½", VG...**400.00**
Sweet-Orr Pants/Shirts/Overalls, ps, logo on yel, 6x28", EX...**1,050.00**
Three (3) Bros Cigars, cigar cutter, wood base, image on front, EX+...........**650.00**
Tiger Chewing Tobacco, bin, 5 Cent Pkgs, gold on dk bl, rnd, 12", EX....**1,000.00**
Topsy Hosiery, match holder, tin, beach girl, Black boy logo, 5", VG+ **700.00**
Town Crier Coffee, tc, pry lid, bl graphics, 1-lb, VG....................**425.00**
Toyland Peanut Butter, pail, mc graphics on bl, 1-lb, EX+..........**300.00**
Trout-Line Burley Cut, pocket tin, vertical, gr, 3¾", EX+ **775.00**
Tums, dc Baby Snooks toy, Tums ad/radio show on bk, 1950, 16", EX...**50.00**
Uncle Sam Quick Cooking Oats, cb container, 1¼-lb, 7", EX+ .**325.00**
Uniform Cut Plug, tc, rnd w/slip lid, graphics on red, 6", EX+....**1,250.00**
Van Houten's Cocoa, paper sign, little girl, 29x21", EX **345.00**
Van Melles Toffees, tc, birds on 3 sides, bl, 11½", EX **200.00**
Vantine's Sana-Dermal Talcum, tc, mother & child image, 5", EX+ ..**825.00**
Velvet Tobacco, ts, dog/fireside/3 generations, 28x22", VG **500.00**
Virginia Dare American Wines, tray, couple in forest, 12" dia, EX+...**185.00**
Walkover Shoes, flange ts, oval, man/woman images, 28x17", EX+ .**1,500.00**
Waterman's Ideal Fountain Pen, dc cb sign, Santa/globe, 15", EX........**600.00**
Waterman's Ideal Fountain Pen, door push, globe graphics, 9x3", EX+ **500.00**
Waverly Pure Rye, alto-plaster plaque, Black minstrel trio, 33x26", EX ..**950.00**
Weddles Tea, tc, slip lid, early autos on all sides, 3x5x3", EX........**50.00**
Westminster Rye Whiskey, sf ts, driver negotiates for dead pig, 25x37" ..**1,265.00**
Wheatlet Cereal, dc cb stand-up, Uncle Sam before crowd, 6x4", EX+ .**170.00**
Whistle, bottle topper, cb, lady in yel, 8", unused, NM...............**100.00**
Whistle, fan hanger, cb, 11½x2½", NM..**55.00**
White House Coffee, dc tin flange, hand-held can, rare, 14x9", EX+..**4,600.00**
White House Coffee, thermometer, wood, curved top, blk on wht, 15", VG...**275.00**
White Rock Beverages, door pull, name above bottle, 1940s, 14x4", NM+...**250.00**
Whiz Fly Fume, display shelf, tin w/ad marquee, 30x18", EX+ ...**425.00**
Williams Khush-Amadi Talc, tc, fairy graphics, 5", EX+..........**1,600.00**
Winner Plug Tobacco, litho, jockeys on horseback, ca 1900, 10", VG...**65.00**
Wm J Moxley Margarine, ts, family uses product, rstr, 27x39" **500.00**
Woods' Radiator, paper sign, Too Hot To Bear/graphics, 30x21", EX..**1,450.00**
Woods Improved Lollacapop Mosquito Antidote, tc, 3x2x¾", EX+.......**100.00**
Wrigley's, tray, Happy To Serve You..., red/yel, 13x11", EX+ **450.00**
Wrigley's Nips, display box, cb, 9x13x6", VG+..............................**475.00**
Yellow Cabs, pocket mirror, 1920s cab on wht, yel trim, 3½" dia, EX........**700.00**
Yellow Kid, cigar box, wood, hinged lid, gold-stamped image, 9x5", EX......**170.00**

Zeno Chewing Gum, jar, glass, ground neck, orig lid, sq, 5x5x8", EX.......**550.00**
Zipp's Cherri-o, tray, bird on branch, 12" dia, EX+......................**800.00**

Advertising Cards

Advertising trade cards enjoyed great popularity during the last quarter of the nineteenth century when the chromolithography printing process was refined and put into common use. The purpose of the trade card was to acquaint the public with a business, product, service, or event. Most trade cards range in size from 2" x 3" to 4" x 6"; however, many are found in both smaller and larger sizes.

There are two classifications of trade cards: 'private design' and 'stock.' Private design cards were used by a single company or individual; the images on the cards were designed for only that company. Stock cards were generics that any individual or company could purchase from a printer's inventory. These cards usually had a blank space on the front for the company to overprint with their own name and product information.

Four categories of particular interest to collectors are:

Mechanical — a card which achieves movement through the use of a pull tab, fold-out side, or movable part.

Hold-to-light — a card that reveals its design only when viewed before a strong light.

Diecut — a card in the form of something like a box, a piece of clothing, etc.

Metamorphic — a card that by folding down a flap shows a transformed image, such as a white beard turning black after use of a product.

For a more thorough study of the subject, we recommend *Reflections 1* and *Reflections 2* by Kit Barry; his address can be found in the Directory under Vermont. Values are given for cards in near-mint condition.

Alden Fruit Vinegar, Priscilla..**12.00**
American Breakfast Cereal, hummingbird on wheat **20.00**
Austen's Forest Flower Cologne, gypsy cherub w/violets................**9.00**
Austen's Forest Flower Cologne, man & woman on swing **9.00**
Boss Watch Case, deep-sea diver, sunken ship, watch case............**15.00**
Bousemeem Spices, nymph dropping flowers on man....................**12.00**
Burrows Clothing House, sailor boy w/bouquet in hand **8.00**
Demorest's Reliable Patterns, rose stem through banner.................**6.00**
Enterprise Mfg, bone/shell/corn mill, mill w/corn **45.00**
Fairbank Canning Co, dressed lion serving product......................**45.00**
Fisk, Clark & Hagg Mufflers, man & woman, outdoor wear..........**10.00**
Glenwood Stove, girl in red dress & hat w/bouquet......................**8.00**
Hagan Magnolia Balm, woman & cherub w/2 bottles **35.00**

Huntley & Palmers Biscuits, Reading & London, natives in boat with spears approach hippopotamus, $25.00. (Photo courtesy Dave Cheadle)

Imperial Egg Food, chicken in eggshell on water **20.00**
John Wanamaker Clothes, boy hanging sign.................................**12.00**
Keystone Watch Case, diecut keystone, monkey on clock **15.00**
Lea & Perrin Sauce, chef using product on salad **35.00**
Max Stadler Clothes, children on swing, tricycle, horse................**10.00**
Mennen Talcum Powder, 3 children, 1 w/flag, & product **25.00**
Mme Demorest Maison de Patrons, 2 roses & banner.....................**6.00**

National Line Steamships, SS Egypt................................**45.00**
Peckham Justice Stove, justice leaning on sword, stove................**35.00**
Penn Mutual Life Ins Co, 2 roses **8.00**
Petrie Face Powder, man w/woman sitting by tree **9.00**
Ritter Preserved Fruit, jam, man & woman, stove, window...........**15.00**
Shuman Co Clothier, beach scene, ocean scene **6.00**
Spencerian Pen, girl writing at desk w/collie dog.....................**30.00**
Ta-Ka Kake, girl holding cupcake **25.00**
Thurber Flavoring Extract, 2 roses **12.00**
Universal Fashion Co, 3 panels of country scenes **10.00**
Weir Stove Co, woman in hat looking to left **12.00**
Yates Clothes, 2 fox hunters w/dog pack **13.00**
Yates Clothes, 2 men jumping horses, Am flag on pole.................**12.00**

Advertising Dolls and Figures

Whether your interest in ad dolls is fueled by nostalgia or strictly because of their amusing, often clever advertising impact, there are several points that should be considered before making your purchases. Condition is of utmost importance; never pay book price for dolls in poor condition, whether they are cloth or of another material. Restoring fabric dolls is usually unsatisfactory and involves a good deal of work. Seams must be opened, stuffing removed, the doll washed and dried, and then reassembled. Washing old fabrics may prove to be disastrous. Colors may fade or run, and most stains are totally resistant to washing. It's usually best to leave the fabric doll as it is.

Watch for new dolls as they become available. Save related advertising literature, extra coupons, etc., and keep these along with the doll to further enhance your collection. Old dolls with no marks are sometimes challenging to identify. While some products may use the same familiar trademark figures for a number of years (the Jolly Green Giant, Pillsbury's Poppin' Fresh, and the Keebler Elf, for example), others appear on the market for a short time only and may be difficult to trace. Most libraries have reference books with trademarks and logos that might provide a clue in tracking down your doll's identity. Children see advertising figures on Saturday morning cartoons that are often unfamiliar to adults, or other ad doll collectors may have the information you seek.

Some advertising dolls are still easy to find and relatively inexpensive, ranging in cost from $1.00 to $100.00. The hard plastic and early composition dolls are bringing the higher prices. Advertising dolls are popular with children as well as adults. For a more thorough study of the subject, we recommend *Advertising Character Collectibles* by Warren Dotz and *Advertising Dolls with Values* by Myra Yellin Outwater (Schiffer). Values apply only to examples in the condition given in the descriptions; you may have to adjust your prices up or down. Just be sure to discount prices for soil, missing parts, wear, or damage of any type.

Archie Archway, compo, Archway Cookies, 1970s, 5", NM.........**60.00**
Bazooka Joe, stuffed cloth, Bazooka Bubble Gum, 1973, EX **20.00**
Betty Crocker, stuffed cloth, Kenner, 1974, 13", VG....................**20.00**
Campbell Kid, girl, Campbell's, Ideal, 1955, 8", EX, minimum value ..**125.00**
Campbell Kids, Colonial boy & girl, Campbell's Soups, 1976, 10", ea...**60.00**
Cap'n Crunch, plush, Quaker Oats, 1990, 18", EX **20.00**
Charlie Tuna, vinyl, w/arms up (rare), Star-Kist Tuna, 1973, 7½", M...**75.00**
Cheerleader, Texaco, 11½", NMIB...**65.00**
Chiquita, stuffed cloth, Chiquita Bananas, 1974 premium, NM, minimum ...**40.00**
Chucky Cheese, bank, vinyl, Chucky Cheese Pizza, 7", EX **10.00**
Colonel Sanders (puppet), plastic, Kentucky Fried Chicken, 1960s, EX.**20.00**
Count Chocula, squeeze vinyl, General Mills, 1977, 8", NM......**125.00**
Diaparene Baby, vinyl, orig diaper, 1980s, M, from $50 to **75.00**
Dunkin Munchkin, stuffed cloth, Dunkin' Donuts, 15", EX, from $15 to .**20.00**
Elsie the Cow, plush w/vinyl head, brn & yel, Borden, 16", M ...**120.00**
Ernie, plush, Keebler, 1981, 24", EX.......................................**45.00**

Ernie, rubber, Keebler, 6½", NM...............................18.00
Eskimo Pie Boy, stuffed cloth, Chase Bag Co, 1964-74, 15", EX...20.00
Fresh-Up Freddie, stuffed cloth w/rubber head, Seven-Up, 15", EX...75.00
Gerber boy & girl, squeak vinyl, Atlanta Novelty, 1985, 8", EX, ea ..20.00
Green Giant, cloth, 1966 premium, 16", M (in orig mailer), from $25 to ...35.00
Helping Hand, plush, Hamburger Helper, 14", M.........................10.00
Jack Frost boy, stuffed cloth, 17", M 50.00
Jeans man, Jordache, Mego, 12", MIB.............................30.00
Little Sprout, inflatable, Green Giant, 1970s, 24", MIP, from $35 to ..65.00
Lotta Light, cloth, uncut, Westinghouse, 17", NM.........................85.00
Lysol Kid, stuffed cloth, Trudy Corp, 1986, NM, minimum value.30.00
M&M man, plain M&M shape, plush, 12" 10.00
Michelin Man, Mr Bib holding baby, rubber, 7", EX 125.00
Miss Tastee Freeze, hard plastic, Tastee Freeze, 1950s, 7", NM......20.00
Mr Bubble, squeeze vinyl, Dow, 1990, 8", NM 35.00
Mr Fleet, vinyl, all-wht version, Chrysler, 10", VG, from $150 to ..200.00
Mr Wiggle puppet, red vinyl, Jell-O, 1966, M..................75.00
Mr Zip, wooden pop-up, US Postal Service, 1960s, 6½", EX 75.00
Orange Bird, bank, vinyl, Florida Oranges, 1974, MIP.................40.00
Pizza Pizza man, plush, Little Caesar's Pizza, 1990, EX 5.00
Poppin' Fresh, stuffed cloth, talker, Pillsbury, Mattel, 16", NM ..100.00
Rastus, stuffed cloth, Cream of Wheat, Rastus, NM+ 150.00
Spot, plush w/suction cups on hands, Seven-Up, 6", MIB.............10.00
Taped Crusader, vinyl, Curad Band-Aids, 1975, 7½", NM............30.00

African Art

African art does not consist of a single class of objects. Rather, these often-powerful images and objects are carved by many varying African tribes and groups across the central continent; each item represents specific cultural and spiritual functions and meanings. Many kinds of materials are used including wood, metal, fiber, ivory, and bone. Large numbers of these items are now being produced and sold to the tourist trade, but 'authentic' African art is generally considered to consist of objects which were used in cultural and/or religious activities. The items listed here are authentic, in good condition, without provenance, and considered to be of average aesthetic quality. Scott Nelson, a collector of African art, is our advisor; his address is listed in the Directory under New Mexico.

Basket, Nigeria, open fiber w/cowrie shells, 8x10".................175.00
Beads, trade; ceramic, string of 20 ....100.00
Bracelet, Ashanti, bronze, knobs.......................................35.00
Cloth, Kuba, geometric design, 18" sq.............................175.00
Comb, Ashanti, bird's head surmount, 4".........................200.00
Container, Luba, gourd, wooden figural stopper.....................90.00
Divination board, Yoruba, animals, 20" dia.......................475.00
Doll, Ashanti, figural, 7"...275.00
Doll, Mossi, abstract human figure 275.00
Door, Dogon, granary, human figures, 26".......................1,200.00
Drum, Hemba, geometric designs, 22".............................275.00
Earrings, Masai, beaded, 6"...175.00
Figure, Dogon, crouched male, 10".................................650.00
Figure, Senufo, standing female, 12"...............................275.00
Figure, Yoruba, pnt colonial, 12" 175.00
Goldweight, Ashanti, bronze figure 125.00
Hat, Kuba, fibre, blk pnt 175.00
Headdress, Bamana, Tchi-wara (antelope), horizontal................675.00
Heddle pulley, Senufo, bird surmount, 5"..........................275.00
Ibejis, Yoruba, 9", pr 375.00
Lock, Bamana door, 2 figural surmounts, 14" 675.00
Mask, Bamana, N'Tomo, 14" 375.00
Mask, Dan, human face, 15"...375.00

Mask, Dogon, Kanaga, 26" 500.00
Mask, Karumba, polychrome, antelope, 21"......................475.00
Mask, Mende, helmet, female initiation, 12"....................875.00
Mask, Pende, human face, 8"...375.00
Pendent, Yoruba, ivory human figure, 4".........................900.00

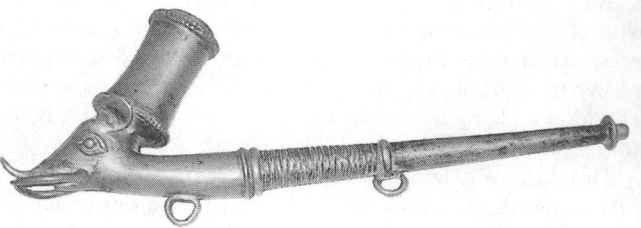

Pipe, Cameroons, elephant, brass, 14", $900.00. (Photo courtesy Scott Nelson)

Ring, Dogon, bronze, horse & rider................................275.00
Slingshot, Baule, animal head, 5"...................................85.00
Stool, Lega, human figural supports, 13"..........................675.00
Whisk, Yoruba, human figure, wood & horsehair, 12".............275.00

Agata

Agata is New England peachblow (the factory called it 'Wild Rose') with an applied metallic stain which produces gold tracery and dark blue mottling. The stain is subject to wear, and the amount of remaining stain greatly affects the value. It is especially valuable (and rare) on satin-finish items when found on peachblow of intense color. Caution! Be sure to use only gentle cleaning methods.

Currently rare types of art glass have been realizing erratic prices at auction; until they stabilize, we can only suggest an average range of values. In the listings that follow, examples are glossy unless noted otherwise. A condition rating of 'EX' indicates that the stain shows a slight amount of wear. Our advisors for this category are Betty and Clarence Maier; they are listed in the Directory under Pennsylvania. See also Green Opaque.

Bowl, ruffled, spittoon shape, fair stain, 3x5¼"...........................750.00
Bowl, spittoon form w/scalloped edge, VG stain/mottling, 2½x5½" ..1,265.00
Cruet, trifold top, gold int decor, pk hdl, wht ball stopper, 6" .1,600.00
Finger bowl, ruffled top, 2½x5¼", from $600 to.......................700.00
Finger bowl, 2½x5¼", +6½" underplate 975.00
Tumbler, EX stain & mottling, 3¾", from $750 to 1,000.00
Vase, much gold tracery, petal top, thin walls, 4½" 685.00
Vase, satin finish, EX stain & mottling, 6" 2,325.00
Vase, wide ruffled top, 4-pinch body, EX stain & mottling, 4¾"...1,150.00
Vase, 4-sided rim, pinched sides, 6"...................................1,500.00

Akro Agate

The Akro Agate Company operated in West Virginia from 1914 until 1951, and in addition to their famous marbles they made children's dishes, powder jars with Scottie dogs on top, candlesticks, and ashtrays, for instance — in many colors and patterns. Though some of their glassware was made in solid colors, their most popular products were made of the same swirled colors as their marbles. Though many pieces are not marked, you will find some that are marked with their distinctive logo: a crow flying through the letter 'A' holding an Aggie in its beak and one in each claw. Some novelty items may instead carry one of these trademarks: 'J.V. Co., Inc.,' 'Braun & Corwin,' 'N.Y.C. Vogue Merc Co. U.S.A.,' 'Hamilton Match Co.,' and 'Mexicali Pickwick Cosmetic Corp.'

Color is a very important worth-assessing factor. Some pieces may be common in one color but rare in others. Occasionally an item will have exceptionally good colors, and this would make it more valuable than an example with only average color. When buying either marbles or juvenile tea sets in original boxes, be sure the box contains its original contents.

Note: Recently unearthed original written information has discounted the generally accepted attribution of the Chiquita and J.P. patterns to the Akro company, proving instead that they were made by the Alley Agate Company.

For more information we recommend *The Complete Line of the Akro Agate Co.* by our advisors, Roger and Claudia Hardy (available from them); they are listed in the Directory under West Virginia. Our advisor for miscellaneous Akro Agate is Albert Morin, who is in the Directory under Massachusetts.

Concentric Rib

Creamer, dk gr, 1⁵⁄₁₆"	15.00
Cup, wht opaque, 1⁵⁄₁₆"	90.00
Pitcher, dk & med bl, 2⅞"	40.00
Plate, purple (rare), 3¼"	45.00
Saucer, wht opaque, 2¾"	4.00
Set, dk gr & ivory, 8-pc, MIB	110.00
Sugar bowl, lt bl, 1⁵⁄₁₆"	20.00
Teapot w/lid, Canary Yellow	30.00
Tumbler, pk or dk ivory, 2"	10.00

Concentric Ring

Creamer, lg, bl transparent, 1¾"	75.00
Creamer, sm, ivory or wht opaque, 1⅜"	20.00
Cup, lg, purple, 1¾"	100.00
Cup, sm, Canary Yellow, 1⅜"	95.00
Pitcher, sm, med or Royal Blue, 2⅞"	125.00
Plate, lg, bl/wht marbleized, 4¼"	70.00
Plate, sm, purple, 3⁵⁄₁₆"	45.00
Saucer, sm, bl transparent, 2¾"	30.00
Set, lg, bl & ivory marbleized, 21-pc, M (no box)	2,000.00
Set, sm, bl transparent, 8-pc, MIB	375.00
Sugar bowl, lg, wht opaque, 2⅜"	20.00
Sugar bowl, sm, Apple or dk gr, 1⅜"	20.00
Teapot, lg, Royal Blue, no lid, 2¾"	125.00
Teapot, sm, med or Royal Blue, no lid, 2⅜"	65.00
Teapot lid, sm, ivory or wht, 2⅜"	20.00
Tumbler, bl transparent, 2" (1 sz only)	32.00

Interior Panel

Set, green and white, 21-piece, MIB, $300.00.
(Photo courtesy Roger and Claudia Hardy)

Bowl, cereal; lg, med bl lustre, 3⅜"	40.00
Bowl, cereal; lg, topaz transparent, 3⅜"	26.00
Creamer, sm, Canary Yellow, 1⁵⁄₁₆"	70.00
Creamer, sm, Royal Blue, 1⁵⁄₁₆"	35.00
Plate, lg, oxblood & wht marbleized, 4¼"	30.00
Plate, lg, pk lustre, 4¼"	20.00
Plate, sm, pk lustre, 3⁵⁄₁₆"	15.00
Saucer, sm, topaz transparent, 2¾"	12.00
Set, lg, med bl or Canary Yellow, 21-pc, M (no box)	815.00
Set, lg, topaz transparent, 21-pc, MIB	550.00
Set, sm, Canary Yellow, 16-pc, M (no box)	560.00
Sugar bowl, lg, Royal Blue, 1½"	60.00
Sugar bowl, sm, dk gr lustre, 1⁵⁄₁₆"	95.00
Teapot, lg, lemonade & oxblood, no lid, 2¾"	300.00
Teapot, lg, Royal Blue, no lid, 2¾"	80.00
Teapot, sm, gr & wht marbleized, 2½"	65.00
Teapot lid, lg, gr transparent, 2¹¹⁄₁₆"	20.00
Teapot lid, lg, pk lustre, 2¹¹⁄₁₆"	25.00
Tumbler, gr transparent (1 sz made, used w/lg & sm sets)	18.00
Water set, sm, topaz or gr, pitcher+6 tumblers, 7-pc	155.00

Miss America

Creamer, wht w/decal, 1¾"	70.00
Plate, gr transparent, 4½"	50.00
Set, gr transparent, 8-pc, M (no box)	560.00
Set, red transparent red, serves 4, 17-pc, M (no box)	2,330.00
Set, wht opaque, serves 2, 11-pc, MIB	632.00
Sugar bowl lid, wht opaque, 2⅝"	50.00
Teapot, red onyx, 2½"	150.00
Teapot lid, red transparent, 2⅞"	225.00

Octagonal

Bowl, cereal; lg, dk gr, 3⅜"	18.00
Bowl, cereal; lg, wht or ivory, open hdls, 3⅜"	18.00
Creamer, lg, lemonade & oxblood, 1½"	70.00
Creamer, sm, pale bl, open hdl, 1¼"	30.00
Creamer, sm, pale bl, closed hdl, 1¼"	30.00
Cup, lg, dk gr, 1½"	15.00
Cup, sm, orange, 1¼"	40.00
Cup, sm, wht opaque or ivory, open hdl, 1¼"	45.00
Plate, lg, Apple Green, 4¼"	10.00
Plate, lg, turq or lt bl, 4¼"	25.00
Saucer, sm, Canary Yellow, 2¾"	12.00
Set, lg, dk gr/pk/orange, 17-pc, MIB	400.00
Set, sm, Apple Green/orange/Canary Yellow/pale bl/ivory, 16", MIB	435.00
Sugar bowl, lg, med or dk bl, open hdl, 1½"	40.00
Sugar bowl, lg, wht opaque or ivory, 1½"	20.00
Teapot, lg, dk gr, no lid, 3⅝"	25.00
Teapot, lg, med or dk bl, no lid, open hdl, 3⅝"	65.00
Teapot, sm, pale bl, open hdl, 3⅜"	40.00
Teapot, sm, Royal Blue, no lid, 3⅜"	40.00
Teapot lid, lg, pk, 2¾"	20.00
Teapot lid, lg, wht or ivory, 2¾"	20.00
Teapot lid, sm, ivory, 2"	15.00
Tumbler, sm, Apple Green, 2"	20.00

Raised Daisy

Creamer, sm, dk turq or dk bl, 1⁵⁄₁₆"	100.00
Plate, sm, dk turq or dk bl, 3"	28.00
Set, dk bl/dk gr/yel, serves 4, 19-pc, M (no box)	867.00
Sugar bowl, sm, lt or dk yel, 1⁵⁄₁₆"	35.00

Teapot, sm, dk gr, no lid, 2⅜" 50.00
Teapot lid, sm, dk turq or dk bl, 2¹⁄₁₆" 75.00
Tumbler, sm, Daisy, lt or dk yel, 2" 25.00
Tumbler, sm, plain, dk turq or dk bl, 2" 100.00
Water set, sm, Daisy, dk turq & yel, 7-pc 195.00

Stacked Disc

Creamer, sm, dk gr, 1⁵⁄₁₆" 15.00
Cup, sm, Canary Yellow, 1⁵⁄₁₆" 95.00
Pitcher, sm, med or dk bl, 2⅞" 90.00
Set, sm, dk bl/dk gr/Canary Yellow, serves 2, 8-pc, MIB.............120.00
Set, sm, dk gr/dk bl/pk/orange/wht, serves 4, 21-pc, MIB............335.00
Sugar bowl, sm, pk or dk ivory, 1⁵⁄₁₆" 25.00
Teapot lid, sm, dk gr, 2⁵⁄₁₆" 5.00
Tumbler, sm, wht opaque, 2" 7.00
Water set, sm, dk gr & wht, 7-pc, MIB..130.00

Stacked Disc and Interior Panel

Bowl, cereal; lg, dk gr, 3⅜" 50.00
Creamer, sm, med or Royal Blue, 1⅜" 20.00
Cup, lg, bl transparent, 1¾" 60.00
Pitcher, sm, bl transparent, 2⅞" 75.00
Saucer, sm, bl & wht marbleized, 2¾" 40.00
Set, lg, bl transparent, serves 4, 21-pc, MIB 1,200.00
Set, sm, bl & wht marbleized, serves 2, 8-pc, M (no box)...........520.00
Set, sm, bl transparent, serves 4, 21-pc, MIB 940.00
Sugar bowl, lg, med or Royal Blue, 1¾" 40.00
Teapot, lg, bl & wht marbleized, no lid, 2¾" 225.00
Tumbler, sm, gr transparent, 2" 18.00
Water set, sm, bl transparent, 6-pc, M (no box) 267.00

Stippled Band

Bowl, cereal; lg, gr transparent, rare, 3⅜" 125.00
Creamer, sm, gr transparent, 1¼"...85.00
Cup, lg, Azure Blue transparent, 1½" 45.00
Pitcher, sm, topaz transparent, 2⅞" 35.00
Plate, lg, gr transparent, 4¼"..10.00
Set, lg, Azure Blue transparent, serves 4, 17-pc, MIB.............1,050.00
Set, lg, topaz, serves 4, 17-pc, M (no box) 395.00
Set, sm, gr transparent, serves 2, 8-pc, M (no box).....................135.00
Set, sm, topaz transparent, serves 6, 28-pc, MIB 600.00
Sugar bowl, sm, gr transparent, 1¼" 85.00
Sugar bowl lid, lg, topaz transparent, 2" 50.00
Teapot, lg, Azure Blue transparent, 2⅝" 175.00
Teapot, sm, topaz transparent, no lid, 2⅜" 28.00
Teapot lid, lg, topaz transparent, 2⅝" 45.00
Teapot lid, sm, topaz transparent, 2⅜" 25.00
Tumbler, lg, topaz or gr transparent, 2⅛" 100.00
Tumbler, sm, topaz transparent, 1¾" 15.00
Water set, sm, topaz transparent, 7-pc, MIB 175.00

Miscellaneous

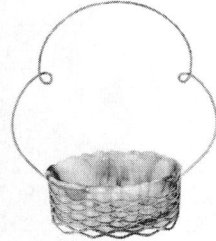

Basket, green and white marbleized, 3½x6", in 10½x9" metal frame, $28.00.

Ashtray, Hexagonal, marbleized, from $20 to..............................60.00
Ashtray, marbleized, 5" sq, from $60 to 90.00
Ashtray, shell form, marbleized, 2 to 4 colors, ea from $5 to.........15.00
Ashtray/match holder, Mexicali Hat, 3¼", from $25 to 30.00
Flowerpot, #1307, 5¼", from $350 to..400.00
Flowerpot, #1310, 4" 250.00
Flowerpot, Ribbed Top, #291½", any color, 2¼", from $8 to 10.00
Flowerpot, Ribbed Top, #294, any color, 4"..................................25.00
Jardiniere, Graduated Dart (Type I) #306, sq mouth, marbleized, 5"..50.00
Jardiniere, Ribs & Flutes #306CF, sq mouth, solid color, 5" 35.00
Powder jar, Concentric Ring (Type 1), #760, marbleized, 3-toed..40.00
Powder jar, Ivy #323, solid or crystal 100.00
Powder jar, Sawtooth, solid orange, from $300 to.......................350.00
Puff box, Colonial Lady, amber 1,200.00
Puff box, Colonial Lady, Royal Blue..225.00
Puff box, Scottie Dog, lt bl...110.00
Puff box, Scottie Dog, med bl 125.00
Tray, Victory Safety, marbleized, 8-pointed star shape, 6"...........400.00
Vase, Cornucopia, marbleized, plain ft, 3¼", from $6 to 10.00
Vase, Floral, tab hdls, marbleized, 3¼", from $10 to 15.00
Vase, Graduated Dart, #312, marbleized, 8¾", from $75 to..........100.00
Vase, Graduated Dart Type II, scalloped, marbleized, 6¼", $110 to...125.00
Vase, Grecian urn, marbleized, 6-sided ft, 3¼"..............................10.00
Vase, Ribs & Flutes, #311, solid color, 8", from $165 to 195.00
Vivaudou, apothecary jar, lt bl...100.00
Vivaudou, mortar & pestle, blk..18.00
Vivaudou, powder puff box, bl or pk 90.00
Vivaudou, powder puff box, marbleized 300.00
Vivaudou, shaving mug, blk..45.00

Alamo Pottery

Alamo art pottery (1945 – 1951) was a division of the Alamo Pottery of San Antonio, Texas, which was primarily a maker of sanitary ware (bathroom fixtures). The art pottery division was founded by Jake Rowe, Richard Potter, and Bruce Blunt, and produced vitreous china items which have survived the decades without crazing and with the high gloss glazes still gleaming as if new. (Mrs. Potter was a valuable resource in compiling information about Alamo history.)

Rowe, Potter, and Blunt developed glazes, processes, and mold shapes from which came styles and colors that ran the gamut from elegant, classically styled vases to whimsical figurals, and from pale translucent aquas and yellows to bold primary greens, blues, and yellows. The vast majority of the pieces are monochromatic, and the rare sponge- or spatter-ware pieces are at a premium.

Alamo is usually marked with a mold number (from 701 to 908, and P-2, P-3, and presumably P-1). Many also have an oval Alamo Pottery ink stamp in either black or blue. Bottoms are generally unglazed, although a few pitchers with glazed bottoms exist. Flea bites in the glaze are fairly common and unless excessive are tolerated by most collectors. Crazing and staining are nonexistent, and virtually all interiors are fully glazed. These items were originally intended for the floral trade, and most sold for less than $3.00.

The art pottery division of Alamo closed in 1951 due to high costs of storing and shipping. Rowe, Potter, and Blunt moved to Gilmer, Texas, and founded Gilmer Pottery (see Gilmer listing), which produced many items often mistaken for Alamo. Our advisor for this category is Suzanne Knight; she is listed in the Directory under Texas.

Bowl, #245, 3x6" 9.00
Bowl, pet feeding; #730, duck, bear & bunny on sides, 7" dia.......33.00
Figurine, swan, #725, 5½x5"..30.00
Flowerpot, #829-5, diagonal waves, 5"...12.00

Flowerpot, #829-9, diagonal waves, 8½" 30.00
Flowerpot, #902-5, ribbed, 5x6x4" 18.50
Pitcher, #757, 4¼" 20.00
Pitcher, water, #760, diagonal waves, 7½" 35.00
Vase, #718, rnd base, sq top, 8½x5½" 40.00
Vase, #722, ruffled, 7¼" 15.00
Vase, #740, 10¾" 60.00
Vase, #742, 7x12" 45.00
Vase, #773, scalloped sides & top 16.50
Vase, #829-6, 5x6" dia 16.50
Vase, #829-7, diagonal waves, 7" 30.00
Vase, #900-7, flares to 7" at top, 7" 23.00
Vase, P-2, lt gr, 6¾" 48.00
Vase, 15" 110.00

Alexandrite

Alexandrite is a type of art glass introduced around the turn of the century by Thomas Webb and Sons of England. It is recognized by its characteristic shading, pale yellow to rose and blue at the edge of the item. Although other companies (Moser, for example) produced glass they called alexandrite, only examples made by Webb possess all the described characteristics and command premium prices. Amount and intensity of blue determines value. Our advisors for this category are Betty and Clarence Maier; they are listed in the Directory under Pennsylvania.

Bowl, ruffled, 2½x5" 900.00
Pitcher, Honeycomb, amber hdl, mini, 2½" 1,800.00
Plate, Honeycomb, ruffled, 5½" 850.00
Vase, floriform, 8 optic ribs, scalloped/flared rim, ftd, 6½" 1,345.00

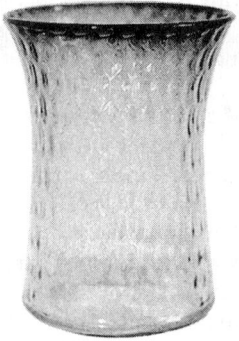

Vase, Honeycomb, EX blue edge, 4", $1,950.00. (Photo courtesy Betty and Clarence Maier)

Vase, ovoid w/6-sided rim, 2½" 1,000.00

Almanacs

The earliest evidence indicates that almanacs were used as long ago as Ancient Egypt. Throughout the Dark Ages they were circulated in great volume and were referred to by more people than any other book except the Bible. *The Old Farmer's Almanac* first appeared in 1793 and has been issued annually since that time. Usually more of a pamphlet than a book (only a few have hard covers), the almanac provided planting and harvesting information to farmers, weather forecasts for seamen, medical advice, household hints, mathematical tutoring, postal rates, railroad schedules, weights and measures, receipts, and jokes. Before 1800 the information was unscientific and based entirely on astrology and folklore. The first almanac in America was printed in 1639 by William Pierce Mariner; it contained data of this nature. One of the best-known editions, Ben Franklin's *Poor*

Richard's Almanac, was introduced in 1732 and continued to be printed for twenty-five years.

By the nineteenth century, merchants saw the advertising potential in a publication so widely distributed, and the advertising almanac evolved. These were distributed free of charge by drug stores and mercantiles and were usually somewhat lacking in information, containing simply a calendar, a few jokes, and a variety of ads for quick remedies and quack cures.

Today their concept and informative, often amusing text make almanacs popular collectibles that may usually be had at reasonable prices. Because they were printed in such large numbers and often saved from year to year, their prices are still low. Most fall within a range of $4.00 to $15.00. Very common examples may be virtually worthless; those printed before 1860 are especially collectible. Quite rare and highly prized are the Kate Greenaway 'Almanacks,' printed in London from 1883 to 1897. These are illustrated with her drawings of children, one for each calendar month. See also Greenaway, Kate.

1693, Apollo Anglicanus, The English Apollo, 45-pg, G.............90.00
1847, Boston Almanac w/Business & Railroad Directory, 192-pg, VG ..40.00
1863, Ayer's American Almanac, VG 25.00
1885, The Old Farmer's Almanac, VG 20.00
1892, The World Almanac & Bureau of Information, VG...........70.00
1895, Warner's Safe Cure Almanac, 32-pg, 6x8½", VG 20.00
1898, Courier-Journal Almanac, Louisville, 448-pg, 5x7", VG 25.00
1898, Kickapoo Almanac, 32-pg, 6x8", VG+ 45.00
1902, Dr D Jayne's Medical Almanac & Guide to Health, 36-pg, VG...18.00
1902, The World Almanac & Encyclopedia, 608-pg, VG 20.00
1904, Studebakers Farmer's Almanac & Weather Forecast, 60-pg, VG...35.00
1917, International Harvester Almanac, 48-pg, VG+ 45.00
1919, Health Almanac, US Public Health Service, 48-pg, VG 15.00
1921, Brooklyn Eagle Almanac, 482-pg.............................85.00
1924, World Almanac & Book of Facts, VG+ 20.00
1927, Bell System Telephone Almanac, 30-pg, 7x10", VG+.........22.00
1927, Spaulding's Athletic Almanac #9, 250-pg+, VG+ 25.00
1936, Shell Olympics Sports Almanac, 48-pg, 6x3", VG 15.00
1939, Dr Kilmer's Swamp-Root Almanac & Dream Book, VG.....14.00
1946, American Nautical Almanac, 318-pg, VG+ 17.50
1961, National Catholics Almanac, EX 15.00

Aluminum

Aluminum, though being the most abundant metal in the earth's crust, always occurs in combination with other elements. Before a practical method for its refinement was developed in the late nineteenth century, articles made of aluminum were very expensive. After the process for commercial smelting was perfected in 1916, it became profitable to adapt the ductile, nontarnishing material to many uses.

By the late '30s, novelties, trays, pitchers, and many other tableware items were being produced. They were often handcrafted with elaborate decoration. Russel Wright designed a line of lovely pieces such as lamps, vases, and desk accessories that are becoming very collectible. Many who crafted the ware marked it with their company logo, and these signed pieces are attracting the most interest. Wendell August Forge (Grove City, PA) is a mark to watch for; this firm was the first to produce hammered aluminum (it is still made there today), and some of their examples are particularly nice. Upwardly mobile market values reflect their popularity with today's collectors. In general, 'spun' aluminum is from the '30s or early '40s, and 'hammered' aluminum is from the '30s to the '60s.

For further information, refer to *Collectible Aluminum, An Identification and Value Guide* (2000 updated values) by Everett Grist, listed in the Directory under Tennessee; *Affordable Art Deco* by Ken Hutchison and Greg Johnson; *Vintage Bar Ware* by Stephen Visakay; and *Collector's*

Encyclopedia of Russel Wright by Ann Kerr. Another excellent reference is *Hammered Aluminum, Hand Wrought Collectibles,* by our advisor, Dannie Woodard, see the Directory for Texas.

Ashtray, daisies, 3 rests, Everlast, 6" dia.................................**20.00**
Ashtray, pine cone, center 3-bar rest, fluted, W August Forge, 6" dia...**65.00**
Basket, acorns/leaves, rolled rim, braided hdl, Continental, 12" ...**25.00**
Basket, mums, sq w/upturned rim, finger-wave hdl, Continental, 8"..**25.00**
Basket, sailing ship, fluted rim, sq-knot dbl hdl, Federal Silver, 9"...**35.00**
Basket, tulip, hexagon w/serrated rim, dogwood cut-out hdl, R Kent, 7"..**35.00**
Beverage spoons, Tallstirs, anodized, Color Craft, 6 on card **40.00**
Bookends, leaping bass figures w/water sprays, Bruce Cox, 7", pr...**185.00**
Bowl, bamboo, serrated rim, Everlast, 1x8" dia **10.00**
Bowl, dogwood, fluted/crimped rim, W August Forge, 7" dia........**20.00**
Bowl, dogwood/butterfly, ribbon/bead rim, anodized, A Armour, 8" sq..**25.00**
Bowl, ducks in flight, scalloped rim, W August Forge, 10" dia......**65.00**
Bowl, tulip/hammered, serrated, loop hdls, ped ft, R Kent, 2x10 dia.....**35.00**
Candle holder, oak leaf shape w/acorn cup & decor, B Fox, 10" L...**35.00**
Candy dish, dbl butterfly dishes w/center loop hdl, anodized, Everlast...**15.00**
Candy dish, leaf form w/sailing ship, scrolled hdl, World Hand Forge...**15.00**
Casserole, dogwood & butterfly, ring finial, tab hdls, A Armour, 10".....**50.00**
Casserole, hammered, marble finial & 3 ft, ribbon hdls, unmk, 6" dia...**10.00**
Chocolate pot, mums, hinged lid w/petal finial, Continental, 10"...**85.00**
Cigarette box, duck applied to lid, L Argental, 1½x3x5" **75.00**
Coasters, bamboo, set of 4 on ftd trivet, Everlast, 3½" dia...........**20.00**

Coffee urn, Chrysanthemum pattern, Continental Silver, EX, $85.00; Coaster set, from $25.00 to $35.00.

Coffee urn, mums, glass ball finial, spigot, Continental, 15" **75.00**
Compote, hammered w/tulip-&-ribbon finial, open ribbon stem, unmk...**15.00**
Compote, wild rose, stem ft, serrated rim, Continental, 5x5" dia..**20.00**
Creamer & sugar bowl w/tray, dbl loop hdls & finial, Buenilum ...**15.00**
Crumb tray & brush, grapevine, Lucite brush w/hammered hdl, Everlast...**10.00**
Double boiler, polished w/wood hdl & finial, Pyrex insert, Buenilum .**10.00**
Dresser dish, single rose on lid, sq beaded glass dish, Farberware ..**10.00**
Fondue pot w/sterno cup & base, beaded lip, wood hdl, Buenilum .**5.00**
Gravy boat w/plate, mums, spouted bowl w/hdl, serrated, Continental..**25.00**
Hurricane lamp, grape & leaf, loop hdl, glass chimney, Everlast, 9".......**20.00**
Ice bucket, tulip, lid attached by chain to hdl, ftd, unmk, 7x8" dia.........**40.00**
Ice bucket (open), hammered, fluted rim, barbell hdls, Everlast, 5x10"..**15.00**
Key chains, various patterns, DeMarsh Forge, ea **12.00**
Lazy Susan, tulip sprays/hammered, flower/ribbon decor, R Kent, 18" ..**15.00**
Matchbox covers, pine cone or bittersweet, W August Forge, ea..**65.00**
Napkin holder, flower & ribbon, 4-ftd fan shape, serrated, unmk, 6" L..**15.00**
Paperweight, ducks in flight, W August Forge, 3x5" L **75.00**
Pitcher, acorn & leaf, bulbous, coiled hdl, Continental, 8"...........**30.00**
Pitcher, bamboo, ice lip, rolled rim, Everlast, 8" **35.00**
Pitcher, wild rose/hammered, sm ice lip, ear hdl, Continental, 8" ...**40.00**
Plate, alphabet edge, unmk, 7" dia..**30.00**
Plate, dogwood & butterfly, fluted rim, A Armour, 10" dia **45.00**

Popcorn popper, ducks on hinged lid, W August Forge, 9" dia......**75.00**
Sherbets, anodized bases w/fluted glass inserts, unmk, set of 6 ......**35.00**
Silent butler, bird on branch, fluted, open wire hdl, NS Co, 6" dia.**15.00**
Strainer, woven wire basket, red wood hdl, 8"...............................**8.50**
Tidbit, ducks in flight, 2-tier rectangles, Everlast, 12" **35.00**
Tray, bar; anchor & rope w/sea gulls, Everlast, 9x15"....................**30.00**
Tray, bar; water lilies, self-hdld, A Armour, 8x17" **45.00**
Tray, bread; mums, 2 leaves on scalloped rim, Continental, 8x11" ..**25.00**
Tray, bread; wild rose, oval/serrated, tab hdls, Continental, 6x13"...**15.00**
Tray, relish; geese in flight, 4-part, self-hdld, A Armour, 5x16" **75.00**
Tray, sandwich; bittersweet, W August Forge, 8x11" **35.00**
Tray, serving; fisherman/hammered, fluted, Hand Forged, 18" dia.**65.00**
Tray, serving; goldfish fr by beading, walnut hdls, unmk, 10x14" ..**45.00**
Tray, serving; hinged folding w/center open hdl, Everlast, 13½x12" ..**25.00**
Tray, serving; horse heads/hammered, bar hdls, Everlast, 12x16" ..**25.00**
Tray, serving; polished w/fox hunt scenes on hdls, Kensington, 14x23"...**20.00**
Tray, serving; sailing ship/hammered, bar hdls, A Armour, 9x13".**65.00**
Tray, snack; quail in flight on scalloped oval, W August Forge, 7x9" ...**60.00**
Trivit, pine cones, oval, Everlast, 8x11"...**5.00**
Vase, mums, cylindrical w/serrated incurvate rim/ft, Continental, 10" ...**85.00**
Wastebasket, pine cones, flared fluted rim, W August Forge, 11" ...**150.00**
Water set, anodized, 7" pitcher+6 5" tumblers **75.00**

AMACO, American Art Clay Co.

AMACO is the logo of the American Art Clay Co. Inc., founded in Indianapolis, Indiana, in 1919, by Ted O. Philpot. They produced a line of art pottery from 1931 through 1938. The company is still in business but now produces only supplies, implements, and tools for the ceramic trade.

Values for AMACO have risen sharply, especially those for figurals, items with Art Deco styling, and pieces with uncommon shapes. Our advisor for this category is Virginia Heiss; she is listed in the Directory under Indiana.

Bowl, med bl, #145, 2½x11¾"..**150.00**
Bowl, yel gloss, hdls, 3 ball feet, #167, 5¼x8¾" **175.00**
Figurine, male dancer, wht, #156, 14¾".....................................**350.00**
Ginger jar, bl, w/lid, #131, 9"...**275.00**
Vase, dk bl gloss, hdls, #39, 6½" **95.00**
Vase, dk gr matt, hdls, 4 buttress ft, #19, 12½".........................**350.00**
Vase, lt gr matt, swollen bottom, #44, 7½" **95.00**
Vase, tan matt, hdls, swollen middle, #34, 11" **150.00**
Vase, wht matt, w/scroll hdls, #49, 10".......................................**125.00**
Vase, yel gloss, #S-5, 5½"..**65.00**

Amberina

Amberina, one of the earliest types of art glass, was developed in 1883 by Joseph Locke of the New England Glass Company. The trademark was registered by W.L. Libbey, who often signed his name in script within the pontil.

Amberina was made by adding gold powder to the batch, which produced glass in the basic amber hue. Part of the item, usually the top, was simply reheated to develop the characteristic deep red or fuchsia shading. Early amberina was mold blown, but cut and pressed amberina was also produced. The rarest type is plated amberina, made by New England for a short time after 1886. It has been estimated that less than 2,000 pieces were ever produced. Other companies, among them Hobbs and Brockunier, Mt. Washington Glass Company, and Sowerby's Ellison Glassworks of England, made their own versions, being careful to change the name of their product to avoid infringing on Libbey's patent. Prices realized at auction seem to be erratic, to say the least, and dealers appear to be 'testing the waters' with prices that start out very high only to be reduced later if the item does not sell at the original asking price. A lot of amberina glassware is of a more recent vintage — look for evidence of an early production, since the later wares are worth much less than glassware that can be attributed to the older makers. Generic amberina with hand-painted flowers will bring lower prices as well. Our values are taken from auction results and dealer lists, omitting the extremely high and low ends of the range. See also Libbey.

Key: NE — New England Glass Company

Bowl, Daisy & Button, triangular, Hobbs & Brockunier, 4x10x8½"..175.00
Bowl, Dmn Quilt, tricorner, 4½" 80.00
Bowl, ruffled, NE, 2½x5" 375.00
Bowl, Swirl, Mt WA, 2¾x4½"..295.00
Bowl, Venetian Dmn, raised on int/ext, EX color, NE, 2¼x8"....690.00
Butter dish, Dmn Quilt, amber pigtail finial, crimped 6½" base, NE...2,500.00
Centerpiece, Daisy & Button, boat shape, Hobbs & Brockunier, 14" L .950.00
Creamer, Venetian Dmn, EX color, str flaring sides, NE, 4⅜".....635.00
Cup, punch; Dmn Quilt, amber reeded hdl, 2½" 75.00
Cup, punch; Dmn Quilt, ribbed hdl, NE.......................................185.00
Goblet, deep color, ball connector, deep amber & red stem, 8½" ...450.00
Mug, Int Rib, bulbous bottom, Mt WA, 3x3¾" 275.00
Mustard pot, Pillar Ribbed, ovoid, SP lid (worn), NE, 3x2"........750.00
Pitcher, #131 (lg Hobnails), tankard form, Mt WA, rare, 5½" ...3,000.00
Pitcher, Invt T'print, EX color, 5¾x5" 345.00
Pitcher, Swirl, amber hdl, 8" 275.00
Pitcher, Venetian Dmn, str/flaring sides, amber hdl, NE, 8½x5"..690.00
Plates, Daisy & Button, sq w/shaped corners, Hobbs, 5½", set of 6.........450.00
Rose bowl, Dmn Quilt, amber rigaree at neck, pinched sides, NE, 4¾" .635.00
Rose bowl, Dmn Quilt, flashed color, 3 scroll ft, Midwestern, 3x5" 175.00
Rose bowl, Dmn Quilt, 4 appl 'wishbones'/prunts, NE, 4¾x5"...2,250.00
Shade, ruffled, Mt WA, 4¼" 575.00
Shaker, Int Rib, 2-pc lid (worn/dent), 4x1¾" 285.00
Shakers, Honeycomb, cylindrical w/dome lids, NE, 3¾x1½", pr...380.00
Shakers, Pillar Ribbed, NE, 4x1½", pr 690.00
Spittoon, hourglass form w/ruffled rim 450.00
Sugar bowl, Invt T'print, sq mouth, ogee sides w/amber hdls, open, 4" ..375.00
Syrup pitcher, Invt T'print, bulbous, SP top has spout/hdl, NE, 5½"...1,200.00
Toothpick holder, Baby Invt T'print, bbl shape, 2½" 225.00
Toothpick holder, Baby Invt T'print, fuchsia, 2¼x2½" 350.00
Toothpick holder, Baby Invt T'print, sq top, NE, 2¼" 295.00
Toothpick holder, Dmn Quilt, wide tightly crimped flaring rim, NE, 4"...750.00
Toothpick holder, hat shape w/tricon rim, 2¼" 285.00
Tumbler, champagne; Int Rib, NE, 4x2½" 125.00
Tumbler, lemonade; diagonal ribs, gold leaves, amber reed hdl, 5¼"...225.00
Vase, gold butterflies, amber rigaree, 7¾"....................................100.00
Vase, Invt T'print, folded rim, 3 amber reed ft, EX color, NE, 7x5" ..1,500.00
Vase, lily; Optic Rib, rim w/3 shaped lobes, EX color, NE, 12½x5" 575.00
Vase, lily; Optic Rib, 3-lobe rim, NE, w/short collar rim, 7½" 500.00
Vase, lily; 15" 825.00
Wine glass, optic ribs, EX color, stemmed, NE, 4½x2½" 200.00

Plated Amberina

Bowl, 5 inverted lobes, Aurora/NE Glass Works label, 7½" 3,500.00
Lemonade, amber hdl..1,800.00
Pitcher, water; outstanding color, deep amber hdl, 7x7" 10,350.00
Punch cup, bbl shape, 2¾x3¾" 2,250.00
Tumbler, EX color, 4" 2,800.00
Tumbler, 3¾" 1,600.00
Vase, lily form, 6¼" 2,800.00

American Encaustic Tiling Co.

A.E. Tile was organized in 1879 in Zanesville, Ohio. Until its closing in 1935, they produced beautiful ornamental and architectural tile equal to the best European imports. They also made vases, figurines, and novelty items with exceptionally fine modeling and glazes. For a more thorough study we recommend *American Art Pottery* by Dick Sigafoose. See also Tiles.

Figure, woman with urn, ivory with black and gold accents, signed Griffin, paper label, 11x8x6", $750.00.

Bookends, putti play w/rabbit, matt blk & silver, mk 325.00
Box, Oriental scene emb on orange crystalline matt, 7½" 200.00
Inkwell, matt blk & silver, dbl, w/logo 255.00
Plaque, cavalier w/sword, pk majolica, fr, 5x18".........................325.00
Plaque, lion & lioness, dusty rose, 12x6", pr 695.00
Tile, forest landscape (detailed), 6", in fr 300.00
Trivet, AETCo logo in center, 8-sided, mc, 6" dia.......................140.00
Vase, red-brn semigloss, 4 full-length buttresses, 8", NM 350.00

American Indian Art

That time when the American Indian was free to practice the crafts and culture that was his heritage has always held a fascination for many. They were a people who appreciated beauty of design and colorful decoration in their furnishings and clothing; and because instruction in their crafts was a routine part of their rearing, they were well accomplished. Several tribes developed areas in which they excelled. The Navajo were weavers and silversmiths, the Zuni, lapidaries. Examples of their craftsmanship are very valuable. Today even the work of contemporary Indian artists — weavers, silversmiths, carvers, and others — is highly collectible. Unless otherwise noted, values are for items with no obvious damage or excessive wear (EX/NM). For a more thorough study we recommend *Arrowheads and Projectile Points*; *Indian Axes and Stone Related Artifacts*; *Indian Artifacts of the Midwest, Books I through IV*; and *Collector's Guide to Indian Pipes, Identification and Values*. All have been written by our advisor, Lar Hothem; you will find his address in the Directory under Ohio.

Key:
bw — beadwork   p-h — prehistoric
dmn — diamond   s-s — sinew sewn

Apparel and Accessories

Before the white traders brought the Indian women cloth from which to sew their garments and beads to use for decorating them, clothing was made from skins sewn together with sinew, usually made of animal tendon. Porcupine quills were dyed bright colors and woven into bags and armbands and used to decorate clothing and moccasins. Examples of early quillwork are scarce today and highly collectible.

Early in the nineteenth century, beads were being transported via pony pack trains. These 'pony' beads were irregular shapes of opaque glass imported from Venice. Nearly always blue or white, they were twice as large as the later 'seed' beads. By 1870 translucent beads in many sizes and colors had been made available, and Indian beadwork had become commercialized. Each tribe developed its own distinctive methods and preferred decorations, making it possible for collectors today to determine the origin of many items. Soon after the turn of the century, the craft of beadworking began to diminish.

Belt, Crow, leather w/brass tacks in panel design, ca 1930, 39x1½"...**70.00**
Collar & tie, Crow, full bw, ca 1950..**550.00**
Dress, Blackfeet, bw & bugle beads on red wool, 1890s, 46x35"..**2,000.00**
Garters, Chippewa, loomed, mc bw, w/drops, 9x3".....................**200.00**
Gauntlets, Plateau, floral bw & fringe, 1930s, 12x6½"................**250.00**
Hat, Karok, tightly woven fez type, ca 1920, 3x7".......................**475.00**
Hat, Nez Perce, woven cornhusk/bear grass/& hemp, 1920s, 7½x8"..**800.00**
Leggings, Cheyenne, s-s bw on tanned/ochred antelope hide, 1870s, 18"..**1,100.00**
Leggings, Nez Perce, trade cloth panels w/bw & trim, 1900s, 31x22"..**180.00**
Leggings, Ute, wide & narrow bw strip on ea, 1930s, 30x20".....**475.00**
Moccasins, Arapaho, s-s buffalo hide, ca 1890, 9"....................**1,200.00**
Moccasins, Cree, buckskin, mc floral bw toes, high vamps, 1920s, 10"..**160.00**
Moccasins, Cree, s-s buckskin w/bw tradecloth insert/toes, 1890s, 10"....**225.00**
Moccasins, Crow, bw on yel ochred buckskin, buffalo soles, 1890s, 10"..**900.00**
Moccasins, Crow, full geometric bw on wht, 1910s, 10"..............**800.00**
Moccasins, Crow, s-s buffalo hide, ornate geometric bw, 1900, 10"..**250.00**
Moccasins, Crow lady's, high-top buckskin w/floral bw, 10"........**160.00**
Moccasins, Potowatomi, buckskin w/bw flaps & toes, 1890s, 9½"..**250.00**
Moccasins, Sioux, s-s, full bw, rawhide soles, 1930s, 10"............**275.00**
Moccasins, Sioux, wht roses w/mc stems on dk red, rpr, 10½"........**440.00**
Outfit, Iroquois, bw on velvet, 1910s, jacket+pants+feather bonnet..**325.00**
Robe, Plains, buffalo hide w/EX pnting (faded), 19th C, 36x31"...**400.00**
Sash, Chippewa, full bw belt w/red wool fringe, 1910s, 33x5"....**650.00**
Sash, Hopi, hand woven, fringed & embr traditional style, 1950s, 36"..**275.00**
Shawl, Sioux, trade cloth, by Jessie American Horse, 1940s, 72x54"......**225.00**
Shirt, war; Blackfoot, geometric bw strips & bibs, fringe, 1880s, 56"...**8,000.00**

Bags and Cases

The Indians used bags for many purposes, and most display excellent form and workmanship. Of the types listed below, many collectors consider the pipe bag to be the most desirable form. Pipe bags were long, narrow, leather and bead or quillwork creations made to hold tobacco in a compartment at the bottom and the pipe, with the bowl removed from the stem, in the top. Long buckskin fringe was used as trim and complemented the quilled and beaded design to make the bag a masterpiece of Indian art.

Apache, hide w/mc bw stars, fringe, 1890s, 6x6"..........................**500.00**
Apache, throw-over style, shell & tin dangles, 1890s, 36x8½"..**1,700.00**
Arapaho, dispatch case, bw on wht leather, bugle beads/fringe, 1880s.**1,900.00**
Arapaho, medicine, parfleche, pnt, 1880s....................................**300.00**
Crow, medicine pouch, bw on ochred buckskin, 20th C, 11x3"..**110.00**
Crow, parfleche, mineral pnt, 20th C, 11x19"............................**700.00**
Crow, tepee, bw on tanned elk hide, ca 1910, matched pr.......**6,500.00**
Great Lakes, bandolier, trade cloth, contour/floral bw, 1880s, 35x14".**1,600.00**
Mandan, pipe, yel ochred, s-s buffalo hide w/quillwork, 1860s, 16x8"....**225.00**
Nez Perce, bandolier, bw on red stroud strap, 20th C, 12x14".**4,750.00**
Nez Perce, flat cornhusk w/trade yarn design, ca 1900, 6½x7½"..**1,100.00**
Nez Perce, twined cornhusk, muted geometrics/pines, 1900s, 10x12"..**650.00**
Plateau, awl, conical w/bw, w/cvd bone awl, 1930s, 8x1"...........**300.00**
Plateau, belt pouch, bird bw on pk w/contour bw, 1890s, 5x4½"...**850.00**

Sioux, flap, much bw, made from war shirt bib, ca 1900, 13x6½"...**600.00**

Baskets

In the following listings, examples are basket form and coiled unless noted otherwise.

Apache, bowl, finely coiled, butterfly & cross design, 3x10".......**800.00**
Apache, canteen, embedded pitch, latigo hdl, ca 1900, 8x3"......**500.00**
Atsugewi, bowl, full twist o/l w/linear designs, maidenhair fern, 3x5"..**165.00**

California Mission (probably Diegueño), olla, natural and dyed juncas with grass, April 1, 1907, woven with floral design, 17x16", $8,250.00. (Photo courtesy Garth's Auctions)

Chemehuevi, tray, simple dbl-ring pattern, 1920s, 2¼x8".......**1,200.00**
Chitimacha, bowl, chain link design, vegetal dyes, L Darden, 4½".**1,150.00**
Chitimacha, ox-heart shape, alligator entrails design, 1890s, 9"......**5,750.00**
Chitimacha, ox-heart shape, blk bird's eye pattern, 1890s, 3x4"......**2,000.00**
Karok, bowl, half-twined o/l stepped design, red stain, 4x6½"....**600.00**
Maidu, natural & peeled redbud, stepped/paneled design, 4x6"..**770.00**
NE Woodlands, rectangular, red/bl decor, cvd hdls, 1850s, 13x33x20"..**865.00**
Nootka/Makah, bottle cover w/lid, whaling scene, 1950s, 4½x1¾".......**120.00**
Ojibway, bark/sweetgrass, red & wht quillwork, w/lid, 1940s, 3x5".........**275.00**
Ojibway, porcupine quills on bark, eagle design on lid,1940s, 4x8"........**450.00**
Papago, bowl, str sides, Saguaro cactus decor, 1970s, 7x12"........**100.00**
Papago, owl form w/wings, horns/etc, Alice Juan, ca 1965, 8x8"..**60.00**
Pima, allover geometrics, ca 1930, 11x13"...................................**600.00**
Pima, bowl, classic fret & cross design, 1930s, 4½x15"...............**650.00**
Pima, bowl, expanding sides, geometrics, 1950s, 5x9½"..............**200.00**
Pima, bowl, hourglass designs, ca 1935, 2x11"............................**250.00**
Pima, bowl, stacked arrow point & cross motif, 1960s, 4x9½"....**275.00**
Pima, bowl, V designs, matching star-design lid, 1935, 1¾x2½"...**850.00**
Pima, chicken-scratch dancers, w/lid, ca 1935, 1¼x1¼"...........**700.00**
Pima, swastikas & negative triangle decor, 1930s, 2½x12½".......**500.00**
Pima, tray, central star/stair/triangle designs, 1930s, ½x6¼".......**200.00**
Pima, tray, old turtlebk pattern, 1920s, 2½x11½" **450.00**
Pima, 5 dancers interspersed w/crosses, 1900s, 4½x7½".............**325.00**
Pit River, bottle cover, traditional design, gr bottle, 1930s, 8"....**300.00**
Pomo, bottle cover, traditional design, 1920s, 12x4"..................**325.00**
Pomo, burden, traditional conical form, ca 1870, 18x21"........**1,400.00**
Pomo, fully feathered, ca 1960, mini, ½x1½"...............................**180.00**
Quinault, gathering, banded design, ca 1900, 9x6".....................**150.00**
Salish, trunk, woven imbrications, lid w/fringe, 1935, 8x12x6½"......**160.00**
Tlingit, spruce root w/dyed beargrass & fern false embr, 5x8".....**600.00**
Tlingit, twined, mc geometrics, ca 1910, sm rpr, 4x3".................**160.00**
Ute, mc human faces all around, 1980s, 4x18"...........................**550.00**
Ute, tray, Corn Maiden Kachina pattern, 1970s, 19½" dia.........**425.00**
Wakeshan, twined, branching design, w/lid, 3x4".......................**275.00**
Yavapai Apache, deer/butterflies/cactus/etc decor, 1935, 13x13" ...**1,300.00**
Yurok, twined, mc quail topknot design, 1910, 3x5½".................**250.00**
2nd Mesa Hopi, plaque, Kachina figure, 1940s, 13½"................**325.00**

2nd Mesa Hopi, plaque, red/blk/yel radiating design, 1940s, 16" ...**275.00**

Blades and Points

Relics of this type usually display characteristics of a general area, time period, or a particular location. With study, those made by the Plains Indians are easily discerned from those of the West Coast. Because modern man has imitated the art of the Indian by reproducing these artifacts through modern means, use caution before investing your money in 'too good to be authentic' specimens. For a more thorough study we recommend *Field Guide to Flint Arrowheads and Knives of the North American Indian* by Lawrence N. and Steven N. Tulley, *Arrowheads and Projectile Points*, and *Indian Artifacts of the Midwest, Books I through IV*, by Lar Hothem.

Bi-pointed, gray flint, minor edge rstr, Mississippian, 8x1¾" ...**1,000.00**
Bifurcated, colored chert, Archaic, IN, 2½x1½" ...**50.00**
Clovis, gr & tan hornstone, fluted, early Paleo, 2½" ...**725.00**
Clovis, wht Burlington chert, fluted, early Paleo, 3⅜" ...**850.00**
Corner-notched, dk Upper Mercer flint, early Archaic, OH, 4" .**225.00**
Dovetail/St Charles, reddish hornstone, Archaic, IN, 4½x1¾" ..**375.00**
Hardin, swirly gray flint, Archaic, IL, 11⅛x5x⅜" ...**400.00**
Lanceolate, speckled chert, late Paleo, IN, 5⅜x1⅛" ...**250.00**
Leaf shape, caramel chert, thin, edge work, Adena, IL, 5½x2½" ..**275.00**
Palmer, chert, corner notches, serrated edges, Archaic, KY, 3¼" ...**400.00**
Pine Tree, bl-gray flint, basal granding, serrated, Archaic, 2¼" ..**250.00**
Robbins Adena, striated Flintridge, early Woodland, OH, 4⅜" ..**350.00**
Sedalia, mottled Burlington chert, late Archaic, MO, 3½x1⅛" ...**40.00**
Side-notch, chert, Archaic, IA, 3¼" ...**25.00**
Stanfield (Cobb triangular), bl-gray flint, EX patina, Archaic, KY, 4" ...**425.00**
Stilwell, caramel chert, serrated, early Archaic, IA, 3½" ...**175.00**
Turkey-tail, gray & cream flint, early Woodland, IL, 6¼" ...**400.00**

Blankets

Chimayo, geometrics on turq ground, ca 1940, 46x70" ...**200.00**
Lakota, strip, s-s w/full bw on buffalo hide, 1880s, 63x3½" ...**2,750.00**
Navajo, dbl-weave, hand loomed, ca 1920, 31x62" ...**110.00**
Navajo, natural wool transitional w/stripes, 1930s, 57x54" ...**225.00**
Navajo, saddle, hand-spun wool, geometrics, 1950s, 30x33" ...**190.00**
Navajo, saddle, Sunday type w/mc fringe, ca 1970, 30x28" ...**225.00**
Navajo, saddle (dbl), traditional hand spun wool, 1930s, 32x58" ..**225.00**
Navajo transitional, line & sq designs, 1920s, 69x72" ...**325.00**
Navajo, woman's wearing; striped, 1890s, 48x65" ...**325.00**

Ceremonial Items

Amulet, Plains, fringed hide with allover multicolor beadwork, 5¼" (excluding fringe), $700.00.

Bandolier, Sioux, 2-row brass beads w/medicine ball, 1900s, 62" ...**225.00**
Basket, Tlingit, 9 whirling log swastikas, w/lid, 1910s, 2½x4" ...**450.00**
Club, Plains style, rawhide-wrapped stone w/bw hdl, dangles, 20th C ...**225.00**
Dance wand, Plains style, horn w/hawk bells, bw hdl, 20th C, 26x8" ...**150.00**
Drum, Plains style, rawhide w/EX pntings, full bw beater, 20th C, 15" ..**425.00**
Drum, Taos NM, wood/leather, heads/sides in mc pnt, ca '20s, 11x13" ..**875.00**
Feast dish, NW Coast, cvd/pnt, bird & animal form, 1930s, 22x10" ...**325.00**
Headdress/mask, Apache Devil Dancer, pnt wood, ca 1935, 17x20" ...**250.00**
Necklace, Yacqui, shell dance, ca 1900, 38x2" ...**110.00**
Rattle, Blackfoot, buffalo scrotum w/red ochre, bw hdl, 19th C, 12" ..**300.00**
Rattle, NW Coast, finely cvd/pnt, ca 1970, 10x5" ...**425.00**
Roach, dancer's headdress, porcupine & horsehair, 1960s, 15½" ..**50.00**
Spoon, cvd horn, animal effigy head, bw hdl, 20th C, 15½x3½" ..**250.00**

Dolls

Blackfoot, hide face, shell-decor dress, bw moccasins, 1930s, 12" ...**550.00**
Hopi, Kachina, Black Ogre, cottonwood, w/cane & knife, ca 1940, 13" ...**350.00**
Hopi, Kachina, Chaveyo, 1st Mesa depiction, Paul Mendez, 15" ..**135.00**
Hopi, Kachina, cvd/pnt, lg tabletta, C Pongyesvia, 1960, 9½" ...**90.00**
Hopi, Kachina, Hana Clown, seated w/watermelon, C Yestewa, 1960, 11x6" .**160.00**
Hopi, Kachina, Nayaiyataka, case mask w/red ears, feathers, 9½" ..**685.00**
Hopi, Kachina, Snake Dancer, w/snake in mouth & feather, 1970s, 11" ..**200.00**
Hopi, Kachina, Sunface, cvd cottonwood root, 1940s, 9" ...**550.00**
Nisqually, twined basketry w/facial features, 1900, 8x5" ...**265.00**
Papago, basketry female w/arms, removable hat, 1940s, 11½x4" ...**350.00**
Sioux, bw hide face, bw dress/leggings/moccasins, 1900s, 9x5" ...**500.00**
Zuni, fully beaded, traditional attire/squash, 1970, 7" ...**100.00**

Domestics

Bowl, Eastern Woodlands, burlwood, deeply cvd w/hdls, 1800s, 8x12x15" ...**4,600.00**
Box, Micmac, bark & wood w/pnt flower cvd on top, 1850s, 2x3x4" .**275.00**
Box, trinket; Chippewa, cut/pierced birchbark, 1930s, 3x3" ...**150.00**
Cradle, Kootenai, board-bked buckskin w/bw Canadian flags, 1920s, 30" .**1,100.00**
Cradle, Paiute, hooded basketry w/yarn laces, geometrics, 1970s, 19" ..**100.00**
Pestle, Columbia River, cvd phallic form, p-h, 9x4" ...**550.00**
Pestle, Columbia River, stone w/horn hdl, 18th C, 15x2" ...**160.00**
Pestle, gr rock, hand-tooled phallic form, p-h, 6x2¼" ...**160.00**
Saddle, Crow, dbl-end, full bw & floral panel drops, 1960s, 25" .**600.00**
Scraper, L-shaped bone, forged steel blade, rawhide wrap, 1930s, 12x2" ..**1,400.00**

Jewelry and Adornments

As early as 500 A.D., Indians in the Southwest drilled turquoise nuggets and strung them on cords made of sinew or braided hair. The Spanish introduced them to coral, and it became a popular item of jewelry; abalone and clam shells were favored by the Coastal Indians. Not until the last half of the nineteenth century did the Indians learn to work with silver. Each tribe developed its own distinctive style and preferred design, which until about 1920 made it possible to determine tribal origin with some degree of accuracy. Since that time, because of modern means of communication and travel, motifs have become less distinct.

Quality Indian silver jewelry may be antique or contemporary. Age, though certainly to be considered, is not as important a factor as fine workmanship and good stones. Pre-1910 silver will show evidence of hammer marks, and designs are usually simple. Beads have sometimes been shaped from coins. Stones tend to be small; when silver wire was used, it is usually square. To insure your investment, choose a reputable dealer.

Arm bands, Kiowa, hand-cvd brass, att J Caesar, 1920s, 10x3½" ...**150.00**
Belt, Navajo silver w/14 2x2½" conchos, ca 1970 ...**200.00**
Belt drop, Crow, full bw w/arrow designs, 1940s, 33x2" ...**350.00**
Bolo tie, Apache Head #2, Jesse Monongye, ca 1977, 2x2¼" ..**2,750.00**
Bolo tie, Zuni, MOP w/bear claw tips, Ray & Eva Wyaco, 1970, 3¼x3" .**600.00**
Bracelet, Navajo, silver w/21 Morenci turq, 1970s, 1¼" W ...**130.00**

Bracelet, Navajo man, Old Pawn, silver/turq in 3 rows, 1960s....**275.00**
Bracelet, Navajo silver w/1 bl turq, sgn TK Johnson, ca 1960, 1" W..**100.00**
Brooch, Navajo, turq & silver, classic style, ca 1940, 4x1½" **225.00**
Hairpins, Hopi, silver w/turq inlay, 1950s, pr.................................**110.00**
Necklace, Blackfeet, beaded 10-strand loop w/shells/teeth, 1900s ..**1,100.00**
Necklace, Plains, buffalo tooth, brass & glass beads, 20th C, 40"..**110.00**
Necklace, Pueblo, silver cross w/cast silver naja, 1940s, 28" **550.00**
Necklace, Santo Domingo, 6-strand coral heshi w/squaw wrap, 1950s, 26"....**190.00**
Necklace, Zuni, inlay spinner pendant on handmade chain, 1940s, 34" ..**450.00**
Necklace, Zuni, silver & jet inlaid bear w/silver feather drips, 1970 ...**400.00**
Pendant, Navajo, sandcast silver kachina w/turq eyes/tummy, 1940s, 3" ..**40.00**
Roach pin, Sioux, wood w/quillwork & hawk bells, 1910s, 8x2½" ..**200.00**
Squash blossom, Zuni, turq & silver, ca 1940, 31½x1½" **750.00**

Pipes

Pipe bowls were usually carved from soft stone, such as catlinite or red pipestone, an argilaceous sedimentary rock composed mainly of hardened clay. Steatite was also used. Some ceremonial pipes were simply styled, while others were intricately designed naturalistic figurals, sometimes in bird or frog forms called effigies. Their stems, made of wood and often covered with leather, were sometimes nearly a yard in length. For more thorough study we recommend *Collector's Guide to Indian Pipes* by Lar Hothem.

Basalt, fr-tube type, from Warner Valley OR, p-h, 1¾x1¾" **35.00**
Catlinite, disc, red w/pk flecks, polish, 1¾" dia, 3½" **565.00**
Catlinite, L-shaped, serrated ridge, 2⅜", minimum value **650.00**
Catlinite, sq cvd design, w/stem, Dakota, 1920s, 17x3½"+tamper..**450.00**
Catlinite, T-shape Plains type, EX polish, 4x8"............................**500.00**
Cherokee, cvd stone, flat head, NC, ca 1910, 9x3½" **100.00**
Cherokee, cvd stone w/human effigy, NC, ca 1900, 5x2¾" **90.00**
Cherokee, red pottery, sinew-wrapped stem, 18th C, 9½x1".......**150.00**
Council, reddish-gray, stump type, p-h, 4¼" dia **750.00**
Cvd, blk hardstone, Hopewell, extended hand holding bowl, p-h, 6x2".**250.00**
Cvd stone, protruding bowl w/zoomorphic figure, ca 1900, 6¾x2¾" **50.00**
Effigy, bird, greenish stone, Mississippian, 2x2⅛" **400.00**
Effigy, frog, shell-tempered clay, Mississippian, 2½x3" **350.00**
Effigy, owl, brn-gr sandstone, Mississippian, 2x1¼x3¼"..............**600.00**
Effigy, pinched-faced blower, Huron-Petun, 1500-1650, 2¾" ..**1,000.00**
Effigy, raccoon (?) on platform, dolomite, ca 200 BC-400 AD, 4"...**1,050.00**
Effigy, turtle, tan pipestone, Mississippian, 2⅜"........................**2,200.00**
Pipestone, disc, polished, late p-h, OH, 1½x4½" **1,000.00**
Pipestone, tubular, blocked end, sm stem hole, Adena, 1x4¼" ..**1,600.00**
Pipestone (gray), bullet shape, Pre-Iroquois, 2¼", from $375 to.**600.00**
Pottery, elbow type, late p-h, OH, 1¾" **200.00**
Sandstone, tubular w/blocked ends, Adena, OH, 4¼".................**700.00**
Steatite (blk), elbow, ca 1000-1500 AD, 1⅝x1¼"......................**250.00**
Steatite (gr), obtuse angle, ca 450-700 AD, VA, 2½x7".........**1,000.00**
Trumpet, red & brn pottery w/decor, Iroquois, ca 1600-50, 4¾" stem..**450.00**

Pottery

Indian pottery is nearly always decorated in such a manner as to indicate the tribe that produced it or the pueblo in which it was made. For instance, the designs of Cochiti potters were usually scattered forms from nature or sacred symbols. The Zuni preferred an ornate repetitive decoration of a closer configuration. They often used stylized deer and bird forms, sometimes in dimensional applications.

Acoma, bowl, geometrics & avian figures, scalloped rim, 1½x7½" ...**230.00**
Acoma, bowl, mc geometric design, pie-crust rim, ca 1920, 4x9½" ..**180.00**
Acoma, jar, mc geometrics, well used, 1930s, 9x6" **325.00**
Acoma, jar, 2-color design, 1960, 7½x10"....................................**50.00**

Anasazi, pitcher, blk on wht, checkerboard & geometrics, p-h, 7x6" ...**750.00**
Anasazi, pitcher, blk on wht, crosshatch design, p-h, 6¾x5¾" ...**425.00**
Casas Grandes, bowl, blk/red ochre linear decor on gray-buff, 4x8" ..**125.00**
Casas Grandes, olla, swirling/intersecting triangles, 10x12" **300.00**
Four Mile, olla, linear decor, p-h, 5x9½" **325.00**
Gila, bowl, geometrics, squarish, p-h, 2¾x6"..............................**250.00**
Ho Ho Kam, red on buff fret design, p-h, 3¼x5½"......................**250.00**
Mata Ortiz, pot, polychrome, Nat Ortiz, 20th C, 9x7½".............**275.00**
San Juan, dough bowl, redware, JA Trujillo, ca 1950, 6¼x13", EX..**500.00**
Santa Clara, bear effigies, Margaret & Luther, 1960s, mini, pr ...**225.00**
Santa Clara, bowl, shiny blk, Margaret Tafoya, 1940s, 2½x7½".**700.00**
Santa Clara, wedding jar, Avanu, Margaret & Luther, 1960s, 9½"....**3,000.00**
Zia, bowl, geometrics, sgn w/bell (Sarafina Bell), 1950s, 5x10" .**250.00**
Zuni, jar, sq neck, relief frog & heartline deer, 1930s, 6½x6¼" ..**425.00**

Pottery, San Ildefonso

The pottery of the San Ildefonso pueblo is especially sought after by collectors today. Under the leadership of Maria Martinez and her husband Julian, experiments began about 1918 which led to the development of the 'black-on-black' design achieved through exacting methods of firing the ware. They discovered that by smothering the fire at a specified temperature, the carbon in the smoke that ensued caused the pottery to blacken. Maria signed her work (often 'Marie') from the late teens to the 1960s; she died in 1980. Today pieces with her signature may bring prices in the $500.00 to $4,500.00 range.

Jar, blkware, butterflies, sgn Marie & Julian, 7x9"....................**2,200.00**
Jar, blkware, feathers, Santana & Adam, 1960s, 4¾x4¾" **850.00**
Jar, blkware, stylized feathers around shoulder, Ada Kai, 4x7½".**415.00**
Olla, 3-color, shouldered form, Maria Martinez, 1930s, 8½x9" ..**1,300.00**
Plate, polished gunmetal finish, Maria Poveka, 1960s, 5½" **700.00**

Rugs, Navajo

Storm pattern with feather design border, ca 1930, 72x45", $715.00.

Bands of hourglass shapes w/central dmns, 6-color, 45x56".........**415.00**
Big Rock area, stepped geometrics/crosses, tight weave, 1960s, 55x36"...**450.00**
Crystal area, central lozenge, geometrics, 1935, 62x38" **600.00**
Dbl & twill weave, neutral colors, ca 1935, 62x32".....................**225.00**
Ganado, expanding dmn, serrated scallop border, spirit line, 37x60" ...**330.00**
Ganado, hand loomed, 1930s, 40x66"......................................**1,800.00**
Ganado, lg X in red/wht on gray, 3-color terraced border, 55x57"..**200.00**
Geometric border & central dmn, red/blk/gray, 1930s, 88x46"...**1,000.00**
Geometrics in 4 bands, natural gray/blk & wht wool, ca 1935, 58x36" ..**325.00**
Pictorial: spider/toad/lightning, att 2 Grey Hills, 58x83" **600.00**
Red open field w/blk border, 1930s, 80x52" **3,250.00**
Red/natural dk wool stripes, rprs, 19th C, 41x67"......................**275.00**

Serrated Dmns, natural & vegetal dyes, 1940s, 64x32" 300.00
Storm pattern, natural hand-spun wool, 1940s, 66x45" 1,100.00
Tan central field w/stepped fret mc borders, 35x55" 495.00
Teec Nos Pos, geometrics, analine colors, tightly woven, 1950s, 36x34"....800.00
Teec Nos Pos, red/blk/gray/wht geometrics, 1940s, 68x42"...........850.00
Transitional, simple stripes, corner fringe, rpr, 36x52" 685.00
Two Grey Hills, all natural, hand-spun, ca 1960, 49x34" 700.00
W Reservation, red/blk/gray geometrics, ca 1935, 54x76" 850.00
Yei figures in center, vegetal dye, 1940s, 51x36" 700.00
2 bands w/stepped devices, mc on carded gray, holes to 1 end, 48x76" ...1,200.00

Shaped Stone Artifacts

Bannerstone, butterfly, gr banded slate, Archaic, KY, 2⅞x4"......400.00
Bannerstone, butterfly/single-notch, banded slate, Archaic.....1,000.00
Bannerstone, butterfly/unnotched, banded slate, Archaic, OH, 6" ...2,000.00
Bannerstone, butterfly/unnotched, glacial slate, Archaic, 1¾x4½" 350.00
Bannerstone, extended wing, brn banded slate w/EX polish, IN, 7" 500.00
Bannerstone, hourglass, hardstone (4-color), Archaic, OH 2,500.00
Bannerstone, notched ovate type, banded slate, OH, 3x4½"....2,000.00
Bannerstone, ridge-edged triangle, gr/wht hardstone, 2½x1¾"...800.00
Bannerstone, tubular, banded slate, Archaic, IN, 1½x5½" 350.00
Bannerstone, winged dbl-notch, gr glacial slate, Archaic, 3⅜x4⅞" ..1,800.00
Bannerstone, winged/unnotched, gr banded slate, Archaic, OH, 3x5¼"...750.00
Boatstone, granite gneiss w/dk spots, Woodland, 1x5⅝x¾"........600.00
Effigy stone, lizard, banded slate, middle Archaic, IN, 5½" 800.00
Gorget, gr-blk slate, eng elk figure, Woodland, 3¾" 275.00
Gorget, rectangular, banded slate, polished, Woodland, OH, 5".195.00
Gorget, reel shape, banded slate, Woodland, OH, 3" 800.00
Gorget, tool grade hematite, Archaic, MO, 1¾x2½"....................250.00
Pendant, anchor type, banded slate, Woodland, IN, 4" 550.00
Pendant, blk hardstone, 21 tally mks, incising, MO, 2⅛x1¼"....150.00
Pendant, keyhole, gr banded slate, polished, Woodland, 4⅛x2".425.00

Tools

Adz, gray-brn Dover flint, flat face, TN, 7¾x2" 350.00
Adz, mottled hardstone, rectangular, polish, OH..........................85.00
Adz, tan hardstone, OH, 6½x2" 85.00
Axe, blk hardstone, ½-groove, EX polish, IN, 6½x11½" 1,300.00
Axe, crystalline, full groove, fine edge, OH, 2¼x7x1⅞" 150.00
Axe, dk gray slate, ¾-groove, G polish, OH, 3¾x8½"................800.00
Axe, granite, full groove, IL, 2¾x4⅛x1⅝"................................110.00
Axe, hematite, full groove, G polish, MO, med-lg 250.00
Axe, speckled tan granite, full groove, EX polish, PA, 4x7x3"....425.00
Celt, blk hardstone, polished, SC, 2½x5½x1½" 175.00
Celt, flint or chert, AL, late p-h, 6⅞x2x¾" 100.00
Celt, greenstone, MI, 8¼x2¼", from $350 to 450.00
Chisel, polished flint, IL, 7x1½"..225.00
Drill, lt flint, T-top, Archaic, IN, 2¼"...50.00
Gouge, dk hardstone, well scooped, MI, 5⅞"............................175.00
Gouge, hardstone, ME, 9¼x1½", from $375 to 450.00
Hammerstone, grooved, IN or IL, 3x2", from $40 to 60.00
Maul, ¾-groove & full groove, WI, 4"..150.00
Pestle, quartzite, knobbed, highly polished, Archaic, OH, 7" ...1,000.00
Saw, gray flint w/cortex, Paleo, KY, 1x2¾" 100.00
Spud, blk & wht hardstone, WI, 6x2⅞"......................................650.00

Weapons

Bow, Pueblo, sinew string, 19th C, +3 sinew-wrapped arrows 325.00
Bow, S Plains, pnt Bois de Arc, sharp ends for war, 19th C, 60"..........225.00
Bow, Sioux, recurved, gr pigment, orig sinew string, 19th C, 50" 425.00
Club, Plains, hide over stone, bw/fringe hdl, 20th C, 26x2" 150.00

Lance, forged steel point, gr tradecloth cover, 1880s, 80" 1,100.00
Tomahawk, Am, spike-bk belt type, 19th C, 10x6¼"..................200.00
Tomahawk, iron w/brass tacks, wire-wrapped hdl, 1880s, 14x7" .700.00
War club, Great Lakes, ball head, EX patina, 1870, 24x7" 1,600.00

Miscellaneous

Canoe model, Kwakiutl, cvd/pnt, 1910s, 18" 375.00
Game, Cheyenne, pin & bone, 1930, 11x1½" 200.00
Martingale, Crow, full bw, ca 1920, 54x45".............................500.00
Mirror board, Sioux, pnt/tacked geometrics, 1910s, 18½x7".......700.00
Paddle, acorn mush; Hupa, wooden classic form, 1900s, 22½x2¼"..475.00
Peace medal, King George, brass colored, dtd 1757, 1¾" 150.00
Saddle drape, Klamath, fringed buckskin w/geometric bw, 1930s, 78x14"..350.00
Sand painting, Navajo, Crying Fawn, sgn CW, 1980, 16x16" 90.00
Tepee, Crow, sun/moon/hands design, full liner, ca 1900, 15x25'...1,500.00
Toy horse, Crow, leather w/bw accessories, 1920s, 11x12½" 180.00

American Painted Porcelain

The American china-painting movement can be traced back to an extracurricular class attended by art students at the McMicken School of Design in Cincinnati. These students, who were the wives and daughters of the city's financial elite, managed to successfully paint numerous porcelains for display in the Woman's Pavilion of the 1876 United States Centennial Exposition held in Philadelphia — an amazing feat considering the high technical skill required for proficiency, as well as the length of time and multiple firings necessary to finish the ware. From then until 1917 when the United States entered World War I, china painting was a profession as well as a popular amateur pursuit for many people, particularly women. In fact, over 25,000 people were involved in this art form at the turn of the last century.

Collectors and antique dealers have discovered American hand-painted porcelain, and they have become aware of its history, beauty, and potential value. Until now, there was no all-inclusive source to turn to for information on this subject. *American Painted Porcelain: Collector's Identification & Value Guide, Antique Trader's Comprehensive Guide to American Painted Porcelain,* and *Painted Porcelain Jewelry and Buttons: Collector's Identification & Value Guide* by Dorothy Kamm are the culmination of a decade of research; we recommend them highly for further study.

Though American pieces are of high quality and commensurate with their European counterparts, they are much less costly today. Generally, you will pay as little as $10.00 for a 6" plate and less than $50.00 for many other items. Values are based on aesthetic appeal, quality of the workmanship, size, rarity of the piece and of the subject matter, and condition. Age is the least important factor, because most American painted porcelains are not dated. (Factory backstamps are helpful in establishing the approximate time period an item was decorated, but they aren't totally reliable.) See Clubs, Newsletters, and Catalogs for information regarding *Dorothy's Kamm's Porcelain Collector's Companion,* each issue of which contains comprehensive material expounding on artists, patterns, dating, and functions of china.

Our advisor for this category is Dorothy Kamm; she is listed in the Directory under Florida.

Bar pin, brass-plated bezel, 1½" W, from $25 to.............................45.00
Belt buckle brooch, oval, 1¾x2⅛", from $90 to 125.00
Bonbon bowl (depending on size), from $18 to 85.00
Bowl, fruit; from $60 to 80.00
Box, 4¾ dia, from $50 to 75.00
Brooch, brass-plated bezel, oval, 2x1½", from $55 to 75.00
Brooch, gold-plated bezel, 1½" dia, from $35 to 55.00
Brooch/pendant, heart shape, gold-plated bezel, 2x1¾", from $50 to....85.00

Cake plate, from $35 to..**75.00**
Candlestick, from $45 to...**125.00**
Celery tray, from $35 to..**75.00**
Condiment set, poppy, tray/shakers/toothpick, 1891-1914, from $45 to..**55.00**
Cruet, from $60 to..**80.00**
Cuff pin, rectangular, brass-pated bezel, ¼x1⅛", from $12 to **18.00**
Cup & saucer **45.00**
Cup & saucer, bouillon; from $35 to..............................**45.00**
Ewer (depending on size), from $100 to **175.00**
Gravy boat, from $55 to **75.00**
Handy pin, brass-plated bezel, 1½", from $30 to...........**40.00**
Hatpin holder, from $88 to **125.00**
Jam jar, from $30 to...**50.00**
Jardiniere (depending on size), from $65 to **375.00**
Mug, from $40 to **75.00**
Napkin ring, from $10 to...**25.00**
Pendant, gold-plated bezel, 1" dia, from $50 to...............**75.00**
Pin tray, from $30 to..**50.00**
Pitcher, lemonade; from $175 to....................................**225.00**
Plate, 6", from $10 to...**35.00**
Plate, 8", from $45 to...**65.00**
Salt cellar, from $20 to **40.00**
Scarf pin, medallion, brass-plated bezel & shank, 1¼" dia, $35 to **65.00**
Shakers, pr, from $25 to **40.00**
Shirtwaist button, 1" dia, from $20 to **40.00**
Shirtwaist set, brooch, brass-plated mts, 1¾"+ cuff links, $150 to ..**350.00**
Stein, from $75 to **115.00**
Tea or coffee set, ea set, from $175 to............................**300.00**
Whiskey set, ears of corn, sgn, Surquist, 1903-17, 8-pc, $300 to.**400.00**

Amphora

The Amphora Porcelain Works in the Teplitz-Turn area of Bohemia produced Art Nouveau-styled vases and figurines during the latter part of the 1800s through the first few decades of the twentieth century. They marked their wares with various stamps, some incorporating the name and location of the pottery with a crown or a shield. Because Bohemia was part of the Austro-Hungarian empire prior to WWI, some examples are marked Austria; items marked with the Czechoslovakia designation were made after the war. All decoration described in the listings that follow is hand painted unless otherwise indicated.

Our advisor for this category is John Cobabe; he is listed in the Directory under California.

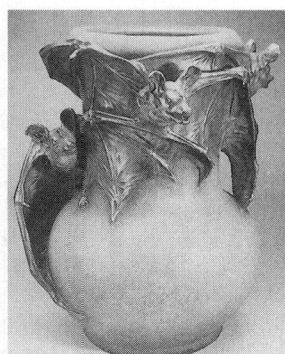

Vase, high-relief bats in gold iridescent and dark red on lemon skin ground, #4660 6, impressed mark with crown, minor restoration, 22¼x18", $7,250.00.

Bowl, shell form w/woman sitting on edge w/cherub at shoulder, 14x12"..**1,100.00**
Bowl, woman's head above pond of nymphs, 12x16" **1,300.00**
Figurine, polar bear, naturalistic, #8283, 10x12¾"..................**495.00**
Pitcher, Art Nouveau foliage, integral hdl, 10x7" **1,000.00**

Pitcher, emb fruit & leaves, oval mk, 12x6", NM.....................**600.00**
Planter, maiden relaxing on edge looking up at orange flower, 12x14"...**2,700.00**
Pot, floral, 4 hdls, crown mk, 7¼x12" **700.00**
Sculpture, tigers (2) w/prey, dk bl mk, 11x20x11" **450.00**
Vase, appl acorns & leaves on branches, #d, 14½", NM...........**1,100.00**
Vase, cat & mouse on ea end w/flowered vine design, 5x13" **360.00**
Vase, coal miner figural, earth tones w/gold trim, mk, 16½"....**1,400.00**
Vase, Deco-style flowers, Tegel-en Fayencefabriek Amphora, 1925, 17x9"..**1,750.00**
Vase, emb swirls & panels, red on gr w/irid, 9½" **700.00**
Vase, geometric cutouts & appl jewels, Dachal, hdls, 15½", NM...**2,000.00**
Vase, gr & gold w/vertical gray panels w/cutouts, 8-sided, 9" **550.00**
Vase, grapes & flowers, trophy form w/wide angular hdls, 14x11", EX .**450.00**
Vase, grapes appl on mottled bl, 3½", NM **95.00**
Vase, maiden in woods, gilded, pinched opening, 12x6"..........**2,750.00**
Vase, Nouveau florals, neck-to-hip hdls, oval mk, 9" **2,100.00**
Vase, Nouveau geometrics, bird hdls, 8½x4½" **150.00**
Vase, Nouveau grapes, integral hdls, ftd, 13".............................**400.00**
Vase, random & controlled lines w/faux jewels, #2024 56, 7", EX...**1,900.00**

Animal Dishes With Covers

Covered animal dishes have been produced for nearly two centuries and are as varied as their manufacturers. They were made in many types of glass (slag, colored, clear, and milk glass) as well as china and pottery. On bases of nests and baskets, you will find animals and birds of every sort. The most common was the hen.

Some of the smaller versions made by McKee, Indiana Tumbler and Goblet Company, and Westmoreland Specialty Glass of Pittsburgh, Pennsylvania, were sold to food-processing companies who filled them with prepared mustard, baking powder, etc. Occasionally one will be found with the paper label still intact identifying the product and processing company.

Many of the glass versions produced during the latter part of the nineteenth century have been recently reproduced. In the 1960s, the Kemple Glass Company made the rooster, fox, lion, cat, lamb, hen, horse, turkey, duck, dove, and rabbit on split-ribbed or basketweave bases. They were made in amethyst, blue, amber, and milk glass, as well as a variegated slag. Kanawha, L.G. Wright, and Imperial made several as well. It is sometimes necessary to compare items in question to verified examples of older glass in order to recognize reproductions. Reproduction is continued today.

For more information, we recommend *Covered Animal Dishes* by Everett Grist, whose address is in the Directory under Tennessee; *Collector's Encyclopedia of Milk Glass* by Betty and Bill Newbound; *Westmoreland Glass* by Charles West Wilson; and *American Slag Glass* by Ruth Grizel. In the listings below, when only one dimension is given, it is the greater one, usually length. See also Greentown and other specific companies.

Bird, milk glass, rnd basketweave base, Vallerysthal **95.00**
Cat, milk glass, split-rib base, 1 pc mk McKee, 5½" **275.00**
Cat, wht w/bl opaque head, wide-rib base, Westmoreland.............**85.00**
Dog, bl opaque, wide-rib base, Westmoreland................................**70.00**
Dolphin, milk glass, on sauce-dish base, att Westmoreland, 7¼"...**100.00**
Dolphin, transparent (clear or colored), sawtooth rim (+)............**45.00**
Duck, Atterbury; milk glass, Patent Apld For, 11".......................**245.00**
Duck, clear, wavy base, Challinor Taylor, 8" **65.00**
Duck, Swimming; amber, Vallerysthal, 5" **120.00**
Elephant, clear, Co-operative Flint, Indiana or Taiwan, 9" **25.00**
Elephant w/Rider, milk glass, Vallerysthal, 7" **400.00**
Fish, Entwined; milk glass, glass eyes, Atterbury, dtd lid, 6".......**225.00**
Fish, Flat; gr transparent...**75.00**
Frog, milk glass, split-rib base, unmk McKee, 5½"......................**550.00**
Hen, Straight Headed; amber, Indiana Glass **15.00**

Hen, Straight Headed; bl carnival, Indiana Glass.........................**25.00**
Hen, transparent (clear or colored), dmn basketweave nest, Greentown...**300.00**
Hen on Sleigh, milk glass, Westmoreland Specialty, 5½" (+).......**85.00**
Hen w/Chicks, milk glass, split-rib base, unmk McKee, 5½" **165.00**
Lion, British; milk glass, emb title on base, 6¼" **195.00**
Lion, Ribbed; milk glass, glass eyes, ribbed base, dated................**275.00**
Rabbit, Atterbury; milk glass, Pat Aug 6, 1889 on base, 9" **300.00**
Rabbit, milk glass, wheat base, unmk Flaccus **350.00**
Rabbit, Mule Eared; milk glass, picket base, Westmoreland (+)....**40.00**
Rat on Egg, milk glass, Vallerysthal **225.00**
Robin, bl opaque, ped base, Vallerysthal (+)..................................**90.00**
Rooster, bl opaque w/wht head, wide-rib base, Westmoreland **95.00**
Rooster, clear w/pnt, Challinor Taylor, 7" **95.00**
Rooster, milk glass/bl opaque, wide-rib base, Westmoreland, 5¼".**95.00**
Rooster, purple opaque, wide-rib base, Westmoreland, 5" **125.00**
Squirrel, milk glass, split-rib base, unmk McKee, 5½".................**185.00**
Swan, Block; clear frosted, Challinor Taylor, 7"............................**120.00**
Swan, Closed-Neck; bl opaque, Westmoreland...........................**100.00**
Swan, Raised-Wing; milk glass, eye sockets, Atterbury **225.00**
Turkey, milk glass, split-rib base, 1 pc mk McKee, 5½" **220.00**

Appliances, Electric

Antique electric appliances represent a diverse field and are always being sought after by collectors. There were over one hundred different companies manufacturing electric appliances in the first half of the twentieth century; some were making over ten different models under several different names at any given time in all fields: coffeepots, toasters, waffle irons, etc., while others were making only one or two models for extended periods of time. Today collectors and decorators alike are seeking those items to add to a collection or to use as accent pieces in a period kitchen. Refer to *Toasters and Small Kitchen Appliances* published by L-W Book Sales for more information. If you're especially interested in vintage fans, we recommend *The Collector's Guide to Electric Fans* by John Witt. Toaster collectors will enjoy *Collector's Guide to Toasters & Accessories* by Helen Greguire. (The latter two books are published by Collector Books.)

Always check the cord before using and make sure the appliance is in good condition, free of rust and pitting. The prices below are for appliances in good to excellent condition. Prices may vary around the country.

If you have any questions regarding antique appliances, feel free to contact our advisor, Jim Barker; he is listed in the Directory under Pennsylvania.

Blender, Nutone In-Built, pk triangular shape w/gray lid, 9", EX..**50.00**
Blender, Waring #702B Deluxe, copper base, Pat 2109501, 14", NM..**125.00**
Can opener, Dazey Push Button, 1950s, MIB................................**32.50**
Can opener, Sunbeam, yel plastic body, EX chrome **40.00**
Chafing dish, SP, International Silver Co, alcohol burner, lg........**55.00**
Coffee urn, DeLonghi Ultimate, stainless steel, thermostat, 60-cup, EX...**65.00**
Coffee urn, Farberware, stainless steel, ped ft, 55-cup, EX.............**70.00**
Coffee urn, Manning-Bowman, chrome w/Bakelite hdls, 1920s, 14"...**75.00**
Coffee urn, Manning-Bowman #3593, stainless steel, dtd 1911, EX....**75.00**
Coffee urn, Westinghouse, chrome, ca 1918, 14", NM..................**50.00**
Egg cooker, Hankscraft, aluminum, ca 1940s, MIB.......................**30.00**
Egg cooker, Sunbeam, aluminum, holds 3, 8"..............................**25.00**
Fan, Air Castle, aluminum blades, Deco styling, 18" w/14" cage, EX .**200.00**
Fan, Colonial Fan & Motor Co...OH USA, Pat April 27 '09, EX ...**215.00**
Fan, EKC Dynamo & Motor Co Type 21 #J3597, brass blades, 11", NM..**1,250.00**
Fan, Emerson, 4 brass blades, 3-speed, orange cage, 10"............**150.00**
Fan, General Electric, brass blades, gr enameling, 17".................**190.00**
Fan, General Electric, oscillating, 1920s-30s, 16", VG **95.00**
Fan, Polar Cub type G, CI base, brass blades, 8" w/6½" cage **95.00**
Fan, Roto-Beam, chrome, Deco style, 20" w/15" cage, EX **160.00**

Fan, Vornado #24C3-1, 2-tone gray, 2-speed, EX **100.00**
Fan, Western Electric W-168557, 4-blade, brass, 3-speed, EX.....**137.50**
Fan, Westinghouse Riviera R-2021, 20" **145.00**
Food warmer, Dominion #1414, 4" dia coil, 7¾" base, EX **35.00**
Heater, Superior, brass & copper, 15x14" **80.00**
Heater, water; Karikeen, adjustable air flow, 1930s, EX.................**65.00**
Hot plate, Great Northern, single, 1930s, EX **25.00**
Iron, KM Knapp Monarch, travel, ca 1940, 6⅜", from $30 to **50.00**
Iron, Minneapolis Minn, gr porc, ca 1925, 6½", from $100 to....**150.00**
Iron, Steam Electric Corp, aluminum surface, ca 1925, 9⅛" **30.00**
Kettle, General Electric #K49A, stainless steel, 8½" **68.00**
Kettle, Groen #TDB7-20, stainless steel, tilting, 20-qt, from $325 to...**400.00**
Kettle, Hamilton Beach Cordless Electric, 10-cup, EX.................**35.00**
Kettle, Streamline, Bakelite hdls, 8x8½" dia, EX...........................**30.00**
Mixer, Braun KM32, multi-function, Rams & Gugelot era, NM...**190.00**
Mixer, Hobart C10, 3-speed, w/bowl & whisk attachment, 10-qt, 28"..**325.00**
Mixer, Kitchenaid (Hobart) Model G, ca 1920s, EX...................**135.00**
Mixer, Oster #210, blk enamel on CI, stainless containers, EX...**100.00**
Mixer, Star-Right Magic Maid Model B, Jadite bowls, 3 beaters, M.....**150.00**
Percolator, Farberware, chrome w/glass finial, Bakelite ft, 1930s, 12" ...**175.00**
Percolator, Hotpoint, chrome w/wood hdls, cr/sug, NM **40.00**
Percolator, Manning-Bowman, copper, plated int, 1914, cr/sug........**100.00**
Percolator, Universal, chrome, 1930s, 8-cup, EX **40.00**
Percolator, Westinghouse, stainless steel, Deco style, 8-cup **50.00**
Popcorn popper, K-M Knapp Monarch, glass lid, wood hdls, 10", NM..**35.00**
Popcorn popper, Kwikway, aluminum w/Fire-King glass lid, 1940s, EX..**40.00**
Skillet, Corning Ware Electromatic, Blue Cornflower, M **55.00**
Skillet, Farberware #344A, high dome, NM **125.00**
Skillet, Sunbeam, aluminum, 11½" sq, EX....................................**35.00**
Skillet, West Bend #7230E, Nutri-Seal on lid, stainless steel, EX.**35.00**
Skillet/buffet server, Farberware #335A, stainless steel, 12" **50.00**
Toaster, Auto-Toastmaker #73 Pat Pending, wood hdls/knob, EX ..**120.00**
Toaster, General Electric D12, porc, Pat Oct 20, 1908, EX.........**325.00**

Toaster, Gold Seal, 1924, EX, $90.00.

Toaster, Leslie Press-To-Matic, chrome & Bakelite, EX.................**60.00**
Toaster, McGraw Electric Co #1B8, chrome & Bakelite, 7x10", EX..**55.00**
Toaster, Penn-Air #280, drop style, wht enamel, EX **70.00**
Toaster, Samsun, 3 side slots, chrome w/blk trim, NM **125.00**
Toaster, Sunbeam AT-A, glass front w/leaves, M **70.00**
Toaster, Sunbeam T-9, chrome, Deco-style curved 2-slot top, EX.**70.00**
Toaster, Toast-O-Later, Bakelite base, 1936-40s, EX...................**295.00**
Toaster, Torrid Push-O-Matic, red knobs, Pat Feb 15, 1927, 7".....**62.50**
Toaster, Universal #E948T, 8x7", G..**75.00**
Vacuum, Regina, Pneumatic Cleaner, tank type, EX.....................**140.00**
Waffle iron, Bersted #211, switch on cord, EXIB..........................**30.00**
Waffle iron, General Electric, chrome w/Bakelite lid, 12" dia.......**35.00**
Waffle iron, Lady Hibbard #344, chrome/ceramic/Bakelite, EX **70.00**
Waffle iron, Sunbeam Wafflewitch #F3, Bakelite hdls, EX............**95.00**

Arc-En-Ciel

The Arc-En-Ciel Pottery Company operated in Zanesville, Ohio, from 1903 until 1907. Artware was produced only until 1905, typically finished in a high lustre gold glaze. Though not always marked, those pieces that are carry the half-circle rainbow logo containing the company name.

Vase, allover gold lustre, integral hdls, mk, lt wear, 5½x 4" **185.00**
Vase, cream mottle on gold, gourd shape, 6¾".............................**175.00**
Vase, gold irid, twisted stem, 7" **100.00**

Arequipa

The Arequipa Pottery operated from 1911 until 1918 at a sanitorium near Fairfax, California. Its purpose was two-fold: therapy for the patients and financial support for the institution. Frederick H. Rhead was the originator and director. The ware, made from local clays, was often hand thrown, simply styled and decorated. Marks were varied but always incorporated the name of the pottery and the state. A circular arrangement encompassing the negative image of a vase beside a tree is most common.

Examples are evaluated according to quality of artwork; size and shape are less important. Those done by Rhead himself are most desirable.

Bowl, bl/gr semimatt emb w/grass motif, octagonal, 1½x7".........**350.00**
Scarab, maroon matt, 5"..**700.00**
Vase, vining leaves (at shoulder), yel/wht/bl on purple, 6", NM..**4,500.00**

Argy-Rousseau, G.

Gabriel Argy-Rousseau produced both fine art glass and quality commercial ware in Paris, France, in 1918. He favored Art Nouveau as well as Art Deco and in the '20s produced a line of vases in the Egyptian manner, made popular by the discovery of King Tut's tomb. One of the most important types of glass he made was pate-de-verre. Most of his work is signed. Items listed below are pate-de-verre unless noted otherwise.

Ashtray, amethyst w/purple criss-cross devices centering red dmns, 6"..**800.00**
Bowl, ivy, gr/bl on frost, ftd, mfg flaw, 4x5" **1,925.00**
Lantern, red shell at base on gray/red-streaked ovoid, 7" **4,250.00**
Pendant, flowers, purple/red in amethyst ribbed vase on frost, 2½"..**1,500.00**
Pendant, wht flowers w/blk stamens, 2x1½" **950.00**
Vase, Thebes, notched ribs, red/bugundy cvd hdls & border, 6" ...**6,300.00**

Art Deco

To the uninformed observer, Art Deco evokes images of chrome and glass, streamlined curves and aerodynamic shapes, mirrored prints of pink flamingos, and statues of slender nudes and greyhound dogs. Though the Deco movement began in 1925 at the Paris International Exposition and lasted to some extent into the 1950s, within that period of time the evolution of fashion and taste continued as it always has, resulting in subtle variations.

The French Deco look was one of opulence — exotic inlaid woods, rich material, lush fur, and leather. Lines tended toward symmetrical curves. American designers adapted the concept to cover every aspect of fashion and home furnishings from small inexpensive picture frames, cigarette lighters, and costume jewelry to high-fashion designer clothing and exquisite massive furniture with squared or circular lines. Vinyl was

a popular covering, and chrome-plated brass was used for chairs, cocktail shakers, lamps, and tables. Dinnerware, glassware, theaters, and train stations were designed to reflect the new 'Modernism.'

The Deco movement made itself apparent into the '50s in wrought iron lamps with stepped pink plastic shades and Venetian blinds. The sheer volume of production during those twenty-five years provides collectors today with fine examples of the period that can be bought for as little as $10.00 or $20.00 up to the thousands. Chrome items signed 'Chase' are prized by collectors, and blue glass radios and tables with blue glass tops are high on the list of desirability in many areas.

Those interested in learning more about this subject will want to read *Collector's Guide to Art Deco* by Mary Frank Gaston and *Affordable Art Deco, Identification and Value Guide*, by Hutchinson and Johnson. (Both are published by Collector Books.) See also Bronzes; Chase; Frankart; Jewelry; Lalique; Radios; etc.

Bookcase, Frankl, maple/ebonized trim, 3-step Skyscraper, '20s, 80" ...**32,500.00**
Buffet, Macassar ebony w/ivory inlay, granite top, 82" L...........**2,300.00**
Bust, lady's head on tall sq ped, wht, De Vegh by Lamberton China, 10" ...**210.00**
Carpet, Follot, hand-knotted wool, geometric, Made in France, 132" sq....**2,000.00**
Chair, lounge; wood arms & fr, uphl bk & seat, 34", pr...............**375.00**
Figurine, Egyptian lady, cold-pnt cast metal, holds crystal ball, 10"...**200.00**
Figurine, man, standing w/flowers, wht, De Vegh/Lamberton China, 17"...**140.00**
Hall tree, Fr, wrought iron, mirror/planter/umbrella holders, 83x63"...**2,500.00**
Lamp, 'J' stems w/blk disc terminals on chrome disc base, 2 rnd shades....**275.00**
Lamp, draped nude kneels by pk textured globe, patinated metal, 19"...**250.00**
Lamp, Suet et Mare (att), alabaster, ginger jar form, 18x10", pr **6,000.00**
Lamp base, California Porcelain, stepped geometric, brn/gray, 11"....**700.00**
Rug, Matisse Mimosa, Alexander Smith & Sons, ltd ed, 58x36"...**2,800.00**
Sconce, half-rnd aluminum shade on frosted glass column, 19x14" ..**375.00**

Sculpture, stylized woman and fawn in alabaster, marked Italy, 14x14x5", $500.00.

Sideboard, mahog w/radiating veneer in 4 drw fronts, 82" L ...**2,300.00**
Table, blk shelves, red Bakelite hdl, 2-tier, 28x22" dia **550.00**
Table, center; mahog w/ebony trim, 5-part pedestal, 54" L **1,600.00**
Torchere, ovoid cameo shade, 4-ftd pencil std, 66", EX, pr......**5,200.00**
Vase, bl & brn drip, 4 masks on shoulder, Primavera 4826, 10" ..**460.00**
Vase, Hull House, stylized antelopes, brn on yel, bulbous, 6½".**1,300.00**

Art Glass Baskets

Popular novelty and gift items during the Victorian era, these one-of-a-kind works of art were produced in just about any type of art glass in use at that time. They were never marked. Many were not true production pieces but 'whimsies' made by glassworkers to relieve the tedium of the long work day. Some were made as special gifts. The more decorative and imaginative the design, the more valuable the basket. For more information, we recommend *Collector's Encyclopedia of American Art*

Glass by John A. Shuman, III (Collector Books).

Note: Prices on art glass baskets have softened due to the influence of the Internet which has made them much more accessible.

Amberina overshot w/amber twist hdl, ruffled, Sandwich, 6½" ..**150.00**
Apricot w/gold spangle stripes, rose int, sq top, clear loop hdl, 6x6"...**325.00**
Caramel & yel o/l w/HP flowers & gold, clear twist hdl, 8x7x6" ...**195.00**
Clear, hdl & ft w/pk & wht latticinio stripes, 8¾x7½" **850.00**
Clear w/wht opal flowers, cranberry rim, 9½" **95.00**
Cranberry w/crystal hdl, petticoat shape, ruffled rim, ca 1890, 7x5" .**250.00**
Dmn Quilt, wht w/pk int, clear reeded hdl, 6½" **100.00**
Hobnail, bl satin, dbl pinched rim, frosted U-hdl, 5½" **150.00**
Hobnail, cased bl opal, melon ribs, lobed ruffled top, Xd hdl, 11x11"...**375.00**
Opal w/pk int, amber rim, appl tree trunk amber hdl, 9" **200.00**
Orange satin w/mint gr int, ruffled, wishbone thorn hdl, 7x7"....**275.00**
Orange w/HP chick & eggs/bk: floral, clear ruffle w/rosettes, 7x6"...**450.00**
Spangle, mc/silver, clear edge/rope hdl, ruffled, 10x10x9"..........**325.00**
Spatter, bl, bl thorn hdl, 4-fold ruffled rim, 7½x6½" **110.00**
Spatter, bl/wht, bl thorn hdl, rim pinched to form 8-point star, 6x6"...**225.00**
Spatter, brn/gr on yel, wht int, ruffled edge pulled down twice, 7x7"...**195.00**
Spatter, brn/jade, wht int, clear thorn hdl, 7-point star rim, 7x6".........**275.00**
Spatter, pk/yel, clear thorn hdl, top pinched to form 8-point star, 6"...**250.00**
Spatter, pk/yel on wht, triangular, twist in hdl forms top loop, 8x5".....**225.00**
Spatter, yel/pk, wht int, clear thorn hdl, 6x6".............................**165.00**
Yel-gr w/gold flowers, wht int, clear pointed hdl, E Webb mk, 5x4" ...**495.00**

Art Nouveau

From the famous 'L'Art Nouveau' shop on the Rue de Provence in Paris, 'New Art' spread across the continent and belatedly arrived in America in time to add its curvilinear elements and asymmetrical ornamentations to the ostentatious remains of the Rococo revival of the 1800s. Nouveau manifested itself in every facet of decorative art. In glassware Tiffany turned the concept into a commercial success that lasted well into the second decade of this century and created a style that inspired other American glassmakers for decades. Furniture, lamps, bronzes, jewelry, and automobiles were designed within the realm of its dictates. Today's market abounds with lovely examples of Art Nouveau, allowing the collector to choose one or several areas that hold a special interest. Our advisor for this category is Steven Whysel; he is listed in the Directory under Florida. See also Bronzes; Galle; Jewelry; Loetz; Tiffany; Silver; specific manufacturers.

Armchair, back and seat formed as flowers and leaves, female heads as arm terminals, rockwork base, Ecole de Nancy, $1,495.00.

Candelabrum, pewter, 3-light, whiplash stems/roots base, 11½"..**2,000.00**
Candlestick, pewter, swirling organic form w/3 'stem' arms, 11" .**800.00**
Fire screen, brass fr: leaves/whiplash stems, heart-shape mirror, 31" ...**2,100.00**
Lamp, brass etched shade w/lg jewels, 2-stem std, European, 26x15", EX...**1,150.00**
Lamp, bronze, nude child pulls chain, slag petal shade, Bofill, 26" **2,900.00**
Lamp, bronze nymph riding wave, shell beneath her, Germany, 8½x7"...**1,300.00**
Lamp, lg shell in leafy cup on spiral stem, copper, EE Burton, 18" **2,600.00**
Table, marquetry scenic in exotic woods, France, 20x30x18"......**750.00**
Tray, silver, 3-D nude w/wings standing on lily pad, 6½x6¼" **200.00**
Vase, bronze, branch hdls, pine cones on shoulder, Gorham, 4" .**975.00**
Vase, pewter w/inset jewels, whiplash hdls, Tudric #O29, 10" .**1,300.00**

Arts and Crafts

The Arts and Crafts movement began in England during the last quarter of the nineteenth century, and its influence was soon felt in this country. Among its proponents in America were Elbert Hubbard (see Roycroft) and Gustav Stickley (see Stickley). They rebelled against the mechanized mass production of the Industrial Revolution and against the cumulative influence of hundreds of years of man's changing taste. They subscribed to a theory of purification of style: that designs be geared strictly to necessity. At the same time they sought to elevate these basic ideals to the level of accepted 'art.' Simplicity was their virtue; to their critics it was a fault.

The type of furniture they promoted was squarely built, usually of heavy oak, and so simple was its appearance that as a result many began to copy the style which became known as 'Mission.' Soon factories had geared production toward making cheap copies of their designs. In 1915 Stickley's own operation failed, a victim of changing styles and tastes. Hubbard lost his life that same year on the ill-fated *Lusitania*. By the end of the decade the style had lost its popularity.

Metalware was produced by numerous crafts people, from experts such as Dirk van Erp and Albert Berry to unknown novices. Metal items or hardware should not be scrubbed or scoured; to do so could remove or damage the rich, dark patina typical of this period. Collectors have become increasingly fussy, rejecting outright pieces with damage or alteration to their original condition (such as refinishing, patina loss, repairs, and replacements). As is true for other categories of antiques and collectibles, premium prices have been paid for objects in mint original and untouched condition. Our advisor for this category is Bruce Austin; he is listed in the Directory under New York. See also Limbert; Roycroft; Silver; Stickley; specific manufacturers.

Note: When no condition is noted within the description lines, assume that values are given for examples in excellent condition. That is, metal items retain their original patina and wooden items are still in their original finish. Values for examples in conditions other than excellent will be indicated in the descriptions with appropriate condition codes.

Key: h/cp — hammered copper

Armchair, Harden, 5-slat bk/4 ea side, thru-tenons/arch seat rail, 38"...**850.00**
Armchair, Liberty, oak w/blk inlay, rush bk panels/seat, 34x28" **2,100.00**
Armchair, Shop o/t Crafters, side posts w/inlay, 4-slat bk, no mk, 39"...**650.00**
Armchair, Shop o/t Crafters #331, inlay, sqs/rectangles ea side, 44"...**6,500.00**
Bed, Luce, mahog, central slat w/inlay, cut-out top rail, 62x78x45" **850.00**
Bookcase, Lifetime, 3 9-pane doors, worn orig finish, 55x61x12"........**2,300.00**
Bookends, Forest Craft Guild, h/cp, sq w/sm sq cutouts, 4½x6" .**500.00**
Bookends, h/cp, pointed top w/appl cut-out 'GAW,' new patina, 6½"...**375.00**
Bowl, Benedict, h/cp, 4 appl fan devices extend to pad ft, 3x8½"....**325.00**
Bowl, h/cp, heavy gauge, 23" **1,500.00**
Bowl, h/cp w/emb leaves & stems, hdls, 8½" **425.00**
Bowl, Jarvie, h/cp, slightly rolled rim, 8" **750.00**
Bowl, Kalo, hammered silver, w/dome lid, 4½x4½" **1,800.00**

Bowl, Los Castillo, hammered silver w/brass/copper cat decor, 8x13"..**1,000.00**
Bowl, sterling w/emb floral at rim on hammered ground, 5" **260.00**
Bowl, van Erp, h/cp (warty motif), D'Arcy Gaw, incurvate, 10" **6,000.00**
Box, Christofle, silver floral on wood, stems form even panels, 6½" **425.00**
Box, Dixon, h/cp w/appl initial, lacquered int, 4x3"..................**200.00**
Box, Hurley, bronze w/2 sea horses on top, gr/brn patina, 5" L **750.00**
Box, Hurley, bronze w/5 emb sea horses on rnd lid, dtd 1924, 5½" ...**1,600.00**
Box, Japanese, bamboo, parquet top, ftd, 5x4½"..........................**150.00**
Box, Japanese, woven reeds, 12x9" **450.00**
Box, van Erp, h/cp, imp open box mk, 3½x3¼" **425.00**
Box, van Erp, h/cp, overhanging lid, 6" L **850.00**
Breakfront, Liberty & Co, arched top, 2 drw, 2 doors, rfn, 58x60x24"..**2,200.00**
Candelabra, Jarvie, 2 conical holders, slim std w/pyriform finial, 11"...**7,000.00**

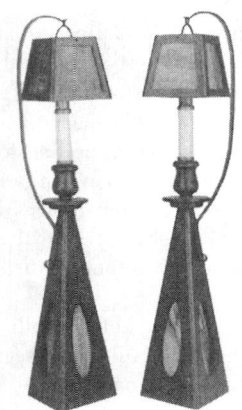

Candle lamps, four-sided green slag shades, curved wrought-iron straps over triangular oak bases with green slag glass inserts, unmarked, 25½", $600.00 for the pair.

Candlestick, ET Hurley, bronze w/sea horses, flared base, cleaned, 13"..**600.00**
Candlestick, FJR Gyllenberg, bronze, 9½" **180.00**
Candlestick, Jarvie, Alpha model, h/cp, 11" **600.00**
Candlestick, Jarvie, Beta, bulbous cup, wafer above wide ft, 12½".**2,100.00**
Candlestick, Preston, bronze, very slim trumpet form on wide ft, 14"..**1,400.00**
Candlesticks, h/cp, twisted stem, rolled flat base, 8½", VG, pr...**200.00**
Candlesticks, h/cp, 3 flared straps form stem, wishbone cups, 9", pr..**700.00**
Candlesticks, Jarvie, bronze, pencil stems, wide disk ft, 11", pr...**475.00**
Candlesticks, Jarvie, h/cp, 11", pr.....................................**400.00**
Candlesticks, Kipp, h/cp, 2-strap stem on raised sq base, 8", pr...**800.00**
Candlesticks, Liberty (att), emb design, mk English #023, 5½", pr.....**400.00**
Candlesticks, oak, sq stem w/corbels, cruciform base, #17, 8", VG, pr..**80.00**
Candlesticks, Preston, bronze, torch shape w/pencil std, 12", pr.......**2,100.00**
Cellarette, Rholfs (att), ash wood, pierced decor, 56x18x7" **950.00**
Chair, desk; Barden Bros, top rail, 3-slat bk, saddle seat, 37" **425.00**
Chairs, 2 wide slats form bks, wooden seats, rfn, 37", 2 arm+5 sides .**1,200.00**
Chalice, Jarvie, hammered silver, tubular pedestal w/wide ft, 11" **2,600.00**
Chamberstick, Gorham, bronze w/silver o/l, 3½x8" **350.00**
Chamberstick, Onondaga, h/cp, 4½"..................................**200.00**
Chandelier, 4 Steuben gold irid shades on chains hang from bronze ring..**1,600.00**
Charger, Voulkos, loops/dots, brn/olive/gray mottle, 15½" **3,250.00**
China cabinet, door w/6 sq panes at top, base drw, 58x34x16", VG .**2,000.00**
Clock, Dutch, hammered wrought iron w/enamel hr mks, 10x8".......**1,300.00**
Clock, grandfather; slats at side, cabinet below, copper hdw, 76", G......**160.00**
Clock, Liberty, pewter, Tree of Life design w/enameling, 8x5".**4,500.00**
Clock, tooled leather front, invt acorn shape, Roycroft style, 5½" ..**375.00**
Costumer, Lifetime #535, sq pole w/4-leg tepee base, no mk, 67", VG...**375.00**
Costumer, thick pole w/4 flared legs, orig hooks, 67x21" **500.00**
Desk, Shop o/t Crafters #274, paneled slant front/drw/shelf, 48x30" **600.00**
Desk, Shop o/t Crafters #279, ldgl ea side slant front, drw, 46x42"....**1,200.00**
Desk, Shop o/t Crafters #281, leather top/1-drw/bk gallery, 42x29" **325.00**
Dinner gong, Liberty, hammered pewter, mk Tudric, 18x20"...**2,500.00**
Dresser, English, mirror bk w/copper details, 4-drw, rfn, 63x36" ...**2,200.00**

Dresser, Luce, oak w/pewter/ebony inlay, orig mirror, 67x45x22" .**1,700.00**
Firescreen, Japan, bamboo reeds & slats, thru tenons, 41x36½".**425.00**
Footstool, leatherette top, flared sides w/appl key-tenons, 16x18x14" ...**100.00**
Frame, bronze w/appl strapwork designs, rnd w/hexagonal opening, 8x6"..**550.00**
Frame, English, h/cp w/emb trefoils, shaped sides, 10½x8½" **700.00**
Frame, Friedell, hammered silver w/monogram initials, 8½x6½" ..**250.00**
Frame, Lebolt, hammered silver, 11x9" **900.00**
Frame, Liberty, pewter w/Tree of Life design, 10x8" **1,400.00**
Frame, Silvercrest, textured bronze w/banded devices, #2216, 7x6" **150.00**
Frame, Wm Hutton, h/silver w/flowing lines & enamel inlay, 8x6½" ..**1,700.00**
Frame, wood w/delicate silver o/l floral, 4½x2½" **500.00**
Hall tree, oak w/hc/p heart amid gr tiles, drw, English, 77x48x15" ...**2,800.00**
Hall tree, Shop o/t Crafters, single pole w/hooks, stepped ft, 66" ...**325.00**
Jardiniere & ped, Liberty, oatmeal/gray, stylized roses/leaves, 37"...**2,300.00**
Lamp, h/cp, shade w/4 mica panels, inkwell base w/curving arm, 19" ..**4,600.00**
Lamp, Heintz, bronze w/appl silver birds, harp std, 11", VG **500.00**
Lamp, Heintz, sterling on bronze, cut-out floral shade, 9½x9"...**1,100.00**
Lamp, van Erp, h/cp, conical shade w/4 mica panels, globe base, 12x10" **7,000.00**
Lamp, van Erp, h/cp, conical 11" 4-panel mica shade; bulbous base, 11"..**11,000.00**
Lamp, van Erp, h/cp, 18" mica shade w/copper cap/straps; flared base.**9,500.00**
Lamp, van Erp, h/cp, 21" shade w/rpl mica; can neck, angular width..**9,000.00**
Lamp, van Erp, h/cp cylindrical base, 12" mica shade w/4 straps, 14".**12,000.00**
Lamp, 6-panel mica shade, squat h/cp vasiform base w/hdls, 16x16" ...**2,150.00**
Magazine stand, 4-shelf, cut-out sides w/rnd tops, dk finish, 36x19"........**300.00**
Mirror, Bugatti, wood/pewter inlay, rtcl copper ring w/silk drops, 23"..**4,250.00**
Mirror, Fr, wrought iron w/snail device ea side, 18½" dia............**700.00**
Mirror, hammered pewter w/orig design, 17½x22½"................**1,250.00**
Music stand, mahog, 4-shelf, arched gallery, rfn, 39x20x14"....**1,000.00**
Nightstand, Michigan Chair Co, 1-drw, lower shelf, label, 30", VG...**950.00**
Portfolio cover, tooled leather w/landscape, 14x17", VG **200.00**
Print, woodblock; Asian boy/butterflies, H Hyde, oak fr, 8x3½" ..**550.00**
Print, woodblock; Asian lady atop waves, B Lum, oak fr, 9½x2½" ..**400.00**
Print, woodblock; Asian lady/child, H Hyde, oak fr, 17x14" **650.00**
Print, woodblock; Fishing Boats, E Norton, fr, 4½x6½"..............**550.00**
Print, woodblock; girl/flowers in pots, H Hyde, matted/fr, 11x6½" ..**700.00**
Print, woodblock; landscape, G Kampmand, oak fr, 15½x11½" .**500.00**
Rocker, Harden, 2 narrow+1 wide vertical bk slats, slated sides, 38" ..**950.00**
Rocker, reuphl seat/bk, cleaned orig finish, 27x32x32", VG **250.00**
Rug, Caucasian, geometrics in bl/red/gr/ivory/camel, 34x140".**2,500.00**
Rug, Drugget, brn diagonals border gr floral on oatmeal, 136x74", EX..**350.00**
Rug, Hamadan, red & bl geometrics, 44x67" **250.00**
Rug, Oriental geometric design, bl/tan/burgundy, 82x50" **650.00**
Sconce, CA Art Tile, landscape/garden in architectural frwork, 14", pr..**2,700.00**
Server, Lifetime, Puritan, 1 drw, arched rail, paper label, 36x40x19"...**1,800.00**
Settle, even arms, wide/thin vertical slats alternate in bk/sides, 84" **2,500.00**
Sideboard, oak, mirror bk w/inlay, 2 drw/2 doors, rfn, 75x54" .**2,700.00**
Smoking set, Heintz, sterling/bronze w/appl golfer, 9½' tray+6 pcs ...**475.00**
Spoon, TC Shops, hammered silver, 12½"..................................**100.00**
Table, arched apron, X stretchers, lt wear to top, 29x36" dia......**475.00**
Table, English, 16-tile (gr) top, arched aprons, rstr finish, 18" sq..**1,000.00**
Table, Lifetime, apron, 4 flared legs, thru tenons, rfn, 26x18" dia..**2,300.00**
Table, oak w/wicker apron & base, 29x20" dia............................**425.00**
Table, tea; Rittenhouse, lower shelf, rfn, 24x24" dia **1,500.00**
Table, trestle; Ford & Johnson, shelf, shoe-ft base, label, 48", VG..**850.00**
Tea set, J Henrichs, copper & brass, 6-pc set...............................**425.00**
Teapot, Gorham, h/cp w/appl silver floral, wood hdl, bronze stand, 11"..**3,250.00**
Tray, hammered silver, 2 open hdls, compartments, 15½x7½" ...**150.00**
Tray, van Erp, h/cp, extended rim hdls w/raised devices, 16½" L ...**650.00**
Tray, van Erp, h/cp, raised hdls, 13½" **500.00**
Umbrella stand, Benedict Studios, cylindrical, riveted hdls, 24x10" ...**700.00**
Umbrella stand, h/cp, 16" **200.00**
Vase, Craftsman, h/cp, 4-sided w/2 rim-to-base angled strap hdls, 8" ...**300.00**
Vase, h/cp, appl floral stems, slim classic form, w/liner, 15", VG ...**550.00**
Vase, h/cp, 2 horizontal bands, horizontal hdls, wide/conical, 14", VG ..**750.00**

Vase, h/cp w/raised device, crimped top, sq w/riveted ribs, 11" ...650.00
Vase, Heintz, copper w/silver o/l trees & flowers, mk, 12" 375.00
Vase, Kipp, h/cp, 3-buttress form, 7½" 1,800.00
Vase, Maija Grotell, fishscale devices, ivory on brn/tan, 12x12"...7,500.00
Vase, Paul Cox, hand-trn, red gloss, 4½" 90.00
Vase, Sadlacek, hammered silver, floriform w/petal rim, 10" 425.00
Vase, Silvercrest, bronze w/silver o/l, 7" 150.00
Vase, Spaulding, hammered silver, eng floral sprig, trumpet form, 7"...750.00
Vase, van Erp, h/cp, shouldered, drilled, 8½" 1,300.00
Vase, van Erp, h/cp, str/flared sides, 4½" 900.00
Vase, Voulkos, 4-sided w/pnt faces, gray/brn/tan, shouldered, 9"...4,250.00
Wall bowl, Hairnian, h/cp, melon ribbed w/arched bkpc, 8x13".900.00
Wardrobe, English, cvd panel w/linen-fold motif & coat of arms, 71x23"...1,900.00

Attwell, Mabel Lucie

Born in London in 1879, Mabel Lucie Attwell put her talent in illustration and design toward many outlets. Merchandise ranging from children's books and dinnerware, postcards, advertising, dolls, calendars, and greeting cards were marketed under her direction. She also designed a line of china called Nursery Ware for the Shelley China Company (see also Shelley). Our advisor for this category is David Ehrhard; he is listed in the Directory under California.

Biscuit tin, boy w/fairies, 5" dia...25.00
Book, Alice in Wonderland, L Carroll, Tuck & Sons, 12 plates .165.00
Book, Grimm's Fairy Tales, Piccola Pan Books, 1977, EX..............45.00
Book, Lucie Attwell's Annual, Dean & Son, EX 45.00
Bowl, Fisherman Joe..., Simpsons Ambassador Ware, 5½" 80.00
Chamber pot, Nursery Ware, scenes w/girl & pixies, 3½x6⅜" dia..350.00
Cup & saucer, Nursery Ware, girl & boy w/pixies, Shelley..........165.00
Figurine, Sam w/dog, 1959-61, 3" 265.00
Figurine, Sarah running w/dog, Wade, 1959-61 ....175.00
Handkerchief, pixies, children & owls, bl & wht, 8½" sq 40.00
Milk jug, Boo-Boo, little pixie-like boy w/hand to head, Shelley, 6"...310.00
Plaque, Please Remember, Never Leave..., Valentine, 12x8".........65.00
Plate, Look at the Fairies..., Simpsons Solian Ware, 6" 80.00
Plate, Nursery Ware, When Will I Grow Up 70.00
Postcard, Up to My Neck in Things, boy in dad's pants, 1940s.....35.00
Puzzle, jigsaw; Peter Pan & Wendy, Rainbow Designs, 56-pc, 1921...40.00
Trinket dish, heart shaped, glass lid, Enesco, 1989, 3x3½"............35.00

Austrian Ware

From the late 1800s until the beginning of WWI, several companies were located in the area known at the turn of the century as Bohemia. They produced hard-paste porcelain dinnerware and decorative items primarily for the American trade. Today examples bearing the marks of these firms are usually referred to by collectors as Austrian ware, indicating simply the country of their origin. Of those various companies, these marks are best known: M.Z. Austria; Victoria, Carlsbad, Austria (Schmidt and Company); and O. & E.G. (Royal) Austria. Of these three companies, Victoria, Carlsbad, Austria, is the most highly valued.

Though most of the decorations were transfer designs which were sometimes signed by the original artist, pieces marked Royal Austria were often hand painted and so indicated alongside the backstamp.

Collectors should note that in our listings transfer decorations showing 'signatures' (sgn), such as 'Wagner,' 'Kauffmann,' 'LeBrun,' etc., were not actually painted by those artists but were merely based on their original paintings. Our advisor for this category is Mary Frank Gaston.

Biscuit jar, florals on ribbed bulbous body, #933, MZ, 6" 80.00

Bowl, console; plums & currants, sgn Hilda, Royal Austria, 1919, 16"...550.00
Chocolate pot, roses on wht w/much gold, 12" 315.00
Chocolate pot, 2 lovers in garden/roses, artist sgn, gold hdl........365.00
Cruet, roses allover, gold stopper, MZ Austria mk, ca 1900, 8½"....395.00
Dresser set, floral w/gold, O&EG mk, 1900s, 13" tray+box+hair receiver....395.00
Dresser set, roses on pk, sgn Mrs Schaexer, tray+box+hair receiver 395.00
Ewer, roses on wht w/gold, sgn Weyron, 10¼" 450.00
Lamp, 3 girls dance around floral column, 2-light, 22" 385.00
Pitcher, Nouveau lady w/grape clusters form hdl, Wahliss, 13⅜".2,800.00
Rose bowl, poppies, gold ft, ruffled rim, 5x4¼" 165.00
Rose bowl, violets, gold ft & ruffle, 4" 168.00
Rose bowl, wild roses on lav to cream, ftd, 1898-1908, 5¼" 235.00

Tankards: Grapes and leaves, artist signed, Vienna Hand Painted China, 14¼", $350.00; Classical couple on cream and pink, 13½", from $250.00 to $350.00.

Vase, irises (EX art), sgn B Woody, cylindrical, stamped, 16" 825.00
Vase, lilacs, gold angle hdls, crown mk, 18½" 1,195.00
Vase, mums w/heavy raised gold, shouldered, OE&G mk, 15" 550.00
Vase, roses, artist sgn, gold rim, ca 1900, 12", NM 450.00
Vase, roses, mc on lt bl, trumpet neck, crown mk, 12½" 665.00
Vase, roses, pk on bl, bulbous, Royal Austria mk, 9½" 350.00
Vase, roses allover, gold 3" opening, Royal Austria mk, 4½x6½" ..450.00
Vase, roses on gr to lt bl, globular, bottle neck, 7¾" 600.00
Vase, roses on lt gr to bl, cylindrical, ca 1914, 12½" 450.00
Vase, roses w/gold, sgn L Brown, angle hdls, crown mk, ca 1900, 18"..1,400.00

Autographs

Autograph collecting, also known as 'philography' or 'love of writing,' used to be a hobby shared by a few thousand dedicated collectors. But in recent years, autograph collecting has become a serious pursuit for more than 2,000,000 collectors worldwide. And in the past decade, more investors are adding rare and valuable autograph portfolios to their traditional investments. One reason for this sudden interest in autograph investing relates to the simple economic law of supply and demand. Rare autographs have a 'fixed' supply, meaning that unlike diamonds, gold, silver, stock certificates, etc., no more are being produced. There are only so many Abraham Lincoln, Marilyn Monroe, and Charles Lindbergh autographs available. In the meantime, it's estimated that more than 20,000 new collectors enter the market each year, thus creating an ever-increasing demand. Hence, the rare autographs generally rise steadily in value each year. Because of this scarcity, a serious collector will pay over $10,000.00 for a photograph signed by both Wilbur and Orville Wright, or as much as $25,000.00 for a handwritten letter of George Washington.

But by far, the majority of autograph collectors in the country do it for the love of the hobby. A polite letter and self-addressed, stamped envelope sent to a famous person will often bring the desired result. And occasionally one receives not only an autograph but a nice handwritten letter thanking the fan as well!

In terms of value, there are five general types of autographs: 1) mere signatures on an album page or card; 2) signed photographs; 3) signed documents; 4) typed letters signed; and 5) handwritten letters. The signatures are the least valuable, and handwritten letters the most valuable. The reasoning here is simple: with a handwritten letter, not only do you get an autograph but the handwritten message of the person as well. And this content can sometimes increase the value many times over. A handwritten letter of Babe Ruth's thanking a fan for a gift might fetch a few thousand dollars. But if the letter were to mention Ruth's feelings on the day he retired, it could easily sell for $10,000.00 or more.

Today the Internet has become a popular way to buy and sell autographs. A word of warning: Be very careful when buying over the Internet. It is an easy way for unscrupulous forgers to sell their fakes and disappear. Teenagers need to be especially aware that many of the 'signed' photos on the Internet of Sarah Michelle Gellar, Brad Pitt, Katie Holmes, Leonardo DeCaprio, Kate Winslett, and many others are either signed by secretaries or are outright forgeries. Make sure the Internet dealer offers a full money-back guarantee of authenticity and belongs to one of the major autograph organizations. Ask how long the dealer has been in business and for personal references if possible. Remember the old Latin warning, 'caveat emptor,' let the buyer beware.

There are several major autograph collector organizations where members can exchange celebrity addresses or buy, sell, and trade their autographed wares. Philography can be a fun and rewarding hobby. And who knows! In ten or twenty years, those autographs you got for free could be worth a small fortune!

In the listings below, photos are assumed black and white unless noted color. Our advisor for autographs is Tim Anderson; he is listed in the Directory under Utah.

Key:
ANS — handwritten note signed
ins — inscription
ISP — inscribed signed photo
LS — signed letter, typed or written by someone else
sig — signature
SP — signed photo

Aaker, Lee; SP as Rusty w/Rin Tin Tin, color, 8x10" 30.00
Bergen, Edgar; sig on album pg, also signed Charlie 65.00
Bogart, Humphrey; sig on album pg...950.00
Brook, Phyllis; SP, sepia, 1937, 5x7" 50.00
Burton, Richard; sig on 3x5" card, 1954...125.00
Calhoun, Rory; sig on album pg...42.00
Carter, Jimmy; sig on thank you card to television station 75.00

Charlie Chaplin, silver gelatin signed photo, 9x7", $575.00.

Churchill, Marguerite; ins/sig on album pg 40.00
Coburn, Charles; sig on album pg..50.00
Connelly, Walter; sig on 1½x2½" album pg.....................................45.00
Crippen, ISP, official standard-issue NASA photo 1970s, 8x10"...55.00
Davis, Rufe; ISP, sepia, 4¼x7" 35.00
Dempsey; Jack; sig on album pg 75.00
Dodd, Jimmie; sig on 4x5" album page 65.00

Dove, Billie; ISP, blk & wht, ca 1960s, 3½x5" 45.00
Eastman, George; DS, receipt for securities, 1921, 11x8½" 1,300.00
Evans, Muriel; SP, blk & wht, sepia, 1934, 5x7" 60.00
Ferebee, Tom; Enola Gay Bombardier, SP of mushroom cloud......25.00
Forest, Frank; ISP, sepia, 8x10" 40.00
Gielgud; Sir John; sig on 3x5" paper..40.00
Gish, Lillian; SP, blk & wht, 8x10" 85.00
Greene, Lorne; ISP, blk & wht, 8x10" 145.00
Haley, Jack; ISP, sepia, 1930s, 8x10"..275.00
Hardie, Russell; ISP, sepia, 1930s, 5x7"...60.00
Harvey, Laurence; sig on 3x5" card...75.00
Hayward, Louis; sig on lt bl album pg...35.00
Holmes, Oliver Wendell; ANS, reply to request, 1857, w/envelope .275.00
Hope, Bob; sig on album pg 45.00
Ives, Burl; sig on 3x5" card 40.00
Jenkins, Allen; ISP, sepia, movie scene, 8x10".................................55.00
Johnson, Luci; LS on White House stationary 45.00
King, John 'Dusty'; SP, sepia, 5x7" 60.00
Knight, June; ISP, sepia, movie scene, 10x8".....................................40.00
Lane, Lola; sig on album pg..35.00
Leonov, Aleksei A; sig on 3½x6" card 185.00
Logan, Ella; SP, sepia, w/top hat & cane, 1938, 5x7".....................60.00
MacRae, Gordon; sig on 3x5" card 45.00
March, Hal; ISP, blk & wht, 1950s, 8x10" 45.00
Mitchum, Robert; sig on album page 50.00
Montgomery, Robert; sig on 3x5" card 40.00
Nagel, Conrad; SP, sepia, ca 1920s, 5x7" 45.00
Nelson, Ozzie; sig on album pg...50.00
Nixon, Richard; sig copy of his book Six Crises 395.00
Oberon, Merle; SP, sepia, 5x7"..70.00
Parks, Bert; sig on 3x5" card..37.00
Paulsen, Pat; sig on 3x5" card..35.00
Quinn, Anthony; sig on 3x5" card..45.00
Remick, Lee; sig on 3x5" card..45.00
Richenbacker, Eddie; SP, sepia, 5x7" 195.00
Rogers, Ginger; sig on album pg...55.00
Romero, Cesar; ISP, blk & wht, 7½x9½"...60.00
Roosevelt, Eleanor; sig on album pg, 1961 ....75.00
Rutherford, Ann; SP, sepia, 1930s-40s, 8x10" 50.00
Scott, Fred; SP, blk & wht, cowboy attire w/2 guns drawn, 8x10".45.00
Skala, Lilia; ISP, blk & wht, 8x10" 40.00
Smith, Kate; sig on album pg 50.00
Stedman, Myrtle; ISP, sepia, 8x10" 75.00
Strasberg, Susan; sig on 3x5" card...40.00
Taylor, Elizabeth; ISP, blk & wht, 8x10" 250.00
Thaxter, Phyllis; SP, color, 1940s, 5x7"..45.00
Thomas, Danny; sig on 3x5" card...35.00
Vaughn, Alberta; ISP, sepia, 1920s, 7½x9½" 70.00
Walston, Ray; sig on 3x5" index card, 1964 ....40.00
Whitney, Eleanore; SP, blk & wht, 1937, 5½x7" 50.00
Wolfe, Ian; ISP, blk & wht, 8x10" 40.00

Automobilia

While some automobilia buffs are primarily concerned with restoring vintage cars, others concentrate on only one area of collecting. For instance, hood ornaments were often quite spectacular. Made of chrome or nickel plate on brass or bronze, they were designed to represent the 'winged maiden' Victory, flying bats, sleek greyhounds, soaring eagles, and a host of other creatures. Today they often bring prices in the $75.00 to $200.00 range. R. Lalique glass ornaments go much higher!

Horns, radios, clocks, gear shift knobs, and key chains with company emblems are other areas of interest. Generally, items pertaining to the classics of the '30s are most in demand. Paper advertising material, manuals, and catalogs in excellent condition are also collectible.

License plate collectors search for the early porcelain-on-cast-iron examples. First year plates (e.g., Massachusetts, 1903; Wisconsin, 1905; Indiana, 1913) are especially valuable. The last of the states to issue regulation plates were South Carolina and Texas in 1917, and Florida in 1918. While many northeastern states had registered hundreds of thousands of vehicles by the 1920s making these plates relatively common, those from the southern and western states of that period are considered rare. Naturally, condition is important. While a pair in mint condition might sell for as much as $100.00 to $125.00, a pair with chipped or otherwise damaged porcelain may sometimes be had for as little as $25.00 to $30.00.

Our advisor for this category is Leonard Needham; he is listed in the Directory under California. For more information we recommend *American Automobilia: An Illustrated History and Price Guide* by Jim and Nancy Schaut. See also Gas Globes and Panels.

Trophy, Chevrolet, Spirit of St. Louis, Quota Trophy – October 1927, $900.00.

Ad, Excelsior Auto Cycle, paper, circular graphics, fr, 15x23", EX ..80.00
Auto Mapometer, silver w/blk hdl, Mapometer Mfg Co, EX (VG box)...80.00
Badge, Chalmers Motor Co, bl & wht enameled, 2¾", EX 80.00
Badge, chauffeur; Manitoba, 1922, VG+ 25.00
Badge, chauffeur; 1938, EX 18.50
Badge, 1919 Port Huron Auto Club, radiator shape, enameled, EX..875.00
Binder, Ford Service Bulletin, 1939-40, Canadian, VG+ 105.00
Blotter, Dodge Brothers Trucks, 1929, 9x4", EX...........................35.00
Book, Blue Book of Custom Restyling, 110 pgs, 1949, VG+ 50.00
Book, Corvair Owner's Handbook of Maintenance & Repair, 1964-65, EX...20.00
Booklet, Mille Miglia, MG's effort in 1933 race, 48 pgs, VG+....210.00
Brochure, Aston Martin DB44, 1960s, 9x6", EX...........................35.00
Brochure, sales; 1966 Lincoln Continental, 18 pgs, EX 20.00
Brochure, 1958 Lincoln & MKIII Deluxe, 24 pgs, 15x10", NM....35.00
Bulb & Fuse Kit (Emergency), Ford, tin, w/contents, 2½x3½", VG+..85.00
Catalog, Alco/American Locomotive Co, 1913, 32 pgs, EX 350.00
Catalog, Martin-Semour Paint Color Directory, 1962, 12 pgs, EX...15.00
Catalog, Special Parts; Chrysler, Direct Connections, 1976, EX...15.00
Chart, Tune-Up; 1956 Cadillac Eldorado, EX 25.00
Clock, dash; for Hudson Super 6, Waltham Clock Co, EX 250.00
Clock, GMC Sales/Service, neon, octagonal, 18½", EX+...........300.00
Clock, Packard, neon, 21" dia, EX...725.00
Crank, Model A, G 35.00
Decanter, Motorcraft Spark Plugs, plug shape, 12½", EX 60.00
Flyer, 1959 Studebaker Lark, 2-sided, EX 8.00
Handbook, 1975 MG Midget Driver's; 79 pgs, VG+......................15.00
Hood ornament, Bentley Motors, lg 'B' w/wings, for 1938-55, EX..310.00
Hood ornament, Packard Goddess of Speed, 1940, EX 175.00
Hood ornament, 1952 Rolls Royce Spirit of Ecstasy, EX 250.00
Horn, brass, Dixie Model T, 1872 Edwards Pat Pending, 9½".....120.00
Hubcaps, 1955 Oldsmobile, EX, pr 15.00
Lamp, Chevrolet, plastic, bl bow-tie logo on wht shade, 15", EX .45.00
License plate, 1915 Connecticut, porc, yel on blk, EX 65.00

License plate attachment, Auto Assoc of NJ, die-cut porc, 5x10", EX+...175.00
License plate attachment, Canadian Travel Club, triangle w/beaver, EX ...15.00
License plate fr, Harry Mann Corvette, 1960s, NM......................85.00
Lighter, metal bluebird racer w/wht plastic wheels, 1940s, 3⅛", EX+..40.00
Manual, owner's; Cadillac, 1963, VG 30.00
Manual, owner's; Mercedes-Benz 190 SL, 1959, EX 195.00
Manual, 1940 Hudson, EX 30.00
Manual, 1943 Motors Truck Repair, 914 pgs, 1st edition, EX........35.00
Manual, 1951 Plymouth, 36 pgs, 8½x5½", VG 30.00
Manual, 1954 Holden FJ, 44 pgs, VG+ 35.00
Medallion, AAA, Cincinnati, some wear & rpt, 3x4½" 25.00
Mirror, Indian Motorcycle, bl-tinted glass w/chrome, EX............625.00
Mirror, rear-view; brass, beveled glass, for early auto, 8x10"........275.00
Pin, Peerless, silver eagle w/bl & red shield, enameled, EX 10.00
Playing cards, Pontiac Sales & Service, 2 complete decks in box, EX...30.00
Program, 1970 Laguna Seca Trans Am Auto Racing, 40 pgs, NM...45.00
Road sign, Route 66, yel sunflower design on blk, Kansas, EX....205.00
Screwdriver, Triple-Bit; White Truck Motor Co, EX (orig box)....25.00
Sign, BMW, porc concave disc, geometric center, wht/bl, 24" dia, EX..400.00
Sign, Effecto Auto Finishes, steel, 7" dia, VG 35.00
Sign, Ford The Universal Car, porc winged triangle, 2-sided, 30" L, EX ..1,800.00
Sign, Ford V8, neon, V8 at bottom of Ford oval, 26x27½", EX+ ..200.00
Sign, Maryland Casualty Co Auto Ins..., porc, graphics, 61x28", G.....450.00
Sign, Masury's Automobile Colors, celluloid on metal, wood fr, 18x23".650.00
Sign, Mercedes Benz, porc concave disc, bl & wht, 23½" dia, VG 700.00
Sign, Motorola Car Radio/Authorized Service, tin, 2-sided, 20x28", EX+..350.00
Sign, Rolls/RR/Royce, emb fiberglass, wht on maroon, 85x50x2¼", EX ..160.00
Speedometer, Corbin Indian/Harley, 100 MPH, EX.................1,000.00
Suicide knob, w/lady in bikini inside, Rainbow Plastics, EX 80.00
Tire guage, brass, A Schrader's Son...NY 20.00
Tire pump, wheel driven, A Wissler, 9" L, VG (orig wood box) .110.00

Autumn Leaf

In 1933 the Hall China Company designed a line of dinnerware for the Jewel Tea Company, who offered it to their customers as premiums. Although you may hear the ware referred to as 'Jewel Tea,' it was officially named 'Autumn Leaf' in the 1940s. In addition to the dinnerware, frosted Libbey glass tumblers, stemware, and a melmac service with the orange and gold bittersweet pod were available over the years, as were tablecloths, plastic covers for bowls and mixers, and metal items such as cake safes, hot pads, coasters, wastebaskets, and canisters. Even shelf paper and playing cards were made to coordinate. In 1958 the International Silver Company designed silverplated flatware in a pattern called 'Autumn' which was to be used with dishes in the Autumn Leaf pattern. A year later, a line of stainless flatware was introduced. These accessory lines are prized by collectors today.

One of the most fascinating aspects of collecting the Autumn Leaf pattern has been the wonderful discoveries of previously unlisted pieces. Among these items are two different bud-ray lid one-pound butter dishes; most recently a one-pound butter dish in the 'Zephyr' or 'Bingo' style; a miniature set of the 'Casper' salt and pepper shakers; coffee, tea, and sugar canisters; a pair of candlesticks; an experimental condiment jar; and a covered candy dish. All of these china pieces are attributed to the Hall China Company. Other unusual items have turned up in the accessory lines as well and include a Libbey frosted tumbler in a pilsner shape, a wooden serving bowl, and an apron made from the oilcloth (plastic) material that was used in the 1950s tablecloth. These latter items appear to be professionally done, and we can only speculate as to their origin. Collectors believe that the Hall items were sample pieces that were never meant to be distributed.

Hall discontinued the Autumn Leaf line in 1978. At that time the date was added to the backstamp to mark ware still in stock in the Hall warehouse. A special promotion by Jewel saw the reintroduction of basic dinnerware and serving pieces with the 1978 backstamp. These pieces have made their way into many collections. Additionally, in 1979 Jewel released a line of enamel-clad cookware and a Vellux blanket made by Martex which were decorated with the Autumn Leaf pattern. They continued to offer these items for a few years only, then all distribution of Autumn Leaf items was discontinued.

It should be noted that the Hall China Company has produced several limited edition items for the National Autumn Leaf Collectors Club (NALCC): a New York-style teapot (1984); an Edgewater vase (1987, different than the original shape); candlesticks (1988); a Philadelphia-style teapot, creamer, and sugar set (1990); a tea-for-two set and a Solo tea set (1991), a donut jug, and a large oval casserole. Later came the small ball jug, 1-cup French teapot, and a set of four chocolate mugs. Other special items over the past few years made for them by Hall China include a sugar packet holder, a chamberstick, and an oyster cocktail. Additional items are scheduled for production. All of these are plainly marked as having been made for the NALCC and are appropriately dated. A few other pieces have been made by Hall as limited editions for an Ohio company, but these are easily identified: the Airflow teapot and the Norris refrigerator pitcher (neither of which was previously decorated with the Autumn Leaf decal), a square-handled beverage mug, and the new-style Irish mug. A production problem with the square-handled mugs halted their production. The company then issued a regular conic-style mug with a round handle. Additional items available now are a covered onion soup, tall bud vase, china kitchen memo board, and egg drop-style salt and pepper shakers with a mustard pot. They have also issued a deck of playing cards and Libbey tumblers. See *Garage Sale & Flea Market Annual* (Collector Books) for suggested values for club pieces. Our advisor for this category is Gwynne Harrison; she is listed in the Directory under California. For more information we recommend *Collector's Encyclopedia of Hall China, Third Edition,* by Margaret and Kenn Whitmyer.

Baker, cake; Heatflow clear glass, Mary Dunbar, 1½-qt	85.00
Baker, French, 2-pt	175.00
Baker, oval, Fort Pitt, 12-oz ind	225.00
Baker/souffle, 4⅛"	12.00
Bean pot, 1-hdl	1,000.00
Bean pot, 2-hdl, 2¼-qt	250.00
Blanket, Autumn Leaf color, Vellux, full sz	175.00
Blanket, bl, Vellux, full sz	200.00
Book, Mary Dunbar Cookbook	30.00
Bottle, Jim Beam, w/stand	130.00
Bowl, cream soup	40.00
Bowl, flat soup; 8½"	20.00
Bowl, fruit; 5½"	6.00
Bowl, grease; w/lid	20.00
Bowl, mixing; New Metal, 3-pc set	325.00
Bowl, Royal Glas-Bake, set of 4	500.00
Bowl, salad; 9""	20.00
Bowl, soup; Melmac	20.00
Bowl, vegetable; divided, oval	125.00
Bowl, vegetable; oval	25.00
Bowl, vegetable; rnd, 9"	175.00
Bowl, vegetable; Royal Glasbake, milk wht, divided	150.00
Bowl cover set, plastic, 8-pc: 7 assorted covers in pouch	100.00
Bread box, metal, from $400 to	800.00
Butter dish, ¼-lb, regular, ruffled top, from $175 to	250.00
Butter dish, ¼-lb, sq top, rare	2,000.00
Butter dish, ¼-lb, wings top	2,000.00
Cake plate	28.00
Cake safe, metal, motif on top or sides, 5", ea	50.00
Candle holder, Chamber, club gift, 1991	125.00

Candle holder, club pc, 892 made, 1989, pr	250.00
Candy dish, metal base	550.00
Canister, Autumn Leaf color/pattern, wht plastic lid, Douglas	10.00
Canister, brn & gold, wht plastic lid	30.00
Canister, metal, rnd, w/coppertone lid, set of 4, from $600 to	1,000.00
Canister, metal, rnd, w/matching lids, set of 3, from $200 to	300.00
Casserole, Heatflow, w/lid, rnd, 2-qt	85.00
Clock, electric	550.00
Clock, salesman's award	450.00
Coaster, metal, 3⅛"	8.00
Coffee percolator, electric, all china, 4-pc	400.00
Coffeepot, Jewel's Best, 30-cup	600.00
Coffeepot, percolator, electric	400.00
Coffeepot, Rayed, 8-cup	45.00
Coffeepot, 9-cup, Rayed	45.00
Cookie jar, Tootsie, 'Rayed'	310.00

Cookie jar, Zeisel, 1957 – 69, from $275.00 to $300.00.

Cookware, New Metal, 7-pc set	650.00
Creamer & sugar bowl, Rayed, 1930s style	80.00
Cup, St Denis	50.00
Cup & saucer, regular, Ruffled-D	9.00
Custard cup, Heatflow clear glass, Mary Dunbar, from $40 to	60.00
Custard cup, Radiance	10.00
Dutch oven, metal, porc, w/lid, 5-qt	175.00
Flatware, sp, ea	35.00
Fry pan, Mary Dunbar, top stoveware glass	175.00
Gravy boat, w/underplate (pickle dish)	55.00
Hot pad, metal, oval, 10¾", from $12 to	15.00
Hot pad, metal, red or gr felt-like bking, rnd	20.00
Hurricane lamp, Douglas, w/metal base, pr, minimum value	500.00
Jug, ball form, #3	40.00
Jug, batter; Sundial (bowl), rare	5,500.00
Jug, utility; Rayed, 2½-pt, 6"	25.00
Loaf pan, Mary Dunbar, from $90 to	125.00
Mug, chocolate; club pc, 1,500 made, 1992, 4-pc set	100.00
Mug, Irish coffee	150.00
Napkin, ecru muslin, 16" sq	50.00
Pickle dish or gravy liner, oval, 9"	25.00
Pickle dish/platter, 6"	25.00
Pie plate, Heatflow, clear glass, Mary Dunbar, from $45 to	60.00
Pie plate, 9½"	35.00
Place mat, paper, scalloped, set of 8, from $150 to	325.00
Plate, 8"	18.00
Plate, 9"	12.00
Plate, 10"	18.00
Platter, oval, 13½"	28.00
Pressure cooker, Mary Dunbar, metal	225.00
Range set, shakers & grease jar w/lid	60.00
Saucepan, w/lid, metal, 2-qt	100.00
Shakers, Casper, ruffled, regular, pr	30.00
Shelf liner, paper, 108" roll	50.00

Stack set, 4-pc 125.00
Tablecloth, cotton sailcloth w/gold stripe, 54x54" 140.00
Tablecloth, cotton sailcloth w/gold stripe, 54x72" 140.00
Tablecloth, muslin, 56x81" 300.00
Tablecloth, plastic 150.00
Teapot, Newport, dtd 1978, from $175 to 250.00
Teapot, Rayed, long spout, 1935 ....95.00
Teapot, Rayed, long spout, 1978, from $800 to 1,600.00
Teapot, Solo, club pc, 1,400 made, 1991 ....100.00
Tidbit tray, 2-tier 100.00
Tin, fruitcake; wht or tan 10.00
Toaster cover, plastic, Mary Dunbar 50.00
Towel, tea; cotton, 16x33" 60.00
Toy, Jewel Truck, gr, from $350 to 425.00
Toy, Jewel Truck Semi Trailer, brn, from $1,000 to 1,500.00
Toy, Jewel Van, brn, Buddy L, from $400 to 650.00
Tray, glass, wood hdl 140.00
Tray, metal, oval 100.00
Tumbler, Brockway, 9-oz, 13-oz or 16-oz, ea 45.00
Tumbler, Libbey, frosted, 9-oz, 3¾" 32.00
Tumbler, Libbey, frosted, 14-oz, 5½" 20.00
Tumbler, Libbey, gold & frost on clear, 10-oz 75.00
Tumbler, Libbey, gold frost etched, flat or ftd, 10-oz, ea 65.00
Tumbler, Libbey, gold frost etched, flat or ftd, 15-oz, ea 65.00
Vase, bud; regular decal, 6" 275.00
Vase, Edgewater, club pc, 626 made, 1987 ....350.00
Warmer, rnd 160.00

Aviation

Aviation buffs are interested in any phase of flying, from early developments with gliders, balloons, airships, and flying machines to more modern innovations. Books, catalogs, photos, patents, lithographs, ad cards, and posters are among the paper ephemera they treasure alongside models of unlikely flying contraptions, propellers and rudders, insignia and equipment from WWI and WWII, and memorabilia from the flights of the Wright Brothers, Lindbergh, Earhart, and the Zeppelins. Our advisor for this category is John R. Joiner; he is listed in the Directory under Georgia. See also Militaria.

Badge, worker's; Curtiss Wright, brass, WWII era, pin-bk, EX 50.00
Binder, WWII Instrument Manuals (5), dtd 1944, 11½x9½", EX..50.00
Book, The Aircraft Handbook, F&H Colvin, 415 pgs, 1921, VG+ ...60.00
Booklet, BAOC VC10 Wonder Aircraft of the Age, 16 pgs, 1965, EX...25.00
Booklet, Pan Am World Airways Route Maps, 1950s-60s, EX 20.00
Booklet, TWA, Travel Tips to Switzerland, 130 pgs, 1963, EX 12.00
Brochure, adv Braniff International flying Concorde, 1979, EX ...35.00
Brochure, Pan Am World Airlines New Dbl-Decker Clipper, 1949, EX ..30.00
Brochure, sales; Taylor Cub, Taylor Aircraft Co, 1940s, EX 60.00
Calendar, Grumman Aviation, spiral bound, photos & info, EX...30.00
Cards, cigarette; Aircraft of the RAF, complete set of 50, 1938, EX...20.00
Cup, coffee; US Air, gr w/burgundy letters, M 15.00
Cup & saucer, TWA, wht w/red stripe & logo, Rosenthal, 1960s, EX ..30.00
Decanter, sake; Continental, Tokyo gift, 1978, 17", EX..............35.00
Kit, BOAC Junior Jet Club; complete in orig pkg, 1957, EX 40.00
Label, Grand Central Air Terminal, Curtiss Wright, 1940s, M 80.00
Label, luggage; Panagra, N & S America in blk & wht, 3½" dia ..45.00
Label, luggage; Pan Am/CIA Mexicana De Aviacion, 1940s, 4x5½"..30.00
Label, luggage; SCADTA, Columbian Airlines, 1930s, NM 20.00
Label, luggage; UAT French Airlines, luggage shape, 1940s, EX...12.00
Magazine, Western Flying, November 1940, EX 12.50
Manual, owner's; Cessna Model 172 & Skyhawk, 1968, VG 15.00
Oil can, Archer Lubricants, 1-qt, full, EX 15.00

Packet, Compimentary Flight; Continental Airlines, 1959, EX 25.00
Pennant, Welcome Lindy, wht letters on bl, 10x14¾", EX 350.00
Photo, aerial; American Airlines DC3 US Mail Express, 1930s, EX..30.00
Photo, female passenger of TWA Sleeper Flight w/stewardess, EX ..25.00
Photo, WWI Allied camouflaged biplane in flight, matted & fr, 8x6"...400.00
Pin, Safety Member, Rohr Aircraft, wht & gr enameled, EX.........30.00
Plaque, Iran Air, ornate w/flying horse symbol, pewter, 8" dia 15.00
Postcard, United Airlines, Boeing Transport w/travel route, EX ...65.00
Poster, Disneyland Travel, TWA, rocketship & castle, 40x25", VG..600.00
Poster, TWA, Visit Switzerland, shows the Matterhorn, 35x28" ...20.00
Poster, Western Airlines LA, silk-screened, 1970s, 25x39", EX 30.00
Safety card, United Airlines, DC-6B, plastic coated, 1962, EX.....60.00
Scarf, Quantas Air Lines, graphics & logos, 1950s, 30x31", EX 55.00
Schedule, Texas International Airlines, 1975, EX 10.00
Schedule, Western Airlines, 1943, 8x9", EX 23.00
Slide rule, Model MK-6B, Kane Aero Co, w/case, 1957, EX.........20.00
Tickets, Northern Consolidated Airlines, 1963, EX, pr 30.00
Timetable, Bahamas Airways, 1963, VG 30.00
Timetable, EL AL Israel Airlines, 1951, VG+ 155.00
Timetable, GUEST Airlines, 1961, VG 35.00
Timetable, KLM & British Continental Airways, 1936, VG+ 15.00
Timetable, Sabena Belgian World Airlines, 1965, VG 18.50

Baccarat

The Baccarat Glass company was founded in 1765 near Luneville, France, and continues to this day to produce quality crystal tableware, vases, perfume bottles, and figurines. The firm became famous for the high-quality millefiori and caned paperweights produced there from 1845 until about 1860. Examples of these range from $300.00 to as much as several thousand. Since 1953 they have resumed the production of paperweights on a limited edition basis. Our advisors for this category are Randall Monsen and Rod Baer; their address is listed in the Directory under Virginia. See also Bottles, Commercial Perfume; Paperweights.

Vase, crystal, octagonal tapered form, 12", $600.00.

Bottle, scent; Swirl, Rose Tiente, 6½", pr 175.00
Bowl, cameo (stylized), gr on etched clear, star-cut bottom, 6" L ..175.00
Box, dmn-cut design, bronze gilted, w/lid, 5½x5½x4", EX 650.00
Candlestick, Massena, 6", pr 80.00
Carafe, Swirl, Rose Tiente, 10" 225.00
Champagne, Capri, 5¼" 55.00
Compote, Swirl, Rose Tiente, 3¼x4¾" 60.00
Cruet set, 1950s, 5½x2x4", w/chrome fr 180.00
Decanter, Harmonie, w/stopper 200.00
Dice, beveled edge, 1½" sq, w/orig box, pr 100.00
Dish, jam; 5", w/5½" spoon 90.00
Figurine, butterfly on base, lav, 4" 135.00
Figurine, cat, blk, 6" 225.00
Figurine, crouching tiger, 2x6" 175.00
Figurine, eagle, 6¾x5" 150.00

Figurine, elephant, lg..**350.00**
Figurine, elephant, 5¼x5¼"...**225.00**
Figurine, frog, 5x2½x3¼"...**120.00**
Figurine, nude lady, kneeling w/hands behind head, sgn, 6"........**200.00**
Figurine, owl, 4x2"...**100.00**
Figurine, polar bear, sgn, 4½x6½"..**200.00**
Figurine, woman jogging, 10"..**150.00**
Glasses, Harcourt, set of 12, 5⅛x3¾"..**525.00**
Goblet, red wine; Massena, 7x3"...**90.00**
Goblet, water; Capri, 6⅝", set of 6..**350.00**
Goblet, water; Massena, 5½"...**70.00**
Goblet, water; Neptune, etched, 9"...**260.00**
Goblet, wine; St Remy, 5⅞", set of 6...**225.00**
Hurricane lamps, etched globe, prisms, cherub stem, 25", EX, pr...**1,000.00**
Ice bucket, Massena, 5x5⅜"...**160.00**
Lamp, oil; Rose Tiente, brass gilt, 6½"......................................**165.00**
Obelisk, blk glass, sq base, 10"...**250.00**
Salt, open; dbl, w/center hdl, 5¼x2⅛".....................................**100.00**
Trylon, pyramid shape, 10"...**200.00**
Tumbler, cordial; Tallyrand, 2¼", set of 8.................................**225.00**
Tumbler, old fashioned; Tallyrand, etched mk, set of 12, 3½".....**500.00**
Tumbler, Rose Tiente, 4"..**60.00**
Vase, cameo floral, cranberry on frost, 6"..................................**225.00**
Vase, grasshopper on base supports vase, 8⅜".........................**125.00**
Vase, leaves & berries, ruby to etched clear w/gold, baluster, 12x5"..**1,850.00**
Vase, snake coils frosted bamboo-like body, beetle on rim, ftd, 9".........**350.00**

Badges

The breast badge came into general usage in this country about 1840. Since most are not marked and styles have changed very little to the present day, they are often difficult to date. The most reliable clue is the pin and catch. One of the earliest types, used primarily before the turn of the century, involved a 't-pin' and a 'shell' catch. In a second style, the pin was hinged with a small square of sheet metal, and the clasp was cylindrical. From the late 1800s until about 1940, the pin and clasp were made from one continuous piece of thin metal wire. The same type, with the addition of a flat back plate, was used a little later. There are exceptions to these findings, and other types of clasps were also used. Hallmarks and inscriptions may also help pinpoint an approximate age.

Badges have been made from a variety of materials, usually brass or nickel silver; but even solid silver and gold were used for special orders. They are found in many basic shapes and variations — stars with five to seven points, shields, disks, ovals, and octagonals being most often encountered. Of prime importance to collectors, however, is that the title and/or location appear on the badge. Those with designations of positions no longer existing (City Constable, for example) and names of early western states and towns are most valuable.

Badges are among the most commonly reproduced (and faked) types of antiques on the market. At any flea market, ten fakes can be found for every authentic example. Genuine law badges start at $30.00 to $40.00 for recent examples (1950 – 1970); earlier pieces (1910 – 1930) usually bring $50.00 to $90.00. Pre-1900 badges often sell for more than $100.00. Authentic gold badges are usually priced at a minimum of scrap value (karat, weight, spot price for gold); fine gold badges from before 1900 can sell for $400.00 to $800.00, and a few will bring even more. A fire badge is usually valued at about half the price of a law badge from the same era and material. Our advisor for this category is Gene Matzke; he is listed in the Directory under Wisconsin.

Alert Affiliated League of Emergency Radio Teams, gold-tone shield, 3"...**25.00**
Boston Press, gold-plated, eng florals, oval, 1890s, 2x1", EX.........**45.00**
C&A RR Police, 6-point star, silver, saddle-type pin-bk.............**185.00**

CA Dept of Corrections, state seal, 7-point star, Blackinton, 2¾"..**60.00**
Chicago Fire Patrol Committee, bl enamel on brass, 1¾x2¾"...**500.00**
Chicago Special Police, NP, 6-point star, ca 1920s.....................**125.00**
Cleveland Police Sergeant, gold-tone metal shield, 3"................**35.00**
DC Pippenger Dec 5th 1862 Knapp Wis, silver shield, orig pin-bk..**600.00**
Deputy Sheriff, Racine WI, 6-point star, 1925-26, 1⅞"..............**60.00**
Deputy Sheriff Juneau Co, gold-plated metal, 1940s, 2½"............**45.00**

Deputy U.S. Marshall, 1920s, type #3 variation, worn original finish, safety-pin style clasp, $770.00.

Final Encampment, Sons of Union/Confederate Veterans, 1949, NMOC.**380.00**
Fountain City FD, silver metal, eagle on shield.............................**35.00**
Interborough Rapid Transit Employee, NP, 2¼" dia....................**28.00**
Kansas City Fireman, 4-leaf clover shape, 1910s, 1⅞".................**85.00**
Licensed Chauffeur 1951...Illinois, 1¾x1¼"...............................**25.00**
Master At Arms, USS Dauphin, 6-point star, 1940s......................**75.00**
Metropolitan Police Asst Chief DC, gold shield, 2¼x2⅛".........**195.00**
Minnesota Chauffeur, 1917, pin-bk, EX......................................**325.00**
Pinkerton Special Services, shield w/eagle, hallmk.......................**35.00**
Port Huron Auto Club, radiator shape, enameled, 1919, 2½x4"...**775.00**
Post Office, Philadelphia, pin-bk, Peiffer Bros, 2⅜"...................**375.00**
Texas Rangers, silver w/hallmark, Dept of Public Safety, EX.......**465.00**
US Customs Watchman, gold-plated, circular, mk Mayer, EX....**985.00**
US Inspector, Steam Vessels, silver, 2x2", EX...............................**825.00**
2nd Asst Chief Boston PA, eagle atop shield, lt wear, 2¼"...........**35.00**

Banks

In general, bank values are established on the auction block and sales between collectors and dealers, and the driving force that determines the final price is condition. The spread between the price of a bank in excellent condition and the identical model in only good condition continues to widen. In order to be a seasoned collector in the pursuit of wise investments, one must learn to carefully determine overall condition by assessing the amount and strength (depth) of the paint, and by checking for breaks, repairs, and replaced parts; all bear heavily on value. Paint and casting variations are other considerations the collector should become familiar with.

Banks continue to maintain their value. Mechanicals often bring astronomical prices, making it imperative that collectors understand the market. Let's take a look at the price variations possible on an Uncle Sam mechanical bank. If you find one with considerable paint missing but with some good color showing, the price would be around $1,000.00. If it has repairs or restoration, the value could drop to somewhere near $800.00 or less. Still another example with two thirds of its original paint and no repairs would probably bring $1,800.00. If it had only minor nicks, it could go as high as $3,500.00. Should you find one in 95% paint with no repairs $5,000.00 or more would not be out of line. After considering all of these factors, remember: the final price is always determined by what a willing buyer and seller agree on for a specific bank.

Mechanical banks are the 'crème de le crème' in the arena of cast-iron toy collecting. They are among the most outstanding products of the Industrial Revolution and are recognized as some of the most successful of the mass-produced products of the nineteenth century. The earliest mechanicals were made of wood or lead. In 1869 John Hall introduced Hall's Excelsior, made of cast iron. It was an immediate success. J. & E. Stevens produced the bank for Hall and as a result soon began to make their own designs. Several companies followed suit, most of which were already in the hardware business. They used newly developed iron-casting techniques to produce these novelty savings devices for the emerging toy market. The social mores and customs of the times, political attitudes, racial and ethnic biases, the excitement of the circus, and humorous everyday events all served as inspiration for the creation of hundreds of banks. Designers made the most of simple mechanics to produce models with captivating actions that served not only to amuse but promote the concept of thrift to the children. The quality and detail of the castings were truly remarkable. The majority of collectible banks were made from 1870 to 1910; however, they continued to be manufactured until the onset of WWII. J & E. Stevens, Shepard Hardware, and Kyser and Rex were some of the most prolific manufacturers of mechanicals. They made still banks as well.

Still banks are widely collected. Various materials were used in their construction, and each material represents a subfield in still bank collections. No one knows exactly how many different banks were made, but upwards of three thousand have been identified in the various books published on the subject. Cast-iron examples still dominate the market, but lead banks from Europe are growing in value. Tin and early pottery banks are drawing more interest as well. American pottery banks which were primarily collected by Americana collectors are becoming more important in the still bank field.

To increase your knowledge of banks, attend shows and auctions. Direct contact with collectors and knowledgeable dealers is a very good way to develop a feel for prices and quality. It will also help you in gaining the ability to judge condition, and you'll learn to recognize the more desirable banks as well.

Both mechanical and still banks have been reproduced. One way to detect a reproduction is by measuring. The dimensions of a reproduced bank will always be fractionally smaller, since the original bank was cast from a pattern while the reproduction was made from a casting of the original bank. As both values and interest continue to increase, it becomes even more important to educate ourselves to the fullest extent possible. We recommend these books for your library: *The Bank Book* by Norman, *The Dictionary of Still Banks* by Long and Pitman, *The Penny Bank Book* by Moore, *Penny Banks Around the World* by Don Duer, and *Penny Lane* by Davidson, which is considered the most complete reference available. It contains a cross-reference listing of numbers from all other publications on mechanical banks. Other books to consider are *Collector's Guide to Glass Banks* by Charles V. Reynolds, *Ceramic Coin Banks* by Tom Stoddard, and *Collector's Guide to Banks* by Beverly and Jim Mangus which covers modern pottery, porcelain, and composition banks.

Our advisor for mechanical and still banks is Clive Devenish, who is listed in the Directory under California.

All banks are assumed to be complete and original unless noted otherwise in the description. A number of banks are commonly found with a particular repair. When this repair is reflected in our pricing, it will be so indicated. When traps (typically key lock, as in Uncle Sam) are an integral part of the body of the bank, lack of such results in a severe reduction in the value of the bank. When the trap is underneath the bank (typically a twist trap, as in Eagle and Eaglets), reduction in value is minimal.

To most accurately represent current market values, we have used condition codes in our listings that correspond with guidelines developed by today's bank collectors.

NM — 98% paint	VG — 80% paint
PR (pristine) — 95% paint	G — 70% paint
EX — 90% paint	

Key:
CI — cast iron	NP — nickel-plated

Advertising

Chevrolet Globe, M-798 variant, tin, 4¼", EX	80.00
Decker's Iowana (pig), M-603, CI, 2¼", EX	150.00
Gem Heater, M-1364, CI, 4¾", G	90.00
Indiana Silo, M-1247, CI w/gold pnt, 3½", EX	1,150.00
Kelvinator Refrigerater on Legs, M-1338 variant, CI, 4⅜", VG	150.00
Reliable Parlor Stove, M-1356, CI, 6¼", EX	450.00
Singer Electric Sewing Machine, M-1369, tin/CI, 5⅛", EX	400.00
York Stove, M-1351, CI, 4", EX	275.00

Book of Knowledge Banks

Book of Knowledge Banks were produced by John Wright (Pennsylvania) from circa 1950 until 1975. Of the thirty models they made during those years, a few continued to be made in very limited numbers until the late 1980s; these they referred to as the 'Medallion' series. (Today the Medallion banks command the same prices as the earlier Book of Knowledge series.) Each bank was a handcrafted, hand-painted duplicate of an original as was found in the collection of The Book of Knowledge, the first children's encyclopedia in this country. Because the antique banks are often priced out of the range of many of today's collectors, these banks are being sought out as affordable substitutes for their very expensive counterparts. It should also be noted that China has reproduced banks with the Book of Knowledge inscription on them. These copies are flooding the market and affecting prices. Buyers should take extra caution when investing in Book of Knowledge banks and purchase them through a reputable dealer who offers a satisfaction guarantee as well as a guarantee that the bank is authentic. Our advisor for Book of Knowledge banks is Dan Iannotti; he is listed under Michigan.

Artillery Bank, NM	295.00
Butting Buffalo, M	295.00
Cabin, NM	265.00
Cow (kicking), NM	295.00
Dentist, EX	175.00
I Always Did 'Spise a Mule, NM	250.00
Leap Frog, NM	295.00
Milking Cow, NM	275.00
Owl (turns head), NM	225.00
Tammany, NMIB	250.00
Teddy & the Bear, NM	265.00
Uncle Remus, M	285.00
US & Spain, NM	265.00

Mechanical

Boy on Trapeze, N-1350, cast iron, J. Barton & Smith Co., 9½", EX, $3,800.00.

Acrobat, N-1010, CI, EX....6,800.00
Always Did 'Spise a Mule (bench), N-2940, CI, G....600.00
Arch-Top Clown, N-1860, tin, EX....275.00
Archie Anderson, aluminum, EX....225.00
Bill E Grin, N-1230, CI, EX....3,500.00
Bill E Grin, N-1230, CI, old rpt, no trap, rpl screw....375.00
Boy Robbing Bird's Nest, CI, J&E Stevens, PR....15,000.00
Bulldog (coin on nose), N-1430, CI, EX....3,000.00
Cat & Mouse, N-1700, CI, rpl plate, EX....2,500.00
Clown (rnd trap), tin, Chein, postwar, EX....125.00
Clown (sq trap), tin, Chein, EX....400.00
Darktown Battery, N-2080, arms rstr, VG....1,800.00
Darktown Battery, N-2080, CI, EX....4,800.00
Dinah, N-2150, CI, EX....900.00
Dog on Turntable, N-2170, CI, VG....550.00
Eagle & Eaglets, N-2230, CI, EX....1,500.00
Elephant, Man in Howdah; N-2280, CI, EX....800.00
Elephant & 3 Clowns, N-2250, CI, EX....2,800.00
Hall's Lilliput, N-2740, CI, EX....750.00
Humpty Dumpty, N-2900, CI, VG....1,250.00
Indian Shooting Bear, N-2980, CI, J&E Stevens, orig feathers, EX..3,800.00
Joe Socko, N-3050, tin, EX....400.00
Jolly N, CI, EX, all orig (many variations), from $200 to....900.00
Jolly N w/High Hat, N-3250, CI, VG....600.00
Lion & Monkeys, N-3650, CI, Kyser & Rex, orig monkey, VG..2,800.00
Magician, N-370, CI, EX....3,600.00
Monkey & Parrot, N-3950, tin, EX....500.00
Monkey Bank, N-3960, CI, Hubley, EX....600.00
Mule Entering Barn, N-4030, CI, VG....1,400.00
Novelty, N-4260, CI, EX....2,200.00
Octagonal Fort, N-4280, CI, G....1,850.00
Owl Turns Head, N-4380, CI, G....475.00
Pistol, N-4600, NP sheet metal, EX....650.00
Presto, N-4650, CI, EX....375.00
Professor Pug Frog, N-4690, CI, J&E Stevens, EX....15,000.00
Snappit, N-5160, CI, VG....450.00
Speaking Dog, N-5170, CI, EX....3,000.00
Stump Speaker, N-5370, CI, VG....3,000.00
Tammany, N-5420, CI, VG....500.00
Teddy & Bear, N-5460, CI, EX....2,800.00
Trick Dog, N-5630, CI, Hubley, VG....400.00
Trick Dog (6-part base), N-5620, CI, Shepard, EX....2,800.00
Uncle Sam, N-5740, CI, EX....3,800.00
Uncle Tom, N-5770, CI, EX....600.00
US Bank (building), N-5810, CI, rare, EX....12,000.00
Watch Dog Safe, N-5890, CI, worn pnt, no bellows....200.00
William Tell, N-5940, CI, VG....650.00

Registering

Superman Dime Register Bank, tin, 2½" square, EX, from $225.00 to $250.00.

Bean Pot, M-951, CI, 3", EX....250.00
Beehive Registering Savings Bank, CI/NP, 5⅜", EX....275.00
Bestmaid, tin, 4¾", EX....75.00
Buddy (L) Savings & Recording Bank, sheet metal, 6⁵⁄₁₆", EX...125.00
Dandy Self Registering Savings Bank, tin, 4¾", NM....360.00
Donald Duck Clock Vault, tin, Spanish sayings on drum, EX....140.00
Keene Savings Bank, tin, EX....350.00
Penny Saver, CI, 5⅛", VG....80.00
Popeye Dime Register (pocket), M-1573, silver pnt on tin, 2½", EX..75.00
Prudential Registering Savings Bank (10¢), CI/NP, 7¼", EX....350.00
Snow White Dime Register (pocket), M-1567, tin, 2½" sq, EX.150.00
Uncle Sam, M-1290, sheet steel w/blk & gold, 6¼", EX....80.00

Still

$100,000 Money Bag, M-1262, CI, 3⅝", EX....400.00
Amish Boy & Pig on Bale, M-195, wht metal, 4¾", EX....45.00
Arcade Steamboat, M-1460, CI, 2⅜" H, EX....460.00
Baby Bird, M-670, lead, w/touched-up pnt, 3", EX....260.00
Baseball Player, M-18, CI, 5¾", VG....160.00
Baseball Player, M-19, CI, 5¾", EX....525.00
Baseball Player, M-19, CI, 5¾", NM....1,025.00
Bear Stealing Honey (on base), M-1308 variant, CI, 7¾", EX...360.00
Bear Stealing Pig, M-693, CI, rpl screw, 5½", G....550.00
Billiken, M-74, CI, 4¼", EX....65.00
Billy Bounce (Give Billy a Penny), M-15, CI, 4¾", VG....350.00
Billy Possom, M-563, CI, Harper, rpl screw, 3", EX....2,200.00
Blackpool Tower, M-984, CI, partial rpt, rpl screw, 7⅜"....100.00
Blackpool Tower, M-984, CI, 7⅜", EX....300.00
Buffalo, M-560, CI w/gold pnt, 3⅛", EX....130.00
Building w/Belfrey, M-1233, CI, hairline, rpl posts, VG....2,300.00
Building w/Eagle Finial, M-1134, CI, 9¾", EX....850.00
Bulldog (seated), M-396, CI, 3⅞", EX....185.00
Bulldog (seated), M-396, CI, 3⅞", NM....400.00
Bulldog (standing), M-403, CI, 2¼", EX....380.00
Bulldog w/Sailor Cap, M-363, lead, 4⅜", EX....400.00
Bungalow, M-999, CI, 3¾", EX....360.00
Buster Brown & Tige, M-241, CI, gold & red pnt, 5½", VG....160.00
Buster Brown & Tige, M-241, CI, 5½", G....95.00
Buster Brown & Tige, M-242 variant, CI, 5½", NM....850.00
Buster Brown & Tige Good Luck, M-508, CI, 4¼', VG....300.00
Cadet, M-8, CI, crack at slot, 5¾", VG....150.00
Cadet, M-8, CI, 5¾", NM....650.00
Camel (kneeling), M-770, CI, 2½", EX....750.00
Camel (lg), M-767, CI, 7¼", EX....350.00
Campbell Kids, M-163, CI, gold pnt, 3¾", EX....300.00
Campbell Kids, M-163, CI, rpl screw, 3¾", G....140.00
Captain Kidd, M-38, CI, 5⅝", G....130.00
Castle With Two Towers, M-1114, CI, 7", EX....1,000.00
Cat on Tub, M-358, CI, gold pnt, 4⅛", EX....160.00
Cat w/Long Tail, M-369, CI, rpl screw, 4⅜", EX....725.00
Charles Russell, M-247, wht metal, gold pnt, 6¼", EX....50.00
Charlie Chaplin, M-290, glass/tin, 3¾", EX....125.00
Charlie McCarthy on Trunk, M-207, compo, 5¼", M....430.00
Circus Elephant, M-462, CI, 3⅞", EX....160.00
City Bank w/Chimney, M-1101, CI, old rpt, 6¾"....1,450.00
City Bank w/Crown, M-1095, CI, 5½", NM....7,000.00
City Bank w/Teller, M-1097, CI, 5½", NM....570.00
Clown, M-211, CI, 6¼", EX....230.00
Columbia Bank, M-1070, CI, 5¾", EX....560.00
Columbia Bank, M-1073, CI, no trap, 8¾", EX....490.00
Columbia Tower, M-1118, CI, rpl turnpin, 6⅞", VG....675.00
Columbian Safe Deposit, CI, 6½", NM....600.00
Coronation, M-1319, CI, 6¼", EX....700.00
County Bank, M-1110, CI, 4¼", G....160.00

Cow, M-553, CI, 3⅜", EX..............................290.00
Crown Building, M-1225, CI, 5", NM.............3,000.00
Crown Building on Legs, M-1151, CI, 4⅞", NM..........1,450.00
Cupola, M-1146, CI, 4⅛", EX........................340.00
Cupola Building, M-1145, CI, 5½", NM.............1,375.00
Dog by Ball, M-390, lead/tin, 2⅛", VG.............230.00
Dog w/Floppy Ears, M-410, lead, 5¾", EX..........500.00
Dolphin, M-33, CI, gold pnt, 4½", EX..............800.00
Domed Mosque, M-1176, CI, 5⅛", EX................330.00
Donkey w/Saddle & Reins, M-497 variant, lead, 4", EX...........110.00
Double Decker Bus, M-1490, CI, bl pnt, 2¼", NM.......1,025.00
Duck (rnd), M-619, CI, red/gr/yel pnt, NM.............570.00
Duck on Tub, M-616, CI, 5⅜", EX...................200.00
Dutch Girl (standing), M-16, CI, gold pnt, 6½", NM.........950.00
Dutch Girl w/Flowers, M-181, CI, 5¼", EX..........110.00
Elephant on Tub (decorated), M-484, CI, 5⅜", NM.........460.00
Elephant on Wheels, M-446, CI, 4⅛", EX............330.00
Elephant w/Howdah, M-476 variant, porcelainized CI, 4¾".......115.00
Eureka Trust & Savings Safe, CI, 5¾", EX..........425.00
Fala (dog), M-430, CI, 2¾", EX.....................295.00
Feed My Sheep (lamb), M-596, lead, gold pnt, 2¾", VG.........140.00
Fez w/Tassle (Syria Potentate), M-1396, steel, w/key, 2⅜", EX.....90.00
Flat Iron Building, M-1159, CI, 8¼", EX...........2,400.00
Flat Iron Building, M-1160, CI, no trap, 5¾", EX......370.00
Forlorn Dog, M-408, wht metal, 4¾", G..............75.00
Fortune Ship, M-1457, CI, 4⅛", NM...............1,600.00
Foxy Grandpa, M-320, CI, 5½", EX..................340.00
Foxy Grandpa, M-320, CI, 5½", G...................195.00
Frowning Face, M-12, CI, 5⅝", EX.................1,650.00
General Grant, M-115 variant, CI, Harper, 5⅝", EX.........3,400.00
Give Me a Penny, M-166 variant, CI, 5¾", EX........400.00
Globe, M-812, CI, 5", VG...........................250.00
Globe on Arc, M-789, CI, red pnt, 5¼", EX..........380.00
Globe on Arc, M-789, CI, 5¼", G....................125.00
Globe Savings Fund, M-1199, CI, 7⅛", EX.........3,000.00
Golliwog, M-85, CI, 6¼", EX........................500.00
Graf Zeppelin, M-1428, CI, 1¾" H, EX...............220.00
Grizzly Bear, M-703, lead, pnt worn in bk, 2¾"......100.00
Hansel & Gretel, M-1016, tin, 2¼", EX.............125.00
Harper Stork Safe, M-651, CI, hdl missing, 5½", EX.........850.00
High Rise, M-1217, CI w/japanning, 5½", EX.........300.00
High Rise, M-1219, CI, 4⅝", EX.....................390.00
High Rise Tiered, M-1215, CI, 5¾", EX..............350.00
Home Savings, M-1126, CI, 5⅞", EX.................290.00
Horse on Tub (decorated), M-509, CI, 5¼", VG.......155.00
Horse on Wheels, M-512, CI, 5", EX.................425.00
Horseshoe, Wire Mesh; M-524, CI/tin, G- Arcade label, 3¼", VG..95.00
I Made Chicago Famous (pig), M-629, CI, Harper, 2⅛", EX.....220.00
I Made St Louis Famous (mule), M-489, CI, Harper, 4¾", EX..1,950.00
Independence Hall, M-1244, CI, 8⅞", EX.............600.00
Iron Master's Cabin, M-1027, CI, 4¼", EX.........3,300.00
Labrador Retriever, M-412, CI, 4½", EX.............270.00
Litchfield Cathedral, M-968, CI, 6⅝", EX...........450.00
Main Street Trolley (no people), M-1469, CI, gold pnt, 3", EX.300.00
Maine (battleship), M-1439, CI, 6" H, NM.........4,000.00
Mammy w/Basket, M-175, wht metal, 5¼", NM........280.00
Mammy w/Spoon, M-168, CI, 5⅞", EX................225.00
Mary & Lamb, M-164, CI, 4¾", VG...................700.00
Mary & Lamb, M-164, CI, 4⅜" (EX Moore collection), NM. 3,800.00
Mean Standing Bear, M-713, CI, 5½", EX............260.00
Metropolitan Safe, CI, 5⅞", NM...................2,200.00
Mickey Mouse Post Office, tin, cylindrical, 6", NM.......140.00
Middy, M-36, CI, w/clapper, 5¼", G.................135.00
Minuteman, M-44, CI, 6", NM......................1,350.00

Model T (2nd version), M-1483, CI, 4", NM........1,050.00
Monkey w/Removable Hat, M-740, brass, 3⅞", EX........900.00
Mulligan, M-177, CI, 5¾', EX.......................160.00
Mutt & Jeff, M-157, CI, gold pnt, 4¼", EX..........150.00
Newfoundland (dog), M-440, CI, 3⅝", EX.............300.00
Ocean Liner, M-1444, lead, 2¾" H, VG..............140.00
Oregon (battleship), M-1450, CI, rpl guns, 3⅞", G......230.00
Oregon (battleship), M-1452, CI, rpl turnpin, VG......400.00
Oriental Camel, M-769, CI, 3¾", G.................325.00
Pass Round the Hat (Derby), M-1381, CI, 1⅝", EX......200.00
Peaceful Bill/Harper Smiling Jim, M-109, CI, 4", EX......2,400.00
Pearl Street Building, M-1096, worn gold overpnt, 4¼"......380.00
Pig (standing), M-478, CI, 3", EX..................240.00
Policeman, M-182, CI, Arcade, 5½", EX.............1,100.00
Porky Pig, M-264, CI, 6", EX+......................400.00
Porky Pig, M-264, CI, 6", VG.......................175.00
Professor Pug Frog, M-311, CI, 3¼", EX.............330.00
Puppo, M-416, CI, 4⅞", VG..........................155.00
Quilted Lion, M-758, CI, 3¾", EX...................300.00
Reindeer, M-376, CI, 6¼", NM.......................280.00
Rhino, M-721, CI, 2⅝", NM........................1,050.00
Roof Bank Building, M-1122, CI, 5¼", G.............300.00
Rooster, M-548, CI, 4¾", EX........................130.00
Rumplestiltskin, M-27, CI, 6", VG..................200.00
Sailor, M-27, CI, 5¼", G............................85.00
Sailor, M-28, CI, 5½", G...........................125.00
Sailor, M-29, CI, 5⅝", NM..........................800.00

Santa With Tree, cast iron, Hubley, 6", PR, $950.00; EX, $650.00.
(Photo courtesy Dunbar Gallery)

Scottie (standing), M-435, CI, 3¾", VG.............140.00
Seal on Rock, M-732, CI, 3½", EX...................600.00
Squirrel w/Nut, M-660, CI, 4⅛", VG.................470.00
State Bank, M-1078, CI, w/key, 8", NM.............1,350.00
State Bank, M-1083, CI, 4⅛", EX....................250.00
State Bank, M-1085, CI, 3", EX.....................300.00
Stop Sign, M-1479, CI, 4½", G......................220.00
Tank, M-1436, lead, 3", VG.........................725.00
Temple Bar Building, M-1163, CI, 4", EX............600.00
Transvaal Money Box, M-1, CI, recast pipe, 6¼", VG......3,200.00
Triangular Building w/Clock, M-1235, CI, 6", EX......650.00
Two-Faced Black Boy (lg), M-83, CI, EX.............300.00
Two-Faced Black Boy (sm), M-84, CI, 3⅛", EX........200.00
Two-Faced Devil, M-31, CI, 4¼", EX.................700.00
US Army/Navy Safe, electroplated CI, 6⅛", EX......1,200.00
USA Mail Mailbox w/Eagle, M-851, CI, 4⅛", EX........75.00
Watch Me Grow, M-279 variant, tin, 5¾", EX..........70.00
Westminster Abbey, M-973, CI, old gold pnt, 6¼"......250.00
White City Barrel #1, M-908, NP, EX...............150.00
World Time Bank, M-1539, CI, orig paper, 4⅛", EX......500.00

Yellow Cab, M-1493, CI, 4¼", VG **1,200.00**
1882 Villa, M-959, CI, 5⅞", VG **800.00**
1890 Tower Bank, M-1198, CI, 6⅞", EX **1,200.00**
1893 World's Fair Administration Building, M-1072, CI, 6", EX ..**650.00**

Barber Shop Collectibles

Even for the stranger in town, the local barber shop was easy to find, its location vividly marked with the traditional red and white striped barber pole that for centuries identified such establishments. As far back as the twelfth century, the barber has had a place in recorded history. At one time he not only groomed the beards and cut the hair of his gentlemen clients but was known as the 'blood-letter' as well, hence the red stripe for blood and the white for the bandages. Many early barbers even pulled teeth! Later, laws were enacted that divided the practices of barbering and surgery.

The Victorian barber shop reflected the charm of that era with fancy barber chairs upholstered in rich wine-colored velvet; rows of bottles made from colored art glass held hair tonics and shaving lotion. Backbars of richly carved oak with beveled mirrors lined the wall behind the barber's station. During the late nineteenth century, the barber pole with a blue stripe added to the standard red and white as a patriotic gesture came into vogue.

Today the barber shop has all but disappeared from the American scene, replaced by modern unisex salons. Collectors search for the barber poles, the fancy chairs, and the tonic bottles of an era gone but not forgotten. See also Bottles; Razors; Shaving Mugs.

Sterilizer, Sanitary, glass body with enamel letters, brass front, ca 1910, 9½x7¼x10¾", NM, $150.00.

Bank, Dandy Dan, barber pole body w/blk hat, plastic, 6¾" **17.50**
Book, The Barber's Manual, AB Moler, 262 pgs, 1956, VG+ **16.00**
Booster seat, metal w/red vinyl seat, 1940s, EX **60.00**
Catalog, Koch's/The Buerger Bros Supply Co, 1926, EX **150.00**
Chair, Berninghaus Hercules, porc base & armrests, 1920s, VG+ ..**675.00**
Chair, child's; pedal car as seat, hydraulic, EX rstr, 44x36" **2,100.00**
Chair, Koken, CI/porc, burgundy w/gilt, brass trim, new leather, 53".**1,200.00**
Chair, Takara Chukosho #560, Belmont on metal frwork, 1956, EX.....**650.00**
Dispenser, balm; Campana's Italian Balm, brass w/glass bottle, EX ..**45.00**
Display, Charlex razor & case, celluloid & metal, 26½" L, EX ...**450.00**
Hair-Vac, Oster #215, NMIB **125.00**
Photo, 2 barbers w/customers, sepia-tone, ca 1910, 11x14", EX **17.50**
Pole, glass cylinder, Marvy, 36" **350.00**
Pole, glass/chrome, red & wht, Emil J Paidar Co, rstr, 22" **280.00**
Pole, Marvy Model 55, chrome/glass, working, EX **425.00**
Pole, porc light-up, red/wht/bl, w/wht globe, electric, 87", EX ...**2,200.00**
Pole, thinning shears, Craftsman Taper #145, 7", EXIB.................**16.00**
Pole, trn wood, red & wht rpt, tin cover on top, 76".....................**550.00**
Postcard, Hyki Dandruff Remedy, FH Schwann Barber Supply, NM...**17.50**
Razor, straight; Greens Barber Supply, nickel silver bolsters, VG..**17.50**
Razor hone, Boss Barber, VG+ (G box) **18.00**

Scalp massager, Stim-U-Lax Junior, Oster, 1950s, EXIB...............**60.00**
Sign, Ask for Wildroot, red/wht/bl on wht w/pole, 1949, EX........**85.00**
Sign, porc, Barber Shop w/red, wht & bl striped border, 12x24", EX ...**125.00**
Sign, porc, Barber Shop/pole design, die-cut top, red/wht/bl, 30x7", EX ..**225.00**
Sterilizer, Nu-Vita Products Co, 4 trays, 1940s, EX......................**80.00**

Barometers

Barometers are instruments designed to measure the weight or pressure of the atmosphere in order to anticipate approaching weather changes. They have a glorious history. Some of the foremost thinkers of the seventeenth century developed the mercury barometer, as the discovery of the natural laws of the universe progressed. Working in 1644 from experiments by Galileo, Evangelista Torrecelli used a glass tube and a jar of mercury to create a vacuum and therefore prove that air has weight. Four years later, Rene Descartes added a paper scale to the top of Torrecelli's mercury tube and created the basic barometer. Blaise Pascal, working with Descartes, used it to determine the heights of mountains; indeed, only later was the correlation between changes in air pressure and changes in the weather observed and the term 'weather-glass' applied. Robert Boyle introduced it to England, and Robert Hook modified the form and designed the wheel barometer.

The most common type of barometer is the wheel or banjo type. Second is the stick type. Modifications of the plain stick would be the marine gimballed type, followed by the laboratory or Kew or Fortin type. Others are the Admiral Fitzroys of which there are twelve or more types. The above all have mercury contained in either glass tubing or wood-box cisterns.

Another type of barometer is the aneroid, working on atmospheric pressure changes. They come in all sizes ranging from 1" in diameter to 12" or larger. They may be in metal or wood cases. There is a Barograph which records on a graph that rotates around a drum powered by a seven-day clock mechanism. Pocket barometers (altimeters) vary in sizes from 1" diameter up to 6" diameter. One final type of barometer is the sympiesometer, a modification of the stick barometer used for a limited time and not as accurate as a conventional marine barometer. Our advisor for this category is Bob Elsner; he is listed in the Directory under Florida.

Key:
dl — dial
s — stick type
w — wheel type (banjo)

American

Andrew J Lloyd & Co Boston, s, oak, w/thermometer, 41" **375.00**
Charles Wilder, NH/Woodruff's...1860, s, mahog, 38", EX **3,100.00**
Charles Wilder, Peterboro NH, rosewood, Woodruff/Pat **950.00**
DE Lent, Rochester NY, s, allover cvd case, 36" **300.00**
Leoni, NY, w, mahog w/eng eagle, ca 1840 ....**1,850.00**
Simmons & Sons, Fulton NY **950.00**

English

A Marinone Co, band-inlay mahog w/SP gauge, broken arch pediment, 38" .**1,300.00**
Admiral Fitzroy's, mercury tube, thermometer, 38x6¾" **365.00**
Bianchi, w, mahog w/shell inlay, 8" dl, thermometer, 1820s, up to ..**800.00**
Cary-Strand St London, s, mahog, silver dl, mid-19th C, from $1,500 to .**1,700.00**
CW Dixey Optician to Queen..., mahog bow-front, early 1800s, 42" ...**4,500.00**
Dollond London, s, Georgian mahog w/inlay, 19th C, 37" **1,850.00**
Fraser...London, s, mahog bow-front, 1790s, 36", EX **9,000.00**
G Terza Norwich, mahog over pine w/inlays, 38", VG **385.00**
Geo Adams, London, s, mahog, 1790s, NM **6,000.00**
Harris & Sons, mahog bow-front, swan-neck/silvered dl, thermometer, to ..**3,300.00**

J Della Toree Perth, w, Georgian mahog/walnut, 39", VG **685.00**
J Tory & Co London, mahog w/silver dl, exposed mercury tube, $800 to ..**950.00**
Josh Long...London, mahog veneer bow-front, 1820s, NM......**7,000.00**
Lione Somalvico Co 125....London, w/temperature/hydrometer/etc, 39" ..**460.00**
Richardson & Son, s, mahog w/silvered brass scales, 1830s, 53".........**9,000.00**
Rosewood, w, 10" dl, w/thermometer/mirror/hygrometer/level, up to.**1,000.00**
Wm Adler, s, rosewood w/ivory scale, brass mts, early, 37" **3,800.00**

Other Barometer Types

Aneroid, brass case, from $150 to...**200.00**
Aneroid, Gaunt & Arnsley, marquetry, thermometer, 1910, 33" ...**465.00**
Aneroid, Napoleon III, cvd owl, hunting dog & rabbits, 1855-70, 28" .**1,725.00**
Aneroid, w/exposed ½-rnd thermometer, from $200 to **250.00**
Barograph reading barometer, mahog, Negretti & Zambra..........**950.00**
Barograph recording barometer, sgn, from $450 to **950.00**
Barograph recording barometer, unsgn, from $250 to **350.00**
Pocket (altimeter), no case **100.00**
Pocket (altimeter), w/case, from $150 to...............................**200.00**
Sympiesometer, from $1,500 to **2,000.00**

Barware

Back in the thirties when social soirees were very elegant affairs thanks to the influence of Hollywood in all its glamour and mystique, cocktails were often served up in shakers styled as miniature airplanes, zeppelins, skyscrapers, lady's legs, penguins, roosters, bowling pins, etc. Some were by top designers such as Norman Bel Geddes and Russel Wright. They were made of silverplate, glass, and chrome, often trimmed with colorful Bakelite handles. Today these are hot collectibles, and even the more common Deco-styled chrome cylinders are often priced at $25.00 and up. Ice buckets, trays, and other bar accessories are also included in this area of collecting.

For further information we recommend *Vintage Bar Ware Identification & Value Guide* by Stephen Visakay, our advisor for this category; he is listed in the Directory under New Jersey.

See also Bottle Openers.

Shakers: Dumbbell, cobalt glass, West Virginia Specialty, 13", $400.00; Rooster's head, silver-plated brass on clear base, with strainer, 1920s, 11", $1,650.00; Lady's Leg, ruby glass with chrome, Derby Shelton Silver, $1,250.00.
(Photo courtesy Stephen Visakay)

Bar towel, cloth w/Black caricature motif, 1940s, oblong........ ......**35.00**
Book, The Savoy Cocktail Book, H Craddock, 1930, M......... ...**150.00**
Canape tray, satin chromium over brass, 1935, 4½x6¾" **10.00**
Cigarette dispenser, brass & Bakelite bartender, Art Metal, 8" ...**550.00**
Cocktail cup, glass insert, mk Farber Bros, Pat, 4¼" **11.00**
Cocktail cup, SP, golf bag form, Derby, 1920s, 3".........................**65.00**
Cocktail dish, bar scene w/drink names, 1930s, 8"........................**90.00**

Cocktail glass, frosted glass w/sterling rings, ftd, 1930s, 3⅜" **7.00**
Cocktail glass, rooster scenes, ftd, 1930s, 3½x3¼"...........................**8.00**
Cocktail glass, SP ftd rooster figural holder w/cut glass insert **125.00**
Cocktail set, bowling ball container/decanter/6 glasses, 1940-50s....**65.00**
Cocktail set, chrome/glass gyroscope, shaker/4 tumblers/24" dia tray.**750.00**
Cocktail set, NP, hammered, shaker/10 stemmed cups/tray, 1927..**175.00**
Ice bowl w/tongs, chrome, Russell Wright/Chase, 1930s-40s, 7" dia ..**35.00**
Ice bucket, chrome-plated copper, w/tray, Keystone, 1930s........**95.00**
Ice chopper, cobalt glass w/silk-screened recipes, 1930s, 11½" **65.00**
Ice tongs, NP, ca 1928, 1x7½" **40.00**
Martini spike/Vermouth dispenser, syringe shape, 1950s, 6½".......**25.00**
Mixer, chrome pitcher w/jade Catalin trim, 1928, 52-oz, 10¾" ..**250.00**
Mixer, outboard motor shape, b/o, Swank, 6"..............................**50.00**
Picks, bottle forms in wood 'bar' w/chrome, 4½x5" **45.00**
Pitcher, martini; stainless steel w/walnut hdl, Italy, 9¼".................**45.00**
Shaker, aluminum, cylindrical w/blk plastic top, 1940s, 12"..........**55.00**
Shaker, chrome, Connoisseur w/cover knob, Manning-Bowman, 1930s, 12"...**95.00**
Shaker, chrome, incised bands, Manning-Bowman, 8" **50.00**
Shaker, chrome, skyscraper, blk enamel cap & base, 12¼"...........**60.00**
Shaker, glass, dumbbell w/ribbing, 12", VG **160.00**
Shaker, glass, gr w/crystal hdl, chrome trim, Cambridge, 1930s, 11" ...**105.00**
Shaker, glass, gr w/eng rooster, SP top, 1926, 10½" **75.00**
Shaker, glass, lantern form, cranberry w/SP trim, English, mk, 1930s ..**400.00**
Shaker, glass, ribbed w/pnt blk bands, Czech, 1930s...................**100.00**
Shaker, glass, ruby w/applied sterling trim, 9½" **150.00**
Shaker, glass, World's Fair, bl letters etched on opaque, 5" **325.00**
Shaker, leather on wood, pnt/lacquer, France, 1930s, 11¾x3⅛".**275.00**
Shaker, NP, hammered, Bernard Rice & Sons, 1920s, 13¾" **75.00**
Shaker, SP, bell shape, Asprey & Co, 1937, 11x6" **315.00**
Shaker, SP, bell shape, Dunhill, 11"......................................**90.00**
Shaker, SP, cylindrical, Italy, 11½".......................................**115.00**
Shaker, SP, milk pail form, Reed & Barton, 1957, 10", VG **100.00**
Shaker, sterling, Modernist pitcher, allover relief sqs, Gorham, 12" ..**4,500.00**
Shot jigger, graduated, stemmed, Napier, 4" **85.00**
Snack tin, triangular, gold w/blk dots, martini pictures, 1930s......**12.00**
Soda siphon, chrome w/enameled top, Bel Geddes, mk, Pat, 10" ..**160.00**
Swizzle sticks, glass, tuxedoed men, 1930s, 7¼", ea **15.00**
Swizzle sticks, glass w/mc fruit tops, 6-pc, Bohemian, 1930s, 8" **18.00**
Traveling bar, NP shaker form, 9-pc, mk Germany, ca 1928, 8"....**85.00**
Traveling bar, SP zeppelin, 19-pc set, Germany, ca 1928, 12"..**2,500.00**
Tray, metal, Here's How, flappers w/drinks, J Held Jr art, 12x17", NM..**100.00**
Tumbler, glass, dice sealed in bottom, 4" **6.00**
Tumbler rack w/4 tumblers, gyroscope, 20x4½" dia rings **125.00**

Baskets

Basket weaving is a craft as old as ancient history. Baskets have been used to harvest crops, for domestic chores, and to contain the catch of fishermen. Materials at hand were utilized, and baskets from a specific region are often distinguishable simply by analyzing the natural fibers used in their construction. Early Indian baskets were made of corn husks or woven grasses. Willow splint, straw, rope, and paper were also used. Until the invention of the veneering machine in the late 1800s, splint was made by water-soaking a split log until the fibers were softened and flexible. Long strips were pulled out by hand and, while still wet and pliable, woven into baskets in either a cross-hatch or hexagonal weave.

Most handcrafted baskets on the market today were made between 1860 and the early 1900s. Factory baskets with a thick, wide splint cut by machine are of little interest to collectors. The more popular baskets are those designed for a specific purpose, rather than the more commonly found utility baskets that had multiple uses. Among the most costly forms are the Nantucket Lighthouse baskets, which were basically copied from those made there for centuries by aboriginal Indians. They were designed in the style of whale-oil barrels and named for the South Shoal Nantucket Lightship where many were made during the last half of the nineteenth century. Cheese baskets (used to separate curds from whey), herb-gathering baskets, and finely woven Shaker miniatures are other highly-prized examples of the basket-weaver's art.

In the listings that follow, assume that each has a center bentwood handle (unless handles of another type are noted) that is not included in the height. Unless another type of material is indicated, assume that each is made of splint. Prices are subjective and hinge on several factors: construction, age, color, and general appearance.

See also American Indian; Eskimo; Sewing; Shaker.

Apple, oak staves, trn pine solid bottom, wrapped rim, 9x15" **175.00**
Bark, splint threadings on seams/rim/hdls, 14x23x17" **770.00**
Berry, stave/wire construction, swing hdls, dk finish, 4½x3⅜"....**385.00**
Buttocks, flat arched hdl, 8x9" **55.00**
Buttocks, woven bl bands, 9x9x14" **120.00**
Buttocks, 26-rib, EX color, sm breaks, 9x15x13" **110.00**
Buttocks, 26-rib, wide center band over weaving, lt wear/damage, 7" L..**165.00**
Buttocks, 28-rib, tight weave, bl-gr pnt, 14x17x14", EX..........**1,295.00**
Buttocks, 30-rib, tight weave, alligatored finish, 8x11x9" **195.00**
Buttocks, 64-rib, fine weave, twist hdl, brn/red woven stripes, 20" L..**400.00**
Canted sides w/geometric hoops around center, sq base, 13¾", EX.....**360.00**
Double lid, rnd/ftd, fixed hdl, bands of bl splints, 11x10", EX **335.00**
Feather, mc pnt dmns, Am, 19th C, 25½x20½" dia **1,380.00**
Gathering, rnd sides curve in to base, cvd hdl, 15" H **100.00**
Gathering, woven bl stripes on natural, minor breaks, 10x12x9"..**70.00**
Gathering, 2 side hdls, EX patina, rectangular, 6x8x16" **275.00**
Gathering, 3 oak runners on woven bottom, strap hdl.................**155.00**
Grain, rye straw, wrapped rim, iron hdl, 7x11" **200.00**
Half buttocks, brn pnt, 5x8" **195.00**
Half buttocks, 28-rib, EX color, minor breaks, 13x13"...............**245.00**
Laundry, deep rectangle, 2 cvd hdls, 19th C, 15x28x20", EX......**300.00**
Market, gr pnt w/wear, oval, wood base, few breaks, 14x16" **165.00**
Melon, 18-rib, flat base, tightly woven, 7¼" **165.00**
Melon, 20 radiating ribs, EX patina, 10½" **85.00**
Melon, 34-rib, oval top slightly misshapen, 14x15" **195.00**
Melon, 35-rib, sq top, woven covering on hdl, breaks, 10" **110.00**
Mini, bl pnt, single hdl, 2x1¾"..**545.00**
Mini, buttocks, Eye-of-God hdl, 2 lowest ribs form base, 3"........**200.00**
Mini, buttocks, 38-rib, 2½x5"...**550.00**
Mini, dk stain, dbl strand braided rim, very old **75.00**
Mini, melon, blk over gr pnt, 19th C..**500.00**
Mini, melon, 12-rib, wide bentwood hdl forms center rib, 2x3½", VG...**105.00**
Mini, rectangular, ca 1900, 5½x5x5½" **175.00**
Mini, rectangular, 2x3x3⅞"..**220.00**
Nantucket, D-shaped hdl, wood base, CM Lewis, 5x6¾" **1,600.00**
Nantucket, EX patina, CM Lewis, graduated set of 5, 7¾" to 13", EX..**15,250.00**
Nantucket, hdls, EX patina, 12x20" dia, EX................................**5,175.00**
Nantucket, hdls (rpr), ca 1900, 3¾x10x7½" **575.00**
Nantucket, inscr: made by JG Fisher...1893, 7½x7½".............**1,850.00**
Nantucket, purse w/swing hdl, appl ivory medallion on lid, 7x8x6" ...**3,100.00**
Nantucket, swing hdl, checkerboard inlaid finial & peg, 6" **700.00**
Nantucket, swing hdl, trn base, TS Lowe, early 1900s, 10x9¾"..**1,380.00**
Nantucket, swing hdl, trn ivory pegs/closure, cvd whale medallion, 10" ..**325.00**
Nantucket, swing hdl, trn/scribed wood base, 19th C, 11x11".**1,600.00**
Nantucket, swing hdl, wooden base, JF Reyes, ca 1945, 13x10½" .**2,070.00**
Nantucket, swing hdl, 9⅝x7½"..**1,725.00**
Pantry, loose weave, single-wrap hickory rim, 1800s, 4½x11½" .**165.00**
Pnt, dk red over wht, sq bottom, 1850s, 3¾x12" dia **175.00**
Pnt, med gr, att Amish, lt damage, 8x14x20" **2,000.00**
Pnt, red/brn/bl striped splints, brn lacing, sq base, 19th C, 13x14"..**575.00**
Pnt, salmon, fixed hdl, single-wrapped rim, 19th C, 5½x10½" ..**515.00**
Potato-stamped decor, w/lid, sq, 11x14x19" **415.00**

Round, sq base, EX patina, 8¾"...**275.00**
Round, sq base, worn, 9" **85.00**
Swing hdl, kick-up base, 8x12" **275.00**
Swing hdl, open weaving (made like cheese basket), 8" dia..........**55.00**

Battersea

Battersea is a term that refers to enameling on copper or other metal. Though originally produced at Battersea, England, in the mid-eighteenth century, the craft was later practiced throughout the Staffordshire district. Boxes are the most common examples. Some are figurals, and many bear an inscription. Values are given for examples with only minimal damage, which is normal. Our advisor for this category is John Harrigan; he is listed in the Directory under Minnesota.

Box, The Constitution on lid, mirror inside, made for American market, late eighteenth century, ⅞x2x1⅜", EX, $2,415.00. (Photo courtesy Skinner Inc.)

Box, Colonial family fish from river bank, lt gr bkground, 2" **600.00**
Box, Have Communion w/...+floral ribbons on lt bl, mirror, 1⅝", VG.....**330.00**
Box, hound/rabbit on lid, mc on cobalt, mirror, 2", EX...............**495.00**
Box, lovebirds, wht/gold on brn/blk marbleized, mirror, 1¾" **300.00**
Box, Mother's Gift in wht circle on bl, mirror, 1¾", VG **350.00**
Box, Token of Regard & foliage on lt bl, mirror missing, 1½" **220.00**
Box, Trifle from York, dk bl w/wht lid trimmed in red & bl, 1¾", VG..**350.00**
Box, Trifles Shew (sic) Respect, wht beading on aqua w/blk, 1¾", EX..**465.00**
Candlesticks, floral, mc on wht panels on bl, 9", pr, VG **2,500.00**
Knob, Gen Lafayette portrait, blk on wht, Bilston, 2", pr (1 w/damage) ..**880.00**
Knob, girl w/canary, mc, Bilston, 1⅞", pr......................................**985.00**
Knob, ship, Admiral Duncan, Venerable 74 guns...1797, mc, 1½", pr ...**985.00**

Bauer

Originally founded in Paducah, Kentucky, in 1885, the J.A. Bauer Company moved to Los Angeles where it was re-established in 1910. Until the 1920s their major products were terra cotta gardenware, flowerpots, and stoneware and yellow ware bowls. During prohibition they produced crocks for home use. A more artful form of product began to develop with the addition of designer Louis Ipsen to the staff circa 1915. Some of his work, a line of molded vases, flowerpots, bowls, etc., was awarded a bronze medal at the Pacific International Exposition in 1916.

In 1930 the first of many dinnerware lines was tested on the market. Their initial pattern, Plain Ware, was well accepted and led the way to the introduction of the most popular dinnerware in their history and with today's collectors, Ring Ware. It was produced from 1932 into the early 1960s in solid colors of jade green, royal blue, dusty burgundy, ivory, Chinese Yellow, Delph Blue, orange-red, and (in very limited quantities) black or white. Its simple pattern was a design of closely spaced concentric ribs, either convex or concave. Over the years, more than one hundred shapes were available. Some were made in limited quantities, resulting in rare items to whet the appetites of Bauer buffs today. Other patterns were La Linda, produced during the 1940s and 1950s, and Monterey Moderne, introduced in 1948 and remaining popular into the 1950s (made in pink, black, gray, brown, and green).

After WWII a flood of foreign imports and loss of key employees drastically curtailed their sales, and the pottery began a steady decline that ended in failure in 1962. Prices listed below reflect the California market. For more information we recommend *Collector's Encyclopedia of Bauer Pottery: Identification & Values* (Collector Books) and *The Collector's Encyclopedia of California Pottery, Second Edition*, both by Jack Chipman, our advisor for this category. Mr. Chipman's address may be found in the Directory under California.

In the lines of Ring and Plain ware, pricing depends to some extent on color. Use the low end of our range of values for light brown, Chinese Yellow, orange-red, jade green, red-brown, olive green, light blue, turquoise, and gray; the high-end colors are Delph Blue, ivory, dusty burgundy, cobalt, chartreuse, papaya, and burgundy. Black is 50% higher than the high end; to evaluate white, double the high side. Use the low end of the range to evaluate Monterey items in all colors but Monterey Blue, burgundy, and white — those are high-end colors. You'll need to double the high end for black in this line as well as Monterey Moderne. An in-depth study of colors may be found in the books referenced above.

Art Pottery

Bowl, gr glaze #2, low, 10" 200.00
Jar, carnation; gr glaze #1, cylindrical vase shape, 24" 1,800.00
Jardiniere, emb filigree design, gr glaze #2, 10" 750.00

Brusche Al Fresco and Contempo

Bowl, divided; Al Fresco, gray speckled, 2x9" 35.00
Bowl, fruit; Al Fresco, burgundy, str sides, 5" 15.00
Bowl, fruit; Al Fresco, chartreuse, str sides, 5" 10.00
Casserole, Al Fresco, chartreuse, w/lid 27.50
Coffeepot, Al Fresco 30.00
Creamer, jumbo; Al Fresco, Olive Green 15.00
Cup, Al Fresco, burgundy 10.00
Cup, Al Fresco, pk speckled 10.00
Plate, dinner; Al Fresco, burgundy, 10" 10.00
Plate, dinner; Al Fresco, gray, 10" 10.00
Platter, Al Fresco, pk speckled, rectangular, 12⅝" 22.00
Saucer, Al Fresco, chartreuse 2.50
Saucer, Al Fresco, Olive Green 2.50
Shaker, Al Fresco, burgundy 10.00
Teapot, Contempo, dk gr, 7x10" 65.00

Matt Carlton

Ashtray, Mexican; sombrero form, Delph Blue, 3¾x6", from $175 to ...250.00
Bowl, Jade Green, 3x6" sq 85.00
Jar, cactus; red, 4x9½" 345.00
Vase, California, cobalt, 10", from $500 to 575.00
Vase, Delph Blue, hand thrown, twist hdls, 12⅛x7" 1,000.00
Vase, Jade Green, ribbed, ruffled rim, 12" 375.00
Vase, Rebekah, hand decor, Chinese Yellow, 18" 1,750.00
Vase, Rebekah, gr glaze #2, shoulder hdls, ogee sides, 24" 2,500.00
Vase, wht, ruffled, 5½" 110.00
Vase, wht, ruffled rim, 7", from $200 to 250.00

Florist and Garden Pottery

Bowl, Indian, #8, orange-red, 5½x10", minimum value 300.00
Pot, dbl ped; wht matt, 21x11" 175.00
Pot, Dome; speckled brn, 11" in brass fitted stand 135.00
Pot, Spanish; speckled gr, 4" 30.00

Pot, Swirl, Cal-Art, 3" 25.00
Pot, Swirl, Cal-Art, 5" 40.00
Pot, Swirl, Cal-Art, 6" 55.00
Pot, Swirl, Cal-Art, 12" 150.00

La Linda and Glass Pastel Kitchenware

Bowl, vegetable; oval, 8" 35.00
Bowl, vegetable; oval, 10" 45.00
Cookie jar, from $130 to 165.00
Creamer, old or new style 15.00
Cup & saucer, from $35 to 45.00
Gravy boat 30.00
Pitcher, ice water; 2-qt, 6½x10", glossy pk 95.00
Plate, bread & butter; gr, 6" 8.00
Plate, chop 75.00
Plate, 10", from $40 to 55.00

Monterey

Footed fruit bowl, 12", from $150.00 to $225.00. (Photo courtesy Jack Chipman)

Bowl, batter 90.00
Custard baking set, 6 custard cups (various colors) in metal fr 275.00
Custard cup, orange-red 45.00
Egg cup 650.00
Ramekin 30.00
Refrigerator beverage dispenser, w/lid, from $250 to 325.00
Teapot, old style, 6-cup 85.00

Monterey Moderne and Related Kitchenware

Bowl, fruit; 4½" 12.50
Bowl, mixing; #12 ....60.00
Bowl, mixing; #18 ....35.00
Bowl, mixing; #36 ....20.00
Bowl, salad; low, 8½" 35.00
Buffet server 15.00
Casserole, brass-plated metal fr, 2-qt 50.00
Coffee server 48.00
Creamer 20.00
Cup, coffee 20.00
Pitcher, 1½-pt 35.00
Plate, bread & butter; 6½" 10.00
Platter, rectangular, 12" 35.00
Saucer 6.00
Tidbit tray, 3-tiered, pk, bottom plate: 9½" 50.00

Plain Ware

Bean pot, ind 135.00
Bean pot, ½-gal, from $185 to 200.00
Bowl, mixing; yel (late period), #3, 6¾x14¼" 175.00
Butter pat, blk, 4½" 125.00
Coffee server 115.00
Goblet (not handmade) 175.00
Pitcher, Dutch; orange-red, Carlton, 12", from $300 to 350.00

Pitcher, 5" 195.00
Ramekin, from $15 to..20.00

Ring Ware

Ashtray, 4", from $65 to 90.00
Bowl, batter; 2-qt, from $125 to 175.00
Bowl, low salad; burgundy, 12".................................250.00
Bowl, mixing; #9, from $175 to 235.00
Bowl, mixing; #12, from $145 to 180.00
Bowl, mixing; #18, from $110 to 165.00
Bowl, mixing; #30, from $90 to 120.00
Bowl, mixing; #36, from $50 to 75.00
Bowl, vegetable; oval, 8", from $95 to 135.00
Butter dish, rnd, from $250 to 350.00
Casserole, w/lid, 8½", in holder, from $165 to 250.00
Coffee server, wooden hdl, 6-cup, from $75 to............100.00
Coffee server, wooden hdl, 8-cup, from $135 to..........185.00
Cookie jar, from $450 to 700.00
Creamer & sugar bowl, midget 250.00
Cup, coffee; from $35 to...55.00
Mug, beer; from $300 to 375.00
Pitcher, 2-qt, from $165 to 200.00
Pitcher, 3-qt, from $250 to 325.00
Plate, chop; 14", from $100 to 150.00
Plate, dinner; 10½", from $100 to 125.00
Plate, luncheon; 9", from $30 to 55.00
Platter, 12", from $75 to 100.00
Platter, 15" 125.00
Punch bowl, 14", from $600 to.................................1,000.00
Shaker, squat...65.00
Sherbet, from $100 to 150.00
Stacking refrigerator set, 3-color, 3 pcs+lid, from $225 to..........300.00
Teapot, 6-cup, from $250 to 325.00
Tumbler, w/hdls, 12-oz, from $50 to 75.00

Bavaria

Bavaria, Germany, was long the center of that country's pottery industry; in the 1800s, many firms operated in and around the area. Chinaware vases, novelties, and table accessories were decorated with transfer prints as well as by hand by artists who sometimes signed their work. The examples listed here are marked with 'Bavaria' and the logos of some of the various companies which were located there.

Bowl, oranges with blossoms and leaves, gold trim at rim, 9½", $75.00.

Cache pot, poppies w/gold, artist sgn, 9½"................................525.00
Ewer, blackberries & buds, looped gold hdl, 12", NM 450.00
Ewer, pansies w/much gold, ca 1900, 5½x8" 365.00
Plate, gr irid w/children, animals & toys, child sz, 7½" 45.00

Sugar shaker, roses on wht, artist sgn, mk, 4½" 168.00
Sweetened condensed milk set, roses on gr, JC Bavaria, 1900, 3-pc..240.00
Tankard, roses on gr to wht, artist sgn, ca 1900-15, 13½" 425.00
Tea set, Elegant Rose w/gold, teapot, creamer & sugar, 6 c/s.......225.00
Teacup set, grapes w/gold, A&C, 4 w/lids+8½" sq tray, EX.........250.00
Teapot, emb scroll w/pk Briar Rose motif, Schumann #30, 8¼" ...80.00
Teapot, Empress, gold trim, Schumann, EX 300.00
Teapot, wht w/bl floral transfer, silver trim, 8" 125.00
Vase, chrysanthemums (vibrant), gold hdls, 1900-15 mk, 11¾" .450.00
Vase, pansies, artist sgn, globular, dtd 1912, 5½" 168.00
Vase, pillow; lilacs w/gold (EX art), dragon hdls, J&C mk, 1902, 11"...1,250.00
Vase, pillow; roses allover, sgn JHM, dtd 1893, 9½x10½"............550.00
Vase, roses, mc on wht, waisted cylinder, H&C Selb mk, 12" 395.00
Vase, roses on lt bl, bottle neck, shouldered, RXC w/crown mk, 12" .450.00
Vase, roses on wht, artist sgn, ovoid, ZS&Co mk, 8¾" 415.00

Beer Cans

In the early 1930s one of America's largest can-manufacturing companies approached an East Coast brewery with a novel concept — beer in cans. The brewery decided to take a chance on the idea, and in January, 1935, the beer can was born.

The 'church key' style can opener was invented at the same time, and early flat top cans actually had instructions on how to use it to open a can.

Canned beer soared in popularity, and breweries scrambled to meet the canning challenge. Since many companies did not have a machine to fill a flat-top can, the cone top was invented. Brewery executives believed its shape would be more acceptable to consumers used to buying bottled beer, and it easily passed through existing bottling machinery. The more compact flat-top can dominated sales, and by the 1950s cone tops were obsolete.

About values: Condition is critical when determining the value of a beer can. Prices quoted are for like-new condition cans, free of rust, dents, scratches, and other damage. Like any collectible, value drops in direct proportion to condition, and off-grade cans are often worth no more than one-half of retail value. Information in our descriptions is given in this specific order: 1) name of brew; 2) company — may be simply repetitive; and 3) city/state or state.

Altes Lager Beer, Tivoli, Detroit MI, crowntainer, VG..................37.50
Ballantine Export, Ballantine, Newark NJ, cone top, 32-oz, VG+ ..87.50
BCCA Convention, BCCA, St Louis MO, 3rd convention, cone top, NM ...35.00
Beverywick, Beverwyck, Albany NY, cone top, G 40.00
Beverywick Ale, Beverwyck, Albany NY, cone top, NM 150.00
Black Pride Lager, West Bend Lithia, West Bend WI, pull tab, NM...8.00
Blatz Pilsner, Blatz, Lawrence MI, J spout, VG+ 90.00
Brauck's Jubilee, Bruckman, Cincinnati OH, cone top, EX...........70.00
Canadian Ale, Canadian Ace, Chicago IL, cone top, VG 25.00
Champagne Velvet, Champagn Velvet, Chicago IL, cone top, EX..30.00
Champale Velvet, Terre Haute, Terre Haute IN, EX 32.00
Colt 45 Premium, National, Baltimore MD, 1970s test can, NM .68.00
Copper Club Pilsner, Haas, Hancock MI, cone top, EX 72.50
CV Gold Label, Terre Haute, Terre Haute IN, 16", VG...............60.00
Dakota, Dakota, Bismark ND, zip top, 1960s, NM 46.00
Duquesne Can O Beer, Duquesne, Pittsburgh PA, cone top, VG..85.00
F&S Premium, Fuhrmann & Schmidt, Shamokin PA, flat top, 1950s, EX...12.50
Falstaff, Falstaff, St Louis MO, vinyl label mock-up can, NM+.....47.50
Fehr's XL, Fehr, Louisville KY, crowntainer, VG+ 37.50
Fort Schuylar Lager, Utica Brg, Utica NY, cone top.....................105.00
Gluek's Sitte, Gluek, Minneapolis MN, flat top, 8-oz, NM 28.00
Goebel Bantam, Goebel, Detroit MI, flat top, 7-oz, VG..................6.00
Gold Crest 51, Tennesssee, Memphis TN, cone top, EX 90.00

Hudepohl, Hudepohl, Cincinnati OH, cone top, G **40.00**
Keglet, Esslinger, Philadelphia PA, flat top, 1950s, EX **25.00**
Krueger Finest, Krueger, Newark NM, crowntainer, NM...............**80.00**
Krueger Premium, Krueger, Newark NJ, flat top, 1590s, NM **12.50**
Lebanon Valley Pilsner, Lebanon Valley, Lebanon PA, cone top, VG....**87.00**
Lucky Lager, Lucky Lager, San Francisco CA, flat top, 1930s, G ..**21.00**
Narragansett Light Ale, Narragansett, Cranston RI, flat top, 1950s, VG..**66.00**
Neuweiler's Pilsner, Neuweiler, Allentown PA, crowntainer, NM ...**70.00**
Old Dutch, Metropolis, New York NY, cone top, EX **65.00**
Old Export, Cumberland, Cumberland MD, cone top, NM **78.00**
Old Milwaukee Genuine Draft, Schlitz, Milwaukee WI, ring pull, NM..**78.00**
Old Reading Beer, Old Reading, Reading PA, cone top, EX.......**150.00**
Old Style Lager, Heilmann, Lacrosse WI, high profile cone top, VG ...**40.00**
Old Topper Snappy Ale, Rochester, Rochester NY, J spout cone top, VG.**47.50**
Ortleib's Premium Lager, Ortlieb, Philadelphia PA, flat top, VG..**15.00**
Pabst Blue Ribbon Export, Pabst, Milwaukee WI, flat top, NM....**44.00**
Pfeiffer Famous, Pfeiffer, Detroit MI, ring tab, 1960s, NM.............**5.00**
Pickwick Ale, Haffenreffer, Boston MA, cone top, EX.................**50.00**
Pilsner Supreme, Maier, Los Angeles CA, flat top, EX.................**15.00**
Rainier Club, Rainier, San Francisco CA, flat top, 1940s, EX **55.00**
Ram's Head Ale, Adam Scheidt, Norristown PA, flat top, EX....**112.00**
Reingold Genuine Bock, Leibmann, Orange NJ, flat top, 1950s, VG...**38.00**
Reisch Gold top, Reisch, Springfield IL, high profile, VG **40.00**
Rib Mountain Lager, Wausau, Wausau WI, flat top, 1950s, NM **215.00**
Royal, Reno, Reno NV, cone top, G..**25.00**
Royal Bru, Union, New Castle PA, cone top, VG......................**135.00**
Schlitz, Schlitz, Milwaukee WI, cone top, VG **21.00**
Schmidt's Ale, Schmidt's, Philadelphia PA, cone top, VG............**65.00**
Schmidt's Bock, Schmidt's, Philadelphia PA, flat top, G+ **35.00**
Sigraa, Reno, Reno NV, cone top, G+......................................**40.00**
Standard Sparkling Ale, Standard, Rochester NY, J spout, cone top, EX.**92.00**
Star, G Western, Belleville IL, high profile cone top, VG............**40.00**
Steiwerbru, Atlantic, Atlanta GA, G..**85.00**
Sunshine Extra Light, Barbey's, Reading PA, cone top, EX........**137.50**
United Milwaukee Lager, Fuhrmann & Schmidt, Shamokin PA, flat top, NM ...**75.00**
Valley Brew Pale, El Dorado, Stockton CA, cone top, G.............**46.00**

Bellaire, Marc

Marc Bellaire, originally Donald Edmund Fleischman, was born in Toledo, Ohio, in 1925. He studied at the Toledo Museum of Art under Ernest Spring while employed as a designer for the Libbey Glass Company. During World War II while serving in the Navy, he travelled extensively throughout the Pacific. As a result of this experience, he developed an even broader and enriched sense of design and color.

Marc settled in California in the 1950s where his work attracted the attention of national buyers and agencies who persuaded him to create ceramic lines of his own, employing hand-decorating techniques throughout. He built a studio in Culver City, and there he produced high-quality ceramics, often decorated with ultramodern figures or geometric patterns and executed with a distinctive flair. His most famous line was Mardi Gras, decorated with slim dancers in spattered and striped colors of black, blue, pink, and white. Other major patterns were Jamaica, Balinese, Beachcomber, Friendly Island, Cave Painting, Hawaiian, Bird Isle, Oriental, Jungle Dancer, and Kashmir. Kashmir usually has the name Ingle on the front and Bellaire on the reverse.

It is to be noted that Marc was employed by Sascha Brastoff during the 1950s. Many believe that he was hired for his creative imagination and style.

During the period from 1951 to 1956, Marc was named one of the top ten artware designers by *Giftwares Magazine*. After 1956 he taught and lectured on art, design, and ceramic decorating techniques from

coast to coast. Many of his pieces were one of a kind, commissioned throughout the United States.

During the 1970s he set up a studio in Marin County, California, and eventually moved to Palm Springs where he opened his final studio/gallery. There he produced large pieces with a Southwestern style. Mr Bellaire died in 1994. Our advisor for this category is Marty Webster; he is listed in the Directory under Michigan.

Ashtray, Bird Isle, blk birds on cream, 8" **85.00**
Ashtray, Clown, mc on cream, 7" **65.00**
Ashtray, Jamaica, musicians on brn, 10x14".................................**85.00**
Ashtray, Mardi Gras, figures on blk, rolled rim, 9" **100.00**
Ashtray, Mardi Gras, figures on blk, 4x8½"................................**35.00**
Ashtray, Mardi Gras, figures on blk, 14x14".............................**225.00**
Ashtray, Still Life, matt fruits & leaves, 10x15"...........................**100.00**
Bowl, Beachcomber, low teardrop shape, 12" L..........................**100.00**
Bowl, Cotillian, lady w/bl bird, 13x9" **125.00**
Bowl, Fruit - Three Pears, yel & gr **45.00**
Bowl, Jungle Dancer, 11½x5½"...**150.00**
Box, African figures on lid, 6"..**95.00**
Box, Jamaica, man w/guitar, free-form, B46, 8".........................**115.00**
Box, Mardi Gras, w/lid, 10" dia..**150.00**
Candlestick, Jamaica, man, 10½"...**125.00**
Charger, stylized bird on branch, 15"...**165.00**
Compote, Cave Painting, 4-ftd, 6x12" **100.00**
Compote, Cotillian, 4-ftd, 8x17"..**200.00**
Cookie jar, Stick People, wood lid, 10" **150.00**
Ewer, Mardi Gras, figures on blk, hdl, 18" **400.00**
Figurine, bird w/long neck, 17"...**250.00**
Figurine, buffalo, brn & blk, 9½" L...**465.00**
Figurine, bull, 9" **345.00**
Figurine, Jamaica, man playing guitar...**300.00**
Figurine, Mardi Gras, reclining man, very slim, 18" **800.00**
Figurine, Mardi Gras, standing man, very slim, 24" **700.00**
Figurine, Polynesian, standing man, 12"......................................**500.00**

Figurine, primitive horse, green and brown, 8½x6", $275.00.

Lamp, Mardi Gras, long neck vase on wood base, 28" **450.00**
Platter, fisherman w/net, 16" dia..**150.00**
Platter, Friendly Island, 10"..**135.00**
Platter, Hawaiian, 3 figures on orange, 7x13"..............................**55.00**
Platter, Mardi Gras, figures on blk, 12x18" **250.00**
Platter, Polynesian dancer, egg-shaped, 11x15"...........................**250.00**
Platter, underwater design in sea gr, 16" **100.00**
Switch plate, dancer on blk, B-26, 3x4¾"..................................**150.00**
Tray, Black man, dancing, triangle, 8½x17"................................**75.00**
Tray, Hawaiian figures, peach & blk, 10x14" **145.00**
Tray, Jungle Dancer, figure on blk/gr, 12" dia.............................**145.00**
Vase, Balinese women, hourglass shape, 8"................................**100.00**
Vase, Black Cats, hourglass shape, 8"...**100.00**
Vase, Indian on Horseback, mk Bellaire 89, 10" **150.00**

Vase, Mardi Gras, figures on blk, 18".............................250.00
Vase, Mardi Gras, hourglass shape on 3 ft, 11".............125.00
Vase, Polynesian woman, 9"...100.00
Vase, Stick People, irregular beak-like opening, 12"....................250.00

Belleek, American

From 1883 until 1930, several American potteries located in New Jersey and Ohio manufactured a type of china similar to the famous Irish Belleek soft-paste porcelain. The American manufacturers identified their porcelain by using 'Belleek' or 'Beleek' in their marks. American Belleek is considered the highest achievement of the American porcelain industry. Production centered around artistic cabinet pieces and luxury tablewares. Many examples emulated Irish shapes and decor with marine themes and other naturalistic styles. While all are highly collectible, some companies' products are rarer than others. The best-known manufacturers are Ott and Brewer, Willets, The Ceramic Art Company (CAC), and Lenox. You will find more detailed information in those specific categories. Our advisor for this category is Mary Frank Gaston.

Key:
AAC — American Art China   CAP — Columbian Art Pottery

Bell, Independence Hall bl transfer, CAP, 4½"...........................600.00
Bowl, cream soup; Bouquet, Coxon, w/underplate.......................225.00
Creamer, floral border, sponged gold, ornate hdl, AAC, 4".........300.00
Cup & saucer, demitasse; Tridacna, gold trim, CAP....................140.00
Cup & saucer, floral reserves in red border, Morgan...................250.00

Ewer, hand-painted roses, branch handle, red mark, $1,200.00. (Photo courtesy Mary Frank Gaston)

Plate, peacocks & mixed florals w/gold, Gordon, 7" 65.00
Plate, workers in wheat field, man at gate, AAC, 6¼"................250.00
Teapot, dragon form, gold paste leaves, CAP, 7½x9" 1,550.00
Vase, floral on wht, gold emb hdls, AAC, 12", pr 1,650.00

Belleek, Irish

Belleek is a very thin translucent porcelain that takes its name from the village in Ireland where it originated in 1859. The glaze is a creamy ivory color with a pearl-like lustre. The tablewares, baskets, figurines, and vases that have always been made there are being crafted yet today. Shamrock, Tridacna, Echinus, and Thorn are but a few of the many patterns of tableware which have been made during some periods of the pottery's history. Throughout the years, their most popular pattern has been Shamrock.

It is possible to date an example to within twenty to thirty years of crafting by the mark. Pieces with an early stamp often bring prices nearly triple that of a similar but current item. With some variation, the marks have always incorporated the Irish wolfhound, Celtic round tower, harp, and shamrocks. The first three marks (usually in black) were used from 1863 to 1946. A series of green marks identified the pottery's offerings from 1946 until the seventh mark (in gold/brown) was introduced in 1980 (it was discontinued in 1992). The eighth mark was blue and closely resembled the gold mark. It was used from 1993 to 1996. The ninth, tenth, and eleventh marks went back to the simplicity of the first mark with only the registry mark (an R encased in a circle) to distinguish them from the original. The ninth mark, which was used from 1997 to 1999, was blue. A special black version of that mark was introduced for the year 2000 and a Millennium 2000 banner was added. The tenth or Millennium mark was retired at the end of 2000, and the current green mark was introduced as the eleventh mark. Belleek Collector's International Society limited edition pieces are designated with a special mark in red. In the listings below, numbers designated with the prefix 'D' relate to the book *Belleek, The Complete Collector's Guide and Illustrated Reference, Second Edition*, by Richard K. Degenhardt (published by Wallace-Homestead Book Company, One Chilton Way, Radnor, PA 19098-0230). The numbers designated with the prefix 'B' are current production numbers used by the pottery. Our advisor for this category is Liz Stillwell; she is listed in the Directory under California.

Key:
A — plain (glazed only)	I — 1863 – 1890
B — cob lustre	II — 1891 – 1926
C — hand tinted	III — 1926 – 1946
D — hand painted	IV — 1946 – 1955
E — hand-painted shamrocks	V — 1955 – 1965
F — hand gilted	VI — 1965 – 3/31/1980
G — hand tinted and gilted	VII — 4/1/1980 – 1992
H — hand-painted shamrocks and gilted	VIII — 1/4/1993 – 1996
	IX — 1997 – 1999
J — mother-of-pearl	X — 2000 only
K — hand painted and gilted	XI — 2001 – current
L — bisque and plain	
M — decalcomania	
N — special hand-painted decoration	
T — transfer design	

Further information concerning Periods of Crafting (Baskets):
1 — 1865 – 1890, BELLEEK (three strand)
2 — 1865 – 1890, BELLEEK CO. FERMANAGH (three strand)
3 — 1891 – 1920, BELLEEK CO. FERMANAGH IRELAND (three strand)
4 — 1921 – 1954, BELLEEK CO. FERMANAGH IRELAND (fourstrand)
5 — 1955 – 1979, BELLEEK® CO. FERMANAGH IRELAND (four strand)
6 — 1980 – 1985, BELLEEK® IRELAND (four strand)
7 — 1985 – 1989, BELLEEK® IRELAND 'ID NUMBER' (four strand)
8 – 12 — 1990 to present (Refer to *Belleek, The Complete Collector's Guide and Illustrated Reference, 2nd Edition*, Chapter 5)

Aberdeen Tea Ware Tea & Saucer, D489-II, B.............................550.00
Aberdeen Vase, Flowered, D59-III, J, sm, 6" 525.00
Achilles Vase, Flowered, D1154-V, A...350.00
Ampanida Open Cream, D1291-I, C 400.00
Artichoke Tea Ware Teapot, D710-I, F...750.00
Bamboo Teapot, D515-I, A, lg..750.00
Beer Tankard, D2075-VII, F, 5¼" 125.00
Belleek Easter Egg, 1972, D1632-VI, B 250.00
Bird's Nest Basket, D123-4, D...325.00
Blarney Tea Ware Coffee & Saucer, D579-II, C 375.00
Boat Ash Tray, D229-V, B 85.00
Bonbonniere, Flowered, 1980, D1812-VII, K...............................190.00
Boston Basket, Flowered, D1249-5, A..1,200.00
Boudoir Candlestick, Flowered, D1506-I J.................................1,400.00

Bust of Queen of the Hops, D1130-III, L&B, 11½" 4,000.00
Charter Member Trademark Plaque, 1979, D1810-VI, K 175.00
Coral Bell, D2078-VI, B...90.00
Cottage Cheese Dish, D2079-V, B..150.00
Custard Cup & Saucer, D680-I, A...275.00
Daisy Spill, D178-VI, E..70.00
Double Shell Flowerpot, Flowered, D1674-II, J 550.00
Earthenware Plate, D890-I, T, 8" 80.00
Echinus Tea Ware Egg Cup, D666-IV, B......................................70.00
Erne Vase, D83-III, C..400.00
Fan Tea Ware Tea & Saucer, D694-I, K......................................450.00
Fermanagh Vase, D139-V, G..120.00
Finner Tea Ware Dejeuner Set, D674-I, K...............................5,200.00
Floral Treasures Elephant, B2389-XI, A 180.00
Flowered Crate, D268-II, B...450.00
Gladstone Chamber Pot, D2082-I, T.......................................1,500.00
Gospel Plates, D1811-VI, 1813, 1815 & 1817-VII, M&F, set of 4 .650.00
Grass Mug, D214-VI, D..90.00
Harebell Vase, D180-VI, K, 8" 70.00
Heart Plate, D634-V, B, sz 1...40.00
Heart Shape Basket, Flowered, D1259-5, A, sm 400.00
Indian Corn Spill, D190-V, A, 6"...90.00
Irish Cottage Condiment Set, D2089-III, B................................750.00
Ivy Sugar & Cream, D241-III, B, sm...175.00
Ivy Tea Ware Bread Plate, D1410-III, B.....................................325.00
Killarney Biscuit Jar, D1981-VII, D...125.00
Killarney Candlestick, D1982-VII, D...110.00
Lace Tea Ware Sugar & Cream, D801&802-I, G 700.00
Leprechaun, D1142-VII, K, 5¼"..175.00
Lifford Cream, D301-VI, B..70.00
Lily Tea Ware Tray, D540-II, C 1,800.00
Mask Tea Ware Coffeepot, D1477-IV, B 300.00
Milk Maid Lithophane, B2436-XI, L&B, 9.2x11.1" 175.00
Oak Leaf Vase, B2020-XI, F, 8"..60.00
Pierced Spill, Flowered, D1179-II, J, sm, 2¼" 425.00
Pig, D230-V, B, sm, 2"..90.00
Pig, D231-III, E, lg, 3"..195.00

Richard K. Degenhardt Basket, D, 1995, 8", $525.00. (Made to commemorate the significant role Mr. Degenhardt played in the founding of the Belleek Collectors International Society.)

Root Centre, D1159-III, D...900.00
Round Tumbler, D281-III, A, sz 2..175.00
Shamrock Salt, D273-II, A 90.00
Shamrock Tea Ware Kettle, D387-III, E, sm...............................550.00
Shamrock Ware Hurricane Lamp, D2010-VII, E 85.00
Shamrock Ware Sandwich Tray, D1334-III, E 450.00
Shell Plateaux, D790-V, B, sm, 4½" dia......................................70.00
St John Gospel Plate, 1984, D1817-VII, M&F............................300.00
St Luke Gospel Plate, 1982, D1815-VII, M&F............................150.00
St Mark Gospel Plate, 1981, D1813-VII, M&F............................150.00
St Matthew Gospel Plate, 1979, D1811-VI, M&F.......................150.00
Summer Briar Trinket Box, D2054-VII, 3"...................................85.00

Swan, D254-VI, B, lg, 4¼"..90.00
Swan, D255-II, B, sm, 3¼" 210.00
Sydney Tea Ware Teapot, D608-II, G...700.00
Toy Shamrock Sugar & Cream, D234-II, E..................................160.00
Tree Trunk Vase, D1786-V, B, 6½"..70.00
Triple Flower Holder, D172-II, C...550.00
Victoria Tea Ware Tea & Saucer, D593-II, G 550.00

Bells

Some areas of interest represented in the study of bells are history, religion, and geography. Since Biblical times, bells have announced morning church services, vespers, deaths, christenings, school hours, fires, and community events. Countries have used them en masse to peal out the good news of Christmas, New Year's, and the endings of World Wars I and II. They've been rung in times of great sorrow, such as the death of Abraham Lincoln.

Dorothy Malone Anthony is the author of a series of ten books entitled *World of Bells*. Her address is in the Directory under Kansas. All have over two hundred colored pictures covering many bell categories. See also Nodders; Schoolhouse Collectibles.

Bell metal, emb From Meneely's West, Troy NY, 1852, lg...........130.00
Brass, ceremonial w/ornate etching, pointed finial, 4⅞x2½" dia ..40.00
Brass, lady in pilgrim-style hat w/purse in hand, 3½" 45.00
Brass, patriotic theme w/emb eagles, 5½"....................................60.00
Brass, school type, trn wood hdl w/incised rings, heavy, 10" 185.00
Brass, school type, wood hdl, EX patina, 8½" 65.00
Call, onyx/brass, brass rtcl gallery w/8 abalone shells, 4½x4¼" ..135.00
China, wht w/HP floral decor, Florence Ceramics, 4½x3" dia 110.00
Communion, 4 bells w/bird finials on branch-like arm, brass........60.00
Figurine, lady holding flower to chest, brass, 4⅜".....................165.00
Glass, clear w/gr hdl, oval panels w/3 etched birds, 10"..............175.00
Glass, custard w/HP roses, advertising, Jefferson Glass, 1910, 6½"...160.00
Glass, Save Time Telephone, cobalt, 2¼" 60.00
Grave, brass w/bronze hdl, mk 1818, 9x6½" dia 100.00
Hotel desk, brass support & wheel on wood base, 5½x3½" dia ..125.00
Sleigh, brass, set of 23, ea 1½", on strap, EX..............................200.00
Sleigh, NP brass, set of 70, ea 1½", on 41" strap.........................185.00
Sterling, Tiffany, monogramed, 2¾" 225.00
Sterling silver, Gorham, hand-hammered finish, ca 1879, 4¼"...215.00
Temple, Hindu inscription on front, ornate decor, 8¼x6" dia.......55.00

Bennington

Although the term has become a generic one for the mottled brown ware produced there, Bennington is not a type of pottery, but rather a town in Vermont where two important potteries were located. The Norton Company, founded in 1793, produced mainly redware and salt-glazed stoneware; only during a brief partnership with Fenton (1845 – 47) was any Rockingham attempted. The Norton Company endured until 1894, operated by succeeding generations of the Norton family. Fenton organized his own pottery in 1847. There he manufactured not only redware and stoneware, but more artistic types as well — graniteware, scroddled ware, flint enamel, a fine parian, and vast amounts of their famous Rockingham. Though from an esthetic standpoint his work rated highly among the country's finest ceramic achievements, he was economically unsuccessful. His pottery closed in 1858.

It is estimated that only one in five Fenton pieces were marked; and although it has become a common practice to link any fine piece of Rockingham to this area, careful study is vital in order to be able to distinguish Bennington's from the similar wares of many other American and Staffordshire potteries. Although the practice was without the permission of the proprietor, it was nevertheless a common occurrence for a potter to take his molds with him when moving from one pottery to the next, so particularly well-received designs were often reproduced at several locations. Of eight known Fenton marks, four are variations of the '1849' impressed stamp: 'Lyman Fenton Co., Fenton's Enamel Patented 1849, Bennington, Vermont.' These are generally found on examples of Rockingham and flint enamel. A raised, rectangular scroll with 'Fenton's Works, Bennington, Vermont,' was used on early examples of porcelain. From 1852 to 1858, the company operated under the title of the United States Pottery Company. Three marks — the ribbon mark with the initials USP, the oval with a scrollwork border and the name in full, and the plain oval with the name in full — were used during that period.

Among the more sought-after examples are the bird and animal figurines, novelty pitchers, figural bottles, and all of the more finely modeled items. Recumbent deer, cows, standing lions with one forepaw on a ball, and opposing pairs of poodles with baskets in their mouths and 'coleslaw' fur were made in Rockingham, flint enamel, and occasionally in parian. Numbers in the listings below refer to the book *Bennington Pottery and Porcelain* by Barret. Our advisors for Bennington (except for parian and stoneware) are Barbara and Charles Adams; they are listed in the Directory under Massachusetts.

Key: c/s — cobalt on salt glaze

Book flask, Bennington Companion C, flint enamel, brn/gr, 7¾" ..**935.00**
Book flask, Coming Thro' the Rye, bl gloss, 5" **550.00**
Book flask, Departed Spirits, flint enamel, brn/gr, no mk, 4" **595.00**
Book flask, Departed Spirits, flint enamel, lt brn w/teal gr, 7¾" .**595.00**
Book flask, Departed Spirits, flint enamel w/brn & teal, rpr, 5½".........**330.00**
Book flask, Departed Spirits G, flint enamel w/brn & teal, rpr, 5½" **385.00**
Book flask, flint enamel, tan w/bl-gr pages, mk Enamel Pat 1849, 6" ..**950.00**
Candlestick, flint enamel w/some dk bl, firing flaws, lines, 7½" .**595.00**
Candlestick, flint enamel w/some dk gr, 8" **825.00**
Coachman bottle, Rockingham, wrapped in cloak/has cup, mk, 10½", NM ...**1,095.00**
Flask, eagle w/banner 1 side, bk: morning glory, med brn, 7" **275.00**
Humidor, Rockingham, Lyman Fenton & Co, ca 1849-58, 8", EX ..**495.00**
Inkwell, Rockingham, shoe shape, ca 1880, 5½" **250.00**
Marble, bl & lt brn mottle, minor flaw, 1⅞" **110.00**
Pipkin, Rockingham, Lyman Fenton & Co, w/lid, 7¼" **695.00**
Toby bottle, Old Tom, Rockingham, astride bbl/holding 2 cups, 8½" .**1,250.00**

Stoneware

Butter churn, floral spray, c/s, E&LP Norton, 1861-81, 17½", EX .**575.00**
Crock, #2/plume, c/s, E&LP Norton, line, ca 1880, 7" **175.00**
Crock, #4/floral spray, c/s, E&LP Norton, rprs, ca 1880, 11".......**100.00**
Jar, preserve; #2/floral, c/s, E&LP Norton, prof rstr, 1880s, 11"...**415.00**
Jar, preserve; #2/floral, c/s, J&E Norton, chip, ca 1861, 11" **600.00**
Jar, preserve; #2/floral spray, c/s, J&E Norton, ping, ca 1855, 11" ..**745.00**
Jar, preserve; #3/flowers in compote, c/s, J&E Norton, 1850s, 13", EX...**880.00**
Jar, preserve; #3/thistle floral, c/s, J&E Norton, ca 1855, 12", VG ..**415.00**

Jug, large dotted bird on branch with worm in beak, J&E Norton & Co., professional restoration to handle, two-gallon, ca 1859, 13½", $1,980.00.

Jug, #1/bird, c/s, J Norton & Co, rstr, ca 1861, 10"....................**770.00**
Jug, #1/bird on stump, c/s, J&E Norton, chips, ca 1855, 11".......**650.00**
Jug, #2/accent, ochre/s, Norton & Fenton..., pings, 1840s, 11"...**300.00**
Jug, #2/bird on twig, c/s, J Norton & Co, drilled, ca 1861, 12"...**465.00**
Jug, #2/deer standing, c/s, J&E Norton, rstr, ca 1855, 14"........**6,600.00**
Jug, #2/floral, c/s, J&E Norton, spider/mks, ca 1855, 13"............**360.00**
Jug, #3/flower (ornate), c/s, J&E Norton, ca 1855, 15".............**600.00**
Jug, #3/triple flower, c/s, Julius Norton, stain/line, ca 1848, 16" .**165.00**
Jug, #4/floral (stylized), c/s, E&LP Norton, chip, 1880s, 17½" ...**1,045.00**

Beswick

In the early 1890s, James Wright Beswick operated a pottery in Longston, England, where he produced fine dinnerware as well as ornamental ceramics. Today's collectors are most interested in the figurines made since 1936 by a later generation Beswick firm, John Beswick, Ltd. They specialize in reproducing accurately detailed bone-china models of authentic breeds of animals. Their Fireside Series includes dogs, cats, elephants, horses, the Huntsman, and an Indian figure, which measure up to 14" in height. The Connoisseur line is modeled after the likenesses of famous racing horses. Beatrix Potter's characters and some of Walt Disney's are charmingly re-created and appeal to children and adults alike. Other items, such as character Tobys, have also been produced. The Beswick name is stamped on each piece. The firm was absorbed by the Doulton group in 1973.

Beatrix Potter, Amiable Guinea Pig, B3 ....**450.00**
Beatrix Potter, Apply Dappley, bottle out **250.00**
Beatrix Potter, Babbity Bumble, B6 ....**250.00**
Beatrix Potter, Benjamin Bunny, ears out, shoes in, 3B.............**195.00**
Beatrix Potter, Cecily Parsley, 3B...**95.00**
Beatrix Potter, Chippy Hackee, B3 ....**85.00**
Beatrix Potter, Cottontail, 3B **45.00**
Beatrix Potter, Diggory Diggory Delvet, 3B **75.00**
Beatrix Potter, Flopsy, Mopsy, Cottontail, B3 ....**65.00**
Beatrix Potter, Gentleman Mouse Made Bow, B6a.....................**200.00**
Beatrix Potter, Goody & Timmy Tiptoes, C3 ....**275.00**
Beatrix Potter, Hunca Muncca, 2B gold......................................**175.00**
Beatrix Potter, Jemima Puddleduck, B3 ....**55.00**
Beatrix Potter, Jemima Puddleduck/Nest, B6 ....**45.00**
Beatrix Potter, John Joiner, B6..**55.00**
Beatrix Potter, Johnny Townmouse/Bag, B6...............................**325.00**
Beatrix Potter, Little Black Rabbit, B3 ....**65.00**
Beatrix Potter, Little Pig Robinson Spying, B6 ....**150.00**
Beatrix Potter, Mittens & Moppet, B6..**250.00**
Beatrix Potter, Mr Benjamin Bunny/Peter Rabbit, B3 ....**75.00**
Beatrix Potter, Mr Jackson, B3..**55.00**
Beatrix Potter, Mr Jeremy Fisher Digging, B4 ....**195.00**
Beatrix Potter, Mrs Rabbit, umbrella out, 2B.............................**450.00**
Beatrix Potter, Mrs Rabbit w/Peter, P3646 ....**80.00**
Beatrix Potter, Mrs Tiggy Winkle, B3 ....**55.00**
Beatrix Potter, Mrs Tittlemouse 3B...**45.00**
Beatrix Potter, Old Mr Brown B3 ....**60.00**
Beatrix Potter, Old Woman in Shoe Knitting, B6 ....**95.00**
Beatrix Potter, Peter Rabbit, B3...**65.00**
Beatrix Potter, Peter Rabbit, P1098 ....**95.00**
Beatrix Potter, Pickles, 3A...**450.00**
Beatrix Potter, Pigwig, B3..**550.00**
Beatrix Potter, Rebecca Puddleduck, B3 ....**40.00**
Beatrix Potter, Samuel Whiskers, B3 ....**45.00**
Beatrix Potter, Squirrel Nutkin, red/brn, B3.................................**65.00**
Beatrix Potter, Tabitha Twitchit, B3 ....**75.00**
Beatrix Potter, Thomasina Tittlemouse, B6 ....**110.00**

Beatrix Potter, Timmy Willie, B3..45.00
Beatrix Potter, Tom Kitten, 1st version, 3B.............................85.00
Beatrix Potter, Tom Kitten w/Butterfly, 3C.........................325.00
Beatrix Potter, Tommy Brock, 2nd version, lg patch, 3B.............65.00
Bird, Budgie parakeet, #1216, w/orig sticker 200.00
Bird, Bullfinch, #1042 ....49.00
Bird, Cardinal, #927, 6¼" 150.00
Bird, Chickadee, #929, 5½x3¾"..195.00
Bird, Goldcrest, #2145 ....49.00
Bird, Grey Wagtail, #1041 ....49.00
Bird, Parrot, yel & gr, perched on stump, #980, 5" 195.00
Bird, Robin, #980 ....49.00
Bird, Whitethroat, #2106 ....49.00
Cat, Siamese, seated, 9½" 125.00
Cat, Siamese, standing, #1897, 6½" 45.00
Cat, Siamese pr, recumbent, #1296, 3x4¼x4¼", NM...................48.00
Character jug, Captain Cuttle, 1948-73, 4¾"..........................130.00
Character jug, Mr Micawber, #310, 1970-73, 8½"....................125.00
Character jug, Sairey Gamp, #371, 1936-73, 6½"....................125.00
Creamer & sugar bowl, Pecksniff, #1117/#1129 ....85.00
Disney, Owl, from Winnie the Pooh, 3" 125.00
Disney, Winnie the Pooh, 1968-90, 2½".....................................99.00
Dog, Airedale, CH Cast Iron Monarch, 5½"............................165.00
Dog, Chihuahua on pillow, 2⅝"...45.00
Dog, Corgi, 2¾"..35.00
Dog, Dachshund, begging, red, 4"...175.00
Dog, Doberman Pinscher, Annastock Lance, 5¾".......................85.00
Dog, German Shepherd, CH Ulrica of Brittas, 5¼" 145.00
Dog, German Shepherd, recumbent, D3378, 2½".......................50.00
Dog, Golden Labrador, Wendover, 5¾x8" 110.00
Dog, Pekinese, begging, #1059, 4½"..175.00
Dog, Springer Spaniel, 5x7" 65.00
Dog, Welsh Corgi, Black Prince, 5½".......................................175.00
Duck, mallard ashtray, postwar mk, 4x4".................................52.00
Horse, Bois Racehorse, #701, 2nd version, 8" 95.00
Horse, Clydesdale, 8½x9¾x3"..125.00
Horse, Dales Pony, #1671, 6½x8"..195.00
Horse, Foal #763, 2st version, 3¼" 75.00
Horse, Foal #996, 1943-76, 3"...75.00
Horse, Foal #997, 3¼"..75.00
Horse, Palomino, #1261, 1st version, 6¾" 135.00
Horse, Palomino, Arab Xayal, #1265, 6½".................................145.00
Horse, Palomino, 7½x8½x3"...200.00
Horse, Spirit of Nature, wht matt, #2935 ....95.00
Horse, Swish Tail Horse, #1182, 8½x10"..................................195.00
Pitcher, Palm Tree, #1074...175.00
Shakers, Laurel & Hardey, 4", 3¼", on tray...............................75.00
Teapot, Sairey Gamp, #691, 5½" 300.00
Vase, shell form, gr/cream to beige, 7¼x10"..............................95.00

Bicycles

The time frame of collecting cycling items extends from the days of ancient manumotive transport to the present. The eras most interesting to collectors are (simplistically) the 1860s, with the Velocipede; 1875 – 89, famous for the High Wheel; 1890 – 1900, when the Safety bicycle was developed; 1920 – 1955, for the Balloon Tire. Virtually every aspect of collecting is encompassed — everything from late eighteenth-century prints to jerseys worn in last year's Tour de France. The collector can break the field down to a particular category, medium, or history. One can make special collections of cycling photographs, the bikes themselves, porcelains, lithographs, related toys, etc. There are over fifteen different circa 1819 Hobby horse plates which in themselves would make a most

wonderful and challenging collection. Cycliana encompasses virtually every aspect of art, antiques, and collectibles. Any one of these fields could relate to social, sport, financial, or mechanical history. Below is a select group of items from a few of these categories.

Our advisor for this category is Lorne Shields; he is listed in the Directory under Ohio. (Mr. Shields is interested in the acquisition of early cycliana and offers to help evaluate early bicycle-related items.)

Bicycles

Cinelli Super Coursa, Campagnolo Super Record Road Racing, 1977, G....1,000.00
Elgin Motor Bike, 26" wheels, light/horn/rack, 1927, as found ...500.00
Evinrude Streamflow Deluxe, balloon tire, ca 1938, EX orig (not rstr)..15,000.00
Hard Tired Safety, Elliott Hickory, wood & metal fr, ca 1888, VG...5,000.00
High wheel/Penny Farthing, 52" front wheel, G orig saddle, ca 1884, VG...1,750.00
Pierce Arrow racer, Buffalo NY, 28" wood wheels/spring fork, 1900s, EX......1,750.00
Remington, men's std pattern, 28" wooden wheels, ca 1896, VG..350.00
Rollfast Club, balloon tires, w/tank & light, 26" wheels, 1937, EX...1,200.00

Rudge High-wheeler, 52" front wheel, brake mechanism, complete with nameplate, EX, $2,600.00. (Photo courtesy Lorne Shields)

Schwinn Liner, balloon tires, w/accessories, 1954, rstr 600.00
Velocepede/boneshaker, front-wheel driven, orig pnt/saddle, 1870s, EX..2,000.00

Related Memorabilia and Ephemera

Bell, Boy Scout emblem, ca 1930, as found, working....................35.00
Bell, front wheel lever driven, Hill & Tollman, ca 1884, EX...1,000.00
Board game, Wheeling, 29x15" board w/playing pcs, ca 1900, VG...150.00
Book, The Am Bicycler, CE Pratt, Boston, 2nd ed, 1880, VG....150.00
Book, The Wheelmen + Outing, 1st 5 vols, bound, Oct 1882-Mar 1885, EX....325.00
Bottle, stoneware, man on high-wheeler, Emerson's Stout, EX 75.00
Brooch, British, silver hallmk, ca 1900, EX...............................150.00
Buttons, cello, various ads, Whitehead & Hoag, ca 1896, from $5 to ..100.00
Calendar, Columbia, litho, 1915, 14x10", G orig 100.00
Camera, Cycle Poco #3 w/all fittings, Rochester Camera, ca 1900, VG..150.00
Catalog, Columbia, Westfield MA, 1885, NM 150.00
Catalog, Gormulley & Jeffrey, Chicago, 1896, VG 75.00
Chandelier, cherubs riding high-wheelers, electrified/rstr, ca 1885 ..7,500.00
Cigar box top label, racer, M..35.00
Cigar cutter, modeled as high-wheel bike, ca 1885, EX...............250.00
Cigarette package, Cycle Brand, some cigarettes inside, ca 1910, VG ..75.00
Clock, Automata, high-wheel cyclist, barometer/thermometer, 1890s, EX...1,000.00
Clock, man/bicycle, gilt bronze, British United Clock, 1893, 7", VG..600.00
Cyclometer, McDonnell, for high-wheel bike, ca 1886, VG....1,000.00
Cyclometer, NY Standard, ca 1896, MIB 125.00
Figurines, bsk, 15" male & female bicyclists, Heubach, EX, pr ...1,800.00
Humidor, porc, Velocipede Accident, figural hdl, ca 1870s, 7x6x4", EX..1,000.00

Lamp, carbide, P&H, w/much orig nickel, ca 1925, VG **65.00**
Lamp, Lucas King of the Road, oil burner, ca 1900, EX **100.00**
Lithograph, Monark Bicycle Works, Chicago, ca 1895, 16x22" ..**750.00**
Match safe, sterling, hand-eng cyclist, 1895.....................................**350.00**
Medal, gold, figural, hand eng, bike race, 1st place, 1886, EX **500.00**
Medal, silver, Participants, group outing, Freehold NJ, 1896, G ...**45.00**
Paperweight, Yale Bicycle, sulfide flag inside, ca 1900, G- **150.00**
Photo, cabinet card, high-wheel racer, ca 1882, VG **100.00**
Photo, carte de visite, lady w/new Safety Bike, ca 1897, EX **20.00**
Photo, tintype, outside group, 8th-plate, ca 1900, EX **35.00**
Pipe, meerschaum, man on high-wheeler, ca 1890, in orig case ..**750.00**
Plate, Hobby Horse, bl transfer, English, ca 1819, VG **350.00**
Plate, majolica, ca 1900, 7", EX **65.00**
Playing cards, Goodall #973, full deck of 52+Joker, ca 1900, EXIB........**50.00**
Poster, Peugeot, military cyclist w/letter, Fr, WWI era, 35x48", VG .**2,500.00**
Poster, Wolfe Am Bicycles, Art Nouveau lady, ca 1897, 57x41", G..**3,000.00**
Print, Hobby Horse, hand-colored etching, Tegg, Mar 1819, 12x18", NM...**350.00**
Print, lady velocipedist, hand colored, Fr, ca 1870, 12x18", EX ..**500.00**
Razor, str; Tandem Cyclists on blade, VG in box **75.00**
Sheet music, Daisy Daisy, 1930s, EX..**10.00**
Sign, Schwinn, paper board, 1960s, 14x25", VG **100.00**
Spoon, Victor Bicycles, sterling silver, 3¾", EX.............................**50.00**
Stein, high-wheel racer, HP, German, ca 1885, 19", EX **1,000.00**
Stein, Safety Cyclist w/lady, lithophane in base, German, ca 1900..**125.00**
Stereoptic view, The Boulevard NY City, VG.................................**15.00**
Stevengraph, The Last Lap, woven silk, orig bk, English, ca 1878, VG....**300.00**
Thermometer, Safety Cyclist, metal on wood, 8", EX..................**125.00**
Trade card, Tuck, man & lady on Sociable Trike, chromo litho, 1885, EX..**50.00**
Trade card, W Duke & Sons, Lady High-Wheel Tricks, 1895, 1 of 25, EX .**40.00**
Trophy, SP, full-figure cyclist, awarded, Germany, ca 1900, 17", VG....**450.00**
Watch, nickel w/cyclist pattern, open face/stem wind, 1910, nonworking..**150.00**
Watch, silver open face w/clamp for handlebar, Lucas, 1900s, VG ..**350.00**

Big Little Books

The first Big Little Book was published in 1933 and copyrighted in 1932 by the Whitman Publishing Company of Racine, Wisconsin. Its hero was Dick Tracy. The concept was so well accepted that others soon followed Whitman's example; and though the 'Big Little Book' phrase became a trademark of the Whitman Company, the formats of his competitors (Saalfield, Goldsmith, Van Wiseman, Lynn, and World Syndicate) were exact copies. Today's Big Little Book buffs collect them all.

These hand-sized sagas of adventure were illustrated with full-page cartoons on the right-hand page and the story narration on the left. Colorful cardboard covers contained hundreds of pages, usually totaling over an inch in thickness. Big Little Books originally sold for 10¢ at the dime store; as late as the mid-1950s when the popularity of comic books caused sales to decline, signaling an end to production, their price had risen to a mere 20¢. Their appeal was directed toward the pre-teens who bought, traded, and hoarded Big Little Books. Because so many were stored in attics and closets, many have survived. Among the super heroes are G-Men, Flash Gordon, Tarzan, the Lone Ranger, and Red Ryder; in a lighter vein, you'll find such lovable characters as Blondie and Dagwood, Mickey Mouse, Little Orphan Annie, and Felix the Cat.

In the early to mid-'30s, Whitman published several Big Little Books as advertising premiums for the Coco Malt Company, who packed them in boxes of their cereal. These are highly prized by today's collectors, as are Disney stories and super-hero adventures.

For more information we recommend *Big Little Books, A Collector's Reference and Value Guide*, by Larry Jacobs; and *Collector's Guide to Children's Books, Volumes 1, 2*, and *3*, by Dian McClure Jones and Rosemary Jones (Collector Books). Our advisor for this category is Ron Donnelly; he is listed in the Directory under Alabama.

Note: At the present time, the market for these books is fairly stable — values for common examples are actually dropping. Only the rare, character-related titles are increasing.

Alice in Wonderland, Whitman #759, NM **55.00**
Arizona Kid on the Bandit Trail, Whitman #1192, EX **15.00**
Betty Boop in Show White, Whitman #1119, VG **45.00**
Blondie, Baby Dumpling & All, Whitman #1487, EX **25.00**
Buck Jones in Ride 'Em Cowboy, Whitman #1116, EX **25.00**
Buck Rogers Vs Fiend of Space, Whitman #1409, EX **65.00**
Captain Easy Behind Enemy Lines, Whitman #1474, G **10.00**
Chester Cump Finds the Hidden Treasure, Whitman #766, EX....**35.00**
Convoy Patrol, Whitman #1446, EX...**10.00**
Dan Dunn Secret Operative 48 & Underworld Gorillas, Whitman #1417, EX ...**30.00**
Danger Trails in Africa, Whitman #1151, NM **35.00**
Dick Tracy & the Boris Arson Gang, Whitman #1163, EX...........**30.00**
Dick Tracy Out West, Whitman #723, NM **100.00**
Dirigible-ZR 90 & the Disappearing Zeppelin, Whitman #1464, NM..**40.00**
Don Winslow & the Giant Girl Spy, Whitman #1408, EX **30.00**
Donald Duck Is Here Again, Whitman #1484, EX **40.00**
Erik Noble & the Forty-Niners, Whitman #772, EX **20.00**
Flying the Sky Clipper Winsie Atkins, Whitman #1108, NM **30.00**
G-Man on the Crime Trail, Whitman #1118, NM **30.00**
Gene Autry & the Mystery of Paint Rock Canyon, Whitman #1425, VG...**15.00**
George O'Brien & the Hooded Riders, Whitman #1457, G............**5.00**
Harold Teen Swinging at the Sugar Bowl, Whitman #1418, EX....**15.00**
International Spy, Dr Doom Face Death of Dawn, Whitman #1148, EX...**15.00**
Invisible Scarlet O'Neil Vs the King of the Slums, Whitman #1406, NM ..**40.00**
Jungle Jim, Whitman #1138, VG...**15.00**
Kayo & Moon Mullins & the One Man Gang, Whitman #1415, EX.**25.00**
Li'l Abner Among the Millionaires, Whitman #1401, EX **25.00**
Little Miss Muffet, Whitman #1120, EX **20.00**
Little Orphan Annie, Whitman #708 (2nd BLB), NM................**200.00**
Mary Lee & the Mystery of the Indian Beads, Whitman #1438, EX..**20.00**
Mickey Mouse, The Mail Pilot, Whitman #731, EX **65.00**
Mickey Mouse & the Sacred Jewel, Whitman #1187, EX **40.00**
Mickey Mouse on Sky Island, Whitman #1417, NM...................**75.00**
Popeye, The Super Fighter, Whitman #1406, VG **15.00**
Popeye & the Quest for the Rainbird, Whitman #1459, EX **35.00**
Porky Pig & Petunia, Whitman #1408, EX **30.00**
Ray Land of the Tank Corps, Whitman #1447, NM.....................**30.00**
Roy Rogers at Crossed Feathers Ranch, Whitman #1494, EX.......**30.00**
Shadow & the Living Death, Whitman #1430, VG **45.00**
Skeezix at the Military Academy, Whitman #1408, NM...............**35.00**
Smilin' Jack & the Escape From Death Rock, Whitman #1445, VG..**10.00**
Smoky Stover All Pictures Comics, Whitman #1413, EX.............**25.00**
Tailspin Tommy, The Weasel & His Skywaymen, Whitman #1410, EX ..**25.00**
Tarzan & the Ant Men, Whitman #1444, EX...............................**40.00**
Tarzan of the Screen, Whitman #778, NM **100.00**
Tim McCoy on the Tomahawk Trail, Whitman #1436, EX...........**25.00**
Tom Mix & Tony Jr in Terror Trail, Whitman #762, NM.............**70.00**
Tom Swift & His Magnetic Silencer, Whitman #1437, EX...........**35.00**
Uncle Ray's Story of the United States, Whitman #722, VG **15.00**

Uncle Wiggily's Adventures, 1946, Howard Garis, EX, $30.00.

Walt Disney's Bambi, Whitman #1469, NM 70.00
Walt Disney's Dumbo, Only His Ears Grew; Whitman #1400, EX ...40.00
West Point of the Air, Whitman #1164, EX 20.00
Wings of the USA, Whitman #1407, NM 35.00

Bing and Grondahl

In 1853 brothers M.H. and J.H. Bing formed a partnership with Frederick Vilhelm Grondahl in Copenhagen, Denmark. Their early wares were porcelain plaques and figurines designed by the noted sculptor Thorvaldsen of Denmark. Dinnerware production began in 1863, and by 1889 their underglaze color 'Copenhagen Blue' had earned them worldwide acclaim. They are perhaps most famous today for their Christmas plates, the first of which was made in 1895. See also Limited Edition Plates.

Bowl, cereal; Sea Gull, #45 ....50.00
Bowl, fruit; Sea Gull, #21A, 5⅜" 45.00
Bowl, Sea Gull, ruffled edge, #40B, 1⅜x5¾" dia 110.00
Bowl, serving; Sea Gull, #43, 2¾x9¾" dia 70.00
Bowl, vegetable; Sea Gull, sea horse hdls, w/lid, 7x10¼" dia 200.00
Butter pat, Sea Gull, shell shape, 3½x3" 20.00
Coffeecup, Sea Gull, #103 ....75.00
Coffeepot, Sea Gull, #91, w/lid 175.00
Coffeepot, Sea Gull, #91A, w/lid 280.00
Compote, Sea Gull, #206, lg, 9½" 110.00
Creamer, Sea Gull, #85B, open 135.00
Cup & saucer, Christmas Rose 20.00
Dish, nut; Sea Gull, star shape, #42A, 5" 40.00
Dish, Sea Gull, shell shape, #42, 6¾" 80.00
Figurine, boxer, lying down, #3635, 3½x6" 85.00
Figurine, boy & girl dancing, #1845, 8⅜" 265.00
Figurine, boy & girl on bench w/drinking cups, #2176, 5¾" 150.00
Figurine, boy & girl standing bk-to-bk, #2373 ....110.00
Figurine, boy blowing trumpet, #1792, 7½" 145.00
Figurine, boy holding puppy, #1747, 6¾" 90.00
Figurine, boy kissing girl, #2162, 7½" 85.00
Figurine, boy on rock, 7½" 175.00
Figurine, children playing, #1568, 5x5" 145.00
Figurine, couple lying on ground, #1644T, 9½x12½" 400.00
Figurine, crow, head turn slightly, #1714, 11x5⅞" 250.00
Figurine, girl holding kitten, #1779, 6¾" 110.00
Figurine, girl on bench w/tulips, #229, 5½" 105.00
Figurine, girl w/cat in lap, #2329, 5¼" 210.00
Figurine, lady in bl dress feeding chickens, #2220S 165.00
Figurine, lady milking cow while cat watches, #2017, 5x7" 260.00
Figurine, mother in chair reading to 2 children, #1644, 9x6¼" ..400.00
Figurine, pointer puppy chasing tail, #2026, 4½x6½" 110.00
Figurine, rabbit, #1592, 3½x4¾" 90.00
Figurine, Siamese cat sitting w/1 paw raised, #2308, 5½" 80.00
Figurine, spaniel, #2172, 4½x3" 80.00
Figurine, wire-haired fox terrier, #1998, 5½x5½" 160.00
Gravy boat, Sea Gull, attached tray 130.00
Nappy, leaf shape, bl flowers & vines, 9x7" 75.00
Plate, Blue Fluted, 9½" 30.00
Plate, bread & butter; Sea Gull, #28, 6⅞" 30.00
Plate, cake; Sea Gull, triangular, #40, 9¼" 110.00
Plate, salad; Sea Gull, #26, 8½" 55.00
Plate, tea; Sea Gull, #27, 7½" 45.00
Saucer, Sea Gull, #305 ....10.00
Smoke set, Sea Gull, 2½" cigarette urn, 3½" ind ashtray, w/gold .40.00
Sugar bowl, Sea Gull, #94, w/lid 80.00
Sugar bowl, Sea Gull, #94A, w/lid 160.00

Teacup and saucer, Bute cup with sea gull design and handle, ca 1948, from $50.00 to $60.00. (Photo courtesy Jim and Susan Harran)

Teacup, Sea Gull, #108 ....75.00
Teapot, Sea Gull, #238, w/lid 280.00
Teapot, Sea Gull, #654, w/lid 200.00
Tray, Sea Gull, gold trim, 8½x5⅛" 85.00
Vase, Blue Fluted, #208/32, 2½x2" 40.00
Vase, Sea Gull, 2¾" 20.00
Vase, sea shore w/waves along sandy beach, #72-2, 4½" 90.00

Binoculars

There are several types of binoculars, and the terminology used to refer to them is not consistent or precise. Generally, 'field glasses' refer to simple Galilean optics, where the lens next to the eye (the ocular) is concave and dished away from the eye. By looking through the large lens (the objective), it is easy to see that the light goes straight through the two lenses. These are lower power, have a very small field of view, and do not work nearly as well as prism binoculars. In a smaller size, they are opera glasses, and their price increases if they are covered with mother-of-pearl (fairly common but very attractive), abalone shell (more colorful), ivory (quite scarce), or other exotic materials. Field glasses are not valuable unless very unusual or by the best makers, such as Zeiss or Leitz. Prism binoculars have the objective lens offset from the eyepiece and give a much better view. This is the standard binocular form, called Porro prisms, and dates from around 1900. Another type of prism binocular is the roof prism, which at first resembles the straight-through field glasses, with two simple cylinders or cones, here containing very small prisms. These can be distinguished by the high quality views they give and by a thin diagonal line that can be seen when looking backwards through the objective. In general, German binoculars are the most desirable, followed by American, English, and finally French, which can be of good quality but are very common unless of unusual configuration. Japanese optics of WWII or before are often of very high quality. 'Made in Occupied Japan' binoculars are very common, but collectors prize those by Nippon Kogaku (Nikon). Some binoculars are center focus (CF), with one central wheel that focuses both sides at once. These are much easier to use but more difficult to seal against dirt and moisture. Individual focus (IF) binoculars are adjusted by rotating each eyepiece and tend to be cleaner inside in older optics. Each type is preferred by different collectors. Very large binoculars are always of great interest. All binoculars are numbered according to their magnifying power and the diameter of the objective in millimeters. Optics of 6 x 30 magnify six times and have 30 millimeter objectives.

Prisms are easily knocked out of alignment, requiring an expensive and difficult repair. If severe, this misalignment is immediately noticeable on use by the double-image scene. Minor damage can be seen by focusing on a small object and slowly moving the binoculars away from the eye, which will cause the images to appear to separate. Overall cleanliness should be checked by looking backwards (through the objective) at a light or the sky, when any film or dirt on the lenses or prisms can easily be seen. Pristine binoculars are worth far more than when dirty or misaligned, and broken or cracked optics lower the value far more. Cases help keep binoculars clean but do not add materially to the value.

As of 2002, any significant changes in value are due to Internet sales. Some of the prices listed here are lower than would be reached at an online auction. Revisions of these values would be inappropriate at this point for these reasons: First, values are fluctuating wildly on the Internet; 'auction fever' is extreme. Second, some common instruments can fetch a high price at an Internet sale, and it is clear that the price will not be supported as more of them are placed at auction. In fact, an overlooked collectible like the binocular will be subject to a great increase in supply as they are retrieved from closets in response to the values people see at an online auction. Third, sellers who have access to these Internet auctions can use them for price guides if they wish, but the values in this listing have to reflect what can be obtained at an average large antique show. The following listings assume a very good overall condition, with generally clean and aligned optics.

Our advisor for this category is Peter Abrahams, who studies and collects binoculars and other optics. Please contact, especially to exchange reference material (SASE required with written questions). Mr. Abrahams is listed in the Directory under Oregon.

Field Glasses

Fernglas 08, German WWI, 6x39, military gr, many makers.........**50.00**
Folding, modern, hinged flat case, oculars outside **10.00**
Folding or telescoping, no bbls, old **125.00**
Ivory covered, various sm szs & makers...**200.00**
LeMaire, bl leather/brass, various szs, other Fr makers same **25.00**
Metal, emb hunting scene, various sm szs & makers.....................**45.00**
Pearl covered, various sm szs & makers **90.00**
Porc covered, delicate painting, various sm szs & makers............**200.00**
US Naval Gun Factory Optical Shop 6x30.....................................**75.00**
Zeiss 'Galan' 2.5x34, modern design look, early 1920s **120.00**

Prism Binoculars (Porro)

Barr & Stroud, 7x50, Porro II prisms, IF, WWII **120.00**
Bausch & Lomb, 6x30, IF, WWI, Signal Corps..............................**50.00**
Bausch & Lomb, 7x50, IF, WWII, other makers same **90.00**
Bausch & Lomb Zephyr, 7x35 & other, CF...................................**140.00**
Bausch & Lomb/Zeiss, 8x17, CF, Pat 1897 ....**140.00**
Crown Optical, 6x30, IF, WWI, filters **50.00**
France, various makers & szs, if not unusual **30.00**
German WWII 10x80, eyepcs at 45 degrees **500.00**
German WWII 6x30, 3-letter code for various makers..................**60.00**
Goertz Trieder Binocle, various szs, unusual adjustment................**85.00**
Huet, Paris 7x22, other sm szs, unusual shapes.............................**80.00**
Leitz 6x30 Dienstglas, IF, good optics **75.00**
Leitz 8x30 Binuxit, CF, outstanding optics...................................**150.00**
M19, US military 7x50, ca 1980..**150.00**
Nikon 9x35, 7x35, CF, 1950s...**100.00**
Nippon Kogaku, 7x50, IF, Made in Occupied Japan....................**150.00**
Ross Stepnada, 7x30, CF, wide angle, 1930s **250.00**
Ross 6x30, standard British WWI issue **50.00**
Sard, 6x42, IF, very wide angle, WWII..**900.00**
Toko (Tokyo Opt Co) 7x50, IF, Made in Occupied Japan.............**45.00**
Universal Camera 6x30, IF, WWII, other makers same.................**50.00**
US Naval Gun Factory Optical Shop 6x30, IF, filters, WWI **70.00**
US Naval Gun Factory Optical 10x45, IF, WWI...........................**200.00**
US Navy, 20x120, various makers, WWII & later **2,200.00**
Warner & Swasey (important maker) 8x20, CF, 1902.................**200.00**
Wollensak 6x30, ca 1940..**50.00**
Zeiss Deltrintem 8x30, CF, 1930s..**95.00**
Zeiss DF 95, 6x18, sq shoulder, very early **160.00**
Zeiss Starmorbi 12/24/42x60, turret eyepcs, 1920s **2,500.00**
Zeiss Teleater 3x13, CF, bl leather **120.00**
Zeiss 15x60, CF or IF, various models **700.00**

Zeiss 8x40 Delactis, CF or IF, 1930s **230.00**

Roof Prism Binoculars

Hensoldt Dialyt, various szs, 1930s-80s **140.00**
Hensoldt Universal Dialyt, 6x26, 3.5x26, 1920s...........................**120.00**
Leitz Trinovid, 7x42 & other, CF, 1960s-80s, EX.........................**500.00**
Zeiss Dialyt, 8x30, CF, 1960s **400.00**

Bisque

Bisque is a term referring to unglazed earthenware or porcelain that has been fired only once. During the Victorian era, bisque figurines became very popular. Most were highly decorated in pastels and gilt and demonstrated a fine degree of workmanship in the quality of their modeling. Few were marked. See also Heubach; Nodders; Dolls; Piano Babies.

Victorian boy and girl, intaglio eyes, pastels with gold trim, Germany #1268/#1266, 12", EX, $140.00 for the pair. (Photo courtesy McMasters Auctions)

Boy & girl in fancy chairs, much gold, 6½", pr...........................**165.00**
Boy w/basket, bl shorts/lav shirt, Germany, 14" **250.00**
Boy w/grapes & sickle; girl w/sheaf of wheat, 9", pr....................**100.00**
Cherubs support rtcl vase, gold trim, 9" **200.00**
Clowns (2) playing leapfrog, EX quality, 7½" **125.00**
Grecian lady w/cornucopia (w/dagger, resting on post), 13½", pr **220.00**
Lamp, boy & girl w/dancing bear figural, Germany, 11"..............**200.00**
Wall pocket, boy & girl in balcony, scrolling, mc, 7".....................**75.00**

Black Americana

Black memorabilia is without a doubt a field that encompasses the most widely exploited ethnic group in our history. But within this field there are many levels of interest: arts and achievements such as folk music and literature, caricatures in advertising, souvenirs, toys, fine art, and legitimate research into the days of their enslavement and enduring struggle for equality. The list is endless.

In the listings below are some with a derogatory connotation. Thankfully, these are from a bygone era and represent the mores of a culture that existed nearly a century ago. They are included only to convey the fact that they are a part of this growing area of collecting interest. Black Americana catalogs featuring a wide variety of items for sale are available; see the Directory under Clubs, Newsletters, and Catalogs for more information. We also recommend *Black Collectibles* by P.J. Gibbs (Collector Books). See also Cookie Jars; Postcards; Posters; Sheet Music.

Ashtray, brn/blk-pnt aluminum face w/lg wht open mouth, 1920s, 5", NM ...**165.00**
Ashtray, ceramic, Come Seven, pup watches boy shoot craps, 1940s, M..**50.00**

Baby dish, 3-part set in silver, hot water spout, graphics, VG+ **55.00**
Baby rattle, clown face w/sterling trim, cvd bone hdl, 1870s, 4".......**175.00**
Banjo, plastic & celluloid, river showboat graphics, 22", EX+ **75.00**
Bank, pot metal, Mammy w/laundry basket, EX **150.00**
Bank, red/wht/bl-pnt wood figure w/blk fur hair, Germany, 1910, 5", EX .**125.00**
Bank, Watch Your Savings Grow register, golly litho on tin, 5", EX+........**220.00**
Book, Adventures of Two Dutch Dolls, Upton reprint, 1966, 65 pgs, M ...**100.00**
Book, Kemble's Pickaninnies, hardcover, USA, 1901, rare, VG .**450.00**
Book, Little Black Sambo, Helen Bannerman/Platt & Munk, 1935, 63 pgs.**100.00**
Book, Little Brown Koko, 1st ed, 1940, 96 pgs, EX **85.00**
Candy jar, amber glass head shape w/pnt hat & features, 1920s, NM .**200.00**
Cigarette holder, boy cutting melon holder, pnt bsk, 1880s, 4", M ..**110.00**
Clock, alarm; Little Black Sambo, rnd, metal fr, 1940s, 3½", EX.**170.00**
Clock, die-cut pnt wood figure w/dial on chest, Germany, 7¼", NM+.**560.00**
Coat rack, pnt bronze w/J Griffin head, 5 filigree hooks, 1880s, EX+..**425.00**
Cookbook, Aunt Caroline's Dixieland Recipes, 1922, EX+ **55.00**
Cookie jar, Aunt Jemima, plastic, F&F, M **650.00**
Crank toy, wood, Old Kentucky Home, w/Lime Kiln Club, EXIB...**4,500.00**
Creamer & sugar bowl, Aunt Jemima & Uncle Mose, plastic, F&F ..**175.00**
Decanter set, 5 minstrels, ceramic, Italy, 5¼", M, ea **55.00**
Display, bakery chef figure, rubber-type compo, 18", VG+ **325.00**
Display, boy figure in tattered clothing, automated, 1930s, EX+.**900.00**
Display, boy on base, plaster w/wood hands & base, clockwork, 23" .**1,900.00**
Display, boy sitting, nude, toothy grin, clockwork, 18x16x7", EX+...**1,500.00**
Display, Smoking Sambo figure, die-cut paperbrd, 16", EX+ **85.00**
Doll, Beloved Belindy, stuffed cloth, Georgene Novelties, 13½", EX...**700.00**
Doll, Grumpy, Effanbee, 12", EX **375.00**
Egg cup, plastic, Robertson Golden Shred Golliwog, 3¼", NM..**125.00**
Figure, pipe-smoking banjo player in twig chair, plaster, 21", VG+ .**1,500.00**
Figure, porter/usher in walking stride, paper over tin, 47", VG+...**70.00**
Figure, shoeshine boy looking up woman's shirt, pnt bsk, 1880s. 5", NM.**150.00**
Figure, 3 boys eating watermelon, pnt plaster, 1920s, 12x17", EX ..**140.00**
Fishing lure, Sam-Bo, plastic, 4½", EX (VG box)..........................**55.00**
Game, bean bag, cb, figure w/open mouth, 3 cups, 1900s, 16", EX+...**125.00**
Game, Chuckler's Game, Rosebud, 1931, NMIB.......................**100.00**
Game, Darky Five Pins, Milton Bradley, 1890s, complete, NMIB..**350.00**
Game, Sambo ring toss, die-cut image, ca 1921, EX (VG box)...**100.00**
Game, Skillets & Cakes, Milton Bradley, 1946, complete, EXIB...**200.00**
Game, Snap, 46 golliwog cards, England, late 1920s, NMIB.........**75.00**
Handkerchief, Best To Ask Mom/Dad for the Rest, images on wht, 9", NM...**110.00**
Humidor, waist-length gent in hat/coat/vest, HP porc, 7", NM ..**400.00**
Lamp, ceramic, lady's head w/brn skin & elaborate hair, 7", EX .**175.00**
Lawn ornament, CI boy w/watermelon, 1955, 20-lb, NM **150.00**
Lighter, Deco head, flames shoot out mouth, pnt metal, 1930s, 3", NM..**80.00**
Magazine, Black Panther, 1971 The Year of the Youth, EX+ **70.00**
Marionette, boy in cloth overalls/shirt, Effanbee, 1930s, 14", EX+....**175.00**
Mask, Mammy features, pnt pressed canvas/cotton, 1930s-40s, NM....**45.00**
Mask, Mardis Gras-type head w/red lips in top hat, papier-mache, VG+....**875.00**
Measuring spoon holder, chalkware Mammy figure, NM................**50.00**
Note pad, Aunt Jemima, F&F, 1950s **95.00**
Pamphlet, WWI gov't issue of 'Negro & Flag,' EX+ **20.00**
Pegbrd, pnt die-cut wood Mammy shape, 9x5¾", NM **100.00**
Pepper mill, ceramic cone-shaped chef in red/wht/bl apron, 10", NM ..**85.00**
Photo, Seven Com 'Leven, 5 men rolling dice/playing cards, ca 1910.**100.00**
Pin-bk button, Uncle Remus Club around Brer Rabbit, 1910s, 1¼", NM ..**120.00**
Pincushion, litho-on-wood Mammy figure w/skirt cushion, 4½", NM ..**55.00**
Pitcher, ironstone w/transfer of minstrel band, Wish I Was ..., 8½" **325.00**
Planter, ceramic Mammy figure w/bk side as extra-lg planter, M...**75.00**
Poster, House-Rent Party/Pigmeat Alamo Markham, linen bk, 40", EX+ .**125.00**
Poster, Jes yo come along an' laff at Uncle Tom's Cabin, 3-sheet, EX .**2,185.00**
Poster, Ragtime Jubilee/Big Time Minstrel Revue, fr, 23x15", EX.**35.00**
Pull toy, Mammy pushing buggy, pnt plaster/compo/tin, 10x5x11", VG+..**150.00**
Puppet toy, die-cut Jim Dandy ad pc, Crudoform Liniment, 8", NM..**300.00**
Shakers, Aunt Jemima & Uncle Mose, plastic, F&F, 3½", pr........**55.00**

Shakers. Aunt Jemima & Uncle Mose, plastic, F&F, 5", pr...........**75.00**
Shakers. Mammy & farmer, pnt wood, 2½", EX, pr....................**40.00**

Shakers, Mammy with coffeepot and cup, green striped skirt, plastic, F&F Die Works, 5¼", $225.00 for the pair.

Shaving mug, blk head, soap top/cream bottom (mouth), 1880s, NM+...**330.00**
Shoehorn, man's head at tip of hdl, EX **30.00**
Slave tax badge, copper, mid-19th C, 1½x1½" **1,150.00**
Snow dome, figure w/watermelon, Atlas Crystal Works, 4", NM .**250.00**
Song book, My Old Savannah Home, slaves on cover, 1880, 13¼x10¼" .**200.00**
Tape measure, ceramic head in bow tie/bowler hat, Germany, 1910, 2"....**300.00**
Tip tray, Clover Brand Shoes..., boy w/watermelon, oval, 1880s, VG+ **240.00**
Toaster cover. Mammy doll w/stuffed body, 1940s, 18", EX **45.00**
Token, slave auctioneer, brass, dtd 1846, EX.................................**55.00**
Toy figure, Be-Bop Jigger, plastic figure on tin drum, Marx, 10", EX+..**225.00**
Toy figure, Dancing Dan walker, pnt wood, M&R Novelty, 13", EX+ ...**55.00**
Valentine, Jest Horning In on Valentine's Day..., heart shape, EX...**20.00**
Vase, bud; girl w/melon against tree trunk, majolica, 1880s, 8", M ..**235.00**

Black Cats

Made in Japan during the '50s, these novelty cats may be found bearing the labels of several different importers, all with their own particular characteristics. The best known and most collectible of these cats are from the Shafford line. Even when unmarked, they are easily identified by their red bows, green eyes, and white whiskers, eyeliners, and eyebrows. Relco/Royal Sealy cats are tall and slender, and their bow ties are gold with red dots. Wales is a wonderful line with yellow eyes and gold detailing; Enesco cats have blue eyes, and there are other lines as well. When evaluating your black cats, be sure to inspect their paint and judge them accordingly. Fifty percent paint should relate to 50% of our suggested values, which are given for cats in mint (or nearly mint) paint. Enthusiastic bidding on Internet auctions have resulted in much higher prices on the more hard-to-find items as reflected in our listings.

Ashtray, flat face, Shafford, hard-to-find sz, 3¾"..........................**45.00**
Ashtray, 3-D head, open mouth w/cigarette rest, Shafford **22.00**
Bank, upright, Shafford-like features, mk Tommy, 2-part, from $150 to .**175.00**
Cigarette lighter, sm cat stands on book by table lamp..................**85.00**
Condiment set, 6" oil/vinegar cruets, 2¾" shakers in metal fr.......**85.00**
Cookie jar, lg head, Shafford, from $80 to **100.00**
Creamer & sugar bowl, Shafford...**45.00**
Cruets, he w/O eyes, she w/V eyes & hair bow, Shafford, pr, $60 to ..**75.00**
Decanter set, upright cat w/yel eyes, 6 plain wines **35.00**
Demitasse pot, tail hdl, bow finial, Shafford, 7½" **110.00**
Desk caddy, pen forms tail, spring body holds letters, 6½"..............**8.00**
Fork, emb cat face, gr eyes, from wall-hanging utensil set, Shafford ..**125.00**
Ice bucket, cylindrical w/emb yel-eyed cat face, 2 szs, ea..............**75.00**
Mug, Shafford, rare lg sz, 4¼", from $70 to **80.00**

Paperweight, head on stepped chrome base, open mouth, yel eyes, rare ..**75.00**
Pincushion, cushion on bk, tongue measure **25.00**
Pot holder caddy, 'teapot' cat, 3 hooks, Shafford, from $170 to ..**195.00**
Shakers, rnd-bodied 'teapot' cat, Shafford, pr, from $125 to **140.00**
Spice set, 6 sq shakers in wooden fr, yel eyes **175.00**
Teapot, ball-shaped body, gr eyes, Shafford, 4-4½" **30.00**
Teapot, ball-shaped body, head lid, Shafford, med sz **45.00**
Teapot, yel eyes, 1-cup **30.00**
Tray, flat face, wicker hdl, Shafford, rare **185.00**
Wall pocket, flattened 'teapot' cat, Shafford, scarce, $125 to......**150.00**

Black Glass

Black glass is a type of colored glass that when held to strong light usually appears deep purple, though since each glasshouse had its own formula, tones may vary. It was sometimes etched or given a satin finish; and occasionally it was decorated with silver, gold, enamel, coralene, or any of these in combination. The decoration was done either by the glasshouse or by firms that specialized in decorating glassware. Crystal, jade, colored glass, or milk glass was sometimes used with the black as an accent. Black glass has been made by many companies since the seventeenth century. Contemporary glasshouses produced black glass during the Depression, seldom signing their product. It is still being made today.

To learn more about the subject, we recommend *A Collector's Guide to Black Glass, Books I* and *II*, written by our advisor, Marlena Toohey; she is listed in the Directory under Colorado. Look for her newly updated value guide. See also Tiffin, L.E. Smith, and other specific manufacturers.

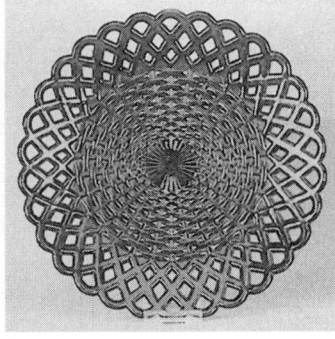

Plate, Wickerwork, Sowerby's Ellison Glass Works, ca 1920s, 9", $45.00. (Photo courtesy Marlena Toohey)

Bowl, console; oval, unknown maker, 12½" **20.00**
Bowl, HP Maytime decor, hdls, Imperial #320, 1930s, 6" W **20.00**
Bowl, shallow, unknown maker, 1920s, 9" **25.00**
Bowl/nutcracker, rnd bowl w/chrome nutcracker, 1920s-30s, 8¾" dia..**185.00**
Box, cigarette; New Martinsville, 1930s, 7" L **65.00**
Box, cigarette; w/match-holder finial, Victorian, 7¼" **75.00**
Box, cylindrical w/hinged lid, gold design, Victorian, 4½"..........**135.00**
Box, glove; scalloped, Victorian, 4x10½" **145.00**
Candlestick, hdld, satin, US Glass, #319, 2¾" **25.00**
Candlestick, sq tapered cup w/yel & gr rose decal, 1920s-30s, 2" **15.00**
Candlestick, Wigwam, LE Smith, 1935, 3¼" **20.00**
Candlesticks, twisted stems, H Northwood Co, #725, 1920s, 10", pr...**150.00**
Canister, floral pattern, Tiara Exclusive, 7¼" **30.00**
Clock, desk; resembles watch in triangular form, Germany, 1980s, 3"..**75.00**
Compote, Thumbprint, ftd, #4429, Fenton label, 1968-74, 5½" **35.00**
Creamer & sugar bowl, Old Quilt, Summit Art Glass, 1993, ea ...**20.00**
Cup & saucer, plain, Hazel Atlas, 1930s, 5½" saucer.....................**10.00**
Decanter, bulbous w/thumbprint pattern, pewter decor/top, 1930s, 9½"..**95.00**
Decanter, high relief ribs, teardrop stopper, elongated hdl, ftd, 12" **85.00**
Doorknob, unknown maker, 1920s-30s, 2½" **20.00**
Flower frog, mk Patent Applied for April 11, 1916, 2½" dia.........**10.00**

Frame, smooth w/rnd curved corners, Mikasa, 1980s, 7½x5½" **25.00**
Honey dish, Beehive pattern, Tiara Exclusives, 6" **45.00**
Ice bucket, Top Hat, Stelvia, 1987, 12x7"..**125.00**
Ladle, punch; hand blown, unmk, USA, 12" L................................**100.00**
Lamp, hurricane; frosted bowl atop blk base, DG&L, Findley Ohio, 1897 ...**250.00**
Pitcher, bulbous hobnail w/twisted neck, Tiara Exclusives, 1½-qt ...**35.00**
Planter, emb lion & lattice decor, 4-ftd, McKee, 1930s, 5x9" **48.00**
Planter, sq w/penguins in relief on sides, gold trim, 4" **32.00**
Plate, Ebon (embellished), Morgantown, 7½" **22.00**
Plate, Mary Gregory decor, Forget-Me-Not Border, Westmoreland, 8"..**75.00**
Platter, ribbed rim & inner circle, 18½" dia...................................**95.00**
Punch bowl, Tom & Jerry, silver writing, McKee, 1950s, 11½" ..**200.00**
Razor blade sharpener, unknown maker, 3" L................................**15.00**
Soap dish, swan figure at 1 end of fluted dish, Titan, 5¼"............**35.00**
Swizzle stick, mk Buffalo Statler Hotel Brooklyn, 7½" **8.00**
Tray, playing card; 1930s **45.00**
Tray, rnd w/satin figural dolphin center, scalloped rim, Viking, 11" ...**60.00**
Tumble-up decanter, unknown maker, 6½" (w/o tumbler) **15.00**
Vase, bud; tapering, pnt floral decor, Maryland Glass Co, 1929-33, 10" ..**35.00**
Vase, emb daffodils, flared rim, low tab hdls, base, 1930s, 4¾" **28.00**
Vase, fluted, unknown maker, 1930s, 6¼" **30.00**
Vase, sq w/raised nudes on panels, satin, US Glass, 1924-34, 9½" ...**95.00**
Vase, 4-ftd tapered sq w/Fern & Holly pattern, Victorian, 3½".....**38.00**

Blown Glass

Blown glass is rather difficult to date; eighteenth and nineteenth century examples vary little as to technique or style. It ranges from the primitive to the sophisticated, but the metallic content of very early glass caused tiny imperfections that are obvious upon examination, and these are often indicative of age.

In America, Stiegel introduced the English technique of using a patterned, part-size mold, a practice which was generally followed by many glasshouses after the Revolution. From 1820 to about 1850, glass was blown into full-size three-part molds. In the listings below, glass is assumed clear unless color is mentioned. Our advisor for this category is Mark Vuono; he is listed in the Directory under Connecticut. See also Bottles and specific manufactures.

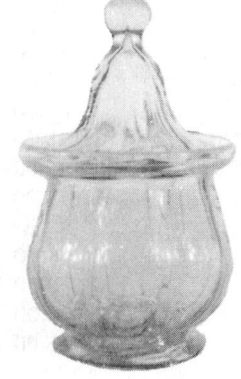

Sugar bowl, Pillar mold, tooled and folded rim, applied foot, knob on rim, pontil scar, American, 1885 – 1870, 7¼", $1,450.00. (Photo courtesy Glass Works Auctions)

Bottle, mini demijohn, aqua, pontil scar, appl mouth, 3" **50.00**
Celery vase, cut w/dmns & sprigs, Bakewell & Pears, 8" **700.00**
Compote, hollow stem, tooled rim, orig lid, 9" **300.00**
Decanter, Pineapple Diamond, cobalt, smooth base, orig stopper, 10" ...**120.00**
Fishbowl on stand, spherical body, 1800s, 16x11".........................**635.00**
Flip glass, etched sunburst/medallion/bird/flowers, w/lid, 1800s, 11" ..**2,000.00**
Fly trap, etched bamboo decor, w/stopper, 1850s, 12" **1,035.00**
Fly trap, Riege a Mouche..., tooled base, appl seal, 6¾", EX............**120.00**
Fly trap, tooled base, appl lip, 3 ft, 7" dia **210.00**

Food cover, appl knob hdl/folded rim, 6x11½" dia 300.00
Master salt, cobalt, swirled ribs, appl ft, att Phila, 2¾x2¾" 250.00
Pan, milk; dk bl-aqua, pontil scar, folded rim, 5x9½" 200.00
Pan, pale bottle gr, pontil scar, folded down rim, 2x3⅝" 65.00
Pitcher, amber, appl hdl, crimped base, open pontil, 1790s, 9" ...1,955.00
Pitcher, lt aqua, appl threading at neck, trefoil hdl, NY, 1844-60, 9" ..2,000.00
Pitcher, med gr, pontil scar, tooled rim w/pour spout, 6⅛" 425.00
Pitcher, med purple amethyst, 12-dmn pattern, potstone, 9½" ...750.00
Pitcher, typical form w/shaped spout, Am, 1825, 8" 500.00
Stemware, air twist stem, conical bowl, English, 1700s, 6", set of 6 ..2,350.00
Sugar bowl, dk amethyst, milk-glass banded rim, 1825-45 ....825.00
Vase, lt gr w/opal loopings, cylindrical, 1850s, 11¾" 115.00

Blown Three-Mold Glass

A popular collectible in the '20s, '30s, and '40s, blown three-mold glass has again gained the attention of many. Produced from approximately 1815 to 1840 in various New York, New England, and Midwestern glasshouses, it was a cheaper alternative to the expensive imported Irish cut glass.

Distinguishing features of blown three-mold glass are the three distinct mold marks and the concave-convex appearance of the glass. For every indentation on the inner surface of the ware, there will be a corresponding protuberance on the outside. Blown three-mold glass is most often clear with the exception of inkwells and a few known decanters. Any colored three-mold glass commands a premium price.

The numbers in the listings that follow refer to the book *American Glass* by George and Helen McKearin. Our advisor for this category is Mark Vuono; he is listed in the Directory under Connecticut.

Bottle, toilet water; GI-3 type 2, cobalt, pontil scar, 6⅛" 210.00
Bottle, toilet water; GI-7 type 4, cobalt, pontil scar, 5⅞" 190.00
Bottle, toilet water; GI-7 type 4, med lav-bl, pontil scar, 5¾" 180.00
Bottle, toilet water; GI-19, lt cobalt, pontil scar, 5⅜" 275.00
Decanter, GI-29, med smoky cobalt, pontil scar, flared lip, 5¼" .300.00
Decanter, GII-18 (similar), smoky clear, pontil scar, 7⅞" 210.00
Decanter, GIII-2 Type I, dk olive gr, ribbed lower body, 6¾" ..2,875.00

Blue and White Stoneware

Salt glaze or molded stoneware was most commonly produced in a blue and white coloration, much of which was also decorated with numerous 'in-mold' designs (some 150 plus patterns). It was made by practically every American pottery from the turn of the century until the mid-1930s. Crocks, pitchers, wash sets, rolling pins, and other household wares are only a few of the items that may be found in this type of 'country' pottery, now one of today's popular collectibles.

Logan, Brush-McCoy, Uhl Co., and Burley Winter were among those who produced it; but very few pieces were ever signed. Naturally, condition must be a prime consideration, especially if one is buying for resale; pieces with good, strong color and fully molded patterns bring premium prices. Normal wear and signs of age are to be expected, since this was utility ware and received heavy use in busy households.

In the listings that follow, crocks, salts, and butter holders are assumed to be without lids unless noted otherwise. Items are in near-mint condition unless noted otherwise. Though common pieces seem to have softened to some degree, scarce items and those in outstanding mint condition are stronger than ever. For further information we recommend *Blue and White Stoneware* by Kathryn McNerny and *Collector's Encyclopedia of Salt Glaze Stoneware* by Terry Taylor, our advisor for this category (see Directory, North Carolina), and Terry and Kay Lowrance. See also specific manufacturers.

Salt crock, Daisy on Snow Flake, dark blue, with lid, from $275.00 to $300.00. (Photo courtesy Terry Taylor)

Bank w/Money Bank stencil, coin slot, break to open, 4x3" 1,500.00
Bean pot, Boston Baked Beans, Swirl, heavy diffused pattern 500.00
Bowl, Apricot, 9½" 95.00
Bowl, Daisy on Lattice, 10¾" 100.00
Bowl, milk; Flying Bird shoulder, 3¾x9½" 525.00
Bowl, milk; Flying Bird shoulder, 3¾x9½", w/matching lid 1,200.00
Bowl, mixing; Flying Bird, 4x7½" 350.00
Bowl, Reverse Pyramids w/Reverse Picket Fence, 2½x4½" 65.00
Bowl, Wedding Ring, 6 szs, $150 ea, or set of 6 for 800.00
Bowl, Wildflower (stenciled), 4½x7" 125.00
Bowl (milk crock), Apricot, w/hdl 225.00
Box, powder; Wildflower & Fishscale, w/lid 275.00
Butter crock, Apricot, appl wood & wire hdl, w/lid, 4x7" 275.00
Butter crock, Basketweave & Morning Glory, w/lid, 4x7½" 500.00
Butter crock, Butterfly, orig lid & bail, 6½" 225.00
Butter crock, Cows, appl wood & wire hdl, w/lid, 4½x7¼" 500.00
Butter crock, Daisy & Trellis, orig lid & bail, 4½" 175.00
Butter crock, Daisy & Waffle, 4x8", NM 175.00
Butter crock, Dragon Fly & Flower, no lid, 4½x7" 125.00
Butter crock, Draped Windows, 4½x8" 235.00
Butter crock, Eagle, orig lid & bail, M 1,080.00
Butter crock, Grapes & Leaves, dbl ring around rim, 3x6½" 175.00
Butter crock, Lovebirds, w/lid 5½x6", M 600.00
Butter crock, Peacock, w/lid, 6x6" 800.00
Butter crock, Wild Flower (stenciled), w/lid, 6½x7¼" 175.00
Butter jar, Wildflower, appl wood & wire hdl, 5x7" 275.00
Canister, Basketweave, Cloves, orig lid, 4½" 200.00
Canister, Basketweave, Coffee, orig lid, 7½" 350.00
Canister, Basketweave, Pepper, orig lid, 4½" 200.00
Canister, Basketweave, Put Your Fist In, orig lid, 7½" 750.00
Canister, Basketweave, Salt, orig lid, 7½" 350.00
Canister, Basketweave, Sugar, orig lid, 7½" 350.00
Canister, Basketweave, Tobacco, orig lid, 7½" 750.00
Canister, Snowflake (stenciled), rpl lid, 6½x5¾" 150.00
Canister set, Basketweave, 9-pc 5,000.00
Chamberpot, Fishscale & Wild Rose, no lid, 5½x9¼" 250.00
Chamberpot, Peacock, 9¾" 1,250.00
Chamberpot, Wildflower, stenciled pattern, 6x11" 135.00
Chamberpot, Wildflower & Fishscale, w/lid 400.00
Coffeepot, Bull's Eye, rim chips, 9¾x3¾" (base) 2,550.00
Coffeepot, Oval, Diffused Blue, bl-tipped knob, str sides, 11x4" ..2,500.00
Coffeepot, Peacock, patterned sloped sides, 7x10" 4,000.00
Coffeepot, Swirl, w/lid & metal base plate 900.00
Cookie jar, Brickers, flat button finial, 8x8" 725.00
Cooler, iced tea; Blue Band, flat lid, complete, 13x11" 295.00
Cooler, water; Apple Blossom, brass spigot, 17x15" 2,500.00
Cooler, water; Blue Band, orig lid 250.00

Cooler, water; Cupid, brass spigot, patterned lid, 15x12" 700.00
Cooler, water; Polar Bear, brass NP spigot, rare, 1-gal, 17x15" ...3,100.00
Cooler, water; Polar Bear, Ice Water, w/lid, hairlines, 6-gal, 15¼" ...1,000.00
Crock, Lovebird, rstr bail & handgrip, 5½x9" 400.00
Cup, Wildflower w/emb Ribbon & Bow, 4½x2½" 85.00
Cuspidor, Basketweave & Morning Glory, 5x7½" 150.00
Cuspidor, Butterfly & Shield, 6x7½" 175.00
Cuspidor, Flower Panels & Arches, 7x7½" 275.00
Custard cup, Fishscale, 5x2½" 150.00
Egg storage crock, Barrel Staves, bail hdl, 5½x6" 200.00
Grease jar, Flying Bird, orig lid, 4x4½" 1,200.00
Ice crock, Barrel Staves, rope/tongs/ice block emb, 4½x6" 225.00
Jardiniere, Flowers, hairline, 7⅞" (complete w/stand & crock) 800.00
Meat tenderizer, Wildflower 650.00
Mug, Basketweave & Flower, 5x3" 150.00
Mug, beer; advertising, Diffused Blue, sqd hdl 150.00
Mug, Flying Bird, 5x3" 200.00
Mug, plain 65.00
Mug, Windy City (Fannie Flagg), Robinson Clay Products 200.00
Pie plate, Blue Walled Brick-Edge star emb base, 10½" 225.00
Pitcher, Acorns, stenciled, 8x6½" 175.00
Pitcher, American Beauty Rose, 10" 500.00
Pitcher, Apricot, 8" 250.00
Pitcher, Barrel, +6 mugs 395.00
Pitcher, Basketweave & Morning Glory, 9" 325.00
Pitcher, Blue Band, plain 200.00
Pitcher, Blue Band Scroll, emb design 300.00
Pitcher, Bluebird, 9x7" 450.00
Pitcher, Butterfly, 9x7" 500.00
Pitcher, Castle & Fishscale, 8" 195.00
Pitcher, Cattails, stenciled design, bulbous, 7" 225.00
Pitcher, Cattails, 10" 300.00
Pitcher, Cattails, 9½" 275.00
Pitcher, Cherry Band, w/adv date 1914, 9½" 1,425.00
Pitcher, Cherry Cluster, 7½" 650.00
Pitcher, Cherry Cluster & Basketweave, 10" 375.00
Pitcher, Columns & Arches, 8¾x5" 425.00
Pitcher, Daisy Cluster, rare, 7x7" 800.00
Pitcher, Doe & Fawn, bl, 8½" 185.00
Pitcher, Dutch Boy & Girl by Windmill, 9" 200.00
Pitcher, Dutch Landscape, stenciled, Diffused Blue, tall 225.00
Pitcher, Eagle w/Shield & Arrows, rare, 8" 800.00
Pitcher, Fishscale & Wild Rose (part of wash set), 10" 160.00
Pitcher, Flying Bird, 9" 625.00
Pitcher, Garden Rose, 9" 500.00
Pitcher, Garden Rose Sponge, 9" 800.00
Pitcher, Girl & Dog, regular bl, 9" 800.00
Pitcher, Girl & Dog, sponge, 7" 1,000.00
Pitcher, Grape & Shield, 8½x5" 150.00
Pitcher, Grape w/Rickrack, any sz 250.00
Pitcher, Grazing Cows, bl, 7½" 400.00
Pitcher, Grazing Cows, bl, 8" 250.00
Pitcher, Grazing Cows, 6½" 500.00
Pitcher, hot water; Wildflower & Fishscale, sm 150.00
Pitcher, Indian Boy & Girl (Capt John Smith & Pocahontas), 6" ...300.00
Pitcher, Indian Good Luck (Swastika), 8½" 200.00
Pitcher, Iris, 9" 375.00
Pitcher, Leaping Deer, sponge, 8" 1,500.00
Pitcher, Leaping Deer, 8½" 375.00
Pitcher, Leaping Deer in 1 oval, Swan in other (mfg error), 8" ...1,500.00
Pitcher, Lincoln, allover deep bl, 4¾x4¾" 250.00
Pitcher, Lincoln, allover deep bl, 6x4" 300.00
Pitcher, Lincoln, allover deep bl, 7x5" 400.00
Pitcher, Lincoln, allover deep bl, 8x6" 730.00

Pitcher, Lovebird, arc bands, deep color, 8½", EX 500.00
Pitcher, Lovebird, pale color, 8½" 300.00
Pitcher, Monk, dk cobalt 350.00
Pitcher, Peacock 2,000.00
Pitcher, Pine Cone, sponge, rare, 9½" 2,000.00
Pitcher, Pine Cone, 9½" 1,500.00
Pitcher, Poinsettia, 6½" 275.00
Pitcher, Rose on Trellis, 8x5½" 225.00
Pitcher, Scroll & Leaf, advertising, 8" 450.00
Pitcher, Shield, prof rpr, 8" 200.00
Pitcher, Stag & Pine Trees, 9" 450.00
Pitcher, Swan, in oval, deep color, 8½", EX 400.00
Pitcher, Tulip, 8x4" 325.00
Pitcher, Wild Rose, solid bl, 9x6" 450.00
Pitcher, Wild Rose, sponged bands, 9" 500.00
Pitcher, Windmill & Bush, 9" 225.00
Pitcher, Windmills, 7¼", EX 195.00
Pitcher, Windy City (Fannie Flagg), Robinson Clay, 8½" 450.00
Roaster, Diffused Blue, appl hdls, flat finial, 9x19" 225.00
Roaster, Wildflower, domed lid, 8½x12" 225.00
Rolling pin, Blue Band, advertising, Andka, Nebr, 14x4" 900.00
Rolling pin, Blue Band, no advertising, 14x4" 375.00
Rolling pin, Swirl, baker's sz, 16" 1,600.00
Rolling pin, Swirl, orig wooden hdls, 13" 1,600.00
Rolling pin, Wild Flower, advertising, Analomink PA, dtd 1905 .1,100.00
Rolling pin, Wildflower, plain 375.00
Rolling pin, Wildflower, w/center decor, 15x4½" 650.00
Salt crock, Apricot, no lid 130.00
Salt crock, Butterfly, orig lid 350.00
Salt crock, Eagle, w/lid 800.00
Salt crock, Grapevine on Fence, pale bl, orig lid, 6½x6¾" 300.00
Salt crock, Peacock, w/lid 1,000.00
Soap dish, Beaded Rose 150.00
Soap dish, cat's head 200.00
Soap dish, Indian in War Bonnet 250.00
Soap dish, Wildflower & Fishscale 150.00
Spice set, Basketweave, 6-pc, w/lids 2,000.00
Teapot, Swirl, dbl wire bail hdl, ball shape, 9x6½" 1,200.00
Toothbrush holder, Bow Tie, stenciled flower 50.00
Toothbrush holder, Wildflower & Fishscale 325.00
Vinegar cruet, rare, 4½x3" 375.00
Wash bowl & pitcher, Rose on Trellis 300.00
Wash bowl & pitcher, Wildflower & Fishscale 500.00
Wash set, Wildflower & Fishscale, complete, 7-pc 2,500.00
Washboard, sponge 400.00
Water bottle, Diffused Blue Swirl, stopper w/cork, 10x5½" 800.00
Whipped cream jar, 4¾x6¾" 550.00

Blue Ridge

Blue Ridge dinnerware was produced by Southern Potteries of Erwin, Tennessee, from the late 1930s until 1956 in twelve basic styles and two thousand different patterns, all of which were hand decorated under the glaze. Vivid colors lit up floral arrangements of seemingly endless variation, fruit of every sort from simple clusters to lush assortments, barnyard fowl, peasant figures, and unpretentious textured patterns. Although it is these dinnerware lines for which they are best known, collectors prize the artist-signed plates from the '40s and the limited line of character jugs made during the '50s most highly. Examples of the French Peasant pattern are valued at double the prices listed below; very simple patterns will bring 25% to 50% less.

Our advisors, Betty and Bill Newbound, have compiled three lovely books, *Blue Ridge Dinnerware, Revised Third Edition*, and *The Collector's Ency-*

clopedia of Blue Ridge, Volumes I and *II,* all with beautiful color illustrations and current market values. They are listed in the Directory under North Carolina. For information concerning the National Blue Ridge Newsletter, see the Clubs, Newsletters, and Catalogs section of the Directory.

Ashtray, advertising, Railroad, from $65 to 75.00
Ashtray, ind, from $20 to 24.00
Ashtrays, Mallard, box shape, 3½x2½", from $40 to.....................45.00
Baking dish, divided, 8x13", from $25 to....................................30.00
Baking dish, plain, 8x13", from $22 to 25.00
Basket, aluminum edge, 10", from $30 to....................................35.00
Bonbon, Charm House, china, from $100 to 125.00
Bonbon, flat shell, china, from $80 to...85.00
Bowl, cereal soup (coupe); 6", from $14 to.................................16.00
Bowl, fruit; 5¼", from $6 to 8.00
Bowl, hot cereal; from $14 to 17.00
Bowl, mixing; med, from $20 to 25.00
Bowl, vegetable; w/lid, from $60 to...65.00
Box, Mallard, from $650 to...700.00
Box, Sherman Lily, from $700 to 750.00
Butter dish, from $40 to 45.00
Cake lifter, from $30 to 35.00
Casserole, w/lid, from $50 to..55.00
Child's play tea set, complete, from $400 to 425.00
Chocolate tray, from $475 to 500.00
Creamer, Charm House, china, from $70 to.................................85.00
Creamer, Colonial, lg, open, from $18 to 22.00
Creamer, regular shape, from $15 to 18.00
Cup & saucer, demitasse; earthenware, from $40 to 45.00
Cup & saucer, demitasse; premium, from $60 to...........................65.00
Cup & saucer, Turkey & Acorns, from $60 to...............................65.00
Egg cup, dbl, from $25 to 30.00
Jug, character; Daniel Boone, Indian or Paul Revere, ea, from $725 to 750.00
Jug, character; Pioneer Woman, from $575 to 600.00
Lamp, china, from $250 to...300.00
Lazy susan center bowl, w/lid, from $150 to 180.00
Leftover w/lid, sm, med or lg, ea, from $25 to 30.00
Pitcher, Abby, china, from $175 to 180.00
Pitcher, Antique, china, 5", from $90 to 95.00
Pitcher, Chick, china, from $125 to 135.00
Pitcher, Sculptured Fruit, petite, from $80 to..............................85.00
Pitcher, Watuga, from $375 to...400.00

**Pitcher, yellow and pink tulips,
8½", $190.00.**

Plate, advertising, lg, from $400 to 450.00
Plate, artist sgn, 10¼", from $575 to 626.00
Plate, Christmas Tree, from $75 to 80.00
Plate, dinner; premium, 10½", from $55 to 60.00
Plate, party; w/cup & well, premium, from $80 to 85.00
Plate, 11½-12", from $45 to 50.00
Platter, Turkey pattern, lg, from $260 to 275.00

Platter, 12½-13", ea, from $25 to...27.00
Ramekin, w/lid, 5", from $25 to 30.00
Relish, deep shell, china, from $80 to..85.00
Relish, Mod Leaf, china, from $75 to 80.00
Salad fork, china, from $45 to...50.00
Server, wood or metal hdl, from $25 to 30.00
Shakers, Apple, 1¾", pr, from $25 to 30.00
Shakers, Bud Top, pr, from $50 to...55.00
Shakers, Chickens, pr, from $140 to 150.00
Shakers, Mallard, pr, from $300 to 350.00
Shakers, range; pr, from $45 to 50.00
Shakers, Skyline, pr, from $20 to 25.00
Shakers, Twig, pr, from $20 to 22.00
Sugar bowl, Charm House, china, from $75 to 85.00
Sugar bowl, Colonial, sm, from $20 to 22.00
Sugar bowl, regular shape, w/lid, from $22 to..............................25.00
Tea tile, rnd or sq, 6", ea, from $50 to 60.00
Teapot, ball shape, premium, from $200 to................................225.00
Teapot, Good Housekeeping, from $175 to.................................180.00
Tidbit, 3-tier, from $40 to...45.00
Toast, w/lid, premium, from $210 to..225.00
Tray, demi; Skyline, 9½x7½", from $90 to...................................95.00
Vase, boot form, 8", from $95 to 100.00
Vase, tapered, china, from $100 to 125.00

Blue Willow

Blue Willow, inspired no doubt by the numerous patterns of the blue and white Nanking imports, has been popular since the late eighteenth century and has been made in as many variations as there were manufacturers. English transfer wares by such notable firms as Allerton and Ridgway are the most sought after and the most expensive. Japanese potters have been producing Willow-patterned dinnerware since the late 1800s, and American manufacturers have followed suit. Although blue is the color most commonly used, mauve and black lines have also been made. For further study we recommend the book *Blue Willow,* with full-color photos and current prices, by Mary Frank Gaston, our advisor for this category. Another source of information is *Collecting Blue Willow* by M. A. Harman (Collector Books). In the following listings, if no manufacturer is noted, the ware is unmarked. See also Buffalo.

Bowl, chestnut; rtcl lattice sides, hdls, English, no mk, 10" 1,000.00
Bowl, divided vegetable; Allerton, oval, 7¼" L 130.00
Bowl, flat soup; Eagle, 8" 12.50
Bowl, flat soup; Royal China, 8½" 10.00
Bowl, Maestricht, 2¾x9⅞"..120.00
Bowl, ped ft, John Tams Ltd, English, 5x9¼"...............................160.00
Bowl, vegetable; oval, Japan...35.00
Bowl, vegetable; sqd/shaped, English, mk Ye Olde Willow, 9¾" .120.00
Bowl, vegetable; variant center pattern, pictorial border, 10" 25.00
Bowl, vegetable; w/lid & hdls, Myott Son & Co, 9½" 175.00
Bowl, vegetable; Woods Ware, 10" 40.00
Chamberstick, scalloped edge, w/gold, Gibson & Son, 5" dia 17.50
Cheese dish, sq plate w/canted corners, sq lid, Wiltshaw & Robinson ..250.00
Condiment shaker, pierced silver lid, Taylor Tunnicliffe & Co, 2" ...55.00
Creamer, Japan...10.00
Creamer, Japan, child sz 25.00
Creamer, red, Royal China...15.00
Creamer & sugar bowl, w/lid, Bakewell Bros, 3", 5½" 150.00
Cup, chili; Japan, 3½x4" 50.00
Cup, chili; red, 5" 45.00
Cup, chili; w/liner plate, Japan 75.00
Cup, demitasse; red, restaurant ware..10.00

Cup, Petris Ragout-Maestricht 20.00
Cup & saucer, Meakin for Nieman-Marcus, 1970s 30.00
Egg cup, dbl, 3½" 30.00
Egg cup, dbl, 4¼" 30.00
Gravy boat, Wood & Sons, 7" L 65.00
Horseradish dish, Doulton, 5½" 65.00
Jug, batter; frosted glass, Hazel Atlas, 10" 100.00
Leaf dish, no mk, English, 6" L 175.00
Mug, bbl shape, unmk 15.00
Pitcher, Chicago Jug, Doulton, 1907, 3-pt 500.00
Pitcher, Mandarin pattern, dagger border, Edge Malkin & Co, 5" ..125.00
Pitcher, milk; Homer Laughlin, 5" 45.00
Pitcher, w/lid, Japan, 11" 125.00
Plate, Booth's Willow, Meakin for Nieman-Marcus, 1970s, 7" 20.00
Plate, bread & butter; Royal China 3.00
Plate, dessert/bread & butter; Japan 5.00
Plate, dinner; Booth's Willow, Meakin for Nieman-Marcus, 1970s .30.00
Plate, dinner; Imperial, 9¾" 27.00
Plate, dinner; Japan, 9" 10.00
Plate, dinner; Linder & Carter, 9½" 24.00
Plate, dinner; Moriyama, 9¼" 12.00
Plate, grill; Booths center pattern, Bow Knot border, 10¾" 30.00
Plate, grill; heavy, Japan 18.00
Plate, salad; red, Jackson China Restaurant Ware 8.00
Plate, salad; red, unmk 8.00
Plate, salad; red, Wallace China 8.00
Plate, salad; Steventon 6.00
Plate, traditional center & border, Charles Meigh & Son, 9¼" 85.00
Platter, Homer Laughlin, 13" 25.00
Platter, tab hdls, unmk Royal China, 11¾" 20.00
Punch bowl, tall ped base, hdls, Wedgwood, 6x9" 1,000.00
Relish tray, Booths center pattern, Bow Knot border, Wood & Sons, 9" ..30.00
Shakers, wood bottoms, Japan, 3¾", pr 12.00
Sugar bowl, w/lid, Japan 15.00
Sugar bowl, w/lid, Japan, child sz 30.00
Tankard, pewter lid, Burleigh, scroll/flower border, English, 7" ...350.00
Tea bowl, Pountney & Co, 3½" dia 85.00
Teapot, Two Temples II, butterfly border, Malkin mk: MIE, 3½" ..125.00
Tumbler, glass, Hazel Atlas, 5" 20.00
Tumbler, juice; glass, Jeannette, 3½" 12.00
Tumbler, juice; Japan 25.00
Tumbler, water; glass, Jeannette, 5½" 12.00
Tureen, ftd/bar hdls, w/ladle, English, no mk, 6x9" 550.00
Wash set, Wedgwood, bowl & pitcher 1,700.00

Bluebird China

Made from 1910 to 1934, Bluebird China is lovely ware most often decorated with bluebirds flying among pink flowering branches. The origins of this decal are unknown and will probably always remain a mystery. Like many decals of this period, they were never exclusive and appeared on the dinnerware of a dozen manufactures. Another style depicts larger, more slender bluebirds in flight. The latter variety was made by Knowles, Taylor, Knowles; W.S. George (Derwood); French Co.; Sterling Colonial; and Pope Gosser. All of it was inexpensive dinnerware and reached the height of its popularity during the 1920s. Many potteries produced it, and shapes differ from one manufacturer to another. Besides the companies we've already mentioned, you'll find the trademarks of Cleveland; Carrolton; Homer Laughlin (today the most expensive, most collected, and most available of all the lines); Limoges China of Sebring, Ohio; Salem; Taylor, Smith, Taylor; and there are others.

Our advisor for this category is Kenna Rosen; she is listed in the Directory under Texas.

Bowl, berry; Cleveland, ind..12.50
Bowl, deep, Derwood, WS George, 4¾" 25.00
Bowl, deep, Homer Laughlin, 5½" 35.00
Bowl, gravy; Hopewell China, w/saucer......................................50.00
Bowl, sauce; SP Co, 4½" 12.50
Bowl, soup; PMC Co, 8" 30.00
Bowl, vegetable; Cleveland, 9¾" 45.00
Butter dish, Buffalo, 5" dia 100.00
Butter dish, Carrollton, 6¼" sq 85.00
Butter dish, Steubenville, 4½" holder w/in 7" dish....................175.00
Butter pat, unmk 15.00
Calendar plate, 1921 advertising pc, ELP Co, 8" 95.00
Canister set, rnd, unmk, 6½x5", 6 for 300.00
Casserole, Buffalo, w/lid 175.00
Casserole, CP Co, child's, 8x3" 75.00
Casserole, Empress, Homer Laughlin, rnd, w/lid, 8½" 150.00
Casserole, Ostro China, 10½" dia..95.00
Casserole, Pope Gosser, w/lid, 10½x10½" 100.00
Casserole, Royal China International, 7x11½" 125.00
Casserole, Taylor Smith & Taylor, w/lid, 11x7½" 130.00
Casserole, The Potters Cooperative, E Liverpool, rnd, 8½" 125.00
Chocolate cup, ftd, no mk, 3½" 35.00
Coffeepot, Sterling Colonial...150.00
Covered platter/food warmer, Buffalo, 19x13" 125.00
Cream & sugar bowl, SP Co, w/lid 85.00
Cream & sugar bowl, TA McNichol, w/lid...................................75.00
Creamer, Derwood, WS George...30.00

Creamer, unmarked, 4", $25.00.

Creamer & sugar bowl, Homer Laughlin, w/lid............................100.00
Creamer & sugar bowl, Knowles Taylor Knowles..........................75.00
Creamer & sugar bowl, TA McNichol, w/lid.................................75.00
Cup, coffee; unmk, 3½" 25.00
Cup, tea; unmk 15.00
Cup & saucer, Buffalo...50.00
Cup & saucer, from $25 to..45.00
Cup & saucer, Owen China, St Louis..25.00
Custard cup, KT&K, 3½"..35.00
Dish, oval, Hudson, Homer Laughlin, 1x5¼x4" 20.00
Egg cup, Buffalo, very rare, 2½" 75.00
Gravy w/underplate, Homer Laughlin, 4x9¾" 75.00
Ladle, sauce; gold scrolling 40.00
Pitcher, water; Buffalo, 7" 175.00
Pitcher, water; Harker Pottery Co, ca 1890, 8x9" 200.00
Pitcher, water; Salem China, 10" 125.00
Plate, baby; ELP Co China, 7½x7½" 150.00
Plate, bread; hdls, gold trim, unmk, 10" 150.00
Plate, dessert; Limoges, 6"..8.00
Plate, dinner; Cleveland, 9" 25.00
Plate, dinner; Knowles Taylor Knowles, 9¾" 22.50
Plate, dinner; Wilmer Ware 20.00

Plate, Homer Laughlin, 8½"	35.00
Plate, National China, 8"	22.50
Plate, rtcl, sq, unmk, 9"	35.00
Plate, scalloped, Homer Laughlin, 7¼"	35.00
Plate, Steubenville, 9"	22.50
Platter, Carollton, sqd oval, 17¾x12¾"	95.00
Platter, Edwin M Knowles, 14½x11"	75.00
Platter, Hopewell China, 13x10"	75.00
Platter, Hopewell China, 17½x13"	100.00
Platter, Pope Gosser, 17x13"	125.00
Platter, Thompson Glenwood, 13x10"	75.00
Platter, unmk, 9x7"	45.00
Platter, West End Pottery Co, 15½x11"	100.00
Platter, 10 bluebirds, gold trim at rim, DE McNichol, 15¼x11¼"	75.00
Saucer, Homer Laughlin	5.00
Sugar bowl, Illinois China Co, w/lid, 7x6"	50.00
Syrup, Homer Laughlin, 6½"	150.00
Syrup, unmk, 4"	35.00
Tea set, CPCo, child sz, 21-pc	400.00
Teapot, Carollton	250.00
Teapot, ELP Co, 8½x8½"	250.00
Teapot, Homer Laughlin	400.00
Teapot, KT&K mk, 3½x7¼"	250.00

Boch Freres

Founded in the early 1840s in La Louviere, Boch Freres Keramis became the foremost producer of art pottery in Belgium. Though primarily they served a localized market, in 1844 they earned worldwide recognition for some of their sculptural works on display at the International Exposition in Paris.

In 1907 Charles Catteau of France was appointed head of the art department. Before that time, the firm had concentrated on developing glazes and perfecting elegant forms. The style they pursued was traditional, favoring the re-creation of established eighteenth-century ceramics. Catteau brought with him to Boch Freres the New Wave (or Art Nouveau) influence in form and decoration. His designs won him international acclaim at the Exhibition d'Art Decoratif in Paris in 1925, and it is for his work that Boch Freres is so highly regarded today. He occasionally signed his work as well as that of others who under his direct supervision carried out his preconceived designs. He was associated with the company until 1950 and lived the remainder of his life in Nice, France, where he died in 1966. The Boch Freres Keramis factory continues to operate today, producing bathroom fixtures and other utilitarian wares. A variety of marks have been used, most incorporating some combination of 'Boch Freres,' 'Keramis,' 'BFK,' or 'Ch Catteau.' A shield topped by a crown and flanked by a 'B' and an 'F' was used as well.

Box, geometrics w/yel & pk flowers on wht, 4x5x2"	210.00
Box, stylized flowers, brass hinge & border, 1½x5½x4"	300.00
Charger, antelope grazing, C Catteau, D493, 14½"	1,150.00
Vase, antelope grazing, Catteau, #899, ca 1925, 10¼"	1,600.00
Vase, antelope grazing, Catteau, ovoid, ca 1925, 13¼"	2,400.00
Vase, antelope grazing, flattened heart shape, #1291, 9"	1,265.00
Vase, birds among vines, ovoid, D4507, 11½"	925.00
Vase, central band of irregular ovals & 6 vertical lines, Catteau, 10"	750.00
Vase, circles/stylized moons/lines, shouldered, #485, 10¾"	460.00
Vase, deer (2) in various poses, bl on wht, Catteau, 9¼"	1,100.00
Vase, flower baskets & swags in 3 sections, slim neck, 8½"	400.00
Vase, flower clusters in 3 sections, mc on ivory crackle, #267, 10"	800.00
Vase, flower on flattened heart shape, #1293, 9¼"	800.00
Vase, flowers & floral borders, bulbous, #909, 12"	800.00
Vase, flowers & stripes, emb brass band at rim, #897, 10½"	435.00

Vase, flowers/berries/branches & mc stripes, #2813, 9½"	925.00
Vase, repeating flowers separated by mc bands, spherical, 7"	925.00
Vase, repeating scrolls & scallops, invt rim, bulbous, 9"	550.00
Vase, repeating triangles/trapezoids/circles, #960, 12½"	750.00
Vase, sunburst flowers on ivory crackle, #899, 10½"	575.00
Vase, trailing floral bands (5), #704, att, 9⅛"	400.00
Vase, tulips, bl borders, #899, 10½"	700.00
Vase, yel roses on arbor bkground w/gold stars, Catteau, 18½"	1,000.00

Boehm

Boehm sculptures were the creation of Edward Marshall Boehm, a ceramic artist who coupled his love of the art with his love of nature to produce figurines of birds, animals, and flowers in lovely background settings accurate to the smallest detail. Sculptures of historical figures and those representing the fine arts were also made and along with many of the bird figurines, have established secondary-market values many times their original prices. His first pieces were made in the very early 1950s in Trenton, New Jersey, under the name of Osso Ceramics. Mr. Boehm died in 1969, and the firm has since been managed by his wife. Today known as Edward Marshall Boehm, Inc., the private family-held corporation produces not only porcelain sculptures but collector plates as well. Both limited and non-limited editions of their works have been issued. Examples are marked with various backstamps, all of which have incorporated the Boehm name since 1951. 'Osso Ceramics' in upper case lettering was used in 1950 and 1951. Our advisor for this category is Leon Reimert; he is listed in the Directory under Pennsylvania.

Red-Shouldered Hawk, #40251, 1984, limited edition, 26¼", $975.00.

Alec's Red Rose, #56, 1980, 6¾x9x6"	460.00
American Avocet, 15¾x11x7½"	750.00
Arabian Stallion, #49, 1983, 15½x15x4½"	700.00
Blue Jay, 17¼x14¼x9"	750.00
Blue Jay Fledgling, 5x5½x5"	150.00
Bluebird Fledgling, #400-75, 4¾x4x4½"	235.00
Bluebird Fledgling, #442A, 4½x3½"	145.00
Broad-Billed Hummingbird on Morning Glory, #40519, 7"	355.00
Cardinal pr, male & female on rocks w/wht flowers, #149, 12x14"	700.00
Common Tern, #40297, 6½x4"	280.00
Crested Flycatcher Fledgling, mouth open, on branch, #458, 5x3"	160.00
Dalmatian, Anheuser-Busch's mascot Mike, #126, ltd ed, 3x1"	260.00
Emmet Barnes Camellia, 7½x11½x8"	230.00
Flamingo, Wading Bird Series, #40294, 8½"	160.00
Gardenia, 2¾x5½x4"	200.00
Gold Rose, #67, 3½x11¾x4¾"	160.00
Honeysuckle w/Butterflies, 186, 1979, 11½x7x5½"	200.00
Hoopoe, Judaic Collection honoring State of Israel, #65, 12x4x8"	575.00
Hoopoe Fledgling, 6½x4x3½"	175.00

Kestril, #492, limited edition, 14½" **1,010.00**
Kingfisher Fledgling, 6x3¾" dia..**145.00**
Madonna, wht, mk Queen of Peace, 13" **340.00**
Magnolia Grandiflora, #88, 1980, 6x15x7" **635.00**
Marigolds, #75, 1982, 5x8x6" **300.00**
Morning Doves, male & female on branch, #443, 15½" **565.00**
Mute Swan, #67, 20x15¾x10½" **1,785.00**
Mute Swan, #67, 21¼x17x17" **2,185.00**
Parrot Tulip, #24, 1980, 10½x9x4½" **345.00**
Peach Rose w/Daisies, #48, 1980, 15½x7x7" **260.00**
Pink Lotus, #42, 1978, 5x9¾x8½" **615.00**
Rabbit at Rest, 3½x4¼" **215.00**
Red Poppies, #242, 9x9x5" **665.00**
Redstart w/Hazel, 7½x4x3½" **300.00**
Roadrunner, #40239, 7½x14" **290.00**
Sow & Piglet, 3x5½x3½" **285.00**
Spanish Iris, #297, 1978, 8¼x8½x3" **230.00**
Spirit of Bethlehem, Mary, Joseph & Christ Child, MIB **360.00**
Spirit of Bethlehem, 3 angels, Christian Era Collection, MIB **420.00**
Swan, 5x6½x3¼" **115.00**
Tropical Fish w/Staghorn Coral, #35, 1983, 14½x12x8½" **800.00**
Western Bluebird Fledgling, #494, 4¾x4" dia.............................**175.00**
White Rose, #200-55-W, 5¾" **180.00**
White-Throated Sparrow on Branch, #430, 9½" **255.00**
Yellow Rose, 12¾x9x8½" **345.00**

Bohemian Glass

The term 'Bohemian glass' has come to refer to a type of glass developed in Bohemia in the late sixteenth century at the Imperial Court of Rudolf II, the Hapsburg Emperor. The popular artistic pursuit of the day was stone carving, and it naturally followed to transfer familiar procedures to the glassmaking industry. During the next century, a formula was discovered that produced a glass with a fine crystal appearance which lent itself well to deep, intricate engraving, and the art was further advanced.

Although many other kinds of art glass were made there, collectors today use the term 'Bohemian glass' to often indicate clear glass overlaid or stained with color through which a design is cut or etched. (Unless otherwise described, the items in the listing that follows are of this type.) Red or yellow on clear glass is common, but other colors may also be found. Another type of Bohemian glass involves cutting through and exposing two layers of color in patterns that are often very intricate. Items such as these are sometimes further decorated with enamel and/or gilt work.

Beaker, bl, good luck/health/fortune symbols, ca 1880, 5"...........**150.00**
Beaker, red, 3 spa scenes, ca 1860, 6" **275.00**
Decanter, cobalt, sq panels around girth & on stem, gilt, 19th C, 12" ..**330.00**
Decanter, ruby, deer in woods w/fence, late 19th C, 15", EX **275.00**
Goblet, blk enamel, hunt scene, 1920, 7" **150.00**
Pokal, amber, horses/dogs/deer, late 19th C, 15", EX..................**750.00**
Stein, red, Carlsbad scene, late 19th C, ½-litre...........................**250.00**

Bookends

Though a few were produced before 1880, bookends became a necessary library accessory and a popular commodity after the printing industry was revolutionized by Mergenthaler's invention, the linotype. Books became abundantly available at such affordable prices that almost every home suddenly had need for bookends. They were carved from wood; cast in iron, bronze, or brass; or cut from stone. Chalkware and glass were used as well. Today's collectors may find such designs as ships,

animals, flowers, and children. Patriotic themes, art reproductions, and those with Art Nouveau and Art Deco styling provide a basis for a diverse and interesting collection.

Currently, figural cast-iron pieces are in demand, especially examples with good original polychrome paint. This has driven the value of painted cast-iron bookends up considerably.

For further information we recommend *Collector's Guide to Bookends, Identification and Values*, by Louis Kuritzky, our advisor for this category; he is listed in the Directory under Florida. See also Arts and Crafts; Bradley and Hubbard.

American Legion, emblem above soldiers, bronze, ca 1939, 8" ...**115.00**
Angelus Call to Prayer, CI, Hubley, ca 1925, 5½" **65.00**
Asleep at Mid-Story, man in chair, gray metal, K&O, ca 1929, 4¼"....**165.00**
Castle Lichtenstein, CI, Bradley & Hubbard, ca 1925, 5"...........**150.00**
Child Reading, holds open book, gray metal, Frankart, 1928, 6½" ..**300.00**

Classical Men, bronze on marble base, ca 1925, 6", $150.00. (Photo courtesy Louis Kuritzky)

Crane, in flight, gray metal, Dodge, ca 1946, 6¾" **75.00**
Dancing Girl, gray metal, polychrome, Ronson, ca 1924, 5"..........**375.00**
Dante & Beatrice Books, gray metal, Jennings Bros, ca 1935, 6"...**195.00**
Doe, looking skyward, gray metal, Frankart, ca 1934, 5¼" **125.00**
Dogwood, 2 flowers, gray metal, PM Craftsman, ca 1965, 5¼" **40.00**
Egyptian Camel, CI, Connecticut Foundry, 1928, 6" **95.00**
Foo Dogs, CI, ca 1920, 5"..**175.00**
German Shepherd, standing, CI, ca 1928, 4¾".................................**45.00**
Girl, Dancing; gray metal, Ronson, ca 1924, 5" **295.00**
Gleaners, 3 figures in field, gray metal, K&O, ca 1925, 4¼".......**125.00**
Horse in Horseshoe, gray metal, Ronson, ca 1930, 4⅝" **95.00**
Horse, Jumping; glass, ca 1940, 8" **100.00**
Hound & Bird, dog w/bird in mouth, gray metal, Frankart, ca 1934, 5".**210.00**
Indian Archer, stands behind onlooker, bronze, WB, ca 1925, 5½"........**125.00**
Indian Scout, figure on horse, gray metal, Jennings Bros, ca 1927, 5"....**170.00**
Indiana Pigeon, Indiana Glass, ca 1940, 5½" **75.00**
Kingfisher, bronze in marble enclosure, ca 1928, 5¾" **195.00**
Latticework & Dog, CI, C Company, 1930, 6" **200.00**
Librarian, gray metal on marble base, JB Hirsch, ca 1932, 6¼" ..**195.00**
Lincoln Profile, CI, ca 1925, 5¼" **65.00**
Lincoln's Cabin, CI, Judd, ca 1925, 3¾" **50.00**
Lion of Lucerne, CI, Judd, ca 1920, 5" **175.00**
Lyre, glass, Fostoria Glass, 1942-1944, 7" **150.00**
Mermaid, gold on gray metal, ca 1930, 6" **250.00**
Nude w/Dogs, CI, #269, ca 1929, 7"...**195.00**
Parrot on book, mc on gray metal, K&O, ca 1928, 6" **125.00**
Pharoah, sits on throne, bronze clad, Armor Bronze, sgn L Cudebrod, 7" .**175.00**
Pilot Wheel, gray metal, Ronson, ca 1930, 4¾" **110.00**
Sailboat, CI, Littco, ca 1929, 7½" **100.00**
Serenade, figure holds guitar & wears sombrero, CI, ca 1929, 4¼"..**100.00**
Servant of Knowledge, gray metal on stone base, JB Hirsch, ca 1930, 5"...**250.00**
Shriner Camel, camel at rest w/Shriner emblem, brass, ca 1930, 4½" **110.00**
Sir Galahad, gray metal, ca 1923, 6½" **125.00**

Stag, lying, figure patented, gray metal, #508, 1925 ....275.00
Tiger, glass, New Martinsville, ca 1940, 6½"................................325.00
Toadstool & Frog, gray metal, McClelland Barclay, ca 1922, 4¼".......195.00
Treasure Ship, bronze clad, Armor Bronze, Vanderoge, ca 1927, 7½".110.00
Tripod Eagle, gray metal, Frankart, ca 1934, 6¾" 135.00
Trouble Underfoot, hippo under elephant, CI, Littco, ca 1926, 4¼"..110.00
Trout, standing on tail fin, gray metal, PM Craftsman, ca 1965, 4".....50.00
Two Lions, 1 facing & 1 in profile, CI, ca 1926, 5".......................50.00
Ultra-modern Elephants, brass & plastic, Chase, ca 1933, 4¾" ..450.00
Washington Bust, CI, ca 1920 ....75.00
Wisdom Well, nude female kneels holding bowl, ca 1929, CI, 5½"..95.00

Bootjacks and Bootscrapers

Bootjacks were made from metal or wood. Some were fancy figural shapes, others strictly business. Their purpose was to facilitate the otherwise awkward process of removing one's boots. Bootscrapers were handy gadgets that provided an effective way to clean the soles of mud and such. Our advisor for this category is Louis Picek; he is listed in the Directory under Iowa.

Bootjacks

Brass, sunflower, Musselman's Plug advertising 150.00
CI, Am Bull Dog, pistol shape, blk pnt, 8"..................................90.00
CI, baroque scrollwork set in marble block, 14" 95.00
CI, beetle, orig pnt, Reading PA, 4x11x3", EX 120.00
CI, Boss emb on shaft, lacy design, 15" L...................................150.00
CI, cat silhouette, blk, 10½x10"..295.00
CI, cricket, no pnt, Webster Bros, Reading PA, 11" 55.00
CI, dachshund, full bodied, EX pnt, 21" L 330.00
CI, lyre on oval scalloped base, 9x11"..125.00
CI, pig silhouette w/cut-out eye, 8½x12"....................................215.00
CI, V-shaped, ornate, VG..48.00
CI & wood, lever action, EX 150.00
Wood, hickory, bentwood hdl, hinged folds, use w/out bending over..85.00
Wood w/leather trim, Lee Riders advertising, EX 75.00
Wrought iron, scrolled top, granite base, early...........................280.00

Bootscrapers

CI, Aunt Jemima figure atop, orig pnt, 15x16x9", VG...............425.00
CI, beetle form, orig pnt, 10½" 85.00
CI, Black boy finial, brushes mtd in brackets, blk rpt, 12½" 250.00

Cast iron, Black man sits above base, some rust and soiling, 13x10", EX, $225.00. (Photo courtesy Collectors Auction Services)

CI, dog silhouette, blk pnt, 10½x10" 295.00
CI, eagle relief & classical lady in oval, Portland Foundry 300.00

CI, griffins, jtd at wings & tails, marble base, 18" 880.00
CI, harp (scrolled) form, 7⅞x7¼" 40.00
CI, pan base w/flared rim w/emb decor, pitting, 17x13x16" 195.00
Steel, dog form, simple tooling, blk pnt, 13" 140.00
Wood, pine w/sq nails, lg early...80.00
Wrought iron, detailed scroll finial, 21x24" 500.00
Wrought iron, ram's-horn scrolls, marble block 150.00
Wrought iron, ribbon curls at top of ea end, 7x7", EX.................40.00
Wrought iron, twisted posts w/star-emb faceted knobs, 12x8".....150.00

Borsato, Antonio

Borsato was a remarkable artist/sculptor who produced some of the most intricately modeled and executed figurines ever made. He was born in Italy and at an early age enjoyed modeling wildlife from clay he dug from the river banks near his home. At age eleven, he became an apprentice of Guido Cacciapuotti of Milan, who helped him develop his skills. During the late '20s and '30s, he continued to concentrate on wildlife studies. Because of his resistance to the fascist government, he was interred at Sardinia from 1940 until the end of the war, after which he returned to Milan where he focused his attention on religious subjects. He entered the export market in 1948 and began to design pieces featuring children and more romantic themes. By the 1960s his work had become very popular in this country. His talent for creating lifelike figures has seldom been rivaled. He contributed much of his success to the fact that each of his figures, though built from the same molded pieces, had its own personality, due the unique way he would tilt a head or position an arm. All had eyelashes, fingernails, and defined musculature; and each piece was painted by hand with antiquated colors and signed 'A. Borsato.' He made over six hundred different models, with some of his groups requiring more than one hundred and sixty components and several months of work to reach completion.

Borsato died in 1982. Today, some of his work is displayed in the Vatican Museum as well private collections.

Prices vary according to size and the amount of work involved. Single figures often fetch $1,200.00. Larger pieces, for instance, 'Gypsy Camp' or 'Revelry,' may go from $15,000.00 to as high as $20,000.00. 'Play Gypsy Play' was originally made in the early '30s; a second version followed in the late '40s, and a limited edition was created to mark the thirtieth anniversary of the date he began his work. Though he planned to make thirty of these limited edition groupings, he died after only thirteen had been completed. This version was larger than the first two and has sold on the secondary market for more than $50,000.00. Various pieces were made in two mediums, gres and porcelain, with porcelain being double the cost of gres. In the listings that follow, our suggested values should be regarded as conservative.

Our advisor for this category is Elizabeth Langtree, she is listed in the Directory under California.

Boulevardier, man seated on bench, 5½x6¼"............................1,350.00
Canine Casualty, man applies first aid to dog, 9x9"..................2,560.00
Child's Prayer, child on lady's lap w/hands folded, 8x6x9½"....1,925.00
Cobbler's Dilemma, man & boy at bench, 10½x7½x8½" 2,900.00
Coffee counter, 3 figures surrounding coffee urn, 10x9" 4,000.00
Comfort & Love, 3 figures in fancy parlor, 12x22"................13,600.00
Dog Trainer, man working w/upright poodle, 6x9½"...............1,600.00
Elders' Delight, couple gathering snails, 8x11" 3,240.00
Elegant Harmony, man at piano, 2nd w/violin, lady beside, 13x15"...9,600.00
Fagoters, man w/bundle on bk w/goat & dog, 11½x8½".........2,100.00
Farmer's Twilight, man offers produce to lady, 7x10"...............3,475.00
Fiddler's Revelry, man seated/playing fiddle, 6x10" 2,140.00
Grandma's Well, lady/child/goose at well, 10x12" 5,125.00
Lover's Lane, figures in horse-drawn carriage on base, 11x24".8,775.00

Nomads, 2 figures w/loaded pack horse & sheep on rocky base, 13x22"..**11,240.00**
Psyche & Eros, classical couple on base, 7¾x8" **1,575.00**
Siesta's Price, fruit card, peddler asleep while cash drw is robbed..**3,200.00**
St George, man on rearing stallion facing dragon, 17¼x11¾" ...**6,625.00**

Bossons Artware in the 21st Century

Bossons closed operations December 1996. The late William Henry Bossons founded the company (formerly located in Congleton, England) in 1944; his son, W. Ray Bossons (deceased 1999) was manager from 1951 until his retirement in 1994. The company was always owned and managed by the Bossons family, who have stored the only remaining molds (many have been destroyed) and at the present time have no intention of selling them or the Bossons' name.

With the company's closing in 1996, all Bossons are now categorized as discontinued; as stock holdings are depleted, some are appreciating at a very fast rate. Noteworthy are the values of some Seafarers, mainly Clipper Captain (1993), issue price $45.00, now $275.00 to $350.00, and Barbarossa (1994), issue price $65.00, now $185.00 to $250.00. Many of the B heads that sold in the US for under $5.00 are now in the range of $100.00 to $300.00. The Character Studies or 'Masks' (Dickens and all the Seafarers) have always been the most popular. However, in the past couple of years even the Wildlife Collections and many of the descriptive High Relief plaques are becoming extremely popular, including the Floral Plaques and depictions of English life and historical monuments. The lifelike animal studies of dogs and cats are coveted by animal enthusiasts. In the past few years added interest has been given to most all Bossons subjects. Because Bossons were exported to nearly forty countries around the globe with Canada and the U.S. being the most important importers, collector interest is widespread. In addition to the U.K., Australia, New Zealand, and South Africa, to mention a few, have become primary havens for collectors wanting to find the rarest specimens.

Major points to remember: 1) Not all will have the name incised under the collar (e.g., Syrian, Smuggler, Tibetan, and Tyrolean, see *Schroeder's* seventeenth edition for pictures).

2) Many character studies in gypsum plaster are produced in England that are not Bossons; to be specific, Legends, Naturecraft, and those incised with only 'Made in England.' Fraser-Art products are Bossons, so are products marked Briar Rose. Osborne Ivorex is not Bossons. Though all rights to Osborne products were purchased by Bossons in 1971, the appearance and coloring were changed and then issued under the Bossons name. For pictures and technical details about plaster faces that are *not* Bossons, typical trademarks, Bossons Ivorex, and Bossons Briar Rose Products, link on the net directly to www.donsbossons.com.

3) Except in very rare cases, all carry the incised copyright: 'Bossons, Congleton, England, World copyright reserved' on the back *and* in most cases under the collars, along with that particular Bossons' specific name. The Fraser-Art Division (named for Mrs. Ruth Fraser Bossons) is becoming one of the most popular areas of collecting for experienced and avid Bossons collectors. Invented by Ray Bossons, Fraser-Art was termed to be 'five-star wall ornaments' for these reasons: 1) exhibition, quality models; 2) bold designs for effect; 3) fine detail to add interest; 4) shockproof and lightweight (made of hard PVC/Stonite® substance; 5) colorfully hand painted as are all Bossons. **Important:** The copyright date is most often a mold date and can help determine value. An exception is Sardinian; it carries the date 1959 copyright incised on the back; however, it wasn't released or introduced to the public until 1962, and it was discontinued in 1969. This 1959 example is called the 'blue hat' Sardinian. It has a filled-in back and an incised 1961 (c) under the collar to the left of the model name. However, the blue hat model was also released with the same coloring

and an exterior wire hanger, but with the back hollowed out to lessen the shipping weight. Though it has a 1961 (c) incision, there is no 1959 (c) on the back. Later in 1989, Bossons decided to release another version of Sardinian with a green hat. To further confuse the issue of copyrights, several models of the green hat were released with the original 1961(c) incision. Under advisement from Bossons collectors, the company agreed to include an additional 1988 copyright incision on the back, the year of introduction. So it has the 1961 (c) under the collar and 1988 incised on the back.

Contradiction in Values: Originally, the older blue 1959 model with filled-in back was rare and valued at $175.00 to $200.00 and the 1961 green model about $145.00 to $165.00. However, the 1988 green model was only produced for four years, so fewer examples were made, and this has now given it a commanding lead. It's valued at $185.00 to $225.00 and the 1959 edition at about $85.00 to $125.00. This is only one of several examples where the Bossons copyright serves to confuse rather than help determine values.

Though they can be used for authentication, painted initials on the underside are of interest but are not a critical consideration when determining value. Incised initials, e.g. FW (Fred Wright), AB (Alica Brindley), and WRB (W. Ray Bossons) are sculptors/modelers and are extremely important in authenticating Bossons and in some cases for determining value. Mold makers incised initials on the backs of Bossons are extremely important when authenticating Bossons. A few examples include: K (Ken Potts), P (George Proudlove), and D (Damen Smith).

Suggestions for evaluating Bossons based on rarity and condition: A. Attempt to determine the copyright (release) date from under the collar and/or on the back. (Refer to Sardinian example above.)

B. Length of production helps determine rarity. With few exceptions, the earlier Character Heads (1958 – 63) and latest (1986 – 98) are found in fewer numbers. Production dates can be found in *Imagical World of Bossons, Vol. 1, 1946 – 82*, and *Vol. II, 1982 – 94*, by Dr. Robert E. Davis. (See advisor's Directory listing for information on this publication.) The final productions from 1994 to 1996 can be viewed in Bossons yearly brochures or by contacting our advisor. Examples in rare color combinations may be valued at 200% to 300% of retail. (See Harry Wheatcroft example on page 60.)

C. Condition is a major factor. If in 'new' condition and in original colors, a Bossons is worth 100% of its retail value. Premium prices are obtained for only pristine, perfect Bossons, either in factory new condition and in their original boxes or perfectly returned to their original structural and coloring beauty by a professional restoration artist recommended by Bossons.

Beware of fakes and look-alikes; above all, know your dealer. Be aware that Internet auctions are flooded with plaster 'faces' and figures claiming to be Bossons in mint condition which are neither mint nor Bossons. A frequently copied fake Bossons is Harry Wheatcroft, the famous English rose grower who developed the Peace Rose in his Nottingham gardens. Photos that follow emphasize the importance of evaluating and owning only authentic Bossons.

See Clubs, Newsletters, and Catalogs in the Directory for International Bossons Collectors' Society (IBCS). Our advisor for this category is Dr. Don Hardisty; since 1984 he has been recommended by Bossons to restore their products. He is listed in the Directory under New Mexico. For restoration and purchasing questions, the Do's and Don'ts of Bossons repairing, visit his website at www.donsbossons.com.

Abduhl, 1961-86, widely available today, M, minimum value.......**55.00**
Aruja Barbarossa, 1994-96 (2-yr production), MIB, from $145 to.**250.00**
Espana (male & female), very desirable, poor condition **600.00**
Espana (male & female), very desirable, prof rstr, minimum value ..**6,000.00**
Examples originally valued at $5, many models, from $100 to....**300.00**
Examples released ca 1959, rare, from $500 to **1,000.00**

Examples released ca 1959, very rare (few examples), minimum value ...10,000.00

Left: Harry Wheatcroft, blue eyes (standard color), new/original condition and coloring, typical back cavity and recessed wire hanger, from $900.00 to $1,000.00; average condition, from $500.00 to $600.00; poor condition, from $100.00 to $200.00. (Very rare coloring with brown eyes, filled-in back, recessed wire hanger, minimum value, $1,200.00.) **Right:** Fake Harry Wheatcroft, back has flimsy wire hanger, pock marks, crude finish and sloppy overlap of colors; there is no Bossons copyright on the base, value, none. (Photo courtesy Dr. Don Hardisty)

Punjabi, gr hat (standard color), from $65 to................100.00
Punjabi, yel hat (rare), from $200 to.............................300.00
Snake Charmer, 1959-64 (once $700-900), EX, now from $300 to ..500.00

Bottle Openers

At the beginning of the nineteenth century, manufacturers began to seal bottles with a metal cap that required a new type of bottle opener. Now the screw cap and the flip top have made bottle openers nearly obsolete. There are many variations, some in combination with other tools. Many openers were used as means of advertising a product. Various materials were used, including silver and brass.

A figural bottle opener is defined as a figure designed for the sole purpose of lifting a bottle cap. The actual opener must be an integral part of the figure itself. A base-plate opener is one where the lifter is a separate metal piece attached to the underside of the figure. The major producers of iron figurals were Wilton Products, John Wright Inc., Gadzik Sales, and L & L Favors. Openers may be free-standing and three-dimensional, wall hung or flat. They can be made of cast iron (often painted), brass, bronze, or aluminum.

Numbers within the listings refer to a reference book printed by the FBOC (Figural Bottle Opener Collectors) organization. Those seeking additional information are encouraged to contact FBOC, whose address can be found in the Directory under Clubs, Newsletters, and Catalogs. The items below are all in excellent original condition unless noted otherwise.

Ballerina's leg & slipper, flat metal, Gilt Top...Beer, 1914, 3¼" 85.00
Baseball player about to throw, flat, shiny metal, Ringler, 3¼" 60.00
Black face, bronze-pnt pot metal, F-401a, 5³⁄₁₆x4⅝"...................300.00
Bulldog head, pnt CI, F-425, VG..45.00
Clown, CI w/mc pnt, F-417, 3 screw holes for wall mt, 4x4", G ...45.00
Cowboy w/guitar, pnt CI, F-27, 4¾", EX.....................................75.00
Donkey, pnt CI, F-60, 3⅝", VG...35.00
Donkey, pnt CI, Hubley, F-61, 3", EX..38.00
Double-Eyed man, bald, CI, EX pnt, Wilton 327, F-414, 3¾", NM...65.00
Elephant, pnt CI, F-49, 3", VG...40.00

Elephant, walking, red pnt on CI, Wilton, F-46, 2½x3¼" 35.00
Goat, pnt CI, flat bk, F-71, 4¼", EX..60.00
Golf bag & clubs, silver, mk 925 Chaney, clubs are corkscrew, 4¼"..215.00
Lady beside lamppost w/rolling pin, pnt CI, unmk, F-7, 4" 40.00
Mallard duck, pnt CI, unmk, F-106, 2½x3½".............................80.00
NHL hockey skate (Bruins colors), diecast, Scott Prod, 1968, 5½x5"...52.50
Nude, brass, mk Eerage England, 1920s, 4⅛" 30.00
Nude, brass, Russwood c 1946, F-171, 4½" 35.00
Old Snifter, NP brass, removable hat, corkscrew in bk, 6¾", EX ..50.00
Parrot, CI w/mc pnt, F-109, 5", NM..35.00
Parrot, CI w/mc pnt, plain stand, Wright, F-108, 5½", EX...........45.00
Parrot, CI w/mc pnt & can punch, F-113, 5" 75.00
Patty Pep, pnt CI, L&L Favors, F-36, 1950s, 4", EX...................500.00
Pelican, CI, worn yel pnt, F-29, 3½" 45.00
Pink flamingo, hollow mold, pnt wht metal, Wright, F-119, 4" ..100.00
Polly Parrot, chrome, Deco style, corkscrew in bk, 5", MIB.........40.00
Pretzel, pnt CI, F-230, 1930-50, 3½" W, EX................................40.00
Trout, CI w/speckled mc pnt, F-159, 5", EX, from $60 to...........100.00

Bottles and Flasks

As far back as the first century B.C., the Romans preferred blown glass containers for their pills and potions. Though you're not apt to find many of those, you will find bottles of every size, shape, and color made to hold perfume, ink, medicine, soda, spirits, vinegar, and many other liquids. American business firms preferred glass bottles in which to package their commercial products and used them extensively from the late eighteenth century on. Bitters bottles contained 'medicine' (actually herb-flavored alcohol), and judging from the number of these found today, their contents found favor with many! Because of a heavy tax imposed on the sale of liquor in seventeenth-century England by King George, who hoped to curtail alcohol abuse among his subjects, bottlers simply added 'curative' herbs to their brew and thus avoided taxation. Since gin was taxed in America as well, the practice continued in this country. Scores of brands were sold; among the most popular were Dr. H.S. Flint & Co. Quaker Bitters, Dr. Kaufman's Anti-Cholera Bitters, and Dr. J. Hostetter's Stomach Bitters. Most bitters bottles were made in shades of amber, brown, and aquamarine. Clear glass was used to a lesser extent, as were green tones. Blue, amethyst, red-brown, and milk glass examples are rare. (Please note that color is a strong factor when pricing bottles. For example, an amber Hostetter's bitters sells for $25.00 or less, but a green variant can bring hundreds of dollars. An aqua scroll flask may bring $50.00, but a cobalt blue variation will command over $1,000.00.)

Perfume or scent bottles were produced abroad by companies all over Europe from the late sixteenth century on. Perfume making became such a prolific trade that as a result beautifully decorated bottles were fashionable. In America they were produced in great quantities by Stiegel in 1770 and by Boston and Sandwich in the early nineteenth century. Cologne bottles were first made in about 1830 and toilet-water bottles in the 1880s. Rene Lalique produced fine scent bottles from as early as the turn of the century. The first were one-of-a-kind creations done in the cire perdue method. He later designed bottles for the Coty Perfume Company with a different style for each Coty fragrance.

Spirit flasks from the nineteenth century were blown in specially designed molds with varied motifs including political subjects, railroad trains, and symbolic devices. The most commonly used colors were amber, dark brown, and green.

Pitkin flasks were the creation of the Pitkin glass works which operated in East Manchester, Connecticut, from 1783 to 1830. However, other glasshouses in New England and the Midwest copied the Pitkin flask style. All are known as Pitkins.

From the twentieth century, early pop and beer bottles are very collectible as is nearly every extinct commercial container. Dairy bottles are a relatively new area of interest; look for round bottles in good condition with both city and state as well as a nice graphic relating to the farm or the dairy.

Bottles may be dated by the methods used in their production. For instance, a rough pontil indicates a date before 1845. After the bottle was blown, a pontil rod was attached to the bottom, a glob of molten glass acting as the 'glue.' This allowed the glassblower to continue to manipulate the extremely hot bottle until it was finished. From about 1845 until approximately 1860, the molten glass 'glue' was omitted. The rod was simply heated to a temperature high enough to cause it to afix itself to the bottle. When the rod was snapped off, a metallic residue was left on the base of the bottle; this is called an 'iron pontil.' (The presence of a pontil scar thus indicates early manufacture and increases the value of a bottle.) A seam that reaches from base to lip marks a machine-made bottle from after 1903, while an applied or hand-finished lip points to an early mold-blown bottle. The Industrial Revolution saw keen competition between manufacturers, and as a result, scores of patents were issued. Many concentrated on various types of closures; the crown bottle cap, for instance, was patented in 1892. If a manufacturer's name is present, consulting a book on marks may help you date your bottle. For more information we recommend *Bottle Pricing Guide, 3rd Edition*, by Hugh Cleveland.

Among our advisors for this category are Madeleine France (see the Directory under Florida), Mark Vuono (Connecticut), Steve Ketcham (Minnesota), Monsen and Baer (Virginia), and John Shaw (Florida/Maine). In the listings that follow (most of which have been taken from auction catalogs), glass is assumed to be clear unless color is indicated. See also Advertising, various companies; Blown Glass; Blown Three-Mold Glass; California Perfume Company; Czechoslovakia; De Vilbiss; Fire Fighting; Lalique; Steuben; Zanesville Glass.

Key:

am — applied mouth	grd — ground pontil
bbl — barrel	GW — Glass Works
bt — blob top	ip — iron pontil
b3m — blown 3-mold	ps — pontil scar
cm — collared mouth	rm — rolled mouth
fl — filigree	sb — smooth base
fm — flared mouth	sl — sloping
gm — ground mouth	sm — sheared mouth
gp — graphite pontil	tm — tooled mouth

Barber Bottles

Bay Rum in gold on milk glass w/mc bird, sb, tm, 8⅞".................350.00
Bohemian cut decor, ruby o/l, sb, Am, 1890-1925, 8" 200.00
Cobalt frost w/mc florals (lg/overall), sb, sm, 8½" 180.00
Cobalt w/mc florals, ps, tm, lt stain, 7¾" 275.00
Coinspot, dk teal-bl, melon sides, sb, tm, 8½" 170.00
Emerald gr w/mc florals, ps, rm, 8"..160.00
Hair Oil in gold, powder bl opaque w/mc florals, ps, am, 8¾" 350.00
Invt T'print, lt cobalt, wht & yel florals, ps, rm, 8¼" 160.00
Mallet, med gr w/mc florals, ps, rm, 7⅝" 180.00
Mallet, med purple-amethyst w/mc decor, ps, rm, 7½" 160.00
Mary Gregory boy on med gr, ps, rm, 8"......................................275.00
Mary Gregory lady & Vegederma on med amethyst, ps, rm, 8⅛" ..400.00
Milk glass w/dk brn neck & yel bkground w/mc florals, sb, 8" 185.00
Purple-amethyst w/mc florals, ps, rm, 8¼"..................................90.00
Ribbed, cobalt, mc florals, sb, rm, 7⅛".......................................100.00
Ribbed, cobalt, silver & yel Persian decor (worn), ps, sm, 6⅝".....80.00
Ribbed, cobalt, wht & gold enamel, ps, sm, 6⅞" 170.00
Ribbed, cobalt bell form w/mc decor, ps, sm, 7⅞" 325.00

Ribbed, cranberry w/mc floral, ps, sm, 7¼" 475.00
Ribbed, grape-amethyst bell form w/mc floral, ps, tm, 7" 375.00
Ribbed, lt purple-lav w/mc florals, ps, rm, 7" 190.00
Ribbed, med turq-bl bell form w/mc florals, ps, tm, 7".................250.00
Ribbed, turq-bl w/mc florals, ps, tm, 6¾" 80.00
Ribbed, yel-gr bell form w/mc florals, ps, sm, lt stain, 6¾"..........170.00
Stars & Stripes, opal on turq-bl, sb, rm, 7"...................................300.00
Toilet Water, lav-bl opaque w/florals, ps, rm, 8⅞" 500.00
Wht fiery opal w/HP horses jumping fence & florals, ps, tm, 7½"..275.00
Wht fiery opal w/mc florals & cherub, ps, sm, 7¾" 400.00
Yel-gr w/gold & mc Nouveau decor, ps, rm, 7¾".........................400.00

Bitters Bottles

American Stomach...Rochester NY, amber, sb, tm, 1890-1900, 8"...**95.00**
AMS2 1864 Constitution...Buffalo NY, amber, sb, sl cm, 9½"....**875.00**
Atwood's Jaundice...Moses Atwood..., dk bl-aqua, 12-sided, 6¼", NM.**140.00**
Baker's Orange Grove, golden yel w/amber & olive tone, 9⅝", NM **575.00**
Bavarian...Hoffheimer Brothers, olive gr, sb, sl cm, 9¼" **1,100.00**
Bell's Cocktail...Jas M Bell & Co New York, amber lady's leg, 10⅜".**400.00**
Brown's Celebrated Indian Herb...1868, yel-amber queen, 12¼".**675.00**
BT 1865 SC Smith's Druid..., root beer-amber bbl, sb, am, 9⅜"..**1,400.00**
Burgundy...Trade Registered...Burwell, med amber, sb, tm, 8¼", EX.**85.00**
Burton's Ginger Wine..., aqua, sm, tm, stain/flake, 4⅛" **350.00**
Campbell's Scotch..., golden amber, strap-side flask, sb, 6¼", EX.**110.00**
Canton w/star, med amber, lady's leg, sb, am, some dullness, 12¼" ...**400.00**
Cognac...Steinfield Sold Agent for US, dk yel-olive gr, sb, 11⅛"..**1,450.00**
Dandelion...Trade (dandelion) Mark, med amber, sb, tm, 7¼", NM.**400.00**
Didier's..., honey amber, sb, tm, 7⅞" **150.00**
Digestine PJ Bowlin Liquor Co..., golden amber, sb, tm, 8¼" **325.00**
Doyle's Hop..., med citron 6-log cabin, sb, sl cm, 10" **300.00**
Dr Bishop's Wa-Hoo Bitters..., med yel-amber semi-cabin, 10¼", NM...**600.00**
Dr Gilberts Rock & Rye Stomach..., teal-bl, sb, tm, 7⅝" **2,200.00**
Dr Loew's Celebrated...Cleveland O, med yel-gr, sb, tm, 9⅜".....**300.00**
Dr Med Koch's Universal Magen... (waffle pattern), yel-olive gr, 8".**525.00**
Dr Simons' Indian..., bright yel-gr, cylindrical, sb, tm, 5¼" **800.00**
Dr Soule's Hop...1872 (berries/leaves), yel-olive semi-cabin, sb, 10".**475.00**
Dr Tompkins' Vegetable, med teal-bl, sb, tm, recut lettering, 9".**625.00**
Dr Varena's Japan..., med amber, sb, tm, 9⅜".............................**100.00**
Eagle Angostora Bark..., amber, sb, tm, 4"..................................**275.00**
General Bolivar..., 7-Up gr, sb, tm, 6½" **400.00**
Geo Benz & Sons Appetine, amber, 3 labels/contents, 3½"........**475.00**
Geo Benz & Sons Appetine..., dk red-amber, Pat Nov 23 1897 on sb, 8"...**275.00**
Golden Seal..., golden amber, sb, sl cm, bruise, 9" **350.00**
Great Tonic Dr Caldwell's Herb..., med amber, sb, sl dbl cm, 12½" ..**180.00**
Greeley's Bourbon Whiskey..., reddish puce bbl, sb, am, 9⅜" **550.00**
Greeley's Bourbon..., dk smoky puce bbl, sb, am, 9¼", NM **275.00**
Greeley's Bourbon..., med smoky topaz bbl, sb, am, chip, 9¼"....**140.00**
Hagan's..., med amber, triangular, sb, sl cm, 9⅞", NM **375.00**
Hall's...EE Hall New Haven...1842, amber bbl, sb, am, stain, 9⅛".**200.00**
Herkules...CA (monogram) 1 Qt, dk 7-Up gr, sb, tm, 7½"......**1,200.00**
Herkules...CA (monogram) 4 Fl Oz, dk 7-Up gr, sb, tm, 4¼"..**1,250.00**
Hertrichs Bitter Hilt Verdauen, bright gr, orig neck seal, sb, 5⅝"..**130.00**
Highland...& Scotch Tonic, dk amber bbl, sb, am, 9⅝"...........**1,650.00**
HP Herb Wild Cherry...Reading PA Wild Cherry..., yel-amber cabin, 10"...**850.00**
John Moffat Phoenix...Price...NY, olive gr w/amber tone, 5½"...**700.00**
John Root's...Buffalo NY 1834, med bl-gr semi-cabin, sb, am, 10", NM.**750.00**
Johnson's Calisaya...VT, red-amber, sb, sl cm, bubbles, 9¾"........**400.00**
Keystone, med amber bbl, sb, sl cm, haze/bruise, 10".................**325.00**
Kimball's Jaundice...Troy NH, med yel-amber, ip, sl cm, flake, 7".......**575.00**
Ko-Hi...Koehler & Hinrichs St Paul, med amber, sb, tm, haze, 9"......**220.00**
Lediard's Celebrated Stomach..., teal-bl, sb, sl dbl cm, bruise, 10"......**525.00**
Moulton's Oloroso...Trademark (pineapple), bl-aqua, sb, dbl cm, 12"..**700.00**
National..., dk strawberry-puce ear of corn, Pat 1867 on sb, 12½"..**1,850.00**

Newman's Golden Fruit..., med amber, sb, sl cm, 10¾" 400.00
Old Homestead Wild Cherry...Patent, med apricot-puce cabin, 9⅜" 5,000.00
Old Sachem...Wigwam Tonic, med straw yel w/olive bbl, sb, chip, 9¼" .1,550.00
Original Pocahontas...Y Ferguson, pale ice bl bbl, sb, am, 9¼", NM 3,500.00
Penn's Pony...Philadelphia PA, amber, sb, tm, 9" 250.00
Schroeder's...Louisville KY, amber lady's leg, sb, tm, stain, 5¼" ..325.00
Seaworth...Co Cape Way New Jersey, med amber lighthouse, sb, 6⅜" .3,000.00
Simon's Centennial...Trade Mark, red-amber Geo Washington bust, 10" .1,650.00
Snyder's Celebrated...Philada PA, amber, sb, sl dbl cm, 9⅝" 125.00
Sol Frank's Panacea...New York, dk amber lighthouse, sb, cm, 10" ..1,250.00
ST Drake's 1860 Plantation X...1862, yel-olive, 4-log, sb, 10", EX......800.00
Suffolk...Philbrook & Tucker Boston, golden yel-amber pig, sb, am, 10" ..575.00
Victor Roberg's Prussian..., honey amber case gin form, sb, 10" ..625.00
Wampoo...Blum Siegel & Bro New York, olive-yel, sb, dbl cm, chip, 10" ...575.00
Warner's Safe Tonic... (safe) Rochester NY, med amber, sb, tm, 7½" ...625.00
Wryghte's...London London, dk olive gr, ps, rm, 5¾" 775.00

Black Glass Bottles

Many early European and American bottles are deep, dark green or amber in color. Collectors refer to such coloring as black glass. Before held to light, the glass is so dark it appears to be black.

Hexagonal wine, dk olive-amber, ps, am, ½-sz, 6½x2½" 1,000.00
Mallet, dk olive-amber, ps w/deep kick-up, appl string lip, 9x4⅜" ..200.00
Onion, dk olive-amber, appl string lip, chip, ½-sz, 6" 250.00
Onion, dk olive-amber, ps w/kick-up, am, chips, 6x3¾" 350.00
Onion, yel-olive gr, ps, am, lt stain, 6½x4¾" 90.00
Seal: AB, dk olive-amber, ps, appl string lip, magnum, 14¾" 975.00
Seal: GB (arm holding sword), dk olive gr, ps kick-up, am, 8¾" ...375.00
Seal: I Tweed 1720, dk olive-amber pancake onion, 6¾", NM...4,000.00
Seal: Ino Hawkins 1741, olive-amber bladder, ps, chip, 7⅛" ...4,300.00

Seal: John Winn Jr., H. Ricketts Co Glass Works Bristol on base, dark olive-amber, pontil scar, double collar mouth, 1830 – 50, 8⅞", $225.00.

Seal: Joseph King 1735, olive gr mallet, ps, am, stain, 8", NM...1,850.00
Seal: Loop 1777, olive gr, ps, appl string lip, 8¾x3¾" 8,750.00
Seal: RT 1789, dk olive gr w/amber tone, ps, am, 9⅜x4¼" 1,250.00
Seal: Saml Faro Roach 1785, olive-amber, ps, am, chip, 9x4¼" ...2,250.00
Seal: W Gildas Esq Barton 1773, dk olive gr, stain, 10¾" 1,350.00
Seal: W Leman Chard 1771, dk olive gr, Pat on shoulder, mk base, 11" ..350.00

Blown Glass Bottles and Flasks

Chestnut flask, lt apple gr, ps, am, 5⅞" 200.00
Chestnut flask, med peach puce, 24 right-swirl ribs, label, ps, 9" ...350.00
Chestnut flask, pale bl-gr, ps, sm, 6¼" 95.00
Chestnut flask, yel-olive w/amber tone, ps, am, bubbles, 8⅜" 220.00
Pitkin flask, med bl-gr, 32 broken right-swirl ribs, ps, sm, 6¾" ...400.00
Pitkin flask, olive gr w/some yel, 16 right-swirl ribs, ps, 6" 425.00

Cologne, Perfume, and Toilet Water Bottles

Bead & Rib, clambroth opal, sb, am, 5⅝" 180.00
Bl w/icicle trim, crystal ft, icicle stopper, Sandwich, 9" 375.00
Clear/faceted w/brass mts, dbl (hinged), Savory & Moore, 1900, 4½" .200.00
Coin Spot, med purple-amethyst, sb, rm, Am, 1855-70, 5¾" 325.00
Corseted, cobalt, ps, fm, made to take glass stopper, 5⅜" 110.00
Corseted, 6-sided, cobalt w/gold traces, Sandwich type, 3½" 130.00
Corseted, 8-sided, med teal-gr, sb, tm, 4⅝" 700.00
Cylindrical, cobalt, ps, fm, Am, 1845-55, 8⅜" 170.00
Cylindrical, pk puce, ps, rm, Am, 1845-60, 7" 170.00
Elongated loop, dk bl-gr, faceted stopper, 1840-70, 7¾" 865.00
Herringbone corners, dk purple-amethyst, sb, rm, 6¼" 230.00
Herringbone corners, pale ice bl, sb, rm, 6¼" 240.00
Hexagonal, amberina, paneled neck & body w/oval printies, 1850s, 8" ..635.00
Polygonal, cobalt, sb, rm, 4¾" 250.00
Polygonal, teal-bl, sb, rm, 4⅞" 275.00
Purple-amethyst w/wheel-cut vintage, ps, Eau De Cologne label, 11¾" ...650.00
Sq w/vertical center rib, med pk-amethyst, sb, dbl cm, 12¼" 850.00
Thumbprint & Herringbone, med turq-bl, sb, rm, haze, 9" 475.00
6-sided, amethyst, waisted/faceted body, w/stopper, 1840-70, 7" .635.00
6-sided, bl opaque, enamel decor, petal rim, w/stopper, 6x4" 315.00
6-sided, dk frosted sapphire bl, orig stopper, Sandwich type, 4¾" ...150.00
6-sided, G&B emb on cobalt, petal-style base, ps, rm, 4¼" 130.00
6-sided, lt gr, mold-blown, faceted stopper, 1840-70, 6½" 285.00
8-sided, sapphire bl, sb, ring tm, flake, 7½" 275.00
8-sided w/fluted shoulders, cobalt, fm, dug, 3¾" 130.00
11-sided (cut/polished), powder bl opaque, ps, fm, 2⅝" 130.00
12-sided, dk purple-amethyst, sb, rm, 4⅞" 110.00
12-sided, dk sapphire bl, ps, fm, 9¼" 600.00
12-sided, dk sapphire bl, sb, tm, whittled/crude, 5⅝", NM 160.00
12-sided, lav-amethyst, sb, rm, 6⅜" 300.00
12-sided, med cobalt, sb, rm, 7½" 170.00
12-sided, smoky sapphire bl, ps, tm, tiny bubbles, 7⅜" 775.00
12-sided, turq bl opal, sb, fm, lt haze, 3" 95.00
12-sided, turq bl opal, sb, rm, lt haze, 4¾" 300.00
12-sided w/horizontal ribs on alternating panels, purple, sb, 5½" ..150.00
12-sided w/sl shoulders, clear, ps, rm, 4" 95.00
12-sided w/sl shoulders, cobalt, sb, rm, 4⅛" 100.00
12-sided w/sl shoulders, dk amethyst, ps, rm, flake, 4" 150.00
12-sided w/sl shoulders, dk gr, ps, rm, 10" 625.00
12-sided w/sl shoulders, dk teal, sb, Eau De Cologne label, 6⅝" .700.00
12-sided w/sl shoulders, lt amethyst, sb, rm, 4¾" 90.00
12-sided w/sl shoulders, med emerald gr, sb, rm, 6⅛" 300.00
12-sided w/sl shoulders, pk-amethyst, sb, rm, 7½" 230.00
12-sided w/sl shoulders, purple-amethyst, ps, rm, 6⅜" 230.00
12-sided w/sl shoulders, teal-bl, sb, tm, 4⅞" 140.00

Commercial Perfume Bottles

One of the most popular and growing areas of perfume bottle collecting is what are called 'commercial' perfume bottles. They are called commercial because they were sold with perfume in them — in a sense one pays for the perfume and the bottle is free. Collectors especially value bottles that retain their original label and box, called a perfume presentation If the bottle is unopened, so much the better. Rare fragrances and those from the 1920s are highly prized. 'Tis a sweet, sweet hobby. Our advisors are Randy Monsen and Rod Baer; they are listed in the Directory under Virginia.

Bourjois, Ashes of Roses, clear w/blk stopper, empty, 2.1", in box ..220.00
Bourjois, Evening in Paris, cobalt flacon, 3.5", M in star box 235.00
Bourjois, Glamour, clear w/gold cap, 1950s, 2.5", MIB 45.00
Bourjois, Kobako, snuff bottle form w/emb leaves, 2.7", +Bakelite box ..320.00

Caron, Voeu de Noel, wht opal w/emb floral, gold name, 3.6"....**495.00**
Ciro, Parfum Maskèe, clear Pierrot shape w/blk/wht top, 8.2" **415.00**
Ciro, Surrender, clear faceted gem form, 3.6", in beige/gold box..**100.00**
Corday, Miss Corday, replica mini w/stopper, 1.7", near empty in box.**110.00**
D'Orsay, Belle de Jour, wht satin, hand holding bow forms top, 3.4"....**400.00**
Duvelle Le Gui, gr teardrop w/button stopper, empty, 3.2", +box..**200.00**
E Arden, Mèmoire Chèrie, frosted female form, 4.4"...................**360.00**
Eroy, Adorèe, cushion w/frosted kneeling nude stopper, 4.4" **175.00**
Estee Lauder, Cinnabar, solid perfume compact, cat lid, 1.4" **360.00**
Evyan, Golden Shadows, clear bell shape, gold label, sealed, 2.9", MIB.**90.00**
Guerlain, Eau de Cologne Impèriale, apothecary shape w/label, 6.2"...**360.00**
H Carnegie, Hypnotic, gold enameled lady's head & shoulders, 4.2" +box..**600.00**
Houbigant, Violette, flask w/gold stopper, purple label, 3.3", +box........**100.00**
J Desprez, Escarmouche, clear sword w/gold cap, tassel, scabbard, 4.8".**110.00**
Merle Norman, Impact, clear w/frosted stopper, decal, 1950s, 2", MIB.**100.00**
Molinard, Xmas Bells, blk glass bell, 6" **155.00**
Mury, Le Narcisse Bleu, hexagon w/emb flowers, label, 2.4", +box..**275.00**
Park Avenue Perfumes, Waldorf, silver label, 2.2", +wht box **125.00**
Revillon, Detchema, invt brandy snifter form, 2.1", +box.............**75.00**
Richard Hudnut, Le Dèbut Vert, gr octagon w/gold stopper & label, 2.2" **180.00**
Schiaparelli, Shocking, solid perfume compact, pk stones, 1.5", in box....**220.00**
Suzy Golden, Laughter, lady's head w/gr enamel hat stopper, 3.1".......**415.00**
Weil, Cassandra, Ionic column w/gold label, sealed, 3", MIB......**450.00**

Dairy Bottles

Alta Crest Ayrshire Dairy, Spencer MA, cow portraits, 10-oz **50.00**
Borden's, emb name, seal on bk, ribbed, heavy squat style, ½-pt ..**15.00**
Borden's, morning glory on shoulder, red pyro, rnd ½-gal **120.00**
Bordon's, Elsie on front & bk, red pyro, short, sq ½-pt..................**15.00**
Country Egg Nog, Shelbourne VT, maroon pyro, sq qt **11.00**
Ferland's, Store - It Whips, blk & orange pyro, sq cream top **55.00**
Green Acre Dairy, farm scene, 'Why Not Use...,' gr pyro, tall, rnd qt...**36.00**
Haskell's Guernsey Milk, Agusta GA, rhyme on bk, gr pyro, rnd pt **55.00**
Hillside Dairy, Huntington Sta, LI, yel pyro, tall, rnd qt, dullness ...**17.50**
Hilton Dairy, Madison ME, red pyro, tall, rnd qt...........................**15.00**
Ideal Farms, Augusta NJ, wide mouth, rnd qt **28.00**
Marshall Dairy Co, Ithaca NY, orange pyro, tall, rnd qt, slightly dull ...**15.00**
Melrose Dairy, Ormond FL, bl pyro, tall, rnd qt, clouding.............**26.00**
Mission Milk, orange pyro, tall, rnd qt **15.00**
Peplau's Dairy, orange pyro, 1-oz creamer.....................................**28.00**
Purity Maid, bl pyro, ¾-oz creamer...**22.00**
Salois Sanitary Dairy, war logos, orange pyro, rnd, 10-oz.............**55.00**
Sealtest, red pyro, ½-oz creamer **28.00**
Smith's Dairy, Erie PA, maroon pyro, rnd ½-pt.............................**15.00**
Sunsett Farm Dairy, Woodstock VT, Brown Swiss cow, orange pyro, sq qt..**60.00**
TeCroney Dairy, Clymer NY, maroon pyro, tall, rnd qt **24.00**
Titusville Dairy Products Co, PA, red & blk pyro, tall, rnd qt **85.00**
Urbandale Guernsey Dairy, Elkhorn WI, orange & blk pyro, rnd ½-pt.....**15.00**
Wauregan Dairy, WT Burns, rhyme, red & blk pyro, rnd qt cream-top **85.00**
Whalens Dairy, Lincoln ME, orange & blk pyro, tall, rnd qt **45.00**
Zenda Farms, Clayton NY, orange pyro, rnd ½-pt **10.00**

Figural Bottles

Alligator, milk glass, ps, sm, Deponiert on side of base, 10", NM.....**1,450.00**
Chinaman sitting, cobalt w/pnt metal head, Oriental emb on sb, 5½" ...**450.00**
Fountain, clear to cranberry red, Depose on ps base, tm, 11¼"...**185.00**
Frog, Deponiert, lt aqua, sb, flake, 5¼" **400.00**
Roller skate, turq-bl w/gold laces, orig metal & wood band, 6⅞"...**1,600.00**
Spiked helmet, clear w/gold pnt, sb, orig pewter screw-on top, 3¼".**170.00**
Stalagmite (or fountain), olive gr, sb, tm, European, 6⅜" **50.00**
Violin, golden amber, Pat Apl'd For on body, sm, chip, 6⅝".........**45.00**
Violin, ice bl, sb, tm, 7¼" **35.00**

Flasks

Baltimore Monument/Corn for the World, golden yel, dbl cm, qt.**900.00**
Bust of Washington/Baltimore GW, GI-23, med yel-gr, ps, qt .**3,700.00**
Coffin & Hay Hammonton/Flag & Eagle, GII-48, aqua, sm, pt...**130.00**
Corn for World/Monument, GVI-4, golden amber, ip, dbl cm, lip rpr, qt...**210.00**
Cornucopia/Urn, GII-4, olive gr, ps, sm, pt...............................**80.00**
Cornucopia/Urn, GIII-17, aqua, seed bubbles, open p, pt, 6½" ..**220.00**
Cornucopia/Urn, GIII-4, olive-amber, sm, ps, pt, NM..................**70.00**
Eagle/Coffin & Hay, GII-48, med bl-gr, ps, sm, qt.....................**2,200.00**
Eagle/Eagle, GII-105, med yel-amber w/olive tone, sb, am, pt, NM..**90.00**
Eagle/Eagle, GII-106, forest gr, sb, am w/ring, pt **210.00**
Eagle/Eagle, GII-81, dk yel-amber, ps, sm, pt, NM **190.00**
Eagle/Horse Pulling Cart, GV-9, olive gr w/amber tone, ps, tm, pt ...**250.00**
Flora Temple/Harness Trot, GXIII-19, med copper-puce, sb, am & hdl, qt.**525.00**
Flora Temple/Harness Trot, GXIII-23, dk reddish puce, sb, am, pt...**220.00**
Flora Temple/Harness Trot, GXIII-23, med bl-gr, sb, am, pt........**300.00**
General Taylor/Monument, GI-73, med amethyst, sm, ps, pt ..**16,000.00**
Hunter/Fisherman, GXIII-4, golden amber, ip, sl cm, calabash...**220.00**
Hunter/Fisherman, med copper-puce, ip, sl cm, calabash **350.00**
Jenny Lind/GW, yel-olive, ps, dbl cm, bubbles, calabash **1,850.00**
LaFayette/Wheeling Knox & McKee, GI-69, gr-aqua, ps, sm, pt, EX ..**725.00**
Masonic Eagle, GIV-1, bl-gr, sm, ps, pt......................................**300.00**
Masonic Eagle, GIV-5, lt yel-gr, wide rm, ps, pt **1,000.00**
P&W/Keen Sunburst, GVIII-10, olive gr, sm, ps, ½-pt, NM **300.00**
Ringold/Taylor, GI-71, lt pk-amethyst, ps, sm, flake, pt **1,000.00**
Scroll, GIX-10, bright yel-olive, ps, sm, pt **1,550.00**
Scroll, GIX-10, citron, ps, sm, bubbles, pt, NM..........................**500.00**
Scroll, GIX-10, dk olive-amber, ps, am, pt...................................**525.00**
Scroll, GIX-10, dk sapphire bl, ps, sm, pt **2,000.00**
Scroll, GIX-10, grass gr, ps, sm, pt, NM...................................**1,800.00**
Scroll, GIX-10, med cornflower bl, ps, sm, pt.............................**1,400.00**
Scroll, GIX-10, med teal, ps, tm, pt...**1,200.00**
Scroll, GIX-10, med yel-gr, ps, sm, crude/bubbles, flake, pt.........**475.00**
Scroll, GIX-10, med yel-olive, ps, sm, pt......................................**800.00**
Scroll, GIX-11, bl-gr, ps, sm, pt **750.00**
Scroll, GIX-11, clear, ps, am, pt..**450.00**
Scroll, GIX-11, dk emerald gr, ps, am, pt..................................**1,800.00**
Scroll, GIX-11, med yel-amber, ps, sm, sm bruise, crude, pt........**400.00**
Scroll, Louisville KY/GW, GIX-8, lt bl-gr, ps, sm, pt..................**475.00**
Success to the RR, GV-I, golden amber, sm, ps, 1849-60, pt ...**4,300.00**
Sunburst, GVIII-10, yel-tobacco amber, ps, sm, ½-pt.................**700.00**
Sunburst, GVIII-29, aqua w/olive streaks through top, sm, ps, ¾-pt...**350.00**
Sunburst, GVIII-29, lt bl-gr, ps, sm, pt **170.00**
Sunburst, GVIII-8, med yel-amber, ps, sm, pt **400.00**
Sunburst, GVIII-9, olive gr w/amber tone, ps, tm, ½-pt..............**500.00**
Taylor/Bragg, GX-6, copper, ps, sm, cleaned, ½-pt...................**1,500.00**
Tree/Tree, GX-18, lt to med yel-olive, open p, dbl cm, bubbles, qt...**1,700.00**
Tree/Tree, GX-18, med bl-gr, open p, dbl cm, lt haze, qt **1,250.00**
Tree/Tree, GX-19, bright yel-olive, ps, dbl cm, tiny chips, qt......**825.00**
Washington/Jackson, GI-33, olive gr, ps, sm, partial label, chip, pt...**130.00**
Washington/Lockport GW, GI-60, med gr, dbl cm, ip, qt........**4,025.00**
Washington/Taylor, GI-37, grape-amethyst, ps, sm, qt.............**4,300.00**
Washington/Taylor, GI-39, dk bl-gr, open p, sm, qt....................**275.00**

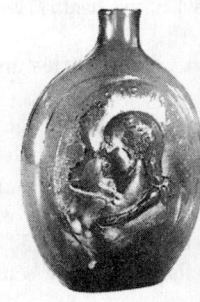

Washington/Taylor, GI-39, smoky topaz with good olive tone, smooth base, tooled mouth, 1850 – 60, pint, $1,200.00.

Washington/Taylor, GI-39, golden yel-amber, open p, sm, crude, qt. 1,700.00
Washington/Taylor, GI-40a, sapphire bl, sm, ps, pt 4,885.00
Washington/Taylor, GI-40c, aqua, seed bubbles, crude, pt, NM..110.00
Washington/Taylor, GI-41, dk olive gr, ps, sm, ½-pt, NM 2,800.00
Washington/Taylor, GI-54, turq-teal, am, crude, qt 750.00

Food Bottles and Jars

Am, lt teal-bl, ip, rm, ca 1840-50, 8⅞" 150.00
Beehive, med amber, ps, tm, 6¼" 210.00
Peppersauce, dk bl-aqua 6-sided cathedral, ip, am, 10⅝" 210.00
Peppersauce, lt to med gr cathedral, open p, dbl cm, 8⅝", NM..185.00
Pickle, bl-aqua 6-sided cathedral, ps, rm, 13" 375.00
Pickle, dk aqua cathedral w/gr tones, sb, rm, 11¼" 400.00
Pickle, Wendell & Espy Phila, aqua, ps, tm, 7⅝" 600.00
Wendell (around shoulder), dk bl-aqua, sb, am, 9¾" 90.00
Wendell & Espy Mince Meat 152 So Front..., aqua, ps, rm, 9" ...400.00
Wide mouth, lt yel-gr, sq, flared tm, 12½x5⅛" 300.00
Wide mouth, med olive gr, ps, sm, seed bubbles, 12⅛" 300.00
Wide mouth, med olive gr w/amber tone, ip kick-up, am, 8" 425.00

Ink Bottles

Barrel, SI Comp, aqua, sb, tm, flakes, 2⅛" 90.00
Barrel, SI Comp, milk glass, sb, tm, 2¼", NM 160.00
Barrel, WE Bonney, aqua, sb, tm, 2¾" 70.00
Carter's, dk cobalt clover, 6-sided, sb, am, 2⅞" 155.00
Carter's med gr, sb, tm, NM labels, master, 6⅛" 190.00
Carter's on sb, cobalt cathedral, am, mid sz, 6¼" 220.00
Carter's Pat Apd For, aqua cone, sb, tm, pan rest in shoulder, 2½" ...65.00
Cone, cobalt, open p, rm, 2½" 750.00
Cone, dk emerald gr, ps, sm, 2⅜" 575.00
Cone, yel-olive, X on ps base, sm, 2⅜" 300.00
Dog figural, clear, hinged collar, sb, pnt details, 3¾" 110.00
E Waters Troy NY, aqua, ps, am, lt stain, 3" 400.00
Geometric, med yel-amber, ps, tm, 1½" 170.00
Geometric, olive-amber, ps, disc tm, chips, 1⅞x2¾" 175.00
Harrison's Columbian, aqua, 8-sided, Patent on shoulder, label, 3"..350.00
Harrison's Columbian, aqua, 8-sided, Patent on shoulder, ps, 2½" ...150.00
Harrison's Columbian, cobalt, ip, disc-type mouth, 7", NM 725.00
Hover Phila, med bl-gr, open p, fm w/tiny flake, 4½" 210.00
J&IEM, lt teal-gr igloo, sb, gm, 1¾" 160.00
JJ Butler Cin O, dk bl-aqua, open p, rm, lt haze, 2⅜" 160.00
JJ Butler Cin Ohio, aqua semi-cabin, open p, rm, 2½" 100.00
JJ Butler Cinct Ohio, gr-aqua cone, ps, sm (unfinished), 2⅜" 250.00
Master, med yel-amber, ip, am w/spout, b3m, 7½" 200.00
Pancake, cobalt, ps, orig glass lid w/appl knob, 2" 140.00
Penn Mfg Works...Philada (on sb), tm, orig stopper, 2⅛" 85.00
Pitkin, olive gr, 36 left-swirl ribs, ps, tm, 1⅝", NM 400.00
Pitkin, yel-olive gr, 36 left-swirl ribs, tm, flake, 1⅞x2⅜" 425.00
Soapstone, blk, sq, single filler hole, 1⅞" 140.00
Soapstone, RSC C 1814, blk, 3 quill holes, filler hole on dome, 2" ..275.00
Teakettle, bl & wht alternating loops, 8-sided, 1¾" 625.00
Teakettle, blk amethyst w/gold traces, sb, gm, 2¼" 375.00
Teakettle, cobalt, 8-sided, sb, gm, orig brass ring, hinged lid, 2" .575.00
Teakettle, cobalt to clear, ribs, brass neck ring/hinged lid, 1⅝" ..875.00
Teakettle, dk sapphire bl, sb, gm, brass neck ring, 2" 350.00
Teakettle, mint gr opal w/enamel, sb, brass ring/hinged lid, 2⅝" ...525.00
Teakettle, wht porc w/gold trim, 3" 350.00
Turtle, bl-aqua, sb, gm, 1½" 80.00
Turtle, purple-amethyst, sb, gr, tiny crack, 2" 650.00
Umbrella, cobalt, reversed 77 on sb, tm, 2¾", NM 190.00
Umbrella, dk red-amber, 8-sided, ps, sm, 2⅜", NM 230.00
Umbrella, golden amber to yel-amber, 8-sided, sb, rm, 2⅝" 145.00
Umbrella, med bl-gr, 8-sided, open p, rm, lt stain, 2½" 85.00
Umbrella, med grape-amethyst, 8-sided, sb, rm, 2⅝" 1,300.00
Umbrella, orange-amber, 8-sided, sb, rm, 2⅝" 170.00
Waters Ink Troy NY, aqua, 6-sided umbrella, ps, rm, lt haze, 2⅝" ..675.00
Wood's Black Ink Portland, aqua cone, ps, rm, 2½" 220.00

Medicine Bottles

Note: Warner's bottles listed below are not American versions, and some are valued higher than those from Rochester, New York.

A.B.L Myers AM/Rock Rose/New Haven, emerald green, crude blob lip, iron pontil, burst bubble, 1860 – 70, 9½", $450.00.

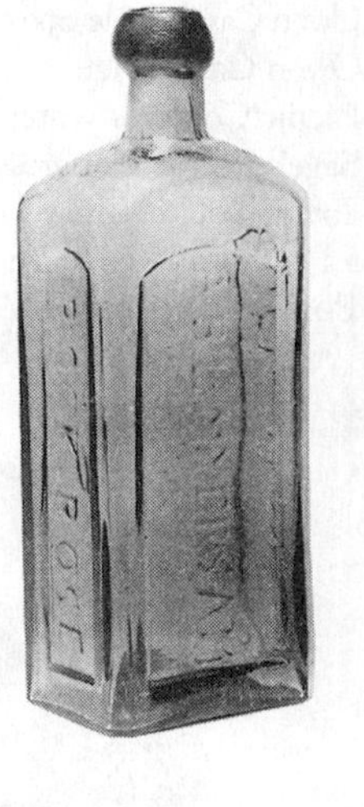

Ayer's Cherry Pectoral Lowell MA, lt bl, am, open p, 7" 30.00
By AA Cooley Hartford CT, olive gr, oval, open p, sm, 4⅝" 600.00
C Heimstreet & Co Troy NY, med sapphire bl, 8-sided, ps, 7" 325.00
Carter's Spanish Mixture, med olive gr, ps, sl dbl cm, 7⅞" 1,200.00
Castor Oil, aqua, ps, rm, flake, 5⅛" 65.00
Compound Chlorine Tooth Wash..., med to dk yel-amber, ps, fm, 6" .4,600.00
Craig's Kidney & Liver Cure..., med amber, sb, dbl cm, 9⅝" 170.00
Dr Elmore's Gheumatine-Goutaline..., med amber, sb, sl cm, 9⅝"...300.00
Dr J McClintock's Family..., lt bl-aqua, fm, 5½" 50.00
Dr Tebbett's Physiological Hair Regenerator, dk purple-amethyst, 7½ ..210.00
Dr Wilson's Hair Restorer, amber, sb, tm, crude, bubbles, 7¾" ...100.00
Dr Wistar's Balsam of Wild Cherry Philada Wms, med gr-aqua, 6¼" ..70.00
Gun WA's Chinese Remedy...Harmless, golden yel, sb, dbl cm, 8⅛" .300.00
H Lake's Indian Specific, bl-aqua, ps, am, 8¼" 1,200.00
I Covert's Balm of Life, dk olive gr, open p, sl cm, 5⅞" 2,600.00
Log Cabin Cough & Consumption Remedy, amber, Pat... on sb, 7" ...120.00
Log Cabin Extract Rochester NY, chocolate amber, sb, tm, 6½" .120.00
Log Cabin Extract...NY, med amber, Pat... on sb, tm, NM label, 6⅜" ..235.00
LQC Wishart's Pine Tree Tar Cordial..., med bl-gr, sb, sl cm, 10¼" 140.00
LQC Wishart's Pine Tree..., dk emerald gr, sb, am, haze, 9⅝" 300.00
LQC Wishart's Pine Tree..., dk teal-gr, sb, sl cm, 9⅝" 400.00
LQC Wishart's Pine Tree..., lt bl-gr, sb, sl cm, potstone, 9⅞" 65.00
LQC Wishart's Pine Tree..., lt teal-bl, sb, sl cm, flake, 7⅞" 155.00
LQC Wishart's Pine Tree..., med amber, sb, tm, label/contents, 9⅝" ..375.00
LQC Wishart's Pine Tree..., med teal, sb, sl cm, 10¼" 140.00
Lyon's Powder B&P NY, grape-amethyst, open p, rm, stain, 4⅜" ..240.00
Peruvian Syrup, aqua, ps, am, NM label, 9⅜" 150.00
Rohrer's Expectoral Wild Cherry..., golden amber, ip, sl dbl cm, 11" ..425.00
Swift's Syphilitic Specific, cobalt, sb, dbl cm, 9½" 725.00
Trade Mark Sparks Perfect Health..., golden amber, sb, tm, 9⅜" ...160.00
True Daffy's Elixir..., olive gr rectangle w/beveled corners, 4⅜" ..775.00
USA Hosp Dept, yel w/amber tone, SDS on sb, dbl cm, 9¼" 675.00
Warner's Safe Cure..., bright yel-gr, sb, tm, 4½" 600.00
Warner's Safe Cure..., med red-amber, sb, bt, 9½" 300.00
Warner's Safe Reumatic Cure..., med amber, st, tm, 9½" 70.00

Mineral Water and Soda Bottles

Bay City Soda Water SF w/star, sapphire bl, whittled.................110.00
Chase & Co...San Francisco...CA, emerald gr, graphite p, NM..375.00
Eel River Valley Soda Wks Springville CA, aqua, Hutchinson ..230.00
GP Morrill, bl-teal, whittled, minor scratches, NM....................400.00
Humboldt Artisan Mineral Water...CA, aqua w/gr streaks, Hutchinson...50.00
John Odea Eureka Cal Bottling Wks, aqua w/much whittling, NM..100.00
O&EM Fremont Factory, aqua, blob top, whittled, minor scratching, NM..100.00
Owen Casey Eagle Soda Wks..., bright sapphire, blob top.............70.00
Owen Casey Eagle Soda Wks..., brilliant gr, blob top, whittled, NM ...120.00
Owen Casey Eagle Soda Wks..., cobalt, blob top, whittled/bubbles......180.00
Owen Casey Eagle Soda Wks..., lt gr-aqua, blob top, bubbles/crude 60.00
Owen Casey Eagle Soda Wks..., steel bl w/bubbles, blob top 160.00
Pacific Congress Water P Caduca, gr-aqua, strong strike, haze, NM ..30.00
Sage's Pacific Congress...California, lime gr, running deer, NM..750.00
Taylor & Co Valpariso..., teal bl, bubbles, ps 250.00

Poison Bottles

Poison - Poison, dark amber, smooth base, NM label, ca 1890, 10¼", $180.00.

Gift! (skull & X bones) Gift!..., med gr, 6-sided, 250 on sb, 6½" ..400.00
Lin Belladon Poison in orange & wht pyro on dk gr, tm, 8" 85.00
Poison, cobalt, dmn hobnails, Davis....USA on sb, tm, 3⅛", EX...750.00
Poison Gift Velend, med yel-gr, emb skull/X bones/t'print, 8⅜"..300.00
Poison Jacobs Bichloride..., amber, emb skull/X bones, 8-sided, 2¼" ..825.00
Poison Jacobs Bichloride..., amber, emb skull/X bones, 8-sided, 3⅜".1,100.00
Poison Pat Appl'd For....1894, cobalt skull, sb, 4⅛" 2,250.00
Poison Poison, amber, sb, triangular w/rnded bk, tm, label, 8¼"...85.00
Vorsicht! Gift! Attenzione!..., med gr, emb skull/X bones/t'print, 9" ..875.00

Saratogas

Artesian Spring Co...Mineral Water, bl-gr, sb, dbl cm, bubbles, pt ..150.00
Champion Spouting Spring...Water, aqua, sb, sl dbl cm, pt 210.00
Clarke & Co New York, med emerald gr, ps, dbl cm, flake, pt....120.00
Congress & Empire Spring Co..., emerald gr, sb, dbl cm, pt........220.00
Congress & Empire Spring Co...NY, med olive gr, sb, sl dbl cm, ½-pt..190.00
Crystal Spring Co...NY, med bl-gr, sb, dbl cm, flake, pt 675.00
Crystal Spring Water CR Brown..., dk emerald gr, sb, bruise, pt..1,000.00
Excelsior Spring...NY, dk teal-bl, sb, sl dbl cm, pt 195.00
Franklin Spring Mineral Water..., emerald gr, sb, dbl cm, pt.......350.00
GW Weston & Co Saratoga NY, dk olive gr, sb, sl dbl cm, bruise, qt..80.00
GW Weston & Co Saratoga NY, dk olive gr, sb, sl dbl cm, pt....140.00
Highrock Congress Spring (rock) C&W..., dk teal-bl, sb, dbl cm, pt....300.00
Highrock Congress Spring (rock) C&W..., emerald gr, sb, dbl cm, pt..235.00
Highrock Congress Spring (rock) C&W..., yel-amber, sb, dbl cm, pt...240.00
Highrock Congress Spring (rock) C&W..., yel-olive, sb, dbl cm, pt..230.00

John Clarke New York, dk olive gr, ps, sl dbl cm, stain, pt..........160.00
John Clarke New York, dk yel-olive gr, ps, sl dbl cm, crude, qt...130.00
Pavilion & United States Spring Co..., dk yel-olive, sb, dbl cm, pt ..180.00
Quaker Springs IW Meader..., emerald gr, sb, dbl cm, pt 1,900.00
Saragoga A Spring Co NY, dk olive-amber, sb, sl dbl cm, pt.......110.00
Saratoga (star) Spring, emerald gr, sb, dbl cm, pt......................450.00
Saratoga Red Spring, emerald gr, sb, dbl cm, w/contents/cork, pt .95.00
Saratoga Seltzer Spring Co...SSS, emerald gr, sb, dbl cm, bruise, pt..2,400.00
Saratoga Seltzer Water, teal-bl, sb, am, ½-pt 110.00
Saratoga Vichy Spouting Spring V..., med amber, sb, dbl cm, pt.450.00
Star Spring Co (star) ...NY, dk yel-amber, sb, dbl cm, crude, pt .150.00
Triton Spouting Spring..., bl-aqua, sb, dbl cm, potstone, pt 775.00
Union Spring..., emerald gr, sb, dbl cm, whittled, pt...............2,900.00
Washington Lithia Well...Ballston Spa NY, aqua, sb, dbl cm, pt...275.00
Washington Spring Co (bust) Ballston..., emerald gr, sb, dbl cm, pt.1,500.00
Washington Spring..., yel-amber, sb, single cm, sm stain/chip, pt..135.00

Sarsaparilla Bottles

Dr Townsend's...Albany NY, dk emerald gr, ip, sl cm, 9½" 475.00
Dr Townsend's...Albany NY, dk yel-olive gr, ip, am, bubbles, 9⅝"...425.00
Dr Townsend's...Albany NY, med bl-gr, sb, sl cm, 9½" 135.00
Dr Townsend's...Albany NY, med emerald gr, ip, sl cm, cleaned, 9⅝"...210.00
Dr Townsend's...Albany NY, med emerald gr, ps, sl cm, 9½" 350.00
Log Cabin...Rochester NY, dk tobacco amber, Pat...87 on sb, 9" 140.00
Old Dr Townsend's...New York, dk bl-aqua, sb, sl cm, 9¾", NM 110.00

Spirits Bottles

AM Bininger & Co...New York, golden amber hdld jug, sb, 8" ..325.00
AM Bininger & Co...Old London Dock Gin, dk yel-olive, sb, cm, 9¾"..250.00
Bininger's (clock face) Regulator..., golden amber, ps, dbl cm, 5⅞".......900.00
CA Richards & Co 99 Washington St..., blood red-amber, sb, 9⅝"......110.00
CA Richards & Co 99 Washington St..., yel, sb, sl cm, 9½" 425.00
Casper's Whiskey...North Carolina People, cobalt, sb, tm, 12" ...425.00
Chestnut Grove...CW, red-amber hdld chestnut, ps, 8⅞" 120.00
Distilled in 1848 Old Kentucky...amber bbl, ps, dbl cm, 8⅛"......150.00
Duffy Crescent Saloon..., bl-aqua pig, sb, open bubble, 7¾"....1,050.00
Duffy Crescent Saloon..., clear pig, sb, gm, 7⅝" 1,550.00
Forest Lawn JVH, med olive gr, ps, am, whittled/bubbles, 7¼"....240.00
Good Old Bourbon in a..., med amber to dk red-amber hog, sb, 6¾"..350.00
James Dingley & Co 99 Washington..., golden amber, sb, sl cm, 9½"..110.00
JH Cutter Old... (crown) E Martin..., golden yel-amber, sb, 11⅝"...300.00
Joseph N Galway New York, amber, sb, am, EX label, 8⅞".........170.00
L&Co (monogram in crown), amber, Pat Apd For on sb, gm, orig cap, 6"...625.00
Lancaster GW Lancaster NY, dk cherry-puce bbl, sb, dbl cm, 9¾"...450.00
Old London Dock Gin AM Bininger...NY, med olive gr, sb, 9⅞", NM..200.00
Perrine's Apple Ginger..., med amber cabin, sb, tm, 9¾" 190.00
Perrine's Apple Ginger..., med amber semi-cabin, sb, tm, 9¾"....170.00
Phoenix (eagle) Bourbon...San Francisco, med amber, sb, tm, 11¾" ...230.00
Phoenix Old (eagle) Trade Mark...Proprts, amber coffin flask, 6⅜" 275.00
Schapin & Gore Sour Mash 1867 Chicago, amber strap-side flask, ½-pt...200.00
Something Good in a Hog's..., clear hog, Pat W on sb, 4⅛" 80.00
Spruance Stanley...Francisco Cal, dk red-amber, sb, sl dbl cm, 11⅝" ...130.00
Taylor & Loyall (star) Fine Liquors...VA, orange-amber, sb, 11½" 350.00
Van Dunck's Genever..., dk red-amber coachman, sb, am, 8¾", NM 90.00
Wormser Bros San Francisco, med amber flask, sb, dbl cm, 8½".325.00

Boxes

Boxes have been used by civilized man since ancient Egypt and Rome. Down through the centuries, specifically designed containers have been made from every conceivable material. Precious metals, papier-mache, Battersea, Oriental lacquer, and wood have held riches from the treasuries of kings, snuff for the fashionable set of the last century, China tea, and countless other commodities. In the following descriptions, when only one dimension is given, it is length. See also Toleware; specific manufacturers.

Alligator covered, ca 1950s, Cuba, 9½x6" 210.00
Bentwood, flowers/leaves, 3-color on mustard, laced seams, 14", VG ..575.00
Bible, grpt w/gilt linear decor, lt wear, 19th C, 10x12x3½" 800.00
Book form, spruce w/inlay bands/star/moon/hearts/etc, sliding lid, 6" ..195.00
Bride's, bentwood w/laced seams, orig floral pnt, German, 7x12x19"...800.00
Bride's, couple in colonial attire on brn stain, inscr/1796, 16", VG......495.00
Bride's, German verse borders lid w/lg litho, mc rose vines, 18" L, EX.700.00
Bride's, laced seams/wooden pegs, orig floral decor, 12x8x5" 600.00
Burl, made from natural form w/cut ends, ring hdl on figured lid, 8" .55.00
Candle, dvtl walnut, slide lid, divided int, 5x18x6¾", EX 195.00
Candle, pine w/old rfn, sq nails, 1-brd sides, slide lid, 8x20x11"..220.00
Candle, poplar w/red over mustard grpt, dvtl w/slant lid, 20th C, 12"...250.00
Candle, slant-lid top w/wire hinges, peaked bk, old bl pnt, 7x5x13" ..10,925.00
Candle, wall mt, sq nail built, curved sides, divided int, rpt, 12"...525.00
Comb, walnut, 2-brd bk w/cut finials top & bottom, 14x9x3" 75.00
Cutlery, bird's-eye maple Georgian w/rosewood bands, 6-sided, 9x11".375.00
Cutlery, dvtl walnut, cvd panels, cut-out hdl, 8x13x8½" 300.00
Cutlery, dvtl walnut, shaped crest w/cut-out hdl, mellow finish, 14" L..440.00
Cutlery, yew or oak w/worn gr pnt, arched divider, cut-out hdl, 13" L ..165.00
Desk, burlwood/ebonized fruitwood, oblong, English, 1850-65, 5x17x11" ..350.00
Document, dvtl pine, brushed decor over earlier salmon, 1-brd top, 12"...220.00
Dome top, grpt, hinged lid, bun ft, fitted int, Am, 19th C, 7x7"...488.00
Dome top, mc swags on grpt, N Europe, 19th C, 12x19x13" 635.00
Dome top, pnt mc floral on bl, T-head nails, 9"...........................495.00
Glass, brass torches/porc medallion w/HP couple on lid, 7" L.....275.00
Grpt flame grain mahog, brass hinges, varnish, 5x7x10", EX 135.00
Jigsaw-work panels w/unicorns, deeply scalloped crest, wall mt, 19x10"...220.00
Pantry, bentwood, cvd compass star/heart, steel/copper tacks, 9", VG 275.00
Pantry, bentwood, orig dk gr pnt, sm chips, 8⅝" 165.00
Pantry, bentwood w/dk red pnt, iron tacks, 8x12"dia 690.00
Pantry, bentwood w/dry red pnt, lid chips, 10¼" 250.00
Pantry, bentwood w/yel pnt, iron tacks, wod pegs at base, 3x7" dia...600.00
Pine w/pnt blk waves on brn, iron lock, 12x15x27", EX 470.00

Ribbon, bentwood with hand-painted tulips and floral designs, laced joining, VG, $210.00; Bride's, painted figures and faint German script, $460.00; Trinket, hand-painted tulips and floral design, laced joining, EX, $300.00. (Photo courtesy Aston Americana Auctioneers & Appraisers)

Rosemalled pine, pots of flowers on gr, floral top, dvtl, wear, 9x18" 385.00
Satinwood vnr, pointed dome top, bun ft, damaged lock/vnr, 7x9x3½"...220.00
Storage, brn pnt circles & quarter trns on pine, 19th C, 17x33x17"......400.00
Storage, pine, red pnt w/floral decor, paper lined, 19th C, 8½" ..635.00
Storage, wallpapered, 1863 label, oval, 3x4x7" 400.00
Tea, rosewood/mahog/satinwood, sarcophagus form, 1820s, 5½" ...635.00
Wallpaper, gray w/wht swirls & gr accents, 2⅞x5" 300.00
Writing, burl walnut, fold-over slanted top w/MOP inlay, 14"....285.00

Boyd Crystal Art Glass

This small but productive glasshouse has more than 300 molds and has produced more than 350 colors. They are very collector oriented and alter their mark every five years. In 1978 they used a simple B in a diamond. Today, with four changes behind them, the original mark is now encompassed by four additional lines. Vaseline collectors have increased in number, and many of Boyd's Vaseline pieces (variations include Firefly and Citron) are increasing in value rapidly. Many of Boyd's colors — Golden Delight, Peridot, Pippin Green, and others — fluoresce under black light, and are now highly sought after.

In the near future, watch for price increases for Joey the Horse, as the mold has recently been converted to a carousel horse, preventing further production. Li'l Joe the Horse has met the same fate and is now very limited. As always, satins and hand-painted pieces are commanding 10 – 50% more than the same items in the regular finish. Also worth mentioning is the fact that when this glasshouse retires a design, they select a color of their choosing once a year and make that item with a 'R' on it so that collectors that choose to can still collect that design.

Internet exposure and the heightened awareness of Boyd collectibles that resulted have caused an increase in prices of from 5% to 85% in some cases. We will wait to see where they level off before endorsing what may be erratic values. Our advisor for this category is Joyce Pringle; she is listed in the Directory under Texas.

Key: (R) — retired

Airplane, Lemon Vaseline (R) 45.00
Airplane, Vaseline, (R) 50.00
Artie the Penguin, Classic Black Carnival, 3" 22.00
Artie the Penguin, Cobalt Blue, 3".......................................20.00
Artie the Penguin, Columbus White, 3"...............................20.00
Artie the Penguin, Moss Green, 3".......................................26.00
Bernie Eagle, Lemon Vaseline 28.00
Bird Salt, Vaseline 22.00
Bow Slipper, Yellow Vaseline, 6" 25.00
Bunny on Nest Salt, Peacock Blue 20.00
Bunny on Nest Salt, Rosie Pink 20.00
Candlewick Cannonball Salt Cellar, Vaseline......................22.00
Candlewick Coaster, Vaseline 15.00
Candlewick Trinket Box, Yellow Vaseline 45.00
Cat Slipper, Yellow Vaseline, 6"..28.00
Chick Salt, Green Vaseline 22.50
Chick Salt, Lemon Vaseline 22.50
Chick Salt, Maverick 50.00
Chick Salt, Pale Orchid 45.00
Chick Salt, Vaseline, Signature Series..................................24.00
Chick Salt, Yellow Opalescent...40.00
Chick Trinket Dish, Vaseline...22.00
Colonial Drape Toothpick, Vaseline.....................................20.00
Daisy & Button Toothpick, Yellow Vaseline 21.50
Doberman Dog Head, Aruba Slag Satin...............................50.00
Eli & Sarah, Amish Farm Couple, Cobalt Blue 18.00
Eli & Sarah, Amish Farm Couple, Marshmallow.................30.00
Forget-Me-Not Toothpick, Vaseline......................................21.50
Gorilla, Yellow Vaseline (R) 24.00
Heart Bewel Box, Vaseline 45.00
Indian Hatchet Tomahawk, Lemon Vaseline 25.00
JB Scotty, Ebony..105.00
JB Scotty, Green Peridot 110.00
Joey the Horse, Alice Blue...35.00
Katie Butterfly, Moss Green Vaseline 12.00
Katie Butterfly, Rosie Pink 12.00

Kewpie Doll, Alpine Blue, 3"...20.00
Kewpie Doll, Rosie Pink Opalescent, 3"...........................20.00
Kewpie Doll, Tangy Lime Green Vaseline (transparent), 3"..........25.00
Lamb Salt, Yellow Vaseline, Signature Series..................24.00
Lamb Tea Party Set, Green Vaseline, MIB......................85.00
Lucky the Unicorn, Alpine Blue....................................15.00
Lucky the Unicorn, Alpine Blue, sgn.............................25.00
Lucky the Unicorn, Lemon Vaseline (R) 35.00
Lucky the Unicorn, Moss Green....................................33.00
Lucky the Unicorn, Rubina..33.00
Melissa Doll, Peacock Blue 10.00
Patrick Balloon Bear, Cashmere Pink (R) 14.00
Patrick Balloon Bear, Windsor Blue (R)........................14.00
Pooch, Aruba Slag Satin, 3"..40.00
Pooch, Fantasia Satin, 3" 40.00
Pooch, Purple Fizz Satin, 3"...35.00
Praying Angel, Lemon Vaseline....................................25.00
Rooster Holder, Vaseline...28.00
Rose Puff Box, White Milk 25.00
Scotty, Nutmeg Chocolate Slag 28.50
Sly Fox, Moss Green, 3" (R) 22.00
Sly Fox, Yellow Vaseline, 3" (R) 25.00
Star Dew Drop Master Salt Cellar, Vaseline.................22.50
Taffy the Carousel Horse, Alpine Blue 24.00
Taffy the Carousel Horse, Avocado Green 20.00
Taffy the Carousel Horse, Cobalt Blue 24.00
Taffy the Carousel Horse, Moss Green 20.00
Taffy the Carousel Horse, Moss Green, sgn 26.00
Taffy the Carousel Horse, Peacock Blue 20.00
Taffy the Carousel Hourse, Rosie Pink 24.00
Tommy the Tiger, Moss Green.......................................25.00
Turkey on Nest Salt, Moss Green Vaseline 22.50
Turtle Salt, Vaseline 35.00

Bradley and Hubbard

The Bradley and Hubbard Mfg. Company was a firm which produced metal accessories for the home. They operated from about 1860 until the early part of this century, and their products reflected both the Arts and Crafts and Art Nouveau influence. Their logo was a device with a triangular arrangement of the company name containing a smaller triangle and an Aladdin lamp. See also Bookends.

Lamps

Banquet, brass-washed w/leaf motif, etched spherical globe, 25x6"..180.00
Desk, NP w/bulbous font, milk glass shade, 22½x9½" 410.00
Gone w/Wind, coppery metal ft bulb font w/3-D griffin hdls, ball shade ...500.00
Student, brass w/faceted base, gr glass shade, 9x5½" 200.00
Table, shade/base wrought in Mediterranean-style filigree, 32x12" ..260.00

Miscellaneous

Clock, George Washington figural, painted cast iron, 16½", $1,200.00.

Ashtray, CI elephant on marble stand, metal tray w/gr patina, 8½x7"..310.00
Ashtray stand, brass w/copper patina, acanthus hdl, 26x7½" 90.00
Ashtray stand, brass w/copper patina & enamel mc flowers, 28x13"...110.00
Ashtray stand, gilt metal, floral & fruit repousse, w/newspaper holder.150.00
Book rack, copper w/gilt wreath, adjustable 100.00
Candleabrum, brass, 5-light, faceted base & bobeches, #193, 14"...110.00
Candlesticks, brass, str stem, rnd ft, paper label, 9½", pr.............70.00
Desk set, brass, classical volutes flank well w/glass liner 10¾" L.100.00
Desk set, brass, sq-in-sq motif, letter holder/calendar, tray, blotter ...240.00
Desk set, brass base centered w/stag head pen holder, 10" L........200.00
Desk set, chrome, Deco style, inkwell, letter holder, ink blotter.130.00
Hall mirror, gilded CI, ornate rtcl devices, 2 candle holders, 20x13"...250.00
Inkwell, brass w/bronze patina, glass liner, 2½x3½" dia 60.00

Brass

Brass is an alloy consisting essentially of copper and zinc in variable proportions. It is a medium that has been used for both utilitarian items and objects of artistic merit. Today, with the inflated price of copper and the popular use of plastics, almost anything made of brass is collectible, though right now, at least, there is little interest in items made after 1950. Our advisor, Mary Frank Gaston, has compiled a lovely book, *Antique Brass and Copper*, with full-color photos. See also Candlesticks.

Ashtray, ind hand-held type, cast, Am, 1920s, 1x1½" dia............25.00
Baker's andiron, copper finish, triangular ft, fluted column, 10", pr...190.00
Box, slipper; emb tavern scene, casters, 14x16½x11"................200.00
Bucket, appl animal designs, English, early 1800s, 11x10½" ...1,000.00
Cabinet pull, ornate, from $25 to 35.00
Cabinet pull, ornate, w/backplate, from $40 to............................50.00
Cabinet pull, simple style, from $15 to.......................................18.00
Cabinet pull, w/backplate & key-hole opening, from $25 to.........30.00
Candelabrum, 3-light, curled design, English, mid-1800s, 20x16" ...1,200.00
Carafe, water; Maxwell Phillips NY, mid-20th C, 8" 75.00
Censer, emb foliage, rtcl lid w/3 cherubs chained to base, 12", EX .190.00
Chisel, red brass, Beryl Co S 108, 7½" 60.00
Coffee service, Deco style, mk Doryln..., 1930s, pot+stand+cr/sug+tray.400.00
Colander, pan w/punched designs, iron hdl................................150.00
Creamer & sugar bowl, pewter hdls..185.00
Curtain tie-back, knob style..45.00
Desk set, Deco style, Am, 1920s, inkwell+letter holder+blotter .250.00
Dipper, 4½" bowl, 13"...90.00
Door handle, ornate pattern, 11" 75.00
Dust pan, emb decor, English, 8½x8" 65.00
Fire dogs, spherical base w/emb florals, European, mid-1800s, 8"...700.00
Flashlight, NP & brass, mk TL-122-A, ca 1930, 7" 45.00
Incense burner, ornate openwork, Oriental, w/hanging chain.....300.00
Jardiniere, emb decor, lion-head hdls, English, early 1700s, 12x17"...1,400.00
Kettle, apple butter, iron hdl, Am, rpr, 10x17" 175.00
Kettle, gooseneck spout, rnded hdl, 19th C, 12"........................300.00
Kettle, jelly; iron bail, Am, mid- to late 1800s, 7x13".................325.00
Kettle, str sides, brass bail, 11x9½"...250.00
Kettle, wooden hdl & finial, 20th C, 8"......................................120.00
Kettle/cauldron, iron bail, Am, mid-1800s, 12x19" 375.00
Ladle, pouring spout on bowl, pierced to hang, Am, late 1800s, 15" ..110.00
Lamp, gooseneck type, bends to direct light, electric 275.00
Letter holder, Victorian, 7½x10x6" 40.00
Magazine rack, tripod base w/tapered spiral legs, mahog base, mk Hall.275.00
Match holder, attached tray, 4"...75.00
Measure, grain; Howe, 8½x4½"..150.00
Pepper mill, Germany, cylindrical, late 1800s-early 1900s, 7½"....90.00
Sconce, Medusa in high relief, English, 1850s, 16x18" 2,200.00
Scoop, sugar/grain; mk Pat Dec 8, 1868 on hdl, from $75 to...........95.00

Shell casing, ca 1915, 5½x2" dia **45.00**
Shoe mold, red brass, 11x9" **35.00**
Shower head, 9½" dia **100.00**
Spittoon, hammered border, 5x7" **65.00**
Sundial, eng coat of arms w/rampant lions, dtd 1665, 8" dia ...**1,175.00**
Teapot, wood & brass hdl, on 3-legged stand, English, early 1800s..**750.00**
Teaspoon, Am, 19th C, VG **18.00**
Tray, emb Nouveau pattern, pierced hdls, 14x9"........**140.00**
Tray, emb scroll & floral border, 10" dia **85.00**
Tray, horseshoe shape, ftd, mid-20th C, 10½x7"...........**85.00**
Tray, stippled design, mid-20th C, 11x16" **80.00**
Umbrella stand, red brass, lion-head hdls, mid-20th C **175.00**
Vase, conical, very heavy, Oriental, mid-20th C, 8½" **85.00**
Vase, emb chariots, blk onyx base inserts: elephants/soldiers, 12", pr ...**660.00**
Vase, emb Nouveau leafy branches Fr, flared ft, 10½", pr............**550.00**

Brastoff, Sascha

The son of immigrant parents, Sascha Brastoff was encouraged to develop his artistic talents to the fullest, encouragement that was well taken, as his achievements aptly attest. Though at various times he was a dancer, sculptor, Hollywood costume designer, jeweler, and painter, it is his ceramics that are today becoming highly regarded collectibles.

Sascha began his career in the United States in the late 1940s. In a beautiful studio built for him by his friend and mentor, Winthrop Rockefeller, he designed innovative wares that even then were among the most expensive on the market. All designing was done personally by Brastoff; he also supervised the staff which at the height of production numbered approximately 150. Wares signed with his full signature (not merely backstamped 'Sascha Brastoff') were personally crafted by him and are valued much more highly than those signed 'Sascha B.,' indicating work done under his supervision. Until his death in 1993, he continued his work in Los Angeles, in his latter years producing 'Sascha Holograms,' which were distributed by the Hummelwerk Company.

Though the resin animals signed 'Sascha B.' were neither made nor designed by Brastoff, collectors of these pieces value them highly. After he left the factory in the 1960s, the company retained the use of the name to be used on reissues of earlier pieces or merchandise purchased at trade shows.

In the listings that follow, items are ceramic and signed 'Sascha B.' unless 'full signature' or another medium is indicated. For further information we recommend *The Collector's Encyclopedia of California Pottery, Second Edition* by Jack Chipman, available from Collector Books or your local book store.

Ashtray, blk wash over gold, #012, 7" dia......................**25.00**
Ashtray, poodle, gold dot accents, #H-1, hooded, 3½x6" dia, $45 to ..**60.00**
Bowl, gold Oriental characters, clam shell shape, 5x5x12"............**50.00**
Bowl, Mosaic, #M-21, free-form, 2½x4x6" **40.00**
Bowl, Star Steed, #C-14, 3 ftd, 2½x9½x8½"..................**115.00**
Bowl (3-ftd) & pitcher, mc fruit on brn, 9¾" dia, 7¼" H **260.00**
Box, fruit & leaf design on lid, 5" **65.00**
Box, Roof Tops, w/lid, #021, 2x5x7⅝" **100.00**
Candle holder, bl-gr resin, dmn criss-cross design, 7¾" **45.00**
Charger, mc fruit on lime gr fading to blk rim, 14"......................**135.00**
Cigarette holder, Jewel Bird, pipe shape, gold mouthpc.................**55.00**
Dish, Aztec or Mayan, gold bird design, 7" sq **55.00**
Dish, gold, egg shape, 3 ftd, 4x7½".................................**50.00**
Dish, gold w/wht drip accents, shell shape, #S-52.............**60.00**
Dish, Jewel Bird, #F-42, 10" dia **80.00**
Dish, Roof Tops, #C-8, 6x13"..**90.00**
Dish, Star Steed, 7½" sq, from $50 to **60.00**
Figurine, hippo, bl resin, 4¼x10", from $450 to **550.00**

Figurine, Merbaby w/shell above head, dk turq w/gold, 13x11" ..**775.00**
Figurine, seal, orange resin, 9½"....................................**300.00**
Pitcher, gold over copper-tone, #068, 10½" **55.00**
Plate, ChiChi bird, 8½" **175.00**
Plate, Roof Tops, folded edge, 11" dia...........................**90.00**
Plate, Star Steed, brass, 11¾", in 13" sq presentation box **190.00**
Plate, Star Steed, folded edge, 11" dia............................**65.00**
Toothpick holder, mc rings on wht, 2½x2½"..................**25.00**

Tray server, fish form, 11½x6",
$75.00 for the set.

Tray, tidbit; Surf Ballet, 10½' sq, from $35 to................**45.00**
Vase, Aztec or Mayan, #082, 8" **75.00**
Vase, Aztec or Mayan, horse on wht, 5½x8½" dia, from $90 to.**120.00**
Vase, Roof Tops, #147, 8½" **100.00**
Vase, Roof Tops, 10" **145.00**
Wall plaque, stylized fish on wht, 12" dia......................**50.00**
Wall pocket, Provincial Rooster, #P-1, 4x5" **80.00**

Brayton Laguna

A few short years after Durlin Brayton married Ellen Webster Grieve, his small pottery, which he had opened in 1927, became highly successful. Extensive lines were created and all of them flourished. Hand-turned pieces were done in the early years; today these are the most difficult to find. Durlin Brayton hand incised ashtrays, vases, and dinnerware (plates in assorted sizes, pitchers, cups and saucers, and creamers and sugar bowls). These early items were marked 'Laguna Pottery,' incised on unglazed bases.

Brayton's childrens' series is highly collected today as is the Walt Disney line. Also popular are the Circus line, Calasia (art pottery decorated with stylized feathers and circles), Webton ware, the Blackamoor series, and the Gay Nineties line. Each seemed to prove more profitable than the lines before it. Both white and pink clays were utilized in production. At its peak, the pottery employed more than 150 people. After World War II when imports began to flood the market, Brayton Laguna was one of the companies that managed to hold their own. By 1968, however, it was necessary to cease production.

For more information on this as well as many other potteries in the state, we recommend *The Collector's Encyclopedia of California Pottery* by Jack Chipman; he is listed in the Directory under California.

Candle holders, Blackamoor, sitting w/legs Xd, 4¾", pr, $130 to...**150.00**
Cookie jar, chicken shape, 10"...**400.00**
Cookie jar, Wedding Ring Granny (+)...............................**500.00**
Creamer, calico cat, 4½", from $50 to..............................**60.00**
Figurine, Ann, seated, 4", from $60 to............................**75.00**
Figurine, bear seated, front legs apart, 1950s, 3½" **75.00**
Figurine, Bedtime (couple), Gay 90s Series, 8¾"...........**160.00**
Figurine, circus horse & ringmaster, pr...........................**155.00**
Figurine, Donald Duck, chest on ground, 4½x3½"...............**195.00**
Figurine, fantasy bird, twisting head & neck, #H-49, 11x9½" **160.00**

Figurine, Figaro, begging, 3½", from $100 to 110.00
Figurine, fox, red, #H-57, scarce, from $100 to 145.00
Figurine, Frances, 8½" 60.00
Figurine, Gay Nineties Bar, 7½x8½", from $95 to 115.00
Figurine, Hillbilly Wedding group, 6-pc set 2,000.00
Figurine, Ivan, 7" 70.00
Figurine, lady w/wolfhounds, 11" 120.00
Figurine, Matilda, peasant woman w/2 baskets over shoulder, 7⅝" ..95.00
Figurine, Patti, Childhood Series 95.00
Figurine, purple cow family: cow, calf & bull (6"), from $350 to ...450.00
Figurine, Sambo, 7¾" 250.00
Figurine, Zizi & Fifi, maroon & gr, pr 500.00
Flower holder, Sally, blond, bl flowered dress 50.00
Jelly jar, Mammy, red, rare 600.00
Planter, Blackamoor, kneeling holding planter 130.00
Planter, camel w/baskets on ea side of hump 60.00
Planter, donkey & cart, ceramic & wood 130.00
Plate, eggplant, hand fluted 75.00
Shakers, Calico Cat & Gingham Dog, pr 85.00
Shakers, mammy & chef, bl & wht, 5", pr 195.00
Shakers, peasant couple, both w/floral decor, pr 65.00
Shakers, rooster & hen, prof rstr, pr 100.00
Vase, bonnet w/bl bow, 3x4" 35.00
Wall hanger w/flowerpot, caballero, maroon & wht 95.00

Bread Plates and Trays

Bread plates and trays have been produced not only in many types of glass but in metal and pottery as well. Those considered most collectible were made during the last quarter of the nineteenth century from pressed glass with well-detailed embossed designs, many of them portraying a particularly significant historical event. A great number of these plates were sold at the 1876 Philadelphia Centennial Exposition by various glass manufacturers who exhibited their wares on the grounds. Among the themes depicted are the Declaration of Independence, the Constitution, McKinley's memorial 'It Is God's Way,' Remembrance of Three Presidents, the Purchase of Alaska, and various presidential campaigns, to mention only a few.

'L' numbers correspond with a reference book by Lindsey. Our advisor for this category is Darlene Yohe; she is listed in the Directory under Arkansas.

Actress, HMS Pinafore, oval, La Belle, 1880s, 11¼" 100.00
Barley (Cable Edge & Stippled) 65.00
Be Industrious, beehive & flowers, oval, 11½" 78.00
Beaded Grape 25.00
Bevelled Diamond & Star 30.00
Black Builders of Bicentennial, 1776-1976 ....35.00
Bunker Hill, L-44, 13½x9" 75.00
Classic, Blane or Cleveland, ea 200.00
Classic, Logan 250.00
Columbia, shield shape, bl, L-54, 11½x9½" 165.00
Columbia, shield shape, vaseline, L-54, 11½x9½" 295.00
Cupid & Venus 45.00
Daisy & Button (Hobbs) 25.00
Eagle, Constitution, motto, oval 60.00
Egyptian, Temple 325.00
Flower Pot, We Trust in God 75.00
Garfield Drape 80.00
Garfield Memorial, L-302, 10" L 40.00
Give Us Our Daily Bread, Dew Drop 65.00
Give Us This Day, Sheaf of Wheat, 13" L 75.00
Give Us This Day, 1776-1876, Continental, oval 90.00

Gladstone, 9" 45.00
Goddess of Hunt, rectangular, hdls 110.00
Hidalgo 25.00
In Remembrance, frosted, 3 Presidents 59.00
Independence Hall 125.00
It Is Pleasant To Labor, grapes & leaf center, 12¾" dia 55.00
Jeweled Band (Scalloped Tape) 25.00
Knights of Labor, amber, oval, L-512, 12" 145.00
Last Supper 40.00
Liberty Bell Signers 95.00
Maltese Cross in Circles 55.00
Memorial Hall 65.00

McCormick's Reaper,
$160.00.

Morman Tabernacle, stippled border, rare 425.00
National, shield shape, rare 85.00
Old State House in Philadelphia, Erected in 1735, 12½" 85.00
Panelled Fishbone 35.00
Pope Leo XIII, 10" 35.00
Rock of Ages, milk glass center, dtd, 8¾" 180.00
Santa Maria Variant 15.00
Sheridan Memorial 40.00
Teddy Roosevelt, dancing bears, L-357, 10" L 145.00
US Grant, Patriot & Soldier, 11" sq 85.00
Volunteer, emerald gr, L-101 ....575.00
Washington, First War/First Peace, L-27, 12x8½" 100.00
Washington Centennial, clear Washington center 125.00
William J Bryan, milk glass 45.00

Bretby

Bretby art pottery was made by Tooth & Co., at Woodville, near Burton-on-Trent, Derbyshire, from as early as 1884 until well into the twentieth century. Marks containing the 'Made in England' designation indicate twentieth century examples.

Vase, blue and black matt,
5½", $75.00.

Bowl, bl turq crackle w/copper variations, 3½x5½" 55.00
Bowl, swirling pattern, bls & yel, #1644, early mk, 3x5½" 40.00
Charger, Dutch scene relief, mc, 1920s, 18" 100.00

Tray, brn/blk mottle, crimped/emb border, #1333, 8¼x6"..............**50.00**
Vase, Clanta, gilt-bronze look, #2352, 9" **110.00**
Vase, gr semi-matt, 6-lobe flower-like form, #12401/2C, 5"...........**50.00**
Vase, Sam Weller, man in top hat, blk/beige/mc, 6x3¼", from $50 to ..**60.00**

Bride's Baskets and Bowls

Victorian brides were showered with gifts, as brides have always been; one of the most popular gift items was the bride's basket. Art glass inserts from both European and American glasshouses, some in lovely transparent hues with dainty enameled florals, others of Peachblow, Vasa Murrhina, satin or cased glass, were cradled in complementary silverplated holders. While many of these holders were simply engraved or delicately embossed, others (such as those from Pairpoint and Wilcox) were wonderfully ornate, often with figurals of cherubs or animals or birds. The bride's basket was no longer in fashion after the turn of the century.

Watch for 'marriages' of bowls and frames. To warrant the best price, the two pieces should be the original pairing. If you can't be certain of this, at least check to see that the bowl fits snugly into the frame. Beware of later-made bowls (such as Fenton's) in Victorian holders and new frames being produced in Taiwan. In the listings that follow, if no frame is described, the price is for a bowl only.

Amberina w/etch griffins/floral scrolls; hdld ormolu Aurora fr, 8x12"..**495.00**
Apricot satin, HP decor int; Meriden SP fr, 15" **800.00**
Apricot to pk w/wht & purple wisteria, yel int, ruffled, 5½x10" .**900.00**
Bl satin w/gold flowers & leaves, frosted ruffled rim, 3¼x9½" **175.00**
Cased w/cranberry shaded int, appl amber rim, SP fr, 12½" **230.00**
Frosted w/cranberry ruffle; ftd emb metal base w/griffin hdls, 12x10" ...**250.00**
Fuchsia/ruby swirl, crimped/ruffled; SP scrolled fr, 3½x10" **190.00**
Hobnail, cranberry opal, ruffled rim; ornate SP fr, 7x14" **350.00**
MOP Dmn Quilt, apricot/wht w/pie-crust ruffle; Rockford ftd fr, 11x8"...**300.00**
Peachblow w/florals w/in & w/out; Meriden holder......................**375.00**

Peach with enameled white roses, pleated rim; gold frame with rope handle and flower decoration, 10¾", $1,600.00.

Pigeon blood w/yel flower & gr stems, 10"; 4-ftd ormolu holder, 14" ..**250.00**
Pk shaded w/floral, wht int, 9½", EX; Brooklyn SP Co ftd fr......**235.00**
Purple shaded satin w/HP flowers & lacy foliage, 3½x10¾" **195.00**
Spatter, cranberry/wht w/clear ruffle, 5x11"; ftd Derby holder w/leaf ..**195.00**
Swirl, yel/pk w/clear rigaree, English, 8"; simple Wilcox fr, EX...**235.00**
Turq on wht w/griffin & urn cameo, Mt WA; SP Pairpoint fr, 9"...**1,100.00**
Wht to cranberry cased, enameled scrolls/flowers, 11" **150.00**

Bristol Glass

Bristol is a type of semi-opaque opaline glass whose name was derived from the area in England where it was first produced. Similar glass was made in France, Germany, and Italy. In this country, it was made by the New England Glass Company and to a lesser extent by its contemporaries. During the eighteenth and nineteenth centuries, Bristol glass was imported in large amounts and sold cheaply, thereby contributing to the demise of the earlier glasshouses here in America. It is very difficult to distinguish the English Bristol from other opaline types. Style, design, and decoration serve as clues to its origin; but often only those well versed in the field can spot these subtle variations.

Bottle, dresser; flowers & leaves on lt bl, gold-trim stopper, 9½" ..**75.00**
Lustres, flowers on bl w/gold, prisms, rpr, 14x6", pr..................**1,150.00**
Vase, bird w/nest & eggs among flowers on wht, hdls, 12x7½" ...**175.00**
Vase, birds & branches on lt gr, worn gold, 1880s, 17"................**225.00**
Vase, flowers & leaves on wht, gold trim, ca 1880, 10¾x4½" **115.00**
Vase, flowers & sm bird on wht, scalloped, ftd, 12½x4" **72.00**
Vase, flowers on gr w/gold, ruffled top, slim, 9" **60.00**
Vase, flowers on ivory, stick neck, worn gold, 7¾".........................**45.00**
Vase, flowers on wht, 1880s, 11" **75.00**
Vase, girl's portrait on wht, 11x5" **225.00**
Vase, hand w/cornucopia form, bl, 10½x5" **150.00**
Vase, lady & cherubs transfer on wht, ca 1880, 8".......................**250.00**
Vase, mill scene & flowers on bl, 9½x5" **110.00**
Vase, roses & mc flowers on lt bl, worn gold, 1870s, 12x4", pr ...**300.00**
Vase, roses w/gold on wht, 7½x5" **90.00**

British Royalty Commemoratives

Royalty commemoratives have been issued for royal events since Edward VI's 1547 coronation through modern-day occasions, so it's possible to start collecting at any period of history. Many collectors begin with Queen Victoria's reign, collecting examples for each succeeding monarch and continuing through modern events.

Some collectors identify with a particular royal personage and limit their collecting to that era, ie., Queen Elizabeth's life and reign. Other collectors look to the future, expanding their collection to include the heir apparents Prince Charles and his first-born son, Prince William.

Royalty commemorative collecting is often further refined around a particular type of collectible. Nearly any item with room for a portrait and a description has been manufactured as a souvenir. Thus royalty commemoratives are available in glass, ceramic, metal, fabric, plastic, and paper. This wide variety of material lends itself to any pocketbook. The range covers expensive limited edition ceramics to inexpensive souvenir key chains, puzzles, matchbooks, etc.

Many recent royalty headline events have been commemorated in a variety of souvenirs. Buying some of these modern commemoratives at the moderate issue prices could be a good investment. After all, today's events are tomorrow's history.

For further study we recommend *British Royal Commemoratives* by our advisor for this category, Audrey Zeder; she is listed in the Directory under Washington.

Key:

A/S — Andrew/Sarah	invest — investiture
ann — anniversary	jub — jubilee
BD — birthday	K/Q — King Queen
C/D — Charles/Diana	LE — limited edition
chr — christening	mem — memorial
Chs — Charles	Pr — Prince
com — commemorative	Prs — Princess
cor — coronation	QM — Queen Mother
EPNS — electro-plated nickel	wed — wedding
silver	Wm — William
ILN — Illustrated London News	vis — visit
inscr — inscribed	

Bank, Elizabeth II cor, mc portrait of Q & Pr Chs, tin **75.00**

Beaker, Edward VII cor, emb portrait on tan stoneware, Doulton...**155.00**
Booklet, C/D wed, Royal Betrothal, Pitkins, 8-pg fold-out............**35.00**
Booklet, Pr Mary/Viscount Lascelles wed, Pitkins, 1922................**25.00**
Bookmark, Elizabeth II, woven silk used in cor robes, 1953 ....**50.00**
Bookmark, Elizabeth II 2002 jub, leather w/gold portrait & decor...**10.00**
Bottle, Elizabeth II 1977 jub, amethyst w/emb portrait & decor ...**45.00**
Bowl, Edward VIII, sepia portrait, mc decal, Made in Japan, 1937, 5"..**35.00**
Bowl, Prs Margaret 1958 Canada visit, sepia portrait, Aynsley ...**195.00**
Bowl, Victoria 1897 jub, blk/wht portrait, WH Goss, 3¼" **90.00**
Cheese dish, Victoria 1897 jub, relief portrait & decor **295.00**
Compote, Elizabeth II 1959 Canada visit, mc decor, Paragon.....**110.00**
Covered dish, Pr Wm birth, relief child lid, Worcester, 5" **150.00**
Cup & saucer, Edward VIII, mc portrait in cor robe, Shelley, 1937 ...**95.00**
Cup & saucer, Elizabeth II 2002 jub, mc portrait/decor, bone china..**30.00**
Doll, Elizabeth II 40th ann as Q, cor robes, Alexander, 8"..........**300.00**
Doll, Prs Elizabeth (as in 1937), bsk, LE, Nesbit, 1978, 16" **525.00**
Ephemera, Elizabeth II '77 jub spiral notebook, unused, 4x3" **15.00**
Ephemera, Victoria, unused prestamped Newfoundland postcard, 1871..**20.00**
Figure, Duke Edinburgh 1874 wed, military uniform, 7"............**115.00**
Figure jug, Elizabeth II cor, figure on throne, Burleigh Ware **345.00**
ILN C/D 10th wed ann, pastel portrait cover, 10-pg article **35.00**
ILN Record No, George V cor, red cover/gold decor, 16x11" **175.00**
Jewel box, Diana 1997 mem, plays Memories, Ercolano.............**175.00**
Jewelry, Elizabeth II cor pin, mc portrait w/rhinestone accent, 2".**25.00**
Jewelry, Prs Diana 1997 earrings, mc portrait, SP **25.00**
Loving cup, C/D 1981 betrothal, mc portrait & decor, Caverswal..**150.00**
Magazine, L'Illustration, 1937, marriage of Duke of Windsor **30.00**
Magazine, Star Weekly, Toronto, George VI Canada Visit, 1939..**25.00**
Medallion, Victoria 1887 jub, brass w/emb silver portrait, 1½".....**45.00**
Miniature, Prs Elizabeth/Margaret teapot, mc portrait w/lustre, 3"...**75.00**
Mug, C/D engagement, blk line portrait, ear hdl, Carlton.............**75.00**
Mug, Edward VIII, sepia portrait, mc decor, molded lion hdl, 1937..**60.00**
Mug, Elizabeth II cor, pk w/emb portrait & floral decor, 4¼"........**40.00**
Mug, Elizabeth II 2002 jub, mc portrait, bone china......................**20.00**
Mug, Prs Anne 50th BD, mc portrait & decor, LE 50, Chown **75.00**
Mug, Prs Diana 21 BD, mc portrait & decor, Caverswall **125.00**
Mug, QM 101 BD (2001), mc portrait & decor, LE 70, Chown ...**75.00**
Newspaper, George V cor, The Times, June 19, 1911 ....**35.00**
Newspaper, QM 100 BD, Daily Express, Tribute, July 19, 2000 ....**15.00**
Novelty, C/D 1981 wed pocketknife, mc decor, unused.................**65.00**
Novelty, Edward VII cor letter opener, emb figure, ivory color **60.00**
Novelty, Elizabeth II 1977 jub bed warmer, copper w/ceramic insert ..**25.00**
Novelty, George V toasting fork, emb portrait on brass, 19½".......**75.00**
Novelty, Pr Albert document clip, relief portrait, 1860, 5x2"........**55.00**
Photograph, Prs Elizabeth 1947 honeymoon, Prs at Broadlands, blk/wht ...**30.00**
Pin-bk button, Pr of Wales, blk/wht portrait, 1936, ¾" **30.00**
Pitcher, Edward VII cor, mc portrait, pk lustre, 6" **150.00**
Plate, C/D wed, mc portrait & decor, mint gr border, 8½" **35.00**
Plate, Edward VII cor, mc portrait, cobalt border, 8½"................**165.00**
Plate, Edward VIII, mc portrait in ermine cor robe, 1937, 6½".....**55.00**
Plate, George VI 1939 Canada vis, K/Q & 2 Prs, Meakin, 6" **35.00**

Playing cards, C/D wed, mc portrait/decor, dbl pack, unused **55.00**
Playing cards, Geo VI, mc portrait/decor, dbl pack, 1937.............**75.00**
Postcard, QM 100 BD, set of 5 picturing royal postage stamps......**20.00**
Pressed glass, Prs Diana mem plate, portrait, irid, 3½" **35.00**
Pressed glass, Victoria 1887 jub chamber candle holder, amber ..**125.00**
Pressed glass, Victoria 1897 jub bowl, clear w/gold portrait, 8½".........**125.00**
Record, Elizabeth II at Frankie Lane show, 1954, Columbia, 33⅓ rpm.......**35.00**
Ribbon, Victoria mem, blk w/gold inscr, attached pin-bk, 5" **135.00**
Sheet music, When the King Goes Riding By, 1937.......................**35.00**
Spoon, George VI cor, annointing decor, SP, 4½" **35.00**
Spoon set, 1936 year of 3 Kings, sterling, set of 6 in orig box **325.00**
Stamp albums, C/D wed, over 800 stamps on decor pgs, pr.........**395.00**
Teapot, George V cor, mc portrait, bl/pk lustre, 2-cup.................**125.00**
Teapot, QM 101 BD, mc young/old portraits, LE 15, Chown **150.00**
Textile, C/D engagement tea towel, blk/wht portrait w/mc decor.**45.00**
Textile, Elizabeth II 2002 jub tea towel, blk/wht portrait w/mc decor ...**10.00**
Textile, QM 100 BD tea towel, mc portrait & decor **15.00**
Thimble, Elizabeth 2002 jub, mc portrait & decor, bone china **10.00**
Thimble, QM 100 BD, mc portrait & decor **15.00**
Tile, C/D wed, blk/wht portrait w/pastel decor, 6" dia **35.00**
Tin, Elizabeth II '77 jub, lt bl w/mc portrait, Jameson, 9" dia........**35.00**
Tin, Geo VI cor, blk/wht family portrait by Vandyk, upright, 5"...**55.00**
Tin, Pr Albert, emb portrait on brass, Cachou, 1860, 1⅝" **95.00**
Tin, Pr Albert 1860, emb portrait on brass, Cachou, 1⅝" **75.00**
Tin, Pr Wales, sepia portrait, orig label, 1930, 9" dia..................**110.00**
Toby mug, Geo VI cor, treacle brn glaze, G hdl, 4" **85.00**

Broadmoor

In October of 1933, the Broadmoor Art Pottery was formed and space rented at 217 East Pikes Peak Avenue, Colorado Springs, Colorado. Most of the pottery they produced would not be considered elaborate, and only a handful was decorated. Many pieces were signed by P.H. Genter, J.B. Hunt, Eric Hellman, and Cecil Jones. It is reported that this plant closed in 1936, and Genter moved his operations to Denver.

Broadmoor pottery is marked in several ways: a Greek or Egyptian-type label depicting two potters (one at the wheel and one at a tile-pressing machine) and the word Broadmoor; an ink-stamped 'Broadmoor Pottery, Colorado Springs (or Denver), Colorado'; and an incised version of the latter.

The bottoms of all pieces are always white and can be either glazed or unglazed. Glaze colors are turquoise, green, yellow, cobalt blue, light blue, white, pink, pink with blue, maroon red, black, and copper lustre. Both matt and high gloss finishes were used.

The company produced many advertising tiles, novelty items, coasters, ashtrays, and vases for local establishments around Denver and as far away as Wyoming. An Indian head was incised into many of the advertising items, which also often bear a company or a product name. A series of small animals (horses, dogs, elephants, lamb, squirrels, a toucan bird, and a hippo), each about 2" high, are easily recognized by the style of their modeling and glaze treatments, though all are unmarked.

Ashtray, bl matt w/wht dog figure in center, 4 rests **45.00**
Bowl, red, incurvate rim, 15" **55.00**
Creamer & sugar bowl, bl, curved hdls, ind, 2" **35.00**
Figurine, squirrel on sq base, brn, stamp, 2" **40.00**
Mug, cylindrical, paper label, 5½" **50.00**
Planter, frog figural, red, open mouth **65.00**
Vase, bl matt, pillow form, 6x9"...**55.00**
Vase, honeycomb glaze, slightly flared cylinder, ftd, 12"............**140.00**
Vase, Mongol Red, waisted, 8" **75.00**

Plate, Victoria 1886 Jubilee, Victoria Queen and Empress, scenes of British Empire, Queen and Prince of Wales on each side, worn gold, 9½", $295.00.

Broadsides

Webster defines a broadside as simply a large sheet of paper printed on one side. During the 1880s, they were the most practical means of mass-communication. By the middle of the century, they had become elaborate and lengthy with information, illustrations, portraits, and fancy border designs. Those printed on coated stock are usually worth more.

Act for filling CT Army quota, 1782, 2-sided, 11¾x8¼", VG ...800.00
Ad for Paddock-Hawley Iron Co, blacksmith's leg vise, 1897, 13x6"...40.00
Ad for Sun Mfg Dbl Decker Show Case, late 1800s, 17x7¼" 100.00
Batallion Orders, sgn in type JE Smith Major, 1818, 18¾x14" ...800.00
Day of Reckoning at Hand, anti-War of 1812, NY, 13x9¼", VG..500.00
Draft in Lebanon Co CT, long list of names, 1862, 19x5" 400.00
General Orders, MA militia, Boston, 1791, 13x7¾", VG 650.00

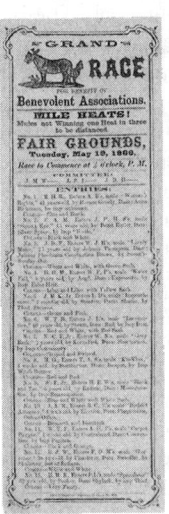

Grand Race for Benefit of Benevolent Association...1868, printed by Paul J. Christian, 14½x5", EX, $300.00.

Grand Union Meeting at Greenville, 1860, 17¼x12", G.............400.00
Meeting to be held in courthouse, MO, 1881, 6x9".......................75.00
Mr Wm Craft Is Notorious Liar..., tan newsprint, 1868, 4¾x9½"...150.00
Nailstone None or Never, horse for stud, 1911, 15¾x11"...........300.00
Nov 28 declared as day of Thanksgiving, MO, 1878, 9x11½" 75.00
Poem to the memory of Anna Roush, 26 verses, 12x9" 75.00
President's Message, Boston Times Extra, Dec 6, 1838, 25x17¾" ..400.00
Public sale of household items/etc, MO, 1868, 12¼x9½" 75.00
Show Your Colors, NY, handwritten manuscript, 1861, 6¼x8" ..450.00
What Jeff Davis Thinks of the War, 2-column, 1864, 11½x9"..1,500.00
1st Message of President Jackson to Congress..., on silk, 1830, 26x20" ..3,000.00

Bronzes

Thomas Ball, George Bessell, and Leonard Volk were some of the earliest American sculptors who produced figures in bronze for home decor during the 1840s. Pieces of historical significance were the most popular, but by the 1880s a more fanciful type of artwork took hold. Some of the fine sculptors of the day were Daniel Chester French, Augustus St. Gaudens, and John Quincy Adams Ward. Bronzes reached the height of their popularity at the turn of the century. The American West was portrayed to its fullest by Remington, Russell, James Frazier, Hermon MacNeil, and Solon Borglum. Animals of every species were modeled by A.P. Proctor, Paul Bartlett, and Albert Laellele, to name but a few.

Art Nouveau and Art Deco influenced the medium during the '20s,

evidenced by the works of Allen Clark, Harriet Frismuth, E.F. Sanford, and Bessie P. Vonnoh.

Be aware that recasts abound. While often esthetically satisfactory, they are not original and should be priced accordingly. In much the same manner as prints are evaluated, the original castings made under the direction of the artist are the most valuable. Later castings from the original mold are worth less. A recast is not made from the original mold. Instead, a rubber-like substance is applied to the bronze, peeled away, and filled with wax. Then, using the same 'lost wax' procedure as the artist uses on completion of his original wax model, a clay-like substance is formed around the wax figure and the whole fired to vitrify the clay. The wax, of course, melts away, hence the term 'lost wax.' Recast bronzes lose detail and are somewhat smaller than the original due to the shrinkage of the clay mold.

Austrian, African boy in rowboat, crocodile, cold pnt, 1890s, 4" L..635.00
Austrian, Dutch boy (& girl), cold pnt, on onyx base, 5", pr ..2,300.00
Austrian, Fawn, brn/blk patina, 3½", on ivory stand...................375.00
Austrian, lamp, Arab holds up carpet for sale, cold pnt, 10" ...1,725.00
Austrian, lamp, nude Cleopatra on litter carried by 2 African men, 13" ..3,450.00
Barye, Antoine-Louis; rearing bull & attacking jaguar, 8½x11x4¼"..4,000.00
Beach, Chester; nude w/fish, arms aloft, 2-step marble base, 9½".......1,200.00
Bonheur, bull, recumbent, Peyrol Foundry, 5¾x11⅜x7¼" 3,100.00
Bonheur, bull charging, mid stride w/head down, 9¾x16¼x4⅝"..1,850.00
Bonheur, bull standing w/head raised, Peyrol Foundry, 6x8½x4"..1,850.00
Bonheur, bull walking up rocky grade, 12¼x13¾x5⅝".............2,100.00
Bouret, Au Clair Dela Lune; boy playing lute, 18" 660.00
Canova, bust of Napoleon, blk patina, on plinth w/N in circle, 16"....2,115.00
Carrier-Belleuse, Diana the Huntress w/hound & putto, no base, 17".1,645.00
Continental, bust of Athena in helmet, on waisted ped, 1875, 8"..........800.00

Couston, Marley Horse, dark brown patina, 14x15x5¾", $1,250.00. (Photo courtesy Neal Auction Company)

Dalou, man w/shovel, Suissi P ETs Paris, 7" 850.00
Demortino, bust of child, on marble base, 1900-05, 5½x5½x3½" ..300.00
Emerite, bird, on marble base, 5x6" 650.00
Encke, bust of Nubian princess, Gladenbeck foundry, 7½" 400.00
Erte, 3 Graces, polychrome, 16" 4,000.00
French, winged maid, breasts exposed, stands by oil lamp, 18", EX, pr ...2,645.00
Frishmuth, nude, gazing upward, 1 arm raised, Gorham #253, 20"...12,000.00
Geschutz, Arab snake charmer on base, Austria, 1890s, 6x2" 400.00
Geschutz, kitten, gray tabby cold pnt, Austria, 1850s, 4½x7¼" .865.00
Giambologna, pr: Mercury atop Boreas' head, Hebe (dancer), 1860, 33"....3,500.00
Godet, bust of water nymph, dk gr-brn patina, 16" 2,650.00
Hartley, JS (after); Whirlwind, nude w/billowing drape, unsgn, 22" 1,725.00
Heuvelmans, cloaked lady kisses baby, ivory face/baby, EX patina, 13"..2,400.00
Lanceray, IA; Bashkir cavalier on horse, wood base, 1880s, 10½" 1,765.00
Lemarquier, C; Nature Boy, Louchet Foundry, 1900, marble base, 18"..2,000.00

Lorenzl, nude on 1 ft, arms extended, 1925, onyx base, 9" **1,150.00**
Moreau, cherub playing hornpipe, seated on broken column, 9" ...**230.00**
Moreau, drunken Bacchus, circular base, 21¼x9¾" **400.00**
Ouline, bust of young man, gr/brn patina, 13" on low plinth......**485.00**
Parhar, ape, slender figure on raised sq base, 4".............................**375.00**
Parhar, bird standing on sq base, 4" **350.00**
Phillip, C; female olympic downhill skier, blk marble base, 14x20" ..**1,400.00**
Remington (after), Cheyenne, warrior on horsebk, marble base, 21" ...**300.00**
Remington (after), cowboy on rearing horse, dmn/circle mk, 23" **450.00**
T Rochard, pheasant, hollow cast, striding, marble base, 12¾x17".......**200.00**
Troubetzkoy, sleeping fox, Petersburg 1904, marble base, 14" L **5,450.00**
Unmk, bust of Mercury, chocolate brn & parcel gilt patina, 20th C, 12" .**400.00**
Valton, C; wounded mountain lion, brn patina, 20th C, 21x34"..**3,800.00**
Vierthaler, Diana, nude w/bow, 1900, 15", on marble column .**1,350.00**

Brownies by Palmer Cox

Created by Palmer Cox in 1883, the Brownies charmed children through the pages of books and magazines, as dolls, on their dinnerware, in advertising material, and on souvenirs. Each had his own personality, among them The Bellhop, The London Bobby, The Chairman, and Uncle Sam. But the oversized, triangular face with the startled expression, the protruding tummy, and the spindle legs were characteristics of them all. They were inspired by the Scottish legends related to Cox as a child by his parents, who were of English descent. His introduction of the Brownies to the world was accomplished by a poem called *The Brownies Ride*. Books followed in rapid succession, thirteen in the series, all written as well as illustrated by Palmer Cox.

By the late 1890s, the Brownies were active in advertising. They promoted such products as games, coffee, toys, patent medicines, and rubber boots. 'Greenies' were the Brownies' first cousins, created by Cox to charm and to woo through the pages of the advertising almanacs of the G.G. Green Company of New Jersey. Perhaps the best-known endorsement in the Brownies' career was for the Kodak Brownie, which became so popular and sold in such volume that their name became synonymous with this type of camera.

Since the late 1970s a biography on Palmer Cox has been written, a major rock band had their concert T-shirts adorned with his brownies, and a reproduction of the Uncle Sam candlestick is known to exist. Bacause of the resurging interest in Cox's Brownies beware of other possible reproductions. Our advisor for this category is Anne Kier; she is listed in the Directory under Ohio.

Ashtray, Brownie scene, RS Germany, 1913 ....**95.00**
Basket, SP, Brownies w/chocolate advertising, Tufts....................**265.00**

Bonbon tray, silver-plated with six engraved Brownies, knob feet, marked Warrented James Tufts, Boston, 6¾", $250.00. (From the collection of Anne Kier)

Book, Another Brownie Book, NY, 1890, 1st ed, w/dust jacket, VG ..**250.00**
Book, Brownies & Goblins, Grosset Dunlap, no date, VG.............**45.00**
Book, Brownies & Other Stories, ca 1900, VG...............................**55.00**
Book, Brownies & Prince Florimel, Century, 1918, VG **95.00**
Book, Brownies at Home, laminated cover, Dover, 1968, EX........**35.00**
Book, Brownies at Home, w/dust jacket, 1942, VG **35.00**
Book, Brownies at Home, 144 pgs, Century Co, 1893, VG...........**85.00**
Book, Brownies in Fairyland, Century Co **45.00**
Book, Funny Stories About Funny People, 1905, EX....................**35.00**
Book, Little Goody Two Shoes, 1903, EX **40.00**
Book, Querie Queers, color plates, EX **145.00**
Book, The Brownies, Their Book, 1897, EX **185.00**
Bottle, soda; emb Brownies, M...**30.00**
Brownie Portrait Cubes, McLoughlin Bros, c Cox 1892, VG......**300.00**
Candlestick, Bobby, majolica, 7½" **300.00**
Candy dish, 15 Brownies, ball ft, Tufts SP, 7x5½" **250.00**
Cigar box, wood w/Our Brownies emb inner lid label, EX+........**185.00**
Cigar holder/ashtray, full-figure Brownie, Pairpoint SP **425.00**
Comic book, The Brownies, Dell Four-Color, #398, 1952, VG.....**20.00**
Creamer, Little Boy Blue verse & 4 Brownies, gold trim, china **95.00**
Creamer, Scottsman head, majolica, 3¼"...................................**100.00**
Cup, SP w/9 enameled Brownies, Middletown Plate Co, 3"........**235.00**
Cup & saucer, demi; comical action Brownies, Ceramic Art Co..**110.00**
Figure, Chinaman, papier-mache head, 9", EX **450.00**
Figures, papier-mache w/stick legs, jtd arms, 1900s, 5", EX, 4 for..**1,500.00**
Fruit crate label, Brownies collect/distribute orange juice, 10" **45.00**
Fruit crate label, harvesting orange juice, 1930s, 10x11", EX.......**25.00**
Game, Mysterio, Vanishing Drawing, Charles Graham, 1929, VG...**45.00**
Game, 9 Pins, litho on wood, w/stands & balls, McLoughlin, EX (EX box)....**2,000.00**
Humidor, Bobby head figural, majolica, 6"................................**225.00**
Ice cream bag, Cox illus, 5¢ orig value, 1930s, M **40.00**
Magazine page, Ladies' Home Journal, Cox illus, ca 1890 ....**18.00**
Match holder, Brownie on striker, majolica **235.00**
Needle book, Brownies, 1892 World's Fair, rare **75.00**
Nodder, Brownies (3) on donkey, bsk, German, 1890s, 6½x6¼" **1,950.00**
Paper doll, Indian Brownie, Lion Coffee, EX **40.00**
Paperweight, Brownie figural, SP...**145.00**
Pencil box, rolling-pin shape, 15 Brownies in boat.......................**95.00**
Pitcher, china, Brownies playing golf on tan, 6" **185.00**
Pitcher, china, 2 Brownies on front, 3 on bk, 4½"........................**110.00**
Plate, porc, mk La Francaise, 7"..**85.00**
Plate, SP, Brownies on rim, 8½"..**95.00**
Print, Brownies fishing, matted, 1895, 13½x15½".......................**55.00**
Print, Brownies' toboggan ride, matted, 1895, 13½x15½" **55.00**
Rubber stamp, set of 12 ....**100.00**
Sheet music, Dance of the Brownies...**35.00**
Sign, emb Brownies on tin, Howell's Root Beer, EX....................**185.00**
Table set, brass, emb Brownies, 3-pc (knife/fork/spoon), no box ...**85.00**
Table set, brass, emb Brownies, 6", in orig box.............................**95.00**
Towels, Days of the Week, cotton, embroidered, set of 7................**45.00**
Toy, Movie Top, litho tin w/3 windows, ca 1927, 1⅞x4¾" dia ...**150.00**
Trade card, Estey Organ Co, playing instruments, 3x5".................**15.00**
Trade card, Mitchell, Lewis & Stave Co, 3x5", VG........................**30.00**
Trade card, Sheriff's Sale Segars, Brownies & product, 5x3" **25.00**
Tray, 2 fencing Brownies, self hdls, china, 6¼x4½"....................**110.00**

Brush-McCoy

George Brush began his career in the pottery industry in 1901 working for the J.B. Owens Pottery Co. in Zanesville, Ohio. He left the company in 1907 to go into business for himself, only to have fire completely destroy his pottery less than one year after it was founded. In 1909 he became associated with J.W. McCoy, who had operated a pottery of his own in Roseville, Ohio, since 1899. The two men formed the Brush-McCoy Pottery in 1911, locating their headquarters in Zanesville. After the merger, the company expanded and produced not only staple commercial wares but also fine artware. Lines of the highest quality such as Navarre, Venetian, Oriental, and Sylvan were equal to that of their larger competitors. Because very little of the ware was marked, it is often mistaken for Weller, Roseville, or Peters and Reed.

In 1918 after a fire in Zanesville had destroyed the manufacturing portion of that plant, all production was contained in their Roseville (Ohio) plant #2. A stoneware type of clay was used there, and as a result the artware lines of Jewel, Zuniart, King Tut, Florastone, Jetwood, Krakle-Kraft, and Panelart are so distinctive that they are more easily recognizable. Examples of these lines are unique and very beautiful, also quite rare and highly prized!

After McCoy died, the family withdrew their interests, and in 1925 the name of the firm was changed to The Brush Pottery. The era of hand-decorated art pottery production had passed for the most part, having been almost completely replaced by commercial lines. The Brush-Barnett family retained their interest in the pottery until 1981 when it was purchased by the Dearborn Company.

For more information we recommend *The Collector's Encyclopedia of Brush-McCoy Pottery* by Sharon and Bob Huxford, and *Sanford's Guide to Brush-McCoy Pottery, Books I and II*, written by Martha and Steve Sanford, our advisors for this category, and edited by David P. Sanford. They are listed in the Directory under California.

Of all the wares bearing the later Brush script mark, their figural cookie jars are the most collectible, and several have been reproduced. Information on Brush cookie jars (as well as confusing reproductions) can be found in *The Collector's Encyclopedia of Cookie Jars* by Joyce and Fred Roerig; they are listed in the Directory under South Carolina. Beware! Cookie jars marked Brush-McCoy are not authentic.

Cookie Jars

Antique Touring Car	700.00
Boy w/Balloons	800.00
Chick in Nest (+)	400.00
Cinderella Pumpkin, #W32	250.00
Circus Horse, gr (+)	950.00
Clown, yel pants	200.00
Clown Bust, #W49	300.00
Cookie House, #W31	125.00
Covered Wagon, dog finial, #W30, minimum value (+)	550.00
Cow w/Cat on Bk, brn, #W10 (+)	125.00
Cow w/Cat on Bk, purple, minimum value (+)	1,000.00
Davy Crockett, no gold, mk USA (+)	300.00
Dog & Basket	250.00

Donkey Cart, ears down, gray, #W33, $400.00. (Photo courtesy Ermagene Westfall)

Donkey Cart, ears up, #W33, minimum value	800.00
Elephant w/Ice Cream Cone (+)	500.00
Elephant w/Monkey on Bk, minimum value	5,000.00
Fish, #W52 (+)	500.00
Formal Pig, gold trim, #W7 Brush USA (+)	475.00
Formal Pig, no gold, gr hat & coat (+)	300.00
Gas Lamp, #K1	75.00
Granny, pk apron, bl dots on skirt	325.00
Granny, plain skirt, minimum value (+)	400.00
Happy Bunny, wht, #W25	225.00
Hen on Basket, unmk	125.00
Hillbilly Frog, minimum value (+)	4,500.00
Humpty Dumpty, w/beany & bow tie (+)	275.00
Humpty Dumpty, w/peaked hat & shoes	225.00
Laughing Hippo, #W27 (+)	750.00
Little Angel (+)	800.00
Little Boy Blue, gold trim, #K25, sm	700.00
Little Boy Blue, no gold, #K24 Brush USA, lg (+)	800.00
Little Girl, #017 (+)	550.00
Little Red Riding Hood, gold trim, mk lg, minimum value (+)	850.00
Little Red Riding Hood, no gold, #K24 USA, sm	550.00
Night Owl	125.00
Old Clock, #W10	150.00
Old Shoe, #W23 (+)	125.00
Panda, #W21 (+)	250.00
Peter, Peter Pumpkin Eater, #W24	300.00
Peter Pan, gold trim, lg (+)	800.00
Peter Pan, no gold, sm	550.00
Puppy Police (+)	585.00
Raggedy Ann, #W16	475.00
Sitting Pig (+)	400.00
Smiling Bear, #W46 (+)	350.00
Squirrel on Log, #W26	100.00
Squirrel w/Top Hat, blk coat & hat	275.00
Squirrel w/Top Hat, gr coat	250.00
Stylized Owl	350.00
Stylized Siamese, #W41	450.00
Teddy Bear, ft apart	250.00
Teddy Bear, ft together	200.00
Treasure Chest, #W28	170.00

Miscellaneous

Bookends, Venetian, Indian chief, Ivotint, 1929, 5x5½", pr	300.00
Bowl, Jetwood, #01, 5" opening, from $225 to	325.00
Bowl, Moss Green, #01, 6", from $20 to	30.00
Candlesticks, Amaryllis Kolorkraft, #026, 9", pr	250.00
Candlesticks, Jewel, #032, 10", ea from $275 to	350.00
Candlesticks, Vogue, blk geometrics on wht, 12", ea	325.00
Casserole, Perfection, 1920s, 4x10", from $25 to	50.00
Clock, Flapper, Onyx (gr), #336, 1926, 4½", from $75 to	150.00
Cuspidor, Willow, bl, #14, 1915, from $75 to	150.00
Decanter, Onyx (bl), 7", from $100 to	150.00
Figurine, Horace Falcon, blk, 7"	160.00
Flower frog, heart shape, Onyx (bl), 2½", from $25 to	45.00
Hanging pot, #168, 1962, 8", from $25 to	40.00
Hanging pot, Floradora, 5x7", from $65 to	100.00
Jar, Ali Baba, yel, 2-hdl, 16½", from $200 to	300.00
Jardiniere, Egyptian, bl, 1923, 5½"	200.00
Jardiniere, Jetwood, #240, type 2, 7½", from $400 to	500.00
Jardiniere, Moderne Kolorkraft, #260, 1929, 10", from $125 to	175.00
Jardiniere, Rockcraft, 7½", from $90 to	140.00
Jardiniere, Zuniart, #240, 10½", from $400 to	700.00
Jewelry caddy, mermaid	150.00

Lamp base, Kolorkraft, 1920s, 10½", from $125 to......................**175.00**
Lamp base, Wise Bird (owl) figure, 1927, 9" **225.00**
Mug, Bluebird, from $75 to..**125.00**
Oil jar, bl to brn drip, 25½", from $400 to....................................**650.00**
Ornament, birdbath; wht, 2 frogs (1 standing, 1 sitting), 7½" **200.00**
Pitcher, Amsterdam, #53, 3 various, from $125 to.......................**195.00**
Pitcher, Cattail, #3315, 1927, 2-pt, from $125 to **175.00**
Planter, cat w/head turned, yel..**60.00**
Planter, swan, mk Brush USA 629..**50.00**
Radio bug, 1927, 9½x3", from $500 to...**950.00**
Umbrella stand, Athenian, shape #75, 17", from $400 to **600.00**
Urn, Onyx (gr), #699, 11½", from $125 to **175.00**
Vase, Bronze Line, palette mk USA 720, 8"....................................**40.00**
Vase, bud; King Tut, #047, 10", from $700 to.........................**1,000.00**
Vase, King Tut, scarab, 12" **2,200.00**
Vase, Krackle-Kraft, #053, 3", from $350 to **450.00**
Vase, Majolica, Amaryllis shape, 6½, from $75 to......................**125.00**
Vase, Onyx (bl), swan hdls, #747, 5" **65.00**
Vase, Onyx (brn), shouldered, 4" **45.00**
Wall plaques, African Masks, mk USA, 10½", pr.....................**300.00**
Wall pocket, duck in flight...**95.00**

Buffalo Pottery

The founding of the Buffalo Pottery in Buffalo, New York, in 1901, was a direct result of the success achieved by John Larkin through his innovative methods of marketing 'Sweet Home Soap.' Choosing to omit 'middle-man' profits, Larkin preferred to deal directly with the consumer and offered premiums as an enticement for sales. The pottery soon proved a success in its own right and began producing advertising and commemorative items for other companies, as well as commercial tableware. In 1905 they introduced their Blue Willow line after extensive experimentation resulted in the development of the first successful underglaze cobalt achieved by an American company. Between 1905 and 1909, a line of pitchers and jugs were hand decorated in historical, literary, floral, and outdoor themes. Twenty-nine styles are known to have been made.

Their most famous line was Deldare Ware, the bulk of which was made from 1908 to 1909. It was hand decorated after illustrations by Cecil Aldin. Views of English life were portrayed in detail through unusual use of color against the natural olive green cast of the body. Today the 'Fallowfield Hunt' scenes are more difficult to locate than 'Scenes of Village Life in Ye Olden Days.' A Deldare calendar plate was made in 1910. These are very rare and are highly valued by collectors. The line was revived in 1923 and dropped again in 1925. Every piece was marked 'Made at Ye Buffalo Pottery, Deldare Ware Underglaze.' Most are dated, though date has no bearing on the value. Emerald Deldare was made on the same olive body and on standard Deldare Ware shapes, featured historical scenes and Art Nouveau decorations. Most pieces are found with a 1911 date stamp. Production was very limited due to the intricate, time-consuming detail. Needless to say, it is very rare and extremely desirable.

Abino Ware, most of which was made in 1912, also used standard Deldare shapes, but its colors were earthy and the decorations more delicately applied. Sailboats, windmills, and country scenes were favored motifs. These designs were achieved by overpainting transfer prints and were often signed by the artist. The ware is marked 'Abino' in hand-printed block letters. Production was limited; and as a result, examples of this line are scarce today.

Commercial or institutional ware was another of Buffalo Pottery's crowning achievements. In 1917 vitrified china production began, and the firm produced for accounts worldwide. After 1956 all of their wares bore the name Buffalo China. Buffalo China (commercial and institu-

tional ware) is being produced today by Oneida Silver Company.

Our advisor for this category is Lila Shrader; she is listed in the Directory under California.

See also Bluebird China.

Abino

Cup & saucer, nautical theme w/sailboats, Harris.....................**440.00**
Plate, Point Abino, Canada, sailing ships, 7¼" **335.00**
Plate, Portland, ME, Portland Head Light, Stuart, 9½"............**490.00**
Plate, windmill overlooking bay, blk lining, Harris, 8¼".............**470.00**
Teapot, nautical theme, Stuart & Harris, 5¼"............................**880.00**
Tray, card w/tab hdls, windmill & boat overlooking inlet, Stuart, 8"...**550.00**
Tray, windmill, farmhouse overlooking bay, Harris, 10½x14" **825.00**
Vase, sailboats on high seas, baluster shape, Harris, 8½"..........**1,650.00**

Deldare

Ashtray/match holder, Scenes of Village Life, 3½x6¼" **715.00**
Bowl, cereal; Ye Olden Days, no rim, 5"..**330.00**
Bowl, cereal; Ye Olden Days, no rim, 6¼"....................................**185.00**
Bowl, fern; Ye Village Tavern, 8" dia **475.00**
Bowl, fruit; Fallowfield Hunt, The Death, 9", from $550 to........**715.00**
Bowl, fruit; octagonal, tab hdls, Emerald, 10"........................**3,445.00**
Bowl, fruit; Ye Olden Days, sm, 5¾"..**180.00**
Bowl, fruit; Ye Village Tavern, 3¾x9¼", from $385 to................**450.00**
Bowl, nut; Ye Lion Inn, 8"..**665.00**
Bowl, soup; Fallowfield Hunt, Breaking Cover, 9", from $250 to...**465.00**
Candle holder/match holder, Village Scene, 5" **495.00**
Candlestick, Village Scene, drilled for wiring, 8½"......................**355.00**
Candlesticks, Village Scene, not drilled, 9", pr **900.00**
Chamberstick, To Advise in a Whisper, shield-bk w/hdl, 6"....**1,250.00**
Chocolate pot, Ye Village Street, w/lid, 10¼"..........................**1,750.00**
Creamer, Fallowfield Hunt, Breaking Cover, angular style, 2¾x4½" ..**495.00**
Cup & saucer, bouillon; Fallowfield Hunt, hdls **935.00**
Cup & saucer, chocolate; Ye Village Street..................................**490.00**
Cup & saucer, Ye Olden Days, from $110 to.................................**185.00**
Humidor, Emerald, Dr Syntax w/Lady Holding a Whip, w/lid, 7"..**1,160.00**
Humidor, Emerald, There Was an Old Sailor, w/lid, 5x8", from $925 to...**1,400.00**
Humidor, Ye Lion Inn, w/lid, 7⅜x6½"..**800.00**
Inkwell set, Emerald, 2 inkwells (1 w/lid), +14" tray...............**6,050.00**
Mug, Emerald, Dr Syntax Again Filled Up His Glass, 4¼".........**455.00**
Mug, Fallowfield Hunt, At the Three Pigeons, 4½", from $220 to..**315.00**
Mug, Fallowfield Hunt, mini, 2½", from $715 to.........................**880.00**
Mug, Fallowfield Hunt, Three Pigeons, w/custom lid, 4½" **580.00**
Mug, Scenes of Village Life, mini, 2½".......................................**1,200.00**
Mug, Village Life in Olden Days, child sz, 2½"............................**475.00**
Mug, Ye Lion Inn, 4¼", from $165 to **245.00**
Pitcher, Emerald, Dr Syntax Amused w/Pat in the Pond, 7x6" ..**1,045.00**
Pitcher, Fallowfield Hunt, Breaking Cover, 9", from $585 to......**660.00**
Pitcher, This Amazed Me, 8¾", from $330 to...............................**465.00**
Pitcher, To Spare an Old Broken Soldier, 7".................................**410.00**
Plaque, Emerald, Dr Syntax Sells Grizzle, 13" **1,435.00**
Plaque, Emerald, peacock in full splendor, 12" **4,675.00**
Plaque, Friday, Monks at Banquet Table, Gerhardt, 12"...........**2,300.00**
Plaque, Thursday, Monks Fishing, M Crooker, 12"...................**2,200.00**
Plate, calendar for 1910, 9½", from $1,550 to **2,100.00**
Plate, chop; Fallowfield Hunt, The Start, 13½", from $330 to ...**580.00**
Plate, Emerald, Dr Syntax Making a Discovery, 10", from $900 to ...**1,050.00**
Plate, Emerald, Dr Syntax Pursued by a Bull, 9½"......................**935.00**
Plate, Emerald, Dr Syntax Star Gazing, 9¼", from $660 to.........**825.00**
Plate, Emerald, Misfortune at Tulip Hall, 8½", from $330 to......**445.00**
Plate, Emerald, Yankee Doodle, 10" **2,090.00**
Plate, Fallowfield Hunt, Breaking Cover, 7¼" **110.00**

Plate, Fallowfield Hunt, 6¼" **135.00**
Plate, Ye Olden Times, 9¼" **100.00**
Plate, Ye Town Crier, 8¼", from $125 to **165.00**
Plate, Ye Village Gossips, 10" **185.00**
Punch bowl, Fallowfield Hunt, Breaking Cover, Death…, 14½".......**10,725.00**
Punch cups, cottage scene, 2¼", set of 8........................**4,675.00**
Shaving cup, Ye Razor, 3½x6½", NM **1,425.00**
Sugar bowl, Fallowfield Hunt, open, 6-sided, 4" dia **375.00**
Tankard, Emerald, Dancing Mice & Owl, 12¼"........**4,950.00**
Tankard, Emerald, Dr Syntax Entertained…, 10½", from $2,000 to...**2,585.00**
Tankard, Fallowfield Hunt, The Hunt Supper, 12¼", from $1,270 to .**1,750.00**
Tankard, The Great Controversy, 12½", from $660 to....**1,185.00**
Tea tile, Traveling in Ye Olden Days, 6" dia, from $250 to **440.00**
Teapot, Scenes of Village Life in Ye Olden Days, w/lid, 3¾" **390.00**
Teapot, Scenes of Village Life in Ye Olden Days, w/lid, 5¾" **510.00**
Tiles, Fallowfield Hunt, Breakfast 3 Pigeons, 6 8" form table top..**3,850.00**
Tray, card; Fallowfield Hunt, w/tab hdls, 7".......................**385.00**
Tray, Dancing Ye Minuet, 9¼x12" **620.00**
Tray, Emerald, w/hdls, companion to octagonal bowl, 13" **1,840.00**
Tray, relish; Ye Olden Times, 2x12"..................................**648.00**
Tray, tea; Heirlooms, 10½x12", from $495 to **565.00**
Vase, Village Scene, w/3 men in conversation, corset shape, 7"..**490.00**
Vase, 3 fashionable ladies/lady & gentleman, 9"......................**1,245.00**

Miscellaneous

Bowl, Bonrea, rich bl w/rich gold trim, oval, 9" **45.00**
Bowl, cereal; Blue Willow, 6" **38.00**
Bowl, cereal; Gaudy Willow, 6"......................................**110.00**
Bowl, salad; Blue Willow, sqd, 3x7½"..............................**280.00**
Bowl, serving; Roycroft, 1926, 7½x6x1⅞"......................**179.00**
Bowl, soup; Oneida, gr & wht stripes, w/rim, 9"....................**6.00**
Bowl, soup/cereal; Roycroft, 1990s, from $12 to **22.00**
Butter pat, Blue Willow, 3", from $22 to **42.00**
Butter pat, desert cactus, comical rabbit, full color, 1930s, 3" **45.00**
Butter pat, First Baptist Church/Vallejo in script, 1921 ....**28.00**
Butter pat, Forget-Me-Not, rich gold, scalloped edge, 3"............**28.00**
Butter pat, Gaudy Willow, 3" **85.00**
Butter pat, gr floral border design, 1922, 3" **9.00**
Butter pat, HC against shoreline scene, 1926, 3" **29.00**
Butter pat, ICC w/crossed golf clubs & tennis rackets, 1920s, 3" ..**48.00**
Butter pat, Masonic emblem, Gaithersburg MD, 1920s, 3" **19.00**
Butter pat, red rooster serving cocktails, Chicago in blk, 3¼".......**56.00**
Butter pat, US Forest Service logo, gr on wht, 3" **65.00**
Butter pat, Vienna, 3", from $8 to **20.00**
Butter pat, WBH interlocking script, blk & wht, '20s-30s, 3¼" ..**20.00**
Cake plate, pk & yel roses w/greenery & rich gold, rtcl hdls, 10½" ...**40.00**
Canisters, Cinnamon/Cloves/(1 plain), no mk, brn letters, 3", 3 for .**65.00**
Canisters, Coffee/Sugar/Flour, blk letters on ivory, 6½", 3 for.....**185.00**
Catalog, Larkin, 224 pgs, Fall/Winter 1929, 8x10¾" **35.00**
Chamber pot, Chrysanthemum, teal gr, hdl, w/lid, 6¾" **120.00**
Chamber pot, wht w/gold trim, hdl, no lid, 5¼" **45.00**
Child's cup & saucer, Roosevelt Bears, G gold.............................**435.00**
Child's feeding dish, Campbell's Kids, gold trim, no alphabet, 7¾"...**110.00**
Child's tea set, pot+cr+sug w/lid, +2 c/s+1 4" plate **265.00**
Chocolate pot, wht w/rich gold, initials HC, w/lid, 8"...................**75.00**
Condiment jar, narrow gr stripe on ea pc, w/lid, 2¾" **20.00**
Creamer, Blue Willow, 4" **70.00**
Creamer, ind; Blue Willow, no hdl, 1920 ....**45.00**
Creamer, ind; Fairview, no hdl, 1920s..............................**22.00**
Creamer, ind; gr floral border, no hdl, 2¾" **9.00**
Creamer, ind; HFH, gr on wht, no hdl, 1920s, 2½" **38.00**
Creamer, ind; SCECo in blk on ivory, w/hdl, 1920s, 2½" **40.00**
Creamer, ind; Westover Hotel w/WH intertwined, no hdl, 2¼"...**28.00**

Creamer, Roosevelt Bears, 2¾".......................................**325.00**
Creamer, Yosemite Park, Ahwahnee, geometrics, blk/brn on ivory, 4" ...**28.00**
Cup & saucer, AAA auto club, California, demitasse **26.00**
Cup & saucer, Blue Lune, 1920s......................................**11.00**
Cup & saucer, Blue Willow...**39.00**
Cup & saucer, Blue Willow, demitasse.............................**45.00**
Cup & saucer, Bonrea, from $9 to **18.00**
Cup & saucer, Prince pattern, 1927....................................**9.00**
Egg cup, Blue Willow, pedestal, 2¼".................................**45.00**
Egg cup, Blue Willow, 3¼"...**48.00**
Fish set, ea w/different fish, 15x11" platter+6 9" plates **300.00**
Gravy boat, Blue Willow, 8x5"..**75.00**
Gravy boat, Bonrea, rich bl, 9x5", +8x4" liner....................**42.00**
Jardiniere, Chrysanthemum, rich gold trim, 11⅜x15½".............**660.00**
Jardiniere, Marina Flora design, deep bl on wht w/gold, 10" **220.00**
Jug, Blue Willow, Chicago style, 5" **330.00**
Jug, Cinderella, 6¼", from $360 to **470.00**
Jug, John Paul Jones, bl & wht, 9" **790.00**
Jug, Mason, 8¼"..**440.00**
Jug, Robin Hood, 8¼"...**465.00**
Jug, The Gunner, 6" **340.00**
Mug, advertising; Bing & Nathan, Buffalo NY, 4½" **55.00**
Mug, Roycroft, early issue, 3½" **145.00**
Mug, Roycroft, Oneida, 3" **25.00**
Mustard, Alpine in bl script, 1927, w/lid, 2¾" **25.00**
Pitcher, Geranium, mc, 5½" **220.00**
Pitcher, Geranium, teal gr, 5½" **90.00**
Pitcher, Pilgrim, 9", from $400 to **525.00**
Pitcher, Roosevelt Bears, 8¼"..**2,200.00**
Plaque, The Gunner, hunter w/rifle & dog, teal gr, 9½" **150.00**
Plate, advertising; Toucan, Home Furn Co, Indianapolis, 7½"......**65.00**
Plate, Brown Willow, Oneida, 10" **13.00**
Plate, Brown Willow, 1920s, 10", from $20 to....................**28.00**
Plate, Christmas, Dickens, 1960, 9½", from $19 to **26.00**
Plate, commemorative; Faneuil Hall, Boston, bl & wht, 10¼" ...**55.00**
Plate, commemorative; Main St, Buffalo NY, teal gr, 7¼" **46.00**
Plate, commemorative; Niagara Falls, teal gr & wht, 10¼"..........**35.00**
Plate, Cooperstown, Indian statue, 7½".............................**50.00**
Plate, Dr Syntax Disputing the Landlady, rich bl & wht, 9¼"....**220.00**
Plate, El Morocco, 10"...**50.00**
Plate, Game Bird series, American woodcock, teal gr, 9¼"...........**69.00**
Plate, Lady & the Tramp, 11" **30.00**
Plate, Mandalay pattern, 5½"..**4.00**
Plate, Masonic emblem, 1922, 9½" **11.00**
Plate, New Bedford Fifty Years Ago, scalloped edge, tan on wht, 10¼"..**125.00**
Plate, Niagara Falls, mc on teal gr+gold, 7¼" **95.00**
Plate, Roosevelt Bears, rich gold, 6 lg & 5 sm scenes, 10"..........**785.00**
Plate, Roosevelt Bears, scalloped edge, 7¼" **485.00**
Plate, Roycroft, 1988, 5½" **25.00**
Plate, World's Fair, Obelisk & Sphere logo, gr & wht, 1939, 10½"..**175.00**
Platter, Dogwood, scalloped edge, 1982, 10x13" **25.00**
Platter, Dr Syntax Advertisement for a Wife, rich bl & wht, 14x11"...**330.00**
Platter, LaFrance Rose, border of teal gr roses, 15x11" **22.00**
Platter, Red Willow, Oneida, 5x8½"..................................**11.00**
Platter, Town of Massena logo, bl on wht, 1954, 9¼x13"............**38.00**
Punch bowl, Tom & Jerry, Colorido body, 11" bowl+6 4" hdld cups...**250.00**
Relish dish, Blue Willow, dory (boat shape), 1925, 7½x3½" **20.00**
Sauce boat, Blue Willow, hdls, w/attached liner, 5½x7½" **225.00**
Shakers, Roycroft, early issue, 3", pr...............................**555.00**
Spittoon, Chrysanthemum, teal gr, 9"...............................**225.00**
Spittoon, gold stripes on gold body, 1925, 4¼" **42.00**
Sugar bowl, Blue Willow, hdls, w/lid, 5½"..........................**65.00**
Sugar bowl, Roycroft, 1928, hdls, w/lid **215.00**
Teapot, Blue Willow, sqd, w/lid, 6"...................................**290.00**

Teapot, Gaudy Willow, w/internal tea caddy & lid, 6" 360.00
Teapot w/lid, Argyle w/internal tea infusor, 1925, 6"..................158.00
Toilet set, roses, bowl+pitcher+chamber pot w/lid+sm pitcher+vase ...350.00
Tray, pin, Bowman Hotel, 1922, 3½x5"...7.00
Vase, Geranium, rnd rose-bowl style w/closed mouth, 4" 120.00
Vase, Multifleure, baluster shape, 8"...250.00
Vase, w/2 ornate hdls & ruffled collar, 1905, 10" 90.00

Buggy Steps

In the old West with its horse-drawn vehicles, iron buggy steps were an every day requirement. From cart, buckboard, wagon, and carriage, they were a necessary supplement to daily travel. Many patented styles and designs were manufactured and every approved design was assigned a patent number. Today, these are very collectible.

Steps with embossed names can still be found on rare occasions. Specialty steps, such as those hand forged by blacksmiths and carriage manufacturers, can be and often are considered works of art. Today large surrey steps with folding mud guards are commanding increasingly higher prices. Name or no-name steps have been previously listed in earlier editions; consult those issues for more information. Values suggested in the listings that follow are for quality steps in excellent to good condition. Because type and size are other worth-assessing factors to consider, only general values are given here. Our advisor for this category is John Waddell; he is listed in the Directory under Texas.

Emerson, oval, tee-mount, 5x3½", $75.00; Peru, round, tee-mount, 4½", $70.00; Staver, oval, tri-fork mount, 4½x3½", $70.00. (Photo courtesy John Waddell)

Bolt-on, 2-hole, sm pad, from $10 to...15.00
Carriage, special manufacture, folding stage, rare, from $120 to .210.00
Mtd, tee-mount, from $15 to 25.00
Mtd, tri-fork, from $15 to...25.00
Mtd, 3-point w/branch, from $25 to 35.00
Name, ornate, scarce, from $50 to 75.00
Surrey, bar & branch arm, lg, from $90 to......................................135.00

Burmese

Burmese glass was patented in 1885 by the Mount Washington Glass Co. It is typically shaded from canary yellow to a rosy salmon color. The yellow is produced by the addition of uranium oxide to the mix. The salmon color comes from the addition of gold salts and is achieved by reheating the object (partially) in the furnace. It is thus called 'heat sensitive' glass. Thomas Webb of England was licensed to produce Burmese and often added more gold, giving an almost fuchsia tinge to the salmon in some cases. They called their glass 'Queen's Burmese,' and this is

sometimes etched on the base of the object. This is not to be confused with Mount Washington's 'Queen's Design,' which refers to the design painted on the object. Both companies added decoration to many pieces. Mount Washington-Pairpoint produced some Burmese in the late 1920s and Gundersen and Bryden in the 1950s and 1970s, but the color and shapes are different.

Our advisors for this category are Dolli and Wilfred Cohen; they are listed in the Directory under California. In the listings that follow, examples are assumed to have the satin finish unless noted 'shiny.' See also Lamps, Fairy.

Vase, Mt. Washington, Egyptian desert scene with gold, oviform, 11½", $2,500.00. (Photo courtesy Skinner Inc.)

Bell, shiny w/crystal hdl topped w/3 stacked Burmese balls, 7½" ...375.00
Bonbon, Mt WA, shiny, 3 appl yel prunts, heart-shape rim, hdl, 6½" ...835.00
Bowl, berry; Mt WA, pie-crust rim, 2x9".......................................950.00
Bowl, Mt WA, rectangular rim, very thin, 2x5x4½" 425.00
Bowl, Mt WA, rectangular w/ruffled top, 3½x10½x7" 500.00
Bowl, Pairpoint, loosely ruffled, 1920s, 3½x12½" 495.00
Candlesticks, shiny, 5½", pr...395.00
Cracker jar, acorns/oak leaves w/gilt on yel to peach, SP lid, 7x5"........600.00
Cruet, Mt WA, shiny, squat ribbed body, mushroom stopper, 7" ...1,250.00
Epergne w/4 3½" fairy lamp shades in metal holder, 10" ruffled base.2,000.00
Hall light, Mt WA, Hobnail, w/ceiling mt...................................2,500.00
Pitcher, Gundersen, ftd, strap hdl, 5¾x6" 375.00
Pitcher, Mt WA, tightly ruffled, str flaring sides, 5½" 400.00
Pitcher, tankard; Mt WA, scarce sz, 7¼x4"...................................950.00
Pitcher, Webb, acorns on pine branches, ruffled, 3" 300.00
Plate, Pairpoint, 1920s, 10"...275.00
Rose bowl, Mt WA, ribbed, tightly crimped rim thrusts upward, 5x9" ..750.00
Rose bowl, Mt WA, ruffled, amber ruffled ft, egg shape, 4".........275.00
Rose bowl, Mt WA, ruffled top, 2½" 150.00
Rose bowl, Webb, floral spray, egg shape on wide ruffled ft, 4" ...395.00
Rose bowl, Webb, floral/leaves, 6-sided rim, 3½" 395.00
Rose bowl, Webb, holly berries on leafy stems, 6-sided rim, 3½" ...395.00
Rose bowl, Webb, inverted scalloped rim, spherical, 3"................175.00
Shaker, Mt WA, ribbed cylinder, 2-part metal top, 4¼".............265.00
Sherbet, Pairpoint, 1930s, 3½", +6½" plate..................................295.00
Sugar bowl, Mt WA, petticoat shape w/ruffled top, open, 3x4" ..425.00
Toothpick holder, Mt WA, Dmn Quilt, shiny, tricon rim, 2x2½"...595.00
Toothpick holder, Mt WA, sq top, bulbous bottom, 2¾" 325.00
Toothpick holder, Mt WA, tricorner, 2" 395.00
Tumbler, Mt WA, 3¾" 175.00
Vase, berries/leaves, ruffled, stick neck, Queen's, 3"....................450.00
Vase, florals cascade from wht-dotted rim, stick-neck gourd shape, 8"...750.00
Vase, jack-in-pulpit; Mt WA, pie-crust rim, 9" 685.00
Vase, jack-in-pulpit; Mt WA, prunus blossoms/wht dots/gold, 12½" ..1,450.00
Vase, jack-in-pulpit; Mt WA, tightly crimped, yel trn-down rim, 15"....920.00
Vase, jack-in-pulpit; Mt WA, wild flowers/vines, crimped rim, 14" 1,450.00
Vase, jack-in-pulpit; Pairpoint, 5¼x6¾" 575.00
Vase, lily; Mt WA, scarce sz, 7"..375.00

Vase, lily; Mt WA, shiny, EX color, 12¾" 875.00
Vase, lily; Mt WA, unusual irregular base, 14" 875.00
Vase, lily; Mt WA, 12" 750.00
Vase, lily; Mt WA, 15" 950.00
Vase, lily; Mt WA, 3-lobe rim, EX color w/refired yel lip, 19" .1,000.00
Vase, lily; shiny, on mirrored base w/monogram, 4x4" 225.00
Vase, lily; Webb, mc florals, ormolu base, Queen's, 9½" 1,200.00
Vase, Mt WA, bamboo tubes, gold/brn/gr/tan/rust, gourd form, 11½" 2,250.00
Vase, Mt WA, branch w/2 lg mc flowers & enamel dots, stick neck, 10" ..1,785.00
Vase, Mt WA, daisies, bulbous w/short can neck, 3x3½" 695.00
Vase, Mt WA, egg-shaped w/ruffled top, yel ruffled ft, 4" 325.00
Vase, Mt WA, fern on lily form in Egyptian-style gold Dunham mt, 6"....545.00
Vase, Mt WA, floral sprays ea side, urn w/gold hdls/rim/ft, 6" 750.00
Vase, Mt WA, gourd shape w/stick neck, 8", pr 850.00
Vase, Mt WA, gourd shape w/stick neck, 10x5½" 750.00
Vase, Mt WA, Grecian urn form, hdls extend above rim to shoulder, 7"...1,250.00
Vase, Mt WA, Oriental poppy, maroon/yel/gr/gilt, rnd w/stick neck, 11" ..2,150.00
Vase, Mt WA, ovoid w/sqd top, 2½" 150.00
Vase, Mt WA, ovoid w/6-sided rim, 2¾" 200.00
Vase, Mt WA, shiny, spherical w/stick neck, 6" 350.00
Vase, Mt WA, shiny w/appl Burmese flowers, 4-pinch rim, 5x7", NM....4,250.00
Vase, Mt WA, slim elongated goblet form, 9x1½" 1,150.00
Vase, Mt WA, 8 ribs, ogee sides, petal rim, 4¼x5½" .....,............575.00
Vase, Pairpoint, ftd chalice form, petal rim, dbl-knob stem, '20s, 10"...950.00
Vase, Pairpoint, petal top, incurvate sides, 1920s, 8½" 450.00
Vase, prunus blossoms in bl, tightly crimped/flared rim, 4½x3" ..375.00
Vase, spherical w/waisted neck, ruffled rim, 3", pr 250.00
Vase, Webb, berries/leaves, ruffled, stick neck, Queen's, 3¼"......350.00
Vase, Webb, berries/vines, bulbous w/6-crimp top, ftd, 4¾" 450.00
Vase, Webb, berries/vines, 6-sided pinched-in rim, 3½x3½" 475.00
Vase, Webb, berries/vines in gr/gold, mk Pat, 6¼" 795.00
Vase, Webb, crimped top, bulbous, 3", pr 300.00
Vase, Webb, floral sprays, bottle form, 9¾" 950.00
Vase, Webb, fuchsias/leaves, squat w/flaring trumpet neck, 3x3"...400.00

Butter Molds and Stamps

The art of decorating butter began in Europe during the reign of Charles II. This practice was continued in America by the farmer's wife who sold her homemade butter at the weekly market to earn extra money during hard times. A mold or stamp with a special design, hand carved either by her husband or a local craftsman, not only made her product more attractive but also helped identify it as hers. The pattern became the trademark of Mrs. Smith, and all who saw it knew that this was her butter. It was usually the rule that no two farms used the same mold within a certain area, thus the many variations and patterns available to the collector today. The most valuable are those which have animals, birds, or odd shapes. The most sought-after motifs are the eagle, cow, fish, and rooster. These works of early folk art are quickly disappearing from the market.

Molds

Acorn (dbl) & leaves, 5½x4½" dia 115.00
Anchor, rectangular, 5x4" 195.00
Beaver on log, EX detail, split in hdl, VG....................................79.00
Birds in nests, worm holes, 2-pc, screw eyes ea end, 1⅝x11¾"...130.00
Clover Vale Dairy, Clover Vale in 4 sections, 10⅞x3¾" 60.00
Cow on wavy grass, case has age crack, 4⅝" dia........................110.00
Fish, EX patina, scratch mks, lollipop hdl, 3¼" W 195.00
Flower, plunger-type, walnut, 5¾x4¾" dia 90.00
Flower (dbl) w/2 buds & leaves, crack in case, 4⅛x6"................135.00
Flower (stylized), cvd border, rectangular, 19th C, 2½x8x4¾" ...235.00
Flowers & leaf, 7x5"+hdl, EX...85.00

Flowers & leaves, hinged, ca 1930-40, 2¼x6" sq 150.00
Leaf, 1-lb, 4⅝", VG..80.00
Pineapple, plunger-type, Pat 1866, made of pine, 3½x2" dia 135.00
Sheaths of Wheat, PA Dutch mortise joints, EX 225.00
Sunflower & leaves, plunger-type, 5x3½" dia 75.00
Swan, plunger-type, ca 1920s, 4x3½" dia 70.00
Swan (stylized), 3½" dia...145.00
Turkey, Meadow Gold, Beatrice Creamery Co, 2¾", M (EX box) ...85.00
Wheat, 3½x3¾"+plunger..95.00
Wheat sheaf, dbl, 3-pc, 4⅝x2¾" 85.00
4-leaf clover, mended crack, 1-lb 85.00
4-pattern, hinged, 5⅜x6" sq..215.00

Stamps

Left to right: Floral intaglio design with fluted border, American, 1850s, 4½", $80.00; Double, intaglio star and leaves with fluted border, floral pattern on reverse, small age crack, 5", $220.00; Maltese cross 'klappmodel' mold, five-section with various carvings including lady at pump, 6½", $420.00; Tulip design with carved and chipped border, 1830s, 4", $270.00; Floral over leaf design, deeply carved, lollipop handle, 1830s, 3" diameter, $210.00. (Photo courtesy Aston Macek Auctioneers and Appraisers)

Acorns/oak leaves, EX cvg, name in border, 5" dia 85.00
Deer, buck at fence w/tree, 3½" dia, VG- 295.00
Deer (X-hatched) & sun, zigzag border, no hdl, 4" dia 550.00
Eagle (X-hatched) & sun, 1-pc hdl, lg chip in edge, 4⅝" dia......360.00
Eagle & star, dbl-border, old patina, 4½" dia, EX 350.00
Eagle w/shield, leaf border, 4¼" dia 360.00
Fern & leaves, 4" dia 55.00
Flower (thistle?) inset nailed hdl, age crack, semicircular, 7" L....440.00
Heart w/X-hatching & leaves, pegged hdl, semicircular, 7" L 690.00
Hearts & dmns w/notched edges alternate, 2⅞" dia....................135.00
Maple leaf, EX cvg, 19th C, 3½" 95.00
Pineapple, inset nailed hdl, scrubbed, semicircular, 7" L.............440.00
Roses, leaves in middle, rectangular, 6½x2"................................285.00
Sheaf of wheat, inset hdl, lt wear, semicircular, 7" L 250.00
Sheaf of wheat, rectangular, 4½" L...440.00
Sheaf of wheat, 4¾' dia 160.00
Star flower (shallow) surrounded by hearts, cvd flower on hdl, 4½" ...140.00
Strawberries w/leaf, threaded hdl, well done, age cracks, 3¼" dia.......110.00
Strawberry & leaves, 4" dia 70.00
Tulip & stars on raised panels w/notched edge, hdl missing, 4¾x3"..300.00
Wheat, EX patina & cvg, no splits, 3¾" dia 125.00

Buttonhooks

The earliest known written reference to buttonhooks (shoe hooks, glove hooks, or collar buttoners) is dated 1611. They became a necessary implement in the 1850s when tight-fitting high-button shoes became fashionable. Later in the nineteenth century, ladies' button gloves and men's button-on collars and cuffs dictated specific types of buttoners, some with a closed wire loop instead of a hook end. Both shoes and gloves used as many as twenty-four buttons each. Usage began to wane in the late 1920s following a fashion change to low-cut laced shoes and the invention of the zipper. There was a brief resurgence of use following the 1948 movie 'High Button Shoes.' For a simple, needed utilitarian device, buttonhook handles were made from a surprising variety of materials: natural wood, bone, ivory, agate and mother-of-pearl, plain steel, celluloid, aluminum, iron, lead and pewter, artistic copper, brass, silver, gold, and many other materials, in lengths that varied from under 2" to over 20". Many designs folded or retracted, and buttonhooks were often combined with shoehorns and other useful implements. Stamped steel buttonhooks often came free with the purchase of shoes, gloves, or collars. Material, design, workmanship, condition, and relative scarcity are the primary market value factors. Prices range from $1.00 to over $500.00, with most being in the $10.00 to $100.00 range. Buttonhooks are fairly easy to find, and they are interesting to display.

Our advisor for this category is Richard Mathes; he is listed in the Directory under Ohio. See also The Buttonhook Society listing in the Directory under Clubs, Newsletters, and Catalogs.

Buttonhook/penknife, ivory side plates, man's **50.00**
Collar buttoner, stamped steel, advertising, closed end, 3" **20.00**
Glove hook, gold-plated, retractable, 3" **90.00**
Glove hook, loop end, agate hdl, 2½" **60.00**
Shoe hook, colored celluloid hdl, 8" **15.00**
Shoe hook, lathe-trn hardwood hdl, dk finish, 8" **15.00**
Shoe hook, SP w/blade, repousse hdl, Pat Jan 5 1892, 5" **40.00**
Shoe hook, stamped steel, advertising, 5" **8.00**
Shoe hook, sterling, floral & geometrics, 8" **55.00**
Shoe hook, sterling, Nouveau lady's face, 6½" **75.00**
Shoe hook, sterling, W w/arrow, hammered Florentine decor, mk...**55.00**
Shoe hook/shoehorn, combination, steel & celluloid, 9" **35.00**

Bybee

The Bybee Pottery was founded in 1845 in the small town of Bybee, Kentucky, by the Cornelison family. Their earliest wares were primarily stoneware churns and jars. Today the work is carried on by sixth-generation Cornelison potters who still use the same facilities and production methods to make a more diversified line of pottery. From a fine white clay mined only a few miles from the potting shed itself, the shop produces vases, jugs, dinnerware, and banks in a variety of colors, some of which are shipped to the larger cities to be sold in department stores and specialty shops. The bulk of their wares, however, is sold to the thousands of tourists who are attracted to the pottery each year.

Baking dish, maroon, tab hdls, 2x9½" dia **25.00**
Bowl, dk red, deep, 10" **25.00**
Candle holders, rose, saucer type w/finger hold, pr **15.00**
Creamer, chicken shape, cobalt bl, 5½" **17.50**
Cup, dessert; maroon, 2x3½" dia **8.00**
Flowerpot, navy bl, ruffled rim. 10x7" dia **15.00**
Mug, bl specked top w/HP bluebird on side, bbl shape, 5" **15.00**
Piggy bank, gr sponge, 3x5½" **10.00**
Pitcher, purple sponge on wht, 72-oz **25.00**
Plate, dinner; bl, mk #211, 10½" **25.00**
Skillet, cobalt bl, mk #1313, 1x5½" (w/hdl) **16.50**
Soup tureen, purple, w/lid, 3-qt **40.00**
Teapot, feldspathic moss gr, dome lid, pre-1969, mk BB, 5¾" **50.00**
Vase, brn, 2 loop hdls, 6½" **60.00**

Cabat

From beginning experimentation with pottery in New York City around 1940, through several different types of clay, designs, and glazes, and relocation to Arizona, the Rose Cabat 'Feelie,' so named because 'it feels so good,' evolved into present forms and glazes in the late 1950s. Rose was aided and encouraged through the years by her late husband Erni. Their small 'weed pots' are readily recognizable by their light weight, tiny thin necks, and soft glazes. Pieces are marked with a hand-incised 'Cabat' on the bottom.

Vase, aqua blending to charcoal blk, gourd shape, #841, 3¾x2".**300.00**
Vase, bl & gr matt, 3¾" **190.00**
Vase, charcoal matt w/blk flecks, slender, incised mk/62/XI, 3½x2".**300.00**
Vase, dk bl w/lt gr highlights, 4" **200.00**
Vase, gray to brn matt dripping over unglazed bottom, cylindrical, 6"...**500.00**
Vase, ivory/tan/brn matt, 8" dia **290.00**
Vase, lime gr w/tan highlights, 5½" **475.00**

Vase, lime to medium green with many gray crystals, 3", $300.00. (Photo courtesy Cincinnati Art Galleries)

Vase, mustard yel drips on yel matt, spherical, incised mk/A, 2½"...**195.00**
Vase, pk w/yel & tan crystals, 3½"...**240.00**

Calendar Plates

Calendar plates were advertising giveaways most popular from about 1906 until the late twenties. They were decorated with colorful underglaze decals of lovely ladies, flowers, animals, birds and, of course, the twelve months of the year of their issue. During the 1950s they came into vogue again but never to the extent they were originally. Those with exceptional detailing, or those with scenes of a particular activity are most desirable, so are any from before 1906.

1909, bird w/1909 ribbon in mouth, 8¼" **65.00**
1909, cherries & strawberry blossoms, Imperial, 7½"....................**60.00**
1909, P Cummings Confectionary & Ice Cream, 8" **55.00**
1910, boys swimming, James Whitcomb Riley quote, 9⅞" **65.00**
1910, lighthouse on rocks, gold rim, Pope Gosser China, 8¼".......**55.00**
1910, magnolias w/holly leaves & berries, Am China Co, 8½" **60.00**
1910, man w/creel stream fishing, 7¼" **40.00**
1910, months on pages of open book, gr ivy & forget-me-nots, 6¾".**40.00**
1910, Washington's Old Home at Mt Vernon, 9⅛" **50.00**
1910, 2 winged cherubs ringing bell, Woman's Relief Corp, 8½"..**85.00**
1911, Abe Lincoln center, 9" **150.00**
1911, girl w/buggy walks w/boy tooting horn, 8¾"........................**70.00**
1911, sea & shoreline w/sm boat on beach, 7⅝"............................**60.00**
1911-12, dbl-year, pk ribbons & roses, 8½"....................................**80.00**
1912, fruit & daisies, gold scalloped edge, 7¼"..............................**55.00**
1912, Lincoln, Garfield & McKinley, Am flag, 9¼" **70.00**
1912, Teddy Roosevelt, greenery & snowflakes, 8¾".....................**95.00**
1913, Rainbow Falls, Yosemite Valley, 9⅜"....................................**95.00**
1914, Washington Capitol, gold scalloped rim, 9⅛"......................**65.00**

1917, silver vase w/pk roses, 7" **60.00**
1917, steamship Mayflower, Am flag, +4 other flags, 9¼" **65.00**
1922, grapes & leaves, Pioneer Flour Mills, Texas, 8¼".............**75.00**
1956, windmill w/gold floral, squarish, 10¼" dia.....................**15.00**
1957, Community Grade School, Madison City IL Centennial, 10" .**45.00**
1967, Fox Terrier head, Walter's Auction Gallery, 9" **27.00**

Calendars

Calendars are collected for their colorful prints, often attributed to a well-recognized artist of the period. Advertising calendars from the turn of the century often have a double appeal when representing a company whose tins, signs, store displays, etc., are also collectible. See also Parrish, Maxfield.

1916, girl beside bouquet, sailboat beyond, cardboard diecut, Geo. Weiss, 20½x10½", full pad, EX, $360.00.

1888, Hood's, die-cut girl, 8", NM..................................**165.00**
1888, Hood's, girl in bonnet, 7½", NM+.............................**90.00**
1890, Ivory Soap, months bound together, seasons illus, 9x6", VG..**40.00**
1892, Voltaic Compound, die-cut baby in bassinet, 10", NM **155.00**
1893, Hood's, boy & girl w/globe, 8½", NM.........................**175.00**
1894, CI Hood Co, Sweet Sixteen, girl in wht w/floral hat, EX .**145.00**
1897, Hood's, girl in purple hat, 7", NM.............................**155.00**
1898, Hood's, Sweet Sixteen, 9", EX+.................................**50.00**
1899, Fall River Gasworks, die-cut lady, 'I Cook w/Gas,' 12x7", EX..**150.00**
1900, Fall River Gasworks, mother/daughter make donuts, 15x10", EX .**300.00**
1900, United States Rubbers, diecut, trifold, EX.....................**40.00**
1902, Stillings Bros Flour, 2 girl chefs making bread, 14", EX+ ..**160.00**
1902, The Good Store, diecut, boy/girl/rabbits/wheelbarrow, 16", VG..**135.00**
1905, Hood's, butterfly shape w/2 girls, 8", EX+ **115.00**
1906, diecut, bust image of maiden fr by lilacs, 15", EX+............**145.00**
1906, Model Meat Market, 2 girls & cat in landscape, 18", EX+..**60.00**
1906, Snag-Proof Boots, period lady w/gun & elves, 12", NM **220.00**
1907, diecut, 2 boys on barrel playing in lily pond, 16", EX+ **100.00**
1907, Eichberg, diecut, kids/doves/birdhouse/flowers, 16", EX **100.00**
1907, Hood's, Halcyon Days, 12", EX+ **175.00**
1907, Metropolitan Life Insurance, 4 stages of womanhood, 29x8", EX .**115.00**
1908, Hood's, 2 boys & dog by fence, 8", NM **200.00**
1908, Louis Bell, diecut, girl in gr looking in hand mirror, 14", NM...**160.00**
1909, Hood's, Papa's Coming, 13", EX+...............................**170.00**
1909, JB Plummer, diecut, couple courting, floral border, 17", EX+ ..**160.00**
1909, Milwaukee Harvester Machines, couple w/baby, 20", VG+.**75.00**
1910, Dr Simmons, Indian maiden, 12", EX+.........................**175.00**
1911, diecut w/boy & puppies in basket, floral garland, 14", EX+.**50.00**
1911, Hood's, lady w/roses, 11", EX+.................................**215.00**

1912, Hood's, Donna Inez a Spanish Beauty, 10", EX+ **150.00**
1912, WS, diecut, kids on keg fr by floral vines/sign, 19", EX.....**160.00**
1913, Hood's, kids w/kittens, 7½", EX+ **200.00**
1914, Hood's, woman in red w/baby, 13", EX+ **165.00**
1915, Christmas scene, German litho (?), gilt fr, 20", EX+ **250.00**
1915, Holeproof Hosiery, coy girl in bathing suit, 16x9", VG.....**225.00**
1916, Weed Chains, yard long, 4 portraits fr by chained tires, fr, EX .**1,100.00**
1917, Dutch Boy Paints, famous image, 38x15", EX **90.00**
1918, Hood's, snow falling on girl in red, 10", NM...................**175.00**
1919, Swift's Premium, 4-sheet, working women of WWI, EX ...**145.00**
1921, Sharples, milkmaid w/cows, 22", VG+ **165.00**
1922, De Laval, girl w/rose, Haskell Coffin art, 24", EX.............**215.00**
1924, Western Ammunition, dog pulling blanket off couple, 31", EX+ ...**400.00**
1924, Winchester, duck hunt, 27", VG **150.00**
1926, Round Oak Stoves, emb, Doe-Wah-Jack on river bank, 21", NM- .**2,475.00**
1927, Nehi, beach girl w/bottle, 20", EX+ **250.00**
1932, Ellis Garage, damsels in distress w/car, 22x14", VG..........**125.00**
1932, On Time, Pennsylvania Railroad, complete, EX................**390.00**
1938, Dr Pepper, girl in gold gown, Earl Moran art, 33½", EX+ .**900.00**
1938, Nehi, girl at helm, R Armstrong art, 24", VG+ **365.00**
1940, Dr Pepper, top only, 2 ladies w/bottles, 12x16", NM+ **50.00**
1942, Clicquot Club, lady/boy, NM+ **125.00**
1942, Federal Trucks, girl in skimpy nautical outfit, 34", EX.........**60.00**
1942, McCormick Deering, boy playing horn, 20", EX+ **40.00**
1942, NuGrape, girl holding up bottle, 24x17", VG **100.00**
1942, Seven-Up, pinup girl, EX+ **140.00**
1942, Texaco, Zoe Mozart art, 19", NM **90.00**
1944, Lafayette Pharmacal, hunting & fishing, 18x8½", VG........**40.00**
1945, Dr Pepper, Kathryn Booth, 22", EX.............................**175.00**
1946, Kist, garden girl, 26", NM+......................................**180.00**
1946, Orange-Crush, girl w/toy panda bear, 30", VG...................**80.00**
1947, City Club Brewing Co, portrait of gent, 33", VG+ **35.00**
1947, NuGrape, 6-pg, 22", VG **60.00**
1948, Squirt, girl in red sweater, 23", NM **45.00**
1949, Grapette, formal garden scene, 11", NM **45.00**
1949, Squirt, girl drinking from bottle w/straw, NM **25.00**
1952, US Royal Tires, Medcalf girl in 2-pc on water skis, 33", EX...**60.00**
1953, Esquire, 9x12", w/orig envelope, EX.............................**150.00**
1958, Orange-Crush, couple w/bottles, 26", EX **35.00**

Caliente

Caliente was a line of colored dinnerware made by the Paden City Pottery Company in Paden City, West Virginia. It was produced during the 1930s and 1940s in tangerine, yellow, blue, green, and cobalt blue.

Bowl, cream soup **18.00**
Bowl, salad, 10" **28.00**
Bowl, 5¼" **10.00**
Bowl, 9" **20.00**
Candle holder **20.00**
Casserole **40.00**
Creamer **18.00**
Cup & saucer **15.00**
Plate, 6" **5.00**
Plate, 9½" **10.00**
Plate, 10" **17.50**
Platter, 12" **25.00**
Platter, 14" **28.00**
Shakers, pr **25.00**
Sugar bowl, w/lid **20.00**
Teapot **50.00**

California Faience

California Faience was the trade name used by William V. Bragdon and Chauncy R. Thomas on vases, bowls, and other artware produced at their pottery known as 'The Tile Shop' in Berkeley, California, from 1920 to 1930. Faience tile was the principal product of the business during these years and is the favorite with today's collectors. Items in a glossy glaze are rare and therefore more valuable. Tiles were marked 'California Faience' with a die stamp.

See also Tiles.

Vase, blue, pomegranate form, 11½", minimum value $1,200.00.

Trivet, flower basket, mc on wht w/dk bl border, 5¼" dia 150.00
Vase, bl matt, cylindrical, 6" 250.00
Vase, cobalt bl, smooth sides, 6" 240.00
Vase, glossy bl tones, bulbous bottom, 11" 310.00
Vase, glossy plum, vertical panels & ribs, short collar, 5x7" dia ..300.00
Vase, lt bl gloss, inverted rim, 4½" 120.00
Vase, lt gr on brn clay, conical, 8" 190.00
Vase, multitone bl gloss, 3½" 100.00

California Perfume Company

D.H. McConnell, Sr., founded the California Perfume Company (C.P. Company; C.P.C.) in 1886 in New York City. He had previously been a salesman for a book company, which he later purchased. His door-to-door sales usually involved the lady of the house, to whom he presented a complimentary bottle of inexpensive perfume. Upon determining his perfume to be more popular than his books, he decided that the manufacture of perfume might be more lucrative. He bottled toiletries under the name 'California Perfume Company' and a line of household products called 'Perfection.' In 1928 the name 'Avon' appeared on the label, and in 1939 the C.P.C. name was entirely removed from the product. The success of the company is attributed to the door-to-door sales approach and 'money back' guarantee offered by his first 'Depot Agent,' Mrs. P.F.E. Albee, known today as the 'Avon Lady.'

The company's containers are quite collectible today, especially the older, hard-to-find items. Advanced collectors seek 'go with' items labeled Goetting & Co., New York; Goetting's; or Savoi Et Cie, Paris. Such examples date from 1871 to 1896. The Goetting Company was purchased by D.H. McConnell; Savoi Et Cie was a line which they imported to sell through department stores. Also of special interest are packaging and advertising with the Ambrosia or Hinze Ambrosia Company label. This was a subsidiary company whose objective seems to have been to produce a line of face creams, etc., for sale through drugstores and other such commercial outlets. They operated in New York from about 1875 until 1954. Because very little is known about these companies and since only a few examples of their product containers and advertising material have been found, market values for such items have not yet been established. Other items sought by the collector include products marked

Gertrude Recordon, Marvel Electric Silver Cleaner, Easy Day Automatic Clothes Washer, pre-1915 catalogs, California Perfume Company 1909 and 1910 calendars, and 1916 Calopad Sanitary Napkins.

There are hundreds of local Avon Collector Clubs throughout the world that also have C.P.C. collectors in their membership. If you are interested in joining, locating, or starting a new club, contact the National Association of Avon Collectors, Inc., listed in the Directory under Clubs, Newsletters, and Catalogs. Those wanting a National Newsletter Club or price guides may contact Avon Times, listed in the same section. Inquiries concerning California Perfume Company items and the companies or items mentioned in the previous paragraphs should be directed toward our advisor, Dick Pardini, whose address is given under California. (Please send a large SASE and be sure to request clearly the information you are seeking; not interested in Avons, 'Perfection' marked C.P.C.'s, or Anniversary Keepsakes.) For more information we recommend *Bud Hastin's New 16th Edition Avon Collector's Encyclopedia.*

Note: Our values are for items in mint condition. A very rare item or one in super mint condition might go for 10% more. Damage, wear, missing parts, etc., must be considered; items judged to be in only good to very good condition should be priced at up to 50% of listed values, with fair to good at 25% and excellent at 75%. Parts (labels, stoppers, caps, etc.) might be evaluated at 10% of these prices.

Narcissus Perfume, 1925, 1-oz, M 120.00
Narcissus Perfume, 1929-30, mc box, 1-oz, MIB 160.00
Natoma Rose Perfume, 1914-15, glass bottle/stopper, ½-oz, M ...160.00
Natoma Rose Perfume, 1916, ½-oz, M 155.00
Natoma Rose Talcum Powder, tin container, 1911, 3½-oz, MIB ..250.00

Olive Oil, glass bottle, 1915, eight-ounce, rare, M, $90.00.
(Photo courtesy Dick Pardini)

Perfume Sample Set, 1923, MIB...175.00
Powder Sachet, bottle, ca 1915, M 48.00
Powder Sachets, 1890s, M 90.00
Powder tin, 2 nude babies play w/giant rose ea side, 1912, M 110.00
Radiant Nail Powder, tin container, 1923, M..................................25.00
Rose Pomade, jar, milk glass, 1914, M 55.00
Shampoo Cream, milk glass, 1908, 4-oz, M 75.00
Sweet Sixteen Face Powder, paper container, 1918, M..................50.00
Tooth Tablet, aluminum lid, clear or milk wht bottom, 1920s, M.50.00
Tooth Wash, emb bottle w/label, 1915, M 105.00
Trailing Arbutus Face Powder, paper container, 1925, MIB 40.00
Trailing Arbutus Talcum, tin container, 1914, sample sz, M.........70.00
Trailing Arbutus Talcum, tin container, 1920, 1-lb, M 70.00
Verna Talc, mc container, 1928, 4-oz, MIB 95.00

Vernafleur Face Powder, tin container, 1925, M 20.00
Vernafleur Perfume, 1923, 1-oz, MIB..............................140.00
Violet Almond Meal, tin container, 1923, 4-oz, M....................50.00
Witch Hazel Cream, 1904, 2-oz tube, MIB..................................50.00

Camark

The Camden Art and Tile Company (commonly known as Camark) of Camden, Arkansas, was organized in the fall of 1926 by Samuel J. 'Jack' Carnes. Using clays from Arkansas, John Lessell, who had been hired as art director by Carnes, produced the initial lustre and iridescent Lessell wares for Camark ('CAM'den, 'ARK'ansas) before his death in December 1926. Before the plant opened in the spring of 1927, Carnes brought John's wife, Jeanne, and stepdaughter Billie to oversee the art department's manufacture of Le-Camark. Production by the Lessell family included variations of J.B. Owens' Soudanese and Opalesce and Weller's Marengo and Lamar. Camark's version of Marengo was called Old English. They also made wares identical to Weller's LaSa. Pieces made by John Lessell back in Ohio were signed 'Lessell,' while those made by Jeanne and Billie in Arkansas during 1927 were signed 'Le-Camark.' By 1928 Camark's production centered on traditional glazes. Drip glazes similar to Muncie Pottery were produced, in particular the green drip over pink. In the 1930s commercial castware with simple glossy and matt finishes became the primary focus and would continue so until Camark closed in the early 1960s. Between the 1960s and 1980s the company operated mainly as a retail store selling existing inventory, but some limited production occurred. In 1986 the company was purchased by the Ashcraft family of Camden, but no pottery has yet been made at the factory.

For further information we recommend *Guide to Camark Pottery, Book II,* by David Edwin Gifford. Our advisor for this category is Tony Freyaldenhoven; he is listed in the Directory under Arkansas.

Bowl, Mulberry w/lt overflow, emb ribs, 1st block letter mk, 5x9"..150.00
Box, Iris, bas relief/HP, Rose Pink, Lechner, #847R USA, 5¼x3x4" .140.00
Candlestick, Festoon of Roses, HP, bl, Lechner, unmk, 5¼" 35.00
Candlesticks, Morning Glory II, emb/HP, Lechner, unmk, 5¼", pr .80.00
Candlesticks, pineapple form, mk USA R-51, 3½", pr 40.00
Compote, Circle Nor-So II, speckled yel, ruffled, 4¾"....................30.00
Figurine, horse on base, #567, HP, 8x10".................................160.00
Figurine, Pointer dog, burgundy, Grapette decal, unmk, 2¼".........60.00

Figurine, razor-back hog, maroon, #117, EX, $50.00.

Pitcher, Celestial Blue, parrot hdl, ink stamp, 6½".....................180.00
Pitcher, yel/gr/bl layered look, sticker, 9½" 150.00
Plaque, horse head, Lechner, bl/silver sticker, 7"...........................75.00
Shakers, S&P shapes, Mirror Black w/gold trim, unmk, 2¾", pr..30.00
Stein, Royal Blue, cylindrical, angle hdl, 1st block letter, 5¼" 35.00
Vase, bl w/gr overflow, rnd shouldered, unmk, 2¾" 50.00
Vase, emb flower, leaves form hdls, burgundy, USA 571, 7½" 45.00
Vase, Emerald Green, urn form, Deluxe sticker, 8¼".....................20.00
Vase, fan; Royal Blue, emb decor, 1st block letter, 5½" 35.00
Vase, Festoon of Roses, Rose Pink, hdls, unmk, 9½" 100.00

Vase, gr w/wht overflow, die stamp, 5¼" 85.00
Vase, ivory, trumpet neck, raised ft, 1st block letter, 11¾" 50.00
Vase, Lessell, palm scenic, flared cylinder, die stamp, 9½".......1,000.00
Vase, orange crackle matt, angle hdls, gold ink stamp, 8¼" 400.00
Vase, orange w/gr overflow, shoulders, brn sticker, 4¼" 50.00
Vase, rose w/gr overflow, Deco style, hdls, unmk, 6" 85.00

Cambridge Glass

The Cambridge Glass Company began operations in 1901 in Cambridge, Ohio. Primarily they made crystal dinnerware and well-designed accessory pieces until the 1920s when they introduced the concept of color that was to become so popular on the American dinnerware market. Always maintaining high standards of quality and elegance, they produced many lines that became bestsellers; through the '20s and '30s they were recognized as the largest manufacturer of this type of glassware in the world.

Of the various marks the company used, the 'C in triangle' is the most familiar. Production stopped in 1958. For a more thorough study of the subject, we recommend *Colors in Cambridge Glass* by the National Cambridge Collectors, Inc.; their address may be found in the Directory under Clubs. *Glass Animals and Figural Flower Frogs of the Depression Era* by Lee Garmon and Dick Spencer is a wonderful source for an in-depth view of their particular aspect of glass collecting. They are both listed in the Directory under Illinois. See also Carnival Glass; Glass Animals.

Apple Blossom, crystal, bowl, cereal; 6" 35.00
Apple Blossom, crystal, bowl, 13" 55.00
Apple Blossom, crystal, cup..16.00
Apple Blossom, crystal, plate, bread & butter; sq..........................8.00
Apple Blossom, crystal, plate, bread & butter; 6"...........................8.00
Apple Blossom, crystal, stem, parfait; #1066 ....25.00
Apple Blossom, crystal, tray, relish; hdld, 7"................................25.00
Apple Blossom, crystal, vase, 5"...65.00
Apple Blossom, pk or gr, bowl, baker; 10"...................................110.00
Apple Blossom, pk or gr, comport, tall, 7"....................................95.00
Apple Blossom, pk or gr, pitcher, ball form, 80-oz 495.00
Apple Blossom, pk or gr, saucer..8.00
Apple Blossom, pk or gr, stem, sherbet; #3135, low, 6-oz.............28.00
Apple Blossom, pk or gr, tumbler, #3131, ftd, 10-oz.....................45.00
Apple Blossom, yel or amber, bowl, pickle; 9".............................55.00
Apple Blossom, yel or amber, candelabrum, 3-light, keyhole 50.00
Apple Blossom, yel or amber, pitcher, ftd, flat sides, 50-oz..........275.00
Apple Blossom, yel or amber, plate, service; sq 45.00
Apple Blossom, yel or amber, stem, cocktail; #3130, 3-oz.............32.00
Apple Blossom, yel or amber, tumbler, #3025, 12-oz....................16.00
Candlelight, crystal, bonbon, #3900/130, ftd, 2-hdl, 7" 40.00
Candlelight, crystal, candlestick, #647, 2-light, 6"........................75.00
Candlelight, crystal, cruet, #3900/100, w/stopper, 6-oz...............150.00
Candlelight, crystal, nut cup, #3400/71, 4-ftd, 3" 70.00
Candlelight, crystal, plate, #3900/26, 4-toed, 12" 75.00
Candlelight, crystal, plate, cracker; #3900/135, 13½"...................75.00
Candlelight, crystal, plate, dinner; #3900/24, 10½"......................85.00
Candlelight, crystal, relish, #3900/125, 3-part, 9" 65.00
Candlelight, crystal, shakers, #3900/1177, pr..............................135.00
Candlelight, crystal, stem, cocktail; #7801, 4-oz 35.00
Candlelight, crystal, sugar bowl, #3900/41 ....25.00
Candlelight, crystal, vase, #279, ftd, 13" 165.00
Candlelight, crystal, vase, globe; #1309, 5".................................85.00
Caprice, bl or pk, ashtray, #216, 5" 25.00
Caprice, bl or pk, bowl, fruit; #18, 5"...75.00
Caprice, bl or pk, bowl, salad; #57, 4-ftd, 10" 125.00
Caprice, bl or pk, coaster, #13, 3½"..35.00

Caprice, bl or pk, marmalade, #89, w/lid, 6-oz 225.00
Caprice, bl or pk, oil, #101, w/stopper, 3-oz 85.00
Caprice, bl or pk, plate, cake; #36, ftd, 13" 395.00
Caprice, bl or pk, plate, #30, 16" 125.00
Caprice, bl or pk, saucer, #17 ....5.50
Caprice, bl or pk, stem, sherbet; #300, low, blown, 6-oz 18.00
Caprice, bl or pk, stem, water; #1, 10-oz 47.50
Caprice, bl or pk, tumbler, table; #310, flat, 10-oz 65.00
Caprice, bl or pk, tumbler, tea; #300, ftd, 12-oz 40.00
Caprice, bl or pk, vase, ball; #240, 9¼" 310.00
Caprice, bl or pk, vase, ivy bowl; #232, 5" 225.00
Caprice, crystal, ashtray, #215, 4" 8.00
Caprice, crystal, bottle, bitters; #186, 7-oz 225.00
Caprice, crystal, bowl, pickle; #102, 9" 25.00
Caprice, crystal, bowl, salad; #80, cupped, 13" 75.00
Caprice, crystal, candlestick, #74, 3-light, ea 40.00
Caprice, crystal, cup, #17 ....14.00
Caprice, crystal, nut dish, #93, 2½" 22.00
Caprice, crystal, plate, bread & butter; #21, 6½" 11.00
Caprice, crystal, shakers, ball; #91, pr 40.00
Caprice, crystal, stem, parfait; #300, blown, 5-oz 95.00
Caprice, crystal, stem, wine; #6, 3-oz 40.00
Caprice, crystal, tray, oval, #42, 9" 22.00
Caprice, crystal, tumbler, #10, ftd, 10-oz 20.00
Caprice, crystal, vase, ball; #238, 6½" 65.00
Caprice, crystal, vase, ball; #241, 4¼" 45.00

Caprice, pitcher, juice; #279, 32-ounce, $135.00.

Chantilly, crystal, bowl, oval, 4-ftd, 12" 50.00
Chantilly, crystal, bowl, relish/pickle; 7" 32.00
Chantilly, crystal, butter dish, rnd 145.00
Chantilly, crystal, cup 17.50
Chantilly, crystal, ice bucket, w/chrome hdl 75.00
Chantilly, crystal, plate, dinner; 10½" 60.00
Chantilly, crystal, stem, cordial; #3775, 1-oz 60.00
Chantilly, crystal, stem, water; #3600, 10-oz 28.00
Chantilly, crystal, stem, wine; #3600, 2½-oz 35.00
Chantilly, crystal, sugar bowl 18.00
Chantilly, crystal, syrup 175.00
Chantilly, crystal, tumbler, 13-oz 26.00
Cleo, bl, bowl, fruit; 5½" 40.00
Cleo, bl, candlestick, 1-light, 2 styles, ea 40.00
Cleo, bl, cup, Decagon 30.00
Cleo, bl, stem, wine; #3077, 3½-oz 95.00
Cleo, bl, tumbler, #3077, ftd, 8-oz 60.00
Cleo, pk, gr, yel or amber, bowl, cranberry; 6½" 40.00
Cleo, pk, gr, yel or amber, bowl, oval, 11" 75.00
Cleo, pk, gr, yel or amber, candy box; w/lid 185.00
Cleo, pk, gr, yel or amber, ice tub 125.00
Cleo, pk, gr, yel or amber, plate, 7" 18.00
Cleo, pk, gr, yel or amber, saucer, Decagon 5.00

Cleo, pk, gr, yel or amber, stem, fruit; #3115, 6-oz 16.00
Cleo, pk, gr, yel or amber, syrup pitcher, Drip Cut 195.00
Daffodil, crystal, bonbon, #1181 ....30.00
Daffodil, crystal, celery; #248, 11" 65.00
Daffodil, crystal, cup, #11770 ....25.00
Daffodil, crystal, plate, #1176, sq, 8" 20.00
Daffodil, crystal, plate, cake; #1495, 11½" 75.00
Daffodil, crystal, shakers, #360, squat, pr 65.00
Daffodil, crystal, stem, cordial; #3779, 1-oz 85.00
Daffodil, crystal, stem, water; #1937, 11-oz 45.00
Daffodil, crystal, sugar bowl, #254 ....25.00
Daffodil, crystal, vase, #278, ftd, 11" 125.00
Decagon, bl, bowl, fruit; belled, 5½" 20.00
Decagon, bl, cup 11.00
Decagon, bl, ice tub 65.00
Decagon, bl, plate, 7½" 12.00
Decagon, bl, saucer 4.00
Decagon, bl, tumbler, ftd, 5-oz 20.00
Decagon, pastel colors, bowl, berry; 10" 35.00
Decagon, pastel colors, bowl, cereal; flat rim, 6" 22.00
Decagon, pastel colors, bowl, cream soup; w/liner 22.00
Decagon, pastel colors, plate, grill; 10" 35.00
Decagon, pastel colors, plate, hdls, 7" 9.00
Decagon, pastel colors, tray, pickle; 9" 25.00
Diane, crystal, bottle, bitters 165.00
Diane, crystal, bowl, berry; 5" 30.00
Diane, crystal, bowl, cereal; 6" 35.00
Diane, crystal, cabinet flask 295.00
Diane, crystal, cigarette urn 50.00
Diane, crystal, cup 20.00
Diane, crystal, oil, w/stopper, 6-oz 135.00
Diane, crystal, plate, salad; 8" 14.00
Diane, crystal, plate, torte; 14" 75.00
Diane, crystal, saucer 6.00
Diane, crystal, stem, cordial; #3122, 1-oz 65.00
Diane, crystal, stem, water; #1066, 11-oz 32.00
Diane, crystal, sugar bowl, #3400, scroll hdl 20.00
Diane, crystal, tumbler, tea; #1066, 12-oz 28.00
Diane, crystal, tumbler, 13-oz 35.00
Diane, crystal, vase, flower; 11" 95.00
Diane, crystal, vase, globe; 5" 55.00
Elaine, crystal, basket, 2-hdl, upturned sides, 6" 22.00
Elaine, crystal, bowl, celery & relish; 3-part, 12" 55.00
Elaine, crystal, bowl, pickle or relish; 7" 35.00
Elaine, crystal, candlestick, 5", ea 28.00
Elaine, crystal, comport, blown, 5⅜" 50.00
Elaine, crystal, cup 20.00
Elaine, crystal, plate, salad; 8" 22.00
Elaine, crystal, shakers, hdld, pr 45.00
Elaine, crystal, stem, goblet; #1402 ....28.00
Elaine, crystal, stem, sherbet; #3104, tall, 7-oz 125.00
Elaine, crystal, stem, wine; #3500, 2½-oz 40.00
Elaine, crystal, sugar bowl, ind 20.00
Elaine, crystal, tumbler, tea; #3500, ftd, 12-oz 35.00
Gloria, crystal, bowl, cranberry; 3½" 35.00
Gloria, crystal, bowl, flared rim, 13" 65.00
Gloria, crystal, bowl, salad; tab hdl, 9" 50.00
Gloria, crystal, comport, low, 7" 40.00
Gloria, crystal, pitcher, ball; 80-oz 295.00
Gloria, crystal, plate, salad; sq 14.00
Gloria, crystal, plate, 8½" 16.00
Gloria, crystal, shakers, ftd, metal tops, pr 60.00
Gloria, crystal, stem, water; #3120, 9-oz 28.00
Gloria, crystal, stem, water; #3135, 8-oz 28.00

Gloria, crystal, syrup, tall, ftd **95.00**
Gloria, crystal, tumbler, juice; #3135, 5-oz **18.00**
Gloria, crystal, vase, 11" **100.00**
Gloria, gr, pk or yel, bowl, cereal; rnd, 6" **50.00**
Gloria, gr, pk or yel, candlestick, 6", ea **75.00**
Gloria, gr, pk or yel, cup, rnd or sq **33.00**
Gloria, gr, pk or yel, plate, dinner; 9½" **100.00**
Gloria, gr, pk or yel, saucer, sq **6.00**
Gloria, gr, pk or yel, tumbler, #3115, ftd, 8-oz **40.00**
Gloria, gr, pk or yel, tumbler, tea; #3135, 12-oz **50.00**
Imperial Hunt Scene, colors, bowl, cereal; 6" **40.00**
Imperial Hunt Scene, colors, plate, 8" **25.00**
Imperial Hunt Scene, colors, stem, parfait; #3085, 5½-oz **75.00**
Imperial Hunt Scene, colors, tumbler, #3085, ftd, 8-oz **35.00**
Imperial Hunt Scene, crystal, bowl, 8" **40.00**
Imperial Hunt Scene, crystal, ice bucket **65.00**
Imperial Hunt Scene, crystal, stem, tomato; #1402, 6-oz **45.00**
Imperial Hunt Scene, crystal, sugar bowl, flat, w/lid **50.00**
Marjorie, crystal, bowl, finger; #7606 ....**40.00**
Marjorie, crystal, comport, #4011 ....**45.00**
Marjorie, crystal, jug, #93, 3-pt **155.00**
Marjorie, crystal, night bottle, #4002, w/tumbler, 20-oz **235.00**
Marjorie, crystal, stem, water; #3750, 10-oz **22.00**
Marjorie, crystal, stem, wine; #3750, 3-oz **35.00**
Marjorie, crystal, syrup, #106, w/lid, 8-oz **125.00**
Marjorie, crystal, tumbler, table; #7606, 10-oz **25.00**
Mt Vernon, amber or crystal, ashtray, #68, 4" **12.00**
Mt Vernon, amber or crystal, bowl, cereal; #32, 6" **12.50**
Mt Vernon, amber or crystal, bowl, #135, oval, 11" **25.00**
Mt Vernon, amber or crystal, bowl, #44, flared, 12½" **35.00**
Mt Vernon, amber or crystal, box, #17, sq, w/cover, 4" **32.50**
Mt Vernon, amber or crystal, candlestick, #130, 4", ea **10.00**
Mt Vernon, amber or crystal, celery, #98, 11" **17.50**
Mt Vernon, amber or crystal, coaster, #60, plain, 3" **5.00**
Mt Vernon, amber or crystal, cup, #7 ....**6.50**
Mt Vernon, amber or crystal, ice bucket, #92, w/tongs **35.00**
Mt Vernon, amber or crystal, mustard, #28, w/lid, 2½-oz **25.00**
Mt Vernon, amber or crystal, plate, bread & butter; #4, 6" **3.00**
Mt Vernon, amber or crystal, plate, dinner; #40, 10½" **35.00**
Mt Vernon, amber or crystal, saucer, #7 ....**7.50**
Mt Vernon, amber or crystal, shakers, #28, pr **22.50**
Mt Vernon, amber or crystal, stem, claret; #25, 4½-oz **13.50**
Mt Vernon, amber or crystal, stem, water; #1, 10-oz **15.00**
Mt Vernon, amber or crystal, sugar bowl, #86 ....**10.00**
Mt Vernon, amber or crystal, tumbler, table; #51, 10-oz **12.00**
Mt Vernon, amber or crystal, vase, #58, 7" **30.00**
Number 520 Byzantine, Peach Blo or gr, bowl, fruit; #928, 5¼" **22.50**
Number 520 Byzantine, Peach Blo or gr, butter dish **155.00**
Number 520 Byzantine, Peach Blo or gr, cup, #933 ......**18.00**
Number 520 Byzantine, Peach Blo or gr, plate, sherbet; 6" **10.00**
Number 520 Byzantine, Peach Blo or gr, saucer, #933 ......**7.00**
Number 520 Byzantine, Peach Blo or gr, stem, wine; #3060, 2½-oz **35.00**
Number 520 Byzantine, Peach Blo or gr, sugar bowl, #138, rim ft **20.00**
Number 520 Byzantine, Peach Blo or gr, tumbler, #3060, ftd, 10-oz **25.00**
Number 704 Windows Border, colors, bottle, decanter; #0315 ......**175.00**
Number 704 Windows Border, colors, bowl, finger; #3060 ......**35.00**
Number 704 Windows Border, colors, candlestick, #227½, 2", ea **20.00**
Number 704 Windows Border, colors, cheese plate, #468 ......**35.00**
Number 704 Windows Border, colors, cigarette box, #430 ......**50.00**
Number 704 Windows Border, colors, creamer, #943, flat **22.50**
Number 704 Windows Border, colors, jug, #107 ......**150.00**
Number 704 Windows Border, colors, plate, 8" **15.00**
Number 704 Windows Border, colors, syrup jug, #814, tall **125.00**
Portia, crystal, bowl, finger; #3124, w/liner **45.00**

Portia, crystal, bowl, relish; 2-part, 6" **22.00**
Portia, crystal, bowl, 4-ftd, flared, 10" **50.00**
Portia, crystal, candy box, rnd, w/lid **100.00**
Portia, crystal, cocktail shaker, w/stopper **150.00**
Portia, crystal, creamer, ind **20.00**
Portia, crystal, cup, rnd **20.00**
Portia, crystal, plate, salad; 8" **15.00**
Portia, crystal, plate, torte; 14" **65.00**
Portia, crystal, saucer, sq or rnd **5.00**
Portia, crystal, stem, cocktail; #3121, 3-oz **30.00**
Portia, crystal, stem, goblet; #3124, 10-oz **28.00**
Portia, crystal, stem, goblet; #3130, 9-oz **28.00**
Portia, crystal, tray, celery; 11" **40.00**
Portia, crystal, vase, bud; 10" **65.00**
Rosalie, amber, bowl, 10" **40.00**
Rosalie, amber, candlestick, keyhole, 5", ea **30.00**
Rosalie, amber, plate, dinner; 9½" **40.00**
Rosalie, amber, sugar shaker **225.00**
Rosalie, bl, pk or gr, bowl, cream soup **30.00**
Rosalie, bl, pk or gr, bowl, 11" **70.00**
Rosalie, bl, pk or gr, cup **35.00**
Rosalie, bl, pk or gr, saucer **5.00**
Rose Point, crystal, ashtray, #3500/126, 4" **40.00**
Rose Point, crystal, basket, #3400/1182, 2-hdl, 6" **40.00**
Rose Point, crystal, bowl, #221, 3-part, 8½" **225.00**
Rose Point, crystal, bowl, #3400/1, flared, 13" **85.00**
Rose Point, crystal, bowl, #3400/4, flared, 4-ftd, 12" **75.00**
Rose Point, crystal, bowl, cereal; #3500/11, 6" **110.00**
Rose Point, crystal, bowl, fruit; #3500/10, 5" **85.00**
Rose Point, crystal, butter dish, #508, rnd **195.00**
Rose Point, crystal, candlestick, #627, 4", ea **60.00**
Rose Point, crystal, celery, #3500/652, 12" **65.00**
Rose Point, crystal, cheese dish, #980, 5" **595.00**
Rose Point, crystal, comport, #3900/135, 5" **50.00**
Rose Point, crystal, cup, punch; #488, 5-oz **37.50**
Rose Point, crystal, honey dish, #3500/139, w/lid **350.00**
Rose Point, crystal, hot plate or trivet **125.00**
Rose Point, crystal, ice pail, #3400/851 ....**175.00**
Rose Point, crystal, mayonnaise, #3400/11, 3-pc **75.00**
Rose Point, crystal, pickle/relish dish, #3900/123, 7" **40.00**
Rose Point, crystal, pitcher, ball; #3400/38, 80-oz **250.00**
Rose Point, crystal, plate, dinner; #3400/64, 10½" **165.00**
Rose Point, crystal, plate, salad; #3900/22, 8" **22.00**
Rose Point, crystal, relish, #3400/91, 3-part, 3-hdl, 8" **40.00**
Rose Point, crystal, shakers, #1468, egg shape, pr **95.00**
Rose Point, crystal, stem, claret; #3106, 4½-oz **60.00**
Rose Point, crystal, stem, water; #3121, 10-oz **42.00**
Rose Point, crystal, sugar bowl, #3500/14 ....**22.00**
Rose Point, crystal, tray, #3500/67, rnd, 12" **195.00**
Rose Point, crystal, tumbler, #498, str sides, 10-oz **50.00**
Rose Point, crystal, vase, #274, slim, 10" **65.00**
Rose Point, crystal, vase, #572, 6" **175.00**
Tally Ho, amber or crystal, bowl, 8" **25.00**
Tally Ho, amber or crystal, candlestick, 5", ea **25.00**
Tally Ho, amber or crystal, plate, salad; 8" **15.00**
Tally Ho, Carmen or Royal Blue, bowl, pan; 12" **100.00**
Tally Ho, Carmen or Royal Blue, coaster, 4" **22.50**
Tally Ho, Carmen or Royal Blue, plate, finger bowl **15.00**
Tally Ho, Forest Green, goblet, cocktail **16.00**
Tally Ho, Forest Green, tumbler, 5-oz **17.50**
Valencia, crystal, ashtray, #3500/126, rnd, 4" **16.00**
Valencia, crystal, bowl, #1402/88, 11" **45.00**
Valencia, crystal, perfume, #3400/92, 2-oz **175.00**
Valencia, crystal, relish, #3500/67, 6-pc, 12" **195.00**

Valencia, crystal, stem, goblet; #1402 ....**28.00**
Valencia, crystal, tumbler, #3500, ftd, 10-oz..................**20.00**
Wildflower, crystal, basket, #3400/1182, 2-hdl, ftd, 6" **30.00**
Wildflower, crystal, bowl, relish; #3900/123, 7" **20.00**
Wildflower, crystal, candlestick, #3400/646, 5", ea **27.50**
Wildflower, crystal, creamer, #3900/41 ....**15.00**
Wildflower, crystal, oil, #3900/100, w/stopper, 6-oz **85.00**
Wildflower, crystal, plate, dinner; #3900/24, 10½" **67.50**
Wildflower, crystal, plate, salad; #3900/22, 8" **17.50**
Wildflower, crystal, saucer, #3900/17 or #3400/54............**3.50**
Wildflower, crystal, stem, wine; #3121, 3½-oz **35.00**
Wildflower, crystal, vase, bud; #1528, 10" **40.00**

Cameo

The technique of glass carving was perfected 2,000 years ago in ancient Rome and Greece. The most famous ancient example of cameo glass is the Portland Vase, made in Rome around 100 A.D. After glass blowing was developed, glassmakers devised a method of casing several layers of colored glass together, often with a light color over a darker base, to enhance the design. Skilled carvers meticulously worked the fragile glass to produce incredibly detailed classic scenes. In the eighteenth and nineteenth centuries Oriental and Near-Eastern artisans used the technique more extensively. European glassmakers revived the art during the last quarter of the nineteenth century. In France, Galle and Daum produced some of the finest examples of modern times, using as many as five layers of glass to develop their designs, usually scenics or subjects from nature. Hand carving was supplemented by the use of a copper engraving wheel, and acid was used to cut away the layers more quickly.

In England, Thomas Webb and Sons used modern machinery and technology to eliminate many of the problems that plagued early glass carvers. One of Webb's best-known carvers, George Woodall, is credited with producing over four hundred pieces. Woodall was trained in the art by John Northwood, famous for reproducing the Portland Vase in 1876. Cameo glass became very popular during the late 1800s, resulting in a market that demanded more than could be produced, due to the tedious procedures involved. In an effort to produce greater volume, less elaborate pieces with simple floral or geometric designs were made, often entirely acid etched with little or no hand carving. While very little cameo glass was made in this country, a few pieces were produced by James Gillinder, Tiffany, and the Libbey Glass Company. Though some continued to be made on a limited scale into the 1900s (and until about 1920 in France), for the most part, inferior products caused a marked reduction in its manufacture by the turn of the century. Beware of new 'French' cameo glass from Romania and Taiwan. Some of it is very good and may be signed with 'old' signatures. Know your dealer! Our advisor for this category is Don Williams; he is listed in the Directory under Missouri. See also specific manufactures.

English

Bottle, scent; floral, wht on gr, rnd lay-down style, 2¾" **2,500.00**
Bowl, morning glories/leaves, wht on citron, 2¾x5" **450.00**
Bowl, nut; honeysuckle/bk: butterfly, wht on red, 3" **1,175.00**
Bowl, trumpet flowers, bk: butterfly, cvd border, wht on bl, ftd, 6" ..**700.00**
Compote, daisies, wht on yel, 4-arm ormolu base, 4¼x4¾" **325.00**
Fairy lamp, floral, wht on bl, flaring base mk Clarke's, 5½" **6,250.00**
Finger bowl, branch/border, wht on citron, 2½x3¾" **450.00**
Finger bowl, branch/flowering buds, wht on red, 2½x3¾" **650.00**
Lamp base, butterfly/flowers, wht on purple, metal mts, 4x5½" ..**750.00**
Plaque, floral, wht on citron, oval, 5½x3½" **1,275.00**
Sweetmeat, flowers, aqua w/gilt on cream, sgn Pat, metal mts, 5½" ..**950.00**
Vase, cascading floral front/bk, 3-color, stick neck, 3½" **800.00**

Vase, collar/floral branches/butterfly, wht on yel to lime, bottle, 7" ..**3,900.00**
Vase, floral, wht/lav on lt bl, floral neck, squat w/stick neck, 3" ...**1,450.00**
Vase, floral stems, rim/ft bands, wht on Prussian bl, shouldered, 5"..**950.00**
Vase, flowers/wheat stalks, wht on rose, shouldered, 4½" **1,000.00**
Vase, fruit branches/insect on peachblow color, ovoid, 5½"........**950.00**
Vase, leafy branches, wht/rose on bright yel, long neck, low flare, 6"..**2,250.00**
Vase, lily blossoms/honeycombs, amber/gold on clear, Richardson, 8".**1,350.00**
Vase, str branches form latticework, wht on lt cranberry, bulbous, 6" **525.00**
Vase, 2 butterflies/tree branches, mc on frost, ovoid, pinched rim, 8"..**1,200.00**

French

Bowl, iris, orange/pk on textured citron w/gilt, St Louis, 2x5" **300.00**
Champagne, honeysuckle, purple/gr on yel, Richard, 4½" **300.00**
Lamp, floral on base/shade, bl/umber on pk/frost, Lyon, 15x11"..**1,250.00**
Night light, forest/lake, gr/yel on umber & yel, Arsall, 15" **900.00**
Sugar bowl, floral, purple/gr on frost, w/lid, emb silver mts, 5½"..**300.00**
Vase, bud; thistles, cranberry on needlepoint etch, 3-ftd metal fr, 8" ..**225.00**
Vase, columbine, pk on X-hatch clear/pk, gilt rim/details, Depose, 10"...**385.00**
Vase, day lilies, purple/dk gr on wht, Arsdale, ovoid, 12" **650.00**
Vase, floral, bk: tree branch, cut/pnt/gilt, St Denis, ftd, 12" **225.00**

Vase, flowers, buds, and leafy stems, marquetry, purple on clear martele, BS&C Verrerie D'Art De Lorraine, 7", $5,500.00.

Vase, fuchsia, burgundy/gr on wht frost, ovoid, Arsall, 12" **600.00**
Vase, landscape/birds, dk gr on rust, mk:2 arrows in rectangle, 4¾"..**450.00**
Vase, leaves, gr on amber frost, squatty, sgn Muller, 5x6¼".........**350.00**
Vase, leaves/buds, gr/amethyst on frost, flat-sided, Arsall, 10".....**600.00**
Vase, leaves/cascading fruit, amethyst on lav, Michel de Nancy, 2"...**175.00**
Vase, pine needles/acorns, brn on orange, ovoid, Richard, 8½"..**650.00**
Vase, sunflower, red/yel/brn on gr frost, D'Aurys, ovoid, 12" ...**1,200.00**
Vase, trees/far shoreline, dk gr on ruby/orange/lime, Chouvenin, 8"...**300.00**
Vase, trees/lake, orange on frost, bottle form, Richard, 3½"........**225.00**
Vase, village/lake/trees, dk on med gr, Michel, 8" **325.00**

Candle Holders

The earliest type of candlestick, called a pricket, was constructed with a sharp point on which the candle was impaled. The socket type, first used in the sixteenth century, consisted of the socket and a short stem with a wide drip pan and base. These were made from sheets of silver or other metal; not until late in the seventeenth century were candlesticks made by casting. By the 1700s, styles began to vary from the traditional fluted column or baluster form and became more elaborate. A Rococo style with scrolls, shellwork, and naturalistic leaves and flowers came into vogue that afforded the individual silversmith the opportunity to exhibit his skill and artistry. The last half of the eighteenth century brought a return to fluted columns with neoclassic motifs. Because they were made of thin sheet silver, weighted bases were used to add stability. The Rococo styles of the Regency period were heavily encrusted with applied figures and flowers. Candelabra with six to nine branches became popular. By the Victorian era when lamps came into general use, there was less innovation and more adaptation of the earlier styles. For more information, we recommend *Glass Candlesticks of the Depression Era* by Gene Florence (Collector Books). See also Silver; Tinware; specific manufacturers.

Amber glass w/diaper cuttings, fluted shafts, Van Dyke cups, 11", pr ...**575.00**
Brass, baluster shaft, mid-drip pan, flared base, rprs, 17th C, 9", pr ...**2,185.00**
Brass, baluster w/ring trn/stepped base, polished, 8½" **250.00**
Brass, beehive, w/pushup, mk England, 6", pr **165.00**

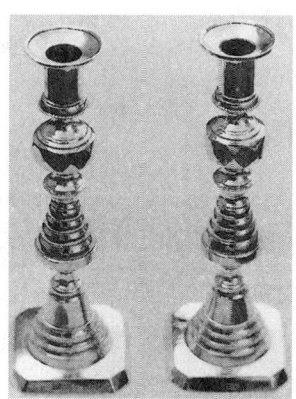

Brass, beehive and diamond design, with push rods and brass ejector buttons, marked England, 1890s, 9¾x3½", from $200.00 to $225.00 for the pair. (Photo courtesy Mary Frank Gaston)

Brass, capstan, raised rings around socket, early, 4¾", VG **495.00**
Brass, capstan, rnd base w/ring trn at ft, 4¾" **875.00**
Brass, capstan, thin bell base, flared pan under socket, early, 4½" ..**850.00**
Brass, dome trn base, trn column, dished mid-drip pan, 7⅜" ...**1,100.00**
Brass, extractor, cylindrical stem, appl band, H-shaped hdl, 1850s, 5"..**230.00**
Brass, fluted columns/acanthus leaves, 1830s, 10x4¼", pr...........**460.00**
Brass, octagonal/scalloped step-down base, 2 soldered pcs, 9½", pr..**825.00**
Brass, old SP traces, baluster w/stepped & paneled base, 9½" **220.00**
Brass, QA, petal base/socket, ring trns, early/2-pc, 7½", pr......**2,000.00**
Brass, QA, scalloped base w/relief rings, trn baluster stem, 9" **770.00**
Brass, QA style, scalloped base, trn columns, pushup missing, 7".**110.00**
Brass, ring-trn baluster on sq pan base, late 17th C, 5⅝", VG....**230.00**
Brass, ring-trn shaft, hex interval on sq base, late 17th C, 4¾" ..**750.00**
Brass, ring-trn stem, dome base w/3 raised & stepped rings, 8" ...**350.00**
Brass, solid/trn stem, sq base w/half-rnd ft & dome top, 9½", pr.**275.00**
Brass, spiral stem, octagonal base w/raised ring & tooling, 7", VG...**440.00**
Brass, spiral stem, saucer base, early, soldered rpr/lt dents, 6" **220.00**
Brass, thin finely trn stem, sm trn drip pan/sockets, scalloped ft, 9"..**80.00**
Brass, w/pushup, Birmingham, 1825-40, 7½", pr..........................**315.00**
Brass, wide sq ftd base w/raised rim & incised rings, trn stem, 7", EX...**330.00**
Brass, 2 scroll/leaf arms w/sockets+center socket, marble ft, 10", pr......**200.00**
Brass, 3-knob stem, octagonal base, minor wear, early, 5½" **330.00**
Bronze, water lily form, open center forms socket, 10⅝", pr **440.00**
Bronze/cloisonne, Louis XV-style, 5-light, 1880s, 20", pr.........**2,000.00**
Candelabra, gilt bronze Late Regency style, 6-arm, ca 1835, 25x12", pr.**1,265.00**
Candelabra, gilt metal, 6-light, cherub masks, foliage, 28x17", pr....**1,380.00**
Giltwood, cvd in Greek Classical style, faux marble base, 29", pr...**2,000.00**
Giltwood, trumpet shafts in ebonized clenched-fist supports, 31", pr...**1,100.00**
Hogscraper, Ecclesiastical, SP, w/pushup, England, 19th C, 20"..**430.00**
Sconce, brass, openwork foliage/satyr heads, 3-arm, 17', pr **225.00**
Sconce, brass, ribbon & acanthus leaf bracket w/3 arms, 14¼", pr **300.00**
Sconce, brass, 3 scroll arms, crenelated cups, quatrefoil bk, 13", pr...**1,095.00**
Sconce, Rococo pnt/parcel gilt, 2-light, electrified, 32x10", pr...**1,950.00**
Sconce, tin, emb ribs, crimped hanger, fluted cup, 1800s, 13¼"..**1,265.00**
Taper jack, wrought iron, scroll legs under rectangular stand, 7½" ..**800.00**
Wrought iron, 3 penny ft, drip pan w/adjustable socket, 9½" **495.00**

Candlewick

Candlewick crystal was made by the Imperial Glass Corporation, a division of Lenox Inc., Bellaire, Ohio. It was introduced in 1936, and though never marked except for paper labels, it is easily recognized by the beaded crystal rims, stems, and handles inspired by the tufted needlework called candlewicking, practiced by our pioneer women. During its production, more than 741 items were designed and produced. In September 1982 when Imperial closed its doors, thirty-four pieces were still being made.

Identification numbers and mold numbers used by the company help collectors recognize the various styles and shapes. Most of the pieces are from the #400 series, though other series numbers were also used. Stemware was made in eight styles — five from the #400 series made from 1941 to 1962, one from #3400 series made in 1937, another from #3800 series made in 1941, and the eighth style from the #4000 series made in 1947. In the listings that follow, some #400 items lack the mold number because that information was not found in the company files.

A few pieces have been made in color or with a gold wash. At least two lines, Valley Lily and Floral, utilized Candlewick with floral patterns cut into the crystal. These are scarce today. Other rare items include gifts such as the desk calendar made by the company for its employees and customers; the dresser set comprised of a mirror, clock, puff jar, and cologne; and the chip and dip set.

Ashtray, #400/172, heart shape, 4½" **10.00**
Ashtray, #400/653, sq, 5¾" **50.00**
Bottle, bitters; #400/117, w/tube, 4-oz **65.00**
Bowl, #400/10F, rnd, 9" **50.00**
Bowl, #400/104B, belled, 14" **80.00**
Bowl, #400/231, sq, 5" **100.00**
Bowl, #400/5F, rnd, 7" **25.00**
Bowl, #400/73H, heart shape w/hdl, 9" **175.00**
Bowl, #400/75F, cupped edge, 10" **45.00**
Bowl, #400/92B, rnd, 12" **45.00**
Bowl, baked apple; #400/53X, rolled edge, 6"...............................**30.00**
Bowl, butter/jam; #400/262, 3-part, 10½" **195.00**
Bowl, finger; #3800 ....**35.00**
Bowl, float; #400/92F, 12" **40.00**
Bowl, lily; #400/74J, 4-ftd, 7" **75.00**
Bowl, pickle/celery; #400/57, 7½" **27.50**
Bowl, sauce; #400/243, deep, 5½" **40.00**
Bowl, vegetable; #400/65/1, w/lid, 8"...**325.00**
Butter, #400/161, w/bead top, ¼-lb...**30.00**
Butter & jam set, #400/204, 5-pc..**395.00**
Cake stand, #400/67D, low ft, 10" **60.00**
Candle holder, #400/280, flat, 3½", ea **50.00**
Candle holder, #400/40C, flower, 5", ea **35.00**
Candle holder, #400/86, mushroom, ea **35.00**
Cigarette holder, #400/44, bead ft, 3" **35.00**
Clock, rnd, 4" **295.00**
Coaster, #400/226, w/spoon rest..**16.00**
Compote, #400/66B, low, plain stem, 5½" **22.00**
Creamer, #400/31, plain ft **9.00**
Cup, coffee; #400/37 ....**7.50**
Cup, tea; #400/35 ....**8.00**
Deviled egg server, #400/154, center hdl, 12" **125.00**
Fork & spoon, #400/75, set **38.00**
Hurricane lamp, #400/76, 2-pc, hdl, candle base **195.00**
Ice tub, #400/168, hdls, 7"...**225.00**
Jam set, #400/1589, 5-pc, oval tray w/2 marmalade jars w/ladles ...**115.00**
Ladle, punch; #400/91 ....**30.00**
Marmalade set, #400/1989, 3-pc, beaded ft, w/lid & spoon **40.00**

Mayonnaise set, #400/49, 3-pc, plate, heart bowl & spoon 35.00
Mustard jar, #400/156, w/spoon 33.00
Oil, #400/121, w/stopper, etched 'Oil' 65.00
Pitcher, #400/18, beaded ft, 80-oz 235.00
Pitcher, #400/416, plain, 20-oz 40.00
Plate, #400/124, oval, 12½" 85.00
Plate, #400/169, oval, 8" 25.00
Plate, bread/butter; #400/1D, 6" 8.00
Plate, dinner; #400/10D, 10½" 40.00
Plate, luncheon; #400/7D, 9" 13.50
Plate, salad; #400/3D, 7"..8.00
Plate, salad; #400/5D, 8"..9.00
Plate, torte; #400/113D, hdls, 14" 40.00
Platter, #400/131D, 16" 225.00
Salad set, buffet; #400/17, rnd tray+2-part bowl+2 spoons, 4-pc...95.00
Salt spoon, #400/616, 3" 11.00
Saucer, after dinner; #400/77AD..6.00
Shakers, #400/247, bead ft, str sides, chrome top, pr......................16.00
Shakers, #400/96, bead ft, bulbous, chrome top, pr.......................15.00
Stem, claret; #3800 ....75.00
Stem, cocktail; #400/190, 4-oz 18.00
Stem, oyster cocktail; #3400, 4-oz 15.00
Stem, parfait; #3400, 6-oz 58.00
Stem, tea; #4000, 12-oz 25.00
Stem, wine; #3400, 4-oz 26.00
Sugar bowl, #400/18, domed ft...135.00
Tray, condiment; #400/148, 5¼x9¼"...45.00
Tray, fruit; #400/68F, center hdl, 10½" 125.00
Tray, lemon; #400/221, center hdl, 5½" 35.00
Tray, tidbit; #400/2701, 2-tier, cupped 50.00
Tumbler, #3800, 9-oz 26.00
Tumbler, juice; #400/18, 5-oz 45.00
Tumbler, juice; #400/19, 5-oz 10.00
Tumbler, water; #400/18, 9-oz 45.00
Vase, #400/143C, flat, crimped edge, 8" 70.00
Vase, #400/193, ftd, 10" 185.00
Vase, fan; #400/287F, 6" 30.00

Candy Containers

Figural glass candy containers were first created in 1876 when ingenious candy manufacturers began to use them to package their products. Two of the first containers, the Liberty Bell and Independence Hall, were distributed for our country's centennial celebration. Children found these toys appealing, and an industry was launched that lasted into the mid-1960s.

Figural candy containers include animals, comic characters, guns, telephones, transportation vehicles, household appliances, and many other intriguing designs. The oldest (those made prior to 1920) were usually hand painted and often contained extra metal parts in addition to the metal strip or screw closures. During the 1950s these metal parts were replaced with plastic, a practice that continued until candy containers met their demise in the 1960s. While predominately clear, they are found in nearly all colors of glass including milk glass, green, amber, pink, emerald, cobalt, ruby flashed, and light blue. Usually the color was intentional, but leftover glass was used as well and resulted in unplanned colors. Various examples are found in light or ice blue, and new finds are always being discovered. Production of the glass portion of candy containers was centered around the western Pennsylvania city of Jeannette. Major producers include Westmoreland Glass, West Bros., Victory Glass, J.H. Millstein, J.C. Crosetti, L.E. Smith, Jack Stough, and T.H. Stough. While 90% of all glass candies were made in the Jeannette area, other companies such as Eagle Glass, Play Toy, and Geo. Borgfeldt Co. have a

few to their credit as well.

Buyer beware! Many candy containers have been reproduced. Some, including the Camera and the Rabbit Pushing Wheelbarrow, come already painted from distributors. Others may have a slick or oily feel to the touch. The following list may also alert you to possible reproductions:

Amber Pistol, L #144 (first sold full in the 1970s, not listed in E&A)

Auto, D&P #173/E&A #33/L #377

Auto, D&P #163/E&A #60/L #356

Black and White Taxi, D&P #182/L #353 (A number of metal roofs have appeared. They are different from originals because the white section is more silvery in color than the original cream. These closures are put on original bases and often priced for hundreds of dollars.)

Camera, D&P #419/E&A #121/L #238 (original says 'Pat Apld For' on bottom, reproduction says 'B. Shakman' or is ground off)

Carpet Sweeper, D&P 296/E&A #133/L #243 (currently being sold with no metal parts)

Carpet Sweeper, E&A #132/L #242 (currently being sold with no metal parts)

Charlie Chaplin, D&P 195/E&A #137/L #83 (original has 'Geo. Borgfeldt' on base; reproduction comes in pink and blue)

Chicken on Nest, D&P #10/E&A #149/L #12

Display Case, D&P #422/E&A #177/L #246 (original should be painted silver and brown)

Dog, D&P #21/E&A #180/L #24 (clear and cobalt)

Drum Mug, D&P #431/E&A #543/L #255

Happifats on Drum, D&P #199/E&A #208/L #89 (no notches on repro for closure to hook into)

Fire Engine, D&P 258/E&A #213/L #386 (repros in green and blue glass)

Independence Hall, D&P #130/E&A #342/L #76 (original is rectangular; repro has offset base with red felt-lined closure)

Jackie Coogan, D&P #202/E&A #345/L #90 (marked inside 'B')

Kewpie, D&P #204/E&A #349/L #91 (must have Geo. Borgfeldt on base to be original)

Mailbox, D&P #216/E&A #521/L #254 (repro marked Taiwan)

Mantel Clock, D&P #483/E&A #162/L #114 (originally in ruby flashed, milk glass, clear, and frosted only)

Mule and Waterwagon, D&P #51/E&A #539/L #38 (original marked Jeannette, PA)

Naked Child, E&A 546/L #94

Owl, D&P #52/E&A #566/L #37, (Original is found in clear only, often painted. Repro is found in clear, blue, green, and pink with a higher threaded base and less detail.)

Peter Rabbit, D&P #60/E&A #618/L #55

Piano, D&P #460/E&A #577/L #289 (original in only clear and milk glass, both painted)

Rabbit Pushing Wheelbarrow, D&P #72/E&A #601/L #47 (eggs are speckled on the repro; solid on the original)

Rocking Horse, D&P #46/E&A #651/L #58 (original in clear only, repro marked 'Rocky')

Safe, D&P #311/E&A #661/L #268 (original in clear, ruby flashed, and milk glass only)

Santa, D&P 284/E&A #674/L #103 (original has plastic head; repro [1970s] is all glass and opens at bottom)

Santa's Boot, D&P #273/E&A #111/L #233

Scottie Dog, D&P #35/E&A #184/L #17 (Repro has a ice-like color and is often slick and oily.)

Station Wagon, D&P #178/E&A #56/L #378

Stough Rabbit, D&P #53/E&A #617/L #54

Uncle Sam's Hat, D&P #428/E&A #303/L #168

Wagon, U.S. Express D&P #530 (glass is being reproduced without any metal parts)

Others are possible. If in doubt, do not buy without a guarantee from the dealer and return privilege in writing.

Our advisor for glass containers is Jeff Bradfield; he is listed in the

Directory under Virginia. You may contact him with questions, if you will include an SASE. See Clubs, Newsletters, and Catalogs for the address of the Candy Container Collectors of America. A bimonthly newsletter offers insight into new finds, reproductions, updates, and articles from over four hundred collectors and members, including all authors of books on candy containers. Dues are $25.00 yearly. The club holds an annual convention in June in Lancaster, Pennsylvania, for collectors of candy containers.

'L' numbers used in this guide refer to a standard reference series, *An Album of Candy Containers, Vols 1 and 2*, by Jennie Long. 'E&A' numbers correlate with *The Compleat American Glass Candy Containers Handbook* by Eikelberner and Agadjanian, revised by Adele Bowden. D&P numbers refer to *The Collector's Guide to Candy Containers* by Doug Dezso and Leon and Rose Poirier (Collector Books). For additional information, another fine reference is *Modern Candy Containers & Novelties* by Jack Brush & William Miller, also from Collector Books.

Airplane, Army Bomber; mk JH Millstein Co, D&P 76/E&A 6/L 328...**40.00**
Airplane, P-38 Lightning; Victory Glass, D&P 82/E&A 12/L 326 ..**225.00**
Airplane, Red Plastic Wing; musical toy, D&P 83/E&A 3 ....**50.00**
Amos & Andy, in auto, Victory Glass, D&P 187/E&A 21/L 77.**500.00**
Apothecary Jar, Old Fashion #2; Stough, D&P 116/L 558 ....**12.00**
Baseball Player by Barrel, D&P 190/E&A 77/L 80 ....**800.00**
Baseball Player on Base, shaker top, D&P 191/E&A 78/L 81 .....**800.00**
Binoculars, Victor, brass-plated tin fr & box, D&P 98/E&A 560/L 624 ...**600.00**
Blimp, heavy glass, D&P 88.....................**300.00**
Boat, Cruiser; JH Millstein, D&P 102 ....**30.00**
Boat, Queen Mary; heavy glass, emb, D&P 103 ....**400.00**
Boat, Submarine; Geo Borgfeldt & Co, D&P 104/E&A 101/L 337 ..**550.00**
Bottle, Dairy Sweets; w/metal fr, D&P 108/E&A 532/L 501 ....**200.00**
Bottle, Dolly's Milk; VG Co, D&P 109/E&A 527/L 66.............**60.00**
Bottle, Milk; German, wire closure at neck, D&P 111 ....**90.00**
Bottle, Seltzer; w/hdl & spout, D&P 112 ....**500.00**
Bucket, Kid Kandy; yel tin/blk silhouettes, D&P 418.................**275.00**
Bureau, slide-on closure, real mirror, D&P 294/E&A 112/L 125 ...**200.00**
Bus, Greyhound w/Luggage Rack; Victory Glass, D&P 151/E&A 113/L 342 ...**300.00**
Bus, Victory Lines Special, D&P 156/E&A 115/L 347 ....**90.00**
Bus w/Screw-On Closure, D&P 153.....................**350.00**
Camel, Shriner's; clear or amber glass, sitting; D&P 4...................**50.00**
Candelabrum, shaker tops w/base, D&P 317/E&A 174-1/L 202 ...**40.00**
Cannon, US Defense Field Gun; tin barrel, D&P 387/E&A 128/L 142 ..**300.00**
Cannon, 2-Wheel Mount #2; cobalt, D&P 385/E&A 124/L 536 ...**500.00**
Car, Boyd; various colors, D&P 159 ....**25.00**
Car, Electric Coupe — Pat Feb 18, 1913; D&P 162/E&A 48/L 355 ..**100.00**
Car, Four Door; mk West Bros Co, D&P 168/E&A 41/L 348..**1,000.00**
Car, Large Flat Top Hearse; D&P 166.....................**600.00**
Car, Little Touring; Stough, D&P 172.....................**30.00**
Car, Minature Streamlined; D&P 173/E&A 33/L 377 (+).............**25.00**
Car, Station Wagon; JH Millstein, D&P 178/E&A 56/L 378 (+) .**40.00**
Car, Yellow Taxi; D&P 184/E&A 43.....................**1,300.00**
Carpet Sweeper, Baby; wire hdl, D&P 295/E&A 132/L 242 (+).**475.00**
Chicken on Oblong Basket, Victory Glass, D&P 11/E&A 147/L 10..**75.00**
Clock, Candy Bank; all plastic, D&P 479 ....**50.00**
Clock, Mantel; stippled w/scrollwork, D&P 482/E&A 164/L 116 ...**200.00**
Coal Car w/Couplers, rivet border, D&P 515 ....**375.00**
Condiment Set, Rainbow Candy; metal base, D&P 297/E&A 175/L 503...**50.00**
Die, glass box w/1 to 6 pips on faces, D&P 421/E&A 175-1/L 268...**25.00**
Dirigible, Mu-Mu; Bakelite closure, D&P 90.....................**200.00**
Dog, Bulldog w/Oblong Base; Stough, D&P 17/E&A 186/L 16 ...**40.00**
Dog, Hot Doggie; HE Widmer, D&P 23/E&A 320/L 14..........**1,100.00**
Dog, Hound w/Lg Glass Hat; seated, D&P 27/E&A 182/L 22 ......**20.00**
Dog, Little Doggie in the Window; Stough, D&P 30/E&A 178/L 483 ..**30.00**
Dog by Barrel, LE Smith, D&P 19/E&A 190/L 13 ....**250.00**
Duck on Rnd Base (basket), D&P 40/E&A 200/L 26 ....**625.00**

Elephant, Genteel; dressed/standing, D&P 42/E&A 207/L 33 ....**350.00**

Felix on Tub, Copyright 1922 – 24 by Pat Sullivan Pat Appld For, gold-tone screw-on closure, D&P 201/E&A 211-1, 3¼x2⅛", from $3,000.00 to $3,500.00. (Photo courtesy Doug Dezso)

Fire Engine, Ladder Truck; Victory Glass, D&P 254/E&A 216/L 384...**250.00**
Fire Engine, Little Boiler #2; D&P 257/E&A 218-1/L 381 ....**100.00**
Fire Engine, Three Dot USA; D&P 260/E&A 220/L 380...........**100.00**
Fish, smiling/tail up, D&P 44.....................**150.00**
Flapper, paper face glued inside, D&P 203/E&A 227 ....**75.00**
Flat Iron, snap-on bottom, D&P 306/E&A 344/L 249 ....**625.00**
Golf Club, German, D&P 425/E&A 244 ....**70.00**
Gun, Beaded Border Grip; D&P 390/E&A 246 ....**20.00**
Gun, Sm Revolver; grip w/dmn emb, D&P 398/E&A 253 ....**30.00**
Gun, Stough's Whistling Jim — Straight Grip; D&P 402 ....**20.00**
Harmonica, Sweetone; harp shape, 13-note, D&P 447 ....**125.00**
Helicopter, attached rotor, Stough, D&P 91/E&A 306/L 329.....**300.00**
Horn, Millstein 1948; plastic bell & mouthpc, D&P 449/E&A 311 ..**20.00**
Horn, Musical Clarinet 55; cb tube/tin whistle cap, D&P 451......**30.00**
Horn, 3 Valve; gilt valves, D&P 455/E&A 312/L 281.................**175.00**
House w/Chimney, front dormer, D&P 129/E&A 324/L 75 ....**250.00**
Jack O'Lantern, Big Straight Eyes; D&P 264/E&A 347/L 160....**350.00**
Kettle on 3 Feet, horizontal ribs/orig closure, D&P 307/E&A 355/L 251 .**45.00**
Koala, stippled, mk San Diego Zoo, D&P 49/L 467.....................**20.00**
Lamp, Candlestick Base; waxed paper-cup shade, D&P 322/E&A 370/L 559...**325.00**
Lamp, Hurricane; pyramid shape/oblong base, D&P 330/E&A 366/L 561 .**425.00**
Lamp, Kerosene w/Swizzle Stick; D&P 333.....................**75.00**
Lamp, Metal Shade; Stough, D&P 335/L 464 ....**50.00**
Lamp, Monkey; mk See Speak Hear No Evil, D&P 338/E&A 533/L 214 ...**350.00**
Lamppost, glass globe/pewter stand, D&P 341/L 553 ....**100.00**
Lantern, Aluminum Top & Bottom; beaded ribs, D&P 343/E&A 449/L 560...**30.00**
Lantern, Japanese Paper Type; w/candle holder inside, D&P 354/E&A 389...**425.00**
Lantern, Squat Six Rib; metal cap w/bail, D&P 363/E&A 401.....**30.00**
Lantern, 16 Hole; D&P 376/E&A 444/L 190 ....**35.00**
Lantern on Stand, shaker closure, ruby stain, D&P 358/L 571......**50.00**
Lanterns, Twins on Anchor; hang on metal fr, D&P 370/E&A 385/L 186...**25.00**
Liberty Bell, pewter closure, D&P 93/E&A 86/L 227.................**200.00**
Liberty Bell w/Hanger, D&P 95/E&A 85/L 229.....................**45.00**
Locomotive, Curved Line 888; D&P 490/E&A 483 ....**55.00**
Locomotive, Dbl Window w/Rear Screw Cap; D&P 525 ....**200.00**
Locomotive, Little 23; open at cab end, D&P 496 ....**125.00**
Locomotive, Stough's Musical Toy; D&P 506 ....**30.00**
Locomotive, 2-Stacker #23; D&P 512/E&A 479/L 603 ....**150.00**
Mug, Child's; false bottom/base holds candy, D&P 432/E&A 541/L 256.**325.00**
Nurse, Waisted; Crosetti, D&P 125/E&A 548/L 71 ....**25.00**
Oil Can, Independence Bell; w/oil-can spout, D&P 435/E&A 556 ..**550.00**
Owl, sitting on base, D&P 52/E&A 566/L 37 (+) **200.00**
Pencil, Kiddies Candy; w/box; D&P 217.....................**50.00**
Peter Rabbit, pnt, JH Millstein, D&P 60/E&A 618/L 55 (+).........**30.00**
Phonograph w/Glass Horn, gold pnt trim, D&P 458/E&A 576/L 286 (+)...**450.00**
Piano, coin-slot closure, milk glass, D&P 460/E&A 577/L 289 (+) ..**400.00**
Pipe, Germany, cork closure, D&P 437/E&A 585 ....**60.00**
Powder Horn, D&P 411/E&A 589/L 265.....................**80.00**

Pumpkin Head Mounted Policeman, no pnt, D&P 269...........**1,600.00**
Pumpkin Head Witch, pnt, wire bail, D&P 272/E&A 594/L 165...**900.00**
Rabbit Family, stippled, mk VG Co, D&P 56/E&A 604/L 43 .**1,000.00**
Racer, Plastic; clear w/gr wheels, D&P 472 ....**30.00**
Racer #12, Victory Glass, D&P 476/E&A 642/L 432 ....**200.00**
Rolling Pin, Victory Glass, D&P 310/E&A 660/L 267 ....**300.00**
Rooster, Crowing; Victory Glass, G pnt, D&P 73/E&A 151.......**350.00**
Safe, Dime; CD Kenny, D&P 312/E&A 661B/L 268...................**100.00**
Santa Claus in Long Coat, base closure, D&P 279......................**300.00**
Santa Claus Leaving Chimney, Victory Glass, D&P 281/E&A 673/L 102...**150.00**
Santa's Boot — Glass, emb strap, D&P 273/E&A 111/L 233 (+).**30.00**
Santa w/Skis, all plastic; D&P 287 ....**20.00**
Settee, Rocking; gilt edge/arms/risers, D&P 313/E&A 653/L 134...**650.00**
Snowman w/Pipe, all plastic, D&P 290..**15.00**
Soldier, Doughboy; emb helmet/uniform, D&P 209/L 525..........**200.00**
Soldier w/Sword, on base, D&P 210/E&A 682/L 107 ....**1,400.00**
Stop & Go, metal post/blades, D&P 441/E&A 706/L 317 ....**525.00**
Suitcase, milk glass, D&P 377/E&A 707.....................................**150.00**
Table, emb drw w/center knob, D&P 316/E&A 714/L 136.........**850.00**
Tank, Man in Turret; emb treads, D&P 412/E&A 722/L 437........**45.00**
Telephone, Desk; metal ear/mouthpcs, D&P 222/L 581...........**1,200.00**
Telephone, Glass Receiver — USA; D&P 226/E&A 736/L 290...**70.00**
Telephone, Kiddies Bank; metal, Stough, D&P 230 ....**90.00**
Telephone, Pay Station; plastic w/glass bottle, D&P 235/E&A 120/L 239...**275.00**
Telephone, Stough's Ringed Base; D&P 247 ....**30.00**
Tomahawk & Gun, wood hdl, cb head, glass gun, D&P 416.........**50.00**
Top, Lg; wood spring-loaded winder, Eagle Glass, D&P 442/E&A 775 ..**125.00**
Toy Assortment, Christmas; 4 toys, D&P 469 ....**100.00**
Toy Assortment, Kiddies Candy Filled; 5 toys, D&P 470 ....**475.00**
Trojan Horse, plastic, mk Rosbro Plastics Prov RI, D&P 48..........**25.00**
Uncle Sam by Barrel, slot in closure, 95% pnt, D&P 215/E&A 801/L 112 ...**800.00**
Village City Garage, tin w/insert, D&P 136/E&A 811/L 76G ...**140.00**
Village School House, tin w/insert, D&P 143/E&A 808/L 76J ...**170.00**
Wagon, Tin; bed notched for seat, D&P 529/E&A 820.................**60.00**
Wheelbarrow, Victory Glass, tin snap-on closure, D&P 531/E&A 832/L 273 ...**90.00**
Windmill, Dutch; 4-blade wheel, D&P 534/E&A 843/L 448........**80.00**
Windmill, Plastic Bank; D&P 536...**30.00**
Windmill, Teddy; crisscross tower, tin cap, D&P 537/E&A 845/L 444...**850.00**
World Globe, mtd on pewter stand, D&P 445/E&A 860/L 276 .**500.00**

Miscellaneous

These types of candy containers are generally figural. Many are holiday related. Our advisor for this category is Jenny Tarrant; she is listed in the Directory under Missouri. See also Christmas; Easter; Halloween.

Key: pm — papier-mache

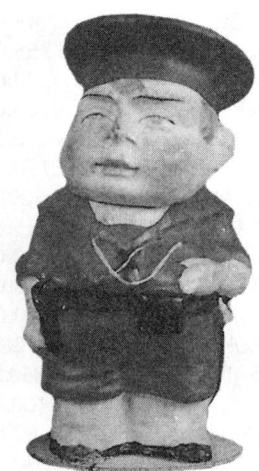

Boy in blue uniform with black belt, knife case, and sword, papier-mache, unmarked German, 6", EX, $265.00.

Bulldog, compo, cream w/orange hat, Germany, 4", VG **100.00**
Cat, pm w/gesso, mc pnt, glass eyes, red ribbon, rpr, 6" **190.00**
Cat, seated, pm w/gesso, worn flocking, glass eyes, old rpr, 4".....**175.00**
Cat in shoe, compo & gesso w/mc pnt, rpr to ears, 4" **150.00**
Cat in shoe, pm & gesso, mc pnt, glass eyes, rprs, 4"...................**150.00**
Doll, bsk open dome head, crepe-paper/cb cylinder body, Germany, 6"..**225.00**
Dove, compo w/gray pnt, pk-pnt metal ft, orange glass eyes, 4½x8" **150.00**
Elephant, pm, glass tusks, Germany, ca 1885-1920, 6" L...........**155.00**
English Bobby, pm, EX pnt, Pat No 208063, 12" **160.00**
Geo WA, compo, stands on rnd box w/silk flag, Germany, 5".....**225.00**
Geo WA bust, bottom plug, compo, 2-3" **125.00**
Geo WA bust, bottom plug, compo, 4-6" **150.00**
Geo WA w/tree stump, compo, Germany, 3-4"...........................**150.00**
Geo WA w/tree stump, compo, Germany, 5-7"...........................**225.00**
Horse, pm, head removes, 4½", VG **85.00**
Pig, pm, gr w/HP features, Made in Germany, 5¼x5½x3" **135.00**
Pig, pm, sleeping, worn/soiled pk flocking, 5⅝"..........................**165.00**
Pigeon, compo w/metal ft, gray/wht/irid purple, 4½x6" **150.00**
Rooster, compo w/metal ft, yel/red/brn pnt, lt ft wear, 4½x4¾" .**195.00**
Rooster, pm, lg red comb, Made in Japan, 1950s, 7", EX..............**75.00**
St Patrick's Day, Irish man bust, w/plug, compo, Germany, 3-4".**125.00**
St Patrick's Day, Irish man bust, w/plug, compo, Germany, 5-6".**150.00**
St Patrick's Day, Irish man on candy box, compo, Germany, 3½" .**155.00**
St Patrick's Day, pig, flocked gr, plug in tummy, wood legs, 3-5".**165.00**
St Patrick's Day, pig, pk w/shamrock, compo, Germany, 4-6"......**155.00**
St Patrick's Day, potato, compo, Germany, 3-4".........................**75.00**
Stag, compo w/metal rack, brn flocked/yel glass eyes, Germany, 10", VG..**465.00**
Stork w/baby, spun cotton & paper, lifts leg, Germany, 1950s, 6½" ...**95.00**
Turkey, compo w/metal ft, head removes, Germany, 5" **195.00**
Turkey, compo w/metal legs, head removes, Germany, 3½" **125.00**
Turkey, pm, cb base, 5½", EX **170.00**
Watermelon w/face, molded cb, Made in Austria, 4¼x2¾", EX.**160.00**

Canes

Fancy canes and walking sticks were once the mark of a gentleman. Hand-carved examples are collected and admired as folk art from the past. The glass canes that never could have been practical are unique whimseys of the glass-blower's profession. Gadget and container sticks, which were produced in a wide variety, are highly desirable. Character, political, and novelty types are also sought after as are those with handles made of precious metals.

For more information we recommend *American Folk Art Canes, Personal Sculpture*, by George H. Meyer, Sandringham Press, 100 West Long Lake Rd., Suite 100, Bloomfield Hills, MI 48304. Other possible references are *Canes in the United States* by Catherine Dike and *Canes From the 17th – 20th Century* by Jeffrey Snyder. For information concerning the Cane Collectors Club, see the Directory under Clubs, Newsletters, and Catalogs. Our advisor for this category is Bruce Thalberg; he is listed in the Directory under Connecticut.

Boxwood, lady's leg w/garter & boot hdl, chestnut shaft, 1870s..**125.00**
Brass plated, elephant sword hdl, mahog shaft, brass ferrule, 1900s .**200.00**
Cigarette lighter in malacca crook, Ronson De-Light, 1930s...**4,750.00**
Ear trumpet in blk enamel metal hdl, gold collar, bamboo shaft, 1860s.**2,500.00**
Ebony pug dog w/glass eyes, on pillow hdl silver collar, ebony shaft.......**1,000.00**
Folk art, wood, cvd satyr's head w/porc eyes, chain-cvd shaft, 1860s...**325.00**
Folk art, wood, cvd tobacco leaves, alligator, 2-tone, 1870s........**600.00**
Harmonica, bec de corbin hdl, mahog w/ivory inlay, 1890s.....**2,000.00**
Horn, elephant w/glass eyes hdl, malacca shaft, metal/iron ferrule...**200.00**
Imari porc ball w/chrysanthemums, gold-plated collar, English, 1880s...**1,500.00**
Ivory, cat w/gr glass eyes finial, gilt collar, ebony shaft, 1900s.....**300.00**
Ivory, horse-head w/glass eyes hdl, silver collar/malacca shaft, 1880s....**750.00**

Ivory, Lady Liberty L-shaped hdl, malacca shaft, ca 1886............**500.00**
Ivory, Noh masks hdl w/stained details, bamboo shaft, England, 1890s..**600.00**
Ivory, rabbit w/glass eyes hdl, silver collar, malacca shaft, Am.**1,700.00**
Ivory, ram w/glass eyes hdl/sterling collar/ebony shaft, London, 1885....**1,500.00**
Ivory, rose hdl, coconut wood shaft, brass/ivory ferrule................**450.00**
Ivory, skull w/o lower jaw, hdl silver collar, ebony shaft, 1890s.**1,000.00**
Ivory, 2 faces of man hdl, malacca shaft, horn ferrule, 1900s **650.00**
Ivory hand hdl removes for 12½" sword, bamboo shaft, 1840s ...**1,200.00**
Ivory hdl w/inlay, blk pnt hardwood shaft, horn ferrule, 1920s...**1,200.00**
Jade knob, rock crystal ring, silver collar, ebony shaft, 1900s......**900.00**
Meissen, bl & wht porc hdl w/monarch reserve, dk hardwood shaft, 1860s ...**850.00**
Porc, lady & flowers, pk on wht hdl, gold collar, malacca shaft, 1880s..**375.00**
Rhino hoof w/tortoise shell & brass pins, malacca shaft, 1880s ..**600.00**
Rhino horn L hdl, solid 1-pc w/brass ferrule, 1880s....................**700.00**
Rose quartz w/amethyst & seed pearls, pnt hardwood shaft, Fr, 1900s..**3,750.00**
Sard agate, sq hdl, silver collar, bamboo shaft, London, ca 1900 ...**200.00**
Silver, Am Indian hdl, partridgewood shaft, Unger Bros, 1890s ...**3,000.00**
Silver, eagle's head hdl, horn ferrule, hardwood shaft, Tiffany .**7,000.00**
Silver, wavy lines & eng name, Gorham/mk Sterling, hardwood shaft...**300.00**
Silver, whistle in ornate scroll L hdl, exotic palmwood shaft, 1890s **500.00**
Tortoiseshell & silver pistol hdl, malacca shaft, horn ferrule, 1890s........**750.00**
Wedgwood, bl & wht slightly curved hdl, partridgewood shaft, 1920s..**2,600.00**
Whale ivory & bone w/cvd fist, baleen cuff button, brass tip, 19th C **800.00**

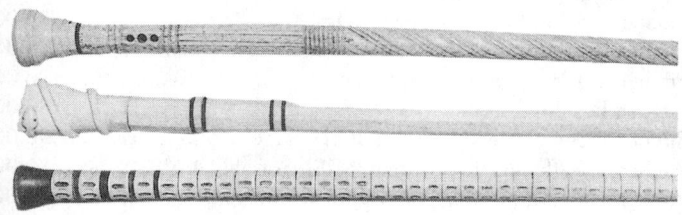

Whalebone with ring, reeded and twisted carved details, ivory knob, black baleen (?) inlay, 35", $2,200.00; Whalebone, carved ivory handle in form of hand with snake, inlaid black rings, 37½", $1,750.00; Fish vertebrae with baleen or horn inlaid rings and knob (chipped), 34", $195.00. (Photo courtesy Garth's Auctions Inc.)

Whalebone w/cvd whale tail on crook hdl, baleen separators, 1850s ..**1,000.00**
Wood, Am Indian chief hdl, de-barked natural wood hdl, 1885.**375.00**
Wood, belt cvd on hdl, shaft: snake w/vining ivy, 35" **450.00**
Wood, bulldog w/ivory inlay/glass eyes, silver collar, wood shaft ..**550.00**
Wood, cvd Airedale w/glass eyes, silver collar, malacca shaft, 1895........**500.00**
Wood, cvd dog w/wagging tongue w/glass eyes hdl, cherrywood shaft....**400.00**
Wood, cvd fist hdl, detailed rattlesnake enwines length, 35" **300.00**
Wood, geometric-inlay balloon hdl, 3-color shaft w/Masonic motif, 33" ...**100.00**
Wood, primitive bird hdl, red/gr stain w/bead eyes, burned dots, 33" ..**50.00**
Wood, sheepdog w/glass eyes pistol hdl, malacca shaft, rpl ferrule.....**350.00**

Canton

Canton is a blue and white porcelain that was first exported in the 1790s by clipper ships from China to the United States. Importation continued into the 1920s. Canton became very popular along the East Coast where the major ports were located. Its popularity was due to several factors: it was readily available, inexpensive, and (due to the fact that it came in many different forms) appealing to homeowners.

The porcelain's blue and white color and simple motif (teahouse, trees, bridge, and a rain-cloud border) have made it a favorite of people who collect early American furniture and accessories. Buyers of Canton should shop at large outdoor shows and up-scale antique shows. Collec-

tions are regularly sold at auction and many examples may be found on eBay. Collectors usually prefer a rich, deep tone rather than a lighter blue. Cracks, large chips, and major repairs will substantially affect values. Prices of Canton have escalated sharply over the last twenty years, and rare forms are highly sought after by advanced collectors. Our advisor for this category is Hobart D. Van Deusen; he is listed in the Directory under Connecticut.

Bowl, fruit; rtcl rim, end hdls, 10¾", NM **850.00**
Bowl, scalloped rim, 4½x10¼" **925.00**
Bowl, serving; sq, 8¾", pr..**460.00**
Creamer, flat spout, 3½" **165.00**
Mug, cylindrical, twisted hdl, 4¼", EX...................................**515.00**
Mug, cylindrical, twisted hdl, 5½", EX...................................**750.00**
Pitcher, 7¾", EX...**500.00**
Plate, 19th C, 10" **85.00**
Platter, octagonal, rim rprs, 17", VG **165.00**
Platter, octagonal, 19th C, 14¾x11¾", EX **400.00**
Platter, scalloped border, 19th C, 10⅛" **400.00**
Shrimp dish, 19th C, 10¼x9½" **515.00**
Syllabub, cup, 3⅜" **160.00**
Teapot, domed lid, hairline in hdl, 8x9¼" **575.00**
Tureen, boar's head hdls, stem finial, ftd, 7¾x14x9¾".............**1,265.00**
Tureen, gravy; boar's head hdls, fruit finial, 3½x5", +underplate ...**495.00**

Capodimonte

The relief style, highly colored and defined porcelain pieces in this listing are commonly called and identified in our current marketplace as Capodimonte. It was King Ferdinand IV, son of King Charles who opened a factory in Naples in 1771 and began to use the mark of the blue crown N (BCN). When the factory closed in 1834, the Ginori family at Doccia near Florence, Italy, acquired what was left of the factory and continued using its mark. The factory continued until 1896 when it was then combined with Societa Ceramica Richard of Milan which continues today to manufacture fine porcelain pieces marked with a crest and wreaths under a blue crown with R. Capodimonte.

Boxes and steins are highly sought after as they are cross collectibles. Figurines, figure groupings, flowery vases, urns, and the like are also highly collectible, but most items on the market today are of recent manufacture. In the past several years, Europeans have been attending U.S. antique shows and auctions in order to purchase Capodimonte items to take back home, since many pieces were destroyed during the two world wars. This has driven up prices of the older ware. Our advisor for this category is James Highfield; he is listed in the Directory under Indiana.

Floral Style

Basket of flowers, 10x8x14"...**55.00**
Carriage w/2 horses, 21x30"..**295.00**
Ewer, single flower, 13" **10.00**
Vase, wide hdls, 22x16"..**40.00**
Vase, 15x8" **30.00**
Wall clock, 19x15" **40.00**

Relief Style

Bottle, scent; child & dragonfly, crown stopper, BCN, 3x½" **65.00**
Bowl, peasants around royal lady (sitting), BCN, 2x14".............**150.00**
Box, frolicking cherubs w/grape harvest, BCN, 3½x3x6"............**180.00**
Box, grand piano w/brass legs, BCN, 5½x5½x9" **400.00**
Box, Leda & swan on lid, raised ft, BCN, 3¼x3x5" **100.00**
Cake platter, center family crest, BCN, 7x10½"........................**200.00**

Candlesticks, 3 draped maidens, BCN, 13½", pr 250.00
Card holder, cherubs & children, BCN, 2⅝" dia 20.00
Card holder, peasant figural, BCN, 3⅜" H 17.00
Figurines, dwarf band, BCN, set of 4 ....73.00
Plaque, deer & dogs in woods, BCN, 9½x5½" 145.00
Plaques, mtd in jeweled & bronze wood fr, 19x12", pr 650.00
Plates, floral center, signed presentation, 9¼", set of 6............600.00
Stein, grape harvesting, bird finial, BCN, 12"......................400.00
Stein, monkey finial lid, camel-face hdl, BCN, 9".................450.00
Teapot, country & mtn scenes, BCN, 8x5x5".........................100.00
Urn, Roman soldiers, dbl mask hdls, Keramos mk, 10x6½" dia 50.00
Wine pitcher, drunken men & satyrs, grapevine hdl, BCN, 6" ...100.00

Carlton Ware

Carlton Ware was the product of Wiltshaw and Robinson, who operated in the Staffordshire district of England from about 1890. During the 1920s, they produced ornamental ware with enameled and gilded decorations such as flowers and birds, often on a black background. In 1958 the firm was renamed Carlton Ware Ltd. Their trademark was a crown over a circular stamp with 'W & R, Stoke on Trent,' surrounding a swallow. 'Carlton Ware' was sometimes added by hand.

Ashtray, New Mikado, Rouge Royale ground, 5x5" 68.00
Ashtray, Rouge Royale, Deco shape, 7" L 40.00
Basket, cream w/floral on ea side, MIE/Australia, 4"..............90.00
Biscuit bbl, floral on cream, SP rim, lid & hdl, ca 1895, 6" 495.00
Bookends, Polka Dot, Deco shape, 5", pr 175.00
Bowl, Apple Blossom, dbl leaf, 2x9½x6".............................45.00
Bowl, Apple Blossom, leaf form, 10x6"..............................37.00
Bowl, Bleu Royale, #17359, 2¾x9¼".................................85.00
Bowl, Flowers & Basket (Springtime), oblong, 2¾x10¾x8" ...60.00
Bowl, Foxglove, 2x8x5¾"...32.00
Bowl, Foxglove, 10½"..45.00
Bowl, gr & blk tree w/orange blooms, orange mottled hdls/ft, 3¼x7" ..295.00
Bowl, Grape & Leaf, 2½x9½x9".....................................95.00
Bowl, Lobster/Langouste, 3-lobe, 11x11½" 75.00
Bowl, Magnolia, 12½x6¾"...22.00
Bowl, Oak Tree, 2½x11x7"..110.00
Bowl, orange lustre w/bl bird in wht center, W&R mk, 11x7"....325.00
Bowl, Poppy, shape #2289, 2½x9½x9"...............................95.00
Bowl, Poppy, 2x8½x5½"..45.00
Bowl, Primula, triangular, shape #2036, 4¾x4"....................18.00
Bowl, Rouge Royale, Mandarin, 2x10½x8¼"........................195.00
Bowl, Rouge Royale, shape #2149/2, 2x8½" sq......................49.00
Bowl, salad; Foxglove, gr, w/servers 125.00
Bowl, salad; leaf shape, dk gray/gray-wht, 10", +gray & wht servers...37.50
Bowl, salad; Lettuce (Tomato), 3x9" +8" servers.....................70.00
Bowl, salad; Primula, shape #2005, 3x9¼"...........................48.00
Bowl, salad; Wild Rose (Dog Rose), ftd, 4x11x8½" 95.00
Bowl, serving; Hazelnut, 13½x8½"...................................37.00
Bowl, serving; Hazelnut, 17x10½"...................................65.00
Bowl, Spring, gr w/flowers, ftd, conical Deco shape, 2x7" 140.00
Bowl, Thistle, 2x9½x6½" 40.00
Bowl, Water Lily, dbl leaf, 2x8¼x5½" 70.00
Bowl, Wild Rose (Dog Rose), leaf shape, 2x8½x5" 30.00
Bowl, Wild Rose (Dog Rose), 2x9¾x6"...............................38.00
Butter dish, Buttercup, pk, 4½x3¾"..................................30.00
Cheese plate, Apple Blossom, leaf shape, 7x4¾".....................38.00
Cheese plate, Red Currants, 7x6"....................................43.00
Coffeepot, bright orange w/ringed bottom, 12", +6 matching cups..100.00
Coffeepot, lilac w/wht lids & int, +cr/sug & 6 c&s.................300.00
Comport, Buttercup, yel, 2¼x5"....................................75.00

Comport, Hydrangea, 1½x6¾x4¼".....................................95.00
Comport, Primula, ftd, 2x6x4¾"....................................50.00
Creamer, Lettuce (Tomato), 2½x5⅝"..................................30.00
Creamer & sugar bowl, Apple Blossom, shape #1670, 3¾", 2¼" 110.00
Creamer & sugar bowl, Foxglove, yel ground........................110.00
Cruet, Twin Tone, burgundy/cream, 7" L............................40.00
Cup & saucer, demi; mustard yel w/blk & gold border, 1910-15 .115.00
Cup & saucer, Foxglove..70.00
Cup & saucer, Lace Heritage.......................................25.00
Cup & saucer, Oriental design, gilted hdl/int on cup & saucer border ...70.00
Cup & saucer, Primula, 3x3", 5½"..................................80.00
Cup & saucer, Wild Rose...45.00
Cup plate, leaf shape, gr, 7¾x7"...................................30.00
Egg cup, 2 legs as ft, gr shoes w/mustard polka-dot socks, from $50 to..65.00
Egg cup set, Apple Blossom, 4 cups+shakers+tray 200.00
Ginger jar, lyre-tail bird, flowers & fruit, #2969, 8".............100.00
Ginger jar, Rouge Royale, Mikado, gilded, w/lid, 3½"..............130.00
Honey pot, Foxglove, gr...80.00
Honey pot, Hydrangea..95.00
Humidor, Oriental birds/trees, brass closure/finial, gold trim, 4¼" ..295.00
Knife, Apple Blossom, yel...25.00
Marmalade pot, Apple Blossom, 4¾".................................65.00
Marmalade pot, Foxglove, 4¼"......................................90.00
Mug, hangman scene, 1940, 3"......................................45.00
Nut dish, gr w/purple grapes & gr leaves, w/matching spoon........90.00
Pitcher, Apple Blossom, gr, ped ft, 3½"...........................55.00
Pitcher, Apple Blossom, oval, 2¼x5¼"..............................45.00
Pitcher, bl flowers on lt bl, sq hdl, 6½"..........................300.00
Pitcher, Foxglove, 2¼"..50.00
Pitcher, French Blue, '9'-shape hdl in gold, 6" 90.00
Pitcher, gr w/florals, flower finial, MIE/Australia, 4½"..........210.00
Pitcher, Hazelnut, 6"...45.00
Pitcher, Oak Tree, shape #1191, 5¼"...............................155.00
Pitcher, Poppy, purple on lt gr, Art Deco style, ca 1930s, 6" 250.00
Pitcher, Rabbits at Dusk, rabbits under tree on orange, gr int, 7"....260.00
Pitcher, Rock Garden (Garden Wall), Deco style, 3½"...............80.00
Plate, Apple Blossom, triangular leaf form, 7¼x7¼"................38.00
Plate, Buttercup, shape #1395, MIE, 3¾x4½"........................40.00
Plate, Buttercup, shape #1482, 7x6½"..............................60.00
Plate, Buttercup, yel, 9½x8½".....................................90.00
Plate, Flowers & Basket (Springtime), hdl, 11½x7"................60.00
Plate, Foxglove, leaf shape, 5¾x5"................................25.00
Plate, Lettuce (Tomato), shape #2095/2, 10¾x6"...................28.00
Plate, Magnolia, 13½x5"...38.00
Plate, Morning Glory, lav, 10¾x6¾"................................30.00
Plate, Morning Glory, teal, 14x5".................................30.00
Plate, Poppy, 3-ftd, shape #2257/8, 9x8¼".........................85.00
Plate, Water Lily, shape #1783/8, 9x8"............................68.00
Plate, Wild Rose (Dog Rose), 8¼"..................................35.00
Plate, Wild Rose (Dog Rose), 10x9"................................50.00
Platter, egg; Lobster/Langouste, 12"..............................80.00
Sauce boat, gray/gray-wht leaf shape, 1950s, +tray 26.00
Sauce boat & tray, Buttercup......................................75.00
Sauce boat & tray, Water Lily, WWII era...........................50.00
Shakers, English Beefeater forms, orange mks, 4", pr..............40.00
Shakers, Lobster/Langouste, 3½", pr...............................65.00
Shakers, policemen cylindrical forms, vintage, 4", pr.............40.00
Sugar bowl, Wild Rose, gr, w/lid..................................45.00
Tea set, Windstream, brn & beige, 5x9" pot+jam jar+cr/sug........250.00
Teapot, Foxglove, 4"..210.00
Teapot, Primula, flowers/leaves, flower finial & hdl, 5½"........160.00
Teapot, Willow, bl pagodas on wht, ca 1894, W&R mk, w/lid....265.00
Toast rack, Foxglove, MIE, 3½"....................................95.00
Vase, Autumn Leaf, Pattern #3766, shape #464, 4½"................145.00

Vase, birds on branches & florals, incurvate rim, ped ft, 6".........210.00
Vase, Bleu Royale, gold twist at rim & above ped ft, bulbous, 5" ..95.00
Vase, Fantasia, fantasy flowers on bl w/gilt, 4⅜" 310.00
Vase, Fantasia, fantasy flowers on dk bl bkground, int decor, 6x5"...625.00
Vase, Hollyhocks (Deco style), lustre, orig label, 4½".................295.00
Vase, Persian scenes w/gold on cobalt, 10½x4¾"....................345.00
Vase, Primula, simplistic flowers, bulbous, 3½".........................135.00
Vase, Rock Garden (Garden Wall), shape #1244, 5"...................125.00
Vase, Rouge Royale, gold trim, 4x4"...35.00
Vase, Rouge Royale, Mikado, w/gold, 5½" 150.00
Vase, spider web & flowers on wht, gold rim & hdls, 4"..............185.00
Vase, Tulip, mauve & pk on cream, sq, hdls, 5x5" 90.00

Carnival Collectibles

Carnival items from the early part of this century represent the lighter side of an America that was alternately prospering and sophisticated or devastated by war and domestic conflict. But whatever the country's condition, the carnival's thrilling rides and shooting galleries were a sure way of letting it all go by — at least for an evening.

For further information on chalkware figures, we recommend *The Carnival Chalk Prize* by our advisor, Thomas G. Morris, who is listed in the Directory under Oregon.

In the shooting gallery target listings below, items are rated for availability from 1, commonly found, to 10, rarely found (these numbers appear just before the size), and all are made of cast iron. Our advisors for shooting gallery targets are Richard and Valerie Tucker; their address is listed in the Directory under Texas.

Chalkware Figures

Alice the Goon, ca 1930-40, 10" 165.00
Apache Babe, ca 1936, 15" 75.00
Barney Google, ca 1930-40, 6½" 100.00
Bell Hop, ca 1946, 13"...85.00
Buddy Lee w/hands in pockets, ca 1930-40, 13½" 95.00
Canadian Mountie standing w/1 arm up, mk 1937, 16" 150.00
Cat sitting looking into fishbowl, ca 1940-50, 9½" 75.00
Charlie McCarthy sitting w/hands in pockets, no hat, ca 1935-45, 13" ..90.00
China boy, mk 1948, 13"...120.00
Dead End Kid, ca 1935-45, rare, 15" 165.00
Dog sitting (No Body Loves Me), mk 1917, 5" 35.00
Donald Duck standing, ca 1930-40, 9¾"....................................85.00
Dopey standing w/drum, bank, ca 1937-50, 7½"..........................65.00
Elephant sitting, flat bk, ca 1930-45, 4¼" 15.00
Eugene the Jeep, all chalkware, ca 1930-40, rare, 12" to 14", ea ..350.00
Felix the Cat standing w/hands behind bk, ca 1922-40, 12½" 245.00

Freckles w/finger to mouth, ca 1935-45, 6x8x5¾" 25.00
Frog sitting on log raft, ca 1935-45, 6x8x5¾" 25.00
Girl (Frenchie), mk 1924, 15" 245.00
Girl bathing beauty standing w/hands on head, ca 1920-35, 12" ..95.00
Good Time Willie, mk 7/1939, 9"..70.00
Horse w/sad face, ca 1945-50, 5"..20.00
Hula girl playing ukulele, ca 1935-45, 12¾" 145.00
Human skull, ca 1935-45, 6"...45.00
Humpty Dumpty sitting on fence smiling, ca 1940-50, 11"...........45.00
Jockey on horse jumping over barrier, ca 1935-45, 9¼"................45.00
Lady in evening dress, ca 1935-45, 13½" 75.00
Lady in full skirt w/Afghan dog, ca 1930-40, 11¼"......................55.00
Lighthouse lamp, w/light inside, ca 1935-45, 15½" 115.00
Little Red Riding Hood, mk 1930/Connie Mamat, 14" 55.00
Mae West standing holding flower, ca 1935-45, 13" 145.00
Majorette holding baton, ca 1940-50, 15½".................................55.00
Matador w/hands up, mk 1939, 14"...120.00
Mexican taking a siesta, ashtray, mk 1936, 6½"...........................45.00
Nude Lady (Hubba Hubba), mk 1947, 14"................................185.00
Olive Oyl standing w/hands at sides, ca 1935-45, 8½" 110.00
Oriental lady sitting w/hands around knees, ca 1935-40, 5½".......45.00
Owl, flat bk, ca 1935-50, 5½"...10.00
Pappy Yokum w/arms crossed, ca 1935-45, 13" 125.00
Parrot perched on stump, ca 1935-40, 13½" 45.00
Pig standing wearing apron & cap, ca 1940-50, 5½".....................15.00
Pluto sitting, ca 1930-40, 6"..55.00
Porky Pig standing wearing top hat, ca 1940-50, rare, 11" 75.00
Rabbit sitting, bank, ca 1940-50, 11¾"..55.00
Rattlesnake coiled, ashtray, ca 1935-45, 3½" 20.00
Sailing schooner, 3-D, ca 1930-40, 10½" 45.00
Sailor at ease holding rifle, ca 1935-45, 13½"............................110.00
Santa Claus w/bag of toys on shoulder, ca 1935-45, 12½"............65.00
Scottie dog sitting w/ears pointed, ca 1935-45, 7" 25.00
Shirley Temple, ca 1935-45, 14½"..240.00
Snow White standing holding her dress, ca 1937-50, 14" 85.00
Snuffy Smith in lg floppy hat, ca 1934-45, 9¼" 95.00
Sweater girl w/hands in pockets wearing tam, ca 1930-40, 11½" ..45.00
Three Little Pigs sitting together, ca 1935-45, 5x5½" 30.00
Uncle Sam w/sleeves rolled up, ca 1935-45, 15" 135.00
Wimpy eating hamburger (You Bring the Ducks), mk 1929, 13" 175.00

Shooting Gallery Targets

Battleship, worn wht pnt, Mangels, 5, 6¼x11⅜", $200 to..........300.00
Birds (8) on bar, worn pnt, Mangels, 9, 3½x41½", $700 to........800.00
Bull's-eye w/pop-up duck, old pnt, Quakenbush, 7, 12" dia, $500 to....600.00

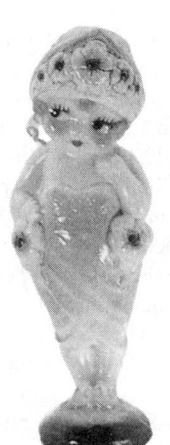

Flapper-era 'Sheba Girl,' copyright Jenkins, ca 1925, 13½", $175.00. (Photo courtesy Thomas G. Morris)

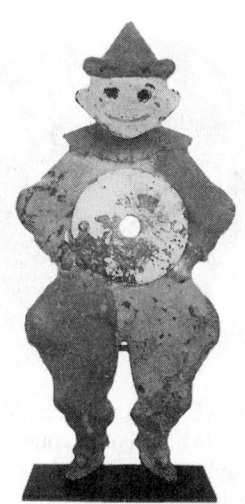

Clown, standing with attached bull's eye, cast iron with multicolor paint, H.C. Evans or Emil R. Hoffmann, Chicago, IL, 7, rare, 20½x9¾x¾", $1,000.00+. (Photo courtesy Richard and Valerie Tucker)

Clown, worn red/wht pnt, Mangels, 9, 19x9½"+movable arms, minimum...**1,000.00**
Dbl star spinner, worn mc pnt, WF Mangels, 6, 8x2¾", $200 to..**300.00**
Dog running, worn wht pnt, Smith or Evans, 6, 6x11", $100 to.**200.00**
Duck, detailed feathers, old pnt, Parker, 8, 3¾x5½", $100 to.....**200.00**
Duck, detailed feathers, worn pnt, Evans, 4, 5½x8½", $100 to ..**200.00**
Eagle w/wings wide, mc pnt, Smith or Evans 6, 14¾", $650 to...**750.00**
Elephant, worn red pnt, King, 10, 17x19", minimum value.....**1,000.00**
Greyhound, bull's-eye, old patina, Parker, 8, 26" W, minimum ..**1,000.00**
Indian chief, worn mc pnt, Hoffmann or Smith, 10, 20x15", minimum..**1,000.00**
Monkey, standing, worn pnt, 10, 9¾x8½", $300 to.....**400.00**
Owl, bull's eye, wht traces, Evans, 6, 10¾x5⅛", $400 to **500.00**
Pipe, old patina, Smith, 1, 5⅜x1¾", value less than **50.00**
Rabbit running, bull's-eye, old patina, Parker, 8, 12x25x1", minimum ...**1,000.00**
Rabbit standing, worn pnt, Smith or Mueller, 8, 18x10", $900 to.....**1,000.00**
Reindeer (elk), wht pnt (worn/rusty), 7, 10x9", $300 to.............**400.00**
Saber-tooth tiger, old patina, Mangels, 7, 7¾x13", $300 to **400.00**
Soldier w/rifle, pnt traces/old patina, Mueller, 5, 9x5", $100 to..**200.00**
Squirrel running, old patina, Smith, 4, 5⅛x9¼", $100 to...........**200.00**
Swan, worn wht pnt, Mueller, 7, 5¾x5", $100 to.......................**200.00**

Carnival Glass

Carnival glass is pressed glass that has been coated with a sodium solution and fired to give it an exterior lustre. First made in America in 1905, it was produced until the late 1920s and had great popularity in the average American household, for unlike the costly art glass produced by Tiffany, carnival glass could be mass produced at a small cost. Colors most found are marigold, green, blue, and purple; but others exist in lesser quantities and include white, clear, red, aqua opalescent, peach opalescent, ice blue, ice green, amber, lavender, and smoke.

Companies mainly responsible for its production in America include the Fenton Art Glass Company, Williamstown, West Virginia; the Northwood Glass Company, Wheeling, West Virginia; the Imperial Glass Company, Bellaire, Ohio; the Millersburg Glass Company, Millersburg, Ohio; and the Dugan Glass Company (Diamond Glass), Indiana, Pennsylvania. In addition to these major manufacturers, lesser producers included the U.S. Glass Company, the Cambridge Glass Company, the Westmoreland Glass Company, and the McKee Glass Company.

Carnival glass has been highly collectible since the 1950s and has been reproduced for the last twenty-five years. Several national and state collectors' organizations exist, and many fine books are available on old carnival glass, including *The Standard Encyclopedia of Carnival Glass* by Bill Edwards, *Dugan & Diamond Carnival Glass, 1909 – 1931, Imperial Carnival Glass,* and *Northwood Carnival Glass, 1908 – 1925,* all by Carl O. Burns.

Flowers and Frames, bowl, oxblood, triangular, $275.00.
(Photo courtesy Carl Burns)

Acorn (Fenton), bowl, gr, 6¼-7½"..**185.00**
Acorn (Millersburg), compote, amethyst, rare........................**2,000.00**
Amaryllis (Northwood), compote, marigold, sm........................**300.00**
Angela, perfume, marigold **50.00**

Apple Blossom (Diamond), bowl, marigold, 6-7½" **25.00**
Apple Tree (Fenton), pitcher, marigold......................................**300.00**
Arched Flute (Fenton), toothpick holder, Celeste Blue **125.00**
Art Deco (English), bowl, marigold, 4" **35.00**
Australian Diamond (Crystal), creamer, amethyst......................**80.00**
Autumn Acorns (Fenton), plate, amethyst, very scarce...........**1,200.00**
Balloons (Imperial), perfume atomizer, marigold........................**60.00**
Band of Stars, wine, marigold, stemmed **50.00**
Banded Diamonds (Crystal), flower set, marigold, 2 pcs...........**150.00**
Banded Drape (Fenton), tumbler, wht..**95.00**
Banded Laurel Wreath, juice tumbler, marigold, ftd **25.00**
Basketweave (Northwood), compote, marigold...........................**60.00**
Beaded Acanthus (Imperial), milk pitcher, gr **260.00**
Beaded Cable (Northwood), candy dish, bl **185.00**
Beaded Panels (Imperial), bowl, marigold, 8"............................**45.00**
Beaded Shell (Dugan), creamer or spooner, marigold **75.00**
Beads (Northwood), bowl, amethyst, 8½".....................................**60.00**
Bellaire Souvenir (Imperial), bowl, marigold, scarce **125.00**
Bells & Beads (Dugan), hat shape, amethyst................................**60.00**
Big Basketweave (Dugan), basket, marigold, lg...........................**75.00**
Big Fish (Millersburg), banana bowl, gr, rare **1,900.00**
Blackberry, Miniature (Fenton), plate, bl, stemmed, scarce **450.00**
Blackberry (Fenton), vase, whimsey, marigold, rare...................**800.00**
Blackberry Spray (Fenton), bonbon, marigold **35.00**
Blossom & Palm (Northwood), bowl, gr, 9"..................................**70.00**
Blueberry (Fenton), pitcher, bl, scarce......................................**900.00**
Border Plants (Dugan), bowl, amethyst, flat, 8½"......................**125.00**
Bouquet (Fenton), tumbler, bl **100.00**
Brand Furniture (Fenton), basket, advertising, marigold, open edge...**100.00**
Britt (Kahula), tumbler, bl, rare...**1,000.00**
Brocaded Acorns (Fostoria), ice bucket, ice bl **255.00**
Brocaded Daises (Fostoria), wine goblet, ice gr.........................**200.00**
Brocaded Palms (Fostoria), bowl, dome, ice gr............................**85.00**
Brocaded Summer Gardens, cake plate, ice bl, w/center hdl.......**135.00**
Broken Arches (Imperial), punch bowl, marigold, w/base...........**400.00**
Bud Vase Whimsey (Fenton), vase, bl, 2 or 4 sides up **100.00**
Bull's Eye (US Glass), oil lamp, marigold...................................**210.00**
Butterflies (Fenton), bonbon, bl **65.00**
Butterfly (Fenton), ornament, ice bl, rare..................................**650.00**
Butterfly & Berry (Fenton), bowl, wht, ftd, 5"............................**95.00**
Butterfly & Fern (Fenton), pitcher, marigold, variant (no ferns)...**2,000.00**
Buzz Saw, shade, marigold **40.00**
Buzz Saw & File, pitcher, marigold..**350.00**
Cameo Medallion Basket (Westmoreland), basket, marigold, 3 szs, $35 to...**75.00**
Cane (Imperial), pickle dish, clambroth......................................**20.00**
Cane & Daisy Cut (Jenkins), basket, marigold, hdld, rare **220.00**
Capitol (Westmoreland), bowl, bl, ftd, sm **70.00**
Caroline (Dugan), banana bowl, marigold, 7-10"........................**70.00**
Cartwheel, #411 (Heisey), goblet, marigold **75.00**
Chatham (US Glass), candlesticks, marigold, pr **90.00**
Cherokee, tumbler, bl...**65.00**
Cherries & Little Flowers (Northwood), pitcher, marigold.........**175.00**
Cherry (aka Hanging Cherries) (Millersburg), bowl, marigold, 9"..**150.00**
Cherry (aka Hanging Cherries) (Millersburg), creamer, marigold ..**150.00**
Cherry Chain (Fenton), plate, marigold, 6-9".............................**115.00**
Cherry Smash (US Glass), bowl, marigold, 8" **65.00**
Chesterfield (Imperial), candlesticks, marigold, pr.....................**60.00**
Chesterfield (Imperial), champagne, marigold, 5½".....................**35.00**
Chrysanthemum (Fenton), bowl, bl, flat, 9" **125.00**
Coin Spot (Dugan), compote, aqua opal.....................................**375.00**
Coin Spot (Dugan), compote, peach opal....................................**175.00**
Columbia (Imperial), vase, marigold **45.00**
Connie (Northwood), pitcher, wht **750.00**
Connie (Northwood), tumbler, wht...**150.00**

Corn, cruet, wht, rare..1,100.00
Cornflowers, bowl, marigold, ftd............................125.00
Cornucopia (Fenton), candlesticks, marigold, pr 75.00
Cosmos & Cane (US Glass), chop plate, marigold, rare.........1,200.00
Cosmos & Cane (US Glass), sugar bowl, marigold, w/lid 100.00
Covered Frog (Cooperative Flint), ice gr 325.00
CR (Argentina), ashtray, marigold 175.00
Crackle (Imperial), bowl, gr, 9".............................30.00
Crackle (Imperial), bowl, marigold, 5" 15.00
Crucifix (Imperial), candlestick, marigold, rare, ea...........600.00
Curtain Time, vase, marigold, 9½" 35.00
Curved Star/Cathedral, compote, marigold, 2 szs..............60.00
Cut Crystal (US Glass), water bottle, marigold 185.00
Cut Sprays (Imperial), vase, marigold, 10½"..................45.00
Dahlia (Dugan), bowl, wht, ftd, 5" 95.00
Daisy & Cane (Brockwitz), epergne, marigold.................175.00
Daisy & Plume (Northwood & Dugan), candy dish, amethyst, ftd 90.00
Daisy Dear (Dugan), bowl aqua 225.00
Daisy Dear (Dugan), plate, whimsey, peach opal, rare.................325.00
Dandelion (Northwood), tumbler, ice bl......................150.00
Davenport, lemonade tumbler, marigold 35.00
Deep Grape (Millersburg), compote, marigold, rare 1,800.00
DeVilbiss, atomizer, marigold, complete 125.00
Diamond & Fan, cordial set, marigold, 7-pc..................350.00
Diamond & File (Fenton), plate, marigold, 2 sides up, scarce, 9½"...150.00
Diamond Cut (Crystal), bowl, marigold, 10"...................90.00
Diamond Flutes (US Glass), parfait, marigold.................55.00
Diamond Lace (Imperial), bowl, gr, 5".........................50.00
Diamond Point Columns (Fenton), vase, bl.....................90.00
Diamond Point Columns (Late), powder jar, marigold, w/lid........40.00
Diamond Star, vase, marigold, 8".............................80.00
Double Daisy (Fenton), pitcher, marigold, bulbous 200.00
Double Daisy (Fenton), tumbler, gr 40.00
Double Loop (Northwood), sugar bowl, bl......................60.00
Doughnut Bridle Rosette, amethyst 95.00
Dozen Roses, A (Imperial), bowl, amethyst, ftd, rare, 8-10" 900.00
Dragon & Lotus (Fenton), nut bowl, bl, scarce 425.00
Drapery (Northwood), vase, marigold 65.00
Drapery Variant (Northwood), vase, bl, scarce 175.00
Dugan's Many Ribs (Dugan), hat shape, peach opal.............95.00
Dugan's Many Ribs (Dugan), vase, peach opal 125.00
Early American (Duncan & Miller), plate, marigold...............75.00
Egg & Dart, candlesticks, marigold, pr 90.00
Elks (Millersburg), bowl, amethyst, rare...................2,100.00
Embroidered Flower & Urn (Jain), tumbler, marigold 90.00
Enameled Crocus, pitcher, marigold 125.00
Enameled Crocus, tumbler, marigold 20.00
Enameled Freesia, pitcher, marigold 125.00
Enameled Iris (Fenton), pitcher, bl.........................650.00
Engraved Floral (Fenton), tumbler, gr 95.00
Etched Deco (Standard), bowl, marigold, 3-ftd, 7" 35.00
Evelyn (Fostoria), bowl, gr, 1940s........................1,000.00
Fan (Dugan), gravy boat, amethyst, ftd......................175.00
Fan (Dugan), sauce bowl, peach opal, 5".....................150.00
Fan-Tail (Fenton), bowl, marigold, ftd, 9"..................125.00
Fashion (Imperial), butter dish, amethyst 200.00
Feathered Serpent (Fenton), bowl, gr, tri-corner, 6" 150.00
Feldman Bros (Fenton), basket, open edge, marigold, very scarce ...55.00
Fenton's #9, candy jar, marigold, w/lid......................35.00
Fenton's #643, candy jar, marigold, w/lid....................70.00
Fenton's #888, vase, bl......................................70.00
Fentonia Fruit (Fenton), pitcher, marigold, rare 600.00
Fern (Northwood), compote, marigold..........................75.00
Field Flower (Imperial), milk pitcher, gr, rare 220.00

Field Thistle (US Glass), bowl, ice bl, 6-10"................250.00
File (Imperial & English), bowl, amethyst, 7-10"..............50.00
Fine Cut & Star, banana boat, marigold, 5"..................150.00
Fine Rib (Fenton), vase, marigold, w/base, 2⅞"...............35.00
Fine Rib (Northwood), vase, bl, 7-14".......................165.00
Fishscale & Beads (Dugan), bowl, amethyst, 6-8"..............45.00
Five Panel, candy jar, marigold, stemmed.....................70.00
Flashing Stars, tumbler, bl, rare...........................275.00
Florabelle, pitcher, ice gr.................................500.00
Floral & Grape Variant (Fenton), tumbler, bl.................30.00
Floral & Wheat (Dugan), bonbon, bl, stemmed, 2 styles 250.00
Flowers & Spades (Dugan), bowl, amethyst, scarce, 5".........75.00
Flute (Fenton), vase, red, 7-12"............................325.00
Flute (Northwood), butter dish, marigold 135.00
Flute (Northwood), ring tree, marigold, rare................175.00
Flute & Cane (Imperial), compote, marigold, lg...............75.00
Flute & Honeycomb (Imperial), bowl, marigold, rare, 8½"........150.00
Folding Fan (Dugan), compote, peach opal 125.00
Footed Drape (Westmoreland), vase, marigold or wht..................50.00
Four Pillars (Northwood & Dugan), vase, ice gr..............250.00
Free Fold (Imperial), vase, wht 70.00
Fruit & Berries (English), bean pot, bl, w/lid, rare........425.00
Fruit Jar (Ball), marigold 50.00
Fruits & Flowers (Northwood), bowl, gr, 7" 65.00
Gaelic (Indiana Glass), butter dish, marigold 165.00
Garden Path (Dugan), bowl, wht, 5-7" 100.00
Georgia Belle (Dugan), card tray, amethyst, ftd, rare...............80.00
Goddess of Harvest (Fenton), bowl, marigold, very rare, 9½" .6,000.00
Golden Bird, nappy, marigold, ftd w/hdl 300.00
Golden Oxen, mug, marigold...................................20.00
Golden Thistle, tray, marigold, rare, 5" 350.00
Gooseberry Spray (US Glass), bowl, marigold, scarce, 10" 65.00
Graceful (Northwood), vase, marigold 45.00
Grape & Cable (Northwood), bonbon, gr.......................100.00
Grape & Cable (Northwood), bowl, ice cream; amethyst, 5-6" 75.00

Grape and Cable (Northwood), bowl, blue, ruffled, 10 – 11½", $250.00.
(Photo courtesy Bill Edwards)

Grape & Cable (Northwood), plate, marigold, 2 sides up...........150.00
Grape & Cable (Northwood), punch cup, wht, 2 szs....................70.00
Grape & Cherry, bowl, bl, rare, 8½" 200.00
Grape & Gothic Arches (Northwood), bowl, marigold, 5"...........15.00
Grape Delight (Dugan), nut bowl, marigold, ftd, 6" 50.00
Grape Leaves (Dugan), bowl, bl, w/3-in-1 edge, 8½".............185.00
Grapevine Lattice (Dugan), plate, lav, 6½-7½".................375.00
Grapevine Lattice (Dugan), plate, wht, 6½-7½"................150.00
Hamburg (Sweden), jardiniere, bl 195.00
Handled Vase (Imperial), marigold, 3 shapes..................45.00
Harvest Poppy, compote, gr..................................400.00
Hatpin, Flying Bat, amethyst 125.00
Hatpin, Honeycomb Ornament, bl..............................125.00
Hatpin, Rooster, ice bl 110.00
Hatpin, Salamanders, amethyst................................75.00
Hattie (Imperial), plate, gr, rare..........................475.00

Hawaiian Lei (Higbee), sugar bowl, marigold 75.00
Heart Band Souvenir (McKee), mug, marigold, sm 85.00
Heavy Diamond (Imperial), creamer, marigold............................30.00
Heavy Grape (Imperial), plate, marigold, 6".............................300.00
Heavy Heart (Higbee), tumbler, marigold.................................150.00
Heavy Iris (Dugan), tumbler, amethyst......................................95.00
Heavy Prisms (English), celery vase, bl, 6"...............................100.00
Heavy Vine, shot glass, marigold 80.00
Heisey #357, water bottle, marigold 190.00
Heisey Colonial, dresser tray, marigold....................................100.00
Heisey Floral Spray, candy, ice bl, stemmed, w/lid, 11"..............100.00
Hex Base, candlesticks, gr, pr..110.00
Hickman, castor set, marigold, 4-pc..250.00
Hobnail & Cane (Crystal), compote, marigold............................85.00
Hobstar (Imperial), fruit bowl, marigold, w/base......................100.00
Hobstar & Cut Triangles (English), plate, gr............................110.00
Hobstar & Feather (Millersburg), creamer, amethyst, rare 700.00
Hobstar & Tassels (Imperial), bowl, marigold, scarce, 7-8" 150.00
Hobstar Reversed (English), frog & holder, marigold 50.00
Hoffman House (Imperial), goblet, red, very scarce....................350.00
Holly Sprig (Millersburg), bonbon, marigold, 2 shapes.................50.00
Holly Whirl (Millersburg), bonbon, amethyst, 2 shapes...............80.00
Honeycomb & Clover (Fenton), bonbon, bl..................................40.00
Honeycomb & Hobstar (Millersburg), vase, amethyst, rare, 8¼"...7,300.00
Horseshoe, shot glass, marigold 35.00
Humpty-Dumpty, jar, mustard; marigold...................................75.00
Ice Crystals, bowl, wht, ftd 85.00
Illinois Daisy (English), cookie jar, marigold, w/lid....................60.00
Imperial #499, sherbet, gr...30.00
Imperial #499, sherbet, marigold..15.00
Imperial Grape (Imperial), wine, gr...35.00
Imperial Jewels (Imperial), plate, amethyst, 7"...........................75.00
Intaglio Daisy (Diamond), bowl, marigold, 4½"..........................30.00
Interior Rib, vase, marigold...50.00
Interior Swirl, tumbler, gr...70.00
Inverted Strawberry (Cambridge), bowl, marigold, 5" 40.00
Inverted Strawberry (Cambridge), tumbler, gr, rare...................200.00
Iris (Fenton), buttermilk goblet, marigold.................................25.00
Ivy, claret, marigold, stemmed...85.00
Jester's Cap (Dugan/Diamond), vase, amethyst..........................75.00
Jewel Box, inkwell, gr...200.00
Jewels (Dugan), bowl, gr, various szs.......................................150.00
Jewels (Dugan), candlesticks, marigold, pr................................100.00
Kingfisher & Variant (Australian), bowl, amethyst, 9½".............325.00
Kittens (Fenton), plate, amethyst, scarce, 4½"..........................500.00
Kokomo (English), rose bowl, bl, ftd...50.00
Laco, oil bottle, marigold, 9¼"..80.00
Lacy Dewdrop (Westmoreland), tumbler, irid moonstone...........250.00
Late Enameled Strawberry, lemonade tumbler, marigold 75.00
Lattice (Dugan), bowl, amethyst, various szs...............................70.00
Lattice & Prisms, cologne, marigold, w/stopper 65.00
Laurel, shade, marigold...40.00
LBJ Hat, ashtray, marigold..25.00
Leaf & Beads (Northwood), nut bowl, gr, ftd, scarce..................110.00
Leaf Swirl (Westmoreland), compote, amethyst 70.00
Leaf Tiers (Fenton), pitcher, marigold, ftd, rare.........................525.00
Little Beads, bowl, marigold, 8" 20.00
Long Leaf (Dugan), bowl, peach opal, ftd.................................175.00
Long Thumbprint Hobnail (Fenton), vase, bl, 7-11"..................130.00
Long Thumbprint Variant, creamer or sugar bowl, marigold, ea ...40.00
Louisa (Westmoreland), candy dish, marigold, ftd.......................40.00
Love Birds (Phoenix), vase, ice gr, very rare.............................450.00
Lustre & Clear (Fenton), fan vase, ice gr....................................90.00
Lustre Flute (Northwood), bonbon, amethyst or gr 50.00

Lustre Rose (Imperial), centerpiece bowl, gr, ftd 200.00
Magnolia Drape (Fenton), pitcher, marigold............................275.00
Malaga (Dugan), bowl, marigold, scarce, 9" 75.00
Maple Leaf (Dugan), sugar bowl, marigold.................................70.00
Massachusetts (US Glass), mug, marigold, rare.........................150.00
Maypole, vase, gr, 6¼"..60.00
Melon Rib, powder jar, marigold, w/lid......................................35.00
Mexican Bell, goblet, flashed, marigold.....................................40.00
Milady (Fenton), tumbler, marigold...70.00
Millersburg Grape, bowl, marigold, rare, 5"...............................60.00
Miniature, flower basket (Westmoreland), peach opal 150.00
Mirrored Lotus (Fenton), plate, marigold, rare, 7½"..................500.00
Mirrored Peacocks (Jain), tumbler, marigold, rare.....................325.00
Moderne, cup or saucer, marigold..15.00
Moonprint (Brockwitz), butter dish, marigold 100.00
Moonprint (Brockwitz), milk pitcher, marigold, scarce 175.00
Moxie, bottle, wht, rare..90.00
Mystery, perfume bottle, marigold...50.00
Napoli (Italy), glass, wine, bl..25.00
Nell (Higbee), mug, marigold..75.00
Niagara Falls (Jeannette), milk pitcher, marigold 35.00
Nippon (Northwood), bowl, wht, 8½"......................................225.00
Northwood's #657, candlesticks, gr, 2 szs, pr............................100.00
Notches, plate, marigold, 8"...50.00
Number 2176 (Sowerby), lemon squeezer, marigold....................60.00
Octagon (Imperial), pitcher, marigold, 2 szs.............................225.00
Omera (Imperial), plate, marigold, 8"...50.00
Omnibus, tumbler, bl, rare..550.00
Open Edge Basket (Basketweave) (Fenton), bowl, ice bl, lg.......250.00
Optic & Buttons (Imperial), bowl, marigold, hdls, 12"................45.00
Optic & Buttons (Imperial), salt cup, marigold, rare..................200.00
Orange Peel (Westmoreland), custard cup, marigold, scarce 25.00
Orange Tree (Fenton), breakfast set, bl, 2 pcs..........................200.00
Orange Tree & Scroll (Fenton), tumbler, marigold......................50.00
Oval & Round (Imperial), plate, amber, scarce, 10"...................110.00
Oval & Round (Imperial), plate, marigold, scarce, 10" 65.00
Palm Beach (US Glass), bowl, marigold, 9"................................55.00
Panama (US Glass), goblet, marigold, rare 150.00
Paneled Dandelion (Fenton), tumbler, amethyst 60.00
Paneled Diamond & Bow (Fenton), vase, bl, 5-14".....................125.00
Paneled Tree Trunk (Dugan), vase, peach opal, rare, 7-12".........375.00
Panels & Ball (Fenton) (aka Persian Pearl), bowl, wht, scarce, 11" ..175.00
Parlor Panels (Imperial), vase, gr, 4-14"...................................200.00
Parlor Panels (Imperial), vase, marigold, 4-14"...........................50.00
Peach Blossom, bowl, amethyst, 7½"...75.00
Peaches, wine bottle, marigold..45.00
Peacock (Millersburg), bowl, ice cream; gr, 5"..........................400.00
Peacock & Urn (Fenton), compote, marigold.............................30.00
Peacock at the Fountain (Northwood), bowl, ice bl, 5" 75.00
Peacock Tail (Fenton), bonbon, bl, stemmed..............................65.00
Pearl & Jewels (Fenton), basket, wht, 4"..................................200.00
Pearly Dots (Westmoreland), bowl, gr..70.00
Pennsylvania Dutch (Jeannette), milk pitcher, marigold...............35.00
Persian Garden (Dugan), berry bowl, wht, 5" 70.00

Persian Garden, plate, amethyst, basket edge, rare, 7", $450.00.
(Photo courtesy Carl Burns)

Persian Medallion (Fenton), bowl, marigold, 5" 40.00
Persian Medallion (Fenton), hair receiver, marigold.................70.00
Petals (Dugan), banana bowl, peach opal 100.00
Phlox (Northwood), tumbler, marigold......................................65.00
Pillar & Drape, shade, wht...90.00
Pin-Ups (Australian), bowl, amethyst, rare, 4-6" 80.00
Pinched Swirl (Dugan), vase, peach opal 80.00
Pineapple (English), sugar bowl, marigold, stemmed or flat 75.00
Plain Jane, paperweight, marigold...90.00
Plain Jane (Imperial), bowl, gr, 4"...35.00
Plutec (McKee), vase, marigold...190.00
Pompeian (Dugan), vase, hyacinth; peach opal 200.00
Poppy (Northwood), pickle dish, ice bl, oval..........................400.00
Premium (Imperial), candlesticks, amethyst, pr.......................175.00
Premium (Imperial), candlesticks, red, pr.................................425.00
Primrose & Ribbon, light shade, marigold.................................90.00
Prism, shakers, marigold, pr...60.00
Prism Band (Fenton), tumbler, bl 45.00
Prisms (Westmoreland), compote, amethyst, scarce, 5" 90.00
Pulled Loop (Dugan), vase, peach opal, squat, 5-7".................200.00
Pulled Loop (Dugan), vase, peach opal, 8-16" 65.00
Question Marks (Dugan), bonbon, wht......................................60.00
Ragged Robin (Fenton), bowl, gr, scarce, 8¾".........................175.00
Ranger (Mexican), milk pitcher, marigold...............................150.00
Raspberry (Northwood), gravy boat, amethyst, ftd...................150.00
Rays & Ribbon (Millersburg), banana boat, gr, rare................1,250.00
Regal Cane, goblet, marigold 70.00
Ribbed Swirl, pitcher, gr...225.00
Ribs (Czechoslovakia), puff box, marigold 95.00
Ribs (Czechoslovakia), soap dish, marigold 60.00
Rock Crystal (McKee), punch bowl, amethyst, w/base, rare 800.00
Rococo (Imperial), bowl, gr, ftd, 5" 150.00
Rosalind (Millersburg), compote, marigold, ruffled, rare, 8" 1,000.00
Rose, bottle, wht...125.00
Rose Garden (Sweden & Germany), vase, marigold, oval, 2 szs .375.00
Rose Spray (Fenton), compote, ice gr 145.00
Rosettes (Northwood), bowl, marigold, ftd, 7-9" 75.00
Royal Lustre (Dugan), bowl, console; red.................................135.00
Royal Lustre (Dugan), candlesticks, marigold, pr......................80.00
Sailboats (Fenton), goblet, marigold 225.00
Scale Band (Fenton), bowl, wht, 6"..90.00
Scepter, candle holder, marigold, scarce, pr...............................95.00
Scotch Thistle (Fenton), compote, gr...90.00
Scroll & Flower (Imperial), vase, smoke, old only, 10" 2,000.00
Scroll Embossed (Imperial), dessert, marigold, stemmed 65.00
Seaweed, lamp, marigold, 2 szs...250.00
Serpentine Rose (English), rose bowl, marigold, ftd 90.00
Shell & Jewel (Westmoreland), creamer, marigold, w/lid..............55.00
Ship & Stars, plate, marigold, 8" 25.00
Shrine (US Glass), toothpick holder, amethyst 650.00
Singing Birds (Northwood), mug, marigold, stippled................200.00
Single Flower (Dugan), hat, marigold...30.00
Six Petals (Dugan), bowl, wht, 8½"..85.00
Small Blackberry (Northwood), compote, amethyst...................65.00
Small Palms, shade, marigold..45.00
Smooth Rays (Dugan), bowl, amethyst 75.00
Snow Fancy (Imperial), bowl, gr, 5"...60.00
Snowflake (Cambridge), tankard, marigold, very rare.............2,000.00
Souvenir Miniature, marigold, lettering 50.00
Sowerby Flower Block (English), flower frog, marigold 60.00
Spearhead & Rib (Fenton's #916), vase, bl, 8-15"......................95.00
Spider Web (Northwood, Dugan), vase, marigold, 2 shapes........55.00
Split Diamond (English), bowl, marigold, scarce, 8" 40.00
Springtime (Northwood), bowl, gr, 5"...80.00

Star, buttermilk goblet, marigold 25.00
Star & File (Imperial), ice cream dish, marigold, stemmed 60.00
Star & File (Imperial), iced-tea tumbler, marigold....................70.00
Star Medallion (Imperial), celery tray, marigold........................60.00
Starbright, vase, amethyst, 6½"...45.00
Starbright, vase, bl, 6½"...50.00
Starfish (Dugan), bonbon, hdld, peach opal, rare.....................165.00
Stars & Stripes (Old Glory), plate, marigold, rare, 7½".............150.00
Stippled Acorns (Jeannette), candy dish, amethyst, w/cover, ftd..35.00
Stippled Flower (Dugan), bowl, peach opal, 8½"........................85.00
Stippled Rays (Northwood), bonbon, gr......................................45.00
Stork & Rushes (Dugan), punch cup, bl......................................35.00
Strawberry (Fenton), bonbon, marigold 50.00
Strawberry (Millersburg), compote, marigold, rare 525.00
Strawberry Scroll (Fenton), tumbler, bl, rare 135.00
Strawberry w/Checkerboard (Jenkins), spooner, marigold............45.00
String of Beads, gr..40.00
Strutting Peacock (Westmoreland), sugar bowl, gr, w/lid.........100.00
Sun Punch, bottle, marigold..30.00
Sun Punch, bottle, wht..35.00
Sunflower & Diamond, vase, bl, 2 szs.......................................125.00
Sunken Daisy (English), sugar bowl, marigold 30.00
Sunray, compote, amethyst...45.00
Swirl Variant (Imperial), plate, wht, 6-8¼".................................70.00
Swirled Morning Glory (Imperial), vase, smoke.........................90.00
Ten Mums (Fenton), tumbler, bl, rare 80.00
Texas, tumbler, bl, giant...250.00
Thistle (Fenton), bowl, marigold, 8-10" 50.00
Thistle & Lotus (Fenton), bowl, gr, 7" 75.00
Thistle Banana Boat (Fenton), marigold, ftd, scarce 200.00
Threaded Six Panel, bud vase, marigold, 7¾"............................75.00
Three Roll, tumble-up, marigold, complete................................90.00
Thumbprint & Spears, creamer, gr..60.00
Tiered Thumbprint, candlesticks, marigold, pr 120.00
Tomato Band (Czech), liquor set, marigold, complete...............175.00
Top Hat, vase, wht, 9½"..50.00
Tree Bark (Imperial), pickle jar, marigold, 7½"..........................55.00
Tree Bark Variant, candle holder marigold, w/stand 75.00
Triplets (Dugan), bowl, amethyst, 6-8" 30.00
Tulip (Millersburg), compote, gr, rare, 9"................................1,100.00
Twelve Rings, candlesticks, marigold, ea 45.00
Twisted Rib (Dugan), vase, bl, various szs................................150.00
Two Flowers (Fenton), rose bowl, amethyst, rare......................150.00
Two Forty Nine, candle holders, red, pr....................................700.00
Two Handled Swirl (Imperial), vase, marigold............................50.00
US Diamond Block (US Glass), compote, peach opal, rare..........90.00
Vera, vase, bl...155.00
Vineyard (Dugan), tumbler, marigold 20.00
Vining Twigs (Dugan), bowl, gr, 7½"...50.00
Vintage (Fenton), punch cup, gr...40.00
Vintage (Millersburg), bowl, marigold, rare, 9".........................625.00
Waffle Block (Imperial), plate, marigold, 6"...............................30.00
Waffle Block (Imperial), tumbler, clambroth, scarce 350.00
Water Lily (Fenton), bowl, amethyst, ftd, 5"..............................90.00
Water Lily & Cattails (Fenton), bonbon, marigold 60.00
Weeping Cherry (Dugan), bowl, marigold, ftd............................90.00
Western Daisy (Westmoreland), hat, amethyst 60.00
Westmoreland's #1776, compote, amethyst, tall stemmed 95.00
Whirling Hobstar, punch bowl & base, child's, marigold 125.00
Wide Panel (Fenton), lemonade glass, wht, hdld........................70.00
Wide Panel (Imperial), plate, red, 6"..200.00
Wide Panel Bouquet, basket, marigold, 3½"...............................75.00
Wide Panel Shade, light shade, marigold 95.00
Wild Berry, powder jar, marigold, w/lid....................................250.00

Wild Flower (Northwood), compote, bl, plain int......................450.00
Wild Rose (Northwood), bowl, marigold, ftd, open edge, 6".........75.00
Windmill (Imperial), bowl, marigold, 9".................................35.00
Windmill (Imperial), pickle dish, marigold..............................30.00
Wishbone (Northwood), tumbler, gr, scarce 135.00
Wishbone & Spades (Dugan), bowl, amethyst, 10" 400.00
Wreathed Bleeding Hearts (Dugan), vase, marigold, 5¼" 125.00
Wreathed Cherry (Dugan), bowl, bl, oval, 10½-12"....................300.00
Zig Zag (Millersburg), bowl, amethyst, rnd or ruffled, 9½" 450.00
Zip Zip (English), flower frog holder, marigold 60.00
Zippered Heart (Imperial), Queen's vase, marigold, rare..........4,200.00
474 (Imperial), goblet, marigold 50.00
49'er, pitcher, marigold, squat 225.00

Carousel Figures

For generations of Americans, visions of carousel horses revolving majestically around lively band organs rekindle wonderful childhood experiences. These nostalgic memories are the legacy of the creative talent from a dozen carving shops that created America's carousel art. Skilled craftsmen brought their trade from Europe where American carvers took the carousel animal from a folk art creation to a true art form. The golden age of carousel art lasted from 1880 to 1929.

There are two basic types of American carousels. The largest and most impressive is the 'park style' carousel built for permanent installation in major amusement centers. These were created in Philadelphia by Gustav and William Dentzel, Muller Brothers, and E. Joy Morris who became the Philadelphia Toboggan Company in 1902. A more flamboyant group of carousel animals was carved in Coney Island, New York, by Charles Looff, Marcus Illions, Charles Carmel, and Stein & Goldstein's Artistic Carousel Company. These park-style carousels were typically three, four, and even five rows with forty-five to sixty-eight animals on a platform. Collectors often pay a premium for the carvings by these men. The outside row animals are larger and more ornate and command higher prices. The horses on the inside rows are smaller, less decorated, and of lesser value.

The most popular style of carousel art is the 'country fair style.' These carousels were portable affairs created for mobility. The horses are smaller and less ornate with leg and head positions that allow for stacking and easy loading. These were built primarily for North Tonawanda, New York, near Niagara Falls, by Armitage Herschell Company, Herschell Spillman Company, Spillman Engineering Company, and Allen Herschell. Charles W. Parker was also well known for his portable merry-go-rounds. He was based in Leavenworth, Kansas. Parker and Herschell Spillman both created a few large park-style carousels as well, but they are better known for their portable models.

Horses are by far the most common figure found, but there are two dozen other animals that were created for the carousel platform. Carousel animals, unlike most other antiques, are oftentimes worth more in a restored condition. Figures found with original factory paint are extraordinarily rare and bring premium amounts. Typically, carousel horses are found in garish, poorly applied 'park paint' and are often missing legs or ears. Carousel horses are hollow. They were glued up from several blocks for greater strength and lighter weight. Bass and poplar woods were used extensively.

If you have an antique carousel animal you would like to have identified, send a clear photograph and description along with a LSASE to our advisor, William Manns, who is listed in the Directory under New Mexico. Mr. Manns is the author of *Painted Ponies*, containing many full-color photographs, guides, charts, and directories for the collector.

Key:
IR — inside row   OR — outside row

MR — middle row   PTC — Philadelphia Toboggan
                                   Company

Coney Island-Style Horses

Carmel, IR jumper, unrstr..4,800.00
Carmel, MR jumper, unrstr...8,500.00
Carmel, OR jumper w/cherub, rstr................................20,000.00
Illions, IR jumper, rstr...5,200.00
Illions, MR stander, rstr...9,200.00

Illions, outside row jumper, original paint, horsehair tail, ca 1910, $9,000.00.

Looff, IR jumper unrstr 3,200.00
Looff, OR jumper, unrstr 16,000.00
Stein & Goldstein, IR jumper, unrstr.............................4,700.00
Stein & Goldstein, MR jumper, rstr...............................9,000.00
Stein & Goldstein, OR stander w/bells, unrstr.................20,000.00

European Horses

Anderson, English, unrstr 2,500.00
Bayol, French, unrstr...2,500.00
Heyn, German, unrstr..3,000.00
Hubner, Belgian, unrstr..2,000.00
Savage, English, unrstr...2,500.00

Menagerie Animals (Non-Horses)

Dentzel, bear, unrstr..20,000.00
Dentzel, cat, unrstr...22,000.00
Dentzel, deer, unrstr...13,500.00
Dentzel, lion, unrstr..35,000.00
Dentzel, pig, unrstr..8,000.00
E Joy Morris, deer, unrstr...10,000.00
Herschell Spillman, cat, unrstr....................................11,000.00
Herschell Spillman, chicken, portable, unrstr....................7,000.00
Herschell Spillman, dog, portable, unrstr........................6,500.00
Herschell Spillman, frog, unrstr 15,000.00
Looff, camel, unrstr..10,000.00
Looff, goat, rstr..13,500.00
Muller, tiger, rstr..32,000.00

Philadelphia-Style Horses

Dentzel, IR 'topknot' jumper, unrstr.............................4,500.00
Dentzel, MR jumper, unrstr 9,500.00
Dentzel, OR stander, female cvg on shoulder, rstr.............22,000.00
Dentzel, prancer, rstr...9,500.00
Morris, IR prancer, rstr..7,000.00
Morris, MR stander, unrstr......................................9,500.00
Morris, OR stander, rstr...13,500.00

Muller, IR jumper, rstr.......................................5,700.00
Muller, MR jumper, rstr 8,500.00
Muller, OR stander, rstr...................................20,000.00
Muller, OR stander w/military trappings............40,000.00
PTC, chariot (bench-like seat), rstr 8,900.00
PTC, IR jumper, rstr 4,000.00
PTC, MR jumper, rstr 12,800.00
PTC, OR stander, armored, rstr 35,000.00
PTC, OR stander, unrstr...................................20,000.00

Portable Carousel Horses

Allan Herschell, all aluminum, ca 1950 ....500.00
Allan Herschell, half & half, wood & aluminum head 1,300.00
Allan Herschell, IR Indian pony, unrstr.............2,200.00
Allan Herschell, OR, rstr..................................3,200.00
Allan Herschell, OR Trojan-style jumper 3,600.00
Armitage Herschell, track-machine jumper 2,800.00
Dare, jumper, unrstr 3,000.00
Herschell Spillman, chariot (bench-like seat) 3,800.00
Herschell Spillman, IR jumper, unrstr.................2,400.00
Herschell Spillman, MR jumper, unrstr................2,900.00
Herschell Spillman, OR, eagle decor 4,500.00
Herschell Spillman, OR, park machine 10,000.00
Parker, MR jumper, unrstr.................................4,200.00
Parker, OR jumper, park machine, unrstr.............6,500.00
Parker, OR jumper, rstr 5,800.00

Cartoon Art

Collectors of cartoon art are interested in many forms of original art — animation cels, sports, political or editorial cartoons, syndicated comic strip panels, and caricature. To produce even a short animated cartoon strip, hundreds of original drawings are required, each showing the characters in slightly advancing positions. Called 'cels' because those made prior to the 1950s were made from a celluloid material, collectors often pay hundreds of dollars for a frame from a favorite movie. Prices of Disney cels with backgrounds vary widely. Background paintings, model sheets, storyboards, and preliminary sketches are also collectible — so are comic book drawings executed in India ink and signed by the artist. Daily 'funnies' originals, especially the earlier ones portraying super heroes, and Sunday comic strips, the early as well as the later ones, are collected. Cartoon art has become recognized and valued as a novel yet valid form of contemporary art. In the listings below all cels are gouache on celluloid unless noted otherwise.

Key:
WB — Warner Brothers　　　　WD — Walt Disney Productions

Animation Cels, Full Color

Raggedy Ann, original production cel from 1990, 12x15" in frame, with certificate of authenticity, $125.00.
(Photo courtesy June Moon)

Bugs Bunny in baseball gear, sgn Friz Freleng, ltd ed...............1,500.00
Bugs Bunny waking up, WB, repro bkground, 12½x10½" 350.00
Dirk the Daring & Princess Daphne, Dragon's Lair II 850.00
Fiver, Watership Down, c Nepenthe 495.00
Hazel, Fiver, Big-Wig & Blackberry, Watership Down, Nepenthe ..495.00
Joker behind bars, Batman, 12x15".................................150.00
Littlefoot, Land Before Time, c UCS & Amblin 995.00
Pepe Le Pew & love interest Kitty Catch, sgn Chuck Jones, ltd ed ..1,050.00
Pickachu & Ash, Pokemon, blk bkground 500.00
Pink Panther w/horn, Mancini music behind, sgn Freleng, ltd ed....850.00
Speedy Gonzalez, detailed bkground, Warner Bros 200.00
Wizzer McQuaff & Wickersham Brother, MGM/UA 1,100.00
Yogi, Boo Boo, Snagglepuss & Wally Gator, Hanna-Barbera, unfr 350.00

Animation Drawings

Bashful, Snow White & 7 Dwarfs, Disney, graphite/orange pencil, 1937 ...950.00
Heffalump, Winnie the Pooh...Day, Disney, graphite, 1958, 11x12"...275.00
Jiminy Cricket, Mickey Mouse Club, Disney, in fr 725.00
Mickey as sorcerer's apprentice, Fantasia, mc pencil, '40, 6" image ...5,800.00
Mickey Mouse, Mickey's Circus, Disney, 1936, 4½" image on 10x12" ..850.00
Oswold the Lucky Rabbit, Disney, graphite, ca 1930, 4½" image...1,800.00
Peter Pan, in headdress, red/bl pencil, 1953, on 14x16" sheet .1,600.00
Timothy Mouse Dumbo, Disney, graphite on paper, 1941, 4x5½" image ...375.00

Miscellaneous

Daily comic strip, Li'l Abner, India ink on Strathmore paper, 1938, 5½x22¼", in frame, $600.00.

Model cel, Yogi's Treasure Hung, w/Quick Draw in wagon, Hanna-Barbera....400.00
Model sheet, Gossamer, colored figure amid drawings, Warner Bros 795.00
Model sheet, Legionnaire Sargent, c Jay Ward 295.00
Model sheet, Shakespeare, Jay Ward 295.00
Production cel, Bacchus, Fantasia, Courvoisier ground, 1940..4,800.00
Production cel, boy in cave, Walter Lantz.................................600.00
Production cel, Bugs Bunny in top hat at curtain, Warner Bros .400.00
Production cel, Flash Gordon, running w/lady, Filmation/King Features ...350.00
Production cel, Jessica Rabbit, Roller Coaster Rabbit, Disney.2,100.00
Production cel, Jiminy Cricket, Mickey's Christmas Carol, Disney..995.00
Production cel, Pinocchio on orig bkground, Disney 16,000.00
Production cel, Snagglepuss, Hanna-Barbera 150.00
Publicity cel, Batman & Robin on blk w/batmobile & moon, filmation ...450.00
Storyboard, Jacques & Gus, Cinderella, graphite on paper, 1950, 6x8" ..1,600.00
Storyboard, Nightmare Before Christmas, pastels on blk paper, 1994.....3,300.00

Cartoon Books

'Books of cartoons' were printed during the first decade of the twentieth century and remained popular until the advent of the modern comic book in the late '30s. Cartoon books, printed in both color and black and white, were merely reprints of current newspaper comic strips. The books, ranging from thirty to seventy pages and in sizes from 3½" x 8" up to 11" x 17", were usually bound with cardboard covers and were often distributed as premiums in exchange for coupons saved from the daily paper. One of the largest of the companies who printed these books was Cupples and Leon, producer of nearly half of the two hundred titles on record. Among the most popular sellers were *Mutt and Jeff, Bringing Up Father,* and *Little Orphan Annie.*

Barnaby, Crockett Johnson, 1st edition, 1943, G- 65.00
Beau Peep, 2nd in series, Daily star, VG..45.00
Blondie, #17, Chick Young, David McKay, NM 110.00

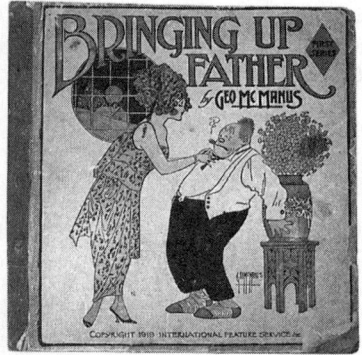

Bringing Up Father, #1, Geo. McManus, VG, $100.00.

Bringing Up Father, #4, Cupples & Leon, EX+ 110.00
Buster Brown, F Stokes, 1902-03, 25-pg, 16x11", EX 150.00
Captain & the Kids, Whitman, ca 1934, EX................................75.00
Dear Gertrood, 1st edition, Ehret/McBride & Co, 11x8", w/dust jacket..22.50
Diary of Snubs Our Dog, Carmack, Belden Press, 1926, VG.........20.00
Ella Cinders, Whitman, ca 1934, VG..25.00
Freckles & His Friends, Whitman, ca 1934, EX.............................65.00
I Go Pogo, Walt Kelly, Simon & Schuster, 1952, VG 17.50
Little Orphan Annie Never Say Die, Cupples & Leon, VG 50.00
Moon Mullins, 3rd in series, Kayo cover, 1920s, NM 95.00
Mutt & Jeff, 3rd in series, Bud Fisher/Ball Co, 1912, 5½x15½", G....55.00
Popeye, King Features, Saalfield, 1934, VG+...............................130.00
Popeye, King Features, Saalfield, 1934, 13x8½", NM..................365.00
Tillie the Toiler, #4, Cupples & Leon, EX 70.00

Cash Registers

From 1884 until 1916, the National Cash Register Company dominated the field with a massive over-choice of styles and functions. Before the termination of the 'antique styles,' 1,600,000 registers had been built an inexpensive, painted-on woodgrain patterned steel cabinet replaced the ornate plates, though the mechanisms remained unchanged. Serial numbers were consecutive, making dating simple. Many registers were chopped up for brass shell casings in the two world wars, and as a result, those that remained became more attractive to collectors. Of the NCRs, scholars speculate that about half of them survive. Add to that the many other existing brands, and it is estimated that there are nearly two million registers to discover.

Register values are fixed by a machine's scarcity and charm, including add-on fixtures such as brass or glass topsigns, clocks, and personalized nameplates. National used eight designs on metal registers and four on inlaid wood machines.

The condition code of registers in this column is quite simple: good (G), very good (VG), and mint (M), restored by a professional. About 20% variation in prices can be attributed to geography and buyer/seller differences.

Internet web pages have jumped into the pricing fray, sometimes creating a carnival-like frenzy when prices aren't fixed. *Schroeder's* will provide a standard but also be mindful of permanent changes generated by the 'Net. For further information we recommend *Antique Cash Registers, 1880 – 1920,* by Bartsch and Sanchez.

Dial, emb brass, emb pattern on drw, 25", EX.....................6,500.00
Monitor #1A, wood w/CI Amount of Sale sign, ca 1900, 9x13x14", VG...415.00
NCR #1, Am detail adder, VG...2,650.00
NCR #2 or #3, inlaid oak or mahog, scarce 2,250.00
NCR #3, mahog inlay, deep wood drw, ca 1886, VG 4,500.00
NCR #5, narrow scroll, glass topsign, M 2,750.00
NCR #7 or #8, detail adder, fleur-de-lis, VG..............................850.00
NCR #13 or #14, Ionic CI, 1899, G 750.00
NCR #30, bronze, total adder, 13 keys, VG..........................2,000.00
NCR #33, 1903, VG...900.00
NCR #47, oak w/mahog inlay, up to $6, VG 2,250.00
NCR #50, Renaissance design, orig clock, M 2,500.00
NCR #52, Renaissance design, orig clock, extended base, VG...2,900.00
NCR #52 or #52¼, Renaissance design, extended base, no clock, VG...2,500.00
NCR #64, Bohemian pattern, iron, 25-key, 1901, VG 600.00
NCR #78, custom built to eliminate bk window, NP, 1902, VG.950.00
NCR #129-130, bronze, VG 950.00
NCR #130, Art Nouveau cabinet, M..1,600.00
NCR #135, Art Nouveau pattern, CI, 31-key, 1905, VG............600.00
NCR #215 or #216, bronze fleur-de-lis, VG..........................1,200.00
NCR #226, rare bilingual topsign, VG 900.00
NCR #250 or #251, bronze, VG..1,200.00
NCR #312, #313, or #317, dolphin pattern, VG 800.00
NCR #322, #323, or #327, marble 3 sides, extended base, M..2,500.00
NCR #322, #323, or #327, marble 3 sides, extended base, VG..1,500.00
NCR #324, bronze plated, wood base, $2 till, rstr, 21x16x13½".920.00
NCR #324, VG...700.00
NCR #332, #333 or #349, orig topsign, M...............................1,150.00
NCR #332, #333 or #349, orig topsign, VG..............................550.00
NCR #336, brass, M..950.00
NCR #337, dolphin design, M..950.00
NCR #338, dogwood pattern, English numerals, CA, 1910-16, VG ..475.00
NCR #359-G, fleur-de-lis pattern, brass w/marble tray, 1906, EX+.....200.00
NCR #360, 37 keys, rings to $60, 1908-09, M...........................1,500.00
NCR #441 or #442, Empire design w/quartered-oak base, M...1,750.00
NCR #441E, electric, VG..1,250.00
NCR #442E-L, EX orig 1,800.00
NCR #452E, electric, M 2,000.00
NCR #522, 2-drw, electric bar model, 1910-16, M...................2,500.00
NCR #522, 2-drw, electric bar model, 1910-16, VG...............1,800.00

National Cash Register #593-E-L-9-F, nine oak drawers, floor model with lights, M, $8,200.00.

NCR #711-#717, mahog-grain finish on steel, M **275.00**
NCR #1054, glass automatic w/box attachment, 1910-16, M..**1,200.00**

Cast Iron

In the mid-1800s, the cast-iron industry was raging in the United States. It was recognized as a medium extremely adaptable for uses ranging from ornamental architectural filigree to actual building construction. It could be cast from a mold into any conceivable design that could be reproduced over and over at a relatively small cost. It could be painted to give an entirely versatile appearance. Furniture with openwork designs of grapevines and leaves and intricate lacy scrollwork was cast for gardens as well as inside use. Figural doorstops of every sort, bootjacks, trivets, and a host of other useful and decorative items were made before the 'ferromania' had run its course. For more information, we recommend *Antique Iron* by Kathryn McNerney (Collector Books). See also Kitchen, Cast-Iron Bakers and Kettles; and other specific categories.

Bathtub, wht porc, claw ft, 60x30x16"+ft **475.00**
Bed headbrd, oval/rnd tubing w/scroll & cross, foliate medallions, 61"...**550.00**
Bench, allover openwork vintage, scrolled seat, wht pnt, 29x26", pr......**330.00**
Bench, Am Rococo, crescent moon shape, laurel bk, wht pnt, 1870s, 44" ...**2,750.00**
Bench, bk w/hunting dog in oval, scroll arms/legs, slat seat, 31x50"......**500.00**
Bench, demilune, scalloped bk, berry decor, griffin armrests, 42", pr..**3,450.00**
Bench, random twig design w/leaves, Kramer Bros Fdry, rstr/rpt, 38" **700.00**
Chair, side; scrolled bk, rnd dished seat, dk gr pnt, 33", VG **85.00**
Fern stand, Mid-Eastern Revival, ornate/rtcl, worn NP, 32x15" dia....**350.00**
Finial, eagle, 2-part, old gold rpt, 9x16" **110.00**
Finial, pineapple, old gr rpt, 20½" **220.00**

Fountain, attributed to J.W. Fiske, late nineteenth century, minor losses and surface rust, 40", $1,100.00.

Fountain, child w/basket (basin), stands on rockwork, 1860s, 35", pr..**6,465.00**
Hall tree, naturalistic tree form w/7 hooks & mirror, old blk pnt, 72".....**925.00**
Herb grinder, boat shaped w/roller-grinder, wood hdl, pitting, 5x16" **300.00**
Hitching post, lion's head finial, old mc pnt w/gold, 1890s, 45" **2,500.00**
Hitching post, tapered tree trunk w/grapevines & stars, 70", VG ..**600.00**
Kettle, CI w/wrought iron bail hdl, tripod ft, 19th C, 13x9" dia....**230.00**
Ornament, rabbit, seated, mc pnt traces, late 1800s, 11⅝x10" ...**345.00**
Plaques, Ramses V & Cleopatra, Peerless Mfg, 22½x20", pr ...**2,750.00**
Settee, openwork branches & leaves, arched arms, 33x44"......**1,500.00**
Table, ice cream; shell & acanthus leaf decor, tripod base, old rpt .**110.00**
Terrarium, glass sides, gr pnt w/gilt finials, slate base, 16x25x15" ..**300.00**
Top hat (container), enameled int mk Standard Mfg, rpt ext, 7x9x11"..**375.00**
Urn, amphora shape w/classic motifs, dk gr pnt, 29x24".........**1,000.00**
Urn, Classical Revival, dk gr pnt, Am, 1870s, 21x25", pr........**2,400.00**
Urn, Classical Revival, on plinth, dk gr pnt, 40x20", pr..........**2,000.00**
Urn, flared rim, bas-relief leafage, dk gr pnt, 21x17", pr **1,000.00**
Urn, leaf motif on flared lip/base, egg/dart bowl, scroll hdls, 10x12"...**290.00**

Urn, lobed sides, everted lip, sq plinth, 1875, 38x26" **2,645.00**
Urn, lotus form, everted petal rim, ped base, sq plinth, 19", pr...**400.00**

Castor Sets

Castor sets became popular during the early years of the eighteenth century and continued to be used through the late Victorian era. Their purpose was to hold various condiments for table use. The most common type was a circular arrangement with a center handle on a revolving pedestal base that held three, four, five, or six bottles. A few were equipped with a bell for calling the servant. Frames were made of silverplate, glass, or pewter. Though most bottles were of pressed glass, some of the designs were cut, and on rare occasion, colored glass with enameled decorations was used as well. To maintain authenticity and value, castor sets should have matching bottles. Prices listed below are for those with matching bottles and in frames with plating that is in excellent condition (unless noted otherwise). Note: Watch for new frames and bottles in clear, cranberry, cobalt, and vaseline Inverted Thumbprint as well as reproductions of Czechoslovakian cut glass bottles. These have recently been appearing on the market.

Six-piece silver and cut glass castor set, engraved PH 1777, 36 troy ounce, auctioned with material originally owned by Patrick Henry, $4,000.00.

5-bottle, Bristol glass, floral on pk; cherub SP fr, 1890s, 15x5" ...**975.00**
5-bottle, cranberry Invt T'print; SP fr, 14½" **600.00**
5-bottle, cut glass; pewter fr & lids, 11½" **350.00**
5-bottle, cut glass; SP fr, VG..**100.00**
5-bottle, cut/eng glass; Webster quadruple SP fr, 15x7" **265.00**
5-bottle, pressed glass; rstr Meriden, fr w/cherub on hdl.............**525.00**
5-bottle, vaseline glass; Meriden #827 SP fr, 13¾" **775.00**
6-bottle, cut glass (plain); Sheffield-type fr w/gadrooned edges, 8x7" **275.00**
6-bottle, cut glass; Mermod SP fr w/wolf, grapes/birds, 18x7" **450.00**
6-bottle, cut glass; SP ftd fr w/emb vintage, Fr/Tete-Leroy **200.00**
6-bottle+bud vase, pressed glass; rstr SP #2114 fr, revolves **750.00**

Catalina Island

Catalina Island pottery was made on the island of the same name, which is about twenty-six miles off the coast of Los Angeles. The pottery was started in 1927 at Pebble Beach, by Wm. Wrigley, Jr., who was instrumental in developing and using the native clays. Its principal products were brick and tile to be used for construction on the island. Garden pieces were first produced, then vases, bookends, lamps, ashtrays, novelty items, and finally dinnerware. The ware became very popular and was soon being shipped to the mainland as well.

Some of the pottery was hand thrown; some was made in molds. Most pieces are marked Catalina Island or Catalina with a printed incised stamp or handwritten with a pointed tool. Cast items were sometimes marked in the mold, a few have an ink stamp, and a paper label was also used. The most favored colors in tableware and accessories are 1) black (rare), 2) Seafoam and Monterey Brown (uncommon), 3) matt blue and green, 4) Toyon Red (orange), 5) other brights, and 6) pastels with a matt finish.

The color of the clay can help to identify approximately when a piece was made: 1927 to 1932, brown to red (Island) clay (very popular with collectors, tends to increase values); 1931 to 1932, an experimental period with various colors; 1932 to 1937, mainly white clay, though tan to brown clays were also used on occasion.

Items marked Catalina Pottery are listed in Gladding McBean. For further information we recommend *Catalina Island Pottery Collectors Guide* by Steven and Aisha Hoefs, and *The Collector's Encyclopedia of California Pottery, Second Edition,* by Jack Chipman (Collector Books). Our advisor for this category is Steven Hoefs; he is listed in the Directory under Georgia.

Dinnerware and Accessories

Bowl, clam-shell shape, ivory, ftd, 5x7¼x11"..............................190.00
Bowl, serving; oval 125.00
Bowl, Toyon Red, tab hdls, 2¼x6¼" dia 60.00
Casserole, w/lid, lg..275.00
Coffee server, Catalina Blue, wooden hdl, 8¼".............................175.00
Creamer & sugar bowl...100.00
Cup, demitasse; 2⅝"...35.00
Pitcher, matt gr satin, 7½", from $300 to...................................325.00

Pitcher, 2-quart, 7", $325.00.
(Photo courtesy Steven and Aisha Hoefs)

Plate, chop; Mandarin Yellow, 1930s, 14" dia, from $80 to 90.00
Plate, 3-sections, scalloped edge, 8¾" dia 110.00
Tumbler, wht clay, 4" 50.00

Miscellaneous

Ashtray, cowboy hat form, Catalina Blue....................................175.00
Candlesticks, pearly wht, 3¼", pr 175.00
Candlesticks, satin bl, 4¼", pr 70.00
Plate, Moorish design, Monterey Brown/Obsidian Black, 10½"..500.00
Vase, fluted, ftd, 6¼" 150.00
Vase, gourd shape w/hdls, 9" 425.00
Vase, stepped top, sm angle hdls, 5" 375.00
Vase, tan w/gr int, scalloped rim, 9x7" 125.00
Vase, Toyon Red, red clay, 7½x5½"..355.00
Vase, turq, 8-sided, horizontal ribs on every other side, #619, 7½" ..195.00
Vase, wht w/bl int, leaf-shape sides, #335, 6½" 40.00
Wall pocket, basketweave, 9½"..525.00

Catalogs

Catalogs are not only intriguing to collect on their own merit, but for the collector with a specific interest, they are often the only remain-

ing source of background information available, and as such they offer a wealth of otherwise unrecorded data. The mail-order industry can be traced as far back as the mid-1800s. Even before Aaron Montgomery Ward began his career in 1872, Laacke and Joys of Wisconsin and the Orvis Company of Vermont, both dealers in sporting goods, had been well established for many years. The E.C. Allen Company sold household necessities and novelties by mail on a broad scale in the 1870s. By the end of the Civil War, sewing machines, garden seed, musical instruments, even medicine, were available from catalogs. In the 1880s Macy's of New York issued a 127-page catalog; Sears and Spiegel followed suit in about 1890. Craft and art supply catalogs were first available about 1880 and covered such varied fields as china painting, stenciling, wood burning, brass embossing, hair weaving, and shellcraft. Today some collectors confine their interests not only to craft catalogs in general but often to just one subject. There are several factors besides rarity which make a catalog valuable: age, condition, profuse illustrations, how collectible the field is that it deals with, the amount of color used in its printing, its size (format and number of pages), and whether it is a manufacturer's catalog verses a jobber's catalog (the former being the most desirable).

Key:
F/W — Fall/Winter   S/S — Spring/Summer

AA Cutter Co, men's boots/shoes, 1920, 40 pgs, VG 45.00
AB Barnes, farm machinery & supplies, 1881, 66 pgs, G+ 38.00
AC Gilbert Co, toy construction sets, 1962, 16 pgs, VG+ 45.00
AE Russ Co, brewery products, 1915, 73 pgs, VG........................45.00
American Decalcomania Co, all-purpose transfers, 1928, 12 pgs, VG ..25.00
American Ironing Machine Co, 1920, 17 pgs, G+.........................40.00
Army & Navy Supply Co, 1936, 36 pgs, G 40.00
Blue Star Products, woodworking equipment, 1940, 39 pgs, VG+...35.00
Bob Brown's Hunting Supplies, 1959, 62 pgs, VG 30.00
Bramhall Deane Co, household, 1914, 121 pgs, G+ 90.00
Butler Hard Rubber Co, 1892, 91 pgs, VG+ 70.00
Carbone Inc, decorative arts imports, 1927, 116 pgs, G 42.00
Carolina Sporting Goods Co, S/S, 1926, 62 pgs 120.00
CE Ward Co, fraternal, 1921, 128 pgs, VG..................................65.00
Charles W Story, musical supplies, 1888, 52 pgs, G.....................65.00
Chas C Navlet Co, gardening, 1921, 32 pgs, EX...........................25.00
Christy Gunworks, 1958, 102 pgs, VG 45.00
Colonial Candle Co, 1924, 22 pgs, VG.......................................20.00
Colorado Sporting Goods, 1920, 194 pgs, G+..............................40.00
Colt Firearms Co, 1930, 36 pgs, VG...100.00
Continental Products, general/toys, 1960, 742 pgs, EX.................75.00
Coyte, McCandlish Co, wholesale grocery, 1888, 16 pgs, G..........50.00
Crafstman Wood Service Co, woodworking, 1939, 136 pgs, G+...25.00
Emil Braude & Sons, jewelry/appliances/watches, etc, 1949, 174 pgs, VG....65.00
Fisher Scientific Co, lab appliances, 1958, 1,028 pgs, VG............60.00
Fostoria Glass Co, 1925, 40 pgs, EX+ 38.00
Gordon Novelty Co, 1958, 174 pgs, VG+....................................80.00
Hartman Trunk Co, baggage/cases, 1922, 88 pgs, VG+ 45.00
Henry Hesse, sewing, 1908, VG..20.00
Horrocks Ibbotson, fishing, 1948, 128 pgs, VG...........................25.00
Imperial Steel Range Co, #87, 1900, 64 pgs, VG+ 100.00
International Harvester, 1935, 384 pgs, G...................................35.00
James A Biddle, electrical, 1910, 12 pgs, G+ 15.00
JI Case Co Inc, 1939, 12 pgs, G..20.00
John T Tower, tools, 1883, 12 pgs, G...32.00
Johnson Motors, Sea Horse Outboards, 1961, 24 pgs, EX.............40.00
Johnson Smith Co, novelties/toys, 1944, 320 pgs, VG 80.00
Lafayette Radio, #82, 1941, 192 pgs, G 50.00
Lamson Bros Co, baby items, 1915, 70 pgs, VG...........................36.00
Lane Bryant, F/W, 1933, 76 pgs, G 25.00
Lane Bryant, S/S, 1928, 112 pgs, VG 50.00

Larkin Co Inc, premiums, 1933, 184 pgs, G+ 35.00
Leonard Refrigerator Co, 50th Anniversary, 1931, 8 pgs, VG+ 20.00
LL Bean, outdoor clothing/camping, Fall 1953, 108 pgs, VG........50.00
Logmans, Green & Co, telescopes, 1896, 112 pgs, G+ 45.00

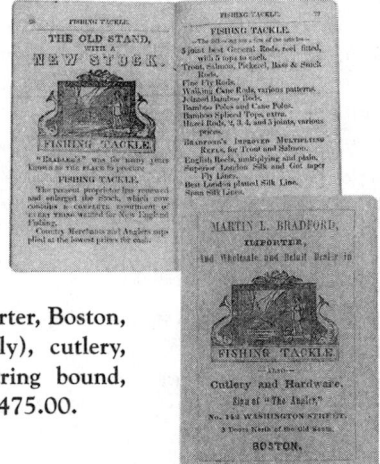

Martin L. Bradford Exporter, Boston, fishing tackle (very early), cutlery, and hardware, 1847, string bound, 32-page, 4x2½", EX, $2,475.00.

McLean, Black & Co Inc, jewelry/silverware, 1924, 160 pgs, VG.52.00
Milton Bradley Co, games, 1957, 16 pgs, EX...................................30.00
Montgomery Ward, groceries, Sept/Oct 1910, 74 pgs, G 40.00
Montgomery Ward, outdoor sporting/camping supplies, 1960, 128 pgs, VG...40.00
Montgomery Ward, Wardway Homes plans/kits, 1927, 96 pgs, VG ...75.00
Mutual Fabric Co, clothing, 1932, 24 pgs, VG+ 55.00
Norge Electric Ranges, 1938, 16 pgs, VG......................................25.00
Ohio Carriage Mfg Co, 1909, 172 pgs, G+......................................55.00
P&K Inc, fishing supplies, 1947, 48 pgs, VG.................................75.00
Perry Dame Co, clothing, F/W, 1920, 178 pgs, G 100.00
Plastics Catalog Corp, 1943, 852 pgs, VG....................................150.00
Pritzlazz, tools/hardware/housewares, etc 1957, 1,570 pgs, EX 80.00
Red Wing Shoe Co, ladies' shoes, 1947, 8 pgs, VG 25.00
Roberts Bros, tents & canopies, 1884, 24 pgs, G+ 35.00
Rogers, Peet & Co, men's/boy's clothing, 1898, 99 pgs, VG...........50.00
Rudolph Wurlitzer Co, musical, 1930s, 120 pgs, G......................125.00
Sears, Roebuck & Co, #1, baby carriages/go-carts, 1903-04, 74 pgs, G ..80.00
Sears, Roebuck & Co, #119, fashions/furniture, 1909, 1,183 pgs, G- ...200.00
SF Meyers Co NY, #32, jewelry, 1891, 312 pgs, hardbk, EX........275.00
Sidney Shepard & Co, household goods, 1998, 36 pgs, G.............50.00
Silver Truss Corp, medical, 1940, 66 pgs, VG 20.00
Singer Bros, novelties/general, 1914, 204 pgs, VG 150.00
Standard Mail Order Co, clothing, July/Aug 1915, 80 pgs, G 50.00
Star Rare Coins, 1930, 208 pgs, VG..40.00
Strombecker, toys, 1954, 12 pgs, VG...75.00
Sutherland & Co, sewing supplies, 1901, 74 pgs, G......................65.00
Thorn Wire Hedge Co, 1884, 16 pgs, VG.......................................55.00
Visalia Stock Saddle Co, 1938, 128 pgs, G+ 90.00
Walgreen Agency Drug Stores, Christmas, 1960, 244 pgs, EX 100.00
Wally Frank Smoking Pipes & Tobacco, Christmas 1957, 48 pgs, VG...20.00
Weaver-Ebling Auto Parts, NY City, 1926, 270 pgs, G 100.00
Webster & Perks Tool Co, 1917, 35 pgs, VG+...............................30.00
Western Robe Co, 1905, 48 pgs, VG...180.00
Wheeler-Okell Co, furniture, 1927, 39 pgs, G 32.00
Winchester Repeating Arms, 1950, 116 pgs, G.............................40.00
Wm T Wood & Co, ice equipment/supplies, 1904, 80 pgs, VG..130.00
Woodward Iron & Hardware, 1883, 44 pgs, VG 52.00
Work Bros & Co, men's/boys' clothing, 1893, 64 pgs, EX 30.00

Ceramic Art Company

Jonathan Coxon, Sr., and Walter Scott Lenox established the Ceramic Art Company in 1889 in Trenton, New Jersey, where they produced fine belleek porcelain. Both were experienced in its production, having previously worked for Ott and Brewer. They hired artists to hand paint their wares with portraits, scenes, and lovely florals. Today artist-signed examples bring the highest prices. Several marks were used, three of which contain the 'CAC' monogram. A green wreath surrounding the company name in full was used on special-order wares, but these are not often encountered. Coxon eventually left the company, and it was later reorganized under the Lenox name. See also Lenox. Our advisor for this category is Mary Frank Gaston.

Bowl, Nouveau lady w/flowing hair profile on lid, FM Brooks, 7½"....310.00
Bowl, roses all around, ruffled rim, 1889-1896, 3¼x6¼" 495.00
Cup, line of bl enameled dots w/gold bands, ped ft.......................55.00
Inkwell on scalloped tray, pk roses/gr leaves on wht, gilt, 3½x9" .280.00
Loving cup, commemorative w/initials, much gold, 8x6" 225.00
Mug, monk on shaded brn (china-pnt type), 3-hdl, 7x7"...........250.00
Pitcher, cider; apples & leaves on purple to apricot, 1894-1906, 6"...550.00
Pitcher, cider; blackberries, sgn Craub, palette mk, 6"................665.00
Pitcher, cider; roses (lg, mc), angular hdl w/emb dots, 5½".........495.00
Pitcher, grapevines, bl on bl, 6x7½" 160.00

Pitcher, violets on white with gold trim, double-spouted, brown CAC mark, 3", $225.00. (Photo courtesy Mary Frank Gaston)

Powder jar, roses, mc w/gold netting & bl beading, 1889-1906, 2¾" ..245.00
Stein, monks drinking in cellar, sterling lid, CAC, ½-litre 500.00
Tankard, grapes & vines, cylindrical, palette mk, 14", from $650 to...725.00
Tankard, nude/grape arbor & golden chalice, EI Beck, 1896, 15"..550.00
Tankard, seated monk, flow blue, DL Kemp, 14½".....................180.00
Vase, birds & herons, shouldered, 10¼" 250.00
Vase, chrysanthemums, bulbous, tiny neck, 1894-1906, 7½" 725.00
Vase, chrysanthemums, sgn, globular, sm neck, ruffled rim, 1894-06, 8"...725.00
Vase, flowers, AJ Frill, stick neck, ca 1894-1906, 12x6", NM 495.00
Vase, mums, red on peach to brn, sgn AD, 16x8".......................320.00
Vase, nude among holly, wht on dk gr, sgn, 11½x4¼" 410.00
Vase, roses, bulbous w/stick neck, sm ruffled rim, 8¼x7¼" 635.00
Vase, roses, ornate gold hdls at shoulders, flared neck, 18" 2,200.00
Vase, roses & foliage, bottle neck, flat gold rim, 11"...................595.00
Vase, spider mums, stick neck, gold twig hdls, ca 1889-1906, 10½"..650.00
Vase, tea roses on lt ground w/gilt, ornate shape w/hdls, 19x8"...675.00
Vase, trumpet flowers (china-pnt style), tiny rim, 11½x4¼" 300.00
Vase, wild roses, H Wright, bottle shape, 1898, 12½x6" 270.00
Vase, wisteria, purple/wht on shaded purple, gold int/hdls, 12x8"...550.00

Ceramic Arts Studio, Madison

The Ceramic Arts Studio Company began operations sometime

prior to the 1940s, but it was about then that Betty Harrington started marketing her goods through this company. Betty Harrington was the designer primarily responsible for creating the line of figurines and knickknacks that has become so popular with collectors. There were two others — Ulli Rebus, who not only designed several of the animals and various other pieces but taught Betty the art of mold-making as well; and Ruth Planter, who's work may have been limited to 'Sonny' and 'Honey.' About 65% of these items are marked, but even unmarked items become easily recognizable after only a brief study of their distinctive styling and glaze colors. At least eight different marks were used, among them the black ink stamp and the incised mark: 'Ceramic Arts Studio, Madison, Wisc.' A paper sticker was used in the early years.

After the 1955 demise of the company in Madison, the owner (Ruben Sand) went to Japan where he continued production under the same name using many of the same molds. After a short time, the old molds were retired, and new and quite different items were produced. Most of the Japanese pieces can be found with a Ceramic Arts Studio backstamp. The Japanese identification was often on a paper label and can be missing. Japanese pieces are never marked Madison, Wisc., but not all Madison pieces are either. Red or blue backstamps are exclusively Japanese.

Another company that also produced figurines operated at about the same time as the Madison studio. It was called Ceramic Art (no 's') Studio; do not confuse the two.

A second and larger building in the C.A.S. complex in Madison was for the exclusive production of metal accessories. The creator and designer of this related line was Zona Liberace, Liberace's stepmother, who was art director for the line of figurines as well. These pieces are rising fast in value and because they weren't marked can sometimes be found at bargain prices. They were so popular that other ceramic companies bought them to complement their own lines, so they may also be found with ceramic figures other than C.A.S.'s.

Our advisor for this category is BA Wellman; his address can be found under Massachusetts. Mr. Wellman encourages collectors to e-mail him with any new information concerning company history and/or production. See also Clubs, Newsletters, and Catalogs.

Bank, Mr & Mrs Blankety Blank, 4½", pr	295.00
Bank, Paisley Pig, 3"	150.00
Bank, Skunky, 4"	195.00
Birdbath, 4½"	100.00
Candle holder, Bedtime Girl, 4¾"	95.00
Candle holder, Triad Girl, center, 5"	150.00
Candle holder, Triad Girl, right or left; from $90 to	110.00
Figurine, Adonis & Aphrodite, 9¼", 8", pr	795.00
Figurine, Alice, sitting on knees, 4½"	295.00
Figurine, Archibald, dragon, 8", minimum value	325.00
Figurine, Autumn Andy, 5"	90.00
Figurine, Bali-Hai, standing, topless	200.00
Figurine, Bali-Hai, standing, 8"	100.00

Figurine, Balinese Dance Man, 9½", $145.00.

Figurine, Caddy, mountain goat, 5¼"	200.00
Figurine, Chinese Boy & Girl, 3"	50.00
Figurine, Cinderella & Prince, bl, 6½", pr, from $175 to	185.00
Figurine, Comedy & Tragedy, 10", pr	235.00
Figurine, Cupid on flower	75.00
Figurine, Daisy, donkey, 4¾", from $130 to	150.00
Figurine, Dutch Boy & Girl, 4½", pr, from $50 to	65.00
Figurine, Dutch Love Boy & Girl, kissing, pr	85.00
Figurine, fawn, from Indian group, 4¼"	50.00
Figurine, Frisky the colt, 3¾"	125.00
Figurine, Gay '90s Man, dog at side, 7"	60.00
Figurine, Hansel & Gretel, 1-pc, 3"	100.00
Figurine, Harem Girl, kneeling, 4½"	80.00
Figurine, Japanese Kubaki Man, rare, 8½"	300.00
Figurine, King's Flutist & Lutist Jesters, pr	325.00
Figurine, lamb, plain	50.00
Figurine, Lightning the stallion, 5¾"	190.00
Figurine, longhorn ox, 3" L	90.00
Figurine, Madonna w/golden halo	145.00
Figurine, Mary & lamb w/bow, 6¼", 4", pr	80.00
Figurine, mermaid mother on rock, 4"	185.00
Figurine, Minnehaha	125.00
Figurine, Modern Colt, stylized, 7½"	200.00
Figurine, Mop-Pi & Smi-Li, pr	65.00
Figurine, Our Lady of Fatima	90.00
Figurine, Palomino Colt, 5¾"	90.00
Figurine, panda w/hat	60.00
Figurine, Pekingese, 3"	95.00
Figurine, Peter Pan & Wendy, 5¼", pr	250.00
Figurine, Petrov & Petrushka, 5½", 5", from $90 to	100.00
Figurine, Pioneer Sam & Suzie, 5½", 5", pr	95.00
Figurine, Polish Boy & Girl, 6½", pr	120.00
Figurine, Promenade Man & Woman, pr	175.00
Figurine, Rose, ballerina tying shoe	95.00
Figurine, shepherd, 8½", from $100 to	135.00
Figurine, Square Dance Boy & Girl, 6½", 6"	225.00
Figurine, squirrel w/jacket, 2¼"	45.00
Figurine, St Agnes w/lamb, 1-pc	65.00
Figurine, St Francis w/extended arms, 7"	150.00
Figurine, St George on charger, 8½", from $225 to	295.00
Figurine, Temple Dancer, from $75 to	165.00
Figurine, tortoise w/hat, crawling, 2½" L	125.00
Figurine, Water Man & Woman, 11½", pr	495.00
Head vase, African Man, 8"	325.00
Head vase, Becky, 5¼"	165.00
Lamp, Fire Man on base, very scarce	500.00
Pitcher, Adam & Eve, 3"	60.00
Pitcher, George Washington & stars, wht on bl	65.00
Plaque, Attitude & Arabesque, pr, from $135 to	150.00
Plaque, Dancing Dutch Boy & Girl, pr	130.00
Plaque, Hamlet, 8"	225.00
Plaque, Harlequin & Columbine, pr	225.00
Plaque, Manchu & Lotus, 8", pr	190.00
Plaque, striped fish mother, 9"	90.00
Razor blade bank, Tony, #319, 4¾"	95.00
Shakers, baby chick in nest, snuggle, pr	50.00
Shakers, Black boy & alligator, pr	275.00
Shakers, Blackamoor, 4¾", pr	95.00
Shakers, boy & chair, pr	70.00
Shakers, Calico Cat & Gingham Dog, 3", 2¾", pr	125.00
Shakers, covered wagon & oxen, ea 3" L, pr	80.00
Shakers, dog & doghouse, snuggle, pr	150.00
Shakers, fox & goose, snuggle, 3¼", 2¼", pr	225.00
Shakers, kangaroo mother & joey, snuggle, 4¾", 2½", pr	160.00

Shakers, monkey mother & baby, snuggle, pr 100.00
Shakers, Oak Sprite & Spring Leaf, pr 70.00
Shakers, Paul Bunyan & tree, pr......................................200.00
Shakers, Sabu (Black boy) & elephant, pr 275.00
Shakers, Santa Claus & Christmas tree, 2¼", pr 150.00
Shakers, Sooty & Taffy, Scotty dogs, pr..................................65.00
Shelf sitter, Banjo Girl, 4", from $80 to.................................100.00
Shelf sitter, Berty & Bobby, pr 380.00
Shelf sitter, Budgie, bird 40.00
Shelf sitter, Collie mother, 5"...65.00
Shelf sitter, Dutch Boy, 4½"..35.00
Shelf sitter, En Pos & En Repos, 4½", pr...............................195.00
Shelf sitter, Fluffy & Tuffy, cats, 7", pr................................185.00
Shelf sitter, Maurice & Michelle, 7", pr 165.00
Shelf sitter, Pete & Polly, parrots, chartreuse, pr.......................185.00
Shelf sitter, Sun-Li & Su-Lin, chubby, 5½", pr.........................95.00
Shelf sitter, Winney & Willy, pr...295.00
Shelf sitter, Young Love Couple, kissing boy & girl, 4½", pr.........90.00
Vase, bud; bamboo, 6"..25.00
Vase, Wing-Sang & Lu-Tang, wht w/gr trim, vase behind, 7", pr..95.00

Metal Accessories

Arched window for religious figure, 6½" 75.00
Artist palette w/shelves, left & right, 13" W...............................95.00
Beanstalk for Jack, rare..165.00
Birdcage w/perch, 14"..85.00
Box, dmn shape, 15½x14" 55.00
Corner spider web for Miss Muffet, flat blk, 4"...........................95.00
Frame w/shelf, 22" sq 55.00
Garden shelf, for Mary Contrary, 4x12".................................95.00
Musical score, flat blk, 14x12" 90.00
Pocket step shelf, w/planter, rnd, 8"....................................75.00
Pyramid shelf..75.00
Rainbow arch w/shelf, blk, 13½x19x5½".............................120.00
Sofa, for Maurice & Michelle, from $60 to 80.00
Star for angel, flat blk...80.00
Triple ring for birds (shelf sitting), 15" 75.00

Chalkware

Chalkware figures were a popular commodity from approximately 1860 until 1890. They were made from gypsum or plaster of Paris formed in a mold and then hand painted in oils or watercolors. Items such as animals and birds, figures, banks, toys, and religious ornaments modeled after more expensive Staffordshire wares were often sold door to door. Their origin is attributed to Italian immigrants. Today regarded as a form of folk art, nineteenth century American pieces bring prices in the hundreds of dollars. Carnival chalkware from this century is also collectible, especially figures that are personality related. For those, see Carnival Collectibles.

Poodles, hollow with solid base, original paint, $525.00. (Photo courtesy Aston Macek Auctioneers and Appraisers)

Bust, lady in elegant clothes, pnt losses, 19th C, 10" 1,495.00
Cat, seated, yel & blk stripes w/red details, sm rpr, 19th C, 10"...4,600.00
Cat, w/grn, blk spots, yel collar, gr base, wear/glued rpr, 6" 550.00
Dog, free-standing front legs, lt brn ears, gr/red-stripe base, 6", EX 275.00
Dog, molded fur, tail curves over bk, brn w/mc on gr base, 8x6", EX....935.00
Dog, red/gr/blk pnt on base/collar/head, blk ears, yel eyes, 5", EX.........245.00
Dog, seated w/basket in mouth, red/gr/blk details, stepped base, 6" 600.00
Dog (poodle?), pk/brn pnt, blk ears/mouth/collar/base, 6½" L....330.00
Dove bank on base w/branches & leaves pnt gr & brn, brn wings, 11", EX ...330.00
Lamb, recumbent, curly coat, lt olive base, red/blk details, 5" L .275.00
Lamb, recumbent on molded base, 4" L 165.00
Ram on grassy base, early, 2⅛x2½", EX 45.00
Spaniel, molded fur/collar/chain, cleaned w/pnt traces, 12", facing pr...135.00
Squirrel, eating nut, red/gr on wht, 6" 360.00

Champleve

Champleve, enameling on brass or other metal, differs from cloisonne in that the design is depressed or incised into the metal, rather than being built in with wire dividers as in the cloisonnè procedure. The cells, or depressions, are filled in with color, and the piece is then fired.

Vase, engraved and enameled bands, pelmet-shaped panels below, dragon handles, dark brown patina, 36x22", $2,500.00. (Photo courtesy Neal Auction Company)

Garniture, enamel/gilt, 1890s, 16" clock+2 2-light torcheres ..3,000.00
Jardiniere, wide oval w/loose ring hdls, ftd, F Barbedienne, 9x7x11"...2,300.00
Tazza, Moorish design, atop brass stem w/2 lion-capped warriers, 7x7"...200.00
Vase, Islamic motif, ftd/hdls, F Barbedinne, 10½"....................1,265.00

Chase Brass & Copper Company

Chase introduced this logo in 1928. The company incorporated in 1876 as the Waterbury Manufacturing Company. It was located in Waterbury, Connecticut. This location remained Chase's principal fabrication plant, and it was here that the 'Specialties' were made.

In 1900 the company chose the name Chase Companies Inc., in honor of their founder, Augustus Sabin Chase. The name encompassed Chase's many factories. Only the New York City sales division was called Chase Brass and Copper Co., but from 1936 on, that name was used exclusively.

In 1930 the sales division invited people to visit their new Specialties Sales Showroom in New York City 'where an interesting assortment of decorative and utilitarian pieces in brass and copper in a variety of designs and treatments are offered for your consideration.' Like several other large companies, Chase hired well-known designers such as Walter Von Nessen, Lurelle Guild, the Gerths, Russel Wright, and Dr. A Reimann. Harry Laylon, an in-house designer, created much of the new line.

From 1930 to 1942 Chase offered lamps, smoking accessories, and housewares similar to those Americans were seeing on the Hollywood screen — generally at prices the average person could afford.

Besides chromium, Chase manufactured many products in a variety of finishes, some even in silver plate. Many objects were polished or satin-finished brass and/or copper.

After World War II Chase no longer made the Specialties line. It had represented only a tiny fraction of this huge company's production. Instead they concentrated on a variety of fabricated mill items. Some dedicated Chase collectors even have shower heads, faucet aerators, gutter pipe, and metal samples. Is anyone using Chase window screening?

Chase products are marked either on the item itself or on a screw or rivet. Because Chase sold screws, rivets, nails, etc. (all with their logo), not all items having these Chase-marked components were actually made at Chase. It should also be noted that during the 1930s, China produced good quality chromium copies; so when you're not absolutely positive an item is Chase, buy it because you like it, understanding that its authenticity may be in question. Remember that if a magnet sticks to it, it's not Chase. Brass and copper are not magnetic, and Chase did not use steel.

Prior to 1933 Chase made smoking accessories for the Park Sherman Co. Some are marked 'Park Sherman, Chicago, Illinois, Made of Chase Brass.' Others carry a Park Sherman logo. It is believed that the 'heraldic emblem' was also used during this period. Many items are identical or very similar to Chase-marked pieces. Produced in the 1950s, National Silver's 'Emerald Glo' wares look very similar to Chase pieces, but Chase did not make them. It is very possible that National purchased Chase tooling after the Chase Specialties line was discontinued.

For further study we recommend *Chase Complete, Chase Catalogs 1934 & 1935, 1930s Lighting – Deco & Traditional by Chase;* and *The Chase Era, 1933 and 1942 Catalogs of the Chase Brass & Copper Co.* all by Donald-Brian Johnson and Leslie Pina (Schiffer); *Art Deco Chrome, The Chase Era,* by Richard Kilbride (Mrs. Kilbride is listed in the Directory under Connecticut); and *Art Deco Chrome* by James Linz (Schiffer).

In the listings that follow, examples are polished unless noted satin. A co-advisor for this category is Barbara Endter; she is listed in the Directory under New York. Donna and John Thorpe are our advisors for Chase lighting; they are listed in the Directory under Wisconsin.

Key:
LG — designed by Lurelle Guild   VN — designed by Von Nessen

Bookends, Davy Jones, wheel, brass/walnut/Bakelite, #90142 ....**60.00**
Bookends, Moderne, brass/riveted copper/panels, #11246, 6½", G **775.00**
Candlesticks, Bubble, copper/orange Catalin, #17063, 1935, 2½", pr ...**110.00**
Candlesticks, Taurex, chrome or copper, VN, #24003, 7", pr, $150 to ..**160.00**
Centerpiece, Architext, rectangular, #27009, from $50 to **60.00**
Cigarette holder, Bubble, open chromium sphere on sq, #860, 2¼"...**50.00**
Cocktail set, Doric, chrome, 12½" shaker+6 3" cups+12" tray ...**350.00**
Cocktail set, Gaiety, chrome/Bakelite, shaker+4 cups+tray, $100 to...**110.00**

Cocktail Set, Holiday; #90064, shaker, four cocktails and tray, designed by Howard Reichenbach and Harry Laylon, complete, from $100.00 to $110.00. (Photo courtesy Steven Visakay)

Coffee set, Comet, chrome/Bakelite, VN, pot+cr/sug+tray, #90120....**325.00**

Coffee set, Continental, chrome/Bakelite, VN, #17052, 3-pc. $210 to...**250.00**
Coffee set, Coronet, VN, pot+cr/sug+tray, #90121, from $600 to......**650.00**
Coffee set, Diplomat, chrome, Bakelite hdl, VN, #17029, 1932, $280 to..**300.00**
Creamer & sugar bowl, Savoy, w/tray, #26008, 1936, from $55 to...**65.00**
Cruet set, ribbed glass w/chrome trim, #26009, 8", from $250 to...**275.00**
Dish, Tulip, polished chromium, scroll hdl, #90005, from $45 to .**50.00**
Fruit basket, wireware, LG, #27028, 12½", from $200 to **300.00**
Ice bowl, chrome, Russel Wright, #28002, 1934, w/tongs...............**80.00**
Ice bowl, copper w/Bakelite hdls, Russel Wright, #28002, w/tongs ..**135.00**
Ice drink cup, chromium, #90085, 5¼", from $25 to **35.00**
Lamp, Glow, copper & brass, cone shade, #01001, 8", from $70 to....**80.00**
Lighter, Fire Ball, chrome, Schulze, #851, 2½", 1936 ....**45.00**
Pitcher, water; Sparta, chromium, wht plastic hdl, #90055, 8', $75 to **85.00**
Pretzelman (pretzel holder), copper, LG, #90038, 1934, from $100 to ..**120.00**
Shakers, chrome spheres, Russel Wright, #28004, 1932, pr...........**65.00**
Skewers, chromium plated, #90075, set of 4, ea 9¼", MIB **135.00**
Smoking stand, Stratosphere, chromium, VN, #17076, 1937, VG, $350 to..**400.00**
Sugar shaker, chromium, #90057, from $50 to **60.00**
Table bell, Manchu, chrome & Catalin, #13006, 1936..................**65.00**
Tea infuser, chrome, Bakelite hdl, #90118, 5", MIB **110.00**
Tray, Festivity, chrome, stepped hdls, #09018, 19⅝"x12¼", EX ...**275.00**
Vase, bud; 4-tube, copper w/ivory Bakelite, #3010, 1940, from $45 to.....**55.00**
Vase, Minerva, chrome, ribbed, ivory Bakelite stem, #03C12, 6⅜".....**50.00**
Watering can, copper & brass, #11173, 1934, G, from $65 to.......**75.00**
Wine cooler, chromium, child Bacchus in relief, R Kent, #27015, 9"..**600.00**

Chelsea Dinnerware

Made from about 1830 to 1880 in the Staffordshire district of England, this white dinnerware is decorated with lustre embossings in the grape, thistle, sprig, or fruit and cornucopia patterns. The relief designs vary from lavender to blue, and the body of the ware may be porcelain, ironstone, or earthenware. Because it was not produced in Chelsea as the name would suggest, dealers often prefer to call it 'Grandmother's Ware.'

For more information we recommend *Collector's Encyclopedia of English China* by Mary Frank Gaston (Collector Books), our advisor for this category.

Sprig, coffeepot, six-sided, 9½", NM, $110.00.

Grape, bowl, 8" **35.00**
Grape, cake plate, emb ribs, 10" dia, from $25 to **30.00**
Grape, cake plate, w/copper lustre, 10" sq, from $25 to **30.00**
Grape, coffeepot, stick hdl, 2-cup, 7"...**75.00**
Grape, creamer, 5½"...**55.00**
Grape, cup & saucer, from $25 to **35.00**
Grape, egg cup, 2¼", from $35 to **50.00**
Grape, pitcher, milk, 40-oz...**60.00**
Grape, plate, 6", from $12 to..**15.00**
Grape, plate, 7"...**18.00**
Grape, plate, 8", from $22 to..**25.00**
Grape, plate, 9½" **22.50**

Grape, sugar bowl, w/lid 55.00
Grape, teapot, octagonal, 10"...165.00
Grape, teapot, octagonal, 8½", from $125 to 150.00
Grape, teapot, 2-cup..75.00
Grape, waste bowl..40.00
Sprig, cake plate, 9" 40.00
Sprig, cup & saucer..40.00
Sprig, pitcher, milk...60.00
Sprig, plate, dinner 25.00
Sprig, plate, 7" 18.00
Thistle, butter pat...15.00
Thistle, cake plate, 8¾", from $25 to 30.00
Thistle, cup & saucer, from $30 to...35.00
Thistle, plate, 6", from $6 to 8.00
Thistle, plate, 7" 15.00
Thistle, sugar bowl, 8-sided, w/lid, 7½" 45.00

Chelsea Keramic Art Works

The Chelsea Keramic Art Works Robertson and Sons Pottery was established in 1872 in Chelsea, Massachusetts, by several members of the Robertson family, including Hugh C. Robertson who later formed the Dedham Pottery. Though their very early artware utilized a redware body, by the late 1870s it was replaced with yellow or buff burning clay. A line called Bourg-la-Reine (underglazed slip-decorated ware with primarily blue and green backgrounds) was produced, though not to any great extent. Other pieces were designed in imitation of Asian metalware, even to the extent that surfaces were 'hammered' to further enhance the effect. Occasionally live flora was pressed into the damp vessel walls to leave a decorative impression. They also made glazed plaques and tiles. Hugh C. Robertson ran the pottery alone after 1884 and labored to re-create the ancient Ming-era blood-red glaze. Although world acclaim greeted his rediscovery of what he then called 'Robertson's Blood,' his red-glazed vases cost too much to produce and bankruptcy followed in 1889. Supported by wealthy Boston art patrons, Hugh's pottery reopened in 1891 as the Chelsea Pottery U.S., and began using his other 1880s rediscovery, the crackle glaze, producing cobalt blue-decorated dinnerware. When this firm moved to Dedham in 1895 the ware became known as Dedham Pottery. From 1875 to 1880 the pottery was marked Chelsea Keramic Art Works Robertson and Sons in either two or three impressed lines. Earlier pieces were not marked. The impressed mark CKAW in a diamond formation was also used between 1875 and 1889. From 1891 through 1895 the impressed letters CPUS in a cloverleaf was utilized for the new firm. After the move to Dedham, only new Dedham Pottery marks were used. See also Dedham Pottery.

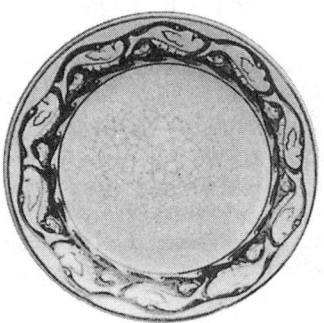

Plate, Upside Down Dolphin and Baby, impressed CPUS mark, 8½", $700.00.

Vase, cvd floral, baluster, flecks on steel bl, CKAW, 11¼" 900.00
Vase, emb bee & florals on khaki gr, Chelsea Keramic & Sons, 7" ..600.00
Vase, floral incised/cvd on steel bl w/cobalt/khaki flecks, CKAW, 11"..935.00
Vase, scrolls at shoulders, bl-gr w/gray & brn streaks, ftd, 5⅛"....450.00

Cherokee Pottery

Made and sold in Oklahoma through tribal-owned facilities at an industrial development sponsored in part by the Bureau of Indian Affairs, this pottery may be marked Cherokee in angular-style lettering or with the outline of an Indian head.

Cup, red w/Indians around campfire, mk 9-9-77 w/arrow, 4¼" 15.00
Lamp, blk, triangular w/3 pinched sides, 22" 85.00
Pitcher, multi-gr drip glaze, mk 9-21-77 w/arrow, 11½".................15.00
Vase, bl, 3 hdls w/rim pinch above ea, Indian head mk, 8" 65.00
Vase, bl w/gr, red, orange & wht drip, mk w/arrow & 3-5-92, 5"...15.00

Children's Books

Children's books, especially those from the Victorian era, are charming collectibles. Colorful lithographic illustrations that once delighted little boys in long curls and tiny girls in long stockings and lots of ribbons and lace have lost none of their appeal. Some collectors limit themselves to a specific subject, while others may be far more interested in the illustrations. First editions are more valuable than later issues, and condition and rarity are very important factors to consider before making your purchase. For further information we recommend *Collector's Guide to Children's Books, Volumes I, II,* and *III,* and *Boys' and Girls' Book Series,* all by Diane McClure Jones and Rosemary Jones; *Whitman Juvenile Books Reference & Value Guide* by David and Virginia Brown; and *Big Little Books* by Larry Jacobs. All are available from Collector Books or your local bookstore.

Key:
brd — board   ed — edition
dj — dust jacket

Freaky Friday, Mary Rodgers, Harper & Row, 1972, Edward Gorey illustrated dust wrapper, book club issue, NM, $200.00.

Adventures of Prince Melonseed, ME Chaffey, Briggs, 1916, 1st ed ..60.00
Animal Story Book, A Lang, Longmans, 1896, hardcover 110.00
Bambi, Disney/Heath, 1944, hardcover 75.00
Bandit Jim Crow, L Bancroft, Reilly Britton, ca 1906, hardcover .85.00
Belle's Pink Roots, J Mathews, Dutton, 1881, hardcover...............85.00
Brushwood Boy, R Kipling, Doubleday, 1907 ....40.00
Child in the Bamboo Grove, R Harris, Faber & Faber, 1972, 1st ed........65.00
Child's Book of Abridged Wisdom, C Harold, Elder, 1905, rope-ringed..45.00
Child's Garden of Verses, RL Stevenson, Saalfield, 1929, softcover.........65.00
Complete Cheerful Cherub, R McCann, Covivi Friede Inc, 1932, hardcover...20.00
Donald Duck & His Ups & Downs, WDE, 1930s, hardcover 100.00
Enchanted Castle, E Nesbit, Coward McCann, 1933, hardcover..25.00
Fairy Gold, E Kovar, Whitman, 1931 ....60.00

Famous Fairy Tales, Eulalie, Platt, 1923, hardcover 70.00
Fight of the Pueblo, CJ Cannon, Houghton, 1934, hardcover 25.00
Flying Scotsman, D Crockford, Oxford University Press, ca 1937..35.00
Folk Tales of Flanders, J DeBosschere, Dodd, 1918, hardcover ...110.00
G-Man's Son, W Robinson, Goldsmith, 1936, hardcover w/dj 30.00
Hansel & Gretel & Other Stories, Bros Grimm, Doran, 1925, 1st Am ed...400.00
Hunting of the Snark, L Carroll, Harper, 1903, hardcover..........225.00
In Colonial Times, ME Wilkins, Lothrop, 1899..............................25.00
Inger Johanne's Lively Doings, D Zwilgmeyer, Lothrop, 1940.......40.00

Jack the Giant Killer, Raphael Tuck, ca 1900, four color plates, stiff color wrappers, 11x8", VG, $60.00. (Photo courtesy Marvelous Books)

JoJo/A Glowing-Eye Book, M Barrows, Rand McNally, 1944, hardcover...50.00
Kate Douglas Wiggin As Her Sister Knew Her, NA Smith, Houghton, 1925 .15.00
Little Match Man, L Barzini, Penn, 1917, cloth-over-brd 50.00
Little Minister, J Barrie, Russell, 1898, Maude Adams ed, hardcover....30.00
Little Miss Ducky Daddles, E McCandlish, Stoll & Edwards, 1926,......25.00
Little Pig's Picnic & Other Stories, Disney/Heath, 1939, hardcover 75.00
Little Red Riding Hood & the Big Bad Wolf, D McKay, 1934, softcover...50.00
Little Robinson Crusoe, CD Fox, Charles Renard, 1925, hardcover..65.00
Luck & Pluck, B Nolan, Heath, 1942, hardcover 20.00
Mickey Mouse Fire Brigade, Disney, 1930s, hardcover 75.00
Mickey Mouse Movie Stories, 1931, hardcover 200.00
Mother Goose, E Osgood Grover, Volland, 1915, 1st ed.............200.00
My Land & Water Friends, ME Bamford, Lothrop, 1996, hardcover...20.00
Nan in the City, M Hamlin, Roberts, 1897, hardcover 20.00
New Baby, Ruth & Harold Shane, Golden, 1948, 1st ed, cloth cover ..65.00
Nils, Ingri & Edgar Parin D'Aulaire, Doubleday, 1948, 1st ed.......45.00
Noah & the Rabbit, H McKay, Dutton, 1932, hardcover..............30.00
Old Fashioned Fairy Tales, MF Washburne, Rand McNally, 1928...60.00
Once Upon a Time, M Craigie, Putnam, 1876, gilted hardcover ..25.00
Painted Moccasin, C Moon, Stokes, 1931, hardcover 35.00
Peter Teeter Stories, Prof OHL Schwetzky, Thompson, 1904, hardcover...75.00
Raggedy Ann's Lucky Pennies, J Gruelle, MA Donohue, 1932, hardcover 45.00
Riley Fairy Tales, James Whitcomb Riley, Bobbs Merrill, 1923 .....25.00
Round the Mulberry Bush, M McNeil, Saalfield, 1933, hardcover ..75.00
Star of Hansi, M Vance, Harper, 1936, 1st ed, hardcover..............25.00
Stories From Uncle Remus, J Chandler Harris, Saalfield, 1934, w/dj ...125.00
Stories of the Pilgrims, MB Pumphery, McNally, 1912, hardcover....30.00
Stork Book, N Newkirk, Caldwell, 1907, hardcover......................20.00
Tale of Benjamin Bunny, Beatrix Potter, Warne, 1932, hardcover...60.00
Tammy & Pepper, Big Golden, 1st ed, hardcover 40.00
Tigers & Things, A Kauffman, Macmillan, 1929, hardcover.........30.00
Tommy w/the Big Tent, HW Root, Harper, 1924, hardcover 20.00
Tortilla Girl, MF McElravey, Whitman, 1946, hardcover..............10.00
Tubby the Tuba, Treasure Books, 1950s 20.00
Uncle Terry, CC Munn, Lee & Shepard, 1901, hardcover 20.00
Vagabond in Velvet, C Newcomb, Longmans, 1942, hardcover.....15.00
Willie Woodchuck, Bonnie Books, 1954, EX.................................30.00
Wynken Blynken & Nod, E Field, Whitman, 1941, softcover 40.00
Young Hickory, S Young, Farrar, 1940, hardcover, w/dj 25.00
Zeke, M White Ovington, Harcourt, 1941, hardcover 20.00

Children's Things

China

Nearly every item devised for adult furnishings has been reduced to child size — furniture, dishes, sporting goods, even some tools. All are very collectible. During the late seventeenth and early eighteenth centuries, miniature china dinnerware sets were made both in China and in England. They were not intended primarily as children's playthings, however, but instead were made to furnish miniature rooms and cabinets that provided a popular diversion for the adults of that period. By the nineteenth century, the emphasis had shifted, and most of the small-scaled dinnerware and tea sets were made for children's play.

Late in the nineteenth century and well into the twentieth, toy pressed glass dishes were made, many in the same pattern as full-scale glassware. Today these toy dishes often fetch prices in the same range as those for the 'grown-ups'!

Our advisors for this category are Margaret and Kenn Whitmyer; you will find their address in the Directory under Ohio. See also A B C Plates; Blue Willow; Clothing; Stickley; etc.

Bowl, Blue Marble, oval, England, 4½" 55.00
Bowl, Bluebird, ftd, Choisy & LeRoi, 5¼" 55.00
Bowl, soup; Blue Acorn, RSR (Ridgway, Sparks & Ridgway), 4½"...18.00
Bowl, soup; Fancy Loop, England, 3¾"..15.00
Bowl, soup; Flow Blue Dogwood, Minton, 4⅛"............................48.00
Bowl, soup; Maiden-Hair-Fern, Ridgway's, 4½" 18.00
Bowl, Twin Flowers, oval, England, 5" 100.00
Bowl, vegetable; Kite Fliers, w/lid, England, 3½" 132.00
Canister, Blue Banded, Germany, 3⅝" 34.00
Casserole, Bears, w/lid, Made in Japan, 2¼"..................................25.00
Casserole, Blue Willow, Occupied Japan 65.00
Casserole, Forget-Me-Not, England, 4¾".....................................175.00
Casserole, Gold Floral, England, 5½" 55.00
Casserole, Little Orphan Annie, Made in Japan 45.00
Casserole, Maiden-Hair-Fern, Ridgway's, 5¼" 42.00
Casserole, Tan Lustre Floral, oval, Made in Japan, 1⅝"..................22.00
Casserole, Twin Flowers, England, 5" 132.00
Chamber pot, Pink Floral, 2¼" 42.00
Cocoa pot, Otter, w/lid, Noritake 180.00
Compote, Blue Banded Ironstone, mk Iron Stone, 3¼" 42.00
Compote, Walley Ironstone, England, 5¾" 420.00
Creamer, Angel w/Shining Star, Germany, 3¾".............................45.00
Creamer, Blue Dot, Occupied Japan 8.00
Creamer, Butterfly, England, 3¼" 12.00
Creamer, Dutch Children, Made in Japan 13.00
Creamer, Dutch Figures, Edwin M Knowles, 2⅛" 15.00
Creamer, Elephant Lustre, figural, Made in Japan, 2" 22.00
Creamer, Flow Blue Basket, England 65.00
Creamer, Gaudy Ironstone, England, 2⅜" 48.00
Creamer, Green Lustre Standing Pony, Germany, 3¼".....................18.00
Creamer, Gumdrop Tree, Southern Potteries, 3" 33.00
Creamer, Lady Standing by Urn, England 60.00
Creamer, Mary Had a Little Lamb, England, 1½"..........................15.00
Creamer, Pink Lustre, Hunt Scene, Germany 33.00
Creamer, Pink Lustre Merry Christmas, Germany, 2⅞"..................33.00
Creamer, Silhouette, Noritake 22.00
Creamer, Stick Spatter, Staffordshire, 3⅛"....................................46.00
Cup, birds & nest charcoal transfer w/lustre bands, 1840s, 2½"..120.00
Cup, Blue Onion, England...12.00
Cup, Buster Brown, Germany, 5"..36.00
Cup, Dr Franklin's Maxims, bl transfer, unmk, 2¼x3", EX..........480.00

Cup, Silhouette Children, Victoria/Czechoslovakia, 1⅞" 10.00
Cup, Snow White, WD Ent, Made in Japan, ca 1937, 1½" 18.00
Cup, Water Hen, England, 2" 22.00
Cup & saucer, Chinaman, Japan, 1⅛", 2⅞" 25.00
Cup & saucer, Circus, Edwin M Knowles, 2⅛", 4¾" 12.00
Cup & saucer, Holly, Germany 33.00
Cup & saucer, Nursery Rhyme, Germany, 1¾", 3¾" 18.00
Cup & saucer, Nursery Rhymes, W&Co Hanley, 2", 5" 30.00
Cup & saucer, Orient, England, 3", 4¼" 35.00
Cup & saucer, Teddy Bear, Germany, 2", 4¼" 42.00
Egg whip, Blue Onion, Germany, 4½" 180.00
Gravy boat, Athens, England, 1¾" 40.00
Gravy boat, Rosamond, Bistro, 2½" 65.00
Ladle, Greek Key, RSR (Ridgway, Sparks & Ridgway), 5" 18.00
Mug, blk transfer 'William' in beaded/vine fr, Staffordshire, 1830 ...220.00
Mug, March (verse), mother/child/dog, pk transfer, 2½", NM....190.00
Plate, Father Christmas & the Children, Germany, 5" 25.00
Plate, Flow Blue Dogwood, Minton, 4" 27.00
Plate, Flowers That Never Fade, children, blk transfer, 5", EX ...180.00
Plate, Franklin's Proverb, Silks & Satins..., pk lustre/mc, 6", EX..100.00
Plate, Franklin's Proverb, 3 Removes Are As Bad..., pk lustre, VG 100.00
Plate, He That by the Plough Would Thrive..., pk lustre/mc, 5", NM ..130.00
Plate, I Never Saw an Oft Removed Tree..., pk lustre/mc, JKK, 5", EX ..90.00
Plate, Present for Elizabeth, florals, blk transfer, 1820s, 5" 260.00
Plate, Robinson Crusoe, blk transfer/mc, 1920s, 6", EX................75.00
Platter, Blue Banded Ironstone, mk Iron Stone, 4¼" 22.00
Platter, Forget-Me-Not, England, 6½" 115.00
Platter, Gold Floral, England, 7" 40.00
Platter, Greek Key, RSR (Ridgway, Sparks & Ridgway), 8"...........33.00
Platter, Lively Fern & Floral, England, 5" 30.00
Platter, Myrtle Wreath, JM&S, 5¾" 30.00
Platter, Pembroke, Bistro, 4½" 11.00
Platter, Rodesia, Ridgway's, 5" 12.00
Platter, Rosamond, Bistro, 4¼" 48.00
Platter, Spirit of Children, England, 5" 24.00
Saucer, Dimmock's Blue Banded, England, 4" 4.00
Saucer, Punch & Judy, England, 4¼"..15.00
Stein, character, Bavaria, 1⅞" 22.00
Sugar bowl, Floral Medallion, w/lid, Made in Japan, 2½" 15.00
Sugar bowl, Flow Blue Basket, England, w/lid, 3¾" 90.00
Sugar bowl, Gaudy Ironstone, England, w/lid, 4" 72.00
Sugar bowl, Girls w/Pets, Allerton & Sons, w/lid, 4½" 28.00
Sugar bowl, Green Lustre Merry Christmas, w/lid, Leuchtenburg, 3⅝' ...40.00
Sugar bowl, House That Jack Built, w/lid, Germany, 3½" 28.00
Sugar bowl, Humphrey's Clock, Ridgway's England.....................33.00
Sugar bowl, Old Moss Rose, w/lid 30.00
Sugar bowl, Pagoda on White, w/lid, Made in Japan 8.00
Sugar bowl, Pink Open Rose, England, 1¾" 12.00
Sugar bowl, Saint Nicholas, w/lid, Germany, 5½" 190.00
Tea set, Dolly Dimple, porc, 11-pc (sugar missing) in orig box, G...180.00
Teapot, Amherst Japan, w/lid, England, 4¼" 190.00
Teapot, Barnyard Animals, w/lid, Germany, 5¾" 70.00
Teapot, Blue Willow, w/lid, Made in Japan, 3¾".........................75.00
Teapot, Butterfly, w/lid, Made in Japan, 3⅜" 35.00
Teapot, Dutch Windmill, w/lid, Germany, 6½"............................95.00
Teapot, Friends, w/lid, Germany, 5½" 110.00
Teapot, Godey Print, w/lid, Salem China 55.00
Teapot, Joseph, Mary & the Donkey, w/lid, Germany, 5½".........150.00
Teapot, Roman Chariots, Cauldon England, w/lid, 3⅜".............135.00
Teapot, Silhouette Children, w/lid, Victoria/Czechoslovakia, 3⅝" ...40.00
Teapot, Water Hen, England, w/lid, 5¼" 90.00
Toothbrush holder, Pink Lustre, England, 1¾x3⅛" 55.00
Tray, Bluebird & Floral, hdls, England, 4¾" 48.00
Tray, Dimity, rectangular, England, 4⅞" 28.00

Tray, Mickey Mouse, c Walt Disney, Made in Japan, 6"................35.00
Tray, Phoenix Bird, hdls, Made in Japan, 6¼".............................68.00
Tureen, Blue Acorn, RSR (Ridgway, Sparks & Ridgway), 6½".....42.00
Tureen, Fishers, CE&M, 3½" 60.00
Tureen, Myrtle Wreath, MJ&S, 4½" 85.00
Tureen, Rhodesia, Ridgway's, 4¾"..65.00
Tureen stand, Livesley Fern & Floral, England, 5½".....................28.00
Underplate, Athens, England, 4¼" 15.00
Underplate, Blue Marble, England, 5½" 60.00
Underplate, Pembroke, Bistro, 6¾" 27.00
Waste bowl, Lady Standing by Urn, 2⅞" 48.00
Waste bowl, Stick Spatter, Staffordshire, 2½"............................80.00

Furniture

Examples with no dimensions given are child size unless noted doll size.

Key: ds — doll size

Highchair, Windsor, arrow-back with shaped seat, splayed legs, early red paint, New England, 1830s, 36x21½", EX+, $2,875.00.

Armchair, Windsor sack-bk, repro by David Smith, pnt w/faux wear, 29" ..660.00
Bed, cherry, chip-cvg, rolled ft/head brds, ball finials, Zoar OH, 43"..2,400.00
Bed, cherry cannon-ball rope type, trn posts, rfn, ds, 14x22" 200.00
Bed, mahog, trn posts, scrolled head/ft brds, ds, 12x19x12", G...385.00
Bureau, bl w/red & pnt birds, ornately cut mirror fr, Pat 1881, 28" 700.00
Chair, commode; Windsor bow-bk, orig blk pnt, ca 1800, seat: 7½"...315.00
Chair, ice cream; bent wire, rpl seat, ca 1920, 22", pr...................75.00
Chair, potty; rabbit-ear style, orig blk pnt w/gold pinstriping, 21"....110.00
Chair, potty; wide pine brd w/old red pnt, sq nails, 23½" 110.00
Chair, walnut, 3-slat bk, cowhide seat, varnish traces, LA, 1830-50 ....575.00
Chair, Windsor birdcage, bamboo trn, shield seat, 1890s, rpt, 21", pr..600.00
Chair, 4-spindle bk, plank seat, pnt strawberries, ds, 9¼" 600.00
Chest, curly maple/pine Hplwht style, fan inlay, 28x27"..........1,300.00
Chest, dk umber feather grpt on mustard, 3-drw, wood pulls, 16x12", EX..275.00
Chest, mahog Classical, 3 grad drws/trn ft, rpl pulls rfn, 18x14" 900.00
Chest, manog/cherry Emp, scrolled columns, stepped-out top drw, 25x23" ..2,900.00
Chest, pnt maple Classical, 4-drw, 1825-35, 22x17x11" 1,850.00
Chest, walnut top bank of drws stepped out, trn columns, 1855, 26x18" ..2,800.00
Chest, 2 short over 2 long drw, bun ft, red stain, Am, 19th C, 16"...3,000.00
Cradle, curly maple, cut-out hdls, dvtl corners, 20x41" 385.00
Cradle, hooded, pine, sq & t-head nails/some dvtl, rockers, 13x16", VG.......140.00
Cradle, joined & paneled oak, NE, ca 1700, rfn, 30x39x20" 1,800.00
Cradle, mahog Am, Gothic arch hanger, trestle base, 1840s, 48x39x21"..1,435.00
Cradle, poplar w/orig red grpt, scalloped head/ft brds, ds, 11x17"..220.00
Cradle, red w/yel & wht scrolls, Lucy pnt ea side, ds, 12x27x12", VG..165.00
Cradle, rnded head/ft, gr pnt w/mustard & brn int faux bois, PA, 40"...800.00

Crib, birch, tall slender posts, 4 urn splats ea side, 70" H............220.00
Cupboard, oak w/alligatored finish, panel do, dvtl drw, 30x20x12"..375.00
Cupboard, step-bk, base w/2 drws over 2 doors, wht pnt.............250.00
Cupboard, step-bk, cherry, cornice, shelves, 2 doors, 1850s, 37x24"..1,725.00
Desk, birch & maple QA, slant lid, compartments, old rfn, 26x28"...2,800.00
Highchair, aluminum fr, red vinyl seat & bk, wht tray, 1950s, NM..........70.00
Highchair, pnt Windsor, 5-spindle bk, bamboo trn stiles, worn pnt, 36"....460.00
Highchair, trn maple & ash, urn finials, old red wash, 37"..........315.00
Highchair, Windsor, old blk rpt, trn legs, shaped seat w/G- caning 330.00
Rocker, walnut, cvd bk rest w/woven cane panel, cane seat, Vict, 30"..350.00
Stand, Federal tiger maple, drw, ball ft, early 19th C, 19x17x15".......3,000.00
Table, drop-leaf; cherry Sheraton style, 6 trn legs, 18x30"+2 leaves...1,000.00
Table, work; pine, tapered/splay legs, mortise/tenon built, 13x15x28"...135.00

Glass

Acorn, creamer, crystal frost, 3⅜" 250.00
Acorn, sugar bowl, w/lid, 4¾" 200.00
Arched Panel, pitcher, Westmoreland, 3¾" 35.00
Arched Panel, tumbler, pk, gr or cobalt, Westmoreland, 2", ea.....30.00
Austrian No 200, butter dish, crystal, Greentown, 2¼" 200.00
Austrian No 200, spooner, canary, Greentown, 3" 200.00
Baby Thumbprint, cake stand, 2" 125.00
Bead & Scroll, butter dish, dk gr, bl or amber, 4", ea..................300.00
Beaded Swirl, butter dish, Westmoreland, 2⅜" 52.00
Beaded Swirl, spooner, amber or cobalt, Westmoreland, 2¼", ea....150.00
Betty Jane, baker, oval, McKee, 4¼x6⅜" 12.00
Betty Jane, bread baker, crystal w/red trim, rectangular, #256 ....30.00
Betty Jane, ramekin, McKee, #294..6.50
Block, butter dish, amber, 3" 185.00
Braided Belt, creamer, wht w/decor, 2⅝"....................................115.00
Bucket (Wooden Pail), sugar bowl, Bryce Bros, 3¾" 200.00

Button and Arches, butter dish, 3½x5", $150.00 to $180.00. (Photo courtesy Doris Anderson Lechler)

Button Panel No 44, butter dish, crystal w/gold, Geo Duncan's Sons ..125.00
Button Panel No 44, spooner, crystal (no gold), Geo Duncan's Sons.....62.00
Cherry Blossom, cup, pk, 1½" (+) 30.00
Cherry Blossom, sugar bowl, Delphite, 2⅝" (+)............................35.00
Chimo, spooner, 2" (+) 50.00
Clear & Diamond Panel, butter dish, gr, 4" 130.00
Clear & Diamond Panel, sugar bowl, bl, w/lid, 3½" 55.00
Colonial Flute, pitcher, 3¼"..22.00
Colonial Flute, punch cup, 1⅞"...14.00
Dewdrop, butter dish, bl or amber, Columbia, 2⅝", ea................170.00
Dewdrop, spooner, Columbia, 2¾" 70.00
Doric & Pansy, creamer, pk, 2¾" 35.00
Doric & Pansy, plate, ultramarine, 5⅞" 9.00
Doyle No 500, butter dish, amber, 2¼" 110.00
Doyle No 500, tray, bl, 6⅝" 80.00
Drum, mug, 2"...40.00
Dutch Boudoir, pitcher, bl opaque, 2¼" 130.00

Dutch Boudoir, pomade, milk glass, 1½" (+) 125.00
Flattened Diamond & Sunburst 'Thumbelina,' creamer, Westmoreland...20.00
Galloway No 15071, pitcher, crystal w/gold, US Glass, 3⅞" 35.00
Galloway No 15071, water set, blush, US Glass, 7-pc 315.00
Grapevine w/Ovals, creamer, McKee, 2" (+)...................................67.00
Hobnail w/Thumbprint Base No 150, tray, bl or amber, Doyle, 7⅜"...60.00
Homespun, plate, 4½" 7.00
Homespun, teapot, pk, w/lid 150.00
Inverted Strawberry, bowl, master berry; Cambridge, 1⅝"............65.00
Jade-ite, canister, blk lettering, Jeannette, 3" 300.00
Kidibake, casserole, clear opal, w/lid, #1938, 4½" 85.00
Kidibake, ramekin, clear opal, #1923, 2½" 22.00
Laurel, plate, Scottie decal, 5⅞" 40.00
Laurel, sugar bowl, French Ivory, 2⅜"...35.00
Liberty Bell, mug, 2" 125.00
Liberty Bell, spooner, milk glass, 2⅜"...150.00
Little Tots, creamer, gr, England, 1⅜"...10.00
Michigan, butter dish, flashed w/red or gr, US Glass, 3½" 175.00
Moderntone, plate, wht, 5¼" 7.00
Moderntone, set, beige/aqua/rose/Sunny Yellow, 16-pc 220.00
Nursery Rhyme, creamer, US Glass, 2½" 55.00
Nursery Rhyme, punch bowl, milk glass, US Glass, 3¼" 135.00
Pattee Cross, bowl, berry; US Glass, 1" 12.00
Peacock Feather, cake stand, US Glass, 3" 95.00
Pennsylvania, creamer, US Glass, 2½" 45.00
Pennsylvania, spooner, gr, US Glass, 2½" 95.00
Plain Pattern No 13, butter dish, milk glass, King, 1⅞" 175.00
Pyrexette, bread baker, Corning, 3x4¾" 22.00
Rex/Fancy Cut, butter dish, Co-Operative Flint Glass, 2⅜".........42.00
Rex/Fancy Cut, tumbler, Co-Operative Flint Glass, 1⅝"..............18.00
Sawtooth, creamer, 3½" 32.00
Sawtooth, sugar bowl, w/lid, 4⅞" 50.00
Standing Lamb, butter dish...900.00
Standing Lamb, spooner, frosted..1,100.00
Stippled Diamond, creamer, bl or amber, 2¼", ea........................100.00
Stippled Diamond, sugar bowl, w/lid, 3⅛".....................................85.00
Stippled Vines & Beads, butter dish, teal or amber, 2⅜", ea.......140.00
Stippled Vines & Beads, butter dish, 2⅜".....................................110.00
Sultan, butter dish, gr or gr frosted, McKee, 3¾".........................300.00
Sultan, sugar bowl, w/lid, McKee, 4½"...125.00
Sunny Suzy, casserole, w/lid, Anchor Hocking, 10-oz...................10.00
Sunny Suzy, custard cup, Anchor Hocking, 5-oz............................3.00
Tulip & Honeycomb, bowl, oval, Federal, 1¾"...............................65.00
Tulip & Honeycomb, sugar bowl, w/lid, Federal, 3¾".....................35.00
Twin Snowshoes, spooner, US Glass..110.00
Two Band, butter dish 75.00
Two Band, sugar bowl, w/lid, 3¾"..65.00
Wheat Sheaf No 500, bowl, master berry; 2¼" 45.00
Wheat Sheaf No 500, wine set, Cambridge, 7-pc 170.00
Wild Rose, butter dish, milk glass, Greentown, 3½".....................75.00
Wild Rose, candlestick, Greentown, 4⅛".....................................125.00

Miscellaneous

Buggy, wood, bl/mustard pnt, blk lines on wood spokes, cloth top, ds..385.00
Noah's Ark, 6 cvd/pnt animals, Noah & 2 ladies, 12x19", EX 700.00
Riding horse, Mobo, pressed steel, Sebel/London, all orig, 30", NM.........460.00
Rocking horse, wood w/orig pnt, wht scrollwork on base, partial saddle...660.00
Sled, old red rpt w/blk & yel stripes, runners w/swans' heads, 34" 330.00
Sled, worn orig pnt, bentwood runners w/cast gooseneck finials, 36"........275.00
Stroller, metal w/wood hdl, mk Sturgis on footrests & fenders, 53", VG..100.00
Stroller, pnt pressed steel w/oak seat & hdls, rear storage, rstr, 27"...........290.00
Trunk, covered in 19th-C wallpaper, dome top, ds, 10x16½" 85.00
Wagon, pressed steel w/battery-op headlights, streamlined, rstr, 32"......635.00

Wheelbarrow, blk over red w/gold, wooden pnt wheel, sq nails, 38" L..415.00

Chintz

'Chintz' is the generic name for English china with an allover floral transfer design. This eye-catching china is reminiscent of chintz dress fabric. It is colorful, bright, and cheery with its many floral designs and reminds one of an English garden in full bloom. It was produced in England during the first half of this century and stands out among other styles of china. Pattern names often found with the manufacturer's name on the bottom of pieces include Florence, Blue Chintz, English Roses, Delphinium, June Roses, Hazel, Eversham, Royalty, Sweet Pea, Summertime, and Welbeck, among others.

The older patterns tend to be composed of larger flowers, while the later, more popular lines can be quite intricate in design. And while the first collectors preferred the earthenware lines, many are now searching for the bone china dinnerware made by such firms as Shelley. You can concentrate on reassembling a favorite pattern, or you can mix two or more designs together for a charming, eclectic look. Another choice may be to limit your collection to teapots (the stacking ones are especially nice), breakfast sets, or cups and saucers.

Though the Chintz market remains very active, prices for some pieces have been significantly compromised due to their having been reproduced. For further information we recommend *Charlton Book of Chintz, I, II,* and *II,* by Susan Scott. Our advisor is Mary Jane Hastings; she is listed in the Directory under Illinois. See also Shelley.

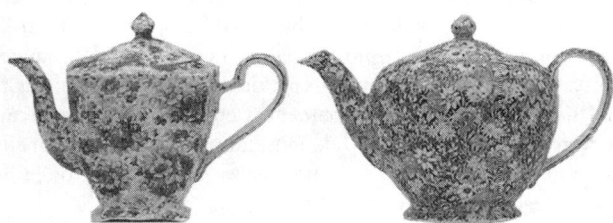

Summertime, teapot, Ascot shape, four-cup, $600.00; Balmoral, teapot, Albans shape, six-cup, NM, $650.00.

Anemone, plate, Lord Nelson, 8½" sq..............................95.00
Balmoral, bowl, mayonnaise; Saville shape, Royal Winton.........125.00
Bedale, canoe, pattern on int/ext, Royal Winton 145.00
Beeston, cake stand, ped ft...350.00
Cheadle, butter pat, Ascot shape, Royal Winton........................125.00
Cheadle, comport, oval, Royal Winton..................................175.00
Cheadle, sandwich tray, 12x7"..135.00
Chelsia, egg cup, ftd..135.00
Clevedon, sugar bowl, Ascot shape, Royal Winton 145.00
Cotswold, shakers, Fife shape, Royal Winton, pr......................175.00
Crocus, sauce boat & stand, Era shape, Royal Winton..............145.00
Crocus, trio, Athena shape, Royal Winton 165.00
Delphinium, comport, Lily shape, Royal Winton, 2¾" H..........125.00
Delphinium, teapot, Countess shape, Royal Winton, 6-cup, prof rstr ..325.00
DuBarry, ashtray, rectangular, James Kent, 4⅞x3¾"................45.00
DuBarry, bowl, mayonnaise; James Kent, 2½x5"......................55.00
DuBarry, cake plate, molded tab hdls, James Kent, 10x9½" 135.00
DuBarry, creamer, Granville shape, James Kent, 3¼" 85.00
DuBarry, cup & saucer, James Kent 130.00
DuBarry, teapot, Diamond shape, James Kent, lg........................600.00
Eleanor, coffee can & saucer, demi; Royal Winton.......................55.00
Eleanor, creamer & sugar bowl, Albans shape, Royal Winton, sm...95.00
Eleanor, toast rack, Era shape, 2-slice, Royal Winton...............125.00
English Rose, bowl, oval w/cut-out hdls, Royal Winton, 5½x4½" ...135.00

English Rose, plate, Ascot shape, Royal Winton, 5¼" 85.00
English Rose, sauce boat & stand, Era shape, Royal Winton 245.00
Ester, trivet, Royal Winton 165.00
Evesham, butter pat, Trefu shape, 4¾x4" 115.00
Evesham, creamer & sugar bowl, Ascot shape, Royal Winton 225.00
Evesham, plate, Ascot shape, Royal Winton, 5¼" 85.00
Floral Feast, teapot, Norman shape, Royal Winton, 3-cup 495.00
Florita, bowl, fluted rim, James Kent, 5"..................................60.00
Florita, creamer & sugar bowl, James Kent, 1¼", 2".................125.00
Florita, plate, Granville shape, James Kent, 9".........................175.00
Florita, sweet dish, sq Chelsea shape, tab hdls, James Kent, 5⅜" ..75.00
Hazel, breakfast set, Royal Winton, 6-pc 1,350.00
Hazel, bud vase, Clywd shape, Royal Winton, 3¾" 295.00
Hazel, cup & saucer, demitasse; Ascot shape, Royal Winton 95.00
Hazel, sandwich tray, Royal Winton.......................................190.00
Hazel, sauce boat & stand, Era shape, Royal Winton 165.00
Hydrangea, creamer, Granville shape, James Kent, 3⅛" 85.00
Hydrangea, plate, Granville shape, James Kent, 6½".....................35.00
Julia, bowl, Ascot shape, Royal Winton, 6⅝"............................145.00
Julia, nut dish, Ascot shape, cut-out hdls, Royal Winton, 6¾x5¼" ..245.00
Julia, sandwich plate, Ascot shape, Royal Winton, 5¼"...............85.00
Julia, sugar bowl, Albans, Royal Winton, 4½" 145.00
Julia, toast rack, Queen shape, 4-slice, Royal Winton 425.00
June Roses, sugar bowl, Norman shape, Royal Winton..................85.00
Kew, breakfast set, Royal Winton, 6-pc...............................1,200.00
Kew, cup & saucer, demitasse; Albans shape, Royal Winton.......125.00
Kew, sauce boat & stand, Era shape, Royal Winton 145.00
Kew, trio, Athena shape, Royal Winton.................................145.00
Kinver, compote, Lily shape, Royal Winton, 3x6" 245.00
Lilac Time, coffeepot, Empire shape......................................750.00
Majestic, butter dish, rectangular, Ascot shape, Royal Winton...295.00
Majestic, cake plate, Ascot shape, Royal Winton.......................450.00
Marguerite, plate, Ajax shape, 10-sided, Royal Winton, 6¾".......30.00
Marguerite, plate, Orleans shape, Royal Winton, 6" 35.00
Marigold, plate, Granville shape, James Kent, 9" 95.00
Marina, cake plate, Lord Nelson, 8½"...................................85.00
Marina, cake plate, Lord Nelson, 10⅝x9⅛".............................95.00
Marina, teapot, stacking; 3-pc, Lord Nelson.............................495.00
Mauve Chintz, bud vase, Crown Ducal...................................145.00
Pansy, creamer & sugar bowl, Lord Nelson...............................95.00
Pansy, cup & saucer, demitasse; Lord Nelson............................60.00
Pansy, trio, Lord Nelson..115.00
Peony, bowl, Crown Ducal, 5¼"...65.00
Primula, bowl, mayonnaise; w/liner, Crown Ducal.......................85.00
Primula, bowl, oval, Crown Ducal, 9¾x8¾".............................125.00
Primula, jug, Crown Ducal, 3¾"...125.00
Primula, plate, Crown Ducal, 9"..45.00
Primula, teapot, Crown Ducal, 2-cup.....................................375.00
Primula, toast rack, 2-slice, Crown Ducal................................125.00
Rapture, bowl, cereal; James Kent, 1¼x6"................................42.00
Rosalynde, plate, Granville shape, James Kent, 10"......................95.00
Rosalynde, plate, James Kent, 9"...80.00
Rosalynde, toast rack, 4-slice, James Kent...............................395.00
Rosetime, cake plate, Lord Nelson, 8½"...................................65.00
Rosetime, creamer & sugar bowl, Ascot shape, Lord Nelson.........95.00
Rosetime, nut dish, cut-out hdls, Lord Nelson, 6⅞x5⅝" 95.00
Rosetime, plate, Lord Nelson, 8½" sq......................................95.00
Rosetime, trio, Lord Nelson..95.00
Royalty, basket, Hampton shape, Royal Winton, 4x4¼"................495.00
Royalty, bowl, salad; chrome lid, Royal Winton 450.00
Royalty, cake plate, on chrome stand, 9" sq.............................149.00
Shrewsbury, sugar bowl, Albans shape, Royal Winton, sm...........65.00
Somerset, plate, Ascot shape, Royal Winton, 6⅛" 85.00
Somerset, plate, octagonal, Royal Winton, 5⅛" 85.00

Somerset, trio, Ascot shape, Royal Winton 155.00
Spring, cheese keeper, Rex shape, Royal Winton 350.00
Spring, plate, Ascot shape, Royal Winton, 5¼" 70.00
Summertime, bonbon, Royal Winton, 1¼x6x5" 45.00
Summertime, butter pat, Royal Winton, 4¼" sq..........................37.00
Summertime, cup & saucer, King shape, Royal Winton..............140.00
Summertime, nut dish, Royal Winton.......................................135.00
Summertime, trio, Athena shape, Royal Winton 125.00
Sunshine, bowl, dessert; Ascot shape, Royal Winton, 6¾" 60.00
Sunshine, condiment set, Royal Winton...................................395.00
Sunshine, sauce boat & stand, Era shape, Royal Winton............145.00
Sweet Pea, bowl, Crown shape, Royal Winton, NM 695.00
Sweet Pea, tennis set...165.00
Victorian, lamp, Royal Winton 1,400.00
Welbeck, compote, Royal Winton..725.00
Welbeck, plate, Saville shape, Royal Winton, 4¼"......................95.00
Welbeck, toast rack, Queen shape, 4-slice, Royal Winton 395.00

Chocolate Glass

Jacob Rosenthal developed chocolate glass, a rich shaded opaque brown sometimes referred to as caramel slag, in 1900 at the Indiana Tumbler and Goblet Company of Greentown, Indiana. Later, other companies produced similar ware. Only the latter is listed here. See also Greentown. Our advisors for this category are Jerry and Sandi Garrett; they are listed in the Directory under Indiana.

Aurora, pickle dish, violin shape 225.00
Bottle, barber; Venetian, McKee 650.00
Bowl, Beaded Triangle, 4½" 350.00
Bowl, Chrysanthemum Leaf, smooth rim, 4⅜" 275.00
Bowl, Geneva, oval, 10½" 450.00
Bowl, Rose Garland, 7½" 2,750.00
Box, dresser; rectangular, 4¼x3½"...375.00
Box, powder; Orange Tree, Fenton, rnd 425.00
Butter dish, File, Royal Glass...2,500.00
Butter dish, Fleur-de-Lis, Royal Glass 750.00
Butter dish, White Oak 6,000.00
Butter dish, Wild Rose w/Bowknot..550.00
Carafe, Chrysanthemum Leaf 2,500.00
Compote, jelly; Majestic, McKee...800.00
Compote, Melrose, Royal Glass, 7¾" 300.00
Creamer, Aldine..1,300.00
Creamer, Chrysanthemum Leaf 650.00
Cruet, Shield w/Daisy & Button, Royal Glass 5,000.00
Dish, Honeycomb, rectangular, Royal Glass, 6¾x4"....................425.00
Mug, Serenade, 4¾" 175.00
Nappy, Chrysanthemum Leaf...675.00
Nappy, Navarre, hdl, McKee..300.00

Pitcher, File, $2,000.00.

Pitcher, Fleur-de-Lis, Royal Glass...1,250.00
Shaker, Big Rib...500.00
Shaker, Geneva 350.00
Spooner, Chrysanthemum Leaf..600.00
Sugar bowl, Aldine, w/lid 1,750.00
Sugar bowl, File, w/lid, Royal Glass, 4" dia 1,045.00
Toothpick holder, Geneva...600.00
Tray, Wild Rose w/Bowknot, 10½x8"...400.00
Tumbler, Chrysanthemum Leaf..550.00

Christmas Collectibles

Christmas past . . . lovely mementos from long ago attest to the ostentatious Victorian celebrations of the season.

St. Nicholas, better known as Santa, has changed much since 300 A.D. when the good Bishop Nicholas showered needy children with gifts and kindnesses. During the early eighteenth century, Santa was portrayed as the kind gift-giver to well-behaved children and the stern switch-bearing disciplinarian to those who were bad. In 1822 Clement Clark Moore, a New York poet, wrote his famous *Night Before Christmas,* and the Santa he described was jolly and jovial — a lovable old elf who was stern with no one. Early Santas wore robes of yellow, brown, blue, green, red, white, or even purple. But Thomas Nast, who worked as an illustrator for *Harper's Weekly,* was the first to depict Santa in a red suit instead of the traditional robe and to locate him the entire year at the North Pole headquarters.

Today's collectors prize early Santa figures, especially those in robes of fur or mohair or those dressed in an unusual color. Some early examples of Christmas memorabilia are the pre-1870 ornaments from Dresden, Germany. These cardboard figures — angels, gondolas, umbrellas, dirigibles, and countless others — sparkled with gold and silver trim. Late in the 1870s, blown glass ornaments were imported from Germany. There were over 6,000 recorded designs, all painted inside with silvery colors. From 1890 through 1910, blown glass spheres were often decorated with beads, tassels, and tinsel rope.

Christmas lights, made by Sandwich and some of their contemporaries, were either pressed or mold-blown glass shaped into a form similar to a water tumbler. They were filled with water and then hung from the tree by a wire handle; oil floating on the surface of the water served as fuel for the lighted wick.

Kugels are glass ornaments that were made as early as 1820 and as late as 1890. Ball-shaped examples are more common than the fruit and vegetable forms and have been found in sizes ranging from 1" to 14" in diameter. They were made of thick glass with heavy brass caps, in cobalt, green, gold, silver, red, and occasionally in amethyst.

Although experiments involving the use of electric light bulbs for the Christmas tree occurred before 1900, it was 1903 before the first manufactured socket set was marketed. These were very expensive and often proved a safety hazard. In 1921 safety regulations were established, and products were guaranteed safety approved. The early bulbs were smaller replicas of Edison's household bulb. By 1910 G.E. bulbs were rounded with a pointed end, and until 1919 all bulbs were hand blown. The first figural bulbs were made around 1910 in Austria. Japan soon followed, but their product was never of the high quality of the Austrian wares. American manufacturers produced their first machine-made figurals after 1919. Today figural bulbs (especially character-related examples) are very popular collectibles. Bubble lights were popular from about 1945 to 1960 when miniature lights were introduced. These tiny lamps dampened the public's enthusiasm for the bubblers, and manufacturers stopped providing replacement bulbs.

Feather trees were made from 1850 to 1950. All are collectible. Watch for newly manufactured feather trees that have been reintroduced.

For further information concerning Christmas collectibles, we recommend *Christmas Ornaments, Lights, and Decorations, A Collector's*

Identification and Value Guide, Volumes I through *III*, by George Johnson, available from Collector Books or your local bookstore.

Note: Values are given for bulbs with good paint, with no breaks or cracks, and in working order. Examples termed 'mini' measure no more than 1½". When no condition is mentioned in the description, assume values are for examples in EX/NM condition except paper items; those should be assumed NM/M.

Bulbs

Acorn, clear, std base, 3", from $25 to..30.00
Angel standing in long robe, clear, Japan, ca 1925, 2½"..............70.00
Angelfish, milk glass, short & wide, Japan, 2"................................60.00
Ball, plain, Glo-Ray by Noma, from 50¢ to....................................75
Banana, clear, Japan, ca 1925, 2¾"..30.00
Bear sitting on haunches, milk glass, Japan, ca 1950, 2¾"............35.00
Bubble light, Made by USA Light, 1949-56, from $4 to..................6.00
Bubble light, Noma Snap On, ca 1949-50, from $8 to...................10.00
Bubble light, World Wide, 1970, from $3 to....................................5.00
Cat in suit w/glasses, clear, Japan, 2¼"..175.00
Chick w/wings folded, clear, 1½"..35.00
Choir girl, milk glass, Japan, 2½"...30.00
Chrysanthemum, clear, 2½", from $30 to..40.00
Dog in basket (frowning), milk glass, Japan, 2¾"..........................35.00
Elephant sitting on ball, milk glass, Japan, 2¾".............................40.00
Grapes, milk glass, wide bunch, 2½", from $10 to..........................15.00
Indian chief standing in long robe & headdress, Europe, 3¼"....275.00
Lamp, hurricane; Czechoslovakia, recent, 2¼", from $5 to...........10.00
Lion w/tennis racket, milk glass, Japan, ca 1935 & 1955, 2¾"......30.00
Moon Mullins, milk glass, Japan, ca 1935 & 1955, 2¾"................35.00
Olympic Torch, milk glass, Japan, 2½"...35.00
Owl in vest & top hat, milk glass, Japan, 2¼"..............................110.00
Parakeet, milk glass, Japan, sm, 3¾", from $8 to...........................10.00
Peach, clear, ca 1920, 2"..25.00
Pine cone, clear, fat, 2", from $5 to..10.00
Queen of Hearts, milk glass, Paramount, from $15 to....................25.00
Rabbit playing banjo, milk glass, Japan, 2¾"..................................25.00

Santa, German style with bag, tree, and toys, EX detail, 9", NM, $250.00.

Santa face on bell (type II), milk glass, Japan, 1¾"......................15.00
Santa head, milk glass, lg chimney, Type 1, 2½", from $15 to.......20.00
Snowman w/stick, clear, Japan, 2½"...30.00
Star w/crescent moon, milk glass, 1950s, 2", from $15 to..............20.00
Street lantern, clear, 2", from $15 to...20.00
Tadpole, milk glass, Japan, 2½"...100.00
Walnut, clear, ca 1920, 1¾"...30.00
Zeppelin, clear, Am, lg, 2¾", from $35 to.......................................50.00

Candy Containers

Acorn, Dresden, gold/silver, flat, 2⅜", from $30 to........................40.00
Barrel w/dog & geese, printed paper on cb, opens at end, 2", $70 to..90.00
Basket, wicker; paper, appl Dresden trim, leather strap, 2¼" dia.200.00
Canteen, paper, US the Old Canteen, cork top, 3½" dia, $125 to ..150.00
Cockatiel head, Dresden, gold/silver or natural, 3-D, 2½"..........400.00
Cougar head, Dresden, gold/silver, 3-D, 2¼", from $475 to........525.00
Ear of corn, Dresden, natural, 3-D, 4¾", from $95 to..................120.00
Elephant head, Dresden, gold/silver, 3-D, sack in head, 3"..........425.00
Hot air balloon, printed paper on cb, 3-D, 5", from $200 to.......225.00
Mummy, Dresden, natural, 3-D, 4", from $300 to........................350.00
Parrot head, Dresden, natural, 3-D, 1¾", from $325 to...............350.00
Rooster, Dresden, natural, 3-D, 2¾", from $300 to......................325.00
Santa, cloth coat, fur beard, tree in hand/bluebird on other, 15"..1,050.00
Santa, felt coat, fur beard, opens at waist, compo, Germany, 7"..475.00
Santa, felt coat, fur beard, opens at waist, compo, Germany, 9"..575.00
Santa in Luffa (moss) car, cloth/compo Santa, tree on bk, Germany, 8"..500.00
Santa on skis, hard plastic, mc, Am, ca 1955, 3½", from $12 to...15.00
Santa's boots, papier-mache, Germany, 3", from $20 to................30.00
Santa waving, hard plastic, wht opaque/red/clear, 1960s, 3½"......15.00
Swan, Dresden, natural, 3-D, 2¾x3", from $225 to......................250.00
Trunk, printed paper, curved top, 3", from $25 to..........................35.00
Watering can, printed paper on cb, riveted hdl/spout, 2½", $200 to...250.00

Ornaments

Anchor, colored paper on cb, ca 1870s to 1910s, 3-6", ea, $25 to.35.00
Angel, die-cut paper w/cotton skirt, 21" overall, from $190 to ...210.00
Angel, scrap only, generic head, full body, 2-3½", ea, from $3 to....8.00
Angel head, scrap only, short wings fr face, 3", from $5 to..............7.00
Baby carriage, Dresden, gold/silver, 3-D, 4", from $450 to..........500.00
Ball, hard plastic, openwork & holly leaves, Bradford Plastics, 1955....2.50
Ball, plastic, molded in 2 parts, loop at top, 1930s, 2¾", $5 to........6.00
Bell, Dresden, gold/silver & pnt, flat, 5½x4½", from $110 to.....125.00
Bell, honeycomb paper, Am, 1920s-60s, 3-4", ea, from $2 to..........3.00
Boy clown, scrap only, w/in gold oval fr, 3½", from $3 to...............8.00
Butterfly, layered cb w/Venetian dew, 3", from $25 to 35.00
Carriage, Dresden, flat, 6½", from $60 to......................................75.00
Christ (adult), scrap w/tinsel, 7½", from $20 to............................30.00
Clown, Dresden-like, pnt, 3-D, conical hat, 3½", from $15 to 20.00
Duck, fluorescent, Glow-in-the-Dark, USA, 3¾", from $15 to.....17.00
Eagle, Dresden, on branch w/wings wide, gold/silver, flat, 5½"...100.00
Girl w/doll, die-cut paper, w/cotton batting skirt, 10x8", $80 to.100.00
Girl w/tree, scrap w/tinsel, Type II, 9½", from $55 to...................65.00
Icicle, twisted, colored acrylic, ca 1930, 5¾", from $4 to 5.00
Lion, Dresden, stalking, gold/silver, 3-D, 4¾", from $395 to.......450.00
Lion, fluorescent, Glow-in-the-Dark, USA, 3¼", from $6 to..........8.00
Owl, Dresden, natural, single sided, 3", from $75 to......................90.00
Rose, Dresden-like, pnt, ball w/emb petals, 1910s, 2" dia, $40 to .50.00
Santa, die-cut paper, spun glass skirt, Type IV, 3", from $35 to 45.00
Santa in wht fur coat w/cane, scrap w/tinsel, 4½", from $50 to 60.00
Santa w/child & toys, scrap w/tinsel, 1890s, Germany, from $35 to..50.00
Snow girl bust, scrap w/tinsel, Germany, 4½", from $20 to...........30.00
St Nicholas head, scrap w/tinsel, jeweled hat & collar, 3¾", $15 to ..25.00
Star, Dresden, gold/silver, dbl, 2-3¼", from $65 to 85.00
Teardrop, hard plastic, silvered, Jewel Brite, 3½", from $1 to.........1.50
Wreath, Dresden, gold/silver, flat, 4¼", from $50 to......................65.00

Miscellaneous

Beads, plastic, rnd or oval, Japan or China, 1960-70s, 108", $2 to..3.00
Candle holder, acorns on leaf, tin litho, 3-2½", ea, from $60 to...65.00
Candle holder, angel w/anchor, heavy tin, clip, 2", from $80 to ...90.00

Candle holder, angel/cherub w/rose, tin litho, clip, 2", from $80 to..**90.00**
Candle holder, butterfly, tin reflecter counterweight, 2½", $75 to...**85.00**
Candle holder, cherries, emb heavy tin, clip, 1½", from $55 to..**65.00**
Candle holder, marigold glass shade, clip, 2¼", from $50 to **60.00**
Candle holder, raspberries, tin litho, clip, 2", from $80 to............**85.00**
Christmas light, bust of King Edward, purple amethyst, Eclipse, 4¼"...**625.00**
Christmas light, bust of Queen Mary, root beer-amber, Eclipse, 4¼"....**400.00**
Christmas light, Harlequin, cobalt, 1890-1910, 3¾" **110.00**
Christmas light, Dmn Quilt, cranberry, 3¾", from $110 to.........**120.00**
Christmas light, Dmn Quilt, ruby, Brock's Crystal..., Made in Austria ..**125.00**
Christmas light, pineapple, aqua, lt stain, 1890-1910, 4⅛" **65.00**
Christmas light, strawberry, clear, 1890-1910, 3⅜" **100.00**
Christmas light, tulip, bright yel-gr, Hearn Wright..., 3½"...........**135.00**
Decoration, church, silvered plastic, Shiny Brite, 1950s, 4¼".......**10.00**
Decoration, deer w/raised leg, celluloid, Japan, ca 1950s, 6½" **7.00**
Decoration, Santa w/lantern, celluloid, Made in Japan, 4¾" **45.00**
Fence, CI, dmns/semicircle motif, fleur-de-lis finials, 12" L **165.00**
Fence, wood pickets w/gr rpt, wire nails, hinged corners, 11x22x22"...**60.00**
Fence+2 gates, CI, dmns/semicircular sections, gr/gold pnt, 11" L.....**495.00**
Kugel, ball, bl, 5-10", from $70 to..**100.00**
Kugel, ball, gold, 2-3", from $25 to **35.00**
Kugel, ball, silver, 1-1¾", from $15 to **20.00**
Kugel, dk sapphire bl, brass hanger, 4½" **110.00**
Kugel, early shape w/pike, hanger held by cork, 1½-3", $40 to **75.00**
Kugel, egg, pear or teardrop, gr, 1¾-2", from $60 to **70.00**
Kugel, grape cluster, bl, 3-4", from $175 to................................**200.00**
Kugel, grapes w/emb leaves, bl, 2¾-3", from $175 to....................**200.00**
Kugel, pine cone, cobalt, leaf-like cap, 4½" dia, from $500 to....**600.00**
Kugel, ribbed egg or pear, gold, 2-2¾", from $95 to.....................**125.00**
Kugel, ribbed egg or pear, silver, 3-4", from $175 to **200.00**
Kugel, Schecken, spotted appearance, from $125 to....................**150.00**
Lantern, all metal (no inserts), 4-sided, 1930s, 3½x5", $30 to......**35.00**
Lantern, stained glass in metal fr, 6-sided, 1890s, 3½", $50 to......**60.00**
Light, grapes cluster, clear, Hearn Wright & Co..., 3⅞"............**40.00**
Light, tulip, med yel-gr, Hearn Wright & Co..., 3⅝"...................**200.00**
Light, tulip, teal bl, Hearn Wright & Co..., 3½" **375.00**
Light, tulip, turq bl, Hearn Wright & Co..., 3⅝".......................**220.00**
Light cover, dog, clear glass, blown, Germany/USA, 3¾", $75 to.**90.00**
Light cover, rose, clear glass, blown, Germany/USA, 2½", $50 to...**60.00**
Light reflector, Dmn Ray Jeweled..., ca 1927, 3", set, MIB **9.00**
Light reflector, single layer foil, Natti, 3½", MIB of 8 ....**3.00**
Light shade, plastic, Christmas scene, Noma Bell, from $5 to **7.00**
Santa, Belsnickle, compo w/feather tree, red robe, glitter, 7", NM...**385.00**
Santa, Belsnickle, holds basket/moss tree, bells as belt, 12", EX...**2,100.00**
Santa, Belsnickle, papier-mache, w/feather tree, mc, 8", VG **275.00**
Santa, celluloid w/cb bk, lights up, 24", NMIB **65.00**
Santa, compo, lt brn robe w/wool trim, feather tree, 7½", EX **245.00**
Santa, compo & cb w/squeaker (silent), Germany, 7" **125.00**
Santa, compo w/bl cloth pants & bag, red robe, feather tree, MIJ, 7" ...**55.00**
Santa, papier-mache, w/tree, mc w/gold glitter, ca 1900, 14¼" ..**3,250.00**
Santa, papier-mache & cb, paper belt, Japan, 13", EX...................**85.00**
Santas on teeter-totter, wood/cloth (gr pants)/compo, w/up, 7x3", NM+ ..**450.00**
Sheep, compo w/wht pnt & yellowish covering, 4¾x6", VG **80.00**
Sucker holder, snowman tipping hat, plastic, Am, ca 1955, 3¼"..**15.00**
Tree, feather; Germany, Japan or US, 24-31", from $125 to........**180.00**
Tree, feather; Germany, Japan or US, 38-46", from $220 to........**295.00**
Tree stand, Cameo, musical, steel, electric, 1960s, 13", from $20 to **25.00**
Tree stand, CI, tree trunk/foliage/stairway motif, worn mc pnt, 10x10"...**85.00**
Tree stand, cone shape, metal, Noma, ca 1928, 13", from $175 to.........**200.00**
Tree stand, metal, 4-leg, electrified, 1920-30s, 12" dia, $30 to **40.00**
Tree stand, sheet metal house w/chimney, red/wht pnt, 10½x13x11" ..**110.00**
Tree stand, steel, 3 detachable legs, 8-light, Noma, 1948, 19".......**25.00**
Tree top, angel, scrap, Silvestre/Printed in Germany, old, 15".......**90.00**
Tree top, angel, wax, fabric & feathers, Germany, 1930s, 10", $175 to...**200.00**

Tree top, star, Color Point Star, Glo-Lite, 8", from $8 to **12.00**
Tree top, star, metal w/plastic 'gem,' Krystal Star, 4½", $8 to........**10.00**
Tree top, storks at fountain, free-blown, Italy, 1950s, 16", $150 to...**175.00**

Chrysanthemum Sprig, Blue

This is the blue opaque version of Northwood's popular pattern, Chrysanthemum Sprig. It was made at the turn of the century and is today very rare, as its values indicate. Prices are influenced by the amount of gold remaining on the raised designs. Our advisors for this category are Betty and Clarence Maier; they're listed in the Directory under Pennsylvania.

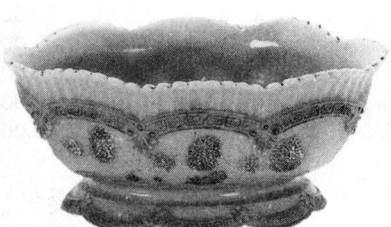

Bowl, master fruit; 10½", $600.00.

Bowl, berry; sm **325.00**
Butter dish **1,250.00**
Butter dish, lt in color **500.00**
Celery, from $400 to..**550.00**
Compote, jelly **600.00**
Condiment tray, rare, VG gold **750.00**
Creamer, from $285 to..**350.00**
Cruet, EX gold, from $975 to **1,200.00**
Pitcher, water **1,100.00**
Shakers, pr **450.00**
Spooner, from $300 to..**350.00**
Sugar bowl, M gold, w/lid, 7", from $350 to **450.00**
Toothpick holder **450.00**
Tumbler, 3¾", EX gold **182.00**

Circus Collectibles

During the 1890s, the golden age of the circus, Barnum and Bailey's parades transformed mundane city streets into an exotic never-never land inhabited by trumpeting elephants with jeweled gold headgear strutting by to the strains of the calliope that issued from a fine red- and gilt-painted wagon extravagantly decorated with carved wooden animals of every description. It was an exciting experience. Is it any wonder that collectors today treasure the mementos of that golden era? See also Posters.

Key:
B&B — Barnum & Bailey   RB — Ringling Bros.

Bedspread, clowns, red border, mk 1969 RB, 101x72", EX **70.00**
Book, RB B&B, clown cover, info on acts/animals/etc, 1932, 10x7", EX..**65.00**
Book, route; RB & B&B, 1942, 74 pgs, 4x6"EX............................**45.00**
Book, route; RB & B&B, 1952, EX+ **30.00**
Carousel mirror, elaborate wood fr w/electric lights, 1905, 40x28", VG...**1,325.00**
Handkerchief, clowns & animals printed on cotton, 8¾" **16.00**
Metrocard, RB B&B, unused, M (sealed) **90.00**
Photo, lady w/snake around neck & 1 around arm, tin-type, 3⅜x2⅞" ..**280.00**
Photo, man giving shave in B&B tent, tin-type, 3½x2½" **300.00**
Pin-bk button, Souvenir of the Circus, clown on bl, 1¾", EX **10.00**
Postcard, circus train photo, 5½x8¾" **7.00**

Postcard, 2 elephants w/trainer, Real-Photo, unused, VG+ **65.00**
Poster, Congress of Athletes, We Meet All Comers, canvas, 7x24", G...**500.00**
Poster, RB B&B, giraffe-necked women, 1930s, 24¾x17", VG+ ..**60.00**
Program, RB, 1975, full color, 96-pg w/centerfold poster, NM **35.00**
Program, RB B&B, 1921, EX **38.00**
Program, RB B&B, 1950, EX **32.00**
Program, RB B&B, 1971, 101st edition, w/2 lg reissue posters, EX..**25.00**
Program, RB B&B, 1985, Centennial Souvenir Edition, 10x13", EX ...**10.00**
Ring, Al Tomaini Giant, gray metal, giveaway **49.00**
Route schedule, RB B&B Tour Route #9, 1951, EX.......................**5.00**
Toy souvenir, King Tusk (stuffed elephant), RB, 21" L, NM **48.00**

Ring holder, bulldog w/tail up (holder), peach & wht, from $35 to..**45.00**
Salt & pepper shakers, 2 eggs in a basket, 3 pcs **40.00**
Shakers, pixies, ea seated holding rnd shaker, pr..........................**60.00**
Sock darner, girl w/red hair, gr bow & sleeves, orig ribbon............**50.00**
Sprinkler bottle, Chinaman, w/stopper, 1940s, 8¼"....................**45.00**
String holder, heart shape, You'll Always Have a 'Pull' w/Me.......**45.00**
Toothpick holder, butler figural, 4½"...**40.00**
Tray, bread; Distlefink, bird form, 12½" L **25.00**
Wall pocket, Antoine, chef's face, 7¼" **75.00**
Wall pocket, coffeepot, w/verse, 3x5½x8½" **35.00**
Wall pocket, teapot, Take Time for Tea, 7x7½"...........................**55.00**

Cleminson

A hobby turned to enterprise, Cleminson is one of several California potteries whose clever hand-decorated wares are attracting the attention of today's collectors. The Cleminsons started their business at their El Monte home in 1941 and were so successful that eventually they expanded to a modern plant that employed more than 150 workers. They produced not only dinnerware and kitchen items such as cookie jars, canisters, and accessories, but novelty wall vases, small trays, plaques, etc., as well. Though nearly always marked, Cleminson wares are easy to spot as you become familiar with their distinctive glaze colors. Their grayed-down blue and green, berry red, and dusty pink say 'Cleminson' as clearly as their trademark. Unable to compete with foreign imports, the pottery closed in 1963. For more information we recommend *The Collector's Encyclopedia of California Pottery, Second Edition*, by Jack Chipman (Collector Books).

Bell, dinner; French Maid, wht & bl dress, 6¼"..............................**40.00**
Bobby pin holder, Bobby Guard, guard figural, hat is lid **40.00**
Box, trinket; Miss in a Bathtub, 3½x5" **55.00**
Butter dish, Distlefink, bird form **35.00**
Card holder, divided tray w/center handle w/flowers **35.00**
Cleanser shaker, Katrina, hand-decorated, 6¼".............................**35.00**
Cookie jar, Christmas Cookie House, 7" **35.00**
Cookie jar, Mother's Best **375.00**

Cookie jar, Potbellied Stove, $225.00.

Clewell

Charles Walter Clewell was a metal worker who perfected the technique of plating an entire ceramic vessel with a thin layer of copper or bronze treated with an oxidizing agent to produce a natural deterioration of the surface. Through trial and error, he was able to control the degree of patina achieved. In the early stages, the metal darkened and if allowed to develop further formed a natural turquoise-blue or green corrosion. He worked alone in his small Akron, Ohio, studio from about 1906, buying undecorated pottery from several Ohio firms, among them Weller, Owens, and Cambridge. His work is usually marked. Clewell died in 1965, having never revealed his secret process to others.

Prices for Clewell have advanced rapidly during the past few years along with the Arts and Crafts market in general. Right now, good examples are bringing whatever the traffic will bear.

Vases (left to right): Bulbous with flared rim, brown to verdigris patina, #290-2-6, 7½x3½", $600.00; Buttressed handles, bronze to verdigris patina, #408-2-6, 5½x7", EX, $700.00; Classic shape, bronze to verdigris patina, #378-26, NM, $2,200.00; Ovoid, fine verdigris to bronze patina, #321-24, 6¼x3½", $580.00; Flat shoulder, striated gold, green, and copper patina, 11x7¾", NM, $950.00. (Photo courtesy David Rago)

Creamer & sugar bowl, PA Dutch decor **17.50**
Cup, clown's head figural, lid is conical hat, red/gr/bl on wht **80.00**
Cup & saucer, jumbo...**25.00**
Dispenser, lotion; lg gr overlapping leaves w/daisies, 5½".............**35.00**
Egg dish, 2 indents for eggs & 1 w/rooster for scraps, 1¼x6" **15.00**
Figurine, Granville the Elf, trimmed in brn, 3¼"............................**40.00**
Jar, vitamin; Daily Dose, w/lid, 5" **80.00**
Pie bird, wht w/striped tail, 4½" **60.00**
Plate, crowing rooster, 9½"...**60.00**
Razor blade bank, wht w/man's face in brn & beige, 4" **40.00**

Bowl, brn w/some gr & bl patina, minor stress lines, 9½" **475.00**
Lamp base, #440-41, rust over gr patina, swollen, 1-socket, 9" ...**635.00**
Lamp base, incised floral on copper, flaring/ftd, 14" **800.00**
Vase, #331-25, orange/gr/bl patina, 5¾".......................................**850.00**
Vase, #465, orange/dk red/gr/bl patina, 4½" **1,100.00**
Vase, brn over gr, elongated ovoid w/short collar rim, 12½", NM ...**1,700.00**
Vase, bud; bronze patina w/free-form & cut-bk motif, 8½" **375.00**
Vase, dk brn patina, squat & wide w/sm loop hdls, 3¾" W........**270.00**
Vase, gr w/areas of brn (exceptional patina), classic form, 15"..**2,200.00**
Vase, gr/brn exceptional patina, shouldered, 11½"..................**1,600.00**
Vase, gr/brn patina, hdls, broad shoulders, 9"..............................**750.00**

Vase, rust shoulder to EX gr on lower ⅔, sm neck, 6½", NM **375.00**

Clews

Brothers Ralph and James Clews were potters who operated in Cobridge in the Staffordshire district from 1817 to 1835. They are best known for their blue and white transfer-printed earthenwares, which included American Views, Moral Maxims, Picturesque Views, and English Views. A series called *Three Tours of Dr. Syntax* contained thirty-one different scenes with each piece bearing a descriptive title. Another popular series was *Pictures of Sir David Wilkie* with seven prints. (Though we once thought that the Don Quixote series was made by Clews, new information seems to indicate that it was made instead by Davenport.) Both printed and impressed marks were used, often incorporating the pattern name as well as the pottery. See also Staffordshire, Historical.

Bowl, soup; Chase After a Wolf, ca 1825, 9½" **595.00**
Bowl, vegetable; Dr Syntax Setting Out on His First Tour, 11" sq ...**950.00**
Coffeepot, Water Girl, bl transfer, ca 1825, 10½", NM **1,500.00**
Plate, Dr Syntax Returned From His Tour, dk bl transfer, 8¾" ..**550.00**
Plate, Dr Syntax Turned Nurse, dk bl transfer, 1825, 7⅞"..........**575.00**
Plate, Escape of the Mouse, dk bl transfer, 10"............................**450.00**
Plate, Italian Series, bl transfer, 1818-34, 9¾" **260.00**
Plate, Valentine, bl transfer, ca 1825, 10" **525.00**

Platter, Dr. Syntax Gazing, dark blue transfer, minor restoration to back, 9", $200.00.

Sauce tureen, Errand Boy, bl transfer, ca 1825, w/Rabbit on Wall tray....**1,450.00**
Sugar bowl, Basket & Urn, med bl transfer..................................**375.00**
Tea bowl & saucer, Bird's Nest, bl transfer, 1830s......................**110.00**
Teapot, Basket & Urn, med bl transfer, prof rpr...........................**425.00**
Teapot, shepherd w/dog & sheep, dk bl transfer, lg.....................**750.00**
Vase, Chameleon Ware, Lava, bls/grs w/wht, Deco style, #252, 4½x4"..**95.00**

Cliff, Clarice

Between 1928 and 1935 in Burslem, England, as the director and part owner of Wilkinson and Newport Pottery Companies, Clarice Cliff and her 'paintresses' created a body of hand-painted pottery whose influence is felt to the present time.

The name for the oevre was Bizarre Ware, and the predominant sensibility, style, and appearance was Deco. Almost all pieces are signed. There were over 160 patterns and more than 400 shapes, all of which are illustrated in *A Bizarre Affair — The Life and Work of Clarice Cliff*, published by Harry N. Abrams, Inc., written by Len Griffen and Susan and Louis Meisel.

Note: Non-hand-painted work (transfer printed) was produced after World War II and into the 1950s. Some of the most common names are 'Tonquin' and 'Charlotte.' These items, while attractive and enjoyable to own, have little value in the collector market. Our advisors for this category are Wilfred and Dolli Cohen; they are listed in the Directory under California.

Biscuit barrel, Celtic Harvest, 6½x6½"..................................**395.00**
Bone dish, Tonquin, purple **28.00**
Bowl, Celtic Harvest, 3½x11" **395.00**
Bowl, Delecia, HP int/ext, 4x9", NM.......................................**345.00**
Bowl, Delecia Citrus, oranges & lemons, stamped, 4x8¾", NM .**440.00**
Bowl, Orange Chintz, stamped, 2¼x7", NM.............................**330.00**
Bowl, vegetable; Duvivier, w/lid..**75.00**
Cheese keeper, Monumental Landscape, dtd 11-30, 10x8x6½" **1,000.00**
Clog (Dutch shoe), Bizarre, Aureau & Rodanthe design, 2¼x4¼" ...**545.00**
Clog (Dutch shoe), Red Roof, stamped, 5½" **465.00**
Coffeepot, Crocus, bl & orange flowers over brn w/yel top, Bizarre **595.00**
Cup & saucer, Fantasque, Melon, 1930-33, 2¼x3½", 5¾", NM ..**500.00**
Cup & saucer, Sunshine, Bizarre, 2¼x2¼", 4¼"........................**400.00**
Demitasse set, Pompadour, coffeepot+cr/sug+6 c/s......................**750.00**
Dish, Biarritz, shallow, 9x7½" **245.00**
Jam pot, Celtic Harvest, 3x4" dia **250.00**
Jam/honey pot, banded design, Bizarre, 3x3"............................**325.00**
Jardiniere, Red Autumn, 3-ftd, 9x9" dia....................................**800.00**
Jug, Celtic Harvest, #57A/s, 8½", NM **245.00**
Jug, geometrics, Bizarre, 4¼x5½"..**625.00**
Jug, Isis; Petunia, flowers on brn & yel, stamped, 9¾x8" **1,650.00**
Jug, Isis; Trees & House (Alpine), stamped, 12x9"....................**1,980.00**
Jug, Sungold, geometric & bands, 2-hdl, 11"............................**2,800.00**
Pitcher, Autumn (Balloon Tree), angular hdl, 5⅞" **1,100.00**
Plaque, Pine Grove, pines among swirling center, stamped, 10" .**495.00**
Plate, Autumn, trees & house on hill, scalloped rim, stamped, 6" ...**525.00**
Plate, Autumn, trees & path, red border, stamped, 9", NM **950.00**
Plate, Blue Chintz, stamped, 6¾" **600.00**
Plate, Broth, mc flowers & abstracts, stamped, 7¾", NM............**300.00**
Plate, Buckingham Palace, artist sgn, 1930s, 11" **75.00**
Plate, Crocus, Bizarre, octagonal Athens shape, 5½" **195.00**
Plate, Fantasque, Melon (Picasso fruit), 9".................................**525.00**
Plate, geometrics around concentric rings, Bizarre, 10" **320.00**
Plate, Inspiration Intarsio, cascading Deco flowers, stamped, 9½"..**995.00**
Plate, Moonflower, flowers & abstracts, stamped, 10½", NM ..**1,000.00**
Plate, Star, scalloped/red, w/red border, stamped, 5½"................**415.00**
Plate, Turkey, mc on brn bkground, 10" **75.00**
Service set, Nasturtium, pitcher+cr/sug, 5½", 3", 2¼" **770.00**
Tea set, batchelor's; Rodanthe, Bizarre, 1934, sm pot+cr/sug+c/s..**1,500.00**
Teapot, Celtic Harvest, 6½"..**250.00**
Toby jug, Clarice Cliff, Kevin Francis ltd ed, 1980s, 10"..........**1,500.00**

Vase, Lotus, multicolor geometrics, twin handles, 11⅜", $2,000.00; Lotus jug, Fantasque, cottages and trees, 9⅜", $2,500.00; Wall plate, Secrets, houses in landscape, 18", $2,000.00; Jug, Inspiration, lotus shape with stylized trees and hills, 11½", $2,500.00; Lotus jug, Fantasque, stylized fruit on diapered ground, 11½", $2,000.00.

Vase, Blue-Eyed Marigolds, 2-hdl, 11½" **2,500.00**

Vase, Dbl-Diamond, mc dmns w/orange band at top, ped ft, 6½" ..2,000.00
Vase, Delecia Feaches, #342, Bizarre, 8".......................................975.00
Vase, Inspiration, Bizarre, 5½"...650.00
Vase, Inspiration Nasturtium, floral on aqua, 7x3½" 990.00
Vase, Linquist, 2-hdld/3-ftd cauldron shape, 3x3" dia................580.00
Vase, Nouveau magnolias, 8"...495.00
Wall pocket, 2 parrots perched on bench, 1936...........................600.00

Clifton

Clifton Art Pottery of Clifton, New Jersey, was organized ca 1903. Until 1911 when they turned to the production of wall and floor tile, they made artware of several varieties. The founders were Fred Tschirner and William A. Long. Long had developed the method for underglaze slip painting that had been used at the Lonhuda Pottery in Steubenville, Ohio, in the 1890s. Crystal Patina, the first artware made by the small company, utilized a fine white body and flowing, blended colors, the earliest a green crystalline. Indian Ware, copied from the pottery of the American Indians, was usually decorated in black geometric designs on red clay. (On the occasions when white was used in addition to the black, the ware was often not as well executed; so even though two-color decoration is very rare, it is normally not as desirable to the collector.) Robin's Egg Blue, pale blue on the white body, and Tirrube, a slip-decorated matt ware, were also produced.

Vase, Crystal Patina, gr, flowing color, mfg flaw, 9½x3¼"...........200.00
Vase, Crystal Patina, gr, rim-to-shoulder hdls, mfg flaw, 6½x8" ..350.00
Vase, Crystal Patina, gr, squat, 2¼x4" 210.00
Vase, Crystal Patina, gr/khaki, broad banded form, 1906, 11" .1,200.00
Vase, Indian Ware, blk/tan/red, sgn Arizona, 7½" W 200.00

Vase, Indian Ware, incised and painted design, buff and black on brown, 9½" wide, $400.00.

Vase, Indian Ware, geometric shoulder band, collared rim, 4½x6¾" 90.00
Vase, Tirrube, mums, wht/yel on plum, att Haubrich, mfg flaw, 5"......200.00

Clocks

In the early days of our country's history, clock makers were influenced by styles imported from Europe. They copied the European's cabinets and reconstructed their movements — needed materials were in short supply; modifications had to be made. Of necessity was born mainspring motive power and spring clocks. Wooden movements were made on a mass-production basis as early as 1808. Before the middle of the century, brass movements had been developed.

Today's collectors prefer clocks from the eighteenth and nineteenth centuries with pendulum-regulated movements. Bracket clocks made during this period utilized the shorter pendulum improvised in 1658 by Fromentiel, a prominent English clock maker. These smaller square-face clocks usually were made with a dome top fitted with a handle or a decorative finial. The case was usually walnut or ebony and was sometimes decorated with pierced brass mountings. Brackets were often mounted on the wall to accommodate the clock, hence the name. The banjo

clock was patented in 1802 by Simon Willard. It derived its descriptive name from its banjo-like shape. A similar but more elaborate style was called the lyre clock.

The first electric novelty clocks were developed in the 1940s. Lux, who was the major producer, had been in business since 1912, making wind-up novelties during the '20s and '30s. Another company, Mastercrafter Novelty Clocks, first obtained a patent to produce these clocks in the late 1940s. Other manufacturers were Keebler, Westclox, and Columbia Time. The cases were made of china, Syroco, wood, and plastic; most were animated and some had pendulettes. Prices vary according to condition and rarity.

Except for the novelty clocks whose values are on the increase, clock prices have been stable for several years. Unless noted otherwise, values are given for eight-day time only clocks in excellent condition. Clocks that have been altered, damaged, or have had parts replaced are worth considerably less.

Our advisor is Bruce A. Austin; he is listed in the Directory under New York. Our novelty clock advisors is Anita Levi (Allegheny Mountain Antiques Gallery); she is listed in the Directory under Pennsylvania.

Key:

br — brass	reg — regulator
dl — dial	rswd — rosewood
esc — escapement	TS — time & strike
mcr — mercury	wt — weight
mvt — movement	vnr — veneer
OG — ogee	2nds — seconds
pnd — pendulum	

Calendar Clocks

Fr, dbl-dl perpetual, 4-glass crystal reg case, pnd, 1895, 18".....8,250.00
Ithaca #1 Reg, rpl cvgs & dl mask, rstr, 1884, 72"..................15,000.00
Ithaca #20 Farmer's, walnut, dbl dl w/rpl paper/pnd, rfn, VG 400.00
Ithaca #8 Shelf Library, walnut, repapered dl, rpr crest, 1880, 26" ...700.00
Ithaca Cottage #5 Variant, walnut panels, 1875, 20½"............1,000.00
LF & WW Carter, CT; rswd, BB Lewis calendar mechanism, 1865, 32"...2,000.00
Seth Thomas, walnut Am Renaissance, dbl dl, Pat Feb 15 1876, 32" ..750.00
Seth Thomas #1, rswd vnr w/losses, poor dl rstr, 1866, 33", G....525.00
Seth Thomas #3, rswd vnr, repapered dl, ca 1875, 26¾", VG+ ..600.00
Seth Thomas #5, walnut, minor pnt loss to dl, rstr/rpl, ca 1886, 20" .750.00
Seth Thomas #9 Parlor, walnut w/burl vnrs, prof rstr, 1886, 29½"..5,500.00
Seth Thomas #10 Office, oak w/label, rfn, 1875, 49", VG.......5,200.00
Southern Fashion #2, walnut vnr, rpt dl, rpl finials, 1875, 30½", G....650.00
Southern Fashion #4, dbl-dl, walnut, rfn, 1878, 32", VG.........1,850.00
Welch Arditi, dbl dl, EX patina/labels, 1885, 27"....................1,700.00
Welch Arditi, walnut, prof rfn, 1885, 27", VG.........................1,500.00
Welch Spring & Co #1 Reg, rswd, upside-down 2-wt mvt, 1878, 53"..5,750.00
Welch Spring & Co #5 Reg, 30-day, club-ft esc, 1878, 39", VG..........6,000.00

Novelty Clocks

Ansonia Lock & Key #35, orig thermometer (key), 1886, 6", VG....950.00
Ansonia Locomotive #44, dk dl, wht metal castings, 1886, 7¾", G .1,100.00
Fr, Windmill, Industrial series, 1880, 17½", VG.......................2,700.00
Fr Aboriginal, spelter figure w/clock in tummy, 1910, 11½", VG ..900.00
Fr Jester, bell ringer alarm, 1900, 11½", G..............................2,000.00
Griesbaum, whistling drunk at lamppost, 1935, 18½", VG.........650.00
Horseshoe, Waterbury Derby, NP, paper dl, 1-day, 1890, 5¾", VG..185.00
Kit Kat, eyes move, tail wags, red & wht, 1950s 95.00
Lux, banjo, NP, 30-hr rear-wind mvt, ca 1930, 6", M.................250.00
Lux, Bobbing Bird #314 cuckoo, 1940, 9", NMIB 175.00
Lux, violin, NP, 30-hr rear-wind mvt, ca 1930, 6½", M..............400.00

New Haven, gr/gray slag glass, strut supports, 1920, 8" **325.00**
Regent Mfg, bronzed CI cow, 30-hr, advertising pc, 1930, 8½" ..**500.00**

Shelf Clocks

Ansonia Arabia, porc, bright colors, porc dl (M), 1902, 10½" ...**350.00**
Ansonia Eagle, Ansonia Dollar watch suspended from mouth, 1910, 9", VG...**535.00**
Ansonia Greenwich, copper/bronze finish, ca 1901, rprs, 8½" **165.00**
Ansonia Huntress & Fisher swinger, G tin can arm, orig dl, 1890, 25"...**4,200.00**
Ansonia La Bretagne, Royal Bonn porc, roses, 1915, 15" **1,650.00**
Ansonia La Clair, Royal Bonn porc, floral, 1910, rstr, 15", VG...**1,900.00**
Ansonia La Cruz, Royal Bonn porc, floral on gr, 1900, 11½" **475.00**
Ansonia La Layon, Royal Bonn porc, 3-color, 1905, 14½" **1,500.00**
Ansonia La Lorne, Royal Bonn porc, floral w/gold, 1905, 11½".**600.00**
Ansonia La Nord, Royal Bonn porc, floral, 1905, 11¾" **1,200.00**
Ansonia La Orne, Royal Bonn porc, floral, 1908, 11¼", VG......**550.00**
Ansonia La Rita, Royal Bonn porc, gong, 1900, 11½", VG........**900.00**
Ansonia La Vogue, Royal Bonn porc, open esc, 1900, 12¾", VG....**950.00**
Ansonia Symbol Extra, crystal reg, porc dl, 1894, 15½", G **475.00**
Austrian, Royal Vienna porc, 8 cameos, 1895, 11½", NM **4,000.00**
Austrian Kingwood Bracket, Louis XIV style, 2-day/2-bell, 1775, 29"..**3,500.00**
Black Forest, cvd game-birds figural, bell-strike Fr mvt, 1875, 19" **1,500.00**
Boston Delphus, crystal reg, porc dl, worn gilt, 1890s, 10½", VG.............**850.00**
Brewster & Ingraham, steeple w/cone finials, 30-hr, 1845, 20", VG.........**250.00**
Brewster & Ingraham Beehive, rswd vnr, 1845, 19" **450.00**
Chelsea Willard ship's banjo, ships tablet, 1938, ¾-sz, 34", VG......**850.00**
Chelsea/Tiffany Babro #32, mahog tambour, 1916, 11x24" **975.00**
Chelsea/Tiffany Mahog Gothic, rstr 8" silvered dl, 1912, 18", VG....**900.00**
Chelsea/Tiffany Tambour #3, 5½" dl, br case, 1917, 8⅞".........**1,400.00**
Chelsea/Tiffany Yacht Wheel, br/mahog, 6" dl, 1922, 18½", VG **1,800.00**
Chelsea/Walk Tambour #4, ship's strike, 6½" copper dl, 1920, 12x24".......**700.00**
E Downes for G Mitchell, mahog vnr Pillar & Scroll, rpl rvpt, 31".........**2,200.00**
E Terry & Sons, mahog Fed Pillar & Scroll, 34-hr, rvpt tablet, 30x17"...**1,600.00**
Eli & Samuel Terry, mahog Fed Pillar & Scroll, 30-hr, rvpt tablet, 32"...**4,600.00**
Forestville Hdw, mahog/rswd vnr steeple, 30-hr, 1854, 12¾", VG+ **1,000.00**
Fr, patinated spelter La Nuit figure, swing arm, 1890, 32" **8,000.00**
Fr carriage, rstr gold-plate case-on-case, 2-tune, 1900, 9" **6,500.00**
Fr lyre, ebony vnr gilt ormolu, bell strike mvt, ca 1860, 20½"..**2,500.00**
Fr Masonic Tools (Industrial series), platform mvt, 1890, 14" .**1,675.00**
Fr octagonal crystal reg, mrc pnd, 8-pane, 1900, 12"................**1,150.00**
Fr Skeleton, rpl silk thread pnd, gilt hands, marble base, 1830, 12"..**1,500.00**
Fr 4-column Emp style, repousse br/ebony, rstr, 1870, 20½" **1,225.00**
German, bronzed spelter Batboy, swing arm, porc dl, 1905, 17" **1,500.00**
German, bronzed spelter swing arm, onyx/ormolu stand, 1800, 14".**2,750.00**
Gilbert Egyptian #58, TS/alarm, orig dl, 1900, 23½" **200.00**
Heyndricky-Vankerm a Burxelles, gilt bronze military man, 1850s, 28" **3,200.00**
Ingraham, 30-hr, ripple door, clear tablet, all orig, 1856, 17", G.**450.00**
Ingraham Admiral Dewey, emb oak, orig stencil on glass door, 1899, 23" ...**450.00**
Ingraham Dakota, weak paper dl, rswd vnr w/worn gilt, 1880, 15¾" ..**700.00**

Isidore Grenot Paris, Classical ormolu mantel type with winged figure, enamel dial, ca 1815, 19x14x4½", EX, $5,000.00.

Ives Internal Column OG, br bk mvt, orig dl, 1845, 30", VG **600.00**
Japy & Cie, blk marble, porc dl, gold trim, pnd, 1890s, 10"........**225.00**
Jerome Fusee, Emp style, upper mvt, wooden dl, 1845, 23" **1,650.00**
Junghans, swing arm, onyx/ormolu stand, 1910, 10¼" **1,200.00**
Junghans Elephant swinger, jewel bar/bronze bezel/ball, porc dl, 1910....**700.00**
Junghans patinated spelter elephant, swing arm, porc dl, 1905, 11"...**1,700.00**
Lord & Taylor France, gr marble w/gilt, pnt face, 9½".............**275.00**
MA, mahog/flame birch vnr, arched crest, pnt dl, central reserve, 34".**6,900.00**
New Haven mini 30-hr steeple, orig dl, star tablet, stripped, 14½" **275.00**
New Haven Thoreau, porc dl, open esc, gold pnt, 1911, 15" **375.00**
New Haven Wardrop, porc dl, orig finish/tablets, ca 1915, 24½" ..**250.00**
Pool, Executive, trn base, spring intact, ca 1928, 12" w/glass dome ..**380.00**
S Thomas, Adamantine, 4 columns ea side, paper dl, 1898, 11".**225.00**
S Thomas, mahog tambour, 89-L mvt, 2-note, rfn, ca 1920, 9½" **125.00**
S Thomas #00, 4-bell Sonora, silvered dl/faux mahog, 1915, 10" ..**600.00**
S Thomas Celtic, bronzed wht metal, 51-style mvt, SP dl, 1913, 9" **150.00**
S Thomas Chime #11, 5-bell Sonora, mahog, clean mvt, rstr, 1920, 13"...**550.00**
S Thomas Chime #72, #113 solid plate mvt, 1920, 14¾" **650.00**
S Thomas Column & Cornice, rswd vnr, rpt dl, 1850, 32½", VG.**275.00**
S Thomas Emp #200, crystal reg, porc dl, 1917, 9½", VG+........**275.00**
S Thomas mini cottage, 1-day/TS, rswd vnr, rpl/rfn, ca 1878, 9" .**180.00**
S Thomas Naples, oak w/EX cvg, prof rstr, 1902, 12" **700.00**
S Thomas Pillar & Scroll, Terry's Pat mvt, Mt Vernon tablet, 1825, 32"..**1,400.00**
S Thomas Queen Anne, walnut, orig dl, damascene pnd, 1890, 36".**800.00**
S Thomas Tudor #3 cottage, rswd case, ca 1870s, rpr/rfn, 9½" ...**300.00**
SB Terry, 30-hr cigar box/cottage, figured mahog, gong, 1852, 12" ...**1,300.00**
Simplex Timerecorder, oak time-punch, orig tablet, 1920, 31" ...**575.00**
Smith & Bros, vnr, 8-day OG, rack-striking mvt, rstr/rfn 1841, 31" .**600.00**
Terry, Downs & Burwell, CI w/orig finish & MOP, mk mvt, 1851, 10½" ..**400.00**
Terry & Andrews, steeple on steeple, rpl dl/hands/glasses, 1850s, 25" ..**850.00**
Tiffany, cobalt porc lyre w/swinging brilliants, porc dl, 1890, 14"...**5,000.00**
Waterbury Cottage Extra, rswd, 8-day, alarm, 1881, 12¾" **170.00**
Welch, blk marble/red onyx, Gothic case, porc dl, open esc, 1890, 15"....**325.00**
Whiting short transitional, paw ft, lion/carriage tablet, 1830, 26" ..**2,100.00**
Yale, CI front w/open esc, lt pnt wear, 1883, 4¼".......................**525.00**

Tall Case Clocks

Aaron Willard, Fed mahog w/inlay, 3 brass finials/rvpt, 93" ..**23,500.00**
Abraham Lower, mahog & tiger maple Fed w/inlay, 1800s, rfn/rstr, 91".**9,775.00**
Chpndl to Hplwht transitional, figured mahog, rfn/rprs, 91"..**2,500.00**
Edw Spalding, hardwood w/some figure, eng steel face, rpl finials, 84" ...**3,000.00**
English, mahog w/swan's neck broken ped, twist colonnettes, 1840s, 98"...**3,500.00**
Gilbert #7 Reg, walnut, gold sunburst, lyre pnd, 1881, 102"..**12,000.00**
Grpt, hood w/3 trn pillars & arched fretwork, wooden works, 90" ..**1,800.00**
Henry Ober, cherry Fed, castle top w/reeded plinths, 96" **4,900.00**
J Mulliken, MA; mahog Chpndl, enamel dl, old rfn, 94" **20,000.00**
John Guild (att), tiger maple Chpndl, old rfn, 18th C, 97"...**20,000.00**
John J Krause, PA; cherry Fed, tombstone door, enamel dl, 30-day, 84" **4,850.00**
L Bailey...Yarmouth, birch Chpndl, fretwork crest, tombstone door, rfn...**17,250.00**
L Watson Cincinnati, cherry & burl vnr, wooden works, rfn, 92½" **8,745.00**
Nathan Hale (att), cherry Fed w/inlay, solid crest, rfn, 1810, 86" ..**9,200.00**
Oscar Onken Co Cincinnati, mahog, moon dl/eng br face, rpr, 95"..**2,100.00**
Pine Co, HP face w/roses, Masonic panel in arch, wood wts, 91"........**1,650.00**
S Thomas #15 reg, walnut & burl vnrs, rubbed dl, 1880, 100", VG.**21,000.00**
Samuel Best, cherry Chpndl, hood: free-standing columns/rosettes, 99".**9,900.00**
Simon Willard, MA, Fed mahog, pierced fret above arch, ca 1800, 93" .**36,800.00**
Simon Willard, mahog Fed w/inlay & br mts & finials, 1800-10.......**37,950.00**
Thos Cross, oak/mahog vnr panels w/string & fan inlay, 83" **2,900.00**
Tiffany & Co, mahog, ped w/cvd frieze, moon-phase dl, 1900s, 99" ..**16,000.00**
Waterbury #65 reg, oak, mrc pnd, porc dl, 1903, 81½"............**10,750.00**
Waterbury #71 reg, quarter-sawn oak, orig pnd, 1905, 96¼" **10,500.00**
Waterbury #8 reg, jeweler's, cherry w/burl accents, 1890, 96".....**9,000.00**
Winterhalder & Hofmeier, 9-tube, 2-tune, rpl hood, rstr, 1910, 95"....**2,900.00**

Wm Cummens, Boston; mahog Fed, pierced fretwork, old rfn, 86"..**10,350.00**

Wall Clocks

Abel Chandler, Classical mahog & gilt gesso lyre banjo, 1825, 40"..**4,500.00**
Ansonia A reg, long drop, walnut, rpl pnd/bezel, 1920, 32", VG.........**400.00**
Ansonia Santa Fe, blk walnut, paper dl, 2-wt mvt, 1904, 52", G **3,600.00**
Austrian Grand Sonnerie Picture Fr, porc dl, music box, 1820, 22½" ...**1,550.00**
Baird, advertising on red, sgn dl, G label, 1890, 30½", EX orig.........**1,350.00**
Becker Alt Deutech-style reg, walnut, 3-color dl, 1-wt, 1890, 56".....**1,150.00**
Brewster & Ingraham, CI front w/EX pnt decor, minor rstr, 1850, 17".**750.00**
Chelsea/Ball Tambour #5, ship's strike, 6½" special dl, 1922, 11"......**1,800.00**
Colonial Willard banjo, TS, silkscreen tablets, 1950, 40" **350.00**
E Howard #4 banjo, rfn case, rstr dl, touched-up tablets, 1885, 32"..**1,700.00**
E Howard #5 banjo, rpt tablets, broken spring, ca 1900, 29", G ...**2,500.00**
E Howard #12 reg, walnut, clear front glass, rpt dl, 1875, 60", VG+..**5,200.00**
E Howard #27, marble dl, presentation pc, NP mvt, 1900, 35" ..**4,700.00**
E Howard #59-8 reissue, sgn mvt, 1977, 46" **1,100.00**
G Becker late Biedermeyer-style reg, 2-wt, eng dl, rstr/rpl, 1860, 47" ...**900.00**
G Becker reg, box style, walnut vnr, 6-pane door, 2-wt, 1910, 36" **450.00**
G Becker Vienna reg, oak/walnut vnr, sgn dl, 2-wt, 1901, 48", VG.....**875.00**
Geo A Jones Pinwheel reg, rfn walnut, rstr, 1880, 55", VG.....**3,750.00**
German, walnut wall reg, br pnd, 5" bell, 1900, 34", G...............**350.00**
German, Westminster chimes, Deco style, oak case, 1930s, 34½" ..**450.00**
German, 2-wt reg, Viennese style, rfn walnut, rstr, 1900, 46" **700.00**
Gilbert #11 reg, rfn walnut, spring for T/2 wts for T, 1891, 50", G....**3,200.00**
Gilbert #3022 Store reg, crude orig tablets, 1925, 34½"..............**275.00**
Herschede Willard banjo, Perry's Victory tablets, wt drive, 1925, 42" .**1,800.00**
Ingraham Corrugated Gallery, chestnut, rstr, 1875, 25½" dia..**2,350.00**
Ingraham Northwestern store reg, oak, w/calendar, 1910, 39", G **300.00**
JC Brown, 2-wt OG, rswd/mahog, wood dl, 1849, 29", G+.........**300.00**
Kienzle, fancy walnut Berlin-style free swinger, 1905, 39½" **1,700.00**
Lenzkirch, oak, 7" rnd glass dl, coiled wire gong, 1870, 12" **375.00**
Lenzkirch Berlin-style open-well swinger, walnut/bronze, 1900, 34"..**2,000.00**
Morbier, 2-wt wag, lg iron bell, prayer repeat, 1860, 53", VG.....**750.00**
R Muller & Son Vienna-style reg, walnut, celluloid dl, 1905, 57" **1,550.00**
S Thomas #2 reg, oak, orig dl & hdw, 1920, 34", VG **1,100.00**
S Thomas #6 reg, cherry, prof rstr, 1884, 49" **4,300.00**
S Thomas #19 reg, oak, rstr dl, prof rfn, 1890, 75", VG.........**26,000.00**
S Thomas Empire #4 Crystal reg, porc dl, pnd, 1910, 10½"........**525.00**
S Thomas Marcy, 3-train, 2 bells/gong, rstr, 1886, 46" **4,550.00**
S Thomas Signet, rfn walnut, geometric tablet, rstr, 1884, 23"...**800.00**
Sessions Star Pointer, rstr dl/rpl bezel/rfn, 1910, 32"....................**425.00**
Simon Willard, Fed mahog w/inlay banjo, T-bridge mvt, 1805, rfn, 33".**4,000.00**
Stephenson, Howard & Davis banjo, mahog, rvpt oval, 1840s, rfn, 39".**5,750.00**
Waterbury #3 reg, walnut, rfn, sm rpr to pnd, 1891, 46", VG..**2,400.00**
Waterbury #9 reg, walnut, pinwheel mvt, lyre pnd, rstr, 1880, 88"....**14,000.00**
Waterbury Galesburg, oak, pnd, NM label, 1905, 52" **1,000.00**
Welch, Spring & Co, blk walnut w/gold leaf, orig 18" dl, 1880, 30" ..**4,900.00**
Welch, Spring & Co #8 reg, blk walnut, rprs, 1885, 66", VG.....**9,000.00**
Welch, Spring & Co #9 reg, 30-day T, porc dl, all orig, 1889, 39"....**4,700.00**

Cloisonne

Cloisonne is a method of decorating metal with enameling. Fine metal wires are soldered onto the metal body following the lines of a pre-determined design. The resulting channels are filled in with enamels of various colors, and the item is fired. The final step is a smoothing process that assures even exposure of the wire pattern. The art is predominately Oriental and has been practiced continuously, except during war years, since the sixteenth century. The most excellent examples date from 1865 until the turn of the century. The early twentieth century export variety is usually lightweight and the workmanship inferior. Modern wares are of good quality and are produced in Taiwan as well as China.

Several variations of the basic art include plique-a-jour, achieved by removing the metal body after firing, leaving only the transparent enamel work; foil cloisonne, using transparent or semitranslucent enameling over a layer of embossed silver covering the metal body of the vessel; wireless cloisonne, made by removing the wire dividers prior to firing; and cloisonne executed on ceramic, wood, or lacquer rather than metal.

Box, scrolling flowers on teal, brass ft, ca 1925, 1½x3¾x3" **65.00**
Chamberstick, flowers & honeybee, gilt hdl, 20th C, 1¼x4¼".....**95.00**
Desk set, Nouveau style, Austria, 9-pc **1,500.00**
Inkwell, frog figural, hinged lid, 6x4" **475.00**
Jardinieres, floral on turq, foo dog hdls, 1880s, 15½x23¼", pr......**4,250.00**
Plate, 2 phoenix birds/clouds/central spiraling chrysanthemum, 12"...**350.00**

Teapot, stylized phoenix and dragon on black field of reserves and medallions on gilt copper, late nineteenth century, 5½", $450.00.

Umbrella hdl, bl w/wht dragon & flowers, overall length: 40" **80.00**
Vase, chrysanthemums/foliage on bl w/gold flecks, 25"+wooden stand...**500.00**
Vase, cranes/flowers in bamboo panels, Japan, 2⅞" **465.00**
Vase, dragons & pheasants w/gold flecks, autumn tones, Japan, 7½"...**285.00**
Vase, floral on cobalt, bottle form, Edo (1615-1868), 4¾x3¼" ..**325.00**

Clothing and Accessories

The field of collectible, vintage, and antique clothing is often confusing, especially for the novice collector or nonspecialty dealer. Prices vary enormously, depending on where you are — the Midwestern and Southern states still harbor the best deals, sometimes as much as 70% below book value — and the individual article of clothing in question. Prior to 1940 almost all apparel was custom made, therefore each garment is unique in both design and quality of construction. Specialty gowns, i.e. dresses which can be worn by modern-day brides or for special events, fetch the highest prices. Civil War re-enactors have driven up the prices of authentic Civil War apparel. Dresses with intact bustles continue to be rare finds. Young collectors are creating a demand for wearable 1950s – 1970s clothing, although prices in these categories still remain reasonable. A first-time collector needs to do thorough research to understand vintage clothing construction techniques before venturing into this field because of the many reproductions and mismarked items now finding their way onto the market. For example, reproductions of Victorian dresses usually close with a zipper instead of the traditional hooks and eyes. Zippers were not commonly used until after 1935.

For further information we recommend *Collector's Guide to Vintage Fashions* by Kristina Harris (an easy-to-use guide for dating women's clothing); *Vintage Hats and Bonnets, 1770 – 1970,* by Susan Langley; *Ladies' Vintage Accessories,* by LaRea Johnson Bruton; and *Antique & Vintage Clothing: A Guide to Dating and Valuation of Women's Clothing, 1850 – 1940,* by our advisor, Diane Snyder-Haug, available from Collector Books or your local bookstore. (Ms. Snyder-Haug is listed in the

Directory under Florida.) Our values are for items of ladies' clothing unless noted 'man's' or 'child's.' Assume them to be in excellent condition unless otherwise described.

Key:
cap/s — cap sleeves	ms — machine sewn
embr — embroidery	n/s — no sleeves
hs — hand sewn	plt — pleated
l/s — long sleeves	s/s — short sleeves

Blazer, man's, tan linen, Howard, 1940s **145.00**
Bloomers, child's, wht, button style w/embr & cutwork, 1920s **6.00**
Blouse, abstract print knit, s/s, jewel neck, bk zipper, 1970s **16.50**
Blouse, acetate satin floral print, l/s, dog-ear collar, 1960s.............**20.00**
Blouse, cotton broadcloth, mandarin collar, s/s, 1960s **18.50**
Blouse, cotton broadcloth, midriff style w/front ties, l/s, 1970s **16.50**
Blouse, cotton paisley print, s/s, roll-up cuffs, 1960s **17.00**
Blouse, linen w/floral embr & tiny tucks, high neck, l/s, ca 1905, EX **235.00**
Blouse, polyester twill, l/s, ruffled bodice, Le Mond, 1970s **17.50**
Blouse, see-thru crinkle crepe, l/s, ruffled neck/bodice, 1960s **18.50**
Blouse, sheer organdy print, s/s, covered buttons, collar, 1950s.....**15.00**
Blouse, silk w/floral embr/lace inserts/ruching, w/cuffs, 1905, EX....**225.00**
Blouse, wool jersey w/rayon chevella trim, ¾/s, bow tie, 1950s.....**23.50**
Cape, beaded velvet w/foliate applique & fur trim, 1880s **885.00**
Cape, evening; blk beaded velvet, 1940s....................................**415.00**
Cape, opera; gold metallic brocade, Stern Bros, 1920s **895.00**
Cloak, evening; bl/gold metallic brocade w/wht fur trim, 1920s .**975.00**
Coat, blk wool, Battenberg lace appliques, ca 1900 ....**1,050.00**
Coat, brn linen, dbl cape collar, plt bk, full length, 1890s **455.00**
Coat, evening; cut velvet w/mink collar & cuffs, metallic trim, 1920s ...**995.00**
Coat, evening; metallic brocade w/velvet collar & cuffs, 1920s...**1,085.00**
Coat, Irish lace, cutaway style, ca 1900 ....**975.00**
Coat, leather & suede, A-line, pockets, hip-length, 1970s.............**75.00**
Coat, opera; gold metallic brocade w/blk velvet & fox details, 1920s..**1,025.00**
Coat, silk tape lace w/inset mesh panels & embr, fringe, ca 1910 ....**635.00**
Coat, trench; man's, poly-cotton, wool lined, Christian Dior, 1960s..**90.00**
Coat, wht linen w/overall embr, ca 1915......................................**865.00**
Coat, wool, attached cape/belted bk/soutache trim, 1900s........................**1,095.00**
Coat, wool w/soutache & satin, swing bk, full/s, Paris label, 1900s....**1,250.00**
Coat jacket, brn leather, 2 patch pockets, mid-calf length, 1970s.**72.50**
Coat jacket, wool twill, 1-button swing type, lg shoulder pads, 1940s...**40.00**
Corset, gold & blk stripes, 1870s-80s, EX......................................**765.00**
Dress, abstract floral polyester, ruffled neck/hem, n/s, mini, 1960s...**27.50**
Dress, aqua silk w/much embr/beading/metallic lace, puff/s, ca 1904.**1,675.00**
Dress, beaded blk velvet, beaded mesh/s, sequined bodice, 1890s.......**1,685.00**
Dress, beaded metallic mesh w/ribbon appliques, n/s, 1920s **895.00**
Dress, bias-cut brn silk chiffon, draped/s w/open shoulders, 1930s..**465.00**
Dress, bias-cut satin w/draped bodice, train, l/s, 1930s **425.00**
Dress, bias-cut silk velvet w/rhinestones at neck & cuffs, 1930s .**450.00**
Dress, bl tulle w/irid beadwork torso, n/s, ca 1928.....................**2,680.00**
Dress, bl tulle w/matching stole, Hattie Carnegie, 1940s **535.00**
Dress, blk & gold cut lamè, draped low bk, n/s, full length, 1930s........**585.00**
Dress, blk beaded silk chiffon, V neck, s/open at shoulder, ca 1927......**895.00**
Dress, blk beaded tulle over gr satin, lace s/s, designer label, 1900s ...**2,200.00**
Dress, blk Chantilly lace over pk satin w/embr hip detail, l/s, 1920s.....**565.00**
Dress, blk silk chiffon w/metallic gold flowers, n/s, ca 1926 ....**795.00**
Dress, blk silk georgette, n/s, V neck & bk, 3-tier skirt, 1960s **37.50**
Dress, blk silk velvet w/Oriental beaded roses, n/s, ca 1923 .....**1,095.00**
Dress, blk tulle & beading over silver metallic lace, n/s, 1915.**1,565.00**
Dress, blk velvet w/beading & embr, l/s, J Marsh Co, ca 1924.**1,025.00**
Dress, child's, cotton print, bk buttons, tie waist, s/s, 1930s **18.00**
Dress, child's, plaid cotton, button-bk, tie belt, s/s, collar, 1950s ..**18.00**
Dress, child's, plaid/navy cotton, scalloped waist, Cinderella, 1940s..**12.00**
Dress, child's, yel linen w/ornate buttons, ties at waist, 1940s **20.00**

Dress, cotton seersucker, n/s sheath w/bolero jacket, 1950s...........**36.00**
Dress, day; taupe satin w/embr & plt trim, s/s, ca 1927 ....**345.00**
Dress, evening; beaded net, low neck, n/s, 1890s, EX **1,650.00**
Dress, evening; bias-cut floral satin w/low bk, s/s, full length, 1930s.....**395.00**
Dress, evening; bias-cut silk chiffon, flowing bk panel, n/s, 1930s.......**425.00**
Dress, evening; bias-cut silk chiffon, rhinestones allover, n/s, 1930s ...**525.00**

Dress, evening; gold beaded and silk chiffon flapper style, ca 1926, EX, $1,430.00. (Photo courtesy Neal Auction Company)

Dress, evening; satin, trained tunic over plt skirt, mink trim, 1930s ...**875.00**
Dress, floral silk, V neck, s/s, 1850s..**950.00**
Dress, floral/polka-dot knit, n/s, scoop neck, flared skirt, 1970s **26.50**
Dress, Fr beaded satin tea gown, l/s, sm collar, 1890s **1,985.00**
Dress, Fr beaded silk chiffon, n/s, flapper style, ca 1925 ....**985.00**
Dress, Fr satin w/embr bodice, half/s, train, Paris label, ca 1910 ..**2,100.00**
Dress, Fr watered silk w/cream lace swags, l/s, ca 1904.............**1,775.00**
Dress, geometric print polyester dbl knit, n/s, slit skirt, 1970s..........**32.00**
Dress, gold beads & sequins w/long fringe hem of silver beads, 1920s ..**950.00**
Dress, Hawaiian floral print, tent style, 1960s.................................**30.00**
Dress, Hawaiian print, n/s, mini w/Watteau bk, Evelyn Margolis, 1960s .**32.00**
Dress, ivory lace w/beaded bodice, n/s, ca 1915 ....**1,365.00**
Dress, lined rayon crepe, s/s, scoop neck, ¾/s bolero jacket, 1950s.....**35.00**
Dress, nylon lace & taffeta, V neck, n/s, collar, full skirt, 1950s ...**36.00**
Dress, pk floral, ruched/s, lace neckline, velvet trim, 1890s **595.00**
Dress, pk polyester, tulip/s, crossover bodice, belt, 1970s.............**30.00**
Dress, promenade; striped cotton, high neck, l/s, ca 1869 ....**950.00**
Dress, red silk w/beaded stand-out pockets, n/s, 1950s.............**325.00**
Dress, silk chiffon w/bead work, flapper style, n/s, ca 1925..........**765.00**
Dress, silk chiffon w/beads/sequins, handkerchief hem, Sho Max, 1980s ..**95.00**
Dress, silk chiffon w/glass beads, s/s shift style, 1980s................**57.50**
Dress, silk lace w/bias-cut ruffles, l/s lace jacket, 1930s.................**565.00**
Dress, striped organdy, trained/ruffled skirt, s/s, jacket, 1860s **965.00**
Dress, taupe linen w/pin tucks & lace inserts, l/s, ca 1910 ....**685.00**
Dress, tea; embr tulle, V neck, ruffled half/s, ca 1915 ....**865.00**
Dress, tea; wht linen w/lace inserts, l/s, ca 1915...........................**585.00**
Dress, velvet w/lamè & silver metallic lace, train, s/s, 1920s.........**950.00**
Dress, walking; linen w/soutache & linen lace, l/s, 1800s............**985.00**
Dress, walking; wht embr linen, l/s, 3-pc, ca 1902 ....**895.00**
Dress, walking; wht linen w/floral embr, l/s jacket, ca 1897 ....**895.00**
Dress, wedding; ruffled organdy, bustle bk, high neck, l/s, 1870s...**1,250.00**
Dress, wedding; satin & lace, cowl neck, train, lace/s, 1930s.........**585.00**
Dress, wht batiste w/embr & soutache bands, l/s, 1920s **575.00**
Dress, wht batiste w/Irish lace inserts, tucks, l/s, 1890s, EX.........**565.00**
Dress, wht embr tulle & lace w/satin piping, train, s/s, ca 1910...**1,625.00**
Dress, wht gauze & lace, puff/s, train, ca 1902......................**1,595.00**
Dressing gown, lame & silk chiffon, wide/s, bow at waist, 1930s ...**750.00**
Dressing gown, silk chiffon, wide/s, train, 1930s **425.00**
Fur coat, Braunstein, blk mink, full length, w/leather tie belt, EX..**600.00**

Hat, ivory tulle w/ostrich feathers on wire fr, ca 1900, EX 465.00
Hat, lace crown w/wide silk brim & roses on wire fr, 1920s, EX .365.00
Jacket, beach; man's, lined terry cloth, pockets, s/s, 1950s.............30.00
Jacket, beaded velvet, cutaway style w/applique & embr, 1890s..835.00
Jacket, blk leather w/wht trim, 5-button, no lapel, 2 pockets, 1960s..45.00
Jacket, blk silk tape lace, full/s, ca 1905 ....395.00
Jacket, blk wool w/scallop & button detail, l/s, ca 1915 ....395.00
Jacket, dacron polyester boucle, gold buttons, s/s, 1960s 20.00
Jacket, evening; maribou feathers w/ostrich feather trim, 1940s .465.00
Jacket, motorcycle; blk horsehide leather, 1930s-40s, EX............925.00
Jacket, riding; man's, blond deerskin, Pioneer Wear, 1940s.........350.00
Jacket, shantung w/taffeta lining, 3-button, ruffled V neck, 1960s..25.00
Jacket, shooting; man's, game pockets at front & hips, 1940s 145.00
Jacket, suede, no lapel, l/s, padded shoulders, A&F orig, short, 1980s..42.50
Jacket, textured polyester dbl knit w/rhinestones, l/s, short, 1980s....20.00
Jacket, wool flannel, 49er style, shell buttons, patch pockets, 1950s..30.00
Jeans, blk denim, 5-pocket, 21" bell bottoms, Mudd Jeans, 1980s.20.00
Jeans, cotton denim, 5-pocket, str legs, Gloria Vanderbilt, 1980s.18.00
Jeans, denim, star embr on bk pocket, 3-pocket flares, Shades, 1980s...20.00
Jeans, Levi Big E Redline 502, zipper, all orig labels, ca 1966, M...575.00
Jeans, Levi 501 XX, Big E, orig button fly, hidden rivets, NM.1,100.00
Jumpsuit, nylon tricot knit leopard print, City of Paris, 1960s 47.50
Jumpsuit, polyester knit, bolero jacket, 27" bell bottoms, 1970s ...30.00
Mantle, silk brocade w/passementerie, accomodates bustle, 1880s...875.00
Nightgown, Fr silk w/embr/ribbons/appliques, 1930s 525.00
Overdress, blk beaded net, wide/s, fringe, ca 1921....................1,275.00
Overdress, silver pcs on wht mesh tunic style, 1920s..................725.00
Pants, cotton corduroy, tapered-leg capris, Carol Brent, 1960s 20.00
Pants, cotton polyester twill, str legs, Dittos, 1970s 17.50
Pants, dbl knit, 24" bell bottoms, elastic waist, Alec Colman , 1970s...24.00
Pants, golf; man's, wht rayon, lg bk pockets, fitted waist, 1950s....75.00
Pants, man's, gray flannel, plt front, Hollywood waistline, 1950s..45.00
Pants, man's, poly-rayon blend, Campus, 1960s 35.00
Pants, man's, Western Chinos, pearl snaps, wht piping, 1960s......45.00
Pants, polyester twill, flat front, no pockets, Levis Bend Over, 1960s...25.00
Pants, printed cotton denim, 2-pocket, tapered legs, zipper, 1950s ..65.00
Pants, Quiana nylon knit, 29" bell bottoms, Ship 'n Shore, 1970s.22.50
Pants, turq stretch denim capris, Erwin, 1960s..............................27.50
Pants, wool/nylon stretch twill, ski stirrups, Made in Italy, 1960s.18.50
Pantsuit, cotton polyester seersucker, n/s, stovepipe legs, 1960s ...25.00
Pantsuit, floral-print cotton, ¾/s top, str-leg pants, 1970s 27.50
Pantsuit, polyester cotton w/floral border, ¾/s, str legs, 1970s.......27.50
Peacoat, man's, bl velvet w/brass buttons, Stratojac, 1960s 90.00
Riding habit, fitted jacket & divided skirt, ca 1895 ....1,285.00
Shawl, aqua silk tulle w/metallic gold embr, ca 1900....................525.00
Shawl, blk satin w/woven metallic gold pattern, 1920s............1,000.00
Shawl, Deco floral printed silk, rectangular, 1920s 300.00
Shawl, ecru silk ribbon, long fringe, ca 1925 ....275.00
Shawl, finely woven paisley w/scalloped blk center, 19th C, 125x61"..375.00
Shawl, paisley, machine woven, minor wear, 64x69" 100.00
Shawl, paisley, machine woven, 66x72" 200.00
Shawl, paisley, red w/woven borders in gr/bl/gold/blk, lt wear, 64"..275.00
Shawl, silk chiffon w/paisley design & metallic lace & embr......965.00
Shawl, silk floss flowers in crewel-type embr, blk fringe, ca 1900..1,000.00
Shawl, silk w/Chinese bird & tree pattern, ca 1900....................950.00
Shawl, silk w/Chinese hand-embr flowers, wht fringe, ca 1900...785.00
Shawl, silver & gold lamé w/cabbage roses & fringe, 1920s.....1,000.00
Shawl, silver metallic lace, rounded triangle, ca 1900 ....645.00
Shawl, velvet w/stenciled flowers, blk fringe, rectangular, 1920s ...765.00
Shirt, blk corduroy w/gold lurex stripes, cuffs, gold buttons, 1950s..19.00
Shirt, bowling; man's, pk rayon w/embr pocket, Empire.................45.00
Shirt, bowling; man's, 2-tone rayon w/embr across bk, 1950s........85.00
Shirt, Hawaiian print cotton, gold-tone buttons/mandarin collar, 1960s ..24.00
Shirt, man's, bl gabardine, collar, l/s, Godchaux's, 1950s.............125.00

Shirt, Hawaiian print with bird-of-paradise flowers on polyester, bright colors, Holiday Sportswear, 1950s, M, $200.00. (Photo courtesy Manion's International Auction House, Inc.)

Shirt, man's, Hawaiian crests & flowers cotton print.....................30.00
Shirt, man's, Hawaiian Tiki cotton print, Surfside 45.00
Shirt, man's, rayon handkerchief print, s/s, Manhattan, 1940s......80.00
Shirt, man's, Tapa print cotton, plastic buttons, s/s, 1950s 40.00
Shirt, printed crepe, s/s, button bk, Laura Mae Life Press, 1960s ..15.00
Shirt, sequined nylon chiffon, stretch waist/cuffs, Lady Helene, 1980s...34.00
Shoes, high-laced, 2 shades of brn, 1890s, EX...............................325.00
Shorts, man's, Oxford cloth, Bermudas, flat front, 4-pocket, 1960s...17.50
Shorts, men's, Hawaiian cotton print w/knit inner liner, 1970s 14.00
Shorts, suede leather w/lining, plt front, pockets, 1980s................25.00
Skirt, cotton print, beyond-circle, 1950s......................................27.50
Skirt, cotton print, circle swing style, 1950s................................27.50
Skirt, plaid flanel, flared, slightly gathered waist, 1970s 20.00
Skirt, rayon velvet print, long, gathered at waist, 1960s.................25.00
Skirt, silk chiffon w/lining, knee-length, plt, 1960s 22.50
Skirt, silk shantung print, lined, mini, 1960s 18.50
Slacks, man's, gray pinstripe flannel, cinch-bk waist, 1960s 45.00
Slip, 2-layer crinoline, 5-tiered, nylon tricot/net/organdy, 1980s ..25.00
Stole, stenciled/beaded silk chiffon w/birds/foliage, Gallenga, 1920s...985.00
Stole jacket, acrylic fake mink w/satin lining, 1950s 32.50
Suit, knit, lapel shirt jacket, knife-plt skirt, Koret of CA, 1960s...22.50
Suit, leisure; plaid wool, flare-leg pants, built-in belt, 1960s 22.50
Suit, lined wool, ¾/s, crocheted buttons/str skirt, Lilli Ann, 1960s....55.00
Suit, plaid wool, capris+plt skirt+vest+dbl-breasted jacket, 1960s...85.00
Suit, rayon check weave, ⅞/s 3-button jacket w/str skirt, 1950s ...30.00
Sundress, child's, cotton w/pique trim, elastic bk waist, 1940s 10.00
Sweater, acrylic w/beading, ¾-sleeve, Gloria Swanson/Forever Young ...30.00
Sweater, cardigan, acrylic knit w/embr front, l/s, Dove, 1960s......27.50
Sweater, cardigan, boucle knit, l/s, 1960s 25.00
Sweater, cardigan, wool, mc stripes, pockets, Gino Paoli, 1960s ...18.00
Sweater, child's, wool knit, handmade, plastic buttons, 1940s.........6.00
Sweater, gray heather knit, Robert Mackie, 1950s.........................32.00
Sweater, lambswool & nylon w/bugle beads, long midriff, l/s 28.50
Sweater, man's, Collegiate style, wht wool w/red/bl stripes, 1950s...65.00
Sweater, mohair, crewneck pullover, popcorn yoke, Bobbie Brooks, 1960s ...30.00
Sweater, ski; man's, red & blk striped acrylic, Ski Togs.................35.00
Sweater, striped acrylic, s/s, buttoned turtleneck pullover, 1960s..16.00
Sweater vest, orlon acrylic w/arrows pattern, scoop neck, 1970s...19.00
Teddy, child's, wht cotton, cutwork, open lace, 1920s 20.00
Vest, man's, wht linen, lined, EX...25.00
Waistcoat, man's, embr silk w/appl roundels, rstr, 1790s..............230.00

Cluthra

The name cluthra is derived from the Scottish word 'clutha,' meaning cloudy. Glassware by this name was first produced by J. Couper and Sons, England. Frederick Carder developed cluthra while at the Steuben Glass Works, and similar types of glassware were also made by Durand and Kimball. It is found in both solid and shaded colors and is characterized by a spotty appearance resulting from small air pockets trapped between its two layers.

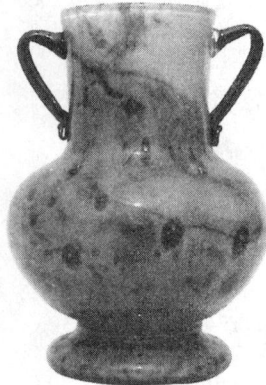

Vase, variegated orange and white mottling with bubbles, charcoal handles, Kimball, K20144-12 Dec - 7, 11", $425.00.

Bowl, wht w/pk int, no mk, 10" 100.00
Vase, clear w/yel-orange & wht, ovoid w/flaring rim, #20164-8, 8x8" ..**275.00**
Vase, gr mottle, bulbous w/flared rim, Kimball, #1986-6K, 6" **175.00**
Vase, red/yel/wht mottle on clear, trumpet form, Kimball, 10¾" ...**600.00**
Vase, royal bl, spherical, Kimball, 4x4", pr **475.00**
Vase, turq to gr decor on wht, crystal ft, shouldered, Kimball, 9" ..**300.00**

Coalport

In 1745 in Caughley, England, Squire Brown began a modest business fashioning crude pots and jugs from clay mined in his own fields. Tom Turner, a young potter who had apprenticed his trade at Worcester, was hired in 1772 to plan and oversee the construction of a 'proper' factory. Three years later he bought the business, which he named Caughley Coalport Porcelain Manufactory. Though the dinnerware he produced was meant to be only everyday china, the hand-painted florals, birds, and landscapes used to decorate the ware were done in exquisite detail and in a wide range of colors. In 1780 Turner introduced the Willow pattern which he produced using a newly perfected method of transfer printing. (Wares from the period between 1775 and 1799 are termed 'Caughley' or 'Salopian'; see section on Caughley.) John Rose purchased the Caughley factory from Thomas Turner in 1799, adding that holding to his own pottery which he had built two years before in Coalport. (It is from this point that the pottery's history that the wares are termed 'Coalport.') The porcelain produced there before 1814 was unmarked with very few exceptions. After 1820 some examples were marked with a '2' with an oversize top loop. The term 'Coalbrookdale' refers to a fine type of porcelain decorated in floral bas relief, similar to the work of Dresden.

After 1835 highly decorated ware with rich ground colors imitated the work of Sevres and Chelsea, even going so far as to copy their marks. From about 1895 until the 1920s, the mark in use was 'Coalport' over a crown with 'England A.D. 1750' indicating the date claimed as the founding, not the date of manufacture. From the 1920s until 1945, 'Made in England' over a crown and 'Coalport' below was used. Later the mark was 'Coalport' over a smaller crown with 'Made in England' in a curve below.

Each of the major English porcelain companies excelled in certain areas of manufacture. Coalport produced the finest 'jeweled' porcelain, made by picking up a heavy mixture of slip and color and dropping it onto the surface of the ware. These 'jewels' are perfectly spaced and are often graduated in size with the smaller 'jewels' at the neck or base of the vase. Some ware was decorated with very large 'jewels' resembling black opals or other polished stones. Such pieces are in demand by the advanced collector.

It is common to find considerable crazing in old Coalport, since the

glaze was thinly applied to increase the brilliance of the colors. Many early vases had covers; look for a flat surface that would have supported a lid (just because it is gilded does not mean the vase never had one). Pieces whose lids are missing are worth about 40% less. Most lids had finials which have been broken and restored. You should deduct about 10% for a professional restoration on a finial.

In 1926 the Coalport Company moved to Shelton in Staffordshire and today belongs to a group headed by the Wedgwood Company. See also Indian Tree.

Bowl, Queen Elizabeth Silver Jubilee, 1977 ltd ed, 4½x10" **265.00**
Cottage, Old Curiosity Shop, retired, 5" **200.00**
Cottage, Toll House, 1974-81, 5¼" **200.00**
Cottage, Windmill, 5½x4" **225.00**
Cup & saucer, Fluted, flowers w/gold, 1891-1920, mini, 2", 3½" ..**75.00**
Cup & saucer, pate-sur-pate, cobalt, gold & wht, 1891-1920......**195.00**
Figurine, Doris, yel & gr skirt, 1915-49, 4½" **110.00**
Vase, temple; Indian Tree, gold rams' heads hdls, 9"...................**200.00**

Coca-Cola

J.S. Pemberton, creator of Coca-Cola, originated his world-famous drink in 1886. From its inception the Coca-Cola Company began an incredible advertising campaign which has proven to be one of the most successful promotions in history. The quantity and diversity of advertising material put out by Coca-Cola in the last one hundred years is literally mind-boggling. From the beginning, the company has projected an image of wholesomeness and Americana. Beautiful women in Victorian costumes, teenagers and schoolchildren, blue- and white-collar workers, the men and women of the Armed Forces, and even Santa Claus have appeared in advertisements with a Coke in their hands. Some of the earliest collectibles include trays, syrup dispensers, gum jars, pocket mirrors, and calendars. Many of these items fetch prices in the thousands of dollars. Later examples include radios, signs, lighters, thermometers, playing cards, clocks, and toys — particularly toy trucks.

In 1970 the Coca-Cola Company initialed a multimillion-dollar 'image-refurbishing campaign' which introduced the new 'Dynamic Contour' logo, a twisting white ribbon under the Coca-Cola and Coke trademarks. The new logo often serves as a cut-off point to the purist collector. Newer and very ardent collectors, however, relish the myriad of items marketed since that date, as they often cannot afford the high prices that the vintage pieces command. For more information we recommend *Petretti's Coca-Cola Collectibles Price Guide* (available from Nostalgia Publications whose address you will find under Auctions in the Directory); *B.J. Summers' Guide to Coca-Cola*, *Third Edition*, and *B.J. Summers' Pocket Guide to Coca-Cola*, *Third Edition*; also *Coca-Cola Commemorative Bottles*, *Second Edition*, by Bob and Debra Henrich. You may wish to call our advisor for this category, Craig Stifter, at 630-789-5780; he is listed in the Directory under Illinois.

Key:
CC — Coca-Cola   sf — self-framed
dc — diecut   tm — trademark

Reproductions and Fantasies

Beware of reproductions! Prices are given for the genuine original articles, but the symbol (+) at the end of some of the following lines indicate items that have been reproduced. Warning! The 1924, 1925, and 1935 calendars have been reproduced. They are identical in almost every way; only a professional can tell them apart. These are *very* deceiving! Watch for frauds: genuinely old celluloid items ranging from combs, mirrors, knives, and forks to doorknobs that have been recently etched with a new double-lined trademark. Still another area of concern deals with reproduction and fantasy items. A fantasy item is a novelty made to appear authentic with inscriptions such as 'Tiffany Studios,' 'Trans Pan Expo,' 'World's Fair,' etc. In reality, these items never existed as originals. For instance, don't be fooled by a Coca-Cola cash register; no originals are known to exist! Large mirrors for bars are being reproduced and are often selling for $10.00 to $50.00.

Of the hundreds of reproductions (designated 'R' in the following examples) and fantasies (designated 'F') on the market today, these are the most deceiving.

Belt buckle, no originals thought to exist (F), up to 10.00
Bottle, dk amber, w/arrows, heavy, narrow spout (R)....................10.00
Bottle carrier, wood, yel w/red logo, holds 6 bottles (R)...............10.00
Clock, Gilbert, regulator, battery-op, ¾-sz, NM+ (R) 175.00
Cooler, Glascock Jr, made by Coca-Cola USA (R) 350.00
Doorknob, glass etched w/tm (F) 3.00
Knife, bottle shape, 1970s, many variations (F), ea........................5.00
Knife, fork or spoon w/celluloid hdl, newly etched tm (F)..............5.00
Letter opener, stamped metal, Coca-Cola for 5¢ (F)......................3.00
Pocket watch, often old watch w/new face (R) 10.00
Pocketknife, yel & red, 1933 World's Fair (F) 2.00
Sign, cb, lady w/fur, dtd 1911, 9x11" (F) 3.00
Soda fountain glass holder, word 'Drink' on orig (R) 5.00
Thermometer, bottle form, DONASCO, 17" (R)........................10.00
Trade card, copy of 1905 'Bathtub' foldout, emb 1978 (R)............25.00

The following items have been reproduced and are among the most deceptive of all:
    Pocket mirrors from 1905, 1906, 1908, 1909, 1910, 1911, 1916, and 1920
    Trays from 1899, 1910, 1913, 1914, 1917, 1920, 1923, 1925, 1926, 1934, and 1937
    Tip trays from 1907, 1909, 1910, 1913, 1914, 1917, and 1920
    Knives: many versions of the German brass model
    Cartons: wood versions, yellow with logo
    Calendars: 1924, 1925, and 1935
    These items have been marketed:
    Brass thermometer, bottle shape, Taiwan, 24"
    Cast-iron toys (none ever made)
    Cast-iron door pull, bottle shape, made to look old
    Poster, Yes Girl (R)
    Button sign, has 1 round hole while original has 4 slots, most have bottle logo, 12", 16", 20" (R)
    Bullet trash receptacles (old cans with decals)
    Paperweight, rectangular, with Pepsin Gum insert
    1930 Bakelite radio, 24" tall, repro is lighter in weight than the original, of poor quality and cheaply made
    1949 cooler radio (reproduced with tape deck)
    Tin bottle sign, 40"
    Fishtail die-cut tin sign, 20" long
    Straw holders (no originals exist)
    Coca-Cola bicycle with cooler, fantasy item: the piece has been totally made-up, no such original exists
    1914 calendar top, reproduction, 11¼x23¾", printed on smooth-finish heavy ivory paper
    Countless trays — most unauthorized (must read 'American Artworks; Coshocton, OH.')

Centennial Items

The Coca-Cola Company celebrated its 100th birthday in 1986, and amidst all the fanfare came many new collectible items, all sporting the 100th-anniversary logo. These items are destined to become an important part of the total Coca-Cola collectible spectrum. The following pieces are among the most popular centennial items.

Bottle, gold-dipped, in velvet sleeve, 6½-oz...................................75.00
Bottle, Hutchinson, amber, Root Co, ½-oz, 3 in case.................375.00
Bottle, International, set of 9 in plexiglas case............................500.00
Bottle, leaded crystal, 100th logo, 6½-oz, MIB..........................150.00
Medallion, bronze, 3" dia, w/box...100.00
Pin set, wood fr, 101 pins...300.00
Scarf, silk, 30x30"...40.00
Thermometer, glass cover, 14" dia, M..35.00

Coca-Cola Originals

Menu board, 1934, tin, 28x19", NM, $650.00.
(Photo courtesy Craig Stifter)

Ashtray, porc, oblong/center rests, features 12 languages, 12½", NM...100.00
Ax, For Sportsman, pnt inlay on blade, pnt logo on wood hdl, NMIB....3,425.00
Banner ...Edgar Bergen w/Charlie McCarthy..., canvas, 1950s, 42x60" ...1,100.00
Banner, Drink CC From Bottle Through Straw/bottle, 1910, 16x70", VG+...4,000.00
Blotter, Coke Knows No Season, 1947, NM 11.00
Blotter, Drink CC Delicious & Refreshing, 1951, NM 12.00
Blotter, How About a Coke, 1944, NM+ 28.00
Blotter, 50th Anniversary, 1886-1936, NM...................................20.00
Bottle carrier, aluminum, bail hdl w/wood grip, 6-pack, NM 60.00
Bottle carrier, wood w/stamped lettering, holds 12 1-qt bottles, VG...100.00
Bottlers 75th Anniversary set, complete w/case, NM 50.00
Calendar, 1915, complete, G+..1,000.00
Calendar, 1921, incomplete, EX+ 2,100.00
Calendar, 1924, complete, NM 3,200.00
Calendar, 1926, incomplete, EX+ 450.00
Calendar, 1931, complete, NM 1,250.00
Calendar, 1933, complete, EX+ 775.00
Calendar, 1938, complete, VG+ 500.00
Catalog, Merchandising Equipment for CC, 3-ring binder, 1958-62, EX+ ...300.00
Clock, Drink CC, bottle/yel dot, Pam, 1950s, 15" dia, EX+ 220.00
Clock, Drink CC in Bottles on red dot, light-up, Swihart, 15" dia..925.00
Clock, Drink CC on red serrated disc, aluminum fr, 21" dia, EX...450.00
Clock, Drink CC red dot on maroon w/gold #s, 17" dia, EX.......150.00
Clock, neon w/octagonal logo (bottle on yel dot), 1942, 16" sq, VG+...800.00
Coffee cup, wht china w/red Drink CC logo, 1930s, NM...........400.00
Coin changer, Have a Coke, red/chrome, 12x15x4", VG...........425.00
Cookie jar, Hollywood Polar Bear, 2nd in series, 1996, from $30 to....40.00
Cookie jar, 6-pack form, ceramic, Enesco, 1996, from $40 to........50.00
Cooler, airline, Drink CC in Bottles, red, 12x18x8", EX............275.00
Cooler, stainless steel, Northwest Airlines, 1940-50s, 10", VG...200.00
Coupon, Lillian Nordica, 1904, 9½x6½", NM 250.00
Cutout for Children, Circus, fr, 1921, 10x15", NM 200.00
Dispenser, plastic w/paper cup holder, top carry hdl, 1940s, 2-gal, EX......800.00
Display, cb trifold, Jackie Cooper/Wallace Berry, 1934, 32x42", NM ..7,700.00
Display, 3-D cb, girl at lunch, No After-Lunch Drowsiness, 1933, EX+..3,400.00
Display, 3-D cb, girl w/glass seated at fountain, 1929, EX+....11,000.00

Display bottle, clear glass w/tin cap, Ill Glass Co, 1930s, 20", EXIB....**750.00**

Doll, Buddy Lee as delivery man, 1950s, rpl uniform, NM..........**290.00**

Door handle, aluminum bottle form w/red disk, 11", EX..............**325.00**

Door handle, button on wht tin bk plate, D&R, 12", NM..........**350.00**

Door handle, plastic bottle on red metal mount, Have a Coke, NM.....**275.00**

Door push, tin, Be Really Refreshed, vertical fishtail on wht, 8", NM ..**300.00**

Door push bar, porc, Drink CC panel on wrought iron bar, EX ..**300.00**

Festoon, Howdy Pardner/Pause...Refresh, 3-pc, 1950s, EX+ **2,530.00**

Festoon, Poppies, 5-pc, 1938, unused, M (orig envelope) **1,050.00**

Festoon, snowmen soda jerks on dk bl, 5-pc, 1936, NM+........**7,500.00**

Festoon, Verbena, yel flowers/billbrd logos/lady in center, 5-pc, 1932 ...**2,700.00**

Festoon, water lilies, 5-pc, 1935, NM+ **1,800.00**

Frame, Kay Displays, gold-pnt wood w/metal bottle, for 21x36" sign, EX ..**225.00**

Glass, flared, frosted 5¢ arrow logo, lg, G **475.00**

Glass, flared, frosted 5¢ arrow logo, sm, EX+ **750.00**

Glass, pewter w/emb logo, w/leather pouch, 1930s, EX **625.00**

Glass holder, silver cut-out vertical bar pattern, early 1900s, NM+...**2,400.00**

Magazine, Red Barrel, Jackie Cooper cover, 1934, NM **65.00**

Match striker/door push, porc, 4x4", EX **300.00**

Matchbook cover, color image of girl drinking from glass, 1913, EX...**660.00**

Matchbook cover, leather w/gold lettering, 1907, NM+..............**380.00**

Menu board, tin, fishtail above chalkbrd w/wht lines, 1959, EX+....**180.00**

Menu board, tin, oblong w/rnd ends/slots/center button, 1950s, 62", VG .**450.00**

Menu board, tin, oval atop chalkbrd w/rnd corners, 26x18", VG ..**150.00**

Menu board, tin, sf chalkbrd, Refresh Yourself, 1930s, VG **325.00**

Miniature, plastic case w/12 bottles, red on yel, 1950s, VG+ **75.00**

Paperweight, bottle caps encased in plastic, 4x4½", NMIB...........**50.00**

Pin, 60-yr service, 10kt w/12 diamond chips, cloisonne detail, MIB..**1,800.00**

Pocket mirror, 1910 Hamilton King girl, EX+ **300.00**

Postcard, Hamilton King girl, 1909, matted & fr, EX **225.00**

Radio, floor cooler form, red plastic, 1950s, 10", EX+ **600.00**

Salesman's sample, Glascock Jr cooler, w/case, 1929, rare, EX+ .**28,000.00**

Salesman's sample, Standard Ice cooler (1939), w/tin insulator, EX+..**2,750.00**

Sign, aisle marker, sq ad panel flanked by #d circular panels, 29", EX....**175.00**

Sign, bottle, dc tin, Trade Mark Registered, 1950s, 17", NM......**150.00**

Sign, button, porc, CC over bottle on red, 24", EX **250.00**

Sign, button, porc, Drink CC in Bottles, wht on red, 36", VG...**200.00**

Sign, button, tin, Drink CC/Sign of Good Taste on red, 12", NM **375.00**

Sign, cb, Add Zest, trail of party people on yel, 1951, 27x16", NM+ .**875.00**

Sign, cb, clown/boy/performing dog/girl, Sundblom art, 1936, 49", NM+...**8,500.00**

Sign, cb, Good/Pause, girl on trapeze, fr, 1954, 28x57", EX **350.00**

Sign, cb, Lillian Nordica, 1905, 46x26", VG...............................**4,100.00**

Sign, cb, Mind Reader, girl reaching for bottle, 1944, 28x56", VG.....**200.00**

Sign, cb, Pause for a Coke, archery scene, gold fr, 1948, 27x16", EX ..**675.00**

Sign, cb, Play Refreshed, girl on carousel horse, 1940s, 50x29", VG...**500.00**

Sign, cb, Refreshed Through 70 Years, 2-sided, 1955, 28x56", VG **150.00**

Sign, cb, Refreshment, girl w/food cart, orig fr, 1949, 27x16", VG......**275.00**

Sign, cb, The Best of Taste, girl offered bottle, 1956, 50x30", NM+...**850.00**

Sign, cb, Welcome Home, couple at open fridge, 1944, 28x56, VG ...**250.00**

Sign, cb, Your Thirst Takes Wings, girl pilot, 1940, 16x27", VG...**475.00**

Sign, cb, 1886-1936, 2 period girls w/bottles, 50x29", VG+ **1,390.00**

Sign, cb dc, couple at sundial, 1911, 36x29", EX+ **4,000.00**

Sign, cb hanger, Featuring Hot Bar-B-Q Platter..., 28x22", EX...**100.00**

Sign, cb hanger, 3-D bottle/hotdog/billbrd logo/phrase, 1932, 20", NM...**2,500.00**

Sign, cb stand-up, Chewing Gum, bow/bag/flowers/portrait, 1903, NM+..**14,520.00**

Sign, cb stand-up, couple/6-pack, Take Some Home, 1947, 24x18", NM........**225.00**

Sign, cb stand-up, Military girl w/bottle, 1943, 17", EX+.............**425.00**

Sign, cb stand-up, Santa w/toy bag at feet, button logo, 1945, 13", EX.**250.00**

Sign, cb stand-up, waitress, Coke Brightens Every Bite, 1959, 36", VG ...**275.00**

Sign, cb trolley, Work Refreshed, work whistle, 1941, 11x21", NM+....**875.00**

Sign, celluloid disc, CC/D&R, gold/wht on red, gold border, 9", EX+ ..**200.00**

Sign, counter-top light-up, Lunch With Us/Drink..., Price Bros, 1950s....**900.00**

Sign, flange, tin, button w/Ice Cold & bottle arrow, 1953, 23", EX......**475.00**

Sign, flange, tin, Enjoy CC in Bottles, red, 1950s, 18" dia, NM .**770.00**

Sign, Kay Displays, dc plywood US map on wire rings w/NSEW, 16", EX ...**950.00**

Sign, Kay Displays, wood emblem, Drink CC, gold/red, 1930s, 6x14", VG .**225.00**

Sign, light-up, Drink CC fishtail on wht w/gr border, 1963, oblong, EX....**625.00**

Sign, masonite dmn, Drink.../bottle on yel dot on red, 1946, 42" **400.00**

Sign, neon, CC on red plastic fishtail, 15x28", NM **300.00**

Sign, neon, Enjoy in sm letters above CC w/tail, sq fr, 15x27", NM+ ..**350.00**

Sign, paper, Pause..., girl's profile w/bottle, 1920s, 20x12", EX+ ...**1,250.00**

Sign, paper, Refreshing, bottle/button in snow/icicles, 1950s, 18x58" ...**950.00**

Sign, paper, 5¢/Drink CC button/lg bottle/boy at window, 11x25', NM ...**120.00**

Sign, porc, bottle on yel disc, 15" dia, VG **175.00**

Sign, porc, Fountain Service/Drink CC, red/gr ground, 12x28", VG.....**250.00**

Sign, porc, Lunch/Pause Refresh, yel, 2-sided, 1950s, 26x28", EX+ ...**2,000.00**

Sign, porc shield, Fountain Service/Drink CC, 2-sided, 1936, 25", EX .**950.00**

Sign, school crossing policeman, dc tin, 1950s, EX **3,000.00**

Sign, sidewalk, fishtail logo w/menu brd, metal fr, 28x20", VG ..**125.00**

Sign, tin, Betty, sf, 1914, 41x31", VG+......................................**4,700.00**

Sign, tin, Big King Size, fishtail/bottle, gr stripes, 28x20", NM...**425.00**

Sign, tin, Drink CC 5¢ Ice Cold, bottle on yel dot, 1940, 54x18", VG+ ..**300.00**

Sign, tin, Drink CC/D&R, bottle at left, Dasco, 1929, 11x35", VG.......**235.00**

Sign, tin, Drink upper left/CC over bottle on red, wood fr, 60" L, VG...**150.00**

Sign, tin, Gas Today/Drink CC While You Wait, 1930, 20x28", EX...**4,500.00**

Sign, tin, New Betty w/bottle/Drink..., red/gr sf, 1940, 12x34", EX+ **825.00**

Sign, tin, Take Home a Carton/6-pack/Drink..., silver sf, 1941, 54x18" ...**1,200.00**

Sign, tin, Things Go Better..., button/bottle on wht, 1964, 54x18", NM ..**350.00**

Sign, tin pilaster, Pick Up 12, 12" button atop wht panel, NM ..**2,065.00**

Sign, tin triangle hanger/bracket, Drink CC Ice Cold/bottle, 1933, VG ...**990.00**

Sign, 6-pack, dc tin, D&R, 1954, NM **1,800.00**

Sign, 6-pack, dc tin, King Size, 1963, 36x30", VG+ **925.00**

Silverware, 6-pc set w/knife, 2 forks, 3 spoons, NM+..............**1,275.00**

Syrup bottle, etched logo w/filigree border, aluminum cap, 1920s, NM..**300.00**

Thermometer, dial, Drink CC, red w/wht detail, 12", dia, EX **130.00**

Thermometer, dial, Things Go Better w/Coke, 1960s, 18" dia, NM+ **650.00**

Thermometer, tin, button at top, Quality Refreshment, 1950s, 9', EX...**300.00**

Thermometer, tin, cigar shape, red & wht, 1950s, 30", EX–.......**425.00**

Thermometer, tin, emb gold bottle on red, rnd ends, 1930s, 16", VG+....**120.00**

Toy dispenser bank, red, Linemar, EXIB **1,330.00**

Toy truck, Smitty Toys on door, red-pnt wood, Smith Miller, 1940s, EX .**1,300.00**

Toy truck, Sprite Boy sign on yel stake bed, Marx, 1950s, NMIB..**1,300.00**

Whistle, dc cb bottle form, 1920, EX **450.00**

Trays

Values are given for trays in excellent plus condition (C8+). Those that have been reproduced are marked with a (+). The 1934 Weismuller and O'Sullivan tray has been reproduced at least three times. To be original, it will have a black back and must say 'American Artworks, Coshocton, Ohio.' It was not reproduced by Coca-Cola in the 1950s.

All 10½x13½" original serving trays produced from 1910 to 1942 are marked with a date, Made in USA, and the American Artworks Inc., Coshocton Ohio. All original trays of this format (1910 – 40) had REG TM in the tail of the C.

1897, Victorian Lady, 9¼" dia, VG..**15,000.00**

1901, Hilda Clark, 9¾", VG...**4,000.00**

1903, Hilda Clark, oval, 18½x15", EX.......................................**6,000.00**

1905, Lillian Russell, glass or bottle, 10½x13¼", EX **3,500.00**

1906, Juanita, glass or bottle, oval, 13¼x10½", EX....................**2,200.00**

1907, Relieves Fatigue, 10½x13¼", NM **4,000.00**

1907, Relieves Fatigue, 13½x16½", EX **3,600.00**

1908, Topless, Wherever Ginger Ale..., 12¼" dia, NM **11,500.00**

1909, St Louis Fair, 10½x13¼", EX **1,800.00**

1909, St Louis Fair, 13½x16½", NM **3,000.00**

1910, Coca-Cola Girl, Hamilton King, 10½x13¼", VG.............**850.00**

1914, Betty, oval, 12¼x15¼", EX+ **475.00**

1914, Betty, 10½x13¼", EX..................................600.00
1916, Elaine, 8½x19", NM...............................600.00
1920, Garden Girl, oval, 10½x13¼", EX+............800.00
1921, Autumn Girl, oval, 10½x13¼", EX+ 800.00
1922, Summer Girl, 10½x13¼", NM.................1,100.00
1923, Flapper Girl, 10½x13¼", NM 500.00
1924, Smiling Girl, brn rim, 10½x13¼", EX..........650.00
1924, Smiling Girl, maroon rim, 10½x13¼", EX...1,050.00
1925, Party, 10½x13¼", NM..............................600.00
1926, Golfers, 10½x13¼", EX.............................700.00
1927, Curbside Service, 10½x13¼", EX................750.00
1928, Bobbed Hair, 10½x13¼", EX+....................650.00
1929, Girl in Swimsuit w/Glass, 10½x13¼", EX+ 450.00
1930, Swimmer, 10½x13¼", EX..........................425.00
1930, Telephone, 10½x13¼", NM........................650.00
1931, Boy w/Sandwich & Dog, 10½x13¼", NM....1,100.00
1932, Girl in Swimsuit on Beach, Hayden, 10½x13¼", EX+ 625.00
1933, Francis Dee, 10½x13¼", NM......................800.00
1934, Weismuller & O'Sullivan, 10½x13¼", NM 1,100.00
1935, Madge Evans, 10½x13¼", NM....................575.00
1936, Hostess, 10½x13¼", NM............................600.00
1937, Running Girl, 10½x13¼", NM.....................350.00
1938, Girl in the Afternoon, 10½x13¼", NM.........275.00
1939, Springboard Girl, 10½x13¼", NM...............350.00
1940, Sailor Girl, 10½x13¼", NM........................400.00
1941, Ice Skater, 10½x13¼", NM.........................450.00

**1942, Roadster, 10½x13¼",
NM+, $500.00.**

1950s, Girl w/Wind in Hair, screen bkground, 10½x13¼", M....100.00
1950s, Girl w/Wind in Hair, solid bkground, 10½x13¼", NM ...225.00
1955, Menu Girl, 10½x13¼", M 65.00
1957, Birdhouse, 10½x13¼", NM.........................125.00
1957, Rooster, 10½x13¼", NM.............................175.00
1957, Umbrella Girl, 10½x13¼", M......................375.00
1961, Pansy Garden, 10½x13¼", NM......................30.00

Vendors

Though interest in Coca-Cola machines of the 1949 – 1959 era rose dramatically over the last few years, values currently seem to have leveled off and actually dropped 15% to 20%. The major manufacturers of these curved-top, 5¢ and 10¢ machines were Vendo (V), Vendorlator (VMC), Cavalier (C or CS), and Jacobs. Prices are for machines in excellent or better condition, complete and working. They vary greatly according to geographical location.

Cavalier, model #CS72, EX orig..........................1,600.00
Cavalier, model #CS72, M rstr.............................3,200.00
Cavalier, model #C27, M rstr...............................2,800.00
Cavalier, model #C27, orig..................................1,200.00

Cavalier, model #C51, EX orig...............................950.00
Cavalier, model #C51, M rstr..............................2,000.00
Jacobs, model #26, EX.......................................1,200.00
Jacobs, model #26, M rstr 2,500.00
Vendo, model #23, EX orig.....................................900.00
Vendo, model #39, EX orig..................................1,100.00
Vendo, model #39, M, rstr..................................2,700.00
Vendo, model #44, EX orig..................................2,500.00
Vendo, model #44, M rstr...................................3,750.00
Vendo, model #56, EX orig..................................1,400.00
Vendo, model #56, M rstr...................................3,200.00
Vendo, model #80, EX orig.....................................600.00
Vendo, model #80, M rstr...................................1,250.00

**Vendo, model #81, 1950s,
58x27x16", EX original,
$1,900.00.** (Photo courtesy B.J. Summers/Mike and Debbie Summers)

Vendo, model #81, M rstr....................................3,200.00
Vendorlator, model #27, EX orig.........................1,200.00
Vendorlator, model #27, rstr (w/stand) 2,750.00
Vendorlator, model #27A, EX orig..........................900.00
Vendorlator, model #27A, M rstr.........................2,000.00
Vendorlator, model #33, EX orig..........................1,100.00
Vendorlator, model #33, M rstr............................2,250.00
Vendorlator, model #44, EX orig..........................1,500.00
Vendorlator, model #44, M rstr............................3,200.00
Vendorlator, model #72, EX orig..........................1,000.00
Vendorlator, model #72, M rstr............................1,800.00

Coffee Grinders

Coffee mills, also called grinders, are becoming more and more popular with eager collectors and those simply wishing to add to their antique kitchen motif. Coffee mills fall into several basic types and the same mill can sometimes be referred to in various ways. Box mills, also called lap, or table mills are generally made of wood. True wall mills are usually of iron and have a cup or receiver of some kind to catch the ground coffee. Side mills, really made to be mounted to a post or the side of a cabinet, are usually made completely of iron or iron with a tin hopper. Canister mills have grinding mechanisms made of iron and can have hoppers made of either tin, sheet metal, glass, or porcelain. Upright iron mills can have one wheel, two wheels, one wheel and one crank, or just one crank alone and can range in height from around twelve inches up to six or seven feet in height and weigh in excess of three hundred pounds. Some mills were made to be clamped to the edge of a table. And of cource, the final incarnation came with the advent of electricity in the form of small electric mills available to the homemaker up to the large industrial models for commercial use.

The advent of the Internet and online auctions has brought out both the good and bad among collectible coffee mills. Doing your homework is the most important factor when purchasing coffee mills online. Many reproductions and modern examples are found online that are represented as genuine old coffee mills. It should also be remembered that many companies produced certain models in the hundreds of thousands that still exist in vast numbers and therefore are quite common. Few mills are actually scarce or rare, and there are no known miniature salesmen's samples. Mills most often identified as salesmen's samples are in fact toys. This does not, however, diminish their desirability. Grist mills, for corn or other grains, are often incorrectly identified as coffee mills. While generally not as valuable as coffee mills, they are often found in the collections of coffee mill enthusiasts. Our advisor for this category is Shane Branchcomb; he is listed in the Directory under Virginia.

Key: adj — adjustment

Left to right: National Specialty Mfg. Co., cast-iron upright, ca 1910, 12", EX, $475.00; Peck, Stow, and Wilcox #3600, cast-iron side mill, original bronze color, NM, $175.00; Royal Blue tin canister, wall mount, ca 1910, 12", EX, $225.00.

A Kenrick & Sons No 1, lap, CI w/brass hopper, CI drw, EX 125.00
Adams Pat, lap, pewter hopper, wood w/orig knob 155.00
Arcade, glass catchers, mk Arcade Freeport Illinois....................125.00
Arcade Crystal #9010, CI, Art Deco, glass hopper, EX 175.00
Arcade Crystal #9010, CI, w/orig mk cup, NM 285.00
Arcade Favorite No 7, side, CI w/orig lid, grind adj front, VG 95.00
Arcade Imperial, lap, CI, closed hopper, wood box, EX 110.00
Arcade Imperial No 200, lap, CI hopper w/eagle, Pat 88, 89 ......155.00
Arcade Imperial No 999, decal, 1-lb box, EX 155.00
Arcade IXL, table, ornate CI hopper, hdl on side, 1-lb, EX 350.00
Arcade Jewel, canister, rectangular glass hopper, w/lid, EX 695.00
Arcade No 3, canister, CI w/glass hopper, orig lid, EX 155.00
Arcade No 4, canister, CI, glass hopper, orig lid, wall mt, EX.....175.00
Arcade No 5, side, CI, Pat June '94, VG..................................95.00
Arcade No 700, lap, w/dust cover, Sears 1908 catalog, EX..........155.00
Arcade Our Baby (toy), label, mini, EX 95.00
Arcade Queen, glass canister & receiver, CI works, EX 350.00
Arcade Royal, canister, CI cup, tin hopper, EX...........................85.00
Arcade Telephone, canister, CI front, Pat Sept 25, '88, EX 525.00
Arcade Telephone, early motif, CI & wood, EX 600.00
Arcade X-Ray, CI works, wood hopper w/glass, EX 155.00
Bell, canister, similar to Golden Rule, CI & wood, EX 595.00
Belmont, Lightning No 23, canister, tin & CI, EX.....................225.00
Blacksmith-made, funnel shape, 1-hdl, open hopper, wall mt.....345.00
Blacksmith-made, funnel shape, 2-hdl, wall mt to 2x4", VG 375.00
Bronson-Walton Ever Ready No 2, w/cup, Pat 1905, EX 165.00
Bronson-Walton Monitor, table, tin, w/cup, ca 1909, EX.............80.00
Bronson-Walton Silver Lake, canister, glass hopper, EX 595.00
Caravan, canister, CI works, tin hopper, ca 1910, VG/EX 165.00
Cavanaugh Bros, table, front fill, 1-lb, EX 265.00

Cavanaugh's, table, CI, ornate legs, wood box, EX.....................525.00
Clawson & Clark No 1, CI, dbl grind, Pat 1886, 6" wheel 685.00
Coles Mfg No 7, counter, CI, Pat 1887, 16" wheels, 27", EX......825.00
Coles No 00, CI, wall mt w/CI cup, NM 295.00
Crescent, CI, Rutland VT, orig pnt, 15" wheels, EX....................675.00
Daisy No 867 (toy), CI top, wood box & drw, orig decal, mini, EX...85.00
Elgin Nat'l, floor, silver hopper, 24" wheels 1,500.00
Elgin Nat'l No 44, CI, red, w/eagle & pan, 15" wheels, 24" 775.00
Elgin Nat'l No 46, orig pnt/decals, 12" wheels, EX....................675.00
Enterprise, floor, CI, CI hopper, Pat 1898, 39" wheels, 72", VG.2,500.00
Enterprise Baby No 2, orig pnt & decals, 2 wheels, 7½", EX...1,050.00
Enterprise Boss, floor, CI, closed hopper, 1873, 39" wheels......3,675.00
Enterprise No 1, counter, open hopper, hdl, Pat 1873, 11", VG .245.00
Enterprise No 1, counter, orig pnt/decals, side hdl, 1898.............255.00
Enterprise No 2, orig pnt/decal, 2 8¾" wheels, EX.....................825.00
Enterprise No 3, counter, CI, wood drw, orig pnt/decals 785.00
Enterprise No 7, counter, CI, orig pnt, 17" wheel w/eagle, VG ..850.00
Enterprise No 16, floor, CI, orig pnt, CI hopper......................4,100.00
Enterprise No 50, single-wheel grist mill, NM...........................100.00
Enterprise No 212, floor, CI, 2 wheels, orig pnt, 30½", EX 3,000.00
Enterprise No 300, very heavy, wall mt, w/catcher, EX 495.00
Fairbanks Morse, floor, CI, brass hopper, 2 wheels, 27", EX.....3,100.00
Golden Rule, canister, w/orig glass, CI front, wood box, EX.......375.00
Grand Union Tea, table, CI sq base, rnd hopper, mfg Griswold..595.00
Hart, Henry C; Detroit Mich, CI, wall mt, NM.........................95.00
Hobart No 265, electric, covered hopper 295.00
J Fisher Warranted, lap, dvtl walnut, pewter hopper, unique.......265.00
Juvenile (toy), lap, CI top, wood box, orig drw & decal, EX.......115.00
L'il Tot (toy), CI hopper & drw front, wood box, decal, mini 95.00
Landers, Frary & Clark, canister, CI & tin, Pat 1905, VG 80.00
Landers, Frary & Clark, CI, rnd, sq base, ornate, Pat 1875 ....600.00
Landers, Frary & Clark Crown No 11, CI, decals, side crank, EX ..225.00
Landers, Frary & Clark Crown No 20, counter, 8" wheels, EX ...900.00
Landers, Frary & Clark No 24, w/orig mk hopper, NM 155.00
Landers, Frary & Clark No 50, counter, CI, 12" wheels, EX+.....995.00
Landers, Frary & Clark Regal, canister, wall mt...........................85.00
Landers, Frary & Clark Universal No 10, table, tin.......................85.00
Landers, Frary & Clark Universal No 14, table, Pat 1905, VG.....85.00
Logan & Strobridge, Franco-American, lap, ornate CI hopper...125.00
Luther, side, CI, tin hopper, brass plate, Pat 1843....................275.00
MJB, tin canister, wall mt w/lid & cup, EX..............................175.00
Nat'l Specialty, CI, brass hopper, 2 12½" wheels.....................1,100.00
Nat'l Specialty No 0, table, CI, covered hopper, clamps on........165.00
Nat'l Specialty No 7, CI, 16½" wheels, EX 1,000.00
New Model, lap, CI w/CI drw, bottom open all 4 sides, EX.......125.00
None Such, Bronson Co Cleveland OH, table, tin, pnt, EX.......125.00
Olde Thompson, lap, orig drw, EX...65.00
Parker, side, CI, grind adj front, Pat 1876, orig brd....................75.00
Parker (mk CPCo) No 1350, CI, wall mt, NM............................85.00
Parker Challenge Fast Grind No 555, table, orig, 1-lb, EX 125.00
Parker Eagle No 50, side, CI, Pat 1860, EX...............................85.00
Parker No 60, side, tin hopper, brass eagle medallion lid...............85.00
Parker No 260 Columbia, table, side grind, 1-lb, EX..................350.00
Parker No 350, side, orig lid, Pat 4/1876, EX 165.00
Parker No 400 series, lap, split-covered top, ornate.....................135.00
Parker No 446, wall mt...175.00
Parker No 449, canister, CI, orig lid & catcher, EX....................145.00
Parker No 700, counter, CI, wood drw, 17" wheels, G 885.00
Parker No 3000, drw, eagle on top, 11" wheels, orig...................725.00
Parker Union, side, CI, gear drive, Pat 1855, EX.......................125.00
Parker Victor No 535, table, wood/tin hopper, hdl 135.00
Peck, Stow & Wilcox Internat'l #360, lap 175.00
PS&W No 3500, side, CI, orig lid, EX.......................................155.00
PS&W Standard No 31, lap, CI open hopper, wood box............125.00

PS&W Vortex No 40, lap, wood box, CI hopper 175.00
PSW&Co No 5, side, orig CI lid, EX 75.00
Queen (toy), CI hopper & drw front, wood box, decal, mini........95.00
Richmond, side, CI, Chatham Conn (2 szs made), EX, ea..........345.00
Russell & Erwin Diamond, CI, bronze finish, rare 395.00
Russell & Erwin Mfg Co No 1008, CI hopper, wood box............115.00
S&H, counter, CI, w/drw, 19" wheels, 21", VG......................675.00
Selsor, Cook & Co, lap, name on hdl, Pat 1859 ....185.00
Silvers No 1, CI, dbl-grind, w/cup, EX.................................725.00
Simmon's Defiance, label, CI fill lid, 1-lb box, EX 125.00
Simmon's Hdwe, Delmar Coffee, table, CI cover.....................295.00
Star, canister, tin w/CI works, Pat 1910, VG..........................120.00
Star, floor, brass hopper, 2 CI wheels.................................1,100.00
Star No 12, CI, brass hopper, 2 wheels, rstr, EX 2,500.00
Star No 7, counter, CI, w/pan, 2-wheel, VG............................650.00
Steinfield, canister, CI works, glass jar, orig lid, EX 175.00
Stuttle, Henry, #2, CI, tin hopper, Pat 2/20/77, EX...................345.00
Sun Mfg No 1080, orig lid & drw, 1-lb box, EX/NM..................125.00
Sun No 94, side, CI, Greenfield OH, VG 75.00
Sun Success No 25, cylinder, 2 different szs, EX, ea....................295.00
Swift, drug mill, CI, open hopper, Pat June 30, 1874 ....525.00
Swift No 12, Lane Brothers, 9" wheel 550.00
Swift No 13, counter, orig tin drw, red pnt, 12" wheels, 19" 475.00
Swift No 15, counter, orig decals/pnt, Pat 1875, 19" wheels....1,100.00
Swift No 26, Lane Brothers, floor, CI, 2 wheels 2,500.00
Tillmann's, Hawaiian Coffee, CI, wall mt, EX 215.00
Universal No 109, blk tin w/gr decal, Pat 1905, NM...................75.00
Vandergrift, side hinged, CI, ca 1870, complete, EX 265.00
Waddel, A-9, orig drw & label, box type, EX 125.00
Waddel, A-17, CI, sunflower design, wall mt, EX......................280.00
Wilson Increase, side, CI & tin...75.00
Wright, John, CI, red or gr, ca 1968, 2 6¾" wheels, NM 350.00
Wrightsville Hdwe Brighton, label, 1-lb box, EX.....................110.00
Wrightsville Hdwe Peerless No 200, canister, CI/glass, EX 160.00
WW Weaver Warranted, dvtl walnut, pewter hopper, ca 1830...225.00

Coin-Operated Machines

Coin-operated machines may be the fastest-growing area of collector interest in today's market. Many machines are bought, restored, and used for home entertainment. Older examples from the turn of the century and those with especially elaborate decoration and innovative features are most desirable.

The www.GameRoomAntiques.com website and *Antique Amusements, Slot Machine, and Jukebox Gazette* are excellent sources of information for those interested in coin-operated machines; see the Clubs, Newsletters, and Catalogs section of the Directory for publishing information. Jackie and Ken Durham are our advisors; they are listed in the Directory under the District of Columbia.

Arcade Machines

Advance 1¢ Electric shocker, battery operated, EX...................1,495.00
Bat A Ball, flip ball, rpt case, rstr bk door, 25x16x11" 1,650.00
Bulldozer, 1950s, EX...995.00
Caille 1¢ Happy Home Peep Show, early 1900s, EX 1,495.00
Coast Baseball w/pinball feature, gumball vendor, 1950s, rstr 495.00
Erie Digger, floor model, new cabinet & castings, 1930s, EX...2,995.00
Erie Digger, on pine carnival crate, 1930s, EX orig 1,950.00
Exhibit Supply 1¢ Little Gypsy, yes/no answers, 1920s, 17x8x5", EX .1,295.00
Exhibit Supply 5¢ Crane, steam shovel, floor model, 1930s, VG ..3,300.00
Helicopter Trainer, 1960s, EX..995.00
Hercules Midget Baseball, 1931, EX..................................3,995.00

Internat'l Mutoscope Harem Dancer, tin on CI base, #53HWH, 72", M rstr....800.00
Irritating Maze, SNK, EX...1,995.00
Junior Deputy Pistol Range, 5¢ for 10 shots, 1940s-50s, G..........895.00
Marionette Puppet, WC Frank (dancing frankfurter), EX 1,250.00
Merchandiser Digger, floor model w/marquee, EX.................3,795.00
Mills Perfect Muscle Developer, strength tester, owl's head bezel, VG ..1,700.00
Mills Seal Flip, skill game, 1930s, rpt case, 32"......................2,495.00
Punt Return 5¢, move rod w/o touching bar, 1950s, VG.............795.00
Rally Driving, Atari, 1950s, gumball vendor, EX....................1,495.00
Super Ice Chexx, rstr 2,500.00
Underwater Marionette Puppet, EX 995.00

Jukeboxes

The coin-operated phonograph of the early 1900s paved the way for the jukeboxes of the 1920s. Seeburg was first on the market with an automatic eight-tune phonograph. By the 1930s Wurlitzer was the top name in the industry with dealerships all over the country. As a result of the growing ranks of competitors, the '40s produced the most beautiful machines made. Wurlitzers from this era are probably the most popularly sought-after models on the market today. The model #1015 of 1946 is considered the all-time classic and often brings prices in excess of $8,000.00.

Mills Panoram Movie, 16mm film, 1930s, rstr.......................17,000.00
Rockola #1422, EX orig 6,000.00
Rockola #1426, reconditioned.......................................6,000.00
Scopitone Movie, 1950s, rstr...4,000.00
Seeburg #100, EX orig..4,000.00
Seeburg #100C, cherry veneer, new chrome, 1952, rstr 6,000.00
Seeburg #201, EX orig..5,695.00
Seeburg #222, reconditioned 5,700.00
Seeburg DS-160, 1962, VG orig.....................................2,300.00
Seeburg J-100, 1955, VG orig..3,795.00
Seeburg M-100C, 1952, EX orig....................................3,495.00
Seeburg M-100C, 1952, rstr. 4,950.00
Seeburg Q-100, VG orig 2,295.00
Seeburg Q-160, 1959, VG orig......................................1,800.00
Seeburg R, 1954, VG orig..4,000.00
Seeburg Trashcan, ca 1946-48, rstr, 57x36x26" 2,600.00
Seeburg 100B/100BL, 45 rpm, 100 selections; 1951, EX.........2,500.00
Wurlitzer #41, counter-top, 1940s, rstr..............................7,500.00
Wurlitzer #61, counter-top, rstr 7,500.00
Wurlitzer #600, EX orig 4,295.00
Wurlitzer #750, reconditioned 9,300.00
Wurlitzer #850, Peacock, rstr.......................................19,850.00
Wurlitzer #1015, EX orig 9,000.00
Wurlitzer #1015, VG...7,500.00
Wurlitzer #1100, EX orig 7,295.00

Wurlitzer #1900 Centennial, two hundred selections, 55", VG original, $3,000.00.

Wurlitzer #2304, 104 selections, 1959, EX orig **3,000.00**
Wurlitzer #2610, 100 selections, 1962, VG **2,400.00**
Wurlitzer Carousel Cassette, 1972, 41x22x19", EX **3,000.00**

Pinball Machines

Allied Leisure Sea Hunt, 1972, EX...**400.00**
Bally Bally Hoo, 1969, rstr..**450.00**
Bally Carnival Queen, 1958, VG...**450.00**
Bally Centaur, 1981, working, VG...**600.00**
Bally Fireball Classic, 1985, EX..**800.00**
Bally Vampire, 2-player, 1971, EX...**650.00**
Bally 4 Million BC, 1971, VG...**1,600.00**
Bally 8 Ball Deluxe, 1981, EX..**1,600.00**
Gottlieb Aloha, 2-player, bonus build-up, 1961, VG.................**495.00**
Gottlieb Astro, add-a-ball game, ltd production, 1971, EX........**495.00**
Gottlieb Big Brave, 1973, VG..**1,000.00**
Gottlieb Big Hit, wedge head, orig pnt, 1977, EX orig..............**500.00**
Gottlieb Cover Girl, wedge head, 1962, rstr.............................**750.00**
Gottlieb Crossroads, 1940s-early '50s, rstr, 65".....................**1,000.00**
Gottlieb Fair Lady, 1956, EX+...**1,300.00**
Gottlieb Haunted House, 1982, M rstr...................................**1,500.00**
Gottlieb Incredible Hulk, 1978, EX orig..................................**800.00**
Gottlieb King Pin, 1973, EX orig..**350.00**
Gottlieb Volley, 1976, EX..**550.00**
Sonic Prospector, Laurel & Hardy, 4-player, 1977, EX..............**575.00**
Stern Wild Fyre, 1979, EX orig...**400.00**
Williams Alien Poker, 3-flipper, 1980, EX................................**600.00**
Williams Banzai Run, 1988, EX..**1,350.00**
Williams Base Hit (pitch & bat), rstr.....................................**1,950.00**
Williams Beat the Clock, multi-ball, 1 player, invt wedge head, EX...**750.00**
Williams Comet, 1985, EX+...**1,295.00**
Williams Deluxe Short Stop (pitch & bat), 1958, rstr.............**1,950.00**
Williams Olympic Hockey, 1972, EX.......................................**600.00**
World Cup Soccer, EX...**3,600.00**

Slot Machines

Color wheel, 45-slot, early, rstr...**19,500.00**
Jennings Victoria Jackpot, NP table-top model w/oak sides, 1930s, EX...**2,400.00**
Jennings 1¢ Little Duke, w/side gumball vendor, 1933, EX......**4,000.00**
Jennings 25¢ Sun Chief, front lights up, 1949, EX..................**3,495.00**
Mills $1 Golden Nugget, 1947, prof rstr................................**6,000.00**
Mills Novelty 50¢, bl front, rstr..**3,000.00**
Mills 5¢ High Top, 1940s, EX orig..**2,595.00**
Mills 5¢ QT, cast alumninun/wood, 1935, 18x12", VG..........**1,150.00**
Mills 5¢ skyscraper, 1936, old rstr.......................................**3,195.00**
Mills 5¢ Vest Pocket, 1938, 8" cube w/hidden reel strips, EX.....**800.00**
Mills 10¢ High Top, old rstr...**2,695.00**
Mills 25¢ Bursting Cherry, working jackpot, 1938-42, rstr.......**3,195.00**
Mills 25¢ Extra Bell, rstr...**3,195.00**
Mills 25¢ High Top, chrome front, 1940s, EX........................**2,795.00**
Mills 25¢ Lion Head (Wolf's head), str-drop, 1932, rstr...........**3,000.00**
Mills 25¢ War Eagle, 5-coin visible escalator, 1931, rstr..........**3,195.00**
Pace 10¢ Blue Pocket-Rocket comet, rejects slugs, 1940, EX..**2,695.00**
Puck, color wheel, upright, 1900s.......................................**16,000.00**
Watling Dewey, upright, ca 1902-16, EX..............................**14,995.00**
Watling 5¢ Roll-A-Top, dtd 1934, rstr...................................**4,000.00**

Trade Stimulators

Ad Lee's King's Horses, horse race, 1933, VG+.......................**1,950.00**
Daval Penny Pack, emb cigarette on front, 1939, rstr, 12x9x9"..**650.00**
Free Play, reel strips, 1940s, 13x10x9", EX..............................**495.00**

Groetchen Pok-o-Reel, card reels, gum vendor, 1930s, EX.........**775.00**
Indoor Striker, flip ball, wood case, gumball vendor, rstr.........**1,250.00**
Lattimore Game-o-Skill, 1890s, rstr, 14x17x10"....................**1,950.00**
Nugget, award card front, like punchboard, 11x7x6", EX...........**395.00**
Reliance Card, card flip, 1900s, EX..**3,995.00**
Rocola Radio Wizard, 2-reel, playing cards, 1930s, EX orig........**850.00**
Rolletto, roulette-type, ca 1933, 7x13x14", EX.........................**950.00**
Try It Dice, nickel play, rpt case, 1920s, 8x11x7"......................**495.00**
Twico Dice, w/gumball vendor, 1950s, 12x11x21", EX.............**395.00**

Vendors

    Vending machines sold a product or a service. They were already in common usage by 1900 selling gum, cigars, matches, and a host of other commodities. Peanut and gumball machines are especially popular today. The most valuable are those with their original finish and decals. Older machines made of cast iron are especially desirable, while those with plastic globes have little collector value. When buying unrestored peanut machines, beware of salt damage.

Acorn 1¢, gumball, CI w/clear globe, decal, 14½", w/key, G........**85.00**
Advance Big Mouth, peanuts, rolled steel/NP brass, ca 1925, rstr...**395.00**
Advance 1¢, match, CI w/glass dome, dk gr pnt base w/gilt, rstr, 18"..**575.00**
Atlas Bantam, bulk vendor, ca 1947, rstr, 11¼x8x10"..............**395.00**
Columbus M 1¢, gumball, CI base & lid, paneled globe, rstr, 14⅛"..**395.00**
Columbus Model A, CI & glass, rstr, 16½"................................**595.00**
Columbus Model 21, peanuts, metal & glass, 8-sided globe, ca 1934, 13"..**595.00**
Ford 1¢, gumball, aluminum w/clear flat-top globe, decal, 11⅓", EX...**165.00**
Master 1¢/5¢, gumball, metal/porc/glass, Pat 1923, rstr, 16x8x8"..**595.00**
Master/Norris 1¢ gumball, aqua/tan porc, ca 1923, rstr, 16x8"..**395.00**
Mills Automatic, gumball, stainless, 6-column, 1936, 16¼", VG..**150.00**
Northwestern #33, porc/glass, 1933, rstr.................................**395.00**
Northwestern Corp #31AP, stamps, porc, w/marquee, rstr, 15¾x9x8¼"..**395.00**

Smilin' Sam From Alabam Salted Peanuts, coin drop, painted cast iron with minor scratches, working, 13", $4,000.00.

Sun Nut's, cast aluminum & glass, rstr, 13¾x7¾x9¾"..................**175.00**
Victor Topper, metal & glass, rpt base, rstr, 16¼x6½x6½".........**185.00**
Yu Chu Ball Gum, CI, clear sq globe w/paper label, Pat 1925....**160.00**
Zeno 1¢, gum, oak w/press lettered side panels, 17x11", VG.......**950.00**

Cole, A. R.

    A second generation North Carolina potter, Arthur Ray Cole opened his own shop in 1926, operating under the name Rainbow Pottery until 1941 when he adopted his own name for the title of his business. He remained active until he died in 1974. He was skilled in modeling the pottery and highly recognized for his fine glazes.

Bowl, Chinese Blue w/red highlights & purple areas, flaring, 9".**600.00**

Jardiniere, red & blk streaks, hdls, 12½" 400.00
Pitcher, wht w/gr mottle, w/lid, ca 1950-60, 10¼x6" 225.00
Vase, brn/gr crystalline, elongated teardrop form, 8" 140.00
Vase, brn/gr matt, lg dbl wishbone hdls, bulbous, att, 8" 250.00
Vase, poppies on whiplash stems, pk/rose, shouldered, ca 1915, 7", NM ..325.00
Vase, textured lt bl/brn, bottle shape w/shoulder hdls, mfg line, 18" ...200.00
Vase, yel/gold/brn crystalline, classic form w/hdls, att, 12" 300.00

Comic Books

    For almost sixty years, the American public has been thrilled by the monthly adventures of everyone's favorite comic book heroes such as Superman, Captain Marvel, and Spiderman. Each 10¢ comic book issue, featuring a new saga of adventure and mystery, were usually met with excitement and anticipation by the youngsters who eagerly purchased them from their neighborhood candy store or newsstand. Unfortunately, the vast majority of these comic books were eventually discarded in favor of other worldly pursuits. Due to this fact, most comic books from the '30s and '40s did not survive, making them a very scarce and desirable collectible in today's world. Many comic books are worth very little, a few of the better examples are listed here.

Incredible Hulk, Marvel #102, 1968, Big Premiere Issue, EX, $80.00.

Adventures of Bob Hope, Dell #30, VG...25.00
Adventures of the Jaguar, #1, VG...35.00
Al Capp's Wolf Gal, #2, 1952, VG+..55.00
Alvin & His Pals Merry Christmas, Dell 1963, NM 20.00
Annie Oakley & Tagg, Dell #575, EX..30.00
Avengers, Marvel #1, 1963, G+...225.00
Bat Masterson, Dell Four-Color #1013, 1959, VG.........................15.00
Beatles, Dell Giant #1, 1964, EX, from $75 to............................125.00
Best of Donald Duck & Scrooge, #2, 1967, EX.............................40.00
Bewitched, Dell #1, 1965, NM, from $75 to.................................100.00
Bugs Bunny Christmas Funnies, Dell #7, NM 50.00
Captain Marvel Adventures, Dell #24, 1943, EX 175.00
Challengers of the Unknown, #28, EX...40.00
Christmas in Disneyland, Dell #1, NM 95.00
Christmas w/Mother Goose, Dell #201, EX..................................35.00
Daredevil, Marvel #1, 1964, VG...155.00
Dark Shadows, Gold Key #15, 1972, EX 15.00
Dick Tracy, Dell #4, NM..100.00
Doc Savage, #12, 1943, NM 300.00
Don Winslow, #61, 1948, EX 25.00
Donald Duck Beach Party, Dell Giant #1, EX.............................35.00
Donald Duck in Mathmagicland, Dell #1198, EX........................45.00
Dr Who & the Daleks, Dell #1, 1966, VG....................................15.00
F-Troop, Dell #4, 1967, VG...20.00

Family Affair, Gold Key #1, 1970, NM...40.00
Felix the Cat, Toby Press #58, 1954, VG 25.00
Flash, Why?, DC Comics, 1965, NM..40.00
Flintstones, Gold Key Giant, #1, 1965, EX...................................50.00
Flipper, Gold Key #2, 1966, photo cover, EX 35.00
Garrison's Gorillas, Dell #5, 1967, VG...20.00
George of the Jungle, Dell Giant #1, EX 40.00
Get Smart, Dell #1, 1965, NM...35.00
Hawkman, DC Comics #1, 1964, NM...500.00
Howdy Doody, Dell #15, 1952, EX...25.00
HR Pufnstuf, Gold Key #2, 1971, EX 40.00
Human Torch Battling Submariner, #8, NM 2,600.00
Incredible Hulk, Marvel #6, 1963, VG+ 200.00
Jetsons, Gold Key #6, 1963, VG+...15.00
Josie & the Pussycats, Archie Comics #6, 1964, NM 20.00
Little Audrey TV Funtime, Harvey Giant #1, 1962, VG 10.00
Lone Ranger, March of Comics #310, photo cover, EX 45.00
Looney Tunes Merrie Melodies, Dell/Leon Schlesinger, 1940s, EX...60.00
Marvel Super Heroes Tales Annual, #1, 1964, EX 65.00
Mod Squad, Dell #1, 1969, NM...40.00
Munsters, Gold Key #1, VG+ 45.00
Nancy & Sluggo, Dell #145, EX+ 15.00
Nick Fury Agent of Shield, Marvel Comics, EX 15.00
Oswald Rabbit, Dell Four-Color #102, 1946, VG..........................25.00
Pat Boone, DC Comics #4, 1960, rare, EX....................................80.00
Phantom, Gold Key, 1964, EX..25.00
Playful Little Audrey, Dell #1, 1957, EX+....................................60.00
Rat Patrol, Dell #1, EX..17.00
Red Ryder, Dell #69, 1949, NM...35.00
Regards From Captain Wonder, Kid Comics #1, NM 2,000.00
Restless Gun, Dell Four-Color #1146, VG 25.00
Rifleman, Dell #5, 1960, photo cover, EX.....................................30.00
Ruff & Reddy #7, EX..35.00

Saint, Avon Periodicals #6, EX, $65.00.

Savage Sword of Conan, Marvel #1, NM......................................65.00
Silly Symphonies, Dell #7, NM 75.00
Soldiers of Fortune, Dell #1, 1951, VG 35.00
Space Busters, Dell #2, 1952, EX..150.00
Star Trek, Gold Key, 1968, M 150.00
Superboy, Dell #22, 1952, VG..50.00
Superman, DC Comics #1, 1939, NM, minimum value 10,000.00
Superman's Pal Jimmy Olsen, Dell #23, VG................................20.00
Tales From the Crypt, Dell #28, VG..75.00
Tarzan Saves the Proud Princess From Enemy Raiders, Dell, 1960, EX...25.00
Terry & the Pirates, Dell #101, 1945, EX......................................80.00
Tex Ritter, Fawcett #17, 1953, photo cover, EX............................30.00
That Darn Cat, Movie Comics, NM..45.00

Three Stooges, Dell #1170, 1961, VG.............................30.00
Tom & Jerry Back to School, Dell Giant #1, 1956, NM..............100.00
Tweety & Sylvester, Dell #11, NM.................................20.00
Two-Gun Kid, Marvel Comics, 1964, NM.............................18.00
Underworld Crime, Dell #3, 1952, EX..............................35.00
Untouchables, Dell #207, EX......................................40.00
Vacation in Disneyland, Dell Giant #1, 1959, NM.................150.00
Walt Disney's Picnic Party, Dell Giant #8, 1957, VG..............50.00
Walt Disney's Treasure Island, Dell #624, 1955, EX..............22.00
Yogi Bear Jellystone Jollies, Gold Key #11, 1963, EX............15.00
Young Man, Atlas #27, 1954, EX+.................................225.00
Zane Grey's Outlaw Trail, Dell Four-Color #511, 1954, EX........25.00
Zorro, Gold Key #3, 1966, EX+...................................15.00

Compacts

The use of cosmetics before WWI was looked upon with disdain. After the war women became liberated, entered the work force, and started to use makeup. The compact, a portable container for cosmetics, became a necessity. The basic compact contains a mirror and a powder puff.

The vintage compacts were fashioned in a myriad of shapes, styles, materials, and motifs. They were made of precious metals, fabrics, plastics, and in almost any other conceivable medium. Commemorative, premium, patriotic, figural, Art Deco, plastic, and gadgetry compacts are just a few of the most sought-after types available today. Those that are combined with other accessories (music/compact, watch/compact, cane/compact) are also very much in demand. Vintage compacts are an especially desirable collectible since the workmanship, design, techniques, and materials used in their execution would be very expensive and virtually impossible to duplicate today.

Our advisor, Roselyn Gerson, has written five highly informative books: *Ladies' Compacts of the 19th and 20th Centuries; Vintage Vanity gatgs and Purses; Vintage and Contemporary Purse Accessories; Vintage & Vogue Ladies' Compacts;* and *Estèe Lauder Solid Perfume Compact Collection.* She is listed in the Directory under the state of New York. For further information we recommend *Collector's Encyclopedia of Compacts, Carryalls, and Face Powder Boxes, Volumes I* and *II* by Laura M. Mueller. See Clubs, Newsletters, and Catalogs for information concerning the compact collectors' club and their periodical publication, *The Powder Puff.*

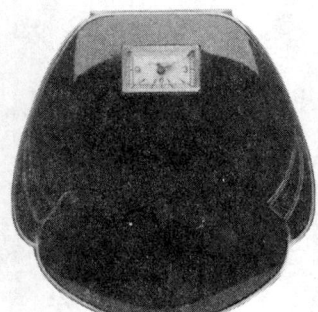

Art Deco watch/compact, black and gold enamel on shell form with watch marked Illinois Watch Case Co., 3½", $300.00.

Animal heads: cat, fox or owl, gold-tone w/faux stone eyes, Italy, ea ...400.00
Bolster, gold-tone, Dorset Fifth Ave 60.00
Bolster, silver-tone w/carrying chain, Winnie Winkle, 1920s, 1¾"..275.00
Book, gold-tone w/emb grid pattern, polished border, Coty, 1940s..60.00
Bracelet, silver-tone resembling belt & buckle w/gold-tone insignia 325.00
Carryall, oblong w/carrying chain, silver w/eng design, Germany.........200.00
Carryall, oblong w/mesh strap, MOP ribbed inlay w/zigzag border........275.00
Carryall, oblong w/mesh strap, pk/yel/wht metal basketweave, Evans..150.00
Carryall, oblong w/mesh strap, watch centered on gold sunburst, Evans...300.00
Carryall, sq w/carrying chain, silvered w/oval cameo, DF Briggs.225.00

Chair, gold-tone w/coin-top seat, cabriole legs, Robt Orig, 3½".400.00
Clamshell, frosted milk glass w/gold-tone trim, Russia, 3"...........250.00
Compass, gold-tone w/working compass under beveled glass dome, 2¾"...175.00
Crown, gold-tone w/emb king's crown motif, Stratton, 1940-50s ...200.00
Envelope, sterling w/antique finish, Tiffany & Co, Italy 275.00
Fan, MOP w/floral decor & rhinestones, Japan, mini 50.00
Fan, petit-point landscape scene w/house, swivel mirror 175.00
Finger-ring chain, arrowhead, silvered metal w/enamel inlay, 1920s...50.00
Finger-ring chain, rnd, silver-tone w/pnt roses on yel enamel, 1⅞"...100.00
Half-moon, bl enamel w/diagonal gold-tone band & trim, Rex, 5½" ..75.00
Half-moon, petit-point w/gold-tone scalloped rim, 1930s............100.00
Hand mirror, ivory celluloid, hinged lid reveals compact, 5x2¾" dia...125.00
Heart, pk & yel gold-tone puffy basketweave, Evans, ca 1946 ....200.00
Horseshoe, leather w/gold-tone decor, possibly Spain...................80.00
Mask, lt bl harlequin shape, 1940s................................150.00
Music box, gold-tone w/applied sheet music of 'Star Dust,' 1920s ..125.00
Music box, MOP w/gold-tone musical notes & G-clef, Stratton.175.00
Oblong, brass & blk enamel allover receeding triangle design, Volupte .40.00
Octagonal, gr enamel w/HP wooded stream, gold-tone trim, 2¼" 175.00
Octagonal, w/carrying chain, pk/yel/bl abstract Deco design, 1920s.....175.00
Oval, gold-tone w/blk enamel harlequin mask motif, Dorothy Gray, 1940s...100.00
Oval, MOP w/faux sapphires & rhinestones, K&K, 1930-40s........75.00
Oval, petit-point floral design w/blk enamel trim, Rowenta..........50.00
Padlock, rnd w/gold-tone lock motif on wht enamel 100.00
Painter's palette, copper-tone w/HP pansies, eng brushes, HA La Pensee ...300.00
Pendant, ball form, sterling w/eng filigree design, w/chain, 1" 225.00
Pendant, rnd gold-tone w/filigree, pearl & turq stone decor, Fr, 2" ...250.00
Picture hat, blk & pk fabric w/MOP & beaded flower decor, 3" .250.00
Picture hat, silver-tone w/emb ribs/flowers/bow, Dorothy Gray...150.00
Pocket watch, gold-tone w/encircled floral decor, Volupte, 1940s...........100.00
Purse, brushed gold-tone w/mc stones in filigree plaque, w/chain, 2x3"..150.00
Rnd, aluminum cut-out bird design on orange, Roger & Gallet, 3" 225.00
Rnd, bl enamel w/pnt scene on locket center, scalloped rim, Kigu ..75.00
Rnd, blk matt w/gold & silver inlayed floral scene, Amita, 1920s ..125.00
Rnd, celluloid, 2-tone silhouette head image, Antonin of/Fr, 3".175.00
Rnd, cork & gold-tone w/bl/orange/cream abstract design, 3".......65.00
Rnd, gold-tone w/allover mc & multi-shaped prong-set stones, 3½"....100.00
Rnd, gold-tone w/emb polished leaping gazelles & cloud design, 5⅞"..325.00
Rnd, sterling gold-wash w/pk/yel/wht basketweave, Evans, 5" 225.00
Rnd, sterling w/red/yel/gr/bl/gold swirls, 2¾" 300.00
Shamrock coin purse shape, gunmetal.................................80.00
Souvenir, Canada, rnd, gold-tone w/colorful maple leaf on bl, 2¾" ...100.00
Souvenir, San Francisco, sq, gold-tone w/engraved points of interest..45.00
Sq, bl ribbed silk w/bl stone clasp, England...............................125.00
Sq, gold-tone covered w/blk & clear crystal flowers, 2" 45.00
Sq, gold-tone mesh w/buckle closure, Volupte 100.00
Sq, gold-tone w/clear plastic waffle top, Wadsworth, 1930s 125.00
Sq, gold-tone w/wht Schiaparelli logo on hot pk enamel, 2½" 125.00
Sq, leather w/envelope coin holder, rnd corners, Lin-Bren, 1940s 100.00
Sq, silvered metal w/allover embossed 'Adam & Eve' motif, Volupte ...80.00
Sq, Simplicity Printed Pattern 25 Cents, Wadsworth, from $225 to...400.00
Sq, Until We Meet Again in script above military couple, wood, 1940s ...100.00
Sq, Yes/No in gr & red on wht enamel................................125.00
Suitcase, brn lizzard w/2 carrying hdls, zippered...........................150.00
Tandem, dbl octagons (powder/rouge) w/chain-attached lipstick, enamel ..525.00
Triangular, bowed sides, brass w/cameo on filigree, rope border 85.00
Triangular, gold-tone w/gr & yel checked design, Volupte.............80.00
Vanity, acorn w/lipstick in tassel, carrying cord, cvd plastic, 2¼" ...1,000.00
Vanity, camera, silver, Van-Mist, Filkwik Co, 1930s....................150.00
Vanity, clutch, wht & gold fabric w/tree of life decor, Richard Hudnut..100.00
Vanity, oblong w/carrying chain, pnt flower basket on gr enamel 250.00
Vanity, octagon w/lipstick on chain, silver-tone w/enameled Deco motif....250.00
Vanity, oval w/lipstick on chain, gold-tone w/enameled Deco motif.....250.00
Vanity, pouchette w/pk & gr trim, mirror on outside base, 1920s ..100.00

Vanity, purse w/carrying cord, polished sterling, England, early 1900s...**500.00**
Vanity, rnd, petit-point top w/gold-tone mesh ruffled border, Evans......**200.00**
Vanity, saddlebag w/lamé fabric cover, gold-tone & blk trim, 4".**150.00**

Consolidated Lamp and Glass

The Consolidated Lamp and Glass Company of Coraopolis, Pennsylvania, was incorporated in 1894. For many years their primary business was the manufacture of lighting glass such as oil lamps and shades for both gas and electric lighting. The popular 'Cosmos' line of lamps and tableware was produced from 1894 to 1915. (See also Cosmos.) In 1926 Consolidated introduced their Martele line, a type of 'sculptured' ware closely resembling Lalique glassware of France. (Compare Consolidated's 'Lovebirds' vase with the Lalique 'Perruches' vase.) It is this line of vases, lamps, and tableware which is often mistaken for a very similar type of glassware produced by the Phoenix Glass Company, located nearby in Monaca, Pennsylvania. For example, the so-called Phoenix 'Grasshopper' vases are actually Consolidated's 'Katydid' vases.

Items in the Martele line were produced in blue, pink, green, crystal, white, or custard glass decorated with various fired-on color treatments or a satin finish. For the most part, their colors were distinctively different from those used by Phoenix. Although not foolproof, one of the ways of distinguishing Consolidated's wares from those of Phoenix is that most of the time Consolidated applied color to the raised portion of the design, leaving the background plain, while Phoenix usually applied color to the background, leaving the raised surfaces undecorated. This is particularly true of those pieces in white or custard glass.

In 1928 Consolidated introduced their Ruba Rombic line, which was their Art Deco or Art Moderne line of glassware. It was only produced from 1928 to 1932 and is quite scarce. Today it is highly sought after by both Consolidated and Art Deco collectors.

Consolidated closed its doors for good in 1964. Subsequently a few of the molds passed into the hands of other glass companies that later reproduced certain patterns; one such reissue is the 'Chickadee' vase, found in avocado green, satin-finish custard, or milk glass. Our advisor for this category is Jack D. Wilson, author of *Phoenix and Consolidated Art Glass, 1926 – 1980*; he is listed in the Directory under Arizona.

Bird of Paradise, candy box, purple wash, oval............................**325.00**
Bird of Paradise, vase, orange wash, 10" **235.00**
Bird of Paradise, vase, pk cased, 10" **300.00**
Bird of Paradise, vase, pk wash, fan shape, 6"..............................**175.00**
Bird of Paradise, vase, sepia wash, fan form, 6"...........................**135.00**
Bird of Paradise, vase, yel wash, fan shape, 10".............................**275.00**
Bittersweet, vase, amber irid over milk glass casing, rare............**325.00**
Bittersweet, vase, bl/gr/orange on satin milk glass.......................**120.00**
Bittersweet, vase, gr cased **275.00**
Blackberry, umbrella vase, wht wash..**550.00**
Catalonian, candlestick, yel **45.00**
Catalonian, plate, russet finish (rare color), 6" **150.00**
Catalonian, vase, purple wash, pinched, 6" **225.00**
Catalonian, vase, red **150.00**
Catalonian, violet vase, ruby stain...**75.00**
Chickadee, vase, gr wash on crystal..**110.00**
Chickadee, vase, sepia wash on crystal..**200.00**
Chickadee, vase, 3-color highlights on satin custard **195.00**
Chrysanthemum, vase, bl on creamy milk glass, 12"......................**115.00**
Chrysanthemum, vase, red, 12" **350.00**
Chrysanthemum, vase, ruby-stain highlights in crystal, metal surmount..**225.00**
Chrysanthemum, vase, ruby stain on crystal **200.00**
Chrysanthemum, vase, 3-color highlights on satin milk glass **175.00**
Cockatoo, candlestick, yel wash **125.00**

Cockatoo, vase, yel cased..**425.00**
Dancing Girls, lamp, pk & bl on creamy custard, 12"+mts **550.00**
Dancing Girls, vase, bl highlights on satin milk glass, 12" **525.00**
Dancing Girls, vase, straw opal, rare color, 12" **750.00**

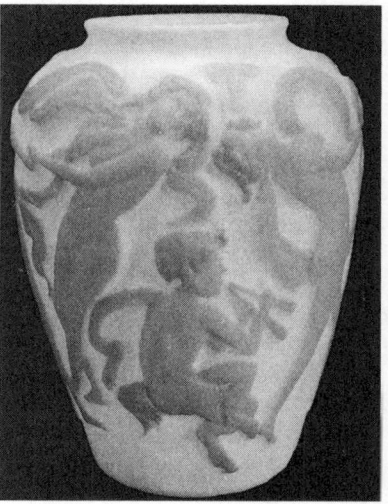

Dancing Girls, vase, tricolor on satin custard, 11⅝", $550.00. (Photo courtesy Skinner, Inc.)

Dancing Nymph, goblet, pk frosted..**125.00**
Dancing Nymph, plate, frosted, 8"...**75.00**
Dancing Nymph, vase, crystal, fan shape **125.00**
Dogwood, lamp, 3-color highlights on satin milk glass...............**125.00**
Dogwood, vase, gold highlights on glossy milk glass, 11" **150.00**
Dogwood, vase, yel cased, 11"...**300.00**
Dragon Fly, vase, gold on glossy custard, 7"..................................**175.00**
Dragon Fly, vase, gr cased, orig Martele label...............................**175.00**
Dragon Fly, vase, yel cased, 7"...**125.00**
Fish, bowl, gr wash w/frosted design, 15"......................................**425.00**
Fish, tray, yel wash..**200.00**
Five Fruits, bowl, berry; purple wash...**30.00**
Five Fruits, goblet, yel wash **35.00**
Five Fruits, plate, purple wash, 14" **150.00**
Florentine, vase, coffee brn, etched **250.00**
Florentine, vase, gr, tumbler shape..**50.00**
Foxglove, lamp, wht w/lav-bl flowers & gr leaves, orig mts, 10¼" ..**145.00**
Hollyhock, lamp vase, reverse gr highlights on crystal **150.00**
Hummingbird, vase, amber wash **75.00**
Hummingbird, vase, 3-color highlights on satin milk glass **110.00**
Iris, bowl, console; pk wash, 10¾"..**145.00**
Iris, bowl, mayonnaise; purple wash..**40.00**
Iris, console set, pk wash, 10¾" bowl+2 candlesticks **375.00**
Iris, jug, sepia wash...**250.00**
Jonquil, vase, gold highlights on milk glass...................................**110.00**
Katydid, ashtray, bl wash, very rare..**300.00**
Katydid, vase, bl on satin milk glass, ovoid **165.00**
Katydid, vase, purple wash, tumbler shape.....................................**170.00**
Katydid, vase, reverse purple highlights on straw opal, ovoid......**325.00**
Line 700, vase, Fr crystal highlighting, 10" **325.00**
Line 700, vase, satin blk, 6½"...**475.00**
Love Bird, banana bowl, reverse highlighting on crystal **450.00**
Love Bird, glove box, gr wash, very rare..**350.00**
Love Bird, vase, gold highlights on straw opal **400.00**
Love Bird, vase, pk wash, 10x8"...**275.00**
Love Bird, vase, yel cased...**425.00**
Nuthatch, planter vase, sepia cased..**250.00**
Nuthatch, planter vase, 3-color highlights on satin milk glass....**225.00**
Olive, bowl, purple wash, 4" **125.00**
Olive, lamp, 3-color highlighting (very rare)................................**300.00**
Olive, vase, gr & yel highlighting on satin custard.......................**165.00**

Olive, vase, ruby-stain highlights on crystal.................................135.00
Orchids, bowl, console; gray wash (rare color)............................275.00
Pine Cone, vase, purple cased...250.00
Pine Cone, vase, ruby-stain highlights on crystal.........................150.00
Pond Lily, candy box, purple wash, oval.....................................235.00
Poppy, vase, purple cased..400.00
Regent Line, cookie jar, ash-rose pk on wht opal casing 250.00
Regent Line, vase, aqua bl over wht opal....................................125.00
Regent Line, vase, violets decor..45.00
Ruba Rombic, nut dish, Jungle Green (very rare)........................225.00
Ruba Rombic, plate, Jungle Green, rare, 15" 1,500.00
Ruba Rombic, plate, service; Jungle Green, 10".........................275.00
Ruba Rombic, plate, smoky topaz, 8"..135.00
Ruba Rombic, tumbler, lav, 9-oz..300.00
Ruba Rombic, vase, silver, 9½" 4,450.00
Ruba Rombic, vase, smoky topaz, 9½".....................................2,900.00
Screech Owls, vase, gr wash on crystal 75.00
Screech Owls, vase, orange w/gr reeds on satin custard...............145.00
Screech Owls, vase, sepia cased...250.00
Sea Gull, vase, orange highlighting on satin custard 275.00
Sea Gull, vase, yel cased, 11"..450.00
Spanish Knobs, candlestick, yel...45.00
Spanish Knobs, sundae, yel 30.00
Tropical Fish (Gold Fish), vase, gr wash on crystal, 9" 300.00
Tropical Fish (Gold Fish), vase, orange on gr satin, 9" 325.00
Tropical Fish (Gold Fish), vase, straw opal, 9"...........................480.00

Cookbooks

Cookbooks from the nineteenth century, though often hard to find, are a delight to today's collectors both for their quaint formats and printing methods as well as for their outmoded, often humorous views on nutrition. Recipes required a 'pinch' of salt, butter 'the size of an egg' or a 'walnut,' or a 'handful' of flour. Collectors sometimes specialize in cookbooks issued as advertising premiums. Especially desirable are the figurals that were shaped like a jar, a slice of bread, or some other form relative to the product. Others with unique features such as illustrations by well-known artists or references to famous people or places are priced in accordance. Cookbooks written earlier than 1874 are the most valuable and when found command prices as high as $200.00; figurals usually sell in the $10.00 to $15.00 range.

As is true with all other books, if the original dust jacket is present and in nice condition, a cookbook's value goes up by at least $5.00. Right now, books on Italian cooking from before circa 1940 are in demand, and bread-baking is important this year. For further information we recommend *A Guide to Collecting Cookbooks* by Col. Bob Allen and *Price Guide to Cookbooks and Recipe Leaflets* by Linda Dickinson. Our advisor for this category is Charlotte Safir; she is listed in the Directory under New York.

Key:
CB — cookbook   dj — dust jacket

The Ad-ven-tur-ous Billy and Betty, 1923, $25.00. (Photo courtesy Colonel Bob Allen)

American CB, Mrs FL Gillette, 1886-89, hardbk, VG 75.00
American Pure Food CB, Sears & Roebuck Co, 1889, hardbk, VG ..75.00
Art of Cookery Made Plain & Easy, Glasse, 1799, VG...............170.00
Better Homes & Gardens CB, Home Service Bureau, 1930-37, 3-ring, VG ..30.00
Bettina's Best Desserts, L Weaver, 1923, hardbk, VG 20.00
Betty Furness Westinghouse CB, Kiene, 1st print, 1954, hardbk, VG..25.00
Bread & Bread Making, ST Rorer, Arnold & Co, 1887, hardbk, VG...75.00
Canning & Preserving, ST Rorer, 1887, hardbk, VG 60.00
Chafing Dish Possibilities, F Farmer, 1898, 1909, hardbk, 161 pgs, VG .125.00
Common Sense Papers on Cookery, Payne, ca 1920, EX.............30.00
Cooking for Profit, Alice Bradley, 1933, hardbk, VG 35.00
Dishes for All Year Round, ST Rorer, 1903, leaflet, EX 6.00
Duncan Hines Dessert Book, 1955, hardbk, VG 20.00
Edith Barber's CB, 1940, hardbk, VG..35.00
Enterprising Housekeeper, Johnson, 1898, paperbk, EX 25.00
Favorite Recipes of Famous Women, F Stratton, 1925, EX 12.00
Feeding the Family, MS Rose, 1925, hardbk, VG 35.00
French Cooking for All, Voison, 1932, hardbk, VG 35.00
Genuine German Cooking & Baking, Lina Meier, 1930, cloth cover, VG...35.00
Good Housekeeping Book of Good Meals, K Fisher, 1st ed, VG...35.00
Granite Ironware CB, 1887, VG 110.00
Green Mountain CB, 1941, VG 12.50
Heinz Recipe Book, HJ Heinz Co, 1939, spiral-bound, VG 25.00
Hershey — The Chocolate Town, Compliments of..., 1923, paperbk, VG...20.00
Home CB, E Ives, 1928, hardbk, 750 pgs, VG 18.00
Ida Bailey Allen's Money-Saving CB, 1st ed, 1940, hardbk, VG ..35.00
International CB, Heywood, 1929, hardbk, EX............................12.00
James Beard CB w/Isabel E Calvert, 1959, 1961, hardbk, VG.......20.00
Jams, Jellies, Marmalades Certo Surejell, Bradley, 1924, paperbk, VG....15.00
Jell-O America's Most Famous Dessert, bride cover, 1916, leaflet, EX....40.00
Knox Gelatin Recipes, 1896, Black person on cover, EX 30.00
Ladies' New Book of Cookery, S Hale, 1852, 5th ed, hardbk, VG .40.00
Libby's Fancy Red Alaska Salmon, 1935, paperbk can shape, VG..15.00
Lowney's CB, MW Howard, WM Lowney Co, 1907/1908/1912, hardbk, VG ..30.00
Made Over Dishes, Sarah Tyson Rorer, 1898, hardbk, VG............55.00
Magic Chef Cooking, American Stove, 1937, hardbk, EX 10.00
Metropolitan CB, Metropolitan Life Ins Co, 1918, paperbk, VG .20.00
Mrs Hale's New CB, Sarah J Hale, 1851, hardbk, VG.................140.00
New Home CB, Illinois State Register, 1925, VG 8.00
New Perfection Oil Stove, 1914, paperbk, EX 15.00
Picture CB, Betty Crocker, 1950, 1st ed, EX 20.00
Pure Food CB, M Maddock, 1914, EX.......................................20.00
Quality Grocer, March 1931, paperbk, EX 11.00
Quantity Cooking, Woman's Home Companion, 1927, paperbk, VG..14.00
Ralston Recipes, 1920, woman in shoe on cover, leaflet, EX.........12.00
Royal Baker & Pastry Cook, Chefs of NY Cooking School, 1902, VG 25.00
Savory Prize Recipe Book, Republic Metalware Co, 1909, paperbk, VG..25.00
Service CB #1, I Allen, 1933, hardbk, EX..................................12.00
Simplified Cooking, A Peterson, Ill, 1926, hardbk, EX 18.00
Table Decorations & Delicacies, H Prices, 1914, hardbk, EX........15.00
Tribune CB, Jane Eddington, Chicago Tribune, 1925, paperbk, 1925, VG...20.00
Tyson Baking Book, Marion, 1916, VG......................................15.00
Union Gs & Electric Co CB, Cincinnati, 1907, paperbk, VG.......10.00
Vitality Demands Energy, General Mills, 1934, paperbk, EX.........65.00
Watkins Salad CB, B Allen, 1946, hardbk, EX 15.00
Woman's World Calendar CB, Mrs Ida Bailey Allen, 1922, paperbk, VG...20.00
Yankee CB, I Wolcott, 1939, EX...8.00
Young American CB, 1938, hardbk, VG 6.00
Your Mexican Kitchen, NV Scott, 1935, hardbk, VG 35.00

Cookie Cutters

Early hand-fashioned cookie cutters have recently been command-

Cookie Cutters

ing stiff prices at country auctions, and the ranks of interested collectors are growing steadily. Especially valuable are the figural cutters; and the more complicated the design, the higher the price. A follow-up of the carved wooden cookie boards, the first cutters were probably made by itinerant tinkers from leftover or recycled pieces of tin. Though most of the eighteenth-century examples are now in museums or collections, it is still possible to find some good cutters from the late 1800s when changes in the manufacture of tin resulted in a thinner, less expensive material. The width of the cutting strip is often a good indicator of age; the wider the strip, the older the cutter. While the very early cutters were 1" to 1½" deep, by the '20s and '30s, many were less than ½" deep. Crude, spotty soldering indicates an older cutter, while a thin line of solder usually tends to suggest a much later manufacture. The shape of the backplate is another clue. Later cutters will have oval, round, or rectangular backs, while on the earlier type the back was cut to follow the lines of the design. Cookie cutters usually vary from 2" to 4" in size, but gingerbread men were often made as tall as 12". Birds, fish, hearts, and tulips are common; simple versions can be purchased for as little as $12.00 to $15.00. The larger figurals, especially those with more imaginative details, often bring $75.00 and up. The cookie cutters listed here are tin and handmade unless noted otherwise.

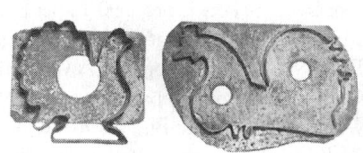

Eagle, flat back, 6" $50.00; Turkey, flat back, 6", $50.00; Peacock, flat back, marked Germany, 4", $65.00. (Photo courtesy Garth's Auctions, Inc.)

Angel, aluminum w/cut-out hdl, 5"	5.00
Barnyard Animals, 12 figures, Montgomery Wards, MIB	20.00
Bearded man w/slouch hat carrying book, 9¾", EX	400.00
Bird, aluminum, red riveted hdl, Holey Tole	18.00
Bird, flat bk, 5x2¾"	25.00
Bunny, flat bk, 1920s, 2⅝"	22.50
Chicken, early, 4½x3¼"	22.50
Chicken, flat bk, 1920s, 2x2"	18.00
Deer, lg antlers w/many points, strap hdl, 7"	440.00
Deer, running; 19th C, 4½x4"	80.00
Dmn w/scalloped edge, aluminum w/gr wood hdl, 3⅜"	12.50
Donald, Mickey, Minnie & Pluto, Walt Disney Characters, 1950s, MIB	70.00
Donald Duck, aluminum, flat bk	35.00
Donkey, Democratic, metal, M (EX box)	75.00
Dutch man & lady, 6⅞", pr	125.00
Elephant, aluminum w/gr wooden hdl, 1930s-40s, 2¾x3¼"	30.00
Fish, flat bk, 6½x2½"	20.00
Friar Tuck, Robin Hood Flour, 3¾"	20.00
Gingerbread boy, red plastic, Betty Crocker Gingerbread Mix, 4"	10.50
Gingerbread boy, red plastic, Design Pat 127026, 4¾"	12.00
Goat, flat bk, 3⅛x2"	25.00
Heart, aluminum w/wood hdl, crinkled edges	12.00
Heart, Swans Down, aluminum, flat bk, riveted hdl, 2½x2¾"	15.00
Heart, 19th C, 3½"	20.00
Holly leaves & brrries, red plastic, Aunt Chicks	6.00
Horse, Davis Baking Powder, 3x3¾"	34.50
Horse, no hdl, 5¾x5⅞"	30.00
Lion, aluminum, flat bk, red hdl, Holey Tole, 2½x4½"	12.00

Man, open bk, strap hdl, Germany, 5¾"	45.00
Man dancing, wearing hat, 10"	120.00
Man w/flat-top hat, lg oval hdl, 7½"	220.00
Man w/rnd top hat & long coat, minor rust, 7¾"	175.00
Meeko (Lion King), c Disney Treasure Craft, from $45 to	55.00
Nina, Pinta & Santa Maria, Christopher Columbus' ships, MIB	40.00
Pig, long snout, flat bk, 5¼x2½"	38.00
Pig, 5x3"	55.00
Pretzel, metal w/wood hdl, 4¼x3"	20.00
Rabbit, 'Formay' on front, heavy tin, 3x6"	32.00
Rabbit, aluminum, gr metal hdl, 4" L	12.50
Rabbit running, appl hdl, 7¼"	50.00
Reindeer, aluminum w/cut-out hdl, 3¼"	5.00
Rnd w/scalloped edge, aluminum w/gr wood hdl, 2⅝"	12.50
Rnd w/serrated edge, steel, ½-circle strap hdl	4.25
Roller, aluminum, makes rnd cookies, dtd July 4 1922, 6" L	18.50
Rolling type w/5 shapes, mk P DRGM Made in W Germany, 3½x2¼"+hdl	33.00
Rooster, early, 4¾x3¼"	32.00
Santa, aluminum, loop hdl, unmk, 4x2"	7.00
Santa carrying Christmas tree, mk Germany #148, ca 1900, 4x8"	110.00
Santa's boot, flat bk, 19th C, 3x2"	60.00
Santa w/bag, aluminum, gr wood hdl, 3½"	15.00
Scary cat (Halloween), aluminum, 4¼x3"	18.00
Scottie dog, aluminum, cut-out hdl, 2¼x2¾"	6.00
Squirrel, 3⅝x2⅝"	25.00
Star, early, 3¼x3"	20.00
Trick or Treat, bat, cat, pumpkin, witch, owl & broom, MIB	28.00
Troll, Wrigley's Chewing Gum promo, Mirro Aluminum, 1966, 3¾"	25.00
Tulip, 2x3½"	16.50
Turkey, aluminum, cut-out hdl, 3x4"	5.00
Whale, flat bk, 3¾"	28.00
Witch on broomstick, copper-colored aluminum, unmk, 5¼x5"	17.00
12 Days of Christmas set, Chilton, 1978, MIB	26.00
6 sided (6 shapes), Made in Holland	18.00

Cookie Jars

The appeal of the cookie jar is universal; folks of all ages, both male and female, love to collect 'em! The early '30s heavy stoneware jars of a rather nondescript nature quickly gave way to figurals of every type imaginable. Those from the mid to late '30s were often decorated over the glaze with 'cold paint,' but by the early '40s underglaze decorating resulted in cheerful, bright, permanent colors and cookie jars that still have a new look fifty years later.

Stimulated by the high prices commanded by desirable cookie jars, a broad spectrum of 'new' cookie jars are flooding the marketplace in three categories: 1) Manufactures have expanded their lines with exciting new designs specifically geared toward attracting the collector market. 2) Limited editions and artist-designed jars have proliferated. 3) Reproductions, signed and unsigned, have pervaded the market, creating uncertainty among new collectors and inexperienced dealers. One of the most troublesome reproductions is the Little Red Riding Hood jar marked McCoy. Several Brush jars are being reproduced, and because the old molds are being used, these are especially deceptive. In addition to these reproductions, we've also been alerted to watch for cookie jars marked Brush-McCoy made from molds that Brush never used. Remember that none of Brush's cookie jars were marked Brush-McCoy, so any bearing the compound name is fraudulent. For more information on cookie jars and reproductions, we recommend *The Collector's Encyclopedia of Cookie Jars, Books I, II, and III* by Fred and Joyce Roerig; they are listed in the Directory under South Carolina. Another good source is *An Illustrated Guide to Cookie Jars, Books I and II,* by Ermagene Westfall. Our advisors for this category are Fred and Joyce Roerig; they are listed in the Directory under South Carolina.

The examples listed below were made by companies other than those found elsewhere in this book; see also specific manufacturers.

Adam & Eve Apple Tree, Fitz & Floyd, mk c FF 1987, minimum value ...**300.00**
After School Cookies Bus, Am Bisque, from $150 to **175.00**
Angel (Black), Wihoa's Cookie Classic #29-91 c G931-0999.....**150.00**
Animaniacs Chocolate Cookies, TM & c 94 WB Made In China, from $75 to....**95.00**
Blue Bonnet Sue, Nabisco, from $60 to................................**80.00**
Caterpiller, butterly finial, CA Originals, mk 853, from $75 to **95.00**
Circus Wagon, Sierra Vista Ceramics Pasadena Cal, from $75 to .**85.00**
City Cab, yel w/'chrome' detail, wht tires, mk Japan, from $175 to....**225.00**
Clown, Cookie incised on base, Ungemach, USA on bk, from $275 to ..**325.00**
Clown, Maurice c Calif USA **225.00**
Clown Head, Enesco Imports Japan E-5835, from $125 to..........**150.00**
Coach Lamp, Am Bisque, mk USA..**125.00**
Cookie Bakery, gr roof, CA Originals, mk 863 USA, from $35 to...**45.00**
Cookie Chef Head, blk ear hdls, Marsh Industries, unmk, from $125 to....**135.00**
Cookie King, Deforest of CA c 1957, from $400 to.....................**425.00**
Cookie Monster, Enesco/Jim Henson Productions, 1993, from $55 to ...**85.00**
Cookie Planet, rocket finial, Hirsch, mk WH 55 c, from $90 to ..**100.00**
Cookie Safe, Cardinal 309 c USA, from $60 to...........................**70.00**
Cool Cookie Penguin, Hallmark Cards Inc, from $300 to **350.00**
Corvette, North Am Ceramics, mk ACC J9 c 1986 NAC USA, from $100 to ..**125.00**
Cotton Pickers in Wagon, Wihoa's Cookie Classic #1-90, minimum value ...**150.00**

Cow Jumped Over the Moon, American Bisque, marked 806 USA, from $500.00 to $550.00.
(Photo courtesy Joyce Roerig)

Cow on Moon, Doranne of CA, mk J2 USA...............................**325.00**
Disney Channel, Treasure Craft, cylinder, from $100 to **125.00**
Dopey (Snow White), c Disney Treasure Craft, from $100 to.....**125.00**
Dragon, Doranne of CA, mk USA, from $150 to.......................**175.00**
Elephant, Sierra Vista CA, from $100 to **125.00**
Elephant w/Ball & Glove, Cara Marks for Sigma..., from $100 to ..**125.00**
Elvis w/Guitar, Happy Memories Collectibles, limited ed, from $300 to ..**375.00**
Ernie the Keebler Elf, c 1898 Keebler Co.....................................**80.00**
ET, wood-tone, unmk, from $45 to...**50.00**
Fat Cat, Sigma Tastesetter MCMLXXXV, from $225 to..............**275.00**
Fat Lady, Fitz & Floyd, mk c OCI, from $125 to..........................**150.00**
Foghorn-Leghorn, TM & c 1993 Warner Bros Inc...Taiwan, from $125 to..**150.00**
Frog Sitting, bow/flowers, CA Originals, mk 877 USA, from $40 to...**50.00**
Gingerbread Man, Jay Import Co Inc, 1996, from $20 to.............**30.00**
Goodies Pig, DeForest of CA c 1956, from $95 to.....................**110.00**
Gumball Machine, 1¢ Each, CA Originals, mk 890 USA, from $45 to ..**60.00**
Haunted House, Fitz & Floyd c FF 1987, from $150 to **175.00**
Henny (Dandee Hen), DeForest of CA USA, from $200 to.......**225.00**
Herman Munster, Star Jars/Treasure Craft c 1996..., from $225 to...**275.00**
Hobby Horse, 1956 WM Hirsch CA, from $100 to......................**125.00**
Hortense, Sigma, Designed by David Straus, from $125 to **150.00**
Humpty Dumpty, CA Originals, mk 882, from $100 to **125.00**
Humpty Dumpty, Clay Art, 1991, from $100 to **125.00**
Italian Couple, A Little Co c 1991..**180.00**

Jack-'O-Lantern w/Bat, Exclusively for Lotus...1989, from $60 to.**70.00**
James Dean, James Dean Foundation/Clay Art, 1996, from $65 to.......**75.00**
Kooky Klown, c By Newhauser Pat Pending Green Prod Cleveland..**125.00**
Las Vegas Jackpot Slot Machine, Doranne of CA, mk J 64 c USA **50.00**
Mammy w/Watermelon Slice (Bernadine), artist sgn TF, from $65 to..**75.00**
Michael Jordan & Bugs Bunny Space Jam, TM & c 1996 WB, $125 to......**150.00**
Mickey Mouse Club House, c Walt Disney Prod, from $100 to ..**125.00**
Nun, WH Hirsch Mgc Co CA USA, from $200 to.....................**225.00**
Owl, Fitz & Floyd Inc c MCMLXXVIII FF, from $40 to...............**50.00**
Owl, Whoo's eating 'owl' cookies?, Enesco E-9227 c 1997, from $20 to..**30.00**
Owl w/Guitar, Maurice c CA USA 1976 PG 62, from $90 to **110.00**
Peck O' Cookies Hen, William H Hirsch Mfg Co, from $90 to..**110.00**
Pig Clown, Cara Marks for Sigma..., from $125 to **150.00**
Pirate Bust, Treasure Craft c Made in USA, from $275 to **325.00**
Poodle, 1960 DeForest of CA USA, from $45 to..........................**55.00**
Queen, Maddux of CA USA c 210, from $100 to **125.00**
Radio, Tune In a Cookie, CA Originals, mk 888 USA, from $40 to ..**45.00**
Rudolph, Am Bisque, mk c RLM, minimum value......................**400.00**
Santa in Airplane, Exclusively for Lotus...China 1991, $25 to **35.00**
Scarecrow, CA Originals, mk 871 USA, from $100 to...............**125.00**
School Bus, Doranne of CA CJ 120 USA, from $100 to **125.00**
Sherman on the Mount, Am Greeting Corp, from $250 to **275.00**
Snoopy (World War I Flying Ace), Benjamin & Medwin Inc, from $55 to...**65.00**
Snowman, Doranne of CA, mk J 52 USA, from $200 to **225.00**
Soccer Ball, Treasure Craft c Made in USA, from $40 to..............**45.00**
Speedy Gonzales, TM & c 96 WB Made In China, from $75 to...**85.00**
Teakettle, emb colonial couple in profile, Am Bisque, from $25 to ..**35.00**
Teapot w/Flowers, CA Originals, mk 737, from $25 to.................**35.00**
Tom & Jerry, Harry James, c 90 Turner Entertainment Co, from $225 to...**250.00**
Tommy Pickles (Rugrats), Viacom Created By Klasky/Csupo, 1996....**75.00**
Treasure Chest w/Octopus, CA Orig, mk 878 USA, from $100 to ...**125.00**
Vegetable House, Department 56 1990, from $50 to **60.00**
Walt Disney Cookie Bus, c 1961 Walt Disney Prod, from $475 to..**500.00**
Wolf Head, Paw Print Wolfe Original Limited Ed, from $85 to..**100.00**
Woody Woodpecker Head, c 1967 Walter Lantz, minimum value...**750.00**
Yogi Bear, Harry James, c 1990 Hanna Barbera Prod Inc, from $300 to...**325.00**

Cooper, Susie

A twentieth-century ceramic designer whose works are now attracting the attention of collectors, Susie Cooper was first affiliated with the A.E. Gray Pottery in Henley, England, in 1922 where she designed in lustres and painted items with her own ideas as well. (Examples of Gray's lustreware is rare and costly.) By 1930 she and her brother-in-law, Jack Beeson, had established a family business. Her pottery soon became a success, and she was subsequently offered space at Crown Works, Burslem. In 1940 she received the honorary title of Royal Designer for Industry, the only such distinction ever awarded by the Royal Society of Arts solely for pottery design. Miss Cooper received the Order of the British Empire in the New Year's Honors List of 1979. She was the chief designer for the Wedgwood group from 1966 until she resigned in 1972. After 1980 she worked on a free-lance basis until her death in July 1995.

Berry set, Nosegay, 2½x9¼"+6 2x5½" bowls...............................**500.00**
Bowl, Longleaf, 7½" **60.00**
Bowl, Patricia Rose, 7¾" **50.00**
Bowl, soup; Tigerlily, 4¾" dia, w/6½" underplate.........................**35.00**
Breakfast set, Concentric Circles, earth tones, 10-pc, serves 2....**500.00**
Candle holders, Cornpoppy, 1½x3¾", pr **90.00**
Coffee can & saucer, Venetia, C2039 ....**45.00**
Coffee set, Tigerlily, Kestral-shape pot+cr/sug+6 demi c/s...........**750.00**
Coffeepot, #505 pattern, stylized floral, Kestrel shape **315.00**
Coffeepot, Nosegay, Kestral shape, 1932, 7".................................**450.00**

Coffeepot, Swansea Spray, Kestral shape, 7"	400.00
Cup, Asterix	42.00
Cup, Nosegay, #1163	42.00
Cup, Talisman, C1139	39.00
Cup & saucer, Glen Mist	62.00
Cup & saucer, Nosegay	75.00
Cup & saucer, Patricia Rose, Spiral shape	230.00
Cup & saucer, Printemps	80.00
Cup & saucer, Swansea Spray, 4 for	320.00
Cup & saucer, Wedding Ring	30.00
Gravy jug, Susan's Red, 6" to end of hdl	60.00
Gravy jug & plate, Swansea Spray, plate 6½" dia	75.00
Jug, Dresden Spray, 4½"	100.00
Jug, Gardenia, #2283, 4½", NM	99.00
Jug, Harmony, yel/orange/blk/gray bands, w/4 matching beakers	390.00
Jug, Longleaf, Kestrel shape, gr, 2½"	80.00
Jug, milk; Susan's Red, 4", NM	80.00
Jug, Tigerlily, Kestrel shape, 4¼"	67.00
Jug, water; Crescent Sgraffito, Kestrel shape, 7", NM	300.00
Mug, 3 emb designs on salmon-colored band, 19th C	120.00
Plate, Corinthian, 10½"	22.50
Plate, dinner; Antoinette	20.00
Plate, Longleaf, 7"	40.00
Plate, Patricia Rose, 10"	75.00
Plate, Romance Pink, 6"	10.00
Snack set, Deco Rooster, 3½x7½" tray, +2½" cup	140.00
Tea set, Nosegay, Kestral-shape 5" teapot+milk jug+sugar bowl	700.00
Tea set, Printeps, Kestral shape, 3-pc	250.00
Trio, Crescent Sgraffito, c/s+plate, NM	65.00
Trio, Glen Mist, c/s+plate	85.00
Trio, Romance Pink, c/s+plate, NM	45.00
Trio, Sunflower, c/s+plate	85.00

Coors

The firm that became known as Coors Porcelain Company in 1920 was founded in 1908 by John J. Herold, originally of the Roseville Pottery in Zanesville, Ohio. Though still in business today, they are best known for their artware vases and Rosebud dinnerware produced before 1939.

Coors vases produced before the late '30s were made in a matt finish; by the latter years of the decade, high-gloss glazes were also being used. Nearly fifty shapes were in production, and some of the more common forms were made in three sizes. Typical colors in matt are white, orange, blue, green, yellow, and tan. Yellow, blue, maroon, pink, and green are found in high gloss. All vases are marked with a triangular arrangement of the words 'Coors Colorado Pottery' enclosing the word 'Golden.' You may find vases (usually 6" to 6½") marked with the Colorado State Fair stamp and dated 1939. For such a vase, add $10.00 to the suggested values given below.

Our advisor for this category is Jo Ellen Winther; she is listed in the Directory under Colorado.

Rosebud

Ashtray	175.00
Bake pan, 12¼x8¼"	75.00
Bowl, mixing; 3-pt	45.00
Bowl, mixing; 6-pt	45.00
Bowl, oatmeal	35.00
Bowl, pudding; 7-pt	75.00
Cake knife	85.00
Casserole, Dutch; sm	72.00
Casserole, str sides, 5"	50.00

Casserole, str sides, 7"	55.00
Casserole, str sides, 8"	65.00
Casserole, w/lid, 9½"	100.00
Cup & saucer	45.00
Dish, vegetable; deep	35.00
Egg cup	50.00
Honey pot, w/spoon	300.00
Jar, utility; w/lid	85.00
Loaf pan, from $40 to	50.00
Pie plate	35.00
Pitcher, w/lid, sm	95.00
Plate, 5"	8.00
Plate, 8"	25.00
Ramekin, hdld	35.00
Shakers, kitchen; pr	45.00
Sugar bowl, w/lid	40.00
Teapot, 6-cup, from $160 to	185.00
Tumbler, ftd or w/hdl, from $105 to	130.00

Miscellaneous

Cake knife, Hawthorne, decalcomania	90.00
Casserole, Open Window, decalcomania, str sides, w/lid, lg	125.00
Creamer, Mello-Tone or Rockmount	15.00
Cup & saucer, Mello-Tone or Rockmount	15.00
Mortar & pestle, cobalt	55.00
Pitcher, Open Window, decalcomania, w/lid, lg	125.00
Shakers, Coorado, gr, pr	50.00
Shakers, Mello-Tone or Rockmount, pr	15.00
Teapot, Tulip, decalcomania	150.00
Vase, Beehive, orange matt, sm rings, 6"	45.00
Vase, Brighton, yel matt, bulbous, 8"	70.00
Vase, bud; yel high gloss, 8"	30.00

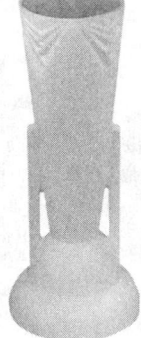

Vase, Deco style, white, 12", $345.00.

Vase, Golden, bl matt, integral hdls, 6"	55.00
Vase, Golden, burgundy high gloss, integral hdls, 6"	45.00
Vase, Leadville, gr matt, angle hdls, 8"	70.00
Vase, Matchless, gr matt, emb ribs, 8"	70.00
Vase, Trinidad, wht matt w/turq int, hdls, 12"	125.00

Copper

Handcrafted copper was made in America from early in the eighteenth century until about 1850, with the center of its production in Pennsylvania. Examples have been found signed by such notable coppersmiths as Kidd, Buchanan, Babb, Bently, and Harbeson. Of the many utilitarian items made, teakettles are the most desirable. Early examples from the eighteenth century were made with a dovetailed joint which was hammered and smoothed to a uniform thickness. Pots from the nineteenth century were seamed. Coffeepots were made in many shapes and sizes and along with mugs, kettles, warming pans, and measures are easiest to find. Stills ranging in sizes of up to fifty-gallon are popular with collectors today. Mary Frank Gaston has compiled a lovely book, *Antique Brass and Copper*, with many full-color photos and current market values.

Candy pan, iron hdls, 14" dia 195.00
Chestnut roaster, punched design on lid, iron hdl, 23"................160.00
Coffeepot, hinged brass spout cover, wood hdl, Majestic, 11½"...140.00
Coffeepot, hinged spout cover, wood hdl & finial, emb fleur-de-lis, 9"...140.00
Dipper, brass, hdl, 7½" dia, 26"..100.00
Funnel, 6x6"...35.00
Hot water container, rectangular, iron hdls.................................350.00
Jardiniere, appl brass decor, 3-legged brass stand, English, Victorian ..400.00
Jug, syrup; funnel spout, New England, 19th C............................225.00
Kettle, fancy wood & brass hdl, brass finial, China, 9x6½" dia ..250.00
Kettle, hinged lid, brass hdl & finial, European, 19th C, 8½x6" ...250.00
Kettle, preserving; iron hdls, 26" dia 350.00
Kettle, stewing; dvtl, 8½x13½" 175.00
Measure, ½-cup, 2½"...25.00
Pitcher, hammered, curved hdl riveted to rim, 8" 95.00
Pitcher, syrup; dvtl, 19th C, 6"...95.00
Planter, brass lions' heads, brass paw ft, English, 19th C, 15x13"..1,400.00
Plaque, emb roses, fluted border, 14"...90.00
Saucepan, dvtl on base, iron hdl, 19th C, 5½x9" dia 175.00
Saucepan, dvtl, w/lid, GF Baker Phila, 11" dia 245.00
Saucepans, dvtl, HP/Harrods Stores Ltd London, 4" to 8", w/lids, 6 for ..1,100.00
Shoehorn, from hammered sheet, handmade, early 1800s, 8⅞" 40.00
Skimmer, iron hdl, 7½" dia, 34" 100.00
Skimmer, pierced bowl, 5" W, 22" 100.00
Steamer, iron hdl, English, 19th C, 10x24x15"............................650.00
Teakettle, dvtl, brass/copper hdl, brass acorn finial, sm dents, 12"..195.00
Teakettle, gooseneck, dvtl, fixed brass hdl w/trn wood grip.........135.00

Teakettle, gooseneck spout, hinged copper handle, brass finial, dovetailed, signed Henry Trottmann, early nineteenth century, 11⅝x7½", EX, $500.00. (Photo courtesy Horst Auctioneers)

Tray, spun, ca 1900, 12" dia...80.00
Tub, crude soldering around top, 12x14" 75.00
Warming pan, walnut trn hdl, 44" L..175.00
Wash boiler, Sullivan Geiger Co Indianapolis, 13x24"................170.00

Copper Lustre

Copper lustre is a term referring to a type of pottery made in Staffordshire after the turn of the nineteenth century. It is finished in a metallic rusty-brown glaze resembling true copper. Pitchers are found in abundance, ranging from simple styles with dull bands of color to those with fancy handles and bands of embossed, polychromed flowers. Bowls are common; goblets, mugs, teapots, and sugar bowls much less so. It's easy to find, but not in good condition. Pieces with hand-painted decoration and those with historical transfers are the most valuable.

Bowl, bl band w/floral decor, 3½x6¼" dia, from $35 to 45.00

Creamer, church w/bell tower & cottage motif, 4", from $70 to ...80.00
Master salt, beaded rim w/cobalt band, relief decor, 2⅝"..............40.00
Mug, floral decor, 3", from $60 to 75.00
Pitcher, dolphin hdl, Neptune mask spout, emb flower basket, 5½" ...160.00
Pitcher, mother & daughter transfer on ea side, 7" 275.00
Sugar bowl, over-glazed enamel floral decor, w/lid, sq body, 6" 90.00
Vase, cobalt bands w/ applied decor, fluted top, 6".......................80.00
Vase, cottage/tower, scalloped rim w/emb mc flowers, 5½"...............65.00

Coralene Glass

Coralene is a unique type of art glass easily recognized by the tiny grains of glass that form its decoration. Lacy allover patterns of seaweed, geometrics, and florals were used, as well as solid forms such as fish, plants, and single blossoms. (Seaweed is most commonly found and not as valuable as the other types of decoration.) It was made by several glasshouses both here and abroad. Values are based to a considerable extent on the amount of beading that remains. Our advisors for this category are Betty and Clarence Maier; they are listed in the Directory under Pennsylvania.

Cracker jar, lt cranberry w/yel seaweed (losses), SP mts, 7x5¾" .300.00
Mug, amber satin w/orange seaweed, turq hdl, 2" 150.00
Pitcher, bl satin w/yel seaweed, wht int, sq top, water sz 975.00
Sugar shaker, bl Raindrop MOP w/pk seaweed, spherical, 6"...1,000.00
Tumbler, pk Dmn Quilt w/wht bellflowers & daisies, 3¾" 230.00
Tumbler, pk to wht Dmn Quilt MOP w/wht floral, 3¾" 175.00
Vase, bl Dmn Quilt w/yel flowers & gr leaves, stick neck, 5¾" 90.00
Vase, bl Herringbone w/alternating gold dots & stripes, 7½" 150.00
Vase, cranberry w/mc floral & gold, 3-ftd, 10¼x4⅝"...................515.00
Vase, peachblow w/yel seaweed, wht int, ovoid, Webb, 9½".......425.00
Vase, pk w/yel seaweed, ovoid w/short collar neck, 5x3½"..........260.00

Cordey

The Cordey China Company was founded in 1942 in Trenton, New Jersey, by Boleslaw Cybis. The operation was small with less than a dozen workers. They produced figurines, vases, lamps, and similar wares, much of which was marketed through gift shops both nationwide and abroad. Though the earlier wares were made of plaster, Cybis soon developed his own formula for a porcelain composition which he called 'Papka.' Cordey figurines and busts were characterized by old-world charm, Rococo scrolls, delicate floral appliques, ruffles, and real lace which was dipped in liquefied clay to add dimension to the work.

Although on rare occasions some items were not numbered or signed, the 'basic' figure was cast both with numbers and the Cordey signature. The molded pieces were then individually decorated and each marked with its own impressed identification number as well as a mark to indicate the artist-decorator. Their numbering system began with 200 and in later years progressed into the 8000s. As can best be established, Cordey continued production until sometime in the mid-1950s. Boleslaw Cybis died in 1957, his wife in 1958.

Due to the increased availability of Cordey on the Internet over the last year, values of the more common pieces have fallen off. Our advisor for this category is Sharon A. Payne; she is listed in the Directory under Washington.

Key: ff — full figure

#313, bust of woman, sgn MB Cybis..225.00
#324, courting mallards, 14", pr..495.00
#914, clock, rococo scrolls & appl roses w/gold, Lanshire, 9½"......95.00

#1023, console bowl, lg roses w/gold, oblong, 6x15x8" 85.00
#1047, vase, rtcl top w/appl flower band, 12", EX 75.00
#3003/#4005, man & lady, elaborate hair, appl flowers, 7", pr.......90.00
#4027, lady w/parasol, 8" 90.00
#4034-G, lady, ff, many lace ruffles, appl flowers, long curls, 8" ..110.00
#4049-P, lady, ff, 10" 110.00
#4073, Victorian lady w/lace top & blk dress, 13" 150.00
#5011, bust of lady, lace collar, long curls, common, 6" 60.00
#5015, bust of lady, 6" 60.00
#5025, bust of lady, ruffled bodice, lg hat, blk hair, 6¾" 60.00
#5027, bust of lady, long curls, lace & appl flowers, 7½", NM 50.00
#5028, lady, ff, blond ringlets, Jr Colonial group, 6¾" 60.00
#5036, lady, ¾-figure, pk & bl, hands away, 8¾" 70.00
#5042, Monsieur DuBarry, man in fine clothes, long curls, ff, 11" ...95.00
#5045, boy figure w/basket of breadsticks, 9½" 75.00
#5047/#5048, man & lady, ff, she w/grapes/jar, he w/flowers, 11", pr ..125.00
#5069, Marcele, ¾-bust, much lace & roses, scarce......................125.00
#5084, Madam DuBarry, Victorian lady, ff, 11" 110.00
#5088-A, lady, ff, hat w/lg feathers, lace sleeves, 10¾" 75.00
#5091, man, ff, holds coattail wide as if to bow, 10½" 55.00
#6004, bluebird on stump, lg...75.00
#7028, wall shelf, Art Nouveau nude w/cornucopia, 8x6½"..........85.00
#8021, trinket box, appl flowers, 3x6½x4¾"..................................55.00
#9009, clock, appl roses, clockworks mk Lanshire, 13x11½" 150.00
Box, appl roses & buds on lid, ftd, common, 4½x5" sq 50.00
Bust, Neopolitan squire, 14" 150.00
Cat, wht w/gr eyes, pk bow & flower at neck, sitting, 8" 95.00
Dish, Cupid among bed of roses w/lace shawl, gold trim, 8½x6"...110.00

Corkscrews

The history of the corkscrew dates back to the mid-1600s, when wine makers concluded that the best-aged wine was that stored in smaller containers, either stoneware or glass. Since plugs left unsealed were often damaged by rodents, corks were cut off flush with the bottle top and sealed with wax or a metal cover. Removing the cork cleanly with none left to grasp became a problem. The task was found to be relatively simple using the worm on the end of a flintlock gun rod. So the corkscrew evolved. Endless patents have been issued for mechanized models. Handles range from carved wood, ivory, and bone to porcelain and repousse silver. Exotic materials such as agate, mother-of-pearl, and gold plate were also used on occasion. Celluloid lady's legs are popular.

For further information, we recommend *The Ultimate Corkscrew Book* and *Bull's Pocket Guide to Corkscrews* by Donald Bull, our advisor for this category. He is listed in the Directory under Virginia. In the following descriptions, values are for examples in excellent condition, unless noted otherwise.

Figural, devil with corkscrew tail, red-painted cast iron, 3½", EX, $75.00.

Artistic style, kissing birds hdl, Just Anderson, Denmark, $125 to...150.00
Bow, folding, cap lifter frets, from $60 to.....................................80.00

Bow, simple, folding type w/corkscrew only, from $10 to..............50.00
Champagne tap, New Century, Williamson Co, from $50 to........75.00
Codd bottle opener added to boxwood hdl, J&W Roper Birmingham 125.00
Columbus split fr, metal hdl, mk Lamgbein Germany, from $100 to........150.00
Cvd tusk resembling toucan's head, bell cap, Walker, 1900, $300 to........400.00
Dbl lever, A1, Pat James Heeley & Sons...England, 1888, from $125 to .175.00
Dbl lever, Barman, Party Bottle Opener on shirt front, 1959, orig box 150.00
Dbl lever, Hootch Owl, Pat #, Mar 17, 1936, from $1,000 to..1,500.00
Figural, fish, cast metal, detailed, lg, from $75 to.........................100.00
Figural, Kirby, SP, Jolly Good Mixer, from $150 to 200.00
Figural, lion (prancing), cap-lifter mouth, Made in Israel, $50 to .75.00
Figural, mermaid, cast metal, waiter's friend, Davis Improved Pat..1,200.00
Finger pull, full grip (Cellarman's Corkscrew), simple, unmk, up to....20.00
Finger pull, 2- or 3- finger, w/cap lifter, various mks, from $5 to....50.00
Finger pull, 3-finger, leather-wrapped hdl, from $75 to 100.00
Flynut, fixed to fr, mk J Prille Depose Paris/Helice JHP Depose....80.00
Frame, Farrow & Jackson type, unmk butterfly hdl w/centering button ...250.00
Lazy tong, Pullezi, Heeley's Orig Pat, 1902, from $150 to 300.00
Murphy, fr w/locking hdl, mk R Murphy Boston, from $75 to 100.00
Peg & worm, various metals & ends, ea from $75 to 200.00
Picnic, sterling sheath, cap lifter, Muller & Schmidt, from $75 to...125.00
Pocket folder, nickel silver hdls mk Wilson Co, from $175 to 200.00
Prong puller, cap lifter swivels from inside hdl, For Crown Corks..........100.00
Prong puller, Magic Cork Extractor, Lucian Mumford, 1879 or 1892....700.00
Roundlet, sterling threaded case slides apart to release worm, $150 to..300.00
Scissors, ornate design on German silver hdls, from $800 to ...1,000.00
Silver, cap lifter, corkscrew in hdl, from $75 to 125.00
Silver, peanut-shaped hdl ends, from $400 to 500.00
Single lever, Lund & Hipkins, 1854, from $100 to 250.00
Slide out, German or Fr version of Jansen Pat, from $150 to......250.00
Spring, steel, Hercules, from $20 to...30.00
Syroco, man in top hat (Old Codger/Codger/Topper), from $90 to ..150.00
T-hdl, ivory or bone, fr type, mini, from $100 to 300.00
T-hdl, simple trn wood, direct pull, from $10 to 75.00
T-hdl, wood w/narrow worm, mid-sz, from $15 to.........................25.00
Tablespoon w/corkscrew, gold-wash sterling, gold-plated worm, $300 to....350.00
Tools, Nathan Jenkins' 1930 Am Pat, 15 Tools in 1, from $150 to..200.00
Waiter's Friend, Davis Pat, knife blade on top of hdl, from $125 to..175.00
2-pillar fr w/ivory hand gripping bar, early 19th C, from $2,000 to..3,000.00

Cosmos

Cosmos, sometimes called Stemless Daisy, is a patterned glass tableware produced from 1894 through 1915 by Consolidated Lamp and Glass Company. Relief-molded flowers on a finely crosscut background were painted in soft colors of pink, blue, and yellow. Though nearly all were made of milk glass, a few items may be found in clear glass with the designs painted on. In addition to the tableware, lamps were also made.

Bottle, cologne; orig stopper, rare, from $275 to 300.00
Butter dish, 5x8"...275.00
Creamer 150.00
Lamp, bouquet; kerosene, 24" 575.00
Lamp, bouquet; slender base, rnd globe, all orig, 16" 525.00
Lamp, mini, 7½", EX..275.00
Lamp, 10"...450.00
Pickle castor, mk SP fr, from $600 to 700.00
Pitcher, milk; 5"..250.00
Pitcher, syrup; 6"...300.00
Pitcher, water...350.00
Shakers, tall, orig lids, pr..175.00
Spooner...125.00
Sugar bowl, open 150.00

Sugar bowl, w/lid 185.00
Sugar shaker...400.00
Tumbler, 3¾" 75.00

Cottageware

You'll find a varied assortment of novelty dinnerware items, all styled as cozy little English cottages or huts with cone-shaped roofs; some may have a waterwheel or a windmill. Marks will vary. English-made Price Brothers or Beswick pieces are valued in the same range as those marked Occupied Japan, while items marked simply Japan are considerably less pricey. Our advisor for this category is Grace Klender; she is listed in the Directory under Ohio. All of the following examples are Price Brothers/Kensington unless noted otherwise.

Bank, dbl slot, 4½x3½x5"...95.00
Bell, minimum value..150.00
Biscuit jar, wicker hdl, Maruhon Ware, Occupied Japan, 6½" 92.50
Bowl, salad..65.00
Butter dish...65.00
Butter dish, oval, Burlington Ware, 6"......................60.00
Butter dish, rnd, Beswick, England, w/lid, 3½x6", from $75 to...100.00
Butter pat, emb cottage, rectangular, Occupied Japan 20.00
Chocolate pot..148.00
Condiment set, mustard, 2½" s&p on 5" hdld leaf tray 85.00
Condiment set, mustard pot, s&p, row arrangement, 6" 50.00
Condiment set, mustard pot, s&p, tray, row arrangement, 7¾"...50.00
Condiment set, 3-part cottage on shaped tray w/appl bush, 4½" ..85.00
Cookie jar, pk/brn/gr, sq, Japan, 8½x5½" 75.00
Cookie jar, windmill, wicker hdl................................165.00
Cookie jar/canister, cylindrical, rare sz, 8x3¾" 275.00
Cookie jar/canister, cylindrical, 8½x5"......................140.00
Cookie/biscuit jar, Occupied Japan 95.00
Creamer, windmill, Occupied Japan, 2⅝" 30.00
Creamer & sugar bowl, 2½x4½"...................................50.00

Cup and saucer, 3⅜", 5½", $55.00; Chocolate cup and saucer, straight sides, 3¾", 5⅜", $45.00.

Cup & saucer, 2½", 4½" 50.00
Demitasse pot 110.00
Dish w/cover, Occupied Japan, sm..............................40.00
Egg cup set, 4 on 6" sq tray...65.00
Gravy boat & tray, rare 275.00
Grease jar, Occupied Japan, from $25 to 38.00
Hot water pot, Westminster, England, 8½x4" 50.00
Marmalade 45.00
Marmalade & jelly, 2 houses cojoined 85.00
Mug, 3⅞" 55.00
Pin tray, 4" dia 22.00
Pitcher, emb cottage, lg flower on hdl.......................150.00
Pitcher, tankard; rnd, 7⅞"...138.00

Platter, oval, 11¾x7½"...65.00
Reamer, Japan 65.00
Sugar box, for cubes, 5¾" L..50.00
Tea set, Japan, child's, serves 4................................165.00
Teapot, Keele Street, +cr/sug 95.00
Teapot, Occupied Japan, 6½".......................................55.00
Teapot, 6¼"...70.00
Toast rack, 3-slot, 3½"...75.00
Toast rack, 4-slot, 5½"...85.00
Tumbler, Occupied Japan, 3½", set of 6........................65.00

Coverlets

The Jacquard attachment for hand looms represented a culmination of weaving developments made in France. Introduced to America by the early 1820s, it gave professional weavers the ability to easily create complex patterns with curved lines. Those who could afford the new loom adaptation could now use hole-punched pasteboard cards to weave floral patterns that before could only be achieved with intense labor on a draw-loom.

Before the Jacquard mechanism, most weavers made their coverlets in geometric patterns. Use of indigo-blue and brightly colored wools often livened the twills and overshot patterns available to the small-loom home weaver. Those who had larger multiple-harness looms could produce warm double-woven, twill-block, or summer-and-winter designs.

While the new floral and pictorial patterns' popularity had displaced the geometrics in urban areas, the mid-Atlantic, and the Midwest by the 1840s, even factory production of the Jacquard coverlets was disrupted by cotton and wool shortages during the Civil War. A revived production in the 1870s saw a style change to a center-medallion motif, but a new fad for white 'Marseilles' spreads soon halted sales of Jacquard-woven coverlets. Production of Jacquard carpets continued to the turn of the century.

Rural and frontier weavers continued to make geometric-design coverlets through the nineteenth century, and local craft revivals have continued the tradition through this century. All-cotton overshots were factory produced in Kentucky from the 1940s, and factories and professional weavers made cotton-and-wool overshots during the past decade. Many Jacquard-woven coverlets have dates and names of places and people (often the intended owner — not the weaver) woven into corners or borders. In the listings that follow, examples are blue and white and in excellent condition unless noted otherwise. When dates are included, they appear on the coverlet itself as part of the woven design.

Key: mdl — medallion

Jacquard

Basket mdl, swags & flowers, indigo/red/gold, fringe, 1840s, 80x95" ...465.00
Bird border, 3-color, fringe, PA, 1854, lg, EX+.............................800.00
Birds/trees/flowers, 3-color, fringe 2 sides, sgn/1855, 80x96" 525.00
Birds/trees/stars, 4-color, fringe, PA, sgn/1850, 96x76" 750.00
Central mdl w/foliate border, 2-pc, sgn/1850, 86x83"..................460.00
Central mdls, eagle corners, red/wht, fringe, late 1800s, 78x86", VG...275.00
Church center, stars & angels, 3-color, 1860s, 78x85".............475.00
Circles/ovals/fans, red/bl/blk, fringe, 1850s, 72x90" 450.00
Eagle ea corner, center swag mdl, 3-color, fringe, 1850s, 72x82"..450.00
Eagle in ea corner, red/wht, PA, 1840-50, 82x85", EX..............600.00
Floral mdl, Washington corners w/eagles/etc, red/wht, 1-pc, 1869, 74"..525.00
Floral mdl w/geometric ground, 3-color, fringe, PA, 1840s, lg, VG........425.00
Floral mdls/border, 2-pc, 1856, 69x75", VG 440.00
Floral mdls/borders, quail corners, red/gr/bl, summer/winter, 80x86"...470.00
Floral mdls/sunbursts/grid, 3-color, 2-pc dbl, 73x76", VG 250.00

Floral mdls, scrolled tulip border, gr/red/natural, 90x74", EX............385.00
Floral/geometric mdls w/leaf border, rose corners, 3-color, 2-pc ..200.00
Florals & swirls, brn/navy, fringe, ltweight, PA, 1843, 82x98", NM ..825.00
Flower urns, rose/buildings borders, 4-color, 2-pc, 1859, 66x83".350.00
Geometric, bl/lt bl/red/wht, no fringe, MD, 1839, 73x84", VG+ 425.00
Geometric, house border, center seam, OH, 1848, 72x83", VG......325.00
Geometric floral, navy/orange/gr/brn, PA, 1840s?, 90x84" 600.00
Geometrics, eagles on 3 borders, red/wht/bl, PA, 1837, 81x91" ..650.00
Grapevine border w/leaf/heart mdls, red/bl/wht/navy, 2-pc, 69x86"......200.00
Houses/stars/flowers, salmon/gr/wht/navy, 2-pc, single weave, 74x80".300.00
Mdl center, eagles/shields in corners, 4-color, PA, stains, 76x84".250.00
Peacock w/young/flower urns, fringe 1 side, OH, 76x84" 450.00
Rose mdls (4), eagle & tree borders, bl/wht/red/lt bl, 2-pc, 88x76"..550.00
Rose mdls w/branch borders, 2-pc, 1839, 72x90" 300.00
Snow flakes/flower urns, 1-pc, 1859, 73x86" 415.00
Snowball, 2-pc, lt stain, 72x84" 250.00
Star mdl & flowers, red/wht, heavy border, long fringe, 19th C, 90x80"..425.00
Star mdls, oak-leaf border, red/bl/gr/cream, HF Stager...PA, 86" sq ..460.00
Star mdls/tulips, fruit baskets/houses in border, 3-color, 80" 440.00
Urns of flowers, bldgs/palm tree border, 2-pc, 68x80" 440.00

Overshot

Block & 9 Patch, rust/wht, 2-pc, early 1900s, 10x86", VG 300.00
Floral mdls, eagles in border, NY 1833, 79x98", EX......................525.00
Geometrics, bl & wht, 2-pc, minor stains/wear, 19th C, 60x84".250.00
Geometrics, red & wht, 3-pc, 19th C, 88x72", NM 400.00
Lover's knot, dk bl/dk red/natural, by LH Kincheloe, WV, 90x100", VG..385.00
Optical, gr & tan, gr fringe, 3-pc, late 1800s, 97x101" 325.00
Optical, natural/lt gold, 2-pc, 77x92" 110.00
Stripes w/circles & blocks, 2 shades of bl w/red, 2-pc, 90x80" 440.00

Miscellaneous

Linsey-woolsey, indigo bl, floral quilting, 1837, 104" sq...........2,750.00
Linsey-woolsey, pumpkin colored, 2-pc, late 1700s, 95x86".....2,000.00

Cowan

Guy Cowan opened a small pottery near Cleveland, Ohio, in 1913, where he made tile and artware on a small scale from the natural red clay available there. He developed distinctive glazes — necessary, he felt, to cover the dark red body. After the war and a temporary halt in production, Cowan moved his pottery to Rocky River, where he made a commercial line of artware utilizing a highly-fired white porcelain. Although he acquiesced to the necessity of mass production, every effort was made to insure a product of highest quality. Fine artists, among them Waylande Gregory, Thelma Frazier, and Viktor Schreckengost, designed pieces which were often produced in limited editions, some of which sell today for prices in the thousands. Most of the ware was marked 'Cowan,' except for the 1930 mass-produced line called 'Lakeware.' Falling under the crunch of the Great Depression, the pottery closed in 1931.

The use of an asterisk (*) in the listing below indicates a nonfactory name that is being provided as a suggested name for the convenience of present-day collectors. One example is the glaze *Original Ivory, which is a high-gloss white that resembles undecorated porcelain. It was used on many of Cowan's lady 'flower figures' (Cowan's more graceful term for what some collectors call frogs).

Our advisor for this category is Mark Bassett; he is listed in the Directory under Ohio. With Victoria Naumann, Mark is the author of *Cowan Pottery and the Cleveland School*, a detailed history of Cowan Pottery and of Guy Cowan's students, colleagues, and designers. Prices quoted are for examples in mint condition, unless noted otherwise.

Bookends, Boy/Girl, FN Wilcox, *Original Ivory, #521, 6½", pr .250.00
Box, candy, R Josset, *Pippin Green, #X-14, 6¼" 250.00
Candelabra, C-Shaped Triple, April Green, #751, 5", pr 100.00
Candlesticks, low hdls, Larkspur, #528, 3½", pr...........................60.00
Cigarette jar, mtn goat finial, Eckhardt, Oriental Red, #X-9, 7¼".300.00
Figurine, flamingo, W Gregory, Special Ivory, 11½"...................500.00
Flower frog, Anticipation, RG Cowan, *Orig Ivory, #708, 7¾"..800.00
Flower frog, Repose, RG Cowan, *Original Ivory, #712, 6½" 300.00
Flower frog, Triumphant, RG Cowan, *Original Ivory, #717, 15½"...2,500.00
Lamp, Grecian females, 4 panels, Gregory, Parchment Blue, #908, 13½"..350.00
Lamp, molded leaf designs, hdls, Marigold, 10¾" 225.00

Vases, Chinese Bird, designed by R. Guy Cowan, Melon Green, shape #747, 1st Prize (pottery) 1927 Cleveland Museum of Art May Show, 11¼", $700.00 each. (Photo courtesy David Rago)

Vase, Delphinium (?), #571, stamped, 10¾" 300.00
Vase, Pillow, Antique Green, #798, 5" 125.00
Wall plaque, The Hunt, V Schreckengost, mc, #X-44, 11½" ..1,500.00

Cracker Jack

Kids have been buying Cracker Jack since it was first introduced in the 1890s. By 1912 it was packaged with a free toy inside. Before the first kernel was crunched, eager fingers had retrieved the surprise from the depth of the box — actually no easy task, considering the care required to keep the contents so swiftly displaced from spilling over the side! Though a little older, perhaps, many of those same kids still are looking — just as eagerly — for the Cracker Jack prizes. Point of sale, company collectibles, and the prizes as well have over the years reflected America's changing culture. Grocer sales and incentives from around the turn of the century — paper dolls, postcards, and song books — were often marked Rueckheim Brothers (the inventors of Cracker Jack) or Reliable Confections. Over the years the company made some changes, leaving a trail of clues that often help collectors date their items. The company's name changed in 1922 from Rueckheim Brothers & Eckstein (who had been made a partner for inventing a method for keeping the caramelized kernels from sticking together) to The Cracker Jack Company. Their Brooklyn office was open from 1914 until it closed in 1923 The first time the sailor Jack logo was used on their packaging was in 1919. The sailor image of a Rueckheim child (with red, white, and blue colors) was introduced by these German immigrants in an attempt to show America support during the time of heightened patriotism after WW I. For packages and 'point of sale' dating, note that the word 'prize' was used from 1912 to 1925, 'novelty' from 1925 to 1932, and 'toy' from 1933 on.

The first loose-packed prizes were toys made of wood, clay, tin, metal, and lithographed paper (the reason some early prizes are stained). Plastic toys were introduced in 1946. Paper wrapped for safety purposes in 1948, subjects echo the 'hype' of the day — yo-yos, tops, whistles, and sports cards in the simple, peaceful days of our country, propaganda and war toys in the '40s, games in the '50s, and space toys in the '60s. Few of the estimated 15 billion prizes were marked. Advertising items from Angelus Marshmallow and Checkers Confections (cousins of the Cracker Jack family) are also collectible. When no condition is indicated, the items listed below are assumed to be in excellent to mint condition. 'CJ' indicates that the item is marked. Note: An often-asked question concerns the tin Toonerville Trolley called 'CJ.' No data has been found in the factory archives to authenticate this item; it is assumed that the 'CJ' merely refers to its small size. For further information see *Cracker Jack Toys, The Complete, Unofficial Guide for Collectors*, by Larry White. Our co-advisors for this category are Wes Johnson (listed in the Directory under Kentucky) and Harriet Joyce (under Florida). Also look for *The Prize Insider* newsletter listed in the Directory under Clubs, Newsletters, and Catalogs.

Novelty paper cards, pull tab and eyes open and close, came in assortment of people, animals, fruit, and vegetables, ca 1920s, $65.00 each. (Photo courtesy Harriet Joyce)

Dealer Incentives and Premiums

Badge, pin-bk, celluloid, lady w/CJ label reverse, 1905, 1¼"......85.00
Bat, baseball; wood, Hillerich & Bradsby, CJ, full sz......85.00
Blotter, CJ question mk box, yel, 7¾x3¾"......185.00
Book, pocket; jester on cover, CJ Riddles......30.00
Book, pocket; riddle/sailor boy/dog on cover, RWB, CJ, 1919......55.00
Book, recipe; Angelus, 1930s......22.00
Book, Uncle Sam Song Book, CJ, 1911, ea......40.00
Cart w/2 movable wheels, wood dowel tongue, CJ......50.00
Corkscrew/opener, metal plated, CJ/Angelus, 3¾" tube case......85.00
Golf tee set, wood tees in paper 'matchbook' folder, CJ, 1920s...725.00
Harmonica, full scale, emb CJ, early, 5⅛"......365.00
Jigsaw puzzle, CJ or Checkers, 1 of 4, 7x10", in envelope......35.00
Marbles, Akro set of 12 in box w/instructions, CJ, 1929......950.00
Mask, Halloween; paper, CJ, series, 10" or 12", ea......28.00
Match holder, hinged, eng gold-tone case, CJ, 2½x1⅞"......650.00
Mirror, oval, Angelus (redhead or blond) on box......89.00
Palm puzzle, mirror bk, CJ, mk Germany/RWB, 1910-14, 1½"...110.00
Pen, ink; w/nib, tin litho bbl, CJ......485.00
Pencil top clip, metal/celluloid, oval boy & dog logo......220.00
Pencil top clip, metal/celluloid, tube shape w/pkg......220.00
Postcard, bear, 1 of 16, CJ, 1907, ea......35.00
Puzzle, metal, CJ/Angelus, 1 of 15, '34, in envelope, ea......14.00
Riddle card, 2 series of 20, w/pkg/from factory, CJ, 1907, ea......10.00
Tablet, school; CJ, 1929, 8x10"......195.00
Thimble, aluminum, CJ Co/Angelus, red pnt, rare, ea......165.00
Truck, steel, wood wheels for CJ pkg, unmk......100.00
Wings, air corps type, silver or blk, stud-bk, CJ, 1930s, 3", ea......55.00

Packaging

Box, popcorn; Question Mark box end for CJ 'Toy,' 1933-34......250.00
Box, popcorn; red scroll border, CJ 'Prize,' 1912-25, ea......150.00
Box, popcorn; store display, CJ 'Novelty,' 1925-32, ea......90.00
Canister, tin, CJ Candy Corn Crisp, 10-oz......75.00
Canister, tin, CJ Coconut Corn Crisp, 1-lb......55.00
Canister, tin, CJ Coconut Corn Crisp, 10-oz......65.00
CJ Commemorative canister, mc scene, 1990s, ea......9.00
CJ Commemorative canister, wht w/red scroll, 1980s, ea......8.00
Crate, shipping; wood, CJ, Rueckheim Bros Eck, 1902-22, lg......165.00

Prizes, Cast Metal

Badge, shield, CJ Jr Detective, silver, 1931, 1¼"......50.00
Badge, 6-point star, mc CJ Police, silver, 1931, 1¼"......55.00
Button, stud bk, Me for Cracker Jack, boy & dog, oval......55.00
Button, stud bk, Xd bats & ball, CJ pitcher/etc series, 1928......130.00
Chair, T (Tootsie), 3 different sectional pcs, pnt, mini, ea......12.00
Coins, Presidents, 31 series, CJ, 1933, ea......6.00
Dollhouse items; lantern, mug, candlestick, etc; no mk, ea......6.50
Horse & wagon, CJ, 3-D, silver or gold, early, 2½", ea......250.00
Pistol, soft lead, inked, CJ on bbl, early, rare, 2⅛"......180.00
Ring, alphabet letter setting (series), unmk, ea......4.00
Rocking horse, no rider, 3-D, inked, early, 1⅛"......25.00
Rocking horse w/boy, 3-D, inked, early, 1½"......32.00
Spinner, early pkg in center, 'More You Eat...,' CJ, rare......295.00
Tootsietoy series: boats, cars, animals; 1931, ¾"-1½", ea......7.00

Prizes, Paper

Baseball CJ score counter, 3⅜" L......130.00
Book, Animals (or Birds), to color, Makatoy, unmk, 1949, mini...35.00
Book, Bess & Bill on CJ Hill, series of 12, 1937, mini......105.00
Book, Birds We Know, CJ, 1928, mini......105.00
Book, Chaplin flip book, CJ, 1920s, ea......140.00
Book, drawing w/tracing paper, CJ, 1920s, mini......110.00
Book, Twigg & Sprigg, CJ, 1930, mini......105.00
Booklet, stickers/wisecracks/riddles, Borden, CJ, 1965 on......3.00
Decal, cartoon or nursery rhyme figure, 1947-49, CJ......12.00
Disguise, ears, red (out of carrier), unmk, 1950, pr......30.00
Disguise, ears, red (still in carrier), CJ, 1950, pr......65.00
Disguise, glasses, hinged, cello lenses, CJ Where Ever..., 1933......65.00
Disguise, glasses, hinged, w/eyeballs, unmk, 1933......6.00
Disguise, mustache, blk/brn, in carrier, CJ, 1949......55.00
Fan, lady's, folding, mc, unmk......20.00
Fortune Teller, boy/dog on film in envelope, CJ, 1920s, 1¾x2½".80.00
Fortune wheel, 2-pc litho, turn for fortune, CJ, 1¾"......70.00
Game, Midget Auto Race, wheel spins, CJ, 1949, 3⅜" H......25.00
Game spinner, ...baseball at home, rectangle, CJ, 2¾" W......125.00
Game spinner, ...baseball at home, unmk, 1946, 1½" dia......60.00
Hat, fold out, More You Eat/More You Want, CJ, early......75.00
Hat, Indian headdress, CJ, 1931, 2½" H......125.00
Hat, Indian headdress, CJ, 1950s, 5⅝" H......275.00
Hat, Me for CJ, early, ea......120.00
Hat visor, baseball, tie-on string, red or gr, CJ, 1931......120.00
Magic game book, erasable slate, CJ, series of 13, 1946, ea......25.00
Movie, boy at blkboard, turn wheel: draws/erases, CJ, 1931, 2"..175.00
Movie, Goofy Zoo, trn wheel(s): change animals, unmk, 1939......25.00
Movie, pull tab for 2nd picture, series, CJ, 1943, 1¼", ea......105.00
Movie, pull tab for 2nd picture, yel, early, 3", in envelope......125.00
Paper dolls, Boggie, Betty & Billie......125.00
Sand toy pictures, pours for action, series of 14, 1967, ea......55.00
Top, golf game, wood stick center, CJ, 1933......57.00
Top, string; Rainbow Spinner, 2-pc, cb, different designs, ea......45.00
Transfer, iron-on, sport figure or patriotic, CJ, 1939, ea......22.00
Transfer, iron-on, sport figure or patriotic, unmk, 1939, ea......6.00
Whistle, Blow for More, CJ box/boy/dog, yel, 1931, ea......55.00

Whistle, Blow for More, CJ/Angelus pkgs, 1928, '31 or '33, ea.....**45.00**
Whistle, pressed paper, series of 10, 1948-49, CJ, 1¼x2", ea.........**34.00**
Whistle, Razz Zooka, C Carey Cloud design, CJ, 1949.................**32.00**

Prizes, Plastic

Animals, standup, letter on bk, series of 26, Nosco, 1953, ea..........**4.00**
Animals, standup on base, assorted, Nosco or CJ, 1947 on, ea........**2.00**
Baseball players, 3-D, bl or gray team, 1948, 1½", ea.....................**8.00**
Disc, emb comic character, series of 12, 1954, unmk, 1½" **16.00**
Disc, emb fish plaque, oval, series of 10, 1956, unmk, ea...............**14.00**
Dog, 3-D, hollow base, series of 10, CJCO, 1954, ea **6.00**
Figure, circus; stands on base, 1 of 12, Nosco, 1951-54....................**3.00**
Figure on rocking base, semi-flat, 1 of 9, Cloud design, '56 ....**4.00**
Fob, alphabet letter w/loop on top, 1 of 26, 1954, 1½"...................**4.00**
Magnifying glass, many designs/shapes, from 1961, ea **1.00**
Palm puzzle, ball(s) roll into holes, dome or rnd, from 1966...........**6.00**
Palm puzzle, ball(s) roll into holes, rectangle, CJ, 1920s, ea...........**55.00**
Palm puzzle, ball(s) roll into holes, sq, CJ, 1920s, ea **45.00**
Pinball game, lever shoots ball/score in holes, 1964 to recent........**5.00**
Ships in a bottle, 6 different, unmk, 1960, ea...............................**6.00**
Signs, road; Stop, Caution, etc, yel, series of 10, 1954-60, ea..........**5.00**
Spinner, tops varied colors, 10 designs, from 1948, ea...................**2.50**
Toys, take apart/assemble, variety, from '62, assembled, ea **2.00**
Toys, take apart/assemble, variety, from '62, unassembled, ea **5.00**
Whistle, tube w/animals on top, CJ, series, 1950-53, 1⅜" **7.00**

Prizes, Tin

Badge, boy & dog diecut, complete w/bend-over tab, CJ **150.00**
Badge, boy & dog diecut, w/o tab at top, CJ **95.00**
Badge, emb/plated CJ officer, 2⅜" or 1⅝", early, ea....................**110.00**
Badge, litho, red/wht/bl, boy/dog, CJ, 1920s, 1¼" dia **150.00**
Bank, 3-D book form, red/gr/or blk, CJ Bank, early, 2"................**120.00**
Bookmark, dogs, 4 different, 1941, 3", ea................................**18.00**
Brooch or pin, various designs on card, CJ/logo, early, ea...........**125.00**
Cash register, litho, More You Eat, CJ, early, 1⅞" **275.00**
Clicker, 'Noisy CJ Snapper,' pear shape, aluminum, 1949.............**14.00**
Clicker, CJ Telegraph, Pat 1897, inked, 1¾" dia, ea....................**145.00**
Doll dishes, tin plated, CJ, '31, 1¾", 1⅞", & 2⅛" dia, ea...........**35.00**
Fortune Wheel, 2-pc litho, CJ, 1939-41, 1¾" **105.00**
Helicopter, yel propeller, wood stick, unmk, 1937, 2⅝" **27.00**
Horse & wagon, litho diecut, CJ & Angelus, 2⅛"..........................**65.00**
Horse & wagon, litho diecut, gray/red mks, CJ, 1914-23, 3⅛"....**395.00**
Model T Ford, License: NY 1915 #999, blk/wht, CJ, rare, 2"......**410.00**
Pocket watch, silver or gold, CJ as numerals, 1931, 1½" **45.00**
Sled, tin plated, CJ, 1931, 2" L **35.00**
Small box shape; garage litho, unmk, 1⅛" **60.00**
Small box shape: electric stove litho, unmk, 1⅛" **80.00**
Small box shape: radio litho, bl, unmk, 1⅛" **60.00**
Soldier, litho, die-cut standup, officer/private/etc, unmk, ea **17.00**
Spinner, wood stick, Always on Top, red/wht/bl, CJ, 1½" dia.......**25.00**
Spinner, wood stick, Fortune Teller Game, red/wht/bl, CJ, 1½" ...**90.00**
Spinner, wood stick, Question Mark Box at center, CJ **50.00**
Spinner, wood stick, 2 Toppers, red/wht/bl, Angelus/Jack, 1½" **85.00**
Stand up, comic character, 1 of 10, CJ, 1936-46, ea **60.00**
Stand up, oval Am Flag, series of 4, unmk, 1936-45, ea **18.00**
Stand up, rectangle litho, boy & dog, ca 1916, lg or sm, ea **155.00**
Tall box shape: Frozen Foods locker freezer, '47, unmk, 1¾" **75.00**
Tall box shape: Refrigerator Car, CJ, 1947, 1¾" L......................**125.00**
Tall box shape: grandfather clock, unmk, 1947, 1¾" **65.00**
Tall box shape: radio, Tune in w/CJ, brn/yel, 1939, 1¾" **125.00**
Train, engine & tender, litho, CJ Line/512 ....**125.00**
Train, litho coach only, red, unmk, 1941..................................**24.00**

Train, litho engine only, red, 1941, unmk **20.00**
Train, Lone Eagle Flyer cars, unmk **65.00**
Train, Lone Eagle Flyer engine, unmk **60.00**
Tray, emb, litho w/early pkg, 2¼x1¾" **95.00**
Truck, litho, RWB, CJ/Angelus, 1931, ea **65.00**
Wagon shape: Playtime Trailer (auto trailer), unmk, 1947............**50.00**
Wagon shape: Tank Corps No 57, gr & blk, 1941........................**30.00**
Wagon shape: Caterpillar tractor, unmk, 1931, 1¾" L..................**35.00**
Wagon shape: CJ Shows, yel circus wagon, series of 5, ea **175.00**
Wagon shape: tank, orange/red/gr camouflage, unmk **65.00**
Wheelbarrow, tin plated, bk leg in place, CJ, 1931, 2½" L **35.00**

Miscellaneous

Ad, comic book, CJ, ea **14.00**
Ad, Saturday Evening Post, mc, CJ, 1919, 11x14"...........................**18.00**
Hat, ball park vendor cap, CJ, 1930s **30.00**
Lunch box, tin, 2 hdls, CJ, 1980s, 4½x5x6"..............................**40.00**
Lunch box, tin emb, CJ, 1970s, 4x7x9" **30.00**
Medal, CJ salesman award, brass, 1939, scarce **125.00**
Sign, bathing beauty, 5-color cb, CJ, early, 17x22" **460.00**
Sign, boy or girl w/box of CJ, 5-color cb, early, 17x22", ea **460.00**
Sign, Jack & Bingo, die-cut litho, easel standup, CJ, early.........**450.00**
Sign, Jack & Bingo, standing on early CJ pkg, mc cb, rare **520.00**
Sign, Santa & prizes, mc cb, Angelus, early, lg **220.00**
Sign, Santa & prizes, mc cb, Checkers, early, lg.....................**1,000.00**
Sign, Santa & prizes, mc cb, CJ, early, lg **265.00**

Crackle Glass

Though this type of glassware was introduced as early as the 1880s (by the New England Glass Co.), it was made primarily from 1930 until about 1980. It was produced by more than five hundred companies here (by Benko, Rainbow, and Kanawah, among others) and abroad (by such renown companies as Moser, for example), and its name is descriptive. The surface looks as though the glass has been heated then plunged into cold water, thus producing a network of tight cracks. It was made in a variety of colors; among the more expensive today are ruby red, amberina, cobalt, cranberry, and gray. For more information we recommend *Crackle Glass, Identification and Value Guide, Book I* and *Book II* (Collector Books), by Stan and Arlene Weitman, our advisors this category; they are listed in the Directory under New York. See also Moser.

Ashtray, dk topaz, incurvate rim w/3 rests, 1950s-60s, 7¾x3¾"....**35.00**
Bowl, smooth fold-over rim, 6¾x15".......................................**75.00**
Candle holder, sea gr, bulbous/bottle neck, Blenko, 1960s, 5¼" .**60.00**
Candy dish, amberina, flared ruffled rim, Kanawha, 1957-87, 3" .**55.00**
Cream & sugar bowl, bright bl, bulbous, Pilgrim, 1949-69, 3½", pr ...**80.00**
Cruet, sea gr, bulbous/ruffled rim, ball stopper, Pilgrim, 1949-69, 6" ..**85.00**
Cup, amberina, bulbous w/drop-over hdl, Kanawha, 1957-87, 2½" ..**40.00**
Decanter, crystal w/olive-gr stopper, pinched sides, Blenko, 10½"......**125.00**
Decanter, sea gr, bulbous/long neck/ruffle rim, Blenko, 1960s, 13¼"..**125.00**
Decanter, topaz, bulbous w/lg ball stopper, Blenko, 1963, 8¾"......**85.00**
Fish, topaz, upturned body, Hamon, 1940s-70s, 9".........................**95.00**
Goblet, olive gr, str sided, plain rim, 5¾".....................................**75.00**
Hat, amberina, smooth bottom, Kanawha, 1957-87, 2"................**45.00**
Jug, dk amber, bulbous w/tapered bottom, clear hdl, Pilgrim, 6¾" .**80.00**
Pear, pale sea gr, Blenko, 1950s-60s, 5", from $60 to **100.00**
Pitcher, amethyst w/clear drop-over hdl, Pilgrim, 1949-69, 3¼" ...**55.00**
Pitcher, bl w/clear angled hdl, fluted rim, Pilgrim, 1949-69, 3½"..**50.00**
Pitcher, wheat, bulbous, drop-over hdl, sm neck, Blenko, 1960s, 9¾" .**100.00**
Punch bowl, crystal, ftd, Blenko, 1950s, 7x11¾", from $200 to..**250.00**
Tumbler, ruby, pinched, Hamon, 1940s-70s, 6".........................**75.00**

Vase, amberina, bulbous w/flared ruffled rim, Kanawha, 1959-87, 5½" ..60.00
Vase, amethyst, flared dbl-neck rim, Blenko, 1940s-50s, 4" 85.00
Vase, clear w/bl rosettes, flared rim, Blenko, 1940s-50s, 7" 110.00
Vase, emerald gr, bulbous w/long bottle neck, Hamon, 1940s-70s, 9¾"...80.00
Vase, Jonquil, ftd w/ruffle & fluted rim, Blenko, 1950s, 7¼".......145.00
Vase, sea gr w/clear angled hdls on bulbous form, Blenko, 7½"..100.00
Vase, tangerine, bottle neck w/ruffled rim, Rainbow, 1940s-60s, 5¼" .70.00

Cranberry Glass

Cranberry glass is named for its resemblance to the color of cranberry juice. It was made by many companies both here and abroad, becoming popular in America soon after the Civil War. It was made in free-blown ware as well as mold-blown. Today cranberry glass is being reproduced, and it is sometimes difficult to distinguish the old from the new. Ask a reputable dealer if you are unsure.

For further information we recommend *American Art Glass* by John A. Shumann III, available from Collector Books or your local bookstore. See also Cruets; Salts; Sugar Shakers; Syrups.

Basket, clear hdl, petticoat shape w/ruffled edge, 1890s, 7x5".....250.00
Basket, Invt T'print, clear hdl, recent, 8x4¼"........................85.00
Box, HP decor, hinged lid, ormolu base, 5"...........................150.00
Cracker jar, florals/scrolls, melon ribs, w/SP mts: 8¾" 400.00
Creamer, ruffled rim, clear hdl, rigaree at neck, shell ft, 4¼"......145.00
Decanter, cut, orig stopper, slim, recent, 16"........................95.00
Epergne, single trumpet, crystal rigaree, 12".........................230.00
Finger bowl, amber threading on ruffled rim..........................135.00
Mug, Invt T'print, clear hdl, 4" 110.00
Pitcher, bellflower eng, crystal hdl, 1880s, 9".......................375.00
Pitcher, Invt T'print, bulbous, clear hdl, 7x7", +4 3¾" tumblers ...380.00
Plate, 8"..55.00
Smoke bell..120.00
Tumbler, bellflower eng, 1880s, 3¾"..................................125.00
Vase, daisies, pinched sides, quatrafold rim, 11½"....................65.00
Vase, emb vertical ribs w/spiral int, 20th C, 9¾" 50.00
Vase, HP lilies of the valley w/gold leaves, 7½"......................135.00
Vase, Invt T'print, 4¼"...65.00
Vase, ruffled rim, appl serpentine, 10½"..............................200.00
Vase, tulip form w/opal flutes, bronze base, 12x5"....................450.00

Crown Devon

Devon and Crown Devon were trade names of S. Fielding and Company, Ltd., an English firm founded after 1879. They produced majolica, earthenware mugs, vases, and kitchenware. In the 1930s they manufactured an esceptional line of Art Deco vases that have recently been much in demand.

Bowl, emb flower tree, pastels on cream, oblong, hdls, #5029R, 11" ...35.00
Condiment set, Erin, ca 1880-90, 3 pcs in 6" SP fr...................160.00
Decanter, John Peel w/verse, fox hdl, 8½" 275.00
Dish, Mattasung pattern, dragonflies & spider webs, 7½x10" 420.00
Figurine, Woeful Willie, sad-eyed dog, 1930s, 5½".....................75.00
Jug, musical; At Ilkla Moor w/verse, 8x7½"...........................225.00
Jug, musical; floral decor, 9".......................................540.00
Jug, musical; Harry Lauders, w/verse, twist hdl, 9½"..................260.00
Jug, musical; Killarney, MIE, 7¾x7¼".................................495.00
Mug, 2 men & 1 lady by fireplace, Auld Lang Syne words, 4½".110.00
Toby, Chelsea pensioner, ca 1950, 4"..................................60.00
Toby, Guardsman, ca 1960, 8¼"...90.00
Urn, Devonia, #0681, gilded, dbl-hdl, sgn G Cox, w/lid, 7x12"..925.00

Vase, castle w/flowers on reverse, w/hdls, 7"...............140.00
Vase, fruit scene, ovoid w/ruffled sides, 9x4⅜"...............110.00

Vase, geometric circles and Vs in multicolor, Hylan Cooke, 9", $550.00.

Vase, Memphis, 2 gold bands w/blk spaced lines, mk CM5, 9"......90.00
Vase, shaded lime/lemon/mauve, rams' heads hdls, #A1499nn, 7½"..750.00

Crown Ducal

The Crown Ducal mark was first used by the A.G. Richardson & Co. pottery of Tunstall, England, in 1925. The items collectors are taking a particular interest in were decorated by Charlotte Rhead, a contemporary of Suzie Cooper and Clarice Cliff, and a member of the esteemed family of English pottery designers and artists.

Beaker, Little Boy Blue, ca 1936, 4" 175.00
Bowl, chick, ca 1936, 6¾"...140.00
Charger, dragon, brn/tan squeezebag on yel, C Rhead, 17" 100.00
Cream mug, Coaching Days, 2¾"...20.00
Ewer, wind-tossed tulips, Bursley Ware, C Rhead, ca 1946, 13"..275.00
Ginger jar, Pattern #TL95, Bursley Ware, C Rhead, ca 1946, 5½"..280.00
Jardiniere, Pattern #3274, patches/stitches, ca 1933, 9½x8½"....480.00
Jug, Autumn Leaves, C Rhead, 6¼", EX...............................280.00
Jug, Harlequin, 4¼"...55.00
Jug, Harlequin, 7¼"...75.00
Plate, Autumn Leaves, C Rhead, flaw, 10½" 380.00
Plate, Geo Washington Bicentenary Commemorative, 1732-1932, 10½"...88.00
Vase, Autumn Leaves, emb ribs, Rhead, 7"...........................395.00
Vase, Indian Tree, pattern #4795, C Rhead, #136, hairline, 5¾"..180.00
Vase, Lotus Leaves, pattern #2682, C Rhead, ca 1932, 7¾"........440.00

Crown Milano

Crown Milano was a line of decorated milk glass (or opal ware) introduced by the Mt. Washington Glass Co. of New Bedford, Massachussetts, in the early 1890s. It had previously been called Albertine Ware. Some pieces are marked with a 'CM,' and many had paper labels. This ware is usually highly decorated and will most likely have a significant amount of gold painted on it. The shiny pieces were recently discovered to have been called 'Colonial Ware' and have a laurel wreath and a crown. This ware was well received in its day, and outstanding pieces bring high prices on today's market. Advisors for this category are Wilfred and Dolli Cohen; they are listed in the Directory under California.

Bowl, mixed flowers, rolled-out 3-corner rim, 9"; ftd Pairpoint base ..1,750.00
Box, jewel; emb scrolls/medallion/gilt on opal, metal base, 7" dia....595.00
Box, jewel; pansy panels on emb scrolls; pincushion lid, 3¼x5¼"...525.00
Box, poppy/gold scrolls on peach; dome lid, 4x7" dia.................950.00
Candlesticks, portrait on wine w/gold, Pairpoint metal base, 8", pr...1,750.00

Cracker jar, bamboo, gr/gold/brn on pnt burmese, ornate SP mts, 6" ...900.00
Cracker jar, Colonial Ware, dancing pr/gold scrolls, no mk, 6x7" 750.00
Cracker jar, Colonial Ware, 2 children in gold scroll reserves, 7" ..695.00
Cracker jar, dandelions on pnt burmese, simple shape, SP mts, 7" ...575.00
Cracker jar, Dresden-type floral/scrolls, bbl shape, orig hdw 1,150.00
Cracker jar, gold mums on lt tan, sq, mk PCM; SP mts #MW4413, 9x5", EX..595.00
Cracker jar, roses/mums/gold by Frederick, bowl shape, w/fixed hdl: 9" ..985.00
Cracker jar, water lilies on turq to cream, gilt mts, w/hld: 9" 700.00
Creamer, gold-lined floral, melon ribs, silver rim/hdl, 4½" 450.00
Cup & saucer, demi; floral vine w/gold on wht, pk-tinted rim, 2", 5" ..1,750.00
Ewer, Colonial Ware, scrolls/x-hatching/florals on glossy wht, 7x7" ..1,250.00
Ewer, shepherd/cottage w/in gold scrollwork, rope twist at neck, 10"...5,000.00
Lamp, Colonial Ware, florals/swags/etc w/gilt, ball shade/urn base, 23" ..2,950.00
Lamp base, floral on pnt burmese, 2-pc: rnd font atop bottle form, 14" ...575.00
Marmalade, Dmn Quilt w/gold-lined oak leaves & 14 glass berries, 5" ...600.00
Mustard jar, gold floral on beige, str sides, fancy SP lid/hdl, 4", NM 575.00
Pitcher, Colonial, gold bows/3" scroll & leaf band, thorn hdl, 11x5"...1,200.00
Pitcher, wheat stalk on opal, melon ribbed, smooth hdl, crown mk, 9".275.00
Rose bowl, orchid, purple on yel to gr, #619, 3¼x4" 495.00
Sweetmeat, Dmn Quilt w/thistles, SP lid, 5x4¼" 400.00
Vase, acorns/leaves on yel, ribbed gourd w/trifold top, gilt rim, 9"...700.00
Vase, allover Persian flowers/jewels, snake around stick neck, 11x8" ...3,100.00
Vase, Colonial Ware, florals/gold shadow leaves, V-cut rim, 9"...945.00
Vase, Colonial Ware, long stems/lilies, ftd ovoid w/loop hdl atop, 13" ..2,200.00
Vase, fern fronds on tan/wht, gold/beige scrolls at neck, 8¾x6½" 1,200.00
Vase, florals, gold tones w/jewels on cream, squat w/stick neck, 12" ...700.00
Vase, florals/foliage on yel to cream, 4-lobe rim, spherical, 6" .1,350.00
Vase, gold leaves on ivory, dbl-gourd shape, 6½x7½" 520.00
Vase, gold petit-point iris/tan traceries on beige, 8 ribs, 5x4"......875.00
Vase, gold rose branches, rnd w/long trumpet neck, 15x6" 2,275.00
Vase, gold spider mums on gr, oval panels, att Guba, 10x9" 2,250.00
Vase, gold/jeweled daisies on gr-washed beige, melon-rib bottom, 13" ..2,245.00
Vase, gold/silver azaleas & traceries, ovoid w/4-fold cup neck, 14" ..2,500.00
Vase, lg thistles on lt tan w/gold, 12½x5½"...............................1,100.00
Vase, mums, red/yel/bl, globular, stick neck w/extruded gold hdls, 13"...1,800.00
Vase, Oriental flowers w/scrolling stems, long-neck gourd shape, 13" 1,750.00
Vase, pansies on wht w/free-form gold accents, petticoat form, 10½".........750.00
Vase, peonies, lav/wht/yel on lt yel, collar neck w/gold, bulbous, 8" 765.00
Vase, peony, wht w/gold outlines on cream, 24 swirl ribs, bulbous, 6"...1,450.00
Vase, wild roses, pk on yel/wht, long neck pulled to 4 points, 9½"...........750.00

Cruets

Cruets, containers made to hold oil or vinegar, are usually bulbous with tall, narrow throats, a handle, and a stopper. During the nineteenth century and for several years after, they were produced in abundance in virtually every type of glassware available. Those listed below are assumed to be with stopper and mint unless noted otherwise. Our advisor for this category is Elaine Ezell; she is listed in the Directory under Maryland.

See also Specific manufacturers.

Amber, small hand-painted flowers, 8½", $165.00.

Amberette..90.00
Amberina, trifold top, dk amber hdl/ball stopper, 7" 230.00
Amberina Coinspot, trifold top, amber hdl/faceted stopper, 7"...350.00
Arched Ovals..60.00
Arched Ovals, gr..130.00
Art...60.00
Artichoke...65.00
Bead Swag, milk glass w/gold beading 250.00
Beaded Comet Band...45.00
Bethlehem Star...50.00
Bevelled Star...45.00
Brazilian...60.00
Broken Column...60.00
Bubble Lattice Paneled Sprig, wht opal...............................325.00
Cambridge #2660...65.00
Cane Column..45.00
Cathedral..60.00
Chrysanthemum Base Swirl, bl opal....................................250.00
Columbian Coin (US Coin) 70.00
Connecticut...60.00
Cranberry, wht floral/berries on gold twig, ringed body/stopper, 8" ..250.00
Cranberry spatter, ruffled top, clear stopper, 5¾"..................95.00
Crystal Wedding..145.00
Cupid & Venus..165.00
Daisy & Fern, wht opal, Northwood 225.00
Dakota...100.00
Dewey..65.00
Dewey, amber..95.00
Diamond Fan...75.00
Diamond Quilt, bl satin MOP..210.00
Diamond Quilt, cranberry satin..110.00
Duncan Homestead..50.00
Faceted Flower (Swirl)..65.00
Feather, gr...250.00
Fern Burst (Palm Wreath)...65.00
Fleur-de-Lis & Grape...60.00
Florida..60.00
Fostoria's Priscilla...75.00
Galloway...55.00
Gr spatter w/emb leaves...200.00
Heart w/Thumbprint..65.00
Heisey #1250...75.00
Heisey #300 Colonial, made in 5 szs, ea, from $50 to..................85.00
Hobbs Block..65.00
Honeycomb w/Star...50.00
Illinois...55.00
Indiana #123...55.00
Invt T'print, amberina..365.00
Invt T'print, rubena verde, teepee shape, Hobbs & Brockunier, 7"..550.00
Jackson, vaseline opal...225.00
Jacob's Ladder 95.00
Klondike...190.00
Leaf & Star..70.00
Lt bl w/reeded amber hdl, faceted amber stopper w/int teardrop, 6"..185.00
Masonic...45.00
Massachusetts, mini...60.00
Millefiori, lt bl aqua, app hdl, 8"...315.00
Nail...65.00
Nailhead, rose stain..295.00
New Jersey...60.00
Ohio Star..85.00
Opaque wht, att NE Glass, very rare, 6"................................850.00
Paneled Herringbone, gr...125.00
Paneled Sunflower...45.00

Peacock Feather..**50.00**
Persian..**50.00**
Pinwheel...**130.00**
Portland..**65.00**
Punty & Diamond Point..**50.00**
Radiant Daisy, frosted bottom w/clear daisies................**80.00**
Ranson (Gold Band), canary yel vaseline **155.00**
Royal Crystal, ruby stain, sm......................................**295.00**
S-Repeat...**70.00**
Sawtooth...**110.00**
Scroll w/Cane Band..**45.00**
Sextec...**50.00**
Shoshone, gr **65.00**
Snail..**125.00**
Spanish Lace, bl opal, clear cut stopper, Northwood.....**595.00**
Star & Notched Rib..**55.00**
Strawberry Diamond & Fan...**100.00**
Swirl, bl opal, ribbed **200.00**
Tarantum's Virginia...**60.00**
Ten-Pointed Star..**60.00**
Thousand Eye, apple gr **65.00**
Three-In-One..**60.00**
Tile (Optical Cube)...**50.00**
Truncated Cube..**65.00**
Twin Snowshoes...**60.00**
Waffle Block..**65.00**
Wht opal, royal bl wafer above opal ft, royal bl hdl/stopper, 9½" ..**125.00**
Wht opal ribbon swirl w/sapphire bl stopper & hdl, 5½" **285.00**
Wild Bouquet, bl opal, opal hdl, clear stopper, 7¼" **395.00**
Wisconsin..**110.00**

Cup Plates, Glass

Before the middle 1850s, it was socially acceptable to pour hot tea into a deep saucer to cool. The tea was sipped from the saucer rather than the cup, which frequently was handleless and too hot to hold. The cup plate served as a coaster for the cup. It is generally agreed that the first examples of pressed glass cup plates were made about 1826 at the Boston and Sandwich Glass Co. in Sandwich, Cape Cod, Massachusetts. Other glassworks in three major areas (New England, Philadelphia, and the Midwest, especially Pittsburgh) quickly followed suit.

Antique glass cup plates range in size from 2⅝" up to 4¼" in diameter. The earliest plates had simple designs inspired by cut glass patterns, but by 1829 they had become more complex. The span from then until about 1845 is known as the 'Lacy Period,' when cup plate designs and pressing techniques were at their peak. To cover pressing imperfections, the backgrounds of the plates were often covered with fine stippling which endowed them with a glittering brilliance called 'laciness.' They were made in a multitude of designs — some purely decorative, others commemorative. Subjects include the American eagle, hearts, sunbursts, log cabins, ships, George Washington, the political candidates Clay and Harrison, plows, beehives, etc. Of all the patterns, the round George Washington plate is the rarest and most valuable — only four are known to exist today.

Authenticity is most important. Collectors must be aware that contemporary plates which have no antique counterparts and fakes modeled after antique patterns have had wide distribution. Condition is also important, though it is the exceptional plate that does not have some rim roughness. More important considerations are scarcity of design and color.

Our advisor for this category is John Bilane; he is listed in the Directory under New Jersey. The book *American Glass* by George and

Helen McKearin has a section on glass cup plates. The definitive book is *American Glass Cup Plates* by Ruth Webb Lee and James H. Rose. Numbers in the listings that follow refer to the latter. When attempting to evaluate a cup plate, remember that minor rim roughness is normal. See also Staffordshire; Pairpoint.

R-20, VG **30.00**
R-23, G+ **26.00**
R-30, scarce, VG **64.00**
R-31, rare, VG+ **74.00**
R-41, scarce, G+ **38.00**
R-47, VG **30.00**
R-62-A, VG- **48.00**
R-66, VG **76.00**
R-72, rare, VG+ **78.00**
R-79, G **32.00**
R-97, scarce, VG- **48.00**
R-99, rare, VG **70.00**
R-101, scarce, VG **51.00**
R-103, rare, G **62.00**
R-104, VG **35.00**
R-124-A, VG- **37.00**
R-151-A, G- **28.00**
R-158-B, scarce, EX- **50.00**
R-159-A, scarce, G **39.00**
R-164-A, EX **40.00**
R-169-B, EX **40.00**
R-172-A, EX **40.00**
R-174, EX **45.00**
R-176-A, EX **43.00**
R-177, VG **43.00**
R-216, G **53.00**
R-236, G **28.00**
R-255, VG **20.00**
R-257, VG- **32.00**
R-258, VG **30.00**
R-269, VG **30.00**
R-269-B, scarce, G+ **34.00**
R-271-A, VG **30.00**
R-285, VG **34.00**
R-291, VG- **26.00**
R-311, VG- **20.00**
R-313, VG **21.00**
R-323, VG- **18.00**
R-334, G+ **17.00**
R-339, VG **19.00**
R-340, G **15.00**
R-342, G **14.00**
R-343-B, scarce, VG **35.00**
R-379, VG- **12.00**
R-390-A, G+ **11.00**
R-393, G **10.00**
R-396, VG **13.00**
R-402, VG **14.00**
R-425, G **21.00**
R-447, G **22.00**
R-465, G **25.00**
R-465-H, VG **23.00**
R-465-N, G **16.00**
R-467-A, G **15.00**
R-508, G+ **15.00**
R-546, G+ **15.00**
R-565-A, G+ **26.00**
R-590, G **28.00**

R-593, scarce, G 42.00
R-594, VG- 32.00
R-605-A, scarce, G 105.00
R-610-A, VG 34.00
R-610-C, VG- 40.00
R-619, G 35.00
R-619-A, G 39.00
R-628, scarce, G 53.00
R-636, VG- 42.00
R-637, very rare, VG- 260.00
R-642, VG 20.00
R-643, VG 26.00
R-661, VG 39.00
R-665-A, G+ 34.00
R-666, VG 35.00
R-670, scarce, VG- 60.00
R-670-A, VG 39.00
R-676-C, G 47.00
R-677, VG 38.00
R-679, VG 34.00
R-693, G+ 75.00

Cups and Saucers

The earliest utensils for drinking were small porcelain and stoneware bowls imported from China by the East Indian Company in the early seventeenth century. European and English tea bowls and saucers, imitating Chinese and Japanese originals, were produced from the early eighteenth century and often decorated with Chinese-type motifs. By about 1810, handles were fitted to the bowl to form the now familiar teacup, and this form became almost universal. Coffee in England and on the continent was often served in a can — a straight-sided cylinder with a handle. After 1820 the coffee can gave way to the more fanciful form of the coffee cup.

An infinite variety of cups and saucers are available for both the new and experienced collector, and they can be found in all price ranges. There is probably no better way to thoroughly know and understand the various ceramic manufacturers than to study cups and saucers. Our advisors for this category, Susan and Jim Harran, have written two books, entitled *Collectible Cups and Saucers, Identification and Values, Books I and II*, published by Collector Books. Over 800 full-color photos fill book II which is divided into six collectible categories: early years (1700 – 1875), cabinet cups, nineteenth- and twentieth-century dinnerware, English tablewares, miniatures, and mustache cups and saucers. The Harrans are listed in the Directory under New Jersey.

Demitasse cup and saucer, hand-painted flowers with gilt leaves, John Aynsley & Sons, ca 1883, from $100.00 to $125.00. (Photo courtesy Susan and Jim Harran)

Breakfast, floral int/ext, MZ Austria, ca 1900, from $45 to 60.00
Chocolate, floral on wht, scalloped saucer, Limoges, 1891-1914...50.00
Chocolate, gold ferns on wht, 8-fluted cup, Limoges, 1890-25, $100 to .125.00
Coffee, floral w/cobalt & gold, Ridgway, ca 1825, from $80 to ...100.00
Demi, Cattail, Bute cup w/loop hdl, Lenox, 1950s, from $40 to 50.00
Demi, chintz flowers, can w/loop hdl, Crown Staffordshire, 1930s .32.50
Demi, floral majolica w/serpent hdl, Cantagalli, 1878-1901 ....100.00
Demi, gold & jewels on wht & blk, Bute cup, Royal Worcester, 1927..........185.00
Demi, Golden Orchid, artist sgn, Stouffer Co, 1938-46, from $50 to ..60.00
Demi, pk & wht w/gold scrolls & beads, Royal Doulton, 1902-22 ....175.00
Demi, silver o/l on pk, Austria, 1920s, from $125 to 175.00
Mini, floral transfer, loop hdl, Foley, 1921-29, from $100 to.......150.00
Mini, Indian Tree, Coalport, 1920-39, from $150 to 200.00
Mini, Rosebud, str-sided cup w/loop hdl, Shelley, 1945-66, $175 to .200.00
Snack, amateur fruit decor in Pickard style, Bavaria, 1920s, $40 to.....50.00
Snack, forget-me-nots, fan hdl, Limoges, ca 1882-90, from $100 to..125.00
Tea, aqua rose & polka dots, Royal Standard, 1949+, from $40 to.50.00
Tea, Blue Willow w/gold, Booths Ltd, 1912+, from $40 to............50.00
Tea, boy playing flute, bucket-shape cup, HenRiot Quimper, 1920s ...175.00
Tea, courting scenes alternate w/flowers, HP, Dresden, R Klemm, 1900s...100.00
Tea, floral on pearlware, handleless, SE&C Challinor, 1860-90....75.00
Tea, floral transfer, quatrefoil cup w/feathered hdl, Moore Bros, 1891..70.00
Tea, floral transfer, waisted cup w/loop hdl, Foley, 1930-35, $30 to.......40.00
Tea, floral transfer w/cobalt & gold, Paragon, 1957+, from $35 to...45.00
Tea, Florentine, kicked loop hdl, Wedgwood, 1901-19, from $50 to ...75.00
Tea, flowers on cobalt w/hand gilding, Copeland Spode, 1891+, $100 to....125.00
Tea, geometrics, majolica, 8-sided cup, sq hdl, Choisy-le-Roi, 1870s..115.00
Tea, gold border on cream, 6-sided, Lenox, 1920s, from $60 to 75.00
Tea, gold leaves on turq & wht bands, Aynsley, 1950s, from $30 to...40.00
Tea, HP geometrics, Adam Titian Ware, 1896-1920s, from $25 to..35.00
Tea, HP sprig ware, London-shaped bowl, unmk, ca 1830, from $50 to .70.00
Tea, Indian, purple w/gold dots, 12-lobed cup, Meissen, 1860-1924.....275.00
Tea, Rose & Red Daisy, 14-flute, Shelley, ca 1945-66, from $45 to.........65.00
Tea, roses transfer w/gold, ftd/ribbed cup, Colclough China Ltd, 1950+....35.00
Tea, silver o/l on pk, Bavaria/US Zone, 1945-49, from $150 to ..200.00
Tea, Yule Tide, holly & berries, ftd, Queen Anne, 1950+, from $30 to...40.00

Currier & Ives by Royal

During the 1950s dinnerware decorated with transfer-printed scenes taken from prints by Currier and Ives was manufactured by Royal China and given as premiums through A&P stores. Though it was also made in pink and green, the blue is by far the most popular. Pie plates in black and brown can be found, but no china sets in these colors have been reported. Occasionally pieces are being found that have hand-painted colors on them with the same blue backgrounds. It has become a very popular collectible at malls and flea markets around the country. Included in our listings are pieces from Hostess sets, which should be of great interest to collectors. New pieces which have been added to the price list include the clock, coffee mug with round handle, tall cup, snack plate, spoon rest/wall plaque, second-type gravy and underplate, and third-type sugar bowl with no handles. Also, the 11½" round platter with the 'Rocky Mountains' scene has been added (very rare). Currier and Ives by Royal is one of the fastest growing collectibles on the market today. Our advisors for this category are Treva and Jack Hamlin; they are listed in the Directory under Ohio.

Ashtray, 5½", from $15 to...18.00
Bowl, cereal; tab hdl, 6¼" 48.00
Bowl, cereal; 6¼" 15.00
Bowl, dessert; 5½" 5.00
Bowl, soup; 8" 14.00
Bowl, vegetable, 9" 25.00

Bowl, vegetable; deep, 10"	30.00
Butter dish, Fashionable decal	55.00
Butter dish, Road Winter decal	40.00
Casserole, angle hdls	115.00
Casserole, tab hdls, knob turned 90 degrees	250.00
Clock, 10" plate, bl #s, 2 decals	200.00
Creamer, angle hdl	8.00
Creamer, rnd hdl, tall	48.00
Cup, angle hdl	4.00
Cup, rnd hdl, tall, 9"	10.00
Gravy boat, pour spout	20.00
Gravy boat, tab hdls	58.00
Ladle, gravy; all wht	50.00
Lamp, candle; w/globe	300.00
Mug, coffee; reg	35.00
Mug, coffee; rnd hdl	35.00
Pie baker, 9 decals, 10"	30.00
Plate, bread; 6½"	5.00
Plate, calendar; 10"	20.00
Plate, chop; Getting Ice, 11½"	38.00
Plate, chop; Rocky Mountains, 11½"	65.00
Plate, chop; 12¼"	35.00
Plate, dinner; 10"	7.00
Plate, luncheon; 9"	25.00
Plate, salad; 7¼"	15.00
Plate, snack; w/cup well, 9"	75.00
Platter, oval, 13"	35.00
Platter, tab hdls, 10½" dia	22.00
Platter, 13" dia	75.00
Saucer, 6⅛"	2.00
Shakers, pr	35.00
Spoon rest, wall hanging	75.00
Sugar bowl, hdld, w/lid	18.00
Sugar bowl, no hdls, flared top	48.00
Sugar bowl, no hdls, w/lid	35.00
Teapot	150.00
Tidbit tray, 3-tier, orig only	75.00
Tray, gravy boat; like 7" plate	75.00
Tray, gravy boat; regular	20.00
Tumbler, iced tea; 12-oz, 5½"	17.50
Tumbler, juice; 5-oz, 3½"	17.50
Tumbler, old fashioned; 7-oz, 3¼"	17.50
Tumbler, water; 8½-oz, 4¾"	17.50

Hostess Set Pieces

Bowl, candy; 7¾"	25.00
Bowl, dip; 4⅜"	20.00
Pie baker, 11"	45.00
Plate, cake; flat, 10"	40.00
Plate, cake; ftd, 10"	125.00
Plate, serving; 7"	18.00
Tray, deviled egg	150.00

Custard Glass

As early as the 1880s, custard glass was produced in England. Migrating glassmakers brought the formula for the creamy ivory ware to America. One of them was Harry Northwood, who in 1898 founded his company in Indiana, Pennsylvania, and introduced the glassware to the American market. Soon other companies were producing custard, among them Heisey, Tarentum, Fenton, and McKee. Not only dinnerware patterns but souvenir items were made. Today custard is the most expensive of the colored pressed glassware patterns. The formula for producing the luminous glass contains uranium salts which imparts the cream color to the batch and causes it to glow when it is examined under a black light.

Argonaut Shell, bowl, master berry; gold & decor, 10½" L	275.00
Argonaut Shell, bowl, sauce; ftd, gold & decor	75.00
Argonaut Shell, butter dish, gold & decor	350.00
Argonaut Shell, butter dish, no gold	300.00
Argonaut Shell, compote, jelly; gold & decor, scarce	165.00
Argonaut Shell, creamer, no gold	110.00
Argonaut Shell, cruet, gold & decor	850.00
Argonaut Shell, pitcher, water; gold & decor	475.00
Argonaut Shell, shakers, gold & decor, pr	435.00
Argonaut Shell, spooner, gold & decor	250.00
Argonaut Shell, sugar bowl, w/lid, gold & decor	235.00
Argonaut Shell, tumbler, gold & decor	110.00
Bead Swag, bowl, sauce; floral & gold	50.00
Bead Swag, goblet, floral & gold	65.00
Bead Swag, tray, pickle; floral & gold, rare	300.00
Bead Swag, wine, floral & gold	60.00
Beaded Circle, bowl, master berry; floral & gold	275.00
Beaded Circle, butter dish, floral & gold	500.00
Beaded Circle, creamer, floral & gold	180.00
Beaded Circle, pitcher, water; floral & gold	750.00
Beaded Circle, shakers, floral & gold, pr	1,000.00
Beaded Circle, spooner, floral & gold	185.00
Beaded Circle, tumbler, floral & gold, very rare	175.00
Cane Insert, berry set, 7-pc	450.00
Cane Insert, table set, 4-pc	450.00
Cherry & Scales, bowl, master berry; nutmeg stain	145.00
Cherry & Scales, butter dish, nutmeg stain	250.00
Cherry & Scales, creamer, nutmeg stain	125.00
Cherry & Scales, pitcher, water; nutmeg stain, scarce	350.00
Cherry & Scales, spooner, nutmeg stain, scarce	125.00
Cherry & Scales, sugar bowl, w/lid, nutmeg stain, scarce	150.00
Cherry & Scales, tumbler, nutmeg stain, scarce	75.00
Chrysanthemum Sprig, bowl, master berry; gold & decor	300.00
Chrysanthemum Sprig, bowl, master berry; no gold	175.00
Chrysanthemum Sprig, bowl, sauce; ftd, gold & decor	60.00
Chrysanthemum Sprig, butter dish, gold & decor	375.00
Chrysanthemum Sprig, celery vase, gold & decor, rare	700.00
Chrysanthemum Sprig, compote, jelly; gold & decor	150.00
Chrysanthemum Sprig, compote, jelly; no decor	100.00
Chrysanthemum Sprig, creamer, gold & decor	135.00
Chrysanthemum Sprig, cruet, gold & decor, 6¾"	495.00

Chrysanthemum Sprig, water pitcher, decoration and gold trim, 8", $395.00.

Chrysanthemum Sprig, pitcher, water; no decor	350.00
Chrysanthemum Sprig, shakers, gold & decor, pr	300.00

Chrysanthemum Sprig, spooner, gold & decor................................135.00
Chrysanthemum Sprig, spooner, no gold...75.00
Chrysanthemum Sprig, sugar bowl, gold & decor......................250.00
Chrysanthemum Sprig, toothpick holder, gold & decor.............325.00
Chrysanthemum Sprig, toothpick holder, no decor.....................175.00
Chrysanthemum Sprig, tray, condiment; gold & decor, rare 595.00
Chrysanthemum Sprig, tumbler, gold & decor.............................80.00
Dandelion, mug, nutmeg stain...175.00
Delaware, bowl, sauce; pk stain..65.00
Delaware, creamer, breakfast; pk stain...75.00
Delaware, tray, pin; gr stain..85.00
Delaware, tumbler, pk stain...65.00
Diamond w/Peg, bowl, master berry; roses & gold 225.00
Diamond w/Peg, bowl, sauce; roses & gold....................................50.00
Diamond w/Peg, butter dish, roses & gold...................................275.00
Diamond w/Peg, creamer, ind; no decor 35.00
Diamond w/Peg, creamer, ind; souvenir..50.00
Diamond w/Peg, creamer, roses & gold...85.00
Diamond w/Peg, mug, souvenir...50.00
Diamond w/Peg, napkin ring, roses & gold, rare..........................175.00
Diamond w/Peg, pitcher, roses & gold, 5½".................................275.00
Diamond w/Peg, sugar bowl, w/lid, roses & gold.........................175.00
Diamond w/Peg, toothpick holder, roses & gold..........................175.00
Diamond w/Peg, tumbler, roses & gold..75.00
Diamond w/Peg, water set, souvenir, 7-pc....................................650.00
Diamond w/Peg, wine, roses & gold...65.00
Diamond w/Peg, wine, souvenir..55.00
Everglades, bowl, master berry; gold & decor..............................215.00
Everglades, bowl, sauce; gold & decor...60.00
Everglades, butter dish, gold & decor..395.00
Everglades, creamer, gold & decor..155.00
Everglades, cruet, EX gold & decor...1,200.00
Everglades, shakers, gold & decor, pr...375.00
Everglades, spooner, gold & decor..160.00
Everglades, sugar bowl, w/lid, gold & decor 235.00
Everglades, tumbler, gold & decor..100.00
Fan, bowl, master berry; good gold..200.00
Fan, bowl, sauce; good gold..60.00
Fan, butter dish, good gold..345.00
Fan, creamer, good gold...110.00
Fan, ice cream set, good gold, 7-pc...500.00
Fan, pitcher, water; good gold...300.00
Fan, spooner, good gold...100.00
Fan, sugar bowl, w/lid, good gold...175.00
Fan, tumbler, good gold...85.00
Fan, water set, good gold, 7-pc...725.00
Fine Cut & Roses, rose bowl, fancy int, nutmeg stain 100.00
Fine Cut & Roses, rose bowl, plain int...85.00

Geneva, floral decor: butter dish, $250.00; Sugar bowl, with lid, $175.00; Spooner, $100.00; Creamer, $115.00.

Geneva, bowl, master berry; floral decor, ftd, oval, 9" L.............110.00
Geneva, bowl, master berry; floral decor, rnd, 9" 130.00
Geneva, bowl, sauce; floral decor, oval...50.00
Geneva, bowl, sauce; floral decor, rnd..50.00
Geneva, butter dish, no decor...145.00
Geneva, compote, jelly; floral decor 95.00
Geneva, cruet, floral decor..475.00
Geneva, pitcher, water; floral decor...275.00
Geneva, shakers, floral decor, pr...280.00
Geneva, sugar bowl, open, floral decor..85.00
Geneva, syrup, floral decor..500.00
Geneva, toothpick holder, floral w/M gold...................................375.00
Geneva, tumbler, floral decor..60.00
Georgia Gem, bowl, master berry; good gold................................135.00
Georgia Gem, bowl, master berry; gr opaque................................115.00
Georgia Gem, butter dish, good gold...200.00
Georgia Gem, celery vase, good gold...145.00
Georgia Gem, creamer, good gold..100.00
Georgia Gem, creamer, no gold..60.00
Georgia Gem, cruet, good gold...295.00
Georgia Gem, mug, good gold...45.00
Georgia Gem, powder jar, w/lid, good gold....................................80.00
Georgia Gem, shakers, good gold, pr...140.00
Georgia Gem, spooner, souvenir..55.00
Georgia Gem, sugar bowl, w/lid, no gold..95.00
Grape (& Cable), bottle, scent; orig stopper, nutmeg stain.........650.00
Grape (& Cable), bowl, banana; ftd, nutmeg stain.......................350.00
Grape (& Cable), bowl, centerpc; ftd, nutmeg stain 450.00
Grape (& Cable), bowl, master berry; flat, nutmeg stain.............200.00
Grape (& Cable), bowl, nutmeg stain, 7½" 60.00
Grape (& Cable), bowl, orange; ftd, flat top, nutmeg stain.........400.00
Grape (& Cable), bowl, orange; ftd, nutmeg stain 500.00
Grape (& Cable), bowl, sauce; nutmeg stain, ftd............................50.00
Grape (& Cable), butter dish, nutmeg stain 300.00
Grape (& Cable), compote, jelly; open, nutmeg stain...................150.00
Grape (& Cable), compote, nutmeg stain, 4½x8".........................300.00
Grape (& Cable), cracker jar, nutmeg stain...................................850.00
Grape (& Cable), creamer, breakfast; nutmeg stain........................80.00
Grape (& Cable), humidor, bl stain, rare..950.00
Grape (& Cable), humidor, nutmeg stain, rare..............................900.00
Grape (& Cable), nappy, nutmet stain, rare.....................................60.00
Grape (& Cable), pitcher, water; nutmeg stain 550.00
Grape (& Cable), plate, nutmeg stain, 7" 50.00
Grape (& Cable), plate, nutmeg stain, 8" 65.00
Grape (& Cable), powder jar, nutmeg stain....................................350.00
Grape (& Cable), punch bowl, w/base, nutmeg stain...............1,900.00
Grape (& Cable), spooner, nutmeg stain..155.00
Grape (& Cable), sugar bowl, breakfast; open, nutmeg stain 85.00
Grape (& Cable), sugar bowl, w/lid, nutmeg stain........................225.00
Grape (& Cable), tray, dresser; nutmeg stain, scarce, lg.............375.00
Grape (& Cable), tray, pin; nutmeg stain 150.00
Grape (& Cable), tumbler, nutmeg stain..75.00
Grape & Gothic Arches, bowl, master berry; pearl w/gold..........200.00
Grape & Gothic Arches, bowl, sauce; pearl w/gold, rare...............80.00
Grape & Gothic Arches, butter dish, pearl w/gold.......................235.00
Grape & Gothic Arches, creamer, pearl w/gold, rare....................100.00
Grape & Gothic Arches, favor vase, nutmeg stain 80.00
Grape & Gothic Arches, goblet, pearl w/gold.................................75.00
Grape & Gothic Arches, pitcher, water; pearl w/gold 300.00
Grape & Gothic Arches, spooner, pearl w/gold...............................85.00
Grape & Gothic Arches, sugar bowl, w/lid, pearl w/gold 135.00
Grape & Gothic Arches, tumbler, pearl w/gold...............................65.00
Grape Arbor, vase, hat form...90.00
Heart w/Thumbprint, creamer 90.00

Heart w/Thumbprint, lamp, good pnt, scarce, 8" 450.00
Heart w/Thumbprint, sugar bowl, ind.................................95.00
Honeycomb, wine 65.00
Horse Medallion, bowl, gr stain, 7" 85.00
Intaglio, bowl, master berry; gold & decor, ftd, 9" 250.00
Intaglio, bowl, sauce; gold & decor 50.00
Intaglio, butter dish, gold & decor, scarce 300.00
Intaglio, compote, jelly; gold & decor 125.00
Intaglio, creamer, gold & decor 125.00
Intaglio, cruet, gold & decor 475.00
Intaglio, pitcher, water; gold & decor 395.00
Intaglio, shakers, gold & decor, pr 250.00
Intaglio, spooner, gold & decor 135.00
Intaglio, sugar bowl, w/lid, gold & decor 180.00
Intaglio, tumbler, gold & decor 95.00
Inverted Fan & Feather, bowl, master berry; gold & decor..........275.00
Inverted Fan & Feather, bowl, sauce; gold & decor 75.00
Inverted Fan & Feather, butter dish, gold & decor 400.00
Inverted Fan & Feather, compote, jelly; gold & decor, rare 500.00
Inverted Fan & Feather, creamer, gold & decor 175.00
Inverted Fan & Feather, cruet, gold & decor, scarce, 6½" 1,100.00
Inverted Fan & Feather, pitcher, water; gold & decor 700.00
Inverted Fan & Feather, punch cup, gold & decor 250.00
Inverted Fan & Feather, shakers, gold & decor, pr 750.00
Inverted Fan & Feather, spooner, gold & decor 165.00
Inverted Fan & Feather, sugar bowl, w/lid, gold & decor 250.00
Inverted Fan & Feather, tumbler, gold & decor 115.00
Jackson (Alaska Variant), bowl, master berry; good gold, ftd......150.00
Jackson (Alaska Variant), bowl, sauce; good gold 50.00
Jackson (Alaska Variant), creamer, good gold 85.00
Jackson (Alaska Variant), pitcher, water; good gold 250.00
Jackson (Alaska Variant), pitcher, water; no decor..........175.00
Jackson (Alaska Variant), shakers, good gold, pr 195.00
Jackson (Alaska Variant), tumbler, good gold 50.00
Louis XV, bowl, master berry; good gold...........................250.00
Louis XV, bowl, sauce; good gold, ftd.................................50.00
Louis XV, butter dish, good gold 250.00
Louis XV, creamer, good gold 85.00
Louis XV, pitcher, water; good gold 250.00
Louis XV, spooner, good gold 110.00
Louis XV, sugar bowl, w/lid, good gold 165.00
Louis XV, tumbler, good gold 65.00
Maple Leaf, bowl, master berry; gold & decor, scarce 350.00
Maple Leaf, bowl, sauce; gold & decor, scarce.................50.00
Maple Leaf, butter dish, gold & decor 350.00
Maple Leaf, compote, jelly; gold & decor, rare 475.00
Maple Leaf, creamer, gold & decor 150.00
Maple Leaf, cruet, gold & decor, rare............................3,000.00
Maple Leaf, pitcher, water; gold & decor 400.00
Maple Leaf, shakers, gold & decor, very rare, pr...............1,000.00
Maple Leaf, spooner, gold & decor 175.00
Maple Leaf, sugar bowl, w/lid, gold & decor 250.00
Maple Leaf, tumbler, gold & decor 100.00
Panelled Poppy, lamp shade, nutmeg stain, scarce 900.00
Peacock & Urn, bowl, ice cream; nutmeg stain, sm..........80.00
Peacock & Urn, bowl, ice cream; nutmeg stain, 10" 350.00
Punty Band, shakers, pr 175.00
Punty Band, spooner, floral decor 100.00
Punty Band, tumbler, floral decor, souvenir......................65.00
Ribbed Drape, bowl, sauce; roses & gold 45.00
Ribbed Drape, butter dish, scalloped, roses & gold....................400.00
Ribbed Drape, compote, jelly; roses & gold, rare 200.00
Ribbed Drape, creamer, roses & gold, scarce 180.00
Ribbed Drape, cruet, roses & gold, rare...........................700.00

Ribbed Drape, pitcher, water; roses & gold, rare.....................365.00
Ribbed Drape, shakers, roses & gold, rare, pr 400.00
Ribbed Drape, spooner, roses & gold 195.00
Ribbed Drape, sugar bowl, w/lid, roses & gold 250.00
Ribbed Drape, toothpick holder, roses & gold 475.00
Ribbed Drape, tumbler, roses & gold 75.00
Ribbed Thumbprint, wine, floral decor 80.00
Ring Band, bowl, master berry; roses & gold...................200.00
Ring Band, bowl, sauce; roses & gold 50.00
Ring Band, butter dish, roses & gold 300.00
Ring Band, compote, jelly; roses & gold, scarce..............195.00
Ring Band, creamer, roses & gold......................................125.00
Ring Band, cruet, roses & gold, scarce 500.00
Ring Band, cruet, roses decor, clear stopper 175.00
Ring Band, pitcher, roses & gold, 7½" 375.00
Ring Band, shakers, roses & gold, pr 155.00
Ring Band, spooner, roses & gold......................................125.00
Ring Band, syrup, roses & gold, scarce 475.00
Ring Band, table set, 4-pc 450.00
Ring Band, toothpick holder, roses & gold 155.00
Ring Band, tray, condiment; roses & gold 200.00
Singing Birds, mug, nutmeg stain..85.00
Tarentum's Victoria, bowl, master berry; gold & decor...............200.00
Tarentum's Victoria, butter dish, gold & decor, rare 350.00
Tarentum's Victoria, celery vase, gold & decor, rare 300.00
Tarentum's Victoria, creamer, gold & decor, scarce 135.00
Tarentum's Victoria, pitcher, water; gold & decor, rare 375.00
Tarentum's Victoria, spooner, gold & decor 135.00
Tarentum's Victoria, sugar bowl, w/lid, gold & decor.................175.00
Tarentum's Victoria, tumbler, gold & decor......................75.00
Vermont, butter dish, bl decor 195.00
Vermont, toothpick holder, bl decor.................................175.00
Vermont, vase, floral decor, jeweled 125.00
Wide Band, bell, roses 195.00
Wild Bouquet, bowl, sauce; gold & decor...........................60.00
Wild Bouquet, butter dish, gold & decor, rare 750.00
Wild Bouquet, creamer, no gold 145.00
Wild Bouquet, cruet, gold & decor....................................995.00
Wild Bouquet, spooner, gold & decor 175.00
Wild Bouquet, tumbler, no decor......................................100.00
Winged Scroll, bowl, master berry; gold & decor, 11" L.............250.00
Winged Scroll, bowl, sauce; good gold................................50.00
Winged Scroll, butter dish, good gold 235.00
Winged Scroll, butter dish, no decor 175.00
Winged Scroll, celery vase, good gold, rare 400.00
Winged Scroll, cigarette jar, scarce...................................195.00
Winged Scroll, compote, ruffled, rare, 6¾x10¾"....................495.00
Winged Scroll, cruet, good gold, rpl clear stopper 400.00
Winged Scroll, hair receiver, good gold............................135.00
Winged Scroll, pitcher, water; bulbous, good gold.................400.00
Winged Scroll, shakers, bulbous, good gold, rare, pr.................400.00
Winged Scroll, shakers, str sides, good gold, pr......................300.00
Winged Scroll, sugar bowl, w/lid, good gold.........................175.00
Winged Scroll, syrup, good gold 450.00
Winged Scroll, tumbler, good gold......................................75.00

Cut Glass

The earliest documented evidence of commercial glass cutting in the United States was in 1810; the producers were Bakewell and Page of Pittsburgh. These first efforts resulted in simple patterns with only a moderate amount of cutting. By the middle of the century, glass cutters began experimenting with a thicker glass which enabled them to use deeper cuttings, though patterns remained much the same. This period is usually referred to as Rich Cut. Using three types of wheels — a flat edge, a mitered edge, and a convex edge — facets, miters, and depressions were combined to produce various designs. In the late 1870s, a curved miter was developed which greatly expanded design potential. Patterns became more elaborate, often covering the entire surface. The Brilliant Period of cut glass covered a span from about 1880 until 1915. Because of the pressure necessary to achieve the deeply cut patterns, only glass containing a high grade of metal could withstand the process. For this reason and the amount of handwork involved, cut glass has always been expensive. Bowls cut with pinwheels may be either foreign or of a newer vintage, beware! Identifiable patterns and signed pieces that are well cut and in excellent condition bring the higher prices on today's market. For more information, we recommend *Evers' Standard Cut Glass Value Guide* (Collector Books). See also Dorflinger; Hawkes; Libbey; Tuthill; Val St. Lambert; other specific manufacturers.

Basket, Daisy, eng, Pitkins & Brooks, 8", from $475 to 525.00
Basket, Sunbeam, Pitkins & Brooks, 7½", from $250 to 300.00
Bell, call; Buzz Star, from $175 to 225.00
Bell, Jewel, TB Clark & Co, lg, from $275 to 325.00
Bonbon, American Beauty, Averbeck, 5", from $75 to 90.00
Bonbon, Argo, JD Bergen, 7", from $70 to.......................................85.00
Bonbon, Beverly, Pitkins & Brooks, 6", from $75 to......................90.00
Bonbon, Garland, w/lid, Pitkins & Brooks, 5", from $70 to 80.00
Bonbon, Lady Curzon, Averbeck, from $85 to.............................100.00
Bottle, cologne; Carolyn, Pitkins & Brooks, 6-oz, from $85 to ...110.00
Bottle, cologne; Mars, Pitkins & Brooks, 8-oz, from $125 to 150.00
Bottle, tobasco; Delmar, Pitkins & Brooks, from $100 to............125.00
Bowl, Chester, JD Bergen, 10", from $250 to 300.00
Bowl, Corsair, JD Bergen, 9", from $130 to 150.00
Bowl, Desdemona, TB Clark & Co, 10", from $250 to 300.00
Bowl, nappy, Clover, leaf shape, hdl, Higgins & Seiter, from $50 to ..60.00
Bowl, nappy, Kenwood, JD Bergen, 7", from $150 to 175.00
Bowl, nappy, Ruby, no hdl, Averbeck, 5", from $75 to 90.00
Bowl, punch; Carolyn, Pitkins & Brooks, 14", from $1,000 to ...1,200.00
Bowl, punch; Edna, JD Bergen, 14", from $1,200 to.................1,500.00
Bowl, punch; Plymouth, Pitkins & Brooks, 12", from $850 to ..1,000.00
Bowl, Ruby, Averbeck, 7", from $65 to...80.00
Bowl, salad; Carnegie, Pitkins & Brooks, 8", from $150 to 200.00
Bowl, salad; Venice, Pitkins & Brooks, 8", from $150 to.............175.00
Bowl, whipped cream; Liberty, Averbeck, 7x4½", from $125 to .150.00
Box, glove; Delmar, Pitkins & Brooks, 11", from $275 to 300.00
Box, panel cut, star-pattern lid, SP collar, CF Monroe, 6" dia 600.00
Box, panel-cut, swivel mirror in star-cut lid, CF Monroe, 4" dia..350.00
Box, puff; Crete, Pitkins & Brooks, from $150 to 175.00
Butter tub & plate, Ruby, Averbeck, from $250 to 300.00
Butterette, Saratoga, Averbeck, from $20 to 25.00
Candlestick, Albert, JD Bergen, 10", from $150 to.......................175.00
Candlestick, Oro, Pitkins & Brooks, 8", from $150 to.................225.00
Carafe, Gilmore, JD Bergen, qt, from $150 to 175.00
Carafe, Heart Globe, Pitkins & Brooks, from $225 to.................275.00
Carafe, Roland, JD Bergen, qt, from $150 to 175.00
Celery tray, Diamond, Averbeck, 12", from $175 to 200.00
Celery tray, Domino, JD Bergen, 4½x11", from $175 to 225.00
Celery tray, Meadville, Pitkins & Brooks, 11", from $125 to 150.00
Celery tray, Winola, TB Clark & Co, from $75 to 100.00
Cheese dish, Webster, Higgins & Seiter, from $250 to 300.00
Comport, Alexis, Pitkins & Brooks, from $125 to........................150.00
Comport, London, spoon dish w/ft, Overbeck, 7½", from $150 to ..200.00
Comports, Marcus, JD Bergen, 8", from $175 to 225.00
Cordial set, Glenwood, JD Bergen, decanter+6 cordials+tray, $500 to..650.00
Creamer & sugar bowl, Lady Curzon, Averbeck, from $90 to 110.00

Creamer & sugar bowl, Mars, Pitkins & Brooks, from $150 to ...175.00
Creamer & sugar bowl, Washington, Higgins & Seiter, from $70 to...80.00
Cruet, oil; Bermuda, Pitkins & Brooks, 8½", from $175 to.........200.00
Cruet, oil; Prism, JD Bergen, ½-pt, from $75 to...........................90.00
Cup, Electric, JD Bergen, from $22 to...25.00
Cup, Premier, JD Bergen, from $30 to..35.00
Cup, Rajah, Pitkins & Brooks, from $30 to..................................35.00
Decanter, Ansonia, JD Bergen, 1-qt, from $250 to......................300.00
Decanter, Florida, Averbeck, no hdl, pt, from $125 to 150.00
Decanter, Golf, JD Bergen, 1-pt, from $150 to.............................200.00
Decanter, Russian, att Mt WA, 11x5" 975.00
Goblet, Electric, JD Bergen, from $50 to......................................55.00
Goblet, Marie, JD Bergen, from $60 to...70.00
Goblet, Naples, Averbeck, from $40 to 50.00

Fruit bowl and plate, Star pattern, Hawkes, 1890s, 8½", 10", $715.00. (Photo courtesy Neal Auction Company)

Goblet, Winola, TB Clark & Co, from $35 to 40.00
Hair receiver, Esther, Pitkins & Brooks, 5", from $200 to 250.00
Humidor, Glenwood, JD Bergen, holds 50 cigars, from $200 to..250.00
Jar, horseradish; Savoy, JD Bergen, from $125 to 150.00
Jug, claret; Princeton, JD Bergen, 3-pt, from $375 to 425.00
Jug, Desdemona, Priscilla shape, TB Clark & Co, from $350 to.400.00
Jug, Savoy, JD Bergen, 1-qt, from $250 to....................................300.00
Lamp, Arc, electric, Pitkins & Brooks, 12½", from $450 to........500.00
Lamp, Chrysanthemum, eng, 32 prisms, electric, Pitkins & Brooks, 17"....1,350.00
Loving cup, Prism, Averbeck, ½-pt, from $30 to 50.00
Mayonnaise set, Radium, Averbeck, bowl+plate, 5", from $125 to..150.00
Mustard dish & plate, Premier, JD Bergen, from $150 to 170.00
Olive dish, Priscilla, Averbeck, 7¾", from $100 to......................125.00
Pickle dish, Canton, Averbeck, 8", from $150 to 175.00
Pitcher, claret; Syrott, Higgins & Seiter, 3-pt, from $250 to 300.00
Pitcher, Delta, JD Bergen, 1-qt, from $175 to..............................200.00
Pitcher, Goldenrod, JD Bergen, 2-qt, from $300 to 350.00
Pitcher, Vienna, Averbeck, 3-pt, from $225 to 250.00
Plate, American Beauty, Averbeck, 7", from $125 to 150.00
Plate, Lowell, Averbeck, 7", from $70 to..80.00
Plateau, Star, Pitkins & Brooks, 10", from $20 to 25.00
Salad fork & spoon, Manhattan, TB Clark & Co, pr, from $75 to ..100.00
Salt cellar, DeSoto, JD Bergen, from $20 to................................75.00
Salt cellar, Venus, TB Clark & Co, from $15 to............................20.00
Saucer, Beaver, Pitkins & Brooks, 5", from $70 to........................85.00
Shaker, Henry VII, TB Clark & Co, from $20 to..........................25.00
Spoon holder, Jewell, Empress shape, TB Clark K & Co, from $100 to ...125.00
Spooner, Cortez, Pitkins & Brooks, 7½", from $125 to 135.00
Spooner, Diamond, Averbeck, from $175 to 200.00
Spooner, Marietta, Averbeck, from $110 to 135.00
Spooner, Prism, Averbeck, from $60 to 75.00
Sugar bowl, Oregon, JD Bergen, from $40 to..............................50.00
Tray, ice cream; Adonis, TB Clark & Co, from $400 to.............450.00
Tray, ice cream; Kenwood, JD Bergen, 9x16", from $500 to........600.00
Tray, ice cream; Renaissance, Averbeck, 8x12", from $50 to.........65.00
Tub, ice; Napoleon, Higgins & Seiter, w/underplate, from $250 to..300.00

Tumbler, champagne; Gilmore, JD Bergen, from $30 to **35.00**
Tumbler, Florentine, Higgins & Seiter, from $25 to......................**30.00**
Tumbler, Savoy, JD Bergen, from $25 to..**30.00**
Vase, Florida, Averbeck, 10", from $125 to **200.00**
Vase, Henry VIII, TB Clark & Co, 10", from $150 to.................**200.00**
Vase, Naples, Averbeck, 17", from $900 to.................................**1,000.00**
Vase, Queen, JD Bergen, 10", from $150 to **200.00**
Vase, Sheldon, JD Bergen, 14", from $400 to................................**500.00**
Vase, Trophy, JD Bergen, slim, 12", from $80 to **120.00**
Water set, Golf, JD Bergen, pitcher+6 tumblers+tray, from $600 to........**650.00**
Water set, Newport, JD Bergen, carafe+6 tumblers+tray, from $350 to ..**375.00**

Cut Overlay Glass

Glassware with one or more overlying colors through which a design has been cut is called 'Cut Overlay.' It was made both here and abroad. Watch for new imitations!

Bottle, scent; wht cut to bl w/gilt, matching stopper, 6".............**150.00**
Candlesticks, cranberry to clear w/circles, silver mts, 8¾", pr.......**80.00**
Celery, Polka Dot, shaded cranberry over wht & clear, Wheeling, 6¾".**385.00**
Champagne, cobalt to clear w/vintage, base of bowl faceted, 4x3¾" **65.00**
Cup & saucer, wht cut to gr, wht panels remain, gilt trim...........**100.00**
Mustard pot, wht cut to clear w/cloverleaves, gilt trim, hdl, 4½".**135.00**
Spill holder, wht cut to ruby w/windows, HP hunting scenes, gilt, 6"...**110.00**
Vase, cobalt/wht/clear, trefoils/loops/rings, baluster, 12", pr **1,850.00**
Vase, cranberry to clear, oval windows, heavy gold florals, 5½"..**385.00**
Wine, cranberry to clear w/strawberry, dmn & fan, star base, 4½"...**75.00**

Cut Velvet

Cut Velvet glassware was made during the late 1800s. It is characterized by the effect achieved through the execution of relief-molded patterns, often ribbing or diamond quilting, which allows its white inner casing to show through the outer layer.

Cup, Dmn Quilt, pk **130.00**
Finger bowl, Dmn Quilt, bl, 2½" **230.00**
Lamp, Dmn Quilt, rose pk, opal glass ball shade, 17" **495.00**

Pitcher, Diamond Quilt, deep sapphire blue, blue reeded handle, 8¾x6", $400.00.

Vase, Dmn Quilt, dk mauve, bulbous w/stick neck, 6"...................**95.00**
Vase, Dmn Quilt, dk to lt pk, ruffled 4-lobe top, Mt WA, 4¼x3"...**225.00**
Vase, Dmn Quilt, lt gold, dbl-gourd w/curved neck, 13½" **650.00**
Vase, Dmn Quilt, lt to dk gr, stick neck, 9", pr **300.00**
Vase, Dmn Quilt, orange, ruffled/flared top, 9x6" **675.00**
Vase, Dmn Quilt, pk, 11" **250.00**
Vase, Dmn Quilt, royal bl, squat, 2" rim, 3" **200.00**
Vase, Herringbone, ruffled/flared rim trn down on 2 sides, Mt WA, 8" ..**450.00**

Vase, vertical ribs, bl, 8"..**285.00**
Vase, vertical ribs, pk, rnd w/stick neck, 6" **175.00**

Cybis

Boleslaw Cybis was a graduate of the Academy of Fine Arts in Warsaw, Poland, and was well recognized as a fine artist by the time he was commissioned by his government to paint murals in the Polish Pavilion's Hall of Honor at the 1939 World's Fair. Finding themselves stranded in America at the outbreak of WWII, the Cybises founded an artists' studio, first in Astoria, New York, and later in Trenton, New Jersey, where they made fine figurines and plaques with exacting artistry and craftsmanship entailing extensive handwork. The studio still operates today producing exquisite porcelains on a limited edition basis.

Aphrodite, #675, 8½" **740.00**
Baby Brother, duckling, 3½x4x3"...**120.00**
Buffalo, 3x5¼"...**170.00**
Child w/teddy bear & Christmas stocking, 5½"............................**80.00**
Duck, 4¼"...**165.00**
Eskimo chld bust, #466, Children of the World Collection, 10½".....**255.00**
First Flight Girl, girl kneeling w/bird in hand, 4½" **100.00**
Goldilocks & Panda, Children To Cherish Collection, 6" **500.00**
Harlequin, masked, #86, 15½"...**315.00**
Indian colt, kneeling, feather & braid in mane, 4½x8¾" **265.00**
Little Red Riding Hood, 6¾"..**330.00**
Madonna w/bird on wrist, 11½"..**210.00**
Magnolia Blossom, 8x6x5" **255.00**
Mallard ducks, mating pr, 14"..**500.00**
Mary, Children To Cherish Collection, #478, 10½"....................**340.00**
Mr Fluffy Tail, squirrel, Woodland Series, 8" **430.00**
Ophelia (Hamlet), #135, 13" **815.00**
Owl, 4½"...**105.00**
Polyanna, Children To Cherish Collection, #465, 7" **160.00**
Princess Red Feather, Children To Cherish Collection, 10" **810.00**
Queen of Peace, 7" **205.00**
Rabbit, 3¼x4½"...**180.00**
Siamese cat, 6½" **810.00**
Sir Escargot, snail, 3¼x4" **255.00**
Wendy, young girl in nightgown holding doll, 6½" **125.00**
White Cloud, Children To Cherish Collection, 11½" **810.00**

Czechoslovakian Collectibles

Czechoslovakia came into being as a country in 1918. Located in the heart of Europe, it was a land with the natural resources necessary to support a glass industry that dated back to the mid-fourteenth century. The glass that was produced there has captured the attention of today's collectors, and for good reason. There are beautiful vases — cased, ruffled, applied with rigaree or silver overlay — fine enough to rival those of the best glasshouses. Czechoslovakian art glass baskets are quite as attractive as Victorian America's, and the elegant cut glass perfumes made in colors as well as crystal are unrivaled. There are also pressed glass perfumes, molded in lovely Deco shapes, of various types of art glass. Some are overlaid with gold filigree set with 'jewels.' Jewelry, lamps, porcelains, and fine art pottery are also included in the field.

More than seventy marks have been recorded, including those in the mold, ink stamped, acid etched, or on a small metal nameplate. The newer marks are incised, stamped 'Royal Dux Made in Czechoslovakia' (see Royal Dux), or printed on a paper label which reads 'Bohemian Glass Made in Czechoslovakia.' (Communist controlled from 1948, Czechoslovakia once again was made a free country in December 1989.

Today it no longer exists; after 1993 it was divided to form two countries, the Czech Republic and the Slovak Republic.) For a more thorough study of the subject, we recommend *Made in Czechoslovakia* and *Made in Czechoslovakia Book 2*, by our advisor, Ruth A. Forsythe. Other fine books are *Czechoslovakian Glass & Collectibles*, Volumes I and II, by Dale and Diane Barta and Helen M. Rose; *Czechoslovakian Perfume Bottles and Boudoir Accessories* by Jacquelyne Y. Jones North, and *Czechoslovakian Pottery* by Bowers, Closser, and Ellis. In the listings that follow, when one dimension is given, it refers to height; decoration is enamel unless noted otherwise. See also Amphora; Erphila.

Candy Containers

Bl & yel mottle w/yel ruffle rim, jet hdl, 8" 300.00
Blk cased w/silver mica, bl int, blk hdl, 8" 350.00
Lt gr varicolored, matching hdl, 8" 200.00
Mc mottle, crystal str-top thorn hdl, 6½" 200.00
Pk varicolored, matching hdl, 8" 200.00
Red & yel mottle, crystal str-top hdl, 8½" 125.00
Red & yel mottle, twisted crystal thorn hdl, 7" 220.00
Red varicolored w/twisted crystal thorn hdl, 5½" 250.00
Yel opaque w/blk rim, simple crystal hdl, 6½" 200.00

Cased Art Glass

Bowl, mc mottled (autumn colors) satin, amber cased, 3-ftd, 4⅛" ... 175.00
Candlestick, cameo vine, blk on orange, slim w/wide ft, 12½" ... 650.00
Decanter, silver o/l bird on orange, 12" 135.00
Vase, apple gr w/3 cobalt rim-to-hip hdls, cobalt rim, 8¼" 875.00
Vase, bird on branch on orange w/blk trim, shouldered/ftd, 11" . 200.00
Vase, bl, 3 blk buttressed ft, 9" 125.00
Vase, bl opaque, appl red spirals eventually form hdls, 8½" 175.00
Vase, bl w/pk lining, crimped/ruffled top, 8½" 110.00
Vase, fan; red w/gr aventurine, 7½" 195.00
Vase, gr, clear gr ornaments down sides of trumpet neck, 5½" 95.00
Vase, jack-in-the-pulpit; yel w/thin blk trim at rim, 13½" 150.00
Vase, lav, slim w/blk trim on ruffled rim, 8¼" 95.00
Vase, orange & blk varicolored, waisted, ftd, flared rim, 8" 120.00
Vase, red w/blk streaky o/l, 4½" 85.00
Vase, red w/gr aventurine, gourd shape, 7¼" 180.00
Vase, red w/spiraling blk serpentine, 6½" 100.00
Vase, red w/3 cobalt hdls & rim, bulbous, 5½" 575.00
Vase, varicolored w/gr aventurine, trumpet neck, ftd, 7" 150.00
Vase, wht opaque, appl dk amber ornaments, ball form, 4⅝" 125.00
Vase, yel w/blk clovers, 3 blk angle hdls, 3½" 675.00
Vase, yel w/brn mottle at base, slightly shouldered, 6¼" 85.00
Vase, yel w/mc mottle on lower half, flared ft & rim, 8" 95.00
Vase, yel w/silver decor, blk at ft & rim, 9½" 65.00
Wine, red w/blk stem, silver trim, 7½" 65.00

Cut Glass Perfume Bottles

Amber, geometric cutting, shouldered, faceted teardrop stopper, 6" .. 180.00
Amber, geometric cutting on half-circle, figure in stopper, 5½" . 450.00
Amber to clear, geometric cutting, atomizer fittings, 8½" 200.00
Bl, geometric cutting, 3-prong tulip-like stopper, 5" 265.00
Bl, low/wide stepped base, lovers clear/frosted stopper, 6¼" 850.00
Blk opaque, slim stepped form w/crystal crescent stopper, 4⅝" ... 250.00
Blk opaque w/jewels & gold, clear stopper, 4¼" 375.00
Crystal, clear & frosted cranes stopper, 7⅞" 650.00
Crystal, geometric cutting, bl floral stopper, 5⅝" 160.00
Crystal, geometric cutting, shouldered, red stopper w/figure, 5½"... 400.00
Crystal, sm pyramidal base w/slim amber prism stopper, 6½" 165.00
Gr, floral cutting on ball shape, flower stopper, 5⅛" 180.00

Gr, sloped sides, shell-shaped stopper, 4⅞" 150.00
Gr, w/gold & jewels, 4⅝" 400.00
Gr/crystal, 2-pc bottle, gr frosted floral stopper, 6" 475.00
Pk, ornate cutting, shouldered, pk frosted floral stopper, 8" 450.00
Topaz, geometric cutting, geometric shield-shape stopper, 5½" .. 170.00
Topaz, simple cutting, floral spear-shaped stopper, 6⅛" 180.00

Lamps

Beaded glass basket of fruit form, metal fr, 10x8½" 1,035.00
Desk, metal base, acid-cut shade, 10" 600.00
Kerosene, pnt milk glass w/gold trim, 12¾" 200.00
Lamp, Art Deco figure stands by crystal (bubbly) globe on ped, 9" .. 800.00
Lamp, cobalt lustre, classic shape, rpl shade, 13¼" 200.00
Perfume, cut bl shade, 4" 350.00
Perfume, enamel florals, 4" 350.00
Sconce, crystal, 2-arm, prisms, 14½" 300.00
Student, metal shade, acid-cut shade, 21" 1,000.00
Table, Art Deco geometric base, matching conical shade, 9" .. 1,000.00
Table, basket form, mc fruit in bl beaded base, 8" 900.00
Table, basket form, mc nuts & fruit, crystal beaded base, 10¾" ... 1,200.00
Table, lady figural, porc w/glass flower skirt & bodice, 10¼" ... 1,200.00
Table, mc mottled satin base & shade, 12½" 800.00
Table, peacock figural, brass w/beaded glass tail/blk onyx base, 12" ... 1,400.00
Table, pnt church & snow scene, 8¾" 500.00

Mold-Blown and Pressed Bottles

Atomizer, cobalt w/enamel, jewel top, 7¼" 280.00
Atomizer, crystal w/pnt decor, slim, 7¾" 125.00
Atomizer, gr w/appl blk serpentine, 8" 375.00

Black base with molded archer and flying geese, clear stopper with engraved birds, signed Ingrid Czechoslovakia, 5½", $1,250.00. (Photo courtesy Monsen and Baer)

Bl opaque, emb nude & butterfly, 5¼" 1,200.00
Cranberry opal, Hobnail, wht opal stopper, 5½" 225.00
Crystal w/chain dangles & jewels, 3" 185.00
Dk bl enamel w/jewels, gilt metal lid w/chain, scarce, 3" 300.00
Gr, canteen form w/overall jewels, 2⅝" 250.00
Purple lustre, bulbous base, flower stopper, 4½" 200.00

Opaque, Crystal, Colored Transparent Glass

Bl opaque, trumpet neck, 7" 100.00
Decanter, amber w/floral cutting, shouldered cylinder, 8" 150.00
Decanter, gr (bubbly), HP fox hunt scene, 9⅝" 175.00
Martini set, 13" blk tray+4 blk/red glasses w/silver o/l 230.00
Pitcher, bl (bubbly), squat, sm neck/rim, 4-bead stopper, 8⅝" 200.00
Pitcher, exotic bird, mc on cobalt, w/lid, 11¼" 350.00
Tumbler, exotic bird on dk bl, 5½" 65.00
Vase, crystal w/red & blk streaky o/l, ftd, 8¼" 200.00
Vase, fan; orange w/yel o/l, 8" 200.00

Vase, mauve, acid etched, ruffled rim w/blk trim, 5⅝" 125.00
Vase, pk lustre w/lustre threading at top, ftd, 9⅜" 475.00
Vase, red & wht mottle, slim cylinder, 5⅞"...............................65.00
Vase, wht opal w/appl opal balls (5 ea side) forming hdls, 8⅝"...275.00

Pottery, Procelain, Semiporcelain

Bowl, vining floral, mc on blk, wht int, 3" H..............................75.00
Canister, flower basket reserve, Tea, sq sides, 7½" 45.00
Creamer, cow figural, wht w/brn spots, blk tail hdl, 6¾" 110.00
Creamer, moose-head figural, brn tones, antlers form rim, 4⅞" 45.00
Creamer, parrot figural, 4½" 55.00
Creamer, wht w/blk & wht cat hdl, 4⅜" 75.00
Creamer & sugar bowl, pk lustre, w/lid, 3¼", 4"..........................50.00
Flower holder, bird on stump, 5⅜"......................................40.00
Shakers, Mexican man & lady, red/wht/yel, 2¾", pr...................30.00
Wall pocket, bird & apples, 4¾"...65.00
Wall pocket, bird perched beside birdhouse, 5½" 60.00
Wall pocket, peacock, mc on cobalt w/blk trim, 7¼" 125.00
Wall pocket, woodpecker on tree trunk, 7¾"..............................70.00

D'Argental

D'Argental cameo glass was produced in France from the 1870s until about 1920 in the Art Nouveau style. Browns and tans were favored colors used to complement floral and scenic designs developed through acid cuttings. Our advisor for this category is Don Williams; he is listed in the Directory under Missouri.

Cameo

Candy dish, floral, dk gr on orange, w/lid, 5x7" dia..................1,400.00
Vase, floral, brn on yel/red, 7x4½" 750.00
Vase, floral garden, gr/gray on clear, rose top/base, shouldered, 14" ..2,000.00
Vase, flower garden, dk red on sunset ground, shouldered, 4" 325.00
Vase, Grotesque, rectangular body w/4-pointed ruffled rim, 5¾" ...250.00

Vase, landscape scene beyond grasses and trees, butterscotch, red, brown, and black, 13", $1,540.00. (Photo courtesy Jackson's Auctioneers & Appraisers of Fine Art)

Vase, leaves, royal bl on frost, ftd, stick neck, 6" 500.00
Vase, palm trees/island beyond, purple on amethyst frost, 9¾" ...700.00
Vase, trees/castle on mtn beyond, brn on yel, 7¾"..................1,300.00

Daum Nancy

Daum was an important producer of French cameo glass, operating from the late 1800s until after the turn of the century. They used various techniques — acid cutting, wheel engraving, and handwork — to create beautiful scenic designs and nature subjects in the Art Nouveau manner. Virtually all examples are signed. Daum is still in production, producing many figural items. Our advisor for this category is Don Williams; he is listed in the Directory under Missouri.

Cameo

Bottle, liquor; design/label of Grand Marnier on gr, 8½".........1,000.00
Bottle, scent; floral, violet on pk/gr, w/gilt, cvd/gilded stopper, 3" ..950.00
Bowl, columbine cut/pnt on yel frost to wine, 3x8" 2,600.00
Bowl, evening landscape on mottled orange, lobed rim, 2¾x6" ..1,150.00
Bowl, orchids cut/pnt on yel & gr mottle, shaped rim, 7½".....3,450.00
Bowl, ship, cut/pnt on bl & frost, red shoreline, 4½" 800.00
Bowl, summer woodland, 1x2" L 850.00
Bowl, trees & lake/bk & lid: florals, mc/gilt on opal, 1¼x1¾" ...1,400.00
Box, floral stems cut/pnt on yel/purple, dome lid, 4" dia..........1,600.00
Box, fuchsia, cut/pnt on wht mottle, sqd form, dome lid, 3x4"...6,300.00
Cordial, trees/lake/mtns, brn on red-amber, 2" 550.00
Flask, thistles/banner w/motto, cut/pnt on gr w/gold, 7"............475.00
Jar, 4 floral bands w/gold on clear & frost, w/lid, 5¼x2½".......1,300.00
Lamp, trees extend from base, tree-tops mushroom shade, 25"..11,000.00
Pitcher, bleeding hearts cut/pnt on pk/wht, peach hdl, 3" 2,150.00
Pitcher, orchids cut/pnt on orange to tan w/gr ft, 4½" 2,100.00
Pitcher, violets, wine/maroon on gr to pk, gold collar, cvd hdl, 5" .2,000.00
Rose bowl, ducks/flowers allover, cut/pnt on wht, egg shape, 5½"..2,300.00
Salt buckets, 4 seasons, 1¼x1¾", set of 4, MIB......................6,500.00
Salt cellar, holly leaves/berries on vitrified citron, 1⅛x2" L 1,200.00
Salt cellar, rain scene cut/pnt on pk/gr, 1x2", NM...................2,850.00
Salt cellar, summer scene, blk on gr, cut/pnt, 1x2"...................1,300.00
Salt cellar, winter scene on orange, 1¾".................................1,600.00
Tumbler, floral cut/pnt on opal frost, gold trim, 1¾", NM 1,250.00
Tumbler, mistletoe, wht/gold on opal texture, 4¾".....................500.00
Vase, bellflowers, dk/lt purple, martele, in lily-emb silver base, 8" ...2,300.00
Vase, berries cvd/appl, orange on orange to gr w/purple at ft, 13" 4,850.00
Vase, berry clusters, done in vitrified powders, stick neck, ftd, 9".....1,500.00
Vase, blown-out trees/foliage w/buildings beyond, yel/orange, 12x4"..6,300.00
Vase, carnation, purple on bl & pk, pillow form, 1½x2"..........1,100.00
Vase, day lilies, bl/gr on gr to amethyst/bl mottle, spherical, 2½".1,450.00
Vase, Dutch winter scene ea side, cvd/pnt, pillow form, 2¼" .1,350.00
Vase, floral, lt/dk rust w/gr stems on cranberry to yel/wht, 4¾x6"..2,250.00
Vase, floral allover, cvd from vitrified powders, slim form, 20"..5,300.00
Vase, floral spikes cut/pnt on yel to purple, 4-sided, 4¾x2" 1,725.00
Vase, floral stems/geometrics, burgundy/gr on pastel mottle, slim, 20"..5,500.00
Vase, floral w/gold on cranberry frost, rectangular, 4¾"..............700.00
Vase, fuchsia, lav/pk on wht/purple, sqd/waisted, 4½x3½" 1,700.00
Vase, iris, bk: dragonfly, on clear to amethyst, cylindrical, 14"..1,350.00
Vase, leaves/berries, 3-layer on orange/yel/mottle, slim/bun base, 15"..3,500.00
Vase, leaves/tendrils, vitrified yel/orange on turq, stick neck, 27"....4,600.00
Vase, lg oaks/stream/mtn, gr/dk bl on lt bl/frost, pillow form, 5x6"..3,300.00
Vase, lily of the valley, lime w/opal & allover martele, 4¼x3" ..2,850.00
Vase, lily of valley, gr on martele turq, squat w/swollen neck, 5" ..2,000.00
Vase, mushrooms cut/pnt on yel mottle, tapered cylinder w/hdls, 7½"..14,000.00
Vase, poppies, cut/pnt red on orange/yel, 5¾x3½"..................2,100.00
Vase, prairie scene cut /pnt on pk to gr, cylinder w/flattened rim, 8"..10,600.00
Vase, purple flowers/gr/leaves on wht to orange, long can neck, 5x3"..1,600.00
Vase, river/boats/hills, brn on yel/orange, ovoid, 5½" 1,800.00
Vase, sailboat/hills, brn on yel/orange, long neck, ftd, 11½"....2,850.00
Vase, scenic (detailed) cut/pnt on wht w/yel, 4-sided, 4½x2"..2,100.00
Vase, sweet peas, ruby on wht/amethyst/orange, ftd cylinder, 4½"..1,300.00
Vase, trees, lake w/ships beyond, sunset, wide flat-sided neck, 12"..2,650.00
Vase, trees/lake, lav on rust mottle, frosted sky, ftd trumpet, 7"........1,500.00
Vase, trees/lake/rocky shores on bl, cut/pnt, 2½" 950.00
Vase, trees/rocks before lake/mtns, gr/blk on gr/rust/yel, ftd, 17"........3,950.00

Vase, tulips cut/pnt/bk: HP fisherman & windmills on opal, hdls, 11"...**2,800.00**
Vase, turtles/sea horses/coral, crystal w/int mc streaks, cylinder, 13 ...**1,850.00**
Vase, vines/leaves/flowers, purple/yel on rust/ruby/yel, bulbous, 5" ..**2,500.00**
Vase, violet/buds on long stems on bl/wht, bulbous, flared rim, 3¼" .**1,600.00**
Vase, violets on stems cut/pnt on purple/wht, gold motif at base, 16".**9,500.00**
Vase, violets w/gr & gold on wht & amethyst, 3 amethyst loop ft, 4x4"..**4,250.00**
Vase, winter scene on orange/yel, 3-pinch ft & triangular rim, 3¾".**2,250.00**
Vase, winter trees ea side on yel mottle, pillow form, 3¼x4½".**1,900.00**

Miscellaneous

Compote, mottled rust & gr, X of Lorrain cvd on ft, 5x9" **350.00**
Lamp, 15" conical shade & base w/etched triangle borders, smoky gray .**4,000.00**
Vase, bottom shaped as head of garlic, gr/bl/yel/wht mottle, 12"......**4,300.00**
Vase, Deco flower band, heavy 3-color pnt on bl, ftd U form, 8" ..**575.00**
Vase, turq w/wine & gold foil blown into Marjorelle fr w/flowers, 12".**4,850.00**

De Vez

De Vez was a type of acid-cut French cameo glass produced by Cristallerie de Pantin in Paris around the turn of the century. Our advisor for this category is Don Williams; he is listed in the Directory under Missouri.

Cameo

Atomizer, rose garden, dk bl on turq, no sprayer, 6" **350.00**
Bowl, cascading foliage w/mtns/island beyond, gr on yel, lid, 3½" ..**350.00**
Lamp base, 4 sailing ships, bl on gr to wht, 24" **1,800.00**
Rose bowl, grapes/leaves, maroon/red on citron, 4-crimp rim, 3x4½"..**500.00**
Vase, boats/lake, shoreline beyond, lav on sunset sky, slim, 6¾".**850.00**
Vase, bud; ships/overhanging leaves, bls on yel to pk, top ground, 3"...**495.00**
Vase, fish boat/mtn lake/village beyond, bl on amber sky, 5x5" ..**850.00**
Vase, flowers, boats beyond, amethyst/bl on bl/yel, slim form, 9½"..**650.00**
Vase, gondola/ships/Venus harbor, bl on citron w/pastel sky, 12" ..**1,050.00**
Vase, grasses, royal bl on lav/pk, rare sz: 1¼" **325.00**
Vase, island w/distant chalet, florals at bulbous rim on rust, 8"...**700.00**
Vase, lake/islands/shore, bl on lt bl, ftd, bulbous w/pointed rim, 6"..**900.00**
Vase, lake/trees/islands/mtns, bls on yel to pk, shouldered, 6".....**495.00**
Vase, lg tree/cabin on island in mtn lake, mahog on yel/frost, 8"...**880.00**
Vase, lg trees/lake & mtns beyond, purple on orange, slim, 4½".**500.00**
Vase, pines/mtns/cabin, violet on yel/bl, swollen cylinder, 8" ..**1,250.00**
Vase, sm deer/trees/snowy hills, maroon on orange, 6½"............**650.00**
Vase, trees/lake/sailboats, royal bl on pastels, 2¼" **350.00**

De Vilbiss

Perfume bottles, atomizers, and dresser accessories marketed by the De Vilbiss Company are appreciated by collectors today for the various types of lovely glassware used in their manufacture as well as for their pleasing shapes. Various companies provided the glass, while De Vilbiss made only the metal tops. They marketed their merchandise not only here but in Paris, England, Canada, and Havana as well. Their marks were acid stamped, ink stamped, in gold script, molded in, or on paper labels. One is no more significant than another. Our advisor for this category is Randy Monsen; he is listed in the Directory under Virginia.

Atomizer, amber egg shape on curvilinear metal stand, 6¼".......**220.00**
Atomizer, amber trumpet form w/cut flowers, Steuben/De Vilbiss, 7½" ..**350.00**
Atomizer, amber w/etched flower trellis in gold & blk, rpl ball, 9".**440.00**
Atomizer, bl Aurene w/cvd flowers, rpl ball/tassel, 9¾" **1,100.00**
Atomizer, bl enamel w/stencil, ovoid, orig ball/cord, 7¼" **100.00**

Atomizer, bl w/cut leaves/enameled gazelles, rpl ball, 6⅜" **440.00**
Atomizer, blk bullet shape on brass scroll fr, orig ball, 6" **385.00**
Atomizer, blk w/mc leaves & gold, ped ft, orig ball, 9½" **770.00**
Atomizer, clear, asymmetrical, orig ball, Bakelite finial, 2½", MIB..**165.00**
Atomizer, clear w/cut design, rpl ball/tassel, 6½" **110.00**
Atomizer, frosted & clear w/abstract mc design, orig ball, 6" **285.00**

Atomizer, frosted orange with gold enameling, original gold hardware and bulb, marked, 5½", $300.00. (Photo courtesy Monsen and Baer)

Atomizer, frosted w/molded flowers, gold overcap, all orig, 5¼".**145.00**
Atomizer, lt amber w/etched gold windows, petal design ft, 8" ...**285.00**
Atomizer, peach w/gold enameled lady stem, orig ball, 7⅜" **1,650.00**
Atomizer, pk w/gold trellis, orig pk ball, 7½" **770.00**
Bottle, amber, slim w/wide ft, dropper w/blk glass medallion, 6".**175.00**
Bottle, blk streamline style w/chrome attachment, 2¼", EX.......**220.00**
Bottle, blk w/3 orange-enameled flower panels, glass dauber, 4¾"..**185.00**
Bottle, HP roses & leaves, hexagonal, metal shaker top, pre-1920s, 4"..**66.00**
Bottle, lt gr w/enameled gr & gold chevrons, 7¾" **265.00**
Bottle, pk enamel w/blk stencil, dropper w/flat top, 4¾" **120.00**
Bottle & atomizer, blk w/gold leaves, 7½", pr, M in gold box **825.00**
Bottle & atomizer, pk w/cut leaves & gold pheasants, 9¼", pr ..**1,980.00**
Dresser set, HP flowers w/gold trim, 7-pc.................................**1,000.00**
Ginger jar, lt amber w/gold pine needles, 6¼" **415.00**
Lamp, perfume; peacock w/long flowing tail, 7¾" **385.00**
Powder box, blk & gold enamel, 4¼" dia....................................**300.00**

Decanters

Ceramic whiskey decanters were brought into prominence in 1955 by the James Beam Distilling Company. Few other companies besides Beam produced these decanters during the next ten years or so; however, other companies did eventually follow suit. At its peak in 1975, at least twenty prominent companies and several on a lesser scale made these decanters. Beam stopped making decanters in mid-1992. Now only a couple of companies are still producing these collectibles.

Liquor dealers have told collectors for years that ceramic decanters are not as valuable, and in some cases worthless, if emptied or if the federal tax stamp has been broken. Nothing is further from the truth. Following are but a few of many reasons you should consider emptying ceramic decanters:

1) If the thin glaze on the inside ever cracks (and it does in a small percentage of decanters), the contents will push through to the outside. It is then referred to as a 'leaker' and worth a fraction of its original value.

2) A large number of decanters left full in one area of your house poses a fire hazard.

3) A burglar, after stealing jewelry and electronics, may make off with some of your decanters just to enjoy the contents. If they are empty, chances are they will not be bothered.

4) It is illegal in most states for collectors to sell a full decanter without a liquor license.

Unlike years ago, few collectors now collect all types of decanters. Most now specialize. For example, they may collect trains, cars, owls, Indians, clowns, or any number of different things that have been depicted on or as a decanter. They are finding exceptional quality available at reasonable prices, especially when compared with many other types of collectibles.

We have tried to list those brands that are the most popular with collectors. Likewise, individual decanters listed are the ones (or representative of the ones) most commonly found. The following listing is but a small fraction of the thousands of decanters that have been produced.

These decanters come from all over the world. While Jim Beam owned its own china factory in the U.S., some of the others have been imported from Mexico, Taiwan, Japan, and elsewhere. They vary in size from miniatures (approximately two-ounce) to gallons. Values range from a few dollars to more than $3,000.00 per decanter.

Most collectors and dealers define a 'mint' decanter as one with no chips, no cracks, and label intact. A missing federal tax stamp or lack of contents have no bearing on value. All values are given for 'mint' decanters. A 'mini' behind a listing indicates a miniature. All others are fifth or 750 ml unless noted otherwise. Our advisor for this category is Roy Willis; he is listed in the Directory under Kentucky.

Aesthetic Specialties (ASI)

Golf, Bing Crosby 39th	40.00
Truck, Ice Cream	80.00
Truck, Telephone	75.00

Beam

Casino Series, Harold's Club Slot Machine, bl	15.00
Casino Series, Harold's Club Slot Machine, gray	12.00
Casino Series, Smith's North Shore	15.00
Centennial Series, Antioch	5.00
Centennial Series, Chicago Fire	20.00
Centennial Series, Dodge City, Boot Hill	10.00
Centennial Series, Laramie	6.00
Centennial Series, Yellowstone	8.00
Executive Series, 1955, Royal Porcelain	210.00
Executive Series, 1957, Royal Dimonte	40.00
Executive Series, 1960, Blue Cherub	60.00
Executive Series, 1968, Presidential	12.00
Executive Series, 1972, Regency	12.00
Foreign Series, Australia, Queensland	20.00
Foreign Series, Australia, Sydney Opera House	24.00
Foreign Series, Australia, Tigers	16.00
Foreign Series, Germany, Hansel & Gretel	10.00
Foreign Series, Germany, Pied Piper	20.00
Foreign Series, Germany, Wiesbaden	10.00
Organization Series, Ducks Unlimited #1, 1974	35.00
Organization Series, Ducks Unlimited #2, 1975	40.00
Organization Series, Ducks Unlimited #3, 1977	40.00
Organization Series, Ducks Unlimited #4, 1978	45.00
Organization Series, Ducks Unlimited #5, 1979	45.00
Organization Series, Fleet Reserve	5.00
Organization Series, Kentucky Colonel	12.00
Organization Series, Marine Corps Emblem	50.00
Organization Series, Pearl Harbor, 1972	20.00
Organization Series, Shriner, Indiana	6.00
Organization Series, VFW	8.00
People Series, Buffalo Bill	20.00
People Series, Captain & Mate	15.00
People Series, General Stark	15.00
People Series, Hatfield or McCoy	25.00
People Series, Indian Chief	20.00

People Series, Rocky Marciano	45.00
State Series, Arizona	10.00
State Series, Florida Shell	6.00
State Series, Illinois	8.00
State Series, Michigan	12.00
State Series, Nebraska	18.00
Wheel Series, Army Jeep	50.00
Wheel Series, Cadillac Convertible, 1959, pk	65.00
Wheel Series, Chevy, 1957 Bel Air Convertible, turq & wht	65.00
Wheel Series, Chevy, 1957 Bel Air Hardtop, red & wht	95.00
Wheel Series, Corvette, 1953, wht	175.00
Wheel Series, Corvette, 1957, blk	85.00

Wheel Series, 1984 Corvettes, White, $75.00; Red, $90.00.

Wheel Series, Duesenberg, 1934, lt bl	110.00
Wheel Series, Ford, 1903 Model A, blk or red	50.00
Wheel Series, Ford, 1928 Model A Coupe, gr	75.00
Wheel Series, Ford, 1929 Phaeton, gr	65.00
Wheel Series, Ford, 1935 Pickup, Clermont Supply	70.00
Wheel Series, Jewel Tea Wagon	60.00
Wheel Series, Train, Baggage Car	45.00
Wheel Series, Train, Casey Jones Box Car, gr	60.00
Wheel Series, Train, Casey Jones Caboose, red	25.00
Wheel Series, Train, Casey Jones Tank Car, wht	50.00
Wheel Series, Train, Dining Car	90.00
Wheel Series, Train, Grant Coal Tender	65.00
Wheel Series, Train, Grant Locomotive	60.00
Wheel Series, Train, Observation Car	65.00
Wheel Series, Train, Passenger Car	45.00

Brooks

American Legion, Hawaii, 1973	16.00
Amvets Polish Legion	10.00
Bareknuckle Fighter	35.00
Basketball Player	20.00
Betsy Ross	10.00
Cardinal, Virginia	18.00
Cards - Jack, Queen or King, ea	15.00
Clock, Grandfather	10.00
Delta Belle, Riverboat	10.00
Duesenberg	35.00
Equestrienne	12.00
Goldpanner	10.00
Hambletonian	20.00
Harold's Club Dice	15.00
Jayhawk, Kansas	20.00
Kachina #1, Morning Singer	75.00
Kachina #2, Hummingbird	65.00
Kachina #3, Antelope	65.00
Kitten on Pillow	12.00

Lion on Rock	14.00
Owl, Old Ez #1	30.00
Owl, Old Ez #1, mini	20.00
Panda	18.00
Quail	10.00
Shrine, Sphinx	12.00

Dant, J.W.

Fort Sill	8.00
Mount Rushmore	6.00
Paul Bunyan	6.00

Doubles

Cadillac, 1913	30.00
Pierce Arrow, 1915	45.00
Stutz Bearcat, 1919	35.00

Famous Firsts

Locomotive, Dewitt Clinton	35.00
Racer, Marmon Wasp	75.00
Racer, Marmon Wasp, mini	35.00
Racer, National #8	60.00
Racer, National #8, mini	35.00
Spirit of St Louis, lg	150.00
Spirit of St Louis, midi	70.00
Spirit of St Louis mini	45.00

Hoffman

Betsy Ross	50.00
College Series, Helmet, Georgia	40.00
College Series, Helmet, LSU	30.00
College Series, Helmet, Nebraska	45.00
College Series, Mascot, Kentucky Football or Basketball, ea	50.00
College Series, Mascot, LSU, Running or Passing, ea	40.00

Dalmation, 1987, mini, $30.00.

Mr Lucky Series, Mr Carpenter	38.00
Mr Lucky Series, Mr Carpenter, mini	17.00
Mr Lucky Series, Mr Harpist	28.00
Mr Lucky Series, Mr Harpist, mini	15.00
Mr Lucky Series, Mr Photographer	45.00
Race Car, Donahue, Sunoco #66	125.00
Race Car, Rutherford #3	110.00
Wildlife Series, Bobcat & Pheasant	50.00
Wildlife Series, Panda	55.00

Kontinental

Editor	35.00
Editor, mini	20.00
Gunsmith	35.00
Gunsmith, mini	20.00
Innkeeper	30.00
Lumberjack	30.00

Lionstone

Annie Oakley	28.00
Bartender	28.00
Bartender, mini	16.00
Baseball Players	75.00
Basketball Players	50.00
Bath, Saturday Night	75.00
Boxers	70.00
Cowboy	25.00
Cowboy, mini	15.00
Cowgirl	30.00
Custer's Last Stand, set of 4	500.00
Fireman #1, red hat	100.00
Fireman #1, yel hat	130.00
Fireman #2, carrying child	95.00
Goldfinch	25.00
Judge Roy Bean	25.00
Laundryman, Chinese	22.00
Madame	45.00
OK Corral Shootout, set of 3	395.00
OK Corral Shootout, set of 3, mini	225.00
Oriental Workers, 6 different, ea	35.00
Professor	45.00
Professor, mini	20.00
Scout, Cavalry	20.00
Scout, Cavalry, mini	15.00
Telegrapher	28.00
Trapper	30.00

McCormick

Bicentennial Series, Betsy Ross	28.00
Bicentennial Series, Paul Revere	35.00
Bicentennial Series, Spirit of '76	50.00
Elvis, Aloha	180.00
Elvis, Aloha, mini	200.00
Elvis, Bust	50.00
Elvis, Gold Tribute, 1979	180.00
Elvis, Sargeant	290.00
Elvis, 25th Anniversary, 1980	150.00
Ford, Henry	30.00
Ford, Henry; mini	22.00
Grant, US	50.00
King Arthur's Court, Merlin	45.00
King Arthur's Court, Sir Lancelot	35.00
Lindbergh, Charles	50.00
Lindbergh, Charles; mini	18.00
Muhammad Ali	200.00
Rogers, Will	35.00
Rogers, Will; mini	15.00
Roosevelt, Eleanor	30.00
Shrine, Imperial Council	35.00
Shrine, Noble	30.00
Strowger Telephone	35.00

Old Commonwealth

Boot, Western	25.00
Boot, Western, mini	12.00
Coins of Ireland, 1979	25.00
Dogs of Ireland, 1980	30.00
Fisherman, 'A Keeper'	50.00
Golden Retriever	60.00
Leprechaun, Elusive, 1980	45.00
Leprechaun, Irish Minstrel, 1982	40.00
Leprechaun, Lucky, 1983	35.00
Princeton University	30.00
Tennessee Walking Horse	60.00

Old Fitzgerald

Irish Charm, 1977	22.00
Irish Counties, 1973	20.00
Irish Patriots, 1971	18.00
Songs of Ireland, 1969	18.00
Songs of Ireland, 1974	20.00

Ski Country

Badger Family	50.00
Badger Family, mini	25.00
Barnum, PT	50.00
Barnum, PT; mini	30.00
Bluebirds Wall Plaque	85.00
Bull Rider	80.00
Bull Rider, mini	40.00
Cedar Waxwings	55.00
Cedar Waxwings, mini	25.00
Dove, Peace	60.00
Dove, Peace, mini	28.00
Duck, King Eider	65.00
Duck, King Eider, mini	35.00
Ducks Unlimited #3, Mallard, 1980	75.00
Ducks Unlimited #3, Mallard, 1980, mini	50.00
Ducks Unlimited #4, Canbasback, 1981, mini	30.00
Ducks Unlimited #4, Canvasback, 1981	60.00
Ducks Unlimited #5, Wood Duck, 1982	100.00
Ducks Unlimited #5, Wood Duck, 1982, mini	50.00
Eagle, Bald; on water	150.00
Eagle, Bald; on water, mini	45.00
Eagle, Harpy	135.00
Eagle, Harpy, mini	95.00
Flycatcher	130.00
Flycatcher, mini	50.00
Fox on Log	75.00
Fox on Log, mini	140.00
Fox on Log, 1.75 liter	250.00

Holiday Cardinals, 1991, limited edition of 800, $85.00.

Indian, End of Trail	250.00
Indian, End of Trail, mini	110.00
Indian, Great Spirit	110.00
Indian, Great Spirit, mini	25.00
Indian, Lookout	65.00
Indian, Lookout, mini	30.00
Kestrel Wall Plaque	75.00
Lion, Mountain	50.00
Lion, Mountain; mini	30.00
Lion on Drum	48.00
Lion on Drum, mini	26.00
Owl, Barn	75.00
Owl, Barn; mini	30.00
Owl, Screech Family	110.00
Owl, Screech Family, mini	70.00
Owl, Screech Family, 1-gal	350.00
Raccoon Wall Plaque	95.00
Salmon, Landlocked	50.00
Salmon, Landlocked, mini	30.00
Sea Gull Wall Plaque	60.00
Squirrel Wall Plaque	175.00
Trout, Rainbow	70.00
Trout, Rainbow; mini	35.00
US Ski Team	35.00
US Ski Team, mini	18.00

Wild Turkey

Series I, #1, #2, #3 or #4, mini, ea	18.00
Series I, #1, 1971	200.00
Series I, #2	150.00
Series I, #3	70.00
Series I, #4	70.00
Series I, #5	25.00
Series I, #6	25.00
Series I, #7	25.00
Series I, #8	45.00
Series I, set of #5, #6, #7 & #8, mini	175.00
Series II, Lore #1	25.00
Series II, Lore #2	35.00
Series II, Lore #3	45.00
Series II, Lore #4	50.00
Series III, #1, In Flight	110.00
Series III, #1, In Flight, mini	45.00
Series III, #2, Turkey & Bobcat	140.00
Series III, #2, Turkey & Bobcat, mini	55.00
Series III, #3, Fighting Turkeys	150.00
Series III, #3, Fighting Turkeys, mini	60.00
Series III, #4, Turkey & Eagle	95.00
Series III, #4, Turkey & Eagle, mini	85.00
Series III, #5, Turkey & Raccoon	95.00
Series III, #5, Turkey & Raccoon, mini	45.00
Series III, #6, Turkey & Poults	95.00
Series III, #6, Turkey & Poults, mini	45.00
Series III, #7, Turkey & Red Fox	95.00
Series III, #7, Turkey & Red Fox, mini	60.00
Series III, #8, Turkey & Owl	100.00
Series III, #8, Turkey & Owl, mini	60.00
Series III, #9, Turkey & Bear Cubs	100.00
Series III, #9, Turkey & Bear Cubs, mini	60.00
Series III, #10, Turkey & Coyote	95.00
Series III, #10, Turkey & Coyote, mini	50.00
Series III, #11, Turkey & Falcon	95.00
Series III, #11, Turkey & Falcon, mini	60.00

Series III, #12, Turkey & Skunks **110.00**
Series III, #12, Turkey & Skunks, mini...........................**60.00**

Decoys

American colonists learned the craft of decoy making from the Indians who used them to lure birds out of the sky as an important food source. Early models were carved from wood such as pine, cedar, balsa, etc., and a few were made of canvas or papier-mache. There are two basic types of decoys: water floaters and shorebirds (also called 'stick-ups'). Within each type are many different species, ducks being the most plentiful since they migrated along all four of America's great waterways. Market hunting became big business around 1880, resulting in large-scale commercial production of decoys which continued until about 1910 when such hunting was outlawed by the Migratory Bird Treaty.

Today decoys are one of the most collectible types of American folk art. The most valuable are those carved by such artists as Laing, Crowell, Ward, and Wheeler, to name only a few. Each area, such as Massachusetts, Connecticut, Maine, the Illinois River, and the Delaware River, produces decoys with distinctive regional characteristics. Examples of commercial decoys produced by well-known factories — among them Mason, Stevens, and Dodge — are also prized by collectors. Though mass produced, these nevertheless required a certain amount of hand carving and decorating. Well-carved examples, especially those of rare species, are appreciating rapidly, and those with original paint are more desirable. In the listings that follow, all decoys are solid-bodied unless noted hollow.

Key:
CG — Challenge Grade	PDF — Pratt Decoy
DDF — Dodge Decoy Factory	PG — Premier Grade
MDF — Mason's Decoy Factory	RP — repaint
OP — original paint	SG — Standard Grade
ORP — old repaint	WDF — Wildfowler Decoy Factory
OWP — original working paint	WOP — worn original paint

Black Duck, Ben Schmidt, NM OP, early 20th C **1,600.00**
Black Duck, Billy Ellis, NM OP w/EX detail, EX patina, tiny dents...**600.00**
Black Duck, Chauncey Wheeler, trn head, OP w/some RP on head, shot mks....**575.00**
Black Duck, Dan English, OP w/touchup, minor chips.............**1,500.00**
Black Duck, MDF, PG, NM OP, prof rpr, tiny dents...................**950.00**
Black-Bellied Plover, Wm Gibian, relief-cvd wings, NM OP......**325.00**
Bluebill drake, DDF, EX OP w/touchup, minor neck filler missing ..**900.00**
Bluebill drake, DDF, worn OP, scarred body, glue showing..........**225.00**
Bluebill drake, Ezra Hankins, hollow, VG OWP, late 19th C......**400.00**
Bluebill drake, Harvey Stevens, OP on bk, remainder in-use RP, 1880s...**650.00**
Bluebill drake, MDF, PG, EX OP, crack/dents/shot.....................**400.00**
Bluebill hen, Ben Schmidt, NM OP/minor RP on bill, rough spot..**300.00**
Bluebill hen, Davey Nichol, relief-cvd wings, NM OP, seam separation.**500.00**
Bluewing Teal drake, PDF, NM OP, crack/dent/chip **600.00**
Bluewing Teal hen, Billy Ellis, EX OP w/fine detail, structural flaws..**425.00**
Bluewing Teal hen, MDF, SG, glass eyes, EX OP, chips/shot ...**1,000.00**
Bluewing Teal hen, MDF, SG, pnt eyes, EX OP w/touchups, rpl eyes..**800.00**
Brant, MDF, CG, EX OP, sm split/crack/2 low knots................**1,100.00**
Brant, Sam Smith, hollow, EX OP w/wht OP under tail **350.00**
Canada Goose, Ken Harris, cork body, trn head, comb pnt, NM OP, EX....**600.00**
Canada Goose, Ward Bros, balsa body, cedar head trn, 1948, rough...**350.00**
Canada Goose, Ward Bros, trn head, EX OP, ca 1940, crack...**4,300.00**
Canada Goose, Ward Bros, weathered/pnt traces, 1930s, dents/cracks....**3,300.00**
Canada Goose, WDF, unstamped Atlantic model, EX OP, dents...**325.00**
Canvasback drake, HA Stevens, OP w/G comb pnt, prof rpr, 1880s..**800.00**
Canvasback drake, John McLoughlin, EX OP **2,450.00**
Canvasback drake, JR Wells, NM OP w/minor RP, Meredith brand..**2,150.00**
Canvasback drake, MDF, PG, Chesapeake Bay model, EX OP, prof rpr ...**750.00**

Canvasback drake, MDF, PG, NM OP, separation/dents **850.00**
Canvasback drake, MDF, PG Seneca Lake, VG OP, split/hit by shot ..**300.00**
Canvasback drake, Ward Bros, sleeping, balsa/cedar, Lem Ward RP, 1977..**1,250.00**
Canvasback drake, Ward Bros, trn head, Len Ward rpt, 1948 .**1,350.00**
Canvasback hen, Bert Graves, lead keel weight, EX OP w/touchup ..**3,000.00**
Canvasback hen, Charles Shang Wheeler, NM OP w/mellow surface .**9,000.00**
Canvasback hen, JM Hays...Co, Superior model, EX OP, crack, VG **300.00**
Coot, MDF, CG, EX OP (swirl) w/touchup, prof rprs.................**700.00**
Coot, PDF, EX OP, tiny dents/crack in 1 eye, 1925 ....**250.00**
Dowicher, unknown maker, wax eyes, EX OP w/plumage pattern, 1880s...**700.00**
Goldeneye hen, MDF, PG, EX OP w/blk OP traces, sm rpr **500.00**
Goldeneye hen, Rhodes Truex, working ORP, mid-20th C.........**500.00**

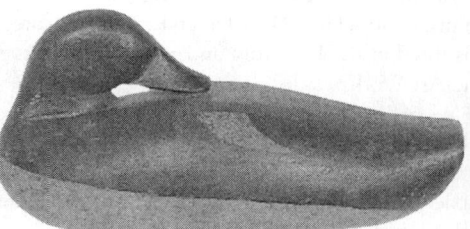

Goldeneye sleeping hen, Ed Parsons, fine original paint, ca 1890 – 1900, rare, $3,000.00.

Goldeneye pr, Ward Bros, slightly trn heads, NM OP, 1966 ....**7,500.00**
Greenwing Teal pr, Davey Nichol, trn heads, drake dtd 1973, NM OP...**1,400.00**
Mallard drake, Artie Bennett, preening, NM OP **300.00**
Mallard drake, DDF, EX OP, old rpr, dents, ca 1880s..................**600.00**
Mallard drake, DDF, EX OP w/mellow surface, thin crack **900.00**
Mallard drake, H Whittington, metal tail spring/trn head, EX OP, 1963...**700.00**
Mallard drake, Robert Elliston, WOP, orig weight, dents.............**400.00**
Mallard hen, Bert Graves, lead keel, NM OP, sm chip.............**3,850.00**
Mallard hen, MDF, PG, snakey head, VG OP, rpr/shot **400.00**
Mallard pr, MDF, PG, EX OP, separated seam, dents................**1,400.00**
Mallard pr, MDF, SG, pnt eyes, EX OP, crack............................**400.00**
Merganser hen, MDF, SG, glass eyes, EX OP, chips/shot............**550.00**
Merganser hen, MDF, SG, tack eyes, VG OP, missing filler/shot...**400.00**
Peep, Mark McNair, relief-cvd wings/eyes, NM OP....................**950.00**
Pintail drake, Ward Bros, EX OP, minor prof rpr, rpl eyes, sm chips...**1,800.00**
Pintail hen, Ward Bros, trn head, Ward Bros rpt, 1936 model..**1,600.00**
Plover, MDF, OP in fall plumage, late 19th C, VG **1,100.00**
Quail, Elmer Crowell, NM OP, tiny flakes, mini **1,500.00**
Redhead drake, Robert Elliston, EX OP, Dupee rig brand traces..**18,000.00**
Ringbill drake, Mark McNair, trn head, OP, My First Rig on underside **1,000.00**
Scoter drake, JM Hays...Co, Superior model, wht winged, EX OP, VG..**550.00**
Snipe, Harry V Shourds, EX OP, lt wear on breast & bill **2,700.00**
Tern, Elmer Crowell, standing, trn head, split tail, NM OP, dent .**4,500.00**
Wigeon drake, MDF, PG, NM OP w/old varnish, split seam/sm crack ...**7,000.00**
Wigeon drake, Ward Bros, trn head, EX OP, ca 1930, hairline/dent..**9,000.00**
Wigeon hen, Ken Harris, NM OP, tiny chip/crack, EX **575.00**
Wigeon hen, MDF, SG, glass eyes, EX OP, prof rpr, shot............**400.00**
Wigeon pr, Geo Kessler, NM OP, slight roughness to drake's bill..**4,600.00**
Wigeon pr, Ward Bros, balsa bodies, sm prof rpr, NM OP, mini....**1,100.00**
Yellowlegs, MDF, tack eyes, EX OP, feather pnt detail, dents ..**1,600.00**

Dedham Pottery

Originally founded in Chelsea, Massachusetts, as the Chelsea Keramic Works, the name was changed to Dedham Pottery in 1895 after the firm relocated in Dedham, near Boston, Massachusetts. The ware utilized a gray stoneware body with a crackle glaze and simple cobalt border designs of flowers, birds, and animals. Decorations were brushed on by hand using an ancient Chinese method which suspended the cobalt within the overall glaze. There were thirteen standard patterns, among them Magnolia, Iris, Butterfly, Duck, Polar Bear, and Rabbit, the latter of which was chosen to represent the company on their logo. On the very early pieces, the rabbits face left; decorators soon found the reverse position easier to paint, and the rabbits were turned to the right. (Earlier examples are worth from 10% to 20% more than identical pieces manufactured in later years.) In addition to the standard patterns, other designs were produced for special orders. These and artist-signed pieces are highly valued by collectors today.

Though their primary product was the blue-printed, crackle-glazed dinnerware, two types of artware were also produced: crackle glaze and flambe. Their notable volcanic ware was a type of the latter. The mark is incised and often accompanies the cipher of Hugh Robertson. The firm was operated by succeeding generations of the Robertson family until it closed in 1943. Our advisor for this category is Dale MacLean; he is listed in the Directory under Massachusetts. See also Chelsea Keramic Art Works.

Dinnerware

Bacon/celery tray, Rabbit, flared rim, stamped/registered, 9¾"....440.00
Bowl, Lotus, registered, 2x5" 425.00
Bowl, nappy, Rabbit, stamped, 1½x6" 400.00
Bowl, Polar Bear, imp, 1⅛x5½" 770.00
Bowl, Rabbit, sq, stamped, 2¾x8½" 450.00
Bowl, Rabbit, stamped, 2x5½" 250.00
Bowl, Rabbit, stamped, 3½x9" 465.00
Bowl, soup; Mushroom & Wicket, stamped, 1½x8½" 900.00
Bowl, Swan, stamped, sgn B, 3¼x7", NM 525.00
Butter pat, Wild Rose, hand-cut petal-like edges, stamped, 3½".325.00
Candle holders, Rabbit, flat-style rim, stamped/registered, 1¾", pr..300.00
Charger, Rabbit, stamped, 12" 575.00
Coffee cup & saucer, Grape, stamped, 2¼", 6¼" 415.00
Compote, Rabbit, stamped, 3¼x5¼" 495.00
Cup & saucer, coffee; Duck, stamped/registered, 2¼x4½", 6"....475.00
Cup & saucer, coffee; Rabbit, stamped/registered, 2¼x5", 6" 250.00
Cup & saucer, demi; Rabbit, vessel-style, stamped, 2", 4¼" 475.00
Cup & saucer, Elephant & Baby, stamped, 2¼x4¼", 6", NM 950.00
Cup & saucer, Rabbit, stamped/registered, 4¼x5¼", 6¾" 385.00
Egg cup, Rabbit, mini ped, unmk, 2½x2" 330.00
Marmalade jar, Rabbit, globular, stamped, 4¾x4½" 550.00

Mug, child's; Elephant, stamped mark, 3½x4¼", $2,200.00.

Pitcher, Rabbit, bulbous, in-making bruise, stamped, 5¼" 360.00
Pitcher, Standing Rabbit on front, sq, stamped/B on base, 4¾"...2,500.00
Pitcher, Swan, bulbous, stamped, 5x6" 600.00
Plate, Azalea, stamped/registered/2 imp rabbits, 8¼" 275.00
Plate, child's, Rabbit, stamped, 1x7½" 550.00
Plate, Clover, stamped/registered/imp, 8½" 1,250.00
Plate, coupe soup; Rabbit, stamped, 1½x7¼" 300.00
Plate, Crab, stamped/registered/imp, 8¾" 770.00
Plate, Day Lily, stamped/imp, 6¼" 850.00
Plate, Double Turtle, stamped/imp, 6"........1,100.00

Plate, Duck, stamped, 6" 300.00
Plate, Elephant & Baby, stamped/registered, 7½" 700.00
Plate, Elephant & Baby, stamped/2 imp rabbits, 9½" 975.00
Plate, Fairbanks, registered/1931/imp, 8½" 2,500.00
Plate, French Mushroom, stamped/imp, 10" 1,500.00
Plate, Grape, stamped, some dimpling, 8½" 195.00
Plate, Grape, stamped, 6" 195.00
Plate, Horse Chestnut, stamped/imp, 10" 360.00
Plate, Horse Chestnut, stamped/imp, 6" 220.00
Plate, In the Potted Orange Tree, imp, 8½" 500.00
Plate, Iris, Maude Davenport, stamped/imp, 6" 275.00
Plate, Iris, stamped/imp, 10" 330.00
Plate, Lion Tapestry, stamped, 8½", NM 1,200.00
Plate, Lobster, stamped/imp, 8" 770.00
Plate, Luna Moth, stamped/imp, rstr, 6" 440.00
Plate, Magnolia, Maude Davenport, stamped, 6" 220.00
Plate, Magnolia, stamped/imp, 10", NM 350.00
Plate, Moth, Maude Davenport, stamped/imp, 8½" 550.00
Plate, Mushroom, stamped/imp, 8½" 600.00
Plate, Mushroom, stamped/imp, 6" 450.00
Plate, Owl & Star, stamped, 6", NM 1,870.00
Plate, Pineapple, stamped, 10" 825.00
Plate, Polar Bear, stamped/imp, 8½" 750.00
Plate, Pomegranate, #98/unidentified initials, 8½" 2,500.00
Plate, Pond Lily, Maude Davenport, stamped/imp, 8½" 275.00
Plate, Poppy, mini buds along border, imp/unidentifed letters, 10¼" ..800.00
Plate, Rabbit, Davenport rebus, stamped/imp, 10" 300.00
Plate, Rabbit, stamped/imp, 6" 200.00
Plate, Rabbit, stamped/registered, 8½", NM 250.00
Plate, Single Ear Rabbit, stamp/imp, 8½" 275.00
Plate, Snow Tree, Maude Davenport, stamped, 9¾" 495.00
Plate, Snow Tree, stamped, 6", NM 275.00
Plate, Swan, stamped/imp, 6¼" 415.00
Plate, Tufted Duck, imp, 8½" 375.00
Plate, Turkey, Maude Davenport, imp, 10" 500.00
Shakers, Rabbit, sgn DP, 3½", NM, pr 450.00
Sugar bowl, Rabbit, domed lid, incised DP, 4¾x4¼" 385.00
Tea tile, Elephant & Baby, stamped/registered, rstr kiln pop, 5½" 950.00
Tea tile, Swan, stamped, faint hairline on bk, 4¾" 300.00
Tureen, Rabbit, dome lid w/knob hdl, stamped, 4x7", NM 700.00

Miscellaneous

Ashtray, Azalea, flat style, stamped/registered, 6½" dia 400.00
Ashtray, Rabbit, flat rim, stamped, mini, 4" 300.00
Flower frog, standing rabbit, stamped, 6½x4½" 1,350.00
Vase, Sang de Boef, burgundy over maroon, ovoid, incised, 8⅛x3" ..700.00

Degenhart

The Crystal Art Glass factory in Cambridge, Ohio, opened in 1947 under the private ownership of John and Elizabeth Degenhart. John had previously worked for the Cambridge Glass Company and was well known for his superior paperweights. After his death in 1964, Elizabeth took over management of the factory, hiring several workers from the defunct Cambridge Company, including Zack Boyd. Boyd was responsible for many unique colors, some of which were named for him. From 1964 to 1974, more than twenty-seven different moulds were created, most of them resulting from Elizabeth Degenhart's work and creativity, and over 145 official colors were developed. Elizabeth died in 1978, requesting that the ten moulds she had built while operating the factory were to be turned over to the Degenhart Museum. The remaining moulds were to be held by the Island Mould and Machine Company, who (complying with her request) removed the familiar 'D in heart' trademark. The factory was eventually bought by Zack's son, Bernard Boyd. He also acquired the remaining Degenhart moulds, to which he added his own logo.

In general, slags and opaques should be valued 15% to 20% higher than crystals in color.

Bicentennial Bell, Vaseline 12.00
Bird Salt, Bittersweet..20.00
Bird Salt, Lavender Green Slag...35.00
Bird Toothpick, Custard Slag...25.00
Bird Toothpick, Milk White 15.00
Bird Toothpick, Vaseline...15.00
Chick Salt, Cobalt, 2"..20.00

Daisy and Button Boot, Custard Slag, 4⅝x4⅛", **$30.00.** (Photo courtesy Earlene Wheatley)

Elephant Toothpick, Cobalt..25.00
Elizabeth Degenhart Portrait Dish, Amethyst, 5½" 30.00
Elizabeth Degenhart Portrait Dish, Crystal, 5½".............20.00
Gypsy Pot, Cobalt...15.00
Heart Jewel Box, Cobalt...25.00
Heart Jewel Box, Ivory 35.00
Heart Toothpick, Amberina..20.00
Heart Toothpick, Milk White 15.00
Hen Covered Dish, Cobalt, 3" 25.00
Hobo Baby Shoe Toothpick, Vaseline 12.00
Kat Slipper, Amethyst...20.00
Owl, Amberina..30.00
Owl, Antique Blue..30.00
Owl, Bloody Mary #4 ....75.00
Owl, Cobalt Carnival...125.00
Owl, Daffodil...30.00
Owl, Dark Rose Marie 25.00
Owl, Emerald Green #1..30.00
Owl, Green Slag 45.00
Owl, Lavender 50.00
Owl, Lemonade...55.00
Owl, Light Bluefire, 3½" 45.00
Owl, Midnight Sun...50.00
Owl, Milk White 20.00
Owl, Opal Variant 75.00
Owl, Sapphire Blue..20.00
Owl, Sunset..40.00
Owl, Tiger, 3½"...45.00
Pooch, Baby Pink Slag..30.00
Pooch, Blue Marble Slag..30.00
Pooch, Buttercup Slag...35.00
Pooch, Canary 15.00
Pooch, Charcoal 20.00
Pooch, Crown Tuscan..20.00
Pooch, Dark Powder Blue Slag...45.00
Pooch, Dark Toffee Slag 22.00
Pooch, Fawn...15.00

Pooch, Lavender Slag..30.00
Pooch, Red..25.00
Pooch, Rose Marie..15.00
Pooch, Tomato #2...30.00
Priscilla Doll, Baby Green..75.00
Priscilla Doll, Crown Tuscan...75.00
Priscilla Doll, Sapphire...40.00
Priscilla Doll, Snow White...50.00
Priscilla Doll, Vaseline..65.00
Skate Boot, Cobalt 30.00
Tomahawk, Amethyst...25.00
Tomahawk, Blue Bell...25.00
Tomahawk, Cobalt Blue Carnival...50.00
Tomahawk, Custard..40.00
Turkey Covered Dish, Amethyst...35.00
Turkey Covered Dish, Caramel Slag......................................75.00

Delatte

Delatte was a manufacturer of French cameo glass. Founded in 1921, their style reflected the influence of the Art Deco era with strong color contrasts and bold design. Our advisor for this category is Don Williams; he is listed in the Directory under Missouri.

Cameo

Vase, pine cones/branches, dk wine/blk on orange, 4-panel, 3x3¾x2" ..275.00
Vase, pine cones/needles, blk on dk gr, ovoid w/sm neck, 9½" ...650.00
Vase, pine cones/needles, dk amethyst over mint gr, 9x7"..........750.00
Vase, roses, dk amethyst on bright pk, slim ovoid, 6¼" 320.00

Delft

Old Delftware, made as early as the sixteenth century, was originally a low-fired earthenware coated in a thin opaque tin glaze with painted-on blue or polychrome designs. It was not until the last half of the nineteenth century, however, that the ware became commonly referred to as Delft, acquiring the name from the Dutch village that had become the major center of its production. English, German, and French potters also produced Delft, though with noticeable differences both in shape and decorative theme.

In the early part of the eighteenth century, the German potter, Bottger, developed a formula for porcelain; in England, Wedgwood began producing creamware — both of which were much more durable. Unable to compete, one by one the Delft potteries failed. Soon only one remained. In 1876 De Porcelyne Fles reintroduced Delftware on a hard white body with blue and white decorative themes reflecting the Dutch countryside, windmills by the sea, and Dutch children. This manufacturer is the most well known of several operating today. Their products are now produced under the Royal Delft label.

For further information we recommend *Discovering Dutch Delftware, Modern Delft and Makkum Pottery,* by Stephen J. Van Hook (Glen Park Press, Alexandria, Virginia). Examples listed here are blue on white unless noted otherwise. See also specific manufacturers. Our advisor is Ralph Jaarsma; he is listed in the Directory under Iowa.

Bowl, English, Chinese man by house & tree, ca 1740, 3½x9" dia ...365.00
Bowl, punch; English, floral & geometric borders, 18th C, 7½" dia .280.00
Charger, Dutch, Chinamen & landscapes, ca 1690, 14".............770.00
Charger, Dutch, chinoiserie, 17th C, 13" dia 350.00
Charger, English, floral, 18th C, 13½" dia 1,215.00
Charger, English, regal lion in pavilion, 14" 925.00

Charger, English, swordsman on horseback, multicolor with three manganese concentric rings on exterior, seventeenth/eighteenth century, 12½", $560.00.

Dish, Dutch, floral, shell rim, 18th C, 8" dia 390.00
Humidor, Dutch, cherubs/banner: Lumbricor, 1700s, 12½" 1,000.00
Lamp base, Oriental figures in landscape, England, 13½", EX 700.00
Mug, Germany, tennis player motif, Royal Bonn, 6½" 675.00
Plate, Dutch, Chinese floral, 18th C, 9" dia...............................170.00
Plate, Dutch, Chinese scene, ca 1750, ¾x8½" dia 210.00
Plate, Dutch, chinoiserie seascape, geometric border, ca 1750, 8⅞" ..280.00
Plate, Dutch, duck pond, 16th C, 6¼" dia 300.00
Plate, Dutch, floral decor, 18th C, 9¼" dia................................130.00
Plate, English, Chinese lotus by fenced garden, 18th C, 9" 150.00
Platter, Germany, windmill & seascape, Rosenthal, 11½x17" dia...250.00
Tile, Dutch, sailing boat, 1930s, 4¾x9"....................................120.00
Tile, Dutch, windmill scene, 6¼x6¼" (in walnut fr)...................250.00
Tile, English, David slaying Goliath, flower corners, 1725-50, 5" sq..110.00
Utensil rack, Dutch, windmill & landscape scene, 18½x13½" ...105.00
Vase, Dutch, floral decor, 6-sided, 19th C, 11¾" 110.00
Vase, Dutch, house at waters edge, Porceleyne Fles, 1886, 9¼" ..145.00
Vase, Dutch, Oriental scenes in oval panels, w/lid, 13", EX........800.00
Vase, Dutch, William of Orange, flared top, 7½" 700.00

Depression Glass

Depression glass is defined by Gene Florence, author of several best-selling books on the subject, as 'the inexpensive glassware made primarily during the Depression era in the colors of amber, green, pink, blue, red, yellow, white, and crystal.' This glass was mass produced, sold through five-and-dime stores and mail-order catalogs, and given away as premiums with gas and food products.

The listings in this book are far from being complete. If you want a more thorough presentation of this fascinating glassware, we recommend *The Collector's Encyclopedia of Depression Glass, Pocket Guide to Depression Glass, Elegant Glassware of the Depression Era, Very Rare Glassware of the Depression Years, Glass Candlesticks of the Depression Era,* and *Kitchen Glassware of the Depression Years,* all by Gene Florence, whose address is listed in the Directory under Kentucky. See also McKee; New Martinsville.

Key:
AOP — allover pattern   PAT — pattern at top

Adam, bowl, dessert; pk or gr, 4¾" 25.00
Adam, bowl, gr, oval, 10" 40.00
Adam, bowl, pk, w/lid, 9" 75.00
Adam, bowl, pk or gr, 7¾" 30.00
Adam, butter dish, pk, w/lid 110.00
Adam, cake plate, gr, ftd, 10" 32.50
Adam, creamer, pk..28.00
Adam, cup, gr 25.00
Adam, pitcher, pk, 32-oz, 8" 45.00
Adam, plate, dinner; pk, sq, 9"...35.00
Adam, platter, pk, 11¾"..33.00

Adam, sugar bowl, gr 35.00
Adam, tumbler, iced tea; pk or gr, 5½" 65.00
Adam, vase, gr, 7½"..95.00
American Pioneer, bowl, console; gr, 10¾" 70.00
American Pioneer, bowl, crystal or pk, hdld, 9" 30.00
American Pioneer, candy jar, crystal or pk, w/lid, 1½-lb.............100.00
American Pioneer, cheese & cracker set, gr, indented platter & comport ...70.00
American Pioneer, creamer, gr, 3½" 22.00
American Pioneer, goblet, wine; crystal or pk, 3-oz, 4"................40.00
American Pioneer, plate, crystal or pk, 8 " 11.00
American Pioneer, plate, gr, 6" 15.00
American Pioneer, saucer, gr 5.00
American Pioneer, tumbler, juice; crystal or pk, 5-oz............40.00
American Pioneer, vase, gr, 4 styles, 7" 135.00
American Pioneer, whiskey, crystal or pk, 2-oz, 2¼"............50.00
American Sweetheart, bowl, berry; cremax, rnd, 9"..............50.00
American Sweetheart, cup, red..120.00
American Sweetheart, plate, bread & butter; smoke or other trims, 6" ...22.00
American Sweetheart, plate, luncheon; monax, 9"................12.00
American Sweetheart, plate, salad; bl, 8".............................130.00
American Sweetheart, tumbler, pk, 9-oz, 4¼".......................95.00
Aunt Polly, bowl, berry; gr or irid, 4¾"..................................8.00
Aunt Polly, bowl, bl, hdl, 5½" 25.00
Aunt Polly, bowl, pickle; gr or irid, oval, hdl, 7¼" 15.00
Aunt Polly, candy dish, bl, hdls, ftd.....................................60.00
Aunt Polly, creamer, bl..60.00
Aunt Polly, sherbet, gr or irid...10.00
Aunt Polly, tumbler, bl, 8-oz, 3⅝"..38.00
Aurora, bowl, cobalt or pk, deep, 4½"..................................65.00
Aurora, cup, cobalt or pk 17.50
Aurora, saucer, gr 2.50
Avocado, bowl, crystal, hdls, 5¼" 10.00
Avocado, bowl, pk, 3¼"x9½" 150.00
Avocado, cup, gr, ftd, 2 styles...38.00
Avocado, plate, sherbet; pk, 6⅜"...16.00
Avocado, sugar bowl, crystal, ftd..12.00
Beaded Block, bowl, ice bl, rnd, 6½".....................................38.00
Beaded Block, bowl, lily; red, rnd, 4½"...............................495.00
Beaded Block, sugar bowl, crystal, pk, gr or amber...............25.00
Beaded Block, vase, bouquet; irid, 6"....................................45.00
Block Optic, bowl, cereal; pk, 5¼"...40.00
Block Optic, bowl, console; amber, rolled edge, 11¾"............45.00
Block Optic, bowl, lg berry; gr or pk, 8½" 35.00
Block Optic, candlesticks, pk, 1¾", pr...................................80.00
Block Optic, cup, yel, 4 styles 8.00
Block Optic, plate, luncheon; yel or pk, 8"..............................8.00
Block Optic, plate, sandwich; gr or pk, 10¼"........................25.00
Block Optic, plate, sherbet; gr, yel or pk, 6"...........................3.00
Block Optic, sherbet, yel, 6-oz, 4¾" 21.00
Block Optic, tumbler, gr, 3"...60.00
Block Optic, tumbler, gr, 3-oz, 2⅝"..25.00
Block Optic, tumbler, pk, flat, 10-11 oz, 5" 18.00
Bowknot, bowl, cereal; gr, 5½"..35.00
Bowknot, plate, salad; gr, 7"..15.00
Bowknot, tumbler, gr, ftd, 10-oz, 5" 25.00
Cameo, bowl, console; pk, 3-leg, 11" 75.00
Cameo, bowl, salad; gr, 7¼" 65.00
Cameo, creamer, yel, 3¼"..22.00
Cameo, plate, dinner; gr, 9½"..25.00
Cameo, plate, salad; crystal, 7"...3.50
Cameo, sugar bowl, yel, 3¼"...20.00
Cameo, tumbler, water; pk, 9-oz, 4" 80.00
Cherry Blossom, bowl, berry; Delphite, 4¾" 16.00
Cherry Blossom, bowl, berry; gr or Delphite, rnd, 8½" 50.00

Cherry Blossom, bowl, cereal; pk, 5¾" 52.00
Cherry Blossom, bowl, gr, hdls, 9" 75.00
Cherry Blossom, butter dish, gr, w/lid........................125.00
Cherry Blossom, creamer, pk....................................25.00
Cherry Blossom, cup, pk...24.00
Cherry Blossom, plate, dinner; pk or gr, 9" 28.00
Cherry Blossom, plate, grill; gr, 10" 125.00
Cherry Blossom, plate, grill; pk, 9" 38.00
Cherry Blossom, plate, sherbet; gr or Delphite, 6" 10.00
Cherry Blossom, platter, pk or gr, oval, 11" 60.00
Cherry Blossom, saucer, gr or Delphite.........................5.00
Cherry Blossom, tumbler, Delphite, scalloped ftd, AOP, 8-oz, 4½" .25.00
Cherryberry, bowl, berry; pk or gr, deep, 7½" 32.00
Cherryberry, bowl, salad; crystal or irid, deep, 6½" 20.00
Cherryberry, creamer, crystal or irid, sm 12.00
Cherryberry, plate, salad; crystal or irid, 7½" 8.00
Cherryberry, tumbler, pk or gr, 9-oz, 3⅝".................40.00
Chinex Classic, bowl, Brownstone or plain ivory, 11" 17.00
Chinex Classic, bowl, salad; decal decor, 6¾"..............20.00
Chinex Classic, bowl, soup; castle decor, 7¾"..............40.00
Chinex Classic, creamer, Brownstone or plain ivory.......5.50
Chinex Classic, plate, dinner; decal decor, 9¾" 9.00
Chinex Classic, sugar bowl, castle decor 20.00
Circle, bowl, gr, 8"..30.00
Circle, cup, pk, 2 styles, ea......................................10.00
Circle, goblet, water; gr, 8-oz...................................11.00
Circle, plate, sandwich; gr, 10"................................14.00
Circle, saucer, pk, w/cup ring....................................3.00
Circle, tumbler, water; gr, 8-oz, 4"..............................9.00
Cloverleaf, bowl, cereal; gr, 5"..................................50.00
Cloverleaf, bowl, deep salad; yel, 7"..........................85.00
Cloverleaf, candy dish, gr, w/lid................................65.00
Cloverleaf, plate, grill; gr, 10¼"...............................25.00
Cloverleaf, plate, sherbet; blk, 6"..............................40.00
Cloverleaf, saucer, pk or gr..3.00
Cloverleaf, sherbet, pk, ftd, 3"..................................10.00
Colonial, bowl, cereal; pk, 5½"..................................65.00
Colonial, butter dish, crystal, w/lid............................42.00
Colonial, plate, dinner; gr, 10"..................................65.00
Colonial, shakers, pk, pr...150.00
Colonial, stem, cordial; gr, 1-oz, 3¾".........................30.00
Colonial, tumbler, juice; crystal, 5-oz, 3".....................15.00
Colonial Block, bowl, crystal, 4"..................................4.00
Colonial Block, butter tub, crystal.............................25.00
Colonial Block, pitcher, pk or gr................................45.00
Colonial Block, sugar bowl, wht...................................8.00
Colonial Fluted, bowl, cereal; gr, 6"...........................16.00
Colonial Fluted, creamer, gr.....................................10.00
Colonial Fluted, saucer, gr...2.00
Columbia, bowl, crystal, ruffled edge, 10½" 22.00
Columbia, bowl, low soup; crystal, 8"..........................25.00
Columbia, cup, crystal...9.00
Columbia, saucer, pk...10.00
Coronation, bowl, berry; pk or Royal Ruby, hdls, 4¼"......7.00
Coronation, bowl, nappy; Royal Ruby, hdls, 6½" 18.00
Coronation, bowl, pk, 8"...195.00
Coronation, plate, luncheon; gr, 8½"..........................60.00
Coronation, tumbler, pk, ftd, 10-oz, 5".......................30.00
Cremax, bowl, vegetable; cremax, 9".............................8.00
Cremax, cup, bl or decal decor....................................5.00
Cremax, plate, dinner; cremax, 9¾".............................4.50
Cremax, saucer, demitasse; bl or decal decor...............10.00
Cube, bowl, salad; pk, 6½".......................................14.00
Cube, cup, gr...9.00

Cube, plate, luncheon; gr, 8"....................................10.00
Cube, shakers, pk, pr...35.00
Cube, tumbler, pk, 9-oz, 4".......................................75.00
Diamond Quilted, bowl, bl or blk, str, 7"......................22.00
Diamond Quilted, bowl, pk or gr, crimped edge, 7" 9.00
Diamond Quilted, candy jar, pk or gr, ftd, w/lid............65.00
Diamond Quilted, plate, sherbet; bl or blk, 6".................8.00
Diamond Quilted, punch bowl, pk or gr, w/stand.........500.00
Diamond Quilted, sandwich server, bl or blk, center hdl....50.00
Diamond Quilted, tumbler, water; pk or gr, 9-oz.............9.00
Diana, bowl, cereal; crystal, 5".....................................6.00
Diana, bowl, salad; pk, 9"...20.00
Diana, candy jar, amber, rnd, w/lid.............................40.00
Diana, plate, pk, 9½"...20.00
Diana, platter, crystal, oval, 12"................................12.00
Diana, sugar bowl, amber, oval, open...........................8.00
Dogwood, bowl, cereal; pk or gr, 5½"..........................35.00
Dogwood, plate, bread & butter; monax or cremax, 6"....22.00
Dogwood, plate, dinner; pk, 9¼"................................36.00
Dogwood, saucer, monax or cremax.............................20.00
Dogwood, sherbet, gr, low ftd..................................115.00
Doric, bowl, berry; Delphite, 4½"...............................55.00
Doric, bowl, pk, hdls, 9"...35.00
Doric, cake plate, gr, 3 legs, 10"...............................35.00
Doric, candy dish, Delphite, 3-pt...............................12.00
Doric, cup, gr...14.00
Doric, relish tray, gr, 4x4"...12.00
Doric, tray, serving; pk or gr, 8x8".............................40.00
Doric & Pansy, bowl, berry; gr or teal, 4½"..................24.00
Doric & Pansy, butter dish, gr or teal, w/lid................495.00
Doric & Pansy, plate, salad; gr or teal, 7"....................40.00
Doric & Pansy, plate, sherbet; pk or crystal, 6"...............7.50
Doric & Pansy, saucer, pk or crystal.............................4.00
Doric & Pansy, sugar bowl, gr or teal, open................110.00
English Hobnail, bottle, toilet; pk or gr, 5-oz...............35.00
English Hobnail, bowl (crimped dish), pk or gr, 6".........18.00
English Hobnail, bowl, nappy, turq or ice bl, rnd, 5".......40.00
English Hobnail, bowl, pickle; pk or gr, 8"....................30.00
English Hobnail, candlestick, turq or ice bl, rnd base, 9"....50.00
English Hobnail, cigarette jar, turq or ice bl, rnd, w/lid....60.00
English Hobnail, cup, pk or gr....................................18.00
English Hobnail, plate, pk or gr, rnd, 8" 12.50
English Hobnail, plate, turq or ice bl, rnd, 10"..............85.00
English Hobnail, shakers, pk or gr, flat, pr.................150.00
English Hobnail, sherbet, turq or ice bl, rnd ft, low.......12.00
English Hobnail, tumbler, iced tea; pk or gr, 10-oz.......25.00
Fire King, bowl, salad; pk or gr, 7¼"...........................80.00
Fire King, cookie jar, crystal, w/lid...........................600.00
Fire King, creamer, bl, ftd, 3¼".................................150.00
Fire King, plate, grill; crystal, 10½"............................40.00
Fire King, plate, salver; pk or gr, 10½".........................95.00
Fire King, plate, sherbet; crystal, 6"...........................40.00
Fire King, sugar bowl, bl, ftd, 3¼".............................150.00
Fire King, tumbler, juice; crystal, ftd, 3½"...................40.00
Floral, bowl, berry; Delphite, 4"................................50.00
Floral, candlesticks, pk, 4", pr...................................90.00
Floral, candy jar, gr, w/lid..42.50
Floral, canister set, Jadite, coffee, tea, cereal, sugar, 5¼", ea........95.00
Floral, plate, salad; pk, 8"...15.00
Floral, tumbler, lemonade; gr, ftd, 9-oz, 5½"...............60.00
Floral & Diamond Band, bowl, lg berry; pk or gr, 8"......20.00
Floral & Diamond Band, compote, pk, tall, 5½" 20.00
Floral & Diamond Band, sugar, gr, sm.........................12.00
Foral & Diamond Band, tumbler, iced tea; pk, 5".........45.00

Floral & Diamond Band, luncheon plate, pink, 8", $45.00. (Photo courtesy Gene Florence)

Florentine No 1, bowl, berry; crystal or gr, 5".............................12.00
Florentine No 1, bowl, cream soup or ruffled nut; cobalt 60.00
Florentine No 1, butter dish, yel, w/lid......................................180.00
Florentine No 1, coaster/ashtray, pk, 3¾".....................................28.00
Florentine No 1, cup, cobalt...85.00
Florentine No 1, plate, grill; yel, 10"...15.00
Florentine No 1, saucer, crystal or gr 3.00
Florentine No 1, tumbler, lemonade (like Floral); pk, 9-oz, 5¼" ...125.00
Florentine No 2, bowl, cereal; crystal or gr, 6" 33.00
Florentine No 2, bowl, crystal or gr, flat, 9" 27.50
Florentine No 2, candy dish, pk, w/lid 145.00
Florentine No 2, gravy boat, yel...65.00
Florentine No 2, plate, salad; crystal, gr or pk, 8½" 8.50
Florentine No 2, tumbler, water; cobalt, 9-oz, 4" 70.00
Florentine No 2, vase or parfait, yel, 6"...65.00
Flower Garden w/Butterflies, ashtray, amber or crystal, w/match holder...165.00
Flower Garden w/Butterflies, creamer, pk, gr or bl-gr.....................75.00
Flower Garden w/Butterflies, plate, amber or crystal, 7" 16.00
Flower Garden w/Butterflies, plate, pk, gr or bl-gr, 10" 42.50
Flower Garden w/Butterflies, saucer, pk, gr or bl-gr.......................25.00
Flower Garden w/Butterflies, vase, Dahlia; blk, cupped, 8" 210.00
Fortune, bowl, berry; pk or crystal, 4" 10.00
Fortune, cup, pk or crystal..12.00
Fruits, pitcher, gr, flat bottom, 7" 95.00
Fruits, plate, luncheon; gr or pk, 8"..12.00
Fruits, tumbler, pk, combo of fruits, 4"...22.00
Georgian, bowl, vegetable; gr, oval, 9"...65.00
Georgian, plate, luncheon; gr, 8" 11.00
Georgian, tumbler, gr, flat, 9-oz, 4"..70.00
Hex Optic, bowl, mixing; pk or gr, 9"...25.00
Hex Optic, butter dish, pk or gr, rectangular, w/lid, 1-lb 90.00
Hex Optic, cup, pk or gr, 2-hdl styles, ea......................................10.00
Hex Optic, plate, luncheon; pk or gr, 8"...5.50
Hex Optic, refrigerator dish, pk or gr, 4x4"..................................18.00
Hex Optic, tumbler, pk or gr, ftd, 7"...12.00
Hex Optic, whiskey, pk or gr, 1-oz, 2"..8.00
Hobnail, goblet, iced tea; crystal, 12-oz 10.00
Hobnail, plate, sherbet; pk, 6"...4.00
Hobnail, tumbler, juice; crystal, 5-oz 4.00
Homespun, bowl, lg berry; pk or crystal, 8¼"...............................30.00
Homespun, cup, pk or crystal..14.00
Homespun, saucer, pk or crystal..5.00
Homespun, tumbler, pk or crystal, ftd, 15-oz, 6¼".........................35.00
Indiana Custard, bowl, berry; French Ivory, 5½".............................12.00
Indiana Custard, butter dish, French Ivory, w/lid..........................65.00
Indiana Custard, cup, French Ivory 37.50
Indiana Custard, plate, salad; French Ivory, 7½".............................20.00
Iris, bowl, berry; irid, beaded edge, 4½"...9.00

Iris, butter dish, irid, w/lid...45.00
Iris, candlesticks, crystal, pr...42.50
Iris, creamer, gr or pk, ftd...150.00
Iris, goblet, wine; crystal, 3-oz, 4½"..16.00
Iris, pitcher, irid, ftd, 9½"..42.50
Iris, vase, crystal, 9"...30.00
Jubilee, bowl, fruit; yel, flat, 11½"...160.00
Jubilee, cheese & cracker set, pk 255.00
Jubilee, plate, salad; pk, 7"...22.50
Jubilee, sherbet, yel, 8-oz, 3"...70.00
Jubilee, tumbler, water; pk, 10-oz, 6"..75.00
Laced Edge, bowl, soup; opal, 7"..90.00
Laced Edge, cup, opal...35.00
Laced Edge, plate, bread & butter; opal, 8½"................................18.00
Laced Edge, sugar bowl, opal..40.00
Lake Como, bowl, cereal; wht, 6"..28.00
Lake Como, creamer, wht, ftd...32.50
Lake Como, platter, wht, 11"...75.00
Lake Como, saucer, wht..12.00
Laurel, bowl, cereal; Poudre Blue, 6"..28.00
Laurel, bowl, lg berry; Jade Green or decor rims, 9".....................40.00
Laurel, cheese dish, White Opal or French Ivory, w/lid................60.00
Laurel, plate, salad; Jade Green or decor rims, 7½"......................20.00
Laurel, sherbet/champagne, White Opal or French Ivory, 5".........50.00
Lincoln Inn, bowl, cobalt or red, crimped, 6"................................15.00
Lincoln Inn, goblet, water; cobalt or red.......................................30.00
Lincoln Inn, shakers, blk, pr...300.00
Lincoln Inn, tumbler, water; amethyst, flat, 9-oz 19.50
Lorain, bowl, cereal; crystal or gr, 6"..50.00
Lorain, cup, yel...15.00
Lorain, platter, yel, 11½"...45.00
Lorain, snack tray, crystal or gr 35.00
Madrid, bowl, berry; amber or pk, 9⅜"..20.00
Madrid, bowl, soup; amber or gr, 7" 16.00
Madrid, bowl, vegetable; bl, oval, 10"..40.00
Madrid, creamer, gr, ftd..12.50
Madrid, Jell-O mold, amber, tall, 2⅛"...10.00
Madrid, plate, grill; gr, 10½"...20.00
Madrid, plate, sherbet; bl, 6"...8.00
Madrid, saucer, pk 5.00
Manhattan, ashtray, crystal, rnd, 4"..12.00
Manhattan, bowl, berry; crystal, 7½"...22.00
Manhattan, candy dish, pk, 3 legs, 6¼"...15.00
Manhattan, shakers, crystal, sq, 2", pr..30.00
Manhattan, sherbet, pk...18.00
Mayfair (Federal), bowl, cream soup; crystal, 5"...........................15.00
Mayfair (Federal), plate, salad; crystal, 6¾"....................................4.50
Mayfair (Federal), sugar bowl, amber, ftd.....................................13.00
Mayfair (Federal), tumbler, gr, 9-oz, 4½"......................................45.00
Mayfair/Open Rose, bowl, bl, low flat, 11¾"..................................72.50
Mayfair/Open Rose, bowl, cereal; gr or yel, 5½".............................85.00
Mayfair/Open Rose, bowl, vegetable; pk, oval, 9½"........................35.00
Mayfair/Open Rose, candy dish, pk, w/lid......................................60.00
Mayfair/Open Rose, celery dish, bl, divided, 10"............................80.00
Mayfair/Open Rose, cup, gr or yel..155.00
Mayfair/Open Rose, goblet, wine; pk, 3-oz, 4½".............................110.00
Mayfair/Open Rose, plate, grill; pk, 9½"...50.00
Mayfair/Open Rose, plate, luncheon; bl, 8½"..................................55.00
Mayfair/Open Rose, sandwich server, gr, center hdl......................40.00
Mayfair/Open Rose, saucer, yel, w/cup ring..................................150.00
Mayfair/Open Rose, sugar bowl, gr or yel, ftd..............................210.00
Mayfair/Open Rose, tumbler, pk, ftd, 10-oz, 5¼".............................48.00
Miss America, bowl, berry; gr, 4½"..15.00
Miss America, bowl, cereal; pk, 6¼"...30.00

Miss America, cake plate, crystal, ftd, 12" 26.00

Miss America, candy dish, pink, $165.00.

Miss America, cup, Royal Ruby 295.00
Miss America, pitcher, crystal, 65-oz, 8" 50.00
Miss America, plate, sherbet; gr, 5¾" 8.00
Miss America, saucer, Royal Ruby 75.00
Miss America, shakers, pk, pr 67.50
Moderntone, bowl, cream soup; amethyst, 4¾" 20.00
Moderntone, bowl, soup; cobalt, 7½" 150.00
Moderntone, plate, salad; cobalt, 6¾" 11.00
Moderntone, platter, cobalt, oval, 12" 85.00
Moderntone, sherbet, amethyst 12.00
Moondrops, bowl, berry; bl or red, 5¼" 25.00
Moondrops, bowl, casserole; pk, 9¾" 125.00
Moondrops, bowl, celery; gr, boat shape, 11" 23.00
Moondrops, candle holders bl or red, ruffled, 2", pr 45.00
Moondrops, cup, bl or red 16.00
Moondrops, goblet, wine; amethyst, 4-oz, 4" 13.00
Moondrops, perfume bottle, crystal, 'rocket' 195.00
Moondrops, plate, dinner; bl or red, 9½" 30.00
Moondrops, platter, smoke, oval, 12" 25.00
Moondrops, tumbler, bl or red, 8-oz, 4⅜" 20.00
Mt Pleasant, bowl, rose; amethyst, blk or cobalt, 4" 27.50
Mt Pleasant, candlesticks, pk or gr, dbl, pr 26.00
Mt Pleasant, plate, amethyst, blk or cobalt, hdls, 12" 33.00
Mt Pleasant, plate, pk or gr, scalloped or sq, 8" 10.00
Mt Pleasant, vase, amethyst, blk or cobalt, 7¼" 35.00
New Century, ashtray/coaster, gr or crystal, 5⅜" 30.00
New Century, decanter, gr or crystal, w/stopper 75.00
New Century, goblet, wine; gr or crystal, 2½-oz 33.00
New Century, plate, grill; gr or crystal, 10" 20.00
New Century, saucer, pk, cobalt or amethyst 7.50
New Century, tumbler, gr or crystal, ftd, 9-oz, 4⅞" 25.00
New Century, tumbler, pk, cobalt or amethyst, 5-oz, 3½" 12.00
Newport, bowl, berry; cobalt, 4¾" 22.00
Newport, creamer, amethyst 14.00
Newport, plate, luncheon; cobalt, 8½" 16.00
Newport, plate, sandwich; amethyst, 11¾" 40.00
Newport, sugar bowl, cobalt or amethyst 16.00
No 610 Pyramid, bowl, berry; yel, 4¾" 55.00
No 610 Pyramid, creamer, crystal 20.00
No 610 Pyramid, relish tray, pk, hdl, 4-part 60.00
No 610 Pyramid, tumbler, gr, ftd, 11-oz 85.00
No 612 Horseshoe, bowl, berry; gr or yel, 9½" 50.00
No 612 Horseshoe, bowl, berry; yel, 4½" 25.00
No 612 Horseshoe, cup, gr 12.00
No 612 Horseshoe, plate, salad; gr or yel, 8⅜" 12.00
No 612 Horseshoe, sugar bowl, gr, open 18.00
No 612 Horseshoe, tumbler, yel, ftd, 12-oz 185.00
No 616 Vernon, creamer, crystal, ftd 12.00

No 616 Vernon, plate, sandwich; gr, 11½" 27.50
No 616 Vernon, tumbler, gr or yel, ftd, 5" 45.00
No 618 Pineapple & Floral, bowl, cereal; crystal, 6" 30.00
No 618 Pineapple & Floral, bowl, vegetable; amber or red, oval, 10" ...20.00
No 618 Pineapple & Floral, cup, crystal, amber or red 10.00
No 618 Pineapple & Floral, plate, sandwich; amber or red, 11½" ...17.50
No 618 Pineapple & Floral, tumbler, crystal, 12-oz, 5" 50.00
Normandie, bowl, berry; pk, 8½" 40.00
Normandie, cup, irid 6.00
Normandie, tumbler, juice; amber, 5-oz, 4" 35.00
Old Cafe, bowl, berry; crystal or pk, tab hdls, 3¾" 14.00
Old Cafe, bowl, Royal Ruby, closed hdls, 9" 18.00
Old Cafe, pitcher, crystal or pk, 80-oz 150.00
Old Cafe, plate, dinner; crystal or pk, 10" 65.00
Old Cafe, sherbet, Royal Ruby, low ftd, 3¾" 12.00
Old English, bowl, fruit; pk, gr or amber, ftd, 9" 40.00
Old English, candy jar, pk, gr or amber, w/lid 60.00
Old English, egg cup, crystal 10.00
Old English, vase, pk, gr or amber, ftd, 12" 75.00
Ovide, cup, decor wht 12.50
Ovide, plate, luncheon; Art Deco, 8" 60.00
Ovide, plate, sherbet; gr, 6" 2.50
Ovide, sugar bowl, blk, open 6.50
Oyster & Pearl, bowl, Royal Ruby, hdl, 5½" 20.00
Oyster & Pearl, candle holders, wht or fired-on gr or pk, 3½", pr.30.00
Oyster & Pearl, relish dish, crystal or pk, oblong, divided, 10½" ..18.00
Parrot, bowl, soup; gr, 7" 55.00
Parrot, creamer, gr, ftd 60.00
Parrot, jam dish, amber, 7" 38.00
Parrot, plate, salad; gr, 7½" 40.00
Parrot, platter, amber, oblong, 11¼" 75.00
Parrot, saucer, amber 17.50
Parrot, tumbler, gr, 10-oz, ¼" 195.00
Patrician, bowl, berry; amber or crystal, 8½" 45.00
Patrician, bowl, cream soup; pk or gr, 4¾" 22.00
Patrician, butter dish, amber or crystal, w/lid 95.00
Patrician, cup, gr 14.00
Patrician, plate, grill; amber or crystal, 10½" 14.00
Patrician, shakers, amber or crystal, pr 60.00
Patrician, tumbler, pk, 14-oz, 5½" 45.00
Patrick, bowl, fruit; yel, hdls, 9" 145.00
Patrick, goblet, water; pk, 10-oz, 6" 80.00
Patrick, mayonnaise, pk, 3-pc 195.00
Patrick, plate, luncheon; yel, 8" 25.00
Petalware, bowl, cream soup; cremax, monax or plain, 4½" 12.00
Petalware, bowl, soup; cremax, monax, florette or fired-on decor, 7" ...100.00
Petalware, cup, red trim or floral 27.50
Petalware, pitcher, crystal, w/decor bands, 80-oz 35.00
Petalware, plate, dinner; pk, 9" 14.00
Primo, bowl, yel or gr, 3-ftd, 11" 60.00
Primo, creamer, yel or gr 12.00
Primo, plate, yel or gr, 7½" 14.00
Primo, sugar bowl, yel or gr 12.00
Primo, tumbler, yel or gr, 9-oz, 5¾" 20.00
Princess, bowl, cereal or oatmeal; gr, pk, topaz or apricot, 5" 40.00
Princess, bowl, vegetable; gr, oval, 10" 32.00
Princess, cookie jar, pk, w/lid 70.00
Princess, cup, topaz or apricot 9.00
Princess, spice shakers, gr, 5½", pr 40.00
Princess, tumbler, iced tea; topaz or apricot, 13-oz, 5¼" 32.00
Princess, tumbler, pk, ftd, 12½-oz, 6½" 90.00
Queen Mary, ashtray, pk, oval, 2x3¾" 5.00
Queen Mary, bowl, cereal; crystal, 6" 6.00
Queen Mary, plate, sandwich; pk, #450, 12" 25.00

Queen Mary, tumbler, juice; crystal, 5-oz, 3½" 4.00
Raindrops, bowl, berry; gr, 7½" 55.00
Raindrops, sherbet, gr 7.00
Raindrops, tumbler, gr, 4-oz, 3" 5.00
Ribbon, bowl, berry; gr, 4" 35.00
Ribbon, bowl, gr, str sides, 8" 75.00
Ribbon, shakers, blk, pr 45.00
Ribbon, sugar bowl, gr, ftd 15.00
Ring, bowl, berry; crystal, 5" 4.00
Ring, cocktail shaker, crystal 20.00
Ring, decanter, gr or w/decor, w/stopper 45.00
Ring, goblet, wine; crystal, 3½-oz, 4½" 13.00
Ring, tumbler, gr or w/decor, 4-oz, 3" 12.00
Rock Crystal, bowl, crystal, scalloped edge, 4" 12.00
Rock Crystal, bowl, red, scalloped edge, 5" 45.00
Rock Crystal, bowl, salad; amber, scalloped edge, 9" 50.00
Rock Crystal, bowl, salad; crystal, scalloped edge, 7" 24.00
Rock Crystal, butter dish, crystal, w/lid 335.00
Rock Crystal, candlesticks, red, tall, 8", pr 475.00
Rock Crystal, comport, crystal, 7" 50.00
Rock Crystal, ice dish, crystal, 3 styles 40.00
Rock Crystal, sandwich server, red, center hdl 145.00
Rock Crystal, shakers, aqua, 2 styles, pr 125.00
Rock Crystal, stem, wine; crystal, 2-oz 25.00
Rock Crystal, sundae, red, low ft, 6-oz 38.00
Rock Crystal, syrup, crystal, w/lid 195.00
Rose Cameo, bowl, berry; gr, 4½" 15.00
Rose Cameo, bowl, gr, str sides, 6" 30.00
Rose Cameo, sherbet, gr 15.00
Rosemary, bowl, cereal; gr, 6" 38.00
Rosemary, bowl, cream soup; amber, 5" 18.00
Rosemary, plate, dinner; amber 10.00
Rosemary, plate, salad; pk, 6¾" 13.00
Rosemary, tumbler, gr, 9-oz, 4¼" 40.00
Roulette, bowl, fruit; crystal, 9" 9.50
Roulette, plate, sherbet; pk or gr, 6" 5.00
Roulette, tumbler, pk or gr, ftd, 10-oz, 5½" 35.00
Roulette, tumbler, water; crystal, 9-oz, 4⅛" 13.00
Round Robin, bowl, berry; irid, 4" 9.00
Round Robin, sugar bowl, gr 12.50
Roxana, bowl, berry; yel, 5" 16.00
Roxana, bowl, wht, 4½x2⅜" 20.00
Roxana, plate, sherbet; yel, 6" 10.00
Royal Lace, bowl, berry; crystal, 5" 15.00
Royal Lace, bowl, cream soup; gr, 4¾" 38.00
Royal Lace, bowl, nut; crystal 295.00

Royal Lace, butter dish, crystal, $80.00.

Royal Lace, creamer, pk, ftd 22.00
Royal Lace, cup, crystal 9.00
Royal Lace, pitcher, bl, w/lip, 68-oz, 8" 310.00
Royal Lace, plate, grill; pk, 9⅞" 22.00

Royal Lace, plate, luncheon; crystal, 8½" 8.00
Royal Lace, plate, sherbet; gr, 6" 12.00
S Pattern, bowl, cereal; crystal, 5½" 5.00
S Pattern, plate, cake; crystal, heavy, 11¾" 40.00
S Pattern, plate, dinner; yel, amber, or crystal w/trims, 9¼" 10.00
S Pattern, tumbler, yel, amber or crystal w/trims, 12-oz, 5" 15.00
Sandwich, bowl, amber or crystal, 6" 4.00
Sandwich, bowl, console; pk or gr, 9" 40.00
Sandwich, cruet, teal bl, w/stopper, 6½-oz 135.00
Sandwich, plate, bread & butter; amber or crystal, 7" 4.00
Sandwich, plate, luncheon; red, 8⅜" 20.00
Sandwich, wine, pk or gr, 4-oz, 3" 25.00
Sharon, bowl, cream soup; pk, 5" 50.00
Sharon, bowl, fruit; gr, 10½" 42.50
Sharon, bowl, vegetable; amber, oval, 9½" 18.00
Sharon, cup, amber 10.00
Sharon, plate, bread & butter; gr, 6" 9.00
Sharon, sugar bowl, pk 14.00
Ships, cocktail shaker, bl & wht 38.00
Ships, pitcher, bl & wht, w/lip, 86-oz 75.00
Ships, plate, salad; bl & wht, 8" 30.00
Ships, saucer, bl & wht 20.00
Ships, tumbler, bl & wht, roly-poly, 6-oz 12.00
Sierra, bowl, cereal; gr, 5½" 18.00
Sierra, creamer, pk 20.00
Sierra, platter, pk, oval, 11" 55.00
Sierra, shakers, pk, pr 45.00
Sierra, tumbler, gr, ftd, 9-oz, 4½" 90.00
Spiral, bowl, berry; gr, 8" 12.50
Spiral, platter, gr, 12" 35.00
Spiral, shakers, gr, pr 35.00
Spiral, tumbler, water; gr, 9-oz, 5" 10.00
Starlight, bowl, pk, closed hdls, 8½" 20.00
Starlight, plate, dinner; crystal or wht, 8" 7.50
Starlight, relish dish, crystal or wht 15.00
Starlight, sugar bowl, crystal or wht, oval 8.00
Strawberry, bowl, deep salad; crystal or irid, 6½" 15.00
Strawberry, butter dish, pk or gr, w/lid 195.00
Strawberry, pickle dish, crystal or irid, oval, 8¼" 9.00
Strawberry, sugar bowl, pk or gr, open, sm 22.00
Sunburst, bowl, berry; crystal, 8½" 18.00
Sunburst, creamer, crystal, ftd 10.00
Sunburst, tray, crystal, oval, sm 12.00
Sunflower, cake plate, pk or gr, 3-leg, 10" 15.00
Sunflower, saucer, gr 10.00
Swirl, bowl, berry; Delphite, 4⅞" or 5¼", ea 14.00
Swirl, bowl, console; pk, ftd, 10½" 20.00
Swirl, bowl, salad; ultramarine, rimmed, 9" 32.00
Swirl, candle holders, ultramarine, dbl branch, pr 60.00
Swirl, candy dish, pk, w/lid 115.00
Swirl, plate, sandwich; pk, 12½" 22.00
Swirl, platter, Delphite, oval, 12" 38.00
Swirl, tumbler, ultramarine, ftd, 9-oz 47.50
Tea Room, bowl, banana split; gr, ftd, 7½" 95.00
Tea Room, bowl, celery; gr, 8¼" 35.00
Tea Room, creamer, pk, rectangular 20.00
Tea Room, ice bucket, pk 55.00
Tea Room, sherbet, gr or pk, tall, ftd 50.00
Tea Room, sugar bowl, pk, flat, w/lid 165.00
Tea Room, tumbler, pk, ftd, 12-oz 70.00
Tea Room, vase, gr, str sides, 9½" 100.00
Thistle, bowl, lg fruit; gr, 10¼" 295.00
Thistle, cup, pk, thin 25.00
Thistle, plate, cake; pk, heavy, 13" 195.00

Thistle, plate, luncheon; gr, 8" 24.00
Tulip, ice tub, amethyst or bl, 3x4⅞" 95.00
Tulip, plate, amethyst or bl, 6" 11.00
Tulip, sugar bowl, crystal or gr 20.00
Tulip, tumbler, whiskey; amethyst or bl 35.00
Twisted Optic, bowl, cereal; bl or canary yel, 5" 16.00
Twisted Optic, bowl, salad; pk, 10" 30.00
Twisted Optic, candy jar, bl or canary yel, flat, w/lid 85.00
Twisted Optic, compote, cheese; bl or canary yel 20.00
Twisted Optic, creamer, gr 8.00
Twisted Optic, cup, amber 5.00
Twisted Optic, plate, luncheon; bl or canary yel, 7" 8.00
Twisted Optic, platter, bl or canary yel, oval 35.00
Twisted Optic, sugar bowl, pk 7.00
Twisted Optic, tumbler, gr, 8-oz, 4½" 6.00
US Swirl, bowl, lg berry; pk, 7⅞" 16.00
US Swirl, comport, gr 35.00
US Swirl, sugar bowl, gr or pk, w/lid 40.00
US Swirl, vase, pk, 6½" 25.00
Victory, bowl, flat soup; blk, amber, pk or gr, 8½" 20.00
Victory, bowl, vegetable; blk, amber, pk or gr, oval, 9" 32.00
Victory, candlesticks, bl, 3", pr 125.00
Victory, goblet, blk, amber, pk or gr, 7-oz, 5" 25.00
Victory, plate, luncheon; bl, 8" 30.00
Vitrock, bowl, cream soup; wht, 5½" 16.00
Vitrock, cup, wht 6.00
Vitrock, plate, dinner; wht, 10" 10.00
Vitrock, plate, salad; wht, 7¼" 4.00
Waterford, bowl, berry; pk, 4¾" 20.00
Waterford, bowl, lg berry; crystal, 8½" 15.00
Waterford, butter dish, crystal, w/lid 30.00
Waterford, cup, pk, Miss America shape 45.00
Waterford, plate, sherbet; crystal, 6" 4.00
Waterford, shakers, crystal, 2 types, pr 9.00
Waterford, sherbet, pk, ftd 20.00
Windsor, bowl, crystal, pointed edge, 8" 18.00
Windsor, bowl, fruit console; crystal, 12½" 30.00
Windsor, bowl, pk, 3 legs, 7⅛" 30.00
Windsor, plate, dinner; gr, 9" 25.00
Windsor, tumbler, crystal, ftd, 4" 8.00

Desert Sands

As early as the 1850s, the Evans family living in the Ozark Mountains of Missouri produced domestic clay products. Their small pot shop was passed on from one generation to the next. In the 1920s it was moved to North Las Vegas, Nevada, where the name Desert Sands was adopted. Succeeding generations of the family continued to relocate, taking the business with them. From 1937 to 1962 it operated in Boulder City, Nevada; then it was moved to Barstow, California, where it remained until it closed in the late 1970s.

Desert Sands pottery is similar to Mission Ware by Niloak. Various mineral oxides were blended to mimic the naturally occurring sand formations of the American West. A high-gloss glaze was applied to add intensity to the colorful striations that characterize the ware. Not all examples are marked, making it sometimes difficult to attribute. Marked items carry an ink stamp with the Desert Sands designation. Paper labels were also used.

Ashtray, mc swirls, 2x8½" 50.00
Ashtray, 7" dia 25.00
Bowl, nut; thumbprint pattern, 1¾x3½" 35.00
Bowl, ped ft, 5x6" 50.00

Bowl, 1¾x4½" 30.00
Bowl, 2x7" 35.00
Candle holder, 1½x5" 35.00
Cup, 3⅜" 20.00
Pitcher, mini, 3" 20.00
Planter, hanging; 3x5½" dia 40.00
Shakers, beehive shape, 1½", pr 25.00
Spoon rest, heart shape, 5" 55.00

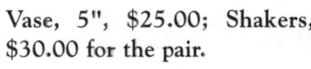

Vase, 5", $25.00; Shakers, $30.00 for the pair.

Vase, invt cylinder, 14" 90.00
Vase, waisted form, flared rim, 8" 70.00
Wall pocket, 3⅜x5¼x5½" 150.00

Documents

Although the word 'document' is defined in the general sense as 'anything printed or written, etc., relied upon to record or prove something. . .,' in the collectibles market, the term is more diversified with broadsides, billheads, checks, invoices, letters and letterheads, land grants, receipts, and waybills some of the most sought after. Some documents in demand are those related to a specific subject such as advertising, mining, railroads, military, politics, banking, slavery, nautical, or legal (deeds, mortgages, etc.). Other collectors look for examples representing a specific period of time such as colonial documents, Revolutionary or Civil War documents, early western documents, or those from a specific region, state, or city.

Aside from supply and demand, there are five major factors which determine the collector-value of a document. These are:

1) Age — Documents from the eastern half of the country can be found that date back to the 1700s or earlier. Most documents sought by collectors usually date from 1700 to 1900. Those with twentieth-century dates are still abundant and not in demand unless of special significance or beauty.

2) Region of origin — Depending on age, documents from rural and less-populated areas are harder to find than those from major cities and heavily populated states. The colonization of the West and Midwest did not begin until after 1850, so while an 1870s billhead from New York or Chicago is common, one from Albuquerque or Phoenix is not, since most of the Southwest was still unsettled.

3) Attractiveness — Some documents are plain and unadorned, but collectors prefer colorful, profusely illustrated pieces. Additional artwork and engravings add to the value.

4) Historical content — Unusual or interesting content, such as a letter written by a Civil War soldier giving an eye-witness account of the Battle of Gettysburg or a western territorial billhead listing numerous animal hides purchased from a trapper, will sell for more than one with mundane information.

5) Condition — Through neglect or environmental conditions, over many decades paper articles can become stained, torn, or deteriorated. Heavily damaged or stained documents are generally avoided alto-

gether. Those with minor problems are more acceptable, although their value will decrease anywhere from 20% to 50%, depending upon the extent of damage. Avoid attempting to repair tears with scotch tape — sell 'as is' so that the collector can take proper steps toward restoration.

Foreign documents are plentiful; and though some are very attractive, resale may be difficult. The listings that follow are generalized; prices are variable depending entirely upon the five points noted above. Values here are based upon examples with no major damage. Common grade documents without significant content are found in abundance and generally have little collector value. These usually date from the late 1800s to mid-1900s. It should be noted that the items listed below are examples of those that meet the criteria for having collector value. There is little demand for documents worth less than $5.00. For more information we recommend *Owning Western History* by our advisor Warren Anderson. His address and ordering information may be found in the Directory under Utah.

Key:
illus — illustrated   vgn — vignette

Agreement, Putah Creek CA/1882, shares in water co, handwritten, 8x9" ..**25.00**
Appointment, 1814, to rank of 2nd sergeant, printed/written, vgn..**150.00**
Appointment certificate, Nat'l Gards of RI, 1929, state seal, EX..**30.00**
Appraisal, SC, 1846, slaves/animals/tools/etc, 10x8" **200.00**
Billhead, AZ Territory, Lexington Livery & Feed Stables, vgn, 1905 ..**20.00**
Billhead, NE/1892, sale of livestock, pre-printed, 8x8" **18.00**
Billhead, NV/1908, Goldfield Daily Tribune, pre-printed, 4x8" **15.00**
Billhead, UT/1896, lumber co vgn w/list of products, pre-printed **20.00**
Check, Bank of Ouray, CO, Chief vgn, to Denver Nat'l, 1904, 4x9", NM ...**25.00**
Condolence, House of Representatives gold seal, death of Pope, 1939.....**100.00**
Court order, AZ Territory/1883, hold men for assault charges, legal sz **35.00**
Declaration of Independence, litho cotton panel, early 1800s, 30x28" .**1,600.00**
Deed, WA Territory/1868, pre-printed/handwritten cancellation, 2-pg **40.00**
Discharge, Continental Army, 1782, handwritten release **200.00**
Envelope, Union/E Pluribus Unum, Civil War era, 3x5½" **250.00**
Final statement, NY, 1864, printed form w/info on killed soldier..**35.00**
Invoice, DE Volunteers, 1860s, belts/scabbards/etc, 9¾x7½" **75.00**
Land grant, Dorchester MA, May 25, 1792, lt stain/fold, 12x7½" ...**115.00**
Land grant, OK/1902, homestead certificate for 160 acres, pre-printed...**35.00**
Letter, CA/1888, re: payment of ranch property, 3 5x7" pgs..........**15.00**
Letter, from IN/1910, re: railroad trip/lectures, 2 8x10" pgs...........**17.00**
Letter, ID Territory/1890, trade of whiskey for cigars, 1 6x9" pg ...**30.00**
Letter, PA, 1865, war news, lined emb stationery, faded, 2-pg **200.00**

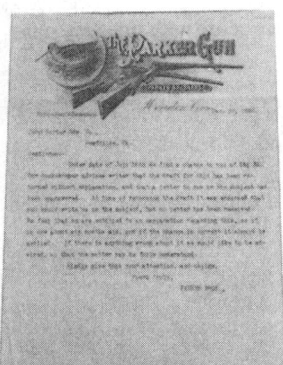

Letter, Parker Gun Co. letterhead, request for payment, December 1895, VG+, $185.00.

Letter, Ray Detective Agency...Secret Service, 1911, typed, 1-pg .**20.00**
Letterhead, MN/1888, factory vgn, re: overdue payment, 6x9".........**15.00**
Order, Sandwich, 1802, delivery of gunpowder, 4x7" **125.00**
Pay order, CT, 1777, feed for Col Hancock's horse, 7¼x3" **225.00**
Pay order, WY/1898, Neponset Land & Live Stock Co, purple printing ..**30.00**

Pay order, 1755, school teacher's wages, 5¼x7½" **175.00**
Playbill, Boston Theatre, Feb 3, 1794, litho on silk, 11x91"+fr ..**315.00**
Promissory note, CA/1877, handwritten for $16,000 to be paid in gold..**18.00**
Prospectus, CA, Banker's Oil Co, ca 1902, 8 8x9" pgs..................**20.00**
Quit-claim deed, CO/1880, pre-printed, 2 lots on main street, 11x17" ..**22.00**
Receipt, West Point, 1778, leather breeches, 3x6" **225.00**
Shipping order, Boston, 1836, vgn, partly printed, 10½x9" **100.00**
Sight draft, Corinne in UT Territory/1875, pre-printed, ornate border ..**20.00**
Time check, Wewissa Mine in CO/1890, pre-printed, pay of $2.50 per day....**18.00**
Voucher, Civil War PA volunteer's discharge, pre-printed, 8x11" .**20.00**

Dollhouses and Furnishings

Dollhouses were introduced commercially in this country late in the 1700s by Dutch craftsmen who settled in the East. By the mid-1800s, they had become meticulously detailed, divided into separate rooms, and lavishly furnished to reflect the opulence of the day. Originally intended for the amusement of adults of the household, by the late 1800s their status had changed to that of a child's toy. Though many early dollhouses were lovingly hand fashioned for a special little girl, those made commercially by such companies as Bliss and Schoenhut are highly valued.

Furniture and furnishings in the Biedermeier style featuring stenciled Victorian decorations often sell for several hundred dollars each. Other early pieces made of pewter, porcelain, or papier-mache are also quite valuable. Certainly less expensive but very collectible, nonetheless, is the quality, hallmarked plastic furniture produced during the 1940s by Renwal and Acme, and the 1960's Petite Princess line produced by Ideal. In the listings that follow, dollhouses are litho paper on wood, unless otherwise noted. For more information, see *Schroeder's Collectible Toys, Antique to Modern*. Our advisor for this category is Barbara Rosen; she is listed in the Directory under New Jersey. See also Miniatures.

Furnishings

Armoire, Tomy Smaller Homes, w/hangers **15.00**
Baby crib, Superior, rust brn or bright bl, ¾" scale, ea **8.00**
Bed, canopy; Tomy Smaller Homes **15.00**
Buffet, Ideal Petite Princess, #4419-8, complete, in orig box.........**25.00**
Buffet, Young Decorator, dk marbleized maroon **25.00**
Cabinet, floor; Nancy Forbes, walnut **4.00**
Cabinet, medicine; Tootsietoy, ivory **25.00**
Chair, barrel; Renwal, med bl w/metallic red base **9.00**
Chair, living room; Marx, hard plastic, tufted, lt gr, ¾" scale **5.00**
Chair, living room; Tootsietoy, gold wicker-look w/cushion **18.00**
Chair, patio; Plasco, bl w/dk ivory legs or bl w/ivory legs, ea **3.00**
Chair, rocker; Kilgore, bl, G- pnt **50.00**
Chair w/ottoman, Strombecker, lt brn flocked, 1" scale **25.00**
Chest of drw, Marx, hard plastic, bl or pk, ¾" scale, ea **5.00**
Clock, kitchen; Renwal, ivory...**20.00**
Counter, Marx, hard plastic, w/molded phone & hot plate, ½" scale..**5.00**
Desk, Wolverine, off-wht or turq, ea..**3.00**
Diaper pail, Young Decorator, yel w/bl **25.00**
Dining room set, Marx, soft plastic, brn, 7-pc, ¾" scale **20.00**
Doll, baby in diaper, Acme/Thomas, 2" **4.00**
Doll, boy or girl sitting, Marx, ea **4.00**
Doll, father, Renwal, metal rivets, bl suit **30.00**
Doll, father, Renwal, plastic rivets, all tan.....................................**25.00**
Dustpan, Renwal, red or yel, ea..**10.00**
Fireplace, Marx Little Hostess, ivory **20.00**
Fireplace, Reliable, rust **45.00**
Highchair, Ideal, collapsible, bl or pk, ea.......................................**25.00**
Lamp, floor; Strombecker, ivory shade, blk base, ¾" scale **15.00**
Mirror, bathroom; Tomy Smaller Homes, standing **15.00**

Piano, Allied/Pyro, blk w/wht keyboard 12.00
Piano, Ideal, w/bench, dk marbleized brn.....................................25.00
Playground seesaw, Renwal, bl w/red & yel or yel w/red & bl, ea..45.00
Playground slide, Renwal, bl w/red steps or yel w/bl steps, ea........22.00
Playpen, Marx, soft plastic, pk, ¾" scale......................................3.00
Radio, table; Renwal, metallic red...18.00
Refrigerator, Young Decorator, wht..55.00
Shoofly, Acme/Thomas, dk bl or red w/yel horse head, ea 18.00
Sink, bathroom; Ideal, bl w/yel...10.00
Sink, bathroom; Superior, med off-gr, ivory or wht, ¾" scale, ea.....5.00
Sink, kitchen; Jaydon, ivory w/blk..15.00
Sofa, game room; Marx, hard plastic, curved, red, ½" scale...........15.00
Sofa, Superior, pale gr, turq or red, ¾" scale, ea 5.00
Stove, Renwal, opening door, ivory w/blk 15.00
Sweeper, Renwal, red w/bl hdl, 1 roller 30.00
Table, dining room; Ideal Petite Princess, #4421-4 ....15.00
Table, gate-leg; Marx Little Hostess, rust...................................15.00
Table, kitchen; Ideal, wht..20.00
Table, kitchen; Reliable, ivory 12.00
Table, lamp; Renwal, reddish brn..8.00
Table, step-end; Marx, hard plastic, bl, ¾" scale 4.00
Table, step-end; Marx, soft plastic, med bl, ¾" scale......................3.00
Telephone, Tootsietoy, gr..45.00
Television, console; Marx, hard plastic, ½" scale 3.00
Tub, Superior, yel, gr, or turq, ¾" scale, ea 5.00
Vanity & bench, Strombecker, walnut, 1936, 1" scale...................30.00
Washer, front load, Marx, hard plastic, wht, ¾" scale.....................6.00

Houses, Shops, and Single Rooms

**Bliss, litho on wood, blue roof, 13", EX,
$900.00.** (Photo courtesy McMasters Auctions)

Bliss, 1½ story w/attic, red roof/dormers/porch w/steps, 20x18", G ...1,800.00
Brumberger, contemporary colonial, 2-story, 5-room, 1970, 20x24", MIB..60.00
Fisher-Price, #280, 3-story, lights up, MIB..................................50.00
German, carriage house, stalls/office/carriage hall/loft, 25x36", VG....1,700.00
German, shop, pnt wood/papered, drws/light/many accessories, EX..1,600.00
German, warehouse, 3-story w/bl roof, hoist, 22x11x9", VG ...2,000.00
Gottschalk, Australian villa, 2-story, 2-room, litho/wood, 31x27", EX..9,200.00
Gottschalk, Victorian, 2-story, 2-room, litho/wood/glass windows, EX..4,300.00
Marx, Little Red Schoolhouse, tin w/plastic furniture & figures, EX.........450.00
Marx, Newlyweds Bathroom, #192, w/furniture, 1925, 3x5x3", NM 225.00
McLoughlin Bros, Dolly's Playhouse, folding 2-story, late 1800s, EXIB.....400.00
Ohio Art, Midget Manor, 2-story, tin, w/furniture, 1949, 8x5½", MIB.....300.00
Schoenhut, bungalow, 2-room, emb cb roof, electric, 17x17x15", EX.....550.00
Schoenhut, 2-room cottage, window boxes on 2 front porch windows, EX..375.00
Superior, modern, 1½-story, tin, MIB...125.00
T Cohn, 2-story, 6-room, tin, dbl patio, red & wht w/gr shutters, VG 200.00
Wolverine, Corner Grocer, tin, w/shelving & grocery items, 13x16", G..350.00

Dolls

To learn to invest your money wisely as you enjoy the hobby of doll collecting, you must become aware of defects which may devaluate a doll. In bisque, watch for eye chips, hairline cracks and chips, or breaks on any part of the head. Composition should be clean, not crazed or cracked. Vinyl and plastic should be clean with no pen or crayon marks. Though a quality replacement wig is acceptable for bisque dolls, composition and hard plastics should have their originals in uncut condition. Original clothing is a must except in bisque dolls, since it is unusual to find one in its original costume.

It is important to remember that prices are based on condition and rarity. When no condition is noted, either in the line listing or the sub-category narrative, dolls are assumed to be in excellent condition. In relation to bisque dolls, excellent means having no cracks, chips, or hairlines, being nicely dressed, shoed, wigged, and ready to to be placed into a collection.

For a more thorough study of the subject, refer to *Modern Collectible Dolls, Volumes II, III, IV, V,* and *Doll Values, Antique to Modern, Fifth Edition,* by Patsy Moyer; *Collector's Guide to Dolls of the 1960s and 1970s* by Cindy Sabulis; *Talking Toys of the 20th Century* by Kathy and Don Lewis; and *Collector's Guide to Celebrity Dolls,* by David Spurgeon. Several other book are referenced throughout this category. All are published by Collector Books. Except for the subcategories where another expert is noted, our general advisor for this category is author Patsy Moyer; she is listed in the Directory under Arizona.

Key:
bjtd — ball-jointed   OC — original clothes
blb — bent limb body   o/m — open mouth
bsk — bisque   p/e — pierced ears
c/m — closed mouth   pnt/e — painted eyes
hh — human hair   pwt/e — paperweight eyes
hp — hard plastic   RpC — replaced clothes
jtd — jointed   ShHd — shoulder head
MIG — Made In Germany   ShPl — shoulder plate
NC — no clothes   SkHd — socket head
o/c/e — open closed eyes   str — straight
o/c/m — open closed mouth   trn — turned

American Character

Annie Oakley, hp walker, embr on skirt, OC, 14", EX...............400.00
Baby, hp/vinyl, w/bottle, OC, 12", MIB.....................................250.00
Bottletot, compo head, cloth body, crier, OC, 1926, 13", EX......250.00
Caroll Ann Berry, all compo Patsy type, o/c/e, OC, 1935, 19½", EX...785.00
Freckles, face changes, OC, 1966, 13", M 40.00
Magic Make Up, vinyl, grow hair, OC, 1965-66, 11½", EX..........75.00
Petite mk baby, compo head, cloth body, OC, 14", EX...............185.00
Petite mk mama, compo head, cloth body, o/c/e, wig, OC, 24", EX..385.00
Sally, compo & cloth, cryer, pnt or o/c/e, OC, 12½"...................225.00
Sweet Sue Sophisticate, vinyl head, tag, earrings, OC, 19", EX..300.00
Teeny Tiny Tear, vinyl, RpC, 12", EX, from $25 to 30.00
Tiny Tears, hp/vinyl, OC, 1950-62, 8", EX................................50.00
Toni, vinyl head, rooted hair, OC, ca 1958, 10½", EX...............195.00
Tressy, in Miss America Character outfit, NM 65.00
Tressy, loose in orig dress, EX 35.00
Tressy, MIB 125.00
Tressy, Pre-Teen; M...75.00

Annalee

Barbara Annalee Davis has been making her dolls since 1950.

What began as a hobby, very soon turned into a commercial venture. Her whimsical creations range from tiny angels atop powder puff clouds to funky giant frogs, some 42" in height. In between there are dolls for every occasion (with Christmas being her specialty), all characterized by their unique construction methods (felt over flexible wire framework) and wonderful facial expressions. Naturally, some of the older dolls are the most valuable (though more recent examples are desirable as well, depending on scarcity and demand), and condition, as usual, is very important. To date your doll, look at the tag. If made before 1986, that date is only the copyright date. (Dolls made after 1986 do carry the manufacturing date.) Dolls from the 1950s have a long white red-embroidered tag with no date. From 1959 to 1964, that same tag had a date in the upper right-hand corner. From 1965 until 1970, it was folded in half and sewn into the seam. In 1970, a satiny white tag with a date preceded by a copyright symbol in the upper right-hand corner was used. In 1975, the tag was a long white cotton strip with a copyright date. This tag was folded over in 1982, making it shorter. Our advisor for Annalees is Jane Holt; she is listed in the Directory under New Hampshire.

1961, bellhop, 25"	550.00
1966, beach girl w/towel, 10"	275.00
1968, donkey, 36"	550.00
1969, snowgirl, 29"	375.00
1972, Mr & Mrs Santa w/laundry basket for cards, 29", set	145.00
1974, leprechaun w/sack, 10"	75.00
1975-76, Colonial boy & girl mouse, 7", pr	125.00
1975-76, Yankee Doodle Dandy, 18", on 18" horse	475.00
1976, Colonial drummer boy, tricorn hat, 18"	225.00
1977, Leprechaun, dk gr body, shamrock vest, 10", NM	70.00
1978, Pilgrim boy & girl, 18", pr	195.00
1981, clown, 42"	350.00
1982, bride & groom mice, 12", pr	300.00
1982, I'm #10, 7"	60.00
1982, skunk boy holds red heart, 12"	115.00

1982, Windsurfer Mouse (Annalee birth date on sail), 7", $115.00.
(Photo courtesy Jane Holt)

1982, Xmas giraffe, w/10" elf, produced 1 yr, 22"	300.00
1984, Mrs Santa w/muff, 18"	50.00
1984-85, Valentine bunny, 7"	55.00
1985, Jazz cat, 3 different instruments, 12", ea	125.00
1985, kid w/sled, 12"	70.00
1985-86, bear, Valentine on shoulder, Be My Honey Bear on shirt, 18"	115.00
1985-87, Indian boy mouse, bl loincloth, brn moccasins, 12"	65.00
1985-89, Indian boy mouse, bl loincloth, bow & arrow, 7"	35.00
1985-89, Pilgrim boy & girl mice, 12", pr	125.00
1985-90, Mrs Santa, velour, 18"	95.00
1986, Victorian Mr Santa, cranberry velour, 18"	150.00
1986-87, pumpkin balloon, 14", w/7" witch mouse	125.00
1987, bride & groom cats, 10", pr	150.00
1987, Cupid kid in hot air balloon, 7"	85.00
1988, kitten on sled, 10"	55.00

1989, Eskimo bear, 10"	75.00
1989, Santa chef w/bowl & spoon, 30"	150.00
1989, Tommy Turkey, tan body, yel ft, 12"	80.00
1989, toy soldier, 30"	125.00
1989-90, Pilgrim couple w/plaque (Giving Thanks), 10", set	140.00
1989-91, dragon kid, 7"	45.00
1989-92, pumpkin kid, 7"	45.00
1991-92, spider, mobile, 12"	50.00
1992-93, ladybug kid, Halloween, 7"	45.00
1993, butterfly kid, yel, Halloween	45.00
1993, girl eating turkey, 7"	65.00
1993-94, Headless Horseman w/horse, 10"	125.00
1994, country girl bunny w/basket, 30"	150.00
1994, Halloween elf, blk, 5"	25.00
1994, skating penguin, 10"	65.00
1994-95, Old World Mrs Santa, beige plaid dress, gr apron, 30"	250.00
1995, girl building snowman, 7"	40.00
1995, girl scarecrow, 12"	70.00
1995, tepee, 17"	50.00
1997, haunted tree, tan, 15"	90.00
1997, Spellbinder, 18"	125.00
1998, Katie O', Paddy O' mice, 7", pr	65.00
1998, mailman elf, 10"	40.00

Armand Marseille

#225, character, SkHd, glass eyes, o/m/teeth, jtd compo, RpC, 14", EX	3,600.00
#251, character face, SkHd, o/c/m, RpC, 13", VG	1,100.00
#345, Kiddiejoy, SkHd, glass eyes, c/m, cloth body, RpC, 16", EX	525.00
#360a, character face, o/m, RpC, ca 1913, 12", EX	400.00
#372, Kiddiejoy, ShHd, pnt hair/eyes, o/c/m/teeth, RpC, 18", EX	650.00
#390, o/m, glass eyes, compo body, OC, 18", EX	375.00
#390, o/m, glass eyes, kid body, RpC, 15", EX	255.00
#449, character face, pnt bsk, RpC, 15", EX	765.00
#500, domed ShHd, molded/pnt hair, pnt intaglio eyes, RpC, 17", EX	1,000.00
#520, domed head, glass eyes, o/m, compo body, RpC, 12", EX	775.00
#570, domed head, c/m, RpC, 12", EX	1,850.00
#700, c/m, pnt/e, RpC, ca 1920, 12½", VG	1,500.00
#701, SkHd, o/c/e, c/m, RpC, 16", EX	2,450.00
Alma, kid body, RpC, 15", VG	150.00
AM #341, My Dream Baby, RpC, 10", EX	250.00
Baby Gloria, solid dome, o/m, pnt hair, 15", RpC, VG	575.00
Baby Phyllis, c/m, pnt hair, RpC, 13", EX	500.00
Baby Phyllis, c/m, pnt hair, RpC, 21", VG	850.00
Columbia, compo body, RpC, 22", EX	565.00

Barbie Dolls and Related Dolls

Though the face has changed three times since 1959, Barbie doll is still as popular today as she was when she was first introduced. Named after the young daughter of the first owner of the Mattel Company, the original Barbie doll had a white iris but no eye color. These dolls are nearly impossible to find, but there is a myriad of her successors and related collectibles just waiting to be found.

For further information we recommend *The Story of Barbie, Second Edition*, by Kittarah B. Westenhouser; *The World of Barbie Dolls* and *The Wonder of Barbie, 1976 – 1986*, by Paris, Susan, and Carol Manos; *Barbie Exclusives, Books 1* and *2*, by Margo Rana; *Barbie Doll Boom, 1986 – 1995*, and *Collector's Encyclopedia of Barbie Doll Exclusives and More*, both by J. Michael Augustyniak; *The Barbie Doll Years* by Patrick C. and Joyce L. Olds; and *Barbie Doll Fashion, Vol I* and *II*, by Sarah Sink Eames, which gives a complete history of the wardrobes of Barbie, her friends, and her family. *Schroeder's Toys, Antique to Modern*, is another good source for current market values. All these are published by Collector Books.

Allan, 1963, pnt red hair, str legs, MIB, from $125 to..................145.00
Barbie, #1, 1958-59, blond or brunette, MIB, ea, from $5,000 to...6,500.00
Barbie, #2, 1959, blond or brunette, MIB, ea, from $5,000 to .6,000.00
Barbie, #3, 1960, blond or brunette, orig swimsuit, NM, ea........950.00
Barbie, #4, 1960, blond or brunette, orig swimsuit, M, ea, $450 to..500.00
Barbie, #5, 1961, red hair, orig swimsuit, NM....................375.00
Barbie, #6, blond, orig swimsuit, EX.............................250.00
Barbie, American girl, 1964, blond, brn or brunette hair, NRFB, ea..1,500.00
Barbie, Beauty Secrets, 1980, Pretty Reflections, MIB.............85.00
Barbie, Bubble-Cut, 1961, any color hair, orig swimsuit, NM.....400.00
Barbie, Color-Magic, 1966, blond or brunette, all orig, NM, ea..750.00
Barbie, Dramatic New Living, 1970, brunette, NRFB.............250.00
Barbie, Fair Hair, 1967, NRFB..................................250.00
Barbie, Fashion Queen, 1963, pnt brunette hair, NRFB.............450.00
Barbie, Free Moving, 1974, NRFB................................165.00
Barbie, Gold Medal Skater, 1976, MIB............................85.00
Barbie, Holiday, 1988, NRFB, minimum value...................1,000.00
Barbie, Holiday, 1989, NRFB....................................250.00
Barbie, Holiday, 1992, NRFB....................................150.00
Barbie, Irish, 1984, Dolls of the World, NRFB...................125.00
Barbie, Korean, 1988, Dolls of the World, NRFB..................60.00
Barbie, Loving You, 1984, MIB...................................40.00
Barbie, Music Lovin', 1986, NRFB................................50.00
Barbie, New Living, 1969, blond, NRFB.........................200.00
Barbie, Oriental, 1981, Dolls of the World, NRFB................150.00
Barbie, Peaches 'n Cream, 1985, MIB.............................35.00
Barbie, Show 'n Ride, 1988, Toys R Us, NRFB...................200.00
Barbie, Spanish, 1983, Dolls of the World, NRFB.................110.00
Barbie, Sun Lovin' Malibu, 1979, MIB............................50.00
Barbie, Swirl Ponytail, 1964, blond or brunette, OC, M, ea, $400 to...500.00
Barbie, Twirly Curls, 1983, MIB.................................45.00
Barbie, Twist 'n Turn, 1971, brunette, NRFB....................500.00

Barbie, Walk Lively, 1972, blond hair, MIB, $125.00. (Photo courtesy Sibyl DeWein and Joan Ashabraner)

Brad, Talking, 1971, MIB.......................................250.00
Cara, Ballerina, 1976, MIB......................................75.00
Christie, Fashion Photo, 1978, MIB..............................95.00
Francie, Twist 'n Turn, 1966, brunette, orig swimsuit, EX........150.00
Francy, Busy, 1972, NRFB.......................................425.00
Ken, Beach Blast, 1989, NRFB....................................25.00
Ken, Bendable Legs, 1965, pnt blond hair, NRFB.................650.00
Ken, Bendable Legs, 1965, pnt brunette hair, MIB...............350.00
Ken, Fashion Jeans, 1982, MIB...................................35.00
Ken, Live Action, 1971, NRFB..................................100.00
Ken, Sun Lovin' Malibu, 1979, NRFB..............................35.00
Ken, Totally Hair, 1991, NRFB...................................50.00
Midge, 1963, bendable legs, blond or red hair, MIB, ea..........500.00
Midge, 1963, str legs, blond hair, EX/NM.......................150.00
PJ, Deluxe Quick Curl, 1976, MIB................................65.00
PJ, Sunsational Malibu, 1982, MIB...............................40.00
Scott, Skipper's boyfriend, 1980, MIB...........................55.00

Skipper, Hollywood Hair, 1993, NRFB.............................30.00
Skipper, Music Lovin', 1985, NRFB...............................65.00
Skooter, Bendable Legs, 1965, blond, MIB.......................225.00
Steffie, Walk Lively, 1968, OC, NM.............................175.00

Barbie Gifts Sets and Related Accessories

When no condition is indicated, the items listed below are assumed to be mint and in the original box or package (if one was issued). Items in only excellent condition may be worth 40% to 60% less.

Case, Barbie & Ken on blk vinyl, 1963, EX.......................65.00
Case, Barbie & Stacey, vinyl, 1967, NM..........................75.00
Case, Barbie in 4 outfits on red vinyl, 1962, EX, from $30 to.......40.00
Clothes, Arabian Nights, Ken, #0774, 1964, NRFB...............200.00
Clothes, Cinderella, Barbie, #872, complete, NM...............150.00
Clothes, Fun Shine, Barbie, #3480, 1972, complete, M..........250.00
Clothes, Long on Leather, Francie, #1769, 1970, NRFB..........155.00
Clothes, Special Date, Ken, #1401, complete, NM................85.00
Fashion Pak, All the Trimmings, Barbie & Stacey, #0050, 1970, MOC..75.00
Fashion Pak, On the Go, Barbie, 1964, NRFP......................85.00
Fashion Pak, Undertones, Skipper, 1970, MIP.....................75.00
Gift set, Barbie & Ken Campin' Out, 1983, MIB..................75.00
Gift set, Happy Birthday Barbie, 1985, NRFB.....................50.00
Gift set, Superstar Barbie & Ken, 1978, MIB....................175.00
House, Barbie Deluxe Family, 1966, complete, VG................135.00
House, Barbie Glamour Home, 1985, MIB..........................125.00
House, Francie, 1966, complete, M..............................150.00
House, Skipper's Deluxe Dream, Sears Exclusive, 1966, MIB.....500.00
Room, Barbie & Ken Little Theatre, 1964, complete, NMIB.....600.00
Shop, Barbie Cafe Today, 1971, MIB............................400.00
Vehicle, Barbie Silver 'Vette, MIB..............................30.00
Vehicle, Beach Bus, 1974, MIB...................................45.00
Vehicle, Starlight Motorhome, 1994, MIB.........................45.00

Belton

Concave head, 2 or 3 hole, EX bsk, o/c/m or c/m, w/wig, 8".......800.00
Concave head, 2 or 3 hole, EX bsk, o/c/m or c/m, w/wig, 10"..1,200.00
Concave head, 2 or 3 hole, EX bsk, o/c/m or c/m, w/wig, 13"..1,600.00
Concave head, 2 or 3 hole, EX bsk, o/c/m or c/m, w/wig, 15"..1,900.00
Concave head, 2 or 3 hole, EX bsk, o/c/m or c/m, w/wig, 16"..2,000.00
Concave head, 2 or 3 hole, EX bsk, o/c/m or c/m, w/wig, 17"..2,400.00
Concave head, 2 or 3 hole, EX bsk, o/c/m or c/m, w/wig, 20"..2,800.00
Concave head, 2 or 3 hole, EX bsk, o/c/m or c/m, w/wig, 22"..3,000.00
Concave head, 2 or 3 hole, EX bsk, o/c/m or c/m, w/wig, 22"..3,000.00
Concave head, 2 or 3 hole, EX bsk, o/c/m or c/m, w/wig, 23"..3,200.00
Concave head, 2 or 3 hole, EX bsk, o/c/m or c/m, w/wig, 26"..3,800.00

Betsy McCall

Am Character, in Town & Country outfit, 8", M..................175.00
Am Character, jtd, OC, 19", MIB, minimum value................500.00
Am Character, Mommy's Helper, 8", EX (at auction)............130.00
Am Character, Sandy McCall, vinyl, o/c/e, OC, 1959, 39", M...350.00
Am Character, vinyl, rooted hair, flirty eyes, 1919, 19", VG......275.00
Horsman, vinyl/hp, o/c/e, c/m, OC, 1974, 12½", MIB.............125.00
Ideal, all orig, MIB...225.00
Uneeda, vinyl, rooted hair, o/c/e, OC, 1964, 11½", minimum......95.00

Boudoir Dolls

Boudoir dolls, often called bed dolls, French dolls, or flapper dolls were popular from the late teens through the 1940s. The era of the 1920s and 1930s was the golden age of boudoir dolls!

More common boudoir dolls are usually found with composition head, arms, and high-heeled feet. Clothes are nailed on (later ones have stapled-on clothes). Wigs are usually mohair, human hair, or silk floss. Smoking boudoir dolls were made in the late teens and early 1920s. More expensive boudoir dolls were made in France, Italy, and Germany, as well as the U.S. Usually they are all cloth with elaborate sewn or pinned-on costumes and silk, felt, or velvet painted faces. Sizes of boudoir dolls vary, but most are around 30". These dolls were made to adorn a lady's boudoir or sit on a bed. They were not meant as children's playthings! Our advisor for this category is Bonnie Groves; she is listed in the Directory under Texas.

Sterling, Halloween pair, composition, nailed-on costumes, lady has strung arms, male is scarce, Sterling Doll Co (marked on back), 26", minimum value for the pair, $900.00. (Photo courtesy Bonnie Groves)

Am, silk face, organdy embr dress & hat, 30", VG 265.00
Anita, compo head & hands, cloth body, EX costume, orig, VG, $250 to ...300.00
Anita, compo head & hands, cloth body, nude, '20s, EX, from $75 to..150.00
Anita, compo head & hands, cloth body, rare hands w/snap fingers, VG....300.00
Anita, compo head & hands, silk floss wig, OC/shoes, VG, $150 to ..200.00
Anita, compo head & hands, sleep eyes, all orig, EX, from $300 to....500.00
Anita, smoker, head only, VG, from $75 to 145.00
Blossom, lady, MIB, minimum value 600.00
Blossom, lady, tagged costume, all orig, VG 300.00
Blossom, Pierrot, mask face/swivel head, OC, 1920s, 30", from $400 to...600.00
Blossom, smoker, Argentine costume, 30", EX, minimum value .650.00
Bride, all orig, 1940s, 29", VG 90.00
Cloth, silk face, mohair wig, nude, shoes & stockings, 30", VG, $85 to....150.00
Compo, common carnival type, all orig, 1940s, 28", VG, $95 to ..160.00
Compo, sleep eyes, bald, nude, 30", G, from $100 to 200.00
Doll head on hat stand, VG, from $65 to 135.00
Egg-head type, mask face, nude, 31", G 60.00
Etta, all cloth, all orig, 30", VG, from $200 to..........................450.00
Finely pnt features, average clothes & quality, 28", from $85 to .150.00
Finely pnt features, average clothes & quality, 32", from $100 to..200.00
Finely pnt features, EX clothes/quality, glass eyes, 28", minimum 250.00
Finely pnt features, EX clothes/quality, glass eyes, 32", minimum 300.00
Finely pnt features, std quality, dressed, 16" 150.00
Fr, cloth, all orig, 30", VG...400.00
Fr, cloth, music box inside, all orig, 30", EX, minimum value.....700.00
Fr, harem lady, silk mask face, all cloth, fine clothes, 31", minimum ..600.00
Fr, Pierrot, all orig, 34", EX 400.00
Fr, silk face, bsk arms/legs, mini, 20", EX, from $200 to 350.00
Fr, silk face, bsk limbs, OC, 30", VG, from $350 to.....................400.00
Fr, silk face & costume, bsk arms/legs, 21", VG, from $150 to 200.00
Fr, silk floss hair, all orig, 31", G 175.00
Glass eyed, 27", EX, from $200 to 250.00
Lenci, Fadette, smoker, 26", VG...2,025.00
Lenci, Fadette, 17", EX 1,050.00
Pattern for boudoir doll costume, orig (not copy), VG.................30.00
Plastic arms & legs, all orig, 1940s, 26", EX 165.00
Shoes for doll, EX, minimum value 45.00
Silk face, unmk, all orig, 30", EX..300.00
Silk face, unmk, wht mohair, RpC (old pattern), orig shoes, 30", EX ..200.00

Smoker, cloth, 16" 285.00
Smoker, cloth, 25" 475.00
Smoker, jtd compo, all orig, EX, from $600 to............................800.00
Smoker, jtd compo, nude/bald, 25", G-, from $100 to 200.00
Standard pillow type (no legs), all orig, 24", VG.........................165.00
Sterling, arms need restringing, EXIB.......................................300.00
Sterling, compo, jtd arms, all orig, 26", VG, from $200 to..........300.00
Sterling, compo, jtd arms, nude, 26", VG 100.00
Sterling, male, dressed as baseball player, all orig, EX, minimum...600.00
Sterling, male, dressed as clown, all orig, EX, minimum value....400.00
W-K-S, common std doll, crazed, EX clothes, 28" 135.00
W-K-S, compo head, hands & high-heeled ft, VG clothes, rpl hat, 30"...175.00
W-K-S, compo ShPl, high-heeled ft, EX clothes, 30" 175.00

Bru

Bebe Brevete, swivel head ShPl, hh, pwt/e, c/m, kid body, OC, 14", EX ..13,750.00
Bebe Brevete, swivel head ShPl, mohair wig, pwt/e, kid body, 19", VG.18,500.00
Bebe Gourmand, o/m w/tongue, food empties from ft, RpC, 16", EX.25,000.00
Bebe Modele, cvd wooden body, RpC, 19", VG, minimum value.....19,000.00
Bru Jne, swivel head, hh, cork pate, pwt/e, o/c/m w/teeth, OC, 12" ...11,500.00
Bru Jne, swivel head, mohair, pwt/e, o/c/m w/teeth, OC, 20" .20,000.00
Bru Jne, swivel head, mohair wig, pwt/e, o/c/m/teeth, p/e, 17", VG..12,750.00
Bru Jne R, swivel head, hh, c/m, compo body, RpC, 21", VG .4,875.00
Bru Jne R, swivel head, hh, pwt/e, o/m w/teeth, compo body, OC, 11".2,500.00
Circle Dot Bebe, swivel head, hh, pwt/e, o/c/m, RpC, 14", VG ...10,500.00
Fashion-type, swivel head, metal stringing device, pnt/e, RpC, 12", VG..2,300.00
Fashion-type, swivel head, metal stringing device, pnt/e, RpC, 15", EX....3,300.00

Celebrity

Barbara Eden as Jeannie, Remco, 1972, 6½", NRFB 100.00
Captain & Tenille, Mego, 1970s, 12", MIB, ea 60.00
Desi Arnaz (Ricky Ricardo), Applause, 1988, 17", MIB................50.00
Fred Gwynne (Herman Munster), Remco, 1964, MIB.................150.00
Jimmy Osmond, Mattel, 1978, 9", MIB......................................75.00
Kristy McNichol (Buddy), Mattel, 1978, w/extra outfit, 9", MIB..45.00
Lenny & Squiggy, Mego, 1977, NRFB, pr 200.00
Marilyn Monroe, Tristar, 1982, 11½", NRFB..............................100.00
Pam Dauber (Mindy), Mattel, 1979, 8½", MIB 50.00
Princess Diana, Goldberger, wedding gown, 1982, 11½", NRFB ...250.00
Richard Taylor, 1990s, 11", MIB...75.00
Sonny & Cher, Mego, 1975, 12", NM, ea 50.00
Twiggy, Mattel, 1967, 11½", rare, MIB......................................400.00
Vince Edwards (Ben Casey), Bing Crosby Productions, 1962, 12", MIB..400.00

China, Unmarked

Boy, short curly blk or blond hair w/exposed ears, 13", VG.........195.00
Child, swivel neck, ShPl, china lower limbs, RpC, 14", EX.....2,850.00
Covered Wagon style, center-part hair, RpC, 10", EX 275.00
Covered Wagon style, center-part hair, RpC, 31", EX, minimum value ...900.00
Covered Wagon style, sausage curls, leather arms, OC, 21", EX.700.00
French, pnt/e, open crown, wig, kid body/china arms, 14", VG....2,350.00
Man or boy, glass eyes, 17", VG...1,975.00
Man w/curls, RpC, 19", EX..1,850.00
P/e w/ornate hairdo, RpC, 17", EX, minimum value 1,550.00
Pk tone w/bun or coronet, RpC, 15", EX.................................2,825.00
Queen Victoria (young), RpC, 16", EX.....................................1,600.00
Sophia Smith, str sausage curls in ridge around head, RpC, 19", EX..1,325.00
Spill curls w/ or w/o headband, nude, 13", VG 325.00
Unmk Japan, blk or blond hair, ca 1910-20, RpC, 10", EX.........125.00
Wood body, jtd hips, covered-wagon hairdo, 1840s-50s, 15" ...1,900.00
1840s style, boy, smiling, side-parted brn hair, RpC, 21", EX...4,600.00

1840s style, ShHd w/long neck, brn hair in bun, RpC, 16", EX.......**3,500.00**
1850s style, Alice in Wonderland, snood/headband, RpC, 12", EX **300.00**
1850s style, flange neck, Motchmann-style body, RpC, 17", EX......**2,650.00**
1860s style, blk flat-top hair w/curls on sides, RpC, 10", EX.......**165.00**
1860s style, blk flat-top hair w/curls on sides, swivel neck, RpC, 15" ...**975.00**
1860s style, Grape Lady, grape cluster & leaves, RpC, 15", EX ..**1,325.00**
1860s style, highbrow, curls, high forehead, rnd face, RpC, 15" ...**535.00**
1860s style, Mary T Lincoln, blk hair, gold snood/bows, RpC, 21", EX..**5,600.00**
1870s style, Acelina Patti, center part, ringlets, RpC, 14", EX ...**250.00**
1870s style, bands across forehead, blond, 14", VG **265.00**
1880s style, Dolly Madison, blk hair w/ribbon & bow, pnt/e, RpC, 14"..**350.00**
1890s style, common/low brow, RpC, 10", EX **115.00**
1890s style, common/low brow, RpC, 23", EX **300.00**

Cloth

A cloth doll in very good condition will display light wear and soiling, while one assessed as excellent will be clean and bright.

Alabama Indestructible, baby, 1900-25, 12", EX **1,500.00**
Alabama Indestructible, barefoot baby, rare, 13", EX **3,000.00**
Art Fabric Mills, color litho, 1899-1910+, 30", EX **400.00**
Babyland Rag, color litho, 1893-1928, 16½", VG **200.00**
Babyland Rag, flat pnt face, 1893-1923, 16½", EX......................**900.00**
Beecher type, needle-sculpted features, ca 1900, 20", VG...........**550.00**
Bing Art, pnt hair, cloth or felt, ca 1921-32, 15", EX..................**650.00**
Bing Art, wigged, 1921-32, 16", EX...**650.00**
Black Mammy style, pnt or embr features, 1910-20s, 12", EX **200.00**
Bruckner Topsy Turvy, 13", EX **875.00**
Chad Valley, Captain Blye, glass eyes, 1917-1930+, 18", EX ...**1,000.00**
Chad Valley, Princess Alexandra, glass eyes, 16", EX...............**1,500.00**
Fangel, baby, printed face, mitten hands, 1920-30+, 13", EX......**425.00**
Mollye's, child, mask face, 1929-30+, 13", EX **130.00**

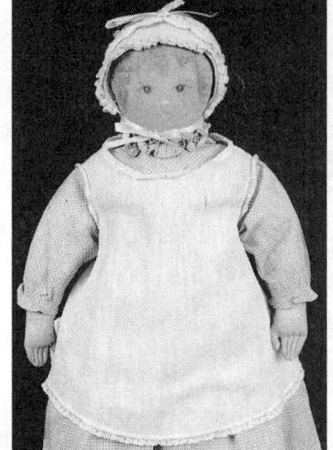

Moravian, nicely dressed, 18", EX, $1,525.00. (Photo courtesy McMasters Auctions)

Raleigh, Shoebutton Sue, flat face, pnt curls, 1921, 15" (auction)....**1,900.00**
Wellings, child, pnt/e, 1926-30+, 18", EX...................................**600.00**

Effanbee

Bernard Fleischaker and Hugo Baum became business partners in 1910, and after two difficult years of finding toys to buy, they decided to manufacture dolls and toys of their own. The Effanbee trademark is a blending of their names, Eff for Fleischaker and bee for Baum. The company still exists today. For more information we recommend *Effanbee Dolls* by Pat Smith.

Baby Grumpy, compo ShHd, pnt/e, c/m, cloth/compo body, OC, 14".......**300.00**
Betty Bounce, compo, o/m/2 teeth/tongue, skin wig, OC, 18" **375.00**
Charlie McCarthy, ShHd, pnt/e, string-op, OC, 20" **775.00**
Mary Ann, compo, o/c/e, o/m, wig, 1932+, OC, 19" **350.00**
Mary Lee as Anne Shirley, compo, o/m/4 teeth, mohair wig, OC, 16"..**500.00**
Patsy, compo, pnt/e, molded hair w/hair band, 1920s, OC, 13½"..**550.00**
Patsy Ann, compo, o/c/e, c/m, 5-pc body OC, 19" **600.00**
Patsy Baby, compo, o/c/e, c/m, bent limbs, OC, 11" **350.00**
Patsy Jr, compo, tin o/c/e, c/m, molded pnt hair, OC, 11", VG...**300.00**
Patsyette, compo, pnt/e, c/m, molded/pnt hair, OC, 9", MIB......**500.00**
Suzanne, jtd compo, o/c/e, wig, c/m, magnets in hands, OC, 14" ..**325.00**
Tinyette Quintuplets, FAO Schwarz..., compo, OC, 7", EX in case...**1,750.00**

Half Dolls

Half dolls were never meant to be objects of play. Most were modeled after the likenesses of lovely ladies, though children and animals were represented as well. Most of the ladies were firmly sewn on to pincushion bases that were beautifully decorated and served as the skirts of their gowns. Other skirts were actually covers for items on milady's dressing table. Some were used for parasol or brush handles or for tops to candy containers or perfume bottles. Most popular from 1900 to about 1930, they will most often be found marked with the country of their origin, especially Bavaria, Germany, France, and Japan. You may also find some fine quality pieces marked Goebel, Dressel and Kester, KPM, and Heubach.

Germany, arms & hands attached, common type, 3" **35.00**
Germany, arms & hands attached, common type, 5" **45.00**
Germany, arms & hands attached, common type, 7" **70.00**
Germany, arms & hands completely away, 4", from $150 to **200.00**
Germany, arms & hands completely away, 6", from $225 to **300.00**
Germany, arms & hands completely away, 8", from $300 to **400.00**
Germany, arms & hands completely away, 12", from $675 to **900.00**
Germany, arms extended, holds item, 4" **185.00**
Germany, arms extended, holds item, 6" **275.00**
Germany, arms extended, maker's mk, 6" **400.00**
Japan mk, 3"..**20.00**
Japan mk, 6"..**50.00**

Handwerck, Heinrich

#69, bsk SkHd, o/m, o/c/e, bjtd body, p/e, wig, RpC, 15", EX **500.00**
#79, bsk SkHd, o/m w/teeth, set eyes, bjtd, wig, RpC, 32", VG....**1,000.00**
#79 or #89, c/m, RpC, 15", VG..**1,275.00**
#89, bsk SkHd, o/m, set eyes, bjtd body, p/e, wig, RpC, 21", VG.....**500.00**
#99, bsk SkHd, o/m, o/c/e, bjtd, p/e, wig, RpC, 14", EX..............**750.00**
#109, bsk SkHd, o/m w/teeth, o/c/e, bjtd, wig, RpC, 36", EX..**2,000.00**
#119, bsk SkHd, o/m w/teeth, o/c/e, bjtd, wig, RpC, 25", EX **850.00**
#199, bsk SkHd, o/m w/teeth, set eyes, bjtd, wig, RpC, 32", VG..**1,000.00**
Kid body, ShHd, o/m, RpC, 14", EX...**235.00**
No #, bsk SkHd, o/m, bjtd, p/e, wig, RpC, 36", EX **1,900.00**

Hertel, Schwab, and Company

#130 or #142, bsk baby, wig, o/m or o/c/m, RpC, 9", EX, ea **325.00**
#131, character face, molded hair, o/c/e, o/m, RpC, 15", VG ..**1,000.00**
#134, character face, o/c/e, c/m, ca 1915, 11", VG...................**3,500.00**
#140, character face, glass eyes, o/c laughing mouth, RpC, 12", VG..**2,550.00**
#141, character face, pnt/e, o/c/m, RpC, 12", EX **3,100.00**
#151, SkHd, o/c/e, o/m/2 teeth, RpC, 11".................................**400.00**
#159, 2 faces, ca 1911, RpC, 10", VG **850.00**
#167, K&H character, o/c/m or o/m, RpC, ca 1912, 15"..........**2,000.00**
Toddler, bsk head, molded hair, o/m, pnt eyes, bent legs, RpC, 14", EX ..**600.00**

Heubach, Ernst

#250, ShHd, o/m, kid body, RpC, 9", VG 125.00
#267, SkHd, o/m, glass eyes, 5-pc compo body, RpC, 11", EX 250.00
#275, ShHd, o/m, kid body, RpC, 23", EX 525.00
#300, SkHd, o/m, glass eyes, wig, 5-pc compo body, RpC, 20", EX.....550.00
#338, newborn, solid dome, pnt hair, glass eyes, c/m, RpC, 13", VG..300.00
#399, newborn, solid dome, pnt hair, glass eyes, c/m, RpC, 15", EX....700.00
#444, Black, RpC, 12", EX...400.00
#1900, child, o/m, glass eyes, kid body, horseshoe mk, RpC, 12", EX ..150.00

Heubach, Gebruder

#5636, character, SkHd, glass eyes/laughing o/c/m/teeth, RpC, 13", EX......2,000.00
#5777, Dolly Dimple, o/m, RpC, 14", EX 2,300.00
#6692, character, sunburst, intaglio eyes, c/m, 1912, RpC, 14", EX 875.00
#6970, SkHd, glass eyes, c/m, sq mk, RpC, 12", EX 2,000.00
#7246, c/m, sunburst or sq mk, ca 1912, RpC, 16", EX 1,300.00
#7647, dome ShHd, intaglio eyes, smiling/m w/teeth, RpC, 20", VG.....2,100.00
#7850, Coquette, o/c/m, ca 1912, RpC, 11", EX......................750.00
#7925, lady, ShHd, glass eyes, smiling o/m, RpC, 15", EX 2,000.00
#7977, Baby Stuart, glass eyes, removable bsk bonnet, 13", EX 1,900.00
#8316, Grinning Boy, glass eyes, o/c/m/8 teeth, RpC, 19", EX......4,800.00
#11010, Revalo, o/c/e, o/m, for Gebr Ohlhaver, RpC, 19", EX ...700.00

Ideal

Two of Ideal's most collectible lines of dolls are Crissy and Toni. For more information, refer to *Collector's Guide to Ideal Dolls, Second Edition,* by Judith Izen (Collector Books).

Ali Fashion Flatsy, NRFP, from $45 to..65.00
Baby Crissy, pk dress, 1973-76, EX 150.00
Baby Snoozie, RpC, 1965, EX, from $50 to.....................................75.00
Bud, MIB...600.00
Casey Flatsy, MIB, from $50 to 75.00
Cinnamon, Curly Ribbons; 1974, EX 45.00
Cinnamon, Hairdoodler; 1973, EX 40.00
Crissy, Magic Hair; 1977, NRFB..100.00
Crissy, Swirla Curla; 1973, EX 35.00
Dodi, MIB 75.00
Gwen Fashion Flatsy, NRFP, from $55 to 75.00
Kissy, 1960s, 22", MIB, from $100 to 125.00
Patti Playful, 1970, 16", EX, from $25 to....................................35.00
Patti Playpal, 1959-62, 35", EX..350.00
Pos'n Pepper, MIB 75.00
Saucy Walker, all orig, 28", NM, from $150 to 225.00
Tammy, MIB 85.00
Tammy's Mom, MIB 75.00
Ted, MIB..50.00
Toddler Thumbelina, 1960s, complete w/walker, NMIB, from $75 to...100.00
Velvet, Swirly Daisies; 1974, MIB..65.00

Jumeau

The Jumeau factory became the best known name for dolls during the 1880s and 1890s. Early dolls were works of art with closed mouths and paperweight eyes. When son Emile Jumeau took over, he patented sleep eyes with eyelids that drooped down over the eyes. This model also had flirty (eyes that move from side to side) eyes and is extremely rare. Over 98% of Jumeau dolls have paperweight eyes. The less-expensive German dolls were the downfall of the French doll manufacturers, and in 1899 the Jumeau company had to combine with several others in an effort to save the French doll industry from German competition.

BL Bebe, SkHd, pwt/e, c/m, jtd compo body, RpC, 18", VG 3,900.00
Depose E (sz #) J, RpC, 15", EX..6,200.00
Depose E (sz #) J, RpC, 23", VG..6,000.00
Depose Jumeau, bsk head, c/m, pwt/e, compo/wood body, RpC, 14", EX..5,000.00
EJ Bebe, bsk SkHd, wig, pwt/e, c/m, jtd body, RpC, 20", EX ..12,000.00
EJ w/sz # between, RpC, 15", EX..6,100.00
EJ w/sz # between, RpC, 17", VG..4,900.00
EJ w/sz # between, RpC, 26", EX..9,000.00
Fashion type, swivel head, c/m, pwt/e, p/e, RpC, 11", EX........6,200.00
Fashion type, wood body, bsk lower arms, RpC, 16", VG 3,800.00
Jumeau Portrait, wood body, RpC, 15", VG.....................................4,300.00
Long Face Triste Bebe, pwt/e, c/m, str wrists, RpC, 19", EX ...18,500.00
Phonograph, bsk head, o/m, player in torso, RpC, 20", EX working .7,800.00
Tete Jumeau, adult, SkHd, glass eyes, o/m, wig, RpC, 21", VG....2,400.00
Tete Jumeau, Bebe, bsk SkHd, c/m, glass eyes, wig, RpC, 32", VG ..6,000.00
Tete Jumeau, child, set eyes, o/m, ca 1907, RpC, 14", EX........1,850.00
Tete Jumeau Bebe, c/m, RpC, 10", EX 5,500.00

Kammer and Reinhardt

#100, character, dome head, intaglio/e, o/c/m, RpC, 15", EX......775.00
#101, Peter or Marie, pnt/e, c/m, ca 1909, RpC, 15", EX, ea...3,200.00
#102, Elsa or Walter, pnt/e, molded hair, c/m, RpC, 14", VG, ea..32,000.00
#109, Elise, pnt/e, c/m, RpC, 14", EX 7,000.00
#114, Hans or Gretchen, pnt/e, c/m, RpC, 13", EX, ea.............3,275.00
#115A, baby, o/c/e, c/m, wig, bent legs, RpC, 12", EX 3,000.00
#115A, toddler, compo, jtd body, RpC, 15-16", EX................5,000.00
#117, Mein Liebling, glass eyes, c/m, RpC, 15", EX 4,400.00
#121, o/c/e, o/m, baby body, RpC, 10", EX.....................................600.00
#127, domed head, toddler body, RpC, 20", VG 1,650.00

#131, googly eyes, 14", $12,000.00 at auction. (Photo courtesy McMasters Auctions)

#191, Dolly Face, o/m, o/c/e, jtd child's body, RpC, 17", VG......650.00
#192, o/m, o/c/e, jtd child's body, RpC, 9", EX 1,000.00
K*R, SkHd, glass eyes, o/m, RpC, 19", EX......................................750.00

Kestner

Johannes D. Kestner made buttons at a lathe in a Waltershausen factory in the early 1800s. When this line of work failed, he used the same lathe to turn doll bodies. Thus the Kestner company began. It was one of the few German manufacturers to make the complete doll. By 1860, with the purchase of a porcelain factory, Kestner made doll heads of china and bisque as well as wax, worked-in-leather, celluloid, and cardboard. In 1895 the Kestner trademark of a crown with streamers was registered in the U.S. and a year later in Germany. Kestner felt the mark was appropriate since he referred to himself as the 'king of German dollmakers.'

#103, mold XI, pouty c/m, RpC, 20", VG **1,950.00**
#128, SkHd, inset eyes, c/m, mohair wig, H/MIG/12, RpC, 19" **1,400.00**
#128, SkHd, pouty c/m, glass eyes, bjtd body, wig, RpC, 15", EX ... **1,000.00**
#142, bsk SkHd, o/m, glass eyes, bjtd, RpC, 8", EX **700.00**
#143, SkHd, o/m, glass eyes, jtd body, RpC, 13", EX **1,000.00**
#145, bsk ShHd, o/m, mohair wig, RpC, 20", EX **400.00**
#171, Daisy, bsk SkHd, o/m, glass eyes, RpC, 18", EX.............. **1,150.00**
#172, Gibson Girl, ShHd, c/m, glass eyes, kid body, RpC, 18", VG .. **1,500.00**
#206, fat cheeks, c/m, glass eyes, child or toddler, RpC, 15", VG **6,700.00**
#211, SkHd, o/m, glass eyes, pnt hair, baby body, RpC, 16", EX . **900.00**
#220, SkHd, o/c/e, o/c/m, RpC, 14", VG **3,225.00**
#247, SkHd, o/c/e, o/m, RpC, 15", EX **1,900.00**
#257, SkHd, o/c/e, o/m, RpC, 17", EX **1,025.00**
Early child w/# only, cm, glass eyes, kid body, wig, RpC, 17", EX .. **800.00**
Early child w/# only, ShHd, o/c/m, kid body, RpC, 15", VG **525.00**
JDK, SkHd, o/m, glass eyes, pnt hair, bent legs, RpC, 14", EX **950.00**
Sz # only, trn ShHd, c/m, RpC, 18", VG **600.00**

Lenci

Characteristics of Lenci dolls include seamless, steam-molded felt heads, quality clothing, childishly plump bodies, and painted eyes that glance to the side. Fine mohair wigs were used, and the middle and fourth fingers were sewn together. Look for the factory stamp on the foot, though paper labels were also used. The Lenci factory continues today, producing dolls of the same high quality. Values are for dolls in excellent condition — no moth holes, very little fading. Dolls from the 1940s, 1950s, and beyond generally bring the lower prices; add for tags, boxes, and accessories. Mint dolls and rare examples bring higher prices. Dolls in only good condition are worth approximately 25% of one rated excellent.

Celebrity, Bach, 17", EX **2,850.00**
Celebrity, Mendel, 22", EX **3,700.00**
Character, Aviator, girl w/felt helmet, 18", EX **3,200.00**
Character, Cupid, 17", EX **5,200.00**
Character, Flower Girl, ca 1930, 20", EX **1,000.00**
Character, Lucia 48, ca 1930, 14", EX **800.00**
Character, Sailor, 17", EX **1,450.00**
Child, hard face, plainer costume, 1940s-50s, 13", EX **400.00**
Child, hard face, plainer costume, 1940s-50s, 17", EX **600.00**
Child, softer face, elaborate costume, 1920s-30s, 13", EX **1,750.00**
Child, softer face, elaborate costume, 1920s-30s, 17", EX **2,500.00**
Ethnic/regional, Bali dancer, 15", EX **1,500.00**
Ethnic/regional, Oriental child, 17", EX **3,600.00**
Ethnic/regional, Spanish girl, ca 1930, 14", EX **800.00**
Eye variation, flirty glass eyes, 20", EX **2,800.00**
Eye variation, glass eyes, 16", EX **1,600.00**
Fadette, adult face, flapper or boudoir body w/long limbs, 17", EX .. **1,050.00**
Mascotte, swing legs, may have loop on neck, 8½", EX **325.00**
Mini, child, 9", EX **400.00**
Mini, Tyrol boy, 9", EX **375.00**

Liddle Kiddles

From 1966 to 1971, Mattel produced Liddle Kiddle dolls ranging in size from ¾" to 4". They were all poseable and had rooted hair that could be restyled. There were various series of the dolls, among them Animiddles, Zoolery Jewelry Kiddles, extraterrestrials, and Sweet Treats, as well as many accessories. Our advisor for this category is Paris Langford; she is listed in the Directory under Louisiana. Please send a SASE for information or contact Paris by e-mail: bbean415@aol.com.

Babe Biddle, #3505, complete, M **60.00**
Beat-A-Diddle, #3510, MIP **500.00**

Chitty Chitty Bang Bang, #3597, 1968, MOC **250.00**
Chocolottie's House, #2501, MIP **40.00**
Cookin' Kiddle, #3846, complete, M **150.00**
Florence Kiddle, #3507, complete, M **75.00**
Flower Ring Kiddle, #3744, MIP **50.00**
Greta Grape, #3728, 1968-69, M **50.00**
Heart Pin Kiddle, #3741, MIP **50.00**
Honeysuckle Kologne, #3704, MIP **75.00**
Jewelry Kiddles Treasure Box, #3735 & #5166, M, ea. **40.00**
Kiddle Kologne Sweet Three Boutique, #3708, NRFB **300.00**
Kola Kiddles Three-Pak, #3734, NRFB **300.00**
Lenore Limousine, #3743, complete, M **60.00**
Liddle Kiddles Kastle, #3522, M **55.00**
Liddle Kiddles Talking Townhouse, #5154, MIB **50.00**
Lime Lou Spoonfulls, #2815, MIP **25.00**
Lolli-Grape, 33656, complete, M **60.00**
Lou Locket, #3537, MIP **75.00**
Luscious Lime, #3733, glitter variation, complete, M **75.00**

Luvvy Duvvy Kiddle, #3596, MIB, $75.00. (Photo courtesy Paris Langford)

Nappytime Baby, #3818, complete, M **75.00**
Rapunzel & the Prince, #3783, MIP **200.00**
Rosemary Roadster, #3642, complete, M **60.00**
Snap-Happy Furniture, #5171, MIP **30.00**
Suki Skediddle, #3767, complete, M **25.00**
Teresa Touring Car, #3644, complete, M **60.00**
Windy Fliddle, #3514, complete, M **75.00**

Madame Alexander

Beatrice Alexander founded the Alexander Doll Company in 1923 by making an all-cloth, oil-painted face, Alice in Wonderland doll. With the help of her three sisters, the company prospered; and by the late 1950s there were over six hundred employees making Madame Alexander dolls. The company still produces these lovely dolls today. For more information, refer to *Collector's Encyclopedia of Madame Alexander Dolls* by Pat Smith; and *Madame Alexander Collector's Dolls Price Guide* and *Madame Alexander Store Exclusives and Limited Editions*, both by Linda Crosey. All are published by Collector Books.

In the listings that follow, values represent dolls in mint to near-mint condition.

Austria Girl, hp, str legs, Wendy Ann, 1973-75, mk Alex, 8" **75.00**
Babs, Skater, hp, Margaret, 1948-50, 15", minimum value **1,100.00**
Best Man, hp, Wendy Ann, #461, 1955 only, 8" **825.00**
Bolivia, hp, bend-knee/bend-knee walker, Wendy Ann, 1963-1966, 8" ... **350.00**
Bridesmaid, compo, Little Betty, 1937-39, 9" **325.00**
Carmen, compo, sleep eyes, Little Betty, 1937-39, 11" **350.00**
Cinderella, compo, Wendy Ann, 1935-37, 13" **375.00**
Cissy, hp, jtd, EX face color, ball gown, 1955-59, 20", minimum ... **900.00**
Country Cousin, cloth, 1940s, 26" **650.00**
Danish, compo, Tiny Betty, 1937-41, 7" **325.00**
Edith the Lonely Doll, plastic/vinyl, Mary-Bel, 1958-59, 16" **375.00**

Elise, hp, jtd ankles/elbows/knees, nylon tulle/veil, 1957, 16½" .**400.00**
Evangeline, cloth, 1930s, 18", minimum value **650.00**
France, compo, Tiny Betty, 1936-43, 7" **300.00**
Godey Lady, hp, Margaret, 1950-51, 18", minimum value **1,500.00**
Hansel, compo, Tiny Betty, 1935-42, 7" **300.00**
Irish, hp, str leg, mk Alexander, 1976-85, 8" **65.00**
Jeannie Walker, compo, jtd legs, 1940s, 13-14", minimum value...**675.00**
Kathy Baby, vinyl, rooted or molded hair, 1954-56, 13-16", from $75 to ...**125.00**
Korea, hp, bend-knee/bend-knee walker, Maggie Mixup, #772, 1968-70, 8"...**225.00**
Lissy, hp, jtd knees/elbows, as bride, 1956-58, 11½-12"...............**450.00**
Little Genius Toddler, hp, caracul hair, Wendy Ann, 1954-55, 8"..**275.00**
Lucinda, plastic/vinyl, Janie, 1969-70, 12" **325.00**
Madeline, hp, jtd elbows/knees, 1950-53, 17-18", minimum value ..**800.00**
Mary Mine, cloth/vinyl, 1977-89, 21" **125.00**
Michael, plastic/vinyl, w/teddy bear, Janie, 1969 only, 11".........**375.00**
Normandy, compo, Tiny Betty, 1935-38, 7" **275.00**
Patty Pigtails, hp, Margaret, 1949 only, 14", minimum value......**675.00**
Polish, compo, Tiny Betty, 1935-36, 7" **275.00**
Princess Elizabeth, compo, c/m (Betty), 1937-41, 13", minimum value..**625.00**
Renoir, hp, Margaret, 1950 only, 14", minimum value **875.00**
Rose Fairy, hp, Wendy Ann, #622, 1956 only, 8", minimum value .**1,400.00**
Scarlett O'Hara, compo, Little Betty, 1938-41, 8" **500.00**
School Girl, compo, Tiny Betty, 1936-43, 7" **285.00**
Sound of Music, Maria, Nancy Drew, 1971-73, 12" **350.00**
Sugar Darlin' cloth/vinyl, 1964 only, 14-18", from $75 to...........**125.00**
Tinker Bell, hp, Cissette, #1110, 1969 only, 11", minimum value ..**475.00**
Treena Ballerina, hp, Margaret, 1952 only, 15", minimum value...**700.00**
Velvet Party Dress, hp, #389, 1957 only, rare, 8", minimum value ..**2,000.00**
Wendy Ann, compo, 1935-48, 11-15", from $325 to.....................**575.00**
Wendy Kin Baby, 1-pc vinyl body w/hp Little Genius head, 1954, 8"...**375.00**
Yolanda, Brenda Star, 1965 only, 12" **375.00**
Zorina Ballerina, compo, Wendy Ann, w/extra makeup, 1937-38, 17".**1,900.00**

Mattel

Baby Beans, several variations, 1970, NM, ea from $15 to............**40.00**
Baby Cheryl, talker, 1965, 16", MIB...**200.00**
Baby Fun, all orig but no accessories, 1968, 7", EX, from $25 to...**30.00**
Baby Small Talk, 1968, MIB **125.00**
Black Chatty Baby, M **650.00**
Black Chatty Cathy, pageboy hair, 1962, M **1,200.00**
Chatty Baby, brunette, red pinafore/wht romper, w/tag, MIB......**250.00**
Chatty Baby, open speaker, blond hair, bl eyes, M........................**250.00**
Chatty Cathy, brunette, bl eyes, early, M **85.00**
Chatty Cathy, brunette, bl eyes, Pat Pending, M..........................**750.00**
Chatty Cathy, mid-year or transitional, brunette, brn eyes, M....**650.00**
Cynthia, talker, M **45.00**
Dancerina, b/o, 1968, 24", MIB, from $75 to..............................**125.00**
Downy Dilly, #3832, NRFB **100.00**
Hairy Hurry Downsy Wizzer, #3838, complete, EX......................**100.00**
Heather, Rockflower, NRFB, from $40 to....................................**50.00**
Lilac, Rockflowers, #1167, NRFB, from $35 to **50.00**
Peachy & Her Puppets, 1972, MIB, from $35 to **50.00**
Singin' Chatty, blond hair, M **250.00**
Sunshine Family Grandparents, 1976, MIB, minimum value........**60.00**
Sunshine Family Sister, complete w/shoes, EX.............................**20.00**
Tickle Pinkle & Her Bugabout Car, MIB, from $75 to **100.00**
Timey Tell, talker, MIB..**110.00**
Tiny Baby Pat-A-Burp, vinyl, RpC, 1965, 14", EX, from $25 to ...**30.00**
Tiny Chatty Twins, M, ea..**250.00**

Papier-Mache

Clown, pnt features, molded hair, 5-pc jtd body, RpC, 1920s+, 8", EX...**235.00**

Fr type, ShHd, glass eyes, bamboo teeth, RpC, 1835-50, 18", EX....**1,750.00**
German, glass eyes, c/m, jtd body, RpC, 1879-1900s, 21", EX.....**900.00**
German type, ShHd, molded hair, pnt eyes, wig, RpC, 13", EX..**900.00**
Glass eyes, cloth body, wooden limbs, OC, 1840-60s, 18", EX ...**1,700.00**

Kid gusseted body, shoulder head, eyes without pupils, open mouth with teeth, mohair wig, original clothes, unmarked (French), 19½", EX, $1,000.00. (Photo courtesy McMasters Auctions)

Molded braids/bun, waisted kid body, wood limbs, OC, 1820-60s, 15", EX ..**1,590.00**
Molded bun, waisted kid body, wood limbs, 1820-60s, OC, 9", EX.....**800.00**
Molded curls, waisted kid body/wood limbs, OC, 1820-60s, 14", EX..**575.00**
Pnt eyes, cloth body, wooden limbs, OC, 1840-60s, 9", EX **450.00**
Pnt eyes, cloth body, wooden limbs, OC, 21", EX....................**1,150.00**
Trn ShHd, glass eyes, c/m, cloth/compo, RpC, 1879-1900s, 16", EX..**700.00**

Parian

Alice in Wonderland, molded headband & comb, RpC, 1850-1900", 19", EX....**750.00**
Empress Eugenie, head-pc snood, RpC, 1850-1900+, 25", EX **750.00**
Lady, fancy hair, glass eyes, p/e, RpC, 1850-1900+, 20", EX **2,700.00**
Lady, fancy hair style, pnt eyes, p/e, RpC, 1850-1900s+, 16", EX..**900.00**
Lady, simple molded hair, RpC, 1850-1900+, 10", EX................**175.00**
Lady, swivel neck, glass eyes, RpC, 1850-1900+, 15", EX **2,700.00**
Man or boy, glass eyes, cloth body, RpC, 1850-1900+, 16", EX..**2,825.00**
Man or boy, pnt eyes, cloth body, RpC, 1850-1900+, 17", EX.**1,000.00**
Mary Todd Lincoln, headband, snood, RpC, 1860s, 25", EX **700.00**
Molded bodice, fancy trim, RpC, 1850s-1900+, 17", EX............**800.00**

Schoenhut

Albert Schoenhut left Germany in 1866 to go to Pennsylvania to work as a repairman for toy pianos. He eventually applied his skills to wooden toys and later designed an all-wood doll which he patented on January 17, 1911. These uniquely jointed dolls were painted with enamels and came with a metal stand. Some of the later dolls had stuffed bodies, voice boxes, and hollow heads. Due to the changing economy and fierce competition, the company closed in the mid-1930s.

#100, girl w/cvd hair, solemn face, RpC, 1911-12, 16", EX minimum...**3,000.00**
#101, girl short cvd hair, rnd eyes, smile, RpC, 1911-12, 16", EX....**2,400.00**
#102, girl, cvd hair w/fine braids in bk, RpC, 1912-6, 20", EX ...**2,100.00**
#105, girl, short cvd bob & ribbon, RpC, 1912-16, 19-21", EX, ea ..**2,100.00**
#107/#107W (walker), bent-limb baby, RpC, 1913-26, 13", EX .**550.00**
#107/107W (walker), toddler, cloth body w/crier, RpC, 14", EX...**600.00**
#108/#108W (walker), toddler, RpC, 1917, 26", EX **850.00**
#110W, bent-limb baby, o/c/e, o/m, RpC, 1921-23, 15", EX **625.00**
#203, boy, cvd hair, grin, comb mks, RpC, 1911-12, 16", EX, minimum..**3,000.00**
#204, boy, cvd hair brushed forward, serious, RpC, 1911-12, 16", EX....**2,400.00**
#207, boy, cvd short curly hair, RpC, 1912-16, 14", EX **2,400.00**
#300, girl, long curly wig, face of #102, RpC, 1911-12, 16", EX.**1,500.00**
#308, girl, braided wig, RpC, 1912-16, 14", EX **800.00**
#312, girl, bobbed wig or curls, RpC, 1917-24, 14", EX...............**775.00**
#317, Miss Dolly, o/c/e, o/m/teeth, wig, RpC, 15-21", EX, ea......**700.00**
#400, boy, short bob, K*R #101 face, RpC, 1911-12, 16", EX .**1,500.00**

#407, boy, wig, face of #310 girl, RpC, 1912-16, 19-21", EX, ea .**825.00**
Max or Moritz, cvd figure, pnt hair, cvd shoes, 8", EX, ea...........**625.00**
Tootsie Wootsie, cvd hair, o/c/m/2 teeth, lg ears, RpC, 15", EX....**3,400.00**

SFBJ

By 1895 Germany was producing dolls at much lower prices than the French dollmakers could, so to save the doll industry, several leading French manufacturers united to form one large company. Bru, Raberry and Delphieu, Pintel and Godshaux, Fleischman and Bodel, Jumeau, and many others united to form the company Society Francaise de Fabrication de Bebes et Jouets (SFBJ).

#60/301, Bluette, bsk SkHd, set eyes, o/m/teeth/wig, RpC, 10⅝", EX.....**1,100.00**
#226, character face, glass eyes, c/m, RpC, 20", EX.................**2,400.00**
#227, character face, glass eyes, o/m/teeth, RpC, 17", EX........**1,900.00**
#235, character face, glass eyes, o/c/m, RpC, 18", EX...............**1,800.00**
#236, character face, glass eyes, toddler, RpC, 15", EX.............**1,350.00**
#238, character face, sm o/m, RpC, 18", EX.......................**2,400.00**
#242, character face, nursing baby, RpC, ca 1910, 15", VG.....**3,000.00**
#251, o/c/m/teeth & tongue, RpC, 15", EX.......................**1,500.00**
#252, character face, glass eyes, pouty c/m, RpC, 15", EX.......**4,000.00**
No mold #, Bluette, Jumeau type, o/m, RpC, 10⅝", EX...........**1,750.00**

Shirley Temple

Prices are suggested for dolls complete and in at least near mint condition. Add up to 25% (depending on her outfit) if mint with box. A played-with doll in only very good condition would be worth only about half of listed values.

Bsk, 6", Japan, unlicensed version, all orig, 6", NM....................**250.00**
Celluloid, 13", Dutch, metal pate, o/c/e, all orig, NM................**350.00**
Celluloid, 5", Japan, unlicensed version, all orig, NM................**185.00**
Compo, 7½", Japan, molded hair, pnt/e, o/c/m/teeth, all orig, NM.....**300.00**
Compo, 13", Ideal, all orig, NM....................................**750.00**
Compo, 18", Baby Shirley, Ideal, all orig, 18", NM..................**1,200.00**
Compo, 18", Hawaiian, Ideal, blk yarn hair, grass skirt, NM.......**950.00**

Composition, 18", Ideal, fully jointed, original mohair wig, hazel sleep eyes, open mouth with upper teeth, in all original Captain January outfit, $850.00; Trunk, $200.00. (Photo courtesy Ursula R. Mertz)

Compo, 22", Ideal, all orig, 1934+, NM....................................**1,200.00**
Compo, 27", Ideal, all orig, 1934+, NM....................................**1,750.00**
Vinyl, 12", o/c/e, rooted wig, o/c/m/teeth, all orig, 1957, NM.....**275.00**
Vinyl, 15", mk ST//15, all orig, 1958-61, NM.............................**375.00**
Vinyl, 16", Stand Up & Cheer outfit, all orig, 1973, NM...........**165.00**
Vinyl, 17", Montgomery Wards reissue, all orig, 1972, M in plain box..**225.00**
Vinyl, 35-36', mk ST-35-38-2, jtd wrists, all orig, 1960, NM ..**2,100.00**
Vinyl, 36", mk Doll Dreams & Love, Hank Garfinkle, all orig, M...**250.00**

Simon and Halbig

Simon and Halbig was one of the finest German makers to operate during the 1870s into the 1930s. Due to the high quality of the makers, their dolls still command large prices today. During the 1890s a few Simon & Halbig heads were used by a French maker, but these are extremely rare and well marked S&H.

#1009, o/c/e, o/m/teeth, kid body, wig, RpC, ca 1889, 19", EX...**525.00**
#1039, bsk head, glass eyes, wig, compo walker, RpC, 13", EX, minimum....**2,000.00**
#1039, SkHd or swivel w/bsk ShPl, glass eyes, o/m, RpC, 9", EX ..**500.00**
#1078, glass eyes, o/m/teeth, mohair wig, 5-pc body, RpC, 1892, 8", EX ...**550.00**
#1109, glass eyes, o/m, RpC, ca 1893, 18", EX **1,050.00**
#1249, Santa, glass eyes, o/m, RpC, ca 1898, 10½", EX **700.00**
#1250, ShHd, dolly face, RpC, ca 1898, 23", EX **800.00**
#1250, ShHd, glass eyes, o/m, kid body, RpC, 19", EX **800.00**
#1294, baby, character face, glass eyes, o/m, RpC, ca 1912, 19", EX ..**1,000.00**
#1428, baby, character face, glass eyes, o/c/m, RpC, ca 1914, 13", EX....**1,600.00**
#1478, c/m, RpC, ca 1920, 15", EX.......................................**9,000.00**
#151, pnt/e, laughing c/m, RpC, ca 1912, EX...........................**5,000.00**
#179, child, o/c/e, o/m, p/e, compo/wood body, RpC, ca 1886, 13", EX...**1,300.00**
#530, child, ShHd, RpC, 1870s, 19", EX................................**685.00**
#729, glass eyes, laughing o/c/m, RpC, ca 1888, 16", EX **2,550.00**
#739, child, glass eyes, o/c/m, compo/wood body, RpC, ca 1888, 15", EX ..**2,100.00**
#905, child, o/m, RpC, ca 1888, 18", EX **1,800.00**
#919, glass eyes, c/m, RpC, ca 1888, 19", EX...........................**8,550.00**
#939, bsk SkHd, glass eyes, o/m, p/e, RpC, 11", EX....................**925.00**
#949, glass eyes, o/m, RpC, ca 1888, 19", EX **1,800.00**
S&H (no mold #), child, ShHd, molded hair, RpC, 1870s, 19", EX..**1,700.00**

Steiner, Jules

Jules Nicholas Steiner established one of the earliest French manufacturing companies (making dishes and clocks) in 1855. He began with mechanical dolls with bisque heads and open mouths with two rows of bamboo teeth; his patents grew to include walking and talking dolls. In 1880 he registered a patent for a doll with sleep eyes. This doll could be put to sleep by turning a rod that operated a wire attached to its eyes.

Baby, Motschmann type, bsk dome, c/m, glass eyes, wig, RpC, 14", EX..**4,800.00**
Bebe le Parisian, SkHd, cb pate, pwt/e, c/m, wig, 1895+, 10", EX **3,600.00**
Bebe w/figure mks, SkHd, glass eyes, c/m, wig, RpC, 1887+, 16", EX **4,900.00**
Bebe w/figure mks, SkHd, o/c/m/dimples, RpC, 1887+, 27", EX..............**4,500.00**
Bebe w/series mks, SkHd w/cb pate, pwt/e, c/m, RpC, 1880s, 27", EX...**9,500.00**
Key-wind kicker, crying Bebe, glass eyes, teeth, wig, RpC, 21", EX.........**2,350.00**
Series mks, SkHd w/cb pate, pwt/e, RpC, 1880s, 14", EX **8,500.00**
Unmk Bebe, SkHd, pwt/e, o/m/teeth, wig, RpC, 1870s, 18", EX ...**6,000.00**

Vogue

This is the company that made the Ginny doll. Composition was used during the '40s, but vinyl was the preferred material throughout the decade of the '50s. An original mint-condition composition Ginny would be worth a minimum of $450.00 on the market today (played-with about $90.00). The last Ginny came out in 1969. Another Vogue doll that is becoming very collectible is Jill, whose values are steadily climbing. For more information, we recommend *Collector's Encyclopedia of Vogue Dolls* by Judith Izen and Carol Stover. Our advisor for Jill dolls is Bonnie Groves; she is listed in the Directory under Texas.

Baby Dear One, 1962, 25", MIB...**250.00**
Ginny, hp, jtd walker, o/c/e, 1957, 8", M......................................**150.00**
Ginny, hp, molded lashes, walker, 1954-57, OC, minimum value ...**300.00**
Ginny, hp, pnt/e, c/m, mohair wig, OC (overalls), 7½" **225.00**

Ginny, hp, pnt lashes, strung, 1953, 8", MIB 325.00
Ginny as Davy Crockett, 1953, 8"...400.00
Ginny Baby, 20", MIB...55.00
Ginny International, vinyl, 1977, OC, minimum value 45.00
Jan, all orig, 10½", G...65.00
Jan (Sweetheart), all orig, 12", MIB, minimum value...................75.00
Jan/Jill desk & chair, gr, VG, from $50 to.............................135.00
Jan/Jill wardrobe, gr, VG, from $50 to..................................135.00
Jeff, vinyl, bl suit, 10", VG..125.00
Jeff, vinyl, shorts outfit, 10", VG, from $65 to 85.00
Jill, hp, in ballerina outfit, all orig, 10½", EX 135.00
Jill, hp, in cotton street dress, all orig, 10½", EX from $85 to.....135.00
Jill, hp, in formal, 10½", EX, from $150 to 200.00
Jill, hp, in leotard, 10½", VG...95.00
Jill, hp, in leotard, 1957, 10½", MIB....................................250.00
Jill, hp, in office dress, incomplete outfit, VG........................75.00
Jill, hp, in peach dress, no earrings, 10½", VG 50.00
Jill, hp, in record hop outfit, 10½", VG 65.00
Jill, hp, in semiformal w/tag, 10½", VG 40.00
Jill, hp, in toreador outfit, all orig, VG.................................85.00
Jill, hp, in 1947 outfit, all orig, 10"...................................145.00
Jill, hp, nude, 10½", G 28.00
Jill, vinyl, History Land, all orig, from $100 to 165.00
Jill bed, VG from $50 to 85.00
Jill chromium head pendant, MIP, from $50 to.......................80.00
Jill cotton dress, from $35 to..50.00
Jill Dream Cozy Bed Set (bedding), MIP, from $35 to................50.00
Jill dress, semiformal, MIP, from $50 to.................................75.00
Jill dress & hat (no doll), #3190, 1959, EX 100.00
Jill formal, #7403, MIB...55.00
Jill harem dress, #3212, EX...45.00
Jill heart necklace, MIB...17.50
Jill high heels, wht, EX...8.50
Jill hostess outfit set (no doll), #3311, 1960, MIB 160.00
Jill jewelry, MIP, from $35 to...50.00
Jill nylons, MOP..27.50
Jill pearl choker & earrings, MIB..15.00
Jill pearl tiara, VG 13.00
Jill poodle purse, EX 39.00
Jill red leotard, w/tag, VG...9.00
Jill semiformal set (no doll), #7511, 1957, MIB......................255.00
Jill shoes, MIP...25.00
Jill wig, MIP 40.00
Toddles Draf-Tee, compo toddler, pnt/e, c/m, mohair wig, OC, 7½".........350.00
Toddles Baby, compo, pnt/e, OC: dress/coat/bonnet, 7" 265.00

Wax, Poured Wax

Over compo, Alice in Wonderland style w/molded headband, RpC, 16", EX ..525.00
Over compo, child w/molded bonnet, RpC, 1860-80, 16", EX....325.00
Over compo, man, trn ShHd, molded hat, set eyes, RpC, 17", VG ..1,000.00
Over compo, molded hair, ShHd, glass eyes, wooden limbs, RpC, 15", EX ..300.00
Over compo, ShHd, o/c/m, glass eyes, RpC, 17", EX...................300.00
Over compo, slit ShHd, glass eyes w/wire closure, RpC, 1830s+, 18", EX...1,400.00
Over compo, 2 faces, Bartenstein, RpC, 1880s+, 15", EX 900.00
Poured, baby, ShHd, glass eyes, c/m, Montanari type, RpC, 17", EX...1,500.00
Poured, child, ShHd, inserted hair, glass eyes, RpC, 13", EX...1,100.00
Poured, lady, RpC, 8", EX 770.00
Poured w/plastic reinforcing, glass eyes, inserted hair, RpC, 14", EX..1,000.00

Door Knockers

Door knockers, those charming precursors of the doorbell, come in

an intriguing array of shapes and styles. The very rare ones come from England. Cast-iron examples made in this country were often produced in forms similar to the more familiar doorstop figures.

Our listings are prices realized at auction. Most were in exceptional condition. See Doorstops for suggestions on pricing examples in lesser conditions.

Aberdeen Terrier, cast metal, EX patina & details, 6" 40.00
Bulldog, brass, unmk, 3" dog on 5" bkplate 75.00
Cat w/arched bk, CI, MIB..275.00
Cobra, coiled w/raised head, on shield, copper, 19th C, 12½x7" ...210.00
Dog's head resting on front paws, cvd wood, lifts at nose, 6½" ...250.00
Eagle, CI, 19th C, minor wear, 8¾".......................................345.00
Elephant head w/boy sitting on top, mk Africa, 7" 70.00
Flower basket, mk #205, rectangular bk, 1⅞x4" 185.00
Flowers in ped vase w/bow at top, mk #124 ....250.00
Head of Mercury, wrought iron, English, ca 1865, separate clapper...185.00
Kewpie, brass, ca 1920, 4¾"...80.00
Lion head, ring in mouth, brass, 6¼"......................................95.00
Owl on branch, oval bkplate, 4x3"...160.00
Pug dog, bronze, mk CB/662, 4¼x1¾".................................235.00
Rabbit, running, brass, 4"...160.00
Russian eagle, dbl-headed, brass, 12¾x12¼" 105.00
Shakespeare, CI, no pnt, ca 1900 ....55.00
Shakespeare bust in wreath w/verse on plaque, brass, 5" 50.00
St Thomas w/Canterbury Cathedral above, brass, 4½x2½" 85.00
Stag, w/crest & castle on bk, crown on top, copper, 2⅜x3¼" 150.00
Tulip, wide fr, aluminum, 8x5¼"...165.00
Woodpecker, Hubley, CI, ca 1930, 3¾x2⅝", from $135 to.........150.00

Doorstops

Although introduced in England in the mid-1800s, cast-iron doorstops were not made to any great extent in this country until after the Civil War. Once called 'door porters,' their function was to keep doors open to provide better ventilation. They have been produced in many shapes and sizes, both dimensional and flat-backed, and in the past few years have become a popular, yet affordable collectible. While cast-iron examples are the most common, brass, wood, and chalk were also used. An average price is in the $100.00 to $200.00 range, though some are valued at more than $400.00. Doorstops retained their usefulness and appeal well into the '30s.

In some areas of the country, it it may be necessary to adjust prices down about 25%. When no condition code is present, items are assumed to be in exceptional original condition, flat-backed unless noted full-figured, and cast iron unless another material is mentioned. To evaluate a doorstop in only very good to excellent paint, deduct at least 35%. Values for examples in poor to good paint drop dramatically. For further information we recommend *Doorstops, Identification and Values*, by Jeanne Bertoia.

Key: ff — full figured

Turkey and heron, each with detailed casting, pristine paint with rubber knobs intact, Bradley & Hubbard, **$6,050.00 (turkey) and $4,500.00 (heron).** (Photo courtesy Bill Bertoia Auctions)

Baby Reaching, nude bkside, 1 arm raised, 17x7", minimum value...1,000.00
Basket of Kittens (3), M Rosenstein....USA, 10x7", from $400 to........475.00
Basket of Tulips, tall woven body, Hubley, 13x9", from $350 to .500.00
Beagle Pup, ff, 8x7½", from $400 to..550.00
Boston Terrier Pup, wedge, 7¾x8½", from $150 to 200.00
Bulldog, ff, porcelainized, 5¾x8½", from $75 to..........................125.00
Camel, ff, 7x9", from $275 to..350.00
Cape Cod Cottage, Hubley, #444, 5½x7¾", from $125 to..........200.00
Cat, glass eyes, sitting, 9¾x4⅜", from $125 to 200.00
Charging elephant, 6½x5⅞", from $100 to 175.00
Cherubs, 2 w/grapes, 10x5⅝", from $375 to...................................450.00
Cinderella Carriage, carriage & 2 horses on base, 9¾x19", $150 to..225.00
Clown, legs wide, conical hat, 11½x5½", from $850 to...........1,000.00
Daisy Bowl, Hubley, #232, 7x6", from $75 to.................................150.00
Doberman Pinscher, ff, Hubley, 8x8½", from $400 to 550.00
Dutch Girl, yoke & pails, Littco Products #33, 13x10", from $375 to...400.00
El Capitan, marching pose, on base, 7¾x5¼", from $175 to 250.00
French Girl, holding skirt wide, Hubley, 9¼x5½", from $250 to...325.00
Frog, standing w/arms akimbo, ff, 14x7", minimum value........1,000.00
Geisha, ff, sitting w/musical instrument, Hubley, 7x6", from $200 to....275.00
George Washington, ff, 15x6½", from $475 to 550.00
Giraffe, wedge, S-110, 13½x5¼", from $250 to..........................300.00
Girl w/Beanie, ff, #663, 8¾x3¼", from $400 to..........................475.00
Grapes & Leaves, Albany Foundry, 7¾x6½", from $125 to........200.00
Japanese Spaniel, begging, CJo, #1267, 9x4½", from $300 to.....375.00
Jill, girl w/water pail, Hubley, #226, 8¾x5¾", from $400 to 550.00
Koala, No 5 c 1930 Taylor Cook, 7¼x5½", from $450 to...........550.00
Lighthouse, cJo, #1290, 7¾x5", from $150 to............................225.00
Lil Red Riding Hood, Hubley, #95, 9½x5", from $425 to 550.00
Little Colonial Lady, tiered skirt, ff, Nat'l Foundry, 4⅝", $75 to...85.00
Little Girl by Wall, ff, Albany Foundry, 5½x3¼", from $175 to ..250.00
Maid, curtsying, CJo #1242, 8⅞x4⅞", from $275 to 350.00
Maid of Honor, lady w/bouquet, skirt held in left hand, Hubley, 8¼" ..350.00
Mary Quite Contrary, girl watering flowers, Littco Products, 11⅜" 900.00
Mayflower, Eastern Specialty Mfg Co, 8¼x9", from $150 to.......225.00
Minuet Girl, lady in dancing pose, cJo, 8½x5", from $225 to.....275.00
Monkey on Barrel, Taylor Cook No 3, 1930, 8⅜x4⅞", from $400 to ..475.00
Mrs Sloper, comic figure w/baby in ea arm, English, 10¾", $400 to......475.00
Old Mill, log building w/flowing water, 6¼x8¼", from $300 to..375.00
Old Salt, Lg; yel slicker, blk hat & boots, 14½", from $325 to ...375.00
Parlor Maid, Hubley, #268, c Fish, 9¼x3½", minimum value .1,000.00
Pirate w/sword, on base, 12x5¾", from $475 to 550.00
Poinsettia, in pot on base, CJo, #1232, 10x5", from $275 to.......350.00
Popeye, ff, Hubley, 1929 King Features..., 9x4½", minimum value....1,000.00
Rabbit Eating Carrot, 8⅛x4⅞", from $400 to............................475.00
Rose Basket, mc flowers, pk bow on hdl, Hubley, #121, 11x8", $150 to...225.00
Scottish Highlander, w/spear on base, 15½x13", from $275 to ...325.00
Snooper, man on tiptoe w/magnifying glass, 13¼x4½", from $750 to....1,000.00
Sophia Smith House, 2-story w/center chimney, 8¼x5½", $325 to......400.00
Spanish Girl w/fan & hair comb, Pat appl for..., 9½", $275 to ..375.00
Squirrel, w/nut on log, 11x9½", from $275 to.............................400.00
Swan, head down, 15¾x6¾", from $275 to 350.00
West Wind, child in billowing clothes, English, 18x7", from $375 to ..450.00
Whippet, facing left, 6¾x7½", from $150 to 225.00
White Caddie, man holding golf bag & clubs, 8x6", minimum value ...1,000.00
Windmill, AA Richardson, 8x5⅝", from $150 to.......................225.00
Wine Man, man w/many bottles, 9½x7", from $650 to..............850.00
Wirehaired Fox Terrier, seated, Hubley, #467, 10½x12¾", $500 to...600.00
Woman Holding Shawl, ff, 8x3½", from $175 to 250.00

Dorchester Pottery

Taking its name from the town in Massachusetts where it was organized in 1895, the Dorchester Pottery Company made primarily utilitarian wares, though other types of items were made as well. By 1940 a line of decorative pottery was introduced, some of which was painted by hand with scrollwork or themes from nature. The buildings were destroyed by fire in the late 1970s, and the pottery was never rebuilt. In the listings that follow, the decorations described are all in cobalt unless otherwise noted. Our advisor for this category is Dale MacLean; he is listed in the Directory under Massachusetts.

Key: CAH — Charles A. Hill (noted artist)

Basket, high-glaze wht, flared rim, paper label, 11¾x9¼"...........200.00
Bottle, scent; Full Scroll, spherical, mk, 5½x4½"........................275.00
Bottle, scent; Tear Drop, CAH/Ricci, 5½x3¾" 325.00
Bowl, Blueberry, sgn CAH, stamped, 2⅛x5¾" 100.00
Bowl, Clematis, spongeware ext, sgn, stamped, 3⅛x8½" 400.00
Bowl, Dragon-Bumblebee-Butterfly, sgn CAH, stamped, 2¼x9" ...275.00
Bowl, Ship & Seascape, sgn K Denisons, stamped, 2x5½"..........175.00
Candy dish, Pussy Willow, sgn, stamped, 1½x6½" 165.00
Candy dish, Whale, sgn CAH, ¾x5½"..150.00
Casserole, Geometric, sgn RT, stamped, 2½x7⅛".........................300.00
Casserole, Pine Cone, hdls, CAH, stamped, 2¾x5¼" 225.00
Charger, Ship, sgn JM/N Ricci, stamped, 12¼" 425.00
Coffee set, Blueberry, sgn CAH, pot+mug+sugar bowl...............400.00
Creamer & sugar bowl, Blueberry, sgn, stamped, 3", 3½"...........250.00
Crock, Berry & Vine, unmk, 9¾x7", NM 165.00
Cup, demitasse; Half Scroll, CAH, stamped, 2x3¾"......................90.00
Cup, Happy Day, clown's face, All Gone in bottom, mk, 2¾"....100.00
Jell-O mold, Fluted Blueberry & Stripe, stamped, 2½x5¼" 125.00
Mug, Anchor, stylized anchor & rope on ivory, stamped, 4½" 90.00
Mug, Grape, sgn CAH, stamped, 3x5¼" 75.00
Mug, Pine Cone & Blizzard, ...Blizzard of 1978, stamped, 4⅛" ...225.00
Mug & saucer, Pine Cone, sgn CAH, stamped, 3", 6¼".............100.00
Pitcher, Grape, sgn CAH, stamped, 5½x7½" 225.00
Pitcher, Nouveau geometric, R Trotter, pinched, 7¼x6", NM....300.00
Pitcher, water; Pine Cone, sgn RB, stamped, 7½" 250.00
Pitcher, Whale, sgn CAH/N Ricci, stamped, 5½x7" 250.00
Plate, Farm Mill & Landscape, sgn K Denisons, stamped, 7½"...200.00
Plate, Ship, Denisons, stamped, 7½", NM 250.00
Plate, Strawberry, sgn RT, stamped, 9¾" 200.00

Plate, Whale, blended blue waves, N. Ricci/Fecit/CAH, 10½", $250.00.

Syrup, Blueberry, bulbous, w/lid, sgn, stamped, 5"........................175.00
Syrup, Half Scroll, striped hdl, w/lid, sgn, stamped, 4¾"............175.00
Toby jug, Quaker Oats replica, early orig label, 8x7½"................275.00
Vase, 2-tone bl, 4-sided, crimped mouth, bulbous, mk, 4½x5"....175.00

Dorflinger

C. Dorflinger was born in Alsace, France, and came to this country when he was ten years old. When still very young, he obtained a job in a glass factory in New Jersey. As a young man, he started his own glass-works in Brooklyn, New York, opening new factories as profits permitted. During that time he made cut glass articles for many famous people including President and Mrs. Lincoln, for whom he produced a complete service of tableware with the United States Coat of Arms. In 1863 he sold the New York factories because of ill health and moved to his farm near White Mills, Pennsylvania. His health returned, and he started a plant near his home. It was there that he did much of his best work, making use of only the very finest materials. Christian died in 1915, and the plant was closed in 1921 by consent of the family.

Dorflinger glass is rare and often hard to identify. Very few pieces were marked. Many only carried a small paper label which was quickly discarded; these are seldom found today. Identification is more accurately made through a study of the patterns, as colors may vary.

Bottle, scent; Marlboro, cut hobstar base, orig stopper	250.00
Bowl, Prince of Wales Plumes, knob stem, hobstar ft, 7x9"	600.00
Compote, Kalana Pansy, ruffled, teardrop stem, 5¼x8"	87.50
Cruet, Kalana Poppy, #1220, w/stopper & star-cut base	95.00
Decanter, cut neck, acid etching, att Honesdale	150.00
Decanter, Renaissance, pr	515.00
Pitcher, water; Colonial, 7½"	300.00
Plate, Picket Fence, 6¼"	55.00
Salt cellar, Parisian, paperweight style, master	140.00
Sherbet, Calla Lily, 3¼x4⅛"	125.00
Tumbler, Chester, gr cut to clear, 4"	300.00
Tumbler, gr cut to clear, att, 4½"	175.00
Tumbler, Old Colony, 3¾"	200.00
Tumbler, whiskey; blk rooster in bottom, 2⅝"	125.00
Vase, cut, waisted, slim, scalloped rim, ca 1890, 12¼"	385.00
Vase, Honeycomb, 24-point hobstar on base, 12x5"	980.00
Wine, gr cut to clear bowl, crystal ft, att, 7½"	195.00
Wine, Parisian, cranberry cut to clear, 4¾"	175.00

Dragon Ware

Dragon ware is fairly accessible and is still being made today. The new dragon ware is distinguishable by the lack of detail in the application of the dragon. In the older pieces, much care is given to the slipwork of the dragon itself, including the eyes, wings, scales, and pearl. The new ware tends to be flat, lacking personality and detail. Many pieces were made for souvenirs, so be aware of many additional markings on the outside of the piece.

The colors that are mentioned refer to the primary color found on the piece. This usually tends to be the black or gray colors. Splashes of pink and blue are found on these pieces. The newer pieces tend to have more shine or gloss than their older counterparts (not including lustreware). Older colors tend to be more vibrant, while many of the newer colors run into the pastel range. In addition to the primary colors, splashes of other colors are often found, creating a cloud effect behind the dragon. At this writing, pieces that are older and not the typical black/gray colors are commanding slightly higher prices and attention than similar pieces in black.

The primary colors are applied in several ways, the most common being a wide band of color on the top and bottom of each piece. The 'cloud' effect is when the primary color (and often the only color besides those of the dragon) is swirled on, creating a cloud-like background for the dragon. The lustreware look is when the primary color is solid throughout the piece creating a very shiny background; the solid color is when the piece is completely one color except for the dragon, clouds, and pearl.

Many cups have lithophanes consisting of the face of a geisha girl.

Nude lithophanes can also be found, although they are more scarce. The newer the lithophane, the less detail that it seems to have.

Items listed below are unmarked unless noted otherwise. Ranges are given to take into consideration the age and quality of the piece. Please examine the pieces carefully and note if the piece is old or new. The Internet auction sites are good places to see various pieces from different areas. Feel free to visit the website: www.Dragonware.com.

Key:
MIJ — Made in Japan	MIOJ — Made in Occupied Japan

Ashtray, blk, rectangular, 3¾x2½", from $5 to	7.50
Ashtray, blk, 4" sq, from $15 to	20.00
Box, wht pearl, rectangular, from $10 to	20.00
Candy dish, blk, scalloped, HP Betson sticker, 6", from $45 to	75.00
Candy dish, blk, 2-tier, HP MIJ TT, 6½" & 9" plates, 12" H, $75 to	125.00
Candy dish, blk, 3-section, w/hdl, HP Japan, 10", from $75 to	175.00
Candy dish, blk, 4-section, w/hdl, from $125 to	150.00
Child's tea set, blk, 17-pc, from $125 to	175.00
Child's teapot+cup & saucer, blk, from $15 to	20.00
Cigarette set, blk, box+2 ashtrays, from $15 to	25.00
Condiment set, blk, 10-pc, from $100 to	150.00
Console set, blk w/lustre, bowl+2 candlesticks, HP Japan, $200 to	325.00
Cup & saucer, bl cloud, from $25 to	35.00
Cup & saucer, blk, no lithophane, Nagoya, from $45 to	75.00
Cup & saucer, brn, lithophane, from $12.50 to	20.00
Cup & saucer, coffee; blk, lithophane, from $25 to	30.00
Cup & saucer, demi; bl, whistler, MIJ, from $25 to	45.00
Cup & saucer, demi; gr cloud w/lustre, MIOJ, from $20 to	30.00
Cup & saucer, demi; bl, nude lithophane, from $40 to	75.00
Cup & saucer, MIOJ, wide low 1¼" cup, 3⅞" saucer, from $25 to	45.00
Cup & saucer, orange, HP butterflies in cup, Japan, from $30 to	50.00
Incense burner, blk, 3", from $7.50 to	12.50
Incense burner, blk, 5", from $10 to	15.00
Jam pot, blk, wrapped rattan hdl, sq, MIJ, 3x3x3", from $35 to	50.00
Jewelry box, blk, HP MIJ Endo China, 6x4x2", from $20 to	30.00
Lamp, blk, wood base, cloth cord, 20", from $75 to	125.00
Lamps, gr, hdls, 25x7½", pr, from $150 to	200.00
Lemon dish, blk, MIJ, 5½" sq, from $20 to	40.00

Pitcher, beige dragon on mother-of-pearl, dragon figural handle, 4½", from $40.00 to $75.00. (Photo courtesy Lee Garmon)

Plate, blk lattice edging, Japan, 6½", from $40 to	75.00
Plate, gray, Japan, 7½", from $15 to	30.00
Relish tray, blk, 4 sections w/wicker hdl, from $25 to	50.00
Rice bowls w/spoons, blk, 4½x2¼", from $75 to	100.00
Saki bbl w/elephant stopper, blk, 6x9½", from $125 to	150.00
Saki dispenser, blk, whistling, from $35 to	50.00
Saki set, orange, lithophane, whistling, MIJ, 5-pc, from $50 to	100.00
Saki set w/4 cups, wht pearl, teapot-shaped decanter, MIJ, from $25 to	75.00
Shakers, bl, ball shape, MIJ, 2⅜", pr, from $15 to	25.00
Snack set, blk, lithophane, Nippon, 13-pc, from $125 to	175.00

Tea set, bl cloud, raised star mk, MIJ, 23-pc, from $250 to..........**375.00**
Tea set, blk, lithophane, ca 1940s-50s, 17-pc, from $75 to............**90.00**
Tea set, brn satsuma style, dragon spouts, 23-pc, from $275 to ...**400.00**
Tea set, demi; red, lithophane, 15-pc, from $100 to **125.00**
Tea set, orange cloud, pot+cr/sug+6 c/s, 15-pc, from $100 to......**175.00**
Teapot, blk, HP MIJ, 3x5", from $25 to...**40.00**
Teapot, blk, moriage on hdl & finial, Nippon, MIJ, 6¼", $35 to ..**50.00**
Teapot, brn, dragon spout, 7½", from $35 to................................**50.00**
Teapot, gray, gold trim, MIJ, mini, 1¾", from $20 to.....................**30.00**
Teapot, pk, Florida souvenir, scalloped, from $30 to......................**40.00**
Teapot set (dbl), blk, 5" pots+5½x7" trivet, HP MIJ TT, $150 to ..**200.00**
Vase, blk, bl eyes, 6-paneled, Noritake, 8½", from $125 to.........**160.00**
Vase, blk, hdld, HP, 10", from $50 to..**75.00**
Vase, blk, hdld, HP Miyako Nippon, 12½", from $250 to...........**450.00**
Vase, blk, hdld, HP Nippon, 11¼", from $175 to **375.00**
Vase, blk, hdld, HP Nippon, 9", from $125 to **225.00**
Vase, blk, hdld, wht flat dragon, Nippon, 12½", from $175 to....**225.00**
Vase, blk, sq, HP MIJ, 7¾", from $150 to.....................................**250.00**
Vase, gray w/gold trim on dragon, hdls & rim, unmk, 7½", $50 to..**125.00**
Vase, red, hdld, 1" thick, 3¾x4", from $20 to **40.00**
Vase, yel, 4", from $10 to..**15.00**
Wall pocket, brn/orange, 5½", from $50 to **75.00**
Wall vases, blk, pr, from $75 to..**150.00**

Dresden

The city of Dresden was a leading cultural center in the seventeenth century and in the eighteenth century became known as the Florence on the Elbe because of its magnificent baroque architecture and its outstanding museums. Artists, poets, musicians, philosophers, and porcelain artists took up residence in Dresden.

In the late nineteenth century, there was a considerable demand among the middle classes for porcelain. This demand was met by Dresden porcelain painters. Between 1855 and 1944, more than two hundred painting studios existed in the city. The studios bought porcelain white ware from manufacturers such as Meissen and Rosenthal for decorating, marketing, and reselling throughout the world. The largest of these studios include Donath & Co., Franziska Hirsch, Richard Klemm, Ambrosius Lamm, Carl Thieme, and Helena Wolfsohn.

Most of the Dresden studios produced work in imitation of Meissen and Royal Vienna. Flower painting enhanced with burnished gold, courting couples, landscapes, and Cupids were used as decorative motifs. As with other hand-painted procelains, value is dependent upon the quality of the decoration. Sometimes the artwork equaled or even surpassed that of the Meissen factory.

Some of the most loved and eagerly collected of all Dresden porcelains are the beautiful and graceful lace figures. Many of the figures found in the maketplace today were not made in Dresden but in other areas of Germany. For more information, we recommend *Dresden Porcelain Studios*, by Jim and Susan Harran, our advisors for this category. They are listed in the Directory under New Jersey.

Bowl, floral on wht w/gold, shallow, F Hirsch, 1893-1930, 13x9" .**95.00**
Compote, 4 Seasons figures/floral bocage, pierced/cvd, 1890s, 19x16x8"...**1,800.00**
Cup, demitasse; gilt bird hdl, cobalt & gold, jeweling, A Lamm 7" L.**375.00**
Cup, tea; HP flowers on wht, burnished gold, F Hirsch..............**115.00**
Figurine, ballerina, lace skirt, arms extended, 3¾", NM.............**125.00**
Figurine, Georgian pr at ft of long staircase, 1890s, 9½x15" **700.00**
Figurine, macaw, bl & gold, on stump w/flowers below, 9½x4"...**250.00**
Figurine, rooster strutting, 8½" **250.00**
Letter holder, floral w/gold, 1900...**225.00**
Plaque, classical maiden, artist sgn, 9½x6½"+ornate 16x20" fr ...**3,200.00**
Plate, courting couple/flowers, cobalt/gold rim, Heufel, 1891, 9"....**275.00**

Plate, courting scene, W Koch, 1928-1949, 10¾" **165.00**
Plate, courting scene, Wesner, floral medallion border, 1890s, 7½"...**115.00**
Plate, floral, sgn A Lamm, cobalt & gold rim, 1880s, 8"..............**95.00**
Relish, courting scenes, A Lamm, 2-part, 1891-1914, 12½" L....**225.00**
Sconce w/mirror, putti/maiden, mid-19th C, minor prof rstr, 26x14".**2,750.00**
Tea set, HP flowers on wht, H Wolfsohn, 1800s, pot+cr/sug w/lid **375.00**

Three children present bouquets to seated lady as couple looks on, 16x24", $2,500.00.

Tray, battle scene, C Thieme, 1888-1901, 15¼x12¼"................**895.00**
Vase, courting scene, scalloped rim w/gold band, 6½x6½" **350.00**
Vase, garden party scene, R Klemm, gold hdls, 1900-10, 5¼".....**250.00**

Dresser Accessories

Dresser sets, ring trees, figural or satin pincushions, manicure sets — all those lovely items that graced milady's dressing table — were at the same time decorative as well as functional. Today they appeal to collectors for many reasons. The Victorian era is well represented by repousse silver-backed mirrors and brushes and pincushions that were used to display ornamental pins for the hair, hats, and scarves. The hair receiver — similar to a powder jar but with an opening in the lid — was used to hold long strands of hair retrieved from the comb or brush. These were wound around the finger and tucked in the opening to be used later for hair jewelry and pictures, many of which survive to the present day. (See Hair Weaving.)

Celluloid dresser sets were popular during the late 1800s and early 1900s. Some included manicure tools, pill boxes, and buttonhooks, as well as the basic items. Because celluloid tends to break rather easily, a whole set may be hard to find today. (See also Plastics.) With the current interest in anything Art Deco, sets from the '30s and '40s are especially collectible. These may be made of crystal, Bakelite, or silver, and the original boxes just as lavishly appointed as their contents.

Box, collar; leather, w/3 Arrow collars, 8½" dia.............................**75.00**
Box, cvd alabaster, lady (cold-pnt metal/ivorene) on lid, 6" L....**275.00**
Box, Victorian ladies in motor car in floral fr on celluloid, 10" L.**195.00**
Clothes brush, Deco lady figural china hdl, unmk, 7", MIB..........**65.00**
Clothes brush, duck figural wooden hdl, England, 1930s, 11½", EX ...**30.00**
Clothes brush, German shepherd dog figural porc hdl, Germany, 7" ..**40.00**
Clothes brush, lady w/dog figural china hdl, brush forms skirt, 8".**50.00**
Eyeglasses holder, ceramic, dog figural, 1950s, 4x3x5" **42.50**
Hair receiver, celluloid, Pearl French Ivory, Deco style, 3¾" dia ..**40.00**
Hair receiver, cut crystal, silver repousse lid, Webster, 3¼x4".......**50.00**
Hair receiver, Persian Medallion, Marigold, sq top, Fenton, 4¼" dia..**45.00**
Hair receiver, porcelain, HP floral, illegible mk, 3x3½" **42.50**
Jar, clear cylinder, silver lid w/emb flower/butterfly, Le Pierre, 4".**135.00**
Jar, cut floral/geometrics, sterling lid w/Oriental decor, 3x4" dia..**215.00**
Jar, cut glass, sterling repousse Cupid & lady on lid, 2x2½"........**225.00**
Jar, wht opaque glass egg w/HP flowers, 3-leg brass base, 1890s, 6"..**160.00**
Mirror, hand; silver, Nouveau scrolls & flowers, hallmk..............**225.00**
Rouge pot, butterscotch Bakelite, screw-on cap, E Arden, 1¼" dia.**65.00**

Set, Elizabeth, flow bl, ca 1885, 7 pcs on 18x7½" tray **685.00**
Set, pearlized pk/blk celluloid w/eng silver floral, 3-pc **85.00**
Set, Shagreen & ivory, England, 1920s, mirror+2 clothes/2 hairbrushes **515.00**
Set, yel/blk/wht Deco pattern, Cauldon, 13 pcs on 12" tray, NM..**675.00**
Shoe spoon, silver, floral pattern, mk Sterling, 8½".......................**28.00**
Tray, Lucite, etched floral, 2 metal rods run length, 1940s, 11x20"...**85.00**

Dryden

Dryden Pottery was founded in 1946 by WWII veteran Jim Dryden. Starting in a Quonset hut and selling molded products from his dad's hardware store, Dryden was soon selling pottery to Macy's of New York and the Fred Harvey Restaurants on the Santa Fe Railroad. He used tan Kansas clay and volcanic ash as a component of his very durable glossy glaze.

After ten years, some six hundred stores stocked Dryden pottery. Direct sales to tourists offered the best profit as he found himself competing with increasing numbers of imports from retooled Japan and Europe. Using a dental drill to make the inscriptions, Dryden began to offer pottery with personalized messages and logos. This handwork was appreciated by customers then and is still admired by collectors today.

To find a broader and larger tourist base, the pottery moved to Hot Springs National Park in 1956. Again, local materials (clay for potting and quartz for glazes) were initially used to make the pottery. Then, in order to improve consistency, they turned to commercial clay which fired bone white and controlled glazes. These improvements were made as part of a competitive move toward the hand-turned original pottery made there today. The ever-growing variety of new and unique shapes and glazes has made Dryden Pottery popular for over fifty-five years.

In 2001 The Book Stops Here published the first catalog and history of Dryden Pottery. The book shows the evolution of Dryden art pottery from molded ware to unique hand-thrown pieces; the studio illustrations show the durable and colorful glazes that make Dryden special. The book includes a complete bibliography and price guide.

Kansas pieces have a golden tan clay base and were made between 1946 and 1956. Arkansas pieces made after 1956 were made from bone white clay. Dryden is as yet unknown to many collectors, and prices vary. A personalized piece with its original label commands about twice the price of the same piece with no inscription. For one-of-a-kind and unusual items rarely seen for sale, prices can exceed $500.00. Early Dryden figurines currently command the highest prices. Our advisor for this category is Robert Miller; he is listed in the Directory under Indiana.

Kansas Dryden (1946 – 1956)

Ashtray, #17A, Kanopolis Lake...**38.00**
Ashtray, Lamer Hotels..**22.00**
Bowl, #7E, 7" **28.00**
Bowl (candy dish), #7B, 2"...**20.00**
Creamer/sugar bowl, #108, Lebanon, Kans......................................**38.00**
Cup, coffee; #2, 2½" **20.00**
Dish, lg apple, #12 ....**30.00**
Dish, sm apple, #C2...**20.00**
Ewer, yel, #715...**28.00**
Figurine, donkey on stand, #7 ....**70.00**
Flowerpot, w/liner, 4" **28.00**
Gravy boat, #7H..**25.00**
Jug, #H3, #H2 or #H1, ea...**20.00**
Jug, bl, Wichita, Kans, #102, 5"...**28.00**
Pitcher, #49, 70-oz...**50.00**
Pitcher, Black Hills, SD, #180..**22.00**
Pitcher, Brookville Hotel, #98, 5½"...**28.00**
Pitcher, ewer shape, #99, mini **25.00**
Pitcher, maroon, #192, 6"...**22.00**

Shakers, jugs, #70, pr...**22.00**
Stein, #7, bbl...**22.00**
Vase, brn, #106, 3½"..**22.00**
Vase, bud; yel, #97...**28.00**
Vase, Bull Shoals Dam, sq, #17...**28.00**
Vase, gr, 3½"..**32.00**
Vase, ivy, #180, 4"..**40.00**
Vase, shamrock, 4-H...**32.00**
Wall pocket, gr, #887..**34.00**
Wall pocket, Grand River, #86...**52.00**
Wall pocket, 3-leaf, #956..**40.00**

Arkansas Dryden (1956 to Present)

Vase with deer, dark green, 9", $24.00.

Ashtray, Ellsworth HS, 1981 ....**22.00**
Bowl, muted, 8½"..**25.00**
Cup, face, JK Dryden...**15.00**
Figurine, fighting cocks, mc, 11"..**42.00**
Mugs, mc, set of 6...**28.00**
Pitcher, folk art, 8½"..**20.00**
Planter, elephant...**16.00**
Vase, cactus...**16.00**
Vase, hole in side...**16.00**
Vase, wheel thrown, mini..**22.00**

Duncan and Miller

The firm that became known as the Duncan and Miller Glass Company in 1900 was organized in 1874 in Pittsburgh, Pennsylvania, a partnership between George Duncan, his sons Harry and James, and his son-in-law Augustus Heisey. John Ernest Miller was hired as their designer. He is credited with creating the most famous of all Duncan's glassware lines, Three Face. (See Pattern Glass.) The George Duncan and Sons Glass Company, as it was titled, was only one of eighteen companies that merged in 1891 with U.S. Glass. Soon after the Pittsburgh factory burned in 1892, the association was dissolved, and Heisey left the firm to set up his own factory in Newark, Ohio. Duncan built his new plant in Washington, Pennsylvania, where he continued to make pressed glassware in such notable patterns as Bagware, Amberette, Duncan Flute, Button Arches, and Zippered Slash. The firm was eventually sold to U.S. Glass in Tiffin, Ohio, and unofficially closed in August 1955.

In addition to the early pressed dinnerware patterns, today's Duncan and Miller collectors enjoy searching for opalescent vases in many patterns and colors, frosted 'Satin Tone' glassware, acid-etched designs, and lovely stemware such as the Rock Crystal cuttings. Milk glass was made in limited quantity and is considered a good investment. Ruby glass, Ebony (a lovely opaque black glass popular during the '20s and '30s), and, of course, the glass animal and bird figurines are all highly valued examples of the art of Duncan and Miller.

Expect to pay at least 25% more than values listed for other colors, for ruby and cobalt, as much as 50% more in the Georgian, Pall Mall, and Sandwich lines. Pink, green, and amber Sandwich is worth approximately 30% more than the same items in crystal. Milk glass examples of American Way are valued up to 30% higher than color, 50% higher in Pall Mall. Chartreuse Canterbury is worth 10% to 20% more than crystal. Add approximately 40% to 50% to listed prices for opalescent items. Etchings, cuttings, and other decorations will increase values by about 50%. For further study we recommend *The Encyclopedia of Duncan Glass*, by Gail Krause; she is listed in the Directory under Pennsylvania. Several Duncan and Miller lines are shown in *Elegant Glassware of the Depression Era* by Gene Florence. Also refer to *Glass Animals and Figural Flower Frogs of the Depression Era* by Lee Garmon and Dick Spencer; they are both listed under Illinois. See also Glass Animals. Our advisor is Roselle Schleifman; she is listed in the Directory under New York.

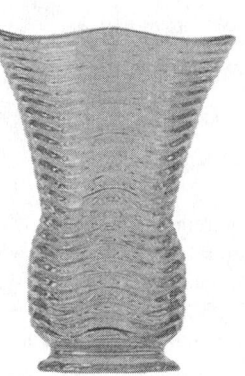

**Canterbury, blue, vase, 10",
$145.00.** (Photo courtesy Gene Florence)

Canterbury, crystal, ashtray, 5"	12.00
Canterbury, crystal, bowl, salad dressing; 2-part, 5x3¼"	12.50
Canterbury, crystal, bowl, sweetmeat; star, hdls, 6x2"	15.00
Canterbury, crystal, bowl, 8½x4"	22.00
Canterbury, crystal, candle holder, 3½"	12.50
Canterbury, crystal, candlestick, 6"	25.00
Canterbury, crystal, candy, w/5" lid, 6½"	32.50
Canterbury, crystal, cigarette jar, w/lid, 4"	20.00
Canterbury, crystal, cup	11.00
Canterbury, crystal, plate, cake; 14"	25.00
Canterbury, crystal, plate, dinner; 11¼"	27.50
Canterbury, crystal, saucer	3.00
Canterbury, crystal, stem, water; 9-oz, 6"	14.00
Canterbury, crystal, tumbler, juice; ftd, 5-oz, 4¼"	7.50
Canterbury, crystal, vase, flared, 12"	85.00
Canterbury, crystal, vase, oval, 4"	17.50
Caribbean, bl, ashtray, 4-indent, 6"	32.50
Caribbean, bl, bowl, 8½"	70.00
Caribbean, bl, candy dish, w/lid, 4x7"	95.00
Caribbean, bl, ladle, punch	100.00
Caribbean, bl, mustard, w/slotted lid, 4"	65.00
Caribbean, bl, plate, salad; 7½"	20.00
Caribbean, bl, saucer	8.00
Caribbean, bl, stem, sherbet; ftd, 4¼"	17.50
Caribbean, bl, tray, relish; rnd, 2-part, 6"	25.00
Caribbean, bl, tumbler, shot glass; 2-oz, 2¼"	60.00
Caribbean, crystal, bowl, finger; 4½"	16.00
Caribbean, crystal, bowl, salad; 9"	30.00
Caribbean, crystal, cup, tea	15.00
Caribbean, crystal, pitcher, syrup; 9-oz, 4¼"	65.00

Caribbean, crystal, plate, bread & butter; 6¼"	5.00
Caribbean, crystal, plate, fruit nappy liner; hdls, 6"	4.00
Caribbean, crystal, plate, 14"	25.00
Caribbean, crystal, sugar bowl	11.00
Caribbean, crystal, vase, ruffled top, ftd, 9"	50.00
First Love, crystal, bottle, oil; #5200, w/stopper, 8"	70.00
First Love, crystal, bowl, #6, 12x3½"	70.00
First Love, crystal, bowl, #126, ftd, flat, 12½"	75.00
First Love, crystal, bowl, olive; #115, oval, 6x2½"	25.00
First Love, crystal, butter/cheese dish, #111, 7" sq	130.00
First Love, crystal, carafe, water; #5200, w/stopper	195.00
First Love, crystal, cruet, #30	90.00
First Love, crystal, ice bucket, #30, 6"	110.00
First Love, crystal, mustard, w/lid & underplate	57.50
First Love, crystal, plate, #111, 7"	17.50
First Love, crystal, plate, #111, 11"	47.50
First Love, crystal, plate, #30, 8½"	20.00
First Love, crystal, plate, cake; #115, hdls, 13½"	50.00
First Love, crystal, shakers, #30, pr	30.00
First Love, crystal, stem, wine; #5111½, 3-oz, 5¼"	32.50
First Love, crystal, sugar bowl, #115, ind, 2½"	15.00
First Love, crystal, vase, #506, ftd, 10"	115.00
First Love, crystal, vase, #507, 6"	55.00
First Love, crystal, vase, bud; #506, 9"	80.00
Lily of the Valley, crystal, creamer	25.00
Lily of the Valley, crystal, plate, 8"	20.00
Nautical, bl, creamer	30.00
Nautical, bl, plate, 10"	60.00
Nautical, bl, tumbler, cocktail	22.00
Nautical, crystal, cigarette jar	25.00
Nautical, crystal, cocktail shaker, fish design	60.00
Nautical, crystal, ice bucket	55.00
Nautical, opal, decanter	650.00
Sandwich, crystal, ashtray, sq, 2¾"	8.00
Sandwich, crystal, basket, oval, w/loop hdl, 11½"	250.00
Sandwich, crystal, bowl, console; oblong, 12"	40.00
Sandwich, crystal, bowl, cupped nut; 11"	55.00
Sandwich, crystal, bowl, fruit salad; 6"	12.00
Sandwich, crystal, bowl, fruit; 5"	10.00
Sandwich, crystal, bowl, nut; 3½"	10.00
Sandwich, crystal, cake stand, plain ped, ftd, 13"	80.00
Sandwich, crystal, candlestick, 2-light, 5"	37.50
Sandwich, crystal, candy box, flat, w/lid, 5"	40.00
Sandwich, crystal, coaster, 5"	12.00
Sandwich, crystal, oil bottle, 5¾"	35.00
Sandwich, crystal, plate, deviled egg; 12"	55.00
Sandwich, crystal, plate, salad; 8"	12.50
Sandwich, crystal, shakers, w/metal tops, 2½", pr	18.00
Sandwich, crystal, stem, wine; 3-oz, 4¼"	20.00
Sandwich, crystal, sugar bowl, 5-oz	7.50
Sandwich, crystal, tray, fruit epergne; 12"	52.00
Sandwich, crystal, tray, relish; oblong, 3-part, 10"	27.50
Sandwich, crystal, urn, w/lid, ftd, 12"	175.00
Sandwich, crystal, vase, fan; ftd, 5"	45.00
Sandwich, crystal, vase, hat shape, 4"	22.00
Sandwich, plate, jelly; ind, 3"	6.00
Spiral Flutes, amber, gr or pk, bowl, bouillon; 3¾"	15.00
Spiral Flutes, amber, gr or pk, bowl, cereal; sm flange, 6½"	32.50
Spiral Flutes, amber, gr or pk, bowl, nappy; 5"	6.00
Spiral Flutes, amber, gr or pk, bowl, nappy; 9"	27.50
Spiral Flutes, amber, gr or pk, candle holder, 7½"	55.00
Spiral Flutes, amber, gr or pk, cup	9.00
Spiral Flutes, amber, gr or pk, plate, luncheon; 8⅜"	4.00
Spiral Flutes, amber, gr or pk, sugar bowl, oval	8.00

Spiral Flutes, amber, gr or pk, tumbler, flat, 8-oz, 4¼" **30.00**
Spiral Flutes, amber, gr or pk, tumbler, soda; flat, 7-oz, 4¾" **35.00**
Spiral Flutes, amber, gr or pk, vase, 8½" **30.00**
Tear Drop, crystal, ashtray, ind, 3" **6.00**
Tear Drop, crystal, bowl, finger; 4¼" **7.00**
Tear Drop, crystal, bowl, flower; oval, 8x12" **50.00**
Tear Drop, crystal, bowl, salad; 12" **40.00**
Tear Drop, crystal, cup, tea; 6-oz **6.00**
Tear Drop, crystal, plate, bread & butter; 6" **4.00**
Tear Drop, crystal, plate, lazy susan; 18" **90.00**
Tear Drop, crystal, plate, salad; 7½" **5.00**
Tear Drop, crystal, plate, torte; rolled edge, 16" **37.50**
Tear Drop, crystal, stem, cordial; 1-oz, 4" **32.00**
Tear Drop, crystal, stem, wine; 3-oz, 4¾" **18.00**
Tear Drop, crystal, sugar bowl, 6-oz **6.00**
Tear Drop, crystal, sugar bowl, 8-oz **8.00**
Tear Drop, crystal, sweetmeat, hdls, star shape, 7" **40.00**
Tear Drop, crystal, tray, relish; 3-part, 12" **27.50**
Tear Drop, crystal, tumbler, iced tea; flat, 12-oz, 5¼" **15.00**
Tear Drop, crystal, tumbler, juice; flat, 3½-oz, 3¼" **6.00**
Tear Drop, crystal, urn, w/lid, ftd, 9" **135.00**
Terrace, cobalt or red, cup **40.00**
Terrace, cobalt or red, plate, 7" **35.00**
Terrace, cobalt or red, stem, saucer champagne; #5111½, 5-oz, 5" .**50.00**
Terrace, cobalt or red, tray, relish; hdls, 2-part, 6x1¾" **50.00**
Terrace, crystal or amber, bowl, ftd, 9x4½" **42.00**
Terrace, crystal or amber, butter or cheese dish, 7" sq **120.00**
Terrace, crystal or amber, plate, sq, 9" **35.00**
Terrace, crystal or amber, relish, hdls, 5-part, 12" **50.00**
Terrace, crystal or amber, stem, cordial **42.50**
Terrace, crystal or amber, tray, relish; 4-part, 9" **35.00**

Durand

Durand art glass was made by the Vineland Flint Glass Works of Vineland, New Jersey. Victor Durand Jr. was the sole proprietor. The division called the 'fancy shop' was geared to the production of fine hand-blown art glass in the style of Tiffany and Steuben. Crystal, ambergis, and opal glass were each used as a basis to create such patterns as King Tut, Heart and Vine, Peacock Feather, and Egyptian Crackle. Cased glass was used to produce cut designs. Production of art glass began in 1924 and continued until 1931. Although much of this art glass was unsigned, when it was, it was generally signed within the pontil 'Durand' or 'Durand' written across the top of a large letter V, all in silver script. The numbers that sometimes appear along with the signature indicate the shape and height of the object. Owner Victor Durand employed the owner and several workers from the failed Quezal Art Glass and Decorating Co. This is why early Durand may sometimes look similar to Quezal art glass. In 1926 Durand art glass was awarded a medal of honor at the Sesquicentennial International Exposition in Philadelphia, Pennsylvania. Our advisor for this category is Edward J. Meschi, author of *Durand — The Man and His Glass* (Antique Publications); he is listed in the Directory under New Jersey.

Bowl, finger; ambergris w/gr trim, 2½x5", w/6½" underplate **225.00**
Bowl, finger; Optic Rib, bl, 2x4½" **100.00**
Bowl, peacock feathers, opal/gr on gr over crystal, 4x9½" **725.00**
Candlesticks, King Tut, bl on marigold, gold int, 10", pr **2,750.00**
Candlesticks, leaf & flower cutting, yel lustre, 3½x3½", pr **525.00**
Candlesticks, peacock feathers, opal/gr on gr, flared top, 3½", pr **675.00**
Candlesticks, ruby w/Spanish Yellow cup/stem, ruby ft, 6", pr **725.00**
Champagne, ruby flashed w/Spanish Yellow stem & ruby ft, 6" **275.00**
Compote, Optic Rib, ruby w/Spanish Yellow stem, ruby ft, 4x7½" ...**625.00**

Compote, peacock feathers, opal/gr on gr on clear, ambergris ft, 6" ..**575.00**
Ginger jar, feathers, gr on gold w/gold threading, w/lid, 8" **1,800.00**
Ginger jar, King Tut, gr on orange gold, 8" **3,700.00**
Goblet, feathers, opal on gr over crystal, crystal stem/ft, 6½" **350.00**
Goblet, feathers, wht on ruby w/ambergris stem, 6¼" **350.00**
Goblet, Optic Rib, bl w/Spanish Yellow stem, bl ft, 8½" **375.00**
Goblet, Optic Rib, bl w/Spanish Yellow stem, ruby ft, 8½" **375.00**
Goblet, peacock feathers, opal/bl on bl to clear, yel stem/ft, 7" ...**325.00**
Jar, feathers, opal/bl on gold, thread-wrapped, 7" **1,700.00**
Plate, salad; Optic Rib, yel lustre w/gr trim, scalloped, 8½" **125.00**
Plate, salad; peacock feathers, opal/ruby, 8" **275.00**

Rose bowl vase, green coil decor on orange-gold iridescent, applied gold iridescent foot with blue highlights, 5", $1,750.00.
(Photo courtesy Edward J. Meschi)

Torchiere, Egyptian Crackle, striated w/gold irid, electrified, 12".**850.00**
Torchiere, Optic Rib, gr w/gold irid int, bronze base, table sz, pr ..**1,750.00**
Tumbler, iced tea; ambergris w/gr trim, 6" **100.00**
Tumbler, lemonade; Optic Rib, ruby, 5½" **135.00**
Vase, allover gold threading on orange-gold irid, bl/gold ft, 10", EX **500.00**
Vase, ambergris w/bl & wht banding & Thelma floral cutting, 10" **875.00**
Vase, ambergris w/wht single-line 'feather,' 3 panels cut w/grapes, 7" ..**650.00**
Vase, amethyst, Optic Rib, ovoid w/ruffled top, 4¼" **225.00**
Vase, bl irid, ovoid, #20172, 5" **700.00**
Vase, bl irid w/bl threading overall, #1710-6, 6½" **800.00**
Vase, bl w/random silver/bl threading, urn form, 8x8" **1,035.00**
Vase, cameo, gold irid w/acid-cut woodland scene, sgn, 14" **4,200.00**
Vase, cut o/l, red to clear, 9" **2,250.00**
Vase, cut o/l, 4-color geometric floral on clear, sgn/1971-10, 10½" **2,700.00**
Vase, feathers, bl/gold on wht w/threading (losses), gold ft, 12" **1,200.00**
Vase, feathers, opal/gold w/gr tips on gold, threading, stick neck, 10" **1,050.00**
Vase, feathers, wht/gold w/bl tips on gold, gold threading, ftd, 10" **950.00**
Vase, gold irid, squat ovoid w/tapered neck, bl flared rim, 8x9" ..**800.00**
Vase, gold irid, squat w/trumpet neck, #1986-6, 7½x9" **550.00**
Vase, gold irid, wide mouth, #V-1968-6, 6" **350.00**
Vase, gold irid w/much gold threading, wide-mouth cylinder, 8¾", EX ..**650.00**
Vase, gold w/pk hightlights, str incurvate sides, 6x4" **550.00**
Vase, gold w/red highlights, flaring neck, 7x4" **350.00**
Vase, gr crystal crackle w/lustre, 10½" **1,300.00**
Vase, hearts/vines, opal on bl irid, ovoid, #1968-6, 6" **1,100.00**
Vase, hearts/vines, wht on bl irid, shouldered cylinder, 10½" ..**1,450.00**
Vase, King Tut, bl irid on orange/gold irid, bulbous, #1964, 10" ..**1,600.00**
Vase, King Tut, gold on gr, sgn, 1968, 8" **1,150.00**
Vase, King Tut, gold on Lady Gay Rose, 9" **2,100.00**
Vase, King Tut, gold on opal, gold int, shouldered, 8¾" **1,200.00**
Vase, King Tut, gr on gold, amber-bl base, trumpet form, 14" ..**1,850.00**
Vase, King Tut, silver bl on gr w/gold int, wide ruffled rim, 5¾x4" ..**1,100.00**
Vase, opal w/gr & gold coil decor, 10" **1,300.00**
Vase, Optic Rib, lt amethyst, 6" **450.00**
Vase, peacock feathers, opal w/bl top, 8" **1,050.00**
Vase, peacock feathers, opal w/emerald gr top, 13" **1,050.00**
Vase, red-gold irid, ftd, bulbous w/stick neck, att, 8¾" **450.00**

Easter

In the early 1900s to the 1930s, Germany made the first composition candy containers in the shapes of Easter rabbits, ducks, and chicks. A few were also made of molded cardboard. In the 1940s West Germany made candy containers out of molded cardboard. Many of these had spring necks to give a nodding effect. From the 1930s and into the 1950s, United States manufacturers made Easter candy containers out of egg-carton material (pulp) or pressed cardboard. Ducks and chicks are not as high in demand as rabbits. Rabbits with painted-on clothes or attached fabric clothes bring more than the plain brown or white rabbits. When no condition mentioned in the description, assume that values reflect excellent to near mint condition for all but paper items; those assume to be in near mint to mint condition. Our advisor for this category is Jenny Tarrant; she is listed in the Directory under Missouri.

Note: In the candy container section, measurements given for the rabbit and cart or rabbit and wagon containers indicate the distance to the tip of the rabbit's ears.

Candy Containers

German, begging rabbit, brn w/glass eyes, compo, 1900-30s, 5" **95.00**
German, begging rabbit, brn w/glass eyes, compo, 1900-30s, 6" ..**125.00**
German, begging rabbit, brn w/glass eyes, compo, 1900-30s, 7" ..**150.00**
German, begging rabbit, brn w/glass eyes, compo, 1900-30s, 8" ..**175.00**
German, begging rabbit, brn w/glass eyes, compo, 1900-30s, 9" ..**250.00**
German, begging rabbit, mohair covered, compo, 1900-30s, 4" ..**150.00**
German, begging rabbit, mohair covered, compo, 1900-30s, 5" ..**175.00**
German, begging rabbit, mohair covered, compo, 1900-30s, 6" ..**250.00**
German, begging rabbit, mohair covered, compo, 1900-30s, 7" ..**275.00**
German, duck, yel w/glass eyes, compo, 1900-30s, 5" **110.00**
German, duck or chick, pnt-on clothes, compo, 1900-30s, 3-4" .**125.00**
German, duck or chick, pnt-on clothes, compo, 1900-30s, 5" **145.00**
German, duck or chick, pnt-on clothes, compo, 1900-30s, 6" **185.00**
German, duck or chick, pnt-on clothes, compo, 1900-30s, 7" **200.00**
German, egg, molded cb, 1900-30, 3-7", from $65 to **85.00**
German, egg, molded cb, 1900-30, 8" **65.00**
German, egg, tin, 1900-10, 2-3", EX, from $65 to **75.00**
German, rabbit (dressed) in car, compo, 1900-30s, from $250 to ..**325.00**
German, rabbit (dressed) in shoe, compo, 1900-30s, from $250 to ..**325.00**
German, rabbit (dressed) on egg, compo, 1900-30s, from $250 to ...**325.00**
German, rabbit (dressed) on log, compo, 1900-30s, from $200 to....**250.00**
German, rabbit pulling cart, mohair covered, 1900-30s, 6" **300.00**
German, rabbit pulling cart, mohair covered, 1900-30s, 7" **375.00**
German, rabbit pulling wood cart, mohair covered, 1900-30s, 4" .**250.00**
German, rabbit pulling wood cart, mohair covered, 1900-30s, 5" .**275.00**
German, rabbit pulling wood wagon, brn compo, 1900-30s, 4" ...**195.00**
German, rabbit pulling wood wagon, brn compo, 1900-30s, 5" ...**250.00**
German, rabbit pulling wood wagon, brn compo, 1900-30s, 6" ...**275.00**
German, rabbit w/fabric clothes, compo, 1900-30s, 4" **250.00**
German, rabbit w/fabric clothes, compo, 1900-30s, 5" **300.00**
German, rabbit w/fabric clothes, compo, 1900-30s, 6" **350.00**
German, rabbit w/fabric clothes, compo, 1900-30s, 7" **400.00**
German, rabbit w/glass beading, compo, 1900-30s, 6" **150.00**
German, rabbit w/pnt-on clothes, compo, 1900-30s, 4" **150.00**
German, rabbit w/pnt-on clothes, compo, 1900-30s, 5" **200.00**
German, rabbit w/pnt-on clothes, compo, 1900-30s, 6" **250.00**
German, rabbit w/pnt-on clothes, compo, 1900-30s, 7" **300.00**
German, sitting rabbit, brn w/glass eyes, compo, 1900-30s, 5" **95.00**
German, sitting rabbit, brn w/glass eyes, compo, 1900-30s, 6" **110.00**
German, sitting rabbit, brn w/glass eyes, compo, 1900-30s, 7" **125.00**
German, sitting rabbit, mohair covered, compo, 1900-30s, 4" **150.00**
German, sitting rabbit, mohair covered, compo, 1900-30s, 5" **175.00**

German, sitting rabbit, mohair covered, compo, 1900-30s, 6" **225.00**
German, standing rabbit (Ma), pnt-on clothes, molded cb, 10½" ..**340.00**
German, standing rabbit (Pa), pnt-on clothes, molded cb, 10½" .**340.00**
German, walking rabbit, brn w/glass eyes, compo, 1900-30s, 5" ..**110.00**
German, walking rabbit, brn w/glass eyes, compo, 1900-30s, 6" ..**125.00**
German, walking rabbit, brn w/glass eyes, compo, 1900-30s, 7" ..**150.00**
German, walking rabbit, brn w/glass eyes, compo, 1900-30s, 8" ..**175.00**
German, walking rabbit, brn w/glass eyes, compo, 1900-30s, 9" ..**250.00**
German, walking rabbit, mohair covered, compo, 1900-30s, 4" ..**195.00**
German, walking rabbit, mohair covered, compo, 1900-30s, 5" ..**225.00**
German, walking rabbit, mohair covered, compo, 1900-30s, 6" ..**250.00**
German, walking rabbit, mohair covered, compo, 1900-30s, 7" ..**275.00**
German, walking rabbit, wht compo, 1900-30s, 6" **125.00**
German, walking rabbit, wht w/pnt on clothes, compo, 1900-30s, 3" ..**125.00**
US, begging rabbit, pulp, 1940-50, w/base................................**55.00**
US, sitting rabbit, pulp, brn w/glass eyes, Burk Co, 1930 ....**85.00**
US, sitting rabbit, pulp, no basket, 1940-50 ....**45.00**
US, sitting rabbit next to lg basket, pulp, 1930-50 ....**75.00**
US, sitting rabbit w/basket on bk, pulp, 1940-50 ....**75.00**

US, Walking Duck Cart, Fisher-Price, #305, 1957 – 64, $40.00. (Photo courtesy Linda Baker)

W German/US Zone, dressed chick, cb, spring neck, 1940-50......**65.00**
W German/US Zone, dressed rabbit, cb, spring neck, 1940-50 .....**80.00**
W German/US Zone, egg, molded cb, 1940-60, 3-8", from $25 to.**40.00**
W German/US Zone, plain rabbit, cb, spring neck, 1940-50 ....**60.00**

Miscellaneous

Celluloid chick or duck, dressed, 3-5", M....................................**45.00**
Celluloid chick or duck, dressed, 6-8", M....................................**75.00**
Celluloid chicken pulling wagon w/rabbit, M **125.00**
Celluloid rabbit, dressed, 3-5", M...**65.00**
Celluloid rabbit, dressed, 6-8", M...**75.00**
Celluloid rabbit, plain, 3-5", M...**20.00**
Celluloid rabbit, plain, 6-7", M...**30.00**
Celluloid rabbit & chick in swan boat, M....................................**150.00**
Celluloid rabbit driving car, M **150.00**
Celluloid rabbit pulling wagon, M...**125.00**
Celluloid rabbit pushing or pulling cart, lg, M.............................**125.00**
Celluloid rabbit pushing or pulling cart, sm, M...........................**75.00**
Celluloid windup toy, Japan or Occupied Japan, M **150.00**
Celluloid windup toy, Japan or Occupied Japan, MIB **195.00**
Cotton batten rabbit w/paper ears, Japan, 1930-50, 2-5" **30.00**
Cotton batten rabbit w/paper ears, Japan, 1930-50, 6" **45.00**

Egg Cups

Egg cups, one of the fastest growing collectibles, have been traced back to the ruins of Pompeii. They have been made in almost every country and in almost every conceivable material (ceramics, glass, metal, papier-mache, plastic, wood, ivory, even rubber and straw). Popular categories include Art Deco, Black Memorabilia, Chintz, Characters/Personalities, Golliwoggs, Railroadiana, Steamship, Souvenir Ware, etc.

Still being produced today, egg cups appeal to collectors on many levels. Prices can range from quite inexpensive to many thousands of dollars. Those made prior to 1840 are scarce and sought after, as are the character/personality egg cups of the 1930s.

For a more thorough study of egg cups we recommend that you refer to *Egg Cups: An Illustrated History and Price Guide* (Antique Publications) by Brenda Blake, our advisor. You will find her address listed in the Directory under Maine.

Key:
bkt — bucket, a single cup without a foot
dbl — 2-sided with small end for eating egg in shell, large end for mixing egg with toast and butter
fig — figural, an egg cup actually molded into the shape of an animal, bird, car, person, etc.
hoop — hoop, a single open cup with waistline
inst dbl — large custard cup shape
set — tray or cruet (stand, frame, or basket) with 2 to 8 cups
sgl — single, with a foot; goblet shaped

American China/Pottery

Bkt, chicks on bl border, Paul Revere Pottery.............................325.00
Dbl, Brittany, Homer Laughlin 17.00
Dbl, Chick, Juvenile, Roseville, ca 1917....................................235.00
Dbl, Country Garden, Stangl..15.00
Dbl, Harlequin, Eva Zeisel, Hall, 1950s.......................................28.00
Dbl, Homespun, plaid, Vernon Kilns, 1950s..................................25.00
Dbl, Homestead, Provincial, Metlox, 1965 ....35.00
Dbl, Lu Ray, Persian Cream 25.00
Dbl, Lu Ray, Windsor Blue..22.00
Dbl, Ming, Lenox, ca 1930..40.00
Dbl, Pear, gr, MA Hadley...20.00
Dbl, Red Rooster, Provincial, Metlox, 1965..................................35.00
Dbl, Ring Ware, bl, Bauer..475.00
Dbl, Ring Ware, blk, rare, Bauer 4,000.00
Dbl, Rooster, Pennsbury 25.00
Dbl, ship design, bl, Rookwood, ca 1922.....................................250.00
Dbl, Virginia Rose, Homer Laughlin 75.00
Fig, Rooster, rare, Metlox..350.00
Fig, Sneakers, red high tops, Dept 56, current...............................10.00
Inst dbl, Rosebud, Coors, 1940s...55.00
Set, Apple, 2 dbl cups on tray, Winfield, ca 1940 ....50.00
Sgl, Apple, Franciscan..32.00
Sgl, Blue Willow, Buffalo...60.00
Sgl, Hawaiian Flowers, Vernon Kilns...85.00
Sgl, Pacific Ware, early, Pacific Clay Products, ca 1930s 48.00
Sgl, Vistosa, red, Taylor, Smith & Taylor, ca 1940 ....35.00

Characters/Personalities

Bkt, Donald Duck, yel & bl, 1940s...45.00
Bkt, Holly Hobbie, in kitchen, Japan 16.00
Bkt, Katzenjammer Kids, color illus..100.00
Dbl, The Virginian, Robt E Lee on horse.....................................28.00
Fig, Elvis Presley, bl sunglasses...15.00
Fig, Fergie, Spitting Image, 1980s 62.00
Fig, Grumpy, WD Ent, 1937 ....175.00
Fig, Mickey Mouse, pulling rickshaw..60.00
Fig, Mickey Mouse, sombrero...130.00
Fig, Popeye, lying down hoisting cup, Japan 125.00

Fig, Popeye, squatting, w/pipe, Japan...100.00
Fig, Popeye, standing, Japan...200.00
Fig, Princess Di, Spitting Image, 1980s..80.00
Fig, Sneezy, WD Ent, 1937..150.00
Fig, Sooty, playing criquet, Keele St 35.00
Fig, Swee' Pea, yel, KFS, 1980 ....70.00
Fig, Thumper, pushing cup...85.00
Sgl, Anne of Green Gables, Crown Ashton, recent 10.50
Sgl, Donald Duck, Good Morning series 16.00
Sgl, Elvis Presley, single view 28.00
Sgl, Elvis Presley, 2 views in circle...35.00
Sgl, Garfield, Good Morning series..16.00
Sgl, Snoopy, Good Morning series...14.00
Sgl, The Phantom...15.00

Figurals

Swan, orange and white lustre, black Japan mark, 2½"; Chick, yellow and white lustre, black Japan mark, 2¼", each from $12.00 to $18.00. (Photo courtesy Carole Bess White)

Fig, blk boy sits on pot, attached to orange lustre cup, Japan, 1930s...160.00
Fig, blk face, earrings, bow tie, foreign, early 1900s.....................125.00
Fig, Bluebird, Lefton...48.00
Fig, brn face, blk bow tie, ca 1920s...75.00
Fig, cat, Miss Priss, Lefton..40.00
Fig, Financial Times newspaper, soap egg....................................18.00
Fig, frog, gr, Ganz, China, recent 9.00
Fig, Golly, standing with Afro, attached to lustre cup, Japan, 1930s...200.00
Fig, Harrod's Doorman, Wade 28.00
Fig, pirate w/eye patch, Japan, 1980s 12.00
Fig, rooster, blk & wht, Cog Rouge..16.00
Fig, rooster, br drip, glazed, Pfaltzgraff......................................30.00
Fig, running legs, Carlton..58.00
Fig, Sergeant Chimp, plastic, w/lid..25.00
Fig, Volkswagen, Devon Ceramics, ca 1959 ....22.00
Fig, walking leg w/peg leg, Carlton...65.00
Fig, Wellies, Carlton..85.00
Fig, Whistler, bear, lustre, foreign 120.00
Fig, Whistler, duck, yel, foreign 85.00
Set, Cottage Ware, 4 cottage-shaped cups on sq tray, Price Bros, 1930s..60.00
Set, Muppets, Statler, Waldorf, Zoot, Sam, Sigma, ca 1981 ....200.00

Foreign

Bkt, Cardinal Tuck, red robe, Goebel, 1960s................................150.00
Bkt, Friar Tuck, brn robe, Goebel, 1960s....................................45.00
Dbl, gold & wht, Noritake..40.00
Dbl, Regency, red, rooster, Quimper, 1950s.................................30.00
Dbl, Rooster, Holt Howard, 1961 ....16.00
Dbl, Rose Chintz, Lefton...25.00
Dbl, Soleil, yel, male peasant, Quimper.......................................45.00
Dbl, Tree in the Meadow, Noritake 35.00

Set, chicken on ped, 12 ftd cups, HP bsk, Bing & Grondahl, ca 1865..**600.00**
Sgl, Blue Flower, Royal Copenhagen, ca 1940 ....**25.00**
Sgl, Canton, bl & wht, ca 1850..**150.00**
Sgl, Chinese Bouquet, Herend **56.00**
Sgl, floral, mc, gilding, Sevres, ca 1789 ....**400.00**
Sgl, sea gull, Bing & Grondahl **20.00**
Sgl, Shamrock, Belleek, 3rd gr mk **45.00**
Sgl, silver w/enameling, Russian **750.00**
Sgl, Tridacna, coral base, 2nd blk mk, Belleek...................**225.00**

Glass

Dbl, Chalaine Blue, McKee **20.00**
Dbl, English Hobnail, amber, Westmoreland, 1930s...................**32.00**
Dbl, Hobnail, Duncan & Miller, ca 1935 ....**20.00**
Dbl, Jadite, gr...**32.00**
Dbl, milk glass, flared base, Hazel Atlas.................................**9.00**
Dbl, Peloton, bl filaments, ca 1890..................................**185.00**
Fig, chick, gr, Portieux **20.00**
Sgl, Bristol, bl, fluted, ca 1810 ....**250.00**
Sgl, Burmese, pk to wht, Thomas Webb..............................**150.00**
Sgl, Candlewick, beaded ft, Imperial **70.00**
Sgl, Cremax, bl to wht...**7.50**
Sgl, Greek Key, Heisey, ca 1911-38......................................**95.00**
Sgl, Nailsea, pk looping...**250.00**
Sgl, Rock Crystal, ruby, McKee...**60.00**
Sgl, slag, Hobnail, purple...**75.00**
Sgl, spangle, cased, variegated color streaks w/silver mica..........**125.00**

Souvenir

Bkt, Cumberland Hotel, bl logo, Royal Doulton, ca 1890.............**13.00**
Bkt, Raffles Hotel, maroon bands, Churchill, ca 1995...................**13.00**
Dbl, Calgary Petroleum Club, CPC, Maddock............................**30.00**
Dbl, Chateau Laurier, Grand Trunk Rwy, bl & wht shield, T Haviland **490.00**
Dbl, DYC Yacht Club, Lenox, 1920s-30s **45.00**
Dbl, Hotel Tivoli, Panama Canal Zone **65.00**
Dbl, Macy's, printed across cup, ca 1930s.............................**45.00**
Dbl, Sigma Alpha Epsilon, purple Greek letters **25.00**
Dbl, YMCA, bl seal...**26.00**
Sgl, Great Lakes Expo, Cleveland, 1936, transfer, Czechoslovakia ..**30.00**
Sgl, So Shore Country Club, 1930s **25.00**
Sgl, Stanhope, ivory, Exhibit of Foreign Arts & Mfgrs, Boston, 1883 ..**150.00**
Sgl, The Patriotic Fowl, Lloyd George, ca 1920............................**50.00**

Staffordshire

Bkt, Golfer, Royal Doulton **300.00**
Dbl, Argyle, flow bl, Grindley..**200.00**
Dbl, Cornishware, bl bands, TC Green, 1930s...........................**55.00**
Dbl, Ferrara, red transfer, Wedgwood....................................**36.00**
Dbl, Iris, flow bl, Royal Staff, ca 1907 ....**90.00**
Dbl, Monarch, flow bl, Myott **150.00**
Dbl, Mr Snowman w/dish hat, Royal Doulton......................**100.00**
Dbl, Old Britain Castle, Johnson Bros...................................**22.00**
Dbl, Summertime, Chintz, Royal Winton..............................**140.00**
Dbl, Watteau, purple transfer, Masons..................................**35.00**
Dbl, Wicker Lane, Copeland/Spode **22.00**
Sgl, Italian, bl, Spode, 1990s...**16.00**
Sgl, Jasperware, Dance of the Hours, Wedgwood, 1995.................**32.00**
Sgl, Lady Hamilton, Royal Albert **32.00**
Sgl, Madris, flow bl, New Wharf, ca 1900.............................**200.00**
Sgl, Old Leeds Spray, Royal Doulton....................................**40.00**
Sgl, Pomegranate, Moorcroft..**350.00**

Sgl, Tower, red, Copeland/Spode, ca 1930...................................**35.00**

Steamship/Cruise Ship

Bkt, Belgium Maritime, orange & bl flag, Corabel.......................**25.00**
Bkt, Princess Cruise, floral, Dudson, 1999 ....**6.00**
Bkt, Salen Line, bl flag, Rorstrand, ca 1932 ....**28.00**
Dbl, Eastern Steamship Lines, ca 1920s.................................**80.00**
Dbl, Imperial Oil, Pearsons Steiner **110.00**
Dbl, Luckenbach Lines..**40.00**
Dbl, Red Cross Line, ca 1920-30 ....**80.00**
Dbl, United States Line, Lamberton **100.00**
Hoop, Court Line **75.00**
Hoop, Dominion Line, bl transfer, ca 1890 ....**175.00**
Hoop, Hamburg-American Line (HAPAG)................................**40.00**
Hoop, Manchester Lines **75.00**
Sgl, Cornuba, antique shape, Spode **150.00**
Sgl, Holland American..**50.00**
Sgl, NV Mancora, SP w/crest..**32.00**
Sgl, Polska Morska Handlowa, ca 1960 ....**20.00**
Sgl, Scotia Prince, 2001..**6.00**

Elfinware

Made in Germany from about 1920 until the 1940s, these miniature vases, boxes, salt cellars, and miscellaneous novelty items are characterized by the tiny applied flowers that often cover their entire surface. Pieces with animals and birds are the most valuable, followed by the more interesting examples such as diminutive grand pianos, candle holders, etc. Items covered in 'spinach' (applied green moss) can be valued at 75% to 100% higher than pieces that are not decorated in this manner. See also Salts, Open.

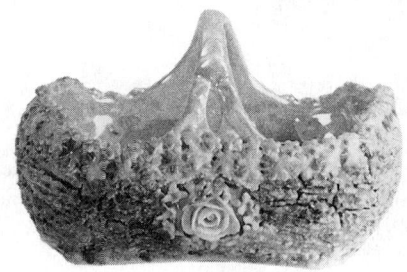

**Basket, applied flowers and much 'spinach,'
stamped Germany, 3x5", $135.00.**

Basket, appl flowers, 3½x4½" **85.00**
Basket, appl mc sprig w/gr spinach, bl flowered hdl, 2⅛" **65.00**
Boot, appl flowers, mk Germany, 3"......................................**27.50**
Boot, HP floral w/flared petal top, mk Germany, 3".....................**35.00**
Box, appl flowers, fan-shaped lid, Germany, sm **25.00**
Box, trinket; HP floral on fan-shaped lid, sticker on bottom.........**30.00**
House, appl spinach, 4¼x1⅜x3¼"...**125.00**
Pot, appl flowers & spinach, Germany, 1¾x1¾" **25.00**
Shoe, Brogan style, appl purple flowers & forget-me-nots, 4"........**75.00**
Shoe, curled toe, appl flowers, unmk, 2¼x5¼"...........................**100.00**
Shoe, high-heel; appl flower on toe, gr spinach & bl trim, 3" **70.00**
Shoe, pointed toe, appl flowers, 2¼x5¼"..................................**100.00**
Vase, appl flowers all over & spinach, hdls, 3"...........................**125.00**
Vase, appl flowers at rim, spinach, Germany, 2½x1" **58.00**
Vase, oval reserve w/HP bouquet, gr spinach w/bl floral rim, 2½x1"..**65.00**

Epergnes

Popular during the Victorian era, epergnes were fancy centerpieces often consisting of several tiers of vases (called lilies), candle holders, dishes, or a combination of components. They were made in all types of art glass, and some were set in ornate plated frames.

Amberina w/appl amber serpentine, 3-lily, red ruffled base, 1880s, 14"...**1,495.00**
Amethyst w/etched vintage, 1-trumpet, marble base w/ornate holder, 14" ...**500.00**
Bl opal, 3-lily, ruffled bl opal base, 17½".....................................**1,450.00**
Bl opaque to milk glass, 4-lily, wht ruffled base, 16x14" **450.00**
Bl satin, 1-lily w/HP florals, ruffled top & base, 10¾x7" **600.00**
Bl w/wht flowers, ruffled bowl on ftd base, 13x10".........................**190.00**
Clear to bl, 2-lily, clear ruffled base on mirrored pier, 11" **600.00**
Cranberry opal to vaseline, 3-lily, 21¾"....................................**1,200.00**
Cranberry opal w/candy ribbon edge, 3-lily, ca 1890, 19" **1,425.00**
Cut crystal, tazza base w/central lily, ca 1890...........................**1,675.00**
Gr opaque, 2-tier, SP base, 14" **400.00**
Lt gr to opal to cranberry, 3-lily, 21"...**950.00**
Pk opal swirl, 1-lily, wht base, 2-pc, 13¼"....................................**375.00**
Pk opaque w/appl threading, 4-lily, mirror base, 13½x10½" **2,400.00**
SP, 3 floral cups w/glass bowls, Reed & Barton, 1900s, 15x22x9"...**1,150.00**
SP (E Barker), comport+4 sm bowls or candle holders (interchange), 20" ...**1,495.00**

Sterling silver and silver-gilt maiden support, engraved base with water scenes and 'Americus Club,' Gorham, 1870s, 19½x15", $8,800.00.

Vaseline, Rib Optic, 5-trumpet, ruffled bowl, 20".....................**1,350.00**
Vaseline opal, 3-lily, ruffled base, 18x12"................................**1,694.00**
Wht opal w/appl gr serpentine, 3-lily, 19x11"..........................**1,750.00**

Erickson

Carl Erickson of Bremen, Ohio, produced hand-formed glassware from 1943 until 1960 in artistic shapes, no two of which were identical. One of the characteristics of his work was the air bubbles that were captured within the glass. Though most examples are clear, colored items were also made. Rather than to risk compromising his high standards by selling the factory, when Erickson retired, the plant was dismantled and sold.

Bottle, scent; amethyst, w/crystal stopper, 7½x4", NM **150.00**
Bowl, whimsey; clear crackle, 1940s, 6x5" **165.00**
Decanter, clear crackle, flared sides w/teardrop stopper, 15½" **150.00**
Tumbler, dbl old fashioned; clear to gr, 4x2¾", w/gr muddler **80.00**
Vase, champagne color, bubbles, incurvate rim, sticker, 11".......**185.00**
Vase, crystal over smoke w/controlled spiral bubbles, 15"...........**140.00**
Vase, gr, orig label, 8¾x4¾"...**95.00**
Vase, gr trumpet neck w/clear base w/controlled bubbles, 12".....**150.00**
Vase, gr w/controlled rows of bubbles, bulbous sides, 7"..............**65.00**
Vase, lav w/horizontal rows of bubbles, clear base, 15" **165.00**

Vase, smoke, teardrop w/flared rim, 13".....................................**180.00**

Erphila

The Erphila trademark was used by Ebeling and Ruess Co. of Philadelphia between 1886 and the 1950s. The company imported quality porcelain and pottery from Germany, Czechoslovakia, Italy, and France. Pieces more readily found are from Germany and Czechoslovakia. A variety of items can be found and pieces such as figural teapots and larger figurines are moving up in value. There are a variety of marks, but all contain the name Erphila. One of the earlier marks is a green rectangle containing the name Erphila Germany. In general Erphila pieces are scarce, not easily found.

Basket, floral chintz, 4¾" **100.00**
Bookends, ram's head, wht porc, Czech, 6x8", pr.........................**140.00**
Bottle, scent, emb swirls on wht w/gilt stopper & rim, 1930s, 5" ..**36.00**
Bowl, Warwick, Cheery Chintz, basketweave border, 2¼x8½".....**90.00**
Bowl, wide latticework border, #9411/3, 2⅝x8" sq **78.00**
Cake plate, Cheery Chintz, #6599, MIG, 11"..................................**55.00**
Cake plate, flower garlands & gold on wht, 11¼" **80.00**
Cigarette holder, elephant, MIG, 4½"..**75.00**
Covered dish, hen on nest, wht w/mc & gold trim, Czech, 5½" ...**55.00**
Creamer, cream, wht & blk cat climbing side forms hdl, 5½x3" ...**90.00**
Creamer, mc floral decor, Czech, 2¾x3½" **70.00**
Figurine, beagle, brn & wht, sitting, MIG, 5" **60.00**
Figurine, Bengal tiger, Germany, #2109/11, 6x14".......................**125.00**
Figurine, bloodhound, paper label, 5x7" **75.00**
Figurine, Borzoi hound, MIG, 2½x5½"...**65.00**
Figurine, Boxer dog, 4½x7"..**55.00**
Figurine, dachshund & cat at play, Germany, #d, 6x5".................**95.00**
Figurine, dog w/head cocked to side, gray, gr mk, 4½x5"..............**32.00**
Figurine, fox, recumbent, 9½"..**40.00**
Figurine, huskie, blk, brn & wht, standing, MIG, 4" **50.00**
Figurine, Madonna, bl & tan, bust prayer pose, MIG, 10"............**80.00**
Figurine, man & lady, Gerold & Co, #5800B/#5800A, 13", pr ...**180.00**
Figurine, Russian wolfhound, MIG, 7"..**35.00**
Figurine, Samoyed dog, MIG, 3¼x3¾"..**40.00**
Figurine, zebra, Germany, 6x6"...**80.00**
Flower frog, scarf dancer w/leg bk, wht faience, 7x5" **195.00**
Honey pot, beehive w/bee finial, 5x4", w/6" underplate..............**140.00**
Inkwell, lady in orange/wht/gr, front pen rest, ca 1920................**275.00**
Pitcher, rooster, yel/red/bl, Czech, NM..**245.00**
Pitcher, toucan, off-wht w/red & blk features, 5¾".......................**135.00**
Plate, condiment; Cheery Chintz, #6583-27, 4-part, 10½" dia **50.00**
Pot, orange ext w/wht int, cats hanging onto ea side, 1¾"............**95.00**
Reamer, orange w/reamer top, Czecho-Slovakia, pre-1917, 6" **285.00**
Teapot, beagle, sitting up, MIG, 8½"...**150.00**
Teapot, cat, blk & wht w/red bow, tail hdl, #6700B, 8"..............**185.00**
Teapot, dachshund begging, Made in US Zone Germany, #6703B, 8" ..**195.00**
Teapot, dog begging, #6702B, 7½" **225.00**
Teapot, pig shape, 7" **190.00**
Teapot, poodle dog, #734, 8¼"...**225.00**
Vase, cream w/celadon gr int, flowing Deco rim, 1930s, 10⅝" **75.00**
Wall pocket, gr w/red & blk berries & red bird on top, MIG **60.00**

Eskimo Artifacts

While ivory carvings made from walrus tusks or whale teeth have been the most emphasized articles of Eskimo art, basketry and woodworking are other areas in which these Alaskan Indians excel. Their designs are effected through the application of simple yet dramatic lines and almost stark decorative devices. Though not pursued to the extent of American Indian art, the unique work of these northern tribes is beginning to attract the serious attention of today's collectors.

Awl, cvd bone, 6x½", ca 1900, w/orig sealskin pouch 40.00
Basket, coiled grasses w/embr & wrapped decor, late 1800s, 7x7½" 395.00
Basket, fine-weave split grass w/cross design & lid, 1920s, 6x8½" 275.00
Basket, symmetrical weave, dyed seal gut imbrications, 1900s, 11x12" 300.00
Blanket, sewn/beaded story type on bl wool, 1950s, child's, 36x60" ...600.00
Cribbage board, cvd ivory w/salmon/hunters/etc, 1930s, 18" 425.00

Doll, Greenland (or Lapland), carved wood, with baby, complete leather costume, ca 1900, 15x4", $250.00. (Photo courtesy Allard Auctions Inc.)

Harpoon, hand-forged head, wooden shaft, 36" 675.00
Postcard, Eskimo seal hunters, Hewitts, mailed 1949, EX..............25.00
Sculpture, cvd bone, lady w/baby, ca 1970, 5½x2" 160.00
Sculpture, cvd ivory, walrus, EX detail, ca 1970, 2½x6".............375.00
Sculpture, cvd ivory, 7-dog sled team, sled & driver, 1950s, 16" L...550.00
Sculpture, cvd stone, Inuit hunter, ca 1970s, 4¼" 295.00
Shuttle, weaving; cvd whalebone, 19th C, set of 3, largest: 8"....145.00
Spoons, cvd fossil ivory, 1850s, 5 for 120.00
Ulu, stone, orig hdl, ca 1900, 4x5" 475.00

Face Jugs, Contemporary

The most recognizable form of Southern folk pottery is the face jug. Rich alkaline glazes (lustrous greens and browns) are typical, and occasionally shards of glass are applied to the surface of the ware which during firing melts to produce opalescent 'glass runs' over the alkaline. In some locations clay deposits contain elements that result in areas of fluorescent blue or rutile; another variation is swirled or striped ware, reminiscent of eighteenth-century agateware from Staffordshire. Collector demand for these unique one-of-a-kind jugs is at an all-time high and is still escalating. Choice examples made by Burlon B. Craig and Lanier Meaders sometimes bring over $1,000.00 on the secondary market. If you're interested in learning more about this type of folk pottery, contact the Southern Folk Pottery Collectors Society; their address is in the Directory under Clubs, Newsletters, and Catalogs. Our advisor for this category is Billy Ray Hussey; he is listed in the Directory under North Carolina.

China teeth, contorted features, dbl-faced, C Hewell, 12⅝".......360.00
China teeth, mustache, alkaline glaze, C Lisk, 11½"...................135.00
China teeth, pierced eyes, mc swirl colors, B Craig, 1980s, 13" ..440.00
China teeth, protruding features, brn mottle, B Craig, 16" 430.00
China teeth, 2-color swirl w/crushed glass glaze, Craig, 4" 265.00
Dbl, grotesque, alkaline gr w/gravel teeth, Lanier Meaders, 9"..2,750.00
Dbl, wht-glazed teeth/eyes, gr over Albany slip, M Rogers, 7¼"..300.00
Devil's face, uprn blk brows, red glaze, shard teeth, Brown's, 15".1,200.00

Grotesque, fat cheeks, olive gr, Lanier Meaders, 10" 825.00
Grotesque, rnd mouth w/shard teeth, cross-eyed, gr/wht swirl, CL, 12"..360.00
Grotesque, 2 short rows of shard teeth, gr/bl, DD Craig Vale NC, 17" ...275.00
Man w/big nose & cigar, brn/orange, Brown's, 8½" 360.00
Open mouth w/4 teeth, eyes down-cast, alkaline gr, L Meaders, 9¾" 935.00
Pebbles (2) form teeth, grotesque features, brn mottle, L Meaders, 11"..800.00
Porc clay teeth & eyes, glossy copper-blk lustre, BH XIX, 1992, 3⅝" 400.00
Relaxed closed eyes, closed smile, Frogskin, BH XVI..., 1991, 9½"..350.00
Rock quartz teeth, horns & pointy ears, dk gr alkaline, QL Meaders, 9".1,500.00
Wht clay teeth, cobalt pupils, dk brn, R Meaders, 11x22" dia 185.00

Fairings

Fairings are small, brightly colored nineteenth-century hard-paste porcelain objects, largely figural groups and boxes. Most figural fairings portray amusing (if not risque) scenes of courting couples, marital woes, and political satire complete with appropriate base captions.

Fairing boxes, also referred to as trinket boxes, sometimes had captions similar to figural fairings, and often the same figures on top. It was originally assumed that fairings were made in the Staffordshire area and were referred to as Staffordshire fairings for many years. The European market soon followed producing fairings and boxes since they could be made very inexpensively. England encouraged these markets by not charging import duties. Both the figural fairings and the trinket box fairings were made with the same consumer in mind.

Conta & Boehme of Poessneck, Germany, became the leading maker of both types of fairings. Not all fairings were marked. Those that were had an incised model number, a Roman numeral size number, and the painter's number. By 1850 the Conta shield was impressed or raised on the porcelain (with model #), followed by the paper label (1900s). Their mark depicts a bent arm holding a sword inside a shield. After 1891 all wares shipped into the U.S. had to be clearly marked with the country of origin, thus the word Germany was added. The words 'Made in...' were added in 1921.

For more information, we recommend *Victorian Trinket Boxes* by Janice and Richard Vogel, and their latest book *Conta & Boehme Porcelain*, published by the authors (see Directory, Florida). Other good 'out of print' references are *Victorian Fairings* by W.S. Bristowe and *Victorian Fairings and Their Values* by Margaret Anderson. Items listed below reflect values for very good to excellent condition.

Fairings

An Awkward Interruption, #2875, from $125 to 200.00
Broken Hoop, #3343, from $200 to 300.00
Don't Awake the Baby, #3367, from $300 to 400.00
How Bridget Served the Tomatoes Undressed, #3362, minimum value..400.00
Landlord in Love, #3309, from $200 to 300.00
Looking Down Upon His Luck, #2863, from $125 to.................200.00
Off You Please Sir, #3314, from $300 to 400.00
Returning at One O'clock in the Morning, #2857, from $75 to .125.00
Tea Party, #3365, from $125 to 200.00
Walk In, #2866, from $300 to...400.00
Welsh Tea Party, #3371, from $75 to..................................125.00
Which Is Prettiest, #3366, from $125 to 200.00

Trinket Boxes

Dresser, A Little Turk, #3679, from $225 to................................275.00
Dresser, boy & girl on teeter-totter, #2988, from $100 to............150.00
Dresser, cat on fireplace mantel, #3520, from $125 to.................175.00
Dresser, cats play on dresser top, #3564, from $175 to.................225.00
Dresser, child in highchair, #2196, from $100 to 150.00

Dresser, girl & doll, #3591, from $150 to **225.00**
Dresser, girl & goose, #3621, from $175 to..................................**225.00**
Dresser, girl holds hoop for sm dog, #57, from $100 to **150.00**
Dresser, girl w/sheep, #255, from $50 to **125.00**
Dresser, Kaiser Wilhelm I on lid, #2954, from $150 to...............**200.00**
Dresser, Kiss Me Quick, bicyclists on lid, #2883, from $200 to ...**250.00**
Dresser, Little John in Trouble, boy & dog on mantel, #3559, $225 to...**275.00**
Dresser, monkey & drum, #3570, from $150 to **225.00**
Dresser, Piano mk Steck & Comp, #1327, from $100 to **125.00**
Figural, boy & girl in basket, #3617, 4¼x3½", from $75 to **150.00**
Figural, Kaiser Wilhelm II, #2948, 5½x5", from $150 to.............**200.00**
Lg, boy & girl at checkerboard, #3639, 7x6¼", from $400 to **500.00**
Lg, figural, lady stands beside vanity, #2939, 4½", from $85 to...**125.00**
3-spot, Sleeping Beauty, from $150 to **200.00**
3-spot, Zouave soldiers (3), from $200 to **300.00**

Fans

The Japanese are said to have invented the fan. From there it went to China, and Portuguese traders took the idea to Europe. Though usually considered milady's accessory, even the gentlemen in seventeenth-century England carried fans! More fashionable than practical, some were of feathers and lovely hand-painted silks with carved ivory or tortoise sticks. Some French fans had peepholes. There are mourning fans, calendar fans, and those with advertising.

Fine antique fans (pre-1900) of ivory or mother-of-pearl are highly desirable. Those from before 1800 often sell for upwards of $1,000.00. Examples with mother-of-pearl sticks are most desirable; least desirable are those with sticks of celluloid. Our advisor for this category is Vicki Flanigan; she is listed in the Directory under Virginia.

Blk Chantilly lace w/sequins, bone ribs, 1750s, 10⅝", EX **1,100.00**
Blk lacquer w/HP design, Chinese Export, late 19th C, VG **125.00**
Brussel's lace on blk gauze, cvd abalone/MOP sticks, 11", EX **600.00**
French paper, aristocratic scenes, rtcl, MOP sticks, 14x8"...........**500.00**
HP cherubims/sequins on batiste, nacré ribbing, 1920s, 18", EX..**1,950.00**
HP silk, gold-pnt wooden sticks, plush red maribou feathers, ca 1900...**230.00**
Ivory, floral cvgs, cord tied, Continental, late 1700s, 7¾"...........**460.00**
Lace on silk, MOP sticks, Tiffany & Co, 9½", +case, minimum value..**800.00**
MOP & paper brise, HP figures in garden scene, European **1,000.00**
Ostrich feathers, bl on celluloid base, EX......................................**100.00**
Paper on vellum, HP cherubs, cvd MOP sticks, fr, sgn, EX.......**1,000.00**
Pk feathers, celluloid splines, 15x20"..**150.00**
Silvered filigree w/enamel chinoiserie, silver sticks, China, rare..**2,500.00**
Tortoise shell w/gilt-lacquered scholars & landscape, 8".............**500.00**
Watercolor Oriental scene on paper, ivory ribs, 17", EX **1,300.00**

Farm Collectibles

Country living in the nineteenth century entailed plowing, planting, and harvesting; gathering eggs and milking; making soap from lard rendered on butchering day; and numerous other tasks performed with primitive tools of which we in the twentieth century have had little firsthand knowledge. Our advisor for this category is Lar Hothem; his address is listed in the Directory under Ohio. See also Cast Iron; Lamps, Lanterns; Woodenware; Wrought Iron.

Bag, Funk's G Hybrid Seed Corn Is Here, EX **5.00**
Bee smoker bellows, generic type, 1940s, EX **20.00**
Blueberry picker, metal prongs w/iron fr, Fr, 7½x5x2" **55.00**
Bucket, well; galvanized iron w/twisted wire bail, 1800s................**35.00**
Corn dryer, iron, 10-prong, braided rope ring on top, 19" **17.50**

Corn planter lid, Hayes Mfg...Il, emb words, mk H73 ....**30.00**
Corn sheller, Little Iowa S1, metal, hand held................................**95.00**
Corn shucker, CI, Fulton CS 10, 12x12x11" w/hdl.........................**40.00**
Corn stalk cutter, CI, Parker's Clipper...Dec 1 '74, VG **55.00**
Dryer, seed corn; metal shaft w/spikes, hangs ears to dry **20.00**
Feed sack, McMillen Feed Mills, red/wht/bl ad on wht, 38x20", EX..**5.00**
File, for horse's teeth, 3¼" on 19" wooden hdl.............................**50.00**
Grain fork, pnt wood, 3-tine, long hdl, 19th C, 82x11" **700.00**
Grain measure, wood w/metal bands, wood hdls, 11x14" **35.00**
Grain measure, wooden, side hdl, 7" dia **250.00**
Grain measure, wooden w/iron bands, factory made, 1800s, 8x12" dia ..**85.00**
Hames, wrought iron, complete w/wooden shafts, 1890s, 25" **20.00**
Handbook, Corn in Industry, Corn Industries Research, 1937, 64-pg ..**5.00**
Harness hook, CI, 10" **28.00**
Hog holder, iron bar w/ring, Dr Rimsharp Handy...Nov 1931, 22" L .**20.00**
Hook, hay; wrought iron, made from 1 pc, 10½" **10.00**
Hook, wrought iron, 14", w/orig 14" wood hdl.............................**15.00**
Implement seat, Clarks, CI, EX..**100.00**
Implement seat, Deering, CI, VG...**35.00**
Implement seat, Emerson No 1, metal, EX.....................................**20.00**
Implement seat, Milwaukee, CI, EX...**50.00**
Implement seat, no name, CI, VG...**30.00**
Implement seat, Peters, CI, w/latch, EX.......................................**275.00**
Implement seat, Toledo, CI...**245.00**
Implement seat, Western L Roller Co Hastings Neb, CI, EX........**50.00**
Knife, field; iron hdl w/wood extension, sharp blade, 16½" **25.00**
Lantern, CT Ham Mfg No 0 Clipper, all orig, tall globe **50.00**
Lantern, wooden w/glass slides, tin candle socket, 10"+hdl **525.00**
Lard squeezer, hardwood, grooved pincers type, 49½x27½" **75.00**
Mister, brass, pump style, mk Whitney Boston Mass **125.00**

Muzzle, calf; hand-carved wood and rope, late 1800s, 12", $45.00. (Photo courtesy Kathryn McNerney)

Scoop, cranberry; tin, lapped edges, steel teeth, early..................**145.00**
Scoop, grain; copper, dvtl, iron hdl, 8x15".................................**265.00**
Scoop, grain; hand-cvd wood, English, 18x7" +38" hdl................**80.00**
Scoop, grain; wood & metal, EX old patina, 6½x15" **22.50**
Shovel, grain; bird's-eye maple, cvd scallop on hdl, ca 1800, 13" ..**575.00**
Shovel, grain; hand-cut lt wood w/curved hdl, 50" L, minimum value...**225.00**
Silage cutter, curved blade, hardwood hdls....................................**75.00**
Wagon seat, maple & hickory, mushroom arms, splint seat, pegged, dbl ..**550.00**
Wagon seat, walnut w/worn red/blk decor, wrought-iron hdw, 8x14x45" ...**75.00**
Wagon seat, wood w/metal base, orig pnt, 30x38x21" **500.00**
Yoke, calf's; bentwood branch w/poke (hits fences & gates) **45.00**
Yoke, cow; EX old patina..**50.00**
Yoke, oxen; single, wood w/bent hickory hoop, 29"....................**100.00**

Fenton

Frank and John Fenton were brothers who founded the Fenton Art

Glass Company in 1906 in Martin's Ferry, Ohio. The venture, at first only a decorating shop, began operations in July of 1905 using blanks purchased from other companies. This operation soon proved unsatisfactory, and by 1907 they had constructed their own glass factory in Williamstown, West Virginia. John left the company in 1909 and organized his own firm in Millersburg, Ohio.

The Fenton Company produced over one hundred thirty patterns of carnival glass. They also made custard, chocolate, opalescent, and stretch glass. This company has always been known for its various colors of glass and has continually changed its production to stay attune with current tastes in decorating. In 1925 they produced a line of 'off-hand' (handmade) items that incorporated the techniques of threading and mosaic work in four patterns: hanging heart, hanging vine, pulled feather, and mosaic. Because the process proved to be unprofitable, the line was discontinued after one year. Today the prices paid for these pieces are becoming astronomical. Even their glassware made in the past twenty-five years is already regarded as collectible. Various paper labels have been used since the 1920s; only since 1970 has the logo been stamped into the glass. For further information we recommend *Fenton Art Glass, 1907 – 1939*, and *Fenton Art Glass Patterns, 1939 – 1980*, by Margaret and Kenn Whitmyer; *Fenton Glass, The Third Twenty-Five Years*, by William Heacock (with 1998 value guide); and *Fenton Glass: The 1980s Decade* by Robert E. Eaton, Jr. (1997 values). For information concerning Fenton Art Glass Collectors of America, Inc., see the Clubs, Newsletters, and Catalogs section of the Directory. See also Carnival Glass; Custard Glass; Stretch Glass.

Apple Blossom, bowl, 1960-61, 10" 82.50
Apple Tree, vase, Moonstone, crimped, #1561, 1933, 10"...........145.00
Aqua Crest, bowl, cupped, flared, #203, 1941-43, 4½"................22.00
Aqua Crest, vase, tulip; triangular, #192, 1942-43, 6" 60.00
Basket Weave w/Open Edge, bonbon, ruby, #1093, 1932, 6½" 24.00
Basket Weave w/Open Edge, bowl, gr, #1092, 1936, 5½".............14.00
Basket Weave w/Open Edge, plate, ruby, 9" 22.00
Big Cookies, basket, amber, #1681, 1933, 10½" 100.00
Big Cookies, basket, blk, #1681, 1933-34, 10½"........................115.00
Big Cookies, macaroon jar, amber, #1681, 1933-34, 7"................215.00
Black Rose, candle holder, 2-pc, 1954-55..................................375.00
Blue Ridge, bowl, crimped, oval, 10" 80.00
Blue Ridge, top hat, #1921, 10"..225.00
Blueberry, vase, gr, #1562, 1933, 10" 42.50
Blueberry, vase, Royal Blue, #1562, 1935, 10"...........................150.00
Bubble Optic/Honeycomb, vase, 1961-62, 11½" 195.00
Cameo Opal, comport, rnd, flared, #1533, 1929, 6"......................75.00
Coin Dot, basket, cranberry opal, #203, 1947-65, 7", from $85 to..115.00
Coin Dot, creamer, lime opal, #1924, 1952-54 ....75.00
Coin Dot, tumbler, French Opal, str, #1353, 1948-53, 9-oz...........16.00
Coin Dot, vase, bl opal, crimped, #194, 1948-53, 6" 42.50
Coin Dot, vase, cranberry opal, dbl crimped, 1952-62, 11".........145.00
Daisy & Button, cup, Royal Blue, 1937-39..................................12.00
Daisy & Button, slipper ashtray, ruby, 1937-39 ....20.00
Dancing Ladies, bowl, Chinese Yellow, oval, #900, 1932-35, 11"..235.00
Dancing Ladies, vase, Chinese Yellow, hdls, #901, 6"..............115.00
Dancing Ladies, vase, Jade Green, hdls, #901, 1933, 6"..............50.00
Dancing Ladies, vase, Mongolian Green, #901, 1934, 9" sq........300.00
Diamond Lace, basket, French Opal w/Aqua Crest, 1948-50, 12" ...185.00
Diamond Lace, comport, Blue Opal w/Silver Crest, #1948, 1949-50...115.00
Diamond Optic, bonbon, Jade Green, flared, #1502, 1927, 6" 45.00
Diamond Optic, bonbon, Tangerine, dolphin hdls, #1502, 7½"..28.00
Diamond Optic, candlestick, Mulberry, squat, #192, 1942 ....85.00
Diamond Optic, creamer, ruby, #1502, 1927 ....28.00
Diamond Optic, cup, Celeste Blue, #1502 ....27.50
Diamond Optic, finger bowl, Rose, #1502, 1928...........................15.00
Diamond Optic, ice tub, gr or Rose, #1502, 1927-38, 4".............22.50

Diamond Optic, ivy ball & base, cranberry opal, 1952-54 ....150.00
Diamond Optic, shaker, Rose, #1502, 1928...................................44.00
Diamond Optic, sugar bowl, blk, #1502, 1930 ....30.00
Diamond Optic, tumbler, aquamarine, #1636, 1928, 12-oz 14.00
Diamond Optic, vase, Tangerine, #1502, 1927, 8½" 100.00
Diamond Optic, vase, tulip; #192, 1943-49, 5½" 22.50
Dolphin, bonbon, Royal Blue satin, etched, #1621, 5½" sq 45.00
Dolphin, comport, Jade Green, ftd, #1533, 6" dia.........................45.00
Dolphin, tray, sandwich; Rose, #1502-A, 10"................................50.00
Dot Optic, vase, French Opal, crimped, #1354, 10".....................110.00
Elizabeth, jug, batter; blk, w/lid, 1930-33 ....165.00
Emerald Crest, bowl, deep dessert; #680, 1949-56 ....26.00
Emerald Crest, comport, low ft, 1945-56.......................................52.50
Emerald Crest, vase, dbl crimped, #711, 1949-52, 5½".................45.00
Flame, candlestick, bl base, #649, 1924, 10" 155.00
Flower Windows, tumbler, iced tea; ruby, #1720, 1937-38............52.50
Georgian, cocktail shaker, ruby..90.00
Georgian, mug, aquamarine or Jade Green, 10-oz.........................38.00
Gold Crest, hand vase, 1943-44, #193, 11"..................................200.00
Gold Crest, vase, dbl crimped, 1943-44, #192, 5"........................22.50

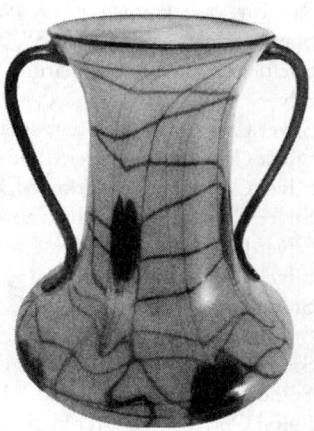

Hanging Heart, vase, #3010, green and black, 1925 only, $3,000.00.
(Photo courtesy Frank W. Ford)

Hobnail, ashtray, French Opal, fan shape, 1941-55 ....18.00
Hobnail, basket, cranberry, 1940-57, 4½" 60.00
Hobnail, bowl, topaz opal, flared, 1941-44, 7"..............................37.50
Hobnail, cake plate, bl opal, ftd, 1941-44, 12"............................135.00
Hobnail, candle bowl, blk, 1968-75, 6" 17.50
Hobnail, goblet, wine; Plum Opal, 1961 ....37.50
Hobnail, jug, syrup; Apple Green o/l, 1961-62, 12-oz...................27.50
Hobnail, jug, turq, squat, 1955-57, 32-oz......................................42.50
Hobnail, relish, amber, 1959-60 ....8.00
Hobnail, vase, bl opal, flared, scalloped, 1941-44, 9"....................87.50
Hobnail, vase, bl pastel, dbl crimped, 1954-55, 4½".....................18.00
Hobnail, vase, cranberry, bottle shape, 1941-44, 10" 215.00
Hobnail, vase, gr opal, dbl crimped, 1940-41, 8" 100.00
Hobnail, vase, lime gr opal, 1953-54, 8".......................................265.00
Hobnail, vase, Orchid Opal, 1940s, 6" 75.00
Ivory Crest, rose bowl, 1940-41, #201, 5"......................................30.00
Ivory Crest, vase, tulip; triangular, #1923, 1940-42, 7" 32.00
Lacy Edge, bowl, banana; gr pastel, 1955-56 ....52.50
Lacy Edge, plate, rose pastel, 1954-57, 9".....................................20.00
Leaf Tiers, bowl, Jade Green, cupped, #1790, 1935, 8"................120.00
Leaf Tiers, cake plate, Royal Blue, early 1940s, 10-12".................165.00
Lilac, flowerpot, w/underplate, #1554, 1933 ....140.00
Lilac, vase, fan; #857, 1933, 8"...60.00
Mandarin Red, cake plate, #1790, 1934, 12".................................85.00
Mandarin Red, vase, #184, 1933-34, 10".....................................115.00
Ming, bonbon, gr satin, crimped, dolphin hdls, #1621, 1935-36, 6½" ..12.50
Ming, mayonnaise jar, crystal satin, 1935-36................................75.00

Mosaic, bottle, cologne; #53 ....**1,100.00**
Mosaic, vase, bud; #3021, 11¼" **500.00**
Peach Crest, basket, #711, 1949-52, 7½" **155.00**
Peach Crest, bowl, 8-point, #1522, 1940-41, 10" **80.00**
Peach Crest, candle holder, 1956-62 ....**40.00**
Peach Crest, top hat, #1922, 1940-41, 8" **110.00**
Peacock, vase, Mongolian Green, flared, 1933-35, 8" **175.00**
Peacock, vase, Periwinkle Blue, flared or cupped, #791, 1935, 8" ...**175.00**
Pekin Blue, candlestick, #549, 1924, 8½" **82.50**
Pineapple, bonbon, Rose satin, triangle, 1938, 6½" **27.50**
Pineapple, candle holder, dbl branch; Rose, #2000, 1938, 5½" **55.00**
Pineapple, comport, crystal satin, crimped, 1938, 7" H **40.00**
Plymouth, goblet, wine; Stiegel Green, 4-oz **25.00**
Plymouth, tumbler, French Opal, 6", 12-oz **24.00**
Poinsettia, basket, crystal satin, hdl, #1616, 1938-39, 9½" **70.00**
Priscilla, basket, bl, 1950s, 12" **135.00**
Rib Optic, cruet, bl satin, #815, 1952-55 ....**225.00**
Rib Optic, hat, gr opal, #1522, 1939, 10" **70.00**
Rose Crest, jug, #192-A, 1946-48, 9" **135.00**
Rose Crest, vase, dbl crimped, #1924, 1946-48, 5" **27.50**
San Toy, ginger jar, crystal, w/lid, #893, 1936 ....**120.00**
San Toy, vase, gr, oval, #349, 1936 ....**85.00**
Sheffield, plate, ruby, 1936-38, 8" **12.50**
Sheffield, tumbler, aquamarine, 1936-38, 9-oz **12.00**
Silver Crest, basket, conical, #36, 1943-47, 4½" **30.00**
Silver Crest, planter, 2-tier, #680, 1950-52 ....**60.00**
Silver Crest, tidbit, 3-tier, 1956-60 ....**70.00**
Silver Crest, vase, dbl crimped, #711, 1949-72, 6" **27.00**
Silver Crest/Violets in the Snow, bowl, 1976, 9½" **70.00**
Silver Jamestown, vase, 1957-59, 5" **50.00**
Silver Rose, relish, heart shape, hdld, 1956-58 ....**55.00**
Snowcrest, bowl, amber, #1522, 11" **55.00**
Snowcrest, bowl, ruby, #1522, 1951-54, 11" **110.00**
Snowcrest, vase, dk gr, #3005, 150-53, 7½" **82.50**
Spiral Optic, bowl, gr, flared, #1503, 1927-30, 10" **25.00**
Spiral Optic, bowl, Orchid, dolphin hdls, #1503, 1928, 10" **48.00**
Spiral Optic, pitcher, cranberry, #187, 1938-40 ....**450.00**
Spiral Optic, top hat, bl opal, #1924, 1939, 4" **45.00**
Spiral Optic, vase, cranberry, pinched, 1954-56, 8" **85.00**
Stretch, basket, Celeste Blue, ftd, #1093, ca 1920s, 6½" **375.00**
Stretch, candlestick, Persian Pearl w/blk base, #549, 8½" **100.00**
Stretch, plate, Grecian Gold, octagonal, #758, 1920s, 8½" **7.50**
Stretch, vase, Celeste Blue, fan shape w/dolphins, #1533, 6" **185.00**
Stretch/Diamond Optic, basket, Velva Rose, metal hdl, #1615, 6" ...**95.00**
Stretch/Diamond Optic, vase, aquamarine, #1502, ca 1930, 8" **90.00**
Stretch/Rib Optic, pitcher, topaz, ribbed, 10¼" **575.00**
Sung Ko, ginger jar, #893, ca 1935, 8½" **1,500.00**
Swirl, bowl, gr pastel, 1954-56, 11" **55.00**
Venetian Red, vase, bud; #251, 1924-25, 10" **70.00**
Wisteria, candlestick, etched satin, #349, 1937-38 ....**60.00**
Wisteria, plate, #103, 1924, 6" **5.00**
Wisteria/Silvertone, cake plate, #1003, 1934-38, 10" **38.00**

Fiesta

Fiesta is a line of dinnerware that was originally produced by the Homer Laughlin China Company of Newell, West Virginia, from 1936 until 1973. It was made in eleven different solid colors with over fifty pieces in the assortment. The pattern was developed by Frederick Rhead, an English Stoke-on-Trent potter who was an important contributor to the art-pottery movement in this country during the early part of the century. The design was carried out through the use of a simple band-of-rings device near the rim. Fiesta Red, a strong red-orange glaze color, was made with depleted uranium oxide. It was more expensive to produce than the other colors and sold at higher prices. During the '50s the color assortment was gray, rose, chartreuse, and dark green. These colors are relatively harder to find and along with medium green (new in 1959) command the highest prices.

Fiesta Kitchen Kraft was introduced in 1939; it consisted of seventeen pieces of kitchenware such as pie plates, refrigerator sets, mixing bowls, and covered jars in four popular Fiesta colors.

As a final attempt to adapt production to modern-day techniques and methods, Fiesta was restyled in 1969. Of the original colors, only Fiesta Red remained. This line, called Fiesta Ironstone, was discontinued in 1973.

Two types of marks were used: an ink stamp on machine-jiggered pieces and an indented mark molded into the hollow ware pieces.

In 1986 HLC reintroduced a line of Fiesta dinnerware in five colors: black, white, pink, apricot, and cobalt (darker and denser than the original shade). Since then yellow, turquoise, seafoam green, 'country' blue, lilac, persimmon, sapphire blue, chartreuse, gray, juniper, cinnabar, plum, and sunflower yellow have been added. Collectors have found that the new line poses no threat to their investments.

In the listings below, 'original colors' indicates only three of the original six — light green, turquoise, and yellow (or those remaining after specific original colors have been priced). Red, ivory, and cobalt values are listed separately. Turquoise was the last original color to be introduced, so the items that were discontinued in 1946 are harder to find in that color (since it had a shorter production run), and values fall into the price range of red, cobalt, and ivory. These are designated with an asterisk.

For more information we recommend *The Collector's Encyclopedia of Fiesta, Harlequin, and Riviera, 9th Edition* (values updated in 2001), by Sharon and Bob Huxford, and *Post86 Fiesta* by Richard Racheter, both by Collector Books.

Dinnerware

Sauce boat: '50s colors, $78.00; medium green, $155.00; original colors, $45.00; red, cobalt, or ivory, $75.00.

Ashtray, '50s colors **88.00**
Ashtray, orig colors **48.00**
Ashtray, red, cobalt or ivory **65.00**
Bowl, covered onion soup; cobalt or ivory **725.00**
Bowl, covered onion soup; red **750.00**
Bowl, covered onion soup; turq, minimum value **8,000.00**
Bowl, covered onion soup; yel or lt gr **650.00**
Bowl, cream soup; '50s colors **75.00**
Bowl, cream soup; med gr, minimum value **4,200.00**
Bowl, cream soup; orig colors **45.00**
Bowl, cream soup; red, cobalt or ivory **62.00**
Bowl, dessert; '50s colors, 6" **52.00**
Bowl, dessert; med gr, 6" **600.00**
Bowl, dessert; orig colors, 6" **40.00**
Bowl, dessert; red, cobalt or ivory, 6" **52.00**
Bowl, fruit; '50s colors, 4¾" **40.00**
Bowl, fruit; '50s colors, 5½" **40.00**
Bowl, fruit; med gr, 4¾" **525.00**
Bowl, fruit; med gr, 5½" **80.00**

Bowl, fruit; orig colors, 4¾" 28.00
Bowl, fruit; orig colors, 5½" 28.00
Bowl, fruit; orig colors, 11¾" 275.00
Bowl, fruit; red, cobalt or ivory, 4¾" 35.00
Bowl, fruit; red, cobalt or ivory, 5½" 35.00
Bowl, fruit; red, cobalt or ivory, 11¾" * 340.00
Bowl, ftd salad; orig colors 340.00
Bowl, ftd salad; red, cobalt or ivory * 400.00
Bowl, ind salad; med gr, 7½" 120.00
Bowl, ind salad; red, turq or yel, 7½" 90.00
Bowl, nappy; '50s colors, 8½" 65.00
Bowl, nappy; med gr, 8½" 145.00
Bowl, nappy; orig colors, 8½" 42.00
Bowl, nappy; orig colors, 9½" 52.00
Bowl, nappy; red, cobalt or ivory, 8½" * 58.00
Bowl, nappy; red, cobalt or ivory, 9½" * 65.00
Bowl, Tom & Jerry; ivory w/gold letters 260.00
Bowl, unlisted salad; red, cobalt or ivory 1,200.00
Bowl, unlisted salad; yel 110.00
Candle holders, bulb; orig colors, pr 110.00
Candle holders, bulb; red, cobalt or ivory, pr * 140.00
Candle holders, tripod; orig colors, pr 485.00
Candle holders, tripod; red, cobalt or ivory, pr * 650.00
Carafe, orig colors 255.00
Carafe, red, cobalt or ivory * 340.00
Casserole, '50s colors 300.00
Casserole, French; standard colors other than yel 725.00
Casserole, French; yel 300.00
Casserole, med gr 900.00
Casserole, orig colors 165.00
Casserole, red, cobalt or ivory 225.00
Coffeepot, '50s colors 350.00
Coffeepot, demi; orig colors 425.00
Coffeepot, demi; red, cobalt or ivory * 550.00
Coffeepot, orig colors 195.00
Coffeepot, red, cobalt or ivory 255.00
Compote, orig colors, 12" 150.00
Compote, red, cobalt or ivory, 12" * 200.00
Compote, sweets; orig colors 80.00
Compote, sweets; red, cobalt or ivory * 100.00
Creamer, '50s colors 40.00
Creamer, ind; red 365.00
Creamer, ind; yel 80.00
Creamer, med gr 90.00
Creamer, orig colors 22.00
Creamer, red, cobalt or ivory 35.00
Creamer, stick hdld, orig colors 48.00
Creamer, stick hdld, red, cobalt or ivory * 72.00
Cup, demi; '50s colors 375.00
Cup, demi; orig colors 68.00
Cup, demi; red, cobalt or ivory 80.00
Egg cup, '50s colors 160.00
Egg cup, orig colors 60.00
Egg cup, red, cobalt or ivory 72.00
Lid, for mixing bowl #1-#3, any color, minimum value 770.00
Lid, for mixing bowl #4, any color, minimum value 1,000.00
Marmalade, orig colors 245.00
Marmalade, red, cobalt or ivory * 325.00
Mixing bowl, #1, orig colors 180.00
Mixing bowl, #1, red, cobalt or ivory * 245.00
Mixing bowl, #2, orig colors 115.00
Mixing bowl, #2, red, cobalt or ivory * 130.00
Mixing bowl, #3, orig colors 125.00
Mixing bowl, #3, red, cobalt or ivory * 135.00

Mixing bowl, #4, orig colors 130.00
Mixing bowl, #4, red, cobalt or ivory * 160.00
Mixing bowl, #5, orig colors 160.00
Mixing bowl, #5, red, cobalt or ivory * 185.00
Mixing bowl, #6, orig colors 215.00
Mixing bowl, #6, red, cobalt or ivory * 275.00
Mixing bowl, #7, orig colors 350.00
Mixing bowl, #7, red, cobalt or ivory * 410.00
Mug, Tom & Jerry; '50s colors 100.00
Mug, Tom & Jerry; ivory w/gold letters 65.00
Mug, Tom & Jerry; orig colors 60.00
Mug, Tom & Jerry; red, cobalt or ivory 82.00
Mustard, orig colors 210.00
Mustard, red, cobalt or ivory * 265.00
Pitcher, disk juice; gray, minimum value 3,000.00
Pitcher, disk juice; Harlequin yel 60.00
Pitcher, disk juice; red 600.00
Pitcher, disk juice; yel 48.00
Pitcher, disk water; '50s colors 280.00
Pitcher, disk water; med gr, minimum value 1,200.00
Pitcher, disk water; orig colors 125.00
Pitcher, disk water; red, cobalt or ivory 170.00
Pitcher, ice; orig colors 140.00
Pitcher, ice; red, cobalt or ivory * 160.00
Pitcher, jug, 2-pt; '50s colors 150.00
Pitcher, jug, 2-pt; orig colors 88.00
Pitcher, jug, 2-pt; red, cobalt or ivory 120.00
Plate, '50s colors, 6" 9.00
Plate, '50s colors, 7" 13.00
Plate, '50s colors, 9" 22.00
Plate, '50s colors, 10" 52.00
Plate, cake; orig colors 900.00
Plate, cake; red, cobalt or ivory * 1,000.00
Plate, calendar; 1954 or 1955, 10" 45.00
Plate, calendar; 1955, 9" 50.00
Plate, chop; '50s colors, 13" 100.00
Plate, chop; '50s colors, 15" 145.00
Plate, chop; med gr, 13" 375.00
Plate, chop; orig colors, 13" 42.00
Plate, chop; orig colors, 15" 50.00
Plate, chop; red, cobalt or ivory, 13" 60.00
Plate, chop; red, cobalt or ivory, 15" 80.00
Plate, compartment; '50s colors, 10½" 75.00
Plate, compartment; orig colors, 10½" 40.00
Plate, compartment; orig colors, 12" 55.00
Plate, compartment; red, cobalt or ivory, 10½" 45.00
Plate, compartment; red, cobalt or ivory, 12" 60.00
Plate, deep; '50s colors 58.00
Plate, deep; med gr 140.00
Plate, deep; orig colors 38.00
Plate, deep; red, cobalt or ivory 60.00
Plate, med gr, 6" 20.00
Plate, med gr, 7" 32.00
Plate, med gr, 9" 45.00
Plate, med gr, 10" 135.00
Plate, orig colors, 6" 5.00
Plate, orig colors, 7" 9.00
Plate, orig colors, 9" 12.00
Plate, orig colors, 10" 32.00
Plate, red, cobalt or ivory, 6" 7.00
Plate, red, cobalt or ivory, 7" 10.00
Plate, red, cobalt or ivory, 9" 18.00
Plate, red, cobalt or ivory, 10" 40.00
Platter, '50s colors 58.00

Platter, med gr	175.00
Platter, orig colors	35.00
Platter, red, cobalt or ivory	45.00
Relish tray, gold decor, complete	250.00
Relish tray base, orig colors	75.00
Relish tray base, red, cobalt or ivory *	100.00
Relish tray center insert, orig colors	50.00
Relish tray center insert, red, cobalt or ivory *	60.00
Relish tray side insert, orig colors	50.00
Relish tray side insert, red, cobalt or ivory *	60.00
Saucer, '50s colors	6.00
Saucer, demi; '50s colors	110.00
Saucer, demi; orig colors	18.00
Saucer, demi; red, cobalt or ivory	22.00
Saucer, med gr	12.00
Saucer, orig colors	4.00
Shakers, '50s colors, pr	45.00
Shakers, med gr, pr	185.00
Shakers, orig colors, pr	22.00
Shakers, red, cobalt or ivory, pr	30.00
Sugar bowl, ind; turq	365.00
Sugar bowl, ind; yel	125.00
Sugar bowl, w/lid, '50s colors, 3¼x3½"	75.00
Sugar bowl, w/lid, med gr, 3¼x3½"	225.00
Sugar bowl, w/lid, orig colors, 3¼x3½"	48.00
Sugar bowl, w/lid, red, cobalt or ivory, 3¼x3½"	58.00
Syrup, orig colors	375.00
Syrup, red, cobalt or ivory *	425.00
Teacup, '50s colors	38.00
Teacup, med gr	60.00
Teacup, orig colors	25.00
Teacup, red, cobalt or ivory	35.00
Teapot, lg; orig colors	210.00
Teapot, lg; red, cobalt or ivory *	260.00
Teapot, med; '50s colors	325.00
Teapot, med; med gr, minimum value	1,200.00
Teapot, med; orig colors	165.00
Teapot, med; red, cobalt or ivory	225.00
Tray, figure-8; cobalt	100.00
Tray, figure-8; turq or yel	400.00
Tray, utility; orig colors	38.00
Tray, utility; red, cobalt or ivory *	42.00
Tumbler, juice; chartreuse, or dk gr	600.00
Tumbler, juice; orig colors	40.00
Tumbler, juice; red, cobalt or ivory	60.00
Tumbler, juice; rose	65.00
Tumbler, water; orig colors	65.00
Tumbler, water; red, cobalt or ivory *	85.00
Vase, bud; orig colors	85.00
Vase, bud; red, cobalt or ivory *	125.00
Vase, orig colors, 8"	600.00
Vase, orig colors, 10"	850.00
Vase, orig colors, 12", minimum value	1,100.00
Vase, red, cobalt or ivory, 8" *	700.00
Vase, red, cobalt or ivory, 10" *	950.00
Vase, red, cobalt or ivory, 12", minimum value *	1,300.00

Kitchen Kraft

Bowl, mixing; lt gr or yel, 6"	72.00
Bowl, mixing; lt gr or yel, 8"	85.00
Bowl, mixing; lt gr or yel, 10"	115.00
Bowl, mixing; red or cobalt, 6"	78.00
Bowl, mixing; red or cobalt, 8"	95.00

Bowl, mixing; red or cobalt, 10"	125.00
Cake plate, lt gr or yel	55.00
Cake plate, red or cobalt	65.00
Cake server, lt gr or yel	145.00
Cake server, red or cobalt	155.00
Casserole, ind; lt gr or yel	150.00
Casserole, ind; red or cobalt	160.00
Casserole, lt gr or yel, 7½"	85.00

Casserole, 8½", light green or yellow, $100.00; red or cobalt, $110.00.

Casserole, red or cobalt, 7½"	90.00
Covered jar, lg; lt gr or yel	320.00
Covered jar, lg; red or cobalt	325.00
Covered jar, med; lt gr or yel	280.00
Covered jar, med; red or cobalt	295.00
Covered jar, sm; lt gr or yel	285.00
Covered jar, sm; red or cobalt	300.00
Covered jug, lt gr or yel	280.00
Covered jug, red or cobalt	290.00
Fork, lt gr or yel	125.00
Fork, red or cobalt	135.00
Metal frame for platter	26.00
Pie plate, lt gr or yel, 9"	45.00
Pie plate, lt gr or yel, 10"	45.00
Pie plate, red or cobalt, 9"	48.00
Pie plate, red or cobalt, 10"	48.00
Pie plate, Spruce gr	305.00
Platter, lt gr or yel	70.00
Platter, red or cobalt	75.00
Platter, spruce gr	350.00
Shakers, lt gr or yel, pr	100.00
Shakers, red or cobalt, pr	110.00
Spoon, ivory, 12", minimum value	500.00
Spoon, lt gr or yel	135.00
Spoon, red or cobalt	145.00
Stacking refrigerator lid, ivory	225.00
Stacking refrigerator lid, lt gr or yel	75.00
Stacking refrigerator lid, red or cobalt	85.00
Stacking refrigerator unit, ivory	210.00
Stacking refrigerator unit, lt gr or yel	48.00
Stacking refrigerator unit, red or cobalt	58.00

Fifties Modern

Postwar furniture design is marked by organic shapes and lighter woods and forms. New materials from war research such as molded plywood and fiberglass were used extensively. For the first time, design was extended to the masses and the baby-boomer generation grew up surrounded by modern shape and color, the perfect expression of postwar optimism. The top designers in America worked for Herman Miller and Knoll Furniture Company. These include Charles Eames, George Nelson, and Eero Saarinen.

Unless noted otherwise values are given for furnishings in excellent condition; glassware and ceramic items are assumed to be in mint condition. This information was provided to us by Richard Wright. See also Italian Glass.

Key:
alum — aluminum
fbrg — fiberglass
lcq — lacquered
lm — laminated
plwd — plywood
ss — stainless steel
uphl — upholstered
vnr — veneer

Armchair, Cherner/Plycraft, bentwood arms/legs, triangle bk, 31", pr.**1,900.00**
Armchair, Eames/Miller, X-based fbrg shell, tubular chrome, 29"..**450.00**
Armchair, Emeco, ltweight anodized alum fr w/vinyl uphl, VG, 4 for....**600.00**
Armchair, Jacobsen/Hansen, Egg, brn vinyl, alum X-base, 42"..**2,600.00**
Armchair, lounge; Weber/Lloyd, chrome tube fr w/rnd reuphl seats **350.00**
Armchair, Nelson/Miller, Pretzel, lm birch plwd legs/1-pc arms & bk.**2,500.00**
Armchair, Platner/Knoll, blk wire fr/base, wrap-around bk w/red wool...**700.00**
Armchair, Rohde/Troy Sunshade, Spring, chrome w/new vinyl cushions, pr.**200.00**
Armchair, Wormley/Dunbar, tan leather seat/T-bk w/cutouts, 31"......**500.00**
Bar stool, Cherner/Plycraft, molded plwd, purple uphl triangle bk/seat **600.00**
Bench, Nelson/Miller, cane top w/ebonized fr, folding chrome legs, 48" ...**1,100.00**
Bench, Nelson/Miller, Primavera, slat top, birch legs, 103" **1,400.00**
Bench, Nelson/Miller, Primavera, slat top, blk legs, rfn, 73", VG......**650.00**
Bench, Widdicomb, lt & dk mahog w/cvd detail, +cushion, 72x16x17" **800.00**
Bench, Wormley/Dunbar, mahog w/brass details, uphl, 66" L.**2,200.00**
Bench, Wormley/Dunbar, walnut w/bentwood U-legs, 12x19x42"...**700.00**
Bench/table, Danish style, teak w/raised lip, no mk, 18x23x71".**170.00**
Breakfront, McCobb/Calvin, Irwin Collection, mahog/glass, 68x66"..**1,000.00**
Buffet/breakfront, McCobb/Calvin, mahog shelving unit/cabinet, 84x60" ...**2,000.00**
Cabinet, Nakashima, walnut, 8 drw behind 2 sliding panel doors, 60" L..**7,000.00**
Cabinet, Nelson/Miller, Steel Fr, blk/yel/olive drws, glass top, 34" L..**1,500.00**
Cabinet, Nelson/Miller, Steel Fr, orange drw/2 avocado doors, 34" L..**1,000.00**
Cabinet, Saarinen/Johnson, birch vnr, 5-drw, alum pulls, 46x32"..**1,700.00**
Cabinet, Scandinavian, rosewood w/some inlay, no mk, 32x20x83"..**1,800.00**
Cabinet, Wormley/Dunbar, mahog w/oval cut-out pulls, 24x30x30", VG .**800.00**
Chair, Bertoia/Knoll, Diamond, chrome wire fr/base w/vinyl seat, 30"..**260.00**
Chair, Bertoia/Knoll, rpt vinyl-coated steel rods, orig seat pad, 30"..**75.00**
Chair, C&R Eames/Miller, molded plwd, mk LCW, pr **1,000.00**
Chair, Castle/Stendig, Molar, molded wht fbrg w/blk base trim, 35"..**475.00**
Chair, Eames/Miller, ash plwd seat/bk/fr, oval shock mt, 29" **600.00**
Chair, Eames/Miller, DCM, molded plwd seat/bk, chrome fr, VG ..**160.00**
Chair, Eames/Miller, DCW, molded birch bk/fr, 29", pr **500.00**
Chair, Eames/Miller, LCW, birch plwd fr w/shaggy yel seat/bk, 26"...**1,600.00**
Chair, Eames/Miller, LCW, molded ash plwd seat/bk/fr, 27", NM **1,200.00**
Chair, Eames/Miller, LCW, plwd w/red aniline dye, mc period fabric, VG ..**2,600.00**
Chair, Eames/Miller, Soft Pad, high-bk, leather uphl, anodized fr, 40" ..**1,300.00**
Chair, Ekselius/Stendig, Jan, bent tubular foam-covered fr+ottoman **1,100.00**
Chair, Jacobsen/Hansen, Swan, fbrg w/red wool uphl, alum X-ped, pr..**3,000.00**
Chair, Joffman, Kubus, sq w/tufted blk leather, 28x36", +ottoman, VG .**1,250.00**
Chair, Juhl/Baker, Chieftain, tan leather U-bk on walnut fr, 36" **2,800.00**
Chair, lounge; Eames/Miller, #670, orange leather, 33", +ottoman..........**2,000.00**
Chair, lounge; Laszlo, sculptural bk/sides, tan wool w/oak legs, 28" **650.00**
Chair, lounge; Nakashima, walnut spindle-bk, armless, 30x24x31".........**1,600.00**
Chair, Maly/Linge Roset, Swing, alum fr w/removable uphl, +ottoman .**1,100.00**
Chair, Mathsson, Eva, birch plwd, rpl webbing, 33x24x27" **325.00**
Chair, Nelson/Miller, Coconut, steel shell, reuphl, +ottoman, G...**4,250.00**
Chair, Nelson/Miller, Kangaroo, molded seat/bk, chrome fr, 40x36"...**4,250.00**
Chair, Panton/Miller, Panton, orange plastic, 1974, sgn/dtd, 33" .**325.00**
Chair, Paulin/Arifort, Tongue, foam-covered steel fr w/mc fabric......**3,000.00**
Chair, Rietveld, zigzag style comprised of 4 wood planks, 29x19x14"......**2,600.00**
Chair, rocker; Eames/Miller, RAR, yel rope-edge Zenith shell, 27x27"...**1,200.00**
Chair, side; Breuer, tubular chrome w/blk leather seat & bk, 26x24x25"..**275.00**
Chair, swivel lounge; C&R Eames, rosewood shell/blk leather, +ottoman..**2,300.00**
Chair, Wegner/Hansen, Peacock, ash/teak, thru-tenons, paper cord seat ..**1,500.00**

Chair, womb; Saarinen/Knoll, fbrg form w/metal fr, reuphl, +ottoman...**650.00**
Chair set, Bertoia/Knoll, child's, webbed wire w/red vinyl seat, 4 for......**500.00**
Chair set, Cherner/Plycraft, molded walnut plwd, 2 arm/4 sides...**2,600.00**
Chair set, Eames/Miller, DAR, fbrg on Eiffel Tower base, 4 for..**1,300.00**
Chair set, Eames/Miller, DAX, parchment fbrg on zinc H-base, 4 for...........**450.00**
Chairs, style of Wegner, teak, 1-pc even arms/bk, cane seat, 29", pr **25,000.00**
Chaise lounge, Mourgue/Airbourne, Djinn, bent steel tube fr, 65", VG..**1,000.00**
Charger, Werner Drews, ceramic, mc abstracts w/varied texture, 16" L..**4,250.00**
Chest, Robsjohn-Gibbings/Widdicomb, mahog w/caned pulls, 4-drw, 41"..**1,500.00**
Clock, Nelson/Miller, Ball, 12 blk-pnt balls around brass center, 12"....**650.00**
Clock, Nelson/Miller, 12 birch balls on spikes, brass center, 23" dia......**2,100.00**
Credenza, Robsjohn-Gibbings/Widdicomb, mahog, 3-drw, 68", VG **900.00**
Daybed, Nelson/Miller, birch fr & bkrest, alum hairpin legs, 75"...........**2,100.00**
Daybed, Probber/Probber Inc, mahog w/slat bkrest, w/pad/bolsters, VG...**700.00**
Daybed, Stein/Knoll, birch fr w/loose seat cushion, orig uphl, 76"........**1,200.00**
Desk, Nelson/Miller, Drop-front Pull-out, ebonized, 3-drw, 40x40", VG...**1,100.00**
Desk, Nelson/Miller, Executive L, walnut, 80", +72" L w/gr lm top ...**2,200.00**
Desk, Nelson/Miller, Modern Management, 48" walnut vnr top, 3-drw, VG..**5,500.00**
Desk, Nelson/Miller #4658, dk gr lcq w/gr leather top, chrome legs, VG....**10,000.00**
Dresser, McCobb, Planner Group, 6-drw, 48" L, on matching bench...**600.00**
Dresser, Nelson/Miller, teak, 4 over 6 drw, metal knobs, 67" L, VG .**2,100.00**
Dresser, Robsjohn-Gibbings/Widdicomb, mahog 6-drw w/rnded pulls+mirror ...**800.00**
Dresser, Robsjohn-Gibbings/Widdicomb, 12-drw w/4 arch sections+mirror ..**1,700.00**
Figurine, Wayland Gregory, doves, olive gr w/sgraffito, 4½x7", pr...**50.00**
Figurine, Waylande Gregory, rooster, bl w/wht sgraffito, 14x14".**150.00**
Hang-It-All, Eames/Tigrett, 15 pnt wood balls on plastic/metal fr, VG ..**850.00**

Inkwell and rocker blotter, Wayland Gregory, brown and cream, Dunhill, US Patent numbers, $375.00.

Lamp, desk; Teague/Polaroid, Bakelite/alum w/streamline shade, 13" **850.00**
Lamp, floor; Guariche, brass counterweight base in wht metal fr, 77" .**1,700.00**
Lamp, floor; Von Nessen/Nessen, Lucite shelf, 16" wht plastic shade ..**200.00**
Lamp, Grossman, 3 glass cylinder shades, enamel base, 61" **750.00**
Lamp, Nelson/Koch & Lowy, Half Nelson, chrome w/disc diffuser, 19", VG.....**1,300.00**
Lamp, Nelson/Miller, Bubble, wht vinyl over steel wire fr, 14", EXIB..**250.00**
Lamp, Nelson/Miller, Fishnet Bubble, hourglass shape w/webbing, 24x11" ..**500.00**
Lamp, Nelson/Miller, Lantern Collection, 16" formed vinyl shade, 20"....**400.00**
Mirror, Robsjohn-Gibbings, caned w/brass corner trim, 34" sq, VG ...**400.00**
Night stand, Nakashima, walnut, 3-drw, 25x19x16", pr...........**4,250.00**
Night stand, Wormley/Dunbar, mahog w/oval cut-out pulls, 25", pr...**700.00**
Ottoman, Jacobsen/Hansen, for Egg chair, brn vinyl, on alum X-base .**950.00**
Plaque, Waylande Gregory, Madonna & Child, ivory, 7½x4¾" .**100.00**
Rocker, molded birch plwd bk, uphl seat, blk rod base, birch runners..**170.00**
Rug, Calder, abstract in primary colors, sgn CA 74, 84x16", VG **3,000.00**
Rug, Fields, abstract in orange/rust/tan 100% virgin wool, 84x6", G ...**300.00**
Rug, geometric gray & beige pile, 89x67" **750.00**
Screen, folding; Eames/Miller, FSW-6, blk finish/orig canvas, VG....**2,000.00**
Sculpture, Fantoni, fish, bronze w/orig patina on wood base, 14½" L ..**260.00**
Sculpture, Loredano Rosin, female torso, clear w/int red/bl/yel, 13".....**750.00**
Sculpture, Nelson, bird, pebble eye, copper ft & branch, 12x13" **1,600.00**
Sculpture, Rosenthal-Netter, 4 stacked elephants, dripping gr, 13" **125.00**
Sideboard, McCobb/Calvin, walnut, 3-drw, 2 sliding doors, 36x66".....**550.00**

Sideboard, Nelson/Miller, Thin Edge, rosewood vnr, 4-drw/3-door, 80".....**2,900.00**
Sofa, Eames/Miller, Aluminum Group #3743, blk leather, alum fr, VG.....**4,500.00**
Sofa, Jacobsen, Swan, contour bk & arms, blk fabric, chrome base, 57"..**2,500.00**
Sofa, Maly/Ligne Roset, Swing, alum/steel w/removable uphl, 64"..**1,300.00**
Sofa, Nelson/Miller, Marshmallow, wht-pnt fr w/18 orig cushions, 53"..**18,000.00**
Sofa, Nelson/Miller, Sling, blk leather w/chrome fr & legs, 87", VG.......**3,000.00**
Sofa, Wormley/Dunbar, curved fr on mahog base, +4 loose cushions, 81"..**2,500.00**
Sofa bed, Schultz/Knoll, Convertible, blk-pnt tubular steel fr, reuphl .**3,750.00**
Table, bedside; Nelson/Miller, walnut, drw, 4 trapezoidal legs, 18x19"....**200.00**
Table, coffee; McCobb/Winchendon, maple, 36" dia top, 4 legs.**260.00**
Table, coffee; Nakashima, walnut slab on dowel-joined 2-slab base, 60"..**6,000.00**
Table, coffee; Robsjohn-Gibbings/Widdicomb, mahog w/darker edge, 54"...**800.00**
Table, coffee; Wormley/Dunbar, burled wood vnr, rfn, 54" L..**1,500.00**
Table, coffee; Wormley/Dunbar, wht lm top, 88" W, VG **450.00**
Table, coffee; Wormley/Dunbar, 48" dia travertine top, dk 6-leg base .**1,000.00**
Table, coffee; 3-pc glass construction w/chrome joints, 50" L **300.00**
Table, dining; Nelson/Miller, Lazy Susan, 48" dia gr plastic top..**400.00**
Table, dining; Nelson/Miller #5259, Oval Soft-Edge, X-legs, 78x42", VG..**500.00**
Table, dining; Robsjohn/Gibbings, lt walnut, Xd end supports, 6' L........**1,150.00**
Table, Eames/Miller, It-1 Incidental, walnut, chrome folding legs, 22" ..**1,100.00**
Table, end; Nelson/Miller, wht lm top, walnut drw/shelf, chrome fr, VG ..**260.00**
Table, magazine; Wormley/Dunbar, walnut/mahog 3-leg, 2 receptacles, VG....**850.00**
Table, Nakashima, Conoid, blk walnut slab, 4 rosewood butterfly joints...**17,000.00**
Table, Nelson/Miller, 28" dia blk lm w/birch trim, alum ped base....**550.00**
Table, occasional; Wormley/Dunbar, walnut, 20" dia top/shelf w/drw, VG ...**650.00**
Table, occasional: Saarinin/Knoll, 20" dia wht marble top, wht base **500.00**
Table, side; Planter/Knoll, 16" dia glass top on chrome wire base, 18" **700.00**
Table, Wormley/Dunbar, mahog flip-top, console when closed, 48" L....**650.00**
Table, 2-tier; Sorenson/Knoll, birch plwd, uptrn sides, 25x24x23" **700.00**
Tray, Nelson/Miller, molded walnut plwd, 15½" sq.........................**30.00**
Vanity, Nelson/Miller, teak, 4 drw ea side, 78", +23" W stool, VG ...**2,500.00**
Vase, Gambone, wht drips on turq, flat ovoid, 17¼x7"............**1,300.00**
Vase, Holmegaard, stoneware w/brn & gray, ribbed/spherical, AB #6, 5"....**350.00**
Vase, Voulkos, bl/brn stylized bands on caramel, bulbous w/sm neck, 9"..**3,250.00**

Finch, Kay

Kay Finch and her husband, Braden, operated a small pottery in Corona Del Mar, California, from 1939 to 1963. The company remained small, employing from twenty to sixty local residents who Kay trained in all but the most requiring tasks, which she herself performed. The company produced animal and bird figurines, most notably dogs, Kay's favorites. Figures of 'Godey' type couples were also made, as were tableware (consisting of breakfast sets) and other artware. Most pieces were marked, but ink stamps often came off during cleaning.

After Kay's husband, Braden, died in 1962, she closed the business. Some of her molds were sold to Freeman-McFarlin of El Monte, California, who soon contracted with Kay for new designs. Though the realism that is so evident in her original works is still strikingly apparent in these later pieces, none of the vibrant pastels or signature curliques are there. Kay Finch died on June 21, 1993.

For further information we recommend *Kay Finch Ceramics, Her Enchanted World* (Schiffer), written by our advisors for this category, Mike Nickel and Cynthia Horvath; they are listed in the Directory under Michigan. *The New Kay Finch Ceramics Identification Guide* (published in 1996), containing many reprints of original catalog pages, is available from Frances Finch Webb; she is listed in the Directory under California. See also Clubs, Newsletters, and Catalogs.

Note: Original model numbers are included in the following descriptions — three-digit numbers indicate pre-1946 models. After 1946 they were assigned four-digit numbers, the first two digits representing the year of initial production. Unless otherwise described, our prices are for figurines decorated in multiple colors, not solid glazes.

Bank, Lion, #5921, 8" **400.00**
Bank, Smiley, flowers, 6¾x8" **375.00**
Brooch, Afghan head, 2x3" **250.00**
Cup, Missouri Mule, natural colors, 4¼" **125.00**
Egg box, 9x8" **175.00**
Figurine, Afghan Angel, natural colors, #4911, 2½x2½" **400.00**
Figurine, Armour, mare, #474, 12" **650.00**

Figurine, Baby Ambrosia, kitten, pink and white, #5165, 5½", $200.00.

Figurine, Baby Bunny, #5303, 3½" **125.00**
Figurine, Baby Giraffe, woodtone, #835, 7½x8¼" **400.00**
Figurine, Banu, Afghan dog (head only), #476, 12" **2,500.00**
Figurine, Beggar, poodle, #5262, 8" **600.00**
Figurine, Bull, #6211, 6½" **300.00**
Figurine, Casey Jones Jr, #5013, 5½" **200.00**
Figurine, Chanticleer, rooster, #129, 11" **300.00**
Figurine, Circus Baby Elephant, #5365, 2¼" **350.00**
Figurine, Cockatoo, #5401, 15" **750.00**
Figurine, Cocker, cocker spaniel, sitting, #5201, 8" **450.00**
Figurine, Cocker, cocker spaniel, sitting, #5260, 4½" **350.00**
Figurine, Dog Show Boxer, #5025, 5x5" **500.00**
Figurine, Dog Show Maltese, #5833, 2½" **500.00**
Figurine, Dog Show Westie, #4833.............................**400.00**
Figurine, Dog Show Yorkie, #4851 ....**500.00**
Figurine, Doggie, bow at neck, #5301, 4½x5½" **400.00**
Figurine, Donkey, #4776, 28" **3,500.00**
Figurine, Ducky-Wucky & Ducky-Wucky w/Lustre Hat, #5006/#5006L, 6", pr ...**500.00**
Figurine, Grumpy, pig, #165, 6x7½" **275.00**
Figurine, Guppy, #173, 2½" L **125.00**
Figurine, Hannibal, angry cat, #180, 10½"..................**600.00**
Figurine, Hear No Evil, kitten, #4836, 3"....................**125.00**
Figurine, Jezebel, contented cat, #179, 6x9"...............**275.00**
Figurine, Jocko & Socko, clothed monkeys, #4842/#4841, 4", pr.....**450.00**
Figurine, Kneeling Madonna, #4900, 6".......................**100.00**
Figurine, Life-Size Lamb, #167, 20"........................**3,500.00**
Figurine, Listening Bunny & Carrots (bunny), #452/#473, 8¼", pr ..**600.00**
Figurine, Long-eared Dog, #5926, 6" **175.00**
Figurine, Mehitable, playful cat, #181, 8½".................**350.00**
Figurine, Mitzi, Pomeranian, #465, 10x10" natural colors, rare ..**2,500.00**
Figurine, Mouse, rare, 3" **350.00**
Figurine, Peasant Boy & Girl, #113/#117, 6¾", pr **100.00**
Figurine, Pekingese, #154, 14" L.................................**600.00**
Figurine, Persian Hunter & Dancer, #5162/#5163, 9½", pr.........**500.00**
Figurine, Pheasant, pk lustre w/gold, rare, #5020, 18" L, pr.........**750.00**
Figurine, Porky Pig, #5055, 2¾x3".............................**450.00**
Figurine, Prancing Lamb, #168, 10½" **575.00**
Figurine, Princess (Camellia/Pong-Jee), no crown, 38" **6,000.00**
Figurine, Seababy, #162, 2½x3½" **175.00**
Figurine, Singing Angel, #4802, 4½" **175.00**
Figurine, Skunks, #4774/#4775, 4¼", 3", pr................**550.00**
Figurine, Sleepy Bear, #5004, 4½".............................**200.00**

Figurine, Squirrel Family, #108A/B/C), 3½" parents, 1¾" baby..150.00
Figurine, St Francis, mottled tan, #5456, 24" 1,000.00
Figurine, Standing Donkey, Florentine White, #839, 9½" 300.00
Figurine, Swallow, on perch, 5" 175.00
Figurine, Turkey, #5843, 4½" 175.00
Figurine, Whippet, gold-leaf, #836, 12½" 500.00
Figurine, Windblown Afghan, pewter-like glaze, #5757, 6x6".....650.00
Figurine, Winkie Pig, #185, 3¾x4" 95.00
Figurine, 3 Wise Men, mottled tan, #5590/#5591/#5592), 10", set of 3....350.00
Plaque, Butterfly, #5720, 14"..225.00
Plaque, Starfish, #5790, 9" 250.00
Stein, attached poodle, #5458 ....450.00
String holder, dog w/bow over left ear, wall mt, 4½x4" 400.00
Table fountain, Sea Nymph, single color, #6064, w/fount & stand ...2,000.00
Tea tile, Yorkshire Terrier emb, 5½" sq......................................95.00
Toby jug, Santa w/hat lid, 5½" 150.00
Tumbler, emb Afghan design, mk Kay & Brayden, 6" 250.00
Wall pocket, Girl, gold gloss 250.00

Findlay Onyx and Floradine

Findlay, Ohio, was the location of the Dalzell, Gilmore, and Leighton Glass Company, one of at least sixteen companies that flourished there between 1886 and 1901. Their most famous ware, Onyx, is very rare. It was produced for only a short time beginning in 1889 due to the heavy losses incurred in the manufacturing process.

Onyx is layered glass, usually found in creamy white with a dainty floral pattern accented with metallic lustre that has been trapped between the two layers. Other colors found on rare occasions include a light amber (with either no lustre or with gilt flowers), light amethyst (or lavender), and rose. Although old tradepaper articles indicate the company originally intended to produce the line in three distinct colors, long-time Onyx collectors report that aside from the white, production was very limited. Other colors of Onyx are very rare, and the few examples that are found tend to support the theory that production of colored Onyx ware remained for the most part in the experimental stage. Even three-layered items have been found (they are extremely rare) decorated with three-color flowers. As a rule of thumb, using white Onyx prices as a basis for evaluation, expect to pay five to ten times more for colored examples.

Floradine is a separate line that was made with the Onyx molds. A single-layer rose satin glassware with white opal flowers, it is usually valued at twice the price of colored Onyx.

Chipping around the rims is very common, and price is determined to a great extent by condition. Our advisors for this category are Betty and Clarence Maier; they are listed in the Directory under Pennsylvania. Unless otherwise noted, our values are for examples in near-mint condition.

Floradine

Bowl, fluted, squat bulbous base, 4" 950.00
Celery vase, fluted cylinder neck, bulbous body, 6½", EX........1,000.00
Celery vase 1,800.00
Mustard pot...1,550.00
Spooner, 4¾"...1,285.00
Sugar bowl, bulbous, w/lid, 5½" 1,200.00
Sugar shaker 1,500.00
Syrup pitcher...2,500.00
Toothpick holder, 2½" 1,500.00
Tumbler, slightly bulbous, 3⅝"...1,000.00

Onyx

Bowl, wht w/raspberry decor, fluted top, 2½x4½" 2,000.00

Bowl, wht w/silver decor, 2¾x8"..350.00
Butter dish, wht w/silver decor, 3x6".....................................1,250.00
Covered dish, wht w/silver decor, 5½" 1,000.00
Creamer, wht w/silver decor, 4½"..485.00
Mustard, wht w/raspberry decor, hinged metal lid, 3¼" 2,900.00

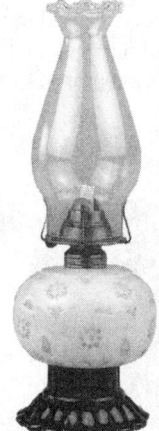

Oil lamp, black opaque base, small repair to collar, 7¼", $6,500.00. (Photo courtesy Early Auction Co.)

Pitcher, apricot w/orange decor, 4½"......................................4,200.00
Pitcher, water; wht w/silver decor, 8" 1,200.00
Shaker, wht w/silver decor, minor wear, 2¾" 650.00
Shaker, wht w/silver decor, Pat 2/23/1889, 2⅝" 800.00
Spooner, raisin w/wht decor, rare color, 4½"...........................2,250.00
Spooner, raisin w/wht decor 4", EX 1,250.00
Spooner, wht w/orange decor, 3¾"..1,500.00
Spooner, wht w/silver decor 4½", EX 250.00
Spooner, wht w/silver decor 4½"..525.00
Sugar bowl, wht w/silver decor, 5½", EX...................................475.00
Sugar shaker, wht w/silver decor, 5½", from $400 to 550.00
Syrup, gr (unusual color) w/silver decor 3,000.00
Syrup, wht w/silver decor, 7¾", from $850 to..........................1,150.00
Toothpick holder, wht w/silver decor, from $425 to 500.00
Tumbler, wht w/apricot decor, lt line unseen from w/in, bbl....2,300.00
Tumbler, wht w/silver decor, bbl shape, 3½", EX........................450.00
Tumbler, wht w/silver decor, thin str sides (rare), 3¾"............1,250.00

Fire Marks

The earliest American fire marks date back to 1752 when 'The Philadelphia Contributionship for the Insurance of Houses from Loss by Fire' (the official name of this company, who is still in business) used a plaque to identify property they insured. Early fire marks were made of cast iron, sheet brass, lead, copper, tin, and zinc. The insignia of the insurance company appeared on each mark, and they would normally reward the volunteer fire department who managed to be the first on the scene to battle the fire. (Altercations occasionally broke out between firefighting companies vying for the chance to earn the reward!)

Fire marks were first used in Great Britain about 1780 and were more elaborate than U.S. marks. The first English examples were made of lead and carried a policy number. They were used to identify insured property to the fire brigades maintained by the insurance companies. Most copper and brass fire marks are of European origin.

During the latter half of the nineteenth century, municipalities replaced the volunteer fire companies and fire brigades with paid fire departments. No longer was there a need for fire marks, so the companies discontinued their use (though some companies still use fire marks for advertising purposes). See *The Fire Mark Circle of America*, listed under Clubs, Newsletters, and Catalogs in the Directory.

Prices listed are for legitimate fire marks in good to excellent condition. Reproductions are identified when possible. Many fire marks have been and continue to be widely reproduced in cast iron and aluminum. They are sold legitimately as decorator items and collectible reproductions. Fantasy items, on the other hand, are not reproductions, as they depict items that never existed in the first place. They are twentieth century fabrications and never existed in their present form prior to this recent production. They appear in cast iron, aluminum, and other mediums.

Clockwise: **Fire Association of Philadelphia, 1860 – 1870, minor paint loss, 11¾", $400.00; Associated Firemen's Insurance Company of Baltimore, Maryland, running figure, 1847 – 1849, minor paint loss, 11¾", $320.00; Valiant Hose #2, nineteenth century, minor paint loss, 10⅝", $400.00; UF with spread eagle, nineteenth century, minor paint loss, 11", $300.00.**

Baltimore Equitable Society, clasped hands/1794, pnt CI, 10x8x9" ..1,380.00
City Insurance Co Cin, CI, 12½" L 850.00
German Freeport III, pnt tin, 2½x7", EX, from $100 to..............150.00
Green Tree Mutual Assurance, CI, NM orig pnt, 3¼" 125.00
Hands clasped (4) & #906, unmk fantasy item, 7x10½" 15.00
Insured Home New York, tin, 5¼x8⅛", VG 80.00
Invicta & famous wht horse of Kent, lead, 8¾x6½" 385.00
Mutual Assurance of Phila, gr tree type on wooden shield..........100.00
Mutual Insurance, angel flying over Charleston, 9½x7½" 750.00
Northwestern National Service Strength Safety, tin, 3" 55.00
Philadelphia Contributorship, metal hands on wooden shield, EX ...75.00
Phoenix, copper, many varieties, worn 90.00
Protector Fire Ins Co London, copper, 1835, VG 85.00

Firefighting Collectibles

Firefighting collectibles have always been a good investment in terms of value appreciation. Many times the market will be temporarily affected by wild price swings caused by the 'supply and demand principle' as related to a small group of aggressive collectors. These collectors will occasionally pay well over market value for a particular item they need or want. Once their desires are satisfied, prices seem to return to their normal range. It has been noticed that during these periods of high prices, many items enter the marketplace that otherwise would remain in collections. This may (it has in the past) cause a price depression (due again to the 'supply and demand principle' of market behavior).

The recent phenomena of Internet buying and selling of firefighting collectibles and antiques has caused wild swings in prices for some fire collectibles. The cause of this is the ability to reach into vast international markets. It appears that this has resulted in a significant escalation in prices paid for select items. The bottom-line items still languish price wise,

but at least continue to change hands. This marketplace continues to be active, and many outstanding items have appeared recently in the fire antiques and collectibles field. But when all is said and done, the careful purchase of quality, well-documented firefighting items will continue to be an enjoyable hobby and an excellent investment opportunity.

Today there is a large, active group of collectors for fire department antiques (items over 100 years old) and an even larger group seeking related collectibles (those less than 100 years old). Our advisors for this category (except grenades) are H. Thomas and Patricia Laun; they are listed in the Directory under New York. (SASE required.)

Fire grenades preceded the pressurized metal fire extinguishers used today. They were filled with a mixture of chemicals and water and made of glass thin enough to shatter easily when thrown into the flames. Many varieties of colors and shapes were used. Not all the grenades listed contain salt-brine solution, some, such as the Red Comet, contain carbon tetrachloride, a powerful solvent that is also a health hazard and an environmental threat. (It attacks the ozone layer.) It is best to leave any contents inside the glass balls. The source of grenade prices are mainly auction results; current retail values will fluctuate. Our fire grenades advisor is Willy Young; he is listed in the Directory under Nevada.

Alarm, Belcher & Loomis. . .RT, 4-needle, brass bell, oak case, 8x13"..280.00
Axe, hand; steel w/wood hdl mk Hartwele Hickory, EX..............150.00
Axe, parade; Viking style, NP, EX 125.00
Badge, brass, Volunteer Fireman's Assoc NY City 227, EX............85.00
Badge, Chicago Relief Engineer..., CH Hanson, silver-tone, 2⅛"..130.00
Badge, LI City FD Exempt 42, eagle atop, gold-tone metal, EX....95.00
Badge, West Parke/Stowe Twp, SP brass, 1930s, 1¾", EX..............35.00
Bell, apparatus; after-market style, 12", NM................................500.00
Bell, apparatus; brass, 11" dia, w/bracket 400.00
Bell, apparatus; NP, 10" dia, EX 495.00
Bell, muffin type, brass w/trn wood hdl, 5½" dia, NM................550.00
Belt, leather, 2-pc brass buckle w/eagle center, SFHC, VG..........175.00
Box, alarm; Auto Call, CI, industrial style 25.00
Box, alarm; Gamewell, CI, telegraph door, operational, early 1900s, EX....245.00
Box, alarm; Holtzer Cabot, CI/brass, institutional style 75.00
Box, alarm; Safa, street type, complete & working......................125.00
Box, ballot; walnut (worn), wooden blk & wht balls....................120.00
Bucket, leather, hand stitched, orig pnt banner: name/'06, EX ...650.00
Bucket, leather, old blk w/faded gold letters; B&A, 12" 465.00
Bucket, leather w/old gr rpt, gilt letters/foliate, red int, 19", VG ...880.00
Bucket, rubberized canvas, EX 95.00
Catalog, Am LaFrance Motor Cars, w/FD testimonials, 1914.....115.00
Certificate, Dover Fire Department, 1874, orig seal, fr: 19x24" ..110.00
Certificate, Fireman's Membership FDNY, 1927, 22x17½", w/fr...70.00
Extinguisher, apparatus; Seagrave Foam, EX 275.00
Extinguisher, Fireen, tin tube, dry powder, 11¾x3¼", G..............20.00
Extinguisher, Phomene, Pyrene Mfg Co, chrome, 25" 45.00
Extinguisher, SOS Defender, brass pump type, CCL4, 12½x3", w/mt...20.00
Gauge, sprinkler; Am Fire Extinguisher, NP brass, 6"..................30.00
Gong, Gamewell, oak case, flat top, 15" brass bell, VG..........2,350.00
Gong, Gamewell, turtle type w/6" steel bell, EX........................110.00
Gong, Gamewell Bliss, chrome, steel bell, chain wind, 10" 125.00
Grenade, Am, clear w/pk contents 650.00
Grenade, B&ORR, gr 1,200.00
Grenade, Babcock's, smoky gr, Chicago IL 1,200.00
Grenade, Harden Improved, amber, petal design 950.00
Grenade, Harden Quilted, lt cornflower bl, pt............................450.00
Grenade, Harden Quilted, turq w/Patented & no dates, ½-pt 250.00
Grenade, Harden's Improved, cobalt, seed bubbles, 1880-90, 6½"...1,600.00
Grenade, Harden's Star, med bl, qt..500.00
Grenade, Harden's Star (flat), aqua, English, pt 350.00
Grenade, Harden's Star..., turq-bl, qt, 7⅞"................................200.00
Grenade, Harden Tubular, lines around Star, turq 850.00

Grenade, Harkness, Lapis Blue 550.00
Grenade, Hayward's Diamond, aqua-gr, pt 300.00
Grenade, Hayward's Pleated, amber, ⅔-qt 1,000.00
Grenade, Hayward's Pleated, cornflower bl, pt............500.00
Grenade, Hayward's Round Panel, plum amethyst, pt.............1,800.00
Grenade, Hayward Victory, aquamarine w/emb dmns, 6½" 2,900.00
Grenade, Hayward...NY, clear, w/contents, NM label, 7½" 400.00
Grenade, Hayward...NY, cobalt, smooth base, w/contents, 6".....275.00
Grenade, Healy's Hand Fire Extinguisher Co, yel-olive, 11"....1,050.00
Grenade, Little Giant, aqua, 1887-90, NM label & contents, pt, 6½"..1,950.00
Grenade, Nutting, HSN Diamond, amber 2,000.00
Grenade, Patented, lt sapphire bl, w/contents, pt 210.00
Grenade, Rockford Kalamazoo...Applied For, cobalt, w/contents, 11¼"...675.00
Harness, hinged metal, FDNY, ca 1900, EX 425.00
Helmet, aluminum w/high eagle, Asst Chief NFD, EX 210.00
Helmet, fiberglass w/leather front, EX 60.00
Helmet, leather, high eagle, #1 on frontispc, VG 350.00
Helmet, leather, high eagle, fancy frontispc, 4-comb, 1840s, EX ...500.00
Helmet, leather, high eagle, H&L #3 shield, Wilson, VG...........300.00
Helmet, leather, high eagle, lacks frontispc, VG.....................185.00
Helmet, leather, high eagle, Vineland NJ, VG+ 300.00
Helmet, leather, high eagle, Wilson of NY, 1870s, VG 425.00
Helmet, leather, New Yorker style, Cairnes, 1988, NM..............195.00
Helmet, leather, OSHA New Yorker, Company 3 MLFD, w/eye shield...250.00
Hose clamp, Akron, cast aluminum.......................................65.00
Lantern, Bridgeport Brass Co, hand type, 1870s-80s, EX 425.00
Lantern, Dietz Fire King, EX..175.00
Lantern, Dietz Fire King, Seagrave, slide-off cage, complete 500.00
Lantern, Dietz King Fire Dept, red globe, mixed metals, VG......175.00
Lantern, Dietz Queen Fire Dept, NP brass, hand sz 710.00
Lantern, wrist; spring-loaded candle burner, fixed globe, 1870s ..525.00
Lantern globe, for Dietz King, cobalt.....................................85.00
Lantern globe, for Dietz King, red (or bl or gr) over clear 450.00
Nozzle, brass, from pc of chemical apparatus, w/shut-off, early......80.00
Nozzle, Flame Buster, Ginnell, 2½" w/2 hdls, scarce.....................85.00
Nozzle, Handline, brass, leather hdls, 1950s, 2½", 20" H 275.00
Nozzle, Handline, NP brass, Akron-Worcester, Ohio..., 1930, 2" ...110.00
Nozzle, Powhatan, brass, booster sz......................................37.50
Nozzle, spinning cellar; Bresnan, brass, 2½".............................265.00
Plaque, builder's, brass, Standard Fire Dept, 5¼x7" 25.00
Plaque, builder's, NP brass, built by RS Nochols...VT 400.00
Pole, pike, trn hdl, 46½", VG 60.00
Register, Nonpareil, Gamewell, VG 235.00
Ribbon, Houtzpale PA convention, 1897, EX 15.00
Rule book, Chicago, ca 1925, 79+ pgs, G 35.00
Siren, Siren Signal Corp NJ, 12-volt, red pnt, G..........................40.00
Tool chest, wood w/pnt decor, Waltham WFA, 16x36x17", EX .400.00
Torch, apparatus; brass, mtd on wood base, 1850s, 9", EX..........220.00
Torch, parade; brass, on swivel, no burner, 8", VG 60.00
Trumpet, brass, worn, VG 425.00
Trumpet, pewter, Woodbury Pewters repro, eagle & shield, 19", EX...150.00
Trumpet, presentation; SP w/eng steamer, 1892, 21", NM 1,300.00
Wrench, Boston Coupling Co, combination spanner, 9½", EX 10.00

Fireplace Accessories and Implements

In the colonial days of our country, fireplaces provided heat in the winter and were used year round to cook food in the kitchen. The implements that were a necessary part of these functions were varied and have become treasured collectibles, many put to new use in modern homes as decorative accessories. Gypsy pots may hold magazines; copper and brass kettles, newly polished and gleaming, contain dried flowers or green plants. Firebacks, highly ornamental iron panels that once reflected heat and protected masonry walls, are now sometimes used as wall decorations. By Victorian times the cook stove had replaced the kitchen fireplace, and many of these early utensils were already obsolete; but as a source of heat and comfort, the fireplace continued to be used for several more decades. See also Wrought Iron.

Andirons, bell metal & iron, Fed style, 1800s, pr 1,000.00
Andirons, brass, Fed, urn finial, ball & claw ft, 1800-15, 22"..1,850.00
Andirons, brass w/EX detail & paw ft, reeded/tapered columns, 20th C ..325.00
Andirons, bronze w/gilt, sphinx forms w/openwork, 16½" 1,725.00
Andirons, CI, Geo WA, standing in waistcoat & boots, pnt, 15"..1,765.00
Andirons, CI, Hessian soldier, rpr, 8⅞x5¾x10¼" 460.00

Andirons, cast iron, Neo-Classical style with Liberty bearing fruit, ram's head drape-and-swag bases, American, late nineteenth century, 17½", $715.00 for the pair.

Andirons, CI w/emb sunflowers, polychromed, late 1800s, 21" ...1,500.00
Bellows, dk mustard w/4-color fruit stencil, 18", VG 110.00
Bellows, turtle-bk; mustard w/red & gold stencil tulips, gr bands, 17" ..220.00
Bellows, wood, leather & brass w/mc pnt, Am, 1800s, 18½" 750.00
Coal bucket, dvtl copper, Dutch, 10x9" 275.00
Coal bucket, hand-hammered copper, wrought-iron hdl, 18"......175.00
Crane, wrought iron, swinging, 1840-50, 14¾", minimum value...175.00
Fender, brass, Late Regency, pierced frieze/gadrooning, 47" 575.00
Fender, brass & wire w/ring-trn finials, D form, 1840s, 15x44"...1,325.00
Fender, brass D-form rim w/ball finials, vertical wire scrolls, 44" ..2,000.00
Fender, brass/wire D form, ca 1800, 10½x39½x13" 800.00
Fender, steel & iron, scalloped w/rtcl & ornate lining, 12x40x14"......865.00
Fireback, sheet copper w/emb peacock, in wrought-iron fr, 28x17".....275.00
Fork, toasting; brass, pierced design, from 18-20".......................60.00
Grate, pierced/eng brass & CI, urn finials, 1780s, 28x25x13"...2,750.00
Kettle shelf, wrought iron, penny ft, twisted iron X-member, 12"...190.00
Kettle stand, wrought iron & brass, trn wood hdl, 7x15x9" 550.00
Log bin, hammered copper, brass paw ft, early 1800s, 27x22"..2,700.00
Poker, CI w/brass top 28.00
Roaster, iron w/tin hood, hinged door, wide spout, 19th C, 22x26x12"..800.00
Screen, cvd rosewood w/needlepoint hawk scene, 1850s, 43x28" ..1,100.00
Scuttle, hammered copper w/emb florals at top, Vict, 18"...........300.00
Scuttle, japanned tin, hinged lid, chinoiserie panel, 1880s, 15x10" .400.00
Toaster, wrought iron, rotary type, dbl arch & scroll decor, 16x16"...260.00
Toaster, wrought iron, 2 wide stubby ft, curled hdl rest, 16" L 295.00
Tongs, brass, scissors type, 10½"...75.00
Trivet, brass, folding style, 7½x24" 800.00

Fishing Collectibles

Collecting old fishing tackle is becoming more popular every year. Though at first most interest was geared toward old lures and some reels, rods, advertising, and miscellaneous items are quickly gaining ground. Values are given for examples in excellent or better condition and should be used only as a guide. For more information we recommend *19th-Century Fishing Lures* by Arlan Carter; *The Fishing Lure Collector's Bible* by

R.L. Streater with Dudley Murphy and Rick Edmisten; *Fishing Lure Collectibles* by Dudley Murphy and Rick Edmisten; *Collector's Encyclopedia of Creek Chub Lures and Collectibles, Second Edition*, by Harold E. Smith, MD; *Commercial Fish Decoys* by Frank R. Baron; *The Heddon Legacy* by Bill Roberts and Rob Pavey; and *Modern Fishing Lure Collectibles* by Russel Lewis. All are published by Collector Books. Our advisor for this category is Dave Hoover; he is listed in the Directory under Indiana.

Key:
BE — bead eyes   PE — painted eyes
GE — glass eyes   TE — tack eyes

Bucket, minnow; Climax Lifesaver, pnt tin, bail hdl, 7½x9", EX .40.00
Bucket, minnow; copper, perforated lid, bail hdl, oval, 7" 50.00
Creel, classic split willow, slant lid, rawhide hinges, 8x12x9" 300.00
Creel, turtle; tooled leather/tight rattan, bulbous, EX 2,600.00
Creel, woven splint, plywood lid, leather shoulder strap, 7x16x10" ..165.00
Creel harness, Ray Salminen, horsehide w/brass hdw, EX 65.00
Decoy, catfish, cvd/pnt w/metal fins & weight, 1900, 2x8" 400.00
Decoy, LeRoy Howell, blk on wht w/metal fins & tail, 7¾" 550.00
Decoy, LeRoy Howell, sunfish w/metal fins, wooden tail, 4¼" ...825.00
Decoy, turtle, cvd/pnt wood w/metal fins, BE, 1910, 8" 880.00
Gaff, brass, telescoping, retractable hook guard, extended: 34"...135.00
Gaff, Hardy Bros Ltd, collapsible alloy, brass hook guard, open: 37" ..55.00
Lure, Coast Minnow, single hook, 5¼", from $300 to 350.00
Lure, Creek Chub, #7000, blk bead eyes, 2 trebles, 2¾", $40 to ...60.00
Lure, Creek Chub, Dinger #5600, 1 treble, 2", from $50 to 60.00

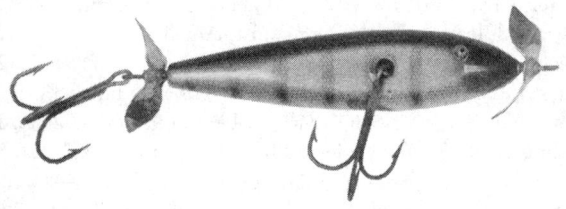

Lure, Creek Chub Musky Injured Minnow, perch scale finish, glass eyes, treble hooks, handmade props, 5", NM, $1,500.00.

Lure, Creek Chub, Pikie Minnow #700, 3 trebles, 4¼", from $40 to ..60.00
Lure, Creek Chub, Sinful Sal #S20, 1 treble, 2¾", from $40 to 50.00
Lure, Creek Chub, Weed Bug #2800, 2 single weed guards, 2", $100 to..150.00
Lure, Fred C Keeling & Co, Bearcat, 2 trebles, ca 1920, 3⅞", $40 to ..50.00
Lure, Heddon, Black Sucker #1300, 3 trebles, L rig, 5¾", $750 to ...800.00
Lure, Heddon, Crazy Crawler, 2 trebles, movable wings, 2½", $30 to.......40.00
Lure, Heddon, Darting Zara #660, 3 trebles, 3⅝", from $100 to..125.00
Lure, Heddon, Dowagiac Minnow #20, 3 trebles, prop cup rig, 2¼".125.00
Lure, Heddon, Husky Minnow #300, 6 trebles, 3¾", from $250 to...300.00
Lure, Heddon, Killer #450, 3 trebles, brass hdw, 2⅝", from $300 to..400.00
Lure, Heddon, River Runt #110, 2 trebles/2-pc hook rig, 2⅝", $40 to.65.00
Lure, Heddon, Surface #200, 4 trebles, L hook rig, 4¾", $250 to ..300.00
Lure, Heddon, Wiggle-King #2000, 3 dbls, 3¾", from $50 to........75.00
Lure, Jamison, #1 Coaxer, 1 fixed single hook, felt wings, 1½" 45.00
Lure, Jamison, Fly Rod Wiggler, 1 dbl hook, 2⅛", from $40 to 60.00
Lure, Jamison, Smacker, single dressed hook, 6", from $10 to 25.00
Lure, Keeling, Bass Crawfish, 2 trebles, 2½", from $60 to 75.00
Lure, Keeling, Long Tom, 3 trebles, 4", from $50 to 75.00
Lure, Keeling, Round Expert, 3 special trebles, 2½", from $150 to..175.00
Lure, Moonlight, Great Injured Minnow, 2 trebles, late 1920s, 4"...100.00
Lure, Moonlight, Underwater Minnow, 2 trebles, ca 1912, 2¾".350.00
Lure, Moonlight, Wobbler, 3 trebles, ca 1923, 4", from $50 to 75.00
Lure, Paw Paw, Pike Caster, 3 trebles, 1940, 4", from $50 to.........75.00

Lure, Pflueger, Bender, 2 trebles, 4⅛", from $150 to....................200.00
Lure, Pflueger, Champion Minnow, 5 trebles, 3¾", from $75 to ...125.00
Lure, Pflueger, Competitor Minnow, 3 trebles, 2½-5", from $125 to 175.00
Lure, Pflueger, Conrad Frog, single hook, airbrushed, 3", from $30 to 50.00
Lure, Pflueger, Flocked Mouse, 2 trebles, Mustang lip, 2¾", $150 to 200.00
Lure, Pflueger, Kent Floater, 3 trebles, Dmn P on propellers, 2¼".........250.00
Lure, Pflueger, Kornish Frog, 1 treble, 1910, 2", from $25 to.........40.00
Lure, Pflueger, Muskellunge Minnow, 3 singles, ca 1895, 7", $300 to...400.00
Lure, Pflueger, Surprise Minnow #3900, 3 trebles, 1915, 3¾", $75 to...125.00
Lure, Shakespeare, Bass-A-Lure #6591, 2 trebles, GE, 3⅜", $75 to 100.00
Lure, Shakespeare, Floating Wooden Minnow #31, 2 trebles, 1907, 2¾"..125.00
Lure, Shakespeare, Injun Joe #6593, 1 feathered treble, 2¼", $45 to...75.00
Lure, Shakespeare, Jim Dandy Surface Bait, 2 trebles, 1930, 2¾".75.00
Lure, Shakespeare, Kazoo Minnow #44, 5 trebles, 3¾", from $75 to ..125.00
Lure, Shakespeare, Midget Underwater #6600, 1 treble, 1930, 2" ...100.00
Lure, Shakespeare, Musky Minnow #64, 5 trebles, 5¼", from $500 to.600.00
Lure, Shakespeare, Revolution, 3 trebles, 1902, 3½", from $150 to......200.00
Lure, Shakespeare, Rubber Frog, 1 treble, pnt rubber, 2⅜", $75 to 100.00
Lure, Shakespeare, Sure Lure, 1 treble, pnt rubber, 2¾", $300 to ..400.00
Lure, South Bend, Bass-Oreno, 3 trebles, red/wht, 3½", from $80 to ..90.00
Lure, South Bend, Fish-Oreno #953, 2 trebles, 3½", from $15 to .30.00
Lure, South Bend, Gulf-Oreno #983, 2 trebles, 1926, 3½", $50 to..75.00
Lure, South Bend, Min-Buck Minnow #945, 5 trebles, 1919, 3⅝" ..115.00
Lure, South Bend, Surface Minnow, 3 trebles, 3⅝", from $125 to ...150.00
Lure, South Bend, Troll-Oreno #978, 3 trebles, 1920, 5⅞", $40 to....60.00
Lure, South Bend, Two-Oreno #975, 2 trebles, TE, 3¾", from $15 to ...30.00
Lure, South Bend, Underwater Minnow #903, 3 trebles, 3", from $50 to...75.00
Lure, Wilson, Bassmerizer, 2 trebles, 3⅝", from $100 to..............150.00
Lure, Wilson, Cupped Wobbler, 3 trebles, 1915, 4", from $30 to ..40.00
Lure, Wilson, Sizzler, 2 singles, 1915, 2¼", from $50 to 100.00
Reel, Julius Von Hofe NY, crank hdl, sz 3, plain hard rubber plates ..880.00
Reel, Julius Von Hofe Pat Oct 8 89, sz 3, silver & hard rubber ...550.00
Reel, Talbot Reel & Mfg Co..., German silver, EX 385.00
Rod, bass; HL Leonard/Leonard & Mills Co, 3-pc, 2-tip, rattan hdl, 6' ..275.00
Rod, fly; Heddon #13, 3-pc, 2-tip, ca 1936, 9'6", EX...................110.00
Rod, fly; Ron Kusse Grilse Model, mirror finish, 8' 990.00
Rod, salmon; Orvis-Wes Jordan, 2-pc 2-tip, 8'6", M in orig case ...635.00
Rod, trout; EF Payne Rod Co, 3-pc, 2-tip, 9'6", EX rstr...............330.00
Rod, trout; GH Howells #3944, 2-pc, 2-tip, 8'9", MM in bag..1,700.00
Rod, trout; Heddon #10, 3-pc, 2-tip, #2½ ferrule, 9', VG...........160.00
Rod, trout; Phillipson Paragon #59, 3-pc, 2-tip, 8'6", NM 385.00
Rod, trout; Wright & McGill Granger Special, 3-pc, 2-tip, 9', EX..230.00

Flags of the United States

Over the past few years the popularity of vintage flags has grown dramatically, and prices have risen greatly as a result. The pending restoration of the Fort McHenry Flag (The Star Spangled Banner) has also created greater public interest in flag collecting.

The brevity and imprecise language of the first Flag Act of 1777 allowed great artistic license for America's early flag makers. This resulted in a rich variety of imaginative star formations which coexisted with more conventional row patterns. In 1912 inviolate design standards were established for the new 48-star flag, but the banners of our earlier history continue to survive:

The 'Great Star' pattern — configured from the combined stars of the union, appeared in various star denominations for about 50 years, then gradually disappeared in the post-Civil War years.

The utilitarian 'scatter' pattern — created through the random placement of stars, is traceable to the formative years of our nation and remained a design influence through most of the nineteenth century.

The 'wreath' pattern — first appearing in the form of simple single-wreath formations, eventually evolved into the elegant double- and triple-wreath medallion patterns of the Centennial period.

Acquisition of specific star denominations is also a primary consideration in the collecting process. Pre-Civil War flags of 33 stars or less are very scarce and are typically treated as 'blue chip' items. Civil War-era flags of 34 and 35 stars also stand among the most sought-after denominations. Market demand for 36-, 37-, and 38-star flags is strong but less broad-based, while interest in the unofficial 39-, 40-, 41-, and 42-star examples is largely confined to flag aficionados. The very rare 43 remains in a class by itself and is guaranteed to attract the attention of the serious collector.

Row-patterned flags of 44, 45, and 46 stars still turn up with some frequency and serve as a source of more modestly priced vintage flags. Ordinary 48-star flags flood the flea markets and are priced accordingly, while the short-lived 49 is regarded as a legitimate collectible. Flags with 13 stars, produced over a period of more than 200 years, surface in many forms and must be assessed on a case-by-case basis.

Many flag buffs favor sizes that are manageable for wall display, while others are attracted to the more monumental proportions. Allowances are typically made for the normal wear and tear — it goes with the territory. But severe fabric deterioration and other forms of excessive physical damage are legitimate points of negotiation.

The dollar value of a flag is by no means based upon age alone. The wide price swings in the listing below have been influenced by a variety of determining factors related to age, scarcity, and aesthetic merit. In fact, almost any special feature that stands out as unusual or distinctive is a potential asset. Imprinted flags and inscribed flags; 8-point stars, gold stars, and added stars; extra stripes, missing stripes, tricolor stripes and war stripes are all part of the pricing equation. And while political and military flags may rank above all others in terms of prestige and price, any flag with a significant and well-documented historical connection has 'star' potential (pardon the pun). Our advisor for this category is Ryan Cooper; he is listed in the Directory under Massachusetts.

13 stars, circular pattern, hand sewn, 1860s.............................**2,800.00**
13 stars, hand/machine sewn, Centennial...................................**850.00**
13 stars, printed glazed muslin, 1880s, 7x11"..............................**200.00**
13 stars, US Naval boat insignia, 1880, 50x96"...........................**750.00**
15 stars, union jack from War of 1812, rare, 35x62".............**23,000.00**
15 stars, 15 stripes, all machine sewn, ca 1912, 48x72"..............**375.00**

16 stars, Great Star, hand sewn, 1850s, 54x78", 9,500.00.

19 stars, 16 orig+3, sewn scrap fabric, 39x66"............................**7,500.00**
20 stars, oval pattern, ship's flag, 1818, worn, 64x128"............**6,500.00**
21 stars, Commissioning pennant, ship 'Herald,' 1819, 50'......**8,500.00**
25 stars, oval pattern w/central star, ship's flag, 96x200".........**6,700.00**
25 stars, row pattern, Civil War, 90x175".................................**2,200.00**
26 stars, Great Star, embr on sewn silk, 30x43".......................**8,500.00**

29 stars, entirely hand sewn, poor condition, 43x68"..............**3,500.00**
30 stars, gold stars/fringe, silk, delicate, 52x68".......................**4,500.00**
31 stars, Great Star, hand-sewn silk, 14'...................................**4,000.00**
31 stars, row pattern, hand-stitched bunting, 104x247".........**2,500.00**
32 stars, dbl wreath of inset stars, hand sewn, 36x48".............**5,200.00**
33 stars, Great Star, hand-sewn muslin, 60x96".......................**5,000.00**
33 stars, hand-/machine-sewn wool bunting, 66x92"...............**2,250.00**
33 stars, in rows, printed bunting, 28x44", G-...........................**1,000.00**
34 stars, dbl-wreath pattern, printed silk, 18x28"...................**1,200.00**
34 stars, Great Star, from Albany RR Depot, 116x175"..........**4,500.00**
34 stars, printed linen, 3 sewn sections, 22x48"...........................**600.00**
34 stars, random pattern, hand sewn, 66x140"........................**1,200.00**
35 stars, dbl-wreath pattern, printed, sized muslin, 19x28"......**1,200.00**
35 stars, recruiting flag, sewn bunting, 50x116".......................**1,800.00**
35 stars, row pattern, hand/machine sewn, 96x180"...............**1,200.00**
36 stars, cut-in, in rows, machined stripes, 25x50"...................**1,000.00**
36 stars, inscr parade flag, muslin print, 6x9"..............................**250.00**
36 stars, sailing ship's, inscr & dtd, 75x142".................................**950.00**
37 stars, medallion pattern, printed/sewn muslin, 48x87"...........**550.00**
37 stars, printed silk, 32x40"...**300.00**
37 stars, row pattern, hand-sewn silk, poor, 60x80".....................**350.00**
37 stars, row pattern, stitched bunting, 30x48"............................**600.00**
38 stars, medallion-wreath pattern, printed cotton, 12x17"........**325.00**
38 stars, printed silk w/ribbon ties, 30x47".................................**350.00**
38 stars, row pattern, clamp dyed in 3 sections, 60x120"............**325.00**
38 stars, row pattern, hand/machine-stitched bunting, 71x116".**350.00**
38 stars, unique wreath pattern, sewn, 89x134"...........................**800.00**
38 stars, 1776-1876 pattern, printed linen, 27½x46"..............**1,800.00**
39 stars, Centennial 'International Flag,' 16x24".........................**200.00**
39 stars, row pattern, all machine-stitched bunting, 40x84".......**350.00**
39 stars, row pattern variation, printed silk, 12x24"...................**125.00**
39 stars (6-5 pattern), printed gauze bunting, 19x34"................**125.00**
40 stars, row pattern, hand-sewn bunting, lg, 98x204"...............**270.00**
40 stars, row pattern, printed/sewn British import, 55x106".......**185.00**
41 stars (rare), printed cotton sheeting, 15x24"..........................**275.00**
42 stars, sewn cotton, from Ft Hamilton NY, 120x177".............**275.00**
42 stars, 7-row pattern, printed cotton, 12x17"..........................**125.00**
43 stars, machine-sewn bunting, extremely rare, 29x70".........**1,200.00**
44 stars, machine-sewn cotton bunting, 53x82".........................**200.00**
44 stars, triple-wreath pattern, printed cotton, 23x26"..............**350.00**
45 stars, HP w/sewn stripes, 38x70"..**120.00**
45 stars, machine-sewn cotton bunting, 80x108"..........................**55.00**
45 stars, printed silk w/red ribbon ties, 32x46"............................**45.00**
45 stars, row pattern variant, printed muslin, 9x13"......................**25.00**
46 stars, machine-sewn wool bunting, 72x138"............................**60.00**
46 stars, printed silk, GAR Post in gold, 32x45"..........................**350.00**
47 stars, unofficial, sewn bunting, 108x137"...............................**350.00**
48 stars, all crocheted, dtd 1941, 20x38"......................................**85.00**
48 stars, machine-sewn cotton bunting, 60x96"............................**50.00**
48 stars, printed cotton w/GAR surprint, 11x16"..........................**40.00**
48 stars, sewn to form 'USA,' unauthorized WWI, 45x69".........**300.00**
48 stars, USN Union Jack, machine-sewn wool, 23x33"...............**35.00**
48 stars in gold, sewn WWII casket flag, 58x118"........................**95.00**
49 stars, embr, sewn stripes, 36x60"..**45.00**
49 stars, 3 uncut flags, printed cotton sheet, 37x36"....................**25.00**
50 stars, early prototype 'June 1959,' 52x66".............................**220.00**
50 stars, hand-knitted coverlet w/fringe, 30x51"..........................**30.00**
51 stars, printed flaglette for DC statehood, 4x6".........................**15.00**

Florence Ceramics

Figurines marked 'Florence Ceramics' were produced in the '40s and '50s in Pasadena, California. The quality of the ware and the attention given to detail are prompting a growing interest among today's collectors. The names of these lovely ladies, gents, and figural groups are nearly always incised into their bases. The company name is ink stamped. Examples are evaluated by size, rarity, and intricacy of design. For more information we recommend *The Collector's Encyclopedia of California Pottery, Second Edition,* by Jack Chipman, who is listed in the Directory under California; *The Florence Collectibles* by Doug Foland, and *The Complete Book of Florence Ceramics: A Labor of Love* by Sue and Jerry Kline and Margaret Wehrspaun. Our advisor for this category is Jerry Kline; he is listed in the Directory under Tennessee.

Anita, brocade, rare, 15", from $2,750 to	3,000.00
Bea, 7¼", from $135 to	150.00
Blondi & Sandy, rare, 7½", pr, from $2,500 to	3,000.00
Blue Boy, 12", from $400 to	450.00
Butch, 5½", from $175 to	200.00
Camille, plain, 8½", from $225 to	250.00
Carmen, rare, 12½", from $2,750 to	3,000.00
Caroline, brocade, rare, 15", from $3,000 to	3,500.00
Clarissa, lamp, 7¾", from $500 to	550.00
Colleen, 8", from $275 to	300.00
David, 7½", from $125 to	140.00
Dear Ruth, TV lamp, rare, 9", from $1,200 to	1,400.00
Delia, yel, hand showing, 7¼", from $325 to	375.00
Denise, 10", from $800 to	850.00
Don, prom boy, 9½", from $425 to	475.00
Dot & Bud, rare, 7½", pr, from $1,400 to	1,500.00
Elaine, Godey girl, matt, 6", from $60 to	70.00
Emily, flower holder, 8", from $50 to	60.00
Eugenia, 9", from $450 to	500.00
Eve, 8½", from $375 to	425.00
Fair Lady, rare, 11½", from $3,250 to	3,500.00
Fern, flower holder, no gold, 7", from $115 to	125.00
Georgia, brocade, rare, 13½", from $2,750 to	3,000.00
Halloween Child, rare, 4", from $600 to	700.00
Jennifer, 7¾", from $450 to	500.00
Jim, child, 6¼", from $60 to	70.00
John Alden, 9¼", from $250 to	275.00
Jose, peasant man w/cart, rare, from $650 to	700.00
Joy, child, 6", from $175 to	200.00
Julie, 7¼", from $200 to	250.00
Karla, ballerina, 9¾", from $450 to	500.00
Kiu & She-Ti, 10¼", pr, from $450 to	500.00
Lady Diana, 10", from $1,250 to	1,400.00
Lea, flower holder, 6", from $80 to	100.00
Lillian Russell, rare, 15", from $2,700 to	2,900.00
Little Don, pajamas, rare, 5½", from $2,250 to	2,500.00
Lorry Young Teen, rare, 8", from $1,200 to	1,400.00
Love Letter, rare, 10", from $2,250 to	2,500.00
Madonna, 10", from $150 to	175.00
Madonna & Child, bust, 4¾", from $400 to	450.00
Margaret, rare, 9¾", from $1,600 to	1,750.00
Marie Antoinette, 10", from $375 to	400.00
Martha, 8¼", from $600 to	650.00
Master David, rare, 8", from $500 to	550.00
Memories, 5¾x6½", from $1,250 to	1,400.00
Merry Maids, Betty, Jane or Rosie, shell bowl, ea, $200 to	225.00
Mimi, flower holder, 6", from $70 to	80.00
Nell Gwenn, rare, 10", from $2,500 to	2,750.00
Patsy, flower holder, 6", from $50 to	60.00
Peter, rare, 9¼", from $500 to	550.00
Pinkie, 12", from $400 to	450.00
Reggie, 7½", from $400 to	450.00
Rosalie, 9½", from $1,000 to	1,100.00

Sarah Bernhardt, very rare, 13¼", from $3,500 to	4,000.00
Story Hour, w/boy & girl, 8", from $1,100 to	1,250.00
Summer, 6¼", from $400 to	450.00
Toy, 9", from $325 to	350.00

Victoria, from $575.00 to $625.00. (Photo courtesy Doug Foland)

Virginia, brocade, rare, 15", from $3,000 to	3,500.00
Vivian, lamp, 10", from $550 to	650.00
Yvonne, plain, 8¾", from $425 to	450.00

Florentine Cameo

Although the appearance may look much like English cameo, the decoration on this type of glass is not wheel cut or acid etched. Instead a type of heavy paste — usually a frosty white — is applied to the surface to create a look very similar to true cameo. It was produced in France as well as England; it is sometimes marked 'Florentine.'

Vase, pk w/daffodils, 5", pr	125.00
Vase, pk w/robin & berry bush, 10"	145.00

Flow Blue

Flow Blue ware was produced by many Staffordshire potters; among the most familiar were Meigh, Podmore and Walker, Samuel Alcock, Ridgway, John Wedge Wood (who often signed his work Wedgewood), and Davenport. It was popular from about 1825 through 1860 and again from 1880 until after the turn of the century. The name describes the blurred or flowing affect of the cobalt decoration, achieved through the introduction of a chemical vapor into the kiln. The body of the ware is ironstone, and Oriental motifs were favored. Later issues were on a lighter body and often decorated with gilt. For further information we recommend *The Collector's Encyclopedia of Flow Blue China* (1st and 2nd series) by Mary Frank Gaston (Collector Books).

Abbey, chocolate pot, Geo Jones, 10"	235.00
Abbey, wash bowl & pitcher, Geo Jones	2,000.00
Amoy, bowl, berry; Davenport, 5¼"	175.00
Amoy, pitcher, att Adams, 7"	800.00
Amoy, pitcher, WE & Co (Wm Emberton & Co), mid-1800s, 6½"	550.00
Amoy, platter, Davenport, 12½x9¼", NM	350.00
Amoy, sugar bowl, octagonal, 8", EX	500.00
Amoy, tea bowl & saucer, Davenport, 3", 6¼"	150.00
Argyle, tray, 6-sided, Ford & Sons, 9x6¼"	200.00
Arundel, salad fork & spoon, Doulton, pr	225.00
Astoria, pitcher, New Wharf Pottery, 6¾"	350.00
Auld Lang Syne, cup, R&M Co, 3½x5½"	95.00
Beauties of China, pitcher, Mellor Venables & Co, 7½"	900.00
Beauties of China, plate, Mellor Venables & Co, 9½"	150.00
Belmont, plate, Weatherby & Sons, 9"	90.00
Belmont, waste jar, w/lid, Meakin, 16x14"	850.00

Blue Danube, saucer, gold trim, Johnson Bros, 6½" 25.00
Bouquet, cuspidor, Furnival, 2½x8" 900.00
Bouquet, plate, Alcock, 9" 90.00
Brunswick, cup & saucer, New Wharf Pottery, 3½", 5¾" 90.00
Burleigh, platter, Burgess & Leigh, 16" 450.00
Cambrian, cup plate, 4", NM 80.00
Cambridge, cup & saucer, Meakin, 3", 6" 100.00
Cambridge, relish, Meakin, 8½x5¼" 125.00
Carlton, platter, Ford & Sons, 12½x9", NM 170.00
Cashmere, jam dish & underplate, lions' head hdls, Ridgway & Morley....850.00
Chapoo, tea bowl & saucer, John Wedge Wood, 3", 6" 200.00
Chinese, pitcher, Dimmock, 9" 550.00
Chinese, plate, Bourne & Leigh, 9½" 200.00
Chinese, sugar bowl, ftd, Dimmock, 8x6¾" 600.00
Chinese, vase, Wedgwood Etruria, 12" 900.00
Chiswick, cup & saucer, Ridgway, 1912-20, 2½x3¾", 6⅛" 155.00
Chiswick, saucer, smooth rim, Ridgway 20.00
Chusan, punch bowl, unmk, 7x12" 1,800.00
Chusan, saucer, att Peter Holdcroft & Co 50.00
Chusan, sugar bowl, w/lid, Clementson, 8" 750.00
Chusan, teacup, hdld, Holdcroft, ca 1830 ....195.00
Coburg, plate, John Edwards, 8" 125.00
Coburg, platter, att Barker & Kent, 13x10½" 300.00
Colonial, bowl, vegetable; w/lid, Meakin, 7x10" 275.00
Colonial, plate, 8⅞" 80.00
Coral, plate, soup; Johnson Bros, 9" 65.00
Coral, sugar bowl, w/lid, Johnson Bros, 5½" 175.00
Crescent, bowl, vegetable; rectangular, Grindley, 10x8" 165.00
Crescent, cake plate, Grindley, 14x13¼" 150.00
Crumlin, pitcher, Myott, 10" 450.00
Crumlin, plate, Myott, 9" 85.00
Dahlia, platter, att E Challinor, 10¾x8¼" 300.00
Dahlia, sugar bowl, w/lid, att E Challinor, 7½" 500.00
Davenport, plate, Hollinshead & Kirkham, 6½" sq 40.00
Devon, platter, Meakin, 14x10" 275.00
Dorothy, bone dish, Upper Hanley, 6½", EX, 6 for 200.00
Douglas, bowl, vegetable; w/lid, Ford & Sons, 11x8" 325.00
Dundee, creamer, Ridgway, 5½" 180.00
Eclipse, bowl, berry, Johnson Bros, 5¼" 32.50
Elsie, creamer, New Wharf Pottery 95.00
Empress, platter, Wedgwood, 15¼x12¼" 285.00
Ferrara, pitcher, Wedgwood, 6" 325.00
Florida, bowl, vegetable; w/lid, Johnson Bros 450.00
Florida, platter, 6-sided, Johnson Bros, 15x10" 400.00
Forget-Me-Not, bowl, vegetable; w/lid, 12x6", NM 595.00
Geisha, bowl, Upper Hanley Pottery, 10" 170.00
Geisha, plate, bread & butter; Ford & Sons, 7" 50.00
Gironde, bowl, berry; Grindley, 6" 27.50
Gironde, bowl, sauce; scalloped rim, Grindley, 6" 40.00
Gironde, cup & saucer, Grindley, 2", 6" 85.00
Haddon, charger, Grindley, 12½" 395.00
Haddon, platter, oval, Grindley, 16¼x11½" 275.00
Hollyhock, plate, Wedgwood, 10½" 80.00
Hollyhock, platter, Wedgwood, 10x7¼" 175.00
Hong Kong, bowl, Meigh, 8" 300.00
Indian Tree & Flower, cup plate, paneled rim, 4¼" 70.00
Indian Vase, platter, S&EH, 12½x10" 500.00
Iris, bowl, soup; Staffordshire, 8" 78.00
Iris, plate, dinner; Staffordshire, 9" 85.00
Iris, plate, sponged gold around fluted rim, Cauldon, 10" 85.00
Iris, plate, wide cobalt border, W&E Corn, 9" 75.00
Japan, plate, mc o/l w/gold, 9¼" 80.00
Japan, platter, Fell, 10¼x8", NM 80.00
Japan, teapot, ped ft, T Fell 900.00

Jedo, plate, W Adams & Sons, 10" 140.00
Jedo, tea bowl & saucer, Adams, 3", 6" 180.00
Jewel, plate, Bourne & Leigh, 8" 35.00
Jewel, saucer, Johnson Bros, 6½" 15.00
La Belle, bowl, serving; scalloped rim, Wheeling, 3x11¼x9¼", EX ..175.00
La Belle, bowl, serving; Wheeling, 3x11¼x9¼" 275.00
La Belle, compote, 4-ftd, Wheeling, 5¾x13½x10¾", NM 550.00
La Belle, ice cream tray, Wheeling, 13" 350.00
La Pavot, bowl, vegetable; w/lid, Grindley, 11x7" 300.00
Ladas, gravy boat & underplate, emb decor/gold trim, Ridgway, 8¾" ...165.00
Lakewood, cup & saucer, gold o/l, Wood & Son, 2", 4" 90.00
Lakewood, tureen, w/lid & ladle, Wood 750.00
Lonsdale, cup & saucer, Royal Semi Porcelain 110.00
Lonsdale, gravy boat, gold trim, Samuel Ford & Co 90.00
Lonsdale, tray, SF&Co, 11½x9¼" 250.00
Lorne, bowl, vegetable; oval, Grindley, 9¼" 135.00
Lorne, creamer & sugar bowl 400.00
Madras, pitcher, Royal Doulton, 8½" 700.00
Madras, platter, Doulton, 16" 500.00
Magnolia, cup & saucer 60.00
Magnolia, platter, 11x8" 275.00
Manhattan, plate, soup; Alcock, 9" 70.00
Marechal Neil, bowl, fruit/cereal; Grindley, 6" 50.00
Marechal Neil, sugar bowl, w/lid, Grindley 165.00
Melbourne, bowl, Grindley, 9½" sq 100.00
Melbourne, bowl, oval, 10" 95.00
Melrose, bowl, soup; New Wharf Pottery, 9" 65.00
Melrose, plate, Doulton, 8½" 70.00
Nankin, plate, Doulton, 10½" 95.00
Nankin, teapot, ped ft, att Cauldon 900.00
Non Pareil, bowl, vegetable; rectangular, Burgess & Leigh, 9½" ...350.00
Non Pareil, butter dish, wht drainer insert, 4x8x7¼", EX 275.00
Non Pareil, cup saucer, punch; Burgess & Leigh, NM 150.00
Non Pareil, pitcher, milk; Burgess & Leigh, 7¾" 650.00
Non Pareil, waste bowl, Burgess & Leigh, 3x5¾" 225.00
Oregon, bowl, vegetable; oval, ftd, w/lid, Johnson Bros, 11½x9½" ...300.00
Oregon, plate, Mayer, 7½" 75.00
Oregon, sugar bowl, w/lid, ped ft, Mayer 650.00
Ormonde, cup & saucer, Meakin, 3", 6" 100.00
Ormonde, waste jar, Meakin, 13½" 750.00
Osborne, bone dish, Ridgway, 3½x6" 48.00
Osborne, creamer, Ridgway, 4" 150.00
Paris, bowl, New Wharf Pottery, 9" 155.00
Paris, plate, New Wharf Pottery, 9" 80.00
Peach, bowl, berry; Johnson Bros, 5" 25.00
Peach, platter, Johnson Bros, 17x14" 350.00
Pekin, platter, Jones, 12½" 250.00
Pekin, tea bowl & saucer, Dimmock 150.00
Penang, plate, Ridgway, 9¼" 175.00
Penang, platter, rectangular, Ridgway, 16x12" 850.00
Regent, plate, unidentified manufacturer, 9" 75.00
Regent, soup tureen, w/lid, Meakin, 8½x12½", +13" ladle 1,500.00
Roseville, compote, ftd, gold trim, Maddock, 4x9" 425.00
Roseville, platter, Maddock, 14½x10" 300.00
Savoy, platter, Empire Porcelain, 13½x10½" 250.00
Savoy, sugar bowl, w/lid, Johnson Bros 185.00
Scinde, bowl, Alcock, 1¼x9½" 125.00
Scinde, bowl, sauce; Alcock, 5", NM 60.00
Scinde, bowl, soup; Alcock, 10½", from $125 to 175.00
Scinde, bowl, vegetable; Alcock, 2¾x11¾x9", NM 375.00
Scinde, bowl, vegetable; rectangular, Alcock, 1¾x9½x7" 250.00
Scinde, cup plate, Alcock, 4¼" 150.00
Scinde, plate, Alcock, 8¼" 175.00
Scinde, plate, Alcock, 10½", NM 150.00

Scinde, platter, Alcock, 12½x10½"...................................600.00
Scinde, platter, Alcock, 16¼x12½", NM.........................500.00

Seville, teapot, $495.00.

Shanghae, relish, 1-hdl, Furnival.....................................250.00
Shanghae, sugar bowl, ped ft, w/lid, Furnival................750.00
Shanghae, teapot, oval, Furnival, 5¼", NM.....................250.00
Shanghai, plate, paneled shape, Adams, 9¼"...................150.00
Shapoo, cup & saucer, Hughes, 2¼", 4½"........................90.00
Shapoo, cup plate, Thomas Hughes, 4⅛"..........................90.00
Shapoo, plate, T&R Boote, 10"..150.00
Temple, cup & saucer, Podmore Walker, 3", 6".............165.00
Temple, plate, Podmore Walker, 10"..............................175.00
Tonquin, platter, Adams & Sons, 13½x10¼", NM.........250.00
Tonquin, platter, Clementson & Young, 18x14"...........1,100.00
Tonquin, platter, Heath, 14"...600.00
Touraine, bowl, soup; Stanley, 1½x8¾", pr....................125.00
Touraine, bowl, vegetable; w/lid, 12x7", NM..................550.00
Touraine, pitcher, milk; sm...450.00
Touraine, plate, Alcock, 10", EX......................................75.00
Trent, plate, New Wharf Pottery, 10".............................80.00
Trent, tureen, rpr to hdl, w/lid, Ford & Son, 6x11".......110.00
Turin, plate, dessert; Johnson Bros, 6¼".......................32.00
Turin, plate, dinner; Johnson Bros, 10"..........................78.00
Turin, plate, luncheon; Johnson Bros, 8".......................55.00
Turkey, plate, unmk, 9½"...110.00
Turkey, platter, unmk, 18x13½".....................................450.00
Vermont, plate, soup; Burgess & Leigh, 9"......................65.00
Vermont, soup tureen, gold trim, Burgess & Leigh.......450.00
Wagon Wheel, mug, 3"...125.00
Wagon Wheel, pitcher, 3¼", NM......................................80.00
Wagon Wheel, tea set, child sz, 5½" pot+cr/sug+6 ea: c/s+plates, EX..1,000.00
Waldorf, bowl, New Wharf Pottery, 3x9".......................135.00
Waldorf, plate, New Wharf Pottery, 10"..........................95.00
Waldorf, platter, New Wharf Pottery, 11x9"..................275.00
Watteau, bowl, berry; Doulton, 5½"................................45.00
Watteau, bowl, vegetable; rectangular, w/lid, Doulton, 12".......450.00
Watteau, chocolate pot, Doulton, 8"...............................450.00
Watteau, saucer, full pattern, 5½"...................................35.00
Windsor, plate, gold trim, CT Maling, 9".........................70.00

Flue Covers

When spring housecleaning started and the heating stove was taken down for the warm weather season, the unsightly hole where the stovepipe joined the chimney was hidden with an attractive flue cover. They were made with a colorful litho print behind glass with a chain for hanging. In a 1929 catalog, they were advertised at 16¢ each or six for 80¢. Although scarce today, some scenes were actually reverse painted on the glass itself. The most popular motifs were florals, children, animals, and lovely ladies. Occasionally flue covers were made in sets of three — one served a functional purpose, while the others were added to provide a more attractive wall arrangement. They range in size from 7" to 14", but 9" is the average.

For further information we recommend *Flue Covers, Collector's Value Guide*, by Jim Meckley II, available from Collector Books or your local bookstore.

Annalisse, Victorian lady w/long brn flowing hair, 7½", from $85 to....95.00
Blueberries & Tomatoes, on shelf, 9½", from $70 to....................80.00
Box of Violets, 9½", from $75 to..85.00
Branch of Cherries, girl w/brn curls holds branch, 7x8½", $75 to...85.00
Buddies, 3 Black boys on cotton bale, 9½", from $250 to...........300.00
Carla in cape, girl w/hood over blond hair, 7¾", from $55 to.......65.00
Cherub & Stars, pensive pose, stars in border, 8", from $55 to......60.00
Clara & Kitten, girl in bl, 9½", from $60 to..................................70.00
Comforting, mother & father w/child, blk & wht, 9½", $75 to....85.00
Daddy's Girls, blond & burnette girls in pk & yel, 9½", from $60 to...70.00
Feline Love, lady w/rose in hair holds cat, 7¾", from $90 to......100.00
Fisherman, sailboat scene, 9¼", from $60 to...............................70.00
Flapper, portrait of lady in 1920s-style hat, 7¾", from $75 to.......85.00
Gift, flowers & strawberries in basket, 12", from $75 to..............85.00
Green Biretta, girl in gr hat w/flowers at ea ear, 4¾", from $55 to .65.00
Heaven's Pleasure, classical lady on swing, cherubs, 8¾", $85 to..95.00
Hunt, fox hunt scene w/riders & dogs, 9½", from $80 to.............90.00
Lassie, Collie portrait, 9½", from $75 to......................................85.00
Linda's Fruit, child w/cherries, fancy hat & curls, 9½", $75 to......85.00
Master's Son, young dandy stands beside table, 8½", from $65 to.75.00
My Friend Barney, girl in red embraces dog, 8", from $85 to........95.00
Old Gray Mare, head in profile, w/bridle, 7¾", from $70 to.........80.00
Over the Fence, couple talk at fence, 9½", from $60 to...............65.00
Parasol, Oriental child w/colorful parasol, 9½", from $50 to........60.00
Pink Chapeau, girl in lg pk hat, long curling brn hair, 7¾", $65 to ...75.00
Rebecca in Red, girl in fancy red outfit w/hat, holds flowers, 9½" ...100.00
Red Roses in Vase, 8¼x7", from $85 to......................................95.00

The Reflection, girl and cat before mirror, 9½", from $100.00 to $110.00. (Photo courtesy Jim Meckley II)

Rose Bonnet, Victorian lady in flowered hat, 9½", from $90 to .110.00
Serenade, man plays guitar to lady in interior scene, 10¼", $50 to ..60.00
Springtime, lady w/flowers in hair w/in flowered arch, 8", $55 to....65.00
Swans, group of swans on lake, landscape beyond, 10¼", from $70 to ...80.00
Teeter-Totter, 3 children & dog at play, 9½", from $70 to............80.00
Thinking, lady stands in thoughtful pose, 7¾", from $55 to.........65.00
Tresses, lady w/long flowing hair & low-cut bodice, 7¾", $55 to..65.00
Waltz, boy & girl dancing, 6½x9", from $75 to.............................85.00
Winter Magic, boy & girl in winter scene, 9½", from $85 to........95.00

Folk Art

That the creative energies of the mind ever spark innovations in functional utilitarian channels as well as toward playful frivolity is well documented in the study of American folk art. While the average early settler rarely had free time to pursue art for its own sake, his creative energy exemplified itself in fashioning useful objects carved or otherwise ornamented beyond the scope of pure practicality. After the advent of the Industrial Revolution, the pace of everyday living became more leisurely, and country folk found they had extra time. Not accustomed to sitting idle, many turned to carving, painting, or weaving. Whirligigs, imaginative toys for the children, and whimsies of all types resulted. Though often rather crude, this type of early art represents a segment of our heritage and as such has become valued by collectors.

Values given for drawings, paintings, and theorems are 'in frame' unless noted otherwise. See also Baskets; Decoys; Frakturs; Samplers; Trade Signs; Weather Vanes; Wood Carvings.

Armchair, notched & bent twigs, slat seat, 45", EX......................165.00
Birdhouse, Noah's Ark, pnt pine, 6 portholes, 1890s, 17½x26x10", VG..600.00
Calligraphic drawing, horse & dog, pen/ink on paper, 15¾x22½" 460.00
Calligraphy, bird/banner: May We Live & Be Happy, 3-color ink, 7x10".165.00
Collage on paper, eagle & shield, pnt/feathers, 13x15" 195.00
Cvg, bust of woman, limestone IN, 20th C, 15¼x15x9" 1,380.00
Cvg, head of man w/long beard, sandstone, pnt eyes, E Popeye Reed, 12" ...440.00
Cvg, Indian lady's head, limestone, E Popeye Reed, glue rpr, 12" ..220.00
Cvg, Venus stands on shell/covers herself w/her hair, limestone 17" ..1,650.00
Diorama: Adirondack cabin/shack/sawbuck on wood slab, tin roofs, 24" L.110.00
Frame, Xd corners, overall appl wood fragments suggest florals, 15x18" .1,700.00
House, made of bottle caps, 3-color pnt, 18x16x18"....................475.00
Paper cutout, concentric circles w/hearts/tulips/scrolls, PA, 10x10".......770.00
Paper cutout, squirrels/birds in tree, wht on dk bl, SS Lindsay, 8x7" ..2,800.00
Rooster, sheet iron, 3-D w/flat tail, copper rivets, w/stand: 24"...770.00
Theorem on paper, fruit bowl, Am School, 19th C, 15½x11½", VG+ ..1,265.00
Theorem on paper, watercolor, rose/columbine w/pen & ink verse, 12x10".195.00
Theorem on velvet, flower basket, unsgn, 1850s, 17x23½"+fr ...1,840.00
Theorem on velvet, fruit basket, sgn, 20th C, 11x14", +gilt fr....220.00
Theorem on velvet, fruit spilling from basket, unsgn, 19th C, 7x8"+fr...700.00
Theorem on velvet, magnolia & lilies w/foliate, EX art, 13x14".525.00
Whirligig, bathing beauty, sm sq blade ea hand, mc pnt, 9", +base...2,000.00

Whirligig, Black man waves arms, hand carved, early metal tacks for buttons, original paint, chips/cracks, 17", $1,100.00. (Photo courtesy Collectors Auction Service)

Whirligig, cottage birdhouse, mc pnt on wood, ca 1900, 13x8x18" 230.00
Whirligig, horse trotting, articulated legs, weathered pnt, 28x22x29"..375.00
Whirligig, witch on broom, pnt traces, on stand, 14x25¾" 6,300.00

Fostoria

The Fostoria Glass Company was built in 1887 at Fostoria, Ohio, but by 1891 it had moved to Moundsville, West Virginia. During the next two decades, they produced many lines of pressed patterned tableware and lamps. Their most famous pattern, American, was introduced in 1915 and was produced continuously until 1986 in well over two hundred different pieces. From 1920 to 1925, top artists designed tablewares

in colored glass — canary (vaseline), amber, blue, orchid, green, and ebony — in pressed patterns as well as etched designs. By the late '30s, Fostoria was recognized as the largest producer of handmade glassware in the world. The company ceased operations in Moundsville in 1986.

Many items from both the American and Coin Glass lines have been reproduced by Lancaster Colony. In some cases the new glass is superior in quality to the old. Since the 1950s, Indiana Glass has produced a pattern called 'Whitehall' that looks very much like Fostoria's American, though with slight variations. Because Indiana's is not handmade glass, the lines of the 'cube' pattern and the edges of the items are sharp and untapered in comparison to the fire-polished originals. Three-footed pieces lack the 'toe' and instead have a peg-like foot, and the rays on the bottoms of the American examples are narrower than on the Whitehall counterparts. The Home Interiors Company offers several pieces of American look-alikes which were not even produced in the United States. Be sure of your dealer and study the books suggested below to become more familiar with the original line.

Coin Glass reproductions are flooding the market. Among items you may encounter are an 8" round bowl, 9" oval bowl, 8¼" wedding bowl, 4½" candlesticks, urn with lid, 6¼" candy jar with lid, footed comport, sugar, and creamer; there could possibly be others. Colors in production are crystal, green, blue, and red. The red color is very good, but the blue is not the original color, nor is the emerald green. Buyer beware!

For further information see *Elegant Glassware of the Depression Era* by Gene Florence; *Fostoria Glassware, 1887 – 1982*, by Frances Bones; *Fostoria Stemware, The Crystal for America Series* (there are four books), by Milbra Long and Emily Seate; and *Fostoria, Volume II*, by Ann Kerr. *Glass Animals and Figural Flower Frogs of the Depression Era* by Lee Garmon and Dick Spencer offers an in-depth look at that particular aspect of Fostoria's production. (See also Glass Animals.) Their addresses are listed in the Directory under Illinois. Items with (+) at the end of the lines have been reproduced; prices are for original issues.

American, crystal, ashtray, oval, 5½"................................20.00
American, crystal, ashtray, sq, 2⅞" 7.50
American, crystal, bowl, banana split; 3½x9"....................495.00
American, crystal, bowl, boat; 2-part, 9" 12.50
American, crystal, bowl, deep, 8"..................................60.00
American, crystal, bowl, deep, 10"................................35.00
American, crystal, bowl, float; 10".................................45.00
American, crystal, bowl, fruit; shallow, 13" 75.00
American, crystal, bowl, lemon; w/lid, 5½"......................60.00
American, crystal, bowl, olive; oblong, 6" 12.00
American, crystal, bowl, oval, 4½"................................15.00
American, crystal, bowl, punch; w/low-ftd base, 3¾-gal, 18"......400.00
American, crystal, box, candy; w/lid, 3-part, triangular 90.00
American, crystal, box, jewel; w/lid, 5¼x2¼"......................375.00
American, crystal, candlestick, octagon ft, 6" 25.00
American, crystal, candlestick, twin, 4⅛x8½" 60.00
American, crystal, coaster, 3¾".....................................9.00
American, crystal, creamer, ind, 4¾-oz............................9.00
American, crystal, creamer, 9½-oz..................................12.50
American, crystal, decanter, w/stopper, 24-oz, 9¼"..........85.00
American, crystal, goblet, claret; #2056, 7-oz, 4⅞"........60.00
American, crystal, hat, 3"..27.50
American, crystal, ice tub, w/liner, 5⅝" 90.00
American, crystal, napkin ring......................................12.50
American, crystal, picture fr......................................15.00
American, crystal, plate, cake; hdls, 10" 27.50
American, crystal, plate, salad; 7"................................10.00
American, crystal, platter, oval, 12"..............................55.00
American, crystal, ring holder 200.00
American, crystal, rose bowl, 3½" 20.00
American, crystal, spooner, 3¾" 35.00

American, crystal, toothpick holder 25.00
American, crystal, tray, sq, 4-part, 10" 85.00
American, crystal, tumbler, iced tea; hdld...........................350.00
American, crystal, urn, sq, ped ft, 6" 30.00
American, crystal, vase, swung; 12" 250.00

American, crystal wedding bowl, 8", $110.00.

Baroque, bl, bowl, hdld, 10" 95.00
Baroque, bl, bowl, pickle; 8"..30.00
Baroque, bl, sugar bowl, ind, 3"...27.50
Baroque, crystal, bowl, cream soup 35.00
Baroque, crystal, comport, 4¾" 15.00
Baroque, crystal, cup..10.00
Baroque, crystal, oil, w/stopper, 5½" 85.00
Baroque, crystal, plate, 7½"...5.00
Baroque, crystal, sweetmeat, w/lid, 9" 75.00
Baroque, crystal, tumbler, juice; 5-oz, 3¾"...........................12.00
Baroque, yel, bowl, celery; 11" 25.00
Baroque, yel, candlestick, 4"..35.00
Baroque, yel, cup...20.00
Baroque, yel, plate, 8½"...17.50
Baroque, yel, vase, 7"...120.00
Brocade, #287 Grape, gr, bowl, #2362, Saturn rings, low, 12" 90.00
Brocade, #287 Grape, gr, sweetmeat, #2375, hexagonal, hdls........40.00
Brocade, #289 Paradise, gr/Orchid, candlestick, #2324, 4" 35.00
Brocade, #289 Paradise, gr/Orchid, vase, #4100, 8" 95.00
Brocade, #290 Oakleaf, crystal, bonbon, #2375 ....30.00
Brocade, #290 Oakleaf, crystal, cheese & cracker, #2368 ....65.00
Brocade, #290 Oakleaf, crystal, pail, whip cream; #2375..............105.00
Brocade, #290 Oakleaf, crystal, plate, #2283, 8" 22.00
Brocade, #290 Oakleaf, gr or rose, urn, #2413, w/lid 175.00
Brocade, #72 Oakwood, Orchid or Azure, bowl, finger; #869 ....75.00
Brocade, #72 Oakwood, Orchid or Azure, comport, pulled stem, #2400, 8"...115.00
Brocade, #72 Oakwood, Orchid or Azure, sherbet, low, #877, 6-oz .45.00
Brocade, #73 Palm Leaf, rose or gr, lemon dish, bow hdl, #2375...40.00
Coin, amber, ashtray, #1372/123, 5" 17.50
Coin, amber, creamer, #1372/680 ....10.00
Coin, bl, ashtray, #1372/114, 7½" dia.................................40.00
Coin, bl, condiment set, #1372/737, tray+2 shakers+cruet 335.00
Coin, bl, decanter, w/stopper, #1372/400, pt, 10³⁄₁₆"..................250.00
Coin, bl, salver, ftd, #1372/630, 6½"..................................225.00
Coin, bl or ruby, sugar bowl, #1372/673, w/lid 45.00
Coin, crystal, cigarette box, #1372/374, 5¾x4½" 40.00
Coin, crystal, nappy, #1372/459 ....22.00
Coin, crystal, punch bowl base, #1372/602 ....165.00
Coin, crystal, stem, sherbet, #1372/7, 9-oz., 5¼" 25.00
Coin, crystal, tumbler, iced tea/highball; #1372/64......................37.50
Coin, gr, candy jar, w/lid, #1372/347, 6⁵⁄₁₆"..................................100.00
Coin, gr, vase, bud; #1372/799, 8" 60.00
Coin, olive, bowl, wedding; w/lid, #1372/162 ....32.50

Coin, olive, pitcher, #1372/453, 32-oz....................................55.00
Coin, ruby, creamer, #1372/680 ....16.00
Colony, crystal, ashtray, rnd, 3"..7.00
Colony, crystal, bowl, bonbon; 5" 9.00
Colony, crystal, bowl, celery; 11½"..30.00
Colony, crystal, bowl, olive; oblong, 7"..................................12.00
Colony, crystal, butter dish, ¼-lb..40.00
Colony, crystal, cheese & cracker 50.00
Colony, crystal, cigarette box...45.00
Colony, crystal, mayonnaise, 3-pc..35.00
Colony, crystal, oil, w/stopper, 4½-oz....................................37.50
Colony, crystal, plate, dinner; 9"..25.00
Colony, crystal, saucer...2.00
Colony, crystal, vase, cupped, 7"..40.00
Fairfax, amber, ashtray, 5½"..13.00
Fairfax, amber, bowl, 12"..25.00
Fairfax, amber, candlestick, 3"..12.00
Fairfax, amber, nut cup, blown...22.00
Fairfax, amber, platter; oval, 12" 22.00
Fairfax, amber, sugar pail..30.00
Fairfax, gr or topaz, bottle, salad dressing 110.00
Fairfax, gr or topaz, cigarette box..25.00
Fairfax, gr or topaz, ice bowl 20.00
Fairfax, gr or topaz, plate, salad; 8¾"......................................8.00
Fairfax, gr or topaz, saucer, AD..5.00
Fairfax, gr or topaz, tumbler; ftd, 5-oz, 4½"..........................11.00
Fairfax, rose, bl or Orchid, bowl, cereal; 6" 30.00
Fairfax, rose, bl or Orchid, bowl, 12" 50.00
Fairfax, rose, bl or Orchid, butter dish..................................135.00
Fairfax, rose, bl or Orchid, cup, AD.......................................30.00
Fairfax, rose, bl or Orchid, mayonnaise ladle 35.00
Fairfax, rose, bl or Orchid, plate, cake; 10" 22.00
Fairfax, rose, bl or orchid, stem, cordial; ¾-oz, 4" 70.00
Fuchsia, crystal, candlestick, #2395½, 5" 55.00
Fuchsia, crystal, cup, #2440 ....20.00
Fuchsia, crystal, lemon dish, #2470..32.00
Fuchsia, crystal, sweetmeat, #2470...38.00
Fuchsia, crystal, tumbler, #833, 12-oz 30.00
Fuchsia, Wisteria, bowl, #2440, 11½"...................................165.00
Fuchsia, Wisteria, stem, claret; #6004, 4-oz..........................75.00
Hermitage, amber, gr or topaz, decanter, #2449, w/stopper, 28-oz ...110.00
Hermitage, amber, gr or topaz, plate, crescent salad; #2449, 7⅜"..17.50
Hermitage, Azure, ashtray, #2449..8.00
Hermitage, Azure, plate, sandwich; #2449, 12".....................20.00
Hermitage, Azure, tumbler; #2449, ftd, 5-oz, 4" 12.00
Hermitage, crystal, bowl, soup; #2449½, 7".............................8.00
Hermitage, crystal, tray, condiment; #2449, 6½" 6.00
Hermitage, Wisteria, cup, #2449, ftd......................................22.00
Hermitage, Wisteria, saucer, #2449..8.00
Horizon, Cinnamon, crystal, or Spruce Green, plate, dinner; 10".15.00
Jamestown, bl, pk or ruby, sugar bowl, #2719/679, ftd, 3½" 25.00
June, crystal, ashtray...25.00
June, crystal, cream soup, ftd...22.00
June, crystal, cup, AD...25.00
June, crystal, plate, bread/butter; 6" 7.00
June, crystal, plate, chop; 13"...25.00
June, crystal, sugar pail...70.00
June, crystal, vase, 2 styles, 8", ea..80.00
June, rose or bl, bowl, bonbon..30.00
June, rose or bl, bowl, finger; w/liner.....................................75.00
June, rose or bl, goblet; cordial; ¾-oz, 4"..............................155.00
June, topaz, comport; #2400, 5" 50.00
June, topaz, ice bucket...100.00
June, topaz, oil, ftd...350.00

June, topaz, sauce boat 125.00
Kashmir, bl, bowl, fruit; 5" 25.00
Kashmir, bl, ice bucket 90.00
Kashmir, bl, saucer, AD; rnd 15.00
Kashmir, bl, vase, 8" 145.00
Kashmir, yel or gr, ashtray 25.00
Kashmir, yel or gr, bowl, baker, 9" 37.50
Kashmir, yel or gr, candlestick, 5" 22.50
Kashmir, yel or gr, cup 15.00
Kashmir, yel or gr, plate, dinner; 10" 45.00
Kashmir, yel or gr, sandwich server, center hdl...................35.00
Kashmir, yel or gr, stem, parfait; 5½-oz 30.00
Kashmir, yel or gr, stem, wine; 2½-oz 32.00
Kashmir, yel or gr, tumbler, 11-oz 22.50
Lafayette, burgundy, cup..35.00
Lafayette, crystal or amber, bowl, cereal; 6" 20.00
Lafayette, crystal or amber, bowl, pickle; 8½" 18.00
Lafayette, crystal or amber, cup 15.00
Lafayette, crystal or amber, plate, 10" 35.00
Lafayette, Empire Green, relish, 3-part, 7½" 45.00
Lafayette, Regal Blue, bonbon, hdls, 5" 35.00
Lafayette, rose, gr or topaz, bowl, cream soup.....................35.00
Lafayette, rose, gr or topaz, cake plate, oval, hdls, 10½"........45.00
Lafayette, rose, gr or topaz, plate, 6" 12.00
Lafayette, Wisteria, bowl, nappy, 8" 85.00

Lido, vase, footed, 5", $75.00.
(Photo courtesy Gene Florence)

Navarre, crystal, bowl, finger; #869, 4½"...........................75.00
Navarre, crystal, bowl, floating garden; #2496, oval, 10".........55.00
Navarre, crystal, candlestick, #2472, dbl, 5".......................50.00
Navarre, crystal, candlestick, #2496, 4"............................25.00
Navarre, crystal, cup, #2440..20.00
Navarre, crystal, plate, bread/butter; #2440, 6"..................11.00
Navarre, crystal, plate, cracker; #2496, 11".......................50.00
Navarre, crystal, relish, #2496, sq, 2-part, 6"....................32.50
Navarre, crystal, saucer, #2440.......................................5.00
Navarre, crystal, shakers, flat, #2364, 3¼", pr 75.00
Navarre, crystal, stem, cocktail; #6106, 3½-oz, 6" 25.00
Navarre, crystal, sugar bowl, #2496, ind 16.00
Navarre, crystal, tidbit, #2496, 3-ftd, turned-up edge, 8¼" 22.00
New Garland, amber or topaz, bowl, fruit; 5" 10.00
New Garland, amber or topaz, candlestick, 3".......................17.50
New Garland, amber or topaz, decanter 125.00
New Garland, amber or topaz, nut, ind 10.00
New Garland, amber or topaz, saucer..................................3.00
New Garland, amber or topaz, stem, cocktail; #4120, 3½-oz.........20.00
New Garland, amber or topaz, stem, water goblet; #4120.............22.00
New Garland, amber or topaz, tumbler, #4120, 10-oz 14.00
New Garland, rose, bowl, soup; 7" 30.00
New Garland, rose, ice bucket 70.00
New Garland, rose, platter, 15" 75.00

New Garland, rose, relish, 4-part 27.50
New Garland, rose, stem, wine; #6002 ....25.00
New Garland, rose, vase, 8" 60.00
Pioneer, Azure or Orchid, ashtray, deep, lg........................25.00
Pioneer, Azure or Orchid, relish, rnd, 3-part 17.50
Pioneer, bl, bowl, pickle; oval, 8" 22.50
Pioneer, bl, bowl, salad; 10"..40.00
Pioneer, bl, plate, cream soup.......................................7.00
Pioneer, bl, plate, 8" 15.00
Pioneer, crystal, amber or gr, bowl, soup; rnd, 7" 15.00
Pioneer, crystal, amber or gr, celery, oval, narrow, 11" 20.00
Pioneer, crystal, amber or gr, sugar bowl, flat.....................9.00
Pioneer, Ebony, ashtray, deep, lg...................................18.00
Pioneer, rose or topaz, creamer, ftd 12.00
Pioneer, rose or topaz, egg cup 25.00
Pioneer, rose or topaz, relish, 3-part, rnd 15.00
Rogene, crystal, almond, #4095, ftd..................................8.00
Rogene, crystal, bowl, finger; #766 ....20.00
Rogene, crystal, bowl, jelly; #825, w/lid...........................37.50
Rogene, crystal, mayonnaise ladle...................................22.50
Rogene, crystal, plate, salad; #2283, 7".............................10.00
Rogene, crystal, plate, w/cut star, 11"..............................27.50
Rogene, crystal, plate, 5" 6.00
Rogene, crystal, stem, parfait; #5082, 6-oz.........................22.50
Rogene, crystal, stem, wine; #5082, 2½-oz 25.00
Rogene, crystal, tumbler, ftd, #4095, 10-oz.........................15.00
Rogene, crystal, tumbler, whiskey; #887, 2½-oz......................15.00
Royal, amber or gr, ashtray, #2350, 3½" 22.50
Royal, amber or gr, bowl, cereal; #2350, 6½" 25.00
Royal, amber or gr, bowl, fruit; #2350, 5½" 15.00
Royal, amber or gr, bowl, salad; #2350, 10" 35.00
Royal, amber or gr, butter dish, #2350.............................295.00
Royal, amber or gr, candy dish, ftd, w/lid, ¼-lb 195.00
Royal, amber or gr, egg cup, #2350 ....27.50
Royal, amber or gr, ice bucket, #2376...............................65.00
Royal, amber or gr, plate, bread/butter; #2350, 6" 3.00
Royal, amber or gr, plate, cheese; w/lid, #2276, 11"...............150.00
Royal, amber or gr, plate, chop; #2350, 13".........................30.00
Royal, amber or gr, plate, salad; #2350, 7½"........................4.00
Royal, amber or gr, shakers, #5100, pr..............................60.00
Royal, amber or gr, stem, parfait; #869, 5½-oz 32.50
Royal, amber or gr, stem, water; #869, 9-oz.........................23.00
Royal, amber or gr, tumbler, flat, #869, 5-oz.......................22.50
Royal, amber or gr, vase, flared, #2292.............................125.00
Seville, amber, bowl, cereal; #2350, 6½" 18.00
Seville, amber, bowl, ftd, 10".......................................35.00
Seville, amber, bowl, grapefruit; molded, #2315....................25.00
Seville, amber, candlestick, #2324, 2"..............................18.00
Seville, amber, cup, AD; #2350 ....25.00
Seville, amber, pickle, #2350, 8"....................................13.50
Seville, amber, plate, #2350, rnd, 15"..............................45.00
Seville, amber, plate, cheese & cracker; #2368, 11".................40.00
Seville, amber, platter, #2350, 12".................................40.00
Seville, amber, stem, cordial; #870.................................65.00
Seville, amber, urn, #2324, sm 75.00
Seville, gr, bowl, bouillon; #2350, flat 16.00
Seville, gr, bowl, vegetable; #2350.................................27.50
Seville, gr, candlestick, #2324, 9".................................50.00
Seville, gr, comport, #2350, 8".....................................35.00
Seville, gr, egg cup, #2350...35.00
Seville, gr, pitcher, #5084, ftd...................................295.00
Seville, gr, sauce boat, #2350......................................75.00
Seville, gr, vase, #2292, 8"..75.00
Sun Ray, crystal, ashtray, sq.......................................10.00

Sun Ray, crystal, coaster, 4" 6.00
Sun Ray, crystal, plate, torte; 15" 65.00
Sun Ray, crystal, tray, sq, 10" 35.00
Sun Ray, crystal, vase, 7" 50.00
Trojan, rose, bottle, salad dressing; #2983 ....595.00
Trojan, rose, bowl, cereal; #2375, 6½" 60.00
Trojan, rose, bowl, cream soup; #2375, ftd 35.00
Trojan, rose, bowl, whipped cream; #2375.........................23.00
Trojan, rose, comport, #2375, 7" 65.00
Trojan, rose, goblet, water; #5299, 10-oz, 8¼" 40.00
Trojan, rose, mayonnaise ladle 30.00
Trojan, rose, plate, luncheon; #2375, 8¾" 22.00
Trojan, rose, vase, #2417, 8" 175.00
Trojan, topaz, ashtray, #2350, lg 40.00
Trojan, topaz, candlestick, #2394, 2" 24.00
Trojan, topaz, cup, #2375½, ftd 18.00
Trojan, topaz, ice bucket, #2375 ....65.00
Trojan, topaz, sauce plate, #2375 ....45.00
Trojan, topaz, sherbet, #5099, 6" 25.00
Trojan, topaz, sugar pail, #2378...165.00
Versailles, bl, ashtray, #2350..50.00
Versailles, bl, bowl, lemon 22.00
Versailles, bl, bowl, mint; 3-ftd, 4½" 45.00
Versailles, bl, candlestick, scroll, #2395½, 5" 65.00
Versailles, bl, plate, chop; #2375, 13" 90.00
Versailles, bl, sweetmeat, #2375 ....25.00
Versailles, pk, gr, or yel, bowl, bonbon; #2375 ....25.00
Versailles, pk, gr, or yel, bowl, grapefruit; #5082½.........75.00
Versailles, pk, gr, or yel, plate, luncheon; #2375, 8¾" 15.00
Versailles, pk or gr, candlestick, #2395, 3" 25.00
Versailles, pk or gr, sauce boat, #2375 ....150.00
Versailles, pk or gr, vase, #4100, 8" 195.00
Versailles, yel, bowl, #2394, 3 ftd, 6" 40.00
Versailles, yel, bowl, whipped cream; #2375 ....25.00
Versailles, yel, comport, #5098, 3" 30.00
Versailles, yel, ice bucket, #2375 ....80.00
Versailles, yel, sugar bowl, ftd, #2375½ 20.00
Vesper, amber, bowl, soup; deep, 8¼" 45.00
Vesper, amber, candlestick, #2324, 4" 25.00
Vesper, amber, egg cup, #2350 ....45.00
Vesper, amber, shakers, #5100, pr...90.00
Vesper, amber, tumbler, #5100, ftd, 5-oz 22.00
Vesper, bl, bowl, baker; #2350, oval, 9" 100.00
Vesper, bl, bowl, fruit; #2350, 5½" 30.00
Vesper, bl, celery, #2350 ....45.00
Vesper, gr, bowl, #2329, rolled edge, 14".............................55.00
Vesper, gr, bowl, soup; #2350, shallow, 7¾" 30.00
Vesper, gr, pickle, #2350...26.00
Vesper, gr, platter, #2350, 12" 65.00

Fostoria Glass Specialty Company

The Fostoria Glass Specialty Company was founded in Fostoria, Ohio, in 1899. In 1910 they were purchased by General Electric. The new owners had an interest in developing a high-quality lustre-type art glass able to compete with the very successful glassware produced by Tiffany. They hired Walter Hicks, who had previously worked for Tiffany, to help develop the line they called Iris. Their efforts were extremely successful. The art glass they developed was cased and iridescent, very similar to Steuben's Aurene. Colors included green, tan, white, blue, yellow, and rose. It was made in several patterns, including Heart and Leaf, Leaf and Tendrils, Heart and Spider Webbing, and Lustred Dot. Although the main thrust of their production was lamp shades, vases, and bowls were

made as well. Iris was made for only four years, since gold was required in its production and manufacturing costs were very high. It was marked with only a paper label, without which identification is sometimes difficult. Look for a pronounced, well-finished pontil that shows the glass layers represented. Most items show a layer of white, which Fostoria called Calcite, as did Steuben. Very little has been written on the history of this company, but for more information refer to *The Collector's Encyclopedia of Art Glass* by John Shuman (Collector Books), and *Fostoria Ohio Glass, Vol II*, by Melvin L. Murray (self published).

Our advisor for this category is Frank W. Ford; he is listed in the Directory under Massachusetts.

Rose bowl, Iris, gold lustre leaves on opal, ovoid 500.00
Shade, festoons, gr on opal, 7" 250.00

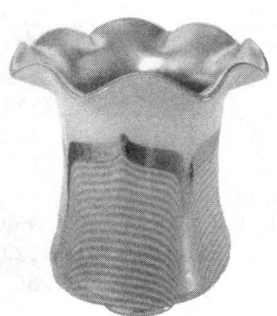

Shade, green pulled feathers on opal, gold lining, $300.00. (Photo courtesy Frank W. Ford)

Shade, Iris, gold lustre leaves on opal, 4½" 300.00
Shade, leaves & vines, gr & gold on opal, 4-sided......................250.00
Shade, leaves & vines on pearly wht, gold int, bell form, 4½" ...300.00
Vase, Iris, gold lustre, pinched-in sides, narrow neck, ftd, 4½" ...600.00
Vase, Iris, gold lustre w/gr leaves/vines, sq top, 12" 2,000.00

Frakturs

Fraktur is a German style of black letter text type. To collectors the fraktur is a type of hand-lettered document used by the people of German descent who settled in the areas of Pennsylvania, New Jersey, Maryland, Virginia, North and South Carolina, Ohio, Kentucky, and Ontario. These documents recorded births and baptisms and were used as bookplates and as certificates of honor. They were elaborately decorated with colorful folk-art borders of hearts, birds, angels, and flowers. Examples by recognized artists and those with an unusual decorative motif bring prices well into the thousands of dollars; in fact, some have sold at major auction houses well in excess of $10,000.00. Frakturs made in the late 1700s after the invention of the printing press provided the writer with a prepared text that he needed only to fill in at his own discretion. The next step in the evolution of machine-printed frakturs combined woodblock-printed decorations along with the text which the 'artist' sometimes enhanced with color. By the mid-1800s, even the coloring was done by machine. The vorschrift was a handwritten example prepared by a fraktur teacher to demonstrate his skill in lettering and decorating. These are often considered to be the finest of frakturs. Those dated before 1820 are most valuable.

The practice of fraktur art began to diminish after 1830 but hung on even to the early years of this century among the Pennsylvania Germans ingrained with such customs. Our advisor for this category is Frederick S. Weiser; he is listed in the Directory under Pennsylvania. (Mr. Weiser has provided our text, but being unable to physically examine the frakturs listed below can not vouch for their authenticity, age, or condition. When requesting information, please include a self-addressed stamped evelope.) These prices were realized at various reputable auction galleries in the East and Midwest. Unless otherwise noted, values are for examples in excellent condition. Note: Be careful not to confuse frakturs with prints, calligraphy, English-language marriage certificates, Lord's Prayers, etc.

Key:
lp — laid paper   wc — watercolored
pr — printed   wp — wove paper
p/i — pen and ink

Birth Record

P/i, hearts/flowers/text, PA, 1738, 8x 12½", G.............................750.00
P/i/wc, birds & flowers, yel border, Killian, PA, 1869, 7x4¼" 135.00
P/i/wc, mantel+2 urns, 2 full-length ladies, 1838, att H Young, 17x15" ...2,750.00
P/i/wc, memorial, 3 hearts/sun/moon, name/1861, 19x16", VG...1,200.00
P/i/wc, urn w/vining roses atop sq w/verse, 1840, 12x15", EX..3,100.00
P/i/wc, vines fr text, birds/baskets of flowers, 1862, rstr, 14x11"..850.00
P/i/wc, 2 lg flowers/wreath/stars in corners, att H Young, 1858, 14x11..1,300.00
P/i/wc, 2 parrots/flowers/political poem, Berks Co 1848, 12x10", VG..2,250.00
P/i/wc/lp, Am eagle w/arrows/flowers/swag, PA, late 18th C, 11x11"..485.00
Pr/p/i/wc, Lady Liberty/Plenty/lion/eagle/cherub, ca 1880, 21x18"..2,500.00
Pr/p/i/wc, Welentines, flanking primitive parrots, 1831, 8x10", G...1,900.00
Pr/wc, angel/cherub/birds, 1885, Eagle Book Store, 17x14"........110.00
Pr/wc, angels/cherubs/birds/etc, Ritter, 1837, 16½x13¼"............225.00
Pr/wc, Gerburts und Taufschein/angels/bird, PA/1806, 19x15"...250.00
Pr/wc, heart w/text, tulips/flowers, 1796, 17x20", VG..............1,595.00
Pr/wc, lg+2 sm hearts, sgn F Krebs, 1796, rstr/stains, 16x19"......825.00
Pr/wc, wreath/angels/tulips/roses, 1835, 15x18", VG..................600.00
Pr/wc/lp, lg/sm hearts, p/i parrots, 1791, 12x16", VG...............1,500.00
Wc/lp, heart w/pious verse/flowers/etc, PA, ca 1800, 4¾x3½"+fr 260.00

Miscellaneous

Birth letter and marriage certificate, green, orange, and brown watercolor on wove paper, dated 1765, some paper loss, discoloration, and abrasions, 8x13", $900.00.

Bookplate, wc/lp, flowers/geometrics, 1863, 7¼x5¼"+fr..........1,650.00
Family register, pencil/wc/lp, angel/rose, OH/1850s, 14x11½"+fr...770.00
Haus-Segen, pr/wc/p/i, bird/flowers/fans, sgn HW Billie, 18x15", EX..1,375.00
Map, p/i/wc/lp, Lancaster Co PA, dtd 1827, 12x8"+fr.................440.00
Penmanship, marriage record/1830, 12x19", in contemporary fr.330.00

Frames

Styles in picture frames have changed with the fashion of the day, but those that especially interest today's collectors are the deep shadow boxes made of fine woods such as walnut or cherry, those with Art Nouveau influence, and the oak frames decorated with molded gesso and gilt from the Victorian era.

As is true in general in the antiques and collectibles fields, the influence of online trading is greatly affecting prices. Many items once considered difficult to locate are now readily available on the Internet; as a result, values have declined. Our advisor for this category is Michael Hinton; he is listed in the Directory under Pennsylvania.

Note: Unless another date is given, frames described in the following listings are from the nineteenth century.

Beadwork birds & flowers, scalloped top, easel bk, 7½", EX 175.00
Bird's-eye maple w/gilt liner (damage), 4" W, 20x25".................440.00
Bird's-eye veneer ogee, gilt liner, 33x27"..............................250.00
Brass, florals/leaves, oval, Fr, 1860s, 6x4½", EX.......................75.00
CI w/gilt, rtcl leaves, metal bk, desk type, 11½x8¼".................65.00
Clear glass rod w/topaz caning, brass holder, Italy, 1930s, 13x11"...625.00
Curly maple, appl half-trn, raised corner blocks, 15x12".............220.00
Gesso/gilt, foliate/floral-molded, 37x32", EX...........................260.00
Gessoed corners w/fruits & flowers, Vict, 45x36", VG...............100.00
Giltwood, cvd bellflower, acanthus & reeded decor, 37x42", pr..750.00
Micro mosaic floral, arched top, new velvet bk, Italy, 5x3¾" 375.00
Pressed yel metal, designed for tintype, 1860s, 3½x5½", EX.......185.00
Sterling, dbl w/hinged top, 2 glass inserts, lion hall mk, 4¾x3"..250.00
Sterling, oval, easel bk, eng monogram, 2 ball supports, 7x5⅝"....65.00
Walnut, worn, 3" W, 13x11", pr...40.00
Walnut Vict crisscross, cvd leaves at corners, 22x18".................150.00

Frances Ware

Frances Ware, produced in the 1880s by Hobbs, Brockunier and Company of Wheeling, West Virginia, is a term refering to the decoration or finish used in the production of some of their glassware lines. Hobnail (Dewdrop) is the most commonly found of these lines, though Swirl and on occasion Quartered Block with Stars were also finished with the frosted surface and amber-stained band that defines the Frances Ware indication. Though in general collectors also tend to regard examples in crystal with simply an amber-stained band as Frances Ware, according to *Hobbs, Brockunier & Co. Glass* by Nelia and Tom Bredehoft (Collector Books), this is incorrect. The company called this finish 'decorated #7.' To evaluate examples in crystal with amber stain, deduct 10% from the values given below, which are strictly for the frosted finish. Our advisors for this category are Betty and Clarence Maier; they are listed in the Directory under Pennsylvania.

Hobnail, bowl, ftd, berry pontil, 6x10"..................................150.00
Hobnail, bowl, no flange, 9" sq...85.00
Hobnail, bowl, oblong, 8"...75.00
Hobnail, bowl, shell ftd, 8"...250.00
Hobnail, bowl, 2½x5½"..30.00
Hobnail, bowl, 7½" sq...70.00
Hobnail, bowl, 7½", from $65 to..75.00
Hobnail, bowl, 8"...75.00
Hobnail, bowl, 8" sq..75.00
Hobnail, bowl, 10"...90.00
Hobnail, butter dish, from $80 to.......................................120.00
Hobnail, celery vase...125.00
Hobnail, chandelier, amber font, brass fr, 14" dia......................950.00
Hobnail, creamer, from $40 to..60.00
Hobnail, cruet, from $425 to..500.00
Hobnail, finger bowl, 4", from $25 to....................................35.00
Hobnail, molasses can..375.00
Hobnail, nappy, 4½" sq..25.00
Hobnail, pickle jar...175.00
Hobnail, pitcher, milk..175.00
Hobnail, pitcher, water; sq top, 8½"....................................195.00
Hobnail, sauce dish, sq, 4"..28.00
Hobnail, shakers, very rare, pr...300.00
Hobnail, sugar bowl, w/lid, from $65 to..................................80.00
Hobnail, syrup, pewter lid..375.00
Hobnail, toothpick holder/toy tumbler....................................60.00

Hobnail, tray, cloverleaf, 12", from $90 to 125.00
Hobnail, tumbler, water...45.00
Hobnail, vase, ruffled top..165.00
Quartered Block w/Stars, bowl, oval, 10" 65.00
Quartered Block w/Stars, butter dish 95.00
Quartered Block w/Stars, goblet 140.00
Quartered Block w/Stars, sugar bowl, w/lid 75.00
Swirl, bowl, 4"...25.00
Swirl, bowl, 8"...90.00
Swirl, butter dish 95.00
Swirl, celery, ind 35.00
Swirl, cruet, from $250 to 295.00
Swirl, mustard jar, from $90 to 125.00
Swirl, pitcher, water 225.00
Swirl, plate, 6"...30.00
Swirl, shakers, pr...165.00
Swirl, sugar bowl, w/lid...80.00
Swirl, sugar shaker, orig lid..195.00
Swirl, syrup, Pat dtd 295.00
Swirl, toothpick holder 160.00
Swirl, tumbler 45.00

Franciscan

Franciscan is a trade name used by Gladding McBean and Co., founded in northern California in 1875. In 1923 they purchased the Tropico plant in Glendale where they produced sewer pipe, gardenware, and tile. By 1934 the first of their dinnerware lines, El Patio, was produced. It was a plain design made in bright, attractive colors. El Patio Nouveau followed in 1935, glazed in two colors — one tone on the inside, a contrasting hue on the outside. Coronado, a favorite of today's collectors, was introduced in 1936. It was styled with a wide, swirled border and was made in pastels, both satin and glossy. Before 1940 fifteen patterns had been produced. The first hand-decorated lines were introduced in 1937, the ever-popular Apple pattern in 1940, Desert Rose in 1941, and Ivy in 1948. Many other hand-decorated and decaled patterns were produced there from 1934 to 1984.

Dinnerware marks before 1940 include 'GMcB' in an oval, 'F' within a square, or 'Franciscan' with 'Pottery' underneath (which was later changed to 'Ware'). A circular arrangement of 'Franciscan' with 'Made in California USA' in the center was used from 1940 until 1949. At least forty marks were used before 1975; several more were introduced after that. At one time, paper labels were used.

The company merged with Lock Joint Pipe Company in 1963, becoming part of the Interpace Corporation. In July of 1979 Franciscan was purchased by Wedgwood Limited of England, and the Glendale plant closed in October 1984.

Note: Due to limited space, we have used a pricing formula, meant to be only a general guide, not a mechanical ratio on each piece. Rarity varies with pattern, and not all pieces occur in all patterns. Our advisors for this category are Mick and Lorna Chase (Fiesta Plus); they are listed in the Directory under Tennessee. See also Gladding McBean.

Ivy, TV plate, $245.00; ten-ounce tumbler, $45.00.

Coronado

Both satin (matt) and glossy colors were made including turquoise, coral, celadon, light yellow, ivory, and gray in satin; and turquoise, coral, apple green, light yellow, white, maroon, and redwood in glossy glazes. High-end values are for maroon, yellow, redwood, and gray. Add 10 – 15% for gloss.

Bowl, casserole; w/lid, from $85 to 125.00
Bowl, cereal; from $15 to 20.00
Bowl, cream soup; w/underplate, from $40 to...............................50.00
Bowl, fruit; from $12 to 18.00
Bowl, nut cup; from $16 to...18.00
Bowl, onion soup; w/lid, from $45 to 60.00
Bowl, rim soup; from $28 to 32.00
Bowl, salad; lg, from $35 to 50.00
Bowl, serving; oval, 10½", from $30 to.......................................45.00
Bowl, serving; 7½" dia, from $20 to...25.00
Bowl, serving; 8½" dia, from $18 to...20.00
Bowl, sherbet/egg cup; from $15 to 18.00
Butter dish, from $35 to 45.00
Cigarette box, w/lid, from $75 to 90.00
Creamer, from $12 to..15.00
Cup & saucer, demitasse; from $28 to 45.00
Cup & saucer, jumbo 35.00
Demitasse pot, from $125 to 195.00
Fast-stand gravy, from $28 to 40.00
Jam jar, w/lid, from $65 to 80.00
Pitcher, 1½-qt, from $35 to..60.00
Plate, chop; 12½" dia, from $25 to 35.00
Plate, chop; 14" dia, from $35 to 45.00
Plate, crescent hostess; w/cup well, no established value
Plate, crescent salad; lg, no established value
Plate, ind crescent salad; from $25 to 35.00
Plate, 6½", from $6 to 10.00
Plate, 7½", from $9 to 12.00
Plate, 8½", from $12 to 15.00
Plate, 9½", from $15 to 18.00
Plate, 10½", from $20 to 25.00
Platter, oval, 10", from $20 to 25.00
Platter, oval, 13", from $30 to 45.00
Platter, oval, 15½", from $45 to 60.00
Relish dish, oval, from $20 to 35.00
Shakers, pr, from $20 to 35.00
Sugar bowl, w/lid, from $15 to 25.00
Teacup & saucer, from $12 to 15.00
Teapot, from $65 to 95.00
Tumbler, water; no established value
Vase, 8", no established value

Desert Rose

Ashtray, ind 20.00
Ashtray, oval..125.00
Ashtray, sq 295.00
Bell, Danbury Mint 125.00
Bell, dinner 125.00
Bowl, bouillon; w/lid 395.00
Bowl, cereal; 6" 15.00
Bowl, divided vegetable..45.00
Bowl, fruit..7.00
Bowl, mixing; lg..195.00
Bowl, mixing; med...185.00
Bowl, mixing; sm...175.00

Bowl, porringer 200.00
Bowl, rimmed soup 28.00
Bowl, salad; 10" 115.00
Bowl, soup; ftd 32.00
Bowl, vegetable; 8" 32.00
Bowl, vegetable; 9" 40.00
Box, cigarette 125.00
Box, egg 195.00
Box, heart shape 165.00
Box, rnd 165.00
Butter dish 45.00
Candle holders, pr 145.00
Candy dish, oval 295.00
Casserole, 1½-qt 85.00
Casserole, 2½-qt, minimum value 495.00
Coffeepot 125.00
Coffeepot, ind 395.00
Compote, lg 75.00
Compote, low 125.00
Cookie jar 295.00
Creamer, ind 40.00
Creamer, regular 22.00
Cup & saucer, coffee 85.00
Cup & saucer, demitasse 55.00
Cup & saucer, jumbo 65.00
Cup & saucer, tall 45.00
Cup & saucer, tea 15.00
Egg cup 35.00
Ginger jar 225.00
Goblet, ftd 195.00
Gravy boat 32.00
Heart 145.00
Hurricane lamp 495.00
Jam jar 125.00
Long 'n narrow, 15½x7¾" 495.00
Microwave dish, oblong, 1½-qt 285.00
Microwave dish, sq, 1-qt 215.00
Microwave dish, sq, 8" 245.00
Mug, bbl, 12-oz 50.00
Mug, cocoa; 10-oz 135.00
Mug, 7-oz 32.00
Napkin ring 65.00
Piggy bank 295.00
Pitcher, jug 195.00
Pitcher, milk 75.00
Pitcher, syrup 95.00
Pitcher, water; 2½-qt 125.00
Plate, chop; 12" 75.00
Plate, chop; 14" 175.00
Plate, coupe dessert 65.00
Plate, coupe party 195.00
Plate, coupe steak 195.00
Plate, divided; child's 195.00
Plate, grill 125.00
Plate, side salad 40.00
Plate, TV 175.00
Plate, 6½" 6.00
Plate, 8½" 12.00
Plate, 9½" 20.00
Plate, 10½" 18.00
Platter, turkey; 19" 295.00
Platter, 12¾" 45.00
Platter, 14" 65.00
Relish, oval, 10" 35.00

Relish, 3-section 75.00
Shaker & pepper mill, pr 295.00
Shakers, rose bud, pr 18.00
Shakers, tall, pr 75.00
Sherbet 25.00
Soup ladle 95.00
Sugar bowl, open, ind 125.00
Sugar bowl, regular 32.00
Tea canister 225.00
Teapot 125.00
Thimble 75.00
Tidbit tray, 2-tier 195.00
Tile, in fr 75.00
Tile, sq 45.00
Toast cover 195.00
Trivet, fluted, rnd 325.00
Tumbler, juice; 6-oz 55.00
Tumbler, 10-oz 32.00
Tureen, soup; flat bottom 495.00
Tureen, soup; ftd, either style 695.00
Vase, bud 75.00

For other hand-painted patterns, we recommend the following general guide for comparable pieces (based on current values):

Daisy	-20%
October	-20%
Cafe Royal	Same as Desert Rose
Forget-Me-Not	Same as Desert Rose
Meadow Rose	Same as Desert Rose
Strawberry Fair	Same as Desert Rose
Strawberry Time	Same as Desert Rose
Fresh Fruit	Same as Desert Rose
Bountiful	Same as Desert Rose
Desert Rose	Base Line Values
Apple	+10%
Ivy	+20%
Poppy	+50%
Original (small) Fruit	+50%
Wild Flower	200% or more!

Apple Pieces Not Available in Desert Rose

There are several Apple items that are so scarce they command higher prices than fit the above formula. The Apple ginger jar is valued at $600.00+, the 4" jug at $195.00+, and any covered box in Apple is at least 50% more than Desert Rose.

There is not an active market in Bouquet, Rosette, or Twilight Rose, as these are scarce, having been produced only a short time. Our estimate would place Bouquet and Rosette in the October range (-20%) and Twilight Rose in the Ivy range (+40%).

El Patio, 1934 – 1954

This line includes a few pieces not offered in Coronado, and the colors differ; but per piece these two patterns are valued about the same.

Bowl, batter; minimum value 450.00
Bowl, str sides, lg 55.00
Bowl, str sides, med 45.00
Casserole, stick hdl & lid, ind 65.00
Coaster 65.00
Jam jar, redesigned 425.00
Shaker & pepper mill, wooden top, pr 395.00
½-apple baker, from $195 to 225.00

Franciscan Fine China

The main line of fine china was called Masterpiece. There were at least four marks used during its production from 1941 to 1977. Almost every piece is clearly marked. This china is true porcelain, the body having been fired at a very high temperature. Many years of research and experimentation went into this china before it was marketed. Production was temporarily suspended during the war years. More than 170 patterns and many varying shapes were produced. All are valued about the same with the exception of the Renaissance group, which is 25% higher.

Bowl, vegetable; serving, oval	50.00
Cup	20.00
Plate, bread & butter	18.00
Plate, dinner	30.00
Plate, salad	25.00
Saucer	12.00

Starburst

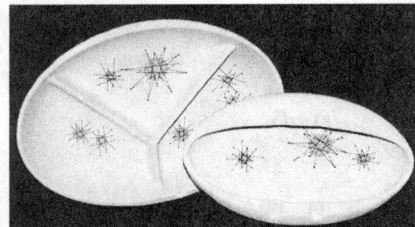

Relish, three-part, 9", $35.00; Ashtray, oval, large, $50.00.

Ashtray, ind	20.00
Bonbon/jelly dish	35.00
Bowl, crescent salad	40.00
Bowl, divided, 8"	25.00
Bowl, fruit; ind	13.00
Bowl, salad; ind	25.00
Bowl, soup/cereal	13.00
Bowl, vegetable; 8½"	45.00
Butter dish	45.00
Candlesticks, pr, from $175 to	200.00
Casserole, lg	100.00
Coffeepot	150.00
Creamer	15.00
Cup & saucer	25.00
Gravy boat, from $20 to	30.00
Gravy boat, w/attached undertray	40.00
Gravy ladle	30.00
Jug, water; 10"	90.00
Mug, sm	60.00
Mug, tall	95.00
Oil cruet	75.00
Pepper mill	150.00
Pitcher, water; 10"	85.00
Pitcher, 7½", from $50 to	75.00
Plate, chop; from $55 to	65.00
Plate, dinner	12.00
Plate, 6"	6.00
Plate, 8"	8.00
Plate, 11"	45.00
Platter, 15"	80.00
Shakers, bullet shape, lg, pr	50.00
Shakers, sm, pr	20.00
Snack/TV tray w/cup rest, 12½", from $75 to	100.00
Sugar bowl	25.00

Tumbler, 6-oz, from $40 to	50.00
Vinegar cruet	75.00

Frankart

During the 1920s Frankart, Inc., of New York City, produced a line of accessories that included figural nude lamps, bookends, ashtrays, etc. These white metal composition items were offered in several finishes including verde green, jap black, and gunmetal gray. The company also produced a line of caricatured animals, but the stylized nude figurals have proven to be the most collectible today. With few exceptions, all pieces were marked 'Frankart, Inc.' with a patent number or 'pat. appl. for.' All pieces listed are in very good original condition unless otherwise indicated. Our advisor for this category is Walter Glenn; he is listed in the Directory under Georgia.

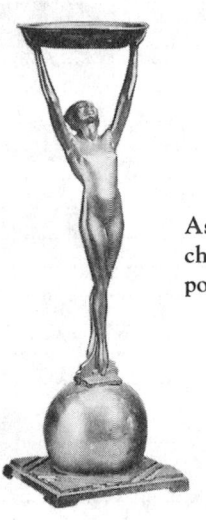

Ash stand, nude stands on chromed metal sphere, lacking pottery insert, 24", $850.00.

Aquarium, 3 kneeling nudes encircle 10" aqua bowl, 10"	1,500.00
Ashtray, nude dancing, holds tray on hip, box on base, 10"	750.00
Ashtray, nude grows from leaves to hold tray above, 25"	1,550.00
Ashtray, nude on horseshoe base holds tray aloft, 23"	1,150.00
Ashtray, nude stands, 3" ashball on geometric base, 10"	750.00
Ashtray, nudes (3) joined at hips hold 6" pottery bowl, 25"	2,200.00
Ashtray, stylized dachshund spans 4½" sq ashtray, 5"	350.00
Bookends, nude fan dancer holds books, 10", pr	625.00
Bookends, nude sits atop human skull, 8", pr	900.00
Bookends, nude sits atop mushrooms, 8", pr	650.00
Bookends, nudes in headstand support books, 10", pr	600.00
Bookends, Roman-inspired masks, 7½", pr	600.00
Clock, nudes (2) kneel & hold 10" dia glass clock, 12½"	2,100.00
Lamp, nude holds rod above, glass panel hangs by rings, 13"	1,600.00
Lamp, nude holds 6" glass cylinder on ea shoulder, 17"	1,200.00
Lamp, nude stands, arms bk, glass butterfly wings, 10¼"	1,950.00
Lamp, nude stands atop frost glass panel, light below, 10"	950.00
Lamp, nudes (2) stand & face ea other through amber glass rods, 12"	1,650.00
Lamp, nudes (4) stand & surround sq glass cylinder, 13"	1,550.00
Smoke set, seated nude, cigarette box on base, tray in ea arm, 9"	850.00
Smoke stand, nude stands atop ball, holds tray aloft, 25"	750.00
Vase, dancing nude holds 10" vase to side, 12½"	1,500.00
Vase, nudes (2) stand bk-to-bk, hold 7" glass vase, 13"	950.00
Wall sconce, nude sits on floral framework, 6"	850.00

Frankoma

The Frank Pottery, founded in Oklahoma in 1933 by John Frank, became known as Frankoma in 1934. The company produced decorative figurals, vases, and such, marking their ware from 1936 – 1938 with a pacing leopard 'Frankoma' mark. These pieces are highly sought. The entire operation was destroyed by fire in 1938, and new molds were cast — some from surviving pieces — and a similar line of production was pursued. The body of the ware was changed in 1955 from a honey tan (called 'Ada clay,' referring to the name of the town near the area where it was dug) to a red brick clay (known as Sapulpa), and this, along with the color of the glazes (over fifty have been used), helps determine the period of production. A Southwestern theme has always been favored in design as well as in color selection.

In 1965 they began to produce a limited-edition series of Christmas plates, followed by a bottle vase series in 1969. Considered very collectible are their political mugs, bicentennial plates, Teenagers of the Bible plates, and the Wildlife series. Their ceramic Christmas cards are also very popular items with today's collectors.

Frankoma celebrated their 50th anniversary in 1983. On September 26 of that same year, Frankoma was again destroyed by fire. Because of a fire-proof wall, master molds of all 1983 production items were saved, allowing plans for rebuilding to begin immediately.

Frankoma filed for Chapter 11 in April 1990, and eventually sold to a Maryland investor in February of 1991, thereby ending the family-ownership era. For a more thorough study of the subject, we recommend that you refer to *Frankoma Treasures* and *Frankoma and Other Oklahoma Potteries* by Phyllis and Tom Bess, our advisors; you will find their address in the Directory under Oklahoma.

Ashtray, Teardrop, Desert Gold, 13"...10.00
Bookends, Charger Horse, Desert Gold, Ada clay, 1934-60, pr...250.00
Bookends, Setter, Prairie Green, 7", pr..200.00
Bowl, mint; Prairie Green, Beauceant Okla 34 City mk..............250.00
Bowl, mint; White Sand, Ada clay, #35, NM 25.00
Bowl, vegetable; Plainsman, Desert Gold, sq...............................18.00
Christmas card, 1944, from $400 to...500.00
Christmas card, 1947-48, from $95 to 115.00
Christmas card, 1949, from $85 to...95.00
Christmas card, 1950-51, from $125 to.......................................150.00
Christmas card, 1952, Donna Frank, from $150 to.....................200.00
Christmas card, 1952, from $125 to...140.00
Christmas card, 1953, from $90 to...110.00
Christmas card, 1954...110.00
Christmas card, 1957...70.00
Christmas card, 1958-60..65.00
Christmas card, 1969-71..40.00
Christmas card, 1972...35.00
Christmas card, 1973-75..30.00
Christmas card, 1976-77..25.00
Christmas card, 1978-79..25.00
Christmas card, 1980-82..25.00
Christmas plate, 1965, mk First Issue, M....................................185.00
Creamer & sugar bowl, Wagon Wheel, Desert Gold, Ada clay, NM...40.00
Dealer sign, brn satin, Sapulpa clay, #3DS..................................110.00
Lazy susan, Wagon Wheel, tan, Ada clay, complete 60.00
Leaf dish, Gracetone, aqua, #125, 9"..20.00
Leaf dish, Prairie Green, #227, lg...40.00
Mug, dbl coffee; Westwind, Peach Glow 18.00
Mug, Plainsman, dk brn satin, 12-oz..15.00
Mug, Plainsman, Prairie Green, 12-oz 15.00
Mug, Wagon Wheel, Desert Gold, 16-oz...18.00
Pin, employee service; Pacing Panther 110.00
Pitcher, Plainsman, dk brn satin, ice lip, 2-qt 60.00
Pitcher, Plainsman, White Sand, w/ice lip, 2-qt, NM....................35.00
Plate, dinner; Prairie Green, 10", 6 for...120.00
Plate, salad; Westwind, White Sand, 7"...7.50

Platter, Plainsman, dk brn satin, 13"..25.00
Platter, steak; Westwind, Desert Gold, shallow, 11".....................15.00
Ramekin, Desert Gold, Sapulpa clay, bbl w/lid, 1950-61 ....35.00
Sculpture, Gardener Boy, mc (no overalls), #702, 1950-52, 7" ...325.00
Sculpture, Gardener Girl, bl dress, #701, 5¾" 125.00

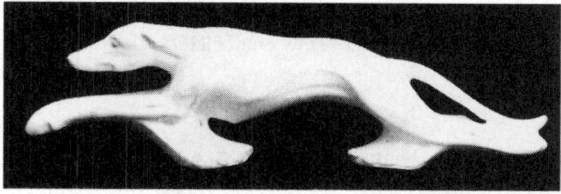

Sculpture, Greyhound, creamy ivory, modified base, 14" long, $125.00.

Sculpture, Indian Bowl Maker, Prairie Green, Sapulpa clay, 6".....90.00
Sculpture, Miniature Walking Elephant, White Sand, #169, 1¾"..110.00
Sculpture, Nude, Desert Gold, sgn Gerald Smith, #d, 11¾" 185.00
Sculpture, Puma, seated, blk gloss, Ada clay, #114, 6½".............95.00
Sculpture, Setter, Desert Gold, Sapulpa clay, 5¼x8" 185.00
Sculpture, Setter, Onyx, Ada clay, #163, 2¾x4¼" 210.00
Sculpture, Swan, Desert Gold, Ada clay, #168, 3" 60.00
Sculpture, Swan, open tail, blk, #229 ....90.00
Shakers, Bull, Prairie Green, Ada clay, pr....................................245.00
Shakers, Bull, Red Bud, pr..315.00
Shakers, Mayan-Aztec, White Sand, pr, NM 20.00
Shakers, Snail, Peacock Blue, Ada clay, 2", pr..............................75.00
Teacup, Plainsman, dk brn satin, 5-oz..10.00
Teacup, Plainsman, Prairie Green, 5-oz..10.00
Teapot, Plainsman, Prairie Green, 12-cup.......................................75.00
Trivet, Arizona Biltmore, sgn FLLW, bsk/blk bloss, 6¼" sq 70.00
Vase, Boot, White Sand, 4"..18.00
Vase, bud; Snail, Flame, Sapulpa clay, #31....................................29.00
Vase, collector; V-1, from $125 to 150.00
Vase, collector; V-2, 1970, 12", from $80 to....................................90.00
Vase, collector; V-4, 1972..85.00
Vase, collector; V-5, 1973, 13" 85.00
Vase, collector; V-6, from $80 to...90.00
Vase, collector; V-7, 13"...80.00
Vase, collector; V-8, w/stopper, 13"..75.00
Vase, collector; V-9, w/stopper, 13"..75.00
Vase, collector; V-10 & V-11, ea from $40 to..................................50.00
Vase, collector; V-12, 13" 65.00
Vase, collector; V-14, from $75 to...85.00
Vase, collector; V-15, 13", from $85 to..100.00
Vase, Fish, shiny blk, 2⅝x3¾"..235.00
Vase, Flat, Prairie Green, Ada clay, #39, puma mk, sm 385.00
Vase, Indian, Royal Blue, Ada clay, #70, 1938-42, 6"..................165.00
Vase, Prairie Green, hdls, #71, 10½" 67.50
Vase, Red Bud, Ada clay, #43, 8"..85.00

Fraternal Organizations

Fraternal memorabilia is a vast and varied field. Emblems representing the various organizations have been used to decorate cups, shaving mugs, plates, and glassware. Medals, swords, documents, and other ceremonial paraphernalia from the 1800s and early 1900s are especially prized. Our advisor for Odd Fellows is Greg Spiess; he is listed in the Directory under Illinois. Information on Masonic and Shrine memorabilia has been provided by David Smies, who is listed under Kansas. Assistance concerning Elks collectibles was provided by David Wendel; he is listed in the Directory under Missouri.

Elks

Ashtray, Bakelite, Model #313 Autopoint Co, mk PA State Elks 1951 ..20.00
Bowl, logo w/purple band, BPOE #23, Buffalo China, 5½" 10.00
Charm, elk head on teardrop enameled clock w/14k wht gold tooth ..40.00
Medal, 1902 Salt Lake Reunion, elk head w/IL Delegate, 3-part ..45.00
Tie tack, enameled w/14k gold elk head attached to elk tooth 50.00
Watch fob, 14k gold elk head below enameled clock on elk tooth ..80.00

Masons

Apron, HP symbols on silk, bl silk band/fringe, wear, 15x15" 55.00
Apron, needlework symbols on silk, early 1800s, 18x18", in fr ...635.00
Ashtray, wht w/logo in center & gold edge, 5¼" dia 15.00
Badge, Knights Templar, Bidderford Commandrey #4, 2-pc, 3¼" L ...25.00
Belt buckle, Masonic Kilt, pewter, eng, emb in center...................30.00
Book, History of Freemasonry Among Negroes in America, Davis, 1946...25.00
Bowl, Masonic Temple in Rochester NY, MIG, Jonrith & Co, 5¼" ..15.00
Cuff links, 10k gold w/logo, ½x⅝", pr.......................................33.00
Flask, Al Malaikah Temple, eng desert & pyramid scene, dtd 1912..50.00
Flyer, Masonic & Eastern Star Gifts & Novelties, 1930s...............25.00
Money clip, cabachon, enameled w/gold flecks & logo, 1⅛x1⅝" .17.50
Necklace, 5 rhinestone-centered stars below gold-plated logo, w/chain ..25.00
Pendant, gold w/logo in circle, 3x4" dia 30.00
Pin, delegate; Eastern Star, 32nd Triennial Assembly, 1967 ....15.00
Pin, fez shape, red enamel w/torch & emblem, ⅞" 15.00
Pin, Shriner emblem, 14k gold w/7 dmns, ¾" 40.00
Pin, 50 Year Member, star in center, gold-tone 15.00
Plate, 1912 Defender of the Cross, gold trim, 8¼"..........................20.00
Ring, 14k gold w/bl enameled 'G' & logo w/sm dmn ea side.........70.00
Tac pin, Past Patron, emblem & Eastern Star, gold-tone, ½"........12.50

Odd Fellows

Book, Forms & Ceremonies, 65 pgs, 1927, 5½x8¼".......................20.00
Book, Ritual Lodge, 209 pgs, 1961, 5½x8¼" 20.00
Doorstop, CI, crescent moon/7 stars/bird/3 rings w/FLT over lg R, #81 ..230.00
Hat, blk velvet w/silver embr design, EX.......................................35.00
Oil on brd, hand/tree/heart/card, 19th C, 7¾x15" 920.00
Paperweight, Rebekah, w/moon, stars, dove & chain, glass, EX....20.00
Pin, hammer hangs from 3-link chain w/star below, 10k gold, EX 40.00
Reflector, 3-link chain & eye on plastic front, 3½" dia.................25.00

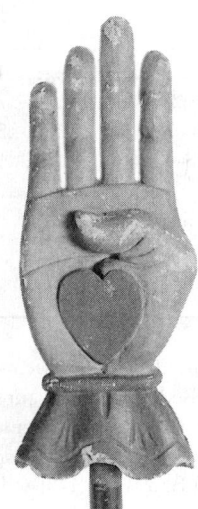

Staff, carved and painted heart in hand, $1,100.00. (Photo courtesy Aston Macek Auctioneers and Appraisers)

Staff, cvd wood w/mc pnt, top: hand w/cuffed sleeve, 64" 2,300.00

Sword, faux ivory hdl w/knight's head on top, 27" blade, w/sheath...80.00
Tunic, biege w/metallic trim, silver metal discs, cotton, EX 70.00
Turban, blk w/Brown Race tag inside, EX 35.00
Wall hanging, 24 symbols/etc in ovals on cloth, NY, 19th C, 48x75" ...3,000.00

Shrine

Badge, Prefection, brass/celluloid, w/maroon & yel ribbon, 4¾" ...30.00
Badge, SP brass, Imperial Council...Atlantic City NJ...1904, w/ribbon ..25.00
Money clip, NP brass, 1980s, 2⅝x1⅜" 10.00
Mug, gold & blk transfer on wht ceramic, ca 1910, 3⅛", NM 35.00
Paperweight, glass, mirror bk w/Shrine Jewel photo, 4¼x2¾x1" ..40.00
Picture, fr, grpt steel, early 20th C, early rvpt symbolic mat, 13x11"..70.00
Pin, enamel & 14k gold, ½x¼", EX...35.00

Miscellaneous

Eagles, doorknob in eagle shape, brass, 2½" dia, pr........................60.00
Knights of Pythias, medal, knight w/Xd axes, sterling w/brass o/l 25.00
Lions Club, plate, emblem on wht, Balfouc Ceramics, 10½" 12.50
Loyal Order of Moose, trivet, moose stands in grass, bronze, EX...14.50
Loyal Order of Moose Member Sponsor Award, mug, wht w/moose, EX..13.50
VFW, pin, lapel; wht van w/red trim w/VFW New Jersey, w/cross, plastic ...20.00

Fraunfelter

Charles Fraunfelter organized his company in Zanesville, Ohio, in 1915. It was known as the Ohio Pottery Company until 1923. During this period their main product was a line of utilitarian articles for chemical laboratories made of hard-paste porcelain. In 1918 they used the same body to produce a brown and white line called 'Petruscan.' By 1920 a line of hotel ware was added. The company organized in 1923 and became known and Fraunfelter China Company; but after the death of Fraunfelter in 1925, the business fell into hard times and eventually closed altogether in 1939.

Casserole, HP pheasants & flowers, steam vent in lid, 1¾x9" 95.00
Coffeepot, emb/pnt floral on wht, Therm-O-Proof........................38.00
Creamer, Bird of Paradise, silver trim, #2632 ....20.00
Creamer, cobalt w/fluer-de-lis, gold int, #289, 2⅝x2⅝" 35.00
Creamer, gr & wht Deco style w/platinum trim 15.00
Creamer & sugar bowl, HP Nouveau decor, gold hdls, #80 ....45.00
Dripolator, cream w/gr trim, aluminum parts mk Enterprise..........30.00
Dripolator, wht-over-red w/central silver band, +cr/sug.................90.00
Percolator set, lustreware, +cr/sug...125.00
Plate, wht w/Coronado Hotel crest & brn & bl band, 7½"...........15.00
Platter, pale bl, oval, 13¼" 15.00
Teapot, cream w/gold trim, 4-cup..55.00
Teapot, gr & wht Deco style w/platinum trim, S-88, 8-cup...........65.00
Teapot, teal w/gold decor, gold spout & hdl, #376?.....................65.00
Teapot, wht daises on gr, metal hinged lid w/eng dmn band, 6½" ...45.00
Teapot, wht-over-red w/silver band, 9" 50.00
Vase, pearlized purple, #93, 4½" 35.00

Fruit Jars

As early as 1829, canning jars were being manufactured for use in the home preservation of foodstuffs. For the past twenty-five years, they have been sought as popular collectibles. At the last estimate, over four thousand fruit jars and variations were known to exist. Some are very rare, perhaps one-of-a-kind examples known to have survived to the present day. Among the most valuable are the black glass jars, the amber

Van Vliet, and the cobalt Millville. These often bring prices in excess of $20,000.00 when they can be found. Aside from condition, values are based on age, rarity, color, and special features. For further information, we recommend *1000 Fruit Jars* by Bill Schroeder. Our advisor for this category is John Hathaway; he is listed in the Directory under Maine.

A Kline Pat'd Oct 27 63 Use Pin on Stopper, aqua, pt, NM 58.00
A Kline Use Pin Pat's Oct 27, 1863 on stopper, aqua, pt 80.00
Alston, The; qt, w/repro lid 250.00
American (over eagle & flags) Fruit Jar, lt gr, qt.........................125.00
Atlas Can or Freeze, ½-pt..20.00
Atlas E-Z Seal, amber, qt..55.00
Atlas E-Z Seal, aqua, ½-pt..20.00
Atlas E-Z Seal, gr, w/gr lid, pt..18.00
Atlas Junior Mason, ½-pt...18.00
Atlas Mason's Patent, apple gr, qt..20.00
Atlas Mason's Patent Nov 30th 1858, aqua, ½-gal...........................9.00
Ball Ideal Ball, bl, full wire bail, ½-pt...55.00
Ball Ideal Pat'd July 14, 1908, lt gr, qt...6.00
Ball Improved (dropped A), pt..9.00
Ball Mason, apple gr, qt..35.00
Ball Perfect Mason, amber, 6 ribs, ½-gal 45.00
Ball Perfect Mason, aquamarine, ½-gal...25.00
Ball Perfect Mason, bl, rnd, old, ½-pt..135.00
Ball Perfect Mason, bl, sq, qt..10.00
Ball Perfection, bl, pt, no closure..100.00
Banner (in stippled banner), ½-pt..150.00
Banner encircled by Pat dates, aqua, qt...150.00
BBGMCo, aqua, ½-gal...175.00
Bosco Double Seal, qt, NM..33.00
Boston Trade Mark Dagger (dagger) Brand, lt gr, qt 250.00
Bostwick Perfect Sealer, pt..100.00
Brighton, ½-gal, repro clamp..130.00
Canton Domestic Fruit Jar, orig wire, qt..120.00
Canton Fruit Jar, ½-gal...150.00
Caroll's True Seal, pt..58.00
Clark Fruit Jar Cleveland O, aqua, qt, orig 100.00
Clark's Peerless, aqua, qt..6.00
Cohansey (arched), strong emb, aqua, pt 75.00
Crown (crown), deep sun-colored amethyst, clear lid, qt 14.00
Crown (crown)/T Eaton Co...Toronto..., bl, qt.................................58.00
Crown (Sweet Heat Crown) Imperial, aqua, pt................................35.00
Crown Mason, ribbed, ½-pt..20.00
Dexter (circled by fruit), aqua, qt, orig closure................................95.00
Doolittle (script), aqua, no lid, ½-gal...50.00
Double Seal, qt..15.00
Durham (in circle), aqua, pt...30.00
Easy Co BJCMono Vacuum Jar, aqua, orig lid, 3-prong clamp, qt.40.00
EC Hazard & Co Shrewbury NJ, aqua, tall qt...................................20.00
Electric World Globe, aqua, repro clamp, qt...................................135.00
Empire, The; aqua, repro clamp, ½-gal...98.00
Eureka 12 Patd Dec 27th 1864, aqua, qt 80.00
Fruit Commonwealth Jar, qt...88.00
Fruit Keeper GCCO, aqua, orig clamp, pt...75.00
Gem, aqua, midget...40.00
Gem Rutherford & Co, The; aqua, qt 20.00
Gimbel Bros Pure Food Store Phil, pt...48.00
Globe, amber, qt..125.00
Golden Crown (crown) Table Syrup, pt...30.00
Haines's Patent March 1st 1870, aqua, orig wire, qt......................130.00
Haines's 3 Patent March 1st 1870, aqua, repro wire, qt.................100.00
Hero, The; aqua, orig 2-pc lid, qt...95.00
Hero (over cross), aqua, qt...55.00
Hero Improved, The; aqua, qt..35.00

Honest Mason Jar Pat 1858, dk sun-colored amethyst, qt 40.00
Ideal, The; aqua, qt..25.00
Ideal Imperial, The; aqua, qt 35.00
Jewel Bar (in block letters in fr), qt..15.00
Kemp Day & Company New - York, aqua, qt...................................125.00
Kerr Self Sealing Mason, sky bl, ½-gal...75.00
King Pat Nov 2, 1869, The; aqua, repro clamp, qt, lid chip........188.00
Knox (K in Keystone), ½-pt, w/unmk zinc lid..................................25.00
Lafayette (in script), qt..190.00
Leader, The (1 line); aqua, repro metal, pt 100.00
Leader, The (2 lines); amber, repro of lower half metal, qt 200.00
LeGrand Ideal (monogram) Pat'd 7-5-98 Vacuum Jar, aqua, orig lid ..200.00
Lockport Mason, aqua, pt...4.00
Lynchburg Standard Mason, aqua, qt..30.00
Manufactured for JT Kinney Trenton, NJ, aqua qt, NM 250.00
Mason, teal gr, qt..45.00
Mason (arched) Improved (5 dots below Mason), apple gr, qt......30.00
Mason (over Q G), sun-colored amethyst, qt..................................150.00
Mason's (cross) Improved, reverse: circle, aqua, qt........................25.00
Mason's CFJ Improved, midget 25.00
Mason's Cross Improved Ghost Trade Mark, lt apple gr, qt 48.00
Mason's Cross Patent Nov 30th, aqua, midget, flake 42.00
Mason's Cross Patent Nov 30th 1858, lt apple gr, qt 69.00
Mason's Jar of 1872 (ghost Improved), aqua, qt, ground chips 58.00
Mason's Patent Nov 30th 58, aqua, midget......................................60.00
Mason's Patent Nov 30th 58 Christmas Mason, aqua, pt............100.00
Mason's 2 Patent Nov 30th 1858, aqua, midget...............................50.00
Mason's 7 (sm) Patent Nov 30th 1858, gr, qt...................................22.00
Mountain Mason, rnd, qt..22.00
Newark Special Extra Mason Jar, lt gr, qt..30.00
Pacific (script) Mason, qt...35.00
Pat'd Mrch 26th 1867 BB Wilcox 17, aqua, qt, all orig...............125.00
Pet, aqua, ½-gal...150.00
Presto, ½-pt...35.00
Protector (arched), aqua, repro lid, qt..43.00
Protector (panels not recessed), aqua, ½-gal...................................43.00
Putnam (base), amber, qt...50.00
Royal (below crown) TM Full Measure, amber, w/amber lid, qt .100.00
Smalley's (crown) Royal Trademark Nu-Seal, base: Smalley, ½-pt ...75.00
Solidex (in oval on lid only), lt gr, qt...32.00
Star (above star), aqua, repro closure, ½-gal...................................150.00

Trade Mark Advance (overlaid on JW monogram) Pat. Apl'd For, aqua, smooth base, correct glass lid (also marked), quart, $450.00. (Photo courtesy Glassworks Auctions)

Star (circled by fruit), aqua, repro closure, ½-gal..........................145.00
Trade Mark Lightning, amber, pt...125.00
Trade Mark Lightning, amber, ½-gal...120.00
Trade Mark Lightning, gr, qt..125.00
Trade Mark Lightning Putnam (all on base), amber, 24-oz 135.00
Trade Mark the Dandy, amber, qt..250.00
Trademark No 1 Lightning, aqua, qt 135.00
Trademark VR Lightning (fancy letters), aqua, ½-gal 225.00
Winslow Jar, aqua, ½-gal, all orig 125.00

Fry

Henry Fry established his glassworks in 1901 in Rochester, Pennsylvania. There, until 1933 when it was sold to the Libbey Company, he produced glassware of the finest quality. In the early years they produced beautiful cut glass; and when it began to wane in popularity, Fry turned to the manufacture of occasional pieces and oven glassware. He is perhaps most famous for the opalescent pearl art glass called 'Foval.' It was sometimes made with blue or jade green trim in combination. Because it was in production for only a short time in 1926 and 1927, it is hard to find. For further information, we recommend *Collector's Encyclopedia of Fry Glassware* by the H.DC. Fry Glass Society. Our advisor for this category is Ron Damaska; he is listed in the Directory under Pennsylvania. See also Kitchen Collectibles, Glassware.

Baker, pearl ovenware, oval, 6", from $35 to 38.00
Baker, pearl ovenware, 9" sq..30.00
Bean pot, mk Fry Ovenware #1924-1, w/lid, 1-qt 85.00
Bell, amber, needle etched, 7½"..45.00
Bonbon, cut dmns & fans, sgn, 5¾" 60.00
Bottle, scent; Foval, Delft Blue stopper w/etched flower, 7½".....385.00
Bowl, console; blk w/crystal swirl ball stem & ruffled ft 280.00
Bowl, cut, Lyton, sawtooth rim, 4x8"..80.00
Bowl, cut, 3 flowers in bottom fans around stars, sawtooth rim, 7"..95.00
Bowl, cut stars/fans/X-hatching, notched rim, 3x7", NM 100.00
Bowl, Foval, int gold/bl bands, Delft Blue ped ft, 4x8" 200.00
Bowl, fruit; cut, Orient, ftd, 9"..175.00
Bowl, ice cream; Rose etch..17.50
Brown betty, pearl ovenware, 9", from $55 to 65.00
Cake plate, Sunnybrook, pk, ftd, 12"...48.00
Candle holder, blk, wide flat ft, 3" 18.00
Candlesticks, Foval ft/cup, bl threads on alabaster stem, 11", pr.200.00
Casserole, pearl ovenware, emb grapes, w/lid, 7" dia, from $55 to.65.00
Casserole, pearl ovenware, w/lid, 7" sq, in metal holder, from $85 to..95.00
Casserole, pearl ovenware, w/lid & metal fr, 8½" 25.00
Casserole, pearl ovenware, 2-part, shallow, 9" 40.00
Compote, cut, Orient, 7⅜x6", NM 125.00
Compote, wht w/lt gr stem, 6⅞"..460.00
Creamer & sugar bowl, Foval, Delft Blue hdls, sm........................70.00
Cup, coffee; pearl ovenware 27.50
Cup, custard; eng, 6-oz, from $10 to 12.00
Cup, custard; pearl ovenware 16.00
Cup, lemonade; Foval w/Jade Green hdl, 5⅜" 65.00
Dish, cut, heart shape, sgn, 5¾" 160.00
Goblet, amber w/gold-encrusted rim, 9-oz, 6⅝" 25.00
Goblet, Dmn Optic, azure, 7"..35.00
Ice bucket, pk, w/lid, from $225 to 245.00

Little Mother's Kidibake Set, two ramekins, pie plate, casserole, loaf pan, and recipe booklet, $250.00.

Jar, jelly/marmalade; Foval, w/hdls & lid, 1924, 9-oz, ...60.00
Loaf pan/bread baker, pearl ovenware, 3x9½x5¼"...........................40.00
Nappy, cut, Lyton, 1¼x6"...80.00
Percolator, Ovenglass, complete, 10", NM 375.00

Pie plate, eng, 9½", in holder, from $45 to............................50.00
Pie plate, pearl ovenware, #1916, 9" 30.00
Pie plate, pearl ovenware, 10" 15.00
Pitcher, Celeste Blue, bubbles/rim threading, bl hdl, 9", +underplate....150.00
Pitcher, crystal w/gr hdl & knob finial, crackle glass, 9¼" 240.00
Pitcher, Foval, ftd, Delft Blue hdl, 7" 125.00
Pitcher, smoke gray, crackle glass, pinched spout, 11" 135.00
Plate, cut, Brighton, 7" sq 245.00
Plate, grill; pk, 8½", from $30 to...50.00
Plate, sherbet; Rose etch, plain center, 6" 20.00
Plate, sherbet; Rose etch, star-cut center, 6" 25.00
Platter, fish; eng, 11", from $60 to..65.00
Platter, meat; gr, Not Heat Resisting Glass, 13", from $115 to....125.00
Platter, tree & well; Ovenglass, w/matching SP holder, 16¾x12"..55.00
Ramekin, pearl ovenware, 3", from $15 to 18.00
Roaster, pearl ovenware, dome lid, 7½x14x10", from $200 to 225.00
Saucer, Foval, 4½" 20.00
Saucer champagne, Rose etch, str sides 20.00
Server, eng, 8-sided oval, 6½x9" w/holder, from $65 to 75.00
Sherbet, Foval, Delft Blue stem & ft 120.00
Sherbet, Rose etch, flared top 20.00
Shirred egg dish, pearl ovenware, 7½" dia, from $30 to 35.00
Snack set, Foval, 6x9" plate w/cup, from $45 to 50.00
Snack set, Royal Blue, 6x9" plate w/cup, from $95 to 110.00
Stem, wine; crystal w/gold band at rim w/flower pattern, 7"..........20.00
Sugar bowl, cut, Pershing, 4x3"..60.00
Sugar bowl, Foval w/Jade Green hdls, open, 3x5½" 240.00
Teapot, Foval w/Jade Green hdl, spout & finial, EX 365.00
Trivet, Foval, #1959, 8" dia...35.00
Tumbler, crystal w/blk scalloped ft, red fired-on band, 13-oz, 5½" ...45.00
Tumbler, crystal w/fired-on yel & gold trim, hdl, 12-oz, 4¾".........50.00
Tumbler, iced tea; cut, Japanese Maid, cherry blossom hdl, ftd, 5"...115.00
Tumbler, Panel Optic, Rose Pink, 6" 25.00
Vase, clear crackle glass, amethyst appl rosettes 75.00
Vase, cut, Daisy Flora, cylindrical w/flared top, 10" 90.00
Vase, Dmn Quilt w/blk glass threading, 9½x7x4¾" 195.00

Fulper

Throughout the nineteenth century (for perhaps as long as one hundred years) the Fulper pottery in Flemington, New Jersey, produced utilitarian and commercial wares. But it was during the span from 1909 to 1935 (the Arts & Crafts period in particular) that they became prominent producers of beautifully glazed art pottery. Although most pieces were cast and not hand decorated, their graceful, classical shapes together with wonderful experimental glaze combinations made each piece a true work of art.

The company also made dolls' heads, Kewpies, figural perfume lamps and powder boxes. Examples prized most highly by collectors today are those that were produced before the devastating fire of 1929 and the subsequent takeover by Martin Stangl. (See Stangl Pottery.)

Several marks were used: a vertical in-line 'Fulper' being the most common, a horizontal mark, Flemington, Rafco, Prang, and paper labels (on earlier pieces). Most Fulper is marked although unmarked pots that surface can be identified by shape and glaze characteristics. Values are determined by size, desirability of glaze, and rarity of form. Lamps with colored glass inserts are rare and avidly sought by collectors. Our advisor for this category is Douglass White; he is listed in the Directory under Florida.

Bookends, book form, oatmeal on Copperdust crystalline, 4⅞", pr ...700.00
Bowl, bl-gr crystalline, scalloped rim, 4⅝x9¾".............................150.00
Bowl, Chinese Blue Flambe, ink stamp, 3½" H 160.00
Bowl, panels w/emb peacock feathers or florals, cream/bl/brn drip, 10"...250.00

Candlestick, Mirror Black on Copperdust crystalline, 2⅜" 200.00
Chamber stick, Wisteria, hdl, racetrack ink stamp, 7¼" 160.00
Console set, Chinese Blue flambe, 16" bowl+2 candlesticks, NM ..300.00
Flower frog, scarab, gr over bl flambe, 1⅜x3¼", NM....................70.00
Jar, Mirror Black, str/flaring sides, w/lid, 7" 425.00
Lamp, brn matt fluted base/10" shade w/daffodils & inset slag pcs, 17" ..7,500.00
Lamp, Flemington Gr, 16" #22 shade w/30 bl & gr inset sqs, sgn/#d base ...17,000.00
Urn, indigo bl snowflake crystals on bl flambe, 4 ear hdls, 13"...4,700.00
Vase, Ashes of Rose, angle hdls, wide hip shape, 7¾" 400.00
Vase, Ashes of Rose crystalline on Elephant's Breath, hdls, 6¼"..375.00
Vase, bl crystalline over brn, squat ftd pear form, 7½" 600.00
Vase, bl drip w/bl & gr matt over lt gr matt, bulbous/shouldered, 10" ..475.00
Vase, bl snowflake crystalline, 6-sided, #511, 7⅝" 700.00
Vase, bl w/gray drip, angle shoulder, geometric neck band, 9", NM......475.00
Vase, bl/brn drip w/dk crystalline highlights, squat w/wide collar, 6" 220.00

Vases, each with original label (which adds value) from Panama Pacific Exposition of 1915: Blue and green crystalline, open handles, 11½", $3,750.00; Blue and brown flambe, bulbous with banded neck and flared rim, 15", $1,800.00. (Photo courtesy Treadway Gallery, Inc.)

Vase, blk streaks on gr over bl gloss, sq/tapering, Prang, 9" 400.00
Vase, bright bl drip over gr, flared top, ogee sides, 13", NM........300.00
Vase, brn/yel flambe w/some lt bl at base, spherical, 7", NM 250.00
Vase, butterscotch flambe, flared ft, die-stamp mk, 12" 550.00
Vase, Cat's Eye Flambe, #576, racetrack mk, 11½" 950.00
Vase, Cat's Eye Flambe, angle hdls, racetrack mk, 8"...................400.00
Vase, Cat's Eye Flambe, squat pear form w/rim-to-width hdls, 6"...250.00
Vase, Chinese Blue Flambe over silvered crystalline Mirror Black, 10"..1,500.00
Vase, Copperdust crystalline, single arched hdl, #571, 11¾" ...3,500.00
Vase, Copperdust on gr flambe, low angle width, conforming hdls, 10" ...650.00
Vase, cream to olive to bl flambe, bullet form, 10" 600.00
Vase, cucumber crystalline, bulbous w/can neck, rim-to-width hdls, 8"..550.00
Vase, dk shades of bl gloss, ovoid, 6½" 260.00
Vase, emb mushrooms, creamy yel flambe w/mocha highlights, #444, 10"....1,400.00
Vase, Flemington Green drip on oatmeal speckle, buttressed rim, 5"..425.00
Vase, Flemington Green on rose, 4 buttresses, 8⅛" 350.00
Vase, frothy bl crystalline, 2 loop hdls, #574, 13" 650.00
Vase, gloppy bl-gr flambe over Famille Rose, 3-hdl, 6⅝"............550.00
Vase, gloppy gr matt, vertical mk, classic shape, 5⅞" 275.00
Vase, gr on teal over streaky Wisteria, oval mk, 16½" 3,300.00
Vase, gr w/minute crystals, flambe at flaring neck, 12x8".........3,000.00
Vase, gr/brn metallic, 6¾" 425.00
Vase, gunmetal/brn/gr flambe, can w/4 molded buttresses, bulb base, 9"...350.00
Vase, mint gr crystalline, rnd w/can neck, rim-to-width hdls, 7½"...260.00
Vase, mint gr crystalline w/lt irid, rnd w/3 sm rim hdls, disc ft, 8"....450.00
Vase, Mirror Black, brn & ochre flambe, #588, 11⅜" 2,900.00
Vase, Mirror Black, bulbous w/ped ft, flared neck, hdls, 12"........650.00
Vase, Mirror Black over Flemington Green crystalline, hdls, 2⅞" ...150.00
Vase, Mirror Black w/flowing Copperdust, #536, 13" 1,700.00
Vase, multi-tone bl crystalline, rim-to-shoulder hdls, 9x4½" 600.00
Vase, multi-tone bl crystalline on red matt, wide urn form w/hdls, 9" ...1,600.00
Vase, pk to gray crystalline, slim/4-sided w/raised sq base, 8½"...260.00
Vase, red/ivory mingling matt, darker toward base, bulbous, flaw, 12"...600.00
Vase, variegated grs on bl, #15, ink mk, 11" 1,600.00

Vase, Wisteria, angle hdls, 4½", NM..160.00
Vase, 2-tone Wisteria, rim-to-hip hdls, ink mk, 5¾" 200.00
Vase, 3-color flambe (umber & 2 bls), unmk, 5⅝" 425.00

Furniture

Aside its obvious utility, furniture has always been a symbol indicating wealth, taste, and social position. Each period of time has wrought distinct changes in style, choice of wood, and techniques — all clues that the expert can use to determine just when an item was made. Regional differences as well as secondary wood choice give us clues as to country and locale. The end of the Civil War brought with it the Industrial Revolution and the capability of producing man-made furniture. With this came the Victorian period and the many revival styles.

Important to the collector (and dealer) is the ability to recognize furniture on a 'good, better, best' approach. Age alone does not equal value. During a recessionary market the 'best' of forms always seem to do well. The 'better' or middle market will show a drop in value, and the 'good' or lower end of the marketplace will suffer the most. Many of this year's values emphasize what has been going on in the marketplace. Auction estimates for part of the year were way off the mark due to unforeseen economic factors. But the market is recovering, and at the time of this writing, prices realized at auction continue to show promise. Value is based on scarcity, form, and technique, as well as what is fashionable in the marketplace at the time. Some pieces are timeless classics and will always have a place in the antiques marketplace. Others are strictly fashionable at the time, and value is speculative at best.

Still popular and continuing to rise are the mahogany classic copies from the early twentieth century. This includes the styles of Queen Anne, Duncan Phyfe, Chippendale, Sheraton, and Hepplewhite. The English counterparts are also enjoying popularity. Turn-of-the-century European inlaid and carved furniture is still rising in value. Stronger in the marketplace is the 'decorator trade,' who realize this type of furniture is a sound investment and can be refinished (without any loss of value) to suit the client's needs. Upholstered pieces that are 'floor ready' are bringing stronger prices at auction. Frames for sofas, chairs, and benches needing new upholstery and some work are being sold reasonably to eager collectors and dealers. They realize that when the work is completed, they will have a unique, well-made item at a reasonable price.

Items that have sold at auction for at least 25% lower than their normal market values will be designated with (*). Items listed in the lines that are designated with (**) are pieces in the best of form and of museum quality.

Please note: If a piece actually dates to the period of time during which its style originated, we will use the name of the style only. For example: 'Hepplewhite' will indicate an American piece from roughly the late 1700s to 1815. The term 'style' will describe a piece that is far removed from the original time frame. 'Hepplewhite style' refers to examples from the turn of the century. When the term 'repro' is used it will mean that the item in question is less than thirty years old and is being sold on a secondary market. When only one dimension is given for blanket chests, dry sinks, tables, settees, sideboards, and sofas, it is length.

Condition is the most important factor to consider in determining value. It is also important to remember that *where* a piece sells has a definite bearing on the price it will realize, due simply to regional preference. Our advisor for this category is Suzy McLennan Anderson, ISA CAPP, of Heritage Antiques and Anderson Auctions, LLC, whose address is listed in the Directory under New Jersey. (Photo and SASE required; no phone appraisals.) To learn more about furniture, we recommend *The Collector's Encyclopedia of American Furniture* (there are three in the series) and *Furniture of the Depression Era* by Robert and Harriet Swedberg; *Heywood-Wakefield Modern Furniture* by Steve and Roger Rouland; *Antique Oak Furniture* by Conover Hill; *American Oak Furni-*

ture and *Victorian Furniture, Our American Heritage, Books I* and *II*, by Kathryn McNerney; *Collector's Guide to Oak Furniture* by Jennifer George; *Early American Furniture* by John Obbard; and *Antique Furniture*. See also Art Deco; Art Nouveau; Arts and Crafts; Fifties Modern; Limbert; Nutting, Wallace; Shaker; Stickley.

Key:

Am — American	Geo — Georgian, George
bj — bootjack	grpt — grainpainted
brd — board	hdbd — headboard
Chpndl — Chippendale	hdw — hardware
Co — Country	Hplwht — Hepplewhite
cvd — carved	mar — marriage
cvg — carving	NE — New England
c&b — claw and ball	QA — Queen Anne
do — door	rswd — rosewood
drw — drawer	trn — turning, turned
Emp — Empire	uphl — upholstered/upholstery
Fed — Federal	vnr — veneer
Fr — French	Vict — Victorian
ftbd — footboard	W/M — William and Mary
G — good	: — over (example: 1 do: 2 drw)

Armoires, See Also Wardrobes

Cherrywood Am w/inlay, rpl cornice:frieze:2 panel do, LA, 1790s......**10,350.00**
Mahog Am, beaded cornice:mirror do, LA, 19th C, 99x48x26"...........**3,450.00**
Mahog Am Classical, 2 panel do:fluted pilasters:cvd knees:paw ft, 90"..**7,500.00**
Mahog Am Late Classical, cornice:dbl panel do:stepped ftd base, 96"..**7,000.00**
Mahog Anglo-Indian, dbl mirror do, fitted int drws, 19th C, 84x45"...**1,600.00**
Mahog Fed w/cvg & gilt mts, att Duncan Phyfe, ca 1815, 86x66".........**9,775.00**
Walnut Fr Provincial, molded cornice:cvd frieze:dbl do:cvd apron, 93"..**3,750.00**

Beds

Burl walnut Am Renaissance w/vnr panels, much cvg, 92x64x84"...**8,000.00**
Cherry Co Sheraton w/pine hdbd, high posts/urn finials, rpl rails, 65".**990.00**
Cherry tall post w/acanthus cvg & EX trn, pine hdbd, w/tester, 62" H..**800.00**
Cherry w/cvg, 4-poster, scrolled hdbd, red wash traces, 93"................**3,795.00**
Cherry/pine Southern Fed, low posts, scrolled hdbd, 66x54"...........**1,850.00**
Curly maple, trn posts/blanket roll, urn finials, 43x50" * **880.00**
Mahog, tall-post w/tester, pineapple/urn/spiral cvgs, 92x54x75" .**3,275.00**
Mahog Am, tall octagonal posts, molded full tester, 1840s **2,300.00**
Mahog Am w/cove half-tester:scroll brackets:arched hdbd, 105" **5,175.00**
Mahog Am w/Gothic vnr panels, cvd posts, tester, 1850s, 104x76x58"...**4,000.00**
Mahog Classical, low posts w/ball finials, scrolling hdbd, 46x56" **1,150.00**
Mahog Emp w/flame vnr, tall posts, acanthus cvg, pineapple finials ..**2,200.00**
Mahog Sheraton style, trn ft w/tall urn posts & reeding, 42" W, pr.......**650.00**
Rope, curly maple w/poplar hdbd insert, ball finials/bold trns, 54" H....**935.00**
Rswd Louis Philippe style, rnded hdbd & ftbds, 1840-50s, 52x58".....**3,750.00**
Sheraton, tall-post w/canopy, brass bolt-hole covers, 89x50x72".......**4,000.00**
Sleigh, mahog Am Late Classical w/Gothic cvg, plinth ft, 41x64"...**3,735.00**

Benches

Bucket, pine Co, truncated sides, grad shelves, rfn, 44x36x15" ..**495.00**
Bucket, step-down, pine w/gr over early red, 4-shelf, C ends, 48", EX..**1,900.00**
Ebonized English Regency, uphl crest:spindles:uphl seat:trn legs, 58" .**1,600.00**
Giltwood Regency style, scrolled arms, reeded seat rail, reuphl, pr.**2,650.00**
Kneeler, walnut English Vict, velvet uphl w/beading, 1890s, 46" L...**575.00**
Mahog Geo III style w/cvg, serpentine seat, scroll arms, 42".......**515.00**
Mammy's, blk rpt w/EX stencil decor, rprs, 30x52" **770.00**
Pine w/worn mustard rpt, bj ends, 2-brd top w/shaped aprons, 56"..**135.00**
Red pnt, bj ends, water stains, 17x15x43"..................................**350.00**

Settle, oak Geo w/cvg, paneled bk, curved seat, 60x66" **3,200.00**
Water, pine w/bl on base, scrubbed top, bj ends, wear, 20x12x47"..**325.00**
Window, fruitwood Louis XV style, foliate cvgs, cabriole legs, 25x24"...**250.00**
Windsor, bamboo trn, 29-spindle bk, arms, rpr/rpt, 78" **2,000.00**

Blanket Chests, Coffers, Trunks, and Mule Chests

Dower, PA pnt/decor, dvtl, appl moldings, dtd 1795, 22x48x20"..**3,000.00**
Fruitwood Fr Provincial, Ionic capitals, block ft, 30x46x24" **1,035.00**
Immigrant's, pine, rpt tombstone panels w/unicorns, 40" L, VG.**800.00**
Ohio, poplar w/blk over red, 1-brd top, scalloped apron, 23x38x19" ...**1,925.00**
Pine, dvtl, old salmon rpt, 1-brd top, rpl ft, 20x38x16" **330.00**
Pine, 6-brd, dvtl bracket ft, orig bl pnt, NY, 1790s, 21x44x22"..**5,175.00**
Pine down to red traces, 1-brd top, 2-drw, rpl hinges, rpr, 42x40x17"...**770.00**
Pine w/brn over salmon decor, dvtl, dtd 1850, rprs/rpl hinges, 38" **715.00**
Pine 6-brd, orig smoke & bl-gr smoke decor, 1800s, 22x37x16".....**3,735.00**
Pnt pine, PA, molded top:till:dvtl box:cut-out ft, old gr pnt, 39" **865.00**
Pnt/decor PA, 6-brd, dvtl, iron hdls, 1790s, 18x48x20"..............**800.00**
Poplar w/PA red-brn over orange, dvtl, 1-brd top, till, rstr hinge ..**330.00**
Sheraton Co w/early red rpt, pegged, trn ft, 25x39x20" **550.00**
Steamer trunk, Louis Vuitton, emb leather, fitted int, EX **4,000.00**
Walnut PA, wrought-iron bear trap lock, 2-drw, 26x48x24" **1,800.00**

Bookcases

Breakfront, mahog Geo III style w/cvg, 6 glass do:6 panel, 94x156" ..**8,625.00**
Cypress, 2 glazed do:2, shelved int, 86x52x14".........................**1,265.00**

Lawyer's bookcase, five-section, quartersawn oak with beveled leaded glass doors, $2,200.00.

Mahog Am, 3 Gothic-pane do:base of 3 drw:4 panel do, 1840s, 102x79"...**6,000.00**
Mahog Am Gothic, cornice: dbl glazed do:2 panel drw:plinth, 92x50" ..**3,165.00**
Mahog Geo III style, 4 mullioned do:4 panel do, 108x95x16".**6,000.00**
Oak Am Rococo, cvd central do & scroll glazed do:2 drw & 2 do, 77x93"..**1,600.00**
Rswd Vict, cvd crest:dbl do:4 drw w/cvd escutcheons, 93x59x24" **..**11,785.00**
Walnut Am, arched top w/compass & globe:dbl do:skirt, 1850s, 105x55"....**3,450.00**
Walnut Am Modern Gothic, gallery:3 shelves:2-drw base, att Pabst...**2,000.00**
Walnut Am Rococo, crest w/shell:do:shaped skirt, appl tracery, 92x38"..**2,650.00**
Walnut Am Rococo, scrolling pediment w/cvd bust:dbl do:2 drw, 113x73"..**11,500.00**
Walnut Dutch bombe, arched pediment w/crest, 2-part, c&b ft, 109x72".......**8,625.00**
Walnut Vict step-bk, cvd crest:glass do:drw, 86x33".................**2,400.00**

Bureaus, See Chests

Cabinets

Apothecary, blk stain, 48-drw, scalloped bj ends, wire nails, 62x43" ..**4,000.00**
Apothecary, 16-drw, rfn, 30x39"...**1,100.00**

Bombe, cvd mahog, cornice:panel do:3-drw base, Dutch, 1800s, 101x71"...**13,800.00**
Breakfront, pine Geo III, 3 mullioned dbl do:3 dbl panel do, 94x109"..**11,500.00**
China, mahog w/inlay, crest:2 mullioned do:2 drw:apron, 19th C, 65"....**1,150.00**
Corner, pine Chpndl, 2 arched raised-panel do, rfn/rpl/rpr, 1760s, 94" **7,500.00**
Corner wall; mahog English fluted demilune, shaped top rail, 38x18x18" ..**500.00**
Curio, Fr gilt w/ormolu trim, HP floral, cabriole legs, 20th C, 50x27"......**800.00**
Curio, Fr-style gilt rpt w/gesso detail, serpentine glass, 44x25", EX............**770.00**
Curio, mahog w/inlay on base do, glazed do in top, arch crest, 67x25"....**550.00**
Display, Geo III style, blk/gilt/red japanned Oriental decor, 81x31" **4,885.00**
Hanging, pine w/dk red finish, pumpkin rpt on do panel, 5 int drw, 25' ..**300.00**
Press, mahog Fed, vnr frieze, 3-part, 1820-25, 83½x48"............**7,000.00**
Record, oak, 5-drw, w/pegs...**450.00**
Spice, pine/poplar, wire nails, 15-drw, mustard sponged pnt, 19x11x4"...**2,200.00**
Vitrine, cherrywood & ebony Biedermeier style, gilt capitals, 76x46".....**3,500.00**

Candlestands

Butternut/maple Fed, canted-corner top, tripod base, 1800s, 29x20x16"..**2,000.00**
Cherry Chpndl, trn baluster:tripod:cabriole legs, rfn, 27x18x18" **600.00**
Cherry Co, sq top:vase & ring-trn shaft:tripod, rfn, 1790s, 25x17" sq....**1,265.00**
Cherry Fed, tilt-top:tripod w/curving legs, partial rfn, 27x21x16".........**635.00**
Cherry Fed, 8-sided beaded tray top:tripod, early 1800s, 28x16x22"....**575.00**
Cherry Hplwht, octagonal 13x18"top, high 3-leg base, 28".........**600.00**
Cherry QA, swelled pedestal:tripod:pad ft, sm rpr, 26" **1,725.00**
Mahog Fed, tilt-top, tripod cabriole legs, rfn, 29½x24x16" **1,850.00**
Maple Fed, dish top on vase & ring-trn post:tripod legs, rfn, 29x15"....**2,000.00**
Oak, primitive, 3 chamfered legs/column on sq platform base, 34".........**550.00**
Tiger maple & maple dish-top, ring-trn post:tripod, old rfn, 27x16"..**2,000.00**

Chairs

Arm, bamboo Regency, lattice dmn medallion bk:uphl seat:splayed legs .**1,150.00**
Arm, cherry/maple QA, cvd crest:scroll-cvd arms:leather seat:trn legs **1,600.00**
Arm, mahog Chpndl w/much cvd, slip seat, c&b ft **575.00**
Arm, mahog Fed w/ogival wings, reuphl, old rfn, early 1800s, 47"....**6,250.00**
Arm, mahog Fed wing-bk, sq seat, tapered legs, reuphl, rfn, 47".....**3,000.00**
Arm, mahog Geo III, bowed crest:pierced splat:sq legs **1,150.00**
Arm, maple QA, yoke crest:vasiform splat:rpl seat:trn legs, red stain ..**4,200.00**
Arm, Old Hickory, spindled bow-bk, woven seat, 36" **325.00**
Arm, Old Hickory, woven splint seat/bk, orig finish, 36", VG **450.00**
Arm, pnt banister bk w/stag horn crest:rush seat:trn legs, 44"....**3,000.00**
Arm, rswd Am Rococo, foliate crest:pierced stiles:cabriole legs reuphl...**2,400.00**

Armchair, rosewood (carved and laminated) American Rococo, John Henry Belter, shaped back with ribbon-tied rose crest and foliage, cabriole legs, brass casters, fine upholstery, 1850 – 60, $3,400.00.

Arm, rswd/vnr Vict, leaf-cvd arms, cvd crest/apron, rstr, 43" **800.00**
Arm, walnut Vict, finger-cvd detail, uphl, rprs, 41"....................**440.00**
Arm, Windsor, blk-pnt bow-bk, J Oldham brand, 1790-1835 ** ..**6,500.00**
Chaise, Louis XVI style, mechanical bk/damask uphl, 19th C, 32x68x28"..**1,600.00**

Corner, Co w/alligatored pnt, trn legs, rpl crest rail/rush seat, 30" ...**440.00**
Corner, mahog Chpndl, cvd bk splats:uphl seat:apron:claw ft, 34"..**635.00**
Corner, mahog Geo III style, Gothic pierced splats, arms **460.00**
Corner, maple Co, shaped crest:scrolled splats:rpl rush seat, 31" **1,600.00**
Corner, maple Co, trn stretchers/legs, scroll hand holds, shaped crest.....**330.00**
Corner, walnut QA, cabriole front leg, EX trn supports, U splats ** ...**5,000.00**
Library, mahog Geo III style, serpentine padded bk, damask uphl........**1,950.00**
Library, walnut Am Renaissance, reclines, much cvg, leather uphl, 51" .**2,500.00**
Recamier, mahog Am Classical, cvd bk, dolphin-cvd ft, reuphl, 73" ...**7,000.00**
Recamier, mahog Am Classical w/cvg, paw ft w/cvd brackets, 34x86", G..**7,765.00**
Rocker, arm; bent twig arms, 4-slat bk, shaped twig seat, pnt, 42"....**550.00**
Rocker, arm; Old Hickory, woven bow-bk & seat, 35" **325.00**
Rocker, arm; tiger maple Classical, caned bk rest & seat, 45"....**975.00**
Roundabout commode, walnut QA, pillow bk:sq seat:cabriole legs, rstr..**3,100.00**
Savonarola, oak Renaissance style, cvd bk:lion arm terminals:paw ft....**500.00**
Side, birch Co Chpndl, ribbon-bk, pegged, sq legs, rpl seat, 37".**110.00**
Side, English QA walnut, vase splat, cabriole front legs, rstr, VG...**880.00**
Side, hardwood, banister bk, yoke crest:trn ft/legs, rfn, 19th C, 43" ..**165.00**
Side, mahog Am, serpentine crest rail, cabriole legs, NY, 1850s....**175.00**
Side, mahog Chpndl w/cvd crest rail:pierced splat:slip seat:c&b ft....**575.00**
Side, mahog English QA, cvd/rtcl scrolls on ornate bk splat, rstr, 39" ...**1,000.00**
Side, mahog Geo III, yoke crest:pierced splats:sq legs..................**500.00**
Side, QA style mahog, Spanish ft, rush seat, 42" **385.00**
Side, S Badlam/SF, mahog Fed foliage-cvd shield bk, 37" **1,700.00**
Side, walnut Am, mask crest:minotaur-flanked splat:cvd seat/apron **425.00**
Side, walnut Chpndl, serpentine crest:slip seat:cabriole legs, rfn ** **4,600.00**
Side, Windsor, maple & ash 7-spindle fan-bk, dk brn w/gold, 36"......**1,600.00**
Side, Windsor, maple & ash 7-spindle sack-bk, old rfn, 37".....**3,000.00**
Side, Windsor, 7-spindle, bamboo trn, blk pnt, 34" **425.00**
Side, Windsor, 7-spindle, bamboo trn, 36"................................**275.00**
Slipper, rswd Am Renaissance, pierced foliate crest, silk uphl, 41"....**185.00**
Walnut Am Gothic w/much cvg, painted columns, arched bk, 48" ..**375.00**
Walnut Italian Neoclassical, ram's head terminals, uphl bk/seat....**2,000.00**

Chair Sets

Arm, beechwood Charles II style, needlepoint uphl, brass nails, pr ..**575.00**
Arm, mahog Napoleon III w/gilt bronze mts, sq bks, reuphl, pr.....**4,850.00**
Arm, walnut Am Neo-Greco w/incising & inlay, lady's, NY, 1850s, pr...**1,500.00**
Dining, mahog Chpndl style, pierced/cvd splats, c&b ft, 2 arm+6 side ...**3,000.00**
Dining, mahog Geo III style w/cvg, uphl seat, 1 arm+5 side....**3,000.00**
Kitchen, pnt Am Classical, gold on gr w/shaped crest, trn legs, 6 for ..**2,000.00**
Side, balloon bk, 3-color fruit/foliage, rstr/minor rpt, 4 for..........**750.00**
Side, beechwood Louis XVI style, padded bks/seats, cvd legs, 6 for....**2,300.00**
Side, cherry Chpndl style, rtcl bk bars/5-arch crest, Kittinger, 6 for ...**2,300.00**
Side, mahog Chpndl, beaded serpentine crests, rstr, 38", 5 for....**6,300.00**
Side, mahog Chpndl, crest:vasiform splat:slip seat:sq legs, 37", 5 for....**5,465.00**
Side, mahog Chpndl, ribbon bks, reuphl seat, sq legs, rstr, 8 for.........**19,550.00**
Side, mahog Chpndl, serpentine crests:uphl seat:sq legs, old rstr, pr **2,185.00**
Side, mahog English Hplwht style, cvd wheel bks/saddle seats, 6 for....**2,875.00**
Side, mahog Fed, 5 reeded slats:uphl seat w/bowed front, 37", 4 for.....**2,000.00**
Side, mahog Fr Emp, molded crest:lyre splat:bow front:cvd legs, 6 for.**8,625.00**
Side, mahog Wm IV w/cvg, Corinthian capital stiles, crest, 6 for........**3,500.00**
Side, satinwood Geo III style w/decor crest/apron, uphl seat, 4 for.......**2,750.00**

Chests (Antique), See Also Dressers

Bachelor's, mahog Geo III, dressing slide:3 grad drws, 32x33x19"..**4,600.00**
Blk japanned Geo III style bow-front w/chinoiserie, 2 short:2 drw, 44"..**2,000.00**
Campaign, hardwood Anglo/Indian, 2 short:3 long drw, 2-pc, 19th C, 42" ...**2,300.00**
Cherry Chpndl, 4-drw, 2-brd top, bracket ft, rstr/rpl, 35x38"..**3,850.00**
Cherry Co w/red wash, 6-drw, att PA, some pulls rpl, 49x43" **900.00**
Cherry Fed w/mahog vnr, bow-front, 4 grad drws, Fr ft, rfn/rpl, 39x41" ...**1,850.00**
Cherry/mahog vnr inlay Sheraton, 4-drw, reeded/trn pilasters, 42x43" ...**2,750.00**

Curly maple Co Sheraton, 2 short drw:3, rfn/rpl brasses, 44x43" .2,400.00
Dower, oak English, lift top:cvd frieze:block ft, ca 1800, 26x57x25" ..1,265.00
Dressing, mahog Am Late Fed, 2 sm drw:4 long:cvd paw ft, 52x45" 1,600.00
Japanned Geo I style w/gilt landscape, 2 short:3 grad drw, 40x40"...3,735.00
Mahog Fed, ogee top:4 drw:scalloped apron:tapered legs, 49x40" 1,850.00
Mahog Fed w/inlay, 4 grad drw:bracket ft, old rstr, 35x38x19" ...8,625.00
Mahog Geo III, shaped top:2 short:3 grad drw:bracket ft, 38x42x21" 2,300.00
Mahog Geo III style, 3 drw w/inlay:apron:Fr splayed ft, 34x43x19".......4,000.00
Mahog Hplwht w/inlay, 4 grad drw, flame vnr apron, Fr ft, 41x40" 3,750.00
Mahog Louis XV style, gray marble top:drw:cabriole legs:sabots, 36x40"..2,875.00
Maple/birch Co Hplwht, cornice:5 grad dvtl drw:bracket ft, 43x39".........6,600.00
Maple/pine Co Chpndl, stepped cornice, high bracket ft, rstr, 48x36".....1,500.00
On chest, cherrywood Am, 2 short:3 drws:2-drw base, 18th C, 60x44"....7,185.00
On chest, maple Chpndl, 2 short drw: 4 grad:base of 4 grad drw, 71" 14,950.00
On-chest, mahog Geo III style w/inlay, dentil-molded cornice, 71x40"..1,500.00
Tall, birch, cornice:cvd drw:4 grad:bracket ft, orig red, 54x36" ** 48,875.00
Tall, tiger maple Chpndl, cornice:6 grad drw:bracket ft, rfn, 58" 5,750.00
Tiger maple Chpndl, faux 3-drw facade:5 grad drw, rfn/rpl, 1789s, 55".8,000.00
Tiger maple Fed, 4 scratch-beaded grad drw:skirt, rfn, 39x39x18"..........4,300.00
Walnut Chpndl, cornice:2 short:6 grad drws:bracket ft, 53x40x22".......2,645.00
Walnut Chpndl, long:3 short drw:shell-cvd legs:c&b ft, rstr, 37x41x20"....4,300.00
Walnut Chpndl, 4 grad drw, fluted quarter columns, old rfn, 33x38" 6,900.00
Walnut Chpndl, 4 grad drw, rpl brass, old rfn, 1760-80, 37x35x21" 5,750.00
Walnut Fed w/inlay, 5 cockbeaded drw, lamb's tongue corners, 46x38".4,850.00
Walnut Geo I w/inlay, 2 short:3 grad drw:bracket ft, 35x38x23" 6,000.00

Cupboards, See Also Pie Safes

Bird's-eye maple step-bk, 3-drw:2 panel do:bracket ft, repro, 89x54"...2,300.00
Chimney, poplar, sides unfinished, 2-do, int shelves, 92x20"...1,100.00
Corner, cherry, 2 glazed do:2 panel do, stepped cornice, 78x17" 1,600.00
Corner, walnut Chpndl, 12-pane do:4-panel do, rpl/rfn, PA, 1780s, 84"..14,950.00
Corner, walnut Co, 2-pc, cornice:12-pane do:3 drw:2 do, 44x47"..3,300.00
Hanging, red pnt/int: mustard, scalloped crest, paneled do, 42x26"....1,000.00
Jelly, walnut, 2-do w/5 int shelves, molded cornice, att Zoar, 55x40"................1,200.00
Pewter, pine w/red rpt, inner edge of 'window' is scalloped, 80x34", G ..2,750.00
Pnt pine, dvtl w/arched/molded opening w/2 shelves, PA, 34x20x9"......8,000.00
Step-bk, pine Fed, cornice:2 8-pane do:drw:2 do, old rfn, 85x51x19"....7,000.00
Step-bk, pnt/glazed pine, cornice:2 6-pane do:3 drw:2 do, PA, 84x52"....9,775.00
Tall, hard pine, cornice:2 4-panel do:molded base:bracket ft, rfn, 69" 3,000.00
Tall, pnt pine, cornice:2-do:bracket base, RI, 1780s, 76x42x11"......6,900.00
Wall, pine Co, crest:dbl do:appl molded base, old rfn, 23x25x7" 2,645.00
Walnut Italian w/floral cvg, do:drw, canted sides, 18th C, 36x29"..3,300.00

Desks

Cherry Chpndl, oxbow slant lid, 4 grad drws:ogee ft, rfn, 45x39x22"......8,000.00
Cherry Chpndl, slant lid, reeded ¼-columns, int w/cvd shells, 45x40".14,850.00
Curly maple/pine Co, slant lid, 7 int drws, base molding, 40x38"............3,850.00
Davenport, burl walnut w/cvg, mechanical top w/leather insert, 36x22"....5,175.00
Davenport, burled walnut w/inlay, leather lift top, 1850s, 30x22"............1,955.00
Lap, mahog Geo IV w/brass inlay, leather top, 1820-25, 7x19x11" 1,500.00
Mahog Chpndl, block front drws, cvd lid, c&b ft, 43x39x20"..8,000.00
Mahog Chpndl serpentine, slant lid, 4 grad drw, rpl brasses, 44x42"..4,600.00
Mahog Fed inlaid tambour, bookcase top, MA, ca 1816, 82x40x20" ** ..34,500.00
Mahog Geo IV style, tooled leather top, dbl pedestals ea w/4 drws....6,000.00
Mahog Georgian, slant lid, fitted int, 2 short:3 grad drws, 43x38" 2,000.00
Oak Chpndl, slant lid, exposed dvtl top, bracket ft, 1850s, 38x22"..2,000.00
Oak English, gallery & sides w/cvgs, hinged lid, fitted int, 44x26"....1,600.00
Oak Geo III, slant lid, orig brass pulls, 4 long drws, 42"...........3,000.00
Plantation, walnut Am, bookcase top:folding flap:2 drw:trn legs, 79" ...1,500.00
Tiger maple Chpndl, drop-front, fitted int, grad drws, 41x36" ** 76,200.00
Tiger maple Chpndl, slant lid, fitted int & lid:3 drw, rfn, 40x36".........5,175.00
Walnut Chpndl, slant lid, fitted int, rpl brass, old rfn, 42x40" ..4,600.00

Walnut QA, slant lid, fitted int, 2 short:2 grad drw, rstr, 41x38"...2,500.00

Dressers (Machine Age), See Also Chests

Mahog, mirror:2 short:2 long drw, G Baver NY Pat, 7x52x23" ..1,450.00
Walnut Am Rococo w/figure, marble:4 grad drw, EC Peck, 39".1,400.00

Dry Sinks

Cherry/maple w/some curl, 2 raised poplar do, bracket ft, rpl bkbrd..935.00
Chestnut, gallery top:cupbrd do w/shaped recessed panels:3 drw, 71x36"...650.00
Grpt, yel/brn w/bl int, 2 dvtl drw w/sunken panels, 45" 2,300.00
Mixed woods w/dk brn rpt over varnish, angle ft, 1 drw, 30x25" ...880.00
Pine Co w/red alligatored rpt, 2 panel do/bracket ft, sq nails, 36x48"..1,200.00
Pnt Co, orig dk brn, 1-brd ends, 2 dvtl drw, OH, 32x42x18" 990.00
Poplar/pine w/grpt, bracket ft, 2-do base, step-bk top, 51x48x19" 2,100.00
Red-pnt pine, exposed tenons, shelf w/later copper insert, 19th C..2,645.00
Walnut/ash, old grpt, crest:3 drw:sink:2 panel do, rpr, 68x48x18" 5,775.00
Walnut/poplar w/old red pnt, 2 panel do, dvtl drw, 32x43x19", EX..1,750.00

Hall Piece

Chair, oak English, arched bk w/cvd shield:shaped seat:spike ft..250.00
Chair, oak Gothic, pierced arches:cvd apron:spade ft, 1860s, 52" 865.00
Chair, rswd Am, foliate scroll crest; pierced splat:trn stiles, 42" * 175.00
Cupboard, oak Jacobean style, arched panel do, 1890s, 72x30x23"....1,500.00

Hall tree, American golden oak, arched crest with applied carvings, beveled mirror back, storage bench, paw feet, original hardware, ca 1900, 89x48x18", $2,200.00.

Pier table, cvd giltwood, stenciled mahog, bronze mts, paw ft, 40x44" ..10,350.00
Pier table, mahog Am Late Fed, marble top, scroll supports, mirror bk....2,750.00
Pier table, rswd Late Fed, marble:apron:tapered legs:sq ft, 36x43x21".....1,600.00
Stand, walnut & rswd-grained Am Gothic, marble top center, 102" ** ...15,400.00

Highboys

Cherry Chpndl, 5 grad drw:drw:3:cabriole legs, orig brasses, rfn, 71" 23,000.00
Cherry QA, cornice:4 grad drw:base of long drw:3:cabriole legs, 70" 30,000.00
Mahog QA, cornice:2 short:3 grad drw:drw:cabriole legs:pad ft, 58" 4,000.00
Maple/cherry QA, 3 short:4 grad drw:3, orig brasses, rprs, 63x39"...........3,575.00
Tiger maple QA, 5 grad drw top:2 drw:skirt:cabriole legs, rfn, 77x37"..43,125.00
Walnut/pine QA, fan cvgs, broken arch ped w/urn, minor loss, 80" 27,500.00

Lowboys

Mahog Chpndl style, 4 drw:cvd fan:cabriole legs, Hankel-Harris, 31x31"...550.00
Oak Geo w/X-banding, 3 drw:skirt:cabriole legs, 27x32x19" 2,300.00

Pie Safes

Mixed woods, pegged, sides & 2 do punched tin, 45x39x18" **1,400.00**
Poplar w/old blk pnt, high ft w/bj ends, dvtl drw at center, 85x42x16"..**1,980.00**
Poplar w/old blk rpt, 12 tins w/stars & circles, 59x42x17" **2,100.00**
Sideboard type w/old vrn over mustard grpt, screen inserts, 51x61x18" ...**1,320.00**
Walnut Co, old gold rpt on punched tin panels, high trn ft, 57x40"..**1,550.00**
Walnut w/old rfn, str legs, 2 do, arched tin panels, 2 drw, 54x41".........**550.00**

Secretaries

Fruitwood Fr Emp, marble top:drw:fall front:2 do:bronze bases, 54x37" ...**2,300.00**
Mahog Am Gothic, bookcase top:shelf:2 drw, OH, 101x47x25" ...**4,600.00**
Mahog Fr Provincial style, 2 do bookcase top:slant lid:3 drw, 51"....**500.00**
Oak Louis XVI style, slant front, reeded stiles, 46x41x21"..........**800.00**
Walnut Vict, 2 glass do:slant front desk:3 drw, 84x41x19" **700.00**
Walnut Vict, 3 do:slant lid:3 drw overhang base w/cvg, 87x43" ...**3,200.00**

Settees

Fr giltwood, cvd fr/floral uphl, +2 side & 2 armchairs, set **2,145.00**
Giltwood Louis XVI style, serpentine crest, floral cvgs, 28x56x24"....**1,725.00**
Mahog Geo III style, serpentine crest:acanthus legs: c&b ft, 35x62"..**1,150.00**
Mahog Geo III style, triple chair-bk w/cvd crests, c&b ft, uphl seat ..**2,875.00**
Mahog/ebony Edwardian, pin-prick florals, padded arms, mohair uphl, 53".**700.00**
QA style, relief-cvd cabriole legs, scrolled arms, high 3-step bk, 45"..**2,000.00**
Satinwood Biedermeier w/ebony decor, scrolled arms, 1840, 33x82".**3,450.00**
Walnut Geo II w/marquetry inlay, dbl chair-bk, c&b ft, 41x51x19"..**4,300.00**
Windsor w/PA pnt decor, 12 spindles:plank seat, pnt touchups, 35x71"..**1,725.00**

Settles, See Benches

Shelves

Bracket, parcel-gilt Rococo-style cvg, 18th C, 16x14x4¾", pr..............**700.00**
Bracket, mahog Geo style, shelf:demilune body:pendant, 13x22x12"..........**1,150.00**
Etagere, walnut Am Gothic, grad open shelves w/pierced bks, 73x30x19"..**4,000.00**
Plate rack, mahog w/cvd head & acanthus supports, 33x58x9"...**875.00**
Wall, pine w/comb grpt, D-shaped ends, grad shelves, wear, 20x32"..**1,200.00**
Wall, walnut serpentine crest:3 shelves, old rfn, PA, 1800s, 30x30x8"..**865.00**

Sideboards

Burl walnut Am Renaissance, 2 shelves/mirrors:marble:2 drw:2 do, 92".**6,000.00**
Corner, mahog Neoclassical, scrolled bkbrd:3 drw:2 do, 42x60" ** **55,000.00**
Credenza, Venetian style w/pnt decor, 4 drw:4 do, bracket ft, 43x85".....**3,675.00**
Hunt, pine English, gallery:2 frieze drw:sq legs w/shelf, 40x58" ..**1,380.00**
Mahog & satinwood Fed w/inlay, 3 drw: dbl do & side drws, 41x72x29"..**26,450.00**
Mahog Am Classical, splashbrd w/cvd pineapples:3 drws:cabinet, 71x67"....**5,000.00**

Mahogany Classic sideboard, center shelf above mirror flanked by carved columns, marble top center, three drawers, four doors, paw feet, 1830s, 59x67x25", $3,200.00.

Mahog Classical, 3 short:long dr:2 panel do:scroll ft, rpl hdw, 44"......**1,000.00**

Mahog English Vict, eagle crest, foliate moldings, ped ends, 67x84"..**2,300.00**
Mahog Fed w/inlay, rpl brass/old rfn, ca 1810, 41x64x23" **2,185.00**
Mahog Regency w/inlay, bksplash/2 drw:bow-front top:2 ped:paw ft, 94"....**8,000.00**
Mahog/bird's eye maple/rswd vnr Fed, att T Seymour, rfn/rpl, 61" **...**31,000.00**
Mahog/flame vnr Emp, 4 panel do divided w/reeded columns, gallery, 47"..**1,800.00**
Mahog/pine Sheraton, dvtl drws, high trn ft, 41x73x23".........**3,850.00**
Walnut & mahog Southern, 3 frieze drw:4 panel do:trn ft, 49x71"..**5,750.00**
Walnut Am Fed w/inlay, later sq tapered legs w/brass cuffs, 44x72"..**4,600.00**
Walnut Am Renaissance, appl trn, 2 drw:3 do, 55x59x19"......**1,650.00**

Sofas

Chesterfield, Edwardian style, leather uphl, trn ft, 28x84x33".**1,500.00**
Chesterfield, leather, overstuffed arms/bk, brass nailheads, 88" .**3,000.00**
Chesterfield, tooled leather, scroll arms, bun ft..........**700.00**
Curule, mahog Regency style, rope-cvd crest & fr, reuphl, 31x82"..**865.00**
Mahog Am Classical, scrolled bk/crest:cvd/rolled arms:vasiform ft, 89"..**4,885.00**
Mahog Am Classical w/cornucopia arms, paw ft, 31x86x25"..**5,465.00**
Mahog Classical, leaf-cvd crest & ft, eagle's head supports, rstr, 82"...**1,955.00**
Mahog Fed, rolled crest w/4 inlaid panels, brass paw ft, reuphl, 75"..**4,700.00**
Mahog Fed, scrolled vnr crest w/foliate cvg, horsehair uphl, 90"..**1,400.00**
Mahog Fed style, sq bk w/sloping arms & reeded supports, reuphl, 75"..**3,100.00**
Mahog Geo III style camel-bk, scroll arms, pierced fretwork, 70" **460.00**
Mahog vnr Fed, 3-section crest, reuphl/rfn/rprs, 36x75" **3,000.00**
Rswd Am Rococo, Rosalie pattern, tripartite crest, Belter, 80"..**6,600.00**
Walnut Beidermeier style TX cvd scroll, plank seat, 1850s, 32x81"..**3,900.00**
Walnut English, tufted bk:gadrooned rail:cvd legs, reuphl, 1880s, 89".**700.00**

Stands

Bedside, mahog Geo style, bow-front, drw:dbl do, 28x26x16" **575.00**
Canterbury, mahog Geo, trn balusters, old rfn, 21x20x15" **2,185.00**
Canterbury, mahog Wm IV, pierced anthemion, drw, scroll ft.**1,725.00**
Canterbury, rswd Wm IV w/ornate gallery, 2 drw:trn ft **1,850.00**
Canterbury, walnut Am Renaissance, pierced ends, 4 dividers, 26x20x20" ..**500.00**
Canterbury, Wm IV, ornate, tiered, concealed base drw, 1830s........**1,380.00**
Cherry/poplar Sheraton, 2-drw, stacked rings+other EX cvgs, EX rstr.....**3,500.00**
Curly maple Hplwht, 1-drw w/line detail, orig hdw, 1-brd 17" sq top......**4,300.00**
Dressing, mahog Fed, mirror:stepped marble top:3 drws:arrow ft, 79x41"..**1,100.00**
Mahog Sheraton, 2-drw, fluted legs, tooled brass knobs, top: 20x17".........**650.00**
Maple w//bird's eye facings Co Sheraton, 2 curved-front drw, 22" W **660.00**
Music, mahog, sq w/support bar for top, drw:4 shelves, rfn, 1800s, 46" ...**2,875.00**
Music, walnut Am, gallery:3 tiers w/lyre dividers:drw, 41x23x15"............**1,000.00**
Sewing, mahog, Martha WA style, trn/reeded legs, Cowan label, 27" **110.00**
Sewing, Sheraton mahog/flame vnr, EX trn/reeded, 17x17" top, VG ...**1,700.00**
Tray-top, pine Am, drw, ring-trn tapered legs, rfn/rpl pull, 27x19x18"........**750.00**
Twig, tripod log base, split log apron, dk w/alligatoring, 30x14" .**220.00**
Twig, tripod twig base w/crisscrossed twigs ea side, pnt, 27x12" sq...**330.00**
Twig, 3-twig arches form crown on sq top, bent twigs in base, 24x12" ...**85.00**
Walnut Emp, 1-drw, EX trn legs, 19x18" top **600.00**
Work, mahog/maple Fed, ovolo corners, reeded/tapered legs, 39x19x21"..**6,325.00**

Stools

Backstool, oak Geo, open bk, molded plank seat, trn legs...........**230.00**
Footstool, Louis XVI-style cvd giltwood w/uphl top, 21x18x14".**800.00**
Footstool, Louis XVI-style giltwood w/uphl top, 8½x15x13" **350.00**
Footstool, mahog Fed, molded fr on bracket ft, uphl top, 16x17x17"...**350.00**
Footstool, mahog vnr Emp, lift lid, needlework uphl, 14x27x25" **300.00**
Footstool, Napoleon III, faux Morocco leather, uphl top, 1850s, 8x12"..**175.00**
Footstool, oak English, bun ft, shaped X-stretchers, trn legs, 14" sq ..**330.00**
Footstool, walnut Am Late Fed, needlepoint uphl, 13x21" sq.....**515.00**
Footstool, walnut European, pierced X-stretcher, trn legs/ft, 18x22"..**550.00**
Piano, mahog Am Fed, dolphin supports:swivel:cvd legs:paw ft......**2,300.00**

Tables

Banquet, mahog Fed w/inlay, 3-part, center w/drop leaves, 104"..........**2,185.00**
Banquet, mahog/vnr English Hplwht w/inlay, 3-part, rfn/rpl, 124"......**3,000.00**
Bedside, mahog Am Late Fed, adjustable, 8-sided ped, 28x32x23".....**2,300.00**
Breakfast, mahog Duncan Phyfe, faux drw, cvd legs, brass paw ft, 38".**7,475.00**
Breakfast, mahog Fed w/inlay, hinged leaves, rpl brasses/rfn, 37" **1,600.00**
Breakfast/tilt-top, burlwood & mahog Rococo-style cvg, 1860s, 46" dia..**2,000.00**
Card, mahog Am Fed, fold-over swivel top, paw ft, 30x35x19".........**2,300.00**
Card, mahog Am Late Fed, fold-over top:foliate ped:paw ft, 40x20"..**2,500.00**
Card, mahog Fed, fold-over swivel top:4 supports:paw ft, 29x36x18"..**3,450.00**
Card, mahog Fed, fold-over top:apron:gilt supports:plinth:4 legs, 40"..**4,600.00**
Card, mahog Fed demilune w/inlaid fold-over top, 28x36x18" .**1,150.00**
Card, mahog Fed w/string inlay & conch shells, NY, 39x36x17"............**7,000.00**
Card, mahog Louis Philippe w/cvg, fold-over serpentine top, 19th C **1,265.00**
Center, mahog Am Fed w/figured top:ped:3 cvd ball ft, 29x39"...............**2,875.00**
Center, mahog Baltimore Late Fed, tilt-top, trn shaft:arched legs, 41"....**7,765.00**
Center, rswd Am, marble top:ornate cvd apron:caryatid supports, 1870s..**4,875.00**
Center, rswd Rococo, 12-sided marble top:skirt:4 supports:cvd ft, 47"..**5,500.00**
Center, walnut Continental, tilt-top:3 supports:cvd ft, 29x45".....**4,000.00**
Console, mahog Adams-style demilune, central frieze, 36x67x20".....**2,500.00**
Console, mahog Am Rococo, cvd apron & knees, scroll ft, 35x53x23"..**6,000.00**
Console, mahog Fed, marble top:drw:do:scroll ft, 37x30x19" ..**2,000.00**
Console, oak English, center drw in frieze, cvd front legs, 36x84x24"..**4,600.00**
Dining, mahog Fed, 2 parts ea w/drop leaf & ped base, NY, 90".....**3,000.00**
Dining, mahog Regency style, 3 fluted peds, 2 leaves, 20th C, 86"....**800.00**
Dining, oak, oval, fruit & floral cvd ped **840.00**
Dough, oak Fr Provincial w/star inlay, drw:apron:trn legs, 31x47x39"...**2,300.00**
Dressing, mahog Am Rococo Duchesse, crest:mirror:marble:drw:cvg legs..**5,175.00**
Dressing, mahog Rococo Duchesse , shaped mirror:drw:cabriole legs, 72"...**3,735.00**

Dressing table, second period Empire with acanthus-carved pedestal base and claw feet, ca 1885, $1,600.00.

Dressing, walnut Chpndl, rpl top, old rfn/rpl brass, 30x28x18"....**5,465.00**
Drop-leaf, mahog Fed, beaded top:faux drw:reeded legs, old rfn, 30"..**2,200.00**
Drop-leaf, mahog Fed, 2 drw:lyre:molded plinth:scroll ft, 22x19"..**800.00**
Drop-leaf, mahog Fed w/inlay, oval top, old rstr, 43" open.......**4,600.00**
Drop-leaf, mahog Late Geo III w/inlay, rnded leaves, 57x35"..**3,675.00**
Drop-leaf, maple w/lt curl, transitional Chpndl to Hplwht, top: 16x47" ..**825.00**
Gate-leg, oak W/M, top w/D-shaped ends:trn stretchers & ft, 37x40x21" ..**4,000.00**
Harvest, Hplwht-style cherry, 2-brd 23x72+10" drop leaves, 20th C...**1,000.00**
Hutch, pine w/birch legs, rectangular top: 42x40" **650.00**
Library, cherrywood Am Aesthetic Movement, relief cvg, c&b ft, 36"....**800.00**
Library, mahog Fed, wht marble:cvd apron:scroll legs, att Meeks..........**1,500.00**
Nesting, mahog Regency style w/ebony inlay, trn legs, set of 4 ...**515.00**
Pembroke, mahog/vnr/inlay English Hplwht, false drws, rstr, 33" dia......**1,750.00**
Sewing, Fed mahog/vnr, 2-drw, EX trn/reeded legs w/ring detail, 29x23"..**2,475.00**
Side, cherrywood Fr, drw, tapered legs, 1840s, 28x49x27"...........**865.00**
Side, gilt Renaissance w/pietra-dura, red marble, cvd griffins, 32x23"..**5,800.00**
Side, mahog Geo III, 2 short:long drw:sq legs, 28x30x19" **1,265.00**
Side, mahog/mahog vnr, rtcl brass gallery, Fine Art Furniture, 26" dia.....**495.00**

Side, Majorelle, att; mc fruitwood w/inlay floral, splay legs, 30", VG..**2,000.00**
Side, maple Fed, scalloped top:drw:tapered legs, 27x21x24" **460.00**
Side, oak Geo II w/cvg, 2 drw:trn legs:pad ft, 28x35x21".........**2,750.00**
Side, rswd & parquetry Rococo style, drw, cabriole legs, 32x34x22"......**800.00**
Side, walnut Am Aesthetic, tile top, spindled gallery & shelf, 19x19"..**460.00**
Sofa, mahog Classical, drop leaves, inlaid drw, 29x36x55" (open) **7,000.00**
Sofa, mahog Fed style, hinged book rest:frieze drws:lyre trestle base...**1,380.00**
Tea, mahog Am Chpndl w/cvg, birdcage:c&b ft, 1760s, 30x34x34" ** ..**10,925.00**
Tilt-top, maple Charles X style w/cvd urn ped, 29x36" dia **1,150.00**
Tilt-top, rswd Wm IV, column support, 3 paw ft, 28x47" dia...**3,900.00**
Work, mahog Am Classical w/rswd bands, att Quervelle, 30x23x17" **5,465.00**
Work, rswd Am cvd, molded top:drw, Alexander Roux label, 32x26x16" ...**3,000.00**
Work, walnut PA, trn legs w/sq ft, stretcher base, 1 drw, 30", VG ...**2,000.00**
Writing, mahog Geo III, drw w/bail hdl, sq tapered legs, 1800s, 28x34"...**700.00**

Wardrobes

Linen press, mahog Wm IV, cornice:arched panel dbl do:2 short drw:2...**2,600.00**
Mahog Georgian, panel do, orig brasses, on stand, 81x51x22" ...**4,000.00**
Pine Geo IV style, 4 arched do:3 drw:plinth, 88x90x24".........**2,000.00**
Walnut/poplar/chestnut Co, old red pnt, pegs/sq nails, 81x42x23"...**3,025.00**

Washstands

Corner, mahog English, bow-front, gallery:shelf:drw, rpr/rfn, 38x22"..**330.00**
Corner, mahog Geo III w/inlay, drw:sq legs w/splayed ft, 32x24x17"..**750.00**
Rswd Am, marble top:drw:do, ca 1860, 30x18½x17½"...............**400.00**
Tinned iron, wht pnt w/nautical transfer, ca 1900, 15½" L.........**460.00**

Miscellaneous

Basket tree, cherry/birch, spiral-trn column, 14-arm, 78".........**2,300.00**
Bed steps, mahog Geo III style, leather inserts, 27x16x27", pr......**1,850.00**
Bed steps, mahog/oak/pine English, trn legs/leather inserts, 25x28x17"..**600.00**
Bed steps, walnut, jtd stool-type construction, vase supports, 12x18" **660.00**
Bed/library steps, fruitwood Provincial, cut-out hand hold, 24" ..**400.00**
Butler's tray on folding stand, mahog Vict, 1850s, 35x30x18¼".**700.00**
Cellarette, mahog Wm IV sarcophagus, scrolled bracket ft, 1840s........**3,735.00**
Cellarette, poplar w/old wash, hinged lid, fitted int, sq legs, 19th C ...**2,400.00**
Easel, ebonized Am Renaissance, Celtic cross crest, 1870s, 72x24x10" ..**800.00**
Easel, walnut Am Renaissance, mid-19th C **1,265.00**
Glider, Old Hickory, splint seat/bk on platform base, mk, 34x51", VG ..**4,000.00**
Mantel, walnut Am Aesthetic, foliate cvg/spindled mirror bk, 50x64x16"..**3,165.00**
Pedestal, gr marble, octagonal tops, Corinthian capitals, 47x13", pr ...**1,500.00**
Pedestal, marble fluted Ionic column w/8-sided top & vase, 27x12".......**550.00**
Pedestal, walnut Am Modern Gothic w/much cvg, 1870s, 38x16" sq.**1,265.00**
Peg brd, pine w/worn dk finish, beaded edges, 9 pegs, 60"............**220.00**
Podium, pine, sq top:box base w/drw, brn grpt:earlier bl, early 1800s......**865.00**
Screen, oil on leather, English, 4 pnt panels w/reserves, 73x86".........**4,800.00**
Set, burl walnut Am Renaissance, bed+armoire+bureau+commode **5,175.00**
Set, dining; mahog, RJ Horner, late 19th C, 15-pc set...........**31,625.00**
Set, Fr giltwood, cvd fr/floral uphl, 2 armchirs+2 side+settee ..**2,145.00**
Set, mahog Am w/cvg, bed+2 dressers+armoire, 1850s.....................**6,600.00**
Set, parlor; cvd/laminated rswd Am Rococo, att Meeks, 4-pc **27,500.00**
Set, Rustic Hickory Furniture Co, settee+2 armchairs+2 ottomans, VG..**2,100.00**
Swing, Old Hickory, bk/arms/A-fr support of poles, woven seat, 93x67" ..**1,600.00**
Torchere, mahog Geo III style, shelf:lattice:3 cabriole legs, 44", pr..**3,225.00**
Umbrella stand, walnut Neoclassical style w/cvg, 1890s, 38x17x18"....**500.00**
Window seat, mahog Am Late Fed, needlework uphl, 46"........**1,150.00**

Galle

Emile Galle was one of the most important producers of cameo glass in France. His firm, founded in Nancy in 1874, produced beautiful cameo in the Art Nouveau style during the 1890s, using a variety of techniques. He also produced glassware with enameled decoration, as well as some fine pottery — animal figurines, table services, vases, and other objets d' art. In the mid-1880s he became interested in the various colors and textures of natural woods and as a result began to create furniture which he used as yet another medium for expression of his artistic talent. Marquetry was the primary method Galle used in decorating his furniture, preferring landscapes, Nouveau floral and fruit arrangements, butterflies, squirrels, and other forms from nature. It is for his furniture and his cameo glass that he is best known today. All Galle is signed.

In the listings below, 'fp' indicates items that have been fire polished. Our advisor for this category is Don Williams; he is listed in the Directory under Missouri.

Cameo

Bottle, scent; floral, purple on amethyst frost, flat sides, 3¾" 525.00
Bowl, cranberries/leaves, ruby on frost, 2¼x7" 425.00
Bowl, fuchsia, cvd/mc pnt w/gilt on aquamarine texture, 4x7" ...1,800.00
Bowl, 4-layer oxblood cvg representing conch shell, 5¾x6" 4,600.00
Inkwell, flowers, amber on frost, matching stopper, 2x4" 800.00
Vase, berries, ruby on frost to yel, bulbous w/stick neck, 6" 700.00
Vase, berry branches, lt red on amber, cylinder w/bun base, 13" ...2,875.00
Vase, berry branches, wine on citron, heart shape w/short neck, 9" ..2,875.00
Vase, berry cascade, red on orange/frost, stick neck, 12" 1,700.00
Vase, bleeding hearts on dk amber w/amethyst ft, chalice shape, 7¾" .1,900.00
Vase, blown-out apples on branch, red/brn on yel frost, ovoid, 12" ...10,350.00
Vase, blown-out flower pods, amber on dk umber, bulbous/ftd, 7"......6,000.00
Vase, bluebells/heart leaves, brn on yel fr, U-shape, 4½" 2,300.00
Vase, cherries/leaves, red on amber & frost, camphor hdls, 3¾" .950.00
Vase, crocus/lilies, lav/pk on clear, short ft, 8x3½"..................1,800.00
Vase, day lilies, royal bl on dk gr branches on amber-rose, 5x10" .3,900.00
Vase, ferns, burgundy/gr on pk-tinged frost, long neck, 15" 2,300.00
Vase, fisherman on lake/island cottage, bl on amber, ftd, 4¼" 425.00
Vase, flock of birds/hill/mtns, dk/lt bl on amber, bulbous, 11x9" ...7,500.00

Vase, floral, amber, orange, and maroon on gray, 10⅞", $3,500.00; Vase, trees beside water, chartreuse and brown on blush to gray, narrow mouth, 9", $1,725.00. (Photo courtesy Skinner, Inc.)

Vase, floral, cranberry on yel, slim, 7" 900.00
Vase, floral, lav-bl/gr w/wht outlines on peach, sm flared neck, 7"...825.00
Vase, floral, orange on frost, banjo shape w/collar neck, 5½x4¾" ..750.00
Vase, floral, purple on lt yel, shouldered, narrow at base, 3¾" 440.00
Vase, floral, yel/burgundy on pk/rose frost, cylindrical, 9¾".....1,150.00
Vase, floral stalk, wine/wht on frost, sqd/slim w/sqd bun base, 29" .8,600.00
Vase, floral stems, ruby on citron, ftd/flat sided, stick neck, 7" ...450.00
Vase, flower garden, red on amber frost, red rim, ped ft, 8"......1,650.00
Vase, grapes/leaves, fp orange on crystal w/int silver flecks, 7½"...1,000.00
Vase, honeysuckle, umber on citron, conical, 4¼" 550.00
Vase, impatiens, gr/lav/wht on pk-tinged frost, cylindrical, 9½" ..3,165.00
Vase, iris/leaves, amethyst on frost, stick neck, 3¼" 360.00
Vase, leaves, dk amethyst on peach/bl frost, banjo form, 5½".....400.00
Vase, leaves/berries, dk amethyst on frost, bulbous, 2½" 290.00
Vase, leaves/flowering stem, amber on pk/citron, stick neck, 6"..525.00
Vase, leaves/fruit, umber on pk frost, shouldered, 3" 300.00
Vase, lg trees/lake/distant mtns, purple/bl tones, 4-petal top, 5x4"...1,950.00
Vase, lily pads/dragonfly, amber/bl on bl frost, banjo shape, 6½"......2,400.00
Vase, morning glories overall, bl on yel frost, ringed neck, 6"..1,200.00
Vase, oak leaves/acorns hang from rim, gr on apricot, 12" 1,250.00
Vase, phlox, amethyst on pk/frost, shouldered, 2½x3" 325.00
Vase, pond lilies, dk amethyst on gr/lav/frost, 6x4" 1,000.00
Vase, pond lilies/reeds, lav on citron, flat-sided stick neck, 10" 1,900.00
Vase, poppies, red on yel/wht, ftd/bulbous w/short collar neck, 9"..2,650.00
Vase, spider mum, dk maroon on peach-orange, 6x4" 690.00
Vase, stems/leaves, amethyst on frost/yel, stick neck, 6".............450.00
Vase, trees w/air-infused blown-out trunks, wine on bl/amber, 11½"..8,500.00
Vase, trees/forest beyond, dk gr on frost, slim/ftd, 9½"............1,500.00
Vase, windblown leaves allover, maroon on frost/orange, 4¾x3¾" 800.00
Vase, wisteria, amethyst on amber & frost, stick neck, 10" 750.00
Vase, wisteria, orange on frost, squat w/stick neck, 4" 250.00
Vase, wisteria cascades, amethyst on yel & frost, cylindrical, 15" .1,400.00
Vase, wisteria cascades, lime/olive gr on apricot frost, slim, 18" 1,500.00
Vase, wisteria cascades, wine/rose on amber, banjo form, 6¾" 650.00

Enameled Glass

Bowl, boy picks fruit on amber, 2 sides fold, 3rd w/petals, unmk, 9" ..345.00
Decanter, grape harvesters/gilt on olive, ribbed/bulbous, 13" 300.00
Dish, chartreuse, fish encircle lid, ftd, 4½x4" 650.00
Rose bowl, orchids, purple on gr texture, 3½x4½"...................1,600.00
Vase, bud; floral, pk/rose on clear swirl, tubular, ruffle disc ft, 8" ...900.00
Vase, ivory w/bl top & base, floral/stars in red/gold, cylinder, 12" ..2,750.00
Vase, lily, pk/red on lt amber w/gold foil, 5 'stacked' lobes, 12" ..1,256.00

Pottery

Pitcher, Fr peasant, J-shape body w/loop hdl, prof rstr spout, 8x6"...865.00
Pitcher, swirl ribs w/bird-head spout, twist hdl, brn tones, 9" ..1,000.00
Vase, floral swag, pastels on lt gray, side festoons, cut rim, ftd, 5" ..690.00
Vase, tulips/beetle relief on tan mottle, bottle shape w/long hdl, 8" ..840.00

Gambling Memorabilia

Gambling memorabilia from the infamous casinos of the West and items that were once used on the 'Floating Palace' riverboats are especially sought after by today's collectors.

Chip rack, Catalin, ice-block style, with two hundred Catalin chips, $250.00. (Photo courtesy Robert Eisenstadt)

Ashtray, blk amethyst glass, Barney's Tahoe, 3 rests, 3⅜" 7.50
Ashtray, clear glass, Cactus Pete's Howdy Folks in red & gr, 3¼" .22.00
Ashtray, clear glass swan, Harrah's Reno...1968...Headliner Room ...68.00
Ashtray, Exchange Club, clear w/logo in red center 75.00
Ashtray, Rainbow Club, Casino Henderson, blk w/gold letters, 3½"...15.00
Brochure, Primadonna Casino, Star Dust ad, EX 10.00

Card, membership; Aladdin Casino, aerial view of hotel, EX **30.00**
Card shuffler, metal fr w/wood hdls, Nestor Johnson, NMIB.........**30.00**
Chip, Balinese Room, blk center w/red border, $100, 1½"..........**150.00**
Chip, Club Forest, New Orleans, wht w/18 stars in bl border **45.00**
Chip, Four Queens Hotel & Casino, Golden Retriever.................**12.50**
Chip, Old Southport Club, yel w/red & blk border, $1, 1⅝".........**40.00**
Chip, Pussycat a' Go Go, blk & wht w/gr & purple border, $5 .....**55.00**
Chips, plastic w/70 ea in 7 colors, unmk, 1¼", w/orig case, 7x11"...**45.00**
Dice, Cactus Pete's, red plastic w/cactus on 2 sides, pr......................**6.50**
Dice, Dunes Casino, red w/logo & Genie, mk 1956, EX **75.00**
Dice, Spirit Mountain, dk red plastic, pr **7.00**
Draw poker display, hands illustrated, Shakespearean quote, 20x24" ...**200.00**
Game, Chuck-a-Luck, wire cage dice game, 5x10", EX..............**100.00**
Game, Game of Lotto, McLoughlin Bros, home gambling, EXIB...**225.00**
Game, Play Poker, unused punch-out sheet, Brady, 1949, 11½x8¼" ...**100.00**
Guide, gaming; Riviera Hotel, 1955, 12 pgs, EX............................**28.00**
Keno goose, Clover Club, Honduran mahog, 23¼", w/100 pills **2,000.00**
Punch board, Big Stakes, 25¢ 1,700 hole, 8¾x11½", unpunched, M..**40.00**
Punch board, Boomtown TX Charley, 25¢ 1,200-hole, unpunched, M...**15.00**
Punch board, Champ, 10¢ 1,200-hole, 10¾x13", unpunched, NM **40.00**
Punch board, Diamond Dust, 5¢ 600-hole, 5¾x8⅞", unpunched, NM...**75.00**
Shakers, Harold's Club, frosted w/logo in bl, 3½", pr....................**50.00**
Token, Primm Valley Resort & Casino, $10, Bonnie & Clyde center ..**17.50**
Wheel, pnt wood, steel spokes, New England, 19th C, 24" dia...**450.00**
Wheel, roulette; wooden, mini, worn pnt, 2x10x5"......................**275.00**

Game Calls

Those interested in hunting and fishing collectibles are beginning to take notice of the finer specimens of game calls available on today's market.

Crow, Jim Crow, MIB **70.00**
Crow, wooden w/bone top, 3", EX **125.00**
Dove, Herter's, maple, crest decal **75.00**
Duck, Alvin Taylor, ebony & silver, rare, EX...............................**360.00**
Duck, Browning, #5013, EX..**165.00**
Duck, CH Amaden, Hambone, walnut, 5"....................................**345.00**
Duck, Charles Perdew, checkered walnut, ca 1920, EX............**1,600.00**
Duck, D Tucker, dk walnut w/brass reed, 3-panel checkering, EX...**155.00**
Duck, Doug Porter, gun-sight stopper, unvarnished, EX **375.00**
Duck, John 'Sandy' Morrow, checkered, 2nd quarter 20th C, 7", EX ..**1,100.00**

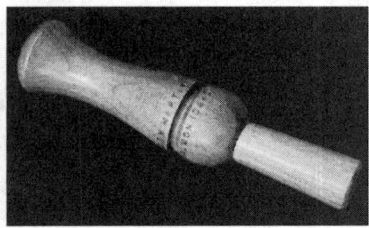

Duck call, Ken Martin, Salmon Idaho, walnut, from $100.00 to $125.00.

Duck, Olt, mk Perfect Mallard Call, Model #C-3 Deluxe **115.00**
Duck, Tom Turpin, Cajun, walnut, EX..**500.00**
Duck, Walter Dreenen, birds-eye maple, plastic reed, 5".............**200.00**
Goose, Herter's, #377, MIB...**50.00**
Squirrel, Herter's, Famous 99, walnut w/brass plate, MIB..............**30.00**
Squirrel, Olt, Model #P-17, MIB **35.00**
Turkey, Ben Lee Slate, sgn, 1970s-80s, EX **290.00**
Turkey, Dick Kirby, trough style, 5½"..**200.00**
Turkey, Gibson, paddle box, Pat January 5 1897, NMIB..........**3,200.00**
Turkey, Lynch, #101 Foolproof, scratch box type........................**340.00**
Turkey, Lynch World Champion, box style, eng, w/instructions .**680.00**

Turkey, ML Lynch, Model #102, NMIB..............................**140.00**
Turkey, Stevenson's, scratch type, late 1950s-early 1960s, EXIB ...**95.00**

Gameboards

Gameboards, the handmade ones from the eighteenth and nineteenth century, are collected more for their folk art quality than their relation to games. Excellent examples of these handcrafted 'playthings' sell well into the thousands of dollars; even the simple designs are often expensive. If you are interested in this field, you must study it carefully. The market is always full of 'new' examples. Well-established dealers are often your best sources; they are essential if you do not have the expertise to judge the age of the boards yourself. Our advisor for this category is Louis Picek; he is listed in the Directory under Iowa.

Unknown game, hinged board with multicolor paint, America, ca 1900, 19¼" square, EX, $2,645.00.

Checkers, blk/gr/red worn rpt, worn gallery, edge damage, 16x19"...**300.00**
Checkers, blk/red sqs on red, yel border w/fleur-de-lis, 25" L **675.00**
Checkers, blk/wht checks w/in molded fr, ochre grpt border, 24x20".**1,100.00**
Checkers, blk/wht pnt w/dk bl border, 19th C, 17x20" **635.00**
Checkers, breadboard ends w/salmon/blk/bl-gray orig pnt, 1875-90...**1,825.00**
Checkers, cvd & pnt red & wht, card suits on corners, 28x29" ..**150.00**
Checkers, gr/iron red/blk, yel grpt on bk, 19th C, 14x14", EX ..**1,380.00**
Checkers, inlaid, maple/cherry w/pine, 20x20" **110.00**
Checkers, mustard w/blk sqs, wide pine brd/oak trim, sq nails, 19x19"...**1,000.00**
Checkers, pine, red/blk sqs, wear/losses, ca 1800, 17⅜x23¼" **865.00**
Checkers, pine w/blk pnt sqs, 27½x18x1"....................................**95.00**
Checkers, pine w/6-color pnt, inlaid butternut scallops, 18x18" ..**1,200.00**
Checkers, pine/maple w/orig blk/wht pnt, 19th C, 18x24"..........**390.00**
Checkers, poplar, blk/gr blocks on gray, bk: orange, sgn/1901, 17x18" ..**500.00**
Checkers, poplar w/red/blk pnt, relief-cvd sqs, gallery, 13x23"....**600.00**
Checkers, red/gr, rpt gold line design, gallery edge worn, 21x13"..**1,200.00**
Checkers, salmon-red w/ocher & blk sqs, Am, 19th C, 18x18"..**750.00**
Checkers, walnut, old varnish w/blk sqs, folds, 14x14"................**275.00**
Checkers, 4-color pnt, stamped CA Brown 1852 on bk, 22x22" **1,380.00**
Checkers/backgammon, pnt wood w/grpt borders, 19th C, 17½x18" .**865.00**
Checkers/parcheesi, blk/mustard/gr on red, gallery, rpt, 19x19"........**2,000.00**
Checkers/parcheesi, mc pnt on wood, appl molding, late 1800s, 24x25".**1,375.00**
Checkers/parcheesi, pine w/orig pnt, dbl-sided, ca 1860, 19x28"...**2,750.00**
Checkers/parcheesi, pnt wood, cvd outline, Am, 19th C, 24x24"..**1,600.00**
Parcheesi, pine w/5-color pnt, stencil: Home, 19x20" **3,575.00**
Parcheesi, 5-color pnt, minor loss/grime, 19th C, 17¾" sq **1,725.00**
Tic-Tac-Toe, pine w/orig pnt, 10 pcs fit into pegs, 1½x13x13" **65.00**

Games

Collectors of antique games are finding it more difficult to find their treasures at shows and flea markets. Most of the action these days seems to be through specialty dealers and auctions. The appreciation of the art on the boards and boxes continues to grow. You see many of the early games proudly displayed as art, and they should be. The period from the 1850s to 1910 continues to draw the most interest. Many of the games of that period were executed by well-known artists and illustrators. The quality of their lithography cannot be matched today. The historical value of games made before 1850 has caused interest in this period to increase. While they may not have the graphic quality of the later period, their insights into the social and moral character of the early nineteenth century are interesting.

Twentieth-century games invoke a nostalgic feeling among collectors who recall looking forward to a game under the Christmas tree each year. They search for examples that bring back those Christmas-morning memories. While the quality of their lithography is certainly less than the early games, the introduction of personalities from the comic strips, radio, and later TV created new interest. Every child wanted a game that featured their favorite character. Monopoly, probably the most famous game ever produced, was introduced during the Great Depression.

For further information, we recommend *Schroeder's Collectible Toys, Antique to Modern,* available from Collector Books.

All American Skittle Score-Ball, Aurora, 1974, EXIB 35.00
Amazing Dunninger Mind Reading Game, Hasbro, 1976, NMIB. 32.00

Barnyard Tiddly Winks, Parker Bros., 1930, complete, MIB, $95.00.

Battleboard, Ideal, 1972, NMIB 30.00
Boots & Saddles, Gardner, 1958, EXIB 50.00
Cabby, Selchow & Righter, 1950s, EXIB 75.00
Camp Granada, Milton Bradley, 1965, MIB 45.00
Camp Runamuck, cards, Ideal, 1965, EXIB 25.00
Candyland, Milton Bradley, 1962, VG (VG box) 50.00
Carl Hubbell Mechanical Baseball, Gotham, 1948, EXIB 250.00
Championship Baseball, Lansing, 1966, EXIB 35.00
Chase Back, Milton Bradley, 1962, MIB (sealed) 15.00
Chutes Away, Gabriel, 1978, EXIB 65.00
Cold Feet, Ideal, 1967, EXIB 35.00
Diver Dan Tug-O-War, Milton Bradley, 1961, EXIB 50.00
Don't Spill the Beans, Schaper, 1967, MIB (sealed) 25.00
Electric Baseball, Electric Game Co, 1940s, EXIB 35.00
Fireball XL5, Milton Bradley, 1964, EXIB 95.00
Flea Circus, Mattel, 1964, EXIB 35.00
Frantic Frogs, Milton Bradley, 1965, EXIB 30.00
Game of Politics, Parker Bros, 1952, VG (VG box) 40.00
Game of Steeplechase, McLoughlin Bros, 1889, EX (G box) 275.00
Game of Transatlantic Flight, 1920s, EXIB 300.00
Gang Busters, Whitman, 1939, EXIB 75.00
Gang Busters Target, Marx, NMIB 200.00
Garroway's Game of Possessions, Remco, 1955, EXIB 45.00
Gusher, Carrom, 1946, EXIB 75.00
Hight Dice, Bettye-B, 1956, EXIB 40.00
Indian Trail Game, 1920s, EXIB 250.00

King of the Cheese, Milton Bradley, 1959, EXIB 40.00
Knuckle Busters, Hasbro, 1967, EXIB 55.00
League Parlor Baseball, Bliss, c 1885, EX 1,200.00
Let's Face It, Hasbro, 1955, EXIB 30.00
Lost Heir, Milton Bradley, 1905, EX (G box) 135.00
Major League Indoor Base Ball, Philadelphia Game Mfg Co, oak case. 1,700.00
Mentor, Hasbro, 1961, EXIB 40.00
Monopoly Deluxe, Parker Bros, 1964, EXIB 45.00
Monstermania, Marx, 1977, MIB 30.00
Moon Tag, Parker Bros, 1957, EXIB 85.00
Mr Machine, Ideal, 1961, EXIB 75.00
Mystery Date, Milton Bradley, 1965, EXIB 125.00
Official Baseball, Milton Bradley, 1966, EXIB 100.00
OK Telegraph, 1910, EX (VG box) 300.00
Pathfinder, Milton Bradley, 1977, EXIB 20.00
Pirate Plunder, All-Fair, VG (VG box) 50.00
Pirates of the Caribbean, Parker Bros, 1967, EXIB 25.00
Poison Ivy, Ideal, 1969, VG (VG box) 40.00
Pop-Za-Ball Target, Mattel, 1961, EXIB 40.00
Pro Football, Milton Bradley, 1964, VG (VG box) 45.00
Pro League Basketball, Gotham, 1958, EXIB 75.00
Psychic Baseball Game, Barker Bros, 1935, EXIB 300.00
Ride the Surf, 1963, EXIB 65.00
Seven Seas, Cadaco, 1960, EXIB 35.00
Sharpshooter, Cadaco, 1965, EXIB 65.00
Shenanigans, Milton Bradley, 1964, EXIB 50.00
Sheriff of Dodge City, Parker Bros, 1966, EXIB 25.00
Shooting Gallery, Wyandotte, 1940s, EXIB 150.00
Silly Safari, Topper, 1966, EXIB 50.00
Singing Bone, Hasbro, 1964, EXIB 45.00
Sinking Titanic, Ideal, 1976, EXIB 45.00
Slap Trap, Ideal, 1967, EXIB 30.00
Space Age, Parker Bros, 1953, EXIB 75.00
Space Pilot, Cadaco, 1951, EXIB 75.00
Square Mile, Milton Bradley, 1962, EXIB 45.00
Stock Exchange, Milton Bradley, 1964, EXIB 50.00
Sub Attack, Milton Bradley, 1965, EXIB 35.00
Super Crow Shoot, Jaymar, 1958, EXIB 40.00
Talking Football, Mattel, 1971, EXIB 100.00
Tic-Tac Dough, Transogram, 1956, EXIB 40.00
Tiddly Winks Barrage Game, Corey, WWII era, EXIB 90.00
Tin Can Alley, Ideal, 1976, EXIB 50.00
Top Secret, National Games, 1956, EXIB 65.00
Toy Town, Milton Bradley, 1962, EXIB 50.00
Tradewinds, Parker Bros, 1960, VG (VG box) 75.00
Trapped, Bettye-B, 1956, EXIB 40.00
Treasure Island, Harett-Gilmar, 1955, EXIB 45.00
Win, Place & Show, Milton Bradley, 1949, EXIB 40.00
Wolfman Mystery, Hasbro, 1963, EXIB 150.00
World's Fair, Milton Bradley, 1964, EXIB 40.00

Personalities, Movies, and TV Shows

Adventures of Davy Crockett, Harett-Gilmar, 1955, EXIB 75.00
Alien, Kenner, 1979, EXIB 50.00
Amazing Spider-Man, Milton Bradley, 1966, EXIB 250.00
Batman & Robin Marble Maze, Hasbro, 1966, EXIB 100.00
Batman Batarang Toss, Pressman, 1966, EXIB 175.00
Batman Shooting Arcade, Marx, 1966, EXIB 250.00
Brady Bunch, Whitman, 1973, MIB 100.00
Bugaloos, Milton Bradley, 1971, MIB, from $50 to 60.00
Captain America, Milton Bradley, 1966, MIB 100.00
Captain Kidd, Lowell, 1950s, EXIB 50.00
Cinderella, Parker Bros, 1964, EXIB 50.00

Dark Shadows, Milton Bradley, 1969, NMIB 40.00
Dating Game, Hasbro, 1967, EXIB 30.00
Davy Crockett Rescue Race, Gabriel, EXIB, from $55 to 75.00
Dick Tracy Crimestopper, Ideal, 1963, NM (EX box) 75.00
Donald Duck's Tiddley Winx, Jaymar/WDP, EXIB 75.00
Dracula, Hasbro, 1963, EXIB 150.00
Eliot Ness & the Untouchables, Transogram, 1961, EXIB 65.00
Felix the Cat, target game, Lido, 1960, EXIB 60.00
Fugitive, Ideal, 1964, EXIB 125.00
Game of Snow White..., Milton Bradley/WDE, 1930s, NMIB 50.00
Gilligan's Island, Games Gems/T Cohn, 1965, EXIB 225.00
Gunsmoke Target, Park Plastics, 1958, EXIB 100.00
Hopalong Cassidy, Milton Bradley, 1950, EXIB 125.00
Howdy Doody's Own Game, Parker Bros, 1949, EXIB 100.00
Ironside, Ideal, 1967, EXIB 100.00
Land of the Giants, Ideal, 1968, NMIB 200.00
Lone Ranger Double Target, Marx, 17", EXIB 200.00
Man From UNCLE, target game, Marx, 1966, EXIB 300.00
Melvin Pervis' G-Men Detective Game, Parker Bros, 1930s, NMIB ..175.00
Mickey Mantle Big 6 Sports Gardner, 1950s, VG (VG box) 150.00
Mickey Mouse Bagatelle, Marks Bros, NM 700.00
Mickey Mouse Circus, Marks Bros, EXIB 650.00
Mickey Mouse Roll 'Em, Marks Bros, NM 600.00
Mighty Hercules, Hasbro, 1963, NMIB 300.00
Mission Impossible, Ideal, 1966, EXIB 75.00
Mr Ed, Parker Bros, 1960s, EXIB 65.00
New Adventures of Pinocchio, Lowell, 1960, EXIB 50.00
Newlywed Game, Hasbro, 1969, NMIB 20.00
Peter Gunn, Lowell, 1965, EXIB 75.00
Peter Potamus, Ideal, 1964, EXIB 185.00
Phantom of the Opera, Mystery, Hasbro, 1963, EXIB 225.00
Pin the Nose on Pinocchio, Parker Bros, 1939, EXIB 250.00
Put the Tail on Ferdinand the Bull, Whitman/WDE, 1938, VG.125.00
Raggedy Ann, Milton Bradley, 1954, EXIB 35.00
Rat Patrol Desert Combat, Transogram, 1966, NMIB 125.00
Robinson Crusoe, Lowell, 1961, EXIB 50.00
Rocky & His Friends, Milton Bradley, 1960, EXIB 65.00
Sam Snead Tee Off, 1973, VG (VG box) 35.00
Sleeping Beauty, Parker Bros, 1952, EXIB 50.00
Snagglepuss, Transogram, 1961, EXIB 40.00
Snoopy & the Red Baron, Milton Bradley, 1970, MIB 40.00
Snuffy Smith Time's a Wastin', Milton Bradley, 1963, EXIB 35.00
Steve Canyon, Lowell, 1959, EXIB 60.00
Superman Match II, Ideal, 1978, MIB 85.00
That Girl, Remco, 1969, EXIB 70.00
Thunderball, Milton Bradley, 1965, EXIB 50.00
Tom & Jerry, Parker Bros, 1948, EXIB 50.00
Tom Mix Shooting Gallery, Parker Bros, 1930s, EXIB 250.00
Untouchables, target game, Marx, 1960, EXIB 200.00

Voyage to the Bottom of
the Sea, Milton Bradley,
MIB, $70.00.

Wanted Dead or Alive, Marx, 1959, NM (G box) 300.00

Woody Woodpecker Ring Toss Game, 1958, MIB 100.00
Yogi Bear Score-A-Matic Ball Toss, Transogram, EXIB 65.00

G. A. R. Memorabilia

The 'The Grand Army of the Republic' was first conceived by
Chaplain W.J. Rutledge and Major B.J. Stephenson early in 1864 when
they were tent-mates during our own Civil War. These men vowed to
each other that if they were spared they would establish an organization
that would preserve friendships and memories formed during this time.
Shortly after the war ended, Rutledge and Stephenson made their desires
a reality. The first National Convention of the Grand Army of the
Republic was held in Indianapolis, Indiana, on November 20, 1866. The
purpose of the organization was to provide aid and assistance to the wid-
ows and orphans of the fallen Union dead and to care for the hospital-
ized veterans as needed. The last comrade of the G.A.R. died in 1949.

Many items are surfacing from the early encampments which were
held on both state and national levels and resulted in a wide variety of
souvenir items having been made.

Badge, canteen; We Drank From the Same Canteen, 2-pc w/ribbon 90.00
Badge, Post Officer, bl on insignia bar, bl ribbon over star 150.00
Badge, Reunion 1st Missouri Engineers Indiana, ladder style, VG+ ..410.00
Badge, reunion; Union Ex-Prisoners of War Assoc, 31st Anniversary, EX ...190.00
Banner, Welcome VFW, GAR, & Allied Groups, gold on blk silkscreen, EX ...35.00
Belt buckle, GAR Multi-Service, Xd swords/cannons/rifles, +anchor, EX ...40.00
Book, Civil War Roster, Gordon Post #90, Donnelly #307, Gage #375, EX ..160.00
Booklet, Rules & Regulations Nat'l Encampment GAR 1884, 40 pgs, VG 25.00
Card, Member in Good Standing; dtd 2/17/1869, 6⅜x3¼", EX ...60.00
Centerpc, presentation; Lincoln...1900, Reed & Barton, 4x11½" 240.00
Chart, badge insignia ID, 1920s, 4½x7", EX 25.00
Flag stand, WRC 1883 Auxilary to GAR, 4-legged, mk 1924, EX ..30.00

Flask, multicolored transfers of presidents Lincoln, Garfield, and
McKinley (all assassinated while in
office), G.A.R. medal on reverse, ca
1901, 5¾", NM, $475.00.

Handbook, Grand Army Manual & Soldier Citizen; 402 pgs, VG+ ..42.00
Medal, Honorable Discharge; bronze w/red/wht/bl ribbon, 3" 625.00
Medal, Nat'l Encampment Representative, eagle w/coin pendant, 1925..300.00
Medal, reunion; Contributing Member, Post 290, 3-pc 40.00
Pin, Gold Membership, eagle-over-flag w/star underneath, EX 75.00
Postcard, Lincoln Funeral Car, 42nd Nat'l Encampment, 1908, EX...15.00
Postcard, Union soldier standing guard, emb, ca 1910, EX 25.00
Postcard, 46th Annual Encampment, Springfield OH, 1912, EX..40.00
Ribbon, Welcome to Kearny's 1st Brigade...1907, purple, 4½x1½" 75.00
Shield, papier-mache, wht/bl w/gilt highlights, Welcome GAR, 18x14" ...250.00
Special orders, Memorial Day, Post #2 NH, 8x6", EX 5.00
Stickpin, 46th Encampment, OH, gold w/bl enamel, GAR in wht center, EX...100.00

Garden City Pottery

Founded in 1902 in San Jose, California, by the end of the 1920s this pottery had grown to become the largest in Northern California. During that period production focused on stoneware, sewer pipe, and red clay flowerpots. In the late '30s and '40s, the company produced dinnerware in bright solid colors of yellow, green, blue, orange, cobalt, turquoise, white, and black. Royal Arden Hickman, who would later gain fame for the innovative artware he modeled for the Haeger company, designed not only dinnerware but a line of Art Deco vases and bowls as well. The company endured hard times by adapting to the changing needs of the market and during the '50s concentrated on production of garden products. Foreign imports, however, proved to be too competitive, and the company's pottery production ceased in 1979.

Because none of the colored-glazed products were ever marked, to learn to identify the products of this company, you'll need to refer to *Sanford's Guide to Garden City Pottery* by Jim Pasquali, who is listed in the Directory under California. Values apply to items in all colors (except black) and all patterns, unless noted otherwise. Due to relative rarity, 20% should be added for any item found in black.

Bowl, bulb; solid color, 5"...15.00
Bowl, low, ribbed, solid color, 14"..............................45.00
Bowl, mixing, wide rings, solid color, #3 (mid sz) 30.00
Bowl, Succulent, conical, solid color, 9"........................35.00
Canister, Ring, sm...35.00
Casserole, narrow or wide rings, solid color, 7", ea........35.00

Deco vase, 4½x10", $65.00; Candle holders, pair, $35.00.
(Photo courtesy Jim Pasquali)

Jardiniere, ribbed, solid color, 10" 45.00
Mug, solid color 20.00
Nappy, solid color, #6, lg 35.00
Plate, artichoke; solid color 40.00
Plate, bread & butter; solid color, 5" 5.00
Ramekin, solid color, 3" 20.00
Teapot, Deco style, solid color, 4-cup 75.00

Gardner Porcelain

Models of wonderfully complicated and detailed subjects illustrating people of many nations absorbed in day-to-day activities were made by this company from the turn of the nineteenth century until well past the 1850s. The factory was founded in 1765 near Moscow, Russia, by an Englishman by the name of Francis Gardner. They are still in business today.

Figure, bear mother feeding cub on her lap, ca 1840, rstr, 6¼" ...750.00
Figure, bearded man by tree-trunk inkwell, bsk, 1840s, 5½" 700.00
Figure, boy w/crab about to awaken friend, ca 1840, 5½" 975.00
Figure, coachman w/hands to hips, ca 1840, 7½" 920.00
Figure, dancing peasant girl, 1 hand up, 1 on hip, porc, 1830s, 5¼" ...800.00
Figure, dancing peasant lady, bsk, ca 1860, 8¼" 550.00
Figure, dancing peasant man, hands to hips, bsk, 1850s, 9½" 920.00
Figure, drunken husband w/wife & child, bsk, 1860s, rstr, 9"...1,035.00
Figure, female water carrier w/yoke & pails, 1820s, 9¾" 6,325.00

Figure, fish seller man w/wooden basket on head, early 1800s, rstr, 9"...1,035.00
Figure, girl by trunk w/baby (lid of matchbox), bsk, 1875, 5¾" ..375.00
Figure, glazier w/palette & cloth, ca 1845, 4½" 1,100.00
Figure, ice breaker w/ice pick & bbl on sled, bsk, ca 1850s, 10⅝" 975.00
Figure, Jewish man w/potbelly, bsk, 1880s, rstr, 8¼" 920.00
Figure, Jewish man w/umbrella, bsk, 1860s, flaw, 9" 2,300.00
Figure, lady w/baby drags drunken husband, bsk, 1860s, 6½" ..1,100.00
Figure, lady w/berry baskets & cup, early 1800s, 7½" 1,380.00
Figure, lady w/flower & berry basket, early 1800s, rstr, 7" 1,495.00
Figure, lady w/2 berry baskets, ca 1820, rstr, 7⅜" 1,035.00
Figure, maiden w/wooden basket & flower wreath, late 1800s, 8"....575.00
Figure, male dandy w/nest of eggs in hand, bsk, mid-1800s, 11" .865.00
Figure, man seated holding up child, bsk, mid-1800s, 9" 920.00
Figure, man sits & plays accordion, mid-1800s, 7"......................865.00
Figure, man sweeping w/broom, early 1800s, 6⅝" 1,150.00
Figure, man w/arms crossed, strap on bk, early 1800s, 8", EX......920.00
Figure, man w/child on shoulder, dead deer at ft, bsk, 1850s, 11" ..1,150.00
Figure, man w/kettle & straw bag, 1830, rstr, 7½"...................1,100.00
Figure, old lady carding wool, bsk, ca 1850s, 5⅛" 750.00
Figure, old lady w/shawl & scarf carries bundle, bsk, 1860, 8¼" ..1,265.00
Figure, old man (Tolstoy?) seated, high boots, bsk, 1860s, 6½" ..575.00
Figure, old woman stands w/walking stick & basket, mid-1800s, 6½"..750.00
Figure, peasant boy pushes wheelbarrow w/keg, early 1800s, rstr, 6" .1,150.00
Figure, peasant girl w/basket, early 1800s, rstr, 7⅜" 1,035.00
Figure, peasant lady & child w/accordion, ca 1850s, 3⅞"...........635.00
Figure, peasant lady prepares meal, bsk, 1850s, rstr, 5½" 865.00
Figure, peasant lady w/close-wrapped baby, bsk, 1850s, 9½", EX...550.00
Figure, peasant man w/wheelbarrow, bsk, rstr gold, 1820s, 5¾" ..545.00
Figure, peddler in fur-trimmed coat, tray on head, mid-1800s, 7½" ..700.00
Figure, Polish couple in regional clothes, late 1800s, 10⅜", EX 1,100.00
Figure, Siberian lady w/baby on bk, hooded tunics, late 1800s, 9½".575.00
Figure, soldier w/sword in hand, 19th C, rstr, 8" 1,100.00
Figure, tea & pastry vendor w/urn & basket, bsk, 1850s, rstr, 7" .635.00
Figure, tea vendor w/kettle & bag, ca 1840, rstr, 7½" 1,100.00
Figure, tea vendor w/urn & cup, bbl inkwell behind, 1830s, rstr, 10" ..1,265.00
Figure, tea vendor w/urn under arm, ca 1825, rstr, 7⅝" 920.00
Figure, Turk w/cane & handkerchief, mid-1800s, rstr, 8" 1,380.00
Figure, uniformed man tended by cobbler, ca 1855, rstr, 7¼" 920.00
Figure, woman modeled as sphinx, Miklashevskii factory, 1850, 6¾"..1,380.00
Figure, 2 boys play w/eggs, bsk, 1850s, 5½" 1,035.00
Figure, 2 boys seated by well, dog beside, ca 1850s, 3½" 750.00
Figure, 2 children by child in broken cart, bsk, 1870s, 5½" 800.00
Figure, 2 children on trestle, 3rd w/horn, 1850s, rstr, 4¾" 750.00
Figure, 2 men conversing, rectangular base, mid-1800s, 8¼"....1,035.00
Figure, 3 men w/bottle, accordion & overcoat, bsk, 1860s, 10", EX...2,400.00
Figure, 4 children by well, bsk, 1860, 3¼" 1,035.00

Gas Globes and Panels

Gas globes and panels, once a common sight, have vanished from the countryside but are being sought by collectors as a unique form of advertising memorabilia. Early globes from the 1920s (some date back to as early as 1912), now referred to as 'one-piece globes,' were made of molded milk glass and were globular in shape. The gas company name was etched or painted on the glass. Few of these were ever produced, and this type is valued very highly by collectors today.

A new type of pump was introduced in the early 1930s; the old 'visible' pumps were replaced by 'electric' models. Globes were changing at the same time. By the mid-teens a three-piece globe consisting of a pair of inserts and a metal body was being produced in both 15" and 16½" sizes. Collectors prefer to call globes that are not one-piece or plastic 'three-piece glass' (Type 2) or 'metal body, glass inserts' (Type 3). Though metal-body globes (Type 3) were popular in the 1930s, they were common in the 1920s, and some were actually made as early as 1915. Though rare in numbers, their use spans many years. In the 1930s Type 2 and Type 3 globes became the replacements of the one-piece globe. The most recently manufactured gas globes are made with a plastic body that contains two 13½" glass lenses. These were common in the '50s but were actually used as early as 1932.

In the listings that follow, values are for examples with both sides in excellent condition: no chips, wear, or other damage.

Note: Standard Crowns with raised letters are one-piece globes that were made in the 1920s; those made in the 1950s (no raised letters), though one-piece, are not regarded as such by today's collectors. Our advisor for this category is Scott Benjamin; he is listed in the Directory under Ohio.

Type 1, Plastic Body, Glass Inserts (Inserts 13½") — 1931 – 1950s

Conoco Ethyl Gasoline, 13½", NM, $500.00.

D-X Marine, rare, EX	1,200.00
Dixie, plastic band, EX	250.00
DX Lubricating Gasoline, tan body, EX	300.00
Frontier Gas, Rarin' To Go, w/horse, EX	1,000.00
Kendal Deluxe, Capcolite body w/red pnt, 13½", EX	350.00
Kendall Polly Power, Capcolite body, 13½", EX	400.00
Marathon, no runner, EX	200.00
Never Nox Ethyl, EX	450.00
Spur, Oval body, EX	350.00
Texaco Diesel Chief, Capcolite body, 13½", EX	1,350.00
Viking, pictures Viking ship, EX	1,750.00

Type 2, Glass Frame, Glass Inserts (Inserts 13½") — 1926 – 1940s

Aerio, gr gill ripple body, 13½", EX	7,500.00
American, gill body, 12½", EX	400.00
Amoco, gill body, 13½", EX	400.00
Atlantic, glass body, 13½", EX	325.00
Atlantic Imperial, gill body, 13½", EX	450.00
Derby, EX	450.00
Esso, EX	325.00
Frontier Gas, Double Refined, EX	400.00
Guyler Brand, milk glass, EX	850.00
Pitman Streamlined, bl gill rippled body, 13½", EX	7,000.00
Pure, EX	500.00
Sinclair Dino, milk glass, EX	300.00
Sinclair Pennant, EX	1,000.00
Sky Chief, gill body, 13½", EX	500.00
Standard Crown, bl, EX	800.00
Standard Crown, gr, EX	1,000.00
Standard Crown, gray, EX	1,200.00
Standard Crown, wht, red or gold, EX, ea	400.00
Standard Flame, EX	400.00
Texaco Ethyl, EX	1,600.00
White Flash, gill body, EX	450.00

WNAX, w/radio station pictured, EX	2,500.00

Type 3, Metal Frame, Glass Inserts (Inserts 15" or 16½") — 1915 – 1930s

Aero Mobilgas, new metal body, rare, 15", EX	2,500.00
Atlantic Ethyl, 16½", EX	750.00
Atlantic White Flash, 16½", EX	750.00
General Ethyl, 15" fr, complete, EX	1,200.00
Kendal Gasoline, airplane, metal body, rare, 15", EX	6,000.00
Marathon, low profile metal body, 15", EX	1,300.00
Mobilgas Ethyl, 16½", EX	600.00
Oil Creek Gas, drake well & derrick, 15", EX	3,000.00
Phillips Benzo, low profile metal body, 15", EX	3,500.00
Purol Gasoline, w/arrow, porc body, EX	900.00
Red Crown Ethyl, EX	950.00
Royal Maine, high profile metal body, 15", EX	2,500.00
Signal, old stoplight, 15", EX	4,500.00
Stanolined Aviation, rare, 16½", EX	5,000.00
Texaco Leaded, glass panels, complete globe, EX	5,000.00
White Star, 15" fr, complete, EX	1,300.00

Type 4, One-Piece Glass Globes, No Inserts, Company Name Etched, Raised or Enameled — 1912 – 1931

Atlantic, chimney cap, EX	3,000.00
Dixie, etched	2,000.00
Mobil Gargoyle, gargoyle pictured, oval, EX	2,200.00
Pierce Pennant, etched, EX	3,200.00
Republic, 3-sided, EX	2,200.00
Shell, rnd, etched, EX	800.00
Super Shell, clam shape, EX	1,800.00
Super Shell, rnd, etched, EX	4,000.00
Texaco, etched letters, wide body, EX	3,000.00
Texaco Ethyl, EX	2,200.00
That Good Gulf..., emb, orange & blk letters, EX	1,200.00
White Eagle, blunt nose, 20¾", EX	1,600.00
White Eagle, detailed eagle, 20¾", EX	2,000.00
White Rose, boy pictured, pnt, EX	3,000.00

Gaudy Dutch

Inspired by Oriental Imari wares, Gaudy Dutch was made in England from 1800 to 1820. It was hand decorated on a soft-paste body with rich underglaze blues accented in orange, red, pink, green, and yellow. It differs from Gaudy Welsh in that there is no lustre (except on Water Lily). There are seventeen patterns, some of which are War Bonnet, Grape, Dahlia, Oyster, Urn, Butterfly, Carnation, Single Rose, Double Rose, and Water Lily. For further information we recommend *The Collector's Encyclopedia of Gaudy Dutch & Welsh* by John A. Shuman, III, available from Collector Books. Unless otherwise noted, values are given for items with minimal wear and no obvious damage.

Butterfly, creamer	1,450.00
Butterfly, plate, butterfly on side, 7¼"	825.00
Butterfly, teapot	2,530.00
Butterfly, waste bowl	1,400.00
Carnation, cup plate	715.00
Carnation, plate, yel dot border, 9¾"	1,050.00
Carnation, plate, 8"	660.00
Cybis, cup plate, butterfly to side, unmk	165.00
Dahlia, plate, 8"	880.00
Dahlia, tea bowl & saucer	825.00
Double Rose, creamer	660.00

Double Rose, plate, deep, 9¾"	850.00
Double Rose, platter, slightly mellowed, 10½"	3,000.00
Double Rose, teapot	880.00
Dove, creamer	770.00
Dove, creamer, helmet shape, rare	1,400.00
Dove, plate, 9¾"	880.00
Grape, cream pitcher	770.00
Grape, cup & saucer	515.00
Grape, plate, minor stains, 8"	440.00
Grape, platter, 15"	990.00
Grape, waste bowl	400.00
Leaf, sugar bowl, w/lid	1,100.00
Oyster, creamer	440.00
Oyster, sugar bowl, orange, w/lid	1,500.00
Oyster, waste bowl, 6¼"	1,200.00
Primrose, tea bowl & saucer	770.00
Single Rose, coffeepot, dome lid, EX	1,500.00
Single Rose, sugar bowl, oblong, shell hdls	825.00
Strawflower, plate, mk Riley, 8¼"	880.00
Strawflower, plate, 9¼"	915.00
Sunflower, plate, 7½"	600.00
Sunflower, plate, 8¼"	660.00
Urn, plate, scup; 8⅞"	550.00
Urn, waste bowl, 5½"	900.00
War Bonnet, plate, 8"	715.00
War Bonnet, sugar bowl, w/lid, sm rpr	925.00
War Bonnet, toddy plate, 5¼", M	1,040.00
War Bonnet, waste bowl, 5"	1,100.00
Zinnia, plate, 6⅜"	660.00

Gaudy Welsh

Gaudy Welsh was an inexpensive hand-decorated ware made in both England and Wales from 1820 until 1860. It is characterized by its colors — principally blue, orange-rust, and copper lustre — and by its uninhibited patterns. Accent colors may be yellow and green. (Pink lustre may be present, since lustre applied to the white areas appears pink. A copper tone develops from painting lustre onto the dark colors.) The body of the ware may be heavy ironstone (also called Gaudy Ironstone), creamware, earthenware, or porcelain; even style and shapes vary considerably. Patterns, while usually floral, are also sometimes geometric and may have trees and birds. Beware! The Wagon Wheel pattern has been reproduced.

Our advisor for this category is Cheryl Nelson; she is listed in the Directory under Minnesota. For further information we recommend *The Collector's Encyclopedia of Gaudy Dutch & Welsh* by John A. Shuman, III, available from Collector Books.

Note: Prices are rising, as collector demand continues to increase. For the first time, British auction houses are picturing and promoting Gaudy Welsh. However, demand for Columbine, Grape, Tulip, Oyster, and Wagon Wheel is slow. We should also mention that the Bethedsa pattern is very similar to a Davenport jug pattern. No porcelain Gaudy Welsh was made in Wales.

Plates (from left to right): Rocking Urn, $250.00; Cherry Tree, $240.00; Basket of Flowers, $235.00.
(Photo courtesy Cheryl Nelson)

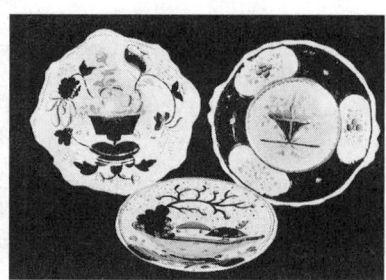

Aster, plate, 9"	235.00
Basket of Flowers, jug, 4"	325.00
Beanstock, jug, 5¼"	670.00
Billingsley Rose, cup & saucer	225.00
Bittersweet, plate, 6"	325.00
Cardiff, jug, 7'	700.00
Castle, jug, 3"	475.00
Chinoserie, mug, 3"	195.00
Columbine, cup & saucer	95.00
Conwy, jug, 7"	700.00
Coral, waste bowl	425.00
Crest, jug, 6"	680.00
Daffodil, jug, 6"	725.00
Dahlia, teapot	735.00
Dancing Leaves, plate, 8"	350.00
Dotted Circle, plate, 8"	375.00
Elfin Cap, plate	345.00
Ewer, teapot	875.00
Floret, cup & saucer	98.00
Fruit, sugar bowl	800.00
Geranium, toddy plate, 4"	295.00
Grape, sugar bowl, mk Imperial	425.00
Grape & Lily, creamer, 4"	475.00
Ivy, bowl, 9½"	1,100.00
Japan, jug, 8"	750.00
Lantern, jug, 7"	800.00
Lotus, plate, 6"	300.00
Marigold, creamer, 4"	325.00
Nebula, teapot	795.00
Oyster, cup & saucer	75.00
Penllyn, plate, 8"	350.00
Poinsettia, cup & saucer	225.00
Poppy, jug, 8'	595.00
Rainbow, jug, 6"	675.00

Geisha Girl

Geisha Girl porcelain was one of several key Japanese china production efforts aimed at the booming export markets of the U.S., Canada, England, and other parts of Europe. The wares feature colorful, kimono-clad Japanese ladies in scenes of everyday Japanese life surrounded by exquisite flora, fauna, and mountain ranges. Nonetheless, the forms in which the wares were produced reflected the late nineteenth- and early twentieth-century Western dining and decorating preferences: tea and coffee services, vases, dresser sets, children's items, planters, etc.

Over a hundred manufacturers were involved in Geisha Girl production. This accounts for the several hundred different patterns, well over a dozen border colors and styles, and several methods of design execution. Geisha Girl Porcelain was produced in wholly hand-painted versions, but most were hand painted over stenciled outlines. Be wary of Geisha ware executed with decals. Very few decaled examples came out of Japan. Rather, most were Czechoslovakian attempts to hone in on the market. Czech pieces have stamped marks in broad, pseudo-Oriental characters. Items with portraits of Oriental ladies in the bottom of tea or sake cups are *not* Geisha Girl porcelain, unless the outside surface of the wares are decorated as described above. These lovely faces, formed by varying the thickness of the porcelain body, are called lithophanes and are collectible in their own right.

The height of Geisha Girl production was between 1910 and the mid-1930s. Some post-World War II production has been found marked Occupied Japan.

The ware continued in minimal production during the 1960s, but the point of origin of the later pieces was Hong Kong. These productions are discerned by the pure whiteness of the porcelain; even, unemotional borders; lack of background washes and gold enameling; and overall sparseness of detail. A new wave of Nippon-marked reproduction Geisha emerged in 1996. If the Geisha Girl productions of the 1960s – 80s were overly plain, the mid-1990s repros are overly ornate. Original Geisha Girl porcelain was enhanced by brush strokes of color over a stenciled design; it was never the 'color perfectly within the lines' type of decoration found on current reproductions. Original Geisha Girl porcelain was decorated with color washes; the reproductions are in heavy enamels. The backdrop decoration of the current reproductions feature solid, thick colors, and the patterns feature too much color; period Geisha ware had a high ratio of white space to color. The new pieces also have bright shiny gold in proportions greater than most period Geisha ware. The Nippon marks on the reproductions are wrong. Some of the Geisha ware created during the Nippon era bore the small precise decaled green M-in-Wreath mark, a Noritake registered trademark. The reproduction items feature an irregular facsimile of this mark. Stamped onto the reproductions is an unrealistically large M-in-Wreath mark in shades of green ranging from an almost neon to pine green with a wreath that looks like it has seen better days, as it does not have the perfect roundness of the original mark. Reproductions of mid-sized trays, chunky hatpin holders, an ornate vase, a covered bottle, and a powder jar are among the current reproductions popping up at flea and antique markets.

Many of our descriptions contain references to border colors and treatments. This information is given immediately preceding the mark and/or size. Our advisor for this category is Elyce Litts; she is listed in the Directory under New Jersey.

Basket vase, Bamboo Trellis, gold trim, 8½", pr............................150.00
Biscuit jar, Leaving the Teahouse, fluted, bulbous, red w/gold.......45.00
Bondon dish, Battledore, mum shaped, olive gr.............................22.00

Bouillon cup and saucer, Garden Bench J, with lid, multicolor border, $55.00.
(Photo courtesy Elyce Litts)

Bowl, berry; Dragonboat, cobalt w/gold, master+6 ind..................85.00
Bowl, berry; Lady in Rickshaw, red w/gold, scalloped, master........35.00
Bowl, berry; Oni Dance A, 9-lobed, scalloped, red-orange w/gold, ind ..12.00
Bowl, Garden Bench I, red-orange w/int gold lacing, 6"................12.00
Bowl, master nut; Basket A, 9-lobe, 3-ftd, dk apple gr, 6"............30.00
Bowl, rice; Carp D: Fish Bowl, red....................................15.00
Bowl, salad; Garden Bench A, 9-lobed, red, 7¼"........................25.00
Bowl, sauce; Her Master's Keeper, lobed pierced hdl....................8.00
Box, Parasol E, egg shape, red-orange, 4½x3¾x3½".....................35.00
Box, puff; Field Laborers, red w/gold.................................20.00
Butter pat, Basket of Mums B, red-orange w/gold, 3¼"..................10.00
Celery dish, Battledore, apple gr w/gold..............................38.00
Cocoa pot, Pillar Print, red-brn w/gold, cylindrical..................65.00
Cocoa set, Bamboo Trellis, pine gr, pot+6 c/s........................150.00
Cocoa set, Temple B, red/orange w/gold, pot+6 c/s....................175.00
Cracker jar, Spider Puppet, ftd, lobed, cobalt w/gold.................65.00
Creamer, Chinese Coin, Battledore & scenic reserves...................25.00
Creamer, Long-Stemmed Peony, bl w/gold, slim, fluted..................12.00

Creamer, Porch, red-orange, modern....................................10.00
Creamer & sugar bowl, Basket A, dk apple gr w/gold, fluted/scalloped..32.00
Creamer & sugar bowl, Kite A, brn w/gold..............................30.00
Cup, toy; Boy w/Doll, red, 2"...10.00
Cup & saucer, AD; Basket B, dk apple gr w/gold, str side..............15.00
Cup & saucer, AD; Chrysanthemum Garden, foliate shape, gold lacing ..20.00
Cup & saucer, AD; Parasol B: Torii & Parasol, red-orange w/gold...15.00
Cup & saucer, cocoa; Bamboo Tree, pine gr line border................12.00
Cup & saucer, cocoa; Basket B, dk apple gr w/gold, fluted............25.00
Cup & saucer, cocoa; Child Wearing E-Boshi, cobalt bl-gray wash....20.00
Cup & saucer, tea; Bamboo Trellis, dk gr.............................12.00
Cup & saucer, tea; Blue Hoo..14.00
Cup & saucer, tea; Geisha in Sampan A, maroon........................10.00
Cup & saucer, tea; Writing B, bl w/gold..............................15.00
Gravy boat & underplate, Rice Harvesters, leaf shape w/gold.......28.00
Hair receiver, Carp A: Watching the Carp, cobalt w/gold.............30.00
Hair receiver, Sake Time, ruffled rim, reserves.....................35.00
Jar, sachet; Fan C, red w/gold, hdls, ftd, 6½".......................75.00
Lemonade set, Bellflower, brn w/gr details, pitcher+5 mugs........125.00
Nappy, Mother & Daughter, lobed, gold lacing, fan-shaped reserves 30.00
Plate, cake; Duck Watching B, red-orange, floriated/pierced edge...45.00
Plate, Parasol K: Parasol & Basket, swirled flutes, cobalt w/gold, 7"...22.00
Plate, Torii, golden brn w/red buds/gr leaves & gold, 6"............13.00
Plate, Wait for Me, floriate shape, red-orange w/gold buds, 8¾"...26.00
Pot, demitasse; Court lady, HP geisha reserve, mini, 1½".............20.00
Ramekin w/saucer, Checkerboard, cobalt bl w/gold.....................55.00
Relish, Courtesan Processional, 8x5"..................................28.00
Shakers, Dressing, red, pr..10.00
Teapot, Fan Dance, red w/gold...40.00
Toothbrush holder, Flute, red-orange, 4".............................25.00
Tray, condiment; Meeting A, red-orange w/gold, HP decor, 6x4¼"..20.00
Tray, dresser; Garden Bench D, HP gr & red w/gold....................55.00

Georgia Art Pottery

In Cartersville, Georgia, in August 1935, W.J. Gordy first fired pottery turned from regional clays. By 1936 he was marking his wares 'Georgia Art Pottery' (GP) or 'Georgia Art Pottery' (GAP) and continued to do so until 1950 when he used a 'Hand Made by WJ Gordy' stamp (HM). Since 1970 he has signed his pottery. Known throughout the world for his fine glazes, he won the Georgia Governor's Award in 1983. Examples of his wares are on display in the Smithsonian. His father W.T.B. and brother D.X. are also well-known potters.

Vase, swirl ware, unglazed exterior with medium green glazed interior, signed Gordy, ca 1970 – 93, 2⅝x4¼", $125.00. (Photo courtesy Southern Folk Pottery Collectors Society)

Ashtray, med cobalt, 2 rests, 3½" dia.................................35.00
Pencil holder, deep teal gr, 19-hole, 4½x5¼".........................75.00
Pitcher, feldspathic sky bl, ice lip, 7½x7".........................225.00
Pitcher, mauve, flaw, 5½x3"...50.00

Vase, plum, dimpled/fluted, hand-trn, 3x3", NM 70.00

German Porcelain

Unless otherwise noted, the porcelain listed in this section is marked simply 'Germany.' Products of other German manufacturers are listed in specific categories. See also Bisque; Pink Paw Bears; Pink Pigs; Elfinware.

Compote, roses on peach to cream w/much gold, ca 1882, 4½x12x8" ..335.00
Figural group, seated lady & man by fountain, 1900s, 7x8¼" 430.00
Figurine, lady on horse w/market baskets, gold trim, 10x10".......415.00
Plaque, lady's portrait, sgn Sontag, ca 1870, 6x4½" in 14x12" fr ..1,800.00
Plaque, Roman couple in rocky flower garden, sgn, 6¼x4½"......500.00
Plaque, Solitude, sgn Wagner, 5¾x3¾"+13x11" orig gilt-metal fr ...1,800.00
Tray, roses, sgn L Gitti, Alboth & Keiser mk, 12¾x12½" 395.00
Vase, roses allover on shaded pastels, mk AK w/crown, 1920s, 14x6" ..475.00

Gladding McBean and Company

This company was established in 1875 in Lincoln, California. They first produced only clay drainage pipes, but in 1883 architectural terra cotta was introduced, which has been used extensively in the United States as well as abroad. Sometime later a line of garden pottery was added. They soon became the leading producers of tile in the country. In 1923 they purchased the Tropico Pottery in Glendale, California, where in addition to tile they also produced huge garden vases. Their line was expanded in 1934 to included artware and dinnerware.

At least fifteen lines of art pottery were developed between 1934 and 1942. For a short time they stamped their wares with the Tropico Pottery mark; but the majority was signed 'GMcB' in an oval. Later the mark was changed to 'Franciscan' with several variations. After 1937 'Catalina Pottery' was used on some lines. (All items marked 'Catalina Pottery' were made in Glendale.) For further information we recommend *The Collector's Encyclopedia of California Pottery, Second Edition*, by Jack Chipman (Collector Books). See also Franciscan Ware.

Bowl, flower; wht w/bl int, mk Catalina Pottery, 4x18" 180.00
Candy jar, Contour artware, Dawn, minimum value 150.00
Plate, ivory satin, fluted, Catalina Pottery, 14" 70.00
Plate, Montecito, gray satin, 14"..90.00
Platter, Montecito, coral, 12x16" 90.00
Shell tray, Contour artware, gray, teardrop shape, minimum value ..75.00

Statue, nude cherub with bouquet of water lilies, frog resting at his feet, opaque aqua to medium blue matt over tan clay, with factory hole for fountain, attributed, 28", $500.00.

Tile, Siamese cat on wht, artist sgn, ca 1940s-50s, 6" sq, EX.........20.00
Vase, Capistrano Ware, plum & ivory, shape #148 ....90.00
Vase, Montebello, bl w/wht int, apple shape #132, sm 90.00
Vase, Montebello, bl w/wht int, shape #105...............................90.00

Vase, Reseda Art Ware, gold, shape #464 ....100.00
Vase, shell, wht w/turq int, 8"...135.00

Glass Animals and Figurines

These beautiful glass sculptures have been produced by many major companies in America, in fact, some are still being made today. Heisey, Fostoria, Duncan and Miller, Imperial, Paden City, Tiffin, and Cambridge made the vast majority, but there were many others involved on a lesser scale. Some, but not all, marked their animals.

As many of the glass companies went out of business, molds were often sold to others still active who used them to reproduce their own line of animals. While some are easy to recognize, others can be very confusing. For example, Summit Art Glass now owns Cambridge's 6½", 8½", and 10" swan molds. We recommend *Glass Animals of the Depression Era* by Lee Garmon and Dick Spencer, if you're thinking of starting a collection or wanting to identify and evaluate the glass animals you already have. Both are our advisors for this category and are listed in the Directory under Illinois.

Note: Heisey Collectors of America stopped using the plug horse and have adopted the rabbit paperweight as the new yearly mascot. Viking collectors should also be made aware that crystal Viking pieces are much harder to find than colored ones.

Cambridge

Bashful Charlotte, flower frog, crystal, 11½".............................175.00
Bashful Charlotte, flower frog, Dianthus, 6½" 175.00
Bashful Charlotte, flower frog, gr, 11½" 375.00
Bashful Charlotte, flower frog, Moonlight Blue, 11½" 575.00
Bashful Charlotte, flower frog, Moonlight Blue satin, 11½" 800.00
Bird, crystal satin, 2¾" L..35.00
Bird on stump, flower frog, gr, 5¼" 375.00
Blue jay, flower holder, crystal...160.00
Bridge hound, ebony, 1¼" 50.00
Buddha, amber, 5½" 250.00
Draped Lady, flower frog, amber, 8½" 195.00
Draped Lady, flower frog, crystal frost, 13¼" 175.00
Draped Lady, flower frog, Dianthus, 8½" 175.00
Draped Lady, flower frog, Dianthus, 13¼" 225.00
Draped Lady, flower frog, Gold Krystol, 8½"..........................250.00
Draped Lady, flower frog, gr frost, 8½" 150.00
Draped Lady, flower frog, ivory, oval base, 8½"......................800.00
Draped Lady, flower frog, lt emerald, 8½" 175.00
Draped Lady, flower frog, Moonlight Blue, 13" 860.00
Eagle, bookend, crystal, 5½x4x4", ea...................................95.00
Frog, crystal satin...35.00
Heron, crystal, lg, 12"..135.00
Lion, bookend, crystal, ea 185.00
Mandolin Lady, flower frog, crystal.....................................250.00
Mandolin Lady, flower frog, dk amber 450.00
Mandolin Lady, flower frog, lt emerald.................................400.00
Melon Boy, flower frog, Dianthus 450.00
Owl, lamp, ivory w/brn enamel, ebony base, 13½"....................1,100.00
Rose Lady, flower frog, amber, 8½".....................................225.00
Rose Lady, flower frog, crystal satin, tall base, 9¾".................225.00
Rose Lady, flower frog, Dianthus, 8½"..................................250.00
Rose Lady, flower frog, dk amber, tall base, 9¾" 275.00
Rose Lady, flower frog, gr, 8½"...200.00
Scottie, bookends, crystal, hollow, pr 175.00
Sea gull, flower block, crystal..60.00
Swan, amber, #1 style, 10½" 875.00
Swan, Apple Green, #1 style, 13½".....................................850.00

Swan, Carmen, #3 style, 8½"................................350.00
Swan, Carmen, 6½"...225.00
Swan, Crown Tuscan, 3".......................................50.00
Swan, Crown Tuscan, 8½"....................................125.00
Swan, crystal, #1 style, 10½"................................140.00
Swan, dk gr, #3 style, 8½"...................................175.00
Swan, ebony, 3"..65.00
Swan, ebony, 8½"..165.00
Swan, ebony, 10½"...250.00
Swan, ebony, 12½"...300.00
Swan, emerald, 3"..40.00
Swan, emerald, 8½"..125.00
Swan, milk glass, #3 style, 8½"..............................350.00
Swan, milk glass, 6½"..125.00
Swan, milk glass, 8½"..275.00
Swan, punch bowl, Pearl Mist.............................2,900.00
Swan, yel, 8½"...175.00

Turkey, amber, with lid, $450.00.
(Photo courtesy National Cambridge Collectors, Inc.)

Turkey, bl, w/lid...550.00
Turkey, pk, w/lid..400.00
Turtle, flower holder, ebony................................225.00
Two Kids, flower frog, amber, oval base, 9¼"...........350.00
Two Kids, flower frog, amber satin, 9¼".................400.00
Two Kids, flower frog, crystal, 9¼".......................200.00

Duncan and Miller

Bird of Paradise, crystal.....................................700.00
Donkey, cart & peon, crystal, 3-pc set..................525.00
Dove, crystal, head down, 11½" L.........................175.00
Duck, ashtray, crystal, 4".....................................20.00
Duck, ashtray, red, 7"...275.00
Duck, cigarette box, red, 6"..................................425.00
Goose, crystal, fat, 6x6".....................................375.00
Heron, crystal...150.00
Heron, crystal satin, 7".......................................120.00
Mallard duck, cigarette box, crystal, #30, w/lid, 3½x4½"......60.00
Swan, bl opal, W&F, spread wings, 10x12½".............245.00
Swan, candle holder, red, 7", ea.............................80.00
Swan, crystal, solid, 5"..35.00
Swan, crystal, wheat cutting, 11"..........................200.00
Swan, milk glass w/red neck, 10½".........................450.00
Swordfish, bl opal, rare.......................................500.00
Swordfish, crystal..275.00
Sylvan swan, bl or pk, 5½"...................................125.00
Sylvan swan, yel opal, 5½"...................................120.00
Sylvan swan, yel opal, 7½"...................................140.00
Tropical fish, ashtray, pk opal, 3½".........................50.00

Fenton

Airedale, Rosalene, 1992 issue for Heisey 75.00

Alley cat, pk carnival, mk, 11".............................100.00
Alley cat, Teal Marigold, 11"................................85.00
Bear, carnival, sitting..30.00
Bunny, lt bl..16.00
Bunny, pale yel...25.00
Butterfly, candle holder, ruby carnival, 1989 souvenir, 7½", ea.....95.00
Cardinal head, ruby, 6½" 150.00
Donkey, custard, HP daisies, 4½"...........................45.00
Elephant, periwinkle, whiskey bottle, 8"................450.00
Filly, Rosalene, head front, 1992 issue for Heisey........75.00
Fish, bookend, Rosalene, ea..................................65.00
Fish, paperweight, red carnival, ltd ed, 4½"...............65.00
Fish, red w/amberina tail & fins, 2½".......................55.00
Fish, vase, milk glass w/blk tail & eyes, 7"...............425.00
Gazelle, Rosalene...95.00
Giraffe, Rosalene...95.00
Happiness Bird, Rosalene 40.00
Hen, Rosalene, 1992 issue for Heisey 65.00
Peacock, bookends, crystal satin, 5¾", pr................175.00
Plug Horse, HCA, Rosalene..................................50.00
Rabbit, paperweight, Rosalene, 1992 issue for Heisey....55.00
Turtle, flower block, amethyst, 4" L.........................85.00

Fostoria

Bird, candle holder, crystal, 1½"............................20.00
Buddha, bookends, blk, pr...................................525.00
Cardinal head, Silver Mist, 6½"...........................175.00
Cat, lt bl, 3¾"...35.00
Chanticleer, blk, 10¾".......................................600.00
Chinese Lute, ebony w/gold, 12½".........................300.00
Colt, Silver Mist, standing 45.00
Deer, bl, sitting or standing, ea.............................55.00
Deer, milk glass, sitting or standing, ea....................55.00
Dolphin, bl, 4¾"..35.00
Duck, mama, crystal 30.00

Duck family, amber: mama and three ducklings, $75.00 for the set. (Photo courtesy Ann Kerr)

Duckling, crystal, head down (+)............................20.00
Eagle, bookend, crystal, 7½", ea 150.00
Elephant, bookend, ebony, 6½", ea 150.00
Frog, bl, lemon or olive gr, 1⅞", ea.........................40.00
Goldfish, crystal, horizontal, rare.........................145.00
Goldfish, crystal, vertical...................................110.00
Horse, bookend, crystal, 7¾", ea............................45.00
Lady bug, bl, lemon or olive gr, 1¼", ea...................35.00
Madonna, Silver Mist, orig issue, 10" (+).................50.00
Madonna & Child, Silver Mist, lighted base optional, 13½"......325.00
Mermaid, crystal, 11½".......................................125.00
Owl, bl, lemon or olive gr, 2¾"..............................35.00
Pelican, amber, 1991 commemorative 55.00
Penguin, crystal, sq base, 4⅝"...............................75.00
Polar bear, crystal, 4⅝".......................................65.00
Polar bear, topaz, 4⅝".......................................125.00
Rebecca at Well, candle holder, crystal frost, ea........125.00

Sea horse, bookend, crystal, 8", ea.....125.00
Seal, topaz, 3⅞".....125.00
Squirrel, amber, running or sitting, ea.....45.00
St Francis, Silver Mist, orig issue, 13½" (+).....325.00
Stork, bl, lemon or olive gr, 2", ea.....35.00

Heisey

Airedale, crystal.....775.00
Asiatic pheasant, crystal, 7½" L.....325.00
Bull, crystal, sgn, 4x7½".....1,800.00
Bunny, crystal, head down, 2½".....250.00
Chick, crystal, head down or up, ea.....95.00

Clydesdale, crystal, 7½x7", $475.00. (Photo courtesy Lee Garmon and Dick Spencer)

Colt, amber, kicking.....650.00
Colt, amber, rearing.....650.00
Colt, cobalt, kicking.....1,500.00
Colt, cobalt, rearing.....1,500.00
Colt, crystal, kicking.....200.00
Colt, crystal, rearing.....200.00
Colt, crystal, standing.....100.00
Cygnet, baby swan, crystal, 2½".....225.00
Doe head, bookend, crystal, 6¼", ea.....850.00
Dolphin, candlesticks, crystal, #110, pr.....400.00
Dolphin, candlesticks, Moongleam, #110, pr.....800.00
Donkey, crystal.....295.00
Duck, ashtray, crystal.....100.00
Duck, ashtray, Marigold.....400.00
Duck, flower block, crystal.....140.00
Duck, flower block, Flamingo.....200.00
Duck, flower block, Hawthorne.....295.00
Elephant, amber, lg or med, ea.....1,950.00
Elephant, amber, sm.....1,800.00
Elephant, crystal, lg or med, ea.....450.00
Elephant, crystal, sm.....275.00
Filly, crystal, head bkwards.....1,800.00
Filly, crystal, head forward.....1,000.00
Fish, bookend, crystal, ea.....160.00
Fish, bowl, crystal, 9½".....550.00
Fish, candlestick, crystal, 5", ea.....200.00
Fish, match holder, crystal, 3x2¾".....180.00
Flying Mare, crystal.....3,500.00
Frog, cheese plate, Marigold.....285.00
Gazelle, crystal, 10¾".....1,200.00
Giraffe, crystal, head bk.....275.00
Giraffe, crystal, head forward.....240.00
Giraffe, crystal, head to side.....275.00
Goose, crystal, wings down.....450.00
Goose, crystal, wings half.....100.00
Goose, crystal, wings up.....130.00
Hen, crystal, 4½".....375.00
Horse head, bookend, crystal, ea.....175.00
Horse head, cigarette box, crystal, #1489, 4½x4".....60.00
Horse head, frosted, bookend, ea.....140.00
Irish setter, ashtray, crystal.....30.00
Irish setter, ashtray, Flamingo.....45.00
Kingfisher, flower block, Flamingo.....225.00
Kingfisher, Moongleam, flower block.....250.00
Mallard, crystal, wings down.....350.00
Mallard, crystal, wings half.....200.00
Mallard, crystal, wings up.....200.00
Piglet, crystal, sitting.....100.00
Piglet, crystal, standing.....100.00
Plug horse, amber.....600.00
Plug horse, cobalt.....1,200.00
Pouter pigeon, crystal, 7½" L.....900.00
Rabbit, paperweight, crystal, 2¾x3¾".....225.00
Rabbit mother, crystal, 4½x5½".....1,600.00
Ram head, stopper, crystal, 3½".....160.00
Ringneck pheasant, crystal, 11¾".....175.00
Rooster, amber, 5⅝".....2,500.00
Rooster, crystal, 5½x5".....350.00
Rooster, Fighting; crystal frost, 7½x5½".....200.00
Rooster, vase, crystal, 6½".....110.00
Rooster head, cocktail, crystal.....60.00
Rooster head, cocktail shaker, crystal, 1-qt.....75.00
Rooster head, stopper, crystal, 4½".....45.00
Scotty, crystal.....170.00
Sea horse, cocktail, crystal.....160.00
Show horse, crystal.....1,250.00
Sow, crystal, 3x4½".....1,200.00
Sparrow, crystal.....120.00
Swan, crystal.....1,300.00
Swan, ind nut, crystal, #1503.....25.00
Swan, master nut, crystal, #1503.....45.00
Swan, pitcher, crystal.....1,400.00
Tiger, paperweight, crystal, 2¾x8".....900.00
Tropical fish, crystal, 12".....2,200.00
Wood duck, crystal, floating.....225.00
Wood duck, crystal, mother.....800.00
Wood duck, crystal, standing.....225.00

Imperial

Airedale, caramel slag.....115.00
Airedale, Ultra Blue.....75.00
Bull, amber, very rare.....725.00
Bulldog-type pup, milk glass, 3½".....65.00
Champ terrier, caramel slag, 5¾".....95.00
Chick, milk glass, head down.....10.00
Chick, milk glass, head up.....10.00
Clydesdale, Salmon.....275.00
Clydesdale, Verde Green.....170.00
Colt, amber, balking.....140.00
Colt, amber, standing.....125.00
Colt, caramel slag, balking.....140.00
Colt, Horizon Blue, kicking.....35.00
Colt, Sunshine Yellow, standing.....75.00
Cygnet, blk, 2½".....55.00
Cygnet, caramel slag.....65.00
Cygnet, Horizon Blue.....25.00
Donkey, caramel slag.....55.00
Donkey, Meadow Green carnival.....85.00
Donkey, Ultra Blue.....65.00
Elephant, caramel slag, med.....65.00

Elephant, caramel slag, sm 85.00
Elephant, Meadow Green carnival, #674, med 85.00
Elephant, Nut Brown, sm...120.00
Filly, satin, head forward...85.00
Fish, bookend, ruby, ea..340.00
Fish, candlestick, Sunshine Yellow, 5" 40.00
Fish, match holder, Sunshine Yellow satin, 3".................20.00
Flying mare, amber, NI mk, extremely rare.................1,500.00
Gazelle, blk, 11"...300.00
Giraffe, amber, ALIG mk, extremely rare........................350.00
Horse head, bookend, pk, rare, ea....................................300.00
Mallard, caramel slag, wings down....................................200.00
Mallard, caramel slag, wings half...35.00
Mallard, caramel slag, wings up...40.00
Mallard, Horizon Blue, wings down, HCA, 4½" 35.00
Mallard, lt bl satin, wings down 35.00
Marmote Sentinel (woodchuck), caramel slag, 4½" 60.00
Owl, Hootless; caramel slag..50.00
Owl, Jade Green slag, shiny 85.00
Owl, jar, caramel slag, 16½" 75.00
Owl, milk glass..48.00
Owl, purple slag, shiny 95.00
Piglet, amber, sitting..40.00
Piglet, amber, standing 40.00
Piglet, ruby, standing 35.00
Plug horse, pk, HCA, 1978..40.00
Rabbit, paperweight, Horizon Blue, 2¾" 110.00
Ring-neck pheasant, amber, extremely rare......................320.00
Rooster, amber..475.00
Rooster, pk, fighting...175.00
Scolding bird, Cathay Crystal 175.00
Scottie, milk glass, 3½" 55.00
Swan, purple slag, shiny 95.00
Terrier, Parlour Pup, amethyst carnival, 3½"....................45.00
Terrier, Parlour Pup, Sunshine Yellow carnival 50.00
Tiger, paperweight, caramel slag 150.00
Tiger, paperweight, Jade Green, 8" L 95.00
Wood duck, caramel slag...65.00
Wood duck, Ultra Blue satin...55.00
Wood duckling, caramel slag, sitting, 4½" 75.00
Wood duckling, floating, Sunshine Yellow satin 20.00
Wood duckling, standing, Sunshine Yellow satin 20.00
Wood duckling, standing, Ultra Blue..................................45.00

L.E. Smith

Camel, crystal 50.00
Cock, fighting; bl, 9" 55.00
Elephant, crystal, 1¾" 20.00
Goose, crystal, 2½"..25.00
Goose Girl, crystal, orig, 6" 25.00
Goose Girl, gr or flame, 6", ea 40.00
Horse, bookend, amber, rearing, ea.....................................38.00
Horse, bookend, blk, rearing, ea...65.00
Horse, bookend, ruby, rearing, ea 55.00
Horse, crystal, bookend, rearing, ea 35.00
King fish, aquarium, gr, 7¼x15"..275.00
Queen fish, aquarium, gr, 7x15"..225.00
Rooster, butterscotch slag, ltd ed, #208 ....85.00
Scottie, pipe rest, fired-on blk, 5½" L..................................20.00
Sparrow, crystal, head up, 3½"..15.00
Swan, milk glass w/decor, 8½"...45.00
Swan, soap dish, crystal 25.00
Thrush, bl frost 20.00

New Martinsville

Bear, baby, crystal, head trn or str, 3" 60.00
Bear, mama, crystal, 4x6"...225.00
Bear, papa, crystal frost..225.00
Bunny, crystal, head up, scarce, 1" 60.00
Chick, frosted, 1" 25.00
Chick, orange-red...65.00
Elephant, bookend, crystal, 5½", ea.....................................90.00
Gazelle, crystal w/frosted base, leaping, 8¼" 65.00
German shepherd, lamp base, pk..125.00
Hen, crystal, 5" 75.00
Horse, crystal, head up, 8"..95.00
Nautilus shell, bookend, crystal frost, 6", ea 35.00
Pelican, crystal 95.00
Pig, mama, crystal 325.00
Piglet, crystal, standing 125.00
Porpoise on wave, crystal, orig 750.00
Rabbit, mama, crystal..350.00
Rooster w/crooked tail, crystal, 7½" 85.00
Seal, baby w/ball, crystal..60.00
Seal, candlesticks, crystal, lg, pr...150.00

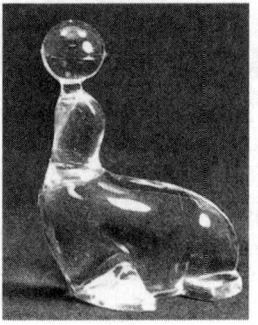

Seal with ball bookends, crystal, 7", pair (one shown), $150.00.

Ship, bookend, crystal, ea..45.00
Starfish, bookends, crystal, pr 200.00
Swan, candle holders, ruby, pr..70.00
Swan, sweetheart candy dish, red, 5" 35.00
Tiger, crystal frost, head down, 7¼"....................................200.00
Wolfhound, crystal, 7" 95.00
Woodsman, crystal, sq base, 7⅜"..135.00

Paden City

Bunny, cotton-ball dispenser, bl frost, ears bk.................150.00
Bunny, cotton-ball dispenser, crystal frost, ears bk.........110.00
Bunny, cotton-ball dispenser, milk glass, ears bk.............125.00
Bunny, cotton-ball dispenser, pk frost, ears up 200.00
Dragon swan, crystal, 9¾" L 225.00
Eagle, bookends, crystal, pr 300.00
Horse, crystal, rearing...150.00
Pelican, crystal 600.00
Pheasant, Chinese; bl..180.00
Pheasant, Chinese; crystal, 13¾" 100.00
Pheasant, Chinese; med bl, 13¾", from $175 to 180.00
Pheasant, crystal, head bk, 12" 110.00
Pheasant, lt bl, head bk, 12" 195.00
Polar bear on ice, crystal, 4½" 65.00
Pony, blk, 12"..350.00
Pony, crystal, 12" 100.00
Pouter pigeon, bookend, crystal, 6¼" 95.00
Rooster, Barnyard; bl, 8¾" 200.00

Rooster, Barnyard; crystal, 8¾" 85.00
Rooster, Chanticleer; bl, 9½" 200.00
Rooster, Chanticleer; crystal, 9½" 95.00
Rooster, Elegant; lt bl, 11" 225.00
Squirrel on curved log, crystal, 5½" 65.00

Tiffin

Pheasant paper-weights, female with head down, upright male, crystal, $300.00. (Photo courtesy Lee Garmon and Dick Spencer)

Cat, blk satin, raised bumps, #9445, 6¼" 140.00
Cat, Sassy Suzie, blk satin w/pnt decor, #9448, 11" 175.00
Cat, Sassy Suzie, milk glass 300.00
Fawn, flower floater, Citron Green 375.00
Fawn, flower floater, Copen Blue 500.00
Fish, crystal, solid, 8¾x9" 350.00
Frog, candle holders, blk satin, pr 225.00
Owl, lamp, cobalt, 1934-29 ....1,250.00
Pheasants, Copen Blue, paperweight bases, male & female pr 650.00

Viking

Angelfish, amber, 7x7" 90.00
Angelfish, blk, 6½" 150.00
Angelfish, milk glass, pr 175.00
Bird, candy dish, med gr, w/lid, 12" 50.00
Bird, med dk bl, 9½" 45.00
Bird, moss gr, tail up, 12" 35.00
Bird, orange, #1311, 10" 40.00
Bird, Orchid, 9½" 50.00
Bird, ruby, #1310, 12" 85.00
Cat, gr, sitting, 8" 55.00
Dog, orange 50.00
Dolphin, candle holders, pk, hexagonal ft, 9½", pr 150.00
Duck, crystal, fighting, head up or down, Viking's Epic Line, ea...50.00
Duck, crystal, standing, Viking's Epic Line, 9" 65.00
Duck, dk teal, Viking's Epic Line, 9" 50.00
Duck, orange, rnd, ftd, 5" 35.00
Duck, ruby, rnd, ftd, 5" 40.00
Duck, vaseline, 5" 40.00
Egret, amber, #1315, 12" 50.00
Egret, orange, 12" 50.00
Horse, aqua bl, 11½" 125.00
Hound dog, crystal, 8" 50.00
Jesus, crystal w/crystal mist, flat bk, 6x5" 65.00
Owl, amber, Viking's Epic Line 45.00
Owl, paperweight, amber 50.00
Penguin, crystal, 7" 45.00
Rabbit, amber, 6½" 45.00
Rabbit (Thumper), crystal, 6½" 45.00
Rooster, avocado, Viking's Epic Line 55.00
Seal, Persimmon, 9¾" L 25.00
Swan, bowl, amber, 6" 45.00
Swan, orange, fluted, 6½x4" 45.00
Swan, Yellow Mist, paper label, 6" 50.00

Westmoreland

Bird in flight, Amber Marigold, wings out, 5" W 35.00
Butterfly, Blue Mist, 2½" 25.00
Butterfly, crystal, 4½" 45.00
Butterfly, Green Mist, 2½" 25.00
Butterfly, pk, 2½" 25.00
Butterfly, Smoke, 3½" 25.00
Cardinal, Green Mist 20.00
Owl, dk bl, shiny eyes, 5½" 65.00
Penguin on ice floe, Brandywine Blue Mist 45.00
Pig, amberina 85.00
Pig, milk glass, fired pnt, orig label 37.50
Porky Pig, milk glass, hollow, 3" L 25.00
Pouter pigeon, any color, 2½", ea 25.00
Robin, crystal, 5⅛" 20.00
Robin, pk, 5⅛" 25.00
Robin, red, 5⅛" 27.50
Starfish, candle holders, milk glass, 5", pr 45.00
Turtle, ashtray, crystal 15.00
Turtle, cigarette box, crystal 45.00
Turtle, flower block, gr, 7 holes, 4" L 55.00
Turtle, paperweight, Green Mist, no holes, 4" L 25.00
Wren, Crystal Mist, 2½" 20.00
Wren, lt bl, 2½" 25.00
Wren, Pink Mist, 2½" 25.00
Wren, red, 2½" 25.00
Wren, smoke, 2½" 25.00
Wren on perch, lt bl on wht, 2-pc 45.00

Miscellaneous

American Glass Co, horse, crystal, jumping...............................65.00
Co-Operative Flint, elephant, crystal, 13" 375.00
Co-Operative Flint, elephant, pk, tusks rpr, 13" 400.00
Co-Operative Flint, elephant, pk, 4½x7" 85.00
Federal, Mopey dog, crystal, 3½" 10.00
Haley, horse, crystal, jumping, 9½" L 65.00
Haley, horse, milk glass, jumping 75.00
Haley, Lady Godiva, bookend, crystal, 1940s, ea 45.00
Haley, thrush, crystal 30.00
Haley, thrush, Robins' Egg Blue 85.00
Indiana, horse head, bookends, milk glass, 6", pr 65.00
Indiana, panther, amber, walking 300.00
Indiana, panther, bl, walking 400.00
Indiana, pouter pigeon, bookend, crystal frost, ea 40.00
LG Wright, trout, crystal 150.00
LG Wright, turtle, amber 125.00
New Martinsville by Mirror Images, baby bear, ruby.......................95.00
New Martinsville by Mirror Images, baby seal, ruby 95.00
New Martinsville by Mirror Images, mama bear, ruby 150.00
New Martinsville by Mirror Images, police dog, ruby 150.00
New Martinsville by Mirror Images, wolfhound, ruby carnival ...150.00
Pilgrim, whale, crystal, #924, w/labels, in 1964 World's Fair box ..45.00

Glass Knives

    Glass knives were manufactured from about 1920 to 1950, with distribution at its greatest in the late 1930s and early 1940s. Colors generally followed Depression glass dinnerware: crystal, light blue, light green, pink (originally called rose), and more rarely amber, forest green, and white (opal). Many glass knives were hand painted in fruit or flower designs. Knife blades were ground to a sharp edge. Today knives are usually found with blades nicked through years of use or bumping in silverware drawers or reground, which is acceptable to collectors as long as the original knife shape is maintained.

Many glass knives were engraved for gift-giving, personalized with the recipient's name and, on occasion, with a greeting. Originally presented in boxes, most glass knives were accompanied by a paper insert extolling the virtues of the knife and describing its care.

Boxes printed with World's Fair logos are fun to find, though not rare. Butter knives, which are smaller than other glass knives, typically were made in Czechoslovakia and sometimes match the handle patterns of glass salad sets. Knife lengths often vary slightly because the knives were snapped off the molded glass and the end ground during manufacture.

Several styles of knives (i.e. Vitex, Dur-X, Cryst-O-Lite) were manufactured by the thousands and are therefore found more often. Prices have become volatile due to the popularity of online, Internet auctions and the competition that results.

Values reflect knives with minor blade roughness or resharpening.

Aer-Flo, Forest Green, 7½" 350.00
Aer-Flo, gr, 7½" 70.00
BK Co, gr, 9¼" 60.00
Block, gr, 8¼" 55.00
Cryst-O-Lite, crystal, 8½", MIB......................................12.00
Dagger, crystal, 9¼" 175.00
Dur-X, 3 leaf, crystal, M in red box................................25.00
Dur-X, 3-leaf, gr, 8¼" 40.00
Dur-X, 3-leaf, pk, 9¼" 35.00
Plain hdl, gr, 9¼" 35.00
Steel-ite, pk...90.00
Stonex, amber, 8½" 250.00
Vitex, pk, 8½" 28.00
Vitex (Star & Diamond), crystal.....................................15.00
Westmoreland, thumbguard, crystal, pnt hdl, 9¼", from $40 to....45.00

Glass Shoes

Little shoes made of glass can be found in hundreds of styles, shapes, and colors. They've been made since the early 1800s by nearly every glasshouse, large and small, in America. To learn more about them, we recommend *Shoes of Glass II* (newly updated) by our advisor Libby Yalom, who is listed in the Directory under Maryland. Numbers in the listings refer to her book. Another reference is *Collectible Glass Shoes, Second Edition*, by Earlene Wheatley, published by Collector Books. See also Boyd; Degenhart.

Daisy and Button, amber match slipper, Diamond Quilt over sole, U.S. Glass, ca 1880, $175.00.
(Photo courtesy Libby Yalom)

#137, boot, w/cuff & spur, purple/bl/wht slag, 3¼x4" 90.00
#162, skate shoe, high bk, dmn block, lg (can hold cologne) 125.00
#181, boot, alligator or snakeskin pattern, amber 75.00
#207A, bootee, knitted effect/scalloped, apple gr, King, 3⅝" L....75.00
#233A, bootee, milk glass w/yel-pnt flowers, 4" L..........................55.00
#248B, man's, milk glass w/bl-pnt flowers & gold trim, 3⅞" L......65.00
#257A, boot, dk gr w/emb leaf & heart, silver-banded rim, 4¼".120.00
#264B, clear w/fancy gold-tone metal bow & rim, 5" L..............125.00
#289A, high-button, w/base, patterned w/textured toe, apple gr, 5½" ...100.00
#316, slipper, clear over cobalt w/gold-pnt trim..........................150.00

#339A, uptrn toe, crystal over cranberry, decor, 5⅜" L 150.00
#432, Dutch shoe, frosted w/gold-pnt decor 45.00
#458A, bottle boot, high-button, dk amber, 4½"..........................85.00
#555, bottle shoe, uptrn toe is bottle neck, clear w/emb decor......60.00
#574, high-button, w/base, purple slag, 6½"...............................175.00
#748, high-heel, stylized w/lg flower, teal, Czech, 6x6" 300.00
#757, pump, clear w/emb sleek gold-tone bow, 5½" L 40.00
#761, boot, low cut, bl w/wht coralene effect, gold trim, 7" L .1,000.00
#774, shoe, clear w/opaque bl rigaree at ankle-high opening, 3" T 175.00
#778, high-heel slipper, pointed toe/ruffle, striped, Venetian, 5" L......110.00
#797, boot, ribbed majorette-type, opaque bl w/gold trim, Gillinder ..130.00

Glidden

Genius designer Glidden Parker established Glidden Pottery in 1940 in Alfred, New York, having been schooled at the unrivaled New York State College of Ceramics at Alfred University. Glidden pottery is characterized by a fine stoneware body, innovative forms, outstanding hand-milled glazes, and hand decoration which make the pieces individual works of art. Production consisted of casual dinnerware, artware, and accessories that were distributed internationally.

In 1949 Glidden Pottery became the second ceramic plant in the country to utilize the revolutionary Ram pressing machine. This allowed for increased production and for the most part eliminated the previously used slip-casting method. However, Glidden stoneware continued to reflect the same superb quality of craftsmanship until the factory closed in 1957. Although the majority of form and decorative patterns were Mr. Parker's personal designs, Fong Chow and Sergio Dello Strologo also designed award-winning lines.

Glidden will be found marked on the unglazed underside with a signature that is hand incised, mold impressed, or ink stamped. Interest in this unique stoneware is growing as collectors discover that it embodies the very finest of mid-century high style. Our advisor is David Pierce; he is listed in the Directory under Ohio.

Ashtray, Green Mesa, #274-U...35.00
Ashtray, High Tide, #272-U..30.00
Ashtray, Loop Artware, #904-U..65.00
Bowl, Engobe, Leaf, #27 ....15.00
Bowl, free-form, Charcoal & Rice 100.00
Bowl, fruit; Feather, #271 ....12.00
Bowl, lug soup; Viridian, #467 ....18.00
Bowl, salad; Sage & Sand, #17...15.00
Bowl, salad; Viridian, oval, #417..30.00
Candlebench, Chi Chi Poodle..40.00
Candlebench, Mexican Cock...45.00
Casserole, Counterpane, #165..38.00
Casserole, Feather, #167...15.00
Casserole, Pear, #165, w/lid...50.00
Casserole, Turquoise Matrix, #163 ....30.00
Casserole, Viridian, #163...35.00
Charger, dk cobalt, Leaf, #68..150.00
Creamer, Alfred Stoneware, #802...55.00
Creamer, Boston Spice, #1430 ....30.00
Creamer, Sage & Sand, #1430 ....20.00
Cup & saucer, Pear, #141 & #142...28.00
Cup & saucer, Sage & Sand, #441A & #442 ....15.00
Cup & saucer, Turquoise Matrix, #141 & #143.......................18.00
Cup & saucer, Viridian, #441A & #442 ....20.00
Pitcher, Feather, #617, 3-qt...65.00
Pitcher, Turquoise Matrix, #615, 1-qt....................................58.00
Planter, Ivy, bird form, Charcoal & Rice...............................175.00
Plate, Handsome Fish, #410...50.00

Plate, luncheon. Sage & Sand, #433...........................8.00
Plate, salad; Plaid, #65..25.00

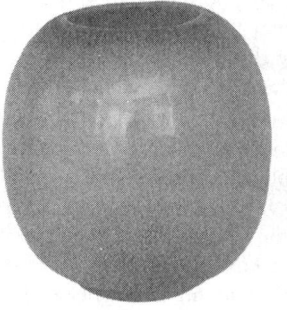

Vase, cobalt, ball form, #49, $60.00. (Photo courtesy David Pierce)

Vase, Turquoise Matrix, #49....................................35.00
Vase, Yellowstone, #86..40.00

Goebel

F.W. Goebel founded the F&W Goebel Company in 1871, located in Rodental, West Germany. They produced thousands of different decorative and useful items over the years, the most famous of which are the Hummel figurines first produced in 1935 based on the artwork of a Franciscan nun, Sister Maria Innocentia Hummel.

The Goebel trademarks have long been a source of confusion because all Goebel products, including Hummels, of any particular time period bear the same trademark, thus leading many to believe all Goebels are Hummels. Always look for the Hummel signature on actual Hummel figurines (these are listed in a separate section).

There are many, many other series — some of which are based on artwork of particular artists such as Disney, Charlot Byj, Janet Robson, Harry Holt, Norman Rockwell, M. Spotl, Lore, Huldah, and Schaubach. Miscellaneous useful items include ashtrays, bookends, salt and pepper shakers, banks, pitchers, inkwells, perfume bottles, etc. Figurines include birds, animals, Art Deco pieces, etc. The Friar Tuck monks and the Co-Boy elves are especially popular.

The date of manufacture of a particular piece is determined by the trademark. The incised date found underneath the base on many items is the mold copyright date. Actual date of manufacture may vary as much as twenty years or more from the copyright date.

Most Common Goebel Trademarks and Approximate Dates Used
1.) Crown mark (may be incised or stamped, or both): 1923 – 1950
2.) Full bee (complete bumble bee inside the letter 'V'): 1950 – 1957
3.) Stylized bee (dot with wings inside the letter 'V'): 1957 – 1964
4.) 3-Line (stylized bee with three lines of copyright info to the right of the trademark): 1964 – 1972
5.) Goebel bee (word Goebel with stylized bee mark over the last letter 'e'): 1972 – 1979
6.) Goebel (word Goebel only): 1979 – Present

Our advisors for this category are Gale and Wayne Bailey; they are listed in the Directory under Georgia.

Cardinal Tuck (Red Monk)

Creamer, TMK-4, 4¼x2½" dia.................................75.00
Egg cup, E 95/4, TMK-2, 2".................................135.00
Mug, TMK-2, 5¼", NM..155.00
Mustard pot, w/lid, 4¾"...125.00
Pipe stubber, TMK-2, 2"...175.00
Shakers, hands on tummy, 2½", pr.............................75.00
Shakers, holding books under arms, TMK-2, 3¼", pr......125.00
Stein, #7407443, metal flip lid, TMK-6.....................150.00

Charlot BYJ Redheads and Blonds

Baby Sitter, BYJ-66, 1970.....................................130.00
Bachelor Degree boy, BYJ-69, TMK-5, NM................45.00
Bibitzer, BYJ-23, 4¼"...70.00
Boy playing bongos, BYJ-65, 1970, NM......................95.00
Boy pulling girl's hair, BYJ-40, 1958.........................65.00
Boy w/arms full of apples, some fallen behind, BYJ-20, 4½"........75.00
E-E-E-EK, girl running from dog who has caught her pants, BYJ-9, 1957...65.00
Forbidden Fruit, BYJ-20, 4¼"...................................85.00
Fore, BYJ-83, TMK-5..90.00
Gangway, BYJ-28, 4½"...95.00
Girl being pursued by blond boy, BYJ-40, 4¾".............75.00
Kibitzer, BYJ-23, TMK-5, NM...................................55.00
Little Shopper, BYJ-3, 1967......................................65.00
Nurse, BYJ-63, 1970, 5¼"...90.00
Off Key, BYJ-22, 3¾"...85.00
Skating & Dating, boy & girl hold hands/skate, BYJ-52, 1967, 4¾"...115.00
Soap, BYJ-8, 5¼"...70.00
Stolen Kiss, BYJ-18, 1957, 5½"..................................85.00
Super Service, BYJ-39, 5".......................................120.00
Young Man's Fancy, BYJ-6, 4½".................................75.00

Co-Boy Figurines

Bert the Soccer Player, orig.....................................65.00
Bit the Bachelor, mk WELL503, TMK-6......................60.00
Brum the Lawyer, 7⅝"...75.00
Carl the Chef, 1979, 7¼"...60.00
Chris the Shoe Cobbler, TMK-6, 6½"..........................55.00
Conny the Night Watchman, 1972, 7⅜".......................85.00
Erik the Marksman, 4"..65.00
George holding baked bird, 1980, 6⅜".........................80.00
Greg the Gourmet, 1980, 6".......................................80.00
Greta Die Hausfrau, 6½"..80.00
Hermann the Butcher, #17-548-18, TMK-6, 7½".........175.00
Homer the Bad Driver, #17-555-16, 6½".......................85.00
Jack the Pharmacist, 1972, 7¼"...................................60.00
Jim the Bowler, 7½"..40.00
John the Hunter, 7¼"...65.00
Neils the Strummer, 1980, 7"......................................55.00
Pat the Baseball Player, #17-529-16, 6½"......................45.00
Paul the Dentist, #17-554-17, TMK-6...........................85.00
Petri the Fisherman, 1972, 7"......................................55.00
Plum the Baker, 7½"...55.00
Porz the Mushroom Grower, 1972, 7½".........................50.00
Ric the Fireman, TMK-7, #17-549-18, 7"......................150.00
Robby cutting lg carrot, 1970, 7¾"...............................65.00
Rosi & Rolf, TMK-6, 4¼"..110.00
Sepp the Beer Man, 8x4', MIB.....................................65.00
Ted the Tennis Player, #17-531-17...............................45.00
Tommy the Football Player, 6¾"...................................40.00
Utz the Banker, 1970, 8"...50.00

Friar Tuck (Brown Monk)

Bank, SD-29, w/key, 5"..75.00
Bottle, KL-92, head stopper, 10½"...............................85.00
Calendar, complete tiles, 1956...................................135.00
Cigarette holder, RX-110...72.50
Condiment set, toes, 1950s, shakers+mustard+tray........135.00
Cookie jar, TMK-6..315.00
Creamer, S-141/0, TMK-2, 4"......................................25.00
Creamer & sugar bowl, TMK-2, 5"................................95.00

Decanter, KL-95, TMK-2, 10x4" 85.00
Decanter/music box, KL-93, 10¾" 375.00
Display sign, #59002 10, 1959, 4x5" 90.00
Egg cup, E-95/A, TMK-2 ....50.00
Egg timer, dbl, E-96 ....85.00
Egg timer, timer sits in well beside monk, 3" 80.00
Flask, TMK-6, 3¾x1x3½" 100.00
Liquor tot, KL-94, 2" 35.00
Mug, T-74/0, TMK-3, 4" 40.00
Mug, 2¼" 25.00
Mustard pot, S-183, 3¾" 25.00
Shakers, hands on stomach, 2½". pr......................................25.00
Shakers, w/red & tan Bibles, TMK-3, pr 75.00
Sugar bowl, Z-37, w/lid, 4½" 25.00
Thermometer, figure stands beside, on base, 4¼" 150.00
Wine goblet, 5½" 65.00

Shakers

Clowns, #73 182 07/#73 183 07, 2¾", pr 25.00
Dutch boy & girl, TMK-6, 2¾", pr...25.00
German boy & girl, TMK-6, 2¾", 2½", pr.............................25.00
Onion & radish tops, TMK-3, 3", pr......................................35.00
Quail, B-125A & B, 1950s, pr..25.00
Rooster & hen, B-10110A & B, TMK6, 3", pr 30.00

Miscellaneous

Perfume lamp, Nightwatch-man, marked TMK-6 58-0550-22, 8¼", $150.00. (Photo courtesy Tom and Linda Millman)

Figurine, bird, crested, mc, sgn Selim/#38-938-25, 1984, 10½", NM....100.00
Figurine, Eleanor, #1442, 8¾" 75.00
Figurine, Elisabeth, gold trim, #1601, 8¾" 75.00
Figurine, Isabella, gold trim, #1503, 8⅝" 75.00
Figurine, Katharina, gold trim, #1772, 8½" 75.00
Figurine, owl, #38-137-16, 1975 ....54.00
Figurine, pelican, 3" 28.00
Figurine, redstart, TMK-5, 3½x3" 39.00
Figurine, sea lion, #3350708, TMK-6, 3¼x5" 28.00
Figurine, sparrow, mustard yel, CV-72 ....32.00
Figurine, titmouse, TMK-5, 6x4½" 48.00
Mug, clown, #74 315 14, TMK-6, 5½" 30.00
Mug, clown playing accordion, #74-011-12, TMK-6, 5", NM.......22.00
Mug, lady, #74 016 12, TMK-6, 5" 29.00
Plaque, horse pulling beer wagen, Munchen on base, TMK-6, 6x7" ..28.00

Goldscheider

The Goldscheider family operated a pottery in Vienna for many

generations before seeking refuge in the United States following Hitler's invasion of their country. They settled in Trenton, New Jersey, in the early 1940s where they established a new corporation and began producing objects of art and tableware items. (No mention was made of the company in the Trenton City Directory after 1950, and it is assumed that by this time the influx of foreign imports had taken its toll.) In 1946 Marcel Goldscheider established a pottery in Staffordshire where he manufactured bone china figures, earthenware, etc., marked with a stamp of his signature. Larger artist-signed examples are the most valuable with the Austrian pieces bringing the higher prices.

A wide variety of marks has been found: 1.) Goldscheider USA Fine China; 2.) Original Goldscheider Fine China; 3.) Goldscheider USA; 4.) Goldscheider-Everlast Corp.; 5.) Goldscheider Everlast Corp. in circle; 6.) Goldscheider Inc. in circle; 7.) Goldcrest Ceramics Corp. in circle; 8.) Goldcrest Fine China; 9.) Goldcrest Fine China USA; 10.) A Goldcrest Creation; and 11.) Created by Goldscheider USA.

Our co-advisors are Randy and Debbie Coe (listed in the Directory under Oregon) and Darrell Thomas (listed under Wisconsin).

Bust, lady w/brn hair, gr hat/jacket, lace collar/cuffs, 15", $575 to.........**650.00**
Bust, lady w/curls, hands beneath face, #7653, 1920s-30s, 15", $850 to..**1,100.00**
Bust, nude w/hands over breasts, #7542/11/20, 14⅞", from $875 to..**1,100.00**
Figurine, boy & girl skaters, #31, 1920-54, 8" **500.00**
Figurine, boy w/top hat & girl w/flowers, #836, 1930s, 8¾", $200 to..**250.00**
Figurine, bulldog, blk & wht w/red collar, #4997/108/8, 6x8", $175 to ...**265.00**
Figurine, dachshund, #4080, 3½x5" **135.00**
Figurine, Deco lady holds skirt up & bk, Dakon, 1930, 10", $475 to ...**550.00**
Figurine, Delores del Rio, Spanish garb, Lorenzl, '30s, 18", $2,000 to....**2,300.00**
Figurine, draped nude w/peacock, #4488/12/35, 1920-25, 16" .**2,000.00**
Figurine, equestrienne on leaping horse, 1920s, 15x16x7", $550 to........**700.00**
Figurine, Europa (nude) beside bull, #3785/36/1, 14x18x6½", $650 to ..**800.00**
Figurine, lady/sewing machine, plays Anniversary Waltz, 1951, $400 to....**450.00**
Tobacco jar, skull form, 7½x6½", from $450 to **550.00**
Vase, lg figure of Victorian maid stands on low width, coppery, 28"....**2,000.00**

Gonder

Lawton Gonder grew up with clay in his hands and fire in his eyes. Gonder's interest in ceramics was greatly influenced by his parents who worked for Weller and a close family friend and noted ceramic authority, John Herold. In his early teens Gonder launched his ceramic career at the Ohio Pottery Company while working for Herold. He later gained valuable experience at American Encaustic Tile Company, Cherry Art Tile, and the Florence Pottery. Gonder was plant manager at the Florence Pottery until fire destroyed the facility in late 1941.

After years of solid production and management experience, Lawton Gonder established the Gonder Ceramic Art Company, formerly the Peters and Reed plant, in South Zanesville, Ohio. Gonder Ceramic Arts produced quality art pottery with beautiful contemporary designs which included human and animal figures and a complete line of Oriental pottery. Accentuating the beautiful shapes were unique and innovative glazes developed by Gonder such as flambe (flame red with streaks of yellow), 24k gold crackle, antique gold, and Chinese crackle. (These glazes bring premium prices.)

All Gonder is marked with the company name and mold number. They include 'Gonder U.S.A' in block letters, 'Gonder' in script, 'Gonder Original' in script, and 'Gonder Ceramic Art' in block letters. Paper labels were also used. Some of the early Gonder molds closely resemble RumRill designs that had been manufactured at the Florence Pottery; and because some RumRill pieces are found with similar (if not identical) shapes, matching mold numbers, and Gonder glazes, it is speculated that some RumRill was produced at the Gonder plant. In 1946 Gonder started another company which he named Elgee (chosen for his initials LG) where he manufactured lamp bases until a fire in 1954 resulted in his shifting lamp production to the main plant. Operations ceased in 1957.

Bowl, bl wash over pk, irregular rim, 10½x8" 32.00
Bowl, console; red flambe, 16" 65.00
Candle holders, fish, pk to bl, #561, pr.....................................82.50
Ewer, gray w/burgundy streaks, H-606, 9" 45.00
Figurine, goose, 5½" 40.00
Figurine, Hawaiian girl w/yoke & 2 pots, gr, 13¼" 85.00
Figurine, panther, streaky tan, #217, 5x15" 80.00
Figurine, rooster, aqua crackle, #525, 11" 115.00
Flower arranger, dk gr, 3-tiered 120.00
Planter, dolphin ea side, turq, #556, 5x11½x4½" 42.00
Vase, bl & brn streaks, pk int, cornucopia form, J-6, 8½x8½" 40.00
Vase, fawn's head, pk mottle, #518, 9½x6" 85.00
Vase, flowing vegetation, yel & gr w/touches of brn, 14½x5x5" ...82.50
Vase, gold crackle, #E-3, 7" 48.00
Vase, gray w/wht sponging, urn shape, #718, 8" 30.00
Vase, leaves & twigs, chartreuse, #599, 16" 130.00
Vase, nautilus shell form, starfish at base, pk-gray, 13"................65.00
Vase, sea gull on front, wht on brn tones, #514, 11¾" 75.00
Vase, streaky brn & tan, sq sides, ftd, #598, 14¾x4½x6" 57.50
Vase, swallows, wht matt, 12" 110.00
Vase, Swirl, gr, bottle neck, waisted, H-607, 9½", pr...................135.00
Vase, 4 tubes tied together in center, turq, H-605, 8¾x6½" 32.00

Goofus Glass

Goofus glass is American-made pressed glass with designs that are either embossed (blown out) or intaglio (cut in). The decorated colors were aerographed or hand applied and not fired on the pieces. The various patterns exemplify the artistry of the turn-of-the-century glass crafters. The primary production dates were ca 1908 to 1918. Goofus was produced by many well-known manufacturers such as Northwood, Indiana, and Dugan.

When no condition is given, our values are for examples in mint original paint. Our advisor for this category is Steve Gillespie of the *Goofus Glass Gazette*; he is listed in the Directory under Missouri. See also Clubs, Newsletters, and Catalogs.

Basket, Diamond & Daisy, hdld, 6½", EX 55.00
Bowl, Butterfly, red & gold, ruffled, 2½x10½", EX+ 75.00
Bowl, Cherry, red & gold, Dugan, 2¼x10⅛"...............................85.00
Bowl, Cherry, ruffled rim, 3¼x10", NM.....................................95.00
Bowl, Jeweled Heart, 2x9", NM...70.00
Bowl, Poppy, red & gold, ftd, 4x9", EX 60.00
Compote, Butterfly, 6⅞x10¼", EX 80.00
Lamp, oil; Grape & Leaf, minor flaking, 13¼" 275.00
Lamp, oil; Wild Rose, Riverside, finger loop, 15" overall 250.00
Plate, Chrysanthemum, frosted ground, 6¼", EX........................60.00
Plate, Little Bo Peep, minor gold flaking, 6½"..........................135.00
Plate, rose in base amid 8 long-stem roses, red/gold, 10¾", EX 55.00
Plate, Temple of Music, Pan Am Expo Buffalo NY, 7¼", EX......120.00
Shakers, Vintage, dk gr & gold on milk glass, G orig lids, 3¼", pr..55.00
Vase, Corn, Dugan, 1905, 7¾", NM..110.00
Vase, Crested Love Birds, Indiana Glass, 10½x5", EX..................60.00
Vase, Dogwood, baluster, 15", EX+ 90.00
Vase, Flower Bouquet, wine & gr, 15½", NM 110.00
Vase, flowers (2) & leaves, red/gr/gold, 9½", EX.........................110.00
Vase, Iris, purple on gr, 12½x5", NM..85.00
Vase, Parrot, 12½", EX...75.00
Vase, Peaches, gold/red/gr, 9", EX 50.00

Vase, Peacock in a Tree, green with gold, 15", NM, $150.00.

Vase, Peacock in Tree, red/gr/gold, 15", EX.................................195.00
Vase, Statue of Liberty, gold/gr, cylindrical, 12½x5" 85.00
Vase, Water Lily, 12", EX 65.00

Goss and Crested China

William Henry Goss received his early education at the Government School of Design at Somerset House, London, and as a result of his merit was introduced to Alderman William Copeland, who owned the Copeland Spode Pottery. Under the influence of Copeland from 1852 to 1858, Goss quickly learned the trade and soon became their chief designer. Little is known about this brief association, and in 1858 Goss left to begin his own business. After a short-lived partnership with a Mr. Peake, Goss opened a pottery on John Street, Stoke-on-Trent, but by 1870 he had moved to his business to a location near London Road. This pottery became the famous Falcon Works. Their mark was a spread-wing falcon (goss-hawk) centering a narrow, horizontal bar with 'W.H. Goss' printed below.

Many of the early pieces made by Goss were left unmarked and are difficult to discern from products made by the Copeland factory, but after he had been in business for about fifteen years, all of his wares were marked. Today unmarked items do not command the prices of the later marked wares.

Adolphus William Henry Goss (Goss's eldest son) joined his father's firm in the 1880s. He introduced cheaper lines, though the more expensive lines continued in production. Shortly after his father's death in 1906, Adolphus retired and left the business to his two younger brothers. The business suffered from problems created by a war economy, and in 1936 Goss assets were held by Cauldon Potteries Ltd. These were eventually taken over by the Coalport Group, who retained the right to use the Goss trademark. Messrs. Ridgeway Potteries bought all the assets in 1954 as well as the right to use the Goss trademark and name. In 1964 the group was known as Allied English Potteries Ltd. (A.E.P.), and in 1971 A.E.P. merged with the Doulton Group. Now it remains to be seen if Goss ware will ever be produced again. Values are all for items in mint condition.

Ancient Carafe, Lillanberis...52.50
Ancient Lamp, Lake Clay Pits, Hamworthy Poole, 1½x4x2½" 50.00
Ancient Pipkin, Southampton..45.00
Bust of Shakespeare, 4" 110.00
Colchester Vase, England..55.00
Elizabethan Measure, Eppleby crest, 1⅜x2¼" 65.00
Exeter Vase, City of London 55.00
Irish Mather, Lytham..27.50
Lincoln Vase, Battle Abbey...55.00
Match Holder/Striker, Arms of Berwick Upon Tweed, 3"............55.00
Ostend Vase, Henley on Thames..55.00
Pilgrim Leather Bottle, Chalfront St Giles..................................27.50
Pompeian Ewer, Suffolk & Bury St Edmonds 60.00
Queen Phillipa's Crest, Derry..90.00

Roman Urn, Hereward the Wake 36.00
Roman Urn, Killarney 55.00
Roman Vessel, WWI Allies Flags, 3" 165.00
Urn, Pensans Domini 1614, Tresvannack, St Paul, Cornwall........70.00
Vase, Model of Ancient Jar...Southwold..., 3¼" 85.00
Vase, RHYL, 3⅛" 25.00

Crested China

Arcadia, Clifton Suspension Bridge, 6½" W 150.00
Arcadia, urn, Tublin 55.00
Carlton, Coleen, Dublin 150.00
Carlton, Irish Spinning Wheel, Belfast 150.00
Carlton, mug, Dolgelly, 1½" 29.00
Carlton, swan, Salcombe...27.50
Carlton, vase, Arms of Lymington, 2½" 29.00
Coronet, shell, City of London 32.00
Grafton, hen, Swindon...55.00
Shelly, Ancient Lights, Deal...100.00
Shelly, dog in kennel, Dover...190.00
Tuscan China, wall pocket, Nose of Brasenose, 3¾x3" 110.00

Gouda

Gouda is an old Dutch market town in the province of South Holland. Famous for its cheese, Gouda's ceramics industry had its beginnings in the early sixteenth century and was fueled by the growth in the popularity of smoking tobacco. Initially learning their craft from immigrant potters from England who had settled in the area, the clay pipe makers of Gouda were soon regarded as the best. While some authorities give 1898 (the date the Zuid-Holland factory began operations) as the initial date for the manufacturing of decorative pottery in Gouda, C.W. Moody, author of *Gouda Ceramics*, indicates the date was ca 1885. Gouda was not the only town in the Netherlands making pottery; Arnhem, Schoonhoven, and Amsterdam also had earthenware factories, but technically the term 'Gouda pottery' refers only to pieces made within the town of Gouda. Today, no Gouda-style factories are active within the city's limits, but in the first quarter of the twentieth century there were several firms producing decorative pottery there — the best known being Zuid, Regina, Zenith, Ivora, and Goedewaagen. At present Royal Goedewagen is making three patterns of limited editions. They are well marked as such.

This information was provided to us by Adela Meadows; she is listed in the Directory under California.

For further information we recommend *The World of Gouda Pottery* by Phyllis T. Ritvo (Front & Center Press, Weston, Massachussets).

Clock garniture, Zuid, Holland, clock with painted ceramic face, four arm supports, baluster body, and floral decor, early 1900s, 20½", with two similar-form 16¾" candle holders, $2,875.00. (Photo courtesy Skinner, Inc.)

Bowl, Bejo, bird & elements, PZH, 1920, 3½x6½", NM 360.00
Bowl, Darla, w/lid, Regina, ca 1928, 6x4" 250.00

Cake plate, Priza, Deco-style floral, ftd, Holland, 1915, 2x8" 190.00
Candlestick, Paris w/brn & blk bands, PZH, 1928, 8½x5½".......330.00
Candlestick, Simona, Holland, #1242, ca 1920, 6¾" 195.00
Candy dish, Orchis, 3-lobe, Regina, 2½x6" 165.00
Chalice, Romeo, much blk, orange & bl scrolling bands, PZH, 1930, 7"...440.00
Covered dish, grapes & flowers, Holland, 4x6½" 150.00
Humidor, Collier, abstract shapes, PZH, 1925, 6x4½" 330.00
Jardiniere, Carlos, floral on wht w/blk waves, PZH, 1935, 5x13x5"...140.00
Jardiniere, wide floral band w/in bl & wht borders, Zumer, 1920s, 5x6"...185.00
Lamp, boats & Nouveau flowers, PZH, flaw, 17½x5½"..............825.00
Pitcher, floral on wht gloss, bulbous, Holland, 1930s, 5x4" 230.00
Pitcher, Peggy Royal, slim neck, 6¼x3¼" 75.00
Plate, abstract swirl pattern, mc w/cobalt, PZH, 1935, 2x13¾" ..360.00
Plate, Unique Metalique, scalloped edge, ca 1950, 8¼" 350.00
Tazza, floral w/abstract elements, gr bands, ca 1927, 5½x9" 220.00
Tazza, Sonny, abstract pattern on cream, PZH, 1927, 5½x9" 220.00
Tray, Marko, Deco swirls w/blk, Plateelbakkerij Zenith, 1935, 15½"...550.00
Tray, Nouveau floral w/blk border, PZH, 1921, 16½x12", NM ...330.00
Vase, Deco floral on blk, blk tub hdls, Metz Royal, ca 1932, 6¼"...185.00
Vase, Juliana Ivora, European, #207, ca 1920, 10¼" 1,200.00
Vase, Nouveau geometric on blk, 4 blk hdls, PZH, 1924, 7½x7", NM..415.00
Vase, Paris, Deco geometrics, flared cylinder, Holland #4201, 8½"..245.00
Vase, repeating florals w/blk & turq, PZH, 1910, 13"..............1,100.00
Vase, swirling abstract, Breetvelt finish, PZH, 1926, 6x3"..........275.00
Vase, Trix, floral w/yel/bl rectangles/blk borders, PZH, 1927, 12" ...415.00

Graniteware

Graniteware, made of a variety of metals with enamel coatings, derives its name from its appearance. The speckled, swirled, or mottled effect of the vari-colored enamels may look like granite — but there the resemblance stops. It wasn't especially durable! Expect at least minor chipping if you plan to collect.

Graniteware was featured in 1876 at Phily's Expo. It was mass produced in quantity, and enough of it has survived to make at least the common items easily affordable. Condition, color, shape, and size are important considerations in evaluating an item; cobalt blue and white, green and white, brown and white, and old red and white swirled items are unusual, thus more expensive. Pieces of heavier weight, seam constructed, riveted, and those with wooden handles and tin or matching graniteware lids are usually older. Pieces with matching granite lids demand higher prices than ones with tin lids.

For further study we recommend *The Collector's Encyclopedia of Graniteware, Book II*, by our advisor, Helen Greguire. It is available from the author and Collector Books. For information on how to order, see her listing in the Directory under South Carolina. For the address of the National Graniteware Society, see the section on Clubs, Newsletters, and Catalogs.

Note: Unless noted otherwise, our values are for pieces in mint or near-mint condition; appropriate deductions must be made if damage is present.

Batter jug, dk bl & wht med mottled relish w/cobalt trim, 10¼"...825.00
Bell, mc roses w/lav & blk bands on wht, brass hdl/clapper, 5¼", VG.........295.00
Biscuit sheet, bl & wht swirl w/blk, 12 cups, Columbian Ware, 11x8"...5,500.00
Biscuit sheet, brn & wht med mottle, Onyx Enamel Ware, 24 cups, VG ...1,100.00
Bowl, fruit; ped ft, cobalt & wht lg mottle, wht int, 7½x8" dia....1,350.00
Bowl, vegetable/pudding; brn & wht lg swirl, wht int, 9½" L......295.00
Bucket, Snow on the Mtn, gr trim, seamless, Elite, w/lid, 5x3⅛" ..525.00
Bucket, water; violet shading to lt lav, Thistle Ware, sm 225.00
Butter dish, wht w/cobalt trim, seamless, L&G Mfg Co, 8⅞" dia ..325.00
Can, cream; bl & wht lg mottle w/blk trim, wht int, w/lid, 7½"...625.00
Can, cream; dk gr & wht lg swirl w/blk trim, seamless, 7¾", VG ..975.00

Can, milk; bl & wht med mottle, lt gray int w/bl flecks, 9½", VG **375.00**
Can, milk; sea gr shading to moss gr, Shamrock Ware, 9¼x5", VG ..**395.00**
Candlestick, red w/blk trim, shell shape, finger ring, 1½x5¾" **195.00**
Canister, cobalt & wht lg mottle, cobalt trim, seamless, 6⅝", VG ...**325.00**
Canister, wht w/dk bl trim & lettering, 7½x5" **110.00**
Carrier, butter; gray med mottle, strap hdl, wooden knob, med sz **275.00**
Chick feeder, cobalt w/wht int, Hoeft...1914, 2¼x8¾", VG **235.00**
Coffee biggin, bl & wht checkered w/cobalt trim, 4-pc, 10½" **425.00**

Coffee biggin, blue and white swirl, M, $495.00. (Photo courtesy Helen Greguire)

Coffee biggin bl & wht fine mottle, squatty, 4-pc **395.00**
Coffee biggin red & off-wht lg mottle w/red trim, 3-pc, 9⅝" **695.00**
Coffee boiler, bl & wht med swirl w/blk trim, seamed, 11¾" **325.00**
Coffee carrier, bl & wht checkered w/cobalt trim, Depose, 8¼" .**395.00**
Coffeepot, aqua w/blk trim & hdl, wht int, Pyrex insert, 1930, 9" ...**95.00**
Coffeepot, bl & wht wavy mottle w/blk trim, wht int, 9¼" **425.00**
Coffeepot, cream w/blk trim & hdl, ...King Volrath Ware, 6¾" ..**130.00**
Coffeepot, dk gray med mottle **225.00**
Coffeepot, dk sea gr shading to moss gr, wht int, seamless, 9" **395.00**
Coffeepot, lav & wht lg mottle, metal mts/bands, 8½", VG **395.00**
Coffeepot, lt bl & wht lg swirl, wht inside, seamless, 10½" **495.00**
Coffeepot, old red & wht med swirl w/cobalt, wht inside, 9½", VG.**1,995.00**
Coffeepot, red & wht med swirl w/cobalt trim, seamless, 9½", VG ...**1,995.00**
Colander, dk gr & wht lg mottle w/cobalt, ftd, deep **425.00**
Colander, gr veins w/wht lumpy effect/gr trim, fancy piercing, 11¾" **165.00**
Corn pot, yel w/brn trim/hdls/lid, Ceramic on Steel...1988, 1½" dia **25.00**
Creamer, solid bl w/wht bands, blk trim **95.00**
Cup & saucer, roses & violets on wht w/blk trim & name, ca 1900, VG ...**95.00**
Cuspidor, mc lg swirl w/orange trim & bottom, wht int, 8¼" dia, VG ..**1,250.00**
Double boiler, bl & wht lg swirl w/blk trim, seamed, 7¼" **475.00**
Fry pan, bl & wht lg swirl, blk trim/hdl, sm, EX **225.00**
Fry pan, gray-bl & wht lg mottle w/blk hdl/trim, 9⅞" dia, VG ...**140.00**
Fry pan, gray-lav & wht lg swirl, wht int, iron base, 10½" dia, VG ...**350.00**
Funnel, cobalt & wht lg swirl w/blk trim & hdl, wht int, sm **275.00**
Funnel, gr & wht lg swirl w/cobalt trim, wht int, 4x5¾" **675.00**
Gravy boat, bl & wht lg swirl w/cobalt trim, triple-coated, ½-pt ..**2,950.00**
Griddle, gray med mottle, riveted ears, wire bail, 16¼" dia, VG.**225.00**
Kettle, cream w/gr trim, 16 ribs, w/lid, 6x7⅜" **55.00**
Kettle, Maslin style, bl & wht lg swirl w/blk trim, Azure Ware...**265.00**
Ladle, soup; lt bl & wht lg mottle w/blk hdl/trim, wht int, 3⅞" dia **65.00**
Measure, aqua & wht lg swirl w/cobalt trim, riveted spout/hdl, 4⅞" ...**450.00**
Measure, bl & wht lg swirl w/blk trim, riveted spout, lg **310.00**
Measure, deep sea gr to moss gr, seamless, Shamrock Ware, 7⅝", VG ...**395.00**
Measure, lav-bl & wht lg swirl w/blk trim, seamed, 9⅞", VG **435.00**
Measure, oyster; gray lg mottle, seamed, emb: 1 qt liq'd, 4⅛", VG ..**395.00**
Mold, rnd tube, bl & wht fine mottle **225.00**
Muffin pan, lav-cobalt & wht med swirl w/blk trim, 14¼x7¼" ..**650.00**
Muffin pan, lt bl & wht fine mottle w/cobalt trim, wht int, 13⅜" L...**595.00**
Mug, brn & wht lg swirl w/cobalt trim, seamless, 4" dia, VG **155.00**
Mug, mush; dk & gr wht mottle w/cobalt trim, Chrysolite, 6" dia, G **150.00**
Mug, mush; camp; bl & wht lg swirl w/blk trim, wht int **235.00**
Pail, water; wht w/bl scallop design, wht int, Bonny Blue, 9½", VG ..**160.00**

Pan, lady fingers; cobalt & wht lg swirl, wht int **2,975.00**
Pan, pudding; blk & wht lg swirl w/blk trim, seamed, 6¾" dia ...**310.00**
Pan, pudding; red & wht lg swirl, cobalt trim/wht int, 8½" dia, VG ...**625.00**
Pie plate, red & wht lg mottle w/cobalt trim, wht int, 9¾" **595.00**
Pitcher, water; bl & wht lg swirl w/blk trim, seamless, 9x4", VG ...**625.00**
Pitcher, water; brn & wht relish w/cobalt trim **275.00**
Pitcher, water; brn/wht/cobalt lg swirl, gray int w/cobalt, 10½" ...**595.00**
Pitcher, water; dk burgundy w/mc veining, Elite Austria, 8⅜" ...**1,250.00**
Pitcher, water; gr & wht lg swirl w/cobalt trim, seamless, 7½", VG ...**895.00**
Platter, bl & wht lg swirl w/blk trim, wht int, oval, 13⅞", VG ...**430.00**
Platter, bl & wht med mottle, wht int, bl trim, oval, 20½", VG.**255.00**
Potty, gray lg mottle, EL-AN-GE, Absolute Safety..., 3¾x6½" ...**145.00**
Ring mold, yel w/wht int, 2¼x8⅛", VG **65.00**
Roaster, bl to lt bl to bl, blk trim, seamless, 12¼" dia, VG **185.00**
Roaster, blk & wht fine mottle, Lisk, 4-pc, 16½" L, VG **85.00**
Scoop, grocer's; cobalt & wht lg swirl/wht int, riveted hdl, 8¾", G ...**650.00**
Scoop, solid cobalt w/wht int, lg **145.00**
Scoop, wht, seamless, 9¼' L, VG **135.00**
Spittoon, wht w/cobalt trim, Sweden, salesman's sample, 2-pc, 2⅜x8" ...**265.00**
Spoon rest, horse-head form, brn w/blk mane, 7" W, VG...........**225.00**
Sugar bowl, mc flowers on wht w/bl trim/hdls, w/lid, 1980, 5¼"...**60.00**
Syrup, cobalt & wht lg swirl, Azurelite, 7½x3⅝" **1,050.00**
Teakettle, dk gr & wht med swirl, wht int, 7¼", VG **1,050.00**
Teakettle, pk & wht lg marbleized w/blk trim, Bakelite knob, 6¾"..**525.00**
Teakettle, red & wht lg swirl w/blk, Bakelite knob, 1950s, 5" **295.00**
Teakettle, red w/blk trim, wht int, gooseneck, 7½x8¾" **110.00**
Teakettle, redipped dk gr & wht speckled over brn & wht swirl, 7½"...**325.00**
Teapot, bl & wht lg swirl, wht int, cobalt trim, Blue Dmn Ware, 9", VG...**425.00**
Teapot, bl/cobalt/wht lg mottle, wht int w/cobalt trim, 9", VG ..**495.00**
Teapot, dk bl shading to lt bl, blk trim/hdl, 8¼", VG **325.00**
Teapot, dk violet to lt, wht int, seamed, 10x5⅝" **325.00**
Teapot, fine bl & wht mottle, wood hdl, brass-plated lid/bottom, G...**195.00**
Teapot, gray med mottle, metal mts/lid/hdl, 10x5⅜" **295.00**
Teapot, lt gray lg mottle, seamed spout, seamless body, 4"..........**295.00**
Teapot, pk & wht lg swirl w/pk trim, wht int, 8¼", VG.............**475.00**
Teapot, pk/wht/gr/bl/dk bl lg mottle, pk int, blk hdl/trim, 8½", VG ...**525.00**
Teapot, red & wht lg swirl w/cobalt trim, seamed, 1960s, 8"........**165.00**
Teapot, wht & lt bl lg swirl, blk hdl/trim, seamless, 9", VG **275.00**
Tray, gray lg mottle, mk L&G Mfg Co, 13⅜x9½" **175.00**
Tub, foot; dk gray med mottle, seamed, hdls, oval, 18¾" L, VG.**195.00**
Tumbler, red-brn & wht lg swirl w/cobalt trim, wht int, 4¾x3½" **350.00**
Wash basin, bl & wht lg mottle w/bl, wht inside, eyelet, 12⅜", VG...**135.00**
Wash basin, bl & wht lg spatter w/blk trim, wht int, 10¼", VG.**145.00**
Water carrier, gray lg mottle, seamless, pouring lip, 8x8½" **550.00**
Wine cooler, yel & wht lg swirl w/blk trim, ca 1960, 7" dia........**325.00**

Green Opaque

Introduced in 1887 by the New England Glass Works, this ware is very scarce due to the fact that it was produced for less than one year. It is characterized by its soft green color and a wavy band of gold reserving a mottled blue metallic stain. It is usually found in satin; examples with a shiny finish are extremely rare. Values depend to a large extent on the amount of the gold and stain remaining.

Bowl, EX gold & mottling, w/lid, 4x6" **1,250.00**
Bowl, EX mottling & gold, 3½x8" **995.00**
Bowl, M stain & gold, 4x8" **1,150.00**
Bowl, VG mottling & gold, w/lid, 4x6⅜" **900.00**
Celery vase, worn satin & gold, 6½" **450.00**
Cruet, M stain & gold, orig stopper **1,950.00**
Cruet, VG stain..**1,500.00**
Mug, EX stain & gold, 2¼' **500.00**

Mug, M stain & gold, 2½" 700.00
Punch cup, M stain & gold 750.00
Punch cup, worn stain & gold, 2½" 225.00
Shaker, M stain & gold, 2½" 400.00
Toothpick holder, EX gold 900.00
Toothpick holder, M gold 1,150.00
Tumbler, lemonade; w/hdl, M stain & gold, 5" 950.00

Tumbler, stain and gold, 3½", $800.00.

Vase, flared, M stain & gold, 6" 900.00

Greenaway, Kate

Kate Greenaway was an English artist who lived from 1846 to 1901. She gained worldwide fame as an illustrator of children's books, drawing children clothed in the styles worn by proper English and American boys and girls of the very early 1800s. Her book, *Under the Willow Tree,* published in 1878, was the first of many. Her sketches appeared in leading magazines, and her greeting cards were in great demand. Manufacturers of china, pottery, and metal products copied her characters to decorate children's dishes, tiles, and salt and pepper shakers as well as many other items.

What some collectors/dealers call Kate Greenaway items are not actual Kate Greenaway designs but merely look-alikes. Genuine Kate Greenaway items (metal, paper, cloth, etc.) must bear close resemblance to her drawings in books, magazines, and special collections. See also Napkin Rings.

Biscuit jar, ceramic, boy w/tinted features, w/lid 165.00
Book, A Apple Pie, Warne, 1940, w/dust jacket, VG 28.00
Book, Almanack for 1884, printed by Edmund Evans, EX 135.00
Book, Birthday Book for Children, 1880, VG 160.00
Book, Day in a Child's Life, Routledge, 1st ed, VG 150.00
Book, Greenaway's Babies, Saalfield Muslin Book, 1907, G+ 40.00
Book, Kate Greenaway Pictures, London, Warne, 1st ed, 1921, VG ..300.00
Book, Kate Greenaway's Alphabet, London, 1880, EX 190.00
Book, Kate Greenaway's Book of Games, Routledge, 1st ed, 1889, NM..475.00
Book, Language of Flowers, Routledge, 1st ed, picture brd, VG..100.00
Book, Little Ann & Other Poems, by Taylor, VG 50.00
Book, Marigold Garden, London, 1888, VG 60.00
Book, Mother Goose, London, later print of 1st ed, VG 150.00
Book, Pied Piper of Hamlin, NM 85.00
Book, Sunshine for Little Children, 1884, EX 80.00
Book, Under the Willow, Routledge, 1st ed, orig cloth 165.00
Bowl, Daisy & Button, amber; Reed & Barton SP fr w/girl & dog...525.00
Butter pat, children playing transfer, pre-1910 ....40.00
Calendar, chromolithograph, 1884, Routledge, 7⅜x9½", EX........60.00
Combination set, shakers/napkin ring/stand, Middleton Plate, $350 to..500.00
Cup & saucer, children transfer, pk lustre trim, pre-1910...........125.00
Engraving, Harper's Bazaar, Jan 1879, full-pg 25.00
Figurine, seated girl tugs on lg hat, bsk, pre-1910, sm........75.00
Handkerchief, ca 1890-1900, 17x16", VG.....................55.00
Hatpin holder, SP, figural girl, Meriden, 4" 125.00

Inkwell, boy & girl, bronze.................................215.00
Match holder, ornate SP, girl in fancy clothes, Tufts 195.00
Paperweight, CI, girl in lg bonnet, pre-1910, 3x2¾" 110.00
Pencil holder, pnt porc, pre-1910 ....100.00
Pickle castor, bl; SP fr w/2 girls, blown-out florals 455.00
Plate, ABC, girl in lg hat, Staffordshire, 7" 105.00
Plate, children at play, fruits, birds & flowers, 9" 100.00
Salt cellar, Little People, bsk, arms over basket, 3¾".........10.00
Scarf, children on silk, early, EX 65.00
Tea set, semi porc, floral motif, pre-1910, 3-pc, child sz 95.00
Toothpick holder, bsk, girl sits on stump, basket on bk........40.00
Toothpick holder, clear glass, 2 girls by basket 100.00
Toothpick holder, SP, girl holds amberina cup, ornate base, 5" ...785.00
Wall pocket, ceramic, 6 girls on open book form, 6x9x3" 137.00

Greentown Glass

Greentown glass is a term referring to the product of the Indiana Tumbler and Goblet Company of Greentown, Indiana, ca 1894 to 1903. Their earlier pressed glass patterns were #75 (originally known as #11), a pseudo-cut glass design; #137, Pleat Band; and #200, Austrian. Another line, Dewey, was designed in 1898. Many lovely colors were produced in addition to crystal. Jacob Rosenthal, who was later affiliated with Fenton, developed his famous chocolate glass in 1900. The rich, shaded opaque brown glass was an overnight success. Two new patterns, Leaf Bracket and Cactus, were designed to display the glass to its best advantage, but previously existing molds were also used. In only three years Rosenthal developed yet another important color formula, Golden Agate. The Holly pattern was designed especially for its production. The dolphin covered dish with a fish finial is perhaps the most common and easily recognized piece ever produced. Other animal dishes were also made; all are highly collectible. There have been many repros — not all are marked! The symbol (+) at the end of some of the following lines was used to indicate items that have been reproduced.

Our advisors for this category are Jerry and Sandi Garrett; they are listed in the Directory under Indiana. See the Pattern Glass section for clear pressed glass; only colored items are listed here.

Animal dish, bird w/berry, Nile Green...................2,000.00
Animal dish, bird w/berry, teal bl 375.00
Animal dish, cat on hamper, amber, tall 350.00
Animal dish, cat on hamper, chocolate, low 700.00
Animal dish, dolphin, beaded, cobalt 1,000.00
Animal dish, dolphin, beaded, emerald gr.................800.00
Animal dish, dolphin, sawtooth, teal bl (+).............800.00
Animal dish, dolphin, smooth, chocolate 450.00
Animal dish, fighting cocks, Nile Green 2,500.00
Animal dish, fighting cocks, teal bl...................1,900.00
Animal dish, hen, amber.................................225.00
Animal dish, hen, cobalt...............................600.00
Animal dish, rabbit, amber (+).........................225.00
Animal dish, rabbit, cobalt 600.00
Austrian, bowl, canary, rectangular, 8¼x5¼" 250.00
Austrian, butter dish, canary, child sz................525.00
Austrian, cake stand, canary 400.00
Austrian, creamer, emerald gr, 4¼" 215.00
Austrian, plate, canary, sq............................225.00
Austrian, sugar bowl, chocolate, w/lid, 2½" 195.00
Brazen Shield, cake stand, bl, 9⅜" or 10⅜", ea 250.00
Brazen Shield, creamer, bl.............................150.00
Brazen Shield, goblet, bl..............................175.00
Brazen Shield, sugar bowl, bl, w/lid 200.00
Cactus, bowl, chocolate, 6¼".............................135.00

Cactus, butter dish on pedestal, chocolate, $850.00.

Cactus, celery, chocolate, 7½" 500.00
Cactus, syrup jug, chocolate, metal lid 225.00
Cactus, tumbler, iced tea; chocolate, 5" 95.00
Cord Drapery, bowl, amber, hand fluted, ftd, 8¼" 225.00
Cord Drapery, bowl, cobalt, 8" 225.00
Cord Drapery, compote, cobalt, w/lid, 4½" 400.00
Cord Drapery, mug, emerald gr, ftd 280.00
Cord Drapery, toothpick holder, amber 350.00
Cupid, butter dish, wht opaque 150.00
Cupid, creamer, Nile Green 425.00
Cupid, spooner, chocolate 350.00
Cupid, sugar bowl, wht opaque, w/lid 150.00
Dewey, butter dish, emerald gr, 4" dia 85.00
Dewey, creamer, canary, 4" 60.00
Dewey, mug, Nile Green 200.00
Dewey, sauce bowl, amber 40.00
Dewey, tumbler, canary 80.00
Early Diamond, dish, cobalt, rectangular, 8x5" 200.00
Early Diamond, tumbler, canary 200.00
Greentown Daisy, butter dish, wht opaque 110.00
Greentown Daisy, creamer, chocolate 225.00
Greentown Daisy, sugar bowl, frosted emerald gr 115.00
Herringbone Buttress, bowl, emerald gr, 7¼" 250.00
Herringbone Buttress, cake stand, emerald gr 500.00
Herringbone Buttress, nappy, emerald gr 225.00
Herringbone Buttress, tumbler, emerald gr, type 1 or type 2, ea ..275.00
Herringbone Buttress, wine, olive gr, 4" 210.00
Holly, sugar bowl, White Agate base, clear lid 750.00
Holly, toothpick holder, Rose Agate 4,500.00
Holly Amber, bowl, 7½" 650.00
Holly Amber, butter dish 2,100.00
Holly Amber, cake stand 2,600.00
Holly Amber, cruet, w/stopper 2,250.00
Holly Amber, pickle dish, hdls 425.00
Holly Amber, vase, ped ft, 8" 2,200.00
Leaf Bracket, butter dish, wht opaque 850.00
Leaf Bracket, nappy, chocolate 85.00
Leaf Bracket, sugar bowl, chocolate, w/lid 165.00
Mug, deer & oak tree, chocolate 750.00
Mug, indoor drinking scene, chocolate, handleless 425.00
Mug, pepperbox, chocolate 350.00
Mug, Serenade, emerald gr 125.00
Novelty, corn vase, amber, 4⅝" 250.00
Novelty, Dewey bust, teal bl, w/base 250.00
Novelty, dust pan, chocolate 750.00
Novelty, mitted hand, Nile Green 650.00
Novelty, trunk, amber (+) 250.00
Novelty, wheelbarrow, Nile Green (+) 325.00
Pattern No 75, bowl, cobalt, 6¼" 200.00
Pattern No 75, bowl, emerald gr, 8" 100.00
Pleat Band, compote, chocolate, plain stem, smooth rim, 4¼" ...175.00
Ruffled Eye, pitcher, water; amber 200.00
Scalloped Flange, tumbler, chocolate 165.00
Scalloped Flange, vase, Nile Green 350.00
Shuttle, butter dish, chocolate 1,250.00
Shuttle, champagne, chocolate 900.00
Shuttle, mug, emerald gr 450.00
Shuttle, spooner, chocolate 500.00
Teardrop & Tassel, butter dish, Nile Green 500.00
Teardrop & Tassel, butter dish, wht opaque 200.00
Teardrop & Tassel, compote, Nile Green, open, 7½" dia 375.00
Teardrop & Tassel, relish, amber, oval 175.00
Teardrop & Tassel, spooner, chocolate 350.00
Teardrop & Tassel, tumbler, Nile Green, type 1 ....300.00
Toothpick holder, dog head, bl frost 350.00
Toothpick holder, dog head, Nile Green (+) 225.00
Toothpick holder, picture fr, teal bl 300.00
Toothpick holder, witch head, chocolate (+) 900.00

Grueby

William Henry Grueby joined the firm of the Low Art Tile Works at the age of fifteen and in 1894, after several years of experience in the production of architectural tiles, founded his own plant, the Grueby Faience Company, in Boston, Massachusetts. Grueby began experimenting with the idea of producing art pottery and had soon perfected a fine glaze (soft and without gloss) in shades of blue, gray, yellow, brown, and his most successful, Cucumber Green. In 1900 his exhibit at the Paris Exposition Universelle won three gold medals.

Grueby pottery was hand thrown and hand decorated in the Arts and Crafts style. Vertically thrust tooled and applied leaves and flower buds were the most common decorative devices. Tiles continued to be an important product, unique (due to the matt glaze decoration) as well as durable. Grueby tiles were often a full inch thick. Many of them were decorated 'en cuenca,' a technique very similar to cloisonne. Instead of copper 'cloisonnes,' however, the tiles had a dust-pressed wall pushed into their surface. Then glazes of appropriate color were laid into the channels between them. This had the effect of stylizing the design in a way appropriate to the Arts and Crafts style.

Incompatible with the Art Nouveau style, the artware production ceased in 1907, but tile production continued for another decade. The ware is marked in one of several ways: 'Grueby Pottery, Boston, USA'; 'Grueby, Boston, Mass.'; or 'Grueby Faience.' The artware is often artist signed. Our advisor for this category is David Rago; he is listed in the Directory under New Jersey.

Vase, tooled and applied leaves and stems extend to yellow trefoils around the neck, superior leathery green matt, much detail, Wilhemina Post, marked/WP/188A, 17¾x8½", $92,000.00. (Photo courtesy Craftsman Auctions)

Lotus bowl, gr (glossy int), leaves, rnd mk/ER, 6x7", NM........1,610.00
Plaque, elephant group, blk on bl-gray, 6-pc, 14x23", in fr, EX ..9,775.00
Scarab, bl, 4" L 850.00
Scarab, gr, 2¾" L 450.00
Tile, angel, ivory on blk, chip to bkside, no mk, 6" 190.00
Tile, floor; knight on horse (2nd w/heart) on wht, mk, 6", lot of 2..975.00

Tile, Grueby Tile/chamberstick w/candle, yel/gr, MD, 6x4½"....**10,925.00**
Tile, man on bench, bl & mustard w/veining, red clay, unmk, 6" ...**330.00**
Tile, Orientalist figure w/vase fr w/lg G, gr/sienna, MK, 8x8", EX ..**16,100.00**
Tile, tulip, pk/gr, 6", in bronze Tiffany trivet, Seaman, wear, 6"...**8,625.00**
Tile, 8 geese around perimeter, brn/tan on gr, 9", NM **10,000.00**
Vase, bl-gray/oatmeal, leaves/buds/quatrefoils, Post, 5x10", VG ..**6,900.00**
Vase, Cerulean Blue w/cobalt speckles, baluster, rpr, 4x2¼" **550.00**
Vase, Cerulean Blue w/cobalt speckles, trumpet form, 6½x5" .**1,200.00**
Vase, Cucumber Green (curdled w/gr veins), mahog int, ribbed, 7½".**1,870.00**
Vase, gr, bulbous w/raised ribs resembling fluting, 3", NM **550.00**
Vase, gr, leaves, Erickson, #101, gourd form, 8x4½", EX..........**2,070.00**
Vase, gr, leaves, ridged floriform, faience mk/MS/1152, 13x8", NM..**11,500.00**
Vase, gr, leaves & buds, label, 7" **2,600.00**
Vase, gr, leaves & buds, rstr chip, 11½" **4,250.00**
Vase, gr, vertical ribs, bulbous w/short collar, 7x9" **6,000.00**
Vase, gr, 4 wide distinct leaves w/central vein, shouldered, 4½"..**6,500.00**
Vase, gr (curdled), leaves, watermelon form, orig tag:#36A, 10x7"..**5,750.00**
Vase, gr (curdled) w/ivory accents, conical, 8x3¾" **1,100.00**
Vase, gr (EX glaze) w/yel buds between pointed leaves, sm rpr, 8"..**5,500.00**
Vase, gr (exceptional/leathery), sq leaves/buds, MD, 13x13", NM..**40,250.00**
Vase, gr (leathery), leaves, F Liley, faience mk, #144, 8x7", NM **4,025.00**
Vase, gr (leathery), leaves/tall buds, rstr base chip, #200, 15x8" **10,350.00**
Vase, gr (leathery), rows of leaves, mk/ER, 4¾x5½", NM **2,645.00**
Vase, ivory (leathery), rnd mk, 15x10", EX **2,415.00**
Vase, med gr, rnd leaves & buds, obscured mk, 7½x4½", NM.**2,875.00**
Vase, ochre, cvd vertical ribs, waisted shoulder, faience mk/BA, 10x5"..**7,475.00**
Vase, yel, leaves, wide onion shape, 7x7", NM **2,600.00**
Vase, yel/brn, 4 veined leaves, cylindrical, sgn, 9"................**13,000.00**

Gustavsberg

Gustavsberg Pottery, founded near Stockholm, Sweden, in the late 1700s, manufactured faience, creamware, and porcelain in the English taste until the end of the nineteenth century. During the twentieth century, the factory has produced some inventive modernistic designs, often signed by their artists. Wilhelm Kage (1889 – 1960) is best remembered for Argenta, a stoneware body decorated in silver overlay, introduced in the 1930s. Usually a mottled green, Argenta can also be found in cobalt blue and white. Other lines included Cintra (an exceptionally translucent porcelain), Farsta (copper-glazed ware), and Farstarust (iron oxide geometric overlay). Designer Stig Lindberg's work, which dates from the 1940s through the early 1970s, includes slab-built figures and a full range of tableware. Some pieces of Gustavsberg are dated.

Bowl, Argenta, fish & bubbles, silver trim, #1094III, 6"..............**225.00**
Bowl, Argenta, silver flowers, ridged sides, silver rim, #59, 6¼" .**185.00**
Bowl, Argenta, silver flowers & rim, ftd, #1094 LV, 7" **185.00**
Bowl, Argenta, 2 silver rings on gr mottle, Kage, 1936, 3⅞".........**75.00**
Bowl, Argenta, 5 silver stripes on gr mottle, #B2, 1⅛x2"............**100.00**
Bowl, bl haresfur, ftd, Friberg, 1955, 1½x2⅜" **390.00**
Bowl, complex grs & reds, Friberg, 1970, 2½x9¾" **450.00**
Bowl, Farsta, olive gr mottle w/incised decor, Kage, 1956, 3x4¼"....**950.00**
Bowl, Farsta, stoneware w/yel & rust nude, Kage, 1950, #902 GM..**325.00**
Bowl, ivory w/pk int, Stig Lindberg, #Y.56.171, 6¼x8¼"............**250.00**
Bowl, ochre/brn mottle, triangular, Friberg, 2⅛x3⅝" **625.00**
Bowl/vase, Sureea, gold on wht, high ft, Kage, 1940s, 4x5⅜" **350.00**
Chalice, incised dominos on tan/brn mottle, Lindberg, 5¾".......**175.00**
Figurine, cat, Larson, ca 1960, 4½x13" **185.00**
Figurine, male & female camel, Larson, 4½x5" **155.00**
Figurine, rhino, baby, gr w/wht 'saddle,' 7½x4½"........................**110.00**
Jar, Argenta, Cupid, w/lid, 6½"...**510.00**
Vase, Argenta, silver Deco stripes on gr, shouldered, Kage, 1930, 8"...**350.00**

Vase, Argenta, silver fern-like design on gr matt, Kage, #1044, 7¾"...**700.00**
Vase, Argenta, silver fish on gr, #55, Kage, 2½" **145.00**
Vase, Argenta, silver flowers & ring on gr, Kage, 1934, 4¼x3¼" ..**250.00**

Vase, Argenta, silver mermaid in grasp of large fish, impressed and applied marks, 10", $2,100.00. (Photo courtesy Cincinnati Auction Gallery)

Vase, Argenta, silver mermaid on gr, #978, 8" **850.00**
Vase, bl to brn matt, Friberg, 1962, 3½x2¾" **900.00**
Vase, bl/brn/gr mottle, waisted, Lindberg, 1961, 8¼x2" **475.00**
Vase, Carrara, wht matt, ftd, Kage, 5x4¾" **225.00**
Vase, complex red/gr/brns w/touches of bl, Friberg, 1964, 3x3½" ...**725.00**
Vase, dk brn mottle w/wht circles, Sundell, 9½x3½" **275.00**
Vase, earth tones w/bl at base, Friberg, ca 1944-47, 7x2¼".........**725.00**
Vase, Egg series, lt to med brn, Friberg, 1951, 4¼x3¼"..............**975.00**
Vase, emb rings, tan to wht, Lindberg, 1967, 4¾x3⅛" **175.00**
Vase, Farstagods, brn/tan w/incising, Kage, 1955, 8x3⅜" **1,600.00**
Vase, mint gr, stick neck, Kage, 1940, 6¾x3½" **550.00**
Vase, red/bl/gr mottle, shouldered, Friberg, 1965, 5⅛x3" **850.00**
Vase, red/gr mottle, waisted, Lindberg, 1967, 7⅞x2" **800.00**
Vase, Reptil, wht, 9x2½" dia **110.00**
Vase, Reptil Carrara, bl, slim, Lindberg, 1940s, 12".....................**275.00**
Vase, silver floral on wht, 5¾" **160.00**
Vase, silver nature motif on wht, Lindberg, #963, 3¼".................**310.00**
Vase, stoneware w/bl & gr hare's fur glaze, Friberg, 1964, 12½"...**1,100.00**
Vase, stoneware w/brn glaze, thrown/sculpted, Lilefors, 4½".......**160.00**
Wall tile, bird, Larsson, ca 1963, 7x10" **125.00**

Gutta Percha

Gutta percha is the plastic substance from the latex of several types of Malaysian trees. It resembles rubber but contains more resin. A patent for the use of this material in manufacturing an early type of plastic was issued in the 1850s.

Brooch, tiered dome w/cloverleaves, cvd castle in center, 1¾" dia ..**80.00**
Earrings, mourning; cvd drops, 1800s, 2½x1", pr........................**180.00**
Frame, molded acorns & branches, brass liner, oval, 4x5½", EX ...**190.00**
Frame, molded floral, rectangular, holds ¼-plate daguerrotype ...**140.00**
Golf ball, line cut, lt overall wear, Eclipse style, 1890s................**170.00**
Golf ball, wht w/emb Silver Town **315.00**
Tape measure, geometrics & sunburst, cloth 60" tape, 1¾" dia, EX..**110.00**

Hadley, M.A.

Founded by artist-turned-potter Mary Alice Hadley, this Louisville, Tennessee, company has been producing handmade dinnerware and decorative items since 1940. Their work is painted freehand in a folksy style with barnyard animals, baskets, whales, and sailing ships in a pastel palette of predominately blues and greens. Each piece is signed with Hadley's first two initials and her last name. She is responsible for creating each design; among collectors, horses and pigs are popular subject matter. Older pieces are generally heavier and along with the more unusual items command the higher prices.

Bowl, Country series, pig, 7", pr..................................24.00
Bowl, Country series, rabbit, 7"..................................16.00
Bowl, lug soup; Country series, house, w/lid, ind 32.50
Butter dish, Country series, cow, 4x6½"..........................38.00
Casserole, Country series, cow & pig, lug hdl, w/lid, 9½".........50.00

Casserole, cow and pig, 'The End' inside, 10" diameter, $45.00.
(Photo courtesy Mike Sissman)

Casserole, Harvest, no bl, w/lid, low, 10".......................40.00
Cooler, farmer & wife, w/lid & base, 21½" 135.00
Cup, julep; New Bird, 8-oz, 4 for................................48.00
Decanter, sherry; Sherry in bl, jug-like shape, ball stopper, 9".......45.00
Mug, Country series, cow, 4¾"....................................30.00
Mug, whale, flared sides...30.00
Pitcher, Christmas, 6½" 32.00
Pitcher, grapes in compote, 5"...................................22.50
Plaque, frog figural, 8x7½"......................................50.00
Plate, Country series, cow, 11"..................................27.50
Plate, Country series, duck, 11".................................27.50
Plate, Country series, pony, 11".................................27.50
Plate, Halloween, ghost, 4" 15.00
Platter, Christmas tree, 12¾"....................................45.00
Refrigerator magnet, Country series, lamb.......................16.50
Shakers, Country series, bird, 3½", pr...........................22.50
Shakers, Country series, pig & sow, lg, 4½", pr..................25.00
Shakers, Harvest, pears, 4½x2½", pr..............................20.00
Soap dish, cupped hands, 4½x6"...................................45.00
Teapot, house & lady, 4½"..35.00
Tile, 2-story house w/yard, 6x6".................................20.00
Utensil jar, Country series, duck 50.00
Vase, cat shape, 14"...95.00

Hagen-Renaker

Best known for their line of miniature animal figures, Hagen-Renaker was founded in Monrovia, California, in 1946. It is estimated that perhaps as many as eighty different dogs were produced. In addition to the animals, they made replicas of characters from several popular Disney films under license from the Disney Studio. The firm relocated in San Dimas in 1962, where they remain active to the present time. Their wares are sometimes marked with an incised 'HR,' a stamped 'Hagen-Renaker' or part of the name, or paper labels. For more information, we recommend *The Collector's Encyclopedia of California Pottery, Second Edition*, by Jack Chipman; *Charlton Standard Catalog of Hagen-Renaker, Second Edition; Disneyana Collector's Guide to Californian Pottery, 1938 – 1960*, by Devin Frick and Tamara Hodge; and *Hagen-Renaker Pottery: Horses and Other Figurines* by Nancy Kelly (Schiffer). Another source of information is Hagen-Renaker Collectors Club (HRCC), listed in the Directory under Clubs, Newsletters, and Catalogs.

Figurine, American Saddle Bred Horse, 3¼".......................90.00
Figurine, Baron, German shepherd, 1953, 3½x5" 50.00
Figurine, Bedouin, 1956, 11x10".................................800.00
Figurine, Belgian, Designer's Workshop/Sespe Violette, 1953 .....900.00
Figurine, Benny, basset hound, 1954, 4x7" 60.00
Figurine, Crusader, alabaster 825.00

Figurine, Dick, Siamese cat, DW sticker, B-728, 1960, 6½".........40.00
Figurine, duck mother & 2 ducklings, matt, 1980s, 4x6"............40.00
Figurine, Grumpy (Snow White & the 7 Dwarfs), Disney, ca 1958, 1"..60.00
Figurine, Gypsy, pointer dog, 1954-55 ....60.00
Figurine, Hamlet, Great Dane, 1954, 4½x7½"......................100.00
Figurine, Horace, caterpillar papa, 3"...........................36.00
Figurine, King Cortez, rearing horse, ltd ed, 9", MIB............120.00
Figurine, King Hubert or Stefan, 1959-60, ea....................56.00
Figurine, Lady & Tramp, dogs, Disney, 1955, 1½", 2¼", NM 100.00
Figurine, Lippett, Morgan stallion, 6¼" 150.00
Figurine, Lippizan stallion, performing Levade, 6"...............325.00
Figurine, Little Horribles vulture, 1958, 1½"+branchy perch......57.50
Figurine, monkeys in a tree, 4½", 3-pc set.......................40.00
Figurine, Nana, St Bernard dog, Disney, foil label, 1950s, 1½" 95.00
Figurine, Nobby, bulldog, 1955, 2x3".............................40.00
Figurine, Skywalker, palomino, 2000 ltd ed, #5284, 4¾"...........80.00
Figurine, Skywalker, red dun, 2000 ltd ed, #3284, 4¾"............40.00
Figurine, Stoneware Elephant, gray & brn shades, #2053, 1989, 2¾" ...40.00
Figurine, Tiger, dachshund pup, DW sticker, 2¼" L 38.00
Figurine, unicorn, trn head, gold horn, B-682, 5" 95.00
Figurine, Vanguard, bay foal, DW sticker, 1961-72, 4¾", EX+ ...200.00
Figurine, Von, German shepherd dog, DW sticker, rpr..............50.00
Figurine, Welsh pony, head up, wht mat, DW sticker, 1981, lg...110.00

Hair Weaving

A rather unusual craft became popular during the mid-1800s. Human hair was used to make jewelry (rings, bracelets, lockets, etc.) by braiding and interlacing fine strands into hollow forms with pearls and beads added for effect. Wreaths were also made, often using hair from deceased family members as well as the living. They were displayed in deep satin-lined frames along with mementoes of the weaver or her departed kin. The fad was abandoned before the turn of the century. The values suggested below are for mint condition examples. Any fraying of the hair greatly lowers value. For further information, we recommend *Collector's Encyclopedia of Hairwork Jewelry* by C. Jeanenne Bell (Collector Books). See also Mourning Collectibles.

Key:
p-w — palette work   t-w — table work

Bracelet, p-w in dome, 6 braided t-w rows, 1840-60, ⅞x7" 585.00
Bracelet, t-w braided rows (3), gold locket clasp, 1850-70 ....525.00
Bracelet, t-w pattern w/gold-filled box clasp w/yel stone, 1850-80 ....325.00
Bracelet, t-w rows (5) in 2 weaves, gold clasp w/pk stone, 1850-80...450.00
Bracelet, t-w rows (7) in 4 weaves, gold/enamel clasp, ca 1845 ..700.00
Brooch, p-w basketweave, jet mt, 1850-60s, 2x1¼"....................225.00
Brooch, p-w basketweave under glass, hollow gold mt, 1840s, 1¾" .350.00
Brooch, p-w curls/flowers on milk glass, hollow gold fr, 1850s, 1⅞".450.00
Brooch, p-w flowers on milk glass ground in gold oval, 1850s, 2" 325.00
Brooch, p-w flowers/curls on milk glass, gilt brass mt, 1850s, 2¼" ...295.00
Brooch, p-w hair revolve in gilt brass fr, 1860-70s, 1½" 350.00
Brooch, p-w under crystal, faceted jet surround, ca 1830s, 1¾" ..350.00
Brooch, p-w under crystal, seed pearls form crescent, ca 1800, 1¾"....350.00
Brooch, p-w under crystal, seed-pearl surround, Georgian, 1¼x½" 300.00
Brooch, p-w wheat sheaf under crystal in gold fr, 1790-1810, 1¾x1"..575.00
Brooch, t-w bow, gold mts w/blk enamel leaf, 1850s-70s, 2x3" ...400.00
Brooch, t-w bow w/gold stamped 1¼x½" mts, 1850s-70s............325.00
Brooch, t-w w/gold-filled mts, 2-color drops, 1850-70s, EX........295.00
Brooch, t-w 2-color horsehair, gold mts, 1860-80s, 2x1½" 195.00
Brooch, tintype front/p-w hair on bk, rolled gold mt, 1860s, 1¼"...150.00
Earrings, t-w close-weave w/gold mts, 1840-70, 1¾" 295.00
Earrings, t-w openweave bells w/gutta percha embellishments, 1850-70s ..475.00

Earrings, t-w teardrops shape w/gold mts, 1840-70, 3¾"..............**420.00**
Earrings, t-w w/openweave dangles, gold mts, 1850s-70s, 2½x1"...**550.00**
Medallion, p-w basketweave under glass, gold mt, 1790-1840 ....**250.00**
Necklace, t-w chain w/gold mts, heart drop w/dangles, 1850-80, 18"..**400.00**
Necklace, t-w choker, gold snake head & tail clasp, 1840-60 .....**540.00**
Necklace, t-w choker w/2 weaves in 3 rows, 1840-60, ¾x14" **450.00**
Necklace, t-w w/2" t-w cross on hard core, 1850s-70s, 16" chain ..**550.00**
Necklace, t-w 2-weave, orig rnd locket, 1860-80, 20" **350.00**
Pendant, gold cross w/compartment for braided hair, 1850-80s, 2½".**650.00**
Ring, p-w basketweave, eng gold oval mt, 1780s, ⅞" **500.00**
Ring, p-w on milk glass, gold navette mt, 1780-1800, 1⅛".........**995.00**
Ring, t-w inset, gold band, 1850-80s, ¼" W **285.00**

Hall

The Hall China Company of East Liverpool, Ohio, was established in 1903. Their earliest products were whiteware toilet seats, mugs, jugs, etc. By 1920 their restaurant-type dinnerware and cookingware had become so successful that Hall was assured of a solid future. They continue today to be one of the country's largest manufacturers of this type of product.

Hall introduced the first of their famous teapots in 1920; new shapes and colors were added each year until about 1948, making them the largest teapot manufacturer in the world. These and the dinnerware lines of the '30s through the '50s have become popular collectibles. For more thorough study of the subject, we recommend *The Collector's Encyclopedia of Hall China, Third Edition*, by Margaret and Kenn Whitmyer; their address may be found in the Directory under Ohio.

Blue Bouquet, bowl, Radiance, 6", from $14 to..............................**18.00**
Blue Bouquet, cake plate, from $40 to..**45.00**
Blue Bouquet, canister, metal, 6" dia, from $20 to.........................**25.00**
Blue Bouquet, creamer, modern, from $25 to..................................**30.00**
Blue Bouquet, drip jar, Radiance, from $150 to.............................**200.00**
Blue Bouquet, pie paker, from $60 to..**70.00**
Cameo Rose, bowl, cream soup; E-style, 5", from $85 to **90.00**
Cameo Rose, creamer, E-style, from $9 to **11.00**
Cameo Rose, plate, E-style, 8", from $8 to **9.50**
Cameo Rose, tidbit, 3-tier, E-style, from $65 to **75.00**
Christmas Tree & Holly, bowl, E-style, oval, from $55 to **60.00**
Christmas Tree & Holly, tidbit, 2-tier, E-style, from $100 to **125.00**
Crocus, bowl, cereal; D-style, 6", from $18 to **20.00**
Crocus, bread box, metal, from $110 to **130.00**
Crocus, coffeepot, Deco, from $700 to **850.00**
Crocus, coffeepot, drip; Jordan, from $450 to **500.00**

Crocus, coffeepot, Terrace shape, silver trim, 8", $65.00.

Crocus, gravy boat, D-style, from $32 to **37.00**
Crocus, jug, Simplicity, from $300 to **350.00**
Crocus, leftover, sq, from $100 to **120.00**
Crocus, plate, D-style, 7¼", from $9 to...**12.00**

Crocus, platter, oval, D-style, 11¼", from $28 to.............................32.00
Crocus, sugar bowl, Medallion, w/lid, from $30 to...........................40.00
Crocus, teapot, Boston, from $190 to...225.00
Game Bird, bowl, Thick Rim, 6", from $25 to..................................30.00
Game Bird, cup, E-style, from $22 to..27.00
Game Bird, platter, E-style, oval, 13¼", from $65 to 75.00
Game Bird, teapot, Windshield, from $255 to...............................315.00
Heather Rose, bowl, salad; E-style, 9", from $14 to.........................16.00
Heather Rose, creamer, E-style, from $8 to 10.00
Heather Rose, pie baker, E-style, from $22 to 25.00
Heather Rose, teapot, Flare shape, from $35 to...............................45.00
Mums, baker, French; D-style, from $30 to 40.00
Mums, bowl, oval, D-style, 10¼", from $40 to 50.00
Mums, casserole, Radiance, from $45 to...50.00
Mums, creamer, Medallion, from $22 to...25.00
Mums, teapot, Boston, from $225 to...300.00
No 488, bowl, flat soup; D-style, 8½", from $30 to...........................35.00
No 488, bowl, Radiance, 10", from $45 to.......................................50.00
No 488, casserole, Sundial, from $45 to..50.00
No 488, cup, D-style, from $18 to..20.00
No 488, mug, Tom & Jerry; from $25 to..30.00
No 488, plate, D-style, 9", from $18 to..20.00
No 488, platter, oval, D-style, 13¼", from $45 to.............................50.00
Orange Poppy, bowl, flat soup; 8½", from $30 to.............................35.00
Orange Poppy, coffeepot, Bellevue, 2-cup, from $1,600 to.......**1,800.00**
Orange Poppy, cup, from $25 to..30.00
Orange Poppy, match safe, metal, from $85 to..............................100.00
Orange Poppy, plate, 9", from $25 to...30.00
Orange Poppy, teapot, Donut, from $350 to 425.00
Pastel Morning Glory, bowl, cereal; D-style, 6"..............................15.00
Pastel Morning Glory, bowl, Radiance, 9", from $35 to...............40.00
Pastel Morning Glory, custard, Radiance, from $25 to 30.00
Pastel Morning Glory, plate, D-style, 9", from $10 to..................15.00
Pastel Morning Glory, pretzel jar, from $195 to 225.00
Pastel Morning Glory, teapot, New York, from $200 to...............260.00
Primrose, ashtray, E-style, from $8 to..10.00
Primrose, bowl, E-style, oval, 9¼", from $22 to 25.00
Primrose, plate, E-style, 10", from $10 to 12.00
Red Poppy, ball jug, #3, from $100 to...120.00
Red Poppy, cake safe, metal, from $40 to.......................................45.00
Red Poppy, creamer, modern, from $22 to......................................25.00
Red Poppy, gravy boat, D-style, from $35 to 40.00
Red Poppy, leftover, rectangular, from $150 to 200.00
Red Poppy, platter, D-style, 13¼", from $28 to...............................32.00
Red Poppy, soap dispenser, metal, from $140 to...........................185.00
Red Poppy, sugar bowl, Daniel, w/lid, from $22 to..........................25.00
Sears' Arlington, bowl, vegetable; w/lid, E-style, from $30 to 35.00
Sears' Arlington, platter, E-style, oval, 13¼", from $18 to 22.00
Sears' Fairfax, creamer, E-style, from $6 to 8.00
Sears' Fairfax, plate, E-style, 6½", from $2.50 to..............................3.50
Sears' Monticello, bowl, cream soup; E-style, 5", from $80 to 90.00
Sears' Monticello, plate, E-style, 10", from $9 to 11.00
Sears' Mount Vernon, cup & saucer, E-style, from $7 to.................9.00
Sears' Mount Vernon, sugar bowl, w/lid, E-style, from $15 to 18.00
Sears' Richmond/Brown-Eyed Susan, plate, E-style, 6½", from $3 to..3.50
Sears' Richmond/Brown-Eyed Susan, plate, E-style, 10", from $7 to..9.00
Serenade, casserole, Radiance, from $30 to 40.00
Serenade, coffeepot, drip; Jordan, all china, from $300 to...........400.00
Serenade, plate, D-style, 8¼", from $6 to.......................................8.50
Serenade, teapot, Aladdin, from $250 to 300.00
Silhouette, bowl, salad; 9", from $16 to..18.00
Silhouette, bowl, vegetable; D-style, 9¼", from $30 to...................32.00
Silhouette, jug #3, Medallion, from $22 to......................................27.00
Silhouette, plate, D-style, 9", from $16 to.......................................18.00

Silhouette, shakers, Medallion, pr, from $50 to................................60.00
Springtime, bowl, salad; D-style, 9", from $12 to 14.00
Springtime, bowl, Thick Rim, 8½", from $15 to................................17.00
Springtime, pie baker, from $18 to...20.00
Springtime, plate, D-style, 7¼", from $5 to...6.00
Teapot, Adele, gr, from $175 to...200.00
Teapot, Aladdin, Golden Glo, from $180 to......................................225.00
Teapot, Albany, blk, from $35 to..45.00
Teapot, Albany, cobalt w/gold, from $65 to..70.00
Teapot, Albany, mahog, gold label, from $50 to.................................65.00
Teapot, Automobile, maroon, from $475 to......................................525.00
Teapot, Baltimore, Chinese Red, from $250 to.................................300.00
Teapot, Baltimore, ivory w/pk rose decal, from $200 to...................225.00
Teapot, Basket, Citrus, from $250 to...300.00
Teapot, Basketball, turq w/gold, from $525 to.................................575.00
Teapot, Birdcage, Emerald Green w/gold, from $620 to 670.00
Teapot, Boston, gr lustre, gold label, from $95 to............................115.00
Teapot, Boston, Warm Yellow w/gold, from $50 to............................55.00
Teapot, Cleveland, Emerald Green, from $45 to.................................55.00
Teapot, Danielle, maroon, from $185 to..200.00
Teapot, Donut, cobalt w/gold, from $400 to.....................................450.00
Teapot, Football, Canary, from $500 to..600.00
Teapot, French, Dresden, gold label, 10- to 12-cup, from $65 to ..70.00
Teapot, French, turq w/gold, 1- to 3-cup, from $45 to.......................65.00
Teapot, Globe, Camellia, from $45 to...55.00
Teapot, Hollywood, Chinese Red, from $185 to.................................225.00
Teapot, Hollywood, pk w/gold, from $60 to 75.00
Teapot, Hook Cover, Delphinium, from $40 to 45.00
Teapot, Illinois, blk w/gold, from $165 to..190.00
Teapot, Indiana, ivory w/gold, from $250 to 275.00
Teapot, Kansas, Emerald Green, from $400 to..................................500.00
Teapot, Los Angeles, Canary, from $45 to..50.00
Teapot, Manhattan, cobalt, from $160 to..180.00
Teapot, Melody, ivory, from $75 to 85.00
Teapot, Moderne, Marine Blue, from $45 to.......................................55.00
Teapot, Musical, Canary, from $155 to..170.00
Teapot, Nautilus, maroon w/gold, from $275 to................................300.00
Teapot, New York, Cadet Blue, gold label, from $50 to......................60.00
Teapot, New York, Orchid, from $200 to...250.00
Teapot, Ohio, maroon, from $200 to...225.00
Teapot, Parade, Mustard, from $50 to..55.00
Teapot, Philadelphia, cobalt, gold loop design, 1- to 4-cup, $60 to...65.00
Teapot, Philadelphia, Stock Brown w/gold, 10-cup, from $30 to ..35.00
Teapot, Rhythm, turq, from $120 to...140.00
Teapot, Sani-Grid, Cadet Blue, from $18 to.......................................20.00
Teapot, Star, Delphinium w/gold, from $110 to................................125.00
Tulip, bowl, cereal; D-style, 6", from $14 to 16.00
Tulip, casserole, tab hdls, from $100 to 125.00
Tulip, plate, D-style, 10", from $55 to...65.00
Tulip, stack set, Radiance, from $95 to...110.00
Wildfire, creamer, Sani-Grid, from $25 to..30.00
Wildfire, cup, D-style, from $12 to 14.00
Wildfire, platter, D-style, oval, 13¼", from $25 to.............................28.00
Wildfire, shaker, Teardrop, ea from $18 to 22.00
Yellow Rose, coffeepot, Norse, from $75 to..85.00
Yellow Rose, gravy boat, D-style, from $30 to 35.00
Yellow Rose, plate, D-style, 8¼", from $8 to.......................................9.00
Yellow Rose, teapot, New York, from $150 to....................................200.00

Zeisel Designs, Hallcraft

Century Fern, bowl, divided vegetable; from $28 to 32.00
Century Fern, jug, from $28 to...32.00
Century Fern, ladle, from $18 to..22.00

Century Fern, teapot, 6-cup, from $150 to.......................................185.00
Century Garden of Eden, bowl, soup/cereal; 8", from $8 to..........10.00
Century Garden of Eden, gravy boat, from $28 to 32.00
Century Garden of Eden, relish, 4-part, from $30 to 35.00
Century Sunglow, casserole, from $55 to...65.00
Century Sunglow, plate, 8", from $7.50 to..9.50
Century Sunglow, platter, 15", from $32 to..37.00
Tomorrow's Classic Arizona, bowl, open baker; 11-oz, from $18 to...22.00
Tomorrow's Classic Arizona, butter dish, from $145 to 175.00
Tomorrow's Classic Arizona, plate, 11", from $11 to........................13.00
Tomorrow's Classic Bouquet, candlestick, 4¼", from $35 to 45.00

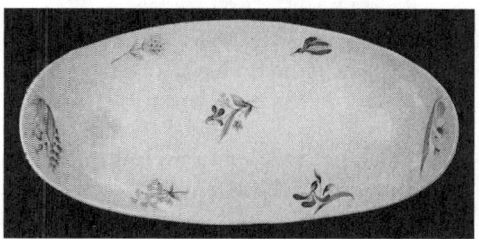

Tomorrow's Classic Bouquet, celery tray, $25.00.

Tomorrow's Classic Bouquet, egg cup, from $55 to 60.00
Tomorrow's Classic Bouquet, jug, 3-qt, from $40 to.........................45.00
Tomorrow's Classic Bouquet, vase, from $80 to.................................95.00
Tomorrow's Classic Buckingham, ashtray, from $8 to 10.00
Tomorrow's Classic Buckingham, casserole, 2-qt, from $55 to.......65.00
Tomorrow's Classic Buckingham, sugar bowl, w/lid, from $20 to ..22.00
Tomorrow's Classic Caprice, bowl, vegetable; 8¾" sq, from $22 to...25.00
Tomorrow's Classic Caprice, marmite, w/lid, from $27 to.............32.00
Tomorrow's Classic Caprice, vinegar bottle, from $65 to..............75.00
Tomorrow's Classic Dawn, bowl, coupe soup; 9", from $9 to.........11.00
Tomorrow's Classic Dawn, butter dish, from $160 to..................190.00
Tomorrow's Classic Dawn, plate, 11", from $12 to..........................14.00
Tomorrow's Classic Fantasy, bowl, lg salad; 14½", from $32 to 37.00
Tomorrow's Classic Fantasy, creamer, AD: from $10 to..................12.00
Tomorrow's Classic Fantasy, platter, 15", from $30 to.....................35.00
Tomorrow's Classic Flair, candlestick, 4½", from $30 to.................35.00
Tomorrow's Classic Flair, gravy boat, from $42 to............................45.00
Tomorrow's Classic Flair, shaker, ea from $15 to.............................18.00
Tomorrow's Classic Frost Flowers, butter dish, from $140 to.......160.00
Tomorrow's Classic Frost Flowers, casserole, 2-qt, from $45 to......55.00
Tomorrow's Classic Frost Flowers, onion soup, w/lid, from $35 to.37.00
Tomorrow's Classic Harlequin, celery bowl, oval, from $22 to......24.00
Tomorrow's Classic Harlequin, cookie jar, Zeisel style, from $250 to..300.00
Tomorrow's Classic Harlequin, plate, 8", from $8.50 to..................9.50
Tomorrow's Classic Holiday, bowl, fruit; ftd, lg, from $40 to.........45.00
Tomorrow's Classic Holiday, plate, 11", from $10 to........................12.00
Tomorrow's Classic Lyric, bowl, coupe soup; 9", from $8.50 to......11.00
Tomorrow's Classic Lyric, candlestick, 4½", from $28 to..............32.00
Tomorrow's Classic Lyric, egg cup, from $50 to................................55.00
Tomorrow's Classic Lyric, platter, 12¼", from $20 to......................22.00
Tomorrow's Classic Mulberry, casserole, 2-qt, from $45 to 55.00
Tomorrow's Classic Mulberry, ladle, from $20 to.............................22.00
Tomorrow's Classic Mulberry, sugar bowl, w/lid, from $20 to 22.00
Tomorrow's Classic Peach Blossom, bowl, coupe soup; 9", from $9 to...11.00
Tomorrow's Classic Peach Blossom, coffeepot, 6-cup, from $85 to...105.00
Tomorrow's Classic Peach Blossom, platter, 12¼", from $22 to 28.00
Tomorrow's Classic Pinecone, cup, from $9 to 11.00
Tomorrow's Classic Pinecone, platter, 11¼", from $22 to...............25.00
Tomorrow's Classic Pinecone, tidbit, 3-tier, from $55 to 65.00
Tomorrow's Classic Spring, candlestick, 8", from $35 to...............40.00

Tomorrow's Classic Spring, egg cup, from $42 to **45.00**
Tomorrow's Classic Spring, plate, 11", from $11 to **13.00**

Hallmark

Hallmark introduced a line of artplas (molded plastic) ornaments in 1973 which quickly became popular with collectors. The Hallmark Keepsake Ornament Collectors Club was organized in 1987 and offered exclusive limited edition ornaments to club members only. Hallmark has produced miniature ornaments since 1988 and added a line of Easter (now known as Spring) ornaments beginning in 1991. All these ornaments are very collectible.

Our advice for this category is from the Baggage Car; you will find them listed in the Directory under Iowa. Values are for ornaments in mint condition and with their original boxes.

1973, XHD-102-2, Manger Scene, wht glass ball **80.00**
1973, XHD106-2, Christmas Is Love, glass ball **70.00**
1974, QX101-1, Elf, yarn..**25.00**
1974, QX107-1, Snowgoose, wht glass ball **80.00**
1975, QX132-1, Joy, Nostalgia, handcrafted, rare **235.00**
1975, QX166-1, Norman Rockwell Santa, satin ball **60.00**
1976, QX182-1, Yesteryears Santa, dtd **175.00**
1977, QX133-5, Merry Christmas 1977, Disney, satin ball, dtd **50.00**
1977, QX191-5, Twirl-About Weather House.................................**90.00**
1978, QX250-3, Yesterday's Toys, gold glass ball, dtd....................**35.00**
1979, QX134-7, A Christmas Treat, candy cane............................**70.00**
1979, QX147-6, Bellswinger #1, dtd...**400.00**
1979, QX150-7, Outdoor Fun, handcrafted **120.00**
1980, QX143-4, Santa's Express #2, dtd......................................**200.00**
1980, QX158-4, Checking It Twice, handcrafted **180.00**
1980, QX207-4, Christmas Love, wht glass ball, dtd **38.00**
1981, QX439-5, Sailing Santa, handcrafted.................................**240.00**
1982, QX460-3, Tin Locomotive #1, dtd, pressed tin **650.00**
1983, QX401-7, Thimble Elf #6, handcrafted **35.00**
1984, QX250-1, Currier & Ives, glass ball.....................................**22.50**
1985, QX264-2, Baby-Sitter, glass ball, MIB **12.50**
1985, QX372-5, Special Friends, acrylic medallion, dtd................**12.00**
1986, QX401-3, Ten Years Together, porc bell, dtd **25.00**
1986, QX402-6, Mr & Mrs Claus #1: Merry Mistletoe Time, dtd...**100.00**
1987, QX442-7, Porcelain Bear #5, HP..**38.00**
1987, QX452-7, Reindoggy **35.00**
1988, QX404-1, Wooden Airplane #5, Wooden Childhood **22.50**
1989, QXC581-2, Sitting Purrty, dtd..**40.00**
1990, QX466-6, Polar Jogger, handcrafted **18.00**
1991, QX411-9, Fabulous Decade #2, handcrafted, dtd................**40.00**
1993, QX104-5, Riding the Wind, Folk Art Americana, dtd........**52.00**
1994, QX573-6, Secret Santa, handcrafted **12.00**
1995, QXC404-9, Christmas Bake-Off...**105.00**
1997, QX1681-7, Wedding Day Barbie & Ken **50.00**
1998, QX652-3, The Holy Family, Blessed Nativity, 3-pc **45.00**
1999, QX642-9, 1949 Cadillac Coupe DeVille (50th Anniversary) ..**25.00**
2000, QXI414-4, Angel of Promise...**24.00**

Halloween

Though the origin of Halloween is steeped in pagan rites and superstitions, today Halloween is strictly a fun time, and Halloween items are fun to collect. Pumpkin-head candy containers of papier-mache or pressed cardboard, noisemakers, postcards with black cats and witches, costumes, and decorations are only a sampling of the variety available.

Here's how you can determine the origin of your jack-o'-lantern:

American
1940 – 1950s

German
1900 – 1930s

— items are larger
— made of egg-carton material
— bottom and body are one piece

— items are generally small
— made of cardboard or composition
— always has a cut-out triangular nose; simple, crisscross lines in mouth; blue rings in eyes
— have attached cardboard bottoms

For further information we recommend *More Halloween Collectibles, Anthropomorphic Vegetables and Fruits of Halloween*, by Pamela E. Apkarian-Russell (Schiffer). Other good reference books are *Halloween in America* by Stuart Schneider, and *Halloween Collectables* by Dan and Pauline Campanelli.

Our advisor for this category is Jenny Tarrant; she is listed in the Directory under Missouri. See Clubs, Newsletters, and Catalogs for information concerning *Trick or Treat Trader*, a quarterly newsletter. Unless noted otherwise, values are for examples in excellent to near mint condition except for paper items, in which case assume the condition to be near mint to mint.

American

Most American items were made during the 1940s and 1950s, though a few date from the 1930s as well. Lanterns are constructed either of flat cardboard or the pressed cardboard pulp used to make the jack-o-lantern shown on the left above.

Jack-o'-lantern, pressed cb pulp w/orig face, 4" **95.00**
Jack-o'-lantern, pressed cb pulp w/orig face, 4½" **125.00**
Jack-o'-lantern, pressed cb pulp w/orig face, 5" **145.00**
Jack-o'-lantern, pressed cb pulp w/orig face, 5½" **165.00**
Jack-o'-lantern, pressed cb pulp w/orig face, 6" **185.00**
Jack-o'-lantern, pressed cb pulp w/orig face, 6½" **195.00**
Jack-o'-lantern, pressed cb pulp w/orig face, 7" **225.00**
Jack-o'-lantern, pressed cb pulp w/orig face, 8", minimum value ...**275.00**
Lantern, cat, pressed cb pulp w/orig face **245.00**
Lantern, cat (full body), pressed cb pulp, 7x6½" **350.00**
Lantern, cb w/tab sides, any **95.00**
Lantern, pumpkin man (full body), pressed cb pulp **350.00**
Plastic Halloween car...**250.00**
Plastic pumpkin stagecoach, witch & cat..**450.00**
Plastic witch holding blk cat w/wobbling head, 7" **150.00**
Plastic witch on rocket, upright, 7" **450.00**
Plastic witch on rocket, 4" **95.00**
Plastic witch on rocket, 5" **350.00**
Tambourine, tin litho/paper, Ohio Art, 1930s, 6" dia....................**75.00**
Tin noisemaker, bell style **38.00**
Tin noisemaker, can shaker **38.00**
Tin noisemaker, clicker..**35.00**

Tin noisemaker, fry pan style..55.00
Tin noisemaker, horn..55.00
Tin noisemaker, sq spinner 38.00
Tin noisemaker, tambourine, Chein 150.00
Tin noisemaker, tambourine, Kirkoff 95.00

Celluloid (German, Japanese, or American)

Blk cat, plain, M..150.00
Egg-shape house, M...400.00
Long-leg veggie rattle, M 300.00
Owl, plain, M 150.00
Owl on pumpkin, M..175.00
Owl on tree, M 200.00
Pumpkin-face man, M..350.00
Pumpkin-face pirate, M..400.00
Scarecrow, M 175.00
Witch, plain, M 300.00
Witch in auto, M...450.00
Witch in corncob car, M 500.00
Witch pulling cart w/ghost, M 400.00
Witch pulling pumpkin cart w/cat, M 400.00
Witch sitting on pumpkin, M 350.00

German

As a general rule, German Halloween collectibles date from 1900 through the early 1930s. They were made either of composition or molded cardboard, and their values are higher than American-made items. In the listings that follow, all candy containers are made of composition unless noted otherwise.

Candy container, anthropomorphic pear, composition, 3", $425.00; Pumpkin man, jointed bisque, 7", $825.00; Veggie man, composition, 5", $675.00.
(Photo courtesy Jennie Tarrant)

Candy container, blk cat walking, glass eyes, head removes, 3-4"...225.00
Candy container, blk cat walking, glass eyes, head removes, 5-6"...250.00
Candy container, cat, glass eyes, 4-6", from $250 to....................325.00
Candy container, cat, w/mohair, 5" 350.00
Candy container, cat, 3-5", from $175 to 285.00
Candy container, lemon-head man, pnt compo, 7" 575.00
Candy container, pumpkin-head man (or any vegetable), on box, 3"..175.00
Candy container, pumpkin-head man (or any vegetable), on box, 4"..185.00
Candy container, pumpkin-head man (or any vegetable), on box, 5"..225.00
Candy container, pumpkin-head man (or any vegetable), on box, 6"..275.00
Candy container, witch, pumpkin people, devil, ghost, etc, 3" ...225.00
Candy container, witch, pumpkin people, devil, ghost, etc, 4" ...300.00
Candy container, witch, pumpkin people, devil, ghost, etc, 5" ...325.00
Candy container, witch, pumpkin people, devil, ghost, etc, 6" ...375.00
Candy container, witch or pumpkin man, head removes, 4".......225.00
Candy container, witch or pumpkin man, head removes, 5".......250.00
Candy container, witch or pumpkin man, head removes, 6".......300.00
Candy container, witch or pumpkin man, head removes, 7".......350.00
Diecut, bat, emb cb, from $95 to 125.00
Diecut, cat, emb cb, from $55 to..95.00
Diecut, devil, emb cb, from $95 to 150.00
Diecut, jack-o'-lantern, emb cb...65.00
Diecut, pumpkin man or lady, emb cb, 7½" 125.00

Jack-o'-lantern, compo w/orig insert, 3" 225.00
Jack-o'-lantern, compo w/orig insert, 3½".............................250.00
Jack-o'-lantern, compo w/orig insert, 4" 250.00
Jack-o'-lantern, compo w/orig insert, 4½".............................275.00
Jack-o'-lantern, compo w/orig insert, 5" 350.00
Jack-o'-lantern, molded cb w/orig insert, 3" 110.00
Jack-o'-lantern, molded cb w/orig insert, 3½".......................120.00
Jack-o'-lantern, molded cb w/orig insert, 4" 155.00
Jack-o'-lantern, molded cb w/orig insert, 4½".......................165.00
Jack-o'-lantern, molded cb w/orig insert, 5" 200.00
Jack-o'-lantern, molded cb w/orig insert, 5½".......................225.00
Jack-o'-lantern, molded cb w/orig insert, 6" 275.00
Jack-o'-lantern, molded cb w/orig insert, 6½", minimum value ..300.00
Lantern, cat, cb, molded nose, bow under chin, 3-5", from $275 to..375.00
Lantern, cat, cb, simple rnd style..225.00
Lantern (ghost, skull, devil, witch, etc), molded cb, 3-4", minimum ..375.00
Lantern (ghost, skull, devil, witch, etc), molded cb, 5"+, minimum ...425.00
Lantern (skull, devil, witch, etc), compo, 3", minimum value 375.00
Lantern (skull, devil, witch, etc), compo, 4", minimum value 425.00
Lantern (skull, devil, witch, etc), compo, 5", minimum value 550.00
Noisemaker, cat (3-D) on wood rachet 150.00
Noisemaker, cb figure (flat) on rachet....................................125.00
Noisemaker, db paddle w/die-cut face.....................................95.00
Noisemaker, devil (3-D) on wood rachet 175.00
Noisemaker, pumpkin head (3-D) on wood rachet....................150.00
Noisemaker, tin frying pan paddle, 5" L 125.00
Noisemaker, tin horn, 3" 75.00
Noisemaker, veggie (3-D) horn (w/pnt face) 150.00
Noisemaker, veggie or fruit (3-D) horn (no face), ea...................65.00
Noisemaker, witch (3-D) on wood rachet 175.00
Noisemaker, wood & paper tambourine 250.00

Hampshire

The Hampshire Pottery Company was established in 1871 in Keene, New Hampshire, by James Scollay Taft. Their earliest products were redware and stoneware utility items such as jugs, churns, crocks, and flowerpots. In 1878 they produced majolica ware which met with such success that they began to experiment with the idea of manufacturing art pottery. By 1883 they had developed a Royal Worcester type of finish which they applied to vases, tea sets, powder boxes, and cookie jars. It was also utilized for souvenir items that were decorated with transfer designs prepared from photographic plates.

Cadmon Robertson, brother-in-law of Taft, joined the company in 1904 and was responsible for developing their famous matt glazes. Colors included shades of green, brown, red, and blue. Early examples were of earthenware, but eventually the body was changed to semiporcelain. Some of his designs were marked with an M in a circle as a tribute to his wife, Emoretta. Robertson died in 1914, leaving a void impossible to fill. Taft sold the business in 1916 to George Morton, who continued to use the matt glazes that Robertson had developed. After a temporary halt in production during WWI, Morton returned to Keene and re-equipped the factory with the machinery needed to manufacture hotel china and floor tile. Because of the expense involved in transporting coal to fire the kilns, Morton found he could not compete with potteries of Ohio and New Jersey who were able to utilize locally available natural gas. He was forced to close the plant in 1923.

Interest is highest in examples with the monochrome glazes, and it is the glaze, not the size or form, that dictates value. The souvenir pieces are not particularly of high quality and tend to be passed over by today's collectors.

Bowl, bl mottle w/tooled leaves, #132, S, 2⅞x5⅞", EX 450.00

Bowl, gr, emb floral at shoulder, 5½"............................200.00
Bowl, gr matt, leaves, #132, 3x5¾", NM.......................275.00
Bowl vase, matt, cvd Greek Key rim band on gr, sgn, 6", NM 260.00
Candle holder, lav-pk matt sections over dove-gray, long stem, 5½"...450.00
Ewer, brn/gr/gunmetal, folded rim, loop hdl, 6" 150.00
Lamp, gr matt, cvd floral, wide/squat, +gr glass 6-panel shade.1,600.00
Lamp, gr matt, cvd water lilies, squat, 6-panel glass shade, 16" ..3,000.00
Lamp, gr matt, wide/squat w/panels in lower half, +15" ldgl shade ...1,400.00
Lamp base, gr matt, protruding neck, sticker/mk, 6½x9" 375.00
Pitcher, gr matt, curved hdl, spherical body on ped, 6" 250.00
Teapot, pk, Oriental floral, w/orig insert, 4½x8" 550.00
Tumbler, cerulean bl mottle/spatter, prof rstr, 7" 200.00
Vase, bl matt, vertical panels, 4¾" 260.00
Vase, bl/gr speckled, broad form w/vertical leaves, 8"...............1,300.00
Vase, blk matt w/lt irid, swollen form, 8" 450.00
Vase, brn matt, broad form, 9" 550.00
Vase, brn tones, leaves separated by stems & buds, 7" 500.00
Vase, bud; gr matt, sq panels, long neck, #155, 5" 300.00
Vase, cream to salmon pk matt w/brn mottling, #18-1, 5"...........400.00
Vase, deep cerulean bl, Grecian style, #120, 5" 425.00
Vase, gr matt, ears of corn, 6" 650.00
Vase, gr matt, geometrics, 2 cut-out hdls, cylindrical neck, 15"...1,800.00
Vase, gr matt, Greek Key, shouldered, #59, 5½x5¾"..............800.00
Vase, gr matt, squat/bulbous w/long trumpet neck, 4¼" 180.00
Vase, gr matt, tooled leaves/flower, 4½" 550.00
Vase, gr matt, vertical leaves, broad, #132, 3" 475.00
Vase, gr matt, vertical leaves alternate w/buds & stems, 7½"......850.00
Vase, gr matt, vertical ribs, 3½" 270.00
Vase, gr matt, 3 lg loop hdls w/emb notches, unmk, 5" 200.00
Vase, gr matt w/frothy wht, emb foliage, #52/2, 6¼x3½"............400.00
Vase, gr mottle, leather purse w/drawstring form, 11⅛".............550.00
Vase, gr mottle (experimental), vertical leaves, shouldered, 4¼"...375.00
Vase, gr to brn matt (experimental), wide leaves, 3¾" 650.00
Vase, gr/brn mottle, 6"...................400.00
Vase, lt bl mottle at shoulder on dk bl, 3x5½"...................550.00
Vase, mahog, integral hdls, 6" 190.00
Vase, oatmeal to mustard-yel matt, cylindrical, #131, 7½"..........650.00
Vase, suspended bl matt, emb geometrics, #59, 5" 400.00
Vase, volcanic-style matt, Earthen Gourd, #46, 3¾" 425.00
Vase, yel/gr mottled matt, leaves, 6¾" 600.00

Handel

Philip Handel was best known for the art glass lamps he produced at the turn of the century. His work is similar to the Tiffany lamps of the same era. Handel made gas and electric lamps with both leaded glass and reverse-painted shades. Chipped ice shades with a texture similar to overshot glass were also produced. Shades signed by artists such as Bailey, Palme, and Parlow are highly valued.

Teroma lamp shades were created from clear blown glass blanks that were painted on the interior (reverse painted), while Teroma art glass (the decorative vases, humidors, etc. in the Handel Ware line) is painted on the exterior. This type of glassware has a 'chipped ice' effect achieved by sand blasting and coating the surface with fish glue. The piece is kiln fired at 800 degrees F. The contraction of the glue during the cooling process gives the glass a frosted, textured effect. Some shades are sand-finished, adding texture and depth.

Both the glassware and chinaware decorated by Handel are rare and command high prices on today's market. Many of Handel's chinaware blanks were supplied by Limoges.

Key:
A/C — Arts & Crafts   chp — chipped/lightly sanded

Handel Ware

Fernery, spider mums on wht opal, ftd, 4x9" 1,800.00
Shade, Nouveau leaves/berries, gr/red on tan to yel, shouldered, 12" ...260.00
Vase, Teroma, mtn lake w/birch in foreground, sgn Broggi, 8x4"..1,200.00
Vase, Teroma, tree scene, Bedegie, 9½x5¼"...................1,600.00

Lamps

Table lamp, 8" slag glass shade w/cut-out floral design, marked; bronzed metal base with mushroom cutouts, original patina, 14", $4,750.00.

Boudoir, HP 8" winter scene sgn shade; bronzed trunk w/roots std, 14"..1,200.00
Boudoir, rvpt 7" roses shade #5609 w/emb weave (EX); trunk base, 15".1,900.00
Boudoir, rvpt 7" Venetian scene shade #6450 (EX); metal std, 15"...1,725.00
Boudoir, rvpt 7" wild roses #6452 shade; bulbous bronze base, 15"...1,750.00
Boudoir, rvpt 7½" meadow/butterfly #6560 shade; mk bronze std, 14"...2,185.00
Desk, chp gr-pnt 8" cylinder shade; bronze base, 14"...................1,150.00
Desk, etched brn #d shade w/gr highlights; metal std, 12x9½"...1,600.00
Desk, metal o/l gridwork & lyre 9" cylinder shade; fancy base, 14"........1,200.00
Desk, rvpt moon/forest cylinder shade #6577; coppery finish std, 13"...3,735.00
Desk, rvpt 8½" trees/lake cylinder shade, acanthus-band on base 3,500.00
Floor, art glass 14" shade w/pulled hearts; bronze std, 60" 950.00
Floor, chp 10" brn shade; bronze harp base, #6068½, 57", VG...2,600.00
Floor, gold w/platinum zig-zag Steuben 10" shade; bronzed std, 56"...3,750.00
Floor, ldgl 26" mottled gr shade; fluted bronzed metal base, 64" ...5,500.00
Hanging, 10x10" shade of ldgl sqs w/overhanging conical top, mts, 42"...800.00
Piano, rvpt floral shade; bronze std w/articulated arm, 14"...500.00
Shade only: gr ext simulating chipped ice, wht int, +brass ring, 10" 700.00
Student, dbl; chp 10" gr #6047 shades on wht; bronze std w/wide ft, EX ...2,760.00
Table, HP 14" #6585 ribbon/flower-band dome shade; metal std, 21"...1,800.00
Table, ldgl 18" roses shade w/leafy apron; quatrefoil base, 23"..11,165.00
Table, o/l 18" shade w/landscape panels; cut-bk floral on bronze std........5,000.00
Table, o/l 18" 8-panel bent-glass shade w/geometrics; Nouveau, 25".2,000.00
Table, pnt metal o/l 18" roses/lattice 8-panel shade; vasiform base..........4,500.00
Table, rvpt 15" #6391 ships at sea/palm trees shade; lobed/flared std.......9,500.00
Table, rvpt 15" red/gr thistles shade; ribbed bronzed base, 21½"..............8,000.00
Table, rvpt 15" Treasure Island shade #6391; fluted/flaring std, 24" 9,500.00
Table, rvpt 18" daffodil shade #5648; bronze shouldered base w/wide ft..7,475.00
Table, rvpt 18" ruins/palm trees #6825 shade; fluted urn std, 23".............8,500.00
Table, rvpt 18" shade #6636 w/mc floral band; EX bronze A/C base, 26"..12,000.00
Table, rvpt 18" sunset/palm trees sgn #6322 shade; tree-emb std, 23"..12,000.00
Table, rvpt 18" Treasure Island shade #6391A; fluted/flared sgn std........7,000.00
Table, rvpt/chp 14" shore/cabin shade #3075 (EX); metal std, 22"..........1,900.00
Table, rvpt/chp 18" rose-band shade; open 3-scroll bronzed std, 24" 7,500.00
Table, rvpt/chp 18" Treasure Island sgn shade #6391; lobed flared std.....12,000.00
Table, slag glass w/floral cutouts 8" shade, bronzed metal std, 14".......3,750.00
Table, slag glass 14" 4-panel shade (1 cut w/birds); rtcl #2175D std ..2,500.00

Harker

The Harker Pottery was established in East Liverpool, Ohio, in

1840. Their earliest products were yellow ware and Rockingham produced from local clay. After 1900 whiteware was made from imported materials. The plant eventually grew to be a large manufacturer of dinnerware and kitchenware, employing as many as three hundred people. It closed in 1972 after it was purchased by the Jeannette Glass Company. Perhaps their best-known lines were their Cameo wares, decorated with white silhouettes in a cameo effect on contrasting solid colors. Floral silhouettes are standard, but other designs were also used. Blue and pink are the most often found background hues; a few pieces are found in yellow. For further information we recommend *The Best of Collectible Dinnerware* by Jo Cunningham (Schiffer). Our advisor for this category is Ted Haun; he is listed in the Directory under Indiana.

Amy, rolling pin, from $70 to 80.00
Colonial Lady, sugar bowl, w/lid 32.00
Countryside, jug, Arches, w/lid, 5¾" 315.00
D'Ware, shakers, yel, pr 38.00
Dainty Flower, batter jug, powder bl, w/lid, 8½" 60.00
Dainty Flower, gravy boat 45.00
Dainty Flower, teapot, w/lid, 5½" 35.00
Deco Dahlia, casserole, dbl stacking; w/lid, 4½" 35.00
Ivy, pitcher, disc; w/lid 45.00
Mallow, pie plate, 10" 30.00
Mallow, refrigerator dish, w/lid, 5x4¼" 90.00
Mallow, rolling pin, 15" 185.00
Oriental Poppy, bowl, custard; 2½x4" 35.00
Oriental Poppy, casserole, w/lid, 2¾x6½" 55.00
Oriental Poppy, pitcher, Arches, 32-oz 105.00
Oriental Poppy, platter, meat; indents for drainage, 15¾x11¾" .210.00
Petit Point, bowl, batter; 9¾" 60.00
Petit Point, bowl, deep, 5½x12¼" 40.00
Petit Point, drip jar, w/lid, skyscraper style 30.00
Petit Point, rolling pin, 15¼", from $100 to 120.00
Petit Point, water jug, w/lid, 8¼", from $65 to 75.00
Red Apple I, plate, serving; 11" 35.00
Red Apple I, platter 35.00
Red Apple I, teapot, 6" 70.00
Red Apple II, bowl, vegetable; 8½" 30.00
Red Apple II, casserole, w/lid, 4x8½" 60.00
Red Apple II, drip jar, skyscraper style, 3x5x5" 40.00
Red Apple II, pitcher, w/lid, 10" 160.00
Red Apple II, plate, serving; sq, 10¾x12" 40.00
Red Apple II, plate, sq, 8¾" 50.00
Red Apple II, plate, 10¼" 30.00
Red Apple II, shakers, skyscraper style, 4¼", pr 50.00
Red Apple II, shakers, skyscraper style, 5", pr 60.00
Rockingham, mug, emb stag on side w/hound dog hdl, #1840, 5"..35.00
Ruffled Tulip, cheese plate, 11" 55.00
Ruffled Tulip, pie plate, 9¾" 40.00
Ruffled Tulip, pitcher, w/lid, 32-oz 70.00
Tea For Two, casserole, w/lid, 3½x8⅜" 55.00
White Rose, pitcher, bl, 7¾" 55.00
Wild Rose, teapot 70.00

Harlequin

Harlequin dinnerware, produced by the Homer Laughlin China Company of Newell, West Virginia, was introduced in 1938. It was a lightweight ware made in maroon, mauve blue, and spruce green, as well as all the Fiesta colors except ivory (see Fiesta). It was marketed exclusively by the Woolworth stores, who considered it to be their all-time bestseller. For this reason they contracted with Homer Laughlin to reissue Harlequin to commemorate their 100th anniversary in 1979.

Although three of the original glazes were used in the reissue, the few serving pieces that were made were restyled, and collectors found the new line to be no threat to their investments.

The Harlequin animals, including a fish, lamb, cat, penguin, duck, and donkey, were made during the early 1940s, also for the dime-store trade. Today these are very desirable to collectors of Homer Laughlin china.

In the listings that follow, use the values designated 'high' for all colors other than turquoise and yellow. Unless priced, for medium green, double the 'high' values on all items other than flat items and small bowls. *The Collector's Encyclopedia of Fiesta* (Collector Books, 2001 values) by Sharon and Bob Huxford contains a more thorough study of this subject and includes specific pricing for many medium green examples.

Pitcher, service water;
High, $105.00; Low,
$75.00.

Animals, maverick, gold trim..50.00
Animals, non-standard color..325.00
Animals, standard color 195.00
Ashtray, basketweave, high 60.00
Ashtray, basketweave, low 40.00
Ashtray, regular, high 53.00
Ashtray, regular, low 38.00
Ashtray/saucer, high 68.00
Ashtray/saucer, low 55.00
Bowl, '36s oatmeal; high 28.00
Bowl, '36s oatmeal; low 16.00
Bowl, '36s; high 40.00
Bowl, '36s; low 28.00
Bowl, cream soup; high 32.00
Bowl, cream soup; low 25.00
Bowl, cream soup; med gr, minimum value 900.00
Bowl, fruit; high, 5½" 11.00
Bowl, fruit; low, 5½" 8.00
Bowl, ind salad; high 42.00
Bowl, ind salad; low 28.00
Bowl, mixing; Kitchen Kraft, mauve bl, 8"...........................125.00
Bowl, mixing; Kitchen Kraft, red or lt gr, 6", ea 90.00
Bowl, mixing; Kitchen Kraft, yel, 10".....................................125.00
Bowl, nappy; high, 9" 40.00
Bowl, nappy; low, 9" 28.00
Bowl, oval baker, high 42.00
Bowl, oval baker, low 27.00
Butter dish, cobalt, ½-lb 300.00
Butter dish, high, ½-lb 135.00
Butter dish, low, ½-lb 115.00
Candle holders, high, pr 300.00
Candle holders, low, pr 250.00
Casserole, w/lid, high 160.00
Casserole, w/lid, low 95.00
Creamer, high lip, any color, ea 135.00
Creamer, ind; high 35.00
Creamer, ind; low 20.00
Creamer, novelty, high 42.00
Creamer, novelty, low 28.00
Creamer, regular, high 20.00
Creamer, regular, low 14.00

Cup, demitasse; high 110.00
Cup, demitasse; low 42.00
Cup, lg, any color, ea 185.00
Cup, tea; high 11.00
Cup, tea; low 9.00
Egg cup, dbl, high 28.00
Egg cup, dbl, low 20.00
Egg cup, single, high 35.00
Egg cup, single, low 25.00
Marmalade, high 265.00
Marmalade, low 225.00
Nut dish, basketweave, high 20.00
Nut dish, basketweave, low 15.00
Perfume bottle, any color, ea 140.00
Pitcher, 22-oz jug, high 70.00
Pitcher, 22-oz jug, low 50.00
Pitcher, 22-oz jug, med gr 800.00
Plate, deep; high 30.00
Plate, deep; low 20.00
Plate, deep; med gr 90.00
Plate, high, 6" 5.50
Plate, high, 7" 8.00
Plate, high, 9" 14.00
Plate, high, 10" 40.00
Plate, low, 6" 4.00
Plate, low, 7" 6.00
Plate, low, 9" 10.00
Plate, low, 10" 24.00
Platter, high, 11" 27.00
Platter, high, 13" 34.00
Platter, low, 11" 20.00
Platter, low, 13" 24.00
Platter, med gr, 11" 210.00
Platter, med gr, 13" 300.00
Relish tray, mixed colors 335.00
Sauce boat, high 35.00
Sauce boat, low 22.00
Saucer, demitasse; high 30.00
Saucer, demitasse; low 18.00
Saucer, demitasse; med gr, minimum value 175.00
Saucer, high 4.00
Saucer, low 2.00
Shakers, high, pr 26.00
Shakers, low, pr 18.00
Sugar bowl, w/lid, high 32.00
Sugar bowl, w/lid, low 20.00
Sugar bowl, w/lid, med gr, minimum value 135.00
Syrup, red or yel 250.00
Syrup, spruce gr or mauve 340.00
Teapot, high 155.00
Teapot, low 90.00
Tumbler, car decal 65.00
Tumbler, high 58.00
Tumbler, low 45.00

Hatpin Holders

Most hatpin holders were made from 1860 to 1920 to coincide with the period during which hatpins were popularly in vogue. The taller types were required to house the long hatpins necessary to secure the large hats that were in style from 1890 to 1914. They were usually porcelain, either decorated by hand or by transfer with florals or scenics, although some were clever figurals. Glass examples are

rare, and those of slag or carnival glass are especially valuable.

If you are interested in collecting or dealing in hatpins or hatpin holders, you will enjoy *Hatpins and Hatpin Holders* by Lillian Baker, with beautiful color illustrations and current market values. For information concerning the International Club for Collectors of Hatpins and Hatpin Holders, see the Clubs, Newsletters, and Catalogs section of the Directory. Our advisor for this category is Robert Larsen; he is listed in the Directory under Nebraska. (SASE required.)

Bsk, swan figural, Germany, ca 1900, 7¼x5" 185.00
Carnival glass, Grape & Cable, amethyst, Northwood, 7x2½" ...350.00
Carnival glass, Orange Tree, cobalt, Fenton 325.00
China, classical lady & peacock, Limoges, 7-hole, 3⅝" 225.00
China, Cockerel, I'll Take Care of the Pins, Longpark Torquay, 4¾" ...125.00
China, HP bl flowers on wht, Willets mk, 5⅛", NM 175.00
China, HP cottage scene, Royal Doulton, 5½" 295.00
China, HP flowers w/gold, RS Germany, NM 125.00
China, HP roses, scalloped base, Rosenthal, early 1900s, 6x2½" ...150.00
China, Ophelia portrait, Royal Doulton, 7-hole, 5x3½" 300.00
China, portrait tapestry, Royal Bayreuth, bl mk, 15-hole, 4½" ...525.00
China, strawberries on brick tower, Schafer & Vater mk, 5" 250.00
Chocolate glass, floral decor, ftd, ca 1905, 7⅞x2⅝" 500.00
Flow Blue, gold rim, 12-hole, 8-sided base, 5¼" 155.00

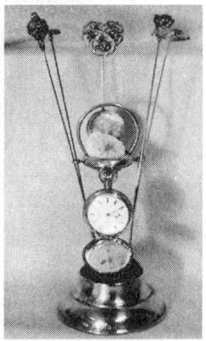

Combination hatpin holder with watch and compact, from $1,800.00 to $2,000.00. (From the collection of Robert V. Larsen)

Silver, parrot on perch, English hallmks, 1911, 4" 195.00
Silver, Scottish thistle motif w/amber glass head, Sterling, ca 1906 ....195.00
Silver, 9-section ring, loop top, cushion base, England, ca 1913, 5"....195.00
Silver base & velvet cushion w/2 ring holders, Derby Silver, 6½" ...85.00
SP, flowers & scrolls, Meriden/Wilcox Quadruple Plate, 5¾" 165.00
Wht metal, Kewpie w/umbrella on floral base, mk Kewpie, 3½" ...175.00

Hatpins

A hatpin was used to securely fasten a hat to the hair and head of the wearer. Hatpins, measuring from 4" to 12" in length, were worn from approximately 1850 to 1920. During the Art Deco period, hatpins became ornaments rather than the decorative functional jewels that they had been. The hatpin period reached its zenith in 1913 just prior to World War I, which brought about a radical change in women's headdress and fashion. About that time, women began to scorn the bonnet and adopt 'the hat' as a symbol of their equality. The hatpin was made of every natural and manufactured element in a myriad of designs that challenge the imagination. They were contrived to serve every fashion need and complement the milliner's art. Collectors often concentrate on a specific type: hand-painted porcelains, sterling silver, commemoratives, sporting activities, carnival glass, Art Nouveau and/or Art Deco designs, Victorian gothics with mounted stones, exquisite rhinestones, engraved and brass-mounted escutcheon heads, gold and gems, or simply primitive types made in the Victorian parlor. Some collectors prefer the long pin-shanks while others select only those on tremblants or nodder-type pin-shanks.

If you are interested in collecting or dealing in hatpins, see the information in the Hatpin Holders introduction concerning a national collectors' club. For further study we recommend *Hatpins and Hatpin Holders* by Lillian Baker available at your local bookstore or from Collector Books. Our advisor for this category is Robert Larsen; he is listed in the Directory under Nebraska. (SASE required.)

Key: cab — cabochon

Brass Nouveau style w/4 topaz glass stones, 2¾" on 12" brass pin......**225.00**
Brass panels w/floral accents/topaz glass stone, 2", on 10" brass pin ..**245.00**

Bug hatpins (considered good luck in Victorian times), each from $450.00 to $600.00. (From the collection of Virginia Woodbury, president of the American Hatpin Society)

Cab-cut garnet, 1" overall head, atop 5½" gilt pin **165.00**
Ceramic HP scene in button-sleeve brass mt, 1913, 1½" on steel pin ...**160.00**
Faux sapphires & clear brilliants, ca 1895, 1½"x2" on 8" steel pin ...**175.00**
Horn butterfly w/mc stones/2 peacock eyes, 3⅜", on steel pin....**150.00**
Ivory, elephant on ball cvg, 1⅛", 7⅜" steel pin **175.00**
Molded plastic feather & flame w/molded/pnt bugle beads, 3¼", 1920s...**115.00**
Mosaic in brass button sleeve w/gold wire, 1870s, 1", on brass pin......**150.00**
Oxidized brass Nouveau 4-panel mt w/amethyst brilliant, 3", brass pin ...**175.00**
Oxidized silver alloy w/amethyst glass stones, 1½" on steel pin ..**150.00**
Peacock-eye glass, bezel-set in sterling cage, CH (Charles Horner) ..**185.00**
Porc, HP Victorian couple w/gold o/l, 1¾", 7½" gilt pin.............**225.00**
Porc ball w/ceramic transfer & gold o/l, ca 1895, 1¼", on steel pin ..**245.00**
Satsuma, HP birds & leaves, 1½", on 10½" steel pin **235.00**
Satsuma, HP Japanese women, gold beading, 1¾" on 10" pin **250.00**
Sterling Gibson Girl figural, ca 1900, ½x1¼" **150.00**
Sterling lady suffragette w/repousse, ½x1", on 8" steel pin..........**150.00**
Sterling Nouveau lady w/repousse, ca 1905, 1" on 8¾" steel pin...**140.00**
Sterling sweet pea form, 1¼", on 8" steel shank mk Delamothe.**140.00**
Vanity, red stone/rhinestones on brass mt, mirror, Pat Pend, 1½" ..**2,000.00**

Haviland

The Haviland China Company was organized in 1840 by David Haviland, a New York china importer. His search for a pure white, nonporous porcelain led him to Limoges, France, where natural deposits of suitable clay had already attracted numerous china manufacturers. The fine china he produced there was translucent and meticulously decorated, with each piece fired in an individual sagger.

It has been estimated that as many as 60,000 chinaware patterns were designed, each piece marked with one of several company backstamps. 'H. & Co.' was used until 1890 when a law was enacted making it necessary to include the country of origin. Various marks have been used since that time including 'Haviland, France'; 'Haviland & Co. Limoges'; and 'Decorated by Haviland & Co.' Various associations with family members over the years have resulted in changes in management as well as company name. In 1892 Theodore Haviland left the firm to start his own business. Some of his ware was marked 'Mont Mery.' Later logos included a horseshoe, a shield, and various uses of his initials and

name. In 1941 this branch moved to the United States. Wares produced here are marked 'Theodore Haviland, N.Y.' or 'Made In America.'

Though it is their dinnerware lines for which they are most famous, during the 1880s and 1890s they also made exquisite art pottery using a technique of underglaze slip decoration called Barbotine, which had been invented by Ernest Chaplet. In 1885 Haviland bought the formula and hired Chaplet to oversee its production. The technique involved mixing heavy white clay slip with pigments to produce a compound of the same consistency as oil paints. The finished product actually resembled oil paintings of the period, the texture achieved through the application of the heavy medium to the clay body in much the same manner as an artist would apply paint to his canvas. Primarily the body used with this method was a low-fired faience, though they also produced stoneware. Numbers in the listings below refer to pattern books by Arlene Schleiger. For further information we recommend Mary Frank Gaston's *Encyclopedia of Limoges Porcelain, Third Edition* (the first two editions are out of print), which offers examples and marks of the Haviland Company.

Bowl, brn flowers w/gold, H&Co, 1880s, 12x8", from $75 to........**95.00**
Bowl, leaf; garden theme w/brushed gold, fluted border, TR Davis, 12"..**7,000.00**
Cake plate, Dubarry, Dresden-type floral, Theodore, 10¾".........**175.00**
Chamber stick, Moss Rose, bl trim, ring hdl, H&Co, late 19th C...........**225.00**
Charger, Oriental scene in lg wht flower on turq w/gold, H&Co, 13¾".**700.00**
Coffeepot, mc floral, braided hdl & finial, H&Co, late 19th C, 9½".....**350.00**
Compote, flowers & berries w/gold, sgn Andrew, ftd, H&Co, 9x10" **750.00**
Cruets, co-joined ducks, Sandoz, Limoges, #33, 1917, 6½".........**225.00**
Cup & saucer, bl roses, Napkin Fold shape, H&Co, 1876-86, from $75 to...**90.00**
Cuspidor, roses on tinted bl w/gold, H&Co, 7x9", from $400 to ...**500.00**
Gravy boat, mc flowers w/gold, w/lid & tray, H&Co, from $145 to....**165.00**
Pitcher, penguin figural, Sandoz, Theodore Haviland, 7", from $500 to..**600.00**
Plate, game birds in brush, H&Co for Tynedale Co..., 9½".........**120.00**
Plate, hunting scene, monochrome, Napkin Fold shape, H&Co, 9½" sq....**275.00**
Plate, mc bouquets w/brushed gold, Theodore Haviland, 10", from $60 to...**75.00**
Plate, oyster; pk flowers, 5 shells, H&Co, late 19th C, 7¼"........**240.00**
Plate, pk roses w/gold beading, scalloped, H&Co, 10", from $40 to........**50.00**
Platter, wht w/gold trim, w/well, Theodore, 12x14½", from $300 to **350.00**
Sugar bowl, roses on pastel, 3 gold hdls, w/lid, H&Co, from $150 to...**170.00**
Tea set, floral transfer, Ivy mold, H&Co, 1865-75, 3-pc set **475.00**
Teapot, bird & leaves, Basket-Weave mold, H&Co, 6" L, from $245 to...**265.00**
Teapot, red roses/gold fleur-de-lis, bl trim, gold spout/etc, +cr/sug..........**250.00**
Vase, Morning Glory; gold trim, H&Co, 1850s, 6", from $1,000 to ...**1,200.00**
Vase, putti w/grapes, lion-face hdls, Limoges, 12⅞", NM.........**1,000.00**

Hawkes

Thomas Hawkes established his factory in Corning, New York, in 1880. He developed many beautiful patterns of cut glass, two of which were awarded the Grand Prize at the Paris Exposition in 1889. By the end of the century, his company was renowned for the finest in cut glass production. The company logo was a trefoil form enclosing a hawk in each of the two bottom lobes with a fleur-de-lis in the center. With the exception of some of the very early designs, all Hawkes was signed. (Our values are for signed pieces.)

Bottle, scent; amethyst w/cut floral scrolls, silver trim, ftd **150.00**
Bowl, Carnation, 2x7½"...**90.00**
Bowl, Chrysanthemum, 2¼x4½"...**200.00**
Candelabrum, raised center socket+2, all w/prisms, 15" **575.00**
Compote, Graphic, dandelions/foliage, sculptured disc ft, 5x12"...**175.00**
Compote, Verre de Soie w/floral eng, 5x7" **320.00**
Cruet, Cyprus, faceted stopper, 6⅝" **180.00**
Frame, floral cuttings in border, 6½x5" **175.00**

Plate, Gladys, 6" 70.00
Plate, Napoleon, 6" 360.00
Plate, Russian, 9¾" 130.00
Vase, allover floral/scrolls etched on crystal w/gr ft, fan form, 11" ..250.00
Vase, gr, etched floral, ftd fan shape, 7½" 100.00
Vase, 3 mallards/bands/puntys, ovoid, Hawkes Sterling ft, 9¾x7"...950.00

Head Vases

Vases modeled as heads of lovely ladies, delightful children, clowns, Madonnas — even some animals — were once popular as flower containers. Today they represent a growing area of collector interest. Most of them were imported from Japan, although some American potteries produced a few as well.

For more information, we recommend *Head Vases, Identification and Values*, by Kathleen Cole; and *The World of Head Vase Planters* by Mike Posgay and Ian Warner.

Baby, blond draped in bl blanket, Samson Import Co #5359, 1966, 7½"...65.00
Baby, blond draped in bl holding kitten, unmk, 6" 40.00
Baby, pk bonnet w/bl bow, pearl necklace, w/phone, Enesco #2185, 5"......45.00
Boy, blond dressed in bl & wht w/cap, Relpo #2010, 7" 70.00
Boy fireman, #5 on hat, Inarco label, 5" 75.00
Clown, red & wht hat, hand up, Napco #IH-2243, 6¼" 50.00
Clown, red conical hat, ruffled collar, Inarco, 7" 55.00
Clown, wht face w/red & blk, bald head, Inarco #E5071, 4½" 40.00
Girl, blond curls w/pk bow, gold & wht ruffled collar, Japan, 5½"....45.00
Girl, blond dressed in pk, holds gift, gold trim, Japan, 5½" 50.00
Girl, blond w/hands in prayerful pose, Inarco #E1579, 6"..............45.00
Girl, blond w/umbrella dressed in bl & wht, unmk, 4¼" 75.00
Girl, pigtails, yel scarf & bodice, Inarco #E2965, 7" 58.00
Girl, winking, bl hat, bl & wht bow at neck, unmk, 6" 50.00
Holy Mother & Child, pastels, unmk, 5½" 22.50
Jackie Kennedy Onassis, all wht, Inarco #E1853, 6½" 450.00
Lady, bl hat w/bow, gold lashes & jewelry, unmk, 4"....................25.00
Lady, blk hair, detailed dk eyes, gr bodice w/appl trim, unmk, 7¼"....50.00
Lady, blk/bodice, pearl necklace/earrings, hand up, Inarco #E190/L, 7"..125.00
Lady, blond, pearl earrings, gold trim, Napcoware #CF6060, 3½".35.00
Lady, blond in pk, hand up, Lefton's #2705, 6½" 75.00
Lady, blond ponytail, brn derby hat, pearls, hand up, unmk, 6½".60.00
Lady, blond ringlets, pearls, gr/wht bodice, hand up, Relpo #2055, 6"..140.00
Lady, blond ringlets, pearls, Inarco #E5623, 6½" 85.00
Lady, blond w/bl bow, pearls, yel bodice, hand up, Nancy Pew, 6".........125.00
Lady, blond w/bl bow in hair, bl & wht bodice, Inarco #E3663, 7½" 200.00
Lady, blond w/bow in hair, pearls, bl bodice, Napcoware #C8501, 8"...250.00
Lady, blond w/braid around head, pearls, Rubens #501, 1959, 6½"...50.00
Lady, blond w/Elizabethan collar, porc, unmk, 6"..........................80.00
Lady, blond w/flower in hair, pearls, wht gloved hand up, unmk, 7"...125.00
Lady, blond w/gold lashes, bl bodice, Japan, 6½" 65.00
Lady, blond w/heavy lashes, flowers on shoulder, Napcoware #C6431, 6"....50.00
Lady, blond w/pearl earrings, flowers at neck, Napcoware #C6427, 5"...55.00
Lady, blond w/pearls, gr & wht hat & bodice, hand up, Rubens #476, 5"...45.00
Lady, blond w/pearls, gr bodice, Parma #A219, 8½"....................300.00
Lady, blond w/pk hat, pearl earrings, hand up, Vcagco, 5½".........75.00
Lady, blond w/pk tam, wht gloved hand up, Relpo #K1964/S, 5½"...150.00
Lady, blond w/rose in hair, hand up, Inarco #E480, 1961, 3½" 40.00
Lady, blond w/side-swept hair, pearls, Lark label, 5" 85.00
Lady, brn flip, gloved hand up, Lefton's #624, 6½" 65.00
Lady, brn hair, flat-rim hat, yel bodice, unmk, 6"..........................45.00
Lady, brn hair, flat-rim hat w/flowers, pearls, Napco #C4556C, 6¼"....75.00
Lady, brn streaky hair, blk bodice, Napcoware #C7313, 4½" 30.00
Lady, flower in brn hair, print bodice, Relpo #K936B, 6" 55.00
Lady, flower on hat, strapless bodice, hands up, Lefton's #2900, 6" 85.00

Lady, flowered pillbox hat, gloved hands up, Relpo, #A1373S, 4½" ..45.00

Lady, frosted hair, pearl earrings and four-strand necklace, black scalloped bodice, Inarco #E2966, 11", $150.00.

Lady, frosted hair, lg hat, pearls, Napcoware #C7494, 6" 75.00
Lady, hat w/bow at chin, pearl necklace, gr bodice, unmk, 5½"....60.00
Lady, hat w/bow in front, pearls, pk bodice, Enesco label, 5" 90.00
Lady, lg flower at right temple, pearls, Napco #C3141A, 1958, 6½"...125.00
Lady, lt brn ringlets, bl hat, thick blk lashes, Japan, 6¼"...............55.00
Lady, pale bl overall w/gold trim, hand up, Japan, 6½"..................45.00
Lady, peek-a-boo bang, pearl necklace, hand up, Inarco #E2104, 7"....350.00
Lady, scarf covers hair, hand up, blk lashes, Inarco #E1904, 6½"...250.00
Lady, side-swept hair, gold lashes, yel bodice, Velco #10759, 5½"....75.00
Lady, side-swept hair, pearls, ruffled bodice, #3854, 6½".............150.00
Lady, wht hair, pk hat, bl & wht bodice w/flower, Margo, 6" 50.00
Lady, wht hat, blond curls, 1 pearl earring, Relpo #K1836, 7" 350.00
Lady, wht hat w/gold band, pearls, wht floral bodice, unmk, 5" 40.00
Lady, wht ringlets, ruffled sq neckline, Napco #C5708, 1962, 6"...200.00
Lady, wht w/gold trim, mk Glamour Girl, 6½"...........................20.00
Nun, prayerful pose w/hands crossed, thick lashes, Relpo, 6½".....35.00
Nun w/hymn book, Inarco #E188/M, 1961, 6" 4,250.00
Oriental lady, Japanese headdress, gold trim, #3237, 7½".............50.00
Oriental lady, ornate headdress & bodice, unmk, 8½" 125.00
Teen girl, blond braids, flat pk bow, #4796, 5¾" 50.00
Teen girl, blond w/bl head band & bodice, Inarco #E2967, 5½"...80.00
Teen girl, blond w/orange hair bows, pearl earrings, Relpo #2004, 7"....200.00
Teen girl, brunette w/yel hair bow, flower at shoulder, Enesco, 5½" ..50.00

Heisey

A.H. Heisey began his long career at the King Glass Company of Pittsburgh. He later joined the Ripley Glass Company which soon became Geo. Duncan and Sons. After Duncan's death Heisey became half-owner in partnership with his brother-in-law, James Duncan. In 1895 he built his own factory in Newark, Ohio, initiating production in 1896 and continuing until Christmas of 1957. At that time Imperial Glass Corporation bought some of the molds. After 1968 they removed the old 'Diamond H' from any they put into use. In 1985 HCA purchased all of Imperial's Heisey molds with the exception of the Old Williamsburg line.

During their highly successful period of production, Heisey made fine handcrafted tableware with simple, yet graceful designs. Early pieces were not marked. After November 1901 the glassware was marked either with the 'Diamond H' or a paper label. Blown ware is often marked on the stem, never on the bowl or foot.

For more information we recommend *Collector's Encyclopedia of Heisey Glass, 1925 – 1938*, by Neila Bredehoft and *Heisey Glass, 1896 – 1957* by Neila and Tom Bredehoft.

For information concerning Heisey Collectors of America, see the Clubs, Newsletters, and Catalogs section of the Directory. See also Glass Animals.

Charter Oak, crystal, bowl, finger; #3362 ....10.00
Charter Oak, crystal, plate, salad; #1246 (Acorn & Leaves), 6" 5.00
Charter Oak, Flamingo, bowl, floral; #116 (oak leaf), 11" 45.00
Charter Oak, Hawthorne, stem, cocktail; #3362, 3-oz 45.00
Charter Oak, Hawthrone, candlestick, Tricorn, #129, 3-light, 5" ..140.00
Charter Oak, Marigold, tumbler, flat, #3362, 10-oz 30.00
Charter Oak, Moongleam, stem, parfait; #3362, 4½-oz 35.00
Chintz, crystal, bowl, mint; ftd, 6" 20.00
Chintz, crystal, creamer, ind 12.00
Chintz, crystal, oil, 4-oz 60.00
Chintz, crystal, stem, wine; #3389, 2½-oz 25.00
Chintz, crystal, tray, celery; 10" 15.00
Chintz, Sahara, bowl, cream soup 35.00
Chintz, Sahara, bowl, pickle & olive; 2-part, 13" 35.00
Chintz, Sahara, stem, claret; #3389, 4-oz 50.00
Chintz, Sahara, stem, water; #3389, 9-oz 35.00
Crystolite, crystal, bonbon, shell, 7" 22.00
Crystolite, crystal, bowl, gardenia; shallow, 12" 65.00
Crystolite, crystal, bowl, preserve; 5" 20.00
Crystolite, crystal, bowl, punch; 7½-qt 120.00
Crystolite, crystal, candlestick, 1-light, ftd 25.00
Crystolite, crystal, coaster, 4" 12.00
Crystolite, crystal, cup 22.00
Crystolite, crystal, ladle, punch; glass 35.00
Crystolite, crystal, plate, sandwich; 14" 55.00
Crystolite, crystal, plate, torte; 11" 40.00
Crystolite, crystal, sugar bowl, ind 20.00
Crystolite, crystal, tray, celery; rectangular, 12" 38.00
Empress, Alexandrite, bowl, cream soup 110.00
Empress, Alexandrite, bowl, nut; ind, dolphin ft 170.00
Empress, Alexandrite, plate, sq, 6" 40.00
Empress, Alexandrite, plate, sq, 10½" 335.00
Empress, Alexandrite, plate, 8" 75.00
Empress, cobalt, bowl, nappy, dolphin ft, 7½" 300.00
Empress, cobalt, plate, sq, 7" 60.00
Empress, Flamingo, ashtray 175.00
Empress, Flamingo, bowl, floral; flared, 9" 70.00
Empress, Flamingo, bowl, nappy, 8" 35.00
Empress, Flamingo, plate, 6" 11.00
Empress, Flamingo, platter, 14" 40.00
Empress, Flamingo, tray, celery; 13" 30.00
Empress, Moongleam, bowl, jelly; ftd, hdls, 6" 30.00
Empress, Moongleam, bowl, vegetable; oval, 10" 75.00
Empress, Moongleam, comport, oval, 7" 80.00
Empress, Moongleam, cup 35.00
Empress, Moongleam, saucer, rnd 15.00
Empress, Moongleam, tumbler, iced tea; ground bottom, 12-oz 75.00
Empress, Sahara, bonbon, 6" 25.00
Empress, Sahara, candlestick, dolphin ft, 6" 100.00

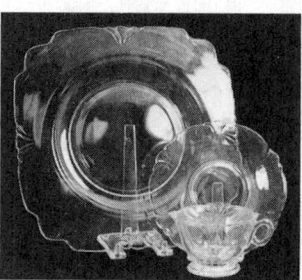

**Empress, Sahara, plate, dinner;
10½", $100.00; Matching cup
and saucer, $40.00.**

Greek Key, crystal, bowl, banana split; flat, 9" 45.00
Greek Key, crystal, bowl, finger 40.00

Greek Key, crystal, bowl, jelly; low ft, w/lid, 5" 110.00
Greek Key, crystal, bowl, orange; 12" 500.00
Greek Key, crystal, cheese & cracker set, 10" 150.00
Greek Key, crystal, creamer 50.00
Greek Key, crystal, egg cup, 5-oz 80.00
Greek Key, crystal, jar, celery; tall 140.00
Greek Key, crystal, plate, 5" 25.00
Greek Key, crystal, plate, 8" 70.00
Greek Key, crystal, stem, cocktail; 3-oz 50.00
Greek Key, crystal, stem, low ft, 9-oz 110.00
Greek Key, crystal, sugar bowl 50.00
Greek Key, crystal, tumbler, flared rim, 12-oz 100.00
Greek Key, crystal, tumbler, water; 5½-oz 50.00
Greek Key, crystal, water bottle 220.00
Ipswich, Alexandrite, stem, goblet; knob in stem, 10-oz 750.00
Ipswich, cobalt, candlestick, 1-light, 6" 400.00
Ipswich, crystal, bowl, floral; ftd, 11" 80.00
Ipswich, crystal, tumbler, soda; ftd, 12-oz 40.00
Ipswich, gr, stem, saucer champagne; knob in stem, 5-oz 70.00
Ipswich, pk, sugar bowl 70.00
Ipswich, Sahara, candy jar, w/lid, ½-lb 300.00
Lariat, crystal, ashtray, 4" 15.00
Lariat, crystal, basket, ftd, 10" 195.00
Lariat, crystal, bowl, mayonnaise; 2-part, 7" 24.00
Lariat, crystal, bowl, salad; 10½" 40.00
Lariat, crystal, candlestick, 2-light 40.00
Lariat, crystal, cheese dish, w/lid, 8" 60.00
Lariat, crystal, coaster, 4" 12.00
Lariat, crystal, creamer 20.00
Lariat, crystal, ice tub 75.00
Lariat, crystal, plate, cookie; 11" 35.00
Lariat, crystal, plate, deviled egg; oval, 15" 220.00
Lariat, crystal, plate, salad; 7" 14.00
Lariat, crystal, stem, wine; blown, 2½-oz 25.00
Lariat, crystal, sugar bowl 20.00
Lariat, crystal, tumbler, iced tea; ftd, 12-oz 28.00
Lariat, crystal, tumbler, juice; ftd, 5-oz 22.00
Lariat, crystal, vase, swung 135.00
Lodestar, Dawn, bowl, crimped, 11" 100.00
Lodestar, Dawn, bowl, sauce; #1626, 4½" 40.00
Lodestar, Dawn, candy jar, w/lid, 5" 135.00
Lodestar, Dawn, celery, 10" 60.00
Lodestar, Dawn, plate, 14" 90.00
Lodestar, Dawn, tumbler, juice; 6-oz 40.00
Minuet, crystal, bowl, finger; #3309 ....50.00
Minuet, crystal, bowl, pickle & olive; 13" 45.00
Minuet, crystal, bowl, salad dressing; 7" 40.00
Minuet, crystal, candlestick, #142 Cascade, 3-light 90.00
Minuet, crystal, cup 30.00
Minuet, crystal, plate, luncheon; 8" 30.00
Minuet, crystal, stem, wine; #5010, 2½-oz 50.00
Minuet, crystal, tumbler, water; #5010, low ft, 9-oz 35.00
New Era, crystal, ashtray or ind nut 50.00
New Era, crystal, cup 12.00
New Era, crystal, plate, 10x8" 42.50
New Era, crystal, stem, claret; 4-oz 20.00
New Era, crystal, stem, wine; 3-oz 30.00
New Era, crystal, tumbler, soda; ftd, 12-oz 15.00
Octagon, crystal, bonbon, #1229, sides up, 6" 10.00
Octagon, crystal, plate, 10½" 17.00
Octagon, Flamingo, bowl, mint; #1229, 6" 20.00
Octagon, Flamingo, Sahara or Moongleam, tray, #500, oblong, 6" ...15.00
Octagon, Flamingo, sugar bowl, #500 ....25.00
Octagon, Hawthorne, bowl, #500, 6" 35.00

Octagon, Hawthorne, plate, 6" 15.00
Octagon, Marigold, bowl, nut; ind, hdls 65.00
Octagon, Moongleam, ice tub, #500 ....80.00
Octagon, Sahara, bowl, vegetable; 9" 25.00
Octagon, Sahara or Moongleam, creamer, #500 ....35.00
Old Colony, Sahara, bouillon cup, hdls, ftd 25.00
Old Colony, Sahara, bowl, grapefruit; 6" 30.00
Old Colony, Sahara, bowl, salad; rnd, hdls, 10" ..60.00
Old Colony, Sahara, bowl, Triplex, 7" 35.00
Old Colony, Sahara, bowl, vegetable; oval, 10" 42.00
Old Colony, Sahara, comport, #3368, ftd, 7" 70.00
Old Colony, Sahara, cup 32.00
Old Colony, Sahara, plate, cream soup 12.00
Old Colony, Sahara, plate, rnd, 7" 20.00
Old Colony, Sahara, plate, sq, 10½" 70.00
Old Colony, Sahara, shakers, pr 125.00
Old Colony, Sahara, stem, champagne; #3380, 6-oz ..20.00
Old Colony, Sahara, stem, claret; #3380, 4-oz 30.00
Old Colony, Sahara, stem, cocktail; #3390, 3-oz ...20.00
Old Colony, Sahara, sugar bowl, ind 40.00
Old Colony, Sahara, tray, celery; 13" 40.00
Old Colony, Sahara, tumbler, bar; #3390, ftd, 2-oz ..20.00
Old Colony, Sahara, tumbler, iced tea; #3380, 12-oz ..22.00
Old Colony, Sahara, tumbler, juice; #3390, ftd, 5-oz ..20.00
Old Colony, Sahara, vase, ftd, 9" 150.00
Old Sandwich, cobalt, ashtray, ind 45.00
Old Sandwich, cobalt, stem, claret; 4-oz 150.00
Old Sandwich, crystal, beer mug, 14-oz 45.00
Old Sandwich, crystal, catsup bottle, w/#3 stopper ..70.00
Old Sandwich, crystal, cup 40.00
Old Sandwich, crystal, plate, sq, 8" 15.00
Old Sandwich, crystal, tumbler, iced tea; ftd, 12-oz ..20.00
Old Sandwich, Flamingo, candlestick, 6" 120.00
Old Sandwich, Flamingo, plate, sq, 7" 27.00
Old Sandwich, Flamingo or Sahara, parfait, 4½-oz ..50.00
Old Sandwich, Flamingo or Sahara, sundae, 6-oz 30.00
Old Sandwich, Flamingo or Sahara, tumbler, 10-oz ..40.00
Old Sandwich, Moongleam, bowl, floral; rnd, ftd, 11" ..100.00
Old Sandwich, Moongleam, creamer, oval 50.00
Old Sandwich, Moongleam, shakers, pr 85.00
Old Sandwich, Sahara, oil bottle, w/#85 stopper, 2½-oz ..140.00
Old Sandwich, Sahara, sugar bowl, oval 55.00
Old Sandwich, Sahara or Moongleam, bowl, finger ...60.00
Orchid, crystal, ashtray, 3" 30.00
Orchid, crystal, bell, dinner; #5022 or #5025 ....135.00
Orchid, crystal, bowl, deep salad; 10" 125.00
Orchid, crystal, bowl, finger; #3309 or #5025 .....92.50
Orchid, crystal, bowl, floral; 13" 115.00
Orchid, crystal, bowl, fruit or salad; ftd, 9" ...135.00
Orchid, crystal, bowl, gardenia; 13" 70.00
Orchid, crystal, bowl, jelly; Waverly, ftd, 6½-oz ..65.00
Orchid, crystal, bowl, nappy; Queen Ann, 8" 70.00
Orchid, crystal, bowl, relish; oblong, 3-part, 11" ..70.00
Orchid, crystal, bowl, salad; 7" 60.00

Orchid, crystal, candlestick, Trident, 2-light, 5" ..55.00
Orchid, crystal, candy dish, w/lid, bow-knot finial, 6" ..175.00
Orchid, crystal, cigarette holder, #4035 ....85.00
Orchid, crystal, comport, blown, 5½" 95.00
Orchid, crystal, creamer, ind 35.00
Orchid, crystal, marmalade, w/lid 235.00
Orchid, crystal, mayonnaise, ftd, 5½" 55.00
Orchid, crystal, plate, cheese & cracker; 14" 155.00
Orchid, crystal, plate, salad; 7" 22.00
Orchid, crystal, plate, sandwich; 11" 75.00
Orchid, crystal, shakers, pr 85.00
Orchid, crystal, stem, sherbet; #5022 or #5025, 6-oz ..25.00
Orchid, crystal, stem, wine; #5022 or #5025, 3-oz ..80.00
Orchid, crystal, sugar bowl, ftd 35.00
Orchid, crystal, vase, ftd, 7" 140.00
Plantation, crystal, bowl, celery; 13" 70.00
Plantation, crystal, bowl, dressing; 2-part, 8½" ..70.00
Plantation, crystal, bowl, jelly; flared, 6½" 60.00
Plantation, crystal, bowl, punch; Dr Johnson, 9-qt ..625.00
Plantation, crystal, butter dish, oblong, ¼-lb ...115.00
Plantation, crystal, candle block, 1-light 115.00
Plantation, crystal, cheese dish, w/lid, ftd, 5" ..90.00
Plantation, crystal, coaster, 4" 60.00
Plantation, crystal, cup 40.00
Plantation, crystal, marmalade, w/lid 190.00
Plantation, crystal, plate, salad; 7" 25.00
Plantation, crystal, plate, sandwich; 14" 120.00
Plantation, crystal, saucer 10.00
Plantation, crystal, stem, wine; blown, 3-oz 75.00
Plantation, crystal, sugar bowl, ftd 40.00
Plantation, crystal, tumbler, juice; ftd, blown, 5-oz ..40.00
Pleat & Panel, crystal, bowl, vegetable; oval, 9" ..12.50
Pleat & Panel, crystal, plate, dinner; 10¾" 15.00
Pleat & Panel, Flamingo, bowl, chow chow; 4" 11.00
Pleat & Panel, Flamingo, cup 15.00
Pleat & Panel, Flamingo, tumbler, iced tea; ground bottom, 12-oz ..25.00
Pleat & Panel, Moongleam, marmalade, 4¾" 35.00
Pleat & Panel, Moongleam, plate, bread; 7" 10.00
Pleat & Panel, Moongleam, tray, spice; compartments, 10" ..30.00
Provincial, crystal, ashtray, sq, 3" 12.50
Provincial, crystal, bottle, oil & vinegar 65.00
Provincial, crystal, bowl, gardenia; 13" 40.00
Provincial, crystal, bowl, nappy, 4½" 15.00
Provincial, crystal, cup, punch 10.00
Provincial, crystal, mustard 110.00
Provincial, crystal, plate, bread; 7" 10.00
Provincial, crystal, plate, torte; 14" 45.00
Provincial, crystal, stem, 10-oz 20.00
Provincial, crystal, vase, sweet pea; 6" 45.00
Provincial, Limelight Green, bonbon, upturned sides, hdls, 7" ..45.00
Provincial, Limelight Green, candy box, ftd, w/lid, 5½" ..550.00
Provincial, Limelight Green, creamer, ftd 95.00
Provincial, Limelight Green, tumbler, iced tea; ftd, 12-oz ..80.00
Provincial, Limelight Green, tumbler, juice; ftd, 5-oz ..60.00
Queen Ann, crystal, bonbon, 6" 12.00
Queen Ann, crystal, bowl, frappe; w/center 25.00
Queen Ann, crystal, bowl, vegetable; oval, 10" 30.00
Queen Ann, crystal, creamer, ind 20.00
Queen Ann, crystal, cup 15.00
Queen Ann, crystal, cup, AD 20.00
Queen Ann, crystal, plate, 4½" 5.00
Queen Ann, crystal, plate, 8" 9.00
Queen Ann, crystal, shakers, pr 50.00
Queen Ann, crystal, tray, celery; 13" 20.00

Orchid, crystal, butter dish, Cabochon, quarter pound, $335.00.
(Photo courtesy Gene Florence)

Ridgeleigh, crystal, ashtray, rnd, 4" 22.00
Ridgeleigh, crystal, bottle, cologne; 4-oz 130.00
Ridgeleigh, crystal, bowl, punch; 11" 200.00
Ridgeleigh, crystal, bowl, salad; 9" 40.00
Ridgeleigh, crystal, cup 16.00
Ridgeleigh, crystal, mustard, w/lid 80.00
Ridgeleigh, crystal, plate, rnd, 6" 12.00
Ridgeleigh, crystal, stem, cocktail; blown, 3½-oz 35.00
Ridgeleigh, crystal, stem, wine; pressed 40.00
Ridgeleigh, crystal, vase, 8" 75.00
Rose, crystal, bell, dinner; #5072 ....150.00
Rose, crystal, bowl, gardenia; Waverly, 10" 75.00
Rose, crystal, bowl, honey; Waverly, ftd, 7" 60.00
Rose, crystal, bowl, salad; Waverly, 9" 145.00
Rose, crystal, bowl, Waverly, oval, 4-ftd, 11" 150.00
Rose, crystal, chocolate, Waverly, w/lid, 5" 210.00
Rose, crystal, cocktail shaker, Cobel, #4225 ....245.00
Rose, crystal, ice tub, Waverly, hdls..........................475.00

Rose, crystal, pitcher, #4164, 73-ounce, $595.00. (Photo courtesy Gene Florence)

Rose, crystal, plate, salad; Waverly, 8" 30.00
Rose, crystal, stem, cocktail; #5072, 4-oz..................45.00
Rose, crystal, stem, water; #5072, 9-oz......................42.00
Rose, crystal, tray, celery; Waverly, 12"......................65.00
Rose, crystal, vase, #4198, 8" 195.00
Saturn, crystal, bowl, baked apple 25.00
Saturn, crystal, bowl, pickle; 7" 35.00
Saturn, crystal, creamer 25.00
Saturn, crystal, sugar bowl 25.00
Saturn, crystal, tumbler, 10-oz.....................................20.00
Saturn, Limelight Green, bowl, nappy; 5" 90.00
Saturn, Limelight Green, mayonnaise 80.00
Saturn, Limelight Green, plate, 6" 35.00
Stanhope, crystal, bowl, salad; 11" 90.00
Stanhope, crystal, plate, 7".......................................20.00
Stanhope, crystal, saucer 10.00
Stanhope, crystal, stem, goblet; #4083, 10-oz.............22.50
Stanhope, crystal, vase, ball, 7"................................100.00
Twist, Alexandrite, ice bucket 425.00
Twist, crystal, bowl, floral; 9" 25.00
Twist, crystal, sugar bowl, ind, unusual 30.00
Twist, Flamingo, bottle, French dressing.......................90.00
Twist, Flamingo, Marigold or Sahara, ice tub..............125.00
Twist, Flamingo, saucer...5.00
Twist, Flamingo or Moongleam, tray, celery; 10".........50.00
Twist, Marigold, claret, 4-oz..50.00
Twist, Marigold, plate, relish; 3-part, 13" 35.00
Twist, Moongleam, bowl, nut; ind.................................40.00
Twist, Moongleam or Marigold, stem, luncheon; 1-block stem, 9-oz..70.00
Twist, Moongleam or Sahara, plate, ground bottom, 8" 20.00
Victorian, crystal, bottle, oil; 3-oz................................65.00
Victorian, crystal, bowl, finger 25.00
Victorian, crystal, decanter, w/stopper, 32-oz..............70.00
Victorian, crystal, plate, sandwich; 13" 90.00

Victorian, crystal, stem, claret; 3-oz............................28.00
Victorian, crystal, tumbler, old-fashioned; 8-oz 35.00
Waverly, crystal, bowl, salad; 7" 20.00
Waverly, crystal, bowl, vegetable; 9" 35.00
Waverly, crystal, box, candy; w/bow-tie knob, 6" 45.00
Waverly, crystal, cup 14.00
Waverly, crystal, plate, sandwich; 11" 20.00
Waverly, crystal, vase, ftd, 7".......................................35.00
Yeoman, crystal, bowl, fruit; oval, 9" 20.00
Yeoman, crystal, plate, 7" 5.00
Yeoman, crystal, tray, celery; 13"..................................20.00
Yeoman, Flamingo, bowl, banana split; ftd....................23.00
Yeoman, Flamingo, comport, deep, low ft, 6" 30.00
Yeoman, Flamingo, saucer 5.00
Yeoman, Flamingo, tumbler, iced tea; 12-oz.................20.00
Yeoman, Hawthorne, bowl, vegetable; 6" 20.00
Yeoman, Hawthorne, platter, oval, 12" 33.00
Yeoman, Marigold, parfait, 5-oz 35.00
Yeoman, Marigold, plate, 6" 15.00
Yeoman, Moongleam, cup 25.00
Yeoman, Moongleam, tray, celery; 9" 15.00
Yeoman, Sahara, stem, oyster cocktail; ftd, 2¾-oz 10.00
Yeoman, Sahara, stem, 8-oz...18.00

Herend

Herend, Hungary, was the center of a thriving pottery industry as early as the mid-1800s. Decorative items as well as tablewares were made in keeping with the styles of the times. One of the factories located in this area was founded by Moritz Fisher, who often marked his wares with a cojoined MF. Items described in the following listings may be marked simply Herend, indicating the city, or with a manufacturer's backstamp.

Bonbonniere, cat finial, 8-sided, 2½x2½" 55.00
Bowl, lug soup; pk on wht w/rose finial, lug hdl, 3x4"+hdl 67.50
Box, potpourri; egg shape, castle mk, #5048-1, 3x4½" 70.00
Dessert set, pk floral on wht, cake plate+6 sm plates................165.00
Figurine, boy w/dog, Austrian attire, Deco era, 6¼" 165.00
Figurine, cat, bl & wht w/orange ball, 4½x5¼" 165.00
Figurine, rabbit sitting on leaves, #158, 1¾x3" 42.50
Platter, Queen Victoria, plants & butterflies, #1171, 1943, 14½" ...250.00
Teapot, pk floral w/gold, rose finial, 8x6¼" 295.00
Tray, flowers & butterflies, 9x7½"...85.00
Tray, pk floral on wht, pierced hdls, gold trim, 12½" 85.00
Tray, sweets; mixed flowers, 4-compartment, 1942, 6¾"...............95.00

Heubach

Gebruder Heubach is a German company that has been in operation since the 1800s, producing quality bisque figurines and novelty items. They are perhaps most famous for their doll heads and piano babies, most of which are marked with the circular rising sun device containing an 'H' superimposed over a 'C.' Items with arms and hands positioned away from the body are more valuable, and color of hair and intaglio eyes affect price as well. Our advisor for this category is Grace Ochsner; she is listed in the Directory under Illinois. See also Dolls, Heubach.

Baby, bl ribbon in blond curls, smiling mouth w/teeth, wht gown, 10"...700.00
Baby girl (nude) on knees, blond hair, 6½" 500.00
Baby in diaper & top hat, intaglio eyes, 1 arm extended, #876, 6"....475.00
Baby seated in pk dress, 5" 325.00
Baby sitting, detailed dress, intaglio eyes, 2 teeth, 8½", NM 375.00

Boy in dk bl sweater, tan pants, on tummy holding ball, 5" L.....**425.00**
Boy in gr knicker suit w/pocket linings trn out, 9" **525.00**
Boy in nightshirt w/pug dog, 7" **1,700.00**
Boy on sled, opens at waist (candy container), NM **450.00**
Child in bunny outfit by egg, 6x3¼" **625.00**
Dutch boy & girl stand bk to bk, unmk, 5¼x3"...........................**250.00**
Girl curtsying in nightie, roses at ft, sunburst mk, 11"................**475.00**
Girl in bunny costume before lg pk egg, eyes to side, 7½" **525.00**
Girl leaning on elbows, bust only, sunburst mk, 6" **400.00**
Girl sitting on stone wall, holding blanket, 9½"...........................**425.00**
Man & lady, fine pk attire w/gold trim, #62/#00, 14", pr............**775.00**
Pierrot, seated, 1 leg extended, Vera Bartels, ca 1920, 15¼x6½"...**550.00**
Santa sitting on log (candy container), bl intaglio eyes, 1910s, 8x6" ...**600.00**

Hickman, Royal Arden

Born in Willamette, Oregon, Royal A. Hickman was a genius in all aspects of design interpretation. Mr. Hickman's expertise can be seen in the designs of the lovely Heisey figurines, Kosta crystal, Bruce Fox aluminum, Three Crowns aluminum, Vernon Kilns, and Royal Haeger Pottery, as well as handcrafted silver, furniture, and paintings.

Hickman (as a designer), Harvey Hamilton (his son-in-law), and Frank Petty (also as a designer), all worked for Haeger potteries from 1939 through 1944. Hickman and his son-in-law left Haeger, moved to Tennessee in 1944 and started Royal Hickman Industries. Frank Petty left Haeger in 1938 and founded Petty Pottery in Louisiana. He returned to Haeger in 1940 and then joined Hickman and Hamilton in Tennessee.

The Petty glazes are fantastic! Watch for them. Frank Petty has really not received the recognition he truly deserves, as he was an extremely talented artist. Hickman noted this and was the one who started the practice of putting the Petty Glaze sticker on those designs.

Because Mr. Hickman moved around during much of his lifetime (as with all designers), his influence has been felt in all forms of the media. Designs from his independent companies include 'Royal Hickman Pottery and Lamps' (sold through Ceramic Arts Inc., of Chattanooga, Tennessee), 'Royal Hickman's Paris Ware,' 'Royal Hickman — Florida,' and 'California Designed by Royal Hickman.' The following listings will give examples of pieces bearing the various trademarks.

Our advisor for this category is Lanette Clarke; she is listed in the Directory under California. See also Garden City Pottery; Royal Haeger.

Bruce Fox Aluminum

Bowl, leaf shape, stem hdl, 8¾x16¼" **55.00**
Candle holders, triple; curved ribbon-like base, 5¾" high end, pr ..**100.00**
Candlesticks, daffodil blossom w/2 leaves, 10⅜x3", pr **110.00**
Tray, charging bull, SP-77, 9x14½" **110.00**
Tray, fish form, 22½x7" **85.00**
Tray, leaf form, long/slender, 4 cast ft, RH-5, 15½x6" **75.00**
Tray, leaf form, 5-lobe w/long stem (hdl), 5-ftd, 9½x11"+stem.....**80.00**
Tray, lobster, sgn Bruce For-RH #73, lg.......................................**85.00**
Tray, pineapple shape, leaf hdl, 13x6½" **32.00**
Tray, serving; banana-leaf shape, 5 petals, 21x9"..........................**65.00**
Tray, serving; basketweave w/maple-leaf edging, 8¾x15¾" **60.00**
Tray, wood w/aluminum fr & horse's head in center, 27½x18"......**75.00**
Tray, 2-acorn oak, 14½" **45.00**

California, Designed by Royal Hickman

Figurine, deer, apple gr w/wht spots, appl eyes, 15" **75.00**
Lamp base, flying geese, 17" **250.00**
Swan, red & blk highlights, #643, #17 ....**125.00**
Vase, fish on wave, brn w/frosty wht, orig label, 9" **157.50**

Royal Hickman — Guadalajara, Mexico

Vase, three dolphin figures, 14k gold decoration, gold tall crown signature label, 13", $300.00.
(Photo courtesy Doris Frizzell)

Tray, silver, banana-leaf hdls, 15" L **220.00**
Vase, classic ftd shape w/very ornate hdls, pk mottle, #342, 12" .**145.00**

Miscellaneous Signatures

Lamp base, Petty Crystal Glaze, mauve/purple/maroon, unmk, 14½" .**95.00**
Tray, 3 heart-shaped leaves, center blossom, SP metal, 3x8½"....**167.50**
Vase, angelfish, Royal Hickman Florida, #521, 9½" **75.00**
Vase, bl mottle, shouldered, Royal Hickman USA, #544, 11½" .**165.00**
Vase, crystal, sea horse figural, Royal Hickman USA, #468, 8".....**75.00**
Vase, dk red w/shades of gr, shouldered, USA mk, #202, 7½".....**275.00**
Vase, fish figural, Petty Crystal Glaze, #467 ....**75.00**
Vase, Fluted, dusty mauve w/seafoam gr drip, USA mk, 1940, 7"..**100.00**
Vase, Petty Crystal Glaze, bl & cream mottle, ftd, #458, USA mk, 8"..**75.00**
Vase, swan form, Petty Crystal Glaze, Royal Hickman USA #475, 16⅝" ...**125.00**

Higgins

Contemporary glass artists Frances and Michael Higgins designed high-quality glassware from the late 1940s until his death on February 13, 1999. (Frances continues with her staff.) Their designs were often created by fusing layers of glass together, though sometimes colored ground glass was used to 'paint' the decoration onto the surface. Molds were used, and through a process called 'slumping,' the glass was fired to a very high temperature, causing it to soften and take on the predetermined shape. Their work is ultramodern and is more readily found in metropolitan areas.

The earliest mark was an engraved signature on the bottom of the glass — either 'Frances Stewart Higgins' or 'Michael Higgins' or both, which was dropped in favor of just 'Higgins' with a raised 'Higgins Man.' From approximately 1957 to 1964, the Higgins signature was embossed in gold on the top. After 1964 the signature again appeared on the bottom and was engraved in the glass. Recent items produced at the Higgins studio in Riverside, Illinois, are marked 'Higgins' and dated (Higgins 99 for example). For more information we recommend *Higgins, Adventures in Glass*, by Donald-Brian Johnson and Leslie Pina (Schiffer). Our advisor is Dennis Hopp; he is listed in the Directory under Illinois.

Ashtray, birdcages, birds in reserves on red, molded to form, 8" L ..**160.00**
Ashtray, Deco abstract, orange/blk/gray/brn w/gold, 7x5".............**80.00**
Ashtray, fish, gr & bl on gray w/gold, free-form, 10x7"...............**100.00**
Ashtray, geometric, gr tones w/gold triangles & circles, 6" **82.50**
Ashtray, gr & gold radiant pattern, 7½" sq **260.00**
Ashtray, jewels, mc on smoke gray, much gold, 1⅛x8¼"...............**65.00**
Ashtray, keys, 4-color on smoke w/gold, 1x7x5" **45.00**
Ashtray, mc patches (mainly turq) w/gold, 10x7" **70.00**
Ashtray, peacock feathers, purple & bl w/gold spirals, 10x7" **110.00**
Ashtray, Siamese Purple, gr & bl spokes on purple, 7x10" **100.00**
Bowl, bl & gr stripes on purple, flared rim, 8"..............................**160.00**

Bowl, Deco-like pattern in turq/bl/lime gr/orange, 1½x5½" 82.50
Bowl, mc vertical ribs w/raised air bubbles, 15" 180.00
Bowl, pop-art flowers, orange/gr/bl, 3-part, 2x9" 160.00
Bowl, red & yel 'spindles' on turq, ruffled/crimped rim, 2½x12" ...215.00
Bowl & underplate, turq & orange woven look, 6⅜", 7⅜" 130.00
Box, purple wood base, glass mc geometric design top, 7½".......130.00
Box, red & gold geometric lid on clear base, 1⅛x7½x3¾" 350.00
Charger, Thistledown, 12⅛" 140.00
Dish, radiating yel/gr/blk bands w/gold spiraling, 1¼x10¼x13"..215.00
Figure, angel, muted shades except for pk face, gold trim, 11¾x5" ..135.00
Plaque, hen & chicks, clear 'chicken wire' bkground, 14x7".......335.00
Plaque, lg owl in rectangle, incised sgn, 5x9"..............................450.00
Plate, Classic Line, chartreuse or pk, 7½", pr...............................160.00
Plate, flowers, orange, wht & gold on speckled gold, 8½" 95.00
Plate, lt gr, controlled bubbles, sgn Glen Lukens, 14½" 210.00
Plate, mc scrolling abstract design, 7½" 125.00
Tray, abstract linear pattern w/mc dots & gold on clear, 15" dia.265.00
Tray, fused patches & gold work on bl, 14x10" 395.00
Tray, geometric, Mandarin Red, 14x6½" 72.50
Tray, gr & wht abstract w/gold spirals & rays, 3-compartment, 9½"...95.00
Tray, radiating pattern in bl & gr tones, 13½" sq..........................160.00
Tray, raised & scrolled design on purple, 10½" sq..........................100.00
Tray, turq & wht blotches w/blk lines, stickman mk, 10" sq........120.00
Vase, abstract linear pattern, yel & wht, wide flat rim, 3¾x4¾".....150.00
Vase, lime gr & wht stripes, rolled rim, appl drip on trunk, 7"....495.00

Historical Glass

Glassware commemorating particularly significant historical events became popular in the late 1800s. Bread trays were the most common form, but plates, mugs, pitchers, and other items were also pressed in clear as well as colored glass. It was sold in vast amounts at the 1876 Philadelphia Centennial Exposition by various manufacturers who exhibited their wares on the grounds. It remained popular well into the twentieth century.

In the listings that follow, L numbers refer to a book by Lindsey, a standard guide used by many collectors. Our advisor for this category is Darlene Yohe; she is listed in the Directory under Arkansas. See also Bread Plates; Pattern Glass.

Bottle, Century of Progress 1833-1933, skyscraper/cabin, 6x6" 38.00
Bowl, berry; Liberty Bell, sm 35.00
Bowl, berry; Lindbergh, sm..15.00
Bowl, Industry, log cabin center w/cider bbl at right, 6½", NM..125.00
Bust, MJ Owens, frosted, 4¾" 138.00
Butter dish, Liberty Bell 165.00
Butter dish, Lincoln Drape...145.00
Butter dish, Log Cabin 325.00
Butter dish, US Grant, Patriot & Soldier 60.00
Butter dish, Washington Centennial 90.00
Celery vase, HMS Pinafore, Actress 170.00
Champagne, Washington Centennial......................................55.00
Compote, Actress, Jenny Lind 85.00
Compote, Lincoln Drape, w/lid, 8½".....................................175.00
Creamer or spooner, Washington Centennial 70.00
Egg cup, Lincoln Drape 50.00
Goblet, Liberty Bell, Gillinder, 1876, 6⅛x3½" 48.00
Goblet, Lincoln Drape, 2 szs, ea, from $125 to 165.00
Goblet, Philadelphia Centennial, 6¼x3" 65.00
Marmalade jar, Log Cabin, w/lid...325.00
Mug, Our Country's Martyrs, Lincoln & Garfield, 2⅝x2¼" 110.00
Mug, Protection & Plenty 50.00
Mug, Protection & Prosperity, Maj Wm McKinley below portrait, 3¼" ...75.00
Pickle dish, E Pluribus Unum & eagles, 5¾x10", NM 42.50
Pickle dish, US Grant, Patriot & Soldier 20.00
Pitcher, Lincoln Drape 400.00
Pitcher, Washington Centennial 155.00
Plate, Admiral Dewey, 7" 95.00
Plate, California (bears) Mid-Winter Fair, milk glass, 9½", NM...95.00
Plate, Egyptian Pyramids 125.00
Plate, flag w/eagles & fleur-de-lis border, milk glass, 7¼", NM 30.00
Plate, Garfield, 101 border, tab hdls, 9¾"..................................85.00
Plate, General Fitzhugh Lee transfer, 5½" 45.00
Plate, Last Supper 55.00
Plate, Liberty Bell, 100 Years Ago on rim, twig hdls, 8", NM 80.00
Plate, Lincoln Drape, 6" 100.00
Plate, Louisiana Purchase Exposition, 7½"..................................90.00
Plate, Old State House (Philadelphia) 85.00
Plate, Protection & Plenty, 8½" 65.00
Plate, Union, 5½"..60.00
Platter, HMS Pinafore, Actress 100.00
Salt cellar, Liberty Bell 40.00
Shaker, Washington Centennial...55.00
Spill, Lincoln Drape 60.00
Sugar bowl, Log Cabin 300.00
Sugar bowl, US Grant, Patriot & Soldier.....................................25.00
Tumbler, iced tea; Louisiana Purchase Exposition.........................35.00
Tumbler, Lincoln Drape..60.00
Wine, Washington Centennial 45.00

Hobbs, Brockunier & Co.

Hobbs and Brockunier's South Wheeling Glass Works was in operation during the last quarter of the nineteenth century. They are most famous for their peachblow, amberina, Daisy and Button, and Hobnail pattern glass. The mainstay of the operation, however, was druggist items and plain glassware — bowls, mugs, and simple footed pitchers with shell handles.

For further information we recommend *Hobbs, Brockunier & Co. Glass, Identification and Value Guide,* by Neila and Tom Bredehoft (Collector Books). See also Frances Ware.

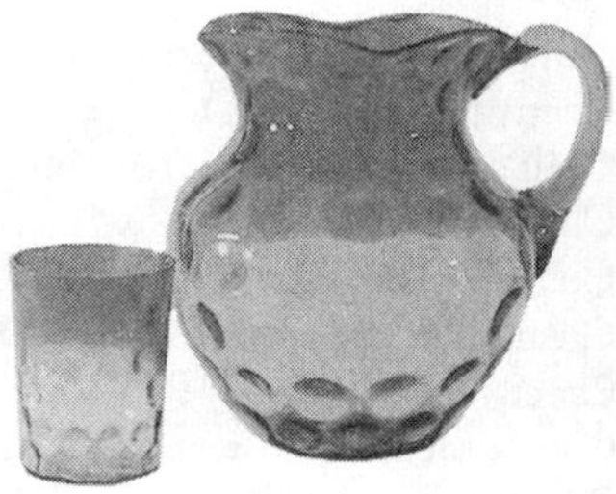

Tumbler, Polka Dot, ruby amber, #236, $70.00; Matching pitcher, #319, $400.00. (Photo courtesy Neila and Tom Bredehoft)

Bottle, bar; Marine Green, #76...225.00
Bowl, cranberry; Daisy & Button, canary 35.00
Bowl, Daisy & Button, crystal w/amber stain, 10"..........................70.00
Bowl, finger; Craquelle, amber, melon ribs 30.00
Bowl, finger; Spangled...220.00
Bowl, Windows, ruby opal, 4" 55.00
Canoe, Daisy & Button, sapphire 100.00
Celery vase, Murano, ruby alabaster, diagonal swirls, #20..............70.00
Cheese dish, Polka Dot, ruby, #101 ....240.00
Decanter, Spangled, horizontal swirls, bulbous w/flared rim, 8½" .75.00
Jug, Venetian, wht loopings w/bl threading, minimum value...1,800.00
Molasses can, Dew Drop, canary...375.00
Pickle jar, Dew Drop, sapphire, w/lid...175.00
Pitcher, tankard; Coin Spot, vaseline, 3-strand air-twist hdl, 8½" ...500.00

Sugar bowl, Craquelle, ruby, #216......................................**50.00**
Tumbler, champagne; Polka Dot, ruby amber, #247 ....**85.00**
Tumbler, Windows, sapphire opal **185.00**
Vase, Dew Drop, Marine Green, ruffled rim......................**165.00**
Vase, Spangled, ring neck, lg **400.00**

Holt Howard

Novelty ceramics marked Holt Howard were produced in Japan from the 1950s into the 1970s, and these have become quite collectible. They're not only marked, but most are dated as well. There are several lines to reassemble — the rooster, the white cat, figural banks, Christmas angels, and Santas, to name only a few — but the one that most Holt Howard collectors seem to gravitate toward is the pixie line. For more information see *Garage Sale and Flea Market Annual* (Collector Books).

Ashtray, golfer figural, 5½" **95.00**
Ashtray, Kozy Kitten on sq plaid base, 4 corner rests, $60 to **75.00**
Ashtray, old lady w/liquor bottle, skirt forms tray, ft show.............**40.00**
Ashtray, Rooster, open body w/rectangular opening, w/rest...........**15.00**
Ashtray, Santa in plane mk N Pole Jet stream, trays in wings, 6½"..**110.00**
Bank, Dandy Lion, bobbin' head, from $100 to **135.00**
Butter dish, Kozy Kitten peeking out on side, ¼-lb, rare.............**150.00**
Butter dish, Rooster, emb, ¼-lb, from $50 to **65.00**
Cake stand, musical: Jingle Bells, wht w/3-D holly leaves & berries..**85.00**
Candle holder, 2 stacking Santas, mk #6007, 8¼" **38.00**
Candle holders, bride & groom, 4", pr......................................**50.00**

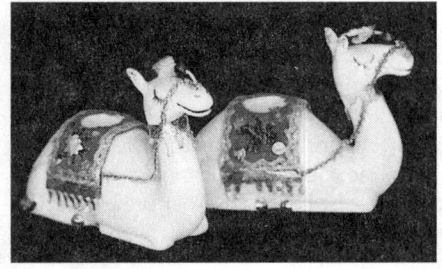

Candle holders, Christmas camels, pair, $20.00. (From the collection of Pat and Ann Duncan)

Candle huggers, figural snowmen w/Christmas tree hats/red scarfs, pr ..**35.00**
Cherry jar, Cherries If You Please on sign held by butler, minimum ...**250.00**
Chili sauce, Pixieware, rare, minimum value **400.00**
Christmas tree, electric, 10"......................................**70.00**
Coffeepot, Rooster, electric, from $60 to......................................**85.00**
Creamer & sugar bowl, Kozy Kitten, stackable, from $125 to **150.00**
Cruets, oil & vinegar; Pixieware, Sally & Sam, pr......................**275.00**
Cup & saucer, Rooster......................................**20.00**
Decanter, Whiskey, Pixieware, winking head stopper, minimum value ...**225.00**
Desk accessory, cat w/hole in head for pencil, wire bk for papers, 6" ..**40.00**
Figurines, Santas shaped as N, O, E & L, 3⅞", set of 4 ....**65.00**
Honey, Pixieware, very rare, from $400 to **500.00**
Italian dressing bottle, Pixieware, from $160 to......................**175.00**
Jam & jelly jar, Rooster, emb **60.00**
Ketchup jar, tomato-face finial w/leaf hair, 6" **60.00**
Lipstick holder, Ponytail Princess, from $50 to **65.00**
Match holder, pk mouse w/cane, unmk, 6"......................................**48.00**
Match holder, Santa w/bongo drum, 4½"......................................**30.00**
Mustard jar, Pixieware, yel head finial, from $75 to......................**100.00**
Mustard jar, Rooster, emb on front, w/lid **35.00**
Paper clip, pnt sq faces w/blk bk clip, rare, pr......................................**50.00**
Pitcher, Rooster, emb on front, indents for gripping, no hdl, tall ..**50.00**
Planter, angel w/hands in muff, silver trim, mk 1958, 4" **40.00**
Planter, bull, wht w/ring in nose **35.00**

Plate, Rooster, emb, 8½", from $20 to **25.00**
Powdered cleanser shaker, Kozy Kitten figural, w/broom, from $100 to..**125.00**
Punch bowl, holly sprig on wht, paneled, w/ladle & 8 cups **65.00**
Relish jar, Pixieware, gr flat head on lid......................................**200.00**
Shakers, goose & golden egg, pr......................................**40.00**
Shakers, Kozy Kitten head, 1 in plaid cap, pr, in wire fr **75.00**
Shakers, poodle & cat, 4½", 4", pr......................................**40.00**
Shakers, Rooster, figural, tall, pr, from $30 to **40.00**
Shakers, Santa & his bag, Santa: 3", pr......................................**35.00**
Shakers, Santa standing, 5½", pr......................................**18.00**
Shakers, tiger, big smile, 3½", pr......................................**25.00**
Spice set, Kozy Kitten, stacking, from $150 to......................................**175.00**
Spice Set, Pixieware, stacking, from $150 to **175.00**
String holder, Kozy Kitten, head only, from $50 to......................**60.00**
Super scooper, Hot Stuff, red & wht, w/lid, 6" **50.00**
Taper holder, elf in sleigh w/candy-cane runners, 'spaghetti' trim, 5" ..**28.00**
Tray, butler (Jeeves), 4¾" W......................................**150.00**
Tray, Rooster, facing left, from $15 to......................................**20.00**
Votive candle holder, pig, pastel, dtd 1958, 5½"......................................**45.00**
Votive candle holder, Santa, dtd 1968, 3" **20.00**
Wall pocket, Kozy Kitten, head only, from $60 to **75.00**

Homer Laughlin

The Homer Laughlin China Company of Newell, West Virginia, was founded in 1871. The superior dinnerware they displayed at the Centennial Exposition in Philadelphia in 1876 won the highest award of excellence. From that time to the present, they have continued to produce quality dinnerware and kitchenware, many lines of which are becoming very popular collectibles. Most of the dinnerware is marked with the name of the pattern and occasionally with the shape name as well. The 'HLC' trademark is usually followed by a number series, the first two digits of which indicate the year of its manufacture. For further information we recommend *The Collector's Encyclopedia of Fiesta, Ninth Edition,* by Sharon and Bob Huxford; *The Collector's Encyclopedia of Homer Laughlin China* by Joanne Jasper; and *Collector's Guide to Homer Laughlin's Virginia Rose* by Richard G. Racheter (all available from Collector Books) and *Homer Laughlin, A Giant Among Dishes,* by Jo Cunningham; and *Homer Laughlin China, Guide to Shapes and Patterns,* by Jo Cunningham and Darlene Nossaman (both by Schiffer). Our advisors for Virginia Rose are Jack and Treva Hamlin; they are listed in the Directory under Ohio.

Our values are base prices. Very desirable patterns on the shapes named in our listings may increase values by as much as 70%. See also Blue Willow; Fiesta; Harlequin; Riviera.

Debutante

Bowl, coupe soup; from $6 to **8.00**
Coffeepot, from $45 to......................................**55.00**
Creamer, from $10 to......................................**14.00**
Dish, 15", from $18 to......................................**25.00**
Egg cup, dbl; from $10 to **15.00**
Plate, 9", from $7 to......................................**8.00**
Teapot, from $35 to......................................**45.00**

Eggshell Georgian

Baker, 9", from $20 to......................................**26.00**
Creamer, from $15 to......................................**18.00**
Plate, sq, 8", from $12 to **15.00**
Plate, 8", from $10 to......................................**12.00**
Platter, 11", from $18 to......................................**26.00**
Saucer, cream soup; from $6 to......................................**8.00**

Teapot, from $55 to 95.00

Eggshell Nautilus

Baker, 10", from $22 to...26.00
Bowl, fruit; from $6 to 8.00
Bowl, onion soup (lug); from $12 to....................................16.00
Creamer, from $13 to...17.00
Cup & saucer, AD; from $20 to...26.00
Dish, 13", from $22 to...30.00
Plate, 8", from $8 to..10.00

Empress

Baker, 9", from $18 to..20.00
Bowl, cream soup; from $12 to..16.00
Bowl, nappy, 9", from $18 to...20.00
Cup, bouillon; 6-oz, from $10 to...14.00
Jug, 30s, 18-oz, from $30 to..35.00
Plate, deep; 7", from $8 to..10.00
Sauce boat, from $20 to...28.00
Teapot, from $75 to...95.00

Marigold

Bowl, deep, 6", from $12 to...14.00
Bowl, oatmeal; from $6 to..8.00
Dish, 13", from $25 to...35.00
Plate, sq, 8", from $12 to...15.00
Sauce boat, from $24 to...30.00
Teacup & saucer, from $11 to 15.00

Nautilus

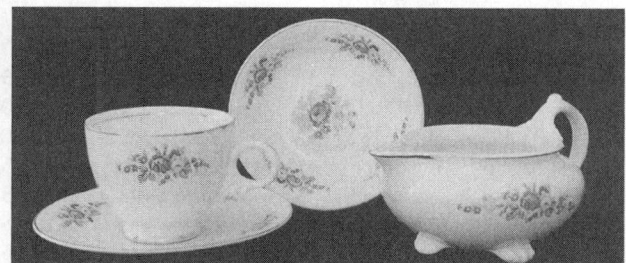

Bouquet pattern: Teacup and saucer, from $10.00 to $13.00; Plate, 6", from $5.00 to $7.00; Creamer, from $12.00 to $18.00. (Photo courtesy Joanne Jasper)

Bowl, deep, 5", from $8 to...12.00
Bowl, onion soup (lug); from $12 to......................................14.00
Coffee mug, Baltimore, from $18 to......................................25.00
Dish, 13½", from $18 to..26.00
Plate, 7", from $6 to..8.00
Sauce boat, fast stand, from $30 to.......................................35.00

Rhythm

Bowl, cereal/soup; 5½", from $7 to.......................................10.00
Cup & saucer, tea; from $9 to...12.00
Dish, 13½", from $18 to..24.00
Plate, 6", from $4 to..6.00
Plate, 9", from $7 to..10.00
Shakers (Swing), pr, from $15 to...20.00
Teapot, from $35 to...50.00

Swing

Bowl, nappy, from $22 to...28.00
Cup & saucer, tea; from $13 to..17.00
Muffin lid, from $45 to..75.00
Plate, deep (rim soup); from $10 to.......................................13.00
Platter, 11", from $20 to..26.00
Saucer, soup; from $8 to..10.00
Shakers, pr, from $15 to...35.00

Wells

Baker (oval bowl), 9", from $20 to...26.00
Bowl, cream soup; from $8 to...10.00
Bowl, fruit; from $5 to...7.00
Butter dish, from $75 to...85.00
Cup, coffee AD; from $20 to..28.00
Sugar bowl, w/lid, from $22 to...26.00
Teapot, from $75 to...125.00

Yellowstone

Baker (oval bowl), 5½", from $10 to......................................12.00
Butter dish, ind, from $4 to...6.00
Cup, coffee; AD, from $14 to...20.00
Jug, 30s, from $30 to...35.00
Plate, 5', from $4 to...6.00
Plate, 9', from $9 to...12.00
Sauce boat stand, from $6 to..8.00

Hull

The A.E. Hull Pottery was formed in 1905 in Zanesville, Ohio, and in the early years produced stoneware specialities. They expanded in 1907, adding a second plant and employing over two hundred workers. By 1920 they were manufacturing a full line of stoneware, art pottery with both airbrushed and blended glazes, florist pots, and gardenware. They also produced toilet ware and kitchen items with a white semi-porcelain body. Although these continued to be staple products, after the stock market crash of 1929, emphasis was shifted to tile production. By the mid-'30 interest in art pottery production was growing, and over the next fifteen years, several lines of matt pastel floral-decorated patterns were designed, consisting of vases, planters, baskets, ewers, and bowls in various sizes.

The Red Riding Hood cookie jar, patented in 1943, proved so successful that a whole line of figural kitchenware and novelty items was added. They continued to be produced well into the '50s. (See also Little Red Riding Hood.) Through the '40s their floral artware lines flooded the market, due to the restriction of foreign imports. Although best known for their pastel matt-glazed ware, some of the lines were high gloss. Rosella, glossy coral on a pink clay body, was produced for a short time only; and Magnolia, although offered in a matt glaze, was produced in gloss as well.

The plant was destroyed in 1950 by a flood which resulted in a devastating fire when the floodwater caused the kilns to explode. The company rebuilt and equipped their new factory with the most modern machinery. It was soon apparent that the matt glaze could not be duplicated through the more modern processes, however, and soon attention was concentrated on high-gloss artware lines such as Parchment and Pine and Ebb Tide. Figural planters and novelties, piggy banks, and dinnerware were produced in abundance in the late '50s and '60s. By the mid-'70s dinnerware and florist ware were the mainstay of their business. The firm discontinued operations in 1985.

Our advisor, Brenda Roberts, has compiled a lovely book, *The Collector's Encyclopedia of Hull Pottery,* with full-color photos and current values, available from Collector Books.

Special note to Hull collectors: reproductions are on the market in all categories of Hull pottery — matt florals, Red Riding Hood, and later lines including House 'n Garden dinnerware.

Blossom Flite, basket, #T-2, 6", from $55 to 80.00
Blossom Flite, candle holder, #T-11, 3", from $45 to 65.00
Bow-Knot, basket, ornate rim, bow on hdl, #B-29, 12", from $1,600 to...2,400.00
Bow-Knot, flowerpot, attached saucer, #B-6, 6½", from $225 to ...275.00
Bow-Knot, vase, bow at neck, bl to gr, #B-14, 12½", from $1,300 to...1,600.00
Bow-Knot, vase, cornucopia; pk to gr, #B-5, 7½", from $200 to .265.00
Bow-Knot, wall pocket, iron shape, unmk, 6¼", from $300 to ...385.00
Butterfly, ashtray, #B-3, 7", from $30 to..45.00
Butterfly, vase, 3-ftd, #B-10, 7", from $50 to....................................75.00
Calla Lily, vase, cornucopia; bl to wht, #570-33, 8", from $120 to...150.00
Calla Lily, vase, gr to pk, hdls, #540/33, 6", from $135 to 160.00
Camellia, basket, #107, 8", from $315 to 385.00
Camellia, hanging basket, #132, 7", from $260 to 325.00
Camellia, vase, lamp shape, #139, 10½", from $350 to 450.00
Camellia, vase, swan form, #118, 6½", from $165 to....................210.00
Capri, basket, #70, 6½", from $60 to..90.00
Cinderella Kitchenware (Blossom), creamer, #28, 4½", from $45 to .65.00
Cinderella Kitchenware (Blossom), sugar bowl, w/lid, #27, 4½"...65.00
Cinderella Kitchenware (Bouquet), pitcher, #22, 64-oz, from $175 to.230.00
Cinderella Kitchenware (Bouquet), pitcher, #29, 32-oz, from $60 to 85.00
Continental, basket, #55, bl & wht, 12¾", from $145 to...........215.00
Continental, candle holder/planter, unmk, 4", from $25 to...........35.00
Continental, planter, gr & wht, #41, 15½", from $25 to...............40.00
Continental, vase, bud; #66, 9½", from $30 to 40.00
Dogwood, ewer, pk to bl, #516, 11½", from $500 to....................625.00
Dogwood, teapot, #507, 6½", from $350 to 450.00
Dogwood, vase, cornucopia; yel to bl, #522, 3¾", from $95 to ...125.00
Dogwood, vase, pk to bl, ornate hdls, #510, 10½", from $290 to ..375.00
Early Art, jardiniere, stoneware, 1920s, 6½".................................125.00
Early Art, vase, emb rings, #39, 1920s, 8", from $115 to 150.00
Early Utility, pitcher, yel w/brn band, #107/30, 1920s, 4¾" 60.00
Early Utility, spice jar, gr, block H in dmn, 1920s, 3½", from $70 to 95.00
Early Utility, stein, American Legion, #498, 6½", from $70 to.....90.00
Ebb Tide, ashtray, from $125 to 165.00
Ebb Tide, basket, unmk, 6¼", from $125 to 165.00
Ebb Tide, vase, cornucopia; 11¾", from $90 to 145.00
Fiesta, flowerpot, blk, #40, 4¼", from $20 to 30.00
Fiesta, jardiniere, #43, 6", from $35 to..45.00
Fiesta, vase, cornucopia; #49, 8½", from $90 to...........................125.00
Fiesta, vase, #50, 9", from $70 to 95.00
Heritageware, mug, #A-8, 3¼", from $8 to 10.00
Heritageware, shaker, 3½", from $10 to..14.00
House 'n Garden Serving-Ware, butter dish, avocado, 7¾", $20 to........25.00
House 'n Garden Serving-Ware, canister set, brn, 6, 7, 8, 9", $350 to..450.00
House 'n Garden Serving-Ware, carafe, olive gr, 6½", from $30 to.........40.00
Imperial, Madonna, wht, #F-7, 7", from $30 to...............................40.00
Imperial, planter, praying hands, #F-475, 6", from $20 to.............30.00
Imperial, vase, urn form, blk, #454, 5", from $16 to.......................22.00
Iris, candle holder, pk to bl, hdls, #411, 5", from $120 to...........145.00
Iris, ewer, pk to bl, ornate hdl, #401, 13½", from $500 to...........575.00
Iris, rose bowl, yel, #412, 7", from $170 to 210.00
Iris, vase, yel, hdls, #403, 4¾", from $90 to 125.00
Iris, vase, yel to pk, hdls, #402, 7", from $160 to 200.00
Kitchenware (Crescent), bowl, #B-1, 9½", from $25 to 35.00
Kitchenware (Crescent), creamer, #B-15, 4¼", from $16 to 22.00
Kitchenware (Debonair), cookie jar, yel, #0-8, 8¾", from $70 to .95.00
Kitchenware (Floral), pitcher, #46, 6", from $40 to 55.00

Kitchenware (Floral), shaker, #44, 3½", from $15 to.....................20.00
Lusterware, candle holder, wht, unmk, 1928, 3", from $70 to 90.00
Magnolia, gloss; basket, #H-14, 10½", from $350 to 425.00
Magnolia, gloss; candle holder, #H-24, 4", from $40 to 60.00
Magnolia, gloss; ewer, #H-11, 8½", from $140 to...........................175.00
Magnolia, gloss; sugar bowl, #H-22, 3¾", from $40 to...................60.00
Magnolia, gloss; vase, #H-17, 12½", from $225 to.........................290.00
Magnolia, matt; basket, #10, 10½", from $350 to..........................410.00
Magnolia, matt; candle holder, #27, 4", from $55 to.......................75.00
Magnolia, matt; vase, dbl cornucopia; #6, 12", from $175 to 225.00
Magnolia, matt; vase, low hdls, #20, 15", from $425 to................515.00
Magnolia, matt; vase, open hdls, #21, 12½", from $370 to 470.00
Marcrest, ashtray, dk gr, 8½x4½", from $15 to 20.00
Marcrest, mug, 3¼", from $8 to 10.00
Marcrest, pitcher, 7½", from $40 to...55.00
Mardi Gras/Granada, bowl, mixing; pk, unmk, 1940, 10¼", from $40 to...55.00
Mardi Gras/Granada, ewer, wht to pale pk, #31, 10", from $145 to 175.00
Mardi Gras/Granada, vase, pk to bl, hdls, #48, 1947, 9", from $50 to...75.00
Mardi Gras/Granada, vase, wht, #216, 1947, 9", from $45 to........65.00
Mardi Gras/Granada, vase, wht, low hdls, #215, 1947, 9", from $45 to...65.00
Mayfair, wall pocket, mandolin, #84, 7", from $65 to 80.00

Mirror Brown, gingerbread man tray, $75.00.

Novelty, baby shoes, unmk, 3½", from $80 to.................................125.00
Novelty, Bandana Duck, #76, 3½x3½", from $30 to 40.00
Novelty, bear, wht, unmk, early to mid-1940s, 1½", from $70 to ..100.00
Novelty, piggy bank, solid-color satin, 1958, 3½".........................425.00
Novelty, planter, baby, #62, mid-1940s, 6¼", from $30 to............45.00
Novelty, planter, kitten, #61, mid-1940s, 7½", from $45 to...........75.00
Novelty, planter, parrot, #60, 6x9½", from $45 to 65.00
Novelty, planter, pheasant, #61, 6x8", from $45 to.........................65.00
Novelty, planter, pig, #60, mid-1940s, 5", from $30 to 45.00
Novelty, planter, poodle, #114, 8", from $45 to 65.00
Novelty, rooster, #951, early 1940s, 7", from $45 to......................75.00
Novelty, shrimp planter, yel, #201, 1940, 5½", from $30 to...........40.00
Orchid, bookends, #316, 7", pr, from $950 to.............................1,350.00
Orchid, jardiniere, bl, #317, 4¾", from $140 to 165.00
Parchment & Pine, basket, #S-8, 16½" L, from $175 to 225.00
Parchment & Pine, candle holder, unmk, 5" L, from $25 to 35.00
Parchment & Pine, vase, cornucopia; #S-2-R, 7¾", from $45 to .65.00
Poppy, basket, cream to pk, #601, 9", from $800 to..................1,100.00
Poppy, planter, ornate rim, #602, 6½", from $220 to....................270.00
Poppy, wall pocket, cornucopia form, pk to bl, #609, 9", from $325 to...425.00
Rainbow, leaf dish, 12¼", from $30 to...40.00
Regal, planter, #301, 3½", from $10 to..15.00
Rosella, ewer, all wht, #R-9, 6½", from $70 to 105.00
Rosella, ewer, pk & gr on wht, #R-7, 9½", from $1,200 to......1,500.00
Rosella, lamp base, #L 3, 1946, 11", from $350 to 475.00
Rosella, vase, #R-2, 5", from $70 to...95.00
Royal Ebb Tide, vase, spiraling shell shape, unmk, 10¾", $80 to...100.00
Royal Woodland, bowl, console; turq w/gray, #W-29, 14½", $75 to..115.00

Royal Woodland, vase, cornucopia; pk w/gray, #W-10, 11", from $60 to ..**75.00**
Serenade, candy dish, #S-3, 8¼", from $140 to **175.00**
Serenade, pitcher, #S-21, 10½", from $185 to **250.00**
Serenade, vase, #S-12, 14", from $130 to.................................**175.00**
Sueno Tulip, basket, bl, curvy hdl, #102-33, 6", from $300 to **395.00**
Sueno Tulip, vase, bl, hdls, #101-33, 9", from $300 to **340.00**
Sueno Tulip, vase, cream to bl, hdls, #106-33, 6", from $125 to .**145.00**
Sunglow, bowl, #50, 9½", from $35 to.....................................**45.00**
Sunglow, casserole, w/lid, #51, 7½", from $55 to **80.00**
Sunglow, flowerpot, #97, 5½", from $30 to **40.00**
Sunglow, pitcher, #52, 24-oz, from $40 to....................................**60.00**
Thistle, vase, pk, angle hdls, #52, 6½", from $130 to.................**150.00**
Tokay/Tuscany, ewer, #13, 12", from $240 to **295.00**
Tokay/Tuscany, vase, cornucopia; #10, 11", from $55 to...............**80.00**
Tokay/Tuscany, vase, urn form, #5, 5½", from $40 to **60.00**
Tropicana, basket, #55, 12¾", from $750 to.............................**850.00**
Tropicana, vase, #54, 12½", from $450 to................................**525.00**
Utility, bowl, Banded, bl & tan bands, unmk, 7", from $25 to......**40.00**
Water Lily, teapot, #L-18, 6", from $210 to..............................**265.00**
Water Lily, vase, dbl cornucopia; pk to bl, #L-27, 12", from $235 to ..**265.00**
Water Lily, vase, pk to bl, hdls, #L-A, 8½", from $165 to...........**185.00**
Water Lily, vase, rim-to-hip hdls, #L-16, 12½", from $355 to.....**455.00**
Wildflower, basket, pk to bl, #W-16, 10½", from $350 to **410.00**
Wildflower, ewer, yel to pk, high hdl, #W-19, 13½", from $440 to ..**520.00**
Wildflower, vase, pk to yel, hdls, #W-1, 5½", from $45 to **65.00**
Wildflower, vase, pk to yel to bl, hdls, #W-17, 12½", from $265 to ..**310.00**
Wildflower (≠ series), bowl, console; pk, #70, 12", from $375 to .**475.00**
Wildflower (# series), vase, cornucopia; pk, #58, 6¼", from $165 to.......**215.00**
Woodland, matt (post-1950); basket, 2-tone, #W-22, 10½", $235 to.....**280.00**
Woodland, matt (post-1950); vase, 2-tone, hdls, #W-16, 8½", $195 to..**275.00**
Woodland, matt; candle holder, #W-30, 3½", from $130 to **165.00**
Woodland, matt; ewer, ornate hdl, #W-6, 6½", from $165 to.....**215.00**
Woodland, matt; vase, cornucopia; #W-1, 5½", from $75 to **100.00**
Woodland, matt; vase, low twig hdls, #W-16, 8½", from $195 to **275.00**

Hummel

Hummel figurines were created through the artistry of Berta Hummel, a Franciscan nun called Sister M. Innocentia. The first figures were made about 1935 by Franz Goebel of Goebel Art Inc., Rodental, West Germany. Plates, plaques, and candy dishes are also produced, and the older, discontinued editions are highly sought collectibles. Generally speaking, an issue can be dated by the trademark. The first Hummels, from 1935 to 1949, were either incised or stamped with the 'Crown WG' mark. The 'Full Bee in V' mark was employed with minor variations until 1959. At that time the bee was stylized and represented by a solid disk with angled symetrical wings completely contained within the confines of the 'V.' The Three-Line mark, 1964 – 1972, utilized the stylized bee and included a three-line arrangement, 'c by W. Goebel, W. Germany.' Another change in 1972 saw the 'Stylized Bee in V' suspended between the vertical bars of the 'b' and 'l' of a printed 'Goebel, West Germany.' Collectors refer to this mark as the 'Last Bee' or 'Goebel Bee.' The mark in use from 1979 to 1990 omits the 'bee in V.' The New Crown mark, in use from 1991 to 1999 is a small crown with 'WG' initials, a large 'Goebel,' and a small 'Germany' signifying a united Germany. The current Millennium Mark came into use in the year 2000 and features a large bee. For further study we recommend *Hummel, An Illustrated Handbook and Price Guide*, by Ken Armke; *Hummel Figurines and Plates, A Collector's Identification and Value Guide*, by Carl Luckey; *The No. 1 Price Guide to M.I. Hummel* by Robert L. Miller; and *The Fascinating World of M.I. Hummel* by Goebel. These books are available through your local book dealer. See also Limited Edition Plates.

Key:
ce — closed edition	MM — Millennium Mark
CM — Crown Mark	NC — New Crown Mark
cn — closed number	oe — open edition
FB — Full Bee	SB — Stylized Bee
LB — Last Bee	tw — temporarily withdrawn
MB — Missing Bee	3L — Three-Line mark

#II/111, Wayside Harmony, table lamp, CM, ce, 7½" **430.00**
#II/112, Just Resting, table lamp, CM, ce, 7½" **430.00**
#III/110, Let's Sing, box, CM, ce, 6¼" **540.00**
#III/38/I, Angel, Joyous News w/Lute, candle holder, FB, ce, 2½" ..**180.00**
#III/57, Chick Girl, box, CM, ce, 6" **540.00**
#III/58, Playmates, box, MB, tw, 5½" **145.00**
#III/69, Happy Pastime, box, CM, ce, 6½" **540.00**
#1, Puppy Love, LB, ce, 5' **250.00**
#3/I, Book Worm, SB, ce, 5½" **340.00**
#5, Strolling Along, FB, ce, 5¼" **360.00**
#7/I, Merry Wanderer, 3L, ce, 7½" **360.00**
#9, Begging His Share, CM, ce, 5½" **540.00**
#11 2/0, Merry Wanderer, CM, ce, 4½" **325.00**
#12/I, Chimney Sweep, CM, ce, 6" **505.00**
#14 A&B, Book Worm, boy & girl, bookends, CM, ce, 5½", pr......**865.00**
#16 2/C, Little Hiker, FB, ce, 4" **180.00**
#18, Christ Child, SB, ce, 3¾x6½" **160.00**
#20, Prayer Before Battle, FB, ce, 4¼" **250.00**
#22/0, Angel w/Bird, font, CM, ce, 3x4" **180.00**
#24/I, Lullaby, candle holder, CM, ce, 3½x5" **395.00**
#26/0, Child Jesus, font, FB, ce, 2¾x5¼" **90.00**
#28/II, Wayside Devotion, CM, ce, 7".......................................**865.00**

#30/0 A&B, Ba-Bee-Ring, plaque, red rings, Crown Mark, small repairs, 4¾x5", $2,590.00.

#32/0, Little Gabriel, CM, ce, 5¼"..**325.00**
#34, Singing Lesson, ashtray, LB, ce, 3½" to 6¼"........................**135.00**
#36/0, Child w/Flowers, font, CM, ce, 3¼x4¼" **160.00**
#42/0, Good Shepherd, 3L, ce, 6½" **235.00**
#44/A, Culprits, table lamp, CM, ce, 8¾"..................................**360.00**
#46/I, Madonna w/o Halo, wht, FB, ce, 12" **120.00**
#48/V, Madonna, plaque, CM, ce, 8¾x10¾"..................**1,080.00**
#49/I, To Market, FB, ce, 6½"...**865.00**
#50/0, Volunteers, LB, ce, 5¾" **260.00**
#52/0, Going to Grandma's, 3L, ce, 4¾" **235.00**
#54, Silent Night, candle holder, SB, ce, 3½x4¾" **340.00**
#56, Culprits, CM, ce, 6½" **610.00**
#56/B, Out of Danger, SB, ce, 6½" **325.00**
#59, Skier, SB, ce, 5½" **235.00**
#6/I, Sensitive Hunter, FB, ce, 5¾"..**360.00**
#60 A&B, Farm Boy & Goose Girl, bookends, LB, ce, 4¾", pr.....**290.00**
#62, Happy Pastime, ashtray, CM, ce, 3½x6¼" **325.00**
#63, Singing Lesson, FB, ce, 3" **180.00**
#64, Shepherd's Boy, FB, ce, 5¾" **290.00**
#65/C, Farewell, FB, ce, 4" **4,320.00**
#67, Doll Mother, FB, ce, 4½" **290.00**
#69, Happy Pastime, CM, ce, 3½" **360.00**
#71, Stormy Weather, CM, ce, 6½" **790.00**
#72, Spring Cheer, FB, ce, 5¼" **235.00**
#73, Little Helper, FB, ce, 4½" **180.00**

#75, White Angel, font, FB, ce, 4" 90.00
#78/VIII, Blessed Child, FB, ce, 14" 360.00
#80, Little Scholar, SB, ce, 5½" 235.00
#82, School Boy, CM, ce, 5" 450.00
#84/V, Worship, FB, ce, 13" 1,080.00
#86, Happiness, FB, ce, 4¾" 180.00
#88, Heavenly Protection, SB, ce, 9" 790.00
#89/I, Little Cellist, 3L, ce, 5¾" 200.00
#91 A&B, Angels at Prayer, font, CM, ce, 3⅜x5", pr 290.00
#92, Merry Wanderer, plaque, SB, ce, 4½x5" 160.00
#94 3/0, Suprise, FB, ce, 4" 200.00
#96, Little Shopper, FB, ce, 4¾" 200.00
#97, Trumpet Boy, FB, ce, 4¾" 180.00
#99, Eventide, CM, ce, 4¼x5" 685.00
#100, Shrine, table lamp, CM, ce, 7½" 5,760.00
#109, Happy Traveler, SB, ce, 5" 160.00
#114, Let's Sing, ashtray, FB, ce, 3½x6¼" 180.00
#118, Little Thrifty, bank, FB, ce, 5¼" 290.00
#123, Max & Moritz, CM, ce, 5¼" 470.00
#124/0, Hello, SB, ce, 6" 250.00
#126, Retreat to Safety, plaque, 3L, ce, 4¾x4¾" 160.00
#128, Baker, LB, ce, 5" 175.00
#130, Duet, FB, ce, 5¼" 395.00
#131, Street Singer, SB, ce, 5¼" 215.00
#134, Quartet, plaque, FB, ce, 5½x6¼" 380.00
#136/I, Friends, SB, ce, 5¼" 235.00
#138, Tiny Baby in Crib, wall plaque, FB, cn, 2¼x3" 2,160.00
#140, The Mail Is Here, plaque, CM, ce, 4¼x6¾" 470.00
#142/X, Apple Tree Boy, FB, ce, 30" 18,720.00
#143/0, Boots, FB, ce, 5¼" 265.00
#145, Little Guardian, FB, ce, 4" 200.00
#146, Angel Duet, font, FB, ce, 3½x4¾" 90.00
#151, Madonna Holding Child, bl, FB, ce, 12½" 1,440.00
#152 B, Umbrella Girl, CM, ce, 8" 2,880.00
#154/0, Waiter, FB, ce, 6" 270.00
#163, Whitsuntide, FB, ce, 6¾" 610.00
#166, Boy w/Bird, ashtray, CM, ce, 3¼x6" 325.00
#167, Angel w/Bird, font, CM, ce, 3¼x4⅛" 180.00
#168, Standing Boy, wall plaque, FB, ce, 4⅛x5½" 395.00
#169, Bird Duet, SB, ce, 4" 150.00
#171 4/0, Little Sweeper, MB, ce, 3" 90.00
#173/0, Festival Harmony (flute), SB, ce, 8" 360.00
#174, She Loves Me, She Loves Me Not, CM, ce, 4¼" 395.00
#177, School Girls, FB, ce, 9½" 2,880.00
#179, Coquettes, CM, ce, 5¼" 575.00
#180, Tuneful Goodnight, wall plaque, FB, ce, 5x4¾" 290.00
#183, Forest Shrine, FB, ce, 9" 720.00
#185, Accordion Boy, CM, ce, 5½" 395.00
#187, MI Hummel Plaque (in English), CM, ce, 5½x4" 900.00
#188, Celestial Musician, SB, ce, 7" 305.00
#193, Angel Duet, candle holder, CM, ce, 5" 970.00
#195 2/0, Barnyard Hero, SB, ce, 4" 200.00
#196/0, Telling Her Secret, FB, ce, 5¼" 430.00
#197 2/0, Be Patient, LB, ce, 4½" 170.00
#199/0, Feeding Time, FB, ce, 4½" 290.00
#200/0, Little Goat Herder, LB, ce, 4½" 175.00
#201 2/0, Retreat to Safety, 3L, ce, 4" 195.00
#203 2/0, Signs of Spring, FB, ce, 4" 305.00
#205, MI Hummel Dealer's Plaque (in German), CM, ce, 5½x4¼" ..1,010.00
#207, Heavenly Angel, font, CM, ce, 3x5" 250.00
#217, Boy w/Toothache, FB, ce, 5½" 305.00
#218/0, Birthday Serenade, FB, ce, 5¼" 630.00
#219 2/0, Little Velma, FB, cn, 4" 2,880.00
#222, Madonna Plaque, metal fr, FB, ce, 4x5" 540.00
#224/I, Wayside Harmony, table lamp, FB, ce, 7½" 395.00
#226, The Mail Is Here, SB, ce, 4¼x6" 610.00
#227, She Loves Me, She Loves Me Not, table lamp, LB, ce, 7½" ..290.00
#230, Apple Tree Boy, table lamp, FB, ce, 7½" 650.00
#231, Birthday Serenade, table lamp, FB, ce, 9¾" 1,440.00
#235, Happy Days, table lamp, FB, ce, 7¾" 650.00
#238 A, Angel w/Lute, SB, ce, 2¼" 70.00
#239 A, Girl w/Nosegay, SB, ce, 3½" 110.00
#239 C, Boy w/Horse, 3L, ce, 3½" 60.00
#240, Little Drummer, SB, ce, 4" 175.00
#241, Angel Joyous News w/Lute, font, FB, cn, 3x4½" 1,080.00
#246, Holy Family, font, SB, ce, 3⅛x4½" 70.00
#248/0, Guardian Angel, font, SB, ce, 2⅜x5⅜" 145.00
#251 A&B, She Loves Me, She Loves Me Not, bookends, FB, ce, 5", pr ...395.00
#262, Heavenly Lullaby, 3L, ce, 3½x5" 470.00
#264, Heavenly Angel, annual plate, 1971, 3L, ce, 7½" 360.00
#266, Globe Trotter, annual plate, 1973, LB, ce, 7½" 110.00
#269, Apple Tree Girl, annual plate, 1976, LB, ce, 7½" 35.00
#278, Chick Girl, annual plate, 1985, MB, ce, 7½" 35.00
#301, Christmas Angel, MB, ce, 6" 210.00
#305, The Builder, SB, ce, 5½" 720.00
#307, Good Hunting, SB, ce, 5" 720.00
#308, Little Tailor, 3L, ce, rare, 5½" 720.00
#310, Searching Angel, wall plaque, LB, ce, 3¾" 215.00
#314, Confidentially, 3L, ce, 5½" 720.00
#317, Not For You, SB, ce, 5½" 540.00
#321, Wash Day, SB, ce, 5¾" 540.00
#322, Little Pharmacist, 3L, ce, 6" 230.00
#327, The Run-A-Way, 3L, ce, 5¼" 790.00
#328, Carnival, 3L, ce, 6" 200.00
#331, Crossroads, 3L, ce, 6¾" 540.00
#332, Soldier Boy, SB, ce, 6" 720.00
#334, Homeward Bound, 3L, ce, new style, 5¼" 340.00
#336, Close Harmony, SB, ce, 5½" 720.00
#338, Birthday Cake, candle holder, MB, ce, 3½" 120.00
#340, Letter to Santa Claus, 3L, ce, 7¼" 540.00
#342, Mischief Maker, 3L, ce, 5" 540.00
#344, Feathered Friends, 3L, ce, 4¾" 540.00
#346, The Smart Little Sister, SB, ce, 4¾" 720.00
#351, The Botanist, LB, ce, 4" 1,080.00
#353/I, Spring Dance, SB, ce, 6¾" 720.00
#360A, Boy & Girl, wall vase, SB, ce, 4½x6" 380.00
#363, Big Housecleaning, SB, ce, 4" 1,440.00
#369, Follow the Leader, 3L, ce, 7" 1,225.00
#371, Daddy's Girl, MB, ce, 4¾" 190.00
#374, Lost Stocking, 3L, ce, 4½" 720.00
#377, Bashful, LB, ce, 4¾" 175.00
#378, Easter Greetings, 3L, ce, 5" 720.00
#380, Daisies Don't Tell, LB, ce, 5" 720.00
#383, Going Home, LB, ce, 5" 1,440.00
#384, Easter Time, 3L, ce, 4" 720.00
#386, On Secret Path, 3L, ce, 5¼" 720.00
#388, Little Band, candle holder, 3L, ce, 3x4¾" 250.00
#390, Boy w/Accordion, 3L, ce, 2½" 125.00

Hutschenreuther

The Porcelain Factory C.M. Hutschenreuther operated in Bavaria from 1814 to 1969. After the death of the elder Hutschenreuther in 1845, his son Lorenz took over operations, continuing there until 1857 when he left to establish his own company in the nearby city of Selb. The original manufactory became a joint stock company in 1904, absorbing several other potteries. In 1969 both Hutschenreuther firms merged, and that company still operates in Selb. They have distributing centers in both France and the United States.

Bowl, vegetable; Fontainebleau, w/lid 230.00
Candle holders, nude boy w/holder on ea shoulder, US Zone, 8½", pr ...535.00
Charger, wild roses, artist sgn, etched gold border, hdls, 1915, 12" 250.00
Coffeepot, Empress, platinum trim..90.00
Coffeepot, Fontainebleau 200.00
Coffeepot, Viktoria 195.00
Cup & saucer, Coburg 135.00
Cup & saucer, Revere 87.00
Figurine, Borzoi dogs running, Lorenz, 12x13¾x3½" 525.00
Figurine, dancer w/mandolin, wht/bl/gold, ca 1925, 6¼" 240.00
Figurine, draped nude Deco lady on tiger, K Tutter, 14¾x22½" ...2,700.00
Figurine, Finale, dancer, pastels, K Tutter, 11⅛x11½" 475.00
Figurine, Frightened Horses, stallions (2), 11½x15x6" 925.00
Figurine, girl w/doe & flowers, mc pastels, 1920s, 9½x7" 485.00
Figurine, girls (3) clasp hands/dance in circle, mc pastels, 9x9½"....825.00
Figurine, golden retriever puppy, 2⅝".......................................120.00
Figurine, greyhound on plinth, head down, blanc-de-chine, 4¼x10"...295.00
Figurine, Mephistopheles, sinister face, in red & blk, 11½" 650.00
Figurine, Skye Terrier dog, HP, ca 1916-38, 5x5".....................215.00
Figurine, tabby cat, Achtziger stamp, 3½x6"..............................210.00
Figurine, whippet stands w/head up, brn spots, 5¼x6½" 275.00
Figurine, whippets at play, MH Fritz, ca 1916-38, 11x9½".........465.00
Plaque, Hunter's Assistant w/Pheasant, rich color, 15¾" sq........495.00
Plaque, Renaissance lady, ¾-portrait, Krause, 1900, 9x7", +fr.2,900.00
Plate, dessert Edgerton, much gold, 8¼" sq, 5 for 150.00
Platter, Fontainebleau, sm..120.00
Platter, Maple Leaf, med 138.00

Imari

Imari is a generic term which covers a broad family of wares. It was made in more than a dozen Japanese villages, but the name is that of the port from whence it was shipped to Europe. There are several types of Imari. The most common features a design with panels of birds, florals, or people surrounding a central basket of flowers. The colors used in this type are underglaze blue with overglaze red, gold, and green enamels. The Chinese also made Imari wares which differ from the Japanese type in several ways — the absence of spur marks, a thinner-type body, and a more consistent control of the blue. Imari-type wares were copied on the continent by Meissen and by English potters, among them Worcester, Derby, and Bow. Unless noted otherwise, our values are for Japanese ware.

Charger, floral arrangement center, wide pictorial ehon rim with cobalt and gold, floral and bamboo exterior, deep, eighteenth century, 18½", $1,500.00.

Bowl, geometrics, red/wht/gr w/cobalt & gold borders, 20th C, 5x12".300.00
Charger, floral panels, mc w/gold traces, 18½" 330.00
Charger, kyln medallion, people in scenic panels w/gold, 1890s, 18"..1,500.00
Charger, lg vase of flowers in center, panel/geometric rim, 15" ...140.00
Charger, pagoda/birds/dragons/etc (EX detail), red character mk, 16" ...220.00
Charger, scalloped rim w/geometric panels & flowers, 13" 440.00
Charger, scalloped rim w/4 lg floral reserves & red lattice, gilt, 12"...325.00
Charger, screen/lady, floral border, overglaze gold, sm rpr, 15½".220.00
Charger, 3 scenes in rim, center w/vase of flowers, appl gold, 19"...360.00
Charger, 6-part rim w/birds, flowers etc, pheasant in center, 18"......330.00
Jar, paneled sides w/gilt, dome lid w/dog finial, character mk, 8", pr.825.00
Plate, basket w/bonsai tree, sc w/canted corners, 10x10" 245.00
Platter, paneled rim, floral & gilt detail, 14½x12"......................165.00
Vase, bottle shape w/appl dragon (rpr), florals, 12"....................325.00
Vase, bud; floral, rnd ribbed body w/long thin neck, 8", pr 385.00

Imperial Glass Company

The Imperial Glass Company was organized in 1901 in Bellaire, Ohio, and started manufacturing glassware in 1904. Their early products were jelly glasses, hotel tumblers, etc., but by 1910 they were making a name for themselves by pressing quantities of carnival glass, the iridescent glassware that was popular during that time. In 1914 NuCut was introduced to imitate cut glass. The line was so popular that it was made in crystal and colors and was reintroduced as Collector's Crystal in the 1950s. From 1916 to 1920 they used the lustre process to make a line called Imperial Jewels. Free-Hand ware, art glass made entirely by hand using no molds, was made from 1922 to 1928.

The company entered bankruptcy in 1931 but was able to continue operations and reorganize as the Imperial Glass Corporation. In 1936 Imperial introduced the Candlewick line, for which it is best known. In the late thirties the Vintage Grape milk glass line was added, and in 1951 a major ad campaign was launched, making Imperial one of the leading milk glass manufacturers.

In 1940 Imperial bought the molds and assets of the Central Glass Works of Wheeling, West Virginia; in 1958 they acquired the molds of the Heisey Company and in 1960 the molds of the Cambridge Glass Company of Cambridge, Ohio. Imperial used these molds, and after 1951 they marked their glassware with an 'I' superimposed over the 'G' trademark. The company was bought by Lenox in 1973; subsequently an 'L' was added to the 'IG' mark. In 1981 Lenox sold Imperial to Arthur Lorch, a private investor (who modified the L by adding a line at the top angled to the left, giving rise to the 'ALIG' mark). He in turn sold the company to Robert F. Stahl, Jr., in 1982. Mr. Stahl filed for Chapter 11 to reorganize, but in mid-1984 liquidation was ordered, and all assets were sold. A few items that had been made in '84 were marked with an 'N' superimposed over the 'I' for 'New Imperial.'

For more information, we recommend *Imperial Glass Encyclopedia, Vols I, II,* and *III,* edited by James Measell; and *Imperial Carnival Glass* by Carl O. Burns.

Our advisor for this category is Kathy Doub; she is listed in the Directory under Maryland. See also Candlewick; Carnival Glass; Glass Animals and Figurines; Stretch Glass.

Ashtray, Cape Cod, crystal #160/134/1, 4" 14.00
Ashtray, heart shape, ruby slag, #294, 4½" 25.00
Baked apple, Cape Cod, ruby 25.00
Basket, Crocheted Crystal, 9" 45.00
Basket, Monticello, crystal 10"...20.00
Bottle, bitters; Reeded, any color, 3-oz 35.00
Bottle, cologne; Cape Cod, crystal, w/stopper, #1601 ....60.00
Bottle, condiment; Cape Cod, crystal, #160/224, 6-oz.................65.00
Bottle, cordial; Cape Cod, crystal, #160/256, 18-oz 90.00
Bowl, Amelia, Clambroth, sq, 5½"...25.00
Bowl, Atterbury Scroll, crystal, 3-toed 25.00
Bowl, Beaded Block, crystal, pk, gr or amber, rnd, flared, 7¼" 30.00

Bowl, Cape Cod, crystal, hdls, #160/51F, 6" 33.00
Bowl, Cape Cod, crystal, oval, divided, #160/125, 11" 80.00
Bowl, console; Crocheted Crystal, 11"...30.00
Bowl, console; Twisted Optic, amber, 10½".................................25.00
Bowl, cream soup, Twisted Optic, bl or yel, 4¾"........................25.00
Bowl, Dmn Quilt, blk, crimped, 7"...20.00
Bowl, finger; Mt Vernon, crystal, 5" 12.00
Bowl, Hobnail, purple slag, #641, 8½"..95.00
Bowl, Laced Edge, opal, 5½"...37.50
Bowl, Monticello, crystal, rnd, 7"...12.50
Bowl, nappy, Amelia, smoke, rnd, 6"..40.00
Bowl, nappy, Fancy Colonial, any color, 6".................................20.00
Bowl, nappy, Pansy, caramel slag, hdl, 5"....................................35.00
Bowl, Pipe, ruby slag, #1605, 7½"...40.00
Bowl, Rose, jade slag, #52c, 8"...65.00
Bowl, Rose, jade slag, #62c, 9"...75.00
Bowl, salad; Crocheted Crystal, 10½"...27.50
Bowl, salad; Twisted Optic, bl or yel, 9¼".....................................40.00
Bowl, soup; Katy, gr opal, 7"...80.00
Bowl, Twisted Optic, gr, crimped, 7"...20.00
Box, dog, purple slag, #822...185.00
Box, squirrel, purple slag, #821, 5½"...180.00
Butter dish, Cape Cod, crystal, #160/161, ¼-lb, w/lid 45.00
Butter dish, Fancy Colonial, any color, w/lid 75.00
Butter tub, Mt Vernon, crystal, 5"...15.00
Cake salver, Dmn Quilt, pk or gr, tall, 10" dia 60.00
Cake stand, Cape Cod, crystal, #160/103D, 11"..........................85.00
Cake stand, Crocheted Crystal, ftd, 12" 40.00
Candle holder, Cape Cod, crystal, #160/170, 3"..........................26.50

Candle holder, Crocheted Crystal, Laced Edge #78C, 2", $20.00. (Photo courtesy Gene Florence)

Candle holder, Crocheted Crystal, Narcissus bowl shape 25.00
Candlestick, Free-Hand, heart/vine, wht on clear, bl cup, 10"....400.00
Candlesticks, Dolphin, caramel slag, #779, 5", pr 65.00
Candy box, Reeded, any color, ftd, w/cone lid 50.00
Carafe, wine; Cape Cod, crystal, #160/185, 26-oz.......................195.00
Celery, Crocheted Crystal, oval, 10"...25.00
Celery, Flute & Cane, crystal, oval, 8½".......................................25.00
Celery tray, Huckabee, pk, oval, 8¼"..32.50
Champagne, Cape Cod, amber, #1602...18.00
Cigarette holder, Cape Cod, crystal, ftd, #1602 ....12.50
Claret, Cape Cod, Azalea, #1602...20.00
Claret, Cape Cod, crystal, #1602, 5-oz 12.00
Claret, Fancy Colonial, any color, deep, 5-oz...............................30.00
Coaster, Cape Cod, crystal, flat, #160/1R, 4½"...............................9.00
Coaster, Cape Cod, crystal, w/spoon rest, #160/76.......................10.00
Cocktail, Cape Cod, crystal, #160b...12.00
Cocktail, Cape Cod, ruby, #160...27.00
Comport, Cape Cod, crystal, #160F, 5¼"......................................27.50
Comport, Katy, milk glass, 4¾"...45.00
Cookie jar, Cape Cod, crystal, wicker hdl, w/lid, #160/195, 6½"...100.00
Cordial, Collector's Crystal, #612 ....14.00
Cordial, Fancy Colonial, pk, #582, 1-oz 50.00
Creamer, Amelia, crystal 20.00

Creamer, Crocheted Crystal, ftd 20.00
Creamer, Fancy Colonial, any color, ftd 25.00
Cruet, Collector's Crystal, caramel slag, #505 ....50.00
Cruet, Octagon, jade, w/stopper, #505 ....75.00
Cup, coffee; Cape Cod, crystal, #160/37 ....7.00
Cup, coffee; Mt Vernon, crystal 8.00
Cup, punch; Crocheted Crystal, closed hdl 5.00
Cup, punch; Crocheted Crystal, open hdl 7.00
Cup, Reeded, any color 20.00
Cup, Square Hazen, crystal, pk or gr 15.00
Decanter, bourbon; Cape Cod, crystal, #160/260 ....80.00
Decanter, Cask #1, Antique Blue...50.00
Decanter, Grape, Heather, #8 ....55.00
Egg cup, Cape Cod, crystal, #160/225...32.50
Goblet, cafe parfait; Fancy Colonial, any color, low ft.................25.00
Goblet, Cape Cod, Evergreen, #160, 14-oz....................................55.00
Goblet, Chroma, amber (Maderia), #123 ....24.00
Goblet, Mt Vernon, crystal, 9-oz...10.00
Goblet, water; Monticello, crystal..15.00
Goblet, wine; Amelia, Rubigold 50.00
Goblet, wine; Atterbury Scroll, milk glass....................................12.00
Goblet, wine; Crocheted Crystal, 4½-oz, 5½"................................25.00
Goblet, wine; Dmn Quilted, pk or gr, 2-oz...................................12.00
Ice bucket, Cape Cod, crystal, #160/63, 6½"...............................195.00
Ice tub, Reeded, any color 55.00
Jar, pokal; Cape Cod, crystal, #160/128, 11" 85.00
Jelly, Beaded Block, crystal, pk, gr or amber, stemmed/flared, 4½".25.00
Ladle, punch; Cape Cod, crystal 35.00
Lamp, hurricane; Crocheted Crystal, 11" 65.00
Mayonnaise, Monticello, crystal, 3-pc..30.00
Mayonnaise, Twisted Optic, bl or yel..50.00
Mint dish, Cape Cod, crystal, heart shape, #160/49, 5".................25.00
Muddler, Reeded, any color, 4½"...10.00
Mug, Cape Cod, crystal, hdls, #160/188, 12-oz 50.00
Nut dish, Cape Cod, crystal, hdls, #160/184, 4".............................30.00
Parfait, Cape Cod, crystal, #1602, 6-oz...12.00
Pickle jar, Mt Vernon, crystal, w/lid...35.00
Pickle tray, Fancy Colonial, any color, oval, 8" 30.00
Pitcher, Atterbury Scroll, milk glass 60.00
Pitcher, Cape Cod, crystal, #160/24, 2-qt....................................100.00
Pitcher, Dew Drop, opal, #624, 56-oz..65.00
Pitcher, Windmill, red slag, satin 55.00
Plate, Beaded Block, yel, sq, 7¾"..30.00
Plate, bread & butter; Cape Cod, #160/1D, 6½".............................8.00
Plate, buffet; Twisted Optic, gr, 14" 25.00
Plate, Cape Cod, crystal, #160/3D, 7"..8.00
Plate, Crocheted Crystal, 17"...40.00
Plate, dinner; Cape Cod, crystal, #160/10D, 10"...........................37.50
Plate, Flute & Cane, 6"...20.00
Plate, luncheon; Dmn Quilted, bl or blk, 8"..................................15.00
Plate, Monticello, crystal, rnd, 12"...35.00
Plate, Mt Vernon, crystal, rnd, 8" 10.00
Plate, salad bowl liner; Crocheted Crystal, 13".............................22.50
Plate, salad; Katy, bl opal, 8"...32.00
Plate, salad; Laced Edge, opal, 8"..35.00
Plate, salad; Reeded, any color, belled rim, 8" 20.00
Plate, sandwich; Twisted Optic, bl or yel, 10"...............................20.00
Plate, sherbet; Twisted Optic, pk, 6"...3.00
Plate, torte; Cape Cod, crystal, #1608F, 13"..................................37.50
Puff box, Cape Cod, crystal, #1601, w/lid.....................................50.00
Punch bowl, Crocheted Crystal, 14"..65.00
Relish, Cape Cod, crystal, 5-part, #160/102, 11"...........................70.00
Relish, Crocheted Crystal, 3-part, 11½"...25.00
Rose bowl, Wide Panel, marigold on milk glass..........................210.00

Salt cellar, ruby slag, 4-ftd, #61 ....20.00
Shakers, Atterbury Scroll, crystal, ea................................15.00
Shakers, Cape Cod, crystal, sq, #160/109, pr...................25.00
Shakers, Cape Cod, Fern Green, #160/117, pr................35.00
Shakers, Monticello, crystal, w/glass tops, ea.................20.00
Shakers, Mt Vernon, crystal, pr...22.00
Sherbet, Crocheted Crystal, 6-oz, 5"...............................10.00
Sherbet, Dmn Quilted, bl or blk...16.00
Sherbet, Huckabee, pk, ftd..30.00
Sherbet, Twisted Optic, bl or yel.......................................10.00
Sugar bowl, Crocheted Crystal, ftd....................................20.00
Sugar bowl, Fancy Colonial, any color, w/lid....................30.00
Tidbit, Laced Edge, opal, 2-tier, 8" & 10" plates.............110.00
Toothpick holder, Octagon, caramel slag, #505...............25.00
Tumbler, Fancy Colonial, any color, 10-oz......................18.00
Tumbler, Flute & Cane, crystal, 9-oz...............................30.00
Tumbler, fruit juice; Crocheted Crystal, ftd, 6-oz, 6".......10.00
Tumbler, iced tea; Cape Cod, crystal, #160, 12-oz.........12.50
Tumbler, iced tea; Crocheted Crystal, 12-oz, 7⅛"...........25.00
Tumbler, iced tea; Mt Vernon, crystal, 12-oz.................12.50
Tumbler, Katy, gr opal, 9-oz...55.00
Tumbler, water; Atterbury Scroll, milk glass...................15.00
Tumbler, whiskey; Cape Cod, #160, 2½-oz.....................12.50
Vase, ball; Reeded, any color, 4"......................................17.50
Vase, bud; Free-Hand, hearts/vines, lt gr on opal, 8½"...350.00
Vase, Cape Cod, crystal, ftd, #160/21, 11½"...................70.00
Vase, Cape Cod, crystal, urn form w/hdls, #160/186, 10½".........195.00
Vase, Crocheted Crystal, 8"...20.00
Vase, Free-Hand, bl irid w/opal pulled swags, cylindrical, 11½"..350.00
Vase, Free-Hand, bronze w/waves of bl & orange, waisted shape, 10½"..750.00
Vase, Free-Hand, draped swags, gr-bl on marigold irid, 11½" ..1,000.00
Vase, Free-Hand, hearts/vines, bl on orange, ruffled, 5x6¾".......400.00
Vase, Free-Hand, hearts/vines, lt bl on clear irid, bl rim, 10"...1,100.00
Vase, Free-Hand, hearts/vines, orange on dk bl, 5¾" 900.00
Vase, Free-Hand, leaves, gr on cream w/gold irid, ca 1925, 10½" ...800.00
Vase, Free-Hand, loops, bl on wht, baluster, att, ca 1925, 6¾" ...300.00
Vase, Free-Hand, mc swirls in cobalt, orange int, stick neck, 9¾"..500.00
Vase, Free-Hand, swags, bl on opal, orange int, shouldered, 7½"...550.00
Vase, Free-hand, wht/bl/gray marbleized w/bl int, cylindrical, 9" ...500.00
Vase, Katy, red, #743b, 5¼"..65.00
Vase, Mosaic, cobalt shaded & swirled w/opal, orange int, 6½"..490.00
Vase, Nuart, irid aquamarine, shouldered/incurvate, 6¾"............125.00
Vase, Reeded (Spun), red, 9" 75.00

Imperial Porcelain

The Blue Ridge Mountain Boys were created by cartoonist Paul Webb and translated into three-dimension by the Imperial Porcelain Corporation of Zanesville, Ohio, in 1947. These figurines decorated ashtrays, vases, mugs, bowls, pitchers, planters, and other items. The Mountain Boys series were numbered 92 through 108, each with a different and amusing portrayal of mountain life. Imperial also produced American Folklore miniatures, twenty-three tiny animals one inch or less in size, and the Al Capp Dogpatch series. Because of financial difficulties, the company closed in 1960.

American Folklore Miniatures

Cat, 1½", from $95 to...125.00
Cow, 1¾", from $95 to..125.00
Hound dogs, from $95 to..125.00
Plaque, store ad, Am Folklore Porcelain Miniatures, 4½"...........450.00
Sow, from $95 to...125.00

Blue Ridge Mountain Boys by Paul Webb

Ashtray, #92, 2 men by tree stump, for pipes...............125.00
Ashtray, #101, man w/jug & snake..................................120.00
Ashtray, #103, hillbilly & skunk......................................120.00
Ashtray, #105, baby, hound dog & frog..........................135.00
Ashtray, #106, Barrel of Wishes, w/hound.....................115.00
Box, cigarette; #98, dog atop, baby at door, sq.............165.00

Dealer's sign, Paul Webb, 8¼x9", $700.00.

Decanter, #100, outhouse, man & bird.........................125.00
Decanter, #104, Ma leaning over stump, w/baby & skunk.........145.00
Decanter, man, jug, snake & tree stump, Hispch Inc, 1946........125.00
Figurine, #101, man leans against tree trunk, 5"..............125.00
Figurine, man on hands & knees, 3"...............................130.00
Figurine, man sitting, 3½"...145.00
Figurine, man sitting w/chicken on knee, 3"....................130.00
Jug, #101, Willie & snake 95.00
Mug, #94, Bearing Down, 6"..95.00
Mug, #94, dbl baby hdl, 4¼"..95.00
Mug, #94, man w/bl pants hdl, 4¼"....................................95.00
Mug, #94, man w/yel beard & red pants hdl, 4¼"...............95.00
Mug, #99, Target Practice, boy on goat, farmer, 5¾"...........95.00
Pitcher, lemonade...200.00
Planter, #81, man drinking from jug, sitting by washtub.......95.00
Planter, #100, outhouse, man & bird...............................125.00
Planter, #105, man w/chicken on knee, washtub.............130.00
Planter, #110, man, w/jug & snake, 4½" 95.00
Shakers, Ma & Old Doc, pr...115.00

Miscellaneous

Items in this section that are designated 'IP' are miscellaneous novelties made by Imperial Porcelain; the remainder are of interest to Paul Webb collectors, though made by an unknown manufacturer. Prints on calendars and playing cards are signed 'Paul Webb.'

Artist board, babies or mtn women, sgn Paul Webb, 30x30" 275.00
Artist board, mtn boys only, sgn Paul Webb, 30x30"................275.00
Calendar, 1954, 12 sgn scenes, Brown & Bigelow, complete.........65.00
Figurine, cat in high-heeled shoe, 5½" L.............................65.00
Hot pad, Dutch boy w/tulips, rnd, IP...................................30.00
Ink blotters, sgn scenes, ea...15.00
Mug, #29, man hdl, sgn Paul Webb, 4¾"...........................50.00
Planter, #106, dog sitting by tub, IP...................................95.00
Playing cards, ad: Rafe Oiling Gun, Brown & Bigelow, MIB.........75.00
Shakers, pigs, 5", pr..95.00
Shakers, standing pigs, IP, 8", pr....................................110.00

Indian Tree

Indian Tree is a popular dinnerware pattern produced by various potteries since the early 1800s to recent times. Although backgrounds and borders vary, the Oriental theme is carried out with the gnarled, brown branch of a pink-blossomed tree. Among the manufacturers' marks, you may find represented such notable firms as Coalport, S. Hancock and Sons, Soho Pottery, and John Maddock and Sons. See also Johnson Brothers.

Pieces by Maddock: 8" plate, $8.00; 10" plate, $12.50; 6" plate, $5.00; Cup, $22.50.

Bonbon, fluted, Coalport, 6¼"..20.00
Bowl, Aynsley, 2¾x8¾"..60.00
Bowl, cream soup; scalloped, Spode...45.00
Bowl, fruit; Johnson Bros, 5"..9.00
Bowl, fruit; Morley, sm...8.00
Bowl, fruit; Spode, 5¼", set of 6..95.00
Bowl, Myott, 8"...20.00
Bowl, scalloped, Coalport, 1½x6"..40.00
Bowl, soup; Johnson Bros, 7¼"...13.00
Bowl, vegetable; John Maddock & Sons, ca 1935, w/lid, 8" dia....55.00
Bowl, vegetable; Johnson Bros, 8½"..25.00
Bowl, vegetable; Noritake, ca 1930s, w/hdls & lid, 10½" W.........50.00
Butter pat, scalloped, #2/916, 4¼"..18.00
Candy dish, scalloped edge, gr mk, 5¼" L.....................................20.00
Coffee can & saucer, Maddock, 2¼"...18.00
Creamer & sugar bowl, Coalport, bone china mk, late..................40.00
Cup & saucer, AD; Minton..25.00
Cup & saucer, Spode..35.00
Dinner service, Coalport, serves 10+8 serving pieces, 144-pc.....750.00
Egg cup, flat base, Johnson Bros, 1¾", set of 4.............................70.00
Gravy boat, w/attached underplate, Spode.....................................88.00
Jar, Sadler, fancy shape, w/lid, 4½"..55.00
Pitcher, Coalport, 4¾"...65.00
Plate, cookie; Coalport, 10½"...55.00
Plate, Copeland Spode, 9", 12 for...425.00
Plate, dessert; ruffled rim, 8"..30.00
Plate, dinner; scalloped, Coalport, 10"..40.00
Plate, luncheon; Minton, #5185, 9¼", set of 8.............................100.00
Plate, salad; scalloped, Coalport, 7¾", set of 6..............................85.00
Plate, sandwich; closed scroll hdls, Coalport, sq, 10" W..............55.00
Plate, Staffordshire, 9"..12.00
Platter, Ashworth, 14½"..90.00
Platter, John Maddock & Son, 14"...35.00
Platter, well & tree, 21"..305.00
Tazza, scalloped ft, Coalport, 3¼x8"..75.00
Teacup & saucer, cone shape, scalloped, Coalport, gr mk.............32.00
Teapot, Burgess & Lee...60.00
Tray, mc w/gold accents, Coalport, 10¾x8½"................................85.00
Tray, octagonal, scalloped rim, Copeland, 8".................................65.00
Tray, serving; fluted, w/hdls, 10½", EX..48.00

Inkwells and Inkstands

Receptacles for various writing fluids have been used since ancient times. Through the years they have been made from countless materials — glass, metal, porcelain, pottery, wood, and even papier-mache. During the eighteenth century, gold or silver inkstands were presented to royalty; the well-known silver inkstand by Philip Syng, Jr., was used for the signing of the Declaration of Independence, and impressive brass inkstands with wells and pounce pots (sanders) were proud possessions of men of letters. When literacy vastly increased in the nineteenth century, the dip pen replaced the quill pen, and inkwells and inkstands were widely used and produced in a broad range of sizes in functional and decorative forms from ornate Victorian to flowing Art Nouveau and stylized Art Deco designs. However, the acceptance of the ballpoint pen literally put inkstands and inkwells 'out of business.' But their historical significance and intriguing diversity of form and styling fascinate today's collectors.

For further information we recommend *Collector's Encyclopedia to Inkwells*, Books I and II, by Veldon Badders (Collector Books). See also Bottles, Ink.

Brass, cast chestnut leaf & nut, hinged lid, glass insert, 1900s....250.00
Brass, piano form w/flip top, tray/insert inside, European, 1840s, 9"..550.00
Brass (sheet), dome shape w/glass insert, Am, ca 1910, 3¼" dia...50.00
Brass w/swivel lid, distressed look, contour style, ca 1890, 2½".....60.00
Bronze, Spirit of Oceans, figure among waves, unsgn, 7¾x15¾"...865.00
Bronze-finished sheet metal, Deco style, glass well, ca 1900, 4½" W..50.00
Ceramic, red glaze, mk 552.7 W Germany, 20th C, 2" sq, from $30 to...40.00
CI, blk pnt, Rococo style, pressed glass well, ca 1900, 5¼" W....140.00
CI, oak leaves surround elk head, pattern glass well, Am, 1900..200.00
CI stand w/flip top cover at bk, 2" pressed glass well, ca 1890....140.00
Copper, hammered, Arts & Crafts style, ca 1915, 3½" dia............45.00
Faience, HP Deco decor w/floral border, 8-sided, France, 1920s...125.00
Glass, bl, blown & cut, faceted, HP floral, silver lid, ca 1880.....800.00
Glass, bottle gr, mold blown w/funnel top, Am, 1830s-40s, 1⅝" dia...250.00
Glass, brilliant bl, cut, hinged brass mts, 8-sided, Am, 1900s, 2¾"....450.00
Glass, Cane cutting, brass mts, Am?, ca 1900, 2" sq...................145.00
Glass, cobalt, mold-blown melon form, Am, 1860s, 2¾" dia......200.00
Glass, Daisy & Button, lt gr, Am, ca 1900, 2¼" sq........................75.00
Glass, emb metal lid & ormolu base, 2½x4"..................................90.00
Glass, Galouch (pressed), brass flame finial, Fr, ca 1890, 3" sq......95.00
Glass, pk/bl/red swirled, 4-ftd ormolu stand, metal collar/finial, 6"....225.00
Glass, Sandwich Star (pressed), hinged Britannia floral top, ca 1900 .95.00
Glass, vaseline, blown/cut, faceted octagon, pyramid top, ca 1900 ..550.00
Glass, wht opal, 6 bulbous panels, brass mts, Am, 1890s, 2¼" dia...175.00
Ironstone, Gothic shape, R Arthur...1854..., 2½x3" dia.............220.00
Porc, bl bamboo, pierced sides, Japan, late 1800s, 2¼" sq, $160 to..190.00
Porc, gold plumes on wht, Limoges, 5½" dia, from $90 to..........110.00
Porc, HP decor, horseshoe-shaped base, Japanese export, 3½x4⅝"...100.00
Porc, mc floral on emb swirl, brass mts, Fr, late 19th C, 3½x2⅜".....110.00
Porc, 16th-C couple on lid, Rococo style, Old Paris, 1840-50, 5½"...650.00
Pottery, gr-bl & tan bell form, lid w/finial, Newcomb, 4⅛"........300.00
Pottery, man's face, open mouth, brn, 1 hole, Doulton, 1880s, 2½"..250.00
Pottery, swan/egg/tree trunk w/gold, Staffordshire, 1860, 2½" H...300.00
Pottery, thrown, circular contour, sgn KM, Am, 20th C, 3¼" dia.40.00
SP, Rococo edges/ft, 2 faceted bottles, candle holder w/snuffer, 11" L.690.00
SP base w/2 cut o/l wells w/SP lids, Rococo, att Germany, ca 1880....400.00
SP copper w/emb 16th-C figures, domed hinged lid, 1920s.........175.00
Stone, dk moss gr to pale gr, brass mts, ca 1900, 4" dia..............130.00
Stone, lt gr onyx, rnded top w/opening, China, ca 1870, 2¼" dia..110.00
Treen, grpt w/gilt leaves, glass well, S Sillman & Co, wear, 3x4½"..220.00
Trn wood w/HP cherries, pressed glass insert, ca 1900, 3½" dia...150.00
Wht metal, Nouveau lady w/mandolin, glass insert, ca 1900, 4½x7"...180.00

Insulators

The telegraph was invented in 1844. The devices developed to hold the electrical transmission wires to the poles were called insulators. The telephone, invented in 1876, intensified their usefulness; and by the turn of the century, thousands of varieties were being produced in pottery, wood, and glass of various colors. Even though it has been rumored that red glass insulators exist, none have ever been authenticated. There are amber-colored insulators that appear to have a red tint to the amber, and those are called red-amber. Many insulators are embossed with patent dates.

Of the more than 3,000 types known to exist, today's collectors evaluate their worth by age, rarity of color and, of course, condition. Aqua and green are the most common colors in glass, dark brown the most common in porcelain. Threadless insulators (for example, CD #701.1), made between 1850 and 1865, bring prices well into the hundreds, sometimes even the thousands, if in mint condition.

In the listings that follow, the CD numbers are from an identification system developed in the late 1960s by N.R. Woodward.

Those seeking additional information about insulators are encouraged to contact Line Jewels NIA #1380 (whose address may be found in the Directory under Clubs, Newsletters, and Catalogs) or attend a club-endorsed show. (For information see Directory under Florida for Jacqueline Linscott Barnes.) In the listings that follow those stating 'no name' have no company identification, but do have embossed numbers, dots, etc. Those stating 'no embossing' are without raised letters, dots, or any other markings.

Key:
* (asterisk) — Canadian
BE — base embossed
CB — corrugated base
CD — Consolidated Design
FDP — flat drip points
RB — rough base
RDP — round drip points
SB — smooth base
SDP — sharp drip points

CD 103, Gayner, SB, aqua 500.00
CD 106, Birmingham/No 10, RDP, straw 40.00
CD 106, Good, SB, aqua 15.00
CD 106, McLaughlin/No 9, USA, SDP, lt gr 2.00
CD 113, Whitall Tatum/No 13, lt straw 5.00
CD 119, W Brookfield, NY/Pat Apr 28 1885, SB, aqua..........3,500.00
CD 121, C&P Tel Co, SB, aqua 8.00
CD 121, Maydwell-16W/USA, SDP, straw 35.00
CD 122, Armstrong/No 2, made in USA, SB, clear 2.00
CD 122*, Dominion-16, RDP, lt peach 2.00
CD 125, Hemingray/No 15, SDP, gr 75.00
CD 127, H Brooke's, Pat Jan 25 1870, BE, lt aqua.............85.00
CD 133, California, SB, aqua......................................10.00
CD 133, California, SB, peach 325.00
CD 133, OVG Co, SB, aqua 40.00
CD 134, KCGW, SB, gr-aqua......................................18.00
CD 134, T-H E Co, SB, lt bl-aqua 10.00
CD 136, B&O, SB, gr-aqua...20.00
CD 136.5, Boston Bottle Works, Pat Oct 15 1972, SB, aqua...3,500.00
CD 141.8, JF Buzby/Pat May 6 1890, SB, aqua 20,000.00
CD 145, BGM Co, SB, lt purple....................................250.00
CD 145, GTP Tel Co, SB, aqua 15.00
CD 145, HG Co/Petticoat, SB, aqua 2.00
CD 154, Hemingray-42, Hemingray Blue.........................30.00
CD 154, Hemingray-42, RDP, aqua 1.00
CD 154, Maydwell-42/USA, RDP, straw 2.00
CD 158, Boston Bottle Works/Pat Applied For, SB, aqua.........650.00
CD 160, Brookfield/NY, SB, gr 5.00
CD 160.6, AT&T Co, SB, lt yel-gr..............................2,500.00

CD 161, California, SB, purple...................................30.00
CD 162, BGM Co, SB, purple 300.00
CD 162, California, SB, sage gr..................................10.00
CD 162, Hamilton Glass Co, RB, lt aqua......................25.00
CD 190/191, Hemingray-50, SB, aqua.........................15.00
CD 190/191, Transposition, SB, milky aqua, 2-pc 400.00
CD 194/195, Hemingray-54-A, SB, purple....................150.00
CD 197, Hemingray-53, CB, clear 2.00
CD 208, Hemingray/No 44, SDP, aqua.........................12.00
CD 214, Armstrong's No 10, SB, clear 2.00
CD 217, Armstrong's No 51, C3, SB, root beer amber.........10.00
CD 221, Hemingray-68, SB, golden amber....................500.00
CD 231, Hemingray-820, CB, clear..............................25.00
CD 238, Hemingray-514, CB, honey amber 325.00
CD 250, NEGM Co, SB, aqua..................................1,250.00
CD 252, No 2 Cable, RB, orange-amber........................300.00
CD 254, No 3 Cable, SB, aqua 30.00
CD 262, No 2 Columbia, SB, lt bl-aqua........................175.00
CD 267.5, NEGM Co, SB, emerald gr............................200.00
CD 269, Jumbo, SB, aqua 500.00
CD 292.5, Boston/'Knowles 6', SB, aqua 300.00
CD 297, FM Locke Victor NY/No 16, SB, dk aqua 15.00
CD 317, Chambers/Pat Aug 14 1877, SB, lt aqua 500.00
CD 729.4, Mulford & Biddle/83 John St NY, SB, aqua 1,250.00

CD 731, Tillotson, crown embossed in arc, smooth base, sapphire blue, $2,500.00. (Photo courtesy Jacqueline Linscott Barnes)

CD 734.8*, no embossing, SB, olive blk glass..................300.00
CD 735, Chester/NY, SB, aqua...................................600.00
CD 736, NY & ERR, SB, lt gr-aqua...........................3,000.00
CD 742.3, MT Co, BE, lt teal-bl 600.00
CD 1038, Cutter, Pat April 26 1904, SB, aqua 300.00

Irons

History, geography, art, and cultural diversity are all represented in the collecting of antique pressing irons. The progress of fashion and invention can be traced through the evolution of the pressing iron.

Over seven hundred years ago, implements constructed of stone, bone, wood, glass, and wrought iron were used for pressing fabrics. Early ironing devices were quite primitive in form, and heating techniques included inserting a hot metal slug into a cavity of the iron, adding hot burning coals into a chamber or pan, and placing the iron directly on hot coals or a hot surface.

To the pleasure of today's collectors, some of these early irons, mainly from the period of 1700 to 1850, were decorated by artisans who carved and painted them with regional motifs typical of their natural surroundings and spiritual cultures.

Beginning in the mid-1800s, new cultural demands for fancy wearing apparel initiated a revolution in technology for types of irons and methods to heat them. Typical of this period is the fluter which was essential for producing the ruffles demanded by the nineteenth-century ladies. Hat irons, polishers, and numerous unusual iron forms were also used during this time, and provided a means to produce crimps, curves, curls, and special fabric textures. Irons from this time are characterized by their unique shapes, odd handles, latches, decorations, and even revolving mechanisms.

Also during this time, irons began to be heated by burning liquid and gaseous fuels. Gradually the new technology of the electrically heated iron replaced all other heating methods, except in the more rural areas and undeveloped countries. Even today the Amish communities utilize gasoline fuel irons.

In the listings that follow, prices are given for examples in best possible as-found condition. Damage, repairs, plating, excessive wear, rust, and missing parts can dramatically reduce value. For further information we recommend *Irons by Irons*, *More Irons by Irons*, and *Even More Irons by Irons* by our advisor Dave Irons; his address and information for ordering these books are given in the Directory under Pennsylvania.

Billiard table, Brunswick Blake..., twist hdl, late 1800s, 9½" **200.00**
Box, Dutch, all brass, openwork top, mid-1800s, 8½", $300 to...**500.00**
Box, European, lift-up gate, all iron, mid-1800s, 7¾", $150 to ...**200.00**
Box, Junior Carbon...1911...Appld For, top lifts off, 6", $200 to.**300.00**
Box, Laundry Queen #2, top lifts off, late 1800s, 6¼", $200 to ..**300.00**
Box, Scottish, brass posts/latch/trivet, after 1850, 6¼", over **750.00**
Cap, LT (French), late 1800s, 3⅞", from $30 to **50.00**

Combination sadiron/fluter with wire latch, $90.00.

Egg, electric, standing, Therma, early 1900s, egg: 5¾" **150.00**
Egg, European, cast on rod w/iron hdl, late 1800s, egg: 2¼" **20.00**
Flatiron, cast, Landr_ss, New Yo_k...'67, #5, 5½", from $30 to **50.00**
Flatiron, cast (anchor), late 1800s, 6", from $20 to **30.00**
Flatiron, cold hdl, Special Hardware, ca 1900, 6¼", from $70 to ...**100.00**
Flatiron, cold hdl, WH Howell...Oct 11 05, 6½", from $70 to ...**100.00**
Flatiron, Le Gaulois #5 (warrior), ca 1900, 6¼", from $70 to **100.00**
Flatiron, wrought iron, 1-pc, rnd ends, mid-1800s, 5", from $150 to...**200.00**
Fluter, combination, charcoal, Eclipse Pat Aut 25 1903, 6½" **150.00**
Fluter, combination, Patented July 24, '74, clamps on sadiron, 8½"...**500.00**
Fluter, Crown North Bros Mfg...USA, electric, belt driven, 1890s, over..**750.00**
Fluter, roller, Clark's Ptd '73 in script, blk pnt, 6¼", $150 to......**200.00**
Gasoline, Standard Gas Iron, ca 1900, 7¼", from $150 to **200.00**
Goffering, dbl, English, brass w/marble base, mid-1800s, 10¼", over.....**750.00**
Goffering, dbl, English, slug in center well, ca 1800, 14¾", over...**750.00**
Goffering, dbl, European, iron w/ornate cast base, mid-1800s, 11½" ..**500.00**
Goffering, W Bullock & Co #10, S-style std, rnd base, ca 1900, 6¼"....**100.00**
Hat, steam heated, curved sides/rnded edges/insulated top, late 1800s..**150.00**
Meta fuel, British Boudoir..., body revolves, ca 1900, 5¼", 150 to.........**200.00**
Natural gas, Johnson Iron Racine Wis..., 1900s, 6¼", from $100 to **150.00**
Natural gas, JW Right Co, Burmingham, w/chimney/copper shield, 1900s...**30.00**
Natural gas, Schreiber & Goldberg NY, early 1900s, 6", from $100 to..**150.00**
Polisher, Geneva IL, WH Howell, smooth bottom, late 1800s, 5".........**150.00**
Polisher, Repose #2, ridged bottom parallel to bk edge, late 1800s, 7"...**200.00**
Seam, Pat Apd For, hdl opens up & folds bk, late 1800s, 6¾" **300.00**
Sleeve, all cast, rib hdl, late 1800s, 5¼", from $30 to....................**50.00**

Sleeve, Pat'd June 15 1897, long flat toe, 9⅞", from $150 to......**200.00**
Slug, drop-in-bk, European, made in pcs, leather hdl, 1700s, 5½"...**300.00**
Slug, European, brass w/Delft hdl, late 1800s, 7¼", from $500 to **700.00**
Smoothing stone, European, hand blown w/hdl, gr-blk, 1800s, 6x4¾"....**50.00**
Swan, CI, red w/blk pinstriping, late 1800s, 1⅞", from $200 to..**300.00**
Velvet polisher, Fr, w/stand, late 1800s, 14", from $150 to..........**200.00**

Ironstone

During the last quarter of the eighteenth century, English potters began experimenting with a new type of body that contained calcinated flint and a higher china clay content, intent on producing a fine durable whiteware — heavy, yet with a texture that would resemble porcelain. To remove the last trace of yellow, a minute amount of cobalt was added, often resulting in a bluish-white tone. Wm and John Turner of Caughley and Josiah Spode II were the first to manufacture the ware successfully. Others, such as Davenport, Hicks and Meigh, and Ralph and Josiah Wedgwood, followed with their own versions. The latter coined the name 'Pearl' to refer to his product and incorporated the term into his trademark. In 1813 a 14-year patent was issued to Charles James Mason, who called his ware Patented Ironstone. Francis Morley, G.L. Asworth, T.J. Mayer, and other Staffordshire potters continued to produce ironstone until the end of the century. While some of these patterns are simple to the extreme, many are decorated with in-mold designs of fruit, grain, and foliage on ribbed or scalloped shapes. In the 1830s transfer-printed designs in blue, mulberry, pink, green, and black became popular; and polychrome versions of Oriental wares were manufactured to compete with the Chinese trade. See also Mason's Ironstone. Our advise for this category comes from Home Place Antiques, whose address is listed in the Directory under Illinois.

Baker, Sydenham, 8-sided, T&R Boote, 1853, 10x8" **95.00**
Bowl, Artichoke, #971, w/lid, 7x13"...**145.00**
Bowl, emb ribs, J&G Meakin, 1890s, 3¼x8¼", NM.....................**75.00**
Bowl, fruit/punch; Warranted...Mercer..., 5½x9½" **190.00**
Bowl, Hebe, ftd, Alcock, 4½x7½", EX..**60.00**
Bowl, Potomac (Blackberry), W Baker & Co, ca 1862, 10" **60.00**
Bowl, sauce; Laurel Wreath, Elsmore & Forster, 5" **40.00**
Bowl, serving; Flower Garden Border, Grindley, 1890s, 4¼x6" **55.00**
Bowl, vegetable; Sydenham, T&R Boote, w/lid, 9x11½x9" **215.00**
Bowl, Wheat & Daisy, Bishop & Stonier, 1890s, 9" **45.00**
Bowl, 8-sided, TJ & J Mayer, ca 1845, 10½", EX.......................**195.00**
Butter dish, 3-pc, H Meakin, 4¾x6" dia **165.00**
Child's tea set, Imperial Ironstone John Alcock, 1850s, 11-pc, VG ..**795.00**
Coffeepot, Niagara, Walley, 1856, 11"...**175.00**
Coffeepot, octagonal, paneled, rosette finial, TJ & J Mayer, 9", EX ...**295.00**
Creamer, Ceres, Elsmore & Forster, 5x6½", NM **165.00**
Creamer, Fuchsia, unmk, 5½" **85.00**
Creamer, Reeded Grape, branch hdl, Pankhurst & Dimmock, 5"....**195.00**
Cup & saucer, Budded Vine, Meakin..**32.00**
Mug, Chain of Tulips, J&G Meakin, 1890s, 3", NM.....................**95.00**
Pitcher, Baltic, ped ft, GF Bowers, ca 1855, 11¼" **285.00**
Pitcher, Ceres, Elsmore & Forster, 1850s, 10" **265.00**
Pitcher, Draped Leaf, Ceres-like shape, 12".....................................**95.00**
Pitcher, Hyacinth, 8"..**225.00**
Pitcher, Jacob Furnival & Co, 1850-70, 10½x7", EX.....................**95.00**
Pitcher, Laurel Wreath, Elsmore & Forster, sm rpr, 8" **165.00**
Pitcher, Lily of the Valley, H Burgess, 12x8½", EX.......................**95.00**
Pitcher, milk; octagonal w/paneled sides, sqd hdl, Edwards, 1846, 8" .**395.00**
Pitcher, milk; President, J Edwards, ca 1856, 7½"........................**245.00**
Pitcher, Nouveau arches on body, Johnson Bros, 1883-1913, 8¾"...**140.00**
Pitcher, scalloped hdl, flared spout, Johnson Bros, England, 11" **220.00**
Pitcher, scroll & lion detail to hdl, John Edwards, ca 1900, 12½" ..**175.00**

Pitcher, Shaw's Fan, Anthony Shaw, ca 1856, 11¼" 195.00
Pitcher, Tulip shape, Wedgwood, ca 1880, 13x8" 135.00
Pitcher, Wheat & Blackberry, Ceres, Meakin, 1860s, 9", NM 145.00
Plate, dinner; President, 10⅝" 40.00
Plate, Gothic, Alcock, 1850s, 8½" 57.50
Plate, Laurel Wreath, Elsmore & Forster, 9¾" 60.00
Plate, seashell shape, Harvey, 7¼x6½" 75.00
Plate, Sydenham, T&R Boote, 9⅜" 35.00
Plate, Victor, F Jones, 1868, 9" 55.00
Plate, Wheat, Wilkinson, 9¾", 12 for 135.00
Platter, Framed Leaf, Pankhurst, ca 1850, 17", NM 95.00
Platter, Gothic border w/everted ribs, T Goodfellow, 1850s, 15x11½"..150.00
Platter, Grapevine, Centennial, W&E Corn, 14¾x10½".............60.00
Platter, President, John Edwards, 15½" 110.00
Platter, Square Ridged, Johnson Bros, 1880s, 13¾x10", EX 85.00
Platter, Wheat, Royal Patent Ironstone, Turner Goodard, 18½", NM..70.00
Relish, Wheat & Clover, Tomkinson Bro & Co, 9" L 70.00
Sauce boat, Fig, Davenport, 9½" L 95.00
Sauce tureen, Athena, w/lid, 6½x7¾" 265.00
Sauce tureen, emb scrolls, Mayer & Elliot...1865, +tray/ladle.....200.00
Soap dish, Cable & Ring, w/insert, Meakin, 1890s, 6½", EX......145.00
Soap dish, Tea Berry, copper lustre trim, 4x5½x3¾x4" 295.00
Soup ladle, Chinese, 12" 150.00
Sugar bowl, Iona, w/lid, Powell & Bishop, 1886, 7½" 90.00
Tea set, Sharon/Arch, Wedgwood, child sz, 5" pot+cr/sug+6 c/s.....650.00
Teapot, Ceres, bl trim, Elsmore & Forster, 11¼" 395.00
Teapot, Ceres, Elsmore & Forster, EX...180.00
Teapot, Fig, Wedgwood, 9½", EX 225.00
Teapot, Wheat, Wilkinson, 8½" 245.00
Tureen, Fluted Pearl, J Wedgwood, ca 1847, w/lid, 12¼" L, EX..225.00
Tureen, Portland, trumpet flower finial, Elsmore Forster, 13½" L..195.00
Tureen, vegetable; Early Swirl, Morley, 1845, 11" L, NM...........225.00
Tureen, vegetable; President, J Edwards, w/lid, 9x10" 235.00
Tureen, vegetable; Wheat, w/lid, W&E Corn, 7¼x13", EX 195.00
Undertray, Trailing Ivy, Maddock & Son, ca 1850, 8⅜x6"............60.00
Wash bowl & pitcher, Wheat 375.00
Waste jar, Ribbed Bud, bud finial, Pankhurst, 1850-52, 16"........875.00

Patterned Ironstone

Bowl, Aurora, purple transfer/mc, Morley, rectangular, 11" L 120.00
Pitcher, landscape transfer w/gold on red, Senator... below spout, 10"...460.00
Plate, Excelsior, 12-sided, Wolliscroft, 10" 50.00
Platter, Seine, purple transfer, Wedgwood, 13½" 160.00
Platter, well & tree; Tobacco Leaf w/Imari-like border, Ashworth, 21"..650.00
Soup tureen, Japanese flowers, w/lid, Copeland, 1855-70, 11x10½".......345.00
Sugar bowl, Medina, bl transfer, octagonal, leaf hdls, w/lid, mk, 8" ..175.00
Vase, floral 'Imari' pattern, corseted, Edwardian, 1900s, 12x6", pr....350.00

Italian Glass

Throughout the twentieth century, one of the major glassmaking centers of the world was the island of Murano. From the Stile Liberte work of Artisi Barovier (1890 – 1920s) to the early work of Ettore Sottsass in the 1970s, they excelled in creativity and craftsmanship. The 1920s to 1940s featured the work of glass designers like Ercole Barovier for Barovier and Toso and Vittorio Zecchin, Napoleone Martinuzzi, and Carlo Scarpa for Venini. Many of these pieces are highly prized by collectors.

The 1950s saw a revival of Italy as a world-reknown design center for all of the arts. Glass led the charge with the brightly colored work of Fulvio Bianconi for Venini, Dino Martens for Aureliano Toso, and Ercole Barovier for Barovier and Toso. The best of these pieces are extremely desirable. The '60s and '70s have also seen many innovative

designs with work by the Finnish Tapio Wirkkala, the American Thomas Stearns, and many other designers.

Unfortunately, amongst the great glass, there was a plethora of commercial ashtrays, vases, and figurines produced that, though having some value, do not compare in quality and design to the great glass of Murano.

Venini: The Venini company was founded in 1921 by Paolo Venini, and he led the company until his death in 1959. Major Italian designers worked for the firm, including Vittorio Zecchin, Napoleone Martinuzzi, Carlo Scarpa, and Fulvio Bianconi. After his death, his son-in-law, Ludovico de Santillana, ran the factory and employed designers like Toni Zucchieri, Tapio Wirkkala, and Thomas Stearns. The company is known for creative designs and techniques including Inciso (finely etched lines), Battuto (carved facets), Sommerso (controlled bubbles), Pezzato (patches of fused glass), and Fascie (horizontal colored lines in clear glass). Until the mid-'60s, most pieces were signed with acid-etched 'Venini Murano ITALIA.' In the '60s they started engraving the signatures. The factory still exists.

Barovier: In the late 1920s, Ercole Barovier took over the Artisti Barovier and started designing many different vases. In the 1930s he merged with Ferro Toso and became Barovier and Toso. He designed many different series of glass including the Barbarico (rough, acid-treated brown or deep blue glass), Eugenio (free-blown vases), Efeso, Rotallato, Dorico, Egeo (vases incorporating murrine designs), and Primavera (white etched glass with black bands). He designed until 1974. The company is still in existence. Most pieces were unsigned.

Aureliano Toso: The great glass designer Dino Martens was involved with the company from about 1938 to 1965. It was his work that produced the very desirable Oriente vases. This technique consisted of free-formed patches of green, yellow, blue, purple, black, and white stars and pieces of zanfirico canes fused into brilliantly colored vases and bowls. His El Dorado series was based on the same technique but was not opaque. He also designed pieces with alternating groups of black and white filigrana lines. Pieces are unsigned.

Seguso: Flavio Poli became the artistic director of Seguso in the late 1930s and remained until 1963. He is known for his Corroso (acid-etched glass) and his Valve series (elegant forms of two to three layers of colored glass with a clear glass casing).

Archimede Seguso: In 1946 Archimede Seguso left the Seguso Vetri D'Arte to open a new company and designed many innovative pieces. His Merlatto (thin white filigrana suspended three dimensionally) series is his most famous. The epitome of his work is where a colored glass (yellow or purple) is windowed in the merlotti. His Macchia Ambra Verde is yellow and spots on a gold base encased in clear glass. The A Piume series contained feathers and leaves suspended in glass. Pieces are unsigned.

Alfredo Barbini: Barbini was a designer known for his sculptures of sea subjects and his amorphic-shaped vases with an inner core of red or blue glass with a heavy layer of finely incised outer glass. He worked in the 1950s to the 1960s, and some pieces are signed.

Vistosi: Although this glassworks was started in the 1940s, fame came in the 1960s and 1970s with the birds designed by Allesandro Pianon and the early work of the Memphis school designer, Ettore Sottsass. Pieces may be signed.

AVEM: This company is known for its work in the 1950s and 1960s. The designer, Ansolo Fuga, did work using a solid white glass with inclusions of multicolored murrines.

Cenedese: This is a postwar company led by Gino Cenedese with Alfredo Barbini as designer. When Barbini left, Cenedese took over the design work and also used the free-lanced designs of Fulvio Bianconi. They are known for their figurines and vases with suspended murrines.

Cappellin: Venini's original partner (1921 – 25), Giacomo Cappellin, opened a short-lived company (1925 – 32) that was to become extremely important. His chief designer was the young Carlo Scarpa who was to create many masterpieces in glass both for Cappellin and then Venini.

Ettore Sottsass: Sottass founded the Memphis School of Design in the 1970s. He is an extremely famous modern designer who designed several series of glass for the Vistosi Glass Company. The pieces were created in limited editions, signed and numbered, and each piece was given a name.

Our advisor for this category is Howard Lockwood, publisher of *Vetri: Italian Glass News*. For further information concerning Mr. Lockwood or this publication, see the Directory under New Jersey.

Venini Glass

A Machie vase, sgn, 9½"	11,000.00
Battuto lt bl vase	4,315.00
Battuto purple dbl-gourd vase	11,325.00
Battuto yel bowl	800.00
Bird, gr irid	720.00
Bird, tan & wht lattimo	8,360.00
Bolle, vase, orange & amber	920.00
Bollicine vase, gr cylinder w/gr disc ft	3,885.00
Canoe, red & blk murrines w/inner bl core	7,550.00
Cinesi wht vase	540.00
Colletto amber vase w/deep amber collar	865.00
Cylindrical vase w/mc vertical canes	2,115.00
Demode marbleized vase w/sq top	485.00
Fasce orrizontalli gr bottle w/2 red bands	1,150.00
Fasce orrizontalli gr vase w/yel lattimo fasce	645.00
Fasce orrizontalli gray bottle w/yel & maroon bands	1,265.00
Fasce orrizontalli gray bottle w/yel band	415.00
Fasce orrizontalli wht bowl w/smoked bands	195.00
Fasce vertical gr lattimo & red transparent vase	7,280.00
Fasce verticale gr & bl vertical stripes bottle	1,035.00
Fasce verticale gr/clear/red striped pitcher	1,150.00
Fasce verticale red & violet vertical caned vase	1,495.00
Fascemurrine gray vase w/band of murrines	1,780.00
Fazzoletto aubergine & wht latticino	880.00
Fazzoletto blk ext/gray int	1,380.00
Fazzoletto orange int/cream ext	565.00
Fazzoletto red & wht zanfirico	430.00
Fazzoletto red/gr/clear glass canes	610.00
Figurine, Mrs Tartaglia	2,922.00
Figurine, pezzato man	1,765.00
Fish, various colors, Ken Scott, 3 for	1,215.00
Flared cylindrical vase, bl/gr/red canes	4,465.00
Forato bl pitcher w/single lg hole	1,300.00
Giada bl bottle w/matching stopper	1,500.00
Hourglass, gray/bl	865.00
Hourglass, red/bl	1,150.00
Hourglass, yel/gray	1,150.00
Incalmo bl base, violet top bottle	555.00
Incalmo gr w/red stripes w/stopper bottle	1,240.00
Incalmo straw base, gr top bottle	55.00
Incalmo transparent bl bottle w/wht latticino band	700.00
Inciso deep bl vase	1,500.00
Inciso gr triangular bottle	1,200.00
Inciso gr waisted vase w/vertical inciso	29,665.00
Inciso lt gr stoppered bottle	635.00
Inciso metallic bl stoppered bottle	1,185.00
Lattimo bl bowl w/wht ft	4,745.00
Mezza filigrana flacon, aubergine w/clear stopper	1,080.00
Mezza filigrana flared wht cylindrical vase	7,120.00
Mezza filigrana sqd vase, orange & clear filigrana	2,115.00
Mezza filigrana wht vase w/rnd to sq top	5,550.00
Mosaico zanfirico gray w/wht zanfirico vase	3,125.00
Murrine battuto bowl in opaque murrines, red w/blk	26,950.00

Murrine bl murrine rectangular dish	5,985.00
Murrine bowl, red & orange murrines	3,545.00
Murrine vase, blk & wht murrines	4,855.00
Nautilus shell, clear irid	7,000.00
Occhi gr & wht triangular vase	17,800.00
Pezzato bottle vase, red/bl/wht	9,775.00
Pezzato cigar-shaped vase, red/bl/gr/aubergine	3,235.00
Pezzato pinched cylinder-shaped vase	3,290.00
Pezzato sq vase in gr/red/bl/clear	1,715.00
Pezzato triangular bowl	4,875.00
Pezzato vase, aubergine/gr/straw/clear patches	8,900.00
Pezzato vase, red/bl/straw/gr	10,785.00
Pulegoso gr 2-hdld vase	1,220.00
Rilievi rose-colored vase w/bubbles & serpent ft	1,888.00
Rooster, blk murrines, red crop	4,315.00
Sirene, rose, arms over head	6,425.00
Sommerso bl 4-sided scalloped bowl w/bubbles	278.00
Sommerso bollicine brn vase	1,525.00
Sommerso bollicine red flared vase	4,315.00
Sommerso gr bird w/gold inclusions	833.00
Sommerso gr 4-sided bowl w/bubbles	310.00
Spicchi vase, lt bl/aubergine/pk canes	3,525.00
Tessuto gr/plum flared bowl	8,630.00
Tessuto vase: red/wht, red/plum	865.00
Transparante straw-colored Veronese vase	595.00
Zanfirico wht latticino vase	1,235.00

Non-Venini Glass

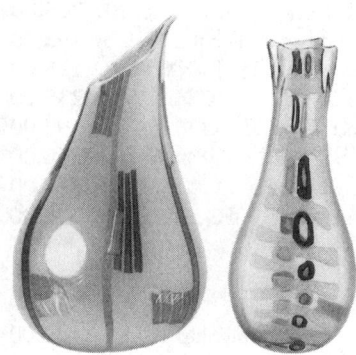

AVEM Vases by Ansolo Fuga: Pitcher form with fused white opaque canes with long sections of red, blue, yellow, and green, cased clear, ca 1955, 17", $3,750.00; Clear with applied vertical bands and zanfirico segments alternating with red, yellow, blue, and amber murrines, ca 1958, 16", $3,500.00.

A Seguso, A Piume cylindrical vase w/feathers	4,725.00
A Seguso, clear vase w/red core	465.00
A Seguso, Filigrana lt bl bowl	430.00
A Seguso, Laguna pk vase	1,075.00
A Seguso, Losanghe red bowl	2,375.00
A Seguso, Macchia Ambre Verde vase & bowl	735.00
A Seguso, Merletto bowl, brn	970.00
Aldo Nason Hokohama: 2 spouts	4,315.00
Aldo Nason Reazione Policrome vase w/gr murrines	3,950.00
Aureliano Toso, Bianca Nera ashtray	475.00
Aureliano Toso, Bianca Nera elongated bowl	775.00
Aureliano Toso, Cactus: 4 appl uplifted arms	2,350.00
Aureliano Toso, El Dorado vase, model #5215	12,000.00
Aureliano Toso, Frammentati vase, mc	4,200.00
Aureliano Toso, Lattimo yel vase	485.00
Aureliano Toso, Oriente vase, no pinwheel	900.00
Aureliano Toso, Oriente vase w/pinwheel	7,900.00
Aureliano Toso, Oriente 2-hdld pitcher	9,700.00
AVEM Ferro Anse Volante irid violet vase	1,883.00
AVEM Fuga incalmo murrine vase	3,776.00
AVEM Fuga 2-spouted vase w/red/bl murrines	8,882.00

AVEM Nason vase w/3 spouts & internal decor 3,220.00
AVEM Reazione polychrome bird 1,080.00
AVEM Reazione polychrome sm pitcher w/bl murrines 2,415.00
AVEM Reazione polychrome sm vase w/bl murrines 1,150.00
Barbini, charger, clear w/2 fish in center 725.00
Barbini, Inciso Sasso, red core, ftd. 4,465.00
Barbini, Inciso Sasso, red core, no base 3,235.00
Barbini, Martinuzzi figure: bull, dk blk scavo 1,385.00
Barbini, Martinuzzi inciso triangular gray vase 1,055.00
Barbini, Martinuzzi inciso triangular red vase 2,300.00
Barbini, Martinuzzi triangular orange vase 1,221.00
Barovier, Ambrato vase w/pinched int 2,155.00
Barovier, Argo wht & aubergine cylindrical vase 5,551.00
Barovier, ashtray, gold decor 500.00
Barovier, Barbarico pinched vase 1,265.00
Barovier, Cordonato D'Oro gr bowl 345.00
Barovier, Crepuscolo bucket-shaped vase 4,315.00
Barovier, Dorico Acquamarine, bl & wht murrines 9,170.00
Barovier, Dorico Corniola cylindrical vase 4,045.00
Barovier, Eugenio pitcher w/gr trim 975.00
Barovier, Graffito gr & clear vase 1,945.00
Barovier, Intarsio red & bl triangles vase 1,725.00
Barovier, Lenti irid clear vase 4,045.00
Barovier, Neomurrine yel & blk bowl 2,695.00
Barovier, Pelugoso 2-hdld pk vase 335.00
Barovier, Porpora bowl, rose 395.00
Barovier, Primavera vase w/blk lip wrap 23,500.00
Barovier, Seguso Ferro, lion, brn 6,475.00
Barovier, Spacchi vase, blk w/wht fold 5,125.00
Cenedese, DaRos bird-shaped vase, 4 rows of murrines 665.00
Cenedese, DaRos Il Momento clear w/amber core 978.00
Cenedese, Filigrana clear & wht bottle-form vase 665.00
Cenedese, Fish block w/2 fish 450.00
Cenedese, Fish block w/2 fish & seaweed 750.00
Cenedese, Fish block w/6 sm fish 2,498.00
Cenedese, Sommerso sqd bottle form 845.00
Cenedese, Sommerso vase, lime yel & bl 550.00
Fratelli Toso, E Toso Kiku red vase w/blk & yel 5,895.00
Fratelli Toso, E Toso Millepunti bl vase w/gr 5,050.00
Fratelli Toso, E Toso Nerox A Petoni bottle vase 1,055.00
Fratelli Toso, E Toso Tiffany vase of sqd murrines 11,865.00
Fratelli Toso, Murrine teapot 445.00
Fratelli Toso, Murrine 2-hdld vase 555.00
Fratelli Toso, Nero A Giallo blk waisted vase 6,475.00
Fratelli Toso, Perelda Stellato cylindrical vase 5,895.00
Fratelli Toso, Perelda Stellato red/yel/gr vase 9,595.00
Fratelli Toso, Zanfirico lg cylindrical ftd vase 2,115.00
IVR Mazzega Gino Mazzega ashtray, deep straw 140.00
IVR Mazzega Scarpa Croce vase, clear w/internal decor 1,350.00
Salviati, Abstract figural sculpture 400.00
Salviati, Asti Clio red filigrana vase 730.00
Salviati, Obelisk, mc 425.00
Salviati Gaspari Sasso: clear vase w/red & aubergine 1,565.00
Seguso Vetri D'Arte, Sommerso bl/amber vase 1,500.00
Seguso Vetri D'Arte, Sommerso gr bowl 800.00
Seguso Vetri D'Arte, Sommerso orange/gr vase 750.00
Seguso Vetri D'Arte, Sommerso red w/amber decanter 400.00
Sottsass sculpture, blk base w/wht decor 6,203.00
Sottsass stepped vase, blk w/gr top 1,150.00
Tagliapietra Incalmo vase 3,235.00
Tagliapietra vase, yel w/canes 1,575.00
Tagliepietra, aubergine fishnet filigree vase 3,235.00
Vistosi, Incalmo squashed apple-shaped vase 915.00
Vistosi, lamp, inverted hat-shaped shade 455.00

Vistosi, Pulcino, J-shaped, gr 1,495.00
Vistosi, Pulcino: bl w/murrines 2,700.00
Vistosi, Pulcino: globular model: orange w/prunts 1,775.00
Zecchin-Martinuzzi, Pulegoso wht vase 2,425.00
Zecchin-Martinuzzi, Rosso e Nera vase 16,185.00

Ivory

Ivory has been used and appreciated since Neolithic times. It has been a product of every culture and continent. It is the second most valuable organic material after pearls. Ivory is defined as the dentine portion of mammalian teeth. Commercially the most important ivory comes from elephant and mammoth tusks, walrus tusks, hippo teeth, and sperm whale teeth. The smaller tusks of boar and warthog are often used whole.

Ivory has been used for artistic purposes as a palette for oil paints, as inlay on furniture, and especially as a medium for sculptures. Some are in the round, others in the form of plaques. Ivory also has numerous utilitarian uses such as cups and tankards; combs; handles for knives and medical tools; salt and pepper shakers; chess, domino, and checker pieces; billiard balls; jewelry; shoehorns; snuff boxes; brush pots; and fans.

There are a number of laws domestically and internationally to protect endangered animals including the elephant, walrus, and whale. However ivory taken and used before the various enactment dates is legal within the country in which it is located, and can be shipped internationally with a permit. Ivory from mammoths, hippopotamus, wart hog, and boar is excepted from all bans.

Prices have been stable for the last ten years, rising slightly in the last year. Prices are highest for European, Japanese, and Chinese ivories. Prices are lowest for African and Indian ivories. As with all collectibles, the very best pieces will appreciate most in the years to come. Small, poorly carved pieces will not appreciate to any extent. Our advisor for this category is Robert Weisblut; he is listed in the Directory under Maryland.

Woman with weaving implements, Chinese, early twentieth century, 9", $675.00. (Photo courtesy Robert Weisblut)

Bust of Voltaire on marble plinth, France, 19th C, 10" 7,500.00
Children, carving, Communist Chinese era, 9½" 1,250.00
Goddess, multi-armed, w/sitar, Indian, 20th C, 6½" 125.00
Grouping of gods & children, Chinese, early 20th C, 10" 2,650.00
Hippo tooth carving of village scene, Chinese, 1980s, 16" 325.00
Hornbill ivory ear ornament, Borneo, early 20th C, 4" 750.00
Narwhal tusk shakers, scrimshawed, 2½", pr 350.00
Snuff bottle, deep relief, China, 19th C, 5" 1,250.00
Study of rose branch, Japan, early 20th C, 13" 1,750.00
Table screen on stand, Ming Era, 11" 2,200.00
Tusk, full, cvd procession of people, African, mid-19th C 775.00
Vases, set of 2, w/basket, early 19th C, Chinese, 8" 2,000.00
Village scene, Japanese, ca 1900, 5½" 2,000.00

Walrus sailing vessel w/full sails, Eskimo, 1950s, 10".................**1,500.00**

Jack-in-the-Pulpit Vases

Popular novelties at the turn of the century, jack-in-the-pulpit vases were made in every type of art glass produced. Some were simple, others elaborately appliquéd and enameled. They were shaped to resemble the lily for which they were named.

Clear w/amber shadings, amethyst lily of the valley, 6½"............**160.00**
Frosted o/l w/ribs, appl gr leaves & ruby Xmas cactus, 13"..........**750.00**
Gr Dmn Quilt body, ruby/opal top w/silver flecks, 9½".................**60.00**
Lt gr to mottled gr w/cranberry rim, 8¾"...................................**50.00**
Peachblow colors, Mt WA, 7"...**100.00**
Pk Hobnail, crimped rim, opal cased, 7"...................................**125.00**
Rainbow, tooled crimped camphor ft, ruffled rim, 8"..................**250.00**
Wht w/yel to rose quilted int, HP base/int w/daisies, ruffled, 9".**550.00**

Jewelry

Jewelry as objects of adornment has always been regarded with special affection. Today prices for gems and gemstones crafted into antique and collectible jewelry are based on artistic merit, personal appeal, pure sentimentality, and intrinsic value. Note: In general, diamond prices have gone up more than 20% in the past year, and platinum is becoming popular again, so retail prices are rising. Diamond prices vary greatly depending on cut, color, clarity, etc., and to assess the value of any diamond of more than a carat in weight, you will need to have information about all of these factors. Values given here are for diamond jewelry with a standard commercial grade of diamonds that are most likely to be encountered.

Our advisor for fine jewelry is Rebecca Dodds; her address may be found in the Directory under Florida. Marcia 'Sparkles' Brown is our advisor for costume jewelry and the author of *Unsigned Beauties of Costume Jewelry* and *Signed Beauties of Costume Jewelry* (Collector Books); she is also the host of the video *Hidden Treasures, A Collector's Guide to Antique and Vintage Jewelry of the 19th and 20th Centuries*. Mrs. Brown is listed in the Directory under Oregon. Other good references are *Collectible Costume Jewelry* by Cherri Simonds; *Costume Jewelry, A Practical Handbook & Value Guide*, and *Collectible Silver Jewelry* by Fred Rezazadeh; *100 Years of Collectible Jewelry*, and *Fifty Years of Collectible Fashion Jewelry* by Lillian Baker; *Vintage Jewelry for Investment and Casual Ware* by Karen L. Edeen; and *Painted Porcelain Jewelry and Buttons* by Dorothy Kamm (all available from Collector Books). See also American Painted Porcelain; Hair Weaving.

Key:
cab — cabochon	g-t — gold-tone
ct — carat	k — karat
dmn — diamond	plat — platinum
dwt — penny weight	r/stn — rhinestone
Euro — European cut	stn — stone
fl — filigree	tw — total weight
gf — gold filled	wg — white gold
gp — gold plated	yg — yellow gold
grad — graduated	ygf — yellow gold filled
gw — gold washed	

Bar pin, plat, 35 mine-cut 1.25ct tw dmns, yg bks, pr..............**1,495.00**
Bracelet, bangle; 18k pk gold, seed pearls & turq-set flowers & leaves...**1,035.00**
Bracelet, charm; Tiffany, 14k yg, 8 gold charms+1915 5 peso Cuban coin.**2,300.00**
Bracelet, Glen Yank, sterling, 1 side w/raised panel, 2 are triangular..**400.00**
Bracelet, plat, 45 baguette dmns 6ct tw (H-J/VSI-VS2)..........**7,000.00**

Bracelet, silver gilt wide band w/eng medallions, English, 1870s....**160.00**
Bracelet, tennis; wg, rnd dmns, 1.75ct tw (G-H, VS2-SI1).........**920.00**
Bracelet, Tiffany, 14k yg, retro style, 33mm W, 48.33 dwt.......**1,950.00**
Bracelet, Wm Spratling, sterling, 1" W................................**1,265.00**
Bracelet, 14k rose/pk & yg, retro style, 34.9 grams, 7½".............**895.00**
Bracelet, 14k yg, stiff plain wide hollow band w/half pearls, 1870s..**600.00**
Bracelet, 14k yg, stiff twisted wire hollow band w/knot, 1890s...**975.00**
Bracelet, 14k yg & blk onyx stiff band w/half pearls, ca 1865.**1,035.00**
Bracelet, 14k yg flat curb links w/14 yg charms, ca 1880.........**2,750.00**
Bracelet, 14k yg flexible mesh, eng/enamel decor, 5 pearls, 40.5 dwt...**1,495.00**
Bracelet, 14k yg slide w/buckle & blk enameling, Vict.................**575.00**
Bracelet, 14k yg stiff band w/3 mine-cut dmns 1.35ct tw, 1880s....**2,500.00**
Bracelet, 15k yg stiff twig-like band w/garnet in leafy center, 1860s..**800.00**
Bracelet, 18k heavy links, Italian stirrup design..........................**440.00**
Brooch, dragonfly, enameled, 40 sm rose-cut dmns w/oval .50ct sapphire.**1,380.00**
Brooch, Frost, hammered/etched brass w/gr wash, dmn shape, 3¾" L..**450.00**
Brooch, Kalo, hammered silver w/cherries & leaves, 2" dia........**260.00**
Brooch, Margot De Taxo, sterling fish, cvd detail/amethyst cab, 1¾".....**80.00**
Brooch, Spratling, sterling bow w/lg amethyst, bead bezel/trim, 4½"...**325.00**
Brooch, Wm Spratling, owl, silver w/lg amethyst eyes, 2¼".....**1,100.00**
Brooch, Wm Spratling, silver feather w/lg inset amethyst, 2½"..**400.00**
Brooch, yg, 7 old mine-cut dmns 1ct tw (H-J, VS2-S12), 50 seed pearls...**375.00**
Brooch, yg spider, oval amethyst body w/1 pearl, 1880s, 4.75 dwt...**185.00**
Brooch, 14k wg, full-cut 1.80ct dmns (I, VS1) in circle...........**1,100.00**
Brooch, 14k yg bee, 20 rnd 2.35ct tw rubies................................**300.00**
Brooch, 14k yg bumblebee w/2 1.15ct tw sapphires+19 4.50ct tw rubies..**800.00**
Brooch, 14k yg fleur-de-lis w/53 5ct tw mine-cut dmns, 1870-80s..**4,350.00**
Brooch, 14k yg lizard w/175 sm dmns (1.5cts), 29 sq rubies (.75cts)..**1,200.00**
Brooch, 14k yg w/.30 mine-cut dmn, English, ca 1890, from $200 to..**300.00**
Brooch, 15k yg w/raised fl, oval dome center, 1860s....................**460.00**
Brooch, 18k yg, cab 19ct lapis lazuli+45 .45ct tw dmns+2 sm cab rubies..**2,185.00**
Brooch, 18k yg flower w/24 pave-set 3.40ct tw dmns & 2 10mm pearls...**2,600.00**
Brooch & earrings, Tiffany, 14k yg, 15 7.50ct amethysts+3 sm dmns....**860.00**
Brooch & earrings, Tiffany, 18k yg sunbursts w/17 .90ct tw dmns......**3,000.00**
Brooch & earrings, 14k yg w/sm cab turq & rnd-cut dmns .30ct tw......**630.00**
Brooch/pendant, plat w/many single & mine-cut dmns tw 5ct, Deco style.**3,000.00**
Brooch/pendant, 14k yg cross w/40 mine-cut dmns, 8.5ct tw, 1860s.**6,000.00**
Earrings, cab rose tourmaline/cultured pearl clusters, clips, pr.....**460.00**
Earrings, shell warrior cameos, gold openwork, 8 sm dmns, 1880s, pr..**1,000.00**
Earrings, 14k gold half-hoops w/8 1.5ct tw triangular tanzanites, pr.........**175.00**
Earrings, 14k yg, blk/wht onyx cameo pendant, 1870s, pr...........**800.00**
Earrings, 14k yg pendants w/buckle ends, pr...............................**75.00**
Earrings, 14k yg w/.35ct mine-cut dmn solitaire, screw bks, pr...**300.00**
Earrings, 14k yg w/teardrop-shaped cameos, ca 1941, pr.............**150.00**
Earrings, 18k wg, 7x4mm cab jadeite+7 .20ct tw dmns+11 .25tw dmns, pr...**1,500.00**
Earrings, 18k yg, .03ct rnd dmn amid 6 .40 tw rubies, button style, pr.......**750.00**
Earrings, 18k yg bees, ea w/91 sm dmns+92 tiny emeralds+2 rubies, pr..**2,750.00**
Earrings, 20k yg hoops, beveled edge, pr....................................**280.00**
Locket, 14k yg, cross on top w/decor, 1870-80, 10 dwt.............**515.00**
Necklace, angel skin coral beads, 1-strand, 14k yg fl clasp..........**350.00**
Necklace, cultured pearls, 7x7½mm, matinee length.................**750.00**
Necklace, Kalo, silver 2" leaf/berry pendant on chain................**450.00**
Necklace, pearls, 2 strands of 7-7.5mm w/14k yg/jade clasp, matinee..**2,000.00**
Necklace, Tiffany, sterling silver cross & rope chain (29½").......**150.00**
Necklace, Tiffany, 18k yg & oxblood coral choker..................**1,495.00**
Necklace, 14k yg, rnd gold & dmn ornament on clasp, 22 dwt, 28"..**1,495.00**
Necklace, 14k yg chain w/blk enamel/gold slide, 2 tassels, 30 dwt, 41"..**2,400.00**
Necklace, 14k yg links w/centerpc of 132 2.5ct tw dmns (IJ VS1)..**2,000.00**
Necklace, 14k yg rope, 14.75 dwt, 24¼"...................................**375.00**
Necklace, 15k yg anchor links w/spring ring clasp, 22.4 dwt, 1890s..**1,725.00**
Necklace, 18k yg curb link chain, marked AMC in oval, 34 dwt, 16"..**800.00**
Necklace, 18k yg w/71 30ct tw prong-set rnd sapphires...........**3,500.00**
Pendant, Merle Bennett, sterling, chain w/linked 2-part pearl-set drop........**950.00**
Pendant, plat, 1ct mine-cut dmn+15 sm dmns (H-J, S12-II), Deco style.**1,840.00**

Pendant, 14k yg heart w/16 .03ct rnd dmns, on dainty 14k gold chain........**300.00**
Pendant, 14k yg w/5mm rnd amethyst & 16 seed pearls, 4mm garnet drop...**250.00**
Pendant, 15k yg Bishop's cross, flat casing/bead ends, 1870s, 7.6 dwt....**800.00**
Pendant, 18k yg cross w/fl, scalloped ends, Mexico, 13.75 dwt ...**430.00**
Ring, plat, emerald-cut 2.90ct emerald w/20 full-cut 1 ct tw dmns+2 sm...**4,800.00**
Ring, plat w/.25 sq dmn+15 sm dmns tw .75ct (VSI, H).............**625.00**
Ring, plat w/4.86ct Euro dmn (VS)+4 dmn tw .66 ....**23,000.00**
Ring, Tiffany, 18k yg, 2ct tw finest dmns in cluster, 1950s.......**4,000.00**

Ring, yellow gold, old-mine cut 2.0 carat oval diamond (I-J color, I quality), six baguettes and forty single-cut round diamonds, Art Deco style, $8,500.00.

Ring, 10k yg band w/3 rubies & 2 sm dmns **210.00**
Ring, 10k yg w/3 marquise rubies+2 dmn chips............................**75.00**
Ring, 14k rose gold w/lg oval topaz, scrolled motif......................**90.00**
Ring, 14k rose/pk gold dome w/sm dmns & rubies, 1940s **675.00**
Ring, 14k wg, oval faceted 19x13mm pk topaz w/6 1.5ct tw dmns ..**375.00**
Ring, 14k wg cluster: 10 pearls+4 sm dmns & bands of 10 accent dmns ...**200.00**
Ring, 14k yg, lg emerald-cut tourmaline+36 sm+5 .20ct dmns ...**600.00**
Ring, 14k yg, oval bl 3ct sapphire amid 14 1.25 tw mine-cut dmns..**2,750.00**
Ring, 14k yg, 1ct dmn (IZ, K), man's **1,200.00**
Ring, 14k yg, 3 dmns (¼ct+2 at .10ct, VVSI, F) man's...............**400.00**
Ring, 14k yg, 7x5mm oval tanzanite amid 25 sm .50 ct tw dmns (H-J) ...**400.00**
Ring, 14k yg w/chrysoberyl cat's eye 6½x7mm, man's **285.00**
Ring, 14k yg w/handmade cvd floral w/angel skin coral w/openwork...**200.00**
Ring, 18k, 13mm South Sea pearl+4 princess-cut dmns tw .80+18 sm dmns....**3,680.00**
Ring, 18k wg, cab 2ct bl sapphire amid 52 .65ct tw dmns...........**925.00**
Ring, 18k wg, Eastern Star, mc stones+21 sm dmns **300.00**
Ring, 18k wg, oval 11x9mm cab ruby+10 sm rubies+174 1ct tw dmns....**2,000.00**
Ring, 18k wg, sq sapphire 2½mm+2 dmns .25ct tw.....................**525.00**
Ring, 18k yg, center rose-cut dmn amid 12 sm rose-cut dmns, 1820s..**2,400.00**
Ring, 18k yg, octagonal 25ct amethyst solitaire **260.00**
Ring, 18k yg, w/13mm gray pearl...**865.00**
Ring, 18k yg w/12ct sq-cut emerald, 6 princess-cut dmns ea side..**1,700.00**
Ring, 18k yg w/8.5mm pearl amid 12 sm rnd .60ct tw dmns **575.00**
Stickpin, gp Indian's profile in relief, Deco era, from $25 to **45.00**
Stickpin, gp w/bl & wht enamel beads, late Vict, from $10 to.............**20.00**
Stickpin, silver & copper pharaoh's head w/enameling, Nouveau, $25 to.....**45.00**
Stickpin, 14k wg, cvd shell lady's face cameo, Vict, $150 to **200.00**
Stickpin, 14k wg fl w/2mm single-cut dmn, Vict, from $100 to **150.00**

Costume Jewelry

Rhinestone jewelry is a very popular field of collecting. Rhinestones are foil-backed, leaded crystal, and faceted stones with a sparkle outshining diamonds. Copyrighting jewelry came into effect in 1955. Pieces bearing a copyright mark (post-1955) are considered 'collectibles,' while pieces (with no copyright) made before then are regarded as 'antiques.' Fur clips are two-pronged, used to anchor fur stoles. Dress clips have a spring clasp and are used at the dress neckline. Look for signed and well-made, unmarked pieces for your collections and preserve this American art form. Our advisor for costume jewelry is Marcia Brown (see introductory paragraphs for information on her books and videos).

Bracelet, Accessocraft, pottery/metal rings on chain, from $45 to..**55.00**
Bracelet, Bakelite, blk/brn w/foliage cvg, 1½", VG, from $375 to....**425.00**
Bracelet, Bakelite, geometric cvg, cream, ¾"+, VG, from $85 to..**90.00**
Bracelet, Bakelite, geometric cvg, gr, 1"+ wide, VG, from $100 to ..**175.00**

Bracelet, Bakelite, marbled apricot w/simple cvg, 1¼", VG, up to...**160.00**
Bracelet, Bakelite, 8-sided, bl w/red & wht ring inserts, up to.......**70.00**
Bracelet, bangle; Bakelite, blk w/heavy floral cvg, ¾", VG, up to.**350.00**
Bracelet, bangle; Bakelite, cream w/marbled yel dots, EX **850.00**
Bracelet, bangle; Bakelite, cream w/6 brn marbled dots, from $200 to ..**275.00**
Bracelet, bangle; Bakelite, orange w/geometric cvg, from $30 to ..**50.00**
Bracelet, bangle; Bakelite, red bow ties on cream, ¾" wide, VG ..**3,000.00**
Bracelet, bangle; Bakelite, 3 cvd/pnt segments w/brass insert, up to .**140.00**
Bracelet, clear r/stns in 3 rows..**45.00**
Bracelet, cuff; mc r/stns **85.00**
Bracelet, cuff; plastic, tan w/injected orange free-form, 2¾", VG .**90.00**
Bracelet, faux pearls, 2-strand, hook fastener, from $15 to **25.00**
Bracelet, fringed bow knot w/gr baguette tassel/irid chatons **185.00**
Bracelet, gilt brass fl w/mc marquise stones, 1900s, from $65 to....**95.00**
Bracelet, gold & wht r/stns in 11 rows, 2¼" W **110.00**
Bracelet, hand-set clear r/stns in single row, from $18 to...............**28.00**
Bracelet, red chatons w/sm r/stns in 2 outer rows..........................**30.00**
Bracelet, tennis; clear r/stn chatons amid 2 rows of gp chains.......**38.00**

Bracelet, two rows of small white chaton rhinestones and three inner rows of baguettes, unsigned, $66.00. (Photo courtesy Marcia Brown)

Bracelet, Trifari, silver-tone metal & faux pearls, from $35 to.......**50.00**
Bracelet & earrings, enamel leaves w/irid r/stns & pearl clusters ..**68.00**
Bracelet & earrings, Florenza, floral design w/plastic beads & r/stns ..**85.00**
Brooch, Art, MOP & antiqued metalwork w/faux pearls/turq/r/stns ..**60.00**
Brooch, Austrian, floral nosegay w/mc r/stns..................................**85.00**
Brooch, Bakelite, Air Raid Patrolman, hinged/articulated, 3½" **1,300.00**
Brooch, Bakelite, cream w/cvd & rtcl hand/flowers, pnt details, 3¼"...**300.00**
Brooch, Bakelite, cvd/pnt floral apple juice pc on yel, 2¾", up to.........**250.00**
Brooch, Bakelite, googly eye 'Aunt Jemima,' red/yel/pnt details, 2" ..**1,000.00**
Brooch, Bakelite, turtle, cream w/brass studs, 3" **60.00**
Brooch, Bakelite, 3 cvd beets, red string stems/gr leaves, 4" **2,500.00**
Brooch, Bakelite, 3 strawberries attached to bar w/celluloid chain, 2"...**350.00**
Brooch, Bakelite, 4 lg cvd orange carrots on gr bar, 4¾", VG.....**850.00**
Brooch, Balinese goddess face w/r/stns in headpc & gr earrings, $80 to **90.00**
Brooch, Boucher, swirl form w/ruby & clear r/stns, early MB mk, up to .**350.00**
Brooch, Ciner, owl, gold-tone metal w/faux emerald eyes **100.00**
Brooch, Eisenberg Ice, topaz/clear r/stns, from $150 to................**190.00**
Brooch, eternal circle w/rows of gold & topaz r/stns **35.00**
Brooch, gp outlined wings w/shaded pk r/stns, lg **75.00**
Brooch, gp 5-leaf clover w/emerald gr chatons................................**48.00**
Brooch, Hattie Carnegie, fish w/faux turq & pearls, from $90 to...**100.00**
Brooch, Hattie Carnegie, silver bug w/trembler wings, from $95 to ..**135.00**
Brooch, Hobe, tree form w/gold-tone wire branches & faux pearls...**150.00**
Brooch, Judy Lee, gr & citrine r/stns, lg, from $45 to **65.00**
Brooch, Lisner, leaf form made of sculptured plastic pk & wht stones.......**40.00**
Brooch, Martha Sleeper, Bakelite, Cactus, apple juice in pnt tan pot..**1,000.00**
Brooch, peacock w/watermelon tourmaline body, aurora borealis r/stns ..**95.00**
Brooch, r/stn duck **65.00**
Brooch, r/stn cluster, lg, 3½" **85.00**
Brooch, r/stns of varied shapes w/chaton center stone, 4½"........**135.00**
Brooch, Weiss, fct r/stns of varied shapes, lg, from $90 to..........**120.00**
Brooch, wht goldfish w/clear r/stns **28.00**
Brooch & earrings, Austrian, yel & red r/stns w/gold leaves **65.00**
Brooch & earrings, Beaujewels, marquise/sculptured stones, lg **75.00**
Brooch & earrings, Boucher, gold-metal knot w/turq & r/stns **350.00**

Brooch & earrings, gr cab w/dk gr chatons, Austrian......................**48.00**
Brooch & earrings, Jomaz, metal leaves w/lg central bl stone, $90 to.....**110.00**
Brooch & earrings, Krammer, crescents w/amethyst r/stns, from $100 to....**150.00**
Brooch & earrings, openwork w/amber cab & fct stones, from $55 to......**70.00**
Cameo set, Whiting & Davis, plastic, pendant+bracelet+earrings...**175.00**
Clip, V shape w/glued clear chaton r/stns.................................**20.00**
Clips, Eisenberg Original, vermeil king & queen w/stones, $1,000 to .**1,800.00**
Cuff links & tie tack, Hickok, fishing theme, from $25 to **35.00**
Earrings, aurora borealis r/stn cluster, pr **38.00**
Earrings, Bakelite, orange/butterscotch segments, teardrops, 2", pr ..**150.00**
Earrings, Claudette, speckled cab stone amid irid r/stns, pr **40.00**
Earrings, Coro, aurora borealis stones on silver-tone, pr **25.00**
Earrings, Coro, lg aquamarine stones, drop style, pr.......................**25.00**
Earrings, Danecraft, sterling silver, pr, from $25 to **40.00**
Earrings, emerald-cut clear r/stns w/chatons & sm r/stns, pr..........**65.00**
Earrings, faux pearl decor on button shape, pr, from $20 to **35.00**
Earrings, Hobe, pearls suspended on gold rings, pr, from $25 to....**45.00**
Earrings, japanned aurora borealis drop from gold chain, pr..........**48.00**
Earrings, Lisner, sculptured plastic stones & r/stns, pr, from $35 to....**50.00**
Earrings, pk r/stns surround pearl, pr...**28.00**
Earrings, Rosenstein, pavé-set r/stns w/central turq stones, pr.......**70.00**
Earrings, Schiaparelli, sculptured stones w/pearl accents, pr.........**75.00**
Earrings, Vendome, beads & r/stns, pr, from $25 to **40.00**
Earrings, Weiss, 3 bl r/stns form drop, pr, from $25 to **35.00**
Earrings, 3 baguette r/stns w/6 sm chaton guards, pr **54.00**
Necklace, Bakelite, dk brn w/3 lg cvd segments, celluloid chain, 10" ...**40.00**
Necklace, faux pearls, 3-strand w/faux pearl center/gr r/stns **25.00**
Necklace, faux pearls, 4-strand, r/stn clasp w/dangles...................**175.00**
Necklace, gilded brass festoon w/faux pearls & fct stones, 1900s ..**80.00**
Necklace, gold & brn cabs on brn r/stn chain................................**30.00**
Necklace, gr carnival glass/gold metallic beads on chain...............**35.00**
Necklace, Nouveau rhodium floral w/navettes/chatons, clear teardrop ...**95.00**
Necklace, Pam, floral w/irid stones/enamel leaves, from $35 to **50.00**
Necklace, Richelieu, faux pearls, 2-strand, from $75 to...............**100.00**
Necklace, Tara, floral design w/clear r/stns, from $35 to................**50.00**
Necklace, Trifari, baguette r/stns, from $80 to **110.00**
Necklace, 3 deep bl pear-shaped stones on r/stn strand **90.00**
Necklace & bracelet, wht enamel fans w/sm r/stn florets & faux pearls...**48.00**
Necklace & earrings, bl plastic beads drop from bl r/stns **30.00**
Necklace & earrings, BsK, plastic pastel inserts, from $50 to........**85.00**
Necklace & earrings, Coro, gold-tone leaves w/mc stones, from $100 to...**150.00**
Necklace & earrings, melon-shaped metal beads, long, screw-bks.....**250.00**
Necklace & earrings, Star, silver-tone w/bl plastic inserts **45.00**
Necklace & earrings, Trifari, enamel leaves w/turq plastic inserts.**75.00**
Necklace & earrings, wht glass cabs w/chaton r/stns......................**40.00**
Pendant, gilt brass w/faceted Bohemian beads, 1900s, from $85 to..**100.00**
Ring, bl chaton encircled in clear r/stns **35.00**
Ring, blk cab oval w/circle of wht r/stns & outer blk r/stns...........**32.00**
Ring, clear r/stns imitate dmn cluster, adjustable **23.00**
Ring, Eisenberg Ice, yel topaz stone, from $95 to.........................**140.00**
Ring, gp w/7 topaz r/stns..**38.00**
Ring, opaline clusters on gp **45.00**
Ring, topaz chatons form chrysanthemum....................................**55.00**

Johnson Brothers

A Staffordshire-based company operating since well before the turn of the century, Johnson Brothers has produced many familiar lines of dinnerware, several of which are becoming very collectible. Some of their patterns were made in both blue and pink transfer as well as in polychrome. One of the more familiar patterns is Friendly Village, which is still being produced, though the pattern is much more limited than it once was.

Values below range from a low base price for patterns that are still in production (i.e., Friendly Village) or less collectible to a high that would apply to very desirable patterns such as Old Britain Castles, Wild Turkeys, Strawberry Fair, Historic America, Rose Chintz, Chintz, etc. Mid-range lines include Coaching Scenes, Millsteam, Old English Countryside, Rose Bouquet (and there are others).

For more information on marks, patterns, and pricing, we rcommend *Johnson Brothers Dinnerware Pattern Directory and Price Guide* by Mary J. Finegan, who is listed in the Directory under North Carolina.

Bowl, cereal/soup; rnd, sq or lug, ea, from $10 to.........................**12.00**
Bowl, soup; rnd or sq, 7", from $12 to..**14.00**
Bowl, vegetable; oval, from $30 to...**40.00**
Chop/cake plate, from $50 to..**70.00**
Coffee mug, from $15 to..**25.00**
Coffeepot, from $80 to **100.00**
Covered butter dish, from $50 to...**60.00**
Demitasse set, 2-pc, from $20 to...**24.00**
Pitcher/jug, from $45 to...**60.00**
Plate, buffet; 10½-11", from $26 to...**35.00**
Plate, dinner; from $14 to...**20.00**
Plate, salad; sq or rnd, from $10 to...**14.00**
Platter, med, 12-14", ea, from $45 to...**55.00**
Sauce boat/gravy, from $40 to...**48.00**
Sugar bowl, open, from $30 to..**35.00**
Teacup & saucer, from $15 to..**20.00**
Teapot, from $80 to **100.00**
Turkey platter, 20½", from $200 to...**300.00**

Josef Originals

Figurines of lovely ladies, charming girls, and whimsical animals marked Josef Originals were designed by Muriel Joseph George of Arcadia, California, from 1945 to 1985. Until 1960 they were produced in California, but costs were high and copies of her work were being made in Japan. To remain competitive, she and her partner, George Good, found a company in Japan to build a factory and produce her designs to her specifications. Muriel retired in 1982; however, Mr. Good continued production of her work and made some design changes on some figurines. The company was sold in late 1985; the name is currently owned by Dakin/Applause, and a limited amount of figurines with the Josef Originals name are being made. Those made during the ownership of Muriel are the most collectible. They can be recognized by these characteristics: The girls have a high-gloss finish, black eyes, and most are signed on the bottom. As of the late 1970s, bisque finish was making its way into the lineup, and by 1980 glossy girls were fairly scarce in the product line. Brown-eyed figurines date from 1982 through 1985. Applause uses a red-brown eye, although they are starting to release 'copies' of early pieces that are signed Josef Originals by Applause or by Dakin. The animals were nearly always done in a matt finish and bore paper labels only. In the mid-1970s they introduced a line of fuzzy flocked-coat animals with glass eyes. Our advisors, Jim and Kaye Whitaker (see the Directory under Washington, no appraisal requests please) have written three books: *Josef Originals, Charming Figurines, Revised Edition*; *Josef Originals, A Second Look*; and *Josef Originals, Figurines of Muriel Joseph George*. These are all currently available, and each has no repeats of items shown in the other books. Please note: All figurines listed here have black eyes unless specified otherwise. As with many collectibles, values have been impacted to a measurable extent since the advent of the Internet.

Aquarius, Zodiac Girls series, Japan, 4¾" **45.00**
Birthstone dolls, January through December, jewels, Japan, 3½", ea..**25.00**

Boxer dog, Champions series, Japan, 5" 22.00
Buggy Bugs series, various wire antenna, Japan, 3¼", ea 25.00
Cat wall plaque, gray, California 50.00
Cherie, poodle, Kennel Club series, 3½" 25.00
Christmas music box girl decorating tree, Japan, 7" 65.00
Doll of the Month (tilt head), Jan through Dec, California, 3¼", ea ..55.00
Elephant w/tusks, Japan, 6¾" 50.00
Farmer's Daughter, girl w/hen & basket of eggs, Japan, 5" 50.00
First Love Series, Tony, Tina, Japan, 5" 50.00
Girl w/straw hat, Gigi series, 7" 50.00

Greece, in rose toga, California, 10¼", $110.00. (Photo cour-
tesy Jim and Kaye Whitaker)

Happy Anniversary music box, Japan, 7¼" 70.00
Happy Home w/Dove Greeting Angel, Japan, 3¾" 45.00
Hunter, Beautiful, standing horse, Japan, 6" 25.00
International series, various countries, 4¾", ea 50.00
It's a Wonderful World Series figurines, Japan, 3½", ea 35.00
Italian Aristocrats, lady & escort, Japan, 7", ea 90.00
Jeanne, Colonial Days series, Japan, 9" 135.00
Kennel Club series, Yorkshire, etc, Japan, 3", ea 20.00
Love Letter from Love Story, Romance series, Japan, 8" 125.00
Make Believe series, Japan, 4½", ea 35.00
Mama Ballerina, California, 7" 85.00
Mary Ann & Mama, California, 4", 7", pr 145.00
Mermaid lipstick holder, wht/beige trim, Japan, 4" 85.00
Mice, various styles, 2¾", ea 12.00
Miss Mary, Nursery Rhymes series, Japan, 4" 45.00
Missy, girl in bonnet, several colors, California, 4" 45.00
Monday, Days of the Week series, California, 3½" 75.00
Monkeys Mama & Papa, Japan, 3" 15.00
Nanette, half doll w/jewels, several colors, California, 5½" 65.00
New Hat from 'First Time,' Japan, 4½" 40.00
Nurse, Career Girls series, in yel, holding baby, Japan, 5¾" 60.00
Parasol Girl, series 3 in set, Japan, 6¾" 75.00
Pixies, various poses, gr w/red & gold trim, Japan, 2" to 4¼", ea ..30.00
Poodle, from Poodle & Siamese, Japan, 4¼" 30.00
Rose, Flower Girl series, girl w/flower hat, Japan, 4¼" 40.00
Rose Garden series, brn eyes, 6 different, Japan, 5¼", ea 65.00
Ruby, Little Jewels series, girl w/crown w/'ruby,' Japan, 3½" 35.00
Santa, kiss on forehead, Japan, 4¾" 60.00
Secret pal, girl w/fan, various colors, California, 3½" 40.00
Skunks w/wht hair tuft on head, Japan, 2½" 18.00
Sports Angels series, playing various sports, Japan, 2¾", ea 35.00
Tawny, Siamese character cat, Japan, 4" 12.00
Three Kings (set of 3), Japan, 8½" to 11", set 70.00
Watusi Luau series, hunter in pot, natives, etc, Japan, 5" 65.00
Wee Ching, Wee Ling, boy & girl w/dog & cat, California (copied) 65.00
Wee Folk, various poses, Japan, 4½", ea 20.00
World Greatest series, bowler, boxer, etc, Japan, 4½", ea 25.00

Judaica

The items listed below are representative of objects used in both the secular and religious life of the Jewish people. They are evident of a culture where silversmiths, painters, engravers, writers, and metal workers were highly gifted and skilled in their art. Most of the treasures shown in recently displayed exhibits of Judaica were confiscated by the Germans during the late 1930s up to 1945; by then eight Jewish synagogues and fifty warehouses had been filled with Hitler's plunder. Judaica is currently available through dealers, from private collections, and the annual auction held in Israel, New York City, and Boston.

Candlesticks, sabbath; brass, ftd baluster, Morocco, 19th C, 12", pr .1,000.00
Candlesticks, sabbath; silver, chased flowers, Poland, 19th C, 12", pr ...1,380.00
Candlesticks, sabbath; silver, eng, Austro-Hungary, 1890s, 18", pr .1,265.00
Candlesticks, sabbath; silver, eng/trn, Germany, 19th C, 12", pr ...650.00
Canopy, marriage; red/bl velvet w/embr, Am, 19th C, 104x122" w/poles..2,875.00
Gavel, shul klopfer; cvd folk art, 19th C, 10½" 1,000.00
Knife, Challah; silver, eng/inscr hdl, Germany, 19th C, 10¾" 400.00
Lamp, eternal; silver & brass, openwork arms, ca 1900, 20" 230.00
Lamp, Hanukka; brass, 8-part star oil section, Germany, 1800s, 15" 700.00
Lamp, Hanukka; bronze, pierced scrolls, 8 oil pans, Italy, 17th C, 7" ..1,250.00
Lamp, Hanukka; silver, bench-style menorah, Vienna, 1858, 6¾" 2,000.00
Lamp, Hanukka; silver, chased fruit/flowers, Germany, 19th C, 6" 4,850.00
Lamp, Hanukka; silver, emb scrolls/etc, clay ft, Germany, 1900s, 9" 700.00
Lamp, Hanukka; silver Ball Shem Tov type, Ukranian, 1895, 10" 3,450.00
Lamp, sabbath; brass, 8-point star, bell drip pan, Germany, 1800s, 18" .700.00
Lamp, sabbath; cast bronze, 8-pointed star, Italy, 19th C, 22" .2,500.00
Laver, wall; brass, hinged lid, dedication, Poland, 1830, 18" 3,000.00
Plate, bread; silver, emb depictions, Lowenthal, early 20th C, 8¼" ..4,000.00
Plate, SP, for redemption of firstborn, Am, 20th C, 21¾" 2,000.00
Spice box, pewter, sliding lid, loop hdl, Germany, mid-18th C, 6" .575.00
Spice container, silver, fruit form, S-stem, Prague, 1861, 6" 1,265.00
Spice container, silver, ovoid fruit form, Polish, ca 1700, 5¾" 1,035.00
Spice container, silver filigree hemispheres/pennant, Prague, 1845, 5"..375.00
Spice container, SP fruit form on plate, Prague, 1850s, 5½" 1,265.00
Spice tower, gilded silver, castle w/openwork, Russia, 1900s, 16"..2,875.00
Spice tower, ivory/silver, openwork, bells, Turkish, 1890s, 9¼" ..1,035.00
Spice tower, silver, emb/chased flowers, Germany, 1900s, 8½" ...1,265.00
Spice tower, silver, lions/birds/bells, skirt, Riedel, 1864, 11" ...1,850.00
Spice tower, silver filigree, lions/pennant, Berlin, 1850s, 9¼" .1,150.00
Torah breastplate, silver shield form, Poland, 1859, 10" 800.00
Torah breastplate, silver-gilt, E Europe, 1890s, 9¾" 1,000.00
Torah crown, silver, classic design, Continental, 1781, 7¼" ...2,875.00
Torah finial, silver rtcl crown w/foliage/bell, Hungary, 1600s, 12"...23,000.00
Torah finials, silver fruit form, Austro-Hungary, ca 1900, 11¾", pr 545.00
Torah pointer, silver filigree, central knop/finial, London, 1897, 11" ...925.00
Torah pointers, silver, scalloped cuff/hand, Russia, 1800s, 12", pr........925.00
Torah pointers, silver, spiral stem w/leaf tip, Poland, 1900s, 10".525.00
Tray, Seder; SP, emb scene/fruit, ruffled rim, 20th C, 16½".........800.00

Jugtown

The Jugtown Pottery was started about 1920 by Juliana and Jacques Busbee, in Moore County, North Carolina. Ben Owen, a young descendant of a Staffordshire potter, was hired in 1923. He was the master potter, while the Busbees experimented with perfecting glazes and supervising design and modeling. Preferred shapes were those reminiscent of traditional country wares and classic Oriental forms. Glazes were various: natural-clay oranges, buffs, Tobacco-Spit Brown, Mirror Black, white, Frog Skin Green, a lovely turquoise called Chinese Blue, and the traditional cobalt-decorated salt glaze. The pottery gained national recognition, and as a result of their success, several other local potteries were established. The pottery closed for a time in the late 1950s due to the ill health of Mrs. Busbee (who had directed the business after her husband died in 1947) but reopened in 1960. Jugtown is still in operation; however, they no longer use their original glaze colors which are now so collectible and the circular mark is slightly smaller than the original.

Vase, Chinese Translation, white opaque matt, bulbous with four strap handles, marked, 8½x6", $400.00.

Bowl, Chinese Blue w/red highlights, 7½" 425.00
Bowl, Chinese White w/cobalt rim, V Owens, 1960s, 2¼x5¾" 80.00
Bowl, feldspathic satin wht, HP flowers (V Brady), N Sweezy, 1970s, 5" ..60.00
Bowl, Frogskin w/t'prints, V Owens, 1960s, 4x7⅝" 70.00
Bowl, Ox Blood, Korean, Ben Owen, 1930s, 3¼x9¾" 700.00
Bowl, Tobacco-Spit Brown, dbl cord-style hdls, Ben Owen, 1930s, 2x6"....30.00
Catalog & price list, 82 blk & wht photos on parchment, 1960s, 6x9"....100.00
Creamer & sugar bowl, Tobacco-Spit Brown, w/lid, V Owens, 1960s, 3" ...60.00
Figurine, chicken on ped, glossy red-brn, Boyd Owens, 1959-60, 7x7" 500.00
Flyer, Jugtown Ware: An Am Craft..., 3-fold, 1960s, 7½x10½" 25.00
Inkwell, Chinese Blue, Ben Owen, late 1930s, 2⅞" 250.00
Jar, apothecary; Albany slip Frogs Skin, Ben Owen, flat hdls, 1930s, 6" .175.00
Jug, speckled beige semimatt w/cvd shoulder lines, mk/1977, 5¾" ..70.00
Pie dish, bright orange red lead glaze, Ben Owen, X, 1930s, 2½x11" ..70.00
Pie dish, red lead w/spots, Ben Owen, 1930s, 2⅛x10" 100.00
Pie dish, Tobacco-Spit Brown, Ben Owen, late 1930s, 2¼x10½" .70.00
Pitcher, gray w/cobalt int & decor, 3¼" 40.00
Pitcher, red lead w/orange spotting, ca 1920s, 8", NM 120.00
Teapot, orange earthenware, 6½" 390.00
Vase, Chinese Blue, incurvate rim, 4½x3¼" 370.00
Vase, Chinese Blue, ovoid, 5" 475.00
Vase, Chinese Blue, tapered cylinder, 6" 650.00
Vase, Chinese Blue, tapered shoulder, 4x2¾" 310.00
Vase, Chinese Blue w/lt irid, exposed clay around widening base, 6" ...700.00
Vase, Chinese Blue w/red, rnd tapered form, 6" 600.00
Vase, Frogs Skin Green, B Owen, 1930s, 6¾x5¼" w/2¾" opening.155.00
Vase, Mirror Black, Oriental Translation, Ben Owen, 1930s, 3¾"...50.00
Vase, orange/gr/yel mottle, bulbous w/3 hdls, stamp mk, 6x6" 675.00
Vase, Ridge Blue, short neck, wide shoulder, tapered cylinder, 5x6" ...515.00

K. P. M. Porcelain

The original KPM wares were produced from 1823 until 1847 by the Konigliche Porzellan Manfaktur, located in Berlin, Germany. Meissen used the same letters on some of their porcelains, as did several others in the area. In addition to the initials, the mark sometimes contains a crowned eagle with a scepter. Watch for items currently being imported from China; they are marked KPM with the eagle, but the scepter is not present. Our advisor for this category is Don Williams; he is listed in the Directory under Missouri.

Basket, floral sprays w/much gold, 2-part, 4x12½x8½" 140.00
Group, sm girl w/bouquet being crowned by another, 1925, 8" ...725.00
Jar, ovoid w/floral & gilt on ivory, supported by 3 3-D cherubs, 16"...1,200.00
Plaque, German officer, 5" dia+gilt fr w/laurel & helmet.........4,300.00

Plaque, lady's portrait, att Wagner, 9x7"+ornate gilt metal 15x13" fr ..3,200.00
Plaque, men talking at table, sgn Knoeller, 8½x10¾"+fr.........3,500.00
Plaque, monk looking at glass while eating, Sckerfechte, 10x13"+fr..4,850.00
Plaque, peasant tavern scene w/village beyond, 6¼x9¼"........2,185.00
Plaque, Ruth, after Bouguereau, late 1800s, 12¾x7⅞"............2,300.00
Plaque, woman/child at storefront, after Douw, Schmidt, 21x15", pr..18,800.00
Plaque, 2 peasant boys w/dog, fruit & vegetables, KPM/H/15-13, 16x13" ...8,625.00
Plate, floral HP on wht, ca 1840, 10" 37.50
Teapot, cobalt & gold decor in Rococo taste, 1850-65, 6½", EX...200.00

Kayserzinn Pewter

J.P. Kayser Sohn produced pewter decorated with relief-molded Art Nouveau motifs in Germany during the late 1800s and into the 1900s. Examples are marked with 'Kayserzinn' and the mold number within an elongated oval reserve. Items with three-dimensional animals, insects, birds, etc., are valued much higher than bowls, plates, and trays with simple embossed florals, which are usually priced at $100.00 to about $200.00, depending on size.

Bowl, iris relief, butterfly emb on lid, ftd/hdls, #41-4125, 8x9½"...165.00
Bowl, tulips/lily of the valley relief, dome base/hdls, +lid, 7x8", EX 135.00
Candlesticks, flowers/leaves relief, invt trumpet form, #4328, 10", pr ..125.00
Charger, battleship/lighthouse relief, SMS Aegir, #4122, 20" 135.00

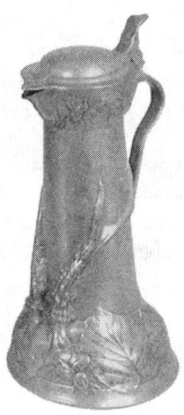

Tankard, flowers and leaves with stag horns at base (all in relief), marked Kayserzinn 20 4035 P, with original sand bag inside, 15", $1,600.00.

Tray, floral emb, w/hdls, #4284, 15½" sq........................900.00
Tray, underwater scene/fish, floral border, #4143, 22" L 135.00
Tureen, flowers/insects relief on body & lid, ftd, #4121, 10x12" .400.00

Keeler, Brad

Keeler studied art for a time in the 1930s; later he became a modeler for a Los Angeles firm. By 1939 he was working in his own studio where he created naturalistic studies of birds and animals which were marketed through giftware stores. They were decorated by means of an airbrush and enhanced with hand-painted details. His flamingo figures were particularly popular. In the mid-'40s, he developed a successful line of Chinese Modern housewares glazed in Ming Dragon Blood, a red color he personally developed. Keeler died of a heart attack in 1952, and the pottery closed soon thereafter. For more information, we recommend *The Collector's Encyclopedia of California Pottery, Second Edition*, by Jack Chipman (Collector Books).

Bowl, lobster on cabbage head, w/lid, +spoon/undertray, 5½" 100.00
Casserole, lobster finial, hdls, 12" 80.00
Charger, fish w/2 fishing lures & line, #141, 11" dia...................160.00

Creamer & sugar bowl, fish, standing on tails.............................260.00
Dish, leaf shape w/lobster center, 3-part, 12"..........................55.00
Figurine, barn swallow, spread-wing bluebird w/split tail, #706, 8"....80.00
Figurine, bird on branch, #720, 4⅜"..........................60.00
Figurine, bird on branch, rose colored, #17, 6".........................70.00
Figurine, cats, blk & wht features, #772 & #773, 7" & 8", pr 150.00
Figurine, cockatoo, 8¾"..60.00
Figurine, flamingo, #31, 8¾", from $85 to 100.00
Figurine, flamingo, head down, #2, 7½", from $125 to...............150.00
Figurine, flamingo, head up, #1, 12", from $165 to.....................200.00
Figurine, pheasant w/1 ft raised, #22, 7" 65.00
Figurine, rooster, rose comb, high fanned-out tail, 9" 85.00
Figurine, Siamese cat, sitting, 3⅜".......................................35.00
Plate, fish shape, 8", from $40 to 45.00
Platter, turkey shape, mc, oval, 15x20¾"................................265.00
Serving fork & spoon, wood w/red lobster claw handles, 11", pr ...165.00
Shakers, fish, standing on tails, #149, 4", pr............................130.00
Tray, cabbage leaf w/tomato-shaped covered bowl in center, 14"..55.00
Tray, gr leaves w/lg red lobster as hdl, 5-section, #864, 15x16" 85.00
Tray, gr leaves w/lg red lobster in center, 2-section, 15" L 70.00

Keen Kutter

Keen Kutter was the brand name chosen in 1870 by the Simmons Firm for a line of high-grade tools and cutlery. The trademark was first applied to high-grade axes. A corporation was formed in 1874 called Simmons Hardware Company. In 1922 Winchester merged with Simmons and continued to carry a full line of hardware plus the Winchester brand. The merger terminated in March of 1929 and converted back to the original status of Simmons Hardware Co. It wasn't until July 1, 1950, that Simmons Hardware Co. was purchased by Shapleigh Hardware Company. All Simmons Hardware Co. trademark lines were continued, and the business operated successfully until its closing in 1962. Today the Keen Kutter logo is owned by the Val-Test Company of Chicago, Illinois. For further study we recommend *Collector's Guide to E. C. Simmons Keen Kutter Cutlery Tools*, an illustrated price guide by our advisors for this category, Jerry and Elaine Heuring, available at your favorite bookstore or public library. The Heurings are listed in the Directory under Missouri. See also Knives.

Axe, fireman's, lg logo, overall: 12¼"....................................475.00
Axe box, sliding top, for bevel axe head, 9¼x5¾x2" 175.00
Bit, gimlet, single cut to fit a brace, sz 5, 7, 9, 12, ea 9.00
Bit brace, ratchet, #KR16, 16" sweep.......................................50.00
Bit set, auger, set of 13, in canvas emblem-shaped pouch............275.00
Buck saw, logo on right-hand side of wood 100.00
Calendar, tin, pad-type, w/hardware store name & location, ea..175.00
Calendar, 1940, scissors ad w/Scott Hardware Co.......................250.00
Calipers, inside firm joint type, 15" 75.00
Carpenter pencils, set of 12, w/cb sleeve, unused, M..................375.00
Carving set, 3-pc w/stag hdls, mk on knife only..........................55.00
Catalog, 1935, No V, cloth cover, 2,118 pgs w/index 425.00
Chisel, butt; tanged beveled edge w/rosewood hdl........................75.00
Clock, Shapleigh, rnd plastic, electric, 10" 350.00
Coping saw, #K50, heavy pattern w/logo..................................30.00
Corn mill, SH Co No 1½ Korn Krusher, cast iron.......................150.00
Display, scissor counter brd, emblem-shaped, wood.....................175.00
Display tire holder, metal, 12¾x7¼".......................................375.00
Display, tool rack, 4'10"x2'4", w/tool outline & number 200.00
Drill, electric, #KK243B, w/sanding pad & drill bits, complete...150.00
Files, tapered, for filing hand saws, 7 different, w/logo, ea............15.00
Flashlights, set of 3, octagonal, 2-, 3- & 5-cell, logo on end cap.125.00
Gouge, hdld socket firmer, various szs, ea 60.00

Hack saw, for 12" blades, heavy, non-adjustable, 20" 70.00
Hair clippers, #S521AK, in original box....................................45.00
Hair cutting set, electric, in display box, w/papers, missing comb...100.00
Hammer, blacksmith riveter, str-pein 125.00
Hammer, claw; Shapleigh, steel shank, rubber hdl.......................35.00
Hammer, ECS Blue Brand, stamped 1 side, etched on other.......100.00
Hand saw, ECS #88, fancy flags & writing on 22" blade 125.00
Hatchet, lathing; chromed w/gauge, logo both sides....................100.00
Hoe, garden or field...35.00
Horse clippers, #K940 or #K950, 10½", ea...............................75.00
Knife, hunting; Shapleigh, unmk sheath, w/logo & leather hdl, 4½"...175.00
Knife, kitchen; steel logo-shaped guard 45.00
Knife pick, used to open pocketknives, w/logo 250.00
Lawn mower, #KKRA18855, gas powered...............................100.00
Letterhead, Simmons Hardware Co...15.00
Level, masonry; #KK25, adjustable, brass button w/logo...............95.00
Level, pocket or torpedo; #F3764GK, wood, 9" 75.00
Mallet, wooden, 4 szs, lg sz w/dbl KK stamp, ea from $45 to.........90.00
Nail apron, cloth, Shapleigh, 21½x16".....................................110.00
Padlock, KK logo-shaped, regular sz..200.00
Padlock, trunk lock w/key..225.00
Plane, #K5 jack w/fence, smooth bottom, adjustable 75.00
Plane, iron block, #K9½, in orig box w/papers, 6"......................200.00
Plane, iron w/smooth bottom, #K2..750.00
Plane, smooth wood bottom, #K22, adjustable, 1¾" blade, 8" 75.00
Pliers, diagonal cutters, #K45-5, in orig box...............................150.00
Pliers, pistol grip, #KK7, mk Pat Applied For Shapleigh Hardware Co...175.00
Plumb bob, hexagon, orig red pnt, 8-oz.....................................125.00
Postcard, 1913 night scene, Boardwalk, Atlantic City, NJ 45.00
Razor, safety; 4 styles, ea from $10 to.......................................20.00
Razor, str; gold-etched blade w/MOP on end 50.00
Receipt pad, carbonized, 6x3½"...35.00
Replacement hdls for various hammers, many w/part of orig label....30.00
Rule, zigzag, #K504, 8-fold, yel enamel, Pat date, 4' 250.00
Saw, 1-man crosscut; #309 w/emblem on blade 200.00
Scissors, old version w/Pat date & KK written out, 8" 12.00

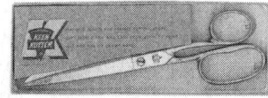

Scissors, S128AK, EX in original cardboard box, $75.00. (Photo courtesy Jerry and Elaine Heuring)

Scoop shovel, all wood hdl...50.00
Screwdriver, #KPA3, torx tip, tenite plastic hdl, 4½" blade..........15.00
Sewing kit, KK logo & hardware store on front, thread/needle/thimble...175.00
Slaw cutter...85.00
Square, tri & miter, CI hdl w/KK & logo, 6" blade.......................50.00
Staple puller, #K1946, different mks, 10¼"................................40.00
Tape line, #K62, steel w/KK on tape, 50'...................................75.00
Thermos, mk Shapleigh Keen Kutter on bottom w/slogan.........150.00
Tomahawk belt axe, logo on head...85.00
Tool box, leather, w/logo stamped in leather, orig decals inside, G ..350.00
Waffle iron, CI, 4-section w/sm logo, Simmons emb on lid 175.00
Wagon, boy's, Jet or Rocket, w/KK on side 250.00

Water jug, Shapleigh, insulated, faucet-spigot type 100.00
Wheelbarrow, w/logo on inside...150.00
Wrench, alligator; adjustable, Pat 5-26-03 ....150.00

Kellogg Studio

Stanley Kellogg (1908 – 1972) opened the Kellogg Studio in Petoskey, Michigan, in 1948. It remained in operation until 1976, producing a wide range of both decorative and functional ceramics including dinnerware, vases, and figurines. Most pieces are glazed in rich, solid colors and are marked 'Petoskey' as well as 'S. Kellogg Studio' or 'Kellogg's.' Stanley Kellogg began as a sculptor, and it was while working on an outdoor monument with the great Swedish-American sculptor, Carl Milles, that Stanley suffered the back injury which forced him to turn to studio work. In addition to naturalistic treatments of Michigan wildlife, Kellogg developed some angular, architectural forms in his molded art pottery. Our co-advisors for this category are Walter P. Hogan and Wendy L. Woodworth; they are listed in the Directory under Michigan. See Kellogg Studio website: www.emunix.emich.edu/~whogan/kellogg/index.html.

Ashtray, yel, sq, 4" 15.00
Bowl, brn w/wht int, 1" 8.00
Bowl, shadow type, gr, bulbous, cut-out kingfishers, 7"...............150.00
Box, ceramic w/metallic glaze, w/lid, 3x5" 55.00
Dish, teardrop shape, lt gr w/tiny flower frog insert, 3½" 15.00
Figurine, crouching rabbit, blk, 2" 95.00
Flower frog vase, yel, spherical, 3¼", w/separate 4" rnd base........55.00
Mug, bl, sq hdl, 5"..20.00
Pitcher, purple, curved hdl, 9"..40.00
Plate, gr, w/flowers & personalized name, 11" 12.00
Vase, bl, bulbous w/cylindrical neck & slanted rim, 3" 35.00

Kelva

Kelva was a trademark of the C.F. Monroe Company of Meriden, Connecticut; it was produced for only a few years after the turn of the century. It is distinguished from the Wave Crest and Nakara lines by its unique Batik-like background, probably achieved through the use of a cloth or sponge to apply the color. Large florals are hand painted on the opaque milk glass; and ormolu and brass mounts were used for the boxes, vases, and trays. Most pieces are signed. Our advisors for this category are Dolli and Wilfred Cohen; they are listed in the Directory under California.

Jar, floral, pink on marbled gray-green, hinged ormolu collar, beveled mirror, ca 1905, 4½x6", $1,250.00. (Photo courtesy Neal Auction Co.)

Biscuit jar, daisies on peach, SP lid/hdl, rare............................1,250.00
Box, floral, pastel w/beading, hexagon, 3x3¼".............................495.00
Box, floral on bl w/beading, 3½x8"..495.00
Box, floral on dk gr w/beading, oval, 2¾x5¼"..............................650.00
Box, lilies, wht on pk, 5¾" sq..635.00
Box, lily on lid, 6-sided, orig lining, mirror, 3¼x5" dia 650.00
Box, roses on bl & cream w/gold, 8" sq....................................1,150.00

Fernery, floral on fuchsia, 4¼x7½" 650.00
Humidor, Cigars/flowers on bl, metal mts/lid/hdl, 4½x8¾" 1,250.00
Match holder/ash receiver, floral on gr w/beading, ftd.................500.00
Shakers, floral on gr, gr enamel top, 3", pr 850.00
Vase, floral on dk gr, slender form, 16".................................1,250.00
Vase, floral on gr, SP ormolu ft, 14" 1,500.00
Vase, floral on red to russet w/beaded ribbon, shouldered, 7¾"...795.00
Vase, lg floral bouquet on gr/pk (shiny), 8x3" 950.00
Vase, roses, pk/wht on moss gr random stripes, 4-ftd ormolu stand, 11"..950.00
Vase, roses w/wht dots on marbled bl, hexagonal, 13".............1,250.00

Kenton Hills

Kenton Hills Porcelain was established in 1940 in Erlanger, Kentucky, by Harold Bopp, former Rookwood superintendent, and David Seyler, noted artist and sculptor. Native clay was used; glazes were very similar to Rookwood's of the same period. The work was of high quality, but because of the restrictions imposed on needed material due to the onset of the war, the operation failed in 1942. Much of the ware is artist signed and marked with the Kenton Hills name or cipher and shape number.

Bust, woman's head, Art Deco, coral gloss, mk KH, 6½x4½" 310.00
Vase, lion on prowl, David Seyler, 8¼"...................................1,300.00

Kentucky Derby Glasses

Kentucky Derby glasses are the official souvenir glasses sold at Churchill Downs filled with mint juleps on Derby Day. Many folks from all over the country who attend the Derby take home the souvenir glass, and thus the collecting begins. The first glass (1938) is said to have either been given away as a souvenir or used for drinks among the elite at the Downs. This one, the 1939 glass, two glasses from 1940, the 1940 – 41 aluminum tumbler, the 'Beetleware' tumblers from 1941 to 1944, and the 1945 short, tall, and jigger glasses are the rarest, most sought-after glasses, and they command the highest prices. Some 1974 glasses incorrectly listed the 1971 winner Canonero II as just Canonero; as a result, it became the 'mistake' glass for that year. Also, glasses made by the Federal Glass Company (whose logo, found on the bottom of the glass, is a small shield containing an F) were used for extra glasses for the 100th running in 1974. There is also a 'mistake' and a correct Federal glass, making four to collect for that year.

The 1956 glass has four variations. On some 1956 glasses the star which was meant to separate the words 'Kentucky Derby' is missing making only one star instead of two stars. Also, all three horses on the glass were meant to have tails, but on some of the glasses only two have tails making two tails instead of three. To identify which 1956 glass you have, just count the number of stars and tails.

In order to identify the year of a pre-1969 glass, since it did not appear on the front of the glass prior to then, simply add one year to the last date listed on the back of the glass. This may seem to be a confusing practice, but the current year's glass is produced long before the Derby winner is determined.

The prices took a bit of a jump this year as more and more collectors are searching for the older glasses which are becoming extremely hard to locate. Our advisor for this category is Betty Hornback; she is listed in the Directory under Kentucky.

1938...4,000.00
1939...6,500.00
1940, aluminum..800.00
1940, French Lick, aluminum 800.00
1940, glass tumbler, 2 styles, ea, minimum value..................10,000.00

1941-44, Beetleware, from $2,500 to	**4,000.00**
1945, jigger	**1,000.00**
1945, regular	**1,600.00**
1945, tall	**450.00**
1946-47, ea	**100.00**
1948, clear bottom	**225.00**
1948, frosted bottom	**250.00**
1949	**225.00**
1950	**450.00**
1951	**650.00**
1952, Gold Cup	**225.00**
1953	**175.00**
1954	**200.00**
1955	**150.00**
1956, 1 star, 2 tails	**275.00**
1956, 1 star, 3 tails	**400.00**
1956, 2 stars, 2 tails	**200.00**
1956, 2 stars, 3 tails	**250.00**

1957, gold and black on frosted glass, $125.00.

1958, Gold Bar	**175.00**
1958, Iron Leige	**225.00**
1959-60, ea	**100.00**
1961	**110.00**
1962-63, Churchill Downs, red, gold & blk on clear	**80.00**
1964, ea	**55.00**
1965	**75.00**
1966	**60.00**
1967-68, ea	**60.00**
1969	**65.00**
1970	**70.00**
1971	**50.00**
1972	**45.00**
1973	**55.00**
1974, Federal, regular & mistake, ea	**200.00**
1974, Libbey, mistake, Canonero in 1971 listing on bk	**18.00**
1974, regular, Canonero II in 1971 listing on bk	**16.00**
1975	**16.00**
1976	**16.00**
1976, plastic	**16.00**
1977	**14.00**
1978-79, ea	**16.00**
1980	**22.00**
1981	**14.00**
1982	**14.00**
1983-85, ea	**12.00**
1986	**14.00**
1986 (1985 copy)	**20.00**
1987-89, ea	**12.00**
1990-92, ea	**10.00**
1993-95, ea	**9.00**

1996-97, ea	**8.00**
1998-99, ea	**6.00**
2000-02, ea	**5.00**

Keramos

Keramos (Austria) produced a line of decorative items including vases, bowls, masks, and figurines that were imported primarily by the Ebeling & Ruess Co. of Philadelphia from the late 1920s to the 1950s. The figurines they manufactured were of high quality and very detailed, similar to those made by other Austrian firms. Their glazes were very smooth, though today some crazing is present on older pieces.

Most items were marked and numbered, and some bear the name or initials of the artist who designed them. In addition to Ebeling & Ruess (whose trademark includes a crown), other importers' stamps and labels may be found as well. Knight Ceramics employed a shield mark, and many of the vases produced through the 1940s are marked with a swastika; these pieces are turning up with increasing frequency at shops as well as Internet auction sites. Although the workmanship they exhibit is somewhat inferior, the glazes used during this period are excellent and are now attracting much attention among collectors.

Detail is a very important worth-assessing factor. The more detailed the art figures are, the more valuable. Artist-signed pieces are quite scarce. Many artists were employed by both Keramos and Goldscheider. The molds of these two companies are sometimes very similar as well, and unmarked items are often difficult to identify with certainty.

Items listed below are considered to be in excellent, undamaged condition unless otherwise stated. Our advisor for this category is Darrell Thomas; he is listed in the Directory under Wisconsin.

Bowl, quails inside, 5"	**35.00**
Bowl, terra cotta, glazed top, Italy mk, 4"	**45.00**
Ewer, beige & brn Swastika mk, 12½"	**650.00**
Ewer, molten red, mk, 4½"	**150.00**
Ewer, robin bl, shield mk, w/matching bowl	**125.00**
Figurine, angel (½-bust), w/label, pr	**350.00**
Figurine, beagle, w/brn & wht markings, E&R label, 6½"	**85.00**
Figurine, cherub w/wings, matt finish, sgn Dakon, mk, 4½", pr	**725.00**
Figurine, fawn, mk, 6"	**125.00**
Figurine, lady dancer, Art Deco, Schwetz-Lehmann, #2930/6, 8½"	**950.00**
Figurine, lady w/basket, EX detail/color, #802, sgn LG, shield mk	**475.00**
Figurine, man, well dressed, 1920s, mk	**550.00**
Figurines, springer spaniel pr: 1 points/1 sits, EX detail, 10½"	**600.00**
Vase, art glaze, earthy colors, 6½"	**250.00**
Vase, bl & gold, Swastika mk, 8½"	**125.00**
Vase, ferns on brn tones, Swastika mk, 12½"	**350.00**
Vase, poppies, Swastika mk, 12¼"	**345.00**
Wall mask, Art Deco, terra cotta w/pastels, no mk, #885, 11"	**875.00**
Wall mask, little boy w/curly hair, singing, matt glaze, 1940s	**650.00**
Wall mask, little girl, sleeping, matt-glaze terra cotta, 1940s glaze	**675.00**
Wall mask, matt-glazed terra cotta, bright colors, 1940s, 8"	**750.00**

Kew Blas

The Union Glass Company was founded in 1854, in Somerville, Massachusetts, an offshoot of the New England Glass Co. in East Cambridge. They made only flint glass — tablewares, lamps, globes, and shades. Kew Blas was a trade name they used for their iridescent, lustered art glass produced there from 1893 until about 1920. The glass was made in imitation of Tiffany and achieved notable success. Some items were decorated with pulled leaf and feather designs, while others had a monochrome lustre surface. The mark was an engraved 'Kew Blas' in an arching arrangement.

Rose bowl, vertical chains, gr irid/gold on butterscotch, 3½" **950.00**
Tumbler, irid gold, 3½x3" **480.00**
Vase, diagonal wavy bands, gold/pk/gr, 8" **990.00**
Vase, feathers, gr & wht on gold irid, 7"...**750.00**
Vase, feathers, gr irid w/gold tips on ivory, incurvate cylinder, 5"...**1,000.00**
Vase, floriform; gold/bronze, bulbous top, wide base, 13x4".........**800.00**
Vase, swirls, irid on gr, 8" **540.00**

Kindell, Dorothy

Yet another California artist that worked during the prolific years of the 1940s and 1950s, Dorothy Kindell produced a variety of household items and giftware, but today she is best known for her nudes. One of her most popular lines consisted of mugs, a pitcher, salt and pepper shakers, a wall pocket, bowls, a creamer and sugar set, and champagne glasses, featuring a lady in various stages of undress, modeled as handles or stems (on the champagnes). In the set of six mugs, she progresses from wearing her glamorous strapless evening gown to ultimately climbing nude, head-first into the last mug. These are relatively common but always marketable. Except for these and the salt and pepper shakers, the other items from the nude line are scarce and rather pricey. Collectors also vie for her island girls, generally seminude and very sensuous.

Ashtray, 2 nudes under 7½" beachcomber's hat, common, from $50 to ..**75.00**
Champagne glass, blk w/gold-colored nude stem, 6x4½" dia **275.00**
Champagne glass, nude stem..**150.00**
Creamer & sugar bowl, nude hdls, 3½x3" dia **290.00**
Figurine, foal, grazing, 3½"...**30.00**
Figurine, island girl in form-fitting strapless dress, 8"...............**75.00**
Figurine, nude on bk w/legs extended upwards, 9x9"................**135.00**
Head vase, Black native girl, red lips & necklace, 6", from $65 to....**75.00**
Ice bucket, nude on ea side, 5x11" dia **185.00**
Mug, nude hdls, 1 of series of 6, common, 5¼-6", ea from $35 to ...**40.00**
Mug, old cowboy w/wht hair/beard/mustache, gray hat, 4½" **135.00**
Shakers, nude hdls, 3x1¼", pr, from $50 to..................................**65.00**
Shelf sitter, nude w/red cold-pnt head band & towel at waist, 11" **390.00**
Turtle box, 12" W...**165.00**
Wall pocket, nude from mug series, rare....................................**295.00**

Kitchen Collectibles

During the last half of the 1850s, mass-produced kitchen gadgets were patented at an astonishing rate. Most were ingeniously efficient. Apple peelers, egg beaters, cherry pitters, food choppers, and such were only the most common of hundreds of kitchen tools well designed to perform only specific tasks. Today all are very collectible.

For further information we recommend *Kitchen Glassware of the Depression Years* and *Anchor Hocking's Fire-King & More, Second Edition,* both by Gene Florence; and *Kitchen Antiques, 1790 – 1940,* by Kathryn McNerney. See also Appliances; Butter Molds and Stamps; Cast Iron; Cookbooks; Copper; Glass Knives; Molds; Pie Birds; Primitives; Reamers; String Holders; Tinware; Trivets; Wooden Ware; Wrought Iron.

Key:
FW — full writing   TM — trade mark

Cast Kitchen Ware

Be aware that cast-iron counterfeit production is on the increase. Items with phony production numbers, finishes, etc., are being made at this time. Many of these new pieces are the popular miniature cornstick pans. To command the values given below, examples must be free from

damage of any kind or excessive wear. Waffle irons must be complete with all three pieces and the handle. The term 'EPU' in the description lines refers to the **Erie PA, USA** mark. The term 'block mark' refers to the lettering in the large logo that was used ca 1920 until 1940; 'slant logo' refers to the lettering in the large logo ca 1900 to 1920. Victor was Griswold's first low-budget line (ca 1875). Skillets #5 and #6 are uncommon, while #7, #8, and #9 are easy to find. For further information contact our advisor, Grant S. Windsor (SASE required); he is listed in the Directory under Virginia. See also Keen Kutter; Clubs, Newsletters, and Catalogs.

Skillet lid, Griswold #12, Self Basting Skillet Cover, $250.00.

Ashtray, Griswold #770, sq, from $20 to **30.00**
Ashtray, Wagner C# 1050, from $5 to..**10.00**
Cake mold, bundt pan, Griswold, from $800 to...........................**900.00**
Cake mold, lamb, Griswold #866, from $75 to **100.00**
Cake mold, Santa, Griswold, from $400 to **500.00**
Display rack, Griswold Griddle, Griswold plate, metal, from $450 to.....**500.00**
Display rack, Griswold Skillet, Griswold plate, brn wood rails,$300 to .**350.00**
Dutch oven, Favorite Piqua Ware #7, Stylized TM, from $40 to ..**60.00**
Dutch oven, Griswold #6, Tite-Top, Block TMs/FW lid, from $250 to......**300.00**
Dutch oven, Griswold #8, Early Tite-Top, Block TMs, FW lid, $40 to.........**60.00**
Dutch oven, Griswold #8, Erie TM, flat top, from $40 to **60.00**
Dutch oven, Griswold #9, Early Tite-Top, Block TMs, FW lid, $40 to.....**60.00**
Dutch oven, Griswold #10, Tite-Top Baster, Slant/EPU TM, from $125 to...**150.00**
Griddle, Griswold #8, Slant/Erie TM, X reinforcement, hdl, $35 to **45.00**
Griddle, Griswold #12 Gas or Vapor, mk Erie Gas Griddle, from $275 to...**325.00**
Griddle, Griswold #14 Bailed, Block TM, from $50 to **75.00**
Griddle, Wagner #8, Stylized TM, C# 1108, hdl, from $20 to **30.00**
Griddle, Wapak #8, oval, Early TM, from $50 to...........................**75.00**
Kettle, Wagner, deep fat fryer, w/basket, C# 1265, from $50 to **75.00**
Kettle, Wagner, rimmed pot, mk Wagner, from $75 to.................**100.00**
Loaf pan, Griswold #877, w/lid #859, from $800 to....................**900.00**
Muffin pan, Filley #1, 14 cups, from $275 to **325.00**
Muffin pan, Filley #4, 8 cups, from $300 to **350.00**
Muffin pan, Filley #6, 11 cups, from $150 to **200.00**
Muffin pan, Filley #10, 11 cups, from $75 to **100.00**
Muffin pan, Griswold #1, Slant/EPU TM, 11 cups, from $200 to **250.00**
Muffin pan, Griswold #3, mk #3 & #943 only, 11 cups, from $150 to **175.00**
Muffin pan, Griswold #8, mk Erie & 946, 8 cups, from $75 to ...**100.00**
Muffin pan, Griswold #11, French roll, wide band, 12 cups, from $30 to..**40.00**
Muffin pan, Griswold #11, French roll, 12 cups, from $25 to........**35.00**
Muffin pan, Griswold #18, popover, wide hdl, 6 cups, from $50 to **75.00**
Muffin pan, Griswold #32, Danish cake, fully mk, 7 cups, from $30 to..**40.00**
Muffin pan, Griswold #34, plett, sm TM, 7 cups, from $15 to **25.00**
Muffin pan, Griswold #50, heart & star, 6 cups, from $1,000 to ...**1,500.00**
Muffin pan, Griswold #100, heart & star, 5 cups, from $600 to.....**800.00**
Muffin pan, Griswold #273, corn stick, 7 cups, from $15 to...........**25.00**
Muffin pan, Wagner I, Vienna roll, 6 cups, from $50 to **75.00**
Muffin pan, Wagner Senior Krusty Korn Kobs, 7 cups, from $35 to ..**50.00**
Patty molds, Griswold #2, MIB, set, from $25 to **35.00**

Pitcher, Griswold, bailed, aluminum, from $225 to **275.00**
Roaster, Griswold #3, oval, Block TMs, w/lid mk Oval Roaster, $475 to...**525.00**
Roaster, Griswold #5, oval, Block TMs, FW lid, from $300 to....**350.00**
Roaster, Griswold #9, oval, Block TMs, FW lid, from $425 to...**475.00**
Roaster, Wagner #3, oval, Stylized TM, raised writing lid, from $150 to..**200.00**
Roaster, Wagner #7, oval, Stylized TM, incised writing lid, $175 to.**225.00**
Skillet, Favorite #12, Stylized TM, from $50 to **100.00**
Skillet, Griswold, sq utility, P# 768, from $25 to **50.00**
Skillet, Griswold, toy, Use Erie Ware the Best, from $225 to......**275.00**
Skillet, Griswold #2, Block TM, heat ring, from $1,800 to......**2,200.00**
Skillet, Griswold #2, Block TM, no heat ring, from $300 to.......**350.00**
Skillet, Griswold #2, Rau Brothers, from $500 to **600.00**
Skillet, Griswold #2, Slant/EPU TM, heat ring, from $375 to....**425.00**
Skillet, Griswold #3, Block TM, no heat ring, from $10 to...........**20.00**
Skillet, Griswold #3, Slant/Erie TM, from $30 to **40.00**
Skillet, Griswold #3, sm TM, early hdl, from $10 to....................**20.00**
Skillet, Griswold #3, Square Fry, from $75 to **125.00**
Skillet, Griswold #4, Block TM, heat ring, from $375 to **425.00**
Skillet, Griswold #4, Block TM, no heat ring, from $40 to...........**60.00**
Skillet, Griswold #5, Block TM, heat ring, from $375 to **425.00**
Skillet, Griswold #5, Block TM, no heat ring, from $10 to...........**20.00**
Skillet, Griswold #5, sm TM, grooved hdl, from $10 to **15.00**
Skillet, Griswold #6, Block TM, heat ring, from $50 to **75.00**
Skillet, Griswold #6, Block TM, no heat ring, from $10 to...........**20.00**
Skillet, Griswold #6, Slant/EPU TM, from $40 to **60.00**
Skillet, Griswold #7, Block TM, heat ring, from $45 to **55.00**
Skillet, Griswold #7, Block TM, no heat ring, from $10 to...........**20.00**
Skillet, Griswold #7, Erie TM, inset heat ring, from $25 to **50.00**
Skillet, Griswold #7, sm TM, grooved hdl, from $10 to **15.00**
Skillet, Griswold #8, Block TM, no heat ring, from $10 to...........**20.00**
Skillet, Griswold #8, extra deep, Block TM, no heat ring, $50 to.....**75.00**
Skillet, Griswold #8, Slant/Erie TM, from $15 to **25.00**
Skillet, Griswold #8, Victor, fully mk, from $35 to **45.00**
Skillet, Griswold #9, Block TM, no heat ring, from $20 to...........**30.00**
Skillet, Griswold #9, Victor, fully mk, from $35 to **45.00**
Skillet, Griswold #10, Block TM, no heat ring, from $40 to.........**60.00**
Skillet, Griswold #11, Block TM, from $125 to.............................**175.00**
Skillet, Griswold #11, Erie TM, inset heat ring, from $125 to **175.00**
Skillet, Griswold #11, Slant/EPU TM, from $250 to....................**300.00**
Skillet, Griswold #12, Block TM, from $75 to..............................**100.00**
Skillet, Griswold #12, Erie TM, from $100 to...............................**150.00**
Skillet, Griswold #12, Slant/EPU TM, from $125 to....................**175.00**
Skillet, Griswold #13, Block TM, from $1,400 to **1,600.00**
Skillet, Griswold #14, Block TM, from $125 to.............................**175.00**
Skillet, Griswold #15, oval, from $250 to....................................**300.00**
Skillet, Griswold #55, sq, made in Sidney OH, from $25 to..........**35.00**
Skillet, unnamed, Corn Bread Skillet, 8 cups, 9" dia, from $10 to....**15.00**
Skillet, Vollrath #5, from $15 to **25.00**
Skillet, Wagner, Bacon & Egg Breakfast; Stylized TM, from $15 to **25.00**
Skillet, Wagner, Sizzle Server, C# 1095, from $15 to.....................**25.00**
Skillet, Wagner #3, Stylized TM, from $5 to................................**10.00**
Skillet, Wapak #5, Z TM, from $35 to **45.00**
Skillet, Wapak #8, Early TM, from $25 to **35.00**
Skillet, Wapak #8, Indian Head Medallion TM, from $75 to...**100.00**
Skillet, Wapak #9, Tapered TM, from $25 to................................**35.00**
Skillet lid, Griswold, sq glass, Block TM knob, 9½x9½", $50 to...**100.00**
Skillet lid, Griswold #6, high dome smooth, Block TM, from $50 to.....**75.00**
Skillet lid, Griswold #7, high dome smooth, Block TM, from $40 to....**60.00**
Skillet lid, Griswold #8, high dome smooth, sm TM, from $20 to **30.00**
Skillet lid, Griswold #8, high dome top logo, Block TM, from $30 to....**40.00**
Skillet lid, Griswold #8, low, top writing, from $30 to.....................**50.00**
Skillet lid, Griswold #10, high dome smooth, Block TM, from $40 to....**60.00**
Skillet lid, Griswold #15, oval, sm TM, P# 1013C, from $500 to..**600.00**
Skillet lid, Wapak #9, mk 9 only, recessed basting dots, from $30 to...**50.00**

Teakettle, Griswold, toy, Use Erie Ware the Best, from $300 to .**325.00**
Trivet, Griswold, Family Tree, P# 1726, lg/decorative, from $10 to....**20.00**
Trivet, Griswold, Grapes, P# 1729, lg/decorative, from $10 to......**20.00**
Trivet, Griswold, Old Lace, P# 1738, sm, from $200 to...............**250.00**
Trivet, Griswold #9, Dutch oven, P# 207, from $20 to.................**30.00**
Trivet, Wagner #9, Dutch oven, aluminum, C# 249, from $25 to.**35.00**
Waffle iron, Griswold #0, toy, Alaska coil hdls, from $2,000 to...**2,500.00**
Waffle iron, Griswold #2, sq, from $650 to **750.00**
Waffle iron, Griswold #2 Savory, sq...**425.00**
Waffle iron, Griswold #7, finger hinge, low hdl base, from $100 to ..**125.00**
Wax ladle, Griswold, Erie TM, P# 964, from $125 to..................**150.00**

Egg Beaters

Egg beaters are unbeatable. Ranging from hand-helds, rotary-crank, and squeeze power to Archimedes up-and-down models, egg beaters are America's favorite kitchen gadget. A mainstay of any kitchenware collection, in recent years egg beaters have come into their own — nutmeg graters, spatulas, and can openers will have to scramble to catch up! At the turn of the century, everyone in America owned an egg beater. Every household did its own mixing and baking — there were no pre-processed foods. And every inventor thought he/she could make a better beater. Thus American ingenuity produced more than one thousand egg beater patents, dating back to 1856, with several hundred different models being manufactured over the years. As true examples of Americana, egg beaters have risen in value over the past couple of years, with a half dozen mixers valued at $2,750.00 and more, including the cast-iron, rotary crank 'Dodge Race Course egg beater.' But the vast majority stay under $50.00, while the values of the super rare beaters continue upward, especially those from Internet auctions. And just when you think you've seen them all, new ones always turn up, usually at flea markets or garage sales. For further information, we recommend our advisor (author of the definitive book on egg beaters) Don Thornton, who is listed in the Directory under California (SASE required).

Star egg beater, April 19, 59 Oct 16, 60, cast-iron rotary crank, 10½", $1,000.00. (Photo courtesy Diane Thornton©1999)

A over D, dbl-action rachet, Pat Nov 19, 1929, 12½" **100.00**
A&J, 1-handed archimedes type, 12½" **25.00**
A&J High Speed Super Center Drive, 11½" **6.00**
A&J Round Dasher, archimedes type, 13½" **25.00**
Archimedes type, mk Made in America Pat Pend **65.00**
Beauty, aluminum **15.00**
Dover, 4-hole wheel, 12½"...**60.00**
Dover Egg beater USA, no date, 9½"...**45.00**
Dover Tumbler, pinion gear, 10" **85.00**
Dunlap's Egg & Cream Whip, No Spatter No Waste, 1906-1907, 11½"..**40.00**
Eagle Precision Tool Co....NY, 1-hand whip, 12⅓" **30.00**

F/S Dover, CI, Pat May 6th, 1873...Nov 24th 1891 ....**75.00**
Holt's, flared dashers, 10½" **65.00**
Holt's Improved, 10½" **50.00**
Holt-Lyon Co No 0 Tarrytown NY, 9" **60.00**
Horlick's, archimedes type **35.00**
Landers Frary & Clark, CI rotary, 10¼" **70.00**
Lyon, propeller, mk USA **160.00**
Maynard, chrome body, stainless beaters, yel hdls, 1950s **9.00**
One-Hand Whip Pat Pend Eagle Precision..., 12½" **40.00**
Rhineland, archimedes type, all metal hdl, 10¼" **65.00**
T&S No 10 Made in USA, 9¾" **50.00**
Taplin Dover, Pat April 14, 1903, 8¾" **35.00**
Taplin Pattern Improved April 14, 1903, bl wooden hdl, 11¾" **40.00**
Taplin's Dover Pattern, Pat April 14, 1903, 12¼" **55.00**

Glass

Baking dish, chicken shape, fired-on colors, Glasbake, McKee **20.00**
Batter bowl, Ribbed, gr, Anchor Hocking, from $40 to **45.00**
Batter jug, blk, Fenton, from $175 to **200.00**
Batter jug, cobalt, McKee, from $150 to **160.00**
Batter jug, Liberty 'American Pioneer,' gr, from $225 to **250.00**
Bowl, drippings; Ships, red on wht, Hazel Atlas, 8-oz, from $50 to....**55.00**
Bowl, flower decor on Jade-ite, Hocking, 7½", 2-qt, from $300 to...**350.00**
Bowl, mixing; Butter-print Cinderella, Pyrex, 6¾" **10.00**
Bowl, mixing; Delphite Blue, 7⅜", from $60 to **75.00**
Bowl, mixing; Hex Optic, pk, flat rim, 9", from $25 to **30.00**
Bowl, mixing; Jade-ite, 9", from $28 to **30.00**
Bowl, mixing; Jennyware, pk, Jeannette, 10½", from $85 to **95.00**
Bowl, mixing; Modern Tulip, Anchor Hocking, 3-qt **20.00**
Bowl, mixing; Paneled, gr transparent, 11½", from $55 to **60.00**
Bowl, refrigerator; Crisscross, gr, 5½" dia, w/lid **190.00**
Butter dish, cobalt, Hazel Atlas, from $300 to **325.00**
Butter dish, custard, rectangular, McKee, from $45 to **50.00**
Butter dish, gr, Butter Cover emb on lid, Hazel Atlas, from $60 to....**65.00**
Butter dish, gr transparent, Hocking, from $50 to **55.00**
Butter dish, pk, bow finial, rectangular, from $65 to **75.00**
Butter dish, red w/crystal top, rectangular, from $120 to **130.00**
Canister, caramel, blk lettering, tin lid, 48-oz, from $100 to **125.00**
Canister, milk glass, Cereal in blk letters, McKee, 48-oz, $125 to....**135.00**
Canister, Red Dots on custard, Mckee, rnd, 48-oz, from $35 to **40.00**
Canister, Sugar, Delphite Blue, 40-oz, from $400 to **425.00**
Canister, Tavern scene, gr on clear, lg, from $40 to **45.00**
Casserole, dk amber, oval, Cambridge, w/lid, from $50 to **55.00**
Casserole, fired-on color, stick hdl, Glasbake, McKee, w/lid, ind..**14.00**
Egg cup, amber, Paden City, from $15 to **18.00**
Egg cup, yel, Hazel Atlas, from $5 to **8.00**
Funnel, ribbed or plain gr, 4½", from $35 to **40.00**
Funnel, Tufglas, from $75 to **85.00**
Gravy boat, pk, Imperial, from $50 to **55.00**
Ice bucket, blk, Fostoria #2543, from $60 to **65.00**
Ice bucket, Hex Optic, gr, reamer top, Jeannette, from $40 to **45.00**
Jar, blk fired-on color, oval, 7", from $20 to **25.00**
Measuring cup, amber, 3-spout, open hdl, Federal, 1-cup, from $35 to...**40.00**
Measuring cup, Chalaine Blue, 2-spout, from $800 to **900.00**
Measuring cup, cobalt, 3-spout, Hazel Atlas, 1-cup, from $350 to..**400.00**
Measuring cup, crystal, Glasbake, McKee, 1-cup, from $20 to **25.00**
Measuring cup, Delphite Blue, Jeannette, 1-cup, from $75 to **85.00**
Measuring cup, fired-on gr, 2-cup, from $25 to **30.00**
Measuring cup, Fluffo, Be Sure of Success..., from $30 to **38.00**
Measuring cup, gr, 1-spout, Hocking, 1-cup, from $30 to **35.00**
Measuring cup, Jennyware, crystal, Jeannette, 1-cup, from $40 to ...**45.00**
Measuring cup, McKee Glasbake Scientific, from $20 to **25.00**
Measuring cup, Sapphire Blue, 1-spout, Anchor Hocking, 8-oz **28.00**

Measuring cup, Seller's, Pat Dec 8, 1925, from $30 to **38.00**
Measuring cup, Seville Yellow, no hdl, McKee, 4-cup, from $500 to ..**600.00**
Measuring pitcher, Delphite Blue, McKee, 4-cup, from $600 to .**650.00**
Measuring pitcher, Jade-ite, Jeannette, 4-cup, from $75 to **85.00**
Measuring pitcher, yel opaque, 2-cup, from $130 to **140.00**
Measuring pitcher/batter jug, custard, McKee, 4-cup, from $50 to ..**55.00**
Mug, gr opaque, from $35 to **40.00**
Mug, Jade-ite, Hocking, 7-oz, from $12 to **14.00**
Pitcher, Chesterfield, amber, Imperial #600, from $120 to **125.00**
Pitcher, utility; pk, from $65 to **75.00**
Pretzel jar, pk, Hocking, from $125 to **150.00**
Refrigerator dish, Blue Dots on custard, McKee, 4x5", from $25 to..**28.00**
Refrigerator dish, gr opaque, Hocking, oval, 8", from $45 to **50.00**
Refrigerator dish, pk, rnd, tab hdl, from $40 to **45.00**
Refrigerator dish, red, Pyrex, 4¼x6¾", from $135 to **150.00**
Refrigerator dish, yel, Hazel Atlas, 4½x5", from $35 to **40.00**
Refrigerator dish, yel opaque, 7¼" sq, from $30 to **35.00**
Relish, dbl; Emerald-Glo, w/holder, from $60 to **70.00**
Rolling pin, clambroth, wooden hdls, from $125 to **135.00**
Shaker, nutmeg; Chalaine Blue, from $165 to **185.00**

Spice jars, Hoosier patented swing-away lids, NM, eight for **$380.00.**

Stack set, Skating Dutch, red on wht, Hazel Atlas, 3-pc set **75.00**
Syrup jug, pk, Paden City, from $50 to **60.00**
Water bottle, Forest Green, Hocking, w/top, from $65 to **75.00**
Water bottle, Forest Green, Owens-Illinois, from $20 to..............**22.50**
Water bottle, red, plain or ribbed, from $225 to **250.00**
Water dispenser, cobalt, LE Smith, from $450 to **500.00**

Miscellaneous

Apple cider press, Buckeye, Superior Drill...OH, CI, 1890-1910, heavy...**450.00**
Apple parer/corer/slicer, Castellos, Pat Aug 26, 1913, VG **25.00**
Apple peeler, Reading Hardware Co Reading PA, CI, blk wood hdl...**48.00**
Apple peeler, unmk, CI, clamps to table, 11½x6" **70.00**
Apple peeler, White Mountain, gr pnt, VG **40.00**
Apple slicer, trn wooden hopper & ft, pierced hdl, Am, 19th C, 5x17" ..**1,950.00**
Bread box, metal w/pk & blk lid, 1950s, 8½x14x10", EX..............**35.00**
Cake turner, coating on metal parts, cream wood hdl......................**8.00**
Cake turner, red wood hdl, 1950s, 7½" **10.00**
Can opener, CI bull figural, EX patina, 6½" **30.00**
Can opener, Dazey DeLuxe Model 80, wall mt, red hdls, 1950s, EX ..**25.00**
Can opener, Edlund Co Edland Junior, red wood hdl **7.00**
Can opener, Never Slip May 17, 1892, loop-hdl version..............**15.00**
Can opener, Vaughan's Safety Roll Junior, MOC............................**5.00**
Canister set, polished chrome, sq sides, Garner Ware, 1950s, 4 for **25.00**
Canister set, Rubbermaid, red & wht hard plastic turntable type, 1950s ..**20.00**
Cherry seeder, New Standard, wobbly wheel................................**85.00**
Cherry seeder, Rollman #3 ....**75.00**
Chopper, bell-shaped metal, red wood hdl, 6" **18.50**
Chopper, Chop-O-Matic, aqua top, clear plastic base, 1950s **17.50**
Chopper, curved blade, wishbone shank, wood hdl **30.00**
Chopper, dbl steel rocker blade, CI shanks, wood hdl, 5x6"..........**22.00**
Chopper, hand-forged blade riveted to wood hdl, 5¾x5½"..........**30.00**
Chopper, hand-forged curved blade riveted to wood hdl, 6½x7⅛" **60.00**

Chopper, New Standard No 1½, w/grinder blade **20.00**
Chopper, nut; Hazel Atlas measure, metal lid, red wood ball hdl..**10.00**
Chopper, Rollman #22, w/5 cutter plates, EX **25.00**
Chopper, Roto Chop, turq plastic **6.00**
Chopper, steel blade, CI hdl, dtd Dec 20, 1902...New Haven CT, 6"...**18.50**
Chopper, up & down action to red wood hdl, Hazel Atlas glass base ...**20.00**
Churn, Dazey #10, beveled edge, 1-qt **750.00**
Churn, Dazey #10, bull's eye, 1-qt **700.00**
Churn, Dazey #20 ....**200.00**
Churn, Dazey #30, Pat 1922 ....**225.00**
Churn, Dazey #40 ....**150.00**
Churn, Dazey #60 ....**165.00**
Churn, Dazey #80 ....**250.00**
Churn, Lightning Butter Machine, Pat Feb 6, 1917, 2-qt **120.00**
Cleanser dispenser, Kleanser Kate, lady figural, ceramic **30.00**
Cutter, biscuit; tin, appl clip-on hdl, 2½" dia **13.00**
Cutter, French fry; Ekco, red hdl, 2 blades, 9" **25.00**
Cutter, tart; metal, spring action, Tart Master, late 1930s, 4" **35.00**
Cutter, tart; metal, spring action, 1930s, 3" dia **20.00**
Donut maker, Sears Maid of Honor, metal, M in G box................**15.00**
Flour sifter, Androck Handi-Sift, mother & children tin litho, M **50.00**
Flour sifter, Bromwell's Flour, metal w/gr wood hdl, 6¼" **15.00**
Flour sifter, Bromwell's Measuring Sifter, tin, gr hdl, 1930s **18.00**
Flour sifter, chrome w/pk wood crank hdl, NM..............................**25.00**
Flour sifter, tin litho, flowers on wht w/yel gingham border, NM..**30.00**
Grater, nutmeg; wood/CI/tin, hand-held, 7" **185.00**
Grinder, Griswold #1, CI, w/4 blades, 40" **25.00**
Grinder, herb; CI disc-shaped crusher, wood hdl, ca 1800, 4x16x4½"...**975.00**
Grinder, nut; glass container, blk hdl, 1950s **18.50**
Grinder, nut; Red Top Nut Grinder, Federal Tool Corp, 5½" **18.50**
Grinder, nut; Red Top Nut Grinder, Hazel Atlas glass base, 6" **18.50**
Juicer, aluminum, Knapps, crank squeezing action, EX.................**35.00**
Juicer, Juice King #JK-54-6, red & chrome, 1950s **30.00**
Knife sharpener, red wood hdl, from $12 to **15.00**
Ladle, metal w/red wood hdl **4.00**
Lard/fruit press, Griswold Classic No 24, EX................................**100.00**
Masher, twisted heavy wire, red wood hdl, made in USA **8.00**
Pastry blender, Androck made in USA, red wood hdl **8.00**
Pastry blender, gr wooden hdl, EX **4.00**
Pea sheller, Vaughan, hand-crank table model, EX........................**55.00**
Pie marker/trimmer, Aunt Evelyn's, Pat 1921 ....**12.50**
Ricer, metal w/red hdl, 11" **2.45**
Rolling pin, cherry wood, 18", EX..**25.00**
Rolling pin, cherry wood, 21x3" **30.00**
Rolling pin, poplar, EX patina, 19" **15.00**
Rolling pin, tin wood, 1-pc, 16¼" **22.50**
Rolling pin, wood w/gr pnt hdls, 15x1½" **15.00**
Rolling pin, wood w/pnt red hdls...**20.00**
Slicer, cheese, wire type w/red wood hdl, 8½" **8.00**
Slicer, Handy Fruit & Vegetable Slicer #6, 12" **18.00**
Spatula, red hdl, 11" **8.00**
Spoon, serving; Androck Stainless...USA, brn Bakelite hdl, 11½" .**8.00**
Sprinkler bottle, elephant w/shamrock on tummy, ceramic, from $100 to..**150.00**
Sprinkler bottle, iron, gr plastic, from $35 to **55.00**
Sprinkler bottle, Myrtle, ceramic, Pfaltzgraff................................**250.00**
Sprinkler bottle, poodle, gray & pk or wht, ceramic, from $200 to..**300.00**
Strainer, woven wire, wood hdl, 8¾", VG...**6.00**
Straw holder, styrene plastic, berries pattern, 10½" **17.50**
Whisk, blk tin & wire, coiled & str, 1880s, 7½" **10.00**

Knife Rests

Knife rests were used to prevent the tablecloth from becoming soiled by used knives. Individual, carving, and even children's rests were produced. Some toy dinnerware sets contained knife rests as well. Several scholars feel that knife rests originated in Germany and France with usage spreading to England and later America as travel between countries became more commonplace. European workers carried designs to other countries. Knife rests have been documented from 1720 through 1839. They are being made yet today by porcelain manufactures and glasshouses to match their tableware patterns. Some of the present-day producers are located in France, Germany, and Poland.

Knife rests of pressed glass, cut crystal, porcelain, sterling silver, plated silver, wood, ivory, and bone have been collected for many years. Signed knife rests are especially desirable. It was not until the Centennial Exhibition in Philadelphia in 1876 that the brilliant new cut glass rests, deeply faceted and shining like diamonds, appeared in shops by the hundreds. There were sets of twelve, eight, or six that came in presentation boxes. Sizes vary from 1¼" to 3¼" for individual knives and from 5" to 6" for carving knives. Glass knife rests were made in many colors such as purple, blue, green, vaseline, pink, and cranberry. It is important to note that prices may vary from one area of the country to another and from dealer to dealer. For further information we recommend our advisor, Beverly Schell Ales; she is listed in the Directory under California.

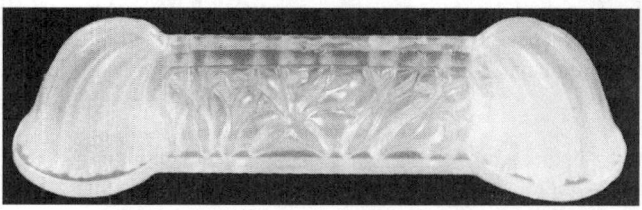

Verlys (unmarked), blue glass, 4", from $100.00 to $150.00.
(Photo courtesy Beverly Schell Ales)

China, Bing & Grondahl, sea horse, bl & wht, 1870-90, 3¾" H, lg...**145.00**
China, Meissen, mk X w/sword logo on end, pr..........................**165.00**
China, Royal Copenhagen, 1/134, Denmark, bl & wht **150.00**
Glass, Art France, horse, pr...**100.00**
Glass, Bimini, gr striped, ftd, early 1990s, 4¾", from $30 to **50.00**
Glass, cut; 8-sided bar, w/dmn, cut on ball end, 5½" **60.00**
Glass, cut; dmns & clear bands w/star-cut ends, 4", NM **145.00**
Glass, cut; Hawkes, prisms, 1889 catalog, 3½", from $100 to **150.00**
Glass, cut; Hoare, prisms, 1853 catalog, 5¾", from $100 to **200.00**
Glass, cut; Libbey, lapidary ends, 3¾", from $50 to **100.00**
Glass, cut; overall Brilliant cuttings, knob ends, 5½" **185.00**
Glass, cut; squash form **75.00**
Glass, cut; star on end of ball, 3" **70.00**
Glass, cut; Waterford, rnd shaft, sq ends, 2½x1⅞", from $100 to..**150.00**
Glass, Imperial, milk glass, mk IG, from $35 to **50.00**
Glass, Lalique France, mk, frosted end **95.00**
Glass, pressed; Baccarat, clear, 4¾", from $25 to **50.00**
Glass, pressed; gr, 3½", pr..**60.00**
Glass, pressed; Heisey, dmn & H mk, 3¼", from $100 to............**150.00**
Glass, pressed; IRENA, Poland, doorknob, 24%, from $10 to.......**20.00**
Glass, Sabino, bl w/duck end **50.00**
Glass, Val St Lambert Belquigue, amber, 1963.............................**100.00**
Metal, fruit & flowers, 3¾", set of 6 (ea different)........................**85.00**
Metal, gold-tone, horse on base, 2¾" L...**75.00**
Pottery, compare Quimper, bl, Hb, #797, ca 1883........................**75.00**
Pottery, Quimper, #499, 1950s, from $40 to **65.00**
SP, children hopping over stile **125.00**
SP, sphinx ea end **75.00**
SP, squirrel w/lg bar on tail, Simpson, Hall & Miller..................**195.00**

Knives

Knife collecting as a hobby began in earnest during the 1960s when government regulations required for the first time that knife companies mark their product with the country of origin. The few collectors and dealers cognizant of this change at once began stockpiling the older knives made before this law was enacted. Another impetus to the growing interest in this area came with the Gun Control Act of 1968, which severely restricted gun trading. Frustrated gun dealers transferred their attention to knives. Today there are collectors' clubs in many of the states.

The most sought-after pocketknives are those made before WWII. However, Case, Schrade, and Primble knives of a more recent manufacture are also collected. Most collectors prefer knives 'as found.' Do not attempt to clean, sharpen, or in any way 'improve' on an old knife.

Please note: The prices quoted here are for knives in mint condition. If a knife has been used, sharpened, or blemished in any way, its value decreases. Knives in excellent condition generally are valued at half the prices listed below. The newer the knife, the greater the reduction in value. For further information refer to *The Standard Knife Collector's Guide, 3rd Edition; Cattaraugus Cutlery, Identification and Values;* and *The Big Knife Book* by Ron Stewart and Roy Ritchie; and *Sargent's American Premium Guide to Knives and Razors, Identification and Values, 3rd Edition,* by Jim Sargent. Our advisor for this category is Bill Wright, author of *Theatre Made Military Knives of WWII* (Schiffer); he is listed in the Directory under Indiana.

Key:
bd — blade   jack — jackknife
imi — imitation

American Knife Co, Winsted, CT, 124, ebony hdl, iron bolster, 2-bd ..50.00
American Knife Co, Winsted, CT, 134, ebony hdl, iron bolster, 1-bd ..40.00
American Knife Co, Winsted, CT, 274, German silver, w/shield ..75.00
American Knife Co, Winsted, CT, 532, German silver bolster, 4-bd ...500.00
Belknap, C1-5600, office, grained ivory hdl, 2-bd, 3⅜" 42.00
Belknap, C1-6264S, carpenter, bone hdl, 3-bd, 3½" 80.00
Belknap, C1-7028-G, pen, bone hdl, 2-bd, 3¼" 60.00
Belknap, C1-704S, premium stock, bone stag hdl, 3-bd, 3½" 90.00
Boker, C3-7614, pen, eng stainless steel hdl, 2-bd, 3⅜" 52.00
Boker, 6113, Congress, stag hdl, 4-bd, 3½" 125.00
Boker, 7083, stag hdl, 2-bd, 3¼" 85.00
Bruckmann, senator, pearl hdl, 2-bd, 3⅝" 75.00
Case, GS1095SAB, gold-stone hdl, 1-bd, Case Bradford PA, 5".350.00
Case, M3102RSS, stainless steel hdl w/bail, 3-bd, XX, 2¾" 50.00
Case, 11031SH, walnut hdl, 1-bd, XX, 3¾" 45.00
Case, 2220, blk compo hdl, 2-bd, XX, 2¾" 100.00
Case, 31048, jack, yel compo hdl, 1-bd, XX, 4⅛" 125.00
Case, 3254, trapper, yel compo hdl, 2-bd, XX, 4⅛" 300.00
Case, 4200SS, melon tester, wht compo hdl, 2-bd, XX, 5½" 800.00
Case, 5172, skinner, stag hdl, 1-bd, XX, 5½" 500.00
Case, 52131, canoe, stag hdl, 2-bd, XX, 3⅝" 500.00
Case, 5299½, stag hdl, 2-bd, USA, 4⅛" 175.00
Case, 53047, stag hdl, 3-bd, USA, 3⅞" 200.00
Case, 5332, stag hdl, 3-bd, XX, 3⅝" 200.00
Case, 61011, hawkbill, bone hdl, 1-bd, USA, 4" 110.00
Case, 6111½L, lock bk, bone hdl, 1-bd, XX, 4¾" 600.00

Case, 6185, jack, bone hdl, 1-bd, USA, 3⅝" 175.00
Case, 62048SpSSP, bone hdl, 2-bd, USA, 4⅛" 70.00
Case, 6207, bone hdl, 2-bd, XX, 3½" 150.00
Case, 62087, bone hdl, 2-bd, XX, 3¼" 100.00
Case, 6246RSS, bone hdl, 1-bd+Marlin SS spike, XX, 4⅜" 200.00
Case, 6254 SSP, trapper, bone hdl, 2-bd, USA, 4⅛" 250.00
Case, 6333, bone hdl, 3-bd, USA, 2⅝" 65.00
Case, 6383, whittler, bone hdl, 3-bd, USA, 3½" 200.00
Case, 6392, gr bone hdl, 3-bd, XX, 4" 500.00
Case, 82058, pearl hdl, 2-bd, Case Bros Cut Co, 2⅞" 250.00
Case, 9333, imi pearl hdl, 3-bd, XX, 2⅝" 50.00
Holley, 26842, sleeve board, German silver lined, 2-bd 210.00
Keen Kutter, KS323, pen, ivory hdl, 2-bd, 3" 40.00
Keen Kutter, Senator, pearl hdl, 2-bd, EC Simmons, 3" 125.00
Maher & Grosh, 050, old timer, cocobola hdl, 2-bd, shield 55.00
Maher & Grosh, 15, bone hdl, 1-sheepfoot bd 47.00
Maher & Grosh, 58, stag hdl, 3-bd 130.00
Queen, 54, pearl hdl, 3-bd, Queen Steel, 2⅝" 30.00
Queen, 8420, mini-trapper, genuine stag hdl, 2-bd, Queen Steel..35.00
Remington, RS3333, stag hdl, 3-bd+punch, 3¾" 310.00
Remington, R22, bone hdl, 2-bd, 3⅜" 225.00
Remington, R161, redwood hdl, 2-bd, 3½" 170.00
Remington, R213, easy opener, bone hdl, 2-bd, 3⅝" 310.00
Remington, R243, easy opener, bone hdl, 2-bd, 3⅝" 310.00
Remington, R609, nickel silver hdl, 2-bd, 3⅜" 190.00
Remington, R1005, pyremite hdl, 2-bd, 3⅝" 230.00
Remington, R1063, bone hdl, 2-bd, 3⅜" 230.00
Remington, R1306, hunter, stag hdl, 1-bd, bullet shield, 4½" .2,600.00
Remington, R1495, pyremite hdl, 2-bd, 3⅛" 200.00
Remington, R1773, easy opener, bone hdl, 2-bd, 3½" 150.00
Remington, R1863, bone hdl, 2-bd, 3⅜" 255.00
Remington, R2505B, pyremite hdl, 2-bd, 3⅜" 125.00
Remington, R3183, bone hdl, 2-bd+punch, 3½" 375.00
Remington, R3513, bone hdl, 3-bd, 3⅜" 300.00
Remington, R4023, bone hdl, 3-bd, 3⅜" 510.00
Remington, R4124, pearl hdl, 2-bd+punch, 3⅞" 500.00
Remington, R4605W, pyremite hdl, 2-bd+punch, 3¼" 240.00
Remington, R6249, nickel silver hdl, 2-bd, 3⅛" 145.00
Remington, R6439, nickel silver hdl, 3-bd, 2¾" 145.00
Remington, R6623, bone hdl, 2-bd, 3⅛" 250.00
Remington, R6835, pyremite hdl, 3-bd, 3⅛" 390.00
Remington, R6864, pearl hdl, 2-bd, 2½" 175.00
Remington, R6883, bone hdl, 2-bd, 3⅛" 260.00
Remington, R6904, pearl hdl, 2-bd, 2½" 170.00
Remington, R7054, solid pearl shadow hdl, 2-bd, 2½" 135.00
Remington, R7094, pearl hdl, 3-bd, 2⅝" 100.00
Remington, R7104, pearl hdl, 3-bd, 3¼" 150.00
Remington, R7344, pearl hdl, 2-bd+corkscrew, 3⅛" 315.00
Remington, R7584, pearl hdl, 3-bd, 3⅜" 315.00
Remington, R7624, pearl hdl, 2-bd, 3⅛" 175.00
Remington, R7825, pyremite hdl, 2-bd+punch, 3⅜" 165.00
Remington, R7854, pearl hdl, 2-bd, 3" 200.00
Remington, 6785W, office, pyremite hdl, 2-bd, 3⅜" 125.00
Remington, 8333, equal end, brn bone hdl, 2-bd, 3¾" 375.00
Robeson, 612407, jack, bone stag hdl, 1-bd, 5" 275.00
Robeson, 622027, jack/easy opener, bone stag hdl, 2-bd, 3⅝" 220.00
Robeson, 622064, pen, bone stag hdl, 2-bd, 2¾" 90.00
Robeson, 622183, jack, bone stag hdl, 2-bd, 2¾" 100.00
Russell, 44H12, pruning, cocobola hdl, 1-bd, 4¼" 145.00
Russell, 65, Barlow, bone hdl, 1-bd, 3⅜" 300.00
Russell, 601, Big Barlow, bone hdl, 1-bd, 5" 500.00
Schrade, 2014S, jack/easy opener, tortoise shell hdl, 2-bd, 3⅝" 75.00
Schrade, 2019BR, jack/easy opener, brass compo hdl, 2-bd, 3⅝" ..60.00
Schrade, 2063½, jack, bone stag hdl, 2-bd, 3⅝" 60.00

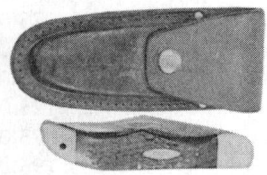

Case 6165SAB, bone stag handle, single blade, USA, two dots, open: 9", EX in leather sheath, $40.00.

Schrade, 2203¾, jack, bone stag hdl, 2-bd, 3½" 180.00
Schrade, 2271, jack, cocobola hdl, 2-bd, 3½" 90.00
Schrade, 8116, sleeveboard, MOP hdl, 3-bd, 3⅜" 110.00
Shapleigh, A150, Grandaddy Barlow, brn bone hdl, 1-bd, 5" 200.00
Shapleigh, B387, bone stag hdl, 2-bd, 5¼" 200.00
Shapleigh, B400, imi stag hdl, 2-bd, 3¼" 55.00
Shapleigh, S105, bone stag hdl, 1-bd, 5" 215.00
Shapleigh, S261, bone stag hdl, 1-bd, 5¼" 350.00
Shapleigh, 1S449½C, lock press-button, celluloid horn hdl 1-bd, 4" ...300.00
Shapleigh, 2S0, bone hdl, 2-bd, 3⅜" 70.00
Stiletto, 6J2009, serpentine skinner, brn stag hdl, 1-bd, 4" 175.00
Stiletto, 6J2011, serpentine jack, blk stag hdl, 2-bd, 3½" 100.00
Stiletto, 6J2017, premium stock, blk stag hdl, 2-bd+punch, 3½"...250.00
Union, 575, jack/easy opener, stag hdl, 2-bd, 3¾" 350.00
Union, 1025T stag hdl, 2-bd, 3¼" 300.00
Western, 3274, premium stock, golden shell pyralin hdl, 2-bd, 3⅞" ...170.00
Western, 6211, Barlow, brn bone hdl, 2-bd, 3¼" 130.00
Western, 162C7, serpentine, stag hdl, 2-bd, 2⅞" 110.00
Western, 92033, swell grip, pearl pyralin hdl, 2-bd, 3⅛" 70.00
Winchester, 1704, Father Barlow, bone hdl, 1-bd, 5" 495.00
Winchester, 1923, dagger jack, bone hdl, 1-bd, 4⅛" 345.00
Winchester, 1937, curved jack, bone hdl, 1-bd, 3⅞" 275.00
Winchester, 1938, bone hdl, 1-bd, 3⅜" 220.00
Winchester, 2303, sm Senator, pearl hdl, 2-bd, 2⅝" 125.00
Winchester, 2317, serpentine pen, pearl hdl, 2-bd, 3" 225.00
Winchester, 2549, jack, ebony hdl, 2-bd, 3¾" 265.00
Winchester, 2344, bone hdl, 2-bd, crest shield 320.00
Winchester, 2932, Congress, bone hdl, 2-bd, 3¼" 275.00
Winchester, 2951, bone hdl, 1-bd+punch, crest shield................250.00
Winchester, 2959, swell end jack/easy opener, bone hdl, 2-bd, 3⅜"..265.00
Winchester, 2988, jack, bone hdl, 2-bd, 4" 325.00
Winchester, 2996, congress, bone hdl, 2-bd, 3¾" 240.00
Winchester, 2997, serpentine pen, bone hdl, 2-bd, 3" 360.00
Winchester, 2998, bone hdl, 2-bd..265.00
Winchester, 3002, swell center, irid celluloid hdl, 3-bd, 3⅝" 385.00
Winchester, 3016, cattle, celluloid hdl, 3-bd, 3¾"........................300.00
Winchester, 3377, sleeveboard pen, pearl hdl, 3-bd, 3⅜" 300.00
Winchester, 3378, sleeveboard pen, pearl hdl, 3-bd, 3" 325.00
Winchester, 3992, slim Senator, bone hdl, 3-bd, 3⅜" 300.00

Miscellaneous

Bolo, US Model 1911, 12" spatula-type bd, brass S-shaped guard, VG...260.00
Bowie, 7" clip point blade, Joseph Allen, German silver cross guard.......195.00
Bowie type, 10¼" clip-point bd mk Solingen Germany, w/scabbard, EX ..70.00
Camp, I Wilson, 12½" bd, stag horn hdl, G, w/orig sheath.........350.00
Fighting, Confederate, 14" bd, forged D guard, VG 2,875.00
Hunting, US Model 1884, 8½" bd w/brass cross guard, VG........635.00
WWII theater, 5" bd, aluminum hdl, w/sheath, EX 75.00
WWII theatre, 6" bd, plexiglass hdl, w/sheath, EX.....................100.00
WWII theatre, 7" bd, micarta hdl, w/sheath, EX 175.00
WWII theatre, 8" bd, wood hdl, w/sheath, EX............................150.00

Kosta

Kosta glassware has been made in Sweden since 1742. Today they are one of that country's leading producers of quality art glass. Two of their most important designers were Elis Bergh (1929 – 1950) and Vicke Lindstrand, artistic director from 1950 to 1973. Lindstrand brought to the company knowledge of important techniques such as Graal, fine figural engraving, Ariel, etc. He influenced new artists to experiment with these techniques and inspired them to create new and innovative designs. Today's collectors are most interested in pieces made during the 1950s and 1960s. Our advisor for this category is Abby Malowanczyk; she is listed in the Directory under Texas.

Bowl, cameo trefoils inside, clear w/purple int layer, Ehrner, 5x7" ...300.00
Bowl, clear w/red/blk/wht treading, ½" thick, 4½x6¾"................260.00
Paperweight, bl swirls in clear, w/bubbles, Bergh #90962, 2¾" dia...125.00
Vase, blk-to-purple & wht crisscross, LH1261, 9¼".....................635.00
Vase, clear & bl w/bubbles, Lindstrand, #41825, 7½"..................425.00
Vase, clear w/bl int curtain, teardrop form, 1950s, 7½"..............120.00
Vase, clear w/dk amethyst band, LH1270, 3x2¼".......................135.00
Vase, clear w/etching of girl jogging, Lindstrand, 8" 175.00
Vase, clear w/gr int curtain & bubbles, #1718, 1950s, 6¼" 100.00
Vase, clear w/purple & bl feathered striations, #47672, 1950s, 7½"..450.00
Vase, clear w/trapped bubbles, Lindstrand, #41011, 12" 220.00
Vase, eng fishing boat/waves/nets, Lindstrand, LG166, 12".........400.00
Vase, horizontal tire-like lobes, ovoid w/disk ft, Bergh, 1935, 10"...350.00
Vase, Pictograph, cut o/l, eng scene, Warff, #46735, 5" 400.00
Vase, 6 cameo-cut moths, purple/clear, Boman, 1900, 9" 2,800.00

Kutani

Kutani, named for the Japanese village where it originated, was first produced in the seventeenth century. The early ware, Ko Kutani, was made for only about thirty years. Several types were produced before 1800, but these are rarely encountered. In the nineteenth century, kilns located in several different villages began to copy the old Kutani wares. This later, more familiar type has large areas of red with gold designs on a white ground decorated with warriors, birds, and flowers in controlled colors of red, gold, and black.

Bowl, geometric landscape, mc, Edo era, ca 1840, 3x14½"......2,000.00
Bowl, poem, birds in branchs ext, birds & clouds int, 5½x10" ...300.00
Bowl, red & wht w/flowers & birds, 5-sided, 3x6" dia...................60.00
Figurine, cat, sleeping, blk/red/wht w/gold lustre, 1x2x2¾"...........75.00
Pitcher, wht flying cranes on red, 5" 95.00
Plate, mother & daughter w/parasols, ca 1895-1900, 9⅞"...........165.00
Teabowl, sunflower w/orange & gr, mk RIJU, 3x5".....................110.00
Teapot, wht w/trees & flowers, gold trim, #391, 4-cup, 8" 50.00
Vase, chickens w/winter landscape, Meiji period, 12x7½" 165.00
Vase, cranes/peacocks/geisha. Foo dog finial, Meiji period, 13"...200.00
Vase, emb mums, wht on wht, 7¼" 100.00
Vase, pine tree landscape w/2 cranes, sgn Sanyu, 8½"................210.00

Labels

Before the advent of the cardboard box, wooden crates were used for transporting products. Paper labels were attached to the crates to identify the contents and the packer. These labels often had colorful lithographed illustrations covering a broad range of subjects. Eventually the cardboard box replaced the crate, and the artwork was imprinted directly onto the carton. Today these paper labels are becoming collectible — primarily for the art, but also for their advertising appeal. Our advisor for this category is Cerebro; their address is listed in the Directory under Pennsylvania.

Can, Acco Spinach, Atlas w/sphere/spinach, M 10.00
Can, Butterfly Stringless Beans, butterfly, ornate graphics, M 8.00
Can, Helmet Mixed Fruit, fruit vignette/armor helmet, emb, M...16.00
Can, Highland Peaches, gazebo/tree/people/peach, emb, M 12.00
Can, JH Hunt Blackberries, fruits across full length, Schmidt litho, M..40.00
Can, Meadowlark Plums. lark on blossom branch/plums, M 10.00
Can, Mojave Apricots, Indian portrait, stone litho, M..................14.00

Can, Narragansett Cranberries, Indian shooting bow & arrow/teepee, M....10.00
Can, Powhatan Apple Sauce, Indian in profile, M 10.00
Can, Sea Bird Salmon, bird/salmon jumping on wht, M 10.00
Can, Three Sisters Tomatoes, 3 ladies, ornate, M 35.00
Can, Valley View Pineapple, Yosemite Valley/poppies/pineapple, M 10.00
Cigar box, inner; American Rattler, Indian on horse/vignettes, NM..300.00
Cigar box, inner; Freedom, eagle against mountains, EX 690.00
Cigar box, inner; Good Policy, document/lighted cigar, EX 600.00
Cigar box, inner; King Dodo/Solid Success 5¢, cartoon bird, EX ..425.00
Cigar box, inner; Pebble/The Only Pebble on the Beach, beach scene, EX..3,200.00
Cigar box, inner; Snow Belle, portrait against snow scene, NM .550.00
Cigar box, inner; Stork, stork w/baby in basket, NM...................275.00
Cigar box, inner; Van Buren, portrait, EX.....................................170.00
Cigar box, outer, The Logger, man seated on log, EX.................225.00
Cigar box, outer; Andy Gump, profile, EX+ 180.00
Cigar box, outer; Gen Harrison, portrait, EX 80.00
Cigar box, outer; Grandby Smelter, mining country, NM 160.00
Cigar box, outer; Grandmother, grandmother at cradle, M.........180.00
Cigar box, outer; I've Got You, couple, EX 120.00
Cigar box, outer; King of Hearts, playing card on yel, M 140.00
Cigar box, outer; Nathan Hale/Schoolhouse, bl/red graphics, NM..90.00
Crate, apple, Anchor, lg ship's anchor on bl/yel logo, M................30.00
Crate, apple, Buckaroo, rider on bucking horse on prairie, M 25.00

Crate, apple, Red Label Apples, $10.00. (Photo courtesy Cerebro)

Crate, apple, Yankee Doll, '40s red sweater girl on bl/wht logo, M ..30.00
Crate, CA Orange, Airship, 4-prop airliner, red logo, M...............30.00
Crate, CA Orange, Reindeer, reindeer on yel ground/groves/etc, M ..20.00
Crate, CA Orange, Rosa de Oro, fancy lettering/orange/rose/ranch, M ..20.00
Crate, CA Orange, Shasta, oranges/blossoms/red ground, M 40.00
Crate, FL Citrus, Blue & the Gray, Civil War vets, M 15.00
Crate, FL Citrus, Florida Cowboy, rider on bucking horse, M 20.00
Crate, FL Citrus, On Top, bl top on orange circle, bl ground, M..25.00
Crate, FL Citrus, Prairie Garden, orange groves/palm trees/river, M..35.00
Crate, lemon, Las Fuentes, vignette of pool/fountain/lemons, M ..15.00
Crate, lemon, Montecito Valley, Las Fuentes Rancho/groves/hills, M ..40.00
Crate, lemon, Pacific Maid, blond girl in skipper's hat, M.............16.00
Crate, pear, Bear Creek, snarling bear, M....................................65.00
Crate, pear, Tipsy Bee, bee on floating pear, M 25.00

Labino

Dominick Labino was a glass blower who until mid-1985 worked in his studio in Ohio, blowing and sculpting various items which he signed and dated. A ceramic engineer by trade, he was instrumental in developing the heat-resistant tiles used in space flights. His glassmaking shows his versatility in the art. While some of his designs are free-form and futuristic, others are reminiscent of the products of older glasshouses. Because of problems with his health, Mr. Labino became unable to blow glass himself; he died January, 10, 1987. Work coming from his studio since mid-1985 has been signed 'Labino Studios, Baker,' indicating ware made by his protegee, E. Baker O'Brien. In addition to her own compositions, she continues to use many of the colors developed by Labino.

Paperweight, cloud-like decor w/clear pearl in gr tint, 1969, 2½" ..300.00
Paperweight, pulled yel/gr/bl on lt bl w/purple tint, 1968, 5½"...600.00
Pitcher/vase, Grotesque, gr, pulled hdl/spout, 1965 ....125.00
Sculpture, Objects in Space, sulphurous yel w/air traps, 1966, 4¼"..3,500.00
Vase, alexandrite (bl to fuchsia), flared, 1968, 4½" 750.00
Vase, Ariel, purple-brn glass w/abstract air traps, 1971, 6¼".......700.00
Vase, dk red striated, pleated base, 1966, 3x6¾"........................550.00
Vase, dk to lt red, uptrn sides, 1971, 3¼x7¼"...........................550.00
Vase, dull red sphere w/twisted prunts, #7, 1971, 5½" 550.00
Vase, pk sphere w/gr-yel prunts, Labino 8-1978, 4¼" 550.00

Lace, Linens, and Needlework

Two distinct audiences vie for old lace and linens. Collectors seek out exceptional stitchery like philatelists and numismatists seek stamps or coins — simply to marvel at its beauty, rarity, and ties to history. Collectors judge lace and linens like figure skaters and gymnasts are judged: artist impression is half the score, technical merit the other. How complex and difficult are the stitches and how well are they done? The 'users' see lace and linens as recyclables. They seek pretty wearables or decorative materials. They want fashionable things in mint condition, and have little or no interest in technique. Both groups influence price.

Undiscovered and underpriced are the eighteenth-century masterpieces of lace and needle art in techniques which will never be duplicated. Their beauty is subtle. Amazing stitches often are invisible without magnification. To get the best value in any lace, linen, or textile item, learn to look closely at individual stitches, and study the design and technique. The finest pieces are wonderfully constructed. The stitches are beautiful to look at, and they do a good job of holding the item together. Our advisor for this category is Elizabeth M. Kurella, author (Krause) of books related to this subject; she is listed in the Directory under Indiana.

Key: embr — embroidered

Am flag, woven/crocheted, red/wht/bl, border of yel/bl tassels, 25x15"...425.00
Bedcover, wht Egyptian cotton w/embr, ca 1900, 90x95"............295.00
Bedcover, wht Irish linen w/embr & drawnwork, 1890s, 78x90" ...295.00
Bedcover, wht Marcella, embr, ca 1890, 86x86" 285.00
Bedspread, net lace, scalloped ruffle, ca 1920-40, 71x10"............180.00
Bolster, bl/wht homespun, hand-sewn seams, 18x55" 135.00
Breakfast set, bl organdy w/applique & embr, 1920s, 14x20"+2 napkins...75.00
Buffet cloth, cotton w/1½" hand lace edge, ca 1900, 23½x31".....75.00
Buffet cloth, wht linen w/Bedfordshire lace inserts, ca 1900, 20" sq........65.00
Cape/collar, Venetian Point hand lace, ca 1880, 10" cape, 36" front ...385.00
Collar, crocheted lace, 1920s, 5" deep 45.00
Collar, Irish crocheted lace, ca 1885, 4x12" bk, 15" L front..........85.00
Coverlet, cotton chintz, brn/red/natural, hand quilted, 1850s, 91x79"..2,100.00
Coverlet, gold-quilted linsley-woolsey, early 1800s, 98x99" 4,850.00
Curtain, wht cotton w/Tambour work embr, 1900s, 64x70"........135.00
Curtains, embr tulle ecru lace, 2 panels: 77x36", M 165.00
Doily, linen center w/embr & 1½" lace edging, ca 1900, 10½", pr ..65.00
Doily, linen center w/wide hand-made lace border, 1890s, 8" 25.00
Doily, linen w/4" crochet lace edge, ca 1900, 12" dia, pr...............65.00
Family register, birds/foliage/verses/trees/etc, sgn/1809, 22x23", EX...3,735.00
Featherbed cover, bl/wht homespun plaid, EX color, patched, 56x68"....85.00
Handkerchief, silk w/bobbin lace insertions.................................20.00
Lingerie bag, wht linen w/wht embr, ca 1900, 14x19" 55.00
Mat, linen w/embr & lace edging, ca 1900, 22½" dia...................55.00
Mat, Madeira linen w/floral openwork, 1920s, 8", 6 for................55.00
Mat, wht linen w/embr & cutwork baskets, ca 1900, 19" dia 55.00
Napkin, linen w/embr & organdy inserts, 12x12", 12 for 85.00
Napkin, wht Irish linen damask, ca 1900, 22x22", 12 for............135.00

Needlework panel, Am eagle w/shield & arrows, China Trade?, 23x21"..**700.00**
Needlework panel, couple in garden, silk embr, oval fr, 11x9", pr..**1,295.00**
Needlework panel, eagle/banner/wreath, dtd 1875, OH, 13⅝x26" ...**195.00**
Needlework panel, Geo WA at Battle of Trenton, silk embr, sgn/1850, 34x25"..**1,175.00**
Needlework panel, peasant lady w/basket, silk on silk embr, 1850s, 16" ...**500.00**
Needlework panel, pk rose w/long stem embr on blk silk, 18x10".**95.00**
Pillow sham, damask Irish linen, M monogram, ca 1900, 30x30" .**90.00**
Pillowcase, wht linen w/frilly 6" filet lace trim, 1900s, 39"............**85.00**
Pillowcases, wht linen w/pale bl embr, ca 1920, 34x20", pr...........**75.00**
Place mat, Madeira hand embr, ca 1920, 5x10½", 4 for **40.00**
Runner, cream linen w/embr/cutwork roses ea corner, 1930s, 40x14"...**65.00**
Runner, Irish linen w/3" hand lace trim, ca 1900, 37x12" **65.00**
Runner, wht linen w/embr, scalloped edge, ca 1900, 42x18" **65.00**
Runner, wht linen w/embr/cutwork corners, 1900s, 47x15" **70.00**
Shawl, blk Spanish bobbin lace, ca 1895, 76x76" **255.00**
Sheets, cotton/linen mix, embr monogram, 1920s, 82x112", pr..**185.00**
Sheets, wht Irish linen, ca 1890, pr: 70x84", +lg pillowcase **135.00**
Show towel, 3 trees w/birds, petit-point detail, sgn/1864, 52x18", EX...**250.00**
Table topper, Irish linen, lace inserts/4" lace edge, 1890s, 30" sq...**130.00**
Tablecloth, bl organdy & fine linen w/embr, 1920s, 42" sq, +6 napkins...**135.00**
Tablecloth, cream linen w/cutwork & embr, 1920s, 60x96", +6 lg napkins....**225.00**
Tablecloth, Fr lace w/Venice scene, ca 1900, 72x111", +12 napkins ..**1,850.00**
Tablecloth, homespun, bl/wht checked, tatted inner bands, 66x54".........**50.00**
Tablecloth, Irish linen w/much crochet filet lace, 1890s, 46"sq ..**175.00**
Tablecloth, ivory linen w/embr, 4" lace edge, ca 1920, 44" sq.....**125.00**
Tablecloth, linen, red/wht, fern & foliage border, wear, 83x62"..**100.00**
Tablecloth, wht linen w/crochet lace edge w/roses, ca 1900, 42" sq..**145.00**
Tablecloth, wht linen w/cutwork & embr, ca 1900, 69x96" **220.00**
Tablecloth, wht linen w/embr, ca 1930, 70x10", +6 embr 16" sq napkins...**165.00**
Tea cloth, wht linen w/embr butterflies, ca 1900, 34x34".............**95.00**
Tea cozy, Battenburg lace cover, ca 1900, 12x10" **55.00**
Towel, gray linen w/embr & fringe ea end, 1920s, 32", pr **40.00**
Towel, Irish linen damask w/5" crochet lace trim, 1890s, 50" **65.00**
Towel, linen w/embr monogram, 4" crochet lace trim, 1890s, 46", pr..**110.00**
Towel, linen w/lg woven flowers, embr monogram, 1890s, 41" **60.00**
Towel, linen w/printed pastel flowers & embr letter, 1920s, 37x23", pr...**75.00**
Towel, wht damask w/embr monogram, 7" scalloped lace edge, 1890s, 53"...**70.00**
Towel, wht Irish linen w/embr & 2" crochet lace trim, 1890s, 51"....**65.00**
Towel, wht linen huckaback, 4" lace at 1 end, ca 1900, 42"..........**55.00**
Towel, wht linen w/monogram, 4" scalloped lace trim, 1890s, 44"...**60.00**
Tray cloth, embr flowers w/cutwork, 3 rows of drawnwork, 1900s, 16x19"...**50.00**
Tray cloth, linen w/drawnwork, 1930s, 12½x8" **40.00**
Tray cloth, linen w/embr flower baskets & butterflies, 1900s, 14x19" ...**55.00**
Tray cloth, wht Irish damask w/3" lace trim, 1900s, 28x22" **70.00**
Tray cloth, wht Irish linen w/5" crochet dbl-dmn edge, 1895, 28x40" ..**75.00**
Tray cloth, wht linen w/Battenburg lace edge, 1920s, 13x26" **55.00**
Tray cloth, wht linen w/embr & tatted edge, ca 1900, 10x15" **50.00**
Veil, wht needlepoint applique lace, ca 1890, 48x50" **245.00**

Lalique

Having recognized her son's talent at an early age, Rene Lalique's mother apprenticed him at the age of 21 to a famous Paris jeweler. In 1885 he opened his own workshop, and his unique style earned him great notoriety because of his use of natural elements in his designs — horn, ivory, semi-precious stone, pearls, coral, enamel, even plastic and glass.

At the Paris Universal Exposition in 1900 at the age of 40, he achieved the pinnacle of his success in the jewelry field. Already having experimented with glass, he decided to focus his artistic talent on that medium. In 1907 after completing seven years of laborious work, Lalique became a master glassmaker and designer of perfume bottles for Francois Coty, a chemist and perfumer who was also his neighbor in the Place Vendome area in Paris. All in all he created over two hundred fifty per-

fume bottles for Roger et Gallet, Coty, Worth, Forvil, Guerlain, D'Orsay, Molinard, and many others. In the commercial perfume bottle collecting field, Rene Lalique's are those most desired. Some of his one-of-a-kind experimental models have gone for over $100,000.00 at auction in the last few years.

At the height of production his factories employed over six hundred workers.

Seeking to bring art into every day life, he designed clocks, tableware, stemware, chandeliers, inkwells, bowls, statues, dressing table items, and, of course, vases. Lalique's unique creativity is evident in his designs through his polishing, frosting, and glazing techniques. He became famous for his use of colored glass in shades of blue, red, black, gray, yellow, green, and opalescence. His glass, so popular in the 1920s and 1930s, is still coveted today.

Lalique's son Marc assumed leadership of the company in 1948, after his father's death. His designs are made from full lead crystal, not the demi-crystal Rene worked with. Designs from 1948 on were signed only Lalique, France. The company was later taken over by Marc's daughter, Marie-Claude, and her designs were modern, clear crystal accented with color motifs. The Lalique company was sold in 1995, and Marie-Claude Lalique retired shortly thereafter.

Condition is of extreme importance to a collector. Grinding, polished out chips, and missing perfume bottle stoppers can reduce the value significantly, sometimes by as much as 80%.

Czechoslovakian glassware bearing fradulent Lalique signatures is appearing on all levels of the market. Study and become familiar with the various Lalique designs before paying a high price for a fraudulent piece. Over the past five years Lalique-designed glass has been showing up in a deep purple-gray color. These are clear glass items that have been 'irradiated' to change their appearance. Buyer beware.

Our advisor for this category is Madeleine France; she is listed in the Directory under Florida.

Key:
cl/fr — clear and frosted   RL — signed R. Lalique
L — signed Lalique   RLF — signed R. Lalique, France
LF — signed Lalique France

Vase, Ronsards, opal, 8", $8,000.00. (Photo courtesy Jackson's Auctions, Inc.)

Bell, bird finial, cl/fr, LF, pre-1940 ....**110.00**
Bottle, scent; Cinq Fleure, 5 flowers, cl w/blk & gold, RLF, 2¾" ...**750.00**
Bottle, scent; Deux Fleurs, cl/fr, RL, ca 1935, 3½" **350.00**
Bottle, scent; Deux Fleurs (2 flowers), cl/fr, RLF, 4x4" **450.00**
Bottle, scent; Illusion, Lalique/D'Orsay, cl, tan fr stopper, 3½"...**450.00**
Bottle, scent; La Belle Saison, lady w/in leafy spires, 4", MIB..**2,400.00**
Bottle, scent; Oree, gown, cl/fr, Claire, early, 3¼"....................**2,100.00**
Bottle, scent; Perles, graduated beads, cl/fr, RL, 5½" **325.00**
Bowl, center; Marguerites, daisies, cl w/bl-gr wash, RLF, 13" **575.00**
Bowl, Dandelion, cl/fr, RLF N 3104, 1⅞x5⅛", 6 for **500.00**
Bowl, Flora-Bella, overlapping leaves, cobalt, RLF, rim shaved, 15"...**3,000.00**
Bowl, Graines D'Asperges, twigs & berries, cl/opal, RLF 3222, 6¼"......**285.00**

Bowl, Poissons No 1, fish & bubbles, opal, RLF, 11⅞" **575.00**
Bowl, Pornic, half-shells along rim, cl/fr, LF, 2x8" **350.00**
Box, dresser; finely ribbed, rabbit/medallion of doves on lid, RL, 3" ...**400.00**
Box, powder; D'Orsay le Lys, cl/fr w/sepia wash, RLF, 2x4" dia ...**750.00**
Box, powder; Vaucluse, cl/fr w/sepia wash, RLF, 1932, 1½x3" **895.00**
Box, 2 ladies in garden, brn patina, RLF, 1¾x2¾" dia, EX **500.00**
Charger, Pivoines, peonies, bl enamel on fr, ca 1920, 14½" **7,000.00**
Clock, 2 etch figures in cl/fr, metal base, RL, Marcilhac #726, 13x14" ...**8,000.00**
Figurine, cat, sitting, fr, LF, 8" **1,200.00**
Figurine, Christ on cross, cl, RLF, 6¾" **460.00**
Figurine, lady holds flowers at waist, fr, RL, 4½", in clear bowl ..**600.00**
Figurine, nude (fr) on clear rock base, LF, 9" **400.00**
Figurine, nude kneeling, fr, LF+paper MIF label, 5x6" **300.00**
Figurine, nude w/lamb, paper label: LF, 4½" **150.00**
Figurine, 2 dancing female nudes, cl/fr, LF, 10" **750.00**
Goblet, Gourgueil, conical, ftd, RLF, ca 1930, 5", 3 for..............**195.00**
Hood ornament, Cinq Chevaux, 5 horses, lt amethyst, RL/F4", EX ..**5,000.00**
Liqueur set, Pouilly, fish, bl wash, RL, decanter+8 2¾" goblets **4,300.00**
Mascot, Comet, trailing star on platform, RL, #1134, 1938, 4x8" **10,000.00**
Mascot, dragonfly, cl/fr, RLF, 8¼x8", pr....................................**5,000.00**
Mirror, Narcisse Couche, sepia wash, RLF 675, 11¾", NM **2,600.00**
Pin tray, 2 birds, cl/fr, LF in script, 4" dia **90.00**
Plate, bird portrait, 1973, cl/fr, LF, MIB **95.00**
Plate, nude encircled w/random flowers in pinwheel, amber, 7" .**150.00**
Plate, swirled lines of opal dots on cl, RL, 10¾" **480.00**
Tumbler, Jaffa, cactus, cl/fr, cylindrical, LF, 4⅝", 12 for..............**925.00**
Vase, Bacchantes, nude maidens, opal, RLF, chip, 8½"..........**25,000.00**
Vase, Beautrellis, bl wash, RLF, 5½x7¼" **1,200.00**
Vase, Canards, ducks, cl/fr w/blk enameling, ca 1931, 5¼"......**1,600.00**
Vase, Chardons, leaves, cl/fr, RL, ca 1930, 7½x6½"...................**800.00**
Vase, Elms, cl/fr, RLF, ca 1935, 10x7½", pr............................**7,500.00**
Vase, Enfants, 2 putti w/grapes, cl/fr, disc ft, RL, 1931, 10½" ..**1,035.00**
Vase, Milan, aspen branches, cobalt, RL, 11⅛".....................**20,000.00**
Vase, Moissac, raised leaves w/bl wash, RLF, 5¼x6" **980.00**
Vase, Oleron, fishes, brn wash, RLF, 3½"..................................**1,380.00**
Vase, Penthievre, fish, blk stain, 1928, 10¼"............................**9,600.00**
Vase, Perruches, parakeets, red-amber fr, spherical, RLF, 10"..**17,250.00**
Vase, Perruches, parrots, brilliant bl, RL, 10", NM **12,000.00**
Vase, Plumes, opal, sloped shoulder, RL, ca 1920, 8⅜"................**975.00**
Vase, Ronces, allover bramble thorns, fr, ovoid, RL, 9½" **1,300.00**
Vase, Ronces, brambles, cherry red, drilled, 9", on wood stand....**1,840.00**
Vase, Sauterelles, grasshoppers, cl/fr w/bl & gr wash, RLF, 10½" ..**7,500.00**

Lamps

The earliest lamps were simple dish containers with a wick that hung over the edge or was supported by a channel or tube. Grease and oil from animal or vegetable sources were the first fuels used. Ancient pottery lamps, crusie, and Betty lamps are examples of these early types. In 1784 Swiss inventor Ami Argand introduced the first major improvement in lamps. His lamp featured a tubular wick and a glass chimney. During the first half of the nineteenth century, whale oil, burning fluid (a highly explosive mixture of turpentine and alcohol), and lard were the most common fuels used in North America. Many lamps were patented for specific use with these fuels.

Kerosene was the first major breakthrough in lighting fuels. It was demonstrated by Canadian geologist Dr. Abraham Gesner in 1846. The discovery and drilling of petroleum in the late 1850s provided an abundant and inexpensive supply of kerosene. It became the main source of light for homes during the balance of the nineteenth century and for remote locations until the 1950s.

Although Thomas A. Edison invented the electric lamp in 1879, it was not until two or three decades later that electric lamps replaced kerosene household lamps. Millions of kerosene lamps were made for every purpose and pocketbook. They ranged in size from tiny night or miniature lamps to tall stand or piano lamps. Hanging varieties for homes commonly had one or two fonts (oil containers), but chandeliers for churches and public buildings often had six or more. Wall or bracket lamps usually had silvered reflectors. Student lamps, parlor lamps (now called Gone-With-the-Wind lamps), and patterned glass lamps were designed to complement the popular furnishing trends of the day. Gaslight, introduced in the early nineteenth century, was used mainly in homes of the wealthy and public places until the early twentieth century. Most fixtures were wall or ceiling mounted, although some table models were also used.

Few of the ordinary early electric lamps have survived. Many lamp manufacturers made the same or similar styles for either kerosene or electricity, sometimes for gas. Top-of-the-line lamps were made by Pairpoint, Phoenix, Tiffany, Bradley and Hubbard, and Handel. See also these specific sections.

When buying lamps that have been converted to electricity, inspect them very carefully for any damage that may have resulted from the alterations; such damage is very common, and when it does occur, the lamp's value may be lessened by as much as 50%. Lamps seem to bring much higher prices in some areas than others, especially the larger cities. Conversely, in rural areas they may bring only half as much as our listed values. One of our advisors for lamps is Carl Heck; he is listed in the Directory under Colorado. Advise for miniature lamps comes from Bob Culver (who is listed in the Directory under Michigan), and Jeff Bradfield (in Virginia) is our advisor for pattern glass lamps. See also Stained Glass.

Key: col — cut overlay

Aladdin Lamps, Electric

From 1908 Aladdin lamps with a mantle became the mainstay of rural America, providing light that compared favorably with the electric light bulb. They were produced by the Mantle Lamp Company of America in over eighteen models and more than one hundred styles. During the 1930s to the 1950s, this company was the leading manufacturer of electric lamps as well. Still in operation today, the company is now known as Aladdin Mantle Lamp Co., located in Clarksville, Tennessee. For those seeking additional information on Aladdin Lamps, we recommend *Aladdin — The Magic Name in Lamps*, *Aladdin Electric Lamps Collector's Manual & Price Guide #3*, and *Aladdin Collector's Manual and Price Guide #19*, all written by our advisor for Aladdins, J. W. Courter; he is listed in the Directory under Kentucky. Mr. Courter has also published a book called *Angle Lamps, Collector's Manual and Price Guide*.

Bed, B-45, Whip-o-Lite shade, from $75 to **100.00**
Bedroom, P-70, metal & ceramic, from $20 to.............................**30.00**
Bedroom, P-71, ceramic, from $25 to **35.00**
Boudoir, G-15, floral base, crystal, 1938-52, from $150 to **200.00**
Boudoir, M-158, metal, 1937, from $30 to **40.00**
Figurine, M-123, lady, metal, from $175.....................................**225.00**
Floor, #3348, Type A, from $150 to...**200.00**
Floor, F-203, metal, 3-way, from $60 to......................................**100.00**
Magic Touch, MT-520, cherry & brass base, from $400 to..........**500.00**
Pin-Up, G-351, wall medallion, Alacite, from $125 to **150.00**
Pin-Up, P-57, Gun-n-Holster, ceramic, 1938-56, from $125 to ..**150.00**
Table, E-200, Vogue Pedestal, gr, from $700 to **800.00**
Table, G-034, from $100 to..**150.00**
Table, G-178, Opalique, from $150 to...**250.00**
Table, G-179, Opalique, from $125 to...**175.00**
Table, G-213A, Alacite, closed urn, from $250 to......................**300.00**
Table, G-221, Alacite, from $75 to..**125.00**
Table, G-309, Alacite, illuminated base, tall harp, from $70 to **90.00**

Table, M-454, ceramic & metal base, from $25 to **35.00**
Table, M-458, ceramic w/blk iron base, from $30 to **40.00**
Table, P-480, planter lamp, ceramic, from $75 to **100.00**
TV, M-367, blk iron base, w/shade, from $30 to **40.00**
TV, M-469, metal, w/shade, from $25 to **30.00**

Aladdin Lamps, Kerosene

Aladdinette, glass chimney, 2 different shapes, from $150 to **250.00**
Caboose Model B, B-400, brass font, w/shade, from $200 to.......**300.00**
Floor Model #12, bl & gold, 1928-29, from $200 to **350.00**
Floor Model B, bronze, 1934-35, from $150 to **225.00**
Floor Model B, ivory & gold, from $150 to..................................**250.00**
Foreign Model #9, table model, London, from $75 to **100.00**
Foreign Model C, Brazil, C-164, glass font, shelf model, $100 to....**125.00**
Foreign Super Aladdin, Bakelite, Australia #1653, pk or bl, $600 to ...**700.00**
Foreign Table Model 12, London, nickel, from $75 to **125.00**
Hanging Model #23, brass w/glass shade, several types, from $60 to.......**100.00**
Hanging Model #3, single chandelier, w/#205 shade, from $3,500 to..**4,500.00**
Shelf Model 23, Lincoln Drape, clear, oil fill, from $100 to.......**125.00**
Table Model #12, str side, bronze or nickel, from $75 to.............**100.00**
Table Model #12 Crystal Vase, Variegated Verde, 12", from $200 to..**250.00**
Table Model #9, nickel, 2 knob variations, ea from $100 to **150.00**
Table Model B, Cathedral #107, clear crystal, from $100 to **150.00**
Table Model B, Oriental B-130, ivory, from $150 to **200.00**
Table Model B, Queen B-96, wht moonstone, from $375 to.......**425.00**
Table Model B, Quilt B-86, gr moonstone, from $200 to **400.00**
Table Model B, Short Lincoln Drape #B62S, ruby crystal solitaire ft.**5,500.00**
Table Model B, Washington Drape B-53P, pk-tint crystal, $175 to **250.00**
Table Model B, Washington Drape B-52, amber crystal, from $125 to .**175.00**

Table, Model #7, satin brass,
original finish, 1917 – 1919,
from $250.00 to $300.00.
(Photo courtesy J.W. Courter)

Table Model 21C, B-139, aluminum font, from $35 to..................**50.00**
Wall bracket Model 7 or 8, from $500 to **600.00**
Wall bracket Practicus, from $425 to **475.00**

Angle Lamps

The Angle Lamp Company of New York City developed a unique type of kerosene lamp that was a vast improvement over those already on the market; they were sold from about 1896 until 1929 and were expensive for their time. Nearly all Angle lamps are hanging lamps and wall lamps. Table models are uncommon. Our Angle lamp advisor is J.W. Courter; he is listed in the Directory under Kentucky. See the narrative for Aladdin Lamps for information concerning popular books Mr. Courter has authored.

Note: Old glass pieces for Angle lamps are scarce to rare; unless noted otherwise the lamp values that follow are for examples with no glass.

Barn lantern, #115, tin, complete **1,000.00**

Hanging, #203, 2-burner, NP tin, EX **300.00**
Hanging, #352, 3-burner, polished brass, EX..............................**600.00**
Hanging, 3-burner, emb grapes, nickel, EX **675.00**
Wall, #125, pinwheel emb, 1-burner, NP brass, EX **400.00**
Wall, #163, polished brass, EX..**275.00**
Wall, Leaf & Vine, nickel, EX...**400.00**

Banquet Lamps

Brass std w/3-D cherub & lg fish, emb metal font, rpl shade, 38", VG ..**800.00**
Col, opal cut to cranberry, globe cut w/florals, ormolu base, 20".**400.00**
Cranberry w/emb ribs, blk stem, wht metal ft, foreign burner, 22", VG..**400.00**
Cut ball shade/font/stem, clear ft, foreign burner, 28" **575.00**
Gilt cherub on base holds font, wht shade w/HP cherubs, 34"....**150.00**
Nickel Plate 101, wht opal font, 12" **500.00**
Poppies emb on red satin, brass fitting, CI base/claw ft, 1890s, 26"...**1,200.00**
Violet-bl opaque base, clambroth font, scalloped ft, 14¾" **300.00**

Chandeliers

Brass, 6 scroll arms, central orb w/pendant drop, 21½x23" dia ...**250.00**
Brass Neo-Classical style, etched/frosted teardrop shades, 65x33"..**2,300.00**
Bronze Emp style, verde patina & gilt, 9-light, 36x26" dia **3,200.00**
Caramel slag 24" shade w/metal o/l: houses/deer/etc, crown, EX.......**1,000.00**
Cut glass prisms & swags w/gilt bronze mts, Louis XV style, 46x31".**2,900.00**
Gilt & bronze Fr Restoration style, 10-light w/leaf decor, 44x28" **5,465.00**
Gilt brass Fr Gothic style, 12-light, electrified, 1880s, 35x35".**1,150.00**
Gilt bronze, 5-light, arms ending in irises/foliage, 1900, 45"....**3,165.00**
Gilt bronze Neo-Greco w/etched & eng globes, prisms, 1870s, 50x32" dia ..**5,300.00**
Gilt bronze Regency style, 12 scrolled/foliate arms, 30x24" dia..**2,500.00**
Gilt bronze w/acanthus & eagle heads, 6-arm, 1880s, 26"........**2,350.00**
Gilt metal & bronze Emp style, flame finial, 6-light, 36x24" dia ..**2,000.00**
Gilt metal & cut glass Neoclassical style, 18-light, 54" **2,750.00**
Gilt metal Neoclassical, 6 branches above 6 dbl, drops, 54x44" ..**3,450.00**
Pnt/parcel giltwood, 2-tier, ea w/6 candle arms, Italy, 1700s, 41x38"...**2,645.00**
Pressed glass Louis XV style, 8-light, prisms, 48" H..................**2,100.00**
Tin band w/9 fluted candle holders, 3 wire chains, 19th C, 17¼" dia ..**4,000.00**
Wrought iron & rock crystal Louis XVI style, 8-light, 44x34", pr...**4,600.00**

Decorated Kerosene Lamps

When only one color is given in a two-layer cut overlay lamp description, the second layer is generally clear; in three-layer examples, the second will ususally be white, the third clear. Exceptions will be noted.

Bl opaline font/stem, 2-step marble base, 9 cut prisms, Oregon shade...**1,150.00**
Bl satin ribbed stem & sm font, cut velvet shade, metal mts, 17"..**550.00**
Col (2-layer), bl, bl hex std on sq base w/gilt, 13½" **1,950.00**
Col (2-layer), cobalt, windows, brass stem, marble ft, 9", pr **975.00**
Col (2-layer), cobalt w/paw prints, to top of shade w/transfers, 18"...**1,100.00**
Col (2-layer), cranberry, windows/floral, gold-trim milk glass ft, 19" **800.00**
Col (2-layer), gr, geometrics, cut Oregon shade, brass/marble std, 20"...**800.00**
Col (2-layer), gr w/gold, ribbed std, opal base, NE Glass, 13"..**1,100.00**
Col (2-layer), peacock bl, reeded std, baroque base, 14" **1,600.00**
Col (2-layer), ruby, brass std, marble base, NE Glass, 13" **1,150.00**
Col (2-layer), ruby, font/stem, marble base, ring w/8 prisms, 13", VG **500.00**
Col (2-layer), ruby, opal fluted std on sq base w/gold, Sandwich, 14"..**1,000.00**
Col (2-layer), wht, mercury-flash std int, brass base, 17" **1,265.00**
Col (2-layer), wht, windows, fluted brass/2-step marble std, 11", EX **390.00**
Col (2-layer), wht/cranberry w/Moorish windows, clambroth base, 13"...**575.00**
Col (3-layer), cobalt, brass std, stepped marble base, Sandwich, 12"...**2,000.00**
Col (3-layer), cranberry, brass std, marble base, NE Glass, 14" **2,000.00**
Col (3-layer), gr, col std, marble base w/gold, Sandwich, 16" ..**7,000.00**
Col (3-layer), pk, reeded brass std, stepped base, Sandwich, 12"...**2,000.00**

Col (3-layer), red, reeded std, marble base, Sandwich, 12" **865.00**
Col (3-layer), red w/rnd & oval windows, brass/marble ft, 12"....**690.00**
Col (3-layer), ruby, pressed glass std, baroque base, 13½" **1,380.00**
Cranberry pear font w/wht threads, brass stem, marble ft, 8½"...**1,265.00**
Cut font on clambroth stem, dbl-step marble base, 15" **460.00**
Ruby-flashed hairpin shapes on clear onion font & flaring ft, 10" ...**110.00**

Fairy Lamps

Bl Dmn Quilt MOP, clear Clarke cup, Cricklite shade, 8½" **350.00**
Bl MOP shade, Clarke porc base, on metal bracket w/mirrored base, 6" **450.00**
Bl satin, crimped top/ruffled bottom, set w/ormolu-fr jewels, 5½" **325.00**
Burmese, Clarke cup, Tunnicliffe bowl base w/floral band, 4¾x6"...**1,250.00**
Burmese, clear base mk Clarke's Pyramid Fairy, Webb, 3¾"........**335.00**
Burmese, floral spray, in Clarke porc base mk Fairy, 5¾" **700.00**
Burmese, on ftd Clarke cup w/SP collar 9¼" **525.00**
Burmese, pyramid shade in Clarke Et Al cup, 4-ftd fr w/4 Burmese vases....**1,350.00**
Burmese, ruffled base, matching shade, Clarke cup, Webb, 5½"...**1,000.00**
Burmese, satin glass insert mk Webb/Clarke, 6"...........................**450.00**
Burmese, Tapestry Ware base, Clarke cup, #1439, 6¼x7½".....**2,000.00**
Burmese, textured Clarke base, 4¼" **175.00**
Burmese, 3 bud vases+2 shades on brass holder, 10x9" **900.00**
Burmese epergne, 2 decor shades, crystal holders, 3-lily stem, 8" ...**3,600.00**
Dk pk to wht w/clear edge, petal base, ruffled-top chimney, 8x6" **165.00**
English cameo, floral, wht on bl, flaring cameo base mk Clarke, 5½"...**6,250.00**
English cameo, floral stems, wht on citron, ovoid w/flared shade, 11" ...**3,250.00**
English cameo, 2 borders/floral, rose/wht on citron, in satin base, 6" **1,400.00**
Florentine Cameo, bl/wht, in frosted holder w/leaf rigaree, 5½".....**200.00**
Gr satin Swirl on gr satin stick base w/camphor rigaree & 4 ft, 12"...**550.00**
Nailsea, bl w/wht loopings, on Clarke crystal base **225.00**
Nailsea, citron w/wht loops, crimped bowl base, Clarke cup, 5x5½" **985.00**
Nailsea, citron w/wht loops, in SP Meriden holder w/3-D cherub, 12"...**750.00**
Nailsea, red w/wht loops, loosely ruffled base, Clarke cup, 5¾" ..**300.00**
Owl figural, bsk w/brn & gold pnt, Noritake, 7" **400.00**
Pk rib satin shade, gold-wash Clarke base 'for burning pyramid'..., 4" ...**500.00**
Rainbow MOP, slim ruffled shade on 8" ruffled base, crystal insert, 8" ..**650.00**
Wht satin cased w/pk, dish-like base w/HP florals, 3-pc, 5½" **200.00**

Gone-With-the-Wind Lamps

Brass emb font: ornate ft/dragon hdls, 9" pnt milk glass shade, 20"..**300.00**
Chrysanthemums on globe shade & base, all orig, 21½" **1,550.00**
Chrysanthemums on wht opaque ball shade & body, Consolidated, 25½"...**1,800.00**
Copper-plated w/3-D griffin hdls, curlicue ft, 10" griffin shade, 21".......**300.00**
Floral on wht ball shade, unusually shaped base, Consolidated, 30"...**1,800.00**
Floral on yel ball shade & base, all orig, 26¾" **1,350.00**
Milk glass pnt w/Greenaway figures/florals, rpl shade, no burner, 20"...**350.00**
Milk glass w/bl Delft ball shade/font/bottle std, cast ft, 34" **635.00**
Milk glass w/carnations on ball shade/vasiform std, fancy cast ft, 28"...**700.00**
Milk glass w/fruit-pnt 11" ball shade (rpl)/squat vasiform base, 27"......**500.00**
Milk glass w/heavy gold & floral ball shade/font/bottle std, 22", EX **300.00**
Milk glass w/overall floral on shade (rpl)/vasiform base, 31½"....**650.00**
Milk glass w/11" roses ball shade (rpl)/shouldered base, fancy ft, 26"......**460.00**
Roses on wht opaque ball shade & base, Parker, Meriden Conn, 27"...**1,800.00**
Wht metal/marble fancy base, brass section w/Miller font, 8½" shade....**460.00**
Yel opaline w/gilt decor, 2-step marble base, cut Oregon shade, 24"....**1,900.00**
Yel w/mc roses: ball shade/ovoid base, plated ornate ft, Larkin, 29"......**1,500.00**

Hanging Lamps

Burmese, shiny, swirled cylinder, 9x7", EX, fancy metal hdw **650.00**
Cranberry Optic Expanded Bull's Eye shade, red brass fr, 11½" ..**135.00**
Dk to lt pk satin glass pillar-rib str-side shade, brass mts, 10"......**575.00**
Hall, 12" pk globe w/gold lions, pulley system joins mts, total: 16"..**250.00**

Pk opal bell-shaped shade, clear orig font, brass fr, 14"................**250.00**
Wht opaque w/HP dome shade, ornate brass fr, prisms, 48" **575.00**

Lanterns

Triangular painted tin barn lantern with two glass panels (one hinged), hanging loops on back, ca 1850s, 19", VG, $345.00.

Barn, mortised wood fr w/4 glasses, bentwood hdl, tin vent , 9", VG...**825.00**
Brass & etched glass, acanthus & reeded finials, cylindrical, 38x15"......**350.00**
Candle, pnt pine, pierced top, 3 glass panes, 19th C, 16x10x10"....**2,400.00**
Carriage, brass, hexagonal, eagle surmount, dbl canopy, 1850-70, 32"....**235.00**
Carriage house, brass, ogee dome w/pineapple finial on ball, 23x9", pr..**440.00**
Hall, brass mt, blown glass, smoke bell, S-link chains, 10" dia....**375.00**
Skater's, brass-plated base & top, chain w/ring, mini, 4½" **525.00**
Tin, Parker's Pat 1855, 4 glass panels w/wire protectors, star cutouts...**525.00**
Tin, Paul Revere type, overall punching, rnd w/cone top, VG....**275.00**
Tin top/base band w/punchings, cobalt globe, rpl burner, 10½"..**575.00**
Tin w/verdigris, canted dome top w/mushroom finial, tapering, 28x17"...**330.00**

Lard Oil/Grease Lamps

CI, rnd pan base w/twist stem & sm ftd reservoir at top, pitting, 8" ..**100.00**
Iron, rush, tripod base/penny ft, spiral column, counterweight, 15"...**275.00**
Pottery, deep saucer base, long spout, grainy tan glaze, 7", EX **165.00**
Wrought iron, pan, tripod base, scalloped collar, wick guide, 25" ..**600.00**
Wrought iron, pan, tripod base w/scroll ft, octagonal pan adjusts, 21"...**385.00**
Wrought iron, rush, wood base, candle socket, 11"......................**385.00**
Wrought/CI, rnd font w/rooster finial, bail top, 23" **440.00**

Miniature Lamps, Kerosene

Miniature oil lamps were originally called 'night lamps' by their manufacturers. Early examples were very utilitarian in design — some holding only enough oil to burn through the night. When kerosene replaced whale oil in the second half of the nineteenth century, 'mini' lamps became more decorative and started serving other purposes. While mini lamps continue to be produced today, collectors place special value on the lamps of the kerosene era, roughly 1855 to 1910. Four reference books are especially valuable to collectors as they try to identify and value their collections: *Miniature Lamps* by Frank and Ruth Smith, Schiffer Publishing, 1968 (referred to as SI); *Miniature Lamps II* by Ruth Smith, Schiffer Publishing, 1982 (SII); *Miniature Victorian Lamps* by Margorie Hulsebus, Schiffer Publishing, 1996 (source of the H numbers below); and *Price Guide for Miniature Lamps* by Marjorie Hulsebus, Schiffer Publishing, 1998 (contains 1998 values for all the above books). References in the following listings correlate with each lamp's plate number in the these books. Our advisor is Bob Culver; he is listed in the Directory under Michigan.

Amethyst, sm pear-shape shade/base w/disk ft, H-124.................**345.00**
Amethyst w/emb panels, gold decor, HP flowers, SI-126, 8¾"....**125.00**
Artichoke, amber satin, rnd shade/shouldered base, S-Fig III, EX...**900.00**
Artichoke, milk glass w/fired-on gr to yel, SI-33............................**175.00**

Artichoke, milk glass w/pk & gr decor, S-Fig III 345.00
Basket, emb yel cased satin, wide shouldered shade, ball base, S-279 ...975.00
Beaded Swirl, cranberry, SI-162, 8½" 180.00
Bl, ribbed, w/attached basketweave match holder w/hdl, SI-52 ..690.00
Bl marbleized/cased w/clear shade/base ruffle, H-404, 8", EX...1,500.00
Bl opaline, emb ball shade/canister base, S-409, NM................1,000.00
Bl w/wht & orange floral, umbrella shade/ftd bulbous base, S-2-475..1,150.00
Bl w/wht enamel floral, U-shape shade w/petal top, urn base, S-460.....690.00
Centennial, ball-shaped chimney-type shade, SI-106, 8" 75.00
Cobalt flaring 3-step base w/hdl, swirl chimney, S-435 variant, EX...375.00
Cobalt w/brass saucer base, hand lamp, SII-81, 4½" dia, EX.........85.00
Cobalt w/emb incurvate cylinder base/squat teardrop top, S-262/255..125.00
Cone, bl cased satin, nutmeg burner, S-394, rpr fitter, 8"............345.00
Cosmos, yel cased, inv't bowl shade, shouldered base, S-286, EX..400.00
Cranberry, 4 amber berry prunts on raised mid band of bell base, 9"...275.00
Cranberry to clear, ovoid base w/clear leaves & shell ft, S-536 ..3,100.00
Cranberry w/gold & orange decor, ball shade/pear base, S-440, EX...975.00
Daisy & Button, amber U-shape shade/ped-ft base, amber chimney, S-482 ...700.00
Dk bl satin w/emb scrolls/geometrics, ball shade/can base, H-193 ......1,200.00
Dk gr w/floral-emb rnd base, bottle neck shade w/faint panels, S-449...250.00
Dk to lt pk cased, appl crystal shell ft, foreign burner, S-377, 12" 575.00
Dk to lt pk cased/emb, ruffled shade/paneled ogee base, S-375, NM 900.00
Dmn Quilt cranberry, umbrella shade/rnd base w/clear ft, S-535, NM ..2,000.00
Dmn Quilt MOP rainbow satin, foreign burner, S-V-Right, 9½", EX+...2,000.00
Florette, gr glossy/cased, S-388...750.00
Florette, pk cased, incurvate bowl shade/ball base, S-388............485.00
Hobnail, amber, plain ped base, nutmeg burner, S-477, 7½", EX ..350.00
Lime to wht satin, emb ogee shade/canister base, S-568, EX ...1,265.00
Little Andy, SII-S1 ....80.00
Little Harry's Night Light, SI-42, pr 75.00
Lt bl opal Swirl, umbrella shade/ovoid base, LG Wright, 7½" 285.00
Med bl pyriform panel shade/shouldered base w/wht florals, H-125 ..345.00
Milk glass w/emb acanthus leaves, ball shade, SI-116, 9¾" 75.00
Milk glass w/emb fishnet & floral, HP floral, rnd shade/base, S-229 ..85.00
Milk glass w/emb scroll-fr panels w/HP floral, ball shade, S-234.250.00
Milk glass w/HP florals, umbrella shade, SI-138, 8¾" 90.00
Milk glass w/pnt clear chimney-type shade, SI-112, 8⅝"..............95.00
Pk porc base w/musicians transfers, milk glass ball shade, SI-136..95.00
Prayer, milk glass, ball shade w/HP decor, SI-147, 9½" 150.00
Raindrop MOP bl U-form ruffled shade/ball base w/frosted ft, S-602......3,100.00
Raindrop MOP yel U-shape ruffled shade/ball base w/frosted ft, S-600 ..1,200.00
Rose glossy cased w/gold floral, umbrella shade/cylinder base, S-391.......1,300.00
Rubena overshot, ball shade/acorn base w/clear ft, 9½", EX....1,495.00
Rubena Verde Optic Rib umbrella shade, base w/gr leaves & ft, S-538 ..2,400.00
Skeleton, bsk w/orchid trim, glass eyes, foreign burner, S-490, 5" 7,500.00
Spatter, bl/wht reverse swirl, ball shade/base, frosted ft, S-II-548 .....1,495.00
Thumbprint, vaseline opal, SI-212, 9"..250.00
Tulip, emb tan to clear overshot, frosted int, amber chimney, S-287,EX ..865.00
Yel cased w/orange & gold floral, umbrella shade/can base, S-391 ...1,050.00
Yel swirl, sqd shade/base w/4 emb medallions, shell ft, S-547 ..3,100.00

Motion Lamps

Animated motion lamps were made as early as 1920 and as late as 1980s. They reached their peak during the 1950s when plastic became widely used. They are characterized by action created by the heat of a light bulb which causes the cylinder to revolve and create the illusion of an animated scene. Some of the better-known manufacturers were Econolite Corp., Scene in Action Corp., and LA Goodman Mfg. Co. As with many collectible items, prices are guided by condition, availability, and collector demand. Collectors should be aware that reproductions of lamps featuring cars, trains, sailing ships, fish, and mill scenes are being made. Values are given for original lamps in mint condition. Any damage or flaws seriously reduce the price. As has been true in many areas of

collecting, Internet auctions have affected the prices of motion lamps. Erratic ups and downs in prices realized have resulted in a market that is often unpredictible. For additional information, we recommend *Collector's Guide to Motion Lamps* by Sam and Anna Samuelian. Our advisors for motion lamps are Kaye and Jim Whitaker; they are listed in the Directory under Washington.

Annie, Johnson Co, 1981, 11" 50.00
Antique Autos, Econolite, 1957, 11" (+) 150.00
Bicycles, Econolite, 11" 200.00
Boy & Girl Scouts, Econolite, 10" 175.00
Butterflies, Econolite, 1954, 11" 150.00
Christmas trees, gr, bl, red, wht (paper), 1950s, 10-24", ea $75 to..110.00
Colonial Fountain, Scene in Action, metal, 1930s, 10" 200.00
Davy Crockett 200.00
Disneyland Express, red or yel plastic, Econolite, 1955, 11".......200.00
Elephant Lady Fortune Teller, chalk, S&S, 1930s, 12" 200.00
Elvgrin Pin-up Girls 350.00
Firefighters, LA Goodman, 1957, 11"...250.00
Fireplace, Econolite, 1958, 11" 150.00
Fish, Salt Water; Econolite, 1950s, 11" (+).................................150.00
Forest Fire, Econolite, 1955, 11" 130.00
Forest Fire, Rotovue Jr, 1949, 10" 125.00
Forest Fire, Scene in Action, 1931, 10" 200.00
Fountain of Youth, Rotovue Jr, 1950, 11" 150.00
Indian Warrior, Gritt Inc, 1920s, 11" 120.00
Japanese Twilight, Scene in Action, 1931, 13" 185.00
Jet Planes, Econolite, 1958, 11" 250.00
Merry Go Round, Rotovue Jr, 1949, 10" 100.00
Miss Liberty, Econolite, 1957, 11" 250.00
More here than meets the eye Hawaiian girl, paper front, 1952, 12" ..200.00
Niagara Falls, Econolite, 1955, 11" 95.00
Niagara Falls, Rotovue Jr, 1949, 10" 75.00
Niagara Falls, Scene in Action, glass w/paper wrap picture, 1931, 10"..150.00
Old Mill, Econolite, 1965, 11" (+) 110.00
Op Art Lamp, Visual Effects, 1970s, 13" (reproduced in 1990s) ...55.00
Oriental Fantasy, LA Goodman, 1957, 11" 110.00
Oriental Scene, Econolite, 1959, 11" 165.00
Sailboats, LA Goodman, 1954, 14" 110.00
Sailing ships, Econolite (+)..150.00
Seattle World's Fair, Econolite..200.00

Snow scene, LA Goodman, $95.00.
(Photo courtesy Kaye and Jim Whitaker)

Snow scene (church or cabin), Econolite, 1957, 11"...................160.00
Steamboats, Econolite, 1957, 11" 150.00
Totville Train, Econolite, 1948, 11" 150.00
Trains, Econolite, 1956, 11" (+) 150.00
Tropical Fish, Econolite, 1954, 11" 95.00
Truck & Bus, Econolite, 1962, 11" 200.00
Venice Canal, Econolite, 1963, 11" 200.00

White Christmas, flat front, Econolite, 11"................................**190.00**
Why You Should Never Drink the Water, paper front, 1946-49, 4 szs, ea...**155.00**

Pattern Glass Lamps

The letter/number codes in the following descriptions refer to *Oil Lamps, Books I, II,* and *III,* by Catherine Thuro (book, page, item number or letter). Our advisor for this section is Jeff Bradfield who is listed in the Directory under Virginia.

Acanthus Leaf, bl & clambroth, Sandwich, w/shade, 10¼", EX .**900.00**
Atterbury Shell 1862, stand lamp, T1-126-c, 8" **150.00**
Beaded Eye Band, stand lamp, fluted columnar base, T1-203-j, 7½" ..**125.00**
Berkshire, flat hand lamp, w/hdl, T1-197-g, 2¾"...........................**130.00**
Bull's Eye & Loop, base w/sq platform, T1-93-k, 8⅛"..................**145.00**
Central Beaded Panel, stand lamp, saucer base , T1-209-h, 9" ...**100.00**
Cherry Ripe, stand lamp, opaque glass base, T1-165-i, 9¼"........**150.00**
Chieftain, stand lamp, med bl base w/dk bl streaks, T1-123-b, 10½" **400.00**
Corn, flat hand lamp, w/hdl, dtd, T1-204-b, 3¼" **250.00**
Cottage w/Fleur-d-lis, stand lamp, wht stepped sq base, T1-121-b, 12"...**200.00**
Daisy & Button, stand lamp, patterned base, T1-223-m, 9" **200.00**
Diamond Sunburst, stand lamp, scalloped base, T1-98-c **85.00**
Elson Fourteen, stand lamp, T1-210-d, 6½" **60.00**
Empress, stand lamp, gr stem w/rnd platform, T1-244-c, 9" **225.00**
Feather Duster, flat hand lamp, w/hdl, T1-220-d, 3½" **125.00**
Feather Duster w/Sawtooth Band, stand lamp, T1-173-j, 8"..........**90.00**
Fern & Shield, stand lamp, octagonal base, T1-103-h, 9¾"........**125.00**
Hobbs Plain Band, stand lamp, opaque sq base, T1-157-g, 10" ...**125.00**
Hobbs Star, stand lamp, opaque base w/sq platform, T1-153-g, 8" ...**150.00**
Laurel, stand lamp, T1-96-c, 8⅝" **90.00**
Link Belt, Farm Boy figural stem, T1-177-g, 10½" **200.00**
Lomax, ftd hand lamp, T1-181-e, 5½" **125.00**
Maple Leaf, stand lamp, Chevron stem, sq Maple Leaf base, T1-221-e ..**1,200.00**
Milton w/Flower Band, flat hand lamp, w/hdl, T1-197-j, 3¼" **95.00**
Oesterling, stand lamp, T1-207-l **80.00**
Paneled Block & Bar, Dmn Bead & Rib stem, T1-167-k, 10".....**200.00**
Patience Band, stand lamp, T1-212-c, 8¼" **90.00**
Pleat & Panel, stand lamp, tapered/sq base, T1-202-c, 7" **80.00**
Prism Under Glass, stand lamp, opaque ribbed base, T1-148-c, 10"..**150.00**
Rand Rib, flat hand lamp, T1-134-a..**85.00**
Ribbed Cup, fluted std on pnt slate base, T1-162-c, 8¼" **135.00**
Ribbed Loop, 9-Panel base, stand lamp, T1-139-k, 8¼" **95.00**
Riverside Regal Fancy Panel, stand lamp, T1-245-i, 8½" **125.00**
Riverside Rose, ftd hand lamp, w/hdl, T1-242-c, 5⅝" **175.00**
Sandwich Blackberry, stand lamp, sq base, T1-116-b, 10⅞"........**225.00**
Sawtooth Loop, stand lamp, 8-scallop base, T1-201-k, 9" **95.00**
Scroll, stand lamp, opaque octagonal base, T1-142-i, 12" **170.00**
Stacked Thumbprints, stand lamp, 15-scallop base, T1-200-e, 7" .**90.00**
Triple Peg & Loop, brass stem/sq platform, T1-160-a, 8¾" **200.00**
Waisted Broad Rib, stand lamp, dk bl stem, T1-168-e, 9½"........**175.00**
Waving Wheat, stand lamp, opaque glass base, T1-165-k, 10" ...**150.00**

Peg Lamps

Clear, cut 6-leaf flower band, onion form, EX, pr **250.00**
Col, cranberry, cylinder font, brass stems, marble ft, 9", EX, pr...**865.00**
Col, ruby, windows/floral, wht metal figural holder on brass ft, 13" .**460.00**
Cranberry w/frosted rubena cut shade, orig burner, 13" **315.00**
Dmn Quilt MOP, dk/lt pk, ruffled U-form shade/ball font, brass ft, 12"..**1,265.00**
Robin's egg bl shade & font w/emb decor, brass base, 15" **750.00**

Reverse-Painted Lamps

Jefferson, 16" shade w/scenic in ribbon-like band; bronzed base, 22" ...**1,600.00**

Jefferson, 17" cottage scenic shade; cast metal 2-socket base, 25" **1,850.00**
Jefferson, 18" landscape shade; bronzed metal std, 22" **1,100.00**
Moe Bridges, 15" landscape shade, gr on brn; fluted metal std, 21".....**850.00**

Moe Bridges, 18" chipped and sand-finished shade with exotic birds on flowering branch; black-patinated urn-form standard, 23", $4,890.00.

Moe Bridges, 18" ducks scenic shade, etched ext; enamel hdld std, 24"....**3,750.00**
Moe Bridges, 18" lake shade; bronzed vase std w/hdls & paw ft, 23" **4,000.00**
Phoenix (att), 17" summer scene w/pond & sheep shade; hdld bottle std...**600.00**
Pittsburgh, 16" int/ext pnt shade w/winter trees/moon/mtns; bronze std..**1,500.00**
Pittsburgh, 16" swans in pond shade (EX); simple std, 23" **2,750.00**
Pittsburgh, 6x10" ribbed oval shade w/forest scene; #S1475½ **800.00**
Pittsburgh-type 17" shade/base: snow/castles; base w/metal o/l, 23".**800.00**
Unknown, 17" Dutch scene/village shade; 2-light bronze base ...**800.00**
Unknown, 17" scenic shade w/lg trees (EX); metal std, 21" **800.00**
Unknown, 18" bent-panel shade w/stylized iris (strong colors), EX...**450.00**

Student Lamps, Kerosene

Brass, gr ribbed 7" dia shade, Manhattan, electrified, 22"............**450.00**
Brass, milk glass shade, K Brenner, 18"...**365.00**
Cast brass Harvard type, Aladdin lamp font, W&W, orig, no shade, 22"...**1,950.00**
NP brass, gr cased shade, 1-light, 20½", NM **675.00**
Yel brass, dbl, cased shades, electrified, 27x23", EX....................**500.00**

TV Lamps

When TV viewing became a popular pastime during the 1940s, TV lamps were developed to provide just the right amount of light — not bright enough to compromise the sharpness of the picture, but just enough to prevent the eyestrain it was feared might result from watching TV in a darkened room. Most were made of ceramic, and many were figurals such as cats, owls, ducks, and the like, or made in the shape of Conestoga wagons, sailing ships, seashells, etc. Some had shades and others were made as planters. Few were marked well enough to identify the maker without some study. *TV Lamps* by Tom Santiso (Collector Books) provides more information.

Our advisors for this category are John and Peggy Scott who are listed in the Directory under Missouri. All lamps listed below are ceramic unless otherwise described. Values are for mint condition examples in working order. See also Maddux; Morton Pottery; Rosemeade; other specific manufacturers

Boy on dolphin, gold pnt, Lane & Co, from $95 to....................**105.00**
Bulldog w/flock coating, eyes glow, from $60 to.............................**80.00**
Dancer leaping, draped long skirt, gold flecks, from $55 to...........**75.00**
Deco horse head on front of planter, brn/gr wash, from $60 to **75.00**
Deer & fawn, both recumbent on wooden base w/Fiberglas shade, $75 to...**90.00**
Donkey pulling cart planter, gr, from $65 to **80.00**
Dove pr, bl w/gold speckles, orig plastic flowers, from $75 to........**95.00**
Duck (flying) w/planter, Lane, w/orig plastic plants, mini, $75 to ...**100.00**
Exotic bird w/planter, mc, porc-like material, from $85 to **100.00**

Grehound pr cn base, shiny wht, from $72.50 to............................**85.00**
Horse prancing, holes above stone wall light up, mc porc, $95 to ..**110.00**
Madonna & Child, plaster, bulb lights up faces, from $150 to....**175.00**
Oriental figure (removable) ea side of well w/removable top, $120 to ..**135.00**
Panther crouching, blk or brn, no base, from $75 to **100.00**
Panther crouching, planter on bk, 22k gold decor, Royal China......**150.00**
Ship, ceramic w/metal sails, portholes light up, from $75 to **80.00**
Ship, plaster w/rvpt bkground, Duquesne Statuary, from $125 to ..**130.00**
Stag, standing among curling grasses, gr, from $75 to **95.00**
Swan pr, plaster w/Fiberglas shade, sgn M Fielack, from $110 to ...**125.00**

Whale Oil/Burning Fluid Lamps

Amethyst, blown sphere w/hdl, short stem w/wide disc ft, 3", pr, EX......**1,150.00**
Amethyst, tapered loop font, octagonal std on sq base, #2110, 8", VG ..**1,375.00**
Brass, saucer base, fluted stem, dolphin hdls, gilt bands, 7", pr....**250.00**
Canary, 3 printy block designs on hexagonal base, 8½", pr.........**920.00**
Clear, 'flying saucer' font on 3-bead stem w/hdl, saucer ft, 5½"....**475.00**
Clear, free-blown cone font, stem w/wafer & invt cone in saucer, 7" **1,000.00**
Clear, free-blown rnd font, stem w/wafers & beads, petticoat base, 9" ..**3,250.00**
Clear, free-blown rnd hdld font on lg cone stem, saucer base, 7½"........**2,185.00**
Clear, free-blown vintage-eng font, ornate pressed stem, 12", pr ...**500.00**
Clear, mini finger lamp, lg loop hdl w/flip terminal, ribbed, 3" ...**775.00**
Clear, rnd font, reverse-emb sq base, 5", EX, pr **450.00**
Clear, rnd font, 4-step sq base, 4½", EX, pr...............................**450.00**
Clear, rnd font on wine-glass stem, pressed cup-plate base, 6" .**1,300.00**
Clear, rnd/ringed font, high stepped 4-lobe base, 9½", VG, pr ...**3,600.00**
Clear, teardrop font, stepped base, 5", EX, pr **635.00**
Clear, teardrop font/5-step 4-lobe base, 6½", VG, pr...................**450.00**
Clear w/fine wht lines, rnd font on lg wafer, ogee stem, saucer ft, 9"..**575.00**
Cobalt, Loop, hand lamp w/hdl, #2107, 3¼", EX **700.00**
Dk amethyst, free-blown, shouldered/disc ft, hdl w/curl terminal, 3"..**6,000.00**
Teal, tapered loop font, octagonal std on sq base, #2110, 9", VG **2,400.00**
Vaseline, pressed/waisted Loop font, hex base, #2111, 9", EX, pr.........**1,000.00**
Wht opaque font w/gilt scrolls, clambroth base, NE Glass, 14" ..**460.00**

Miscellaneous

Argand, patinated bronze w/foliate tripod base, 3-arm, 18", pr **2,300.00**
Astral, A Cornelius & Co, cast brass w/fruit basket decor, 23x9" ...**975.00**
Astral, Am Classical, polished brass, Corinthian capital, 35x13" ..**2,865.00**
Brass, tall/conical w/ring hdls, ornate cast base, rpl shade, 29" ...**235.00**
Floor, red marble w/cream striations & gilt, ornate cvgs, silk shade...**1,900.00**
Marriage, clear fonts, sapphire bl base, mk Pat, no lid, 13½" ..**1,725.00**
Porc vase std w/dk bl & gold floral, cast base, etched 10" ball shade............**575.00**
Sinumbra, Am Late Classical gilt brass & marble, 1850s, 29x12" dia **3,900.00**
Slag glass bent-panel 18" shade (EX) w/metal sunflower border; urn std .**1,150.00**
Slag glass 20" shade w/Deco metal o/l, 2 tiers of panels; fancy std **780.00**
Solar, brass/marble Am Classical, pear-shaped font, marble column, 25"..**2,400.00**
Tea caddy, dragon relief on metal base, also etched on 10" ruby shade.....**1,265.00**
Wht metal ftd bulbous base w/3-D cherub ea side, rpl shade, 22"................**460.00**

Lang, Anton

Anton Lang (1875 – 1938) was a German studio potter and an actor in the Oberammergau Passion Plays early in the twentieth century. Because he played the role of Christ three times, tourists brought his pottery back to the U.S. in suitcases, which accounts for the prevalence of smaller examples today. During 1923 – 1924 Anton Lang and the other 'Passion Players' toured the U.S. selling their crafts. Lang would occasionally throw pottery when the cast passed through a pottery center such as Cincinnati, where Rookwood was located. The pots thrown at Rookwood are easy to identify as Lang hand signed the side of each

piece and they have a 1924 Rookwood mark on the bottom. Lang visited the U.S. only once, and contrary to popular belief, he was never employed by Rookwood. His pottery, marked with his name in script, is fairly scarce and highly valued for its artistic quality. His son Karl (1903 – 1990), also a gifted potter, designed most of the Art Deco shapes and conducted glaze experiments. Only pieces bearing a hand-written signature (not a facsimile) are certain to be Anton Lang originals instead of the work of Karl or the Langs' assistants. Anton and Karl also made pieces together; Karl might design a piece and Anton decorate it. Postcards, programs, prints, and photographs depicting Lang are also collectible. Karl was managing the day-to-day operations of the pottery by 1934, and he continued to operate it as Anton Lang Pottery after his father's death in 1938. The pottery is now owned and operated by Karl's daughter, Barbara Lampe, who took over for her father in 1975. The facsimile 'Anton Lang' signature was used until 1995 when the name was changed to Barbara Lampe Pottery. Her mark is an interlocked 'BL' in a circle. Pieces with a facsimile signature and an interlocked 'UL' in a circle were made by Lampe's former husband, Uli Lampe, and date from 1975 to 1982. The 'Anton Lang' mark is not sharp on pieces made in 1975 and later. The bottoms are brick red clay with three lighter circular tripod marks. The later pieces are considerably heavier than the earlier work. Our advisor for this category is Clark Miller; he is listed in the Directory under Minnesota.

Book, Reminiscences, paperbk, sgn 1st ed, dtd 1934, EX **32.00**
Bowl, gazelle in relief in center, orange, crimped rim, ¾x6½" **25.00**
Chamberstick, aqua w/brn highlights, 2x4½".............................**47.50**
Flowerpot w/saucer, script signature, mini, 2⅛" **42.50**
Lantern slides, from passion play w/actor's portraits, ca 1910, 50 for...**135.00**
Photo, Crucifixion, blk & wht, sgn & dtd 1910, 11¼x8¼" **25.00**
Pitcher, oxblood w/gr at top, pewter lid, 8" **80.00**
Stein, floral faience, pewter lid, ½-litre.................................**220.00**

Vase, blue with yellow flowers, hand signed, 15¾x6½", $1,250.00. (Photo courtesy Clark Miller)

Vase, mottled jug shape w/pinched body, 1 hdl, 5", NM................**32.00**
Vase, Oberammergau incised along rim, flowers on cream, 2¼x3¼" .**22.50**
Vase, 6-color w/triangles/dots, ftd cylinder w/hdls, 6¾", NM......**185.00**

Le Verre Francais

Le Verre Francais was produced during the 1920s by Schneider at Epinay-sur-Seine in France. It was a commercial art glass in the cameo style composed of layered glass with the designs engraved by acid. Favored motifs were stylized leaves and flowers or geometric patterns. It was marked with the name in script or with an inlaid filigrane. Our advisor for this category is Don Williams; he is listed in the Directory under Missouri.

Cameo

Bowl, berry vines on gr/rust mottle, ½-moon shape, 3½x8½" **350.00**
Lamp shade, thorny branches/roses, gr/red on pk mottle, lily form, 6" **400.00**

Pitcher, mushrooms/grasses, brn/dk red on amber mottle, turq hdl, 8"..**1,000.00**
Rose bowl, Deco flowers, purple/amethyst on pk/frost mottle, 3x4" **550.00**
Vase, dahlias, lav on pk mottle, elongated w/bun ft, 17".........**2,400.00**
Vase, Deco floral, lt amethyst on pk/bl mottle frost, slim/ftd, 12" **950.00**
Vase, Deco leaves, maroon/red w/orange rim on yel, ftd, bulbous, 17"..**950.00**
Vase, floral, bright rose on yel mottle, slim w/bun ft, 18".........**2,475.00**
Vase, grapes/leaves/vines, red-brn on yel frost, lip hdls, ftd, 15"................**3,450.00**
Vase, hanging fruit, rust/brn on orange, brn hdls, flared sides, 10" **2,650.00**
Vase, mushrooms/foliage, red/brn on gray-gr mottle, gourd form, 9".........**2,400.00**
Vase, oak/acorns, maroon/umber on orange/yel, ftd trumpet form, 12" ...**1,200.00**
Vase, roses, pk/gr on pk frost, 5½".........**500.00**
Vase, sunbursts/honeycomb, gr/red on orange, honeycomb neck, 4x6" **400.00**
Vase, 3 stems of cockle shells, maroon/red on pk/wht/frost, ftd, 19".........**2,100.00**

Leeds, Leeds Type

The Leeds Pottery was established in 1758 in Yorkshire and under varied management produced fine creamware, often highly reticulated and transfer printed, shiny black-glazed Jackfield wares, polychromed pearlware, and figurines similar to those made in the Staffordshire area. Little of the early ware was marked; after 1775 the impressed 'Leeds Pottery' mark was used. From 1781 to 1820, the name 'Hartley Greens & Co.' was added. The pottery closed in 1898.

Today the term 'Leeds' has become generic and is used to encompass all polychromed pearlware and creamware, wherever its origin. Thus similar wares of other potters (Wood for instance) is often incorrectly called 'Leeds.' Unless a piece is marked or can be definitely attributed to Leeds by confirming the pattern to be authentic, 'Leeds-Type' would be a more accurate nomenclature.

Key:
cw — creamware   pw — pearlware

Coffeepot, Tea Party and Shepherd black transfers on pearlware, entwined strap handle, floral finial, late eighteenth century, 10¼", EX, $865.00.

Coffeepot, pw, mc floral, baluster, dome lid, ca 1800, 13", EX **150.00**
Creamer, floral, 4-color on wht, molded leaf hdl ends, 4¾".........**440.00**
Creamer & sugar bowl, flower, bl w/gr & brn buds, 2¾", 2½" **330.00**
Cup & saucer, grid design in gr w/orange dots & bl circles, mini, NM ...**220.00**
Figure, cw, crowned nude male child atop bear, 18th C, 5¼", pr...**700.00**
Mug, scrolling floral, 5-color, hairlines, 6" **500.00**
Pitcher, floral, 4-color, prof rpr/wear, 6½" **495.00**
Pitcher, foliage/grape-leaf/peacocks band, 5-color, 9", VG **550.00**
Pitcher, HP/red transfer drinking scenes w/verses, name/1809, 6", EX.**1,400.00**
Plaque, pw, Harvest, female figure, mc decor, late 1700s, 12x8½" **430.00**
Plate, cw, fretted lacy border, ca 1790, 9".........**350.00**
Platter, cw, splashed gray & gr on sponged brn, feather edge, 15"......**1,100.00**
Punch bowl, pw, floral bands w/central medallion, late 1700s, 9⅝" ..**1,265.00**
Salt cellar, cw w/bl feather edge, w/lid, from $475 to **550.00**

Sugar bowl, floral, 5-color, shell/ring hdls, acorn finial, 6", EX ...**600.00**
Tea bowl & saucer, floral in yel/bl/gr, mini, EX...........................**275.00**
Tea bowl & saucer, strawberry in yel/gr/brn, old rpr, mini **220.00**
Teapot, cw, ocher to sponged bl, globular, 1780, rstr, 3½"............**460.00**
Teapot, cw, tree trunk form, rstr hairlines, ca 1775, 5¼".............**485.00**
Teapot, yel bands & 4-color sprigs, 4", +matching creamer (flakes)..**550.00**
Tureen, cw, florals/urns/etc, feather edge, w/lid, late 1700s, 8½"....**975.00**
Tureen, pw, flower finial, cobalt decor, feather edge, 7x13".........**430.00**

Lefton China

The Lefton China Company was the creation of Mr. George Zoltan Lefton who migrated to the United States from Hungary in 1939. In 1941 he embarked on a new career and began shaping a business that sprang from his passion for collecting fine china and porcelains. Though his funds were very limited, his vision was to develop a source from which to obtain fine porcelains by reviving the postwar Japanese ceramic industry, which dated back to antiquity. As a trailblazer, George Zoltan Lefton soon earned the reputation as 'The China King.'

Counted among the most desirable and sought-after collectibles of today, Lefton items such as Bluebirds, Miss Priss, Angels, all types of dinnerware, and tea-related items are eagerly acquired by collectors. As is true with any antique or collectible, prices may vary, dependent on location, condition, and availability. For additional information on the history of Lefton China, its factories, marks, products, and values, readers should consult the *Collector's Encyclopedia of Lefton China, Books I, II,* and *III,* and *Lefton Price Guide* by our advisor, Loretta DeLozier, who is listed in the Directory under Florida. All are published by Collector Books.

Ashtray, Forget-Me-Nots, 1 rest, #4080, 3½" **35.00**
Bank, lion wearing glasses, #13384, 6"..**58.00**
Bank, pig w/rhinestone eyes, #90465, 7" **52.00**
Bird, Bird of Paradise, #140, 6¾" **85.00**
Bird, mallard duck, #7555, 11½" **105.00**
Bird, toucan, #1056, 8½" **155.00**
Bowl, Green Holly, w/hdl, #5175, 5½"...**25.00**
Box, candy; Della Robbia, #2089, 6½x7" **36.00**
Box, candy; Poinsettia, bsk, #8026, 5½" **33.00**
Box, Spring Bouquet, hinged lid, #8134, 4"..................................**50.00**
Box, Tiffany Rose, musical, plays Anniversary Waltz, #979, 6¼" ..**60.00**
Butter dish, Gingham **20.00**
Candle holders, Country Squire, #1613, 5½", pr **28.00**
Candle holders, pk roses & sponge gold, #208, 4¾", pr................**55.00**
Canisters, Rustic Daisy, #4115, 4-pc set **105.00**
Cigarette lighter, Gold Wheat, #40111, 3"....................................**38.00**
Cigarette urn, Lily of the Valley, #987, 3½" **40.00**
Coffeepot, Gingham, 8-cup **95.00**
Compote, Rose Chintz, #650, 7"...**42.00**
Compote, violets w/sponged gold, #20406, 10½"..........................**80.00**
Cookie jar, Bluebird, #289, 7¼"...**400.00**
Cookie jar, Dainty Miss, #040, 7½"..**200.00**
Cookie jar, Woodland Cookies, #7858, 10"...................................**55.00**
Creamer & sugar bowl, Fleur de Lis, #1800...................................**38.00**
Creamer & sugar bowl, Green Holly, #1355...................................**35.00**
Creamer & sugar bowl, Rose Chintz, #794, ind **35.00**
Creamer & sugar bowl, Rustic Daisy, #3856..................................**32.00**
Cup & saucer, AD; Elegant Rose, #634 ....**36.00**
Cup & saucer, tea; Americana, #973 ....**40.00**
Cup & saucer, tea; Heavenly Rose, #2758.....................................**42.00**
Figurine, angel in flower plays instrument, #1699, 3¼", set of 3.**150.00**
Figurine, beaver, bsk, #4747, 5"..**38.00**
Figurine, bride & groom on sofa, #4645, 3-pc set.........................**45.00**
Figurine, cat on pillow, #2540, 4½" **20.00**

Figurine, Christmas angel, #1419, 3¼" 20.00
Figurine, Colonial lady, #877, 12" 185.00
Figurine, dachshund w/jewel eyes, matt, #3213, 5" 25.00
Figurine, drummer on horse, #4989, 11" 225.00
Figurine, flower girl, #110, 4¾" 22.00
Figurine, girl w/flowers & 2 pk poodles, #692, 5¼" 42.00
Figurine, graduate w/golden book & wings, #809, 4" 45.00
Figurine, Hi Diddle Diddle, #1257, 4¾" 135.00
Figurine, lady w/hat & flower basket, bl, #1859, 6¼" 60.00
Figurine, lady w/shawl, #1888, 7¾" 80.00
Figurine, Little Miss Mistletoe, #102, 4½" 45.00
Figurine, Provincial man & woman carrying flowers, #7223, 7", pr ..100.00
Figurine, raccoon, bsk, #4752, 5" 48.00
Figurine, squirrel, bsk, #4749, 5" 38.00
Figurine, There Was an Old Woman, #1103, 5¾x6½" 180.00
Figurine, tiger, blk, wht & gold, #8743, 8½" 85.00
Jar, jam; Lilac Chintz, #202 ....40.00
Jar, jam; strawberries on lid, #2661, 5½" 22.00
Leaf dish, Green Heritage, #1860 ....30.00
Mug, Robert E Lee, #2365, 4¼" 55.00
Night light, boy praying, #6625, 6½" 45.00
Pitcher, Brown Heritage, Floral, #1873 ....58.00
Pitcher, Mushroom Forest, #6466, 6¾" 21.00
Pitcher, violets on wht w/gold, 32565, 4½" 35.00
Planter, elf on wht sleigh, #313 ....22.00
Planter, fish figural, #709, 10¼" L 24.00
Planter, girl w/wide-brim hat, #6094, 6¾" 32.00
Planter, kitten w/polka-dot tie, #5741, 7" 20.00
Planter, lady holding skirt wide, #423, 6½" 65.00
Planter, Mardi Gras, 3-leg bucket, #50441, 4¾" 45.00
Plate, Christmas tree, #1096, 8" 32.00
Plate, Eastern Star, 3105, 8" 15.00
Plate, Holly Garland, #1804, 9" 35.00
Plate, 25th Anniversary, #1130, 10¼" 15.00
Shakers, Bossie the Cow, #6510, 3½", pr 25.00
Shakers, Fruits of Italy, #1207, pr 15.00
Shakers, Gingham, pr 18.00
Shakers, owls, #6836, pr 10.00
Snack set, Rose Heirloom, #1074, 9" 32.00
Snack set, To a Wild Rose, #2580, 8" 28.00
Soap dish, flowers on ftd shell shape, #5066 ....12.00
Switch plate, violets, #197, 5½x3½" 20.00
Teapot, Cabbage Cutie, #1213, 6-cup 100.00
Teapot, Elegant Rose, #2275 ....180.00
Teapot, Magnolia, #2519 ....195.00
Teapot, Miss Priss, #1516 ....195.00
Teapot, Silver Wheat, #2156, 8¼" 70.00
Tidbit tray, Elegant Rose, 3-compartment, center hdl, #2351, 6" ..35.00
Tidbit tray, Fruit Fantasia, 2-tier, #6279 ....60.00
Toothbrush holder, French Rose, #2646, 3¾" 20.00
Vase, bud; appl flowers & stones on pk, #70541, 6¾" 45.00
Vase, Lily of the Valley, #198, 3¼" 38.00
Vase, Only a Rose, #382, 5½" 85.00
Vase, pine cones on ewer form, #2461, 6" 35.00
Wall pocket, Dainty Miss, #6767, 5" 125.00
Wall pocket, frying pan w/fruit design, #2112, 9¼" 22.00
Wall pocket, Rustic Daisy on lady's hat, #4360, 8" 25.00
Wall pocket, violin w/rose & sponge gold, #369, 7" 32.00

Legras

Legras and Cie was founded in St. Denis, France, in 1864. Production continued until the 1930s. In addition to their enameled wares,

they made cameo art glass decorated with outdoor scenes and florals executed by acid cuttings through two to six layers of glass. Their work is signed 'Legras' in relief and in enamel. Our advisor for this category is Don Williams; he is listed in the Directory under Missouri.

Vases: Enameled floral medallion on frosted body, etched rim with cobalt enamel, 13¾", $460.00; Cameo berries, maroon on pink and clear, 5¼", $300.00; Enameled poppies on bright green satin with gold accents, 12", $635.00.

Cameo

Bowl, floral cluster, red on crystal w/star-shaped texture, 14" 400.00
Vase, autumn leaves, lime/dk red on opal & burgundy, ftd, 21" ..950.00
Vase, holly/berries, gr/red/amber on citron & sienna, cylindrical, 13" .1,600.00
Vase, lake/skiff beached on island cut/pnt on mottled color, 6x3½" 1,050.00
Vase, leafy vines, lt/dk gr on citron frost & wht, rectangular, 6½" 500.00
Vase, seaweed, maroon/gr on amber-orange, stick neck, 10" 225.00
Vase, shepherd/sheep cut/pnt on sunset-colored ground, oval form, 4x5".440.00
Vase, ships/mtns veiwed from veranda w/flower-ladden lattice, 4x5"....650.00
Vase, trees/boats cut/pnt on orange & gr, sqd swollen cylinder, 12" 460.00
Vase, trees/lake/distant mtns, flat sided, 14" 350.00
Vase, trees/lake/mtns, cut/pnt, hdld ormolu rim, cylindrical, 10" 300.00
Vase, wispy plants, gr/maroon on caramel opaque, 2 gold neck hdls, 11"...800.00

Enameled Glass

Rose bowl, winter scene on orange frost, ruffled, 6x6" 350.00
Vase, berries/leaves on orange to yel, 4½x5" 90.00
Vase, Deco floral, red/blk on textured frost, ovoid, 12" 350.00
Vase, leaves on ovoid shape represent an artichoke, mc, 5¼" 300.00
Vase, trees/lake, gr on amber/citron, cylindrical, mk, 16" 275.00

Lenox

Walter Scott Lenox, former art director at Ott and Brewer, and Jonathan Coxon founded The Ceramic Art Company of Trenton, New Jersey, in 1889. By 1906 Cox had left the company, and to reflect the change in ownership, the name was changed to Lenox Inc. Until 1930 when the production of American-made Belleek came to an end, they continued to produce the same type of high-quality ornamental wares that Lenox and Coxon had learned to master while in the employ of Ott and Brewer. Their superior dinnerware made the company famous, and since 1917 Lenox has been chosen the official White House China. Our advisor for this category is Mary Frank Gaston. See also Ceramic Art Company.

Bowl, berry; Ming, old blk mk, 5¼" 15.00
Bowl, vegetable; Winslow Castle, w/lid, lg 110.00
Cake plate, Mandarin, ped ft, 1½x9" 155.00
Coffee set, Deco irises w/blk & gold bands, pot+cr/sug+6 c/s ..1,900.00
Creamer & sugar bowl, Belleek, roses, helmet creamer, open bowl..200.00
Creamer & sugar bowl, Carolina, Cosmopolitan Collection, w/lid..130.00
Creamer & sugar bowl, Imperial, gold trim, /wlid 130.00

Cup & saucer, bouillon; Autumn, 2 hdls..**65.00**
Cup & saucer, Brookdale, 4" dia, 5¾" dia **22.50**
Cup & saucer, Weatherly **17.50**
Mug, 3 irises, lustred purple on bronze & ivory, Hoyt, 3-hdl, 8" .**300.00**
Pitcher, cider; apples & leaves, +6 cups....................................**950.00**
Plate, dessert; Mandarin Square, 8¼" **70.00**
Plate, dinner; Eclipse, gold trim, 10½" **35.00**
Plate, dinner; Imperial, 10½", 6 for **75.00**
Plate, dinner; Windsong **48.00**
Plate, salad; Weatherly, 8" **16.00**
Plate, salad; Windsong **35.00**
Platter, Castle Garden, oval, 17" **155.00**
Platter, Eternal, 16¼x11¾"...**90.00**
Platter, Weatherly, platinum trim, 16x11", NM.......................**175.00**
Vase, irises, shoulded, sm neck, flared rim, palette mk, 15".........**895.00**
Vase, roses, mc on wht, globular, tiny neck, flat rim, 11".........**1,400.00**
Vase, roses on gr to wht, shouldered, 10" **895.00**
Vase, roses on lav-pk, globular, tiny neck & ruffled rim, 9½" ..**1,295.00**
Vase, roses on lt gr, shouldered, sm neck, flared rim, early mk, 16" ...**1,295.00**

Letter Openers

Made in a wide variety of materials and designs, letter openers make an interesting collection, easy to display and easy on the budget as well. For further information we recommend *Collector's Guide to Letter Openers, Identification & Values,* by Everett Grist (Collector Books); Mr. Grist is listed in the Directory under Tennessee.

Alpaca & abalone, coral eye, fish-shaped bottle opener **20.00**
Aluminum, Great Smoky Mountains, w/letter holder in hdl **12.00**
Bakelite, blk & transparent w/encapsulated sea horse....................**20.00**
Bone, pnt w/southwest scene, mk Mexico, purple wood hdl **15.00**
Brass, contoured w/Art Nouveau holly motif **30.00**
Brass, knight in armor, stamped England.......................................**10.00**
Brass, Lady Godiva forms hdl...**15.00**
Brass, pnt bird & peace, mk Terra Sancta Guild 1968, Israel **8.00**
Brass, unicorn, made in Taiwan **10.00**
Brass, WWII cartridge, Trench Art, South Pacific, ca 1942 ....**25.00**
Brass & turq, mosaic hdl, made in India...**15.00**

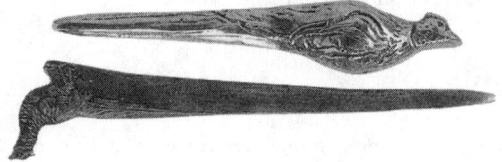

Bronze pheasant, $8.00; Brass pheasant, H.K. Austria, $35.00. (Photo courtesy Everett Grist)

Cast iron, rifle..**10.00**
Copper, swordfish, Florida, made in Japan.....................................**8.00**
Enamel, brass & steel, bl & yel flowers on red, dagger shape **25.00**
Enamel/chrome, sword w/mc dragon motif, gr tassel.....................**25.00**
Genuine alligator head, wood blade, mk Clark Hill Dam, SC **25.00**
Glass & steel, reverse pnt, New York City **12.00**
Gold-colored pot metal figural, red pnt lobster **8.00**
Gold-tone pot metal, magnifier, mk Florida **3.00**
Gr onyx hdl/sterling blade w/open design, Latin American motif..**35.00**
Horn, thistle motif, Dykehead Horncraft, made in Scotland.........**18.00**
Ivory, cvd burro pulling wagon..**40.00**
Lucite, reverse cvd & filled rose, magnifier blade...........................**25.00**

Lucite, 2-1976 US pennies, Las Vegas **12.00**
MOP blade, sterling hdl, Art Nouveau, Victorian............................**70.00**
Mottled tortoise, elephant-head motif, Santo Domingo, Victorian...**85.00**
Nickel, fleur-de-lis, Italy **6.00**
Pewter, dancing frog, Metzke 1979 ....**12.00**
Pewter plate figural, butterfly, Metzke 1975.....................................**6.00**
Plastic, bl, full-length mermaid on hdl, made in USA.....................**6.00**
Plastic, owl figural on branch, made in Italy **8.00**
Plastic, red, souvenir of Knoxville, TN, hdl w/1948-49 calendar insert...**10.00**
Plastic & steel, Niagara Falls scene pnt atop hdl, made in Japan **4.00**
Porcelain, HP pk rose motif, sgn R Riddle **45.00**
Silver plated, continental eagle & stars, mk Gorham Stainless.....**15.00**
Steel, dragon's head in geometric design, Italy **8.00**
Sterling & enamel, Victoria's crest, stamped Sterling, Victorian...**45.00**
White metal, caduceus w/Rexall symbol..**25.00**
Wood, Royal Canadian Mounted Police bust, Windsor, Canada ..**35.00**
Wood & steel, gold stamp praying hands, stainless, Hong Kong **3.00**

Libbey

The New England Glass Company was established in 1818 in Boston, Massachusetts. In 1892 it became known as the Libbey Glass Company. At Chicago's Columbian Expo in 1893, Libbey set up a ten-pot furnace and made glass souvenirs. The display brought them world-wide fame. Between 1878 and 1918, Libbey made exquisite cut and faceted glass, considered today to be the best from the brilliant period. The company is credited for several innovations — the Owens bottle machine that made mass production possible and the Westlake machine which turned out both electric light bulbs and tumblers automatically. They developed a machine to polish the rims of their tumblers in such a way that chipping was unlikely to occur. Their glassware carried the patented Safedge guarantee. Libbey also made glassware in numerous colors, among them cobalt, ruby, pink, green, and amber. Our advisors for this category are Don and Anne Kier; they are listed in the Directory under Ohio.

Basket, amberina, wide fan-flared rim, tall hdl, 8¼x6x4" **2,695.00**
Bottle, scent; amberina, long-neck form w/ball stopper, 6½x3" ..**690.00**
Bottle, scent; amberina, ovoid, complete, 7½x2½".................**1,150.00**
Bowl, amberina, swirled w/6-pinch ruffled rim, mk, 4½" H **900.00**
Bowl, center; alternating starbursts & geometric bands, ca 1895, 12"..**575.00**
Bowl, Cluthra, pk/crystal, 3¾x11"...**395.00**
Bowl, cut, allover pattern w/4 lg hobstars, 9", EX.......................**240.00**
Bowl, cut, Glenda, 2x9"...**550.00**
Bowl, cut, hobstar & fan, mk, shallow, 7"....................................**50.00**
Bowl, cut, hobstar & flute-cut panels alternate, fan, X-hatch, 8"..**75.00**
Bowl, cut, hobstar panels & flutes alternate, block & fan center, 8"...**100.00**
Candlestick, air-twist stem, 8" **225.00**
Celery, cut, Harvard, 11"...**190.00**
Comport, amberina, wafer base, appl std, #3023, 4x8" **625.00**
Compote, clear w/pk Nailsea loops, flaring rim flange, 10x4" **595.00**
Creamer & sugar bowl, cut, Chrysanthemum **300.00**
Creamer & sugar bowl, cut, Colonna **95.00**
Cup & saucer, amberina, World's Fair 1893, 2¼x2½", 4¾" **700.00**
Jar, HP daisies on satin, ribbed melon form, 3" **475.00**
Knife rest, barbell shape w/cut glass ends, ca 1896-1910, 4"..........**75.00**
Maize, bowl, gr husks on wht opaque, 4x8¾" **275.00**
Maize, butter dish, bl husks on irid..**650.00**
Maize, butter dish, bl husks w/gold outlines, 6½x7"................**1,000.00**
Maize, butter dish, gr husks on custard **165.00**
Maize, celery vase, gold leaves, 6½x4½" **225.00**
Maize, celery vase, gr husks on custard **165.00**
Maize, celery vase, gr husks on wht opaque..................................**195.00**

Maize, condiment set, custard, 3 pcs on tray w/metal lid.. ....600.00
Maize, pickle castor, amber stain 595.00
Maize, pickle castor, gr husks on custard, SP fr 495.00
Maize, pitcher, bl husks on clear w/amber irid, clear hdls, 9" 600.00
Maize, pitcher, gold-yel husks on wht, 8¾x5½" 525.00
Maize, shakers, gold edge, bl husks on custard, pr 200.00
Maize, sugar shaker, yel/gold husks on custard, 5¾" 295.00
Maize, syrup, pewter lid, gold irid cob, bl husks, 6" 600.00
Maize, toothpick holder, gold-edge gr husks on custard..........345.00
Maize, tumbler, bl husks on gold irid 150.00
Maize, tumbler, bl husks on irid 125.00
Maize, tumbler, gr husks w/gold tips, 4" 450.00
Maize, tumbler, gr husks w/yel-brn tips, 4" 100.00
Maize, vase, yel/gold husks on custard, 6½" 250.00
Plate, cut, Empress, 12" 700.00
Stem, champagne, squirrel stem, wht opal, 6" 165.00
Stem, champagne flute, bear stem, wht opal, 5½" 185.00
Stem, claret, bear stem, blk, 5½" 155.00
Stem, claret, bear stem, wht opal 175.00
Stem, cordial, Embassy, tall 100.00
Stem, cordial, monkey stem, wht opal, 5" 145.00
Stem, cordial, whippet/greyhound stem, wht opal 175.00
Stem, goblet, cat stem, wht opal 200.00
Stem, goblet, monkey stem, wht opal, 1930s 180.00
Stem, sherbet, rabbit stem, wht opal, 2½" 160.00
Stem, sherbet w/underplate, amberina, 5½", 8½" 750.00
Stem, wine, kangaroo stem, wht opal 230.00
Stem, wine, lt yel-gr threading on bowl, opal ft, unmk, 6⅞"..........30.00
Stem, wine, monkey stem, frosted, 5" 85.00
Sugar bowl, lt bl satin, World's Fair 1893 in gilt, open, 2⅝" 500.00
Vase, amberina, corseted neck w/wide undulating rim, 6x6"....1,200.00
Vase, amberina, flared rim, slim w/wafer base, #3004, ca 1917....725.00
Vase, amberina, Optic Rib, flared rim, wafer/ball ft, 8x3' 1,300.00
Vase, amberina over amber, flared top, 4½" 650.00
Vase, bud; amberina, average color, 12x1½" 595.00
Vase, bud; amberina, elongated, ft attached w/wafer, 11" 550.00
Vase, bud; amberina, intense color, 12x1½" 750.00
Vase, bud; amberina, shouldered, ftd, long slender neck, 9x1½"....575.00
Vase, clear w/t'prints, int wavy gr threads, flared cylinder, 8½" ..250.00
Vase, cut, Brilliant pattern, 4-scallop top, 12x5" 450.00
Vase, jack-in-pulpit; amberina, ribbed bulbous body, sgn, 5" 900.00
Vase, jack-in-pulpit; amberina, Wold's Fair 1893/apple blossoms, 7x4"....1,000.00
Vase, Optic Dmn, crystal w/bl threading, ca 1932, 8" 300.00

Lightning Rod Balls

Used as ornaments on lightning rods, the vast majority of these balls were made of glass, but ceramic examples can be found as well. Their average diameter is 4½", but it can vary from 3½" up to 5½". Only a few of the many available pattern-and-color combinations are listed here. The most common measure 4½" and are found in sun-colored amethyst and milk glass. Our advisor is Rod Krupka, author of a book on this subject. Anyone interested in his book may write to him for more information; he is listed in the Directory under Michigan.

Amber, D&S, unemb, 10-panel, flake 135.00
Amber, Electra Cone, emb, 4½" 185.00
Amber, Swirl, EX collars, 1 cap, tube inside 190.00
Cobalt, Barnett, full collars 125.00
Cobalt, Plain Pendant, rpl cap 160.00
Emerald gr, Pleat-Round, 4½x5" 170.00
Mercury glass, Hawkeye, starbursts on bottom, 5" 315.00
Milk glass, Maher, rpl caps, 4½x5" 275.00

Milk glass, Quilt-Raised, 5x5½", pr 115.00
Milk glass, 6 stars & draped flag emb, 5¼x4" 80.00
Orange Opaque, Didie Blitzen, 3¾x4" 595.00
Red, Electra Cone, unemb, rpl caps 120.00
Red, Plain Pendant, rpl cap 165.00
Slag glass, Electra Cone, unemb 120.00
Sun-colored amethyst, Electra, emb 125.00
Sun-colored amethyst, Swirl, w/metal tube 150.00

Limbert

Charles Limbert was a proponent of the Arts and Crafts style of furniture, emphasizing both quality materials and impeccable workmanship. He became interested in the furniture industry through his father, who owned and operated his own very successful furniture business. Limbert first worked as a salesman, but in 1894 he opened a small business where he made his own line of chairs. In 1902 he began making the furniture for which he is most famous, locating his shop in Grand Rapids, Michigan, where he was born. He hired William Gohlke, an Austrian designer, and Paul Horti, who once worked for Shop of the Crafters. Limbert moved the factory to Holland, Michigan, in 1906. Due to health problems, Limbert retired in 1922. Our advisor for this category is B.A. Austin; he is listed in the Directory under new York.

Key: b — brand

Armchair, #818, massive w/wide front legs, bk/seat cushions, b, VG 3,500.00
Book cabinet, #347, 2-shelf, arch slab sides w/cutout, unmk, 47", VG ...3,500.00
Bookcase, #340, 2-door, ea w/divided pane over 1, b, 46x32x11" ...1,800.00
Bookcase, #366, 5 tiers of shelves, sq cutouts ea side, b, 50"....4,500.00
Cellarette, #751, 1-drw, bottle rack behind door, b, 36x25x17", VG...2,800.00
Chair, #500, sq bk w/cutout, sq cutout at sides, slanted arms...8,500.00

Chair, bicycle; #79, hall chair with original leather back, shaped seat over slab leg, branded, 42", EX, $1,100.00.

Chair, cafe; #500, angle arms over 2 sq cutouts ea side, b, 34x26x22" ...3,500.00
Chair, Morris; #519, bent arms over 2 wide slats, b, 37x40x32"....4,500.00
Chair, side; #911, T-bk, saddle seat, rfn, b, 37", 6 for..................850.00
Chair set, dining; 2 vertical slats, rstr seat, 1 arm+4 side 1,500.00
Chair set, like #581, 3-slat ladderbk, leather seat, b, VG, 6 for ..1,600.00
China cabinet, #473, shelves at sides w/corbel supports, b, 58x45", VG..6,500.00
Desk, #602, drop-front, 2 open shelves, caned gallery, sgn, 46x26", VG..1,800.00
Desk, drop-front, cane panel in bkboard, b, rfn, 47x26" 1,500.00
Desk, slant front over 1 drw, int complete, b, 30x37x14"..........1,000.00
Footstool, #204½, cutout in top, shaped slab sides, 18" L 300.00
Footstool, #224, new leather on top & arched seat rail, 13x18x12", VG...500.00
Hall seat, #81, triangle cutout in tall tapered bk/slab sides, b, 45" ...3,500.00
Hall tree, #230, tapered pole, 4 corbel ft, rfn, b, 68", VG 250.00
Magazine stand, #801, ebon oak w/3 shelves, rfn, 29x30x11" ..1,600.00

Parlor set, settle+armchair+arm rocker, no cushions, VG........**2,300.00**
Pedestal, #244, 16" dia top w/4 arch legs over shelf, rfn, 26", VG.......**3,000.00**
Plant stand, #239, octagonal top, slab sides ea w/2 cutouts, rfn, 28" ...**1,300.00**
Plant stand, #251, 8-sided top, slab sides w/cutouts, 24" H......**1,600.00**
Rocker, #588, 5-slat bk w/curved top rail, rfn, b, 38x29", VG.....**600.00**
Rocker, #822, 4-slat bk, reuphl seat, label, 32x22x30" **600.00**
Rocker, #826, 5-slat bk, drop-in seat, 40x25", VG......................**500.00**
Server, #413, 1-drw, corbels support 42" top, b, rpl hdw, 41", VG....**2,800.00**
Sideboard, #421, wide top: mirror/sq cutouts/full-length corbels, VG....**4,500.00**
Sideboard, #425, angled front/low shelf, copper pulls, 41x59".**7,500.00**
Sideboard, #451½, mirror, corbels ea side base w/6 drw & 2 doors, b..**8,000.00**
Sideboard, #451½, shelf/mirrored bk, orig hdw, rfn, 58x60" **6,000.00**
Stool, #61, low bk w/1 slat, arched seat rail, b, 24x12x15", VG .**425.00**
Stool, #213¾, apron, orig finish, 18x14x14" **1,000.00**
Table, #117, splayed legs, thru tenons, b, 29x36" dia.................**900.00**
Table, #146, oval top, slab sides w/cutouts, shelf, rfn, 45" **2,000.00**
Table, #146, 45" oval top, flared sides w/cutouts, b **2,600.00**
Table, #148, 30" rnd top, wide vertical X-stretchers w/cutouts, b, VG ..**3,750.00**
Table, #153, turtle top, blind drw, slab sides, rfn, 48x30".........**3,250.00**
Table, #211, 12" sq top, splay legs w/low stretchers, b, 16", VG..**200.00**
Table, console; 2 cut corners, 2-drw, 6-leg, rfn, b, 66", VG......**5,000.00**
Table, dining; #423, 54" rnd top/8-side apron, 4-leg+center post, VG..**4,250.00**
Table, dining; #1487, 54" rnd top, base: corbels, ext columns, b, VG..**5,500.00**
Table, library; leather top, flared legs w/corbels, w/tag, 45", VG............**2,100.00**
Tabouret, #251, 8-sided top, 4 slab sides w/corbels & cutouts, b, VG ...**2,100.00**
Washstand, ash, copper top, from Old Faithful Inn, 42x42x18" **6,000.00**

Limited Edition Plates

Current values of some limited edition plates have risen while others have fallen. Prices charged by plate dealers in the secondary market vary greatly; we have tried to suggest an average.

Since Goebel Hummel plates have been discontinued, values have started to decline. While those who are trying to complete the series continue to buy them, few seem interested in starting a collection. As for the Danish plates, Royal Copenhagen and Bing and Grondahl, more purchases are for plates that commemorate the birth year of a child or a wedding anniversary than to add to a collection.

Bing and Grondahl

1975, The Old Water Mill, $30.00.

1895, Behind the Frozen Window..**6,250.00**
1896, New Moon **2,300.00**
1897, Christmas Meal of Sparrows...**1,500.00**
1898, Roses & Star **850.00**
1899, Crows Enjoying Christmas...**1,800.00**
1900, Church Bells Chiming..**1,200.00**
1901, 3 Wise Men **495.00**
1902, Gothic Church Interior..**425.00**
1903, Expectant Children **425.00**
1904, View of Copenhagen From Fredericksberg Hill **210.00**

1905, Anxiety of the Coming Christmas Night.....................**205.00**
1906, Sleighing to Church..**135.00**
1907, Little Match Girl..**195.00**
1908, St Petri Church **110.00**
1909, Yule Tree..**125.00**
1910, Old Organist...**125.00**
1911, Angels & Shepherds...**110.00**
1912, Going to Church...**110.00**
1913, Bringing Home the Tree...**110.00**
1914, Amalienborg Castle...**105.00**
1915, Dog on Chain Outside Window **155.00**
1916, Prayer of the Sparrows..**105.00**
1917, Christmas Boat..**105.00**
1918, Fishing Boat..**105.00**
1919, Outside the Lighted Window.......................................**95.00**
1920, Hare in the Snow **95.00**
1921, Pigeons..**95.00**
1922, Star of Bethlehem..**95.00**
1923, Hermitage **95.00**
1924, Lighthouse...**105.00**
1925, Child's Christmas..**105.00**
1926, Churchgoers...**105.00**
1927, Skating Couple..**155.00**
1928, Eskimos...**95.00**
1929, Fox Outside Farm..**105.00**
1930, Tree in Town Hall Square..**115.00**
1931, Christmas Train...**115.00**
1932, Lifeboat at Work **115.00**
1933, Korsor-Nyborg Ferry...**95.00**
1934, Church Bell in Tower..**95.00**
1935, Lillebelt Bridge **95.00**
1936, Royal Guard...**95.00**
1937, Arrival of Christmas Guests...**115.00**
1938, Lighting the Candles..**175.00**
1939, Old Lock-Eye, The Sandman.......................................**215.00**
1940, Delivering Christmas Letters **265.00**
1941, Horses Enjoying Meal..**325.00**
1942, Danish Farm on Christmas Night.................................**275.00**
1943, Ribe Cathedral **235.00**
1944, Sorgenfri Castle...**145.00**
1945, Old Water Mill..**165.00**
1946, Commemoration Cross..**135.00**
1947, Dybbol Mill **165.00**
1948, Watchman..**115.00**
1949, Landsoldaten..**125.00**
1950, Kronborg Castle at Elsinore **155.00**
1951, Jens Bang...**125.00**
1952, Old Copenhagen Canals & Thorsvaldsen Museum............**135.00**
1953, Royal Boat **135.00**
1954, Snowman...**145.00**
1955, Kaulundborg Church..**145.00**
1956, Christmas in Copenhagen..**175.00**
1957, Christmas Candles...**175.00**
1958, Santa Claus..**140.00**
1959, Christmas Eve..**155.00**
1960, Village Church **205.00**
1961, Winter Harmony..**135.00**
1962, Winter Night..**125.00**
1963, Christmas Elf...**145.00**
1964, Fir Tree & Hare...**65.00**
1965, Bringing Home the Tree...**55.00**
1966, Home for Christmas...**45.00**
1967, Sharing the Joy..**45.00**
1968, Christmas in Church...**35.00**

1969, Arrival of Guests 30.00
1970, Pheasants in Snow..27.00
1971, Christmas at Home..27.00
1972, Christmas in Greenland....................................27.00
1973, Country Christmas 30.00
1974, Christmas in the Village....................................30.00
1976, Christmas Welcome...30.00
1977, Copenhagen Christmas 30.00
1978, A Christmas Tale 30.00
1979, White Christmas 40.00
1980, Christmas in the Woods....................................40.00
1981, Christmas Peace...40.00
1982, The Christmas Tree 57.00
1983, Christmas in Old Town 47.00
1984, Christmas Letter 75.00
1985, Christmas Eve, Farm..65.00
1986, Silent Night..70.00
1987, Snowman's Christmas...55.00
1988, In King's Garden...75.00
1989, Christmas Anchorage 60.00
1990, Changing Guards...65.00
1991, Copenhagen Stock Exchange 65.00
1992, Pastor's Christmas..105.00
1993, Father Christmas in Copenhagen 100.00

M. I. Hummel

The last issue for M.I. Hummel annual plates was made in 1995. Values listed here are for plates in mint condition with original boxes.

1971, Heavenly Angel..395.00
1972, Hear Ye, Hear Ye 40.00
1973, Glober Trotter...60.00
1974, Goose Girl...45.00
1975, Ride Into Christmas 47.00
1976, Apple Tree Girl 47.00
1977, Apple Tree Boy..55.00
1978, Happy Pastime 35.00
1979, Singing Lesson...35.00
1980, School Girl 40.00
1981, Umbrella Boy..70.00
1982, Umbrella Girl 85.00
1983, The Postman..125.00
1984, Little Helper 50.00
1985, Chick Girl...60.00
1986, Playmates..100.00
1987, Feeding Time...130.00
1988, Little Goat Herder..85.00
1989, Farm Boy...100.00
1990, Shepherd's Boy 165.00
1991, Just Resting..125.00
1992, Meditation...160.00
1993, Doll Bath...150.00
1994, Doctor...150.00
1995, Come Back Soon...170.00

Royal Copenhagen

1908, Madonna & Child 3,500.00
1909, Danish Landscape..240.00
1910, Magi...185.00
1911, Danish Landscape..185.00
1912, Christmas Tree..185.00
1913, Frederik Church Spire..170.00

1914, Holy Spirit Church 195.00
1915, Danish Landscape..210.00
1916, Shepherd at Christmas.......................................155.00
1917, Our Savior Church...135.00
1918, Sheep & Shepherds..135.00
1919, In the Park...135.00
1920, Mary & Child Jesus..130.00
1921, Aabenraa Marketplace.......................................125.00
1922, 3 Singing Angels..125.00
1923, Danish Landscape..125.00
1924, Sailing Ship..150.00
1925, Christianshavn Street Scene...............................125.00
1926, Christianshavn Canal 115.00
1927, Ship's Boy at Tiller...175.00
1928, Vicar's Family...125.00
1929, Grundtvig Church..125.00
1930, Fishing Boats..155.00
1931, Mother & Child..150.00
1932, Frederiksberg Gardens.......................................150.00
1933, Ferry & Great Belt...185.00
1934, Hermitage Castle..195.00
1935, Kronborg Castle...275.00
1936, Roskilde Cathedral...240.00
1937, Main Street of Copenhagen...............................295.00
1938, Round Church of Osterlars................................425.00
1939, Greenland Pack Ice..495.00
1940, Good Shepherd..595.00
1941, Danish Village Church.......................................425.00
1942, Bell Tower...495.00
1943, Flight Into Egypt 650.00
1944, Danish Village Scene...395.00
1945, Peaceful Scene...565.00
1946, Zealand Village Church......................................275.00
1947, Good Shepherd..300.00
1948, Nodebo Church..275.00
1949, Our Lady's Cathedral...295.00
1950, Boeslunde Church..295.00
1951, Christmas Angel...450.00
1952, Christmas in Forest 175.00
1953, Frederiksberg Castle...170.00
1954, Amalienborg Palace..185.00
1955, Fano Girl..230.00
1956, Rosenborg Castle..210.00
1957, Good Shepherd..150.00
1958, Sunshine Over Greenland..................................155.00
1959, Christmas Night...175.00
1960, Stag..140.00
1961, Training Ship..165.00
1962, Little Mermaid..165.00
1963, Hojsager Mill..75.00
1964, Fetching the Tree..70.00
1965, Little Skaters..70.00
1966, Blackbird..55.00
1967, Royal Oak..45.00
1968, Last Umiak...50.00
1969, Old Farmyard...45.00
1970, Christmas Rose & Cat..55.00
1971, Hare in Winter..35.00
1972, In the Desert...27.00
1973, Train Home Bound..37.00
1974, Winter Twilight...36.00
1975, Queens Palace..30.00
1976, Danish Watermill..45.00
1977, Immervad Bridge..30.00

1978, Greenland Scenery **32.00**
1979, Choosing Tree..**70.00**
1980, Bringing Home Tree **35.00**
1981, Admiring Tree **45.00**
1982, Waiting for Christmas **95.00**
1983, Merry Christmas **75.00**
1984, Jingle Bells **70.00**
1985, Snowman **70.00**
1986, Wait for Me **67.00**
1987, Winter Birds **80.00**
1988, Christmas Eve Copenhagen **82.00**
1989, Old Skating Pond **95.00**
1990, Christmas in Tivoli..**145.00**
1991, St Lucia Basilica **75.00**
1992, Royal Coach **80.00**
1993, Arrival Guests by Train.......................................**95.00**
1994, Christmas Shopping **90.00**

Limoges

From the mid-eighteenth century, Limoges was the center of the porcelain industry of France, where at one time more than forty companies utilized the local kaolin to make a superior quality china, much of which was exported to the United States. Various marks were used; some included the name of the American export company (rather than the manufacturer) and 'Limoges.' After 1891 'France' was added. Pieces signed by factory artists are more valuable than those decorated outside the factory by amateurs. The listings below are hand-painted pieces unless noted otherwise.

For a more thorough study of the subject, we recommend you refer to *The Collector's Encyclopedia of Limoges Porcelain, Third Edition* (with beautiful illustrations and current market values), by our advisor, Mary Frank Gaston.

Please note: Limoges porcelain is totally French in origin, but one American china manufacturer, The Limoges China Company, marked its earthenware 'Limoges' to reflect its name. For information concerning this American earthenware, we recommend *American Limoges* by Raymonde Limoges. Both this book and Mrs. Gaston's are available from Collector Books.

Basket, lilacs w/gold, artist sgn, T&V, ca 1907, 4x7½"...............**185.00**
Biscuit jar, pansies on shaded purple, early mk, 9x5½"...............**550.00**
Bottle, scent; roses w/gold on wht, unmk, 6¼x2¾".....................**155.00**
Box, dresser; roses w/ornate gold, T&V, ca 1894-1907, 2¾x5" dia...**210.00**
Cake plate, roses, artist sgn, T&V, ca 1907, 10½".....................**295.00**
Candlesticks, forget-me-nots, sgn T King, T&V, 8", pr **335.00**
Candlesticks, roses on gr w/gold trim, T&V, ca 1907, 6", pr **335.00**
Candlesticks, roses on wht w/gold, sgn Pejeau, unmk, 5½", pr ...**265.00**
Charger, fruit, gold scalloped rim, 1890-1930s mk, 12½"............**450.00**
Charger, peaches in basket, gold trim, 1908-30, 13½".................**495.00**
Chocolate pot, roses, gold finial & hdl, T&V, ca 1907, 10½".....**550.00**
Chocolate pot, violets, artist sgn, dtd 1902, unmk, 9" **450.00**
Cup & saucer, currants & gold leaves, dbl mk, ca 1910 ....**125.00**
Decanter, carnations on wht w/gold, Giraud mk, 1920s, 9".........**275.00**
Egg cup, chick w/daisy, gold trim, Tressman/Voght mk, 1907, 3½" ..**125.00**
Flask, violets & lake scene, artist sgn, 5¾" **295.00**
Jardiniere, gilt lilies on lt bl w/gold bands, 8¼x9¼"....................**250.00**
Jardiniere, roses (lg, mc, open), Guerin mk, ca 1800, 11" **1,600.00**
Jardiniere, roses w/much gold, sgn Frieburg, T&V, ca 1907, 9x9".....**1,400.00**
Jardiniere & ped, roses w/much gold, gold hdls, 1900-30, 13¾x13"..**2,800.00**
Pitcher, blackberries & buds, T&V, ca 1907, 12", NM................**550.00**
Pitcher, cider; grapes & roses w/gold, Guerin, 1900-32, 6¼" **600.00**
Pitcher, roses & lilacs, sgn Roby, dbl Elite mk, 10¾"..................**600.00**
Plaque, cherubs at play, 6" dia, +ornate 14x14" fr, pr **665.00**

Plaque, yel roses, artist sgn, 11½x6"+simple fr............................**495.00**
Punch bowl, grapes w/gold, artist sgn, T&V, ca 1907, 14", +9" ped..**1,750.00**
Tankard, apples w/gold dragon hdl, mk JPL, 11¼" **775.00**
Tankard, Nouveau flowers on aqua, dbl Elite mks, pre-1914, 12¼"...**550.00**
Tea strainer, floral (dainty) on wht w/gold, unmk.......................**155.00**
Tray, forget-me-nots, kidney shape, Guerin mk, 1900-32, 13x8½" ..**295.00**
Tray, roses, mc on wht, gold side hdl, Guerin mk, dtd 1906, 11x7"..**225.00**
Tray, roses on wht w/gold, hdls, T&V, ca 1907, 10x7⅝" **175.00**
Vase, currants, artist initialed, loving-cup form, T&V, dtd 1912, 7".**450.00**
Vase, hydrangeas on cream/couple dancing, bottle neck, ca 1900, 22" ...**2,100.00**
Vase, pillow; roses, gold hdls on heart shape, JPL mold, 7¼x9½" **525.00**
Vase, poppies on lt bl, gold hdls & scrollwork, 1891-1900, 13⅛"..**775.00**
Vase, roses allover, artist sgn, T&V, ca 1907, 22" **2,500.00**
Vase, roses allover, gold rim-to-hip hdls, JPL mk, 13½"...........**1,400.00**

Lithophanes

Lithophanes are porcelain panels with relief designs of varying degrees of thickness and density. Transmitted light brings out the pattern in graduated shading, lighter where the porcelain is thin and darker in the heavy areas. They were cast from wax models prepared by artists and depict views of life from the 1800s, religious themes, or scenes of historical significance. First made in Berlin about 1803, they were used as lamp shade panels, window plaques, and candle shields. Later steins, mugs, and cups were made with lithophanes in their bases. Japanese wares were sometimes made with dragons or geisha lithophanes. See also Dragon Ware; Steins.

Lamp, white porcelain with four lithophane panels, 7x5" square, $850.00.

Candle holder, 3 mc courting scenes, cylinder, 5½x4" **350.00**
Panel, boy & dog, 7x5" **135.00**
Panel, child/dog, bl/red stained glass border, 8x10"....................**300.00**
Panel, courting couple, KPM, 6x4¾" **175.00**
Panel, girl playing w/dog & puppies, PPM, 7x5½" **190.00**
Panel, Medieval lady in cathedral/service in session, metal fr, 13x11"...**400.00**
Panel, monther & child, mc attire, 4½x5¾", in ornate fr, 17" ...**410.00**
Panel, mother holding fr up to daughter, HPM, 7x6" **175.00**
Panel, young maiden, KPM, wood fr, 6x4" **275.00**
Shade, 3 panels of various buildings & views, spherical, 5¾" **300.00**
Water font, child/rabbit, opal bowl/panel in emb metal ftd stand, 9"...**200.00**

Little Red Riding Hood

Though usually thought of as a product of the Hull Pottery Company, research has shown that a major part of this line was actually made by Regal China. The idea for this popular line of novelties and kitchenware items was developed and patented by Hull, but records show that to a large extent Hull sent their whiteware to Regal to be decorated. Little Red Riding Hood was produced from 1943 until 1957.

For further information we recommend *The Collector's Encyclopedia of Hull Pottery* by Brenda Roberts and *The Collector's Encyclopedia of Cookie Jars* by Joyce and Fred Roerig. Both are published by Collector Books.

Bank, standing, from $650 to..750.00
Butter dish, from $325 to..350.00
Canister, cereal..1,375.00
Canister, coffee, sugar or flour; ea from $600 to..................700.00
Canister, salt..1,100.00
Canister, tea..700.00
Cookie jar, closed basket, from $350 to..................................375.00
Cookie jar, full skirt, from $750 to..................................850.00
Cookie jar, open basket, from $300 to..................................350.00
Cracker jar, ur mk, from $600 to..................................700.00
Creamer, side pour, from $150 to..................................175.00
Creamer, top pour, no tab hdl, from $400 to..................425.00
Creamer, top pour, tab hdl, from $350 to..................375.00
Lamp, from $1,300 to..1,500.00
Match holder, wall hanging, from $800 to..................850.00
Mustard jar, w/orig spoon..................................350.00
Pitcher, 7", from $325 to..................................350.00
Pitcher, 8"..375.00
Planter, wall hanging, from $375 to..................450.00
Shakers, Pat design 135889, med sz, pr (+), from $800 to..........900.00
Shakers, 3¼", pr, from $60 to..................................90.00
Shakers, 5½", pr, from $175 to..................................200.00
Spice jar, sq base, ea, from $650 to..................750.00
String holder, from $1,800 to..................................2,500.00
Sugar bowl, crawling, no lid, from $300 to..................350.00
Sugar bowl, standing, no lid, from $150 to..................175.00
Sugar bowl, w/lid, from $350 to..................................425.00
Sugar bowl lid, minimum value..................................175.00
Teapot, from $325 to..375.00
Wolf jar, red base, from $925 to..................................975.00
Wolf jar, yel base, from $750 to..................................800.00

Liverpool

In the late 1700s Liverpool potters produced a creamy ivory ware, sometimes called Queen's Ware, which they decorated by means of the newly perfected transfer print. Made specifically for the American market, patriotic inscriptions, political portraits, or other States themes were applied in black with colors sometimes added by hand. (Obviously their loyalty to the crown did not inhibit the progress of business!) Before it lost favor in about 1825, other English potters made a similar product. Today Liverpool is a generic term used to refer to all ware of this type. In our listings, information following the slash mark describes the transfer on the reverse side.

Jug, Apotheosis, dedication to Geo WA, blk transfer, 9½"......2,575.00
Jug, In God Is Our Trust/farmyard, blk transfer, Herculaneum, 9"..800.00
Jug, Masonic panel/Am vessel, eagle at spout, blk transfer w/mc, 10" .1,725.00
Jug, Masonic scenes/Success to Delemere, blk transfer w/gilt, 9½" ..875.00

Jug, Massacre of the French King, La Guillotine...Jan'y 20th 1793, reverse: Marie Anne Charlotte LaConcorde..., black transfers, restored spout, early nineteenth century, 7¾", $3,250.00.

Jug, Noted Tooth Drawer/Man & Machine Make Old..., blk transfer, 7½..900.00
Jug, Prosperity Attend..., blk transfer, 1800s, 9"..................545.00
Jug, Shipwrights Arms/Ship Caroline, blk transfer, HP Am flag, 8", EX ..220.00
Jug, WA in Glory/Am in Tears, blk transfer, 1800s, 9¼" 1,725.00
Mug, James Lawrence... portrait, blk transfer w/mc, 6¼" 3,000.00
Mug, Masonic panel w/symbols, blk, 6", EX..................375.00
Tureen, figure w/coat-of-arms shields, blk transfer, 9½x12¼"..1,095.00

Lladro

Lladro porcelains are currently being produced in Labernes Blanques, Spain. Their retired and limited edition figurines are popular collectibles on the secondary market.

At the Ball, #5398, 14", MIB..................................700.00
Boy w/Drum, #4616, 5x6", MIB..................................625.00
Boy w/Goat, #4506, 10¾"..................................335.00
Christmas Bell, angels, wht w/gold trim, 1989, 3x3½", MIB.......130.00
Collie w/Puppy, #6459, 10x5½"..................................375.00
Doctor, #4602, 15¾", MIB..................................185.00
Dreams of Peace..1,000.00
Family Roots, #5371, 12"..................................850.00
Galloping Horse, 11½x14"..................................810.00
Garden of Dreams, #7634, 13"..................................1,775.00
Girl w/Balloons, 10½"..................................220.00
Girl w/Bonnet, #1147, 8½"..................................240.00
Golfer, #450, 9½x5", MIB..................................150.00
Hebrew Student, #4684, 1970, 11½"..................................775.00
Indian Brave, #3562, ltd ed, 16½" 4,500.00
Julia, ballerina, #1361, 9', MIB..................................240.00
Little Gardener, holding umbrella & basket, 10½"..................385.00
Little Pals, #1985, 9"..................................2,400.00
Little Traveler, #7602, Collector's Society, 9", MIB..................810.00
My New Pet, #5549, 4x8", MIB..................................235.00
Othello & Desdemona, #1145, 13" 3,500.00
Pekingese, 6½"..310.00
Pensive Clown, #5130, 12x9", MIB..................................500.00
Pharmacist, #4844, 12½'..................................640.00
Plate, Christmas, 1972, #7012M, 8" 160.00
Plate, Dia de la Madre, 1972..................................50.00
Shelley, #1357, 1978, 7"..................................240.00
Skye Terrier, 1969, 5½x6¼"..................................725.00
St Nicholas, #5427, 15½"..................................570.00
The Artist, #4732, 14"..................................850.00
Trail Boss, #3561, 20" 4,500.00
Venus & Cupid, #134, 23" 1,280.00
Voyage of Columbus, #5847..................................685.00
Winter Scene, Seasons Series, #5287, 10¼" 440.00

Lobmeyer

J. and L. Lobmeyer, contemporaries of Moser, worked in Vienna, Austria, during the last quadrant of the 1800s. Most of the work attributed to them is decorated with distinctive enameling; favored motifs are people in eighteenth-century garb. Our advisor for this category is Don Williams; he is listed in the Directory under Missouri.

Cordial, pk band, gilt rim on quatrefoil bowl, leaf decor stem, 4⅜"...200.00
Creamer & sugar, village/pheasants, 3 hollow ft, sgn, 3¼", 2¼".....1,250.00
Goblet, man/florals, w/gold, mk VII, unsgn..................235.00
Goblet, mc florals, gold rim/ft borders of U-shape devices, 5".....350.00

Locke Art

By the time he came to America, Joseph Locke had already proven himself many times over as a master glassmaker, having worked in leading English glasshouses for more than seventeen years. Here he joined the New England Glass Company where he invented processes for the manufacture of several types of art glass — amberina, peachblow, pomona, and agata among them. In 1898 he established the Locke Art Glassware Co. in Mt. Oliver, Pittsburgh, Pennsylvania. Locke Art Glass was produced using an acid-etching process by which the most delicate designs were executed on crystal blanks. All examples are signed simply 'Locke Art,' often placed unobtrusively near a leaf or a stem. Some pieces are signed 'Jo Locke,' and some are dated. Most of the work was done by hand. The business continued into the 1920s. For further study we recommend *Locke Art Glass, Guide for Collectors*, by Joseph and Janet Locke, available at your local bookstore.

Our advisor for this category is Richard Haigh; he is listed in the Directory under Virginia.

Champagne, Poppy etch, 6" **95.00**
Cherry dish, Pansy etch, concave ft for pits, flint, 2¾" **150.00**
Cup, punch; Poppy etch **95.00**
Goblet, 3 flowers/buds on random stems, 4¼" **100.00**
Pitcher, Vintage Grape etch, corseted, etch hdl, 8½", +6 tumblers ...**590.00**
Plate, Poinsettia etch, 7" **135.00**
Salt cellar, Vintage, ped ft, 2¼x1¼" **100.00**
Sherbet, Vintage, saucer base **125.00**
Tray, ice cream; eng flowers, 16x8" **460.00**
Tumbler, Grape & Vine **95.00**
Tumbler, water lily & cattail etch, 3½" **100.00**
Vase, Poppy etch, 6x3" **350.00**
Wine, floral etch, dbl-knob stem, rnd ft, 5¾" **125.00**

Locks

The earliest type of lock in recorded history was the wooden cross bar used by ancient Egyptians and their contemporaries. The early Romans are credited with making the first key-operated mechanical lock. The ward lock was invented during the Middle Ages by the Etruscans of Northern Italy; the lever tumbler and combination locks followed at various stages of history with varying degrees of effectiveness. In the eighteenth century the first precision lock was constructed. It was a device that utilized a lever-tumbler mechanism. Two of the best-known of the early nineteenth-century American lock manufacturers are Yale and Sargent, and today's collectors value Winchester and Keen Kutter locks very highly. Factors to consider are rarity, condition, and construction. Brass and bronze locks are generally priced higher than those of steel or iron. Our advisor for this section is Joe Tanner; he is listed in the Directory under Washington.

Key:
bbl — barrel   st — stamped

Brass Lever Tumbler

USBIR, Slaymaker, seal type with window, 4", $60.00.

Ames Sword Co, Perfection st on shackle, 2¾" 65.00
Automatic, emb, flat key, 2⅛" 20.00
Bingham's Best Brand, BBB emb on front, 3¼" 150.00
Blue Grass, emb, 3" 85.00
Cleveland 4 Way, Cleveland 4 Way emb on front, 3⅝" 90.00
Cotterill, st High Security key, 5⅛x3⅛" 350.00
Cotterill Birmingham Eng, st, 5⅛" 400.00
Duplex Yale & Towne Mfg Co, st, 2⅞" 200.00
Eagle Lock Co, word Eagle emb on front, scrolled, 3" 60.00
Geo B Bahr & Co Lou Ky, st, 3⅛" 70.00
Good Luck, emb, 2¾" 45.00
GW Nock, fancy etch, st, 2⅞" 200.00
Jackson's, st Jackson's on front, 2½" 20.00
Keen Kutter, shape of KK emblem, KK emb on front, 4¾" 125.00
Motor, Motor emb on body, 3¼" 35.00
Our Very Best, OVB emb on body, 2⅞" 200.00
Roeyonoc, Roeyonoc st on body, 3¼" 30.00
Ruby, Ruby emb in scroll on front, 2¾" 30.00
Safe, Safe emb in scroll on front, 2⅜" 20.00
Siberian, Siberian emb on shackle, 2½" 110.00
Simmons, emb, 2¼" 18.00
Sphinx, sphinx & pharaoh head emb on front, 2¾" 35.00
Tooker & Reeves (seal lock), st, 5¼" 400.00
Tower & Lyon NY, st, 3" 25.00
W Bohannan & Co, SW emb in scroll on front, 2⅜" 30.00

Combinations

Chicago Combination Lock Co, st on front, brass, 2¾" 60.00
Clark, st, brass, 2¼" 300.00
Corbin Sesamee 4-Dial Brass Lock, st Sesamee, 2¾" 15.00
Junkunc Bros Mfrs, all st on bk, brass, 1⅞" 35.00
Karco st on body, 2½" 50.00
Miller Keyless, st, iron, 3¼" 70.00
No Kee, st, brass, 2" 45.00
Number or letter disk, st, 3-disk, brass, 2½" 100.00
Number or letter disk, st, 3-disk, iron, 2" 20.00
Number or letter disk, st, 4-disk, brass, 4½" 250.00
Number or letter disk, st, 4-disk, iron, 4½" 275.00
Permutation Lock Den Co, emb, brass, 3⅝" 600.00
Quaint Mfg Co, st on lock case, 4¼" 200.00
Sorel Limited Canada, st, brass, 3¼" 200.00
Sq lock case of steel, st Pat Germany, 4-wheel, 3¼" 110.00
Vulcana Push Lock Corp, st on lock case, 3¼" 50.00
WA Harrison, Inc, st, brass, 2½" 100.00
Your Own st on body, 3⅞" 400.00

Eight-Lever Type

Blue Chief, st, steel, 4½" 25.00
Excelsior, st, steel, 4¾" 30.00
Mastadon, st, steel, 4½" 15.00
Reese, st, steel, 4¾" 15.00

Iron Lever Tumbler

Airplane, st, 2¾" 60.00
Automobile, st, 2⅞" 50.00
Bear, emb, 2⅝" 25.00
Bull, word Bull emb on front, 2⅝" 30.00
Bulldog, word Bulldog & face of dog emb on front, 2¾" 35.00
Dan Patch, Dan Patch emb on front, horseshoe on bk, 2¾" 150.00
Dragon, word Dragon & dragon emb on front, 2⅞" 25.00
Eagle, 4 dice emb on front, 2¾" 40.00

G Merkel, st, 3" 30.00
HC Jones (trick lock), st, 4¼" 600.00
Indian Head, Indian head emb on front, 3" 140.00
Jupiter, word Jupiter/star & moon emb on front, 3¼"............18.00
Karo, word Karo emb on front, CI, 3⅛" 25.00
Lever Buckle Co, emb, 4½" 90.00
Mars, emb, 2¼" 20.00
Moose head, emb, 2¾" 20.00
Nineteen O Three, 1903 emb on front, 3⅞" 90.00
Owl, emb, 2¼' 30.00
Red Chief, words Red Chief emb on body, 3¾" 150.00
Rough Rider (horse & rider), emb, 3" 90.00
Rugby, football emb on body, 3" 20.00
Star Lock Works, st, 3⅛" 50.00
Thoroughbred, emb, 2⅛" 35.00
Unique, word Unique emb on front, 3¼" 120.00
Victory, emb, 3⅛" 45.00
W Hall & Co, st, 4½" 400.00
Woodland, emb, 2⅜" 30.00
Yale & Towne, lion face emb on front, shackle mk Y&T, 3".......150.00

Lever Push Key

Achilles, emb, iron, 3⅝" 80.00
Aztec, emb 6-Lever, 2⅛" 100.00
Belknaps 6-Lever, emb, iron, 2¼" 40.00
California, emb, brass, 2½" 100.00
Celtic Cross, emb cross on face, brass, 2¼" 150.00
Champion, emb Champion 6-Lever, brass push-key type, 2¼" 25.00
Cherokee, emb, 6-Lever, iron, 2½" 170.00
Climax, emb Climax 6-Lever, iron push-key type, 2¼" 35.00
Crank, emb, iron, 2⅞" 25.00
Crescent, 4-Lever, emb, iron, 2" 40.00
Dash, emb Dash 6-Lever, iron push-key type, 2¼" 25.00
Duke, emb 6-Lever, 2⅛" 65.00
Eagle, 3-Lever, emb, brass, 2" 50.00
Eclipse, 4-Lever, emb, brass, 2½" 20.00
Elm City 4-Lever, emb, brass, 3" 35.00
Excelsior, emb Excelsior 6-Lever, brass push-key type, 2¼"...........25.00
Fordloc, emb, iron, 3¼" 40.00
Harvard, emb Harvard 4-Lever, brass push-key type, 2" 50.00
HS&Co, 6-Lever, emb, brass, 2¼" 100.00
IXL, emb IXL on body, 2¼" 110.00
Jewett Buffalo, emb, brass, 2¼" 200.00
Keystone, emb Keystone 6-Lever, brass push-key type, 2¼" 40.00
McIntosh, emb, 6-Lever, iron, 2½" 150.00
Morley, emb, iron, 2½" 150.00
National Lock Co, emb, brass, 2½" 120.00
Smith & Egge Mfg Co, Smith & Egge st on front, 3" 75.00
Supplee, emb, iron, 2½" 100.00
Ten Star, emb Ten Star 6-Lever, 2¼" 60.00

Logo — Special Made

Anaconda, st, brass, 2⅞" 60.00
Brass pancake push key emb US Internal Revenue, 2¼" 225.00
Canada Custom, emb, iron, 2¾" 200.00
City of Boston Dept of Schools, st, brass, 2⅞" 40.00
Coca-Cola, st, brass, 2⅝" 50.00
D&H, emb, brass, 2½" 170.00
Delco Products, st, brass 20.00
Hawaiian Elec, st, brass, 3" 30.00
Heart-shape brass lever type emb Shults Co, bbl key, 2¾" 55.00
International Harvester Co, emb, brass, 2½" 100.00

Lilly, st, brass, 2½" 15.00
Okla State Pen, st, brass, 2⅝" 50.00
Ordinance Dept, st, brass, 2⅞" 20.00
Property of Syracuse Univ, st, brass, 2⅝" 40.00
Sq brass pin-tumbler case st Regd US Mail, int counter, 2¾".....140.00
Sq Yale-type brass pin tumbler, st US/A/tree/Forest Svc, 2⅞" 200.00
Standard Oil Co, st, brass, 2⅝" 25.00
Swift & Co, st, iron, 2¼" 20.00
Texaco, emb, brass, 2¾" 60.00
University of Notre Dame, emb, brass, 2½" 300.00
USBIA, st, brass, 3¾" 80.00
USMC, st, brass, 2½" 100.00
West Baking Co, emb, brass, 2½" 200.00
Zoo, st, iron, 2½" 25.00

Pin-Tumbler Type

Corbin, emb, iron, 2¾" 20.00
Eagle, emb, iron, 2¾" 20.00
Fulton, emb Fulton on body, 2⅝" 30.00
Hickory, emb, iron, 2¾" 150.00
Il-A-Noy, emb, iron, 2¾" 40.00
Pearl, brass, emb Pearl on body, 2⅛" 30.00
Rich-Con, emb, iron, 2⅞" 50.00
Sargent, emb, iron, 2¾" 15.00
Segal, iron, emb Segal on shackle, 3¾" 30.00
Yale, brass, emb Yale on body, Made in England on shackle, 3"....30.00
Yale, emb, iron, 2¼" 70.00

Scandinavian (Jail House) Type

Backalaphknck (Russian), st, iron, 5" 400.00
Bull Dog, emb, brass, 2½" 150.00
Corbin, st, brass, 2½" 50.00
Nrarvck (Russian), st, iron, 4" 250.00
Pear, emb, iron, 3½" 40.00
Romer, st, iron, 4" 70.00
Star, emb line on bottom, iron, 3¾" 150.00
Star, iron, 2½" 70.00
99 Miller, emb 99, brass, 1¾" 80.00

Six-Lever Type

Bon-Ton, st, iron, 3" 15.00
Eagle, brass, Eagle Six-Lever st on body 18.00
Miller, Six-Lever, st, brass, 3⅞" 20.00
Safe, brass, Safe st on body 18.00
Yale, brass, Yale emb on front 12.00

Story and Commemorative

AYPEX Seattle (Alaska Yukon Pacific Expo), emb tin/iron, 3" ..235.00
Canteen, US emb on lock, lock: canteen shape, 2" 700.00
CI, emb ornate scroll motif throughout body of lock, 3½"..........250.00
CI, emb skull/X-bones w/florals, NH Co on bk, 3¼" 200.00
Dan Patch, iron, 1⅞" 125.00
Eagle & stars/shield & stars, emb CI, Eagle Liberty, 2½" 300.00
Missouri Seal, brass, 2¼" 150.00
National Hardware Co (NHCo), emb Mercury figure, iron, 2" ..250.00
National Hardware Co (NHCo), emb SK, iron, 3½" 600.00
North Pole, brass, 2⅞" 150.00
Russell & Erwin (R&E), emb Aztec figure, iron, 2¼" 200.00
Russell & Erwin (R&E), emb bird, iron, 2⅞" 500.00
Russell & Erwin (R&E), emb mailbox, iron, 3⅛" 600.00

Russell & Erwin (R&E), emb vase, iron, 3¼" 800.00
1901 Pan Am Expo, brass, emb w/buffalo, 2⅝" 450.00
1904 World's Fair, iron & brass, 3⅝" 400.00

Warded Type

Aetna, emb, brass, 2¼" 35.00
Army, iron pancake ward key, emb letters, 2½" 40.00
Enders, st, brass, 1½" 25.00
Globe, iron sq lock case, emb US on bk, 2⅜" 20.00
Hex, iron, sq lock case, emb US on bk, 2⅛" 95.00
Kirby, emb, brass, 2¼" 20.00
Lucky, emb, brass, 2½" 45.00
Red Cross, brass sq case, emb letters, 2" 10.00
Red Seal, emb, brass, 2" 20.00
Rex, steel case, emb letters, 2⅝" 18.00
Ruby, emb, brass, 2⅛" 20.00
Safety First, brass pancake type, emb letters, 2¾" 15.00
Sampson, emb, iron, 2½" 20.00
Secure, iron pancake type, emb letters, 2⅝" 20.00
Shapleigh, st, brass, 2" 18.00
Sprocket, brass oval shape, emb letters, 2⅛" 50.00
Try Me, iron pancake type, emb letters, 2½" 25.00
Van Guard, emb, iron, 2⅞" 18.00
Winchester, brass sq case, st letters, 2¾" 135.00

Wrought Iron Lever Type (Smokehouse Type)

DM&Co, bbl key, 4¼" 20.00
Improved Warranted, 3½" 35.00
MW&Co, flat key, 3½" 20.00
VR, 3½" 30.00
Waines, 4⅜" 40.00

Loetz

The Loetz Glassworks was established in Klostermule, Austria, in 1840. After Loetz's death the firm was purchased by his grandson, Johann Loetz Witwe. Until WWII the operation continued to produce fine artware, some of which made in the early 1900s bears a striking resemblance to Tiffany's, with whom Loetz was associated at one time. In addition to the iridescent Tiffany-style glass, he also produced threaded glass and some cameo. The majority of Loetz pieces will have a polished pontil. Our advisor for this category is Don Williams; he is listed in the Directory under Missouri.

Bowl, orange/bl irid striated bands, oval rim w/pinched ends, 4x7" ...420.00
Bowl, purple/bl wavy irid, ribbed w/irregular ruffled top, 5x7½" .375.00
Candlestick, gold, wide bobeche, 'trn' stem, dome ft, 14" 460.00
Candlesticks, gold w/bl highlights, traditional shape, 11", pr 595.00
Compote, bl irid w/oil spots, ball stem, w/lid, 8½" 650.00
Compote, cranberry irid w/bl-gold oil spots, ruffled, 8¾x7" 350.00
Compote, dk forest gr w/irid bl-gr oil spots, ruffled, 9" 300.00
Goblet, floriform; gold cup, gr stem w/2 appl leaves, rnd base, 9" ...200.00
Inkwell, lime gr w/diagonal raised drape pattern, 2x5¼" 275.00
Lamp base, Titania, gr leaves on bl cased in clear, ovoid, 8" 1,500.00
Rose bowl, gr/amber irid swirl decor, incurvate lobed rim, 4¼" ..285.00
Rose bowl, lav to gold w/bl waves & dots, pinched incurvate rim, 5x6" ..1,950.00
Shade, gr irid texture & bl oil spots, rolled rim, ruffled top, 5" 90.00
Vase, bl irid w/wide waves & 3 appl trailing prunts, dimpled, 4x3"..2,000.00
Vase, bl w/gold feathers, pinch-sided gourd shape w/hdl, 8" 300.00
Vase, bl w/gold/gr/purple irid oil spots, ornate metal collar, 8x4" ...400.00
Vase, bl/gr irid w/turtle shell finish, Nouveau ormolu hdls, slim, 11" ..400.00

Vase, bl/rose/gold/purple pulls on yel w/oil spots, 3-hdl, 9" 8,000.00
Vase, bright pk above amethyst irid, waves at junction, 8½x3½" ..1,265.00
Vase, bright pk above dk amethyst irid w/waves at junction, ftd, 8x4" ...1,600.00
Vase, brn w/wht 'octopus,' wht int, bulbous, 4-lobe rim, 8x6½".....2,100.00
Vase, cameo apples (4 on branch) on pk frost, 10¾" 1,900.00
Vase, cameo buds/stems, brn on yel, 4¾" 350.00
Vase, cameo cherries/leaves on bl, ftd, oval mk: Czecho-Slovakia, 4" 350.00
Vase, cobalt w/4-dimple shoulder & swirl ribs, 4-crimp top, 8½" 2,000.00
Vase, floral inlaid in purple/gr/bl/gold EX irid, top w/3 dimples, 8"..11,000.00
Vase, gold irid w/bl highlights, waisted, 7" 150.00
Vase, gold irid w/pk & bl oil spots, slim w/low flare, 12" 500.00
Vase, gold w/bl irid feathers, 5 dimples in shoulder, 10x5".......3,165.00
Vase, gold w/bl oil spots, ruffled/cylindrical, 7" 125.00
Vase, gold w/bright bl waves, flange on tubular throat, cone base, 12"....3,000.00
Vase, gold w/gr waves, pinched/lobed top, 11½x5" 500.00
Vase, gold w/pulled waves, flange rim/tube neck, raised cone base, 13" ..1,725.00
Vase, gold/bl irid w/allover swirls, silver rim, 6" 350.00
Vase, gr irid cased in crystal w/appl silver flowers, stick neck, 6" 225.00
Vase, gr irid crackle w/metal rim cut in grapevines & leaves, 6½" .125.00
Vase, gr irid ribs cased in crystal, 5" 650.00
Vase, gr irid w/oil spots, bottle form w/flat flared lip, 8" 300.00
Vase, gr w/bl oil spots, bulbous w/4 dimpled sides, 7¼" 345.00
Vase, gr w/3 rim-to-base teardrops, flared rim, 6½x4" 1,045.00
Vase, gr/bl diagonal striations, quatrafold top, 7x8" 300.00
Vase, ivory w/twisted gold waves w/3 lg pk/ivory trailing prunts, 7"..7,000.00
Vase, lt amethyst/gold w/feathers, very irid, swollen form, 6x3½"..3,000.00
Vase, lt bl w/gr irid oil spots, squatty, pinched sides, 6¾x5½".....175.00
Vase, marble: pk/purple/yel, enameled top, 7"..........................150.00
Vase, olive gr irid w/bl irid waves, low width, 5x4" 2,125.00
Vase, olive gr texture w/acid-cut irid bl Nouveau motif, slim, 8" ...500.00
Vase, opal w/bl/pk/gr leaves/petals, 4-lobe, shouldered, 8" 3,500.00
Vase, orange cased in crystal w/gr/silver feathers, 4½" 2,700.00
Vase, Papillon, red irid w/wht & chartreuse irid, waisted, 6".......500.00
Vase, peach opal w/gold undulations, stick neck, 8½" 200.00
Vase, Rusticana, gr irid w/sm pigtail pulls, cylindrical, 7" 90.00
Vase, salmon pk irid w/bkground waves & bold loops & peaks, 6x4" ..2,000.00

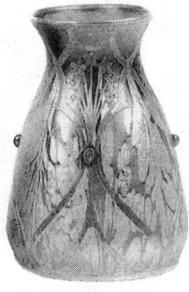

Vase, silver overlay floral on bronze iridescent with green oil-spot splashes, four blossoms set with cabochon orange hard stones, broad base, 7", $4,750.00.

Vase, silver o/l floral on gold w/gr/bl leaves/vines, 4 dimples, 7" ...6,000.00
Vase, silver o/l floral on lt gr irid, ogee sides, flaring rim, 4¼" 575.00
Vase, silver o/l leaves/vines exposes rnd areas of cobalt, 5x3" 700.00
Vase, silver o/l on gr irid, silver rim, ruffled trumpet neck, 11" ...500.00
Vase, silver o/l stems/leaves on amber irid, shouldered, 5½x3" ...2,000.00
Vase, turq irid w/brn/silver/bl feathers half way up, 6x6"..........2,100.00
Vase, wht w/gold waves & 4 wine/platinum trailing prunts, 4"....2,700.00

Lomonosov Porcelain

Founded in St. Petersburg in 1744, the Lomonosov porcelain factory produced exquisite porcelain miniatures for the Czar and other Russian nobility. One of the first factories of its kind, Lomonosov produced mainly vases and delicate sculptures. In the 1800s Lomonosov became closely involved with the Russian Academy of Fine Arts, a connection which has continued to this day as the company continues to supply the world with these fine artistic treasures. In 1992 the backstamp was changed to read 'Made in Russia,' instead of 'Made in USSR.'

Bathing beauty, ca 1960, 7" **45.00**
Bear & cello, late 1940s, 5" **70.00**
Boy & Teddy bear, ca 1948, 8" **55.00**
Boy bathing from bowl, 1950s **70.00**
Boy w/dog, USSR, 3¾x5¾x4¼" **28.00**
Bull moose, LFZ, lg **75.00**
Bulldog, Made in USSR, 8x7x4", NM...............................**25.00**
Dachshund, Made in Russia, 4½x5½" **30.00**
Deer w/antlers, LFZ **52.50**
Fox & beaver, USSR, 1950s, 5" **27.50**
Girl kneels & holds bird, 1940s, bl mk **55.00**
Great Dane, Made in Russia, 5x9¾" **25.00**
Hen & rooster, shakers, USSR, 3¾", pr **45.00**
Hippo, Made in Russia, 3x9½" **35.00**
Hockey player, 1950s, USSR **40.00**
Horse, standing, #974, Made in Russia, 8x10", from $55 to **75.00**
Ice skater, lady, 1960s, USSR..**80.00**
Lenin bust, red mk, ca 1955-60, 7x6" **25.00**
Leopard, playful seated pose, LFZ, lg **65.00**
Lion & rabbit, ca 1948 ....**50.00**
Musician & dancer, #2384, Made in USSR, 6½" **40.00**
Panda bear, USSR, 5x3"..**30.00**
Pelican, ca 1960, USSR, 7" **65.00**
Penguin, USSR mk, 6x3x3"..**24.00**
Poodle, wht, playing, USSR, 3x4" **26.00**
Tiger cub, wht, Made in Russia, 4½x5" **24.00**
Woman in red scarf, 1940s, USSR......................................**40.00**

Longwy

The Longwy workshops were founded in 1798 and continue today to produce pottery in the north of France near the Luxembourg-Belgian border under the name 'Societe des Faienceries de Longwy et Senelle.' The ware for which they are best known was produced during the Art Deco period, decorated in bold colors and designs. Earlier wares made during the first quarter of the nineteenth century reflected the popularity of Oriental art, cloisonne enamels in particular. The designs were executed by impressing the pattern into the moist clay and filling in the depressions with enamels. Examples are marked 'Longwy,' either impressed or painted under glaze.

Charger, peacocks on gold branch w/flowers on turq to dk bl, 14½"..**1,100.00**
Compote, floral band, mc on ivory crackle, #88, 4¼x9¾" **250.00**
Compote, repeating floral clusters, blk borders, 8-sided base, 12" ...**300.00**
Egg, mk Circus #97/150, stylized elephant & leopard, #97/150, 5" .**230.00**
Ewer, wht crackle w/floral & birds, bl rope hdl, 10" **1,040.00**
Figurine, elephant, wht crackle w/Art Deco saddle, 1925-40 ......**240.00**
Tray, mc floral cloisonne-like design, ¾x6x7"...............................**310.00**
Vase, bl butterfly & floral on wht, 2½x5" **160.00**
Vase, bud; flowers/leaves, wine/wht/bl, 3 joined cylinders, #793, 6"..**325.00**
Vase, cloisonne floral decor, #2096, 4x9" **385.00**
Vase, incised/pnt stylized design in blk on bl, bulbous, 11", NM ..**1,000.00**
Vase, peacocks & birds among flowers, blk/bl/yel, rpr, 10¾" **850.00**

Lonhuda

William Long was a druggist by trade who combined his knowledge of chemistry with his artistic ability in an attempt to produce a type of brown-glazed slip-decorated artware similar to that made by the Rookwood Pottery. He achieved his goal in 1889 after years of long and dedicated study. Three years later he founded his firm, the Lonhuda Pottery Company. The name was coined from the first few letters of the last name of each of his partners, W.H. Hunter and Alfred Day. Laura Fry, formerly of the Rookwood company, joined the firm in 1892, bringing with her a license for Long to use her patented airbrush-blending process. Other artists of note, Sarah McLaughlin, Helen Harper, and Jessie Spaulding, joined the firm and decorated the ware with nature studies, animals, and portraits, often signing their work with their initials. Three types of marks were used on the Steubenville Lonhuda ware. The first was a linear composite of the letters 'LPCO' with the name 'Lonhuda' impressed above it. The second, adopted in 1893, was a die-stamp representing the solid profile of an Indian, used on ware patterned after pottery made by the American Indians. This mark was later replaced with an impressed outline of the Indian head with 'Lonhuda' arching above it. Although the ware was successful, the business floundered due to poor management. In 1895 Long became a partner of Sam Weller and moved to Zanesville where the manufacture of the Lonhuda line continued. Less than a year later, Long left the Weller company. He was associated with J.B. Owens until 1899, at which time he moved to Denver, Colorado, where he established the Denver China and Pottery Company in 1901. His efforts to produce Lonhuda utilizing local clay were highly successful. Examples of Denver Lonhuda are sometimes marked with the LF (Lonhuda Faience) cipher contained within a canted diamond form.

Ewer, spaniel on brown, restored handle, 7", $425.00.

Box, floral, sgn AH, LF mk, #244, 2", EX **120.00**
Ewer, daisies, Amelia Sprague, #11, ca 1893, 4" **400.00**
Ewer, scenic, sgn ADF, LF mk, ca 1895, rprs, 12¼" **450.00**
Vase, pansies, 3-hdl, 3 bun ft, LF mk, #280, 3⅝" **140.00**

Lotton

Charles Lotton is a contemporary glass artist. He began blowing glass and developing original designs thirty years ago and now has work on display in many major glass museums and collections, among them the Smithsonian, the Art Institute of Chicago, the Museum of Glass, and the Chrysler Museum. He has become famous for his unique lamps. Every piece is signed and dated. His three sons, David, Daniel, and John, each work in their own studios. All four artists produce distinctive work. They sell their glass at antique shows and in their showroom in Crete, Illinois. For further information read *Lotton Art Glass* by Charles Lotton and Tom O'Conner; see the Directory under Illinois. The values that follow are actual prices realized from a recent auction.

Bowl, Cypriot, pk leaves on lav, J Heer, 3x3½" **185.00**
Bowl, Multi Flora Sunset, Charles, 8x12" **3,500.00**

Bowl, Sunset, Jerry Heer, 3x3½".................................185.00
Paperweight, ruby fruit w/gold irid, Darby Graham, 2½x3½".....190.00
Vase, bl irid w/ bl & silver draped swags, sgn Lotton, 7¾"..........200.00
Vase, Cypriot, gold lustre lava draping/split lip, Charles, 8"....1,100.00
Vase, Draped Webb, Selenium Red w/bl lustre, Charles, 8x7"....795.00
Vase, flowers, pk on muted bl, 5"...................................450.00
Vase, flowers/foliage, pk on dk red, 1987, 9"...............500.00
Vase, hearts/vines allover, silver on amber/red, Charles/1988, 8x7"...450.00
Vase, irid stylized broad leaves on ruby, 3x3½" dia.....................390.00
Vase, Multi Flora, pk/wht on cobalt bl, Charles, 7½x5".............435.00
Vase, paperweight; Multi Flora, 5"................................900.00
Vase, Pulled Feather, bl/gr/gold on wht, red int, 7½"................985.00

Lotus Ware

Isaac Knowles and Issac Harvey operated a pottery in East Liverpool, Ohio, in 1853 where they produced both yellow ware and Rockingham. In 1870 Knowles brought Harvey's interests and took as partners John Taylor and Homer Knowles. Their principal product was ironstone china, but Knowles was confident that American potters could produce as fine a ware as the Europeans. To prove his point, he hired Joshua Poole, an artist from the Belleek Works in Ireland. Poole quickly perfected a Belleek-type china, but fire destroyed this portion of the company. Before it could function again, their hotel china business had grown to the point that it required their full attention in order to meet market demands. By 1891 they were able to try again. They developed a bone china, as fine and thin as before, which they called Lotus. Henry Schmidt from the Meissen factory in Germany decorated the ware, often with lacy filigree applications or hand-formed leaves and flowers to which he added further decoration with liquid slip applied by means of a squeeze bag. Due to high production costs resulting from so much of the fragile ware being damaged in firing and because of changes in tastes and styles of decoration, the Lotus Ware line was dropped in 1896. Some of the early ware was marked 'KT&K China'; later marks have a star and a crescent with 'Lotus Ware' added. Our advisor for this category is Mary Frank Gaston.

Bowl, appl floral branches, netting, 3¾x4¾"...............175.00
Bowl, gold appl florals on tan matt, beaded rim, pk int, 4½"......350.00
Bowl, lady's portrait, swirled/scalloped rim w/gold, 3x10"........1,100.00
Chocolate jug, emb florals, no enameling or gold, 9"..................550.00
Cracker jar, emb fishnet & beadwork panels, 7½".......................550.00
Cup & saucer, tea; Sonoma, sculpted leaves, ftd cup...................135.00
Ewer, rtcl, melon ribs, beaded slim neck, 10".................1,850.00
Jardiniere, yel roses/gold on wht, scrolled edge, 7"...................800.00
Jug, Globe, roses w/much gold, 5x7".................................750.00
Pitcher, netting, 2¾"..100.00
Rose jar, rtcl ovals, dbl-bead rim, rtcl lid, 4½".......................700.00
Syrup, acanthus leaf shoulder, scroll hdl, floral rim, 4½".............225.00
Vase, appl jewel medallions, gold Nouveau hdls, mk, 10"........1,300.00
Vase, lily form, bl/pk/ivory shaded w/gold trim, 8".................1,100.00
Vase, 2 rtcl ovals, beaded florals, ftd/scroll hdls, 9½".............1,200.00

Lu Ray Pastels

Lu Ray Pastels dinnerware was introduced in the early 1940s by Taylor, Smith, and Taylor of East Liverpool, Ohio. It was offered in assorted colors of Persian Cream, Sharon Pink, Surf Green, Windsor Blue, and Chatham Gray in complete place settings as well as many service pieces. It was a successful line in its day and is once again finding favor with collectors of American dinnerware. For further information we recommend *Collector's Guide to Lu Ray Pastels* by Bill and Kathy Mee-

han. Our advisor for this category is Shirley Moore; she is listed in the Directory under Oklahoma.

Chocolate pot, straight sides, $400.00; Individual creamer and sugar bowl with lid (goes with chocolate set), $92.00 each; Chocolate cup, $80.00; Saucer, $30.00.

Bowl, '36s oatmeal...60.00
Bowl, coupe soup; flat..18.00
Bowl, cream soup...70.00
Bowl, fruit; Chatham Gray, 5".......................................16.00
Bowl, fruit; 5"...5.00
Bowl, lug soup; tab hdld...24.00
Bowl, mixing; 5½"...125.00
Bowl, mixing; 7"..125.00
Bowl, mixing; 8¾"...100.00
Bowl, mixing; 10¼"...150.00
Bowl, salad; any color other than yel.............................65.00
Bowl, salad; yel..55.00
Bowl, vegetable; oval, 9½"..20.00
Butter dish, any color other than Chatham Gray, w/lid.............50.00
Butter dish, Chatham Gray, rare color, w/lid......................90.00
Calendar plates, 8", 9" & 10", ea.................................40.00
Casserole...125.00
Coaster/nut dish...65.00
Coffee cup, AD...20.00
Coffeepot, AD...200.00
Creamer..8.00
Creamer, AD, ind...40.00
Egg cup, dbl...24.00
Epergne...125.00
Jug, water; ftd..150.00
Muffin cover...125.00
Muffin cover, w/8" underplate......................................145.00
Nappy, vegetable; rnd, 8½"..20.00
Pitcher, any color other than yel, bulbous w/flat bottom.........125.00
Pitcher, juice...200.00
Pitcher, yel, bulbous w/flat bottom...............................95.00
Plate, cake..70.00
Plate, Chatham Gray, rare color, 7".............................16.00
Plate, chop; 15"...38.00
Plate, grill; compartment...35.00
Plate, 6"..3.00
Plate, 7"..12.00
Plate, 8"..20.00
Plate, 9"..10.00
Plate, 10"..20.00
Platter, oval, 11½"...20.00
Platter, oval, 13"...24.00
Relish dish, 4-part...95.00
Sauce boat...28.00
Sauce boat, any other color than yel, fixed stand.................35.00
Sauce boat, yel, fixed stand...22.50
Saucer, coffee; AD...8.50
Saucer, cream soup..28.00
Saucer, tea..3.00

Shakers, pr 18.00
Sugar bowl, AD; w/lid, from chocolate set 92.00
Sugar bowl, AD; w/lid, ind 40.00
Sugar bowl, w/lid 15.00
Teacup 8.00
Teapot, curved spout, w/lid 125.00
Teapot, flat spout, w/lid 160.00
Tray, pickle 28.00
Tumbler, juice 50.00
Tumbler, water 80.00
Vase, bud 400.00

Lunch Boxes

Early twentieth-century tobacco companies such as Union Leader, Tiger, and Dixie sold their products in square, steel containers with flat, metal carrying handles. These were specifically engineered to be used as lunch boxes when they became empty. (See Advertising, specific companies.) By 1930 oval lunch pails with colorful lithographed decorations on tin were being manufactured to appeal directly to children. These were made by Ohio Art, Decoware, and a few other companies. In 1950 Aladdin Industries produced the first 'real' character lunch box — a Hopalong Cassidy decal-decorated steel container now considered the beginning of the kids' lunch box industry. The other big lunch box manufacturer, American Thermos (later King Seely Thermos Company) brought out its 'blockbuster' Roy Rogers box in 1953, the first fully lithographed steel lunch box and matching bottle. Other companies (ADCO Liberty; Landers, Frary & Clark; Ardee Industries; Okay Industries; Universal; Tindco; Cheinco) also produced character pails. Today's collectors often tend to specialize in those boxes dealing with a particular subject. Western, space, TV series, Disney movies, and cartoon characters are the most popular. There are well over five hundred different lunch boxes available to the astute collector. For further information we recommend *Collector's Guide to Lunch Boxes* by Carole Bess White and L.M. White (Collector Books), and *The Illustrated Encyclopedia of Metal Lunch Boxes* by Allen Woodall and Sean Brickell. In the following listings, lunch boxes are metal unless noted vinyl or plastic, and values include thermoses only when they are mentioned within the descriptions.

As indicated in the lines, most of our values are for examples in exceptional condition; remember to discount sharply for wear and damage beyond the stated conditions.

Action Jackson, w/thermos, 1973, EX 175.00
Addams Family, 1974, EX 50.00
Astrokids, plastic, w/thermos, 1988, M 25.00
Ballerina on Lily Pad, vinyl, 1960s, EX 100.00
Banana Splits, vinyl, w/thermos, 1969, NM 450.00
Barbarino, vinyl brunch bag, 1977, NM 125.00
Battle of the Planets, 1979, EX 40.00
Beatles, bl, 1965, VG 200.00
Bonanza, 1963, VG 85.00
Brave Eagle, w/thermos, 1957, NM 400.00
Bullwinkle & Rocky, bl, 1962, NM 600.00
Bullwinkle Lunch Kit, vinyl, 1962, NM 285.00
Cable Car, dome top, 1962, NM 125.00
California Raisins, vinyl, 1988, EX 20.00
Cartoon Zoo Lunch Chest, 1962, EX 175.00
CHiPs, plastic, dome top, 1977, NM 30.00
Dick Tracy, w/thermos, 1967, NM 200.00
Dr Seuss, 1970, VG+ 70.00
Dudley Do-Right, bl rim, 1962, NM 1,000.00
Ewoks, plastic, 1983, EX 15.00
Family Affair, w/thermos, 1969, EX 135.00

Flags of the United Nations, w/thermos, 1954, NM 250.00
Flintstones & Dino, w/thermos, 1962, NM 250.00
Gene Autry Melody Ranch, w/thermos, 1954, NM 500.00
Get Smart, 1966, EX 200.00
Ghostbusters, plastic, purple, 1988, EX 20.00
Great Wild West, 1959, EX 375.00
Green Hornet, w/thermos, 1967, M 500.00
Guns of Will Sonnet, 1968, EX 100.00
Hansel & Gretel, 1982, EX 100.00
Hector Heathcote, w/thermos, 1964, NM 200.00
Holly Hobbie, plastic, w/thermos, 1989, M 25.00
Home Town Airport, dome top, w/thermos, 1966, EX 200.00
How the West Was Won, w/thermos, 1978, EX 55.00
Huckleberry Hound & Friends, 1961, VG 75.00
Hulk Hogan, plastic, 1989, EX 10.00
Incredible Hulk, 1978, EX 40.00
Knight Rider, 1983, EX 35.00
Land of Giants, 1968, VG 75.00
Laugh-In, w/thermos, 1968, EX 150.00
Li'l Jodie, vinyl, 1985, EX 50.00
Lost in Space, dome top, w/thermos, rare, 1967, NM 60.00
Marvel Super Heroes, 1976, EX 45.00
Mary Poppins, vinyl, 1973, VG 50.00
Mickey Mouse Club, 1976, yel, EX 45.00
Mighty Mouse, plastic, 1979, EX+ 20.00
Mod Tulip, dome top, 1962, EX 100.00
Munsters, w/thermos, 1965, NM 250.00
Nancy Drew Mysteries, 1977, VG 35.00
Partridge Family, w/thermos, 1971, EX 50.00
Peanuts, vinyl, w/thermos, 1965, NM 150.00
Planet of the Apes, 1974, VG 60.00
Popeye, plastic, dome top, 1979, EX 30.00
Popeye, w/thermos, 1962, NM 400.00
Road Runner, 1970, EX 75.00
Robot Man, plastic, 1984, EX 15.00

Roy Rogers and Dale Evans, red shirt, with thermos, 1957, VG, $150.00.

Roy Rogers, vinyl, cream, w/thermos, NM 350.00
Scooby Doo, w/thermos, 1973 ....175.00
Secret Agent T, 1968, VG 60.00
Six Million Dollar Man, plastic, 1974, M 35.00
Smokey Bear, 1975, NM 350.00
Superman, w/thermos, 1967, NM 200.00
Tarzan, w/thermos, 1966, NM 150.00
Three Little Pigs, 1982, EX 100.00
Tic Tac Toe, vinyl, 1970s, EX 50.00
Tom & Jerry, plastic, w/thermos, 1992, M 20.00
Wagon Train, 1964, VG 60.00
Wild Bill Hickok & Jingles, w/thermos, 1965, NM 250.00
Winnie the Pooh, plastic, w/thermos, 1990, M 25.00
Woody Woodpecker, w/thermos, 1972, NM 200.00
World of Barbie, vinyl, pk, 1971, EX 35.00
Yosemite Sam, vinyl, EX 235.00
Ziggy, vinyl, 1979, EX 85.00

Zorro, 1958, VG **90.00**

Lutz

From 1869 to 1888, Nicholas Lutz worked for the Boston and Sandwich Company where he produced the threaded and striped art glass that was so popular during that era. His works were not marked; and since many other glassmakers of the day made similar wares, the term Lutz has come to refer not only to his original works but to any of this type.

Basket, pk threading, appl pk & clear tooled hdl, 6" **235.00**
Cup & saucer, yel/wht/gold striping, gold in hdl, 2½", 4½" **80.00**
Flask, bl/wht/gold striping, ovoid w/flattened sides, 4¾" **130.00**
Smoke bell, pk/wht/gold striping, ruffled, triangular, iron mt......**100.00**
Tumbler, lemonade; cranberry threads, 2 appl berries.................**150.00**
Wine, pk/wht/gold striping, trumpet-shape base, 4⅛" **115.00**

Maddux of California

One of the California-made ceramics now so popular with collectors, Maddux was founded in the late 1930s and during the years that followed produced novelty items, TV lamps, figurines, planters, and tableware accessories.

Ashtray, #7001, 12" dia **10.00**
Ashtray, fish, #7134, 6" L...**20.00**
Ashtray, pig form, natural colors, #7204, 7" L...............................**12.00**
Ashtray, triangular, gunmetal gray, #731, 10½"............................**20.00**
Bank, smiling pig, red or gr, 12" L...**25.00**
Bowl, cabbage leaf design, 4x13" L..**25.00**
Bowl, creamy wht, flared rim, #3093, 2x5½" **16.00**
Bowl, ftd, #2102..**10.00**
Bowl, ped w/6 ind servers, #3095A...**25.00**
Bowl, shell form, wht, #3017..**15.00**
Bowl, vegetable; emb swirls, wht w/turq lid, #3066B, 4½x7¾" **25.00**
Bowl set, Contempo, wht satin, #1047, 16½" **20.00**
Clock, astrology design, Westclox, #718R, 12" dia **75.00**
Cookie jar, Baby Birds on Bough, from $45 to **55.00**
Cookie jar, Chipmunk on Stump, C Romanelli, from $130 to ...**145.00**
Cookie jar, Queen, #2104, from $150 to **175.00**
Cookie jar, Strawberry **25.00**
Figurine, bulls, head up/head down, #972/973, 11" L, pr **75.00**
Figurine, Chinese pheasant, #527, 11½".......................................**20.00**
Figurine, doe, #907, 12½"...**15.00**
Figurine, elephant sitting, #984, 18"..**25.00**
Figurine, flamingo flying, natural colors, #970, 11".......................**45.00**
Figurine, flamingos, #400/401, pr...**50.00**
Figurine, horses rearing/charging, #925/926, pr.............................**20.00**
Figurine, parrots (2) on branch, yel on dk gr, 10x9½x4" **75.00**
Figurine, puppy, #300, 6x5½"...**15.00**
Figurine, rooster, #932, 10½"...**30.00**
Figurine, stag standing, natural, #914, 12½" **20.00**
Planter, bird, #3304 ....**20.00**
Planter, bird in flight, #536, 11½"..**20.00**
Planter, birds (2) in flight, pk & blk, #528, 10" **20.00**
Planter, Chinese Bell Tower, #206A, 8" **20.00**
Planter, cockatoo, pk & bl, #612..**25.00**
Planter, flamingos, pk, #515, 10½"...**75.00**
Planter, swallow, pk & gray, #628...**35.00**
Planter, swan, #150, 11" **18.00**
Planter, swan, blk #510, 11"...**18.00**
Relish, gr pepper, w/lid & side bowls, #3275 ....**15.00**

TV lamp, bassett hound, #896, 12" **140.00**
TV lamp, deer running (2), natural, #829, 10½".............................**45.00**
TV lamp, head of Christ, 3-D planter, #841...................................**45.00**
TV lamp, mallard flying, natural, #839, 11½".................................**45.00**
TV lamp, prairie schooner (covered wagon), #844, 11" **35.00**
TV lamp, rooster, orange, #519, 13"..**75.00**
TV lamp, shell, pearl tone, #808, 13"..**40.00**
TV lamp, shell (Malibu), pearl tone, 10½"....................................**25.00**
TV lamp, swan planter, wht porc, #828, 12½"...............................**50.00**
TV lamp, Toro (bull), ft on mound, #859, 11½".............................**50.00**
TV lamp, Toro (bull) charging, walnut, #894, 11½".......................**40.00**
Vase, flamingos (2), #529, 5"...**40.00**
Vase, horse's head top, str-sided body, aqua, #225, 12"................**20.00**
Vase, swan, wht, #221, 12"...**20.00**

Magazines

Magazines are collected for their cover prints and for the information pertaining to defunct companies and their products that can be gleaned from the old advertisements. In the listings that follow, items are assumed to be in very good condition unless noted otherwise. See also Movie Memorabilia; Parrish, Maxfield.

Key:
M — mint condition, in original wrapper
EX — excellent condition, spine intact, edges of pages clean and straight
VG — very good condition, the average as-found condition

Time, 1945, May 21, Emperor Hirohito cover, NM, $22.00.

Air Stories, 1928, August, G..**25.00**
Atlantic Monthly, 1921, June, Maxfield Parrish, EX **40.00**
Baseball Digest, 1951, April, Joe DiMaggio cover, VG..................**30.00**
Behind the Scene, 1955, July, Marilyn Monroe cover, VG **25.00**
Boy's Life, 1937, July, HC Christy cover, VG................................**10.00**
Caberet Quarterly, 1967, #14, VG..**16.00**
Collier's, 1945, June, Truman cover, VG **6.00**
Collier's, 1955, November, Bette Davis cover, EX **20.00**
Cosmopolitan, 1952, November, Queen Elizabeth II cover, EX **20.00**
Country Song Roundup, 1957, August, Elvis cover, VG **15.00**
Crawdaddy, 1979, #14, Jimi Hendrix, EX......................................**78.00**
Daredevil Aces, 1942, November, NM..**35.00**
Esquire, 1941, November, Vargas & Petty art, EX **20.00**
Evergreen, 1969, June, Bobby Kennedy cover, EX **20.00**
Fortune, 1948, railroad cover, EX **30.00**
Gentleman's Companion, 1980, May, VG......................................**10.00**
Holiday, 1946, March, VG **20.00**
Ladies' Home Journal, 1930, October, Maxfield Parrish's 'Arizona,' EX.**50.00**
Ladies' World, 1913, June, Gibson girl, EX **25.00**
Life, 1936, December 14, Archbishop Canterbury, EX **42.00**
Life, 1937, January 4, FD Roosevelt, EX.......................................**30.00**
Life, 1938, October 10, Carole Lombard cover, VG **20.00**

Life, 1939, May 1, Joe DiMaggio, Petty art, EX............................75.00
Life, 1940, September 2, Dionne Quintuplets, EX.......................30.00
Life, 1942, March 30, Shirley Temple Grows Up, EX...................27.00
Life, 1947, November 17, Howard Hughes, EX.............................15.00
Life, 1950, June 12, Hopalong Cassidy cover, EX 50.00
Life, 1953, July 20, Senator Kennedy cover, EX...........................12.00
Life, 1955, January 10, Greta Garbo, EX 20.00
Life, 1964, August 28, Beatles, EX...40.00
Life, 1969, December 12, Apollo 12 article, VG............................10.00
Life, 1971, July 23, Clint Eastwood cover, VG.............................12.00
Life, 1971, March 19, Ali/Frazier, EX 35.00
Life, 1972, February 25, Liz Taylor at 40, EX...............................25.00
Look, 1927, December, Shirley Temple/Santa cover, EX..............35.00
Look, 1939, July 18, Vivian Leigh, EX...28.00
Look, 1963, January 9, Beatles article, EX....................................28.00
Look, 1966, December 13, John Lennon cover, VG+....................28.00
Look, 1971, April 6, Mickey Mouse cover, VG.............................10.00
Look, 1972, May, Vol 1 #5, Jean Harlow article, EX....................40.00
Modern Photography, 1954, Marilyn Monroe, EX 60.00
Modern Priscilla, 1925, July, flapper girl, VG..............................15.00
Musical Digest, 1928, March, Icart cover, VG..............................60.00
National Geographic, 1915-16, ea..15.00
National Geographic, 1917-24, ea..9.00
National Geographic, 1925-29, ea..8.00
National Geographic, 1930-45, ea..7.00
National Geographic, 1946-55, ea..6.00
National Geographic, 1956-57, ea..5.50
National Geographic, 1968-89, ea..4.50
National Geographic, 1990-present, ea 2.00
Needlecraft, 1924, October, Quaker ad, VG.................................18.00
New Movie, 1934, April, Joan Crawford cover, EX 30.00
Newsweek, 1941, September 8, Hitler cover, VG 10.00
Newsweek, 1957, July 1, Stan Musial cover, EX 15.00
Playboy, 1955, February, Jayne Mansfield, EX............................150.00
Playboy, 1964, January, Marilyn Monroe tribute, EX 50.00
Playboy, 1967, March, Fran Gerard/Sharon Tate, Vargas art, EX ..20.00
Playboy, 1974, April, Jane Fonda, EX..15.00
Popular Photography, 1937, August, swimsuit cover, VG.............15.00
Rave, 1969, September, Paul McCartney article, VG.....................12.00
Rolling Stone, 1967, #1, John Lennon cover, VG 60.00
Rolling Stone, 1969, #37, Elvis Presley, EX.................................20.00
Saturday Evening Post, 1946, March 2, Rockwell cover, EX 10.00
Saturday Evening Post, 1966, July 30, Bob Dylan, EX..................12.00
Sports Illustrated, 1955, April 11, Willie Mays, EX....................200.00
Sports Illustrated, 1956, June 18, Mickey Mantle, EX..................80.00
Sports Illustrated, 1961, October 2, Roger Maris, EX 25.00
Sports Illustrated, 1964, Koufax cover, EX 32.00
Sports Illustrated, 1980, February 4, Christie Brinkley cover, EX..40.00
Time, 1935, April 15, Dizzy Dean, EX..65.00
Time, 1948, May 17, Eddie Arcaro cover, VG+ 25.00
True Confessions, 1938, February, Carole Lombard, Zoe Mozart art, EX ..35.00
True Story, 1935, April, Zoe Mozart art cover, EX 30.00
True Story, 1938, September, Deanna Durbin cover, VG 16.00
True Story, 1951, November, Marilyn, EX.....................................35.00
TV Guide, 1954, June 25, Howdy Doody & Buffalo Bob, NM ...450.00
TV Guide, 1961, January 28, Ronnie Howard & Andy Griffith, EX...175.00
TV Guide, 1956, June 11, cast of Gilligan's Island, EX 125.00
Vogue, 1940, January, swimsuit cover, EX....................................14.00
Yachtsman's Magazine, 1942, May, EX 20.00

Majolica

Majolica is a type of heavy earthenware, design molded and deco-

rated in vivid colors with either a lead or tin type of glaze. It reached its height of popularity in the Victorian era; examples from this period are found in only the lead glazes. Nearly every potter of note, both here and abroad, produced large majolica jardinieres, umbrella stands, pitchers with animal themes, leaf shapes, vegetable forms, and nearly any other design from nature that came to mind. Not all, however, marked their ware. Among those who sometimes did were Minton, Wedgwood, Holdcroft, and George Jones in England; Griffin, Smith, and Hill (Etruscan) in Phoenixville, Pennsylvania; and Chesapeake Pottery (Avalon and Clifton) in Baltimore.

Color and condition are both very important worth-assessing factors. Pieces with cobalt, lavender, and turquoise glazes command the highest prices. For further information we recommend *The Collector's Encyclopedia of Majolica* by Mariann Katz-Marks (see Directory, Pennsylvania). Unless another condition is given, the values that follow are for pieces in mint condition. Our advisor for this category is Hardy Hudson; he is listed in the Directory under Florida.

Ashtray, sailor bulldog figural..150.00
Basket, Pond Lily, Holdcroft, 5¾".......................................500.00
Basket, Strawberry, 4-part, Geo Jones 1,800.00
Bowl, salad; Shell & Seaweed, Etruscan.............................450.00
Bowl, sauce; yel wicker, Etruscan, 5".................................100.00
Bowl, Shell, cobalt, 10"..350.00
Butter dish, Cow, Etruscan...750.00
Butter pat, Begonia Leaf, Etruscan.....................................125.00
Butter pat, fan shape w/yel ground 125.00
Butter pat, Pansy, mc, Etruscan...175.00
Butter pat, Pond Lily, Etruscan...100.00
Cake stand, Napkin on Basketweave, cobalt accents 300.00
Cake stand, Pond Lily, ftd, 9¼"...350.00
Candle holder, girl figural, Continental, 6½"........................90.00
Celery vase, Aster, 7¼" 250.00
Centerpiece, shell supported by Black lady, Continental, 13" .1,600.00
Centerpiece, 2 putti support bowl, Geo Jones, 15x11"............3,200.00
Cheese keeper, floral, ribbon & bow, Albino, Victoria Pottery, 8" 300.00
Cheese keeper, Picket Fence, turq, Geo Jones, 7" 3,200.00
Cheese keeper, putti w/instruments in swags, Holdcroft, 9"...........1,500.00

Cheese keeper, Daisy and Picket Fence on turquoise, George Jones, 10", $8,000.00. (Photo courtesy Michael Strawser)

Comport, bird & prunus, low, 9" dia 275.00
Comport, fish w/shell base, 10"..400.00
Comport, maple leaves on pk, lav int, Etruscan, 8" 350.00
Comport, Shell & Seaweed, Etruscan 950.00
Creamer, goat figural, 3¼'..275.00
Creamer, Overlapping Shells 200.00
Creamer, Wild Rose w/Butterfly, 3½"..................................150.00
Creamer & sugar bowl, Strawberry, Geo Jones.....................600.00

Decanter, parrot figural, St Clement, 12½"...............175.00
Figurine, lady vintager w/basket, Minton, EX...............1,000.00
Figurine, rooster, signed Louise Carrier Belleuse, Minton, 21".3,800.00
Flower frog, hedgehog, mottled, Wedgwood, 6x9½"...............650.00
Game dish, animals at sides, quail w/empty nest finial, G Jones, 13"...3,000.00
Game dish, game on lid, basket base w/oak leaves & acorns, Minton, 14"...4,500.00
Game dish, Lobster, Minton, ca 1870...............15,000.00
Game dish, lovebirds, Wedgwood, 11½"...............2,000.00
Garden seat, Bird & Fan, Argenta, Wedgwood, 17"...............4,000.00
Garden seat, Passion Flower on cobalt, Minton...............8,000.00
Humidor, Black man w/turban figural, EX color, 7½"...............250.00
Humidor, man w/top hat figural, 9¼"...............250.00
Jardiniere, tritons/mermaids/putti/dolphins on turq, G Jones, 23"...............6,250.00
Match striker, Black man artist...............550.00
Match striker, Black man seated w/bundle of cigars...............325.00
Match striker, Black man w/ear of corn sitting on bridge...............350.00
Match striker, bulldog w/pk hat...............300.00
Match striker, cowboy w/rifle, 10"...............250.00
Pickle dish, Ribbon & Bow, cobalt, Fielding...............250.00
Pitcher, Acanthus Leaves & Wheat, pk w/yel rope, Geo Jones, 7¼"...6,000.00
Pitcher, Barrel & Blackberry, Geo Jones, 5½"...............500.00
Pitcher, Bird & Fan, Argenta, Wedgwood, 5½"...............400.00
Pitcher, cucumber figural, 9¼"...............350.00
Pitcher, Dogwood, cobalt, Holdcroft, 5½", EX...............300.00
Pitcher, duck figural, Onnaing, 9"...............350.00
Pitcher, Fan & Scroll, yel ground, 7"...............300.00
Pitcher, Floral & Basket, yel w/ribbon & bow, 7"...............300.00
Pitcher, Floral & Fan, EX color, 7"...............50.00
Pitcher, frog w/pipe figural, Fives-Lille, 10"...............500.00
Pitcher, Hummingbird, Fielding, 7½"...............350.00
Pitcher, Legionnaire figural, Frie Onnaing, 11"...............525.00
Pitcher, owl figural, 7"...............400.00
Pitcher, pig figural, Fr, 8½"...............500.00
Pitcher, Pond Lily, Holdcroft, 4½"...............175.00
Pitcher, Primrose, cobalt, 6½"...............350.00
Pitcher, pug dog figural, 8½"...............350.00
Pitcher, Ribbon & Bow Leaf, Fielding, 5"...............225.00
Pitcher, Stork in Marsh, cobalt, 9½"...............1,000.00
Pitcher, Stork w/Eel, cobalt, 10½"...............750.00
Pitcher, syrup; Coral, Etruscan...............500.00
Pitcher, syrup; Leaf & Fern, pewter top, 5"...............375.00
Pitcher, syrup; Picket Fence & Floral, pewter top, 4"...............200.00
Pitcher, syrup; Sunflower, cobalt, Etruscan...............600.00
Pitcher, syrup; Water Lily, turq, 6½"...............250.00
Pitcher, Wild Rose w/Butterfly, cobalt rim, 7½", EX...............325.00
Plaque, creatures on heavy grass, Palissy, 10½"...............800.00
Plate, bird & branch, Eureka, 8¼"...............250.00
Plate, Bird in Flight, Holdcroft...............300.00
Plate, Cauliflower, Etruscan, 8"...............250.00
Plate, Cauliflower, Etruscan, 9"...............275.00
Plate, Crane in Cattails, rtcl border, Wedgwood, 9"...............950.00
Plate, Overlapping Leaf & Fern, Geo Jones, 8¼"...............850.00
Plate, oyster; malachite, Minton...............1,750.00
Plate, oyster; turq wells & center, 5 shell ft, 10"...............450.00
Plate, Pineapple, 9"...............300.00
Plate, Shell & Seaweed, Wedgwood, 8¾"...............400.00
Plate, Strawberry & Apple on cobalt, Etruscan, 9"...............375.00
Plate, Strawberry & Apple on wht, Etruscan, 9"...............275.00
Platter, Asparagus, French, 17"...............250.00
Platter, Bird & Fan w/Bamboo, 13"...............275.00
Platter, Classical Urn & Sunflower, Samuel Lear, 14"...............450.00
Platter, Corn, 13½"...............375.00
Platter, Dog & Stag, 11"...............275.00
Platter, Fan & Scroll w/pebble ground, Fielding, 13"...............350.00

Platter, Ocean, turq, Wedgwood, 12½"...............900.00
Platter, salmon/vegetation, Argenta, Wedgwood, 1877, 25"...1,850.00
Platter, turtle, frog, crawfish, snake & shells, Palissy, 16"...1,250.00
Salt cellar, boy holds basket, Minton, 8"...............750.00
Sardine box, fish on lid, Geo Jones, 3-pc oval basket...............2,800.00
Sardine box, Pelican, Geo Jones...............3,500.00
Sardine box, Pineapple, fish on lid, fish hdl...............600.00
Sardine box, pointed leaves, pk, Geo Jones...............1,800.00
Sardine box, Swan & Water Lily on pk, Etruscan, EX...............800.00
Shakers, Coral, Etruscan, pr...............500.00
Spittoon, floral, 6"...............250.00
Spittoon, Shell & Seaweed, Etruscan...............900.00
Spoon warmer, conch shell, turq, Geo Jones, 5"...............1,500.00
Spoon warmer, 2 putti atop bbl, Wedgwood...............2,250.00
Sugar bowl, Cauliflower, Etruscan...............375.00
Sugar bowl, Shell & Waves, fish hdls...............325.00
Teapot, Bird & Iris, cobalt, Etruscan...............350.00
Teapot, Cherub rowing boat, cobalt, Holdcroft, rare, 5½"...6,000.00
Teapot, Chinaman, figural, mottled, 6"...............800.00
Teapot, drum shape w/snails on lid & sides, twig hdl...............500.00
Teapot, Heron in Cattails, EX color...............400.00
Teapot, Leaf, turq, Wardle...............350.00
Teapot, Shell & Coral on pebble ground, fish hdl, 6"...............450.00
Teapot, Shell & Seaweed, str spout, Etruscan...............750.00
Tray, Basketweave & Strawberry, 10"...............350.00
Tray, bread; Begonia & Wicker, Etruscan...............300.00
Tray, grapes on turq, 3 twig hdls, Wedgwood, 10"...............600.00
Tray, leaves & fern, 12"...............350.00
Urn, laurel swags, rams handles, Wedgwood...............1,500.00
Vase, Art Nouveau lady & floral, 8½"...............200.00
Vase, Black man w/basket of fruit figural, Continental, 11½"...300.00
Vase, stork figural, 11½"...............250.00
Wall pocket, Oak Leaf & Acorn on Basket, Etruscan, rare...............900.00

Malachite Glass

Malachite is a type of art glass that exhibits strata-like layerings in shades of green, similar to the mineral in its natural form. Some examples have an acid-etched mark of Moser/Carlsbad, usually on the base. However, it should be noted that in the past fifteen years there have been reproductions from Czechoslovakia with a paper label.

Box, vining floral, 4x5½"...............55.00
Dish, turtle, shell is lid, Ingrid series by Riedel, 8½" L...............145.00

Perfume bottle, cherries mold, bird on cherry branch stopper with original green dauber, unsigned Ingrid, 4½", $660.00.
(Photo courtesy Monsen & Baer)

Powder jar, entwined nudes, Czech, 2½x3⅞", NM...............400.00
Vase, nudes & grapes, ftd, att Moser, ca 1940, 9½"...............1,300.00

Mantel Lustres

Mantel lustres are decorative vases or candle holders made from all types of glass, often highly decorated and usually hung with one or more rows of prisms. In the listings that follow, values are given for a pair.

Brass, cast base w/squirrels in tree, wht marble base, cut prisms, 14"...**100.00**
Cranberry glass, 6 5" prisms, unmk Fenton, 1950s, 10x6½" **575.00**
Cut overlay, ruby cut to clear, 5" prisms, Egermann, 10" **875.00**
Cut overlay, ruby cut to clear, 5 wide 10" prisms, 15" **1,700.00**
Cut overlay, wht to gr w/gilt, 10 lg cut prisms, 10", EX **800.00**
Gr glass w/HP gold & silver decor, rpl prisms, Fr, 1880s, 10" **575.00**
Pk opaque, pontil mk, 8 7½" prisms, 1880s, 14x7"...................**1,350.00**
Pk opaque w/gold, blown, 5" prisms, 1880s, 9½" **795.00**
Ruby glass w/dbl row of prisms, HP floral w/gold, 14½" **1,450.00**
Ruby glass w/floral & gold, unmk Moser style, prisms, 14" **2,200.00**
Ruby glass w/gold trim, 7" prisms, 10½" **650.00**

Maps and Atlases

Maps are highly collectible, not only for historical value but also for their sometimes elaborate artwork, legendary information, or data that since they were printed has been proven erroneous. There are many types of maps including geographical, military, celestial, road, and railroad. Nineteenth-century maps, particularly of U.S. areas, are increasing in popularity and price. Rarity, area depicted (i.e. Texas is more sought after than North Dakota), and condition are major price factors. World globes as a form of round maps are increasingly sought after. Our advisor for this category is Murray Hudson; he is listed in the Directory under Tennessee.

Key: hc — hand colored

Atlases

Account of European Settlements in Am, Burke, 1758, 2 volumes ..**650.00**
Beers...Worcester County MA, 1870, 99-pg, 13x16", EX **350.00**
Grand Universal..., Dufour, 40 dbl pgs, 1868, leather binding, EX...........**725.00**
Johnson's Family, Johnson & Browning, 1862, 15x18", 92 maps, VG+..**1,550.00**
Mexico/US border, Bartle, WA, 1890, 19 dbl-pg maps, elephant folio **450.00**
Mitchell's Universal, Cowperthwait, 1850, 129 maps, 17½x4", EX.....**3,500.00**
N America/Canada/Mexico, Shell, 90+ maps, notebook style, 1960, 19x14"....**35.00**
Official Topographical...MA, Walling/Gray, 1871, 118-pg, 13x18"..**625.00**
Peoria IL City & County, hc, Ogle, 1896, 148-pg+30 supplements, oversz ..**425.00**
Toutes les Parties...Globe Terrestre, Bonne, Geneva, 1780, 49 maps, EX..**2,100.00**

Maps

Asia, hand tinted, Germany, 1793, 23x20", +mat & fr **200.00**
Auvergne, mc, Guillaume/Blaeu, Amsterdam, 1640, 17¾x21", VG.**600.00**
Calais Ville Fort de Picardie, Nicolas, Paris, 1693, 7¾x10¾", EX.....**250.00**
Cart Maritima del Reyno de Tierra..., Lopez, Spain, 1785, 14x15"....**300.00**
Carte de Deux Continents, Buffon, Paris, 1760, 9¼x11¾" **125.00**
Carte General Des Etats-Unis, Paris, 13 states shown, 1806, 15x19" ...**400.00**
Carte Generale...Polaires Boreales, Brue, outline color, 1821, 14x20".**250.00**
Carte...Nordquest...Amerique...1792, Vancouver, 1800, 25x20".**500.00**
City of Fall River, MA, CH Bogt/OH Bailey/JC Hazen, 1877, 29x46"..**430.00**
Coast of New England, Nova Scotia..., Jefferys, London, 1746, 14x19".**600.00**
CT, Mitchell, Thomas, Cowperthwait, Phila, 1850, 10¾x13⅜", VG **85.00**
District of Columbia, Tanner, Melish, Phila, 1822, 6½x4", G **175.00**
Engagement of Wht Plains...1776, Martin/Smith, 1808, 7¾x8½" ...**900.00**
Hydrographisk Kaart Ober Europa..., Tuxen/Copenhage, 1833, 19x22" ..**250.00**

IL, Sinclair, 5-panel display, ca 1937, folded: 9x4"........................**15.00**
IN & OH, Bradford, Ticknor, Wiley & Long Boston/NY/1835, 1¾x10", G....**120.00**
Johnson's Georgetown & City of WA, hc, Ward, 1863, 12x15" .**150.00**
Johnson's United States, Johnson, NY, 1864, 15¾x22", EX........**275.00**
Mappe Monde Par Le Sr R De Vaugondy, Paris, 1781, frontispc.**175.00**
N America, mc, Jefferys, Ballard, London, 1758, 7¼x9", G........**225.00**
N L'Afrique, Desbruslins, Buffier, Paris, 1744, 5½x7", G.............**125.00**
NE, Cram, Chicago, PPC Litho, vest pocket series, ca 1900, 17x24", VG ...**200.00**
New & Correct Map of World..., Senex, London, 1720, 6x11½" **600.00**
Parte de Chile, Lopez, Spain, copper eng, 1777, 15x11" **275.00**
Plan de la Ville de Quebec, copper eng, 1750, 8¼x13½"............**425.00**
Rand McNally Railway Guide, FPC Litho, Chicago, ca 1901, 30¼x42", G...**375.00**
Ruiner...Fastning I Tenessee..., uncolored, Danish, 10½x7¼" **70.00**
TX, Mitchell, Phila, 1850, c 1846, browned/frayed, 10½x8" **125.00**
Typus Orbis Terrarum, J Hondius/Fetherstone, London/1625, 5¼x7¾"....**900.00**
United States, Roswell, Lippincott, Phila, 1861, 9¾x12", VG ...**185.00**
Virginiae Item et Floridae, Hondius, Amsterdam, 1600s, 13¼x19"...**2,800.00**
Virginiae...Et Floridae..., Jansson, Amsterdam, 1639, 15x19¾" ..**2,000.00**
World at One View, color, Ensign/Bridgman/Fanning, 1847, 23x31"...**375.00**
Ye French Louisiana, H Moll, hc, Gulf Coast/Carolinas/TX, 9x13" **575.00**

Marblehead

What began as therapy for patients in a sanitarium in Marblehead, Massachusetts, has become recognized as an important part of the Arts and Crafts movement in America. Results of the early experiments under the guidance of Arthur E. Baggs in 1904 met with such success that by 1908 the pottery had been converted to a solely commercial venture. Simple vase shapes were sometimes incised with stylized animal and floral motifs or sailing ships. Some were decorated in low relief; many were plain. Simple matt glazes in soft yellow, gray, wisteria, rose, tobacco brown, and their most popular, Marblehead blue, were used alone or in combination. The Marblehead logo is distinctive — a ship with full sail and the letters 'M' and 'P.' The pottery closed in 1936.

Unless noted otherwise, all items listed below are marked and in the matt glaze.

**Vase, stylized trees in black on blue, impressed mark, 6",
$5,000.00.** (Photo courtesy Treadway Gallery, Inc.)

Bookends, ship w/full sail, 6-color, triangular sides, 6x6", NM ...**3,250.00**
Bowl, lav, low, incurvate rim, 6" **230.00**
Bowl, lt rose, flaring sides, deep, 8½" **600.00**
Bowl vase, brn, petticoat shape, 5½" **500.00**
Bowl vase, brn, spherical, 5" dia **450.00**
Bowl vase, gr, 5" dia...**375.00**
Bowl vase, lt gray, 3½" dia **160.00**
Bowl vase, tan, angled body, 6½" dia **400.00**
Candlestick, gold/brn/yel mottle, saucer base, loop hdl, 4" **350.00**
Chamber stick, olive gr, tall/slim w/saucer base & hdl, 7½"........**800.00**
Tile, Arts & Crafts lg tree flanked by slender trunks, 2-color, 6", fr **5,500.00**

Vase, aqua mottled sections w/cobalt veining, ship logo, 8¾x4", NM.1,320.00
Vase, bl, closed form, mk, 7" W 800.00
Vase, blk w/bl accents, chicory bl at mouth, ovoid, ship logo, 5¼"..440.00
Vase, brn, incurvate cylinder, 3½" 290.00
Vase, brn, tapered cylinder, 5" 350.00
Vase, dk bl, swollen cylinder, 3½" 210.00
Vase, dk gr, widens toward base, 6x5"....................................420.00
Vase, flowers (cvd), dk gr on lt gr, invt rim, cylindrical, 9⅞"...17,250.00
Vase, flowers on leafy tree froms, yel/bl/gr/bl-gray, bulbous, 3½" ...2,400.00
Vase, flying geese & band, bl on dove gray, ships logo, 3½" 2,100.00
Vase, geometrics, sage gr/dk bl/blk speckles, ship logo, 4½", NM...1,045.00
Vase, gr, cylindrical, 3½"..200.00
Vase, gr, incurvate cylinder, 4½" 500.00
Vase, gr mottle on red clay, 11⅝"..1,600.00
Vase, gr w/dk specks, ovoid, 5½"...375.00
Vase, gray, cylinder w/slightly incurvate rim, 3½" 300.00
Vase, gray, swollen shoulder, squat, 5½" W 400.00
Vase, lav, waisted, 4¾"..350.00
Vase, lav-bl, stick neck, faint mk, paper label, 5½" 170.00
Vase, lt purple, widens toward base, 8½"................................700.00
Vase, mauve, tapered cylinder, 3½".......................................240.00
Vase, mocha w/lav hue & brn speckles, bulbous, 4½x4½"..........140.00
Vase, mustard mottle on tan matt, oval paper label, 3¼"............350.00
Vase, neck band, dk on med bl, Baggs, squat pear form, 4"......3,250.00
Vase, pk, ovoid, 5"..425.00
Vase, purple, flared lip, bulbous, 5½" 550.00
Vase, repeating flowers, bl on speckled gray, H Tutt, 5¼"........3,450.00
Vase, sea horses & seaweed, 4-color, Hanna Tutt, cylindrical, 7"...10,000.00
Vase, stems/leaves cross at top & form 4 panels, gray/gr, Tutt, 8x7"..7,500.00
Vase, trees repeat 8X, blk on med bl, tapered, 3½" 5,000.00
Vase, trees w/leaves & fruit on bl, cylindrical, 7" 3,250.00
Vase, trefoils crown arched panels, brn on gr, 5½" 5,000.00
Vase, tulip repeats, dk brn on gr mottle, 5x7"..........................5,500.00
Vase, upright plants, charcoal on bl/gr, sgn, EX art/contrast, 7"....6,000.00
Vase, yel, swollen cylinder, 5½"..700.00
Vase, 4 floral devices w/vertical trails, bls on ivory, Tutt, 5½" 800.00

Marbles

Marbles have been popular with children since the mid-1800s. They've been made in many types from a variety of materials. Among some of the first glass items to be produced, the earliest marbles were made from a solid glass rod broken into sections of the proper length which were placed in a tray of sand and charcoal and returned to the fire. As they were reheated, the trays were constantly agitated until the marbles were completely round. Other marbles were made of china, pottery, steel, and natural stones. Below is a listing of the various types, along with a brief description of each.

Agates: stone marbles of many different colors — bands of color alternating with white usually encircle the marble; most are translucent.

Ballot Box: handmade (with pontils), opaque white or black, used in lodge elections.

Bloodstone: green chalcedony with red spots, a type of quartz.

China: with or without glaze, in a variety of hand-painted designs — parallel bands or bull's-eye designs most common.

Clambroth: opaque glass with outer evenly spaced swirls of one or alternating colors.

Clay: one of the most common older types; some are painted while others are not.

Comic Strip: a series of twelve machine-made marbles with faces of comic strip characters, Peltier Glass Factory, Illinois.

Crockery: sometimes referred to as Benningtons; most are either blue or brown, although some are speckled. The clay is shaped into a sphere, then coated with glaze and fired.

End of the Day: single-pontil glass marbles — the colored part often appears as a multicolored blob or mushroom cloud.

Goldstone: clear glass completely filled with copper flakes that have turned gold-colored from the heat of the manufacturing process.

Indian Swirls: usually black glass with a colored swirl appearing on the outside next to the surface, often irregular.

Latticinio Core Swirls: double-pontil marble with an inner area with net-like effects of swirls coming up around the center.

Lutz Type: glass with colored or clear bands alternating with bands which contain copper flecks.

Micas: clear or colored glass with mica flecks which reflect as silver dots when marble is turned. Red is rare.

Onionskin: spiral type which are solidly colored instead of having individual ribbons or threads, multicolored.

Peppermint Swirls: made of white opaque glass with alternating blue and red outer swirls.

Ribbon Core Swirls: double-pontil marble — center shaped like a ribbon with swirls that come up around the middle.

Rose Quartz: stone marble, usually pink in color, often with fractures inside and on outer surface.

Solid Core Swirls: double-pontil marble — middle is solid with swirls coming up around the core.

Steelies: hollow steel spheres marked with a cross where the steel was bent together to form the ball.

Sulfides: generally made of clear glass with figures inside. Rarer types have colored figures or colored glass.

Tiger Eye: stone marble of golden quartz with inclusions of asbestos, dark brown with gold highlights.

Vaseline: machine-made of yellowish-green glass with small bubbles.

Prices listed below are for marbles in near-mint condition unless noted otherwise. When size is not indicated, assume them to be of average size, ½" to 1". Polished marbles have greatly reduced values. (We do not list tinted marbles because there is no way of knowing how much color the tinting has, and intensity of color is an important worth-assessing factor.)

For a more thorough study of the subject, we recommend *Antique and Collectible Marbles, 3rd Edition*; *Machine-Made and Contemporary Marbles, 2nd Edition*; and *Big Book of Marbles, Second Edition*; all by Everett Grist (published by Collector Books); you will find his address in the Directory under Tennessee. Our advisors for this category are Robert and Stan Block; they are listed in the Directory under Connecticut.

Agate, contemporary, carnelian, 1¾" 20.00
Akro Agate, bl slag...1.00
Akro Agate, corkscrew...2.00
Akro Agate, egg yoke/oxblood swirls on custard, ⅝"+, NM........150.00
Akro Agate, Popeye corkscrew 25.00
Akro Agate, Popeye corkscrew, red/wht/bl (rare), ⅝" 125.00
Akro Agate, sparkler 45.00
Banded Opaque, gr & wht, 2" 1,200.00
Banded Opaque, gr w/red bands, wht & bl streaks, 1¾", EX.......160.00
Banded Opaque, red & wht, 1¾"..1,200.00
Banded Opaque, red & wht, ¾"...125.00
Banded Transparent Swirl, bl, ¾"..45.00
Banded Transparent Swirl, lt gr, 1¾"..300.00
Bennington, bl, 1¾" 15.00
Bennington, bl, ¾" 1.00
Bennington, brn, 1¾"...15.00
Bennington, fancy, 1¾"..40.00
Bennington, fancy, ¾"..2.00
China, decorated, glazed, apple, 1¾"..750.00
China, decorated, glazed, rose, 1¾"..750.00
China, decorated, glazed, wht w/geometrics, 1¾".............................75.00
China, decorated, unglazed, geometrics & flowers, ¾"..................125.00

Christensen Agate, Bloodie..80.00
Christensen Agate, clear Cobra, ⅝", NM+........................145.00
Christensen Agate, flame..400.00
Christensen Agate, Guinea..500.00
Christensen Agate, slag..25.00
Christensen Agate, swirl..25.00
Clambroth, opaque, bl & wht, 1¾"...............................1,500.00
Clambroth, opaque, bl & wht, ¾"...................................200.00
Clambroth, pk (red)/bl/gr swirls, ⅝", EX.........................130.00
Comic, Andy Gump..80.00
Comic, Betty Boop..250.00
Comic, Cotes Bakery, advertising....................................900.00
Comic, Kayo, rare..450.00
Comic, Little Orphan Annie...150.00
Comic, Moon Mullins...300.00
Comic, set of 12..1,500.00
Comic, Skeezix..80.00
End of Day, bl & wht, 1¾"...450.00
Goldstone, ¾'...12.50
Indian Swirl, 1¾"..2,500.00
Indian Swirl Lutz-type, gold flakes, ¾"..........................1,200.00

**Joseph swirl, ⅝",
$150.00 each.** (Photo
courtesy Everett Grist)

Line Crockery, clay, 1¾"...20.00
Lutz type, clear/bl/gold swirls, 1⁵⁄₃₂"..............................300.00
MF Christensen, bl opaque...250.00
MF Christensen, bl slag...5.00
Mica, bl, ¾"...30.00
Mica, gr, 1¾"...500.00
Millefiori flowers, tight pattern, pontil mk, 1½", EX........575.00
Onionskin, w/mica, 1¾"...1,200.00
Onionskin, w/mica, ¾"...110.00
Onionskin, 16-lobe, unusual, 1¾"................................3,000.00
Onionskin, 2 wht panels w/bl streaks & 2 yel w/red streaks, 2¼"...1,125.00
Onionskin, ¾"..80.00
Opaque Swirl, gr, ¾"..40.00
Opaque Swirl, red/yel/bl/wht, pontil mk, 2⅜", EX............995.00
Opaque Swirl Lutz-type, bl/yel/gr, ¾".............................325.00
Peltier Glass, Golden Rebel..500.00
Peltier Glass, National line...25.00
Peltier Glass, NLR Revel, much aventurine, ¹¹⁄₁₆", M.......200.00
Peltier Glass, Peerless Patch..5.00
Peltier Glass, slag...15.00
Peltier Glass, Superman..150.00
Peppermint Swirl, opaque, red/red/wht/bl, 1¾"...........2,000.00
Peppermint Swirl, opaque, red/wht/bl, ¾".....................125.00
Pottery, 1¾"...20.00
Ribbon Core Lutz-type, red, 1¾".................................1,500.00
Solid Opaque, gr, 1¾"...300.00
Solid Opaque, ¾"...40.00
Sulfide, angel, full body, w/halo, little detail, 1¾"...........750.00
Sulfide, angel face w/wings, 1¾"..................................1,200.00
Sulfide, baboon playing bass fiddle, 2⅛"......................1,200.00
Sulfide, baby in basket (Moses in Bullrushes), 1¾".........800.00

Sulfide, bear cub on all 4s, detailed, 1¼".........................100.00
Sulfide, billy goat, 1½"...100.00
Sulfide, bird, 2"..100.00
Sulfide, boar, 1⅞"...165.00
Sulfide, boy in short pants in crawling-like position, 1¾"....600.00
Sulfide, boy in top hat & dress clothes, gr glass, 1¾"....4,000.00
Sulfide, buffalo, little detail, 1¾".....................................300.00
Sulfide, camel, 1-hump, on grassy mound, 1½"...............200.00
Sulfide, child (girl) w/hammer, EX detail, 1¾".................600.00
Sulfide, child sitting, 1¾"...600.00
Sulfide, circus bear, 2"..140.00
Sulfide, coin, face ea side, 1¾"......................................1,500.00
Sulfide, crane w/fish, 1¾"...250.00
Sulfide, crucifix, 1¾", M..600.00
Sulfide, deer, 1¼"...175.00
Sulfide, dog howling, 1⅜"...140.00
Sulfide, dog on grass mound, HP/3-color, pontil, 1¼"...3,500.00
Sulfide, dog w/bird in mouth, 1¾"...................................400.00
Sulfide, dove, 1⅝"...165.00
Sulfide, doves (facing pr), EX details, gr glass, 1¾".......5,000.00
Sulfide, eagle w/closed wings, 1⅞"...................................200.00
Sulfide, elephant, head erect, 'bang' tail, 1¾".................300.00
Sulfide, elephant standing, sea gr glass, 1¾"...................400.00
Sulfide, elephant w/long trunk, 1¼".................................140.00
Sulfide, fish, 1¾"..175.00
Sulfide, fox, 1½", EX..130.00
Sulfide, George Washington, bust, 2⅜"........................2,000.00
Sulfide, gnome, 1½", EX..615.00
Sulfide, hen, 1⅛"..150.00
Sulfide, horse rearing, 1⅞"..175.00
Sulfide, horse standing, 2", EX..130.00
Sulfide, lamb, 1¾"..125.00
Sulfide, lion, standing male, 1½".....................................125.00
Sulfide, Little Boy Blue, 1¾", M......................................450.00
Sulfide, monkey seated on drum, 1⅜"..............................200.00
Sulfide, Nipper dog, 1¾", EX...200.00
Sulfide, numeral 1, 1¾"...400.00
Sulfide, owl, wings spread, detailed feathers, 1¾"...........350.00
Sulfide, owl w/closed wings, 1¾".....................................150.00
Sulfide, papoose, 1¾"...300.00
Sulfide, parrot, 1½", EX...100.00
Sulfide, peacock, tricolor in clear glass, 1¾"................8,000.00
Sulfide, pony, trotting through grassy field, EX detail, 1¾"....200.00
Sulfide, poodle on hind legs, 1⅛".....................................100.00
Sulfide, rabbit, crouching, EX detail, 1¾".......................250.00
Sulfide, rabbit running, lg/offset/sm bubble, 1½", M-......110.00
Sulfide, razor-bk hog, 1½'...150.00
Sulfide, rooster, 1¾"...150.00
Sulfide, sheep grazing, 1¼"..150.00
Sulfide, squirrel standing, 1¾", EX...................................170.00
Sulfide, woman (Kate Greenaway), 1½"...........................300.00
Transitional, Leighton, 1"..1,000.00
Transitional, oxblood, ¾"...2,500.00

Marine Collectibles

Vintage tools used on sea-going vessels, lanterns, clocks, and memorabilia of all types are sought out by those who are interested in preserving the romantic genre that revolves around the life of the sea captains, their boats and their crews; ports of call; and the lure of far-away islands. See also Steamship Collectibles; Telescopes; Scrimshaw; Tools.

Ashtray, brass ship's wheel & compass on top..................35.00

Bag, canvas, EX knot-work carrying hdls, brass gromets, VG......**450.00**
Bell, brass, mk Esso, Liverpool, 1959, 7" **110.00**
Binnacle, Hand Philadelphia, w/compass, 43x25" (usually sm), EX...**1,400.00**
Binnacle, solid brass dome, w/orig compass & light source, 11"...**250.00**
Book, Book of Whales, Beddard, 1900, EX **30.00**
Box, chart; cherry & poplar, dvtl, old gr pnt, early 1800s, 7x34x8" **700.00**
Busk, whalebone, eng couple/eagle/flag/mermaid/etc, mc stain, 13".**3,335.00**
Chest, champhor wood w/brass hdls/mts, 15x33x14", EX...........**275.00**
Chest, sailor's; ropework beckets, cvd decor on top, EX...........**1,700.00**
Chronometer, Riggs & Bro London, 56-hr, brass gimball, EX..**1,300.00**
Chronometer/watch, Longines, 56-hr up/down indicator, 2-tier case...**775.00**
Clock, Seth Thomas, USLH Service, brass, 7¼", EX...............**1,000.00**
Clock, ship's striking; Seth Thomas, brass, VG...........................**300.00**
Compass, dry card; S Thaxter & Son Boston, brass, EX..............**300.00**
Desk, captain's; camphorwood, brass hardware/hdls, China Trade, G ..**450.00**
Dividers, anvil proportional, silver/steel, Germany, 7½", MIB......**80.00**
Figurehead, cockatoos & nest of oranges, cvd wood w/rpt, 55" .**3,500.00**
Figurehead, cvd female w/flowers, mc/gold decor, Germany, 19th C, 27"..**5,175.00**
Figurehead, female w/wings, cvd wood w/orig pnt traces, ca 1880, 48"...**6,500.00**
Fog horn, Powers Bros..., pnt wood, working, 12"+hdl **650.00**
Gun, flare; brass w/wooden grips, unmk, VG **100.00**
Gun, harpoon; CC Brand Norwich Conn, iron bomb type, 1850s, EX..**4,250.00**
Gyroscope, Gyro Sperry...London Mark V VI, brass, 56" on wood base.....**500.00**
Harpoon, dbl flute w/movable barbs, mk W Smith & Son Redditch, 21"..**475.00**
Harpoon, dbl swivel head, spear point, iron, 32", EX **275.00**
Harpoon, Temple type toggle w/reverse barb, 35½", EX..............**600.00**
Hydrometer/thermometer, G Atkins Fenchurch St London, 1807-14, +case ...**450.00**
Instrument, optical device, JH Steward Ltd London, 3", EX in case ..**80.00**
Knife, diver's; EX in orig brass sheath...**375.00**
Lamp, Sherwoods Ltd Trademk Sound, brass w/brass & wood swing hdl ..**100.00**
Lantern, anchor; copper/glass, Seahorse GB TM 35413-Anchor, 13x9½"..**315.00**
Lantern, Beaded Dbl Bull's Eye globe, pnt/pierced tin fr, 1850s, 12".**2,300.00**
Lantern, cabin; brass w/clear globe, Pat 1864, 9" **150.00**
Lantern, Davey & Co London, brass/beveled glass, complete, 17", pr ...**675.00**
Lantern, masthead; brass, red/gr/clear bulbous lenses, burner, 10"...........**175.00**
Lantern, masthead; Perco, brass w/red & bl lenses, 9", VG.........**120.00**
Lantern, wing lights, w/burners, red/bl lenses, port/starboard, pr.....**900.00**
Model, half-hull builder's model of work boat, 12 lifts+keel, 29"....**525.00**
Octant, ebony/brass/ivory, late 18th C, 18" swing arm, EX......**1,100.00**
Octant, O Filby Hamburg, ebony brass & ivory, 1906, EX..........**725.00**
Oil on board, 3-masted ship, RJ Neary, 22x28", +matt & fr........**125.00**
Platter, US Light House Service, bl borders, 12¼x8½"...............**600.00**
Protractor, Lennel...Paris 1777, semicircular arc w/dbl scale, 12x11"....**750.00**
Quadrant, wood w/wood scale/ivory vernier, brass arm, 1880s, 18"...**1,600.00**
Rule, Gunter, boxwood, multiple scales ea side, 24", VG.............**160.00**
Sextant, brass w/blk pnt, 2 eyepcs/7 colored lens, N Beck Pedersen, 9" **495.00**
Sextant, Bufs & Upper East Smithfield London, brass, 3 eyepcs, VG........**400.00**
Sextant, C Plath Hamburg, brass micrometer, 1965, + Bakelite case.........**225.00**
Sextant, ebonized wood w/brass & ivory, 5-colored lens, McGregor, 11".**440.00**
Sextant, Iver C Weilbach & Co...1927, uncleaned/complete, w/case ..**325.00**
Sextant, John Bruce...NY, brass w/silver scales, EX in dvtl case..**700.00**
Sextant, T Wegener Berlin #1948, brass w/silver scales, 10" dia.**1,800.00**
Sextant, Troughton & Simms London, brass, 1826-31, 5¼", +case..**4,000.00**
Telegraph, Bendix Aviation...Alt US & sm anchor, 3" H **600.00**
Telegraph, Swan Hunter & Wigham..., dbl-faced, w/lamp, 42" .**1,950.00**
Tower, engine room communicating; brass w/lamp housing on side, 39"...**1,045.00**
Uniform, yacht club worker's; Croney & Leni NY label, 2-pc, EX **100.00**
Wind meter, W&LE Gurley, nickel/brass, 23".................................**375.00**

Martin Bros.

The Martin Bros. were studio potters who worked from 1873 until 1914, first at Fulham and later at London and Southall. There were four

brothers, each of whom excelled in their particular area. Robert, known as Wallace, was an experienced stonecarver. He modeled a series of grotesque bird and animal figural caricatures. Walter was the potter, responsible for throwing the larger vases on the wheel, firing the kiln, and mixing the clay. Edwin, an artist of stature, preferred more naturalistic forms of decoration. His work was often incised or had relief designs of seaweed, florals, fish, and birds. The fourth brother, Charles, was their business manager. Their work was incised with their names, place of production, and letters and numbers indicating month and year.

Though figural jars continue to command the higher prices, decorated vases and bowls have increased a great deal in value. Our advisor for this category is David Rago; he is listed in the Directory under New Jersey.

Bird couple, mc slips, sgn/dtd, 8½"..**8,800.00**
Bird jar, head cocked, mustard/bl/gr/brn matt, 1898, 10½"....**12,250.00**
Bird vessel, grotesque, brn/bl/gr/gray, wood base, 8x3½" **7,475.00**

Bird vessel, grotesque, large beak, sleepy expression, green, light blue, and black, 1897, 10x8", $12,000.00. (Photo courtesy David Rago)

Clock case, Gothic style w/bizarre creature over dial, 11"........**5,000.00**
Jug, dbl-face, gr/brn salt glaze, brn spout, RW Martin, 1909, 5x4" ...**2,900.00**
Paperweight, dragon w/curled tail, brn/gr, 1882, 2½x4½" **1,400.00**
Spoon warmer, cylinder modeled as cockerel head, comb as hdl ...**875.00**
Toby jug, seated man, brn & caramel, RW Martin, 1903, 10x5½"..**4,900.00**
Vase, coral-like branches in sgraffito on brn, hdls, 9x4"...........**1,200.00**
Vase, incised snails/jellyfish, mc on gray & brn, 1903, 9¼" **3,250.00**
Vase, 5 cvd grotesque dragons, gr/brn on tan & bl, 10x8"........**5,000.00**

Mary Gregory

Mary Gregory glass, for reasons that remain obscure, is the namesake of a Boston and Sandwich Glass Company employee who worked for the company for only two years in the mid-1800s. Although no evidence actually exists to indicate that glass of this type was even produced there, the fine colored or crystal ware decorated with figures of children in white enamel is commonly referred to as Mary Gregory. The glass, in fact, originated in Europe and was imported into this country where it was copied by several eastern glasshouses. It was popular from the mid-1800s until the turn of the century. It is generally accepted that examples with all-white figures were made in the U.S.A., while gold-trimmed items and those with children having tinted faces or a small amount of color on their clothing are European. Though amethyst is rare, examples in cranberry command the higher prices. Blue ranks next; and green, amber, and clear items are worth the least. Watch for new glass decorated with screen-printed children and a minimum of hand painting. The screen effect is easily detected with a magnifying glass.

Bottle, scent; amethyst, child w/balloon, ball stopper, 3½" **175.00**
Decanter, clear, children, gold bands, 10", +6 cordials **200.00**
Decanter, clear, lady, gold ft/rim/stopper/etc, 14" **80.00**

Pitcher, gr, girl catching butterflies in landscape, 6¼"................**275.00**
Tankard, lime gr, girl, 12¼x5½" **245.00**
Tumbler, clear, children w/enamel faces, 3½" **50.00**
Vase, amber w/wht spatter, boy (girl)/foliage, 7x2½", pr **550.00**
Vase, blk, boy w/toy cow tied to stick, mid-1800s, 13" **385.00**
Vase, cobalt, lad/foliage, gold trim, 2½x1½" **325.00**
Vase, cranberry, lady seated on limb, 12¼" **145.00**
Vase, lt amber, girl/trees, bk: flowers, 6¾x3" **225.00**
Vase, sapphire bl, boy, cylinder w/dbl rings above & below decor, 8"...**195.00**
Vase, sapphire bl, boy w/flower, faint ribs, 9x5" **225.00**
Vase, sapphire bl, girl, 8" **170.00**

Mason's Ironstone

In 1813 Charles J. Mason was granted a patent for a process said to 'improve the quality of English porcelain.' The new type of ware was in fact ironstone which Mason decorated with colorful florals and scenics, some of which reflected the Oriental taste. Although his business failed for a short time in the late 1840s, Mason re-established himself and continued to produce dinnerware, tea services, and ornamental pieces until about 1852, at which time the pottery was sold to Francis Morley. Ten years later, Geo. L. and Taylor Ashworth became owners. Both Morley and the Ashworths not only used Mason's molds and patterns but often his mark as well. Because the quality and the workmanship of the later wares do not compare with Mason's earlier product, collectors should take care to distinguish one from the other. Consult a good book on marks to be sure. The Wedgwood Company now owns the rights to the Mason patterns and is reproducing Vista. Note: Blue Vista is generally valued at 15% to 20% above prices for pink/red.

Ashtray, Vista, red, sq, 1925-30 mk, 3½x2½" **20.00**
Bowl, cereal; Vista, red, 1825-30 mk, 6"...................................**18.50**
Bowl, Double Landscape, 1890 mk, 12½" dia............................**200.00**
Bowl, Flowering Bush, mc w/gold, scalloped, 1840 mk, 2x9¼x9" **250.00**
Bowl, Fruit Basket, sq, 1925-30 mk, 2x5½x5½" **100.00**
Bowl, serving; Vista, red, 1925-30 mk, 3¼x9¼" **70.00**
Bowl, serving; Vista, red, 1925-30 mk, 3x8" **60.00**
Cake dish, Vista, red, 1890-1900 mk, 12¼" **175.00**
Compote, Strathmore, scalloped, ftd, 1925-30 mk, 4x9" **200.00**

Covered meat dish, Vista, brown transfer, 11½", $300.00.

Creamer, Vista, red, 1925-30 mk, 3½".......................................**60.00**
Cup & saucer, Fruit Basket, 1925-30 mk, 3¼", 6¾", NM **80.00**
Cup & saucer, Vista, red, 1925-30 mk **22.50**
Egg cup, Vista, red, ftd, 1890-1900 mk, 2x2", 4 for...................**125.00**
Ginger/potpourri jar, Fruit Basket, 1925-30 mk, 5½" **225.00**
Jardiniere, Scroll Chinoiserie, 1830s mk, 4½" **1,495.00**
Jug, Double Landscape, hexagonal, serpent hdl, 1840 mk, 7¾" ..**800.00**
Jug, Fruit Basket, octagonal, serpent hdl, 1925-30 mk, 6¼" **200.00**
Jug, Landscape Scroll, hexagonal, man's-head hdl, 1845 mk, 5¾" ...**300.00**
Jug, Mandarin, 1825 mk, 5¾" **1,195.00**
Jug, Pagoda, 1845 mk, 7¼", NM **500.00**
Jug, Sacrificial Lamb, 1825 mk, 4¾" **1,195.00**
Jug, Strathmore, octagonal, serpent hdl, 1925-30 mk, 4¾" **200.00**
Jug, Vista, red, octagonal, serpent hdl, late 1900s, 6½" **425.00**

Plate, dinner; Vista, red, turkey center, 1925-30 mk, 10¾", 4 for.....**400.00**
Plate, dinner; Vista, red, 1925-50 mk, 10¾", 3 for......................**100.00**
Plate, Flowerpot & Table, 1815-25 mk, 9½" **395.00**
Plate, Mandarin, 1840 blk mk, 8" **175.00**
Plate, Scroll Chinoiserie, 1825 mk, 9⅝" dia..............................**395.00**
Plate, Swansea, mid-1800s mk, 10"...**30.00**
Platter, Asiatic Pheasant, ca 1813-25, 17x13¼" **1,550.00**
Platter, Asiatic Pheasant, 1820 mk, 8x6", NM............................**525.00**
Platter, Vista, red, late 1900s mk, rpr, 15x12¼" **100.00**
Sauce tureen, Fruit Basket, 1925-30 mk, 8¾", +tray & ladle......**300.00**
Sugar bowl, Vista, red, bulbous, 1925-30 mk, 4½" **80.00**
Tazza, Japan, 1840 mk, 3½x9¾x8½" **1,000.00**
Teapot, Vista, red, 1925-30 mk, 7½"...**275.00**
Tray, Fruit Basket, sq w/hdls, late 1900s mk, 10½x9¼"..............**150.00**
Tray, Vista, red, hdls, late 1900s mk, 12¼x6½" **70.00**
Waste bowl, Vista, red, 1925-30 mk, 2¼x4".................................**80.00**

Massier

Clement Massier was a French artist-potter who in 1881 established a workshop at Golfe Juan, France, where he experimented with metallic lustre glazes. (One of his pupils was Jacques Sicardo, who brought the knowledge he had gained through his association with Massier to the Weller Pottery Company in Zanesville, Ohio.) The lustre lines developed by Massier incorporated nature themes with allover decorations of foliage or flowers on shapes modeled in the Art Nouveau style. The ware was usually incised with the Massier name, his initials, or the location of the pottery. Massier died in 1917.

Bowl, mc irid, molded as sirens in ocean waves, rstr, 14" **2,400.00**
Vase, butterflies, gold irid, flaring toward base, 9".....................**900.00**
Vase, flower pods, red lustre, CM, 1891, 4¼" **1,000.00**
Vase, metallic irid swirl pattern, 13¼" **1,400.00**

Match Holders

John Walker, an English chemist, invented the match more than one hundred years ago, quite by accident. Walker was working with a mixture of potash and antimony, hoping to make a combustible that could be used to fire guns. The mixture adhered to the end of the wooden stick he had used for stirring. As he tried to remove it by scraping the stick on the stone floor, it burst into flames. The invention of the match was only a step away! From that time to the present, match holders have been made in amusing figural forms as well as simple utilitarian styles and in a wide range of materials. Both table-top and wallhanging models were made — all designed to keep matches conveniently at hand. The prices in this category are very volatile due to increased interest in this field and the fact that so many can be classified as a cross or dual collectible.

Caution: As prices for originals continue to climb, so do the number of reproductions. Know your dealer. Our advisor for this category is Ron Damaska; he is listed in the Directory under Pennsylvania. See also Advertising.

Black Forest, figural, gnome w/basket, mk Chamonix, 4"............**200.00**
Brass, lady's high top shoe, 4"...**50.00**
Brass, Oriental floral/bird motifs, hinged lid, 2¼x1¼" **95.00**
Bsk, 3 children playing hide-&-seek w/basket behind, 4x3"........**190.00**
Ceramic, Coon Chicken Inn, Black man's smiling face form, M...**335.00**
CI, Amish farmer's face, hollow for matches, 4x6" (+)................**220.00**
CI, andirons & fireplace grating, mk Wayne, 3" **55.00**
CI, box w/scrolled backplate, 2x7½" **135.00**
CI, dbl basket w/floral backplate, wall hanging, 6x7" **85.00**

CI, eagle sits on edge of box, bends over to pick match, 4¾x3¼" ..125.00
CI, pig under basket, 2x3¼x1¼" 75.00
Glass, threaded; wht rnd globe, 2" dia on sterling silver base 70.00
Majolica, beetle w/amber glaze, T mk on base, 5¾" L 300.00
Majolica, Black boy plays accordion, baskets at sides, #8620, 5".550.00
Majolica, frog playing banjo, unmk, 5x6" 310.00
Marble, cvd dog seated by stump, Am, 19th C, 5⅛x4¾x6⅜", EX .260.00
Porc, pale pk flower w/wht dove, wall hanging, 3x3" 135.00
Pot metal, 2 Black men standing by cotton bale (+) 175.00
Silver, nautical motif, snail ft w/supporting shells, Tufts, 4¾" 215.00
Soapstone, See..., Hear..., Speak No Evil monkeys around base, 2¼" ...35.00
SP, chick on wishbone supporting half-egg, Best Wishes eng 80.00
SP, rabbit hugging egg, mk Jennings Brothers, ca 1900 ....175.00
Tin, Juicy Fruit, Wrigley's portrait, 3½x4½" 200.00

Match Safes

Before the invention of the safety match in 1855, matches were carried in small pocket-sized containers because they ignited so easily. Aptly called match safes, these containers were used extensively until about 1920, when cigarette lighters became widely available. Some incorporated added features (hidden compartments, cigar cutters, etc.), some were figural, and others were used by retail companies as advertising giveaways. They were made from every type of material, but silverplated styles abound. Both the advertising and common silverplated cases generally fall in the $50.00 to $100.00 price range.

Beware of reproductions and fakes; there are many currently on the market. Know your dealer. Our advisor for this category is Ron Damaska; he is listed in the Directory under Pennsylvania. See also Advertising.

Advertising, Indian Motorcycle, emb graphics on brass, tarnish, 2½" ...300.00
Advertising, Neverslips Horseshoes, celluloid 125.00

Advertising, REO Speedwagons, brass, winged tire on front, Harrisburg Auto Co., Harrisburg, PA, tarnished, $125.00.

Brass, emb horse head & horseshoe, 2⅝x1½x2½" 45.00
NP brass, camera case form, 2½x1¼" 135.00
NP brass, outhouse figural, door opens to show man w/in, 2" 265.00
NP brass w/MOP sides & HP florals, 1⅜x2⅝", EX 45.00
Porc, ram's head form, brass collar, hinged lid, 3" 635.00
Silver, roulette wheel w/enameling, ca 1900, EX 500.00
SP, dog lying w/head on paws, Gorham, 2" L 425.00
Sterling, Nouveau sea serpent & lobster, late 1800s 1,100.00
Sterling, playing cards in relief, Tiffany, 1890s, EX 900.00
14k gold, fancy, Victorian 400.00

Mauchline Ware

Mauchline ware is the generic name for small, well-made, and useful wooden souvenirs and giftware from Mauchline, Scotland, and nearby locations. It was made from the early nineteenth century into the 1930s. Snuff boxes were among the earliest items, and tea caddies soon followed. From the 1830s on, needlework, stationery, domestic, and cosmetic items were made by the thousands. Today, needlework items are the most plentiful and range from boxes of all sizes made to hold supplies to tiny bodkins and buttons. Napkin rings, egg cups, vases, and bowls are just a few of the domestic items available.

The wood most commonly used in the production of Mauchline ware was sycamore. Finishes vary. Early items were hand decorated with colored paints or pen and ink. By the 1850s, perhaps even earlier, transfer ware was produced, decorated with views associated with the place of purchase. These souvenir items were avidly bought by travelers for themselves as well as for gifts. Major exhibitions and royal occasions were also represented on transferware. An alternative decorating process was initiated during the mid-1860s whereby actual photos replaced the transfers. Because they were finished with multiple layers of varnish, many examples found today are still in excellent condition.

Tartan ware's distinctive decoration was originally hand painted directly on the wood with inks, but in the 1840s machine-made paper in authentic Tartan designs became available. Except for the smallest items, each piece was stamped with the Tartan name. The Tartan decoration was applied to virtually the entire range of Mauchline ware, and because it was favored by Queen Victoria, it became widely popular. Collectors still value Tartan ware above other types of decoration, with transferware being their second choice. Other types of Mauchline decorations include Fern ware and Black Lacquer with floral or transfer decorations.

When cleaning any Mauchline item, extreme care should be used to avoid damaging the finish! Mauchline ware has been reproduced for at least twenty-five years, especially some of the more popular pieces and finishes. Collectors should study the older items for comparison and to learn about the decorating and manufacturing processes.

Box, letter; Aberstwith Castle, EX 75.00
Box, sewing; Edinburgh Castle, 2x4½x11", EX 90.00
Box, stamp; Nubble Light House, 2⅜x1¾x1½", EX 105.00
Box, trinket; blk transfer of Church of the Holy Trinity, 2x5⅜x4" ..125.00
Compass slip case, Fort Mansfield, EX 150.00
Egg cup, Burns Monument, verse on reverse, 3¼x1¾" dia, EX 80.00
Goblet, East Coast Railway, Key West FL, blk transfer, 3¼" 160.00
Letter holder, Poets of America, 2x5¼", EX 85.00
Thimble case, Broughty Ferry, blk transfer, wedge shape, EX 95.00
Thread holder, Lytham Hall, 3", EX 100.00
Tray, castle scene, scalloped rim, 2-part, ca 1880, 5" 90.00
Tray, pin; Natural Arch Torquay, 2½x4" dia, EX 70.00

McCoy

The third generation McCoy potter in the Roseville, Ohio, area was Nelson, who with the aid of his father, J.W., established the Nelson McCoy Sanitary Stoneware Company in 1910. They manufactured churns, jars, jugs, poultry fountains, and foot warmers. By 1925 they had expanded their wares to include majolica jardinieres and pedestals, umbrella stands, and cuspidors, and an embossed line of vases and small jardinieres in a blended brown and green matt glaze. From the late '20s through the mid-'40s, a utilitarian stoneware was produced, some of which was glazed in the soft blue and white so popular with collectors today. They also used a dark brown mahogany color and a medium to dark green, both in a high gloss. In 1933 the firm became known as the Nelson McCoy Pottery Company. They expanded their facilities in 1940 and began to make the novelty artware, cookie jars, and dinnerware that today are synonymous with 'McCoy.' More than two hundred cookie jars of every theme and description were produced.

More than a dozen different marks have been used by the company; nearly all incorporate the name 'McCoy,' although some of the older items were marked 'NM USA.' For further information consult *The Collector's Encyclopedia of McCoy Pottery* (with recently updated values) by

Sharon and Bob Huxford; or *McCoy Pottery Collector's Reference & Value Guide, Vol. I, II,* and *III,* by Margaret Hanson, Craig Nissen, and Bob Hanson (all published by Collector Books). Also available is *Sanfords Guide to McCoy Pottery* by Martha and Steve Sanford. (Mr. Sanford is listed in the Directory under California.)

Alert! Stimulated by the high prices commanded by desirable cookie jars, a broad spectrum of 'new' cookie jars are flooding the marketplace in three categories: 1) Manufacturers have expanded their lines with exciting new designs to attract the collector market. 2) Limited editions and artist-designed jars have proliferated. 3) Reproductions, signed and unsigned, have pervaded the market, creating uncertainty among new collectors and inexperienced dealers. After McCoy closed its doors in the late 1980s, an entrepreneur in Tennessee tried (and succeeded for nearly a decade) to adopt the McCoy Pottery name and mark. This company reproduced old McCoy designs as well as some classic designs of other defunct American potteries, signing their wares 'McCoy' with a mark which very closely approximated the old McCoy mark. Legal action finally put a stop to this practice, though since then this company has used other fraudulent marks as well: Brush-McCoy (the compound name was never used on Brush cookie jars) and B.J. Hull.

Note: Still under pressure from Internet exposure, the cookie jar market remains somewhat soft, and dealers report that the high-end cookie jars are often slow to sell.

Cookie Jars

Apollo, #260, 1970 – 1971, minimum value, $1,000.00.
(Photo courtesy Joyce Roerig)

Animal Crackers 100.00
Apple, 1950-64 ....50.00
Apple, 1967 ....60.00
Apple on Basketweave 70.00
Asparagus 50.00
Astronauts, from $750 to 850.00
Bananas 125.00
Barnum's Animals 150.00
Barrel, Cookies sign on lid 75.00
Baseball Boy 200.00
Basket of Eggs 40.00
Basket of Potatoes 40.00
Bear, cookie in vest, no 'Cookies', from $75 to 85.00
Betsy Baker (+), from $250 to 300.00
Black Kettle, w/immovable bail, HP flowers 40.00
Blue Willow Pitcher 75.00
Bobby Baker 65.00
Bugs Bunny, cylinder, from $165 to 150.00
Burlap Bag, red bird on lid 50.00
Caboose 150.00
Cat on Coal Scuttle 175.00
Chairman of the Board (+) 550.00
Chef, donut (+) 250.00
Chilly Willy 85.00

Chipmunk 125.00
Christmas Tree, minimum value 800.00
Churn, 2 bands 35.00
Circus Horse, blk 250.00
Clown Bust (+) 75.00
Clown in Barrel, yel, bl or gr 85.00
Clyde Dog 250.00
Coalby Cat 375.00
Coca-Cola Can 100.00
Coca-Cola Jug 85.00
Coffee Grinder 45.00
Coffee Mug 45.00
Colonial Fireplace 85.00
Cookie Bank, 1961 ....165.00
Cookie Boy 225.00
Cookie Cabin 80.00
Cookie Jug, dbl loop 35.00
Cookie Jug, single loop, 2-tone gr rope 35.00
Cookie Jug, w/cork stopper, brn & wht 40.00
Cookie Log, squirrel finial, from $35 to 45.00
Cookie Mug 45.00
Cookie Pot, 1964 ....40.00
Cookie Safe 65.00
Cookstove, blk or wht 35.00
Corn, row of standing ears, yel or wht, 1977 ....85.00
Corn, single ear 175.00
Covered Wagon 95.00
Cylinder, w/red flowers 45.00
Dalmatians in Rocking Chair (+) 275.00
Davy Crockett (+) 500.00
Dog on Basketweave, from $75 to 90.00
Drum, red 90.00
Duck on Basketweave, from $75 to 90.00
Dutch Boy 65.00
Dutch Girl, boy on reverse, rare 250.00
Dutch Treat Barn 50.00
Eagle on Basket, from $35 to 50.00
Early American Chest (Chiffoniere) 85.00
Elephant 200.00
Elephant w/Split Trunk, rare, minimum value 300.00
Engine, blk 175.00
Flowerpot, plastic flower on top 500.00
Football Boy (+), from $245 to 275.00
Forbidden Fruit, from $65 to 90.00
Freddy Gleep (+), minimum value 500.00
Friendship 7 ....200.00
Frog on Stump 75.00
Frontier Family 55.00
Fruit in Bushel Basket, from $65 to 80.00
Gingerbread Boy 75.00
Globe 275.00
Grandfather Clock 90.00
Granny 120.00
Hamm's Bear (+) 225.00
Happy Face 80.00
Hen on Nest, from $85 to 95.00
Hillbilly Bear, rare, minimum value (+) 900.00
Hobby Horse (+), from $125 to 150.00
Hocus Rabbit 45.00
Honey Bear, rustic glaze, from $65 to 80.00
Hot Air Balloon 40.00
Ice Cream Cone 45.00
Indian, brn (+) 350.00
Indian, majolica 400.00

Jack-O'-Lantern 500.00
Kangaroo, bl 300.00
Keebler Tree House 70.00
Kettle, bronze, 1961 .... 40.00
Kissing Penguins, from $100 to 125.00
Kitten on Basketweave 90.00
Kittens (2) on Low Basket, minimum value 600.00
Kittens on Ball of Yarn 85.00
Koala Bear 85.00
Kookie Kettle, blk 35.00
Lamb on Basketweave 90.00
Leprechaun, minimum value (+) 1,800.00
Liberty Bell 75.00
Little Clown 75.00
Lollipops 80.00
Mac Dog 95.00
Mammy, Cookies on base, wht (+) 150.00
Mammy w/Cauliflower, G pnt, minimum value (+) 1,100.00
Milk Can, Spirit of '76 .... 45.00
Modern 65.00
Monk 50.00
Mother Goose 150.00
Mouse on Clock 40.00
Mr & Mrs Owl, from $75 to 90.00
Mushroom on Stump 55.00
Nursery, decal of Humpty Dumpty, from $70 to 80.00
Oaken Bucket, from $25 to 45.00
Orange 55.00
Owl 50.00
Pear, 1952 .... 85.00
Pears on Basketweave 70.00
Penguin, yel or aqua, from $175 to 200.00
Pepper, yel 40.00
Picnic Basket, from $65 to 75.00
Pig, winking 300.00
Pineapple 80.00
Pineapple, Modern 90.00
Pirate's Chest, from $125 to 145.00
Popeye Cylinder 200.00
Potbelly Stove, blk 30.00
Puppy, w/sign 85.00
Quaker Oats, rare, minimum value 700.00
Raggedy Ann 110.00
Red Barn, cow in door, rare, minimum value 350.00
Rooster, wht, 1970-1974 .... 60.00
Rooster, 1955-1957 .... 95.00
Round w/HP Leaves 45.00
Sad Clown 85.00
Snoopy on Doghouse (+), mk United Features Syndicate 200.00
Snow Bear, from $65 to 75.00
Spaniel in Doghouse, bird finial 250.00
Stagecoach, minimum value 800.00
Strawberry, 1955-57 .... 65.00
Strawberry, 1971-1975 .... 45.00
Teapot, 1972 .... 60.00
Tepee, slat top 350.00
Tepee, str top (+) 300.00
Tilt Pitcher, blk w/roses 50.00
Timmy Tortoise 45.00
Tomato 60.00
Touring Car 100.00
Traffic Light 50.00
Tudor Cookie House 125.00
Tulip on Flowerpot 150.00

Turkey, gr, rare color 300.00
Turkey, natural colors 250.00
Upside Down Bear, panda 50.00
WC Fields 200.00
Wedding Jar 90.00
Windmill 100.00
Wishing Well 40.00
Woodsy Owl, from $250 to 300.00
Wren House, side lid 175.00
Yosemite Sam, cylinder 150.00

Miscellaneous

Wall pocket, purple grape cluster on leaves, 7x6", from $100.00 to $175.00.

Ashtray, Feb 20 Space Capsule, from $40 to 50.00
Ashtray, top hat form, yel, from $20 to 25.00
Basket planter, Floraline, wht, #561L, 7x7½", from $25 to 35.00
Bowl, Garden Club, scalloped rim/ped ft, 1950s-60s, 7x7", from $30 to 35.00
Canisters, Bamboo, 1974, set of 3, from $75 to 100.00
Canisters, Blue Windmill, 1974, 4-pc set, from $75 to 100.00
Centerpiece, antelope on blk or gr base, 1955, 12" W, from $350 to .. 450.00
Coffee server, Sandstone, 1978, from $30 to 50.00
Creamer, Mediterranean Line, 1980, from $12 to 15.00
Cup & saucer, Brown Antique Rose, 1959, from $25 to 35.00
Deviled egg plate, chicken shape, yel, 1973, from $20 to 30.00
Dutch oven, gr gloss w/emb rings, stoneware, 1920s-30s, 9¾", $75 to .. 100.00
Flowerpot, wavy lines on gr, w/saucer, 1960s, 4-6", ea from $25 to .. 40.00
Jar, oil; burgundy mottle, stoneware, unmk, 1920s-30s, 25", $400 to .. 500.00
Jar, oil; drip-style glaze, stoneware, unmk, 1920s-30s, 18", $350 to 400.00
Jar, porch; leaves & berries on blended matt, 14", from $1,200 to .. 1,500.00
Jardiniere, emb swirling pattern, Model 431L, 6½x8½", $25 to ... 35.00
Jardiniere, gr onyx, unmk, 1930s-40s, 6", from $35 to .. 40.00
Jardiniere, Holly, brn onyx, unmk, 1930s, 10½", from $85 to 100.00
Jardiniere & ped, Basketweave, gr or wht, 8½", 12½" 250.00
Jardiniere & ped, Holly, brn & gr, 8½", 12½", from $200 to 250.00
Jardiniere & ped, Leaves & Berries, brn/gr, unmk, 10½, 18½" ... 650.00
Jug, Happytime Line, children decal, 1974, from $20 to .. 25.00
Matchbox holder, wht w/bl speckles, mk, 1970s, 5¾x3¼" 40.00
Mug, beer advertising on wht w/gold rim, from $25 to .. 30.00
Mug, Similac for Ross Coffee, yel or gr, from $10 to .. 20.00
Novelty, hands tray, wht w/non-production decor under glaze, 1940s ... 55.00
Pitcher, donkey form, gr or yel, 1940s, 7", from $250 to 300.00
Pitcher, fish figural, gr/brn blended, 1949, 7", from $650 to 800.00
Pitcher, Western Wear, brn woodgrain look, 1979, 2½-qt, $50 to ... 75.00
Planter, Artisan Line, wht, mk, 1965, 7½", from $35 to 45.00
Planter, caterpillar figural, wht, Model 416L, 13½" L, from $30 to ... 45.00
Planter, Happy Face, 1970s-80s, from $25 to 35.00
Planter, lamb, wht w/gold bow, 1954, 8½", from $90 to 110.00
Planter, leaves emb on gr, mk, 1950s, 7" L, from $35 to .. 45.00
Planter, Sunburst gold, mk, 1950s-60s, 9½", from $30 to 35.00
Planting dish, Capri, bl w/pk int, 1950-60s, 14½", from $40 to 50.00
Shoe planter, Floraline, yel, #530, 3x8½", from $18 to 25.00
Stein, Schlitz Malt Liquor, #6020, 1973, from $25 to 35.00
Tankard, emb floral, stoneware, unmk, 1920s-30s, 8½", from $70 to .. 90.00

Tea set, Pine Cone, bl (unusual color), 1940s-50s, 3-pc, $100 to ..**125.00**
Tidbit tray, Morano Line, 2-tier, #915, 1966, from $35 to.............**40.00**
Tumbler, gr, emb rings, flared, stoneware, 1920s-30s, 5", from $40 to...**50.00**
Vase, bud; bird details, blended gr & brn, 1940s-50s, 8", $35 to ...**50.00**
Vase, bud; Floraline, turq, 6", from $12 to.......................................**18.00**
Vase, bud; Vesta, yel w/trim, unmk, 1963, 8", from $20 to **25.00**
Vase, Crestwood, yel w/gold, cylindrical, mk, 1964, 14½", $60 to **70.00**
Vase, Floraline Fineforms, dk mauve, unmk, #0488FF, 12½x9", $50 to ...**75.00**
Vase, gr w/emb rings, hdls, shield mk, 7½", from $80 to **100.00**
Vase, gr w/scrolling ft, 1959, 14", from $75 to...........................**100.00**
Vase, hand form, opening in palm, cold-pnt fingernails, 1940s, 6½" ..**175.00**
Vase, peacock emb on gr, hdls, 1948, 8", from $50 to....................**60.00**
Vase, red roses decal on wht, hdls, 1950s, 8", from $35 to.............**45.00**
Vase, Ribbed Pedestal, dk gr, #407, 6½x3¾", from $15 to **20.00**
Vase, Square Top, any standard color, #446, 9", from $20 to.........**25.00**
Vase, yel w/low gold hdls, 1950s, 9", from $85 to **120.00**
Wall pocket, fan form, bl, mid-1950s, 8½x8", from $75 to............**90.00**
Wall pocket, leaves w/berries, mk, 1940s, very rare, 9" **1,000.00**

McCoy, J. W.

The J.W. McCoy Pottery Company was incorporated in 1899. It operated under that name in Roseville, Ohio, until 1911 when McCoy entered into a partnership with George Brush, forming the Brush-McCoy Company. During the early years, McCoy produced kitchenware, majolica jardinieres and pedestals, umbrella stands, and cuspidors. By 1903 they had begun to experiment in the field of art pottery and, though never involved to the extent of some of their contemporaries, nevertheless produced several art lines of merit. Their first line was Mt. Pelee, examples of which are very rare today. Two types of glazes were used, matt green and an iridescent charcoal gray. Though the line was primarily mold formed, some pieces evidence the fact that while the clay remained wet and pliable it was pulled and pinched with the fingers to form crests and peaks in a style not unlike George Ohr.

The company rebuilt in 1904 after being destroyed by fire, and other artware was designed. Loy-Nel Art and Renaissance were standard brown lines, hand decorated under the glaze with colored slip. Shapes and artwork were usually simple but effective. Olympia and Rosewood were relief-molded brown-glaze lines decorated in natural colors with wreaths of leaves and berries or simple floral sprays. Although much of this ware was not marked, you will find examples with the die-stamped 'Loy-Nel Art, McCoy,' or an incised line identification.

Corn Line, mug, unmk, from $50 to..**70.00**
Corn Line, tankard, unmk, 1910, from $300 to **350.00**
Liberty Bell, umbrella stand, sgn Cusick, unmk, 1910, 23" **900.00**
Loy-Nel-Art, jardiniere, floral, 1905, 6", from $250 to................**300.00**
Loy-Nel-Art, jardiniere, Halley's Comet, 1910, 4", from $350 to ..**400.00**
Loy-Nel-Art, vase, cylindrical, 6", from $250 to.........................**300.00**
Loy-Nel-Art, vase, rim-to-hip hdls, 1905, 8", from $250 to **300.00**
Loy-Nel-Art, vase, waisted, no hdls, 1905, 8", from $200 to.......**250.00**
Matt Green, umbrella stand, unmk, 21", from $500 to................**550.00**
Mt Pelee, ewer, from $1,000 to...**1,200.00**
Olympia, mug, 1905, from $150 to...**200.00**
Olympia, punch bowl, 1905, from $500 to....................................**600.00**
Olympia, vase, rim-to-hip hdls, 1905, 5", from $250 to...............**350.00**
Rosewood, ewer, cylinder neck, 1905, 10", from $350 to **450.00**
Rosewood, vase, flared neck, bulbous base, unmk, pre-1903, 9"..**250.00**

McKee

McKee Glass was founded in 1853 in Pittsburgh, Pennsylvania.

Among their early products were tableware of both the flint and non-flint varieties. In 1888 the company relocated to avail themselves of a source of natural gas, thereby founding the town of Jeannette, Pennsylvania. One of their most famous colored dinnerware lines, Rock Crystal, was manufactured in the 1920s. Production during the '30s and '40s included colored opaque dinnerware, Sunkist reamers, and 'bottoms up' cocktail tumblers as well as a line of black glass vases, bowls, and novelty items. All are popular items with today's collectors, but watch for reproductions. The mark of an authentic 'bottoms up' tumbler is the patent number 77725 embossed beneath the feet. The company was purchased in 1916 by Jeannette Glass, under which name it continues to operate. See also Animal Dishes with Covers; Carnival Glass; Depression Glass; Kitchen Collectibles; Reamers.

Coaster, for Bottoms Up tumbler, custard.....................................**50.00**
Comport, amethyst, rolled top, 6x8" dia top **55.00**
Goblet, wine; Rainbow, cut crystal, 4⅛" **25.00**
Pin tray, milk glass, 2x4¾" **13.50**
Punch bowl, Aztec, +base & 12 cups w/metal holders, MIB.......**130.00**
Punch bowl, Tom & Jerry, wht w/blk trim, +8 matching cups **140.00**
Punch bowl, Tom & Jerry; couple in sleigh in winter on wht, +6 cups....**90.00**
Punch mug, Jade-ite, plain **35.00**
Punch mug, Tom & Jerry, clambroth, 3½x4" **25.00**
Punch mug, Tom & Jerry, wht w/blk trim......................................**30.00**
Tumbler, Bottoms Up, Jade-ite, w/coaster, from $165 to **185.00**
Vase, yel, bulbous base, trumpet neck, scalloped rim, 17" **140.00**

Medical Collectibles

The field of medical-related items encompasses a wide area from the primitive bleeding bowl to the X-ray machines of the early 1900s. Other closely related collectibles include apothecary and dental items. Many tools that were originally intended for the pharmacist found their way to the doctor's office, and dentists often used surgical tools when no suitable dental instrument was available. A trend in the late 1800s toward self-medication brought a whole new wave of home-care manuals and 'patent' medical machines for home use. Commonly referred to as 'quack' medical gimmicks, these machines were usually ineffective and occasionally dangerous. Our advisor for this category is Jim Calison; he is listed in the Directory under New York.

Quack machine, Davis and Kidder's Patent Magneto Electric Machine, mahogany case with ivory handle, brass interior, ca 1854, 4½x10x4½", EX, $350.00.

Apothecary cachet machine, Konseal Apparatus, 1800s, 8½x5⅝" ..**30.00**
Apothecary jar, etched/cut vintage, blown, folded rim, ftd, 19"..**385.00**
Bed pan, cream, Homer Laughlin, mid-1800s, 14x10x4", EX........**25.00**
Blood lancet, automatic, Adams, adjustable guard, 4" **15.00**
Book, A Text-book of Medicine, Strumpell, 1895, 2nd Am edition, VG+...**85.00**
Book, Diseases of the Ear, Appleton's Medical Library, 1894, VG ...**25.00**
Book, Diseases of the Nervous System, Gowers, 2nd edition, 1892....**60.00**
Book, Embalming by a New Principle & a New Method, Eckels, 1900s, VG ...**55.00**
Book, Practical Dissections, Hodges, 254 pages, 1858, EX **95.00**

Book, Principles & Practice of Medicine, Osler, 2nd edition, 1896 ....**110.00**
Book, Surgical Instruments, Krohne & Sesemann, London, 1901, VG ..**315.00**
Book, Transfusion of Human Blood, Roussel/Paget, 1877, VG ...**175.00**
Book, 1887 Bray's Anatomy, 1,100 pages, VG+ **85.00**
Button, General Nursing Council for England & Wales, enameled, 1" **40.00**
Eye chart, paper rolled between 2 wooden dowels, FA Hardy #969, VG..**30.00**
Eye cup, cobalt bl glass, Justrite WBM Co, 2½" **110.00**
Glass eye, gray iris, brn pupil, Germany, 1930s, ⅞", VG+ **30.00**
Hearing aid, Zenith Miniature 75, clip-on (for belt) case, VG......**15.00**
Hydrometer set, Sykes, 1830-50, complete in velvet-lined case, EX **460.00**
Invalid feeder, wht w/Red Cross emblem, mk JS/Germany, porc, EX....**30.00**
Leech/bleeding cup, clear glass, bell shape, 2⅛x1½" **18.00**
Scale, NP brass, Fitches, 1885, 2⅞x1½x⅞", VG **40.00**
Stethoscope, monaural; wooden 7"...**200.00**
Tablets, Gessler's Magic Headache Wafers, dtd 1888, in 3x1⅞" box...**235.00**
Thermometer, mk KOH-1-NOOR, +aluminum case w/chain, 4½", EX..**25.00**
Tonsilotomes, mk Betz Germany, 10", EX **35.00**
Trocar, SP brass & steel, 3-pc, unmk, 5"..**20.00**

Meissen

The Royal Saxon Porcelain Works was established in 1710 in Meissen, Saxony. Under the direction of Johann Frederick Bottger, who in 1708 had developed the formula for the first true porcelain body, fine ceramic figurines with exquisite detail, and tableware of the highest quality were produced. Although every effort was made to insure the secrecy of Bottger's discovery, others soon began to copy his ware; and in 1731 Meissen adopted the famous crossed swords trademark to identify their own work. The term 'Dresden ware' is often used to refer to Meissen porcelain, since Bottger's discovery and first potting efforts were in nearby Dresden. See also Onion Pattern.

Bowl, centerpc; Cupid astride lg swan on oval base, 1880-95, 11x13"...**2,185.00**
Bowl, floral (dainty) on wht w/gold, Xd swords, 11¼" **390.00**
Box, 2 cherubs on lid, 1 w/harp, 11½x9½"..............................**1,300.00**
Bust, girl in kerchief w/floral corsage, early 1900s, 6" **635.00**
Charger, floral w/3 reserves, cobalt/gold border, Xd swords, 12"..**665.00**
Clock, children & flowers, Augustus Rex, 19th C, 12x19"......**3,400.00**
Clock, 4 putti (4 seasons), H Marc movement, Xd swords, 1862, 18x11"..**5,000.00**
Coffeepot, flower sprays on wht & yel, snake spout, Xd swords, 10½"..**650.00**

Compote on base, two figures form stem, reticulated bowl with shell base, blue and white floral, 22", EX+, $2,400.00. (Photo courtesy Garth's Auctions)

Figurine, Apollo & Daphne on base, 1845-60, 9¼x5½"..........**1,000.00**
Figurine, boar attacked by hounds, X swords, bicentennial pc/1910, 9"..**1,265.00**
Figurine, children in woods try to catch birds, Xd swords, 6", NM........**875.00**
Figurine, Chinese man measures distances on globe, Xd swords, 5x2"..**750.00**
Figurine, couple under tree w/lamb & dog, rococo-style base, 9½" **900.00**
Figurine, Cupid, outstretched arms, rpr, 7¼" **800.00**
Figurine, Cupid, seated on elaborate plinth w/flowers, 4½" **625.00**
Figurine, Cupid holding 2 flaming hearts, Je Les Balance, 1855-70, 6"...**400.00**

Figurine, Diana the Huntress, w/2 males/dogs & boar, 1880, 14½" **7,000.00**
Figurine, Die Schauende, nude sits, Xd swords, 1935-45, 12½x11½"....**1,150.00**
Figurine, dog, wht w/blk features, purple collar, #1057, 5½x10"....**825.00**
Figurine, Greek pr at table, child in front, Xd swords, 8x7", NM..**1,050.00**
Figurine, lady beside spinning wheel, #2685, 6⅛x6¼"..............**1,525.00**
Figurine, lady drops cherry into cherub's hand, 12½" **575.00**
Figurine, lady sits at table, lap/basket of flowers, Xd swords, 6"...**425.00**
Figurine, lady street vender selling a rabbit, 5½" **825.00**
Figurine, Malabar man & woman, Xd swords, 14x6½", pr........**4,600.00**
Figurine, man & lady, ea w/hunting dogs, 1875-90, 3½", pr **285.00**
Figurine, man w/flower & lady w/basket, after Kaendler, 1875, 19", pr...**6,600.00**
Figurine, pastry chef, Cris de Paris series, ca 1860, 5" **1,000.00**
Figurine, putto wrestling goat, 6½x10x8"................................**575.00**
Figurine, putti (2) artists w/drawing panel/palette, 1855-70, 4¾" ...**700.00**
Figurine, putti (4) around fire on ped, #2753, 3¾x3" **850.00**
Figurine, Triton Catchers, 2 seminudes w/net, 1880s, 13"........**2,100.00**
Pitcher, figures & flowers, gold hdl, Xd swords, 5¼" **175.00**
Plate, figures & floral reserves (4), scalloped rim, Xd swords, 9"..**185.00**
Plate, floral, bl on wht w/gold, rtcl rim, Xd swords, 9¼" **450.00**
Plate, seminude w/Cupid, floral rim, Xd swords, 9½" **200.00**
Plate, serving; floral w/gilt vintage clusters, Xd swords, 11¼" **200.00**
Platter, grapes on cobalt w/gold, Xd swords, 13½x10½"..............**625.00**
Sugar basin, Blackamoor vendor by basket w/flowers on lid, 1850-70, 7"....**1,950.00**
Teapot, couple on path, tree/mountain background, 18th C, 4" ...**1,250.00**
Tureen, modeled as cabbage, magenta/gr, 8x7", +7" underplate ...**3,450.00**
Vase, floral on wht, smooth gold trim, ftd, Xd swords, 5½"........**450.00**
Vase, floral reserve, cobalt w/gold, waisted cylinder, Xd swords, 10"..**665.00**
Vase, stylized florals, gourd shape, Xd swords, 7¼" **350.00**

Mercury Glass

Silvered glass, commonly called mercury glass, was a major scientific achievement of the nineteenth century. It was developed by the glass industry, who was searching for an inexpensive substitute for silver. Though very fragile, it was lightweight and would not tarnish. Mercury glass was made with two thin layers, either blown with a double wall or joined in sections, with the space between the walls of the vessel filled with a silvering compound, the perfecting of which involved much experimentation. Colored glass was also silvered. Green, blue, and amber were favored. Occasionally, colors were achieved using clear glass by adding certain chemicals to the compound. Besides hollow ware items, flat surfaces were silvered as well, through a process whereby small facets were cut on the underneath side, then treated with the silvering compound. Sometimes mercury glass was decorated by engraving; it was also hand painted. Besides decorative items such as vases and candlesticks, for instance, utilitarian items — doorknobs, curtain tiebacks, and reflectors for lamps — were also popular. Silvered Christmas ornaments were produced in large quantities.

Condition is an issue, though opinions are divided. While some prefer their acquisitions to be in mint condition, others accept items with flaked silvering. Watch for reproductions marked Made in China. In the listings that follow, all examples are silver unless noted another color.

Bowl, ftd, 5x8½" **25.00**
Candle holder, etched floral palm tree, 10½"................................**90.00**
Candlestick, gold wash, domed base, stemmed teardrop shape, 6¼" ..**75.00**
Compote, gold-amber int, knobbed stem, 8¼" H **150.00**
Drawer pulls, 1¼" dia, matching set of 6................................**80.00**
Match holder **70.00**
Mug, clear hdl, 3" **40.00**
Rolling pin...**120.00**
Sugar bowl, HP floral, knob finial on dome lid, low ft, 6¼"..........**55.00**
Toothpick holder from $40 to **50.00**

Vase, HP bird, 7½" 70.00
Vase, HP bird & tropical scene, slender, 9¼" 215.00
Vase, HP floral, gold int, gold ext bands, 11" 95.00
Vase, HP orange bird w/yel wings, flowers, 9½" 90.00
Vase, HP red & bl flower w/gold, ftd, 12" 160.00
Vase, HP red rose w/3 gr leaves, 7½" 115.00

Merrimac

Founded in 1897 in Newburyport, Massachusetts, the Merrimac Pottery Company primarily produced gardenware. In 1901, however, they introduced a line of artware that is now attracting the interest of collectors. Marked examples carry an impressed die-stamp or a paper label, each with the firm name and the outline of a sturgeon, the definition of the Indian word Merrimac.

Lamp, gr drip over yel, thick/textured, w/wicker shade, 13" 1,600.00
Vase, cucumber gr feathering on hunter gr, 2¾x3½" 385.00
Vase, teal gr lustre w/blk, tooled leaves, ochre int, 4½x5¼" 1,430.00

Metlox

Metlox Potteries was founded in 1927 in Manhattan Beach, California. Before 1934 when they began producing the ceramic housewares for which they have become famous, they made ceramic and neon outdoor advertising signs. The company went out of business in 1989.

Well-known sculptor Carl Romanelli designed artware in the late 1930s and early 1940s (and again briefly in the 1950s). His work is especially sought after today.

Some Provincial dinnerware lines can be confusing. There are two 'rooster' lines, Red Rooster (red, orange, and brown) and California Provincial (dark green and burgundy), and there are three 'homestead' lines, Colonial Heritage (red, orange, and brown like the Red Rooster pieces), Homestead Provincial (dark green and burgundy like California Provincial), and Provincial Blue (blue and white). For further information we recommend *Collector's Encyclopedia of Metlox Potteries, Second Edition*, by our advisor Carl Gibbs, Jr.; he is listed in the Directory under Texas.

Cookie Jars

Apple, Golden Delicious, 9½", from $150 to 175.00
Barn, Mac's, from $250 to 275.00
Barrel, w/gr apple lid, from $100 to 125.00
Barrel, w/red apple lid, (aka Apple Barrel), 3¾-qt, 11" 75.00
Basket, Natural; w/cookie lid (aka Cookie Basket), 10½", $40 to 50.00
Basket, wht. w/basket lid, from $35 to 45.00
Bear, Ballerina, from $100 to 125.00
Bear, Beau, from $60 to 75.00
Bear, Panda, w/lollipop, from $400 to 450.00
Bear, Teddy, wht, 3-qt, from $40 to 45.00
Beaver, Bucky, from $125 to 150.00
Bluebird on Stump, stain finish, from $65 to 75.00
Calf, Ferdinand, minimum value 900.00
Cat, Calico, gr w/pk ribbon, from $175 to 200.00
Children of the World, Cookie Creations Series, 2-qt, from $125 to 150.00
Cookie Boy, 9", from $275 to 300.00
Debutante, minimum value 400.00
Dina-Stegosaurus, Year of the Dinosaur Series, from $150 to 175.00
Dog, Bassett, from $325 to 350.00
Dog, Gingham, cream w/bl collar, from $150 to 175.00
Duck, Francine, from $225 to 250.00
Duck Blues. from $100 to 125.00

Dutch Girl, minimum value 350.00
Egg Basket, from $175 to 200.00
Flamingo, minimum value 350.00
Frog, the Prince, from $175 to 200.00
Goose, Lucy, from $125 to 150.00
Granada Green, 3-qt, from $35 to 45.00
Grape, from $200 to 250.00

Hen, blue, from $250.00 to $300.00. (Photo courtesy Joyce and Fred Roerig)

Hen & Chick, minimum value 350.00
Humpty Dumpty, no ft, 11", minimum value 500.00
Humpty Dumpty, seated, w/ft, from $250 to 275.00
Kangaroo, 11¼", minimum value 1,000.00
Kitten, says Meow (aka Tattle-Tale), 2¾-qt, 10", from $125 to ..150.00
Lighthouse, from $275 to 300.00
Little Red Riding Hood, minimum value 1,250.00
Loveland, from $65 to 75.00
Mammy, Cook, bl, from $475 to 500.00
Mammy, Cook, red, from $725 to 750.00
Mediteree, 2½-qt, from $35 to 45.00
Merry Go Round, from $250 to 275.00
Mona-Monoclonius, Year of the Dinosaur, aqua or rose, ea from $150 to ...175.00
Mouse, Chef Pierre, from $75 to 100.00
Mushroom Cottage, from $225 to 250.00
Nun, minimum value 1,000.00
Owl, brn, 2½-qt, from $90 to 95.00
Pear, from $125 to 150.00
Penguin, Frosty, short or long coat, from $150 to 175.00
Pig, Slenderella, from $125 to 150.00
Pineapple, 3¾-qt, from $75 to 100.00
Pretty Anne, 2½-qt, from $175 to 200.00
Pumpkin, boy on lid, minimum value 500.00
Rabbit, Easter Bunny, solid chocolate, minimum 350.00
Rabbit on Cabbage, 3-qt, 10", from $125 to 150.00
Raccoon, Cookie Bandit, bsk, 2¾-qt, from $125 to 150.00
Rag Doll, girl, 2½-qt, from $175 to 200.00
Rex-Tyrannosaurus Rex, French Blue or yel, ea 175.00
Rex-Tyrannosaurus Rex, Year of the Dinosaur Series, from $150 to ..175.00
Rocking Horse, 11", minimum value 450.00
Santa Head, from $350 to 375.00
Schoolhouse (aka Little Country Schoolhouse), 11", minimum value ..400.00
Scout, Brownie or Cub, ea from $475 to 500.00
Squirrel on Pine Cone, stain finish, 3-qt, 11", from $85 to 95.00
Strawberry, 3½-qt, 9½", from $85 to 95.00
Sunflowers, Cookie Creations Series, 2-qt, from $65 to 85.00
Topsy, red polka dots, minimum value 800.00
Topsy, solid bl apron, from $425 to 450.00
Walrus, brn & wht, from $350 to 375.00
Wells Fargo, 11x9", from $500 to 550.00
Whale, wht, from $300 to 350.00
Woodpecker on Acorn, 3-qt, from $375 to 400.00

Dinnerware

Antique Grape, bowl, vegetable; w/lid, med, 1-qt, from $80 to.....**85.00**
Antique Grape, coffeepot, 8-cup, from $100 to **110.00**
Antique Grape, oval baker, 10¼", from $50 to **55.00**
Antique Grape, platter, oval, 14¼", from $50 to **55.00**
Autumn Berry, bowl, divided vegetable; 10¾", from $45 to..........**50.00**
Autumn Berry, mug, 8-oz, from $20 to **22.00**
Autumn Berry, plate, bread & butter; 6½", from $8 to **9.00**
California Aztec, bowl, lug soup; from $42 to **45.00**
California Aztec, celery dish, from $75 to **80.00**
California Aztec, plate, dinner; from $32 to...................................**35.00**
California Aztec, platter, 13", from $85 to **90.00**
California Confetti, bowl, divided vegetable; from $60 to............**65.00**
California Confetti, butter dish, from $70 to **75.00**
California Confetti, gravy, from $40 to..**45.00**
California Confetti, pitcher, milk; from $75 to **85.00**
California Freeform, coaster, from $35 to **38.00**
California Freeform, cup, juice; from $60 to...................................**65.00**
California Freeform, plate, chop; from $90 to..............................**100.00**
California Freeform, plate, salad; from $25 to **28.00**
California Ivy, bowl, fruit; 5¼", from $14 to..................................**16.00**
California Ivy, bowl, vegetable; w/lid, 11", from $80 to...............**85.00**
California Ivy, butter dish, from $60 to **65.00**
California Ivy, cup & saucer, from $16 to.......................................**18.00**
California Ivy, shakers, sm, pr, from $28 to....................................**30.00**
California Ivy, soup tureen, w/lid, minimum value **850.00**
California Ivy, teapot, 6-cup, from $115 to...................................**125.00**
California Provincial, bowl, soup; 8", from $28 to **30.00**
California Provincial, cruet set, 2-pc, complete, from $120 to....**130.00**
California Provincial, mug, no lid, 1-pt, from $40 to.....................**42.00**
California Provincial, pepper mill, from $55 to.............................**60.00**
California Provincial, sugar bowl, w/lid, 8-oz, from $35 to **38.00**
California Provincial, tumbler, 11-oz, from $45 to.........................**50.00**
Colonial Heritage, bowl, lug soup; ind, from $20 to **22.00**
Colonial Heritage, butter dish, from $60 to **65.00**
Colonial Heritage, coaster, from $18 to..**20.00**
Colonial Heritage, egg cup, from $25 to..**28.00**
Colonial Heritage, pitcher, lg, from $75 to.....................................**80.00**
Colonial Heritage, plate, dinner; from $13 to **14.00**
Colonial Heritage, turkey platter, from $190 to **215.00**
Colorstax, banana leaf, 20", from $60 to **65.00**
Colorstax, bowl, mixing; med, 44-oz, from $35 to **40.00**
Colorstax, coffeepot, 6-cup, from $90 to...**95.00**
Colorstax, creamer, 11-oz, from $25 to **28.00**
Colorstax, cup, lg, 16-oz, from $22 to **25.00**
Colorstax, plate, BBQ; 3-part, 11", from $28 to.............................**30.00**
Homestead Provincial, butter dish, from $75 to............................**80.00**
Homestead Provincial, coffee carafe, 44-oz, 7-cup, from $140 to....**150.00**
Homestead Provincial, gravy, 1-pt, from $45 to **50.00**
Homestead Provincial, plate, dinner; 10", from $18 to.................**20.00**
Homestead Provincial, platter, oval, 13½", from $55 to...............**60.00**
Homestead Provincial, shakers, pr, from $30 to **32.00**
Lotus, banana leaf, 15", from $50 to..**55.00**
Lotus, bowl, vegetable; 10", from $45 to...**50.00**
Lotus, cup & saucer, 7-oz, from $15 to **17.00**
Lotus, plate, dinner; 11", from $15 to...**16.00**
Navajo, plate, chop; 13", from $60 to..**65.00**
Navajo, plate, salad; 7½", from $11 to **12.00**
Navajo, platter, rectangular, 11", from $35 to **40.00**
Navajo, tumbler, 10-oz, from $35 to..**38.00**
Provincial Blue, bowl, cereal; 7¼", from $20 to............................**22.00**
Provincial Blue, canister, flour; w/lid, from $95 to......................**100.00**
Provincial Blue, creamer, 6-oz, from $30 to...................................**32.00**

Provincial Blue, egg cup, from $40 to..**45.00**
Provincial Blue, hen on nest, from $145 to...................................**155.00**
Provincial Blue, kettle casserole, w/lid, 2-qt+12-oz, from $140 to ..**150.00**
Provincial Blue, plate, bread & butter; 6⅜", from $10 to.............**11.00**
Red Rooster, bread server, 9½", from $60 to **65.00**
Red Rooster, buffet server, 12½" dia, from $65 to........................**70.00**
Red Rooster, canister, tea; w/lid, from $55 to................................**60.00**
Red Rooster, pitcher, sm, 1½-pt, from $40 to.................................**50.00**
Red Rooster, plate, salad; 7½", from $10 to...................................**12.00**
Red Rooster, platter, oval, 11", from $35 to...................................**40.00**
Sculptured Daisy, bowl, vegetable; divided, 7", from $35 to..........**40.00**
Sculptured Daisy, bowl, vegetable; sm, 7" dia, from $32 to..........**35.00**
Sculptured Daisy, cup & saucer, from $12 to..................................**14.00**
Sculptured Daisy, plate, dinner; 10½", from $12 to **13.00**
Sculptured Daisy, teapot, 7-cup, from $90 to................................**100.00**
Sculptured Grape, butter dish, from $60 to....................................**65.00**
Sculptured Grape, plate, luncheon; 9", from $22 to.......................**25.00**
Sculptured Grape, salad fork & spoon, from $65 to.......................**70.00**
Sculptured Grape, sauce boat, 1-pt, from $45 to............................**50.00**
Tickled Pink, creamer, from $22 to..**25.00**
Tickled Pink, plate, salad; 7½", from $9 to **10.00**
Tickled Pink, relish dish, 3-part, 12¾", from $40 to **45.00**
Tickled Pink, tumbler, 14-oz, from $25 to **28.00**
True Blue, bowl, fruit; 6", from $12 to...**14.00**
True Blue, butter dish, oval, from $50 to...**55.00**
True Blue, plate, dinner; 10¾", from $12 to...................................**13.00**
True Blue, plate, salad; 7½"...**10.00**
Vernon Antiqua, bowl, cereal; 7⅛", from $16 to............................**18.00**
Vernon Antiqua, plate, dinner; 10⅝", from $14 to........................**15.00**
Vernon Antiqua, platter, oval, sm, 9⅝", from $35 to....................**40.00**
Woodland Gold, bowl, lug soup; ind, 6¾", from $20 to **22.00**
Woodland Gold, bowl, salad; 11", from $65 to...............................**70.00**
Woodland Gold, cup & saucer, 7-oz, 6" dia, from $12 to..............**14.00**
Woodland Gold, pitcher, sm, 1½-pt, from $40 to...........................**45.00**

Disney Figurines

Bambi w/butterfly, sm, from $225 to...**250.00**
Bashful, from $200 to **250.00**
Cinderella (peasant), from $450 to..**500.00**
Dachshund, mini, 1¼", from $200 to...**250.00**
Dumbo, seated w/bonnet, front legs down, from $125 to **150.00**
Figaro, mini, 1¼", from $175 to...**225.00**
Jiminy Cricket, from $550 to..**600.00**
Owl, from $175 to **200.00**
Pig #2 (3 Little Pigs), 1¼", from $150 to...**200.00**
Snow White, 3", from $550 to..**600.00**
Timothy Mouse, mini, 1¼", from $200 to..**250.00**
Tinker Bell, from $450 to..**500.00**
Tweedle Dum or Tweedle Dee, ea from $225 to............................**250.00**
Unicorn, Fantasia, from $250 to..**325.00**

Miniatures

Caterpillar, from $100 to...**140.00**
Chimpanzee, sitting, 3½", from $100 to..**140.00**
Elephant, sitting, 3¾", from $125 to **175.00**
Goose, 5", from $40 to...**60.00**
Mexican peasant, comical, minimum value **450.00**

Nostalgia Line

Reminiscent of the late nineteenth and early twentieth centuries, the Nostalgia line contained models of locomotives, gramophones, early autos, stage coaches, and baby carriages. There were also wagons and carts pulled by horses or donkeys, sometimes with separate drivers and passengers. The line was produced from the late 1940s through the 1960s.

American Royal Horse, Clydesdale, 9x9", minimum value 250.00
Cadillac, from $75 to..85.00
Dobbin, 11x9", from $150 to 160.00
Locomotive, from $60 to..65.00
Mary Jane, from $65 to..70.00
Mustang horse, 7x5¼", from $135 to 145.00
Perambulator, from $60 to..65.00
Pony cart, from $55 to..60.00
Train set, 3-pc, from $150 to..165.00
Vanderbilt sleigh, 9", from $65 to..70.00

Poppets

From the mid-'60s through the mid-'70s, Metlox produced a line of 'Poppets,' eighty-eight in all, representing characters ranging from royalty and professionals to a Salvation Army group. They came with a name tag; some had paper labels, others backstamps.

Arnie w/4" bowl, from $60 to...70.00
Elizabeth, queen, from $45 to..55.00
Emma the Cook, 8", from $45 to 55.00
Kitty, sm girl, 6⅝", from $40 to..50.00
Ronnie, choir boy, from $45 to...55.00
Sally, girl w/baby, 6¾", from $40 to...50.00
Salty the Sea Captain, 5¼", from $45 to......................................55.00

Romanelli Artware

Vase, Sagittarius from Zodiac series, 8x4x3", from $175.00 to $200.00.

Flower holder (Dancing Girl), 10", from $250............................275.00
Mug, Pearl Harbor, from $100 to...125.00
Vase, bud; Indian Chief; 9⅛", from $425 to................................500.00
Vase, fan; 9', from $325 to..375.00
Vase, Sail Fish, 9", from $140 to...160.00
Vase, Zodiac Series, 8x4x3" ea from $175 to...............................200.00

Mettlach

In 1836 Nicholas Villeroy and Eugene Francis Boch, both of whom were already involved in the potting industry, formed a partnership and established a stoneware factory in an old restored abbey in Mettlach, Germany. Decorative stoneware with in-mold relief was their specialty, steins in particular. Through constant experimentation, they developed innovative methods of decoration. One process, called chromolith, involved inlaying colorful mosaic designs into the body of the ware. Later underglaze printing from copper plates was used. Their stoneware

was of high quality, and their steins won many medals at the St. Louis Expo and early world's fairs. Most examples are marked with an incised castle and the name 'Mettlach.' The numbering system indicates size, date, stock number, and decorator. Production was halted by a fire in 1921; the factory was not rebuilt.

Key:
L — liter   tl — thumb lift
PUG — print under glaze

#44, beaker, relief: 3 men holding goblet, early style, 7½" 385.00
#62, stein, etch/glaze: repeating floral, inlaid lid, .5L 550.00
#202, stein, relief: choir, pewter lid, horn finial & tl, 1L............880.00
#1044, plaque, HP: bird on branch, 17" 880.00
#1044-5078, plaque, Delft: town scene, 17"...........................2,000.00
#1130, stein, etch/glazed: Prussian eagle, Munich child lid, .5L..770.00
#1146, stein, etch: fraternity students drinking, inlaid lid, .5L....550.00
#1154, stein, etch: hunters & game, gargoyle tl, relief pewter lid, 1L...550.00
#1174, stein, etch/relief: repeating design, inlaid lid, .5L 440.00
#1389, vase, etch/PUG: repeating design, 10½" 500.00
#1526-588, stein, PUG: barmaid, pewter lid, .5L.......................135.00
#1526-7200, stein, PUG: fraternity student/verse, pewter lid, .5L ..285.00
#1591, vase, etch: boys in 4 scenes, floral design, 13"..................350.00
#1665, vase, etch/PUG: repeating florals, 7"...............................230.00
#1708, plaque, relief: birds, Oriental design, 11".........................600.00
#1794, stein, etch: Bismark, orig pewter lid, .5L.........................495.00
#1797, stein, etch: cards, inlaid lid of coins, .5L.........................530.00
#1819, stein, etch: Masonic emblem, inlaid lid, .5L.....................965.00
#1861, stein, etch/PUG: Wilhelm I, SP lid (worn), .5L 445.00
#1893, stein, etch: repeating design, pewter lid, 1L.....................440.00
#1909, stein, HP/transfer: brewer, pewter lid, .4L 770.00
#1909-1038, stein, PUG: frogs in pond, pewter lid, Schlitt, .5L .850.00
#1909-715, stein, PUG: men drinking, pewter lid, .5L................165.00
#1917, stein, threading/relief: hops & wheat, inlaid lid, .25L 330.00
#1982, vase, etch: floral, 3x4½"...175.00
#1995, stein, etch: musician drinking, inlaid lid, .5L..................360.00
#2001F, stein, etch/relief: architecture, inlaid lid, .5L................660.00
#2003, stein, etch: 3 scenes of men, inlaid lid, .5L.....................660.00
#2031, stein, etch: military scene, inlaid lid, .5L......................1,045.00
#2069, stein, character: monkey w/fish, inlaid lid, collar, .5L..4,950.00
#2100, stein, etch: Germans meet Romans, inlaid lid, .5L..........900.00
#2121, stein, etch: children, inlaid lid, .25L 350.00
#2123, stein, etch: knight drinking, inlaid lid, Schlitt, .3L 825.00
#2131, stein, relief: 3 lg scenes of people, inlaid lid, .5L............300.00
#2133, stein, etch: dwarf drinking, Schlitt, inlaid lid, .5L........2,750.00
#2140-783, stein, PUG: I Garde Ulanen Regt, pewter lid w/star, .5L..1,045.00
#2204, stein, etch/relief: Prussian eagle, inlaid lid, 1L..............1,155.00
#2207, vase, etch/relief: lovers, flaw, 15½" 1,100.00
#2235, stein, etch: Schutzenliesl, inlaid lid, 1L..........................745.00
#2237, pass cup, relief: courting scenes, 3-hdld, 6½" 385.00
#2276, stein, etch/relief: Gooseman of Nurnberg, lion/shield lid, .5L....685.00
#2282, stein, etch: man in cellar, inlaid lid, .5L..........................440.00
#2307, candy bowl, relief: dwarfs scene, w/lid, 5¼" 220.00
#2368, beaker, HP: student society, Frankfort 1908, .25L............175.00
#2382, stein, etch/glazed: Thirsty Rider, tower body, inlaid lid, 1L 880.00
#2391, stein, etch: Lohengrin wedding, gargoyle hdl, inlaid lid, 1L ..2,100.00
#2391, stein, etch: Lohengrin wedding, inlaid lid, .5L 900.00
#2489, vase, etch: Nouveau floral, 7½".......................................385.00
#2531, stein, etch: man in house, inlaid lid, .5L.........................600.00
#2537, vase, eng: floral, 12¼", NM 650.00
#2590, plaque, etch: girl w/hoop, sgn Payen, 15½" 4,400.00
#2719, stein, etch/glazed: baker, inlaid lid, .5L 2,750.00
#2725, stein, etch/glaze: artist occupation, inlaid lid, .5L, NM 1,430.00
#2727, stein, etch/glaze: printer occupation, inlaid lid, .5L, NM ..1,200.00

#2752, stein, etch: men drinking at table, inlaid lid, Schlitt, .5L....**700.00**
#2809, stein, etch: Faithful Eckhart (Goethe), Quidenus, .5L **770.00**
#2828, stein, etch/relief: Wartburg, inlaid tower lid, rpr, .5L ...**1,375.00**
#2937, stein, etch: night watchman, inlaid lid, 1L.................**1,200.00**
#2950, stein, cameo: Bavarian crest, pewter crest lid, 1L.........**1,045.00**
#2982, vase, etch: Art Nouveau, 2½x4½" **440.00**
#3001, stein, etch: man w/beer glass, F Ringer, Nouveau lid, .5L ..**660.00**
#3006, vase, cameo: mermaid w/fish, 13" **465.00**
#3079-437, stein, HP/transfer: lovers, inlaid lid, .5L.....................**385.00**
#3087, stein, etch: woman drinking, pewter lid, 1L.....................**685.00**
#3185-1281, stein, PUG: hunter, inlaid lid, .5L...........................**220.00**
#3322 III, pitcher, etch: Nouveau design, 5½".............................**350.00**
#5019-5443, stein, faience: man w/stein by bbl, pewter lid, 1L ..**2,750.00**
#5022, stein, faience: country & harbor scenes, pewter lid, 1L...**1,155.00**
#5023, stein, faience: Prussian eagle, pewter lid, 1L.................**2,585.00**
#7022, pitcher, Phanolith, musicians & dancers, Stahl, 16"........**935.00**

Microscopes

The microscope has taken on many forms during its 250-year evolutionary period. The current collectors' market primarily includes examples from England, surplus items from institutions, and continental beginner and intermediate forms which sold through Sears, Roebuck & Company and other retailers of technical instruments. Earlier examples have brass main tubes which are unpainted. Later, more common examples are all black with brass or silver knobs and horseshoe-shaped bases. Early and more complex forms are the most valuable; these always had hardwood cases to house the delicate instruments and their accessories. Instruments were never polished during use, and those that have been polished to use as decorator pieces are of little interest to most avid collectors.

Baker...London, brass, ca 1880, 12", EX in mahog case **365.00**
Beck, brass, binocular, 1890s, w/many accessories, EX in case **650.00**
Carey London, pocket field type, ca 1835, VG in mahog box **950.00**
Colins, binocular, horseshoe magnet, EX oculars, ca 1870, 19", EX ..**885.00**
E Hartnack...Paris, brass, 1800s, 11¼", NM w/accessories in case.....**450.00**
E Leitz Wetzlar, brass, rack & gear focus, ca 1885, 12½", +case..**650.00**
E Lietz Werzlar, complex polarizing, w/bell jar cover, 1920s, 15", EX...**750.00**
J Swift & Son London, enameled CI base/brass pillar, rack & pinion, EX..**3,100.00**
J Swift & Son London, petrological, rack & pinion, 14", EX......**675.00**
J W Queen & Co Philada 1637, ca 1886, 13½x10", EX **425.00**
Nachet a Paris, 4 lenses, 1-sided mirror, 1880s, EX......................**475.00**
Ross London 5038, binocular, rack & pinion focus, Pat on stage, 1880s...**2,300.00**
Zeiss Zena, brass, ca 1860s, 10", EX in walnut case **1,500.00**

Midwestern Glass

As early as 1814, blown glass was made in Ohio. By 1835 glasshouses in Michigan were producing similar pattern-molded types that have long been highly regarded by collectors. During the latter part of the nineteenth century, all six of the states of the Northwest Territory were mass producing the pressed-glass tableware patterns that were then in vogue. Various types of art glass were produced in the area until after the turn of the century. Items listed here are attributed to the Midwest by certain physical characteristics known to be indigenous to that part of the country. See also Findlay Onyx; Greentown Glass; Libbey; Mantua; Zanesville Glass. Our advisor for this category is Mark Vuono; he is listed in the Directory under Connecticut.

Bottle, red-orange, 12-rib, globular, folded-over rim, pontil, 12½"...**150.00**
Bowl, violet to bl amethyst, flared rim, pontil, 5x11"...............**2,200.00**
Flask, aqua, 24 swirl ribs, 6½" **220.00**

Flask, pocket; golden yel, 21 vertical ribs, flattened ovoid, 7".....**500.00**
Pitkin flask, yel-amber, 30 right-swirl ribs, 1815-40, 6½"...........**425.00**

Militaria

Because of the wide and varied scope of items available to collectors of militaria, most tend to concentrate mainly on the area or areas that interest them most or that they can afford to buy. Some items represent a major investment and because of their value have been reproduced. Extreme caution should be used when purchasing Nazi items. Every badge, medal, cap, uniform, dagger, and sword that Nazi Germany issued is being reproduced today. Some repros are crude and easily identified as fakes, while others are very well done and difficult to recognize as reproductions. Purchases from WWII veterans are usually your safest buys. Reputable dealers or collectors will normally offer a money-back guarantee on Nazi items purchased from them. There are a number of excellent Third Reich reference books available in bookstores at very reasonable prices. Study them to avoid losing a much larger sum spent on a reproduction. Our advisor for this category is Ron L. Willis; he is listed in the Directory under Florida.

Key: insg — insignia

Imperial German

Helmet, spike; Baden Infantry, gray metal furniture, rpl chin strap **445.00**
Helmet, spike; Garde du Corps enlisted, tombak/nickel, complete, M..**6,000.00**
Helmet, spike; Pioneer Battalion enlisted, NP eagle frontispiece ..**550.00**
Manual, Feld-Pionierdienst aller Waffen (engineering), 1911, EX....**45.00**
Medal, Bavarian 40 Yr Long Service, silver/bl & gr enameling.....**45.00**
Medal, Franc-Prussian War, dtd 1870-1872, no ribbon..................**25.00**
Medal, Oldenburg Friedrich August Cross, blk iron, w/ribbon......**38.00**
Medal, Wilhelm I 100 Anniversary, gilt bronze, no ribbon **25.00**
Shako, Prussian enlisted Jager, blk leather/gray metal, EX **800.00**

Third Reich

Arm band, Allgemeine SS, wool with bevo label, SS runes and stick pins, EX, $140.00.

Atlas, SS Taschen Atlas, SS runics covered, 1938, EX................**125.00**
Backpack, Army M1939 style, field gray canvas w/leather straps, NM...**40.00**
Belt buckle, Waffen SS enlisted, aluminum, EX **165.00**
Canteen, Waffen SS, aluminum w/wool cover, Bakelite cap & cup, EX...**75.00**
Carrying case, stick grenade; gray-pnt metal, wood hdl, 18½x14¾" ..**75.00**
Collar tab, Nat'l Railway, 5 brass winged wheel insg, EX **27.50**
Cup, field; Army, folding hdls, side spout..**25.00**
Document, Waffen SS, official communique, Mar 1945, scarce....**95.00**
Helmet, battlefield relic, schrapnel hdl, oxidation..........................**35.00**
Helmet, Luftwaffe M1935/40 style, eagle decal, EX+ **125.00**
Helmet, pith; Africa Corps, olive gr felt cover, eagle/shield, M ..**125.00**
Kit, surgeon's; Army, folding cloth w/9 instruments.......................**70.00**
Leaflet, Eastern Front propaganda, in Russian, EX **100.00**
Medal, Eastern Peoples Bravery, w/swords & gr ribbon..................**40.00**
Medal, Veteran Assn Service, silvered crows/monument, no ribbon..**25.00**
Medal, War Service Cross 2nd Class, bronze w/swords & ribbon..**25.00**

Permit, work Eastern territories, eagle cover, ink stamped............**35.00**
Plate, Army mess; wht porc, eagle proofmk, 1936, 9½"................**26.00**
Rucksack, Army, field gray canvas w/leather fittings, sm, EX............**25.00**
Shell carrier, Army Artillery, woven wicker, red pnt rim, 30" H...**90.00**
Shirt, Waffen SS, gray-gr cotton, long sleeves, rare.....................**400.00**
Stickpin, Veteran Assn, aluminum eagle/Iron Cross motif............**25.00**
Trousers, Navy fatigues, brn linen, fall front, metal buttons, NM...**110.00**

Japanese

Badge, WWII Red Cross Special Membership, aluminum w/ribbon, EX...**40.00**
Belt, trousers; WWII, brn leather, roller buckle, VG....................**55.00**
Cap, visor; WWII, Infantry officer's, wool w/brass star, G.............**90.00**
Coveralls, WWII, Tanker, olive drab, complete, EX...................**150.00**
Flag, WWII era, silk, 'meatball' & rising sun, 24x48", EX...........**200.00**
Hat, visor; Russo-Japanese War, Cavalry Officer, wool, 1904-05, EX..**40.00**
Helmet, Army Civil Defense, pnt steel shell w/liner, VG+............**50.00**
Helmet, flight; brn leather w/wht lining, NM................................**60.00**
Helmet, WWII, Army, steel, w/liner/tie, gr w/star, NM................**695.00**
Helmet, WWII, cloth-covered stiff body w/star on front, EX......**250.00**
Insignia, collar; WWII, aircraft mechanic, brass, pr.....................**26.00**
Leggings, WWII, Navy, button-up spat pattern, field rprs, G......**135.00**
Medal, China Incident, bronze w/orig ribbon, dbl-sided, EX.........**35.00**
Medal, WWII, Order of the Rising Sun, 8th Class, w/ribon, M in case...**55.00**
Overcoat, WWII, olive gr w/gr pile collar, dbl-breasted, EX.......**140.00**
Uniform, dress; Cavalry, dk bl wool w/yel frogs, ca 1886, sm, EX...**1,000.00**
Uniform, field; Infantry private, tunic & trousers, ca 1904-05, VG.....**65.00**
Wing, WWII, aluminum bullion wing portion, sew-on, EX..........**28.00**

Russia/Soviet

Ammo belt, machine gun; Imperial Era, canvas w/brass fittings, 1914..**295.00**
Badge, Imperial Era, Foreman, brass, oval, 1880s.........................**100.00**
Belt buckle, Imperial eagle, brass, dbl-headed eagle, EX..............**120.00**
Boots, WWII Army, high-top, pull-on straps, leather soles, pr...**115.00**
Breastplate, WWI battlefield relic, 2nd pattern, bullet fracture..**325.00**
Canteen, Imperial Era, wooden bbl w/old bl pnt, ca 1900, 7½x4¾"..**260.00**
Cap, Imperial Era Dragoon NCO, gr wool/red piping, w/cockade.....**297.50**
Entrenching tool, WWII, spade head w/pnt traces, wood shaft.....**57.50**
Flashlight, field; WWI Army, blk pnt metal body w/NP fittings....**27.50**
Goggles, WWII pilot, metal fr w/clear curved glass lenses, EX......**85.00**
Hat, visor; Pre-WWII Era Cavalry M1922, gray wool w/star insg..**495.00**
Helmet, WWII battlefield relic, gr pnt traces................................**37.50**
Leaflet, WWII propaganda, written in German............................**75.00**
Map case, WWII Army officer, brn leather, 2-compartment, belt loops.**50.00**
Medal, Cross for Service in Caucasus, bronze, Xd swords/eagle, 1865....**85.00**
Medal, Social Welfare Commemorative, silver, 1841-1891, w/ribbon..**42.00**
Medal, St George Cross 3rd Class, silver, Imperial Era, w/ribbon.....**100.00**
Mess kit, WWII Army, aluminum, hinged hdl & bail, pnt traces, 1936..**48.00**
Photo, Imperial officer in full uniform, 1880s, 4x2½", VG...........**25.00**
Pouch, ammo; WWII, dk leather, 2-pocket, flap tabs, belt loops..**35.00**
Shirt, WWI Army M1943 Rubaha, star buttons, summer weight, EX..**375.00**
Uniform, WWII, snow camouflage, attached hood w/drawstrings, M.....**375.00**

United States

Ax, boarding; Federal period, 12½" head, 5" pike, rpl haft.........**800.00**
Belt, saber; Civil War Cavalry enlisted man's, brn leather+eagle plate...**750.00**
Belt, sword; Spanish Am Naval Officer's, blk leather w/plate, EX..**85.00**
Belt, waist; Civil War era, blk leather, oval brass plate, VG........**285.00**
Book, Artillery & Infantry Instruction, West Point/Kingsbury, 1849......**95.00**
Box, cartridge, Civil War era, std Model 1855, 58-caliber, G leather...**300.00**
Breeches, WWI Army, olive drab wool, metal buttons, sm rpr......**35.00**
Canteen, CW, bull's-eye type, tin, pewter spout, EX.....................**300.00**

Canteen, Indian War, canvas cover mk US, orig stopper, dents.**350.00**
Canteen, NY Militia, wooden w/tin bands, old rust-clored pnt, G..**600.00**
Canteen, WWI, canvas cover mk US/dtd 1906, lt dents, VG...**150.00**
Collar disk, WWI enlisted, bronze, nat'l shield/spoked gear..........**42.50**
Drum, snare; Civil War era, lacquered maple w/tack decor, 17" dia, G.**485.00**
Drum, snare; Civil War era, maple, orig Boston label, VG..........**800.00**
Epaulettes, Indian Wars Era, entwined gold bullion, red silk trim, pr...**115.00**
Fife, Civil War era, rosewood, brass/pewter fittings, 14"..............**145.00**
Flag holder & sling, Militia, leather w/brass buckle, 1850s, G....**175.00**
Hat, visor; WWI Navy officer, dk bl wool w/gold & silver insg..**150.00**
Helmet, spike; Indian Wars Era, cork/wht lacquer, brass eagle, EX..**235.00**
Helmet, WWI-era pilot, brn leather, Real Nappa, flannel lined.**225.00**
Jacket, Civil War Cavalry Uniform, wool lace collar, eagle buttons...**1,150.00**
Knapsack, Civil War era, tarred canvas w/leather flap, 1860-70s, G......**155.00**
Manual, Instruction for Volunteers/Militia, Graham/1851, 742-pg..**65.00**
Manual, Nolan's System for Training Cavalry Horses, 1862, VG..**125.00**
Manual, WWI, Hand Bombers & Hand Grenadiers, 1918, EX.....**65.00**
Medal, Spanish-Am War era, WI State Service, bronze...............**40.00**

Patch, WWII era, 13th Airbourne, black over blue with gold, $15.00.

Saddle valise, Mexican War officer's, leather, brass tacks, 16" L, G.**800.00**
Shell case, WWI Era Artillery, brass, 3½"..**25.00**
Shoes, WWI Army, brn leather ankle boots, metal heels, unissued, pr....**125.00**
Telescope, Civil War Era Navy, brass, Dolland, extends to 36½", EX......**550.00**
Tunic, dress; Korean War Marine Corps, dl bl wool, 4-pocket, chevrons..**40.00**
Tunic, Indian Wars era, dk bl wool, dbl-breasted, gold frogs, G....**50.00**
Tunic, WWII Army Sergeant, olive drab wool, 2-pocket, chevrons...**35.00**

Miscellaneous

Britain, medal, Army Long Service & Good Conduct, silver, type 2....**25.00**
Britain, medal, WWI Peace, gray metal, Britannia figure, ca 1919..**25.00**
Dutch, helmet, Army, NM blk finish, complete, 1940s...............**250.00**
E Germany, helmet, Red Cross, complete, 1980s, NM................**250.00**
France, helmet, WWI Infantry, grenade insg, top comb, visor, EX..**200.00**
France, kepi, 1950s era, bl-gray cotton twill, lacking chinstrap.....**25.00**
Hungary, helmet, WWI style, steel, complete, NM......................**150.00**
Italy, cap, visor; WWI era, blk wool crown w/blk velvet band....**235.00**
Italy, helmet, WWII, camouflage, fascist eagle on front.............**200.00**

Milk Glass

    Milk glass is the current collector's name for milk-white opaque glass. The early glassmaker's term was Opal Ware. Originally attempted in England in the eighteenth century with the intention of imitating china, milk glass was not commercially successful until the mid-1800s. Pieces produced in the U.S.A., England, and France during the 1870 – 1900 period are highly prized for their intricate detail and fiery, opalescent edges.

    For further information we recommend *Collector's Encyclopedia of Milk Glass, An Identification & Value Guide*, by Betty and Bill Newbound. (CE numbers in our listings refer to this publication.) Another highly recommended book is *The Milk Glass Book* by Frank Chiarenza and James Slater. The newest reference, published in 2001, is *Milk Glass Imperial Glass Corporation* by Myrna and Bob Garrison. Our advisor for this category is Rod Dockery; he is listed in the Directory under Texas. See also Animal Dishes with Covers; Bread Plates; Historical Glass; Westmoreland.

Key:
CE — Newbound   G — Garrison
F — Ferson   MGB — Milk Glass Book

Ashtray, barefoot form, unmk, CE-357, 4¾" **12.00**
Ashtray, sailboat w/metal sails, mk Made in USA, CE-424, 6¼"..**20.00**
Biscuit jar, HP w/SP hdl & lid, poppy pattern, CE-180, 5½" **75.00**
Bookends, standing bear, Luna Glass, 1916, CE-192, 8¾", pr.....**300.00**
Bowl, Gothic border, Canton Glass, CE-32, 7½" **20.00**
Butter press, HP flower decor, pineapple impression, CE-415, 4½" ..**85.00**
Cake stand, scalloped edge, Indiana Glass, CE-108, 10⅜" sq.........**35.00**
Candlesticks, Dutch Boudoir, US Glass, 1910, CE-76, 3", pr......**120.00**
Candlesticks, figural dolphins, Westmoreland, CE-65, 9¼", pr.....**75.00**
Candy dish, 3-section, w/HP mc floral lid, CE-45, 6½" dia...........**25.00**
Cigarette box, hobby horse, w/Dutch pnt, G-1950/134, minimum.....**600.00**
Compote, grape leaf w/stem & root-like foot, bl, Vallerysthal, CE-86...**65.00**
Creamer, Cherry Thumbprint, Westmoreland, CE-309, 3½" **20.00**
Creamer & sugar bowl, Betsy Ross pattern, Fostoria, CE-294, 4"..**35.00**
Dish, Battleship Maine, w/orig pnt, MGB-178 ....**150.00**
Dish, Crown Butter, MGB-169, 4⅝x5¾" H **225.00**
Epergne, Ribs & Scallops, single-horn, Vallerysthal/Porteiux, CE-106 ...**100.00**
Figurine, owl ring tree, Fenton, 1950s, CE-196, 4¼" **25.00**
Figurine, standing deer, Fostoria, CE-195, 4¾" **50.00**
Honey jar, Pink Beehive, w/lid, Jeannette Glass, CE-52, 4⅛"........**30.00**
Humidor, 3 bulldogs on front, old pipe on reverse, brass lid, CE-181 ...**300.00**
Lamp, banquet; HP flower trim, lacy metal base, CE-237, 17"....**100.00**
Lamp, electric, reclining nude w/harp as base, CE-226, 5¾" **90.00**
Match holder, baby on blk top hat, whimsical detail, F-534, scarce........**450.00**
Novelty, Uncle Sam hat, wht w/red & bl, Westmoreland, CE-404, 3¾"...**55.00**
Perfume bottle, rose-pk w/wht leaves & flowers, CE-8, 8½" **40.00**
Pickle dish, boat shape w/oars emb along side, CE-333, 9½" **40.00**
Pitcher, allover emb water lilies, Fenton, CE-319, 7" **60.00**
Pitcher, ball style w/ice lip, Cambridge Glass, CE-322, 7".............**50.00**
Pitcher, owl form w/amber glass eyes, Challinor-Taylor, F-587, 7½" ...**185.00**
Plate, Beaded Edge, Iris, HP, Westmoreland, CE-248 ....**15.00**
Plate, eagle & shield, MarCor, CE-251, 15" **45.00**
Plate, Lincoln on backward C border, LE Smith, 1960, CE-272, 9¼"...**60.00**
Plate, sm bear, MGB-192, rare, 3⅛" **125.00**
Plate, south sea island view, HP, wide border, CE-266, 9" **12.00**
Plate, Wyoming Monument, F-18, 7½" **100.00**
Plate, 3 owls form top of plate, Westmoreland, CE-265, 7½" **35.00**
Rolling pin, blown glass w/cork, CE-224, 15" **120.00**
Salt box, emb lettering, wooden lid, CE-59, 5¾"...........................**95.00**
Shakers, Arlington pattern, w/pepper mill, Fostoria, CE-286, pr ..**45.00**
Shakers, tomato shape, w/pewter lids, CE-280, 2¾", pr.................**30.00**
Shaving mug, cathedral arches & roses, gold pnt, CE-209, 3¼" .**100.00**
Sugar bowl, Cactus pattern, w/lid, Fenton, CE-299, 6⅛" **30.00**
Sugar bowl, Lace & Dewdrop, bl pnt, w/lid, Phoenix, CE-305, 6" **40.00**
Toothpick holder, owl w/spread wings, Westmoreland, CE-325, 3" ...**20.00**
Tray, comb & brush, crosshatched, CE-348, 10x6¾" **25.00**
Tray, horseshoe emb w/grapes, Imperial Glass, G-1950/54, pg 133....**20.00**
Tumbler, Drape or Puffed, gold rim, Fostoria, CE-212, 2¾" **30.00**
Vase, cornucopia form on base, Westmoreland, 1933, CE-380......**30.00**
Vase, emb w/wild geese in flight, Consolidated, CE-385, 9¾x11½"...**135.00**
Vase, Mephistopheles, panels w/emb roses, Vallerysthal, CE-368, 9½" ..**60.00**
Watering can, bl, Westmoreland, 1904, CE-190, 4" H **50.00**
Wine decanter, emb grapes, Imperial, G-1950/163 ....**45.00**

Millefiori

Millefiori was a type of art glass produced during the 1800s. Literally the term means 'thousand flowers,' an accurate description of its appearance. Canes, fused bundles of multicolored glass threads such as are often used in paperweights were cut into small cross sections, arranged in the desired pattern, refired, and shaped into articles such as cruets, lamps, and novelty items. It is still being produced, and many examples found on the market today are fairly recent in manufacture. See also Paperweights.

Bottle, scent; clear & faceted w/millefiori base, English, 1850, 6" ..**200.00**
Cup & saucer, 3½", 5¼" **215.00**
Toothpick holder, mc on wht, waisted, ruffled rim, 2⅛x1⅞" **160.00**
Toothpick holder, 2½"...**50.00**
Vase, mc canes on blk, hdls, flared ruffled rim, 9x4½" **315.00**
Vase, trumpet form, satin cased, 7x3½".......................................**165.00**

Miniature Paintings

Miniature works of art vary considerably in value depending on many criteria: as with any art form, those that are signed by or can be attributed to a well-known artist may command prices well into the thousands of dollars. Collectors find paintings of identifiable subjects especially interesting, as are those with props, such as a child with a vintage toy or a teddy bear or a soldier in uniform with his weapon at his side. Even if none of these factors come to bear, an example exhibiting fine details and skillful workmanship may bring an exceptional price. Of course, condition is important, and ornate or unusual frames also add value.

Child (identified), on ivory, att Mrs MB Russell, 2¼"+gilt-metal fr **4,300.00**
Courting scenes on ivory, ivory mosaic fr w/mc agate inlay, 5x6", pr **350.00**
Gentleman, oil on ivory, Anglo/Am School, 1800s, 3x2½", EX, +case...**175.00**
Gentleman, on ivory, 1836, gilt-medal pendant fr, 2¾x2⅛" **200.00**
Gentleman, watercolor on ivory, att Cushman, 1840s, 2¾"+fr w/hair ..**1,095.00**
Gentleman, watercolor on ivory, att PA Peticolas, 3½"+pendant fr **800.00**
Gentleman, watercolor on ivory, att Wm Lewis, 3¼x2½"+pendant fr...**375.00**
Gentleman, watercolor on paper, Anglo-Am school, 1800s, 3½x2½"....**230.00**
Gentleman w/jeweled stickpin, on ivory, 2", in leather case **200.00**
Geo Washington, on ivory, after Trumball, Renny/1830, 3x2¼"+fr..**3,000.00**
Girl, ¾-portrait, sgn Kreuze, on ivory, 3½x3", scrimshaw fr........**325.00**
Girl (identified), watercolor on ivory, Am, 19th C, 2½"+pendant fr...**175.00**
Girl in red dress, watercolor in ivory, 3", +leather photo case.....**400.00**

Girl in white dress, attributed to John Brewster Jr, American, 1766 – 1854, watercolor on ivory, 1¾x1¼", in bright-cut pendant frame with braided hair border, minor pigment loss, $7,500.00.

Girl knits, braids/gilt jewelry, ID, rnd brass liner, 4⅝x4½" **1,200.00**
Lady, Gainsborough copy, watercolor on faux ivory, ornate fr, 3¾x3" ..**275.00**
Lady, watercolor on ivory, in pendant fr w/hair compartment, 3¼".......**250.00**
Lady, watercolor on ivory, 6¼x4", minor fading **200.00**

Lady by memorial urn, on ivory in woven hair surround, 3⅜" **460.00**
Lady in blk cloak, on ivory, Chinese school, 1850s, 2½"+fr........**800.00**
Lady in blk dress w/wht lace collar, on paper, early 1800s, fr, 3⅛"..**750.00**
Lady in dress w/high neck ruffle on ivory, 2¾x2"+bronze doré fr ..**495.00**
Lady in wht headscarf, oil on porc, oval, 2½" W, in gilt fr..........**110.00**
Lady's portrait, sgn H Denis, on ivory, ornate 5½" fr...................**995.00**
Lady w/elegant hair, watercolor on ivory, sgn Hing Qua, 2½"+cvd fr ...**1,095.00**
Lady w/ornate hairdo in lush int, on ivory, sgn J Isabey, 4¼"+fr ..**1,725.00**
Madonna Della Sedia, on porc, German/1890s, in 15x7" gesso fr....**550.00**
Man & lady in blk, watercolor on paper, ea 3½x2¾" in fr, pr .**1,495.00**
Man in frock coat, sunset beyond, oil on wood, identified/1800, 6x5"....**1,200.00**
Man in frock coat, watercolor on paper, identified, 7x6", VG **195.00**
Man in profile, identified, on paper, early 1800s, fr, 3⅛x2⅜" **350.00**
Man w/high collar & tie, detailed, ca 1800, orig gilt-copper case, 3"...**2,875.00**
Mme De Breolles portrait on ivory, 2½"+5⅛x4¼" ornate fr........**995.00**
Mme Elizabeth, rtcl brass Rococo fr, 3¼x2½" **275.00**
Mother & child on ivory, sgn RB, 18th C, in oval pressed brass fr....**700.00**
Mother & son on sofa w/toy, on ivory, early 1800s, in fr, 5x3⅞" ..**4,875.00**
Napoleon & Josephine on ivory, 5½x4½", pr **995.00**
Queen Elizabeth w/in gold wreath on red-pnt porc, 3⅜" **115.00**
Soldier, gray uniform/medals on ivory, Fadis, scrimshaw fr, 3x3".**300.00**

Miniatures

There is some confusion as to what should be included in a listing of miniature collectibles. Some feel the only true miniature is the salesman's sample; other collectors consider certain small-scale children's toys to be appropriately referred to as miniatures, while yet others believe a miniature to be any small-scale item that gives evidence to the craftsmanship of its creator. For salesman's samples, see specific category; other types are listed below. See also Dollhouses and Furnishings; Children's Things.

Armoire, mahog & cherrywood, dbl door, shaped skirt, 1790s, 27x19x11"..**8,625.00**
Band saw, CI, w/blade, pulley, Germany, working, 9", EX **460.00**

Bed, half-tester rosewood, brackets, tapered round columns, scrolled crest, urn finials, New Orleans, ca 1850s, 29x21x16½", $2,000.00.

Bed, 4-poster, mahog Fed, scroll headbrd/tapered posts/tester, 16"..**1,850.00**
Blanket chest, mahog, wire hinges, dvtl, bracket base, 7x14"..**1,000.00**
Blanket chest mahog/oak/pine, dvtl, orange pnt, rpr/rpl, 7x13x8" **275.00**
Blanket chest pine w/2 rnd mustard reserves w/gazelles, 15" L, EX.....**2,900.00**
Blanket chest poplar w/dk red over lt brn pnt decor, rpl ft, 10x17"........**990.00**
Blanket chest poplar w/dry gr pnt, cut-out ft, B Harter, 9x14x7"............**220.00**
Blanket chest poplar w/gr stencil animals/urn of flowers, 14" L, EX ...**1,500.00**
Box, blanket; cvd/pnt scrolled florals, Scandinavia, 19th C, 6x5x10" .**1,955.00**
Candlestick phone, Stromberg Carlson, chrome/hard rubber, 3", EX **145.00**
Chest, curly maple Sheraton style, 3 dvtl drws, 16x16x10".........**715.00**
Chest, dk red pnt, 6-brd, arched sides, hinged lid, 18th C, 8x14x6"..**4,850.00**
Chest, Emp style, figured mahog facings/veneer, wire nails, 13x7x13"....**550.00**
Chest, mahog, 3-drw, molded top & base, wire nails, rfn, 10x14x7"......**415.00**

Chest, mahog veneer w/brass band inlay (loose), Regency, 9½".**225.00**
Chest, pine w/red wash, 3-drw, nailed, 16x14x10"......................**675.00**
Chest, softwood w/molded edges, 2-drw, 12x9½" **175.00**
Chest, walnut, 3-drw w/wooden pulls, att Medina Co OH, rpr, 8¼" ..**300.00**
Chest, walnut Emp, 4-drw, old varnish, trn pulls, 12x12x8" **465.00**
Chest, walnut Wm IV w/inlay, 2 short & 3 long drws, 1835, 20"..**700.00**
Chest, walnut/poplar w/flame veneer, serpentine front, 3-drw, 16", EX ..**470.00**
Cradle, rye straw, open ends, shaped red rockers, PA origin, 13" L..**110.00**
Cupboard, butternut & walnut, sq nails, dvtl drw, 11x11x8" **415.00**
Cupboard, gr/tan grpt, rpt top, scalloped base, panel do, 13x14x9"..**250.00**
Cupboard, pine, step-bk, slant lid over bin, rfn, 22x16x9½"......**440.00**
Cupboard, poplar step-bk, old brn pnt over red, 3-shelf top, 31x18"...**660.00**
Dresser, Eastlake, walnut, cvd crest/drws, blk/gold details, 23x13x6" ..**250.00**
Dresser, wood w/pressed florals, mirror, 2 short/2 L drw, 18x17" .**175.00**
Reaper (horse-drawn), working model of 1831 McCormick, 35" .**3,100.00**
Rocking bench, pine, plank seat, spindle bk, tenons, 1890s, 20" ...**175.00**
Sedan chair, tin w/coppery lacquer & HP cherubs, brocade int, 7", VG ..**290.00**
Sidebrd, pine w/brn pnt, scalloped/rtcl crest, scalloped aprons, 20"...**580.00**
Spinning wheel, wood, trn spindles, 11", VG **55.00**
Stand, walnut & pine, old finish, pegged, 1-brd top, 18x14x14" ...**550.00**
Trunk, pine w/orig mc decor, dome top, open till, wire nails, 6x9x5" **745.00**
Trunk, wood/tin, dome top w/int compartments, hdls missing, 14", G+.**150.00**
Waffle iron, Stover, CI w/wood hdls, 4" dia, EX **500.00**

Minton

Thomas Minton established his firm in 1793 at Stoke on Trent and within a few years began producing earthenware with blue-printed patterns similar to the ware he had learned to decorate while employed by the Caughley Porcelain Factory. The Willow pattern was one of his most popular. Neither this nor the porcelain made from 1798 to 1805 was marked (except for an occasional number series), making identification often impossible.

After 1805 until about 1816, fine tea services, beehive-shaped honey pots, trays, etc., were hand decorated with florals, landscapes, Imari-type designs, and neoclassic devices. These were often marked with crossed 'Ls.' It was Minton that invented the acid gold process of decorating (1863), which is now used by a number of different companies. From 1816 until 1823, no porcelain was made. Through the '20s and '30s, the ornamental wares with colorful decoration of applied fruits and florals and figurines in both bisque and enamel were usually left unmarked. As a result, they have been erroneously attributed to other potters. Some of the ware that was marked bears a deliberate imitation of Meissen's crossed swords. From the late '20s through the '40s, Minton made a molded stoneware line (mugs, jugs, teapots, etc.) with florals or figures in high relief. These were marked with an embossed scroll with an 'M' in the bottom curve. Fine parian ware was made in the late 1840s, and in the 1850s Minton experimented with and perfected a line of quality majolica which they produced from 1860 until it was discontinued in 1908. Their slogan was 'Majolica for the Millions,' and for it they gained widespread recognition. Leadership of the firm was assumed by Minton's son Herbert sometime around the middle of the nineteenth century. Working hand in hand with Leon Arnoux, who was both a chemist and an artist, he managed to secure the company's financial future through constant, successful experimentation with both materials and decorating methods. During the Victorian era, M.L. Solon decorated pieces in the pate-sur-pate style, often signing his work; these examples are considered to be the finest of their type. After 1862 all wares were marked 'Minton' or 'Mintons,' with an impressed year cipher.

Many collectors today reassemble the lovely dinnerware patterns that have been made by Minton. Perhaps one of their most popular lines was Minton Rose, introduced in 1854. The company itself once counted forty-seven versions of this pattern being made by other potteries around the world. In addition to less expensive copies, elaborate hand-enameled pieces were also made by Aynsley, Crown Staffordshire, and Paragon China. Solando Ware (1937) and Byzantine Range (1938) were designed by John Wadsworth. Minton ceased all earthenware production in 1939.

See also Majolica; Pate-Sur-Pate.

Bowl, cereal; Lady Devonish, S520	65.00
Bowl, fruit; Gold Laurentian, H5184, 5¼"	49.00
Bowl, ship reserve w/gold on bl-gr lustre, gold hdls, ca 1900, 4x6"	195.00
Bowl, soup; Gold Laurentian, H5184	70.00
Bowl, vegetable; Ardmore, open rnd, S363	188.00
Bowl, cream soup; & saucer, Chatham, S123	90.00
Bowl, cream soup; & saucer, Corinthian, H5218	105.00
Coffeepot, Lorraine, S561	247.50
Coffeepot, Westminster, K154	470.00
Cup & saucer, Alabaster & Gold	89.00
Cup & saucer, bouillon; B898	60.00
Cup & saucer, bouillon; Eloise, B1010	60.00
Cup & saucer, demitasse; Buckingham, K159	110.00
Cup & saucer, demitasse; Pandora, S693	60.00
Cup & saucer, Gray Cameo, S664	79.00
Cup & saucer, Grosvenor	85.00
Cup & saucer, Haddon Hall, #12295	65.00
Cup & saucer, Stanwood	75.00
Garden seat, entwined rings/flower bands, earthenware, 19th C, 18", pr	1,095.00
Jug, ERVII 1901, Secessionist, 7½", NM	285.00
Mug, Genevese, red & wht, ca 1900 mk, 3¼"	125.00
Plate, bread & butter; Penrose	49.00
Plate, cake; Ripon B981	65.00
Plate, cake; Winter Harvest	85.00
Plate, castles scenes, bone china, sgn JE Dean, ca 1910, 9", 12 for	575.00
Plate, dinner; Alabaster & Gold	99.00
Plate, dinner; Cockatrice, 1916	180.00
Plate, dinner; Dainty Sprays, S511	79.00
Plate, dinner; Gold Rose, H4680	90.00
Plate, dinner; Haddon Hall, #12295	75.00
Plate, dinner; Pandora, S693	70.00
Plate, dinner; Vermont, S365	95.00
Plate, salad; Blue Delft, crescent shape, S766	65.00
Plate, salad; Dainty Sprays, S511	56.00
Plate, salad; Laurentian, S659	56.00
Plate, salad; York, S501	48.00
Platter, Ardmore, S363, lg	335.00
Platter, Bala, S570, lg	295.00
Platter, Lady Devonish, S520, lg	410.00
Platter, Marlow, bone china, MIE, 13½"	85.00
Platter, Saint James, bone china, sm	175.00
Platter, Westminster, K154, med	365.00
Sugar bowl, Ardmore, w/lid	129.00
Teapot, Bridal Veil	250.00
Teapot, Vermont, S365	275.00
Vase, floral on 5-spout fan form w/fish-head ft, celadon, 6¼", NM	200.00

Mirrors

The first mirrors were made in England in the thirteenth century of very thin glass backed with lead. Reverse-painted glass mirrors were made in this country as early as the late 1700s and remained popular throughout the next century. The simple hand-painted panel was separated from the mirrored section by a narrow slat, and the frame was either the dark-finished Federal style or the more elegant, often-gilded Sheraton.

Mirrors changed with the style of other furnishings; but whatever type you purchase, as long as the glass sections remain solid, even broken or flaking mirrors are more valued than replaced glass. Careful resilvering is acceptable if excessive deterioration has taken place. In the listings that follow, items are from the nineteenth century unless noted otherwise. The term 'style' (example: Federal style) is used to indicate a mirror reminiscent of but made well after the period indicated. Obviously these retro styles will be valued much lower than their original counterparts. As with most other items in antiques and collectibles, the influence of online trading is greatly affecting prices. Many items once considered difficult to locate are now readily available on the Internet. Our advisor for this category is Michael Hinton; he is listed in the Directory under Pennsylvania.

Key:
Chpndl — Chippendale	QA — Queen Anne
Emp — Empire	Vict — Victorian
Fed — Federal	vnr — veneer

Brass, finely scrolled vining w/Bacchus crest, candle arms, 21x13"	250.00
Brass, rtcl floral panels top/sides, urn crest w/dolphins, 20x6½"	60.00
Burl wood Fr Emp style, eagle crest, bronze capital/base, 64x36"	2,300.00
Cheval, mahog English Regency, sq columnar supports, urn finials, 56"	1,800.00

Courting, molded frame with shaped crest enclosing reverse-painted panels, etched mirror glass, Northern Europe, late 1700s, 18½x11¼", $3,750.00.

Courting, rvpt marbleized surround, stepped crest w/rvpt bird, 17x12"	1,550.00
Dressing, mahog Fed, rectangular w/lyre supports, 2 drws	515.00
Dressing, silver Aesthetic Movement w/repousse flowers & birds, 20x16"	1,000.00
Figured mahog vnr on pine QA, scalloped crest, rpl trim/glass, 23x12"	700.00
Flame mahog veneer Emp, scalloped top/½-pilasters/ogee base, 51x21"	770.00
Gilt & faux tortoise shell Fed, split balusters, rvpt eagle, 26"	3,000.00
Gilt Am Classic, split baluster trn columns, rosette corners, 20x42"	500.00
Gilt Fed, rnd fr w/spherules, lg eagle/foliage crest, 19th C, 49x30"	3,335.00
Gilt gesso & wood Late Fed, eagle on plinth/grapes, 57x34"	5,175.00
Gilt gesso Geo III style, plume crest, swags, pendant shelf, 66x35"	1,035.00
Gilt gesso Late Fed, molded cornice, acorn drops, appl devices, 37x19"	700.00
Gilt gesso w/projecting cornice w/spherules, rvpt panel: girl, 31x19"	750.00
Gilt/gesso Fed, reeded pilasters, rvpt floral panels, 33x18"	440.00
Giltwood Am Rococo, cvd foliate crest/vintage/fruit/scrolls, 54x26"	2,000.00
Giltwood Baroque w/crest shield, floral scrolling, 44x35"	1,200.00
Giltwood Continental, rvpt lady w/open book in crest, 18th C, 22"	3,000.00
Giltwood cvd/pierced fr, Vict, 52x36"	2,875.00
Giltwood Fed, rosette corner blocks, rvpt, reeded columns, 27x25"	900.00
Giltwood Fed w/rvpt Classical ladies in garden, MA, ca 1815, 48x21"	12,650.00
Giltwood Fed w/rvpt fruit & drapery scene above, 1810-20, 29x14"	1,600.00
Giltwood Louis Philippe w/cvd floral crest & scrolling, 78x33"	1,725.00
Giltwood Louis XV style C scroll w/trailing florals, 51x28"	1,850.00
Mahog Chpndl, arched crest, scrolling bracket, Elliot, 1800s, 46x24"	3,450.00
Mahog Chpndl, scrolling crest w/pine cone ears, rpl glass/rfn, 44x22"	975.00
Mahog Chpndl scroll w/regilded eagle & liner, rstr, 42x23"	880.00
Mahog Chpndl w/gilt ho-ho bird, scrolled pendant, rstr, 1790s, 37x20"	865.00
Mahog Chpndl w/gilt ho-ho bird, 2-part beveled glass, rstr, 55x24"	4,200.00

Mahog Chpndl w/inlay, arched crest, rpl glass/rfn, 40x20" **635.00**
Mahog Chpndl w/scroll, gilt/pierced foliage, 37" **1,100.00**
Mahog Fed, molded cornice, rvpt hunt scene, old rfn, 36x18" ...**2,185.00**
Mahog Fed w/inlaid conch shells, vnr pendant, rstr, 48" **635.00**
Mahog QA, arched crest w/scrolled ears, scalloped base, 30x14" **800.00**
Over-mantel, gilt gesso Fed w/oak leaves, 3-part, 33x55" **1,265.00**
Over-mantel, giltwood Am Fed, 3-part, 24x60" **1,265.00**
Pier, gilt Am Late Fed, orig w/minor rubs, 37x61" **2,750.00**
Pier, gilt gesso Fed, ½-baluster columns, 50x26" **2,415.00**
Pier, giltwood Fed, rectangular molded fr w/orig gilt, 63x33" **700.00**
Pine Regency w/cvd eagle & scroll, cvd leaves below, 1820s, 35x22" ..**1,850.00**
Sterling, shaped oval w/emb florals, cherubs, cartouch, 18x14" **1,035.00**
Walnut, relief-cvd w/fruit/sunflower/rose crest, 6" W, 24x20" **330.00**
Walnut Biedermeier, ogee molded crest, paneled stiles, 1830s, 37x26"...**345.00**
Walnut Chpndl, scrolled crest & ears, drop pendant, 41x22" ..**4,300.00**
Walnut veneer & giltwood Chpndl, cvd ho-ho bird finial, 39¼x22" ..**2,000.00**

Mocha

Mochaware is utilitarian pottery made principally in England (and to a lesser extent in France) between 1780 and 1840 on the then prevalent creamware and pearlware bodies. Initially, only those pieces decorated in the seaweed pattern were called 'Mocha,' while geometrically decorated pieces were referred to as 'Banded Creamware.' Other types of decorations were called 'Dipped Ware.' During the last thirty to forty years the term 'Mocha' has been applied to the entire realm of 'Industrialized Slipware' — pottery decorated by the turner on his lathe using coggle wheels and slip cups.

Mocha was made in numerous patterns — Tree, Seaweed or Dandelion, Rope (also called Worm or Loop), Cat's-eye, Tobacco Leaf, Lollypop or Balloon, Marbled, Marbled and Combed, Twig, Geometric or Checkered, Banded, and slip decorations of rings, dots, flags, tulips, wavy lines, etc. It came into its own as a collectible in the latter half of the 1940s and has become increasingly popular as more and more people are exposed to the rich colorings and artistic appeal of its varied forms of abstract decoration. (Please note: Values hinge to a great extent on vivid coloration, intricacy of patters, and unusual features.)

The collector should take care not to confuse the early pearlware and creamware Mocha with the later kitchen yellow ware, graniteware, and ironstone sporting mocha-type decoration that was produced in America by such potters as J. Vodrey, George S. Harker, Edwin Bennett, and John Bell. This type was also produced in Scotland and Wales and was marketed well into the twentieth century.

Our values are prices realized at auction, where nearly every example was in exceptional condition. Unless another condition code is present in the description line, assume that each example was in at least EX+ to NM condition.

Basin, six-color with cat's eyes, earthworm, and dots decoration, Britain, 1820s, 6⅛x14¼", $9,775.00. (Photo courtesy Skinner Auctions, Inc.)

Beaker, engine-trn pattern below brn slip band, 1790s, 2½" **550.00**
Bough pot, engine-trn & rouletted decor in dk brn & blk, 2-pc, 12" **1,100.00**
Bowl, bl & blk bands w/4 parallel orange wavy lines on wht, 1830s, 6" ..**452.00**
Bowl, cat's eyes, mc on gray w/blk bands, matching lid, 1840s, 6½" **2,500.00**

Bowl, cat's eyes, 3-color on rust w/blk bands, 1820s, 4⅝" **575.00**
Bowl, earthworm, brn & wht on wide blk band, brn/bl/gr bands, 8"...**800.00**
Bowl, earthworm, 2-color on taupe w/mc bands, 1830s, 6¼" **550.00**
Bowl, earthworm, 3-color on tan w/blk borders, 1830s, 7" **750.00**
Bowl, fans, brn/rust/wht on rust w/bl & brn bands, 3⅜x8¼"..**6,325.00**
Bowl, geometrics, brn on wht w/gr reeded rim, 1790s, 6" **865.00**
Bowl, marbled, mc on wht w/gr reeded rim, 1780s, 6⅝" **1,150.00**
Bowl, rouletted bands, orange & bl w/blk, 1800s, 7¼" **800.00**
Bowl, seaweed, bl on cream band, 2 narrow bl bands, 1870s, 6½x14"...**470.00**
Bowl, seaweed, blk on wht band on orange w/gr bands, ca 1795, 7½" ..**575.00**
Bowl, trees on buff w/blk borders, hemispherical, 1810s, 7½".....**750.00**
Can, trees, blk on wht, Fr mk, 1810, 2½", pr...............................**515.00**
Coffeepot, bellflower swags on faux tortoise shell, 1780s, 10¼"....**3,750.00**
Cup & saucer, brick red slip w/cream foliate terminals, 1780s **285.00**
Flowerpot, checkered band, sprigged swags on bl w/stripes, 1800s, 5"..**2,185.00**
Jug, cat's eyes, mc on brn w/wavy trailed lines, rouletted bands, 7"......**8,625.00**
Jug, cat's eyes at neck, earthworm, mc on gray, 6½".................**3,565.00**
Jug, cobalt bands on orange w/combed blk bands, rpl hdl, 1820s, 4¾"..**1,950.00**
Jug, earthworm, complex loops, mc on brn, baluster, 1830s, 4⅞" **5,175.00**
Jug, earthworm, wht/bl/tan on lt bl, wht ft/hdl/spout, 6", EX......**350.00**
Jug, earthworm, 3-color on gray, bl & brn bands, 7¾" **920.00**
Jug, gr bands bracket spiraling combed mc bands, bbl, 1820s, 6" ..**3,450.00**
Jug, rouletting patterns, orange/blk w/blk seaweed, baluster, 7½" ..**3,450.00**
Jug, seaweed, mc on brn w/wht stripes, 19th C, 6" **1,725.00**
Jug, seaweed, mc on ochre (3 bands), emb shells, gr stripes, 8" ..**3,750.00**
Jug, seaweed on tan w/brn borders, gr & wht bands, bbl form, 6½" ..**3,750.00**
Jug, tan, ochre/blk bands, bbl form, 1840s, 6¾"...........................**200.00**
Jug, trees, blk on ochre, rust & gr bands, baluster, ca 1800, 6⅝".......**1,725.00**
Jug, trees, blk on wide ochre band, blk & bl bands, bbl form, 5¾"..**1,840.00**
Jug, trees, blk on yel w/bl bands, baluster, 1790s, 8½".............**8,000.00**
Jug, twigs on bl band, wavy lines on rust bands, 1820s, 8".....**14,950.00**
Jug, waves, brn on wht body w/blk & gr bands, 1835, 6¾".......**5,465.00**
Mug, earthworm, 3-color on bl, foliate hdl, 1840s, 3½" **635.00**
Mug, earthworm, 3-color on olive gr, lt bl & brn bands on wht, 5¾"..**1,150.00**
Mug, gr herringbone rouletted bands, 4-color, foliate hdl, 1830s, 6" **2,300.00**
Mug, mc 4-line waves on blk, wht twigs on rust, 1830s, qt, 5¾"..**5,750.00**
Mug, slip-filled tapestry-like turning, blk & wht, brn bands, pt **1,950.00**
Mug, trees, blk on rust, 2 reeded gr bands, ca 1795, 5½" **1,950.00**
Mug, trees, blk on wide brn band, flared ft, ca 1795, 4½" **978.00**
Mug, 7-point dotted stars, wht on brn band, bl bands, 1840s, 4¾".......**975.00**
Mustard pot, cat's eyes, 3-color on mustard, brn & bl bands, w/lid, 4"...**2,300.00**
Mustard pot, oval recessions on brn band on bl bbl form, 1830s, 3⅝"....**1,850.00**
Sugar bowl, trees, 3-color on rust band, lion-head hdls, w/lid, 5" **3,450.00**
Vase, spill; speckled bl w/gr reeded bands, 1790s, 4¼" **575.00**
Waste bowl, earthworm, bl/wht/tan/brn on gray band, brn lines, 6", EX....**250.00**

Molds

Food molds have become popular as collectibles — not only for their value as antiques, but because they also revive childhood memories of elaborate ice cream Santas with candy trim or barley sugar figurals adorning a Christmas tree. Ice cream molds were made of pewter and came in a wide variety of shapes and styles. Chocolate molds were made in fewer shapes but were more detailed. They were usually made of tin or copper, and then were nickel-plated to keep them from tarnishing or rusting, and also for sanitary reasons. Hard candy molds were usually metal, although primitive maple sugar molds (usually simple hearts, rabbits, and other animals) were carved from wood. (Unless otherwise indicated, the hard candy molds in our listings are cast aluminum or stainless steel.) Cake molds were made of cast iron or cast aluminum and were most common in the shape of a lamb, a rabbit, or Santa Claus. Our advisors for this category are Dale and Jean Van Kuren; they are listed in the Directory under New York.

Chocolate Molds

Apple, mk TC Weygandt New York, Made in Germany, 5" dia....**55.00**
Baby doll, 2-pc hinged metal, 7½" **300.00**
Bear, standing, Eppelscheimer & Co NY, wire spring clip w/roller, 5" ...**100.00**
Bunnies (2) hold lg eg, Eppelscheimer #8194, ca 1934, 8½" **100.00**
Clown, metal, detailed, 4½x10½" **70.00**
Dougle Eagle **135.00**
Easter egg w/rooster in heart, zinc-coated metal, ca 1890, 3⅜"...**135.00**
Father Christmas, European, 2-pc, 7½" **100.00**
Jack-o'-lanterns (3), hinged, 1930s-40s, 12x5" **150.00**
Log, 2-pc, 9" **55.00**
Rabbit, copper w/tin plating, 8¼" **75.00**
Rabbit, running, metal, 2-pc, mk Made in USA #4742, 7½x1⅜" ...**90.00**
Rabbit, seated, long ears, 2-pc, 7" **50.00**
Rabbit, seated, 2-pc hinged metal, 5½" **55.00**
Rabbit, standing, worn plating, brass hinges, 8¾" **50.00**
Rabbit, 2-part, 10½" **150.00**
Santa in boat, Anton Reiche #28233, hinged, 1932, EX **475.00**
Sheep w/long hair, 5x7" **100.00**
Snowman, Letang, 2-pc, clips, 10½x6½" **375.00**
Sqirrel, fat cheeks & big eyes, 2-pc, 4x4½" **95.00**
Turkey, 2-pc, 4x3½" **55.00**
Witches (2) on brooms, 5x5", EX..**125.00**

Ice Cream Molds

Airplane, E-131, 5½" **125.00**
Baby, E&Co NY #1020, 4¾"...**50.00**
Bear, hinged, E&Co #637, 4½x3" **155.00**
Bear, S&Co #222..**42.00**
Bell, July 4 1776 on side, 3¾"..**50.00**
Boar, #637, 2-pc, hinged, 4½"..**45.00**
Bride & groom, E&Co #1148, ca 1900 ....**175.00**
Christmas tree, E-137, hinged, 3¾" **250.00**
Cupid, 3x3¼" **115.00**
Eagle, hinged wings wide, E&Co **90.00**
Flag on shield, E&Co, 3½x4" **200.00**
Flower, hinged, E&Co #457, 4x2¾" **160.00**
Frog & lily pad, #578, 4x3¼" **395.00**
George Washington, hinged, #460..**90.00**
George Washington on hatchet head, E&Co, 3½x3" **110.00**
George Washington on shield, mk #454, 4x4½" **200.00**
Good Luck Horseshoe, #183 ....**37.00**
Liberty Bell, E&Co **35.00**
Liberty Bell, mk #605, 3½x4" **60.00**
Pineapple, CG Grevette Co, 3" **45.00**
Pumpkin, E&Co #1157, 3" dia..**50.00**
Pumpkin, hinged, E&Co, 9" dia..**150.00**
Red Riding Hood, E&Co NY, 5½"..**200.00**
Rocket, hinged, 4½x1¾" **30.00**
Santa, mk #636K..**160.00**
Santa Claus, worn hinges, 4⅜" **175.00**
Ship, hinged, E&Co #1164, 4x5" **160.00**
Shoe, laces, 2½x4¾" **75.00**
Spitz dog, Germany, #807, 4¾" **140.00**
Wedding bell, 3" **50.00**
Whale, hinged, E&Co #602, 5x3¼"..**130.00**
Wicker basket, scalloped edge on bk, worn hinge, 3½" **50.00**
Wishbone, mk #332, 5½x4"..**150.00**

Maple Sugar Molds

Beaver, wood, EX detail, 5x9" **90.00**

Cow in 2 parts, wood, varnished, 4½x7" **67.50**
Flower designs (4), wood, EX patina & detail, 11¼x2½" **55.00**
Heart, maple, 8½x4¼x1¼"..**60.00**
Heart (2, swirling), wood, EX patina, 13x4¼x2" **200.00**
Heart & clover, wood, primitive cvg, 5x17½"..............................**60.00**
House w/cvd-in windows & doors, separate sides & roof, 5½"....**110.00**
Openwork on rnd fluted cups, CI, 1840s, 12 in 11x16" fr..........**115.00**

Miscellaneous

Aluminum, fish, copper colored, 5½-cup, 11"..............................**9.00**
Copper, cross form, English, 19th C, 6" H **300.00**
Copper, emb fruit basket, 20th C, 10" L....................................**140.00**
Copper, ring mold Deco design, English, mk #273, 2½x7" **275.00**
Copper, ring shape, English, 19th C, 6" dia **175.00**
Copper, rose & leaf, English, 7½" H **400.00**
Copper, tube, Germany, late 1800s, 4x8" **240.00**
Copper, tube w/emb ribs, 20th C, 2½x5½" **60.00**
Copper/tin, grapes emb, oval, English, 19th C............................**300.00**

Monart

Scottish glassmaker, John Moncrief was fascinated by the technique of suspending colored enamels within the molten glass during the glass-making process. Recognizing the potential of the process (which he had observed while in France), he began his own business in Perth, Scotland, in 1924. The glassware he created was called Monart. Several commercial lines were among the fine artware pieces designed with scrolls or feathers suspended within the glass. Nearly all examples are unmarked, most having originally carried a paper label.

Bowl, bl w/gold flecks, wavy rim, 3⅞x12¼" **110.00**
Bowl, gr/turq mottle w/silver flecks, ftd, folded rim, 2¼x7½" **240.00**
Bowl, speckled yel, orange, & gr, 2¼x4½" **350.00**
Vase, gr mottle w/int orange splashes, overall gold flecks, squat, 7" ..**200.00**
Vase, swirls at middle, int colors: yel to orange, trifold rim, 8" ...**125.00**

Monmouth

The Monmouth Pottery Company was established in 1892 in Monmouth, Illinois. It was touted as the largest pottery in the world. Their primary products were utilitarian: stoneware crocks, churns, jugs, water coolers, etc. — in salt glaze, Bristol, spongeware, and Albany brown. In 1906 they were absorbed by a conglomerate called the Western Stoneware Company. Monmouth Pottery Co. became their #1 plant and until 1930 continued to produce stoneware marked with the Western Stoneware Company's maple leaf logo. Items marked 'Monmouth Pottery Co.' were made before 1906. Western Stoneware Co. introduced a line of artware in 1926. The name chosen for the artware was Monmouth Pottery. Some stamps and paper labels add ILL to the name.

Churn, Bristol, five-gallon, $250.00.
(Photo courtesy Jim Martin)

Bowl, batter; lt gr, 4¾x8" dia 85.00
Bowl, salt glazed, brn int, base mk, 2-gal....................200.00
Churn, #3/maple leaf, cobalt on salt glaze, 3-gal, 13" 175.00
Churn, #5/maple leaf, cobalt on salt glaze, 5-gal...............225.00
Churn, Bristol, 2-gal...250.00
Churn, salt glaze, mini, 4"..1,200.00
Churn, salt glaze, 3-gal...350.00
Churn, 2 Men in a Crock stencil, 5-gal 1,000.00
Cookie jar, bl & wht 150.00
Cooler, ice water; bl & wht sponge, w/lid & spigot, 8-gal........2,000.00
Cooler, ice water; bl & wht sponge, 5-gal..................2,000.00
Cow & calf, brn, mk Monmouth Pottery Co.............2,000.00
Crock, Bristol, mini, 2½" 600.00
Crock, Bristol, 10-gal 100.00
Crock, Bristol, 20-gal 100.00
Crock, Bristol, 60-gal 1,500.00
Crock, early dull Bristol w/cobalt stencil.....................300.00
Crock, salt glaze, Albany slip int, 3-gal........................95.00
Crock, salt glaze, hand decor, base mk, 2-gal 250.00
Crock, salt glaze, unmk, 2-gal 60.00
Crock, salt glaze, 3-gal...150.00
Crock, stencil, bl on dk brn Albany, 3-gal...................300.00
Crock, stencil, bl on dk brn Albany, 6-gal 400.00
Crock, 2 Men in a Crock stencil, 10-gal 500.00
Floor vase, gr mottle, vertically ribbed, 15x8" dia 45.00
Flower frog, bl, 4¾" 35.00
Hen on nest, bl & wht spongeware................................1,200.00
Jug, Bristol w/Albany top, mini, 2½"............................500.00
Pig, brn, mk Monmouth Pottery Co..........................1,000.00
Pitcher, ball shape, yel, mk #299, pottery cap w/cork, 7x8"...........55.00
Snuff or preserve jar, wax seal......................................350.00
Tobacco jar, monk, brn Albany 300.00
Vase, bl matt, incised shoulder band, 16x10" 495.00
Water cooler, bl & wht spongeware, mini....................1,000.00

Monot and Stumpf

The firm of Monot and Stumpf was organized in 1868, the merger of the E.S. Monot and F. Stumpf glassworks. It was located in Pantin, France. They produced fine art glass of various types until ca 1892, when the company reorganized and became known as the Cristallerie de Pantin.

Bowl, pk opal, incurvate rim, 2¾x4½" dia..................210.00
Rose bowl, peachblow, ribbed, att, 2¾"........................225.00
Vase, pk opal, ribbed, globular w/sqd pinched top, 2¼x2¾" 300.00
Vase, pk/yel opal, squat, ribbed, 4½" 145.00

Mont Joye

Mont Joye was a type of acid-cut French cameo glass produced by Cristallerie de Pantin in Paris around the turn of the century. It is accented by enamels. Our advisor for this category is Don Williams; he is listed in the Directory under Missouri.

Vase, cattails in bl, gold-washed cvd gr leaves on lav to fuchsia, 14"..1,100.00
Vase, dandelions on clear flared cylinder w/gold rim, 11½", pr...925.00
Vase, floral w/gold, gourd form, 4-hdl, 8" 1,150.00
Vase, irises, purple/wht on clear w/gold, 16x6" 2,200.00
Vase, lg flower, wht/pk/yel on purple frost w/gilt, stick neck, 12"....275.00
Vase, lily of the valley etched on lt yel, sq, elongated, 5¾" 200.00
Vase, orchid/gold-flowered tracery on amethyst, bulbous, 11".....300.00
Vase, poppies, pk/yel w/gold on gr frost, gold scroll rim, 12" 725.00

Moon and Star

Moon and Star was originally produced in the 1880s by John Adams & Company of Pittsburgh. In the 1960s, Joseph Weishar of Wheeling, West Virginia, owner of the Island Mould & Machine Company, reproduced some of the original molds and incorporated the pattern into approximately forty new and different items. Two of the largest distributors of this line were L.E. Smith of Mt. Pleasant, Pennsylvania, who pressed their own glass, and L.G. Wright of New Martinsville, West Virginia, who had theirs pressed by Fostoria, Fenton, and Westmoreland. Both companies carried a large and varied assortment of shapes and colors. Several other companies were involved in its manufacture as well, especially of the smaller items.

Over the years the glassware has been pressed in amberina (yellow shading to orange- or ruby-red), green, amber, crystal, light blue, and ruby. Pieces in ruby and light blue are most collectible and harder to find than the other colors, which seem to be abundant. Purple, pink, cobalt, amethyst, tan slag, and light green and blue opalescent were made, too, but on a lesser scale.

In 1992 the Weishar company introduced a new color, teal green, which was followed in 1993 with sapphire blue opalescent, and in 1994 with cranberry ice. These items (and those being made today) carried the Weishar mark and were made primarily for collectors. Currently the company is producing water sets, salt and pepper shakers, creamers and sugars, spoon holders, and various relish trays in Delphite and Delphite carnival, Crown Tuscan and Crown Tuscan carnival, Colonial Blue, Millennium Rose (pink), and various other colors on a more limited basis. Unless another color is noted, our values are given for vintage glassware in ruby and light blue. For amberina, green, and amber, deduct 20%.

Syrup pitcher, 5", from $65.00 to $70.00; Cheese shaker, from $50.00 to $55.00, 20% less in amberina, green, and amber.

Ashtray, allover pattern, moon form scallops at rim, 4 rests, 8" dia....25.00
Ashtray, moons at rim, star in base, 6-sided, 8½" 25.00
Banana boat, allover pattern, moons form scallops at rim, 12"......45.00
Bell, pattern along sides, plain rim & hdl, from $35 to..................45.00
Bowl, allover pattern, ftd, scalloped rim, 12x5", from $35 to........45.00
Butter dish, allover pattern, stars form scallops, star finial, ¼-lb...50.00
Cake salver, allover pattern, scalloped rim, raised ft, 5x12", $50 to ..60.00
Candle holder, allover pattern, bowl style w/ring hdl, 2x5½" 18.00
Candle lamp, patterned shade, clear base, 3-pc, 7½", from $20 to....25.00
Chandelier, dome shape, amber, w/font, 14" dia, from $250 to...300.00
Compote, allover pattern, raised ft, patterned lid & hdl, 7½x6"...40.00
Compote, allover pattern, raised ft on stem, patterned lid, 12x8".75.00
Compote, allover pattern, scalloped rim, ftd, 5x6½", from $15 to .20.00
Creamer, allover pattern, raised ft w/scalloped edge, 5¾x3"..........35.00
Decanter, allover pattern, bulbous, patterned stopper, 32-oz, 12"..90.00
Fairy lamp, cylindrical dome-top shade, 6", from $25 to................35.00
Jardiniere, allover pattern, patterned lid, 7¼", minimum value 65.00
Lamp, miniature; from $165 to 190.00
Lamp, miniature; milk glass, from $200 to 225.00
Lamp, oil or electric, allover pattern, all orig, 24" 325.00
Pitcher, water; patterned body, ice lip, str sides, plain ft, 7½" 75.00
Relish tray, patterned moons form scallops, star in base, rectangular .35.00

Shakers, allover pattern, metal lids, 4x2", pr, from $25 to **35.00**
Spooner, allover pattern, str sides, scalloped rim, ftd, 5¼x4" **50.00**
Toothpick holder, allover pattern, scalloped rim, sm flat ft **10.00**
Tumbler, juice; no pattern at rim or on disk ft, 5-oz, 3½".............**15.00**

Moorcroft

William Moorcroft began to work for MacIntyre Potteries in 1897. At first he was the chief designer but very soon took over their newly created art pottery department. His first important design was the Aurelian Ware, part transfer and part hand painted. Very shortly thereafter, around the turn of the century, he developed his famous Florian Ware, with heavy slip, done in mostly blue and white. Since the early 1900s there has been a succession of designs, most of them very characteristic of the company. Moorcroft left MacIntyre in 1913 and went out on his own. He had already established his name, having won prizes and gold medals at the St. Louis World's Fair as well as in Paris. In 1929 Queen Mary, who had been collecting his pottery, made him 'Potter to the Queen,' and the pottery was so stamped up until 1949. William Moorcroft died in 1945, and his son Walter ran the company until recent years. The factory is still in existence. They now produce different designs but continue to use the characteristic slipwork. Moorcroft pottery was sold abroad in Canada, the United States, Australia, and Europe as well as in specialty areas such as the island of Bermuda.

Moorcroft went through a 'Japanese' stage in the early teens with his lovely lustre glazes, Oriental shapes and decorations. During the mid-teens he began to produce his most popular Pomegranate Ware, and Wisteria (often called 'Fruit'). Around that time he also designed the popular Pansy line as well as Leaves and Grapes. Soon he introduced a beautiful landscape series called variously Hazeldine, Moonlit Blue, Eventide, and Dawn. These wonderful designs along with Claremont (Mushrooms) seem to be the most sought after by collectors today. It would be possible to add many other designs to this list.

During the 1920s and 1930s, Moorcroft became very interested in highly fired Flambe (red) glazes. These could only be achieved through a very difficult procedure which he himself perfected in secret. He later passed the knowledge on to his son.

Dating of this pottery is done by knowledge of the designs, shapes, signatures, and marks on the bottom of each piece; an experienced person can usually narrow it down to a short time frame. Prices escalated for this 'rediscovered' pottery in the late 1980s but has now leveled off. This is true mainly of the pre-1935 designs of William Moorcroft, as it is items from that era that attract the most collector interest. Prices in the listings below are for pieces in mint condition unless noted otherwise; no reproductions are listed here. Advisors for this category are Wilfred and Dolli Cohen; they are listed in the Directory under California.

Golden Iris (light amber), #23 Margaret guest set, handled, with pulled pouring lip, $235.00.

Bonbonnier, rose garland, pk/gold on wht, w/lid & lg hdls, 7".**1,500.00**
Bowl, orchid on cobalt (int), ext: cobalt, incurvate rim, 4" **120.00**

Bowl, pansy on cobalt, orig paper label, 4"...................................**295.00**
Mug, Coronation of King George V, MacIntyre, ca 1911, 3⅝"...**195.00**
Pitcher, Florian, bl w/cream & dk gr bands, WM, water sz, 7"....**850.00**
Pitcher, forget-me-not, WM, MacIntyre, 1902, 6¼" **1,350.00**
Plate, pansy, bl on wht, 6½"...**810.00**
Vase, anemone, mc on cobalt, stick neck, 12x7¾"....................**900.00**
Vase, bl cornflowers, classic shape, 9" **1,950.00**
Vase, cornflowers, cylindrical, tapering toward base, 10" **3,000.00**
Vase, Coronation of King Edward VI, MacIntyre, ca 1902, 5", NM...**150.00**
Vase, Eventide, trees/sunset sky, Tudric pewter base, 6½"........**1,950.00**
Vase, Eventide landscape, shouldered, WM, 1925, 6¼"...........**2,250.00**
Vase, fish on wht, ovoid, WM, 1930, 9½".............................**2,700.00**
Vase, Florian, long-stem poppies, bl w/gr leaves on wht, slim, 10"...**2,000.00**
Vase, Florian, peacock feathers, hdls, 5".............................**1,600.00**
Vase, Florian, peacock feathers, yel/dk & lt bl/gr/wht, ovoid, 4"...**1,500.00**
Vase, hibiscus, red on shaded gr, paper label, 3¾x2½" **200.00**
Vase, hibiscus, shouldered, MIE, 8¼" **525.00**
Vase, Lion's Den, rampant lion on cobalt, ltd edition, 9¾" **300.00**
Vase, mixed flowers on wht, 3 gold hdls, cylindrical, 1904-13, 7¾"...**1,500.00**
Vase, orchids, mc on bl flambe, ftd, flared rim, WM, 1928, 12"....**3,500.00**
Vase, pansies, sgn MacIntyre, hdls, 6" **850.00**
Vase, peony bud, sgn WM, #189, 8½".................................**1,300.00**
Vase, polar bear, S Tuffin, ltd ed, 1988, 6"..........................**1,390.00**
Vase, pomegrenates, mc on cobalt, MIE, 5x3¾".......................**795.00**
Vase, pomegranates, mc on cobalt, shouldered, MIE, 6¼x3¾"...**795.00**
Vase, purple lustre, flared neck, ca 1918-28, 8¼", NM...............**195.00**
Vase, rose garland, WM, MacIntyre, 1906, 7½" **2,850.00**
Vase, waving corn on bl, bulbous, WM, 1930, 4" **850.00**
Vase, windswept corn, ovoid, WM, MIE, 1930s, 9⅝", pr.........**2,000.00**

Morgantown Glass

Incorporated in 1899, the Morgantown Glass Works experienced many name changes over the years. Today 'Morgantown Glass' is a generic term used to identify all glass produced there. Purchased by Fostoria in 1965, the factory was permanently closed in 1971.

Golf Ball is the most recognized design with crosshatched bumps equally distributed along the stem (very similar to Cambridge #1066, identified with alternating lines of dimples between rows of crosshatching). Color identification is difficult and further information is provided by Gene Florence in his book *Stemware Identification*. We also recommend *Elegant Glassware of the Depression Era, Tenth Edition*, by Gene Florence. (Both of these books are published by Collector Books.)

Golf Ball, amethyst; stem, claret; 4½-oz, 5¼" **45.00**
Golf Ball, cobalt/crystal; bell...**60.00**
Golf Ball, cobalt/crystal; urn, 6½" **65.00**
Golf Ball, smoke; stem, oyster cocktail; flared, 4-oz, 4¼" **30.00**
Golf Ball, Steigel Gr, Spanish Red or Ritz Bl; creamer................**175.00**
Golf Ball, Steigel Gr, Spanish Red or Ritz Bl; stem, parfait; 4¼"..**85.00**
Golf Ball, Steigel Gr, Spanish Red or Ritz Bl; sugar bowl............**175.00**
Golf Ball, Steigel Gr, Spanish Red or Ritz Bl; tumbler, juice; ftd, 5"..**28.00**
Golf Ball, Steigel Gr, Spanish Red or Ritz Bl; vase, Charlotte; 8"....**250.00**
Queen Louise, crystal w/pk; bowl, finger; ftd................................**200.00**
Queen Louise, crystal w/pk; plate, salad **150.00**
Queen Louise, crystal w/pk; stem, cocktail; 3-oz..........................**350.00**
Queen Louise, crystal w/pk; stem, parfait; 7-oz **395.00**
Queen Louise, crystal w/pk; stem, water; 9-oz..............................**385.00**
Sunrise Medallion, bl; bowl, finger; ftd...**85.00**
Sunrise Medallion, bl; plate, sherbet; 5⅞"....................................**12.50**
Sunrise Medallion, bl; stem, champagne; 7-oz, 6¼"......................**40.00**
Sunrise Medallion, bl; stem, cocktail; 6⅛"....................................**55.00**

Sunrise Medallion, bl; tumbler, ftd, 5-oz, 4¼" 50.00
Sunrise Medallion, crystal, tumbler, ftd, 4-oz, 2½" 25.00
Sunrise Medallion, crystal; plate, salad; 7½" 12.50
Sunrise Medallion, crystal; stem, wine; 2½-oz 45.00
Sunrise Medallion, crystal; vase, bud; slender, 10" 65.00
Sunrise Medallion, pk or gr; cup 80.00
Sunrise Medallion, pk or gr; sugar bowl....................................250.00
Sunrise Medallion, pk or gr; vase, 6x5" 395.00
Tinkerbell, Azure or gr; bowl, finger; ftd..................................75.00
Tinkerbell, Azure or gr; stem, cordial; 1½-oz 145.00
Tinkerbell, Azure or gr; stem, goblet; 9-oz................................125.00
Tinkerbell, Azure or gr; stem, saucer champagne; 5½-oz 95.00
Tinkerbell, Azure or gr; stem, wine; 2½-oz.................................120.00
Tinkerbell, Azure or gr; vase, #36 Uranus, plain top, ftd, 10" 300.00

Mortars and Pestles

Mortars are bowl-shaped vessels used for centuries for the purpose of grinding drugs to a powder or grain into meal. The masher or grinding device is called a pestle.

Brass, eng decor, 19th C, 6¼x6½", +pestle..................................145.00
Brass, Russian, 19th C, hdls, sm, +pestle 85.00
Bronze, European, 17th C, 4", +9" pestle 225.00
Burled maple, 18th C, 7x5¾" w/9 cvd bands, EX patina, +9" pestle...250.00
CI, minor rust, 7x9", +pestle 55.00
Trn maple, acorn-shaped knop, 19th C, 8¼x6¼" 85.00
Wooden, age cracks, 1800s, 3¾x10¾", +ceramic pestle w/wood hdl...50.00

Mortens Studio

Oscar Mortens was already established as a fine sculptural artist when he left his native Sweden to take up residency in Arizona. During the 1940s he developed a line of detailed animal figures which were distributed through the Mortens Studios, a firm he co-founded with Gunnar Thelin. Thelin hired and trained artists to produce Mortens' line, which he called Royal Designs. More than two hundred dogs were modeled and over one hundred horses. Cats and wild animals such as elephants, panthers, deer, and elk were made, but on a much smaller scale. Bookends with sculptured dog heads were shown in their catalogs, and collectors report finding wall plaques on rare occasions. The material they used was a plaster-type composition with wires embedded to support the weight. Examples were marked 'Copyright by the Mortens Studio' either in ink or decal. Watch for flaking, cracks, and separations. Crazing seems to be present in some degree in many examples. When no condition is indicated, the items listed below are assumed to be in near-mint condition, allowing for minor crazing.

Cat, #395, 4¼x4", $50.00.

Bay, plaque, #651, 7x8½" 135.00
Beagle, standing, #872, 4½x5½"..55.00

Bear, brn, sitting w/1 paw raised, #7121, 6" 110.00
Boston Terrier, 3½x7" 75.00
Boxer, head, plaque, 8" 90.00
Boxer, sitting, brn & cream, #551, 2½x2½"...................................60.00
Chihuahua, seated, ears up, facing bk, 3¾"..................................60.00
Cocker Spaniel, tan, #820B, 2¾x3½" 55.00
Collie, standing, #659, 6x7"...100.00
Collie head, plaque, rare, 6x4½"...140.00
Dachshund, blk & tan, #866B, 3½x6"...65.00
Dachshund, sitting, blk & tan, #867B, 3½x4"................................60.00
Doberman Pinscher, sitting, Royal Design, 6½" 110.00
Horse, American Saddlebred, bay, 8" 110.00
Horse, gray, mane erect, #704, 8x8½"..95.00
Horse, wild stallion on base, #718, 9½"....................................110.00
Irish Setter, 3⅝"...65.00
Springer Spaniel, 5x7½"...115.00

Morton Pottery

Six potteries operated in Morton, Illinois, at various times from 1877 to 1976. Each traced its origin to six brothers who immigrated to America to avoid military service in Germany. The Rapp brothers established their first pottery near clay deposits on the south side of town where they made field tile and bricks. Within a few years, they branched out to include utility wares such as jugs, bowls, jars, pitchers, etc. During the ninety-nine years of pottery operations in Morton, the original factory was expanded by some of the sons and nephews of the Rapps. Other family members started their own potteries where artware, gift-store items, and special-order goods were produced. The Cliftwood Art Pottery and the Morton Pottery Company had showrooms in Chicago and New York City during the 1930s. All of Morton's potteries were relatively short-lived operations with the Morton Pottery Company being the last to shut down on September 8, 1976. For a more thorough study of the subject, we recommend *Morton's Potteries: 99 Years, Vols. I and II*, by Doris and Burdell Hall; their address can be found in the Directory under Illinois.

Morton Pottery Works — Morton Earthenware Co. (1877 – 1917)

Bank, acorn shape, cobalt, 3¼"..65.00
Bank, acorn shape, gr, Acorn Stoves, 3¼" 75.00
Bowl, mixing; brn, Rockingham, 4½"..25.00
Chamber pot, yel ware, mini...50.00
Cuspidor, brn, 7"...50.00
Food mold, Turk's turban, brn, Rockingham 75.00
Jardiniere, brn, Rockingham, 7"...40.00
Jardiniere, gr, 5"..30.00
Jug, milk; brn, Rockingham, 1-pt..55.00
Jug, mini, brn, Rockingham..45.00
Marble, brn, Rockingham, 4¼"..35.00
Marble, cobalt, 4¼" 45.00
Marble, gr, 3"..25.00
Paperweight, buffalo figure, brn, Rock Sand Co, 3" 50.00
Pie baker, yel ware, 7"...75.00
Teapot, brn, restaurant, nesting set of 2, ind 50.00

Cliftwood Art Potteries, Inc. (1920 – 1940)

Bowl, deep bulb, bl/gray, 6' 24.00
Bowl, shallow flower; cobalt, 10" 40.00
Bowl, sq, gr/yel drip over wht, w/lid, 6" 50.00
Bowls, storage; pk/orchid drip over wht, 3 nested, w/lids, set 60.00
Figurine, cat, brn drip, reclining, 4½".....................................35.00

Figurine, cat, brn drip, reclining, 6½"...45.00
Figurine, cat, brn drip, reclining, 8½"...55.00
Figurine, cat, brn drip, reclining, 11"...70.00
Figurine, mini bear, brn, 3x1¾"...45.00
Figurine, mini lion, gold/brn, 4x1¾"...50.00
Figurine, mini tiger, yel w/brn stripes, 4x1½"...55.00
Flower frog, disc, bl/wht drip, 5"...18.00
Flower frog, disc, cobalt, 3"...14.00
Flower frog, disc, herbage gr, 2"...10.00
Flower frog, disc, old rose, 4"...16.00
Flower frog, frog, pk, 5½"...35.00
Flower frog, lily pad, bl, 4"...24.00
Flower frog, lily pad, brn drip, 6"...30.00
Flower frog, Lorelei, bl/mulberry drip, 6½"...75.00
Flower frog, turtle, bl/mulberry drip, 5½"...30.00
Flower frog, turtle, gr, 4"...24.00
Jar, Pretzels emb on brn drip, bbl shape, w/lid...65.00
Jug, wine; brn drip, w/music box in base, 9½"...150.00
Matchbox holder, pk/turq over wht, wall mt, 6¾x3½x4"...70.00
Shakers, stove top, yel/gr drip over wht, 5"...30.00
Teapot, globe shape, bl/mulberry, 8-cup, w/ftd trivet, 7"...125.00

Midwest Potteries, Inc. (1940 – 1944)

Figurine, Afghan hound, wht w/gold decor, 7"...45.00
Figurine, camel, tan, 8½"...30.00
Figurine, cockatoo, yel w/gr drip, on ped, 6"...15.00
Figurine, dancing lady, wht w/gold decor, 8½"...50.00
Figurine, deer, wht w/gold decor, 8-point antlers, 12"...50.00
Figurine, female bust, wht/platinum decor, 8½"...90.00
Figurine, Irish Setter, natural colors, 5"...35.00
Figurine, lady w/Russian wolfhound, wht w/gold decor, 11"...125.00
Figurine, pony, yel w/gold decor, 3½"...24.00
Figurine, sea gull, wht w/gold decor, 12"...45.00
Figurine, tiger, yel w/brn stripes, 6x10"...40.00

Figurine, sunfish, airbrushed brown and yellow, 11", $50.00.
(Photo courtesy Doris and Burdell Hall)

Miniature, boat, yel w/bl sails, 2"...15.00
Miniature, camel, brn, 2½"...18.00
Miniature, goose, wht matt, 1¾"...10.00
Miniature, polar bear, wht, 1¾"...12.00
Miniature, rabbits, wht w/gold decor, kissing, rare, 2½"...30.00
Miniature, squirrel, brn, 2"...12.00

Morton Pottery Company (1922 – 1976)

Ashtray, hexagon, bl, Dirksen, 3¾"...25.00
Ashtray, hexagon, red, Nixon, 3¾"...40.00
Ashtray, ovoid, w/appl pheasant...24.00
Ashtray, rectangle, Mor-Tile, 9x7"...24.00
Ashtray, teardrop, Rival Crock Pot, 6"...12.00
Employee service pin, bronze, 10 yrs...20.00
Employee service pin, bronze w/diamond, 25 yrs...70.00
Employee service pin, bronze w/emerald, 15 yrs...35.00
Employee service pin, bronze w/ruby, 20 yrs...50.00
Figurine, Colonial lady, wht/gold/pk, HP, 10"...50.00
Figurine, Fawn, brn spray, 7x5x2"...15.00
Figurine, oxen pr, brn spray, 5x2¾x3½"...40.00
Grass grower, Christmas tree...15.00
Grass grower, GI, Hi Buddy...25.00
Grass grower, Jake...24.00
Grass grower, Jiggs...30.00
Grass grower, Jolly Jim...20.00
Grass grower, pig...20.00
Grass grower, sailor...30.00
Lamp, Irish Setter, bird in mouth...125.00
Lamp, teddy bear...45.00
TV lamp, buffalo, natural colors...150.00
TV lamp, horse head, brn...60.00
TV lamp, panther, blk...40.00

American Art Potteries (1947 – 1963)

Candlestick, donut shape, gr, #140, w/3 cups, 6x7½"...30.00
Candlestick, free-form, gr, #141, w/3 cups, 8x9"...40.00
Figurine, Afghan hounds, blk, 15", pr...55.00
Figurine, deer, brn w/gr spray, #503, leaping, 11½"...45.00
Figurine, deer w/antlers, brn/gr/wht spray, #502, leaping, 11½"...55.00
Figurine, horse, bl/gray spray, #501, looking over bk, 11½"...30.00
Figurine, horse, brn w/gr spray, #501, rearing, 11½"...30.00
Figurine, parrot on stump, wht w/gold decor, 8"...20.00
Figurine, wild horse, brn spray, #504, 11½"...40.00
Honey jug, 14k gold, #50G, 5½"...25.00
Night light, wall mt, brn/wht spray, rare, 6x3½x3¼"...50.00
Planter, baby shoes, pk, #59D, pr on heart, 3½x6½"...30.00
Planter, deer reclining by stump, gr w/brn spray...24.00
Planter, fish, pk & purple on wht...20.00
Planter, pig, blk w/wht stripe...30.00
Planter, quail, natural colors...35.00
Tray, butterfly shape, pk w/mauve spray, #135G, 1x7x6¼"...25.00
Vase, conch shell, gr/yel spray, #131, 6"...25.00
Vase, deer w/fawn, brn spray, #322, 7½"...35.00
Vase, 4 elephant tusks, gray/wht spray, #215, 12½"...30.00

Moser

Ludwig Moser began his career as a struggling glass artist, catering to the rich who visited the famous Austrian health spas. His talent and popularity grew and in 1857 the first of his three studios opened in Karlsbad, Czechoslovakia. The styles developed there were entirely his own; no copies of other artists have ever been found. Some of his original designs include grapes with trailing vines, acorns and oak leaves, and richly enameled, deeply cut or carved floral pieces. Sometimes jewels were applied to the glass as well. Moser's animal scenes reflect his careful attention to detail. Famed for his birds in flight, he also designed stalking tigers and large, detailed elephants, all created in fine enameling.

Moser died in 1916, but the business was continued by his two sons who had been personally and carefully trained by their father. The Moser company bought the Meyr's Neffe Glassworks in 1922 and continued to produce quality glassware.

When identifying Moser, look for great clarity in the glass; deeply carved, continuous engravings; perfect coloration; finely applied enameling (often covered with thin gold leaf); and well-polished pontils. Our advisor for this category is Don Williams; he is listed in the Directory under Missouri. Items described below are enameled unless otherwise. If no color is mentioned in the line, the glass is clear.

Bowl, amber, 2 8" HP salamanders; lg Wilcox base w/2 ladies, 12x12" ...**1,950.00**
Bowl, cranberry w/mc grape leaves & appl grapes, 2½x5¼" **350.00**
Bowl, gr w/overall mc scrolls/gold tracery, 4 reeded ft, 4½x10½" ..**325.00**
Bowl, Prussian Blue w/farm scene, amber rigaree hdls/rim/ft, 4x3x11"......**600.00**
Champagne flute, reverse amberina, heavy gold w/leaves & vines, 6½"...**325.00**
Cheese dish, cranberry w/ornate gold/wht decor & beading, 9x10", EX...**800.00**
Compote, wine cut to clear, stag/deer, clear ft, paper label, 10" dia..........**200.00**
Cordial, cranberry, acid etched, 2¾" **70.00**
Cordial, 6 'Arabic windows' in gr/wine surrounded by gold, ruffled ft......**60.00**
Creamer & sugar bowl, gr to clear w/silver rim band & gold scrolls, 4".**750.00**
Cup & saucer, crystal & gr w/gold tracery, 2x4½".........................**60.00**
Cup & saucer, cut panels, amber-flashed t'prints, ca 1915...........**115.00**
Cup & saucer, demi; cobalt w/gold floral band on saucer & cup.**160.00**
Dish, gr w/mc fern fronds, leaf shape, 8" **200.00**
Finger bowl, foliage panels (heavy enamel), gold int, 4¾", +plate **750.00**
Goblet, clear w/gold-trim rim, cranberry tulip ft w/encrusted gold, 6"..**250.00**
Goblet, cranberry, gold enamel/pk & bl floral on gold band, 6"..**150.00**
Goblet, Prussian Blue w/mc florals in purple-fr panels, gilt trim, 8"...**1,000.00**
Pitcher, gold w/columns of mc beading, cut dmns, 3½" **300.00**
Sherbet, much gold/HP floral, 3½x4½", +underplate **400.00**
Tumbler, amber w/bl ft, mc flowers on gold branches, 4¼" **500.00**
Tumbler, cameo: water/trees/mtns, gr notched bottom, cranberry rim, 5" ...**200.00**
Tumbler, juice; amber, appl acorns/mc leaves................................**650.00**
Tumbler, whiskey; clear w/jeweled band, 2½" **200.00**
Vase, allover etch, bl/gold/amethyst geometric bands top/base, 6x7".**345.00**
Vase, amber, stalagmites/stalactite cvgs meet at waist, faceted, 12" ...**200.00**
Vase, amber w/heron before silver moon, ribbed, bl hdls, 5" **90.00**
Vase, cameo cut/pnt Romans, cranberry on clear, baluster, 15" ...**1,100.00**
Vase, clear to amethyst w/heavy HP deer/pines/cliffs, triangular, 8"..**3,000.00**
Vase, clear to lime gr w/intaglio decor, 7¼"...............................**1,800.00**
Vase, cranberry opal, 2 children/frog on lily pad, ftd pillow form, 8"..**1,400.00**
Vase, gilt scrolls, appl rigaree hdls, ca 1910, 17" **170.00**
Vase, intaglio scrolled acanthus w/gold, gr rim, ca 1910, 7½".....**100.00**
Vase, lav cut to clear w/iris, rectangular body, 10" **500.00**
Vase, marquetry, yel opal w/red intaglio floral w/vines & petals, 6" **1,100.00**
Vase, orange irid w/blk/gold Persian decor, 3 clear hdls, 16x12", EX ...**2,000.00**
Vase, topaz cut to clear, hunters/bears, conical, 6" **225.00**
Wine, cobalt, allover heavy gold scrolls, 6".................................**210.00**
Wine, Rhine; rainbow gold-enameled bowl, clear ribbed ft, 8½"....**200.00**

Moss Rose

Moss Rose was a favorite dinnerware pattern of many Staffordshire and American potters of the mid-1800s. In America the Wheeling Pottery of West Virginia produced the ware in large quantities, and it became one of their bestsellers, remaining popular well into the '90s. The pattern was colored by hand; this type is designated 'old' in our listings to distinguish it from the more modern Moss Rose design of the twentieth century, which we've also included. It's not hard to distinguish between the two. The later ware you'll recognize immediately, since the pattern is applied by decalcomania on stark white backgrounds. It has been made in Japan to a large extent, but companies in Germany and Bavaria have produced it as well. Today, there is more interest in the twentieth-century items than in the older ware.

Bowl, Japan, 1950s, 4x7" **20.00**
Bowl, soup; Pompadour, Rosenthal, US Zone **42.00**
Bowl, sterling knob on lid, Pompadour, Rosenthal, 3¾x5⅛" **40.00**
Bowl, vegetable; w/lid, Pompadour, Rosenthal............................**150.00**
Cake/sandwich plate, Royal Albert..**45.00**

Candle holders, Japan, 3", pr..**15.00**
Coffeepot, Pompadour, Rosenthal, 11" **150.00**
Creamer & sugar bowl, Haviland & Co, sugar: 7" to finial **90.00**
Cruets, oil & vinegar; Japan sticker, pr....................................**25.00**
Cup & saucer, Japan, 2½", 5½" **10.00**
Cup & saucer, Royal Albert..**22.50**
Egg boiler, electric, NM..**55.00**
Egg coddler, Apco, Japan, paper labels, w/clamp & lid, 3½" **32.00**
Lamp, oil; 2-hdl, Japan, 7½" **30.00**
Mustache cup, gold accents, Haviland, from $225 to **275.00**

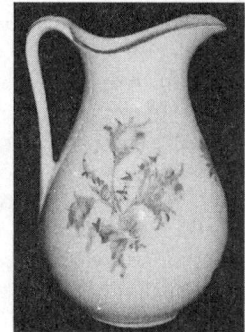

Pitcher, gold trim, Haviland Limoges, 8", from $250.00 to $300.00. (Photo courtesy Mary Frank Gaston)

Place setting, plate+bread plate+berry bowl+c/s, 5-pc set **30.00**
Plate, dinner; Johann Haviland Bavaria, 10", from $10 to **15.00**
Plate, dinner; Royal Albert, 11¼" **15.00**
Plate, 12-sided, Limoges, 9¼" **30.00**
Platter, Pompadour, Rosenthal, 13" dia **70.00**
Platter, Ucagco, rare, 12", from $65 to **85.00**
Shakers, Pompadour, Rosenthal, 5", pr..................................**60.00**
Shakers, Royal Albert, 3", pr...**30.00**
Soap dish, w/lid & drainer, gold trim, Haviland, 5x4", from $175 to....**200.00**
Tea tile, Haviland, 6½" dia, from $125 to..................................**150.00**
Teapot, whistling, electric, Japan, 6"....................................**15.00**
Tidbit, 2-tier, Japan...**20.00**
Tray, Pompadour, Rosenthal, 13x10" **65.00**
Tureen, w/lid, Pompadour, Rosenthal, 7¼x12" **105.00**
Wall pocket, violin shape, marked Japan, 9x4" **58.00**

Mother-of-Pearl Glass

Mother-of-Pearl glass was a type of mold-blown satin art glass popular during the last half of the nineteenth century. A patent for its manufacture was issued in 1886 to Frederick S. Shirley, and one of the companies who produced it was the Mt. Washington Glass Company of New Bedford, Massachusetts. Another was the English firm of Stevens and Williams. Its delicate patterns were developed by blowing the gather into a mold with inside projections that left an intaglio design on the surface of the glass, then sealing the first layer with a second, trapping air in the recesses. Most common are the Diamond Quilted, Raindrop, and Herringbone patterns. It was made in several soft colors, the most rare and valuable is rainbow — a blend of rose, light blue, yellow, and white. Occasionally it may be decorated with coralene, enameling, or gilt. Watch for twentieth-century reproductions, especially in the Diamond Quilted pattern. Our advisors for this category are Betty and Clarence Maier; they are listed in the Directory under Pennsylvania. See also Coralene.

Basket, Dmn Quilt, ivory, 4x4¾" **75.00**
Basket, Dmn Quilt, pk to wht, undulating ruffled top, twist hdl, 8" **275.00**
Basket, Dmn Quilt, rose to pk & wht, rnd w/sq rim, frost loop hdl, 7"..**550.00**
Basket, Herringbone, med to lt bl, crimped camphor rim, Mt WA, 9x8x4" .**675.00**

Basket, Muslin (lg Raindrop), rose, frosted edge/twisted hdl, 9x9x11" ..750.00
Basket/rose bowl, Dmn Quilt, med gr w/rose & mica int, thorn hdl, 9x6" ..950.00
Bowl, Dmn Quilt, bl, 3 frosted ft, 4⅞x6½" 325.00
Bowl, Dmn Quilt, lt moss gr w/mica, short ft, appl clear rim, 4x6½" 575.00
Bowl vase, Flower & Acorn, wht w/gold floral, 4-lobe top, Webb, 4x6".650.00
Box, dresser; Dmn Quilt, bl w/HP flower on lid, Collar & Cuffs, 5½" 175.00
Compote, Herringbone, pk, ruffled top, w/emb metal base, 5½x8½".....150.00
Creamer, irregular airtraps, orange-red w/yel int, satin hdl, 2¾".500.00
Creamer, Raindrop, bl, frosted bl reeded hdl, bulbous, 4½" 175.00
Cruet, Dmn Quilt, rainbow, frosted hdl, faceted stopper, bulbous, 6" ..1,800.00
Cup & saucer, Raindrop, pk to wht, 3", 5" 285.00
Ewer, Herringbone, rose to pk, ruffled rim, dbl-step base, Mt WA, 9"..450.00
Finger bowl, Dmn Quilt, rainbow, ruffled, 2½x5" 325.00
Jug, Polka Dot, peachblow pk, frosted loop hdl, can neck, Mt WA, 6x4" ...475.00
Lamp, Dmn Quilt, pk, ruffled bowl shade/vase-shaped base, 6½" ...800.00
Nappy, Dmn Quilt, wht, crimped triangular rim, w/hdl, 2½x6"..425.00
Pitcher, Coin Spot, rainbow, camphor frost hdl, 7½" 250.00
Rose bowl, Dmn Quilt, bl, incurvate, att Webb, 2¾" 385.00
Rose bowl, Dmn Quilt, rainbow, mk Pat....................................450.00
Rose bowl, Dmn Quilt, turq, ruffled, 3¼" 175.00
Rose bowl, Herringbone, Fr Bl w/pk int, crimped melon form, thin, 3x4"..400.00
Spooner, Dmn Quilt, apricot to wht, 4¾" 135.00
Tumbler, Dmn Quilt, bl to wht w/allover floral, 4" 145.00
Tumbler, Dmn Quilt w/pk/rose/bl floral & bird, mk Rococo Art Glass, 4" ...230.00
Vase, Basketweave, dk to lt bl, upright petal rim, Webb, 7x5" 750.00
Vase, Dmn Quilt, apricot, cupped/petal rim, Mt WA, 6x3".........375.00
Vase, Dmn Quilt, bl, bulbous w/pinched neck & sq top, 10" 200.00
Vase, Dmn Quilt, bl to lt bl, short collar neck, ovoid, 4¾" 165.00
Vase, Dmn Quilt, butterscotch, shouldered, 6" 325.00
Vase, Dmn Quilt, dk apricot, ruffled, stick neck, 8".....................150.00
Vase, Dmn Quilt, lemon yel, ovoid w/ringed collar, bulbous neck, 9"..95.00
Vase, Dmn Quilt, rainbow, shouldered, flared rim, mk Pat, 7x4" 1,250.00
Vase, Dmn Quilt, red-orange w/gold 'dmns,' slightly ruffled, Mt WA, 8"...1,250.00
Vase, Dmn Quilt, rose to pk, frosted ruffled/crimped edge, Mt WA, 9x6"...675.00
Vase, Dmn Quilt, rose to pk w/floral, crimped rim droops on sides, 9"..175.00
Vase, Drapery, yel, frosted ruffled rim, rnd w/long neck, Mt WA, 8x5".650.00
Vase, Federzeichnung, brn w/overall gold tracery, bottle form, 13".....1,600.00
Vase, Federzeichnung, 4-lobe top, Pat #9159, 7x4½" 2,500.00
Vase, Flower & Acorn, wht, pinched ovoid w/3-lobe cupped rim, 6x5".750.00
Vase, Herringbone, lt butterscotch, bulbous w/ruffled top, 10½" ...150.00
Vase, Herringbone, pk, frosted hdls, 8½x3¾" 225.00
Vase, Herringbone, wht w/pk int, allover clear threading, 6" neck, 12"..750.00
Vase, Hobnail, bl to wht, 4 inward rim folds, Mt WA, 5¾x4" 675.00
Vase, Muslin (lg Raindrop), Alice Blue, 3-lobe top, Mt WA, 8x7"..675.00
Vase, Muslin (lg Raindrop), gold, melon ribs, Mt WA, 7¾" 375.00
Vase, Muslin (lg Raindrop), wht, melon rib w/can neck, Mt WA, 6x5½" ..425.00
Vase, Raindrop, bl, fan-shaped top, 5x2¾", pr 295.00
Vase, Raindrop, bl, melon ribs, ruffled rim, 7⅞x6" 210.00
Vase, Raindrop, butterscotch, amber reed hdl, 8½", pr 200.00
Vase, Raindrop, dk gold w/crimped camphor edge, 9x3½" 285.00
Vase, Raindrop, gr, ribbed stick neck w/pinched top, 6"..............120.00
Vase, Raindrop, wht, ruffled 4-lobe top, Mt WA, 11¾x6¾" 550.00
Vase, Swirl, gold to pk-wht, Mt WA, 9x3½"................................425.00
Vase, Swirl, rainbow cased in crystal, 4-lobe gilt rim, 6½" 425.00

Mourning Collectibles

During the eighteenth and early nineteenth centuries, ladies made needlework pictures, samplers, painting on ivory plaques, watercolor drawings, etc., to commemorate the death of a loved one. Elements contained in nearly all examples are the tomb, mourners, a weeping willow tree, and data relating to the deceased. Often plaits of hair were included. Today these are recognized and valued as a valid form of folk art.

Document of resolutions & mourning, pen/ink/watercolor, 1856, EX ...545.00
Locket, gold & blk enamel w/seed pearls, oval................................85.00
Locket, jet w/platinum & dmn figure of Britannia, ca 1878........770.00
Needlework on silk, tomb/urn/trees/lady w/cross, EX work, 1805, 16x14".4,700.00
Needlework on silk, urn/lady/willow/verse, ca 1812, fr, 16½x20⅝"...975.00
Pendant, mourning scene on ivory, feather-shaped locks ea side, 2½"...195.00
Watercolor on velvet, lady at monument, church beyond, 1825, 13x17"..2,000.00

Movie Memorabilia

Movie memorabilia covers a broad range of collectibles, from books and magazines dealing with the industry in general to the various promotional materials which were distributed to arouse interest in a particular film. Many collectors specialize in a specific area — posters, pressbooks, stills, lobby cards, or souvenir programs (also referred to as premiere booklets). In the listings below, a one-sheet poster measures approximately 27" x 41", three-sheet: 41" x 81", and six-sheet: 81" x 81". Window cards measure 14" x 22". Values are for examples in NM condition unless noted otherwise. See also Autographs; Cartoon Art; Magazines; Paper Dolls; Personalities; Rock 'n Roll Memorabilia; Sheet Music.

Window card, *Flying Down to Rio*, Delores Del Rio, 25½x19", EX, $750.00.

Insert, Desert Fury, Burt Lancaster, 1947, VG+ 100.00
Insert, Doctor at Sea, Brigitte Bardot, 1956, EX 65.00
Insert, Don't Knock the Twist, Chubby Checker, 1962 ....65.00
Insert, Eddie Duchin Story, Tyrone Power/Kim Knovak, 1956, EX....50.00
Insert, Her Husband's Affairs, Lucille Ball, 1947, VG+ 75.00
Insert, Johnny Belinda, Jane Wyman, 1948, VG+ 65.00
Insert, Looking for Love, Connie Francis/Johnny Carson, 1964, EX+ ..40.00
Insert, Our Man in Havana, Carol Reed/Alec Guinness/Noel Coward, EX ...35.00
Insert, Step by Step, Lawrence Tierney/Anne Jefferys, 1946, EX ..85.00
Insert, The Day the Earth Froze, 1963, VG+ 50.00
Insert, The Iron Petticoat, Katharine Hepburn/Bob Hope, 1956, EX+..75.00
Insert, Whirlpool, Gene Tierney, 1950, EX....................................50.00
Lobby card, Far Frontier, Roy Rogers, Republic, 1948, EX 40.00
Lobby card, Ghosts, Castle Film, 1960, VG+.................................25.00
Lobby card, House of the Seven Gables, Geo Sanders/V Price, 1940, EX+..25.00
Lobby card, Invasion of the Body Snatchers, cast image, 1956, VG+..125.00
Lobby card, My Boy, Jackie Coogan, 1922, 11x14", EX+ 85.00
Lobby card, The Brown Derby, Johnny Hines, 1926, EX...............75.00
Lobby card, Vertigo, James Stewart/Kim Novak, 1958, VG+........50.00
Lobby card, Voice in the Night, Tim McCoy, 1934, EX 50.00
Lobby card set, Hometown Story, Marilyn Monroe, 1951, EX+ .225.00
Lobby card set, Kill the Umpire, William Bendix, VG................100.00
Lobby card set, Love Nest, Marilyn Monroe, 1951, EX+.............150.00
Lobby card set, Othello, Sir Lawrence Olivier, 1966 ....40.00
Lobby card set, Pushover, Kim Novak/Fred MacMurray, 1954, VG....50.00
Lobby card set, Snows of Kilmanjaro, S Hayward/G Peck/A Gardner, 1952 ....75.00
Poster, Amazing Colossal Man, sci-fi classic, 1957, 3-sheet (linen) ..450.00
Poster, An Act of Murder, Fredric March, 1948, 3-sheet, EX+ 75.00

Poster, Attack of the 50 Ft Woman, Alison Hayes, 1958, 1-sheet (linen) ..**850.00**
Poster, Black Shadows, gorilla/dancing natives, 1949, 1-sheet, VG ...**75.00**
Poster, Breakfast at Tiffany's, Audrey Hepburn, 1961, 3-sheet (linen) ..**600.00**
Poster, Buster Keaton Story, Donald O'Connor, 1957, ½-sheet **35.00**
Poster, China Town, Jack Nicholson, 1974, 1-sheet, EX **150.00**
Poster, Curtain at Eight, stone litho, 1934, 1-sheet (linen).........**300.00**
Poster, Earth Vs the Flying Saucers, Hugh Marlow, 1956, 1-sheet, rare..**450.00**
Poster, Face of Fu Manchu, Christopher Lee, 1965, 1-sheet..........**50.00**
Poster, Family Plot, Bruce Dern, 1976, 1-sheet, EX **40.00**
Poster, Farmer Takes a Wife, Betty Grable, 3-sheet, VG+ **85.00**
Poster, Five of a Kind, Dionne Quints, 1938, ½-sheet, VG **200.00**
Poster, Follow That Dream, Elvis Presley, 1962, 40x60" (rolled), EX....**185.00**
Poster, Girl Hunters, Mickey Spillane as Mike Hammer, 1963, 1-sheet.....**75.00**
Poster, Godzilla King of the Monsters, R Burr, 1956, 1-sheet (linen)..**2,250.00**
Poster, Harvey, James Stewart, 1950, 1-sheet, rstr **1,000.00**
Poster, Have Rocket Will Travel, Columbia, 1959, ½-sheet, VG+..**120.00**
Poster, Heaven Knows Mr Allison, R Mitchum/D Kerr, 1957, 6-sheet, EX....**175.00**
Poster, How To Steel a Million, Audrey Hepburn, 1966, 3-sheet, EX+..**200.00**
Poster, I Walk Alone, B Lancaster/Liz Scott, 1948, 3-sheet (linen) ..**650.00**
Poster, If You Want Susie, Eddie Cantor/Joan Davis, 1947, 3-sheet, VG+ ..**100.00**
Poster, Jungle Drums of Africa, Clayton Moore, 1952, 3-sheet, EX ...**60.00**
Poster, Kansas City Confidential, J Payne/P Foster, 1952, 3-sheet ...**125.00**
Poster, Lady in the Morgue, Preston Foster, 1946 (reissue), 1-sheet...**50.00**
Poster, Little Rascals on Fish Hooky, 1952 (reissue), 1-sheet **125.00**
Poster, Lost City of the Legurian/Human Beasts (#6), 1935, 1-sheet ..**225.00**
Poster, Love Me Tender, Elvis Presley, 1956, 1-sheet (linen) **500.00**
Poster, Macao, Robert Mitchum/Jane Russell, 1952, 3-sheet (linen) ..**850.00**
Poster, Mad Dogs & Englishmen, Leon Russell, 1971, 1-sheet, EX+ **50.00**
Poster, Madame, Sophia Loren, 1962, 1-sheet, EX+ **50.00**
Poster, Magic Town, Jimmy Stewart/Jane Wyman, 1947, 3-sheet, VG+....**100.00**
Poster, Malaya, S Tracy/J Stewart/S Greenstreet, 1949, 3-sheet, EX+ **75.00**
Poster, Manchurian Candidate, Sinatra/L Harvey, 1962, 1-sheet, EX **65.00**
Poster, Mr Belvedere Goes to College, stone litho, 1950, 3-sheet, EX **75.00**
Poster, Munster Go Home, 1966, 3-sheet, VG+ **150.00**
Poster, Painted Veil, Greta Garbo, 1934, 1-sheet (linen).........**1,250.00**
Poster, Passing of Wolf McLean, silent, 1925, 1-sheet, EX..........**500.00**
Poster, Porgy & Bess, S Poitier/D Dandridge/S Davis Jr, 1-sheet, NM...**125.00**
Poster, Raging Bull, Robert DeNiro, 1980, 1-sheet........................**75.00**
Poster, Ride the Wild Surf, Fabian/Tab Hunter, 1964, 1-sheet, VG+ ..**75.00**
Poster, Rob Roy, Richard Todd, 1953, 3-sheet, EX+ **50.00**
Poster, Rock Around the Clock, Bill Haley/etc, 1956, ½-sheet, G+ ...**150.00**
Poster, Sand Pebbles, Steve McQueen, 1967, 40x60" (rolled) **175.00**
Poster, Shadow of the Thin Man, Powell/M Loy, 1941, 1-sheet (linen)...**650.00**
Poster, Sleepers West, Lloyd Nolan, 1942, 1-sheet (linen)..........**225.00**
Poster, Spirit of St Louis, Jimmy Stewart, 1957, 1-sheet, VG+ ...**125.00**
Poster, Summer Storm, Linda Darnell/Geo Sanders, 1944, 1-sheet (linen)....**250.00**
Poster, The Fight Never Ends, Joe Louis/Mills Bros, 1947, 1-sheet **650.00**
Poster, Thoroughly Modern Millie, J Andrews, 1972 (reissue), ½-sheet.....**35.00**
Poster, Thunderball, Sean Connery, 1965, 1-sheet, EX+..............**100.00**
Poster, Virginia, Madeleine Carroll/Fred MacMurry, 1940, 1-sheet, VG ..**100.00**
Poster, You Can't Beat Love, Joan Fontaine, 1937, 1-sheet.........**300.00**
Poster, You're My Everything, D Dailey/Anne Baxter, 1949, 1-sheet, EX...**50.00**
Title card, Give Out Sister, Andrews Sisters/Dan Dailey, 1942, VG+...**25.00**
Title card, Love Crazy, William Powell/Myrna Loy, 1941, EX+ ..**125.00**
Title card, The Black Widow, Ginger Rogers/G Tierney/G Raft, 1954, EX...**25.00**
Window card, Adventures of Robin Hood, Errol Flynn, 1937, EX..**3,000.00**
Window card, Beau Gest, silent version, 22x28", EX **650.00**
Window card, Big Money, E Quillan/R Armstrong/James Gleason, 1930, EX...**75.00**
Window card, Bluebeard's 8th Wife, Gloria Swanson, 1923, rare, VG+ ..**1,250.00**
Window card, Daddy Long Legs, Fred Astaire/Leslie Caron, 1955, VG+ **50.00**
Window card, Girls! Girls! Girls!, Elvis Presley, Paramount, 1962 ..**75.00**
Window card, Kiss Me Kate, Kathryn Grayson/Howard Keel, 1953, VG+ ...**75.00**
Window card, Planet of the Apes, Charlton Heston, 1968, rare.**100.00**
Window card, Swing Time, Fred Astaire/Ginger Rogers, 1936, EX...**1,985.00**

Window card, The Creature Walks Among Us, J Morrow/R Reason, 1956, VG......**125.00**
Window card, The Glenn Miller Story, Jimmy Stewart, 1954, VG ..**65.00**
Window card, The Lost World, Claude Rains, 1960, G+ **35.00**
Window card, The World Changes, Paul Muni, 1933, VG.........**250.00**
Window card, War & Peace, Audrey Hepburn/Henry Fonda, 1956, EX ..**50.00**
Window card, Zorba the Greek, Anthony Quinn, 1965, VG+ **50.00**

Mt. Washington

The Mt. Washington Glass Works was founded in 1837 in South Boston, Massachusetts, but moved to New Bedford in 1869 after purchasing the facilities of the New Bedford Glass Company. Frederick S. Shirley became associated with the firm in 1874. Two years later the company reorganized and became known as the Mt. Washington Glass Company. In 1894 it merged with the Pairpoint Manufacturing Company, a small Brittania works nearby, but continued to conduct business under its own title until after the turn of the century. The combined plants were equipped with the most modern and varied machinery available and boasted a working force with experience and expertise rival to none in the art of blowing and cutting glass. In addition to their fine cut glass, they are recognized as the first American company to make cameo glass, an effect they achieved through acid-cutting methods. In 1885 Shirley was issued a patent to make Burmese, pale yellow glassware tinged with a delicate pink blush. Another patent issued in 1886 allowed them the rights to produce Rose Amber, or amberina, a transparent ware shading from ruby to amber. Pearl Satin Ware and Peachblow, so named for its resemblance to a rosy peach skin, were patented the same year. One of their most famous lines, Crown Milano, was introduced in 1893. It was an opal glass either free-blown or pattern-molded, tinted a delicate color and decorated with enameling and gilt. Royal Flemish was patented in 1894 and is considered the rarest of the Mt. Washington art glass lines. It was decorated with raised, gold-enameled lines dividing the surface of the ware in much the same way as lead lines divide a stained glass window. The sections were filled in with one or several transparent colors and further decorated in gold enamel with florals, foliage, beading, and medallions.

Our advisors for this category are Betty and Clarence Maier; they are listed in the Directory under Pennsylvania. See also Amberina; Cranberry; Salt Shakers; Burmese; Crown Milano; Mother-of-Pearl Glass; Royal Flemish; etc.

Sugar shaker, apple blossoms on egg form with sterling top, 4", $350.00.

Bowl, cameo lady/scrolls/flowers, dk pk on ivory, 4x9" **950.00**
Bowl, fruit; Napoli, pond lilies/gold, 10"; in SP Pairpoint base ...**900.00**
Bowl, mums, varied golds on clear w/gr areas for leaves, 4x7¾" .**285.00**
Condiment: shakers/mustard, floral on ribbed pillar, Pairpoint fr, 8" .**500.00**
Cracker jar, Albertine, dogwood on cream, silver metal mts, jar: 8"..**350.00**
Cracker jar, floral on wht gloss, str sides, w/ornate metal mts: 10" ..**230.00**
Cracker jar, mums on swirled pnt Burmese, emb metal lid, 6½" .**225.00**
Cracker jar, pansies on peach/yel on opal, shouldered, metal mts, 8x6"..**650.00**

Cracker jar, pond lilies on deep gr, egg shape, very rare, SP mts, 10" ...1,750.00
Cracker jar, poppies on blown-out pagoda form; Pairpoint lid #3954, 9" ...1,200.00
Cracker jar, poppies on yel pnt on opal, wide base, Pairpoint mts, 9x8" .525.00
Cracker jar, poppies/gilt on lt gr/wht pnt opal; Pairpoint lid, 6x8x6" 950.00
Cracker jar, roses on tan, 16-panel cylinder, Pairpoint mts, 6½" ...595.00
Cup, punch; Ivy Rose Coin Spot, amber reeded hdl, 2½" 125.00
Humidor, spider mums on shaded yel on opal, cylinder, glass lid, 7x5" 525.00
Lamp, cameo umbrella shade & base, lady/flowers, wht on yel, 21x10" ..8,500.00
Mustard, floral, bl on pk to wht, ribbed ovoid, spike finial, 3¼" .385.00
Nappy, pond lilies, gold/gr on clear, w/hdl, 2x6" 375.00
Salt, chick head, daisies, yel/wht on opal, 2¾" 600.00
Shaker, chick head, foliage, gr on turq to teal (rare colors), 3" L...700.00
Shaker, chick head, trumpet vine/flowers, metal mts...................800.00
Shaker, floral, red/amethyst on bl, lay-down egg shape, 3" L.......110.00
Shakers, Cockle Shell, floral, 1 opal/1 pk, fr: donkey w/saddlebags..5,000.00
Shakers, floral, 1 bl/1 wht, egg shape, in Pairpoint metal fr 300.00
Shakers, floral on cream, fig shape, pr 350.00
Shakers, 4 Lobe, violets on wht, pr...235.00
Sugar shaker, dainty floral on gr to wht, egg shape, 5x4" 375.00
Sugar shaker, daisies on yel, insects emb on lid, melon ribbed, 3x4" ...535.00
Sugar shaker, floral, opal to deep bl top, egg shape, 4½" 450.00
Sugar shaker, violets/leaves on shaded gr, egg shape, 4½" 385.00
Tankard, spider mums/gold traceries on clear, 8x6" 895.00
Vase, cameo mtns/trees/rose bush, purple w/lt bl int, clear casing, 7" ...550.00
Vase, Delft, windmill/man on pk opal w/gold, bottle form, 9x5½".........375.00
Vase, gold storks/florals on blk between dbl horizontal rings, 8", pr 550.00
Vase, jack-in-pulpit, tightly crimped rim, 1 side up/1 down, 8x3½"......200.00
Vase, Lava, mc chips on blk, ovoid w/short trumpet neck, 5½", NM.1,950.00
Vase, Napoli, chicks in rain (gold drops, worn), rim hdls, 8½" .1,250.00
Vase, Napoli, spider mums/gold, long trumpet neck, 8 ribs, 10" .1,350.00
Vase, Verona, florals w/gold/silver outlines on lt pk, #918, 9"..1,250.00

Mulberry China

Mulberry china was made by many of the Staffordshire area potters from about 1830 until the 1850s. It is a transfer-printed earthenware or ironstone named for the color of its decorations, a purplish-brown resembling the juice of the mulberry. Some pieces may have faded out over the years and today look almost gray with only a hint of purple. (Transfer printing was done in many colors; technically only those in the mauve tones are 'mulberry'; color variations have little effect on value.) Some of the patterns (Corean, Jeddo, Pelew, and Formosa, for instance) were also produced in Flow Blue ware. Others seem to have been used exclusively with the mulberry color. Our advisor for this category is Mary Frank Gaston.

Alleghany, plate, 9¼" 75.00
Asiatic Views, plate, Dillian, 9¾" 85.00
Avon, pitcher, 11" 65.00
Avon Cottage, plate, scalloped edges, T Hughes, 9" 48.00
Beauties of China, bowl, Mellor Venables, 1x5⅛" 55.00
Bochara, platter, Edwards, 14x10½" 100.00
Bryonia, cup & saucer 35.00
Bryonia, plate, 8" 32.00
Calcutta, plate, Challinor, 8½" 110.00
Chelsea, plate, Wilkinson, 6½" 35.00
Corean, bowl, shallow, wide flange, Podmore Walker, 5¼" 75.00
Corean, plate, Podmore Walker, 7¾" 60.00
Corean, plate, Podmore Walker, 10" 75.00
Corean, plate, 12-sided, Podmore Walker, 9¾"..........................75.00
Corean, platter, Podmore Walker, 16x12¼", NM.....................325.00
Corean, platter, Podmore Walker, 18x14" 420.00
Corean, posset cup, att Podmore Walker, 3x3½", EX, pr.............90.00

Cumberland Falls, plate, 10" 35.00
Cypress, plate, Davenport, 9¼"..95.00
Cypress, platter, Davenport, rpr, 18x14"......................................85.00
Egina, platter, 8-sided, Challinor, 15½x12" 300.00
Foliage, cup plate, 5¾", set of 4..140.00
Foliage, gravy boat...140.00
Foliage, plate, 7½" 50.00
Foliage, plate, 9" 75.00
Foliage, platter, A Walley, 15¼" 290.00
Foliage, platter, 11"..190.00
Fruit Garden, plate, Hackwood Shelton & Hanley, 8⅝", set of 8...310.00
Hollins College, plate, Wedgwood, 10⅜"......................................70.00
Horticultural, plate, unmk, 9" 140.00
Jeddo, plate, 14-panel, W Adams, 9¼" 140.00
Jeddo, saucer, W Adams, 6" 25.00
Loretta, bowl, Alcock, rpr, 10½" 65.00
Marble, plate, 12-sided, 7½" 30.00
Marble, plate, 9½" 40.00

Medina, teapot, J.F. & Co., pedestal base and coxcomb handle, 10¼x9¼", EX, $700.00.

Moss Rose, plate, 6" 50.00
Neva, cup, handleless; Challinor 50.00
Ning Po, plate, Hall, 9" 110.00
Ning Po, platter, Hall, 10¾x8"...175.00
Non-Pareil, teapot, 7x11"..135.00
Pelew, plate, Challinor, 8½"..120.00
Pelew, plate, 12-sided, E Challinor, dinner sz............................135.00
Pendant Flower, pitcher, mk Kaolin Ware, 12⅛"........................265.00
Peruvian, plate, Wedgwood, 8½"...40.00
Peruvian, platter, Wedgwood, 12½x9½" 175.00
Pomerania, cup plate, Ridgway, 4"..110.00
Pomerania, plate, Ridgway, 10"..165.00
Prize Medal, drainer, TJ&JM mk, 12⅜x9½" 375.00
Rhone Scenery, plate, Mayer, 7½"...60.00
Rhone Scenery, platter, Mayer, 16x12" 310.00
Rhone Scenery, platter, Mayer, 18x14¼", EX 425.00
Rose, creamer, 8-panel, Walker, 5½"..160.00
Rose, plate, Challinor, 10" 75.00
Rose, plate, 8¾"..50.00
Singan, creamer, 8-panel, 5¾" 250.00
Tower, cup & saucer, Copeland Spode, relief molded hdl & edges ..85.00
Venus, plate, Wedgwood, 8¾" 70.00
Vincennes, bowl, soup; Alcock, 2x10⅝".......................................90.00
Vincennes, pitcher, water; John Alcock, 8½" 325.00
Vincennes, plate, Alcock, 7⅛"...55.00
Vincennes, plate, Alcock, 10½"..85.00
Washington Vase, teapot, 8¾"...375.00

Muller Freres

Henri Muller established a factory in 1900 at Croismare, France. He produced fine cameo art glass decorated with florals, birds, and insects in the Art Nouveau style. The work was accomplished by acid engraving and hand finishing. Usual marks were 'Muller,' 'Muller Croismare,' or 'Croismare, Nancy.' In 1910 Henri and his brother Deseri formed a glassworks at Luneville. The cameo art glass made there was nearly all produced by acid cuttings of up to four layers with motifs similar to those favored at Croismare. A good range of colors was used, and some later pieces were gold flecked. Handles and decorative devices were sometimes applied by hand. In addition to the cameo glass, they also produced an acid-finished glass of bold mottled colors in the Deco style. Examples were signed 'Muller Freres' or 'Luneville.' Our advisor for this category is Don Williams; he is listed in the Directory under Missouri.

Cameo

Vase, asters, burgundy/umber on lt bl & yel mottle w/pk, ovoid, 19".6,000.00
Vase, ferns/seed pods, gr on wht frost, 4½" 300.00
Vase, lg pine on hillside overlooking lake/mtns on bl/amber, 10x6".5,000.00
Vase, orchids, lt/dk bl on yel/amber mottle, spherical, 6".........1,500.00
Vase, pines/lake/rocky mtns, bl-blk on dusky orange/bl sky, 12½"..6,000.00
Vase, trees, dk red on bright red, stick neck, 3¾" 500.00
Vase, trees, ruby on rose, att, 3¾"... 250.00
Vase, trees/forest beyond, brn/gr on butterscotch, cylindrical, 2¾"..700.00
Vase, trees/lake/mtns, dk brn/tan on yel/orange, 2¾" 700.00
Vase, trees/lake/mtns, 3-color on yel & frost, flat sides, 4¾"....1,850.00
Vase, trees/man in boat on pnt bkground, flared w/bun ft, 15x4"...2,575.00

Miscellaneous

Ceiling light, 16" purple/yel/wht mottle shade, metal cherub mt....950.00
Sconce, tomato/amber/bl mottle, in vintage CI mt: 21", pr.....1,950.00
Shade, mottle frost to lav, 5¾x4" 75.00

Muncie

The Muncie Pottery was established in Muncie, Indiana, by Charles O. Grafton; it operated there from 1922 until about 1935. The pottery they produced is made of a heavier clay than most of its contemporaries; the styles are sturdy and simple. Early glazes were bright and colorful. In fact, Muncie was advertised as the 'rainbow pottery.' Later most of the ware was finished in a matt glaze. The more collectible examples are those modeled after Consolidated Glass vases — sculptured with lovebirds, grasshoppers, and goldfish. Their line of Art Deco-style vases is called Ruba Rombic by collectors because it bears a remarkable resemblance to the Consolidated Glass Company's Ruba Rombic line. Vases, candlesticks, bookends, ashtrays, bowls, lamp bases, and luncheon sets were made. A line of garden pottery was manufactured for a short time. Items were frequently impressed with MUNCIE in block letters. Letters such as A, K, E, or D and the numbers 1, 2, 3, 4, or 5 often found scratched into the base are finishers' marks. For more information, we recommend *Collector's Encyclopedia of Muncie Pottery* by Jon Rans and Mark Eckelman (Collector Books). Our advisor for this category is Virginia Heiss; she is listed in the Directory in Indiana.

Bulb bowl, 'Ruba Rombic,' #306, matt green drip over lavender, 9" diameter, $375.00; Vase, #404, hand-turned, green drip over lavender, 6", $85.00.

Bottle, #111, molded, matt bl, 4½" 135.00
Canoe, #253, dk matt gr, w/insert, 11½"...................................275.00
Chamber stick, #152, matt gr/rose, 4" 150.00
Dutch shoe, matt pk w/wht drip, 6½"...350.00
Ewer, #136, blk gloss, 12" 150.00
Lamp base, panels w/5 dancing nudes, matt gr over pumpkin, 9⅞".425.00
Vase, #143, gr gloss, w/hdls, 7"..115.00
Vase, #259, blk gloss, trumpet shape, 12"..................................325.00
Vase, Rombic star, #312, dk matt gr, 4x5"...................................375.00

Musical Instruments

The field of automatic musical instruments covers many different categories ranging from watches and tiny seals concealing fine early musical movements to huge organs and orchestrions which weigh many hundreds of pounds and are equivalent to small orchestras. Music boxes, first made in the early nineteenth century by Swiss watchmakers, were produced in both disc and cylinder models. The latter type employs a cylinder with tiny pins that lift the teeth in the comb of the music box (producing a sound much like many individual tuning forks), and music results. The value of a cylinder music box depends on the length and diameter of the cylinder, the date of its manufacture, the number of tunes it plays (four or six is usually better than ten or twelve), and its manufacturer. Nicole Freres, Henri Capt, LeCoultre, and Bremond are among the most highly regarded, and the larger boxes made by Mermod Freres are also popular. Examples with multiple cylinders, extra instruments (such as bells or an organ section), and those in particularly ornate cabinets or with matching tables bring significantly higher prices. Early cylinder boxes were wound with a separate key which was inserted on the left side of the case. These early examples bring a premium. While smaller cylinder boxes are still being made, the larger ones (over 10" cylinders) typically date from before 1900. Disc music boxes were introduced about 1890 but were replaced by the phonograph only twenty-five years later. However, during that time hundreds of thousands were made. Their great advantage was in playing inexpensive interchangeable discs, a factor that remains an attraction for today's collector as well. Among the most popular disc boxes are those made by Regina (USA), Polyphon, Mira, Stella, and Symphonion. Relative values are determined by the size of the discs they play, whether they have single or double combs, if they are upright or table models, and how ornate their cases are. Especially valuable are those that play multiple discs at the same time or are incorporated into tall case clocks.

Player pianos were made in a wide variety of styles. Early varieties consisted of a mechanism which pushed up to a piano and played on the keyboard by means of felt-tipped fingers. These use sixty-five note rolls. Later models have the playing mechanism built in, and most use eighty-eight note rolls. Upright pump player pianos have little value in unrestored condition because the cost of restoration is so high. 'Reproducing' pianos, especially the 'grand' format, can be quite valuable, depending on the make, the size, the condition, and the ornateness of the case. 'Reproducing' pianos have very sophisticated mechanisms and are much more realistic in the reproduction of piano music. They were made in relatively limited quantities. Better manufacturers include Steinway and Mason & Hamlin. Popular roll mechanism makers include Ampico, Duo-Art, and Welte. The market for all types of player pianos has been weak for several years.

Coin-operated pianos (orchestrions) were used commercially and typically incorporate extra instruments in addition to the piano action. These can be very large and complex, incorporating drums, cymbals, xylophones, bells, and dozens of pipes. Both American and European coin pianos are very popular, especially the larger and more complex models made by Wurlitzer, Seeburg, Cremona, Weber, Welte, Hupfeld, and many others. These companies also made automatically playing violins (Mills Violin Virtuoso, Hupfeld), banjos (Encore), and harps (Whitlock); these are quite valuable.

Collecting player organettes is a fun endeavor. Roller organs, organettes, player organs, grind organs, hand organs — whatever the name — are a fascinating group of music makers. Some used wooden barrels or cobs to operate the valves, or metal and cardboard discs or paper strips, paper rolls, metal donuts, or metal strips. They usually played from fourteen to twenty keys or notes. Some were pressure operated or vacuum type. Their heyday lasted from the 1870s to the turn of the century. Most were reed organs, but a few had pipes. Many were made in either America or Germany. They lost favor with the advent of the phonograph, as did the music box. Some music boxes were built with little player organs in them. Any player organette in good working condition with some music and in their original finish should be worth from $200.00 to $600.00, depending on the model. Generally the more keying it has and the larger and fancier the case, the more desirable it is. Rarity plays a part too. There are a handful of individuals who make new music rolls for these player organs. Some machines are very rare, and music for them is nearly impossible to find. For further information on player organs we recommend *Encyclopedia of Automatic Musical Instruments* by Bowers.

Unless noted, prices given are for instruments in fine condition, playing properly, with cabinets or cases in well-preserved or refinished condition. In all instances, unrestored instruments sell for much less, as do those with broken or missing parts, damaged cases, and the like. On the other hand, particularly superb examples in especially ornate case designs and those that have been particularly well kept will often command more. Our advisor for mechanical instruments is Martin Roenigk; he is listed in the Directory under Arkansas.

Key:
c — cylinder   d — disc

Mechanical

Automata, single birdcage, gesso gilt base, 21", G 1,400.00
Box, Bremond, 20" c, 10-tune, alternating tips, G 4,200.00
Box, Bremond-like, 16" c, early orchestral, inlaid case, EX......3,800.00
Box, Capital A, coil spring drive, w/6 cuffs, rstr 4,650.00
Box, Capital A, 1 cuff only, oak, G 3,600.00
Box, Capital B, w/7 cuffs, lt rstr, EX.......................................7,200.00
Box, Jean Billon-Heller, interchangeable 6" c, 9x15½x10¾", G......1,850.00
Box, Mermod Freres, Ideal Sublime...Piccolo, 6 18" c, cvd case, EX....11,500.00
Box, Mermod Freres, keywind, 10¾x3⅛" c, 4-tune, inlaid lid, VG.3,500.00
Box, Mermod Freres, 6 24½" c, cvd oak case w/drws, EX+....46,000.00
Box, Mermod Freres, 9" interchangeable c, coin-op, cvd oak case, VG...2,200.00
Box, Mira, 6¾" d, orig print, mahog case, EX comb....................750.00
Box, Mira, 18½" d, decaled console cabinet, EX orig 11,000.00
Box, Nicole Freres, keywind, 4-tune, 13" c 2,800.00
Box, Nicole Freres, organ, 22-note, 16¼" c, nonworking, VG ...4,800.00
Box, Paillard, interchangeable c, buffet case w/3 drw, 31", VG...12,000.00
Box, Paillard, Sublime Harmonie Tremolo Zither, 17" c, dbl spring, EX..3,700.00
Box, Paillard, 6 17¾" c, 10-tune, full orchestra, walnut, VG.....11,000.00
Box, Regina, 11" dbl c, upright early case, rstr 4,200.00
Box, Regina, 15½" d, dbl comb, coin-op, oak case, VG...........3,500.00
Box, Regina, 15½" d, mahog bow-front, autochanger, EX.....18,500.00
Box, Regina, 15½" d, oak bow-front, auto changer, EX.........19,000.00
Box, Regina #11, 15½" d, dbl comb, cvd mahog case, VG orig....3,400.00
Box, Regina #33 (late style), 27" changer, cvd dragons, EX, +12 d..21,000.00
Box, Regina upright, 27" d single play, dbl comb 14,000.00
Box, Reginaphone #240, console w/cvd dragon heads, EX+ orig ..10,500.00
Box, Reginaphone #240, mahog case w/cvd dragon heads, rstr ..9,800.00
Box, Reuge, c, dbl side-by-side 8¾" comb, 3 dancing girls, EX...950.00
Box, Swiss, rosewood w/mahog & mc inlay, 12" c, 12-tune, 24" L, EX..1,400.00

Box, Symphonion, plays 3 13⅝" d, clock 36,000.00
Box, Symphonion, 11⅞" d, dbl comb, decor case, EX.............2,200.00
Box, Symphonion, 13½" d, dbl comb, G 2,400.00
Box, 17" c, 8-tune, heavily cvd hunt scene case, VG orig 8,250.00
Nickelodeon, Englehardt, w/pipes, art glass, Mission-style case ...9,800.00
Nickelodeon, Peerless #44, rfn oak case, M rstr, +20 rolls 10,500.00
Orchestrion, Pierre Eich Solophone, 102 pipes, old rstr 34,000.00
Organ, Aeolian, 46-note home model, EX orig 1,200.00
Organ, band; Wurlitzer, used on merry-go-round, uses 125 (10-tune) rolls.7,250.00
Organ, band; Wurlitzer #148 Military, natural oak case, EX, +148 rolls..17,000.00
Organ, band; Wurlitzer #153, old partial rstr, VG on trailer..34,000.00
Organ, band; Wurlitzer Caliola, wooden pipes, keyboard, old rstr ..12,750.00
Organ, monkey; Bacigalupo, 43-key, 96 pipes, rstr 9,200.00
Organ, monkey; Zimmerman Harmonipan, exposed pipes, EX+ ..6,500.00
Organ, paper roll; Improved Celestina, EX stencils, +1 roll, EX.900.00
Organ, paper roll; Orguinette Co, R Wurlitzer, no rolls 450.00
Organ, reed; Aeolian Orchestrelle, ca 1900, +14 rolls 3,700.00
Organ, roller; Gem Home Music Box, 6 cobs, ornate case, VG..550.00
Organ, street; Carl Frei, 21-key, 4⅜" rolls, 35 pipes, mini, VG..3,300.00
Organ, street; Richter, 79 key, 350 pipes, rstr 80,000.00
Organ, Wurlitzer #125, brass trumpets, rstr.............................24,000.00
Piano, bbl street; 2 lg drums at top, total rstr..........................1,250.00
Piano, Cremona A, 25¢ play, takes O rolls (10-tune), ca 1920 ..2,900.00
Piano, grand; Baldwin Welte Mignon, 68", w/bench, rstr 8,500.00
Piano, grand; Steinway reproducing Ampico, 78", EX orig......5,500.00
Piano, Melidoca, 30-key, EX, +6 books of music 4,800.00
Piano, Mills Violano Virtuoso, plays piano/violin, working...22,000.00
Piano, Seeburg KT, cabinet style, xylophone, EX orig 10,500.00
Piano, upright; Wurlitzer IX, ldgl front, 5-¢ play, 1915 ....4,650.00
Piano, Wurlitzer CX, 2 ranks of pipes, other instruments, EX orig...18,500.00
Piano/organ combo, Reproduco, Mission-style case, made in Chicago 3,950.00
Pianolin, N Tonawanda, 2 ranks of pipes, oak cabinet-style case, VG ..11,000.00
Pianolin, N Tonwawnda, 2 ranks of pipes/art glass, oak cabinet, EX...12,500.00

Non-Mechanical

Violin, inlaid wood back, late 1800s, 24", EX, $1,700.00. (Photo courtesy Jackson's Auctioneers & Appraisers)

Banjo, 5-string, 16 spreadwing eagle-head tensioners, 1860s, G .300.00
Clarinet, Selmer R1, SP nickel, orig mouthpc, 1920s, NM 1,500.00
Concertina, Henry Silberhorn, Chicago, ornate details, EX 450.00
Drum set, Gresch, champagne sparkle, 1967, 4-pc, w/Beato bags ..950.00
Guitar, Dobro Archtop Electric, 1930s, EX 1,100.00
Guitar, Epiphone Casino E230TD, sunburst, 1960s, EX+ 1,850.00
Guitar, Epiphone Zephyr Regent, 1954, EX w/orig case...........1,500.00
Guitar, Gibson Acoustic J50, 1954, EX...................................2,500.00
Guitar, Gibson Byrdland, 1978, NM w/case 1,900.00
Guitar, Gibson ES 335TD, sunburst, 1966, EX w/brn Lifton-style case ..2,500.00
Guitar, Gibson ES-295, gold, 1952, M in orig case 2,700.00
Guitar, Gibson ES-335, cherry, 1970s, EX 1,800.00
Guitar, Gibson ES-335, left-handed, sunburst, 1975, EX 1,550.00

Guitar, Martin #0021, 1970, NM in hard-shell lined case **1,850.00**
Guitar, Martin D-28, Brazilian bk & sides, 1969, EX **2,500.00**
Guitar, Martin D-28, Indian rosewood/spruce/mahog, 1970, EX+ w/case ...**1,600.00**
Guitar, National Duolian, silver finish, 1930s, EX w/case........**1,475.00**
Guitar Gibson Bowtie, sunburst on resonator, 1960s, EX w/case ..**1,450.00**
Harp, concert; Lion & Healey, tiger maple giltwood & brass, 70" ..**7,000.00**
Keyboard, Moog Prodigy #336a, analog, EX w/case **775.00**
Mandolin, Gibson F2, hand-inlaid German Tuners, ca 1915, EX ..**1,750.00**
Organ, parlor; Beckwith, pump type, upright oak case **200.00**
Organ, parlor; Crown, walnut pump type, high-bk fancy case.....**150.00**
Piano, baby grand; Steinway & Sons S Model, blk ebony, 62x56"..**14,000.00**
Piano, grand; Bechstein, rosewood serpentine case, 1890s, 34x84x62"...**8,000.00**
Saxophone, Selmer MK VI, all orig, relacquered, EX+ w/case ..**2,000.00**
Saxophone, tenor; Selmer New Largebore, Super series, 1931, NM ..**1,600.00**
Trumpet, Besson, ca 1920, NM **1,000.00**
Tuba, Conn, SP, 4-valve, ca 1915, 21" bell, 38", EX...................**975.00**
Ukelele, Roy Smeck Vita, EX in worn case...................................**475.00**
Ukelele, Samual K Kamaka Pineapple, sq frets, Pat 1928, EX .**1,550.00**

Mustache Cups

Mustache cups were popular items during the late Victorian period, designed specifically for the man with the mustache! They were made in silverplate as well as china and ironstone. Decorations ranged from simple transfers to elaborately applied and gilded florals. To properly position the 'mustache bar,' special cups were designed for the 'lefties.' These are the rare ones!

Cherubs emb, serpentine hdl, left-handed Capodimonte type, 1920s.....**160.00**
Floral sprays/beads on pk lustre, Made in Germany, 1880-1910, $60 to....**85.00**
Floral transfer w/overpnt, scalloped rims, Germany, late 1800s, $80 to...**100.00**
Flowers & ferns w/gold beading, 8-flute, Japan, 1875-90, from $150 to.**200.00**
Flowers & Leaves HP, Erdmann Schlegelmilch Suhl, late 1800s ...**225.00**
Flowers HP on yel w/gold, unmk Germany, 1880-1910, from $50 to.........**75.00**
Gold decor on wht, 8-flute, unmk Germany, ca 1880-1910, from $60 to..**75.00**
Longfellow's Wayside Inn in Sudbury MA reserve, Germany, ca 1900......**60.00**
Roses transfer, rustic hdl, Triple Crown China, 1890s, from $150 to.**200.00**
Silver w/etched floral, quadruple plate, Poole Silver, 1890s, $150 to.**200.00**
Water lilies & gilt daisies, gold hdl, Germany, ca 1910-35, $100 to...**125.00**
Yel leafy design along rim, swirled, unmk, ca 1900-30s, from $50 to ..**70.00**

Nailsea

Nailsea is a term referring to clear or colored glass decorated in contrasting spatters, swirls, or loops. These are usually white but may also be pink, red, or blue. It was first produced in Nailsea, England, during the late 1700s but was made in other parts of Britain and Scotland as well. During the mid-1800s a similar type of glass was produced in this country. Originally used for decorative novelties only, by that time tumblers and other practical items were being made from Nailsea-type glass. See also Lamps; Witch Balls.

Flasks: Cranberry with tight white herringbone pattern, pontil scar, double-collar mouth, 7⅛", $925.00; Deep amber with white loopings, pontil scar, sheared lip, 4⅝", $350.00; Medium olive green with white loopings, pontil scar, sheared lip, 6½", $400.00.

Bottle, bellows; wht w/red & bl loopings, rigaree, hdls, 11¾" **460.00**
Bowl, clear w/wht loops & red ruffle, amber rigaree hdls, metal fr, 6" ..**200.00**
Flask, clear w/red/wht/bl loopings, 6½x4¾" **240.00**
Flask, fiery opal w/pk & cobalt loopings, chipped pontil, 7" **110.00**
Rolling pin, clear w/bl & wht loopings, 14¾x2½" dia **200.00**
Salt cellar, cranberry w/rigaree, in SP 3-ftd base **225.00**
Thimble, amber w/red & cream loopings, 1x1".................................**50.00**
Vase, bl w/wht loopings, 8½" **125.00**
Vase, bl/wht loopings, trumpet form w/ruffled rim, metal holder, 9" .**125.00**
Vase, opaque wht w/dk bl loopings & swirls, 9½x6" dia...............**90.00**

Nakara

Nakara was a line of decorated opaque milk glass produced by the C.F. Monroe Company of Meriden, Connecticut, for a few years after the turn of the century. It differs from their Wave Crest line in several ways. The shapes were simpler; pastel colors were deeper and covered more of the surface; more beading was present; flowers were larger; and large transfer prints of figures, Victorian ladies, cherubs, etc., were used as well. Ormolu and brass collars and mounts complemented these opulent pieces. Most items were signed; however, this is not important since the ware was never reproduced. Our advisors for this category are Dolli and Wilfred R. Cohen; their address is listed in the Directory under California.

Ashtray, floral on gr, 3 gilt-metal rests, 6" dia **300.00**
Bonbon tray Dmn Swirl, geometric scrolling/beading on bl **550.00**
Box, Bishop's Hat blank, floral on pk, 6¾" **795.00**
Box, blown-out pansy on bl, 3¾" dia **995.00**
Box, cherubs transfer on lid, 3¾" dia **550.00**
Box, Collars & Cuffs, Gibson girl transfer **2,250.00**
Box, courting couple reserve on peach, 6" dia **1,150.00**
Box, floral on bl & wht w/beading, oval, 2¾x5¼" **495.00**
Box, ladies in Greco-Roman garden transfer, 8" dia.................**2,500.00**
Box, lady's portrait on pk, emb rococo scrolls, 5½x8¼" dia.....**2,750.00**
Box, peach/yel panels alternate, wht dots between, hexagonal, 3¼x3" ..**450.00**
Box, pk rose on lav/pk lid outlined by wht dots, mirror, 3½x5"..**875.00**
Box, robin's egg bl w/tan accents & wht beading, hexagon, 4" ...**515.00**
Box, roses, red & wht on pk to gr w/beading, 6" dia....................**700.00**
Hair receiver, children at tea on bl w/wht beading, dmn shape ..**630.00**
Humidor, Cigars & flowers on bl **775.00**
Humidor, Indian chief on shaded brn, ogee sides, brass lid, 8x6½"..**1,700.00**
Humidor, owl in tree transfer, 5½x4" **1,200.00**
Humidor, Tobacco, frog reading paper on bl, metal lid, 6¾" ...**1,100.00**
Jardinier, pk floral on gr, gold rim...**625.00**
Pin tray, floral, pk wash int, 6-sided, ormolu hdls **225.00**
Smoke set, floral on gr, cigar holder+2 ash bowls+match holder on fr.**800.00**
Sweetmeat, fall leaves on bl, shaped body, metal lid/hdl, 5½" W ..**325.00**

Napkin Rings

Napkin rings became popular during the late 1800s. They were made from various materials. Among the most popular and collectible today are the large group of varied silver-plated figurals made by American manufacturers. Recently the larger figurals in excellent condition have appreciated considerably. Only those with a blackened finish, corrosion, or broken and/or missing parts have maintained their earlier price levels. When no condition is indicated, the items listed below are assumed to be all original and in very good to excellent condition. Check very carefully for missing parts, solder repairs, marriages, and reproductions.

A timely warning: Inexperienced buyers should be aware of excellent reproductions on the market, especially the wheeled pieces and cherubs. However, these do not have the fine detail and patina of the originals and tend to have a more consistent, soft pewter-like finish. These are appearing at the large, quality shows at top prices, being shown along with authentic antique merchandise. Beware!

Key:
gw — gold washed   SH&M — Simpson, Hall &
R&B — Reed & Barton   Miller

Balloon-bk chair w/cushion supports ring, unmk, under..............**200.00**
Bear on base beside scrolled holder, Hamilton #127, from $200 to..**350.00**
Boy crawls behind ring to snare bunny, Meriden SP #0232, minimum..**500.00**
Boy holds treat to begging dog, Aurora SP #29, from $200 to **350.00**
Bull by bright-cut holder on fancy base, Knickerbocker #1250, $200 to ..**350.00**
Cherub amid leaves at side of hexagonal ring, Meriden SP #4650, under...**200.00**
Cherub by ring holds salt cellar aloft, Meriden SP #238, from $200 to..**350.00**
Cherub w/flute on scroll beside ring & sm vase, Rogers & Bro, minimum...**500.00**
Cherubs (2) sit ea side of ring on ftd base, Wilcox SP #10536, $200 to ...**350.00**
Chick ea side of ring on fancy base, Van Bergh #80, under.........**200.00**
Cockatoo on ball before ring, plain raised base, Pairpoint #8, under ..**200.00**
Cockatoo on ped on ftd base beside ring, Tufts, from $200 to.....**350.00**
Cockatoo on sunflower stem, book-shaped ring, Derby #370, from $200 to...**350.00**
Coral & shells form base for ring, Meriden Britannia #227, $200 to ..**350.00**
Cow beside milk bucket-shaped holder, Meriden SP #268, from $200 to..**350.00**
Crane stands w/1 ft up, woodland base, Meriden Britannia #163, $350 to...**500.00**

Croquet mallets (four) encompass ring, Derby #302, 3¾", $225.00.

Dog & goat on base ea side of holder on ped, Webster #148, $200 to..**350.00**
Dog in harness pulls holder on wheels, SH&M #033, from $350 to.....**500.00**
Dog on bk legs views bird atop holder, Aurora SP #27, under **200.00**
Dog w/pail beside bbl-shaped holder, Tufts #1532, from $200 to..**350.00**
Dog w/paw up beside bbl-shaped holder, Rockford SP #125, $200 to ..**350.00**
Dog w/wishbone in mouth on base w/holder on bk, Derby #303, $200 to..**350.00**
Dolphins (2) support ring w/tails, Pairpoint #30, from $200 to...**350.00**
Donkey wearing saddle by plain holder, unmk, from $200 to......**350.00**
Draped child holds vase over head before ring, Wm Rogers #276, $200 to..**350.00**
Eagle (sm) atop ring on ped on base, Meriden Britannia #167, $200 to...**350.00**
Elephant w/trunk up by cloverleaf-shaped ring, unmk, from $200 to **350.00**
Elves balance ring atop fretwork ped on base, R&B #1326, minimum..**500.00**
Eskimo w/ice cutter beside ring, Meriden SP #220, from $200 to ...**350.00**
Faceted ring amid vase & sm bird, Rockford #177, from $200 to ...**350.00**
Fireman's hat rests on ring, earth-like base, Pairpoint #81, minimum ..**500.00**
Flatiron form w/opening in sides, Tufts #1636, under **200.00**
Flowers & leaves support ring, Aurora SP #38, from $200 to......**350.00**
Fox runs beside holder, plain ftd base, Wm Rogers #882, from $350 to..**500.00**
Goat strides away from holder, Meriden Britannia #195, from $200 to ..**350.00**
Greco-Roman male busts support ring, Southington Cutlery #41, $200 to **350.00**
Greenaway-type boy in chair w/book, girl behind, SH&M #036, minimum..**500.00**
Greenaway-type boy in sailor suit atop ring, SH&M, from $200 to **350.00**
Greenaway-type girl in bonnet sits beside ring, Derby #316, $350 to...**500.00**
Greenaway-type girl on toboggan w/ring, Wilcox SP #4342, minimum.....**500.00**
Greenaway-type girl w/dog before ring, unmk, from $350 to.......**500.00**

Long-tailed bird on stem beside ring, Meriden Britannia #202, $200 to.**350.00**
Long-tailed parrot w/wings spread on ring, R&B #1136, from $200 to...**350.00**
Monkey plays horn before ornate ring, #064, from $200 to.........**350.00**
Owl (pepper) sits on sq emb holder, unmk, from $200 to **350.00**
Owl on leaf beside ring, ftd base, Wm Rogers #257, from $200 to..........**350.00**
Pan w/cymbals atop triangular ring, Meriden Britannia #246, $200 to...**350.00**
Pheasant ea side of decor ring, raised base, Meriden SP #271, $200 to...**350.00**
Rabbit w/front ft on holder, unmk, from $200 to......................**350.00**
Rampant lion beside holder, ftd base, Meriden Britannia #153, $200 to....**350.00**
Shakers & cruet surround ring on ftd base, Tufts #1459, from $200 to...**350.00**
Squirrel on base w/emb decor beside ring, Knickerbocker #7, $200 to..**350.00**
Squirrel w/nut faces away from ring, SH&M #09, from $200 to .**350.00**

Nash

A. Douglas Nash founded the Corona Art Glass Company in Long Island, New York. He produced tableware, vases, flasks, etc. using delicate artistic shapes and forms. After 1933 he worked for the Libbey Glass Company.

Bowl, Chintz, red w/silver stripes, 4" **700.00**
Candlesticks, Chintz, Blood Red w/gray, ball stem, 4", pr **775.00**
Cordial, Chintz, bl & gr, 4"..**100.00**
Parfait, gr wavy int threads on crystal ribbed body, disc ft, 4¾" **80.00**
Plate, Chintz, orchid & chartreuse spirals, 6½" **230.00**
Plate, Chintz on gold, purple irid on underside, sgn Nash, 9" **290.00**
Vase, amber irid, flared lip, #544, 4½"...**625.00**
Vase, Chintz, red/gr stripes, red int, sgn/#RD-85X, 12" **1,000.00**
Wine, Chintz, lav/gr alternate, lt bl stem, 6" **175.00**

Natzler, Gertrude and Otto

The Natzlers came to the United States from Vienna in the late 1930s. They settled in Los Angeles where they continued their work in ceramics, for which they were already internationally recognized. Gertrude created the forms; Otto formulated a variety of interesting glazes, among them volcanic, crystalline, and lustre. Our advisor for this category is Abby Malowanczyk; she is listed in the Directory under Texas.

Bowl, cream w/random gr flecks, wide/flaring, 3½x13½".........**4,000.00**
Bowl, peach blossom w/gr/bl/red, fissures/lt irid, deep/ftd, 6½" ..**5,500.00**
Bowl, purple crystalline, oxidation firing, low/flared/ftd, 7¾"..**4,250.00**
Bowl, robin-egg bl, clay exposed at oval rim, #J230, 4½" L **750.00**
Bowl, tiger-eye glaze, reduction firing, low/flared, 6½" **3,000.00**
Bowl, turq w/drips at rim int, rim flattened on 2 sides, 2¼x7"....**2,300.00**
Bowl, wht crater glaze on brn/blk, 7½x9½"...............................**1,600.00**
Bowl, yel crystalline matt over red clay, low/flaring, 11" **3,250.00**
Bowl, yel/lt bl crystalline matt over red clay, #K6167, shallow, 7" ..**1,600.00**
Bowl vase, blk crystalline, wide w/funnel base, 5½" dia...........**1,900.00**
Vase, gr/gray lava glaze w/high & low areas, cylindrical, 13" .**14,000.00**
Vase, random ivory drips reveal terra cotta, ovoid w/funnel neck, 9" ..**5,000.00**
Vase, sky bl gloss (several tones), very bulbous bottle form, 5" ..**4,000.00**
Vase, wht cratered drips expose brn clay, ftd U-form, G&O, 3"....**2,700.00**

Naughties and Bathing Beauties

These daring all-bisque figurines were made in various poses, usually in one piece, in German and American factories during the 1920s. Admired for their fine details, these figures were often nude but were also made with molded-on clothing or dressed in bathing costumes. Items below are all in excellent undamaged condition.

For further information we recommend *Doll Values, Antique to Modern*, by Patsy Moyer (Collector Books). Our advisors for this category are Don and Ann Kier; they are listed in the Directory under Ohio.

Action figure, w/wig, 7", from $450 to 650.00
Action figure, 5", from $350 to over...450.00
Action figure, 7½", from $500 to 650.00
Elderly woman in suit w/legs crossed, 5¼" 2,200.00
Glass eyes, 5", from $300 to 400.00
Glass eyes, 6", from $500 to 650.00
Japan mk, 3", from $50 to 75.00
Japan mk, 5-6", from $65 to 100.00
Japan mk, 9", from $125 to 175.00
Pnt eyes, 3", from $100 to 250.00
Pnt eyes, 6", from $300 to 400.00
Swivel neck, 5", from $500 to 675.00
Swivel neck, 6", from $545 to 725.00
W/animal, 5½", from $1,125 to..1,500.00
2 modeled together, 4½-5½", minimum value 1,600.00

New England Glass Works

Founded in 1818 by Deming Jarves in Boston, Massachusetts, the New England Glass Company produced cut, blown three-mold, free-blown, and pressed glass of the highest quality. They were recognized for their fine decorative accomplishments, using etching, gilding, and engraving to emphasize their wares. For more than fifty years, they produced prize-winning pressed glass tableware sets. Because they refused to compromise the quality of their product by using the cheaper lime-based glass that flooded the market in the 1860s, the company fell into financial trouble and by 1888 was forced to close. However, William Libbey, who had been the sales manager there since 1870, leased the premises and resumed operations with his father, Edward Drummond Libbey, as full partner. In 1892 the firm became known as The Libbey Glass Company. See also Libbey. Our advisor for this category is Elizabeth Simpson; she is listed in the Directory under Maine.

Vase, amethyst, blown trumpet form w/folded rim, 7½"...........1,850.00
Vase, Bull's Eye & Ellipse, emerald gr, att, 7¼x3¼" 1,000.00
Vase, cobalt, blown w/appl rings at rim & neck, 8" 750.00
Vase, Loop, canary, gauffered rim, marble base, 10¾"..................300.00
Vase, 3-Printie Block, emerald gr, gauffered rim, 9¾x3¾" 3,680.00
Vase, 3-Printie Block, lt bl, gauffered rim, hexagonal base, 9¾" ..1,265.00

New Geneva

In the early years of the nineteenth century, several potteries flourished in the Greensboro, Pennsylvania, area. They produced utilitarian stoneware items as well as tile and novelties for many decades. All failed well before the turn of the century.

Creamer, redware w/brn glossy floral, 4¾", EX 600.00
Flowerpot, tan ware w/red-brn florals, ovoid, chips, 8½" 1,100.00
Jar, bl bands/tooling, HP strawberries, stencil: New Geneva, 9½" ...2,750.00
Jug, med brn Albany glaze w/stenciled name, 10⅜" NM.............275.00
Jug, tan ware w/Albany glaze, stenciled label dtd 1880, 6½", NM..275.00
Pitcher, red-tan ware w/brn glossy florals, tooled lines, 8", NM ..600.00
Pitcher, red-tan ware w/red/brn glazed flourishes & lines, 7¾", NM .450.00
Pitcher, tan ware, tooled lines, dk brn glossy floral, 9" 715.00
Pitcher, tan ware w/dk brn glossy lines & florals, 5", NM 450.00
Pitcher, unglazed tan w/dk brn glossy floral, tooled shoulder, 6" .770.00

New Martinsville

The New Martinsville Glass Company took its name from the town in West Virginia where it began operations in 1901. In the beginning years, pressed tablewares were made in crystal as well as colored and opalescent glass. Considered an innovator, the company was known for their imaginative applications of the medium in creating lamps made entirely of glass, vanity sets, figural decanters, and models of animals and birds. In 1944 the company was purchased by Viking Glass, who continued to use many of the old molds, the animals molds included. They marked their wares 'Viking' or 'Rainbow Art.' Viking recently ceased operations and has been purchased by Kenneth Dalzell, president of the Fostoria Company. They, too, are making the bird and animal models. Although at first they were not marked, future productions are to be marked with an acid stamp. Dalzell/Viking animals are in the $50.00 to $60.00 range. Values for cobalt and red items are two to three times higher than for the same item in clear. See also Depression Glass; Glass Animals and Figurines.

Addie, bowl, vegetable; blk, cobalt, jade or red, lg flare rim..........45.00
Addie, cup, crystal or pk, ftd 8.00
Addie, plate, luncheon; bl, cobalt, jade or red 12.50
Addie, tumbler, juice; crystal, ftd, 6-oz 10.00
Janice, basket, crystal, 9x6½" 75.00
Janice, bowl, crystal, oval, 11"...40.00
Janice, bowl, red or bl, cupped, 9½" 65.00
Janice, canape set, crystal, tray w/ftd juice....................................30.00
Janice, celery, crystal, 11" 20.00
Janice, cup, red or bl...23.00
Janice, jam jar, crystal, w/lid, 6" 20.00
Janice, plate, crystal, 13" 30.00
Janice, plate, mayonnaise; bl or red, 6"...12.50
Janice, shakers, red or bl, pr 85.00
Janice, sugar bowl, crystal, tall 15.00
Janice, tumbler, red or bl...30.00
Lions, candy dish, pk or gr, w/lid..55.00
Lions, creamer, blk, #34...30.00
Lions, creamer, crystal, #37...15.00
Lions, plate, pk or gr, 12"...30.00
Meadow Wreath, bowl, relish; crystal, #4228/26, 3-part, 8" 30.00
Meadow Wreath, candy box, crystal, #42/26, 3-part, w/lid............65.00
Meadow Wreath, celery bowl, crystal, #42/26, oval, 10" 35.00
Meadow Wreath, plate, crystal, #42/26, 14"...................................45.00
Meadow Wreath, vase, crystal, #4232/26, crimped, 10".................55.00
Moondrops, bowl, soup; red or bl, 6¾" 75.00
Moondrops, butter dish, colors other than red or bl, w/lid 275.00
Moondrops, comport, red or bl, 4" 32.50
Moondrops, plate, colors other than red or bl, 5⅞" 8.00
Moondrops, plate, sandwich; red or bl, rnd, 14"............................45.00

Prelude, crystal, vase, 10", $75.00.

Radiance, bowl, amber, flared, 10" 25.00
Radiance, bowl, bonbon; red or ice bl, 6" 33.00
Radiance, bowl, pickle; red or ice bl, 7" 35.00
Radiance, candlesticks, amber, 8", pr 95.00
Radiance, comport, red or ice bl, 5" 32.50
Radiance, creamer, red or ice bl 25.00
Radiance, honey jar, red or ice bl, w/lid 125.00
Radiance, plate, luncheon; amber, 8" 10.00
Radiance, tumbler, cobalt, 9-oz 28.00
Top Notch, cup, red, gr, cobalt or amber 20.00
Top Notch, plate, luncheon; red, gr, cobalt or amber 18.00

Newcomb

The Newcomb College of New Orleans, Louisiana, established a pottery in 1895 to provide the students with first-hand experience in the fields of art and ceramics. Using locally dug clays — red and buff in the early years, white-burning by the turn of the century — potters were employed to throw the ware which the ladies of the college decorated. From 1897 until about 1910, the ware they produced was finished in a high glaze and was usually surface painted. After 1905, some carving was done as well. On today's market, even a small piece of carved high glaze ware generally brings a minimum of $4,000.00. After 1912 a matt glaze was favored; these pieces are always carved. Soft blues and greens were used almost exclusively, and decorative themes were chosen to reflect the beauty of the South. The end of the matt-glaze period and the art-pottery era was 1930.

Various marks used by the pottery include an 'N' within a 'C,' sometimes with 'HB' added to indicate a 'hand-built' piece. The potter often incised his initials into the ware, and the artists were encouraged to sign their work. Among the most well-known artists were Sadie Irvine, Henrietta Bailey, and Fannie Simpson.

Newcomb pottery is evaluated to a large extent by era (early, transitional, or matt), decoration, size, and condition. In the following descriptions, unless noted otherwise, all decoration is carved and painted on matt glaze. The term 'transitional' defines a period of two to three years (ca 1910 to 1912) between earlier and later work, and signifies changes to the glazes, colors, and style of decoration. Our advisor for this category is David Rago; he is listed in the Directory under New Jersey.

Key: hg — high glaze

Vase, carved cobalt and yellow irises on moss green, high glaze, exhibition piece, Henrietta Bailey, NC/DL40/HB, 1909, 14x9", $42,000.00. (Photo courtesy Craftsman Auctions)

Bowl, floral rim band, rose/bls, Simpson, #LC73, 10½" 1,300.00
Bowl, water lilies on buff (cvd hg) Roman, 1904, sm rstr, 3x8½" ..4,025.00
Bowl vase, moon/moss/oak trees, Bailey, #IL20, 9" dia, EX 2,700.00
Bud vase, jonquils/leaves (cvd hg), Simpson, 1908, 9x3" 6,900.00
Inkwell, thistles, pk/gr on ivory, w/liner, GR Smith, 1902, 3x4", EX..3,220.00
Jar, moss/oaks, Simpson, 1929, w/lid, label, 5x4½", VG (mfg flaw) 8,625.00
Jardiniere, daffodils, yel/bl-gr on ivory gloss, 8x10", EX 19,550.00
Loving cup, clover blossoms, wht/gr on bl & wht, Kopman, 1902, 4x5", G...2,645.00
Tile, Newcomb fountain/irises, bl/gr, S Irvine/F Ford, #UO53, 6x4½" ..4,800.00
Trivet, crocuses, H Bailey, 1915, flake, 5⅝" dia 1,700.00
Trivet, mossy oak, H Bailey, 1923, 4" 600.00
Trivet, wild roses, AF Simpson, #77, 5¾" dia 1,400.00
Vase, abstract organic designs in bl to gr, RB Kennon, #F33X, 6½" ...3,750.00
Vase, amber, 5-ring neck, ftd, sgn N in circle, 6½" 325.00
Vase, bell flowers/leaves, S Irvine, 1914, 3¼x5¼" 2,300.00
Vase, bell flowers/leaves, Simpson, 1924, 4½x5" 1,840.00
Vase, broad leaves/florals, yel/wht/gr on bl, Chalaron, 1923, 8x4" ...4,315.00
Vase, catfish in swirls (cvd hg), Sabina Elliot Wells, 1902, 9¾" 24,000.00
Vase, crocus blossom hdls (4, cvd), lav, Simpson, 1919, 4½x5½" ...3,450.00
Vase, crocuses, H Bailey, #26, 1929, 4⅝" 1,900.00
Vase, daffodil frieze, S Irvine/JB Hunt, ovoid, 6¾" 4,250.00
Vase, daffodil stems, caramel-lined wht on tan-gold gloss, Joor, 8" ...16,000.00
Vase, Espanol pattern, bl-gr/pk-wht on bl, S Irvine, 1927, 5½x5" 4,025.00
Vase, eucalyptus, waisted, S Irvine, #KZ2, 10½" 3,900.00
Vase, fir trees, bl/gr/ivory, sgn/J Meyer, #BY39, 3" dia 2,200.00
Vase, floral, AF Simpson, 1925, 4½x5" 1,840.00
Vase, floral (cvd hg), Ryan #Y42, rstr, 10" 12,000.00
Vase, floral band, S Irvine, #8, 1925, 3⅝" 1,100.00
Vase, floral band on shaded bl, sgn EAH, 4x3¼", NM 1,870.00
Vase, floral shoulder, CP Littlejohn/J Meyer, #272, 6" 2,800.00
Vase, grapes/leaves, Irvine, 1919, 8¼x6" 5,465.00
Vase, irises (cvd hg), Kennon, 1902, 12½x7", NM 19,550.00
Vase, irises & vertical repeating bands, bl/gr, H Bailey, 4¾x9" ..13,800.00
Vase, moon/moss/oaks, AF Simpson, #3025, 6¾" 3,000.00
Vase, moon/moss/oaks, S Irvine/J Hunt, #35, 1932, 5⅛" 3,600.00
Vase, moon/moss/oaks, S Irvine/K Smith, 1933, 4⅛" 1,800.00
Vase, moon/moss/oaks, S Irvine/Meyer, #QA61, 8½" 5,500.00
Vase, moon/pines, shouldered, AF Simpson, 1918, 8x3½" 4,025.00
Vase, moon/tall pine trees, Bailey, 1931, 9x7" 8,050.00
Vase, morning glories, H Bailey, #179 B, 1913, 9" 5,000.00
Vase, moss/oaks, S Irvine, 1929, 5¼x4¼" 4,300.00
Vase, moss/Spanish oaks (EX art), Simpson, 1929, label, 4x5" ...2,875.00
Vase, pomegranates, E de Hoa Le Blanc, 1903, 8⅝" 10,500.00
Vase, rose band, pk/dk bl on med bl, Irvine/Hunt, 3¾" 1,200.00
Vase, trumpet vines, Simpson, 1921, 9x5" 3,220.00
Vase, tulip buds on curving stems, AF Simpson, 6" 1,700.00
Vase, tulips, dk bl shades on lt bl, M DeLavigne, F78X/JM, 6" ...4,500.00
Vase, vertical leaves swirl at shoulder, bl/gr, A Arbo, #TV24, 9x4" ..4,000.00

Newspapers

People do not collect newspapers simply because they are old. Age has absolutely nothing to do with value — it does not hold true that the older the newspaper, the higher the value. Instead, most of the value is determined by the historic event content. In most cases, the more important to American history the event is, the higher the value. In over two hundred years of American history, perhaps as many as 98% of all newspapers ever published do not contain news of a significant historic event. Newspapers not having news of major events in history are called 'atmosphere.' Atmosphere papers have little collector value. (See price guide below.)

To learn more about the hobby of collecting old and historic newspapers, be sure to visit the mega-website on the Internet at www.historybuff.com/. The e-mail address for the NCSA is help@historybuff.com/. See Newspaper Collector's Society of America in Clubs, Newsletters, and Catalogs for more information.

1800-1820, Atmosphere editions, from $5 to 10.00
1821-1859, Atmosphere editions, from $4 to 8.00

1836, Texas declares independence, from $60 to **85.00**
1845, Annexation of Texas, from $35 to **45.00**
1846, Start of Mexican War, from $25 to **35.00**
1846-1847, Major battles of Mexican War, from $25 to **30.00**
1847, End of Mexican War, from $30 to **40.00**
1848, Gold discovered in California, from $45 to **85.00**
1859, John Brown's raid on Harper's Ferry, from $35 to..............**70.00**
1860, Lincoln elected 1st term, from $125 to **225.00**
1861, Lincoln's inaugural address, from $140 to **275.00**
1861-1865, Atmosphere editions: Confederate titles, from $110 to.**165.00**
1861-1865, Atmosphere editions: Union titles, from $8 to **15.00**
1861-1865, Major battles of Civil War, Union first report, up to ..**120.00**
1862, Emancipation Proclamation, from $85 to **225.00**
1863, Gettysburg Address, from $165 to **380.00**
1865, April 29 edition of Frank Leslie's, from $175 to **225.00**
1865, April 29 edition of Harper's Weekly, from $150 to............**200.00**
1865, Capture & death of J Wilkes Booth, from $85 to **165.00**
1865, Fall of Richmond, from $85 to...**265.00**
1865, NY Herald, Apr 15 (Beware: reprints abound), up to........**900.00**
1865, Titles other than NY Herald, Apr 15, from $125 to **375.00**
1866-1900, Atmosphere editions, from $3 to **5.00**
1876, Custer's Last Stand, 1st reports, from $100 to **250.00**
1881, Billy the Kid killed, from $130 to **250.00**
1881, Garfield assassinated, from $60 to **115.00**
1881, Gunfight at OK Corral, from $175 to **400.00**
1882, Jesse James killed, 1st reports, from $165 to **385.00**
1898, Sinking of Maine, from $25 to..**70.00**
1901, McKinley assassinated, from $45 to **100.00**
1903, Wright Brother's flight, from $200 to **500.00**
1906, San Francisco earthquake, other titles, from $25 to............**50.00**
1906, San Francisco earthquake, San Francisco title, up to **500.00**
1912, Sinking of Titanic, 1st reports, from $100 to **350.00**
1915, Sinking of Lusitania, 1st reports, from $90 to **225.00**
1927, Babe Ruth hits 60th home run, from $50 to **125.00**
1927, Lindbergh arrives in Paris, 1st reports, from $65 to **125.00**
1929, St Valentine's Day Massacre, from $100 to **225.00**
1929, Stock market crash, from $75 to.......................................**180.00**
1931, Al Capone found guilty, from $40 to **80.00**
1931, Jack 'Legs' Diamond killed, from $30 to **45.00**
1933, Machine Gun Kelley captured, from $25 to **45.00**
1934, Baby Face Nelson killed **45.00**
1934, Bonnie & Clyde killed, from $125 to **250.00**
1934, Dillinger killed, from $100 to **250.00**
1934, Pretty Boy Floyd killed, from $25 to **45.00**
1941, Honolulu Star-Bulletin, Dec 7, 1st extra (+), up to...........**600.00**

1948, Chicago Daily Tribune, November 3, Dewey Defeats Truman, up to $800.00. (Photo courtesy Michael McQuillen)

1941, Other titles, Dec 7, w/Pearl Harbor news, from $30 to........**60.00**
1961, Alan Shephard 1st astronaut in space, from $15 to **30.00**
1961, Roger Maris hits 61st home run, from $20 to......................**40.00**
1963, JFK assassination, Nov 22, Dallas title, from $70 to **100.00**
1963, JFK assassination, Nov 22, titles other than Dallas, up to **30.00**
1968, Assassination of Martin Luther King, from $15 to...............**25.00**
1968, Assassination of Robert Kennedy, from $15 to....................**20.00**
1969, Moon landing, from $15 to **30.00**
1974, Nixon resigns, from $15 to...**20.00**

Nicodemus

Chester R. Nicodemus was born near Barberton, Ohio, August, 17, 1901. He started Pennsylvania State University in 1920, where he studied engineering. Chester got a share of a large paper route and attended Cleveland Art School where he studied under Herman Matzen, sculptor, and Frank Wilcox, anatomy illustrator, graduating in 1925. That fall Chester was hired to start the sculpture department at the Dayton Art Institute.

Nicodemus moved from Dayton to Columbus, Ohio, in 1930 and started teaching at the Columbus Art School. During this time he made vases and commissioned sculptures, water fountains, and limestone and wood carvings. In 1941 Chester left the field of teaching to pursue pottery making full time, using local red clay containing a large amount of iron. Known for its durability, he called the ware Ferro-stone. He made teapots and other utility wares, but these goods lost favor, so he started producing animal and bird sculptures, nativity sets, and Christmas ornaments, some bearing Chester's and his wife, Florine's, names as personalized cards for his customers and friends. Chester died in 1990.

His glaze colors were turquoise or aqua, ivory, green mottle, pussy willow (pink), and golden yellow. The glaze was applied so that the color of the warm red clay would show through, adding an extra dimension to each piece. His name is usually incised in the clay in an arch, but paper labels were also used. For more information, we recommend *Sanford Guide to Nicodemus, His Pottery and His Art*, by our advisor for this category, James Riebel; he is listed in the Directory under Ohio.

Ashtray, ram's head figural, bl, 7½x7½" **210.00**
Bank, rabbit, gr crystalline/russet, Ferro-Stone label, 2⅜x4⅜" ...**350.00**
Bottle, turq..**650.00**
Cactus planter, elephant figural, gray w/brn highlights, 2x2½"...**150.00**
Christmas ornament, Holy Night, ivory, 1975, 3¾" **135.00**
Christmas ornament, Merry Christmas, ivory, 1971....................**90.00**
Christmas ornament, tree w/Noel, 1950, 2½" dia.......................**240.00**
Figurine, duck, pussy willow (pk), yel bill & blk eyes, 3x2¾x2" .**225.00**
Figurine, Graduate Owl...**275.00**
Figurine, knight **400.00**
Figurine, owl, 4½x4" **200.00**
Figurine, raccoon, 4½x7" **300.00**
Figurine, robin, yel beak, 4½x3½"...**150.00**
Figurine, squirrel, gray w/brn dots & highlights, 2¾x3⅝" **135.00**
Flower frog, figural, Madonna of the Flowers, 10½x3¼" **250.00**
Planter, bear figural, bl w/brn highlights, 3x4" **175.00**
Punch bowl, bl-gr, Good Cheer/Tom & Jerry on sides.................**260.00**

Niloak

During the latter part of the 1800s, there were many small utilitarian potteries in Benton, Arkansas. By 1900 only the Hyten Brothers Pottery remained. Charles Hyten, a second generation potter, took control of the family business around 1902. Shortly thereafter he renamed it the Eagle Pottery Company. In 1909 Hyten and former Rookwood potter Arthur Dovey began experimentation on a new swirl pottery. Dovey had previously worked for the Ouachita Pottery Company of Hot Springs and produced a swirl pottery there as early as 1906. In March 1910, the Eagle Pottery Company introduced Niloak — kaolin spelled backwards.

During 1911 Benton businessmen formed the Niloak Pottery corporation. Niloak, connected to the Arts and Crafts Movement and known as 'mission' ware, had a national representative in New York by

1913. Niloak's production centered on art pottery characterized by accidental, swirling patterns of natural and artificially colored clays. Many companies through the years have produced swirl pottery, yet none achieved the technical and aesthetic qualities of Niloak. Hyten received a patent in 1928 for the swirl technique. Although most examples have an interior glaze, some early Mission Ware pieces have an exterior glaze as well; these are extremely rare.

In 1934 Hyten's company found itself facing bankruptcy. Hardy L. Winburn, Jr., along with other Little Rock businessmen, raised the necessary capital and were able to provide the kind of leadership needed to make the business profitable once again. Both lines (Eagle and Hywood) were renamed 'Niloak' in 1937 to capitalize on this well-known name. The pottery continued in production until 1947 when it was converted to the Winburn Tile Company, which exists to this day in Little Rock.

Be careful not to confuse the swirl production of the Evans Pottery of Missouri with Niloak. The significant difference is the dark brown matt interior glaze of Evans pottery.

For further information we recommend *Collector's Encyclopedia of Niloak Pottery* by David Edwin Gifford (Collector Books). Our advisor for this category is Lila Shrader; she is listed in the Directory under California. All items listed below bear the Niloak mark unless noted otherwise.

Key:
HN — Hywood by Niloak
N — N mark
NB — Niloak (block letters) mark
NI — Niloak (impressed) mark
NL — Niloak (in low relief) mark

Mission Ware

Ashtray/match holder, 2 rests, unmk, 5x2½" 220.00
Bowl, potty shape, w/o hdl, mk w/Pat Pend, 6x5" 320.00
Bowl, power; w/lid, 6x3¾" 550.00
Candlestick w/4¼" flared ft, 9" 245.00
Chamberstick, w/finger ring, base 5¾x4" 285.00
Child's chamber pot, w/hdl, 6¼x2½" 575.00
Flower frog, 3x1¼" 100.00
Humidor, holder for sponge on underside of lid, 5" 400.00
Humidor, holder for sponge on underside of lid, 6½" 525.00
Mug, barrel shape, 4" 350.00
Pin dish, 3½x2" 77.00
Pitcher, thumb rest on hdl, 2nd art mk, 8" 977.00
Punch cup, predominantly bl, hdl, 1st art mk, 2¾" 165.00
Shot glass, 2nd art mk, 2½" 110.00
Stein, mk w/Pat Pend, hdl, 5¾" 230.00
Tankard, 2nd art mk, grooved base, 10½" 995.00
Tumbler, straight-sided, 3½" 132.00
Vase, baluster shape, flared rim, 10" 350.00
Vase, bowl shape, flared rim, 2nd art mk, 4x2" 76.00
Vase, bowl shape, mk w/Pat Pend, 5½x4¼" 235.00
Vase, bowl shape, rolled rim, 1st art mk, 2½x2" 72.00
Vase, bud; candlestick shape w/flared ft, 6" 155.00
Vase, classic shape, 2nd art mk, 10½" 268.00
Vase, cone shape w/flared ft, 1st art mk, 9" 310.00
Vase, pear shape, unusual teardrop effect in swirls, 7" 245.00
Vase, rose bowl shape, 3½" opening, 6x5¾" 169.00
Vase, squatty, narrow neck w/2" opening, 5¼x3" 228.00
Vase, sundae soda glass shape w/flared ft, 7" 235.00
Vase, wide color bands, 2nd art mk, 3x3½" 88.00
Wall pocket, unmk, rolled rim, 4" flat back at top, 8" 355.00
Water bottle, 1st art mk, ¼" rolled neck rim, 8" 835.00

Miscellaneous

Ashtray, Ozark Dawn, 2 rests, orig Niloak sticker, 4x1" 25.00
Basket, Dolly Varden style, N, 6½" 48.00
Basket, matt, 3" rope-like hdl, HN, 7½" 38.00
Bowl, float; unmk, ruffled edge, 12x2½" 55.00
Bowl, mixing; stoneware, w/lid, 10x4½" 158.00
Candlestick, flower blossom forms candle holder, HN, 3½" 38.00
Candlestick, 5½" base, HN, 3" 36.00
Churn, stoneware, wing-like hdls, w/lid, 11" 155.00
Creamer, cow, tail forms hdl, 4½" 67.00
Cup & saucer, petal shaped, 2¾", 5½" 27.00
Ewer, flared base, graceful hdl, NI, 15" 100.00
Figure, dog, retriever, N, 4½" 55.00
Figure, donkey, ears up & looking bk, no base, 3½" 155.00
Figure, Trojan horse on base, 1 ft raised, 9" 175.00
Head vase, NL, w/hat, 7" 120.00
Indian canoe, NB, 3½x11" 65.00
Lamp base, unmk, bull's eye & open bottom, 7" 435.00
Pitcher, blk, ball shape, hi-gloss, w/cork stopper, 7" 245.00
Pitcher, hi-gloss, mini, 2½-3½", from $10 to 20.00
Pitcher, matt, ball shape, w/cork stopper, 7" 79.00
Pitcher, Memphis, shows ship in relief, 7½" 148.00
Planter, camel or polar bear, w/attached container, N, 3½" 45.00
Planter, circus elephant posed on drum, N, 6" 62.00
Planter, hi-gloss, flowerpot shape w/attached saucer, 4x5" 15.00
Planter, Peter Pan, matt, 7¾" 29.00
Planter, teddy bear, 3¾" 85.00
Plate, dinner; NB, 10" 88.00
Postcard, Home of Niloak Pottery, Benton, Arkansas 17.00
Relish dish, unmk, 3-part, triangular, 9½" 66.00
Shakers, 3" cannon & 2½" tank, N 23.00
Teapot, unmk, Aladdin-like style, w/lid, 6½" 82.00
Vase, hi-gloss, cornucopia, 7" 24.00
Vase, Ozark Dawn, fan shape, ribbing, 14" 135.00
Vase, Ozark Dawn, fine vertical ribbing, NB, 12" 85.00
Vase, pearled gr, flared base, ruffled collar, NB, 7" 55.00
Vase, tulip; hi-gloss, orig Niloak sticker, 7½" 29.00

Nippon

Nippon generally refers to Japanese wares made during the period from 1891 to 1921, although the Nippon mark was also used to a limited extent on later wares (accompanied by 'Japan'). Nippon, meaning Japan, identified the country of origin to comply with American importation restrictions. After 1921 'Japan' was the acceptable alternative. The term does not imply a specific type of product and may be found on items other than porcelains. For further information we recommend *The Collector's Encyclopedias of Nippon Porcelain* (there are seven in the series) by our advisor, Joan Van Patten; you will find her address in the Directory under New York. In the following listings, items are assumed hand painted unless noted otherwise. Numbers included in the descriptions refer to these specific marks:

Key:
#1 — China E-OH
#2 — M in Wreath
#3 — Cherry Blossom
#4 — Double T Diamond in Circle
#5 — Rising Sun
#6 — Royal Kinran
#7 — Maple Leaf
#8 — Royal Nippon, Nishiki
#9 — Royal Moriye Nippon

Bowl, floral, ornate gold 6-sided rim, 3-leg, #2, 7¼" 145.00
Bowl, floral (simple/sm) on wht w/gold, hdls, #2, 9½", $70 to 100.00
Bowl, floral reserves, 8-scallop, bl #7, 7½" 160.00
Bowl, floral w/cobalt & gold, hdls, #2, 8½", from $175 to 235.00
Bowl, gold leaves & berries on wht, scalloped, gr #7, 9¾" 275.00

Bowl, peanuts & leaves in relief, smooth rim, #2, 7", from $125 to ..165.00
Bowl, peanuts in relief inside, hdls, gr #2, 7", from $140 to 180.00
Bowl, roses, mc on wht to cobalt w/gold scalloped rim, #7, 9¾".325.00
Cake plate, floral, pk on wht w/gold, hdls, HP mk, 10½", $80 to...125.00
Cake set, cobalt & floral, #7, 10½" platter+4 6¼" plates............550.00
Candle lamp, palm scenic, gr #2, 12½", from $1,800 to 2,300.00
Cheese dish, Deco decor on wht, slant lid, #2, 7¾" 175.00
Chocolate pot, floral reserve on gr w/gold, ornate hdl, #7, 9¾"..525.00
Chocolate set, moriage dragons, HP mk, 10½" pot+4 c/s, $400 to ..525.00
Cigarette box, Champion Katerfelto (bulldog) on lid, #2, 5½" ..600.00
Condensed milk container, roses on wht w/gold, #7, 6¼", $185 to..235.00
Cookie jar, gold floral on wht, w/underplate, RC mk, 8"............425.00
Cookie jar, roses, mc w/gold, gold ft, bl #7, 7½"..........................575.00
Cracker jar, floral, bl on wht w/gold, hdls, #2, 9½" W 250.00
Creamer & sugar bowl, river scenic, w/lid, #2, from $165 to.......225.00
Cup & saucer, bouillon; floral & bluebird on wht, #7, from $30 to ..50.00
Cup & saucer, river scenic, earth tones, TN mk, from $45 to.......60.00
Demitasse set, pk & gold border on wht, #5, pot+cr/sug+4 c/s+tray ...350.00
Ewer, purple flowers, inv't cone form, #6, 9½", from $175 to 235.00
Ferner, roses, pk on wht w/gold, 4-ftd, #7, 5¾" sq, from $275 to...350.00
Hatpin holder, bl & wht w/gold, attached tray, #7, 4½"..............175.00
Humidor, fox hunt scenic band on gr, sq sides, #7, 6½", $700 to...850.00
Humidor, moriage pipes/etc on shaded mc, bl #7, 7", from $700 to ..850.00
Humidor, mums on gold w/beading, bl #7, 5½"........................1,000.00
Humidor, river scenic, #2, 6", from $350 to 450.00
Humidor, scattered playing cards on bl, 6-sided, #2, 6½" 600.00
Knife rest, floral on wht, #2, 3¾", from $115 to 150.00
Lemon dish, birds, bl on wht, pierced hdls, #5, 5½", from $20 to.30.00
Luncheon set, floral on wht w/gold band, #2, 72-pc set, $1,400 to ...1,800.00
Matchbox holder, gold on wht, rectangular, hangs, #2, 4½" 140.00
Mug, grapes & leaves on brn w/gold, gr #7, 4¾", from $200 to ..275.00
Nappy, lacy gold on wht, hdl, Souvenir of Fair Week 1912, #2, 6¼"...100.00
Nut set, floral on wht, smooth rim, hdls, #2, 9½" bowl+4 ind....180.00
Pitcher, roses on wht w/gold, 6-sided, RC mk, 7", from $235 to .285.00
Plaque, Indian on running horse in relief, gr #2, 10½", $850 to ...1,000.00
Plaque, sampan scenic w/gold rim, #7, 10", from $300 to............375.00
Plaque, squirrel in relief, gr #2, 10½", from $800 to................1,000.00
Plaque, windmill scenic, #2, 10½", from $350 to.........................425.00
Powder box, floral on wht w/gold, #2, 5½" dia, from $60 to 80.00
Punch bowl, grapes, mc on brn, hdls, gr #2, 12¾x13", $1,000 to...1,200.00
Relish, river scenic, 2-compartment, #7, 7½" L, from $120 to....160.00
Sauce dish & underplate, floral on wht w/gold, #7, 2½" H, 7" L...160.00
Server, roses w/gold, 3-compartment, center hdl, #2, 7½" 145.00
Stein, sampan scenic w/pk sky, gold trim, #2, 7", from $600 to...700.00
Sugar shakers, roses on wht w/gold, #7, 4", from $125 to 175.00
Syrup, floral on wht w/gold, 6-sided, gr #2, 5¾", +tray 100.00
Tankard set, elk scenic in relief, #2, 11½" tankard+4 mugs, ...4,400.00
Tea set, Oriental decor w/gold, Pat mk, 5" pot+cr/sug+4 c/s 400.00
Tea set, scenic panels w/gold trim, #2, 6½" pot+cr/sug+4 c/s......525.00
Trinket box, floral on wht heart shape, #2, sm, from $65 to..........90.00
Urn, scenic reserve, gold trim, up-trn hdls, ftd, #7, 10½" 1,750.00
Vase, Anna Potocka portrait reserve on gold & wht w/hdls, #7, 7½"..1,000.00
Vase, cobalt w/gold o/l scenic reserve & band, hdls, #7, 7½"......650.00
Vase, Deco exotic bird panels, gold hdls, #2, 14", from $600 to..725.00
Vase, fisherman scenic in relief, hdls, gr #2, 8¼", $5,500 to 8,000.00
Vase, floral, pk on gr, ruffled rim, bl #7, 10", from $300 to..........400.00
Vase, floral on cobalt w/gold, low hdls, #7, 9½", from $275 to ...350.00
Vase, floral on organic form w/much gold o/l, slim, HP mk, 9¼" .500.00
Vase, floral on wht, bottle neck, cylindrical, #7, 9", from $165 to....250.00
Vase, floral on wht w/gold, ornate/integral hdls, #7, 7½" 350.00
Vase, floral reserve w/cobalt & gold o/l, bottle neck, #2, 7½".....700.00
Vase, floral w/coralene beading, classic form, RS mk, 7" 850.00
Vase, leaves w/gold o/l on brn, cylindrical, bottle neck, #7, 7½"..275.00
Vase, lilies on brn, gold hdls, #2, 9¾", from $300 to 400.00
Vase, mixed flowers, bottle neck, #2, 9", from $300 to................400.00
Vase, moriage landscape, bulbous, hdls, #7, 9" 625.00
Vase, poppies, gold hdls, ft, #2, 10½", from $300 to 400.00
Vase, river scenic, 4 sm rim-to-shoulder angle hdls, #2, 6¾" 300.00
Vase, roses, pk on gold w/turq dots, rim-to-hip hdls, #7, 7" 525.00
Vase, roses, 5-sided, gold hdls, #7, 7¾", from $350 to 425.00
Vase, roses before landscape scene, cylindrical, #7, 12", $500 to ..600.00
Vase, scenic tapestry, #7, 6¼" 800.00
Vase, Wedgwood, cream on bl, rim-to-hip hdls, gr #2, 8"............800.00
Wine jug, English coach scene reserve on gr, #7, 9½"..............1,500.00
Wine jug, river scenic in earth tones, bl #7, 11", $1,000 to 1,400.00

Nodders

So called because of the nodding action of their heads and hands, nodders originated in China where they were used in temple rituals to represent deity. At first they were made of brass and were actually a type of bell; when these bells were rung, the heads of the figures would nod. In the eighteenth century, the idea was adopted by Meissen and by French manufacturers who produced not only china nodders but bisque as well. Most nodders are individual; couples are unusual. The idea remained popular until the end of the nineteenth century and was used during the Victorian era by toy manufacturers.

Anthropomorphic bear w/tennis racket, Dep/#9884, 1879-1954, minimum....1,000.00
Bambi, enameled metal, sturdy, 3¼", minimum value 30.00
Baseball Little Leaguer, clinking eyes, 1950-60s, Japan, 6½" 270.00
Big horn ewe w/suckling lamb, gray celluloid, unmk 20.00
Black man kneeling on chest (bank), pnt wood, Germany, 1920s, 7½x5"....410.00
Black oriental figure w/shoulder yoke, pnt porc, European, 4½".185.00
Bluebird fledgling, pnt zink, Germany, 1900s, worn.......................95.00
Boy w/2 faces, 1 blk & 1 wht, bsk, Germany, 3½" 185.00
Brown nude baby on bk of turtle nodder, pnt bsk, 2¾x3½" 85.00

Chinese couple, brightly decorated bisque, unusual ruffled collars, Germany, early 1900s, 4½", from $200.00 to $250.00 for the pair. **(Photo courtesy Hilma R. Irtz)**

Chinese jester w/tools/teapot/fan, porc, China, 3¾"....................125.00
Dachshund, c NYC Germany, 5¼" L 75.00
Falconer beside planter, Conta & Boehme, #8587, ca 1878-1937 ..250.00
Friar w/potbelly, pnt bsk, Germany, late 1800s, 5½"....................140.00
Hula dancer w/flowers in hair, compo, 6¾"...................................50.00
Japanese elder kneeling w/book, pnt terra cotta, unmk, 6½" 175.00
Jewish man swaying & holding red cloth, Portugal, ca 1900.......150.00
Lady in overcoat carrying sachel & horn, in cap w/goggles, bsk, 3⅛" ..190.00
Oriental man in bl holding bl box, bsk, Germany, 4" 115.00
Paul Bunyan, papier-maché, 1950-60s, 7¾" 140.00
Pig Pen, Peanuts Gang, Lego, M...210.00
Pug & spaniel, porc, on base, 4⅝" 100.00
Pumpkin man, compo on wooden stand, Germany, 1930s, 4¾" .275.00
Santa, neck spring, Vcago Japan, 5¾" 75.00
Scottish terrier w/red coat, plastic, Occupied Japan, 3x4¾" 75.00
Sgt Snorkel (Beatle Bailey), papier-maché, Japan sticker, 7¾" ...120.00
Sultan & sultana, bsk, pk & wht w/gold, #521349, pr 350.00
Victorian boy & girl, pnt bsk, Germany, rpr, 5", pr, from $250 to...350.00

Victorian governess holding slipper, mc details, Germany 195.00
Wise Old Owl, in bl kerchief, orange book under wing, porc 175.00

German Comic Characters

During the early 1930s, Germany produced a collection of small figure dolls, approximately 2" to 4" high, representing the most popular comic strip and cartoon characters of that time. They were made of bisque with brightly painted details and clearly stamped with their appropriate names and 'Germany' on their backs. Generally, their movable heads were attached with an elastic string going through their bodies, hence the name 'nodders,' but there were some characters produced earlier that were frozen with no movable parts. The most popular ones came in boxed sets, but the lesser-known characters were sold separately, making them rarer and harder to find today. We have listed the most valuable characters from the series here; those not mentioned below are valued at $125.00 and under.

Ambrose Potts 350.00
Auntie Blossom 150.00
Auntie Mamie 250.00
Avery..200.00
Buttercup 250.00
Chubby Chaney..250.00
Corky 475.00
Delong Jones..425.00
Dinty Moor (frozen) 500.00
Dock...200.00
Fanny 250.00
Ferina 350.00
Grandpa Teen 350.00
Happy Hooligan 625.00
Harold Teen...150.00
Jeff Regus, med or lg, ea 250.00
Jeff Regus, sm...175.00
Josie...425.00
Junior Nebbs..625.00
Lilacs..425.00
Lillums 150.00
Little Annie Rooney, movable arms, complete 350.00
Little Egypt 350.00
Lord Plushbottom...150.00
Ma & Paw Winkle, ea...350.00
Marjorie 425.00
Mary Ann Jackson...250.00
Matt, med or lg, NM, ea 250.00
Matt, sm...175.00
Max..200.00
Min Gump...150.00
Mr Bailey 150.00
Mr Bibb..400.00
Mr Wicker 250.00
Mushmouth 175.00
Nicodemus..350.00
Old Timer 350.00
Our Gang, 6-pc set, MIB 1,400.00
Pat Finegan 400.00
Patsy..425.00
Perry Winkle, minimum value 100.00
Pete the Dog...250.00
Pop Jenks 200.00
Rudy Nebbs...250.00
Scraps...250.00
Uncle Willie 250.00

Widow Zandor...400.00
Winnie Winkle...150.00

Nordic Art Glass

Finnish and Swedish glass has recently started to develop a following, probably stemming from the revitalization of interest in forms from the 1950s. (The name Nordic is used here because of the inclusion of Finnish glass — the term Scandinavian does not refer to this country.) Included here are Flygsfors, Maleras, Iittala, and Nuutajarvi Glass Works.

Our suggested prices are 'fair market values,' developed after researching the Nordic secondary markets, the current retail prices on items still being produced, and American auction houses and antique stores.

Our advisor for this category is William L. Geary; he is listed in the Directory under Colorado.

Flygsfors Glass Works, Sweden

Flygsfors Glass Works was established in 1888 and continued in production until 1979 when the Orrefors Glass Group ceased operations at this factory.

Flygsfors is well known for art glass designed by Paul Kedelv, who joined the firm in 1949 with a contract to design light fittings, a specialty of the company.

Their 'Coquille' series, which utilizes a unique overlay technique combining opaque, bright colors, and 'Flamingo' have become very desirable on today's secondary market.

Bowl, Coquille, oblong w/flared ends, cranberry/wht, Kedelv, 11"..195.00
Bowl, Coquille, pinched sides, pk w/bl to clear o/l, Kedelv, 5x3"..75.00
Lamp, tall stem form, gr w/clear o/l, flared base, 11" 285.00
Vase, Coquille, flared wings, bl/red, Kedelv, 10¼"......................190.00
Vase, Coquille, flared wings, maroon/gr, Kedelv, 13" 265.00
Vase, Flamingo, teardrop, gr/brn/wht threads w/in, Kedelv, 10½"...245.00
Vase, rectangular form, mold blown, bull & sun motif, Bernt, 8"..55.00

Iittala Glass Works, Finland

This glass works was founded in 1881; it was originally staffed by Swedish workers who produced glassware of very high quality. In 1917 Ahiststrom OY bought and merged Iittala with Karhula Glass Works. After 1945 Karhula's production was limited to container glass. In 1946 Tapio Wirkkala, the internationally known artist/designer, became Iittala's chief designer. Timo Sarpeneva joined him in 1950. Jointly they successfully spearheaded the promotion of Finnish glass in the international markets, winning many international awards for their designs. Today Oiva Toikka leads the design team.

Sculpture, Dancing Leaves, crystal w/paste-on, Sundstrom, 4¾x6"....40.00
Sculpture, Dog Listens to Rain, Marko Salo, 8¼" L....................275.00
Sculpture, Goose, O Toikka, 10x15" 900.00
Vase, Aalto Vase, red, A Aalto, 6¼".......................................1,100.00
Vase, Claritas, blk/opal/clear, T Sarpeneva, 10¼" 1,000.00
Vase, Kantarelle, clear, in production since 1947, 8" 600.00
Vase, Kantarelli, Tapio Wirkkala, 8"...825.00
Vase, Orkidea, clear, in production since 1953, T Sarpaneva 295.00

Maleras Glass Works, Sweden

The first glass works at Maleras was founded in 1890. The city of Maleras was an important railway junction in Smaland, the Kingdom of Crystal, where articles from many of the glasshouses were shipped to the Swedish cities of Stockholm, Goteborg, and Malmo.

During the 1940s, the company built a reputation throughout Sweden as one of the leading manufacturers of lead crystal. In 1975 the company joined the Royal Krona Group. Six years later under the leadership of Mat Jonasson, the glass blowers and members of the community bought the factory from the existing management.

During the last twenty years, the company has produced first-class crystal sculptures of wildlife which are sold around the world. Mat Jonasson is the master designer, and his wildlife images and engraving techniques are superb. Two other designers, artists Erika Hoglund and Lars Goran Tinback, have recently joined the company as well.

Sculpture, Dolphins, ltd ed, clear, Jonasson, 8½" **1,250.00**
Sculpture, Eagle, ltd ed, Jonasson, 12½" **1,250.00**
Sculpture, Giraffes, ltd ed, Jonasson, 9¾" **380.00**
Sculpture, La Madame, amber/grey-bl in clear, Hoglund, ltd ed, 14½" ...**1,595.00**
Sculpture, Plura, E Hoglund, #25004, 9½" **470.00**
Sculpture, Sharks, clear, Jonasson, 7¼" **190.00**
Vase, Igloo, cobalt bl, rough frosting on ext, Jonasson, 4½" **345.00**
Vase, Navarra, red w/blk, teardrop form, Klas-Goran Tinback, 11½" ...**325.00**

Nuutajarvi Glass Works, Finland

Bowl, heart shape, pk, Kaj Franck, 4" **85.00**
Goblet, yel cup on wht stem & ft, Kaj Franck, 8½" **185.00**
Vase, amber underlay/structured bubbles, rnd, Gunnel Nyman, 4" ..**575.00**
Vase, Apple clear w/purple circle, short neck, Saara Hopea, 3½" ...**295.00**
Vase, Kupla, bl to clear base w/turq bubble, Saara Hopea, 7" **400.00**
Vase, Serpentine, clear w/winding wht ribbon, Gunnel Nyman, 18¼" ..**2,950.00**

Noritake

The Noritake Company was first registered in 1904 as Nippon Gomei Kaisha. In 1917 the name became Nippon Toki Kabushiki Toki. The 'M in wreath' mark is that of the Morimura Brothers, distributors with offices in New York. It was used until 1941. The 'tree crest' mark is the crest of the Morimura family.

The Noritake Company has produced fine porcelain dinnerware sets and occasional pieces decorated in the delicate manner for which the Japanese are noted. (Two dinnerware patterns are featured below, and a general range is suggested for others.)

Authority Joan Van Patten has compiled a lovely book, *The Collector's Encyclopedia of Noritake*, with many full-color photos and current prices; you will find her address in the Directory under New York. In the following listings, examples are hand painted unless noted otherwise. Numbers refer to these specific marks:

Key:
#1 — Komaru   #3 — N in Wreath
#2 — M in Wreath

Azalea

The Azalea pattern was produced exclusively for the Larkin Company, who gave the lovely ware away as premiums to club members and their home agents. From 1916 through the 1930s, Larkin distributed fine china which was decorated in pink azaleas on white with gold tracing along edges and handles. Early in the '30s, six pieces of crystal hand painted with the same design were offered: candle holders, a compote, a tray with handles, a scalloped fruit bowl, a cheese and cracker set, and a cake plate. All in all, seventy different pieces of Azalea were produced. Some, such as the fifteen-piece child's set, bulbous vase, china ashtray, and the pancake jug, are quite rare. One of

the earliest marks was the Noritake 'M in wreath' with variations. Later the ware was marked 'Noritake, Azalea, Hand Painted, Japan.' Our advisor for Azalea is Linda Williams; she is listed in the Directory under Massachusetts.

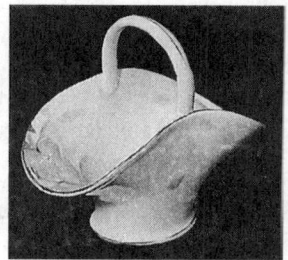

Basket, mint; Dolly Varden, #193, $140.00. (Photo courtesy Linda Williams)

Bonbon, #184, 6¼" **50.00**
Bowl, #12, 10" **42.50**
Bowl, candy/grapefruit; #185 ....**195.00**
Bowl, cream soup; #363 ....**175.00**
Bowl, deep, #310 ....**68.00**
Bowl, fruit; shell form, #188, 7¾" **385.00**
Bowl, oatmeal; #55, 5½" **28.00**
Bowl, soup; #19, 7⅛" **25.00**
Bowl, vegetable; divided, #439, 9½" **295.00**
Bowl, vegetable; oval, #101, 10½" **60.00**
Bowl, vegetable; oval, #172, 9¼" **58.00**
Butter chip, #312, 3¼" **120.00**
Butter tub, w/insert, #54 ....**48.00**
Cake plate, #10, 9¾" **40.00**
Candy jar, w/lid, #313 ....**750.00**
Casserole, gold finial, w/lid, #372 ....**475.00**
Casserole, w/lid, #16 ....**95.00**
Celery tray, closed hdls, 10" **330.00**
Celery/roll tray, #99, 12" **55.00**
Cheese/butter dish, #314 ....**135.00**
Child's set, #253, 15-pc **2,500.00**
Coffeepot, AD; #182 ....**600.00**
Compote, #170 ....**98.00**
Condiment set, #14, 5-pc **65.00**
Creamer & sugar bowl, #7 ....**45.00**
Creamer & sugar bowl, AD; open, #123, from $125 to **140.00**
Creamer & sugar bowl, gold finial, #401 ....**155.00**
Creamer & sugar bowl, ind, #449 ....**395.00**
Creamer & sugar shaker, #122 ....**125.00**
Cruet, #190 ....**160.00**
Cup & saucer, #2 ....**20.00**
Cup & saucer, AD; #183, from $150 to **160.00**
Cup & saucer, bouillon; #124, 3½" **28.00**
Egg cup, #120 ....**40.00**
Gravy boat, #40 ....**48.00**
Jam jar set, #125, 4-pc **155.00**
Mayonnaise set, scalloped, #453, 3-pc **495.00**
Mustard jar, #191, 3-pc **50.00**
Pickle/lemon set, #121 ....**24.50**
Pitcher, milk jug; #100, 1-qt **260.00**
Plate, #4, 7½" **10.00**
Plate, bread & butter; #8, 6½" **10.00**
Plate, breakfast; #98 ....**28.00**
Plate, dinner; #13, 9¾" **22.00**
Plate, grill; 3-compartment, #38, 10¼", from $165 to **175.00**
Plate, salad, 7⅝" sq **75.00**
Plate, scalloped sq, salesman's sample **950.00**
Platter, #17, 14" **60.00**

Platter, #186, 16" 475.00
Platter, #56, 12" 58.00
Platter, cold meat/bacon; #311, 10¼" 195.00
Refreshment set, #39, 2-pc 48.00
Relish, #194, 7⅛" 85.00
Relish, oval, #18, 8½" 20.00
Relish, 2-part, #171 ....58.00
Relish, 2-part, loop hdl, #450, from $390 to 425.00
Relish, 4-section, #119, rare, 10" 160.00
Saucer, fruit; #9, 5¼" 10.00
Shakers, bell form, #11, pr 30.00
Shakers, bulbous, #189, 8" 115.00
Shakers, ind, #126, pr 27.50
Spoon holder, #189, 8" 115.00
Syrup, #97, w/underplate & lid 110.00
Tea tile 40.00
Teapot, #15 ....110.00
Teapot, gold finial, #400 ....495.00
Toothpick holder, #192, from $115 to 120.00
Vase, bulbous, #452 ....1,150.00
Vase, fan form, ftd, #187 ....185.00
Whipped cream/mayonnaise set, #3, 3-pc 38.50

Tree in the Meadow

Another of their dinnerware lines has become a favorite of many collectors. Tree in the Meadow is a scenic hand-painted pattern which features a thatched cottage in a meadow with a lake in the foreground. The version accepted by most collectors will have a tree behind the cottage and will not have a swan or a bridge. The colors resemble a golden sunset on a fall day with shades of orange, gold, and rust. This line was made during the 1920s and 1930s and seems today to be in good supply. A fairly large dinnerware set with several unusual serving pieces can be readily assembled. Our advisor for Tree in the Meadow is Linda Williams; she is listed in the Directory under Massachusetts.

Basket, Dolly Varden 125.00
Bowl, cream soup; 2-hdl 35.00
Bowl, fruit; shell form, #210 ....300.00
Bowl, oatmeal 15.00
Bowl, oval, 9½" 28.00
Bowl, oval, 10½" 45.00
Bowl, soup 28.00
Bowl, vegetable; 9" 35.00
Butter pat 15.00
Butter tub, open, w/drainer 35.00
Cake plate, open hdl 35.00
Candy dish, octagonal, w/lid, 5½" 350.00
Celery dish 35.00

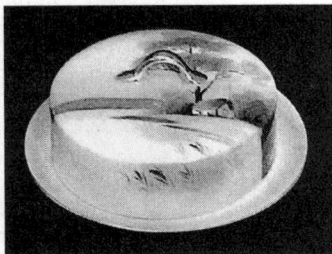

Cheese dish, $75.00. (Photo courtesy Linda Williams)

Coffeepot, demitasse 250.00
Condiment set, 5-pc 45.00
Cruets, vinegar & oil; cojoined, #319 ....325.00

Cup & saucer, breakfast 18.00
Cup & saucer, demitasse 35.00
Demitasse creamer & sugar bowl 58.00
Egg cup 30.00
Gravy boat 50.00
Jam jar/dish, 4-pc 70.00
Lemon dish 15.00
Mayonnaise set, 3-pc 48.00
Plate, dinner; 9¾" 95.00
Plate, salad; 8" 12.00
Plate, 6½" 8.00
Plate, 7⅝" sq 60.00
Platter, 10" 135.00
Platter, 11¾x9" 50.00
Platter, 13¾x10¼" 60.00
Relish, divided 35.00
Snack set (cup & tray), 2-pc 60.00
Sugar bowl, #204 ....25.00
Tea set, 3-pc 135.00

Various Dinnerware Patterns, ca. 1933 to Present

So many lines of dinnerware have been produced by the Noritake company that to list them all would require a volume in itself. In fact, just such a book is available — *The Collector's Encyclopedia of Early Noritake* by Aimee Neff Alden (Collector Books). And while many patterns had specific names, others did not, so you'll probably need the photographs the book contains to help you identify your pattern. Outlined below is a general guide for the more common pieces and patterns. The high side of the range will represent lines from about 1933 until the mid-'60s (including those marked 'Occupied Japan'), while the lower side should be used to evaluate lines made after that period.

Bowl, berry; ind, from $8 to 12.00
Bowl, soup; 7½", from $12 to 16.00
Bowl, vegetable; rnd or oval, ca 1945 to present, from $28 to 38.00
Butter dish, 3-pc, ca 1933-64, from $40 to 50.00
Creamer, from $18 to 28.00
Cup & saucer, demi; from $12 to 17.50
Gravy boat, from $35 to 45.00
Pickle or relish dish, from $18 to 28.00
Plate, bread & butter; from $8 to 12.00
Plate, dinner; from $15 to 30.00
Plate, luncheon; from $10 to 18.00
Plate, salad; from $10 to 15.00
Platter, 12", from $25 to 40.00
Platter, 16" (or larger), from $40 to 60.00
Shakers, pr, from $15 to 25.00
Sugar bowl, w/lid, from $18 to 30.00
Tea & toast set (sm cup & tray), from $18 to 28.00
Teapot, demi pot, chocolate pot or coffeepot, ea, from $45 to 60.00

Miscellaneous

Ashtray, flowers on shaded cream, 4 rests, #2, 5¾" 50.00
Ashtray, Indian chief portrait, geometric rim, 6-sided, #2, 6½" ..225.00
Bowl, exotic birds on wht, Deco-style band, #2, 7¼" 90.00
Bowl, floral reserve w/orange lustre, bl rim, hdls, #2, 9¼" 65.00
Bowl, irises on wht, bl rim w/gold hdls, #2, 10½" 85.00
Bowl, river scenic, 8-sided, red #2, 6½" 50.00
Bowl, roses, pk on wht w/gold border & hdls, gr #2, 11" W 150.00
Bowl, 3 floral reserves w/gold on wht, 3 pierced hdls, #2, 6¼" 50.00
Candlesticks, exotic bird on branch, bl rims & ft, #2, 8¼", pr 240.00
Candy jar, river reserve & band on gold lustre, #2, 6½" 225.00

Celery tray, celery stalks on cream, #2, 12", +6 3¾" salts............**140.00**
Cheese dish, yel band w/Deco flowers on wht, slant lid, #2, 8" L..**125.00**
Chocolate pot, gold o/l on wht, #2, 9" **200.00**
Chocolate set, exotic birds on wht w/gold, #2, 9½" pot+5 c/s **300.00**
Cigarette holder, flowers on bell shape, bird finial, #2, 5" **250.00**
Compote, floral on cream w/gold hdls, ftd, #2, 9¾"......................**80.00**
Compote, swans in river scenic, hdls, #2, 9" W **85.00**
Condensed milk container, Deco floral on wht w/gold, #2, 5¼" ..**160.00**
Condiment set, exotic birds on red, #2, 3 pcs on 6¾" tray..........**150.00**
Egg cup, windmill & river scenic, earth tones, #2, 3½" **40.00**
Humidor, camel scene at sunset, gr #2, 5¾"................................**400.00**
Humidor, owl on branch in relief, #2, 7"......................................**850.00**
Jam jar, bl & gold lustre, rose finial, #2, w/spoon & tray, 5¼".......**80.00**
Lemon dish, flowering branch on yel, red #2, 6½" L **40.00**
Lemon dish, lemons & leaves, tan lustre rim, #2, 5¾" **40.00**
Mantel set, Deco floral on cream w/gold, #2, 9" bowl+pr sticks..**475.00**
Mustard set, roses, pk & yel on wht, #2, 3", 4-pc **35.00**
Napkin ring, mc roses, #2, 2¼" W...**45.00**
Nappy, roses, pastels on cream, 1-hdl, #2, 5" **40.00**
Night light, lady praying figural, lustre dress, #2, 9¾".............**2,700.00**
Plaque, river scenic w/swans, earth tones, #2, 6½" **115.00**
Plate, windmill & river landscape, bright colors, #2, 7½" **65.00**
Playing card holder, horse on tan lustre, ftd, #2, 3¾" **180.00**
Sauce dish, flowers & bird on wht w/tan lustre, #2, 4½", +spoon.**50.00**
Sauce dish, roses on tan w/orange lustre, #2, 5", +ladle & tray **80.00**
Shakers, river scenic, earth tones, #2, 2½", pr..............................**16.00**
Shaving mug, river scenic, earth tones w/gold, #2, 3¾" **120.00**
Spooner, river scenic w/red-roofed cottage, #2, 8" L....................**70.00**
Sugar shaker, floral band on wht, gold top, #2, 6½" **30.00**
Syrup, trees, river & red-roofed cottage scene, #2, 4¼"+tray **85.00**
Tea set, river scenic, #2, child sz, 3½" pot+8 pcs **225.00**
Tile, river scenic, canted corners, #2, 5".......................................**55.00**
Toast rack, bl lustre w/bird finial, #2, 5½" L **125.00**
Tray, river scenic w/swans, bl #1, 12"...**80.00**
Vase, lg open roses, pastel tones w/gold, hdls, #2, 11¼" **250.00**
Vase, peacock feathers on tan, ruffled rim, slim, #1, 8", pr..........**180.00**
Vase, river scenic, jack-in-pulpit shape, #2, 7¾"..........................**200.00**
Vase, roses on long stems on wht, hdls, #2, 8½"..........................**165.00**
Vase, tulip figural, purple & gr, #2, 5¼"......................................**300.00**
Vase, Wedgwood type, wht flowers on bl, hdls, #1, 9½".............**475.00**
Wall pocket, butterflies on tan lustre, red #2, 9"..........................**125.00**

Norse

The Norse Pottery was established in 1903 in Edgerton, Wisconsin, by Thorwald Sampson and Louis Ipson. A year later it was purchased by A.W. Wheelock and moved to Rockford, Illinois. The ware they produced was inspired by ancient bronze vessels of the Norsemen. Designs were often incised into the red clay body. Dragon handles and feet were favored decorative devices, and they achieved a semblance of patina through the application of metallic glazes. The ware was marked with model numbers and a stylized 'N' containing a vertical arrangement of the remaining letters of the name. Production ceased after 1913.

Bowl, 2 serpents incised on side, gr on blk, 3-ftd, 4" **450.00**
Candlestick, cvd tree motif on cylinder shaft, dome ft/hdl, 5½", NM..**550.00**
Chamber stick, cvd edges, high-bk cupped form w/hdl, #69, 6"..**425.00**
Humidor, incised decor on brn, #8, 6½" **750.00**
Jug, sea horses in verdigris on blk metallic, w/stopper, 1903-13, 7"..**900.00**
Pitcher, abstract cvg, blk on gr matt, stoppered, 7", NM.............**750.00**
Vase, angle shoulder w/2 lg dragons as hdls, #6, 7½x14½" **1,500.00**
Vase, grotesque lizard on shoulder, blk matt w/gold & gr, 12"..**1,200.00**
Vase, groups of dots/elongations, gr on blk, #11, 5½x7½" **500.00**

Vase, incised geometrics, gr & blk matt w/gold, 4½x4"..............**500.00**
Vase, 2 creatures w/long tails as hdls, 3 squat ft, 4x6".................**500.00**
Wall pocket, dmn shape w/lizards, #72, very rare, 11".............**2,500.00**

North Dakota School of Mines

The School of Mines of the University of North Dakota was established in 1890, but due to a lack of funding it was not until 1898 that Earle J. Babcock was appointed as director, and efforts were made to produce ware from the native clay he had discovered several years earlier. The first pieces were made by firms in the East from the clay Babcock sent them. Some of the ware was decorated by the manufacturer; some was shipped back to North Dakota to be decorated by native artists. By 1909 students at the University of North Dakota were producing utilitarian items such as tile, brick, shingles, etc., in conjunction with a ceramic course offered through the chemistry department. By 1910 a ceramic department had been established, supervised by Margaret Kelly Cable. Under her leadership, fine artware was produced. Native flowers, grains, buffalo, cowboys, and other subjects indigenous to the state were incorporated into the decorations. Some pieces have an Art Nouveau – Art Deco style easily attributed to her association with Frederick H. Rhead, with whom she studied in 1911. During the '20s the pottery was marketed on a limited scale through gift and jewelry stores in the state. From 1927 until 1949 when Miss Cable announced her retirement, a more widespread distribution was maintained with sales branching out into other states. The ware was marked in cobalt with the official seal — 'Made at School of Mines, N.D. Clay, University of North Dakota, Grand Forks, N.D.' in a circle. Very early ware was sometimes marked 'U.N.D.' in cobalt by hand. Our advisor for this category is William M. Bilsland III; he is listed in the Directory under Iowa.

Vase, Viking ships among waves, carved, dark blue on blue, Julia Mattson, 4¼", $1,400.00.

Bowl, Bentonite, Native Am bird design, Halverson, 1941, 3½x5" ..**950.00**
Bowl, tulips, bl on ivory, 5½"...**700.00**
Bowl vase, floral, red matt, Huck-Prairie Rose, 4" W **450.00**
Bowl vase, 2-tone bl gloss, Huck, 5x7½"....................................**300.00**
Humidor, waves of gr drip on tan, sgn HB, UND mk, 5¾" **400.00**
Plate, flowers & tall conifer, mc on cream, Granther, 1931, 7¼" ..**500.00**
Tile, tulips encircle perimeter, elaborate motif, mc, 5" dia **800.00**
Vase, antelope cvg, gr matt, M Cable, #180 #G 14, 7⅛" **3,400.00**
Vase, bl to gr gloss, swirling ribs, mk, 10"....................................**375.00**
Vase, bl to red, flattened form, 3½" **200.00**
Vase, cvd florals cascade from rim, red/gr on bsk, Huck, 8½"..**1,400.00**
Vase, emb flowers, F Huckfield, mint gr on sandy brn, 3⅞", NM ..**600.00**
Vase, gr matt, sgn, str sides, 4" **450.00**
Vase, gr on brn matt, UND ink stamp, 8⅜".................................**650.00**
Vase, multi-tone gr, sgn J Schroeder, 2½".....................................**60.00**
Vase, prairie roses, F Huckfield, 1930, 4⅞" **600.00**
Vase, prairie roses, F Huckfield/Bridgeman, 1934, #2899, 3⅝" ...**500.00**
Vase, sheaves of wheat relief, F Huckfield, UND mk, 1936, 5x3"...**650.00**
Vase, striated brn, angle hdls, UND mk, 1916, 6⅛" **700.00**

North State

In 1924 the North State Pottery of Sanford, North Carolina, began small-scale production, the result of the extreme fondness Mrs. Rebecca Copper had for potting. With the help of her husband Henry and the abundance of suitable local clay, the pottery flourished and became well known for lovely shapes and beautiful glazes. They shared the knowledge they gained from their glaze experiments with the ceramic engineering department of North Carolina University; and during summer vacation, they often employed some of the university students. Salt glazed stoneware was produced in the early years but was quickly abandoned in favor of Henry's vibrant glazes. Colors of copper red, Chinese Red, moss green, and turquoise blue were used alone and combination, producing bands of blending colors. Some swirl ware was made as well. The pottery was in business for thirty-five years; most of its ware was sold in gift and craft shops throughout North Carolina.

Pitcher, Rebekah, glossy flambe, Walter Owens, 1940s, 7⅞" **375.00**
Vase, chrome red gloss, sloping shoulder, W Owens, 1930s, 8¼"...**200.00**
Vase, cobalt satin gloss, ovoid, att CB Craven, 6x3¼" **275.00**
Vase, fan; flambe dbl-dip, W Owens, 1940s, 4x5½" **175.00**
Vase, gr crystalline flambe over buff clay bottom, 3-hdl, 6x6", EX ...**110.00**
Vase, rust-gr/bright gr/ivory drips on aqua, W Owens, 1930s, 5½"...**225.00**
Vase, turq crystalline flambe, burst bubbles/glaze flecks, 9¾" **170.00**

Northwood

The Northwood Company was founded in 1896 in Indiana, Pennsylvania, by Harry Northwood, whose father, John, was the art director for Stevens and Williams, an English glassworks. Northwood joined the National Glass Company in 1899 but in 1901 again became an independent contractor and formed the Harry Northwood Glass Company of Wheeling, West Virginia. He marketed his first carnival glass in 1908, and it became his most popular product. His company was also famous for its custard, goofus, and pressed glass. Northwood died in 1923, and the company closed. See also Carnival; Custard; Goofus; Opalescent; Pattern Glass.

Berry set, Royal Ivy, rubena, 1 lg+4 sm bowls **275.00**
Bowl, fruit; Royal Ivy, rubena frost, 9" **165.00**
Bowl, Royal Ivy, rubena, 8" **150.00**
Butter dish, Memphis, gr w/gold **200.00**
Butter dish, Royal Ivy, rubena frost...**330.00**
Butter dish, Royal Oak, rubena **400.00**
Candle holder, Swirl, blk, worn gold, pr..**165.00**
Console bowl & candlesticks, Chinese Coral, ca 1924, 10", 8¾" ...**300.00**
Creamer, Leaf Medallion, gr w/gold..**85.00**
Creamer, Memphis, gr **50.00**
Creamer, Royal Oak, rubena frost..**325.00**
Cruet, Royal Ivy, rubena frost **500.00**
Cruet, Royal Oak, rubena frost, orig stopper....................................**525.00**
Pickle castor, Panelled Sprig, rubena, HP decor, SP fr & tongs...**350.00**
Pickle castor, Royal Ivy, rubena frost **265.00**
Pickle castor, Royal Oak, rubena frost; SP fr & lid **420.00**
Pitcher, cranberry spatter, vaseline hdl..**350.00**
Pitcher, Leaf Medallion, amethyst w/gold, water sz.....................**495.00**
Pitcher, red spatter, opal cased w/silver mica..................................**225.00**
Pitcher, water; Royal Oak, rubena **400.00**
Sauce dish, Royal Ivy, rubena..**40.00**
Sauce dish, Royal Oak, rubena...**50.00**
Shakers, Royal Ivy, rubena frost, pr **170.00**
Shakers, Royal Oak, rubena frost, pr **250.00**
Sugar bowl, Memphis, gr w/old **90.00**

Sugar bowl, Royal Ivy, rubena frost...**200.00**
Sugar bowl, Royal Oak, rubena, w/lid..**245.00**
Sugar shaker, Royal Ivy, rubena frost **265.00**
Sugar shaker, Royal Ivy, rubena frost craquelle **325.00**
Syrup, Royal Ivy, rubena **425.00**
Table set, Royal Ivy, rubena frost, 4-pc...**840.00**
Table set, Royal Oak, rubena frost, 4-pc **1,000.00**
Toothpick holder, Royal Ivy, rubena frost..**125.00**
Toothpick holder, Royal Oak, rubena frost **180.00**
Tumbler, Memphis, gr w/gold..**45.00**
Tumbler, Paneled Sprig, rubena, 4"..**65.00**
Tumbler, Royal Ivy, rubena craquelle...**100.00**
Tumbler, Royal Oak, rubena frost **115.00**
Vase, bl MOP w/wht pull-ups, camphor S hdls, stick neck, 8" **375.00**
Vase, bl satin, thin bands of wht pull-ups w/int decor, gourd form, 8" ...**400.00**

Nutcrackers

The nutcracker, though a strictly functional tool, is a good example of one to which man has applied ingenuity, imagination, and engineering skills. Though all were designed to accomplish the same end, hundreds of types exist in almost every material sturdy enough to withstand sufficient pressure to crack the nut. Figurals are popular collectibles, as are those with unusual design and construction. Patented examples are also desirable. Our advisor for this category is Susan Otto; she is listed in the Directory under Ohio. For more information, we recommend *Ornamental and Figural Nutcrackers* by Judith A. Rittenhouse.

Anri lady w/babuska, wood, cvd & pnt **77.00**
Bbl shape, wood w/ivory hdl & rings, screw-type, Fr, 19th C, 3x4"..**700.00**
Bloomer legs, brass lever **100.00**
Breton man, hand-cvd wood..**125.00**
Chamois head, cvd wood w/glass eyes, Swiss, from $89 to **135.00**
Cheshire cat, brass lever, from $10 to **31.00**
Dog, CI, tail lever, Lewisburg Casting, 6x12"................................**35.00**

Dog's head, carved wood with glass eyes and painted details, 7⅞", **$150.00**. (Photo courtesy Garth's Auctions)

Elephant, pnt CI, red w/blk & wht details, 5x9¾" **60.00**
King Ludwig, Germany, lg **3,000.00**
Labrador retriever, bronze pnt CI, 13" L..**655.00**
Man smiling, w/beard & cap, cvd wood, Swiss...............................**65.00**
Mermaid, brass lever..**100.00**
Monkey, hand-cvd wood, figural, jaw opens, 10" **175.00**
Trusty Servant/horse, Winchester, brass lever **30.00**
Vice-type, porc w/brass tooling, screw-type, German...................**400.00**

Nutting, Wallace

Wallace Nutting (1861 – 1941) was America's most famous photographer of the early twentieth century. A retired minister, Nutting took more than 50,000 pictures, keeping 10,000 of his best and destroying the rest. His popular and bestselling scenes included exterior scenes (apple blossoms, country lanes, orchards, calm streams, and rural American countrysides), interior scenes (usually featuring a colonial woman working near a hearth), and foreign scenes (typically thatch-roofed cottages). His poorest selling pictures, which have become today's rarest and most highly collectible, are classified as miscellaneous unusual scenes and include categories not mentioned above: animals, architecturals, children, florals, men, seascapes, and snow scenes. Process prints are 1930s machine-produced reprints of twelve of Nutting's most popular pictures. These have minimal value and can be detected by using a magnifying glass.

Nutting sold literally millions of his hand-colored platinotype pictures between 1900 and his death in 1941. He started in Southbury, Connecticut, and later moved his business to Framingham, Massachusetts. The peak of Wallace Nutting picture production was 1915 – 25. During this period Nutting employed nearly two hundred people, including colorists, darkroom staff, salesmen, and assorted office personnel. Wallace Nutting pictures proved to be a huge commercial success and scarcely an American household was without one by 1925.

While attempting to seek out the finest and best early American furniture as props for his colonial interior scenes, Nutting became an expert in early American antiques. He published nearly twenty books in his lifetime, including his 10-volume *State Beautiful* series and various other books on furniture, photography, clocks, stools, chairs, settles, settees, tables, stands, desks, mirrors, beds, chests of drawers, cabinet pieces, and treenware. He made furniture as well, which he clearly marked with a distinctive paper label that was glued directly onto the piece, or a block or script signature brand which was literally branded into the furniture.

The overall synergy of the Wallace Nutting name — on pictures, books, and furniture — has made anything 'Wallace Nutting' quite collectible.

Our advisor for this category is Michael Ivankovich, author of many books concerning Nutting. Those currently available are *The Collector's Guide to Wallace Nutting Pictures*; *The Wallace Nutting Expansible Catalog*; *The Alphabetical and Numerical Index to Wallace Nutting Pictures*; *The Guide to Wallace Nutting Furniture*, *Wallace Nutting General Catalog, Supreme Edition*; *Wallace Nutting: A Great American Idea*; *Wallace Nutting's Windsors: Correct Windsor Furniture*; and *The Guide to Wallace Nutting-Like Photographers of the Early 20th Century*. Also available through Mr. Ivankovich is *The History of the Sawyer Pictures* by Carol Begley Gray. Mr Ivankovich's address and ordering information are listed in the Directory under Pennsylvania.

Prices below are for pictures in good to excellent condition. Mat stains or blemishes, poor picture color, or frame damage can decrease value significantly.

Wallace Nutting Pictures

Among October Birches, 16x20"	295.00
Ancestral Chamber, 11x14"	350.00
Berkshire Brook, 11x17"	185.00
Bit of Sewing, 11x14"	325.00
Clogheen Bridge, 13x16"	595.00
Cluster of Zinnias, 15x19"	795.00
Cup That Cheers, 11x14"	295.00
Decked as a Bride, 12x14"	185.00
Dream & Reality, 9x15"	175.00
Dream & Reality, 12x20"	195.00
Fleck of Sunshine, 13x17"	350.00
From the Hill, 13x16"	185.00
Fruit Luncheon, 14x11"	275.00
Goose Chase Quilt, 10x15"	325.00
Grandmother's Sheffield, 11x17"	350.00
Harmony, 14x17"	375.00

Heart of Maine, 16x20"	375.00
Honeymoon Blossoms, 13x16"	195.00
Honeymoon Drive, 9x11"	165.00
Honeymoon Stroll, 10x12"	175.00
Informal Call, 13x16"	375.00
June Beautiful, 13x16"	195.00
Little River, 15x22"	225.00
Maple Sugar Cupboard, 12x16"	325.00
Mid-May, 10x13"	165.00

A Natural Bridge, 9x12", $160.00.
(Photo courtesy Michael Ivankovich)

Neighborhhod News, 11x14"	325.00
Nuttinghame Nook, 13x16"	375.00
Pilgrim Daughter, 11x14"	325.00
Priscilla's Cottage, 17x14"	375.00
Private & Confidential, 13x16"	350.00
Providence Pool, 13x16"	1,150.00
Quilting Party, 11x14"	325.00
Romance of the Revolution, 13x15"	375.00
Spring in the Dell, 10x12"	165.00
Story of Chivalry, 10x12"	295.00
Very Satisfactory, 14x17"	350.00
Virginia Reel, 14x16"	325.00
White & Gold, 13x16"	195.00
Winding an Old Tall Clock, 13x15"	325.00
17th Century, 11x14"	295.00

Wallace Nutting Books

England Beautiful, 2nd ed	45.00
Maine Beautiful, 1st ed	45.00
Maine Beautiful, 2nd ed	40.00
New Hampshire Beautiful, 1st ed	45.00
New Hampshire Beautiful, 2nd ed	40.00
New York Beautiful, 2nd ed	45.00
Vermont Beautiful, 2nd ed	40.00

Wallace Nutting Furniture

Brewster armchair, script brand, #411	1,000.00
Brewster rushed 3-legged stool, script brand, #164	385.00
Cross-based candlestand, block brand, #301	525.00
Curly maple candlestick (single), imp brand, #31	175.00
Maple crane bracket table, script brand, #619	685.00
Maple screw (whirling) candlestand, block brand, #21	990.00
Pennsylvania Windsor comb-bk armchair, block brand, #412	1,400.00
Pilgrim side chair, block brand, #393	360.00
Rushed maple stool, block brand, #168, 22"	425.00
Treenware open salt dish, imp brand, #28, 1½"	155.00
Windsor armchair rocker, script brand, #421	1,100.00
Windsor bent-rung bow-bk side chair, bamboo trns, block brand, #305	800.00
Windsor fan-bk side chair, script brand/paper label, #326	550.00

Windsor low-bk armchair, block brand/paper label, #414............**525.00**
Windsor oval stool, paper label, #102................................**250.00**
Windsor rnd stool, block brand, #101 ....**300.00**
Windsor side chair, block brand, #301 ....**525.00**
Windsor slipper side chair, paper label, #310 ....**550.00**
Windsor tripod candlestand, block brand, #17.....................**525.00**
Windsor writing armchair, PA trnings w/drw, block brand, #440..**2,800.00**

Major Wallace Nutting-Like Photographers

Although Wallace Nutting was widely recognized as the country's leading producer of hand-colored photographs during the early twentieth century, he was by no means the only photographer selling this style of picture. Throughout the country literally hundreds of regional photographers were selling hand-colored photographs from their home regions or travels. The subject matters of these photographers was very comparable to Nutting's, including interior, exterior, foreign, and miscellaneous unusual scenes. The key determinants of value include the collectability of the particular photographer, subject matter, condition, and size. Keep in mind that only the rarest pictures in the best condition will bring top prices. Discoloration and/or damage to the picture or matting can reduce value significantly.

Several photographers operated large businesses, and although not as large or well known as Wallace Nutting, they sold a substantial volume of pictures which can still be readily found today. The vast majority of their work was photographed in their home regions and sold primarily to local residents or visiting tourists. It should come as little surprise that three of the major Wallace Nutting-like photographers — David Davidson, Fred Thompson, and the Sawyer Art Co. — each had ties to Wallace Nutting.

David Davidson: Second to Nutting in overall production, Davidson worked primarily in the Rhode Island and Southern Massachusetts area. While a student at Brown University around 1900, Davidson learned the art of hand-colored photography from Wallace Nutting, who happened to be the minister at Davidson's church. After Nutting moved to Southbury in 1905, Davidson graduated from Brown and started a successful photography business in Providence, Rhode Island, which he operated until his death in 1967.

Sawyer: A father and son team, Charles H. Sawyer and Harold B. Sawyer, operated the very successful Sawyer Art Company from 1903 into the 1970s. Beginning in Maine, the Sawyer Art Company moved to Concord, New Hampshire, in 1920 to be nearer their primary market of New Hampshire's White Mountains. Charles H. Sawyer briefly worked for Nutting in 1902 – 03 while living in southern Maine. Sawyer's production volume ranks third behind Wallace Nutting and David Davidson.

Fred Thompson: Frederick H. Thompson and Frederick M. Thompson were another father and son team that operated the Thompson Art Company (TACO) from 1908 to 1923, working primarily in the Portland, Maine, area. We know that Thompson and Nutting had collaborated because Thompson widely marketed an interior scene he had taken in Nutting's Southbury home. The production volume of the Thompson Art Company ranks fourth behind Nutting, Davidson, and Sawyer.

Davidson, Diadem Aisle, 14x17" **150.00**
Davidson, lady & baby carriage (untitled), 8x10".........**250.00**
Davidson, Over the Hills, 7x9" **75.00**
Davidson, Pool, 5x7" **60.00**
Davidson, Red Maple Bend, 5x7" **75.00**
Davidson, River of Lebanon, 5x7" **60.00**
Davidson, River of Peace, 7x9" **65.00**
Davidson, Road Home, 6x8" **75.00**
Davidson, Without a Ripple, 5x7" **60.00**
Sawyer, Along the Country Highway, 9x11"................**145.00**
Sawyer, Echo Lake, 5x6" **75.00**

Sawyer, Flume Falls, 4x6" **60.00**
Sawyer, Storm King Highway, 7x14"..........................**160.00**
Sawyer, To Join the Brimming River, 13x16"...............**160.00**
Thompson, figure in fireside chair, untitled, 5x7".........**110.00**
Thompson, Fireside Fancy Work, 7x9" **110.00**
Thompson, Grandmother's Way, 10x13" **165.00**
Thompson, miniature int: girl at fireplace & spinning wheel, 3x4" ..**75.00**
Thompson, Olde-Tyme Roses, 11x14"..........................**165.00**
Thompson, Paring Apples, 7x9"..................................**125.00**
Thompson, Silent Stream Bridge, 7x14½".....................**125.00**

Minor Wallace-Like Photographers

Hundreds of other smaller local and regional photographers attempted to market hand-colored pictures comparable to Nutting's during the 1900 – 30s time period. Although quite attractive, most were not as appealing to the general public as Wallace Nutting pictures. However, as the price of Wallace Nutting pictures has escalated, the work of these lesser-known Wallace Nutting-like photographers have become increasingly collectible.

A partial listing of some of these minor Wallace Nutting-like photographers include Babcock; J.C. Bicknell; Blair; Ralph Blood (Portland, Maine); Bragg; Brehmer; Brooks; Burrowes; Busch; Carlock; Pedro Cacciola; Croft; Currier; Depue Bros; Derek; Dowly; Eddy; May Farini (hand-colored colonial lithographs); Geo. Forest; Gandara; Gardner (Nantucket, Bermuda, Florida); Gibson; Gideon; Gunn; Bessie Pease Gutmann (hand-colored colonial lithographs); Edward Guy; Harris; C Hazen; Knoffe; Haynes (Yellowstone Park); Margaret Hennesey; Charles Higgins; Hodges; Homer; Krabel; Kattleman; La Bushe; Lake; Lamson (Portland, Maine); M. Lightstrum; Machering; Rossiler Mackinae; Merrill; Meyers; William Moehring; Moran; Murrey; Lyman Nelson; J. Robinson Neville (New England); Patterson; Owen Perry; Phelps; Phinney; Reynolds; F. Robbins; Royce; Fred'k Scheetz (Phila...Pennsylvania); Shelton; Standley (Colorado); Stott; Summers; Esther Svenson; Florence Thompson; Thomas Thompson; M.A. Trott; Sanford Tull; Underhill; Villar; Ward; Wilmot; Edith Wilson; and Wright.

A very general breakdown of prices for works by these minor Wallace Nutting-like photographers would be as follows: larger pictures, greater than 14" x 17", from $75.00 to over $200.00; medium pictures, from 11" x 14" to 14" x 17", from $50.00 to $200.00; smaller pictures, 5" x 7" to 10" x 12", from $10.00 to $75.00.

The same pricing guidelines that apply to Wallace Nutting pictures typically apply to Wallace Nutting-like pictures

1.) Exterior scenes are the most common.

2.) Some photographers sold colonial interior scenes as well.

3.) Subject, matter, condition, and size are all important determinants of value.

Carlock, US Capitol Building, 8x10" **95.00**
Gibson, Pasture Stream, 7x9"...**65.00**
Harris, Cavern Cascade, Watkins Glen NY, 6x10" **65.00**
Harris, Fountain of Youth, St Augustine FL, 4x5" **110.00**
Haynes, Great Falls, Yellowstone Park, 13x18"............................**150.00**
Haynes, Old Faithful, 10x12"...**110.00**
Standley, Bridal Veil Falls CO, 6x11"...**95.00**
Trott, Elbow Beach, Bermuda, 12x14" **75.00**
Villar, Steps to the Road, 7x9" **65.00**
Yates, Bay of Fundy Prime, 6x8" **75.00**
Yates, Princess Helene the Sea God, 7x10" **95.00**

Occupied Japan

Items marked 'Occupied Japan' have become popular collectibles in the last few years. They were produced during the period from the end of World War II until April 18, 1952, when the occupation ended. By no means was all of the ware exported during that time marked 'Occupied Japan'; some was marked 'Japan' or 'Made In Japan.' It is thought that because of the natural resentment felt by the Japanese toward the occupation, only a fraction of these wares carried the 'Occupied' mark. Even though you may find identical 'Japan'-marked items, because of its limited use, only those with the 'Occupied Japan' mark are being collected to any great extent. Values vary considerably, based on the quality of workmanship. Generally, bisque figures command much higher prices than porcelain, since on the whole they are of a finer quality.

For those wanting more information, we recommend *Occupied Japan Collectibles* by Gene Florence; he is listed in the Directory under Kentucky. Our advisor for this category is Florence Archambault; she is listed in the Directory under Rhode Island. She represents the Occupied Japan Club, whose mailing address may be found in the Directory under Clubs, Newsletters, and Catalogs. All items described in the following listings are assumed ceramic unless noted otherwise.

Ashtray, metal, souvenir of Indianapolis Ind, 4¾" 5.00
Basket, pk w/angel on hdl, red mk, 5", from $55 to 60.00
Box, cigarette; bl floral on wht, Rossetti Chicago 20.00
Box, cigarette; emb roses on lid, red mk, from $10 to 12.50
Box, metal, Pegasus emb on lid, rectangular, ftd, sm 17.50
Child's tea set, 2 place settings, 9 pcs 45.00
Child's tea set, 4 place settings, 13 pcs 65.00
Child's tea set, 6 place settings, 23 pcs 100.00
Child's tea set, 6 place settings, 26 pcs 125.00
Crumb butler, metal, souvenir of Washington DC 10.00
Crumb pan, metal, emb NY scene, from $10 to 15.00
Cup & saucer, demitasse; blk w/lacy flower, gr HB in dmn mk 15.00
Cup & saucer, floral on wht w/gold rim, red mk 20.00
Cup & saucer, red hearts w/blk trim on wht, from $7.50 to 15.00
Dinnerware, complete set for 8 +cr/sug+gravy+2 lg/1 sm platter ...350.00
Doll, celluloid, Dutch girl, pnt-on clothes, 8⅝" 50.00
Doll, china, 3" 30.00
Figurine, American children, 6" 75.00
Figurine, ballerina on tiptoe, 5¾" 40.00
Figurine, boy & girl on fence, cat at ft, 4", pr 35.00
Figurine, boy w/horn & girl w/satchel, Hummel type, 4", pr 30.00
Figurine, boy w/truck, 2½" 5.00

Figurine, children under umbrella, 6", $75.00. (Photo courtesy Florence Archambault)

Figurine, Cinderella & Prince Charming on base, Maruyama, 8¼" ..175.00
Figurine, Colonial couple at piano, gold LD in flower face mk, 5½" ...85.00
Figurine, Colonial couple on base, 4¾", from $12.50 to 15.00
Figurine, Colonial lady w/dog & gun, 6" 35.00
Figurine, Colonial man & lady seated, he w/flute, bsk, Andrea, 7", pr ..160.00
Figurine, cowboy, gun on hip, yel hat, 5⅛" 15.00
Figurine, dog w/hat & pipe, red mk, 3½" 12.50
Figurine, East Indian man & woman, 6⅛", pr, from $25 to 40.00
Figurine, East Indian man winding turban, 6" 20.00
Figurine, girl holding doll, Hummel-like, 4¼", from $15 to 18.00
Figurine, girl seated w/book, basket beside, 3¾" 10.00
Figurine, girl w/red feather in hair, pnt bsk, red M over C mk, 4⅜" ..15.00
Figurine, girl w/teddy bear in basket, red mk, 5⅝" 25.00
Figurine, gnome, 1-handed orator, 5⅛", from $12.50 to 15.00
Figurine, horses (2) running, realistic, bl circle T mk, 5" 50.00
Figurine, lady bug w/bat, 4", from $15 to 17.00
Figurine, lady dancer, arms behind head, red mk, 5", from $15 to ...17.50
Figurine, lady holding skirt wide to curtsy, 4¼" 15.00
Figurine, man pushes lady in sled, 5¾" 100.00
Figurine, Oriental lady w/fan, man w/dagger, 8¼" 50.00
Figurine, Oriental lady w/fan, yel skirt, 5", from $10 to 15.00
Figurine, peacock, long flowing tail down, mc, 5", from $17.50 to ..20.00
Figurine, peacock on stump, tail down, 7" 27.50
Figurine, rooster & hen on base, 5", pr 35.00
Lamp base, Colonial couple, bsk, 11" to top of socket 50.00
Planter, couple w/rabbits, bsk, Paulux, 5¼x7¼" 150.00
Planter, East Indian man holding planter, gold trim, 7⅛" 25.00
Planter, lady standing beside lg open flower, bsk, Paulux, 6" 75.00
Plate, fruit center on wht w/gold rim, Ohata China, 6" 20.00
Shoe, cowboy boot, 4⅜", from $6 to 8.00
Shoe, rabbit stands beside, 2⅜", from $6 to 8.00
Tablecloth, linen, paper label, 32" sq, +4 10½" napkins 90.00
Vase, cherub seated beside, pastel w/gold, red mk, 3⅜" 15.00
Vase, cornucopia; silver-tone metal, 8", pr 35.00

Ohr, George

George Ohr established his pottery in the 1880s in Biloxi, Mississippi. The first pottery burned down and was subsequently rebuilt. Ohr, among other things, was a master of the wheel. This mastery enabled him to create unique forms of unbelievable thinness, verging at times on *Abstraction* and looking far ahead toward many art movements of the twentieth century. In addition to Abstraction, by studying Ohr, one can discover elements of Expressionism and Fauvism (the wild use of color often seemingly at odds with the piece being glazed) and Dada (meaning shock the bourgeosie). An Ohr piece may be rooted in the functional form of a teapot, but following his manipulation it becomes a sculpture for which the functional form serves only as a take-off point for the finished piece. Ohr was also a master of glazes. Highly esteemed are his volcanic and gunmetal glazes. He was not well received in his day and sold few pieces of his art pottery — a van Gogh-like tale. Ohr decorated his pieces with snakes and lizards and sometimes with asymmetrical handles. He believed that like all things on earth, no two things should be alike. This dictum was applied to his pottery making. He signed his pieces either in impressed letters or florid script. In the early 1900s Ohr ceased making pottery and became a motorcycle dealer and ultimately sold automobiles. His pottery was stored away to be rediscovered many years later. Ohr died in 1918. Our advisor for this category is Dave Rago; he is listed in the Directory under New Jersey.

Bank, acorn shape, brn lustre/mirror blk, int rattle, 4x2" 1,100.00
Bottle, gr/red/teal leathery matt, twisted/closed-in rim, 7x4" ...7,500.00
Bowl, gr & brn mottle, raised rim/swollen body/tripod base, 2½" H ...750.00
Bowl, gr speckled, down-trn rim, pinched/twisted/swollen body, 2⅝" ..1,850.00
Chalice, blk lustre/umber, flaring base, rstr cup, 6x3¼" 800.00
Cup, mirror mahog w/emb ribs, ochre/brn speckled int, 3½" 350.00
Holder, dk gr w/olive accents, manipulated/dented, wafer ped, 6½" .1,200.00
Inkwell, log cabin, wht & red clay, glued to base, 3x4¼x3½" 865.00
Inkwell, panther, cobalt, firing line to base, mk Biloxi, 3½x4½" .2,425.00
Mug, Joe Jefferson, 1896, dedicated to HR Durant, sheer olive, 3¼" ..2,185.00
Pitcher, cobalt & gunmetal, folded sides, low, rstr, 2½x8" 7,000.00
Pitcher, gunmetal, ovoid, 4x3¾" 2,070.00

Pitcher, gunmetal speckled, 3 lobed openings, rpr hdl/rim, 2½x4" ..5,465.00
Pitcher, mirror blk/eggplant, hourglass form, 5½x3¾" 6,325.00
Plaque, appl crab, dk gr gloss, claws/tips of shell rstr, 1½x8x8" 4,000.00
Puzzle mug, gr/brn gloss, rtcl rim/body, 3½" 950.00
Puzzle mug, gunmetal/brn mottle, snake hdl, 3½x5½".............1,725.00
Snakes, bsk finish, 4", 5", pr 1,200.00
Tyge, dripping gr lustre/gunmetal, 3 ribbon hdls (1 rstr), 4½x5"...5,460.00
Vase, brn & dk gr on caramel, pinched neck, ribbed shoulder, 6¼"..1,430.00
Vase, brn speckled semi-matt, torn rim, 2 sm touch-ups, 2½x4¼"...865.00
Vase, brn-red bsk, deep in-body twist, closed-in rim, 3¾x4"....2,760.00
Vase, brn/gunmetal mottle, collared rim, dimpled, 4½x5¼"....2,800.00
Vase, bsk, deep in-body twist, 3x3¾" 4,325.00
Vase, craters/circles/crimps/etc form face, 4x6", EX 825.00
Vase, forest gr mottled gloss, baluster, rim touch-up, 4¾", EX...3,100.00
Vase, gr/amber speckled, bulbous, lobed rim, in-body twist, no mk, 4"..8,050.00
Vase, gr/brn/blk w/red touches, t'print band in bulbous base, 3½" W 1,300.00
Vase, gray-gr, twisted rim, 2"..2,000.00
Vase, gunmetal, bottle form w/in-body twist, ruffled, EX, 4¾x3¾"..5,465.00
Vase, gunmetal, bulbous w/folded rim, 3x3", NM.....................2,250.00
Vase, gunmetal brn, str sides, notched shoulder, folded rim, 5½x4"..4,025.00
Vase, gunmetal metallic, bulbous w/folded rim, 3x3", NM.......2,530.00
Vase, gunmetal/yel, int: orange, asymetrical rim folds, 5¼", NM ...3,735.00
Vase, khaki gr w/silvery sheen, spherical, raised midsection, 3x3½"..715.00
Vase, mahog speckled above gr/amber sponged base, folded rim, 8x3", VG.10,350.00
Vase, mocha brn w/streaks, flared rim, tapered neck, 3¼x2½" ...715.00

Vase, purple and green leathery matt, in-body twist, 5½x3¾", $6,050.00; Vase, raspberry mottled glaze, crimped and folded rim, ribbon handles, 9½x5¼", $35,750.00. (Photo courtesy Craftsman Auctions)

Vase, raspberry/amber gloss, flared/folded rim, 3¼x3", EX 1,950.00
Vase, raspberry/wht volcanic glaze (some loss) on bl, mfg flaw, 6x3".14,950.00
Vase, red bsk, folded sides/closed-in rim, squat, 3¾x5" 2,875.00
Vase, tiger-eye & brn flambe, in-body twist at shoulder, dimples, 5" .3,500.00
Vase, wht bsk, bulbous w/dimpled shoulder, folded rim, 5x5½", VG..4,300.00

Old Ivory

Old Ivory dinnerware was produced from 1882 to 1920 by Herman Ohme, of Lower Salzbrunn in Silesia. The patterns are referred to by the numbers stamped on the bottom of many items. (Some early patterns are marked Old Ivory and are not numbered, but the vast majority bears the tiny blue fleur-de-lis/crown mark with Silesia or Germany beneath. Handwritten numbers signify something other than pattern.) Patterns #16 and #84 are the easiest to find and come in a wide variety of table items. Values are about the same for both patterns. Other floral designs include pink, yellow, and orange roses; holly; and lavender flowers — all on the same soft ivory background. Our price ranges are intended to represent a nationwide average, though you may have to pay a little more in some areas. Minor damage and gold wear can lower these prices by as much as 25%. Holly pieces command from 50% to 100% more than those listed below. Novice collectors should be aware of copy-cat versions from the turn of the century that are much heavier and of a coarser material. They are marked 'Old Ivory' without the blue trademark. They are not included in this listing.

Another area gaining in popularity is the vases from Ohme usually

featuring portraits of Edwardian children. There are a few other forms with portraits, and these are very pricey, with 4" to 5" vases going in the range of $450.00 to $600.00, and 8" and 9" vases about $800.00 to $1,200.00.

Prices realized on the Internet for Old Ivory now rival RS Prussia. With so many collectors now buying on eBay, prices for common patterns have dropped while the rare patterns and pieces have skyrocketed in price. As prices have risen, many collections have come on the market, resulting in a drop in the prices of common pieces. Because of climbing values for Old Ivory, interest is growing for the clear-glazed pieces by Ohme, which are still reasonable, though escalating in price. In comparison, while an Old Ivory open-handled cake plate might sell for $124.00 to $145.00, a comparable clear-glazed example might go for $45.00 to $55.00 with the same mark and mold. It should be noted that the same items with differing pattern numbers bring widely differing prices. For further information we recommend *Collector's Encyclopedia of Old Ivory China, The Mystery Explored*, by Alma Hillman (our advisor), David Goldschmitt, and Adam Szynkiewicz (Collector Books). Ms. Hillman is listed in the Directory under Maine.

Biscuit/cracker jar, #16, 8", from $400 to 600.00
Bowl, berry; #7, 5", from $25 to 45.00
Bowl, ice cream; #4, 10", from $250 to..450.00
Bowl, porringer; #28 or #75, 6¼", from $125 to 175.00
Bowl, soup; #28, 7½", from $185 to 250.00
Bowl, vegetable; #15, oval, 9½", from $125 to 185.00
Bowl, vegetable; #84, w/lid, 10½" dia, from $900 to.................1,200.00
Cake plate, #12, open hdls, 10" or 11", ea from $125 to 195.00
Chocolate pot, #75, 9½", from $450 to...600.00
Creamer, #16 or #84, 3½", from $60 to...110.00
Cup & saucer, bouillon; #28, 3½", from $200 to 300.00
Cup & saucer, coffee; #16, 3½", from $70 to 90.00
Cup & saucer, mustache; #5, 3½", from $500 to 600.00
Dish, #200, 3-lobed, 8½", from $100 to 175.00
Plate, coupe; #7, 9½" or 10", ea from $200 to.............................300.00
Plate, luncheon; #10, 8½", from $50 to...95.00
Platter, #16, 16½", from $300 to 400.00
Platter, #34, 28", from $800 to 1,000.00
Spooner, #11, 4", from $250 to 400.00
Tazza/cake stand, #137, 9", from $400 to......................................600.00
Tea tile, #11, 6", from $150 to 250.00
Teapot, #200, 8½", from $400 to...600.00
Tray, dresser; #12, 12½", from $200 to 300.00

Old Paris

Old Paris porcelains were made from the mid-eighteenth century until about 1900. Seldom marked, the term refers to the area of manufacture rather than a specific company. In general, the ware was of high quality, characterized by classic shapes, colorful decoration, and gold application.

Chocolate pot, floral reserve on cobalt w/gold, 1890s, 10", +12" tray ..725.00
Coffeepot, birds & flowering branch in blk & gold, 10½" 460.00
Coffeepot, foliate/geometric bands w/gilt, 1830, 11x8"................125.00
Cup & saucer, bsk floral bands, much gilt, rtcl mask hdl, 5", 6¾" ..275.00
Cup & saucer, cobalt & gold panels, Clauss shape, 1835-45 ....175.00
Encrier, appl flowers & rocaille gilt on gr, 19th C, 10x16x8"......635.00
Fruit basket, oval/lattice rtcl to bowl & ft, gilt on wht, 15" W ...345.00
Pitcher, emb ivy & tendrils w/gold, ca 1850, 10x7", pr 400.00
Platter, armorial eagles, claret/wht/gold border, 1860s, 18x12" ...460.00
Platter, fish; Anneau d'Or, 1845-60, 9⅝" 850.00
Spill holders, Spanish gypsy man & lady, ea beside stump, 12", 11", pr..750.00
Tea set, floral w/gold, pot+cr/sug, 1830-50, 3-pc set 345.00
Tureen, armorial eagles, claret/wht/gold borders, 1860s, 7½x13" 750.00

Urn, landscape reserve on cream w/much gold, hdls, no lid, 12", EX, pr .2,350.00
Vase, birds & flowers, ornate gold serpent hdls, 1880s, 13¾", pr ..2,300.00
Vase, floral sprays on bl w/gold, Dutch form, hdls, 1850-65, 14".350.00
Vase, flower heads in relief on bl floriform, 1850-65, 12½", pr...1,035.00
Vase, Greek scene, mc on blk matt, rust hdls w/profile disks, 15", pr...3,800.00
Vase, Italian landscape, 1830s, 8" 285.00
Vase, mc floral panels w/bl & gold, 1850s, 10"............................350.00
Watering can, 2 reserves on pk, 1 floral, 1 mother & child, 1850s...425.00

Old Sleepy Eye

Old Sleepy Eye was a Sioux Indian chief who was born in Minnesota in 1780. His name was used for the name of a town as well as a flour mill. In 1903 the Sleepy Eye Milling Company of Sleepy Eye, Minnesota, contracted the Weir Pottery Company of Monmouth, Illinois, to make steins, vases, salt crocks, and butter tubs which the company gave away to their customers. A bust profile of the old Indian and his name decorated each piece of the blue and gray stoneware. In addition to these four items, the Minnesota Stoneware Company of Red Wing made a mug with a verse which is very scarce today.

In 1906 Weir Pottery merged with six others to form the Western Stoneware Company in Monmouth. They produced a line of blue and white ware using a lighter body, but these pieces were never given as flour premiums. This line consisted of pitchers (five sizes), steins, mugs, sugar bowls, vases, trivets, and mustache cups. These pieces turn up only rarely in other colors and are highly prized by advanced collectors. Advertising items such as trade cards, pillow tops, thermometers, paperweights, letter openers, postcards, cookbooks, and thimbles are considered very valuable. The original ware was made sporadically until 1937. Brown steins and mugs were produced in 1952. Our advisor for this category is Jim Martin; he is listed in the Directory under Illinois.

Barrel, flour; orig paper label, 1920s......................................1,800.00
Barrel, grapevine-effect banding..3,500.00
Barrel, oak w/brass bands 4,500.00
Barrel label, Chief Strong Bakers..., 16", EX+..............................170.00
Barrel label, mk Chief/Strong Bakers, image in center, 16", NM...200.00
Blanket, horse; w/logo, EX..2,500.00
Butter crock, Flemish bl & gray 750.00
Cabinet, bread display; Old Sleepy Eye etched in glass 950.00
Calendar, 1904, NM...375.00
Cookbook, Indian on cover, Sleepy Eye Milling Co, 4¾x4" 300.00
Cookbook, loaf of bread shape, NM 210.00
Coupon, for ordering cookbook 250.00
Dough scraper, tin/wood, To Be Sure, EX...................................435.00
Fan, die-cut image of Old Sleepy Eye, EX+................................200.00
Flour sack, cloth, mc Indian, red letters 345.00
Flour sack, paper, Indian in blk, blk lettering, NM......................125.00

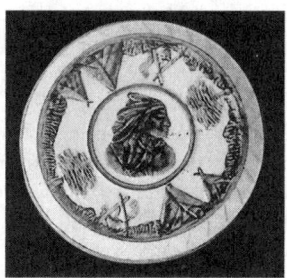

Hot plate, blue and white, $4,500.00. (Photo courtesy Jim Martin)

Ink blotter..125.00
Letter opener, bronze..900.00
Match holder, pnt 1,000.00

Match holder, wht...1,050.00
Mug, bl & gray, 4¼" 360.00
Mug, bl & wht, 4¼" 220.00
Mug, verse, Red Wing, EX...1,625.00
Paperweight, bronzed company trademk 560.00
Pillow cover, Sleepy Eye & tribe meet President Monroe 750.00
Pillow cover, trademk center w/various scenes, 22", NM 1,800.00
Pin-bk button, Indian, rnd face 350.00
Pitcher, #1, 4" 300.00
Pitcher, #2...350.00
Pitcher, #3...315.00
Pitcher, #3, w/bl rim...1,375.00
Pitcher, #4...400.00
Pitcher, #5...435.00
Pitcher, bl & gray, 5" 400.00
Pitcher, bl on cream, 8", M...345.00
Pitcher, brn on yel, Sesquicentennial, 1981, from $100 to..........125.00
Pitcher, standing Indian, good color..1,560.00
Postcard, colorful trademk, 1904 Expo Winner 185.00
Ruler, wooden, 15" 700.00
Salt crock, Flemish bl & gray, 4x6½" 700.00
Sheet music, in fr...300.00
Sign, emb tin litho, ...Flour & Cereal Products, profile, rstr, 28x19"...760.00
Sign, self-fr tin, Old Sleepy Eye Flour, 20x24".......................3,000.00
Sign, sf tin, portrait w/multiple scenes around border, 24x20", G ..2,300.00
Sign, tin litho die-cut Indian, ...Flour & Cereals, 13½"...........1,650.00
Spoon, demitasse; emb roses in bowl, Unity SP..........................105.00
Spoon, Indian-head hdl..125.00
Stein, bl & wht, 7¾"...800.00
Stein, Board of Directors, all yrs, 40-oz......................................265.00
Stein, Board of Directors, 1969, 22-oz..550.00
Stein, brn, 1952, 22-oz..300.00
Stein, brn & wht...1,500.00
Stein, brn & yel, Western Stoneware mk 1,500.00
Stein, chestnut, 40-oz, 1952..325.00
Stein, cobalt..1,250.00
Stein, Flemish, bl on gray..700.00
Stein, ltd edition, 1979-84, ea 125.00
Sugar bowl, bl & wht, 3"...750.00
Thermometer, front rpl 800.00
Vase, cattails, all cobalt..1,450.00
Vase, cattails, bl & wht, good color, 9".......................................800.00
Vase, cattails, brn on yel, rare color 1,500.00
Vase, cattails, gr & wht, rare..5,000.00
Vase, Indian & cattails, Flemish, 8½" 470.00

O'Neill, Rose

Rose O'Neill's Kewpies were introduced in 1909 when they were used to conclude a story in the December issue of *Ladies' Home Journal*. They were an immediate success, and soon Kewpie dolls were being produced worldwide. German manufacturers were among the earliest and also used the Kewpie motif to decorate chinaware as well as other items. The Kewpie is still popular today and can be found on products ranging from Christmas cards and cake ornaments to fabrics, wallpaper, and metal items.

For further information we recommend *Doll Values, Antique to Modern*, by Patsy Moyer (Collector Books). In the following listings, 'sgn' indicates that the item is signed Rose O'Neill. Values are for examples in excellent condition with no chips. The © is also a good mark on items. Unsigned items can be of interest to collectors; many are authentic and collectible, some are too small to sign.

Our advisors for this category are Don and Anne Kier; they are listed in the Directory under Ohio.

Vase, Kewpie with Doodle dog, painted bisque, Germany, very unusual, 3¾", $2,600.00. (Photo courtesy McMasters Auctions)

Book, Loves of Edwy, leather cover, 432 pgs, 1904, VG 850.00
Book, The Goblin Woman, 345 pgs, 1st ed, 1930, VG+ 55.00
Book, They Wanted Jell-O, recipes, 1908, 4½x4½", VG 50.00
Card, The Kewpies Think-That To Win Anything...After It, 1920s......50.00
Christmas plate, Let Joy Be Everywhere You Are, Cameo, 1973, 10¾"..15.00
Creamer, 3 Kewpies w/floral top border, ZS & Co Bavaria, 3x5¼"..85.00
Inkwell, Kewpies (2) stand on sides of glass well, pewter, 3x5" ...165.00
Kewpie, bsk, arms folded, Germany, 6", EX/NM 600.00
Kewpie, bsk, Aviator, Germany, 8½", EX/NM 850.00
Kewpie, bsk, Black, jtd arms, heart label, 11" 160.00
Kewpie, bsk, Black Hottentot, Germany, 5", EX/NM 575.00
Kewpie, bsk, Blunderboo, falling down, Germany, 1¾", EX/NM...425.00
Kewpie, bsk, Cowboy, Germany, 10", EX/NM 800.00
Kewpie, bsk, Doodle Dog, 1½" 275.00
Kewpie, bsk, Farmer, Germany, 6½", EX/NM 575.00
Kewpie, bsk, fly on ft, Germany, 3" 600.00
Kewpie, bsk, Huggers, Germany, 3½", EX/NM 165.00
Kewpie, bsk, immobile, bl wings, pnt hair, Germany, 2", EX/NM 110.00
Kewpie, bsk, immobile, bl wings, pnt hair, Germany, 4½", EX/NM..150.00
Kewpie, bsk, immobile, bl wings, pnt hair, Germany, 6", EX/NM 240.00
Kewpie, bsk, in bl chair holding mandolin, Germany, 4", EX/NM ...925.00
Kewpie, bsk, Jester, wht hat on head, Germany, 4½", EX/NM....700.00
Kewpie, bsk, jtd arms, blond hair, mk, 10½" 575.00
Kewpie, bsk, jtd hips & shoulders, Germany, 10", EX/NM 1,000.00
Kewpie, bsk, jtd shoulders, Germany, 4½", EX/NM....................130.00
Kewpie, bsk, jtd shoulders, Germany, 5¼", EX 275.00
Kewpie, bsk, jtd shoulders, Germany, 7".....................................350.00
Kewpie, bsk, jtd shoulders, Germany, 8½", EX/NM....................400.00
Kewpie, bsk, jtd shoulders, Germany, 10", EX/NM 625.00
Kewpie, bsk, jtd shoulders, Happy New Year on gr ribbon, Germany, 6"..195.00
Kewpie, bsk, jtd shoulders, hips & knees, Germany, 12" 1,550.00
Kewpie, bsk, jtd shoulders, molded clothing, Germany, 6", EX/NM ...330.00
Kewpie, bsk, jtd shoulders, molded clothing, Germany, 8", EX/NM ...375.00
Kewpie, bsk, Mayor, seated in gr wicker chair, Germany, 4½", EX/NM....950.00
Kewpie, bsk, nude holding drawstring bag, #4882, 4½" 1,195.00
Kewpie, bsk, Prussian Soldier, 1913, 5" 1,450.00
Kewpie, bsk, seated w/chick, Germany, 2", EX/NM.....................600.00
Kewpie, bsk, seated w/fly on toe, sgn, 3½" 725.00
Kewpie, bsk, Soldier, bursting from egg, Germany, rare, 4", VG ..6,500.00
Kewpie, bsk, Soldier w/helmet, Germany, 4½", EX/NM 550.00
Kewpie, bsk, stands in front of bl box while sweeping, rpr, 5½" .550.00
Kewpie, bsk, Thinker, Germany, 4-5", EX/NM, ea 275.00
Kewpie, bsk, Traveler, w/umbrella & bag, 1920s, mk, 3½" 220.00
Kewpie, bsk shoulder head, cloth/stockinette body, 7", NM 565.00
Kewpie, celluloid, jtd arms, heart label, 8" 50.00
Kewpie, celluloid, jtd arms, heart label on chest, 12" 275.00
Kewpie, cloth, Richard Krueger Cuddle Kewpie, w/tag, 12"........325.00
Kewpie, compo, jtd body, bl wings, 11", EX/NM 375.00
Kewpie, compo, jtd shoulders, Jesco, 1966, 24", EXIB.................295.00
Kewpie, compo, jtd shoulders, Perky heart label, Cameo, 11".....465.00

Kewpie, compo, jtd shoulders, rnd bl base, 13" 325.00
Kewpie, compo, jtd shoulders, wht dress w/bl trim, Cameo, 12" .365.00
Kewpie, hard plastic, sleep eyes, 5-pc body w/starfish hands, 14", NM ..300.00
Kewpie, soap figure w/cotton batting, RO Wilson, 1917, 4", NM...110.00
Kewpie, soft rubber, Cameo, sgn, 9½" 45.00
Kewpie Doodle Dog, bsk, Germany, 3", EX/NM.......................1,350.00
Lamp, Kewpie (4½") on lamppost, mk, 8" 575.00
Magazine ad, Kewpie Garter Belts, 1915, 10x14½", VG+ 35.00
Magazine article, Kewpies & The Little Mermaid, 3-pg, 8½x11", VG......45.00
Newspaper comic, Tom, Dick & Harry Meet the Kewpies, full-pg, 1918..40.00
Plate, Happy Days Are Here Again, features band, gold trim, 8¼" 25.00
Plate, Kewpies on bl & gr, © on bk, Royal Rudolstadt, 7" dia........75.00
Teapot, angel Kewpies, +cr/sug & 6 c/s, Germany, pot: 5¼", 17 pcs .1,265.00

Onion Pattern

The familiar pattern known to collectors as Onion acquired its name through a case of mistaken identity. Designed in the early 1700s by Johann Haroldt of the Meissen factory in Germany, the pattern was a mixture of earlier Oriental designs. One of its components was a stylized peach, which was mistaken for an onion; as a result, the pattern became known by that name. Usually found in blue, an occasional piece may also be found in pink and red. The pattern is commonly associated with Meissen, but it has been reproduced by many others including Villeroy and Boch and Royal Copenhagen.

Many marks have been used, some of them fraudulent Meissen marks. Study a marks book to become more familiar with them. In our listings, 'Xd swords' indicates first-quality old Meissen ware. Meissen in an oval over a star was a mark of C. Teichert Stove and Porcelain Factory of Meissen; it was used from 1882 until about 1930. Items marked simply Meissen were produced by the State's Porcelain Manufactory VEB after 1972. The crossed swords indication was sometimes added. Today's market abounds with quality reproductions.

Blue Danube is a modern line of Onion-patterned dinnerware produced in Japan and distributed by Lipper International of Wallingford, Connecticut. At least one hundred items are available in porcelain; it is sold in most large stores with china departments.

Bell, shaped hdl, Meissen, #16, 4x3" dia 180.00
Biscuit jar, lg ornate hdls, ped ft, Vienna Woods, 7" 60.00
Bowl, berry; Xd swords, ca 1870, 1½x4½" 100.00
Bowl, rim soup; Xd swords, ca 1870s, 9" 145.00
Bowl, scalloped edge, Blue Danube, Japan, oval, 10" 45.00
Bowl, serving; sq, Meissen, 1¼x8" 135.00
Bowl, serving; triangular, scalloped rim, Meissen, 1¼x8¾".........170.00
Bowl, serving; Xd swords, 7¾" 165.00
Bowl, vegetable; oval, Meissen Xd swords, 6¾x10" 215.00
Bowl, vegetable; twisted finial, gold trim, Meissen, 11½" 160.00
Cache pot, gold borders, Xd swords, 1890s, 5½".........................245.00
Cake stand, Meissen, 4x10½" 290.00
Casserole, Blue Danube, Japan, 8x10½" 65.00
Chamber stick, Old Fashioned, Blue Danube, 4x6" dia, pr............50.00
Cheese dish, Meissen, ca 1900, 7x9" 175.00
Chop plate, Blue Danube, 12" dia...40.00
Compote, rtcl basket-form, swirl ped, Meissen, #19, 4½x7"........400.00
Creamer, restaurant ware, Cauldon Ltd/Albert Pick & Co, 2⅝"...65.00
Cruet set, Blue Danube (old banner mk), corks under lid, 8", pr ..90.00
Cup & saucer, tea; twisted hdl, scalloped edges, Meissen 120.00
Dresser set, pink w/HP porc medallion w/enamel decor, gold trim, 4-pc ..700.00
Egg cup, dbl, Blue Danube, 3¾"..15.00
Jar, tea; w/lid, 7½x3¼" dia 110.00
Lamps, Xd swords, 1870s, electrified, 12½x7", pr 545.00
Leaf nappy, 1-hdl, Xd swords/Germany, 7½"................................85.00

Masher, trn wood hdl, Meissen, 2¼x2½" head w/9" hdl 115.00
Pitcher, long spout, scalloped rim, #35, 6½" 110.00
Plate, dinner; scalloped edge, Blue Danube, Japan, 10⅜" 20.00
Plate, rtcl rim, med bl, Xd swords, 8" 165.00
Plate, salad; scalloped edge, Blue Danube, Japan, 8⅞" 15.00
Platter, Blue Danube, Japan, 14x10", from $60 to........................65.00
Platter, oval, Meissen, 16½x12"..100.00
Platter, oval, scalloped edge, Blue Danube, Japan, 12½" 50.00
Platter, oval, scalloped edge, Meissen w/star, 9¼x14".................190.00
Platter, Xd swords, 13¾" 275.00
Rolling pin, Meissen, 6"+4" hdls 180.00

Rolling pin, wooden handles, 15", EX, $165.00.

Salt box, wooden lid, Salt in blk script, Germany, 6¼x6½" 275.00
Skimmer, 14" L..165.00
Spoon, long wood hdl, 15x2½" 145.00
Stein, Blue Danube, Japan, scalloped rim, 5½" 70.00
Sugar bowl, rosebud finial, unmk Meissen, 2¾x2¼" 235.00
Sugar shaker, slim baluster, unmk (pattern under base), 5" 325.00
Teapot, Blue Danube, Japan, 7x10" 60.00
Teapot, rose finial, Meissen, 19th C, 5½x9¼" 180.00
Tray, bread; Xd swords, 16x11" 175.00
Tray, pierced hdls, rectangular, Blue Danube, Japan, 7x14½", MIB....75.00
Trivet, scalloped edge, Blue Danube, Japan, 6" 20.00
Tureen, shell hdls, dome lid, 1900, 10½" H 665.00
Urn, uptrn hdls, Meissen, 9x6½" dia...180.00

Opalescent Glass

First made in England in 1870, opalescent glass became popular in America around the turn of the century. Its name comes from the milky-white opalescent trim that defines the lines of the pattern. It was produced in table sets, novelties, toothpick holders, vases, and lamps. Note that American-made sugar bowls have lids; sugar bowls of British origin are considered to be complete without lids. For further information we recommend *The Standard Encyclopedia of Opalescent Glass, Fourth Edition*, by Bill Edwards and Mike Carwile (Collector Books).

Acorn Burrs (& Bark), bowl, master; wht 65.00
Acorn Burrs (& Bark), bowl, sauce; wht 45.00
Alaska, sugar bowl, vaseline or canary, w/lid...............................175.00
Argonaut Shell (Nautilus), tumbler, bl 125.00
Beaded Cable, rose bowl, gr, ftd..50.00
Beaded Fan, bowl, gr, ftd 45.00
Beaded Moon & Stars, compote, wht...60.00
Beaded Ovals in Sand, pitcher, bl..425.00
Beaded Stars & Swag, plate, wht 60.00
Beatty Honeycomb, celery vase, wht 70.00
Beatty Rib, sugar shaker, bl 125.00
Beatty Swirl, creamer, wht 60.00
Beaumont Stripe, pitcher, vaseline or canary...............................350.00
Blown Twist, tumbler, cranberry 150.00
Bubble Lattice, sugar bowl, gr 100.00
Cherry, compote, bl, open 90.00
Chrysanthemum Base Swirl, butter dish, wht 200.00
Chrysanthemum Base Swirl, toothpick holder, cranberry.............300.00

Circled Scroll, creamer, gr...95.00
Coinspot, sugar shaker, rubena..265.00
Consolidated Crisscross, celery vase, wht 150.00
Coral Reef, finger bowl, wht 65.00
Daffodils, pitcher, gr..450.00
Daffodils, pitcher, vaseline or canary..500.00
Daisy & Fern, bowl, master; cranberry 250.00
Diamond & Oval Thumbprint, vase, bl..40.00
Diamond Spearhead, butter dish, gr, w/lid...................................250.00
Diamond Spearhead, compote, gr, tall..400.00
Diamond Spearhead, cup & saucer, vaseline or canary..................150.00
Dolly Madison, plate, gr, scarce; 6" 75.00
Double Greek Key, pickle tray, bl 150.00
Duchess, bowl, master; wht 65.00
Duchess, toothpick holder, bl...250.00
Everglades, compote, jelly; vaseline or canary 95.00
Fan, spooner, gr...110.00
Feathers, whimsey nut bowl, bl, rare..150.00
Fern, finger bowl, cranberry 100.00
Flora, tumbler, wht 65.00
Fluted Scrolls (Klondyke), butter dish, vaseline or canary 175.00
Fluted Scrolls (Klondyke), cruet, vaseline or canary...................185.00
Gonderman (Adonis) Swirl, sugar bowl, amber.............................125.00
Greek Key & Ribs, bowl, wht 35.00
Hobnail & Panelled Thumbprint, creamer, bl.................................85.00
Hobnail & Panelled Thumbprint, pitcher, bl.................................300.00
Hobnail in Square (Vesta), tumbler, wht 50.00
Honeycomb & Clover, sugar bowl, gr..110.00
Inside Ribbing, tray, bl 55.00
Inverted Fan & Feather, creamer, bl...145.00
Inverted Fan & Feather, rose bowl, gr 95.00
Jackson, powder jar, vaseline or cranberry 70.00
Jefferson Shield, vase, bl, variant, rare...125.00
Jewel & Flower, novelty bowl, bl 40.00
Jewelled Heart, tray, wht...200.00
Lady Caroline, basket, bl...60.00
Laura (Single Flower Framed), plate, wht, ruffled, rare.................60.00
Leaf & Beads, rose bowl, gr..45.00
Leaf Mold, butter dish, cranberry..425.00
Linking Rings, bowl, vaseline or cranberry....................................65.00
Lustre Flute, pitcher, bl...400.00
Mary Ann, vase, wht, rare..100.00
Meander, bowl, bl 40.00
Northern Star, banana bowl, gr..70.00
Old Man Winter, basket, gr, sm..100.00
Opal Open (Beaded Panels), rose bowl novelty, gr 60.00
Over-All Hob, bowl, master; vaseline or canary..............................70.00
Palisades (Lined Lattice), novelty bowl, gr....................................50.00
Palm Beach, bowl, master; bl 85.00
Panelled Holly, bowl, sauce; bl 75.00
Panelled Holly, pitcher, wht...600.00
Peacock Tail, tumbler, bl, rare..100.00
Piasa Bird, rose bowl, wht..75.00
Picket, planter, bl...75.00
Polka Dot, pitcher, cranberry, rare 350.00
Polka Dot, pitcher, wht, rare..150.00
Prince William, pitcher, vaseline or canary..................................125.00
Princess Diana, compote, bl, metal base.......................................150.00
Pussy Willow, vase, vaseline or canary, 4½" 70.00
Quilted Pillow Sham, creamer, bl 75.00
Reverse Drapery, bowl, bl..45.00
Reverse Swirl, bowl, sauce; bl 25.00
Reverse Swirl, custard cup, cranberry 150.00
Ribbed Lattice, creamer, wht...65.00

Ribbed Lattice, spooner, bl...75.00
Ribbed Spiral, cup & saucer, vaseline or canary 100.00
Ribbed Spiral, vase, funeral; 15-22", wht, ea................................90.00
Ripple, vase, wht..75.00
Rococo, plate, bl, rare, 10"..400.00
Rose (aka Rose & Ruffles), tray, dresser; bl.................................100.00
Roulette, plate, gr..100.00
Ruffles & Rings w/Daisy Band, bowl, gr, ftd..................................40.00
Scroll w/Acanthus, bowl, master; vaseline or canary 50.00
Seafoam, compote, bl..275.00
Seaweed, creamer, cranberry..225.00
Seaweed, rose bowl, wht..95.00
Shell Beaded, pitcher, gr...750.00
Shell Beaded, sugar bowl, wht..135.00
Sir Lancelot, bowl, bl, ftd...45.00
Somerset, bowl, oval, bl, 9"...45.00
Spanish Lace, finger bowl, bl..75.00
Speckled Stripe, barber bottle, wht..200.00
Spokes & Wheels, bowl, gr...50.00
Stars & Stripes, pitcher, wht...250.00
Stripe, tumbler, bl...55.00
Stripe, Wide; pitcher, cranberry...450.00
Sunburst on Shield (Diadem), creamer, vaseline or canary.........145.00
Swag w/Brackets, bowl, wht..30.00

Swag with Brackets, pitcher, white, $135.00; tumbler, white, $30.00.

Swag w/Brackets, tumbler, bl..60.00
Swastika, pitcher, cranberry...1,100.00
Swastika, syrup, wht...350.00
Swirl, cheese dish, wht..150.00
Swirl, shot glass, bl..80.00
Thousand Eye, celery vase, wht 65.00
Thousand Eye, sugar bowl, wht..75.00
Tiny Tears, vase, bl..50.00
Tokyo, tumbler, bl..95.00
Tree of Life, shakers, bl, pr...200.00
Tree of Love, compote, wht...55.00
Twig, vase, bl, panelled, 7"..65.00
Venetian (Spider Web), vase, bl...85.00
Vintage Leaf, bowl, bl, rare...175.00
Waterlily & Cattails, bonbon, amethyst..65.00
Waterlily & Cattails, relish, bl, hdld..65.00
Wheel & Block, novelty plate, bl..45.00
White Chapel, creamer, vaseline or canary 30.00
Wild Bouquet, compote, jelly; bl..175.00
William & Mary, butter dish, vaseline or canary 190.00
Windows (Swirled), bowl, sauce; wht...30.00
Windows (Swirled), sugar shaker, bl...150.00
Wreath & Shell, butter dish, vaseline or canary 225.00
Wreath & Shell, ivy ball, bl, rare...135.00
Wreathed Grape & Cable (carnival), orange bowl, wht, ftd, rare....350.00

Opaline

A type of semiopaque opal glass, opaline was made in white as well as pastel shades and is often enameled. It is similar in appearance to English bristol glass, though its enamel or gilt decorative devices tend to exhibit a French influence.

Bottle, dresser; appl cameo portrait w/gold, ca 1880, 8" 100.00
Compote, shallow bowl, gold scrolls in relief, 1870s, 10x8"........115.00
Pitcher, HP floral, cobalt hdl, ca 1900, 8½", +3 matching cups .525.00

Optical Items

Collectors of Americana are beginning to appreciate the charm of antique optical items, and those involved in the related trade find them particularly fascinating. Anyone, however, can appreciate the evolution of technology apparent when viewing a collection of old eye wear and at the same time admire the primitive ingenuity involved in their construction.

Magnifying glass, brass w/ivory trn hdl, ca 1900, 7" dia, 16" 100.00
Magnifying glass, silver w/ivory hdl, Asprey & Co, 1930s, 13"...635.00
Opera glass, bronze & MOP, Carl Mayer, Austin TX, 1890-1900...175.00
Opera glasses, Aubrey Hammond, blk enamel & morocco, ca 1900, EX .100.00
Opera glasses, fr enameling on cobalt, gold metal, 2¾".............585.00
Opera glasses, Lemaire Paris, gilt-bronze & MOP, EX in leather case ..300.00
Opera glasses, MOP w/pk tinge, brass fittings, Iris Paris, 8½" 275.00
Spectacles, folding, silver fr w/sliding ear pcs, hall mk 100.00
Spectacles, Pince Nez, gutta percha fr, cobalt lenses.....................25.00
Spectacles, slightly wing shaped w/rhinestones, Fr, 1940s 75.00

Orientalia

The art of the Orient is an area of collecting currently enjoying strong collector interest, not only in those examples that are truly 'antique' but in the twentieth-century items as well. Because of the many aspects involved in a study of Orientalia, we can only try through brief comments to acquaint the reader with some of the more readily available examples. We suggest you refer to specialized reference sources for more detailed information. See also specific categories.

Key:
Ch — Chinese	hdwd — hardwood
cvg — carving	Jp — Japan
drw — drawer	Ko — Korean
Dy — Dynasty	lcq — lacquer
E — export	mdl — medallion
FR — Famille Rose	rswd — rosewood
FV — Famille Verte	tkwd — teakwood
gb — guard border	

Bronze

Bell, Western Zhou Dy, 33x23"..480.00
Bird on perch, dragon wrapped around pole, ca 1875, 31x19".5,500.00
Buddha, gilded, Sino-Tibetan style, ca 1900, 18" 1,650.00
Buddha in royal attire, Thailand, 1825, 32".............................3,850.00
Chinese warrior on horse, inset jewels, Guan Yu, 18th C, 10" 2,000.00
Gong, appl gilt Ch characters, on blk lcq stand, ca 1800, 43x26x10" ..285.00
Mongolian horseman, gr patina, 12x19" on wood base 400.00
Syamatara, gilt & silver details, EX patina, 18th C, 8½" 750.00
Teapot, 3 Men of Good Omen, ca 1822, 5¼x4"...........................300.00

Vase, avian decor in relief, patinated, Jp, 1880-90, 12x8½" 200.00
Vase, emb dragons in rings around body, 6" 265.00
Vessel, floral decor & Chinese characters, ca 1900, 2¾x4" 115.00

Furniture

Bench, tkwd, cvd scroll ft/appl openwork details, cushion top, 20x45" ..715.00
Cabinet, blk lcq panel doors w/4 immortals, Jp, 1920s, 27x15x7" 400.00
Cabinet, display; cvd & parcel gilt hdwd, Ch, 33½" 350.00
Chair, side; cvd tkwd w/dragons/leaves, Ch, 19th C, 38", pr.......300.00
Cupboard, fitted int, 2 insert panel doors, pnt finish, Ch, 72x38" ..220.00
Cupboard, pine w/clear lcq/blk pnt designs, South Ch, 2-pc, 72" ..880.00
Cupboard, wedding; openwork w/dragons, 2-door, old red rpt, Ch, 75x55" 700.00
Desk, hdwd, cvd/lcq dragon, ivory/soapstone mts, 19th C, 57x42x28" ..2,000.00
Desk, mixed dk woods, scale & dragons' heads w/wings cvgs, 4-drw, 69" ...1,400.00
Etagere, E, lcq & polychrome, Ch, late 1800s, 58x26" 4,600.00
Hassock, lcq wooden bbl form w/brass filigree, 1920s, 17x15" dia.80.00
Screen, moriage & gold leaf, 2-panel, Jp, ca 1800, 64x62" 1,495.00
Screen, table; cvd ivory flowers/rockwork/cranes, 19th C 575.00
Stand, cvd tkwd, marble top w/floral cvg, Ch, late 1800s, 33x17" dia...285.00
Stand, fern; blk lcq, cvd/pnt florals, People's Republic of Ch, 36".....85.00
Table, alter; elm, high legs, scroll returns, Ch, 1850s, rfn, 33x77"....467.50
Table, blk lcq, pierced aprons, rnd legs, Hebi Province, 1850s, 34x38" .165.00
Table, dk lcq, geometric openwork aprons, mortised, Ch, 32x39x27" ...220.00
Table, E, japanned & gilt decor, Ch, 19th C, 18x36x24".........1,495.00
Table, hardwood plank on table-form supports, Ch, 19th C, 35x76x16"...1,500.00
Table, tkwd w/2 cloisonne medallions, Ch, 16x44x16" 195.00
Vitrine, cvd hdwd w/lcq, early 1900s, 34x20x3" 920.00
Wall bracket, mahog, 3-tier w/gilt lcq & inlay, Meiji, 31x18".....200.00

Hardstones

Crystal, Goddess of Mercy, Kuan Yen Dy, 8" 85.00
Jade, cvd hand, moss-embedded-in-melting-snow color, 8" 150.00
Jade, photo fr, dk gr, 13x10½" 230.00
Lapis Lazuli, eagle & eaglet, Ch, 1950s, 9x8" 1,200.00
Lapis Lazuli, Gama Sennin figure w/toad, 4⅜" 485.00
Nephrite jade, pendant, gray-gr mottle, Chimera, Song Dy, 2"...750.00
Rose quartz, lady w/young girl carrying her train, 8¾", +wood base ..110.00
Rose quartz, 2 women, 9½", on cvd wood base 95.00

Lacquer

Lacquerware is found in several colors, but the one most likely to be encountered is cinnabar. It is often intricately carved, sometimes involving hundreds of layers built one at a time on a metal or wooden base. Later pieces remain red, while older examples tend to darken.

Box, gilt scrolling leafy vines on black, Japan, nineteenth century, 11½" diameter, $715.00.

Box, cricket; cvd dragon & clouds, red on ebonized base, ftd, 21x10"...350.00
Box, jewelry, blk w/HP decor, Jp, 4½x8½x6" 75.00
Box, people/verandas, gilt on blk, scallop sides, brass paw ft, 12" L .950.00
Box, red w/acorns & leaves on wood, 1920-40s, 3x7" dia.............50.00
Box, travel, red lcq w/dragons/pearls/etc, 18th C, 19x15x12"+stand..1,725.00

Tray, blk w/MOP inlay, 13½x9" 40.00
Water bucket, lcq on metal, Jp, ca 1945-53, 9x3"......................200.00

Netsukes

A netsuke is a miniature Japanese carving made with two holes called the Himitoshi, either channeled or within the carved design. As kimonos (the outer garment of the time) had no pockets, the Japanese man hung his pipe, tobacco pouch, or other daily necessities from his waist sash. The most highly valued accessory was a nest of little drawers called an Inro, in which they carried snuff or sometimes opium. The netsuke was the toggle that secured them. Although most are of ivory, others were made of bone, wood, metal, porcelain, or semiprecious stones. Some were inlaid or lacquered. They are found in many forms — figurals the most common, mythological beasts the most desirable. They range in size from 1" up to 3", which was the maximum size allowed by law. Many netsukes represented the owner's profession, religion, or hobbies. Scenes from the daily life of Japan at that time were often depicted in the tiny carvings. The more detailed the carving, the greater the value.

Careful study is required to recognize the quality of the netsuke. Many have been made in Hong Kong in recent years; and even though some are very well carved, these are considered copies and avoided by the serious collector. There are many books that will help you learn to recognize quality netsukes, and most reputable dealers are glad to assist you. Use your magnifying glass to check for repairs. In the listings that follow, netsukes are ivory unless noted otherwise; 'stain' indicates a color wash.

Boy w/puppy, Sairin, late 18th C, 3" 425.00
Bug on leaf, walrus ivory, Meiji, 2½" 225.00
Daruma stretching, mammoth ivory, ca 1920, 2" 250.00
Elephant, 2-pcs joined w/ivory pin, Mizan, Meiji 300.00
Guanyin, dk orange amber, Meiji, 2" 200.00
Horse, color eng, EX details..220.00
Horse, recumbent, ivory nut, Gyokusui, Meiji, 2x½" 225.00
Man & monkey w/jug, color eng, EX detail 220.00
Monkey w/long arms, inlaid shell eyes, Kimehiro, EX patina, lg ..650.00
Musician, EX detail, sgn, 2" 245.00
Octopus w/human face & woman, wood, Shusei, ca 1950, 2".....150.00
Ox, ivory nut w/shell inlay, Meiji, 1½" 155.00
Ram sleeping, amber, Meiji, 1¼" 150.00
Rat on bale, shell inlay, Hiroaki, late 20th C, 1½" 550.00
Sage on horse, ivory, stained 330.00
Sennin & frog, mc stain, Shiro, ca 1900, 2¼" 250.00
Skull w/lizard at top, ivory nut, Meiji, late 19th C, 1½" 250.00
Snails on rock, blk coral, Meiji, 1¾" 200.00
Traveling medicine men, boxwood, sm rpr, Meiji, 2½" 225.00

Porcelain

Chinese export ware was designed to appeal to Western tastes and was often made to order. During the eighteenth century, vast amounts were shipped to Europe and on westward. Much of this fine porcelain consisted of dinnerware lines that were given specific pattern names. Rose Mandarin, Fitzhugh, Armorial, Rose Medallion, and Canton are but a few of the more familiar.

Basin, E, mandarin figures in garden, bl fans, 19th C, 5x16" 750.00
Bowl, E, Armorial, garland border, Ch, 18th C, 9" 100.00
Bowl, E, FR, mandarin reserves, 19th C, 4½x10" 350.00
Bowl, E, FR border on celadon, int: 2 people reading, 12" 325.00
Bowl, E, FV, rock garden/butterflies, Kangxi (1662-1722), 14", EX 365.00
Bowl, punch; Arms of Jongkers, 4 monograms in reserves, 18th C, 16" ..2,875.00
Bowl, punch; E, florals/medallions w/gold & cobalt, late 1700s, rstr.....1,035.00

Bowl, punch; E, mandarin figures in landscape, 1810-20, 10½" ..1,035.00
Box, brush; E, butterflies & flowers w/gold, Ch, 19th C, 7" 635.00
Cache pot & undertray, Rose Canton, hexagonal, Ch, 19th C, 7¼x11" 700.00
Cane stand, E, Hundred Antiques, Ch, 19th C, 24½x9½", pr..3,735.00
Cup & saucer, E, Armorial, Arms of Bishop Impaling Campbell, 18th C...515.00
Ginger jar, E, FV, calligraphy on reverse, 19th C, 14" 165.00
Jardiniere & stand, E, FR, mandarin scenes, carp inside, 24x16"...300.00
Lamp base, E, Hundred Butterflies, cvd ivory elephant finial, 26¾"..460.00
Mantel garniture, FV, 2 vases+2 covered jars w/foo dog finials...2,500.00
Mug, E, 3 people vignettes, sm rpr, 4¾x4" 550.00
Plate, E, garden view w/figures beyond/gold flower border, 14", pr, NM...1,725.00
Plate, E, FR, 8-sided, spearhead border, late 1700s, 9½", pr 295.00
Plate, E, Red Bird & Sacred Flower, Ch, 19th C, 9⅝", 12 for .1,600.00
Plate, E, shield & flowers, vining band w/cobalt, Ch, 1790s, 9¾"..150.00
Plate, Rose Canton, lt wear, 8", 9 for 525.00
Platter, E, Armorial, bl/iron-red/gold shield, 1890s, 15¾"...........460.00
Platter, E, Fitzhugh, 19th C, 16" 750.00
Platter, E, 3 fisherman & lady, scalloped, 19th C, 13½", EX.......250.00
Platter & drainer, E, Red Bird & Sacred Flower, 19th C, 16¾"..920.00
Tureen, Blue Fitzhugh, flower finial, entwined hdls, 11x14"....2,650.00
Tureen, E, floral sprays w/gold insects, w/lid, Ch, 18th C, 7x11"..1,100.00
Tureen, E, Red Bird & Sacred Flower, w/lid & tray, 12x14⅝".2,645.00
Tureen, sauce; Blue Fitzhugh, flower finial, entwined hdls, Ch, 6x8"..925.00
Tureen, sauce; E, butterfly & flowers w/gold, 19th C, w/lid & tray.......375.00
Vase, E, FR, scrolled gilt hdls, 19th C, 24", NM..........................650.00
Vase, peacock bl crackle w/mythical beasts, Ching Dy, 29x7".....700.00

Pottery

Basin, interlacing peony sprays in bl underglaze, Qing-Guan Xu .5,000.00
Bottle, sake; blk, no decor, teardrop shape, 1800s, 13" 150.00
Ginger jar, 5-cloud, ovoid base, Qing..2,400.00
Jar, granary; gr glazed, bear ft, integral lid, Han Dy, 12" 600.00
Model, entertainer dancing/holding tambourine, Sichuan, 17¼" ..2,550.00
Model, horse, std legless 2-part form, Han Dy, 17¾" 725.00
Vase, lt gr w/mc flowers, att Chien Lung (1736-1795), 7"...........245.00

Rugs

The 'Oriental' or Eastern rug market has enjoyed a renewal of interest as collectors have become aware of the fact that some of the semi-antique rugs (those sixty to one hundred years old) may be had at a price within the range of the average buyer.

Aamadan, dk bl border/ground, red/ivory design, 2nd border, 40x70", VG ..330.00
Afghan prayer, red w/multiple borders & design in tan/blk/ivory, 46x31".165.00
Afghanistan, abrash yel/orange w/bl overall design, lt wear, 53x60"...275.00
Afshar, stepped mdl, flower vase pendants on dk bl, ca 1930, 76x57"....400.00
Baluch prayer, tree of life design, mc on camel, ca 1870s, 52x32".......230.00
Bijar, mdls, navy/brick/gr on brick, floral/linear gb, 57x75" 1,035.00
Bijar, stepped dmns/overall floral on brick/bl/cream, 120x180" ...6,670.00
Bijar, trees & flowers on red, meandering red/bl border, 48x82".1,500.00
Caucasian, multiple borders w/ivory primary border on rust, 73x58"..575.00
Feraghan, Herati motif on melon/cream, navy central ground, 115x160" .3,200.00
Genji, ivory/bl/gr borders, mc diagonal stripes, rpr, 38x157"....1,200.00
Hamadan, figural, multiple rust/ivory borders on dk bl, 46x76"..400.00
Heriz, dk bl border, ivory spandrels on dk salmon, 110x134", EX .4,950.00
Heriz, floral on brick, floral on bl border, many colors, 115x140" .3,200.00
Heriz, geometrics, mc on red, mdls in border, 135x100" 1,150.00
Heriz, geometrics in red/bl/ivory/camel, 118x82" 2,500.00
Heriz, gray/blk border, ivory spandrels on lt red, 144x100" 1,265.00
Heriz, lg mdl, rose/bl on rust, ivory borders, wear, 140x200"....7,150.00
Heriz, midnight bl border, salmon spandrels on dk red, 118x144"..1,980.00
Iranian Kashan, floral on burgundy, orange & bl borders, 113x154"...990.00

Karabaugh, ivory border and red-dish ground, light wear and border loss, 105x47", $2,145.00.

Karaja, dk bl border on dk red, lt wear, 100x144" 1,980.00
Kashan, wine w/ivory & bl spandrels, multiple borders, 120x96" .1,000.00
Kazak, keyhole mdl inset w/3 octagons, mc on red, late 1800s, 60x41" ..375.00
Kazak, red w/bl & salmon spandrels, med bl border, 63x65" 495.00
Meshed, pk-red w/dk bl petal spandrels, med bl border, 120x75"..440.00
NW Persia, 6 concentric dmns, mc on blk, 1900s, 134x38"........975.00
Persian, floral, bl/rust/ivory/gr, 10x193" 1,200.00
Quash Quai Shiraz saddle bag, midnight bl w/camel border, 16x18"...470.00
Russian, Kazak, abrash red ground, dk ivory border, 49x73"........250.00
Sarouk, burgundy w/dk bl border, 50x30" 275.00
Sarouk, med bl & camel borders on lt burgundy, 125x135" 4,400.00
Sarouk, midnight bl border on lt burgundy, 49x75"..................1,150.00
Sarouk, red mottled ground w/midnight bl border, 108x144", EX+ ..1,100.00
Senneh, orange w/bl & lt bl spandrels, rewoven ends, 40x58"....275.00
Serapi, sage gr w/dk salmon border & spandrels, 100x120" 330.00
Shiraz, bl spandrels & red grd, ivory border, 62x88" 250.00
Shiraz, geometrics in camel/brn/red/bl, 144x100" 3,750.00
Shirvan prayer, flower lattice, mc on brn, red border, 1890s, 54x41" ...800.00
Tabriz, burgundy w/tan & lt gr spandrels, bl border, 120x94"......440.00
Tabriz, geometrics & florals, red/bl/ivory/camel, att, 144x110" .4,250.00
Tabriz prayer, ivory border, lt bl spandrels & pk-red ground, 24x30"...200.00
Turkoman, 3 columns of 10 guls in mc on rust-red, mid-1900s, 102x66"...635.00

Silver

Hoaching, Canton; cup, dragon hdls, emb floral, late 1800s, 8½" 2,400.00
Hung Chong, tazza, emb bamboo, emb figures/dragons, ca 1900, 6½x8"..460.00
Kaishu script mks, box, chased/emb army scene, late 1800s, 6¾" dia 1,265.00
Kaishu script mks, center bowl, scroll hdls, Ch, 19th C, 7⅛" 865.00
Kaishu script mks, sauce boat, appl mums, late 1800s, 9⅛".........700.00
Kwong Man Shing, tea set, bamboo form w/insects, late 1800s, 3-pc..1,000.00
MK, Canton; rose water bottle, bird dropper, late 19th C, 12¼".315.00
Sunshing, Hong Kong; compote, egret supports, 1860-90, 9¾"..4,300.00
Tuck Chang, epergne, central trumpet, dragon/flower panels, 1900s, 12"..1,150.00
Wang Hing, basket, rtcl flowers, bamboo swing hdl, ca 1900, 10½"...350.00
Wang Hing, bowl, emb/rtcl dragons & clouds, 1900, 8½" 1,100.00
Wang Hing, compote, eng/rtcl prunts, 3-part stem, ca 1900, 7" ..1,100.00
Wang Hing, teapot, dragon head finial, emb battle, ca 1900, 6".700.00
YCCo, Ch; candlesticks, appl dragons, presentation, 1934, 8¼", pr...1,380.00

Orrefors

Orrefors Glassworks was founded in 1898 in the Swedish province of Smaaland. Utilizing the expertise of designers such as Simon Gate, Edward Hald, Vicke Lindstrand, and Edwin Ohrstrom, it produced art glass of the highest quality. Various techniques were used in achieving the decoration. Some were wheel engraved; others were blown through a unique process that formed controlled bubbles or air pockets resulting in unusual patterns and shapes. Our advisor for this category is Abby Malowanczyk; she is listed in the Directory under Texas.

Bottle, scent; starfish/seaweed, amethyst in clear, Hald #214, 6"....**2,100.00**
Bowl, Ariel, trapped bubbles, gr/clear, 583 E Ohrstrom, 4½x9½"..**1,000.00**
Bowl, Graal, aquatic scene, E Hald, 534D, 2¼x7⅝" **800.00**
Bowl, Selena, moonstone opal blown crystal, Palmquist, 2½" H...**300.00**
Bowl vase, bl to gr w/bubbles & bl lines, Palmquist, 6½" dia......**350.00**
Goblet, Pop Glass, 5-color spiral stem on wht ft, Cyren, 1967, 8"..**700.00**
Tray, Kraka, yel/steel-bl crystal w/bubbles, Palmquist #484 ....**325.00**
Vase, apple w/'stem' neck, apple gr, Lundin, 1957, D32-57, 15"..**2,875.00**
Vase, Ariel, guitarist/gondola/lady/flowers, Ohrstrom NR 389A, 6⅜".**3,300.00**
Vase, Ariel, int bl discs/bubbles, heavy sq form, Lundin, 1960, 4½"....**2,200.00**
Vase, clear apple form, mk Expo DU 32-57, Ingevorg Lundin, 14½" **950.00**
Vase, clear w/bubbles & bl lines, Palmquist, 4½"........................**325.00**
Vase, eng nude male diver, Lindstrand, 1934, 10½" **2,000.00**
Vase, eng semi-nude dancer, Lindstrand design, cut by Tydh, 1937, 9".**1,500.00**
Vase, Graal, horses, purple on yel to orange & blk, Johansson, 7x7" **4,750.00**
Vase, Graal, int gr fish/seaweed, Hald, heavy facet-cut body, 7", NM **600.00**
Vase, Kraka, int bl veins w/sm bubbles, heavy body, Palmquist, '60, 4"....**350.00**
Vase, Kraka, yel/steel-bl crystal w/bubbles, Palmquist #349, 8½" ..**600.00**

Ott and Brewer

The partnership of Ott and Brewer began in 1865 in Trenton, New Jersey. By 1876 they were making decorated graniteware, parian, and 'ivory porcelain' — similar to Irish belleek though not as fine and of different composition. In 1883, however, experiments toward that end had reached a successful conclusion, and a true belleek body was introduced. It came to be regarded as the finest china ever produced by an American firm. The ware was decorated by various means such as hand painting, transfer printing, gilding, and lustre glazing. The company closed in 1893, one of many that failed during that depression. In the listings below, the ware is belleek unless noted otherwise. Our advisor for this category is Mary Frank Gaston.

Basket, pk flowers w/gold, cactus-shaped hdl w/appl tulips, mk..**1,200.00**
Bowl, Cactus, gold thistles w/in & w/out, mk, 3¼x10½".........**1,100.00**
Bowl, pk lustre int, gold rim, 3½"..**175.00**
Chocolate pot, floral w/gold dragon-shape spout & hdl, mk, 13" .**1,200.00**
Cup & saucer, bouillon; eggshell, pk int w/gilt, 2½", 6" dia........**175.00**
Cup & saucer, ivory w/gold cup w/pk int, 3¼", pk 5⅜" saucer ...**275.00**
Ewer, gold-paste floral, curved rim & hdl, mk, 5¼" **750.00**
Pitcher, irises etc, bamboo spout/neck, cactus hdl, 8" **1,500.00**
Teapot, HP poppies w/gold, bark top & branch hdl, mk, 8½".....**900.00**
Teapot, Tridacna, yel w/gold, wht loop hdl, mk, 4"......................**500.00**
Vase, gold-paste leaves & butterfly, uptrn hdls, 5½" **700.00**

Overbeck

The Overbeck Studio was established in 1911 in Cambridge City, Indiana, by four Overbeck sisters. It survived until the last sister died in 1955. Early wares were often decorated with carved designs of stylized animals, birds, or florals with the designs colored to contrast with the background. Others had tooled designs filled in with various colors for a mosaic effect. After 1937, Mary Frances, the last remaining sister, favored handmade figurines with somewhat bizarre features in fanciful combinations of color. Overbeck ware is signed 'OBK,' frequently with the designer's and potter's initials under the stylized 'OBK.'

Bowl, rust & maize w/gr drip on red clay, 2¾x5⅞" **230.00**
Figurine, dog, standing w/head up, dk brn matt, OBK, 3¾" **300.00**

Figurines, Spanish-looking couple, bls & pks, 4¼", 4¾", EX **400.00**
Figurines, whimsical musicians, 4½", set of 5 ....**2,100.00**

Vase, cut-back and painted birds in three panels, light rose matt and dull green, signed E.H., 5½", **$3,500.00**.
(Photo courtesy Treadway Gallery, Inc.)

Vase, cvd/pnt floral frieze, gr/olive/cream, EF, mfg flaw, 6".......**3,250.00**
Vase, 3 panels w/cut-bk floral rondels, pk/brn on gray to gr, 7½"..**4,750.00**

Overlay Glass

Art glass having layers of more than one type or color of glass is sometimes called overlay or cased glass. Very often glassware of this type has applied decorations such as fruit, flowers, leaves, or ruffles (rigaree), such as is commonly identified with Stevens and Williams. See also Stevens and Williams.

Bowl, pk on wht w/appl 3-color floral/leaves/ft, 5½" H...............**635.00**
Decanter, pk shaded to wht, clear hdl & stopper, 9¼x4" **260.00**
Pitcher, orange to wht shaded, ruffled, clear hdl, 7¼" **175.00**
Rose bowl, bl, HP florals w/gold, 8-crimp, 3½x4¼" **100.00**
Rose bowl, bl, HP morning glories, frosted ft, 5x4½" **145.00**
Tumbler, pk, 4½x2½"...**50.00**
Vase, cream opaque, appl bl plums, amber ft/leaves/hdl, 6".........**145.00**
Vase, peachblow w/appl crystal flower & branch, bulbous, 9" **275.00**
Vase, yel, tomato red int, sq top, 4¼x3½"......................................**70.00**

Overshot

Overshot glass is characterized by the beaded or craggy appearance of its surface. Earlier ware was irregularly textured, while twentieth-century examples tend to be more uniform.

Basket, amberina, amber twist hdl, ruffled, Sandwich, 6½" **150.00**
Bowl, rubena, on wht metal ped ft, 6½x8½" **180.00**
Jug, claret; rubena w/pewter mts, 12", +4 wines w/pewter bases..**475.00**
Pitcher, appl neck ring, twisted hdl, trefoil rim, 13" **275.00**
Pitcher, tankard; cranberry, clear reeded hdl, 9⅜x4½" **175.00**
Pitcher, tankard; rubena, clear hdl, 9½"..**175.00**
Rose bowl, amethyst, icicle ft, 5x4¼"..**185.00**
Rose bowl, rubena, 6x5"...**185.00**
Tumbler, cranberry...**50.00**
Tumbler, lt gr to clear, emb swirl..**35.00**
Tumbler, rubena..**145.00**

Owen, Ben

Ben Owen worked at the Jugtown Pottery of North Carolina from 1923 until it temporarily closed in 1959. He continued in the business in his own Plank Road Pottery, stamping his ware 'Ben Owen, Master Potter,' with many forms made by Lester Fanell Craven in the late 1960s. His pottery closed in 1972. He died in 1983 at the age of 81.

The pottery was reopened in 1981 under the supervision of Benjamin Wade Owen II. One of the principal potters was David Garner who worked there until about 1985. This pottery is still in operation today with Ben II as the main potter.

Jug, Tobacco-Spit Brown, 2 incised lines at shoulder, 4¼" **90.00**
Tile, goose in flight, low relief, mc faience, 11½x17½" **375.00**
Vase, blk-flecked gr gloss, high shoulder w/4 loop hdls, 5" **265.00**
Vase, Chinese Blue curdled w/wht, 7" **235.00**
Vase, Chinese Red on terra cotta, egg form, Ben Owen III 1984, 5¼" ..**185.00**

Owens Pottery

J.B. Owens founded his company in Zanesville, Ohio, in 1891, and until 1907, when the company decided to exert most of its energies in the area of tile production, made several quality lines of art pottery. His first line, Utopian, was a standard brown ware with underglaze slip decoration of nature studies, animals, and portraits. A similar line, Lotus, utilized lighter background colors. Henri Deux, introduced in 1900, featured incised Art Nouveau forms inlaid with color. (Be aware that the Brush McCoy Pottery acquired many of Owens' molds and reproduced a line similar to Henri Deux, which they called Navarre.) Other important lines were Opalesce, Rustic, Feroza, Cyrano, and Mission, examples of which are rare today. The factory burned in 1928, and the company closed shortly thereafter. Values vary according to the quality of the artwork and subject matter. Examples signed by the artist bring higher prices than those that are not signed. For further information we recommend *Owens Pottery Unearthed* by Kristy and Rick McKibben and Jeanette and Marvin Stofft. Mrs. Stofft is listed in the Directory under Indiana.

Experimental, vase, bl/gr/wht flambe on brn, #1110, 10½" **600.00**
Feroza, vase, hammered blk metallic, prof rpr, 7⅞" **300.00**
Lamp base, rose on brn to olive-tan, mk, 9x4" **200.00**
Matt Green, vase, gunmetal/brn texture, 4 vertical emb devices, 9" **650.00**
Matt Green, vase, spherical shoulder on petticoat-shape body, 10½" ..**600.00**
Matt Lotus, vase, floral on crackle, Owensart, #1073, 10¾" **300.00**
Matt Utopian, vase, floral on twisted shape, #124, 13⅞" **425.00**
Matt Utopian, vase, poppies, #S8, 10½x4¼" **350.00**
Matt Utopian, vase, poppies, #0176, 13" **400.00**
Opalesce, vase, poppies w/burnished gold, #1133, 11⅞", NM.....**800.00**
Tile, Little Bo Peep, scene w/verse, in oak fr, 12x12", NM **2,600.00**
Utopian, ewer, silver o/l, 4" **1,800.00**
Utopian, mug, cherries & stems, sgn FL, tankard form, 5¼", 4 for ..**400.00**
Utopian, vase, chrysanthemums, squatty, #1029, 3¾" **150.00**
Utopian, vase, English ivy, H Larzelere, #852, 3", NM................**125.00**
Utopian, vase, gentleman after Rembrandt, #1052, 11¾" **2,200.00**
Utopian, vase, nasturtiums & vines, A Haubrich, 13"................**500.00**
Utopian, vase, simple floral w/ornate silver o/l, 4½" **1,600.00**

Pacific Clay Products

The Pacific Clay Products Company got its start in the 1920s as a consolidation of several smaller southern California potteries. The main Los Angeles plant had been founded in 1890 to make kitchen stoneware, ollas, and similar items. Terra cotta and brick were later produced.

In 1932 Hostess Ware, a vividly colored line of dinnerware, was introduced to compete with Bauer's Ring Ware. Coralitos, a lighter-weight, pastel-hued dinnerware line was first marketed in 1937, and a similar but less expensive line called Arcadia soon followed. Art ware including vases, figurines, candlesticks, etc., was produced from 1932 to 1942, at which time the company went into war-related work and pot-

tery manufacture ceased. A limited amount of hand-decorated dinnerware was also made. For further information we recommend *The Collector's Encyclopedia of California Pottery, 2nd Edition*, by Jack Chipman; he is listed in the Directory under California.

Bowl, red, 9", $25.00. (Photo courtesy Ted Haun)

Bowl, orange, Ring style, 5x11" **85.00**
Cheese server, orange, 15" dia..**95.00**
Coffee carafe, Apache Red, 9½x7½" **95.00**
Coffee carafe, yel, 9½x7½" **95.00**
Goblet, Hostessware, gr **100.00**
Planter, swan, pk, 6", NM **20.00**
Plate, deep orange, 9" **15.00**
Teapot, sapphire, flat base, 6x12"..**125.00**
Tray, Hostessware, 15" **95.00**
Tumbler, tall, matching set of 5 ....**145.00**
Vase, Blended, cobalt/orange/gr/yel on yel clay, 8" **360.00**
Vase, fan; lt bl, 7½x6" **65.00**
Vase, lime gr, emb leaves on stem & ft, hdls, 8x5" **130.00**
Vase, lt pk, 8x5½" **55.00**
Vase, olive gr & turq, stick neck, 8x4" **150.00**

Paden City

Paden City Glass Mfg. Co. was founded in 1916 in Paden City, West Virginia. It made both mold-blown and pressed wares and is most remembered today for its handmade wares in bright colors with fanciful etchings. A great deal of Paden City's business was in supplying decorating companies and fitters with glass; therefore, Paden City never marked their glass with a trademark of any kind, and the company's advertisements were limited to trade publications, rather than retail. In 1948 the management of the company opened a second plant to make utilitarian, machine-made wares such as tumblers and ashtrays, but the move was ill-advised due to a glut of similar wares already on the market. The company remained in operation until 1951 when it permanently closed the doors of both factories as a result of the losses incurred by Plant No. 2. (To clear up an often-repeated misunderstanding, dealers and collectors alike should keep in mind that The Paden City Glass Mfg Co. had absolutely no connection with the Paden City Pottery Company, other than their identical locale.)

Today Paden City is best known for its numerous acid-etched wares that featured birds, but other ornate etchings were also produced — some of which are well documented in print, while others have yet to be documented in publications that are widely available. Peacock and Rose and Cupid are two of the most commonly found etched patterns. Currently, collectors especially seek out examples of Paden City's most detailed etching, Orchid, and its most appealing etching, Cupid. However, pieces bearing undocumented etchings or documented etchings on shapes and/or colors on which that etching has not previously been seen are fetching the highest prices from advanced collectors. Pieces in the company's plainer pressed dinnerware lines, however, have remained affordable, even though some patterns are quite scarce.

Below is a list of Paden City's colors. Names in capital letters indicate original factory color names where known, followed by a description of the color.

Amber — several shades

Blue — early 1920s color, medium shade, not cobalt

Cheriglo — pink

Copen, Neptune, Ceylon — various shades of light blue

Crystal — clear

Ebony — black

Emeraldglo — thinner dark green, not as deep as Forest Green

Forest Green — dark green

Green — various shades, from yellowish to electric green

Mulberry — amethyst

Opal — white (milk glass)

Primrose — amber with reddish tint (rare)

Rose — dark pink (rare)

Royal or Ritz Blue — cobalt

Ruby — red

Topaz — yellow

Collectors seeking more information on Paden City would do well to consult the following: *Paden City, The Color Company*, by Jerry Barnett (out of print, privately published, 1979); *Colored Glassware of the Depression Era 2* by Hazel Marie Weatherman (Glassbooks, 1974); *Price Trends to Colored Glassware of the Depression Era 2* by Hazel Marie Weatherman (Glassbooks, Editions in 1977, 1979, and 1981). Also available are *Paden City Company Catalog Reprints from the 1920s* (Antique Publications, 2000) and *Paden City Glassware* by Paul and Debora Torsiello and Tom Arlene Stillman (Schiffer, 2002). There is also a quarterly newsletter currently being published by the Paden City Glass Collectors Guild; this group is listed the Directory under Clubs, Newsletters, and Catalogs. Our advisor for this category is Michael Krumme; he is listed in the Directory under California. If no color is listed, the item is crystal.

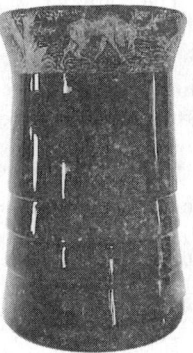

Black Forest (etched), vase, #210, black, 9" from $175.00 to $200.00.
(Photo courtesy Michael Krumme)

Ardith (etched), bowl, console; yel or blk, from $85 to................95.00
Ardith (etched), cake salver, yel or blk, low ft, from $75 to..........85.00
Ardith (etched), candle holders, pk or gr, keyhole style, pr 125.00
Ardith (etched), candy box, yel or blk, sq 150.00
Ardith (etched), cheese & cracker set, pk or gr, from $85 to........95.00
Ardith (etched), comport, yel or blk, from $75 to 95.00
Ardith (etched), creamer & sugar bowl, yel or blk 125.00
Ardith (etched), mayonnaise set, yel or blk, 3-pc........................150.00
Ardith (etched), tray, pk or gr, center hdl....................................85.00
Ardith (etched), tray, yel or blk, hdls, from $75 to 85.00
Ardith (etched), vase, pk or gr, elliptical, sm, 5" 150.00
Ardith (etched), vase, yel or blk, squarish, 9", from $175 to.......200.00
Black Forest (etched), bowl, serving; blk, hdls...........................100.00
Black Forest (etched), cake salver, pk or gr, low ft, from $85 to....95.00
Black Forest (etched), candle holders, pk or gr, mushroom style, pr..125.00
Black Forest (etched), candy dish, blk, ftd 150.00
Black Forest (etched), cheese & cracker set, pk or gr..................110.00
Black Forest (etched), comport, pk or gr, from $85 to 95.00

Black Forest (etched), creamer & sugar bowl, blk, from $85 to 95.00
Black Forest (etched), ice bucket, amber, metal bail 150.00
Black Forest (etched), ice tub, pk or gr, tab hdld.......................125.00
Black Forest (etched), mayonnaise set, pk or gr, 3-pc................150.00
Black Forest (etched), tray, amber, center hdl..............................75.00
Black Forest (etched), tray, pk or gr, hdls, from $65 to 75.00
Black Forest (etched), vase, pk or gr, bulbous, 10", from $150 to ..175.00
Crow's Foot (Round), bowl, serving; ruby or cobalt, hdls.............65.00
Crow's Foot (Round), candle holders, ruby or cobalt, triple, pr ..150.00
Crow's Foot (Round), candle holders, single, pr...........................65.00
Crow's Foot (Round), candy dish, 3-ftd...45.00
Crow's Foot (Round), cheese & cracker set, ruby, from $85 to 95.00
Crow's Foot (Round), comport, ruby or cobalt, tall stem..............65.00
Crow's Foot (Round), console, ruby, flat rim, 3-ftd......................95.00
Crow's Foot (Round), mayonnaise & liner, ruby or cobalt, 3-ftd ..85.00
Crow's Foot (Round), plate, ruby, 6", from $8 to 10.00
Crow's Foot (Round), plate, ruby, 8", from $10 to 12.00
Crow's Foot (Round), plate, ruby, 9", from $25 to 35.00
Crow's Foot (Round), tray, amber, center hdl 50.00
Crow's Foot (Round), tray, amber, hdls..35.00
Crow's Foot (Square), bowl, console; cobalt, from $65 to 85.00
Crow's Foot (Square), bowl, cream soup; ruby 20.00
Crow's Foot (Square), bowl, serving; ruby, hdls, from $45 to 65.00
Crow's Foot (Square), bowl, vegetable; ruby, oval, from $30 to 40.00
Crow's Foot (Square), cake salver, opal, low ft..............................95.00
Crow's Foot (Square), candle holders, blk, mushroom style, pr.....85.00
Crow's Foot (Square), candle holders, ruby, keyhole style, pr........95.00
Crow's Foot (Square), candy dish, ruby or cobalt, cloverleaf shape..150.00
Crow's Foot (Square), candy dish, yel, sq...................................125.00
Crow's Foot (Square), cheese & cracker set, ruby 85.00
Crow's Foot (Square), comport, ruby or cobalt, low stem, from $40 to ..50.00
Crow's Foot (Square), creamer & sugar bowl, amethyst................65.00
Crow's Foot (Square), cup & saucer, ruby, from $15 to.................20.00
Crow's Foot (Square), mayonnaise set, ruby, 3-pc........................95.00
Crow's Foot (Square), plate, ruby, 6", from $8 to 10.00
Crow's Foot (Square), plate, ruby, 8", from $10 to 12.00
Crow's Foot (Square), platter, cobalt, oval 50.00
Crow's Foot (Square), tray, amber, hdls, from $30 to 35.00
Crow's Foot (Square), tray, pk or gr, center hdl............................45.00
Crow's Foot (Square), vase, ruby, cupped, 10"...........................110.00
Cupid (etched), bowl, console; pk or gr, 13" 185.00
Cupid (etched), bowl, pk or gr, oval..295.00
Cupid (etched), candy dish, pk or gr, ftd....................................275.00
Cupid (etched), comport, pk or gr...150.00
Cupid (etched), creamer & sugar bowl, pk or gr..........................175.00
Cupid (etched), ice bucket, pk or gr, metal bail..........................250.00
Cupid (etched), mayonnaise set, pk or gr, 3-pc...........................225.00
Cupid (etched), salver, pk or gr, low ft..150.00
Cupid (etched), tray, center hdl 125.00
Delilah Bird (etched), blk, cylindrical, 9"...................................250.00
Delilah Bird (etched), bowl, console; pk......................................125.00
Delilah Bird (etched), candle holders, pk, keyhole style, pr........150.00
Delilah Bird (etched), comport, low ft 95.00
Delilah Bird (etched), vase, pk or gr, squat, 7"...........................175.00
Eden Rose (etched), top hat 100.00
Eden Rose (etched), vase, blk, cylindrical, 9" 150.00
Eden Rose (etched), vase, gr or pk, bulbous, 12" 175.00
Gazebo (etched), bowl, console; from $45 to 50.00
Gazebo (etched), candy dish, lt bl, ftd...95.00
Gazebo (etched), creamer & sugar bowl, from $40 to....................45.00
Gazebo (etched), mayonnaise bowl & liner, from $35 to 40.00
Gazebo (etched), tray, center hdl..45.00
Gazebo (etched), tray, hdls..40.00
Gazebo (etched), vase, bulbous, 10" 75.00

Gothic Garden (etched), bowl, console; yel or blk, flat rim, $65 to...**75.00**
Gothic Garden (etched), cake salver, pk or gr, low ft...................**95.00**
Gothic Garden (etched), candle holders, yel or blk, keyhole style, pr...**135.00**
Gothic Garden (etched), candy box, pk or gr, sq....................**150.00**
Gothic Garden (etched), cheese & cracker set, yel or blk..........**125.00**
Gothic Garden (etched), comport, pk or gr, from $85 to..............**95.00**
Gothic Garden (etched), creamer & sugar bowl, yel or blk........**125.00**
Gothic Garden (etched), mayonnaise set, yel, 3-pc....................**150.00**
Gothic Garden (etched), tray, pk or gr, hdls, from $75 to..............**85.00**
Gothic Garden (etched), tray, yel or blk, center hdl, from $65 to...**85.00**
Gothic Garden (etched), vase, squarish, 9"...........................**150.00**
Largo, bowl, console; lt bl, 3-ftd.....................................**65.00**
Largo, bowl, serving; lt bl, hdls, from $50 to **65.00**
Largo, cheese & cracker set, ruby....................................**85.00**
Largo, comport, amber...**25.00**
Largo, creamer & sugar bowl, amethyst or forest gr **150.00**
Largo, cup & saucer, ruby..**35.00**
Largo, mayonnaise bowl & liner.....................................**35.00**
Largo, tray, center hdl...**45.00**
Largo, tray, lt bl, hdls...**50.00**
Lela Bird, cake salver, pk or gr, low ft, from $95 to.....................**110.00**
Lela Bird, candle holders, pk or gr, mushroom style, pr **125.00**
Lela Bird, comport, pk or gr, ftd, lg.................................**125.00**
Lela Bird, tray, pk or gr, center hdl, from $75 to......................**85.00**
Lela Bird, vase, blk, elliptical, 8"....................................**125.00**
Lela Bird, vase, blk w/gold etching, bulbous, 12"......................**225.00**
Lela Bird, vase, pk or gr, bulbous, 10", from $125 to...................**150.00**
Maya, bowl, console; 3-ftd...**40.00**
Maya, cheese & cracker set, lt bl, dome lid...........................**75.00**
Maya, comport, ruby, tall..**95.00**
Maya, creamer & sugar bowl...**35.00**
Maya, cup & saucer, lt bl..**30.00**
Maya, tray, lt bl, center hdl...**50.00**
Nora Bird (etched), candle holders, pk or gr, mushroom style, pr...**125.00**
Nora Bird (etched), creamer & sugar bowl, pk or gr...................**150.00**
Nora Bird (etched), mayonnaise set, 3-pc **95.00**
Party Line, banana split dish, gr.....................................**30.00**
Party Line, bowl, console; lt bl, rolled edge...........................**50.00**
Party Line, cake salver, pk or gr, high ft **150.00**
Party Line, candle holders, gr, flat ft, pr.............................**45.00**
Party Line, candle holders, med bl, dome ft, pr.......................**40.00**
Party Line, cocktail shaker, gr.......................................**125.00**
Party Line, cologne bottle, pk, long dauber..........................**65.00**
Party Line, comport, amethyst......................................**40.00**
Party Line, creamer & sugar bowl, pk or gr, from $25 to..............**30.00**
Party Line, ice bucket, pk or gr, metal bail...........................**75.00**
Party Line, ice tub, pk or gr, tab hdl.................................**45.00**
Party Line, pitcher, pk, w/lid..**95.00**
Party Line, powder jar, amber, flat...................................**30.00**
Party Line, shakers, ruby or cobalt, pr...............................**95.00**
Party Line, stem, champagne, pk or gr...............................**15.00**
Party Line, stem, sherbet, pk or gr, low..............................**10.00**
Party Line, stem, tulip sundae, pk or gr **25.00**
Party Line, syrup, gr, metal lid......................................**85.00**
Party Line, tray, pk or gr, center hdl **30.00**
Party Line, tumbler, ftd, 6"...**20.00**
Party Line, tumbler, pk or gr, 4".....................................**15.00**
Party Line, vase, lt bl, fan shape **50.00**
Peacock & Rose (etched), bowl, console; pk or gr, 13" **150.00**
Peacock & Rose (etched), bowl, pk or gr, oval **250.00**
Peacock & Rose (etched), candy dish, pk or gr, ftd....................**225.00**
Peacock & Rose (etched), comport, pk or gr..........................**125.00**
Peacock & Rose (etched), creamer & sugar bowl (no peacock), pk or gr.**200.00**
Peacock & Rose (etched), ice tub, pk or gr, tab hdls..................**125.00**

Peacock & Rose (etched), mayonnaise set, pk or gr, 3-pc...........**175.00**
Peacock & Rose (etched), salver, low ft.............................**125.00**
Peacock & Rose (etched), tray, pk or gr, center hdl...................**95.00**
Peacock & Rose (etched), vase, ebony, bulbous, 10".................**200.00**
Penny Line, bowl, serving; cobalt, hdls **75.00**
Penny Line, creamer & sugar bowl, cobalt **45.00**
Penny Line, creamer & sugar bowl, ruby.............................**30.00**
Penny Line, cup & saucer, ruby **15.00**
Penny Line, decanter, ruby..**85.00**
Penny Line, goblet, ruby, high ft, from $30 to........................**35.00**
Penny Line, goblet, ruby, low ft, from $15 to **20.00**
Penny Line, plate, ruby, 8", from $8 to...............................**10.00**
Penny Line, sherbet, forest gr, low...................................**15.00**
Penny Line, tray, amethyst, center hdl **45.00**
Penny Line, tumbler, ruby, 6".......................................**25.00**
Penny Line, tumbler, shot glass, ruby, from $8 to.....................**10.00**
Spring Orchard (etched), bitters bottle...............................**125.00**
Spring Orchard (etched), cocktail shaker.............................**150.00**
Spring Orchard (etched), decanter, cordial; tilt style, hdld............**50.00**
Spring Orchard (etched), decanter, flat sided, cog stopper............**85.00**
Spring Orchard (etched), stem, cocktail, hourglass shape..............**20.00**
Spring Orchard (etched), stem, cordial **25.00**
Spring Orchard (etched), stem, wine.................................**15.00**
Spring Orchard (etched), tumbler, whiskey...........................**20.00**
Utopia (etched), candy box, heart shape **150.00**
Utopia (etched), relish dish, 3-part..................................**45.00**
Utopia (etched), vase, bulbous, 10"..................................**125.00**
Utopia (etched), vase, squarish, 9"..................................**150.00**

Pairpoint

The Pairpoint Manufacturing Company was built in 1880 in New Bedford, Massachusetts. It was primarily a metalworks whose chief product was coffin fittings. Next door, the Mt. Washington Glassworks made quality glasswares of many varieties. (See Mt. Washington for more information concerning their artware lines.) By 1894 it became apparent to both companies that a merger would be to their best interest.

From the late 1890s until the 1930s, lamps and lamp accessories were an important part of Pairpoint's production. There were three main types of shades, all of which were blown: puffy — blown-out reverse-painted shades (usually floral designs); ribbed — also reverse painted; and scenic — reverse painted with scenes of land or seascapes (usually executed on smooth surfaces, although ribbed scenics may be found occasionally). Cut glass lamps and those with metal overlay panels were also made. Scenic shades were sometimes artist signed. Every shade was stamped on the lower inside or outside edge with 1) The Pairpoint Corp., 2) Patent Pending, 3) Patented July 9, 1907, or 4) Patent Applied For. Bases were made of bronze, copper, brass, silver, or wood and are always signed.

Because they produced only fancy, handmade artware, the company's sales lagged seriously during the Depression, and as time and tastes changed, their style of product was less in demand. As a result, they never fully recovered; consequently part of the buildings and equipment was sold in 1938. The company reorganized in 1939 under the direction of Robert Gundersen and again specialized in quality hand-blown glassware. Isaac Babbit regained possession of the silver departments, and together they established Gundersen Glassworks, Inc. After WWII, because of a sharp decline in sales, it again became necessary to reorganize. The Gundersen-Pairpoint Glassworks was formed, and the old line of cut, engraved artware was reintroduced. The company moved to East Wareham, Massachusetts, in 1957. But business continued to suffer, and the firm closed only one year later. In 1970, however, new facilities were constructed in Sagamore under the direction of Robert Bryden, sales manager for the company since the 1950s.

In 1974 the company began to produce lead glass cup plates which were made on commission as fund-raisers for various churches and organizations. These are signed with a 'P' in diamond and are becoming quite collectible. See also Burmese; Napkin Rings.

Glass

Bottle, scent; clear sphere w/bubbles, exotic bird stopper, 11" **400.00**
Box, dresser; roses/gold scrolls on swirl-emb lt bl, 7½" dia **785.00**
Candlestick, cut floral/leaf, teardrop shape w/cobalt ft, 16", pr...**1,900.00**
Compote, cranberry Dmn Quilt, eng grapes, clear knob bubble stem, 9"...**750.00**
Compote, cut/eng swags & flowers, slim faceted cobalt ped ft, 9x9" **575.00**
Compote, vintage intaglio on lime gr, crystal bubble ball stem, 7x8"...**125.00**
Console bowl, Flambo w/blk ft, 12", +pr mushroom-type candlesticks...**1,950.00**
Console bowl, Tavern glass w/floral, 12", +pr 3" candlesticks **575.00**
Cracker jar, mums in wht reserve on yel, squat, SP mts: 9½" ..**1,000.00**
Decanter, Flambo, orange w/silver o/l, bubble ball stopper, 11x5"..**1,265.00**
Humidor, monk on brn, bk: pipe, cigar finial on metal lid, 6¼x5"....**400.00**
Swan bowl, all crystal, 10½x8½"...**115.00**
Swan bowl, rosaria w/crystal neck, 12x12½"...............................**230.00**
Tumbler, Tavern glass w/whale, 5¼x3¾" **275.00**
Vase, cobalt ft/body w/bubble ball stem, trumpet form, 13".........**125.00**
Vase, flip; Tavern glass w/floral, 8x6"..**275.00**

Lamps

Puffy 6" floral/lg butterflies shade; std #B6134, rpl socket/ring **4,300.00**
Puffy 8" Papillon roses/butterflies sgn shade; sgn gilded std..............**5,000.00**
Puffy 8" Stratford shade w/roses & lattice on yel; bronze std, 14"...**3,275.00**
Puffy 9" Stratford shade w/hollyhocks; sgn std #B6134, 14".....**5,750.00**
Puffy 10" roses/butterfly dome shade; #3047/1/2/7 std w/4 foliate ft..**5,000.00**
Puffy 14" poppies shade; gold doré std w/cutouts & prisms, 20"..**20,000.00**
Puffy 14" Stratford roses/hummingbird shade; SP std w/4 scroll legs ..**8,600.00**
Rvpt 8½" winter trees shade; mk base, missing cap/finial **980.00**
Rvpt 15" horse-drawn wagon/harvest Exeter sgn/rpr shade; hdld urn std ..**2,400.00**
Rvpt 15" lav w/gold floral Murano shade turns bl when lit; #C3014 std .**3,450.00**
Rvpt 17" farm scene shade sgn Fisher (EX); lobed/flared std #D3059 ..**2,500.00**
Rvpt 18" Carlisle shade w/peacocks in garden; 3-part SP std...**8,000.00**
Rvpt 18" Landsdowne shade w/parrots; ornate #3007 std, 18" .**9,200.00**
Rvpt 18" pastel landscape shade w/str sides & open top; 3-part SP std...**3,165.00**
Rvpt 20" seascape/sea gulls sgn shade, glass base pnt to match, 24"..**12,000.00**

Pairpoint Limoges

Limoges china blanks were imported from France in strict accordance with Pairpoint specifications. They were decorated by Pairpoint in designs that ranged from simple to elaborate florals and scenics. Called Crown Pairpoint French China in old Pairpoint and Mt. Washington catalogs, these are easily identified. Look for the Pairpoint name over a crown with the Limoges name below. You may also find similar ware marked 'Pairpoint Minton.'

Tray, Guba ducks on flow blue, #2707/43, 12½x11", $1,500.00. (Photo courtesy James Julia)

Compote, appl Dresden-line flowers on wht, floral-wrapped stem, 8x5" ..**230.00**
Ewer, poppies, yel/rose/gr on pnt brn & gray, #2020/520, 16x8" .**975.00**
Plate, harbor scene w/boat, sgn Tripp, sm rim rstr, 7¼"...............**385.00**
Vase, child in reserve on mahog-red w/gold (worn), ftd, 14".......**485.00**
Vase, mums/gilt on putty, turn-down tulip lip, flowing hdls, 9½" ..**625.00**
Vase, Venetian bldgs reserve/bk: sailing vessel on maroon, hdls, 15" ..**950.00**

Paper Dolls

No one knows quite how or when paper dolls originated. One belief is that they began in Europe as 'pantins' (jumping jacks). During the nineteenth century, most paper dolls portrayed famous dancers and opera stars such as Fanny Elssler and Jenny Lind. In the late 1800s, the Raphael Tuck Publishers of England produced many series of beautiful paper dolls; retail companies used them as advertisements to further the sale of their products. Around the turn of the century, many popular women's magazines began featuring a page of paper dolls.

Most familiar to today's collectors are the books with dolls on cardboard covers and clothes on the inside pages. These made their appearance in the late 1920s and early 1930s. The most collectible (and the most valuable) are those representing celebrities, movie stars, and comic-strip characters of the '30s and '40s.

When no condition is indicated, the dolls listed below are assumed to be in mint, uncut, original condition. Cut sets will be worth about half price if all dolls and outfits are included and pieces are in very good condition. If dolls were produced in die-cut form, these prices reflect such a set in mint condition with all costumes and accessories.

For further information we recommend *Tomart's Price Guide to Lowe and Whitman Paper Dolls* and *Tomart's Price Guide to Saalfield and Merrill Paper Dolls*, both by Mary Young, our advisor for this category; she is listed in the Directory under Ohio. We also recommend *Schroeder's Collectible Toys, Antique to Modern* (Collector Books).

Ann Blyth, Merrill #2550, 1952, uncut, M **135.00**
Annie Oakley, Whitman #1960, 1956, uncut, M..............................**85.00**
Archie's Girls Betty & Veronica, Lowe #2764, 1964, uncut, M **50.00**
Baby Snooks, Whitman #991, 1940, uncut, M **300.00**
Barbie & Ken, Whitman #1527, 1984, uncut, M..........................**15.00**
Betty Grable, Merrill #1558, 1951, 8-pg, uncut, M **200.00**
Blondie, Whitman #974, 1950, uncut, M **125.00**
Bob Cummings Fashion Models, Lowe #2407, 1958, uncut, M.....**75.00**
Bride Doll, Lowe #1043, 1946, uncut, M......................................**60.00**
Carmen Miranda, Whitman #995, 1942, uncut, M **175.00**
Children 'Round the World, Merrill #2565, 1955, uncut, M **40.00**
Cyd Charisse, Whitman #2084, 1956, uncut, M..........................**120.00**
Darlikin Dolls, Whitman #951, 1938, uncut, M **150.00**
Debbie Reynolds, Whitman #1178, 1953, uncut, M......................**150.00**
Dinah Shore, Whitman #977, 1943, uncut, M **200.00**
Dionne Quints, Merrill #3488, 1940, uncut, M **200.00**
Dolls of Other Lands, Whitman #2074, 1963, uncut, M **25.00**
Dr Kildare & Nurse Susan, Lowe #2740, uncut, M....................**65.00**
Dress Alike Dolls, Whitman #2058, 1951, uncut, M....................**25.00**
Elaine Stewart, Whitman #2048, 1955, uncut, M **125.00**
Elizabeth Taylor, Whitman #1177, 1953, uncut, M **150.00**
Esther Williams, Merrill #2553, 1953, uncut, M........................**150.00**
Faye Emerson, Saalfield #2722, 1952, uncut, M........................**100.00**
Finian's Rainbow, Saalfield #4436, 1968, uncut, M...................**50.00**
Gene Autry's Melody Ranch, Whitman #990, 1950, uncut, M ..**100.00**
Grace Kelly, Whitman #2049, 1955, uncut, M **125.00**
Greer Garson, Merrill #4858, 1944, uncut, M **250.00**
Honeymooners, Lowe #2560, 1956, uncut, M.............................**300.00**
Hootenanny, Saalfield #4440, 1964, uncut, M **50.00**
Jane Withers, Whitman #989, 1940, uncut, M **125.00**

Judy & Jack, Lowe #1024, 1940, uncut, M **85.00**
Judy Garland, Whitman #999, 1940, uncut, M **100.00**
King of Swing & Queen of Song, Lowe #1040, 1942, uncut, M .**350.00**
Kitty Goes to Kindergarten, Merrill #1548, 1956, uncut, M **40.00**
Laugh-In Party, Saalfield, #6045, 1969, uncut, M **55.00**
Lennon Sisters, Whitman #1995, 1963, uncut, M **75.00**
Little Women, Lowe #1030, 1941, uncut, M...................................**75.00**
Magazine Cover Girls, Merrill #4856, 1944, uncut, M **100.00**
Mary Ann, Saalfield #268, 1932, uncut, M **75.00**
Mary Martin, Saalfield #2427, 1942, box set, uncut, M **125.00**
Million Dollar Dolls, Lowe #2486, 1958, uncut, M **35.00**
Movie Starlets, Whitman #991, 1942, uncut, M **200.00**
National Velvet, Whitman #1958, 1961, uncut, M **60.00**
Patty Duke, Whitman #1991, 1964, uncut, M **40.00**
Princess Diana, Whitman #1530, 1985, uncut, M **15.00**
Rosemary Clooney, Lowe #1256, 1953, uncut, M......................**100.00**
Roy Rogers Double-R-Bar Ranch, Whitman #1035, 1955, uncut, M..**60.00**
Shirley Temple, Saalfield #1761, 1937, uncut, M **250.00**
Snow White & the Seven Dwarfs, Whitman #1987, 1967 (undtd), uncut, M...**60.00**
Sonja Henie, Merrill #3492, 1940, uncut, M **275.00**
Susan Dey as Laurie, Saalfield #4218, 1972, uncut, M **45.00**
Ten Little Neighbors, Saalfield #204, 1941, uncut, M **30.00**
That Girl, Saalfield #4479, 1967, uncut, M **55.00**
Trixie, Belden-Whitman, 1958, uncut, M **60.00**
TV Tap Stars, Lowe #990, 1952, uncut, M.....................................**35.00**
Twiggy, Whitman #1999, 1967, uncut, M **35.00**
White House Paper Dolls, Saalfield #4475, 1969, uncut, M..........**50.00**
50 Paper Dolls, Saalfield #2313, 1940, uncut, M **75.00**

Paperweights

Glass paperweight collecting has become a feverish passion, growing in intensity in the past few years. Perhaps it is because there many glass artists in the marketplace today who are creating beautiful examples, and a beginning collector can pick up these lovely objets d'art for under $100.00. Hundreds of glass artisans in the U.S. and factories in China, Italy, and Scotland produce 'gift range' paperweights. Collectors have the choice of forming their collections strictly from that price range, or they can choose to select pieces that can run into the thousands of dollars — or anywhere in between. Additionally, astute collectors are beginning to piece together collections of the old Chinese paperweights that were imported into this country during the 1930s. These were basically unrefined imitations of the lovely and unique French weights of the mid-1800s. When viewed some seventy years later, however, one can appreciate the beauty and craftsmanship these weights exhibit. Murano weights, especially those from the 1960s and 1970s, represent another area of concentrated interest. Prices are beginning to escalate in both categories. Collectors who have a larger budget for these exquisite 'glass balls' may form their collection with only antique French paperweights from the classic period (1845 – 1860), the wonderful English or American weights from the 1850s, or choose to collect the high quality contemporary artistry of master glass artists such as Ayotte, Banford, Buzzini, Donofrio, Ebelhare, Grubb, Kontes, S. Lundberg, Rosenfeld, G. Smith, the Trabuccos, or Stankard. The door is wide open for anyone to begin collecting in whatever price range they can afford, and the Paperweight Collector's Association, Inc., with chapters in many states can be of great assistance to collectors at all levels.

Baccarat, St. Louis, Clichy, and Pantin (names synonymous with classic French paperweights) as well as some American factories stopped making paperweights between the 1880s and 1910 due to a decline in their popularity. In the 1950s Baccarat and St. Louis again began paperweight production and continue their lines of high quality, limited pro-

duction weights. In the 1960s many glass studios began to spring up due to the development of smaller glass furnaces, thereby allowing more freedom for the individual glassmaker to design and fabricate a piece of glass from the fire to the annealing kiln. Such success stories are evident in the creative glass produced by Lundberg Studios, Orient & Flume, and Lotton Studios, to name only a few.

Many factors determine value, particularly of antique weights, and auction-realized prices of contemporary weights usually differ from issue price. Competition among new collectors entering the field has greatly influenced prices. As the number of collectors increases, available antique weights decrease per capita, forcing prices upwards. Antique paperweights have steadily increased in value as has the work of many now-deceased glass artists (i.e., Paul Ysart, Joe St. Clair, Charles Kazian, Del Tarsitano). With the demise of Perthshire Paperweights, Ltd., in January 2002, it remains to be seen what will happen with prices on their weights, particularly the limited edition pieces. The dimension given at the end of the line is diameter. Prices are for weights in perfect or near-perfect condition unless otherwise noted. Our advisors for this category are Betty and Larry Schwab, The Paperweight Shoppe; they are listed in the Directory under Illinois.

Key:
con — concentric   jsp — jasper
(d) — deceased   latt — latticinio
fct — faceted   mill — millefiori
gar — garland   o/l — overlay
grd — ground   sil — silhouette

Ayotte, Rick

Butterfly with flowers and branches, 3¼", $1,200.00.

Butterfly among flower branch, 1985, 3¼" **1,200.00**
Sparrow on leafy branch w/yel pods, 1983, 2¾"..........................**700.00**
Thrush w/flower spray on yel, 1985, 3¾" **900.00**
Tiger lilies (4) w/buds & leaves on yel grd, 1-6 fct, 1988, 3⅞"....**900.00**
Yel warbler on branch w/berries & leaves on wht grd, 1983, 3⅛"...**600.00**

Baccarat, Antique

Anemone w/leafy stem, sm star-cut & oval fcts at base, 2¾"...**1,800.00**
Clematis w/gr leaves, bl & wht mill border, star-cut base, 2¾"...**3,200.00**
Close mill w/several animal sils, 1848, 3" **3,200.00**
Pansy & bud on stem, star-cut base, type 2, 3⅛" **3,800.00**

Baccarat, Modern

Close conc mill w/circlets of complex canes, 1969, 3¹/₁₆" **400.00**
Mill carpet, 1968, 3"...**430.00**
Pk pompon w/leaves & stem amid mill ring on clear, star-cut base, 3"....**750.00**
Sagittarius sulfide on cobalt, 1-6 fct, 2⅝"....................................**100.00**
Sam Rayburn sulfide, dbl o/l, clear grid-cut grd, 3⅛" **100.00**

Banford, Bob

Dahlia, red w/6 gr leaves on aqua, 24-point cut rosette base, 3⅛"....800.00
Dahlia/bud, aventurine in clear, complex cane center, 3¼" 600.00
Floral bouquet w/leafy stems, 2⅞" 800.00
Magnum pansy w/mixed flower bouquet, dmn-cut base, 4"......1,700.00
Pears/cherries/leaves on wht lace w/torsade, 2⅞" 600.00
Wheatflower & foliage on cobalt star-cut base, 3" 750.00

Banford, Ray

Basket irises, yel/wht dbl o/l, 3¼"..2,000.00
Cabbage roses, red/wht dbl o/l, grid base, 3¼".........................2,400.00
Lily-of-the-valley, rnd fct top, 6 side fcts, 2¼x2⅞"......................800.00
Pk clematis trellis & buds on blk grd, 1-5 fct, 1971, 2⁷⁄₁₆"..........500.00

Caithness

Floral Fountain, pk multi-petaled layers, 1979, 3⅛" 300.00
Springtime, 3 pk flowers w/gr leaves on dk gr, 1981, 3⅛" 250.00
Venus, Colin Terris, Peter Holmes, 1970, ltd ed, 3"....................800.00

Clichy, Antique

Napoleon III sulfide, 24-point star extends to periphery, 3", NM ..700.00
Pattern pk/bl mill, 2¼" 1,500.00
Spoked gar w/pk & gr rose, 3" 2,000.00

Kaziun, Charles

Con mill w/complex canes w/in mc torsade on bl grd, 2¹⁄₁₆"....1,700.00
Lily, yel on pk grd, ftd, 2¼" 500.00
Trumpet flower & bud on vine w/leaves on amethyst, 2¼" 1,000.00
Yel crimp rose w/4 gr leaves, ped ft, 2⅛"....................................1,200.00

Lundberg Studios

Bl fish on gr w/mica, D Salazar, 1994, 3½" 330.00
Dragonfly/cattails on bl irid, 7-layer 3-D look, Steven, 3½" 400.00
Red rose w/4 leaves, clear dmn-cut shape, Steven, 2"...................400.00

New England Glass, Antique

Fruit cluster in latt basket, 2¾" 950.00
Scramble w/8 whole canes+fragments, repolished, 2⅝"...............270.00

Orient & Flume

Calla lilies (2) on stem w/leaves, S Beyers, 3⅛" 400.00
Drake on water w/fronds, 5-layer, 1985, 3⅛" 350.00
Herons spar as fledglings watch on bl grd, 1983, 3⅛"..................350.00

Perthshire

Butterfly w/in gr complex cane gar, 1988, mini, 2" 300.00
Crocus, amber, 6 curving petals, 1969, 2⅞" 300.00
Mistletoe/holly/poinsettia w/in gr gars on wht, 1-5 fct, 1996 ......400.00
Upright dahlia, pk 4-tier petals, 1972, 3⅛"...................................900.00

Rosenfeld, Ken

Flower bouquet & foliage on sand grd, 1990, 3¼" 575.00
Red & yel rose on stalk w/buds & leaves, 1990, 3" 500.00
Snake, desert grd, rocks, flowers, 1993, 3½" 800.00

Upright bouquet, buds, berries, sculptural cube, 3¼x8½" 850.00

Sandwich Glass

Dahlia w/cane center on stem, wht latt grd, 3⅛".........................800.00
Fruit bouquet on latt, 3⅛" 1,045.00
Poinsettia, red w/gr leaves & stem, 2⅞" 600.00
Weedflower, petals, gold-stone center cane, 2¾"......................1,200.00

St. Louis, Antique

Con mill canes surrounded by pk & gr mill on wht latt bed, 2½"..1,800.00
Mushroom w/lg canes in bl & wht torsade, 1848, 2⅞"............6,000.00
Pansy w/leaves, grid-cut base, 3"..1,500.00
Scramble, undtd, 2¾"...600.00
Turnips w/gr tops on dbl-spiral lattice grd, 2¼" 1,200.00

St. Louis, Modern

Dahlias on bl cut to wht to clear, 5 side fcts, 1975 ....650.00
Lily-of-the-valley w/leaves on garnet red, 1982, 3⅛"..................550.00
Orchid, powder bl opaque, 1994, 3³⁄₁₆".......................................600.00
Pk & gr spirals, egg shape, 2¾x1¾" 225.00
Wht flower w/ruffled mill petals/bud/leaves on orange opaque, 1973...400.00

Stankard, Paul

Chokeberries & wht blossoms on leafy stems, ca 1976, 2⅞"....1,800.00
Flower & 3 buds on stems w/root & bulb, 1989, 3" 2,000.00
Wild rose & foliage on clear, top+5 side fcts, 2½" 1,500.00
Wildflowers & blackberries, 3" 2,300.00

Tarsitano, Debbie

Barberry branch w/berries & 3 buds, 3⁵⁄₁₆" 2,000.00
Red flowers & buds, 6 side fcts, 3" 800.00
Rose w/leaves, star-cut base, 3" 800.00

Tarsitano, Delmo

Gr snake w/open mouth, earth grd, 3¾" 3,800.00
Peaches (2) on branch w/leaves, 7 fcts, 2½" 1,500.00
Snake & fly, earth grd, magnum, 3⅞" 3,600.00
Spider w/vegetation on sandy grd, 3¼".....................................1,500.00

Trabucco, Victor

Flowers & buds among 3 lemons on branch, 1989, 4" 800.00
Flowers & buds w/berries on stems, 1990, 3⅛" 800.00
Red flowers (2) & pk blossom & bud w/gr leafy stems, 1982, 3".600.00

Whitefriars

Christmas angel w/in bl wht stardust canes, 1-5 fct, 1975, 3" 600.00
Close con mill w/circles of canes, 3⅛" 400.00
Close con mill w/complex canes, finger-fct bullet shape, 3"........500.00

Miscellaneous

Buzzini, foxglove bouquet w/morning glory/aster/buds, 1993, 3¼"...1,300.00
Diacons, John; flower w/stardust cane center on spiral latt, 2½" ...275.00
Ebelhare, Drew; bl & wht stave basket w/18 gr & wht posy canes, 2" ..350.00
Gilvey, J; earth mound/4 trees, 2¹⁄₁₆", on 3-tier amber stand 250.00
Gilvey, J; 2 lampwork bees on rock w/moss/plant/6 fronds, 1997, 2¾" ..330.00

Manson, Wm; shark w/bl mica scales on ocean floor, 1981, 2⅞"...**400.00**
Manson, Wm; yel upright rose w/bud & leaves, controlled bubbles, 1999 ..**300.00**
Millville, umbrella, ftd, antique, 3⅛" **500.00**
Pairpoint, 3-tier design w/5 ice-pick bubbles, bubble ball ft, 5½" ..**500.00**
Pairpoint/Gundersen, pk lily on gr grd in clear, 3"..................**250.00**
Simpson, Josh; planet form, grays/bls/brn, 1986, 3x3¼" **200.00**

Papier-Maché

The art of papier-maché was mainly European. It originated in Paris around the middle of the eighteenth century and became popular in America during Victorian times. Small items such as boxes, trays, inkwells, frames, etc., as well as extensive ceiling moldings and larger articles of furniture were made. The process involved building layer upon layer of paper soaked in glue, then coaxed into shape over a wood or wire form. When dry it was painted or decorated with gilt or inlays. Inexpensive twentieth-century 'notions' were machine processed and mold pressed. See also Christmas; Candy Containers.

Figurine, bulldog, glass eyes, nodding head w/hinged jaw, 20" **560.00**
Jewelry box, blk laquer w/inlaid MOP, Vict, 7x4x5¼"..................**210.00**
Lap desk, ornate mc medallions on lid/sides, w/gilt, 1850s, 12" L ...**430.00**
Model, milliner's; mc pnt, 1 w/kidskin skullcap, 15½", pr........**1,100.00**
Music stand, lacquer w/MOP inlay, English Vict, 1850s, 41x17x14"..**1,725.00**
Plate, blk lacquer w/inlaid MOP star center & border, Fr, 6¾" **60.00**
Table, tilt-top, MOP inlay & floral pnt, trn shaft, Vict, 29x23"..**800.00**
Tea caddy, gr & red w/gilt, hinged MOP lid, late 19th C, 4¾x8" ...**500.00**

Tea table, tilt-top with scene of people at harvest time with horse-drawn cart, wood base, Victorian, 28x22" diameter, EX, $550.00.

Tray, flowers & scrolls, mc on blk lacquer, 1840s, 20x24" **550.00**
Tray, Oriental scene w/flowers, 1850s, 23¾x31"......................**1,100.00**

Parian Ware

Parian is hard-paste unglazed porcelain made to resemble marble. First made in the mid-1800s by Staffordshire potters, it was soon after produced in the United States by the U.S. Pottery at Bennington, Vermont. Busts and statuary were favored, but plaques, vases, mugs, and pitchers were also made.

Bust, Albert Edward (King Edward VII), 14½"............................**975.00**
Bust, Clytie, draped bosom, ped base, Art Union of London, 1870s, 14"..**635.00**
Bust, Lord Burton, mk H&L (Hewitt & Leadbeater), dtd 1909, 8½"..**200.00**
Bust, Sir Walter Scott, Robinson & Leadbeater, ca 1875, 7½" ...**225.00**
Figurine, Conquering Jealousy, woman w/2 dogs, HF Libby, 1878, 14x7"..**925.00**
Figurine, Cupid sleeping on tasseled pillow, EX detail, 12" L......**450.00**
Figurine, putto w/seashell at ear, Copeland, 12½" **850.00**
Figurine, standing nude, Minton, dtd Aug 1865, 15" **1,375.00**
Figurine, Sunshine, lady shielding eyes, Copeland, 1858, 19½"..**750.00**

Jug, Grecian figures & Roman columns, bl on wht, 7½x4½" **175.00**
Jug, polychromed enameled birds & floral, 1880s, 8" **300.00**

Parrish, Maxfield

Maxfield Parrish (1870 – 1966), with his unique abilities in architecture, illustrations, and landscapes, was the most prolific artist during 'The Golden Years of Illustrators.' He produced art for more than one hundred magazines, painted girls on rocks for the Edison-Mazda division of General Electric, and landscapes for Brown & Bigelow. His most recognized work was 'Daybreak' that was published in 1923 by House of Art and sold nearly two million prints. Parrish began early training with his father who was a recognized artist, studied architecture at Dartmouth, and became an active participant in the Cornish artist colony in New Hampshire where he resided. Due to his increasing popularity, reproductions are now being marketed.

In our listings, values for prints apply to those that are in their original frames (or very nice and appropriate replacement frames) unless noted otherwise. For further information we recommend *Collector's Value Guide to Early 20th Century American Prints* by Michael Ivankovich. Bobby Babcock, our advisor for this category, is listed in the Directory under Texas.

Key: BB — Brown & Bigelow

Ad display, Hires Root Beer, elf drinking Hires, cb diecut, 29½x24"...**22,500.00**
Ad display, Jell-O/King & Queen Might Eat..., cb trifold, 29x42½".**9,000.00**
Ad poster, Ferry Seeds, Jack & the Beanstalk, 1923, cropped, 19"....**1,800.00**
Ad poster, The Christmas Scribner's, ad for 1899 catalog, 22x14"....**2,000.00**
Book, Golden Treasury, 3rd edition, hardcover, 1941, EX...........**100.00**
Book, Knave of Hearts, spiral-bound, 1925, EX..........................**825.00**
Calendar, Contentment, 1928, no pad, 37½x18", EX..............**1,200.00**
Calendar, Ecstasy, 1930, complete, 19x8½", EX......................**4,300.00**
Calendar, Evening Shadows, B&B, 1940, complete, 10⅜x7⅞" ..**220.00**
Calendar, Lampseller of Bagdad, 1923, complete, 37½x18", EX..**3,900.00**
Calendar, Reveries, 1927, no pad, 19x8½", EX..........................**750.00**
Calendar, Solitude, 1932, complete, 19x8½", EX....................**1,000.00**
Calendar, Spirit of the Night, 1919, partial pad, 37½x18", EX..**3,000.00**
Calendar, Sunrise, 1933, complete, 19x8½", EX.......................**600.00**
Calendar, The Glen, B&B, 1949, complete, 15⅜x11¾" **450.00**
Calendar, Twilight, 1937, complete, 15x10⅞", EX....................**600.00**
Calendar, Vicobello, 1934, complete, rare, 7x4⅞"....................**450.00**
Calendar, Waterfall, 1931, complete, 37½x18", EX................**1,750.00**
Calendar top, Enchantment, 1926, 14⅝x23¼", EX.................**1,600.00**
Calendar top, Golden Hour, 1929, 14½x22⅝", EX.................**1,000.00**
Calendar top, Night Is Fled, 1918, 13⅞x19⅜", EX.................**2,200.00**
Calendar top, Primitive Man, 1921, 6¼x10¾", EX...................**900.00**
Calendar top, Prometheus, 1920, 14⅜x23¾", EX **2,250.00**
Calendar top, Spirit of the Night, 13½x23¼", EX **2,300.00**
Calendar top, Valley of Enchantment, B&B, 1947, 16", EX **275.00**
Calendar top, Venetian Lamplighter, 1924, 14⅛x23⅝", EX....**1,500.00**
Calendar top, Waterfall, 1931, 6½x9", EX................................**650.00**
Catalog, Sterling Bicycles, 24 pgs, 9x6"..................................**450.00**
Chocolate box, Crane, textured cb w/Rubaiyat insert image, 11x7x1", EX ..**650.00**
Letter, handwritten to son Max Jr, 1933, w/eng envelope **625.00**
Magazine cover, Hearst's Magazine, Jack the Giant Killer, 10x7" ..**500.00**
Postcard, The Billboard/A Blot on Nature...., 3½x5⅝"..............**350.00**
Poster, Ex Libris, commemorates 1978 opening of MP Museum, 16x12"...**100.00**
Print, Air Castles, 1904, 16x12" **310.00**
Print, Aucassin Seeks for Nicholette, Scribner, 1903, 17x11½" .**700.00**
Print, Autumn, 1905, 10x12" **450.00**
Print, Cleopatra, House of Art, orig fr, 30x34" overall w/fr **2,300.00**
Print, Dinkey Bird, Scribner, 1905, 16x11" **350.00**

Print, Dreaming, House of Art, 18x30" **1,550.00**
Print, Errant Pan, 1910, 11x9" **600.00**
Print, Eventide, B&B, 1944, 10x12" **250.00**
Print, Garden of Allah, House of Art, 1918, 15x30" **600.00**
Print, Garden of Opportunity, 1925, 11x20½" **500.00**
Print, Hilltop, House of Art, 1927, 12x20" **600.00**
Print, Jason & the Talking Oak, 1908, 11x9" **275.00**
Print, Land of Make Believe, Scribner, 1912, 11x9" **500.00**
Print, Lantern Bearers, Dodge Publishing, 1910, 9½x11½" **600.00**
Print, Lights of Home (Silent Night), 10x12" **400.00**
Print, Moring, House of Art, 1926, 15x12", reproduction **250.00**
Print, Pied Piper, 6¾x21" **1,450.00**
Print, Romance, House of Art, 12x24" **1,300.00**
Print, Rubaiyat, CA Crane, Cleveland, 1917, 8x31" **975.00**
Print, Spirit of Transporation, House of Art, 1923, 20x16" **600.00**
Print, Stars, House of Art, 1927, 10x6" **350.00**

Print, The Century, Midsummer Holiday Number August, 1897, 14x20", EX, $2,000.00.

Print, The Prince (The Knave), 1928, 12x10" **300.00**
Tape measure, Edison Mazda Lamps logo, celluloid, 1920s, 1" **200.00**
Triptych, Daybreak flanked by Stars & Hilltop, fr, 12x32", EX ..**1,000.00**

Pate-De-Verre

Simply translated, pate-de-verre means paste of glass. In the manufacturing process, lead glass is first ground, then mixed with sodium silicate solution to form a paste which can be molded and refired. Some of the most prominent artisans to use this procedure were Almaric Walter, Daum, Argy-Rouseau, and Decorchemont. See also specific manufacturers.

Bust of satyr, amethyst, mk Despret/#1099, 6½" **1,100.00**
Paperweight, top half of human head, wine/pk, Decorchemont, 2x3¼" ...**350.00**
Pendant, lady w/flowing hair, amethyst, gilt mt, 1¼" dia **385.00**
Scarab, gray mottled w/amethyst, sgn Decorchemont, 3x4½" **850.00**
Sculpture, lady's head, yel, sgn Despret, 4" L **550.00**
Vase, 12-panel, cvd geometrics, bubbles, Decorchemont, 7x6" ..**4,600.00**

Pate-Sur-Pate

Pate-sur-pate, literally paste-on paste, is a technique whereby relief decorations are built up on a ceramic body by layering several applications of slip, one on the other, until the desired result is achieved. Usually only two colors are used, and the value of a piece is greatly enhanced as more color is added.

Medallion, cherub, wht on bl, Fr, 19th C, 3⅜x2⅜" **315.00**
Paperweight, classical maiden, Louis Solon, Minton, 6½" **14,375.00**
Vase, cherubs in flight among foliage on brn, 1880s, unmk, 6", pr ...**865.00**
Vase, lady playing harp, bl w/gold trim, ftd, 7½" **475.00**

Vase, putti in flight on teal, Louis Solon, Minton, 1895, 12¼", pr ..**8,000.00**
Vase, putti medallions/flowers on teal, Minton, w/lid, 15¼", pr **11,500.00**
Vase, seated lady, lt gr w/silver hdls, shouldered, 6" **450.00**
Vase, standing female, bl w/gold trim, 7½" **325.00**
Vase, 2 cherubs/mushroom, gr w/4 gold ft, ovoid, 6½" **725.00**

Pattern Glass

Pattern glass was the first mass-produced fancy tableware in America and was much prized by our ancestors. From the 1840s to the Civil War, it contained a high lead content and is known as 'Flint Glass.' It is exceptionally clear and resonant. Later glass was made with soda lime and is known as non-flint. By the 1890s pattern glass was produced in great volume in thousands of patterns, and colored glass came into vogue. Today the highest prices are often paid for these later patterns flashed with rose, amber, canary, and vaseline; stained ruby; or made in colors of cobalt, green, yellow, amethyst, etc. Demand for pattern glass declined by 1915, and glass fanciers were collecting it by 1930. No other field of antiques offers more diversity in patterns, prices, or pieces than this unique and historical glass that represents the Victorian era in America.

Our advisor for this category is Darlene Yohe; she is listed in the Directory under Arkansas. For a more thorough study on the subject, we recommend *Field Guide to Pattern Glass* and by Mollie Helen McCain; *Standard Encyclopedia of Pressed Glass, 1860 – 1930, Identification & Values,* by Bill Edwards and Mike Carwile; and *Early American Pattern Glass* and *Much More Early American Pattern Glass* by Alice Hulett Metz. All are available from Collector Books. See also Bread Plates; Cruets; Historical Glass; Salt and Pepper Shakers; Salts, Open; Sugar Shakers; Syrups; specific manufacturers such as Northwood.

Note: Values are given for open sugar bowls and compotes unless noted 'w/lid.'

Acorn, butter dish **85.00**
Acorn, egg cup **20.00**
Acorn, pitcher **100.00**
Acorn Band, celery vase **20.00**
Acorn Band, egg cup **15.00**
Acorn Band, wine **15.00**
Actress, butter dish **110.00**
Actress, cheese dish **275.00**
Actress, compote, low, 7" **60.00**
Actress, mug **50.00**
Actress, sugar bowl **125.00**
Ada, celery dish **20.00**
Ada, pitcher **95.00**
Ada, sugar bowl **30.00**
Admiral Dewey, See Dewey; See Also Greentown Dewey
Adonis, bowl, berry; sm **10.00**
Adonis, jelly compote **30.00**
Adonis, relish tray **15.00**
Adonis, spooner **25.00**
Alabama, butter dish, ruby stain **145.00**
Alabama, cake stand **40.00**
Alabama, honey dish, w/lid, rare **75.00**
Alaska, celery tray **70.00**
Alaska, pitcher **85.00**
Alaska, spooner **35.00**
Almond, tray, wine **30.00**
Almond, wine, stemmed **25.00**
Amazon, banana stand **50.00**
Amazon, champagne **30.00**
Amazon, cordial **25.00**
Amazon, pitcher **65.00**

Amberette, See Klondike
Amboy, celery dish 15.00
Amboy, goblet...35.00
Amboy, sugar bowl..25.00
American Beauty, bowl, berry; lg 40.00
American Beauty, compote, jelly 30.00
American Beauty, pitcher..75.00
Angular, butter dish..55.00
Angular, pitcher..85.00
Arcadia Lace, candy dish, w/lid.............................35.00
Arcadia Lace, nappy 30.00
Arcadia Lace, plate, 11" 30.00
Arch & Forget-Me-Not Bands, butter dish 45.00
Arch & Forget-Me-Not Bands, creamer 25.00
Arch & Forget-Me-Not Bands, sugar bowl............30.00
Arched Fleur-de-Lis, banana stand 35.00
Arched Fleur-de-Lis, cake stand 40.00
Arched Fleur-de-Lis, plate, 7" sq 20.00
Arched Grape, champagne.......................................25.00
Arched Grape, compote, w/lid 60.00
Arched Grape, tumbler 20.00
Arched Grape, wine 20.00
Arched Ovals, compote..35.00
Arched Ovals, goblet...40.00
Arched Ovals, plate...30.00
Arched Ovals, sugar bowl.......................................25.00

Argent

Argent, butter dish 65.00
Argent, goblet..35.00
Argus, bone dish 15.00
Argus, bottle, bitters 65.00
Argus, bowl, berry; sm..15.00
Argus, champagne 25.00
Argus, egg cup 30.00
Arrowhead-in-Oval, basket.....................................50.00
Arrowhead-in-Oval, celery dish.............................20.00
Arrowhead-in-Oval, plate, 7"..................................20.00
Arrowhead-in-Oval, rose bowl, stemmed 35.00
Art, banana dish 25.00
Art, creamer...20.00
Art, goblet..40.00
Art, mug...30.00
Artichoke, bowl, 7-8" 35.00
Artichoke, cake stand..50.00
Artichoke, finger bowl..45.00
Artichoke, sugar bowl...60.00
Ashman, cake stand...35.00
Ashman, pickle jar...35.00
Ashman, spooner 20.00
Austrian, butter dish..55.00
Austrian, cordial 25.00
Austrian, punch bowl 90.00
Austrian, shaker...25.00
Baby Face, butter dish...275.00

Baby Face, celery dip..65.00
Baby Face, cordial...80.00
Baby Face, sugar bowl...215.00
Balder, See Pennsylvania
Baltimore Pear, butter dish.....................................75.00
Baltimore Pear, goblet 60.00
Baltimore Pear, pitcher...110.00
Baltimore Pear, tray, water.....................................30.00
Bamboo Beauty, creamer or spooner.....................35.00
Bamboo Beauty, pitcher..110.00
Bamboo Beauty, sugar bowl...................................40.00
Banded Buckle, compote, w/lid..............................50.00
Banded Buckle, cordial 20.00
Banded Buckle, pitcher...85.00
Banded Diamond Point, goblet...............................35.00
Banded Diamond Point, sugar bowl 25.00
Banded Fleur-de-Lis, butter dish 65.00
Banded Fleur-de-Lis, egg cup 30.00
Banded Star, celery vase...15.00
Banded Star, pickle dish 15.00
Banded Star, tumbler...20.00
Bar & Block, finger bowl..15.00
Bar & Block, jam jar..35.00
Bar & Block, mustard jar...50.00
Bar & Block, sugar bowl...35.00
Barrel Huber, See Huber
Bead & Scroll, jelly compote 35.00
Bead & Scroll, pitcher...80.00
Beaded Diamond, bowl, berry; sm..........................20.00
Beaded Diamond, butter dish..................................55.00
Beaded Diamond, pitcher..75.00
Beaded Diamond, sugar bowl..................................25.00
Beaded Grape, cake stand..35.00
Beaded Grape, sugar bowl.......................................30.00
Beaded Medallion, egg cup.....................................20.00
Beaded Medallion, sugar bowl................................25.00
Beaded Tulip, cake stand...35.00
Beaded Tulip, ice cream dish..................................20.00
Beaded Tulip, plate..20.00
Bearded Head, See Viking
Bird & Strawberry, butter dish.............................100.00
Bird & Strawberry, chop plate..............................150.00
Bird & Strawberry, plate, sandwich 100.00
Bleeding Heart, honey dish.....................................25.00
Bleeding Heart, waste bowl....................................20.00
Block & Circle, butter dish.....................................55.00
Block & Circle, goblet...40.00
Block & Fan, biscuit jar..50.00
Block & Fan, decanter...45.00
Block & Fan, waste bowl..20.00
Blockade, compote, w/lid, 8"..................................65.00
Blockade, pitcher...85.00
Blue Jay, See Cardinal Bird
Bow Tie, butter pat..20.00
Bow Tie, jam jar..35.00
Bow Tie, salt cellar, master.....................................20.00
Bow Tie, sugar bowl..30.00
Brazen Shield, butter dish.......................................75.00
Brazen Shield, pickle dish.......................................20.00
Brazen Shield, pitcher...95.00
Brazen Shield, sugar bowl.......................................30.00
Brittanic, cracker jar..35.00
Brittanic, custard cup..10.00
Broken Column, biscuit jar......................................80.00

Broken Column, butter dish..........................55.00
Broken Column, cake stand.........................40.00
Broken Column, compote.............................45.00
Broken Column, wine carafe........................50.00
Buckle w/Star, cake stand..........................35.00
Buckle w/Star, goblet..................................30.00
Buckle w/Star, wine....................................15.00
Bull's-Eye & Daisy, butter dish...................65.00
Bull's-Eye & Daisy, tumbler........................20.00
Bull's-Eye & Fan, creamer, sugar bowl or spooner, ea...................30.00
Bull's-Eye & Fan, pitcher............................95.00
Bull's-Eye Band, See Reverse Torpedo
Bull's-Eye in Heart, See Heart w/Thumbprint
Button Arches, cake stand, ruby stain.........175.00
Button Arches, mustard jar..........................25.00
Button Arches, sauce...................................15.00
Buzz-Star, bowl, berry; lg............................45.00
Buzz-Star, goblet...45.00
Buzz-Star, wine..15.00
Cabbage Rose, butter dish...........................65.00
Cabbage Rose, cake plate.............................30.00
Cabbage Rose, champagne............................15.00
Cabbage Rose, egg cup.................................25.00
California, See Beaded Grape
Cane, compote..25.00
Cane, milk pitcher..40.00
Cane, tumbler...20.00
Cane Pinwheel, bowl, various, ea from $10 to.............35.00
Cane Pinwheel, creamer or spooner...............25.00
Cannonball Pinwheel, butter dish.................70.00
Cannonball Pinwheel, pitcher, milk..............55.00
Cannonball Pinwheel, tumbler......................15.00
Cardinal Bird, goblet....................................60.00
Cardinal Bird, honey dish, w/lid....................60.00
Cardinal Bird, sugar bowl..............................35.00
Cathedral, butter dish..................................55.00
Cathedral, cake stand...................................35.00
Cathedral, tumbler.......................................20.00
Centennial, See Liberty Bell
Chain w/Star, bowl, berry; sm.......................20.00
Chain w/Star, creamer...................................27.50
Chain w/Star, plate.......................................25.00
Chain w/Star, sugar bowl..............................25.00
Chandelier, banana stand............................125.00
Chandelier, bowl, finger................................35.00
Chandelier, goblet...75.00
Chandelier, sugar shaker.............................145.00
Cherry & Cable, bowl, berry; sm...................25.00
Cherry & Cable, pitcher..............................100.00
Cherry & Cable, punch cup, scarce................25.00
Cherry & Fig, butter dish.............................85.00
Cherry & Fig, pickle dish.............................20.00
Chippendale, butter dish..............................55.00
Chippendale, shaker......................................30.00
Chippendale, sugar bowl...............................30.00
Church Windows, cake stand........................40.00
Church Windows, sardine dish......................25.00
Classic, celery vase, either style.................125.00
Classic, compote, w/lid, 6½-12½", from $150 to........250.00
Classic, pitcher, water; collared base..........265.00
Cleopatra, See Egyptian
Clio, bowl, fan corners, lg............................40.00
Clio, pitcher...90.00
Coin, See US Coin

Colorado, cheese dish, ftd............................20.00
Colorado, perfume bottle, rare......................65.00
Comet, creamer..165.00
Comet, goblet..40.00
Comet, sugar bowl..25.00
Compact, See Snail
Connecticut, basket......................................35.00
Connecticut, compote, w/lid, from $25 to.....45.00
Connecticut, sherbet cup..............................10.00
Cord Drapery, creamer, bl...........................130.00
Cord Drapery, mug.......................................45.00
Cord Drapery, wine......................................20.00
Cornucopia, bowl, berry; sm.........................20.00
Cornucopia, mug...30.00
Cosmos, creamer or spooner.........................20.00
Cosmos, shaker...20.00
Cottage, bowl, berry; lg................................35.00
Cottage, champagne......................................15.00
Cottage, cup..10.00
Croesus, bowl, purple, 8"............................155.00
Croesus, plate, ftd, 8"...................................25.00
Crossed Shield, butter dish..........................65.00
Crossed Shield, pitcher.................................85.00
Crow's Foot, See Yale
Crown Jewels, See Chandelier

Crystal Queen

Crystal Queen, basket...................................55.00
Crystal Queen, vase.......................................30.00
Crystal Wedding, claret.................................25.00
Crystal Wedding, tumbler..............................30.00
Crystal Wedding, wine..................................98.00
Cube w/Fan, See Pineapple & Fan
Cupid & Venus, cake stand...........................65.00
Cupid & Venus, tumbler................................30.00
Cupids, egg cup...30.00
Cupids, jam jar, w/lid....................................60.00
Cupids, salt cellar, ftd..................................35.00
Currier & Ives, cup & saucer........................40.00
Currier & Ives, tray, Balky Mule...................75.00
Curtain Tie-Back, butter dish.......................45.00
Curtain Tie-Back, compote, w/lid..................35.00
Curtain Tie-Back, plate.................................20.00
Curtain Tie-Back, wine.................................10.00
Cut Log, banana stand..................................40.00
Cut Log, compote, w/lid, 5½-7½"..................65.00
Cut Log, relish dish......................................30.00
Dahlia (Canton), butter dish........................60.00
Dahlia (Canton), cordial...............................20.00
Dahlia (Canton), egg cup..............................20.00
Daisy & Button (Hobbs), butter dish, 2 styles, ea from $55 to....110.00
Daisy & Button (Hobbs), ice tub...................40.00
Daisy & Button (Hobbs), tumbler..................20.00
Daisy & Button w/Crossbars, bowl, 7-9".......30.00

Daisy & Button w/Crossbars, creamer, ind 22.00
Daisy & Button w/Crossbars, mug, 2 szs, ea...............................25.00
Daisy & Button w/V Ornament, bowl, finger............................20.00
Daisy & Button w/V Ornament, celery vase 25.00
Daisy & Button w/V Ornament, sherbet 20.00
Daisy & Scroll, creamer or spooner 25.00
Daisy & Scroll, tumbler..20.00
Daisy-in-Square, bowl, berry; lg 35.00
Daisy-in-Square, pitcher, milk 45.00
Daisy-in-Square, sauce bowl..10.00
Dakota, bottle, cologne 85.00
Dakota, compote, w/lid, 5-12", ea from $65 to.......................140.00
Dart, compote, jelly 35.00
Dart, goblet..50.00
Dart, tumbler 20.00
Deer & Dog, champagne 85.00
Deer & Dog, jar, marmalade 145.00
Deer & Dog, pitcher..175.00
Delaware, basket, silver holder 40.00
Delaware, finger bowl 20.00
Delaware, shade, gas 55.00
Dew & Raindrop, butter dish 45.00
Dew & Raindrop, goblet 35.00
Dew & Raindrop, sherbet...15.00
Dew & Raindrop, tumbler 15.00
Dewey, breakfast set 75.00
Dewey, parfait 30.00
Dewey, See Also Greentown Dewey

Diamond

Diamond, butter dish..70.00
Diamond, pickle dish..15.00
Diamond, tumbler...15.00
Diamond Lattice, creamer or spooner.......................................20.00
Diamond Lattice, plate 25.00
Diamond Lattice, relish (club shape)..35.00
Diamond Medallion, See Grand
Diamond Spearhead, compote, tall 45.00
Diamond Spearhead, mug 25.00
Diamond Spearhead, rose bowl 25.00
Diamond Thumbprint, ale glass..90.00
Diamond Thumbprint, bottle, bitters 450.00
Diamond Thumbprint, cordial...300.00
Diamond Thumbprint, honey dish 35.00
Diamond Thumbprint, tumbler, bar; 3¾" 145.00
Diamond w/Peg, bowl, berry; lg..40.00
Diamond w/Peg, pickle dish 15.00
Diamond w/Peg, sugar bowl..30.00
Doric, See Feather
Double Pinwheel, bowl, 7" 25.00
Double Pinwheel, compote 35.00
Double Pinwheel, pitcher..75.00
Double Ribbon, compote, w/lid 50.00
Double Ribbon, tumbler..25.00

Duncan's #40, butter dish...70.00
Duncan's #40, pitcher...75.00
Duncan's #40, sugar bowl, ind..25.00
Duncan's Late Block, bowl, tricornered.....................................45.00
Duncan's Late Block, ice tub...50.00
Duncan's Late Block, rose bowl...45.00
Egg in Sand, sugar bowl..25.00
Egyptian, compote, 7½" 95.00
Egyptian, plate, Pyramids...125.00
Egyptian, tray, rectangular..95.00
Elephant, See Jumbo
Emerald Green Herringbone, See Florida
English Colonial, claret 10.00
English Colonial, tumbler 15.00
Esther, bowl, berry; lg 45.00
Esther, sugar bowl 30.00
Eyewinker, bowl, berry; sm...15.00
Eyewinker, bowl, vegetable...35.00
Eyewinker, compote, w/lid, 7-9", ea 45.00
Eyewinker, pitcher 150.00
Eyewinker, plate, 7" sq...25.00
Fairfax Strawberry, See Strawberry
Falling Leaves, celery tray 25.00
Falling Leaves, pitcher..70.00
Fan & Star, celery vase 25.00
Fan & Star, plate, 7"..25.00
Fancy Loop, champagne 15.00
Fancy Loop, cracker jar, various, ea from $25 to 45.00
Fancy Loop, tumbler, bar sz..35.00
Fandango, banana stand 45.00
Fandango, cookie jar, tall 50.00
Fandango, custard cup 10.00
Feather, cake stand 50.00
Feather, plate, 10" 40.00
Feather, wine..20.00
Feather Duster, compote, from $20 to 40.00
Feather Duster, egg cup 15.00
Feather Duster, waste bowl...20.00
Festoon, mug..45.00
Festoon, tray, water...40.00
Festoon, tumbler 22.00
File, grape plate..25.00
File, rose bowl, 5½-7"...35.00
File, sugar bowl 25.00
Fine Cut & Block, compote 30.00
Fine Cut & Block, pitcher, amber..88.00
Fine Cut & Block, relish 15.00
Fine Cut & Diamond, See Grand
Fine Cut & Fan, pickle dish, oval..20.00
Fine Cut & Fan, sugar bowl 25.00
Fine Cut & Feather, See Feather
Fishscale, butter dish 65.00
Fishscale, goblet 40.00
Fishscale, relish 20.00
Florida, cake stand..35.00
Florida, celery vase...32.00
Florida, cordial...20.00
Florida, sugar bowl...30.00
Flower Band, celery vase 15.00
Flower Band, goblet..40.00
Flower Pot, cake stand..50.00
Flower Pot, goblet...45.00
Flute, butter dish..65.00
Flute, tumbler...20.00

Flute & Care, butter dish 50.00
Flute & Care, champagne..15.00
Flute & Care, goblet..15.00
Fringed Drape, cordial 15.00
Fringed Drape, sugar bowl 25.00
Fringed Drape, vase, flat, 10-14" 45.00
Frosted Circle, bowl, 7-8", ea 45.00
Frosted Circle, pitcher...125.00
Frosted Circle, tumbler..20.00
Frosted Eagle, bowl, w/lid, 6¼" 175.00
Frosted Eagle, creamer or spooner 45.00
Frosted Ribbon, See Ribbon
Frosted Stork, creamer or spooner 55.00
Frosted Stork, goblet...70.00
Frosted Stork, tumbler 35.00
Galloway, butter dish 65.00
Galloway, cake stand, 3 szs, ea from $65 to 75.00
Galloway, egg cup 50.00
Galloway, Pitcher..100.00
Garfield Drape, cake stand 45.00
Garfield Drape, compote, high or low, w/lid...................70.00
Garfield Drape, honey dish 18.00
Garfield Drape, pitcher, milk 65.00
Gem, See Nailhead
Good Luck, See Horseshoe
Gothic Windows, pickle dish 20.00
Gothic Windows, sugar bowl 30.00
Grand, celery vase 25.00
Grand, decanter...70.00
Grand, sherbet 15.00
Grape & Festoon, compote, w/lid, high std...................110.00
Grape & Festoon, pickle tray 20.00
Grape & Festoon, salt cellar, master 25.00
Grape & Festoon w/Shield, mug, 1⅞" 20.00
Grape w/o Vine, bowl, berry; sm 20.00
Grape w/o Vine, tumbler..20.00
Grape w/Thumbprint, creamer.......................................20.00
Grape w/Thumbprint, cup..10.00
Grasshopper (deduct 50% if no insect is present)
Grasshopper, celery vase..65.00
Grasshopper, marmalade jar 150.00
Grasshopper, pitcher..125.00
Grasshopper, salt cellar 35.00
Hairpin, champagne, flint 78.00
Hand, bowl, oval, 7-10", ea from $20 to.........................35.00
Hand, butter dish...110.00
Hand, honey dish...35.00
Hand, mug...42.00
Hand, wine...20.00
Hartley, cake plate 35.00
Hartley, goblet 50.00
Hartley, sugar bowl 25.00
Heart w/Thumbprint, barber bottle 80.00
Heart w/Thumbprint, compote, 2 szs, ea from $45 to 75.00
Heart w/Thumbprint, ice bucket....................................55.00
Henrietta, bonbon 20.00
Henrietta, cake stand...40.00
Henrietta, sugar bowl, ind 30.00
Herringbone Buttress, See Greentown, Herringbone Buttress
Hickman, compote, jelly 35.00
Hickman, pitcher, water 60.00
Hidalgo, compote, w/lid, high or low std, ea from $40 to 55.00
Hidalgo, cup & saucer 35.00
Hidalgo, waste bowl 15.00

Hobnail, celery vase...30.00
Hobnail, tray..35.00
Hobnail w/Fan, goblet 45.00
Hobnail w/Fan, pitcher 85.00
Hobnail w/Fan, wine 10.00
Hobstar, bowl, fruit; 10½" 35.00
Hobstar, pitcher 75.00
Hobstar & Feather, bowl, applesauce 45.00
Hobstar & Feather, butter dish 200.00
Hobstar & Feather, creamer, spooner or sugar, ea 45.00
Holly, butter dish...165.00
Holly, egg cup..65.00
Holly, goblet 100.00
Holly Amber, See Greentown, Holly Amber
Honeycomb w/Star, cake stand 35.00
Honeycomb w/Star, sauce bowl, flat 10.00
Hops & Barley, See Wheat & Barley
Horseshoe, jam jar 25.00
Horseshoe, plate, 8-10", ea 30.00
Horseshoe, wine, rare 40.00
Huber, butter dish..50.00
Huber, decanter 65.00
Huber, plate 25.00
Hummingbird, cheese plate 35.00
Hummingbird, pitcher..110.00
Hummingbird, tumbler...30.00
Idaho, See Snail
Illinois, basket, hdl 40.00
Illinois, jam jar 30.00
Illinois, olive dish 20.00
Illinois, spoon tray 20.00
Indian Sunset, bowl, berry; lg 40.00
Indian Sunset, creamer or spooner..................................20.00
Indiana, bowl, finger 20.00
Indiana, carafe 35.00
Inverted Feather, celery vase 25.00
Inverted Feather, decanter..75.00
Inverted Feather, punch cup 20.00
Inverted Strawberry, bonbon, ftd 30.00
Inverted Strawberry, goblet 60.00
Inverted Strawberry, vase, sweet pea; stemmed 40.00
Iris w/Meander, See Opalescent Glass
Jacob's Ladder, goblet...70.00
Jacob's Ladder, honey dish 15.00
Jacob's Ladder, marmalade jar 90.00

Jersey Swirl

Jersey Swirl, candlestick 30.00
Jersey Swirl, cup...10.00
Jewel & Dewdrop, cake stand 55.00
Jewel & Dewdrop, mug, 3½"...35.00
Job's Tear, See Art
Jubilee, butter dish...65.00

Jubilee, goblet 45.00
Jubilee, pickle dish 20.00
Jumbo, butter dish, elephant finial, rnd......725.00
Jumbo, butter dish, oblong 500.00
Jumbo, pitcher 700.00
Jumbo, spoon rack 425.00
Kentucky, cake stand 40.00
Kentucky, spooner 35.00
Kentucky, tumbler 20.00
King's Crown, basket, fruit 40.00
King's Crown, cake stand 70.00
King's Crown, compote, 3 szs, ea from $25 to ...40.00
King's Crown, cup & saucer 60.00
King's Crown, plate, 7" 15.00
King's Crown, punch bowl 250.00
Klondike, bowl, 7-8", ea from $60 to 80.00
Klondike, butter dish.....................................150.00
Klondike, creamer...75.00
Klondike, olive dish..40.00
Klondike, relish tray 35.00
Klondike, tumbler 45.00
Kokomo, casserole, w/lid 55.00
Kokomo, compote, jelly 35.00
Kokomo, tumbler 25.00
La Clede, See Hickman
Lacy Dewdrop, bowl, berry; sm 20.00
Lacy Dewdrop, goblet 35.00
Lacy Dewdrop, sugar bowl 25.00
Lattice, celery vase..25.00
Lattice, plate 25.00
Lattice, wine 15.00
Laverne, bowl, oval or rnd, ea from $10 to......45.00
Laverne, creamer or spooner 20.00
Laverne, wine..15.00
Leaf, See Maple Leaf
Leaf & Star, banana boat.................................40.00
Leaf & Star, butter dish 65.00
Leaf & Star, goblet..50.00
Leaf Bracket, See Greentown, Leaf Medallion
Leaf Medallion, See Northwood, Leaf Medallion
Liberty Bell, butter dish.................................165.00
Liberty Bell, pickle dish..................................50.00
Liberty Bell, plate, 3 szs, ea from $70 to 85.00
Lion Head, compote, w/lid, 6-9", ea 125.00
Lion Head, sugar bowl 75.00
Lion w/Cable, butter dish..............................200.00
Lion w/Cable, pitcher....................................275.00
Log Cabin, butter dish...................................325.00
Log Cabin, sugar bowl 300.00
Loop, bottle, bitters 80.00
Loop, cake stand 30.00
Loop, goblet, flint 25.00
Loop, plate 30.00
Loop & Dart w/Diamond Ornament, bottle, water.....50.00
Loop & Dart w/Diamond Ornament, tray, relish; oval 20.00
Loop w/Dewdrop, cake stand..........................40.00
Manhattan, tumbler, iced tea 30.00
Maple Leaf, dish, 10" sq..................................30.00
Maple Leaf, goblet 55.00
Maple Leaf, goblet, vaseline 160.00
Mardi Gras, goblet 35.00
Mardi Gras, sherry 30.00
Maryland, banana dish 35.00
Maryland, pitcher, milk 50.00

Maryland, plate, dinner 25.00
Masonic, cake stand, 9-10", ea from $35 to......45.00
Masonic, relish dish...15.00
Massachusetts, candy dish 25.00
Massachusetts, plate, 8" 30.00
Massachusetts, punch cup 17.50
Medallion Sunburst, cake stand 40.00
Medallion Sunburst, tumbler 15.00
Memphis, bowl, berry; sm 25.00
Memphis, pitcher...275.00
Memphis, punch bowl, w/base, regular 350.00
Michigan, celery vase 25.00
Michigan, goblet, bl stain 42.00
Michigan, plate..30.00

Minerva

Minerva, champagne 25.00
Minerva, waste bowl..55.00
Minnesota, bowl, berry; lg 45.00
Minnesota, mug 25.00
Missouri, cordial..30.00
Missouri, sauce bowl, gr...................................12.50
Moon & Star, cake stand..................................40.00
Moon & Star, champagne.................................15.00
Nail, compote, berry 30.00
Nail, goblet 55.00
Nail, shaker 25.00
Nailhead, butter dish 70.00
Nailhead, creamer..20.00
Nailhead, sugar bowl 25.00
New England Pineapple, champagne...............190.00
New England Pineapple, cordial.....................200.00
New England Pineapple, creamer, flint 275.00
New England Pineapple, sauce bowl, flat or ftd, ea......25.00
New Hampshire, biscuit jar 45.00
New Hampshire, cup, lemonade 10.00
New Hampshire, custard cup...........................10.00
New Jersey, olive dish 25.00
New Jersey, tumbler, 2 styles, ea from $20 to...30.00
Niagara, bowl, berry; lg....................................35.00
Niagara, plate..25.00
Oaken Bucket, See Wooden Pail
Octagon, pitcher, std sz....................................70.00
Octagon, punch bowl 85.00
Ohio Star, pitcher, cider.................................200.00
Ohio Star, punch cup.......................................25.00
One Hundred & One, creamer 55.00
One Hundred & One, pickle dish.....................15.00
One-O-One, See One Hundred & One
Optical Tube, See Tile
Oregon #1, carafe..45.00
Oregon #1, celery vase.....................................20.00
Oregon #1, vase...25.00
Palmette, cake stand 140.00
Palmette, shaker, lg..75.00

Palmette, tumbler, 2 szs, ea from $35 to 60.00
Panelled Diamond Blocks, butter dish...50.00
Panelled Diamond Blocks, sauce bowl..10.00
Panelled Diamond Blocks, sugar bowl 25.00
Panelled Forget-Me-Not, butter dish..50.00
Panelled Forget-Me-Not, mustard jar...42.50
Panelled Strawberry, tumbler..15.00
Panelled Thistle, butter dish..45.00
Panelled Thistle, plate..25.00
Pennsylvania, bowl, berry; sm 15.00
Pennsylvania, goblet...40.00
Persian, cheese dish..65.00
Persian, sugar bowl...35.00
Pineapple & Fan, decanter..35.00
Pineapple & Fan, vase, trumpet form, 10".....................................35.00
Pleat & Panel, creamer or spooner...25.00
Pleat & Panel, tray, water..25.00
Polar Bear, goblet...100.00
Polar Bear, ice bowl..95.00
Portland, cordial...10.00
Portland, cup..20.00
Portland, goblet..30.00
Portland, plate, dinner..20.00
Prayer Rug, See Horseshoe
Pressed Leaf, egg cup...20.00
Pressed Leaf, spooner...25.00
Priscilla, banana stand..50.00
Priscilla, compote, jelly; w/lid 40.00
Priscilla, creamer..20.00
Priscilla, jam jar..50.00
Prism, butter dish...45.00
Prism, champagne...15.00
Queen Anne, pitcher...85.00
Queen Anne, plate...20.00
Raindrop, butter dish..55.00
Raindrop, relish tray...15.00
Raindrop, wine..15.00
Recessed Pillared Red Top, See Nail
Red Block, bowl, rectangular, from $55 to 85.00
Red Block, cup..35.00
Red Block, rose bowl...75.00
Red Top, See Button Arches
Reverse Torpedo, basket, fruit..50.00
Reverse Torpedo, butter dish..70.00
Reverse Torpedo, fruit basket...50.00
Reverse Torpedo, sugar bowl..30.00
Rex, pitcher..95.00
Rex, punch bowl..125.00
Rexford, butter dish..65.00
Rexford, compote..40.00
Rexford, honey jar...45.00
Rexford, wine..20.00
Ribbed Palm, celery vase..20.00
Ribbed Palm, egg cup...15.00
Ribbed Palm, goblet..45.00
Ribbon, cake stand..60.00
Ribbon, compote...50.00
Ribbon, goblet...35.00
Ribbon, tumbler..30.00
Rising Sun, bowl, berry; lg..35.00
Rising Sun, compote...45.00
Robin Hood, pickle dish..15.00
Robin Hood, pitcher..85.00
Roman Key, champagne...15.00

Roman Key, egg cup..20.00
Roman Key, sugar bowl...30.00
Roman Rosette, butter dish...65.00
Roman Rosette, cake stand, 2 szs, ea from $35 to.........................45.00
Roman Rosette, plate..35.00
Romeo, See Block & Fan
Rose in Snow, pitcher..200.00
Rose in Snow, sweetmeat, w/lid..100.00
Rosette, fish relish...35.00
Rosette, plate, w/hdls..35.00
Royal Ivy, See Northwood
Royal Oak, See Northwood
Ruby Diamond, pitcher...125.00
Ruby Diamond, sugar bowl...40.00
Ruby Thumbprint, See King's Crown
S-Repeat, compote, jelly..35.00
S-Repeat, condiment tray, amethyst..40.00
Saint Bernard, bowl, berry; lg...45.00
Saint Bernard, tumbler..20.00
Sawtooth, compote, w/lid, 5-10", ea from $35 to.........................90.00
Sawtooth, gas shade..60.00
Sawtooth, pitcher..165.00
Sawtooth Band, See Amazon
Scalloped Daisy Red Top, See Button Arches
Scroll w/Flowers, cordial..25.00
Scroll w/Flowers, tumbler...20.00
Seneca Loop, See Loop
Sequoia, butter pat..10.00
Sequoia, pickle boat..20.00
Sequoia, tray, brandy...20.00
Sheaf & Block, butter dish..65.00
Sheaf & Block, wine..15.00
Shell & Jewel, pitcher...90.00
Shell & Jewel, shaker..30.00
Shell & Tassel, goblet...60.00
Shell & Tassel, oyster dish..235.00
Shell & Tassel, tray, ice cream..25.00
Shelton Star, butter dish...50.00
Shelton Star, tumbler..15.00
Sheraton, creamer or spooner...20.00
Sheraton, goblet, bl...48.00
Shuttle, bowl, berry; lg..45.00
Shuttle, cordial...15.00

Snail

Snail, banana stand...160.00
Snail, celery tray...35.00
Snail, custard cup..35.00
Snow Flake, butter dish...65.00
Snow Flake, vase, 5-8¼", ea...35.00
Spirea Band, goblet...45.00
Spirea Band, relish..20.00
Spirea Band, tumbler..20.00
Star & Crescent, bowl, berry; sm..10.00
Star & Crescent, pitcher...65.00

Star & File, bowl, 7" 20.00
Star & File, custard cup 15.00
Star & File, tumbler, juice 15.00
Star in Bull's-Eye, goblet 35.00
Star in Bull's-Eye, pitcher 65.00
Star Medallion, bowl, rnd or sq, from $10 to 30.00
Star Medallion, tumbler 15.00
Stars & Stripes, butter dish 65.00
Stars & Stripes, wine 18.00
States, cocktail 27.50
States, cup 15.00
States, nappy, 3-hdl 25.00
Stippled Chain, cake stand 35.00
Stippled Chain, pitcher 85.00
Stippled Chain, sugar bowl 30.00
Stippled Cherry, bowl, berry; lg 50.00
Stippled Cherry, creamer or spooner 25.00
Stippled Forget-Me-Not, butter dish 80.00
Stippled Forget-Me-Not, cordial 20.00
Stippled Forget-Me-Not, pitcher 85.00
Stippled Medallion, butter dish 55.00
Stippled Medallion, plate 20.00
Strawberry, butter dish 55.00
Strawberry, goblet 35.00
Strawberry, honey dish 15.00
Strawberry, pitcher 75.00
Strawberry & Cable, sweetmeat, w/lid, 2 styles, ea 95.00
Strawberry & Cable, wine 15.00
Sunbeam, carafe 35.00
Sunbeam, pitcher 95.00
Sunbeam, sugar bowl 30.00
Sunbeam, tumbler 20.00
Sunk Daisy, carafe 35.00
Sunk Daisy, compote 40.00
Swirl & Ball, cake stand 40.00
Swirl & Ball, candlestick 30.00
Swirl & Ball, jelly dish, ftd 25.00
Tarantum's Virginia, compote 35.00
Tarantum's Virginia, goblet 35.00
Tarantum's Virginia, pitcher 70.00
Teardrop, bowl(s), sq, ea from $20 to 45.00
Teardrop, compote 35.00
Teardrop & Tassel, goblet 75.00
Teardrop & Tassel, relish 36.00
Teasel, cracker jar 40.00
Teasel, honey jar, w/lid 55.00
Texas, cake stand, 8-11", ea 40.00
Texas, horseradish jar, w/lid 55.00
Theatrical, See Actress
Thousand Eye, inkwell 40.00
Thousand Eye, jelly glass 20.00
Thousand Eye, nappy, bl, 5" 45.00
Three Face, compote, w/lid, low std, 6-10", ea 175.00
Three Face, cracker jar 1,350.00
Three Face, goblet 125.00
Three Panel, celery vase, either style 20.00
Three Panel, spooner 16.00
Three Panel, tumbler 20.00
Three-in-One, milk jar, w/lid 70.00
Three-in-One, punch bowl 135.00
Thumbprint, See Argus
Thumbprint Band, See Dakota
Thunderbird, See Hummingbird
Tile, cake stand 35.00

Tile, creamer or spooner 20.00
Tokyo, compote 25.00
Tokyo, plate 25.00
Torpedo, butter dish 65.00
Torpedo, cup & saucer 25.00
Torpedo, saucer bowl 10.00
Tree of Life, See Portland
Truncated Cube, decanter 40.00
Truncated Cube, goblet 50.00
Tulip w/Sawtooth, celery vase 20.00
Tulip w/Sawtooth, creamer, flint 88.00
Tulip w/Sawtooth, pomade jar 40.00
Twin Snowshoes, cake stand 35.00
Twin Snowshoes, creamer or spooner 20.00
Twinkle Star, See Utah
Two Panel, compote 40.00
Two Panel, tray, w/hdls 35.00
US Coin, ale glass 80.00
US Coin, celery vase 80.00
US Coin, claret 80.00
US Coin, epergne 250.00
US Coin, tray, water 150.00
US Sheraton, mustard jar 25.00
US Sheraton, sundae dish 20.00
Utah, cake plate 25.00
Utah, tumbler 20.00
Venus, butter dish 85.00
Venus, plate, Crying Baby 70.00
Viking, celery vase 25.00
Viking, jar, apothecary 75.00
Waffle & Fine Cut, butter dish 65.00
Waffle & Fine Cut, wine 20.00
Waffle Variant, cheese dish, w/lid 60.00
Waffle Variant, sugar bowl 25.00
Wheat & Barley, compote 35.00
Wheat & Barley, mug 30.00
Wheat & Barley, shakers, pr 40.00
Wildflower, cake stand 40.00
Wildflower, salt cellar 10.00
Willow Oak, cake stand 45.00
Willow Oak, celery vase 30.00

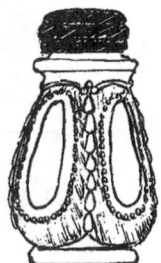

Wisconsin

Wisconsin, banana stand 40.00
Wisconsin, cup & saucer 35.00
Wisconsin, preserve dish, 6-8", ea 25.00
Wooden Pail, butter dish 110.00
Wooden Pail, tumbler 60.00
X-Ray, bowl, berry; lg 55.00
X-Ray, tray, cloverleaf 45.00
Yale, pitcher 85.00
Yale, relish, oval 15.00
Zipper, compote, w/lid 55.00
Zipper, creamer or spooner 25.00

Zippered Heart, butter dish 75.00
Zippered Heart, orange bowl, 12" 85.00
Zippered Heart, sherbet 15.00

Paul Revere Pottery

The Saturday Evening Girls were a social group of young Boston ladies who met to pursue various activities, among them pottery making. Their first kiln was bought in 1906, and within a few years it became necessary to move to a larger location. Because their new quarters were near the historical Old North Church, they chose the name Paul Revere Pottery. With very little training, the girls produced only simple ware. Until 1915 the pottery operated at a deficit, then a new building with four kilns was constructed on Nottingham Road. Vases, miniature jugs, children's tea sets, tiles, dinnerware, and lamps were produced, usually in soft matt glazes often decorated with incised, hand-painted designs from nature. Examples in a dark high gloss may also be found on occasion.

Several marks were used: 'P.R.P.'; 'S.E.G.'; or the circular device, 'Boston, Paul Revere Pottery' with the horse and rider.

The pottery continued to operate; and even though their product sold well, the high production costs of the handmade ware caused the pottery to fail in 1946.

Bowl, ducks & sky, yel/bl/wht/gr, PRP, 5x12", NM...................2,400.00
Bowl, rooster (repeated 4 times), FL/3-26, 2¼x4¼"..................1,980.00
Bowl, rooster & chick, yel/ivory, SEG/241-4-09/FL, 6", NM ...1,200.00
Bowl, steel bl w/tan-wht band, SEG/SG/3-17, 2½x8¼".............360.00
Creamer, rabbits & cabbages, SEG/TB/81.5.11, 2¾x4½"........2,000.00
Mug, rabbits & cabbages, gr/bl/yel, PRP, 1920s, 3¾x4½", NM...990.00
Paperweight, refined lady, octagonal, paper label, 2½", NM....1,100.00
Pitcher, rabbit/grass/sky/Jane, imp logo/FL/12-, 4¼x4¼".............880.00
Pitcher, rooster & chick, SEG/7-16, 3¼x3½" 1,200.00
Plate, duck on hill, bl/ivory/yel/gr, 1920s-30s mk, 7¾" 1,045.00
Plate, rabbit on gr hill, bl & wht sky, imp mk/FL/2-24, 7½" 715.00
Tile, The Common, trees/water/sky, 4-color, FL, 4-1-11, 3¾" sq ..1,750.00
Tile, Washington Street, mc, FL, ca 1910, 3¾" sq, NM 1,250.00
Vase, lotus flowers, SEG, 1900s, 8¾x7", NM...............................770.00
Vase, multitoned bl/gr/pk drip on dk bl, SEG, 5½" 260.00
Vase, sea gr w/aqua hue w/brn flecks, emb swirl, PRP/11-26, 9x6½"...495.00
Vase, sea gr w/metallic blk, streaky mc shoulder, SEG/RB, 12½" ..990.00

Pauline Pottery

Pauline Pottery was made from 1883 to 1888 in Chicago, Illinois, from clay imported from the Ohio area. The company's founder was Mrs. Pauline Jacobus, who had learned the trade at the Rookwood Pottery. Mrs. Jacobus moved to Edgerton, Wisconsin, to be near a source of suitable clay, thus eliminating shipping expenses. Until 1905 she produced high-quality wares, able to imitate with ease designs and styles of such masters as Wedgwood and Meissen. Her products were sold through leading department stores, and the names of some of these firms may appear on the ware. Not all are marked; unless signed by a noted local artist, positive identification is often impossible. Marked examples carry a variety of stamps and signatures: 'Trade Mark' with a crown, 'Pauline Pottery,' and 'Edgerton Art Pottery' are but a few.

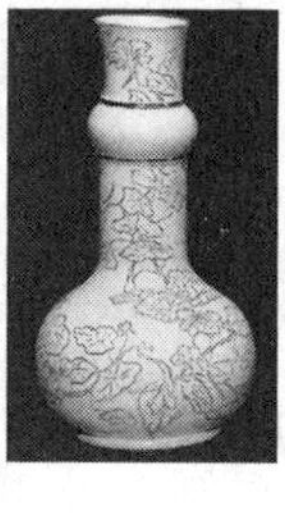

Vase, nasturtiums, Limoges style with fired-on gold highlights, 11⅛", NM, $325.00. (Photo courtesy Cincinnati Art Gallery)

Jar, ginger; abstract mc design w/panels & gold, pierced lid, 9"...550.00
Jar, powder; violets on cream, crown mk, 3¼", NM 225.00
Jardiniere, Nouveau poppies, uptrn sq hdls, unmk, 6⅛", NM 450.00

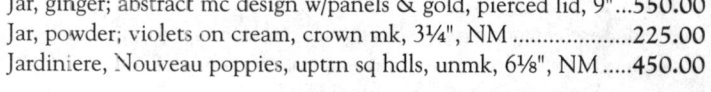

Peachblow

Peachblow, made to imitate the colors of the Chinese Peachbloom porcelain, was made by several glasshouses in the late 1800s. Among them were New England Glass, Mt. Washington, Webb, and Hobbs, Brockunier and Company (Wheeling). Its pink shading was achieved through action of the heat on the gold content of the glass. While New England's peachblow shades from deep crimson to white, Mt. Washington's tends to shade from pink to blue-gray. Many pieces were enameled and gilded. While by far the majority of the pieces made by New England had a satin (acid) finish, they made shiny peachblow as well. Wheeling glass, on the other hand, is rarely found in satin. In the 1950s Gundersen-Pairpoint Glassworks initiated the reproduction of Mt. Washington peachblow, using an exact duplication of the original formula. Though of recent manufacture, this glass is very collectible. Our advisors for this category are Betty and Clarence Maier; they are listed in the Directory under Pennsylvania.

Bowl, Gundersen, slightly flared, short ped ft, 3½x4" 225.00
Bowl, NE Glass, ruffled, 3x9"..500.00
Bowl, NE Glass, thin walls, 1½x4".......................................145.00
Bowl, Webb, gold bird/tree branch, 3 amber reeded ft, EX color, 5x9"....1,600.00
Candlestick, Gundersen, classic shape, rolled socket edge, 8" 375.00
Candlestick, Gundersen, morning glory cup, 8"..........................275.00
Celery, NE Glass, sq petal top, 7x4" 785.00
Creamer, Gundersen, ped ft, 4x5"..295.00
Creamer, Libbey, World's Fair 1893, wht ribs, waisted neck, 3x2¾" ..750.00
Creamer, Wheeling, sq mouth, amber hdl, 4x3½"........................575.00
Cruet, Gundersen, ribbed shell hdl, rnd w/long slim neck, 8x3½"...450.00
Cruet, NE Glass, petticoat form, wht hdl/stopper, 3-lip rim, 6¾".1,950.00
Cruet, NE Glass, shiny, pk-wht hdl, wht ball stopper...............1,500.00
Cruet, Wheeling, amber hdl & faceted stopper, bulbous w/short neck, 7"...1,300.00
Cup & saucer, Gundersen 275.00
Cup & saucer, Italian, ca 1960s, 3¼" 115.00
Decanter, NE Glass, ovoid w/long neck, ball stopper, 12½x4½"......1,450.00
Decanter, NE Glass, rnd w/stick neck, ribbed hdl, rnd stopper, 10" 950.00
Decanter, Wheeling, amber faceted stopper/twist hdl, bulbous, 9x6"...2,500.00
Ewer, claret; Wheeling, amber rigaree at narrow neck/reeded hdl, 10x5"...7,500.00
Goblet, Gundersen, knob stem, 7x4"......................................285.00
Jug, Gundersen, bulbous w/loop hdl, 4½x4"..............................450.00
Pear, NE Glass, 5" L...200.00
Pear, Wheeling, 4¾", NM...900.00
Pitcher, Gundersen, Hobnail, wht w/sm pk area on int, label, ovoid, 6" ..550.00
Pitcher, Gundersen, ogee sides, bun base, fancy hdl, 6x6"...........395.00
Pitcher, mini water; Webb, amber thorn hdl, acid script mk, 5¾"...275.00
Pitcher, NE Glass, petticoat shape, wht loop hdl, 4½x5"............850.00
Pitcher, Sandwich, Hobnail, bulbous w/sq top, 6¾x7½"............550.00
Pitcher, tankard; Wheeling, satin, str flaring sides, reed hdl, 11x4"....1,700.00
Pitcher, water; Wheeling, sq mouth, amber hdl, EX color/thin walls, 7"...1,950.00
Pitcher, Wheeling, Drape, crystal reed hdl, squat w/sqd mouth, 4½" ...345.00
Punch cup, NE Glass..275.00
Rose bowl, NE Glass, ruffled, 3½x3¾".....................................150.00
Rose bowl, Webb, gold stems/butterfly 590.00
Shakers, Wheeling, spherical, 2¾", pr 1,000.00
Spooner, NE Glass, sq top...825.00
Sugar bowl, Wheeling, Drape, w/lid, rare, 6x4", EX.................2,300.00
Sugar bowl, World's Fair 1893/lg mum & pods, lg wht hdls, 2¾x5½"...690.00
Tumbler, Gundersen, 3¾" 275.00
Tumbler, NE Glass, 3¾"...260.00

Tumbler, Wheeling, EX color, 3⅝x2¾"...............................**345.00**
Vase, Gundersen, dimpled body w/very wide crimped ruffled top, 5x6"..**525.00**
Vase, Gundersen, ftd chalice form w/M hdls & sq base, 8½" **550.00**
Vase, Gundersen, long waisted neck, 4x2¾" **135.00**
Vase, Gundersen, ruffled/ftd cornucopia form **525.00**
Vase, lily; NE Glass, outstanding color, 13" **1,950.00**
Vase, lily; NE Glass, shiny, 6½x3" **650.00**
Vase, lily; NE Glass, 7" **785.00**
Vase, lily; NE Glass, 12½" **1,000.00**
Vase, Morgan; Wheeling, orig griffin stand, outstanding color, 10x3" ...**3,150.00**
Vase, Mt WA, daisies, dbl-gourd form w/long neck, 6½" **2,650.00**
Vase, NE Glass, ftd teardrop shape w/trumpet neck, 8", pr **1,275.00**
Vase, NE Glass, rnd w/long neck & cupped rim, 10½" **1,250.00**
Vase, NE Glass, squat/dimpled w/long neck, fuchsia covers ⅔, 11x5"..**1,450.00**
Vase, NE Glass, stick neck, 8¾" **375.00**
Vase, Sandwich, Hobnail, 4-pinch rim, incurvate cylinder, 7x4"...**475.00**
Vase, Webb, gold flowers/rim/ft, stick neck, 6½" **250.00**
Vase, Webb, silver & gold floral/2 insects, frosted loop base, 9½" ..**750.00**
Vase, Wheeling, amber rigaree collar, bulbous w/stick neck, 8" ..**900.00**
Vase, Wheeling, dbl-gourd form, EX color, 7x4½" **3,100.00**
Vase, Wheeling, long neck wider at shoulder, squat ball body, 6⅜x5"..**3,000.00**
Vase, Wheeling, ovoid w/cylinder neck, 13" **975.00**
Vase, Wheeling, stick neck, 8x3" **895.00**
Wine glass, Gundersen, 5" **175.00**

Peking Cameo Glass

The first glasshouse was established in Peking in 1680. It produced glassware made in imitation of porcelain, a more desirable medium to the Chinese. By 1725 multilayered carving that resulted in a cameo effect lead to the manufacture of a wider range of shapes and colors. The factory was closed from 1736 to 1795, but glass made in Po-shan and shipped to Peking for finishing continued to be called Peking glass. Similar glassware was made through the first half of the twentieth century. See also Orientalia.

Bowl, pagodas, wht on red, 8¼", on teak base **175.00**
Bowl, scrolling flowers/bird, amber, early 1900s, 6½" **115.00**
Jar, ginger; Oriental floral, maroon on wht, 9¼" **760.00**
Jar, wild horses, red on wht, teak base, 10½" **1,200.00**
Vase, birds & floral, bl on wht, 10"..**360.00**
Vase, birds & poppies, yel on wht, teak base, 8¼" **660.00**
Vase, dragon, turq on wht, teak base, 9"....................................**410.00**
Vase, lizards & flowering vines, lav on wht, 12" **710.00**
Vase, lotus, gr on wht, hand-cvd, 8¾".......................................**900.00**
Vase, Oriental floral, jade gr on wht, 12" **710.00**
Vase, Oriental scene, gr on wht, baluster, 6" **100.00**
Vase, rabbit & morning glories, gr on wht, teak base, 9" **460.00**

Peloton

Peloton glass was first made by Wilhelm Kralik in Bohemia in 1880. This unusual art glass was produced by rolling colored threads onto the transparent or opaque glass gather as it was removed from the furnace. Usually more than one color of threading was used, and some items were further decorated with enameling. It was made with both shiny and acid finishes.

Bowl, brn/yel strings on wht, ribbed, 3 clear ft, 8-pinch rim, 6x7"..**325.00**
Rose bowl, mc strings on pk, ruffled, 6-ftd crystal base, 3½" **250.00**
Rose bowl, 4-color strings on wht, ribbed, pulled-up rim, 4¼" ...**275.00**
Rose bowl/vase, mc strings on bl, 4-pull rim, sqd, 6 shell ft, 4x4" ...**395.00**
Vase, pk/bl/yel strings on cased crystal, ribbed, 3-fold rim, 5" **300.00**

Pennsbury

Established in the 1950s in Morrisville, Pennsylvania, by Henry Below, the Pennsbury Pottery produced dinnerware and novelty items, much of which was sold in gift shops along the Pennsylvania Turnpike. Henry and his wife, Lee, worked for years at the Stangl Pottery before striking out on their own. Lee and her daughter were the artists responsible for many of the early pieces, the bird figures among them. Pennsbury pottery was hand painted, some in blue on white, some in multicolor on caramel. Pennsylvania Dutch motifs, Amish couples, and barbershop singers were among their most popular decorative themes. Sgraffito (hand incising), was used extensively. The company marked their wares 'Pennsbury Pottery' or 'Pennsbury Pottery, Morrisville, PA.'

In October of 1969 the company closed. Contents of the pottery were sold in December of the following year, and in April of 1971, the buildings burned to the ground. Items marked Pennsbury Glenview or Stumar Pottery (or these marks in combination) were made by Glenview after 1969. Pieces manufactured after 1976 were made by the Pennington Pottery. Several of the old molds still exist, and the original Pennsbury Caramel process is still being used on novelty items, some of which are produced by Lewis Brothers, New Jersey. Production of Pennsbury dinnerware was not resumed after the closing. Our advisor for this category is Shirley Graff; she is listed in the Directory under Ohio. Note: Prices may be higher in some areas of the country — particularly on the East Coast, the southern states, and Texas. Values for examples in the Rooster patterns apply to both black and red variations.

Pitcher, Eagle and E Pluribus Unum, 7¼", from $90.00 to $100.00.

Ashtray, Black Rooster, bellows shape, 10x5½" **30.00**
Ashtray, Folkart, 5" dia...**12.00**
Bookends, eagle figural, 8¼", pr...**100.00**
Bowl, Hex, 9"..**30.00**
Bowl, nappy, Hex, 5" **10.00**
Bowl, Red Rooster, 11"...**25.00**
Bowl, salad; Red Rooster, 13"..**30.00**
Bowl, soup; Folkart, deep..**22.00**
Bread plate, Sheaves of Wheat, rnd...**25.00**
Butter dish, Folkart...**25.00**
Butter dish, Three Tulips...**30.00**
Cake stand, Amish, 4½x11½" **45.00**
Candlestick, Black Rooster, finger style, 2x5" **30.00**
Candlesticks, Hummingbird on Flower, 5", pr.............................**100.00**
Candy dish, Bird over Heart or Folkart, heart shape......................**25.00**
Canister, Black Rooster, wood lid w/rooster figural knob, 4½x7½" ...**90.00**
Canister, Hex, wood lid w/figural knob, 4½x6½" **40.00**
Casserole, Black Rooster, cylindrical, 5"......................................**30.00**
Casserole, Red Rooster, cylindrical, 9"...**40.00**
Cheese & cracker dip set, Black Rooster, 3½x11" **75.00**
Coaster, Fish pattern..**18.00**
Coffeepot, Black Rooster, 2-cup, 6½" **45.00**
Coffeepot, Hex, 6-cup, 8½" **45.00**
Compote, Black Rooster, ftd, 5"...**25.00**
Cookie jar, Folkart, Harvest or Hex, ea **95.00**

Creamer & sugar bowl, Black Rooster, 6", pr 22.00
Cruet, Black Rooster 50.00
Cup & saucer, Black Rooster......................................22.00
Cup & saucer, Hex 12.00
Desk basket, Eagle, 5x5¼x3¼" 35.00
Desk basket, Two Birds over heart, 5x5¼x3¼" 35.00
Egg cup, Red Rooster...20.00
Figurine, Barn Swallow, 6x4½" 80.00
Figurine, Rooster, wht & bl, 12" 200.00
Hot plate, Hex, 6" sq tile in metal fr 50.00
Mug, beer; Barber Shop Quartet, 4½" 20.00
Mug, beverage; Davy Crockett, 4½" 45.00
Mug, coffee; Black Rooster..15.00
Pie plate, Hex Star, 9"...45.00
Pitcher, Amish Man, pt, 5"..20.00
Pitcher, Amish Woman, ½-pt, 3¾" 12.00
Pitcher, Hex, 2-qt, 7¼"..30.00
Pitcher, Tulip, 3-qt, 9¾"..45.00
Plaque, Amish Sayings, 7x5".......................................25.00
Plate, Courting Buggy, 8"..25.00
Plate, Harvest, in factory fr, 11"................................45.00
Platter, Red Rooster, 11x8".......................................35.00
Shakers, Amish, pr...25.00
Shakers, Folkart, pr...25.00
Snack set, Red Rooster, cup+tray..................................14.00
Teapot, Red Rooster, 4-cup...40.00
Tile, Picking Apples, 6" sq 18.00
Tile, Red Rooster, 4" dia..12.00
Tile, Walking to Homestead, 6" sq.................................15.00
Tureen, Black Rooster, w/ladle nook, in metal holder 150.00
Wall pocket, Bellows, 6½x6½" 40.00

Pens and Pencils

The first metallic writing pen was patented in 1809, and soon machine-produced pens with steel nibs gradually began replacing the quill. The first fountain pen was invented in 1830, but due to the fact that the ink flow was not consistent (though leakage was). They were not manufactured commercially until the 1880s. The first successful commercial producers were Waterman in 1884 and Parker with the Lucky Curve in 1888.

The self-filling pen of the early 1900s featured the soft, interior sack which filled with ink as the metal bar on the outside of the pen was raised and lowered. Variations of the filling mechanisms were tried until 1932 when Parker introduced the Vacumatic, a sackless pen with an internal pump.

Prices below are for pens in near mint or better condition which have been professionally restored to full operating capacity. For unrestored as-found pens, approximagely one third should be deducted from the values below.

For more information we recommend *Fountain Pens, Past & Present*, by Paul Erano (Collector Books). Our advisor for this category is Gary Lehrer; he is listed in the Directory under Connecticut. For those interested in purchasing pens through catalogs, both our advisor, Mr. Lehrer and Pen Fanciers (whose address can be found in the Directory under Clubs, Newsletters, and Catalogs) publish extensive catalogs.

Key:

AF — aeromatic filler	HR — hard rubber
BF — button filler	LF — lever filler
CF — capillary filler	NPT — nickel-plated trim
CPT — chrome-plated trim	PF — plunger filler
ED — eyedropper filler	PIF — piston filler

GFM — gold-filled metal	PKF — push knob filler
GFT — gold-filled trim	TD — touchdown filler
GPT — gold-plated trim	VF — vacumatic filler

Fountain Pens

Aiken Lambert, 1900, #2, ED, GF Golpheresque (rare), med, NM .600.00
C Stewart, 1938, #15, LF, gr pearl, NPT, Italic nib, NM 50.00
C Stewart, 1951, #55, LF, gr marble, GFT, stub nib, NM 150.00
C Stewart, 1955, #55, LF, bl marble, GFT, broad nib, NM...........200.00
C Stewart, 1955, #58, LF, gr pearl web, GFT, fine point, NM.....185.00
C Stewart, 1956, #74, twist fill, red herringbone, fretwork band, NM...200.00
C Stewart, 1956, #76, LF, gr herringbone, GFT, med nib, NM ...200.00
C Stewart, 1956, #85, LF, bl pearl w/gold veins, GFT, Italic nib, NM ...150.00
Chilton, 1924, #6, sleeve fill, blk, GFT, med flexible nib, NM...300.00
Conklin, 1918, #2C, CF, blk chased HR, GFT, Xtra-flexible nib, NM...175.00
Conklin, 1927, #2, LF, wht w/blk veins (rare), GFT, med nib, NM....300.00
Conklin, 1927, Endura Large, LF, blk, GFT, med nib, NM 400.00
Conklin, 1927, Endura Large, LF, sapphire bl, GFT, med-fine nib, NM ...650.00
Conklin, 1927, Endura Oversz, blk HR, long cap/section, GFT, NM...700.00
Conklin, 1930, Endura Symetric Oversz, LF, blk/bronze, GFT, NM 350.00
Conklin, 1932, Nozac, PF, gr pearl w/blk stripe, GFT, med nib, NM....300.00
Crocker, 1910, #2, blow filler, GF o/l, med nib, NM 375.00
Crocker, 1932, #2, hatchet fill, blk chased HR, GFT, med nib, NM.150.00
Dunn, 1921, #2, pump fill, ring top, blk chased HR, GFT, red knob, NM..100.00
Eclipse, 1931, #2, LF, Mandarin Yel w/jade ends, GFT, med nib, NM ..75.00
Esterbrook, 1949, LJ Pen, LF, red, NM 25.00
Esterbrook, 1949, SJ Pen, LF, red, NM 20.00
Esterbrook, 1950, Pastel Pen, LF, wht, NM 60.00
Esterbrook, 1950, Relief #12, LF, tiger's eye web, GFT, NM........275.00
Leboeuf, 1928, #4, sleeve fill, ring top, gr pearltex, GFT, NM 250.00
Leboeuf, 1932, #8, sleeve fill, silver pearltex, GFT, med nib, NM ...1,600.00
Mabie Todd, 1925, #44 Eternal, LF, blk, NM..............................100.00
Mabie Todd, 1925, #44 Eternal, LF, jade, NM 175.00
Mabie Todd, 1938, Blackbird Bulb, gr & gold spiral, GFT, NM..175.00
Mabie Todd, 1939, #4, LF, silver pearl snakeskin, NM 175.00
Mabie Todd, 1947, Swan #3240, LF, dk gr, GFT, med nib, NM 95.00
Montblanc, 1927, #1266, PIF, chrome plate fluted, med nib, NM..200.00
Montblanc, 1937, #134, blk w/long window, med nib, NM 450.00
Montblanc, 1937, #333½, PIF, blk, GFT, broad nib, NM.............375.00
Montblanc, 1941, #25 Masterpiece, PIF, 12-sided brn marble, GFT, NM ...1,250.00
Montblanc, 1946, #246 Vest Pocket, BF, tiger's eye, NM.........1,300.00
Montblanc, 1950, #146, PIF, gr stripe, GFT, med nib, NM......1,250.00
Montblanc, 1950, #246, PIF, blk, GFT, short window, NM.........450.00
Montblanc, 1950, #642N, silver striped, brushed chrome cap w/GFT, NM...800.00
Montblanc, 1952, #142, PIF, blk, GFT, flat feed/telescoping filler, NM....300.00
Montblanc, 1955, #124, PF, GF, fluted, med nib, M 250.00
Montblanc, 1955, #82, PIF, GF pinstripe, med nib, M 275.00
Moore, 1941, #2, LF, gr pearl web, GFT, med nib, NM 125.00
Moore, 1946, Fingertip, LF, dk gr, GFT, med nib, M 200.00
Parker, 1918, Black Giant, ED, blk HR, NP clip, med nib, NM...1,500.00
Parker, 1921, Duofold Jr, BF, red HR, bandless cap, med nib, NM...500.00
Parker, 1921, Duofold Sr, BF, red HR, bandless cap, med nib, MIB.1,400.00
Parker, 1928, Duofold Sr, BF, Mandarin Yel, GFT, med nib, NM 1,500.00

Parker, 1930, Duofold Special, red, gold-filled trim, button filler, EX, $250.00. (Photo courtesy Judy and Cliff Lawrence)

Parker, 1932, BF, blk, bandless, med nib, NM 75.00

Parker, 1932, Thrift Time, BF, gray marble, GFT, med nib, NM .200.00
Parker, 1935, Victory, BF, bl marble, GFT, broad nib, NM 300.00
Parker, 1937, Oversz, BF, blk, 14k filigree o/l cap, presentation, NM ...750.00
Parker, 1937, Vacumatic Slender, red laminated, GFT, broad nib, NM..125.00
Parker, 1939, Duofold Jr, BF, silver geometric, NPT, med nib, NM...125.00
Parker, 1945, Vacumatic Major, silver laminated, NPT, dbl jeweled, EX ...150.00
Parker, 1946, #51, AF, forest gr, brushed lustraloy cap, med nib, M ..100.00
Parker, 1946, NS (new style) Duofold, gray, NPT, sgn nib, NM .300.00
Parker, 1948, #51, AF, Buckskin, GF cap w/pinstripe & plain panels, NM...125.00
Parker, 1948, #51, AF, plum, GF cap, fine point, NM 150.00
Parker, 1950, #51 Mark II, AF, rare later version, Italic nib, NM ..125.00
Parker, 1951, #51, AF, plum, brushed lustraloy cap, med nib, NM...125.00
Parker, 1957, #61, wick fill, blk, 2-tone silver cap, med nib, NM .75.00
Parker, 1960, #45, cartridge/converter, bronzed anodized, broad nib, M.100.00
Parker (Valentine), 1935, #2, BF, burgundy pearl web, GFT, rare, NM ..150.00
Pelikan, 1937, #100N, gr pearl, GFT, med nib, NM....................250.00
Pelikan, 1937, #100N, tortoise w/matching cap/derby, Palladium nib, NM ...850.00
Pelikan, 1937, #100N, tortoise w/red cap, med nib, NM.............900.00
Pelikan, 1938, #100N, gr pearl, chased GF band/clip, broad nib, NM ..325.00
Pelikan, 1950, #400, PIF, brn strip, GFT, med nib, NM 185.00
Pelikan, 1950, #400, PIF, gr strip, GFT, med nib, NM................175.00
Pelikan, 1950, #400, PIF, gr V strip, gr turning knob/section, NM...450.00
Salz, 1920, Peter Pan, LF, dk red w/blk veins, GFT, med nib, NM...110.00
Salz, 1925, Peter Pan, LF, blk HR, GFT, rare longer length, NM..70.00
Salz, 1925, Peter Pan, LF, tan/brn Bakelite, GFT, broad nib, NM.75.00
Sheaffer, 1936, Feather Touch #8 Lg Balance, PF, gray marble, NM...450.00
Sheaffer, 1937, Standard Sz Lifetime Balance, LF, blk, GFT, NM.75.00
Sheaffer, 1942, Lifetime, Triumph, PF, silver laminated, NPT, EX...75.00
Sheaffer, 1950, Triumph Snorkel, GF, NM....................................150.00
Sheaffer, 1952, Clipper Snorkel, sage gr, chrome cap w/GFT, MIB..150.00
Sheaffer, 1954, Valiant Snorkel, burgundy, NM............................30.00
Sheaffer, 1954, Valiant Snorkel, pk, NM.......................................75.00
Sheaffer, 1958, Lady Skripsert, gold-plated, jeweled ring, EX........35.00
Sheaffer, 1959, PFM II, blk, chrome cap, broad nib, NM.............175.00
Sheaffer, 1959, PFM III, gray (rare), GFT, med nib, NM 375.00
Sheaffer, 1959, PFM III Demonstrator, transparent, GFT, blk shell, NM...800.00
Soennecken, 1952, 111 Extra, PIF, gr herringbone, NM 600.00
Soennecken, 1952, 111 Superior, PIF, golden weave, NM 400.00
Soennecken, 1952, 222 Extra, PIF, blk.......................................250.00
Soennecken, 1952, 222 Superior, PIF, silver lizard, NM 300.00
Wahl Eversharp, 1920, #0, LF, GF pinstripe, fine nib, NM 55.00
Wahl Eversharp, 1927, Gold Seal, LF, rosewood, med nib, NM..350.00
Wahl Eversharp, 1929, #2, LF, rosewood, GFT, calligraphy nib, NM..150.00
Wahl Eversharp, 1929, Equipoised, LF, blk & pearl, GFT, fine point, NM...350.00
Wahl Eversharp, 1929, Oversz Deco Band, LF, blk, GFT, med nib, NM....450.00
Wahl Eversharp, 1934, #2 Doric, LF, Ice (blk w/pearl veins), NPT, NM....300.00
Wahl Eversharp, 1942, Skyline Jr, LF, bl Moderne stripe, GFT, NM ..100.00
Wahl Eversharp, 1951, Symphony, LF, blk, GFT, med nib, M w/orig label..65.00
Waterman, 1910, #18S Safety, ED, blk HR, rare, M 2,600.00
Waterman, 1915, #14, Ed, blk chased HR, Stanhope cap, NM..1,895.00
Waterman, 1915, #52, LF, blk chased HR, NPT, med nib, NM ..100.00
Waterman, 1915, #452½ LEC, LF, sterling Sheridan, med nib, NM ..450.00
Waterman, 1920, #055½ LEC, LF, GF Gothic, Italic nib, eng, NM...325.00
Waterman, 1920, #52½V, LF, cardinal HR, GFT, med nib, NM.200.00
Waterman, 1924, #54, LF, blk HR, GFT, med nib, NM 110.00
Waterman, 1924, #452, LF, sterling Gothic, med nib, NM 350.00
Waterman, 1925, #58, LF, blk HR, GFT, med nib, NM 875.00
Waterman, 1925, #0552½, ED, Secretary in GF filigree, fine nib, NM..500.00
Waterman, 1926, #5, LF, red ripple w/red band, GFT, med nib, NM+..275.00
Waterman, 1927, #7, LF, red ripple, pk band, 1st yr model, NM 400.00
Waterman, 1929, Patrician, LF, blk HR, GFT, med nib, NM......850.00
Waterman, 1929, Patrician, LF, moss agate 900.00
Waterman, 1940, #2 Model 513, LF (England), GFT, fine nib, NM ..125.00
Waterman, 1941, 100 Yr, blk, smooth cap/bbl, GFT, med nib, NM....300.00

Mechanical

Anonymous, rifle shape, cocking mechanism, eng: Rin Tin Tin, NM ..75.00
Autopoint, 1945, 2-color (blk/bl), w/clip, M................................15.00
Conklin, 1929, Symetric, gr marble, GFT, no clip, EX 40.00
Cross/Tiffany, 1990, sterling silver pinstripe, clip: Tiffany, MIB ..100.00
Eversharp, 1940, blk snakeskin pattern leather cover, GFT, NM...100.00
Montblanc, 1924, #6, octagonal, blk HR, eng bbl, lg, rare, NM.900.00
Montblanc, 1930, #92 Repeater, blk HR, NPT, NM 125.00
Montblanc, 1939, #392 Repeater, blk HR, NM 80.00
Parker, 1929, Duofold Jr, jade, GFT, NM 50.00
Parker, 1929, Duofold Jr, Mandarin Yel, GFT, NM....................150.00
Parker, 1930, Duofold Vest Pocket, burgundy, GFT, w/opener taper, NM...150.00
Parker, 1948, Duofold Repeater, gray, GFT, worn imprint, NM ..150.00
Sheaffer, 1925, Balance, deep jade, GFT, NM+ 50.00
Sheaffer, 1925, Balance, gr marble, GFT, NM+ 40.00
Sheaffer, 1959, PFM III, blk, GFT, M w/orig decal 125.00
Wahl Eversharp, 1929, Oversz Deco Band, blk & pearl, GFT, NM...125.00
Wahl Eversharp, 1939, Coronet, blk w/smooth GF cap, NM 50.00
Wahl Eversharp, 1948, Coronet, bronze pearl, chrome cap w/blk, NM...70.00
Waterman, 1925, blk HR, GFT, M...150.00
Waterman, 1928, #52½ V, olive ripple, GFT, NM........................85.00

Sets

C Stewart, 1951, #27, LF, lav pearl web/GFT, +#37 pencil, NM ...225.00
C Stewart, 1952, #14, LF, bl pearl, GFT, med nib, MIB 60.00
Montblanc, 1972, #1266, PIF, sterling, fluted, 18k wht gold nib, M ..400.00
Parker, 1937, Depression, BF, red pearl, GFT, matching blind caps, NM...175.00
Parker, 1940, Vacuum Jr, gr/bronze/blk stripes, GFT, med nib, NM ...125.00
Parker, 1957, #61, GF, alternating pinstripes & panels, M 200.00
Sheaffer, 1925, #2-25 Tall, LF, blk plastic, GFT, med nib, NM ...100.00
Sheaffer, 1936, Junior, LF, gray marble, NPT, med flexible nib, NM..75.00
Sheaffer, 1952, Clipper Triumph Snorkel, bright red, chrome caps, MIB.175.00
Sheaffer, 1958, Lady Skripsert, GF filigree & bl, MIB 45.00
Sheaffer, 1959, PFM III, blk, GFT, med nib, MIB.......................325.00
Wahl Eversharp, #4, GF w/wave chased pattern, med nib, NM..175.00
Waterman, 1925, #52, LF, red ripple, GFT, med nib, NM...........250.00

Personalities, Fact and Fiction

One of the largest and most popular areas of collecting today is character-related memorabilia. Everyone has favorites, whether they be comic-strip personalities or true-life heroes. The earliest comic strip dealt with the adventures of the Yellow Kid, the smiling, bald-headed Oriental boy always in a nightshirt. He was introduced in 1895, a product of the imagination of Richard Fenton Outcault. Today, though very hard to come by, items relating to the Yellow Kid bring premium prices.

Though her 1923 introduction was unobtrusively made through only one newspaper, New York's *Daily News,* Little Orphan Annie, the vacant-eyed redhead in the inevitable red dress, was quickly adopted by hordes of readers nationwide, and before the demise of her creator, Harold Gray, in 1968, she had starred in her own radio show. She made two feature films, and in 1977 'Annie' was launched on Broadway.

Other early comic figures were Moon Mullins, created in 1923 by Frank Willard; Buck Rogers by Philip Nowlan in 1928; and Betty Boop, the round-faced, innocent-eyed, chubby-cheeked Boop-Boop-a-Doop girl of the early 1930s. Bimbo was her dog and KoKo her clown friend.

Popeye made his debut in 1929 as the spinach-eating sailor with the spindly-limbed girlfriend, Olive Oyl, in the comic strip *Thimble Theatre,* created by Elzie Segar. He became a film star in 1933 and had his own radio show that during 1936 played three times a week on CBS. He obligingly modeled for scores of toys, dolls, and figurines, and especially those from the '30s are very collectible.

Tarzan, created around 1930 by Edgar Rice Burroughs, and Captain Midnight, by Robert Burtt and Willfred G. Moore, are popular heroes with today's collectors. During the days of radio, Sky King of the Flying Crown Ranch (also created by Burtt and Moore) thrilled boys and girls of the mid-1940s. Hopalong Cassidy, Red Rider, Tom Mix, and the Lone Ranger were only a few of the other 'good guys' always on the side of law and order.

But of all the fictional heroes and comic characters collected today, probably the best loved and most well known is Mickey Mouse. Created in the late 1920s by Walt Disney, Micky (as his name was first spelled) became an instant success with his film debut, Steamboat Willie. His popularity was parlayed through wind-up toys, watches, figurines, cookie jars, puppets, clothing, and numerous other products. Items from the 1930s are usually copyrighted 'Walt Disney Enterprises'; thereafter, 'Walt Disney Productions' was used.

For more information we recommend *Schroeder's Collectible Toys, Antique to Modern*, by Sharon and Bob Huxford. For those interested in Disneyana, we recommend *Stern's Guide to Disney Collectibles* (there are three in the series), and *The Collector's Encyclopedia of Disneyana* by David Longest and Michael Stern. *Cartoon Toys & Collectibles* by David Longest; *Collector's Guide to TV Toys & Memorabilia, Second Edition*, by Greg Davis and Bill Morgan; *Roy Rogers and Dale Evans Toys and Memorabilia* by P. Allan Coyle; *Collector's Reference & Value Guide to the Lone Ranger* by Lee Felbinger; and *G-Men and FBI Toys and Collectibles* by Harry and Jody Whitworth are other great publications. All are available from Collector Books. See also Autographs; Banks; Big Little Books; Children's Books; Comic Books; Cookie Jars; Dolls; Games; Lunch Boxes; Movie Memorabilia; Paper Dolls; Pin-Back Buttons; Posters; Puzzles; Rock 'N Roll Memorabilia; Toys.

Alice in Wonderland, figure, ceramic, Japan, 1970s, 6", M 35.00
Alice in Wonderland, pnt book, Whitman, 1951, unused, EX 50.00
Alice in Wonderland, tea set, plastic, 17-pc, Plasco, 1950s, EX+ .65.00
Amos & Andy, figures, bsk, Japan, prewar, 8" & 7", EX, pr 575.00

Andy and Barney from Mayberry, ceramic bobbin' head figures, 1992, 7", $65.00. (Photo courtesy June Moon)

Atom Ant, push-button puppet, Kohner, 1960s, EX 25.00
Bambi, paint book, Whitman/WDP, 1941-42, unused, EX 55.00
Bashful, doll, pnt linen face/felt outfit/plush beard, 1930s, 12", VG+ ... 85.00
Bat Masterson, wallet, Croyder, 1950s, NMIB 75.00
Batman, Batarang, Ideal, 1966, 8", NM 100.00
Batman, Hot-Line Batphone, Marx, 1966, NMIB 500.00
Batman, Official Batman Chute, NPPI, 1966, MOC 40.00
Batman, Switch 'N Go Playset, Mattel, 1966, NMIB, from $800 to .. 1,200.00
Beetle Baily, nodder, NM, from $100 to 150.00
Ben Casey, nodder, NM, from $100 to 125.00
Ben-Hur, coloring book, Lowe #2851, 1959, some pgs colored, EX+ ... 40.00
Betty Boop, bank, ceramic figure, Japan, 7", MIB 45.00

Betty Boop, figure, jtd wood, Jaymar, 1930s, 4¼", M 100.00
Betty Boop, transfers, set of 12, Japan, 1935, NMOC 25.00
Betty Grable, pnt book, Whitman, 1947, unused, EX 55.00
Bionic Woman, Styling Boutique, Kenner, 1977, MIB, from $100 to .. 125.00
Boob McNutt, doll, stuffed cloth w/felt hat, Star Co, 34", VG ... 200.00
Bozo the Clown, doll, Mattel, 1963, talker, 18", VG 45.00
Bozo the Clown, mask, paper litho diecut, Capitol Records, 1950s, VG+ ... 65.00
Buck Rogers, badge, Chief Explorers, NM 400.00
Buck Rogers, school box, Crayon Ship, Am Pencil, 1930s, 5x2", EX .125.00
Buck Rogers, spaceship, Morton Salt, 1940, 3", NM (EX mailer) 175.00
Buffalo Bill, ring, premium, 1950s, VG 45.00
Bugs Bunny, camera, 1976, EXIB 140.00
Bugs Bunny, figure, ceramic, squatting/ears down, Shaw, 1940s, 4", EX .. 65.00
Bugs Bunny, figure, litho tin figure on formed paws base, WBC, 9", G 65.00
Buster Brown, pocket watch, 1928, EX 175.00
Captain Action, flasher ring, variations, Vari-Vue, 1967, EX, ea .. 35.00
Captain America, badge, Sentinels of Liberty, M 850.00
Captain America, kite, plastic, Pressman, 1966, MIP 65.00
Captain Kangaroo, Fun-Damental Activity Set, Lowe, 1977, NM (sealed) .. 20.00
Captain Marvel, club membership card, Fawcett Comics, 1940s, EX ... 30.00
Captain Marvel, comic book, Billy's Big Game, Carnation premium, EX .50.00
Captain Midnight, decoder, w/photo, 1942, NM 225.00
Captain Midnight, ring, Sun God, red plastic stone, 1947, EX .. 1,200.00
Captain Video, ring, Seal, M 550.00
Casper the Friendly Ghost, jack-in-the-box, Mattel, 1960, EX 75.00
Cat in the Hat (Dr Seuss), doll, talker, Mattel, 1970, NM 250.00
Charlie Brown, marionette, wood, Marimo Craft Ltd, 1980s, 7", NM+ .. 85.00
Charlie McCarthy, doll, Effanbee, 1940, 16", NM (EX box) 950.00
Charlie McCarthy, Radio Party, coffee premium, 1938, NM (EX mailer) ... 100.00
Charlie McCarthy, ring, brass, Chase & Sanborn, 1940s, EX 150.00
Charlie McCarthy, scrapbook, spiral, Western Tablet, 1938, VG+ .. 40.00
Charlie's Angels, playset, Toy Factory, 1977, MIB (sealed), from $100 to ... 120.00
CHiPs, bicycle siren, 1970s, M 30.00
Cinderella, doll, Storybook Small Talk, Mattel, MIB, from $125 to ... 175.00
Cinderella, rubber stamp kit, 10-pc w/ink pad, Walt Disney, NMIB .. 20.00
Daffy Duck, bank, pnt metal figure standing next to barrel, 4¼", NM ... 85.00
Daniel Boone, figure, plastic/vinyl, Am Tradition, 1964, 5", NM 100.00
Daniel Boone, Woodland Whistle, Autolite, 1964, NMIB 65.00
Davy Crockett, doll, compo/cloth, open/close eyes, Fortune, 8", NMIB .. 175.00
Davy Crockett, night light, head figure, 1950s, EX 50.00
Davy Crockett, ring, Profile, gr or red enamel on brass, 1950s, NM+ .. 100.00
Davy Crockett, tent, litho on canvas, Empire Mfg, 1950s, NM .. 150.00
Dennis the Menace, doll, Dennis Play Products, 1957, 13", NMIB .. 165.00
Dennis the Menace, hand puppet, cloth/vinyl, EX 40.00
Dick Tracy, Candid Camera, Seymour/NY News, 1950s, EXIB ... 100.00
Dick Tracy, Crimestopper Set, John-Henry, 1930s, MOC, from $75 to .. 100.00
Dick Tracy, figure, pnt lead, 1930s, EX 30.00
Dick Tracy, ring, Post Cereal, MIP 30.00
Dick Tracy, ring, profile/stars on sides, gold-tone metal, 1930s, EX .. 225.00
Dick Tracy, Sparkle Plenty Christmas Tree Lights, unused, MIB ... 115.00
Dizzy Dean, wristwatch, Everbrite/Ingersoll, 1933, scarce, M .. 1,100.00
Dobie Gillis, nodder, NM, from $250 to 300.00
Donald Duck, alarm clock, Bayard, 1930s, 5" dia, NM 250.00
Donald Duck, doll, drum major, Knickerbocker, 1930s, rare, NM ... 1,600.00
Donald Duck, Dress Buttons, emb plastic, set of 3, 1930s, 1" dia, MOC .. 100.00
Donald Duck, figure, bsk, playing violin, Japan, 1930s, 4", NM .300.00
Donald Duck, figure, wood, on sled, Fun-E-Flex/Ideal, NM 1,500.00
Donald Duck, jack-in-the-box, Spear/WDP, 1940, EX 200.00
Donald Duck, nodder, rnd gr base, 1970s, NM 75.00
Donald Duck, plate, ceramic, 3-section, bl trim, Patriot China, 8" ... 75.00
Donald Duck, watering can, litho tin, WDE, c 1938, 3x6x2", EX .. 175.00
Dopey (Snow White), hand puppet, cloth/compo, VG 75.00
Dr Dolittle, doll, talker, Mattel, 1969, 24", NMIB 150.00
Dr Dolittle, party cups, animals/names, Hallmark, M (orig wrappers) ... 20.00

Dr Dolittle, punch-out book, Whitman, 1935, NM......................25.00
Dr Kildare, telephone, plastic, Renzi, 1960s, NM..........................50.00
Dracula, doll, Hamilton Presents, 14", MIB.................................25.00
Dukes of Hazzard, Colorforms, 1981, NMIB...............................30.00
Dumbo the Elephant, hand puppet, cloth/vinyl, Gund, 1955, NM (EX box)....65.00
Edger Bergen, gum wrapper, Better Bubble Gum, waxed paper, 1940s, EX.30.00
Elmer Fudd, bank, pnt metal figure next to barrel, 5½", NM........85.00
Elmer Fudd, planter, pnt metal figure by stump, WBC, 1940s-50s, 6", VG....75.00
Emmet Kelly, Colorforms Circus, 1960, complete, NMIB.............40.00
Emmet Kelly, ventriloquist doll, Juro, 30", NM (w/trunk)..........100.00
ET, night Light, figure w/glowing chest, MIB.............................15.00
Felix the Cat, figure, jtd wood, Schoenhut, rare, 5½", EX.......1,200.00
Felix the Cat, squeak toy, Germany, 6", EX 400.00
Felix the Cat, stencil set, Spears Bavaria/Pat Sullivan, EXIB......200.00
Felix the Cat, windup, cloth/tin, Pat Sullivan, EX+ (EX box)......1,650.00
Ferdinand the Bull, figure, bsk, Japan, 1930s, 3", NM 50.00
Flash Gordon, beanie w/fins & goggles, 1950s, NM 400.00
Flash Gordon, ring, Post Cereal, MIP...85.00
Flash Gordon, space outfit, Esquire Novelties, 1950s, EXIB........350.00
Flash Gordon, wrist compass, silver plastic, FG Inc, 1950s, EX+ ..65.00
Flintstones, coin purse, Barney, 1975, NM 25.00
Flintstones, doll, Pebbles, cloth outfit, Ideal, 1967, 12", MIB.....175.00
Flintstones, Great Big Punchout Book, Whitman, 1961, unpunched, NM...65.00
Flintstones, playset, Marx, 1962, few pcs missing o/w EXIB........200.00
Flintstones, push-button puppet, Bamm-Bamm, Kohner, 1960s, EX..25.00
Flipper, doll, plush w/sailor hat, Knickerbocker, 1976, 17", EX.....30.00
Flipper, riding toy, plastic figure, Irwin, 1965, NM, from $125 to..150.00
Flying Nun, pnt-by-numbers, Hasbro, 1967, complete, MIB........100.00
Foodini, dexterity puzzle, Am Metal, 1950s, rare, NM 125.00
Gabby Hayes, Sheriff Set, John Henry, 1950, MOC, from $100 to..125.00
Garfield, figure, ceramic, tennis player, 4"..................................20.00
Gene Autry, Adventure Story Trail Map, Schafer's Bread, 1950s, EX..100.00
Gene Autry, drum set, 3-pc w/cb figure on lg drum, NMIB 900.00
Gene Autry, poster, cb standup, GA & Co, bust image, 1950s, 14x11", NM....125.00
Gene Autry, stencil book, Stencil Art, 1950, unused, NM.............75.00
Gepetto (Pinocchio), figure, wood, Multi-Products, 1940s, 5½", EX+..100.00
Gepetto (Pinocchio), Story Paint Book, Whitman/WDP, 1939, unused, EX...50.00
Goldilocks, Storykins, Hasbro, 1967, MIP, from $75 to...............100.00
Goofy, doll, Schuco, 1950s, 14", EX 350.00
Goofy, figure, bsk, Japan, 1930s, 3½", EX 135.00
Green Hornet, Electric Drawing Set, Lakeside, 1966, NMIB......250.00
Green Hornet, ring, seal w/glow-in-dark secret compartment, 1947, NM+ ...950.00
Green Hornet, slide-tile puzzle, Roalex, scarce, NMOC 285.00
Gumby & Poky, pnt set, rare, NM...200.00
Happy Hooligan, figure, Elastolin, 11", EX...................................75.00
Hardy Boys, dolls, Kenner, 1978, 12", NRFB, ea..........................50.00
Herman Munster, hand puppet, cloth/compo, Kayro-Vue, 1964, EX.......65.00
Hopalong Cassidy, Bar 20 Ranch Horn, Perlin Products, 1950s, EXIB .250.00
Hopalong Cassidy, belt, Switch-A-Buckle, complete, MOC.......225.00
Hopalong Cassidy, Butter-Nut Bread display loaf, 1950s, 6x12", NM+..85.00
Hopalong Cassidy, dominoes, Milton Bradley, 1950, NMIB........100.00
Hopalong Cassidy, ring, bust image, silver, NM 75.00
Howdy Doody, barette, molded plastic Clarabell figure, 1950s, EX....75.00
Howdy Doody, doll, plastic, Beehler Arts Ltd/Kagran, 1950s, 8", EX+...125.00
Howdy Doody, marionette, Pride Products, 1950s, 15", EXIB.....125.00
Howdy Doody, poster, HD Fudge Bar, mc, Doughnut Corp, 1950s, 12x9", EX ...75.00
Howdy Doody, puppet set, plastic, 5 characters, Tee-Vee, 1950s, EXIB..165.00
Howdy Doody, puppet show punch-out booklet, Whitman, 1952, EX 85.00
Howdy Doody, push puppet, Howdy at microphone, Kohner, 1950s, 6", EXIB..165.00
Howdy Doody, squeeze toy, cowboy sheriff figure, vinyl, 1950s, 13", EX..85.00
Huckleberry Hound, charm bracelet, w/6 charms, 1959, NM (EX card)..35.00
Huckleberry Hound, finger puppet, plastic/cloth, 9", EX+ 15.00
Incredible Hulk, wallet, vinyl, 1976, unused, NM 20.00
Jack Armstrong, Junior Ace First Aid Kit, tin, 1930s, complete, NM...300.00

Jack Armstrong, ring, Siren Whistle, gold-tone w/Egyptian design, EX+ ..150.00
Jackie Coogan, stickpin doll, litho head/pipe-cleaner body, 4", EX+ 40.00
Jerry Mahoney, beanie, wool w/plastic head form, working mouth, 1950s....50.00
Jetsons, Slate & Chalk Set, 1960s, unused, MIB 100.00
Jiminy Cricket, tumbler, plastic head w/flicker eyes, 1950s, 4", NM+...30.00
Joe Palooka, bank/candy container, Little Max figure, 1940s, 4", M 68.00
Katzenjammer Kids, figures, Hans & Franz, 1930s, celluloid, EX, pr...375.00
King Little, doll, compo w/jtd wood limbs, Ideal, 13", EX...........660.00
Knucklehead, ventriloquist doll, Juro, 1960s, 24", NM 360.00
Krazy Kat, doll, stuffed velvet w/appl felt ft/boots, 13", NM 1,000.00
Lady (Lady & the Tramp), pull toy, gr platform, WDP, 1955, NM .125.00
Li'l Abner, bank, Li'l Abner Can O' Coins, litho tin, 4½", EX 30.00
Li'l Abner, flying saucer, bl vinyl, 1954, 9" dia, EX+ 45.00
Little Bo Peep, doll, compo/sleep eyes, Ideal, 1938, 15½", EX....165.00
Little Lulu & Tubby, figures, bsk, 1971, NM, pr 125.00
Little Orphan Annie, bank, tin registering, 1936, 3" dia, EX......450.00
Little Orphan Annie, figure set, bsk, 4-pc, Japan, prewar, M (EX box) ..400.00
Little Orphan Annie (Radio), membership kit, 1945, EX (EX mailer) ..250.00
Little Orphan Annie (Radio), ring, Triple Mystery, VG 500.00
Little Orphan Annie (Radio), Talking Stationery, 1937, NM (NM mailer)....150.00
Little Red Riding Hood, tea set, litho tin, 8-pc, early 1900s, EX...375.00
Lone Ranger, deputy badge, w/secret compartment & code book, NM...175.00
Lone Ranger, doll, compo, Bond Bread badge, Dollcraft, 15", EX+...750.00
Lone Ranger, First Aid Kit, Am White Cross Inc, 1938, complete, EX+ ..100.00
Lone Ranger, harmonica, SP, 1947, NMIB, from $75 to 125.00
Lone Ranger, magic slate, Whitman, 1978, NM 75.00
Lone Ranger, poster, Bond Bread/WABY-WOR radio, blk & wht, 12x8", VG+ ..125.00
Lone Ranger, ring, Filmstrip Saddle, 1950, M.............................265.00
Lone Ranger, telescope, 1946, NMIB, from $150 to....................200.00
Lucy (Peanuts), nodder, UFS, 1970s, 4", NM 65.00

Maggie and Jiggs, dressed papier-maché figures with bendable wire legs, Maggie has real hair, unmarked Germany, 13", EX/NM, $650.00.

Mandrake the Magician, Magic Kit, Transogram, 1949, NMIB, from $250 to ...300.00
Mary Marvel, badge, Club Member, w/cord, rare, NM 450.00
Matt Dillon (Gun Smoke), outfit, Seneca, 1958, complete, EXIB...125.00
Maverick, TV Eras-O-Picture Book, Hasbro, 1959, MIB (sealed)....100.00
Maynard Krebs (Dobie Gillis), nodder, holding bongos, NM, from $250 to...350.00
Mickey Mouse, doll, Dean's Rag, 8", NM....................................900.00
Mickey Mouse, doll, Steiff, orig tags, 11", NM 3,000.00
Mickey Mouse, figure, bsk, w/banjo, Japan, 1930s, 5½" 500.00
Mickey Mouse, flashlight, USA Lite, EX (G box)........................700.00
Mickey Mouse, hand puppet, Steiff, NM 1,500.00
Mickey Mouse, lamp base, metal/decal, Soreng-Manegold, 1930s, 7", EX.....40.00
Mickey Mouse, magic slate, mk Blackboard, Strathmore, 1940s, MIB..100.00
Mickey Mouse, magic slate, WDE, 1930s, NM 100.00
Mickey Mouse, pocket watch, yel shorts, Ingersoll, 1934, rare, NM...2,000.00
Mickey Mouse, pull toy, on scooter, wood & celluloid, VG......1,600.00
Mickey Mouse, push-button puppet, Kohner, 1948, EX 150.00
Mickey Mouse, sand pail & shovel, marching band, Ohio Art, 6", EX....170.00
Mickey Mouse, scissors, die-cut Mickey image, WDE, 1930s, 3", EX......150.00
Mickey Mouse, toy chest/child's seat, wood/cb/cloth, 1930s, 36" L, EX..350.00
Mickey Mouse, wristwatch, rectangular, Ingersoll, 1948, NM (EX box).325.00

Mickey Mouse & Donald Duck, figures in boat, celluloid, WDE, 6" L, EX....**1,775.00**

Mickey Mouse & Minnie, milk bottle, Hilo Dairymen's Center, 5½", EX ...**125.00**

Mickey Mouse Club, TV Bulb, Mickey decal, c Solar Electric Corp, EXIB.**80.00**

Mighty Mouse, squeeze toy, vinyl w/red felt cape, 1950s, 10", EX.**55.00**

Mighty Mouse, sticker book, Whitman, 1967, unused, NM..........**50.00**

Minnie Mouse, doll, cowgirl, Knickerbocker, 1930s, VG.........**2,500.00**

Minnie Mouse, figure, bsk, nightshirt, 1930s, 4", NM.................**150.00**

Minnie Mouse, figure, wood, hobbyhorse, VG **1,500.00**

Minnie Mouse, roly poly, celluloid, Minnie atop ball, NM......**1,200.00**

Morticia (Addams Family), hand puppet, cloth/vinyl, Ideal, 1965, NM...**65.00**

Mortimer Snerd, teeth, Pilo Novelty, 1940s, MIP.........................**60.00**

Mr Ed, hand puppet, talker, Mattel, 1962, MIB.........................**175.00**

Mr Fink (Nutty Mad), water gun, Palmer Plastics, 1960s, MIP.....**60.00**

Munsters, sticker book, Whitman, 1965, unused, M.....................**75.00**

Nancy Drew, fan club kit, FCCA, 1978, complete, NM (NM folder) ..**65.00**

Olive Oyle, hand puppet, cloth/vinyl, 1950s, 10", M, from $50 to ...**60.00**

Oswald Rabbit, doll, cloth/rubber face & hands, Ideal, 1930s, 21", EX...**200.00**

Paladin (Have Gun Will Travel), playset, Multiple, 1960, EXIB...**250.00**

Peanuts, tea set, litho tin, 12-pc, Chein, 1969, MIB, from $200 to..**250.00**

Peter Max, pillow, litho plastic, early 1970s, 15½" sq, EX.............**55.00**

Peter Pan, marionette, Peter Puppet Playthings, 1952, 15", EX+..**65.00**

Phantom of the Opera, nodder, sq base, NM **500.00**

Pink Panther, bank, ceramic, standing w/arms & legs crossed, 7", MIB...**40.00**

Pinky Lee, xylophone, Emenee, complete, NM (EX box)...........**200.00**

Pinocchio, doll, pnt compo w/jtd wooden limbs, Ideal, 1940, 10", VG+..**135.00**

Pinocchio, figure, pnt wood compo, Multi Products, 1940, 2" **65.00**

Pinocchio, figures, ceramic, 7 characters, National Porcelain Co, EX..**110.00**

Pinocchio, lunch pail, tin, blk/wht figures on red, c 1940, 5" dia, EX ..**100.00**

Pinocchio, marionette, Pelham, 1962, 11½", EX.........................**100.00**

Pinocchio, pnt book, Whitman, 1939, unused, NM **15.00**

Pluto, figure, sand-filled celluloid, Japan, 1930s, rare, 3", NM **85.00**

Pluto, nodder, pnt compo, Brechner/WDP/Japan, 1960s, 6", EX+...**65.00**

Popeye, doll, cloth/wood pipe/paper shoes, Japan, prewar, 10", NM...**350.00**

Popeye, figure, celluloid, 1940s, 5", EX **125.00**

Popeye, figure, jtd wood, KFS, 6", EX+ **125.00**

Popeye, pocket watch, Ingersoll, 1935, 2" dia, EX, from $650 to...**850.00**

Porky Pig, wristwatch, Ingraham, mid-1950s, MIB.....................**600.00**

Raggedy Ann, doll, awake/asleep, Georgene, 1940s, 12½", NM.**300.00**

Raggedy Ann, doll, pajama bag, Knickerbocker, 1960s, 27", NM .**80.00**

Raggedy Ann, finger puppet, Bobbs-Merrill, 1977, MOC **20.00**

Rifleman, outfit, Pla-Master, 1959, complete, NM (NM box) **200.00**

Rin-Tin-Tin, Magic Picture Set, Transogram, 1956, complete, NMIB...**65.00**

Rin-Tin-Tin, Wondascope, Nabisco, 1950s, complete, NMIB.......**75.00**

Robin Hood, wristwatch, leather band, Bradley 1956, NM **75.00**

Rocky & Bullwinkle, telescope, Larami, 1970s, MOC...................**25.00**

Rocky Jones Space Ranger, wristwatch, Ingraham, 1950s, MIB ..**750.00**

Roger Wilco, ring, Flying Tiger Rescue w/3-Way Signalling, MIB...**360.00**

Roy Rogers, bandanna, brn/red/bl litho on tan, EX **55.00**

Roy Rogers, bank, metal boot form w/emb graphics, Almar, 1950s, 5", EX...**65.00**

Roy Rogers, pin, Roy Rogers Riders Club, Post Cereal, NM **65.00**

Roy Rogers, slippers, blk & wht, M (VG+ box w/mc paper label)..**165.00**

Roy Rogers, stand, chrome S-curve base w/brass Roy & horse, 25", EX ...**700.00**

Roy Rogers, telescope, Herbert George, 1950s, NM (VG box)...**225.00**

Ruff & Ready, Spelling Game, unused, 1958, M............................**35.00**

Sgt Preston, 10-in-1 Electric Trail Kit, Quaker, complete, rare, EX..**750.00**

Sgt Snorkel (Beetle Baily), nodder, NM, from $100 to **150.00**

Shadow, lapel stud, Shadow Club, NM **400.00**

Shadow, ring, Secret Agent, scarce, MIB **300.00**

Shari Lewis, Electric Drawing Set, 1962, complete, NMIB...........**75.00**

Sherlock Holmes, hand puppet, Kersa (Germany), 1930s, 11½", EX...**100.00**

Sherlock Holmes, souvenir booklet, Garrick Theatre NY, 1900, VG+ **135.00**

Six Million Dollar Man, AM wrist radio, Illco, 1976, MIB, from $200 to ..**350.00**

Sky King, Club Wings, Nabisco, 1959, NM..................................**125.00**

Sky King, Detecto-Microscope, premium, 1950s, complete, EXIB..**250.00**

Sleeping Beauty, coloring book, Magic Forest, 1959, used, NM **25.00**

Sleeping Beauty, figures, King/Queen, Hagen-Renaker, 1930s, 3", M, ea...**525.00**

Smitty, coloring book, McLoughlin Bros, 1931, unused, EX..........**35.00**

Smokey Bear, Junior Forest Ranger Kit, USDA, 1956-57, complete, NM...**65.00**

Snoopy, Camping Set, Determined/Helm Toy, 1975, MIB, from $75 to ..**125.00**

Snoopy, cuckoo clock, Snoopy golfing/Woodstock, Japan, 1983, NM+.....**250.00**

Snow White, alarm clock, Bayard Blanche Neige, 1960, 4½" dia, NM.....**300.00**

Snow White, charm bracelet, 8 cloisonne figures on brass, 1940s, NM..**1,500.00**

Snow White, figure, Hagen-Renaker, 1950s, 2", M **150.00**

Snow White, figure set, bsk, dwarfs w/instruments, 8-pc, VG (VG box)....**550.00**

Snow White, figure set, ceramic, 8-pc, Leonardi, 1939, very rare, M.....**2,100.00**

Snow White, radio, rectangular w/pnt characters, Emerson, 7½", EX ..**1,000.00**

Snuffy Smith, figure set, pk plastic, 4-pc, Marx, 1950s, NM **65.00**

Soupy Sales, marionette, Knickerbocker, 1966, 12", EX...............**75.00**

Soupy Sales, pen, red plastic w/pnt vinyl head topper, 1960s, 7", NM+ **40.00**

Space Patrol, Cosmic Smoke Gun, premium, complete, EX (EX mailer)..**400.00**

Speedy Gonzales, nodder, NM, from $100 to...............................**175.00**

Spider-Man, binder, paper, Mead, 1970s, NM.............................**40.00**

Spider-Man, doll, cloth/vinyl head, Amsco, 1976, 8", EX **40.00**

Spider-Man, Hippity Hop, rubber, G..**100.00**

Steve Canyon, membership card, 1959, EX **20.00**

Straight Arrow, powder horn, 1950s, rare, NM.............................**100.00**

Straight Arrow, ring, Cave Nugget, w/photo, M.........................**225.00**

Superman, horseshoes set, Super Swim, 1950s, complete, EXIB.**100.00**

Superman, Krypton Rocket, National Comics, Kellogg's, 1956, EXIB ..**225.00**

Superman, push-button puppet, Kohner, 1966, NM....................**125.00**

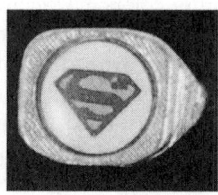

Superman, ring, premium from Post Toasties cereal, 1976, EX in box, $35.00.

Superman, ring, Secret Candy Compartment, 1940s, rare, NM....**8,500.00**

Swee' Pea, squeak toy, rubber, 1930s, 6", VG **75.00**

Tarzan, punch-out book, Whitman, 1967, unpunched, NM..........**45.00**

Tarzan, stamp book, w/95 of 100 orig stamps, Cuba, 1930s, EX ..**500.00**

Thief of Bagdad, coloring book, movie ed, Saalfield, 1940, 12x8", EX+..**50.00**

Three Little Pigs, ashtray, figures on triangular dish, lustre, 3", EX **75.00**

Three Little Pigs, figure set, Seiberling Rubber, rare, EX **1,200.00**

Three Little Pigs, pocket watch, Ingersoll, 1935, NM (EX box)..**2,500.00**

Three Little Pigs, washtub, litho tin, Ohio Art, 1930s, EX.........**125.00**

Three Stooges, finger puppets, molded bust images, 3-pc, 1960s, VG..**300.00**

Thumper (Bambi), figure, pk plastic, Marx, 1950s, 2⅜", NM **75.00**

Tinkerbell, figure, ceramic, Goebel, 1950s, 8½", M.....................**150.00**

Tinkerbell, hand puppet, cloth/vinyl, talker, Gund, EXIB.............**75.00**

Tom Mix, belt, plastic, brass buckle w/secret compartment, 1930s, EX ..**125.00**

Tom Mix, decoder badge, Six-Gun, NM **165.00**

Tom Mix, wristwatch, 100th Anniversary, M **275.00**

Tom Terrific, coloring book, Treasure Books, 1957, unused, EX....**25.00**

Uncle Wiggly, bank, litho tin, Chein, 5", M................................**400.00**

Underdog, sticker book, Whitman, 1973, unused, NM **15.00**

Vincent Price, watercolor set, Sears, 1960s, complete, VG+ (VG+ box)...**75.00**

WC Fields, plaque, head in relief on oval wood-look base, 1970s, 20"..**100.00**

Wild Bill Hickok, Bunkhouse Kit, 1950s, NM (NM envelope) **65.00**

Winnie the Pooh, doll, soft felt plush, Gund, 1964, 6½", VG **30.00**

Winnie the Pooh, jack-in-the-box, Mattel, EX............................**110.00**

Winnie the Pooh, push-button puppet, Kohner, 1960s, EX+ **35.00**

Woodstock, nodder, ceramic, w/bat, Japan, NM **60.00**

Woody Woodpecker, bank, vinyl figure, Imco, 1977, 10½", MIP..**150.00**

Woody Woodpecker, planter, ceramic figure/pot, Napco, 1958, VG+ ..**40.00**

Wyatt Earp, outfit, Yankeeboy, 1950s, complete, VG (VG box).**125.00**

Yogi Bear, guitar, crank-type, Mattel, 1961, EX..............................**65.00**
Yogi Bear, slippers, bl corduroy, 1962, unused, NMIB...................**70.00**
Yosemite Sam, bank, pnt soft vinyl figure, Dakin/WB, 1971, 10", EX+...**45.00**
Zorro, cape, Carnival Creations, NMOC **65.00**
Zorro, Pencil Craft By Numbers, Hassenfeld Bros/WDP, complete, EXIB..**75.00**
Zorro, plate & bowl, plastic, Sun-Valley Melmac, 1950s-60s, EX .**45.00**
Zorro, ring, Z, 1960s, M...**75.00**
Zorro, wallet, brn or wht vinyl w/Zorro & horse, EX, ea **75.00**
Zorro, wristwatch, leather band, US Time, 1955, EX....................**75.00**

Peters and Reed

John Peters and Adam Reed founded their pottery in Zanesville, Ohio, just before the turn of the century, using the local red clay to produce a variety of wares. Moss Aztec, introduced about 1912, has an unglazed exterior with designs molded in high relief and the recesses highlighted with a green wash. Only the interior is glazed to hold water. Pereco (named for Peters, Reed and Company) is glazed in semi-matt blue, maroon, cream, and other colors. Orange was also used very early, but such examples are rare. Shapes are simple with in-mold decoration sometimes borrowed from the Moss Aztec line. Wilse Blue is a line of high-gloss medium blue with dark specks on simple shapes. Landsun, characterized by its soft matt multicolor or blue and gray combinations, is decorated either by dripping or by hand brushing in an effect sometimes called Flame or Herringbone. Chromal, in much the same colors as Landsun, may be decorated with a realistic scenic, or the swirling application of colors may merely suggest one. Vivid, realistic Chromal scenics command much higher prices than weak, poorly drawn examples. (Brush-McCoy made a very similar line called Chromart. Neither will be marked; and due to the lack of documented background material available, it may be impossible make a positive identification. Collectors nearly always attribute this type of decoration to Peters and Reed.) Shadow Ware is usually a glossy, multicolor drip over a harmonious base color but occasionally seen in overall matt glaze. When the base is black, the effect is often iridescent.

Perhaps the most familiar line is the brown high-glaze artware with the 'sprigged'-type designs. Although research has uncovered no positive proof, it has been generally accepted as having been made by Peters and Reed. However, this line has recently been re-attributed to Weller pottery by the Sanfords in their latest book on Peters and Reed pottery. This conclusion was drawn due to the overwhelming number of shapes proven to be Wellery pottery. Several other lines were produced including Mirror Black, Persian, Egyptian, Florentine, Marbleized, etc., and an unidentified line which collectors call Mottled-Marbleized Colors. In this high-gloss line, the red clay body often shows through the splashed-on colors.

In 1922 the company became known as the Zane Pottery. Peters and Reed retired, and Harry McClelland became president. Charles Chilcote designed new lines, and production of many of the old lines continued. The body of the ware after 1922 was light in color. Marks include the impressed logo or ink stamp 'Zaneware' in a rectangle.

Bowl, Landsun, matching turtle flower frog, bl tones, 8" **140.00**
Bowl, Moss Aztec, leaves & branches, flake, 3" H......................**125.00**
Bowl, Pereco, gr matt, emb leafy branches, 3¼x8⅛" **120.00**
Figurine, frog, Marbleized, unmk, 4⅝", NM.............................**200.00**
Figurine, goose, gr matt, unmk, 6" **225.00**
Flower frog, Pereco, lily leaf, unmk, 4" **50.00**
Jar, Landsun, w/lid, 4" **350.00**
Vase, Chromal, dk bl/brn/tan, unmk, 7¾" **500.00**
Vase, Landsun, autumnal earth tones, 9½" **225.00**
Vase, Landsun, bl & pale yel, unmk, 6", NM **150.00**
Vase, Landsun, earth tones w/bl speckles, stick neck, 8", NM.....**125.00**

Vase, Landsun, mc drip, unmk, 11¼"...**350.00**
Vase, Montene, tilt pull, unmk, 3¾" **85.00**
Vase, Montene, variegated grs & tans w/creamy windows, unmk, 4"...**100.00**
Vase, Moss Aztec, emb blkberries, unmk, 7⅞"............................**150.00**
Vase, Moss Aztec, leaves & vines, brn w/gr, Ferrell, 18".............**400.00**
Vase, Moss Aztec, lg flowers, incurvate cylinder, 6"....................**125.00**
Vase, Shadow Ware, mc, bulbous, rolled rim, unmk Zane Ware, 8⅞"...**450.00**
Vase, Shadow Ware, mc, gourd shape, unmk Zane, 5⅛" **325.00**
Vase, Shadow Ware, mc, Zane Ware mk, 8", NM.........................**400.00**

Pewabic

The Pewabic Pottery was formally established in Detroit, Michigan, in 1907 by Mary Chase Perry Stratton and Horace James Caulkins. The two had worked together since 1903, firing their ware in a small kiln Caulkins had designed especially for use by the dental trade. Always a small operation which relied upon basic equipment and the skill of the workers, they took pride in being commissioned for several important architectural tile installations.

Some of the early artware was glazed a simple matt green; occasionally other colors were added, sometimes in combination, one over the other in a drip effect. Later Stratton developed a lustrous crystalline glaze. (Today's values are determined to a great extent by the artistic merit of the glaze.) The body of the ware was highly fired and extremely hard. Shapes were basic, and decorative modeling, if used at all, was in low relief. Mary Stratton kept the pottery open until her death in 1961. In 1968 it was purchased and reopened by Michigan State University; it is still producing today. Several marks were used over the years: a triangle with 'Revelation Pottery' (for a short time only); 'Pewabic' with five maple leaves; and the impressed circle mark.

Ashtray, gray on red, paper label & imp mk, 4x2½" **80.00**
Bowl, burgundy-red irid, recessed vertical panels, shallow, 5¾" ..**165.00**
Vase, bl & gr metallic, shouldered, 7½" **1,500.00**

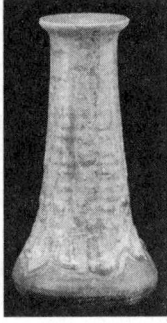

Vase, frothing green celadon and gold lustre, drilled, stamped mark, 10½x5", $2,000.00. (Photo courtesy Craftsmen Auctions)

Vase, gr, cvd geometrics, hand thrown, mk/label, 12½" **3,500.00**
Vase, gr drip on gray-flecked mustard yel, 6¼" **550.00**
Vase, gr/red platinum metallic, shouldered, 11" **3,250.00**
Vase, metallic gray/gold/bl, bulbous, 5½" **750.00**
Vase, purple w/gr inclusions dripping on frothy yel, 6¼" **1,100.00**
Vase, purple/gr/rose metallic w/irid highlights, base flaw, 4" **1,000.00**
Vase, red/platinum gr drip over matt red at bottom, bulbous, 10", EX...**2,300.00**
Vase, tan w/brn flecks & bl accents, blk drip at mouth, 8x4"......**300.00**
Vase, veiled brn areas on yel matt, mfg flaws, 12x7"...................**800.00**

Pewter

Pewter is a metal alloy of tin, copper, very small parts of bismuth and/or antimony, and sometimes lead. Very little American pewter contained lead, however, because much of the ware was designed to be used as tableware, and makers were aware that the use of lead could result in poisoning. (Pieces that do contain lead are usually darker in color and heavier than those that have no lead.) Most of the fine examples of American pewter date from 1700 to the 1840s. Many pieces were melted down and recast into bullets during the American Revolution in 1775; this explains to some extent why examples from this period are quite difficult to find. The pieces that did survive may include buttons, buckles, and writing equipment as well as the tableware we generally think of.

After the Revolution makers began using antimony as the major alloy with the tin in an effort to regain the popularity of pewter, which glassware and china was beginning to replace in the home. The resulting product, known as britannia, had a lustrous silver-like appearance and was far more durable. While closely related, britannia is a collectible in its own right and should not be confused with pewter.

Key: tm — touch mark

Basin, A Griswold tm, wear/scratches, 13⅛".................................**495.00**
Basin, Blakslee Barns eagle tm+B Barns in rectangle, 1½x11", EX+....**465.00**
Basin, G Jones eagle tm, pitting/scratches/sm rpr, 1¾x7¾" **200.00**
Basin, partial London tm, hammered booge & flared rim, 3x13", EX ..**250.00**
Basin, Samuel Pierce eagle tm, dents/pitting, 13¼".....................**220.00**
Bowl, baptismal; R Gleason tm, ftd, 5x8"..............................**650.00**
Bowl, European tm, 11" **350.00**
Bowl, S Griswold eagle tm, rstr booge/rim, 13"..........................**465.00**
Candlesticks, B&P tm, baluster w/rnd bases, rpr, 11¼", pr..........**250.00**
Candlesticks, Ostrander & Norris tm, conical w/flared sockets, 8", pr...**685.00**
Candlesticks, unmk, beaded detail, baluster on domed base, 10", pr...**385.00**
Chalice, Leonared, Reed & Barton tm, polished, 7", pr **385.00**
Charger, J Danforth tm, 1700s, knife mks/lt dents, 12"............**1,265.00**
Charger, J Whitmore tm, 18th C, tooled rim/base lines, rpr, 13"...**400.00**
Charger, unmk, polished, wear, 13" **275.00**
Coffeepot, A Griswold in arch over eagle tm, squat pear form, 10", EX...**575.00**
Coffeepot, Curtis banner tm (partial), squat pear form, 9", VG..**440.00**
Coffeepot, Eben Smith tm, lighthouse form w/eng decor, wood hdl, 12"...**1,380.00**
Coffeepot, Hall & Cotton #2 tm, tall/tapers, enamel hdl, 1840s, rstr, 11"..**525.00**
Coffeepot, HH Graves tm, (4X on base), wide raised band, scroll hdls, 9"....**275.00**
Coffeepot, IC Lewis, 1840s, tapered, tooled rings, pnt scroll hdl, 10"...**330.00**
Coffeepot, unmk (att H Homan), scroll hdl, grape finial, 11".....**165.00**
Deep dish, J Porter eagle tm (2X), 1700s, pitting, 13".................**330.00**
Deep dish, S Danforth tm, early 1800s, pitting, 13" **600.00**
Flagon, Boardman w/rampant lion tm, lt dents, 11½".................**440.00**
Flagon, communion; Reed & Barton tm, 11¼" **220.00**
Inkwell, English tm, wide flat base, bl ceramic insert, 3x9".........**120.00**
Lamp, Capen & Molineux, saucer base, cylinder font, burning fluid, 4"....**110.00**
Lamp, Martin Hyde, baluster w/saucer base, acorn font, minor rpr, 9" ..**220.00**
Lamp, R Gleason tm, whale oil burner, 6½" **400.00**
Measures, European, set of 7, Centilitre to Litre, lt wear, 1½-7".....**220.00**
Measures, 1 mk: Yates, bellied, wear/dents, assembled set of 5, 2-4"..**250.00**
Pitcher, milk; R Dunham tm, tooled rings, 7" **715.00**
Plate, deep; S Hamlin tm, early 1800s, rpr/lt wear, 11½" **365.00**
Plate, deep; Wm Calder tm, lt overall pitting, 11½" **350.00**
Plate, Geo Lightner eagle tm, early 1800s, minor dents, 8".........**400.00**
Plate, London/crown tm w/WW, polished, wear, 12"..................**300.00**
Plate, N Austin tm, shallow dents/pitting, 9½" **325.00**
Plate, R Austin tm, early 1800s, lt pitting/wear, 7¾" **250.00**
Plate, R Gleason tm, ca 1820-70, wear/dents, 9" **275.00**
Plate, RD Boardman eagle tm, 8½"......................................**495.00**
Plate, S Kilbourn tm, rpr, 8½"...**135.00**
Plate, TD Boardman eagle tm, scratches, 7¾".........................**350.00**
Plate, Thomas & Townsend partial tm, rim rpr, 7⅝" **80.00**
Plate, Thomas Danforth Boardman eagle tm, 9"......................**285.00**

Plate, Thos Badger eagle tm, pitting/wear, 8½" **250.00**
Plate, Wm Danforth eagle tm, wear/scratches, 8" **275.00**
Porringer, IG tm, rtcl crown hdl, minor dent, 4¼"......................**330.00**
Porringer, RG crown tm, mini, 2" dia...................................**475.00**
Porringer, S Hamlin Jr tm, rtcl flowered hdl, minor dents, 5⅜"..**550.00**
Porringer, taster; att LC Lewis, rtcl hdl w/damage, 2⅛" **330.00**
Porringer, TD & SB tm, rtcl floral hdl, dent, 5¼"......................**650.00**
Porringer, TD & SB tm, rtcl Old English hdl, 4" **700.00**
Porringer, unmk, att PA, plain hdl w/hanging hole, 5½" **465.00**
Porringer, unmk, cast crown hdl, corroded/pitting, 5¼"..............**220.00**
Porringer, W Calder tm, rtcl floral hdl, 5"..............................**650.00**
Tallpot, F Porter tm, lighthouse form, 10¾" **465.00**
Tallpot, Whitlock Troy NY tm, lighthouse form, pitting/EX rpr, 11"..**330.00**
Tankard, HA & Son int rnd tm, stepped dome lid, rtcl lever, 7"..**1,700.00**
Tankard, J Townsend tm, scrolled hdl, no lid, 4⅜x4"................**280.00**
Teapot, A Porter tm, 1840s, scroll hdl, ftd, rstr, 7" **330.00**
Teapot, A Porter tm, G form, tooled rings, scroll hdl, 7" **300.00**
Teapot, Boardman & Hart 2-line tm, scroll hdl, dome lid, lt dents, 8"..**350.00**
Teapot, E Smith, bulbous, tooled lines, stepped conical finial, 8" **250.00**
Teapot, E Wells, ornate hdl, slightly flaring sides, minor dents, 8"...**135.00**
Teapot, JD Locke NY tm, 9" **415.00**
Teapot, R Dunham, flared neck, scroll hdl, tooled lines, 6½", VG ..**245.00**
Teapot, Sellew & Co tm, rpr, 8½" **300.00**
Teapot, unmk Am, somewhat battered, 8" **250.00**
Teapot, W Humiston Troy NY, flared ft/neck, scroll hdl, 7¾", VG **275.00**
Teapot, W Savage, long waisted neck, blk-pnt hdl, lt pitting, 10" **440.00**
Teapot, Wm Calder, bulbous w/waisted neck & ft, hdl rpr/dent, 7½".**165.00**

Pfaltzgraff

Pfaltzgraff has operated in Pennsylvania since the early 1800s making redware at first, then stoneware crocks and jugs, yellow ware and spongeware in the 1920s, artware and kitchenware in the 1930s, and stoneware kitchen items through the 1940s. To collectors, they're best known for their Gourmet Royal (circa 1950s), a high-gloss dinnerware line of solid brown with frothy white drip glaze around the rims, and their giftware line called Muggsy, comic-character mugs, ashtrays, bottle stoppers, children's dishes, pretzel jars, cookie jars, etc. It was designed in the late 1940s and continued in production until 1960. The older versions have protruding features, while the features of later examples were simply painted on.

Their popular Village line, an almond-glazed pattern with a brown-stenciled folk-art tulip design, was discontinued a few years ago, and is today becoming very collectible. Yorktown and Folk Art are manufactured today only on a very limited basis, so discontinued items in those lines are attracting much interest as well. (In general, use Village prices to help you evaluate those two lines.) For more information on their dinnerware, we recommend *The Flea Market Trader* and *The Garage Sale and Flea Market Annual*, both by Collector Books.

Village, batter bowl, 8", from $35.00 to $42.00.

Gourmet Royale, baker, #321, oval, 7½", from $18 to...................**20.00**
Gourmet Royale, bean pot, #11-3, 3-qt..................................**35.00**
Gourmet Royale, bowl, #241, oval, 7x10", from $15 to.................**18.00**

Gourmet Royale, bowl, salad; tapered sides, 10", from $25 to 28.00
Gourmet Royale, butter dish, #394, ¼-lb, stick type 12.00
Gourmet Royale, casserole, hen on nest, 2-qt, from $75 to 95.00
Gourmet Royale, casserole, stick hdl, 4-qt, from $32 to 40.00
Gourmet Royale, chip 'n dip, #311, molded in 1 pc, 12", from $22 to ...30.00
Gourmet Royale, cup, from $2 to...3.00
Gourmet Royale, gravy boat, w/stick hdl, 2-spout, from $15 to.....20.00
Gourmet Royale, ladle, 3½" dia bowl w/11" hdl, from $18 to 20.00
Gourmet Royale, mug, #392, 16-oz, from $12 to............................14.00
Gourmet Royale, plate, grill; #87, 3-section, 11", from $18 to 20.00
Gourmet Royale, platter, #337, 16", from $25 to 30.00
Gourmet Royale, roaster, #326, oval, 16", from $50 to 60.00
Gourmet Royale, serving tray, rnd, 4-section, upright hdl in center...22.00
Gourmet Royale, teapot, #381, 6-cup, from $18 to.........................22.00
Planter, donkey, brn drip, common, 10", from $15 to 20.00
Village, baker, #24, oval, 10¼", from $8 to 10.00
Village, bowl, serving; #010, 7", from $8 to...................................12.00
Village, butter dish, #028..8.00
Village, coffeepot, lighthouse shape, 48-oz, from $30 to 35.00
Village, flowerpot, 4½", from $15 to...20.00
Village, pedestal mug, #90F, 10-oz..4.50
Village, soup tureen, #160, w/lid & ladle, 3½-qt, from $40 to 45.00

Muggsy Line

Ashtray 125.00
Cigarette server..125.00
Clothes sprinkler bottle, Myrtle, Black, from $275 to 375.00
Clothes sprinkler bottle, Myrtle, wht, from $250 to 350.00
Cookie jar, character face, minimum value 250.00
Jar, utility; Handy Harry, hat w/short bill as flat lid 200.00
Mug, action figure (golfer/fisherman/etc), any, from $65 to 85.00
Mug, character face, shot sz..50.00
Tumbler..60.00

Phoenix Bird

Blue and white Phoenix Bird china has been produced by various Japanese potteries from the early 1900s. With slight variations the design features the Japanese bird of paradise and scroll-like vines of Kara-Kusa, or Chinese grass. Although some of their earlier ware is unmarked, the majority is marked in some fashion. More than 125 different stamps have been reported, with 'Made in Japan' the one most often found. Coming in second is Morimura's wreath and/or crossed stems (both having the letter 'M' within). The cloverleaf with 'Japan' below very often indicates an item having a high-quality transfer-printed design. Among the many categories in the Phoenix Bird pattern are several shapes; therefore (for identification purposes), each has been given a number, i.e. #1, #2, etc. Newer items, if marked at all, carry a paper label. Compared to the older ware, the coloring of the new is whiter and the blue more harsh; the design is sparse with more ground area showing. Although collectors buy even 'new' pieces, the older is, of course, more highly prized and valued.

On today's market, prices fluctuate wildly, based on personal values. While advanced collectors pass up common pieces, they may pay exorbitant amounts for those they need to complete their collections. This creates an artificial high and low price structure. Some of our values are actual selling prices and include examples of both low and high-end sales.

For further information we recommend *Phoenix Bird Chinaware, Books I – V*, written and privately published by our advisor, Joan Oates; her address is in the Directory under Michigan. Join Phoenix Bird Collectors of America (PBCA) and receive the *Phoenix Bird Discoveries* newsletter, an informative publication that will further your appreciation of this chinaware. See Clubs, Newsletters, and Catalogs for ordering information.

Biscuit jar, Border K, 5" dia...91.00
Bouillon, open 60.00
Boullion, w/lid 75.00
Bowl, cereal; 6¼"...18.00
Bowl, fruit; superior quality, 5"...20.50
Bowl, mayonnaise; border outside..92.00
Bowl, soup; 7¼"..35.00
Butter pat 8.75
Cheese/cracker plate..280.00
Chocolate pot, Nippon 400.00
Coffeepot, ring hdl, #3-c 82.00
Creamer & sugar bowl, style #2, child sz....................................46.00
Cup, custard; 2¾x3" 12.50
Cup & saucer, child sz..16.50
Cup & saucer, chocolate; style #2 ....30.00
Cup & saucer, demitasse; 2⅛" H..15.00
Cup & saucer, tea/coffee; common..7.00

Finger bowl, unmarked, 2¼x5⅛x3½", $136.00.
(Photo courtesy Joan Oates)

Gravy ladle, heart border, #3 ....113.50
Hair receiver, 2-pc 92.50
Hair receiver, 2-pc, from $50 to 80.00
Mustard pot, style #7 ....157.50
Mustard pot, style #9 ....122.50
Plate, dinner; 9¾"..56.00
Plate, luncheon; 8½"...24.00
Platter, 7¼"...14.50
Platter, 10x7¼"...40.00
Platter, 12¼"..50.00
Platter, 14¾"..68.00
Platter, 17"...170.00
Reamer & pitcher, rim chips...136.00
Sauce boat, style #2, w/underplate...50.00
Sugar bowl, 6-sided, style #7 ....90.00
Syrup, style #1 ....55.00
Tankard, water..95.00
Tea strainer, style #3 ....70.00
Tea tile, 6" dia..22.50
Teapot, post-1970, mk #25..118.50
Tureen, vegetable...105.00
Vase, post-1970, 3¼"...22.00

Phoenix Glass

Founded in 1880 in Monaca, Pennsylvania, the Phoenix Glass Company became one of the country's foremost manufacturers of lighting glass by the early 1900s. They also produced a wide variety of utilitarian and decorative glassware, including art glass by Joseph Webb, colored cut glass, Gone-With-the-Wind style oil lamps, hotel and barware, and pharmaceutical glassware. Today, however, collectors are primarily interested in the 'Sculptured Artware' produced in the 1930s and 1940s. These beautiful pressed and mold-blown pieces are most often found in white milk glass or crystal with various color treatments or a satin finish.

Phoenix did not mark their 'Sculptured Artware' line on the glass; instead, a silver and black (earliest) or gold and black (later) foil label in the shape of the mythical phoenix was used.

Quite often glassware made by the Consolidated Lamp and Glass Company of nearby Coraopolis, Pennsylvania, is mistaken for Phoenix's 'Sculptured Artware.' Though the style of the glass is very similar, one distinguishing characteristic is that perhaps 80% of the time Phoenix applied color to the background leaving the raised design plain in contrast, while Consolidated generally applied color to the raised design and left the background plain. Also, for the most part, the patterns and colors used by Phoenix were distinctively different from those used by Consolidated.

In 1970 Phoenix Glass became a division of Anchor Hocking which in turn was acquired by the Newell Group in 1987. Phoenix has the distinction of being one of the oldest continuously operating glass factories in the United States. For more information refer to *Phoenix and Consolidated Art Glass, 1926 – 1980*, written by our advisor, Jack D. Wilson, who is listed in the Directory under Arizona. See also Consolidated Glass.

Blackberry, wine glass, irid	145.00
Bluebell, vase, brn shadow, 7"	125.00
Bluebell, vase, lt pk w/pearlized design, 7"	125.00
Bluebell, vase, rose w/pearlized design, 7"	125.00
Cosmos, vase, brn shadow, 7½"	145.00
Cosmos, vase, gr on milk glass, 7½"	145.00
Cosmos, vase, purple pearlized, 7½"	185.00
Daisy, vase, bl over milk glass, 9x9"	450.00
Daisy, vase, tan on frosted, 9x9"	325.00
Dancing Girls, vase, pk shadow, 12"	450.00
Dancing Girls, vase, red pearlized, 12"	625.00
Diving Girl, banana boat, orange w/frosted design	425.00
Diving Girl, banana boat, slate bl shadow on milk glass	375.00
Fern, vase, slate gray pearlized, 7"	155.00
Freesia, vase, bl & frosted, 8"	195.00
Freesia, vase, pk w/frosted design, 8"	150.00
Freesia, vase, yel-tan w/frosted design, fan shape, 8"	175.00
Jewel, vase, wht w/lt bl design, 4¾"	85.00
Jonquil, platter, yel wash over satin ground, 14"	275.00
Lacy Dewdrop, pitcher, gray highlights on milk glass	175.00
Lacy Dewdrop, tumbler, gray highlights on milk glass	45.00
Lily, bowl, console; gr wash w/frosted design	425.00
Lily, vase, aqua wash (rare color), str sides, 8"	225.00
Lily, vase, yel wash, 3-crimp, 9"	295.00
Madonna, vase, gr frost, 10"	175.00
Madonna, vase, lt bl on milk glass, 10"	200.00
Madonna, vase, tan shadow, 10"	225.00
Moon & Stars, fruit holder, heavy caramel irid	250.00
Philodendron, vase, brn shadow	200.00
Philodendron, vase, gray w/frosted design, 11½"	175.00
Phlox, ashtray, slate bl pearlized	225.00
Phlox, box, cigarette; deep burgundy pearlized, w/lid	180.00
Phlox, box, cigarette; gr & milk glass, w/lid	120.00
Phlox, candy dish, bl frosted	200.00
Primrose, vase, gr w/milk glass design, 8¾"	375.00
Reuben Line Screech Owls, vase, bl, orig label	275.00
Ruba Rombic, fish bowl, gr, 6½x12", on metal stand, 36" overall	2,600.00
Star Flower, vase, bl & milk glass, 7"	145.00
Thistle, vase, burgundy pearlized, 18"	750.00
Thistle, vase, med gr pearlized, 18"	550.00
Thistle, vase, tan pearlized, 18"	550.00
Tiger Lily, bowl, pk frosted, 11½"	350.00
Tiger Lily, bowl, wht frosted, 11½"	275.00
Wild Geese, vase, lime gr pearlized, 9x12"	225.00
Wild Rose, vase, slate bl shadow, 10½"	200.00
Zodiac, vase, deep rose over milk glass, 10½"	950.00
Zodiac, vase, slate bl over milk glass	950.00

Phonographs

The phonograph, invented by Thomas Edison in 1877, was the first practical instrument for recording and reproducing sound. Sound wave vibrations were recorded on a tinfoil-covered cylinder and played back with a needle that ran along the grooves made from the recording, thus reproducing the sound. Very little changed to this art of record making until 1885, when the first replayable and removable wax cylinders were developed by the American Graphophone Company. These records were made from 1885 until 1894 and are rare today. Edison began to offer musically recorded wax cylinders in 1889. They continued to be made until 1902. Today they are known as brown wax records. Black wax cylinders were offered in 1902, and the earlier brown wax cylinders were discontinued. These wax two-minute records were sold until 1912. From 1912 until 1929, only four-minute celluloid blue amberol record cylinders were made. The first disc records and disc machines were offered by the inventor Berliner in 1894. They were sold in America until 1900, when the Victor company took over. In the 1890s, all machines played 7" diameter disc records; the 10" size was developed in 1901. By the early 1900s there existed many disc and cylinder phonograph companies, all offering their improvements. Among them were Berliner, Columbia, Zonophone, United States Phono, Wizard, Vitaphone, Amet, and others.

All Victor I's through VI's originally came with a choice of either brass bell, morning-glory, or wooden horns. Wood horns are the most valuable, adding $1,000.00 (or more) to the machine. Spring models were produced until 1929 (and even later). After 1929 most were electric (though some electric-motor models were produced as early as 1910). Unless another condition is noted, prices are for complete, original phonographs in at least fine to excellent condition. Note: Edison coin-operated cylinder players start at $7,000.00 and may go up to $20,000.00 each. All outside-horn Victor phonographs are worth at least $1,000.00 or more, if in excellent original condition. Machines that are complete, still retaining all their original parts, and with the original finish still in good condition are the most sought after, but those that have been carefully restored with their original finishes, decals, etc., are bringing high prices as well. Unless noted, values are for examples in excellent condition, sold at popular, repeated buying prices.

Key:
cyl — cylinder	NP — nickel-plated
mg — morning glory	rpd — reproducer

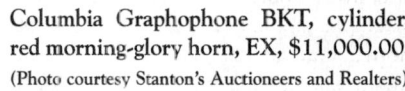

Columbia Graphophone BKT, cylinder, red morning-glory horn, EX, $11,000.00.
(Photo courtesy Stanton's Auctioneers and Realtors)

Amberola VIII, cyl, oak table top	450.00
Amberola 50, cyl, mahog	300.00
Amberola 50, cyl, oak table top, EX	275.00
Bush & Lane, triple rpd, mahog floor model	200.00

Busy Bee, disc, red mg horn 325.00
Chevy, mahog, floor model 200.00
Clark Talk-o-phone, disc, brass bell horn 550.00
Columbia AQ, cyl, blk horn 425.00
Columbia AU, disc, from $450 to 600.00
Columbia BF, cyl, 6" mandrel 600.00
Columbia BM, cyl, mahog case, 6" mandrel................................800.00
Columbia Eagle B, cyl, nickel horn 425.00
Columbia Graphophone AT, cyl..325.00
Columbia Graphophone K, red & gold, disc, w/brass bell horn 1,150.00
Columbia Q, cyl, MIB..450.00
Columbia Q, cyl, w/case, nickel horn 375.00
Columbia 20th Century BC, cyl, 54" brass horn, floor model crane ..1,600.00
Edison Amberola V, cyl, mahog table model................................425.00
Edison Amberola VI, cyl, mahog case 325.00
Edison Amberola X, cyl, table top 300.00
Edison Amberola 75, cyl, mahog floor model 550.00
Edison Amberola 75, oak floor model 550.00
Edison Business C, table model...175.00
Edison Dmn Disc, C-150, oak floor model...................................275.00
Edison Dmn Disc A-100, oak floor model....................................200.00
Edison Dmn Disc A-150, mahog floor model...............................200.00
Edison Dmn Disc B-19, mahog table model.................................400.00
Edison Dmn Disc C-19, floor model..250.00
Edison Fireside B, K rpd, orig brass bell horn 625.00
Edison Gem Black, cyl 400.00
Edison Gem Maroon, cyl, 2-4 min, K rpd, orig Fireside horn ..1,300.00
Edison Home, cyl, 2-min, brass horn 400.00
Edison Home, cyl, 2-4 min, C rpd, brass bell horn 375.00
Edison Home, cyl, 2-4 min, C rpd, gr mg horn 600.00
Edison Home, cyl, 2-4 min, C rpd, mg metal oak grain-pnt horn..625.00
Edison Home, cyl, 2-4 min, K rpd, Edison Standard horn............575.00
Edison Home E, 2-4 min, O rpd, Edison Cygnet horn..................950.00
Edison Home Suitcase, banner top, C rpd, 2-min, sm horn 650.00
Edison S-19, oak floor model...150.00
Edison Standard, cyl, 2-min, C rpd..375.00
Edison Standard, cyl, 2-min, C rpd w/repeater attachment.........650.00
Edison Standard, cyl, 2-4 min, C rpd 375.00
Edison Standard, cyl, 2-4 min, C rpd, earphones.........................475.00
Edison Standard, cyl, 2-4 min, C rpd, mg horn............................650.00
Edison Standard, cyl, 2-4 min, Dmn B rpd...................................500.00
Edison Standard Suitcase, 2-latch case, C rpd 450.00
Edison Standard Suitcase, 4-latch, C rpd, 2-min, sm horn..........550.00
Edison Suitcase Home, banner top, cyl, 2-min, C rpd.................350.00
Edison Triumph, cyl, 2-min, C rpd, 3-spring motor 600.00
Edison Triumph, cyl, 2-4 min, C rpd, 3-spring motor, lg mg horn...900.00
Edison 30, cyl, oak...325.00
Edison 50, cyl, oak table top 375.00
Jeannette, disc, keywind, child's..65.00
Musicalphone by Englewood, disc, front mount, brass bell horn.500.00
Silvertone, disc, oak table top..150.00
Standard, disc, open works, w/horn 500.00
Standard X, disc, brass bell horn...500.00
Standard X, disc, red mg horn 500.00
Victor E, disc, front mount, brass bell horn, from $900 to 1,050.00
Victor I, disc, brass bell horn...1,150.00
Victor II, disc, nickel horn..1,400.00
Victor II, disc, oak case, ribbed/flared horn.................................1,200.00
Victor II, disc, oak horn 2,750.00
Victor II, disc, rear mount, brass bell horn..................................1,200.00
Victor II, humpback, disc, lg brass bell horn...............................1,500.00
Victor IV, disc, mahog w/mahog horn & case..............................4,000.00
Victor M, disc, brass bell horn...1,500.00
Victor P, disc, brass bell horn..1,200.00

Victor R, disc, blk horn..900.00
Victor R, disc, brass bell horn..1,150.00
Victor V, disc, lg brass bell horn 2,300.00
Victor VV-XIA, disc, mahog table top..275.00
Victor VV-215, console, disc...200.00
Victrola Orthophonic, mahog floor model....................................200.00
Victrola VVX, oak floor model..300.00
Windsor, disc, 3-way rpd, mahog floor model 250.00
Zonophone, disc, rear mount, brass bell horn.............................1,400.00
Zonophone, disc, rear mount, oak, red petal horn.....................1,050.00

Photographica

Photographic collectibles include not only the cameras and equipment used to 'freeze' special moments in time but also the photographic images produced by a great variety of processes that have evolved since the daguerrean era of the mid-1800s. For the most part, good quality images have either maintained or increased in value. Poor quality examples (regardless of rarity) are not selling well. Interest in cameras and stereo equipment is down, and dealers report that average-priced items that were moving well are often completely overlooked. Though rare items always have a market, collectors seem to be buying only if they are bargain priced.

Our advisor for this category is John Hess; he is listed in the Directory under Massachusetts.

Albumens

Palace Butte Near Mt Blackore MT, WH Jackson, 13x10"+fr 800.00
Roche Montonnies, Mt of Holy Cross, WH Jackson, 1873, 16x20"..500.00
Warship Monterey Off Astoria in Mouth of Columbia, 19th C, 5x8", G.15.00

Ambrotypes

An ambrotype is a type of photograph produced by an early wet-plate process whereby a faint negative image on glass is seen as positive when held against a dark background.

4th plate, boy in fireman's outfit, hand tinted, 1850s, EX in case..550.00
4th plate, Confederate soldier by table w/shell jacket, +leather case ..550.00
4th plate, Confederate soldier w/hat & gilt buttons, +Union case......550.00
4th plate, sm boy w/pipe in mouth, EX 12.00
6th plate, baby's portrait, ca 1850s, EX in velvet-lined leather case..60.00
6th plate, Confederate soldier, full view, w/slouch hat/etc, +case ..660.00
6th plate, horse-drawn coach, Rufus Anson, +brn leather case ..600.00
6th plate, husband & wife, hand tinted, 1850s, pr, EX in case....250.00
9th plate, Confederate soldier, waist up, coat & kepi, +case.......550.00
9th plate, folk art painting of boy w/flute, compo case 300.00

Cabinet Photos

Black lady (well dressed) holding guitar, G................................395.00
Black lady stands beside climbing rose near house, 7⅞x5⅞", EX..47.50
Boy on lg-wheel tricycle, Terry of Blackpool, EX........................115.00
Buffalo Bill, portrait, signature printed in blk, NM 330.00
Buffalo Bill Cody, w/saddle & Winchester, ca 1890, EX.............500.00
Chinese girls (2) w/bound ft sit w/open book, G 65.00
Cowboy Pianist AO Babel, Nichols, IA, Victorian, 4¼x6⅛" 240.00
Cowgirl w/gun, Carmen Alvarez of Wild West show, EX............150.00
Drummer boy, kepi hat, 1891, 4¼x6½", EX 125.00
Girl w/Jack Russell terrier on chair, 6½x4¼" 60.00
Girls (2) w/dolls, PA, 1892, gilt edges, 6½x4¼", EX 55.00
Girls in fairy costumes, identified/5 & 2 years old, ca 1900, EX....75.00

ID Indian baby, moccasins & Indian blanket, Cummings, VG 65.00
Indian Wars Infantry sergeant in kepi, marksman insignias, 1880s ..75.00
Lady w/10'-long hair, ca 1900, EX 110.00
Lillian Russell, youthful, Sarony, common 75.00
Lillie Langtree, W&D Downey, 1882, NM 200.00
Man (legs amputated) on early tricycle w/lg bk wheels, 6½x4¼" .80.00
Men (4 heavily armed) & 2 ladies, all in western clothes, 1880s?, EX ..385.00
Nebraska Indians baseball team, 1890s, EX...................................219.00
Piegan Chief Curly Bear, 1896, 6½x4¼" 170.00
Sideshow performer, dog-face man, unidentified, pre-1900, EX ..200.00
Snake charmer girl from circus sideshow, Swords Bros PA, 6½x4¼" .65.00
Teacher & 8 girl students at sewing machine, 1880s, 6½x4½", EX....78.00
Yosemite Valley from Mariposa trail, CE Watkins, 3¼x5" 125.00

Cameras

Collecting antique cameras is very popular, and values have continued to move upward as the high-quality items have become harder to find. Most of the pre-1900 cameras will be found in the large format view cameras or studio camera types. There are quite a few of these that can be found in a well-worn condition, but there is a large difference in value between an average-wear item and an excellent or mint-condition camera. It is rare indeed to find one of these early cameras in mint condition.

The types of cameras are generally classified into — large format, medium format, early folding and box types, 35 mm single-lens-reflex (SLR), 35mm rangefinders, twin-lens reflex (TLR), miniature or subminiature, novelty, and even a few others. Collectors may specialize in a type, a style, a time period, or even in high-quality examples of the same camera.

In the 1900 to 1940 period, large quantities of various makes of box cameras and folding bellows type cameras were produced by many manufacturers, and the popular 35mm camera was introduced in the 1930s. Most have low values because they were made in vast numbers, but mint-condition cameras are prized by collectors. In the 1930 to 1955 period, the 35mm rangefinders and the SLR's and TLR's became the cameras of choice. The most prized of these are the early German or Japanese rangefinders such as the Leica, Canon, or Nikon. Earlier, German optics were favored, but after WWII, Japanese cameras and optics rivaled and/or even exceeded the quality of many German optics.

Now there are thousands of different cameras to choose from, and collectors have many options when selecting categories. Quality is the major factor; values vary widely between an average-wear working camera and one in mint condition, or one still in the original box and unused. This brief list suggests average prices for good working cameras with average wear. The same camera in mint condition will be valued much higher, while one with excessive wear (scratches, dents, corrosion, poor optics, nonworking meters or rangefinders) may have little value.

Buying, selling, and trading of old and late vintage cameras on the Internet, both in direct transactions and via e-mail auctions, have affected the number of cameras that are available to collectors. As a result, values have fluctuated as well. Large numbers of old, mass-produced box cameras and folding cameras have been offered; many are in poor condition and have been put up for sale by persons who know nothing about quality. So in general, prices have dropped, except for the mint quality offerings. Many common models in poor to average condition can be bought for $1.00 to $10.00. The collector is advised to purchase only quality cameras that will enhance his collection.

Note: To date, no appreciable collector's market has developed for most old movie cameras or projectors. The Polaroid type of camera has little value, although a few models are gaining in popularity among collectors, and values are expected to increase. Note that many fakes and copies have been made of several of the classic cameras such as the German Leica and caution is advised in purchasing one of these cameras at a price too good to be true. Consult a specialist on high-priced classics if good reference material is not available. Our advisor for this category is

Gene Cataldo; he is listed in the Directory under Alabama (e-mail: genecams@aol.com). SASE required for information by mail.

Agfa, box type, 1930-50, from $10 to..20.00
Alpa, Standard, 1946-52, Swiss, from $1,000 to.......................1,500.00
Ansco, Cadet, from $1 to...5.00
Ansco, Folding, Nr 1 to Nr 10, ea from $8 to..................................30.00
Ansco, Speedex, Standard, 1950..15.00
Ansco, Super Speedex, 3.5 lens, 1953-58...................................150.00
Argoflex, Seventy-five, TLR, 1949-58...7.00
Argus C3 'blk brick,' 35mm, 1940s, from $5 to...............................15.00
Argus C4, 2.8 lens w/flash, from $10 to...25.00
Asahi Pentax, orig, 1957..200.00
Asahiflex 1, 1st Japanese SLR...500.00
Baldi, by Balda-Werk, 1930s, from $20 to.......................................30.00
Bell & Howell Dial-35, from $30 to..50.00
Canon, TX, from $30 to..60.00
Canon AE-1, from $50 to..90.00
Canon AE-1P, from $115 to...150.00
Canon IIB, 1949-53...250.00
Canon IV, 1950-52...325.00
Canon J, 1939-44, from $4,500 to..5,500.00
Canon L-1, 1956-57...400.00
Canon T-50, from $40 to...75.00
Canon TL, from $40 to..70.00
Canon 7, 1961-64...450.00
Compass Camera, 1938, from $1,000 to.......................................1,300.00
Contax II or III, 1936, from $325 to..425.00
Eastman Folding Baby Brownie, Bakelite, from $5 to.....................10.00
Eastman Kodak Box Hawkeye No 2A, from $5 to.............................8.00
Eastman Kodak Hawkeye, plastic, from $5 to....................................8.00
Eastman Kodak Retina IIIc, from $125 to..180.00
Eastman Kodak Retina IIIC, from $200 to.......................................400.00
Eastman Kodak Signet 35...20.00
Eastman Premo, many models exist, ea from $30 to.....................200.00
Eastman View Camera, early 1900, from $100 to..........................200.00
Edinex, by Wirgen, from $20 to...30.00
FED 1, USSR, postwar, from $30 to...60.00
FED 1, USSR, prewar, from $80 to...140.00
Fujica AX-3, from $50 to...90.00
Graflex Pacemaker Crown Graphic, various szs, ea from $80 to .150.00
Hasselblad 1000F, 1952-57, from $500 to..700.00
Konica FS-1, from $50 to..70.00
Kowa H, 1963-67, from $20 to...30.00
Leica II, 1963-67, from $350 to..450.00
Leica M3, 1954-66, from $800 to..1,400.00
Mamiyaflex, TLR, 1951, from $125 to...200.00
Minolta Autocord, TLR, from $75 to..100.00
Minolta SRT-101, from $40 to..70.00
Minolta SRT-202, from $50 to..90.00
Minolta X-700, from $130 to...165.00
Nikon FM...160.00
Olympus OM-1, from $80 to..120.00
Olympus OM-10, from $40 to..65.00
Pentax K-1000..100.00

Pentax Spotmatic, ca 1964, from $50.00 to $150.00. (Photo courtesy C.E. Cataldo)

Polaroid SX-70, from $25 to **35.00**
Praktica Super TL..**50.00**
Regula, King, various models, interchangeable lens, ea **75.00**
Rocoh KR-30, from $60 to **85.00**
Rocoh Singlex, 1965, from $50 to **70.00**
Rolei 35, mini, Germany, 1966-70, from $200 to **275.00**
Rolleiflex SL35M, 1978, from $80 to **100.00**
Spartus Press Flash, 1939-50, from $5 to **10.00**
Topcon Super D, 1963-74, from $100 to **135.00**
Topcon Uni, from $30 to **40.00**
Voighlander Vitessa T, 1957...**200.00**
Yashica FX-70, from $60 to **70.00**
Yashicamat 124G, TLR, from $150 to...................................**250.00**
Zeiss Ikon Juwell, 1927-39 ....**500.00**
Zorki, USSR, 1950-56 ....**50.00**

Carte De Visites

Among the many types of images collectible today are carte de visites, known as CDVs, which are 2¼" x 4" portraits printed on paper and produced in quantity. The CDV fad of the 1800s enticed the famous and the unknown alike to pose for these cards, which were circulated among the public to the extent that they became known as 'publics.' When the popularity of CDVs began to wane, a new fascination developed for the cabinet photo, a larger version measuring about 4½" x 6½". Note: A common portrait CDV is worth only about 50¢ unless it carries a revenue stamp on the back; those that do are valued at about $2.00 each.

Andrew Johnson, head & shoulders only, ca 1865, trimmed, G....**18.00**
Basilica San Marco in Piazza San Marco, early 1800s, VG............**10.00**
Boy on rocking horse, Rice, MO, slight fading..............................**45.00**
CB&Q conductor (identified), lav mt, ca 1880, VG **8.00**
General McPherson, seated, half view, EX...................................**250.00**
Henry Ward Beecher, chest view, Sarcony **50.00**
James Garfield President, advertising for frames/etc, ca 1880, EX.**25.00**
Lady dressed in fine clothes w/scarf & muff, advertising, 1880s, EX...**15.00**
Major General BF Butler, well defined, trimmed **32.50**
Mary Anderson (actress), H Rocher Chicago **35.00**
Men w/product bottle, Rockland ME, AJ Pierce, EX...................**135.00**
Nez Perce lady w/cornhusk, Hanson, 1900s, 6½x4¼" **150.00**
Palace on canal in Venice Italy, Naya & Schoefft, VG...................**9.00**
Robert E Lee, portrait in uniform, in oval, 4x2½"........................**150.00**
Spotted Eagle (Am Indian), sepia, Huffman...MT Territory, 1880s...**350.00**
Stonewall Jackson, facing left, 4x2½", EX **200.00**
Union officer w/kepi/bugle insignia/sword, long mustache, EX **50.00**
Virginia slave girl (identified), hair in long curls, Kellogg............**175.00**
Well-dressed farmer sits w/goat at side, EX...................................**235.00**

Daguerreotypes

Among the many processes used to produce photographic images are the daguerreotypes (made on a plate of chemically treated silver-plated copper) — the most-valued examples being the 'whole' plate which measures 6½" x 8½". Other sizes include the 'half' plate, measuring 4½" x 5½", the 'quarter' plate at 3¼" x 4¼", the 'sixth' plate at 2¾" x 3¼", the 'ninth' at 2" x 2½", and the 'sixteenth' at 1⅜" x 1⅝". (Sizes may vary slightly, and some may have been altered by the photographer.)

4th plate, 3 little girls, gilt-lined mat, +mahog fr........................**140.00**
6th plate, brother & sister possibly twins, pr, +case.....................**495.00**
6th plate, gentleman's portrait vignette, +full case **125.00**
6th plate, lady, fine clothes, seated, hand tinted, +half case..........**65.00**
6th plate, lady w/swollen (deformed?) hand beside husband, +half case...**350.00**

6th plate, man (dignified) in fine clothes, EX, +push-button case..**115.00**
6th plate, man w/rolled-up sleeves, ca 1850, +half case **150.00**
6th plate, mother mourns dead baby in her arms, tinted ribbons...**350.00**
9th plate, elegant lady, tinted cheeks/gold earrings/brooch/etc ...**100.00**
9th plate, man holding quill pen, +ornate rare CI fr.................**415.00**
9th plate, young ladies (2) in shop uniforms, long curls, +case...**495.00**

Photos

Berry Picker, Clayoquot; brn-tone, Curtis, ca 1915, 15½x11" **250.00**
Chief Geronimo, sepia-tone, Hendrick, 1909, 9½x7½" **600.00**
Gen George Patton, blk & wht, WWII era, 9x7" **60.00**
Naranjo family, hand tinted, Santa Clara pueblo, 1910s, 25x16" ..**300.00**
White River Apache, photogravure, Curtis, ca 1903, 7½x5½"+fr ...**140.00**

Stereoscopic Views

Stereo cards are photos made to be viewed through a device called a stereoscope. The glass stereo plates of the mid-1800s and photo prints produced in the darkroom are among the most valuable. In evaluating stereo views, the subject, date, and condition are all-important. Some views were printed over a thirty- to forty-year period; 'first generation' prices are far higher than later copies, made on cheap card stock with reprints or lithographs, rather than actual original photographs.

It is relatively easy to date an American stereo view by the color of the mount that was used, the style of the corners, etc. From about 1854 until the early 1860s, cards were either white, cream-colored, or glossy gray; shades of yellow and a dull gray followed. While the dull gray was used for a very short time, the yellow tones continued in use until the late 1860s. Red, green, violet, or blue cards are from the period between 1865 until about 1870. Until the late 1870s, corners were square; after that they were rounded off to prevent damage. Right now, quality stereo views are at a premium.

Captured Rebel Guns...VA, cannons, very clear, Anthony #2731..**200.00**
Custer w/grizzly bear, Illingworth, 1874, 3½x7" **750.00**
Deserted Rebel Quarters Near Dutch Gap, Anthony #2555 ....**100.00**
Disposing of Horse Thief in WI, hanging scene, 3½x7"..............**400.00**
Lady practices speech before mirror while husband does washing, Weller ...**75.00**
Minneapolis busy street scene, Fearon, EX..................................**30.00**
MN logging scene w/overview of city, Upton, EX.........................**30.00**
MN timber-cutting view w/oxen pulling logs, Upton, EX **35.00**

Oil scene, Spindle Top, Beaumont, Texas, Keystone, EX, $10.00.

Place where Maj Gen JB McPherson was killed..., Anthony #2720..**125.00**
Rebel camp at Chattanooga, lt wear..**110.00**
Ruins of Mayo's footbridge...Richmond VA, Anthony #3271 .....**100.00**
Russian Hill, San Francisco, Soule #1322, VG **45.00**
San Diego farm view w/windmill in foreground, Parker, EX..........**45.00**
St Louis street scene w/trolley/cigar store Indian/etc, EX **35.00**

Tintypes

Tintypes, contemporaries of ambrotypes, were produced on japanned iron and were not as easily damaged.

CDV sz, Union soldiers (2) stand before studio patriotic bkdrop, VG ..**125.00**
Full plate, boy in short pants holds hat w/ribbon, +cvd fr **100.00**
Full plate, Masonic officer in full regalia, ca 1865, +ornate fr **300.00**
Full plate, Union officer w/fancy sword, +ornate gold-pnt fr.......**500.00**
Full plate, Union soldier stands in uniform w/musket & bayonet, 1860s ...**600.00**
Half plate, 2 men on early bicycles, EX **85.00**
Half plate, 3 ladies w/drinks sitting at sm table...........................**135.00**
4th plate, man seated w/dog beside, early, some spotting **125.00**
4th plate, Union officer w/hat & greatcoat, gold details **100.00**
6th plate, boy w/dog in seated studio pose, 1880s **65.00**
6th plate, cavalryman w/Colt pistol & sword, tinted cheeks.......**350.00**
6th plate, Civil War-era lady seated, in fr.......................................**70.00**
6th plate, lady making fishing poles, unusual subject, EX............**285.00**
6th plate, shingle maker at job, EX, +fr..**285.00**
9th plate, carpenters (2) stand w/aprons & tools, EX **125.00**
9th plate, figures in horse-drawn buggy, farm buildings behind, VG ..**40.00**
9th plate, Plateau chief holding pipe, fully costumed **60.00**
9th plate, well-dressed Black man stands in studio pose **80.00**
9th plate, well-dressed man w/amputated arm in studio pose **65.00**

Union Cases

From the mid-1850s until about 1880, cases designed to house these early images were produced from a material known as thermoplastic, a man-made material with an appearance much like gutta percha. Its innovator was Samuel Peck, who used shellac and wood fibers to create a composition he called Union. Peck was part owner of the Scoville Company, makers of both papier-mache and molded leather cases, and he used the company's existing dies to create his new line. Other companies (among them A.P. Critchlow & Company; Littlefield, Parsons & Company; and Holmes, Booth & Hayden) soon duplicated his material and produced their own designs. Today's collectors may refer to cases made of this material as 'thermoplastic,' 'composition,' or 'hard cases,' but the term most often used is 'Union.' It is incorrect to refer to them as gutta percha cases.

Sizes may vary somewhat, but generally a 'whole' plate case measures 7" x 9⅛" to the outside edges, a 'half' plate 4⅞" x 6", a 'quarter' plate 3¾" x 4¾", a 'sixth' 3⅛" x 3⅝", a 'ninth' 2⅜" x 2⅞", and a 'sixteenth' 1¾" x 2". Clifford and Michele Krainik and Carl Walvoord have written a book, *Union Cases*, which we recommend for further study. Another source of information is *Nineteenth Century Photographic Cases and Wall Frames* by Paul Berg. Values are for examples in excellent condition unless noted otherwise.

Half plate, Geometrics, K-16, NM **275.00**
4th plate, Geometric Scroll, K-66, EX+ **135.00**
4th plate, Roger deCoverly & Gypsies Fortune, K-30, EX **125.00**
6th plate, Belt Buckle & Chain, Littlefield Parsons, K-161 ....**110.00**
6th plate, Crossed Cannons & Liberty Cap, K-112, NM **200.00**
6th plate, Geometrics, K-270, VG **150.00**
6th plate, Geometrics/Scrolls, holds 2, Littlefield Parsons, K-267.**90.00**
6th plate, Scrolls, Littlefield Parsons, K-298 ....**80.00**
6th plate, Union & Constitution, K-373, EX **100.00**
9th plate, Geometric, VG **45.00**
9th plate, Geometrics/Scrolls, Littlefield Parsons, K-478.............**50.00**
9th plate, Geometrics/Scrolls, Patent American, K-502 ....**50.00**
9th plate (dbl), Children w/Toys, R-29 ....**135.00**

Miscellaneous

Magic lantern, wood w/lacquered brass fittings, w/illuminant **250.00**
Projector, Carpenter & Westley...London, tin, in orig box w/24 plates...**250.00**
Stereo viewer, Alex Beck, 1870s, damaged veneer **400.00**
Stereo viewer, ebonized/pale wood, folds, Paris, 2¾x11x6¾".......**200.00**

Stereo viewer, folding wood pocket type, lenses fold down, rare.**250.00**
Stereo viewer, Little Rocket, blk pnt, metal stand/wood base, 9"..**75.00**
Stereo viewer, walnut ped type, 1880s, VG.................................**195.00**
Stereographascope, Fr, 3 folding joints, tabs/clasps present, 11x7x3" ..**300.00**
Stereoscope, Mascher's Improved, folding, w/dag 4th-plate portrait, EX ...**375.00**

Piano Babies

A familiar sight in Victorian parlors, piano babies languished atop shawl-covered pianos in a variety of poses: crawling, sitting, on their tummies, or on their backs playing with their toes. Some babies were nude, and some wore gowns. Sizes ranged from about 3" up to 12". The most famous manufacturer of these bisque darlings was the Heubach Brothers of Germany, who nearly always marked their product; see Heubach for listings. Watch for reproductions. These guidelines are excerpted from one of a series of informative doll books by Patsy Moyer, published by Collector Books. Values are for examples in excellent condition.

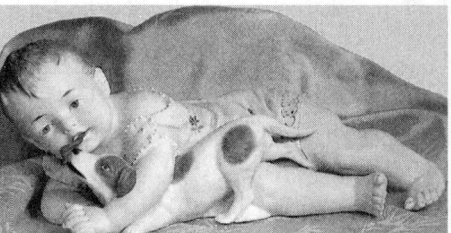

Bisque with painted details, child playing with puppy, intaglio blue eyes, unmarked Germany, 13" long, $800.00.

Blk, bsk, 4', EX quality...**500.00**
Blk, bsk, 4", med quality, unmk **200.00**
Blk, bsk, 5", EX quality...**425.00**
Blk, bsk, 8", EX quality...**600.00**
Blk, bsk, 8", med quality..**295.00**
Blk, bsk, 9", EX quality...**500.00**
Blk, bsk, 12", EX quality...**995.00**
Blk, bsk, 12", med quality..**400.00**
Blk, bsk, 14", EX quality...**900.00**
Blk, bsk, 16", EX quality...**925.00**
Blk, bsk, 16", med quality..**950.00**
Bsk, may not have pnt finish on bk, unmk, 4", med quality........**150.00**
Bsk, may not have pnt finish on bk, unmk, 8", med quality........**275.00**
Bsk, may not have pnt finish on bk, unmk, 12", med quality......**300.00**
Bsk, molded hair, unjtd, molded-on clothes, 4", EX quality **525.00**
Bsk, molded hair, unjtd, molded-on clothes, 4", med quality **400.00**
Bsk, molded hair, unjtd, molded-on clothes, 6", EX quality........**575.00**
Bsk, molded hair, unjtd, molded-on clothes, 8", EX quality........**895.00**
Bsk, molded hair, unjtd, molded-on clothes, 8", med quality **400.00**
Bsk, molded hair, unjtd, molded-on clothes, 9", EX quality........**700.00**
Bsk, molded hair, unjtd, molded-on clothes, 12", EX quality.......**975.00**
Bsk, molded hair, unjtd, molded-on clothes, 16", EX quality...**1,125.00**
Bsk, w/animal/pot/flowers/etc, 4", EX quality....................**425.00**
Bsk, w/animal/pot/flowers/etc, 5", EX quality....................**375.00**
Bsk, w/animal/pot/flowers/etc, 8", EX quality....................**475.00**
Bsk, w/animal/pot/flowers/etc, 10", EX quality **525.00**
Bsk, w/animal/pot/flowers/etc, 12", EX quality **800.00**
Bsk, w/animal/pot/flowers/etc, 16", EX quality, minimum value ..**1,125.00**

Pickard

Founded in 1895 in Chicago, Illinois, the Pickard China Company was originally a decorating studio, importing china blanks from European manufacturers. Some of these early pieces bear the name of those companies as well as Pickard's. Trained artists decorated the wares with hand-painted studies of fruit, florals, birds, and scenics and often signed their work. In 1915 Pickard introduced a line of 23k gold over a dainty floral-etched ground design. In the 1930s they began to experiment with the idea of making their own ware and by 1938 had succeeded in developing a formula for fine translucent china. Since 1976 they have issued an annual limited edition Christmas plate. They are now located in Antioch, Illinois.

The company has used various marks. The earliest (1893 – 1894) was a double-circle mark, 'Edgerton Hand Painted' with 'Pickard' in the center. Variations of the double-circle mark (with 'Hand Painted China' replacing the Edgerton designation) were employed until 1915, each differing enough that collectors can usually pinpoint the date of manufacture within five years. Later marks included the crown mark, 'Pickard' on a gold maple leaf, and the current mark, the lion and shield. Work signed by Challinor, Marker, and Yeschek is especially valued by today's collectors. For further information we recommend *Collector's Encyclopedia of Pickard China* by Alan B. Reed, available from Collector Books.

Bonbon, violets on gr, gold hdls, 1898-1903, JPL France blank, 5½"...150.00
Bowl, roses w/gold over-pnt whiplashes, Motzfelt, 1903-05, 6½"....100.00
Bowl, seashells w/spider web, sgn Krische, 1905-10, 9"...............225.00
Bowl, Yellow Iris Conventional, Beutlich, 1905-10, C&G blank, 9"......200.00
Cake plate, Trumpet Flowers & Trellis, 1905-10, D&C blank, 10½"......125.00
Candy dish, Crab Apple Blossoms, Leach, 1903-05, Haviland blank, 7"..90.00
Charger, apples & foliage, artist sgn, 11¼"................................600.00
Charger, floral sprays on wht, sgn J Sym, gold border, 1906-14...300.00
Charger, Plum Branch, sgn Rean, 1903-05, CA France blank, 12½"...400.00
Charger, Rean Pears, 1903-05, JPL France blank, 13"................500.00
Creamer & sugar bowl, Carnation & Platinum, sgn AP, 1905-10...325.00
Creamer & sugar bowl, Tomascheko Poppy Border, 1905-10, Limoges blank..200.00
Creamer & sugar bowl, Yeschek Raspberries, 1903-06, GDA France blank.....275.00
Cruet, Cyclamen, 1903-05, T&V Limoges blank, 6½"..............350.00
Cup & saucer, Blackberry Conventional, 1903-05, T&V Limoges blank...150.00
Cup & saucer, floral (poinsettias?), sgn Bardos, ca 1910-12........140.00
Cup & saucer, Iris Linear, sgn Lind, 1910-12..............................300.00

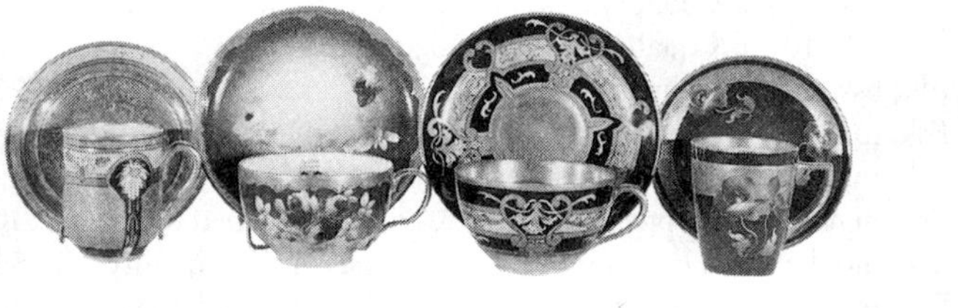

Cups and saucers: Modern Conventional, 1912 – 18, $210.00; Encrusted Linear, 1905 – 10 mark on cup, 1912 – 18 marked saucer, $150.00; Poppies in Gold, 1905 – 10 mark, $250.00; Hand-painted roses, signed Blaha, ca 1903, $225.00. (Photo courtesy Joy Luke Fine Arts Brokers and Auctioneers)

Cup & saucer, raspberries w/gold vines, 1903-05, crown over VB blank..150.00
Cup & saucer, roses on yel w/gold, sgn, 1898-03, JPL France blank..200.00
Ewer, floral, sgn Lind, gold hdl, 10", NM...................................550.00
Hatpin holder, Buttercup Conventional, Beutlich, 1905-10, 4½"....400.00
Pitcher , Alexander, Poinsettia & Lustre, 1905-10, T&V Limoges blank, 8"..525.00
Pitcher, bluebells on wht w/gold, 6-sided, 1910-12, 8¼"............500.00
Pitcher, Dorique, Iris Conventional, 1898-1903, T&V Limoges blank, 7".....550.00
Pitcher, Galois, Arabian, unsgn, 1903-05, JPL France blank, 7½".....625.00
Pitcher, grapes on yel to maroon, 1903-05, AK D France blank, 8"....425.00
Pitcher, lemonade; Autumn Currants, Goess, 1905-10, Limoges blank, 7"....450.00
Pitcher, lemonade; peaches on gr w/gold, 1903-05, CAC blank, 8"...450.00
Pitcher, Pond Lily, Leach, bamboo hdl, 1905-10, AK D blank, 8½"...600.00
Pitcher, Rean Pink Mums, 1903-05, Limoges blank, 5¼"...........300.00
Pitcher, Schoner Lemons, 1903-05, Vienna blank, 6¾".............600.00
Pitcher, White Poppy & Daisy, Gasper, 1910-12, Bavaria blank, 6".........550.00
Plate, chop; Autumn Border, sgn EF, 1903-05, CA France blank, 12½".275.00
Plate, chrysanthemums, sgn Brun, 1905-10, Limoges blank, 8¾" .90.00
Plate, Clover Blossoms & Honey Bee, 1903-05, AKD blank, 8¾"..225.00
Plate, day lilies on wht to gr, 1905-06, 8¾"................................175.00
Plate, Deserted Garden, sgn Rean, JPL Limoges/Pickard, 10⅝+hdls....415.00
Plate, Nasturtium Coventional, 1898-1903, AKD France blank, 8⅝" .200.00
Plate, pheasant scene, sgn Challinor, 1898-1903, Limoges blank..275.00
Plate, roses (sm, dainty) on wht, thin gold border, ca 1910, 8½"...125.00
Plate, Tulip Moderne, sgn, 1898-1903, T&V Limoges blank, 8".200.00
Plate, tulips w/gold, Breidel, 1905-10, Haviland blank, 8½".......175.00
Platter, mc grapes w/etched gold, 1905-10, T&V blank, 12¼"...300.00
Shakers, Marigolds, sgn Schoner, 1905-10, 3¼", pr....................125.00
Tankard, monk peeling turnip, Gasper, 190-510, Limoges blank, 14"...1,350.00
Vase, apple blossoms on blk w/gold, Rean, 1905-10, 8"..............300.00
Vase, Arrow Root on gr lustre, Gifford, cylindrical, 1905-10, 10¼"..350.00
Vase, Aura Mosaic, sgn Rosl, 1910-12, 13"................................850.00
Vase, Calla Lily, sgn Marker, shouldered, 1905-10, 11"..............525.00
Vase, Challinor Hollyhocks, 1903-05, 7"....................................500.00
Vase, Cherokee Rose, sgn Walt, wishbone hdls, 1910-12, 8½"...400.00
Vase, crab apples on gr, slim, pierced rim, gold ft, 1905-10, 9½"...300.00
Vase, Easter Lily, sgn Choner, waisted, D&Co France blank, 9" .400.00
Vase, Japanese lady w/comb, cylindrical, 1903-05, Willets blank, 12"...1,950.00
Vase, Marie, Cornflower Conventional, uptrn hdls, 1903-05, 5½"..550.00
Vase, Moor w/Tiger, Kubash, 1903-05, Limoges blank, 15½" ..1,500.00
Vase, Narcissus on dk gr, Post, 1903-05, #3660 blank, 8"...........400.00
Vase, Nouveau lady/grapes, hdls, 1903-05, WG&Co Limoges blank, 16".3,500.00
Vase, roses on gr to ochre, Lebrun, 1903-05, Willets blank, 13½"..750.00
Vase, St Bernard dog on shaded brn, sgn, teardrop shape, 1898-1903, 8"...3,000.00

Pickle Castors

Affluent Victorian homes seemed to have something for everything, and a pickle castor was not only an item of beauty but of practicality. American Victorian pickle castors can be found in old catalogs dating from the 1860s through the early 1900s. (Those featured in catalogs after 1900 were made by silver manufacturers that were not part of the International Silver Company, which was formed in 1898 — for instance, Reed and Barton, Tufts, Pairpoint, and Benedict.)

Catalogs featured large selections to choose from, ranging from simple to ornate. Inserts could be clear or colored, pattern glass or art glass, molded or blown. Many of these molds and design were made by more than one company as they merged or as personnel took their designs with them from employer to employer. It is common to see the same insert in a variety of different frames and with different lids as viewed in these old catalogs.

Pickle castors are being reproduced today. Frames are being imported from Taiwan. New enameling is being applied to old jars; and new or old tumblers, vases, or spooners are sometimes used as jars in old original frames. The biggest giveaway in this latter scenario is that the replacement insert does not fit properly in the old frame. A good thing to remember is that old glass is not perfect glass.

In the listings below, the description prior to the semicolon refers to the jar (insert), and the remainder of the line describes the frame. Unless a color is mentioned, all glassware is clear. When no condition is indicated, the silver plate is assumed to be in very good to excellent condition, with the fork or tongs present. Glass jars are assumed near mint.

Our advisor for this category is Barbara Aaronson; she is listed in the Directory under California

Albertine w/caladium leaf, Mt WA; ornate Tufts fr.................1,500.00
Albertine w/floral, Mt WA, 4"; in Pairpoint fr, 8½"................2,200.00
Amberina, diagonal ribs; cherub-ftd SP fr..................................850.00

Amberina Rippled Coin Spot w/plums; Meriden fr w/plums, 14", +2 tongs ..1,750.00
Amethyst craquelle w/HP gold orchids; SP fr w/bird finial 950.00
Barrel; ornate Reed & Barton SP fr, +fancy fork 325.00
Bead & Drape, red satin; ftd SP fr 525.00
Bridal Rosette, ruby satin; SP fr 680.00
Cane & Rosette; rstr fr 250.00
Cone, pk cased; ornate pierced SP fr, 10" 650.00
Coreopsis, mc florals on wht satin; SP fr 575.00
Cranberry w/enameled crane in pond; SP fr +bird's-head tong holder ..650.00
Cranberry w/floral; ornate SP fr 650.00
Cranberry w/floral; SP fr w/twisted hdl, Tufts, 10" 650.00
Crown Milano, florals on Hobnail; Pairpoint fr, 9" 2,000.00
Daisy & Button, amber; Webster fr w/emb faces on ft 350.00
Daisy & Button, yel; SP fr, 11" 400.00
Dmn Point, bl, nonflint; orig SP fr & lid 300.00
Electric bl w/etching; Made in Canada SP fr, +10¾" 520.00
Fostoria's Victoria; orig SP fr 350.00
Hobstar, vaseline, Imperial; mk Pairpoint fr, rare 800.00
Honeycomb, rubena w/coralene florals; SP fr w/flower finial 875.00
Invt T'print, amberina, belled body; ornate ornament on SP fr ..750.00
Invt T'print, cranberry w/floral; Holman Eastlake-style fr 650.00
Jacob's Ladder; SP fr, scarce 400.00
MOP, Herringbone, frosted wht to pk; Rogers sq ruffled fr 1,500.00
MOP Dmn Quilt, turq, Mt WA, 6"; mk Knickerbockers 4-ftd ormolu stand ..1,500.00
MOP Raindrop, wht to pk; Simpson Hall Miller fr, 12" 1,500.00
Optic Panel, pk opal, Mt WA; ornate Pairpoint fr 550.00
Paneled; emb SP lid w/sitting dog finial 300.00
Peachblow, ovoid, 4¼"; rope/floral-hdl fr, 9¾" 875.00
Ribbed Pillar, frosted pk spatter, Northwood; orig SP fr 950.00
Rubena, crystal ribs w/gold; SP Reed & Barton fr, 14", +shell tongs...650.00
Spangle, yel/wht w/mica, swirled, flared at base; ornate SP fr 650.00
Torquay, pigeon blood; orig SP fr 650.00
Wht satin, HP rose apple blossoms; rstr fr....................................650.00
Yel-orange mottle w/opal gray, pinched; ornate SP fr, 10" 600.00
Zipper & Beads, emerald gr; SP fr w/birds 550.00

Pie Birds

A pie bird or pie funnel (pie vent) is generally made of pottery, glazed inside and out. Most are 3" to 5" in height with arches at the base to allow steam to enter. The steam is then released through an exit hole at the top.

The English pie funnel was as tall as the special baking dish was deep and held the crust even with the dish's rim, thereby lifting the crust above the filling so it would stay crisp and firm. These dishes came in several different sizes, which accounts for the variances in the heights of the pie birds.

The first deviations from the basic funnels were produced in the mid-1930s to late 1940s: the Clarice Cliff (signed Midwinter or Newport) pie bird (reg. no. on white base) and the signed Nutbrown elephant. Shortly thereafter (1940s – 1960s), figures of bakers and colorful birds were created for additional visual baking fun. From the 1980s to present, many novelty pie vents have been added to the market for the enjoyment of both the baker and collector. These have been made by commercial (including Far East importers) and local enterprises in Canada, England, and the United States. A new category for the 1990s includes an array of holiday-related pie vents. Basic tip: Older pie vents were air brushed, not hand painted.

Incense burners (i.e., elephants and Oriental people), one-hole pepper shakers, dated brass toy bird whistle, egg timers (missing glass timer), and ring holders (i.e., elephant with clover on his tummy) should not be mistaken for pie vents.

Bear in gr jacket, w/hat & shoes, England, 4½" 55.00
Bird, mc details, Morton Pottery, 5" 55.00

Bird, mouth open, arched base, brn, English, 4½" 87.50
Bird, smooth contours w/no details, mouth open, yel, English, 4" ...85.00
Bird, wht w/pk & bl on bl base, Shawnee for Pillsbury, 5½" 55.00
Bird, yel, no details, England, 4" 55.00
Black boy kneeling in prayer, blk pants, England, 4" 55.00
Black chef, shiny blk & wht, 3¼" 55.00
Black chef, yel clothes, 4½" 125.00
Black clown, plain bl top & hat, stands on drum, Made in England, 5"..45.00
Black clown holding pie, emb England on pants, 4½" 45.00
Black lady, bl & wht skirt, gr & wht top, England, 4" 45.00
Black lady w/polka-dot muff, England, 3¾" 45.00
Bugs Bunny, Made in California, 4" 27.00
Bull, brn face & lt brn patches on wht, England, 3¾" 45.00
Bulldog w/baker's hat, wht w/mc details, Made in England, 4½" ..45.00
Bumble Bee, mc, California, 5" 35.00
Chick, yel, Josef Original, 3¼" 65.00
Clown, mc clothes, holds pie & stick, England, 4½" 45.00
Crow, blk, Made in England, 1950s-60s, 4¼" 55.00
Dragon, gr, England, 4¼" 75.00
Dragon, tan w/brn spots, Made in England, 4½" 65.00
Duck, long neck, maroon (hot rose), 5" 75.00
Duck, long neck, med bl, 5" 75.00
Duck, long neck, yel, unmk, 5" 75.00
Elephant, mk Nutbrown Pie Funnel MIE..., 3½" 95.00
Elephant, trunk up, sitting on blk stand, England, 4" 65.00
Fox dressed as detective, England, 4" 45.00
Fox in jacket, cap & tie, mc, emb England, 4" 45.00
Frog, gr mottled head, emb Scotland, 4¼" 65.00
Frog w/bug eyes, gr w/yel tummy, England, 3½" 45.00
Funnel, blk man steals pie from lady w/rolling pin, England, 3½" ...65.00
Golliwog, striped pants, mc, England, 4¾" 55.00
Koala bear, England, 4½" 45.00
Lady badger w/bonnet & apron, mc, England, 3½" 55.00
Meadowlark, ltd ed, Sandhust...Minnesota, 4¾", MIB 70.00
Meadowlark, mc on wht, California, 3½" 35.00
Porky Pig, bl jacket, left arm out, 4¼" 35.00
Rooster, wht w/brn/bl/lav, Cleminson, 4½" 55.00
Rooster, wht w/lt gr/pastel bl/brn, Cleminson, 4½" 55.00
Rooster, wht w/pk/lav/yel, Cleminson, 4½" 55.00
Rooster on stump, wht, Made in England, 4¾" 45.00

Scottie dog, pottery, black, made in England, early 1990s, 4½", from $65.00 to $70.00. (Photo courtesy Candace Sten Davis and Patricia J. Baum)

Squirrel w/nut, mottled brn & wht, England, 3¾" 45.00
Toucan, mc, England, 5¾" 45.00
Turtle, gr bk & spotted underside, England, 4" 45.00
Woodpecker on stump, mc, California, 6¾" 36.00

Pierce, Howard

After Howard Pierce died on February 28, 1994, many values of his pieces increased greatly and items not seen before began to appear on the market. William Manker, a well-known ceramist, hired Mr. Pierce in

1938. This liaison lasted about three years and then Pierced opened a small studio in Laverne, California. He did not want to be in competition with Manker so he began making miniature animal figures, some of which he made into jewelry. Now, pewter miniature brooches, depending on the animal types, are selling for as much as $275.00. Howard married and he and his wife, Ellen (Van Voorhis), opened a small studio in Claremont, California. Polyurethane animals are high on collectors' lists as Howard, after creating in the early years only a few pieces using this material, realized he was allergic to it and had to discontinue its use. Polyurethane was used mostly to create a small number of roadrunners on bases, either standing or running, or birds on small, flat bases. The materials used by Pierce during his long career were varied, probably to satisfy his curiosity and many talents. He experimented with a Jasperware-type body, bronze, concrete, gold leaf, porcelain, Mt. St. Helens ash, and others. In November 1992, Pierce's health had continued to worsen and he and Ellen Pierce destroyed all the molds they had created over the years. Pierce began producing smaller versions of past porcelain wares and developing a few new items.

For further information we recommend *Collector's Encyclopedia of Howard Pierce Porcelain* by our advisor, Darlene Hurst Dommel (Collector Books); she is listed in the Directory under Minnesota.

Figurine, angel, kneeling, holding candle holder, gold, 6x8", pr .120.00
Figurine, birds, lg & 2 sm on branch, wht w/brn highlights, 5¾x8" ..100.00
Figurine, bulldog on USMC base, brn, 5" 210.00
Figurine, cat, stylized, brn & wht, 16½" 400.00
Figurine, coyote, seated, howling, wht w/brn, sgn, 6" 95.00
Figurine, dachshund, brn, 9½" 130.00
Figurine, dog, brn w/wht features, floppy ears, 8¼", 6", pr 170.00
Figurine, doves, bl w/blk, sgn, pr 150.00
Figurine, eagle on log, gray, 7¾" 265.00
Figurine, horse, stylized w/long mane, brn w/wht on mane & tail, 7x8" ...265.00
Figurine, quail (2) in tree, gray 110.00
Figurine, squirrel, gray, 5" 50.00

Figurine, two squirrels peering from stump, brown and white, 11x6½", $250.00. (Photo courtesy Darlene Dommel)

Figurine, St Francis of Assisi, holding bird, gray w/blk, 12" 205.00
Figurines, giraffes, father, mother & baby, 11½", 9½", 5½" 200.00
Figurines, parakeets, aqua bl w/wht & blk, 4", 4½", pr 180.00
Figurines, penguins, mother & baby, blk w/wht chests, 7", 4½", pr..125.00
Figurines, raccoons, 1 on bk, 1 sitting, cream w/brn, pr...............110.00
Flower holder, girl reading book, wht & brn, 6½" 85.00
Flower holder, owls in tree, adult & baby, 7½" 100.00
Planter, roadrunner on rock, gray w/brn, 7x13½" 170.00
Vase, gr w/wht speckled, inserted deer & tree, 5½x3¾x10"........135.00
Whistle, bird shape, brn w/wht on chest, 3½" 100.00

Pietra-Dura

From the Italian Renaissance period, Pietra-Dura is a type of mosaic work used for plaques, table tops, frames, etc., that includes pieces of gemstones, mother-of-pearl, and the like.

Blotter, ebonized wood hdl, 5x2", EX 575.00
Box, cvd florals, 8-sided, scroll ft, late 19th C, 4x5⅜x6" 575.00
Plaque, abstract geometrics, Italy, 20th C, 4¾x3½"+ebony fr 375.00
Plaque, Italian city by river, R Casini, 9¾x5"+ebonized 14x10" fr....485.00
Table, Italian Renaissance style, mc foliage/animals on supports...3,200.00

Pigeon Blood

Pigeon blood glass, produced in the late 1800s, may be distinguished from other dark red glass by its distinctive orange tint.

Bowl, lion head prunts, clear ft/hdls/rim, 7½" H 395.00
Butter dish, Venecia, enameled 5,500.00
Celery vase, Torquay, SP 180.00
Creamer, Venecia, HP decor...200.00
Pitcher, clear hdl, 7"..250.00
Pitcher, milk; melon ribs 175.00
Pitcher, water; Torquay, acid finish, scarce 750.00
Shakers, Flower Band, orig lids, pr...185.00
Spooner, Torquay..100.00
Wine, 6"...55.00

Pigeon Forge

Douglas J. Ferguson and Ernest Wilson started their small pottery in Pigeon Forge, Tennessee, in 1946. Using red-brown and gray locally dug clay and glazes which they themselves formulate, bowls, vases, and sculptures are produced there. Their primary target is the tourist trade.

Figurine, bear, rolling on bk, mk F, 4½x5½" 60.00
Figurine, bear, sitting w/paws in lap, mk, 6½x4¾".......................50.00
Figurine, owl, brn & wht mottled, 4½" 50.00
Figurine, raccoon, brn & wht mottled, Ferguson, 3½x5"...............45.00
Figurine, squirrel, brn & wht mottled, 3½x4" 40.00
Mug, gr w/cvd pine tree, 4½"..270.00
Vase, bl w/brn specks, Ferguson, 1977, 3½"...............................60.00
Vase, bl w/copper drip, Ferguson, 9" 185.00

Pilkington

Founded in 1892 in Manchester, England, the Pilkington pottery experimented in wonderful lustre glazes that were so successful that when they were displayed at exhibition in 1904, they were met with critical acclaim. They soon attracted some of the best ceramic technicians and designers of the day who decorated the lustre ground with flowers, animals, and trees; some pieces were more elaborate with scenes of sailing ships and knights on horseback. Each artist signed his work with his personal monogram. Most pieces were dated and carried the company mark as well. After 1913 the company became known as Royal Lancastrian.

Their Lapis Ware line was introduced in the late 1920s, featuring intermingling tones of color under a matt glaze. Some pieces were very simply decorated while others were painted with designs of stylized leafage, scrolls, swirls, and stripes. The line continued into the '30s. Other pieces of this period were molded and carved with animals, leaves, etc., some of which were reminiscent of their earlier wares.

The company closed in 1938 but reopened in 1948. During this period their mark was a simple P within the outline of a petaled flower shape.

Candlesticks, pk vellum look, Deco style, 1930s, #2224, 2½", pr .90.00
Jardiniere, bl flambe, 1913, 11x11"..250.00
Vase, exotic birds/flowers on cobalt, R Joyce, #2369, ca 1915, 9"...1,400.00
Vase, soft running brn, slightly waisted, #2935, 10"....................125.00
Vase, turq w/brn/gray streaks, shouldered, 1920s, 10" 200.00

Pillin

Polia Pillin was born in Poland in 1909. She came to the U.S. as a teenager and showed an interest and talent for art, which she studied in Chicago. She married William Pillin, who was a poet and potter. They ultimately combined their talents and produced her very distinctive pottery from the 1950s to the mid-1980s. She died in 1993.

Polia Pillin won many prizes for her work, which is always signed Pillin with the loop of the 'P' over the full name. Some undecorated pieces are signed W&P, due to her husband's collaboration.

Her work is prized for its art, not for the shape of her pots, which for the most part are simple vases, dishes, bowls, and boxes. Wall plaques are rare. She pictured women with hair reminiscent of halos, girls, an occasional boy, horses, birds, and fish. After viewing a few of her pieces, her style is unmistakable. Some of her early work is very much like that of Picasso.

Her pieces are somewhat difficult to find, as all the work was done without outside help, and therefore limited in quantity. In the last few years, more and more people have become interested in her work, resulting in escalating prices. Our advisors for this category are Dolli and Wilfred Cohen; they are listed in the Directory under California.

Bowl, stylized horses, mc on mauve, 7⅛" 750.00
Box, lady in wht robe, child in pk leotards, blk shirt, 5½x4"......595.00
Compote, frieze of lady's faces on lt marigold w/turq wash, 5x6" ...650.00
Dish, 2 full-length women, elliptical form, 17½" 2,100.00
Goblet, bust portrait of lady, bl/gr/tan on brn, 9" 750.00
Jug, blistered yel/orn gloss, 7¾x5½" 275.00
Pendant, female portrait on marigold, 3¼x2½" 500.00
Plaque, 5 dancers against gr wall, 15½" L 2,750.00
Plate, lady w/chicken & birds, mc on bl, 8½"...............................800.00
Plate, lady w/3 birds, mc on bl, 10½"..1,400.00

Tray, ballerinas, three in leotards, one in center front in white tutu on blue, 9" square, $850.00.

Tray, Madonna portrait on dk brn w/bl rim, rectangular, lg.........775.00
Tray, 2 cats, free-form, 5" W 750.00
Tray, 2 women & bird, oval, 8½" L 925.00
Vase, avocado gr over lt seaweed gr, onion base, can neck, 6½" .250.00
Vase, cat/rooster, trees/female dancers on marigold, 4½x3¾" 665.00
Vase, chicken/horse/woman, bulbous w/stick neck, 8".................800.00
Vase, fish, 5¼"..450.00
Vase, fish (9) on pastel sea, 6½x6" 495.00
Vase, ladies, mc on bl, rectangular, 9", NM..................................850.00
Vase, ladies (2) & 2 roosters, 6⅞", EX 550.00
Vase, lady, various pastel-colored sqs as bkground, 6x4½".........625.00
Vase, lady & birds/lady w/horse, bottle shape, 6½x2½" 550.00
Vase, lady holding bird, 2nd bird beside; bk: lady, 6¾"................550.00

Vase, lady/horse/goose on brn, 6¼x5", NM.................................550.00

Pin-Back Buttons

Buttons produced up to the early 1920s were made of a celluloid covering held in place by a ring (or collet) to the back of which a pin was secured. Manufacturers used these 'cellos' to advertise their products. Many were of exceptional quality in both color and design. Buttons were produced in sets featuring a variety of subjects. These were given away by tobacco, chewing gum, and candy manufacturers, who often packed them with their product as premiums. Usually the name of the button maker or the product manufacturer was printed on a paper placed in the back of the button. Often these 'back papers' are still in place today. Much of the time the button maker's name was printed on the button's perimeter, and sometimes the copyright was added. Beginning in the 1920s, a large number of buttons were lithographed on tin; these are referred to as tin 'lithos.' Nearly all pin-back buttons are collected today for their advertising appeal or graphic design. There are countless categories to base a collection on.

The following listing contains non-political buttons representative of the many varieties you may find. Our advisor for this category is Michael J. McQuillen; he is listed in the Directory under Indiana.

Babe Ruth, blk & wht, cello, 1930s, 1" EX 50.00
Baby Ruth - Sundae, cello, Geraghty & Co Chicago, 1940s, NM ..110.00
Boy Scout 1928 Round Up, I Roped One, 1³⁄₁₆", M 55.00
Brooklyn Dodgers Football, red & wht, ca 1930-39, NM 55.00
CB Line, Flyer of Great Lakes...While You Sleep, mc, 1¾" 60.00
Ceresota Flour, Bastian Bros, 1¾", NM...55.00
Dead Shot Smokeless Powder, duck in flight, gr border, cello, M .75.00
Dennis the Menace, Cast Your Ballot for Sears, 1968, EX 40.00
Dupont Powders, crow shooting, orig paper in bk, M 80.00
Dupont Powders The Record Breakers, quail, cello, 1", NM.........55.00
Felix, Katz Kitten Club, cello, Parisian Novelty Co, 1930s, EX 45.00
Frank Buck, Bring 'Em Back Alive, ca 1939, 1¾", NM.................35.00
Frankenstein monster, Universal, 1960s, 3½", M 110.00
Gil Hodges, Brooklyn Dodgers, 1950s, 1¾", w/red/wht/bl ribbon ...140.00
Good Humor Ice Cream, ...Safety Club, Whitehead & Hoag, ⅞", EX .50.00
Green Beret Week, Barry Sadler, cello, 1960s, 1¼" 38.00
I Am a Frito Bandito, Frito Lay, ca 1970, 2", EX 42.50
It's Naughty But It's Nice, lovely lady, cello, Whitehead & Hoag.48.00
Jack Dempsey, 1¾" 110.00
Jerry Lucas Day, photo portrait, March 15, 1964, 2¼", NM..........52.50
Jim Piersall, Boston Red Sox, 1950s, NM 115.00
Little Orphan Annie, Los Angeles Express contest, 1930s, 1¼", EX .32.50
Lone Ranger Chief Scout, 1941, NM...52.50
Mickey Mouse w/guitar, enamel on brass, 1930s, 1", EX...............38.00
Mummy monster, Universal, Elwar Ltd NYC, 1960s, 3½" 100.00
Peters Cartridge Co, boy & mallard, M 65.00
Santa Claus, Am Red Cross, 1916, NM 140.00
Santa Claus, Chicago Daily News, Whitehead & Hoag, 1930s, 1¼"...127.50
Santa reading book, Fraser's Store advertising, 1920s, 1¼", NM......120.00
Shirley Temple doll, The World's Darling, cello, Ideal, 1¼", NM......50.00
St Louis Cardinals NL Champions, 1964, 2¼", w/ribbon............130.00
Supermen of Am, Superman, Nat'l Periodicals Publications, 1961, NM ..40.00
Welcome Italian Fleet Rome Chicago New York 1933, aircraft, 1¼" ...60.00

Pine Ridge

In the mid-1930s, the Indian Bureau of Affairs and the Work Progress Administration offered the Native Americans living on the Pine

Ridge Indian Reservation in South Dakota a class in pottery making. Originally, Margaret Cable (director of the University of North Dakota ceramics department) was the instructor and Bruce Doyle was director. By the early 1950s, pottery production at the school was abandoned. In 1955 the equipment was purchased by Ella Irving, a student who had been highly involved with the class since the late 1930s. From then until it closed in the 1980s, Ella virtually ran the pot shop by herself.

The clay used in Pine Ridge pottery was red and the decoration reminiscent of early Indian pottery and beadwork designs. A variety of marks and labels were used. For more information we recommend *Collector's Encyclopedia of the Dakota Potteries* by our advisor, Darlene Hurst Dommel (Collector Books); she is listed in the Directory under Minnesota.

Bowl, flared lip, bl, Ella Irving, 4½x6¾", from $75 to 100.00
Bowl, incurvate rim, avocado gr gloss, mk Reed, 2¼x7", from $40 to...50.00
Creamer & sugar bowl, aqua, Irving, 2" & 2½", from $50 to 75.00
Hanging basket, bulbous urn, brn/cream geometric by Woody, 5x7½"..275.00
Mug, gr, Bernice Talbot, 3½", from $30 to 50.00
Pitcher/4 tumblers, arrow design, Romona Wounded Knee, minimum value ...600.00
Plate, star design, cream on brn, Irving, 7", from $200 to 250.00
Shakers, egg shape, lt gr, Talbot, 2¼", pr, from $25 to...................35.00
Tea set, w/teapot, cr/sug, gr/brn, Cox, from $200 to 250.00
Tumbler, cream geometrics on brn, Woody, 5½", from $75 to 100.00
Vase, airbrushed shaded gloss, mk Palmer '37, 7", from $400 to..500.00
Vase, bulbous w/long bottle neck, gr, Woody, 9½", from $60 to ...85.00
Vase, geometric, milky gloss over terra cotta, Firethunder, 2½"..125.00

Pink Lustre Ware

Pink lustre was produced by nearly every potter in the Staffordshire district in the late eighteenth and first half of the nineteenth centuries. The application of gold lustre on white or light-colored backgrounds produced pinks, while the same over dark colors developed copper. The wares ranged from hand-painted plaques to transfer-printed dinnerware.

Bough pot, House pattern, w/lid, ca 1815, rpr, 9¼"...................1,265.00
Cup & saucer, Moses in Bulrushes, magenta transfer w/mc 40.00
Desk set, Greek Key borders, tray & 3 covered pots, 1810s.........650.00
Jug, commemorative; Princess Charlotte/Prince Leopold, 6" 395.00
Mug, House pattern, emb basketweave, fluted band, 3¾" 175.00
Pitcher, blk transfer: Farmer's Arms, bk: Masonic, HP, 6½", EX.385.00
Pitcher, cottage/ruins, lt bl neck band, leaf hdl/spout, 5", EX 150.00
Pitcher, dog w/bird ea side in pk/gr, emb neck vine, 5¾" 700.00
Pitcher, emb eagle/roses in panels, waisted ft, 5¾" 150.00
Pitcher, 3 ships/verse/names, Queen's Rose, satyr head spout, 9", EX.1,300.00
Pitcher, 4 portrait busts in relief, mc enameling, 6".....................325.00
Punch bowl, HP floral int & ext, ca 1820, 6¾x10¼".................325.00
Tea bowl & saucer, pk lustre rim/leaves, gaudy florals 110.00
Tray, landscape by waterfall, lustre leaf-molded hdls, 15½".........475.00

Pink Paw Bears

These charming figural pieces are very similar to the Pink Pigs described in the following category. They were made in Germany during the same time frame. The cabbage green is identical; the bears themselves are whitish-gray with pink foot pads. You'll find some that are unmarked while others are marked 'Germany' or 'Made in Germany.' In theory, the unmarked bears are the oldest, made prior to 1890 when the McKinley Tariff Act required imports to be marked with the country of origin. Those marked 'Made In' were probably produced after the revision of the Act in 1914.

1 by bean pot...135.00
1 by graphophone...150.00
1 by honey pot...145.00
1 by top hat...125.00
1 in front of basket..135.00
1 in roadster (car identical to pk pig car).................................225.00
1 on binoculars..175.00
1 peaking out of basket...135.00
1 sitting in wicker chair 150.00
2 in hot air balloon..175.00
2 in purse 165.00
2 in roadster..225.00
2 on pin dish...175.00
2 on pin dish w/bag of coins...145.00
2 peering in floor mirror...150.00
2 sitting by mushroom...135.00
2 standing in wash tub..150.00
3 in roadster..250.00
3 on pin dish...160.00

Pink Pigs

Pink Pigs on cabbage green were made in Germany around the turn of the century. They were sold as souvenirs in train depots, amusement parks, and gift shops. 'Action pigs' (those involved in some amusing activity) are the most valuable, and prices increase with the number of pigs. Though a similar type of figurine was made in white bisque, most serious collectors prefer only the pink ones. They are marked in two ways: 'Germany' in incised letters, and a black ink stamp 'Made in Germany' in a circle. The unmarked pigs are the oldest, made prior to 1890 when the McKinley Tariff Act required imports to be marked with the country of origin. Those marked 'Made In' were probably produced after the revision of the Act in 1914.

1 at trough, gold trim, 4½", NM..80.00
1 beside gr drum, wall-mt match holder 95.00
1 beside lg pot emb Boston Baked Beans, match holder, 4" W ...135.00
1 beside purse..115.00
1 beside shoe...115.00
1 beside stump, camera around neck, toothpick holder...............185.00
1 beside tree w/extending branch, emb saying, 4"......................95.00
1 beside wastebasket..95.00
1 coming out of cup, 2½"..95.00
1 coming out of suitcase..95.00
1 coming through gr fence, post at sides, open for flowers...........125.00
1 driving touring car...185.00
1 going through purse...90.00
1 holding binoculars w/case in bk, toothpick holder, 3" W.........125.00
1 holding cup by fence...140.00
1 in barn, arrow on roof, bank, 4¼"..365.00
1 in case looking through binoculars 165.00
1 in gr Dutch shoe..75.00
1 in gr suitcase bank, head 1 side, bk other, gold trim.................110.00
1 in Japanese submarine, Japan imp on both sides......................125.00
1 in money sack bank...95.00
1 on binoculars, gold trim 150.00
1 on cushion chair w/fringe, 3"..195.00
1 on haunches, bottle, blk wood cork top, 2½" 110.00
1 on horseshoe-shaped dish w/raised 4-leaf clover......................110.00
1 on keg playing piano..225.00
1 on shoulder of gr ink bottle..115.00
1 playing accordion on side of tray, wht bear ea side 225.00
1 pushing head through wooden gate 115.00

1 putting letter in mailbox 125.00
1 reclining on horseshoe ashtray.................................85.00
1 riding train, 4½" 225.00
1 sitting by high-top boot..110.00

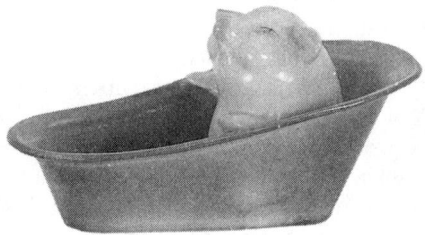

One sitting in bathtub, $135.00.

1 sitting on log, mk Germany 135.00
1 skating on bowling lane, tray, gold trim, 4¾" L 135.00
1 standing in front of cracked open egg....................135.00
1 standing in oversz opera house box, gold trim, 3½"...250.00
1 talking on old-fashioned telephone, gold trim, 3½" 250.00
1 w/basketweave cradle, gold trim, 3½" W 140.00
1 w/front ft in 3-part dish containing 3 dice, 1 ft on dice....175.00
1 w/grandfather clock, 7" 250.00
1 w/hind leg held by lobster, 4½" W, EX 140.00
1 w/lg umbrella, picnic basket & water bucket, 5¼", NM..........150.00
1 w/tennis racket stands beside vase, Lawn Tennis, 3¾" 150.00
1 wearing chef's costume, holds fry pan, w/basket........150.00
2, mother & baby in bl blanket in tub, rabbit on board atop 175.00
2, mother & baby in cradle, Hush a Bye..., gold trim, 3¼x3¼" ..225.00
2, mother in tub gives baby a bottle, lamb looks on, 4x3½" 175.00
2, 1 at telephone booth, 1 inside, 4½" 165.00
2 at confession, 4½" 125.00
2 at pump, bank, Good Old Annual, 3¾"...................170.00
2 at pump & trough, 3¼" W.......................................180.00
2 at wishing well..130.00
2 behind trough, unmk..95.00
2 by eggshell..95.00
2 by washtub, toothpick holder, souvenir of White City, 3¾" W..135.00
2 coming out of woven basket, 3" W, EX 115.00
2 courting in touring car, trinket holder, 4½" W 225.00
2 dancing, in top hat, tux & cane 175.00
2 in basket, gold trim, 3¾" W....................................90.00
2 in basket, Merry Squeelers, 3½x3" 135.00
2 in bed, Good Night on footboard, 4x3x2½" 145.00
2 in carriage 175.00
2 in front of oval washtub w/hdls, 3" W 125.00
2 in open trunk, 3¾"..125.00
2 in purse 115.00
2 looking in phonograph horn, tray, 4½" W.............200.00
2 on basket, head raising lid, plaque on front 145.00
2 on cotton bale, 1 peers from hole, 1 over top.........175.00
2 on seesaw on top of pouch bank.............................175.00
2 on top hat..125.00
2 on tray hugging, 3x4½"..125.00
2 singing, receptacle behind, gold trim, 4½", NM.....365.00
2 sitting at table playing card game 'Hearts'..............225.00
2 sitting by heart-shaped opening, trinket holder, 4" W...............95.00
2 teeter-tottering over log bank, 3½" L, NM.............125.00
2 under toadstool...125.00
2 w/accordion camera, tray, 4½" W..........................150.00
3, mother w/2 babies, The Dinner Bell, planter, 3¾" W.............145.00
3, 1 on lg slipper playing banjo, 2 dancing on side.....195.00
3, 2 sit in front of coal bucket, 3rd inside.................175.00
3 (center pig w/accordion) on tray, gold trim, 6½" L 530.00

3 at trough, 4½" L 150.00
3 dressed up on edge of dish.....................................150.00
3 in horseless carriage, 4½" W...................................150.00
3 sitting at trough, 4½" 100.00
3 sm pigs behind oval trough, mk, 2¾x2½x1¾" 115.00
3 w/baby carriage, father & 2 babies, Wheeling His Own..........225.00
3 w/carriage, mother & 2 babies, Germany 195.00
4, mother pushing cart w/3 babies, clovers on wheels, vase, 3½"...195.00

Pisgah Forest

The Pisgah Forest Pottery was established in 1920 near Mount Pisgah in Arden, North Carolina, by Walter B. Stephen, who had worked in previous years at other locations in the state — Nonconnah and Skyland (the latter from 1913 until 1916). Stephen, who was born in the mountain region near Asheville, was known for his work in the Southern tradition. He produced skillfully executed wares exhibiting an amazing variety of techniques. He operated his business with only two helpers. Recognized today as his most outstanding accomplishment, his Cameo line was decorated by hand in the pate-sur-pate style (similar to Wedgwood Jasper) in such designs as Fiddler and Dog, Spinning Wheel, Covered Wagon, Buffalo Hunt, Mountain Cabin, Square Dancers, Indian Campfire, and Plowman. Stephen is known for other types of wares as well. His crystalline glaze is highly regarded by today's collectors.

At least nine different stamps mark his wares, several of which contain the outline of the potter at the wheel and 'Pisgah Forest.' Cameo is sometimes marked with a circle containing the line name and 'Long Pine, Arden, NC.' Two other marks may be more difficult to recognize: 1) a circle containing the outline of a pine tree, 'N.C.' to the left of the trunk and 'Pine Tree' on the other side; and 2) the letter 'P' with short uprights in the middle of the top and lower curves. Stephen died in 1961, but the work was continued by his associates. Our advisor for this category is R.J. Sayers; he is listed in the Directory under North Carolina.

Creamer & sugar bowl, feldspathic rose, porc, 1934, 2½" **40.00**
Match holder, emb figure/spinning wheel, gr matt w/red areas, 3", EX ...**425.00**
Plate, Cameo, covered wagon/equestrians/dog/etc, wht on brn rim, 9"...**425.00**
Vase, bl into wine at bottom, flared/waisted cylinder, Stephen, 6", pr **150.00**
Vase, Cameo, figures in wht on gr, Stephen, 1959, 13½".........**1,300.00**
Vase, Cameo, Indian scene, dk bl/bright yel, poor mk, 6¾"........**500.00**
Vase, Cameo, neck band: 10 people/Xmas tree, bl/gr/wine body, sgn, 8"..**1,600.00**
Vase, Cameo, teepee/bison/Indians, wht/gray on bl, hdls, Stephen, 19".**1,500.00**
Vase, crystalline, gold on celadon, shouldered, 8½x5" **750.00**
Vase, crystalline, gr on caramel, flaring top, 5" **300.00**
Vase, crystalline, gr/yel, squat/bulbous w/sm rim, 3¾x5" **320.00**
Vase, deep purple, bulbous, Stephen, 8¾".............................**400.00**
Vase, dk bl to shoulder, yel/brn w/gr & silver crystals below, 7x7"..**1,750.00**
Vase, feldspathic sky bl, porc, rim-to-hip hdls, slim, 1934, 9½" ..**325.00**
Vase, mint gr w/areas of wine & yel, 3 rim-to-shoulder hdls, 17", NM....**1,500.00**
Vase, purple & bl matt, bulbous, 1938, 9½"................................**475.00**

Pittsburgh Glass

As early as 1797, utility window glass and hollow ware were being produced in the Pittsburgh area. Coal had been found in abundance, and it was there that it was first used instead of wood to fuel the glass furnaces. Because of this, as many as 150 glass companies operated there at one time. However, most failed due to the economically disastrous effects of the War of 1812. By the mid-1850s those that remained were producing a wide range of flint glass items including pattern-molded and free-blown glass, cut and engraved wares, and pressed tableware patterns.

Our advisor for this category is Mark Vuono; he is listed in the Directory under Connecticut.

Compote, Pillar mold, appl ft, baluster stem, 8 ribs, 6½x7" **350.00**
Compote, Stoddard amber, appl wafer, ftd, ruffled rim, 9x11¼" ...**2,000.00**
Cruet, brilliant bl, 16 vertical ribs, ca 1820-50, hollow hdl/stopper....**1,500.00**
Decanter, cut strawberry dmns & fans, 3 appl rings, 8½" **100.00**
Decanter, Pillar mold, bright yel, pontil, smooth rim, 12"...........**325.00**

Plastics

Plastic was invented in 1868. Since then, many types have been developed, each with unique characteristics and uses. Among the earliest, those most familiar to us today are celluloid and French ivory; they were commonly used to make toiletry articles. In the early years of the century, buttons were made from Casein plastics, which could be made in a wide variety of colors and easily laminated and carved. The plastic jewelry that is so popular today had its heyday in the 1930s. The material used for its production was phenol formaldehyde. Two of the more recognizable tradenames for cast phenolics are Bakelite and Catalin. Buckles, buttons, radio and clock cases, cutlery handles, desk sets, and novelties were also made from this type of plastic. Vinyl and Lucite, acrylic resins, were used during the period between the two World Wars. There were many applications for vinyl, which is still commonly used. Lucite items that are particular interesting to todays collectors are purses and jewelry. (See Jewelry.)

Today's collectors have adopted the term Bakelite to encompass any type of phenoic resin. There are two methods of testing used to identify genuine Bakelite: 1), using a cotton swab and Semichrome or 409, clean an inconspicuous area — oxidation on any color will tint the cotton ivory or light yellow; 2), hold the edge of item under very hot running water for at least twenty seconds; if it's genuine, it will smell like varnish or paint remover.

For more information we recommend *Celluloid Treasures of the Victorian Era* by Joan Van Patten and Elmer and Peggy Williams; *Celluloid Collectibles* by Shirley Dunn; and *Celluloid, Collector's Reference and Value Guide,* by Keith Lauer and Julie Robinson. All are published by Collector Books.

Bakelite/Catalin

Ashtray, blk-speckled brn, Pullman Co, ca 1940s, 5½" dia **80.00**
Box, butterscotch, includes Gem razor & manual, in orig cb box...**350.00**
Box, red lid w/cvd line groupings, blk ft, 3x6" **160.00**
Box, ring; emerald gr w/striations, curved lid, 1¼x2¾" **175.00**
Box, 1933 Century of Progress, blk, 6" L, NM **11.00**
Button, banana shape, orange w/blk, 2½x⅝" **130.00**
Camera, Coronet Midget, gr, 2¼x1" **165.00**
Candle holders, brn marbleized, Deco style, Fr, 6½", pr **165.00**
Candlesticks, funerary; Deco style, inlaid stds, 52", pr.................**425.00**
Chess set, pcs in wht or ivory, in poor orig box **400.00**
Cigar cutter, bust of man, put cigar in mouth, push down hat **95.00**
Cigarette dispenser, dk red w/celluloid lid, Trigerette, 3¾" **125.00**
Crib toy, clown, pk & bl w/apricot & gr, pnt details, 5½", VG...**200.00**
Crib toy, elephant, strung amber spools w/wht 3-D head, 3½" **265.00**
Crib toy, female cat, flat body sections, 3-color, 3½", NM..........**200.00**
Crib toy, Humpty Dumpty, stung amber beads, wht egg head, 4½"..**210.00**
Crib toy, little girl, strung tan/butterscotch beads & chunks, 6" ...**95.00**
Crib toy, man, red hat, rnd/cylindrical shapes for body/arms/legs, 4"..**50.00**
Dice, Caltex w/star on ivory, English, set of 5, MIB......................**70.00**
Dice cup, blk w/gold marbled bottom, 2" **80.00**
Drawer pull, butterscotch swirled, bar style w/chrome bars **15.00**
Figurine, greyhound, gray on gr marbled base, ca 1920s, 8" L **200.00**
Flashlight, Dyna-lite, ivory, streamline styling, EX in box.............**95.00**

Flatware, blk w/inlaid yel teardrop, GH Warranted, 6 sets in box....**500.00**
Flatware, SEB Perma Brite, 2-color hdls, 26 pcs including 2 servers...**1,100.00**
Flatware, yel hdls, service for 6 (4 pcs ea), no serving pcs...........**100.00**
Gavel, mc rings, 7½", EX................................**100.00**
Gearshift knob/clock combo, blk/clear, New Haven, VG **100.00**
Hors d'oeuves set, butterscotch dice hdls, 8 forks in stand **200.00**
Inkwell, streamlined, blk, w/lid................................**25.00**
Jar, amber w/blk & amber lid, emb horizontal rings, 4x3¼" **165.00**
Match holder, cvg of 4 frogs, butterscotch w/red base, 2x2" **195.00**
Mold, cherry, mini............................**85.00**
Napkin ring, bird, assorted colors w/contrasting beaks, set of 6, VG...**400.00**
Napkin ring, donkey, brn, cvd eyes/mouth **95.00**
Napkin ring, rocking horse, olive w/inlaid red eye, 2½", set of 4....**650.00**
Napkin ring, Scottie dog, ivory, no eye **80.00**
Pen holder, blk Deco-style holder on red Lucite base, 3½" L........**55.00**
Pen holder, gr w/chrome accents, Deco styling, 3x2½x4" **135.00**
Pencil sharpener, airplane, butterscotch w/2 insignias **55.00**
Pencil sharpener, Bambi, Walt Disney Productions, 1" dia...........**55.00**
Pencil sharpener, bird, butterscotch marbled w/dk beak, 1½", EX ..**100.00**
Pencil sharpener, Dopey, red w/litho Dopey, Dopey shape, WD .**100.00**
Pencil sharpener, Electro-Pointer, blk, electric, 5¾", NM...........**200.00**
Pencil sharpener, Goofy, rnd & fluted, 1½" **50.00**
Pencil sharpener, mantel clock, Germany 2"......................**50.00**
Pencil sharpener, red marbled in brass bezel, Little Rascals, EX..**285.00**
Pencil sharpener, USA Army plane......................**80.00**
Pencil sharpener, Walt Disney's train, figural, 1¾" **85.00**
Pencil sharpener, 1939 NY WF, butterscotch/blk fair symbols.......**95.00**
Poker chips, butterscotch swirled, 100 in orig box dtd 1932 ....**80.00**
Poker chips, red, gr & butterscotch, in marbled gr holder: 4x3x1⅜" ...**125.00**
Poker chips, 400 swirl-molded chips, in bl, tan, red, EX 14x8x3" case .**450.00**
Powder jar, tortoise-shell look, NM **95.00**
Radio, Addison #2, marbled blk/wht, 1940, 6x5x10", VG.......**1,600.00**
Radio, Addison #2, maroon/tan, 1940, 6x5x10", EX................**2,000.00**
Radio, Addison #2, orange/red, 1940, 6x5x10", EX................**3,750.00**
Radio, Astor, brn, chrome speaker bars, rstr, VG.........................**215.00**
Radio, Automoatic Radio MFG Tom Thumb, marbled gr/tan, 5x4x7", EX..**4,250.00**
Radio, AWA Radiola, blk, tombstone-style case, EX **450.00**
Radio, AWA Radiolette, blk, 'Empire State,' EX **700.00**
Radio, Bendix #115, gr/blk, 1948, 8x6x11", EX..........................**600.00**
Radio, DeWald #A502, marbled brn/yel, 6x6x10", EX.............**1,100.00**
Radio, Emerson, orange w/blk knobs & slats over speaker, 9" W, VG.....**400.00**
Radio, Emerson Aristocrat #400, Geddes design, yel/brn/wht, 11" L, EX..**1,600.00**
Radio, Emerson Patriot, gr-yel w/brn accents, 11" L, EX.............**575.00**
Radio, Emerson Patriot, yel/brn marbleized w/brn knobs, 11" L, EX...**400.00**
Radio, Emerson Tombstone, ivory, nonworking, 10x7", NM **500.00**
Radio, Emerson 5+1 #L573, marbled blk/yel, 8x6x9", VG.......**1,600.00**
Radio, Emerson 5+1 #375, marbled lime/wht, 1941, 6x5x10", VG..**3,250.00**
Radio, Fada #L56, yel/bl, 1939, 6x6x9", EX............................**4,000.00**
Radio, Fada #L56, yel/red/bl, 1939, 6x6x9", EX........................**4,500.00**
Radio, Fada #1000, wine w/orange, EX **1,000.00**
Radio, Fada #52, table model, 1938, minimum value **850.00**
Radio, Fada Dip Top #711, marbled tan/wht, 6x6x9", EX **600.00**
Radio, Fada Prewar Temple #252, yel/bright red, crack, 7x6x11" ..**950.00**
Radio, Farnsworth #BT50, brn, rnded corners, molded speaker bars, EX ...**325.00**
Radio, Garod Commander #6AU1, maroon/yel, 1945, 8x6x11", EX...**1,200.00**
Radio, Garod Commander #6AU1, red/yel, 1945, 8x6x11", NM **1,600.00**
Radio, Garod Drop Handle #1B55L, maroon/yel, 6x8x11", EX....**3,750.00**
Radio, Garod Peak Top #1450, yel/red, 8x6x11", EX **4,250.00**
Radio, Garod Peak Top #1450, yel/tan, 1940, 8x6x11", EX.....**2,100.00**
Radio, Garod 3-Ring #126, maroon/tan, 1940, 8x6x11", EX.**10,000.00**
Radio, General Electric #L573, tan/marbled bl, 7x6x9", VG..**2,800.00**
Radio, General Electric #L573, tortoise/maroon, 1941, 8x6x9", VG...**1,700.00**
Radio, General Television #5B5, blk/gr, 8x6x9", EX **850.00**
Radio, General Television #5B5, blk/red, 8x6x9", EX.............**1,200.00**

Radio, General Television #5B5, lt gr/wht, 8x6x9", EX **6,500.00**
Radio, Majestic #55, dk brn, 1939.................................**250.00**
Radio, Model #41 Kadette Jewel, blk w/scrollwork grill, EX **325.00**
Radio, Motorola #50XC2, Deco table model, 1940, minimum value..**2,000.00**
Radio, Motorola Circle Grill #50SC, marbled yel, 7x6x10", EX..........**2,400.00**

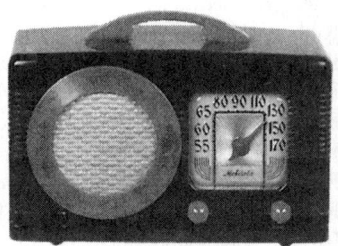

Radio, Motorola Circle Grill, red marble with butterscotch handle, knobs and grill ring, 6x10", EX, $6,000.00.

Radio, Motorola S Grill #51X, blk/red, 1941, 7x6x10", EX **4,750.00**
Radio, Motorola S Grill #51X, tan/gr, 1941, 6x7x10", NM **3,750.00**
Radio, Motorola Vertical Grill #52, marbled yel/tortoise, 6x5x9", EX...**2,400.00**
Radio, Mullard, brn tombstone, bars/circles in grille, EX **250.00**
Radio, RCA Little Nipper #9TX, marbled yel/red, 1939, 4x5x9"...**1,600.00**
Radio, Sentinel #284-NI, table model, AC/DC, 1946, minimum value...**750.00**
Radio, Sonora Coronet #KM, yel/gr, 6x5x9", EX **2,400.00**
Radio, Stewart Warner #62T36, marbled blk/gr/yel, 1945, crack, 13" L...**650.00**
Radio, Stewart Warner Varsity College, dk brn, 1938-1939........**250.00**
Record player, RCA 45-EY-4, tube type, 11x13x8", EX **125.00**
Roulette wheel, mc Catalin chips, wood pack, w/box, 1930s **200.00**
Shakers, gr, bbl shape on flat/ftd 4" L stand, Japan, pr.................**125.00**
Shakers, red or butterscotch, pr fits bk to bk on 1¾" rnd tray.......**85.00**
Shakers, various colors, W Germany, miniature, ½", set of 4......**100.00**
Shakers, 3-pc barbell, shaker ea end, wine & yel, 4⅛" L.............**125.00**
Swizzle stick, butterscotch, star finial, 5¼".....................................**30.00**
Swizzle sticks, assorted styles/colors in case styled as a bar, VG...**300.00**
Table lighter, nude, pnt figure on bronze base, Dunhill..............**165.00**
Tray, Bartels Beer, orange lettering on blk..................................**165.00**

Celluloid

Autograph album, Victorian lady, 4½x6", from $175 to..............**225.00**
Box, collar & cuff; lady's portrait, 6x6¼x6¼", from $300 to.......**350.00**
Box, handkerchief; Mucha print, 3x5½x5½", from $175 to **225.00**
Box, letter; Victorian girls, 2x5x7½", from $100 to....................**150.00**
Box, sewing; harvest scene, 4x9x7½", from $175 to....................**200.00**
Brush, Victorian lady bk, ornate hdl, 8½", from $90 to...............**125.00**
Glove case, Victorian scene, 3¼x11¼x3½", from $250 to **300.00**
Jewel case, mother/child reserve, gilt lock, 3x8x5", from $185 to..**250.00**
Jewel case, Victorian children, velvet trim, musical, 4x10x6".....**250.00**
Manicure set, Victorian scene, 9-pc in 4x13x11" case, from $325 to ...**400.00**
Mirror, hand; ornate bk, 9¾x4", from $100 to............................**150.00**
Mirror, shaving; emb classic figures, trifold, 12¼x20½" **500.00**
Photo album, Victorian child, musical, 12x9½", from $600 to ...**700.00**
Photo album, Victorian scene, upright, 8½x10½", from $450 to ...**525.00**
Shaving set, ivoroid, 5-pc in 3½x9x7" box, from $350 to...........**400.00**
Whisk broom holder, lady in plumed hat, from $125 to..............**175.00**

Playing Cards

Playing cards can be an enjoyable way to trace the course of history. Knowledge of the art, literature, and politics of an era can be gleaned from a study of its playing cards. When royalty lost favor with the people, Kings and Queens were replaced by common people. During the periods of war, generals, officers, and soldiers were favored. In the United States, early examples had portraits of Washington and Adams as opposed to Kings, Indian chiefs instead of Jacks, and goddesses for Queens.

Tarot cards were used in Europe during the 1300s as a game of chance, but in the eighteenth century they were used to predict the future and were regarded with great reverence.

The backs of cards were of no particular consequence until the 1890s. The marble design used by the French during the late 1800s and the colored wood-cut patterns of the Italians in the nineteenth century are among the first attempts at decoration. Later the English used cards printed with portraits of royalty. Eventually cards were decorated with a broad range of subjects from reproductions of fine art to advertising.

Although playing cards are becoming popular collectibles, prices are still relatively low. Complete decks of cards printed earlier than the first postage stamp can still be purchased for less than $100.00. In the listings, below decks are without boxes unless the box is specifically mentioned. Information concerning the American Antique Deck Collectors Club, 52 Plus Joker, may be found in the Directory under Clubs, Newsletters, and Catalogs.

Key:
C — complete   SC — score card
J — joker   XC — extra card

Advertising

Beacon Oil, Colonial Filling Station bks, 1926, 52+special J+XC, EXIB...**85.00**
Hardin Minneapolis Moline, wide, tractors bk, 1943, 52+SC, M..**100.00**

Foreign

Casablanca, Naypes Finos, Camoigne, 40 Spanish suit cards, M...**85.00**
France, Florentin, draped nudes, Becat, 1956, 52+2J+XCs, MIB...**100.00**
France, La Sybille des Salons, Grimaude, 1890, 52+J, NM **85.00**
Germany, Dutch town scenic Aces, Fromman & Morian, 1880, 40C, EX ..**55.00**

Older Wide Decks

Bicycle #808, model bks, ca 1905, 52+J, G **70.00**
Compliments of Am Red Cross Canteen Service, WWI era, NM/VG box ...**80.00**
Congress, English Setter dog, EXIB **18.00**
Congress #606, Lily, ca 1904, 52C, EX...**50.00**
Congress #606, Wanda's Wooing, US Playing Cards, 52+J, EX ..**135.00**
Dougherty #18, kitten w/ball bks, 52+blank card, M in wrapper ...**525.00**
Excelsior, Dougherty, bl eagle bks, 52C, EX **315.00**
Samuel Hart & Co, bl eagle bks, 52C, EXIB **155.00**

Souvenir

Boy Scout 1971 World Jamboree, Coca-Cola/Japan, 52+2 J, MIB..**215.00**
Chicago, Buckingham Fountain at Grant Park, 1950s, 52+2 J, M..**18.00**
I Love Lucy 50th Anniversary, CBS/Desilu, 52C, MIB **55.00**
Las Vegas, Fremont Street at Night, Japan, M in wrapper.............**22.00**
Lone Star bks, view faces of pre-WWI TX, 1915, 52+J, EX/G- box..**32.00**
Mount Rushmore, bridge sz, 42+J, M in (rpl) plastic box..............**18.00**
Rockefeller Center NY (foyer of music hall), Western, 1921, MIB....**55.00**
Southern Pacific, Golden West, ca 1915, 52+2XC+map+booklet, EX..**50.00**
VT Gr Mountain State, 53 views, Chisholm Bros, gold edges, 1910s, EX..**50.00**

Transportation

Choctaw Route RR, c 1899, 52+Choctaw J+map card, EXIB.....**685.00**
TWA Airlines, Connie, 1947, 52+J+SC, M in flocked box............**175.00**
White Pass & Yukon Rte, ca 1900, 52+J+3 info cards, EX in slipcase ..**130.00**

Miscellaneous

American Beauties, Elvgren, 52C, VG **55.00**
Babe Ruth cheering child bks, 1950s, 52+2 J, EX.....................**42.50**
Brotherhood of Light Egyptian Tarot, Church of Light, 1964, MIB..**100.00**
Esquire, pinups on red/bl bks, 1941, dbl deck+60-pg booklet, EXIB....**75.00**
First Moon Ride, Worshipfull, mc bks, 1971, dbl deck, MIB.........**80.00**
Flag bks, Liberty queens/Uncle Sam kings, Mussolina J, Aarco, 53C, M.**50.00**
L Barrymore gold-foil water scene bks, 1960s, dbl deck, MIB........**45.00**
Nile Fortune, gold edges, US Playing Cards, 1897-1904, complete, G ..**50.00**
Trip Trap Drug Info, Spenco, 1970, 52+2 J, gold edges, MIB **38.00**
White Squadron, Fireside Games, 1896, 54C, M/torn box............**45.00**
53 Vargas Girls, plastic coated, poker sz, M in wrapper **55.00**

Political

Many of the most valuable political items are those from any peri-od which relate to a political figure whose term was especially significant or marked by an important event or one whose personality was particu-larly colorful. Posters, ribbons, badges, photographs, and pin-back but-tons are but a few examples of the items popular with collectors of political memorabilia.

Political campaign pin-back buttons were first mass produced and widely distributed in 1896 for the president-to-be William McKinley and for the first of three unsuccessful attempts by William Jennings Bryan. Pin-back buttons have been used during each presidential campaign ever since and are collected by many people. Some of the scarcest are those used in the presidential campaigns of John W. Davis in 1924 and James Cox in 1920.

Contributions to this category were made by Michael J. McQuillen, monthly columnist of *Political Parade*, which appears in *AntiqueWeek* newspapers; he is listed in the Directory under Indiana. Our advisor for this category is Paul J. Longo; he is listed under Mass-achusetts. See also Autographs; Broadsides; Historical Glass; Watch Fobs.

Balloon, Benjamin Harri-son/Levi Morton jugate, 28" wire form with umbrel-la-style central wire, 1888, EX, $400.00.

Badge, mourning; We Mourn Our Martyred President, 33-star flag, 3½"..**300.00**
Ballot, Democratic, Seymour of NY for President, 1868, 9½x6¼"...**125.00**
Bandana, Harrison/Morton jugate, red/tan on off-wht, 22x24½", EX..**150.00**
Booklet, Communist Infiltration in US..., 1946, 40-pg **35.00**
Broadside, Lincoln & Grant on Peace & War, 1864, 11¾x9¼"..**1,500.00**
Broadside, Washington portrait on silk, ca 1800, 11x8", EX....**2,750.00**
Button, clothing; McKinley, $ sign, brass, ca 1896 ....**25.00**
Button, clothing; Zachary Taylor, brass, portrait in relief, NM....**100.00**
Cuff link, Horatio Seymour portrait on milk glass in brass fr **300.00**
Dollar, Dollars for Bread Instead of...Taxes, FDR portrait..............**25.00**
Engraving, US Grant, WE Marshall, 1868, 21x16"+mat & fr.....**500.00**
Engraving, Washington Delivering Inaugural , Sadd, 1849, 22x28" **650.00**
Handkerchief, Grover Cleveland/Allen Thurman, red w/blk, 22x23"....**125.00**
Lapel stud, Our Choice/Bryan & Sewall/1908, emb brass, 1½", EX..**35.00**
Lithograph, Lewis Cass amid 1st 11 presidents, N Currier, 14x10"+fr..**900.00**
Pamphlet, Copperhead Platform!, 1863, 4-pg, 9¼x6", EX **250.00**

Pamphlet, Mr Madison's War, Cutler, Boston, 1812, 62-pg, 9x5½", EX...**300.00**
Pin, Union/flags/shield/eagle on globe, thin brass, Civil War era..**75.00**
Plaque, T Roosevelt profile, Aggressive..., bronze, 1902, 13x10" ...**250.00**
Plate, from JQ Adams presidential service, Paris porc, 9" **2,900.00**
Poem, The Nation Mourns, Lincoln portrait, Magnus, 8x5".......**225.00**
Portrait, FD Roosevelt, portrait on silk in gray tones, 13x11"+fr..**200.00**
Poster, Kennedy for President, portrait, red/wht/bl/blk, 1960, 31x21"...**50.00**
Ribbon, Abraham Lincoln/Martyr President..., silk, 5x2", VG ...**500.00**
Ribbon, Gen Wm H Harrison...1773...1841, lengthy obituary, 8½"...**300.00**
Ribbon, Harrison/Tyler, First in War..., silk, 1840, 7¼x2½" **450.00**
Ribbon, In Memory of Andrew Jackson, portrait on silk, 8x3" ...**300.00**
Ribbon, Lincoln/Hamlin jugate, rpr split, water stains................**900.00**
Ribbon, Washington & Lafayette commemorative, ca 1824-25, 3½x2¼" ...**350.00**
Ribbon, Washington Centennial, blk on gr silk, 8½x2".............**250.00**
Ribbon, Washington Monument, dk print on off-wht silk, 1847, 7x3" ..**250.00**
Ribbon, Zachary Taylor commemorative, eagle/portrait, 1850, 8x4", EX+..**800.00**
Sheet music, Funeral March...Lincoln, Donizetti, 1865, 14x10" ..**300.00**
Song sheet, Nation Mourns Her Martyr'd Son, Hawthorne/Winner, 1865..**400.00**
Stickpin, Benjamin Harrison, brass shell **45.00**
Textile, portraits of 1st 7 presidents printed on cotton, 1829, 16x24"..**2,500.00**
Ticket, Nat'l Union Republican, US Grant/Colfax jugate, 1868, 7½" L....**200.00**
Token, Lucky Tillicum, Rebuild w/Roosevelt, blimp on bk, 1932, 1¼" ...**15.00**
Watch fob, Herbert C Hoover for President, brass/celluloid, ⅞", EX.**85.00**
Watch fob, Parker & Davis, brass, 1½x1¾", EX **60.00**

Pin-back Buttons

Adlai Is OK, red/wht/bl litho, scarce **10.00**
Alfred E Smith for President, gray-tone cello, ⅞".........................**24.00**
Alton Parker w/horseshoe & wishbone swag on wht, 1904, NM, 1¼"..**190.00**
Bryan/Kern held up by Lady Liberty, 1908, 1¼", NM **300.00**
Bush/Lugar/Mutz/Goldsmith Indiana's Winning Team, mc on bl, oval...**5.00**
Carter Mondale 76, candidates face right, blk/wht litho, 1¾".........**5.00**
Charles E Hughes for President, Whitehead & Hoag, 1916, ⅞" ...**33.00**
Confidentially I'm Voting for Roosevelt (Franklin), 1¼" **25.00**
Debs/Seidel 1912 Socialists Candidates, ⅞", VG........................**133.00**
Dewey/Warren, red/wht/bl litho, ⅞" **4.00**
Dewey/Warren, text in curving font, litho, 1948 ....**3.00**
Edith Willkie for First Lady, cello, 1¼" **11.00**
Eisenhower Man of the Hour, cello, 3½" **17.00**
For Freedom Re-Elect Roosevelt, 4FR, red/wht/bl, paper seal, 1¼"..**5.00**
For the Leadership We Need JFK, cello, 1¼".................................**10.00**
Goldwater in '64, blk & wht portrait, bl letters, red rim, 3½"........**15.00**
I Like Ike on wht stripe, red/wht/bl, ⅞" **4.00**
John Kennedy, blk & wht portrait, litho, 1960, 3" **10.00**
Johnson/Humphrey color picture flasher, 2½".............................**10.00**
Kennedy, JFK portrait, cello, scarce, 2¼" **17.00**
Labor for Stevenson, bl-tone photo, cello, 2¼" **23.00**
Landon, brn cello w/sunflower, ⅞" **10.00**
McKinley/Roosevelt w/swagged flag above on gold, 1900, 1¼", NM ..**50.00**
Mondale/Ferraro 1984, red/wht/bl litho, 2¼" **3.00**
Nixon Agnew, portraits, bl & wht, 1¼" **5.00**
Our President Harry S Truman, blk & wht, 1½", 1948, NM.........**56.00**
Reagan/Bush jugate, blk/wht portraits, bl eagle w/ribbon, 1¾" **18.00**
Regan/Bush, eagle w/ribbon, blk/wht/bl, 2¼" oval........................**18.00**
Roosevelt encircled by horseshoe/flag, 1904, 1¼", NM...............**295.00**
Roosevelt/Fairbanks embellished w/flag & eagle, 1904, 1¼", NM ..**225.00**
Roosevelt/Fairbanks w/star, leaf branches & ribbons, 1904, 1¼", NM ..**600.00**
Stevenson for President 1960, bl/wht litho, 1⅛"..............................**6.75**
Taft portrait encircled w/fancy bl & wht border, 1908, 1¼", NM .**85.00**
Thomas E Dewey, sepia portrait, cello, 1¾" **16.00**
Victor Berger/First Socialist Congressman, red/wht/bl, ⅞" **18.00**
Viva Eisenhower, Me Gusta Ike, cream/bl/red cello, 3½" **16.00**
Vote NO on Woman Suffrage, ⅞", NM **33.00**

Warren G Harding for President, sepia photo, cello, ⅞" 17.00
We Want Mamie, cello, 1¼"...12.00
Which Means Me Votee for Willkie, Chinese characters, cello, 1¼" 9.00

Pomona

Pomona glass was patented in 1885 by the New England Glass Works. Its characteristics are an etched background of crystal lead glass often decorated with simple designs painted with metallic stains of amber or blue. The etching was first achieved by hand cutting through an acid resist. This method, called first ground, resulted in an uneven feather-like frost effect. Later, to cut production costs, the hand-cut process was discontinued in favor of an acid bath which effected an even frosting. This method is called second ground. Our advisors for this category are Betty and Clarence Maier; they are listed in the Directory under Pennsylvania.

Bowl, 1st ground, cylindrical, 3x4½" 275.00
Carafe, 2nd ground, cornflowers (wear), 9"...................................690.00
Celery vase, 2nd ground, cornflowers, crimped rim, 5¼" 200.00
Champagne, 2nd ground, 5" 245.00
Creamer, 2nd ground, cornflowers, wishbone ft, pinched rim, 4x5" ..285.00

Cruet, cornflowers, second ground, amber stain, 7¼", $335.00. (Photo courtesy Betty and Clarence Maier)

Finger bowl, 2nd ground, blueberries, crimped, 5", +underplate .485.00
Pitcher, Midwest, red/bl flowers on leafy stems, twist hdl/collar, 8"..225.00
Pitcher, 1st ground, cornflowers, sq top, 6¼" 550.00
Pitcher, 2nd ground, cornflowers, bulbous, amber top, 6¾" 390.00
Punch cup, 1st ground, cornflowers, M bl stain 145.00
Punch cup, 1st ground, lt Invt T'print..45.00
Punch cup, 2nd ground, cornflowers 110.00
Sugar bowl, 2nd ground, cornflowers, open, 2½x5½" 285.00
Sugar bowl, 2nd ground, leaves & berries, hdls, 3" 515.00
Toothpick holder, 2nd ground, gold stained rigaree collar...........425.00
Tumbler, 1st ground, cornflowers, amber top, 3¾".......................200.00
Tumbler, 2nd ground, cornflowers, 4" 95.00

Porcelier

The Porcelier Manufacturing Company, originally from East Liverpool, Ohio, started business in the late 1920s and moved to Greensburg, Pennsylvania, in the early 1930s. The company flourished until the late 1940s and finally closed its doors in 1954.

They produced an endless line of vitrified porcelain products including electric appliances, coffee makers, and light fixtures. These products were sold in many stores under a variety of names and carried over ten different types of marks and labels.

The prices below are for items in excellent condition with no chips, cracks, or excessive wear. For more information, we recommend *Collector's Guide to Porcelier China* by our advisor for this category, Susan E. (Grindberg) Lynn. If you have any questions or information regarding Porcelier, you may contact Mrs. Lynn; she is listed in the Directory under Nevada. (Queries require SASE.)

Beer set, Ringed (solid), 7-pc, from $185 to................................260.00
Boiler, Rope Bow, 8-cup 40.00
Boiler, Sprig, 6-cup, no pan..30.00
Bowl, spaghetti; floral decal 85.00
Canisters, Country Life, ea...35.00
Casserole, Country Life, w/lid, 9½" 85.00
Ceiling fixture, single, rnd basketweave w/emb pnt flower stems..40.00
Coffeepot, Basketweave Floral, w/decorated dripper, 6-cup...........55.00
Coffeepot, Colonial Silhouette, 6-cup dbl.....................................75.00
Coffeepot, Color Band, 8-cup..25.00
Coffeepot, French Dip #566, 6-cup, decorated or undecorated 35.00
Coffeepot, Paneled Orb, 6-cup..30.00
Coffeepot, Serv-All Line, platinum 35.00
Cookie jar, Barock-Colonial, gold..95.00
Creamer & sugar bowl, Golden Fuchsia Platinum, ea....................20.00
Creamer & sugar bowl, Goldfinches, ea 12.00
Creamer & sugar bowl, Scalloped Wild Flowers, ea.......................15.00
Creamer & sugar bowl, Silhouette Hostess, ea..............................12.00
Decanter, Quilted Floral Cameo 40.00
Liqueur set, Ringed, decanter w/6 tall shot glasses........................75.00
Percolator, Antique Rose Deco...65.00
Percolator, Pink Flower Hostess...75.00
Percolator, Scalloped Wild Flowers 110.00
Pitcher, ball form, Beehive Crisscross 70.00
Pitcher, batter; Serv-All Line, gold or red/blk................................40.00
Pitcher, disc; Hearth 70.00
Pretzel jar, Barock-Colonial, gold...95.00
Sandwich grill, Serv-All Line, gold or red/blk, from $175 to 250.00
Shakers, #3020, any, ea...15.00
Syrup jar, Barock-Colonial, ivory, red or bl 45.00
Teapot, Dogwood II, 4-cup, blk..55.00
Teapot, Latticework, 4-cup 30.00
Toaster, Scalloped Wild Flowers, from $900 to........................1,100.00
Urn, Flower Pot Platinum 95.00
Urn, Silhouette Hostess..95.00
Waffle iron, gold or red/blk, #451, from $125 to..........................175.00
Wall sconce, floral decal, w/fluted shade 47.00

Postcards

Postcards are often very difficult to evaluate, since so many factors must be considered — for instance the subject matter or the field of interest they represent. For example, a 1905 postcard of the White House in Washington D.C. may seem like a desirable card, but thousands were produced and sold to tourists who visited there, thus the market is saturated with this card, and there are few collectors to buy it. Value: less than $1.00. However, a particular view of small town of which only five hundred were printed could sell for far more, provided you find someone interested in the subject matter pictured on that card. Take as an example a view of the courthouse in Hillsville, Virginia. This card would appeal to those focusing on that locality or county as well as courthouse collectors. Value: $3.00.

The ability of the subject to withstand time is also a key factor when evaluating postcards. Again using the courthouse as an example, one built in 1900 and still standing in the 1950s has been photographed for fifty years, from possibly a hundred different angles. Compare that with one built in 1900 and replaced in 1908 due to a fire, and you can see how much more desirable a view of the latter would be. But only a specialist would be aware of the differences between these two examples.

Postcard dealers can very easily build up stocks numbering in the 100,000s. Greeting and holiday cards are common and represent another area of collecting that appeals to an entirely different following than the view card. These types of cards range from heavily embossed designs to floral greetings and, of course, include the ever popular Santa Claus card. These were very popular from about 1900 until the 1920s, when postcard communication was the equivalent of today's quick phone call or e-mail. Because of the vast number of them printed, many have little if any value to a collector. For instance, a 1909 Easter card with tiny images or a common floral card of the same vintage, though almost one hundred years old, are virtually worthless. It's the cards with appeal and zest that command the higher prices. One with a beautiful Victorian woman in period clothing, her image filling up the entire card, could easily be worth $3.00 and up. Holiday cards designed for Easter, Valentines Day, Thanksgiving, and Christmas are much more common than those for New Year's, St. Patrick's Day, the 4th of July, and Halloween. Generally, then, they're worth less, but depending on the artist, graphics, desirability, and eye appeal, this may not always be true. The signature of a famous artist will add significant value — conversely, an unknown artist's signature adds none.

In summary, the best way to evaluate your cards is to have a knowledgeable dealer look at them. For a list of dealers, send a SASE to the International Federation of Postcard Dealers, P.O. Box 1765, Manassas, VA 20108. Do not expect a dealer to price cards from a list or written description as this is not possible. For individual questions or evaluation by photocopy (front and back), you may contact our advisor, Jeff Bradfield, 90 Main St., Dayton, VA 22821. You must include a SASE for a reply.

For more information we recommend *Collector's Guide to Post Cards* by Jane Wood and *Vintage Postcards for the Holidays* by Robert and Claudette Reed (Collector Books).

Posters

Advertising posters by such French artists as Cheret and Toulouse-Lautrec were used as early as the mid-1800s. Color lithography spurred their popularity. Circus posters by the Strobridge Lithograph Co. are considered to be the finest in their field, though Gibson and Co. Litho, Erie Litho, and Enquirer Job Printing Co. printed fine examples as well. Posters by noted artists such as Mucha, Parrish, and Hohlwein bring high prices. Other considerations are good color, interesting subject matter and, of course, condition. The WWII posters listed below are among the more expensive examples; 70% of those on the market bring less than $65.00. Values are for examples in excellent condition unless noted otherwise. See also Movie Memorabilia; Rock 'N Roll.

Advertising

Parumerie Distillerie Monaco, color litho on linen, Jules Cheret, 1897, 49x35", EX, $4,000.00.

Anisetta Evangelisti Liquore da Dessert, monkey, Biscaretti, 55x39"....**1,265.00**
Books for Everyone, girl w/book, 1930-30s, 21x12½", NM.........**350.00**
Cachou Lajaunie, lady w/breath freshener, Cappiello, 1920, 59x39", NM...**2,800.00**
Contratto, lady w/lg overflowing champagne glass, Cappiello, 54x38"..**3,165.00**
Cycles Lea, bicyclist, ca 1915-20s, 39x25½", NM **650.00**
Eveready Flashlights, man shines light on globe, 1920s, 30¾x21"...**350.00**
Fine Armagnac, 2 men/glowing bottle, Eugene Oge, 1910, 53x38", EX...**575.00**
Geo Wiedemann Bock Beer, goat, 1900s, 27½x11", NM...........**800.00**
Je ne Fume que le Nil, elephant, Capiello, 1920, linen bk, 46x62".........**500.00**
Liquore Strega G Alberti Benevento, lady in red, Dudovich, 51x35" .**4,800.00**
McLaughlin's XXX Coffee Is a Good Coffee, ca 1900, 21x21½", NM...**550.00**
Persan Export, Nicolitch, 1930, 62x45" **800.00**
Royal Baking Powder, gingerbread man, USA, 1920s, 30x20", NM ...**350.00**
Thermogene, man breathes fire, Cappiello, 1950s, 39x28½", M..**425.00**
Tsung-Li-Yamen's Tea, Oriental w/product, Vercasson, 51x37", G...**275.00**
Veuve Amiot, king in harlequin robe, Cappiello, 64x47" **1,600.00**

Circus

Key:
B&B — Barnum and Bailey   RB — Ringling Borthers

B&B, wide-angle circus view, Strohberg, 1894, 28x75"............**3,200.00**
Christy Bros, 5-Ring Wild Animal Show, Riverside Print, 28x42", VG...**500.00**
Cirque Charles, seals, Friedlander, 1900-10, 27x37", M **900.00**
Cirque Rancy, seals, ca 1900, 54¾x39½", NM.........................**1,500.00**
Haag Bros, elephants/portraits, 1930s, 28x41", M......................**450.00**
Parker & Watts, Kit Carson, lg portrait, laid down on brd, 39x26" **150.00**
Pinder RTF Piste Aux Etoiles, clowns, Grinsson, 1950, 46½x63½" ...**800.00**
RB B&B, snarling leopard, Bailey, ca 1945, 81x53", NM............**950.00**
RB B&B 108th Year, various acts on yel, ca 1978, 40x28", M **125.00**
RB B&B 200 Yrs of Circus in America, elephant on red, ca 1975, 40x28" ..**125.00**

Magic

Alexander the Man Who Knows, face on red, 1920s, 42x28", M..**550.00**
Alexander the Man Who Knows, face on red, 1930, 45x35", M ...**400.00**
Carter the Great, Do the Dead..., ca 1925, 106x81", M...........**2,400.00**
Carter the Great - World's Weird Wonderful Wizard, Otis, 1935, 76x41"....**1,500.00**
Chang & Fak Hong, The Bhuda, sorcerer & serpent, 1930, 24½x17", M..**150.00**
Chang & Fak Hong Japanese Review, ca 1930, 24½x17", M......**150.00**
Kar-mi, stone litho, multiple vignettes, early, 40x27" **400.00**

Theatrical

Blue Jeans, Motto production, Enquire Job Printing, ca 1900, 28x41", M ..**450.00**
Esclarmonde, crowned lady, Choubrac, ca 1890, 47x33", M....**1,100.00**
La Petite Mionne, blond seated at left, ca 1900, 46x60", M **1,500.00**
Les Maris de Ginette, Clerice, ca 1910, 47½x31½", M..............**300.00**
Madame de Pompadour, lady in red, Dola, 1933, 48x32", M **300.00**
Mistinguette - Theatre Morgador, D'Apres JD van Caulaert, 62x45" ..**675.00**
Prison Bait - Louis Beavers, Black cast, 40x26", VG **170.00**
Star Boarder, Enquire Job Printing, ca 1900, 41x28", M **450.00**

Travel

BEA Airlines w/flags, 1940-50s, 38½x24", NM...........................**450.00**
Japan, Autumn in Nikko, 2 Oriental beauties, 1948, 42½x29½", NM .**600.00**
L'Algerie et al Tunisia par la Cie Gle, couple at resort, 40x27" ...**1,200.00**
Nederland, globe/magnifier, 1939, 38¾x23¾", NM **550.00**
Paris, Fr Nat'l Railways, fountain, Cavailles, 1947, 39x25½", NM ..**450.00**
Richmond, Chesapeake & Ohio Ry, Hill, 1950s, 32½x21", NM...**600.00**
See India, 2 men blow long horns, Singh, 1930s, 39x24¾", NM ..**450.00**
Spain, Santander resort, Penagas, 1930, 39x24½", M **950.00**

Switzerland, Lousanne-Ouchy, castle, Hirzel, 1930s, 39¾x25½", NM ..**450.00**
Switzerland, Lucerne, butterfly, Wasserman, 1950s, 40x25", NM ...**525.00**

War

WWI, For Victory Buy WSS (War Saving Stamps), soldier, 28x19", NM ...**225.00**
WWI, Journee de Paris, 4 sm children/wounded soldiers, 1916, 47x31" **400.00**
WWI, Over There...In the Air Service, Fancher, 38½x28", M ..**1,200.00**
WWI, Sur La Terre Ennemie Les Prisoniers...Fam, Steinler, 45x31"...**300.00**
WWI, Uncle Sam Needs That Extra Shovelful, Sindelar, 27½x20", NM ..**225.00**
WWI, War Expo, doughboy w/spike helmet in hands, 40½x27½", NM ..**475.00**
WWI, YMCA Workes Lend Your Strength..., Spear, 27x20", NM ...**200.00**
WWII, I Need Your Skill in a War Job, Uncle Sam points, 28x22"..**175.00**
WWII, If You Tell Where He's Going..., sailor, 28x20" **175.00**
WWII, Is Your Trip Necessary, train car scene, 28x20" **175.00**
WWII, Join the RAAF, men by plane, Jardine, 20x25", NM **625.00**
WWII, RAAF, plane, Rider, ca 1942, 21x26", NM **525.00**
WWII, Stamp Out Waste, hand/stamp, Stahlhart, 36x24", NM.**250.00**

Pot Lids

Pot lids were pottery covers for containers that were used for hair dressing, potted meats, etc. The most common were decorated with colorful transfer prints under the glaze in a variety of themes, animal and scenic. The first and probably the largest company to manufacture these lids was F. & R. Pratt of Fenton, Staffordshire, established in the early 1800s. The name or initials of Jesse Austin, their designer, may sometimes be found on exceptional designs. Although few pot lids were made after the 1880s, the firm continued into the twentieth century.

American pot lids are very rare. Most have been dug up by collectors searching through sites of early gold rush mining towns in California.

In the following listings, all lids are transfer printed; the color(s) mentioned describe the transfer. Minor rim chips are expected and normally do not detract from listed values. When no condition is given, assume that the value is based on an example in such condition.

American

Amandine.. Philadelphia, winter scene, blk/wht, 3⅜", EX..........**600.00**
Compound Ox Marrow...Hauel, Philadelphia, blk/wht, 2⅜", EX ..**160.00**

Cucumber Cream From the Fresh Fruit..., black transfer, 3", M, $200.00.

Eugene Roussel Odontine...Philada, blk/wht, 2¾" sq, M..............**160.00**
For the Cure & Prevention...Amandine..., blk/wht, 7½", EX+base...**140.00**
Genuine Bear's Grease....Philadelphia, blk/wht, 3½", NM+base ...**750.00**
Genuine Lion Pomade...Philadelphia, blk/wht, 2⅞", NM..........**875.00**
Highest Premium Awarded..., 3 ladies pray, blk/wht, 3½", EX+base ..**1,100.00**
Phalon's Ambrosial Shaving Cream...NY, blk/wht, 3⅛", EX.......**200.00**
Phalon's Ambrosial Shaving Cream...NY, purple/wht, 3⅛", VG+ ...**180.00**
Premium Almond Cream..., Franklin bust, red/wht, 3½", NM ...**625.00**
Premium Orris Root...Peters..., red/wht, banner border, 3", NM ...**8,250.00**
R&GA Wright's Gold...Philadelphia, blk/wht, 2½", M **210.00**

Rose Vegetable...Hauel...Gums, blk/wht, 2¾", NM **170.00**
Rose Vegetable...Hauel...Gums, blk/wht, 3¼", NM **170.00**
Saponaceous E Phalon...Compound NY, girl at desk, blk/wht, 3⅞", VG...**180.00**
Wright's Gold Medal..., man at mirror, blk/wht, 4¼", M **650.00**

English

Allied Generals, mc, Pratt, 5", EX................................**145.00**
Atkinson's Cold Cream...London, 6" dia................................**50.00**
Bear Pit, figures view bear, mc, ca late 1820s, EX **120.00**
Bewley & Draper Areca & Rose... Dublin, rectangle, w/base, NM ..**265.00**
Cherry Tooth Paste for Cleansing...Harrogate, 3" **70.00**
Dr Ziemer's Tooth Paste, Alexandra portrait, 3½", EX............**300.00**
Garibaldi, standing w/flag, mc, Pratt, 4½"+fr....................**135.00**
Maws Indian Betel Nut...London, NM **60.00**
Mending the Nets, Pratt, w/jar, 3x3" **95.00**
Poultry Woman, lady dressing chicken, mc, Pratt, 4¼"+fr..........**100.00**
Pretty Kettle of Fish, dogs spill kettle, mc, Pratt, EX+...............**110.00**
Ruined Temple, Pratt, 8' **60.00**
Salifrice...Tooth Paste W Martindale...London, blk/wht, 4x2½" ...**215.00**
Shrimpers, fishing scene, mc, Pratt, 4¼", M **130.00**
Skaters, Victorian figures, mc, Pratt, 4¼", EX....................**125.00**
The Cuts, man & bear seeking lodgings, 3", EX+......................**550.00**
Uncle Toby, man examines lady's eye, Pratt, mid-19th C, 4⅛", EX ..**375.00**
War, downed horse, mc, Pratt, 4", EX **130.00**
Woods Areca Nut Toothpaste..., blk/wht, NM.............................**30.00**

Powder Horns and Shot Flasks

Though powder horns had already been in use for hundreds of years, collectors usually focus on those made after the expansion of the United States westward in the very early 1800s. While some are basic and very simple, others were scrimshawed and highly polished. Especially nice carvings can quickly escalate the value of a horn that has survived intact to as high as $400.00. Those with detailed maps, historical scenes, etc., bring even higher prices.

Metal flasks were introduced in the 1830s; by the middle of the century they were produced in quantity and at prices low enough that they became a viable alternative to the powder horn. Today's collector regards the smaller flasks as the more desirable and valuable, and those made for specific companies bring premium prices.

Flask, brass, Ames, emb star & sunburst, dtd 1838, VG **260.00**
Flask, brass, Ames, fouled anchor over USN ea side, EX+ **925.00**
Flask, brass, Ames, star & sunburst in oval, dtd 1848, G.............**260.00**
Flask, brass, Batty, star & sunburst in oval, dtd 1848, G.............**150.00**
Flask, brass, emb buffalo hunting scene w/rifles/etc, 9" **500.00**
Flask, brass, star & sunburst in circle, G.............................**200.00**
Flask, brass, Stimson, fouled anchor w/USN ea side, VG...........**515.00**
Flask, copper, emb horns & Public Property, VG.......................**200.00**
Flask, copper, Hawksley, fluted bag shape, minor dents, 11" **135.00**
Horn, blk & mottled honey tone w/domed brass stud, no stopper, 6" ...**25.00**
Horn, bone, hunters/deer, tip as bird head w/MOP eyes, 1700s, 11"...**950.00**
Horn, cow's horn, eng West Point scene, dtd 1792, 10"..........**2,275.00**
Horn, cvd rings, brass mts, external spring, brass cap, 1870s, 7½" ...**75.00**
Horn, cvd spout flange, wood base w/trapdoor, 1850s, 9¼".........**150.00**
Horn, flags, crown, cannons, muskets, scalloped edge, 7"............**575.00**
Horn, flat style w/wood spout plug, wood base w/brass brads, 1860s, 7"...**60.00**
Horn, map of Philadelphia/sun/eagles/banner, 18th C, 9", VG...**500.00**
Horn, Montreal scenes/horse/royal coat of arms, sgn/1818, 16"...**2,000.00**
Horn, priming; wood spout plug, 1850s, 3" **45.00**
Horn, scrolls/cannon/ship/owner info, dtd 1750, 13" **3,525.00**
Horn, simple lt cvg, wood base, ca 1870, 6"................................**127.50**

Pratt

Prattware has become a generic reference for a type of relief-molded earthenware with polychrome decoration. Scenic motifs with figures were popular; sometimes captions were added. Jugs are most common, but teapots, tableware, even figurines were made. The term 'Pratt' refers to Wm. Pratt of Lane Delph, who is credited with making the first examples of this type, though similar wares were made later by other Staffordshire potters. Pot lids and other transfer wares marked Pratt were made in Fenton, Staffordshire, by F. & R. Pratt & Co. (See Pot Lids.)

Cradle, typical palette w/pearlware, 1800s, 7"..............................**390.00**
Figurine, lioness, ochre & brn, 1790-1810, 3x4"..........................**450.00**
Pitcher, cream; children in relief reserve, 1810-15, 4¾".............**315.00**
Pitcher, tavern scenes, feather motif at spout/hdl, 9", VG **2,750.00**
Toby jug, Blue Willow w/typical palette coat, 19th C, 5½" **240.00**

Pre-Columbian Artifacts

The term 'pre-Columbian' loosely refers to some time prior to 1492, when Columbus arrived in America. In particular, it indicates pre-1492 artifacts of Central and South America, some of which can be dated as early as 4000 B.C. Artifacts representing the cultures of the Incan, Mayan, and Aztec Indians are avidly sought by the collector. These may be made of precious metals, hardstones, or pottery. Some were used in rituals and religious rites; some such as bowls and other utensils, though strictly utilitarian, nevertheless convey through form and decoration the craftsmanship of these early tribes.

Bowl, Earthenware from Mimbres tribe, black geometrics on red clay, 3x6¾", $1,000.00.

Bowl, pottery, snake design, Mayan, 6x12" **200.00**
Cvg, Olmec head, gr jade-ite, Palenove Mexico, 3¼x2¾"..........**550.00**
Figurine, human, pottery, Columbia, 9x4" **120.00**
Jar, polychrome, oval, sm, Panama, 4½x5"......................................**50.00**
Vessel, blkware w/pornographic human figures, Peru, 7x7" **110.00**
Vessel, cvd blk human effigy pottery, Costa Rica, 5x8½" **180.00**
Vessel, cvd redware effigy, Peru, 6x6" **130.00**
Vessel, human effigy, red on buff geometrics, Costa Rica, 6½x7" ..**110.00**
Vessel, pottery, crab effigy, Chimu, 9x5½" **100.00**
Vessel, pottery, polychrome bird effigy, Incan, 2½x7" **100.00**
Vessel, pottery, polychrome faces all around, 9x5½" **275.00**
Vessel, pottery, stirrup type, human figure effigy, Peru, 6x7¼" **130.00**

Primitives

Like the mouse that ate the grindstone, so has collectible interest in primitives increased, a little bit at a time, until demand is taking bites instead of nibbles into their availability. Although the term 'primitives' once referred to those survival essentials contrived by our American set-

tlers, it has recently been expanded to include objects needed or desired by succeeding generations — items representing the cabin-'n-corn-patch existence as well as examples of life on larger farms and in towns. Through popular usage, it also respectfully covers what are actually 'country collectibles.'

From the 1600s into the latter 1800s, factories employed carvers, blacksmiths, and other artisans whose handwork contributed to turning out quality items. When buying, 'touchmarks,' a company's name and/or location and maker's or owner's initials, are exciting discoveries.

Primitives are uniquely individual. Following identical forms, results more often than not show typically personal ideas. Using this as a guide (combined with circumstances of age, condition, desire to own, etc.) should lead to a reasonably accurate evaluation. For items not listed, consult comparable examples. Authority Kathryn McNerney has compiled several lovely books on primitives and related topics: *Primitives, Our American Heritage*; *Collectible Blue and White Stoneware*; and *Antique Tools, Our American Heritage*. You will find her address in the Directory under Florida. See also Butter Molds and Stamps; Boxes; Copper; Farm Collectibles; Fireplace Implements; Kitchen Collectibles; Molds; Tinware; Weaving; Woodenware; and Wrought Iron.

Bed warmer, brass, eng peacock on flower, stars/foliage surround, 48"..**400.00**
Bed warmer, brass, pierced, English, 12" dia, 45" wood hdl.........**375.00**
Bed warmer, brass w/eng flower on lid, trn wood hdl, 43", G......**255.00**
Bed warmer, copper, pierced, trn poplar wood hdl, ca 1850, 27".**250.00**
Bellows, cvd/pnt wood w/bird, dog & foliage on red, 1830s, 20x10"..**230.00**
Bellows, tortoise shell inlay, burgundy leather sides, 19th C, 16" ...**750.00**
Bucket, oak w/brass bands & swing hdl, Richmond VA Cedar Works Mfg Co....**200.00**
Bucket, sugar; orig bl pnt, plane mks, copper/steel tacks, 15", VG..**440.00**
Bucket, sugar; staved, red-washed bottom, natural top, 13x14" .**195.00**
Bucket, sugar; staved, 1-finger, wire bale hdl, lid split, 7x6½"........**85.00**
Candle mold, pewter in pine fr, 12-tube, nailed, +tin funnel, 19x6x20"..**825.00**
Candle mold, tin, 5-tube, arched base, scroll hdls, x9x3½" **300.00**
Candle mold, tin, 12-tube, dbl hdls, 11x12" **300.00**
Candle mold, tin, 12-tube, ear hdls, 5¾" **385.00**
Candle mold, tin, 24-tube, dbl hdls, ca 1830, 11"......................**250.00**
Cheese curd breaker, wood w/cranked pin-covered cylinder, 1850s..**225.00**
Cheese sieve, hand-molded yel clay w/Albany glaze, 7x10" **300.00**
Churn, pine w/mellow pumpkin color, bootjack ends, 33x16x19"..**220.00**
Dipper, gourd bowl w/wood hdl w/ivory ferrule, some damage, 19" **75.00**
Dough box, cvd oak Fr Provincial, shaped elm panels, 34x41x24"..**2,185.00**
Foot warmer, cherry wood, pierced rectangle, iron swing hdl, 7x12x8"...**300.00**
Foot warmer, cvd yew wood, piercings/1887, age splits/rstr, 8x12x9"..**350.00**
Foot warmer, oak & wrought iron, old brn pnt, 7x9x8" **175.00**
Foot warmer, punched tin panels w/rnd designs, mortised/pegged fr, VG..**195.00**
Foot warmer, wood/tin, punched panels w/circles & hearts, trn posts, G...**250.00**
Keg, staved, wooden bands, old red-brn pnt, 7¼x10"..................**115.00**
Kraut cutter, maple, heart cutout, 26x8" **330.00**
Kraut cutter, poplar, scalloped crest w/heart cutout, 4-blade, PA, 45" ..**220.00**
Kraut cutter, walnut, heart cutout, 19½x10"................................**175.00**
Kraut cutter, walnut, pierced heart-shaped hdl, 19th C, 25" **285.00**
Lamp oil filler, glass, cruet shape, pontil, ground spout, 2¾" **180.00**
Lamp oil filler, glass, short/squatty, hdl w/ball terminal, 2¼x7" ..**975.00**
Lamp oil filler, glass, teardrop, fire-polished spout/hdl, stopper, 6"..**900.00**
Lamp oil filler, glass, teardrop, stopper w/acorn finial, 5" **850.00**
Mallet, chamfered-edge burl head w/paneled curly maple hdl, wear, 11" ...**110.00**
Rack, apple drying; slatted wood base, 4-leg, 1800s, minimum value...**150.00**
Rack, drying; bl pnt, 3 parts w/2 X-arms ea, mortised, 37x84" **310.00**
Rack, drying; curly maple, 2 rows on 3 bars, shoe ft, rfn, 48x36" ..**300.00**
Rack, drying; pine w/3 pegged mortise/tenon X bars, 3-part, ea: 72x36"..**180.00**
Rack, drying; pnt wood, sq nails, arched ft, folds, 19th C, 36x43" ...**635.00**
Rack, quilt; pine tri-fold w/mortise & pin construction, tapered legs ...**400.00**
Snowshoes, pine w/leather strap, 9x32½", pr..............................**110.00**
Sock form, maple, beveled edge, factory made, pr.........................**40.00**

Tub, wooden staves w/iron hoops, D-shape cut-out hdls, 9x19"..**230.00**
Wash tub, pnt pine, staved, pierced hdls, ca 1900, 17x24".........**260.00**
Washboard, Soap Saver, tin w/wooden fr, 24x12" **45.00**
Wood bin, old bl rpt, bracket ft, sq nails, Amish, 45x32x20" ..**1,045.00**
Wood bin, old gray rpt, 1 pc, 3 shelf, open top, 63x31x20" **900.00**

Prints

The term 'print' may be defined today as almost any image printed on paper by any available method. Examples of collectible old 'prints' are Norman Rockwell magazine covers and Maxfield Parrish posters and calendars. 'Original print' refers to one achieved through the efforts of the artist or under his direct supervision. A 'reproduction' is a print produced by an accomplished print maker who reproduces another artist's print or original work. Thorough study is required on the part of the collector to recognize and appreciate the many variable factors to be considered in evaluating a print. Prices vary from one area of the country to another and are dependent upon new findings regarding the scarcity or abundance of prints as such information may arise. Although each collector of old prints may have their own varying criteria by which to judge condition, for those who deal only rarely in this area or newer collectors, a few guidelines may prove helpful. Staining, though unquestionably detrimental, is nearly always present in some degree and should be weighed against the rarity of the print. Professional cleaning should improve its appearance and at the same time help preserve it. Avoid tears that affect the image; minor margin tears are another matter, especially if the print is a rare one. Moderate 'foxing' (brown spots caused by mold or the fermentation of the rag content of old paper) and light stains from the old frames are not serious unless present in excess. Margin trimming was a common practice; but look for at least ½" to 1½" margins, depending on print size.

For more information we recommend *Collector's Value Guide to Early 20th Century American Prints* by Michael Ivankovich. When no condition is indicated, the items listed below are assumed to be in very good to excellent condition. See also Nutting, Wallace; Parrish, Maxfield.

Audubon, John J.

Audubon is the best known of American and European wildlife artists. His first series of prints, 'Birds of America,' was produced by Robert Havell of London. They were printed on Whitman watermarked paper bearing dates of 1826 to 1838. The octavo edition of the same series was printed in seven editions, the first by J.T. Bowen under Audubon's direction. There were seven volumes of text and prints, each 10" x 7", the first five bearing the J.J. Audubon and J.B. Chevalier mark, the last two, J.J. Audubon. They were produced from 1840 through 1844. The second and other editions were printed up to 1871. The bien edition prints were full size, made under the direction of Audubon's sons in the late 1350s. Due to the onset of the Civil War, only 105 plates were finished. These are considered to be the most valuable of the reprints of the 'Birds of America Series.'

In 1971 the complete set was reprinted by Johnson Reprint Corp. of New York and Theaturm Orbis Terrarum of Amsterdam. Examples of the latter bear the watermark G. Schut and Zonen. In 1985 a second reprint was done by Abbeville Press for the National Audubon Society.

Although Audubon is best known for his portrayal of birds, one of his less-familiar series, 'Vivaparous Quadrupeds of North America,' portrayed various species of animals. Assembled in corroboration with John Bachman from 1839 until 1851, these prints are 28" x 22" in size. Several octavo editions were published in the 1850s. In the following listing, all measurements are actual print size unless stated otherwise.

American Sparrow Hawk, Leipzig, 1973, sight: 33½x23½" **150.00**

Canada Otter, Bowen, 1844, Imperial folio **2,500.00**
Downy Woodpecker, JT Bowen, sight: 9x5⅜" **100.00**
Exauimaux Dog, JT Bowen, 1847, Imperial folio....................**2,500.00**
Fork-Tailed Petrel, Havell, 1835, plate CCLX, sight: 12½x20" ...**1,500.00**
Green Shank, Havell, 1835, sight: 15½x24¾" **2,875.00**
Little Chief Hare, Bowen, edge damage/insect specks, 21½x29" ...**150.00**
Lynx Rufus Common American Wild Cat, Bowen, 1842, Imperial folio...**10,000.00**
Nuttall's Hare, Bowen, sight: 6½x9½" **125.00**
Red & White Shouldered Marsh Blackbird, JT Bowen, sight: 9x5¼"...**125.00**
Red-Bellied Nuthatch, JT Bowen, sight: 9x5⅜" **100.00**
Saffron Headed Marsh Blackbird, JT Bowen, sight: 9x5¼" **125.00**
Severn River Flying Squirrel, Bowen, 1844, Imperial folio **2,585.00**
White Wolf, Bowen, 1845, sight: 20⅜x26⅜" **3,500.00**
Worm-Wood Hare, Bowen, sight: 6½x9½" **125.00**

Currier and Ives

Nathaniel Currier was in business by himself until the late 1850s when he formed a partnership with James Merrit Ives. Currier is given credit for being the first to use the medium to portray newsworthy subjects, and the Currier and Ives views of nineteenth-century American culture are familiar to us all. In the following listings, 'C' numbers correspond with a standard reference book by Conningham. Values are given for prints in very good condition; all are colored unless indicated black and white. Unless noted 'NC' (Nathaniel Currier), all prints are published by Currier and Ives. Our advisors for this category are John and Barbara Rudisill (Rudisill's Alt Print Haus); they are listed in the Directory under Maryland.

American Fireman, Always Ready; 1858, C-152, med folio **2,195.00**
American Fireman, Prompt To Rescue; 1858, C-154, med folio...**2,195.00**
American Homestead Winter, 1868, C-172, sm folio.................**850.00**
Ann Maria, NC, 1849, C-236, sm folio...**95.00**
Battle of Coal Harbor VA...1864, C-400, sm folio.....................**275.00**
Best Likeness, 1858, C-505, med folio.......................................**200.00**
Bombardment & Capture of Island Number Ten...1862, C-593, lg folio...**1,300.00**
Bombardment of Fort Pulaski...1862, C-595, sm folio **325.00**
Camping Out, Some of the Right Sort; NC, 1856, C-777, lg folio..**4,000.00**
Central Park, The Drive; 1862, C-951, med folio **2,000.00**
Cherry-Time, 1866, C-1023, med folio **1,200.00**
Clipper Ship Cosmos, C-1142, med folio **1,300.00**
Eliza, NC, C-1688, sm folio...**90.00**
Fall of Richmond VA on...1865, C-1821, lg folio....................**1,900.00**
Fall of Richmond VA on...1865, C-1822, sm folio **300.00**
Fanny, NC, 1846, C-1868, sm folio **75.00**
Farmer's Home - Winter, 1863, C-1892, lg folio......................**6,000.00**
Frozen Up, 1872, C-2155, sm folio...**2,200.00**
Fruits of Intemperance, 1870, C-2193, sm folio **195.00**
Getting In, NC, C-2368, sm folio..**200.00**

Grandest Palace Drawing Room Steamers in the World, Drew and St. John, 1878, C-2541, large folio, $1,800.00.

Grazing Farm, 1867, C-2563, lg folio **1,300.00**
Henry Clay, The Nation's Choice; NC, C-2796, sm folio, VG...**185.00**
Home in the Wilderness, 1870, C-2861, sm folio **650.00**

Home on the Mississippi, 1871, C-2876, sm folio.........................**700.00**
In the Northern Wilds, Trapping Beaver; C-3073, sm folio **525.00**
Julia, NC, 1846, C-3308, sm folio, VG....................................**90.00**
Lakeside Home, 1869, C-3423, med folio **425.00**
Life & Age of Man, Stages...Grave; NC, C-3499, sm folio **250.00**
Life & Age of Woman...Grave; NC, 1850, C-3501, sm folio **250.00**
Life of Fireman - The Metropolitan System, 1866, C-3516, lg folio...**3,500.00**
Life of Sportsman, Coming Into Camp; 1872, C-3524, sm folio.**575.00**
Life of Sportsman, Going Out; 1872, C-3525, sm folio **575.00**
Little Lily, C-3656, sm folio **95.00**
Little Nelly, C-3684, sm folio **95.00**
Lucy, NC, C-3834, sm folio **95.00**
Maiden's Rock, Mississippi River; C-3891, sm folio..................**500.00**
Maj Genl Ambrose E Burnside, 1862, C-3901, sm folio.............**150.00**
Major General Geo G Meade..., 1863, C-3911, sm folio............**195.00**
Major General Wm T Sherman..., C-3931, sm folio **195.00**
Mansion of the Olden Time, C-3969, sm folio **200.00**
Maple Sugaring - Early Spring in...Woods, 1872, C-3975, sm folio ..**1,500.00**
Married, NC, 1845, C-4016, sm folio **125.00**
Martha, NC, C-4017, sm folio **90.00**
Martha Washington, C-4027, med folio **100.00**
Mill Cove Lake Near Po'Keepsie..., C-4123, sm folio.................**400.00**
Mountain Spring Near Cozzen's..., 1862, C-4245, med folio.......**800.00**
Naval Heroes of the US (No 1), NC, 1846, C-4397, sm folio **575.00**
Naval Heroes of the US (No 2), NC, 1846, C-4398, sm folio **575.00**
New England Coast Scene, C-4416, sm folio..............................**325.00**
Old Farm House, 1872, C-4557, sm folio..................................**1,200.00**
Partridge Shooting, 1870, C-4718, sm folio **400.00**
Pet of the Family, On Christmas Morning; C-4757, sm folio **150.00**
Pilot Boat in Storm, C-4782, sm folio **500.00**
President of the United States, C-4903, sm folio........................**175.00**
Ready for Battle, C-5078, sm folio..**225.00**
Ride to School, C-5140, sm folio **2,400.00**
Robert Burns, C-5178, med folio...**145.00**
Sheep Pasture, C-5488, med folio..**370.00**
Shoemaker, C-5494, sm folio..**270.00**
Soldier's Bride, C-5594, sm folio..**150.00**
Squall Off Cape Horn, C-5680, sm folio...................................**800.00**
Stable (No 1), NC, C-5683, med folio **1,200.00**
Staten Island & Narrows From Fort Hamilton, 1861, C-5715, lg folio...**1,800.00**
Steamship Herman, NC, C-5770, sm folio.................................**350.00**
Steamship President..., NC, C-5785, sm folio **340.00**
Straw-Yard, Winter; C-5837, med folio.....................................**1,000.00**
Summer, C-5849, sm folio **95.00**
Summer Morning, C-5870, med folio...**475.00**
Summer Time, C-5879, sm folio **200.00**
Sylvan Lake, C-5940, sm folio **200.00**
Thatched Cottage, C-6002, sm folio **195.00**
Tomb & Shade of Napoleon, NC, C-6099, sm folio...................**150.00**
Trotting Gelding St Julien..., 1881, C-6177, sm folio **350.00**
Trotting on the Road..., 1873, C-6195, sm folio **300.00**
Trout Brook, 1862, C-6227, med folio **1,300.00**
Trout Pool, C-6229, sm folio **1,100.00**
Twilight Hour, C-6253, med folio, sm folio..............................**165.00**
View of Baltimore, NC, 1848, C-6389, sm folio.........................**750.00**
View of New York, NC, 1849, C-6402, med folio......................**1,400.00**
Washington Family, C-6531, sm folio..**85.00**
Water Fowl Shooting, NC, C-6562, sm folio **725.00**
Who's Afraid of You?, 1868, C-6648, sm folio, VG **140.00**
Windsor Castle & Park, C-6720, med folio................................**225.00**
Winter Evening, NC, 1854, C-6734, med folio...........................**2,400.00**
Winter Morning - Feeding the Chickens, 1863, C-6741, lg folio...**6,500.00**
Woodlands in Summer, C-6778, sm folio...................................**300.00**
Yacht Sappho of NY..., C-6814, sm folio **400.00**

Yo-Semite Falls California, C-6829, sm folio **400.00**
Young Brood, C-6840, sm folio..**275.00**
Young Housekeepers, NC, C-6856, sm folio...............................**90.00**
Young Sailor, NC, 1849, C-6867, sm folio.................................**195.00**

Erte (Romain de Tirtoff)

Adam & Eve, emb serigraph, 1982, 37x21" **3,000.00**
Black Rose, serigraph, 1975, 20x15"..**4,400.00**
Columbine, 1983, 32x25" **650.00**
Diva I, emb serigraph w/foil stamping, 36x28" **11,000.00**
Dream, emb serigraph w/foil stamping, 1987, 40x29¾" **4,000.00**
Fox Fur, emb serigraph w/foil stamping, 1986, 33½x26½".......**8,000.00**
Kissing, emb serigraph, 1986, 27x21½" **2,000.00**
Lilies & Lace, emb serigraph w/foil stamping, 1987, 40¾x28½"..**10,000.00**
Marriage Dance, emb serigraph w/foil stamping, 1984, 29x34"....**12,250.00**
Oriental Tale, serigraph, 1982, 30x24".......................................**4,000.00**
Sandstorm, serigraph, 1985, 27¾x20¾"......................................**2,500.00**
Trapeze, serigraph, 1983, 30x22" **4,200.00**
Winter, serigraph, 1975, 13x10"...**1,750.00**
Yvette, lithograph, 1975, 6⅝x2½"..**2,000.00**

Fisher, Harrison

Aprodite, girl in water, ca 1908, 11x7".......................................**65.00**
Dixie, girl w/red scarf & riding crop, ca 1908, 11x7" **65.00**
Hiawatha, head & shoulders of chief in feathered headdress, 10x8" ..**75.00**
Hiawatha, w/maiden beside waterfall, 10x8" **65.00**
His Gift, beauty inspects ring in box, ca 1912, 10x8" **65.00**
Oh! Promise Me, girl at piano, ca 1912, 10x8" **65.00**
Paddling Their Own Canoe, summer camp girls, 10x8" **65.00**
Reflections, lady's profile, ca 1908, 11x7"..................................**65.00**
Under the Rose, girl in flowered hat, 10x8" **65.00**

Fox, R. Atkinson

A Canadian who worked as an artist in the 1880s, R. Atkinson Fox moved to New York about ten years later, where his original oils were widely sold at auction and through exhibitions. Today he is best known, however, for his prints, published by as many as twenty print makers. More than thirty examples of his work appeared on Brown and Bigelow calendars, and it was used in many other forms of advertising as well. Though he was an accomplished artist able to interpret any subject well, he is today best known for his landscapes. Fox died in 1935. Our advisor for Fox prints is Pat Gibson whose address is listed in the Directory under California.

Aces All, #557, 8x12" **265.00**
Blooming Time, #37, 14x18"..**185.00**
Buffalo Hunt, unsgn, #209, 7x10"...**160.00**
By a Waterfall, #144, 10x7"...**100.00**
Challenge, The; #509, elk, ca 1905, 7x5" **100.00**
Clipper Ship, #75, ca 1922, 14x18"...**125.00**
Dawn, girl on bench, #1, 15½x19½"+Deco fr **150.00**
Dreamland, #41, 14x22"...**150.00**
Elysian Fields, lady & flowers, castle beyond, #70, 22½x18½"+fr...**255.00**
Enchanted Steps, #56, ca 1927, 14x17".....................................**195.00**
English Garden, #57, ca 1924, 20x14".......................................**150.00**
Garden of Rest, #143, 10x18"...**155.00**
Garden Realm, #82, unsgn, 10x20"..**140.00**
Good Morning, #553, 1920, 10x12"...**125.00**
Good Shepherd, #29, ca 1927, 12x18" **195.00**
His Last Cartridge, #51, 7⅞x5½"+mat & 1½" Deco fr...............**145.00**
In Moonlight Blue, Indian maiden in canoe, #232, 8x6".............**185.00**

June Morn, girl beside lake, #33, 20x13"+fr 285.00
Lake Louise Alberta, #402, 12x10" 155.00
Love's Paradise, #13, 18x30" 295.00
Majestic Splendor, #93, 18x30" 325.00
Monarch of the North, #613, 16x20" 380.00
Moonlight & Roses, #39, 14x18" 185.00
Nature's Beauty, #16, 10x20" 130.00
Old Fashioned Garden, An; #12, 18x30" 325.00
Poppies, #45, 18x30" 280.00
Proud Mother, A; #430, ca 1920, 10x8" 200.00
Romance Canyon, #32, 13½x9½"+1" fr 195.00
Spirit of Youth, #4, ca 1926, 10x18" 155.00
Wayside House, #48, 33x20"+2" Deco fr 325.00
When Day Is Over, #399, 13½x9½"+fr 195.00
Where Dreams Come True, #202, 1920, 6x7" 145.00

Gutmann, Bessie Pease (1876 – 1960)

Delicately tinted prints of appealing children sometimes accompanied by their pets, sometimes asleep, often captured at some childhood activity are typical of the work of Gutmann; she painted lovely ladies as well and was a successful illustrator of children's books. Her career spanned the five decades, 1900 through 1950.

For further information we recommend *The Gutmann & Gutmann Artists: A Published Works Catalog — Fourth Edition* (Science Press, 2001) by our advisor for this category, Dr. Victor Christie; he is listed in the Directory under Pennsylvania.

Aeroplane, The; #266/#695, 14x21" 800.00
Always, #774, 14x21" 2,500.00
American Girl, The; #220, 13x18" 500.00
Annunciation, #705, 14x21" 1,100.00
Asking for Trouble, #820, 14x21" 250.00
Awakening, #664, 14x21" 125.00
Baby's First Christmas, #158 ....500.00
Bedtime Story, The; #712, 14x21" 800.00
Betty, #787, 14x21" 250.00
Blossom Time, #654, 14x21" 650.00
Blue Bird, The; #265/#666, 14x21" 750.00
Butterfly, The; #632, 14x21" 175.00
Call to Arms, A; #806, 14x21" 800.00
Chip Off the Old Block, #728, 14x21" 600.00
Chuckles, #799, 11x14" 175.00
Chums, #665, 14x21" 300.00
Cupid, 'After All My Trouble,' #608, 16x20" 800.00
Daddy's Coming, #644, 14x21" 500.00
Divine Fire, The; #722, 14x21" 700.00
Double Blessing, A; #643, 14x21" 550.00
Feeling, #19, 6x9" 250.00
Friendly Enemies, #215, 11x14" 175.00
Goldilocks, #771, 14x21" 1,200.00
Good Morning, #801, 14x21" 200.00
Guest's Candle, The; #651, 14x21" 500.00
Hearing, #22, 6x9" 250.00
Home Builders, #233/#655, 14x21" 250.00
In Arcady, #701, 14x21" 675.00
In Disgrace, #792, 14x21" 200.00
In Slumberland, #786, 14x21" 150.00
Kitty's Breakfast, #805, 14x21" 350.00
Knit Two - Purl Two, #657, 14x21" 850.00
Little Bit of Heaven, A; #650, 14x21" 125.00
Little Mother, #803, 14x21" 450.00
Lorelei, #645, 14x21" 2,000.00
Love's Harmony, #791, 14x21" 350.00

Madonna, The; #674, 14x21" 2,100.00
May We Come In, #808, 14x21" 300.00
Message of the Roses, The; #641, 14x21" 400.00
Mighty Like a Rose, #642, 14x21" 160.00
Mischief Brewing, #152, 9x12" 2,200.00

The Mothering Heart, #331, 14x21", $650.00. (Photo courtesy Dr. Victor Christie)

My Honey, #756, 14x21" 1,100.00
New Pet, The; #709, 14x21" 850.00
Nitey Nite, #826, 14x21" 175.00
Now I Lay Me, #620, 14x21" 2,500.00
On Dreamland's Border, #692, 14x21" 165.00
On the Up & Up, #796, 14x21" 190.00
Our Alarm Clock, #150, 9x12" 250.00
Perfect Peace, #809, 14x21" 300.00
Popularity (Has Its Disadvantages), #825, 14x21" 150.00
Priceless Necklace, A; #744, 14x21" 1,200.00
Rosebud, #780, 14x21" 300.00
Seeing, #122, 11x14" 350.00
Smile Worth While, A; #180, 9x12" 800.00
Snowbird, #777, 14x21" 650.00
Sunkissed, #818, 14x21" 150.00
Sympathy, #804, 14x21" 225.00
Symphony, #702, 14x21" 650.00
Thank You, God, #822, 14x21" 175.00
Tom, Tom the Piper's Son, #219, 11x14" 200.00
Touching, #210, 11x14" 180.00
Who's Sleepy?, #816, 14x21" 275.00
Winged, Aureole, The; #700, 14x21" 400.00
Wood Magic, #703, 14x21" 750.00

Icart, Louis

Louis Icart (1888 – 1950) was a Parisian artist best known for his boudoir etchings in the '20s and '30s. In the '80s prices soared, primarily due to Japanese buying. The market began to readjust in 1990, and most etchings now sell at retail between $1,400.00 and $2,500.00. Value is determined by popularity and condition, more than by rarity. Original frames and matting are not important, as most collectors want the etchings restored to their original condition and protected with acid-free mats.

Beware of the following reproduction and knock-off items: 1. Pseudo engravings on white plastic with the Icart 'signature.' 2. Any bronzes with the Icart signature. 3. Most watercolors, especially if they look similar in subject matter to a popular etching. 4. Lithographs where the dot-matrix printing is visible under magnification. Some even have phony embossed seals or rubber stamp markings. Items listed below are in excellent condition unless noted otherwise. Our advisor is William Holland, author of *Louis Icart: The Complete Etchings*, and *The Collectible Maxfield Parrish*; he is listed in the Directory under Pennsylvania.

Arrival, 1941, 21x17", ...1,495.00

Ballerina, 1939, sight: 18¾x22" in ornate giltwood 20x23" fr...**2,500.00**
Departure, 1941, 21x17" **1,495.00**
Fishbowl, 1925, G..**900.00**
He Loves Me, He Loves Me Not, 1926, 19x16", VG **1,265.00**
Lady of the Camelias, 1927, oval: 17x21", VG.......................**1,600.00**
Peonies, 1935, 14x16¾", VG **1,600.00**
Rainbow, 1930, 33x23", EX **5,950.00**
Sofa, 1937, 18½x26½"+fr..**5,500.00**
Speed, 1933, 22x31", EX **3,950.00**
View Over Paris, 1920, 13x20"...**2,900.00**
Waltz Echoes, 1938, 24x24", VG **2,875.00**

Kurz and Allison

Louis Kurz founded the Chicago Lithograph Company in 1833. Among his most notable works were a series of thirty-six Civil War scenes and one hundred illustrations of Chicago architecture. His company was destroyed in the Great Fire of 1871, and in 1880 Kurz formed a partnership with Alexander Allison, an engraver. Until both retired in 1903, they produced hundreds of lithographs in color as well as black and white.

Note: Large folio prints measure 17½" x 25" (image size).

Battle of Antietam, 1888, lg folio **325.00**
Battle of Atlanta, 1888, lg folio **450.00**
Battle of Bunker Hill, Chicago, 1880s, lg folio **700.00**
Battle of Cedar Creek, 1890, lg folio **425.00**
Battle of Champion Hills, Chicago, 1887, lg folio...................**400.00**
Battle of Chancellorsville, 1889, lg folio................................**425.00**
Battle of Franklin, 1891, lg folio **350.00**
Battle of Opequan or Winchester VA, 1893, lg folio...............**325.00**
Gen Ambrose P Hill, Confederate officer, 1865, 28½x22" **250.00**
Gen Geo G Meade, Union officer, 1865, 28¼x22" **250.00**

Gen. G.T. Beauregard, 1865, 28¼x22", EX, $250.00.

Gen Joseph Hooker, Union officer, 1865, 28¼x22" **250.00**
Maj Gen Sterling Price, Confederate officer, 1865, 28¼x22" **250.00**
Siege of Vicksburg, 1888, lg folio...**325.00**

Max, Peter

Born in Germany in 1937, Peter Max came to the United States in 1953 where he later studied art in New York City. His work is colorful and his genre psychedelic. He is a prolific artist, best known for his designs from the '60s and '70s that typified the 'hippie' movement.

Across the Room, lithograph on Arches, 1982, 21x30" **3,000.00**
Angel, serigraph on Fabiano rosa, 1978, 29¾x22" **3,750.00**
Flower at Sea, serigraph on Arches, 1979, 23x30"...................**3,250.00**
In His Garden, lithograph on Arches, 1980, 21½x26⅜" **2,750.00**
Monk & Vase, lithograph on Arches, 1980, 26⅝x21½" **3,500.00**

Pink Silver Flyer, serigraph on Arches, 1981, 22x30" **2,750.00**
Summer Season, serigraph on Arches, 1979, 23x30"................**3,500.00**
76 Jumper, serigraph on Arches, 1975, 26x36" **14,000.00**

McKenney and Hall

Ahyouwaigho, Chief of 6 Nations, 1845, 8½x6½" **415.00**
Ca-Ta-He-Cas-Sa, Black Hoof...Shawnee, Biddle, 1837, full sheet..**375.00**
Foke-Luste-Hajo, Bowen, sight: 9¾x5¾" **250.00**
John Ridge, a Cherokee, FW Greenough, 1838, sight: 17¾x11⅞"..**375.00**
Ka-Ta-Wa-Be-Da, Chippewa Chief, Bowen, 1841, full sheet......**350.00**
Kish-Ke-Kosh, a Fox Brave, Rice, Rutter & Co, sight: 9x5⅝" **250.00**
Lap-Pa-Win-Soe, Delaware Chief, Biddle, 1837, full sheet.........**250.00**
Little Crow, Sioux Chief, Greenough, 1838, lg folio..................**200.00**
Major Ridge, a Cherokee Chief, JT Bowen, 1837, sight: 17¾x11⅞"..**375.00**
Micanopy, Bown, 9¾x5¾"..**250.00**
Nah-Et-Luc-Hopie (Little Doctor), Rice & Clark, 1843, full sheet..**395.00**
O-Hya-Wa-Mince-kee, Chippewa chief, Rice & Clark, 1843, 19x13¼"...**600.00**
Pa-She-Nine, Chippewa chief, Rice & Clark, 1843, 19x13¼" ...**800.00**
Peah-Mas-Ka, Musquawkee Chief, Greenough, 1836, full sheet.**295.00**
Push-Ma-Ta-Ha, EC Biddle, 1833, sight: 14¾x9½" **200.00**
Qua-Ta-Wa-Pea, Shawnee Chief, Greenough, 1838, full sheet...**395.00**
Rant-Che-Wai-Me, Female Flying Pigeon; Greenough, 1838, full sheet ...**450.00**
Red Jacket, EC Biddle, 1834, sight: 14¾x9½" **200.00**
Red Jacket, wearing 1792 Washington Peace Medal, lg folio...**2,000.00**
Takacon, Biddle, 1841, sight 17x12" **715.00**

Prang, Louis

Antietam, battle scene, 1887, 17x23½" **350.00**
Battle of Kenesaw Mountain, battle scene, 1887, 17x23½" **400.00**
Battle of Manilla, colorful sea battle, 1896, 16x20" **125.00**
Battle of Port Hudson, lg folio **170.00**
Harvest Mice, mice among grasses, 1888, 12x9" **30.00**
Miss Christmas, w/greenery, birds in foreground, 1898, 10x8" **125.00**
Miss Patty, girl in bl w/flowers in flower garden, 1895, 10x8"+fr ..**125.00**
Piper & Pair of Nutcrackers, undated, 10x12"+fr.........................**95.00**
Siege of Vicksburg, ca 1888, 15x21½" **425.00**

Yard Longs

Values for yard-long prints are given for examples in near mint condition, full length, nicely framed, and with the original glass. To learn more about this popular area of collector interest, we recommend *Those Wonderful Yard-Long Prints and More*, *More Wonderful Yard-Long Prints, Book 2*, and *Yard-Long Prints, Book 3*, by our advisors Bill and June Keagy, and Charles and Joan Rhoden. They are listed in the Directory under Indiana and Illinois respectively. A word of caution: Watch for reproductions; know your dealer.

At the North Pole, Jos Hoover & Son, Philadelphia, c 1904......**350.00**
Clay, Robinson & Co's Am Beauty Souvenir, ad & 1910 calendar on bk...**450.00**
Dogwood & Violets, Paul DeLongpre..**300.00**
Easter Greetings, Paul DeLongpre, c 1894 ....**425.00**
Girl w/the Laughing Eyes, c 1910 ....**300.00**
Happy Family, 9 monkeys play/relax, 3rd in series, #1037, c 1904.....**400.00**
In Sunny Africa, Jos Hoover & Sons, Philadelphia, #1038, c 1904 ..**450.00**
Kittens w/mother, 8 kittens shown, 1 w/book, 1 w/spool............**275.00**
Lady on balcony facing moonlit waters, flower in hand **300.00**
Morning Glories, Maud Humphrey, c 1892................................**400.00**
Pabst Am Girl, in muted shades of tangerine/yel/gr, 1914 calendar ..**400.00**
Pabst Extract Indian 1906 calendar, Hiawatha's Wooing poem on bk...**500.00**
Pabst Malt Extract Rose Girl, 1909 calendar at bottom **400.00**
Pompeian, attractive couple before grandfather clock, 1915 calendar ...**325.00**

Pompeian art panel, irresistible, Clement Donshea, dtd 1930.....**350.00**
Pompeian by Forbes, M Pickford in bl, sgn Sincerely..., 1916 calendar...**400.00**
Selz Good Shoes, sgn Earl Chambers, 1929 calendar at bottom .**350.00**
Shower of Roses, child at top spilling roses to child below, c 1893 ..**400.00**
Yard of Cherries & Flowers, LeRoy................................**250.00**
4 kittens climbing tree, Helena Maguire **350.00**

Purinton

Founded in 1936 in Wellsville, Ohio, Purinton Pottery relocated in 1941 in Shippenville, Pennsylvania, and began producing hand-painted wares that are today attracting the interest of collectors of 'country-type' dinnerware. Using bold brush strokes of vivid color, simple yet attractive patterns such as Apple, Fruit, Tea Rose, and Pennsylvania Dutch were manufactured in tableware sets and accessory pieces. For more information we recommend *Purinton Pottery* by Susan Morris, our advisor for this category; she is listed in the Directory under Washington.

Ashtray, Apple, center hdl, 5½".......................................**40.00**
Baker, Maywood, 7"..**25.00**
Baker, Turquoise, 7" dia..**45.00**
Bean pot, Mountain Rose, 4½"..**65.00**
Bean pot, Provincial Fruit, w/warming stand, 5¾", 9" w/stand......**65.00**
Biscuit jar, Ivy - Red Blossom, w/lid, 8".....................**55.00**
Bottles, oil & vinegar; Apple, 1-pt, 9½", pr....................**95.00**
Bottles, oil & vinegar; Daisy, 1-pt, 9½", pr....................**75.00**
Bowl, cereal; Normandy Plaid, 5¼"...............................**10.00**
Bowl, cereal; Provincial Fruit, 5¼"................................**10.00**
Bowl, fruit; Normandy Plaid, 12"....................................**35.00**
Bowl, fruit; Petals, 12"..**50.00**
Bowl, fruit; Saraband, 12"..**25.00**
Bowl, range; Grapes, w/lid, 5½".....................................**45.00**
Bowl, salad; Maywood, 11"...**25.00**
Bowl, vegetable; Chartreuse, open, 8½".........................**30.00**
Bowl, vegetable; Intaglio, divided, 10½".........................**30.00**
Bowl, vegetable; Pennsylvania Dutch, divided, 10½"...................**50.00**
Bowl, vegetable; Tea Rose, open, 8½"...........................**40.00**
Butter dish, Apple, 6½"...**65.00**
Candle holder, Intaglio style, star shaped, 6"................**65.00**
Candle holder, Peasant Lady, sgn, minimum value....................**500.00**
Candy dish, Apple, 5¾"..**75.00**
Canister, Apple, half-oval, 5½"...**65.00**
Canister, Fruit, rnd, wooden lid, 7½"...............................**65.00**
Cocktail dish, Desert Flower, 3-D sea horse, bowl ea side, 12"......**75.00**
Coffee server, Seafoam, 9"...**125.00**
Coffeepot, Fruit, drip style, 8-cup, 11"...........................**85.00**
Coffeepot, Fruit, 8-cup, 8"..**65.00**
Coffeepot, Ivy - Red Blossom, 8"...................................**65.00**
Coffeepot, Petals, 8-cup, 8"...**75.00**
Cookie jar, Fruit, red trim, oval, 9"................................**60.00**
Cookie jar, Heather Plaid, oval, 9½"..............................**60.00**
Cookie jar, Normandy Plaid, oval, 9½"..........................**60.00**
Covered dish, Mountain Rose, 9" L.................................**75.00**
Covered dish, Saraband, 9" L..**35.00**
Creamer, Ivy - Yellow Blossom, 3½".................................**15.00**
Creamer & sugar bowl, Chartreuse, mini........................**40.00**
Cup, Turquoise, 2¼x4" dia...**55.00**
Cup & saucer, Maywood, 2½" & 5½"............................**15.00**
Cup & saucer, Petals, 2½" & 5½".................................**22.00**
Decanter, Intaglio, mini, 5"...**35.00**
Dish, jam & jelly; Intaglio, 5½"......................................**40.00**
Grease jar, Fruit, labeled Fats, cobalt trim, 5½".............**60.00**
Grease jar, Normandy Plaid, w/lid, 5½".........................**60.00**

Honey jug, Petals, 6¼"...**45.00**
Honey jug, Shooting Stars, 6¼"......................................**35.00**
Jardiniere, Leaves, 5"...**25.00**
Jardiniere, Windflower, 5"...**30.00**
Jug, Dutch; Fruit, 2-pt, 5¾"...**25.00**

Jug pitcher, Heather Plaid, five-pint, $75.00. (Photo courtesy Susan Morris)

Jug, Kent; Mountain Rose, 1-pt, 4½" **45.00**
Jug, Rebecca; Pennsylvania Dutch, 7½"...........................**75.00**
Marmalade, Mountain Rose, 4½"......................................**65.00**
Mug, Apple, 8-oz, 4"...**35.00**
Mug, beer; Palm Tree, 16-oz, 4¾"..................................**85.00**
Mug, juice; Apple, 6-oz, 2½"...**20.00**
Mug, juice; Fruit, 6-oz, 2½"..**15.00**
Mug, Kent; Normandy Plaid, 1-pt, 4½"...........................**30.00**
Mug, Normandy Plaid, 8-oz, 4"..**25.00**
Pickle dish, Pineapple, sponged edge, 6" **35.00**
Pitcher, beverage; Ivy - Red Blossom, 2-pt, 6¼"..............**55.00**
Pitcher, Petals, 2-pt, 6¼'..**75.00**
Planter, Leaves, 3"..**30.00**
Planter, Ming Tree, 5"..**35.00**
Planter, Tea Rose, 5"...**65.00**
Plate, breakfast; Crescent Flower, 8½"............................**35.00**
Plate, breakfast; Peasant Garden, 8½"...........................**100.00**
Plate, chop; Fruit, 12"...**45.00**
Plate, dinner; Intaglio, 9¾"...**15.00**
Plate, dinner; Saraband, 9¾"..**8.00**
Plate, Intaglio, 12'...**30.00**
Plate, lap; Crescent Flower, 8½".....................................**35.00**
Platr, dinner; Palm Tree, 9¾"...**125.00**
Platter, grill; Apple, 12"...**45.00**
Platter, grill; Chartreuse, 12"..**30.00**
Platter, meat; Apple, 12"..**55.00**
Platter, meat; Ming Tree, 12"..**65.00**
Platter, meat; Seafoam, 12"...**50.00**
Relish, Fruit, 3-part, pottery hdl, 10"..............................**55.00**
Relish, Mountain Rose, 3-part, center ring hdl, 10" **75.00**
Shakers, Apple, range style, 4", pr..................................**50.00**
Shakers, Ivy - Red Blossom, jug style, 2½", pr................**20.00**
Shakers, Peasant Garden, jug style, 2½", pr...................**65.00**
Shakers, Seafoam, 3", pr...**55.00**
Shakers, stacking; Apple, 2¼", pr....................................**50.00**
Sugar bowl, Heather Plaid, w/lid, 4"................................**30.00**
Teapot, Apple, 2-cup, 5"..**40.00**
Teapot, Maywood, 6-cup, 6½"...**45.00**
Teapot, Mountain Rose, 4-cup, 5"....................................**75.00**
Teapot, Saraband, 6-cup, 6½"...**40.00**
Tidbit, Intaglio, 10"...**45.00**
Tray, roll; Apple, 11"...**35.00**
Tray, roll; Tea Rose, 11"...**50.00**
Tumbler, Apple, 12-oz, 5"..**20.00**
Tumbler, Mountain Rose, 12-oz, 5"..................................**35.00**
Tumbler, Provincial Fruit, 12-oz, 5".................................**20.00**

TV lamp, Red Feather, 8½" 75.00
Vase, cornucopia; Ivy - Red Blossom, 6" 25.00
Vase, pillow; Maywood, NAPCO mold, 6¾" 25.00
Vase, Shooting Star, 5" 25.00
Wall pocket, Chartreuse, 3½" 35.00
Wall pocket, Heather Plaid, 3½" 35.00
Wall pocket, Sunny, 3½" 40.00

Purses

Purses from the early 1800s are often decorated with small, brightly colored glass beads. Cut steel beads were popular in the 1840s and remained stylish until about 1930. Purses made of woven mesh date back to the 1820s. Chain-link mesh came into usage in the 1890s, followed by the enamel mesh bags carried by the flappers in the 1920s. Purses are divided into several categories by (a) construction techniques — whether beaded, embroidered, or a type of needlework; (b) material — fabric or metal; and (c) design and style. Condition is very important. Watch for dry, brittle leather or fragile material. For those interested in learning more, we recommend *Antique Purses, A History, Identification, and Value Guide, Second Edition,* by Richard Holiner; *More Beautiful Purses,* and *Combs and Purses,* both by Evelyn Haertigi of Carmel, California; and *Ladies Vintage Accessories* by LaRu Johnson Bruton. An interesting related book is *Vintage Contemporary Purse Accessories* by Roselyn Gerson. Our advisor for this category is Veronica Trainer; she is listed in the Directory under Ohio. See also Plastics.

Key: W&D — Whiting & Davis

Beaded, Arabesque orange, gr & bl decor, Fr, 1930s, 13x8½" ..1,955.00
Beaded, blk, drawstring, Fr, 1920-30, 10x5" 460.00
Beaded, blk & cut steel, checkered design, Fr, 1920-30, 11x9" ...515.00
Beaded, blk & cut steel, silver strips, fringe, Fr, 1920-30, 9x7" ...315.00
Beaded, blk & cut steel miser type w/floral metal slides, Fr, 36" L 865.00
Beaded, floral basket & ribbon, fringe, brass fr w/faux jewels, 11x6" ..575.00
Beaded, floral stripes, fringe, brass fr w/enamel & faux gems, 13x8" ..575.00
Beaded, geometrics, fringe, elephant motif fr, Fr, 1920-30, 6x5" .115.00
Beaded, gold & silver, braided triangular fringe, Fr, 1920-30, 10x5" ..260.00
Beaded, gold & silver geometrics w/tassels, Fr, 1920-30, 9½x5" .515.00
Beaded, gold & silver paisley, fringe, pine-cone brass fr, 12x7½" ..745.00
Beaded, gr & silver Deco design, silver fringe, Fr, 1920-30, 9x6" ..400.00
Beaded, mc fleur-de-lis, amber cabochons in fr, Fr, 1920-30, 7x5" .345.00
Beaded, mc floral, fringe, gilt brass openwork fr w/faux pearls, 11x6" ...400.00
Beaded, mc floral, fringe, ornate brass fr w/mc faux jewels, 15x8" .1,380.00
Beaded, mc floral, fringed saddle style, Fr, 1920-30, 14x7½" 400.00
Beaded, mc floral, jeweled brass fr, fringe, 1920s, 10x5½" 350.00
Beaded, mc floral, jeweled gilt fr & clasp, Fr, 1920-30, 12x9" ...1,850.00
Beaded, mc flower garden, enameled fr w/faux jewels, 11x7" 575.00
Beaded, mc geometrics, fringe, emb dmns on brass fr, 13x7" 635.00
Beaded, mc geometrics, fringe, foliate brass fr, 7x11" 485.00
Beaded, mc geometrics, fringe, SP openwork fr w/faux jewels, 11x6" ...460.00
Beaded, mc red carnation design, ornate gilt fr, Fr, 1920-30, 11x7" .865.00
Beaded, mc urn/etc on bl, jeweled fr & clasp, Fr, 1920-30, 8x6" ...1,100.00
Beaded, silver & blk floral, triple fringe, drawstring, 9x6½" 460.00
Beaded, silver w/blk crochet, fringe, SP floral fr, 6½x4½" 345.00
Beaded, silver w/gold floral, jeweled clasp, tassels, Fr, 8½x5½" ..635.00
Beaded, silver w/kid leather bk, fringe, SP foliate fr, 5½" dia......315.00
Beaded, silver w/mc design, jeweled fr, mc fringe, Fr, 1920-30, 10x9" 2,415.00
Beaded, swans scene, scalloped/fringed, jeweled fr, Fr, 1920-30, 11x6" .1,600.00
Beaded, teal & gold paisley, fringe, plain brass fr, 11x6" 515.00
Beaded, wht irid w/gold trim, Nini Ricci, 1970s, 7½x5¾" 95.00
Cut steel loopy fringe, blk Deco design, Fr, 1920-30, 9½x7" 200.00
Damask brocade, gold embr flowers, trapezoidal, 1950s, 12" 25.00

Fabric, navy w/cvd/jeweled celluloid fr, Guild Orig, 1940s, 9½x9" ..145.00
Leather, alligator, flap w/glass eyes, Cuba, 1950s, 8½x7½" 125.00
Leather, Gothic style w/brass studs & clasp, Coblentz, 6x7½" 75.00
Leather, lizard, gilt brass fittings, Madwed, 1940s, 8x8x2½" 40.00
Leather, lizard, 2-tone metal fr, shoulder strap, Rodo, 5¾x5½" 95.00
Lucite, blk picnic basket type w/brass clasp, 1950s, 3½x8½" 110.00
Lucite, blk w/gold confetti, clear cvd top, brass clasp, 3½x6¾" ..225.00
Mesh, abstract flowers, scalloped/fringed, W&D fr, 8¾x6½" 170.00
Mesh, butterfly & flowers, Mandalian fr, dangles, 6¾x4" 110.00
Mesh, geometric, blk & gold, gold Mandalian fr, 6x3½" 70.00
Mesh, geometric, lav & wht, enameled W&D fr, 6¾x4" 85.00
Mesh, geometric, mc, enamel W&D fr, 6¾x3¾" 110.00
Mesh, geometric design, mc, Mandalian fr, bead drops, 8x4" 115.00
Mesh, gold dmns, scalloped, gold Mandalian fr, 6½x3½" 70.00
Mesh, gold tight weave, gold/enamel W&D fr, 5¾x5" 70.00
Mesh, mc floral, Mandalian fr, fringe, 6½x3¼" 75.00
Mesh, peacocks, mc on wht, Mandalian invt V fr, fringe, 7¾x3¾" ..125.00
Patent leather faux alligator, gold-tone fr, strap hdl, Lennos, 10x8" 95.00
Silk, mc floral w/gold threads, snap closure, 1940s, 5x7" 65.00
Silk faille w/embr flowers/metallic threads, gold-tone fr, 1910s, 8x9" ...225.00
Tapestry, floral w/gold-tone closure, loop hdl, 1950s 45.00
Vinyl, clear clutch w/gold confetti, brass fr, 1950s, 4½x9" 25.00
Wooden basketweave, pnt golf theme, lined, Caro Nan, 8½x6¼" ..65.00

Puzzles

'Jigsaw' puzzles have been around almost as long as games. The first examples were handcrafted from wood, and they are extremely difficult to find. Most of the early examples featured moral subjects just as the board games did. By the 1890s jigsaw puzzles had become a major form of home entertainment. During the Depression years jigsaw puzzles were set up on card tables in almost every home. The early wood examples are the most valuable.

Cube puzzles, or blocks, were often made by the same companies as the board games. Again, early examples display the finest quality lithography. While all subjects are collectible, some (such as Santa blocks) often command prices higher than games from the same period. In the miscellaneous subcategory below, all listing are for jigsaw puzzles (that are complete) unless noted otherwise.

Personalities, Movies, and TV Shows

Little King on Roller Skates, Simon & Schuster, 1933, complete in box, EX, from $125.00 to $175.00. (Photo courtesy Dunbar Gallery)

Aquaman, jigsaw, Whitman, 1968, 100 pcs, MIB 50.00
Batman, jigsaw, Whitman, 1966, 150 pcs, NMIB 30.00
Bionic Woman, fr-tray, APC, 1976, MIP, from $35 to 45.00
Brady Bunch, fr-tray, Whitman #4558, EX 45.00
Captain America, jigsaw, Whitman, 1976, NMIB 30.00
David Cassidy, jigsaw, APC, 1972, MIB, from $35 to 35.00
Donald Duck, jigsaw, Whitman, 1965, 100 pcs, MIB (sealed) 40.00
Eight Is Enough, jigsaw, APC, 1978, MIB 25.00
Fantastic Four, jigsaw, Third Eye, 1971, 500 pcs, MIB................100.00

Farrah Fawcett, jigsaw, APC, 1977, 405 pcs, MIB, from $35 to **40.00**
Green Hornet, fr-tray, Whitman, 1966, set of 4, MIB, from $100 to....**125.00**
HR Pufnstuf, fr-tray, Whitman #4507, 1970, Whitchiepooh's Boat, NM+ ...**35.00**
Jonny Quest, jigsaw, Milton Bradley, 1964, Rescued, EXIB...........**80.00**
Josie & the Pussycats, jigsaw, HG Toys, 1976, MIB **30.00**
KISS, jigsaw, Casse-Tete, 1977, NMIB **25.00**
Liddle Kiddles, fr-tray, Whitman, 1966, M..................................**55.00**
Ludwig Von Drake, jigsaw, Whitman Jr, 1962, 70 pcs, EXIB.........**60.00**
Marvel Super Heroes, jigsaw, Milton Bradley, 1966, 100 pcs, MIB ..**125.00**
Mighty Heroes, fr-tray, Whitman, 1967, M..................................**50.00**
Munsters, jigsaw, Whitman, 1965, 100 pcs, EXIB........................**35.00**
Nancy Drew, jigsaw, APC, 1970s, NM (NM canister)...................**30.00**
Patty Duke, jigsaw, Whitman Jr, 1963, 100 pcs............................**45.00**
Raggedy Ann, fr-tray, Milton Bradley, 1955, NM, from $25 to **35.00**
Roger Ramjet, fr-tray, Whitman, 1966, M...................................**75.00**
Six Million Dollar Man, fr-tray, APC, 1976, MIP.........................**35.00**
Skippy, jigsaw, Consolidated Paper, 1933, set of 3, M (EX box) .**125.00**
Star Wars, jigsaw, Kenner, 1977, Victory Celebration, MIB (sealed)...**25.00**
Starsky & Hutch, jigsaw, HG Toys, 1976, MIB, from $25 to.........**30.00**
Superman, jigsaw, Saalfield/Superman Inc, 1939, set of 6, EXIB ..**1,000.00**
Thunderbirds, jigsaw, Whitman, 1968, EXIB **25.00**
Tom & Jerry, fr-tray, 1965, NM..**20.00**
Uncle Scrooge, jigsaw, Western, 100 lg pcs, MIB (sealed).............**40.00**
Underdog, jigsaw, Whitman, 1975, 100 pcs, MIB.......................**25.00**
Welcome Back Kotter, fr-tray, Whitman, 1977, Kotter portrait, MIP ...**12.50**
Woodsy Owl, jigsaw, Whitman, 1976, 125 pcs, circular, EXIB......**25.00**

Miscellaneous

All on a Summer's Day, plywood, Tuck/Zag-Zaw, 1930s, EXIB ...**140.00**
Bearing the Brunt, plywood, FAO Schwarz, 1950s, EXIB **125.00**
Cathedral of Amiens, plywood, Parker Bros/Pastime, 1930-40, EXIB..**175.00**
Falls at Yellowstone, plywood, J Straus, 1950-60, EXIB...............**125.00**
Game Robber, plywood, Puzzle Port, 1930s-40s, EXIB **300.00**
Geo Washington at Valley Forge, plywood, L Clift/Miloy, 1930s, EXIB...**120.00**
Hazy Hills, plywood, Parker Bros/Pastime, 1950s, EXIB.............**450.00**
Interrupted Supper, plywood, Fuller Novelty, EXIB......................**75.00**
Limit of Wind & Sail, plywood, F Bell, 1930s, EXIB...................**65.00**
Mount Holy Cross, plywood, Sat-Put, 1930s, EXIB.....................**125.00**
Mountain Splendor, cb, Palatial, 1930s, EXIB **15.00**
Nature's Splendor, plywood, Galles, 1930s, EXIB **75.00**
Oven at Bar Harbor, plywood, Hayes/JMH Woodcraft, 1940s, EXIB..**175.00**
Progress of Democracy, plywood, A Lowell, 1920-30, EXIB.........**50.00**
Quiet Retreat, plywood, Atlantic/Kingsbridge, 1950-60, EXIB **30.00**
Raking the Hay, plywood, Parker Bros, early 1900s, EXIB.............**85.00**
Shepherd w/Flock (Untitled), plywood, Parker Bros, EXIB.........**100.00**
There Are Fish Dad, plywood, J Straus, 1950s, EXIB **50.00**
US Map, plywood, Parker Bros, 1915, EX (rpl box) **20.00**
Venice at Eventide, plywood, J Straus, 1930s, EXIB.....................**25.00**
Washington Goes to Church, plywood, Hawkes, 1930s, EX (EX envelope) ...**120.00**
Winter, plywood, Parker Bros, 1938, EXIB.................................**200.00**

Pyrography

Pyrography, also known as wood burning, Flemish art, or poker work, is the art of burning designs into wood or leather and has been practiced over the centuries in many countries.

In the late 1800s pyrography became the hot new hobby for thousands of Americans who burned designs inspired by the popular artists of the day including Mucha, Gibson, Fisher, and Corbett. Thousands of wooden boxes, wall plaques, novelties, and pieces of furniture that they purchased from local general stores or from mail-order catalogs were burned and painted. These pieces were manufactured by companies such

as The Flemish Art Company of New York and Thayer & Chandler of Chicago, who printed the designs on wood for the pyrographers to burn.

This Victorian fad developed into a new form of artistic expression as the individually burned and painted pieces reflected the personality of the pyrographers. The more adventurous started to burn between the lines and developed a style of 'allover burning' that today is known as pyromania. Others not only created their own designs but even made the pieces to be decorated. Both these developments are particularly valued today as true examples of American folk art.

By the 1930s its popularity had declined. Like Mission furniture, it was neglected by generations of collectors and dealers. The recent appreciation of Victoriana, the Arts and Crafts Movement, the American West, and the popularity of turn-of-the-century graphic art has rekindled interest in pyrography which embraces all these styles.

An informative book, *The Burning Passion — Antique and Collectible Pyrography*, by Carole and Richard Smyth, our advisors for this category, is currently available from the authors; they are listed in the Directory under New York.

Key: hb — hand burned

Bank, mechanical, boy next to house, primitive folk art, c 1940 ....**105.00**
Bedroom set, hb/pnt, Wm Rogers/Forusville PA, 1905-07, 3-pc..**4,000.00**
Book rack, hb/pnt girl w/book, 5¾" W, extends to 15¾" L.........**150.00**
Box, flatware; factory burned/pnt poinsettias, Rogers, 9x11x5"...**195.00**
Box, floral decor, stamped design, 14½" sq....................................**40.00**
Box, lady w/flowing hair, Flemish Art Co, 1909, 11¼x4¼" **120.00**
Box, Miller Bros Steel Pens, 1900, stamped to look hb, 7" L, +contents ..**45.00**
Catalog, Thayer-Chandler, Chicago, 1904, 92 pgs, 12 in full color....**27.00**
Chair-table, hb/pnt poinsettias, Rest-Ye... on chair bk, EX **950.00**
Checker/backgammon brd, red & gr decor/glass bead insets, 30x15" ..**1,550.00**
Chest, blanket; hb/pnt swans/lady's head/flowers/etc, ca 1890 ....**850.00**
Chest, medicine; hb/pnt Nouveau lady & vines, wall mt............**450.00**
Coat hanger, hb/pnt poppies & leaves, Mother Dearest **80.00**
Cue holder, hb pool-hall scene, folk art, unique **650.00**
Egg cup, hb/pnt, pr **60.00**
Etching set, Snow White, Disney/Marks, 1938, electric pen, complete..**175.00**
Footstool, hb/pnt allover w/owl/branches/leaves...........................**125.00**
Frame, hb/pnt cherries, standing type, 7½x6", EX **85.00**
Frame, hb/pnt chrysanthemums, Thayer-Chandler, 10½x8", EX ..**85.00**
Frame, hb/pnt flower garland, Thayer-Chandler, 8" dia...............**85.00**
Frame, owls in tree, 2 Is Company, 2 oval cutouts.......................**145.00**
Gameboard, hb/pnt ea side/edges, Flemish Art, 15" sq (open)....**200.00**
Knife rack, hb Lizzie Borden w/axe, 5 hooks below, rare **550.00**
Magazine stand, 4-shelf, burned/pnt florals, Thayer-Chandler, 48" ..**800.00**

Match holders, Gibson-type girl with flowers, hand burned with painted flowers and hair bow, 5¾x4", EX, $95.00; Rising sun on back, Help Yourself burned on lid, painted details, 4¾x4", EX, $95.00; Uncle Sam, A Match for All, burned details, faded paint, 10¾x5¾", $185.00. (Photo courtesy Carole and Richard Smyth)

Mirror, hand; hb/pnt lady's head w/flowing hair, 13¼x6¾" **180.00**
Nut bowl, hb/pnt squirrel on branch, Flemish Art Co #816, 5"...**65.00**
Panel, basswood, hb/pnt orange, Thayer-Chandler, 16x30" **465.00**
Panel, hb after painting: To the Feast, minor gold, 9x34" **500.00**
Pedestal, hb/pnt Nouveau flowers & vines, 45" **400.00**

Plaque, cvd/hb/pnt strawberry basket, 3-ply, 12" dia **70.00**
Plaque, girl bathing puppies, #854, 14½" **125.00**
Plaque, hb orange cat w/bow, paper 1912 calendar, 5¾" dia **50.00**
Plaque, Nouveau lady w/cherries, 19½" **150.00**
Plaque, Oddfellows, hb I O O F in center, early 1900s, 16x10".....**87.00**
Plaque, Victorian couple, Parting by a Wall & flowers.................**145.00**
Ribbon holder, hb/pnt Sunbonnet babies (3), 5x12" **160.00**
Screen, birds & foliage, mc pnt, 3-part, 63x73" **400.00**
Spoon holder, geometric florals, wall hanging, 1915, 10x8" **45.00**
Tie rack, factory stamp, HP soldier/nurse/sailor, WWI motto **125.00**

Quezal

The Quezal Art Glass and Decorating Company of Brooklyn, New York, was founded in 1901 by Martin Bach. A former Tiffany employee, Bach's glass closely resembled that of his former employer. Most pieces were signed 'Quezal,' a name taken from a Central American bird. After Bach's death in 1920, his son-in-law, Conrad Vohlsing, continued to produce a Quezal-type glass in Elmhurst, New York, which he marked 'Lustre Art Glass.' Examples listed here are signed unless noted otherwise.

Cup & saucer, gold irid w/purple highlights, 2½", 4½" **950.00**
Dish, nut; gold irid w/bl-gold int, ribbed w/trifold top, 1½x3½".**250.00**
Parfait, gold w/red & bl irid, conical, disk ft, 5½", set of 6 ......**1,725.00**
Salt cellar, irid, ribbed w/rolled-over rim, 1x3" **250.00**
Shade, feathers, cream on gold, cylindrical, 5"............................**275.00**
Shade, hearts/vines, gr on alabaster, overall threading, 5½" **175.00**
Shade, lily; feathers, cream/gr on gold, 5x5¼" **175.00**
Shade, lily; feathers, gr pastel & gold, gold int, 5" **250.00**
Shade, lily; feathers, gr w/gold on wht, gold int, 4¾", 5 for....**4,000.00**
Vase, bl irid, dbl bulb, stick neck, 9" **1,200.00**
Vase, bl irid, shouldered w/short flared neck, 7¼" **850.00**
Vase, bud; gold, slim cone, tilted/flared rim; metal ft w/flowers, 13"..**1,400.00**
Vase, deep bl w/butterfly irid, waisted neck, 6¾x3½" **800.00**
Vase, feathers, gold/gr on ivory, gold int, trumpet w/ruffle rim, 6" ...**1,850.00**
Vase, feathers (2-layer, 1 red irid w/gold) on cream, squat bottle, 7"..**4,500.00**
Vase, feathers w/hooked band at tips, yel/gr/gold on ivory, #B846, 8"...**2,000.00**
Vase, feathers/swirls, gr/opal/gold, bottle w/flared gold rim, 11" **4,200.00**

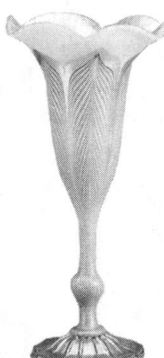

Vase, floriform; feathers, green on opal, gold iridescent domed foot, scalloped rim, bulbed stem, 8¾", $3,450.00. (Photo courtesy Skinner Auctions, Inc.)

Vase, floriform; gold irid, ball on tapered stem, 6-petal top, 5¾" ...**650.00**
Vase, floriform; gold w/red & bl irid, folded/flared rim, 4" **1,200.00**
Vase, gold irid, bulb top on elongated stem, disc ft, 9½"..........**1,450.00**
Vase, gold irid, bulb w/sm neck, 4½" **450.00**
Vase, gold irid, trumpet w/wide ruffled rim, rnd ft w/wafer, 5½" .**825.00**
Vase, gold irid, 12 teardrops on horizontal threading, #C-122, 2x4"..**1,400.00**
Vase, gold irid w/overall opal coils, shouldered, rare label, 10" ...**3,000.00**
Vase, gr/bl irid to dk bl irid, trumpet form w/3-lobe rim & bun ft, 6" ..**1,000.00**
Vase, lily; gold irid, trifold rim, 5¾" **950.00**

Quilts

Quilts, while made of necessity, nevertheless represent an art form which expresses the character and the personality of the designer. During the seventeenth and eighteenth centuries, quilts were considered a necessary part of a bride's hope chest; the traditional number required to be properly endowed for marriage was a 'baker's dozen'! American colonial quilts reflect the English and French taste of our ancestors. They would include the classifications known as Lindsey-Woolsey and the central medallion appliqué quilts fashioned from imported copper-plate printed fabrics.

By 1829 spare time was slightly more available, so women gathered in quilting bees. This not only was a way of sharing the work but also gave them the opportunity to show off their best handiwork. The hand-dyed and pieced quilts emerged, and they are now known as sampler, album, and friendship quilts. By 1845 American printed fabric was available.

In 1793 Eli Whitney developed the cotton gin; as a result, textile production in America became industrialized. Soon inexpensive fabrics were readily available, and ladies were able to choose from colorful prints and solids to add contrast to their work. Both pieced and appliquéd work became popular.

Pieced quilts were considered utilitarian, while appliquéd quilts were shown with pride of accomplishment at the fair or used when itinerant preachers traveled through and stayed for a visit. Today many collectors prize pieced quilts and their intricate geometric patterns above all other types. Many of these designs were given names: Daisy and Oak Leaf, Grandmother's Flower Garden, Log Cabin, and Ocean Wave are only a few. Appliquéd quilts involved stitching one piece — carefully cut into a specific form such as a leaf, a flower, or a stylized device — onto either a large one-piece ground fabric or an individual block. Often the background fabric was quilted in a decorative pattern such as a wreath or medallions.

Amish women scorned printed calicos as 'worldly' and instead used colorful blocks set with black fabrics to produce a stunning pieced effect. To show their reverence for God, the Amish would often include a 'superstition' block which represented the 'imperfection' of Man!

One of the most valuable quilts in existence is the Baltimore album quilt. Made between 1840 and 1860 only three hundred or so still exist today. They have been known to fetch over $100,000.00 at prominent auction houses in New York City. Usually each block features elaborate appliqué work such as a basket of flowers, patriotic flags and eagles, the Oddfellow's heart in hand, etc. The border can be sawtooth, meandering, or swags and tassels.

During the Victorian period the crazy quilt emerged. This style became the most popular quilt ever in terms of sheer numbers produced and popularity. The crazy quilt was formed by random pieces put together following no organized lines and was embellished by elaborate embroidery stitches. Fabrics of choice were brocades, silks, and velvets.

Another type of quilting, highly prized and rare today, is trapunto. These quilts were made by first stitching the outline of the design onto a solid sheet of fabric which was backed with a second having a much looser weave. White was often favored, but color was sometimes used for accent. The design (grapes, flowers, leaves, etc.) was padded through openings made by separating the loose weave of the underneath fabric; a backing was added and the three layers quilted as one.

Besides condition, value is judged on intricacy of pattern, color effect, and craftsmanship. Examine the stitching. Quality quilts have from ten to twelve stitches to the inch. A stitch is defined as any time a needle pierces through the fabric. So you may see five threads but ten (stitches) have been used. In the listings that follow, examples rated excellent have minor defects, otherwise assume them to be free of any damage, soil, or wear. Values given here are auction results; retail may be somewhat higher. For more information, please refer to *Vintage Quilts*,

Identifying, Collecting, Dating, Preserving, and Valuing, by Bobbie Aug, Sharon Newman, and Gerald Roy. Our advisor is Craig Ambrose; he is listed in the Directory under Iowa.

Key:
hs — hand sewn, sewing	mp — machine pieced
hq — hand quilted, quilting	ms — machine sewn

Amish

Birds in the Window, dk mc on blk ground, OH, ca 1900-40, 66x78"..**1,300.00**
Carpenter's Wheel, red/bl/gold/yel/orange cottons, KY, 1920-50, 53x81"..**2,750.00**
Garden Maze, blk/purple/bl, PA, ca 1930-50, 52x79", M.........**2,200.00**
Jacob's Ladder, red/yel/blk/bl (bright), KY, ca 1940, 58x88" **1,750.00**
Log Cabin, salmon/blk, brn cotton bk w/printed flowers, 77x72"..**300.00**
Lonestar, red/turq/gold, triple borders, KY, ca 1960, 66x85", NM....**1,000.00**
Star, blk/burgundy/brn, line hq, PA, ca 1900-30, 72x10", EX **850.00**
Sunshine & Shadows, mc wool/crepe/dbl knit, PA, ca 1970, 86x88", NM..**3,750.00**
Sunshine & Shadows, 5-color, feather hq, PA, 1950s, 80x80", EX ...**1,200.00**
Triple Center Diamond, turq/pk, feather hq, KY, ca 1930, 77x98", NM...**2,950.00**
Tumbling Blocks, 4-color, dmn patch bands, wear/sm holes, 70x75" ..**600.00**
Wild Goose Chase, blk/brn/wht cotton, OH, ca 1900-50, 69x69", VG ...**450.00**
9-Patch, blk & bls, cotton/cotton blends, OH, ca 1970, 74x84", EX ...**950.00**

Appliquéd

Broderie Perse, flower basket/birds w/in floral borders, 93x93"...**6,400.00**
Flags of 42 countries+Geo WA & US shield, 1875, 69x92" **4,400.00**
Floral designs on 9 blocks, mc on wht, EX hq, early 1800s, 90x87"...**1,100.00**
Floral medallions w/leaves, mc on wht, flying geese mc border, 107x87"...**500.00**
Floral wreaths (16), red/yel/gr, simple stitches, faded/lt stain, 74" **385.00**
Flower blossoms & ribbon & bow border, mc cottons, 19th C, 88x89"..**450.00**
Flower borders, eagle in shield, red/gr on cream, 1875, 98x81" ..**4,400.00**
Flower vines, gr & red calico, feather hq, 86" sq.........................**400.00**
Grapes w/leaves & vines, red/gr/wht, red edging, 92x94" **500.00**
Lilies, mc on wht w/wht calico binding, NC, 19th C, 78x84" ..**3,335.00**
Rose Wreath w/meanding vine border, mc on wht, 1850s, 79x68", VG+...**460.00**
Sunflower, goldenrod/gr w/hooked blk centers, swag border, 76x88", EX...**465.00**
Tulips (4 x 4), meandering feathers on int borders, lt stains, 92x92" **1,500.00**
12 stars+eagle w/in row of leafy medallions, swag/ribbon border, 1875....**1,880.00**

Pieced

Basket, yel & gr, fine hq, 1940-45, 82x68", NM **435.00**
Baskets, pk on wht, triangle border, detailed hq, 85x90" **475.00**
Baskets, red on wht w/red block borders, wear/stains, 42x28" **200.00**
Chain, bl/wht, sawtooth border, unwashed, lt stains, 79x90" **330.00**
Crazy, silk/wool/velvet/cotton, thorn-stitch embr, 1850s, 62x88" ...**285.00**
Dbl Irish Chain, red/gr on wht, ca 1860s, 82x82", EX................**525.00**
Diamonds, bl & wht w/dmn hq, lt stain, 69x65" **475.00**
Drunkard's Path, gr/blk & wht polka dot, hs, 1900s, 56x82".......**500.00**
Drunkard's Path, red & wht, hq, 1930s, 71x82", EX....................**425.00**
Fans, mc on burgundy calico, hs, stains, 67x68" **220.00**
Flower Garden, sm prints/solids on lt gr, 1930s, 94x78" **800.00**
Flying Geese, mc silk, bl bands & border, cotton bk, ca 1900, 86x85" ..**350.00**
Garden Maze, burgundy/cream, lt stains, 78x96" **220.00**
Irish Chain, bl/wht print on wht, ms & hq, 1950s, 33x52" **195.00**
Irish Chain variant, bl paisley on wht, bl border, EX quilting, 98x96" ..**350.00**
Log Cabin, sunshine/shadow colors, chevron borders, h/s, 80x82"....**1,485.00**
Log Cabin, wool, deep colors, lt wear, 83x84" **385.00**
Log Cabin Sunshine & Shadow, mc calico w/blk calico bking, 81x81"..**550.00**
Lone Star, bl ground w/yel/pk/red stripes, pinwheel/feather stitches....**495.00**
Lone Star, bl/burgundy/pk/gr/goldenrod on wht, EX hq, 88" sq..**1,100.00**
Lone Star, meandering quilted border, 82x82' **590.00**

Nine Patch, mc w/red grid, ca 1900, 75x21" **230.00**
Nine Patch, mc/off-wht w/red grid, sawtooth border, 1900s, 82x75"..**460.00**
Ocean Waves, bl calico w/wht dmns, 19th C, lt wear, 66x76" **800.00**
Old Maid's Puzzle, red/gr/wht w/yel sqs & gr border, 73x73" **525.00**
Pine Tree (Tree of Life variation), mc cottons, 19th C, 82" sq, VG+ ..**230.00**
Printed floral & Gothic windows in 4 joined pcs, 19th C, 81x82" ..**575.00**
Red leaves w/feathers on wht, 70x87", EX **600.00**
Roman Wall, mc silk & satin, embr signature/1897, 75x68" **460.00**
School House, lg/graphic motif, red on wht & gr, 92x68".........**1,650.00**
Single Irish Chain, magenta/blk/wht, hq shell design, 84x71" **465.00**
Snowflake, red/wht w/red piping border, lt stains, 75x78" **385.00**
Southern Lone Star, red/wht star on med bl, 1920s, lt stains, 74x86" ..**165.00**
Sqs w/various calico patterns on bl grid, 68x81" **700.00**
Star & Block, red on wht, hq, 72x86" **575.00**
Star medallions, red & wht, dbl border, princess feathering, 70x86"...**660.00**
Star of Hope, mc calico, 76x77", EX **575.00**
Stars (30), red on wht, feather wreath between all, 84x73" **690.00**
Wedding Ring, prints & pastels on wht muslin, hs, 1930s, 70x83"...**700.00**
Zig-Zag, yel & gr calico, hs, wht bking w/gr border, 1900, 77x92" **400.00**
30 Cross Sqs, calico/prints/gr w/gold blocks/pk border, hs, 97x83"....**330.00**
9-Patch variation w/triangles, bl/wht, diagonal hq, 69" sq **250.00**

Miscellaneous

Trapunto, mc flowers on wht cotton, pattern hq, 19th C, 72x89" **5,300.00**
Trapunto, red & gr flowers on wht cotton, fine hq, 19th C, 84x85", EX....**1,600.00**

Quimper

Quimper pottery bears the name of the Breton town in northwestern France where it has been made for over three hundred years. Production began in 1690 when Jean-Baptiste Bousquet settled into a small workshop in the suburbs of Quimper, at Locmaria. There he began to make the hand-painted, tin enamel-glazed earthenware which we know today as faience. By the last quarter of the nineteenth century, there were three factories working concurrently: Porquier, de la Hubaudiere (the Grand Maison), and Henriot. All three houses produced similar wares which were decorated with scenes from the everyday life of the peasant folk of the region. Their respective marks are an AP or a P with an intersecting B (similar to a clover), an HB, and an HR (which became HenRiot after litigation in 1922).

The most desirable pieces were produced during the last quarter of the nineteenth century through the first quarter of the twentieth century. These are considered to be artistically superior to the examples made after World War I and II with the exception of the Odetta line, which is now experiencing a renaissance among collectors here and abroad.

Most of what was made was faience, but there was also a history of utilitarian gres ware (stoneware) having been produced there. In 1922 the Grande Maison HB revitalized this ware and introduced the line called Odetta, examples of which seemed to embody the bold spirit of the Art Deco style. The companion faience pieces of this period and genre are classified as Modern Movement examples and frequently bear the name of the artist who designed the mold.

Currently there are two factories still producing Quimper pottery. La Societe Nouvelle des Faienceries de Quimper is owned by Sarah and Paul Jenessens along with a group of American investors. Their mark is a stamped HB-Henriot logo. The other, La Faiencerie d'art Breton, is operated by the direct descendents of the HB and Henriot families. Their pieces are marked with an interlocked F and A conjoined with an inverted B. Other marks include HQF which is the Henriot Quimper France mark and HBQ, the HB Quimper mark. If you care to learn more about Quimper, we recommend *Quimper Pottery: A French Folk Art Faience* by Sandra V. Bondhus, our advisor for this category, whose address can be found in the Directory under Connecticut.

Bell, bagpipe shape, peasant man/floral spray, HQF, 3½" 160.00
Bottle, snuff, book shape, man w/pipe/floral sprays, HB, 2¾x3" .325.00
Bowl, flower garland border, yel & bl bands, HRQ, child sz, 3" 85.00
Bowl, peasant man w/bagpipes, nuts/flower border, Malicorne, 4x11", NM ...400.00
Bowl, red petals/bl dots in garland, geometric center, HBQ, 1½x4" 20.00
Bowl, vegetable; bluets/red dots, w/lid, unmk, 19th C, 5½x14x8½" ...300.00
Butter tub, Normandie man, flower garlands, PB/Lisieux 82, doll sz ...200.00
Candy box, peasant man w/pipe/forest/Crest of Britany, HR 10, 3½x5" ...400.00
Charger, Broderie Breton, man w/son at shore, emb border, HBQ, 12" ...460.00
Charger, geometric snowflakes, bl tones, HQ 90, 11¼" 80.00
Charger, peasant man, faience populaire, scalloped, 19th C, 12", EX ..425.00
Cheese dish, peasant man, gr serpent hdl, 8-sided, HQF 74/99, 8" ..300.00
Creamer, peasant lady/floral sprays, HR 8, 3½", NM...................100.00
Cup & saucer, peasant man, heart shape, HR, 1½x5" 100.00
Figurine, Breton lady w/hands in apron pockets, HB 8, 3¼".......170.00
Figurine, Breton man w/bagpipes, HBQ, flake, 3¼" 170.00
Figurine, peasant lady w/basket, Modern Movement, Galland, HQ, 5¾" ...140.00
Gravy boat, peasant couple/flower branches, dolphin ft, HR, 9", EX......400.00
Jardiniere, swan figural, Breton couple, decor riche, HR 9, 9x16" 1,500.00
Menu card holder, Breton crest/ermine tails, scalloped, Chambord 662 .175.00
Mustard pot, peasant man & plants, gr sponged hdl, w/lid, HR, 3¾" 130.00
Pitcher, biberon; floral sprays, tiny spout, HB, 19th C, 4½" 275.00
Pitcher, biberon; peasant man/flowers, fading, HQF, 7" 170.00
Pitcher, geometric Modern Movement, Breton man hdl, Fouillen, 5½" ..325.00
Plate, bl croisille lattice/stars/mc bands, HBQ, ca 1900, 9⅛"......125.00
Plate, Breton bride & groom/flowers, HQ 155, 9½" 375.00
Plate, cake; Botanique, floral spray/insect, PB, 4½x8" 1,700.00

Plate, couple dancing with Crest of Brittany and crown above, blue acanthus border, decor riche, HR Quimper, 9½", $550.00.

Plate, daisy-like geometric w/lattice, unmk, early/naive, 8½" 120.00
Plate, floral sprigs/dots/petals, faience populaire, unmk, 8½" 240.00
Plate, lady w/bk turned, baby over shoulder, Malicorne, 5".........180.00
Plate, lady w/fish basket, floral sprays, HB, 19th C, 9¾" 275.00
Plate, lady w/grasses ea side/floral sprays, HQ 123, 8½" 80.00
Plate, lady/flower sprays, Malicorne, 9½"............................200.00
Plate, man w/flute/bluets/geometrics, 8-sided, HR, 10" 475.00
Plate, man w/shovel, Le Plu Fort L 'emporte, flakes, 9½" 240.00
Plate, mother w/baby & daughter, decor riche, scalloped, 10" 275.00
Plate, Sevellec Breton Life, peasants & church, HQ 133, 9½" ...200.00
Plate, Ste Marie 1765, Mary w/Christ child, HBx, Malicorne, 9¾" 300.00
Platter, demi-fantasie couple/dogwood, Henriot 103 Camaret, 10½" ..450.00
Sugar bowl, Normandie, Modern Movement, Foillen, rpl lid, 8" 230.00
Trivet, peasant man, florals w/bluets, gr sponging, HQF 122, EX....100.00
Vase, Breton couple/flower spray, prof rstr, PB, 11" 1,700.00
Vase, lady spins/man w/bagpipes, horseshoe form, HB 5, 19th C, 5½" ..850.00
Vase, lady w/flax, demi-fantasie/a la touche florals, HQF, 7¼", EX........250.00
Vase, peasant lady w/jug & milk pail, narrow neck, Henriot, 12", EX...300.00
Vase, peasant lady/Crest of Brittany/fleur-de-lis, HR, 8x7"..........475.00
Vase, quintal; ivoire corbelle, peasant lady, HQ 90, 3½", NM 70.00
Wall pocket, bagpipe shape, man w/arms folded, HQ, 11½".......275.00
Wall pocket, bagpipe shape, man w/bagpipes, HR, chip, 8x6" 200.00
Wall pocket, dbl cornucopia, facing peasant couple, att Malicorne, 5"...195.00
Wall pocket, man w/horn & flower, conical, 19th C, 10½" 180.00
Wall pocket, peasant lady, flowers at top of cone, Malicorne, 12" ..125.00

Radford, Albert

Pottery associated with Albert Radford (1882 – 1904) can be categorized by three periods of production. Pottery produced in Tiffin, Ohio (1896 – 1899), consists of bone china (no marked examples known) and high-quality jasperware with applied Wedgwood-like cameos. Tiffin jasperware is often impressed 'Radford Jasper' in small block letters. At Zanesville, Ohio, Radford jasperware was marked only with an incised, two-digit shape number, and the cameos were not applied but rather formed within the mold and filled with a white slip. Zanesville Radford ware was produced for only a few months before the Radford pottery was acquired by the Arc-en-Ciel company in 1903. Production in Zanesville was handled by Radford's father, Edward (1840 – 1910), who remained in Zanesville after Albert moved to Clarksburg, West Virginia, where the Radford Pottery Co. was completed shortly before Albert's death in 1904. Jasperware was not produced in Clarksburg, and the molds appear to have been left in Zanesville, where some were subsequently used by the Arc-en-Ciel pottery. The Clarksburg, West Virginia, pottery produced a standard glaze, slip-decorated ware, Ruko; Thera and Velvety, matt glazed ware often signed by Albert Haubrich, Alice Bloomer, and other artists; and Radura, a semimatt green glaze developed by Albert Radford's son, Edward. The Clarksburg plant closed in 1912.

Our advisor for this category is James L. Murphy; he is listed in the Directory under Ohio. For pottery marked E. Radford, see Radford, Edward.

Jasper

Bowl, classic figure, prof rstr chip, 5½" 100.00
Bowl, muses & vintage, fluted rim, imp mk 295.00
Box, figure w/cornucopia on lid, prof rpr, ca 1896, 5⅝" H 500.00
Ewer, appl grapes/raspberries, Old Man Winter hdl, #17, 9" 350.00
Letter holder, lady w/bow & target scene, bark trim, #61............500.00
Mug, vintage, gray, #25, 5" 165.00
Pitcher, tankard, vintage, lt bl, #26, 12"...200.00
Vase, bust of Gladstone ea side, twisted form, 3" 125.00
Vase, bust of Washington, bk: eagle, bark trim, #12, 7"..............265.00
Vase, cherubs on flying eagles, #23, 9½"..475.00
Vase, girl running, deep bl, flat & twisted, #53, 3½".....................100.00
Vase, lady kneeling w/bird, gray, #24, 10½x4½"..........................250.00
Vase, lady w/dog, #22, 10x6"...250.00
Vase, lady w/flowers, bk: grapes, #59, 4" 165.00

Miscellaneous

Jardiniere, Ruko, tulips, 8½x9"..250.00
Vase, Radura, 4-hdl, scalloped rim, 10" 400.00
Vase, Thera, floral, mc on gr, #1453, 12½" 700.00
Vase, Thera, nasturtium, A Haubrich, ovoid, 13½", NM...........900.00

Radford, Edward

Pottery marked 'E. Radford, Burslem,' or 'E. Radford, England,' includes a variety of earthenware designed by Edward Radford (1883 – 1968), first for H.J. Wood and later for himself in Burslem (production ending in 1948). A variety of floral patterns, cottage or tavern scenes, and Art Deco motifs distinguish this ware. His father, Edward Thomas Radford, worked at the Pilkington Tile and Pottery Co. in Manchester, England, and appears to have been a brother of Albert Radford. Items in the following listings are hand painted unless noted otherwise.

Ashtray, frog seated st side, England, 3½" 95.00

Basket, peony, 5"..**48.00**
Bowl, trees, earth tones on lt beige mottle, Burslem, 4½x4½"......**95.00**
Bowl, 3-D bird on nest, relief mold, pastels, 5x4¾", NM............**165.00**
Bowl vase, flower stalks, red/bl on pk mottle, Burslem, 2x4½" ...**125.00**
Candle holders, floral, mc on ivory, #94-HZ-F, 3¾", pr.............**150.00**
Candle holders, violets on lt pk, 2¾", pr.......................................**100.00**
Candy dish, morning glories, w/lid, 2x4" **75.00**
Ewer, floral sprays, pastel on lt gr mottle, slim, England, 14" **100.00**
Jug, butterflies/florals relief, str sides, Butterfly/England, 8½" **60.00**
Jug, floral, purple & red on wht, 9¾" **79.00**
Jug, floral spray, mc on ivory, England, WG/H, 9½" **145.00**
Jug, poppies, bl/pk on lt beige mottle, waisted neck, Burslem, 4½"..**100.00**
Shakers, poppies, 4", NM, pr...**54.00**
Tray, dbl; poppy in ea well, Great Britain, 5¾" L......................**60.00**
Vase, bird perched on tree trunk, England, 6x5".........................**200.00**
Vase, clematis, EX color, 5"..**65.00**
Vase, floral, mc on ivory mottle, slightly bulbous, England, 5¾" ...**100.00**
Vase, floral, pk/mc on pk mottle, Great Britain, 3½x3" **85.00**
Vase, poppies, bl/purple on bl mottle, Burslem/232-JGB, 6".......**145.00**
Vase, Sgraffito, lg cvd floral, gr wash on mottled cream, 7½"...**225.00**
Vase, wisteria (4 repeats), red/bl on ivory, #180, England, 8"......**125.00**
Vase, 5-petal flowers, bl/rose on tan mottle, Burslem, 5½"..........**70.00**
Wall pocket, floral spray, mc on pk, sqd cone shape, 7½"..........**125.00**

Radios

    Vintage radios are very collectible. There were thousands of styles and types produced, the most popular of which today are the breadboard and the cathedral. Consoles are usually considered less marketable, since their size makes them hard to display and store. For those wishing to learn more about antique radios, we recommend *Collector's Guide to Antique Radios, Fifth Edition*, by John Slusser, available from your local bookstore or Collector Books. Marty and Sue Bunis are the authors of *Collector's Guide to Transistor Radios, Second Edition*. For information on novelty radios, refer to *Collector's Guide to Novelty Radios* by Marty Bunis and Robert Breed.

    Unless otherwise noted in the descriptions, values are given for working radios in near mint to mint condition. Our advisor for this category is Dr. E.E. Taylor; he is listed in the Directory under Indiana. See also Plastics.

Key:
BC — broadcast	R/P — radio-phonograph
LW — long wave	s/r — slide rule
pb — push button	SW — short wave
phono — phonograph	tbl/m — table model

Philco, #17, wooden cathedral, center front window dial, cloth grill with cutouts, eleven tubes, four knobs, $275.00. (Photo courtesy Sue and Marty Bunis)

Admiral, #15-D5, tbl/m, streamline, plastic, AC/DC, 1940........**100.00**
Admiral, #7C60M, R/P console, wood, BC, AC, 1948..................**60.00**

Air Castle, #106B, tbl/m, streamline, plastic, BC, AC/DC, 1947..**125.00**
Airline, #0BR-514B, tbl/m, Deco style, plastic, BC, 1940............**90.00**
Airline, #74KR-2706B, R/P console, wood, BC, AC, 1947............**50.00**
All-Star, #613, tbl/m, wood, AC, 1938..**65.00**
Am Bosch, #20-L, console, ornate wood, 1931.............................**200.00**
Am Bosch, #575-F, tombstone, wood, AC, 1935...........................**85.00**
Arvin, #1127 (Rhythm King), console, wood, BC, SW, AC, 1936 .**300.00**
Arvin, #8571-1, portable, cloth-covered, BC, AC/DC/battery, 1958.**25.00**
Atwater Kent, #55, console, AC, 1929 ....**125.00**
Atwater Kent, #82D, cathedral, wood, DC, 1931 ....**450.00**
Bendix, #55X4, portable, plastic, BC, AC/DC/battery, 1949.........**40.00**
Brunswick, #T-2580, tbl/m, wood, AC, 1939 ....**75.00**
Brunswick, #21, highboy console, wood, AC, 1929.....................**150.00**
Bulova, #M-701, cathedral w/clock, 1932.....................................**425.00**
Clarion, #TC-2, console, Deco style, wood, 1934.........................**150.00**
Cleveland, tbl/m, wood, battery, 1925...**125.00**
Continental, #1600, tbl/m w/clock, streamline, plastic, BC, AC..**85.00**
Crosley, #02CA, console, wood, BC, SW, 1941............................**150.00**
Crosley, #11-105U, tbl/m, plastic, BC, AC/DC, 1951...................**150.00**
Delco, #R-1230A, tbl/m, plastic, BC, AC/DC, 1947......................**75.00**
Dewald, #522, tbl/m, Deco style, wood, battery, 1936 ....**65.00**
Elgin, #A115 (Super Air Roamer), tbl/m, wood, BC, SW, AC/DC, 1939...**60.00**
Emerson, #25A, tbl/m, wood, AC/DC, 1933................................**100.00**
Emerson, #28, tombstone, walnut, BC, SW, AC, 1934................**110.00**
Eveready, #54, console, wood, AC, 1929 ....**200.00**
Excello, #154, R/P console, wood, 1931.......................................**175.00**
Federal, #57, tbl/m, metal, battery, 1922 ....**650.00**
Firestone, #4-A-23, tbl/m, wood, BC, 2 SW, AC, 1946................**45.00**
Freshman, #6-F-6 (Masterpiece), tbl/m, wood, battery, 1926 ......**100.00**
GE, #E-71, tombstone, 2-tone wood, BC, SW, AC, 1936 ....**110.00**
GE, #K-43-C, cathedral, wood, BC, SW, AC, 1933 ....**175.00**
GE, #M-42, tombstone, wood, AC, 1934......................................**90.00**
GE, #114W, tbl/m, plastic, BC, AC/DC, 1946..............................**35.00**
Grebe, #CR12, tbl/m, wood, battery, 1923...................................**800.00**
Hoffman, #B002, R/P console, wood, BC, FM, AC, 1958............**50.00**
Howard, #225, tbl/m, wood, BC, SW, AC, 1937 ....**65.00**
Jackson-Bell, #62, cathedral, wood, AC, 1930.............................**300.00**
Jewel, #505 (Pin-Up), wall-mt w/clock, plastic, BC, AC, 1947 ....**85.00**
Kadette, #24 (Clockette/Futura), tbl/m, wood, AC, 1937..........**125.00**
Kennedy, #826B, console, wood, 1930 ....**600.00**
Knight, #30, console, wood, battery, 1925....................................**200.00**
Lafayette, #B18, console, wood, BC, SW, AC, 1938 ....**125.00**
Magnavox, #75, console, mahog, battery, 1925............................**275.00**
Majestic, #15A, tombstone, wood, 1932.......................................**125.00**
Majestic, #511, tbl/m, plastic, BC, AC, 1938, minimum value...**800.00**
Mantola, #R-654-PM, tbl/m, plastic, BC, AC/DC, 1946..............**35.00**
Mohawk, #44, tbl/m, wood, battery, 1927 ....**110.00**
Motorola, #55M2, portable, leatherette, BC, AC/DC/battery, 1956..**30.00**
Motorola, #6-T, tbl/m, wood, BC, SW, AC, 1937.......................**90.00**
Motorola, #85K21, console, wood, BC, SW, AC, 1946...............**100.00**
Olympic, #6-606-U, portable, luggage style, BC, AC/DC/battery, 1947..**30.00**
Operadio, #95, cathedral, wood, 1932 ....**500.00**
Packard-Bell, #880-A, R/P chairside, wood, BC, AC, 1948 ....**70.00**
Philco, #15X, console, walnut, AC, 1932 ....**200.00**
Philco, #37-89, cathedral, wood, BC, AC, 1937............................**135.00**
Philco, #39-7, tbl/m, walnut, BC, AC, 1939 ....**60.00**
Philco, #49-1606, R/P console, wood, BC, AC, 1949...................**70.00**
Pilot, #L-8, tbl/m, 2-tone wood, AC, 1933...................................**275.00**
Radiola, #R560P, R/P tbl/m, wood, BC, AC, 1942 ....**25.00**
RCA, #B-411, portable, plastic, BC, battery, 1951 ....**35.00**
RCA, #66BX, portable, aluminum/plastic, BC, AC/DC/battery, 1947...**40.00**
RCA, #96E2, chairside, 2-tone wood, BC, SW, AC, 1939............**200.00**
Remler, #10, cathedral, wood, 1932..**275.00**
Sentinel, #108A, cathedral, wood, AC, 1931 ....**275.00**

Setchell-Carlson, #415, tbl/m, plastic, BC **65.00**
Silvertone, #4464, tombstone, 2-tone wood, AC, 1936 ....**120.00**
Sparton, #71, tombstone, wood, AC, 1933 ....**125.00**
Sparton, #987, console, wood, BC, SW, AC, 1936.....................**200.00**
Stewart-Warner, #07-713H, tbl/m, streamline, plastic, BC, AC, 1939...**85.00**
Stromberg-Carlson, #340-Y, corner console, walnut, BC, SW, AC, 1938 .**150.00**
Trav-Ler, #53, tombstone, wood, AC, 1935 ....**125.00**
Truetone, #D2018, tbl/m, modern, plastic, BC, AC/AC, 1950 ...**175.00**
Westinghouse, #H-203, R/P console, wood, BC, FM, AC, 1949...**60.00**
Westinghouse, #WR-120, tbl/m, plastic, BC, SW, AC/DC, 1937 .**45.00**
Westinghouse, #WR-14, cathedral, 2-tone wood, 1931................**125.00**
Workrite, #17, tbl/m, 2-tone wood, battery, 1927 ....**90.00**
Zenith, #5-G-572, console, wood, BC, SW, AC/DC/battery, 1941 ..**125.00**
Zenith, 4-B-422, tbl/m, plastic, BC, battery, 1940 ....**75.00**

Novelty Radios

Ballantine Ale/Beer, keg form, EX **65.00**
Blizzard/Oreo, 2-sided, M **35.00**
Campbell's Tomato Soup Can, NM **50.00**
Casper the Friendly Ghost, Harvey Cartoons/Sutton, 1972, M.....**65.00**
Champion Spark Plug, MIB..**100.00**
Crayola Crayons, box form w/clock, EX **130.00**
Crest Man, M..**30.00**
Donald Duck, plastic, 2-D head w/open mouth, 1970s, NMIB **75.00**
Excide Ultra Start Battery, AMT, EX...**100.00**
Folgers Coffee Can, plastic, 4", NM..**75.00**
Gumby, Lewco, 1970s, NM...**150.00**
Harley-Davidson Motorcycle, w/cassette player & headphones, M....**75.00**
Hershey Syrup Bottle, MIB **75.00**

Howdy Doody, cloth and vinyl, NM, from $35.00 to $50.00. (Photo courtesy Marty Bunis and Robert F. Breed)

Kent King Size Cigarettes Pack, Japan, EX **250.00**
Manwich Can, EX...**45.00**
Mountain Dew Can, Hong Kong, NM **50.00**
Nestle Nesquik Milk Shake Mix, NM **50.00**
Old Spice Can, Isis, model #105, NM..**100.00**
Planters Cocktail Nuts Can, MIB..**55.00**
Post Grape Nuts Cereal Box, Isis, model #103, M **50.00**
Poweready Batteries, battery shape, M..**75.00**
SOS Detergent Box, 1989, M..**50.00**
Sunoco Gas Pump, EX...**25.00**
Taco Bell, Isis, model #39, M..**50.00**
Tide Detergent, box form w/NASCAR info on bottom, EX..........**40.00**
Tony's Pizza/Pepperidge Farm Distinctive Stuffing, 2-sided, EX **50.00**
V8 Can, NM...**50.00**
Wilson Tennis Balls, can shape, NM **45.00**
Yago Sangria, bottle shape, MIB **65.00**
Yogi Bear, 2-D head, Hanna-Barbera/Markson, M.......................**125.00**

Transistor Radios

Post-World War II baby boomers, now approaching their fiftieth year, are rediscovering prized possessions of youth, their pocket radios. The transistor wonders, born with rock 'n roll, were at the vanguard of miniaturization and futuristic design in the decade which followed their introduction to Christmas shoppers in 1954. The tiny receiving sets launched the growth of Texas Instruments and shortly to follow abroad, Sony and other Japanese giants.

The most desirable sets include the 1954 four-transistor Regency TR-1 and colorful early Sony and Toshiba models. Certain pre-1960 models by Hoffman and Admiral represented the earliest practical use of solar technology and are also highly valued. To avoid high tariffs, scores of two-transistor sets, boys' radios, were imported from Japan with names like Pet and Charmy. Many early inexpensive transistor sets could be heard only with an earphone. The smallest sets are known as shirt-pocket models while those slightly larger are called coat-pockets. Early collectible transistor radios all have civil defense triangle markings at 640 and 1240 on the frequency dial and nine or fewer transistors. Very few desirable sets were made after 1963. Model numbers are most commonly found inside. Our advisor for this category is Mike Brooks; he is listed in the Directory under California and welcomes questions. (Please include a SASE.)

Admiral, #Y2451, horizontal, 10 transistors, AM/FM, AC/battery, 1963..**20.00**
Admiral, #692, horizontal, 5 transistors, AM, battery, 1960..........**30.00**
Aiwa, #AR-670, vertical, 6 transistors, AM, battery, 1964............**35.00**
Arvin, #8576, vertical, 5 transistors, AM, battery, 1958 ....**200.00**
Bulova, #870, vertical, 6 transistors, AM, battery, 1963 ....**30.00**
Commodore, #YTR-601, vertical, 6 transistors, AM **45.00**
Continental, #SW-7, horizontal, 7 transistors, 2 SW, AM, battery, 1959 ...**45.00**
Crown, #TR-333, vertical, 3 transistors, AM, battery, 1959 ....**150.00**
Daltone, Royal #400, vertical, 2 transistors, AM **60.00**
Dewald, #K-544, horizontal, 4 transistors, AM, battery, 1957 .....**65.00**
Eden, #TR-600, vertical, 6 transistors, AM................................**35.00**
Emerson, #842, horizontal, 6 transistors, AM, battery, 1956 ......**45.00**
Emerson, #849, horizontal, AM, battery, 1955...........................**175.00**
Firestone, #4-C-29, horizontal/hybrid, AM, 1955.......................**300.00**
GE, #P840A, horizontal, 7 transistors, AM, battery, 1961...........**20.00**
Hit Parade, #ITR, horizontal, 1 transistor, 1958 ....**100.00**
Hitachi, #WH-761M, vertical, 7 transisors, AM/Marine, battery, 1961 ..**65.00**
Hoffman, #KP707, vertical, 7 transistors, AM, battery, 1962 ......**55.00**
Invicta, #TR-222, horizontal, 6 transistors, AM, battery.............**100.00**
Jeb, #6YR-15A, vertical, AM, battery...**100.00**
Juliette, #TR-91M, horizontal, 9 transistors, AM, battery, 1968 ...**45.00**
Kent, Boy's Radio, vertical, 2 transistors, AM, battery **60.00**
Lafayette, #FS-91, vertical, 9 transistors, AM, battery, 1961.......**200.00**
Maco, #AB-175, horizontal, 7 transistors, SW, AM, battery **30.00**
Magnavox, #AM-805, sq, 7 transistors, AM, battery...................**30.00**
Mantola, #M4D, vertical, 4 transistors, AM, battery, 1957.........**300.00**
Motorola, #X14R, vertical, 6 transistors, AM, battery, 1960 ....**55.00**
Nordmende, Condor, horizontal, 9 transistors, AM/FM, battery, 1963 ..**35.00**
Norelco, #L0X95R/62R, horizontal, 7 transistors, AM, battery, 1961 ....**30.00**
Olympic, #770, horizontal, 6 transistors, AM, battery, 1959 ....**55.00**
Panasonic, #T-13, vertical, 6 transistors, AM, battery, 1962 ....**30.00**
Philco, #T-4J-124, horizontal, 4 transistors, AM, battery, 1959.....**55.00**
Philips, #L1X75T/R, horizontal, 7 transistors, AM, battery..........**45.00**
Queen, #MTR0203, vertical, 2 transistors, AM, battery **60.00**
Raytheon, #T-100-1, horizontal, Am, battery, 1956 ....**350.00**
RCA, #9-BT-9H, horizontal, 6 transistors, AM, battery, 1957 ......**45.00**
Regency, #TR-1, vertical, 4 transistors, mandarin red, 1954 ....**600.00**
Ross, #RE-210 (Micro Solid State), sq, AM, battery **40.00**
Seminole, #801, horizontal, 8 transistors, AM, battery, 1963......**110.00**
Silvertone, #9204, vertical, 6 transistors, AM, battery, 1959.........**50.00**
Sony, #AFM-152, horizontal, 15 transistors, AM/FM, battery, 1965..**50.00**
Summit, #FR-601, vertical, 6 transistors, AM, battery,................**50.00**
Toshiba, #9TM-40, vertical, 9 transistors, AM, battery, 1961 .....**350.00**

Trav-Ler, #TR-284-B, vertical, 6 transistors, AM, battery, 1958 .**100.00**
United Royal, #1050, horizontal, AM/FM, battery **40.00**
Valient, #HT-1221, vertical, 10 transistors, AM, battery...............**25.00**
Westinghouse, #H-589P7, horizontal, 7 transistors, AM, battery, 1957 ...**85.00**
Winston, #W700, vertical, 7 transistors, AM, battery, 1965 ....**40.00**
Zenith, Royal 200, vertical, 7 transistors, AM, battery, 1959 ....**50.00**

Railroadiana

Collecting railroad-related memorabilia has become one of America's most popular hobbies. The range of collectible items available is almost endless; not surprising, considering the fact that more than 185 different railroad lines are represented. Some collectors prefer to specialize in only one railroad, while others attempt to collect at least one item from every railway line known to have existed. For the advanced collector, there is the challenge of locating rarities from short-lived railroads; for the novice, there are abundant keys, buttons, and passes. Among the most popular specializations are dining-car collectibles — flatware, glassware, dinnerware, etc., in a wide variety of patterns and styles. Railroad blankets are also collectible. Most common are Pullman blankets. The early ones had a cross-stitch pattern; these were followed by one in a solid cinnamon color; both are marked clearly with the Pullman name. Pullman, in the 1920s, put out a blue blanket, marked Pullman, specifically for ethnic use. There is one in the Sacramento railroad museum. Other railroads had their own 'marked' blankets that are even more desirable, such as the Soo line, the Chessie, and one marked 'Pheasant' (which was a private car on the Milwaukee Line that was reserved to carry special parties for hunting trips).

Another name among railroad dining collectors is Fred Harvey. From 1893 until after WWII, Fred Harvey masterminded all the dining halls and dining cars on the Santa Fe Railroad System from Chicago to the west coast. (A little known fact, he also had dining facilities on the Frisco railroad.) He had his famous Harvey girls, as portrayed by Judy Garland, and a lot of personal dining china, silver, and linens marked with his 'FH.'

Berth keys have become scarce and expensive as more and more collectors purchase private rail cars. This is also true of 'window lifters,' specially designed pry bars made of wood used to ram the windows open in the old wood coaches.

As is true in most collecting fields, scarcity and condition determine value. There is more interest in some railway lines than in others; generally speaking, it is greater in the region serviced by the particular railroad. American collectors prefer American-made products and items with ties to American railroads. For example, English switch lanterns, though of superior quality, usually sell at lower prices, as does memorabilia from Canadian railways such as Canadian Pacific or Canadian National.

Reproductions abound in railroadiana collectibles — from dinnerware and glassware to lanterns, keys, badges, belt buckles, timetables, and much more. Reproduction hand-executed, reverse-painted glass signs have been abundant throughout the country, most of them read 'Santa Fe,' but some say 'Whites Only.' Lately markets in the East have been inundated with Baltimore & Ohio reproductions: menus, glass water carafes, demitasse sets in the George Washington theme, and more. Beware! Also railroad drumheads are coming out of collections. A drumhead is a large (approximately 24" diameter) glass sign in a metal case. They were used on the back end of all railroad observation cars to advertise a special train or a presidential foray, etc. They're now beginning to surface, and a good one like the Flying Crow from the Kansas City Southern Railroad will go for $2,500.00, as will many others. When items of this value come out, the counterfeiters are right there. It is important to 'Know Thy Dealer.' For a more thorough study, we recommend *Railroad Collectibles, Fourth Edition*, by Stanley L. Baker. The values noted for most of our dinnerware, glassware, linen, silverplate, and timetables are actual

selling prices. However, because prices are so volatile, the best pricing sources are often monthly or quarterly 'For Sale' lists. Two you may find helpful may be ordered from Golden Spike, P.O. Box 422, Williamsville, NY 14221, and Grandpa's Depot, 6720 E. Mississippi Ave., Unit B, Denver, CO 80224. Our co-advisors for this category are Lila Shrader (see Directory, California) and John White (Grandpa's Depot, see Colorado).

Key:
BL — bottom logo	SL — side logo
BS — bottom stamped	SM — side mark
FBS — full back stamp	TL — top logo
NBS — no back stamp	TM — top mark

Dinnerware

Many railroads designed their own china for use in their dining cars or company-owned hotels or stations. Some railroads chose to use stock patterns to which they added their name or logo; others used the same stock patterns without the added identification. For more information, we recommend *Restaurant China, Volumes 1* and *2*, by Barbara J. Conroy (Collector Books).

Ashtray, GN, Mountains & Flowers, 4 rests, BS, 4"......................**55.00**
Bowl, baked apple; ATSF, Adobe, oval, tab hdl, TL, NBS **40.00**
Bowl, berry; ACL, Flora of the South, BS, 5½", from $50 to........**65.00**
Bowl, berry; CI&L (Monon), Hoosier, TL, NBS, 4¾" **160.00**
Bowl, berry; GN, Mountains & Flowers, BS, 5⅛" **149.00**
Bowl, master salad; SP, Prairie Mtn Wildflower, NBS, 3½x9½" **248.00**
Bowl, N&W, Cavalier, oval, TM, NBS, 4½x5½" **35.00**
Bowl, oatmeal; GM&O, Rose w/floral band, TL, NBS, 6" **104.00**
Bowl, rim soup; B&O, Capitol, TL, BS, 9⅞" **78.00**
Bowl, serving; IC, Land O' Corn, rich gold, 7½x10½" **200.00**
Bowl, Winged Streamliner UPRR, Scammell's Trenton China, 6⅜" ..**35.00**
Butter pat, ATSF, Mimbreno, BS, 3⅛", from $125 to..................**160.00**
Butter pat, C&S, Pueblo, TL, NBS, 3⅜" **565.00**
Butter pat, CMStP&P, Peacock, NBS, 3".....................................**74.00**
Butter pat, N&W, Bristol, TL, NBS, 3"..**535.00**
Butter pat, PRR, Congressional, TM, BS, 3¾"..............................**255.00**
Butter pat, Santa Fe, CA Poppy, NBS, 3½".....................................**37.50**
Butter pat, Sante Fe, CA Poppy, BS, 3½", from $100 to..............**125.00**
Butter pat, SP&S, American, NBS, 3⅛"...**42.00**
Butter pat, UP, Winged Streamliner, TL, NBS..............................**38.00**
Children's ware, mug, UP, Zion (monkey), BS, 3¾" ..**175.00**
Chocolate pot, ATSF, Mimbreno, FBS, 5¼".................................**515.00**
Compote, ACL, Carolina, ped ft, BS, 2¾x5¾"...............................**67.00**
Compote, GN, Hill, ped ft, TL, NBS, 5x8¾"............................**1,250.00**
Creamer, Key System, Key Route Inn, w/hdl, SL, NBS, ind, 2¾" ..**360.00**
Creamer, NYC, Depew, BS, 4½" **135.00**
Creamer, RF&P, Tri-Link, no hdl, NSL, NBS, ind, 2"...................**16.00**
Creamer, Wabash, Banner, w/hdl, SL, NBS, ind, 3¼".................**550.00**
Cup, bouillon; CMStP&P, Traveler, no hdls, w/lid, NBS **88.00**
Cup, bouillon; MK&T, Katy Ornaments, hdls, NBS **21.00**
Cup, bouillon; N&W, Cavalier, no hdls, SL, NBS, 3¾"................**76.00**
Cup & saucer, demitasse; ATSF, California Poppy, cup: NBS, saucer: BS...**410.00**
Cup & saucer, demitasse; L&N, Regent, NBS **58.00**
Cup & saucer, demitasse; WP, Feather River, SL & TL, NBS.....**445.00**
Cup & saucer, NP, Monad, cup: NBS, saucer: TM, NBS.............**256.00**
Egg cup, CMStP&P, Traveler, ped ft, NBS, 2⅛" **208.00**
Egg cup, NYC, Mercury, no vertical stripes, ped ft, SM, 2¼".......**182.00**
Egg cup, UP, Winged Streamliner, Trenton, ped ft, SL, NBS, 2½"....**138.00**
Gravy boat, NYC, Vanderbilt (Limoges), BS, 6" **285.00**
Hot food cover, CMStP&P, Peacock, NBS, 5¾"...........................**114.00**
Hot water pot, MP, cobalt, EX gold, w/lid, NBS, ind, 5¼".........**268.00**
Ice cream shell, NYC, Hudson, tab hdl, BS, 4¾" **66.00**

Pitcher, water; SP, Sunset, SL, BS, 8" 525.00
Plate, BC Elec St Ry, Railway Co-Op, TL, NBS, 6½" 52.00
Plate, Boston & Albany (NYC), Berkshire, TL, 7" 150.00
Plate, CP, Garter, TL, NBS, 8½" 356.00
Plate, EH&A St Ry, Hampton, TL, 7" 123.00
Plate, grill; CRI&P, El Reno, TM, NBS, 11½" 126.00
Plate, KCS, Flying Crow, TM, 7¼" 1,025.00
Plate, P&LE, Youngstown, TL, NBS, 10¼" 258.00
Plate, PRR, Mountain Laurel, FBS, 9½" 36.00
Plate, UP, Columbine, BS w/pattern name, 9½" 405.00
Plate, Wabash, Banner, TL, NBS, 9½" 310.00
Platter, ACL, Palmetto, notched corners, TL, NBS 100.00
Platter, D&H, Canterbury, no center seal, TL, 8½x5¾" 136.00
Platter, Northern Alberta, Dunvegan, oval, TL, NBS, 13½" 455.00
Relish dish, CMStP&P, Traveler, NBS, 9½" L 60.00
Relish dish, NYC&StL, Nickel Plate Road, Ft Wayne, TL, 7½x3¾" ..375.00
Sherbet, ATSF, Mimbreno, ped ft, BS, 2½" 255.00
Sugar bowl, GN, Empire, w/lid, NBS, 3¾" 55.00
Teapot, ATSF, Mimbreno, BS, 4⅞" 640.00
Teapot, CRI&P, Hall China, in TL silver fr, NBS, 4" 700.00
Teapot, L&N, Regent, 5½" 130.00
Tray, NYC, Vanderbilt, tab hdls, BS, 8¾x5¾" 50.00

Glass

Ashtray, ATSF, Santa Fe frosted in cursive on bottom, 4½x3¼" ..35.00
Ashtray, ATSF, Turquoise Room, Super Chief, 3¼x4½" 52.00
Ashtray, Erie, 100 Anniversary Great Lakes to..., 1851-1951, 3½" ...22.00
Bar glass, Pere Marquet, 3⅞" 20.00
Bottle, ATSF Chemical Dept emb, narrow neck...........................47.00
Bottle, milk; MP, emb buzz saw logo, 1-qt, 9¾" 85.00
Bottle, milk; PRR, buzz saw logo, ½-pt.....................................30.00
Bottle, NYC w/bl enamel 20th Century Limited logo, orig lid, 6½" ..56.00
Bottle, Old Forester whiskey, 100 proof, Pullman, w/orig screw cap...86.00
Carafe, CPR, acid etch Tremblant Ry logo, appl rings, 7½" 128.00
Carafe, Pere Marquette, 3⅝" 30.00
Champagne, Santa Fe, hock style, heavy base, 5" 60.00
Claret, GN, frosted logo, knob stem, SM, 4¾x2¼" 65.00
Cocktail, GN, w/interlocking GN monogram, 4½" 90.00
Cordial, ATSF, etched Santa Fe w/5 horizontal lines, 3⅛" 110.00
Cruet, GN, etched old goat logo, w/stopper, rare, 5½" 750.00
Decanter, ATSF, SL, w/metal TM lid, 9½" 527.00
Double shot, Pullman in 8-sided base, 3¼" 45.00

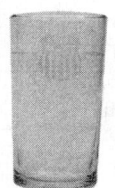

Glassware items with Union Pacific frosted logos: Goblet, 5½", $20.00; Tumbler, 4½", $10.00; Shot glass, 2½", $15.00. (Photo courtesy Stanley Baker)

Highball, PRR, passenger train 4902/clouds/etc, 4½" 18.00
Martini, Pere Marquette, 4⅛" 25.00
Old fashioned, PRR, enamel scene w/train, capitol, NY, 4½" 23.00
Pitcher, D&RG, BS w/speed logo, in SP fr w/hinged lid, 10"......710.00
Shakers, CPR, cylinder w/SP flat tops, 3½", pr............................50.00
Sherbet, CNR, cut stem, pinched sides, etched logo, SM, 4" 50.00
Stem, champagne; Santa Fe on banner w/tassels, 3⅜", pr...........400.00
Swizzle stick, C of NJ, hollow w/CNJ & distiller's ad, 4¾"............21.00
Syrup, SOO Line, cut body w/SP hdl, 1911, rare.........................300.00
Tumbler, C&O For Progress in bl, SM, 4¾".................................18.00

Tumbler, Fred Harvey w/emb intertwined FH, blown, 5⅛" 140.00
Tumbler, Frisco in bl, SM, 5" 15.00
Tumbler, juice; B&O in blk enamel Garrett logo, 5" 15.00
Tumbler, juice; GN, frosted logo, SM, 3½" 35.00
Tumbler, juice; WAB, frosted flag logo, 3¼" 35.00
Tumbler, Santa Fe (script) in wht enamel, 5½" 20.00
Tumbler, SLSF, frosted Frisco logo w/steam loco & coal car, 5½" .12.00
Wine, ATSF, etched Santa Fe & 5 horizontal lines, 6-oz, 4¼"......26.00
Wine, CMStP&P, hollow cut stem, etched logo, SM, 5"...............65.00

Keys

Switch keys are brass with hollow barrels and round heads with holes for attaching to a key ring. They were used to unlock the padlocks on track-side switches when the course of the tracks had to be changed. (Switches were padlocked to prevent them from being thrown by accident or vandals, a situation that could result in a train wreck.) A car key used to open padlocks on freight cars and the like is very similar to the switch key, except the bit is straighter instead of being specifically curved for a particular railroad and its accompanying switch locks. A second type of car key was used for door locks on passenger cars, Pullmans, etc.; this type was usually of brass, but instead of having a hollow barrel, they were shaped like an old-fashioned hotel door key. In order for a key to be collectible, the head must be marked with a name, initials, or a railroad identification, with 'switch' generally designated by 'S' and 'car' by 'C' markings. Railroad, patina 'not polished,' and the presence of a manufacturer's mark other than Adlake all have a positive effect on pricing and collectibility.

A new precedent was set in 1995 when a Denver and South Park car key went at a Missouri auction for $2,500.00. The key was marked DSP&P (an early Colorado road that stopped running in 1898); it was brass and had a hollow barrel and straight bit. Switch keys that only recently brought $15.00 to $17.00 are now bringing $35.00.

Berth, 2-color brass, T-shape, unmk, 3x4" 40.00
Caboose, CNR Mitchel, Canada, long solid bbl, 4".....................15.00
Caboose, unmk, Adlake, solid long bbl, 3¾"..................................8.00
Locker, Pullman F315, flat 12.00
Shanty, GNRR, hollow bbl, 1¾"..15.00
Signal, NPSI, 36 hollow bbl, 2" 28.00
Switch, AARR -749 Adlake 30.00
Switch, BN Inc, Adlake 10.00
Switch, C&O - 3393, Adlake 15.00
Switch, C&S, Adlake #4910..85.00
Switch, CMStPRY B, steel 25.00
Switch, DTRR, Adlake 22.00
Switch, GTR, serifs, steel 30.00
Switch, H&StJ..125.00
Switch, K&IT 1643, Adlake 25.00
Switch, NP, tapered bbl...50.00
Switch, NW, Slaymaker #44037 ....40.00
Switch, Omaha Ry, Adlake 50.00
Switch, PCRR, Adlake, unused 15.00
Switch, SP Ry, big letters & bow, long bbl 25.00

Lanterns

Before 1920 kerosene brakemen's lanterns were made with tall globes, usually 5⅜" high. These are most desirable to collectors and are usually found at the top of the price scale. Short globes from 1921 through 1940 normally measure 3½" in height, except for those manufactured by Dietz, which are 4" tall. (Soon thereafter, battery brakemen's lanterns came into widespread usage; these are not highly regarded by collectors and are generally not railroad marked.)

All lanterns should be marked with the name or initials of the railroad — look on the top, the top apron, or the bell base (if it has one). Globes may be found in these colors (listed in order of popularity): clear, red, amber, aqua, cobalt, and two-color. Any lantern's value is enhanced if it has a colored globe.

Key:
A&W — Adams and Westlake   bb — bell bottom

A&W, C&O, short etched globe, Pat dates **65.00**
A&W, CMStP, red etched short globe, 1923 ....**65.00**
A&W, D&MN, wire ring bottom, clear globe, 1895 ....**185.00**
A&W, hand type, NP brass, clear/gr globe, Dec 26 '64............**1,200.00**
A&W Adams, Rock Island Lines, tall globe, 1897/1908/09........**185.00**
A&W Adams, Santa Fe, clear 5½" globe, bb, 1909 ....**200.00**
A&W Adlake, D&H, short, clear unmk globe **75.00**
A&W Adlake Kero, CRTCo, short amber unmk globe, VG **120.00**
A&W Adlake Kero, Rock Island mk on dome top, unmk short globe..**65.00**
A&W Adlake Kero, SP Lines on rim, electrified, dtd 2-48...........**65.00**
A&W Adlake Kero, TRRA on lid, short clear unmk globe, NM.**65.00**
A&W Adlake Kero, UPRR etched on clear globe, cleaned........**100.00**
A&W Adlake No 250 Kero, M&StL, red short etched globe, dome top..**135.00**
A&W Adlake No 250 Kero, SPCo on dome, gr short globe, 1923 ....**90.00**
A&W Adlake Reliable, CCC&StL, clear 5⅜" globe, wire-ring base..**175.00**
A&W Adlake Reliable, CCC&StL, wire-ring bottom, clear globe, 1912...**175.00**
A&W Adlake Reliable, D&H Co, clear 5½" globe, wire-ring base, 1913 ..**175.00**
A&W Adlake Reliable, K&M RY, tall globe, brakeman's, NM..**185.00**
A&W Adlake Reliable, MCRR, tall mk Corning globe, EX.......**185.00**
A&W Adlake Reliable, OWRR&NCo, tall globe, last Pat 1913 .**500.00**
Armspear, CN, clear short emb globe, Pat Feb 2, 26 on bottom .**150.00**
Armspear, DM&NRy, clear 5½" globe, twist-off bottom w/pot, 1895.....**225.00**
Conductor's, A&W, NP brass, closed bb, gr/clear globe, Pat Dec...64.**1,200.00**
Conductor's, A&W, Pullman, etch globe, Pat...64, EX+ **725.00**
Conductor's, MM Buck & Co, NP brass, gr/clear 5" globe, Pat Dec...65...**1,300.00**
Conger, NP, Pat #s, battery model **20.00**
CT Ham, ERR, clear 5⅜" globe, wire-ring twist-off base, Dec...'93...**175.00**
Dietz, red globe mk Paull S leader, base mk NY USA Royal.........**55.00**
Dietz Acme... NY USA, orig Dietz globe, inspector's, 15"..............**85.00**
Dietz No 1, bl pnt, red globe, mk Made in Hong Kong.................**50.00**
Dressel, J&ERyCo, steel/CI base, oil burner, dome top, 1900 .....**325.00**
ET Wright & Co, GTR, clear 5½" globe, wire-ring base **145.00**
Handlan, MOPAC, clear 5⅜" globe, wire-ring base, single wire guard..**165.00**
Handlan, NYCS, short clear unmk globe **65.00**
Handlan Buck, Frisco, clear 5½" globe, twist-off bb w/pot..........**375.00**
Keystone, PRR, etched 5" red globe, wire-ring base, oil pot, EX.**445.00**
Keystone Casey, B&O, clear 5⅜" globe, wire-ring twist-off base.....**195.00**

Linens and Uniforms

Over the years the many railroad companies took great pride in their dining car table presentation. In the very early years of railroad dining car service, the linens used at the tables were of the finest quality white damask. Most railroads would add their company's logo, name, initials, or even a spectacular scene that would be woven into the cloth (white on white). These patterns were not evident unless the fabric was held at a particular angle to the light. The dining car staff's attire generally consisted of heavily starched blinding white jackets with shiny buttons.

In later years, post-World War II, color began to be used for table linens. Florida railroads created some delightfully colorful items for the table as well as for head-rests. The passenger train crew, the conductor, and the brakemen, were generally attired in black suits, white shirts, and black ties. Their head gear generally bore a badge denoting their position. These items have all become quite collectible. Sadly, however,

replicas of badges and pins have been produced as well as 'fantasy' items (items that do not replicate an older item).

Blanket, CMStP&P, beige/brn checked wool, Greek Key border, 62x86"...**250.00**
Blanket, UP, gray wool, w/blk stripe, logo center, 47x75" **275.00**
Blanket, UP stitched in script on blk & gray wool, Pendleton, 64x80"...**130.00**
Cap, chef's; Santa Fe, logo & DC stamped in blk on wht, folds flat......**22.00**
Hat, conductor's; Amtrak, w/logo hat badge & side buttons **26.00**
Hat, conductor's; B&O, blk wool w/brass hat badge, pre-1940 ...**145.00**
Hat, conductor's; L&N, w/logo hat badge & side buttons **285.00**
Head rest seat cover, ACL, sunbather beach scene, 15x18" **17.00**
Head rest seat cover, Denver Zephyr, blk on gray, 16x19" **31.00**
Head rest seat cover, UP, winged streamliner, red/gray/yel, 14x19"..**17.00**
Jacket, waiter's; SP, mc Daylight ball & wing logo on sleeve, wht ...**58.00**
Napkin, C&NW, wht-on-wht C&NW logo, 23" sq **24.00**
Napkin, CRI&P, wht-on-wht Rock Island logo center, 21" sq **16.00**
Napkin, MP, wht-on-wht buzz saw logo, 20" sq...........................**38.00**
Napkin, SCL, wht-on-wht SCL in center, 19" sq **24.00**
Napkin, SP in script w/ball & wing on ivory w/mc stripes, 17" sq ...**66.00**
Pillowcase, GNRy Co, Pillow Rental 50 Cents..., 19½x30" **12.00**
Pillowcase, Pullman..**12.00**
Pillowcase, UPRR Chair Car, 18½x23" **8.00**
Sheet, Pullman - Property of... stamped repeatedly, 63x85"...........**12.00**
Sheet, South Look Ahead - Look South logo, 81x64" **18.00**
Tablecloth, B&O, wht-on-wht Capitol logo amid bellflowers, 45x54"...**44.00**
Tablecloth, C&NW - The '400,' in gr on yel cotton, 49x51".......**60.00**
Tablecloth, GM&O, wht-on-wht winged logo, 52" sq...................**65.00**
Towel, hand; B&O w/capitol dome woven on bl center stripe......**16.00**
Towel, hand; CN repeated on bl stripe, wht huck, 21x17"............**12.00**
Towel, hand; NYC, New York Central on bl band both ends, 17x21" ...**22.00**
Towel, hand; Property of the Pullman Co in bl stripe on wht, undtd **12.50**
Towel, hand; SMStP&P stamped in blk on wht, 13x19"...............**12.00**
Uniform, conductor's; Milwaukee Road, wool vest, coat & trousers...**175.00**

Locks

Brass switch locks (pre-1920) were made in two styles: heart-shaped and Keen Kutter style. Values for the heart-shaped locks are determined to a great extent by the railroad they represent and just how its name appears on the lock. Most in demand are locks with large embossed letters; if the letters are small and incised, demand for that lock is minimal. For instance, one from the Union Pacific line (even with heavily embossed letters) may go for only $45.00, while the same from the D&RG railroad could go easily sell for $250.00. Old Keen Kutter styles (brass with a 'pointy' base) from Colorado & Southern and Denver & Rio Grande could range from $600.00 to $1,200.00.

Steel switch locks (circa 1920 on) with the initials of the railroad incised in small letters — for example BN, L&H, and PRR — are usually valued at $20.00 to $28.00.

Switch locks described below are all made of brass and are heart shaped.

Switch, P&PU RR, Adlake, 3" wide, with chain, VG, $15.00.

Adlake, C&S, 444 under door cover (late 1944), steel..................**45.00**
Signal, ATSF on bottom edge, Eagle Lock Co...USA on shackle .**35.00**

Signal, CB&Q on front, RACO emb on side, takes hex wrench-type key..**15.00**
Signal, GNRY on front, RACO on side, w/hex wrench-type key .**30.00**
Signal, Rock Island Lines Signal on front, sq **30.00**
Signal, WABASH on front, Yale emb on bk in circle, sq **35.00**
Switch, ATSF on shackle, Slaymaker on key drop, steel w/brass rivets ..**15.00**
Switch, B&MRR on shackle bk, Wilson Bohannon on shackle front....**85.00**
Switch, CM&StP Ry on bk, Loeffelholz & Co on shackle **95.00**
Switch, D&RGW & Pat # on bk, Adlake on key drop, steel **18.00**
Switch, Frisco & Pat # on bk, Adlake on key drop, steel **15.00**
Switch, M&StLRR on shackle front, A&W... on key drop **15.00**
Switch, N&W R'Y Co emb on bk, FS HDW Co on shackle, 1924 ..**125.00**
Switch, N&WRy, Slaymaker, lg S on top of hasp, EX **75.00**
Switch, NP Switch & Pat # on bk, Adlake on key drop, steel **18.00**
Switch, NPR on bk panel, Fraim 1911 Keystone hallmk on shackle ..**265.00**
Switch, SOO on bk panel, Slaymaker...PA on shackle..............**130.00**
Water service, D&RG, F-S Hdw Co, w/key **150.00**

Silverplate

The value of silverplate, hollow ware, or flatware, is influenced by the location of the logo or railroad name and, of course, by condition. A side- or top-marked piece is preferable to one with a bottom mark. Examine a prospective purchase carefully. Some unmarked flatware has been 'enhanced' with a rather crude stamping of the railroad's name. Authentic railway markings were done at the time of manufacture and were generally executed in a flawless manner.

Bouillon cup fr, GN, tab hdls, International, SM, BS, 1964, 4" dia ..**55.00**
Bowl, C&NW, low ft, BS, International, 4¼"................**45.00**
Bowl, CMStP&P, BS, 5¼" **50.00**
Bowl, finger; CB&Q, ftd, R&B, SM, BS, 4¾" **45.00**
Bowl, MP, ftd, flared rim, International, BS, 1926, 2¼x6¼" **45.00**
Butter icer, C&A, tab hdls, 2-pc, R&B, ind, 2¾" **388.00**
Butter pat, GN, International, BS, 3" sq **40.00**
Butter pat, GN, International, TM, BS, 3" sq **30.00**
Change tray, GN on tab hdls, checkered border, International, 6" sq ..**125.00**
Coffee set, ATSF, Deco dmn shapes, R&B, 1937, 6" pot+cr/sug .**625.00**
Coffeepot, ATSF, dmn shape, hinged lid, R&B #3400B, 14-oz **85.00**
Coffeepot, CRI&P, gooseneck spout, Wallace, BS, 1927, 8-oz **150.00**
Coffeepot, GN, hinged lid, ball finial, SM, BS, 1946, 14-oz **75.00**
Coffeepot, GN Ry, beaded edges, Rogers, BS, ca 1910, ½-pt **200.00**
Coffeepot, NYC, hinged lid, International, SL, ind, 5½"............**135.00**
Creamer, B&O, hinged lid, R&B, BM, 8-oz **75.00**
Creamer, GN, hinged lid, hdl, International, SM, BS, 1946, 4-oz ..**85.00**
Creamer, GN, hinged lid, International, SM, BS, ca 1946, 4-oz ...**85.00**
Creamer, IC, hinged lid, International, R&B, BS, 7-oz **86.00**
Fork, cocktail; B&O, Cromwell, International, TM **18.00**
Fork, cocktail; GN, Astoria, Wallace, TM **50.00**
Fork, dinner; NP, Winthrop, Gorham, TM **33.00**
Fork, pickle; NYC, Commonwealth, International, BS, 5¾" **56.00**
Frame, finger bowl; PRR, rtcl sides, BM w/Keystone logo, 4" **188.00**
Hot cake cover, Rock Island Lines, pierced, acorn finial, BS, 5½" ..**85.00**
Knife, dessert; C&NW Ry (script), Modern Art, R&B, BS, 4¾" ..**30.00**
Knife, dinner; PRR, Kings, w/full shell & stainless blade, Adams .**22.00**
Knife, dinner; SP, Broadway, stainless blade, International, BS.....**20.00**
Menu holder, ICRR, pierced side w/2 pencil holders, Wallace, BS ..**135.00**
Nut pick, ATSF, Windsor, International, TM **48.00**
Sauce boat, MP, International, BS, 1926, 2-oz **50.00**
Spoon, condiment; IC, Alden, R&B, TL & BM, 4⅛"............**155.00**
Spoon, demitasse; NP, Alden, R&B, TM, BS................**35.00**
Spoon, demitasse; SPLA&SL, Modern Art, R&B, TL, 4"..........**120.00**
Spoon, soup; MStP&SStM, Empire, Rogers, BM w/SOO, 7⅛".....**32.00**
Sugar bowl, Chicago & Alton, hdls, w/lid, BS, 4x7" **280.00**
Sugar bowl, CRI&P, hdls, w/lid, R&B, BS, 11-oz **135.00**

Sugar bowl, DL&W, hdls, w/lid, International, BS, 8-oz **85.00**
Sugar bowl, GN, hdls, lid removes, International, SM, BS, 1947, 4-oz ...**75.00**
Sugar bowl, MStP&SSM, SOO Line Dollar logo, R&B, ca 1921, 12-oz...**135.00**
Sugar bowl, PRR, Keystone SL, flared base, w/lid, 4½" **175.00**
Sugar bowl, Rock Island, hdls, w/lid, R&B, BS, 11-oz................**135.00**
Sugar tongs, GN, See America First, resembles ice tongs, 4¼" ...**225.00**
Sugar tongs, UP, International, TM, 4½"................**40.00**
Syrup, PRR, Pick Barth, hinged lid, SL, BS, 5½" **230.00**
Tablespoon, GM&O, Broadway, International, TM **22.00**
Tea strainer, SP, TM w/Daylight logo on hdl, R&B, 4¼" **265.00**
Teapot, NP, long spout, hinged lid, Gorham, BS, ca 1890, ¾-pt.**200.00**
Teapot, Santa Fe Route (script) SM, Harrison, 4¾"................**785.00**
Teaspoon, SPLA&SL, Modern Art, R&B, TL................**33.00**
Tray, D&RGW, oval, R&B, BS, 4¾" **75.00**
Tray, ICRR, plain, oval, International, BS, 9x12"................**35.00**

Miscellaneous

Timetables and railroad travel brochures continue to gain in popularity and offer the collector vast information about the glory days of railroading. Annual passes continue to be favored over trip and one-time passes. Their value is contingent upon the specific railroad, its length of run, and the appearance of the pass itself. Many were tiny works of art enhanced with fancy calligraphy and decorated with unique vignettes.

Pocket calendars are popular as well as railroad playing cards. Pins, badges, and uniform buttons bearing the name or logo of a railroad are also sought after. The novice needs to be cautious about signs (metal as well as cardboard) and belt buckles. Reproductions flourish in these areas.

Ashtray, ACL, logo in wht on lg purple circle, 3½" sq..................**17.50**
Ashtray, CN, wht on clear glass, 5½"................**17.00**
Ashtray/table, UP, plunger-type ash disposal w/17" dia table, TM, 27"...**325.00**
Badge, breast; B&O Railway Police, NP shield, 2¼x2½" **230.00**
Badge, breast; Canadian Pacific RR Police, crown & logo, 2¼x2¼" **95.00**
Badge, breast; NPRy Deputy Sheriff, NP 6-pointed star, unmk, 2½" ..**150.00**
Badge, breast; Police 105 Ill Cent RR, 6-pointed NP star, 3"......**175.00**
Badge, cap; GN Ry Brakeman, NP, curved top, 1¼x4"..................**95.00**
Badge, cap; NYC Conductor, NYC bl enamel logo, pebbled gold field...**130.00**
Baggage check, CMStP, Milwaukee Wis, brass w/leather strap, 2" sq....**56.00**
Baggage tag, PARR, lg letterhead on brn, 1949, 2½x5"..................**2.50**
Bell, locomotive; brass w/iron mt, no attribution, 23".............**1,000.00**
Blotter, CB&Q, Combination Tours, Many Glacier Region scene, 4x9"..**15.00**
Blotter, CM&StP, Gallatin Gateway...Yellowstone, 1920s, 3¼x6¼" **20.00**
Blotter, D&LW anthracite logo, fishing cover, 1940s-50s, NM **7.00**
Book, B&O, Rules & Regulations, 1910, 110-pg, 4x6"................**14.00**
Book, Fred Harvey Story of Grand Canyon: How..., 1917, 20th ed, 80-pg ..**15.00**
Book, SP, Rules & Regulations, 1923, 151-pg, 4x6½" **16.00**
Book, Story of Grand Canyon in AZ, Fred Harvey, 1925, M **25.00**
Book, Traveler's Ry Guide, hardbk, HC, 1869, timetables, detailed map..**200.00**
Booklet, CD Midland, Through the Rockies, Hell Gate cover, 7x9", G.....**80.00**
Booklet, child's activity; UP, Yellowstone Bears, 1932, 8½x22"..**110.00**
Brochure, D&RGW, Rocky Mtn Views, string-tied, 1934, 44-pg, 10x12" ...**33.00**
Brochure, GN Glacier Park, 1938, 30-pg+16" sq fold-out map **26.00**
Brochure, Pacific Electric Ry, Mt Lowe Tavern/Cottages+timetable, 1925..**40.00**
Brochure, PRR, NJ Seashore Resorts, 1925, 192-pg+fold-out map .**68.00**
Brochure, Pullman, 9 Ways To Travel, photos, 1964, 4x8"............**15.00**
Brochure, SP, Golden Gate International Exposition, 1939, 20-pg, 8x9" ..**18.00**
Brochure, UP Domeliner, The Challenger, 1961, 9x4"................**12.00**
Builder's plate, Baldwin Westinghouse All Electric..., brass, 1928..**1,800.00**
Button, B&O, brass convex style, Scoville Mfg, ca 1915, lg, EX.....**5.00**
Button, CStPM&0, silver, flat, Chicago Uniform & Cap Co, lg.....**8.00**
Button, D&RGW, brass, sm **20.00**
Button, Gulf, Mobile & OH, brass flat style, Superior Quality, 1890s .**25.00**
Button, Lackawanna RR, brass convex style, Scoville Mfg, ca 1904 ...**10.00**

Button, Pullman, silver, Waterbury Button Co on bk, G, sm **5.00**
Button, vest; ATSF, Cross logo on gold-tone....................................**3.00**
Buttons, POD Ry Mail Service, Scovill Mfg, ⅞", set of 5.............**68.00**
Calendar, ATSF, Navajo Shepherdess, 1954, EX+ **15.00**
Calendar, C&NW, 12 attached sheets on 12x24" sheet w/name trains, 1937...**170.00**
Calendar, perpetual; MP, tin on cb, 19", EX+ **125.00**
Can, kerosene; Erie, bail hdl, long narrow cone top, screw lid, SM ..**90.00**
Can, water; CMStP&P, galvanized, lift-off lid, pouring spout, wire hdl..**30.00**
Canasta score card, CN, red logo, 5½x8½" **3.00**
Check, Memphis & Little Rock, pre-printed date: 18__, #2022, unused..**52.00**
Check, Rio Grande Southern, 1919, cancelled **3.00**
Correspondence, D&RG, memo re use of ballpoint pens, 1947, 7½x8" .**5.00**
Crock, deodorizer; Pullman, 7½" **26.00**
Envelope, Burlington Rte, Aboard the Burlington Zephyr, unused.**2.00**
Guide, D&H, Laurentian cover, blk & wht w/bl, 1950s, 24-pg, EX..**10.00**
Inkwell, NP, Route of Great Baked Potato, full color, no inserts ...**600.00**
Ladder, berth; Pullman, aluminum w/rubber tips, clips, 58" **110.00**
Magazine, C&O Railway Employee's Magazine, Dec 1922, EX.....**15.00**
Map, GN, western section in detail, 1928, 9x12" **15.00**
Map, Gray's RR Map of PA, 1872, 17x26" **57.00**
Map, Plant System, includes FL/SC/Cuba/etc, 1893, unfolds to 19x22"..**50.00**
Map, PRR, state of PA, 55 panels of PA RRs, 9x7" hardcover book, 1910.**105.00**
Map, Puerto Rico RRs, very detailed, 1917, 14x20" **50.00**
Map, RRs of northern MI, Rand McNally, 1904, 28x20" **50.00**
Map, shows routes of NP, CB&Q, SP&S, C&S, GN, 1915, unfolds: 32x36" ..**24.00**
Menu, ATSF Grand Canyon Nat'l Park, WR Leigh cover, 1951 .**22.00**
Menu, Burlington Rte, Denver Zephyr, Supper Being..., 4½x6½" ...**20.00**
Menu, C&CF Ry, Steam Engine No 2 cover, ca 1960s..................**18.00**
Menu, C&NW, Corn King Ltd, single sheet card stock, early 1930s, 8x10"...**37.00**
Menu, CB&Q Burlington Zephyr, child's daily, unfolded: 6x9", NM..**12.00**
Menu, D&RGW, beverages, 4-pg, 1974, 7x4½" **10.00**
Menu, Fred Harvey, dbl fold, no insert, mc scenic cover, 8x11"...**15.00**
Menu, LV passenger terminal on cover, 1928, 10¼x4¼"...............**25.00**
Menu, Rio Grande, Royal Gorge Grill, 1954, 5½x8½" **20.00**
Mirror, GN, frosted Rocky silhouette, beveled edges, 14x28" **980.00**
Notebook daily planner, St Louis SW, The Cotton Belt, 1936 .....**28.00**
Pass, annual; ACL, 1959-60 ....**6.50**
Pass, annual; Galveston, Houston & Henderson, 1881 ....**43.00**
Pass, annual; Gulf, Mobile & Northern, to Superintent IC RR, 1917 ..**48.00**
Pass, annual; Mobile & OH, issued to car tracer, 1889.................**30.00**
Pass, annual; Pontiac, Northern & Oxford to exec of GR&I, 1893 ..**110.00**
Pass, annual; Sandusky, Mansfield & Newark, to B&O agent, 1857 ...**63.00**
Pass, annual; St Louis & Cairo, to exec Memphis & Little Rock RR, 1886 ...**76.00**

Pass, employee's trip; The Missouri Pacific Railway, 1899, EX, $8.50.

Pass, CB&Q, made to President of M&PP RR, card stock, 1909..**15.00**
Pass, Erie RR, countersigned by issuant, 1912-13, EX....................**25.00**
Pass, ICRR, countersigned by issuant, 1912 ....**20.00**
Pin, lapel; ARMMA, steam locomotive on blk enamel, gold letters, ¾" ..**20.00**
Pin, lapel; B of RRC, gr feather, red pencil, gold letters, ½" **15.00**
Playing cards, Burlington Route, logo on cards & case, 52+3, 1925 ..**86.00**
Playing cards, GNRR, Indian figure on box, complete, EX+.........**65.00**
Postcard, Castle Rock CO, train at depot, 1914, VG....................**5.00**
Postcard, Riverside PRR station, postmk 1914............................**28.00**

Prints, C&O, Chessie, Peake, Chessie & kittens, 10x12", +orig envelope ..**47.00**
Semaphore blade, M rstr, 42"..**100.00**
Sewing kit, GN, leather, w/scissors/thread/needles, TM, 3x3" **115.00**
Sheet music, Wabash Cannon Ball, 1933....................................**17.50**
Sign, CB&Q, Burlington Rte, 1-sided porc, grommets, 10x12" ..**200.00**
Sign, Northern Pacific Railway, glass, blk w/gold lettering, 4x34" ..**140.00**
Sign, PRR, Keystone logo, 1-sided porc, 5 grommets, 16x17".....**295.00**
Sign, Railway Express Agency, porc, yel on blk, 12x72", G **145.00**
Sign, RR crossing, 2-sided porc, blk on yel metal, 36"..................**55.00**
Stock certificate, Milwaukee & Pairie Du Chein Ry, 2 stamps, 1864 ..**20.00**
Tallow pot, ATSF, teapot style w/gooseneck spout, 5x7¼x5" **40.00**
Ticket, special excursion to Montague, Yreka RR Co, 1891...........**6.00**
Timetable, Condon, Kinzua & Southern RR, card stock, 1929, 3x4½" .**50.00**
Timetable, CP Annotated...Eastbound Edition, 1903, 97-pg, VG.**55.00**
Timetable, CPRR, The Canadian, 1967, w/system route map.......**12.00**
Timetable, D&RGW, red, 1925 ....**15.00**
Timetable, employee; C&O, 18-pg, June, 1933............................**50.00**
Timetable, employee; WP, Western Division, #28, July 1942 ....**26.00**
Timetable, public; ATSF, 110-pg, 1924...**22.00**
Timetable, public; ATSF, 62 panels, 4-panel system map, 1897 ..**100.00**
Timetable, public; L&N, 2-panel map, unfolds to 18x36" **34.00**
Timetable, public; SP, 4-panel of navigation routes, 72 panels, 1911...**60.00**
Timetable, T&P Ry Co passenger train schedules, 1950s **20.00**
Timetable, WP Feather River box logo, 3-color map, 1949, 8-pg, 1949 ..**14.00**
Trust plate, D&RGW, steel, 8x14½" **45.00**
Wax sealer, Bemidji & No MN Express Co, Bemidji, brass head, wood hdl...**270.00**
Wax sealer, Railway Express Agency, brass head, wood hdl, 3½"..**50.00**
Whistle, CI w/brass valve, 5-chime, 1930s, 20x7" dia, EX.......**1,500.00**
Whistle, Grand Trunk, 5-chime, valve built into brass base, 21"...**100.00**
Whistle, Hancock, 3-chime, step-up, brass, emb Superheat & 300, 25" ..**3,500.00**

Razors

As straight razors gain in popularity, prices of those razors also increase. This carries with it a lure of investment possibilities which can encourage the novice or speculator to make purchases that may later prove to be unwise. We recommend that before investing serious money in razors, you become familiar with the elements which make a razor valuable. As with other collectibles, there are specific traits which are desirable and which have a major impact on the price of a piece.

The following information is based on the second edition of *The Standard Guide to Razors* by Roy Ritchie and Ron Stewart (available from R&C Books, P.O. Box 151, Combs, KY 41729, $9.95 +$2.50 S&H, autographed or from Collector Books). It describes the elements most likely to influence a razor's collector value and their system of calculating that value. (Their book is a valuable reference guide to both the casual and serious collector of razors.)

There are four major factors which determine a razor's collector value. These are the brand and country of origin, the handle material, the art work found on the handles or blades and the condition of the razor. Ritchie and Stewart freely admit that there are other factors that may come into play with some collectors, but these are the major players in determining value. They have devised a system of evaluation which is based on these four factors.

The most important factor is the value placed on the brand and country of origin. This is the price of a common razor made by (or for) a particular company. It has plain handles, probably made of plastic, no art work, and is in collectible condition. It is the beginning value. Hundreds (thousands?) of these values are provided in the 'Listings of Companies and Base Values' chapter in the book.

The second category is that of handle material. This covers a wide range of materials, from fiber on the low end to ivory on the high end. The collector needs to be able to identify the different handle materials when he sees them. This often takes some practice, since there are some very good plastics that can mimic ivory quite successfully. Also, the difference between genuine celluloid and plastic can become significant when determining value. A detailed chart of these values is supplied in the book. The listing below can be used as a general guide.

The third category is the most subjective. Nevertheless, it is an extremely important factor in determining value. This category is artwork, which can include everything from logo art to carving and sculpture. It may range from highly ornate to tastefully correct. Blade etching as well as handle artistry are to be considered. Perhaps what some call the 'gotta have it' or the 'neatness' factors properly fall into this category. You must accurately determine the artistic merits of your razor when you evaluate it relative to this factor. Again, the book we referenced earlier provides a more complete listing of considerations than is used here.

Finally, the condition is factored in. The book's scales run from 'parts' (10% +/-) to 'Good' (150% +/-). Average (100% +/-) is classified as 'Collectible.' See chart D for details concerning condition guidelines for evaluation.

Samplings from charts:

Chart A: Companies and Base Values:

Abercrombie & Finch, NY...14.00
Areial, USA...24.00
Boker, Henri & Co, Germany...14.00
Brick, F, England..12.00
Case Mfg Co, Spring Valley, NY..40.00
Chores, James; England...13.00
Dahlqres, CW; Sweden...14.00
Diane, Japan...10.00
Electric Co, NY..15.00
ERN, Germany...12.00
Fautless, Germany..11.00
Fox Cutlery, Germany...11.00
Fredericks (Celebrated Cutlery), England.................................13.00
Gilbert Bros, England..11.00
Griffon XX, Germany..11.00
Henckels, Germany..15.00
Holly Mfg Co, CT...27.00
International Cutlery Co NY/Germany.......................................11.00
IXL, England...12.00
Jay, John; NY..12.00
KaBar, Union Cut Co, USA...28.00
Kanner, J; Germany...11.00
Kern, R&W; Canada/England..12.00
LeCocltre, Jacque; Switzerland...12.00
Levering Razor Co, NY/Germany..18.00
McIntosh & Heather, OH...12.00
Merit Import Co, Germany...10.00
Monthoote, England...12.00
National Cut Co, OH..11.00
Oxford Razor Co, Germany...10.00
Palmer Brothers, Savannah, GA..20.00
Primble, John; Indian Steel Works, Louisville, KY........................24.00
Queen City, NY...30.00
Querelle, A; Paris, France...12.00
Quigley, Germany...12.00
Radford, Joseph & Sons, England..12.00
Rattler Razor Co, Germany..10.00
Robeson Cut Co, USA..28.00
Salamander Works, Germany..11.00
Söderein, Ekilstuna Sweden...11.00
Taylor, LM; Cincinnati, OH...14.00
Tower Brand, Germany...16.00
Ulmer, Germany...11.00

US Barber Supply, TX...12.00
Vinnegut Hdw Co, IN..11.00
Vogel, Ed; PA..10.00
Wade & Butcher, England..24.00
Weis, JH; Supply House, Louisville, KY...................................15.00
Yankee Cutlery Co, Germany...11.00
Yazbek, Lahod, OH..11.00
Zacour Bros, Germany...10.00
Zepp Germany...10.00

Chart B, as described below, is an abbreviated version of the handle materials list in *The Standard Guide to Razors*. It is an essential category in the use of the appraisal system developed by the authors.

Ivory	550%
Tortoise Shell	500%
Pearl	400%
Stag	400%
Bone	300%
Celluloid	250%
Composition	150%
Plastic	100%

Chart C deals with the artistic value of the razor. As pointed out earlier, this is a very subjective area. It takes study to determine what is good and what is not. Taste can also play a significant role in determining the value placed on the artistic merit of a razor. The range is from superior to nonexistent. Categories generally are divided as follows:

Exceptional	650%
Superior	550%
Good	400%
Average	300%
Minimal	200%
Plain	100%
Nonexistent	0%

Chart D is also very subjective. It determines the condition of the razor. You must judge accurately if the appraisal system is to work for you.

Good   150%

Does not have to be factory mint to fall within this category. However, there can be no visible flaws if it is to be calculated at 150%.

Collectible   100%

May have some flaws that do not greatly detract from the artwork or finish.

Parts   10%

Unrepairable, valuable as salvageable parts.

Razors may fall within any of these categories, ie. collectible + 112%.

Now to determine the value of your razor, multiply A times B, then multiply A times C. Add your two answers and multiply this sum times D. The answer you get is your collector value. See the example below.

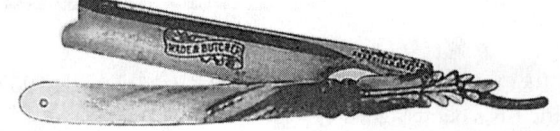

(a) Brand and Origin Base Value	(b) Handle Material % Value	(c) Artwork % Value	(d) Condition % Value	(e) Collector Value
Wade & Butcher England $24.00	Iridescent Pearl Handles 24 x 400% $96.00	Carved handles 24 x 500% $120.00	Cracked handle at pin Collectible- 80%	$96+$120=$216 $216 x 80%= **$172.80**

Reamers

The reamer market is very active right now, and prices are escalating rapidly. They have been made in hundreds of styles and colors and by as many manufacturers. Their purpose is to extract the juices from lemons, oranges, and grapefruits. The largest producer of glass reamers was McKee, who pressed their products from many types of glass — custard; Delphite and Chalaine Blue; opaque white; Skokie Green; black; caramel and white opalescent; Seville Yellow; and transparent pink, green, and clear. Among these, the black and the caramel opalescents are the most valuable.

The Fry Glass Company also made reamers that are today very collectible. The Hazel Atlas Crisscross orange reamer in pink is valued at $300.00 to $325.00 or more — the same in blue, $350.00. Hocking produced a light blue orange reamer and, in the same soft hue, a two-piece reamer and measuring cup combination. Both are considered rare and very valuable with currently quoted estimates at $1,000.00 and up for the former and $1,800.00 and up for the latter. In addition to the colors mentioned, red glass examples — transparent or slag — are rare and costly. Prices vary greatly according to color and rarity. The same reamer in crystal may be worth three times as much in a more desirable color.

Among the most valuable ceramic reamers are those made by American potteries. The Spongeband reamer by Red Wing is valued in excess of $500.00; Coorsite reamers with gold or silver trim are worth $300.00 and up. Figurals are popular — Mickey Mouse and John Bull may bring $600.00 to $1,000.00. Others range from $55.00 to $350.00. Fine china one- and two-piece reamers are also very desirable and command very respectable prices.

A word about reproductions: A series of limited edition reamers is being made by Edna Barnes of Uniontown, Ohio. These are all marked with a 'B' in a circle. Other reproductions have been made from old molds. The most important of these are Anchor Hocking two-piece two-cup measure and top, Gillespie one-cup measure with reamer top, Westmoreland with flattened handle, Westmoreland four-cup measure embossed with orange and lemons, Duboe (hand-held darning egg), and Easley's Diamonds one-piece.

Our advisor for this category is Dee Long; she is listed in the Directory under Illinois. For more information concerning reamers and reproductions, contact our advisor or the National Reamer Collectors Association (see Clubs, Newsletters, and Catalogs). Be sure to include an SASE when requesting information.

Ceramic

Baby's Orange Juice, figural orange, ring hdl, Goebel, 1927 .... 95.00
Child's face, 2-pc, Japan, 3" 120.00
Citrus face, 2-pc, Japan, 1940s, 5½" 100.00
Citrus face (pk, rare), 2-pc, Napco Japan, 5¼" 105.00
Citrus face (yel), 2-pc, Japan, 1940s, 5¼" 90.00
Citrus Fruit face, Japan foil label, 1950s, 5¼" 98.00
Clown, bright orange w/gr on wht, Japan, late 1930s-40s, 7" 145.00
Clown, gr/red/wht, Japan, late 1930s-40s, 5" 115.00

Clown, multicolor, Japan/Sigma, two-piece, 6½", $95.00. (Photo courtesy Bobbie Zucker Bryson)

Clown, mc lustre, ruffled collar, Japan, 1940s, 4¾" 140.00
Clown, mc on wht, Mikori Ware, HP, Made in Japan, 1940s, 7¼" .. 145.00
Clown, orange details on wht, 2-pc, Japan, late 1930s, 5¼" 125.00
Clown, pale gr & wht w/orange hands & ft, Japan, 3½" 50.00
Clown face, mc on wht, reamer hat, Japan, 1940s, 4" 135.00
Duck, bulging bl eyes, orange details, 2-pc, Japan, 2½" 90.00
Duck, mc lustre, Japan, 1940s, 3½" 95.00
Floral, HP w/gold, Noritake, baby's, ca 1906-08, NM 140.00
Floral on wht, 1-pc, Made in Japan, 1940s, 2½" 60.00
Floral on wht, 2-pc, Japan, 1940s, 4" 65.00
Lemon form, HP, Made in Japan, 1940s, 4" 45.00
Lemon form, shiny yel, 3-pc, Made in Japan, 1940s, 5" 60.00
Lemons on wht, 2-pc, mk Italy, 3¼" bowl+2½" stick hdl 15.00
Orange for Baby, orange form, Goebel, C57/2 wide crown mk 40.00
Orange form, orange lustre, 3-pc, Japan, 1940s, 5" 80.00
Orange form, shiny wht, Japan, 3-pc, 1930s-40s, 4¼" 80.00
Orange form, 2-pc, Made in England, 1940s, 3½" 90.00
Orange form, 3-pc, unmk, 4⅞" 70.00
Saucer type w/seed strainer, Goebel, #D-108, stylized bee, NM .. 125.00
Scroll band, bl/orange/beige, Made in Japan, 4½" 40.00
Teapot type, bl & wht, bl-edge reamer top, 4½" 25.00

Glass

Cambridge, gr, flat, from $200 to 225.00
Cambridge, gr, ftd, sm, from $550 to 600.00
Federal, amber, tab hdl, from $300 to 325.00
Federal, gr, pointed cone, from $25 to 28.00
Federal, Panelled, gr, loop hdl, from $30 to 35.00
Federal, pk, ribbed, loop hdl, from $40 to 45.00
Fenton, elephant decor base, 2-pc, from $110 to 125.00
Fleur-de-Lis, milk glass, emb word, from $75 to 85.00
Fry, amber, from $375 to 395.00
Fry, Azure Blue, str sides, from $1,800 to 2,000.00
Fry, canary, fluted 'Jell-O mold,' from $375 to 400.00
Fry, lt gr, from $35 to 85.00
Fry, wht opal, from $35 to 40.00
Hazel Atlas, cobalt, tab hdl, orange reamer, from $295 to 325.00
Hazel Atlas, pk, pitcher & reamer top, 2-cup, from $295 to 325.00
Hazel Atlas, pk (lt or dk), tab hdl, lemon reamer, from $40 to 45.00
Hocking, gr transparent, tab hdl, from $25 to 27.50
Hocking, Vitrock (wht), from $25 to 30.00
Indiana Glass, amber, from $300 to 350.00
Indiana Glass, amber, hdld, spout opposite, from $300 to 325.00
Indiana Glass, amber, 6-sided cone, vertical hdl, from $300 to 350.00
Jeannette, gr transparent, lg, from $30 to 35.00
Jeannette, Jennyware, pk, from $125 to 135.00
Jeannette, lt or dk Jade-ite, from $45 to 50.00
LE Smith, gr, 2-pc, from $325 to 335.00
LINDSAY, pk, from $450 to 500.00
Orange Juice Extractor, blk, from $425 to 450.00
RADNT, crystal, from $135 to 150.00
RADNT, gr, from $450 to 495.00
Saunders, Jade-ite, emb letters, from $1,600 to 1,700.00
Sunkist, blk, from $700 to 750.00
Sunkist, butterscotch, from $375 to 400.00
Sunkist, Chalaine Blue, from $225 to 245.00
Sunkist, Crown Tuscan, from $375 to 400.00
Sunkist, French Ivory, from $45 to 55.00
Sunkist, gray, from $175 to 185.00
Sunkist, turq bl, from $200 to 225.00
Sunkist, yel opaque, from $50 to 55.00
Tricia, blk, from $1,400 to 1,500.00
Tufglass, gr transparent, from $100 to 110.00

Unknown, crystal, Thumbprint, from $45 to **50.00**
Unknown, pk frosted, decor, from $75 to..**85.00**
US Glass, amber, pitcher, set, 2-cup, from $350 to......................**375.00**
US Glass, gr, pitcher set, 4-cup, from $140 to.............................**150.00**
US Glass, pk, pitcher, set, 2-cup, from $55 to................................**60.00**
US Glass, yel opaque, reamer pitcher, from $650 to....................**750.00**
Valencia, milk glass, emb letters, from $120 to............................**150.00**
Westmoreland, amber, from $300 to..**325.00**
Westmoreland, crystal, 2-pc, from $65 to..**70.00**
Westmoreland, crystal w/oranges decor, loop hdl, from $60 to......**65.00**
Westmoreland, pk, 2-pc, from $200 to..**225.00**

Records

Records of interest to collectors are often not the million-selling hits by 'superstars.' Very few records by Bing Crosby, for example, are of any more than nominal value, and those that are valuable usually don't even have his name on the label! Collectors today are most interested in records that were made in limited quantities, early works of a performer who later became famous, and those issued in special series or aimed at a limited market. Vintage records are judged desirable by their recorded content as well; those that lack the quality of music that makes a record collectible will always be 'junk' records in spite of their age, scarcity, or the obsolescence of their technology.

Records are usually graded visually rather than aurally, since it is seldom if ever possible to first play the records you buy at shows, by mail, at flea markets, etc. Condition is one of the most important determinants of value. For example, a nearly mint-condition Elvis Presley 45 of 'Milk Cow Blues' (Sun 215) has a potential value of over $1,500.00. A small sticker on the label could cut its value in half; noticeable wear could reduce its value by 80%. A mint record must show no evidence of use (record jackets, in the case of EPs and LPs, must be equally choice). Excellent condition denotes a record showing only slight signs of use with no audible defects. A very good record has noticeable wear but still plays well. Records of lesser grades may be unsaleable, unless very scarce and/or highly sought-after.

While the value of most 78s does not depend upon their being in appropriate sleeves (although a sleeveless existence certainly contributes to damage and deterioration!), this is not the case with most EPs (extended play 45s) and LPs (long-playing 33⅓ rpm albums), which must have their jackets (cardboard sleeves), in nice condition, free of disfiguring damage, such as writing, stickers, or tape. Often, common and minimally valued 45s might be collectible if they are in appropriate picture sleeves (special sleeves that depict the artist/group or other fanciful or symbolic graphic and identify the song titles, record label, and number), e.g. many common records by Elvis Presley, The Beatles, and The Beach Boys.

Promotional copies (DJ copies) supplied to radio stations often have labels different in designs and/or colors from their commercially issued counterparts. Labels usually bear a designation 'Not for Sale,' 'Audition Copy,' 'Sample Copy,' or the like. Records may be pressed of translucent vinyl; while most promos are not particularly collectible, those by certain 'hot' artists, such as Elvis Presley, The Beach Boys, and The Beatles are usually premium discs.

Many of the most desirable and valuable 45s have been 'bootlegged' (counterfeited). For example, there are probably more fake Elvis Presley *Sun* records in circulation than authentic copies — certainly in higher grades! Collectors should be alert for these often deceptive counterfeits.

Our advisor for this category is L.R. Docks, author of *American Premium Record Guide*, which lists 60,000 records by over 7,000 artists, in its sixth edition. He is listed in the Directory under Texas. In the listings that follow, prices are suggested for records that are in excellent condition; worn or abused records may be worth only a small fraction of the values quoted and may not be saleable at all.

Blues, Rhythm and Blues, Rock 'N Roll, Rockabilly

Adventurers, Rock & Roll Uprising, Columbia 42227, 45 rpm **10.00**
Alexander, Texas; Blue Devil Blues, Okeh 8640, 78 rpm **50.00**
Armstrong, May; Joe Boy Blues, Brunswick 7010, 78 rpm............**100.00**
Avalon, Frankie; Young Frankie Avalon, Chancellor 5002, LP.....**20.00**
Avons, Whisper (Softly), Hull 744, 45 rpm **15.00**
Bailey, Kid; Rowdy Blues, Brunswick 7114, 78 rpm....................**300.00**
Beach Boys, Surfin', Candix 301, 45 rpm......................................**75.00**
Beltones, I Talk to My Echo, Hull 721, 45 rpm **20.00**
Butterbeans & Susie, Contruction Gang, Okeh 8163, 78 rpm....**125.00**
Cannon & Woods, Fourth & Beale, Brunswick 7138, 78 rpm **150.00**
Capris, God Only Knows, Gotham 7304, 45 rpm **40.00**
Carolina Peanut Boys, Spider's Nest Blues, Victor 23319, 78 rpm..**400.00**
Champions, Pay Me Some Attention, Chart 620, 45 rpm **20.00**
Chiffons, He's So Fine, Laurie 2018, LP..**50.00**
Danny & the Juniors, At the Hop, ABC Paramount 11, EP.........**75.00**
Danny & the Juniors, At the Hop, ABC Paramount 9871, 45 rpm...**8.00**
Danny & the Juniors, At the Hop, ABC 9871, 78 rpm.................**30.00**

Darin, Bobby; You're The Reason I'm Living, Capitol 4897, 45 rpm, $12.00.

Davis, Walter; Blue Sea Blues, Bluebird 5038, 78 rpm...................**80.00**
Dells, The; Dreams of Contentment, Vee Jays 166, 45 rpm **30.00**
Down South Boys, The New Stop & Listen Blues, Varsity 6009, 78 rpm..**25.00**
Fabian, Hold That Tiger, Chancellor 5003, LP..............................**40.00**
Fabres, Shelly; The Things We Did Last Summer, Colpix 431, LP..**30.00**
Five Satins, A Million to One, Ember 1028, 45 rpm **10.00**
Foster, Jim; Pork Chop Blues, Champion 15359, 78 rpm............**300.00**
Four Southern Singers, Old Man Harlem, Bluebird 8392, 78 rpm...**15.00**
Franklin, Buck; Crooked World Blues, Victor 23310, 78 rpm.....**100.00**
Gay Notes, For Only a Moment, Drexel 905, 45 rpm....................**80.00**
Georgia Bill, Georgia Rag, Okeh 8924, 78 rpm **300.00**
Glen, Emery; Back Door Blues, Columbia 14472, 78 rpm.............**75.00**
Griffin, Buck; Ballin' & Squallin', Lin 1015, 45 rpm....................**40.00**
Haley, Bill & the Comets; Shake Rattle & Roll, Decca 2168, EP..**30.00**
Hampton, John; Honey Hush, United 210, 45 rpm.......................**20.00**
Heartbreakers, Heartbreaker, RCA Victor 4327, 45 rpm.............**100.00**
Henry, Curtis; G-Man Blues, Bluebird 6845, 78 rpm **20.00**
Holly, Buddy; Peggy Sue, Coral 61885, 45 rpm............................**10.00**
Ink Spots, Something Old Something New, King 535, LP.............**50.00**
Isley Brothers, Don't Be Jealous, Cindy 3009, 45 rpm **20.00**
Jackson Blue Boys, Sweet Alberta, Columbia 14397, 78 rpm.......**150.00**
James, Skip; Cherry Ball Blues, Paramount 13065, 78 rpm **600.00**
James, Sonny; Southern Gentleman, Capitol 779, LP...................**15.00**
Jets, I'll Hide My Tears, Aladdin 3247, 45 rpm.............................**120.00**
Johnson, Frank; Trouble 'Bout My Soul, Herwin 92038, 78 rpm...**250.00**
Johnson, Tommy; Canned Heat Blues, Victor V-38535, 78 rpm...**2,500.00**
Johnson Boys, Violin Blues, Okeh 8708, 78 rpm **100.00**
Junior Blues, Whiskey Head Woman, RPM 320, 78 rpm **15.00**
Kid Stormy Weather, Short Hair Blues, Vocalion 03145, 78 rpm..**125.00**

Kingsmen, One Foolish Mistake, Neil 102, 45 rpm 20.00
Knickerbockers, You Must Know, Natural 3000, 45 rpm.............200.00
Lewis, Archie; Miss Handy Hanks, Champion 16677, 78 rpm....150.00
Lewis, Jerry Lee; Great Balls of Fire, Sun 281, 78 rpm.............50.00
Lillie, Mae; Mama Don't Want It, Okeh 8920, 78 rpm 80.00
Little Richard, Here's Little Richard, Specialty 2100, LP............50.00
Littlefield, Little Willie, Pleading at Midnight, Federal 12110, 45 rpm..150.00
Louisiana Johnny, Whiskey Head Woman, Vocalion 03497, 78 rpm.......30.00
Marquees, The Bells, Grand 141, 45 rpm 75.00
Martin & Robert, Dollar Blues, Brunswick 7007, 78 rpm.............150.00
Mathes, Minnie; Ball Game Blues, Vocalion 04431, 78 rpm.........20.00
McCullum, Robert; Jackson Town Woman, Aristocrat 413, 78 rpm...60.00
Monterays, First Kiss, Dominion 1019, 45 rpm 20.00
Moonglows, Baby Please, Chance 1147, 45 rpm, red plastic 600.00
Muskateers, Deep in My Heart, Roxy 801, 78 rpm 250.00
Nance, Mabel; The Stomps, Silvertone 3547, 78 rpm...............200.00
Nesbitt, Scottie; Troubled & Blue, Bluebird 7155, 78 rpm..........15.00
Neville, Aaron; Show Me the Way, Minit 618, 45 rpm.................10.00
Newman, Jack; Blackberry Wine, Vocalion 04265, 78 rpm 15.00
Ogletree, Louis; Tell It Like It Is, Parrot 822, 45 rpm 40.00
Old Man Oden, Thick & Thin, Decca 7545, 78 rpm...................40.00
One Arm Slim, Crap Shootin' Blues, Vocalion 04676, 78 rpm.....20.00
Orbits, Message of Love, Flair-X 5000, 45 rpm..........................15.00
Orchids, Beginning To Miss You, King 4663, 45 rpm................100.00
Orioles, It Seems So Long Ago, Jubilee 5002, 78 rpm...............15.00
Papa Freddie, Muddy Water Blues, Okeh 8422, 78 rpm...........175.00
Penguins, Cool Cool Penguins, Dooto 242, LP..........................100.00
Peters, Charley; Lord I'm Discouraged, Herwin 92036, 78 rpm...300.00
Pickett, Dan; Lemon Man, Gotham 516, 78 rpm 25.00
Platters, The Platters, King 549, LP 200.00
Presley, Elvis; Blue Suede Shoes, RCA Victor 6636, 45 rpm.........20.00
Presley, Elvis; Blue Suede Shoes, RCA Victor 6636, 78 rpm.........50.00
Prisonaires, My God Is Real, Sun 189, 45 rpm.........................250.00
Richardson 'Mooch'; Helena Blues, Okeh 8611, 78 rpm.............75.00
Rinky Dinks, Mighty Mighty Man, Atco 6128, 45 rpm.................15.00
Robbins, Marty; Long Tall Sally, Columbia 40679, 45 rpm 20.00
Rose, Lucy; Papa You're Too Slow, Champion 15471, 78 rpm 100.00
Sad, Sally; Don't Say Goodbye, Varsity 6033, 78 rpm 20.00
Sam & Oscar, I Done Caught That Rascal Now, Brunswick 7212, 78 rpm....100.00
Scott, Roosevelt; Doctor Bill Blues, Vocalion 05502, 78 rpm 20.00
Scruggs, Irene; My Back to the Wall, Champion 16148, 78 rpm....200.00
Serenaders, Tomorrow Night, JVB 2001, 78 rpm......................100.00
Starr, Andy; I Love My Baby, Arcade 115, 45 rpm......................50.00
Supremes, Could This Be You?, Kitten 6969, 45 rpm..................40.00
Sweet Papa Tadpole, Black Spider Blues, Vocalion 1680, 78 rpm...150.00
Tampa Red, Boogie Woogie Woman, RCA Victor 4275, 45 rpm .30.00
Tarpley, Slim; Alabama Hustler, Paramount 13062, 78 rpm.......200.00
Taylor, Ethel; Empty Bed Blues, Supertone 9285, 78 rpm 100.00
Teardrops, My Heart, Josie 771, 45 rpm 75.00
Terry, Nat; Take It Easy, Imperial 5150, 78 rpm 15.00
Thomas, Rufus; I'm So Worried, Talent 807, 78 rpm.................60.00
Tisdom, James; Throw This Dog a Bone, Universal-Fox 101, 78 rpm...30.00
Turbans, Sister Sookey, Herald 469, 45 rpm.............................12.00
Turner, Bee; Rough Treatin' Daddy, Paramount 13017, 78 rpm ..300.00
Two of Spades, Meddlin' With the Blues, Columbia 14072-D, 78 rpm..30.00
Uptones, I'll Be There, Lute 6025, 45 rpm.................................15.00
Valentines, Tonight Kathleen, Old Town 1009, 45 rpm...............150.00
Van Dykes, The Fixer, Decca 30654, 45 rpm 20.00
Walker, T-Bone; Mean Old World, Capitol 1003, 78 rpm............10.00
Wallace, Sippie; A Jealous Woman Like Me, Okeh 8301, 78 rpm...200.00
Walter & Byrd, Wasn't It Sad About Lemon, Paramount 12945, 78 rpm...175.00
Wayne, James; Sweet Little Woman, Imperial 5258, 45 rpm.........30.00
Whitman, Slim; China Doll, Imperial 8156, 45 rpm...................15.00
Williams, Hank; Ramblin Man, MGM 3219, LP 70.00

Woods, Eva; He's My Man, Silvertone 3557, 78 rpm 100.00
Wrens, Betty Jean, Rama 175, 45 rpm......................................75.00
Yates, Blind Richard; Sore Bunion Blues, Champion 15281, 78 rpm...150.00
Young Lads, Moonlight, Neil 100, 45 rpm..................................20.00
Zircons, Return My Love, Winston 1022, 45 rpm..........................20.00

Country and Western

Arkansas Charlie, Goodbye Old Paint, Vocalion 5270, 78 rpm 15.00
Ashley, Clyde; The Hand Car Yodel, Superior 2636, 78 rpm 25.00
Augusta Trio, Back Up & Push, Champion 15768, 78 rpm...........20.00
Autry, Gene; Oh for the Wild & Wooly West, QRS 1047, 78 rpm, $500 to ..1,000.00

Autry, Gene; That's Why I Left the Mountains, QRS, from $500.00 to $1,000.00. (Photo courtesy Les Docks)

Autry, Gene; Western Classics & Vol 2, Columbia 9001/9002, LP, 10", ea...20.00
Baldwin, Luke; Travlin' Blues, Champion 16343, 78 rpm 25.00
Bang Boys, When Lulu's Gone, Vocalion 03372, 78 rpm 40.00
Bruner, Bill; A Gal Like You, Okeh 45463, 78 rpm 40.00
Carolina Twins, Southern Jack, Victor V40310, 78 rpm................40.00
Carver Boys, Simpson County, Paramount 3233, 78 rpm.............100.00
Davis, Jimmy; The Keyhole in the Door, Bluebird 5156, 78 rpm ..50.00
Delmore Brothers, I'm Leaving You, Bluebird 5258, 78 rpm 15.00
Dixie Mountaineers, Hop Light Ladies, Edison 5207, 78 rpm 20.00
Evans' Old Timers, Honeysuckle Time, Champion 16512, 78 rpm..100.00
Fletcher & Foster, Travelin' North, Champion 16121, 78 rpm 50.00
Freeman & Ashcroft, Alabama Rag, Columbia 15442-D, 78 rpm.50.00
Fruit Jar Guzzlers, Sourwood Mountain, Paramount 3095, 78 rpm ..50.00
Georgia Yellow Hammers, Peaches Down in Georgia, Victor 23683, 78 rpm....100.00
Greene, Amos; Just a Lonely Hobo, Supertone 9709, 78 rpm.......18.00
Hatfield, Overtone; A Gangster's Warning, Columbia 15687-D, 78 rpm..150.00
Honolulu Strollers, Don't Say No, Victor 23600, 78 rpm..............40.00
Jarvis & Justice, Muskrat Rag, Brunswick 358, 78 rpm................15.00
Kelly Brothers, Always Remember, Victor 23833, 78 rpm.............20.00
Kincaid, Bradley; Sourwood Moutain, Superior 366, 78 rpm 50.00
Lone Star Rangers, The Train That Never Arrived, Broadway 8142, 78 rpm....10.00
Long Brothers, Missouri Is Calling, Victor 23637, 78 rpm............30.00
Lullaby Larkers, My Lonely Boyhood Days, Champion 16417, 78 rpm..40.00
Macon, Uncle Dave; One More River To Cross, Bluebird 5842, 78 rpm...30.00
Martin Bros, Don't Marry a Man if He Drinks, Paramount 3248, 78 rpm..50.00
Morris, Zeke; Garden of Prayer, Bluebird 7362, 78 rpm..............10.00
Neal, David; Good Old Turnip Greens, Supertone 9184, 78 rpm .12.00
Nichols Brothers, She's Killing Me, Victor 23582, 78 rpm...........100.00
Oaks, Charlie; Boll Weevil, Vocalion 15342, 78 rpm 10.00
Ozarkers, There's More Pretty Girls Than One, Okeh 45573, 78 rpm...30.00
Perry Country Music Makers, Madaline, Vocalion 5425, 78 rpm..30.00
Pine Knob Serenaders, Apple Cider, Superior 2556, 78 rpm........25.00
Prairie Ramblers, Go Easy Blues, Bluebird 5320, 78 rpm.............30.00
Reed, Blind Alfred; You Must Unload, Victor 20939, 78 rpm.......40.00
Ritter, Tex; Jailhouse Lament, Decca 5306, 78 rpm....................12.00
Rowland, Carter & Son; Cotton-Eyed Joe, Vocalion 5349, 78 rpm..30.00
Scottsdale String Band, Stone Mountain Wobble, Okeh 45118, 78 rpm...15.00
Stanton, Frank; Creole Girl, Superior 2521, 78 rpm....................50.00

Texas Ranger, All Aboard for Blanket Bay, Superior 2792, 78 rpm ..**50.00**
Tubb, Ernest; My Mother Is Lonely, Bluebird 8966, 78 rpm........**100.00**
Vagabonds, The Old Rugged Cross, Victor 23809, 78 rpm.............**30.00**
Wallace, Jerry; Hand Me Down My Walking Cane, Superior 2677, 78 rpm ..**20.00**
Walter Family, Shaker Ben, Champion 16653, 78 rpm...................**60.00**
Wills, Bob & Texas Playboys; Mexicali Rose, Vocalion 03086, 78 rpm....**15.00**
Yates, Ira & Eugene; Sarah Jane, Columbia 15581, 78 rpm.............**50.00**
Young, Clarence; Little Pal, Champion 15924, 78 rpm **15.00**

Jazz, Dance Bands, Personalities

Alabama Washboard Stompers, Pepper Steak, Vocalion 1697, 78 rpm..**50.00**
Alberts, Al & Orch; Building a Nest for Mary, Cameo 9142, 78 rpm....**15.00**
Alston, Ovie & Orch; Junk Man's Serenade, Vocalion 4448, 78 rpm....**10.00**
Ambassadors, The 'Throw-Down' Blues, Vocalion 14933, 78 rpm ..**12.00**
Armstrong, Louis; I'm a Ding Dong Daddy, Okeh 41442, 78 rpm ..**20.00**
Atlanta Syncopators, That Wicked Stomp, Grey Gull 1888, 78 rpm ...**30.00**
Baby Rose Marie, Take a Picture of the Moon, Victor 22960, 78 rpm..**30.00**
Bailey's Dixie Dudes, Go' Long Mule, Gennett 5606, 78 rpm........**10.00**
Banta, Frank; Wild Cherry Rag, Gennett 4735, 78 rpm.................**20.00**
Barker, Tom & Orch; Happy Feet, Parlophone PNY-34084, 78 rpm...**30.00**
Belasco Leon & Orch; Jammin', Vocalion 7863, 78 rpm **30.00**
Campus Boys, I'm Wild About Horns on Automobiles, Banner 6264, 78 rpm...**10.00**
Cardinal Dance Orch, My Mammy Knows, Cardinal 504, 78 rpm......**20.00**
Cellar Boys, Barrel House Stomp, Vocalion 1503, 78 rpm **200.00**
Chicago Footwarmers, Ballin' the Jack, Okey 8533, 78 rpm...........**75.00**
Chicago Hot Five, Oh! What a Thrill, Victor 23326, 78 rpm.......**40.00**
Cliquot Club Eskimos, Hittin' the Bottle, Banner 0779, 78 rpm ..**10.00**
Crosstown Ramblers, River Bottom Glide, Champion 15030, 78 rpm....**60.00**
Dixie Daisies, St Louis Blues, Banner 0839, 78 rpm **12.00**
Dixon, Vance & His Pencils; Hot Peanuts, Columbia 14608-D, 78 rpm..**50.00**
Dubin's Dandies, Gettin' Along, Banner 0505, 78 rpm **10.00**
Dudley, Roberta; Krooked Blues, Nordskog 3007, 78 rpm...........**300.00**
Eaton, Charlie; Bucket of Blood, Herwin 93017, 78 rpm **150.00**
Eddie's Hot Shots, That's a Serious Thing, Victor V-38046, 78 rpm..**50.00**
Ezell, Will; Mixed Up Rag, Paramount 12688, 78 rpm.................**150.00**
Finlay, Lloyd & Orch; Fido Blues, Victor 19644, 78 rpm...............**50.00**
Ford & Ford, I'm Three Times Seven, Paramount 12244, 78 rpm..**125.00**
Gibson, Cleo; Nothing But Blues, Okeh 8700, 78 rpm **50.00**
Goodman, Benny & Orch; Ain'tcha Glad?, Columbia 2835-D, 78 rpm ..**25.00**
Happy Harmonists, Home Brew Blues, Gennett 5286, 78 rpm ...**100.00**
Harlam Trio, Fuzzy Wuzzy, Herwin 93012, 78 rpm......................**200.00**
Harry's Happy Four, Western Melody, Okeh 8266, 78 rpm............**60.00**
Idaho, Bertha; Move It On Out of Here, Columbia 14437-D, 78 rpm..**50.00**
Ideal Serenaders, Dawning, Columbia 1131-D, 78 rpm **10.00**
Indiana Syncopaters, Bees Knees, LaBelle 1418, 78 rpm.............**20.00**
James, Corky & His Blackbirds; Bugahoma Blues, Bell 1182, 78 rpm..**250.00**
Jones, Willie & Orch; Michigan Stomp, Gennett 6326, 78 rpm **200.00**
Kane, Helen; Ain't Cha?, Victor 22192, 78 rpm...........................**12.00**
Kay, Dolly; A Good Man Is Hard To Find, Vocalion 15664, 78 rpm.......**40.00**
King Oliver's Creole Jazz Band, Zulus Ball, Gennett 5275, 78 rpm..**32,000.00**
La Veeda Dance Orch, Strut Yo' Stuff, Columbia 1549-D, 78 rpm...**30.00**
Ladd's Black Aces, Shake It & Break It, Gennett 4762, 78 rpm ...**12.00**
Lee, Ruth; Maybee Someday, Nordskog 3008, 78 rpm.................**300.00**
Mater, Frank; Doin' the Raccoon, Diva 2759-G, 78 rpm **10.00**
McKinney's Cotton Pickers, Cherry, Victor 21730, 78 rpm...........**30.00**
Miami Garden Orch, She Looks Like Helen Brown, Silvertone 5027, 78 rpm..**20.00**
Moonlight Revelers, Memphis Stomp, Grey Gull 1786, 78 rpm ...**50.00**
Moore, Sam; Chain Gang Blues, Okeh 4412, 78 rpm....................**15.00**
Newport Syncopators, Desert Blues, Van Dyke 81854, 78 rpm.....**30.00**
Nicholson, Nick & Orch; True Blue, Champion 15699, 78 rpm ..**35.00**
Original Indiana Five, Sugar, Banner 6008, 78 rpm.....................**12.00**
Pacific Coast Players, Jazzing Around, Radiex 1326, 78 rpm........**12.00**
Parham's Black Patti Band, Un-Te-Da-Da-Da, Black Patti 8038, 78 rpm......**500.00**

Prima, Louis & His New Orleans Gang; Star Dust, Brunswick 7335, 78 rpm....**12.00**
Queen City Blowers, Stomp Off - Let's Go, Champion 15030, 78 rpm ...**75.00**
Quintones, Sly Mongoose, Vocalion 5509, 78 rpm **15.00**
Ramblers, Lonely Eyes, Romeo 315, 78 rpm.................................**8.00**
Red & His Big Ten, At Last I'm Happy, Victor 23033, 78 rpm.....**25.00**
Rhythm Kings, Please Tell Me, Victor 23283, 78 rpm..................**60.00**
Searcy Trio, Kansas Avenue Blues, Okeh 8360, 78 rpm..............**75.00**
Silent Joe & His Boys, Cooler Hot, Champion 15951, 78 rpm......**20.00**
Sioux City Six, Flock O' Blues, Gennett 5569, 78 rpm...............**150.00**
Sizzlers, Diga Diga Doo, Edison 52463, 78 rpm **60.00**
Tampa Blue Jazz Band, Get Hot, Okeh, 4397, 78 rpm.................**10.00**
Tennessee Music Men, Choo Choo, Clarion 5467-C, 78 rpm........**25.00**
Thomas, Hersal; Suitcase Blues, Okeh, 8227, 78 rpm **100.00**
University Eight, Arkansas Blues, Lincoln 2674, 78 rpm **12.00**
Vagabonds, Ukelele Lady, Gennett 3100, 78 rpm **12.00**
Wanderers, Tiger Rag, Bluebird 5887, 78 rpm.............................**15.00**
Washboard Serenaders, Teddy's Blues, V38610, 78 rpm..............**150.00**
Yale Collegians, Blue Again, Okeh 41474, 78 rpm......................**40.00**
Young's Creole Jazz Band, Tin Roof Blues, various labels, 78 rpm, ea ...**150.00**
Zutty & His Band, Look Over Yonder, Decca 431, 78 rpm **10.00**

Red Wing

The Red Wing Stoneware Company, founded in 1878, took its name from its location in Red Wing, Minnesota. In 1906 the name was changed to the Red Wing Union Stoneware Company after a merger with several of the other local potteries. For the most part they produced utilitarian wares such as flowerpots, crocks, and jugs. Their early 1930s catalogs offered a line of art pottery vases in colored glazes, some of which featured handles modeled after swan's necks, snakes, or female nudes. Other examples were quite simple, often with classic styling. After the addition of their dinnerware lines in 1935, 'Stoneware' was dropped from the name, and the company became known as Red Wing Potteries, Inc. They closed in 1967.

The pottery was reopened several years ago, and handmade and decorated salt-glazed stoneware is again being produced. Each piece is stamped with the potters' initials and the year of production.

Our artware advisors are Wendy and Leo Frese (Three Rivers Collectibles); they are listed under Texas. For further study we recommend *Red Wing Stoneware, An Identification and Value Guide*, and *Red Wing Collectibles* by Dan and Gail DePasquale and Larry Peterson; and *Red Wing Art Pottery, Book II*, and *Collector's Encyclopedia of Red Wing Art Pottery* by B.L. and R.L. Dollen. All are published by Collector Books. Another good reference is *Red Wing Art Pottery* by Ray Reiss (privately published).

Commercial Art Ware and Miscellaneous

Vase, applied figures bordered by geometric lines, green and yellow crystalline, #M3103, 14½", $600.00. (Photo courtesy Treadway Gallery, Inc.)

Ashtray, open book form, orange, #863, 5½" **28.00**
Ashtray, rectangular, silver gr, #3002, 12" **32.00**

Bowl, console; emb floral & ribbing, ftd, #1188, 12" 80.00
Bowl, incurvate rim, Greek design, Walnut Green, 10" 135.00
Bowl, Nokomis, strap hdls, 3½x8¾", NM 350.00
Bowl, oak leaf shape, pea gr/caramel, #428, 8x14" 34.00
Bowl, shell shape, #M1567, 9" 56.00
Candle holder, Vintage (grapes), ivory/brn wipe, #622, 5½" 30.00
Compote, cornucopia, cinnamon, #635, 7x11½" 48.00
Compote, fluted, med ped, ivory, #M1597, 7" 36.00
Figurine, bird perched w/tail up, forest gr, 10" 80.00
Flower frog, deer on ped, #531, 10" 60.00
Flowerpot & saucer, emb leaf design, dk gr, 10" dia 155.00
Pitcher, Magnolia, ivory/brn wipe, #1012, 7" 75.00
Planter, birch bark log, #730, 11" 110.00
Planter, deer resting, turq, #1338, 5½" 100.00
Planter, swan form, #259, 6" 68.00
Planter, tulip shape, yel/turq, #896, 7" 46.00
Vase, ball shape, emb, semi-matt wht/gr, #1245, 5½" 50.00
Vase, cylindrical, emb cattail design & ribbing, Walnut Green, 10" .. 150.00
Vase, cylindrical, flower hdls, #1196, 10" 62.00
Vase, cylindrical, spiral design, wht/gr, #1235, 9¾" 46.00
Vase, dbl-hdld, allover emb design, semi-matt ivory/brn wipe, 8¾" 75.00
Vase, Egyptian, gloss gr & wht, #157, 12" 125.00
Vase, emb swirl, yel, #1590, 10" 56.00
Vase, Magnolia, ivory/brn wipe, #1030, 8" 100.00
Vase, modeled as stacked coffee cups, brn/Sagebrush, #1359, 7¾" ... 50.00
Vase, Nokomis, bulbous base, flared rim, mk, 10¼" 400.00
Vase, Nokomis, shouldered, #205, 7⅜", NM 250.00
Vase, 4-sided prism type, Cypress Green, #1633, 7" 48.00
Wall pocket, Magnolia, ivory/brn wipe, #1630, 7" 150.00
Window box, half-circle w/emb bamboo design, #407, 12" 40.00

Cookie Jars

Be aware that there is a very good reproduction of the King of Tarts. Except for the fact that the new jars are slightly smaller, they are sometime difficult to distinguish from the old.

Bob White, unmk 200.00
Carousel, unmk 350.00
Crock, wht 80.00
Dutch Girl (Katrina), yel w/brn trim 175.00
Friar Tuck, cream w/brn, mk 175.00
Friar Tuck, gr, mk 175.00
Friar Tuck, yel, unmk 150.00
Grapes, cobalt or dk purple, ea 275.00
Grapes, gr 135.00

Jack Frost, short, unmarked, $250.00. (Photo courtesy Joyce Roerig)

Jack Frost, unmk, tall 300.00
King of Tarts, mc, mk (+) 325.00
King of Tarts, pk w/bl & blk trim, mk 300.00
King of Tarts, wht, unmk 200.00
Peasant design, emb/pnt figures on aqua 110.00

Peasant design, emb/pnt figures on brn 120.00
Pierre (chef), bl, brn or pk, unmk, ea 150.00
Pineapple, yel 135.00

Dinnerware

Dinnerware lines were added in 1935, and today collectors scramble to rebuild extensive table services. Although interest is obvious, right now the market is so volatile, it is often difficult to establish a price scale with any degree of accuracy. Asking prices may vary from $50.00 to $200.00 on some items, which indicates instability and a collector market trying to find its way. (One guide currently on the market, for instance, lists Midnight Rose dinner plates at $15.00 to $20.00, while another terms them 'rare,' and values them at $145.00 each.) Sellers seem to be unfamiliar with pattern names and proper identification of the various pieces that each line consists of. There were many hand-decorated lines; among the most popular are Bob White, Tropicana, and Round-up. But there are other patterns that are just as attractive and deserving of attention. The Dollen books referenced above both have dinnerware sections, and Ray Reiss has published a book called *Red Wing Dinnerware, Price and Identification Guide*, which shows nearly one hundred patterns on its back cover alone.

Town and Country, designed by Eva Zeisel, was made for only one year in the late 1940s. Today many collectors regard Zeisel as one of the most gifted designers of that era and actively seek examples of her work. Town and Country was a versatile line, adaptable to both informal and semiformal use. It is characterized by irregular, often eccentric shapes, and handles of pitchers and serving pieces are usually extensions of the rim. Bowls and platters are free-form comma shapes or appear tilted, with one side slightly higher than the other. Although the ware is unmarked, it is recognizable by its distinctive shapes and glazes. White (often used to complement interiors of bowls and cups), though an original color, is actually more rare than Bronze (metallic brown, also called gunmetal), which enjoys favored status; Gray is unusual. Other colors include Rust, Dusk Blue, Sand, Chartreuse, Peach, and Forest Green. Pieces have also shown up in Mulberry and Ming Green and are considered quite rare. (These are Red Wing Quartelle colors!) Note: Eva Zeisel recently gave permission to reissue a few select pieces of Town and Country; these are being made by World of Ceramics. In 1996 salt and pepper shakers were reproduced in new colors not resembling Red Wing colors. In 1997 the mixing bowl and syrup were reissued. All new pieces are stamped EZ96 or EZ97 and are visibly different from the old, as far as glaze, pottery base, and weight.

Charles Alexander (who is listed in the Directory under Indiana) advises us on the Town and Country market. Our advisor for the remainder of this category is Brenda Dollen; she is listed in the Directory under Minnesota.

Ardennes, casserole, grip hdl, w/lid 60.00
Ardennes, creamer 25.00
Ardennes, shakers, pr 22.00
Blossom Time, cup 8.00
Blossom Time, saucer 8.00
Bob White, casserole, 2-qt 75.00
Bob White, plate, 11" 22.00
Bob White, tumbler, water 125.00
Brittany, plate, 10" 18.00
Capistrano, plate, 10½" 26.00
Chrysanthemum, bowl, sauce 9.00
Chrysanthemum, creamer 25.00
Chrysanthemum, sugar bowl, w/lid 30.00
Crocus, bowl, vegetable; 2-part 36.00
Crocus, plate, 7½" 20.00
Desert Sun, platter, 13" 50.00

Desert Sun, teapot, w/lid..75.00
Driftwood, platter, 15"...55.00
Ebb Tide, cup & saucer...10.00
Ebb Tide, plate, 10"...18.00
Fantasy, chop plate..40.00
Fantasy, plate, 6½"..15.00
Fantasy, shakers, pr...25.00
Flight, bowl, vegetable; 2-part..60.00
Flight, cup & saucer, rare...55.00
Flight, plate, 10"..100.00
Frontenac, bowl, cereal..10.00
Frontenac, butter dish...20.00
Greenwichstone, bowl, sauce...5.00
Greenwichstone, plate, bread & butter...................................5.00
Greenwichstone, plate, 10"...12.00
Hearthside, relish tray..26.00
Iris, chop plate...40.00
Iris, cup & saucer...25.00
Iris, plate, 10½"..30.00
Iris, spoon rest...40.00
Iris, sugar bowl, w/lid..25.00
Lexington Rose, nappy..15.00
Lexington Rose, plate, bread & butter...................................6.00
Lexington Rose, platter, 13"...35.00
Lotus, butter dish...40.00
Lotus, cup..6.00
Lotus, egg plate, w/lid..90.00
Lotus, plate, 7"...8.00
Lotus, plate, 10½"...20.00
Lotus, saucer...5.00
Midnight Rose, tidbit, 3-tier..28.00
Morning Glory, celery tray...28.00
Nassau, coffee cup...35.00
Normandy, chop plate, 14"..55.00
Orleans, cup & saucer..18.00
Orleans, gravy boat..50.00
Orleans, nappy...35.00
Orleans, plate, 10"..22.00
Orleans, water jug...80.00
Pepe, bean pot, w/lid..32.00
Pepe, bread tray...30.00
Pepe, tray, serving; 1-tier..25.00
Pink Spice, bowl, buffet; 10½"...54.00
Plum Blossom, bowl, sauce...7.00
Plum Blossom, cup...7.00
Plum Blossom, plate, 10½"..18.00
Plum Blossom, saucer..5.00
Pompeii, plate, bread & butter..5.00
Pompeii, plate, salad...6.00
Provincial Oomph, bowl, mixing set; 3-pc, 6" to 10"....................65.00
Provincial Oomph, pitcher, w/lid, 60-oz................................35.00
Provincial Oomph, plate, 10"...15.00
Random Harvest, bowl, dessert; 6¾".....................................10.00
Random Harvest, bowl, soup...10.00
Random Harvest, casserole, w/lid.......................................36.00
Random Harvest, creamer..22.00
Random Harvest, pitcher..40.00
Random Harvest, plate, 10½"..22.00
Random Harvest, relish tray..34.00
Random Harvest, teapot...85.00
Reed, mixing bowl set, 5" to 10", 6-pc................................135.00
Round-Up, butter dish..90.00
Round-Up, plate, 7½"...40.00
Round-Up, saucer...25.00

Round-Up, sugar bowl...30.00
Round-Up, sugar bowl, w/lid..52.00
Smart Set, bowl, soup..18.00
Smart Set, creamer...18.00
Smart Set, plate, 6½"..10.00
Tampico, bowl, fruit; sm...15.00
Tampico, cup & saucer..30.00
Tampico, plate, 10½"...28.00
Tampico, trivet, 6½"...75.00
Tip Toe, plate, 10½"...10.00
Town & Country, basket, 11x7½"...45.00
Town & Country, bean pot, Rust, w/lid, minimum value..................400.00
Town & Country, bowl, soup...27.50
Town & Country, bowl, 5"...15.00
Town & Country, coaster..18.00
Town & Country, creamer & sugar bowl, w/lid, minimum value.............60.00
Town & Country, cup & saucer, tea......................................27.50
Town & Country, lazy susan, mixed colors, complete w/stand............215.00
Town & Country, mug, coffee..75.00
Town & Country, pitcher, 3-pt...100.00
Town & Country, plate, 10½"..45.00
Town & Country, platter, 15x11½".......................................70.00
Town & Country, shakers, Shmoo shape, mixed colors, pr.................75.00
Town & Country, syrup..95.00
Turtle Dove, bowl, cereal..15.00
Turtle Dove, bread tray..55.00
Turtle Dove, shakers, pr...22.00
Two Step, bowl, cereal..8.00
Two Step, plate, 10½"..22.00
Two Step, salt & pepper shakers, pr....................................18.00
Village Green, beverage server, 8-cup..................................30.00
Village Green, mug...20.00
Village Green, pitcher, syrup..18.00
Village Green, pitcher, 10-cup...32.00
Village Green, sugar bowl, w/lid.......................................20.00
Village Green, teapot, 6-cup...40.00
Village Green, water cooler, w/stand, 2-gal...........................600.00
White & Turquoise, bean pot, ftd, wire coiled hdl......................42.00
Willow Wind, plate, dinner; 10½".......................................26.00
Zinnia, creamer..25.00
Zinnia, cup & saucer...15.00
Zinnia, plate, 6½"...18.00

Stoneware

Key:
c/s — cobalt on stoneware   RW — Red Wing
MN — Minnesota   RWUS — Red Wing Union
NS — North Star   Stoneware

Jug, shoulder; white, two-gallon, $75.00.

Bean pot, Albany slip, Boston style, RW, 1-gal....................250.00
Bean pot, Albany slip, MN, ½-gal..................................150.00

Bean pot, Albany slip, NS, 1-gal 135.00
Bowl, batter; Sponge Band, pour spout/bail hdl, RWUS 1,200.00
Bowl, shoulder; wht, RW, 1-pt 55.00
Bowl, Sponge Band on wht, RWUS, 4" 375.00
Butter crock, salt glaze, low, RW, 10-lb 80.00
Butter jar, Albany slip, high, MN, 1-gal 100.00
Butter jar, Albany slip, low, MN, 1-lb 85.00
Butter jar, salt glaze, low, RW, 10-lb 75.00
Butter jar, wht, low, RW, 1-lb 70.00
Casserole, Sponge Band, RWUS, sm 400.00
Chamber pot, wht, fancy hdl, RW, 9", w/lid 150.00
Churn, #3/parrot, c/s, MN, 3-gal 4,500.00
Churn, #4/P, c/s, RW, 4-gal 950.00
Churn, #5/red wing on wht, Union oval, 5-gal 300.00
Churn, #6/butterfly, c/s, RW, 6-gal 1,750.00
Churn, #8/2 birch leaves, c/s, unmk, 8-gal 800.00
Cooler, #4/daisy, c/s, RW, 4-gal 3,200.00
Cooler, #4/2 birch leaves, c/s, RW, 4-gal 2,400.00
Cooler, #5/flower/Ice Water, c/s, RW, 6-gal 9,000.00
Crock, #2/birch leaves, c/s, RWUS, 2-gal 65.00
Crock, #2/dbl P, c/s, MN, 2-gal 200.00
Crock, #25/leaves, c/s, MN, 25-gal 1,250.00
Crock, #5/elephant ear leaves, c/s, MN, 5-gal 125.00
Crock, #5/leaf, c/s, RW, 5-gal 500.00
Crock, #10/leaf, c/s, MN, 10-gal 750.00
Cuspidor, bl & wht sponging, unsgn 650.00
Cuspidor, bl bands on salt glaze, German style, unmk 650.00
Cuspidor, brn & wht, molded seam, unmk 200.00
Cuspidor, molded seam, Albany slip, unmk 125.00
Cuspidor, molded seam, bl & wht sponging, RW, 10" dia 750.00
Flowerpot, Albany slip, geometric decor, NM, 7" 350.00
Jar, packing; wht, bail hdl, RW, 5-lb 75.00
Jar, refrigerator; name outlined in rectangle, w/lid & bail hdl, 5-lb ..300.00
Jar, wax sealer, Albany slip, NS, 1-gal 325.00
Jug, beehive; #3/birch leaves, c/s, RW oval, 3-gal 350.00
Jug, beehive; #3/red wing on wht, Union oval, 3-gal 375.00
Jug, bl bands on wht, cone top, MN, 1-gal 400.00
Jug, common, Albany slip, dome top, MN, 1-gal 75.00
Jug, common, wht, MN, 1-gal 80.00
Jug, fancy, wht w/brn ball top, RW, ½-gal 225.00
Jug, fancy, wht w/brn ball top, RW, ½-pt 175.00
Jug, fruit; Albany slip, wide mouth, MN, ½-gal 100.00
Jug, molded seam, Albany slip, bail hdl, RW, 1-gal 400.00
Jug, molded seam, wht, bail hdl, MN, 1-qt 175.00
Jug, molded seam, wht, bail hdl, RW, 1-gal 150.00
Jug, molded seam; wht, bail hdl, RW, 1-qt 125.00
Jug, shoulder; brn & salt glaze, ball top, RW, 1-gal 225.00
Jug, shoulder; brn & salt glaze, pear top, NS, 1-gal 375.00
Jug, shoulder; wht, cone top, RW, ½-gal 115.00
Jug, shoulder; wht, funnel top, MN, 2-gal 75.00
Jug, shoulder; wht, std top, MN, 1-qt 115.00
Jug, shoulder; wht, std top, RW, 2-gal 75.00
Milk pan, Albany slip, MN, any sz 125.00
Milk pan, bl, RW, 7" 150.00
Pitcher, Albany slip w/emb irises, RW 175.00
Pitcher, mustard; Albany slip, NS 325.00
Umbrella stand, red & bl sponging on wht, unmk 1,300.00
Vase, floor; emb designs, bronze-like finish, RWUS, MN, 22", NM ..300.00
Wash bowl & pitcher, lt bl on wht, emb lily decor, RW 875.00

Redware

The term redware refers to a type of simple earthenware produced
by the Colonists as early as the 1600s. The red clay used in its production was abundant throughout the country, and during the eighteenth
and nineteenth centuries redware was made in great quantities. Intended for utilitarian purposes such as everyday tableware or use in the dairy,
redware was simple in design and decoration. Glazes of various colors
were used, and a liquid clay referred to as 'slip' was sometimes applied in
patterns such as zigzag lines, daisies, or stars. Plates often have a 'coggled'
edge, similar to the way a pie is crimped or jagged, which is done with a
special tool. In the following listings, EX (excellent condition) indicates
only minor damage. Our advisor for this category is Barbara Rosen; she
is listed in the Directory under New Jersey.

Bird whistle, manganese eyes & wings 445.00
Bowl, brn/gr/orange, int: orange/gr, thin, S Miller/dtd, 4x8", EX ..3,300.00

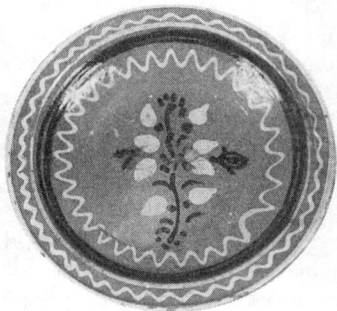

Bowl, slip decorated, shallow, raised bottom, Moravian, nineteenth century, minor flaking, hairline, $500.00. (Photo courtesy Aston Americana Auctioneers & Appraisers)

Bowl, slip squiggles/dots/stars, rim: Liebe Wie, PA, 1890, 6" 585.00
Cookie mold, Colonial trumpeter (coat decor) on horse, Ephrata, 6" ..900.00
Cookie mold, 6 sqs w/harp/birds/urn/deer, 8x5½", EX 440.00
Creamer, dk brn daubed glaze in zigzag pattern, 4½", EX 360.00
Creamer, lt gr runs on burnt orange, 4½" 195.00
Creamer, orange w/gr areas, 3½", VG 110.00
Crock, brn w/ivory runs & splotches, cvd lines, 7" 1,595.00
Dish, brn flecks & sponging around rim, wear/sm chips, 2x4½" ...85.00
Dog, seated, dk olive, coleslaw on head/shoulders, 6" 75.00
Dog, seated, incised collar/chain, sgn Van Vorhis, 7" 195.00
Dog, seated w/free-standing front legs, brn pnt, 9", EX 85.00
Doorstop/grave marker, molded lamp, traces of wht, ca 1880s, 12" ..850.00
Egg cup/master salt, gr splotches, Shenandoah Valley, 3", VG 325.00
Inkstand, emb fruit basket, dk brn, RW Goulding, ca 1830, 2x7x3½" ..345.00
Jar, blk sponging on clear, shoulder ring, flared rim, 6½", EX 55.00
Jar, canning; dk brn splotches on neck/shoulder, incised lines, 9", VG ..330.00
Jar, clear w/brn splotches, ovoid, lug hdls, 10⅝" 460.00
Jar, dk gr w/brn speckles, conical, 2 hdls, ca 1800, 9½" 25,000.00
Jar, moss gr w/brn specks, flat lid, button finial, MA, ca 1800, 7" ...6,900.00
Jar, mottled brn, flared rim, appl hdl, wear, 5⅛x4⅝" 330.00
Jar, reddish w/yel splotches, slightly concave sides, 7x6" 330.00
Jug, clear lead glaze, ovoid, appl ear hdl, chips, 6¼" 300.00
Jug, dk brn brushings, incised ring, ovoid, glued chip, 6¾" 385.00
Jug, dk gr w/lt gr decor, dtd 1888, tricorner spout, 13", NM 165.00
Jug, gr & brn splashes, ovoid, hdl, early 19th C, 9½", EX 1,495.00
Jug, red & brn mottle, early 1800s, 9½" 1,000.00
Jug, vinegar; lt gr-tan & dk brn mottle, ribbed hdl, 1800s, 5" ..9,775.00
Loaf dish, sgraffito farm scene/family history, Mummert, 1982, 19" 325.00
Loaf dish, 3 zigzag yel slip lines flanked by 3 wavy, coggled rim, 17" ...450.00
Loaf pan, 3 sets of yel waves, gr imperfections, coggled, 2x10x13" 770.00
Milk pan, dk brn tree-like sponging, tooled bands, w/hdl, 5x9", EX .600.00
Mold, Turk's head, mottled brn, flakes/chip, 3¾x6⅜" 275.00
Mold, Turk's head, red & brn mottle, ca 1830, 3½x10" 145.00
Mug, 3 yel slip wavy lines, horizontal ribs, 1800s, child sz 3,000.00
Newel post cap, gr/brn mottle, bulbous w/raised spirals ea side, 9x10" ...260.00
Pie plate, cvd peacock/tulips/etc, red on yel/gr, att Medinger, 9" ..2,350.00

Pie plate, yel slip lines, coggled rim, worn/damage, 10¼" **200.00**
Pie plate, yel slip flower/2 wavy lines/Leonore, coggled rim, 12", EX...**2,500.00**
Pie plate, yel slip scrolls at rim, center: Emily, PA, 11" **3,800.00**
Pie plate, yel w/bl wavy lines, rim flakes, 1½x7½" **475.00**
Pie plate, yel/dk brn wavy lines, coggled, rim flake, 6½" **275.00**
Pie plate, 2 sets of sm wavy yel slip lines, 9½", NM **275.00**
Pie plate, 3 str lines amid 6 yel slip waves on gr, 11", NM **385.00**
Pie plate, 3 wavy yel slip lines & 4 tree-like symbols, 10¾", EX.**345.00**
Pie plate, 3 yel slip S-curve lines, coggled, sm rim flake, mini, 4" ...**440.00**
Pie plate, 3-line yel slip S flourish ea side row of scallops, 12", EX.**825.00**
Pie plate, 4-squiggle crossroad-pattern bands in yel, 12", EX **800.00**
Pie plate, 6 wht squiggle bands on gr, crimped edge, 7¾", VG ...**275.00**
Pitcher, brn & gr mottle w/incised str & wavy lines, ca 1800, 11"...**4,600.00**
Pitcher, brn splotches at shoulder, coggled line, ribbed hdl, 6½" ...**345.00**
Pitcher, brn sponging, tooled line at shoulder, 8", EX **385.00**
Pitcher, gr w/orange & brn spots, ovoid, coggled bands, 8", EX ..**935.00**
Pitcher, orange w/blk flecks, incised neck ring, 3⅜", NM **55.00**
Teapot, molded boy-in-tree decor, serpent hdl, 1755, rstr, 3⅜"...**750.00**
Vase, tree stump w/woodpecker on side, some cvg, gr/brn/yel, 4" ..**900.00**

Regal China

Located in Antioch, Illinois, the Regal China Company opened for business in 1938. Products of interest to collectors are James Beam decanters, cookie jars, salt and pepper shakers, and similar novelty items. The company closed its doors sometime in 1993. The Old MacDonald Farm series listed below is especially collectible, so are the salt and pepper shakers.

Note: Where applicable, prices are based on excellent gold trim. (Gold trim must be 90% intact or deductions should be made for wear.) See also Decanters.

Our advisor for this category is Judy Posner; she is listed in the Directory under Florida.

Cookie Jars

Cat, from $340 to **385.00**
Churn Boy **250.00**
Clown, gr collar, from $650 to **675.00**
Davy Crockett, from $450 to **495.00**
Diaper Pin Pig, from $450 to **540.00**
Dutch Girl, from $600 to **655.00**
Dutch Girl, peach trim..**720.00**
FiFi Poodle, from $600 to **655.00**
Fisherman, from $650 to **720.00**
French Chef, from $350 to **405.00**
Goldilocks (+) **340.00**
Harpo Marx..**1,080.00**
Hobby Horse, from $250 to **270.00**
Hubert Lion, from $720 to **855.00**
Humpty Dumpty, red, from $275 to................................**250.00**
Little Miss Muffet, from $315 to......................................**350.00**
Majorette, from $425 to **500.00**
Oriental Lady w/Baskets, from $585 to...........................**630.00**
Peek-a-Boo (+), from $1,350 to **1,440.00**
Quaker Oats..**115.00**
Three Bears..**175.00**
Toby Cookies, unmk, from $675 to **700.00**
Tulip..**270.00**
Uncle Mistletoe..**765.00**

Old McDonald's Farm

Butter dish, cow's head..**220.00**

Canister, flour, cereal, coffee; med, ea, from $225 to **250.00**
Canister, pretzels, peanuts, popcorn, chips, tidbits; lg, ea, $300 to..**350.00**
Canister, salt, sugar, tea; med, ea, from $225 to **250.00**
Canister, soap, cookies; lg, ea, from $350 to..............................**425.00**
Cookie barn, from $295 to...**325.00**
Creamer, rooster, from $120 to..**135.00**
Grease jar, pig, from $200 to...**250.00**
Pitcher, milk; from $425 to..**450.00**
Shakers, boy & girl, pr, from $80 to...**95.00**
Shakers, churn, gold trim, pr..**110.00**
Shakers, feed sacks w/sheep, pr...**195.00**
Spice jar, assorted lids, sm, ea, from $100 to **150.00**
Sugar bowl, hen...**135.00**
Teapot, duck's head, from $250 to **300.00**

Shakers

A Nod to Abe, 3-pc nodder..**300.00**
Bendel, bears, wht w/pk & brn trim, pr, from $125 to.................**150.00**
Bendel, bunnies, wht w/blk & pk trim, pr from $125 to..............**150.00**
Bendel, kissing pigs, gray w/pk trim, lg, pr, from $350 to...........**375.00**
Bendel, love bugs, burgundy, lg, pr, from $150 to **185.00**
Bendel, love bugs, gr, sm, pr...**65.00**
Cat, sitting w/eyes closed, wht w/hat & gold bow, pr **225.00**
Clown, pr...**350.00**
Dutch Girl, pr...**275.00**
FiFi, pr..**450.00**
Fish, mk C Miller, 1-pc...**55.00**
French Chef, wht w/gold trim, pr, from $250 to.........................**350.00**
Humpty Dumpty, pr..**140.00**
Peek-a-Boo, red dots, lg, pr (+), from $475 to............................**525.00**
Peek-a-Boo, red dots, sm, pr, from $250 to................................**275.00**
Peek-a-Boo, wht solid, sm, pr...**200.00**
Pig, pk, mk C Miller, 1-pc..**95.00**
Tulip, pr..**50.00**
Van Tellingen, bears, brn, pr, from $25 to...................................**28.00**
Van Tellingen, boy & dog, Black, pr **125.00**
Van Tellingen, boy & dog, wht, pr...**75.00**
Van Tellingen, bunnies, solid colors, pr, from $28 ....**32.00**
Van Tellingen, ducks, pr...**38.00**
Van Tellingen, Dutch boy & girl, from $45 to.............................**60.00**
Van Tellingen, Mary & lamb, pr..**60.00**
Van Tellingen, sailor & mermaid, pr, from $225 to **260.00**

Relief-Molded Jugs

Early relief-molded pitchers (ca 1830s – 40s) were made in two-piece molds into which sheets of clay were pressed. The relief decoration was deep and well defined, usually of animal or human subjects. Most of these pitchers were designed with a flaring lip and substantial footing. Gradually styles changed, and by the 1860s the rim had become flatter and the foot less pronounced. The relief decoration was not as deep, and foliage became a common design. By the turn of the century, many other types of pitchers had been introduced, and the market for these early styles began to wane.

Watch for recent reproductions; these have been made by the slip-casting method. Unlike relief-molded ware which is relatively smooth inside, slip-cast pitchers will have interior indentations that follow the irregularities of the relief decoration. Values below are for pieces in excellent condition. Our advisor for this category is Kathy Hughes; she is listed in the Directory under North Carolina.

Key: Reg — Registered

Argos, gr, Brownfield, Apr 29, 1864, 8"......................................**175.00**
Bird & Butterfly, tan & wht, Minton, ca 1830, 6"......................**375.00**
Bundle of Faggots, drabware, metal lid, Ridgway, Reg Oct 1, 1835, 8"..**250.00**
Cain & Abel, tan stoneware, Edward Walley, ca 1850, 10" **350.00**
Chelsea Pensioners, wht stoneware, unknown, ca 1845 ....**350.00**
Chrysanthemum, gr & wht, Ridgway, ca 1860, 9¼"....................**275.00**
Cupid at Play, buff & tan, Turner, ca 1800, 9½"..........................**750.00**
Diana, gr stoneware, Edward Walley, Reg June 21, 1850, 10" **425.00**
Diston family/instruments, bl smear/gilt, Alcock, 1840s, 7" **700.00**
Garibaldi, unknown, ca 1870, 13" **300.00**
Good Samaritan, buff & tan, Jones & Walley, 1841, 8" **400.00**
Good Samaritan, wht stoneware, unknown, ca 1850, 9¾"..........**400.00**
Hops, Herbert Minton & Co, wht parian, Reg May 14 1847, 8¼".**900.00**
Idle Apprentices, wht & bl, unknown, 1840, 7" **250.00**
Julius Caesar, gray, appl laurel wreath, Meigh, 1839, 8¼" **450.00**
King Solomon, drabware, Wood & Brownfield, Reg Sept 30 1841, 7½".....**350.00**
Love & War, purple on wht parian, Samuel Alcock, ca 1845, 7¾" **500.00**
Marbleized, Classical, cream & wht, Liverpool Herculaneum, 1805, 7" ..**700.00**
Mermaid & Cupid, Minton, gr & wht parian, ca 1911, 6" **750.00**
Naomi & Daughter-in-Law, lav on parian, Alcock, 1847, 8¾"...**450.00**
Now I'm Grandpa, unknown, ca 1850, 8½"..................................**450.00**
Oxcart & Grapes, unknown, drabware stoneware, ca 1840, 7" ...**350.00**
Peel & Cobden, yel earthenware, unknown, ca 1846 ....**250.00**
Princess Charlotte/Prince Leopold, gold/bl, 2¾" **300.00**
Princess Charlotte/Prince Leopold, minor rstr, 6" **275.00**
Punch, purple on wht parian, Samuel Alcock, ca 1845, 8¾" **700.00**
Robert Burns, Machin & Potts, cream & wht, Reg June 20 1834, 6¼"..**500.00**
Royal Children, bl earthenware, unknown, ca 1848....................**325.00**
Shakespeare, wht on purple parian, Samuel Alcock, ca 1850, 6" ..**700.00**
Sir Robert Peel, tan earthenware, ca 1846 ....**200.00**
Sir Walter Scott commemorative, gray-gr, Minton, 8" **350.00**
Slavery scenes, Ridway & Abington, 1855, 7⅞", minimum value...**1,100.00**
Stag, gray-gr, Enoch & Edward Wood, ca 1840, 9¼"...................**350.00**
Stag, purple on wht parian, Samuel Alcock, ca 1845, 8⅛" **600.00**
Toho, Masons, drabware stoneware, ca 1845, 6½".......................**750.00**
Tulip, bl & wht, Dudson, ca 1860, 7"..**275.00**
Tulip, wht stoneware, Dudson, ca 1860, 8" **250.00**
Youth & Old Age, gray-gr, Copeland-Garret, ca 1845, 8¾"........**300.00**

Restraints

Since the beginning of time, many things from animals to treasures have been held in bondage by hemp, bamboo, chests, chains, shackles, and other constructed devices. Many of these devices were used to hold captives who awaited further torture, as if the restraint wasn't torturous enough. The study and collecting of restraints enables one to learn much about the advancement of civilization in the country or region from which they originated. Such devices at various times in history were made of very heavy metals — so heavy that the wearer could scarcely move about. It has only been in the last sixty years that vast improvements have been made in design and construction that afford the captive some degree of comfort. Our advisor for this category is Joseph Tanner; he is listed in the Directory under Washington.

    Key:
    bbl — barrel   lc — lock case
    d-lb — double lock button   NST — non-swing through
    K — key   ST — swing through
    Kd — keyed   stp — stamped

Foreign Handcuffs

Australian, Saf Lock, ST, takes pin-tumbler K in side, stp **200.00**

Czechalaviak, ST, Ralken flat key, modern ST **150.00**
Deutsche Polizei, ST, middle hinge, folds, takes bbl-bit K............**80.00**
East German, aluminum, single lg hinge, ST, bbl key..................**80.00**
East German, heavy steel, NP single lg hinge, NST, bbl key.......**120.00**
English, Chubb, NST, hi-security 10-slider lock mechanism.......**300.00**
English, Chubb Arrest, steel, ST, multi-bit solid K....................**250.00**
English, Latrobe, aluminum alloy, center chain, ST, dbl-bit K....**200.00**
French Lapegy, ST, aluminum alloys, takes flat bitted K...............**75.00**
French Revolved, oval, ST, takes 2 Ks: bbl & pin tumbler..........**170.00**
German, Swartiger, steel, NST, bbl K goes in at end of cuffs **500.00**
German, 3-lb steel set, 2⅝" thick, center chain, bbl K..............**175.00**
German Clejuso, oval design, ST, dbl-cuff weight, 22-oz **100.00**
German Clejuso, sq lc, adjusts/NST, d-lb on side, bbl K.............**100.00**
German Darby, adjusts, well finished, NST, sm **120.00**
German Hamburg 8, non-adjust NST, center bar/post w/K-way .**275.00**
Hiatt, English Darby, like US CW Darby, stp Hiatt & #d.............**75.00**
Hiatt, solid state, 2 separate cuffs joined bk to bk, stp/#d...........**190.00**
Hiatt English non-adjust screw K Darby style, uses screw K........**120.00**
Hiatt Figure 8, swings open to insert/withdraw wrists.................**150.00**
Italian, stp New Police, modern Peerless type, ST, sm bbl K.........**35.00**
Plug 8, remove plug before inserting external threaded K............**250.00**
Russian modern ST, blued bbl key, unmk, crude........................**80.00**
Spanish, stp Alcyon/Star, modern Peerless type, flat K.................**65.00**
Spanish, stp Alcyon/Star, modern Peerless type, ST, sm bbl K......**45.00**

Foreign Leg Shackles

East German, aluminum, lg hinge, cable amid 4 cuffs, bbl key ...**100.00**
German Clejuso, sq lc, adjusts/NST, d-bl on side, bbl K.............**125.00**
German Clejuso Darby type, adjusts/NST/plated, uses screw K ..**160.00**
Hiatt English combo manacles, handcuff/leg irons w/chain **325.00**
Hiatt English non-adjust screw K Darby style, uses screw K........**100.00**
Hiatt Plug leg irons, same K-ing as Plug-8 cuffs, w/chain **275.00**

U.S. Handcuffs

Romer, non-swing through, takes flat key, resembles padlock, stamped Romer Co., $300.00. (Photo courtesy Joseph Tanner)

Adams, teardrop lc, bbl Kd, NST, usually not stp......................**200.00**
American Munitions, modern/rnd, sm bbl Kd, ST bow, stp..........**45.00**
Bean Giant, sideways figure-8, solid center lc, dbl-bit K.............**550.00**
Bean Patrolman, kidney-bean form, d-lb on lc, NST, stp T **130.00**
Bean-Cobb, sm rnd lc, removable cylinder, d-lb, NST, 1899 ......**100.00**
Cavenay, looks like Marlin Daley but w/screw K, NST...............**180.00**
Civil War padlocking type, various designs w/loop for lock **225.00**
Colt, modern ST bow, sm bbl Kd, stp w/Colt & Co name...........**200.00**
Flash Action Manacle, like Bean Giant w/ST, K-way center......**400.00**
Flexibles, steel segmented bows, NST Darby type, screw K.........**250.00**
Guardian, modern ST, NP steel, bbl K **60.00**
H&R Super, ST, shaft-hinge connector takes hollow titted K **150.00**
Harvard, takes sm bbl K, ST, stp Harvard Lock Co.....................**65.00**
Judd, NST, used rnd/internally triangular K, stp Mattatuck........**150.00**
Lilly Hand Iron, 2" strap iron (8" L), oval bands, NST, sq K......**700.00**
Marlin Daley, NST, bottle-neck form, neck stp, dbl-titted K......**300.00**
Mattatuck, NST, propeller-like K-way, stp Mattatuck/etc **130.00**

Palmer, 2" steel bands, 2 K-ways (top & center), NST stp..........**400.00**
Peerless, ST, takes sm bbl K, stp Mfg'ered by Peerless Co..............**40.00**
Peerless, ST, takes sm bbl K, stp Mfg'ered by S&W Co.................**75.00**
Peerless Big Guy, modern ST, bbl key......................................**50.00**
Phelps, NST, twist chain between cuffs, Tower look-alike **400.00**
Pratt combo, 1 cuff connects w/nipper/claw, ST, mk Pratt **400.00**
Providence Tool Co, stp, NST, Darby screw K style **350.00**
Rankin, steel NST, mk screw K **300.00**
S&W 94 Maximum Security, ST, takes Ace-type K, stp S&W...**120.00**
Strauss, ST, takes lg solid bitted K, stp Strauss Eng Co...............**120.00**
Tower, NST, bottom K, solid/flat-fitted K goes in cuff edge **200.00**
Tower bar cuffs, cuffs separate by 10-12" steel bar.........................**300.00**
Tower Dbl Lock, NST, takes bbl-bitted K, usually stp Tower **110.00**
Tower Detective Pinkerton, NST, sq lc, bbl-bitted K, no stp **165.00**
Tower Single Lock, NST, bbl-bit K, K-way slanted on lc, sm......**125.00**
Tower-Bean, NST, sm rnd lc, takes tiny bbl-bitted K, stp...........**130.00**
Tri-lock, heavy polymer & stainless steel, ST, triple lock............**200.00**
Walden 'Lady Cuff,' NST, takes sm bbl K, lightweight, stp.........**400.00**

U.S. Leg Shackles

American Munitions, as handcuffs **55.00**
Civil War or prison ball & chain, padlocking or rivet type.........**500.00**
Cloc spike, 30" L opening for ankle w/padlock & 2 spikes..........**650.00**
H&R Supers, as handcuffs..**650.00**
Harvard, as handcuffs **125.00**
Judd, as handcuffs **155.00**
Leg lock brace, metal brace, ankle to knee, lever locked.............**225.00**
Oregon boot, break-apart shackle on above ankle support.......**1,200.00**
Palmer, as handcuffs but w/detachable chain, NST **600.00**
Peerless Big Guy, modern ST, bbl key...**60.00**
Providence Tool Co, stp, NST...**250.00**
Strauss, as handcuffs **200.00**
Tower, bottom K, as handcuffs **150.00**
Tower ball & chain, leg iron w/chain & 6-lb to 50-lb ball..........**500.00**
Tower Dbl-Lock, as handcuffs...**130.00**
Tower Detective, as handcuffs...**200.00**

Various Other Restraining Devices

African slave Darby-style cuffs, heavy iron/chain, handmade **200.00**
African slave Darby-style leg shackles, heavy/hand forged..........**220.00**
African slave padlocking or riveted forged iron shackles.............**170.00**
Argus iron claw, twist T to open & close **60.00**
Darby neck collar, rnd steel loop opens w/screw K **400.00**
English figure-8 nipper, claws open by lifting top lock tab **80.00**
Gale finger cuff, knuckle duster, non-K, mk GFC **150.00**
German nipper, twist hdl opens/closes cuff, stp Germany/etc........**75.00**
Hiatt High Security, hinged bbl K & pin-tumbler K (2 key) **150.00**
Jay Pee, thumb cuffs, mk solid body, bbl K **15.00**
Korean, hand chain model, blk, bbl key..**60.00**
Korean, hand hinged model, blk, bbl key.....................................**70.00**
Mighty-Mite, thumb cuffs, solid body, ST, mk, bbl K **110.00**
New Model Russian, chain bbl key, blued....................................**125.00**
New Model Russian, hinged, bbl key, blued.................................**140.00**
Phillips Nipper, claw, flip lever on top to open **80.00**
Thomas Nipper, claw, push button top to open **80.00**
Tower Lyon, thumb cuffs, solid body, NST, dbl-bit center K **200.00**

Reverse Painting on Glass

Verre eglomise is the technique of painting on the underside of glass. Dating back to the early 1700s, this art became popular in the nineteenth century when German immigrants chose historical figures and beautiful women as subjects for their reverse glass paintings. Advertising mirrors of this type came into vogue at the turn of the century.

Chinese Emperor in orange robe, 19x25"......................................**60.00**
Coaching scene: Oxford & London Coach, bird's-eye maple fr, 12x18".**140.00**

John Adams, second President of United States, early nineteenth century, 11½x13¾", $3,450.00.

Karolina, lady in striped/flowered dress, touched up, 14x11" **400.00**
Princess w/attandant; wise man w/boy, Chinese, re-fr, 19x13", pr **250.00**
Statue of Liberty, oval, curved glass, 20½x14", EX **45.00**
Westminster Bridge, London, MOP accents, 24½x20½" **55.00**
White House, 37⅞x15⅞" **210.00**

Ridgway

As early as 1792, the Ridgway brothers, Job and George, produced fine quality earthenwares in Shelton, Staffordshire, marking their products 'Ridgway, Smith, & Ridgway,' and later 'Job & George Ridgway.' Around 1800 the brothers split, and each had his own firm, both at Shelton. They were joined in the business by various members of the Ridgway family, and, in fact, their descendants still operate there today.

The two firms created by the split were the Bell Works and the Cauldon Pottery. Bell produced stone china and earthenware decorated with blue transfer printing. Their mark was 'J. & W. Ridgway' or J. & W.R.' (John and William) until 1848 when 'William Ridgway' was used. The Cauldon Pottery made earthenware, stone china, and high quality porcelains fine enough to win them the distinction of being appointed potters to the Queen. From 1830 their wares attest to this fact, bearing the Royal Arms mark with 'J.R.' within the crest. In 1940 '& Co.' was added. Most examples of Ridgway's wares found today are transfer-printed historical scenes. See also Staffordshire, transferware; and Flow Blue.

Bowl, Indian Scenery, bl transfer, 1830-34, 10½" **150.00**
Cup & saucer, Melisande, chintz **50.00**
Cup & saucer, yel & wht w/fair gold, bone china, 2¾", 5½" **25.00**
Cup plate, Pomerania, purple transfer, 1830, 4" **95.00**
Dish, Pomerania, hdld, ftd, 1830s, oval, 13x10" **230.00**
Pitcher, Oriental, bl transfer, 4" **90.00**
Pitcher , Tyrolean, gr & wht, ca 1835, 4".......................................**225.00**
Plate, Bay of Naples scene, Royal Ambrosial Ware, pierced to hang .**50.00**
Plate, Bridge of St Maurice, Italian series, scalloped edges, 9".......**95.00**
Plate, Japan Opaque, filled-in transfer on pearlware, 1825, 8" **125.00**
Plate, Pomerania, purple transfer, 1840-45, 9" **110.00**
Plate, Pomerania, red-purple transfer, 1830-55, 10".....................**150.00**
Plate, souvenir; Iowa State Capital, brn transfer, 9⅝" **50.00**
Plate, Tuscan Rose, brn transfer, 1840-41, 10" **110.00**
Platter, English Garden #4424, heavy ironstone **75.00**
Platter, Oriental Birds, pearlware, 11" **350.00**
Platter, Pennsylvania Hospital, floral border, 1870, 8-sided, 14x18" ...**575.00**
Platter, Rose & Chain transfer, 1830-40, 14¾" **250.00**
Sugar bowl, Tam O'Shanter scene, hand w/swag hdls, rpl finial..**165.00**

Rie, Lucie

Lucie Rie was born in 1902. She moved to London in 1938 and shared her studio with Hans Coper from 1946 to 1958. Her ceramics look modern; however they are based on shapes from many world cultures dating back to Roman times. Lucie Rie is best known for the use of metallic oxides in her clay and glazes. She specializes in the hand throwing of thin porcelain bowls, which is a very difficult process. Her works are in the world's best museums. All of her ceramics are impressed with a seal mark on the bottom, a cojoined 'L & R' within a rectangular reserve. Recently, when her work is offered at auction, it has been bringing prices that are sometimes double the presale estimates.

Bowl vase, gray w/oatmeal swirled areas, funnel form, 8½" dia...**3,000.00**
Vase, cratered wine/pk/gr, trumpet neck, rnd w/cylinder ft, 10" **9,000.00**

Riviera

Riviera was a line of dinnerware introduced by the Homer Laughlin China Company in 1938. It was sold exclusively by the Murphy Company through their nationwide chain of dime stores. Riviera was unmarked, lightweight, and inexpensive. It was discontinued sometime prior to 1950. Colors are mauve blue, red, yellow, light green, and ivory. On rare occasions, dark blue pieces are found, but this was not a standard color. For further information we recommend *The Collector's Encyclopedia of Fiesta* (2001 values) by Sharon and Bob Huxford, available from Collector Books.

Batter set, complete, from $290 to...**315.00**
Batter set, ivory, w/decals, complete, from $170 to......................**185.00**
Bowl, baker, 9", from $25 to..**30.00**
Bowl, cream soup; w/liner, ivory, from $75 to................................**80.00**
Bowl, fruit; cobalt, 5½", from $34 to **38.00**
Bowl, fruit; 5½", from $12 to..**14.00**
Bowl, nappy, 7¼', from $25 to...**30.00**
Bowl, oatmeal; 6", from $38 to..**42.00**
Bowl, utility; ivory, from $48 to..**52.00**
Butter dish, cobalt, ½-lb, from $300 to...**325.00**
Butter dish, cobalt, ¼-lb, from $250 to...**280.00**
Butter dish, colors other than cobalt, turq or ivory, ¼-lb, $135 to..**150.00**
Butter dish, colors other than cobalt, ½-lb, from $120 to...........**130.00**
Butter dish, ivory, ¼-lb, from $175 to **185.00**
Butter dish, turq, ¼-lb, from $290 to **310.00**
Casserole, from $110 to..**120.00**
Creamer, from $11 to...**13.00**
Cup & saucer, demitasse; ivory, from $80 to **90.00**
Jug, w/lid, from $130 to...**145.00**
Pitcher, juice; mauve bl, from $210 to..**225.00**
Pitcher, juice; yel, from $120 to...**135.00**
Plate, deep, from $22 to **25.00**
Plate, 6", from $7 to..**9.00**
Plate, 7", cobalt. from $35 to...**45.00**
Plate, 7", from $10 to...**14.00**
Plate, 9", from $16 to...**20.00**
Plate, 10", from $55 to...**65.00**
Platter, closed hdls, 11¼", from $24 to..**28.00**
Platter, cobalt, 12", from $70 to..**80.00**
Platter, 11½", from $22 to...**25.00**
Platter, 15", from $55 to..**65.00**
Sauce boat, from $22 to..**27.00**
Saucer, from $4 to...**5.00**
Shakers, pr, from $18 to **20.00**

Sugar bowl, w/lid, from $18 to..**20.00**

Syrup with lid, from $160.00 to $180.00.

Teacup, from $8 to..**11.00**
Teapot, from $155 to..**165.00**
Tidbit, ivory, 2-tier, from $70 to..**75.00**
Tumbler, hdl, from $70 to...**75.00**
Tumbler, hdl, ivory, from $135 to..**145.00**
Tumbler, juice; from $52 to...**55.00**

Robj

Robj was the name of a retail store that operated in Paris for only a few years, from about 1925 to 1931. Robj solicited designs from the best French artisans of the period to produce decorative objects for the home. These were executed mostly in porcelain but there were glass and earthenware pieces as well. The most well known are the figural bottles which were particularly popular in the United States. However, Robj also promoted tea sets, perfume lamps, chess sets, ashtrays, bookends, humidors, powder jars, cigarette boxes, figurines, lamps, and milk pitchers. Robj objects tend to be whimsical, and all embody the Art Deco style. Items listed below are ceramic unless noted otherwise. Our advisors for this category are Randall Monsen and Rod Baer; their address is listed in the Directory under Virginia.

Bookends, leaping greyhounds, wht, #44, 5x6½", pr **450.00**
Bookends, pierrot on 1, pierotte on other, wht, #443, 6¾x8", pr...**295.00**
Bottle, French priest, blk hat forms stopper, 10½x4"...................**365.00**
Condiment jars as people, 1 cleric, 1 veggie man, 3 pcs, EX.......**750.00**
Decanter, musical, Russian man, hat forms stopper, 12"..............**350.00**
Inkwell, Blackamoor in gold/wht robe holds well, no lid, 6".......**275.00**
Inkwell, clown on bk w/legs up, sgn, 7¼x6½" **435.00**
Inkwell, female genie, mc, 5¼"..**180.00**
Perfume burner, wht-robed Oriental, X-legged on steps, 8".........**550.00**

Rock 'N Roll Memorabilia

Memorabilia from the early days of rock 'n roll recalls an era that many of us experienced firsthand; these listings are offered to demonstrate the many and various aspects of this area of collecting. Beware of reproductions! Many are so well done even a knowledgeable collector will sometimes be fooled.

Our advisor for Elvis memorabilia is Rosalind Cranor, author of *Elvis Collectibles* and *Best of Elvis Collectibles* (Overmountain Press); she is listed in the Directory under Virginia. The remainder is under the advisement of Bob Gottuso, author of Beatles, KISS, and Monkees sections in *Garage Sale Gold II* by Tomart; see Pennsylvania. See also Decanters.

Alice Cooper, concert ticket, Jackson MS, June 6, 1975, unused, NM..**25.00**
Andy Gibb, beach towel, The Stigwood Group, 1979, M.............**50.00**
Andy Gibb, jigsaw puzzle, The Stigwood Group, 1978, MIB **25.00**

Beatles, air bed, vinyl, heads w/facsimile signatures, UK, 1964, NM ..900.00
Beatles, apron, heavy wht paper w/blk graphics, US, 1964, EX ..500.00
Beatles, book, Help!, Random House, 1965, hardcover, EX 55.00
Beatles, brooch, guitar shape w/group photo, 1964, M (serrated card) 75.00
Beatles, bubble bath containers, Paul or Ringo only, Colgate, MIB, ea 500.00
Beatles, calendar, Make a Date.., octagonal standup w/knobs, UK, 1964..550.00
Beatles, card, Christmas, apple tree w/candles, mk Klaus 71, M....85.00
Beatles, card, Happy B-Day From All of Us, group, US, 1964, lg, unused ..65.00
Beatles, chair, Yellow Submarine, inflatable vinyl, NM 50.00
Beatles, charm bracelet, The Beatles above heads, Randall, 1964, MOC ...150.00
Beatles, Colorforms Cartoon Kit, 1966, complete, MIB...........1,200.00
Beatles, coloring book, Saalfield #5240, unused, NM 100.00
Beatles, drinking cup, various, Buritte, 1964, 8", NM 130.00
Beatles, drinking glass, group, rubber coated, gold trim, US, 1964, NM ...180.00
Beatles, figures, Swingers Music Set, NMOC..............................140.00
Beatles, flasher rings, set of 4, EX 80.00
Beatles, hanger, die-cut cb bust image w/plastic hook, US, 1968, NM ..175.00
Beatles, key ring, apple on clear Lucite disc on gold-tone metal, NM ...150.00
Beatles, lamp, wooden bead base w/heads on sheet music shade, UK, 1964 ..1,000.00
Beatles, money clip, die-cut apple in sq fr, Apple Records, NM .225.00
Beatles, necklace, 2" wooden disc w/brass figures, Randall, 1964, NM ...225.00
Beatles, pin-bk, I'm Bugs About the 'Beatles,' US, 3½" dia, NM..50.00
Beatles, plaques, HP ceramic heads, Kelsboro Ware, 1964, 5", ea 450.00
Beatles, postcard, Louis Tussad's Wax Museum, color photo, 1960s, NM+ ...25.00
Beatles, poster, Ringo for President, head image, blk on wht, 1964, NM .200.00
Beatles, purse, clutch; vinyl w/leather strap, heads, Dame, 1964, 6x9" ..375.00
Beatles, record tote, vinyl w/dbl plastic hdls, photo image, Seagull 275.00
Beatles, spatter toy, rare, 16", MIP..275.00
Beatles, tote bag, sq vinyl/dbl hdls, variations, tags, Japan, 1966 ...125.00
Beatles, tray, bamboo, blk/wht/red images, Japan, 1964, 3 szs, $100 to ..150.00
Beatles, wig, Lowell, MIP (sealed) 140.00
Bee Gees, notebook, spiral-bound, Rock On, 1979, M, from $35 to..40.00
Bee Gees, patch, cream w/red & blk logo, fan club issue, 1979, M ..35.00
Bee Gees, radio, transistor; Vanity Fair, 1979, 5½", EX 20.00
Bee Gees, wastebasket, Sgt Pepper, Stigwood Group, 1978, M 60.00
Blues Brothers, shopping bag, plastic, movie promo, NM..............20.00
Bobby Darin, ink pen/record, Scripto Wordmaster/Free Record, 1958, MIP....100.00
Boy George & Culture Club, book, ...In His Own Words, Omnibus, 1983, M..20.00
Carpenters, money cube, Lucite w/shredded money, A&M records promo, M ...30.00
Chubby Checker, limbo bar w/record, Whamo, 1962, EX...........125.00
Dave Clark Five, tour book, 1964, lg format, EX 35.00
David Cassidy, guitar, Carnival Toys, 1970s, MIB, from $75 to ..100.00
David Cassidy, slide-tile puzzle, 1970s, M 30.00
Dick Clark, Picture Patch, 1950s, MOC 20.00
Dick Clark/American Bandstand, diary, vinyl, 1958, 4x4", EX...125.00
Dick Clark/American Bandstand, tie clip, cast metal, figural, $45 to..55.00
Donny & Marie Osmond, diary, Continental Plastics, 1977, M....10.00
Donny & Marie Osmond, iron-ons, various, 1970s, ea, from $10 to..15.00
Donny & Marie Osmond, tambourine, Lapin, 1977, 6" dia, M, from $30 to....40.00
Doors, concert ticket, KNRT Theater, Sept 27, 1967, unused, NM..300.00
Doors, stationery, 1960s, NM...100.00
Elton John, card, paper photo, used for pennants, 1970s, M............8.00
Elton John, pennant, Captain Fantastic, paper photo on felt, 1970s, M..25.00
Elvis, autograph book, EP Enterprises, 1956, EX, minimum value ...500.00
Elvis, bracelet, men's; Dog Tag, MOC 40.00
Elvis, coaster, blk & wht photo w/signature, EP Enterprises, 3½" 360.00
Elvis, cookie jar, Elvis in pk Cadillac, Vandor, 1997, MIB 125.00
Elvis, cookie jar, Elvis on Harley by water tower, MIB 100.00
Elvis, fan club kit, complete, 1956, EX, from $300 to 400.00
Elvis, hat, felt w/pictorial band, orig tag, 1950s, NM..................135.00
Elvis, lei w/medallion, Blue Hawaii, EX 200.00
Elvis, lighter, Aloha Elvis/signature & 50 Yrs w/Elvis, Zippo, M..100.00
Elvis, music box, wooden, plays different songs, Japan, 4x6½x12", M ..70.00
Elvis, necklace, Dog Tag, MOC 80.00

Elvis, necklace, heart w/eng image, EP Enterprises, 1956, MIB ..200.00
Elvis, ornament, musical, plays Blue Christmas, Carlton, 1995, MIB..60.00
Elvis, pennant, King of Rock 'N Roll 1935-1977, w/graphics, M ..30.00
Elvis, perfume, Teddy Bear, EP Enterprises, 1956, full, MIB........300.00
Elvis, plate, GI Blues, Delphi, M 40.00
Elvis, postcard, Blue Hawaii scene, unused, M 75.00
Elvis, scrapbook, Solid Gold memories, Ballantine Books, 1977, EX..30.00
Elvis, sheet music, Kentucky Rain, EX 25.00
Elvis, stuffed Hound Dog, Smile Toy Co, NM 250.00
Elvis, ticket stub, Indiana State U, Sept, 16 1977, unused, NM+ .20.00
Elvis, Tie-On Trinket & Gift Enclosure, Rojay Studios, 1950s, MIP ..100.00
Fleetwood Mac, pin, radio promo for 1977 Madison Sq Garden concert, M....12.00
Frank Zappa, tour program, 1980, M 15.00
Genesis, postcard, drawing of man running, blk & wht, Duke, limited ed........5.00
Go Gos, button, We Got the Beat, girls on pk image, 1" dia, M..18.00
Greatful Dead, postcard, BG-263, Dec 31, 1970, NM 30.00
Heart, sheet music, Dog Butterfly, Warner Bros, 1978, NM 12.00
Jackson 5, banner, I Love the Jackson 5, felt, 1960s-70s, 29", NM.30.00
Janis Joplin, photo, blk/wht, singing at mike/blowing hair, 8x10" 5.00
Jefferson Starship, sticker, Spitfire, girl/dragon, Winterland, 1976 ..6.00
Jerry Garcia Band, baseball shirt, 1978 tour, by ABCO, unused, M ...25.00
Jimi Hindrix, photo w/publicity info, Goldstein Organization, 1960s, M ...15.00
John Denver, belt buckle, brass w/color image, Rock Visuals, 1976, EX 25.00
Kinks, booklet, TV Guise (resembles TV Guide), 1975, M 10.00
Kinks, concert ticket, Universal Amphitheater, June 23, 1978, unused ..20.00
KISS, belt buckle, blk w/silver letters & border, 1977, M..............30.00
KISS, costume, Gene Simmons, 1978, EXIB 160.00
KISS, key chain, Aucion, 1977, 4 different, NM, ea 50.00
KISS, lighters, Zippo, set of 4 (ea member), MIB 90.00
KISS, sheet music, various, EX, ea from $10 to..........................20.00
KISS, sleeping bag, Aucoin Management, 1978, EX 500.00
KISS, song book, The Originals or Unmasked, rare, EX, ea........125.00

KISS, waste can, tin litho, P&K Products, 1978, 19x11", EX, $225.00. (Photo courtesy June Moon)

Led Zeppelin, program, Knebworth Park, Aug 11, 1979, VG+ ...200.00
Madonna, lamp, Truth or Dare, Boy Toy, 1992, M, from $200 to..250.00
Meatloaf, poster, concert promo, blk & wht, 1978, M 6.00
Michael Jackson, Electronic Microphone, LJN, 1984, MIB 45.00
Michael Jackson, shoes, blk Billy Jean style, LA Gear, EXIB, $85 to 95.00
Monkees, book, Who's Got the Button, Whitman, 1968, hardcover, EX.20.00
Monkees, bracelet, color photo images on discs, Raybert, 1967, MOC 75.00
Monkees, fan club kit, complete, 1967, EX (EX folder), from $75 to 100.00
Monkees, hand puppet, talker, Mattel, 1968, MIB (sealed) 250.00
Monkees, key ring, guitar shape w/head images, Raybert, 1966.....20.00
Monkees, records, cut-out cb, Colgems/Post Cereal, 1967-68, ea..20.00
Motley Crue, 5 puffy stickers, MIP..5.00
New Kids on the Block, cassette player, Big Step Prod, 1990, MIB.35.00
New Kids on the Block, Colorforms Deluxe Play Set, 1991, MIB.15.00
Osmonds, annual, 1976, NM 25.00

Paul McCartney & Wings, book, by Tony Jasper, hardcover, EX ..20.00
Paul McCartney & Wings, shirt, band photo w/Linda, tour dates on bk, M...20.00
Rick Nelson, Picture Patch, 1950s, MOC...............................20.00
Rolling Stones, dollar bill w/Mick Jager image, M (sealed) 8.00
Rolling Stones, drinking cup, plastic, Voodoo Lounge World Tour 94/94 ..15.00
Rolling Stones, 3-D glasses, promo for Steel Wheels, 1990, M, $20 to ..30.00
Sonny & Cher, pennant, I Love Sonny & Cher, 1970s, NM 35.00
Supremes, arm band, Gammas Invite You to Diana Ross..., 1960s, M ..45.00
Three Dog Night, Picture Patch, 1950s, MOC 20.00

Rockingham

In the early part of the nineteenth century, American potters began to prefer brown- and buff-burning clays over red because of their durability. The glaze favored by many was Rockingham, which varied from a dark brown mottle to a sponged effect sometimes called tortoise shell. It consisted in part of manganese and various metallic salts and was used by many potters until well into the twentieth century. Over the past two years, demand and prices have risen sharply, especially in the East. See also Bennington.

Bowl, brn mottle, ca 1880, 4x9½" 55.00
Bowl, columns & dots emb, ca 1860, 3½x10½" 75.00
Covered dish, mottled, w/lid, ca 1910, 5x8" 85.00
Cow creamer, w/lid, tips of horns broken/base flake, 5½x7" 220.00
Custard cup, lt brn, ca 1870, 2¾" 20.00
Dog, seated, EX detail, scalloped base, rprs, 11".................450.00
Dog, seated, free-standing poodle-like legs, rtcl eyes/nose, 8", EX...495.00
Dog, seated w/chain along 1 leg, rectangular base, 5½" 580.00
Flask, book; chips on spine/edges, 6⅝" 250.00
Flask, boot w/laced side, 6x8¾" 375.00
Flask, boot; laced up 1 side, minor flakes/rim chip, 6x7" 275.00
Flask, dismounted horseman ea side, scalloped neck, 7", VG......385.00
Flask, eagle w/banner 1 side, bk: morning glory, 7" 250.00
Inkwell, boy asleep, holding hat, 4x5½" 325.00
Inkwell, column shape, 1-pc, 3x3⅞" 385.00
Inkwell, reclining dog, alert ears (1 chipped on bk), 4x6"..........450.00
Pitcher, bbl form, ca 1900, 8½" 75.00
Pitcher, hunt scene emb, Am, 1860s, 10"...........................295.00
Pitcher, hunt scene emb, hound hdl, Am, 1860s, 9¾" 550.00
Pitcher, pillar & scroll design, 7¼" 150.00
Pitcher, tulips emb, ca 1890, 5" 195.00
Tray, sq w/molded edge, flared sides, 9".............................85.00
Vase, potpourri; flower bouquets & gold, griffin mk, ca 1835, 11", NM....285.00
Washboard, yel & brn mottle, wood fr, 1870s, 22x12" 850.00

Rockwell, Norman

Norman Rockwell began his career in 1911 at the age of seventeen doing illustrations for a children's book entitled *Tell Me Why Stories*. Within a few years he had produced the *Saturday Evening Post* cover that made him one of America's most beloved artists. Though not well accepted by the professional critics of his day who did not consider his work to be art but 'merely' commercial illustration, Rockwell's popularity grew to the extent that today there is an overwhelming abundance of examples of his work or those related to the theme of one of his illustrations.

The figurines described below were issued by the Rockwell Museum and Museum Collections Inc. (formerly Rockwell Museum). For Rockwell listings by Gorham see last year's edition of *Schroeder's Antiques Price Guide*. Our advisor for this category is Barb Putratz; she is listed in the Directory under Minnesota.

A Walkin' & a Whistlin', 1986...70.00
Adventures Between Adventures, 1986 ....100.00
All Wrapped Up, 1984...100.00
Almost Grown Up, 1982..175.00
America's Artist, ltd ed 5,000, 1983...................................195.00
Another Masterpiece by Norman Rockwell, ltd ed of 5,000, 1985 ..210.00
Apple for the Teacher, Museum Collections Inc, 1986....................70.00
Artist, The; Museum Collections Inc, ltd ed 2,500, 1986 ....195.00
At the Circus, 1982..190.00
Authorized Collector's Center (ad stand), ltd ed 5,000, 1981.....150.00
Baby's First Step, 1979..175.00
Barefoot Boy, Museum Collections Inc, ltd ed 5,000, 1986.........110.00
Bedtime, LCF series, ltd ed 1,000, 1982 ....225.00
Bedtime, 1979..80.00
Bicycle Boys, 1981...120.00

The Big Race, 1984, 4½x5x5", $100.00.

Birthday Party, The; 1980 ....150.00
Bobbing for Apples, 1982...120.00
Bored of Education, 1984 ....95.00
Bottom of the Sixth, Museum Collections Inc, ltd ed 5,000, 1986..200.00
Boy Meets His Dog, A; 1986 ....100.00
Braving the Storm, 1982..115.00
Bride & Groom, 1981..140.00
Bringing Home the Christmas Tree, 1982 ....125.00
Celebration, 1982..190.00
Census Taker, Museum Collections Inc, ltd ed 2,500, 1986........200.00
Checking His List, 1980..90.00
Christmas Prayers, 1985..95.00
Circus Comes to Town, The; 1982 ....125.00
Circus Strongman, 1986...100.00
Cobbler, LCF Series, ltd ed 1,000, 1982 ....225.00
Cobbler, The; 1979...80.00
Collect Fine Porcelain Figurines (ad stand), 1984 ....140.00
Country, Doctor, The; 1982 ....95.00
Courageous Hero, 1982..185.00
Dollhouse for Sis, A; 1979 ....80.00
Downhill Racer, 1981...120.00
Drawing a Blank, Museum Collections Inc, ltd ed 2,500, 1987 ..165.00
Dreams in the Antique Shop, Museum Collections Inc, 1986......80.00
Dreams in the Antique Shop, 1982......................................100.00
Drummer's Friend, The; 1982 ....125.00
Final Touch, A; 1983...95.00
First Car in Town, The; ltd ed 2,500, 1985...........................235.00
First Haircut, The; 1979...150.00
First Prom, The; 1979..125.00
For a Good Boy, LCF series, ltd ed 1,000, 1983 ....225.00
For a Good Boy, 1980...90.00
Freedom of Fear, ltd ed 5,000, 1982..................................350.00
Freedom of Speech, ltd ed 5,000, 1982................................350.00
Freedom of Want, ltd ed 5,000, 1982..................................350.00
Freedom of Worship, ltd ed 5,000, 1982...............................350.00
Giving Thanks, 1982..200.00
Goin' Fishin', 1984..95.00

Going Out, Museum Collections Inc, ltd ed 2,500, 1986............210.00
Good Food Good Friends, 1982......................................225.00
Happy Birthday, Dear Mother, 1979................................140.00
Helping Mother, 1982...120.00
High Hopes, 1983..150.00
High Stepping, 1982...110.00
Home for Fido, A; Museum Collections Inc, 1986......................75.00
Homerun Slugger, 1982...145.00
Kite Maker, The; 1982...135.00
Late Night Dining, Museum Collections Inc, 1986.....................80.00
Letterman, The; Museum Collections Inc, ltd ed 2,500, 1986....165.00
Lighthouse Keeper's Daughter, The; LCF series, ltd ed 1,000, 1982 ..225.00
Lighthouse Keeper's Daughter, The; 1979.............................85.00
Little Mother, 1980...135.00
Little Patient, 1981..120.00
Little Salesman, 1982...185.00
Little Shaver, 1982...185.00
Lovely in Lipstick, Museum Collections Inc, 1988....................75.00
Memories, LCF series, ltd ed 1,000, 1983..........................225.00
Memories, 1980...90.00
Model, The; ltd ed 15,000, 1986...................................150.00
Mom's Helper, ltd ed 15,000, 1986.................................120.00
Mom's Helper, 1986...90.00
Mother's Little Helpers, 1981.....................................140.00
Music Lesson, The; 1980..90.00
Music Master, The; 1980..90.00
Mysterious Malady, Museum Collections Inc, 1986...................100.00
New Arrival, Museum Collections Inc, 1981.........................160.00
No Fishin', No Nothin', Museum Collections Inc, 1986................80.00
Off to School, LCF series, ltd ed 1,000, 1981.....................115.00
Out Fishin', Museum Collections Inc, ltd ed 25,000, 1985 ....100.00
Outward Bound, ltd ed 5,000, 1984.................................200.00
Painter & the Pups, ltd ed 5,000, 1986............................205.00
Partygoers, Museum Collections Inc, ltd ed 2,500, 1984............235.00
Pest, The; 1982...125.00
Playing Pirates, ltd ed 2,500, 1984...............................235.00
Practice Makes Perfect, Museum Collections Inc, ltd ed 2,500, 1987..170.00
Pride of Parenthood, 1986...100.00
Puppy Love, 1983...95.00
Report Card, Museum Collections Inc, 1986...........................80.00
Ringing in Good Cheer, 1981.......................................125.00
Rosie the Riveter, Museum Collections Inc, ltd ed 2,500, 1987 .165.00
Santa Takes a Break, Museum Collections Inc, ltd ed 3,500, 1987..110.00
Saturday's Hero, 1984...105.00
Secrets, ltd ed 5,000, 1986.......................................185.00
Sneezing Spy, Museum Collections Inc, ltd ed 2,500, 1986 ....160.00
Soda Jerk, The; ltd ed 5,000, 1986................................205.00
Space Age Santa, 1984...115.00
Space Pioneers, 1982..185.00
Special Treat, A; 1982..100.00
Spirit of America, The; ltd ed 5,000, 1982.......................185.00
Spring Fever, 1981..100.00
Stereoscope, 1986...100.00
Student, The; 1980..165.00
Summer Fun, 1982..120.00
Sunday Morning, Museum Collections Inc, ltd ed 2,500, 1986 ..225.00
Surprise Treat, 1984...95.00
Sweet Dreams, 1981..190.00
Sweet Sixteen, 1979...125.00
Tattoo Artist, Museum Collections Inc, ltd ed 2,500, 1987 ....170.00
Tipping the Scale, Museum Collections Inc, 1986.....................75.00
Toymaker, The; LCF series, ltd ed 1,000, 1982 ....225.00
Toymaker, The; 1979..95.00
Trumpeter, The; Museum Collections Inc, ltd ed 2,500, 1986 ..2,000.00

Vacation, 1982..115.00
Vacation's Over, 1981 ....120.00
Visiting the Vet, Museum Collections Inc, 1988 ....85.00
Waiting for Santa, 1982...135.00
Washing Our Dog, 1981...140.00
We Missed You Daddy, 1981...190.00
Weighty Matters, ltd ed 5,000, 1986 ....180.00
Wet Behind the Ears, Museum Collections Inc, 1986 ....80.00
While the Audience Waits, 1981....................................100.00
Winter Fun, 1982...95.00
Words of Wisdom, 1982...130.00
Wrapping Christmas Presents, 1980.................................130.00

Rogers, John

John Rogers (1829 – 1904) was a machinist from Manchester, New Hampshire, who turned his hobby of sculpting into a financially successful venture. From the originals he meticulously fashioned of red clay, he had bronze master molds made from which plaster copies were cast. He specialized in five different categories: theatrical, Shakespeare, Civil War, everyday life, and horses. His large detailed groupings portrayed the life and times of the period between 1859 and 1892. In the following listings, examples are assumed to be in very good to excellent condition. Our advisor for this category is George Humphrey; he is listed in the Directory under Maryland.

Balcony...1,500.00
Bath..2,000.00
Bushwacker..2,000.00
Charity Patient...650.00

Checkers Up at the Farm, $575.00.

Chess...1,200.00
Country Post Office...750.00
Courtship in Sleepy Hollow, Pat date................................550.00
Faust & Marguerite, Leaving the Garden 1,200.00
Fetching the Doctor...750.00
First Ride..725.00
Frolic at the Old Homestead, 1887, 22½"..............................800.00
Going for the Cows..450.00
Home Guard..800.00
Mail Day..2,000.00
Matter of Opinion...600.00
One More Shot...550.00
Parting Promise...475.00
Picket Guard..750.00
Referee...800.00
Rip Van Winkle — At Home..325.00
Slave Auction 2,000.00
Taking the Oath & Drawing Rations, sgn, 23" 525.00
Village Schoolmaster..850.00

Wounded Scout, ca 1864 ....750.00

Rookwood

The Rookwood Pottery Company was established in 1879 in Cincinnati, Ohio. Its founder was Maria Longworth Nichols Storer, daughter of a wealthy family who provided the backing necessary to make such an enterprise possible. Mrs. Storer hired competent ceramic artisans and artists of note, who through constant experimentation developed many lines of superior art pottery. While in her employ, Laura Fry invented the airbrush-blending process for which she was issued a patent in 1884. From this, several lines were designed that utilized blended backgrounds. One of their earlier lines, Standard, was a brown ware decorated with underglaze slip-painted nature studies, animals, portraits, etc. Iris and Sea Green were introduced in 1894 and Vellum, a transparent mat-glaze line, in 1904. Other lines followed: Ombroso in 1910 and Soft Porcelain in 1915. Many of the early artware lines were signed by the artist. Soon after the turn of the twentieth century, Rookwood manufactured 'production' pieces that relied mainly on molded designs and forms rather than freehand decoration for their esthetic appeal. The Depression brought on financial difficulties from which the pottery never recovered. Though it continued to operate, the quality of the ware deteriorated, and the pottery was forced to close in 1967.

Unmarked Rookwood is only rarely encountered. Many marks may be found, but the most familiar is the reverse 'RP' monogram. First used in 1886, a flame point was added above it for each succeeding year until 1900. After that a Roman numeral added below indicated the year of manufacture. Impressed letters that related to the type of clay utilized for the body were also used — G for ginger, O for olive, R for red, S for sage green, W for white, and Y for yellow. Artware must be judged on an individual basis. Quality of the artwork is a prime factor to consider. Portraits, animals, and birds are worth more than florals; and pieces signed by a particularly renowned artist are highly prized. For more information we recommend *Rookwood Pottery, Bookends, Paperweights, and Animal Figurals* by Nick and Marilyn Nicholson and Jim Thomas.

Aerial Blue

Ewer, wild roses, A Valentien, #724D, W, 1894, 5½" 3,700.00
Teapot, jonquils, W McDonald, #1022 B, 1896, 4½"................2,000.00
Vase, windmill scenic, JD Wareham, #30F, 1894, 6⅛" 7,000.00

Aventurine

Trivet, sea gull, Aventurine over deep purple, #2351, 1930, 5¾" diameter, $400.00.

Vase, flowers (stylized), L Epply, #2136, 1920, 6⅛"..................1,300.00
Vase, jonquils, E Lincoln, #243, 1922, 9⅞".................................550.00
Vase, pine cones & boughs, L Epply, #1120, 1920, 4⅞" 800.00

Black Opal

Bowl, stylized floral, L Epply, #2287, 1926, 3¾x8¼", NM 500.00
Vase, chevrons & butterflies, S Sax, #2785, 1927, 13¼" 9,250.00
Vase, daisies on cobalt, S Toohey, #589E, W, 1900, rpr, 8⅝"...3,900.00
Vase, pansies, H Wilcox, #2105, 1924, 4⅝"................................700.00

Vase, peonies, S Sax, #S2070, 1926, drilled, 14½"................21,000.00
Vase, poppies, E Lincoln, #30F, W, 1906, 6¼"..........................3,800.00
Vase, poppies & wheat stalks, K Shirayamadani, #925C, X, 1929, 10⅜"....19,000.00
Vase, swan scenic, C Schmidt, #900B, W, 1908, 9½" 45,000.00
Vase, willow & swallows, K Shirayamadani, #951C, 1907, rstr, 10⅜" ...1,200.00

Cameo

Cup & saucer, daisies, A Valentien, #291, W, 1890, 3⅛" dia......300.00
Cup & saucer, wild rose, A Valentien, #291, W, 1890, 3⅛" dia..300.00
Egg dish, daisies, A Sprague, #48, W, 1887, 2¼" 400.00
Egg dish, daisies, S Toohey, #48, W, 1887, 2⅛" 400.00
Plate, floral, scalloped edge, A Sprague, #336BW, 7½" 140.00

French Red

Vase, cherry blossoms, S Sax, #2067, 1920, 7½" 8,500.00
Vase, daisy-like flowers, S Sax, #2191, 1922, 5⅛" 3,500.00
Vase, fuchsias in mat & high glazes, red int, S Sax, #2191, 1922, 5"..6,500.00

High Glaze

Bowl, floral, S Sax, built-in ped, 2 loop hdls, #2950, 1928, 2¾x11" ...950.00
Bowl, rose clusters, L Epply, #2253D, 1928, 2¾x6¾" 425.00
Lamp base, doves & magnolias, J Jensen, #6920, 1948, 12¼"..1,600.00
Lamp base, magnolias, E Becker, #216, 1951, 13⅛" 400.00
Lamp base, Virginia creepers, M McDonald, #S2139, 1936, 11⅞"..1,600.00
Mug, Quick Bear (chief), F King, 1946, 5"..................................400.00
Pitcher, Picasso-like women, J Jensen, #6757, 1949, 7⅛" 1,700.00
Vase, bellflowers, ET Hurley, #614E, 1943, 8⅜"......................1,100.00
Vase, Deco flowers, L Epply, #2914, 1929, 8⅜"......................2,300.00
Vase, deer & foliage, J Jensen, #900C, 1931, 8⅜"..................4,700.00
Vase, deer & woods, J Jensen, #S2180, 1947, sm flaw, 6½" 2,900.00
Vase, exotic birds among trees, ET Hurley, #6079, 1931, 18½" 7,250.00
Vase, exotic flowers & bamboo stalks, S Sax, #1882, 1919, 9⅜" ..6,000.00
Vase, floral band (repeating), S Sax, #2930, 1926, 9¾" 3,100.00
Vase, harbor scenic, ET Hurley, #30E, 1943, 8½" 1,500.00
Vase, irises & gr stems, J Jensen, #6311, 1944, 7¼", NM.........2,900.00
Vase, magnolias, E Barrett, #2783/#3220, 1946, 9⅜", NM..........600.00
Vase, narcissus, K Shirayamadani, #494B, 1925, 4⅞".............2,000.00
Vase, oranges & leaves, A Conant, #295E, 1921, 7¼"............2,800.00
Vase, Oriental-style landscape, L Epply, #2745, X, 1924, 9¼".3,000.00
Vase, peacocks (2) among flowers, ET Hurley, #2033D, 1922, 10" ...5,250.00
Vase, Picasso-like faces, J Jensen, #2720, 1948, 6¼" 9,250.00
Vase, poppies, M McDonald, #1126 C, 1942, 9⅜" 1,900.00
Vase, primroses, S Sax, #892B, 1928, 10¾"...........................3,500.00
Vase, sweet peas, K Shirayamadani, #2006, X 127, 1925, 7⅜" ...3,200.00
Vase, 3 nude women (cobalt) among flowers, J Jensen, S, 1933, 6⅝" ...8,750.00

Iris

Vase, blossoms, gold on lav, OG Reed, #901B, mk as 2nd o/w NM, 12 .....920.00
Vase, Canada geese (5)/water, K Shirayamadani, #1655E, 1909, 7¾" ..18,000.00
Vase, cherry blossoms, L Epply, #283V, mk as 2nd, 1911, 8½x3¾" ...1,035.00
Vase, crocus, F Rothenbusch, 1904, hairline/bruises, 9½x4"....1,380.00
Vase, cyclamens, I Bishop, #922E, W, 1905, 7¼" 1,900.00
Vase, daisies, S Sax, #940C, W, 1903, 11¼"...........................7,000.00
Vase, dandelions (Nouveau), F Rothenbusch, # illegible, W, 1903, 9" ...1,500.00
Vase, dogwood flowers, L Asbury, #614E, W, 1910, 8⅛"..........1,900.00
Vase, floral, E Noonan, #907F, W, 1906, 6⅞" 2,800.00
Vase, goldenrod, H Wilcox, #732D, W, 1896, 7⅜", NM............750.00
Vase, grapes, L Asbury, #1369D, W, X, 1909, 8¾" 1,400.00
Vase, hyacinths, JD Wareham, #925B, W, 1902, 12½"............5,500.00
Vase, hyacinths, OG Reed, #732B, W, 1902, 11" 5,750.00

Vase, jasmine flowers, F Rothenbusch, #860, W, 1901, chip, 6¼" ..**900.00**
Vase, mtn scenic, E Diers, #1369B, W, 1911, 14½" **20,000.00**
Vase, pansies on slate to ivory, I Bishop, #927 F, W, 1906, 5½" **1,100.00**
Vase, paperwhites cluster, R Fechheimer, #938D, W, 1903, 6⅛" ..**2,200.00**
Vase, peacock feathers, blk w/silver mts, M Daly, #S1625, 1900, 10"....**10,500.00**
Vase, poppies, L Asbury, #909BB, W, 1908, 10½" **9,750.00**
Vase, rooks in flight, ET Hurley, #942C, W, X, 1906, 6½", NM....**900.00**
Vase, sailboat scenic band, S Coyne, #1369D, W, 1910, 8⅝"...**12,000.00**
Vase, snowdrops, S Sax, #562, W, 1902, 9½" **2,300.00**
Vase, swans scenic, C Schmidt, #907D, W, 1908, 10½", NM ..**16,500.00**
Vase, thistles, L Asbury, #907DD, W, 1905, drilled/rpr, 9¼"....**1,500.00**
Vase, tulips & gr leaves, blk, E Diers, #796B, W, 1900, 10" **6,250.00**
Vase, water lilies, L Asbury, #320, 1904, 2nd mk, flaw, 11½x4¾" ..**700.00**
Vase wild roses, C Lindemann, #917C, W, X, 1900, 7¼" **1,100.00**

Limoges

Coupe dish, swallows & grasses, A Valentien, 1889, prof rpr, 6⅜"...**180.00**
Ewer, butterfly & grasses, A Valentien, #101, G, 1883, rpr, 11¼"....**400.00**
Ewer, Oriental fisherman at shore, ML Nichols, 1882, 9", NM..**2,500.00**
Jug, perfume; beetle & grasses, M Rettig, #61, G, 1883, 4⅝" **325.00**
Jug, perfume; butterfly/grasses, A Valentien, #61, R, 1883, 4⅝", NM...**225.00**
Jug, perfume; butterfly/tree/etc, NJ Hirschfield, #61, G, 1883, 4¾" **400.00**
Jug, perfume; swallows & bamboo, M Rettig, #61, G, 1883, 4⅝" ..**375.00**
Jug, perfume; swallows & grasses, H Horton, #61, R, 1883, 4⅝" ...**400.00**
Pitcher, swallows (20) & clouds, A Valentien, R, 1882, 6⅜" ..**1,200.00**
Pitcher, swallows & grasses, M Rettig, #200, R, 1883, 7⅞".........**600.00**
Vase, birds & pine boughs, M Daly, #197D, W, 1885, 10½", NM ..**750.00**
Vase, catfish amid crabs & vines, ML Nichols, 1882, 11¼".....**2,800.00**
Vase, lady w/water vessel/ancient ruins, att ML Nichols, G, 1883, 15".**1,200.00**
Vase, 3 scenic panels, ML Nichols, Aladdin shape, 1882, 30", NM....**29,000.00**

Mat

Note: Both incised mat and painted mat are listed here. Incised mat descriptions are indicated by the term 'cvd' within the line; all others are hand-painted mat ware.

Box, sunflowers, K Jones, #2660D, 1922, 2x5¼" **800.00**
Candlestick, gr, organic form w/mushroom hdl, AM Valentien, 4½"...**425.00**
Jug, whiskey; autumn leaves, A Valentien, #273DZ, 1901, 8⅜" .**650.00**
Vase, abstract floral on yel, CS Todd, #1667, 1920, 11", NM **550.00**
Vase, blueberries/leaves, E Barrett, #30F, 1925, 6¾" **750.00**
Vase, cvd apples, gr/red on gr, A Pons, #935D, 1907, 7¼"...**1,600.00**
Vase, cvd cala lilies, R Fechheimer, #943B, 1905, X, 12x7".....**1,725.00**
Vase, cvd fern fronds, gr on bl/maroon, R Fechheimer, 1905, 4½"...**500.00**
Vase, cvd geometrics, gr/brn/tan, W Hentschel, #568, 1914, 4"..**500.00**
Vase, cvd geometrics at shoulder, gr/bl, 1905, 8½" **950.00**
Vase, cvd leaves at neck, brn on brn, S Toohey, #111EZ, 1909, 5" ..**500.00**
Vase, cvd lotus flowers, CS Todd, #763C, 1920, 6½x5¾" **700.00**
Vase, cvd peacock feathers on bl/purple/red/yel, Hentschel, 1915, 8"..**1,500.00**
Vase, cvd poinsettia, tan/red, C Todd, #1654C, 1914, 11".......**3,250.00**
Vase, cvd scrolling pattern, J Harris, #5201D, 1930, rpr, 6¾" **425.00**
Vase, cvd/inlaid/pnt floral, bl/pk mottle, C Todd, #951F, 1920, 6"...**300.00**
Vase, cvd/pnt dandelions, K Shirayamadani, #927E, 1902, 6⅝".**10,000.00**
Vase, daisies, H Wilcox, #51DZ, 1902, prof rpr, 5¼" **2,200.00**
Vase, floral, E Lincoln, #927F, 1922, 6", NM **500.00**
Vase, floral, globular, M McDonald, #6199E, 1931, 3¾" **550.00**
Vase, floral, K Jones, #1930, 1924, 6⅞"....................................**900.00**
Vase, floral band at shoulder, OG Reed, #907F, 1905, 7⅛" **1,200.00**
Vase, Grueby-like leaves below hdls, gr w/red highlights, 1912, 13"...**1,600.00**
Vase, holly, A Sprague, #190CZ, 1901, 8⅞", NM **1,000.00**
Vase, irises, J Jensen, #614D, 1929, 10⅝" **3,400.00**
Vase, irises & buds, J Jenson, #614C, X (mk as 2nd), 1929, 12¾"..**2,000.00**

Vase, leafy branches w/red rose hips, OG Reed, #31D, Z, 1902, 5", NM ...**600.00**
Vase, lotus blossoms & pads, S Coyne, #1910, 1930, 7⅛" **1,700.00**
Vase, pine cones & boughs, L Epply, #1014D, 7⅜" **550.00**
Vase, sculpted leaves, gr/red, K Shiryamadani, 1913, 5½".............**750.00**
Vase, stylized flowers, W Hentschel, #856B, 1914, 16½".........**5,750.00**
Vase, tulips & long leaves, E Lincoln, #2368, 1925, 16⅜"...**2,700.00**
Vase, wild roses, K Jones, #2078, 1928, 4⅞" **700.00**
Vase, wild roses, OG Reed, #924, 1905, 5⅝" **1,300.00**

Porcelain

Vase, columbines, K Shirayamadani, #389, 1925, 3½" **5,000.00**
Vase, English roses & mixed flowers, S Sax, #553C, P, rpr, 10⅛" ...**1,100.00**
Vase, exotic flowers on turq band, L Epply, #2069, P, 1917, 7⅜"....**2,100.00**
Vase, floral, decor neck band, ET Hurley, imp S, 1934, 5"...**2,100.00**
Vase, floral, Turq Bl, CJ McLaughlin, #2367, P, 1917, rpr, 16", pr..**4,000.00**
Vase, floral w/cobalt, W Hentschel, #2820, 1925, 16⅜" **7,750.00**
Vase, Jewel, exotic birds on cobalt, J Jensen, S, 1934, 6x4" **2,070.00**
Vase, Jewel, nudes & flowers, J Jensen, #2969, 1926, X, 7½x7"....**3,750.00**
Vase, leafy band, L Epply, #2189, Y, 1915, 6⅜" **500.00**
Vase, Pan w/flute & wht sheep, A Conant, #2001, P, 4½" **4,100.00**
Vase, wild roses, red/bl on gr w/gunmetal, ET Hurley, 1925, 16" ..**2,600.00**

Sea Green

Pitcher, Brownies & pterodactyls, H Wilcox, #837, G, 1898, 10" **7,500.00**
Tankard, storks/reeds, silver o/l, E Diers, #T 1237, G, 1900, 9⅛".........**9,750.00**
Vase, aquatic plants, drilled, obscured signature, #578B, 1898, 16" ..**2,990.00**
Vase, cvd/pnt grapes, E Diers, silver-on-copper mts, #906D, 1900, 5".**5,000.00**
Vase, fish among waves, ET Hurley, #907D, G, 1903, 10⅛", NM **7,000.00**
Vase, fish on gr, M Daly, #925, 1901, 9½x5" **7,500.00**
Vase, irises, S Laurence, #932B, G, 1902, rpr drill hole, 14⅝" ..**4,300.00**
Vase, Japanese irises, E Lincoln, #952D, G, 1905, 8⅛" **5,000.00**
Vase, maple leaves, A Valentien, #749C, 1895, 6¾" **2,100.00**
Vase, night-blooming cereus, A Valentien, #664 B, 1895, 10⅜" ...**21,000.00**
Vase, ribbons, cvd/plated dragon, Shirayamadani, #S1578, G, 1900, 17"..**14,500.00**
Vase, sea gulls over waves, A Valentien, #346B, 1895, 6½x7", EX **460.00**

Standard

American Indian portrait vases: The Man (Assiniboin), Grace Young, 1900, 8¾", $2,000.00; Conquering Bear — Sioux, Adeliza Drake Sehon, 1901, 9", $5,000.00.

Candle holder, pansies, L Asbury, #635, 1894, 2⅞x5⅛" **600.00**
Creamer, apple blossoms, E Lincoln, E630, W, 1892, 3¼" **375.00**
Creamer, pansies, E Foertmeyer, #548, W, L, 1890 ....**350.00**
Cruet, lily, A Bookprinter, #220, W, L, 1887, rpr, 6" **550.00**
Ewer, floral branch, M Daly, #496A, W, 1891, 12"...................**1,500.00**
Ewer, lilies, A Valentien, #657C, 1894, 8½" **950.00**
Ewer, sweet-pea vines, A Sprague, #495C, W, 1894, 5⅛" **500.00**
Humidor, pipe/matches/cigars/berries, C Steinle, #805, 1903, 5¼".**700.00**
Jug, whiskey; bittersweet, A Sprague, #512C, W, 1893, 5⅞".......**500.00**
Jug, whiskey; poppies & wheat, S Coyne, #673, 1899, 7⅝", NM.**500.00**
Mug, puzzle; portrait of monk, S Lawrence, #711, 1899, 4¾x5", NM ..**635.00**
Pitcher, corn ears on stalks, K Shirayamadani, #838A, X, 1900, 14⅜".**3,900.00**
Pitcher, irises, Schmidt, #456, 1900, 4¼" **1,000.00**

Pitcher, skeleton, silver o/l rim/hdl, Shirayamadani, #564D, 1900, 9", EX .**3,450.00**
Plaque, Dutch gentleman, G Young, after F Hals, 1901, 9⅞x8¼" ..**6,000.00**
Tray, fairies & clouds, H Wilcox, #582, W, LY, 1891, 11⅝" **2,400.00**
Vase, blueberries & leaves, EBI Cranch, #513, L, 1894, 5⅜", NM...**400.00**
Vase, bud; wild roses, E Lincoln, #686, W, 1893, 3⅜" **400.00**
Vase, buttercups, G Hall, #583F, 1903, 4⅞" **475.00**
Vase, carnations, C Baker, #353, 1895, 11½x6¼" **1,375.00**
Vase, carnations, H Wilcox, #771, W, 1892, 7⅝", NM **375.00**
Vase, daisies on gr, L Asbury, #901BB, 1903, 9⅞" **1,400.00**
Vase, day lilies, S Toohey, #803A, 1899, mk as 2nd, 15x6½", NM ..**865.00**
Vase, dogwood branches, ET Hurley, #77A, 1902, 8", NM **550.00**
Vase, floral, H Wilcox, pierced shoulder, hdls, #503, S, 1889, 5"..**850.00**
Vase, floral silver o/l (mk Gorham), A Sprague, #481, 1982, 9".**2,100.00**
Vase, floral silver o/l (mk Gorham), sgn, #724DW, 1984, EX rpr, 5".**2,000.00**
Vase, Geronimo protrait, G Young, silver o/l, #830D, 1899, 6½"...**14,500.00**
Vase, grapes (detailed), ER Felten, #904D, 1904, 7¾" **1,000.00**
Vase, holly silver o/l (extensive), J Zettel, #614FW, 1982, 4½" ...**2,600.00**
Vase, irises, M Nourse, #S1343A, 1897, 9x11" **8,250.00**
Vase, mushrooms, C Schmidt, #534C, 1900, 7x3½", NM **1,600.00**
Vase, nasturtiums, S Coyne, #881D, 1900, 5½" **475.00**
Vase, nasturtiums & leaves, ET Hurley, #927D, 1902, 8¼", NM...**700.00**
Vase, Native American man w/headband, G Young, #707AA, X, 1902, 9⅛"..**6,750.00**
Vase, Nouveau poppies, A Valentien, #690, W, 1893, 9" **2,300.00**
Vase, oak leaves & acorns, A Van Briggle, #468, W, L, 1892, 10¾" ..**1,400.00**
Vase, orchids w/silver floral o/l, JE Zettel, #509, 1891, 5½x4"..**2,300.00**
Vase, Pablino Diaz (sic) portrait, Matt Daly, #732 B, 1900, 10⅜"...**15,000.00**
Vase, pillow; nasturtiums, E Lincoln, #707B, X320X, 1898, 5⅞"...**450.00**
Vase, pillow; violets, M Mitchell, #707B, 1902, 5⅝" **475.00**
Vase, poppies, C Baker, #387, 1897, 10½x5½"..........................**1,375.00**
Vase, poppies, C Baker, #658C, 1900, 7"...................................**475.00**
Vase, poppies, D Cook, strap hdls, #604D, W, 1894, 7" **1,100.00**
Vase, red thistles, J Swing, #829, 1903, 9"..................................**850.00**
Vase, Ute/Suriup, detailed portrait, G Young, #589D, 1898, 11½" ..**20,000.00**
Vase, wild roses, I Bishop, #922E, 1905, 5⅝" **475.00**
Vase, yel wild roses, C Steinle, #614F, 1907, 6½" **700.00**

Tiger Eye

Vase, flying cranes on mahog, MA Daly, #816B, 1900, 14⅜" ..**5,250.00**
Vase, frogs playing, A Valentien, #568E, 1898, 4⅜"...................**500.00**

Vellum

Plaque, birches/water/trees, L Asbury, 1920, 8¾x11"+new fr ..**4,600.00**
Plaque, Early Day, L Epply, 1919, 8x5" +orig fr **3,225.00**
Plaque, Lake Louise, S Sax, 1914, 9x12"+quarter-sawn oak fr .**6,900.00**
Plaque, mtns/trees snow scene, L Asbury, 1927, 8x10"+orig fr ...**8,250.00**
Plaque, Pine Tree, river landscape, L Asbury, 11½x6¾"+gilt fr .**6,325.00**
Plaque, snow scene, F Rothenbusch, 1912, 10⅛x8¼".............**6,500.00**
Plaque, snow scene, S Coyne, V, 1917, 9¼x14¾".................**10,000.00**
Plaque, snow scene w/homestead, K Van Horne, 1915, 7⅛x9¼" .**8,000.00**
Plaque, snow scene w/pines, E Diers, #1916, 9¾x14¾" **7,250.00**
Plaque, summer trees/hills/water, F Rothenbusch, 1920, 12⅜x9⅜"...**6,500.00**
Plaque, summer woodland, F Rothenbusch, 1917, 10½x9½" ...**7,000.00**
Plaque, tree/sky/lake, K Shirayamadani, V, 1912, 8½x12½" **9,000.00**
Plaque, trees & water at dusk, L Asbury, 1918, 8¾x10¾"+new fr ...**6,000.00**
Plaque, Venetian harbor scene, C Schmidt, V, 1916, 9¼x12½" **15,500.00**
Plaque, Venetian harbor sunset scene, C Schmidt, 1918, 9¼x14½"...**11,000.00**
Plaque, woodland scene, ET Hurley, 1921, 9x14¼" **5,000.00**
Plaque, woods at twilight, C Schmidt, 1920, flaw, 8⅛x6⅛" **2,500.00**
Trivet, grapes, mc, #1683, 1929, 5¾x5¾"+recent oak fr.............**450.00**
Vase, apple blossoms, E Lincoln, #915E, V, 1907, 5¾", NM **550.00**
Vase, apple blossoms, illegible signature, #30EZ, 1904, 4½x5" ...**750.00**
Vase, autumn birches & lake, ET Hurley, #6920, 1948, 12¼" .**9,250.00**

Vase, banded scenic, F Rothenbusch, #2040D, V, 1920, 9½" ..**2,600.00**
Vase, birds & flowers, L Epply, #901B, V, 1915, prof rpr, 12⅜" ..**1,100.00**
Vase, carnations, E Diers, #907DD, V, 1907, 10⅜" **1,300.00**
Vase, cherry blossom band, ET Hurley, #913E, 1938, 6⅛" **900.00**
Vase, cherry blossom band, ET Hurley, #915F, V, 1924, 4⅞".......**650.00**
Vase, cherry blossoms, L Asbury, #402, V, 1928, rpr, 6¼" **650.00**
Vase, clouds & trees, ET Hurley, #905D, V, 1907, rstr flaw, 8¼" ..**2,000.00**
Vase, crocus, E Diers, #951D, V, 1907, 9⅛" **900.00**
Vase, cvd pine cones, JD Wareham, #942D, V, 1904, 5⅛"......**2,900.00**
Vase, floral, V Tischler, #357 F, V, 6⅜" **550.00**
Vase, flowers in 3 sections, S Sax, #271A, V, X, 1915, 14" **2,400.00**
Vase, forest/village scene, F Rothenbusch, #514B, V, 1927, 15" .**8,250.00**
Vase, fruit blossom band, E Lincoln, #952F, V, 1908, 6" **600.00**
Vase, fruit blossom band, M McDonald, #1660E, V, 1919, 7½"..**560.00**
Vase, geometrics at shoulder, S Sax, #1064, V, 1904, 3½"...........**850.00**
Vase, hollyhocks, L Asbury, #2441, V, 1925, prof rpr, 14⅛".....**4,500.00**
Vase, hounds running, ET Hurley, #1654, V, X, 1908, 9⅛" **3,600.00**
Vase, hyacinths & wild roses, K Shirayamadani, S, 1933, 8⅜"...**2,500.00**
Vase, irises, E Diers, #2785, V, 1930, 13¼" **7,000.00**
Vase, lady slipper orchids, C Schmidt, #960D, 1905, 8½x3½"...**4,025.00**
Vase, magnolias, K Shirayamadani, #1023C, V, 1925, 10½" .**12,500.00**
Vase, magnolias, K Shirayamadani, #6204C/#6220, 1945, 7⅛"..**2,200.00**
Vase, marine scenic, C Schmidt, #904E, 1922, 7½x3"............**2,415.00**
Vase, misty trees landscape, S Coyne, #2032D, 1915, 10x4¼", NM...**925.00**
Vase, narcissus, ET Hurley, #900D, 1929, 6⅞".......................**1,200.00**
Vase, river scene, L Asbury, #2068, V, 1915, 5½".....................**1,000.00**
Vase, rooks & pines, ET Hurley, #942B, V, 1909, 8½" **3,100.00**
Vase, snow scene, ET Hurley, #952D, V, 1915, 9⅜", NM **850.00**
Vase, spider mums, ET Hurley, #915E, V, 1927, 5⅞".............**2,000.00**
Vase, summer scenic, ET Hurley, #30E, 1940, 8⅜" **3,000.00**
Vase, surf crashing on rocks, ET Hurley, #907B, V, 1909, 17¼" ..**2,400.00**
Vase, swamp w/trees, E Diers, #938C, V, 1908, 8⅜"................**1,700.00**
Vase, thistles, L Asbury, #950D, V, 9⅛" **1,300.00**
Vase, trees & lake, F Rothenbusch, #1658B, V, X, 1910, 14⅝", NM ...**2,000.00**
Vase, trees & lake at twilight, C Smidt, #2032C, V, 1915, 12⅛"...**12,000.00**
Vase, twilight scene, F Rothenbusch, #590D, V, 1907, 9⅜"......**3,100.00**
Vase, Venetian harbor, C Schmidt, #1065B, V, 1916, drilled, 11⅛"...**4,300.00**
Vase, Venetian harbor, C Schmidt, #2066, V, 1924, 7⅜".........**3,200.00**
Vase, water lilies, L Asbury, 1904, rim bruise, 10x7"....................**700.00**
Vase, water lilies & reeds, K Shirayamadani, #950D, V, 1907, 9"...**3,700.00**
Vase, wild roses, E Diers, #2544, V, 1922, 8⅛" **1,100.00**
Vase, wild roses, ET Hurley, #892C, 1930, rpr, 8⅞" **800.00**
Vase, wild roses, F Rothenbusch, #216, V, 1924, prof rpr, 13¼" ..**1,600.00**
Vase, wild roses, F Rothenbusch, #551, V, 1914, 6⅞" **750.00**
Vase, wisteria, ET Hurley, #6867, 1944, 12⅞" **1,800.00**
Vase, wisteria, K Shirayamadani, #2918B, 11⅝"....................**2,700.00**
Vase, woodland at dusk, ET Hurley, #925D, 1917, 8¾" **1,900.00**
Vase, 5 ships/sea gulls, C Schmidt, #950D, 1925, 9" **5,000.00**

Wax Mat

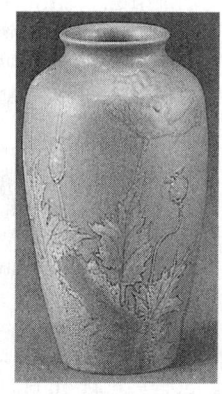

Vase, poppy pods and blossoms, brown and red on red butterfat, Elizabeth Lincoln, 1922, 10½x5¼", $2,400.00.

Bottle, chrysanthemums, E Lincoln, #2825A, 1926, 16½x7" ..**3,750.00**
Vase, cherry blossom panels, E Lincoln, #819, 1922, 5¾x2½" ...**1,265.00**
Vase, crocus on yel butterfat, ET Hurley, S, 1934, 5½x5" **1,035.00**
Vase, dogwood branches on lt brn, Barrett, 1925, 8x4½" **450.00**
Vase, floral abstract on gray-gr mottle, Jensen, 1930, 9x4" **900.00**
Vase, hibiscus, pk on turq, Shirayamadani, 1933, 8x8" **2,300.00**
Vase, magnolia on turq butterfat, J Jensen, S, 1934, 6½x4" **1,265.00**
Vase, nude female, W Hentschel, #5204C, 1931, 7¼" **22,000.00**
Vase, tulips, red on yel, Jensen, lg hdls, 1928, 9x7" **1,500.00**

Miscellaneous

Ashtray, #1084, 1950, owl, gr high glaze, 4¼" **125.00**
Ashtray, #2602, 1934, frog, lt gr high glaze, 3x6½" dia **550.00**
Ashtray, #5524, 1942, retriever puppies, ivory mat, 2⅝" **700.00**
Bookends, #2275, 1923, rooks, slate bl on tan, 5⅛", pr..............**425.00**
Bookends, #2444C, 1919, elephants, bronze tone, 4⅞", NM, pr ...**750.00**
Bookends, #2732, 1926, figureheads, 2-tone gr crystalline, 7", pr..**2,900.00**
Bookends, #2778, 1929, collies, ivory mat, rprs, 6⅛", pr.............**475.00**
Bookends, #6001, 1929, flower baskets, gr on pk, 5⅛", pr, NM, pr ..**350.00**
Bookends, #6124, 1930, brn on gr mat (bronze like), 7⅛", pr .**1,000.00**
Bookends, #6252, 1932, Scarlett w/Fan, aqua mat, 6½", pr **275.00**
Bookends, #6508, 1937, lotus blooms & buds, turq mat, 3⅝", pr ..**375.00**
Bowl, #446B, 1910, cvd geometrics, streaky brns/ivory, 8½" **550.00**
Bowl, #957C, 1906, gr on maroon, Arts & Crafts style, 3x7½", EX..**275.00**
Bowl, #2530, 1930, flowers emb on gr grystalline, 11¼" **150.00**
Candle holders, #2836, 1930, lotus form, gr on pk, 3½", pr........**200.00**
Candlesticks, #1194, 1920, lt bl mat, X, 6¾", pr **140.00**
Candlesticks, #1637, 1921, bl mat, Arts & Crafts style, 9⅜", pr.**300.00**
Candlesticks, #2074, 1922, gr mat, twist hdls, 7¼", pr **400.00**
Candlesticks, #2304, 1920, Egyptian women form, aqua mat, 10¾", pr ...**550.00**
Candlesticks, #6056, 1929, calla lily forms, gr mat, 4⅜", pr........**275.00**
Compote, #2288, 1918, dolphin supports, rose on gr, 10¼" **475.00**
Compote, #2288, 1920, dolphin supports, wht mat, X, 10¼" **275.00**
Figurine, #6164, 1934, nude maiden, ivory, L Abel, 11⅞" **1,700.00**
Inkwell, #1074, 1905, acorn finial, gr mat, 10½" attached tray ..**425.00**
Jar, scent; #1321E, 1927, pk mat, 4" **250.00**
Jug, whiskey; #694, 1906, gr mat, w/stopper, 7⅞" **550.00**
Paperweight, #1623, 1922, rook, bl-gr mottled mat, 3" **300.00**
Paperweight, #2868, 1930, nude, cast monogram of L Abel, 4⅛"...**400.00**
Paperweight, #6156, 1932, gazelle, wht, L Abel, 5⅜"...................**400.00**
Paperweight, #6409, 1933, Mandarin duck, wht mat, 2⅜".........**275.00**
Pencil holder, #1795, 1928, rook, bl mat, 4¾".............................**350.00**
Plaque, landscape comprised of 3 tiles, fr, rstr chips, 12x26"....**7,500.00**
Plates, ca 1920s-30s, bl ship on wht, set of 8................................**350.00**
Platter, ca 1920s-30s, bl ship on wht, 14" **2,600.00**
Sconce, 1919, Arts & Crafts long-stem florals, roots form cup, 9x5" ..**750.00**
Trivet, #M-28, 1925, bl ship, 6" dia..**400.00**
Trivet, #1794, 1927, rook, 5¾" sq+new fr..................................**1,000.00**
Trivet, #3069, 1922, lady w/hoop skirt & parasol, mc, 5¾" sq....**650.00**
Trivet, #3077, 1927, parrot emb on purple, 5⅞" sq **275.00**
Trivet, #3077, 1930, parrot, mc, 5¾x5¾", NM............................**170.00**
Trivet, #3203, 1926, Dutch figures, mc, 5⅞" sq **400.00**
Vase, #654C, 1921, gr on pk, 5½" **130.00**
Vase, #969E, 1904, Native Am design, red mat, 4¼", NM **350.00**
Vase, #1659B, 1911, micro-crystalline gr on tan mat, 13¾" **1,100.00**
Vase, #1681, 1913, lily of the valley emb on bl, 4⅜"...................**225.00**
Vase, #1743, 1920, gr on red, Arts & Crafts style, 7½" **325.00**
Vase, #1824, 1912, bl mat, Arts & Crafts style, 6⅛" **225.00**
Vase, #2326, 1922, rooks emb at base, rust over gr, 5⅞", NM.....**250.00**
Vase, #2330, 1924, gr mat, 3 angular hdls, 4⅞" **200.00**
Vase, #2330, 1929, purple mat, 3 angular hdls, 4⅞" **275.00**
Vase, #2331, 1924, spiraling hdls, gr on pk, 7⅞" **300.00**
Vase, #2380, 1928, gr on pk, 6⅛" **225.00**

Vase, #2428, 1930, hyacinth color, 3-hdl, 5⅜" **275.00**
Vase, #2477, 1920, emb floral, gr on pk, 7¾"...............................**150.00**
Vase, #2556, 1921, Arts & Crafts floral emb on bl-blk mat, 8⅜" ..**400.00**
Vase, #2562, 1921, bl mat, 5¼" **160.00**
Vase, #2616E, 1922, maroon mat, X, 7⅛"....................................**425.00**
Vase, #2716, 1923, crystalline pk mat, 6⅜"..................................**150.00**
Vase, #2930, 1927, Arts & Crafts gr crystalline, 10"....................**750.00**
Vase, #5214, 1941, leaping deer, yel high glaze, 61st Anniv mk, 4½" ..**130.00**
Vase, #6029, 1930, gr mat, 6¼" **200.00**
Vase, #6233, 1931, Deco flowers, yel mat, 5¼"............................**225.00**
Vase, #6315, 1932, bl w/silver on oatmeal crystalline, 6¼" **250.00**
Vase, #6318C, 1932, aqua over slate, 5⅛"....................................**225.00**
Vase, #6350, 1937, bl mat, 4½"..**170.00**
Vase, #6350, 1937, cardinal emb on bl mat, 4½"........................**190.00**
Vase, #6653, 1941, bl crackle, 4¼"...**160.00**
Wall pocket, #2008, 1917, gr on pk, 7⅛"....................................**225.00**

Rorstrand

The Rorstrand Pottery was established in Sweden in 1726 and is today Sweden's oldest existing pottery. The earliest ware, now mostly displayed in Swedish museums, was much like old Delft. Later types were hard-paste porcelains that were enameled and decorated in a peasant style. Contemporary pieces are often described as Swedish Modern. Rorstrand is also famous for their Christmas plates.

Bowl, stoneware w/brn/bl/blk/yel areas, Stalhane, 3x7" **160.00**
Jug, cider; courtyard scenes, w/lid, foo dog finial, ca 1815, 9⅞" **2,900.00**
Vase, bl-gray/wht on stoneware, Gunnar Nylund, '50s, bulbous, 3½" ..**160.00**
Vase, brn/gr/wht areas on stoneware, hand built, Stalhane, 20"..**900.00**
Vase, multitone bl & lt gr, cylindrical, G Nylund, 13" **800.00**
Vase, teal, slender w/trumpet neck, 8¼".......................................**210.00**
Vase, wht w/HP butterfly on ea side, shouldered, 6" **410.00**

Rose Mandarin

Similar in design to Rose Medallion, this Chinese Export porcelain features the pattern of a robed mandarin, often separated by florals, ladies, genre scenes, or butterflies in polychrome enamels. It is sometimes trimmed in gold. Elaborate in decoration, this pattern was popular from the late 1700s until the early 1840s.

Bowl, fruit; oval, ftd, 19th C, 3⅞x15¼x11⅜" **1,100.00**
Bowl, rtcl sides, oval, 8¾"..**250.00**
Bowl, scalloped rim, 9½"...**385.00**
Charger, 6 triangular panels, 16"...**200.00**

Cider jug, foo dog finial, woven double strap handle, nineteenth century, 9½", NM, $3,000.00.

Coffeepot, 19th C, 10¼" **1,500.00**
Plate, dinner; 19th C, 9¾", NM, pr...**315.00**
Platter, well & tree; rstr, 19th C, 17½" **1,150.00**
Platter, 19th C, 14½x11¾"..**975.00**
Platter, 19th C, 17¼x14¾"..**1,600.00**

Sauce boat, intertwined hdl, 19th C, 8¼"....................................**300.00**
Soup plate, 19th C, 10", EX, 3 for...**345.00**
Umbrella stand, wrapped bamboo form, 19th C, 24" **1,495.00**
Vase, court scenes/trellis diapering/foo dog hdls, 24¾", pr, NM...**2,875.00**
Warming dish, 10⅞", EX, pr..**800.00**

Rose Medallion

Rose Medallion is one of the patterns of Chinese export porcelain produced from before 1850 until the second decade of the twentieth century. It is decorated in rose colors with panels of florals, birds, and butterflies that form reserves containing Chinese figures. Pre-1850 ware is unmarked and is characterized by quality workmanship and gold trim. From about 1850 until circa 1860, the kilns in Canton did not operate, and no Rose Medallion was made. Post-1860 examples (still unmarked) can often be recognized by the poor quality of the gold trim or its absence. In the 1890s the ware was often marked 'China'; 'Made in China' was used from 1910 through the 1930s.

Basket, rtcl, hdls, w/undertray, 19th C, 3¾x9¾x7¼", EX...........**315.00**
Bowl, high rtcl sides, flared rim, 4x9x10", NM **440.00**
Bowl, mandarin & floral reserves, 3x8"..................................**285.00**
Bowl, scalloped rim, ribbed, 19th C, 3¾x11"...........................**865.00**
Box, desk; floral reserves, compartments, 1850s........................**350.00**
Canister, mandarin reserves, cylindrical, w/lid, 1850s, 4¾x4".....**260.00**
Garden seat, hex bbl form w/pierced top & sides, 19th C, 18", pr...**4,000.00**
Plate, deep molded, mid-19th C, 8"......................................**250.00**
Plates, court scenes, 19th C, 8", EX, 9 for...............................**975.00**
Platter, mandarin scenes alternate w/birds & flowers, ftd, 3½x15"...**330.00**
Platter, wide border w/dragons, goat, horse, Chinese symbols, 12"...**450.00**
Platter, 6 pie sections, figures w/gold in hari, 10½x13½" **825.00**
Punch bowl, court scenes, cut corners, 19th C, 4¾x10¼" **800.00**
Punch bowl, 19th C, 6x13¼", NM **1,500.00**
Punch bowl, 19th C, 7½x15½"...**2,185.00**
Soup plate, court scene, flowers & butterflies, monograms, 10", 3 for ...**750.00**
Vase, celestial dragons, mandarin reserves, foo dog hdls, 1850s, 10" **575.00**
Vase, figures in garden vignettes, appl dragons, foo dog hdls, 36" **1,850.00**
Vase, flared rim, tapered oval body, foo dog hdls, 25"..................**865.00**
Vase, garniture; butterfly borders, lion mask & ring hdls, 1850s, 16" ..**250.00**
Vase, 19th C, 12¾", NM **515.00**
Wall cone, 19th C, 13½"...**865.00**

Roselane

William and Georgia Fields began Roselane Pottery in their home in 1938. They moved several times over the years, but when William died in 1973, Georgia sold Roselane to Prather Engineering Corporation and the operation moved to Long Beach where it remained until its final closing in 1977.

Roselane had various lines that included several different glazes and treatments. Chinese-Modern is not as popular as some of Roselane's other products. Certain pieces of Chinese-Modern are plentiful and do not bring high values. In the mid-1940s until the early 1950s, Aqua Marine was a buffet serving line with pieces such as large, deep bowls and trays created in a sgraffito technique. The fish or snowflakes motifs are in demand today. The Sparkler series, created in the 1950s, was a popular product for the company. The airbrushed, decorated semi-porcelain children and animals fascinate collectors even though there are some reproductions on the market. Originally the Sparklers had rhinestone eyes, but the later ones were made of plastic. The deer and deer groups on a single base are sought after. Their muted glazes and their lifelike appearances have many collectors trying to amass all of them. William

'Doc' Fields created beautiful animals on walnut bases. The animals were generally a high-gloss white. When they became available the public did not buy them in any quantity and they were discontinued shortly after their introduction. Today collectors avidly look for items in this line and prices reflect that demand.

Bowl, console; brn/blk metallic, 3¼x11¾"............................**42.00**
Bowl, console; lime yel/sand beige, #109, 4x9" sq........................**35.00**
Bowl, console; maroon/gray, #112, 2½x12x7"..........................**28.00**
Bowl, console; wht, 2½x15x8"..**32.00**
Bowl, floral, blk & wht, 2¾x11¼", NM..................................**32.00**
Bowl, pk & blk fish decor, 2x12¾x6½"..................................**75.00**
Bowl, pk & gray, thin walls, 4x14½x5½"................................**39.00**
Bowl, relish; gr & blk w/fish decor, 3-part, wooden ft, 14x12"....**230.00**
Bowl, salad; gr & blk w/fish decor, 14", +lg fork & spoon..........**110.00**
Condiment set, aqua w/blk fish, 2 8¾" cruets+2 5½" shakers.....**185.00**
Figurine, angelfish, Sparkler, 4½", from $20 to **25.00**
Figurine, bulldog, fierce, looking right, Sparkler, 2", from $12 to..**15.00**
Figurine, cat mother holding babies, Sparkler, 5", from $40 to **45.00**
Figurine, cat sitting w/head trn right, tail out, from $25 to **28.00**
Figurine, chicken, gr w/brn, 11", pr......................................**65.00**
Figurine, cockatoo, gray, 8½"...**75.00**
Figurine, deer, leaping, yel, 6"..**40.00**
Figurine, deer, stands w/head trn right, looks down, Sparkler, 5½" ...**25.00**
Figurine, deer, 1 w/nose up, 8", 2nd w/head down, 6", pr..........**40.00**
Figurine, dove, wht, glass eyes, 9½x8".................................**45.00**
Figurine, elephant sitting on hind quarters, Sparkler, 6"............**28.00**
Figurine, exotic bird w/long flowing tail, 9" **45.00**
Figurine, fawn, Sparkler, 4½x1½".......................................**20.00**
Figurine, Oriental dancing couple, shiny wht, 11x8", pr **50.00**
Figurine, Oriental duck, 7½" L...**70.00**
Figurine, Oriental lady, pastel, #185, 7"................................**20.00**
Figurine, Oriental man, soft gray/brn, #207, 8½"......................**20.00**

Figurine, owl, beige and brown, 7½",
$75.00. (From the Dennis Hopp collection)

Figurine, pouter pigeon, Sparkler, 3½" **20.00**
Figurine, rooster, yel, 8½x10½x2¼"....................................**45.00**
Figurine, whippet, sitting, Sparkler, 7½" **28.00**
Planter, bl S shape, 2½x5x13¾" **20.00**
Planter, lady in dress figural, 10" **15.00**
Shaker, Japanese fish, unmk, 5¼", pr...................................**55.00**
Vase, Asian style, wht/turq, #287..**27.50**
Vase, gr w/bl mottle, wht int, #V10, 9⅝x4¼" sq top, NM............**20.00**

Rosemeade

Rosemeade was the name chosen by Wahpeton Pottery Company of Wahpeton, North Dakota, to represent their product. The founders of the company were Laura A. Taylor and R.J. Hughes, who organized the firm in 1940. It is most noted for small bird and animal figurals, either in high gloss or a Van Briggle-like matt glaze. The ware was marked 'Rosemeade' with an ink stamp or carried a 'Prairie Rose' sticker. The pottery closed in 1961. Our advisor for this category is Bryce L. Farnsworth; he is listed in the Directory under North Dakota. For more information we recommend *Collector's Encyclopedia of Rosemeade Pottery* by Darlene Hurst Dommel (Collector Books).

Ashtray, cocker spaniel (head) on side, 7", minimum value **1,000.00**
Ashtray, Minnesota Centennial, state shape, 4½x3¾"................**100.00**
Ashtray, palomino colt at side, 5" **175.00**
Ashtray, Ray (oil derrick) North Dakota, 4¾".............................**175.00**
Bank, fish figural, gr, 3x4¼" **375.00**
Bank, rhinoceros, gr, 3½x6½", minimum value...........................**600.00**
Bowl, bl/blk crackle, hand thrown, 2¼x5" **100.00**
Covered dish, hen on basket, wht on blk, 5½x5½"......................**400.00**
Creamer & sugar bowl, mallard drake & hen, 2¾x6", 2½x6"......**150.00**
Creamer & sugar bowl, Prairie Rose, 2¾", 2".............................**100.00**
Creamer & sugar bowl, twisted hdl, mini, ea 2"..........................**225.00**
Figurine, alligator, 1½x7¾", minimum value.............................**1,000.00**
Figurine, Bluebill drake, mini, 1x1¾"..**175.00**
Figurine, cocks fighting, red & blk, 4¾x6", 5¼x6½", pr.............**200.00**
Figurine, cowboy boot, mini, 2" **100.00**
Figurine, dove, 2¾x2¾", minimum value.....................................**250.00**
Figurine, flamingo, 3", 3¾", pr..**250.00**
Figurine, frog, gr, 1¾x2¾" **175.00**
Figurine, horse, blk gloss, 6¼x4¼"..**200.00**
Figurine, horse, swirl, mk Badlands, 4⅜x3", minimum value **500.00**
Figurine, jackrabbit, solid, pk, 3¼"...**275.00**
Figurine, koala bear on tree trunk, 8½x3½".................................**275.00**
Figurine, mule, gr, 3½x5" **300.00**
Figurine, pheasant cock & hen, mini, 2½", 1¼", pr **300.00**
Incense burner, elephant w/trunk up, rose or aqua, 4¼"...............**175.00**
Jardiniere, Egyptian design/wild ducks, gr, 5x5½"......................**225.00**
Mug, pheasant decal, 4¼" **175.00**
Pick holder, cock, strutting, 3¾x2¾" **125.00**
Pick holder, turkey, 6x6½"...**150.00**
Pitcher, bl, hand thrown, pinched hdl, 2¾"..................................**100.00**
Pitcher, 2-tone swirl, 3¼", minimum value **200.00**
Planter, bird on wood log, 3x6"...**65.00**
Planter, mermaid figural, wht, 4¾x3¾"...**225.00**
Planter, pheasant cock, 3¾x9¼", minimum value.......................**500.00**
Planter, Viking ship form, robin's egg bl, 4¾x10" **250.00**
Plaque, Dakota Centennial, 4" **100.00**
Plaque, walleye fish decal, 6" dia **100.00**
Plaques, sea gulls, set of 3 ....**2,000.00**
Shakers, Black Angus bulls, 1¾", pr..**350.00**
Shakers, bloodhound dog (head), 3", pr **85.00**
Shakers, Bobwhite quail, 2¼", 1½", pr...**75.00**
Shakers, coyote pups, 3¼x2½", pr..**325.00**
Shakers, duck drake & hen, wht, 3½", 2", pr...............................**125.00**
Shakers, grain shocks, bl, 4¾", pr..**150.00**
Shakers, mallard drake & hen, 3½", 2", pr...................................**100.00**
Shakers, mallard ducks, mini, 1x1¾", pr......................................**175.00**
Shakers, obelisk, Geographical Center, 4¼", pr, minimum value ..**250.00**
Shakers, pheasant hen & cock, mini, 2¼x2½", 2¼x2¼", pr **300.00**

Shakers, pheasants, tallest: 3", $75.00 for the pair.

Shakers, skunks, mini, 1½", ¾", pr..**125.00**
Shakers, skunks, 2¾", pr..**50.00**
Shakers, Trojan Seed Corn (ears), 4½", pr...................................**400.00**
Spoon rest, dogwood, wht or pk petals, 3½", minimum value.....**300.00**
Spoon rest, water lily, 4¾" **100.00**
Tray, Indiana state map, 5¼" **125.00**
TV lamp, rooster, wht on gr base, 14½x7¼", minimum value ..**1,500.00**
TV lamp, wolfhound, gray or russet, 6x11¼", ea minimum value...**500.00**
Vase, deer, bl gloss, 8¼"...**75.00**
Vase, mc swirl, unglazed int, shouldered, 8¼", minimum value ..**300.00**
Vase, 3-color swirl, 4¾", minimum value.....................................**200.00**

Rosenthal

In 1879 Phillip Rosenthal established the Rosenthal Porcelain Factory in Selb, Bavaria. Its earliest products were figurines and fine tablewares. The company has continued to operate to the present decade, manufacturing limited edition plates. Our advisor for this category is Raphael Wise; he is listed in the Directory under Florida.

Box, Delft scene of house w/windmill on lid, 1½x4" **110.00**
Box, powder; butterfly w/florals, mc, mk Wendler, 1½x4" **225.00**
Charger, Versace Medusa, 12" **125.00**
Cup & saucer, demi; bl w/silver o/l, 1947 ....**100.00**
Figurine, Blackamoor in wht carrying tray of food, Meisel, 7½" .**360.00**
Figurine, Blackamoor w/accordion, #1056, Meisel, 1951, 8" **360.00**
Figurine, Carmen the dancer, bl & blk outfit, mk #425-1, 9¾" ..**920.00**
Figurine, cat, recumbent, #60, Karner, 1930s, 2x6¾" **320.00**
Figurine, clown w/accordion, #K436/1684, Caasman, 1929, 7¾" ..**320.00**
Figurine, female nude, kneeling/drinking from hands, brn hair, 7x6"..**650.00**
Figurine, naked boy riding bl bird, oval base, 1914-16, #K41, 9" ...**720.00**
Figurine, Neckerei, boy stands in front of lg bird, #523, 1920, 8½" ...**790.00**
Figurine, nude on knees w/bird in hand, #K1016-1, Boess, 1929, 7½" ..**725.00**
Figurine, peacock, wings spread, #1611, 7½" **320.00**
Figurine, stallion, wht, mk, 4x14x14"...**925.00**
Place setting, Flash, 5-pcs..**80.00**
Plate, Floranada, floral & gold, 1921-22, 9¼", set of 6................**145.00**
Plate, mc geometeric design, sgn Emilio, Studio Line, 7½" sq **680.00**
Plate, mermaids/fish/boat, mk Peynet, Studio Lines, 12¾" **165.00**
Powder jar, roses w/much gold, mk **125.00**
Vase, couple on front, Cupid fishing on bk, heart shape, #2568, 4"..**75.00**
Vase, roses allover, shouldered, RXC mk, ca 1900, 13¾".........**1,125.00**
Vase, roses allover w/gold, ovoid, 10½"..**665.00**
Vase, roses on 3 sides, 3-hdld, gourd shape, 11½"......................**450.00**

Roseville

The Roseville Pottery Company was established in 1892 by George F. Young in Roseville, Ohio. Finding their facilities inadequate, the company moved to Zanesville in 1898, erected a new building, and installed the most modern equipment available. By 1900 Young felt ready to enter into the stiffly competitive art pottery market. Roseville's first art line was called Rozane. Similar to Rookwood's Standard, Rozane featured dark blended backgrounds with slip-painted underglaze artwork of nature studies, portraits, birds, and animals. Azurean, developed in 1902, was a blue and white underglaze art line on a blue blended background. Egypto (1904) featured a matt glaze in a soft shade of old green and was modeled in low relief after examples of ancient Egyptian pottery. Mongol (1904) was a high-gloss oxblood red line after the fashion of the Chinese Sang de Boeuf. Mara (1904), an iridescent lustre line of magenta and rose with intricate patterns developed on the surface or in low relief, successfully duplicated Sicardo's work. These early lines were followed by many others of highest quality: Fudjiyama and Woodland (1905 – 06) reflected an Oriental theme; Crystalis (1906) was covered with beautiful frost-like crystals. Della Robbia, their most famous line (introduced in 1906), was decorated with designs ranging from florals, animals, and birds to scenes of Viking warriors and Roman gladiators. These designs were worked in sgraffito with slip-painted details. Very limited but of great importance to collectors today, Rozane Olympic (1905) was decorated with scenes of Greek mythology on a red ground. Pauleo (1914) was the last of the art-ware lines. It was varied — over two hundred glazes were recorded — and some pieces were decorated by hand, usually with florals.

During the second decade of the century until the plant closed forty-years later, new lines were continually added. Some of the more popular of the middle-period lines were Donatello, 1915; Futura, 1928; Pine Cone, 1931; and Blackberry, 1933. The floral lines of the later years have become highly collectible. Pottery from every era of Roseville production — even its utility ware — attest to an unwavering dedication to quality and artistic merit.

Examples of the fine art pottery lines present the greatest challenge to evaluate. Scarcity is a prime consideration. The quality of artwork varied from one artist to another. Some pieces show fine detail and good color, and naturally this influences their values. Studies of animals and portraits bring higher prices than the floral designs. An artist's signature often increases the value of any item, especially if the artist is one who is well recognized.

The market is literally flooded with imposter Roseville that is coming into the country from China. An experienced eye can easily detect these fakes, but to a novice collector, they may pass for old Roseville. Study the marks. If the 'USA' is missing or appears only faintly, the piece is most definitely a reproduction. Also watch for lines with a mark that is not correct for its time frame; for example, Luffa with the script mark, and Woodland with the round Rozane stamp from the 1917 line.

For further information consult the newly revised *Collector's Encyclopedia of Roseville Pottery, First* and *Second Series*, by Sharon and Bob Huxford and Mike Nickel (Collector Books). Other books on the subject include *Collector's Compendium of Roseville Pottery, Volumes I, II*, and *III*, by R.B. Monsen (see Directory, Virginia); and *Roseville in All Its Splendor With Price Guide* by Jack and Nancy Bomm (self-published). Our advisor for this category is Mike Nickel; he is listed in the Directory under Michigan.

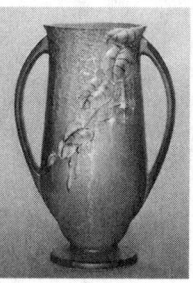

Fuchsia, vase, #903-12, 12½":
in blue, $850.00 to $950.00;
in green, $650.00 to $750.00;
in tan, $550.00 to $650.00.

Apple Blossom, basket, #309, gr or pk, 8", from $275 to.............325.00
Apple Blossom, bud vase, #379, gr or pk, 7", from $150 to.........175.00
Apple Blossom, cornucopia, #321, bl, 6", from $150 to..............175.00
Apple Blossom, ewer, #387, bl, from $325 to................................375.00
Aztec, pitcher, 5", from $350 to.......................................400.00
Aztec, vase cylindrical, sgn C, from $600 to 700.00
Aztec, vase, waisted, 9", from $400 to 500.00
Baneda, center bowl, #237, gr, 13", from $900 to....................1,100.00
Baneda, center bowl, #237, pk, 13", from $750 to.......................900.00
Baneda, vase, #601, gr, 5½", from $600 to 650.00
Baneda, vase, #601, pk, 5½", from $450 to 500.00
Bittersweet, ewer, #816, 8", from $250 to..................................300.00
Bittersweet, planter, #868, 8", from $100 to...............................125.00
Blackberry, center bowl, #228, 13", from $700 to 800.00

Blackberry, jardiniere, #623, 6", from $550 to....................650.00
Blackberry, vase, #569, 5", from $500 to 600.00
Blackberry, wall pocket, #1267, from $2,000 to.................2,500.00
Bleeding Heart, basket, #360, gr or pk, 10", from $325 to..........375.00
Bleeding Heart, ewer, #972, bl, 10", from $650 to...............750.00
Bleeding Heart, wall pocket, #1287, bl, 8", from $600 to..........650.00
Bushberry, bowl, #411, bl, 4", from $150 to.....................175.00
Bushberry, bowl, #411, gr, 4", from $125 to.....................150.00
Bushberry, jardiniere, #657, bl, 3", from $125 to................150.00
Cameo II, flowerpot, 5½", from $350 to 450.00
Cameo II, hanging basket, 4½x7", from $350 to 450.00
Cameo II, jardiniere, 8" tall, from $450 to 550.00
Carnelian I, candle holder, hdld, 3", from $50 to................75.00
Carnelian I, ewer, 15", from $400 to.............................500.00
Carnelian I, loving cup, 5", from $100 to........................125.00
Carnelian II, ewer, 12½', from $600 to............................700.00
Carnelian II, fan vase, 8", from $350 to.........................400.00
Carnelian II, lamp base, ball shape, 8", from $900 to............1,000.00
Carnelian II, vase, sq, hdld, 5", from $150 to...................200.00
Cherry Blossom, candle holders, #1090, brn, 4", pr, from $500 to ..550.00
Cherry Blossom, candle holders, #1090, pk/bl, 4", pr, from $750 to...850.00
Cherry Blossom, jardiniere, #627, brn, 10", from $1,250 to.....1,500.00
Cherry Blossom, jardiniere, #627, pk/bl, 10", from $2,000 to ..2,500.00
Clemana, vase, #123, bl, 7", from $350 to........................400.00
Clemana, vase, #123, gr, 7", from $300 to........................350.00
Clemana, vase, #123, tan, 7", from $250 to.......................300.00
Clematis, basket, #388, brn or gr, 8", from $200 to..............225.00
Clematis, dbl bud vase, #194, bl, 5", from $125 to 150.00
Clematis, wall pocket, #1295, 8", bl, from $225 to...............250.00
Columbine, basket, #368, pk, 12", from $450 to...................500.00
Columbine, bowl, #401, pk, 6", from $150 to 175.00
Columbine, ewer, #18, bl or tan, 18", from $225 to..............250.00
Columbine, ewer, #18, pk, from $275 to...........................300.00
Corinthian, ashtray, 2", from $175 to............................200.00
Corinthian, dbl bud vase, gate-type, 7", from $200 to 225.00
Corinthian, vase, columnar, 8", from $175 to.....................200.00
Corinthian, vase, tapered, 6", from $150 to......................175.00
Cosmos, basket, #358, bl, 12", from $500 to......................550.00
Cosmos, basket, #358, gr, 12", from $450 to 500.00
Cosmos, bowl vase, #376, bl, 6", from $375 to....................425.00
Cosmos, bowl vase, #376, gr, 6", from $325 to....................375.00
Cosmos, bowl vase, #376, tan, 6", from $250 to 300.00
Cosmos, ewer, #957, bl, 15", from $1,100 to......................1,200.00
Cosmos, ewer, #957, tan, 15", from $900 to.......................1,000.00
Cremona, bowl, sq, incurvate rim, 9", from $125 to 150.00
Cremona, flower frog, from $50 to................................75.00
Cremona, vase, tapered, flared rim, ftd, 10½", from $250 to.......300.00
Dahlrose, center bowl, sq hdls, oval, 10", from $175 to..........200.00
Dahlrose, triple bud vase, 6", from $150 to 175.00
Dahlrose, vase, sq, 6", from $300 to.............................350.00
Dawn, vase, #827, gr, 6", from $175 to...........................200.00
Dawn, vase, #827, pk or yel, 6", from $200 to....................250.00
Dogwood I, basket, 6", from $175 to 225.00
Dogwood I, boat planter, 6", from $350 to 400.00
Dogwood I, jardiniere, 8", from $300 to..........................350.00
Dogwood II, bowl, 2½" tall, from $125 to.........................150.00
Dogwood II, vase, urn type, 6", from $175 to.....................200.00
Dogwood II, wall pocket, from $350 to 400.00
Donatello, basket, 15", from $500 to.............................600.00
Donatello, flowerpot, w/saucer, 5", from $225 to.................250.00
Donatello, jardiniere, 8½", from $200 to.........................250.00
Dutch, mug, rare decal, 5", from $150 to.........................200.00
Dutch, mug, 5", from $75 to......................................95.00
Dutch, pitcher, 9½", from $250 to................................350.00

Dutch, soap dish, w/lid, 3", from $250 to 300.00
Egypto, bud vase, 5½", from $450 to 500.00
Egypto, oil lamp, 5", from $1,500 to 2,000.00
Egypto, pitcher, 5", from $750 to...1,000.00
Falline, vase, #644, bl, 6", from $1,300 to 1,500.00
Falline, vase, #644, tan, 6", from $600 to 700.00
Falline, vase, #649, bl, 8", from $1,500 to 1,750.00
Falline, vase, #649, tan, 8", from $800 to 900.00
Ferella, bowl, #212, red, 12", from $1,100 to 1,300.00
Ferella, bowl, #212, tan, 12", from $900 to 1,100.00
Ferella, vase, #497, red, 4", from $475 to 525.00
Ferella, vase, #497, tan, 4", from $400 to 450.00
Florane, bowl, 8" dia, from $75 to..85.00
Florane, vase, cylindrical, sq hdls, 6", from $75 to 95.00
Florentine, basket, 8", from $200 to 250.00
Florentine, compote, ivory, 5", from $100 to..............................125.00
Florentine, wall pocket, 9½", from $225 to 250.00
Foxglove, basket, #373, pk, 8", from $225 to 350.00
Foxglove, ewer, #6, pk/gr, 15", from $850 to 950.00
Foxglove, ewer, #6, 15", from $700 to 800.00
Foxglove, vase, #42, gr/pk, 4", from $95 to 110.00
Freesia, bookends, #15, gr, pr, from $375 to 425.00
Freesia, cornucopia, #198, bl, 8", from $150 to 175.00
Freesia, vase, #122, tangerine, 8", from $200 to...........................225.00
Fuchsia, basket & frog, #350, bl, 8", from $700 to 800.00
Fuchsia, basket & frog, #350, gr, 8", from $550 to 600.00
Fuchsia, pitcher, #1322, w/ice lip, bl, 8", from $750 to...................850.00
Fuchsia, pitcher, #1322, w/ice lip, tan, 8", from $475 to 525.00
Futura, bud vase, #390, bl, 10", from $1,200 to 1,300.00
Futura, bud vase, #422, 6", from $400 to...................................450.00
Futura, vase, #404, bl, 8", from $2,000 to 2,500.00
Futura, vase, #404, gr, 8", from $1,500 to 2,000.00
Futura, vase, #408, 10", from $2,000 to..................................2,500.00
Futura, vase, #428, 6", from $550 to 650.00
Gardenia, basket, #609, 10", from $300 to 350.00
Gardenia, cornucopia, #621, 6", from $100 to 125.00
Gardenia, jardiniere, #600, 4", from $90 to................................110.00
Imperial I, basket, 6", from $150 to 175.00
Imperial I, lamp base, 12", from $200 to 250.00
Imperial I, triple bud vase, 8", from $150 to 175.00
Imperial II, triple wall pocket, from $700 to 800.00
Iris, bowl, #360, bl, 6", from $200 to 250.00
Iris, bowl, #360, pk or tan, 6", from $175 to 225.00
Iris, ewer, #926, pk or tan, 10", from $250 to 300.00
Iris, wall shelf, #2, bl, 8", from $500 to 550.00
Iris, wall shelf, #2, pk or tan, 8", from $450 to 500.00
Ivory II, candelabrum, Velmoss shape, #1116, 5½", from $175 to..225.00
Ivory II, vase, Carnelian shape, 10", from $75 to 95.00
Jonquil, basket, #324, 9", from $600 to 700.00
Jonquil, jardiniere, #621, 6", from $300 to 350.00
Jonquil, vase, #539, 4", from $175 to......................................225.00
Juvenile, bowl, oatmeal; standing rabbit, 5½", from $200 to 225.00
Juvenile, creamer, side-pour, standing rabbit, from $175 to.........200.00
Juvenile, egg cup, chick, very rare, 3", from $700 to...................800.00
Juvenile, mug, 2-hdld, dog sitting, glossy, rare, 3", from $300 to.350.00
Juvenile, plate, rolled edge, 'Little Bo Peep,' 8", from $175 to 200.00
La Rose, bowl, 6" dia, from $100 to..125.00
La Rose, candle holders, 4", pr, from $200 to..............................225.00
Laurel, bowl, #251, gold, 7", from $250 to 275.00
Laurel, bowl, #251, gr, 7", from $300 to 325.00
Laurel, bowl, #251, russet, 7" W, from $275 to 300.00
Laurel, vase, #675, gold, 9", from $550 to 600.00
Laurel, vase, #675, gr, 9", from $700 to 800.00
Lotus, vase, #L3, 10", from $300 to 350.00

Luffa, vase, #685, 7", from $550 to 650.00
Luffa, vase, #691, 12", from $1,000 to...................................1,200.00
Lustre, candle holder, 8", from $50 to.....................................60.00
Lustre, candle holder, 10", from $65 to....................................85.00
Lustre, vase, cylindrical, 10", from $100 to 125.00
Magnolia, basket, #15, 15", from $350 to 400.00
Magnolia, cider pitcher, #1327, 7", from $300 to..........................350.00
Magnolia, planter, #389, 8", from $110 to.................................135.00
Mayfair, bowl, #1110, 4", from $50 to......................................75.00
Mayfair, planter, #1113, 8", from $60 to...................................75.00
Mayfair, tankard, #1107, 12", from $175 to................................200.00
Ming Tree, candle holders, #551, pr, from $100 to 125.00
Ming Tree, ewer, #516, 10", from $150 to 175.00
Mock Orange, jardiniere, #900, 4", from $75 to 100.00
Mock Orange, planter, #981, 7", from $150 to..............................175.00
Montacello, basket, #333, bl, 6½", from $1,200 to.......................1,400.00
Montacello, vase, #555, bl, 4", from $375 to..............................425.00
Montacello, vase, #555, tan, 4", from $350 to 375.00
Morning Glory, bowl vase, #268, gr, 4", from $450 to......................500.00
Morning Glory, bowl vase, #268, ivory, 4", from $350 to 400.00
Moss, center bowl, #294, bl, 12", from $225 to 250.00
Moss, center bowl, #294, pk/gr or orange/gr, 12", from $300 to ..350.00
Moss, vase, #774, pk/gr or orange/gr, 6", from $225 to 250.00
Moss, vase, #774, bl, 6", from $175 to 200.00
Mostique, bowl, glossy beige exterior, 2½", from $125 to...............150.00
Mostique, jardiniere, 10", from $300 to 400.00
Mostique, vase, cylindrical, 6", from $175 to 225.00
Orian, bowl vase, #274, red, 6", from $475 to.............................525.00
Orian, bowl vase, #274, turq, 6", from $375 to............................425.00
Orian, vase, #735, tan, 7", from $200 to 250.00
Orian, vase, #735, yel, 7", from $250 to 300.00
Pauleo, bowl, squatty w/sm upright rim, ftd, floral, 3", from $800 to .1,000.00
Pauleo, vase, cylindrical w/squatty 3-ftd base, 12", from $1,250 to 1,500.00

Pauleo vases: Tulips, multicolor on mottle, shouldered, 19", from $2,000.00 to $2,200.00; Berries and leaves, multicolor on lavender to orange, classic shape with flared rim, 17", from $1,700.00 to $2,000.00.

Peony, bowl, #661, 3", from $95 to 125.00
Peony, ewer, #7, 6", from $100 to 125.00
Peony, wall pocket, #1293, 8", from $250 to 300.00
Persian, bowl, 3 hdls, 3½", from $175 to...................................200.00
Persian, creamer & sugar bowl, w/lid, pr, from $200 to 250.00
Pine Cone, basket, #339, bl, 9x13", from $1,100 to 1,300.00
Pine Cone, cornucopia, #128, bl, 8", from $400 to.....................450.00
Pine Cone, cornucopia, #128, gr, 8", from $200 to 250.00
Pine Cone, fan vase, #472, gr, from $350 to 400.00
Pine Cone, pitcher, #425, bl, 9", from $1,000 to.....................1,250.00
Pine Cone, pitcher, #425, gr, 9", from $550 to............................650.00
Poppy, basket, #347, gray or gr, 10", from $375 to 450.00
Poppy, basket, #347, pk, 10", from $450 to 550.00
Poppy, basket, #347, tan, 10", from $675 to 825.00
Poppy, ewer, #876, gray or gr, 10", from $375 to 450.00
Poppy, ewer, #876, pk, 10", from $450 to 550.00

Poppy, wall pocket/candle holder, #1281, gray or gr, 9", from $800 to ...**900.00**
Poppy, wall pocket/candle holder, #1281, pk, 9", from $900 to.**1,000.00**
Raymor, bean pot, #195, from $50 to **60.00**
Raymor, dinner plate, #152, from $20 to...................................**30.00**
Raymor, hot plate. #159, from $35 to.....................................**40.00**
Rosecraft, bowl, 2½" tall, from $100 to.................................**125.00**
Rosecraft Black, vase, hdld, 10", from $175 to........................**200.00**
Rosecraft Hexagon, bowl vase, brn, 4", from $325 to **375.00**
Rosecraft Hexagon, bowl vase, gr, 4", from $450 to.....................**500.00**
Rosecraft Hexagon, vase, sq hdls, brn, 6", from $250 to.............**300.00**
Rosecraft Hexagon, vase, sq hdls, gr, 6", from $350 to **400.00**
Rosecraft Panel, candlestick, gr, 8", from $300 to.......................**350.00**
Rosecraft Panel, dbl bud vase, gate-type, brn, from $150 to........**175.00**
Rosecraft Panel, dbl bud vase, gate-type, gr, from $200 to...........**250.00**
Rosecraft Vintage, candlestick, 8", from $200 to........................**250.00**
Rosecraft Vintage, jardiniere, 5", from $175 to...........................**200.00**
Rosecraft Vintage, jardiniere, 8", from $350 to...........................**400.00**
Rosecraft Vintage, vase, 8½", from $400 to.............................**450.00**
Rosecraft Vintage, window box, 6x11½", from $550 to **650.00**
Rozane, bowl, #927, 2½", from $100 to **125.00**
Rozane, candlestick, ivory, 6", from $100 to.............................**125.00**
Rozane, ewer, #828, 7", from $300 to.....................................**350.00**
Rozane, pillow vase, #882, sgn F Steele, 9", from $4,000 to.....**5,000.00**
Rozane Light, pitcher, floral, sgn Mary Pierce, 7", from $2,500 to ...**3,000.00**
Rozane Light, vase. floral, gourd form, May Timberlake, 8", $500 to..**550.00**
Rozane 1917, basket, pk, 6", from $175 to **225.00**
Rozane 1917, champagne bucket, ivory, from $300 to.................**350.00**
Russco, bud vase, #695, 8", from $175 to **200.00**
Russco, vase, #703, 15", from $250 to **300.00**
Silhouette, fan vase, #783, 7", from $400 to.............................**450.00**
Silhouette, vase, #763, 8", from $500 to....................................**650.00**
Snowberry, ashtray, #1AT, bl or pk, from $150 to.....................**175.00**
Snowberry, basket, #1BK, gr, 8", from $225 to.........................**250.00**
Snowberry, ewer, #1TK, bl or pk, from $300 to.........................**350.00**
Sunflower, jardiniere, #619, 9", from $2,000 to......................**2,500.00**
Sunflower, vase, #488, 5½", from $1,100 to..........................**1,300.00**
Sunflower, vase, #491, 8", from $1,700 to.................................**1,900.00**
Teasel, basket, #349, dk bl or rust, 10", from $700 to **750.00**
Teasel, basket, #349, lt bl or tan, 10", from $600 to **650.00**
Teasel, ewer, #890, dk bl or rust, 18", from $850 to **950.00**
Teasel, ewer, #890, lt bl or tan, 18", from $700 to **800.00**
Teasel, vase, #644, dk bl or rust, 5", from $200 to......................**225.00**
Teasel, vase, #644, lt bl or tan, 5", from $175 to.........................**200.00**
Thorn Apple, basket, #342, 10", from $350 to............................**400.00**
Thorn Apple, candle holders, #1117, 2½", pr, from $200 to.......**225.00**
Thorn Apple, cornucopia vase, #127, 6", from $150 to..............**175.00**
Thorn Apple, planter, #262, 5", from $150 to **175.00**
Tourmaline, center bowl, #241, 5x12½", from $175 to.............**225.00**
Tourmaline, ginger jar, 9", from $400 to.....................................**450.00**
Tourmaline, rose bowl, #238, 5", from $75 to **100.00**
Tuscany, candle holders, gray/lt bl, 4", pr, from $100 to **125.00**
Tuscany, candle holders, pk, 4", from $125 to............................**150.00**
Tuscany, console bowl, gray/lt bl, 11" W, from $125 to..............**150.00**
Tuscany, console bowl, pk, 11" W, from $150 to.........................**175.00**
Tuscany, fan vase, ftd, pk, 8", from $150 to................................**175.00**
Tuscany, fan vase, gray/lt bl, 8", from $125 to............................**150.00**
Velmoss, dbl bud vase, #116, gr, 8", from $200 to.....................**250.00**
Velmoss, dbl bud vase, bl, #116, 8", from $300 to.....................**350.00**
Velmoss, vase, #716, tan, rare, 7", from $400 to........................**450.00**
Velmoss Scroll, bowl, 2½x9", from $125 to **150.00**
Velmoss Scroll, candlestick, 8", from $175 to.............................**225.00**
Velmoss Scroll, candlestick, 9", from $200 to **250.00**
Water Lily, basket, #380, brn, 8", from $150 to **175.00**
Water Lily, cookie jar, #1, bl, 10", from $600 to **700.00**

Water Lily, ewer, #10, bl. 6", from $175 to.................................**200.00**
Water Lily, jardiniere, #663, brn, 3", from $85 to........................**100.00**
Water Lily, jardiniere, #663, rose/gr, 3", from $125 to **150.00**
White Rose, bowl, #387, 4", from $100 to **125.00**
White Rose, dbl cornucopia, #145, 8", from $125 to..................**150.00**
White Rose, pitcher, #1324, from $225 to.................................**250.00**
Windcraft, tea set (teapot+cr/sug), #271, from $225 to..............**250.00**
Windcraft, vase, #290, 10", from $900 to...................................**1,000.00**
Windsor, candlesticks, #1084, bl, 4½", pr, from $550 to **650.00**
Windsor, candlesticks, #1084, tan, 4½", pr, from $450 to **550.00**
Windsor, flower frog, bl or tan, from $50 to................................**75.00**
Windsor, vase, #549, bl, 7", from $1,100 to..............................**1,300.00**
Windsor, vase, #549, tan, 7", from $900 to................................**1,100.00**
Wisteria, center bowl, #423, bl, 12", from $850 to.....................**950.00**
Wisteria, center bowl, #423, tan, 12", from $500 to...................**550.00**
Wisteria, vase, #681, bl, 9", from $1,500 to..............................**1,750.00**
Wisteria, vase, #681, tan, 9", from $900 to................................**1,000.00**
Woodland, vase, urn, iris, 6½", from $3,000 to.........................**3,500.00**
Woodland, vase, waisted, iris, 8", from $1,250 to **1,500.00**
Woodland, vase, 4-sided twisted shape, floral, 11", from $700 to ..**800.00**
Zephyr Lily, ashtray, #29, gr, from $95 to **110.00**
Zephyr Lily, basket, #393, brn, 7", from $150 to **175.00**
Zephyr Lily, console boat, #475, bl, 10", from $250 to **275.00**
Zephyr Lily, ewer, #24, bl, 15", from $750 to **850.00**

Rowland and Marsellus

Though the impressive back stamp seems to suggest otherwise, Rowland and Marsellus were not Staffordshire potters but American importers who commissioned various English companies to supply them with the transfer-printed crockery and historical ware that had been a popular import commodity since the early 1800s. Plates (both flat and with a rolled edge), cups and saucers, pitchers, and platters were sold as souvenirs from 1890 through the 1930s. Though other importers — Bawo & Dotter and A. C. Bosselman & Co., both of New York City — commissioned the manufacture of similar souvenir items, by far the largest volume carries the R. & M. mark, and Rowland and Marcellus has become a generic term that covers all twentieth-century souvenir china of this type. Their mark may be in full or 'R. & M.' in a diamond. Though primarily made with blue transfers on white, other colors may occasionally be found as well.

Note: Show prices may be as much as 25% higher than our values, which are based on eBay sales. Our advisor for this category is David Ringering; he is listed in the Directory under Oregon.

Key:
r/e — rolled edge   v/o — view of
s/o — souvenir of

Bowl, English castle, floral border, 8½" **40.00**
Creamer, Plymouth, mk as Burbank...**45.00**
Cup & saucer, Alaska-Yukon-Pacific Expo, 1909 ....**120.00**
Cup & saucer, Chicago, s/o...**95.00**
Cup & saucer, farmer's..**45.00**
Cup & saucer, Lemox MA, s/o..**85.00**
Cup & saucer, Niagara Falls NY, s/o **75.00**
Pitcher, American Pilgrims, #527014, 6¼" **250.00**
Pitcher, Declaration of Independence, 7x7½" **350.00**
Pitcher, Discovery of America, 3 major scenes, 7½".................**400.00**
Pitcher, Plymouth Rock, various scenes, 6½".............................**250.00**
Plate, American Authors, 9½"...**65.00**
Plate, Atlantic City, s/o, 9" **78.00**
Plate, Battle of Lake Erie, fruit & flower border..........................**50.00**

Plate, Bethlehem PA, Moravian College, v/o, 9" **35.00**
Plate, Bridgeport CT, s/o, 6-scene border, 10" **55.00**
Plate, Bunker Hill Monument, Ye Olde Historical Pottery, 9" **35.00**
Plate, Cincinnati OH, s/o, State Capital, r/e, 10" **65.00**
Plate, Cleveland OH, s/o, 10" **95.00**
Plate, Countess Grosvenor & Sir Thomas Laurence, 10¼", from $120 to...**150.00**
Plate, coupe; Chicago, Marshall Field & Co, v/o, 6" **45.00**
Plate, coupe; Early Missions CA, s/o, Parmelee/Horham, 6" **40.00**
Plate, coupe; Tucson AZ, 5 scenes, v/o, 6" **40.00**
Plate, famous Musicians & Composers (9), 10" **75.00**
Plate, Hermitage, fruit & flower border, 9¾" **50.00**
Plate, Jackson MS, s/o, New Capitol Building, r/e, 10" **75.00**
Plate, Longfellow, 10" **65.00**
Plate, Lookout Mountain TN, s/o, r/e, 10" **70.00**
Plate, Miami, s/o, Chief Osceola, 10" **70.00**
Plate, Myles Standish, 10" **65.00**
Plate, Niagara Falls, 10" **50.00**
Plate, Plymouth MA, 10" **50.00**
Plate, Richfield Springs NY, r/e, 10" **60.00**
Plate, Theodore Roosevelt, 10" **125.00**
Plate, Topeka KS, s/o, capital w/6-scene border, 10" **75.00**
Plate, Whirlpool Rapids, fruit & flower border, 9¾" **45.00**
Plate, White House, s/o, gr, floral border, 10" **50.00**
Tumbler, Ashville, mc, s/o..**95.00**
Tumbler, Ottawa Canada...**95.00**
Tumbler, Thousand Islands, v/o **85.00**

Royal Bayreuth

Founded in 1794 in Tettau, Bavaria, the Royal Bayreuth firm originally manufactured fine dinnerware of superior quality. Their figural items, produced from before the turn of the century until the onset of WWI, are highly sought after by today's collectors. Perhaps the most abundantly produced and easily recognized of these are the tomato and lobster pieces. Fruits, flowers, people, animals, birds, and vegetables shapes were also made. Aside from figural items, pitchers, toothpick holders, cups and saucers, humidors, and the like were decorated in florals and scenic motifs. Some, such as the very popular Rose Tapestry line, utilized a cloth-like tapestry background. Transfer prints were used as well. Two of the most popular are Sunbonnet Babies and Nursery Rhymes (in particular, those decorated with the complete verse).

Caution: Many pieces were not marked; some were marked 'Deponiert' or 'Registered' only. While marked pieces are the most valued, unmarked items are still very worthwhile. Our advisors for this category are Judy White from California and Dee Hooks from Illinois; they are listed in the Directory under their home states.

Figurals

Wall vase, grapes, white mother-of-pearl, blue mark, $550.00.

Ashtray, elk, bl mk, 2x6"...**295.00**
Bowl, Devil & Cards, 3-D devil in center, bl mk, 7½"............**5,675.00**

Bowl, tomato, bl mk, 3x3"..**45.00**
Bowl, tomato, bl mk, 11¾" L..**315.00**
Box, Queen of Hearts & Devil, bl mk, 2¼x3¾x1¾" **675.00**
Cracker jar, grapes, wht MOP w/lav leaves, no mk, 7½x6", NM...**900.00**
Hatpin holder, owl, unmk...**500.00**
Humidor, elk's head, bl mk, 6x7¾"..**600.00**
Inkwell, elk, glass insert missing, gr mk....................................**350.00**
Match holder, clown, hangs, bl mk, 5", NM..............................**575.00**
Pitcher, bear, mottled blk w/orange int, bl mk, water sz, NM...**675.00**
Pitcher, clown, red, bl mk, cream sz, 3⅝"..................................**265.00**
Pitcher, cow, bl mk, cream sz, 3¾"..**245.00**
Pitcher, crow, blk w/brn beak, bl mk, cream sz...........................**325.00**
Pitcher, crow, gr, Deponiert, cream sz, 4½"................................**700.00**
Pitcher, crow, red w/brn beak, unmk, cream sz, 5" **325.00**
Pitcher, Devil & Cards, bl mk, cream sz, 3½".............................**300.00**
Pitcher, duck, bl, bl mk, milk sz, 4½".......................................**300.00**
Pitcher, duck, Registered, water sz, 6¾"....................................**750.00**
Pitcher, elephant, bl mk, cream sz, 4½" **2,500.00**
Pitcher, fox, unmk, cream sz **4,250.00**
Pitcher, frog, bl mk, cream sz, 3½x5".......................................**345.00**
Pitcher, frog, unmk, ca 1920, cream sz, 4" **245.00**
Pitcher, grapes, unmk, cream sz, 3¾".......................................**245.00**
Pitcher, happy hound, emb Germany on hip, cream sz, 3¾".......**315.00**
Pitcher, ibex, bl mk, cream sz, 4" **575.00**
Pitcher, lamplighter, gr, bl mk, milk sz, 5½", NM....................**425.00**
Pitcher, lemon, bl mk, milk sz, 4¾" **325.00**
Pitcher, lobster, bl mk, cream sz **275.00**
Pitcher, lobster, bl mk, milk sz, 4½" **450.00**
Pitcher, lobster, bl mk, water sz, 6¾" **545.00**
Pitcher, milkmaid, red, bl mk, cream sz, 4" **455.00**
Pitcher, monkey, gr, bl mk, milk sz, 5¼"..................................**530.00**
Pitcher, monkey, unmk, cream sz, 4" **325.00**
Pitcher, mountain goat, bl mk, cream sz...................................**275.00**
Pitcher, Old Man of the Mountain, bl mk, cream sz, 4" **168.00**
Pitcher, owl, bl mk, cream sz, 3¾", NM **325.00**
Pitcher, parakeet, bl mk, milk sz, 5"...**465.00**
Pitcher, parakeet, unmk, cream sz, 4" **225.00**
Pitcher, pig, gray, bl mk, cream sz, 4½".....................................**350.00**
Pitcher, poodle, gray, tail hdl, 4½" **275.00**
Pitcher, poppy, unmk, water sz...**500.00**
Pitcher, rooster, bl mk, cream sz, 4½"..**475.00**
Pitcher, rooster, wht w/red, bl mk, cream sz **415.00**
Pitcher, rose, bl mk, milk sz..**750.00**
Pitcher, rose, unmk, cream sz, 4"..**275.00**
Pitcher, seal, bl mk, cream sz, NM..**235.00**
Pitcher, shell, pearlized, bl mk, cream sz, 4" **285.00**
Pitcher, squirrel, blk, bl mk, cream sz, 5" **3,000.00**
Pitcher, strawberry, bl mk, cream sz, 4".....................................**120.00**
Pitcher, watermelon, bl mk, milk sz, 5" **425.00**
Plate, lobster, unmk, 7½"...**75.00**
Shakers, elk, bl mk, pr..**250.00**
Shaving mug, elk, glossy, bl mk **450.00**
Stirrup cup, chamois, bl mk, very rare, 5⅛"...........................**3,850.00**
Sugar bowl, tomato, bl mk, 3⅞"..**95.00**
Teapot, grapes, pk lustre, bl mk..**415.00**
Tray, lobster, gr mk, 1½x6½x4½"..**75.00**
Wall pocket, grapes, gr, bl mk **250.00**

Nursery Rhymes

Bell, Jack & Beanstalk, w/rhyme & clapper, bl mk.....................**350.00**
Bowl, Jack & Jill, bl mk, 5¾"...**135.00**
Box, Jack & Jill, bl mk, w/lid...**250.00**
Coffeepot, Jack & Jill, bl mk..**365.00**

Dutch shoe, Little Bo Peep, bl mk..375.00
Leaf dish, Little Jack Horner, bl mk.....................................150.00
Mug, Jack & Beanstalk, w/verse, bl mk, lg..........................250.00
Mug, Ring Around the Rosies, bl mk.....................................175.00
Pitcher, Jack in the Beanstalk, bl mk, cream sz, 3½"..........195.00
Pitcher, Little Miss Muffett, bl mk, milk sz........................215.00
Plate, Jack & Beanstalk, bl mk, 6"......................................150.00
Plate, Jack & Jill, bl mk, 6"...150.00
Plate, Little Bo Peep, bl mk, 6¼".......................................175.00
Sugar bowl, Little Boy Blue, bl mk....................................215.00
Vase, Babes in Woods, bl mk, 4"...385.00

Scenics and Action Portraits

Bowl, sheep in landscape, bl mk, 10½".................................250.00
Candlestick, frog & bee, frog on bk, hdl, bl mk, 7", NM............465.00
Candlestick, Musicians, bl mk, 4¾x2¾"..............................275.00
Candy dish, donkey scene, bl mk, ¾x4" sq............................75.00
Creamer & sugar bowl, penguins, ftd..................................420.00
Hair receiver, storks on gr, 2¾"..350.00
Loving cup, cattle in landscape, 3 gold hdls, bl mk, 3¾"............150.00
Pitcher, children playing in circle, bl mk, cream sz, 4½"............135.00
Pitcher, elk in water followed by dogs, bl mk, cider sz, 6"..........145.00
Pitcher, ships, bl mk, cream sz, 3½", NM...............................60.00
Plaque, boy & donkey, bl mk, 8½".......................................135.00
Plaque, men in boat fishing, gold border, bl mk, 9½"................165.00
Plate, girl walking her dog, bl mk, 7½"................................150.00
Plate, soccer players, bl mk, 8¾"...135.00
Teapot, boy & turkeys, bl mk, 3½x6½".................................275.00
Toothpick holder, penguin on yel, tricorner, bl mk, 2¾".............300.00
Tray, Goose Girl, bl mk, 12x9"..165.00
Vase, fox hunt w/riders & horses, bl mk, 4¾".......................150.00
Vase, sailboats, flower borders, bl mk, 8¾".........................215.00

Sunbonnet Babies

Ashtray, scrubbing, dmn shape, bl mk, 5⅝"...........................255.00
Bells, various activities, ltd ed, 3½", 7 for...........................800.00
Pitcher, fishing, bl mk, cream sz, 3½"..................................350.00
Pitcher, ironing, bl mk, cream sz, 3⅛"..................................300.00
Plate, ltd ed, 7 scenes, 13"..250.00
Plates, varied activities, ltd ed of yr 1974, set of 7...................650.00
Sugar bowl, washing, w/lid, bl mk, 3¼"..............................350.00
Vase, fishing, low gold hdls, w/bsk insert, bl mk, 2¾x3½"..........350.00

Tapestries

Powder box, Rose
Tapestry, two-color, blue
mark, 2½x4", $350.00.

Basket, floral, gold trim, bl mk, 5x5½x2¼"...........................265.00
Boot, Rose Tapestry, bl mk, 3¼x4⅝"..................................635.00
Box, dancing couple, bl mk, w/lid, 3½" dia...........................195.00
Box, dancing couple, oval, w/lid, bl mk, 4½" L........................260.00
Creamer, Rose Tapestry, 3¼"..150.00
Hair receiver, dancing couple, w/lid, bl mk, 4½" dia.................590.00
Hair receiver, Rose Tapestry, 3-color, bl mk, 4x2¾".................275.00
Hatpin holder, Rose Tapestry, 3-color, bl mk, 4½"..................525.00

Humidor, goat scene, bl mk, 5½", NM...................................800.00
Pin cushion, Rose Tapestry, slipper form, gr mk, 2½x5".............325.00
Pitcher, lady's portrait, bl mk, cream sz, 3½".........................175.00
Pitcher, Rose Tapestry, bl mk, cream sz.................................250.00
Pitcher, Rose Tapestry, gold trim hdl, bl mk, cream sz, 3"..........285.00
Pitcher, 2 polar bears in Arctic waters, bl mk, 7"......................400.00
Plate, Rose Tapestry, bl mk, 7½"..160.00
Shoe, floral on cream, bl mk, 6" L......................................345.00
Vase, lady w/horse, bl mk, 7½", NM....................................475.00
Vase, Rose Tapestry, bl mk, 4x2¼".....................................200.00
Vase, Rose Tapestry, bl mk, 5¼x3¼"..................................425.00
Vase, Rose Tapestry, unmk, 7x4"..135.00

Royal Copenhagen

The Royal Copenhagen Manufactory was established in Denmark in about 1775 by Frantz Henrich Muller. When bankruptcy threatened in 1779, the Crown took charge. The fine dinnerware and objects of art produced after that time carry the familiar logo, the crown over three wavy lines. For further information we recommend *Royal Copenhagen Porcelain, Animals and Figurines*, by Robert J. Heritage (Schiffer). See also Limited Edition Plates.

Basket, bl floral on wht, lacy edge, prof rpr to hdl, #1/1057, 11"...275.00
Basket, Flora Danica, rtcl openwork sides, gold trim, 7½x9½"..1,900.00
Bowl, crab at rim, wht porc, #3131, 2x6½"...........................250.00
Bowl, Fajance, linear decor w/sharply petaled flowers, 1960s, 4"...75.00
Butter pat, Flora Danica, 3" dia..155.00
Coffeepot, Blue Fluted (half lace), w/lid..............................275.00
Creamer & sugar bowl, Flora Danica, 2¾", 4½" W..................825.00
Cup & saucer, Blue Fluted (plain), from $75 to......................100.00
Cup & saucer, Capanula Hedreacea, lid for cup, sq saucer, #3515, #3514...780.00
Dish, celery, Blue Fluted, #297, 14x5x2"..............................185.00
Dish, Flora Danica, oval, branch-like hdl w/raised flower, 6x8¾"...465.00
Figurine, Amager girl, standing, #1251, 7½", from $190 to........210.00
Figurine, Amager girls, shopping, #1316, 6½x7".....................135.00
Figurine, bassett hound, #4616, 4¾x6"................................160.00
Figurine, bear w/cub, #20193, 5x4½"..................................155.00
Figurine, boxer (dog), #3634, 5½x7½".................................140.00
Figurine, boy w/cow, #772, 6¾x7", from $225 to....................265.00
Figurine, boy w/dog, #782, 7½"...170.00
Figurine, boy w/teddy, #3468, 7", from $160 to......................175.00
Figurine, brn bear, lying on bk, #20271, 4x6½"......................180.00
Figurine, children (2) w/dog, #707, 5¾"...............................165.00
Figurine, children reading, #4670, 5½x8", from $390 to............435.00
Figurine, dachshund, #3140, 4½x3".....................................160.00
Figurine, Fano, #12413, 1950, 5⅞", from $500 to....................575.00
Figurine, faun on ped w/squirrel, #456, 8¾"..........................175.00
Figurine, fox, curled up, #438, 3½x7"..................................390.00
Figurine, fox mother w/kits, #1788, 4½x5"............................425.00
Figurine, geese, male & female, #609, 7¼"............................150.00
Figurine, girl in long dress w/bow in hair, #2444, 8½".............180.00
Figurine, girl w/olive branch, #4527, 6½".............................155.00
Figurine, Girl w/the Golden Horn, #12242, 8½".......................700.00
Figurine, Greenland Boy, #12419, 1952, 4x4½".......................650.00
Figurine, mermaid w/fish, #2348, 2x3".................................135.00
Figurine, mink, #4654, 3½x7"..220.00
Figurine, Nathan the Wise, #1413, 6½"................................195.00
Figurine, nymph w/satyr kneeling at ft, 20th C, 15¼"............1,100.00
Figurine, puppy, brn & wht, #259, 8"...................................200.00
Figurine, sphinx, sitting, #2336, 9"...................................1,650.00
Figurine, Whittler, #905, 7½", from $200 to..........................250.00
Figurine, wht fox, #319/43, 7"..490.00

Plaque, nude & putti w/floral wreath, 5¼"...................................**160.00**
Plate, biscuit; Flora Danica, #3552, 5½"..**380.00**
Plate, Christmas; 1940 ....**520.00**
Plate, dinner; Blue Fluted (plain) **85.00**
Plate, dinner; Flora Danica, 10", from $600 to...........................**650.00**
Plate, luncheon; Flora Danica, 8½"..**340.00**
Plate, salad; Blue Fluted (plain) **65.00**
Plate, salad; Flora Danica, 1⅜x7½", from $400 to.....................**435.00**
Platter, fish, lobster, & water bug on wht, bl border, oval, 10x24" ..**325.00**
Sugar bowl, Blue Fluted (half lace), w/lid **125.00**
Tray, Art Moderne bl/brn/wht faience design, 1950s, 10x6½" **95.00**
Vase, goose on ground watching others fly, #108, 7" **185.00**
Vase, lt/dk gr matt crystalline, shouldered, 3¼" **500.00**
Vase, mother & child standing, #4547, 7"......................................**190.00**
Vase, nude maiden on rock, sailboat beyond, Langeline, #4675, 7"...**115.00**

Royal Copley

Royal Copley is a decorative type of pottery made by the Spaulding China Company in Sebring, Ohio, from 1942 to 1957. They also produced two other major lines — Royal Windsor and Spaulding. Royal Copley was primarily marketed through five-and-ten cent stores; Royal Windsor and Spaulding were sold through department stores, gift shops, and jobbers. Items trimmed in gold are worth 25% to 50% more than the same item with no gold trim.

For more information we recommend *Collector's Guide to Royal Copley Plus Royal Windsor & Spaulding, Books I* and *II*, by our advisor for this category, Joe Devine; he is listed in the Directory under Iowa.

Bank, pig w/bow tie, paper label, hands in front, 6¼", from $45 to ..**50.00**
Figurine, banty rooster, paper label, 6½", from $60 to **75.00**
Figurine, cockatoo, yel, paper label, 7¼", from $30 to...................**35.00**
Figurine, flycatcher, HP details, paper label, 8", from $40 to.........**45.00**
Figurine, kingfisher, 5", from $45 to..**50.00**
Figurine, Oriental boy, 7½", from $20 to...**25.00**
Figurine, rooster, paper label, 8", from $40 to...............................**45.00**
Figurine, spaniel, collar at neck, 6", from $20 to...........................**25.00**
Figurine, titmouse, various colors, paper label, 8", from $25 to **30.00**
Figurine, wren, many colors made, paper label, 6¼", from $20 to..**24.00**
Pitcher, Daffodil, gr stamp, 8", from $33 to....................................**60.00**
Pitcher, Decal (pk floral on wht), gold stamp, 6", from $12 to......**16.00**
Planter, Barefooted Girl, paper label, 7½", from $35 to................**40.00**
Planter, Blackamoor, emb mk, 8", from $40 to...............................**45.00**
Planter, bunting, emb letters, 5", from $30 to **35.00**
Planter, cat & cello, paper label, 7½", from $100 to **125.00**
Planter, cocker spaniel w/basket, paper label, 5½", from $20 to....**25.00**
Planter, deer & doe, wht, 7½", from $45 to **50.00**
Planter, duck & wheelbarrow, paper label, 3¾", from $18 to **20.00**
Planter, elephant w/ball, paper label, 7½", from $25 to.................**30.00**
Planter, girl leaning on bbl, paper label, 6¼", from $20 to............**25.00**
Planter, goldfinch on stump, paper label, 6½", from $30 to **35.00**
Planter, Harmony, tricolor leaves, 4½", from $40 to.....................**45.00**
Planter, Indian boy & drum, paper label, 6½", from $20 to **25.00**
Planter, kitten in picnic basket, paper label, 8", from $70 to.........**75.00**
Planter, Mill, Amsterdam Holland, Ruysdael, 8", from $60 to **70.00**

Planter, Old Colonial Woman, 8",
$60.00. (Photo courtesy Betty Newbound)

Planter, Oriental boy w/basket on bk, paper label, 8", from $40 to ...**45.00**
Planter, pigtail girl, pastel, emb mk, 7", from $35 to.....................**40.00**
Planter, rooster, low tail, paper label, 7⅛", from $30 to................**35.00**
Planter, straw hat w/flowers at band, 7", from $40 to...................**45.00**
Planter, tanager perched on stump, gr stamp or emb mk, 6¼", $20 to ..**25.00**
Planter, teddy bear, chocolate brn, paper label, 6¼", from $40 to ..**45.00**
Planter/wall pocket, girl w/wide-brim hat, emb mk, 7½", from $40 to...**45.00**
Planter/wall pocket, pirate's head, emb letters, 8", from $45 to.....**50.00**
Plaque/planter, rooster, emb letters, 6¾", from $40 to **45.00**
Vase, Bow & Ribbon, ftd, paper label, 6½", from $14 to...............**18.00**
Vase, bud; warbler perched on open stump, 5", from $18 to..........**20.00**
Vase, Carol's Corsage, gr stamp, 7", from $18 to **20.00**
Vase, Decal (pk floral on wht), hdls, gold stamp, 6¼", from $10 to..**14.00**
Vase, Floral Elegance, cobalt, 8", from $28 to **32.00**
Vase, Ivy, ftd, paper label only, 8", from $12 to.............................**14.00**
Vase, Oriental style, dragon, ftd, paper label, 5½", from $12 to....**15.00**
Vase, Trailing Leaf & Vine, paper label, 8½", from $25 to...........**30.00**
Vase/planter, gazelle, gold trim, emb mk, 9", from $40 to.............**45.00**
Vase/planter, mallard on Copley stump, paper label, 8", from $40 to ..**45.00**
Vase/planter, Oriental style, floral, ftd, paper label, 5½", $12 to...**15.00**

Royal Crown Derby

The Royal Crown Derby company can trace its origin back to 1848. It first operated under the name of Locker & Co. but by 1859 had become Stevenson, Sharp & Co. Several changes in ownership occurred until 1866 when it became known as the Sampson Hancock Co. The Derby Crown Porcelain Co. Ltd. was formed in 1876, and these companies soon merged. In 1890 they were appointed as a manufacturer for the Queen and began using the name Royal Crown Derby.

In the early years, considerable 'Japan ware' decorated in Imari style, using red, blue, and gold in Oriental patterns was popular. The company excelled in their ability to use gold in the decoration, and some of the best flower painters of all time were employed. Nice vases or plaques signed by any of these artists will bring thousands of dollars: Gregory, Mosley, Rouse, Gresley, and D'esir'e Leroy. We have observed porcelain plaques decorated with flowers signed by Gregory selling at auction for as much as $12,000.00. If you find a signed piece and are not sure of its value, if at all possible, it would be best to have it appraised by someone very knowledgeable regarding current market values.

As is usual among most other English factories, nearly all of the vases produced by Royal Crown Derby came with covers. If they are missing, deduct 40% to 45%. There are several well illustrated books available from antique booksellers to help you learn to identify this ware. The back stamps used after 1891 will date every piece except dinnerware. The company is still in business, producing outstanding dinnerware and Imari-decorated figures and serving pieces. They also produce custom (one only) sets of table service for the wealthy of the world.

Bowl, Imari #2451, corner hdls, ftd, sq, 1¾x10½"......................**265.00**
Bowl, Red Aves, mk LXI, 5x10" dia **265.00**
Candlesticks, Olde Avesbury, figural dolphins on corners, 10½", pr..**375.00**
Cup & saucer, dblhdld cup, Imari #1128, mk LVI........................**160.00**
Figurine, Budgerigars (birds) on branch, mk XXXIX, 5½" **295.00**
Figurine, dragon, Imari, 3x4½x4⅛"...**210.00**
Figurine, Egyptian cat, Royal Cat series, 8½" **310.00**
Figurine, fox, mk LIII, 2x2¼x3½"...**425.00**
Figurine, hedgehog, mk XLIX, 2½x4½"..**330.00**
Figurine, Russian cat, Royal Cat series, 8½".................................**440.00**
Nut dish, Imari #2451, 8-sided, 1½x6"...**115.00**
Paperweight, koala figural, red, bl & gold, 4½"...........................**350.00**
Place setting, Lombardy, dinner+salad+sm plate+c/s, 5-pc..........**135.00**
Plate, Imari, openwork sterling border, 10¼"................................**160.00**

Plate, Imari, typical palette w/gold, 1939, 10½", 12 for **1,035.00**
Platter, Red Aves, mk LXII, 16x12"..**415.00**
Platter, serving; Asian Rose, 18x14"...**190.00**
Serving set, Imari, meat fork, knife & sharpener, MIB................**225.00**
Teapot, Heraldic, 4-cup, 5x9½"...**240.00**
Teapot, Imari #6299, 2x4"...**285.00**
Urn, bl/wht stripes w/scenic reserve, sq base w/scroll ft, 10" **200.00**

Royal Doulton, Doulton

The range of wares produced by the Doulton Company since its inception in 1815 has been vast and varied. The earliest wares produced in the tiny pottery in Lambeth, England, were salt-glazed pitchers, plain and fancy figural bottles, etc. — all utility-type stoneware geared to the practical needs of everyday living. The original partners, John Doulton and John Watts, saw the potential for success in the manufacture of drain and sewage pipes and during the 1840s concentrated on these highly lucrative types of commercial wares. Watts retired from the company in 1854, and Doulton began experimenting with a more decorative product line. As time went by, many glazes and decorative effects were developed, among them Faience, Impasto, Silicon, Carrara, Marqueterie, Chine, and Rouge Flambe. Tiles and architectural terra cotta were an important part of their manufacture. Late in the nineteenth century at the original Lambeth location, fine artware was decorated by such notable artists as Hannah and Arthur Barlow, George Tinworth, and J.H. McLennan. Stoneware vases with incised animal drawings, gracefully shaped urns with painted scenes, and cleverly modeled figurines rivaled the best of any competitor.

In 1882 a second factory was built in Burslem which continues even yet to produce the famous figurines, character jugs, series ware, and table services so popular with collectors today. Their Kingsware line, made from 1899 to 1946, featured flasks and flagons with drinking scenes, usually on a brown-glazed ground. Some were limited editions, while others were commemorative and advertising items. The Gibson Girl series, twenty-four plates in all, was introduced in 1901. It was drawn by Charles Dana Gibson and is recognized by its blue and white borders and central illustrations, each scene depicting a humorous or poignant episode in the life of 'The Widow and Her Friends.' Dickensware, produced from 1911 through the early 1940s, featured illustrations by Charles Dickens, with many of his famous characters. The Robin Hood series was introduced in 1914; the Shakespeare series #1, portraying scenes from the Bard's plays, was made from 1914 until World War II. The Shakespeare series #2 ran from 1906 until 1974 and was decorated with featured characters. Nursery Rhymes was a series that was first produced in earthenware in 1930 and later in bone china. In 1933 a line of decorated children's ware, the Bunnykin series, was introduced; it continues to be made to the present day. About 150 'bunny' scenes have been devised, the earliest and most desirable being those signed by the artist Barbara Vernon. Most pieces range in value from $60.00 to $120.00.

Factors contributing to the value of a figurine are age, demand, color, and detail. Those with a limited production run and those signed by the artist or marked 'Potted' (indicating a pre-1939 origin) are also more valuable. After 1920 wares were marked with a lion — with or without a crown — over a circular 'Royal Doulton.'

Animals and Birds

Cairn terrier, 2½x2½"...**125.00**
Cocker spaniel puppy in basket, HN2585 ....**125.00**
Cocker spaniels (2), sleeping, HN2590......................................**125.00**
English setter, Maesydd Mustard, Daws, 1931, HN1049, 7½".....**925.00**
Greyhound, HN1067, 4¼x5"..**625.00**
Kitten, licking paw, HN2583, 2"..**75.00**

Lucky, from 101 Dalmatians, 3" **56.00**
Persian cat, wht, seated, HN2539..**285.00**
Pointer dog, HN2624, 5½x11½"..**425.00**
Red Rum, horse, DA218, 12"...**275.00**
Scottish terrier, Champion Albourne Arthur, HN1008, 7½x10¾" ...**525.00**
Siamese, cat, lying, HN2662...**125.00**
Springer spaniel, HN2517, 4x5"..**625.00**
Terrier, Champion Chosen Don of Notts, HN2513....................**925.00**

Bunnykins

Ace, DB42 ....**300.00**
Angel Bunnykins, DB196...**42.00**
Autumn Days, DB5 ....**475.00**
Bedtime, DB63 ....**575.00**
Cheerleader, DB142 ....**325.00**
Christmas Surprise, DB146 ....**49.00**
Detective, DB193 ....**175.00**
Doctor Bunnykins, DB181 ....**49.00**
Fisherman, DB170 ....**90.00**
Fortune Teller, DB218 ....**60.00**
Girl Skater, DB153 ....**50.00**
Groom, DB102...**55.00**
Irishman, DB178 ....**250.00**
Joker, DB171..**495.00**
Mother, DB189..**49.00**
Mountie, DB135 ....**950.00**
Mr Bunnybeat Strum, DB16 ....**220.00**
Mystic Bunnykins, DB197..**60.00**
Pilgrim, DB212 ....**195.00**
Rise & Shine, DB11 ....**150.00**
Schoolmaster, DB60 ....**60.00**
Sleepytime, DB15 ....**90.00**
Susan Queen of the May, DB83 ....**175.00**
Tom, DB72...**90.00**
Touchdown, DB97...**700.00**
Welsh Lady, Db172 ....**400.00**
William, DB69..**150.00**

Character Jugs

Capt. Hook, D6597, large, $490.00.

'Arriet, D6250, mini..**75.00**
'Arriet, D6250, mini, A..**110.00**
Angler, D6866, sm..**145.00**
Ann Boleyn, 06644, lg..**125.00**
Artful Dodger, D6678, tiny...**60.00**
Athos, D6452, sm...**65.00**
Auld Mac, D5824, sm, A...**60.00**
Auld Mac, D6253, mini, A...**50.00**
Auld Mac, D6257, tiny...**215.00**
Beefeater, D6233, sm, ER...**65.00**
Beefeater, D6251, mini...**85.00**
Betsy Trotwood, D6685, tiny...**60.00**
Bill Sykes, D6684, tiny..**60.00**

Blacksmith, D6585, mini 60.00
Buz Fuz, D5838, odd sz 175.00
Cap'n Cuttle, D5842, sm, A 125.00
Capt Ahab, D6522, mini 80.00
Capt Henry Morgan, D6510, mini 65.00
Captain Hook, D6605, mini 350.00
Cardinal, D5614, lg 150.00
Clown, D5610, brn hair, lg 4,250.00
Custer & Sitting Bull, D6712, brn eyes, lg 250.00
David Copperfield, D6680, tiny 95.00
Dick Turpin, D6128, mini, A 60.00
Dick Turpin, D6542, horse hdl, mini 40.00
Edward VII, D7154, lg 310.00
Falstaff, D6287, lg 150.00
Falstaff, D6385, sm 65.00
Fat Boy, D5840, odd sz 300.00
Fortune Teller, D6503, sm 400.00
Fortune Teller, D6523, mini 400.00
Gaoler, D6577, sm 65.00
Gaoler, D6584, mini 60.00
Gardener, D6867, lg, 2nd version 200.00
Genie, D6971, flambe, lg 500.00
Gladiator, D6556, mini 350.00
Granny, D5521, lg 125.00
Gulliver, D6560, lg 680.00
Gunsmith, D6573, lg 140.00
Henry VIII, D6647, sm 60.00
HG Wells, D7095, lg 195.00
Jimmy Durante, D6708, lg 200.00
Jockey, D6625, lg 350.00
John Barleycorn, D5327, lg 250.00
John Barleycorn, D6041, mini, A 100.00
John Doulton, D6656, Big Ben at 8 o'clock, sm 110.00
John Peel, D6130, mini 90.00
Johnny Appleseed, D6372, lg 425.00
Lawyer, D6504, sm 65.00
London Bobby, D6744, lg 350.00
Lord Kitchner, D7148, lg 310.00
Merlin, D6536, sm 65.00
Mikado, D6507, sm 330.00
Mikado, D6525, mini 365.00
Monty, D6202, lg 175.00
Mr Micawber, D6143, tiny 115.00
Mr Pickwick, D5839, odd sz 225.00
Mrs Claus, D6922, mini 125.00
Old Charley, D5144, tiny 145.00
Old Charley, D5420, lg 125.00
Old Charley, D6046, mini 60.00
Old King Cole, D6036, lg 300.00
Old Salt, D6544, sm 85.00
Oscar Wilde, D7146, lg 245.00
Pearly Girl, D6208, lg 1,000.00
Pearly Queen, D6759, lg 225.00
Regency Beau, D6559, lg 1,250.00
Regency Beau, D6565, mini 925.00
Rip Van Winkle, D6463, sm 48.00
Robinson Crusoe, D6539, sm 65.00
Robinson Crusoe, D6546, mini 55.00
Sairey Gamp, D6045, mini 75.00
Sam Weller, D5841, special sz 265.00
Sancho Panza, D6518, mini 60.00
Santa, D6840, red/gr/wht candy cane, lg 1,000.00
Santa Claus, D6705, plain hdl, sm 80.00
Smuggler, D6619, sm 75.00

St George, D6618, lg 325.00
St George, D6621, sm 250.00
Tam O'Shanter, D6632, lg 200.00
Tam O'Shanter, D6636, sm 85.00
Toby Philpots, D5737, A, sm 45.00
Ugly Duchess, D6599, lg 625.00
Ugly Duchess, D6603, sm 300.00
Uriah Heep, D5582, tiny 60.00
Veteran Motorist, D6637, sm 100.00
Veteran Motorist, D6641, mini 125.00
Viking, D6526, mini 175.00
Yachtsman, D6622, lg 150.00

Figurines

A Courting, HN2004 ....750.00
Abdullah, HN2104 ....500.00
Afternoon Tea, HN1747 ....675.00
Alice, HN2158 ....275.00
All Aboard, HN2940 ....250.00
Almost Grown, HN3425 ....60.00
Annabella, HN1871 ....995.00
Antoinette, HN2326 ....245.00
Ascott, HN2356, 5¾" 200.00
Auctioneer, HN2988 ....195.00
Autumn, HN2087 ....575.00
Autumn Breezes, HN1911 ....300.00
Autumn Breezes, HN1913 ....325.00
Autumn Breezes, HN1934 ....350.00
Autumn Breezes, HN2147 ....450.00
Autumntime, HN3621 ....300.00
Babie, HN1679 ....155.00
Babie, HN1842 ....395.00
Babie, HN2121, pk w/gold 95.00
Ballad Seller, HN2266 ....275.00
Ballerina, HN2116 ....325.00
Balloon Seller, HN583 ....1,400.00
Bather, HN1238 ....2,000.00
Beat You to It, HN2871 ....425.00
Belle, HN3703 ....225.00
Bess, HN2002 ....325.00
Beth, HN2870 ....325.00
Blue Beard, HN2105 ....625.00
Boatman, HN2417 ....225.00
Boudoir, HN2542 ....475.00
Buddies, HN2546 ....250.00
Bunny, HN2214 ....225.00
Bunny's Bedtime, HN3370 ....195.00
Camellia, HN2222 ....250.00
Carmen, HN2545 ....350.00
Caroline, HN2112 ....375.00
Centurian, HN2726 ....195.00
Christine, HN1840 ....1,200.00
Christmas Time, HN2110 ....350.00
Clown, HN2890 ....185.00
Cookie, HN1705 ....160.00
Coppelia, HN2115 ....875.00
Countess Harrington, HN3317 ....595.00
Daffy Down Dilly, HN1712 ....425.00
Dainty May, M73 ....800.00
Daisy, HN1961 ....595.00
Darling, HN1319 ....195.00
David Copperfield, M88, bone china, old 100.00
Daydreams, HN1732 ....895.00

Delight, HN1772 ....360.00
Delphine, HN2136 ....425.00
Dinky Do, HN2120 ....80.00
Dinnertime, HN3726 ....125.00
Dolly Vardon, HN1515 ....1,650.00
Dorcas, HN1558 ....350.00
Drummer Boy, HN2679 ....475.00
Dulcie, HN2305 ....220.00
Easter Day, HN2039 ....495.00
Emma, HN2834 ....150.00
Enchantment, HN2178 ....200.00
Ermine Coat, HN1981 ....450.00
Fagin, M49, dk brn, early 100.00
Faith, HN4151 ....235.00
Fiona, HN3252 ....350.00
Flower Seller's Children, HN1342 ....835.00
Flowers for You, HN3889 ....135.00
Francis Duncombe, Gainsborough Ladies, HN3009 ....700.00

Gay Morning, HN2135, 1954 – 1967, $275.00.

General Lee, HN3404 ....1,150.00
Genevieve, HN1962 ....350.00
Gentlewoman, HN1632 ....950.00
Good Catch, HN2258 ....225.00
Gossips, HN2025 ....525.00
Granny, HN1832 ....400.00
Granny's Heritage, HN2031 ....675.00
Greta, HN1485 ....450.00
Gypsy Dance, HN2230 ....325.00
Helen R, HN1572 ....1,150.00
Her Ladyship, HN1977 ....415.00
Honey, HN1963 ....895.00
Jack, HN2060 ....225.00
Janice, HN2165, blk 550.00
Jemma, HN3168 ....250.00
Jessica, HN3850 ....235.00
Jester, HN3236, mini 115.00
Jill, HN2016 ....235.00
Judge, HN2443A 210.00
June, HN1691 ....850.00
Katrina, HN2327 ....285.00
L'Ambitieuse, HN3359 ....395.00
Lady April, HN1958 ....395.00
Lady Charmian, HN1948 ....350.00
Lights Out, HN2262 ....275.00
Lilac Time, HN2137 ....395.00
Little Boy Blue, HN2062 ....195.00
Little Lord Fauntleroy, HN2972 ....50.00
Lobsterman, HN2323 ....175.00
Lorna, HN2311, gr dress, yel shawl 225.00
Lorraine, HN3118 ....250.00

Mantilla, HN2712 ....525.00
Margaret, HN1989 ....495.00
Margery, HN1413 ....1,000.00
Marguerite, HN1928 ....450.00
Mary Had a Little Lamb, HN2048 ....175.00
Mary Mary, HN2044 ....250.00
Masque, HN2554A, midnight bl 325.00
Masquerade, HN2259, red & cream 375.00
Masquerade (male in gold), HN636 ....1,200.00
Maureen, HN1770 ....395.00
May, HN2746 ....275.00
Maytime, HN2113 ....350.00
Micawber, M42, bone china 110.00
Michele, HN2234 ....225.00
Miss Demure, HN1402 ....275.00
Miss Fortune, HN1897 ....750.00
Miss Muffet, HN1936 ....175.00
Modena, HN1845 ....2,350.00
Modesty, NJ2744 ....150.00
Monica, HN1467 ....200.00
Mother's Help, HN2151 ....175.00
Mr Pickwick, M41 ....100.00
Mrs Bardell, M86 ....100.00
My Pet, HN2238 ....195.00
My Pretty Maid, HN2064 ....495.00
My Teddy, HN2177 ....595.00
Natalie, HN3498 ....165.00
Nicola, HN1832 ....375.00
Off to school, HN3768 ....200.00
Once Upon a Time, HN2047 ....450.00
One That Got Away, HN2153 ....550.00
Paisley Shawl, HN1988 ....250.00
Parson's Daughter, HN564 ....575.00
Pearly Boy, HN1482 ....425.00
Pearly Girl, HN2036 ....200.00
Penelope, HN1901 ....450.00
Pensive Moments, HN2704 ....250.00
Picnic, HN2308 ....250.00
Pied Piper, HN2102 ....350.00
Pierrette, HN1749 ....3,500.00
Pillow Fight, HN2270 ....295.00
Prince Charles Wedding, HN2884 ....1,050.00
Princess Diana Wedding, HN2887 ....3,200.00
Priscilla R, HN1495 ....850.00
Punch & Judy Man, HN2765 ....225.00
Queen Elizabeth, HN2502 ....1,800.00
Rachel, HN3976 ....235.00
Rosalind, HN2393 ....250.00
Roseanna, HN1926 ....650.00
Rosebud, HN1983 ....495.00
Sabbath Morn, HN1982 ....325.00
Sara, HN3219, mini 125.00
Shore Leave, HN2254 ....225.00
Simone, HN2378 ....165.00
Southern Belle, HN2229, red & cream 375.00
Special Friend, HN3607 ....85.00
Spring, HN2085 ....450.00
Spring Morn, HN1922 ....250.00
Springtime, HN3477 ....300.00
Stayed at Home, HN2207 ....250.00
Stop Press, HN2683 ....165.00
Summer, HN2086 ....450.00
Summer's Day, HN2181 ....295.00
Summertime, HN3478 ....300.00

Susan, HN2056 ....550.00
Suzette, HN2026 ....500.00
Sweet & Twenty, HN1298 ....500.00
Sweet & Twenty, HN1610 ....625.00
Sweet Maid, HN2092 ....475.00
Sweet Seventeen, HN2734 ....285.00
Teresa, HN3206 ....250.00
Tiny Tim, M56 or HN539 ....100.00
Tom, HN2864 ....250.00
Top o' the Hill, HN2126, mini 125.00
Town Crier, HN3261, mini 125.00
Victoria, HN2471 ....435.00
Vivienne, HN2073 ....240.00
Wayfarer, HN2362 ....250.00
Winter, HN2088 ....450.00
Wintertime, HN3622 ....300.00
Yeoman of the Guard, HN2122 ....1,300.00

Flambe

Figurine, Aladdin's Genie, D6791 ....425.00
Figurine, Alsation dog, HN497 ....650.00
Figurine, bulldog, seated, HN112, 2¾" 900.00
Figurine, collie, seated, K-47, 7½" 865.00
Figurine, elephant, 4¼x6" 275.00
Figurine, foxhound, HN209, ca 1917, 3¾" ...1,000.00
Figurine, owl, 12" 395.00
Figurine, penguin, 6" 260.00
Figurine, penguins (2) snuggling, #103, ca 1922-27, 6", NM 475.00
Figurine, Pride of the Shires, horse, HN2564 ....350.00
Vase, cattle landscape, #1623, 15" 625.00
Vase, sgn Fred Moore, #7754, ca 1909 ....325.00
Vase, Sung, Noke, #1200 (?), 5¾" 400.00
Vase, veined, #1616, 9x7½" 425.00
Vase, veined, #5278, 10½" 340.00

Series Ware

Biscuit box, Simple Simon, Nursery Rhymes, ca 1910 ....200.00
Bowl, Autumn Glory, D5651 ....100.00

Bowl, Deaf scene and Room for One! scene, 4x9" diameter, $900.00. (Photo courtesy Collectors Auction Service)

Bowl, Golfing, Crombie, 1911, 3¼x7¾" 725.00
Bowl, Sam Weller, D6327, sq 225.00
Candlestick, Dutch; Coaching Days, D2716, NM 275.00
Flagon, Uncle Sam, Kingsware 1,050.00
Hatpin holder, Artful Dodger, Dickensware, Noke, 5½" 500.00
Jug, Duke of York, Kingsware 375.00
Jug, Fisherman, Walton Ware, Noke, ca 1910, 6" 275.00
Jug, William Shakespeare, Comedy/Tragedy hdl, Noke, 1933, 10½" ..575.00
Pitcher, Old Curiosity Shop, D5584 ....225.00
Pitcher, Old Peggoty, D2973 ....350.00
Pitcher, Oliver Twist, D5617 ....300.00
Pitcher, Pickwick Papers, D5756 ....325.00
Plate, Bill Sykes, Dickensware, D6327, 10" 125.00
Plate, Mr Pickwick, Dickensware, D2973, 10" 150.00

Plate, Old Moreton Hall, D3858 ....95.00
Plate, Sam Weller, D6327, 10" 150.00
Plate, Tony Weller, D6327, 10" 150.00
Stein, New Cavaliers, D4749 ....295.00
Stein, Night Watchman, D4746 ....1,945.00
Stein, Old Jarvey, D3118 ....295.00
Tea caddy, Fat Boy, Dickensware, 6" 395.00
Teapot, Alfred Jingle, Dickensware, D5175 ......450.00
Tray, Old English Coaching, D6393 ....125.00
Vase, Coaching Days, ca 1925, 3¾x5x1⅝" 300.00
Vase, Poor Jo & Fat Boy, D5864 ....425.00

Stoneware

Coffee mug, #5368, ca 1902 ....75.00
Flagon, Dewar's, Egyptian, #224092, ca 1920 ....295.00
Flagon, Highlan Whiskey, RE4818, ca 1932 ....295.00
Flagon, Scott & Burns, RD224092, ca 1901 .....150.00
Flagon, Wm Grant & Sons 225.00
Foot warmer, Lambeth, ca 1902 ....150.00
Jug, Lord Nelson, Lambeth, 6¼" 750.00
Jug, motto, ca 1914 ....195.00
Jug, Stanley (Emin Pasha Relief Expedition), Lambeth, ca 1889, 7½" ..365.00
Pitcher, hunting scene relief, lt to dk brn, 9½" 200.00
Tankard, Elizabethan figures dining, sterling mts, late 19th C, 6⅞" ..835.00
Teapot, Lord Nelson/Trifalgar, ca 1905, 5x7" 625.00
Vase, Art Nouveau roses, F Jones, Lambeth, ca 1920s, 12¾", pr ...675.00
Vase, birds, Florence Barlow, 11", pr 950.00
Vase, grapes & leaves on gr, Lambeth Faience, 11¾" 425.00
Vase, sheep frieze, Hannah Barlow, 14" 1,150.00
Vase, stylized floral bouquets, ca 1920, 8¾", pr 400.00

Toby Jugs

Happy John, D6070, sm 100.00
Jester, D6910, ltd 235.00
Jolly Toby, D6109, med 140.00
Old Charley, D6030, lg 500.00
Winston Churchill, D6175, sm 100.00

Royal Dux

The Duxer Porzellan Manufactur was established by E. Eichler in 1860. Located in what is now Duchcov, Czechoslovakia, the area was known as Dux, Bohemia, until WWI. The war brought about changes in both the style of the ware as well as the mark. Prewar pieces were modeled in the Art Nouveau or Greek Classical manner and marked with 'Bohemia' and a pink triangle containing the letter 'E.' They were usually matt glazed in green, brown, and gold. Better pieces were made of porcelain, while the larger items were of pottery. After the war the ware was marked with the small pink triangle but without the Bohemia designation; 'Made in Czechoslovakia' was added. The style became Art Deco, with cobalt blue a dominant color.

Bowl, shell shape, 1 lady on top, 1 on side, ca 1900, 15x13" ...1,275.00
Dish, leaf shape, w/lady seated atop, 9x18" 820.00
Figurine, ballet dancer on 1 knee, #22220, 8x5x7" 140.00
Figurine, Bavarian folk dancers, 7x13" 410.00
Figurine, chariot racer speeds through field w/chariot wreckage, 20" L 750.00
Figurine, dancing couple in middle-eastern costumes, Art Deco, 12x8" ...300.00
Figurine, Diana w/Huntress, nude w/Borzoi dog, #717, 14⅜" 350.00
Figurine, Flamenco dancers, 9½x15" 1,275.00

Figurine, koala on branch, #24475, 4x12" **85.00**
Figurine, lady places rose in hair while child hands another, 11x21"...**2,275.00**
Figurine, lady w/2 cats, 9x11" **975.00**
Figurine, nude w/3 lg wht cats, 17⅜" **1,200.00**
Figurine, Pierot w/guitar, #363¾, 8½x14" **775.00**
Figurine, semi-nude harem girl dancer, 13x17".........................**2,025.00**
Figurine, semi-nude snake charmer, #702-2, 9¼" **700.00**
Figurine, shepherdess in pk on rock w/sheep, 9x17½" **515.00**
Figurine, Successful Hunting, dog w/duck in mouth, #2227II, 8½" ..**620.00**
Figurine, zebra, running, 10¼x12"...**200.00**
Figurine, 2 hunting dogs, wht w/gold/brn/lt gr highlights, dmn mk, 16"...**275.00**
Figurines, gypsy boy & girl, both carrying water jugs, #219, #220, pr.....**875.00**
Vase, iris/lady w/flowing hair, bl/wht, w/hdls, 8x3½" **125.00**
Vase, maid, seated, 2 irises rising from long stems at rim, 18", EX...**1,350.00**
Vase, maid in long gown by palm tree, figural, #35/1976, 25", EX ..**1,350.00**
Vase, maiden in gr dress on side w/flowers & leaves, 18" **1,125.00**
Vase, molded as a lg lily w/a lady emerging, bl/wht, pk mk, 14"..**750.00**

Royal Flemish

Royal Flemish was introduced in the late 1880s and was patented in 1894 by the Mt. Washington Glass Company. Transparent glass was enameled with one or several colors and the surface divided by a network of raised lines suggesting leaded glasswork. Some pieces were further decorated with enameled florals, birds, or Roman coins. Our advisors for this category are Betty and Clarence Maier; they are listed in the Directory under Pennsylvania.

Centerpiece, sectioned bowl w/mums & leaves, 12"; on mk cherub base..**4,600.00**
Cracker jar, rose/gold leaves/scrolls, ovoid; ornate metal mts, 10x6" ..**2,750.00**
Cracker jar, sections w/mc flowers, emb lid mk MW, heart-shape hdl, 7"...**1,600.00**
Cracker jar, sq, sectioned/floral panels alternate, lid mk MW, 7x5"...**2,475.00**
Cracker jar, thistles, sq, Pairpoint lid w/rpl hdl, 11" overall **900.00**
Cracker jar, 4 Roman coins/gold-lined sections, metal mts, jar: 7" ..**1,400.00**
Ewer, panels/medallions w/mums & gilt, metal top, 12x5½" ..**7,500.00**
Vase, crowned medallion shield w/2 lions, 5 on neck, loop hdl, 12"..**1,550.00**
Vase, gold peacock w/jewels, bottle form, 13", EX...................**5,700.00**
Vase, gold sections, 3 medallions, 1 w/griffin, long swollen neck, 13" .**2,900.00**
Vase, gold sections w/red dmns/stars, gold foliage/peafowls, 4½x5"......**1,350.00**
Vase, raised gold lines & medallions, red-brn/sienna/gr, 6½"..**3,200.00**
Vase, scrolls/violets/gold lines & daubs, spherical w/sm rim hdls, 7" .**2,200.00**
Vase, snow geese/gold sun & stars, 14½x5" **8,450.00**
Vase, 3 gold coins, 1 w/griffin, squat w/distended decor neck, 11" ...**2,750.00**

Royal Haeger, Haeger

In 1871 David Henry Haeger, a young son of German immigrants, purchased a brick factory at Dundee, Illinois. David's bricks rebuilt Chicago after their great fire in 1871. Many generations of the Haeger family have been associated with the ceramic industry, that his descendants have pursued to the present time. Haeger progressed to include artware in their production as early as 1914. That was only the beginning. In the '30s they began to make a line of commercial dinnerware that was marketed through Marshall Fields. Not long after, Haeger's artware was successful enough that a second plant in Macomb, Illinois, was built.

Royal Haeger was their premium line beginning in 1938 and continued into modern-day production. The chief designer in the '40s was Royal Arden Hickman, a talented artist and sculptor who also worked in mediums other than pottery. For Haeger he designed a line of wonderfully stylized animals, birds, high-style vases, and human figures, all with extremely fine details. His designs are highly regarded by collectors today.

Paper labels have been used throughout Haeger's production. Some items from the teens, '20s, and '30s will be found with 'Haeger' in a diamond shape in-mold script mark. Items with 'RG' (Royal Garden) are part of their Flower-Ware line (also called Regular Haeger or Genuine Haeger). Haeger has produced a premium line (Royal Haeger) as well as a regular line for many years, it just has changed names over the years.

Collectors need to be aware that a certain glaze can bring two to three times more than others. Items that have Royal Hickman in the mold mark or on the label are usually higher valued than without his mark. The current collector trend has leaned more towards the mid-century modern styled pieces of artware. The most desired items are ones done by glaze designers Helmut Bruchman and Alrun Osterberg Guest (presently employed by Haeger). These items are from the late '60s into the very early '80s.

For those wanting to learn more about this pottery, we recommend *Haeger Potteries Through the Years* by our advisor for this category, David Dilley (L-W Books); he is listed in the Directory under Indiana.

R-596, Barnyard Riders planter, silver spray horse with yellow riders, chartreuse base, 13¼", $500.00. (Photo courtesy David Dilley/Snyder's Antiques)

#107, Free Form ashtray, Ebony Cascade, 12½" **15.00**
#312-H, Swan bowl, Persian Blue, 1960, 18" **40.00**
#325-H, Shell bowl, Briar Agate, 1960, 17"......................................**45.00**
#329-H, Pheasant bowl, Gold Tweed, 5½x21¼x7¼" **50.00**
#393, Triple bowl, Oxblood, 1964, 16" **40.00**
#439, vase, Lilac, 1962, 12"...**25.00**
#612, Rooster, Haeger Red, 1962-63, 12¼" **50.00**
#616, Teddy Bear planter, Chartreuse, no mks, ca 1938, 4¾x7x3¼"..**15.00**
#811, Bowl planter, Briar Agate, 3¾x6½"..**10.00**
#845, Bowl planter, green Cascade, 4x10".......................................**45.00**
#857W, jardiniere, Black Mistique, 1955, 16", w/walnut tripod ..**100.00**
#883, console set, emb leaves, 5" sq bowl+matching candle holders..**45.00**
#2094X, ashtray, Brown Earth Graphic Wrap, 9"............................**15.00**
#3112, candle holder, Mirror Gold, 11¾" **65.00**
#3122-A, Ribbed bowl, gr, 2½x7"..**15.00**
#3202, wall pocket, emb leaves, 1946, 7½x9x2½"............................**50.00**
#3205-A, Victory vase, 1942, 6" **40.00**
#3234, Lamb vase, 5¼x2¼" **20.00**
#3291, bowl, Honey/Apricot, low, 10"..**20.00**
#4011, Chalice vase, Peacock, 15"...**50.00**
#4073, vase, Mandarin Orange, emb ribs, 1967, 10" **30.00**
#4185, planter, Green Earth Graphic Wrap, 5½x8" **60.00**
#4187, vase, White Earth Graphic Wrap, bulbous, 13" **85.00**
#5000, planter, Brown Earth Graphic Wrap, 8¼x10"...................**100.00**
#6263, Lilies on Cylinder lamp, 1954, 33½" **225.00**
#8020, Mediterranean fountain, Oyster White, 1955, 17" **350.00**
#8176, Roman Bronze planter, 15" **275.00**
#8181, water pitcher, Peasant Green, 11¾" **50.00**
#8188, pitcher, Brown Earth Graphic Wrap, 8⅞" **55.00**
#8300, Toe Tapper w/flute, brn textured, 8x4¼", minimum value...**40.00**
F-17, Wild Goose, wht matt, unmk, ca 1941, 6½x6¼x2" **15.00**
HT-44, Male candle holder, hand thrown, gray/gr, 15"................**150.00**

R-103, Small Horse, Mauve Agate, 1949, 5½x5½x2½"...............35.00
R-284, Trout flower vase, 1946, 9¾x7¼x4½"...............100.00
R-298, Conch Shell cornucopia, 1946, 11x8¾x4¾"...............75.00
R-318, Russian Wolfhound (head down), Green Briar, 6¼x11½"...75.00
R-390, South American Girl, Manganese stain, 1942, 11".........175.00
R-397, Three Block candle holder, 2¾x3x8¼"...............30.00
R-407, Wren House, Green Briar, 1950...............65.00
R-408, Double Racing Horses, Mallow, 1942, 10".........110.00
R-425, vase, parrot on perch, cylindrical, Manganese & Mallow, 16"..175.00
R-435, Rooster Pheasant, Mauve Agate, unmk, 12x13"...............40.00
R-451, Horse & Colt, Gun Metal or amber, 10x13½"...............150.00
R-453, Peacock planter, Mauve Agate, 10x9¾x3⅛".................40.00
R-466, Curving bowl, lt bl & wht, 3½x14¾x6"...............30.00
R-516, Swan candle holders, Mauve Agate, 8x3⅝", pr...............50.00
R-555, Pei Tung vase, Ebony, 13½"...............40.00
R-563, Elephant planter, Chartreuse & Honey, 1950...............75.00
R-693, Wrap Around vase, gray drip w/wht, 1949, 18"...............75.00
R-711, Chinese Musician, Green Agate, 1950...............65.00
R-721, Indian, on horse before cactus, Desert Red, 1950...........200.00
R-860, ashtray, Oxblood, 3 rests, 1954, 7½"...............15.00
R-869, Gazelle planter, Antique (washed wht), 13¾x17"...............65.00
R-1144, Water Lily bookends, gr w/wht flowers, ca 1952, 7½x5x5", pr...60.00
R-1224, Gypsy Girl flower frog, brn & gr, unmk, 16½x13½".....100.00
R-1257, Lorelei, Platinum Gray, 1953, 15" L...............135.00
R-1354, Edged candle holders, Ebony, 3½x3x2", pr...............30.00
R-1400-C, Fluted bowl, Green Cascade, 1954, 6"...............35.00
R-1466, Basket planter, turq bl, unmk, 9x6½"...............30.00
R-1731, Leaf ashtray, Catseye, 1957, 8½x16½"...............20.00
R-1742, Egyptian Cat, 1957, 20"...............135.00
R-1779, Royal Artware vase, turq gr w/decor, 1957, 8"...............15.00
R-1782, Lamb, White Stone Lace, w/silk ribbon & bell, 15x17"...100.00
R-1796, Classic bud vase, Bittersweet, 1958, 8x3¾"...............15.00
R-1843, candle holder, Pumpkin, 1958, 4", pr...............30.00
RG-56, compote bowl, Black Mistique, 3x9"...............20.00
RG-128, Pleated vase, blk, 14"...............25.00

Royal Rudolstadt

The hard-paste porcelain that has come to be known as Royal Rudolstadt was produced in Thuringia, Germany, in the early eighteenth century. Various names and marks have been associated with this pottery. One of the earliest was a hay-fork symbol associated with Johann Frederich von Schwarzburg-Rudolstadt, one of the first founders. Variations, some that included an 'R,' were also used. In 1854 Earnst Bohne produced wares that were marked with an anchor and the letters 'EB.' Examples commonly found today were made during the late 1800s and early 1900s. These are usually marked with an 'RW' within a shield under a crown and the words 'Crown Rudolstadt.' Items marked 'Germany' were made after 1890.

Biscuit jar, pk/yel roses on wht, gold bow finial, swirled body, 7"...400.00
Bowl, pk roses (2) w/gr leaves, tab hdls, 7"...............75.00
Bowl, wht roses w/gr leaves, 2¼x9½" dia...............135.00
Centerpc, shell shape w/dragon & jaguar climbing sides, 12½x14½".1,675.00
Dish, celery; wht roses w/gr leaves, gold trim, 4x8½"...............50.00
Dish, clover shape, yel roses w/holly, 9x9½"...............150.00
Figurine, boy & girl w/chickens, 7x9½"...............300.00
Plate, cake; pk roses w/gr leaves & vines, gold trim, 8½"...............90.00
Plate, wht daisies w/gr leaves, sm pierced hdls, 10½"...............60.00
Reamer, pk & yel roses, pitcher form, 3x6½"...............135.00
Urn, portrait of couple on cobalt, ornate gold scolls & hdls, 12½"..1,875.00
Vase, birds & flowers, urn shape, sm gold hdls, ca 1905, 8".........140.00
Vase, horn shape supported by elephant head, 7x9½"...............360.00
Vase, 2 Chinese boys hold horn-shape vase, cream, 4½x7"...........70.00

Royal Vienna

In 1719 Claude Innocentius de Paquier established a hard-paste porcelain factory in Vienna where he made highly ornamental wares similar to the type produced at Meissen. Early wares were usually unmarked; but after 1744, when the factory was purchased by the Empress, the Austrian shield (often called 'beehive') was stamped on under the glaze. In the following listings, values are for hand-painted items unless noted otherwise. Decal-decorated items would be considerably lower.

Note: There is a new resurgence of interest in this fine porcelain, but an influx of Japanese reproductions on the market has affected values on genuine old Royal Vienna. Buyer beware! On new items the beehive mark is over the glaze, the weight of the porcelain is heavier, and the decoration is obviously decaled. Our advisor for this category is Madeleine France; she is listed in the Directory under Florida.

Charger, 3 ladies asking Cupid for Love Potion, sgn Ullmer, 12" ..580.00
Compotes, garden scene ea side, w/lid, 10½", pr.....................1,900.00
Cracker jar, pk roses w/sm purple flowers on wht, 6½x9"............630.00
Cup & saucer, maiden/Cupid, gilt int, ped ft, 4x6½"....................90.00
Figurine, Blackamoor w/butterfly, #1522, 3¼"............................710.00
Figurine, Lipizan stallion w/trainer, #1833, 12x10½"...............775.00
Plate, lady's portrait, burgundy/gold rim, 9½"............................450.00
Plate, lady's portrait w/swan border in gold, Wagner, 9¾".......1,500.00
Plate, nude lovers by water's edge, ornate gold border, Wagner, 9½"..1,330.00
Plates, ea w/figural reserves, asst printed signatures, 1900, 12 for..2,900.00
Vase, cobalt w/angel & cherub sitting on cloud, Juno, 5x9½" 185.00
Vase, Countess Litta, wht & lt purple w/gold, 7¼" 1,280.00
Vase, figures at alter transfer, bl/burgundy panels w/gold, 15" 150.00
Vase, ladies in garden, bk: similar, ornate gold hdls, ftd, 13x8"...1,035.00
Vase, lady w/Cupid over shoulder, mc w/gold, 10½" 1,900.00
Vase, lady/cherubs ea side, Wagner, bl/wht/gold, fancy hdls/lid, 12x6"....1,100.00
Vase, Madame Le Brun, bulbous w/flared scalloped rim, gold hdls, 7".....1,200.00

Roycroft

Near the turn of the twentieth century, Elbert Hubbard established the Roycroft Printing Shop in East Aurora, New York. Named in honor of two seventeenth-century printer-bookbinders, the print shop was just the beginning of a community called Roycroft, which came to be known worldwide. Hubbard became a popular personality of the early 1900s, known for his talents in a variety of areas from writing and lecturing to manufacturing. The Roycroft community became a meeting place for people of various capabilities and included shops for the production of furniture, copper, leather items, and a multitude of other wares which were marked with the Roycroft symbol, an 'R' within a circle below a double-barred cross. Hubbard lost his life on the Lusitania in 1915; production at the community continued until the Depression.

Interest is strong in the field of Arts and Crafts in general and in Roycroft items in particular. Copper items are evaluated to a large extent by the condition and type of the original patina. The most desirable patina is either the dark or medium brown; brass-wash, gunmetal, and silver-wash patinas follow in desirability. The acid-etched patina and the smooth (unhammered) surfaced Roycroft pieces are later (after 1925) developments and tend not to be attractive to collectors. Furniture was manufactured in oak, mahogany, bird's-eye maple, and occasionally walnut or ash; collectors prefer oak. Books with Levant binding, tooled leather covers, Japan vellum, or hand illumining are especially collectible; suede cover and parchment paper books are of less interest to collectors as they are fairly common. In the listings that follow, values reflect the worth of items in excellent original condition unless noted to the contrary. Our advisor for this category is Bruce Austin; he is listed in the Directory under New York.

Key: h/cp — hammered copper

Armchair, 1-slat bk, GPI on top rail, leather seat, 41x25" 3,250.00
Ashtray, armchair; h/cp bowl on leather strap tooled w/elephant ea end..750.00
Ashtray, h/cp, 4-strap support riveted to rnd base, 29x8" dia 425.00
Bean pot, copper, 3 sm ft, bail, 5" dia 160.00
Bench, rectangle top/lower stretcher w/dbl-key tenons, 20x42x15"..4,750.00
Blotter, leather, tooled bands/leaves, 7½" L 300.00
Book, Addresses; leather, tooled flowers, 4½x3½" 125.00
Book marker, h/brass w/tooled lines & dots, K Kipp, 4¼", VG 55.00
Bookends, h/cp, arched open strap above short base section, 6½", pr ..350.00
Bookends, h/cp, rnd bkplate w/tooled owl, 5", pr 350.00
Bookends, h/cp, sq w/appl strap & loose rings, Hunter/Kipp, 5", pr ..625.00
Bookends, h/cp, sq w/raised/tooled disc, 'stitched' lines, 5", pr 275.00
Bookends, h/cp, tooled floral on shaped rectangular bkplate, 3", pr ..180.00
Bookends, h/cp w/appl floral device, 8½", VG 160.00
Books, Little Journeys, Homes of the Great, paper sleeves, 14 copies..200.00
Books, Little Journeys, memorial edition, set of 14, EX 190.00
Bookstand, Little Journeys, 2-tier, key-tenons, no mk, 26x26", VG..725.00
Bookstand, Little Journeys, 2-tier, key-tenons, rfn, 26x26x9" 475.00
Bowl, brass/copper, conical w/angle hdls under rim, ped ft, 7", VG..500.00
Bowl, h/cp, incised design at top, lt cleaning, 6½" 270.00
Bowl, h/cp, incurvate rim, 3 sm ft, 10½" 3,750.00
Bowl, h/cp, tooled decor, orig brass patina, unmk, 7" 160.00
Box, cigar; mahog, int w/picture of Hubbard & initials EH, 3x10"..600.00
Box, Goody; mahog w/iron hdw & hdls, orb mk, 23" L, VG 800.00
Box, Roycroft Maple Pecan Patties, paperboard, 7" L, VG 210.00
Brooch, copper w/Roycroft mk, ¾" L 160.00
Candelabra, h/cp, twisted pencil std, 3-arm, V Toothaker, 21", pr...2,000.00
Candle sconce, 4-sided cup on h/cp panel, sq w/emb dogwood above, 10"...550.00
Candlestick, h/cp, 4-sided petal cup on sqd bobeche/stem/ft, 14" .1,400.00
Candlestick, h/cp, 8" 150.00
Candlesticks, h/brass, 2¾x5½", pr 160.00
Candlesticks, h/cp, pencil stem, 8", pr 550.00
Candlesticks, h/cp, 3½", pr 230.00
Chair, side; notched rail, 2 narrow slats, leather seat, 39" 2,100.00
Clock, tooled leather, laced, rnd top w/extended sides, 6x4½" 4,750.00
Desk, oak, drop front, iron strap hinges, 3 drws, 58x43x17" ..20,000.00
Desk organizer, h/cp, 1-pc w/calendar & pen compartment, 5" L..325.00
Desk organizer, h/cp, 2 boxes/inkwell fit behind 10" L pen tray ..1,300.00
Desk set, h/cp w/brass wash, letter rack+inkwell+pen tray+calendar ...350.00
Doll, bean bag; colorful fabrics, 7", EX 200.00
Footstool, mahog, recovered top, rfn, 9x15x9" 475.00
Frame, h/cp, 3½", VG 110.00
Frame, h/cp, 6½x4" 400.00
Frame, leather w/tooled floral, 9x6½" 500.00
Frame, oak, dk finish, 1 row w/6 openings, 11x38" L 3,500.00
Frame, oak, lap-joined corners, 9½x7½" 700.00
Frame, oak, upper corners canted, from Sandy Hubbard estate, 15x11"...400.00
Frame, oak, 2 rows of 3 openings, orb mk, 18x21" 2,500.00
Hat pin, h/cp, sq faceted top w/orb mk, 1" 325.00
Jar, leather covered w/detailed tooled floral on lid, cylinder, 5½" 600.00
Lamp, h/cp, slim std, hammered frosted glass shade, 18½" 2,000.00
Lamp, h/cp, slim std w/twisted extension, parchment shade ea side, 20"..1,500.00
Lamp, h/cp, 2-arm base, orig rawhide 14" shade, 20", VG 1,500.00
Lamp base, h/cp, tulip harp cup, slim std w/flaring ft, 18½" 1,400.00
Lantern, ldgl yel/gr ½-cylinder shade, copper cap/wall bracket, 11"......11,000.00
Magazine rack, #070, 4-shelf, sides taper, script Roycroft, 50x18", VG..7,500.00
Magazine rack, #087½, 3-shelf, slatted bk/sides, orb mk, 39x33" 6,500.00
Mat, leather, tooled/modeled flowers, leaves, vines, 18x12", VG...700.00
Mat, leather, tooled/modeled flowers, oval, 9x6", VG 260.00

Matchbook holder, h/cp, book form w/tooled edge, 2¼" 140.00
Motto, hand colored, Dard Hunter, matted, oak fr, 7½x5½" 90.00
Mousetrap, wood, Better Mousetrap/orb/Roycrofters/East Aurora, NY, 9" ...270.00
Notebook, tooled/modeled leather, brn/tan/gr, 5x3" 125.00
Nut set, h/cp, 7½" ftd bowl+lg spoon & 5 sm trays 2,300.00
Paperweight, leather covered, tooled/modeled device, Bankers Trust 500.00
Pendant, copper disc w/Roycroft mk below hole for hanging, 1½", VG......130.00
Plaque, bronze, emb profile of boy, mk: A Roycrofter/orb, Winsche, 7"..1,000.00
Purse, leather, flower reserve, holds cards/change, laced edges, 4" L..260.00
Ribbon, Southwestern Assoc of Volunteer Firemen East Aurora, 1916, 4" ..350.00
Stick pin, h/brass w/Roycroft mk, 3" L 210.00
Table, lunch; stretcher w/Y ends, rfn, orb mk, 48" L, VG 3,500.00
Thermos, silver w/eng Roycroft Inn & orb, glass lining, 13".........2,000.00
Tray, h/cp, flat rim w/hdls, scratches, 18½" dia, VG 400.00
Tray, h/cp, octagonal w/recessed well, hdls, 12" 400.00
Tray, h/cp, radial hammering, 9" W 260.00
Tray, h/cp, recessed well, 8" 220.00
Tray, h/cp (bold mks), recessed well, hdls, 19", VG 950.00
Tray, h/cp w/polychrome finish, trefoils 3X in rim, recessed well, 10"..1,200.00
Tray, silver wash, hammered border w/trefoils, Jennings design, 7" dia ...475.00
Vase, Am Beauty, h/cp, cleaned, 21", VG 1,400.00
Vase, Am Beauty, h/cp, squat w/long cylinder neck, flaring rim, 19"..1,700.00
Vase, Am Beauty, h/cp, 21½" 2,800.00
Vase, h/cp, cone form w/2 lg loose ring hdls, ped ft, cleaned, 10", VG 425.00
Vase, h/cp, cylinder w/flare rim on squat form, riveted band, 15", VG...3,250.00
Vase, h/cp, hdls, imp mk, 6" 650.00
Vase, h/cp, rim-to-base tooled floral, cylinder w/shaped rim, 10", VG...700.00
Vase, h/cp, tapering toward bottom, 4½", VG 300.00
Vase, h/cp w/polychrome finish, ovoid, 5" 450.00
Wastebasket, mahog w/copper corners, 13x10x10" 1,000.00
Watch fob & cuff links (½" sq), sterling, English Rose motif, K Kipp ...1,100.00

Rozenburg

Some of the most innovative and original Art Nouveau ceramics were created by the Rozenburg factory at the Hague in The Netherlands between 1883 and 1914, when production was ceased. (Several of their better painters continued to work in Gouda, which accounts for some pieces being similar to Gouda.) Rozenburg also made highly prized eggshell ware, so called because of its very thin walls; this is eagerly sought after by collectors. T.A.C. Colenbrander was their artistic leader, with Samuel Schellink and J. Kok designing many of the eggshell pieces. The company liquidated in 1917. Most pieces carry a date code. Our advisor for this category is Ralph Jaarsma; he is listed in the Directory under Iowa.

Cup & saucer, nasturtiums, sgn Schelink, eggshell, octagonal, 1905..1,600.00
Pitcher, exotic birds, brn/ochre on terra cotta, 7" 325.00
Vase, floral, baluster shape, earthenware, 1893, pnt mk, 15"........300.00
Vase, hyacinths on brn, wide shoulder, #374, 8⅝" 500.00
Vase, irises, sqd bottle form, sgn Schelink, eggshell, 1901, 10" ...1,800.00

Rubena

Rubena glass was made by several firms in the late 1800s. It is a blown art glass that shades from clear to red. See also Art Glass Baskets; Cruets; Sugar Shakers; Salts; specific manufacturers.

Bottle, scent; cut body, faceted stopper, 5⅜" 145.00
Bucket, ice; HP decor, SP bail hdl 125.00
Celery vase, Hobnail, cranberry top w/opal hobs, 6½" 110.00
Celery vase, HP floral, SP fr 375.00

Cheese dish, 7x10½" 230.00
Compote, Honeycomb, ftd, 4x8½" 250.00
Cookie jar, melon ribs, 9" 385.00
Cup, punch; reeded hdl 55.00
Pitcher, Invt T'print, sq top, clear twist rope collar/hdl, 4½" 375.00
Pitcher, Wheeling, Drape, amber hdl, 4½" 2,000.00
Rose bowl, vertical ribs, 8-crimp rim, 4½x5" 50.00
Sugar shaker, melon ribs, bulbous, orig lid 165.00
Syrup, Invt T'print, tapered 250.00
Syrup, threaded, orig tin top 480.00
Tumbler, Invt T'print, HP decor 100.00

Rubena Verde

Rubena Verde glass was introduced in the late 1800s by Hobbs, Brockunier, and Company of Wheeling, West Virginia. Its transparent colors shade from red to green. See also Art Glass Baskets; Cruets; Sugar Shakers; Salts. For more information we recommend *Hobbs, Brockunier and Co. Glass* by Neila and Tom Bredehoft.

Bowl, finger; Hobnail, ruffled rim, 4½" dia 110.00
Creamer, Invt T'print, bulbous, reeded hdl, 5" 435.00
Cruet, Invt T'print, teepee shape, Hobbs Brockunier, 7" 550.00
Cruet, Thumbprint, 3-lipped top, 6¾" 550.00
Epergne, central trumpet, hanging baskets, 22" 535.00
Pitcher, Hobnail, vaseline hdl, bulbous, sq top, 8" 450.00
Pitcher, Invt T'print, citron hdl, 7½" 125.00
Pitcher, Invt T'print, rope twist hdl/collar, Hobbs, 7½" 300.00
Syrup, Hobnail, orig lid 150.00
Tumbler, Hobnail, 4" 350.00
Vase, ca 1900, 10" 100.00
Vase, Drape, appl gr ruffled rim, 11" 435.00
Vase, gold floral w/wht outlines, ribbed, ftd, shouldered, 10" 200.00
Wine, Invt T'print, 4¼" 150.00

Ruby Glass

Produced for over one hundred years by every glasshouse of note in this country, ruby glass has been used to create decorative items such as one might find in gift shops, utilitarian bottles and kitchenware, figurines, and dinnerware lines such as were popular in the Depression era. For further information and study, we recommend *Ruby Glass of the 20th Century* by our advisor, Naomi Over; she is listed in the Directory under Colorado.

Banana boat, English Hobnail, Westmoreland, 6¾x9½" 85.00
Basket, clear twisted hdl, Morgantown, 1930-50, 12x10" 110.00
Bottle, Benjamin Franklin portrait, Wheaton, 1980s, 7¾" 40.00
Bowl, Bambu, Imperial, 1960-72, 11" 70.00
Bowl, ruffled rim, Blenco, 1980, 9½" 28.00
Box, jewel; Mary Gregory portrait, Westmoreland, 1983, 2½" 50.00
Cake salver, plain, Viking, 1982, 11¾" 75.00
Candle holder, Barred Oval, Fenton, 1984-86, 6" 70.00
Candle holder, Ring Stem, 1-light, Cambridge, ca 1949-53, 5" 70.00
Candlestick, Iris & Herringbone, ruby flashed, Jeannette, 5½" 85.00
Candlesticks, Heirloom, lustre cut prism design, Cambridge, 10", pr....175.00
Cornucopia candle holders, silver o/l, Paden City, 1920-54, 1¼", pr....105.00
Creamer, ftd, att Cambridge, 2¼" 35.00
Decanter, milk glass stopper, base & hdl, Italy, 17" 85.00
Goblet, Hoffman House, Imperial, 1974-75, 12-oz 30.00
Muddler/stir stick, twist design, Cambridge, 1930s, 4½" 40.00
Plate, Diamond, 8-sided, Imperial, 1920-30, 8" 17.00

Plate, dinner; Rock Crystal, Mckee, 1931, 11½" 85.00
Plate, Maple Leaf, ruffled rim, Westmoreland, 1980s, 14" 110.00
Plate, Spoke & Rim, Duncan & Miller, 1930s, 8¾" 45.00
Platter, Simplicity, Paden City, 1930s, oval 45.00
Relish, w/silver lid, underplate & spoon, 1940s, 2½" H 25.00
Rose bowl, English Hobnail, pinched, Westmoreland, 1980, 8"....75.00
Tray, Regina, Paden City, 1936, 13¼x7¾" 45.00
Tumbler, Georgian, Fenton, ca 1931-38, 9-oz 20.00
Tumbler, juice; waisted, unknown mfg, ca 1927-32...................22.00
Tumbler, water; Standard Glass Co, ca 1940s, 8-oz 7.00
Vase, jack-in-the-pulpit; pnt rose decor, Westmoreland, 1980, 6¼"...30.00
Wine, air-twisted stem, Blenko, 1980, 3-oz 17.00
Wine, crystal ball in stem, Morgantown, 1930s, 5½" 28.00
Wine, twisted stem, unknown mfg, 4-oz 28.00

Ruby-Stained Glass

Ruby-flashed or ruby-stained glass was made through the application of a thin layer of color over clear. It was used in the manufacture of some early pressed tableware and from the Victorian era well into the twentieth century. These items were often engraved on the spot with the date, location, and buyer's name.

Salt shaker, Bead Swag, engraved and dated 1908, 2⅞", $50.00. (Photo courtesy Mildred and Ralph Lechner)

Canoe, Button Arches, Gettysburg 1863, 2¾" 30.00
Creamer, Arched Ovals 35.00
Creamer & spooner, Frost Crystal, Tarentum Glass Co, gold trim ...50.00
Cup, Diamond w/Peg...30.00
Goblet, T'print, allover pattern, Reading PA, 5¾" 35.00
Nappy, Bull's Eye & Daisy, ca 1919...55.00
Pitcher, Heart Band, Compliments of... in gold, McKee, 4", NM .40.00
Pitcher, Souvenir of Caldwell NJ, gold trim, 4" 25.00
Relish, Bull's Eye & Daisy, ca 1909..55.00
Tumbler, Button Arches, Sarasota Springs, 3⅞x3" 35.00
Wine, King's Crown, allover pattern, Renovo PA, 3¾"................26.00

Rugs

Hooked rugs are treasured today for their folk-art appeal. Rug making was a craft that was introduced to this country in about 1830 and flourished its best in the New England states. The prime consideration when evaluating one of these rugs is not age but artistic appeal. Scenes with animals, buildings, and people; patriotic designs; or whimsical themes are preferred. Those with finely conceived designs, great imagination, interesting color use, etc., demand higher prices. Condition is, of course, also a factor. Marked examples bearing the stamps of 'Frost and Co.,' 'Abenakee,' 'C.R.,' and 'Ouia' are highly prized. Note: The rugs listed here are made of rag unless noted otherwise. See also Orientalia, Rugs.

Abstract 'hit or miss' pattern, brn/navy/gr/yel/red, 21x264" **1,600.00**

Autumn leaves & branches on brn, 19th C, 30x53" **800.00**
Butterfly & bird, mc on patterned ground, 19th C, rprs, 29x37" ...**450.00**
Calico kittens & bluebirds on blk w/mc border, 19th C, 28x37" ...**865.00**
Carriage & horses in landscape, sgn CBCM, ca 1935, 39x70" **975.00**
Cat (body comprises entire rug), gray w/bl eyes, cream accents, 29x17" .**495.00**
Concentric free-form shapes on yel w/striped border, 24x36" **375.00**
Dmn chain border, red & gr on cream, red center, 1890s, 18x106", VG ...**315.00**
Dog, recumbent, on striped field, inner border, ca 1900, 27x36" **800.00**
Dog in central panel, wide line/floral borders, Frost, 20x37", EX...**275.00**
Dog on striped ground, geometric border, late 1800s, 28x48" **230.00**
Eagle w/Am shield, border: banners/acorns/leaves, 1910, 36x78" **3,500.00**
Federal house in MA, mc, late 19th C, 22x29", +fr photo of house....**975.00**
Floral bouquet in tan reserve on brn w/mc border, ca 1800, 26x50"...**400.00**
Flower bouquet & card inscribed Mother, 1890s, 33x78" **350.00**
Flower bouquet on gr w/sprig corners, 1890s, 27x44", VG **175.00**
Geometric scroll-like waves & mc chevrons, 1890s, 41x80" **750.00**
Geometric stars & blocks, gr/bl/red/tan, rprs, ca 1900, 36x69" ...**1,150.00**
Grenfell, winter landscape w/dog sled, team & 2 men, 26x44" ...**975.00**
Hunter/dog/cabin/sunset, Newfoundland, 1900s, 27x39" **350.00**
Mill scene w/paddle-wheeler beyond, mc, late 1800s, 22x36" **920.00**
Penny, ea is graduated stack of 3 mc layers, hexagonal, 28x48" **330.00**
Rope pattern, mc (mainly brn), early 1900s, rebound, 39x70"....**400.00**
Water lily, lg/colorful, on red/bl/blk ground, 26x45½"..................**440.00**

RumRill

George Rumrill designed and marketed his pottery designs from 1933 until his death in 1942. During this period of time, four different companies produced his works. Today the most popular designs are those made by the Red Wing Stoneware Company from 1933 until 1936 and Red Wing Potteries from 1936 until early 1938. Some of these lines include Trumpet Flower, Classic, Manhattan, and Athena, the Nudes.

For a period of months in 1938, Shawnee took over the production of RumRill pottery. This relationship ended abruptly, and the Florence Pottery took over and produced his wares until the plant burned down. The final producer was Gonder. Pieces from each individual pottery are easily recognized by their designs, glazes, and/or signatures. It is interesting to note that the same designs were produced by all three companies. They may be marked RumRill or with the name of the specific company that made them. You will find information on RumRill in these books: *Red Wing Art Pottery, Books I* and *II*, by B.L. and R.L. Dollen (Collector Books). Our advisors for this category are Wendy and Leo Frese; they are listed in the Directory under Texas.

Basket, Lovebirds, wht..**80.00**
Basket, Vintage, #615, 12½" **125.00**
Bookends, eagles, Pompeian Brown Antiqued Ivory, #333, pr **235.00**
Bowl, console; Athena, deep bl, #571 ....**1,200.00**
Bowl, gr, #509, 5"...**30.00**
Bowl, Grecian, Dutch Blue, #302, 6"...........................**60.00**
Bowl, lt gr, #E-12 ....**25.00**
Ewer, Vintage, #616L, 11"..**100.00**
Flower frog, Athena, Eggshell, #563............................**1,350.00**
Ivy ball, Suntan w/lt gr, #600-6.....................................**75.00**
Jug, ball; Scarlet & Bay, #A-50, no lid **50.00**
Jug, ball; Scarlet & Bay, #547.......................................**35.00**
Planter, Athena Triple Nude, Suntan w/Seal Brown int, #572/573.**2,500.00**
Vase, Athena Double Nude, Seafoam, #568, 11"....................**350.00**
Vase, Athena Triple Nude, Seafoam, #570 ....**1,500.00**
Vase, bud; Dutch Blue, #290, 9½".....................................**75.00**
Vase, bud; Scarlet & Bay, #510, 8"...................................**50.00**
Vase, dbl cornucopia, wht **35.00**
Vase, fan; Neoclassic, Suntan w/gr int, #669, 10" **100.00**

Vase, floor; Dutch Blue, #T-1..**500.00**
Vase, Fluted, Dutch Blue, #301, 11".................................**350.00**
Vase, Grecian, Dutch Blue, #364, 7" **60.00**
Vase, orange w/yel splotching, #297, octagonal, 5¼"............**100.00**
Vase, Riviera glaze, #686, 11"..**75.00**
Vase, tan w/gr int, elephant-head hdls, #215, 6¾".................**110.00**
Vase, Transition Double Nude, lilac, #249 ....**750.00**
Vase, Trumpet Flower, matt gr drip, #485, 7½x13¼"..............**110.00**
Vase, urn shape, #H-4, off-wht w/pk speckled overglaze, 5½x9".**150.00**
Vase, wht, #629, 7" **30.00**

Ruskin

This English pottery operated near Birmingham from 1989 until 1935. Its founder was W. Howson Taylor, and it was named in honor of the renowned author and critic, John Ruskin. The earliest marks were 'Taylor' in block letters and the initials 'WHT,' the smaller W and H superimposed over the larger T. Later marks included the Ruskin name.

Ginger jar, purple/bl lustre, 1921, 7"...............................**425.00**
Vase, aqua bl opal, shouldered, 1923, 9¼x4".....................**425.00**
Vase, bl crystalline, dimpled ovoid, 5½x5¼".......................**265.00**
Vase, bl over yel to orange, sgn W Howson Taylor, 1933, 8x6" ..**575.00**
Vase, mottled lustre, shouldered, 1914, 9¾x3½".................**350.00**
Vase, pk lustre w/shades of gr & lav, shouldered, 1920s, 10¼x5"...**315.00**
Vase, pk mottle, onion form, 1915, 4x4½"..........................**325.00**
Vase, sang de boeuf w/gr spotting, waisted, 1925, 7½" **625.00**

Russel Wright Dinnerware

Russel Wright, one of America's foremost industrial designers, also designed several lines of ceramic dinnerware, glassware, and aluminum ware that are now highly sought-after collectibles. His most popular dinnerware then and with today's collectors, American Modern, was manufactured by the Steubenville Pottery Company from 1939 until 1959. It was produced in a variety of solid colors in assortments chosen to stay attune with the times. Casual (his first line sturdy enough to be guaranteed against breakage for ten years from date of purchase) is relatively easy to find today — simply because it has held up so well. During the years of its production, the Casual line was constantly being restyled, some items as many as five times. Early examples were heavily mottled, while later pieces were smoothly glazed and sometimes patterned. The ware was marked with Wright's signature and 'China by Iroquois.' It was marketed in fine department stores throughout the country. After 1950 the line was marked 'Iroquois China by Russel Wright.' For those wanting to learn more about the subject, we recommend *The Collector's Encyclopedia of Russel Wright, Third Edition*, by Ann Kerr.

American Modern

To calculate values for American Modern, at the least, double the low values listed for these colors: Canteloupe, Glacier Blue, Bean Brown, and White. Chartreuse is represented by the low end of our range; Cedar, Black Chutney, and Seafoam by the high end; and Coral and Gray near the middle.

Bowl, baker, from $40 to **50.00**
Bowl, divided vegetable; from $135 to **150.00**
Celery, from $38 to **45.00**
Coffeepot, demitasse; from $125 to **150.00**
Creamer, from $15 to...**20.00**
Ice box jar, from $250 to **275.00**

Plate, chop; from $45 to 55.00
Relish, divided, reed hdl, from $250 to 300.00
Saucer, demitasse; from $25 to 30.00
Teapot, from $125 to 135.00

Glass

Morgantown Modern is most popular in Seafoam, Coral, and Chartreuse. In the Flair line, colors other than crystal and pink are rare and expensive. Seafoam is hard to find in Pinch; Canteloupe is scarce, so double the prices for that color, and Ruby Flair is very rare.

Appleman warming tray, rnd or oblong, lg or sm, ea, from $100 to...125.00
Bartlett-Collins Eclipse, hi-ball, 5", from $20 to 25.00
Bartlett-Collins Eclipse, zombie, 7", from $25 to 30.00
Imperial Flare, tumbler, juice; pk or crystal, 6-oz, from $45 to 50.00
Imperial Pinch, tumbler, water; 11-oz, from $25 to........35.00
Imperial Twist, old fashioned, rare, from $35 to.............50.00
Old Morgantown/Modern, chilling bowl, 12-oz, 3", from $150 to ..175.00
Old Morgantown/Modern, iced tea, 15-oz, 5¼", from $20 to........30.00
Old Morgantown/Modern, sherbet, 5-oz, 2¾", from $25 to...........30.00
Theme Formal, cordial, 3-oz, ¾", from $175 to 225.00
Theme Formal, goblet, 8-oz, 5", from $150 to................200.00

Highlight

Bowl, salad/vegetable; rnd, from $100 to 150.00
Bowl, vegetable; oval, from $65 to 75.00
Creamer, from $40 to 55.00
Plate, bread & butter; from $12 to 15.00
Platter, oval, lg, from $55 to 75.00
Shakers, either sz, pr, from $100 to 150.00

Iroquois Casual

To price Sugar White, Charcoal, and Oyster, use the high end of the pricing range. Avocado Yellow, Nutmeg Brown, and Ripe Apricot fall to the low side. Canteloupe commands premium prices, and even more valuable are Brick Red and Aqua.

Bowl, fruit; 9½-oz, 5½", from $12 to 14.00
Butter dish, ¼-lb, rare, from $225 to...........................275.00
Coffeepot, AD; from $100 to 125.00
Creamer, stacking, from $18 to 20.00
Gravy bowl, 12-oz, 5¼", from $15 to 20.00
Pitcher, redesigned, from $175 to 200.00
Shakers, stacking, pr, from $30 to 40.00
Teapot, restyled, scarce, from $200 to..........................225.00

Spun Aluminum

Russel Wright's aluminum ware may not have been especially well accepted in its day — it tended to damage easily and seems to have had only limited market appeal — but today's collectors feel quite differently about it, as is apparent in the suggested values noted in the following listings.

Bain Marie, w/griddle bottom, from $450 to 550.00
Bun warmer, from $75 to...85.00
Flower ring, from $125 to..150.00
Ice bucket, from $75 to 100.00
Muddler, from $75 to...100.00
Relish rosette, med..100.00
Spaghetti set, from $500 to 600.00
Vase, 12", from $150 to 175.00

Sterling

Bowl, fruit; 5", from $8 to...10.00
Bowl, salad; 7½", scarce, from $19 to 24.00
Plate, bread & butter; 6", from $5 to.............................7.00
Plate, luncheon; 9", from $9 to 14.00
Platter, oval, 10½", from $18 to.....................................20.00
Soup, onion; 10-oz, from $25 to....................................30.00

Miscellaneous

Country Garden, cruet, from $300 to...........................350.00
Country Garden, ladle, from $125 to 175.00
Flair, lug soup...12.00
Flair, plate, dinner..10.00
Flair, sugar bowl, w/lid...15.00
Home Decorator, bowl, vegetable; oval, deep, from $15 to 18.00
Home Decorator, cup & saucer, from $9 to 13.00
Ideal Adult Kitchen Ware, bowl, salad; from $20 to......25.00
Ideal Adult Kitchen Ware, tumbler, either, sz, ea, from $20 to 25.00
Knowles Esquire, creamer, from $35 to 45.00
Knowles Esquire, cup & saucer, from $12 to 16.00
Knowles Esquire, plate, salad; 8½", from $10 to............12.00
Meladur, bowl, cereal; rare, from $10 to 12.00
Meladur, plate, dinner; 9", rare, from $10 to 12.00
Naturalistic Bauer, flowerpot, #13A, 7", from $500 to................700.00
Naturalistic Bauer, vase, pillow form, #1A, from $550 to............750.00
Pinch cutlery, iced-tea spoon, from $100 to 125.00
Pinch cutlery, knife, from $125 to 150.00
Residential, bowl, divided vegetable; from $20 to..........25.00
Residential, plate, salad; from $8 to 10.00
Theme Formal, cup & saucer, from $100 to 125.00
Theme Formal, plate, salad; from $75 to 100.00
Theme Informal, mug, from $125 to 150.00
Theme Informal, rice bowl/casserole, w/lid, from $200 to...........225.00
White Clover, clock, General Electric, from $75 to 85.00
White Clover, gravy boat, clover decor, from $40 to....................60.00

Russian Art

Before the Revolution in 1917, many jewelers and craftsmen created exquisite marvels of their arts, distinctive in the extravagant detail of their enamel work, jeweled inlays, and use of precious metals. These treasures aptly symbolized the glitter and the romance of the glorious days under the reign of the Tsars of Imperial Russia. The most famous of these master jewelers was Carl Faberge (1852 – 1920), goldsmith to the Romanovs. Following the tradition of his father, he took over the Faberge workshop in 1870. Eventually Faberge employed more than five hundred assistants and set up workshops in Moscow, Kiev, and London as well as in St. Petersburg. His specialties were enamel work, clockwork automated figures, carved animal and human figures of precious or semiprecious stones, cigarette cases, small boxes, scent flasks, and his best-known creations, the Imperial Easter Eggs — each of an entirely different design. By the turn of the century, his influence had spread to other countries, and his work was revered by royalty and the very wealthy. The onset of the war marked the end of the era. Very little of his work remains on the market, and items that are available are very expensive. But several of his contemporaries were goldsmiths whose work can be equally enchanting. Among them are Klingert, Ovchinnikov, Smirnov, Ruckert, Loriye, Cheryatov, Kuzmichev, Nevalainen, Adler, Sbitnev, Third Artel, Wakewa, Holmstrom, Britzin, Wigstrom, Orlov, Nichols, and Plincke. Most of them produced excellent pieces similar to those made by Faberge between 1880 and 1910.

Perhaps the most important bronze Russian artist was Eugenie Alexandrovich Lanceray (1847 – 87). From 1875 until 1887, he modeled many equestrian groups of falconers and soldiers ranging in height from about 20" to 30". Some of them bear the Chopin foundry mark; they are presently worth from $4,000.00 up. Other excellent artists were Schmidt Felling (nineteenth century), who specialized in mounted figures of cossacks wearing military uniforms, and Nicholas Leiberich (late nineteenth century), who also specialized in equestrian groups. Most of the pieces made by the above artists were signed and had the foundry mark (Chopin, Woerfell, etc.).

Russian porcelain is another field where Imperial connections have undoubtedly added to the interest of collectors and museums worldwide. The most important factories were Imperial Russian Porcelain, St. Petersburg (1744 – 1917); Gardner, Moscow (1765 – 1872); Kuznetsoff, St. Petersburg and Moscow (1800 – 1900); Korniloff, St. Petersburg (1800 – 1900); and Babunin, St. Petersburg (1800 – 1900).

Beaker, silver cylinder mk K Faberge, ca 1896, 2⅞" **675.00**
Belt, silver buckle & 35 links w/niello foliage, ca 1900, 32" **900.00**
Bowl, hammered copper, crowned dbl eagle hdl, mc enamel, 1900s, 7½" ...**335.00**
Censer, silvered bronze, mtd w/cherub, 12" **645.00**
Chalice, silver, eng w/implements of Passion, Moscow, 1819, 10¼" ...**700.00**
Cigar case, silver w/niello horses & wagon, Moscow, 1879, 5¼" **400.00**
Cigarette case, silver, eng geometrics, Moscow, ca 1892, 4¼" **175.00**
Cigarette case, silver & niello, geometrics, Moscow, 1885, 5", EX..**400.00**
Cigarette case, silver & niello trompe l'oeil, Moscow, 1889, 4" ..**450.00**
Claret jug, glass w/silver mt mk K Faberge, ca 1900, 12" **2,240.00**
Creamer & sugar bowl, silver, eng floral, I Sveshnikov **500.00**
Cross, altar; silver, 2-pc, God the Father/Mary/John/etc, 19th C, 12"...**1,600.00**
Cross, priest's, silver, eng w/crucified Christ, Kiev, 1864-97, 4" ..**375.00**
Cross, priest's, silver, emb crucified Christ, Moscow, 19th C, 33" ...**450.00**
Glass, vodka; glass w/silver ft, Soviet control mks, 2", pr **55.00**
Icon, Archangel Raphael, gold leaf ground, ca 1850, 19x15" ..**1,345.00**
Icon, Baptism of Chryst, Mstera or Kholui, ca 1890, 12¼x10½"..**1,000.00**
Icon, Birth of Mother of God, Palekh or Mstera workshop, 1900, 12x11"..**1,120.00**
Icon, Holy John the Forerunner, Palekh School, ca 1800, 14x12"...**1,950.00**
Icon, Holy Prince Vladimir, eng/gilt ground, 1900s, 11x9" **3,650.00**
Icon, Mother of God in prayer w/Christ child, 19th C, 11x9" **785.00**
Icon, Mystic Supper, incised/pnt borders, ca 1890, 21x17¼" **2,350.00**
Icon, Prokrov Mother of God, late Palekh School, 1890s, 12x10"..**725.00**
Icon, Sorrow of Our Lord Jesus Christ, 19th C, 12½x10¼" **450.00**
Icon, St Nicholas, ancient style, 19th C, 12¼x10¼" **1,900.00**
Icon, St Seraphim of Sarov w/prayer rope, ca 1903, 10½x8¾"...**450.00**
Icon, Tikhvin Mother of God, Ural school, early 19th C, 9x7"..**900.00**
Icon, Transfiguration, gold leaf ground, ca 1890, 12x11".............**785.00**
Medallion, enamel, St John, Rostov, 18th C, 3¼" +suspension loop...**435.00**
Medallion, silver, Mystic Supper w/mc paste stones, 19th C, 4½" ...**115.00**
Paperweight, silver lizard w/gr stone eyes, Soviet era, 1x4" **225.00**
Pendant, bronze, Christ as angel, ca 1600, 3¼" **500.00**
Pendant, porc, 2 sides: Tsar Nicholas/Imperial Eagle, 2¼" **395.00**
Samovar, brass, ornate hdls, Batashev, ca 1900, 17" **700.00**
Samovar, SP, grapes & branches, ftd, 19th C, 17" **865.00**
Shot glass, silver-gilt & niello w/emb florals, ca 1940, 3" **55.00**
Vase, gilt silver & enamel, dome base, Alekseev, 1899-1908, 4"...**2,600.00**

Sabino

Sabino art glass was produced by Marius-Ernest Sabino in France during the 1920s and 1930s. It was made in opalescent, frosted, and colored glass and was designed to reflect the Art Deco style of that era. In 1960, using molds he modeled by hand, Sabino once again began to produce art glass using a special formula he himself developed that was characterized by a golden opalescence. Although the family continued to produce glassware for export after his death in 1971, they were never able to duplicate Sabino's formula.

Bottle, scent; emb maidens, opal, ovoid, 1950s, 6" **145.00**
Bottle, scent; La Ronde Fleurie, Sabino Paris, 6" **155.00**
Bottle, scent; lappet leaves on bulbous body, 5¼" **130.00**
Box, emb flowers (various szs), Sabino France, 3½x4" dia **150.00**
Cake toppers, geese, unmk, 1930s, 2½", set of 4 ....**225.00**
Dish, snail shell form, Sabino Paris **155.00**
Knife rest, fish **55.00**
Knife rest, poodle figural, Sabino France **48.00**
Knife rest, squirrel, wht opal, 1¼x3½" **45.00**
Statuette, Capelan (fish) **100.00**
Statuette, Ecureuil (squirrel), Sabino France, 3" **45.00**
Statuette, L'Egyptienne, Sabino Paris **130.00**
Statuette, nude w/2 doves, Sabino France, 6½" **450.00**
Statuette, Reveil, Sabino Paris, 8" **355.00**
Vase, Abondance, Sabino Paris in script, 7"..............................**800.00**
Vase, Carangues (fish), Sabino Paris, 5" **220.00**
Vase, dbl row of arches on clear ftd U-form, outer 1 bl, 2nd gold, 7" ...**500.00**

Salesman's Samples and Patent Models

Salesman's samples and patent models are often mistaken for toys or homemade folk art pieces. They are instead actual working models made by very skilled craftsmen who worked as model-makers. Patent models were made until the early 1900s. After that, the patent office no longer required a model to grant a patent. The name of the inventor or the model-maker and the date it was built is sometimes noted on the patent model. Salesman's samples were occasionally made by model-makers, but often they were assembled by an employee of the company. These usually carried advertising messages to boost the sale of the product. Though they are still in use today, the most desirable examples date from the 1800s to about 1945.

Many small stoves are incorrectly termed a 'salesman's sample'; remember that no matter how detailed one may be, it must be considered a toy unless accompanied by a carrying case, the indisputable mark of a salesman's sample.

Windmill, wood with nickel-plated gears and mechanism, with canvas-covered wooden case fitted to hold blades, etc., 20", NM, $1,900.00.

Anvil, Hercules, steel w/red pnt (worn), 5½" **65.00**
Axe & hammer hdls, Torchbrand, cloth roll-up w/12 wood hdls, EX ..**230.00**
Bathtub, American Standard, CI w/pk ceramic, 1950s styling, 6", EX ..**85.00**
Box car, Herbert's Automatic Brake, wood/brass, sliding doors, 26", VG..**4,000.00**
Cabinet, walnut, ornate crest, mirror bk, 2 glass doors, 32x16x10"..**500.00**
Cane, wood w/bird's-eye maple grpt, bone hdl, unscrews at midway, 17"...**200.00**
Caneo, Kennebec...Co, pnt canvas over wood fr, wicker seats, 63", EX..**7,000.00**
Casket, pressed glass w/HP fixtures, lining intact, 14", VG **3,200.00**
Chair, barber's; Theo A Kochs Co, Chicago, EX....................**12,000.00**
Clothes wringer, Horse Shoe/No 2 Gem, CI/wood/hard rubber, 11", VG...**110.00**
Coffin, Springfield, NP metal w/brass hdls, Pat 1900, 9½", EX-.**980.00**
Coffin, unknown mfg, pine, tapered & shouldered, 13½", EX **800.00**

Disc cart, Cerny, to transport disc harrow, red-pnt metal, 11", VG **350.00**
Fire pumper, RW Chapman Fire King, wood/metal w/pnt, 15" L, EX..**3,300.00**
Furnace, Rogers & Vance, brass, door opens, ash collector, 6" base, EX.**345.00**
Furnace, Williamson, cast aluminum/CI, 13", VG......................**290.00**
Gold bars, Engelhard, case of 6, gold-plated metal, case: 12x9", EX..**225.00**
Hand pump, cast metal/brass on wood block, functional, 5½", EX ...**500.00**
Handsaw, Disston, NP w/company advertising, 7¼", VG.............**60.00**
Louis Cherry Candy, tin box w/42-pc single mold candy display, EX+ **110.00**
Mower, Adriance Buckeye, brass/iron, red/yel pnt, EX detail, 18", VG.**7,500.00**
Paper cutter, Diamond, CI arm, wood cutting surface, 1895, 7x7", EX.....**100.00**
Pitchfork, True Temper, oak/brass/tin, in metal/canvas sheath, 30", EX....**290.00**
Plow (horse-drawn), bronze/wood, inventor: Barr, 1870, 23", VG.........**2,245.00**
Plow, NP CI, horse may pull side to side & plow straight, 16", VG.....**1,265.00**
Police badges, fancy, 8 in 15x9" case, bk mk: Blackinton, M **435.00**
Popcorn popper, hand-held, GD Dudley, dtd 1867, w/paperwork ..**2,500.00**
Rocking recliner, woven wicker, EX workmanship, 17" L, VG ...**230.00**
Snowshoes, varnished rawhide webbing on wood fr, 19½" L, pr.**100.00**
Sofa, Emp, heavy wood fr, uphl, horsehair filled, 1830s, 14", VG.......**2,000.00**
Steam boiler, Continental/Hodge, cut-away view, opening doors, 9", EX ...**400.00**
Stitching device, cast brass/steel/wood w/pnt remnants, complex, 12"..**635.00**
Teller's window, Yale & Town, hand-cvd oak/etched glass, 28x20", EX..**1,400.00**
Toilet seat, Church, lt gr MOP finish w/chrome hdw, 8½" **175.00**
Vacuum cleaner, Hamilton Beach #10, 1934, operational, w/case, 13".**9,000.00**
Voting machine, Shoup, Democrat/Republican names, pressed steel, 10"...**460.00**
Wagon chasis, wood w/brass hubs/rims, spoke wheels, J Wood/1867, 17"..**1,350.00**
Washer, Fairy/Gibson, wood/galvanized metal, red w/yel stencil, 14", G **1,000.00**
Washer, wood/metal bbl, Deluxe Washer Co, ca 1915, 11x10", EX+..**1,850.00**
Water pump, John Best, Pat 1906, cast brass, 20", VG **1,400.00**
Water pump, NP CI, adjustable arm, variable leverage, 11", VG ..**865.00**
Windmill, Rome Deluxe, galvanized metal/screws, litho sign, 17", VG ..**175.00**
Wool carder, brass/wood/bone, 11", VG......................................**290.00**
Yoke, leather, hand stitched w/gr velvet under surface, 12", VG ..**145.00**

Salt Glaze

As early as the 1600s, potters used common salt to glaze their stoneware. This was accomplished by heating the salt and introducing it into the kiln at maximum temperature. The resulting gray-white glaze was a thin, pitted surface that resembles the peel of an orange. We recommend *Collector's Encyclopedia of Salt Glaze Stoneware* by Jerry G. Taylor and Jerry and Kay Lowrance (Collector Books).

Bottle, England, ca 1750s, stain, 9" **535.00**
Pitcher, bl w/hunt scene & grapevines relief, basketweave base, 7½"..**350.00**
Plate, detailed molded surface w/rtcl panels, English, 12" **450.00**
Teapot, emb vintage, heart shape, serpent spout, 1750s, 3¾" ..**2,575.00**
Teapot, mc floral & fence, crabstock hdl, 1750s, 3¼", EX **550.00**
Teapot, morning glories/trellis emb, mk England, 6" **165.00**

Salt Shakers

The screw-top salt shaker was invented by John Mason in 1858. Around 1871 when salt became more refined, some ceramic shakers were molded with perforated tops.

Today's Victorian glass salt shaker collectors' interests primarily encompass art glass of all types and colored glass, with preference given to hand-painted cranberry and ruby glass forms. Also, examples in rubena, opalescent, and custard glass are very desirable in both decorated and undecorated styles.

If you would like to learn more about Victorian glass salt shakers, we recommend *The World of Salt Shakers, Third Edition*, written by Mildred and Ralph Lechner; their address may be found in the Directory

under Virginia. (Mildred and Ralph deal only in Victorian glass shakers. Please do not contact them with questions pertaining to novelty types; written queries require a long self-addressed stamped envelope.) In the following listings, prices are for old, original shakers (one unless noted pair) in excellent condition.

Victorian Glass

Bale, bl w/HP flowers, Pairpoint, 1894-1900, 2⅜".......................**200.00**
Barrel, hobnail w/ribbed base, clear amber, 1885-96, 3¼" **30.00**
Barrel, Inv't Honeycomb; amber/flowers, New England, 1884, 3¼"........**155.00**
Barrel, opaque w/banded design, Challinor/Taylor #14, 1888-91, 2⅜"......**45.00**
Cylinder, honeycomb, clear bl w/HP stemmed flowers, 1885-87, 3½"....**105.00**
Cylinder, Plain Neck; rubena stain w/HP flowers, 1885-1891, 3¾" **215.00**
Diamond Base Lower Half, emerald w/HP flowers, 1901-07, 3¼".**60.00**
Diamonds w/Ribs, ball shape, opaque gr, Dithridge, 1894-1900, 2⅜"..**45.00**
Egg, Flat Bottom; opaque w/HP hen & rooster, 1889-99, pr **400.00**
Fence, 18 vertical ribs, clear bl homogeneous, 1891-1901, 2⅞" **35.00**
Fine Cut & Block, clear ruby-stained, 1890-1900, 3¾" **60.00**
Fleur-de-Lis Spike, clear aqua, 4" **70.00**
Gibson Girl, milk glass cylinder w/HP image, Kokomo, 1904, 3⅜" ...**65.00**
Hex-Curves, tapered barrel, opaque wht, 1899-1910, 2¾" **30.00**
Hexagonal, flared base, emb leaves, opaque w/HP flowers, 1900-08, 3" ..**30.00**
Ice Cube, opaque w/HP flowers, 1896-1904, 2⅛x1⅞" **45.00**
Idyll, curved w/emb design, clear bl w/gold, Jefferson #251, 1907, 3" ..**150.00**
Lobed Heart, cranberry w/HP flowers, Mt WA/Pairpoint, 1894, 2¼"..**175.00**
Marble shaped, HP winter scene, Boston & Sandwich, 1780, 1¾" **200.00**
Melon, opaque w/HP floral swag, Gillinder, 1903-05, 2⅝" **110.00**
Net & Scroll, opaque gr, Dithridge, 1894-1900, 2⅞"....................**55.00**
Optic Ribs, Bulging; clear cranberry w/HP daisies, 1886-90, 2¾" **215.00**
Paneled, 4-sided, tapered, clear dk bl, 2-pc metal top, 1891-1900, 4" .**50.00**
Paneled Hexagon, McKee, 1886, 2¾" **28.00**
Pear, opaque w/HP flowers, Mt WA (?), 1897-1903, 2¾", pr **225.00**
Pillar, Ring Neck; clear bl w/HP flowers or stork, 1886-91, 3⅞" **160.00**
Pillar, Sixteen; cranberry opal, Hobbs, Brockunier, 1885-90, 3⅜" **180.00**
Ribbed Drape, opaque/HP rose, gold trim, Jefferson #2501, 1904, 3¼" ..**225.00**
Ring Neck Variant, bl/opal swirls, Hobbs, Brockunier, 1885-90, 3½" **115.00**
Satina Swirl, frosted vaseline, Hobbs, Brockunier, 1885-90, 3½" ..**190.00**
Scroll, Beaded; opaque w/HP flowers, Helmschmied, 1904, 3¼", pr..**300.00**
Scroll, clear, McKee #402, 1904-1910, 2"......................................**17.00**
Seaweed, wht opal, Hobbs, Brockunier, 1890-91, 3" **85.00**
Slender Neck, wht opaque w/HP flowers, Helmschmied, 1905-07, 3⅜" ..**160.00**
Sphere, Honeycomb Opalescent; clear amber w/opal dots, 1888-1904, 2¼"...**90.00**
Swirl, Dainty; clear reverse rubena, 2-pc top, 1889-94, 3⅜" **210.00**
Swirl, Multi; opaque bl ball form, Dithridge, 1894-1900, 2⅝" **65.00**
Swirl, Spiral; clear cranberry, 1888-94, 3" **105.00**
Tank, Inv't T'print; clear amber w/HP flowers, 1887-84, 3⅛"..........**175.00**
Triplets, opaque wht w/HP floral swags, Flint, 1901-05, 3⅛" **45.00**
Tripod w/Diamond Band, clear canary yel vaseline, 1904-10, 3½"....**130.00**
Twin Variant, wht satin w/HP flowers, Pairpoint, 1886-93, 2⅝", pr..**230.00**
Twisted Cane, opaque bl, 1895-1905, 2⅝" **60.00**
Urn, tapered, translucent custard w/HP floral spray, 1899, 2⅝" **60.00**
Wheel, Hub; clear bl w/HP design, 1894-1900 ....**80.00**
Zippered Borders, ruby-stained thin glass, 1898-1903, 3½" **80.00**

Novelty Shakers

Those interested in novelty shakers will enjoy *Salt and Pepper Shakers, Volumes I, II, III,* and *IV*, by Helene Guarnaccia; *Standard Encyclopedia of Salt and Pepper Shakers, Figural and Novelty, Volumes I* and *II*, by Melva Davern; and *Florence's Big Book of Salt and Pepper Shakers* by Gene Florence. All are available at your local library or from Collector Books. Note: 'Mini' shakers are no taller than 2". Instead of having a cork, the user was directed to 'use tape to cover hole.' Our advisor for novelty salt shakers is Judy Posner; she is listed in the Directory under Pennsylvania. See also Regal; Rosemeade; Occupied Japan; Shawnee; other specific manufacturers.

Novelty Advertising

Borden's Elsie & Elmer (half-figures in chef hats), ceramic, 1940s, pr...150.00
Dooley & Shultz Utica Beer steins, ceramic, taller: 4½", pr........125.00
Fingerhut truck, 2-pc, ceramic, 1¾x3¾" 35.00
Flour Fred (Homepride Flour), hard plastic, 3¼", pr...............55.00
GE refrigerators, plastic, ice maker in door, pr......................25.00
Greyhound buses, pnt metal w/wht tops, bl trim, Japan, pr..........55.00
Hersey's Kiss, ceramic, chocolate color, pr.............................20.00
Hersey's Milk Chocolate mugs, wht/brn/silver candy wrapper middle, pr...20.00
Nugget Sam for Nugget Casino, ceramic, Japan, 1950s, 4", pr......75.00
Peerless Beer men, Hartland Plastic/La Cross Breweries, 1950s, 5", pr...75.00
Prager Beer bottles, glass w/metal tops, pr 28.00
Quaker State Motor Oil cans, heavy cb, 1940s-50s, 1½", pr.........40.00
RCA's Nipper & gramophone, plastic, 1950s, pr......................30.00
Safe-T Cup ice cream cones (vanilla/chocolate), ceramic, 1950s, 4", pr....55.00
Seagrams 7, red plastic, 7 on base, 1950s premium, 3¾", pr..........35.00
St Lawrence Dairy, cream-top glass bottles, metal lids, 3¼", pr, NM...75.00
Sunshine Baker, ceramic, sm, pr 25.00
Tappan ranges, Harvest Gold, dtd 1976, 1-pc 28.00
Waring blender, plastic, pr 20.00

Novelty Animals, Fish, and Birds

Bear artist & easel, ceramic, 3¼", pr....................................45.00
Bears, dressed up, ceramic, orig corks, 3¼", pr 18.00
Brahma bulls walking, ceramic, pr 22.00
Cat on 8-ball, Japan, 4", pr...35.00
Circus horses, Salty & Peppy, ceramic, vintage, 4", pr................24.00
Collie dogs (realistic), ceramic, pr 22.00
Dog & cat in gingham & calico, ceramic, wht w/mc decor, pr......25.00
Farmer & Mrs Pig, ceramic, Enesco, 1980, 3½", pr...................25.00
Fish (realistic w/speckles), glossy porc, vintage, 4¼", pr..............35.00
Giraffes, ceramic, wht w/blk spots & speckles, gold trim, pr..........15.00
Horse heads, ceramic, Japan, 3½", pr 15.00
Horses (stylized), ceramic, wht w/brn manes & tails, pr 10.00
Horses rearing, bone china, 1 blk & 1 tan w/wht accents, pr........15.00
Lions in wide stance (realistic), bone china, pr..........................15.00
Mallard ducks, ceramic, mc, gr Japan mk, 2¾", pr....................10.00
Monkeys, ceramic, Napco/Japan, 1950s, 3⅜", pr 26.00
Pandas (playful), ceramic, red Japan mk, 3½", pr......................12.00
Pig bride & groom, ceramic, red Japan mk, 3¼", pr, NM 36.00
Pig nursing baby pig, ceramic, wht w/blk spots, pr 25.00
Pigs, interlocking, plastic, Fitz & Floyd, 1976, 3x4", pr 40.00
Pigs standing (stylized cartoon features), ceramic, sm, pr 15.00
Purple cows, ceramic, Thames, 1950s, 3⅝x3⅞", pr....................35.00
Rabbit couple (Beatrix Potter style), ceramic, mc on wht, pr........15.00
Rabbit in hat, ceramic, 2-pc...12.00
Raccoons, ceramic, red Japan ink stamp, 1950s, 2½", pr..............15.00
Squirrel w/acorn, pottery (heavier), 3½", pr 10.00
St Bernards (barrels mk S&P), ceramic, pr...............................25.00
Swordfish leaping, ceramic, bright colors, pr............................15.00
Whales w/tails up (toothy smiles), ceramic, pr...........................12.00
Woof & Poof dogs smoking pipes, ceramic, gold trim, 4", pr.........50.00

Miscellaneous Novelties

Alcatraz inmates, ceramic, Exclusive BP Japan paper labels, 4½", pr ..45.00
Apples (realistic), ceramic, red/yel/wht shading, glossy, pr 8.00
Bahama policemen, ceramic, 1950s, 4⅜", pr................................38.00

Baked potatoes w/pats of butter, ceramic, pr 10.00
Bed & pillow, ceramic, glossy, wht w/pk & bl, 2-pc.....................25.00
Beet man (anthroporphic), ceramic, ruffled collar, w/gold, 2½", pr ..32.00
Cigar resting in ashtray, ceramic, 1½x2¼", 2-pc........................30.00
Cigarettes & lighter, ceramic, vintage, pr..................................26.00
Coffee grinder & coffeepot, ceramic, pr...................................20.00
Cow & moon, ceramic, unglazed bottoms, Am, 1950s, 3", pr 30.00
Crab in clam shell, ceramic, clam: 2⅞", smaller crab, 1950s, pr......30.00
Dice & cards, Reno souvenir, ceramic, Exclusive BP Japan, 3½", pr..26.00
Flower kids (anthropomorphic), ceramic, Japan, 1⅞", pr..............19.00
Gun & bullet, ceramic, vintage, 4", pr 24.00
Ham slice in skillet, ceramic, pr..20.00
Kansas (state) & flower, Victoria Ceramics, 1950s, pr.................24.00
Mackinac bridge (MI souvenir), ceramic, Japan label, 2x5¾", 2-pc...45.00
Mermaid & deep-sea diver, ceramic, 3½", pr 75.00
Miss Muffett & spider, ceramic, Poinsettia Studio, pr.................75.00
Nude boy statues, ceramic, Bruxelles, 3⅝", pr...........................49.00
Pear & orange people (anthropomorphic), ceramic, Japan, 2½", pr...24.00
Penguins, pnt wood, 1950s, 2½x2", pr.....................................12.00
Photo album & camera, ceramic, pr 25.00
Pilgrim boy & girl, ceramic, Hallmark, 1970, pr........................15.00
Racing cars, Salty & Peppy, glossy porc, 1¼x3½", pr 35.00
Santa & Mrs Claus in rocking chairs, ceramic, pr.......................15.00
Scarecrow couple, ceramic, vintage, Am, 3", pr.........................28.00
Scottish boy & girl, ceramic, Niagara Falls souvenir, Canada, pr....24.00
Sewing machine & dress form, ceramic, miniature, 2", pr.............95.00
Snowman couple holding letters S&P, bsk w/glazed & gold trim, pr..10.00
Southern Belles, ceramic, glossy, gr PY Japan 'N' in circle, pr.......38.00
Toaster & toast (stacking), ceramic, USA Pottery, 1950s, 3⅞", pr ..20.00
Wrestlers, realistic, ceramic, Japan label, 4¼", pr 45.00

Salts, Open

Before salt became refined, processed, and free-flowing as we know it today, it was necessary to serve it in a salt cellar. An innovation of the early 1800s, the master salt was placed by the host and passed from person to person. Smaller individual salts were a part of each place setting. A small silver spoon was used to sprinkle it onto the food.

If you would like to learn more about the subject of salts, we recommend *5,000 Open Salts*, written by William Heacock and Patricia Johnson, with many full-color illustrations and current values.

Our advisor for this category is Chris Christensen; he is listed in the Directory under California. In the listings below, the numbers refer to the Johnson and Heacock book and *Pressed Glass Salt Dishes* by L.W. and D.B. Neal. Lines with 'repro' within the description reflect values for reproduced salts.

Key:
EPNS — electroplated nickel silver   HM — hallmarked

Animals, Figurals, and Novelties

Bird & Berry, amber or bl, McKee, HJ-931M, old......................55.00
Bird & Berry, unmk Degenhart, HJ-933, colors, minimum............30.00
Chicken, covered, milk glass, Westmoreland, HJ-949 ....25.00
Duck, covered, clear, red beak, HJ-1012.................................45.00
Duck, pressed, heavy, HJ-4677 ....45.00
Elk pulling sleigh, mk 800 silver 600.00
Horseshoe, HJ-3741, ind...25.00
Rabbit, covered, clear, mk Vallerysthal, HJ-3750.......................55.00
Sleigh, Fostoria, HJ-3735, ca 1940......................................45.00
Squirrel on stump, various colors, Boyd, HJ-929-930, repro 12.00
Squirrel on Tree, #3756, ind..55.00

Swan, Crown Tuscan, Cambridge, HJ-936, 1970s, repro 35.00
Swan, str neck, Crown Tuscan, Cambridge, HJ-935 ....100.00
Swan, str neck, gr, pk or amber, Cambridge, HJ-935.....................35.00
Swan pulling cart, bl carnival, HJ-941, 1970s repro......................30.00
Swan pulling cart, clear, HJ-941, ca 1890.......................................65.00
Turtle, amber, bl or milk glass, HJ-4475, 3¼"...............................65.00
Wheelbarrow, chocolate, Greentown, HJ-4669 ....600.00
Wheelbarrow, Nile Green, Greentown, HJ-4669 ....300.00

Cameo, Art Glass, and Miscellaneous

Amethyst glass, tub shape, sgn Sowerby, HJ-413...........................85.00
Bl opal, dbl, ped ft, Fr, HJ-144, ca 1910 ....85.00
Bl slag, tureen shape, Sowerby, HJ-385..85.00
Cased, pk & wht ruffled top, HJ-126...135.00
Cut, Russian pattern, heavy, rnd, HJ-3708, master 35.00
Daum Nancy, windmill scene, HJ-10 ....1,200.00
Daum Nancy, winter scene 1,500.00
English, William & Mary, yel vaseline, HJ-69................................65.00

French, silver with etched glass inserts, 4", $75.00.

Intaglio, animals or butterfly HP, sgn, HJ-159.............................60.00
Intaglio, bl, gr, etc, unsgn, HJ-215..25.00
Intaglio, HP animals/etched butterfly, HJ-145 or HJ-157, ea 60.00
Intaglio, pnt animal center, HJ-160...60.00
Intaglio, 2 in jeweled tree holder, HJ-190...................................125.00
Millefiori, European, HJ-609, ca 1900, 2" dia 450.00
Monot & Stumpf, HJ-19, ca 1900, ind..110.00
Mt Washington, HJ-35 to HJ-44, unsgn.......................................110.00
Opal w/vaseline ruffles, HJ-72..125.00
Plique-a-jour, Viking boat, Norway, 930-S silver, HJ-83, 2½".....850.00
Sowerby, bl slag, HJ-385...110.00
Sowerby, cream opaque, HJ-385...85.00
Sowerby, HJ-385 & HJ-2090, sgn & #d, ea 85.00
Sowerby, purple slag, HJ-385, ca 1880..110.00
Steuben, Calcite, ped ft, HJ-34...295.00
Threaded glass, gr, 'Salt,' sterling rim, HJ-377.............................85.00
Tiffany, bl, ruffled top, sgn, HJ-30...475.00
Tiffany, pulled ears, sgn, HJ-3 ....300.00
Tiffany, witch's pot, sgn, HJ-1 ....300.00
Vaseline, clear rigaree, berry pontil, SP fr, HJ-96........................250.00
Venetian glass, swans..35.00
Webb, Burmese, HJ-75, ca 1890, 1¾" dia 750.00
Webb, 2-color, sgn, HJ-84...1,500.00

China and Porcelain

Austria, HP, mk, HJ-1272, rnd, ind 15.00
Belleek, HP, ruffled top, mk, HJ-1310, rnd, ind.............................35.00
Belleek, star shaped, 3rd blk mk..75.00
Celery salt, HP, HJ-1720, ind...15.00
Dresden, attached flowers, HJ-1689, ind 45.00
Elfinware, heavy decor, Germany, HJ-1270, ind.............................30.00
Elfinware, Japan, HJ-1222, ind...15.00
Elfinware, swan, Germany, ornate, HJ-1039...................................35.00

Elfinware, tub, Germany, HJ-1250, ind...30.00
Elfinware, wheelbarrow, Germany, HJ-1244, ind 65.00
Haviland, HJ-1400, ind..35.00
HP, artist sgn, scalloped ft, HJ-1390, ind.......................................20.00
Limoges, HP, mk, HJ-1275, rnd, ind...15.00
Meissen, HJ-1595, sq, ind...60.00
Nippon, celery salt, HJ-1714, ind 12.00
Nippon, HP, HJ-1365, ind...15.00
Nippon, HP, ped ft, HJ-1495, ind...20.00
Nippon, HP, rnd, 3 legs, #1423-1425...15.00
Nippon, HP floral tub, HJ-1454, ind...20.00
Pickard, HJ-1569, sq, ind..45.00
Royal Bayreuth, animal decor, ped ft, HJ-1666, ind.....................145.00
Royal Bayreuth, figural claw, HJ-1667, ind....................................35.00
Royal Copenhagen, HJ-1332, ind..35.00
Royal Worcester, HJ-1861, ca 1862, ind.......................................150.00
Satsuma, HJ-1932, ca 1940-60, ind..25.00

Lacy Glass

American, non-flint, ca 1920-40, repro, VG...................................45.00
Avon, HJ-3506, repro 10.00
French, amber, non-flint, HJ-1771, ca 1920-40, repro, VG...........65.00
Metro Museum of Art, vaseline, bl, etc, MMA, repro, VG...........20.00
Neal BF-1, basket of flowers, HJ-3462, VG.................................125.00
Neal BF-1s, lt gr, Sandwich, chips..550.00
Neal BS-2, opal, Beaded Scroll, Sandwich, NM..........................175.00
Neal BS-3, chalk wht, Beaded Scroll, Sandwich, EX 500.00
Neal BS-3, dk opaque violet, Beaded Scroll.................................750.00
Neal BT-2, cobalt, boat, Stourbridge, NM 900.00
Neal BT-8, cobalt, boat, Sandwich, VG..600.00
Neal BT-9, opal, boat, NM...500.00
Neal BT-9, violet, boat, NM...600.00
Neal DI-8, dbl, HJ-3460, roughage on bottom..............................175.00
Neal OL-12, NM..175.00

Pottery and Faience

Adams, HM, HJ-1849, ca 1902..120.00
Doulton, Lambeth, sterling HM rim, HJ-1851, ca 1900 ....85.00
Moorcroft, sterling HM rim, London, HJ-1762, ca 1920 ....65.00
Niloak, rnd, HJ-1735, 1½"...65.00
Quimper, dbl, w/dog, HJ-1134 ....110.00
Quimper, HP shoe, Breton figures...75.00
Quimper, pr of shoes, HJ-1162, ca 1940 ....45.00
Royal Doulton, HP animals, HJ-1859, ca 1890..............................85.00
Royal Doulton, pyramid shape, HJ-1870, ca 1873 ....150.00
Royal Doulton, sterling HM rim, HJ-1870, ca 1873 ....115.00
Wedgwood, sterling rim, sgn, HJ-1850, ca 1897..........................160.00

Silver with Cobalt Liners

Bulbous bottom, pierced fr, Sterling, HJ-662.................................75.00
Oval, 4 ball ft, ribbon & garlands, 800, HJ-690 ....75.00
Oval, 4 ball ft, Sterling, HJ-670..65.00
Oval, 4 claw ft, Sheffield, HJ-679, ca 1820 ....110.00
Ped, SP, Bart & Sons, HJ-660 ....70.00
Rnd, flower & leaf in relief, 3-ftd, HJ-685, ca 1850......................85.00
Rnd ped w/appl decor, Sterling, HJ-702, ca 1880 ....100.00

Sterling

Albert Cole, medallion, HJ-4208, ca 1850....................................250.00
American, Lenox insert, lattice holder, HJ-3856 ....45.00

Chinese, mini house w/shaker set, HJ-4743 ....**200.00**
English, boxed set of 2, apostle spoon, HJ-4794.........................**225.00**
French, ornate, HM, matching spoon, HJ-3937, ind **125.00**
German, basket, ped ft, HM 800, HJ-4228 ....**110.00**
German, swan, HM 800, matching spoon, HJ-4299, ca 1890 ....**95.00**
Gorham, medallion, ped ft, HJ-3976, ca 1870 ....**175.00**
Reed & Barton, ped ft, HJ-4226, ca 1900, master, pr **250.00**
Russian, chair, HM, dtd, HJ-4737..**500.00**
Russian, HP over sterling, 3 ball ft, HJ-2004 ....**550.00**
Russian, rnd, ftd, HM, HJ-4053, ca 1893, ind **75.00**
Steiff, chased, w/pepper, HJ-4385, 1918 ....**175.00**
Tiffany, fish, matching spoon, HJ-4324 ....**150.00**
Viking, HP, HM, matching spoon, HJ-2002 to HJ-2005, ea........**125.00**

Samplers

American samplers were made as early as the colonial days; even earlier examples from seventeenth-century England still exist today. Changes in style and design are evident down through the years. Verses were not added until the late seventeenth century. By the eighteenth century, samplers were used not only for sewing experience but also as an educational tool. Young ladies, who often signed and dated their work, embroidered numbers and letters of the alphabet and practiced fancy stitches as well. Fruits and flowers were added for borders; birds, animals, and Adam and Eve became popular subjects. Later houses and other buildings were included. By the nineteenth century, the American Eagle and the little red schoolhouse had made their appearances.

Many factors bear on value: design and workmanship, strength of color, the presence of a signature and/or a date (both being preferred over only one or the other, and earlier is better), and, of course, condition.

ABC rows, info re: name/1817, lt stains/rpr, 15x17" **700.00**
ABCs, homespun, sgn/1843, in recent 10x13" fr **360.00**
ABCs (sm row)+many devices: animals/people/etc, sgn/1768, 21x14", VG.**2,090.00**
ABCs/birds/animals, bright colors, edge damage, 9¼x12¾"+rpt fr ..**385.00**
ABCs/birds/berries w/strawberry border, homespun, 1868, 18x14"+fr...**330.00**
ABCs/checked pattern/flowers, sgn/1796, 11½x8" **2,000.00**
ABCs/convent/vines/flowers, OH, 16¼x20⅝" **770.00**
ABCs/family register, homespun, 1824, minor stains, in 18x19" fr...**385.00**
ABCs/flowering plants/numbers/hearts, 1822, 18x10"+veneer fr .**385.00**
ABCs/fruit baskets/trees/birds/dog, homespun, sgn/1843, 10x11"+fr..**550.00**
ABCs/heart/dmn, homespun, name/1762, 9½x9½"+old fr **770.00**
ABCs/house/birds/strawberries/family history, Welsh, 17x18"+new fr ...**1,200.00**
ABCs/house/flowers/trees/verse, MA, 1825, 15¾x12"..............**1,100.00**
ABCs/memorial scene/geometrics, 1839, 16½x16¾" **635.00**
ABCs/numerals/geometric flowers/baskets/hearts, MA/1825, 17x17"..**1,500.00**
ABCs/trees/verse/flower border, homespun, EX color, 17x12".....**700.00**
ABCs/verse, blk thread, 1818, 17¼x7¾" **460.00**
ABCs/verse//vines, homespun, sgn/1829, in recent 12x13" fr **330.00**
ABCs/verse/dmn border, homespun, sgn/1816, 16x15"..............**800.00**
ABCs/verse/florals, gr homespun, OH/1824, minor stains, 12x13"+fr...**2,400.00**
ABCs/verse/stylized floral urns, sgn Hannah age 10, 19x17", EX..**1,750.00**
ABCs/verses/floral borders, sgn/1809, 17x16¼", EX in fr.........**2,990.00**
ABCs/verses/flower baskets, silk on linen, stains/etc, 18x17"+fr...**1,265.00**
Adam & Eve/ABCs/verse/angel/etc, stains/sm holes, 10x16"+early fr...**1,045.00**
Adam & Eve/apple tree/lions (sm elements), sgn/1815, 12x17"..**1,175.00**
Adam & Eve/manor house/verse, sgn/1854, wool/linen, 15x17"...**2,000.00**
Baskets of flowers/lions/birds/deer/etc, silk/linen, sgn/1816, 17x13"...**1,175.00**
Bird on tree branch, cross/chain stitch on homespun, 9x7", VG...**495.00**
Birds/trees/dogs/verse (sm elements), sgn/1810, 12x8"................**995.00**
Butterflies/flower basket/bird in tree/etc in silk, sgn/1825, 19x19"...**2,090.00**
Castle tower/trees/man in boat, well done, 8x6¾", VG **470.00**
Cross stitch ABCs/#s, house/barn/bldg along bottom, sgn/1819, 17x18"...**2,475.00**

Family register, trees/floral chain border, silk/linen, 1820s, 21x20" ...**5,250.00**
Flowers/trees (Berlin-type work), linen, sgn/mid-1800s, 37x33"+fr.**1,725.00**
Hymn/lg brick manor house, sgn/1818, silk/linen, 23x20" **1,175.00**
Map of England & Wales, silk on linen, sgn/1793, 24½x20½" ..**1,725.00**
Peacock w/strawberry in its mouth, strawberry border, 11x14"....**990.00**
Poem, cat/rooster/flowers/birds/etc, name/1823, color has run, 22x18"...**1,100.00**
Verse/brick/house/sm people/animals, sgn Hannah age 8, 20x20" **1,950.00**
Verse/lg manor house w/sheep & shepherdess, sgn/1846, 24x23" **4,700.00**
Verses (2), vining strawberry borders, silk floss, sgn/1788, 19x19"........**935.00**
World map w/flowers/Capt Cook's voyages, sgn/1785, 18x29", EX ...**4,300.00**

Sandwich Glass

The Boston and Sandwich Glass Company was founded in 1820 by Deming Jarves in Sandwich, Massachusetts. Their first products were simple cruets, salts, half-pint jugs, and lamps. They were attributed with being one of the first to perfect a method for pressing glass, a step toward the manufacture of the 'lacy' glass which they made until about 1840. Many other types of glass were made there — cut, colored, overshot, hobnail, and opalescent among them. After the Civil War, profits began to dwindle due to the keen competition of the Western factories which were situated in areas rich in natural gas and easily accessible sand and coal deposits. The end came with an unreconcilable wage dispute between the workers and the company, and the factory closed in 1888. Today colored Sandwich commands the highest prices.

In 1907 the vacant glasshouse was purchased and refurbished by the Alton Manufacturing Company. They specialized in lighting fixtures, but under the direction of an ex-Tiffany glassblower and former Sandwich resident James H. Grady, they also produced a line of iridescent art glass called Trevaise, examples of which are very rare today. It was often decorated with pulled feathers, whorls, leaves, and vines similar to the glassware produced by Tiffany, Quezal, and Durand. Examples that surface on today's market range in price from $1,500.00 to $2,000.00 and up. Trevaise was made for less than one year. Due to financial problems, the company closed in 1908.

Our advisor for this category is Elizabeth Simpson; she is listed in the Directory under Maine. See also Cup Plates; Lacy Glass; Salts, Open; other specific types of glass.

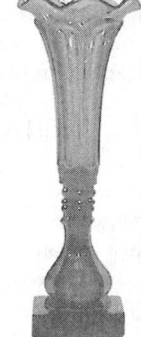

Vase, Loop, sapphire blue, tooled rim, applied by wafer to pressed base, 1840 – 60, 9½", NM, $1,400.00.

Bowl, Plume, dk amber, 1x6" **165.00**
Candlestick, turq, dolphin std, sq base, 10¼" **450.00**
Candlesticks, bl & clambroth, acanthus leaf std, sq base, 11", EX.........**1,265.00**
Candlesticks, clambroth, sq 2-step dolphin base/petal sockets, 10", pr .**1,650.00**
Candlesticks, vaseline, sq dolphin 2-step base/petal sockets, 10", pr **2,000.00**
Candlesticks, vaseline, 1-step dolphin base/petal sockets, 10", VG, pr.....**750.00**
Creamer, cobalt, b3m, paneled & reeded, 1825-40, 4½x2¾" ..**2,875.00**
Decanter, Dmn Quilt, Sunburst & ribs, molded stopper, 9½", pr....**550.00**
Lamp, clambroth, paneled baluster/sq base, pewter caps, att, 10", EX..**700.00**
Sugar bowl, Gothic Arch, canary flint, ca 1840s, att, EX...........**300.00**

Tray, Gothic Arch & Thistle, oblong, ca 1845, 1¾x7x10" **290.00**
Vase, Bigler, amethyst, gauffered rim, 1840-60, 11½"..............**2,185.00**
Vase, Loop, amethyst, gauffered rim, octagonal std, 10"...........**2,000.00**
Vase, tulip; amethyst, scalloped rim, octagonal base, 10" **4,600.00**
Vase, tulip; bl-gr, scalloped rim, octagonal base, 1845-65, 9½"...**4,000.00**
Vase, tulip; emerald gr, scalloped rim, paneled sides, 10", pr....**9,200.00**
Vase, Twisted Loop, amethyst, gauffered rim, hexagonal std, 10"..**3,200.00**
Vase, vaseline, 4-printie, hexagonal base, 1840-60, 11½", pr ..**1,000.00**

Santa Barbara Ceramic Design

Established in 1976 by current director Raymond Markow following three years of refining his decorative process, Santa Barbara Ceramic Design arose with less auspicious beginnings than the Ohio potteries — no financial backing and no machinery beyond that available to ancient potters: wheel, kiln, brushes, and paint.

The company produced intricate, colorful, hand-painted flora and fauna designs on traditional pottery forms, primarily vases and table lamps. Although artistically aligned with turn-of-the-century art potteries, the techniques used were unique and developed within the studio.

Vibrant glaze stains with wax emulsion were applied by brush over a graduated multicolor background, followed by elaborate sgraffito detailing on petals and leaves. In the early 1980s a white stoneware body was incorporated to further brighten the color palette, and during the last few years sgraffito was replaced by detailing with a fine brush.

Early pieces were thrown. Mid-1980 saw a transition to casting, except for experimental or custom pieces. Artists were encouraged to be creative and often given individual gallery exhibitions. Custom orders were welcomed, and experimentation occurred regularly; the resulting pieces are the most rare and seldom appear today. Limited production lines evolved including the Collector Series that featured an elaborate ornamental border designed to enhance the primary design. The Artist's Collection was a numbered series of pieces by senior artists, usually combining flora and fauna.

The company's approach to bold colors and surface decoration influenced many contemporary potters and inspired imitation in both pottery and glass during the craft renaissance of the 1970s and 1980s. Several artists successfully made use of the studio's designs and techniques after leaving. Authentic pieces bear the artist's initials, date, and 'SBCD' marked in black stain and if thrown, the potter's inscription.

Markow employed as many as three potters and twelve decorators at a given time. The ware was marketed through craft festivals and wholesale distribution to art and craft galleries nationwide. An estimated 100,000 art pottery pieces were made before a transition in the late 1980s to silk-screened household and garden items which remain in production today.

Though less than thirty years old, Santa Barbara Ceramic Design's secondary market has seen upwards of 1,000 pieces change hands; these are often viewed as bargains compared to their Rookwood and Weller Hudson counterparts. For artist/potter marks from 1979 to 1989, e-mail johntasha@aol.com or visit the craft café at www.johnguthrie.com. Our advisor is John Guthrie; he is listed in the Directory under South Carolina.

Lamp, #5118, iris, Itoko Takeuchi, 1984, 11"................................**225.00**
Lamp, #5118, iris, unsgn, ca 1984, 11" **195.00**
Lamp, #5119, bouquet, Itoko Takeuchi, 1984, 15½" **592.00**
Lamp, #5119, iris/gladiola, Laurie Linn Ball, 1982, 15½"............**495.00**
Lamp, #5119, morning glory, Laurie Linn Ball, 1986, 15½".......**295.00**
Lamp, #5119lg, bouquet, Laurie Linn Ball, 1982, 17"..................**495.00**
Lamp, #5130, lily of the valley, Itoko Takeuchi, 1984, 7" **128.00**
Lamp, #5130, poppy, Laurie Linn Ball, 1986, 7" **166.00**
Lamp, #7101, apple blossom, Gary Ba-Han, 1984, 13", pr **650.00**
Lamp, #7105, columbine, Margaret Gibson, 1984, 17"................**446.00**

Lamp, #7105, iris, Dorie Knight-Hutchinson, 1984, 17"............**335.00**
Lamp, #7115, fuchsia/bird, Dorie Knight-Hutchinson, 1984, 16"..**485.00**
Lamp, #7115, poppy, Laurie Linn Ball, 1986, 16" **395.00**
Lamp, #7115, tulip, Itoko Takeuchi, 1986, 16" **585.00**
Lamp, #7125, calla lily, Itoko Takeuchi, 1984, 18" **375.00**
Lamp, #7125, iris, Gary Ba-Han, 1984, 18".................................**375.00**
Lamp, #7125, tulip, Itoko Takeuchi, 1988, 18" **305.00**
Mug, #5121, tiger lily, William Pacini, 1984, 5" **82.00**
Oil lamp, #1102, iris, Alvaro Suman, 1980, 6½" **76.00**
Oil lamp, #1102, swan, Barbara Rose, ca 1978, 6½" **72.00**
Pitcher/goblet, #A/C, landscape, Mark MacKay, ca 1978, 9¼"...**128.00**
Plate, #5114, iris, Michelle Foster, 1981, 7"................................**89.00**
Plate, #5114, sweet pea, Michelle Foster, 1982, 7" **133.00**
Platter, #4118, oriental, Itoko Takeuchi, 1984, 15" **243.00**
Teapot, #5109, lily, Anne Fitch, 1982, 8" **427.00**
Vase, #5101, abstract, John Guthrie, 1984, 7".............................**80.00**
Vase, #5101, experimental, Itoko Takeuchi, 1984, 7" **80.00**
Vase, #5101, iris, Mary Favero, 1980, 7"......................................**91.00**
Vase, #5101, iris, Suzanne Tormey, 1981, 7" **180.00**
Vase, #5101, mice, Nancy Looker, 1979, 4¼"..............................**154.00**
Vase, #5101, pansy, Zetta, ca 1982, 6" **100.00**
Vase, #5101, tulip, Itoko Takeuchi, ca 1985, 7" **60.00**
Vase, #5101, water lily, Kat Corcoran, 1980, 5¾"........................**82.00**
Vase, #5102, daffodil, Dorie Knight, 1980, 10"...........................**173.00**
Vase, #5102, daffodil, Laurie Cosca, 1982, 9" **125.00**
Vase, #5102, wisteria, Shannon Sargent, 1985, 9"......................**125.00**
Vase, #5103, experimental, Laurie Linn Ball, 1985, 8".................**104.00**
Vase, #5103, orchid, Mary Favero, 1981, 8"................................**251.00**
Vase, #5103, watercolor, Itoko Takeuchi, 1986, 8".....................**125.00**
Vase, #5104, daffodil, Margaret Gibson, 1984, 14" **225.00**
Vase, #5133, iris, Shannon Sargent, 1984, 20"........................**1,500.00**
Vase, #6112, fuchsia/bird, Dorie Knight-Hutchinson, 1984, 10"..**425.00**
Vase, #6112/7, fuchsia/bird, Dorie Knight-Hutchinson, 1984, 10"..**425.00**
Vase, #6114a, pansy, Dorie Knight-Hutchinson, 1984, 8"..........**275.00**
Vase, #7116, columbine, Suzanne Tormey?, 1980, 14"................**381.00**
Vase, #7116, hibiscus, Laurie Linn Ball, 1985, 12".....................**400.00**
Vase, #7116, iris, Dorie Knight, 1981, 12" **280.00**
Vase, #7116, orchid, unsgn, ca 1981, 12" **298.00**
Vase, #7116cs, bouquet, Itoko Takeuchi, 1986, 12".....................**325.00**
Vase, #7116cs, carnation, Michelle Foster, 1982, 12"...................**446.00**
Vase, #7116cs, morning glory, Mary Favero, 1982, 12"................**298.00**
Vase, #7116ss, tiger/tiger lily, Shannon Sargent, 1984, 12" **650.00**

Sarreguemines

Sarreguemines, France, is the location of Utzschneider and Company, founded about 1880, producers of majolica, transfer-printed dinnerware, figurines, and novelties which are usually marked 'Sarreguemines.' In 1836, under the management of Alexandre de Geiger, son-in-law of Utzschneider, the company became affiliated with Villeroy and Boch. During the 1850s and 1860s, two new facilities with modern steam-fired machinery were erected. Alexandre's son Paul was the next to guide the company, and under his leadership two more factories were built — one at Oigoin and the other at Vitry le Francois. After his death in 1931, the company split but was consolidated again after the war under the name of Sarreguemines-Digoin-Vitry le Francois. Items marked St. Clement were made during the period from 1979 to 1982, indicating the group who owned the company for that span of time. Today the company is known as Sarreguemines-Batiment.

Basket, basketweave w/tomatoes & leaves in bottom, 3x7½x10½"...**145.00**
Compote, gr fern leaves on cream basketweave w/pk rim, 6x11"..**165.00**
Covered dish, basketweave bottom w/fruit on lid, 6½" dia **310.00**

Ewer, howling hound, wht & cobalt w/crackling, 4½x12½" 575.00
Jam jar, strawberries on lid w/basketweave bottom, 3½x4½" 85.00
Jardiniere & ped, cobalt w/emb leaves, gilt highlights, #3672, 47½"..3,475.00
Pitcher, Danish woman's face w/bonnets, ca 1906, 7¾" 475.00
Pitcher, dog figural, brn & wht, 9¾" 575.00
Pitcher, duck figural, yel/orange/gr, mk St Clement, 13" 400.00
Pitcher, ear of corn form, yel & gr, unmk, 9½" 465.00
Pitcher, fish figural, curled-up tail hdl, 9" 385.00
Pitcher, John Bull, #3257, code dtd 1902 ....165.00
Pitcher, leaf on tree bark, 5¾" 175.00
Pitcher, man's dbl face, 'Tu ris quand tu es plein...,' 1901, 8½"..550.00
Pitcher, man's face, rosy cheeks, bl band on forehead, #3181, 8¾"...365.00
Pitcher, man's face, tan hat, #3181, 5", NM................................295.00
Pitcher, parrot figural, mc, mk St Clement France, 13" 435.00
Pitcher, people & tree tops emb, branch-like hdl, 8½" 380.00
Pitcher, rooster figural, bl w/brn chest, purple comb & features, 11".400.00
Pitcher, rooster figural, mc, mk St Clement France, #7516, 13¾" 600.00
Pitcher, Scottish man's face, #3210, 8" 130.00
Plate, oyster 6 wht scallops w/brn edges, turq border 380.00
Platter, grapes & leaves, mk #513F, 9¾x12"................................210.00
Stein, man at table w/baby in relief, pewter lid, #2889, .5-litre ..715.00
Stein, Munich child w/hops & wheat, woman thumblift, #1823, .5 litre.. 770.00

Satin Glass

Satin glass is simply glassware with a velvety matt finish achieved through the application of an acid bath. This procedure has been used by many companies since the twentieth century, both here and abroad, on many types of colored and art glass. See also Mother-of-Pearl; Webb.

Cracker jar, pk w/emb shells & HP flowers, 5½" 85.00
Ewer, pk, 9½" 75.00
Ice bucket, bl, Swirl, metal collar/hdl, 5¼" 70.00
Mug, wht w/pk & gold loopings, frosted hdl, 3½" 175.00

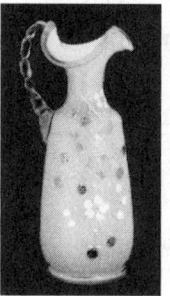

Pitcher, blue with white interior, hand-painted blue and white floral, ruffled top, twist handle, 10", $125.00.

Rose bowl, bl w/scrolling goldenrod & bl floral, diagonal ribs, 5x6"..150.00
Rose bowl, wht to yel w/pk pansies, #617, 5x6" 400.00
Vase, bl to wht, spherical w/long neck, 11x5½"............................265.00
Vase, bl to wht, 4-petal top, wht/orange floral, 11½x4" 185.00
Vase, lav irid, cased, pinched sides, 6", pr.....................................75.00
Vase, peach w/wht daisies, bulbous w/stick neck, 10" 150.00
Vase, tan to wht w/gold & wht game birds, bottle w/cup rim, 10"..165.00

Satsuma

Satsuma is a type of fine cream crackle-glaze pottery or earthenware made in Japan as early as the seventeenth century. The earliest wares, made at the original kiln in the Satsuma province, were enameled with only simple florals. By the late eighteenth century, a floral brocade (or nishikide design) was favored, and similar wares were being made at other kilns under the direction of the Lord of Satsuma. In the early part of the nineteenth century, a diaper pattern was added to the florals. Gold and silver enamels were used for accents by the latter years of the century. During the 1850s, as the quality of goods made for export to the Western world increased and the style of decoration began to evolve toward becoming more appealing to the Westerners, human forms such as Arhats, Kannon, geisha girls, and samurai warriors were added. Today the most valuable pieces are those marked 'Kinkozan,' 'Shuzan,' 'Ryuzan,' and 'Kozan.' The genuine Satsuma 'mon' or mark is a cross within a circle — usually in gold on the body or lid, or in red on the base of the ware. Character marks may be included.

Caution: Much of what is termed 'Satsuma' comes from the Showa period (1926 to the present); it is not true Satsuma but a simulated type, a cheaper pottery with heavy enamel. Collectors need to be aware that much of the of the 'Satsuma' today is really Satsuma style and should not carry the values of true Satsuma.

Bowl, birds & flowers inside & out, pinched sides, mk Genzan, 3x8"..360.00
Bowl, fish; court scenes, geometrics at base, 19th C, 12½x18½"..2,100.00
Bowl, Geisha girls in sq w/floral bkground, floral on wht ext, 6¾" ..860.00
Button, mc landscape, ⅜" dia...315.00
Covered jar (koro), battle scenes, 4-sided, helmet & mask finial, 11"...1,090.00
Cup & saucer, Samari warriors in blk/rust/gold, dragon hdl, Kyoto..160.00
Figurine, Hotei, seated, 5x7" 510.00
Palace urn, figural scene w/raised fruit clusters, 64", pr..........12,500.00
Pin, enameled Chinese man center w/snake motif on sides, 1x3"...150.00
Pin, red/bl/purple flowers w/gold leaves on cream, oval, ½x2"....150.00
Pin dish, floral on wht lid, 3½" dia...100.00
Plate, figural scene w/ornate gold, mk Ganzan Sei, 6½" 1,010.00
Plate, Geisha playing instrument w/incense burning, gold rim, 8¼"...165.00
Vase, birds & floral on cream, cylindrical, Kinkozan, 12x5", pr..1,300.00
Vase, figural scene, gilded, elephant base, 13½x9½", pr 1,650.00
Vase, figural scene w/trees/temples/river, sgn Bizan, 9¾"............410.00
Vase, figural scenes w/2 raised gold tassels, mk Kinkozan, 10x6".775.00
Vase, scholars & children below trellis border, ca 1900, 15", pr...4,000.00
Vase, 2 figural scene panels w/cobalt bkground, 14¼"..............1,000.00

Scales

In today's world of pre-measured and pre-packaged goods, it is difficult to imagine the days when such products as sugar, flour, soap, and candy first had to be weighed by the grocer. The variety of scales used at the turn of the century was highly diverse; at the Philadelphia Exposition in 1876, one company alone displayed over three hundred different weighing devices. Among those found today, brass, cast-iron, and plastic models are the most common. Fancy postal scales in decorative wood, silver, marble, bronze, and mosaic are also to be found.

A word of caution on the values listed: These values range from a low for those items in fair to good condition to the upper values for items in excellent condition. Naturally, items in mint condition could command even higher prices, and they often do. Also, these are retail prices that suggest what a collector will pay for the object. When you sell to a dealer, expect to get much less. The values noted are averages taken from various auction and other catalogs in the possession of the International Society of Antique Scale Collectors members. Among these, but not limited to, are the following: Joel L. Malter & Co., Inc., Encino, CA; *Auktion Alt Technic*, Auction Team, Koln, Germany.

For those seeking additional information concerning antique scales we recommend *Scales, A Collector's Guide*, by Bill and Jan Berning (Schiffer). You are also encouraged to contact the International Society of Antique Scale Collectors, whose address can be found in the Directory under Clubs, Newsletters, and Catalogs. Visit the club website at www.isasc.org.

Key:
ap — arrow pointer
bal — balance
bm — base metal
br — brass
Brit — British
Can — Canadian
Col — Colonial
CW — Civil War
cwt — counterweight
Engl — English
eq — equal arm
Euro — European
FIS — Fairbanks Infallible
    Scale Co.

h — hanging
hcp — hanging counterpoise
hh — hand held
l+ — label with foreign coin values
lb w/i — labeled box with
    instructions
lph — letter plate or holder
pend — pendulum
PP — Patent Pending
st — sterling
tt — torsion type
ua — unequal arm
wt — weight

Analytical (Scientific)

Am, eq, mahog w/br & ivory, late 1800s, 14x16x8", $200 to......**400.00**

Assay

Am, eq, mahog box w/br & ivory, plaque/drw, 1890s, $400 to.**1,000.00**

Coin: Equal Arm Balance, American

Blk japanned metal, eagle on lid, late 19th C, $300 to **400.00**
Col, oak 6-part box, Col moneys, Boston, 1720-75, $600 to ...**1,200.00**
Post Col to CW, oak 6-part box, l+, 1843, $400 to.................**1,000.00**

Coin: Equal Arm Balance, English

Charles I, wooden box w/11 Brit wts, 1640s, $900 to...............**1,500.00**
1-pc wood box, rnd wts, label, Freeman, 1760s, $250 to **450.00**
6-pc oak box, coin wts label, Thos Harrison, 1750s, $200 to......**450.00**

Coin: Equal Arm Balance, French

Solid wood box, 12 sq wts, J Reyne, Bourdeau, 1694, $400 to.**1,000.00**
Solid wood box w/recesses, 5 sq wts, A Gardes, 1800s, $250 to ..**800.00**
1-pc oval box, nested/fractional wts, label, 18th C, $250 to **400.00**
1-pc walnut box, nested wts, Charpentier label, 1810, $275 to...**675.00**

Coin: Equal Arm Balance, Miscellaneous

Amsterdam, 1-pc box, 32 sq wts, label, late 1600s, $850 to.....**2,500.00**
Cologne, full set of wts & full label, late 1600s, $1,200 to.......**2,800.00**
German, wood box, 13+ wts beneath main wts, label, 1795, $650 to ..**900.00**

Counterfeit Coin Detectors, American

Allender Pat, lb w/i, cwt, Nov 22, 1855, 8½", $350 to **650.00**
Allender PP, rocker, labeled box, cwt, 1850s, 8½", $450 to **750.00**
Allender PP, rocker, no box or cwt, 1850s, 8½", $250 to **375.00**
Allender PP, space for $3 gold pc, lb w/i, cwt, 1855, $350 to......**750.00**
Allender PP, space for $3 gold pc, no box or cwt, 1855, $275 to...**375.00**
Allender Warranted, rocker, no box or cwt, 1850s, 8½", $350 to .**475.00**
McNally-Harrison Pat 1882, rocker, cwt & box, FIS, $400 to **750.00**
McNally-Harrison...1882, rocker, CI base, no cwt/box, $250 to .**400.00**
Thompson, Z-formed rocker, Berrian Mfg, 1877 Pat, $175 to.....**350.00**

Counterfeit Coin Detectors, Dutch

Rocker, Ellinckhuysen, brass, +copy of 1829 Patent, $250 to **350.00**

Counterfeit Coin Detectors, English

Folding, Guinea, self-rising, labeled box, 1850s, $175 to.............**225.00**
Folding, Guinea, self-rising, wood box/label, ca 1890s, $125 to ..**175.00**
Folding, Guinea, self-rising, wooden box, pre-1800, $175 to **275.00**
Rocker, simple, no maker's name or cb, end-cap box, $85 to......**125.00**
Rocker, w/maker's name & cb, end-cap box, $120 to **150.00**

Postal

In the listings below an asterisk (*) was used to indicate that any one of several manufacturers' or brand names might be found on that particular set of scales. Some of the American-made pieces could be marked Pelouze, Lorraine, Hanson, Kingsbury, Fairbanks, Troemner, IDL, Newman, Accurate, Ideal, B-T, Marvel, Reliance, Howe, Landers-Frary-Clark, Chatillon, Triner, American Bank Service, or Weiss. European/U.S.-made scales marked with an asterisk (*) could be marked Salter, Peerless, Pelouze, Sturgis, L.F.&C., Alderman, G. Little, or S&D. English-made scales with the asterisk (*) could be marked Josh. & Edmd. Ratcliff, R.W. Winfield, S. Mordan, STS (Samuel Turner, Sr.), W.&T. Avery, Parnall & Sons, S&P, or H.B. Wright. There may be other manufacturers as well.

Brit/Can Bal, eq, br or CI on base, *, 4"-15", $100 to **750.00**
Engl Bal, eq/Roberval, gilt or st, on stand, *, 3"-8", $500 to....**2,500.00**
Engl Bal, eq/Roberval, plain to ornate, *, 3"-8", $100 to **2,500.00**
Engl Spring, candlestick, br or st, *, 3½"-15", $100 to...............**500.00**
Engl Spring, CI, br or NP fr, Salter, ozs/lbs, 7"-10", $25 to..........**200.00**
Engl Steelyard, ua, 1- or 2-beam, h lph, *, 4"-15", $100 to......**1,500.00**
Euro pend, gravity, br, CI or NP fr on base, oz/grams, $75 to **350.00**
Euro pend, gravity, 2-arm, bm, br or NP, *, 6"-9", $50 to **300.00**
Euro/US Spring, br or NP, pence/etc, h or hh, *, 4"-17", $10 to.**100.00**
US Pend, gravity, metal, pnt face, ap, hcp, sm, $20 to **100.00**
US Spring, pnt base metal, *, 2½"-8", $10 to **80.00**
US Spring, pnt bm, *, mtd on inkstand, 2½"-8", $75 to **250.00**
US Spring, pnt bm, rnd glass-covered face, *, 8"-10", $25 to......**100.00**
US Spring, SP, oblong base, *, 2½"-8", $100 to...........................**200.00**
US Spring, st, oblong base, *, 2½"-8", $200 to...........................**500.00**
US Steelyard, ua, CI, *, 5"-13" beam, 4½"-12" base, $25 to.......**100.00**

Schafer and Vater

Established in 1890 by Gustav Schafer and Gunther Vater in the Thuringia region of southwest Germany, by 1913 this firm employed over two hundred workers. The original factory burned in 1918 but was restarted and production continued until WWII. In 1972 the East German government took possession of the building and destroyed all of the molds and the records that were left.

You will find pieces with the impressed mark of a nine-point star with a script 'R' inside the star. On rare occasions you will find this mark in blue ink under glaze. The items are sometimes marked with a four-digit design number and a two-digit artist mark. In addition or instead, pieces may have 'Made in Germany' or in the case of the Kewpies, 'Rose O'Neill copyright.' The company also manufactured items for sale under store names, and those would not have the impressed mark.

Schafer and Vater used various types of clays. Items made of hard-paste porcelain, soft-paste porcelain, jasper, bisque, and majolica can be found. The glazed bisque pieces may be multicolored or have an applied colored slip wash that highlights the intricate details of the modeling. Gold accents were used as well as spots of high-gloss color called jewels. Metallic glazes are coveted. You can find the jasper in green, blue, pink, lavender, and white. New collectors gravitate toward the pink and lavender shades.

Since Schafer and Vater made such a multitude of items, collectors have to compete with many cross-over collections. These include shaving mugs, hatpin holders, match holders, figurines, figural pitchers, Kewpies, tea sets, bottles, naughties, etc.

Reproduction alert: In addition to the crudely made Japanese copies, some English firms are beginning to make figural reproductions. These seem to be well marked and easy to spot. Our advisor for this category is Joanne M. Koehn; she is listed in the Directory under Minnesota.

Ashtray, boy (4") in hat w/cigar, 'And Dad Said, Be a Man'.......280.00
Basket, 3 roses on 'fence,' stem hdl, #6318, 3x4x5½".................140.00
Bottle, clown holding cancan dancer w/liquor bottle, bl, 5½" 185.00
Bottle, man cranking pig's tail, top-hat stopper, 6½"...................245.00
Bowl, brn w/bl band of wht cherubs, 2 ram head hdls, #5660, 3x4¾"...240.00
Cocktail set, figural rooster, Mr Cocktail, w/tray & 3 matching cups 175.00
Creamer, Chanticleer, muted colors, mk, 4¾"..............................135.00
Creamer, figural bear w/coat & muff, bl, mk MIG, 4¾"..............145.00
Figurine, Chamber Maid, #8577, 7⅜"......................................315.00
Figurine, Mr Adam, Black man w/fig leaf, #8242, 7½"..............280.00
Figurine, Naughty in wht dress w/blk stockings, 3".....................60.00
Flask, A Good Sip, kissing couple, unmk, 4¾"...........................165.00
Flask, A Little Scotch, figural Scottsman holds urn, #3024, 5½"..95.00
Flask, Father Christmas in relief, mc on brn, cork stopper, 5½".185.00
Flask, Life Saver, man w/bottle, musical, 11½"...........................185.00
Flask, monkey waiter opening bottle of wine, unmk, 6".............200.00
Flask, One of the Boys, old man w/champagne glass, 7"..............110.00
Hair receiver, woman plays harp to sm angel, bl/wht/irid bronze...175.00
Hat pin holder, seated Oriental lady w/fan, pale gr, 4⅜".............390.00
Match holder, peasant boy w/basket holds cigar to mouth, #5772, 5"...55.00
Pitcher, lady holding fan, 3½"..80.00
Pitcher, Mad Hatter hdl, lovers cameo ea side, #3862, 5¾"........110.00
Pitcher, woman w/upturned umbrella holding pitcher, 5"............110.00
Plaque, Cupid & classical lady, gr/wht, #2892/#82, 7½x6¼"......120.00
Shaving mug, dancer reserve, elephant-head hdl.........................160.00
Shaving mug, emb elk head on brn, wht int, unmk, 3½x3"........110.00
Smoker, bald man, match holes on forehead, 4x3½x2"...............215.00
Smoker, man w/sleeping cap/bug on nose, match holes in forehead..300.00
Sugar bowl, Chanticleer, orange/gr/brn/wht, mk, 3½x5x2½".....120.00
Vase, Castle Walk, couple dance before vase, 6"..........................265.00
Vase, girl holding bird just hatching from egg, bl & wht, 3¾"......35.00

Scheier

The Scheiers began their ceramics careers in the late 1930s and soon thereafter began to teach their craft at the University of New Hampshire. After WWII they cooperated with the Puerto Rican government in establishing a native ceramic industry, an involvement which would continue to influence their designs. In the '50s they retired and moved to Mexico; they currently reside in Arizona.

Charger, black sgraffito figures in a boat with landscape on a blue ground, 15", NM, $1,000.00.

Bowl, bl-gr w/dk bl specks, 3x3¾"..130.00

Bowl, brn w/wht sqs, textured, 3½x5.......................................155.00
Bowl, figures (3) sgraffito in brn on volcanic waves, 8½x8¾"....775.00
Bowl, periwinkle bl to ivory w/cobalt speckles, 6x17"................450.00
Bowl, upsidedown Vs, brn to ivory flambe over caramel, 5x5½"...220.00
Decanter, gray, goat finial, bulbous, 11"..................................300.00
Vase, dk brn w/ribbing, 3¼x4¼"...80.00
Vase, fantasy woman/fish creature, burgundy w/copper dust, 8½".......495.00
Vase, fish sgraffito on charcoal w/bl, teardrop form w/narrow rim, 6"..545.00
Vase, woman engulfed by fish designs, brn w/mocha bands, 7¼x5" ...660.00

Schlegelmilch Porcelain

For information about Schlegelmilch Porcelain, see Mary Frank Gaston's books: *R. S. Prussia Popular Lines* which addresses R. S. Prussia molds and decorations, and *The Collector's Encyclopedia of R. S. Prussia, Fourth Series*, which contains information on the other Schlegelmilch marks, such as Erdman Schlegelmilch (E. S.), Oscar Schlegelmilch (O. S.), and the other R. S. marks (R. S. Germany, R. S. Suhl, R. S. Poland, and R. S. Tillowitz). Both books contain full-color illustrations and current values. Mold numbers appearing in some of the listings refer to these books. Assume that all items described below are marked unless noted otherwise.

R.S. Germany

In 1869 Reinhold Schlegelmilch began to manufacture porcelain in Suhl in the German province of Thuringia. In 1894 he established another factory in Tillowitz in upper Silesia. Both areas were rich in resources necessary for the production of hard-paste porcelain. Wares marked with the name 'Tillowitz' and the accompanying 'R.S. Germany' phrase are attributed to Reinhold. The most common mark is a wreath and star in a solid color under the glaze. Items marked 'R.S. Germany' are usually more simply decorated than R.S. Prussia. Some reflect the Art Deco trend of the 1920s. Certain hand-painted floral decorations and themes such as 'Sheepherder,' 'Man With Horses,' and 'Cottage' are especially valued by collectors — those with a high-gloss finish or on Art Deco shapes in particular. Not all hand-painted items were painted at the factory. Those with an artist's signature but no 'Hand Painted' mark indicate that the blank was decorated outside the factory.

Basket, HP flowers on pearl lustre, simple gold hdl 130.00
Bowl, carnations on shaded gr, pierced hdls, 10¼x9"...................55.00
Bowl, dogwood & pine on brn, ftd, smooth rim, 6¼"...................50.00
Bowl, lily of the valley on wht satin, Lettuce variation mold, 9½" ..350.00
Bowl, Summer Season portrait on wht satin, hdls, mold #25, 8½x13" ...1,900.00
Box, wht lily on club shape..135.00
Cake plate, mums, Carnation mold, unmk, 10½"......................185.00
Cake plate, peonies & snowballs w/gold, pierced hdls, 11".............70.00
Celery tray, cottage scene (thatched roof), 12¾x5¾" 225.00
Celery tray, yel-tinted roses, pierced hdls, 14x6½"......................50.00
Chocolate pot, poppies, wht on tan gloss, angle hdl, ind, 7¼" ...130.00
Coffeepot, floral, wht w/gr on gr to brn, wht hdl, 9" 275.00
Creamer & sugar bowl, pearl lustre, Lettuce mold, w/lid, 2¾" 185.00
Ewer, wht poppies, ornate rim & hdl, RSP mold #640, 5½" 115.00
Mustard pot, pk & wht roses w/gold, 3"......................................85.00
Nappy, roses on pearl lustre, 1 curled hdl 22.50
Plate, apple blossoms, sgn Lenbach, 8".......................................45.00
Plate, sandwich; lilies on shaded ground, center hdl, unmk, 4x10½"..85.00
Plate, surreal dogwood w/gold stems, mold #256, 8½".................55.00
Relish, lilies, fancy gold stencil & pierced work on border...........40.00
Sugar bowl, pk & wht roses, angle hdls, w/lid, 3".......................40.00
Teapot, yel & orange tinted roses, gold stenciled borders, 4½" ...135.00
Tray, dresser; poppies w/gr tint on pearl lustre, 12x7¼".............85.00
Tray, mc peonies, rectangular, pierced work on 2 sides, 4⅛x8" ...110.00

Vase, Peace Bringing Plenty allegorical, red top w/gold, 13"....**1,900.00**

R.S. Poland

'R.S. Poland' is a mark attributed to Reinhold Schlegelmilch's factory in Tillowitz, Silesia. It was in use for a few years after 1945.

Chocolate cup, dogwood & pine on irid, 3" **70.00**
Ewer, Night Watch, scene after Rembrandt on dk gr, mold #900, 6¼"...**550.00**
Vase, Chinese pheasants, slim neck, RS Suhl mold #15, 9" **900.00**
Vase, lady in pastoral scene w/cobalt & gold, hdls, 8½"............**1,500.00**
Vase, roses, gold band at top, 7½", pr..................................**300.00**
Vase, roses on shaded brn, Nouveau hdls, mold #956, 12" **550.00**

R.S. Prussia

Art porcelain bearing the mark 'R.S. Prussia' was manufactured by Reinhold Schlegelmilch in the early 1900s in a Germanic area known until the end of WWI as Prussia. The vast array of mold shapes in combination with a wide variety of decorations is the basis for R.S. Prussia's appeal. Themes can be categorized as figural (usually based on a famous artist's work), birds, florals, portraits, scenics, and animals.

Bowl, fruit on tinted pink, mold #55, 10" **350.00**
Bowl, Lebrun I portrait on Tiffany bronze, unmk, 10".............**1,300.00**
Bowl, lily sprays on pearl lustre, beaded border, mold #156, 11".**250.00**
Bowl, Melon Eaters, undecorated jewels, Point & Clover mold, 10½"...**1,300.00**
Bowl, Old Man in the Mtn, gold trim, mold #14, unmk, 11"......**900.00**
Bowl, pastel flower spray, Sunflower mold, 10½"..........................**235.00**
Bowl, poppies & daisies reflecting, mold #14, 11" **400.00**
Bowl, Potocka portrait, gold trim, mold #29, 10½"....................**1,200.00**
Bowl, roses, mc on lt to dk gr, Grape mold, 11"...........................**375.00**
Bowl, roses & daisies w/gold, Carnation mold variation, 10½"...**325.00**
Bowl, shadow flowers & gold trim, mold #80, 10½".....................**300.00**
Bowl, snowbird scene, Icicle mold, oval, 13½x6¾" **1,700.00**
Bowl, stag scene on satin, gold trim, mold #203, 11" **2,000.00**
Bowl, Summer portrait on pk satin, mold #25, 9½" **2,300.00**
Bowl, swans on lake, oval, mold #7, 13"......................................**650.00**
Box, hairpin; Recamier portrait, mold #826, unmk, 1½x4¼" L.**325.00**
Cake plate, Autumn portrait, Lily mold, pierced hdls, 10¼" ...**2,300.00**
Cake plate, castle scene, Fleur-de-lis mold, 12" **650.00**
Cake plate, poppies w/dk gr touches at border, mold #10c, 10" ...**275.00**
Cake plate, roses, Point & Cover mold, 10¼" **250.00**
Cake plate, roses & snowballs w/cobalt & gold, mold #82, 9¾".**400.00**
Celery dish, clematis on watered silk finish, Lily mold, 12x5" **275.00**
Celery dish, floral w/ladies' (4) cameo portraits in rim, 14x7".**1,300.00**
Celery dish, Melon Eaters, pierced hdls, mold #300, 13½" **600.00**
Chocolate pot, roses on satin w/gold, Iris mold, 11"....................**750.00**
Cup, roses on lt bl to wht, mold #518, 3½".....................................**90.00**
Cup & saucer, calla lily on gr, gold trim, mold #5091.................**115.00**
Ewer, bird of paradise on wht satin, mold #958, 7½" **3,500.00**
Ewer, swan (1) scene, mold #640, 5" **300.00**
Muffineer, lily of the valley on shaded brn, gold trim, unmk **225.00**
Mug, shaving; poppies w/gold, wht hdl, mold #862, 3½" **275.00**
Pitcher, roses & snowballs, Ribbon & Jewel mold variation, 9½"...**525.00**
Plate, Dice Throwers, shadow flowers & gold stencil, mold #300, 8½"..**900.00**
Plate, sailboat scene, gold trim, Popcorn mold, 8½"....................**600.00**
Plate, scattered flowers, Point & Clover mold w/jewels, 9".........**250.00**
Plate, snowbird scene w/gold stencilling, Popcorn mold, 8½" .**1,300.00**
Plate, turkey w/pines, pearlized lustre burder, mold #304, 7½" ...**450.00**
Plate, Winter Season, ornate gold tapestry, mold #343, 9".......**1,900.00**
Sugar bowl, castle scene on turq-gr, mold #568, w/lid **325.00**
Tankard, cottage scene, Stippled Floral mold, 13"...................**1,450.00**
Tankard, Lebrun I portrait on rose finish, Lily mold, 15".........**2,300.00**

Tankard, roses, lav Tiffany finish, gold scrollwork, mold #537, 14"...**1,000.00**
Tankard, roses on pk to wht, mold #525, 14" **900.00**
Tankard, roses on Tiffany irid finish, #643, 15" **1,100.00**
Toothpick holder, swallows & water lilies, hdls, mold #631, 2¼"..**250.00**
Tray, floral on watered silk finish w/pearl lustre, mold #25, 11x7"..**350.00**
Tray, Spring portrait, Carnation mold, pierced hdls, rectangular.**2,100.00**
Urn, mill scene w/cobalt & heavy gold, mold #903, unmk, 11"..**2,600.00**
Vase, cottage scene on dk gr, gold hdls, mold #951, 7"...............**700.00**
Vase, lion & lioness, gold hdls, mold #922, 8½" **1,100.00**
Vase, pheasant on yel to rust, mold #909, unmk, 5¼" **550.00**
Vase, swans & evergreens, mold #922, 9½" **700.00**

R.S. Suhl, Suhl

Porcelains marked with this designation are attributed to Reinhold Schlegelmilch's Suhl factory.

Bowl, lav & wht flowers w/gold, hdls, 8⅛" **150.00**
Bowl, mc mixed flowers, gold trim, scalloped, 1-hdl, 11" **450.00**
Cup & saucer, pk roses, gold stencilling, cup: 1⅞x2" **115.00**
Ewer, peacock scenic, ovoid, unmk, 7".......................................**1,000.00**
Plate, roses on ivory to brn, pierced hdls, 10" **130.00**
Powder jar, pk roses, flat lid, simple rnd shape, 5½" **200.00**
Vase, floral, pk & wht on blk, bulbous, RSP mold #907, bulbous, 5" ...**200.00**
Vase, floral transfer on dk gr w/gold, ornate gold hdls, ftd, 13½" ...**650.00**
Vase, hummingbirds on wht satin, uptrn hdls, unmk, 9½" **4,250.00**

Vase, lavender flowers on green, green mark, 6½", $110.00.

Vase, lilac clematis, waisted, gold angle hdls, 7⅜" **250.00**
Vase, roses, mc on blk, gold hdls, 9¼"...**475.00**
Vase, roses, pk on blk w/gold trim, cylindrical, 7⅛" **400.00**
Vase, roses, wht w/yel on shaded gr, uptrn hdls, 7" **350.00**
Vase, roses & leaves HP underglaze, 6" **225.00**

R.S. Tillowitz

R.S. Tillowitz-marked porcelains are attributed to Reinhold Schlegelmilch's factory in Tillowitz, Silesia.

Bowl, Diana the Huntress, cherubs reserves, Tiffany finish border, 9"..**1,100.00**
Bowl, mc mums, ornate border, gold trim, 10" **225.00**
Bowl, mill scene on mc 'glow' ground w/gold, mold #17, 10¼" ..**500.00**
Bowl, mixed flowers, cobalt & flower border w/gold, 9" **400.00**
Bowl, mixed flowers, floral & bl border w/gold-beaded rim, 7¾" .**250.00**
Bowl, mixed flowers, wide cobalt border w/gold trim, unmk, 10½" .**450.00**
Bowl, roses & buds w/red & gold trim, 10½" **265.00**
Bowl, yel & pk roses, rose-pk border w/gold & flowers, 10¾" **275.00**
Bowl, yel roses w/gold, unmk, 10½" **175.00**
Cake plate, floral from lt to cobalt bl w/gold, mold #11, 9½" **350.00**
Cake plate, flowers & leaves, shadow flowers in border, 10½"......**200.00**
Celery tray, red & wht tulips, gr along outer border, mold #5, 12" ...**150.00**
Chocolate pot, roses, gr & gold decor at top, slim, unmk, 12" **350.00**
Chocolate pot, roses w/gold stems, gold & floral border, mold #8..**400.00**

Chocolate pot, sm pk roses, wide gold border, mold #15, 10" **500.00**

Cup & saucer, floral on wht w/ornate gold rim, cup: 2".................**90.00**

Ferner, mixed flowers w/gold, 4-ftd, 2¾x8½"........................**275.00**

Mug, shaving; floral, pk tint at top border, mold #6, 4"...............**250.00**

Plaque, mill scene w/gold trim on border, mold #19, 11¼".........**150.00**

Plate, poppies & wht flowers w/gold stencilling, mold #6, 9½" ..**300.00**

Syrup & underplate, floral (lt to cobalt bl) on wht w/gold..........**325.00**

Tankard, cottage scene on pk/gr/orange, ornate gold hdl, 14"..**1,300.00**

Tankard, poppies transfer, fancy gold hdl, mold #7, 14¾"...........**750.00**

Toothpick holder, bl floral w/gold highlights, 2¼"......................**150.00**

Tray, dresser; mixed flowers, heavy gold border, unmk, 11½x7½"....**325.00**

Vase, bl & wht flowers & leaves w/gold outlines, bulbous, 5½" ..**300.00**

Vase, Countess Potocka portrait on pearly gr, Tiffany borders, 8¾" ..**800.00**

Schneider

The Schneider Glass Company was founded in 1914 at Epinay-sur-seine, France. They made many types of art glass, some of which sandwiched designs between layers. Other decorative devices were appliqué and carved work. These were marked 'Charder' or 'Schneider.' During the '20s commercial artware was produced with Deco motifs cut by acid through two or three layers and signed 'LeVerre Francais' in script or with a section of inlaid filigrane. Our advisor for this category is Don Williams; he is listed in the Directory under Missouri. See also Le Verre Francais.

Compote, gr w/trapped bubbles, blk ftd base, flared rim, 3¼x8" .**300.00**

Compote, red yel mottle bowl w/wide flange on amethyst ft, 6x15"..**900.00**

Compote, yel to clear mottle on bl ped, 7x10½" **200.00**

Cruet, dk bl to rose mottle spout, sky bl bottom, amethyst hdl, 6½" ..**600.00**

Vase, cobalt, bl ft w/yel wafer, urn shape, 12" **1,550.00**

Vase, Deco cameo floral, pk transparent on texture, 3¾x5"........**600.00**

Vase, gr/yel/orange mottle, ftd cylinder w/flared rim, 12" **300.00**

Vase, int decor: clear panels fr w/amber, bulbous w/stick neck, 4".......**250.00**

Vase, plain & textured clear bands alternate, purple ft, dbl waist, 6" ..**200.00**

Vase, sea-foam gr w/bubbles, swirled ribs, cylindrical, 6¾"..........**975.00**

Vase, yel/orange mottle, upright rim, shouldered, 12½"...........**1,150.00**

Vase, yel/orange spatter on clear, ftd trumpet form, 6½" **85.00**

Schoolhouse Collectibles

Schoolhouse collectibles bring to mind memories of a bygone era when the teacher rang her bell to call the youngsters to class in a one-room schoolhouse where often both the 'hickory stick' and an apple occupied a prominent position on her desk. Our advisor for this category is Kenn Norris; he is listed in the Directory under Texas.

Abacus, wooden mc balls in oak fr on castors, 1940s, 36x65", EX..**175.00**

Bell, polished brass, no eng, rope pull, 12", 19+ lbs.....................**200.00**

Bell recess; brass w/cherry hdl, 8x4½", from $65 to **95.00**

Bell ringer clock, oak w/CI cradle, electric, 31x15x7" **165.00**

Book, Dick & Jane, Fun With; 159 pgs, 1940, VG **75.00**

Book, Dick & Jane, Good Times With Our Friends, 1941, VG **90.00**

Book, Dick & Jane, Grades 1-6, 1950s, set of 12 books, EX........**525.00**

Book, Dick & Jane, Guess Who?, 63 pgs, 1951, VG+ **55.00**

Book, Dick & Jane, Number Stories, Book 2, 1933, NM **110.00**

Book, Dick & Jane, Science Stories, Book 1, 1933, VG................**75.00**

Book, Dick & Jane, teacher's edition, Pre-Primer, 1956, 256 pgs, EX ..**175.00**

Book, Dick & Jane, teacher's edition, 1936, 1st printing, VG+ ..**475.00**

Book, Dick & Jane, The New Fun With; 160 pg, 1956, NM **135.00**

Book, Dick & Jane, The New Look & See, 1951, EX **115.00**

Book, Dick & Jane, The New Our New Friends, 1956, VG..........**70.00**

Book, Dick & Jane, We Look & See, 1946-47, VG+ **110.00**

Book, Dick & Jane, We Work & Play, 1946-47, VG...................**135.00**

Book, Dick & Jane Big Book, 1951, 26 pg, VG+, from $450 to..**750.00**

Book, Mac & Muff Reader, 1950, EX **60.00**

Brochure, School Desk & Furniture, Randolph McNutt, ca 1890, 22x15" ...**30.00**

Cabinet photo, Carlisle Indian school, unidentified girls, 8x10" ...**110.00**

Class ring, Catholic high school, bl stone center, 10k gold, 1960s...**175.00**

Class ring, NY law school, red stone, 14k gold, 1951 ....**165.00**

Clock, General Electric, blk fr, wall hanging, 1940s, 15½" dia...**175.00**

Desk, master's; poplar w/orig red wash, dvtl drw, on fr, 47x39x27"...**660.00**

Desk, oak, swivel top, Angslow-Fowler..NY, 1930s, 31x26x23" ...**185.00**

Desk, seat w/desk on bk, wrought-iron fr...............................**80.00**

Globe, pasteboard w/coated gores, unmk, wire pivot mt, ca 1890, 6" **500.00**

Globe, Peerless, paper over pasteboard, Chicago Heights Ill, 1909, 6"..**650.00**

Globe, Rand McNally, Chicago, 1914, 18" terrestrial, table model....**3,500.00**

Globe, Weber Costello Co, Chicago Heights, 1925, 8" dia in stand..**2,000.00**

Inkwell, for student's desk, Bakelite w/glass well, Am Seating #60 ...**40.00**

Ledger, NY school treasurer's, 1877-81, 6½x4", EX **110.00**

Lesson charts, canvas-reinforced paper on oak hanger, 35x28", EX..**290.00**

Letter sweater, wool knit, maroon w/placket pockets, 1940s, EX ..**27.50**

Pencil sharpener, celluloid, Pinocchio figural, Japan, 3".............**100.00**

Pencil sharpener, CI, baby grand piano, lid opens, EX **35.00**

Pencil sharpener, metal, rabbit sitting upright, Germany, 1¾x1½"..**65.00**

Pencil sharpener, metal, Uncle Sam, full figure, walking, 2x1".....**75.00**

Pencil sharpener, table top, Wizard, shavings drw, 4¼x2¾"..........**25.00**

Photo postcard, Prudence RI school, 1910, unmailed, NM **80.00**

Slate, wood fr, mk made in Pennsylvania, 9x13", from $30 to **35.00**

Souvenir spoon, West Unity High School, silver, 5¼" **110.00**

Stereoview, Shaker schoolroom, 9 girls at desks, Troy NY, EX....**195.00**

Wall map, 9 different maps, cloth w/metal fr w/roller, 48x42, VG+ ..**75.00**

Yearbook, Venice High School, CA, 1966, 8½x11", EX **110.00**

Pencil Boxes

Among the most common of school-related collectibles are the many classes of pencil boxes. Generally from the period of the 1870s to the 1940s, these boxes were made in hundreds of different styles. Materials included tin, wood (thin frame and solid hardwood), and leather; fabric and plastics were later used. Most pencil boxes were in a basic, rectangular configuration, though rare examples were made to resemble other objects such as rolling pins, ball bats, nightsticks, etc. They may still be found at reasonable prices, even though collectors have recently taken a keen interest in them. All boxes listed below are in very good to near-mint condition. Our advisors for pencil boxes are Sue and Lar Hothem, authors of *School Collectibles of the Past*; they are listed in the Directory under Ohio.

Pencil box with sliding, pivoting top, $40.00 (shown with wood-bound slate, mini slate eraser, conical slate pencil sharpener, and slate pencil). (Photo courtesy Sue and Lar Hothem)

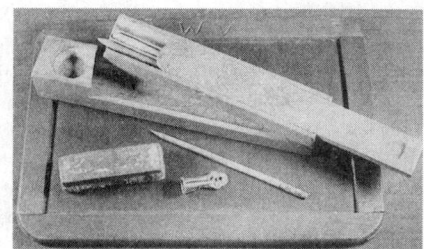

Bakelite, bicycle racing scene, 3-compartment, 8¾x2¼" **110.00**

Boy Scouts, depicts camp scene, tin, Wallace Pencil Co, 3x3x8" .**35.00**

Felix the Cat, Station Broadcasting, fabric, 1935, EX....................**75.00**

Girl Scouts/Campfire Girls, Wallace Pencil Co, 1930s, VG..........**55.00**

Wooden, dachshund figural, rear pulls off, Brodhaven...NY, 10x2" **30.00**

Wooden, depicts children going into 1-room school, brass hinges, 8x5"....**90.00**

Wooden, floral decal, slide lid, sponge compartment, for chalk, 9" **25.00**

Wooden, for slate pencils, 2 gnomes in boat transfer, slide lid, NM...**30.00**
Wooden, Robert F Russell advertising, Am Mfg, ca 1912, 9", EX.**32.00**

Schoop, Hedi

In the 1940s and 1950s one of the most talented artists working in California was Hedi Schoop. Her business ended in 1958 when a fire destroyed her operation. It was at that time that she decided to do free-lance work for other companies such as Cleminson Clay. Schoop was probably the most imitated artist of the time and she answered some of those imitators by successfully suing them. Some imitators were Kim Ward, Ynez, and Yona. Schoop was diversified in her creations, making items such as shapely women, bulky-looking women and children with fat arms and legs, TV lamps, and animals as well as planters and bowls. Schoop used many different marks including the stamped or incised Schoop signature and also a hard-to-find sticker. 'Hollywood, Cal.' or 'California' were occasionally used in conjunction with the Hedi Schoop name. For further information we recommend *The Encyclopedia of California Pottery, Second Edition*, by Jack Chipman; he is listed in the Directory under California.

Ashtray, ballerina doing splits on side, 4x8x8½" **130.00**
Bowl, shell form, ivory w/gold, blk int, 1950s, 12" L.....................**42.50**

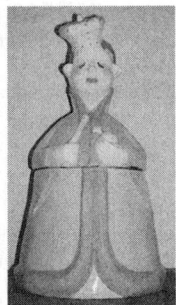

Cookie jar, King, minimum value $400.00. (Photo courtesy Fred and Joyce Roerig)

Dresser box, Deco lady, skirt forms base, hands under chin, 7" **85.00**
Figurine, Balinese dancer, lady in gray w/gold trim, 12½", pr **250.00**
Figurine, Dutch boy & girl, pastel pks & bls, 11½", 11", pr **175.00**
Figurine, girl jumping rope, on base, sgn, 9"................................**160.00**
Figurine, lady on knees w/flowing dress (tray), #140, 8½x11" dia...**110.00**
Figurine, lady w/basket on arm walking collie..............................**210.00**
Figurine, lady w/basket on arm walking poodle, 1950s, 6x10".....**175.00**
Figurine, Marguerita, bowl on head, skirt held out, 12½" **130.00**
Figurine/bowl, lady looking up w/dress skirt (bowl) in hand, 10x17"..**150.00**
Figurine/planter, Balinese dancer w/fan, gold trim, 12".................**95.00**
Figurine/planter, lady w/fan dances in daring gown, open basket, 13"...**95.00**
Figurine/planter, Repose, lady seated, long blk hair, gold trim, 12" **180.00**
Lapel pin, bust of lady in gr/wht striped scarf on head, sgn, 3x1½" **110.00**
Planter, horse, wht w/gr saddle & bow ties, must be sgn, 7" **80.00**
Planter, rooster, orange/gr/brn on blk base, 13" **90.00**
Plate, sailboats at dock, mtns beyond, bl/teal, sgn, sq.................**100.00**
Soap dish, kneeling lady in red w/bowl between legs, sticker, 10½"...**90.00**
Soap dish, lady w/bowl in raised hand, sgn, 10½".......................**130.00**
Vase, rolled flower-petal form, wht w/gold-leaf trim, sgn, 14" **35.00**
Veco, Deco fish on pk sculpted shape, rnd opening at center **75.00**

Schramberg

The Schramberg factory was founded in the early nineteenth century in Schramberg Wuttemberg, Germany. The pieces most commonly seen are those made by Schramberger Majolika Fabrik (SMF) dating from 1912 until 1989.

Some pieces are stamped with the pattern name (i.e. Gobelin) and the number of the painter who executed it. The imprinted number identifies the shape. Marks may also include these names: Wheelock, Black Forest, and Mepoco.

Perhaps the most popular examples with collectors are those from the Gobelin line. Such pieces have a gray background with as many as ten other colors used to create that design. For example, Gobelin 3 pieces will be painted with green and orange leaves and yellow eyes along with other colors specific to that design.

Little is known of the designers who worked for Schramberg; however, Eva Zeisel was employed at the factory for nearly two years starting in the fall of 1928. Her duties included design, production, and merchandising. Our advisors for this category are Ralph Winslow who is listed in the Directory under Missouri and Ann Burton who is listed under Michigan.

Ashtray, peasants dancing, 4x4"...**10.00**
Basket, bl & gr, w/hdl, 5x7½"...**25.00**
Coffeepot, floral, w/lid, 8" **60.00**
Creamer & sugar bowl, w/lid, Gobelin 2 ....**40.00**
Cruet, Gobelin, dbl, 7x8¼"..**45.00**
Pitcher, lily of valley, w/lid, 5⅛"...**30.00**
Planter, floral daisy, 9x4⅛x4¾"...**50.00**
Sugar bowl, Gobelin 4, w/lg hdls, 9¾"..**30.00**
Teapot, ring pattern, att Eva Zeisel...**300.00**
Tray, floral, 5x8¾" **15.00**
Vase, art pottery, floral, 4¾x3⅜" **35.00**
Vase, brn & tan, 6⅛"...**25.00**
Vase, chalet scene, 4½" **65.00**
Vase, floral, mc, 6¼"...**65.00**
Vase, Mondrain, VG, 6"..**130.00**

Scouting Collectibles

Boy Scouts

Scouting was founded in England in 1907 by a retired Major General, Lord Robert Baden-Powell. Its purpose is the same today as it was then — to help develop physically strong, mentally alert boys and to teach them basic fundamentals of survival and leadership. The movement soon spread to the United States, and in 1910 a Chicago publisher, William Boyce, set out to establish scouting in America. The first World Scout Jamboree was held in 1911 in England. Baden-Powell was honored as the Chief Scout of the World. In 1926 he was awarded the Silver Buffalo Award in the United States. He was knighted in 1929 for distinguished military service and for his scouting efforts. Baden-Powell died in 1941. For more information you may contact our advisor, R.J. Sayers, author of *Guide to Scouting Collectibles*, whose address (and ordering information regarding his book) may be found in the Directory under North Carolina. (Correspondence other than book orders requires SASE please.)

Ashtray, National Jamboree, w/logo, 1973..**3.00**
Badge, Wolf, Bear, Lion; Cub Scout, felt, wide border, 1932-40, ea...**4.50**
Bank, Cub Scout, compo bust of Cub..**20.00**
Belt, web type, First Class on buckle w/drawings **10.00**
Belt buckle, World Jamboree, Max Silber limited ed, 1967...........**35.00**
Binoculars, plastic, 12-power, 1950, VG...**12.00**
Book, Boy Scout Life Series, various authors, VG, ea......................**6.50**
Book, Handbook for Scoutmasters, 1st edition, proof copy, 1912, VG..**200.00**
Book, Official Handbook, 1st edition, Baden Powell/ET Seton, 1910...**350.00**
Book, Official Handbook, 2nd edition, 13th to 20th print, 1915, VG, ea ...**45.00**
Book, Official Handbook, 3rd edition, 1927-1937, VG, ea, from $11 to ..**17.00**
Book, Official Handbook, 6th edition, Rockwell cover, 1959-63, VG, ea...**450.00**
Book, Order of the Arrow Handbook, Rucker Newberry, 1948 ..**100.00**

Calendar, 1967 World Jamboree, complete, 42" 20.00
Camera, Kodak, gr, w/case, 1930 ....150.00
Card, membership; plastic, ring at top, 4-pg, 1919.......................15.00
Card, membership; 3-fold, color scout scene, 1922 ....5.00
Catalog, for equipment, ca 1913-40, ea 15.00
Diary, 1915 ....45.00
Diary, 1920s-40s, ea, from $10 to 20.00
Figurine, Baden-Powell bust w/tilted hat, ceramic, 5" 75.00
First Aid kit, Bauer & Black, in khaki case 15.00
Game, Target Ball, marble-shooting game, 1920 ....125.00
Game, The Game of Boy Scouts, Parker Bros, 1912 ....40.00
Greeting card, boy at campfire, Baden-Powell design, 1922 ....10.00
Hat, felt, broad-brimmed, ca 1920-50 ....15.00
Jacket, BS Official, 4-billows pocket, #583, 1918-24 era, EX 50.00
Neckerchief, World Jamboree, US Contingent, 1957 ....10.00
Patch, NJ National Committee, bl felt, wide diamond, 1935......135.00
Patch, NOAC, red twill w/button loop, 1952 ....30.00
Patch, World Jamboree Official, 1955, woven 35.00
Pennant, World Jamboree, 1967, sm or lg, ea...............................7.00
Pin, Eagle Scout, type 1, full feathers 120.00
Pin, Lone Scout Tribe Chief, 1915-24 ....75.00
Pin-bk button, 8-point star w/Baden-Powell in center, bl, w/ribbon ..75.00
Pocket watch, Radiolite, #1269 ....60.00
Pocketknife, Cub Scout, blk hdl, raised emblem on hdl 10.00
Postcard set, World Jamboree, 1957...15.00
Poster, John Glenn — Space Scout, 1960s....................................10.00
Poster, National Jamboree, Rockwell art, 1937, 30x20" 120.00
Ring, full First Class, sterling 10.00
Ring, Sea Scout, w/anchor, sterling 40.00
Sash, Order of the Arrow/Brotherhood, felt, 1930s 25.00
Tin, tea; Maj Gen Baden-Powell bust & scout image on top, 4x4x6" ..60.00
Uniform, Explorer, gr shirt/pants/garrison hat, wht web belt, set ..40.00
Wallet, Cub Scout, National issue, vinyl...4.00
Yearbook, 1st edition, 1915, VG...17.50

Girl Scouts

Collecting Girl Scout memorabilia is a hobby that is growing nationwide. When Sir Baden-Powell founded the Boy Scout movement in England, it proved to be too attractive and too well adapted to youth to limit its great opportunities to boys alone. The sister organization, known in England as the Girl Guides, quickly followed and was equally successful. Mrs. Juliette Low, an American visitor to England and a personal friend of the father of scouting, realized the tremendous future of the movement for her own country, and with the active and friendly cooperation of the Baden-Powells, she founded the Girl Guides in America, enrolling the first patrols in Savannah, Georgia, in March 1912. In 1915 national headquarters were established in Washington, D.C., and the name was changed to Girl Scouts. The first national convention was held in 1914. Each succeeding year has shown growth and increased enthusiasm in this steadily growing army of girls and young women who are learning in the happiest ways to combine patriotism, outdoor activities of every kind, skill in every branch of domestic science, and high standards of community service. Today there are over 400,000 Girl Scouts and more than 22,000 leaders. Mr. Sayers is also our Girl Scout advisor.

Book, Girl Scout Handbook, 1963, new edition, hardcover, 510 pgs ..12.50
Book, Official Leader's Handbook, tan cover, 1920 ....30.00
Calendar, 1920, Brown & Bigelow 100.00
Calendar, 1959, color photos, complete, 16x10" 20.00
Camera, Official GSA, Univex, 1937..50.00
Catalog, uniform; Official GSA, 1930s...15.00
Coin, GSA 60th Anniversary, gold finish, 1972 ....90.00
Compass, Official, Silva System, 1950s-60s, MIB 25.00

Cookie cutter set, GSA, gr hdl, complete, 1950 ....20.00
Doll, GS uniform, gr shorts, Uneeda, 1960-64, 15" 30.00
Flag, Official Brownie, sm, 1930s..25.00
Flashlight, Brownie logo, metal w/chrome finish, 1960s, 3" L.......40.00
Medal, Merit, GSA, w/ribbon, 1920...75.00
Patch, GSA First Class, tan, sq...40.00
Pin, Eaglet, 10k gold, type 2, 1930s...250.00
Postcards, GSA, color, set of 4, 1951-52 ....5.00
Sash, w/badges, patches, & pins, 1970s era 20.00
Sweater, Brownie, brn wool w/insignia patch 10.00
Tin, GSA Peanut Brittle, tin top, 1930s...30.00
Uniform, adult, coat-style dress w/belt, 1939-48 ....45.00
Uniform, wht blouse w/print, brn skirt, M 20.00
Whistle, Official GSA, cylindrical, 1920s.......................................20.00

Scrimshaw

The most desirable examples of the art of scrimshaw can be traced back to the first half of the nineteenth century to the heyday of the whaling industry. Some voyages lasted for several years, and conditions on board were often dismal. Sailors filled the long hours by using the tools of their trade to engrave whale teeth and make boxes, pie crimpers (jagging wheels), etc., from the bone and teeth of captured whales. Eskimos also made scrimshaw, sometimes borrowing designs from the sailors who traded with them.

Beware of fraudulent pieces; fakery is prevalent in this field. Many carved teeth are of recent synthetic manufacture (examples engraved with information such as ships' or captains' names, dates, places, etc., should be treated with extreme caution) and have no antique or collectible value. A listing of most of these plastic items has been published by the Kendall Institute at the Bedford Whaling Museum in New Bedford, Massachusetts. If you're in doubt or a novice collector, it's best to deal with reputable people who guarantee the items they sell. Our advisor for this category is John Rinaldi; he is listed in the Directory under Maine. See also Powder Horns.

Awl, geometrics w/heavy red & blk ink, clasped-hands terminal, ...150.00
Awl, inserted horn rings, lady's leg hdl w/eng high shoe, 5½" .1,265.00
Box, finger construction w/copper tacks, mahog top, 7" L, EX..3,000.00
Busk, vine-edged sqs w/bed, star, tree, ship, etc, red/blk ink, 14" ..4,950.00
Pie crimper, sm heart cutout, 6"...495.00
Snuff box, carpenters w/tools, foliage, 3-color, dtd 1828, 3" L.1,050.00
Snuff box, compass star/sunburst on lid, foliage ea side, 3⅝" L...325.00
Tooth, Am ship by French fort, 2 ladies picking flowers, lt color, 6".5,500.00
Tooth, ship w/Am flag, whaling scene w/men & ship, 2-color, 5" 3,400.00
Tusk, lady in lace dress, girl w/flower, mermaid & deer in blk, 18" 750.00

Sebastians

Prescott W. Baston first produced Sebastian Miniatures in 1938 in his home in Arlington, Massachusetts. In 1946 Baston bought a small shoe factory in Marblehead, Massachusetts, and produced his figurines there for the next thirty years. Over the years Baston sculpted and produced more than seven hundred fifty different pieces, many of which have been sold nationwide through gift shops. Baston and The Lance Corporation of Hudson, Massachusetts, consolidated the line in 1976 and actively promoted Sebastians nationally. Many of Baston's commercial designs, private commissions, and even some open line pieces have become very collectible. Aftermarket price is determined by three factors: 1) current or out of production status, 2) labels, and 3) condition. Copyright dates are of no particular significance with regard to value.

Mr. Baston died in 1984, and his son Prescott 'Woody' Baston, Jr.

continued the tradition by taking over the designing. To date Woody has sculpted over two hundred fifty pieces of his own. After numerous changes in the company that held manufacturing and distribution rights for Sebastians, Woody and his wife Margery are now sculpturing and painting the Sebastian Miniatures out of their home in Massachusetts. By personally producing the pieces, Sebastians are the only collectible line that is produced from design to finished product by the artist. Sebastian Miniatures have come full cycle. Our advisor for this category is Jim Waite; he is listed in the Directory under Illinois.

Adams Academy w/steeple..150.00
Aunt Polly, #7330, 2¾"...30.00
Boy & Pelican, bl label, MIB...35.00
Boy Scout, plaque...200.00
Building Days Boy, bl label...40.00
Carl Moore (WEEI)..350.00
Christopher Columbus, pewter.......................................500.00
Clown, #7342, 4⅛"..45.00
Comm S Decatur - National Bank of Decatur...............195.00
Dame Van Winkle, #7346...40.00
Daniel & Mrs Boone, #21 & #22, Arlington era, 2¾", pr...........100.00
Davy Crockett...200.00
Eskimo, holding fish or bottle...500.00
Eustace Tilley..1,600.00
Ezra, yel label, #8054...35.00
Family of Freemasonry (Ma)..75.00
Family of Freemasonry (Pa)..200.00
Family Reading Aloud, #7345...45.00
Fisherman's Wife..95.00
Gardener Man or Woman...225.00
George & Martha Washington, MIB...................................50.00
George Washington w/cannon, 3⅜"....................................30.00
Icahbod Crane, #7347...30.00
Jean & Catherine Laffite, 3", 2¾", pr................................70.00
Jimmy Fund (schoolboy)...45.00
John & Elizabeth Monroe, 3", pr.....................................140.00
John Alden Cooper...35.00
John F Kennedy, 2⅜"..30.00
Johnny Appleseed, 3¾"..40.00
Jordan March Observer, Marblehead era...........................55.00
Judge Pyncheon..120.00
Judge Thatcher, #7338, 3"...35.00
Leprechaun, ornament or pin...27.00
Long Arm of the Law...40.00
Majorette...450.00
Mayflower, #7333, 3⅞"..30.00
Nativity, music box...750.00
New England Home for Little Wanderers.........................750.00
Old Put Takes a Licking...250.00
Oliver Twist & the Beadle..30.00
Our Lady of Good Voyage (Syn, Wood)...........................250.00
Pilgrims, #7334, 3⅜"..30.00
Pope John XXIII...450.00
Sailing Days Girl, red label...40.00
Scotsman, ltd ed...175.00
Sitzmark...175.00
Smile of the Great Spirit pen stand...................................39.00
Snow Days Girl, girl w/snowman, #6263, MIB....................40.00
Soldier's Farewell..35.00
Speak for It, #7332..30.00
Spirit of '76...35.00
St Joan of Arc..225.00
St Sebastion..300.00
Three Little Kittens (Jell-O)..375.00

Time for Jell-O, man in apron at table w/spoon/mixer/eggs/cups, 1952..375.00
Tom Bowline Ashore, 3⅛"..30.00
Trail to Eagle (Eagle Scout)..125.00
Trick or Treat...55.00
Trumpeting Angel, ornament...22.00
Uncle Sam, #7344, 4⅛"...20.00
Victorian Couple, 1982 fuchsia label, 18"......................160.00
Weaver, #7337, 2¼"...30.00
Weighing the Baby, c 1941...350.00
Will Rogers, 2¾"..40.00
Yankee Sea Captain, #132...35.00
50th Anniversary plaque...75.00

Sevres

Fine-quality porcelains have been made in Sevres, France, since the early 1700s. Rich ground colors were often hand painted with portraits, scenics, and florals. Some pieces were decorated with transfer prints and decalcomania; many were embellished with heavy gold. These wares are the most respected of all French porcelains. Their style and designs have been widely copied, and some of the items listed below are Sevres-type wares.

Basin, Bleu Celeste, putti & floral sprays, 2¼x11½x8¼"........1,100.00
Basket, bird/floral w/in, rtcl, rnd base w/vines on yel, hdls, 11" dia..765.00
Cup & saucer, courting couple/jewels/gold, 2⅞", 5½"............1,500.00
Cup & saucer, floral cartouches on cerulean bl w/gold, 2⅝", 5⅜"..100.00
Cup & saucer, floral roundel in gilt fr, ca 1842, 3⅛", 6"..........1,600.00
Cup & saucer, Letitia Bonaparte portrait on canary w/gold borders, 4"..400.00
Cup & saucer, Louis XIV/Marie Antoinette, faux jewels, late 1800s...1,495.00
Cup & saucer, 18th-C couple reserve w/cobalt & gold, 3", 5⅝".800.00
Lamp, 2 figural reserves, bk: trophies, much gilt, gilt mts, 1875, 23"..2,350.00

Plaque, Josephine in Imperial attire with crown, giltwood Rococo frame with velvet and gold bead liners in shadowbox, 12x11½", $1,250.00. (Photo courtesy Neal Auction Company)

Plate, battle scene, cobalt/gold border, J Morin, 1890s, 9½", pr....3,500.00
Urn, cobalt w/appl Pan heads emerging grape festoons, w/lid, 17x7"...375.00
Urn, couple reserve w/cobalt & gold, fruit finial, 1900s, 26", pr...9,200.00
Urn, courting couple, gilt bands/hdls, E Carelle, now lamps, 20", pr...3,500.00
Urn, lady in woods, ormolu hdls/ft, w/lid, 12x3½"......................345.00
Vase, garniture; Bleu Celeste, putti & gallants reserves, 17", pr....3,000.00
Vase, maiden/rose garden/urn on ped/Cupid, E Broncourt, ftd, 29"..1,850.00

Sewer Tile

Whimsies, advertising novelties, and other ornamental items were sometimes made in potteries where the primary product was simply tile.

Birdhouse, rnd w/conical roof, hand-tooled bark-like texture, 7"...250.00
Cat, elongated/upright, head cocked, tooled eyelashes, metallic, 14"...660.00
Cat, reclining, hand-tooled eyelashes, wht-glazed eyes, 9" L........360.00
Chicken feeder, dk brn, cylindrical, incised decor, 10½"............220.00
Dog, incised designs, G Bagnell, rstr nose/base, 9½"..................880.00
Dog, lt brn glaze, blk eyes/collar, G Bagnell, OH, 10", EX.......1,540.00

Dog, molded detail w/collar & lock, hollow, OH, base chips, 11".....**495.00**
Dog, seated, long hair/bushy tail, partial red-brn glaze, on base, 22".**900.00**
Dog, seated w/collar & chain, metallic flecks in glaze, 8"...........**165.00**
Dog, spaniel, hand-formed/tooled fur, face & collar, open legs, OH, 11"...**360.00**
Frog, glazed, incised 1920 on base, 8¾" L.....................................**525.00**
Groundhog, hand-tooled features, inscribed EJE, OH, 8½".....**1,540.00**
Hobo, made from 8" sq pipe, mc glaze, appl features, Brockway PA, 24".**165.00**
Inkwell, cone form in open-sided sq frwork, on base, no insert, 3½".....**85.00**
Jar, tree trunk w/leaves & ferns, dog on lid, Clay Product, 7x6", VG...**300.00**
Lion, rebument on high rectangular base, full mane, 7x10x5", EX.....**700.00**
Lion, recumbent, facing right, curled tail, edge-molded base, 10", EX.**825.00**
Lion, recumbent, hand modeled & tooled, OH, 6x8¾"..............**550.00**
Lion, recumbent on rectangular base, EX detail/tooled, 3½x5½"....**220.00**
Owl, perched on rnd ped base, EX detail, orange glaze, 10½".....**440.00**
Owl on log, EX detail, heavy glaze, 20th C, 8½".........................**165.00**
Paperweight, emb scowling face wearing hood, metallic flecks, 4" dia...**85.00**
Paperweight, lion's head on disc, Nelsonville Sewer Pipe Co, 3", EX..**165.00**
Planter, appl grapes & leaves, OH, ca 1880, 7", EX.....................**65.00**
Planter, cast w/lions' heads & leaves, triangular base, 23"...........**195.00**
Planter, stump w/memorial inscription, 1888-1920, 39", EX.......**385.00**
Planter, 4 stumps share base, rprs, 17".......................................**220.00**
Plaque, heron w/water plants relief, inscribed on bk: 1890, 11x6", EX.**600.00**
Wall pocket, tree trunk w/sm cut limbs, dk brn glaze, 9x6¼".....**145.00**

Sewing Items

Sewing collectibles continue to intrigue collectors, and fine nineteenth-century and earlier pieces are commanding higher prices due to increased demand and scarcity. Complete needlework boxes and chatelaines in original condition are rare, but even incomplete examples can be considered prime additions to any collection, as long as they meet certain criteria: boxes should contain fittings of the period; the chains of the chatelaine should be intact and contemporary with the style; and the individual holders should be original and match the brooch. As nineteenth-century items become harder to find, new trends in collecting develop. Needle books, many of which were decorated with horses, children, beautiful ladies, etc., have become very popular. Some were giveaways printed with advertisements of products and businesses. Even early pins are collectible; the first ones were made in two parts with the round head attached separately. Pin disks, pin cubes, and other pin holders also make interesting additions to a sewing collection.

Tape measures are very popular — especially Victorian figurals. These command premium prices. Early wooden examples of transferware and Tunbridge ware have gained in popularity, as have figurals of vegetable ivory, celluloid, and other early plastics. From the twentieth century, tatting shuttles made of plastics, bone, brass, sterling, and wood decorated with Art Nouveau, Art Deco, and more modern designs are in demand — so are darning eggs, stilettos, and thimbles. Because of the decline in the popularity of needlework after the 1920s (due to increased production of machine-made items), novelty items were made in an attempt to regain consumer interest, and many collectors today also find these appealing.

Watch for reproductions. Sterling thimbles are being made in Holland and the U.S. and are available in many Victorian-era designs. But the originals are usually plainly marked, either in the inside apex or outside on the band. Avoid testing gold and silver thimbles for content; this often destroys the inside marks. Instead, research the manufacturer's mark; this will often denote the material as well. Even though the reproductions are well finished, they do not have manufacturers' marks. Many thimbles are being made specifically for the collectible market; reproductions of porcelain thimbles are also found. Prices should reflect the age and availability of these thimbles. Our advisor for this category is Kathy Goldsworthy; she is listed in the Directory under Washington. We also recommend *Sewing Tools & Trinkets, Volumes 1* and *2* by Helen Lester Thompson, and *Antique & Collectible Thimbles and Accessories* by Averie Mathes.

Awl, steel & bone, 4¼"..**20.00**
Basket, twisted paper-like cording w/gr plastic trim, w/hdl, sm.....**16.50**
Booklet, Am Thread Co, handkerchief/linen edging, late 1940s, 15-pg...**7.00**
Box, chinoiserie in gilt & cinnabar on blk lacquer, drw, 13x10x5"...**330.00**
Box, rosewood veneer w/brass inlay, fitted int, 10x8x5".............**415.00**
Caddy, Peaseware, 2-pc step-bk, pincushion top, metal posts, 6x4"...**200.00**
Caddy, spool; walnut w/velvet pincushion, 1-drw, 2-tier w/trn ft.**170.00**
Caddy, walnut w/velvet pincushion top, 1-drw.........................**100.00**
Chest, pine w/old grpt, scalloped ft, hinged lid, 12x10x9"..........**600.00**
Clamp, hemming; wrought iron, w/spool holder/clamp/pincushion, 7".**230.00**
Darning egg, blown glass, peachblow, 19th C, 4½"..................**115.00**
Gauge, dressmaker's; Picken, metal, 1915, 6", EX.....................**12.50**
Gauge, sewing/knitting; Singer, older type, 6"............................**7.50**
Knitting stand, maple w/lt curl, ftd rnd base, open center, 1900, 30"...**165.00**
Magazine, Needlecraft, 1926, 51-pg, EX..................................**14.00**
Needle book, Lady Betty, Made in Japan, 1950s, 4¼x3", VG.....**7.00**
Needle book, Liberty, Made in West Germany, EX.....................**8.50**
Needle book, S&H Green Stamps, Queen Victoria Gold Eyed Needles, EX...**10.00**
Needle book, Sun Life Insurance Co promotional, 1960s, 2½x4"...**3.00**
Needle book, Sweetheart, Made in Japan, 3½x5", NM.................**6.00**
Pincushion, ceramic Deco-style bird w/cushion on bk, Japan, 2x3"...**20.00**
Pincushion, NP, shoe roller skate, ca 1895-1910, 2½" L.............**110.00**
Pincushion, porc, figure beside basket w/cushion top, Occupied Japan...**40.00**
Pincushion, silver, elephant figural, Birmingham, 1900, 2¼x2⅝"........**145.00**
Pincushion, silver, pig figural, Birmingham, 1905, 1¾x3¼"..........**75.00**
Pincushion, Sterling, chick figural, Sampson & Mordan, 1905, 2"..**75.00**
Pincushion, vegetable ivory, basket form, Thames Tunnel souvenir...**135.00**
Pincushion/tape measure, Red Riding Hood nodder, 5½", VG...**140.00**
Pinking shears, Compton, M in VG box w/instructions................**12.50**
Scissors, buttonhole; forged steel, screw adjusts, 4⅝"....................**15.00**
Scissors, metal, stork figural, unmk......................................**22.00**
Sewing bird, brass, ornate clamp, EX rstr, 5".........................**135.00**
Sewing bird, brass, Pat Feb 15 8352 at wings, 5x3⅝", EX..........**100.00**
Sewing bird, silver & brass, 2 cushions, Feb 15 1853, EX...........**200.00**
Sewing bird, steel, orig blk pnt, figural worm clamp, 4"............**285.00**
Spool, wood w/bone ends, ca 1900, 1⅜".................................**35.00**
Tatting shuttle, Boy Improved, metal..**10.00**
Tatting shuttle, cvd bone, 1900s, 3"..**20.00**
Thimble, aluminum, bl elephants, bl glass top, ⅞".....................**27.50**
Thimble, bone china, Am Beauty Rose, Royal Albert...................**22.50**
Thimble, bone china, violets, Royal Hampton/Lefton, 1"...........**20.00**
Thimble, Sterling, filigree rim, ¾x⅝".......................................**30.00**
Thimble, Sterling, floral rim, ⅞"..**48.00**
Thimble, Sterling, Forget-Me-Not, fancy top, ¾".......................**48.00**
Tracing wheel, Dritz, Bakelite..**12.50**
Tracing wheel, wood hdl, metal thumb rest, Made in Japan, 6½"...**5.00**

Sewing Machines

The fact that Thomas Saint, an English cabinetmaker, invented the first sewing machine in 1790 was unknown until 1874 when Newton Wilson, an English sewing machine manufacturer and patentee, chanced upon the drawings included in a patent specification describing methods of making boots and shoes. By the middle of the nineteenth century, several patents were granted to American inventors, among them Isaac M. Singer, whose machine used a treadle. These machines were ruggedly built, usually of cast iron. By the 1860s and 1870s, the sewing machine had become a popular commodity, and the ironwork became more detailed and ornate.

Though rare machines are costly, many of the old oak treadle machines (especially these brands: Davis, Home, Household, National, New Home, Singer, Weed, Wheeler & Wilson, and Willcox & Gibbs) have only nominal value. Machines manufactured after 1875 are generally very common as most were mass produced. Values for these later sewing machines range from $50.00 to $100.00. Refer to *Toy and Miniature Sewing Machines, Books I and II*, by Glenda Thomas for more information. Our advisor for this category is Peter Frei; he is listed in the Directory under Massachusetts. In the listings that follow, unless noted otherwise, values are suggested for machines in excellent working order.

Child's, Ideal, cast iron and oak treadle type, 30½", G, $2,000.00.
(Photo courtesy Peter Frei)

Child's, Cornet, heavy metal, wht rabbit in circle, 9" 170.00
Child's, F&W, Gem, manual cam-type crank, 1900s, 7½x5¾" ...350.00
Child's, Genero, Gurlee Stitch Mistress, manual, 1940s-50s, 7" 125.00
Child's, Jones/Meccano Lockstitch, manual/electric, England, 1968..90.00
Child's, Little Modiste, red metal, battery-op, Japan.......................75.00
Child's, Metallograph Corp, Martha Washington Sotoy, manual, 1919 ...225.00
Child's, Muller #12, cast metal, manual, pre-WWII 275.00
Child's, Olympia, manual or battery-op, Japan...............................35.00
Child's, Palitoy, cast metal, manual, England, 6¾x4¼x9"...........160.00
Child's, Singer, Sewhandy Model 20, manual, 1950s, w/box.......150.00
Child's, Singer, Sewhandy Model 50 D, electric, 1960s, w/box 75.00
Child's, Smith & Egge Automatic 1901, CI, manual, ca 1901 ....325.00
Child's, Straco Jet Sew-O-Matic, plastic/metal, manual, 1960s.....50.00
Eldridge, Automatic, 1880s, complete, EX...................................150.00
Florence, CI, belt driven, Pat Nov 12, 1850, fancy stand, EX.....750.00
Goodrich, treadle, quarter-sawn oak cabinet, EX........................200.00
Grover & Baker, last Pat May 27, 1856 ....1,200.00
Singer, Pat 1846, MOP inlay in head, walnut fold-out case 800.00
Singer Featherweight #221, w/attachments, EX in case 465.00
Wheeler & Wilson, 625 Broadway, EX 200.00

Shaker Items

The Shaker community was founded in America in 1776 at Niskeyuna, New York, by a small group of English 'Shaking Quakers.' The name referred to a group dance which was part of their religious rites. Their leader was Mother Ann Lee. By 1815 their membership had grown to more than one thousand in eighteen communities as far west as Indiana and Kentucky. But in less than a decade, their numbers began to decline until today only a handful remain. Their furniture is prized for its originality, simplicity, workmanship, and practicality. Few pieces were signed. Some were carefully finished to enhance the natural wood; a few were painted.

Although other methods were used earlier, most Shaker boxes were of oval construction with overlapping 'fingers' at the seams to prevent buckling as the wood aged. Boxes with original paint fetch triple the price of an unpainted box; number of fingers and overall size should also be considered.

Although the Shakers were responsible for weaving a great number of baskets, their methods are not easily distinguished from those of their outside neighbors, and it is nearly impossible without first-hand knowledge to positively attribute a specific example to their manufacture. They were involved in various commercial efforts other than woodworking — among them sheep and dairy farming, sawmilling, and pipe and brick making. They were the first to raise crops specifically for seed and to market their product commercially. They perfected a method to recycle paper and were able to produce wrinkle-free fabrics. Our advisor for this category is Nancy Winston; she is listed in the Directory under New Hampshire. Standard two-letter state abbreviations have been used throughout the following listings.

Key:
CB — Canterbury
EF — Enfield
NL — New Lebanon
ML — Mt. Lebanon
SDL — Sabbathday Lake
WV — Watervliet

Armchair, maple, #1, 3-slat bk, old tape seat, ML, 1910s, child sz ...750.00
Armchair, tiger maple, scroll arms, 4-slat bk, alligatored, ML.....400.00
Basin stand, maple/pine, tapered legs, shelf, rfn, ca 1800, 35x18x19"...800.00
Basket, feather; blk ash, tall loop hdl, w/lid, 20x14½" 400.00
Basket, fine-weave splint, 2 sm bentwood hdls, red traces, 12" sq, EX 360.00
Bench, apple peeling; pine, 3 trn legs, CI peeler, ca 1847, 26x22x18" 1,750.00
Bench, kneeling; cream pnt, NE, 62" L..350.00
Blanket chest, pine, molded lid, till, lapped/dvtl drw, WV, 1830s, 37".2,600.00
Book, Constitution of Covenant of...Believers..., KY, 1883, EX 1,500.00
Bottle, blown, aqua, emb Shaker Fluid Extract Valerin, pontil, 3½" ..185.00
Bottle, liniment; Faith Whitcomb's Agency, Great Shaker Cure, aqua, 5"...500.00
Bowl & herb pestle, yel birch/maple, orig red on bowl, EF, 15½" dia ...650.00
Box, apple; dvtl pine, orange stain, canted sides, ML, 5½x9½x9" 5,800.00
Box, pine, 2 bins (logs/kindling), yel stain, ML, 28x30x19" 2,100.00
Box, pine w/old yel, dvtl, steel holder on side, ML, 1840s, 25x24x16"....2,750.00
Box, seed; finger-joint construction/2 dividers, ML orig label, 24x12" 190.00
Box, seed; Shaker Choice Vegetable Seeds, labels, 3½x23x11½" 850.00
Box, sewing; dvtl/pegged, hinged lid, brass hdl, w/tray, 1890s, 15" L...........750.00
Box, 2-finger, red stain, 1½x4x2½" 800.00
Box, 3-finger, copper tacks, old worn varnish, 5⅞" L 400.00
Box, 3-finger, copper tacks, 4¾" 575.00
Box, 3-finger, maple/pine, lt bl pnt, 5x11¼" 650.00
Box, 3-finger, worn natural patina, edge damage, 9" L 300.00
Box, 4-finger, fruitwood/pine, orig finish, copper tacks, 2¾x6¾" .2,300.00
Box, 4-finger, maple/pine, natural finish, SDL, 3¾x9¼"..............450.00
Box, 4-finger (left handed), pine & maple, 11½x5½", EX..........750.00
Bucket, red pnt, sgn NF Enfield NH 450.00
Bucket, staved, wire hdl, tin dmns..450.00
Bucket, yel pnt, hang-up tab, sgn NF Enfield NH 450.00
Chair, side; birch, 3 grad slats, rush seat, SDL, 1830s 650.00
Chair, side; 3-slat bk, rpl tape seat, WV, 1840s, 41½", pr 2,185.00
Chair, side; 3-slat bk, trn stiles, splint seat, MA, 1880s, 40" 400.00
Chair, tilter; birch, 3 grad slats, rush seat, EF, 1830s..................1,400.00
Chair, tilter; old rfn, cane seat, MA, 1860s, 39¾" 1,750.00
Chair, tilter; 3-slat bk, tape seat, old red pnt, EF, 40½"............1,750.00
Chair, work; maple, 2-slat bk, rush seat, trn legs, EF, 1850s, 42".635.00
Chest, birch, 4-drw, wood knobs, bksplash, red stain, 47x39x18" 4,000.00
Chest, blanket; breadbrd top, 2 scratch-beaded drws, grpt, NL, 1830s ..1,265.00
Chest, storage; maple/pine, dvtl case, dbl lid, WV, 1830s, 28x60x24"...3,000.00
Chest, work; pine w/old red, 4 dvtl drw, MA, 1830, 15x19x9"...2,300.00
Counter, tailor's; pine w/drop-leaf bk, 3 drws by cupboard, NL, 33x71"...6,000.00
Cupboard, panel do over 2nd, orig red, CI closures, NL, 1840s, 75x38"...7,250.00
Cutlery tray, divided, pierced heart hdl, bl-gray pnt, NH, 6x12½"......635.00
Desk, red pnt, slant lid, drw on fr, sq-to-rnd legs, EF, 49x31x25" 3,000.00
Desk, school; pine/maple, sq-to-rnd legs, slant lid, shelf, 30x41x19"...600.00
Firkin, orig bl pnt, stamped name on lid, 12x12"..........................600.00
Firkin, pine, lapped w/fingered lid, yel over orig gr, w/lid............450.00
Herb carrier, pine w/old red, stationary hdl, CB, 10x21x15".......400.00

Herb dryer, pine tray w/dvtl rim, diagonal slats w/screws, 40x19x2" **400.00**
Match strike, trn maple w/asphalt, w/copper-lidded match holder, 6" ...**550.00**
Measures, hickory/maple/pine, copper nails, ML, 1850s, 3 graduated szs....**800.00**
Mirror holder, butternut & cherry, iron knob, 16x11½" **2,200.00**
Mop, mc lamb's wool, sold in gift shop in 1940s..........................**135.00**
Muzzle, oxen; woven splint, New England, mid-1800s, 14½x14", pr **920.00**
Pail, tongue & groove staves w/iron hoops, birch hdl, NH, 11½x9" **700.00**
Pail, wood staves & iron hoops, bail hdl, Am, 19th C, EX **800.00**
Pen wiper, bsk doll w/patriotic felt, CB **145.00**
Pincushion, maple & red velvet, tomato shape, clamps to table, 1870s....**400.00**
Rack, drying; trestle ft, 4-slat, orig red, EF, 1830s, 35x14x13" .**2,200.00**
Rocker, arm; #4, maple, dk stain, 3-slat bk/shawl bar, tape seat, ML...**450.00**
Rocker, arm; #6, maple, 4-slat bk, orig tape seat, ML, 41½" **1,500.00**
Rocker, arm; #7, ebony finish, rush seat, rpr, ML..........................**500.00**
Rocker, arm; #7, maple, dk stain, 4-slat w/shawl bar, tape seat, ML..**1,000.00**
Rocker, arm; birch, 3-slat bk, ash splint seat, EF, 1830s, 40½".**1,900.00**
Rocker, arm; cherry/maple/birch, 4-slat bk, tape seat, ca 1850.....**1,000.00**
Rocker, armless; #0, maple, orig stain, tape bk/seat, ML, child sz .**3,300.00**
Rocker, armless; #3, ebony stain, orig tape seat & bk, ML **500.00**
Rocker, armless; #3, orig red-brn, rpl tape seat & bk, ML, 35¼" ...**195.00**
Rocker, armless; #3, rfn, rpl rush seat, 34", EX...........................**230.00**
Rocker, armless; 3 flame birch slats, rpl tape seat, EF...............**1,100.00**
Rug, looped/stitched yarn, mc stripes, 30x44" **275.00**
Settee, birch/pine, orig stain, EF, 1840s, 34x59".....................**12,000.00**
Sewing caddy, cherry, ivory-lined thread holes in top of 2 tiers, 6x7"....**220.00**
Sewing carrier, maple/cherry, 3-finger, swing hdl, 9½"+sm tools ...**485.00**
Sewing case, cherry/butternut/poplar, red wash, drw, MA, 1840s, 28" ...**31,000.00**
Shelf, clock; cherry, curved ends, 18x24x5" **800.00**
Sieve, beechwood, finely lapped w/copper nails, copper screen, 6x17"..**200.00**
Sieve, maple/pine, copper nails, EX patina, 3-part, NL, 4x7" L..**500.00**
Spool, sewing; maple or pine, 1" to 3", ea from $45 to **65.00**
Stand, birch, 1-drw, old red stain, 27x20x19", VG.................**2,000.00**
Stand, cherry, swelled ped, tripod base, ML, 1840-50, 25x16¾"...**2,000.00**
Stand, cherry, tripod base, NL, 24x17⅝" dia........................**17,000.00**
Stool, maple, tape top, ML labels, 17x14" sq **700.00**
Stove, CI, 2-pc construction, curved legs, slant top....................**350.00**
Swift, maple, old yel stain, trn wood table clamp, MA, 24½"...**4,500.00**
Swift, maple/beech, old yel stain, 6x22" extended.......................**250.00**
Table, sewing; birch/cherry, drop-leaf, orig red, 2-drw, EF, 38x41x20"..**4,500.00**
Table, sewing; pine/cherry, tray top w/drw, brass mts, 28x26x23"....**2,000.00**
Table, work; birch, dvtl drw, old varnish, trn legs, NH, 1850s.**1,300.00**
Table, work; pine/cherry, drw, drop-leaf bk, ca 1930, 36"+leaf....**6,500.00**
Table, work; tiger maple/cherry/poplar, 2 drws, tapered legs, 28" L.**4,750.00**
Wash stand, pine, natural finish, dvtl drw, tapered sq legs, 31x29x16"..**1,250.00**
Wash tub, staved/lap-fingered hoops, hdls, old red, 1890s, 24" dia......**460.00**
Wheel, walking; maple/oak, pewter collar, FW mk, WV.............**950.00**
Whisk broom, pine w/cvd leather loop for hanging, ML.............**600.00**

Shaving Mugs

Between 1865 and 1920, owning a personalized shaving mug was the order of the day, and the 'occupationals' were the most prestigious. The majority of men having occupational mugs would often frequent the barber shop several times a week, where their mugs were clearly visible for all to see in the barber's rack. As a matter of fact, this display was in many ways the index of the individual town or neighborhood.

During the first twenty years, blank mugs were almost entirely imported from France, Germany, and Austria and were hand painted in this country. Later on, some china was produced by local companies. It is noteworthy that American vitreous china is inferior to the imported Limoges and is subject to extreme crazing.

Artists employed by the American barber supply companies were for the most part extremely talented and capable of executing any design

the owner required, depicting his occupation, fraternal affiliation, or preferred sport. When the mug was completed, the name and the gold trim were always added in varying degrees, depending on the price paid by the customer. This price was determined by the barber who added his markup to that of the barber-supply company. As mentioned above, the popularity of the occupational shaving mug diminished with the advent of World War I and the introduction by Gillette of the safety razor. Later followed the blue laws forcing barber shops to close on Sundays, thereby eliminating the political and social discussions for which they were so well noted.

Occupational shaving mugs are the most sought after of the group which would also include those with sport affiliations. Fraternal mugs, although desirable, do not command the same price as the occupationals. Occasionally, you will find the owner's occupation together with his fraternal affiliation. This combination could add anywhere between 25% to 50% to the price, which is dependent on the execution of the painting, rarity of the subject and detail. Some subjects can be done very simply; others can be done in extreme detail, commanding substantially higher prices. It is fair to say, however, that the rarity of the occupation will dictate the price. Mugs with heavily worn gold lose between 20% and 30% of their value immediately. This would not apply to the gold trim around the rim, but to the loss of the name itself. Our advisor for this category is Burton Handelsman; he is listed in the Directory under New York.

Decorative, bird & flowers w/much gold, Am, 3⅞" **175.00**
Fraternal, BRT (Brotherhood of RR Trainmen) & boxcar, 3⅝" .**220.00**
Fraternal, Foresters of Am, maroon wrap, Vienna Austria, 4".....**140.00**
Fraternal, Knights of Golden Eagle emblem, Am, 3¾"..................**90.00**
Fraternal, Odd Fellows, 3-link symbol w/FLT, branches, 3¾"........**40.00**
Fraternal, Woodsmen of World, emblem/roses, no name, 3⅝"....**100.00**
Occupational, baseball bats & ball by player, bl wrap, Germany ..**2,150.00**
Occupational, blacksmith shoeing horse, horseshoes on wall, D&Co, 4"..**475.00**
Occupational, brewery truck w/bbls, early **1,765.00**
Occupational, bricklayer at wall, flowers ea side, Koken **800.00**
Occupational, cabinetmaker at bench w/tools, name, 3½" **500.00**
Occupational, carriage, detailed, Am, 3⅞", EX **300.00**
Occupational, clarinet above wreath of flowers, Melchior Bros..**350.00**
Occupational, cow & pig, Am, 3¾" **500.00**
Occupational, grocery wagon driver, Limoges, 3¾" **550.00**
Occupational, man driving horse-drawn grocery wagon, much gold, 3⅝" **950.00**
Occupational, man driving horse-drawn sulky, Germany, 3⅝" ...**625.00**
Occupational, man driving touring car, full bl wrap, 3⅝" **1,500.00**
Occupational, man fishing, red/yel w/flowers & banner w/name, 3½" ..**950.00**
Occupational, man hanging wallpaper, name in gold, crack, 4" ..**1500.00**
Occupational, man on steam tractor-driven hay bailer, Am, 3⅞"..**5,200.00**
Occupational, man training Appaloosa horse, purple wrap, Am....**1,500.00**
Occupational, oil derrick scene w/pumping house, Am, 3½" **1,250.00**
Occupational, oil rig, porc w/gold wear, 3¾" **1,100.00**
Occupational, red caboose, name in gold, Bavaria, chip **275.00**
Occupational, restaurant scene, detailed, Austria, 3¾"............**3,800.00**
Occupational, sheep farmer, sheep in pasture, name, 3½"..........**650.00**
Occupational, steeple chase w/crowded stands, name, 4", VG....**400.00**
Occupational, steer's head & butcher's tool, maroon wrap, Limoges...**125.00**
Occupational, 2-seater auto, dtd 1922 ....**1,600.00**
Patriotic, Am eagle on shield, bk: flowers, scuttle type.................**50.00**
Sportsman, duck hunting scene, blk wrap, sm rpr, 3⅝" **130.00**

Shawnee

The Shawnee Pottery Company operated in Zanesville, Ohio, from 1937 to 1961. They produced inexpensive novelty ware (vases, flowerpots, and figurines) as well as a very successful line of figural cookie jars, creamers, and salt and pepper shakers.

They also produced three dinnerware lines, the first of which, Valencia, was designed by Louise Bauer in 1937 for Sears & Roebuck. A starter set was given away with the purchase of one of their refrigerators. Second and most popular was the Corn line. The original design was called White Corn. In 1946 the line was expanded and the color changed to a more natural yellow hue. It was marketed under the name Corn King, and it was produced from 1946 to 1954. Then the colors were changed again. Kernels became a lighter yellow and shucks a darker green. This variation was called Corn Queen. Their third dinnerware line, produced after 1954, was called Lobsterware. It was made in either black, brown, or gray; lobsters were usually applied to serving pieces and accessory items.

For further study we recommend these books: *The Collector's Guide to Shawnee Pottery* by Janice and Duane Vanderbilt, who are listed in the Directory under Indiana; and *Shawnee Pottery, An Identification and Value Guide,* by our advisors for this category, Jim and Bev Mangus; they are listed in Ohio.

Cookie Jars

Bean Pot, snowflake, mk USA 70.00
Cottage, mk USA #6 ....1,500.00
Drum Major, gold trim, mk USA #10 ....700.00
Dutch Boy, cold pnt, mk USA 70.00
Dutch Boy (Happy), bl crisscross stripes w/decals & gold, mk USA ...385.00
Dutch Boy (Happy), patches w/gold, mk USA 525.00
Dutch Girl, bl w/gold decals & trim, mk USA 420.00
Dutch Girl, cold pnt, mk USA 140.00
Dutch Girl, quilted skirt, airbrushed gr, mk Great Northern #1026 ..420.00
Fruit Basket, mk Shawnee #84 ....225.00
Muggsy the Dog, bl scarf, HP blk detail w/gold, mk Pat Muggsy USA ..910.00
Puss 'n Boots, long tail, decals w/gold, mk Pat Puss'n Boots 630.00
Sailor Boy, blk scarf, mk USA 140.00
Sailor Boy, gold scarf w/decals, mk USA 770.00
Smiley the Pig, clover buds, mk Pat Smiley USA 500.00
Smiley the Pig, shamrocks, gr bib, mk USA 280.00
Smiley the Pig, strawberries w/gold, mk USA 700.00
Winnie the Pig, apples w/gold, mk USA 910.00
Winnie the Pig, peach collar, mk Pat Winnie USA 350.00
Winnie the Pig, peach collar w/gold, mk Pat Winnie USA 700.00

Corn Line

Bowl, cereal; King or Queen, mk #94 ....50.00
Bowl, fruit; King or Queen, mk #92 ....48.00
Bowl, mixing; King or Queen, mk #5, 5", from $22 to 25.00
Bowl, mixing; King or Queen, mk #8, 8", from $35 to 45.00
Bowl, vegetable; King, mk #95, 9" 55.00
Butter dish, Queen, w/lid, mk #72 ....55.00
Casserole, King, mk #74 ....40.00
Casserole, Queen, mk #74, lg, from $50 to 55.00
Cookie jar, King or Queen, mk #66 ....350.00
Corn roast set, Queen, #108 ....175.00
Creamer, King, gold trim, mk #70, from $95 to 110.00
Creamer, King or Queen, mk #70 ....25.00
Creamer, White, mk USA 30.00
Mug, King or Queen, mk Shawnee #69, 8-oz 50.00
Pitcher, King or Queen, mk #71, from $60 to 70.00
Pitcher, White, mk USA 65.00
Pitcher, White, w/gold, mk USA 120.00
Plate, Queen, mk #68, 10" 40.00
Platter, King or Queen, mk #96, 12" 55.00
Relish tray, King, mk #79, from $40 to 45.00
Saucer, Queen, mk #91 ....18.00

Shakers, King Indian, pr..80.00
Shakers, King or Queen, lg, pr......................................40.00
Shakers, King or Queen, sm, pr.....................................28.00
Shakers, White, w/gold, sm, pr......................................35.00
Sugar bowl, King or Queen, mk #78, w/lid.....................36.00
Sugar bowl, White, gold trim, mk USA, w/lid.................75.00
Sugar shaker, White Corn, mk USA, from $60 to............70.00
Teapot, King or Queen, mk #65, 10-oz...........................175.00
Teapot, White, gold trim, mk USA, 30-oz........................85.00

Kitchenware

Coffeepot, Pennsylvania Dutch, mk USA #52 ....270.00
Creamer, Pennsylvania Dutch, mk USA #12 ....60.00
Creamer, Puss 'n Boots, gold trim, mk Shawnee USA #85...........140.00
Creamer, Smiley, cloverleaf, gold trim, mk Pat Smiley USA 185.00
Grease jar, cottage, mk USA #8 ....375.00
Jug, ball; Snowflake, mk USA...45.00
Jug, ball; tulip, mk USA...115.00
Pitcher, Bo Peep, gold trim, mk Shawnee #47, 30-oz 175.00
Pitcher, Bo Peep, mk USA Pat Bo Peep, 40-oz................90.00
Pitcher, Chanticleer, all gold, mk Chanticleer................450.00
Pitcher, Chanticleer, plain, mk Pat Chanticleer 90.00
Shakers, Chanticleer, lg, pr..50.00
Shakers, Chanticleer, sm, pr...35.00
Shakers, duck, sm, pr..35.00
Shakers, Dutch Kids, bl & gold, lg, pr, from $85 to..........95.00
Shakers, flowerpot, gold pot & flower, sm, pr..................65.00
Shakers, Jack & Jill, decaled, gold trim, lg, pr, from $200 to.......225.00
Shakers, Muggsy, decals, gold trim, pr, minimum value..............400.00
Shakers, Smiley, bl bib, decals, gold trim, lg, pr.............295.00
Shakers, Smiley, gr bib, lg, pr...135.00
Shakers, Smiley, peach bib, sm, pr...................................50.00
Shakers, Smiley & Winnie, heart set, sm, pr.....................60.00
Shakers, sunflower, sm, pr..35.00
Shakers, Swiss Kids, lg pr...45.00
Shakers, watering can, sm, pr...26.00
Teapot, cottage, 5-cup, mk USA #7, rare, minimum value 650.00
Teapot, fern, emb, peach, yel, bl or gr, 8-cup, mk USA..............60.00
Teapot, hoseshoe design, yel, bl or turq, 8-cup, mk USA 45.00
Teapot, Pennsylvania Dutch, 14-oz, mk USA...................70.00
Teapot, Wave pattern, bl, yel or gr, 5-cup, mk USA..........50.00

Lobsterware

Baker, open, #915 ....40.00
Bean pot, #925...750.00
Bowl, batter; hdld, mk #928..55.00
Butter dish, w/lid, #927...110.00
Casserole, French; #904, 2-qt...30.00
Creamer, jug style, #921 ....50.00
Creamer & sugar bowl, w/lid, mk #910 ....90.00

Hors d'oeuvre holder, marked USA, 7¼", $280.00.

Plate, compartment; #912 ....100.00

Range set, #906, 4-pc **70.00**
Salad set, mk #924, 9-pc **135.00**
Shakers, claw shape, mk USA, pr **40.00**
Shakers, full body, mk USA **225.00**
Spoon holder, dbl, mk USA #935, 8½" **250.00**

Valencia

Ashtray **24.00**
Bowk, fruit; 5" **17.00**
Bowl, mixing; 7" **22.00**
Bowl, mixing; 9" **22.00**
Bowls, nesting; 8 szs, ea **22.00**
Candle holders, bulb, pr **35.00**
Casserole, 7½" **50.00**
Coaster **15.00**
Cup & saucer, AD **22.00**
Cup & saucer, tea **18.00**
Egg cup **18.00**
Fork, 9½" **35.00**
Marmite, 4½" **24.00**
Nappy, 9½" **20.00**
Pie plate, 9¼" **20.00**
Plate, chop; 13" **25.00**
Plate, compartment **24.00**
Plate, 6½" **12.00**
Sugar bowl, w/lid **25.00**
Teapot, regular, 8-cup **65.00**
Tray, relish; compartment **135.00**
Tray, utility **18.00**
Waffle set, 5-pc **100.00**

Miscellaneous

Planter, bull, gold trim, mk #668 ....**25.00**
Planter, circus horse, mk USA **20.00**
Planter, Colonial lady, mk USA #616 ....**35.00**
Planter, cub bear & wagon, gold trim, mk USA #731 ....**50.00**
Planter, deer lying down, mk USA **25.00**
Planter, dove w/planting dish, gold trim, mk #2025 ....**45.00**
Planter, kitten, mk USA #723 ....**35.00**
Planter, Madonna, mk USA **30.00**
Planter, terrier & doghouse, mk USA **25.00**
Vase, cornucopia boy or girl, mk USA #1275 or USA #1265, 5", ea **14.00**
Vase, cornucopia; mk Shawnee USA #865, 5" **16.00**
Wall pocket, clock, w/gold, mk USA #530 ....**45.00**
Wall pocket, red feather, no mk **45.00**

Shearwater

Since 1928 generations of the Peter, Walter, and James McConnell Anderson families have been producing figurines and artwares in their studio at Ocean Springs, Mississippi. Their work is difficult to date. Figures from the '20s and '30s won critical acclaim and have continued to be made to the present time. Early marks include a die-stamped 'Shearwater' in a dime-sized circle, a similar ink stamp, and a half-circle mark. Any older item may still be ordered in the same glazes as it was originally produced, so many pieces on the market today may be relatively new. However, the older marks are not currently in use. Currently produced Black and pirate figurines are marked with a hand-incised 'Shearwater' and/or a cipher formed with an 'S' whose bottom curve doubles as the top loop of a 'P' formed by the addition of an upright placed below and to the left of the S. Many are dated, '93, for example. These figures are

generally valued at $35.00 to $50.00 and are available at the pottery or by mail order. New decorated and carved pieces are very expensive, starting at $400.00 to $500.00 for a 6" pot.

Bowl, matt gr, 2x6" **40.00**
Bowl, streaky bls & grs, half-circle mk, 2x5¼" **48.00**
Candle holder, matt gr, 1⅜x6", pr **65.00**
Candlestick, gr gunmetal, half-circle mk, 2x4" **32.50**
Figurine, At the Races, Black jockey on horse, 4½x9" **60.00**
Figurine, pirate, 6½" **55.00**
Pitcher, matt gr, hdl w/center support, circular stamp, 7x6" **90.00**
Rose bowl, frosty turq & tan, 3½x7" **40.00**
Vase, gr & brn gloss, bulbous on ped, 4x4" **40.00**
Vase, lt bl crystalline, can neck, bulbous, 1930s, 5¾" **215.00**
Vase, streaky gr & brn, shouldered ball form, 5½x7" **70.00**
Vase, tennis players, bl gloss, 9⅝" **700.00**
Vase, tennis players, gr & gunmetal, flared rim, 9½" **1,100.00**

Sheet Music

Sheet music is often collected more for its colorful lithographed covers, rather than for the music itself. Transportation songs (which have pictures or illustrations of trains, ships, and planes), Ragtime and Blues, Comic Characters (especially Disney), Sports, Political, and Expositions are eagerly sought after. Much of the sheet music on the market today is valued at under $5.00; some of the better examples are listed here. For more information refer to *Sheet Music Reference and Price Guide, Second Edition,* by Anna Marie Guiheen and Marie-Reine A. Pafik. Values are given for examples in excellent to near-mint condition unless otherwise noted.

Turkey in the Straw, Otto Bonnell, black cover, VG, $40.00.

All I Care About Is You, Little Jack Little, 1931 ....**5.00**
Angels of Night, Harry J Lincoln, Cover Artist: Starmer, 1909 ....**15.00**
Auto Race, Percy Wenrich, 1908 ....**15.00**
Because, Horwitz & Bowers, 1898 ....**15.00**
Bluebird, Clare Kummer, 1918 ....**10.00**
Buy a Bond Buy a Bond, WB Kernell, WWI, 1918 ....**20.00**
Captive, David H Hawthorne, march, 1909 ....**15.00**
Chicago Express, Percy Wenrich, 1905 ....**15.00**
Cotton Coon's Two Step, CR Harrison, 1903 ....**35.00**
Day By Day, Stanford, 1900 ....**15.00**
Does It Pay?, Zittel & Sutton, 1907 ....**15.00**
Down in Shady Lane, Ballard & Kelly, 1910 ....**5.00**
Drill, Ye Tarriers Drill; Thomas Casey, 1888 ....**15.00**
Fair Debutante, Jules Reynard, 1922 ....**5.00**
For You & the Grand Old Flag, Coleman, 1910 ....**15.00**
Girl on the Automobile, Nathan, 1905 ....**15.00**
Golden Spider, Chas L Johnson, 1910 ....**10.00**
Good Night, Sweet Dreams; Bischoff, 1887 ....**15.00**
Hats Make the Woman, Victor Herbert, 1905 ....**10.00**
He's Such a Wonderful Boy, Motzan, Cover Artist: Pfeiffer, 1915 ...**10.00**
Heaven's Eternal King, Erik Meyer Helmund, 1888 ....**15.00**

Hello Baby, Edward Harrigan & David Braham, 1884..................**15.00**
Honey, I'm Waiting; McKenna, Cover Artist: Pfeiffer, 1913.........**10.00**
I'd Like No Cheap Man, Williams & Walker, 1897.....................**25.00**
I'd Like To Rock a Cradle, Herry F Kissell, 1924 ....**5.00**
I'll Have To Telegraph Another Baby, Manley, 1899.....................**20.00**
I Love You Truly, Carrie Jacobs Bond, 1920 ....**15.00**
I'm Going To Be a Sailor, Wm Heagney, 1906...............................**10.00**
I've Grown So Used to You, Thurland Chattaway, 1901 ....**10.00**
I Went Home With Michael, Felix McGlennon, 1892.....................**15.00**
If I Had You, Irving Berlin, 1914 ....**10.00**
In an Auto Car, Sutton, 1908 ....**15.00**
In Dear Old Saskatoon, Swift, Cover Artist: Pfeiffer, 1914 ....**10.00**
In the Land of Love With the Song Birds, F Wallace Rega, 1915 ...**5.00**
Is He the Only Man in the World, Irving Berlin, 1962 ....**5.00**
It Must Be Love, Meyer, Cover Artist: Pfeiffer, 1912.....................**10.00**
Just Another Kiss, Irving Caesar & N Hilbert, 1919.........................**5.00**
La Pauza, Wilkins, Cover Artist: Pfeieffer, 1914 ....**10.00**
Lady Bird Cha, Cha, Cha; Cover Artist: Norman Rockwell, 1968..**25.00**
Letter From Ireland, JF Mitchell, 1886...**15.00**
Little Toot, Allie Wrubel, Movie: Melody Time, Disney, 1948 .....**10.00**
Maiden's Prayer, Badarzewska, 1914 ....**10.00**
Matrimony Rag, Edgar Leslie & Lewis F Muir, 1911 ....**10.00**
Mid the Bluegrass of Kentucky, Harris, 1909..................................**10.00**
Mona, Sanders, Cover Artist: Pfeiffer, 1909 ....**10.00**
My Coca-Cola Bells, Cover Artist: Pfeiffer **10.00**
My Mobile Gal, MacConnell, 1900...**15.00**
Newport Belles, Ascher, 1901 ....**10.00**
Oh! That Cello, Charlie Chaplin, 1916...**15.00**
On the Sidewalks of Berlin, Clinton Keithley, WWI, 1918 ....**10.00**
Packard & the Ford, Carroll, Transportation, 1915 ....**25.00**
Polar Bear Polka, Albert Berg, 1865 ....**50.00**
Roamin' In the Gloamin', Harry Launder, 1911 ....**10.00**
Rose-Marie, Anne Caldwell & Jerome Kern, 1921 ....**10.00**
Scott Joplin's New Rag, Scott Joplin, 1912 ....**50.00**
Simple Melody, Irving Berlin, 1916..**10.00**
Smiles & the Tears of Killarney, S Carter & N Moret, 1917.........**10.00**
Song That the Anvil Sings, HW Petrie, 1902 ....**10.00**
Sugar Cane Rag, Scott Joplin, 1908...**50.00**
Take Me Back Home Again, Cooper & Millard, 1870 ....**15.00**
There Is a Land of Pure Delight, Haratio W Parker, 1890..............**10.00**
Thinking of You, Frances Lowell & William Dichmont, 1913......**10.00**
Tomahawk, JA McMeekin, Indian, 1916 ....**20.00**
Unknown Soldier Speaks, John McLaughlin, 1940 ....**10.00**
Way Down in Old Indiana, Paul Dresser, 1901 ....**10.00**
Wayside Willies March, Charles L Johnson, 1905 ....**10.00**
Wedding Bells Rag, Miller, Cover Artist: Pfeiffer, 1911 ....**10.00**
What Is This Thing Called Love, Cole Porter, 1929 ....**10.00**
When the Bell in the Lighthouse Rings, Lamb & Solman, 1905..**10.00**
When You Know You're Not Forgotten, J Fred Helf, 1906.............**5.00**
When You Love Her & She Loves You, Kerry Mills, 1907...........**10.00**

Shell-Work Collectibles

Not long after the natural beauty of the shell was discovered, man began to use them for decorative purposes of many types. Shells were used to decorate clothing and household items as well as jewelry, personal gifts, and souvenirs. Remains of shell necklaces have been found that date to a time prior to the great flood!

During Victorian times shell work became a hobby for the middle class. Shell-work jewelry became popular at that time, but very little has survived due to its delicate nature. Examples of love tokens, souvenirs, and whimsies from that era are listed below. For further information we recommend *Neptune's Treasures, A Study and Value Guide*, available from

our advisors, Carole and Richard Smyth (see their listing in the Directory under New York for ordering information).

Box, doghouse w/bsk dog peering out, litho paper, English, Vict, EX...**400.00**
Box, dresser shape, lift-top w/mirror, faux drws, from $250 to.....**385.00**

Box, English Victorian glass and shell, with red silk pincushion on lift top, from $175.00 to $380.00. (Photo courtesy Carole Smyth Antiques)

Box, shoe shape, litho scene at heel, English Vict, EX...............**385.00**
Desk letter holder, shells & litho, young lady, Vict, EX..............**375.00**
Dollhouse, garden of shells, 1930s Am folk art, VG................**1,200.00**
Dresser, w/mirror, 2 silk pincushions & drw, English Vict, EX **300.00**
Inkwell/letter holder, 3 lg shells, pnt ship, Fr Vict, EX.............**185.00**
Mirror, hand; lady's, shells on bk & hdl, Vict, EX.....................**200.00**
Necklace, feather/shell, on animal sinew, Am Indian, late 1800s, G ..**385.00**
Obelisks, shell encrusted, 19th C, pr.......................................**4,500.00**
Pie safe, hearts motif, 19th C Am folk art **3,500.00**
Pincushion, crown shape, shell & silk, Vict, EX, from $125 to...**200.00**
Pincushion, heart shape, 1-sided litho, pins at edge, Vict, EX **185.00**
Roundel, layered shells around bubble glass w/seascape litho, EX....**450.00**
Shadow box, house scene, papier-mache/wire/grasses, Vict English ..**7,000.00**
Thimble holder, sailboat shape, MOP, bsk sailor boy, Vict, EX ...**375.00**
TV lamp, bsk mermaid w/shells & coral, 1950s, EX **55.00**
TV lamp, 3 conch shells w/2 flamingos, 1950s, EX........................**45.00**
West Indies Sailor's Valentine, dbl mahog hex fr w/glass, G-...**8,000.00**

Shelley

In 1872 Joseph Shelley became partners with James Wileman, owner of Foley China Works, thus creating Wileman & Co. in Stoke-on-Trent. Twelve years later James Wileman withdrew from the company, though the firm continued to use his name until 1925 when it became known as Shelley Potteries, Ltd. Like many successful nineteenth-century English potteries, this firm continued to produce useful household wares as well as dinnerware of considerable note. In 1896 the beautiful Dainty White shape was introduced, and it is regarded by many as synonymous with the name Shelley. In addition to the original Dainty (6-flute) design, other lovely shapes were produced: Ludlow (14-flute), Oleander (petal shape), Stratford (12-flute), Queen Anne (with 8 angular panels), Ripon (with its distinctive pedestal), and the 1930s shapes of Vogue, Eve, and Regent.

Though often overlooked, striking earthenware was produced under the direction of Frederick Rhead and later Walter Slater and his son Eric. Many notable artists contributed their talents in designing unusual, attractive wares: Rowland Morris, Mabel Lucie Attwell, and Hilda Cowham, to name but a few.

In 1966 Allied English Potteries acquired control of the Shelley Company, and by 1967 the last of the exquisite Shelley China had been produced to honor remaining overseas orders. In 1971 Allied English Potteries merged with the Doulton group.

It had to happen: Shelley forgeries! Chris Davenport, author of *Shelley Pottery, The Later Years,* reports seeing Mocha-shape cups and saucers with the Shelley mark. However, on close examination it is evident that the mark has been applied to previously unmarked wares too poorly done to have ever left the Shelley Pottery. This Shelley mark can actually be 'felt,' as the refiring is not done at the correct temperature to allow it to be fully incorporated into the glaze. (Beware! These items are often seen on Internet auction sites.)

Some Shelley patterns (Dainty Blue, Bridal Rose, Blue Rock) have been seen on Royal Albert and Queensware pieces. These companies are part of the Royal Doulton Group.

Note: Objects with lids are measured to the top of the finial unless stated otherwise. Be aware that Rose Spray and Bridal Rose are the same pattern. Our advisor for this category is Lila Shrader; she is listed in the Directory under California.

Key:
LF — Late Foley
MLA — Mabel Lucie Attwell
QA — Queen Anne shape
R&RD — Rose & Red Daisy

RPFMN — Rose, Pansy, Forget-Me-Not
Trio — Cup, saucer, and 8" plate unless stated otherwise
W — Wileman, pre-1910

Advertising, ashtray, Greer's OVH Scotch Whiskey, 4½" dia **56.00**
Advertising, ashtray/match holder, The Owl, Fine Spirits, 2½x5"...**90.00**
Advertising, pitcher, Black & White, Scottie dogs, 5" **98.00**
Ashtray, Begonia, Blue Rock, Regency, Stocks, 3½", from $10 to ...**20.00**
Ashtray, Dainty Blue, #051/28, 5" dia **30.00**
Beaker (horn w/o hdl), crested w/2 lions, fine ribs, 4" **23.00**
Bowl, Kingfisher (enamel), 8-sided, blk w/red int, 8½".............**210.00**
Bowl, rim soup; Dainty Blue, #051/28, 8¼" **96.00**
Bowl, vegetable; Black Leafy Trees, QA shape, w/lid, 6x9".........**175.00**
Bowl, vegetable; Blue Rock or Regency, Dainty shape, oval, 4x9"...**110.00**
Bowl, vegetable; Bridal Rose, Dainty shape, dome lid, 6x9".........**395.00**
Bowl, vegetable; Bridal Rose, Rosebud, Dainty shape, oval, 4x9"..**175.00**
Bowl, vegetable; Sheraton, dome lid, #13289, 6x9" dia.............**49.00**
Butter pat, Campanula, #13886, Dainty shape, 3⅞" **95.00**
Butter pat, Dainty Mauve, #051/M, 3⅞" **185.00**
Butter pat, Lowestoft on lt gr w/gr band, #0133, 3¼" **45.00**
Butter pat, Maytime Chintz, #13452, 3¼" **65.00**
Butter pat, Pansy, #13671, Dainty shape, lg, 3⅞" **110.00**
Butter pat, Rosebud, #13426, Dainty shape, 3¾" **67.00**
Butter pat, Rosebud w/lt gr ¼" band on edge, 3¼" **32.00**
Butter pat, Shamrock, #14114, Dainty shape, 3⅞" **72.00**
Butter pat, various mc stylized flowers, 3¼" **26.00**
Cake plate, Glorious Devon, ped ft, #12734, 3x8¼" **166.00**
Cake plate, Heather, tab hdls, #13419, 8x10½" **46.00**
Cake plate, Japan, Imari-like, ped ft, W, 3x8½" **145.00**
Cake plate, Regency, ped ft, Dainty shape, 3x8½", from $65 to .**135.00**
Candlesticks, Art Deco style, no decor, 7½", pr.....................**50.00**
Candy dish, Bluebells, tab hdls, Dainty shape, 5⅞" **30.00**
Candy dish, clam shell shape, various patterns, 4½", from $15 to..**35.00**
Candy dish, Dainty Blue, tab hdls, 5⅞"...............................**53.00**
Chamber stick, enameled butterfly, finger ring, 2¾x5" dia...........**46.00**
Children's ware, cup, MLA, BooBoo riding puppy, 3"...................**80.00**
Children's ware, mug, MLA, boy/girl/BooBoos, 2¾" **178.00**
Children's ware, plate, MLA, BooBoos w/donkey cart, 6" **82.00**
Cigarette holder, Stocks, #13428, Dainty shape, 2⅛"...............**32.00**
Coffeepot, Bridesmaid, Windsor shape, 7" **110.00**
Coffeepot, Chrysanthemum, #2377, Richmond shape, 7¼"........**130.00**
Coffeepot, Dainty Green, 3053/27, 7" **627.00**
Coffeepot, Lily of the Valley, #23822, Dainty shape, 7" **310.00**
Coffeepot, Morning Glory, #13886, Dainty shape, 7¾" **338.00**
Coffeepot, Oleander, Dainty shape, 6½" **185.00**
Coffeepot, pastel, Dainty shape, 7" **165.00**
Coffeepot, Willow, bl, Gainsborough shape, 7½" **265.00**
Coffeepot, Yellow Wild Rose, Warwick shape, 7" **52.00**
Coronation ware, mug, King George & Queen Mary, 1911, W, 3"..**38.00**
Coronation ware, plate, Queen Elizabeth II, 6"........................**22.00**

Cream soup, Ashford, #14091, Oleander shape, hdls, w/underliner..**24.00**
Cream soup, Harebell, Oleander shape, hdls, w/underliner **48.00**
Cream soup, wht w/gold trim, Ludlow shape, hdls, w/underliner ..**26.00**
Creamer, Regency, Dainty shape, mini, 1½" **65.00**
Creamer, Shamrock, Dainty shape, mini, 1½" **90.00**
Creamer & sugar bowl, Melody Chintz, Richmond shape, cr: 3½"..**92.00**
Creamer & sugar bowl, Woodland, #13348, Cambridge shape......**46.00**
Crested ware, Hereford, vase, flattened form w/4 tiny ft, 2½" **7.00**
Cup & saucer, Begonia, #13427, Dainty shape, from $42 to **59.00**
Cup & saucer, blk matt w/pnt birds & flowers, rich gold, Ripon shape ..**170.00**
Cup & saucer, Blue Rock, Westminster shape, mini...................**190.00**
Cup & saucer, Charm, #13862, Westminster shape, mini **155.00**
Cup & saucer, Dainty Mauve, #051/M, from $170 to................**198.00**
Cup & saucer, demitasse; Mocha shape, no hdl, in sterling fr, 1920s..**38.00**
Cup & saucer, demitasse; Wildflowers, Mocha shape.................**56.00**
Cup & saucer, Grey Crystals, #13918, Westminster shape, mini..**200.00**
Cup & saucer, lav w/Summer Glory int, #13418/S20, Oleander shape.........**128.00**
Cup & saucer, Melody, #13452, Cambridge shape, from $35 to....**50.00**
Cup & saucer, mustache; Edmonton, Alberta scene **62.50**
Cup & saucer, mustache; Lord Roberts, Boer War, W, hairline...**345.00**
Cup & saucer, pastel w/Stocks int, ftd Oleander shape................**85.00**
Cup & saucer, Primrose, Canterbury shape, mini **155.00**
Cup & saucer, Primrose, Westminster shape, mini **195.00**
Cup & saucer, Primrose Chintz, #13589, Ripon shape **80.00**
Cup & saucer, Primrose Chintz, Canterbury shape, mini **315.00**
Cup & saucer, R&RD, #13425, Dainty shape, from $45 to...........**58.00**
Cup & saucer, Rock Garden, #13464, Richmond shape.............**65.00**
Cup & saucer, Rosebud, Canterbury shape, mini.....................**130.00**
Cup & saucer, Stocks or Blue Rock, low Oleander shape, from $35 to ...**60.00**
Cup & saucer, Strawberry, #2396, Warwick shape **40.00**
Egg cup, Dainty White w/turq-bl polka dots, Dainty shape, 2⅝"..**43.00**
Egg cup, dbl; Bridal Rose, Rosebud, Dainty shape, 3¾", from $45 to ..**60.00**
Egg cup, dbl; Celandine, Dainty shape, 3¾"..........................**44.00**
Ewer, Persian style w/hdl, dk mauve, w/lid, LF, 9".................**46.00**
Food mold, armadillo shape, W, 4x10x7" **138.00**
Ginger jar, Harmony, w/lid, 4¾".....................................**155.00**
Horn (tall mug w/hdl), Shamrock, #14114, Dainty shape, 4" **65.00**
Hot water pot, Swansea, #11301, bl w/chintz band, 4¼" **185.00**
Jam/honey pot, Begonia, Rosebud, notched lid, Dainty shape, 3¾"...**65.00**
Jam/honey pot, Harmony, notched metal lid, 4" **38.00**
Muffin, Lily of Valley, Stocks, Violets; w/lid, Dainty shape, 7½" ..**125.00**
Mustard pot, Delft lid, 2 tab hdls, no lid, W, 3" **115.00**
Mustard pot, Regency, notched lid, Dainty shape, 2¾" **39.00**
Pitcher, Harmony Ware, shades of bl, 6¼".............................**50.00**
Plate, dessert/salad; Dubarry, Duchess or Georgian, 8¼", from $9 to ...**28.00**
Plate, dinner; Dubarry, Duchess or Sheraton, 10¾", from $28 to..**45.00**
Plate, Imari-like pattern, Snowdrop shape, W, 8¼"...............**105.00**
Plate, Rosebud, RPFMN, Stock, Violets, Dainty shape, 8", from $35 to...**56.00**
Plate, Shamrock, Violets or Wildflower, Dainty shape, 8¼", $39 to ..**52.00**
Plate, various scenes, Dainty shape, 10½", from $48 to.............**85.00**
Plate, various scenes, shapes other than Dainty, 10½", from $32 to...**65.00**
Plate, Wild Anemone, #13977, Dainty shape, 8¼".................**56.00**
Platter, Begonia, Blue Rock or Primrose, Dainty shape, 14½x12"....**165.00**
Platter, Duchess, Cambridge shape, 12x10"..........................**78.00**
Platter, Regency, Dainty shape, 14½x12".............................**135.00**
Posey holder, Melody Chintz, mushroom style, 7¼" dia............**100.00**
Relish dish, Campanula, oval, Dainty shape, 7x4"...................**72.00**
Relish dish, Lilac Time, oval, Dainty shape, 7x4"....................**110.00**
Relish dish, Melody Chintz, 3-section, tab hdls, 10½"...............**112.00**
Sign, Shelley display, Royal Doulton, 1996, 3", from $55 to **96.00**
Smoke set, Lilac, Dainty shape, 2" cigarette holder+2 3" trays **77.00**
Sugar bowl, Autumn Leaves, #13742, Richmond shape, 3¼" **22.00**
Sugar bowl, Blue Iris, QA shape, 2⅝" **67.00**
Tea & toast set, RPFMN, Dainty shape w/indent+cup, 8¼" dia ...**77.00**

Tea & toast set, Rural England, Richmond shape w/indent+cup, 7½"...**55.00**
Tea & toast set, Stocks, #13428, oval, Richmond shape, 5x9" **57.00**
Teapot, Blue Harlequin, #14198, Avon shape, 4½" **55.00**
Teapot, Bridal Rose, Rosebud, RPFMN, Dainty shape, 5", from $260 to...**335.00**
Teapot, Dainty Blue, #051/28, 6"...**395.00**
Teapot, Harebell, #13544, Henley shape, 5"...............................**85.00**
Teapot, Heavenly Pink, #14075/p, Dainty shape, 5"...................**675.00**
Teapot, Old Mill, #13669, Cambridge shape, 5" **145.00**
Teapot, Rambler Rose, #13671, Dainty shape, 6" **490.00**
Teapot, Swansea, #11301, bl w/chintz band, 4⅞"......................**195.00**
Toast rack, Primrose Chintz, 3 panels, tab hdls, 4¾".................**140.00**
Trio, Balloons, #11674, tall QA, 6½" plate................................**225.00**
Trio, bl & wht, Alexandra shape, W, 6" plate, from $85 to.........**110.00**
Trio, Blocks, #11786, Vogue shape **260.00**
Trio, Blue Rock, #13591, Dainty shape, from $110 to.................**125.00**
Trio, Blue Rock, #13591, Henley shape, 6" plate **66.00**
Trio, Crocus, Eve shape, 6¼" plate...**82.00**
Trio, Dainty Yellow, #051/Y...**225.00**
Trio, Flowers of Gold, #14187, Dainty shape **100.00**
Trio, Pansy (lg), #13823, Dainty shape..**145.00**
Trio, Rambler Rose, #13671, Dainty shape **145.00**
Trio, Stocks, Dainty shape, from $65 to **125.00**
Trio, Woodland, #13348, Richmond shape, 7" plate....................**85.00**
Vase, blk matt w/enamel pk roses & gr leaves, 8½" **34.00**
Vase, blk matt w/2" floral band at neck, bottle shape, 9"...............**42.00**
Vase, Oriental-like gr enamel on blk print, lustre, 5½" **56.00**
Vase, wht w/blk/gold/lav/gr Deco decor, 7¼" **86.00**

Silhouettes

Silhouette portraits were made by positioning the subject between a bright light and a sheet of white drawing paper. The resulting shadow was then traced and cut out, the paper mounted over a contrasting color and framed. The hollow-cut process was simplified by an invention called the Physiognotrace, a device that allowed tracing and cutting to be done in one operation. Experienced silhouette artists could do full-length figures, scenics, ships, or trains freehand. Some of the most famous of these artists were Charles Peale Polk, Charles Wilson Peale, William Bache, Doyle, Edouart, Chamberlain, Brown, and William King. Though not often seen, some silhouettes were completely painted or executed in wax. Examples listed here are hollow-cut unless another type is described and assumed to be in excellent condition unless noted otherwise.

Key:
c/p — cut and pasted   p — profile
fl — full length   wc — water color
hc — hand colored

Full-figure of Rodman Wharton mounted on scenic background, signed August Amant Edouart, 1842, $800.00. (Photo courtesy Horst Auctioneers)

Cadet w/cap & dagger, fl, ink w/gold ink features, rvpt metal, 12x8"..**880.00**
Child w/toy, fl, ink/watercolor, 6¾x4¼", gilt fr **3,600.00**

Christian Fritz, p, reverse cut, initials/heart below, 12x10" **900.00**
Colonel Hustler Royal Engineers, fl, c/p, Edouart/1833, 11x7"+fr..**2,185.00**
Dr Hubbard (identified/1772), rvpt, in fr, 5x4½" **300.00**
Family of 4 (child w/toy, girl w/doll), fl, ink w/gold detail, 13x19"...**2,000.00**
Group, p/full-figure: Geo WA/H CLay/etc, 7 in all (1 on horse), 18x14"....**2,645.00**
Horse-drawn carriage, people in foreground, rvpt, ft, 8x10"........**400.00**
Lady, p, blk ink w/gold accents, sausage curls/lace collar, fr, 4x3" ..**165.00**
Lady, p, hair in bun, inked date: 1808, 6½x5½" **360.00**
Lady, p, hair tied up, name/1844, stains/foxing, 6½x5½" **385.00**
Lady, p, ink, blk w/wht details: tall bonnet/flower/hair/collar, 5x4"..**600.00**
Lady sits side-saddle on horse, man stands beside, fl, c/p, 12x14"+fr..**1,100.00**
Lady w/hair comb, p, HP dress w/lace collar & ribbon, glued down, 6x5"...**360.00**
Lady w/hair comb, p, ink detail: hair/fancy collar, inked ground, 6x4"..**440.00**
Lady w/hair up, fancy dress & bouquet, fl, c/p, wc traces, 7x4⅜"+fr...**250.00**
Man in military uniform, hc, wc on paper, E Parmeter, 4x2¾"+fr...**1,380.00**
Man in top hat, fl, c/p, Edouart/1827, 10½x5¾".......................**1,000.00**
Man's head, p, unsgn, ca 1840, 7¼x5¾" in blk & gilt fr.............**200.00**
Peddlers, group of 6 w/wares, rvpt, rvpt mat, bird's eye fr, 7x10"..**440.00**
Pr: sisters, gilt/gouache accents, 4x3", wood fr w/gilt liners.........**630.00**

Silver

Coin Silver

During colonial times in America, the average household could not afford items made of silver, but those fortunate enough to have accumulations of silver coins (900 parts silver/100 parts alloy) took them to the local silversmith who melted them down and made the desired household article as requested. These pieces bore the owner's monogram and often the maker's mark, but the words 'Coin Silver' did not come into use until 1830. By 1860 the standard was raised to 925 parts silver/75 parts alloy and the word 'Sterling' was added. Coin silver came to an end about 1900.

A Himmel/Hyde & Goodrich, pitcher, eng/emb florals, ftd, 1860, 15" **9,775.00**
A Rasch, Phila/New Orleans; fiddle hdl w/single drop, 5½", pr....**115.00**
AC Benedict, NY; punch ladle, fiddle hdl w/wavy shoulders, 13"...**250.00**
Adolphe Himmel, mint julep cup, hand wrought, appl lid & ft, 4-t-oz..**2,530.00**
Am, soup ladle, ca 1835-50, 14⅜"...**230.00**
Asa Blanchard, KY: beaker, plain cylinder w/eng initials, 3⅜"..**3,900.00**
AW Robinson, Philadelphia; sugar urn, chased beadwork, 14-t-oz..**1,495.00**
Ball Black, coffee/tea, spurred scroll hdls, concave panels, 5 pcs...**8,900.00**
Bigelow Bros & Kennard, Boston; tea/coffee set, 2 pots+cr/sug, 92-t-oz...**1,850.00**
Boston, biscuit box, floral finial, fitted int, 19-t-oz..................**1,100.00**
Boston, presentation communion dish w/dome, ca 1815, 24-t-oz...**1,375.00**
Boston, water pitcher, beaded/molded rim, stepped ft, 1855, 23-t-oz..**500.00**
EA Tyler, New Orleans; youth set, Fr Thread, 1835-50, 2-pc......**485.00**
Fletcher, Phila; acanthus calyx, leaf-capped scroll hdl, 1838, 13" **5,175.00**
Gorham, pitcher, classical urn w/reeded band, S-scroll hdl, 34-t-oz ...**2,500.00**
H Hogswell, Salem MA; cup, chased oak leaves/acorns, 1952, 4-t-oz ...**350.00**
Henry Longley, NY; punch ladle, monogram, 1810, 12½", 6-6-oz.........**345.00**
HET, punch ladle, King's pattern, ca 1839-40, 13¾" **3,000.00**
Houghton Perkins, MA; mid-rib hdl, 3-crescent drop on bowl, 14"..**400.00**
JC Moor, NY City; cake basket, 8-sided, rtcl, monogram, 6-6-oz...**700.00**
John Myers, Philadelphia; cream jug, reed loop hdl, 1785-1804, 6-t-oz..**750.00**
Jones Ball & Co, MA; jug, scroll hdl, monogram, 7¼", 11-t-oz..**315.00**
Lincoln & Reed, forks, uncurved w/shoulders, 1835-46, 9 for.....**230.00**
N Harding & Co, Boston; tea set, swag decor, 6" pot+cr/sug, 38-t-oz..**1,600.00**
Robert Shepherd & Robert Boyd, tea set, hinged lids, appl decor, 3-pc..**1,600.00**
S Kirk & Son, Baltimore MD; ladle, monogram, 13", 8-t-oz.......**515.00**
Samuel Ayres, KY; tablespoon, modified coffin, 9¾", pr, 4-t-oz..**630.00**
Scovil & Co, Cincinnati OH; gravy ladle, fiddle hdl, 8½", 2-t-oz...**80.00**
SM Taber, RI; ladle, spatulate end, mid-rib hdl, 1841-50, 4-t-oz..**260.00**

Taylor & Lawrie, Philadelphia; dessert spoon, fiddle hdls, 6 for ..**100.00**
Tyler & Jacks, New Orleans; commemorative cup, 1842, 5-t-oz ...**4,000.00**
Wm G Forbes, NY; tablespoons, monogram, set of 7, 14-t-oz **488.00**
Wm Hollingshead, PA; dessert spoon, eng hdl, ca 1870s, 5 for .**490.00**
Wood & Hughes, pie server, Tuscan, monogram, 9⅝", 2-t-oz **975.00**

Flatware

Silver flatware is being collected today either to replace missing pieces of heirloom sets or in lieu of buying new patterns, by those who admire and appreciate the style and quality of the older ware. Prices vary from dealer to dealer; some pieces are harder to find and are therefore more expensive. Items such as olive spoons, cream ladles, lemon forks, etc., once thought a necessary part of a silver service, may today be slow to sell; as a result, dealers may price them low and make up the difference on items that sell more readily. Many factors enter into evaluation. Popular patterns may be high due to demand though easily found, while scarce patterns may be passed over by collectors who find them difficult to reassemble. If pieces are monogrammed, deduct 20% (for rare, ornate patterns) to 30% (for common, plain pieces). Place settings generally come in three sizes: dinner, place, and luncheon, with the dinner size generally more expensive. In general, dinner knives are 9½" long, place knives, 9" to 9⅛", and luncheon knives, 8¾" to 8⅞". Dinner forks measure 7⅜" to 7½", place forks, 7¼" to 7⅜", and luncheon forks, 6⅞" to 7⅛". Our advisor for this category is Rick Spencer; he is listed in the Directory under Utah.

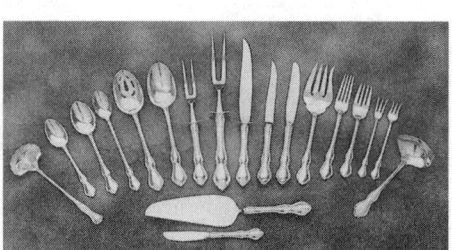

Hampton Court, Reed and Barton, 108-piece set, includes service for twelve along with accessory pieces (partial number of pieces shown), $3,500.00.

Buckingham, Gorham, service for 12, 156 pcs, +cvg set, orig case ..**2,185.00**
Buttercup, Gorham, iced-tea spoon **32.00**
Buttercup, Gorham, luncheon fork **30.00**
Buttercup, Gorham, 4-pc place-sz setting **120.00**
Canterbury, Towle, berry spoon **110.00**
Canterbury, Towle, dinner fork **65.00**
Canterbury, Towle, salad serving fork **135.00**
Canterbury, Towle, salad serving spoon **110.00**
Canterbury, Towle, tablespoon **69.00**
Chantilly, Gorham, cold meat fork **75.00**
Chantilly, Gorham, cream soup **38.00**
Chantilly, Gorham, pie/cake server **42.00**
Chantilly, Gorham, steak knife **38.00**
Chantilly, Gorham, teaspoon **22.00**
Eighteenth Century, Reed & Barton, gravy ladle **88.00**
Eighteenth Century, Reed & Barton, place knife **35.00**
Eighteenth Century, Reed & Barton, sugar spoon **42.00**
Eighteenth Century, Reed & Barton, tablespoon, pierced or plain ..**88.00**
Eighteenth Century, Reed & Barton, 4-pc place-sz setting **125.00**
English King, Tiffany, bouillon spoon **75.00**
English King, Tiffany, cream soup spoon **135.00**
English King, Tiffany, fruit spoon **110.00**
English King, Tiffany, gravy ladle **525.00**
English King, Tiffany, teaspoon **75.00**
Fairfax, Gorham, butter spreader, hollow hdl **24.00**
Fairfax, Gorham, tablespoon, plain **72.00**
Fairfax, Gorham, teaspoon **25.00**
Fairfax, Gorham, 4-pc place-sz setting **129.00**

Francis I, Reed & Barton, cocktail fork **30.00**
Francis I, Reed & Barton, jelly server **42.00**
Francis I, Reed & Barton, luncheon knife **35.00**
Francis I, Reed & Barton, salad fork **39.00**
Francis I, Reed & Barton, teaspoon **27.00**
Frontenac, Simpson, Hall & Miller; grapefruit spoon, fluted rim ..**330.00**
Frontenac, Simpson, Hall & Miller; gumbo soup **89.00**
Frontenac, Simpson, Hall & Miller; master butter knife **125.00**
Frontenac, Simpson, Hall & Miller; teaspoon...................................**28.00**
Grande Baroque, Wallace, cold meat fork **88.00**
Grande Baroque, Wallace, pie/cake server **42.00**
Grande Baroque, Wallace, place/dessert spoon **38.00**
Grande Baroque, Wallace, salad fork **38.00**
Grande Baroque, Wallace, steak knife **38.00**
Grande Baroque, Wallace, teaspoon **27.00**
King Edward, Gorham, demitasse spoon **20.00**
King Edward, Gorham, jelly server **35.00**
King Edward, Gorham, salad fork **32.00**
King Edward, Gorham, service for 12 in orig case, 108 pcs......**3,165.00**
King Edward, Gorham, tablespoon, pierced **75.00**
Lancaster, Gorham, asparagus server **395.00**
Lancaster, Gorham, beef fork, pierced **95.00**
Lancaster, Gorham, bouillon spoon **35.00**
Lancaster, Gorham, sardine server **89.00**
Lancaster, Gorham, sauce ladle **65.00**
Lily, Whiting, berry spoon **425.00**
Lily, Whiting, gravy ladle, shell bowl, 7"...**200.00**
Lily, Whiting, pate spreader **69.00**
Lily, Whiting, salad serving spoon **315.00**
Luxembourg, Gorham, tablespoons, initialed, set of 6 ....**115.00**
Lyric, Gorham, cream soup spoon **35.00**
Lyric, Gorham, flat butter spreader **23.00**
Lyric, Gorham, place fork **34.00**
Lyric, Gorham, sugar spoon **28.00**
Old Colonial, Towle, butter spreader, hollow hdl **29.00**
Old Colonial, Towle, cocktail fork...**39.00**
Old Colonial, Towle, gumbo **69.00**
Old Colonial, Towle, oval soup spoon, sm **29.00**
Old Colonial, Towle, pickle fork..**48.00**
Old Colonial, Towle, teaspoon, 5⅞" **25.00**
Old Colonial, Towle, tomato server **125.00**
Old Lace, Towle, butter spreader, hollow hdl **25.00**
Old Lace, Towle, cream soup spoon **35.00**
Old Lace, Towle, meat fork **65.00**
Old Lace, Towle, place fork...**34.00**
Olympian, Tiffany, asparagus tongs...**2,300.00**
Olympian, Tiffany, baby pusher **225.00**
Olympian, Tiffany, conch spoon, hollow hdl, early **1,300.00**
Olympian, Tiffany, ice cream server, 11½".................................**1,495.00**
Repousse, Kirk, berry spoon, 9" **95.00**
Repousse, Kirk, ice spoon **225.00**
Repousse, Kirk, meat fork, 5-tine **275.00**
Repousse, Kirk, place fork **36.00**
Repousse, Kirk, place knife..**30.00**
Repousse, Kirk, salad serving spoon **275.00**
Repousse, Kirk, service for 4, 24 pcs **425.00**
Rose Point, Wallace, gravy ladle...**69.00**
Rose Point, Wallace, luncheon knife **28.00**
Rose Point, Wallace, salad fork **30.00**
Rose Point, Wallace, tablespoon, pierced **69.00**
Rose Point, Wallace, teaspoon **22.00**
Rose Point, Wallace, 4-pc place-sz setting.......................................**115.00**
Royal Danish, International, butter spreader......................................**25.00**
Royal Danish, International, dessert spoon **39.00**

Royal Danish, International, place fork..**36.00**
Royal Danish, International, salad fork..**39.00**
Royal Danish, International, teaspoon..**25.00**
Savannah, Reed & Barton, berry spoon.......................................**135.00**
Savannah, Reed & Barton, butter spreader, hollow hdl.................**22.00**
Savannah, Reed & Barton, place fork...**38.00**
Savannah, Reed & Barton, sugar spoon..**38.00**
Savannah, Reed & Barton, teaspoon...**28.00**
Silver Flutes, Towle, cream soup spoon..**35.00**
Silver Flutes, Towle, flat butter spreader......................................**23.00**
Silver Flutes, Towle, meat fork..**69.00**
Silver Flutes, Towle, pickle fork...**26.00**
Silver Flutes, Towle, salad fork..**35.00**
Silver Flutes, Towle, tomato server, pierced.................................**99.00**
Strasbourg, Gorham, cold meat fork...**75.00**
Strasbourg, Gorham, luncheon knife..**27.00**
Strasbourg, Gorham, pie/cake server...**42.00**
Strasbourg, Gorham, place knife...**32.00**
Strasbourg, Gorham, place/dessert spoon.....................................**38.00**
Versailles, Gorham, dessert spoon..**85.00**
Versailles, Gorham, gravy ladle...**225.00**
Versailles, Gorham, ladle, 13"...**995.00**
Versailles, Gorham, pastry server, gold wash...............................**550.00**
Versailles, Gorham, tomato server, pierced.................................**495.00**

Hollow Ware

Until the middle of the nineteenth century, the silverware produced in America was custom made on order of the buyer directly from
the silversmith. With the rise of industrialization, factories sprung up
that manufactured silverware for retailers who often added their trademark to the ware. Silver ore was mined in abundance, and demand
spurred production. Changes in style occurred at the whim of fashion.
Repousse decoration (relief work) became popular about 1885, reflecting
the ostentatious preference of the Victorian era. Later in the century,
Greek, Etruscan, and several classic styles found favor. Today the Art
Deco styles of this century are very popular with collectors.

In the listings that follow, manufacturer's name or trademark is
noted first; in lieu of that information, listings are by country or item.
Weight is given in troy ounces. See also Tiffany, Silver.

Key: t-oz — troy ounce

Bailey, Banks & Biddle; tazza, rtcl rim, monogram, ped ft, 2⅜x8".......**135.00**
Black/Starr/Frost, candlesticks, bows/draping, beaded borders, 7", pr.**575.00**
Carl Schon, tray, mollusk shell incased in silver, 3 shell ft, 4½".**300.00**
Continental, beaker, engine-trn cylinder w/molded rim, 1850s, 1-t-oz..**100.00**
Continental, cow creamer, hinged lid, #925, 2x6".....................**375.00**
Continental, sugar castor, Neoclassical, script monogram, 7".....**460.00**
CS&HS, London; sugar castor, pear shape w/emb ribs, dome lid, 5-t-oz..**175.00**
Edward Jay (English), tray, ribbed rim, 3 paw ft, Geo III, 1796, 6"....**275.00**
Fish, candelabra, English Rose, 3-light, 1940s, 12x14", pr...........**750.00**
Frank Smith, bowl, chased/rtcl/emb scrolls & foliage, 20" L, +SP liner..**4,850.00**
Gerrard & Co, London; tapersticks, Baroque-style, 1934, 12-t-oz, pr.......**700.00**
Gorham, bonbon dish, emb thistles at rim, 5⅜", pr...................**115.00**
Gorham, bowl, floral emb everted rim, monogram, 2⅛x10½", 12-t-oz.**230.00**
Gorham, centerpiece basket, cvd/eng, gilt pierced lid, 1919, 15x12"...**1,725.00**
Gorham, covered vegetable bowl, reeded rim, 1912, 24-t-oz.......**300.00**
Gorham, creamer & sugar bowl, bucket form, 1871, 8-t-oz.........**575.00**
Gorham, gravy boat, repousse low form, 2½x6¼"......................**400.00**
Gorham, pitcher, plain urn form w/scroll hdl, initials, modern, 8¾"...**400.00**
Gorham, tea/coffee set, 1913-14, 6-pc w/stand, 115-t-oz............**800.00**
Gorham, water pitcher, reeded band, monogram, 1912, 10⅜", 26-t-oz..**700.00**
Henry Chawner, sugar basket, floral swag/eng border w/deer etc, 5½"....**625.00**

Hester Bateman, London; sugar basket, navette form, 1789, 7-t-oz.....**1,725.00**
IC, London; marrow scoop, Geo II, plain form, 1729, 8⅜", 1-t-oz..........**280.00**
International, fruit bowl, Royal Danish, scroll hdls, 24-t-oz........**315.00**
IW, London; cream pitcher, Geo III, repousse, gilt int, 3½".........**200.00**
JC Ltd, tea/coffee set, 2 pots+cr/sug, ebonized hdls/knobs, 47-t-oz....**1,380.00**
John Lautier, London; marrow scoop, beaded hdl, crest, 1778, 1-t-oz...**175.00**
John Schofield, London; tea caddy, paneled corners/crest, 6-t-oz.......**1,265.00**
John Schofield, London; tureen, urn form w/dome lid, 1785, 73-t-oz...**5,750.00**
John Schofield, London; urn, Geo III, bud finial, 1784, 55-t-oz........**2,400.00**
Kalo, tray, hammered sterling clam shell form, 3" W..................**325.00**
Kirk, teakettle, Nouveau style, mask hdls, heating element, 77-t-oz....**3,750.00**
London, jar, oval, swirl-fluted lid w/vacant reserve, 1890s, 4½".**265.00**
London, waiter, octagonal foliage/shell/gadrooned border, 1783, 8½".....**975.00**
Mexican/Conquistador, coffee service, plain/polished w/blk hdls, 5-pc.**865.00**
Mulholland, bowl, lobed form, hammered, 12½" L......................**160.00**
Paul Storr, plates, Geo III, ca 1815, 10¼", 314-t-oz, 12 for...**23,000.00**
Reed & Barton, coffee set, Hampton Court, 3-pc, 31-t-oz..........**750.00**
Reed & Barton, compote, Francis I, 4¾x8", 13-t-oz...................**460.00**
Shreve, Crump & Low, Boston; AD coffee service, 1890s, pot+cr/sug.**500.00**
Shreve & Co, San Francisco; pitcher, baluster, dtd 1951, 31-t-oz.....**1,000.00**
Shreve & Co, vase, appl/emb Nouveau peonies, trumpet form, 1905, 24"..**4,600.00**
Spaulding, fruit bowl, rtcl rim/foliate scroll border, rnd ft, 10½"...**200.00**
Stone Associates, MA; bowl, ftd, 3¼x7⅜".................................**485.00**
W&J Priest, London; coffeepot, Geo III Rococo, 1770, 18-t-oz.......**1,600.00**
Wilcox/Everston, powder box, plain cylinder w/foliate cover, 1½x3"....**60.00**
Wm B Kerr & Co, Newark; jewel casket, eng monogram, 1885, 3x5x4"...**300.00**
Wm Comyns, London; trumpet vase, repousse floral, 1892, 14", pr.....**1,850.00**
Woodside Sterling, butter dish, emb berries & foliage, ca 1900, 5-t-oz..**285.00**

Silver Overlay

The silver overlay glass made since the 1880s was decorated with a
cut-out pattern of sterling silver applied to the surface of the ware.

Bowl, gr w/daffodil patterned o/l, 3-ftd, 3¼x5"..........................**135.00**
Compote, blk amethyst w/scrolled o/l, ped ft, 7x7"....................**140.00**
Decanter, clear w/grapevine o/l, petticoat shape, 9x7"...............**635.00**
Pitcher, clear w/grapes, leaves & vines o/l, silver spout & hdl, 9"....**450.00**
Vase, cobalt bl w/floral o/l, silver hdls, 3x4".............................**500.00**
Vase, cranberry w/floral o/l, cylindrical, 6½"..............................**585.00**

Vase, floral on deep
emerald green, 3½",
$725.00; Perfume
bottles, scrolls on
emerald green, 4",
4¼", from $350.00 to
$395.00 each.

Vase, gr irid stretch glass w/urn & scroll o/l, fan shape, 6x7½"...**615.00**
Vase, gr irid w/floral o/l, mk Pat, 3¾", pr.................................**575.00**
Vase, gr w/floral o/l, bulbous w/trumpet neck, Alvin Mfg, 7¾"...**770.00**
Vase, gr w/floral o/l, flaring rim, ogee sides, 4", pr....................**630.00**
Vase, red w/floral o/l, bottle form, 3½".....................................**230.00**
Vase, ruby w/floral o/l, squat body w/scalloped trumpet neck, 3½x4"....**395.00**

Silverplate

Silverplated flatware is becoming the focus of attention for many of
today's collectors. Demand is strong for early, ornate patterns, and prices
have continued to rise steadily over the past five years. Our values are

based on pieces in excellent or restored/resilvered condition. Serving pieces are priced to reflect the values of examples in complete original condition, with knives retaining their original blades. If pieces are monogrammed, deduct from 20% (for rare, ornate patterns) to 30% (for common, plain pieces). Our advisor for this category is Rick Spencer; he is listed in the Directory under Utah. For more information we recommend *Standard Encyclopedia of American Silverplate* by Frances M. Bones and Lee Roy Fisher and *Silverplated Flatware, Revised Fourth Edition*, by Tere Hagan. See also Railroadiana, Silverplate.

Flatware

Adam, 1917, Community, berry spoon 45.00
Adam, 1917, Community, butter spreader 8.00
Adam, 1917, Community, cream ladle 20.00
Adam, 1917, Community, dinner fork 12.50
Adam, 1917, Community, sugar tongs 35.00
Ambassador, 1919, 1847 Rogers, cold meat fork 32.00
Ambassador, 1919, 1847 Rogers, dinner fork 8.00
Ambassador, 1919, 1847 Rogers, grapefruit spoon 8.00
Ambassador, 1919, 1847 Rogers, iced-tea spoon 8.00
Ambassador, 1919, 1847 Rogers, teaspoon 4.00
Ancestral, 1924, 1847 Rogers, gravy ladle 35.00
Ancestral, 1924, 1847 Rogers, sugar tongs 40.00
Ancestral, 1924, 1847 Rogers, teaspoon 8.00
Ancestral, 1924, 1847 Rogers, 2-pc carving set 70.00
Anniversary, 1923, 1847 Rogers, cocktail fork 10.00
Anniversary, 1923, 1847 Rogers, dinner fork 12.50
Anniversary, 1923, 1847 Rogers, ice cream spoon 25.00
Anniversary, 1923, 1847 Rogers, rnd soup spoon 10.00
Bird of Paradise, 1923, Community, demitasse spoon 8.00
Bird of Paradise, 1923, Community, jelly server 18.00
Bird of Paradise, 1923, Community, luncheon fork 6.00
Bird of Paradise, 1923, Community, preserve spoon 32.00
Carnation, 1908, WR Keystone Oneida, bouillon soup spoon 17.50
Carnation, 1908, WR Keystone Oneida, ice cream fork 32.00
Carnation, 1908, WR Keystone Oneida, teaspoon 8.00
Cedric, 1906, International, salad fork 16.00
Century, 1923, Holmes & Edwards, cheese server 35.00
Century, 1923, Holmes & Edwards, cocktail fork 10.00
Century, 1923, Holmes & Edwards, dinner fork 12.50
Century, 1923, Holmes & Edwards, pickle fork 10.00
Century, 1923, Holmes & Edwards, rnd soup spoon 10.00
Charter Oak, 1906, 1847 Rogers, butter spreader, flat hdl............40.00
Charter Oak, 1906, 1847 Rogers, cream ladle 70.00
Charter Oak, 1906, 1847 Rogers, dinner knife, hollow hdl, monogram ..45.00
Coronation, 1936, Oneida Community, butter spreader 8.00
Coronation, 1936, Oneida Community, meat fork 22.50
Coronation, 1936, Oneida Community, pie server 42.50
Coronation, 1936, Oneida Community, 4-pc, dinner-sz place setting ...30.00
Eternally Yours, 1941, 1847 Rogers, cream soup spoon 10.00
Eternally Yours, 1941, 1847 Rogers, tablespoon 10.00
Eternally Yours, 1941, 1847 Rogers, teaspoon 4.00
Eternally Yours, 1941, 1847 Rogers, 4-pc viande place setting 27.50
First Love, 1937, 1847 Rogers, cocktail fork...................................12.50
First Love, 1937, 1847 Rogers, dessert place spoon 9.00
First Love, 1937, 1847 Rogers, dinner fork 10.00
First Love, 1937, 1847 Rogers, meat fork 42.50
First Love, 1937, 1847 Rogers, 4-pc dinner-sz place setting 30.00
Grosvenor, 1921, Community, dinner knife 8.00
Grosvenor, 1921, Community, gravy ladle...32.00
Grosvenor, 1921, Community, rnd soup spoon..................................8.00
Grosvenor, 1921, Community, teaspoon..5.00
Heraldic, 1916, 1847 Rogers, cocktail fork 8.00

Heraldic, 1916, 1847 Rogers, iced-tea spoon................................12.00
Heraldic, 1916, 1847 Rogers, salad fork..10.00
Heraldic, 1916, 1847 Rogers, tablespoon..8.00
King Cedric, 1933, Community Plate, cocktail/seafood fork 8.00
King Cedric, 1933, Community Plate, demitasse spoon.................8.00
King Cedric, 1933, Community Plate, dinner fork.............................8.00
King Cedric, 1933, Community Plate, sugar spoon 5.00
Lady Hamilton, 1932, Oneida Community, cocktail fork 8.00
Lady Hamilton, 1932, Oneida Community, dinner fork 10.00
Lady Hamilton, 1932, Oneida Community, sugar tongs 35.00
Lady Hamilton, 1932, Oneida Community, 4-pc dinner-sz place setting ..32.00
Louis XVI, 1911, Oneida Community, berry spoon 35.00
Louis XVI, 1911, Oneida Community, dinner fork 8.00
Louis XVI, 1911, Oneida Community, dinner knife 12.50
Louis XVI, 1911, Oneida Community, flat butter spreader.............8.00
Morning Star, 1948, Community, berry spoon 32.00
Morning Star, 1948, Community, cream soup spoon 8.00
Morning Star, 1948, Community, dinner fork 10.00
Morning Star, 1948, Community, tablespoon 8.00
Mystic, 1903, Rogers & Bros, butter spreader 8.00
Mystic, 1903, Rogers & Bros, dessert place spoon 8.00
Mystic, 1903, Rogers & Bros, dinner fork, hollow hdl 12.50
Mystic, 1903, Rogers & Bros, oyster soup ladle 75.00
Orange Blossom, 1910, Wm A Rogers, dinner fork 12.50
Orange Blossom, 1910, Wm A Rogers, flat butter spreader...........12.50
Orange Blossom, 1910, Wm A Rogers, gravy ladle 42.50
Orange Blossom, 1910, Wm A Rogers, rnd soup spoon 15.00
Orange Blossom, 1910, Wm A Rogers, tablespoon.........................10.00
Patrician, 1914, Oneida Community, butter knife 4.00
Patrician, 1914, Oneida Community, dinner knife 8.00
Patrician, 1914, Oneida Community, grapefruit spoon...................10.00
Patrician, 1914, Oneida Community, jelly server.............................12.50
Patrician, 1914, Oneida Community, pie server, flat hdl...............45.00
Sheraton, 1910, Community Plate, cocktail/seafood fork 8.00
Sheraton, 1910, Community Plate, cold meat fork 17.50
Sheraton, 1910, Community Plate, dinner fork 7.50
Sheraton, 1910, Community Plate, soup ladle, flat hdl 70.00
Tiger Lily, 1901, Reed & Barton, berry spoon, gold-washed bowl .45.00
Tiger Lily, 1901, Reed & Barton, luncheon fork 10.00
Tiger Lily, 1901, Reed & Barton, salad fork 10.00
Tiger Lily, 1901, Reed & Barton, tablespoon...................................8.00
Tuxedo, 1923, Rogers Bros, berry spoon 32.00
Tuxedo, 1923, Rogers Bros, dinner fork 6.00
Tuxedo, 1923, Rogers Bros, gravy ladle...32.00
Tuxedo, 1923, Rogers Bros, rnd soup spoon 10.00
Vintage, 1904, 1847 Rogers, berry spoon...95.00
Vintage, 1904, 1847 Rogers, cream ladle...32.00
Vintage, 1904, 1847 Rogers, dinner fork 16.00
Vintage, 1904, 1847 Rogers, teaspoon 10.00

Hollow Ware

Candlestick, Adams style, Elkington, ca 1900, 11¼", pr.............575.00
Candlestick, scroll-arm cup aside natural tusk, Rodgers Sons, 14", pr..2,500.00
Candlesticks, Rococo, scalloped flower/scroll bases, English, 11", pr....250.00
Centerpiece, 3-D girl sits on rim (2X), mk Perron, Nouveau, 16" L 660.00
Coffee urn, eng detail, brass spout/lg hdls, dome lid, 21", EX......385.00
Coffee/tea set, baluster, gadrooned borders, unmk, 2 pots+cr/sug+tray..500.00
Entree dish, w/lid & warming stand w/dolphins, Elkington, 7x11x8"....400.00
Ice water set, Meriden Britannia, pitcher+goblet+tray...............315.00
Napkin holder, modeled as full-body carp, imp mks, 9" L 300.00
Pitcher, quadruple plate, dbl walled, lady figural hdl, Wilcox, 13"..300.00
Pitcher on stand, tilting, Rogers, Smith & Co, CT; ca 1870, 20" ..635.00
Punch bowl, Reed & Barton, King Frances, 11x16", +ladle+24 cups...750.00

Roast cover, fluted, floral & scroll mts **160.00**
Tea urn, plain, globular w/ring hdls, heating element, Gorham, 15" **500.00**
Tea/coffee, Gorham, Colonial Revival, 5 pcs on hdld 26" tray, 1916 ...**780.00**
Teapot on stand, melon ribed, scroll hdl/spout/legs, English, early **250.00**
Tray, diaper eng, grapevine border, hdls, Meriden Britannia, 33"...**575.00**
Tray, heavy appl grapevines on rim & forming hdls, rectangular, 31"...**250.00**
Vase, repousse floral festoons & scrolls, unmk, 17¾"....................**285.00**
Wine coasters, 2 w/vintage rim, wood base, +wheeled/hdld trolley, 21" ...**750.00**
Wine cooler, floral lift-off rim, branch hdls w/florals, dragon crest **230.00**
Wine cooler, urn form w/lion's-head hdls, 9½x8" **90.00**

Sheffield

Candlesticks, tapered rnd column, dome base w/tooled rings, 11", pr ..**250.00**
Condiment set, 2 salts+2 casters+mustard, cobalt liners, 6-t-oz ..**175.00**
Covered dish, w/shells & gadrooning, 8x14x9", w/warming stand, pr .**1,265.00**
Creamer & sugar bowl, scrolled borders, gadrooned sides, ball ft ..**85.00**
Dish cover, domed oval w/gadrooned band:scrolls/leaves/etc, 9x14x12" ..**460.00**
Entree dish, eng crest, gadrooning, rectangular, 11½x8¼", pr **635.00**
Tea set, Regency style w/gadrooned rims, 5¾" pot+cr/sug, ca 1800...**450.00**
Tea tray, emb vintage, foliate hdls, cast ft, ca 1900, 31x21" **230.00**
Tea urn, Georgian, spherical, ring hdls, sq base, 17" **925.00**
Wine cooler, fluted, gadroon/shell borders, lion hdls, liner, 11", pr....**5,100.00**

Sinclaire

In 1904 H.P. Sinclaire and Company was founded in Corning, New York. For the first sixteen years of production, Sinclaire used blanks from other glassworks for his cut and engraved designs. In 1920 he established his own glass-blowing factory in Bath, New York. His most popular designs utilize fruits, flowers, and other forms from nature. Most of Sinclaire's glass is unmarked; items that are carry his logo: an 'S' within a wreath with two shields.

Bowl, floral etch on canary yel, rolled rim, 13" **230.00**
Bowl, fruit; brilliant cutting, 8x5"...**460.00**
Champagne, Ivy...**70.00**
Compote, glossy blk, Ivorene edge, 7" **420.00**
Flowerpot, geometric cutting, intaglio border **330.00**
Lamp, Flower Basket, cut, 17" **1,500.00**
Pitcher, cut & eng, ped ft, 9" **3,100.00**
Sweetmeat, SP lid & bail hdl...**330.00**
Teapot, Rose...**1,465.00**
Tray, crosscuts, fans & hobstars, oval, 10x7" **325.00**
Vase, eng foliage & flowers, 12"..**200.00**
Vase, silver threads & dmns, 12" **1,500.00**
Vase, Stratford, 16"...**500.00**
Vase, tulips etch, 13½"...**550.00**

Sitzendorf

The Sitzendorf factory began operations in East Germany in the mid-1800s, adopting the name of the city as the name of their company. They produced fine porcelain groups, figurines, etc., in much the same style and quality as Meissen and the Dresden factories. Much of their ware was marked with a crown over the letter 'S' and a horizontal line with two slash marks.

Candle holder, cherubs at base, allover flowers, 1850s, holds 5, 16" ..**975.00**
Figurine, Cinderella's Coach, w/2 horse/driver/footman, 10½" ...**1,425.00**
Figurine, lady in bonnet carrying birdcage **190.00**
Figurine, Officer 1833, soldier in full dress, 9¼" **300.00**

Figurine, Olympian bowed on 1 knee, gold dress & hair, 7x8"....**460.00**
Lamp, 3 cherubs hold up wht basket w/mc flowers, satin shade, 13"...**275.00**

Skookum Dolls

Representing real Indians of various tribes, stern-faced Skookum dolls were designed by Mary McAboy of Missoula, Montana, in the early 1900s. The earliest of McAboy's creations were made with air-dried apple faces that bore a resemblance to the neighboring Chinook Indian tribe. The name Skookum is derived from the Chinook/Siwash term for large or excellent (aka Bully Good) and appears as part of the oval paper labels often attached to the feet of the dolls.

In 1913 McAboy applied for a patent that described her dolls in three styles: a female doll, a female doll with a baby, and a male doll. In 1916 George Borgman and Co. partnered with McAboy, registered the Skookum trademark, and manufactured these dolls which were distributed by the Arrow Novelty Co. of New York and the HH Tammen Co. of Denver. The Skookum (Apple) Packers Association of Washington state produced similar 'friendly faced' dolls as did Louis Ambery for the National Fruit exchange.

The dried apple faces of the first dolls were replaced by those made of a composition material. Plastic faces were introduced in the 1940s, and these continued to be used until production ended in 1959. Skookum dolls were produced in a variety of styles, with the most collectible having stern, lined faces with small painted eyes glancing to the right, colorful Indian blankets pulled tightly across the straw- or paper-filled body to form hidden arms, felt pants or skirts over wooden legs, and wooden feet covered with decorated felt suede or masking tape.

Skookums were produced in sizes ranging from a 2" souvenir mailer with a cardboard address tag to 36" novelty and advertising dolls. Collectors highly prize 21" to 26" dolls as well as dolls that glance to their left. Felt or suede feet predate the less desirable brown plastic feet of the late 1940s and 1950s. Our advisor is Glen Rairigh; he is listed in the Directory under Michigan.

**Males, taped feet, 1940s, 13½",
$275.00; 11½", $150.00.** (Photo
courtesy Glen Rairigh)

Baby, looks left, cradle brd, beaded body/head covering, 10½" ...**1,100.00**
Baby, w/blanket, feather in headband, 3½x3" **200.00**
Baby, w/blanket, leather headband w/pnt decor, 4"......................**30.00**
Baby mailer, 1½¢ postcard attached, feather ribbon binding, 4".**100.00**
Baby mailer, 1½¢ postcard attached, rattan binding, 4" **105.00**
Baby/child in loop basket, blanket wrap, loose hair, 12".............**225.00**
Baby/child in loop basket, blanket wrap, necklace, 14"...............**200.00**
Boy, brn ft pnt decor, Bully Good label, 6½" **100.00**
Boy, brn suede ft w/decor, headband, 10" **150.00**
Boy, w/blanket, felt pants, brn plastic ft w/mk, wood beads, 9½" ..**85.00**
Boy, w/blanket, felt pants, leather shoes, 6½", VG.......................**50.00**
Chief, headdress, paper shoes w/decor, 12½" **250.00**
Family, chief & female w/baby, clothes match, 15" & 14"...........**600.00**
Family, male & female w/baby on bk, w/blankets & many beads, both 22"....**3,180.00**
Family, male w/exposed right arm & female w/baby, 13½" & 12½" ..**900.00**

Female Apache w/baby, w/blanket, ft label, 11", G (orig box) **375.00**
Female w/baby, floral skirt, glass bead necklace, 11½" **300.00**
Female w/baby, w/blanket, beaded headband/necklace/earrings, 16"..**290.00**
Female w/baby, w/blanket, necklace, feather in hair, 16", G **145.00**
Female w/baby, w/blanket, necklace, headband, 12", G..............**115.00**
Female w/baby, w/blanket, purple felt skirt/ft, necklace, 11½" **200.00**
Female w/baby, w/blanket, worn paper ft, 12½", VG..................**150.00**
Girl, cotton-wrapped legs, beaded ft decor, headband, 9½" **150.00**
Girl, cotton-wrapped legs, pnt suede ft covers, Bully Good, 6½"...**100.00**
Girl, w/blanket, felt skirt, decor felt ft, bandana, 10"......................**85.00**
Girl, w/blanket/skirt, leather shoes, feather, label, 6½" **125.00**
Mailer, baby in bl & yel cotton, Grand Canyon 10-1-52................**25.00**
Mailer, baby in patterned cotton on yel cb..................................**25.00**
Mailer, baby in red bandana on yel cb..**55.00**
Male, w/blanket, feather, necklace, leather shoes, 36", EX **1,725.00**
Male, w/blanket, feather in headband, loose hair, felt shoes, 14", VG...**115.00**
Male, w/blanket, headband, necklace, 17½", G............................**635.00**
Twins, feathers tucked in blankets, plastic shoes, 6½", EXIB......**200.00**

Slag Glass

Slag glass is a marbleized opaque glassware made by several companies from about 1870 until the turn of the century. It is usually found in purple or caramel (see Chocolate Glass), though other colors were also made. Pink is rare and very expensive. It was revived in recent years by several American glassmakers, L.E. Smith, Westmoreland, and Imperial among them.

The listings below reflect values for items with excellent color. Our advisor for this category is Sharon Thoerner; she is listed in the Directory under California.

Green, shade, 6 panels in metal fr w/crown, 7¾x13½" **115.00**
Jade Green, honey pot, emb bees, invt funnel-shape lid, Imperial, 5"..**85.00**
Jade Green, toothpick holder, Imperial #505, 1975-77 ....**25.00**
Jade Green, vase, tricornered, Imperial, 3-ftd, 4x9" **185.00**
Pink, #101, toothpick holder, Challinor & Taylor **80.00**
Pink, Invt Fan & Feather, bowl, berry; 6½"............................**1,000.00**
Pink, Invt Fan & Feather, butter dish, 6" dia...........................**1,500.00**
Pink, Invt Fan & Feather, compote, ped ft w/4 toes, 5".............**650.00**
Pink, Invt Fan & Feather, creamer **500.00**
Pink, Invt Fan & Feather, cruet, all orig **900.00**
Pink, Invt Fan & Feather, jelly comport, ribbed stem, 4 ft, 5" **600.00**
Pink, Invt Fan & Feather, pitcher, 8"...................................**2,500.00**
Pink, Invt Fan & Feather, punch cup, from $285 to...................**315.00**
Pink, Invt Fan & Feather, sauce dish, scalloped edge, 4-ftd, 2½x4"...**275.00**
Pink, Invt Fan & Feather, shakers, rare, pr **1,200.00**
Pink, Invt Fan & Feather, spooner **475.00**

Pink, Inverted Fan and Feather, sugar
bowl, with lid, $1,000.00.

Pink, Invt Fan & Feather, toothpick holder, flat **500.00**
Pink, Invt Fan & Feather, toothpick holder, ftd, 2⅜" **1,500.00**

Pink, Invt Fan & Feather, tumbler **235.00**
Purple, bowl, scalloped edge, 2½x10"..**160.00**
Purple, ladies high boot, on base, unmk, 6½" **115.00**
Purple, Majestic Crown, spooner, ftd, 5½x3¾" **135.00**
Purple, pitcher, scroll hdl & ft (3), 4"..**90.00**
Red, basket, Imperial, 10"...**90.00**
Red, compote, scalloped edge, Imperial, 4½x8½"..........................**70.00**
Red, goblet, 1776 Eagle, Imperial, 4"...**25.00**
Ruby, compote, crimped, Imperial #431, 1969-74, 6½", minimum value ...**55.00**

Smith Bros.

Alfred and Harry Smith founded their glassmaking firm in New Bedford, Massachusetts. They had been formerly associated with the Mt. Washington Glass Works, working there from 1871 to 1875 to aid in establishing a decorating department. Smith glass is valued for its excellent enameled decoration on satin or opalescent glass. Pieces were often marked with a lion in a red shield. Our advisors for this category are Betty and Clarence Maier; they are listed in the Directory under Pennsylvania.

Bottle, mums on gr to wht, w/stopper, 11x7¼" **595.00**
Bowl, bride's; 2" band w/birds/flowers on opal; Pairpoint holder, 16"...**1,450.00**
Bowl, moss rose, mc on beige, melon ribs, 4x9" **675.00**
Cracker jar, daisies on cream, melon ribs, metal lid, 7" dia **300.00**
Cracker jar, gold floral allover, melon ribs, 5¾"; w/emb mts #4402 ...**350.00**
Cracker jar, gold floral/girl's face on beige, melon ribs, w/SP mt: 9" ..**665.00**
Cracker jar, ivy/gold on cream, melon ribs, 7" dia **975.00**
Cracker jar, pansies on beige, metal lid, bbl shape, 7x5" **750.00**
Creamer & sugar bowl, pnt burmese w/gold girl's head, SP mts, 3½"...**785.00**
Creamer & sugar bowl, violets on bl to beige, SP tops, 4", 3¾"..**750.00**
Humidor, pansies, bl on cream, melon-rib lid, 6½x4" **850.00**
Jar, gold floral branches w/teal & gold leaves, ribbed, 4x5".........**200.00**
Plate, Santa Maria 1893 World's Fair, anchored ship/sails down, 8"...**600.00**
Powder jar, floral, pk/gr on ivory, melon ribs, w/lid, 3½x5".........**250.00**
Sugar shaker, wild roses on wht, pillar ribs, SP lid (fair), 5¾"....**495.00**
Temple jar, mums on beige, gold-beaded lid, 8¾x6½" **1,675.00**
Toothpick holder, wild roses on wht, pillar ribs, 2¼" **250.00**
Vase, clematis on lt pk, gold-beaded top, 8x4½" **785.00**
Vase, daisies w/red stems on dk ivory w/gilt & wht beads, 3½x5"...**165.00**
Vase, daisy garland on cream, 3 dented sides, 4¾"......................**445.00**
Vase, Easter lilies on emerald gr w/gilt, trumpet form, 10x4¾" ...**450.00**
Vase, Easter lilies w/gold on crystal, 4-lobe rim, 10x5¼".............**375.00**
Vase, ferns, gr/brn on beige, 3 flat sides, 4¾x4" **175.00**
Vase, pond lilies, mc on pk, flaring at base, 7", pr........................**375.00**
Vase, roses/forget-me-nots on wht glossy, canteen form, 8¾x7"..**575.00**
Vase, wild roses on dk to lt to dk gr, ovoid pillow form, 9¾" **795.00**
Vase, winter scene, in ornate Pairpoint SP stand, 7¾x5" **785.00**
Vase, wisteria/gold on apricot, pinched sides, sm rim, 5¼x3½" ..**375.00**
Vase, World's Fair 1893/goldenrod & bl flowers on wht opal, 6" **275.00**

Snow Babies

During the last quarter of the nineteenth century, snow babies — little figures in pebbly white snowsuits — originated in Germany. They were originally made of sugar candy and were often used as decorations for Christmas cakes. Later on they were made of marzipan, a confection of crushed almonds, sugar, and egg whites. Eventually porcelain manufacturers began making them in bisque. They were popular until WWII. These tiny bisque figures range in size from 1" up to 7" tall. Quality German pieces bring very respectable prices on the market today. Beware of reproductions. Our advisor for this category is Linda Vines; she is listed in the Directory under California.

Babies, 2 holding Santa's hands, Germany, 2".................**175.00**
Baby, w/drum & cymbal, mk German US Zone, 2" **90.00**
Baby feeding seal w/baby bottle, Germany, 2".................**175.00**
Baby in sled pulled by huskies, Germany, 2" **165.00**
Baby lying on side, blk face, brn eyes, Germany, 2"..........**250.00**
Baby playing musical instrument, Germany, 2"................**125.00**
Baby sitting, snow ft, pointed hood, EX detail, Germany, 2".......**150.00**
Boy & girl, sliding down the snow on brick wall, Germany, 2½" ..**110.00**
Carollers, 3 w/snow hats & lantern on snow base, Germany, 2" ...**95.00**
Child, no-snow boy or girl pushing lg snowball, Germany, 2".....**110.00**
Santa atop gray elephant, Germany, 2½"......................**175.00**
Santa in yel sailboat, Germany, 2"..........................**125.00**
Santa nodder, Germany, 3" **90.00**
Santa sitting on wht swing, Germany, 3" **135.00**
Snow bear sitting or walking, Germany, 2½" **75.00**
Snow dog, rabbit or cat, Germany, 1", ea **50.00**
Snow man sitting, blk top hat, Germany, 2" **95.00**
Snow mother pushing twins in red charriage-sled, Germany, 2½"...**225.00**

Snuff Boxes

As early as the seventeenth century, the Chinese began using snuff. By the early nineteenth century, the practice had spread to Europe and America. It was used by both the gentlemen and the ladies alike, and expensive snuff boxes and bottles were the earmark of the genteel. Some were of silver or gold set with precious stones or pearls, while others contained music boxes. In the following listings, the dimension noted is length. See also Orientalia, Snuff Bottles.

Blk enamel w/lacquered transfer of naval battle, ca 1812, 3½" ..**1,750.00**
Blk enamel w/lacquered transfer of Treaty of Ghent, ca 1814, 3½" ..**2,000.00**
Blk lacquer burlwood w/HP Napoleon portrait, ca 1812, 1x3½" ..**1,000.00**
Blk lacquer w/France...Ashes of Napoleon transfer, 1840s, 3½"....**1,100.00**
Blk lacquer w/HP Napoleon & Marie Louise portraits, ca 1810, 3½" ...**1,200.00**
Brn marble w/HP scene of soldier & gentleman on lid, ½x2½" .**800.00**
Burl wood, rectangular, 3¼"...................................**100.00**
Ivory, dragon cvg, hinge pin rstr, 4x2½x⅞" **225.00**
Mahog w/HP lid: riverside town/mtns, 3⅛" **80.00**
Sterling, peanut shape, Mexico, 2" L..........................**80.00**

Soap Hollow Furniture

In the Mennonite community of Soap Hollow, Pennsylvania, the women made and sold soap; the men made handcrafted furniture. Rare today, this furniture was stenciled, grain painted, and beautifully decorated with inlaid escutcheons. These pieces are becoming very sought after. When well kept, they are very distinctive and beautiful. The items described in these listings were recently sold through Merle S. Mishlers Auctions, RD 2, Hollsopple, Pennsylvania. All are in excellent condition unless otherwise noted. Our advisor for this category is Anita Levi; she is listed in the Directory under Pennsylvania.

Blanket chest, poplar, red wash/gr rpt, dtd 1855, 20x50" top, att, G...**600.00**
Blanket chest, red/gr pnt w/yel stripes/stencil, SH, 1868, 24x49" ..**19,250.00**
Chest, blanket; feathers on mustard & brn, MB/1897..............**1,400.00**
Chest, blanket; grpt w/blk lid, fruit/florals w/gold, 1882 ....**2,900.00**
Chest, blanket; maroon & gold stencil, rod escutcheon, 1856 ...**2,000.00**
Chest, blanket; poplar, orig red pnt w/blk/gold, att, 22x42".....**3,850.00**
Chest, blanket; red & blk, gold stencil, CW/1874, 25x18x45"......**6,700.00**
Chest, blanket; red & blk, gold stencil, MH/1871, 25x15x10", VG .**6,200.00**
Chest, blanket; red w/floral stencils, rpl hinges, FJ/1892, VG..**3,800.00**
Chest, blanket; rose decals, blk & brn grpt, LK/1890..............**5,000.00**

Chest, 4 lg/2 sm drws w/decor, enamel pulls, sgn, 1951, EX.....**4,600.00**
Chest, 4 lg/3 sm drws, stencil, enamel pulls, sgn, 1883, EX+ ...**5,400.00**
Chest, 6-drw, brn w/mustard & decals, blk top & sides, Sala...**1,900.00**
Chest, 6-drw, cherry w/red stain/ebonized trim, 45x37" **2,750.00**
Chest, 6-drw, no pnt or decor, EX wood, G **475.00**
Chest, 7-drw, foliate stenciling, 1851, 55x41" **1,350.00**
Chest, 7-drw, grpt w/blk, gold stencil, MH 1887, 47½x39½"...**14,500.00**
Chest, 7-drw, maroon w/blk top & sides, rpt, CKM/1879, G **550.00**
Chest of drws, bl brd, hidden lock, stencil, HS/1879 ....**5,500.00**
Chest of drws, brn grpt w/stencil, pnt pulls, 1883, EX+ **5,400.00**
Chest of drws, floral decals/gilt fruit stencil/grpt, MH, 1879....**2,750.00**
Chest of drws, rosewood, 1841...............................**750.00**
Chest of drws, stenciling w/decals, dk brn, fancy bk brd **7,200.00**
Cradle, gilt stencils, mustard trim, maroon grpt **1,100.00**
Cupboard, corner; maroon w/blk, stencil, 1856....................**11,500.00**
Cupboard, Dutch; 4 doors/2 drws, stencil/old rpt, 1875, 84x65" ...**8,000.00**
Cupboard, poplar w/orig red & gr pnt/striping/stencil, 2-pc, 87x64" .**35,200.00**
Cupboard, step-bk; 3 glass doors/2 solid, 3-drw, no decor, 87½x64" ..**20,000.00**
Cupboard, top only, 2 glass doors, no decor, 40x42x13"...........**3,500.00**
Dresser, Emp style, columns on 3 drws, HF/1874....................**2,200.00**
Frame, cross pcs, gr/yel striping, 15½x19¾" **1,000.00**
Frame, gilt edges, stenciled, blk....................................**1,050.00**

Miniature blanket chest, stenciled gold MH 1871, red and black with replaced hinges, crack in lid, 15x25½x10½", $6,200.00 at auction.
(Photo courtesy Anita Levi)

Rope bed, cherry, red & brn finish, rare...................................**2,300.00**
Stand, bedside; rpt mustard brn **400.00**

Soapstone

Soapstone is a soft talc in rock form with a smooth, greasy feel from whence comes its name. (It is also called Soo Chow Jade.) It is composed basically of talc, chlorite, and magnetite. In colonial times it was extracted from out-croppings in large sections with hand saws, carted by oxen to mills, and fashioned into useful domestic articles such as footwarmers, cooking utensils, inkwells, etc. During the early 1800s, it was used to make heating stoves and kitchen sinks. Most familiar today are the carved vases, bookends, and boxes made in China during the Victorian era. For further information we recommend *Collector's Digest of Soapstone* by L-W Book Sales.

Bookends, Foo Dog, ornate cvg, 5x4½x3", pr **160.00**
Figurine, Artic Puffin (bird), deep gr, Inuit, 5x6½" **65.00**
Figurine, bear over seal, on 3x7" base.................................**60.00**
Figurine, elephant w/raised front leg & trunk, glass eyes, 11½" **80.00**
Figurine, grape arbor w/leaves/vines/2 squirrels, gr w/pk base, 5x8"..**100.00**
Figurine, Oriental man w/long mustache holding staff, 1½x4½" ..**50.00**
Figurine, shaman's head, dk gr, 3¼x2½" **55.00**
Figurine, young woman seated, stylized, 4½x10¼" **100.00**
Snuff bottle, Oriental scene, w/spoon in lid, 1960s, 1x3" **85.00**
Vase, birds & flowers, rust/olive/tan/blk, 7½x5½" **135.00**
Vase, cylindrical w/lg mums on side, 6½x3½".........................**60.00**

Soda Fountain Collectibles

The first soda water sales in the United States occurred in the very late 1790s in New York and New Haven, Connecticut. By the 1830s soda water was being sold in drug stores as a medicinal item, especially the effervescent mineral waters from various springs around the country. By this time the first flavored soda water appeared at an apothecary shop in Philadelphia.

The 1830s also saw the first manufacturer (John Matthews) of devices to make soda water. The first marble soda fountain made its appearance in 1857 as a combination ice shaver and flavor-dispensing apparatus. By the 1870s the soda fountain was an established feature of the neighborhood drug store.

The fountains of this period were large, elaborate marble devices with druggists competing with each other for business by having fountains decorated with choice marbles, statues, mirrors, water fountains, and gas lamps.

In 1903 the fountain completed its last major evolution with the introduction of the 'front' counter service we know today. (The soda clerk faced the customer when drawing soda.)

By this time ice cream was a standard feature being served as sundaes, ice cream sodas, and milk shakes. Syrup dispensers were just being introduced as 'point-of-sale' devices to sell various flavorings from many different companies. Straws were commonplace, especially those made from paper. Fancy and unusual ice cream dippers were in daily use, and they continued to evolve, reaching their pinnacle with the introduction of the heart-shaped dipper in 1927.

This American business has provided collectors today with an almost endless supply of interesting and different articles of commerce. One can collect dippers, syrup dispensers, glassware, straw dispensers, milk shakers, advertising, and trade catalogs. (Note: The presence of a 'correct' pump enhances the value of a syrup dispenser by 25%.)

Collectors need to be made aware of decorating pieces that are actually fantasy items: copper ice cream cones, a large copper ice cream dipper, and a copper ice cream soda glass. These items have no resale value. Our advisors for this category are Joyce and Harold Screen; they are listed in the Directory under Maryland. See also Advertising; Coca-Cola.

Candy jar, glass, 3-pc stacking w/lid, 19" overall...........................135.00
Catalog, Confectioners Supplies..., Besco...IN, 1920s, 5x9" 75.00
Catalog, Liquid Carbonic, 1900, 400-pg...400.00
Cone dispenser, metal, Turnball...TN...Pats Pending, 30x8x9", G...150.00
Cone holder, Have Some Ice Cream Now, rpt metal, w/light, EX ...70.00
Dipper, aluminum w/blk ribbed rubber-covered hdl 5.00
Dipper, banana split; Gilchrist #32 ....525.00
Dipper, banana split; Gilchrist #34, 11½", EX 450.00
Dipper, Benedict Indestructo #5, cone shape, sz #6, MIB............140.00
Dipper, Bonny Prod Co NY, aluminum w/stainless gears, yel plastic hdl ..10.00
Dipper, Dover Slicer, dbl lever, NP brass, wood hdl, NM............435.00
Dipper, Erie B-8, de-plated brass & copper, Pat 1908, EX 385.00
Dipper, Fisher Cold Dog, German silver, wood hdl, Canada, 19½" ..925.00
Dipper, Geer Mfg, Clipper Disher Pat Feb 7 05, EX 155.00
Dipper, Gem #9 ....65.00
Dipper, Gilchrist #33, conical, sz #6, 10½", EX 110.00
Dipper, Hamilton Beach #31, polished brass stem 55.00
Dipper, Hamilton Beach #67, 1950s 40.00
Dipper, Kingery, NP brass, wood hdl, 11" 50.00
Dipper, Maryland Baking Co, NP brass, wood hdl, 10", M..........135.00
Dipper, Mayer Mfg, German silver, wood hdl, 12"......................135.00
Dipper, Mosteller #78...160.00
Dipper, Naylor, steel, 8"..65.00
Dipper, Prince Castle...Pat Pend, sq, EX 200.00
Dipper, Quick And Easy, Erie Specialty, aluminum/wood hdl, 10½", NM..135.00

Dipper, sandwich; ICYPI, 10", EX 125.00
Dipper, sandwich; Pat Feb 17 '25, wood hdl, 12½".......................120.00
Dipper, Wendel's Practical Disher, Pat 1927, re-plated, prof rstr ..825.00
Dispenser, Birchola, ceramic ball, 14", EX+..............................1,850.00
Dispenser, Bowey's Hot Chocolate, aluminum w/enameled graphics, EX..135.00
Dispenser, Buckeye Root Beer, blk ceramic/wht logo, 15", EX.1,000.00
Dispenser, Buckeye Root Beer, red metal/chrome box, 12x15", VG ..75.00
Dispenser, Cherry Smash, ceramic ball, 15", EX.....................1,500.00
Dispenser, Cherry Smash, ceramic ball, 5¢ on side, 15", EX+..2,400.00
Dispenser, Chocolate/Hot Fudge/Butterscotch, metal, 13", EX 55.00
Dispenser, Daggett's Florida Punch, intact mixer, 15x9" w/gr base...400.00
Dispenser, Fru-Tola, Morgan-Abbot-Barker, glass/metal, 1911, EX..225.00
Dispenser, Green's Muscadine, 1920s, 13" dia, EX......................110.00
Dispenser, Hall, 3 pumps/3 dip dispensers, 6 flavers noted, M.....100.00
Dispenser, Hires, metal wall-mt w/glass jug, 12", EX 150.00
Dispenser, Horlick's Dumore Malted Milk, porc base, NM 1,800.00
Dispenser, Hot Soda, Manning-Bowman, ca 1890, EX................300.00
Dispenser, Howel's Orange Julep, ceramic ball, 14", EX...........1,800.00
Dispenser, Howel's Orange Julep, pnt steel/ceramic, 24x15" dia, EX ..700.00
Dispenser, Howel's Root Beer, wooden keg, 27x20", EX+ 350.00
Dispenser, Hull Raspberry Syrup, 1920s, 13⅞x4¾x8½" 75.00
Dispenser, iced tea; glass w/wht lettering, lemon finial, 20", EX .165.00
Dispenser, Julep, 2 glass jars in emb metal ftd box, EX+..............450.00
Dispenser, Liberty Root Beer, wood barrel w/claw ft, 14", EX+...700.00
Dispenser, Magnus Root Beer, ceramic keg, gold trim, 15", EX+ ...825.00
Dispenser, malt; Kraft, aluminum w/cobalt emblem, 9", EX........100.00
Dispenser, malt; wall-mt glass & metal jug, 13", NM+ 75.00
Dispenser, Mission Orange, lt gr glass, rubber top, amethyst base, EX ...250.00
Dispenser, Mission Orange, orig labels on yel, 27x12" dia...........700.00
Dispenser, Moxie, clear glass top/wht ceramic base, , NM..........300.00
Dispenser, National Dairy Malted Milk, aluminum, EX 120.00
Dispenser, Stearn's Root Beer, ceramic keg on stump, 17", EX+ .500.00
Dispenser, vaseline glass, brass spigot, 11x8"................................190.00
Dispenser, Ward's Lemon-Crush, ceramic lemon, no pump, 1920, EX ..1,400.00
Dispenser, Ward's Orange-Crush, ceramic orange, orig pump..1,800.00
Dispenser, Zipp's Root Beer, ceramic Robin Hood keg, 1920s, NM..2,700.00
Dispenser, Zipp's 5¢ Cherri-o, wht ceramic keg, 1910s, 14", EX ...3,000.00
Dispenser bottle, Orange-Crush, 1930s-40s, 17x34½"................225.00
Flavor board, Hersey's Ice Cream, emb tin, vertical, EX+ 185.00
Jar, Bovox Bouillon, Whites Utica, w/lid 600.00
Jar, Miner's Beef Bouillon, bull's head, w/lid 500.00
Mixer, malt; Hamilton Beach, marble base, early, 14½", EX.........40.00

Mixer, milk shake; Hamilton Beach #18, stainless steel and porcelain, with cup, VG, $200.00. (Photo courtesy Collectors Auction Services)

Mixer, milk shake; Oster, gr porc, 19", EX 100.00
Mixer, milk shake; Shak Rite, silver Pat 1919 cup, Hazel Atlas glass...425.00
Pitcher, Fro-Joy Ice cream, SP, 6½" 60.00
Rack, sack; Double Cola, mc tin sign above wire rack, wall mt, 16x37"...200.00
Sign, sidewalk; We Serve Gollam's Ice Cream, boy w/cone, EX .415.00
Soda fountain magazine, 1906 ....350.00
Soda fountain magazine, 1912 ....250.00
Soda fountain magazine, 1925 ....150.00
Soda fountain magazine, 1935 ....75.00

Soda glass, Cherry Smash, w/side logo, very rare 800.00
Soda glass, Early California in pk on wht ironstone, 7", 6 for 235.00
Soda glass, milk glass, classic ftd form, 7" 30.00
Straw holder, Benedict, glass, 10-panel sides, metal lifter, 10" 65.00
Straw holder, clear glass, metal lid, Pat Aug 22, 1916, tall/slim ..185.00
Straw holder, clear glass w/threaded metal lid, #37 on base, 9¾"..40.00
Straw holder, Sani Straw, clear glass/metal lid, 1917, 11½" 215.00
Sundae dish, etched glass, ftd, in chrome base, 3½x4", 4 for 30.00
Sundae dish, nickel silver, Wear Brite, Grand Silver Co, 4¾", 6 for..35.00
Sundae dish, stainless, Lily Tulip Cup Corp NY, 3¼", 6 for 30.00
Syrup jar, glass/metal, Johnson's Cold Fudge Syrup, 8", EX+.......200.00
Table, oak top w/wrought iron base, rnd, sm, +4 matching chairs....700.00
Tin container, Snow Sprinkles, sundae graphics, 1937, 10-lb, EX+....55.00
Tray, Eunell's Ice Cream, boy w/arm around girl, 13½" dia, VG+ 500.00
Tray, Hoffman's Ice Cream, girl on blk, red border, 15x11", VG.400.00

Spangle Glass

Spangle glass, also known as Vasa Murrhina, is cased art glass char-acterized by the metallic flakes embedded in its top layer. It was made both abroad and in the United States during the latter years of the nineteenth century, and it was reproduced in the 1960s by the Fenton Art Glass Company.

Vasa Murrhina was a New England distributor who sold glassware of this type manufactured by a Dr. Flower of Sandwich, Massachusetts. Flower had purchased the defunct Cape Cod Glassworks in 1885 and used the facilities to operate his own company. Since none of the ware was marked, it is very difficult to attribute specific examples to his man-ufacture. See also Art Glass Baskets; Fenton.

Creamer, cranberry w/pigeon blood & silver mica, wht lining, clear hdl ...150.00
Cruet, bl w/silver mica, clear stopper & hdl.................................275.00
Mug, amber w/gold mica 125.00
Rose bowl, pk w/maroon splotches & gold flecks, swirl, 4¼" dia...200.00
Syrup, pk mottle w/gold flakes, pewter top, clear hdl, 6½" 240.00
Tumbler, mc w/gold flecks 60.00
Vase, alternating pk/gr w/allover gold mica, ruffled, 6¾"..............75.00
Vase, yel on wht w/silver flecks, wht int, 8½"..............................165.00

Spatter Glass

Spatter glass, characterized by its multicolor 'spatters,' has been made from the late nineteenth century to the present by American glass-houses as well as those abroad. Although it was once thought to have been made entirely by workers at the 'end of the day' from bits and pieces of leftover scrap, it is now known that it was a standard line of produc-tion. See also Art Glass Baskets.

Pitcher, cream and brown with embossed ribs, amber handle, 8½", $150.00; Matching 4" tumbler, $60.00.

Candlestick, pk & clear, ruffled base, 9⅜" 120.00
Celery vase, cranberry & wht 150.00

Pitcher, bl & wht, clear reeded hdl, 6-sided top, 9¼"..................200.00
Rose bowl, pk & bl, 4½" 70.00
Salt cellar, gr & wht, clear petal ft, shell rim rigaree, 1¾" 110.00
Vase, rainbow, clear thorn hdls, 9" 190.00
Vase, wht & rose on pk, stick neck, 10½"...................................175.00

Spatterware

Spatterware is a general term referring to a type of decoration used by English potters as early as the late 1700s. Using a brush or a stick, brightly colored paint was dabbed onto the soft-paste earthenware items, achieving a spattered effect which was often used as a border. Because much of this type of ware was made for export to the United States, some of the subjects in the central design — the schoolhouse and the eagle patterns, for instance — reflect American tastes. Yellow, green, and black spatterware is scarce and highly valued by collectors.

In the descriptions that follow, the color listed after the item indi-cates the color of the spatter. The central design is identified next, and the color description that follows that refers to the design.

Bowl, bl, Adam's Rose, red & gr, 5" dia, VG..............................235.00
Coffeepot, bl, Fort, red/blk/gr, rstr 1,800.00
Creamer, bl, Fort, yel/red/brn/gr, 5¾" 450.00
Mug, bl, Peafowl, 4-color, stain, 3⅛" 725.00
Plate, bl, Dahlia, bl/red/gr, 8½"..330.00
Plate, bl, Eagle, brn, 1850s, 8" 300.00
Plate, bl, Fort, 4-color, 1840s, 9½" 300.00
Plate, bl, Peafowl, 3-color, rpr, 9" 95.00
Plate, bl, Profile Tulip, 3-color, 8¾" 300.00
Plate, bl (paneled border), Adam's Rose, red/gr, minor stains, 9" ..300.00
Plate, purple, Tulip, 4-color, 12-sided, 8¼", VG 270.00
Plate, rainbow, red/bl/yel border, 8½", NM............................3,500.00
Plate, red, Peafowl, 3-color, 9¼" 565.00
Plate, red, Tulip, red/bl/gr, some flaking, 8" 110.00
Plate, red & gr, Columbine, 3-color, 8⅜" 135.00
Plate, red/bl, Bull's Eye & leaves, red & gr, 8¾", EX 165.00
Platter, bl, Castle, 4-color, octagonal, 1840s, 13¾x17½".........5,465.00
Soup bowl, bl (paneled), Peafowl, gr/yel/red, rim flakes, 10½" ...880.00
Sugar bowl, bl, Fort, 3-color, 4½", EX......................................390.00
Sugar bowl, bl, Rose, red/gr/blk, rpl (matching) lid, rpr 395.00
Sugar bowl, gr, Peafowl, red/bl/gr, prof rpr..............................440.00
Sugar bowl, rainbow, red/bl/gr stripes, paneled, no lid, 5½", G...660.00
Tea bowl & saucer, bl, Holly Berry, 3-color, 3", 5⅞".................515.00
Tea bowl & saucer, bl, Rose, red/gr 190.00
Tea bowl & saucer, gr, Columbine, 3-color, NM.........................175.00
Tea bowl & saucer, rainbow (drape) red/yel/gr, sm rpr, lt stain..3,080.00
Tea bowl & saucer, red & bl Rainbow, Open Tulip, 4-color, ½", 6" ..515.00
Teapot, gr, Peafowl, 4-color, child sz, rpl lid 400.00
Teapot, gr t'print spatter (as leaves), Peafowl, 3-color, 7", EX .1,870.00
Teapot, red, Peafowl, 3-color, stains, 7¼"................................495.00
Toddy, red, Tulip, 4-color, 6½", NM..775.00
Wash bowl, bl, Tulip, yel/red/bl, 14", VG 1,200.00

Spelter

Spelter items are cast from commercial zinc and coated with a metallic patina. The result is a product very similar to bronze in appear-ance, yet much less expensive

Bust, Cleopatra, Fr, sgn, 11½"...400.00
Bust, Salome (Salambo), sgn, 11½"...400.00
Ewer, orange detail w/lady figural hdl, ca 1890, 21¼" 400.00

Figurine, Diana the Huntress, woman & dog running, sgn, 23x20x6" ..**2,500.00**
Figurine, Foo Dog, 10¾x12¼x7¼", pr **250.00**
Figurine, Forgeon de la Paix, young ironworker making plow, 1904, 20" ...**500.00**
Figurine, Greek man w/document & pen, gold leaf on face & hands, 13" ..**145.00**
Figurine, Huckleberry Fin, w/cold pnt, 8½" **75.00**
Figurine, Le Moissonneur, man w/candlestick in hand, Fr, 23" ...**275.00**
Figurine, man & woman holding banner behind head, wood base, 19"..**100.00**
Figurine, man stands beside rearing horse, late 19th C, 13x16" ..**150.00**
Figurine, Moses (after Michelangelo), English, 1880s, 10" **900.00**
Figurine, peasant girl feeding rooster, dbl patinated, 1880s, 19"..**175.00**
Figurine, Rebecca at the Well, sgn Henri Plè, 10½x29½" **775.00**

Spode-Copeland

The following is a short cronological history of the Spode company:
1733: Josiah Spode I is born on March 23 at Lane Delph, Staffordshire.
1740: Spode is put to work in a pottery factory.
1754: Spode, now a fully proficient journeyman/potter, works for Turner and Banks in Stoke-on-Trent.
1755: Josiah Spode II is born.
1761: Spode I acquires a factory in Shelton where he makes cream-colored and blue-painted earthenware.
1770: This is the year adopted as the date Spode I founded the business.
1784: Spode I masters the art and techniques of transfer printing in blue under the glaze on earthenware.
1796: This marks the earliest known record of Spode selling porcelain dinnerware.
1800: Spode II produces the first bone china.
1806: Spode is appointed potter to the royal family; this continues past 1983.
1813: Spode produces the first stone china.
1821: Spode introduces Feldspar Porcelain, a variety of bone china.
1833: William Taylor Copeland acquires the Spode factory from the Spode family and becomes partners with Garrett until 1847.
1870: System of impressing date marks on the backs of the dinnerware begins.
1925: Robert Copeland is born. (He presently resides in England.)
1976: The company merges with Worcester Royal Porcelain Company and forms Royal Worcester Spode Limited.
1986: The Spode Society is established.
1989: The holding company for Spode becomes the Porcelain and Fine China Companies Limited.

The price quotes listed in these three categories of Spode are for twentieth-century pre-1965 dinnerware in pristine condition — no cracks, chips, crazing, or stains. Minor knife cuts do not constitute damage unless extreme.

The patterns in the first group are the most common and popular earthenware lines. The second group contains the rarer and higher priced pattern; they are both earthenware and stoneware. Bone china patterns comprise the third group.

Our advisor for this category is Don Haase; he is listed in the Directory under Washington.

First Group:

Ann Hathaway, Billingsley Rose, Buttercup, Byron, Camilla Pink, Chelsea Wicker, Chinese Rose, Christmas Tree (green), Cowslip, Fairy Dell, Fleur de Lis (blue/brown), Florence, Gadroon, Gainsborough, Hazel Dell, Indian Tree, Jewel, Moss Rose, Old Salem, Raeburn, Reynolds, Romney, Rosalie, Rose Brier, Rosebud Chintz, Tower Blue, Valencia, Wickerdale, Wickerdell, Wickerlane.

Bowl, cereal; 6½" **32.00**
Bowl, fruit; 5¼" **28.00**
Bowl, waste; 6" **35.00**
Coffeepot, 8-cup **265.00**

Creamer, lg..**75.00**
Creamer, sm..**65.00**
Cup & saucer, demitasse..**45.00**
Cup & saucer, low/tall..**39.00**
Plate, bread & butter; 6¼" **28.00**
Plate, butter pat..**28.00**

Tower Blue, dinner plate, introduced in 1815 and still being produced today, $39.00.
(Photo courtesy Don Haase)

Plate, luncheon; rnd, 8-9" **35.00**
Plate, salad; 7½" **32.00**
Platter, oval, 13" **140.00**
Platter, oval, 15" **160.00**
Platter, oval, 17" **180.00**
Sauce boat, w/liner **145.00**
Soup, cream; w/liner..**55.00**
Soup, rim, 7½"..**35.00**
Soup, rim, 8½"..**45.00**
Sugar bowl, w/lid, lg **75.00**
Sugar bowl, w/lid, sm **65.00**
Teapot, 8-cup **265.00**
Vegetable, oval, 9-10" **155.00**
Vegetable, oval, 10-11" **165.00**
Vegetable, sq, 8" **145.00**
Vegetable, sq, 9" **155.00**
Vegetable, w/lid **265.00**

Second Group:

Aster, Buchart, Camilla Blue, Christmas Tree (magenta), Italian, Mayflower, Herring Hunt (green/magenta), Patricia, Tower Pink, Wildflower (blue/red), Delhi, Fitzhugh (blue/red/green), Gloucester (blue/red), Ruins (blue/pink/brown), Tradewinds (blue/red).

Bowl, cereal; 6¼" **39.00**
Bowl, fruit; 5½" **35.00**
Bowl, waste; 6" **45.00**
Coffeepot, 8-cup **375.00**
Creamer, lg..**95.00**
Creamer, sm..**85.00**
Cup & saucer, demitasse..**55.00**
Cup & saucer, low/high..**65.00**
Plate, bread & butter; 6¼" **35.00**
Plate, butter pat..**35.00**
Plate, chop; rnd, 13" **295.00**
Plate, dinner; 10½"..**65.00**
Plate, luncheon; rnd, 8-9" **49.00**
Plate, luncheon; sq, 8½" **65.00**
Plate, salad; 7½" **39.00**
Platter, oval, 13" **165.00**
Platter, oval, 15" **180.00**
Platter, oval, 17" **225.00**
Sauce boat, w/liner **185.00**
Soup, rim, 7½"..**45.00**
Soup, rim, 8½"..**55.00**

Sugar bowl, w/lid, lg **95.00**
Sugar bowl, w/lid, sm...**85.00**
Teapot, 8-cup **395.00**
Vegetable, oval, 9-10" **175.00**
Vegetable, oval, 10-11" **195.00**
Vegetable, sq, 8" **165.00**
Vegetable, sq, 9" **185.00**
Vegetable, w/lid **395.00**

Third Group:

Billingsley Rose Savoy, Bridal Rose, Carolyn, Chelsea Garden, Christine, Claudia, Colonel, Dimity, Dresden, Rose Savoy, Fleur de Lis (gray/red/blue), Geisha (blue/pink/white), Irene, Maritime Rose, Primrose (pink), Shanghi, Savoy.

Bowl, cereal; 6¼" **45.00**
Bowl, fruit; 5½" **42.00**
Bowl, waste; 6" **55.00**
Coffeepot, 8-cup **445.00**
Creamer, lg **120.00**
Creamer, sm **110.00**
Cup & saucer, demitasse...**65.00**
Cup & saucer, low/tall **75.00**
Plate, bread & butter; 6¼" **45.00**
Plate, butter pat **39.00**
Plate, chop; rnd, 13" **315.00**
Plate, dessert; 8" **55.00**
Plate, dinner; 10½" **69.00**
Plate, luncheon; rnd, 9" **59.00**
Plate, luncheon; sq, 8½" **69.00**
Plate, salad; 7½" **49.00**
Platter, oval, 13" **195.00**
Platter, oval, 15" **225.00**
Platter, oval, 17" **295.00**
Sauce boat, w/liner **145.00**
Soup, cream; w/liner **145.00**
Soup, rim, 7½" **65.00**
Soup, rim, 8½" **75.00**
Sugar bowl, w/lid, lg **120.00**
Sugar bowl, w/lid, sm...**115.00**
Teapot, 8-cup **445.00**
Vegetable, oval, 9-10" **215.00**
Vegetable, oval, 10-11" **235.00**
Vegetable, sq, 8" **245.00**
Vegetable, sq, 9" **275.00**
Vegetable, w/lid **425.00**

Spongeware

Spongeware is a type of factory-made earthenware that was popular during the last quarter of the nineteenth century and into the first quarter of the twentieth century. It was decorated by dabbing color onto the drying ware with a sponge, leaving a splotched design at random or in simple patterns. Sometimes a solid band of color was added. The vessel was then covered with a clear glaze and fired at a high temperature. Blue on white is the most preferred combination, but green on ivory, orange on white, or those colors in combination may also occasionally be found. As with most pottery, rare forms and condition are major factors in establishing value. Spongeware is still being made today, so beware of newer examples. For further information we recommend *Collector's Encyclopedia of Salt Glaze Stoneware* by Terry Taylor, our advisor for this category, and Terry and Kay Lowrance, available from Collector Books.

Bank, gr/brn, pig figural, pierced eyes, 3½x6", M **200.00**
Bowl, berry; bl/wht, ribbed exterior, mini, 1⅛x2¾" **225.00**
Bowl, bl/wht, heart-shaped panels on sides, 6x12", EX............**300.00**
Bowl, bl/wht, scalloped edge, 1½x9", M.................................**175.00**
Bowl, bl/wht repeating pattern, 4½x9", M, from $85 to............**125.00**
Bowl, milk; brn on yel ware, 9½", EX **100.00**
Bowl, mixing; bl/wht, molded arched panels, 6x13", EX **300.00**
Bowl, mixing; bl/wht pattern sponging, 6x12", M **245.00**
Bowl, mixing; bl/wht w/emb Heart pattern, 5½x10", M, from $175 to ..**225.00**
Bowl, serving; bl/wht, emb columns, 6½x13¼", M **300.00**
Bowl, vegetable; bl/wht, dk sponging, 9" L, M.........................**265.00**
Chamber pot, bl/wht, 5x8½", M, from $225 to **250.00**
Chamber pot, bl/wht w/bl bands, orig domed lid, bail hdl, 12", M...**575.00**
Cookie jar, bl/wht, ball shape, orig lid, 9" **375.00**
Cooler, bl/wht, orig brass spigot, w/rpl lid, 3-gal, 10", NM..........**500.00**
Creamer, bl/wht, 3", M...**285.00**
Creamer, brn/gr on yel ware, mini, 3", M **220.00**
Crock, bl/wht chicken-wire pattern, Butter stencil, chips, 3¾" ..**175.00**
Crock, bl/wht w/Butter stencil, w/orig lid, 4x5½", M...............**350.00**
Crock, milk; bl/wht, 5 sm ft, bail hdl, 5x10", M, from $300 to ...**425.00**
Cuspidor, bl/wht, bl shoulder band, 5x8", M **150.00**
Custard cup, gr/brn on yel ware, 2x4½", M.............................**65.00**
Grandma's Syrup Jug, bl/wht, w/bail, smallest sz, M **1,200.00**
Grandma's Syrup Jug, dk bl/wht, w/bail, sm to med, ea **900.00**
Inkwell, bl/wht, bl stencil: Empire, sq, 1½x1½x1⅜", NM **110.00**
Jardiniere, bl/wht, emb foliage scrolls, worn gold, 9x10½" **250.00**
Mug, bl/wht, dk sponging, 4½", EX **155.00**
Mug, bl/wht, 5x3½", M, from $175 to.....................................**200.00**
Mug, brn on yel ware, raised rings on str sides, emb hdl, 4¾", M ..**275.00**
Mug, lt bl/wht, heavy stoneware, 5¼", NM **165.00**
Piggy bank, bl-gr/tan on cream, 3¾", M **330.00**
Pitcher, batter; bl/wht, rare form, 8x8", M, from $1,700 to......**2,000.00**
Pitcher, bl/brn/red, wide body, 5", M **225.00**
Pitcher, bl/wht, bl-edged wht horizontal bands, ovoid, 9", M......**575.00**
Pitcher, bl/wht, emb daisy & vine w/gold, 9½", EX **165.00**
Pitcher, bl/wht, emb floral & panels, 8½", EX **250.00**
Pitcher, bl/wht, pattern sponging, bulbous, 12", M **395.00**
Pitcher, bl/wht, pattern sponging, upright bar hdl, early, 7", M ..**250.00**
Pitcher, bl/wht, Pine Cone pattern, 9", M...............................**875.00**
Pitcher, bl/wht, strong color & pattern, 9", M **525.00**
Pitcher, bl/wht close pattern, 10x7", M, from $275 to...............**375.00**
Pitcher, bl/wht repeating pattern, Old Fashioned Garden Rose, 9", M..**900.00**
Pitcher, bl/wht repeating pattern, 7x5", M, from $225 to...........**250.00**
Pitcher, brn/bl on cream, 11", EX **200.00**

Pitcher, cobalt sponging on light gray with cobalt accent bands at top and bottom, bulbous, 9¾", M, $575.00.
(Photo courtesy Vicki and Bruce Waasdorp)

Pitcher, gr/wht patterned, emb grapes, 8", M **125.00**
Pitcher, lt bl/wht, Uhl, smallest sz, M..**750.00**
Pitcher, olive gr/wht w/bl edge band, 6½", EX...............................**275.00**
Pitcher, syrup; bl/wht paw prints, 5½x4", M, from $350 to.........**400.00**
Pitcher, tankard; bl/wht, EX sponging, 9", M...............................**395.00**
Plate, bl/wht, scalloped/emb edge, 9", NM **165.00**
Plate, bl/wht, 7", NM **110.00**

Plate, gr/red/wht, 8¼", M.....................................**175.00**
Platter, bl/wht, 13½", M **375.00**
Soap dish, bl/wht, cut-out corners, 3 soap rests in base, 3½x5½" ..**195.00**
Soap dish, bl/wht, raised ribs, 4" dia, M **225.00**
Soap dish, red/bl on wht, 3½x4⅝", M **175.00**
Sugar bowl, gr/wht, 5¼", EX...................................**100.00**
Teapot, bl/wht, w/orig lid, 8½x8½", M, from $1,200 to..........**1,500.00**
Tray, bl/wht, heavy sponging over emb scrolls, gilt edge, 6" dia, M..**225.00**
Umbrella stand, bl/wht w/bl bands at top & bottom, OH, M ..**1,200.00**
Vase, bl/wht, emb ribbon, 7½", EX.............................**110.00**
Washboard **400.00**
Washbowl & pitcher, bl/wht, 5x14", 10x7½", M, from $650 to..**750.00**

Spoons

Souvenir spoons have been popular remembrances since the 1890s. The early hand-wrought examples of the silversmith's art are especially sought and appreciated for their fine craftsmanship. Commemorative, personality-related, advertising, and those with Indian busts or floral designs are only a few of the many types of collectible spoons. In the following listings, spoons are sorted by city, character, or occasion. For further information we recommend *Collectible Souvenir Spoons, Identification & Values*, by Wayne Bednersh (Collector Books).

Key:
B — bowl   ff — full figure
emb — embossed   H — handle
eng — engraved

American Indian, handmade, sm turq gem/stamping on finial, from $20 to.**40.00**
Austrailia, gum leaf/gum nut finial, handmade, J Harris, from $25 to ...**50.00**
Bermuda, tropical fish finial, coat of arms in B, bonbon, from $35 to...**50.00**
Black man carrying a stick w/dead possum, from $100 to............**150.00**
British WWII, 3-pence finial, 6-pence in B, from $35 to **65.00**
CA Mid-Winter Fair, 1894, San Francisco, SP, from $5 to............**15.00**
CA state H w/emb picture of Mt Lowe Incline Railroad, from $40 to ...**75.00**
Cleveland 24th Inaguration, portrait on finial, White House in B..**50.00**
Columbus finial atop movable color globe, transfer-printed ship in B..**600.00**
Dragon, hand-chased, mk w/Chinese characters, from $35 to.......**50.00**
Egyptian, finials open to reveal mummy, Egyptian scene in B, $150 to ..**300.00**
Fairbanks AK skyline ff H, JB Erd, from $125 to **175.00**
Ferris wheel emb in B, 1893 Columbian Exposition on H, from $5 to...**10.00**
Genesee Street, Utica NY eng in B, detail, from $25 to................**50.00**
Harp finial, unusual-shaped B w/eng, unmk, handmade, from $75 to..**125.00**
Heart B w/hand-cut figure of man w/flat-topped hat, from $10 to ...**25.00**
Israel, lion & staff finial, emb Jerusalem UDT in B, from $15 to ..**25.00**
Japanesque, handmade, long H, stork eng in B, from $25 to **50.00**
Kenya on finial, elephants in B, SP, from $5 to..........................**15.00**
Leaning Tower of Pisa, transfer-print finial w/plain B, from $5 to.**10.00**
Los Angeles angel ff H, Mt Lowe railroad emb view in B, from $40 to..**75.00**
Madison WI, multi-scenes emb in B, variety of Hs, ea from $15 to ...**50.00**
Mardi Gras woman (masked), HP in B, state H, from $100 to ...**200.00**
Mechanical windmill finial, cast tavern scene in B, from $75 to...**125.00**
Mexico, Tijuana border monument eng in B, American-made, from $20 to..**45.00**
Montreal skyline emb in B, enameled finial, bonbon, from $15 to..**25.00**
Mormon Tabernacle Salt Lake City in B, elk's tooth finial, $50 to.....**150.00**
Mt Fujiyama scene eng in B, geisha ff H, from $25 to **45.00**
New York stacked skyline ff H, Shepard, from $75 to **150.00**
New Zealand, kiwi bird w/jade-ite body H, NZ finial, from $20 to..**45.00**
Penna Ave & 2nd St, Warren PA acid etched in B, from $20 to..**40.00**
Pinocchio finial, enameled stainless steel, from $5 to...................**10.00**
Pompeian vase replica finial w/print of Mt Vesuvius on B, from $40 to ...**100.00**
Pontiac IL state reformatory eng in B, Towle, from $30 to............**50.00**

Rome, St Peter's Basilica & Vatican, print scenes in B, from $25 to..**65.00**
San Francisco bay emb in B, orange finial, from $15 to................**25.00**
Ship in Panama Canal ff H, San Diego 1915 eng in B, Robbins, $25 to ..**45.00**
Spain, dancing senorita on finial, plain B, demi, from $10 to **20.00**
Switzerland, enamel crossbow w/reclining lion of Lucerne in B, $20 to..**40.00**
Tampa FL skyline ff H, w/pierced bonbon B, Paye, from $150 to ..**300.00**
Thomas Jefferson portrait HP in B; from $300 to **500.00**
Train eng in B, flowered H, Shepard, from $25 to **45.00**
US Army & Navy Hospital, Hot Springs AR, emb on B, state H, $15 to...**50.00**
Utah, angel Moroni finial, Mormon Tabernacle eng in B, from $20 to ...**60.00**
Waikiki HI, cutouts of 4 card suits on H, city eng in B, from $65 to...**90.00**
WC Fields ff H, stainless w/red jeweled eyes, from $25 to **50.00**
3 Wise Men ff H, plain B, lg (server), from $50 to **90.00**

Sports Collectibles

When sports cards became so widely collectible several years ago, other types of related memorabilia started to interest sports fans. Now they search for baseball uniforms, autographed baseballs, game-used bats and gloves, and all sorts of ephemera. Although baseball is America's all-time favorite, other sports have their own groups of interested collectors. Our advice for this category comes from Paul Longo Americana. Mr. Longo is listed in the Directory under Massachusetts. See also Target Balls; Tennis Rackets.

Key: sig — signature

Press pins: N.Y. Yankee, 1923 World Series, NM, $1,700.00; N.Y. Yankees, blue enamel on gold, 1927 World Series, NM/M, $2,750.00.

Baseball, D&M model DB30, mk Special League on sweet spot, VG+..**100.00**
Baseball, Pennant brand, model V3-J340, MIB **150.00**
Bat, Charles Hollocher, Spaulding Autograph series, 33", EX.....**110.00**
Bat, M Mantle sig, Commemorating 536 Lifetime Home Runs, 35", M..**1,500.00**
Bat, Steve Carlton sig, 125 Louisville Slugger model #P89, 34½", M..**175.00**
Bat, 1938 All-Star, players name in gold, 22", NM **160.00**
Boxing gloves, Rocky Marciano endorsed, 1950s, VG+ (VG+ box) ..**300.00**
Catalog, uniform; baseball, D&M, 1913, 13-pg, 6x10", VG+ **200.00**
Catcher's mask, goggle-eyed, Draper-Maynard #305, all orig, EX ..**395.00**
Drawing, Ty Cobb, done in chalk by James Prochauska, 22x26", NM ..**275.00**
Football, The Duke, Wilson, 1960s, MIB.................................**165.00**
Game, Mickey Mouse's Baseball; Post Toasties cutout, EX...........**40.00**
Helmet, football; Goldsmith Wing-front, leather, EX+ **170.00**
Helmet, leather w/face mask, George Reach Co, 1930s, EX **300.00**
Jacket, Dodgers, Timberline, lined, 1950s, NM.........................**150.00**
Jacket, Giants, baseball on chain zipper, 1950s, NM **100.00**
Jersey, Milwaukee Brewers (road), 1981, Paul Molitor, game used, EX+..**1,815.00**
Jersey, New York, wht w/navy pinstripes, Spaulding, EX **300.00**
Jersey, warm-up; Angels, Wilson, knit, 1960s, EX+ **150.00**
Jersey, 1965 Red Sox, road-color gray w/Red Sox on chest, EX+...**500.00**
Nose guard, football, rubber w/head strap, mk Morrill's, 1891, EX...**600.00**
Paperweight, St Louis Cardinals, catcher's mitt shape, leather, 4" ...**40.00**
Pencil holder, bat shape, Columbus eng, wooden, 1900s, 16", EX...**85.00**
Pennant, Hank Aaron, Home Run King, 1974, 30", M.................**25.00**

Pennant, NY Yankees, Am League Championship, 1936, 24", EX ...300.00
Pennant, Princeton Tigers, tiger jumping through letter P, 33", EX ..125.00
Pennant, 1920s Yale, bl w/brn bulldog, 34", EX..........................100.00
Pennant, 1940s Brooklyn Dodgers, My Fan on the letter B, 25", EX...110.00
Photo, American Empire Baseball team, 1900s, 5x7" +fr 95.00
Pillow cover, 1900s couple playing golf, 20x20", EX...................185.00
Postcard, 1911 Portsmouth Team photo, Ohio Baseball League, EX...55.00
Program, 1912 Toledo Baseball, loose binding, VG+.....................35.00
Program, 1938 Sugar Bowl, mc, EX+...................................180.00
Program, 1951 1st Annual Pro Bowl, NM.................................500.00
Puzzle, Centre to Goal, 1904 football, complete, EX+.................570.00
Ticket stub, 1951 World Series, 6th game, EX 95.00
Tickets, 1937 Army/Navy, football, EX+ (in mailer) 35.00
Uniform, basketball, Sioux Indians, wool, maroon w/orange trim, EX+...460.00
Uniform, Bluejays, wht w/gray pinstripes, wool, 1900s, EX+.......155.00

St. Clair

The St. Clair Glass Company began as a small family-oriented operation in Elwood, Indiana, in 1941. Most famous for their lamps, the family made numerous small items of carnival, pink and caramel slag, and custard glass as well. Later, paperweights became popular production pieces; many command relatively high prices on today's market. Weights are stamped and usually dated, while small production pieces are often unmarked. Lamps are in big demand (prices depend on size and whether or not they are signed) as are items signed by Paul or Ed St. Clair. For further information we recommend *St. Clair Glass Collector's Book, Vol. II*, by our advisor Ted Pruitt. He is listed in the Directory under Indiana.

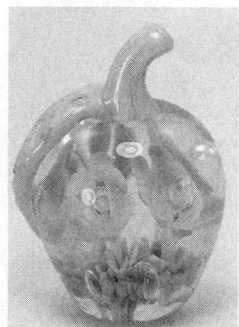

Apple, clear with light blue, 5", $125.00.

Basket, handmade, sm, from $100 to...125.00
Bell, rose, from $1,000 to...1,200.00
Bowl, fluted rim, from $225 to...250.00
Fruit, apple, from $95 to..100.00
Fruit, blueberry, from $140 to 150.00
Goblet, Rose in Snow, from $40 to...50.00
Insulator, handmade, from $100 to.......................................125.00
Lamp, blown ball shape, unsgn, from $275 to.............................300.00
Lamp, TV; unsgn, from $975 to..1,000.00
Lamp, 2-ball w/leaded shade, from $725 to...............................750.00
Marble, baseball player, Ed St Clair, from $125 to......................150.00
Paperweight, crimped, lg, from $60 to.....................................70.00
Paperweight, Kennedy sulfide, windowed, Paul St Clair, mini, $300 to..350.00
Paperweight, lily, wht, Ed St Clair, from $350 to........................400.00
Paperweight, rose, various colors, windowed, ea......................1,200.00
Paperweight, sulfide, Babe Ruth, from $225 to 250.00
Paperweight, sulfide, cat, windowed & etched, from $225 to......250.00
Paperweight, sulfide, Harry S Truman, from $125 to 150.00
Pen holder, handmade, from $65 to..75.00
Picture frame, from $175 to...200.00
Plate, Reagan - Bush, from $25 to 30.00

Ring holder, teapot shape, crimped or flowered, from $75 to 85.00
Statue, Kewpie, from $115 to..125.00
Toothpick holder, Fan & Feather, from $25 to............................30.00
Toothpick holder, fez hat, from $135 to.................................150.00
Toothpick holder, Mrs Degenhart, from $45 to............................50.00
Tumbler, Hollyband, from $40 to..50.00
Vase, blown, waisted, from $175 to......................................200.00
Vase, Butterfly, paperweight base, from $300 to.........................350.00
Wine, Pinwheel, from $35 to..45.00

Staffordshire

Scores of potteries sprang up in England's Staffordshire district in the early eighteenth century; several remain to the present time. (See also specific companies.) Figurines and groups were made in great numbers; dogs were favorite subjects. Often they were made in pairs, each a mirror image of the other. They varied in heights from 3" or 4" to the largest, measuring 16" to 18". From 1840 until about 1900, portrait figures were produced to represent specific characters, both real and fictional. As a rule these were never marked.

Historical ware was made throughout the district; some collectors refer to it as Staffordshire Blue. It was produced as early as 1780, and because much was exported to America, it was very often decorated with transfers depicting scenic views of well-known American landmarks. Early examples were printed in a deep cobalt. By 1830 a softer blue was favored, and within the next decade black, pink, red, and green prints were used. Although sometimes careless about adding their trademark, many companies used their own border designs that were as individual as their names.

This ware should not be confused with the vast amounts of modern china (mostly plates) made from early in the century to the present. These souvenir or commemorative items are usually marketed through gift stores and the like. (See Rowland and Marcellus.)

Our advisor for this category is Jeanne Dunay; she is listed in the Directory under South Carolina. See also specific manufacturers.

Key:
blk — black	l/b — light blue
gr — green	m/b — medium blue
d/b — dark blue	m-d/b — medium dark blue

Figures and Groups

Couple, well dressed, overglaze enamel, earthenware, 1820s, 6½", EX...175.00
Couple under town clock, central relief vase w/flowers, 19th C, 12"......200.00
Cow, creamer, underglaze decor, earthenware, mid-1800s, rstr, 6½" 515.00
Farmer & wife w/wheat, 19th C, 8½"...175.00
Girl & goat, dog at her ft, 8"..175.00
Hen on basketry nest, red/brn/blk enamel, wear, 6x8".................350.00
Highland couple, he sits w/spaniel, she stands, 19th C, 10" 200.00
Highland maidens (3) support watch holder w/upheld arms, 19th C, 11"...200.00
Highland milkmaid & blk-spotted cow, 19th C, 9½", EX...........200.00
Highlands courting couple w/spaniel, 19th C, 13" 75.00
Lions, orange/brn w/blk detail, glass eyes, mc base w/gold, 13" L, pr...400.00
Milkmaid sits beside brn-spotted cow, spill vase, 19th C, 8½" 175.00
Musician playing mandolin for lady, spill vase, 19th C, 8".........175.00
Prince Louis of Hess w/Princess Alice, 19th C, 15" 325.00
Ram, sanded coat w/gray horns, grassy base, 5½" 250.00
Rival, courting couple w/guitar, rival w/knife, 19th C, 12½" 230.00
Scotsman on wht horse w/gold lustre stripes & dogs, 14¼" 440.00
Scotsman w/bagpipe, dog at side, 19th C, 16½" 285.00
Spaniel, red spots, yel flower basket in mouth, mfg flaw/wear, 8".550.00
Spaniels, blk muzzle, yel eyes, copper lustre collar etc, late, 6", pr...110.00

Spaniels, hollow, gold/blk detail, glass eyes (rpr), Sadler, 14", pr ...**350.00**
Spaniels, orange nose, blk & gold detail, yel eyes, 8½", pr..........**200.00**
Spaniels, wht w/rough sanded coat, gray/blk details, w/gilt, 8", pr....**300.00**
Spaniels, yel eyes, gray paws & muzzles, gold lustre over gr, 12", pr...**300.00**
Watch hutch, fox atop, 2 bk-to-bk below, grapes, 8" **550.00**
Whippet w/hare in mouth, bl & gold oval base, 6" **260.00**

Transferware

Bowl, boatmen, Interlachen, bl, scalloped/rtcl, 4x9" **495.00**
Bowl, Luscombe Devonshire, d/b, 12" L, +12" plate, ea rtcl/hdld, NM ..**1,650.00**
Bowl, potato; Italian Buildings, d/b, Hall, 2½x11¾", NM **275.00**
Bowl, soup; Castle, d/b, Clews, 1¼x9¾" **225.00**
Bowl, soup; Fruit & Flowers, Stubbs & Kent, 1½x9¾" **150.00**
Gravy boat, Floral & Grape, d/b, unmk, ca 1850, 4¼x7¾", EX .**225.00**
Pitcher, Boston State House/NY City Hall, d/b, floral band, 6½", EX...**935.00**
Pitcher, girl picks flowers/boy robs bird's nest, d/b, 5½" **495.00**
Pitcher, Middle Eastern scene w/mosque/women/soldiers, d/b, 5½", EX...**250.00**
Pitcher, NY City Hall, bk: Insane Asylum, d/b, unmk Clews, 7", NM..**1,400.00**
Pitcher, Washington Independence, d/b, naval heroes/monument, 5", VG ...**650.00**
Plate, Battery at NY, gr, scalloped/beaded edge, Jacksons Warranted, 8" ..**275.00**
Plate, Boston State House, l/b, Wood (no mk), floral border, 10"....**150.00**
Plate, Commodore MacDonnough's Victory, d/b, Wood, 10", EX....**345.00**
Plate, Death of the Bear, d/b, Spode, 10", pr...............................**865.00**
Plate, East View of LaGrange..., d/b, Woods, 9½" **360.00**
Plate, Fall of Montmorenci Near..., d/b, Wood (eagle mk), 8½".**275.00**
Plate, Fall of Montmorenci Near..., d/b, Wood (eagle/banner mk), 9"..**400.00**
Plate, Harvard College, m/b, acorn & oak leaf border, 10", NM.**300.00**
Plate, Landing of Fathers at Plymouth, d/b, Enoch wood, child sz, 4"..**635.00**
Plate, Landing of Pilgrims, d/b, Am.../WA.../ships border, Wood, 10"..**385.00**
Plate, lion center, d/b, Quadruped series, 10"..............................**450.00**
Plate, Ruins, d/b, scroll feather border, Rogers, 10" **225.00**
Plate, Rustic Scenery, brn, Clementson, 10¼", EX, 10 for **800.00**
Plate, Scott's Illustrations Waverly, d/b, scalloped, 10½" **225.00**
Plate, Village Church, d/b, unmk, ca 1835-45, 9¾" **175.00**
Plate, Wistow Hall Leicestershire, d/b, 2 women in foreground, 8¾"...**160.00**
Platter, Asiatic Pheasants, brn, unmk, ca 1840, 17½x14¾"........**350.00**
Platter, Boston State House, d/b, Rodgers & Son, 19x14½"...**1,500.00**
Platter, Cape Coast Castle on Gold Coast Africa, d/b, Wood, 17"..**2,300.00**
Platter, Church of St Charles, d/b, floral border, R Halls, 19" .**1,000.00**
Platter, elephant, d/b, Quadruped series, Hall, 19x14¾"..........**4,300.00**
Platter, Lake George State of NY, d/b, Wood, 16½x13", VG ..**2,100.00**
Platter, Scroll, gr, ca 1830, 16¾x14¼", NM **550.00**
Platter, Syria, brn, Cochran, ca 1846, 18x14¾", NM..................**750.00**
Platter, tree & well; girl musician, d/b, Riley, 20½x16½" **1,200.00**
Platter, West Point Military School..., red, Adams, 17½x14½" ...**1,500.00**
Soup plate, Pembroke Hall, d/b, morning-glory border, Ridgway, 9¾" ..**175.00**
Tankard, Rhine, brn, Meir & Son, ca 1837-97, 5¾", EX............**125.00**
Tea bowl & saucer, Castle Towards, d/b, Hall, 2¼", 5¼", EX **200.00**
Teapot, Am eagle w/shield, d/b, unmk Clews, scalloped rim, 6½", VG ..**750.00**
Teapot, Asiatic Temples, d/b, Ridgway, 1814-30, 5½" **160.00**
Teapot, Landscape & Floral Urn, red, 1850s, 7½", EX................**450.00**
Tray, Gardener, d/b, att Wood, ca 1818-46, 10¼x8"..................**550.00**
Tray, relish; Savannah Bank, d/b, Ridgway Beauties of Am, 5⅜x8¼" ..**750.00**
Tureen, Sherbourn Castle, d/b, w/lid, Wood, 8¼", +undertray, EX.....**850.00**

Miscellaneous

Bowl, emb bl feather edge, pearlware, 12"....................................**450.00**
Cottage bank, bl/gr sponging, blk details on wht, 3¾", NM **300.00**
Hen on nest, mc bsk, average feather detail, basket base, 8" L....**380.00**
Hen on nest, mc bsk, EX feather detail, basket base, 8" L...........**500.00**
Hen on nest, wht w/gold lustre, red/brn mc on head, 9½x12", EX ..**260.00**
Inkwell, swan form, 3½" **130.00**

Ladle, soup; bl feather edge, from $550 to....................................**650.00**
Mug, emb drinking scene w/3 people & grapevine, 4-color HP, 5" ..**200.00**
Plate, Adams-style floral, scalloped, 1840s, 10¼" **25.00**
Plate, bl feather edge, 10½", from $55 to **85.00**
Plate, brn feather edge w/ship & floral transfer, scalloped, 10" ...**500.00**
Plate, toddy; bl feather edge, blk/mc berries & leaves, octagonal...**500.00**
Platter, bl feather edge, gaudy flowering branch in well, 17" ...**2,000.00**
Platter, Canova, canal/gondola, red, T Mayer, scalloped, 15" **850.00**
Salt cellar, bl feather edge, ftd, master sz, from $350 to..............**450.00**
Sauce boat, bl feather edge, 7" L..**175.00**
Tea bowl & saucer, birds/urn of flowers, d/b, NM **200.00**
Tureen, sauce; gr shell edge decor, w/attached undertray, from $450 to ..**550.00**

Stained Glass

There are many factors to consider in evaluating a window or panel of stained glass art. Besides the obvious factor of condition, intricacy, jeweling, beveling, and the amount of selenium (red, orange, and yellow) present should all be taken into account. Remember, repair work is itself an art and can be very expensive. Our advisor for this category is Carl Heck; he is listed in the Directory under Colorado.

Ceiling Lights

10x24", cobalt w//pk & wht dogwood blossoms, VG...............**4,800.00**
14x21", blown-out fruit in border **300.00**
18", fleur-de-lys border in 3 colors on lt amber w/sq panels **2,300.00**
20", 6 trapezoid panels/geometric apron, Arts & Crafts, VG ...**1,500.00**
24", brickwork w/shaped floral & leaf border, crown, VG........**1,600.00**
24", shouldered form w/grapes & dk latticework on wht, EX...**1,800.00**
27", wide cylindrical apron: raised grapes & leaves, EX **2,000.00**
30", dome w/petal-shaped pcs, gr w/caramel border..................**1,400.00**

Table Lamps

16" bent-panel shade w/stylized floral band (EX), copper std ..**1,800.00**
18" pine-cone border shade: 3-socket std, Bigelow & Kennard, 24" **4,500.00**
18" shade w/abstract dolphins border, gr tones (EX), dolphin std, 29"...**4,800.00**
18" shade w/scroll border, amber on lt opal, pk rose reserve (6X); 23" ..**2,000.00**
19" brickwork/geometric tile shade; reeded std, Duffner/Kimberly, 25" .**3,600.00**
19" geometric shade, 12 jewels in apron (15 panels cracked), Wilkinson....**1,495.00**
20" water lily shade; reeded emb base w/blk patina, Duffner/Kimberly ..**13,800.00**

Windows

Stained, faceted, jeweled, and stain-painted flower and bird scene, floated lead jewel border, originally double-hung sash window, 3rd St. Studios, Cincinnati, Ohio, 1890s, 39x19¾" in frame, from $2,800.00 to $3,200.00. (Photo courtesy Carl Heck)

Chevrons in gr & gold on clear w/frosted border, fr, 55x9½", pr...**1,400.00**
English long-stem rose on twisting upright vine, triple border, 30x14" ...**2,700.00**
Floral center, opal nugget glass jewels, La Farge, 26x29" in fr..**9,200.00**

Geometric pattern in style of L Sullivan w/jewels, fr, 35x25" ..**1,400.00**
Grapevines & trellis, pnt scene beyond, EX/elaborate detail, 44x30"..**1,200.00**
Jeweled Nouveau design, fr, 36x29"......................................**1,400.00**
Lady (pnt) surrounded by magnolias, Nouveau style, fr, 14½x14" **1,500.00**
Lady w/macaw among architectural features/flowers, jewels, fr, 46" sq..**14,000.00**

Miscellaneous

Panel, rondel w/girl, ldgl/HP, tile-like borders, att La Farge, 14x18"...**1,700.00**

Stanford

The Stanford Pottery Co. was founded in 1945 in Sebring, Ohio. One of the founders was George Stanford, a former manager at Spaulding China (Royal Copley). They continued in operations until the factory was destroyed by a fire about 1961. They produced a Corn Line, similar to that of the Shawnee Company, that is today very collectible. Most examples are marked (either Stanford Sebring Ohio or with a paper label), so there should be no difficulty in distinguishing one line from the other.

In addition to their Corn line, they produced planters and figurines, many of which were black trimmed with gold, made to be sold as pairs or sets. Wall pockets and vases were made as well. In 1949 they introduced a line called Tomato Ware, consisting of a cookie jar, grease jar, salt and pepper shakers, creamer and sugar bowl, mustard jar, marmalade jar, etc. These were shaped as bright red tomatoes with green leaves and stems (often used as lid finials), and were marketed under the name 'The Pantry Parade.' Our advisor for this category is Joe Devine; he is listed in the Directory under Iowa.

Ashtray, free-form, orange w/wht 'stucco,' #270-D, mk, 10x7"......**12.00**
Corn Line, butter dish..**60.00**
Corn Line, casserole, 8" L...**50.00**
Corn Line, cookie jar...**100.00**
Corn Line, creamer & sugar bowl.......................................**60.00**
Corn Line, cup..**20.00**
Corn Line, pitcher, 7½"...**65.00**
Corn Line, plate, 9" L..**35.00**
Corn Line, relish tray..**45.00**
Corn Line, shakers, sm, pr..**30.00**
Corn Line, shakers, 4", pr..**35.00**
Corn Line, spoon rest...**30.00**
Corn Line, teapot...**75.00**
Corn Line, tumbler..**35.00**
Planter, Dutch boy or girl by tulip, blk w/gold trim, ea.................**20.00**

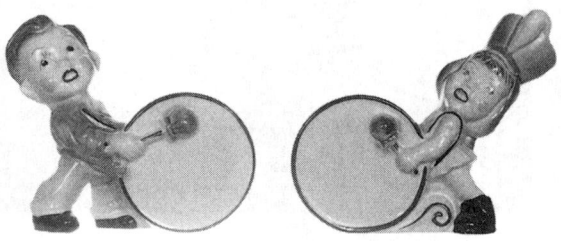

Planters, marching drummer boy and girl, 7", $22.00 each.
(Photo courtesy Glenn Hovinga)

Planter, teddy bear, wht w/pk & bl trim, paper label, 7"...............**35.00**
Tomato Ware, casserole, w/lid, 6x9".....................................**60.00**
Tomato Ware, cookie jar, 8"..**90.00**
Tomato Ware, creamer...**30.00**

Tomato Ware, grease jar, w/lid..**38.00**
Tomato Ware, marmalade jar..**35.00**
Tomato Ware, mustard jar..**35.00**
Tomato Ware, pitcher, 6½"...**65.00**
Tomato Ware, sugar bowl...**30.00**
Wall pocket, bird, bl & cobalt w/gold trim, 7", from $40 to..........**45.00**
Wall pocket, cherry branch, red pie-crust edge, #299, mk, 6¼" **28.00**

Stangl

Stangl Pottery was one of the longest-existing potteries in the United States, having as its beginning in 1814 the Sam Hill Pottery, becoming the Fulper Pottery which gained eminence in the field of art pottery (ca 1860), and then coming under the aegis of Johann Martin Stangl. The German-born Stangl joined Fulper in 1910 as chemical engineer, left for a brief stint at Haeger in Dundee, Illinois, and rejoined Fulper as general manager in 1920. He became president of the firm in 1928. Although Stangl's name was on much of the ware from the late '20s onward, the company's name was not changed officially until 1955. J.M. Stangl died in 1972; the pottery continued under the ownership of Wheaton Industries until 1978, then closed. Stangl is best known for its extensive Birds of America line, styled after Audubon; its brightly colored, hand-carved, hand-painted dinnerware; and its great variety of giftware, including its dry-brushed gold lines. For more information we recommend *Collector's Encyclopedia of Stangl Dinnerware* and *Encyclopedia of Stangl Artware, Lamps & Birds* by Robert Runge, Jr. (Collector Books). Another good reference is *Stangl Pottery* by Harvey Duke; for ordering information refer to the listing for Nancy and Robert Perzel, Popkorn Antiques (our advisors for this category), in the Directory under New Jersey. Also available: *Stangl Pottery, White-Bodied Artware, 1924 – 1942*, by Peter Meissner (Schiffer).

Animals

#1076, piggy bank, sponged wht, not cvd....................................**100.00**
#1076, piggy bank, Terra Rose, brushed finish, hand cvd.............**150.00**
#3243, Wire-Haired Terrier, 3¼"..**350.00**
#3244, Draft Horse, 3"...**200.00**
#3245, Rabbit, 2"..**350.00**
#3246, Buffalo, 2½"...**325.00**
#3247, Gazelle, 3¾"...**450.00**
#3248, Giraffe, 2½"...**600.00**
#3249, Elephant, Antique Gold, 5"...**125.00**
#3249, Elephant, 3"...**350.00**
#3277, Colt, 5"..**1,600.00**
#3278, Goat, 5"..**1,800.00**
#3279, Calf, 3½"...**1,000.00**
#3280, Dog, sitting, 5¼"...**350.00**
#3430, duck, 22"...**8,000.00**
#3433, rooster, blk or wht, 16"...**900.00**
Afghan dog, wht w/blk overglaze, 3½".....................................**150.00**
Burro, blk w/wht overglaze, 3¼"..**150.00**
Cat, Siamese, sitting, decor, 8½"...**500.00**
Cat, sitting, Granada Gold, 8½"...**300.00**
Elephant, wht w/blk overglaze, 2½".......................................**150.00**
Gazelle, wht w/blk overglaze, 3½"...**150.00**
Horse, wht w/blk overglaze, 3½"..**125.00**
Pony, wht w/blk overglaze, 3¾"...**125.00**
Squirrel, wht w/blk overglaze, 3½".......................................**175.00**

Birds

#3250A, Standing Duck, 3¼"..**120.00**

#3250B, Preening Duck, 2¾" 120.00
#3250D, Gazing Duck, 3¾" 120.00
#3273, Rooster, 5¾" 1,000.00
#3274, Penguin, 6" 475.00
#3275, Turkey, 3½" 500.00
#3276D, Bluebird pr, 8½" 160.00
#3281, Duck, mother, 6" 600.00
#3285, Rooster, early, 4½" 120.00
#3286, Hen, late, 3¼" 75.00
#3400, Lovebird, old version, 4" 100.00
#3400, Lovebird, revised, 4" 65.00
#3401, Wren, dk brn, revised, 3½" 55.00
#3401D, Wren pr, tan, old version 725.00
#3402, Oriole, beak down, 3½" 135.00
#3402, Oriole, revised, 3¼" 55.00
#3405, Cockatoo, 6" 45.00
#3406, Kingfisher, 3½" 65.00
#3406D, Kingfisher pr, 5" 165.00
#3407, Owl, 5½x2½" 300.00
#3408, Bird of Paradise, 5½" 125.00
#3420D, Oriole pr, revised, w/leaves, 5½" 125.00
#3432, Duck, running, brn, 5" 900.00
#3432, Duck, standing, brn 700.00
#3432, Duck, standing, grayish wht w/blk spots 1,400.00
#3433, Rooster, natural colors, 16" 4,000.00
#3443, Flying Duck, gray, 9" 275.00
#3444, Cardinal, revised, glossy pk, 7" 90.00
#3444, Cardinal female 180.00
#3445, Rooster, gray, 10" 250.00
#3446, Hen, yel, 7" 180.00
#3447, Prothononatary Warbler 60.00
#3448, Blue-Headed Vireo, 4¼" 65.00
#3449, Parcquet, 5½" 200.00
#3450, Passenger Pigeon, 9x18" 1,700.00
#3451, Willow Ptarmigan 3,000.00
#3452, Painted Bunting, 5" 100.00
#3453, Mountain Bluebird, 6⅛" 2,300.00
#3454, Key West Quail Dove, single wing up, 10" 275.00
#3454, Key West Quail Dove, wings spread, natural colors 1,800.00
#3454, Key West Quail Dove, wings up, wht 600.00
#3455, Shoveler Duck, 12¼x14" 1,800.00
#3457, Pheasant, walking, 7¼x15" 3,100.00
#3458, Quail, 7½" 1,800.00
#3459, Fish Hawk 10,000.00
#3491, Her. Pheasant, 6¼x11" 185.00
#3492, Cock Pheasant 200.00
#3518D, White-Crowned Pigeon pr, bl w/wht heads, 8x14" 1,750.00
#3580, Cockatoo, med, 8⅞" 125.00
#3580, Cockatoo, wht matt, med 500.00
#3581, Chickadees, brn/wht, group of 3, 5½x8½" 200.00
#3582D, Parakeet pr, bl, 7" 220.00
#3582D, Parakeet pr, gr, 7" 260.00
#3583, Parabula Warbler, 4¼" 65.00
#3584, Cockatoo, sgn Jacob, lg, 11⅜" 275.00
#3584, Cockatoo, wht matt, lg 1,050.00
#3585, Rufous Hummingbird, 3" 100.00
#3586, Della Ware Pheasant, natural colors 2,000.00
#3586, Della Ware Pheasant, Terra Rose, gr 650.00
#3589, Indigo Bunting, 3½" 85.00
#3590, Carolina Wren, 4½" 160.00
#3591, Brewer's Blackbird, 3½" 165.00
#3592, Titmouse, 3" 55.00
#3593, Nuthatch, 2½" 65.00
#3594, Red-Faced Warbler, 3" 150.00

#3595, Bobolink, 4¾" 160.00
#3596, Gray Cardinal, 5" 70.00
#3597, Wilson Warbler, yel & blk, 3" 55.00
#3598, Kentucky Warbler, 3" 50.00
#3599D, Hummingbird pr 350.00
#3625, Bird of Paradise, lg 2,400.00
#3626, Broadtail Hummingbird w/bl flower 200.00
#3627, Rivoli Hummingbird, pk flowers, 6" 200.00
#3628, Rieffer's Hummingbird 150.00
#3629, Broadbill Hummingbird, 4½" 150.00
#3634, Allen Hummingbird, 3½" 100.00
#3635, Gold Finches (group) 220.00
#3715, Blue Jay, w/peanut, 10¼" 700.00
#3715, Blue Jay w/peanut, Fulper blk/bl glaze 2,300.00
#3716, Blue Jay, w/leaf, 10¼" 700.00
#3717, Blue Jay pr 2,900.00
#3746, Canary (right), rose flower, 6¼" 260.00
#3747, Canary (left), bl flower, 6¼" 260.00
#3749, Western Tanager, red matt, 4¾" 475.00
#3750, Scarlet Tanager, 8½" 500.00
#3750D, Western Tanager pr, 8" 550.00
#3751, Red-Headed Woodpecker, glossy pk, 6¼" ...475.00
#3751, Red-Headed Woodpecker, red matt, 6¼" 550.00
#3752D, Red-Headed Woodpecker pr, glossy pk, 7¼" 500.00
#3754, White-Wing Crossbill (single) 5,000.00
#3754D, White-Wing Crossbill pr, glossy pk, 9x8" 500.00
#3755, Audubon Warbler, 4¼" 450.00

#3757, Scissor-Tailed Fly-catcher, 11", $1,100.00.

#3758, Magpie-Jay, 10¾" 1,600.00
#3810, Blackpoll Warbler, 3½" 190.00
#3811, Chestnut-Backed Chickadee, 5" 135.00
#3812, Chestnut-Sided Warbler, 4½" 180.00
#3813, Evening Grosbeak, 5" 170.00
#3814, Black-Throated Green Warbler, 3" 165.00
#3815, Western Bluebird, 7' 425.00
#3848, Golden-Crowned Kinglet, 4¼" 125.00
#3849, Goldfinch 120.00
#3851, Red-Breasted Nuthatch, 3¾" 120.00
#3852, Cliff Swallow, 3½" 200.00
#3853, Golden-Crowned Kinglets, 5½x5" 750.00
#3868, Summer Tanager, 4" 750.00
#3921, Yellow-Headed Verdin, 4½" 1,700.00
#3922, European Finch 1,150.00
#3923, Vermillion Fly-Catcher, 5¾" 2,600.00
#3924, Yellow-Throated Warbler, 6" 650.00
#3925, Magnolia Warbler 3,000.00
Stangl Bird dealer sign 1,800.00

Dinnerware

Amber-Glo #3899, bowl, cereal 10.00
Amber-Glo #3899, casserole, skillet shape, 6" 15.00
Amber-Glo #3899, creamer, casual 25.00
Amber-Glo #3899, plate, 11" 20.00

Amber-Glo #3899, tidbit, 10" 8.00
Apple Delight #5161, ashtray, fluted, 5" 12.00
Apple Delight #5161, coffeepot, 8-cup 85.00
Apple Delight #5161, plate, 10" 30.00
Apple Delight #5161, relish 20.00
Bittersweet #5111, bowl, lug soup 10.00
Bittersweet #5111, egg cup 15.00
Bittersweet #5111, gravy boat 15.00
Bittersweet #5111, plate, 10" 15.00
Blue Daisy #5131, bowl, salad; 10" 35.00
Blue Daisy #5131, casserole, w/lid, 8" 50.00
Blue Daisy #5131, plate, 10" 15.00
Blue Daisy #5131, teapot 50.00
Blueberry #3770, bowl, cereal 25.00
Blueberry #3770, bowl, vegetable; 8" 55.00
Blueberry #3770, bread tray 60.00
Blueberry #3770, cruet, w/stopper 50.00
Blueberry #3770, mug, coffee; 2-cup 50.00
Blueberry #3770, plate, picnic; 8" 10.00
Blueberry #3770, warmer 50.00
Carnival #3900, butter dish 35.00
Carnival #3900, coffeepot, 8-cup 75.00
Carnival #3900, egg cup 15.00
Carnival #3900, plate, 10" 15.00
Cosmos #3339, bowl, lug soup 15.00
Cosmos #3339, bowl, salad; low, 12" 75.00
Cosmos #3339, plate, 10" 35.00
Cosmos #3339, platter, oval, 12" 70.00
Country Garden #3943, bowl, lug soup 20.00
Country Garden #3943, cake stand 35.00
Country Garden #3943, mug, stacking 45.00
Country Garden #3943, plate, 9" 35.00
Country Garden #3943, sauce boat 45.00
Daisy #1870, cake stand, high or low, 10" 45.00
Daisy #1870, candle holder 20.00
Daisy #1870, plate, chop; 14" 90.00
Daisy #1870, relish, dbl, lg 30.00
Dogwood #3668 (made for Dellaware), bowl, salad; 10" ...85.00
Dogwood #3668 (made for Dellaware), cup & saucer ...25.00
Dogwood #3668 (made for Dellaware), plate, 10" ...35.00
Festival #3677, bowl, lug soup 20.00
Festival #3677, creamer 20.00
Festival #3677, egg cup 25.00
Festival #3677, plate, 10" 30.00
Festival #3677, teapot 125.00
Festival #5072, cake stand 25.00
Festival #5072, cruet, w/stopper 45.00
Festival #5072, plate, chop; 12½" 95.00
Festival #5072, plate, 11" 45.00
Floral #3342, butter pat 15.00
Floral #3342, cup, coffee 15.00
Floral #3342, teapot 175.00
Fruit & Flowers #4030, bowl, coupe soup 30.00
Fruit & Flowers #4030, bread tray 45.00
Fruit & Flowers #4030, egg cup 25.00
Fruit & Flowers #4030, pickle dish 25.00
Fruit & Flowers #4030, tidbit, 2-tier 35.00
Fruit #3697, bowl, divided, rnd, 10" 75.00
Fruit #3697, bowl, salad; 11" 80.00
Fruit #3697, butter dish 65.00
Fruit #3697, coffeepot, ind 95.00
Fruit #3697, pickle dish 30.00
Fruit #3697, plate, 9" 20.00
Fruit #3697, sugar bowl, ind 30.00

Garden Flower #3700, bowl, salad; 11" 95.00
Garden Flower #3700, candy dish 75.00
Garden Flower #3700, coffeepot, lg 300.00
Garden Flower #3700, plate, 8" 20.00
Golden Blossom #5155, bowl, divided vegetable; oval ...25.00
Golden Blossom #5155, mug, 2-cup 35.00
Golden Blossom #5155, plate, 8" 10.00
Golden Blossom #5155, tidbit, 10" 8.00
Golden Grape #5129, bread tray 25.00
Golden Grape #5129, creamer 10.00
Golden Grape #5129, plate, 7" 12.00
Golden Grape #5129, relish dish 20.00
Golden Harvest #3887, bowl, divided vegetable; oval ...25.00
Golden Harvest #3887, casserole, w/lid, 6" 25.00
Golden Harvest #3887, egg cup 15.00
Golden Harvest #3887, pepper mill, wood top 55.00
Golden Harvest #3887, pitcher, 2-qt 60.00
Grape #3865, coffeepot 150.00
Grape #3865, plate, 9" 30.00
Grape #3865, teapot 150.00
Harvest #3341, bowl, vegetable; 8" 50.00
Harvest #3341, creamer 20.00
Harvest #3341, plate, chop; 14½" 125.00
Harvest #3341, shakers, pr 24.00
Holly #3869, bowl, salad; 12" 150.00
Holly #3869, mug, 2-cup 55.00
Holly #3869, pitcher, ½-pt 35.00
Holly #3869, plate, chop; 12½" 95.00
Kiddieware, bowl, cereal; Indian Campfire #3916 ...125.00
Kiddieware, bowl, cereal; Peter Rabbit 100.00
Kiddieware, bowl, cereal; Pink Fairy #4044 ....125.00
Kiddieware, bowl, cereal; Running Dog 400.00
Kiddieware, bowl, cereal; Wizard of Oz #5159 ......600.00
Kiddieware, cup, Humpty Dumpty #5118, gr 80.00
Kiddieware, cup, Little Bo Peep, #3434, Lunning ...110.00
Kiddieware, cup, Little Boy Blue #3765, Lunning ...100.00
Kiddieware, cup, Ranger Boy #3918 ....75.00
Kiddieware, divided dish, Bluebird #3827 ....350.00
Kiddieware, divided dish, Playful Pups #3920 ....100.00
Kiddieware, mug, Jack & Jill, musical 300.00
Kiddieware, plate, Blocks 150.00
Kiddieware, plate, Goldilocks #3764, 9" 250.00
Kiddieware, warming dish, Alphabet #5085 ....350.00
Magnolia #3870, bowl, cereal 15.00
Magnolia #3870, butter dish 40.00
Magnolia #3870, cigarette box 50.00
Magnolia #3870, coffee server, casual 175.00
Magnolia #3870, plate, 10" 15.00
Orchard Song #5110, bowl, vegetable; w/lid, 8" 65.00
Orchard Song #5110, coffeepot, 8-cup 65.00
Orchard Song #5110, plate, 8" 8.00
Orchard Song #5110, warmer 20.00
Prelude #3769, bowl, lug soup 10.00
Prelude #3769, casserole, ind, 4" 20.00
Prelude #3769, plate, 10" 20.00
Prelude #3769, sugar bowl 15.00
Ranger #3304, ashtray 160.00
Ranger #3304, carafe, w/hdl 750.00
Ranger #3304, plate, 9" 200.00
Ranger #3304, teapot 1,500.00
Rooster #5223, cake stand 30.00
Rooster #5223, pitcher, 2-qt 100.00
Rooster #5223, plate, chop; 12½" 75.00
Rooster #5223, tidbit, 10" 8.00

Sculptured Fruit #5179, candy dish, w/lid 85.00
Sculptured Fruit #5179, plate, 10" 15.00
Sculptured Fruit #5179, saucer 4.00
Sculptured Fruit #5179, teapot, plain, 4-cup 30.00
Star Flower #3864, bowl, lug soup 12.00
Star Flower #3864, casserole, ind, 4" 20.00
Star Flower #3864, mug, coffee 30.00
Star Flower #3864, plate, 10" 20.00
Star Flower #3864, tidbit, 10" 8.00
Thistle #3847, bowl, coupe soup 30.00
Thistle #3847, bowl, vegetable; 8" 50.00
Thistle #3847, cake stand 35.00
Thistle #3847, coffee server, casual 185.00
Thistle #3847, gravy boat & underplate 40.00
Thistle #3847, plate, 11" 35.00
Thistle #3847, tumbler, 12-oz 100.00
Town & Country #5287, baking dish, bl, 7x10" 90.00
Town & Country #5287, cake stand, gr, brn, honey or yel, 10⅝", ea....30.00
Town & Country #5287, cup, bl 20.00
Town & Country #5287, pie plate, blk or crimson, 10½" 50.00
Town & Country #5287, server, dust pan shape, brn or yel 50.00
Town & Country #5287, tile, bl 40.00
Tulip #3365, cup, coffee; Dellansie 35.00
Tulip #3365, plate, chop; 12½" 100.00
Tulip #3365, sugar bowl 30.00
White Dogwood #5167, bowl, vegetable; 8" 30.00
White Dogwood #5167, plate, 8" 12.00
White Dogwood #5167, shakers, floral, pr 50.00
White Dogwood #5167, tile 20.00
Wild Rose #3929, bowl, cereal 20.00
Wild Rose #3929, bowl, vegetable; 8" 45.00
Wild Rose #3929, cake stand 35.00
Wild Rose #3929, mug, 2-cup 50.00
Wild Rose #3929, platter, casual, 13¾" 90.00
Yellow Tulip #3637, bowl, cereal 25.00
Yellow Tulip #3637, bowl, salad; 10" 60.00
Yellow Tulip #3637, creamer, ind 25.00
Yellow Tulip #3637, gravy boat 35.00
Yellow Tulip #3637, pitcher, 1-pt 40.00

Stanley Tools

The Stanley company was founded in Connecticut in 1854, and over the years has absorbed more than a score of tool companies already in existence. By the second decade of the twentieth century, having long since solidified their position as *the* source for tools of the highest grade, the company enjoyed worldwide prestige. Through both World Wars, they were recognized as one of the nation's premier producers of wartime goods. Industrial arts classes introduced baby boomers to Stanley tools and provided yet another impetus to expansion and recognition. Overall, the company's growth and development has kept an easy pace along with the economy of the nation, and it continues today as a leader in the field of tool production.

Three factors to consider when evaluating a tool are these: age, completeness, and condition. One of their earliest trademarks (1854 – 1857) is 'A. Stanley,' found only on rulers. In the early '20s, their now-familiar 'sweetheart' trademark, the letters SW and a heart shape within the confines of a modified rectangle, was adopted. They continued to use this trademark until it was discontinued in 1936. Many other variations were used as well, some of which contain a patent date. A study of these marks will help you determine the vintage of your tools. Condition is extremely important, and though a light cleaning is acceptable, you should never attempt to 'restore' a tool by sanding, repainting, or replac-

ing parts that may be damaged or missing. Unless noted otherwise in the description lines, our values are for tools in average, 'as found' condition, ranging from very good to excellent. Note: Any common number $20.00 rule with the A. Stanley trademark is easily worth $500.00 plus!

For more information, we recommend *Antique and Collectible Stanley Tools*, written by our advisor, John Walter, who is listed in the Directory under Ohio.

Key: tm — trademark

#1 Odd Jobs, with George Hall's Jan. 25, 1887, and Traut and Hall's Sept 18, 1888, patent dates, complete with scribe and vintage No 62 rule, 97% nickel finish, $200.00.
(Photo courtesy The Tool Merchant)

Bevel, #18, blade style, CI body, M 55.00
Bevel, carpenter's; #25, rosewood & brass, 6" 55.00
Bit brace jaws, for #813 or #923, 4½", unused 20.00
Burnishing tool, #185, hardwood hdl, mk Stanley, NMIB 55.00
Chisel, #750, bevel edge, 1¼x9" 35.00
Chisel, socket; #750, bevel edge, ¾x9" 55.00
Cutting iron, #8 jointer plane, 2⅝x7", M 45.00
Cutting iron, for #110 or #130, ca 1930, 5", box of 6 ....125.00
Doweling jig, #59, CI, 6 bit guides, orig box 75.00
Gauge, auger bit depth; #49, NP, 2½", orig box 55.00
Gauge, marking; #72, beech, unfaced, dbl scribe, Sweetheart tm, 8" ...75.00
Gauge, mortise & marking; #77, rosewood, unmk, 6½" 75.00
Hand beader, #69, beech hdl, 4¾", NMIB 935.00
Level sights, #1, 2¼", NMIB 165.00
Plane, block; #103, fixed angle, early Arch tm, 5½" 55.00
Plane, block; #118, low angle, solid steel body, 6", NMIB 110.00
Plane, block; #118P, solid steel, 6", unused 55.00
Plane, chamfer; #72½, w/beading attachment, 6 cutters, 8" 1,285.00
Plane, circular; #113, floral cap, adjustable, 10", M 355.00
Plane, combination; #55, 4 box cutters, NM (orig hinged wood box) 1,335.00
Plane, edge trim block; #95, orig decal, Sweetheart tm, ca 1920s, 6" 295.00
Plane, fibre board beveling; #195, adjustable fence, 8½" 695.00
Plane, fore; #37, Jenny, PAT 16-9-12, 13" 625.00
Plane, fore; #6, rosewood hdl, ca 1950s, 18" 130.00
Plane, fore; #6, Sweetheart tm, 18" 135.00
Plane, jack; #G26, Gage line, 14" 245.00
Plane, jack; #G5, Gage style, PAT 2-17-20, 13½" 215.00
Plane, jack; #5½, Type 11, orig decal, 14½" 185.00
Plane, jointer; #608C, Bedrock, later style, 24" 395.00
Plane, jointer; #7, rosewood hdls, 1950s, 22" 165.00
Plane, jointer; #7C, Sweetheart tm, 1920s, 22" 245.00
Plane, jointer; #8, Type 2, 24", NM 495.00
Plane, jointer; #8C, corrugated sole, rosewood hdls, ca 1935, 24" ..275.00
Plane, junior jack; #5¼, rosewood hdl, 11", NM 155.00
Plane, rabbet; #190, orig decal, 1½x9½" 75.00
Plane, rabbet; #192, CI, Sweetheart tm, 10½", NMIB 265.00
Plane, rabbet; #289, skew blade, Sweetheart tm, 8½" 525.00
Plane, rabbet/dado; #45, Sweetheart tm, 9", NM 325.00
Plane, rabbet/dado; #46, skew blade, floral casting, 9½" MIB..1,985.00
Plane, router; #71, open throat, 3 orig cutters, 1940s, 8" 130.00

Plane, router; #71½, open throat, 2 orig cutters, 8½" **135.00**
Plane, scraper; #12, rosewood hdl, 6" **95.00**
Plane, scrub; #40, rosewood hdl, 1930s, 9½", NMIB...................**295.00**
Plane, smooth; #1, rosewood sapwood hdl, ca 1895, 6"...........**1,845.00**
Plane, smooth; #3, ca 1950, 8" **120.00**
Plane, smooth; #4½, Type 12, V tm, 10½" **255.00**
Plane, smooth; #4C, Type 14, rosewood hdl, Sweetheart tm, 9".**135.00**
Plane, smooth; #605½C, Bedrock, V tm, ca 1915, 14" **395.00**
Plane, tongue & groove; #148, ⅞x9" **175.00**
Plane, transitional; #23, PAT 1892, 9" **65.00**
Plumb & level, #36, 9", NMIB **195.00**
Precision adjustable saw set, #42, 6", w/manual & orig box **65.00**
Rule, zigzag; #856F, Victor, wht enamel finish, 72" **50.00**
Scraper, #0, hand-held, alloy steel, 5", NMIB................................**55.00**
Scraper, wood; #282, Made in Canada, 13½", MIB.....................**75.00**
Spoke shave, rabbit; #68, Sweetheart tm, 11", NM **245.00**

Statue of Liberty

Long before she began greeting immigrants in 1886, the Statue of Liberty was being honored by craftsmen both here and abroad. Her likeness was etched on blades of the finest straight razors from England, captured in finely detailed busts sold as souvenirs to Paris fairgoers in 1878, and presented on colorfully lithographed trade cards, usually satirical, to American shoppers. Perhaps no other object has been represented in more forms or with such frequency as the universal symbol of America. Liberty's keepsakes are also universally accessible. Delightful souvenir models created in 1885 to raise funds for Liberty's pedestal are frequently found at flea markets, while earlier French bronze and terra cotta Liberties have been auctioned for over $100,000.00. Some collectors hunt for the countless forms of nineteenth-century Liberty memorabilia, while many collections were begun in anticipation of the 1986 Centennial with concentration on modern depictions. Our advisor for this category is Mike Brooks; he is listed in the Directory under California.

Bank, Kenton, 1920s, 9⅝" **280.00**
Bookmark, silk, Bartholdi Souvenir, 1886 ....**75.00**
Box, Liberty Hair Clipper, 1930s **25.00**
Box, porc figural, flag at base, Limoges, 4¼x1" **55.00**
Charm bracelet, NY World's Fair...**40.00**
Clock, figural, United, animated, very rare, 1955 ....**350.00**
Cup, pewter, Germany, ca 1904 ....**60.00**
Hanukkah menorah, Liberty-featured candle holders, M Anson..**1,800.00**
Invitation to inauguration, by President Cleveland...................**200.00**
Letter, by Bartoldi, 1866...**225.00**
Magazine, Harper's Weekly, Liberty centerfold, Nov 6, 1886, EX...**125.00**
Magic lantern side, harbor scene..**30.00**
Medal, Belgium relief, bronze, 1916...**70.00**
Medal, Democratic National Convention, NY, 1924 ....**30.00**
Paperweight, glass, rnd, ca 1880s **100.00**
Perfume bottle, Wenck, ca 1910..**325.00**
Photo album, celluloid image on front, velvet bk, 10x8" **275.00**
Pin-bk, No Beer, No Work, prohibition **15.00**
Plate, glass, eng statue, heart shape..**22.00**
Playing cards, Allied Nations, WWI, complete deck....................**20.00**
Postcard, hold-to-light, night scene **45.00**
Puzzle, America, Ellis Island scene, Tuco, 320 pcs, 1940s, 16x20"..**85.00**
Reverse painting on glass, in plaster fr w/orig pnt, 25x19", EX **75.00**
Runner, damask, ca 1890...**85.00**
Scarf, head of Liberty, red/wht/bl, Hermes, 35" sq, NM..............**150.00**
Scissors, emb metal, Liberty 1 side/Woolworth building on reverse, 6"..**55.00**
Smoking stand, figure w/tray on stepped base, patinated metal, 28"..**250.00**
Spoon, figural stem, sterling, Shiebler **75.00**

Statue, American Committee Model, 12", EX...................................**400.00**
Statue, fund-raising, 1885, 6"..**200.00**
Statue, hand cvd, Mexico, 15" **20.00**
Statue, hand-cvd wood (papier-maché mold), Philippines, 1920s..**575.00**
Stereo card, head of Liberty, Paris, 1878..**80.00**
Straight razor, Liberty-etched blade, Sheffield, ca 1880.................**75.00**
Thermometer, key form, Liberty coin top, solid brass, 8½" **50.00**
Ticket, admission to platform for inauguration, 1886 ....**60.00**
Tin, Bartholdi Ribbon Pins, NY City, ca 1890 ....**40.00**
Tin, Liberty Brand Crystallized Ginger, ca 1930 ....**35.00**
Tin, William's American Chewing Nuts, oval, British, 1930s, lg..**65.00**
Tobacco card, Virginia Brights Cigarettes, ca 1887.......................**25.00**
Trade card, Haas' Remedy, 1880s **40.00**
Trade card, satirical, Moline Plow..**30.00**
Trench art, artillery shell vase, WWI **125.00**
Watch fob, 1919 ....**25.00**

Steamship Collectibles

For centuries, ocean-going vessels with their venturesome officers and crews were the catalyst that changed the unknown aspects of our world to the known. Changing economic conditions, unfortunately, have now placed the North American shipping industry in the same jeopardy as the American passenger train. They are becoming a memory. The surge of interest in railroad collectibles and the railroad-related steamship lines has lead collectors to examine the whole spectrum of steamship collectibles.

Reproduction (sometimes called 'replica') and fantasy dinnerware has been creeping into the steamship dinnerware collecting field. Some of the 'replica' ware is quite well done, so one should practice caution and... 'Know Thy Dealer.' Our advisor for this category is Lila Shrader; she is listed in the Directory under California. We also recommend *Restaurant China, Volumes 1* and *2,* by Barbara Conroy.

Key:
BS — back stamped   SL — side logo
hh — hollow handle   SM — side mark
NBS — no back stamp   TL — top logo
R&B — Reed & Barton   TM — top mark

Dining Salon

Bowl, Alaska SS Co Yukon, TL, NBS, 5½" **49.00**
Bowl, American Mail Line, Island Mail, flat soup, TL, 7"...........**110.00**
Bowl, Eastern SS Lines, Eastern Blue, SL, NBS, 2-hdld soup........**36.00**
Bowl, Eastern SS Lines, Eastern Blue, TL, NBS, 4¼"....................**25.00**
Bowl, NY & Cuba Mail Line, brn border, rim soup, BS, 6½"........**38.00**
Bowl, Swedish American Line, Stockholm, 3 crowns SL, 6".........**12.00**
Bowl, US Shipping Board, Granite State, SL shield, 6" **48.00**
Butter pat, Admiral Line, HF Alexander, TL, Bauscher, 3⅛" **56.00**
Butter pat, Canadian Pacific BC Coastal SS, Empress, BS, 3⅛"..**65.00**
Butter pat, Clipper Line, Stella Polaris, TL, NBS, 3" **35.00**
Butter pat, Dalles, Portland & Astoria Nav Co, Regulator, TL, NBS..**179.00**
Butter pat, Matson, Mariposa, NBS, 3⅛" **59.00**
Butter pat, Monticello SS Co, Vallejo, TM, NBS, 3" **375.00**
Butter pat, North German Lloyd, Dresden, TL w/house flag, 3¾"...**66.00**
Butter pat, Puerto Rico Line, Coamo, BS, 3½".............................**45.00**
Butter pat, Red Cross Line, TM w/house flag, 3⅛" **62.00**
Butter pat, Texas Co, Texaco Michigan, TL, BS, 3⅛".................**348.00**
Butter pat, Union SS Co, TL house flag, Art Nouveau border, 3⅛"..**52.00**
Butter pat, White Star Line, Britannic, TM w/house flag, 3x3½"....**115.00**
Cake stand, Royal Mail Steam Packet Co, TM w/house flag, 7" dia..**55.00**
Creamer, Northern SS Co, SS North Western, R&B, 2" **47.00**

Creamer, White Star Line, Brownfield White Star, hdl, 3".........**810.00**
Cruet set w/stoppers, Am President Line, BM metal fr, Internat'l, 7"..**56.00**
Cup & saucer, Canadian Pacific BC Coast SS, Tremblant, TL, SL ..**66.00**
Cup & saucer, demitasse; Furness Steamship Line, flag SL, TL.....**50.00**
Cup & saucer, demitasse; United Fruit Co, Castilla, SL, TL **35.00**
Cup & saucer, Lyle Shipping Co, SL, TM........................**16.00**
Cup & saucer, United States Lines, Gray Star, BS........................**68.00**
Egg cup, Inland SS Co, SL on red dmn, 3¼" **55.00**
Egg cup, New Zealand Shipping Co, SP w/enamel house flag, 2¼" ..**48.00**
Gravy boat, Puerto Rico Line, SL, BS, 5¼" **16.00**
Hot food cover, Levanthian SS Lines, SL, 6" dia......................**34.00**
Hot food cover, United States Shipping Board, Centennial State, SL, 6" ...**65.00**
Menu, Cunard, Queen Mary, luncheon, Deco cover by Stanton, 1936...**52.00**
Menu, Italian Lines, Andrea Doria, S Pollom cover, 1954, 9x12" ...**30.00**
Menu, Los Angeles SS Co, SS Yale, 7/1935, 8½x5½" **18.00**
Menu, Matson Lines, SS Lurline, dinner, captain's signature, 11/1935 ..**43.00**
Menu, White Star Line, RMS Caronia, private party, 1914, 6x4½"..**26.00**
Menu, White Star Line, RMS Olympic, luncheon, 1913 ....**88.00**
Mug, Union Steamship Line, Estates SL, 3½" **120.00**
Plate, Alaska SS Co, Yukon, TL, BS, Buffalo, 9½" **128.00**
Plate, Canadian Pacific SS Lines, Empress, BS, Minton, 9" **42.00**
Plate, New England SS Co, New England, TL, NBS, Buffalo, 9¼"..**68.00**
Plate, oyster French Line (CGT), Normandie, S Lalique, 10" ...**390.00**
Plate, Red Star Line, pattern similar to White Star's Celtic, TL, 9"....**227.00**
Plate, service; Am President Line, Eagle I w/center scenes, 10"..**332.00**
Plate, service; United States Line, Eagle w/rich gold, TL, NBS, 10"...**188.00**
Plate, The Texas Company, Texaco Michigan, TL, 9½" **180.00**
Plate, United States Line, TM: Kosher service, BS, 6½"...............**22.00**
Plate, White Star Lines, Celtic, TL, NBS, 9" **690.00**
Platter, Alcoa SS Co, Alcoa Cavalier, TL, 5x7" **37.00**
Platter, Eastern SS Lines, Eastern Blue, TL, Buffalo, 7x9"...........**52.00**
Shakers, French Line, CGT SL, Christofle, SP lids, 2", pr..........**388.00**
Silver flatware, butter knife, Matson Lines, TL, Internat'l **14.00**
Silver flatware, crumber & crumb tool, SS Normandie, Ercuis, TL, 1935....**98.00**
Silver flatware, dinner fork, Cunard, TM w/house flag, Walker & Hall ..**15.00**
Silver flatware, dinner fork, Matson Lines, TL, Internat'l, 7"........**13.00**
Silver flatware, dinner knife, United Fruit Co, hh, TL, Internat'l ..**18.00**
Silver flatware, napkin ring, White Star Line, #293, SL, Elkington **93.00**
Silver flatware, spoon, White Star Line, TL, Elkington **47.00**
Silver flatware, strawberry 'fork,' Clyde Lines, single tine, TM **18.00**
Silver hollowware, bread tray, United States Line, Gorham, 10x6" ..**128.00**
Silver hollowware, coffeepot, Inter-Island Nav, hinged lid, SL, 4½"..**88.00**
Silver hollowware, creamer, United Fruit Co, SL, Internat'l, 3¼" ..**32.00**
Stem, champagne; Am Export Line, exquisite etching, 4¾" **33.00**
Stem, champagne; SS United States, etched SL, 4½" **52.00**
Stem, cordial; CD&G Bay Transit Co, SS N American, etched, 3¼" ..**38.00**
Stem, cordial; SS Normandie, First Class, CGT SL, Daum, 3½" ..**185.00**
Stem, wine; Red Star Line acid etched, 5" **26.00**
Swizzle stick, CPSS, Empress of Australia, plastic...........................**1.00**
Teapot, Am Export Line, SP fr w/4" Hall ceramic insert **56.00**
Teapot, Northern SS Co, SS North Western, R&B, 4" **85.00**
Vase, bud; Cunard, RMS Ansonia, SP w/enamel SL coat of arms, 6" ..**30.00**

Miscellaneous

Ashtray, Clyde Mallory Line, glass w/silkscreened name & flag, 5"....**20.00**
Ashtray, MV Alberville, SP, detailed ship rendering, 3¼"..............**26.00**
Ashtray, Vacarro Line, Standard Fruit & SS Co, Bakelite, 5" dia .**15.00**
Blanket, American Mail Line logo in center, wool, 62x88" **110.00**
Blanket, Eastern SS Co, Blue Eastern logo ea end, wool, 60x84" ..**87.00**
Block & tackle, wood, #4, 13" L...**23.00**
Book, Americans in Panama, 2nd edition, hardbk, 1913, 256-pg .**24.00**
Book, Sinking of Titanic, memorial edition, hardbk, 1915, 287-pg ...**49.00**
Book, Tragic Story of Empress of Ireland, hardbk, 1914, 351-pg .**100.00**

Book, Travelers' Handbook, hardbk, dust jacket, 1905, 211-pg.....**50.00**
Brochure, Alaska SS, Looking Ahead to..., 1940, 22-pg+map **15.00**
Brochure, Dollar SS Line, Around the World, 1936, 32-pg, 8½x11"..**18.00**
Brochure, Eastern SS Co, w/deck plans/maps/int scenes, 1929 ....**18.00**
Brochure, Italian Line, Andrea Doria, deck plans/int scenes, 1952 .....**38.00**
Button, African Royal Mail SS, gold-tone w/flag logo, dome, 1" ..**12.00**
Button, Dollar Lines, gold-tone w/house flag logo, dome, ⅞" **10.00**
Calendar, pocket; American Mail, celluloid...................................**18.00**
Chronometer, Waltham, gimbaled, silvered dial, mahog case, 5x5x4"..**750.00**
Compass, sighting; brass, Leupold & Stevens, turns 360 degrees, 7x10"..**98.00**
Deck plans, First Class, P&O-Orient Lines, Canberra, 1963.........**16.00**
Deck plans, SS Normandie, Tourist Class, fold-out maps/photos, 1936 ..**210.00**
Dice set, Blue Funnel Line, leather dice cup+6 die+orig box **21.00**
Flag, house; Cunard, flown on Queen Elizabeth II, 1970, 44x66" **148.00**
Hat, Moore-McCormick, Chief Steward enamel badge & braiding **67.00**
Jewelry, souvenir; Anchor Line, enamel pix of Transylvania, 1¼x¾" .**87.00**
Lantern, brass, Durkee Marine Products, electrified, 20½" **100.00**
Lantern, brass, 6-glass sides, Bulpitt burner, 16"+bale w/wood hdl..**88.00**
Lights, bow; Perco, 1 red/1 bl, heavy metal housing, 3¾", pr......**115.00**
Luggage label, Anchor Line, pix of SS Transylvania, 1920s, 4x6".**13.00**
Luggage label, Italian Line, 1st class, 1930s, 4x7½" **11.00**
Luggage label, Munson SS Lines, for stateroom, 1930s, 5" **13.00**
Luggage label, Norddeutscher Lloyd Bremen, very Deco, 1930s....**75.00**
Luggage label, Northern Navigation Co Ltd, 1910, 8" dia **26.00**
Luggage label, NY & Cuba Mail SS Co, 1920s, 3¼" dia **24.00**
Napkin ring, souvenir; Adelaide SS Co, metal w/enamel house flag, 1" H ...**30.00**
Notebook, Hamburg Am Lines, metal, 3x2" (when closed by pencil)..**57.00**
Pass, annual; Bangor & Aroostook SS Co, Vail, Supt B&ARR, 1897..**80.00**
Pass, annual; Northern Pacific SS Co, to Asst Supt NPSS, 1914 .**24.00**
Passenger list, United States Lines, Geo Washington, 1925, 20-pg...**26.00**
Passenger list, Ward Line, Morro Castle, w/tassle, 1931, 5½x7" **36.00**
Playing cards, Cunard, wide, 1900s, 52+Joker+1, in orig case.....**115.00**
Playing cards, Interocean SS Co, dbl deck, 1955, in case **16.00**
Playing cards, Moore-McCormick, dbl deck, 1958, in case **10.00**
Playing cards, United Fruit Co, map of Pacific on bk, 1930s, sealed ..**28.00**
Pocket mirror, American Mail Line, celluloid w/TL, bevel, 3¼" ..**98.00**
Porthole, brass, w/cover & gasket, 8"...**23.00**
Postcard, Baltic, picture & saving of steamship Republic in 1909.**11.00**
Postcard, Grosser Kurfurst Bremen, German & Am flags, 1907....**12.00**
Postcard, shows Adriatid/Aquatainia/Berengaria/Mauretainia, blk/wht..**29.00**
Postcard, SS Celtic at Liverpool, woven silk, postmk 1910...........**83.00**
Poster, Canadian Pacific-Great Atlantic Fleet, 1930s, 36x24" **265.00**
Poster, Holland-America, Statendam, Cassandre art, 1929, 40x30"..**2,450.00**
Poster, White Star Line, Majestic, Aylward art, 1930s, 30x20"...**300.00**
Print, Rex, cb, cut-down calendar top, fr, 30x36" **37.00**
Shakers, souvenir, SS Vandyke, brass w/enamel belt SL, 2¾", pr..**27.00**
Sign, Internat'l Mercantile Marine, porc, 15x17" **565.00**
Stationery, envelope; Detroit & Cleveland Nav Co, 1910, 3¾x6½".......**20.00**
Stationery, letterhead; Armenian SS corp, blk/wht ship's photo, 1920...**56.00**
Tea caddy spoon, souvenir, enamel pix of Queen Elizabeth I, 3¾" ..**22.00**
Tea strainer, souvenir, Cunard, RMS Ansonia, brass w/enamel TM...**18.00**
Timetable, Catskill-Greendale Ferry, single sheet, 1917, 5½x2¾"..**19.00**
Toothpick holder, souvenir, White Star, SP w/SL Majestic house flag...**200.00**
Towel, hand; American Mail Line woven in red stripe on wht huck **28.00**
Towel, hand; D&C Navigation Co, wht huck w/bl stripe, 1943, 17x32".**38.00**
Tray, souvenir, Dayline, emb Hendrick Hudson ship, metal, 8x3"....**180.00**
View folder, Fall River SS, faux leather, 1890, folds out to 72" **28.00**

Steins

Steins have been made from pottery, pewter, glass, stoneware, and porcelain, from very small up to the four-liter size. They may be decorated by etching, in-mold relief, decals, and occasionally they may be hand painted. Some porcelain steins have lithophane bases. Collectors often specialize in a particular type — faience, regimental, or figural, for example — while others limit themselves to the products of only one manufacturer. See also Mettlach.

Key:
L — liter   tl — thumb lift
lith — lithophane

Character, acorn, porc, inlaid lid, .5L, NM 715.00
Character, balloon, zeppelin & Orville Wright on lid, pottery, .5L...1,150.00
Character, barmaid, porc, porc lid, Schierholz, .5L 3,300.00
Character, Bismark, porc, inlaid lid, rpr/chip, .5L.........................450.00
Character, bison, porc, inlaid lid, E Bohne & Sohne, sm rpr, .5L ..3,600.00
Character, Black student, porc, inlaid lid, lith, .5L, NM 600.00
Character, boar, porc, Schierholz, sm rpr, .5L 2,950.00
Character, Bustle Lady, stoneware, pewter lid, flaw, .5L...........1,265.00
Character, cancan dancers, porc, inlaid lid, Schierholz, .5L........685.00
Character, cat holding fish, porc,, porc lid, rpr, .5L 715.00
Character, cavalier, porc, porc lid, Bauer, 1L.............................1,550.00
Character, cucumber, porc, inlaid lid, E Bohne & Sohne, .5L, NM...1,550.00
Character, cucumber, porc, Schierholz, sm prof rpr, .5L.............1,550.00
Character, eagle, stoneware, inlaid lid, .3L.................................400.00
Character, fish, pottery, inlaid lid, Reinhold Merkelbach, #1152, .5L..465.00
Character, Frauenkirche, porc, inlaid lid, lith, Martin Pauson, .5L..1,375.00
Character, Indian chief, porc, inlaid lid, E Bohne & Sohne, .5L...745.00
Character, Iron Cross, glass, blown, enameling, bullet tl, 1914, .5L..850.00
Character, judge, porc, inlaid lid, Schierholz, .5L.....................1,100.00
Character, marksman w/rifle, inlaid lid, Reinemann, .5L 800.00
Character, Max & Moritz, porc, inlaid lid, E Bohne Sohne, rpr, .5L..4,500.00
Character, money bag, porc, inlaid lid, E Bohne & Sohne, .5L..2,500.00
Character, Munich Child, porc, inlaid lid, lith, Schierholz, .5L .880.00
Character, Munich Child, porc, porc lid, 5¾" 350.00
Character, Munich Child, porc w/bsk finish, Reinemann, .25L..500.00
Character, mushroom woman, porc, porc lid, Schierholz, .5L, NM ..2,850.00
Character, Nurnberger Trichter, porc, inlaid lid, Schierholz, .5L..575.00
Character, Sad Radish, porc, inlaid lid, Schierholz, 2.5L 1,300.00
Character, singing pig, porc, Schierholz, .5L................................500.00
Character, skull, porc, inlaid lid, rpr, .5L....................................330.00

Character steins: Hops Lady, pottery with pewter lid, .5 liter, $400.00; Iron Maiden, stoneware, inlaid lid, .5 liter, #500.00; Skull on book, porcelain, inlaid lid, E. Bohne and Sohne, small repair, .5 liter, $485.00.

Faience, HP: lady & trees, pewter base & lid, ca 1800, 1L, NM .990.00
Faience, HP: man on horsebk, pewter lid & base ring, 1792, .5L, NM .1,300.00
Glass, blown, amber, HP: floral, pewter lid & base ring, 1856, 1L ...880.00
Glass, blown, clear, cut decor, eng brewer crest, pewter lid, 1L ..3,200.00
Glass, blown, clear, cut decor, porc man/lady lid, jeweled tl, .5L ...715.00
Glass, blown, clear, eng horse, cut base, prism lid, .5L 335.00
Glass, blown, clear, gr enameling, cut decor, pewter lid, .5L........475.00
Glass, blown, clear, HP: bicyclist, prism inlaid lid, 1900, .4L......550.00
Glass, blown, clear, HP: butterfly, Nouveau pewter lid, .3L 300.00

Glass, blown, clear, transfer/HP: stag at lake, horn tl, .5L 660.00
Glass, blown, pk, Invt T'print, dwarf scene on pewter base & lid, .5L..330.00
Glass, blown/HP: student society crest, pewter base & lid, .5L ...935.00
Military, pottery, HP/transfer: SMS Kaiser Barbarossa, ship, .5L.415.00
Military, stoneware, HP/transfer: 14 Inf Reg..., uniform, .5L.......285.00
Occupational, porc, barber, crest on front, pewter lid, lith, .4L ...660.00
Occupational, porc, bbl maker, pewter lid, lith, .5L 600.00
Occupational, porc, Deutche Amerikanische..., eagle finial, lith, .5L.1,265.00
Occupational, porc, hat maker, crest on front, pewter lid, lith, .5L ...770.00
Occupational, porc, lumberjack, lg scene, pewter lid, lith, .5L...1,045.00
Occupational, porc, nightwatchman, pewter lid, lith, .5L.........1,000.00
Occupational, porc, paper manufacturer, pewter lid, lith, .5L..1,155.00
Occupational, porc, roofer, pewter lid, lith, .5L 440.00
Occupational, porc, saddle maker, pewter lid, lith, .5L, NM.......600.00
Occupational, pottery, HP/transfer: shoemaker, pewter lid, .5L, NM..400.00
Occupational, stoneware, book binder, 2 lg scenes, pewter lid, 1L...1,200.00
Occupational, stoneware, sheepherder, lg scene, pewter lid, 1L..635.00
Porc, HP/transfer: Elsa Und Lohengrin, lith, pewter lid, .5L.......185.00
Porc, HP/transfer: Gambrinus, pewter lid, lith, .5L, NM.............900.00
Porc, HP/transfer: Gambrinus on bl, pewter lid, lith, .5L.........1,150.00
Porc, HP/transfer: guitarist/lady, music box base, pewter lid, .5L.285.00
Porc, HP/transfer: Karl Marx & lady w/torch, pewter lid, lith, .5L...330.00
Porc, HP/transfer: Lohengrin Opera w/swan, lith, pewter lid, .5L....350.00
Porc, HP/transfer: Ludwig II & sm scenes, lion tl, pewter lid, 1L..500.00
Porc, HP/transfer: man on bicycle, pewter lid, 1892, lith, .5L.....500.00
Porc, HP/transfer: Schitzenliesl, porc inlay lid, .5L......................350.00
Pottery, etch: cavalier on horsebk, Hauber & Reuther, #408, .5L...415.00
Pottery, etch: cavaliers drinking, pottery lid, Germscheid, .5L....220.00
Pottery, etch: dwarfs, dwarf on lid, Germscheid, #171, 1L...........300.00
Pottery, etch: dwarfs, pewter lid, Hauber & Reuther, #526, 1L, NM...600.00
Pottery, etch: Gasthaus scene, Hauber & Reuther, #411, .5L......330.00
Pottery, etch: people exit castle, inlaid lid, Marzi & Remy, #1518, 1L ..440.00
Pottery, HP/transfer: Munich Child, pewter lid, Martin Pauson, 1L......525.00
Pottery, HP/transfer: Rheno-Palatia Sei's Panier, pewter lid, 1896, 1L ..550.00
Pottery, HP/transfer: shooting festival, skyline pewter lid, .5L 465.00
Pottery, relief: Adam & Eve figural, snake hdl, pewter lid, .5L, NM...330.00
Pottery, relief: babies & stork, pewter lid, #1276, .5L 525.00
Pottery, relief: coins, inlaid lid w/coin finial, #1262, .5L 275.00
Pottery, relief: Falstaff & Bardolf, animals at base, #536, .5L 265.00
Pottery, relief: Karl Marx/crowd/lady w/flag, pewter lid, .5L, NM..330.00
Pottery, relief: soldiers/horses, pewter lid, Diesinger, #7208, .5L .230.00
Pottery, relief: Vignola Sei's Panier, relief pewter lid, 1989, .5L..465.00
Regimental, porc, Comp Inf...1895-97, soldier/lady finial, lith, .5L....715.00
Regimental, porc, Garde...1906-08, eagle tl w/stanhope, .5L...1,500.00
Regimental, porc, Garde-Schutzen...1903-05, scenes, eagle tl, .5L..2,750.00
Regimental, porc, KUK Div...1901, horse head tl, inlaid lid, lith, .5L.715.00
Regimental, porc, SMS...1906-09, eagle tl, Thuringen hinge, .5L......935.00
Regimental, pottery, Maschinengewehr..., guns, eagle tl, 1905, .5L.1,500.00
Silver, relief: Napoleon & army, 4 ball ft, gold wash int, 9½" .2,850.00
Stoneware, HP/transfer: dachshund, pewter lid, 1L 300.00
Stoneware, HP/transfer: girl w/dog & doll, pewter lid, ⅛-L 165.00
Stoneware, HP/transfer: Hamburg shooting festival, Ringer, 1909, .5L...575.00
Stoneware, HP/transfer: judge & jester, pewter lid, F Ringer, .5L ..385.00
Stoneware, HP/transfer: monks, pewter lid, .5L 275.00
Stoneware, HP/transfer: Munich child, pewter lid, F Ringer, 1L ..440.00
Stoneware, HP/transfer: Munich child & city skyline, pewter lid, 1L...355.00
Stoneware, HP/transfer: mushroom men, eng pewter lid, .5L, NM..330.00
Stoneware, HP/transfer: 4 boys w/flag, pewter lid, 1/8-L 175.00
Stoneware, HP: dachshund/stag, L Hohlwein, pewter lid, lg tl, .5L..2,145.00
Stoneware, HP: knight on horsebk, pewter lid, lg tl, L Hohlwein, .5L...1,595.00
Stoneware, relief: Art Nouveau, pewter lid, Magnussen, 1888, 3L..1,750.00
Stoneware, relief: monkeys & cats, bear hdl, monkey lid, .5L, NM.....440.00
Third Reich, glass, HP/transfer: machine gun scene, helmet finial, .5L..880.00
Third Reich, pottery, HP/transfer: Unteroffizier-Korps..., .5L ..1,000.00

Third Reich, pottery, HP/transfer: 2 Komp...1935-36, helmet lid, .5L...**635.00**

Steuben

Carder Steuben glass was made by the Steuben Glass Works in Corning, New York, while under the direction of Frederick Carder from 1903 to 1932. Perhaps the most popular types of Carder Steuben glass are Gold Aurene which was introduced in 1904 and Blue Aurene, introduced in 1905. Gold and Blue Aurene objects shimmer with the lustrous beauty of their metallic iridescence. Carder also produced other types of 'Aurenes' including Red, Green, Yellow, Brown, and Decorated, all of which are very rare. Aurene also was cased with Calcite glass. Some pieces had paper labels.

Other types of Carder Steuben include Cluthra, Cintra, Florentia, Rosaline, Ivory, Ivrene, Jades, Verre de Soie; there are many more.

Frederick Carder's leadership of Steuben ended in 1932, and the production of colored glassware soon ceased. Since 1932 the tradition of fine Steuben art glass has been continued in crystal.

Our advisor for this category is Thomas P. Dimitroff; he is in the Directory under New York. In the following listings, examples are signed unless noted otherwise.

Key: ACB — acid cut back

Basket, Gold Aurene, hdl attached w/swirl prunts, #483, 8"....**2,500.00**
Bottle, scent; Blue Aurene, teardrop stopper, #1414, 7¾" **1,100.00**
Bottle, scent; clear w/overall gr threading, gr faceted stopper, 5" ...**350.00**
Bottle, scent; crystal w/flower-form stopper, bulbous, 5¼" **400.00**
Bottle, scent; Gold Aurene, ftd urn w/rare diagonal rib stopper, 7".**1,200.00**
Bottle, scent; Gold Aurene, teardrop stopper, #1414, 7¾" **850.00**
Bottle, scent; Matsu-no-ke, clear w/Amethyst ft, sgn Carder, 6" ..**650.00**
Bottle, scent; Rosaline w/Alabaster ft & stopper, slim cone shape, 9"...**550.00**
Bottle, scent; Verre de Soie, ribbed, Celeste Blue flame stopper, 5" **400.00**
Bowl, Blue Aurene, #2851, 3¾x10"................................**750.00**
Bowl, Blue Aurene, incurvate rim, 3 disc ft, #2556, 10" **1,200.00**
Bowl, Blue Aurene, rolled-out rim, 5¼x6¾" **1,250.00**
Bowl, Blue Aurene on Calcite, wide flange, 14"................**1,000.00**
Bowl, gr, swirled 2½" border, shallow, 14"........................**225.00**
Bowl, Rosaline, 2½x5", +7¼" plate................................**150.00**
Bowl, Rose Cintra, on bun base, 6x8"........................**1,700.00**
Bowl, Spanish Green w/controlled bubbles, scalloped bottom, 16"..**175.00**
Candlestick, amber & bl, Venetian style, 10" **350.00**
Candlestick, Ivrene, 2 C-arms, ea w/ribbed rnd cup, heights vary, 8"...**400.00**
Candlestick, Rosaline to Alabaster, 10" **550.00**
Candlestick, Rosaline w/Alabaster ft & finger hdl, #5146, label, 4"..**625.00**
Candlestick, ruby ft/cup, crystal stem, 7"..........................**350.00**
Candlestick, Spanish Green, threading/bubbles, 2-arm, #6533, 5x15"..........**450.00**
Candlesticks, ACB Green Jade on Alabaster, arrowhead leaves, 10", pr...**8,000.00**
Candlesticks, Bristol Yellow, swirl-rib top & ft, 4x3¾", pr..........**450.00**
Candlesticks, Celeste Blue, ribbed, dbl crystal wafer, 10", pr **650.00**
Candlesticks, Celeste Blue cup & ft, clear stem, 10", pr.............**500.00**
Candlesticks, clear w/blk cabochons, blk threaded cups, 12", pr..**2,300.00**
Candlesticks, French Blue, bubbles/random threading, 4x5", pr.**400.00**
Candlesticks, Honeycomb, Topaz, 12", pr **700.00**
Candlesticks, Pomona Green, dbl-ball stem, 12", pr.................**500.00**
Candlesticks, Pomona Green, twist stems, 10", pr....................**450.00**
Candlesticks, Rosaline cup on Alabaster ft sgn Carder, 3¾", pr .**450.00**
Candlesticks, Topaz, twist stem, 12", pr.............................**375.00**
Compote, amber, diagonal swirls, block letter mk, 7x7".............**250.00**
Compote, amber bowl/ft on Celeste Blue swirled stem, pear finial, 7".**1,200.00**
Compote, Honeycomb, Topaz, 6-sided bowl/ft, baluster stem, 6½x12"...**350.00**
Compote, Verre de Soie w/irid, ribbed/ftd, 3x7" **250.00**
Cordials, cranberry w/crystal ft, swirl, 5", set of 6 ....**600.00**

Cordials, Gold Aurene, twist stem, #2361, 4¾", set of 6 ....**2,500.00**
Creamer & sugar bowl, crystal, #7941/#7942 ....**325.00**
Cruet, Verre de Soie w/etched garlands & cornflowers, ftd, 7" ...**175.00**
Darner, Blue Aurene, 6½" L **700.00**
Decanter, Celeste Blue, 4 side indents, clear ball stopper, #1050, 11"..**250.00**
Figurine, Quan Yen, Spanish Green, 8"............................**350.00**
Goblet, etched urns w/flower garlands, sq ped ft, 6½" **200.00**
Goblet, Green Jade w/Alabaster twist stem, #5154, 6" **150.00**
Goblet, Oriental Poppy, pk on gr base & stem, opal ribs, 8" **950.00**
Goblet, Rosaline w/Alabaster stem of 4 interlocking circles, #5120, 6"..**750.00**
Goblet, Rosaline w/eng swags etc; Alabaster twist stem 8" **450.00**
Goblets, crystal w/ruby controlled reeding, swirled, 7", set of 6 .**450.00**
Lamp, ACB floral/gold Aurene dripping on Green Jade, flattened, 10x8"..**3,500.00**
Lamp, Peach Sculptured Quartz w/appl branches, metal base, body: 12".**2,500.00**
Mug, Matsu-no-ke, lav transparent w/bl streaks, lav rim, 6" **275.00**
Nut dish, Gold Aurene, ruffled, #138, 3½" **450.00**
Paperweight, Heart to Heart, by Hilton, #8626, w/case, 2⅜"......**300.00**
Pitcher, Ivory w/blk hdl, paper label, 9¾x7".....................**690.00**
Plaque, Thomas Edison, #C-1929, 7¾x6¾", in acrylic ft...........**950.00**
Powder jar, Gold Aurene, #696, 4¼x4"..............................**850.00**
Salt dish & pepper shaker, crystal, sterling spoon, #7859/7868...**300.00**
Shade, Calcite w/Gold Aurene int, ribbed, petal rim, 5¼" **185.00**
Shade, feathers, gr on gold, 3½x5½"................................**435.00**
Shade, feathers, gr w/gold tips on cream, gold int, 4½"..............**200.00**
Shade, feathers, gr/gold on opal, gold int, ruffled, 4¼x5¼" **300.00**
Shade, Gold Aurene, ribbed, 4½x4¾"................................**190.00**
Shade, Gold Aurene waves/swirls on Calcite, gold int, petal rim, 5"..**300.00**
Shade, Green Aurene w/Intarsia, lg opening 10" **4,400.00**
Shade, King Tut, gr & gold, Gold Aurene int, sgn, Roberts #202, 4½"..**500.00**
Sherbet, Calcite w/Gold Aurene, 4¼", +6" underplate **275.00**
Sherbets, clear w/random Cranberry threading, 3¾", set of 6 .....**390.00**
Sherbets, Cranberry, crystal stem, 5¾", set of 4 ....**390.00**
Table, abstract pcs w/geometric border, wrought iron base, 19x17x17".**7,500.00**
Tazza, gr cut to clear, Crescent #2 pattern, 7x7"....................**450.00**
Tazza, gr ribbed bowl on amber twist stem, 7" **325.00**
Tumbler, high ball; Selenium Red, 6"..................................**125.00**
Tumbler, lemonade; Verre de Soie w/allover irid, bl ft, 6" **300.00**
Vase, ACB birds/flower branches, Green Jade to Alabaster, 10x7" ...**1,900.00**
Vase, ACB Green Jade, 4" floral border, conical on bun ft, 9".**1,800.00**
Vase, ACB Matsu-no-ke, Green Jade to Alabaster, #6078, spherical, 7"...**1,850.00**
Vase, Blue Aurene, bulbous, #2648, 2¾" **900.00**
Vase, Blue Aurene, fan vase w/4 rim openings, #2672, 7½" **1,200.00**
Vase, Blue Aurene, ftd urn shape, #2823 ....**1,400.00**
Vase, Blue Aurene, lg ovoid w/3 pulled V-hdls, #2765, 11", NM..**3,250.00**
Vase, Blue Aurene, ribbed, ftd w/flared rim, 6½"....................**800.00**
Vase, Blue Aurene, ruffled top, #723, 5¼" **650.00**
Vase, Blue Aurene, shouldered, #2645, 2¾" **950.00**
Vase, Blue Aurene, swirled, trumpet form, #6034....................**2,250.00**
Vase, Blue Aurene, waisted w/vertical ribs, scalloped rim, 5¾" ..**900.00**
Vase, Blue Aurene w/3" band of wht leaves & vines, conical, #6298, 10"...**4,500.00**
Vase, Bristol Yellow w/blk reeded rim & t'prints, shouldered, 9" ...**250.00**
Vase, Bristol Yellow w/blk reeding, hdls, #6769, 7½" **400.00**
Vase, bud; Gold Aurene, #2556, 6" **375.00**
Vase, bud; Green Jade w/Alabaster ft, triangular label, 6¼"........**200.00**
Vase, bud; Verre de Soie, flower form w/ruffled top, 16"..............**650.00**
Vase, Celeste Blue, ribbed, ftd, shouldered, 8" **250.00**
Vase, Celeste Blue, threaded rim, controlled bubbles, fan form, 8"..**250.00**
Vase, Cintra, gr/wht on frost, #6031, 6½x6½"......................**1,800.00**
Vase, cornucopia; Celeste Blue w/amethyst ft, 8"....................**400.00**
Vase, crystal w/Pomona Green ft, etched clipper ship, fan form, 8¾"..**350.00**
Vase, crystal w/random gr threading, t'prints, cylindrical, 4".......**125.00**
Vase, floriform; Verre de Soie, twist stem, 8½x5½".................**690.00**
Vase, Gold Aurene, #2556, stick neck, 5¾".........................**300.00**
Vase, Gold Aurene, ftd trumpet form w/rolled rim, #1124, 6" **800.00**

Vase, Gold Aurene, long conical body on rnd base, 5"	875.00
Vase, Gold Aurene, ovoid, #2412, 6"	900.00
Vase, Gold Aurene, shouldered, 10"	1,300.00
Vase, Gold Aurene, squatty, #2792, 3½x5½"	650.00
Vase, Gold Aurene, stump-like tube w/'thorns,' 10½"	750.00
Vase, Gold Aurene, trumpet form w/6-pinch ruffled rim, #723, 6"	750.00
Vase, Gold Aurene, 4-fold rim, bulbous shoulder w/4 indents, #136, 7"	2,800.00
Vase, Gold Aurene w/gr hearts & vines, wht millefiori, #573, 5"	3,400.00
Vase, Gold Aurene w/platinum irid & wht millefiori flowers, 6¾x4"	4,800.00
Vase, Green Jade on Alabaster ft, shouldered, 5"	450.00
Vase, Grotesque, clear to ruffled ruby top, ftd trumpet form, 9"	450.00
Vase, Grotesque, clear to sky bl, 4-pinch top, ftd, 8½"	450.00
Vase, Grotesque, clear w/sqd Cranberry rim, ftd, #7090	700.00
Vase, Grotesque, ivory, trumpet form, ruffled rim, 11"	650.00
Vase, Ivrene, ruffled rim, 8x9"	450.00
Vase, Jade Green, 3-prong stump on Alabaster ft, #2744, 6"	700.00
Vase, Jade Green w/etched fleur-de-lis & floral, Alabaster ft, 5"	800.00
Vase, Light Blue Jade w/Alabaster ft, 5"	1,200.00
Vase, Moonlight, ftd fan shape w/controlled bubbles & threaded rim, 6"	400.00
Vase, Pomona Green, ftd urn shape w/rolled-out rim, 11x8½"	400.00
Vase, Pomona Green, ribbed ftd fan form, 8¾"	200.00
Vase, Rosaline, 6x12½"	575.00
Vase, Rosaline on dbl-ball Alabaster ft, fan form, 8½"	850.00
Vase, Rosaline w/Alabaster, ruffled rim, trumpet form, 8½"	800.00
Vase, Silverina, amethyst w/silver dmn airtraps, flared rim, 12"	650.00
Vase, Spanish Green, swirled ribbing, 10x8"	200.00
Vase, Tyrian, hearts/vines on purple & gr, irid rim, 6¾x3½"	7,500.00
Vase, Verre de Soie, 3-prong stump, 6"	600.00
Vase, Verre de Soie w/swirl ribs, shouldered, 6½"	500.00
Vase, Yellow Cintra, cylindrical w/rolled-out rim, 7¾"	1,200.00
Vse, Bristol Yellow, controlled bubbles, ftd fan form, 9"	250.00
Vse, Cluthra, gr mottle, bulbous w/clear hdls, 12x12"	1,500.00
Vse, Ivrene, ribbed w/flared top, #7307, 9¾"	600.00
Vse, Topaz, 3-prong stump form, #2744, 6"	400.00

Stevengraphs

A Stevengraph is a small picture made of woven silk resembling an elaborate ribbon, created by Thomas Stevens in England in the latter half of the 1800s. They were matted and framed by Stevens, usually with his name appearing on the mat or often with the trade announcement on the back of the mat. He also produced silk postcards and bookmarks, all of which have 'Stevens' woven in silk on one of the mitered corners. Anyone wishing to learn more about Stevengraphs is encouraged to contact the Stevengraph Collectors' Association, whose address can be found in the Directory under Clubs, Newsletters, and Catalogs. Unless noted otherwise, assume our values are for examples in excellent condition.

The Good Old Days, coach and horses, 2x6" plus mat and frame, M, $195.00.

Are You Ready?	300.00
Called to the Rescue, Heroism at Sea	250.00
Columbus Leaving Spain, G	225.00

Coventry, 2 blk & wht scenes, fr, pr	110.00
Crystal Palace (inside), orig matt, G	385.00
Death of Nelson, G	195.00
Declaration of Independence, woven at Columbian Exhibition	225.00
Dick Turpin's Last Ride on His Black Bess, Hogarth, VG	150.00
First Innings, G	325.00
First Point	80.00
First Train Built by Geo Stephenson in 1825, 8⅞x11⅝"	150.00
Full Cry, w/matt	120.00
God Speed the Plow, G	220.00
Grace Darling	200.00
Kenilworth Castle, orig mat & fr, 15½x22½"	175.00
Landing of Columbus, NM	250.00
London & York Mail Coach, 1879 Expo	120.00
Meet, orig mat, old fr, NM	250.00
Mrs Cleveland, VG	135.00
Park in Coventry	75.00
Present Time, 60 Miles an Hour, Lord Howe, orig mat	175.00
Queen Victoria Jubilee, 1837-1887, unfr	55.00
Rescue at Sea, fr, VG	220.00
Start, NM	175.00
Struggle	80.00
Victoria, Queen of Empire on Which the Sun Never Sets, unfr, EX	195.00
Water Jump, fr	225.00
Wellington & Blugher	300.00

Miscellaneous

Bookmark, A Wish O May You E'er in Peace Abide..., 11⅜x2⅛"	50.00
Bookmark, Behold the Man, blk, fr, G	50.00
Bookmark, Friend's Blessings	45.00
Bookmark, Geo Washington, made for Philadelphia Expo, 12x2"	175.00
Bookmark, Home Sweet Home	75.00
Bookmark, Love's Remembrance, VG	75.00
Bookmark, To My Dear Sister	60.00
Bookmark, To My Sons, G	40.00
Postcard, Ann Hathaway's Cottage	40.00
Postcard, RMS Lusitania, VG	75.00
Postcard, Shakespeare's Birthday	45.00

Stevens and Williams

Stevens and Williams glass was produced at the Brierly Hill Glassworks in Stourbridge, England, for nearly a century, beginning in the 1830s. They were credited with being among the first to develop a method of manufacturing a more affordable type of cameo glass. Other lines were also made — silver deposit, alexandrite, and engraved rock crystal, to name but a few. Our advisor for this category is Don Williams; he is listed in the Directory under Missouri.

Cameo

Bottle, scent; allover flowers, umber cut to amber, rnd, 5"	2,500.00
Vase, floral, wht to purple to yel, swollen top, 10⅛"	10,350.00
Vase, Oriental floral branch/bk: butterfly, pk on yel, str sides, 6"	1,450.00
Vase, 4 floral panels, wht on Prussian Blue, stick neck, 10"	6,500.00

Miscellaneous

Basket, pk Pompeiian Swirl, pk, pinched/ruffled, clear twist hdl, 6x5"	800.00
Bottle, scent; Pompeiian Swirl, tan/rust, bl int, cut stopper, rnd, 7"	895.00
Bowl, Matsu-no-ke on yel satin, 3-ftd, 3x6", NM	985.00
Compote, apricot jade w/alabaster ft & lid finial, 10"	200.00

Creamer, cream w/appl strawberry on leafy stem, amber rim/hdl, 4¾" ..**600.00**
Dish, serving; bl jade w/alabaster ft, ball finial, 7½x8" **250.00**
Ewer, Jewel MOP, rose to wht, 3-lobe rim, 10x5½" **695.00**
Pitcher, opal/yel pull-ups w/ruby threading, pk int, clear hdl, 9".**650.00**
Vase, bl w/various appl fruits, rigaree, ftd cornucopia form, 14"..**850.00**
Vase, lemon yel, diagonally swirled air traps, bottle form, 7" **300.00**
Vase, Matsu-no-ke, crystal/rigaree ft on pk w/yel int, U-form, 6", pr...**750.00**
Vase, Matsu-no-ke on lt gr w/thorny protrusions, RD 153553, 5¼"....**485.00**
Vase, Pompeiian Swirl, amber to red, rnd w/stick neck, 11x6½" ..**950.00**
Vase, Pompeiian Swirl, bl w/brn, yel int, bowling-pin form, 12x6½".**1,750.00**
Vase, Pompeiian Swirl, lt brn to gold, dbl-gourd form, 7¾x3¾".**475.00**
Vase, Pompeiian Swirl, MOP diagonal, pk, 7" **500.00**
Vase, Pompeiian Swirl, satin, bl into pk, bulbous w/stick neck, 7¾"...**700.00**

Stickley

Among the leading proponents of the Arts and Crafts Movement, the Stickley brothers — Gustav, Leopold, Charles, Albert, and John George — were at various times and locations separately involved in designing and producing furniture as well as decorative items for the home. (See Arts and Crafts for further information.) The oldest of the five Stickley brothers was Gustav; his work is the most highly regarded of all. He developed the style of furniture referred to as Mission. It was strongly influenced by the type of furnishings found in the Spanish missions of California — utilitarian, squarely built, and simple. It was made most often of oak, and decoration was very limited or non-existent. The work of his brothers display adaptations of many of Gustav's ideas and designs. His factory, the Craftsman Workshop, operated in Eastwood, New York, from the late 1890s until 1915, when he was forced out of business by larger companies who copied his work and sold it at much lower prices. Among his shop marks are the early red decal containing a joiner's compass and the words 'Als Ik Kan,' the branded mark with very similar components, and paper labels.

The firm known as Stickley Brothers was located first in Binghamton, New York, and then Grand Rapids, Michigan. Albert and John George made the move to Michigan, leaving Charles in Binghamton (where he and an uncle continued the operation under a different name). After several years John George left the company to rejoin Leopold in New York. (These two later formed their own firm called L. & J.G. Stickley.) The Stickley Brothers Company's early work produced furniture featuring fine inlay work, decorative cutouts, and leaned strongly toward a style of Arts and Crafts with an English influence. It was tagged with a paper label 'Made by Stickley Brothers, Grand Rapids,' or with a brass plate or decal with the words 'Quaint Furniture,' an English term chosen to refer to their product. In addition to furniture, they made metal accessories as well.

The workshops of the L. & J.G. Stickley Company first operated under the name 'Onondaga Shops.' Located in Fayetteville, New York, their designs were often all but copies of Gustav's work. Their products were well made and marketed, and their business was very successful. Their decal labels contained all or a combination of the words 'Handcraft' or 'Onondaga Shops,' along with the brothers' initials and last name. The firm continues in business today. Our advisor for this category is Bruce Austin; he is listed in the Directory under New York. Note: When only one dimension is given for tables, it is length. Cleaning diminishes values; ours are for furniture and metals with excellent original finishes unless noted otherwise. It is also important to mention that collectors are increasingly fussy about condition. Refinishing lowers value from 15% to 30% (compared to retail). Replaced hardware or wood can likewise dramatically and negatively affect value.

Key:
b — brand   n — no mark

brd — board   p — paper label
d — red decal   t — Quaint metal tag
h/cp — hammered copper
hdw — hardware

Gustav Stickley

Armchair, #2604, curved crest rail, unsgn, ca 1902, pr **2,000.00**
Armchair, #354½, V-bk w/5 slats, p/d, 37" **800.00**
Bed, #912, paneled, peaked top rail, Ellis influence, 51x79x59" **7,000.00**
Bed, #912, paneled head/ftbrds (peaked), d, rprs, 51x79x59", VG...**4,250.00**
Bed, #923, 3 grad vertical slats in head & ftbrd, d, 54" **9,775.00**
Bookcase, #544, 2 16-pane doors, copper pulls, d, rstr bk, 56x62"....**10,000.00**
Bookcase, #703, mahog, 2 doors w/8 sm ldgl sqs at top, n, rfn, 58x54"..**6,500.00**
Bookcase, #715, 1 16-pane door w/copper pull, d/p, 56x36" **6,000.00**
Bookcase, #715, 16-pane door, galleries top, d/p, lt rfn, 46x35" **4,500.00**
Bookcase, #717, 2 8-pane doors, copper pulls, b, 58x48" **8,500.00**
Bookcase, 3 12-pane doors, slab sides w/thru-tenons, d, 56x73" **23,000.00**
Box, h/cp, peaked lid w/4 triangular panels, conforming finial, 10" L ..**1,000.00**
Bridal chest, dbl-strap form w/orig locks, ca 1904, 25x41x20" **30,000.00**
Chair, chalet desk; #2578, wide slat bk, rpl rush seat, 29" **900.00**
Chair, child's; #342, 2-slat bk, worn leather seat, 23" **400.00**
Chair, Morris; #332, flat arm, box mk, 40" **11,000.00**
Chair, Morris; #369, bent arms w/5-slat sides, rfn, n, 37", VG.**7,500.00**
Chair, side; #378, 9-spindle bk, 5-spindle sides, ink mk, 40x17", VG....**700.00**
Chair set, #306½ & 310½, 3-slat ladderbks, 5 side+1 arm, 35"/36"..**4,000.00**
Chair set, #370, 3-slat ladderbks, 5 side+1 arm, n, 36", VG **3,500.00**
Chest, #913, 9-drw, arched toebrd, d, 51x37x20" **8,000.00**
China cabinet, #815, 2 8-pane doors/8-pane sides, b, rfn/rstr, 64", VG...**5,500.00**
China cabinet, #820, 12-pane door, 4-pane sides, b, rfn, 63x36", VG **4,000.00**
China cabinet, #820, 12-pane door, 4-pane sides, b, 63x36"....**6,000.00**
China cabinet, #820½, 2 8-pane doors, d, 56x36" **6,000.00**
Desk, #720, superstructure w/compartments & drws, 2-drw base, d ..**2,000.00**
Desk, chalet; #505, paneled drop front, shoe-ft base, d, 46x24x17" ..**3,500.00**
Desk, leather top w/tacks, drw over kneehole, 4 drw ea side, 54" **6,000.00**
Dresser, #911, lg swivel mirror, 3-drw, arch toebrd, d, 66x48", VG ...**3,500.00**
Footstool, #302, 4 flared legs, poor leather top, d/p, 5x13x13", VG **650.00**
Highchair, #388, 3-slat bk, leather seat, b, 37" **2,000.00**
Lamp, #502, wood stem w/copper band, 16" rpl wicker shade, 19", VG...**600.00**
Lantern, from Yates Hotel, wrought iron w/cutouts/wht glass panes, 31" ...**1,700.00**
Lantern, h/cp, 4-sided/glass-lined, hanger on bk plate w/scrolls, 16" **1,800.00**

Lanterns, hammered copper, nice recent patina, impressed mark, 16", $3,400.00 for the pair. (Photo courtesy Treadway Gallery, Inc.)

Magazine stand, #72, 3-shelf, rfn, p, 42x22", VG **2,500.00**
Magazine stand, #79, no bk, 4-shelf, slab sides w/cutouts, b, 40x14"......**2,600.00**
Magazine stand, open bk, 3-shelf, tacked leather facing, 35x15", G **4,000.00**
Magazine stand (for Toby), 13" sq top, tree-of-life cvd on sides, VG **2,000.00**
Music cabinet, copper/pewter lt wood inlay on panel door, d, 50", VG...**17,000.00**
Rocker, #323, bk w/3 horizontal slats, 5 vertical slats ea side, n, VG **1,500.00**
Rocker, #375, 11-spindle high bk, 9 ea side, sling seat, n, 45x28", VG...**4,000.00**
Rocker, bk: 2 horizontal slats over 5 vertical, d, 43x27x27".....**2,500.00**

Rocker, sewing; #359, 9-spindle bk, worn leather seat, d, 34", VG **425.00**

Rocker, sewing; wide bk splat w/cutout at top/bottom rail, n, 35", VG ...**190.00**

Rocker, 4 horizontal bk slats (top peaked), new leather, d, 38", VG **1,200.00**

Rug, drugget style, Greek Key border, organic design, 101x117"......**4,500.00**

Rug, Nile pattern, mc on oatmeal w/red & blk border, 81x49" ..**2,100.00**

Server, #802, splashbrd, 2-drw, lower shelf, p, rfn, 39x42" **2,000.00**

Server, #819, 3 short drws over 1, iron pulls, b, rfn/rstr, 48", G ..**3,750.00**

Settle, #207, early crib form, 13-slat bk, rfn/rpl rope base, 39x70" **8,000.00**

Settle, #208, 6 wide bk slats, 3 ea end, no cushions, n, 29x32x76" **4,500.00**

Settle, #210, even-arm, wide horizontal bk brd/6-slat sides, d/p, 72".**12,000.00**

Settle, #255, even-arm, 1 horizontal bk brd, 5-slat sides, n, 78", VG...**5,000.00**

Settle, hall; #205, even-arm, 5-slat bk, wide slat ea side, d, 56", VG...**2,400.00**

Shirtwaist box, #95, cedar lined, lift top, iron hdls, p, 16x32x17"........**7,500.00**

Sideboard, #814, door ea side 3 sm drws+long drw, b, 50", G..**4,250.00**

Table, #440, 30" rnd top w/thru-tenons, X-stretcher w/faceted peg, VG ..**3,250.00**

Table, #611, 24" sq cut-corner top, lower shelf, d, 29" **1,500.00**

Table, #648, 36" dia top, arched X-stretchers w/faceted peg, d/p, 30"..**6,000.00**

Table, #677, sq splay legs w/vertical stretcher, d/p, 30x48", VG....**6,500.00**

Table, drop leaf; #638, top: 42x14"+14" cut-corner leaves, p, VG ...**850.00**

Table, library; #401, trestle form, shaped open sides, d, rfn, 48", VG ..**1,100.00**

Table, library; #614, 2-drw, dbl-corbel legs, shelf, d, 48", G **1,500.00**

Table, library; #615, tacked leather top, 2-drw, corbels, d/p, 48", VG..**2,600.00**

Table, library; #624, 3-drw, base shelf, 3-slat sides, d, 54", VG ...**4,000.00**

Table, library; #651, 48x30" tacked leather top, shelf, ink mk, VG...**3,500.00**

Table, lunch; #424, rectangular top, key tenons, d, 29x40x28" ..**2,600.00**

Table, 12 Grueby tiles inset on pegged/thru-tenon top, rfn, 26x24x20" ..**9,500.00**

Tabouret, #603, rnd w/notched X-stretcher, rfn top, 20x18" dia .**600.00**

Tray, h/cp, rim w/4 oval depressions centered w/raised boss, 7" dia ..**325.00**

Tray, h/cp, 2 open hdls, 19" dia **1,300.00**

L. & J.G. Stickley

Armchair, #408, 8 curved bk slats, 6-slat sides, leather seat, n, 32" ...**4,250.00**

Armchair, #422, 6-slat bk, open arms, arched seat, n, 38x28x24", VG ...**475.00**

Bookcase, #638, 2 6-pane doors, arched toe brd, l, 48x48" **4,500.00**

Bookcase, #641, 16-pane door, gallery top, d, lt rfn, 56x30" **8,500.00**

Bookcase, #645, 2 12-pane doors, gallery top, d, 55x48" **9,200.00**

Cellarette, #23, dbl doors, copper strap hinges, 35x32x16"......**8,000.00**

Chair, like #330, 8-spindle bk, new rush seat, p, 36" **750.00**

Chair, Morris; #410, slant arm, 7-slat sides, cushion, d, 38".....**1,000.00**

Chair, Morris; #412, paddle arms, long corbels, new leather, n, 40x39"..**6,000.00**

Chair, Morris; #471, bk adjusts, 6-slat sides, Handcraft, 40", VG .**2,300.00**

Chair, Morris; #497, 5 wide slats, flat arms, thru-tenons, 31" ..**4,750.00**

Chair, side; #304, 8-spindle bk, rstr seat/rfn, d, 39", 6 for **8,000.00**

Chair, side; #330, 7-spindle bk, poor leather seat, 37", G............**170.00**

Chair, side; #424, mahog, 6 slats under V bk, rpl cushion, 36x20"...**425.00**

Chest, #94, 2 half drw:4 full:arched toe brd, rfn, 51x34x20" ...**1,800.00**

China cabinet, #646, 12 ldgl sqs top 2 doors/9 ea side, w, 62x44", VG ..**6,000.00**

Clock, mantel; dk finish, dk face w/wht numbers, Hansen, n, 22"...**11,000.00**

Costumer, #89, single tapered post w/hooks, cruciform base, 72" .**750.00**

Desk, #500, drw over kneehole w/2 half drw ea side, 30x42" **750.00**

Desk, #612 (like), bk gallery:drw:kneehole w/3 drw ea side, rfn......**4,000.00**

Desk, drw pulls out to reveal lift-top writing surface, b, 20x22", VG...**1,700.00**

Footstool, #1292, 7 vertical spindles ea side, 16x18x13", VG **900.00**

Footstool, #391, new leather seat, w, 18x19x14", VG **800.00**

Mirror, dresser; #64, freestanding, label, 30x25x4" **700.00**

Rocker, #336, 4 vertical slats, leatherette seat, 39x26x27" **750.00**

Rocker, #403, thru tenons, w/arms, 37x34x37"...............................**3,750.00**

Rocker, #409, ¾-arms w/4 slats, 4-slat bk, new cushions, 30x28" ..**4,500.00**

Rocker, #436, 6 vertical slats, reuphl cushion seat, 40"...........**1,200.00**

Rocker, #437, 6 vertical slats, w/arms, rstr spring seat, 38" **1,400.00**

Rocker, sewing; 4-slat bk, rush seat, sgn, 30x22x17", VG **200.00**

Settle, #214, 22 curved bk slats, 6-slat arms, d, 62", VG **800.00**

Settle, #221, mahog, even-arm, vertical slats, reuphl seat, 39x60" ..**11,000.00**

Settle, #222, even arm, 20-slat bk/7-slat sides, Handcraft, 76" **14,000.00**

Settle, #281, even arms, 16-slat bk, reuphl leather seat, 34x76"......**11,000.00**

Sideboard, #632, mirror bk, shelf w/corbels, 5-drw/2-door, n, 62x72"...**5,000.00**

Stand, magazine; #46, 4-shelf, 3-slat sides, rfn............................**1,300.00**

Table, #587, 16" sq top, narrow lower shelf, Handcraft, 27", VG.**600.00**

Table, game; #519, folding swivel top, some rstr, open: 30x36x36" **700.00**

Table, game; 48" sq w/cut corners, X-stretcher w/shaped shelf, VG **1,600.00**

Table, lamp; #540, shelf, thru-tenons, cleaned, branded, 29x24" dia ..**1,100.00**

Table, library; 2-drw, dbl key tenons, rfn, 29x48x30" **1,300.00**

Table, library; #520, drw, h/cp hardware, thru-tenons, rfn, 29x36x24"...**1,300.00**

Table, library; #522, mahog, 2-drw, thru-tenons, p, 29x48x30" ..**2,500.00**

Table, library; #531, 48x30" overhang top, shelf w/dbl key tenons, d...**850.00**

Table, library; #822, 2-drw, thru-tenons, stains, 29x48x30" **2,400.00**

Stickley Bros.

Armchair, #323½, rolled arms, reverse tapered legs, n, rpl cushions...**1,300.00**

Armchair, #501½, 3 narrow slats, thru-tenons, reuphl seat, 44" .**800.00**

Bookcase (att), 2 doors w/tulip-shaped lead lines, 60x56", VG ..**10,000.00**

Chair, #481½, 3-slat bk, leather seat, t, 37x18x17" **450.00**

Chair, #841½, low bk w/invt spade, reuphl leather seat, rfn, 29"...**325.00**

Chair, cube; #335, even-arm, vertical slats, d, rfn, 29x26x28" .**2,500.00**

Chair, director's; 8-spindle bk, solid seat, rfn, 43x17x16" **300.00**

Chair, Morris; #354, tapered arms, heavy thru-tenons, n, 37x39x34"..**2,100.00**

Chair, Morris; fixed bk w/2 horizontal slats over 3 vertical, l, 36"....**750.00**

Footstool, #302, notched ft, reuphl top, rfn, 5x12x12" **1,200.00**

Footstool, #324½, tapered legs, arched seat w/new leather, #d, 19"...**160.00**

Gong, dinner; #12, slab sides, chimes, striker missing, 11"..........**140.00**

Hall chair, curved hard leather seat/Xd legs/cut-out top rail, att.**110.00**

Jardiniere, h/cp, vertical panels, 10¼" **1,300.00**

Log holder, #152, 5 vertical slats to sides, cut-out rail, t, VG ..**1,000.00**

Mirror, hall; att, rectangular, 30x36" **850.00**

Mirror, hall; #7572, plate rail, hooks, 28x50" **1,200.00**

Mirror, rectangular, pegs & thru-tenons, att, rfn, 25x39" **900.00**

Plant stand, #550, wide apron, splayed legs, rpr to top, 20x18x18" ..**950.00**

Rocker, arm; #570, reverse bow arms, rpl leather seat, 38" **2,500.00**

Rocker, sewing; 3 horizontal slats, solid seat, b, 20x17x24", VG.**120.00**

Server, #8613, plate rail, drw, shelf, rfn, p, 46x54x22" **1,300.00**

Server, #8701, lower shelf, dk finish, 36x36x20", VG **1,000.00**

Sewing cabinet, 2 lift-top compartments, 3 drws, cleaned, p, 27x27x13"..**1,500.00**

Table, #2577, flared base w/cane inserts, rfn, #d, 29x30" dia ...**1,800.00**

Table, dining; #2670, ped base, cruciform ft, rfn, 30x48" dia **500.00**

Table, dining/conference; #2630, fixed top, refinished, 29x60" diameter, $2,000.00.

Table, drop-leaf; #2817, 30x30x14"+2 9" leaves **200.00**

Tabouret, #111, hexagonal w/fleur-de-lis cutouts, 19x18x18" **800.00**

Tabouret, #111, recovered leather top, 3-leg base w/cutouts, 16" dia..**550.00**

Tabouret, #3138, sq top over Mackmurdo ft, rfn, 18x14x14" **600.00**

Telephone stand, #2886, rectangular, shelf, overcoated, 30x20x18"...**300.00**

Umbrella stand, #7602, trapezoidal w/rnd posts, drip pans, t, 25", VG....**325.00**

Vase, h/cp, bulbous, att, 10" **400.00**

Stiegel

Baron Henry Stiegel produced glassware in Pennsylvania as early as 1760, very similar to glass being made concurrently in Germany and England. Without substantiating evidence, it is impossible to positively attribute a specific article to his manufacture. Although he made other types of glass, today the term Stiegel generally refers to any very early ware made in shapes and colors similar to those he is known to have produced — especially that with etched or enameled decoration. It is generally conceded, however, that most glass of this type is of European origin. Our advisor for this category is Mark Vuono; he is listed in the Directory under Connecticut.

Bride's bottle, mc enameled flowers on clear glass, 5½" **160.00**
Flask, purple amethyst, 18 broken right-swirl ribs, pontil scar, 6"...**1,350.00**
Flip, eng tulips/floral buds, 8"...**400.00**
Flip, reeded/paneled sides, eng scrolls/swags/etc, 6", set of 6 ....**1,880.00**
Tumbler, florals, 3-color, 3½"...**110.00**

Stocks and Bonds

Scripophily (scrip-awfully), the collecting of 'worthless' old stocks and bonds, gained recognition as an area of serious interest around the mid-1970s. Collectors who come from numerous business fields mainly enjoy its hobby aspect, though there are those who consider scripophily an investment. Some collectors like the historical significance that certain certificates have. Others prefer the beauty of older stocks and bonds that were printed in various colors with fancy artwork and ornate engravings. Autograph collectors are found in this field, on the lookout for signed certificates; others collect specific industries.

Many factors help determine the collector value: autograph value, age of the certificate, the industry represented, whether it is issued or not, its attractiveness, condition, and collector demand. Certificates from the mining, energy, and railroad industries are the most popular with collectors. Other industries or special collecting fields include banking, automobiles, aircraft, and territorials. Serious collectors usually prefer only issued certificates that date from before 1910. Unissued certificates are usually worth one-fourth to one-tenth the value of one that has been issued. Inexpensive issued common stocks and bonds dated between the 1940s and 1990s usually retail between $1.00 to $10.00. Those dating between 1890 and 1930 usually sell for $10.00 to $50.00. Those over one hundred years old retail between $25.00 and $100.00 or more, depending on the quantity found and the industry represented. Some stocks are one of a kind while others are found by the hundreds or even thousands, especially railroad certificates. Autographed stocks normally sell anywhere from $50.00 to $1,000.00 or more. A formal collecting organization for scripophilists is known as The Bond and Share Society with an American chapter located in New York City. As is true in any field, potential collectors should take the time to learn the hobby. Prices vary greatly at websites selling old stocks and bonds, sometimes by hundreds of dollars. EBay generally serves as a good source for information regarding current values — search under 'Coins.'

Our advisor for this category is Warren Anderson; he is listed in the Directory under Utah. In many of the following listings, two-letter state abbreviations immediately follow company name. All are in fine condition unless noted otherwise.

Key:
U — unissued   I/U — issued/uncancelled
I/C — issued/cancelled   vgn — vignette

Ahumada Lead Co, miners vgn, 100 shares, ornate border, 1926, I/C ..**20.00**

Allied Telephone Utilities, allegorical vgn, ornate border, 1932, I/C....**30.00**
Alma Lincoln Mining Co, CO, eagle vgn, hand signed, 1936, I/C.......**15.00**
Am Commercial Alcohol Corp, ABNCo, ornate border, 1932, I/C.**15.00**
Am Consolidated Mines, UT, eagle vgn, 1922, I/C **20.00**
Am Kerosene Manifold Co, ME, eagle vgn, 1918, I/C **30.00**
Arkansas Valley Elevator Co, AK, factory vgn, 1882, I/C.............**35.00**
Baltimore City Refrigerating & Heating Co, MD, building vgn, 1902, I/C...**30.00**
Blooming Grove Telephone Co, PA, state seal vgn, 1915, I/C......**40.00**
Burnwell Coal CO, AL, eagle vgn, ornate border, 1909, I/C.......**25.00**
Central Agency Inc, IL, eagle vgn, ornate gr border, 1930, U.......**10.00**
Chicago & E IL RR Co, IL, trains/child vgns, 1888, I/C..............**30.00**
Coronation Mining Co, DE, allegorical vgn, 1945, I/C.................**15.00**
Dando Printing & Publishing, PA, eagle/ship/horses vgn, 1885, I/C.**40.00**
Delaware Lackawana & Western RR, PA, train vgn, 1933, I/C......**9.00**
Dennos Baby Food Sales, AZ, 2 baby vgns, ornate border, 1915, I/C, ..**23.00**
Etta May Mining & Milling, 3 vgns, gold seal, 1920, I/U.............**18.00**
Farmer's Co-operative Assoc Inc, MD, 3 farm scenes, 1940, I/U....**10.00**
Farmer's Deposit Nat'l Bank, PA, dog vgn, gr border, 1903, I/C....**50.00**
Ft Blees Academy, MO, eagle w/shield vgn, 1913, I/C **50.00**
Goldfield United Mines, AZ Territory, ornate border, 1907, I/C...**40.00**
Harlem Independent Hygeria Ice, NY, eagle vgn/gold seal, 1899, I/C.**40.00**
Hudson Food Corp, DE, cloud vgn, ornate border, 1928, I/C........**20.00**
Investors Profit Assoc, CO, eagle vgn, orange stock, 1929, I/U **8.00**
Ione Mining & Milling, workers in tunnel vgn, 1904, I/U............**22.00**
Jumbo Fraction Mining Co, NV, workers/mtn vgns, 1906, I/C......**30.00**
Kenmar Oil Co, DE/1919, 2 vgns, gr printing, I/U **15.00**
Lodi Extension Mining, NV, gold seal, ornate border, 1907, I/C...**30.00**
Lucky Dime Oil Co, Galveston TX, torch/field vgns, 1901, I/C...**40.00**
Mohawk & Malone Ry Co Gold Bond, elk vgn, 1902, I/C...........**30.00**
National Coal Railway, UT, capitol building vgn, sgn FA Sweet, 1926...**35.00**
Nevada Boy Goldfield Mining, NV, allegorical vgn, 1906, I/C **40.00**
Nova Scotian & Mexican Mining Co, 2 vgns, 1901, 200 shares, I/C..**20.00**
NY Central & Hudson River RR, 1897, $1,000 gold bond, ABNCo, vgn, I/C..**25.00**
Option Mining Co, ID, eagle vgn, gold seal, 1925, I/C **20.00**
Pacific Nat'l Bank, LA, EA Wright Bank...Co, ornate border, 1920s, U ..**20.00**
Pittsburgh & Lake Erie RR, 3 vgns, $1,000 gold bond, 1893, +coupons...**27.00**
Price River Irrigation Co, UT, valley vgn, 1918, I/U.....................**18.00**
Raritan River RR, NJ, steamer/sailing ship vgn, 18__, U **20.00**
Rich's Clothes Shop, UT/1916, warrior vgn, orange border, I/U...**12.00**
Robert Emmet Gold & Silver Mining, NV Territory, 1864, vgn, I/U ..**400.00**
Rutland Oil & Gas, AZ Territory, vgn/4 scenes in border, 1905, I/U **18.00**

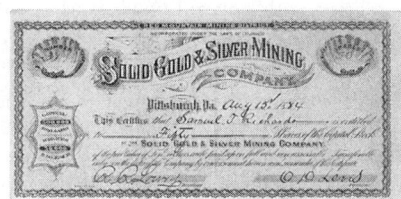

Solid Gold & Silver Mining Company, Colorado, 1884, EX, $100.00. (Photo courtesy America West Archives)

Southern Montana Oil Co, 1919, oilfield vgn, 4 scenes, I/U **14.00**
Stanley Consolidated Mining & Milling, ID, Liberty/eagle vgn, U..**12.00**
Triple Creek Gold Milling Co, CO, mtn vgn on gr, 1925, I/U......**15.00**
Unites States Mining Co, ME, 2 vgns, ABNCo, 1903, I/C...........**25.00**
Utah Patent & Implement Co, UT/1912, eagle vgn, I/U,.............**18.00**
Uvada Consolidated Mines, UT, mining vgn, gr border, 1920, I/U....**20.00**

Stoneware

There are three broad periods of time that collectors of American pottery can look to in evaluating and dating the stoneware and earthenware in their collections. Among the first permanent settlers in America were English and German potters who found a great demand for their individually turned wares. The early pottery was produced from red and yellow clays scraped from the ground at surface levels. The earthenware made in these potteries was fragile and coated with lead glazes that periodically created health problems for the people who ate or drank from it. There was little stoneware available for sale until the early 1800s, because the clays used in its production were not readily available in many areas and transportation was prohibitively expensive. The opening of the Erie Canal and improved roads brought about a dramatic increase in the accessibility of stoneware clay, and many new potteries began to open in New York and New England.

Collectors have difficulty today locating earthenware and stoneware jugs produced prior to 1840, because few have survived intact. These ovoid or pear-shaped jugs were designed to be used on a daily basis. When cracked or severely chipped, they were quickly discarded. The value of handcrafted pottery is often determined by the cobalt decoration it carries. Pieces with elaborate scenes (a chicken pecking corn, a bluebird on a branch, a stag standing near a pine tree, a sailing ship, or people) may easily bring $1,000.00 to $12,000.00 at auction.

After the Civil War there was a need and a national demand for stoneware jugs, crocks, canning jars, churns, spittoons, and a wide variety of other pottery items. The competition among the many potteries reached the point where only the largest could survive. To cut costs, most potteries did away with all but the simplest kinds of decoration on their wares. Time-consuming brush-painted birds or flowers quickly gave way to more quickly executed swirls or numbers and stenciled designs. The coming of home refrigeration and Prohibition in 1919 effectively destroyed the American stoneware industry.

Investment possibilities: 1) Early nineteenth-century stoneware with elaborate decorations and a potter's mark is expensive and will continue to rise in price. 2) Late nineteenth-century hand-thrown stoneware with simple cobalt swirls or numbers is still reasonably priced and a good investment. 3) Mass-produced stoneware (ca. 1890 – 1920) is available in large quantities, inexpensive, and slowly increases in price over the years.

Skillfully repaired pieces often surface; their prices should reflect their condition. Look for a slight change in color and texture. The use of a black light is also useful in exposing some repairs. Buyer beware! Hint: Buy only from reputable dealers who will guarantee their merchandise.

In the following listings, 'c/s' means 'cobalt on salt glaze'; all decoration described before this abbreviation is in cobalt. See also Bennington, Stoneware. Assume that values are for examples in near mint condition with only minimal damage unless another condition code is given in the description.

Batter pail; #2/flowers, c/s, Cowden & Wilcox...PA, 1870s, 11", VG+ .1,200.00
Batter pail; #6/flower, c/s, EW Farrington..., rstr, 1890s, 9½" 465.00
Churn, #2/squiggles, c/s, unsgn, 1840s, short line, 12¾" 175.00
Churn, #4/puppet-like man/cattail, c/s, unsgn, 1850s, 16", EX 2,650.00

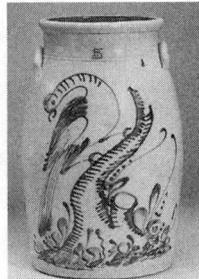

Churn, #5/peafowl on flowering branch, cobalt on salt glaze, possibly upstate New York, nineteenth century, 17½", $5,175.00. (Photo courtesy Skinner Auctions, Inc.)

Churn, #6/vining flowers, c/s, W Roberts...NY, rstr, 1860s, 19" ..800.00
Cooler, Allen Germ Proof Filter, c/s, 14x12", EX 965.00

Cream pot, #2/horse head, c/s, Whites Utica, rpr, ca 1865, 8" ..5,000.00
Cream pot, #4/flower, c/s, Lewis & Cady...VT, ca 1856, 12" 220.00
Crock, #1/bird singing, c/s, unsgn, 1870s, 7¼" 525.00
Crock, #1/leaf, c/s, SL Pewtress...Conn, line, 1880s, 7½" 175.00
Crock, #1/tornado, c/s, NY Stoneware..., chip, 1870s, 9" 200.00
Crock, #2 w/in wreath, c/s, Burger & Lang...NY, chips, 1870s, 9"....165.00
Crock, #2/bird on plume, c/s, Haxstun...NY, chip, 1870s, 9½" ...685.00
Crock, #2/dbl tulips, c/s, Brown Brothers...LI, rstr, 1890s, 9" 165.00
Crock, #2/geometrics, c/s, SB Bosworth...CT, ca 1875, 9½" 135.00
Crock, #3 w/in wreath, c/s, Burger & Co...NY, ca 1877, 10".......415.00
Crock, #3/bird & flower, c/s, WH Farrar..., line, 1850s, 10".....1,925.00
Crock, #3/bird on stump, c/s, Brady & Ryan...NY, 1880s, 10½", EX.700.00
Crock, #3/flower, c/s, Cowden & Wilcox...PA, 1870s, 11½", EX ..525.00
Crock, #3/flower, c/s, N Clark & Co..., 1860s, 12" 275.00
Crock, #3/flower, c/s, SB Bosworth...CT, ca 1890, 10½", EX 90.00
Crock, #3/plume, c/s, JS Taft & Co...NH, ca 1875, 10", EX...........80.00
Crock, #4/dog/birds/tree, c/s, West Troy Pottery, rstr, 1880s, 11½" ..900.00
Crock, #4/dotted flower, c/s, CW Braun...NY, ping, ca 1870, 11"....300.00
Crock, #4/fan-tailed bird, c/s, Whites Utica, ca 1865, 11½", EX .800.00
Crock, #4/parrot (EX art), c/s, SL Pewtress...Conn, ca 1880, 11" 1,870.00
Crock, #4/parrot on plume, c/s, FB Norton...Mass, line, 1870s, 11" ...575.00
Crock, #5/tulip, c/s, S Hart Fulton, ca 1875, 12", EX 110.00
Crock, #6/dbl flower (elaborate), c/s, CW Braun...NY, 1870s, 14", EX..2,650.00
Crock, #6/sunflower, c/s, CW Braun...NY, 1870s, 13½", EX.......250.00
Crock, cake; #11/2/floral, c/s, Frank B Norton..., 1870s, 6½", EX...300.00
Crock, 4 leaves, c/s, 10-gal, 17x14", EX 400.00
Jar, #2 w/sm wreath/dbl flower, c/s, Jordan, prof rstr, 1850s, 11" .200.00
Jar, #2/dancing flower, c/s, John Burger, ca 1865, 11" 415.00
Jar, #2/lg leaf, c/s, Whites Utica NY, minor stain, ca 1865, 11½"...330.00
Jar, #2/plume, c/s, JF Brayton & Co Utica, ca 1835, 8½" 415.00
Jar, #2/starburst, c/s, Jordan, w/orig lid, ca 1850, 10¾"............1,650.00
Jar, #3/running bird, c/s, Whites Utica, prof rstr, ca 1865, 12"....250.00
Jar, preserve; #1½/dbl flower, c/s, Ballard & Bros, line, 1860s, 9".....175.00
Jar, preserve; #1½/tornado, att MacQuoid, 1870s, 10½" 150.00
Jar, preserve; #1/plume, c/s, att NY state, bail hdl, 1860s, 10½" .465.00
Jar, preserve; #2, c/s, John Rietzel...NJ, 1870s, 11½", EX 175.00
Jar, preserve; #2/tulip, c/s, J Fisher & Co...NY, 1880s, 12" 220.00
Jar, preserve; Remmey 1882/Star of David, c/s, ca 1881, 1-qt, 6¾" .1,875.00
Jug, #1/accents, c/s, JB Caire & Co...NY, flaw/stain, 1850s, 9" ...175.00
Jug, #1/flower, c/s, H&G Nash Utica, ca 1832, 11", EX..............220.00
Jug, #1/plumes, c/s, S Hart, tight line, ca 1875, 11".....................110.00
Jug, #1/tulip, c/s, G Apley & Co...NY, 1860s, 11" 465.00
Jug, #1/vine, c/s, unsgn, 1860s, 8½"......................................250.00
Jug, #2/bird on plume, c/s, Ottman Bros...NY, ping, 1870s, 14" ..935.00
Jug, #2/bird on 2-flower branch, c/s, WH Farrar..., rstr, 1850s, 14" ..1,700.00
Jug, #2/clam shell, c/s, Commeraw's... (6-line name), ca 1800, 13", EX....1,925.00
Jug, #2/cloverleaf, c/s, FB Norton...Mass, sm stain, 1870s, 14" ...275.00
Jug, #2/dotted cross, c/s, W Hart Ogdensburg, 1860s, 13½"........965.00
Jug, #2/flower, c/s, J McBurney Jordan, prof rstr, 1850s, 13"........635.00
Jug, #2/flower, c/s, S Hart & Son Fulton, lt stain, ca 1877, 12" ...165.00
Jug, #2/flower, c/s, Whites Utica, ca 1850, 14", EX 110.00
Jug, #2/flower/accents, c/s, SH Addington, 1830s, 14" 685.00
Jug, #2/plume, c/s, ovoid, N Clark & Co..., 1850s, 13½" 465.00
Jug, #2/stripe, ochre/s, Lyman & Clark..., ca 1837, 13", EX 745.00
Jug, #2/tornado, c/s, Geddes NY, 1860s, 14" 660.00
Jug, #2/triple flower, c/s, Lyons, overall staining, 1860s, 14" 360.00
Jug, #2/Venetian sailing ship, c/s, JM Pruden...NJ, 1860s, 13", EX...800.00
Jug, #2/vining flowers, c/s, Edmands & Co, 1870s, 16", EX.........175.00
Jug, #2/wreath, c/s, Jordan, 1840s, 14", EX 650.00
Jug, #2/1853/apple on branch, c/s, Jordan, sm ping ca 1853, 14½" .11,275.00
Jug, #3/brushed decor, c/s, Clark & Co..., hdl missing, ca 1839, 15" 200.00
Jug, #3/dbl bull's-eye flower, c/s, unclear mk, 1870s, 16", EX 575.00
Jug, #4/drooping flower/AE Allen..., c/s, att NY state, 1860s, 17"...200.00
Jug, #4/swags/accents, c/s, G Heiser...NY, rstr, ca 1837, 16" 185.00

Jug, #5/dbl bird, c/s, NY Stoneware Co..., line, 1880s, 19" **1,375.00**
Jug, #5/ribbed orchid, c/s, Whites Utica NY, ca 1865, 18".......**1,925.00**
Jug, John H Sheehan....NY advertising, c/s, 1870s, 2-qt, 9½" **275.00**

Store

Perhaps more so than any other yesteryear establishment, the country store evokes feelings of nostalgia for folks old enough to remember its charms — barrels for coffee, crackers, and big green pickles; candy in a jar for the grocer to weigh on shiny brass scales; beheaded chickens in the meat case outwardly devoid of nothing but feathers. Today mementos from this segment of Americana are being collected by those who 'lived it' as well as those less fortunate!

Our advisor for this category is Charles Reynolds; he is listed in the Directory under Virginia. For more information we recommend *General Store Collectibles, Vols. I* and *II*, by David L. Wilson. See also Advertising; Scales.

Box, cracker; glass cover, old bl pnt, 8½" H...................................**50.00**
Butcher's block, sycamore, rnd top w/3 legs, 31x23½" dia **100.00**
Butcher's block, wooden slab on 3 legs, 19th C, 38x28" dia........**800.00**
Cabinet, oak, 8-sided, metal base, ball/claw ft, revolves, 66" **500.00**
Cabinet, seed; 21 bins, glass fronts, pnt oak, 19x54x120", EX **875.00**
Candy jar, clear glass w/rnd bottom, tilted in metal fr, 5x13½" **40.00**
Case, glass w/tin edges & bottom, sloping hinged lid, 4x10x7"...**330.00**
Case, nickel-bound etched glass, 2 oak doors, 35x28" **350.00**
Case, Utica Forge & Tool Co, tin w/wood drws, 10x14x17" **200.00**

Case, Zeno Gum, oak with graduated glass shelves and mirrored back, embossed lettering on marquee, 18x10", EX, $650.00.

Coffee urn, copper, name plate: Brown's Store..., eagle finial, 32"..**275.00**
Desk, clerk's; walnut, slant front, 4-drw, attached top, 85" **1,450.00**
Dispenser, paper bag; pnt metal, chips, 30x9½" **325.00**
Display jar, clear cylinder, pontil scar, orig tin lid, 4½" **250.00**
Display jar, clear glass, Greek Key pattern at base, neck & lip, 19" **1,900.00**
Display jar, clear glass shouldered cylinder, orig tin lid, 6¼" **140.00**
Display jar, clear globe, smooth bottom, orig stopper, 10" **220.00**
Hat stand, maple, trn...**40.00**
Jar, Nut House emb on clear glass, 9x10½" **85.00**
Scoop, candy; PB Clark & Co, 7", EX..**175.00**
Scoop, metal w/wooden hdl, 11"..**15.00**
Sugar auger, dual trn wood hdl on corkscrew-like end, 15x9½"..**230.00**
Urn, blown clear w/pontil scarred ft, smooth rim, orig lid, 8¼".**100.00**

Stoves

Antique stoves' desirability is based on two criteria: their utility and their decorative merit. It's the latter that adds an 'antique' premium to the basic functional value that could be served just as well by a modern stove. Sheer age is usually irrelevant. Decorative features that enhance desirability include fancy, embossed ornamentation, nickel-plated trim, mica windows, ceramic tiles, and (in cooking stoves) water reservoirs

and high warming closets rather than mere high shelves. The less sheet metal and the more cast iron, the better. Look for crisp, sharp designs in preference to those made from worn or damaged and repaired foundry patterns. Stoves with a pastel porcelain finish can be very attractive; blue is a favorite, white is least desirable. Chrome trim, rather than nickel, dates a stove to circa 1933 or later and is a good indicator of a post-antique stove. Though purists prefer the earlier models trimmed in nickel rather than chrome, there is now considerable public interest in these post-antique stoves as well, and some people are willing to pay a good price for these appliance-era 'classics.' (Note: Remember, not all bright metal trim is chrome; it is important to learn to distinguish chrome from the earlier, more desirable nickel plate.)

Among stove types, base burners (with self-feeding coal magazines) are the most desirable. Then come the upright, cylindrical 'oak' stoves, kitchen ranges, and wood parlors. Cannon stoves approach the margin of undesirability; laundries and gasoline stoves plunge through it.

There's a thin but continuing stream of desirable antique stoves going to the high-priced Pacific Coast market. Interest in antique stoves is least in the deep South. Demand for wood/coal stoves is strongest in areas where firewood is affordable and storage of it is practical. Demand for antique gas ranges has become strong, especially in metropolitan markets, and interest in antique electric ranges is just starting to surface. The market for antique stoves is so limited and the variety so bewildering that a consensus on a going price can hardly emerge. They are only worth something to the right individual, and prices realized depend very greatly on who happens to be in the auction crowd. Even an expert's appraisal will usually miss the realized price by a substantial percent.

In judging condition look out for deep rust pits, warped or burnt-out parts, unsound fire bricks, poorly fitting parts, poor repairs, and empty mounting holes indicating missing trim. Search meticulously for cracks in the cast iron. Our listings reflect auction prices of completely restored, safe, and functional stoves, unless indicated otherwise.

Note: Round Oak stoves carrying the words 'Estate of P.D. Beckwith' above the lower door were made prior to 1935. After that date, the company name was changed to Round Oak Company, and the Beckwith reference was no longer used. In our listings, the term 'tea shelf' has been used to describe both drop and swing shelves, as the function of both types was to accommodate teapots and coffeepots.

Base Burners

Art Amherst #15, NP trim, tiles, 11" urn, 50x25x28", VG......**2,065.00**
Burdett-Smith #44, swivel top, tiles, 38", VG **1,300.00**
Detroit Emerald Jewel #14, NPCI, 1909, 54", +15" brass urn ..**1,700.00**
Favorite #30, Piqua OH, ornate CI, mica windows, 52"+14" urn **2,200.00**
Michigan Stove, Art Garland #400, gargoyles/NP/mica, 1889, rstr...**10,750.00**
Ransom Art Denmark #15, Albany NY, tiles/NP/mica, 1897, VG......**4,950.00**
Thos Caffney Waverly #12, Boston MA, 40x20x22" **6,065.00**
Weir Glenwood #6, NP trim, mica windows, 1909, 68" **965.00**

Franklin Stoves

Acme #18 Orient 1890, 6 tiles, mica windows, fancy..................**315.00**
Iron Foundry...NH, ornate CI, grate missing, 1820s, 37x26x32" .**220.00**
Magee Ideal #3, CI fireplace, 2 side trivets, 1892, 32x28"...........**275.00**
Muzzy & Co Villa Franklin, folding doors, 1830s, 30"+4" urn **195.00**
Noyes & Nutter Kineo #16, fireplace, 1890s, 32x23x20" **200.00**
Southard Robertson Sunny Hearth #2, 1880s, 35x20x29½" **315.00**
Walker & Pratt Good Cheer #22, fireplace, 1850s, 32x27x31"...**330.00**
Wyer & Noble, CI/brass-trim fireplace, old **2,200.00**

Parlor Stoves

The term 'parlor stove' as we use it here is very general and encompasses at least six distinct types recognized by the stove industry: cottage parlor, double-cased airtight, circulator, cylinder, oak, and the fireplace heater.

Bangor Comfort #23, oval w/dome top, Pat 1875, 33"+10" urn..**200.00**
Burdett Smith & Co #44, sq, tiles, mica door, 38"+8" urn..........**385.00**
Co-Op Foundry Sylvan Red Cross #31, tiles, gargoyle legs, Pat 1888-89...**330.00**
Ideal Garland #220, wood/coal cottage, missing urn, ca 1893, rstr ..**1,300.00**
Ilion #5, ornate CI, ca 1853, 33"+13" 2-pc urn **550.00**
JH Shear #2, Albany NY, CI, column style, 56" **935.00**
Johnson, Geer & Cox #4, CI, 4-column, 56" **1,100.00**
Modern Glenwood Wood Parlor, slide top, 1900s, 45x28x24½"...**360.00**
Pratt & Wentworth Peerless, tip-up dome, 1840s, 37x19x15" **150.00**
SH Ransom, ornate CI, rnd air intake, Pat 1846, 26"+14" urn...**300.00**
Somersworth #20, tip-up dome top, 1850s, 39x30x29"................**330.00**
Tyson #1, 2 sheet metal columns, swing doors, 36x17x25"..........**385.00**
Vose & Co #5 Temple, CI, Pat 1854, 44"..................................**880.00**
Warnick & Leibrandt Union Airtight, ornate CI, 1851, 26" **275.00**
Wood/Bishop Royal Clarion #14, mica door, oven, 1890s, 50"...............**275.00**

Ranges (Gas)

Chambers, wht, 4-burner, ca 1949, G...**250.00**
Detroit Jewel, 4-burner, blk/NP, glass oven door, 1918, VG........**550.00**
Magic Chef, wht, 6-burner/2-oven, high closet, 1938, rstr, up to ..**12,000.00**
Magic Chef, wht, 6-burner/2-oven, high closet, 1938, unrstr ..**1,000.00**
Magic Chef, 6-burner/2-oven, warming closet, 1932, EX.........**2,750.00**
O'Keefe & Merritt, 4-burner, cabinet base, ca 1929, G................**110.00**
O'Keefe & Merritt, 6-burner, dual oven/broilers, wht porc, EX ..**500.00**
Quick Meal, 4-burner, bl, cabinet style, 1919, G **925.00**
Quick Meal, 4-burner, gray, canopy/high closet, 1924, unrstr **375.00**
Quick Meal, 4-burner/1-oven, 1928, unrstr..................................**300.00**
Wedgwood, wht porc, complete w/4 burner covers & lifter, 1930s, EX..**900.00**
Wier Insulated Glenwood, 6-burner/2-oven, wht, 1932, rstr......**4,500.00**

Ranges (Wood and Coal)

Noyes & Nutter Kineo C, roll top, water tank, 1900-15 ....**715.00**
Portland Ideal Atlantic 8-20, ornate CI, bk shelf, 1850s...........**1,675.00**
Portland Queen Atlantic, unadorned, 19½x19½x12"..................**685.00**
Taunton Quaker Standard #8-20, NP trim, shelf/tea shelves, 1890s..**945.00**
Walker & Pratt Village Crawford Royal, tea shelves, 1900s........**800.00**
Wood/Bishop Popular Clarion, scrolling, tea shelves, 1890s....**1,150.00**
Wood/Bishop Imperial Clarion #8-20, warming closet, dtd 1898...**1,980.00**

Stove Manufacturers' Toy Stoves

Buck's Jr Range, St Louis MO, new body/pnt/recast parts, 26"....**850.00**
Charter Oak #503, GF Filley, St Louis MO, 14x12x25", EX....**2,050.00**
Dainty, Reading Stove Works, PA, 7x13x8", VG **150.00**
Estate Fresh Air Oven, blk/wht enamel, NP, working gas range, 15"...**2,400.00**
Karr Qualified, bl porc w/NP, Belleville IL, 1925, EX **2,500.00**
Karr Qualified Range, aluminum/tin, dial on door, 21½x13", EX...**775.00**
Karr Range 6, Belleville IL, bl porc, older model, 21½x13x9".**3,000.00**
Little Eva T Southard, NYC, 8½x14x11", VG w/accessories......**575.00**
Little Fanny, Philadelphia Stove Works, ca 1880, CI, minor rust, EX...**300.00**
Royal American, Bridgeford, Louisville KY, 14x12x10", G.........**950.00**

Toy Manufacturers' Toy Stoves

Adams/Pet, CI, cooking, ornate wood burner, 1857, 8½" W base ..**290.00**
Arcade Hotpoint Range, pnt CI, tan & gr, VG **150.00**
Arcade Roper Range, pnt CI, gas type, door opens, 4½", EX........**70.00**
Bing, cookstove, bl steel, brass trim, 16½", VG..........................**600.00**
Crescent, CI, w/shelves, lids, 5 CI pots, 8", EX............................**170.00**

Crescent, cookstove, plated CI & steel, 4-hole, 11½", EX..........**230.00**
Eagle, Hubley, Lancaster PA, NP, recast parts, rstr......................**450.00**
Eagle, Kenton, CI, heavily scrolled, 4-ft, 11½x10", G................**125.00**
Eclipse, J&E Stevens, Cromwell CT, CI, EX................................**175.00**
Kenton Royal, CI & steel, 4-hole, ornate, 10", VG....................**100.00**
Lionel, porc & CI, cream & gr, 4-leg, 32x26", EX......................**550.00**
Little Giant, unmk/unidentified, 7½x8½x11", EX orig..............**675.00**
Novelty, Kenton Hdwe, bl pnt/NP trim, rfn, 13x6½x8½" **600.00**
Pet, The Young Bros, Albany NY, heating type, 10½x6x8½".....**165.00**
Rival, J&E Stevens, Cromwell CT, 14x9x16", M, +2 kettles...**1,350.00**
Rival, no shelves, 12" L, EX..**900.00**
Royal, Kenton, CI & steel, 4-hole/working grates, rpt, 10", G.......**50.00**
Royal, plated CI, stovepipe, shield shape, 16", G........................**85.00**
Spark, CI, heating, int grate, sliding vents, Grey Iron, 14", VG .**115.00**
Triumph, Kenton Hdwe, OH, 14x8½x19", G..............................**195.00**

Strawberry Soft Paste and Lustre Ware

Strawberry lustre is a general term for pearlware and semiporcelain decorated with hand-painted strawberries, veins, tendrils, and pink lustre trim. Strawberry soft paste is decorated creamware without the pink lustre trim. Both types were made by many manufacturers in England in the nineteenth century, most of whom never marked their ware.

Coffeepot, acanthus hdl terminal, emb strawberries, rpr, 12", G.**250.00**
Creamer, emb strawberries/rope-like bands, 4¼x6", EX **100.00**

Plate, strawberries and roses in center, pink border, 8¼", EX, **$80.00**. (Photo courtesy Garth's Auctions)

Plate, basket of red/yel strawberries, flowers, 10", EX **130.00**
Sugar bowl, emb strawberries/rope-like bands, w/lid, 5½x6", VG..**140.00**
Tea bowl & saucer, basket of strawberries on side, EX.................**200.00**
Teapot, emb strawberries/rope-like bands, 5½x9", G...................**250.00**

Stretch Glass

Stretch glass, produced from circa 1916 through 1935, was made in an effort to emulate the fine art glass of Tiffany and Carder. The pressed or blown glassware was sprayed with a metallic salts mix while hot, then reshaped, causing a stretch effect in the iridescent finish. Pieces which were not reshaped had the iridized finish without the stretch, as seen on Fenton's #222 lemonade set and #401 guest set. Northwood, Imperial, Fenton, Diamond, Lancaster, Jeannette, Central, Vineland Flint, and the United States Glass Company were the manufacturers of this type of glass.

For more information we recommend *American Iridescent Stretch Glass* by John Madeley and Dave Shetlar (Collector Books). See also specific companies.

Bonbon, Pearl White (crystal), 4-crimp, Imperial, #38, 2¼x5½" .**70.00**
Bowl, bl, shallow, cupped rim, US Glass, #179, 1¾x7¼" **30.00**
Bowl, Celeste Blue, crimped, 5 rings, Fenton, 2⅛x7½"................**60.00**
Bowl, cobalt, flared smooth rim, Vineland Flint Glass, 4x7½" ...**170.00**

Bowl, dk gr w/marigold irid, crimped, Diamond Glass, 2¾x7½"..175.00
Bowl, gold (lt marigold), flared rim, Jeannette, 3¼x12¼"............55.00
Bowl, gold (marigold), 3-mold, Diamond Glass, 2¾x7⅛".............35.00
Bowl, ivory (custard), 28 optic rays, Northwood, #663, 3¼x9⅝"..160.00
Bowl, Pearl Ruby (marigold), flared, Imperial, #42, 2⅜x7¾"........95.00
Bowl, ruby (red), rolled rim, Fenton, #647, 3⅝x10⅝" 200.00
Bowl, Russet, cupped, Northwood, #670, 2¼x4⅝" 40.00
Candlesticks, Celeste Blue, Fenton, #249, 6½", pr 70.00
Candlesticks, Green Ice (bl-gr), Imperial, #6009, 9", pr.............200.00
Candy jar, Iris Ice (crystal), Optic Rays, 3-ftd, w/lid, Lancaster..120.00
Candy jar, Persian Pearl (crystal) w/blk decor, Fenton, #9, 9x4".150.00
Cheese & cracker set, Topaz w/blk trim, US Glass, #320, 2-pc.....70.00
Comport, amberina (amber stem), 18 rays, Imperial, 7½x7⅝" ...300.00
Comport, Florentine Green, ruffled rim, ftd, Fenton, #9, 4¾x7⅛" 60.00
Comport, Jade Blue, 15-panel, wide bowl, Northwood, #645, 3x6½"...60.00
Comport, Royal Blue (lt cobalt), high ft, US Glass, #314, 7x5⅝"...70.00
Comport, Topaz, openwork rim, ftd, US Glass, #310, 6x11¼"....350.00
Comport, wht lustre (crystal) w/enameling, Lancaster Glass, 4¾x9"...75.00
Comport, Wisteria (lt purple), flared rim, Fenton, #260, 7x5⅞"..140.00
Creamer & sugar bowl, Florentine Green, cobalt hdls, #2 ....225.00
Lamp shade, wht opaque, ribbed, flared, Northwood, 5x5" 65.00
Nut cup, Florentine Green, dolphin stem, Fenton, 4⅝x4⅜x2⅛" ..800.00
Pitcher, Florentine Green, Fenton, #215, 8¼x3½".....................225.00
Pitcher, Topaz w/cobalt hdl, Fenton, #222, 10x4¾" 400.00
Plate, bread; Topaz w/bl trim, US Glass, 7x12"...........................60.00
Plate, Egyptian Lustre (blk opaque), Diamond Glass, 11½"........150.00
Plate, salad; Green Ice (bl-gr), 48 optic rays, Imperial, #805, 8¼"...40.00
Plate, Topaz, Fenton, #631, 11½" 65.00
Puff box, Florentine Green, Fenton, #743, 5x5¼" 75.00
Rose bowl, gr, cupped rim, ftd, Diamond Glass, 3¼x4⅞" 40.00
Sherbet, Russet, ftd, flared, plain, Northwood, #685, 3½x4¼" 45.00
Tumbler, bl, dmn pattern, flat base, Northwood, 3¼x4⅝" 35.00
Vase, bl, flared, US Glass, #151, 3½x8¼" 60.00
Vase, car; Pearl (crystal), crimped, Diamond Glass, 7⅛" 90.00
Vase, fan; Rib Optic, topaz w/etch/gold, Fenton, #570, 5⅞x7" 50.00
Vase, Jade Green (gr opaque), flared rim, US Glass, 5⅞x3½" 60.00
Vase, Pearl Green (gr-yel), crimped, Imperial, #83, 9¾x10⅜"....190.00
Vase, Pearl Ruby (marigold), bulbous, incurvate rim, Imperial, #6 ..125.00
Vase, Ruby (red), hat shape w/crimped sides, Fenton, 3¾x6" 125.00

String Holders

Today, if you want to wrap and secure a package, you have a variety of products to choose from: cellophane tape, staples, etc. But in the 1800s, string was about the only available binder; thus the string holder, either the hanging or counter type, was a common and practical item found in most homes and businesses. Chalkware and ceramic figurals from the 1930s and 1940s contrast with the cast and wrought-iron examples from the 1800s to make for an interesting collection. Our advisor for this category is Charles Reynolds; he is listed in the Directory under Virginia. See also Advertising.

Apple & blueberries, chalkware 50.00
Apple w/face, ceramic, PY, from $100 to 150.00
Ball-shaped openwork cage, CI, on openwork ped base, 6½".........80.00
Beehive, CI, Pat'd Feb'y 14 1860, orig tan pnt, 4x6½"..................95.00
Bird, ceramic, String Nest Pull..65.00
Bird on branch, scissors in head, ceramic, from $85 to................100.00
Black child's face, chalkware, EX..125.00
Boy fishes through whale's mouth, F&F, NM 40.00
Bride & bridesmaids, ceramic, from $75 to 125.00
Campbell's Soup Kid, chalkware, orig pnt, ca 1940, 6½" 260.00
Cat atop ball of red string, chalkware, 7" 45.00

Child sits on globe on beast-head base, brass, 1870s, 14" 350.00
Counter type, CI, Pat Feb 16, 1880, 6" on 6½" base 110.00
Deco girl w/hands in front, flowers, ceramic 95.00
Dutch girl's head, bl dots, chalkware 75.00
Girl, sleeping, ceramic...100.00
Girl w/bl ribbon in hair, chalkware, 8x7".......................................185.00
Gourd, chalkware, from $125 to 150.00
Heinz Pickle, metal ceiling type for cone string 2,500.00
I Hate Housework, ceramic..160.00
Iron w/flowers, ceramic, from $200 to 300.00
Little Chef, Rice Crispy Guy, chalkware, ca 1950s, 7" 170.00
Mammy w/laundry, chalkware, EX..125.00
Man between 2 Southern belles, ceramic 50.00
Monkey on string ball 200.00
Owl, pottery..175.00
Parrot, chalkware, brightly colored, from $125 to..........................150.00
Pig w/flowers, ceramic, from S100 to 125.00
Prince Pineapple, chalkware, from $225 to 275.00
Sailor boy, w/pipe, chalkware 150.00
Snip, cat w/yarn ball, Fitz & Floyd..60.00
Southern belle, ceramic, Japan, 6" 50.00
SSS for the Blood, CI w/top 500.00
Witch in pumpkin, winking, ceramic, from $125 to...................175.00

Sugar Shakers

Sugar shakers (or muffineers, as they were also called) were used during the Victorian era to sprinkle sugar and spice onto breakfast muffins, toast, etc. They were made of art glass, in pressed patterns, and in china. See also specific types and manufacturers (such as Northwood). Our coadvisors for this category are Jeff Bradfield and Dale MacAllister; they are listed in the Directory under Virginia.

Acorn, bl opaque...210.00
Acorn, pk opaque w/mc floral...240.00
Alba, bl opaque 180.00
Argus Swirl, pk (Peach Bloom) 230.00
Beatty Honeycomb, bl opal...250.00
Block & Fan, clear pattern glass..75.00
Blown Twist, gr opal, wide waist...350.00
Bridal Rosette, ruby stain...195.00

Bubble Lattice, blue opal, $450.00.

Bubble Lattice, wht opal 275.00
Challinor's Forget-Me-Not, gr opaque...225.00
Challinor's Forget-Me-Not, pk..175.00
Chrysanthemum Swirl, cranberry opal 495.00
Coin Dot, bl opal, 9-panel 185.00
Cone, bl opaque..135.00
Cone, glossy pk, Consolidated, 5½" 135.00
Creased Teardrop, translucent bl slag 160.00

Crown Milano, fall leaves/bl berries on bsk, floral-emb lid **325.00**
Daisy & Fern, bl opal, wide waist **275.00**
Daisy & Fern, wht opal, wide waist **150.00**
Fern, bl opal...**350.00**
Flower Mold, bl **395.00**
Gillinder Melon..**225.00**
Guttate, pk (+) **325.00**
Hobbs Polka Dot, cranberry **550.00**
Illinois, clear pattern glass **95.00**
Inverted Thumbprint, cranberry **190.00**
Jeweled Heart, bl **275.00**
Late Block, Duncan, clear pattern glass.......................................**75.00**
Leaf Mold, canary spatter...**350.00**
Leaning Pillar, bl opaque **110.00**
Little Shrimp, satin w/decor..**275.00**
Melon, yel floral-decor top, Smith Bros **375.00**
Northwood Venetian, cranberry **225.00**
Panelled Sprig, milk glass, decor **75.00**
Parian Swirl, gr opaque, decor **185.00**
Quilted Phlox, gr transparent **175.00**
Raindrop MOP, royal bl w/pk coralene seaweed, mk Pat, spherical, 6" ...**1,000.00**
Reverse Swirl, cranberry opal..**485.00**
Ribbed Lattice, bl opal..**265.00**
Ribbed Lattice, wht opal...**135.00**
Satin, w/yel floral, melon ribs, Smith Bros **375.00**
Seaweed, cranberry opal..**500.00**
Short Ribbed Lattice, wht, rare **275.00**
Spanish Lace, bl opal, wide waist...**225.00**
Swirl, 9-panel, cranberry opal (reproduced in 1960s) **125.00**
Tomato, wht satin w/decor, Mt WA **375.00**
West Virginia, Optic, cranberry **225.00**
West Virginia, Optic, ribbed milk glass w/HP florals **95.00**

Sunderland Lustre

Sunderland lustre was made by various potters in the Sunderland district of England during the eighteenth and nineteenth centuries. It is often characterized by a splashed-on application of the pink lustre, which results in an effect sometimes referred to as the 'cloud' pattern. Some pieces are transfer printed with scenes, ships, florals, or portraits.

Bowl, Bridge at River Wear/figural scene/2 verses, pk cloud, 5x3¼".**740.00**
Bowl, Ship Caroline blk transfer on wht w/pk cloud border, 4x10" dia ..**435.00**
Cup & saucer, demitasse; pk cloud w/swirl border, mk Staffordshire ...**80.00**
Jug, Mariners Arms, ship/sailors, dk red transfer/mc, 8", NM......**770.00**
Jug, Mason's Arms/Liberty & Justice, ca 1840, 7½".....................**540.00**
Mug, Masonic symbolism, pk & purple lustre, ca 1840, 3⅛x3⅛" ..**265.00**
Mug, Unfortunate London/verse, 3-D frog w/in, yel lustre border....**310.00**
Plaque, Prepare To Meet Thy God, brn transfer w/yel border, 6½"..**500.00**
Plaque, Prepare To Meet Thy God, pk cloud border w/blk trim, 8" dia ..**460.00**
Plaque, Prepare To Meet Thy God, pk cloud w/scalloped border, 7x8"...**540.00**
Plate, pk cloud w/lt bl tint in center, mk w/crown & Allerton's, 7"..**90.00**
Sauce boat, landscape scene in pk, ca 1820, 3¼x5" **110.00**

Surveying Instruments

The practice of surveying offers a wide variety of precision instruments primarily for field use, most of which are associated with the recording of distance and angular measurements. These instruments were primarily made from brass; the larger examples were fitted with tripods and protective cases. These cases also held accessories for the instruments, and these can sometimes play a key part in their evaluation.

Instruments in complete condition and showing little use will have much greater values than those that appear to have had moderate or heavy use. Instruments were never polished during use, and those that have been polished as decorator pieces are of little interest to most avid collectors. Our advisor for this category is Dale Beeks; he is listed in the Directory under Iowa.

Alidade, Gurley, MIB w/sunshade & booklet................................**235.00**
Alidade, plane table; Keuffel & Esser, brass, 10" scope, NMIB ...**415.00**
Alidade, US Navy, telescopic, 1944, NM in 6x14½x14" dvtl case ..**130.00**
Alidade, w/sunshade & booklet, EXIB **240.00**
Chain, Canadian type, ca 1900, 66' **250.00**
Chain, W&LE Gurley, 50 Ft Steel No 10, brass hdls/keys, ca 1900 ..**245.00**
Compass, Benjn K Haggar Baltimore, divided pewter needle, 1818, 7" dia ..**4,100.00**
Compass, Dietzgen, jeweled needle, 2-sight vanes, EX in leather case...**175.00**
Compass, Gurley, vernier, brass, bl steel needle, tripod, 6" dia, +box .**1,800.00**
Compass, J Gargory Fecit, brass, 19th C, EX................................**550.00**
Compass, prismatic; Cooke, Troughton & Simms, EX in leather case ..**115.00**
Compass, Russian military, WW2, dtd 1929, EX **50.00**
Compass, Sawyer & Hobby NY, brass, ca 1840, 17x9", NM in dvtl case.**3,600.00**
Compass, unmk Fr, brass, late 18th C, 4½x3", EX in leather case ...**245.00**
Level, Davis, brass w/NM japanning, 7", NMIB **800.00**
Level, mahog w/brass, triangular, orig tubes, 1850s, 18" base, 9" H..**865.00**
Plane table, compass inset in side, explorer sz, 17x13" **80.00**
Plummet, optical; Topcon, tribrach, fits std theodolite, EX.........**155.00**
Transit, A Berthelemy Ponthus & Therode...Paris, NP brass, 1900s, EXIB..**525.00**
Transit, Buff & Buff Model 21, Boston, ca 1900, w/tripod, EX ...**525.00**
Transit, David Lewis Model 8300 Realist, w/tripod, EX **165.00**
Transit, Dietzgen, brass/blk pnt, WWII era, EX/working in orig case ...**275.00**
Transit, Gurley, leather covered, ca 1900, EX in orig case...........**500.00**
Transit, Heller P Bightly/Philadelphia, brass, w/tripod, EX **825.00**
Transit, J Hale, brass, 10¾" wheel, 1885, w/G- orig tripod **1,050.00**
Transit, Richard Paten & Son, brass w/glass lens & level, 13½".**385.00**
Transit, W&LE Gurley #132-f, ca 1955, 14", w/tripod, EXIB......**425.00**
Transit/theodolite, Path, trough-type compass, w/tripod, 20", EX **350.00**
Tripod, Kueffel & Esser, Johnson head, for alidade, EX **80.00**

Swastika Keramos

Swastika Keramos was a line of artware made by the Owens China Company of Minerva, Ohio, around 1902 – 04. It is characterized either by a coralene type of decoration (similar to the Opalesce line made by the J. B. Owens Pottery Company of Zanesville) or by the application of metallic lustres, usually in simple designs. Shapes are often plain and handles squarish and rather thick, suggestive of the Arts and Crafts style.

Vase, gold/red/lt gr metallic, #5181X, 3x5½" **100.00**
Vase, gr & gold coralene, #509F, ca 1906, 8" **175.00**
Vase, lg flower stem/leaves, wine/gr on gold, 8x3¾" **430.00**
Vase, ruby cobblestone panels & gold swastikas, 7¾".................**250.00**

Syracuse

Syracuse was a line of fine dinnerware and casual ware which was made for nearly a century by the Onondaga Pottery Company of Syracuse, New York. Early patterns were marked O.P. Company. Collectors of American dinnerware are focusing their attention on reassembling some of their many lovely patterns. In 1966 the firm became officially known as the Syracuse China Company in order to better identify with the name of their popular chinaware. Many of the patterns were marked with the shape and color names (Old Ivory, Federal, etc.), not the pattern names. By 1971 dinnerware geared for use in the home was discontinued, and the company turned to the manufacture of hotel, restaurant, and other types of commercial tableware.

Alpine, bowl, vegetable; oval...75.00
Alpine, coffeepot..125.00
Alpine, plate, bread & butter...15.00
Alpine, platter, sm, 12"...40.00
American Songbird, bowl, cream soup; & saucer................50.00
American Songbird, bowl, fruit/dessert..............................40.00
American Songbird, plate, dinner...50.00
American Songbird, plate, salad...35.00
Angelica, creamer...40.00
Angelica, cup & saucer..35.00
Angelica, plate, bread & butter..15.00
Angelica, plate, dinner..40.00
Angelica, plate, salad; 8"..17.50
Apple Blossom, bowl, cream soup...40.00
Apple Blossom, bowl, rimmed soup......................................28.00
Apple Blossom, creamer..40.00
Apple Blossom, cup & saucer...40.00
Apple Blossom, plate, bread & butter...................................22.00
Apple Blossom, plate, dinner...40.00
Apple Blossom, platter, 14"...45.00
Apple Blossom, platter, 16½"...75.00
Athena, bowl, vegetable; oval..68.00
Athena, creamer...48.00
Athena, cup & saucer..26.00
Athena, plate, dinner..34.00
Belcanto, plate, bread & butter..12.00
Belcanto, plate, salad..17.50
Belmont, plate, dinner; platinum trim...................................34.00
Belmont, plate, salad...12.00
Bracelet, bowl, fruit; detailed gold rim.................................22.50
Bracelet, creamer, detailed gold rim......................................52.50
Bracelet, cup & saucer, detailed gold rim............................32.00
Bracelet, gravy boat, detailed gold rim...............................115.00
Bracelet, plate, dinner; detailed gold rim............................42.50
Bracelet, platter, detailed gold rim, med............................130.00
Bracelet, platter, rnd, detailed gold rim..............................100.00
Briarcliff, bowl, vegetable; oval..70.00
Briarcliff, plate, salad; 8"...16.00
Briarcliff, platter, med..110.00
Celeste, creamer...35.00
Celeste, sugar bowl, w/lid...50.00
Diane, plate, dinner..25.00
Diane, plate, salad; 8"..17.50
Gardenia, bowl, cream soup; & saucer..................................40.00
Gardenia, plate, bread & butter..10.00
Gardenia, plate, dinner..36.00
Gardenia, sugar bowl, w/lid...64.00
Lilac Rose, bowl, fruit...27.00
Lilac Rose, coffeepot...195.00
Lynnfield, coffee carafe..28.00
Lynnfield, plate, dinner; 10"...15.00
Lyric, creamer...50.00
Lyric, cup & saucer...30.00
Lyric, plate, dinner..40.00
Lyric, plate, salad; 8"...17.50
Lyric, sugar bowl, w/lid...60.00
Meadow Breeze, cup & saucer..45.00
Meadow Breeze, gravy boat..135.00
Monticello, cup & saucer...30.00
Monticello, gravy boat...130.00
Monticello, sugar bowl, w/lid..65.00

Nocturne, bowl, vegetable; rnd...80.00
Nocturne, plate, dinner..40.00
Nocturne, platter, sm..100.00
Sherwood, bowl, soup..33.00
Sherwood, bowl, vegetable; oval...75.00
Sherwood, creamer..50.00
Sherwood, cup & saucer...30.00
Sherwood, gravy boat...115.00
Sherwood, plate, dinner...42.50
Sherwood, plate, salad..20.00
Sherwood, sugar bowl, w/lid..65.00
Stansbury, bowl, fruit...25.00
Stansbury, bowl, soup..30.00
Stansbury, bowl, vegetable; oval...85.00
Suzanne, bowl, vegetable; gold trim, w/lid........................200.00
Suzanne, creamer, gold trim...50.00
Suzanne, platter, gold trim, lg...150.00
Suzanne, platter, gold trim, med...115.00
Suzanne, platter, gold trim, sm...110.00
Suzanne, sugar bowl, gold trim, w/lid...................................75.00
Victoria, bowl, vegetable; oval, 10¼"......................................70.00
Victoria, creamer...60.00
Victoria, cup & saucer..30.00
Victoria, gravy boat, attached underplate, gold trim.......125.00
Victoria, plate, dinner..42.50
Victoria, plate, salad...20.00
Victoria, platter, med...130.00
Victoria, sugar bowl, w/lid...75.00
Wayside, cup & saucer..25.00
Wayside, platter, sm..80.00

Syrups

Values are for old, original syrups. Beware of reproductions and watch the handle area for cracks! See also various manufacturers (such as Northwood) and specific types of glass. Our coadvisors are Jeff Bradfield and Dale MacAllister; they are listed in the Directory under Virginia. See also Pattern Glass.

Artichoke, clear...75.00
Artichoke, frosted, orig pewter hinged lid..........................165.00
Banded Portland, rose flashed..475.00
Bellflower, clear...500.00
Broken Column, clear..135.00
Buckle w/Star, clear..75.00
Catherine Ann, milk glass, orig lid & hdl...........................115.00
Coin Spot, bl opal, ring neck, dtd lid...................................185.00
Cone, bl..165.00
Cordova, clear...135.00
Coreopsis, milk glass, EX decor...225.00
Currier & Ives, amber..225.00
Dahlia, amber..85.00
Empress, clear...225.00
Esther, clear...300.00
Eyewinker, clear...135.00
Feather, emerald gr...475.00
Flat Flower, bl opaque..350.00
Fostoria's Priscilla, emerald gr w/gold.................................475.00
Galloway, clear..75.00
Guttage, pk cased, metal lid...325.00
Herculese Pillar, blue..250.00
Irid textured crystal w/vertical gr rigaree, Kralik, 7"........90.00
Jacob's Ladder, knight's head finial......................................145.00

Jeweled Heart, blue	400.00
Klondike, clear	200.00
Leaf Umbrella, mauve cased, pewter lid, rare	850.00
Locket on Chain, clear, rare	350.00
Loop, clear	90.00
Michigan, clear	165.00
Moon & Star, orig tin lid	145.00
Red Block, clear w/ruby stain	125.00
Reverse Swirl, cranberry opal, rare	750.00
Ribbed Piller, pk w/wht spatter	300.00
Ring Band, custard w/EX gold	425.00
S-Repeat, gr w/gold	375.00
Shoshone, yel flashed, rare	350.00
Snail, clear	135.00
Solar, clear	80.00
Swan, clear	165.00
Thumbprint (Argus Thumbprint)	150.00
Venetia, cranberry	335.00
Washington Centennial	165.00
Washington Early	175.00
X-Ray, gr w/gold trim	300.00

Target Balls

Prior to 1880 when the clay pigeon was invented, blown glass target balls were used extensively for shotgun competitions. Approximately 2¾" in diameter, these balls were hand blown into a three-piece mold. All have a ragged hole where the blowpipe was twisted free. Target balls date from approximately 1840 (English) to World War I, although they were most widely used in the 1870 – 1880 period. Common examples are unmarked except for the blower's code — dots, crude numerals, etc. Some balls were embossed in a dot or diamond pattern so they were more likely to shatter when struck by shot, and some have names and/or patent dates. When evaluating condition, bubbles and other minor manufacturing imperfections are acceptable; cracks are not. The prices below are for mint condition examples.

Boers & CR Delft Flesschen Fabriek, lt gr, rare, 2⅝"	500.00
Bogardus' Glass Ball Pat'd April 10 1877, amber, Am, 2¾"	400.00
Bogardus' Glass Ball Pat'd April 10 1877, cobalt, 2¾"	800.00
Bogardus' Glass Ball Pat'd April 10 1877, gr, 4-dot variant	1,600.00
Bogardus' Glass Ball Pat'd April 10 1877, olive gr, 2⅝"	1,150.00
C Newman, Dmn Quilt, amber, rare, 2⅝"	825.00
CTB Co, blk pitch, Pat dates on bottom, Am	250.00
Dmn Quilt w/o center band, yel-amber, 2¾"	250.00
Dmn Quilt w/plain center band, clear, ground top, Am	150.00
Dmn Quilt w/plain center band, cobalt, 2⅝"	250.00
Dmn Quilt w/shooter emb in 2 panels, clear, English	300.00
Dmn Quilt w/shooter emb in 2 panels, cobalt, English	725.00
Dmn Quilt w/shooter emb in 2 panels, deep moss gr, English	575.00
Dmn Quilt w/shooter emb in 2 panels, med gr, English	375.00
Dmn Quilt w/shooter emb in 2 panels, purple, English	500.00
EE Eaton Guns & C 53 State St Chicago, golden yel-amber, 2⅝"	1,000.00
For Hockey's Pat Trap, gr, English	850.00
Glashutten Dr A Frank Charlottenburg, yel-olive, 2⅝"	1,200.00
Glashuttenewotte Un Charlottenburg, clear, emb dmns, 2⅝"	700.00
Gurd & Son, London, Ontario, amber, Canadian	500.00
Hobnail w/horizontal ribs along seams, yel-amber, 2¾"	800.00
Hockey's Patent Trap, aqua, English, 2½"	925.00
Horizontal or vertical ribs, amber, either style	150.00
Horizontal ribs (2) intersect w/2 vertical, cobalt, 2⅝"	120.00
Horizontal ribs (7), root beer amber, 3-pc mold, 2⅝"	725.00
Ilmenau (Thur) Sophiehutte, amber, Dmn Quilt, Germany	425.00

Ira Paine's Filled Ball Pat Oct 23 1877, amber, Am	250.00
Ira Paine's Filled Ball Pat Oct 23 1877, cobalt, w/orig feathers	4,000.00
Ira Paine's Filled Ball Pat Oct 23 1877, other than amber, Am	800.00
L Jones Gunmaker Blackburn ___Shire, cobalt, emb dmns, English, 2⅝"	150.00
NB Glass Works Perth, other than pale gr, English	200.00
NB Glass Works Perth, pale gr, English	100.00
Plain, amber w/mold mks	65.00
Plain, clear w/mold mks	1,000.00
Plain, cobalt w/mold mks	150.00
Plain, dk grape amethyst w/mold mks, 2¾" dia	250.00
Plain, dk teal gr w/mold mks, 2¾"	300.00
Plain, olive-yel w/mold mks	375.00
Plain, pk amethyst w/mold mks, 2⅝"	250.00
T Jones, Gunmaker, Blackburn, cobalt, English, 2⅝"	450.00
T Jones, Gunmaker, Blackburn, pale bl, English	150.00
Van Cutsem A St Quentin, cobalt, 2¾" dia	100.00
WW Greener, St Mary's Works, various colors, English, ea	350.00

Related Memorabilia

Ball thrower, dbl; old red pnt, ME Card, Pat...78, 79, VG	900.00
Clay birds, Winchester, Pat May 29 1917, 1 flight in box	100.00
Pitch bird, blk DUVROCK	1.00
Shell, dummy, w/single window, any brand	35.00
Shell, dummy shotgun, Winchester, window w/powder, 6"	125.00
Shell set, dummy, Gamble Stores, 2 window shells, 3 cut out	125.00
Shell set, dummy, Winchester, 5 window shells	175.00
Shell set, dummy shotgun, Peters, 6 window shells+full box	175.00
Shotshell loader, rosewood/brass, Parker Bros, Pat 1884	50.00
Target, Am, sheet metal, rod ends mk Pat Feb 8 '21, set	25.00
Target, blk japanned sheet metal, Bussey Patentee, London	50.00

Targets, Bust-O, black or white breakable wafers, American, each $20.00.

Trap, Chamberlain Cartridge...Nov 7th 05...USA, CI, 21½" L, EX	1,500.00
Trap, DUVROCK, w/blk pitch birds	250.00
Trap, MO-SKEET-O, w/birds	150.00

Tea Caddies

Because tea was once regarded as a precious commodity, special boxes called caddies were used to store the tea leaves. They were made from various materials: porcelain, carved and inlaid woods, and metals ranging from painted tin or tole to engraved silver. Our advisor for this category is Tina Carter; she is listed in the Directory under California.

Blk lacquer w/gold chinoiserie, Chinese Export, 1890s, 5x8x5"	635.00
Fruitwood apple form, English, 19th C	515.00
Ivory w/cvg & inlaid monogram, 3-compartment, ca 1800, 6x12x6"+stand	1,725.00
Mahog Geo III Chpndl, brass mts, 3-compartment, late 1700s, 6x10x5"	500.00
Mahog Geo III sarcophagus form, disc ft, 5½x8x4½"	140.00
Mahog veneer, brass ball ft, beveled sides, early, 5½x7½x4½"	700.00
Mahog veneer w/floral inlay, ivory escutcheon, 1800s, 4½"	515.00
Mahog veneer w/inlay, bureau form w/2 faux drws, ivory pulls	975.00

Mahog veneer w/line & star inlay, int lid w/inlay, 12" L, EX...**1,300.00**
Mahog w/shell inlay in oval cartouch, England, 1800s, 5x8x5"..**460.00**
Tortoise shell, lid: hawk on branch, int lids: birds/flowers, 5x5x7"........**865.00**
Tortoise shell, w/much ivory/MOP/silver inlay, bombe shape, 8" L..**4,750.00**
Tortoise shell w/nacre floral inlay, int shell lids w/ivory knobs, 8" **1,400.00**

Tea Leaf Ironstone

Tea Leaf Ironstone became popular in the 1880s when middle-class American housewives became bored with the plain white stone china that English potters had been exporting to this country for nearly a century. The original design has been credited to Anthony Shaw of Longport, who decorated the plain ironstone with a hand-painted copper lustre design of bands and leaves. Originally known as Lustre Band and Sprig, the pattern has since come to be known as Tea Leaf Lustre. It was produced with minor variations by many different firms both in England and the United States. By the early 1900s, it had become so commonplace that it had lost much of its appeal.

Items marked Red Cliff are reproductions made from 1950 until 1980 for this distributing and decorating company of Chicago, Illinois. Hall China provided many of the blanks. Our advice for this category comes from Home Place Antiques, whose address is listed in the Directory under Illinois.

Bone dish, scalloped edge, Wilkinson, EX.....................................**75.00**
Bowl, mush; Alfred Meakin, 7", EX...**55.00**
Bowl, paneled, scalloped rim, Burgess, 3¼x8¾"............................**75.00**
Bowl, sq w/scalloped rim, Alfred Meakin, 1885, 2⅞x8¼x8½"......**40.00**
Bowl, vegetable; Cable style, Burgess, w/lid, EX **245.00**
Bowl, vegetable; Powell & Bishop, gold lustre, w/lid, 1866-78, 10" L..**195.00**
Bowl, vegetable; Sunburst, ftd, Shaw, w/lid, 11½x5½", EX.........**225.00**
Butter dish, hdls, Wedgwood, 4½x5" sq..**145.00**
Butter dish, vertical ribbing w/leaf finial, Mellor-Taylor, sq.........**195.00**
Butter pat, Alfred Meakin, copper rim **15.00**
Butter pat, ribbed, scalloped edge, Mellor-Taylor, sq...................**18.00**
Coffeepot, Bamboo, Meakin, 9"..**225.00**
Compote, sc, ftd, Wedgwood, 5x8"...**295.00**
Cup & saucer, Chelsea type, Johnson Bros, 3½x2⅝", EX **85.00**
Cup & saucer, handleless; Shaw...**95.00**
Gravy boat, Basketweave rim, Shaw, 3¾x8" **125.00**
Gravy boat, Wedgwood, 3¼x8", +8" underplate...........................**145.00**
Pickle dish, Alfred Meakin, 9½x5"...**75.00**
Pitcher, milk; Bamboo, Meakin, 7½"..**265.00**
Plate, Alfred Meakin, ca 1885, 8⅞", EX..**14.00**
Plate, Meakin, 9¾"..**45.00**
Plate, Tea Berry, Shaw, 9¾"...**65.00**
Plate, Wedgwood & Co, ca 1862-90, 8⅝", EX...............................**12.00**
Plate, Wilkinson, 8"...**16.00**
Platter, rectangular, Alfred Meakin, ca 1898, 14x10" **70.00**
Platter, rectangular, Grindley, 1891-1914, lg................................**70.00**
Platter, sm flaw, Edge Malkin & Co, 10x8¾".................................**85.00**
Sauce dish, rnd, Meakin, 4¾" **18.00**
Shaving mug, leaf on hdl, 12-sided, Shaw......................................**225.00**
Sugar bowl, Fish Hook, Meakin, w/lid, 7" **85.00**
Teapot, Alfred Meakin, 9" **225.00**
Toothbrush holder, Fish Hook, Meakin..**165.00**
Tureen, soup; Shaw, 6x14¼x8", NM, +ladle & underplate **850.00**
Wash bowl, Shaw, 5x14½"...**85.00**

Teapots

Teapots have become popular collectibles in recent years with a surge in tea shops featuring tea, teapots, and serving afternoon tea. Collectors should be aware of modern teapots which imitate older, similar versions. Study the types of pottery, porcelain, and china, as well as the marks. Multicolored, detailed marks over the glaze represent modern pieces. Teapots made in the last thirty years are quite collectible but generally don't demand the same prices as their antique counterparts.

A wide range of teapots can be found by the avid collector. Those from before 1880 are more apt to be found in museums or sold at quality auction houses. Almost every pottery and porcelain manufacturer in Asia, Europe, and America have produced teapots. Some are purely decorative and whimsical, while others are perfect for brewing a pot of tea. Tea drinkers should beware of odd-shaped spouts which sputter and drip. Reproductions to be aware of: majolica styles with modern marks, Blue Willow which has been made continuously for almost two centuries, and those marked Made in China (older teapots have 'chop marks' in Chinese).

Refer to various manufacturers' names for further listings. Our advisor for this category is Tina M. Carter, listed in the Directory under California. Her book, *Teapots*, is available at bookstores or direct from the author.

Bear holding candy cane, paw spout, Made in Korea/Fitz & Floyd..**75.00**
Bluebird & blossoms, Shelley England, 2- to 3-cup, from $130 to..**150.00**
Brew UP Savings Bank, red ceramic, unmk Japan **15.00**
Brn & yel mottle, porc, Victoria Porelite Czechoslovakia, +cr/sug..**75.00**
Brn coralene w/gold, 6-sided, Made in Japan, 1950s......................**22.00**
Brn lustre w/coralene, Gibsons & Sons, registry mk ca 1902.........**65.00**
Brn pottery w/recessed lid, mk USA, ind **25.00**
Butterfly Garden Trellis, majolica style, porc, Japan, Enesco, 1970...**50.00**
Cobalt w/gold, Limoges, mini, 2" **20.00**
Conch shell form, majolica like, unmk Japan, ca 1950..................**45.00**
Crinoline lady, pastels, Sadler, England, ca 1930 ....**95.00**
Cube shape, pk w/Deco designs, Made in Japan, ind **30.00**
Dk teal overlapping design, pottery, mk USA, 1950s, 2-cup **30.00**
Dogwood HP, 2 rings form finial, porc, German blank, 1940s.......**85.00**
Elephant w/man on howdah, HP ceramic, bail hdl, Japan, 1940s-50s...**85.00**
English cottage scene, souvenir, porc, plays music when lifted, 1930s...**65.00**
Floral HP on wht bone china w/bl-gr trim, unmk, mini, 3"...........**25.00**
Floral on wht, handleless, trn-down spout, Japan mk, ind.............**22.00**
Glass, rnd w/blown glass hdl, mk Pyrex USA, 1930s-40s, from $110 to..**125.00**
Glass, shield/initials/floral eng, bird finial, minimum value.........**650.00**
Graniteware, bl & wht mottle, wooden hdl, Manning-Bowman Quality..**125.00**
Holly Ribbons, bone china, Royal Worcester, modern **185.00**
Imari, London shape variation, Coalport, early 1800s..............**1,500.00**

Japan, geometric Art Deco design with multicolor lustre glazes, 7¾" on matching blue tile, $60.00 for the set. (Photo courtesy Carole Bess White)

Japanese scene w/men on journey transfer & HP details, unmk Japan...**50.00**
Lettuce gr & wht stripes w/silver details, McCormic..., 1940s.......**50.00**
Lewis & Clark Expo, Portland OR, scene on cobalt, unmk Germany..**40.00**
Magnolia & forsythia w/much gold, porc, bail hdl, crown mk, England...**125.00**
Monkey w/candy decal on wht, Edwin M Knowles USA **30.00**
Moss Rose, porc, musical (Tea for Two), Japan, 1960 ....**65.00**
Orange lustre, sq, porc, Crooksville China, 1940s **75.00**
Orchard (apple tree design), Wade England, 1980 ....**40.00**
Oriental garden scene w/appl trees/figures, Ardalt...Verithin, 8"...**50.00**
Pursuit (hounds & hunters), semi-porc, Noritake Japan................**95.00**

Red graniteware, curved wood hdl, hinged lid, mk Germany w/lion ..250.00
Rooster HP on brn, pottery, metal bail hdl, Japan, 1960 ....28.00
Roses (tiny) on wht w/emb ribs, porc, Gibsons...England, 1960, ind .28.00
Sailor's smiling face, pastels, Japan, 1950s 55.00
Silver lustre, octagonal, porc, Sutherland...England, 1930 ....85.00
Terra cotta w/clear glaze, Guernsey Cooking Ware, ca 1910, ind..75.00
Tetley Tea, wht porc, figure on lid, Lions-Tetley, modern...............75.00
Toby style, Captain, HMS on cap, Artone England, mini, 2" 25.00
Victorian children decal on heavy china, unmk Germany 45.00
Violet chintz, scalloped edge, Japan, Enesco 140.00
Violets on wht, bamboo hdl, bsk, unmk Japan, mini 25.00
Windmill, HP under glaze, mk Japan, 1940s-50s...........................45.00

Teco

Teco artware was made by the American Terra Cotta and Ceramic Company, located near Chicago, Illinois. The firm was established in 1886 and until 1901 produced only brick, sewer tile, and other redware. Their early glaze was inspired by the matt green made popular by Grueby. 'Teco Green' was made for nearly ten years. It was similar to Grueby's, yet with a subtle silver-gray cast. The company was one of the first in the United States to perfect a true crystalline glaze. The only decoration used was through the modeling and glazing techniques; no hand painting was attempted. Favored motifs were naturalistic leaves and flowers. The company broadened their lines to include garden pottery and faience tiles and panels. New matt glazes (browns, yellows, blue, and rose) were added to the green in 1910. By 1922 the artware lines were discontinued; the company was sold in 1930.

Values are dictated by size and shape, with architectural and organic forms being more desirable. Teco is usually marked with a vertical impressed device comprised of a large 'T' to the left of the remaining three letters.

Bookends, bird & primate, gray semigloss, 6½", pr, NM 600.00
Bowl, gr, #201A, mk, 2⅛x9⅛" 300.00
Bowl, gr, leaf/berry emb on wide inward-folded flange, 2¼x9½" ...685.00
Bowl, gr w/charcoaling, #291, 1⅞x6⅞" 200.00
Candlestick, gr w/charcoaling, floral, hdls, F Albert, #326, 9½".550.00
Jardiniere, gr, bowl cradled in 4 buttress ft, Mundie, 20x28", NM..14,000.00
Pitcher, gr, manipulated mouth, integral hdl, 4x4¾" 385.00
Pitcher, gr w/gun metal, concave cylinder, lg open/split hdl, 8½".3,500.00
Vase, bl, shouldered classic form, Gates, drilled, no mk, 20x11"..1,000.00
Vase, bud; lt mocha w/lav hue, slim neck, spherical base, 5¾" ...715.00
Vase, coral, flowing organic forn, F Moreau, 14" 2,500.00
Vase, experimental bl tones, Wm Gates, cylindrical, 9½", NM..350.00
Vase, gr, bulbous w/can neck, sq open hdls, 3¾x3", EX 600.00
Vase, gr, can neck on bulb body w/lg angle hdls, Gates, rpr, 8" ..5,500.00
Vase, gr, classic shouldered form, Gates, mfg flaw, 11"................700.00
Vase, gr, cone w/flaring base formed by 4 huge open buttresses, 13"..65,000.00
Vase, gr, cut-bk design, 4-pierced low hdls, rpr, 13½" 60,000.00
Vase, gr, cylinder w/2 rim-to-base buttresses, Gates, 6½", NM ...750.00
Vase, gr, dbl gourd, Wm Gates, 7" 650.00
Vase, gr, flared lip, dimpled, bulbous, 2¾x2½" 495.00
Vase, gr, organic form w/bulbous bottom, fluted top, #107, 10"..8,000.00
Vase, gr, ovoid w/sm angle hdls, Gates, 4" 1,000.00
Vase, gr, petticoat shape w/tiny neck, 5x5¾" 635.00
Vase, gr, ribbed teepee shape body w/sm rim, 3¾" 320.00
Vase, gr, right-angle rim-to-base buttress hdls, 3¾x4" 635.00
Vase, gr, rim-to-hip hdls, 9x5" 1,425.00
Vase, gr, 4 open hdls, F Albert, 9" 3,000.00
Vase, gr, 4 sides ea w/recessed arch form sm rim hdls, Albert, 14½"....17,000.00
Vase, gr w/charcoaling, dbl gourd w/4 open-curve hdls, 7", NM..2,600.00
Vase, gr w/charcoaling, geometric collar, emb florals, #154, 10" ...4,000.00

Vase, gr w/charcoaling, organic design, F Moreau, 11¾"..........4,750.00
Vase, gr w/charcoaling, slightly conical w/2 cut-out buttresses, 11"..3,250.00
Vase, gr w/charcoaling, 2 open buttress hdls, Mundie, 11½" ...3,750.00
Vase, gr w/lt charcoaling, 4 open buttresses at top, Albert/#181A, 15"..29,000.00
Vase, gray matt, 4 cut-out hdls, cylindrical, 8", NM................2,500.00
Vase, lt yel-gr, 3-ftd w/cutouts on shoulder, 9", NM 1,400.00
Vase, med gr, bulbous w/ring neck, #203, 3¾x3½"....................280.00
Vase, periwinkle bl, shouldered, 2 imp mks, 4¾x4" 465.00

Teddy Bear Collectibles

The story of Teddy Roosevelt's encounter with the bear cub has been oft recounted with varying degrees of accuracy, so it will suffice to say that it was as a result of this incident in 1902 that the teddy bear got his name. These appealing little creatures are enjoying renewed popularity with collectors today. To one who has not yet succumbed to their obvious charms, one bear seems to look very much like another. How to tell the older ones? Look for long snouts, jointed limbs, large feet and felt paws, long curving arms, and glass or shoe-button eyes. Most old bears have a humped back and are made of mohair stuffed with straw or excelsior. Cute expressions, original clothes, a nice personality, and, of course, good condition add to their value. Early Steiff bears in mint condition may go for a minimum of $150.00 per inch for a small bear up to $300.00 to $350.00 (sometimes even more) per inch for one 20" high or larger. These are easily recognized by the trademark button within the ear. Our advisor for this category is Candace Gunther; she is listed in the Directory under California. For further information we recommend *Teddy Bear Treasury* by Ken Yenke; and *Teddy Bears, Annalee's & Steiff Animals*, by Margaret Fox Mandel. Both are available from Collector Books. See also Toys, Steiff.

Key: jtd — jointed

Bears

Schuco, alpaca wool, painted clear glass eyes, ca 1930s, 11", $2,000.00.
(Photo courtesy Ken Yenke)

Am Strauss, 1907, 15", M..2,000.00
Anker-Munich, MIG, brn mohair/tan velveteen, mitten hands, '40s, 12"..150.00
Bing, cinnamon mohair, long arms, 1920s, 17", minimum value ..3,000.00
Bing, cinnamon mohair, 1925, 14", minimum value 2,500.00
Bing, copper mohair, glass eyes, jtd, excelsior stuffing, 1920s, 18"..8,000.00
Bing, growler, frosted mohair, jtd, 1920, 24", NM (rpl eyes)....7,000.00
Bing, shoe-button eyes, rust-colored nose/claws, ear tag, 12"...........4,000.00
Bing, tag under arm, 1908, 7", minimum value 2,000.00
Bruin/BMC, shoe-button eyes, very early, 10" 2,000.00
Bruin/BMC, squeeze voice, cinnamon mohair, glass eyes, 1907, 14"..3,000.00
Chiltern, brn mohair, amber glass eyes, not jtd, 1960, 26", VG..175.00
Chiltern, tan mohair, amber glass eyes, jtd, squeaker, 1947, 16".325.00
Clemens, growler, glass eyes, w/chest tag, 1948, 15" 500.00
Deans of England, wht mohair, tail twists/head wags, 4 legs down, 5x9"....500.00
Farnell, from 1st Alpha series, ca 1925-30, 12" 1,500.00

German, wind up to swing ball & turn around, plush, 1930s, 8" ...**375.00**
German/Bernhardt & Dorst, preforming (juggles), silk plush, 1910, 6"....**600.00**
Grizzly, pk mohair w/lt snout etc, metal shield in chest, 1960, 15" **225.00**
Gund, cinnamon mohair, egg-shaped ft pads, sewn-in snout, 1920, 15"...**1,000.00**
Gund, thick gold mohair, sewn-in muzzle, felt pads, ID, 1930s, 20" **750.00**
Hecla, wht mohair, 17", EX...**4,000.00**
Hermann, chest tag, mini series from 1950, 5", minimum value....**200.00**
Hermann, growler, lg shoe-button eyes/chubby, 1910, 20", minimum value..**3,500.00**
Ideal, cinnamon mohair, 1906-07, 13", minimum value **1,750.00**
Ideal, tan mohair, shoe-button eyes, jtd, 1903, 18" **5,500.00**
Ideal, yel mohair, glass eyes, ftd, orig romper, 1920s, 17", VG **225.00**
Kamar, panda, blk/wht cotton plush, compo nose, 1950s, 12" **200.00**
Merrythought, brn curly mohair, web embr ft, ftd, 1890, 22", EX....**950.00**
Mizpah, wht mohair, glass eyes, fabric nose, 1908 paper tag, 13"..**1,500.00**
Schuco, no felt on hands or ft, 1950-60s, 4-5", ea **200.00**
Schuco, red, wht or orange mohair, w/felt hands & ft, 2½", ea ..**500.00**
Schuco, skater, mohair key-wind, 1948, 9", minimum value....**1,500.00**
Schuco, Tricky, golden mohair, tail turns head, glass eyes, 1950, 8" ..**950.00**
Schuco, Yes/No, long gold mohair, 1925, 22" **4,400.00**
Schuco, Yes/No Panda, mohair, metal frame, glass eyes, 1950s, 3½"..**1,000.00**
Schuco, 1930s transitional style, 12"...**1,000.00**
Sebastian, cvd wood face/paws, jtd, Raikes/Applause, sgn/#d, 1985, 24"....**275.00**
Steiff, chocolate brn (desirable color), w/button & US Zone tag, 17" **2,000.00**
Steiff, lg head, short str arms, short ft, growler, late '50s, 17" **550.00**
Steiff, panda, blk/wht mohair, 1950s, 6", minimum value **750.00**
Strauss, whistling bear, lt beige mohair, 1907, 16"....................**2,500.00**
Unknown, gold mohair, glass eyes, jtd, 1930s, 15", EX...............**350.00**
Unknown, gold mohair w/red velveteen ears/pads, chubby, post WWII, 11"...**80.00**
Unknown, short str mohair, glass eyes, cotton features, '40s, 9"..**175.00**
Unknown (Am), tan mohair, glass eyes, orig pk ribbon, ftd, 1908, 21"..**450.00**

Miscellaneous

Book, Roosevelt Bears, Vol I, 1907, unread, M, minimum value...**750.00**
Button, brass w/emb Teddy bear, 1907, from $75 to more than ..**100.00**
Chocolate pot, Busy Bear series, vignette of bear on wht w/pk shading..**450.00**
Muff, bear, jtd head, long sewn-on arms/legs, glass eyes, Hecla, NM...**1,500.00**
Sheet music, Will You Be My Teddy Bear, 1907, NM, minimum value .**100.00**
Tea cosy, mohair, stuffed head/arms, body is cover, Steiff, 1913, 15"....**3,500.00**

Telephones

Since Alexander Graham Bell's first successful telephone communication, the phone itself has undergone a complete evolution in style as well as efficiency. Early models, especially those wall types with ornately carved oak boxes, are of special interest to collectors. Also of value are the candlestick phones from the early part of the century and any related memorabilia.

Am Telecom, 1972, EX **40.00**
Automatic Electric, chrome payphone, wired for noncoin use, 1960s..**285.00**
Automatic Electric, str-shaft upright desk stand, dial, NM **275.00**
Bell System, candlestick, operator's issue....................................**90.00**
Candlestick, brass, brass hdl, dial..**325.00**
Connecticut Electric, oak wall-mt intercom, 1901, 17x7x7", VG..**75.00**
Danish Fr, Bakelite, 1913, EX **75.00**
Ericsson, stenciled legs, gr cording, 11x12x6", G.........................**425.00**
Fr, Bakelite, NP brass w/mc transfer, orig wiring, 13½" **110.00**
Gray #50, pay phone, blk...**375.00**
Kellogg, metal, dial wall type, EX **95.00**
Kellogg, wood, oak mt, Pat'd Nov 26, 1901 on speaker, 23", EX ...**290.00**
Leich, hand crank, wall type, EX orig...**225.00**
Leich Magneto...**35.00**

National Cash Register, EX...**145.00**
North Electric H-6, blk, 'Bogart' phone, EX **85.00**
Pay phone, chrome, Western Electric..**275.00**
Stromberg-Carlson, candlestick, NP head.....................................**125.00**
Stromberg-Carlson, desk type, 1930s, EX **40.00**
Stromberg-Carlson, oak wall mt, mk Kellogg, 19x13", EX **225.00**
Table model, oak, metal plate, Long Distance, 40", EX...........**2,650.00**
Western Electric, candlestick type, Pat 1920, 11½", VG **145.00**
Western Electric, dial, desk stand, 1920s, 12", EX **265.00**
Western Electric, oak, candlestick w/dial.......................................**275.00**
Western Electric, school wall intercom, brass/Bakelite, pr.............**50.00**

Blue Bell Paperweights

First issued in the early 1900s, bell-shaped glass paperweights were used as 'give-aways' and/or presented to telephone company executives as tokens of appreciation. The paperweights were used to prevent stacks of papers from blowing off the desks in the days of overhead fans. Over the years they have all but vanished — some taken by retiring employees, others accidentally broken. The weights came to be widely used for advertising by individual telephone companies; and as the smaller companies merged to form larger companies, more and more new paperweights were created. They were widely distributed with the opening of the first transcontinental telephone line in 1915. The bell-shaped paperweight embossed 'Opening of Trans-Pacific Service, Dec. 23, 1931,' in peacock blue glass is very rare, and the price is negotiable. (Weights with 'open' in the price field are also rare and impossible to accurately evaluate.) In 1972 the first Pioneer bell paperweights were made to sell to raise funds for the charities the Pioneers support. This has continued to the present day. These bell paperweights have also become 'collectibles.' For further study we recommend *Blue Bell Paperweights, 1992 Revised Edition*, and its accompanying *1995 Addendum* by Jacqueline Linscott Barnes; she is listed in the Directory under Florida.

American Bell Association, 25th Anniversary, cobalt................**150.00**
Bell System, Chesapeake-Potomac, Ice Blue...............................**150.00**
Bell System/Local & Long Distance, Peacock Blue **225.00**
Break-Up of the Bell System, 1984, Opaline Blue Swirl...............**75.00**
Diamond Jubilee, 1911-1986, 1985, yel..**85.00**
First 50 Years NJ Bell, 1977, Jersey Green **30.00**
Missouri & Kansas Telephone Co, cobalt....................................**175.00**
Nevada Bell, blk glass...**100.00**
Ohio Bell Complete Communications, cobalt **85.00**
Pacific Bell, Nevada Bell, blk glass **75.00**
Pays 7% Mountain States Telephone, Peacock Blue **225.00**
Save Time...Telephone/Save Steps...Telephone, Ice Blue **95.00**
Southwestern Bell Telephone Co, Ice Blue **200.00**
Southwestern Bell Telephone Co, Peacock Blue **200.00**
Southwestern Telegraph & Telephone Co, cobalt **375.00**
TPA, 1979, dk Peacock Blue...**25.00**
TPA, 1981, red **60.00**
TPA, 1986, dk red..**80.00**
TPA, 1988, Neodymium..**80.00**
TPA, 2000, opalescent milk glass..**50.00**
Unembossed, Western Electric, Electric Ink, cobalt **350.00**
West Virginia Centennial, 1863-1963, cobalt..............................**150.00**

Novelty Telephones

Alvin (Alvin & the Chipmunks), 1984, MIB...................................**50.00**
Batmobile, Columbia, 1990, MIB, from $25 to.............................**35.00**
Care Bears, purple, intercom system only, 1983, MIB...................**50.00**
Dale Earnhardt, #3 Goodwrench car, lights flash w/ring, 9x3½", MIB..**600.00**
Flinstones, gray w/red horn-shaped handset, 5-hole dial, 1960s, EX....**80.00**

Garfield, eyes open when receiver is lifted, EX **40.00**
Jeff Gordon, race-car style, Columbia Tel-Com, MIB...................**25.00**
Opus the Penguin, receiver locks onto bk, Tyco, 1987, 14", EX....**60.00**
Power Rangers, NM...**25.00**
Raid Bug, from $90 to **100.00**
Roy Rogers, plastic wall type, 1950s, 9x9", EX................................**50.00**
R2-D2 (Star Wars), top spins when phone rings, 12" **35.00**
Star Trek Enterprise, 1993, NM...**25.00**

Telescopes

Antique telescopes were sold in large quantities to sailors, astronomers, voyeurs, and the military but survive in relatively few numbers because their glass lenses and brass tubes were easily damaged. Even scarcer are antique reflecting telescopes, which use a polished metal mirror to magnify the world. Telescopes used for astronomy give an inverted image, but most old telescopes were used for marine purposes and have more complicated optics that show the world right-side up. Spyglasses are smaller, hand-held telescopes that collapse into their tube and focus by drawing out the tube to the correct length. A more compact instrument, with three or four sections, is also more delicate, and sailors usually preferred a single-draw spyglass. They are almost always of brass, occasionally of nickel silver or silver plate, and usually covered with leather, or sometimes a beautiful rosewood veneer. Solid wood barrel spyglasses (with a brass draw tube) tend to be early and rare. Before the middle of the 1800s, makers put their names in elaborate script on the smallest draw tube, but as 1900 approached, most switched to plain block printing. British instruments from World War One made by a variety of makers are commonly found, sharing a format of a 2" objective, 30" long with three draws extended, a tapered main tube, and sometimes having low- and high-power oculars and beautiful leather cases. U.S. Navy WWII spyglasses are quite common but have outstanding optics and focus by twisting the eyepiece, which makes them weather-proof. The Quartermaster (Q.M.) 16x spyglass is 31" long, with a tapered barrel and a 2½" objective. The Officer of the Deck (O.D.D.) is a 23" cylinder with a 1½" objective. Very massive, short, brass telescopes are usually gun sights or ship equipment and have little interest to most collectors. World War II marked the first widespread use of coated optics, which can be recognized by a colored film on the objective lens. Collectible post-WWII telescopes include early refractors by Unitron or Fecker and reflectors by Cave or Questar. Modern spotting scopes often use a prism to erect the image and are of great interest if made by the best makers, including Nikon and Zeiss. Several modern makers still use lacquered brass, and many replica instruments have been produced.

A telescope with no maker's name is much less interesting than a signed instrument, and 'Made in France' is the most common mark on old spyglasses. Dollond of London made instruments for two hundred years and this is probably the most common name on antiques; but because of their important technical innovations and very high quality, Dollond telescopes are always valuable. Bardou, Paris, telescopes are also of very high quality. Bardou is another relatively common name, since they were a prolific maker for many years, and their spyglasses were sold by Sears. Alvan Clark and Sons were the most prolific early American makers, in operation from the 1850s to the 1920s, and their astronomical telescopes are of great historical import.

Spyglasses are delicate instruments that were subject to severe use under all weather conditions. Cracked or deeply scratched optics are impossible to repair and lower the value considerably. Most lenses are doublets, two lenses glued together, and deteriorated cement is common. This looks like crazed glaze and is fairly difficult to repair. Dents in the tube and damaged or missing leather covering can usually be fixed. The best test of a telescope is to use it, and the image should be sharp and clear. Any accessories, eyepieces, erecting prisms, or quality cases can add significantly to value. The following prices assume that the telescope is in very good to fine condition and give the objective lens (obj.) diameter, which is the most important measurement of a telescope.

Our advisor for this category is Peter Abrahams, who studies and collects telescopes and other optics. Please contact him, especially to exchange reference material. (See his comments concerning online auctions under Binoculars; they are applicable to telescopes as well.) Mr. Abrahams is listed in the Directory under Oregon. (Please include SASE with questions.)

Key:
obj — objective lens   ODD — Officer of the Deck

Adams, George; 2" reflecting, brass cabriole tripod..................**3,500.00**
Bardou & Son, Paris, 4-draw, 50 mm obj, leather, 36"................**250.00**
Bausch & Lomb, 1-draw, 45 mm obj, wrinkled pnt, 17" **90.00**
Brashear, 3½" obj, brass, tripod, w/eyepcs..............................**4,500.00**
Cary, London (script), 2" obj, tripod, w/3 eyepcs **3,000.00**
Clark, Alvan; 4" obj, 48", iron mt on wooden legs...................**7,000.00**
Criterion RV-6 Dynascope, 6" reflector, 1960s...........................**500.00**
Dallmeyer, London (script), 5-draw, 2½" obj, SP, 49" **500.00**
Dollond, London (block), 2-draw, 2" obj, leather cover.............**290.00**
Dollond, London (script), brass, 3" obj, 40", on tripod **2,900.00**
Dollond, London (script), 2-draw, 2" obj, leather cover.............**200.00**
Dollond, London (script), 2-draw, 2" obj, leather cover.............**380.00**
France or Made in France, 3-draw, 30 mm obj, lens cap...............**80.00**
McAlister (script), brass, 3½" obj, 45", tripod......................**3,000.00**
Messer, London Day & Night, brass, mahog hand grip, 2-draw, 1860s, EX..**200.00**
Mogey, brass, 3" obj, 40", on tripod, w/4 eyepcs **3,000.00**
Negretti & Zambra, 2½" obj, equatorial mt, 36", tripod **2,500.00**
Plossl, Wein, 2½" obj, Dialytic optics, 24", table-top tripod....**3,200.00**
Queen & Co (script), 6-draw, 70 mm obj, wood veneer, 50" **700.00**
Questar, reflecting, on astro mt, 1950s, 3½" dia.....................**2,200.00**
R & J Beck, 2" obj, 24", table-top tripod w/cabriole legs **2,200.00**
Short, James; 3" dia reflecting, brass cabriole tripod.................**3,500.00**

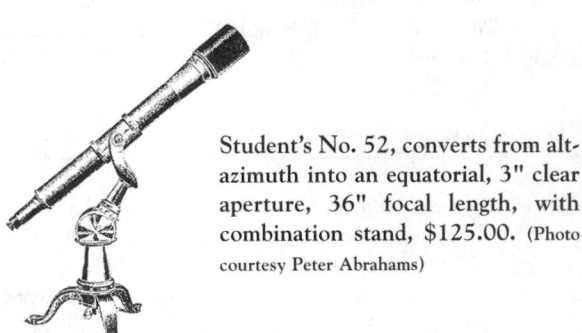

Student's No. 52, converts from alt-azimuth into an equatorial, 3" clear aperture, 36" focal length, with combination stand, $125.00. (Photo courtesy Peter Abrahams)

Tel Sct Regt Mk 2 S (many maker's names), UK, WWI **120.00**
Unitron, 4" obj, wht, 60", on tripod, many accessories **2,500.00**
Unmk, brass, 2" obj, spyglass, leather cover, from $150 to **300.00**
Unmk, brass, 2" obj, stand w/cabriole legs **1,200.00**
US military, brass, very heavy, from $100 to **300.00**
US Navy, QM Spyglass, 16X, MK II, in box **220.00**
US Navy (ODD), Bu. Ships, Mk II, 10-Power, 1943.....................**125.00**
Vion, Paris, 40 mm obj, 3-draw, 40-Power, 21", leather...............**110.00**
Wollensak Mirroscope, 1950s, 12x2" dia, leather case................**200.00**
Wood bbl, rnd taper, 1½" obj, sgn, 1800s....................................**350.00**
Wood bbl, 8-sided, 1½" obj, 1700s, 30" **1,500.00**
Zeiss, brass, 60 mm obj, w/eyepcs & porro prism, tripod **1,700.00**
Zeiss Asiola, 60 mm obj, prism spotting scope, pre-WWII..........**450.00**

Televisions

Many early TVs have escalated in value over the last few years. Pre-1943 sets (usually with only one to five channels) are often worth $500.00 to $5,000.00. Unusually styled small-screen wooden 1940s TVs are 'hot'; but most metal, Bakelite, and large-screen sets are still shunned by collectors. Color TVs with 16" or smaller tubes from the 1950s are valuable; larger color sets are not. One of our advisors for this category is Harry Poster, author of *Poster's Radio & Television Price Guide 1920 – 1990, 2nd Edition*; he is listed in the Directory under New Jersey. Another source of information is *Collector's Guide to Vintage Televisions* by Bryan Durbal and Glenn Bubenheimer (Collector Books).

Key: t/t — table-top

Atwater, mahog wood cabinet, t/t, 1949, 12" 125.00
Bendix, #3030, mahog, console model, 1950, 12" 55.00
Cromwell, #EU-30, console, DuMont RA-119 w/Crosley logo, 1952, 30" ...650.00
Delco, #TV-71A, wood, t/t, Hallicrafters w/Delco name, 1948, 7" ..165.00
DuMont, #RA-119, mahog, console, dbl doors, Royal Sovereign, 1952, 30" ...650.00
Emerson, #619, wood, console, 1948, 10" 75.00
Firestone, #13-G-5, mahog, console, 1948, 10" 60.00
General Electric, #10T6, Bakelite, t/t, 1949, 10" 125.00
General Electric, #807, blond wood, t/t, glass screen, 1949, 10" ...85.00
Hallicrafters, #T-506, mahog, t/t, 12-channel tuner, 1949, 7" 165.00
Majestic, #12C4, wood, console, 1950, 12" 30.00
Motorola, #VT-107B, blond wood, t/t, TS-9 chassis, 1948, 10" 85.00
Motorola, #12VT13B, blond wood, t/t, TS-23 chassis, 1950, 12" .75.00
National, #TV-7M, metal, t/t, 1949, 7" 240.00
Panasonic, #TR-435R, TV-radio, transistor, portable, 1976, 5" 20.00
Pathe, #12-1, mahog, t/t, 1948, 12" 175.00
Philco, #49-1240, wood, console, tall wood legs, 1949, 12" 50.00
RCA, #621TS, blond wood, t/t, 1946, 7" 550.00
RCA, #7T122, blond wood, console, dbl doors, 1951, 17" 95.00
Regal, #16T36, mahog, TV-radio, t/t, 1949, 16" 60.00
Sentinel, #400TV, tan cloth covered, portable, 1948, 7" 125.00
Sparton, #5010, wood, t/t, 1950, 10" 75.00
Stromberg-Carlson, #TV-10L, wood, t/t, 7-chanel tuner, 1947, 10" ..265.00
Sylvania, #21T305, blond wood, t/t, Halolight, 1959, 21" 200.00
Tele-Tone, #TV-208TR, cloth covered, portable, 1948, 7" 85.00
Westinghouse, walnut wood, TV/radio/phonograph, console, 1948, 12" 40.00
Zenith, #G2448Z, walnut, console, 24G26 chassis, Warwick, 1950, 16" ..200.00
Zenith, #L2894H, wood, TV/radio/phonograph, console, 1953, 27" ...100.00

Philco Predictas and Related Items

Made in the years between 1958 and 1960, Philco Predictas have become one of the most sought after lines of televisions in the post-war era. Predictas are now over forty years old, yet their atomic-age styling is just as futuristic today as it was in 1958. As we move into the new millenium, the Predicta line will continue to be highly collectible. Philco Predictas feature a swivel or separate enclosed picture tube and radical cabinet designs.

Please note that recently much has been said about sets equipped with the UHF option. Even though few sets were ordered with this option, it in no way makes the set more rare. Advanced collectors who feel it is important for their collection should not pay more than $50.00 over the price of an equal non-UHF set.

The values given here are for as-found, average, clean, complete, unrestored sets, running or not, that have good picture tubes. Predictas that are missing parts or have damaged viewing screens will have a lower value. Above average Predictas will have much higher values. Please keep in mind that Predictas that have been completely professionally

restored to as new in appearance as well as electronically can easily bring four to five times the stated values. Our advisor for Predicta televisions is David Weddington; he is listed in the Directory under Tennessee.

G4242 Holiday 21" t/t, wood cabinet, blond finish **455.00**
G4242 Holiday 21" t/t, wood cabinet, mahog finish...................**400.00**
G4654 Barber-Pole 21" console, boomerang front leg, blond......**725.00**
G4654 Barber-Pole 21" console, boomerang front leg, mahog **650.00**
G4710 Tandem 21" separate screen w/25' cable, mahog finish ...**625.00**
G4720 Stereo Tandem w/matching 1606S phonoamp, mahog....**1,100.00**
G4720 Stereo Tandem 21" separate screen, 4 brass legs, mahog .**900.00**
H3406 Motel 17" t/t, metal cabinet, cloth grill, no antenna.......**275.00**
H3408 Debutante 17" t/t, cloth grill, w/antenna, charcoal **375.00**
H3410 Princess 17" t/t, metal grill, plastic tuner window............**400.00**
H3410 Princess 17" t/t, orig metal stand, red finish...................**500.00**
H3412 Siesta 17" t/t, w/clock-timer above tuner, gold finish **550.00**

H4730 Danish Modern 21" console, four fin-shaped legs, mahog finish **$950.00.** (Photo courtesy David Weddington)

H4744 Townhouse 21" room-divider, walnut shelves, brass finish.....**1,400.00**
17DRP4 picture tube, MIB, replacement for all 17" t/t Predictas ..**175.00**
21EAP4 or 21FDP4 picture tube, MIB, replacement for all 21" Predictas ...**275.00**

Tennis Rackets

Early tennis rackets (pre-1940) generally exhibit these characteristics: head shape — may be oval, flat-top, transitional flat-top, triangular (or other); throat wedge — the triangular section of wood at the junction of the head and the handle may be concave, convex, solid or laminated; handle — most from this era are not covered by leather and are either combed (grooved) or checkered wood, and some may have cork handles or enlargements at the butt end. Values vary, dependent on age, rarity, style, and condition. Brand and model are important, and all identifying decals should be legible and in good condition. Rackets from 1880 to 1940 range in price from $300.00 to $600.00 for rare models like the Hazel's Streamline down to $10.00 to $20.00 for more common models.

Our advisor for this category is Donald Jones; he is listed in the Directory under Georgia. In the listings that follow, values apply to examples in excellent condition.

Key:
cx-lam — convex laminated   tran — transitional
cx-s — convex solid

AJ Reach, Driver, concave wedge, combed hdl, oval head, 1920..75.00
E Kent, Duchess, concave wedge, bulbous hdl, oval head, 1930.120.00
Hazel's Streamline, branched wedge, leather hdl, oval head, 1935 ..600.00
Horsman, Elberton, concave wedge, smooth hdl, flat-top head, 1885...450.00
Iver Johnson, Special, ex-s wedge, bulbous hdl, tran head, 1900 ...175.00
Magnon, Superior, concave wedge, combed hdl, oval head, 1928.75.00

Slazenger, Demon, cx-lam wedge, fishtail hdl, oval head, 1910 ..**250.00**
Spaulding, Park, cx-s wedge, combed hdl, flat-top head, 1895....**450.00**
Wright-Ditson, Hub, cx-s wedge, checkered hdl, oval head, 1890...**175.00**
Wright-Ditson, Octagon, concave head, combed hdl, oval head, 1895..**120.00**
Wright-Ditson, Star, cs-s wedge, combed hdl, oval head, 1904...**135.00**

Teplitz

Teplitz, in Bohemia, was an active art pottery center at the turn of the century. The Amphora Pottery Works was only one of the firms that operated there. (See Amphora.) Art Nouveau and Art Deco styles were favored, and much of the ware was hand decorated with the primary emphasis on vases and figurines. Items listed here are marked 'Teplitz' or 'Turn,' a nearby city.

Basket, floral on bl irid, dbl hdls, Stellmacher, #d, 4¼" **165.00**
Bust, lady w/long hair on cobalt & gold floral base, 13", EX....**1,600.00**
Compote, draped women w/fruit basket, 2-pc, mk, 15x10" **575.00**
Ewer vase, mc floral w/gold, goldfish lip, beaded hdl, 11x5" **400.00**
Figurine, couple in pillared garden, lace attire, Stellmacher, 20½" ..**350.00**

Vase, Art Nouveau lady's head with flowing hair and flowers with stems forming asymmetrical handles, ochre and green, stamped mark, 13", $450.00.

Vase, flowers & bats in relief, gr/brn matt, #d, sm rstr, 14½" **600.00**
Vase, mushrooms, distant trees, pk/wht on gr/blk/gold, Daschel, 15"..**2,100.00**
Vase, scrolled leafage, gr/tan/ivory w/gold, ca 1905, 6¼".............**260.00**
Vase, wildflowers on baluster w/slim neck, early 20th C, 8" **460.00**

Terra Cotta

Terra cotta is a type of earthenware or clay used for statuary, architectural facings, or domestic articles. It is unglazed, baked to durable hardness, and characterized by the color of the body which may range from brick red to buff.

Griffin, winged creatures seated on base, 42½", pr...................**1,765.00**
Plaque, bust of elderly bearded man, sgn Rigault, 1880s.............**250.00**
Sculpture, 2 street urchins w/lady, HP, Austrian, 14½" **300.00**
Whippet, seated on haunches, hexagonal base, 20th C, 32", EX, pr..**2,350.00**

Thermometers

Few objects man has invented have been so eloquently expressed both functionally and artistically as the ubiquitous thermometer. Developed initially by Galileo in 1593 as a scientific device, thermometers slowly evolved into decorative objet d'art, functional household utensils, and eye-catching advertising specialties. Most American thermometers manufactured early in the twentieth century were produced by Taylor (Tycos), and today their thermometers remain the most plentiful on the market. Decorative thermometers manufactured before 1800 are now

ensconced in the permanent collections of approximately a dozen European museums. Because of their fragility, few devices of this era have survived in private collections. Nowadays most antique thermometers find their way to market through estate sales.

Insofar as sheer beauty, uniqueness, and scientific accuracy, decorative thermometers are far superior to the ordinary and inexpensive versions which carry advertising. Decorative thermometers run the gamut from plain tin household varieties to the highly ornate creations of Tiffany and Bradley and Hubbard. They have been manufactured from nearly every conceivable material — oak, sterling, brass, and glass being the favorites — and have tested the artistry and technical skills of some of America's finest craftsmen. Ornamental models can be found in free-hanging, wall-mounted, or desk/mantel versions.

Since 1994 instrument prices have been escalating at a rate of 35% annually. This is due to their relative scarcity, infrequent trading, and absence of a 'knock-off' (retro) market. Look for this trend to continue indefinitely.

Thermometer prices are based on age, ornateness, and whether mercury or alcohol is used as the filler in the tube. A broken or missing tube will cut at least 40% off the value. Virtually all American-made thermometers available today as collectors' items were made between 1875 and 1940. The golden age of decoratives ended in the early 1940s as modern manufacturing processes and materials robbed them of their natural distinctiveness. Our advisor for this category is Richard T. Porter; he is listed in the Directory under Massachusetts.

Key:
br — brass
Cen — Centigrade
Fah — Fahrenheit
mrc — mercury in tube
pmc — permacolor
R — rare
Rea — Reaumer
sc — scale
stl — stainless
strl — sterling
VR — very rare

Amadio, Fah, Corn Hill, desk, ivory pillar/compass, mrc, 1890, 10"...**850.00**
Anonymous, cvd wood squirrel, glass Rea sc, mrc, 1905, 10"......**800.00**
Anonymous, desk, br conquistador figural, br sc, mrc..................**650.00**
Anonymous, desk, love scene, silver metal, br Rea/Cen sc, mrc, 8"..**830.00**
Anonymous, pendant, strl case, ivory Fah sc, mrc, 1880, 5" **1,250.00**
Anonymous, wall, giltwood fr, ivory Fah sc, 1790, 10x3½" **3,100.00**
Blk/Starr/Frost, desk, barometer, stl, Fah/Cen, mrc, '10, 11"....**2,200.00**
Bradley & Hubbard, desk, br fr & Fah sc, mrc, 1895, 13x6" **2,800.00**
Calley, desk, strl inkwell fr, porc Rea sc, mrc, 1899, 5x6" **3,200.00**
Capendium, desk, handmade br/porc fr, Fah/Cen sc, rnd mrc, 4" ..**850.00**
Carpenter & Westley, desk, ivory w/glass dome mrc, 1880, 6"....**950.00**
Casella London, wall, maxi/minimum, 2 units, wood, plastic sc .**430.00**
Cheshire Silversmiths, desk, br candelabra, mrc, 1875, 10"......**4,500.00**
Chevallier, L'ingre, wall, ivory/mahog, Rea/Cen sc, 1880, 11x3"..**2,350.00**
Clark, desk, ivory ped, crown, mrc, 1904, 7"..............................**400.00**
Cloister, inkwell, stl bk & base w/angels at side, 1901 ....**1,050.00**
Creswel, travel, ivory/case/mirror, removable sc, mrc, 2½" **2,800.00**
CW Wilder...NH, desk, Deco women, br Fah sc, mrc, R, 8"...**1,300.00**
Desk, cvd walrus tusk, 2-tier disc base, inlay sc, 1860, 9" **430.00**
Diamond, wall, br Fah sc on wood, R, 7½x1½"..........................**525.00**
Dixie, W (London); desk, gilt/br, Gothic, SP sc, mrc, 8" **790.00**
Dollard London, desk, strl, br sc, mrc, 1908, R, 6" **750.00**
Dollard London, hanging, mahog fr, strl sc, mrc, 1810, 18" **4,600.00**
Dring & Fage, desk, marble, ivory sc, mrc, 1880, 6" **1,500.00**
England, desk, glass obelisk/8-sided, br Fah sc, mrc, 1880........**1,260.00**
England, desk, marble ped fr, Cen, mrc, 1885, 6½" **930.00**
England, wall, br game bag fr, Fah sc, mrc, 1890, 9x5"............**1,650.00**
England, wall, rectangular wood fr, porc Cen sc, mrc, 1905, 5"..**1,350.00**
Farley, travel, walnut base mt, ivory Fah/Cen sc, mrc, 5" **900.00**
Freeborn, desk, bronze w/3 lead decor, br sc, mrc, 8" **180.00**
G Cooper, desk, bell shape w/cupola, strl, dial, 2x3" **400.00**

Gilbert & Co, travel, silver eng sc, mrc, 1850, 8" 630.00
Gloucenter Scientific, stl case, glass front, pmc, 42" 1,500.00
Heath & Wing, figural calendar, br w/porc sc, mrc, 1870............930.00
J Waldstein, wall, br Rea sc on wood, mrc, 1900s, VR, 10½" 920.00
Kendal, desk, strl obelisk, br Fah sc, mrc, 1890, 8", $1,350 to .1,850.00
Moreau, desk, mahog, Rea/Cen, spiral tube, mrc, 1860, 6½x5½" ..1,725.00
Ohio, wall, CI, 1850, R alcohol, Fah, 10" 350.00
Pairpoint, desk, strl picture fr, mrc, 1907, 5" 650.00
Pig w/branch of tree, Pairpoint #5604, 5¼" 375.00
Reau, desk, sq incline base, floral top, mrc, 1895.......................180.00
Rowley & Sons, travel, ivory sc, mrc, 1894, 4", +case...................350.00
Standard, wall, ivory Fah sc on ebony, mrc, 9" 750.00
Standard..., wall, br fr, enamel dial Fah sc, 1885, 9" dia 950.00
Taylor, chandelier, 3-side, Fah alcohol, 1887, VR, br, 6" 400.00
Taylor, ped, 3-sided, Fah sc, alcohol, 1900, R, 6" 350.00
Thermindex Switzerland, desk, Bakelite stand, Fah sc, 5"...........725.00
Tiffany, desk, strl tetrahedron fr & Fah sc, mrc, 1910, 2x4" 4,000.00
Tiffany, gr glass w/pine needles, br sc/mrc, 1902, 8x12" 2,800.00
Tycos, maxi/minimum, japanned tin/br, mrc, T-5452, 8"............125.00
Unknown, cvd wood squirrel, glass Rea sc, mrc, 1905, VR, 10" .800.00
Unknown, desk, alabaster w/eagle, Rea/Cen sc, mrc, 1895 ....875.00
Unknown, desk, love scene, silver metal, br Rea/Cen sc, mrc, 8"...830.00
Unknown, wall, giltwood fr, ivory Fah sc, 1790, 10x3½".........3,100.00
VJD Inc, wall, clip Fah br sc, mrc, 4", VR 1,650.00
W Pratt, desk, wood inlays, ivory sc, mrc, 1900, 6" 350.00
Warren Foundries, wall, umbrella w/dragon hdl, br sc, mrc, 12" .220.00
West, desk, Gothic design, br, 1900, 12"..................................1,360.00
WG Loveday, wall, Clearside, Fah sc, 5" dia 725.00
Whitehead & Hoag, Lambrecht's Polymeter, mrc, 9"...............1,200.00
Zeradatha, desk, cast metal w/rotate sc, 1926, 7" 140.00

1000 Faces China

A dinner plate from this pattern, it is said, may have as many as 1,000 hand-painted faces, thus the name. Most of what we see today dates from early in the century to midway, but some pieces are even older. Though many pieces are unmarked, the majority carries the marks 'Made in Japan' or 'Japan.' 'Kutani,' 'MIOJ,' and other marks are sometimes seen as well.

There are two primary patterns or colors — Gold and Black Face. Gold is just that — most of the pieces are dominated by gold throughout. Black refers to the fact that in this variation the faces are black, usually against a white background. Many rings and bars of colors make up both primary patterns. Variations include 'Men in Robes' and '1000 Geishas.' All patterns usually feature an inner ring of color surrounded by flashes of multiple colors and an outer ring of color with a pattern painted into it.

Gold was the most popular pattern and seems to be the most available today. Examples with Black faces and the variations are scarce and often command higher prices. Our advisor for this category is Suzi Hibbard; she is listed in the Directory under California.

Bowl, gold, petal shape, 6", from $15 to 25.00
Chocolate set, HP, gold, MIJ, 6-pc, from $75 to 125.00
Creamer & sugar bowl, gold, pear shape, MIJ, from $40 to 60.00
Cup & saucer, blk faces, from $30 to 40.00
Cup & saucer, blk faces, MIJ, from $35 to.......................................55.00
Cup & saucer, demitasse; gold, from $25 to 30.00
Cup & saucer, gold, from $30 to 50.00
Cup & saucer, 1000 Geishas, MIJ, from $35 to 45.00
Egg cup, blk faces, from $20 to..35.00
Ginger jar, gold, from $75 to 125.00
Incense burner, gold, MIJ, from $25 to 40.00

Lamp, gold, 8" vase, from $100 to 150.00
Mustard jar, gold, w/spoon, MIJ, 2¾", from $30 to 40.00
Nappy, gold, 6¾", from $10 to 40.00
Plate, blk faces, 10", from $30 to 50.00
Plate, blk/gold, 6", from $7.50 to 15.00
Plate, blk/gold, 7½", from $15 to 20.00
Plate, Men in Robes, Kutani, 8¼", from $25 to 45.00
Plate, Men in Robes, 6", from $8 to 20.00
Salt cellar, blk faces, from $5 to 15.00
Shakers, blk faces, pr from $10 to 25.00
Snack set, blk faces, kidney-shaped plate, from $20 to 35.00
Snack set, gold w/blk rim, HP, TT MIJ, 16-pc, from $225 to 275.00
Soup set, blk faces, 3-pc, from $50 to 100.00
Sweetmeat, blk faces, 9-pc set in lacquer box, from $150 to 200.00
Sweetmeat set, blk lcq box, blk faces, HP, MIJ, 7-pc, from $125 to...175.00
Sweetmeat set, red lcq box, gold, MIJ, 9-pc, from $150 to 200.00
Tea set, gold, 21-pc, MIJ, from $175 to 250.00
Teapot, blk faces, dragon spout, 7", from $50 to............................75.00
Teapot, blk rim, tomato shape, MIJ, from $35 to 55.00
Teapot, gold, HP Nippon, from $40 to 75.00
Teapot, gold, pear shape, MIJ, from $40 to 75.00
Teapot, gold, dragon spout, 7", from $30 to 75.00
Teapot, gold w/blk rim, bbl shape, HP, MIJ, from $50 to 80.00
Teapot, Men in Robes, 6-sided, Japanese mk, from $40 to 75.00
Teapot, 1000 Geishas, dragon spout, from $50 to 75.00
Vase, blk faces, MIJ, 8", from $50 to..100.00
Vase, detailed w/heavy gold, sm shoulder, flared rim, 12", $100 to...150.00
Vase, gold, 8", from $50 to 100.00
Wall vase, Men in Robes, from $125 to 175.00

Tiffany

Louis Comfort Tiffany was born in 1848 to Charles Lewis and Harriet Young Tiffany of New York. By the time he was eighteen, his father's small dry goods and stationery store had grown and developed into the world-renowned Tiffany and Company. Preferring the study of art to joining his father in the family business, Louis spent the next six years under the tutelage of noted artists. He returned to America in 1870 and until 1875 painted canvases that focused on European and North African scenes. Deciding the more lucrative approach was in the application of industrial arts and crafts, he opened a decorating studio called Louis C. Tiffany and Co., Associated Artists. He began seriously experimenting with glass, and eschewing traditionally painted-on details, he instead learned to produce glass with qualities that could suggest natural textures and effects. His experiments broadened, and he soon concentrated his efforts on vases, bowls, etc., that came to be considered the highest achievements of the art. Peacock feathers, leaves and vines, flowers, and abstracts were developed within the plane of the glass as it was blown. Opalescent and metallic lustres were combined with transparent color to produce stunning effects. Tiffany called his glass Favrile, meaning handmade.

In 1900 he established Tiffany Studios and turned his attention full time to producing art glass, leaded-glass lamp shades and windows, and household wares with metal components. He also designed a complete line of jewelry which was sold through his father's store. He became proficiently accomplished in silverwork and produced such articles as hand mirrors embellished with peacock feather designs set with gems and candlesticks with Favrile glass inserts.

Tiffany's work exemplified the Art Nouveau style of design and decoration, and through his own flamboyant personality and business acumen he perpetrated his tastes onto the American market to the extent that his name became a household word. Tiffany Studios continued to prosper until the second decade of this century when due to changing tastes his influence began to diminish. By the early 1930s the company had closed.

Serial numbers were assigned to much of Tiffany's work, and letter prefixes indicated the year of manufacture: A – N for 1896 – 1900, P – Z for 1901 – 1905. After that, the letter followed the numbers with A – N in use from 1906 – 1912; P – Z from 1913 – 1920. O-marked pieces were made especially for friends and relatives; X indicated pieces not made for sale.

Our listings are primarily from the auction houses in the East where Tiffany sells at a premium. All pieces are signed unless noted otherwise.

Glass

Bottle, barber; gold irid, swollen neck on teardrop body, 7½"......**395.00**
Bowl, deep bl irid w/10 ribs, lt wear, 3¾x9¾"...................**700.00**
Bowl, gold irid, diagonal ribs, crimped rim, #X351, 2½x6½".......**450.00**
Bowl, gold irid, ruffled, ribbed, #X128, 3x7½".....................**500.00**
Bowl, gold irid w/cut & eng vintage, 2½x6", +underplate..........**900.00**
Bowl, gold irid w/onion-skin finish, ruffled, #05599, 6", +underplate..**700.00**
Bowl, gold w/purple irid, etched vintage on wide flange, 3x12"...**1,000.00**
Bowl, Honeycomb, gr irid w/gold irid int, disc ft, flared, #1596, 10"..**750.00**
Bowl, leaves, gold irid w/onionskin, #1925, 2¼" H...................**700.00**
Bowl, lily pads, gr on gold, #4383K, 5x8"..........................**2,645.00**
Bowl, lily pads/vines, gr irid on gold, dbl-rolled rim, 4x6".......**1,500.00**
Bowl, pk & gold irid w/etched branches/leaves, #1848, 10"........**800.00**
Bowl, pond lilies/vines, gr on gold, 5x11", +2-tier flower frog.**2,245.00**
Bowl, stretched aqua irid to opal w/optic ribs, #1898, 2¼x9¾"...**1,035.00**
Bowl, yel/brn pastel w/opal bands, intaglio butterfly, #1699, 10"...**800.00**
Candlestick, bl irid, ribbed w/flared paneled ft, #1286, 12".....**1,600.00**
Compote, amethyst pastel, clear stem, #1871, 2x5¼"................**850.00**
Compote, bl irid, ruffled, ftd, #U1070, 1⅞x4¼".....................**450.00**
Compote, bl irid, 8 prunts on bowl/4 on disc ft, #W619, 3½"....**650.00**
Compote, floriform; gold irid, ribbed, scalloped rim, #6915D, 6"..**950.00**
Compote, gr irid pastel w/opal ribbing, clear ft, #1871, 2x5½"...**475.00**
Compote, pastel bl, opal stem w/intaglio floral stems, #5-1776, 3x6".**1,000.00**
Cordial, bl irid, 4 pinched sides, 2"................................**185.00**
Cordial, gold irid, ribbed w/8 pigtail pulls, #M1394, 2½"............**375.00**
Cordial, gold irid, 4 pinched sides, 2".............................**175.00**
Decanter, gold irid, pinched body & stopper, narrow neck, ftd, 9½"...**900.00**
Dish, gold irid, scalloped vertical rim, shallow 6".................**300.00**
Finger bowl, gold irid, ribbed/ruffled, 4¾", +6" underplate.........**900.00**
Finger bowl, gold irid, 3x4"..**500.00**
Flower frog, bl irid, 4" L..**250.00**
Goblet, gr pastel, ribbed stem, paneled bowl, 8½".................**700.00**
Goblet, pastel w/wide wht opal 'leaves,' purple at rim, 8½".....**1,150.00**
Goblet, pk pastel w/vaseline stem/base, 7½", set of 8.............**4,300.00**
Goblet, turq pastel, opal stripes on bowl & clear reed ft, label, 8"..**900.00**
Nut dish, gold irid, ribbed, 1¼x3"..................................**400.00**
Parfait, lime pastel/opal stripes, crystal disc ft, #688, 9", $600 to...**700.00**
Pitcher, bl irid, bl hdl, 2⅝"......................................**950.00**
Pitcher, leaves/vines, gr on gold, flared cylinder, 5¼".............**1,850.00**
Plate, pk pastel, radiating clear spokes, petal rim, 9", set of 8..**1,800.00**
Salt cellar, bl irid, oval, #1308...................................**575.00**
Salt cellar, gold irid, ftd & ribbed w/tucked neck rim, 1½x2½"..**350.00**
Salt cellar, gold irid, ribbed w/dbl-ruffled rim, ftd, 2x3"........**275.00**
Shade, gold irid, tulip shape, 5"...................................**1,495.00**
Sherbet, Rice, pk irid w/opal ft, #1872, 4½".......................**700.00**
Tumbler, gold irid, bulbous bottom, flared top, 3¾", from $500 to..**550.00**
Vase, agate technique in yel/gray/gr on lt gr, faceted, 7½".......**7,000.00**
Vase, amber w/star millefiori/trailings/cut gr leaves, #Y5909, 5½"....**5,750.00**
Vase, bud; bl irid, bulbous, tapered neck/flared rim, #1502-3663, 10"...**1,800.00**
Vase, bud; leaf tips at base, gr on gold to magenta, long neck, 10"....**1,850.00**
Vase, creamy opal, side-pulled hdls in yel-tinged opal, flattened, 2"....**600.00**
Vase, dk bl irid, ribbed cylinder, flared petal rim, raised ft, 15"...**2,800.00**

Vase, feathers, gold on wht irid & opal, elongated/slender/ftd, 12"..**1,900.00**
Vase, feathers, gold on yel, cylindrical, #F66, 11⅝"...............**1,495.00**
Vase, feathers, gold w/gr tips on cream, gold int, bronze base, 12"..**1,900.00**
Vase, feathers, gr on cream to lt yel, 3-sided, bronze base, 15".**2,500.00**
Vase, feathers, gr on gold cylinder, bronze doré 4-ftd base #715, 25"..**3,500.00**
Vase, feathers, gr on gold irid, corseted, #6582H, 12"............**950.00**
Vase, feathers, gr/gold on irid tan to cream, wide mouth, 1½x2½"....**1,650.00**
Vase, floriform; feathers, elongated body w/plain rim, #2764H, 12"..**7,000.00**
Vase, floriform; feathers, gr on ivory, ribbed, in metal ft #170, 12"....**2,300.00**
Vase, floriform; feathers, wht & mahog on amber, #07661, 10¾"....**16,675.00**
Vase, floriform; gold, deeply pinched rim, 5¾x5½"...................**800.00**
Vase, floriform; gold, elongated ribbed body on knob stem, 15"..**1,850.00**
Vase, floriform; gold w/purple irid, wide cup, pencil stem, 12".**2,100.00**
Vase, floriform; gr/amber/wht pastels, lobed rim, #1743 metal ft, 15"..**3,680.00**
Vase, floriform; hearts/vines, gold w/gr, plain rim, disc ft, 9"....**3,450.00**
Vase, floriform; leaves, gr on gold, bronze artichoke #1043 base, 16"...**925.00**
Vase, floriform; leaves, triangular rim, 4" dia ft, 12"...........**4,700.00**
Vase, flowers/vines, inlaid in orange on gr irid, dbl shoulder, 4"..**2,250.00**
Vase, gold irid, squat ribbed ovoid, #3317B, 5x5"...................**750.00**
Vase, gold irid, trumpet form w/knob stem & ribbed ft, #1533-5458, 11".**1,250.00**
Vase, gold to wht at rim & tops of hdls, #3154A, 2".................**750.00**
Vase, gold w/lime gr irid, dbl-gourd shape, #R5525, 10x5".........**1,495.00**
Vase, gr pastel w/opal zigags, 2-ball opal stem, clear base, #1881, 7"...**900.00**
Vase, hearts/vines, gr on gold, bulbous, #5-8130N, 8¾".............**3,000.00**
Vase, intaglio allover leaves & branches on gold irid, shouldered, 12"..**4,200.00**
Vase, lav pastel, ribbed, disc ft, 6½"..............................**800.00**
Vase, leaves/threaded vines, amber irid on gr, #1732n, 6¾".........**1,500.00**
Vase, leaves/vines, gr on gold, #7793K, bottle form, 3½"..........**1,200.00**
Vase, leaves/vines, gr on gold, w/15 millefiori canes, bulbous, 4"..**2,475.00**
Vase, leaves/vines, inlaid/cvd gr on gold irid, #9715H, 13".......**4,750.00**

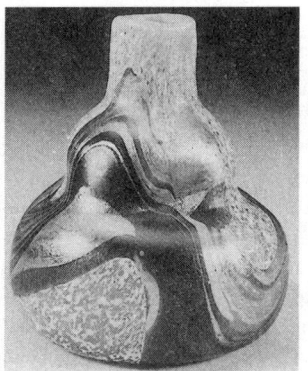

Vase, mottled green, white, and granite gray with green and gold iridescent pulled striations, cased pinched oval body, R1773, 3⅜", $3,565.00.

Vase, pulled swirls suggest long-stem floral, wine/blk/gr on gold, 8"..**6,500.00**
Vase, reactive gold-yel w/abstract motif, #1664P, 5"...............**3,625.00**
Vase, starflowers, gr on gold, gr vines, shouldered, 7x4½".......**1,900.00**
Vase, Tel-Armana gold collar on gr, petticoat shape, #3895J, 7½"...**3,000.00**
Vase, violet-gr w/10 gold-gr irid prunts on disc base, #08736, 11".......**600.00**
Vase, wide irid wavy band on clear aqua, gold-bronze int, #N3071, 5x5".**3,500.00**
Window, forest path/mtns/water/sky, dbl-layered, sgn, 30x22"...**20,700.00**
Wine, gold irid, 4"...**325.00**
Wine, gold irid (EX color), twist stem, 7⅜".........................**550.00**

Lamps

Lamp prices seem to be getting stronger, especially for leaded lamps with brighter colors (red, blue, purples). Bases that are unusual or rare have brought good prices and added to the value of the more common shades that sold on them. Bases with enamel or glass inserts are very much in demand. Our advisor for Tiffany lamps is Carl Heck; he is listed in the Directory under Colorado.

Key: c-b — counterbalance

Base, gilt-bronze, telescoping, knopped reeded std, #684, 63"..2,875.00
Base, gilt-bronze w/acanthus leaves on reeded comumn & base, #655, 28"....2,500.00
Candle, 6½" rnd cased gold shade w/feathers; bronze std w/9 jewels 3,450.00
Candlestick, gold ruffled shade; SP support, label, ca 1900, 16x7½" 1,600.00
Chandelier, twisted/coiled bronze inset w/jewels & ornaments, 38x10"....6,500.00
Chandelier, 24-light, calyx sockets, altered bronze unmk armature, 31".64,500.00
Chandelier, 6 gold lily shades w/gold prisms, rtcl bronze fr, 32x15" 14,000.00
Chandelier, 6-arm, lily shades, gr/brn patina, 18" H.................9,990.00
Desk, damascene brn shade on bronze c-b std #417 (VG) 6,300.00
Desk, damascene cobalt bl dome shade; swivel mt on bronze std, 15".8,000.00
Desk, damascene gr/bl irid 10" shade (EX); petal-ftd harp std adjusts..8,000.00
Desk, feathered 7" caramel shade; c-b std w/single arm, 16......8,000.00
Desk, gold ribbed 6" shade; bronze mk std, 17½" 1,300.00
Desk, gold 6" hanging floriform shade; harp std #419 w/missing ball ft...1,500.00
Desk, ldgl 10" butterscotch/wht dome shade; trumpet std, 18" ...2,300.00
Desk, 7" brn cone shade w/zipper pattern, 3 prunts, cased, 15" ..4,875.00
Desk, 7" damascene gr/wht irid shade; std #322 w/fine fluted ft....4,000.00
Desk, 7" streaky brn dome shade; silvered bronze std #691, 15"....3,450.00
Floor, ldgl 12" acorn-band shade; harp std #423H on 5 high arch ft ..9,750.00
Floor, wht irid shade; harp std #423 w/3 high arch ft 4,300.00
Floor, 10" brn shade w/Intarsia border; harp 3-leg std w/pad ft, 57" 2,600.00
Hall, feathers, gr/wht on amber irid pendant acorn shade, +mts: 41"..6,300.00
Hanging, 14" ball shade blown into bronze lattice w/turtle-bk tile....24,000.00
Lily, 3-light, gold pendant sgn shades; finger loop atop std #306, 16"..3,800.00
Lily, 3-light, ribbed shades, #319 gold doré 3-arm base, 13".....4,500.00
Lily, 6-light (1 rpl); bronze pencil-stem std allows height adjustment....9,200.00
Sconce, 2-light, lily shades; unmk bronze wall mts, 10", NM, pr 10,500.00
Student, dbl; 8" gold damascene sgn shades; trn bronze scroll-arm std ..9,775.00
Student, dome shade w/wavy irid, bronze canister w/appl designs, 24"..5,700.00
Student, 2 etched gold shades (NM); bronze #10914 base, 27" 12,000.00
Table, cameo leaves, gr on 9" dome shade & vasiform base, 16" 8,600.00
Table, cameo roses, wht on gr 12" shade; feathered glass base, 24" 12,000.00
Table, gold 12" ogee shade/trumpet base w/allover gr pattern, 19".........8,000.00
Table, ldgl 15" apple-blossom shade; Grueby base w/appl leaves, 22"..32,500.00
Table, ldgl 15" spider & web gold shade; bronze patina on #337 std ...30,000.00
Table, ldgl 16" acorn-band shade; pencil std w/2 legs, ea w/2 ft............12,000.00
Table, ldgl 16" daffodil shade; 3-socket bronze std, 22" 27,600.00
Table, ldgl 16" pomegranate-band shade; acorn font in 4-leg support....8,500.00
Table, ldgl 16" tulip shade: 3-arm bronze scrolled wire-twist std, 21"...24,000.00
Table, ldgl 17" sq-panel shade w/geometric band; #534 std ...10,000.00
Table, ldgl 18" brickwork shade; font in delicate paw-ft support #5136....18,500.00
Table, ldgl 18" shade: sqs w/leafy band; slim fluted std w/wide base 25,875.00
Table, ldgl 20" dragonfly shade (EX); std #537 w/NM patina, 20".......40,250.00
Table, ldgl 20" red poppy shade (EX); ftd bronze #363 std, 25" 45,000.00
Table, linen-fold 19" caramel shade; 'turtle-bk'/hairpin panel std 13,000.00

Metal Work

Items are bronze unless noted otherwise.

Bookends, Abalone, gold doré, #1173, 5½x5½".....................1,700.00
Bookends, Saints under arches, shaded bl pnt, 6⅛x4½", pr........330.00
Bookends, Zodiac, gold doré, #1091, 6x5" 1,000.00
Bowl, florals in relief, #1707, 1½x9" 275.00
Bowl, geometric banding, gold doré, 9" 285.00
Box, Chinese, gold doré, #1774, 10" L 950.00
Box, Pine Needle, gr/ivory glass bking, ball ft, 6½" L 1,200.00
Box, Spider Web, caramel/ivory glass inserts, 4¼" L 1,000.00
Box, textured gold doré, #1100, 4x6" L 500.00
Bust, Classical maiden w/long hair on base, 1880s, 26½x14x11"..2,000.00
Bust, Victorian lady, detailed bodice & collar, brass, 29" 2,650.00
Candle holder, dbl; blown-in gr glass, 2 cups on organic tray, 6x7" 2,900.00

Candleabrum, 2 cups ea side central spire, blown-in gr glass, 14x15"..4,000.00
Candlestick, cup w/7 jewels, organic stem, wide fluted base, 17½" 3,750.00
Candlestick, flower form, domed base w/glass fragments, 13" ...11,000.00
Candlestick, gold doré, 12 root-shaped ft, #1200, 12½"...........2,100.00
Candlestick, gr glass blown-out artichoke on pencil stem, #27369, 15"..3,750.00
Candlestick, Queen Anne's Lace, gr glass-lined elongated cup, 23½".....4,500.00
Candlestick, 2 bowl cups in tripart supports, central organic stem, 9".....1,900.00
Compote, enamel floral band in bowl/on ft, gold doré, #401, 7x7" 1,200.00
Compote, sun rays, manipulated/rolled rim, #172, 3½x6" 415.00
Desk set, Bookmark, early 1900s, 6-pc set.......................1,500.00
Desk set, Pine Needle, inkwell/tray/blotter ends/sm fr/vase/etc, 9-pc..2,350.00
Frame, Abalone, #1166, 6½x6" 2,300.00
Frame, emb w/coats of arms & heads of knights in armor, #61, 12x10"..1,900.00
Frame, Grapevine, yel/gr glass bking, #949, 7x6¼" 2,200.00
Frame, Indian pattern, EX gr/brn patina, shaped sides, #1187, 7½x6"..2,400.00
Frame, narrow w/abstracts, gold doré, #6, 10x8" 800.00
Frame, Pine Needle, SP w/slag glass inserts, rprs, 7x6" 1,150.00
Frame, Spider Web, gold doré, amber glass bking, 7½x9½", VG...950.00
Frame, Spider Web, gr/brn patina, ivory/gr glass bking, #940, 8x6"...1,300.00
Frame, Spider Web, gr/brn patina, ivory/gr glass bking, 6½x4½"........1,200.00
Frame, Spider Web, gr/brn patina, yel/gr glass bking, #947, 10x8"...2,200.00
Frame, Spider Web, yel/gr/bl glass bking, will hang or stand, 18x16".4,750.00
Inkwell, Pine Needle, gr glass insert, sq, 3¼x3¼" 575.00
Jar, etched gold doré cylinder w/turtlebk tile on lid, #132, 4" 600.00
Letter rack, Zodiac, EX patina, mk, 6¼x9½" 350.00
Paperweight, Pine Needle, gr/wht glass w/in (fractured), 3½" dia....350.00
Smoking stand, bronze, lift-off ashtray w/matchbox holder, #1649, 30"..1,950.00
Thermometer, Zodiac, gold doré, #1014, 8x4½" 650.00
Tray, gold doré, textured, #21810A-411, 14" 120.00
Tray, lacy band at rim, textured/etched ground, 9" 300.00
Tray, lacy band w/opal-type stones, #1670, 7¾"..........................250.00

Pottery

Bowl vase, pumpkins emb on yel-washed ivory pumpkin form, rstr, 13" W ...6,000.00
Vase, cobalt mottle over turq, slim neck, 3-hdl, #7, 12¾" 1,955.00
Vase, cvd leaves on cream matt w/brn wash, #6, 5½", NM......1,100.00
Vase, emb floral on brn matt, 9x11"..............................1,400.00
Vase, organic form, 4-petal body in leafy cup, lt gr/gunmetal, 11", EX ..2,600.00

Silver

Key: t-oz — troy ounces

Bowl, appl vertical fruit bands, 1947-56, 9" dia, 26-t-oz...........2,300.00
Bowl, emb blkberries & scrolls, pierced rim, 1902-07, 18-t-oz.1,150.00
Brooch, bird motif, 1½" L, pr...95.00
Canape tray, emb festoons/rosettes, monogram, 1912-47, 21-t-oz..800.00
Candelabra, floral decor, 5-branch, #32347/95E, pr 7,500.00
Coffee/tea service, ebonized hdls/finials, 2 pots+cr/sug+bowl+tray ..9,775.00
Dish, emb scrolls & shells, eng/rtcl cartouches, ca 1900, 30-t-oz 4,000.00
Flatware, Dunston, service for 8, 1909, 79 pcs, cased 1,265.00

Hot water kettle on stand, chased leafy decoration on pear form, ca 1850, 64-troy ounces, 13¼", $2,300.00.

Jug, floral repousse on textured ground, 1875-91, 35-t-oz **3,750.00**
Jug, water; geometric bands, monogram, 1879, 7¼", 24-t-oz ...**1,600.00**
Napkin rings, oval w/molded edges, eng monogram, 13-t-oz, 12 for..**750.00**
Pill box, walnut form, 1" **270.00**
Platter, meat; foliage & scrolls, reeded sides, 1891-1902, 44-t-oz ..**2,750.00**
Porringer, Little Tom Tucker's Dog molded band, 1907-47, 6-t-oz ...**460.00**
Ring tree, emb, 3x3¾" **130.00**
Salt cellar, 2 coquille bowl centered by putti, 4x5½x2¾" **450.00**
Soup ladle, Chrysanthemum, monogram, 1875-91, 13", 16-t-oz..........**1,850.00**
Tazzae, Chrysanthemum, domed sq bases, 1885-91, 8¾", 47-t-oz, pr...**7,500.00**
Tea tray, Chrysanthemum, 1875-91, 27⅞x17⅞", 215-t-oz.....**18,400.00**
Tea/coffee set, Chrysanthemum, 1875-91, 6-pc w/stand, 232-t-oz ..**26,450.00**
Tray, molded rim, monogram, presentation inscription, 54-t-oz....**1,380.00**
Tureen, Chrysanthemum, floral terminals, 1883-91, 11", 74-t-oz .**9,200.00**
Tureen & underplate, Chrysanthemum, w/lid, 1888, 225-t-oz....**32,000.00**

Tiffin Glass

The Tiffin Glass Company was founded in 1887 in Tiffin, Ohio, one of the many factories composing the U.S. Glass Company. Its early wares consisted of tablewares and decorative items such as lamps and globes. Among the most popular of all Tiffin products was the black satin glass produced there during the 1920s. In 1959 U.S. Glass was sold, and in 1962 the factories closed. The plant was re-opened in 1963 as the Tiffin Art Glass Company. Products from this period were tableware, hand-blown stemware, and other decorative items.

Those interested in learning more about Tiffin glass are encouraged to contact the Tiffin Glass Collectors' Club, whose address can be found in the Directory under Clubs, Newsletters, and Catalogs. See also Black Glass; Glass Animals.

Ashtray, Flanders, crystal, w/cigarette rest, 2¼x3¾" **40.00**
Ashtray, modern cigar; Twilight, #1...**150.00**
Basket, Jungle Assortment, any color, #151, 6" **85.00**
Bowl, bonbon; Flanders, yel, hdls..**45.00**
Bowl, bonbon; Japanese Lily, ftd, #14179, 6" **45.00**
Bowl, celery; Cherokee Rose, oblong, 10½" **55.00**
Bowl, centerpiece; Cherokee Rose, 13" **75.00**
Bowl, console; Cadena, crystal, 12" **45.00**
Bowl, console; Fuchsia, crystal, flared, #5902, 12⅝" **90.00**
Bowl, cream soup; Cadena, crystal..**45.00**
Bowl, finger; Fuchsia, crystal, ftd, #041, 4" **60.00**
Bowl, finger; Water Lily, +plate w/star bottom, #925/#9270 ....**30.00**
Bowl, fruit or nut; Cherokee Rose, crystal, 6" **40.00**
Bowl, fruit or nut; June Night, crystal, 6" **40.00**
Bowl, lily; red & crystal, #6587, 10" **95.00**
Bowl, red & crystal, #6561, 9" **125.00**
Bowl, rose; gr & crystal, #6576, 6"...**125.00**
Bowl, salad; Cherokee Rose, crystal, 7" **45.00**
Bowl, salad; Fuchsia, crystal, #5902, 7¼" **40.00**
Bowl, salad; Fuchsia, crystal, 10" **65.00**
Bowl, whipped cream; Flower Garden/Butterfly, gr, #326, w/ladle ..**150.00**
Candle holders, cobalt, w/bubble, #6125, pr **85.00**
Candle holders, crystal, w/bubble, #6126, pr **50.00**
Candlestick, Citron Green w/Cellini stem, #17423....................**100.00**
Candlestick, Copen Blue w/Cellini stem, #17423....................**125.00**
Candlestick, crystal w/Cellini stem, #17423................................**85.00**
Candlestick, Flanders, crystal, 2 styles **45.00**
Candlestick, Fuchsia, crystal, ball center, 2-light, 5"....................**80.00**
Celery, Flanders, pk, 11"...**75.00**
Celery, June Night, crystal, oblong, 10½" **40.00**
Comport, Copen Blue w/Cellini stem, #17423 ....**70.00**
Comport, crystal w/Cellini stem, #17423 ....**75.00**

Comport, Flanders, yel, 3½"..**60.00**
Comport, Wisteria w/Cellini stem, #17423 ....**125.00**
Creamer, Canterbury, Twilight, #115..**60.00**
Creamer, Classic, crystal, flat **35.00**
Creamer, Fontaine, amber, gr or pk, ftd, #4 ....**35.00**
Creamer, Fuchsia, crystal, ind, #5831, 2⅞".....................................**45.00**
Creamer, Julia, amber **30.00**
Cup, Cadena, crystal..**45.00**
Cup, Flanders, yel, 2 styles **65.00**
Cup, Fontaine, Twilight, #8869 ....**100.00**
Finger bowl, Classic, crystal, ftd...**20.00**
Flower arranger, cobalt & crystal, #6552, 8" **165.00**
Grapefruit, Flanders, pk, w/liner **150.00**
Jug, iced tea; Craquelle, #117, 64-oz..**195.00**
Mayonnaise, Cadena, pk or yel, ftd, w/liner **75.00**
Night lamp, Plum, #9441 ....**95.00**
Nut cup, Flanders, crystal, ftd, blown **40.00**
Oil bottle, Flanders, yel, w/stopper **250.00**
Olive dish, Copen Blue, #6467 ....**75.00**
Olive dish, crystal, #6467..**35.00**
Plate, cake; Fontaine, Twilight, center hdl, #345, 10" **125.00**
Plate, dinner; Classic, crystal, 10" **100.00**
Plate, luncheon; Cherokee Rose, crystal, 8" **15.00**
Plate, luncheon; Classic, pk, 8" **20.00**
Plate, luncheon; Fuchsia, crystal, #5902, 8¼"..............................**17.50**
Plate, luncheon; June Night, crystal, 8"..**12.00**
Plate, sandwich; June Night, crystal, 14" **45.00**
Relish, Cherokee Rose, crystal, 3-part, 6½" **45.00**
Relish, Flanders, crystal, 3-part **45.00**
Relish, Fuchsia, crystal, hdls, 5-part, 10½x12½"...........................**70.00**
Saucer, Classic, crystal..**10.00**
Saucer, Flanders, pk...**15.00**
Shakers, Cherokee Rose, crystal, pr...**150.00**
Shakers, June Night, crystal, pr...**185.00**
Shakers, Jungle Assortment, any color, ftd, #6205 ....**30.00**
Stem, cafe parfait; Julia, amber **35.00**
Stem, claret; Cherokee Rose, crystal, 4-oz **50.00**
Stem, claret; Flanders, crystal...**40.00**
Stem, claret; Fontaine, amber, gr or pk, #033................................**60.00**
Stem, cocktail; June Night, crystal, 3½-oz.....................................**23.00**
Stem, parfait; Fuchsia, crystal, #15083, 6" **40.00**
Stem, saucer champagne; Fontaine, Twilight, #033 ....**55.00**
Stem, sundae; Fontaine, Twilight, #033 ....**45.00**
Stem, water; Classic, pk, 9-oz, 7¼" **55.00**
Stem, wine; Fuchsia, crystal, #15083, 5" **30.00**
Sugar bowl, Cadena, pk or yel **30.00**
Sugar bowl, Classic, crystal, ftd **35.00**
Sugar bowl, Fuchsia, crystal, pearl edge **45.00**
Sugar bowl, Julia, amber **30.00**
Sugar bowl, June Night, crystal...**27.00**
Table bell, Cherokee Rose, crystal **45.00**
Tumbler, Flanders, pk, ftd, 10-oz, 4¾" **45.00**
Tumbler, juice; Cadena, pk or yel, ftd, 4¼"....................................**30.00**
Tumbler, juice; Fuchsia, crystal, flat, 5" **30.00**
Tumbler, water; Cherokee Rose, crystal, ftd, 8-oz...........................**25.00**
Tumbler, water; Craquelle, gr ft, #14185, 12-oz..............................**25.00**
Tumbler, water; June Night, crystal, ftd, 8-oz **22.00**
Vase, bud; Banana, #6116, 9¾"..**65.00**
Vase, bud; Cherokee Rose, crystal, 8" **35.00**
Vase, bud; Fuchsia, crystal, #14185, 8¼".......................................**35.00**
Vase, bud; June Night, crystal, 10" **45.00**
Vase, bud; Plum, #6116, 9¾"...**65.00**
Vase, bud; Wisteria, #6116, 9¾"...**95.00**
Vase, Flanders, yel, Dahlia style...**200.00**

Vase, Globe, crystal, #17350, 9" **65.00**
Vase, Globe, crystal, w/sand cvg, #17350, 9" **125.00**
Vase, Tub, bl w/sand cvg, #17350, 9½" **150.00**
Vase, Tub, crystal, #17350, 9½" **65.00**
Vase, Tub, crystal, w/sand cvg, #17350, 9½" **150.00**
Vase, wall; Jungle Assortment, any color, #320 ....**65.00**
Violet bowl, Twilight, #5551 ....**75.00**

Tiles

The history of tile making dates back to ancient Egypt and Assyria. For centuries tiles have played an important role as a decorative art form, as well as having a utilitarian function. Places such as palace walls, Islamic mosques, Roman floors, and medieval English churches were all adorned with tiles or glazed ceramic surfaces. Remnants of these tile installations can still be seen throughout the world.

The heyday of tile making in England and the United States dates back to circa 1860 through 1930 and envelops the Victorian, Art Nouveau, and Arts & Crafts Movements in both countries. These tiles comprise most of those seen on today's market.

Tiles are being collected today as individual art objects and are increasingly used as decorative accessories. They are also sought in order to restore homes, buildings, and furniture to original period condition. Many people are now incorporating antique and collectible tiles into their home-rebuilding projects for gardens, kitchens, bathrooms, fireplaces, stair risers, and floors.

Tiles must be judged on an individual basis. The condition of the tile face; the quality of the design; the rarity of the artist, company, or series; and the size of the tile or tile panel are just some of the factors to consider when assessing value. People, animals, and scenes are generally more desirable than florals and geometrics. Some glaze colors, such as true pale pink or bright red majolica, add value to Victorian tiles. Tiles may be more difficult to find than many other antiques or collectibles, partly because many were permanently installed. Unfortunately many installations have been destroyed. These factors all have influence on the tile market, and it is not unusual for prices to vary greatly. See also Moravian; Grueby; Rookwood; other specific manufacturers. Our advisor for this category is Karen Guido; she is listed in the Directory under Connecticut.

Key:
maj — majolica glaze   tbld — tube lined
pr mld — press molded   tp — transfer printed
srs — series

Empire, Old Mother Goose, multicolor matt and semigloss on black ground, 12" square, $1,800.00.

American

AETCO, female profile, mottled brn & cream maj, pr mld, 6" ...**195.00**
AETCO, frog & pussy willow fireplace surround, gr maj, 17 6" tiles, G ...**1,800.00**
AETCO, man on horse, mc matt, pr mld, 4" **195.00**

AETCO, rtcl geometric grill, pk matt, 6" **145.00**
Alhambra Tile Co, Art Nouveau faience, 4 flowers, mc, pr mld, 6" ..**295.00**
Batchelder, castle, brn & bl matt, pr mld, 5¾" **225.00**
Batchelder, company ad w/2 birds, matt brn/bl, pr mld, 3", VG ...**525.00**
Batchelder, lion w/curly tail, terra cotta & gr matt, pr mld, 4" ...**175.00**
Batchelder, lovebirds, brn w/bl matt, 5½x17½" **960.00**
Beaver Falls, female profile stove tile, gr maj, 3" dia **110.00**
Boston TC Co, foliage, high molded/cvd relief, unglazed, 4" **50.00**
Calif Art Tile Co, mission/fountain in archway, mc, pr mld, fr, 8x12" ...**1,500.00**
California Faience, ship & waves, bl/gr/gold turq, 7½x11½" ...**3,850.00**
California Faience, stylized floral, red/gr/bl, pr mld, 5½" dia ...**1,050.00**
Claycraft, rtcl geometric grill, brn & turq matt, 7¾" **325.00**
Flint Faience, giraffe, metallic blk w/cream & brn, pr mld, 6" **650.00**
Flint Faience, lantern, orange & gr, pr mld, 3" **45.00**
Franklin Faience, Indian profile, mc, pr mld, 4" **70.00**
Greuby, sea gulls & waves, gr matt, pr mld, fr, 6" **2,600.00**
Grueby, man holding pot w/in a G, mc, 8" **16,000.00**
Hamilton, Victorian lady w/parrot, bl maj, pr mld, 6x12" **325.00**
Handcraft, geometric, terra cotta & gr, 5" **85.00**
Harris Strong, cubist buildings, mc, tbld, fr, 6" **115.00**
Harris Strong, pr 3 tile panels, women, mc, tbld, fr, ea 6" **400.00**
Hartford Faience, water lilies, mc, 9x12" **2,750.00**
Iowa State College, stylized trees, cranberry high glaze w/wht, 3" **400.00**
ITT, female profile w/stars, dk bl maj, pr mld, 6", VG, pr **475.00**
Kensington, female profile, stove tile, brn maj, pr mld, 3" dia **125.00**
Kensington, owl profile, caramel maj, pr mld, 6", VG **300.00**
Low, couple in wagon w/horses, plastic sketch, brn maj, 11x18" ...**3,000.00**
Low, winged cherub & mouse, gr maj, pr mld (high relief), 6" **460.00**
Marblehead, sailing ship, mc, 6¼" dia, VG **590.00**
Mosaic Tile Co, rabbit, mc, raised line, 6" **650.00**
Mosaic Tile Co, rat & fiddle, mc, cuerda seca, 4" **250.00**
Mosaic Tile Co, sandpipers on beach, mc, 48 4" tiles in panel ...**2,800.00**
Mueller Mosaic, oil lamp, unglazed red clay, imp, 6", G **145.00**
Pewabic, flower & leaf, bl/wht high glaze, incised, 3" **100.00**
Robertson Art Tile, geometric, caramel maj, pr mld, 6" **90.00**
S&S, stylized fish, mc, pr mld, 4 6" tiles in panel **2,000.00**
San Jose Potteries, colonial dancing couple, mc, 4" **375.00**
San Jose Potteries, Mexican couple & burro, mc, 8" **425.00**
San Jose Potteries, Mexican courting couple, mc, fr, 7¾" **775.00**
Soriano, goat, gray/wht/yel/bl, label, 6" **30.00**
Sparta Ceramics, Mother Goose, gr/brn matt, molded, 4" **175.00**
Trent, female profile w/bird, gold maj, pr mld, 6" **350.00**
WACO, pinwheel, brn matt w/bl, molded, 4" **80.00**
Wheatley, geometric, mc matt, 4" **235.00**
Wheatley, Zodiac animal, ochre/orange matt, cvd, 5", VT **535.00**
Wheeling, sailing ship, mc, raised line, 4" **185.00**
White Brick TC Co, advertising w/lion, unglazed, 4" **175.00**

English

Brown, Westhead & Moore, Little Boy Blue, brn/wht tp, 6" **165.00**
Burmantofts, 2 mythical birds, brn maj, pr mld, 6", VG **240.00**
Copeland, flower urn, bl/wht, relief molded, 8" **250.00**
Corn Bros, Art Nouveau floral, gr maj, pr mld, 6" **125.00**
Craven Dunnill, peacock feather, brn/gold maj, pr mld, 6", G **125.00**
DeMorgan, flowers & leaves, turq/bl/grs HP, 6" **600.00**
DeMorgan, flowers & leaves, yel/wht/gr HP, 6" **350.00**
Godwin & Thynne, Art Nouveau geometric, mc, tbld, 3x6" **125.00**
H Richards, roses & leaves, mc, tbld, 6" **150.00**
Malkin Edge, water lily, mc, pr mld, 6" **145.00**
Maw, Art Nouveau stylized flower, gold & wht lustre, 6" **200.00**
Minton Hollins, cow w/floral border, brn/cream tp, 6" **155.00**
Minton Hollins, flower set (4), gr maj, pr mld, ea 1½" **60.00**
Mintons ChWks, Aeosop's Fables, monkey & cat, bl/wht, 6" **165.00**

Rhodes Tile Co, Art Nouveau floral, red/gr, pr mld, 6", VG **165.00**
Robert Minton Taylor, man w/goatee, brn/buff encaustic, 6", VG ..**110.00**
Sherwin & Cotton, fruit on branches, brn maj, pr mld, 6" **115.00**
Sherwin & Cotton, woman w/jug, honey-amber maj, intaglio, 12"..**450.00**
T&R Boote, Art Nouveau w/4 red roses, mc, pr mld, 6" **140.00**
Wedgwood, 1918 calendar w/Boston Light, brn & wht tp, 3x4".**125.00**

Other Countries

Belgium, Heximen, Art Nouveau floral, mc, pr mld, 6" **135.00**
France, Martel, lute player, mc HP, 6" **75.00**
France, St Armand-Nord, butterfly, mc, pr mld, 6", VG **180.00**
Germany, Bankel, Art Nouveau floral, mc, pr mld, 6", VG **120.00**
Germany, flowers in pot, mc maj, pr mld, 6"................................**110.00**
Germany, V&B, profiles, gr maj, intaglio, 6", pr **440.00**
Holland, Gouda, Queen Willhelmina commemorative, 1938, 4"..**145.00**
Holland, Westraven Utrecht, galleon, mc, pr mld, 5" **175.00**
Italy, Gambone, stylized deer w/sq, cream/yel/violet/wht, 5" **250.00**
Italy, Ginori, country scene, mc HP, 5½" dia **265.00**
Mexico, Ruggerio, man & donkey, mc HP, 5½"............................**115.00**
Royal Delft Faience, sailboat, mc, ca 1920, 4" **105.00**

Tinware

In the American household of the seventeenth and eighteenth centuries, tinware items could be found in abundance, from food containers to foot warmers and mirror frames. Although the first settlers brought much of their tinware with them from Europe, by 1798 sheets of tin plate were being imported from England for use by the growing number of American tinsmiths. Tinwares were often decorated either by piercing or painted designs which were both freehand and stenciled. (See Toleware.) By the early 1900s, many homes had replaced their old tinware with the more attractive aluminum and graniteware.

In the nineteenth century, tenth wedding anniversaries were traditionally celebrated by gifts of tin. Couples gave big parties, dressed in their wedding clothes, and reaffirmed their vows before their friends and families who arrived bearing (and often wearing) tin gifts, most of which were quite humorous. Anniversary tin items may include hats, cradles, slippers and shoes, rolling pins, etc. See also Primitives and Kitchen Collectibles.

Biscuit cutter, heavy wire hdl..**35.00**
Cheese mold, heart shape, pierced, tubular ft, 3x6x6".................**350.00**
Cheese mold, heart shape, pierced, 3-ftd, strap hanger, 4½" **300.00**

Coffeepot, Pennsylvania origin, punched tulips and urn, brass finial, G, $1,150.00. (Photo courtesy **Aston Americana Auctioneers & Appraisers**)

Coffeepot, stick spout, strap hdl, emb Mason's, 8½", EX...............**90.00**
Cracker pricker/cutter, oblong w/scalloped edge **70.00**
Cup, hinged lid, sm drinking spout w/screw-on cover...................**35.00**
Lunch box, Moore's Pat, folding, red & blk pnt, 1911, EX............**60.00**
Mantel ornaments, cut/molded flowers w/pnt putty, 19th C, 22x9", pr ..**1,955.00**
Measure, raised rings, 1-qt..**20.00**
Mirror fr, punched flower baskets/rnd designs, mirror cracks, 20x20"...**425.00**

Pan, scrapple; Pennsylvania Dutch, ca 1800s, 3x12x14" **65.00**
Pastry sheet, curved bottom, w/tin rolling pin, wood hdls...........**800.00**
Rack, potato baking; 6 rnded points, dtd 1909, 2¼x13½" **45.00**
Roaster, divided, heavy worn hdls, 1800s, 15x12".........................**65.00**
Roaster, oval w/lapped end, wire hdls, PA, 1800s, 4x16x12".........**65.00**
Sconces, bk: molded edges/crimped rnd crest/mirror, 3-socket, 18", pr ..**825.00**
Sconces, ovoid bkplate w/crimped border & drip pan, 13x10", pr ..**825.00**
Sconces, semicircular, crimped crest, added decor, 13", pr.............**350.00**
Skimmer, molasses; wood & dk tin, 10x5¾"+4" hdl.....................**40.00**
Tankard, hinged lid w/heart finial, spade hdl terminal, early, 13" .**50.00**
Teapot, pewter finial, 8" **105.00**

Tobacciana

Tobacciana is the generally accepted term used to cover a field of collecting that includes smoking pipes, cigar molds, cigarette lighters, humidors — in short, any article having to do with the practice of using tobacco in any form. Perhaps the most valuable variety of pipes is the meerschaum, hand carved from hydrous magnesium, an opaque white-gray or cream-colored mineral of the soapstone family. (Much of this is today mined in Turkey which has the largest meerschaum deposit in the world, though there are other deposits of lesser significance around the globe.) These figural bowls often portray an elaborately carved mythological character, an animal, or a historical scene. Amber is sometimes used for the stem. Other collectible pipes are corn cob (Missouri meerschaum) and Indian peace pipes of clay or catlinite. (See American Indian Art.)

Chosen because it was the Indians who first introduced the white man to smoking, the cigar store Indian was a symbol used to identify tobacco stores in the nineteenth century. The majority of them were hand carved between 1830 and 1900 and are today recognized as some of the finest examples of early wood sculptures. When found they command very high prices.

For further information on lighters, refer to *Collector's Guide to Cigarette Lighters* by James Flanagan. Ashtray collectors will enjoy *Collector's Guide to Ashtrays, 2nd Edition*, by Nancy Wanvig. See also Advertising; Snuff Boxes.

Ashtray, brass-coated metal, fly, lift wings for tray, 2 rests, 7"........**28.00**
Ashtray, ceramic, baby bird w/wide mouth, Occupied Japan, 3⅜" ...**18.00**
Ashtray, ceramic, clown head, big-mouth smoker, Japan, 5" **40.00**
Ashtray, ceramic, dog w/big mouth, tongue wags, Japan, 3½".....**160.00**
Ashtray, ceramic, elephant, yel lustre, Japan, 4" **25.00**
Ashtray, ceramic, Snuf-A-Rette, gr, Deco style, 1937....................**75.00**
Ashtray, ceramic, tower, smoker, Berardos Portugal, 5¾" **44.00**
Ashtray, copper, rectangular, mk Gregorian, 4¾" L **12.00**
Ashtray, glass, bl Delphite hat, cord around crown in relief, 6⅛".**42.00**
Ashtray, glass, cobalt w/chrome fretwork fr, Hong Kong, 4" dia....**25.00**
Ashtray, glass, swirled, 3 rests, Lenwile of Ardalt Japan, 4" **23.00**
Ashtray, glass, Terrace, ruby, Duncan & Miller, 1930s, 3½" sq **40.00**
Ashtray, pewter, dog figural hdl, Am, old, 3¾" **28.00**
Ashtray/cigarette holder, ceramic, bellhop in center, 1930s, 4½x4"...**60.00**
Cheroot cutter/charm/fob, gold bird, ruby eyes/dmn nose, 1900, 1½"..**695.00**
Cigar cutter, gold-filled blimp shape, 1x1⅝", w/15" fob chain **110.00**
Cigar cutter, Summons/Brunhoff Mfg, glass/wood/metal, 4¾x8x6½" ..**200.00**
Cigar cutter/clock, Not Left 5¢, CI support, 13", VG **2,150.00**
Cigar cutter/lighter, Santa-Bana, emb brass w/cobalt shade, 10", VG....**1,000.00**
Cigar lamp/lighter, Cressman's Counsellor 5¢, NP CI/tin shade, 7x8",VG...**1,150.00**
Cigar lighter, pewter lady, wick holder ea side, cobalt shade, 11½" .**600.00**
Cigarette card, Jane Russell pinup, Ardath, 1939, EX.....................**4.00**
Cigarette cards, Country Seats & Arms, Player & Sons, 1910, complete .**40.00**
Cigarette cards, Cries of London, Player & Sons, 1903, complete, EX **40.00**
Cigarette cards, Household Hints 2nd Series, Wills, 1930s, complete.......**30.00**
Cigarette case, CI elephant w/trunk up, trn tail for cigarette.......**195.00**

Cigarette case, MOP, Elgin Made in USA, 3x2" **65.00**
Cigarette case, sterling w/eng floral border, Elgin **50.00**
Cigarette dispenser, gold-tone/brass, eng Golden Age, 7x4½x3½" **65.00**
Cigarette dispenser, maroon plastic, music box base, 7½" **125.00**
Cigarette lighter, chromium, butane, Colibri/Ireland, 1960s, 3x⅞" **75.00**
Cigarette lighter, chromium/Bakelite, hula girl on base, Arrow, 1930s..**100.00**
Cigarette lighter, gold-plate & MOP, musical, PAC, 1950s, 2⅝x1⅜"....**100.00**
Cigarette lighter, marble w/brass top, Evans, 1930s, 3¾x2⅛" dia .**35.00**
Cigarette lighter, metal boot, lever at bk, 1920s, 1¾x2⅝" **125.00**
Cigarette lighter, pnt metal elephant, Strikalite, 1940s, 3x3½" **35.00**
Cigarette lighter, Spartan, chromium/metal, Ronson, 1950, 2⅜x3" ...**20.00**
Cigarette lighter, Vara Flame, chromium, butane, Ronson, 1960s, MIB..**40.00**
Cigarette lighter, Zippo, SP w/gold-tone etched wheat, 1994 ....**30.00**
Cigarette lighter/case, chromium/enamel, Magic Case, 1930s, 4¼"......**100.00**
Cigarette lighter/case, chromium/wood slats, Lectrocase, 1930s, 3⅞"...**100.00**
Cigarette papers, Top, RJ Reynolds, 100 in pkg, M........................**10.00**
Figure, Indian, stands/leans on boxes atop keg, 1875, EX pnt, 38" **11,750.00**
Figure, Scotsman w/plumed headdress, cvd oak w/mc pnt, 19th C, 35" ...**6,325.00**
Humidor, brass w/Viking ships & Stonehenge pattern, Edwaagaard, 4"......**37.50**
Humidor, bsk, Black face, realistic, EX color, 6¼" **370.00**
Humidor, Imperial glass, Cube Cut, clear, 7½x5½" **70.00**
Humidor, porc, HP Englishman & horse, England, 1890s, 5¼" ..**230.00**
Humidor, tin litho, Cinco Handy Humidor, Londres.....................**55.00**

Match dispenser, cigar advertising, Universal Match Corporation, metal and glass, 14½x9", VG, $400.00.

Pipe box, 3-slots, keg holder w/lid, pull-out tray, Edwardian, wall mt **265.00**
Pipe box; pine, drw w/rpl pull, old red pnt, 19th C, 20x6x4" ..**4,000.00**
Pipe holder, Syrocco Scottie, 1¾x5¾" **33.00**
Pipe rest, dbl, bronze, EX patina, Denmark, 1½x5½"..................**110.00**
Tobacco cutter, CI horse figural, 18th C, 7⅜", EX **195.00**
Tobacco cutter, Enterprise Mfg...Pat April 13, 1875, VG............**195.00**
Tobacco horn, cvd thistle pattern, sterling top, Scotland, 1850s, 9" ...**450.00**
Tobacco pouch, trn wood w/domed top, 3½" **18.00**
Tobacco rug/felt, Belgium flag on bl, 5¼x8⅛", EX **10.00**
Tobacco rug/felt, collie dog on tan, sm, EX **7.50**
Tobacco rug/felt, French soldier, ca 1914, silk fringe, 4¾x3".........**10.00**
Tobacco rug/felt, Indian w/tobacco leaves in headband, 5½x7¾"+mat & fr....**110.00**
Tobacco rug/felt, WWI American soldier on red, sm, EX..............**18.00**
Tobacco rug/felt, 48-star Am flag on tan, 5¼x8½", EX................**12.00**
Tobacco silk, butterfly, Tokio Cigarettes.....................................**11.00**
Tobacco silk, Col WF Cody on horsebk, 5x7" **130.00**
Tobacco silk, King Kicholas of Montenegro, Nebo Cigarettes, 3¼x5"...**9.00**
Tobacco tin tag, BF Gravely & Sons Cabinet, oval, bl on red, EX **100.00**
Tobacco tin tag, Claw Hammer, hammer shape, bl & wht, EX.....**33.00**
Tobacco tin tag, Elk Horn, rectangular, bl on orange, EX **60.00**
Tobacco tin tag, Hoe Boy, sq, yel, EX...**205.00**
Tobacco tin tag, Knaffle's, scalloped sq, red elephant on yel, EX ..**70.00**
Tobacco tin tag, R Knaffi's Blue Goose, oval, bl on wht, EX.......**165.00**
Tobacco tin tag, Wild Turkey Tobacco, rnd, brn/bl on wht, EX....**75.00**

Pipes

Burl wood, horse head cvg, amber eyes, Bakelite stem, EX............**55.00**

Clay, Uncle Sam, 1876 Centennial, faded pnt, 2¼x6" **125.00**
Meerschaum, Black boy's head cvg, Tarzania on stem, 1½x6½", VG........**175.00**
Meerschaum, Black lady, detailed hair, Austria?, late 19th C, 3½x9" ..**1,250.00**
Meerschaum, clasped hands, amber patina, 19th C, w/stand.......**430.00**
Meerschaum, grapes & leaves cvg, amber stem, 19th C, VG **70.00**
Meerschaum, horses & barking dog cvg, ca 1900, 2x4", M in custom case ..**350.00**
Meerschaum, Indian's face cvg, amber stem, 3" H **475.00**
Meerschaum, sea serpent cvg, sterling silver band, 3¼x7" **385.00**
Meerschaum, 4 cvd rabbits at base of scarecrow, 2⅞x7", NM, +case ..**515.00**
R Barbi, Danish fish shape w/2-color wood insert, NM..............**425.00**
Silver & ivory, begging dog figural, London hallmk, 1860s, 8x15"....**1,600.00**

Toby Jugs

The delightful jug known as the Toby dates back to the eighteenth century, when factories in England produced them for export to the American colonies. Named for the character Toby Philpots in the song *The Little Brown Jug*, the Toby was fashioned in the form of a jolly fellow, usually holding a jug of beer and a glass. The earlier examples were made with strict attention to details such as fingernails and teeth. Originally representing only a non-entity, a trend developed to portray well-known individuals such as George II, Napoleon, and Ben Franklin. Among the most-valued Tobies are those produced by Ralph Wood I in the late 1700s. By the mid-1830s Tobies were being made in America. See also Doulton; Occupied Japan.

Bacchus & Pan, pearlware, rpr, 1800s, 12¾" **1,600.00**
Dr Johnson (Drunken Parson), pearlware, 1830s, 8¼", EX......**1,800.00**
Gin Woman, pearlware, rstr, ca 1840, 10" **1,800.00**
Hearty Goodfellow, pearlware, rpr, 1810s, 11" **750.00**
Lord Howe, ochre, 1820s, 8¾"...**475.00**
Man seated w/hat & jug, cobalt coat, ca 1860, 8½" **275.00**
Man seated w/hat & jug, creamware, rstr chips, 1800s, 9½"....**1,400.00**
Man seated w/hat & jug, turq base, Staffordshire, 1890s, prof rpr, 9" ...**150.00**
Man seated w/hat & jug, yel pants, cobalt coat, 1860s, 8¾".......**275.00**
Man seated w/hat & jug, yel rim, Staffordshire, prof rpr, 1860s, 9" ..**225.00**
Man seated w/jug, pearlware, much rstr, ca 1800, 9¾" **725.00**
Martha Gunn, creamware, stepped base, 1840s, 10½" **2,200.00**
Martha Gunn, pearlware, rpr, 1820s, 9½".................................**2,400.00**
Night Watchman, pearlware, ca 1820, 9½", VG........................**375.00**
Squire type, cobalt coat, red vest, 1890s, 8½"..............................**180.00**
Tar figure w/pipe & pint seated on chest of 'dollars,' 1850s, 10" .**975.00**

Toleware

The term 'toleware' originally came from a French term meaning 'sheet iron.' Today it is used to refer to paint-decorated tin items, most popular from 1800 to 1850s. The craft flourished in Pennsylvania, Connecticut, Maine, and New York state. Early toleware has a very distinctive look. The surface is dull and unvarnished; background colors range from black to cream. Geometrics are quite common, but florals and fruits were also favored. Items made after 1850 were often stenciled, and gold trim was sometimes added.

American toleware is usually found in practical, everyday forms — trays, boxes, and coffeepots are most common — while French examples might include candlesticks, wine coolers, jardinieres, etc. Be sure to note color and design when determining date and value, but condition of the paint is the most important worth-assessing factor. Unless noted otherwise, values are for very good examples with average wear.

Box, deed; dome lid w/yel flowers, 4-color acorns/leaves, 8", EX ...**600.00**
Box, deed; floral, mc on blk, English Made mk, 1¾x3x2⅛".........**75.00**

Box, deed; floral, mc on blk (rubs/fading), 1810s, 5½x9x6½" **155.00**
Box, deed; flowers/berries, red/gr on blk, yel scrolls/stripes, 9½".**435.00**
Box, snuff; floral, mc on blk, scalloped edge, oval, 19th C, 2½" L...**65.00**
Box, spice; gold stencil, 6 sm boxes inside, 1860-70s, 3x9½x6¼".**75.00**
Cabinet, spice; shaped crest, 5 drws w/stenciled names, blk/yel, 14x9"..**420.00**
Clock, leaves, dk gr on mustard yel, wall mt, 1800s, 12" dia.......**350.00**
Coffeepot, floral, mc on blk w/gold, lighthouse shape, 1840s, 9½".**400.00**
Coffeepot, floral on blk japanning, gooseneck spout, 1850s, 10", EX...**750.00**
Coffeepot, floral on blk japanning, str spout, strap hdl, 9", NM **1,380.00**
Coffeepot, tulips/flowers, 3-color in wht circle on blk, 10", NM **1,200.00**
Creamer, floral on blk japanning, 1850s, NY, 4"...........................**175.00**
Creamer, red/gr roses & yel lines on worn japanning, early, 4" ...**330.00**
Pitcher, floral, mc on blk, cylindrical, 10¼", NM......................**460.00**
Planter, floral, mc on blk, wall mt, ET Nash NY, 1940s, EX.........**35.00**
Sugar bowl, lg red fruit/gr leaves on blk, decor lid, 4", NM.........**550.00**
Tea caddy, flowers, 3-color on red w/pk-wht band, flaking/dent, 4"...**495.00**
Tea caddy, red acorns/yel & gr flourishes on blk, some wear, 6"..**495.00**
Tea caddy, red circle w/copper feathers on dk japanning, wear, 6¾"..**350.00**
Tray, floral, mc on blk, scalloped rim, Art Gift...Phila PA, 25x20"......**100.00**
Tray, floral, mc on blk, 1900s, 25x19½", EX **110.00**
Tray, floral, mc on blk japanning, Fr, ca 1900, 29x23"................**225.00**
Tray, flowers & bird, mc on blk, rolled rim, 1920-30s, 17¾x14".**265.00**
Tray, fruit, red w/gr on wht band, yel stripe, wear, octagonal, 9x12"...**330.00**
Tray, roses, mc on lt gr w/gold, Fr, minor crazing, 13½" dia **295.00**
Tray, wavy yel line at rim, red/yel medallion center, oval, 7", NM...**1,750.00**

Tools

Before the Civil War, tools for the most part were handmade. Some were primitive to the point of crudeness, while others reflected the skill of those who took pride in their trade. Increasing demand for quality tools and the dawning of the age of industrialization resulted in tools that were mass produced. Factors important in evaluating antique tools are scarcity, usefulness, and portability. Those with a manufacturer's mark are worth more than unmarked items. When no condition is indicated, the items listed here are assumed to be in excellent condition. Our advisor for this category is Jim Calison; he is listed in the Directory under New York. For more information, we recommend *Antique Tools* by Kathryn McNerney (Collector Books). See also Keen Kutter; Stanley; Winchester.

Auger, wood hdl, 3" bit, 19¾" L **35.00**
Book press, pnt CI, St Louis Book Press Co, Pat 1871, rstr, 14x10x19"..**400.00**
Brace, brass & iron, wood hdl, early, 13¾"..**65.00**
Drawknife, wooden hdls, 14¼" W **25.00**
Drill, beam; 2" w/22" shaft, 17" hdl **32.50**
Drill, brace bit, wood hdl, EX **14.00**
Drill, hand crank, 2-speed, 17"..**48.00**
Gauge, battery; Jewell, 14¼x4x3", in pine container **150.00**
Gauge, shoe; wood & ivory, US Standards Kerby & Bro Makers...NY, 18"...**190.00**
Grease gun, aluminum cylinder, trn wood plunger, 6", EX **30.00**
Lumber tongs, CI, 1850s, 12"...**125.00**
Plane, bench; polished ebony, dbl irons, JH Paul #27 Jointer, EX.**55.00**
Plane, CI, Bailey #3, 8¾"...**55.00**
Plane, mahog w/rosewood hdl, brass mts, unmk, 14x3¼", M **150.00**
Plane, molding; Doscher Plane & Tool...Conn, 9½".......................**55.00**
Plane, molding; wooden, Casey & Co...NY #91, 9½"....................**45.00**
Plane, molding; wooden, Union Warrent...Chapin-Stephens, 9½"....**50.00**
Plane, quarter-sawn oak, unmk, #21, 22x3x7" **110.00**
Plane, rnd eng; Keiffer & Auxer Lancaster Pa, 9½" **30.00**
Plane, wooden, Try (England), ca 1900, 21¾", EX **95.00**
Pliers, fencing; wire cutters in jaw, 12", VG **10.00**
Rule, caliper w/ivory insert in slide, Am Swiss Watch & Supply...OH.**160.00**
Rule, rosewood, brass fittings, 2-fold, unmk, 10¼" closed...........**225.00**

Rule, wood & brass, 4-fold, mk C-S Co, EX **145.00**
Rule/level/angle tool, Chapin-Stephens #086, EX.....................**200.00**
Scribe, wooden, thumbscrew, w/6" ruler, 8" overall....................**25.00**
Spindle beveler, metal, orig blade, EX **30.00**
Sugar devil, iron & wood, Pat 1875, 16½" L **295.00**
Tire pump, brass, wooden hdl, unmk, 12".....................................**42.50**
Trimmer, hoof; PS&L Co USA, 8" **10.00**
Valve grinder, hand operated, twisted center shaft, EX................**10.00**
Vise, pipe; teeth form V on top & bottom, CM Kemp...MD...Climax, EX...**70.00**
Whetstone, Carborundum...NY molded in, 8", M in metal box...**85.00**
Wire stretcher clamp, 1900-30s, 13½x5¼"...................................**30.00**
Wire twister, Yankee style, Bates Valve Bag Corp, 17" **47.50**
Wrench, adjustable, mk 86...B&C...Springfield Mass, 10"............**45.00**
Wrench, carriage; wood & metal, dbl-sided, various szs in set of 4 ..**275.00**
Wrench, monkey; Pat September 7, 1897, EX **35.00**
Wrench, multi; Owatonna, ⅞" to ⅝"..**26.00**
Wrench, open end; CI, Armstrong #2, 5"..**8.00**
Wrench, Reinhard McCabe Model 10, EX.....................................**50.00**

Toothbrush Holders

Most of the collectible toothbrush holders were made in prewar Japan and were modeled after popular comic strip, Disney, and nursery rhyme characters. Since many were made of bisque and decorated with unfired paint, it's not uncommon to find them in less-than-perfect paint, a factor you must consider when attempting to assess their values. Our advisor for this category is Marilyn Cooper, author of *Pictorial Guide to Toothbrush Holders*; she is listed in the Directory under Texas. Plate numbers in the descriptions that follow refer to her book.

Andy Gump & Min, Japan, plate #221, 4", from $85 to **110.00**
Baby Bunting, Germany, plate #1, 6¾" **375.00**
Baker, Japan (Goldcastle), plate #150, 5¼", from $70 to **85.00**
Bear w/Jacket, Japan (Goldcastle), plate #13, 5½", from $80 to ..**90.00**
Bear w/Scarf & Hat, Japan (Goldcastle), plate #16, 5½", from $80 to...**95.00**
Bellhop w/Flowers, Japan, plate #21, 5¼", from $70 to **85.00**
Big Bird, Taiwan (RCC), plate #263, 4¼", from $80 to **90.00**
Boy in Cap & Tie w/Dog, Japan, plate #25, 6¼", from $75 to **85.00**
Candlestick Maker, Japan (Goldcastle), plate #150, 5", from $70 to...**85.00**
Cat Standing on Front Paws, Japan, plate #173, 5⅜", from $90 to ...**100.00**
Cat w/Bass Fiddle, Japan, plate #38, 6", from $130 to **150.00**
Children in Auto, Japan, plate #40, 5", from $80 to.....................**90.00**
Circus Elephant, Japan, plate #56, from $85 to **100.00**
Clown Juggling, Japan, plate #60, from $80 ....**90.00**
Clown w/Mandolin, Japan, plate #61, 6", from $80 to...................**90.00**
Cow w/Bell, Japan, plate #69, 6", from $90 to **100.00**
Crow on Pedestal, Japan (Diamond T), plate #226, 6", from $125 to..**150.00**
Duck, Japan, plate #180, 5½", from $80 to **90.00**
Dutch Boy & Girl Kissing, Japan, plate #88, 6", from $55 to........**65.00**
Fairy, Japan, celluloid, plate #229, 4¾", from $90 to **115.00**
Giraffe, Japan, plate #97, 6", from $115 to..................................**125.00**
Girl w/Umbrella, Japan, plate #45, 4½", from $65 to **75.00**
Humpty Dumpty, Pat Pend, plate #114, bsk, 5½", from $225 to....**250.00**
Kayo, Japan, plate #116, 5", from $100 to...................................**125.00**
Lone Ranger on Silver, Long Ranger Inc, chalk, plate #249, 4", $80 to ..**95.00**
Mickey Mouse & Minnie w/Hands on Hips, Japan, plate #234, 4¼" **300.00**
Old King Cole, Japan, plate #125, 5¼", from $85 to...................**100.00**
Old Mother Hubbard, Germany, plate #3, 6", from $350 to........**375.00**
Peter Rabbit, Germany, plate #4, 6¼", from $350 to...................**375.00**
Pinocchio & Figaro, Shafford, plate #242, 5", from $500 to **525.00**
Popeye, Japan, bsk, plate #244, 5", from $475 to **500.00**
Skippy, jtd arms, plate #245, 5⅝", from $100 to **125.00**
Snow White, plate #246, 6", from $225 to...................................**250.00**

Three Bears w/Bowls, Japan (KIM USUI), plate #248, 4", from $125 to...**150.00**
Tom, Tom the Piper's Son, Japan, plate #154, 5¾", from $95 to..**125.00**
Toonerville Trolley, Japan (Fountain Fox), plate #155, 5½" **550.00**
Traffic Cop, Germany, Don't Forget the Teeth, plate #243, 5", $350 to ...**375.00**

Toothpick Holders

Once common on every table, the toothpick holder was relegated to the china cabinet near the turn of the century. Fortunately, this contributed to their survival. As a result, many are available to collectors today. Because they are small and easily displayed, they are very popular collectibles. They come in a wide range of prices to fit every budget. Many have been reproduced and, unfortunately, are being offered for sale right along with the originals. These 'repros' should be priced in the $10.00 to $30.00 range. Unless you're sure of what you're buying, choose a reputable dealer. In addition to pattern glass, you'll find examples in china, bisque, art glass, and various metals. For further information we recommend *Glass Toothpick Holders, Identification & Values*, by Neila and Tom Bredehoft and Jo and Bob Sanford.

Toothpick holders in the listings that follow are glass unless noted otherwise. Values here are for originals. Our advisor for this category is Judy A. Knauer; she is listed in the Directory under Pennsylvania.

See also specific companies (such as Northwood) and types of glassware (such as Burmese, cranberry, etc.).

Acorn, pk & wht, w/decor, Challinor Taylor & Co, 2¼" **135.00**
Alligator, amber...**95.00**
Arched Fleur-de-Lis..**65.00**
Atlanta...**45.00**
Apollo..**30.00**
Basketweave, amber..**45.00**
Beaded Grape...**40.00**
Beaded Loop...**75.00**
Blazing Cornucopia...**35.00**
Brazilian...**40.00**
Bread & Scroll...**30.00**
Brilliant, amber stain, Riverside, 1895, 2½".............................**145.00**
Buckingham, 3-hdl...**40.00**
Button Panel..**35.00**
Colorado, gr...**40.00**
Column Block/Panel & Star, amber, O'Hara, 1888, 3⅛" **150.00**
Cord Drapery, from $40 to..**100.00**
Croesus, gr w/gold (+)..**95.00**
Croesus, purple w/gold (+)...**120.00**
Dalton..**30.00**
Delaware...**40.00**
Diamond Peg...**35.00**
Diamond Spearhead, vaseline opal...**65.00**
Douglass...**35.00**
Empress, gr..**95.00**
Famous (Panelled T'print) **30.00**
Fandango..**45.00**
Fashion (+) **30.00**
Feather..**75.00**
Florida, ruby & amber stain, Greensburg, 1893, 2¼"...................**325.00**
Galloway...**25.00**
Grated Diamond & Sunburst..**35.00**
Illinois...**40.00**
Inverted Eye..**45.00**
Invt T'print, cranberry, bulging base...**85.00**
Jewel w/Dewdrop..**65.00**
Jeweled Heart (+)..**65.00**
Kentucky...**65.00**

Kitten on a Pillow, amber, Richards & Hartley, 1880s, 3½" (+) ...**75.00**
Klondike, frosted w/amber stain...**225.00**
Ladder w/Diamonds...**35.00**
Leaf Bracket, chocolate..**110.00**
Leafy Scroll...**30.00**
Lion Head (Atlanta), frosted **65.00**
Mardi Gras..**40.00**
Maryland...**160.00**
Memphis...**60.00**
Mikado, bl...**75.00**
Millefiori, 2¾" **50.00**
Ohio Star...**80.00**
Oregon..**75.00**
Orinda...**35.00**
Oval Basket, amber, Adams & Co, 1892, 2¾x2¼".......................**35.00**
Panama...**35.00**
Panelled Sprig, wht opal..**85.00**
Panelled Thistle (+) **45.00**
Peerless...**45.00**
Pride/Beveled Star, amber, Model Flint Glass Co, 1899, 2½" **135.00**
Prize...**45.00**
Rexford..**55.00**
Rising Sun...**35.00**
Royal Lily (Fleur de Lis)...**30.00**
S-Repeat, bl (+)..**55.00**
Sandwich can w/stork in SP holder w/Greenaway figure, 2⅜", NM ..**600.00**
Sawtoothed Honeycomb...**40.00**
Scalloped Six-Point..**40.00**
Scalloped Swirl..**40.00**
Snow Flake..**35.00**
Star in Square, ruby stain, Duncan & Miller, 1909, 2¼".............**225.00**
Stippled Forget-Me-Not..**130.00**
Sunbeam, gr w/gold...**80.00**
Teasel..**40.00**

Texas, $32.50.

Tree (+)...**30.00**
Vogue/Scalloped Skirt, bl w/HP decor, Jefferson Glass, 1904, 2½"...**125.00**
Wreath & Shell, vaseline opal...**225.00**

Torquay Pottery

Torquay is a unique type of pottery made in the South Devon area of England as early as 1867. At the height of productivity, at least a dozen companies flourished there, producing simple folk pottery from the area's natural red clay. The ware was both wheel-turned and molded and decorated under the glaze with heavy slip resulting in low-relief nature subjects or simple scrollwork. Three of the best known of these potteries were Watcombe (1867 – 1962); Aller Vale (in operation from the mid-1800s, producing domestic ware and architectural products); and Longpark (1890 until 1957). Watcombe and Aller Vale merged in 1901 and operated until 1962 under the name of Royal Aller Vale and Watcombe Art Pottery.

A decline in the popularity of the early classical terra-cotta styles (urns, busts, figures, etc.) lead to the introduction of painted and glazed terra-cotta wares. During the late 1880s, white clay wares, both turned and molded, were decorated with colored glazes (Stapleton ware, grotesque molded figures, ornamental vases, large jardinieres, etc.). By the turn of the century, the market for art pottery was diminishing, so the potteries turned to wares decorated in colored slips (Barbotine, Persian, Scrolls, etc.).

Motto wares were introduced in the late nineteenth century by Aller Vale and taken up in the twentieth century by the other Torquay potteries. This eventually became the 'bread and butter' product of the local industry. This was perhaps the most famous type of ware potted in this area because of the verses, proverbs, and quotations that decorated it. This was achieved by the sgraffito technique — scratching the letters through the slip to expose the red clay underneath. The most popular patterns were Cottage, Black Cockerel, Multi-Cockerel, and a scroll-work design called Scandy. Other popular decorations were Kerswell Daisy, ships, kingfishers, applied bird decorations, Art Deco styles, Egyptian ware, and many others. Aller Vale ware may sometimes be found marked 'H.H. and Company,' a firm who assumed ownership from 1897 to 1901. 'Watcombe Torquay' was an impressed mark used from 1884 to 1927.

Our advisors for this category are Jerry and Gerry Kline; they are listed in the Directory under Ohio. If you're interested in joining a Torquay club, you'll find the address of The North American Torquay Society under Clubs, Newsletters, and Catalogs.

Art Pottery

Bottle, scent; Devon Lavender/lav sprig, Crown stopper, 4"..........85.00
Bowl, console; Kingfisher, Royal Torquay, 3x9½".........................175.00
Chamberstick, Persian, Aller Vale, 1891-1902, 10".......................90.00
Cup & saucer, bl scrolls, wht clay, Aller Vale, 2½".......................75.00
Flower vase/holder, True Devon Violets...50.00
Ginger jar, Apple Blossom, SP lid & hdl, Watcombe, 4"............125.00
Jardiniere, Daffodil, Longpark, 1910, 5½x7¼".............................160.00
Jardiniere, Scroll, Aller Vale, early 1900s, 3¾"...........................100.00
Jug, Scandy, Aller Vale, ca 1897-1900, 3½".................................60.00
Jug, stork among rushes on cobalt, Longpark, 1905-10, 10¼x4", pr..525.00
Match holder/striker, boxer dog's head, dog's head on collar, 1898...335.00
Urn, sailing ships, Sepia Ware, Watcombe, 1880s, 12½"............425.00
Vase, berries in leaves, impasto decor, hdl, Watcombe, 1878-80, 6¼"..185.00
Vase, fan; Kerswell Daisy variant, Aller Vale, 1887-1924, 4½".....55.00
Vase, landscape reserve on redware, urn form, Watcombe, pre-1901, 11"...130.00
Vase, Midnight Soloist, cat, hdls, Aller Vale, 1900, 6"...............350.00
Vase, windmill scene, Crown Dorset, motto, early 1900s, 4", pr.270.00

Devon Motto Ware

Cheese keeper, Say Little But Think Much, 3x6", $300.00.

Ashtray, Cottage, 'Don't Go Ashtray'...50.00
Biscuit barrel, Burns Cottage, Watcombe, 'Help Yersel...,' 5½" ..250.00
Bowl, Cottage, 'Never Say Die, Up Man & Try,' lg.......................49.50
Bowl, Scandy, 'Help Yersel...Blate' & 'There's Nain' i' Tae Kitchen,' lg...75.00
Bowl, Scandy, pleated rim, 'Sweeten for Yourself'.........................35.00
Bowl, vegetable; 'Some Ha Meat...Lord Be Thank It' 140.00
Candlestick, Cottage, heart shape, 2½x6".....................................55.00

Candlestick, Sailboat, Longpark, 'Last in Bed.../Hear All...,' pr....55.00
Chamberstick, Scandy, Aller Vale, 'Night Brings...,' 5".................90.00
Chamberstick, Ship, 'Guid Nicht an Joy Be Wi Ye,' 4¼x3½" 85.00
Chocolate pot, Cottage, Watcombe, 'Say Not Always...,' 9"........145.00
Creamer, Cottage, 'Help Yourself to Milk,' 3¾x3½" 65.00
Creamer, Scandy, 'Never Say Die, Up Man & Try'........................67.50
Cup, Cottage, 'Is It to Yer Like,' 4"...65.00
Cup, Cottage, 'Straithes/There's No Wealth But Life'..................52.50
Cup, Jaywick Ship, 'Soft Words Win Hard Hearts' 37.50
Cup & saucer, Cottage, 'Have Another Cup Full,' 3", 5⅜"..............65.00
Flowerpot, 'Be Bold Be Brave'...120.00
Hot water pot, Scandy, Aller Vale, 'Do What You Can...,' 8".....325.00
Jug, cider; Scandy, Devon, 'A Drop of Good Stuff...,' 6¾"..........100.00
Jug, puzzle; 'Within This Jug There Is Good Liqueur...'...............225.00
Jug, puzzle; Ship, 'From a Friend to a Friend' 135.00
Mug, Cherarvon Cottage, 'Leclycl Da (sic)'...................................100.00
Mug, Cottage (snow covered), Royal Watcombe, 'Up to the Lips...'..195.00
Mug, shaving; Cottage, 'The World Looks Brighter...,' 4⅞", EX.230.00
Pen holder, Scandy, 'Just a Scrape of Your Pen' 110.00
Pitcher, Cottage, 'Help Yourself, Don't Be Shy,' 5¼x4½" 95.00
Pitcher, Cottage, 'If You Can't Be Easy...,' 5¼x4"........................110.00
Pitcher, Cottage, 'May the Hinges of Friendship...'.......................75.00
Pitcher, Kerswell Daisy, Aller Vale, motto, ca 1890, 7x5½"........225.00
Plaque, Scandy, Watcombe, 'Work on Hope...Ruling,' 11x7½" ..185.00
Plate, Black Cockerel, Longpark, 'May You Find...,' 8"..................95.00
Plate, Cockerel, Longpark, 'Dauntee 'urry Daunt'ee...,' 7½" 140.00
Plate, Cottage, 'Us Be Always Plaised To Zee 'E'...........................65.00
Ring holder, Scandy, Watcombe, 'All Is Not Gold...,' 3½" 95.00
Shakers, Cottage, ftd egg shape, 'A Necessity.../Hot & Strong,' pr..55.00
Sugar bowl, Cottage, 'Fairest Gems Lie Deepest' 32.50
Sugar bowl, Scandy, 'Take a Little Sugar' 37.50
Sugar bowl, Scandy, 'Wa'al Us Be Main Glad To Ze-E'.................45.00
Teapot, Cockerel, Longpark, 'Take a Cup o' Kindness...,' 6½"....110.00
Teapot, Cottage, 'When You're Up to the Neck...,' 5" 160.00
Teapot, Thistle, Longton, 'Droon Yer Sorrows...,' 4½" 135.00
Tray, Blue, 'A Place for Everything...,' 8x10" 165.00
Tray, Cottage, 3 lobes, ea w/motto, brn border & hdl..................120.00
Tray, dresser; Scandy, Watcombe, 'If You Your Lips...,' 11x7½" ..215.00
Tray, Extended House, Watcombe, 'Do Not Stain To-Day's...,' 11¾"...300.00
Vase, Scandy, slipper form, Aller Vale, no motto, 3¾x4"..............75.00

Tortoise Shell Glass

By combining several shades of glass — brown, clear, and yellow — manufacturers of the nineteenth century were able to produce an art glass that closely resembled the shell of the tortoise. Some of this type of glassware was manufactured in Germany. In America it was made by several firms, the most prominent of which was the Boston and Sandwich Glass Works.

Paperweight, pear shape, gilt leaf, att Boston & Sandwich............95.00
Vase, str sides, 12½x4" sq...90.00

Toys

Toys can be classified into at least two categories: early collectible toys with an established history, and the newer toys. The antique toys are easier to evaluate. A great deal of research has been done on them, and much data is available. The newer toys are just beginning to be studied; relative information is only now being published, and the lack of production records makes it difficult to know how many may be available. Often warehouse finds of these newer toys can change the market. This has happened with battery-operated toys and to some extent with robots. Review past issues of this guide. You will see the changing trends for the newer toys. All toys become more important as collectibles when a fixed period of manufacture is known. When we know the numbers produced and documentation of the makers is established, the prices become more predictable.

The best way to learn about toys is to attend toy shows and auctions. This will give you the opportunity to compare prices and condition. The more collectors and dealers you meet, the more you will learn. There is no substitute for holding a toy in your hand and seeing for yourself what they are. If you are going to be a serious collector, buy all the books you can find. Read every article you see. Knowledge is vital to building a good collection. Study all books that are available. These are some of the most helpful: *Schroeder's Collectible Toys, Antique to Modern*, by Sharon and Bob Huxford; *Collector's Encyclopedia of Disneyana* by David Longest and Michael Stern; *Modern Toys, 1830 – 1980*, by Linda Baker; *Cartoon Toys & Collectibles* by David Longest; *Collectible Male Action Figures* by Paris and Susan Manos; *G-Men and FBI Toys and Collectibles* by Harry and Jody Whitworth; *Breyer Animal Collector's Guide* by Felicia Browell; *Collector's Guide to TV Toys and Memorabilia, 1960s & 1970s, Second Edition*, by Greg Davis and Bill Morgan; *Collectors Guide to Tootsietoys, Second Edition*, by David Richter; *Fisher-Price Toys* by Brad Cassity; *Matchbox Toys, 1974 – 1998, Second Edition, Collector's Guide to Diecast Toys and Scale Models*, and *Toy Car Collector's Guide*, all by Dana Johnson; and *Collector's Guide to Battery Toys, Second Edition*, by Don Hultzman. All are published by Collector Books. Other informative books are *Collecting Toys, Collecting Toy Soldiers*, and *Collecting Toy Trains, An Identification & Value Guide #3*, by Richard O'Brien; and *Toys of the Sixties, A Pictorial Guide*, by Bill Bruegman. In the listings that follow, toys are listed by manufacturer's name if possible, otherwise by type. Measurements are given when appropriate and available; if only one dimension is noted, it is the greater one — height if the toy is vertical, length if it is horizontal. See also Children's Things; Personalities. For toy stoves, see Stoves.

Key:
b/o — battery operated
cl — celluloid
jtd — jointed
NP — nickel plated
w/up — wind-up

AC Gilbert, Charlie Chaplin String Rider, counterweight, tin, 8", EX...300.00
AC Gilbert, Hobo on Unicycle, string rider, tin, 8", EX 600.00
Alps, Happy Life, w/up, tin/cl, 9½", NMIB..................................475.00
Alps, Packard Sedan, friction, tin, blk/chrome, 1953, 16", EXIB..7,200.00
Alps, Reading Bunny, w/up, tin/plush/cloth outfit, 7", MIB........175.00
Alps, Roaring Lion, w/up, tin/plush, 7", MIB................................100.00
Alps, Traveling Boy, w/up, tin/cl, 4½", NMIB 175.00
Althof Bergmann, Side-Wheeler Atlantic, pnt tin, NM..........4,500.00
Arcade, John Deere Model A Tractor (w/driver), CI, 7½", MIB...........2,100.00
Arcade, Pontiac Ladder Truck (2 fireman), CI/rubber tires, 8", NM.....1,650.00
Arcade, White Moving Van (Union Supply), CI, rare, 13½", NMIB.2,800.00
Arnold, Mac 700 Motorcycle, w/up, tin, 8", NM 1,000.00
Asahi, Northwest Airlines DC-7, b/o, litho tin, 19" W, EX (EX box)...650.00
ASC, Batmobile, friction, litho tin, rare, 11", NM (EX box) ..1,200.00
ASC, USAF Sabre Jet Fighter, friction, litho tin, 9" L, NM (EX box) ...250.00
Bandai, Jaguar XKE, friction, tin, metallic bl, wht walls, 8", NM ..150.00
Bandai, Lincoln Continental Convertible, 1958, friction, 11½", NMIB...525.00
Bandai, Messerschmitt Car, friction, tin, rubber tires, 8", NMIB...600.00
Bandai, Porsche (w/driver), b/o, tin/chrome, opening doors, 10", NMIB...150.00
Bing, Limousine, w/up, tin, opening doors, 8", VG 1,250.00
Bing, Yellow Taxi (driver), w/up, tin, disc wheels, 8½", EX.....1,500.00
Bliss, B&M Railroad, 4-pc train, litho paper on wood, 23", VG...1,700.00
Bliss, Cinderella Coach, litho paper on wood, 26", EX 1,650.00
Bliss, Jackson Park Horse-Drawn Trolley, litho paper on wood, 27", EX..5,250.00
Borgfeldt, Donald Duck, w/up, cl, 1936, 5", NM (EX box) 1,700.00

Borgfeldt, Mickey Mouse Whirligig, w/up, cl, prewar, 9", NMIB.............3,000.00
Bremer, Whirlwind Racer #8, gas-powered, ca 1940, 18", EX..2,300.00
Breyer, Fighting Stallion, glossy palomino, 1961-67 ....100.00
Breyer, Indian Pony, buckskin, 1970-72 ....250.00
Breyer, Morgan, woodgrain, 1963-85.....................................750.00
Breyer, Silky Sullivan, flea-bit gray, 1991-92..........................25.00
Breyer, Western Horse, glossy chestnut pinto, 1956-67 ....50.00
Buddy L, Transport Plane, pressed steel, 4-prop, 27" W, VG.......275.00
Carpenter, Tally Ho Wagon (figures/4 horses), EX, 28", VG ...7,100.00
Champion, Wrecker, CI w/NP crank & bbl, 8", NMIB 1,500.00
Chein, Clown w/punching bag, 1930s, 8½", EX.........................600.00
Chein, Disneyland Ferris Wheel, 17", EX.................................500.00
Chein, Popeye Shadow Boxer, rare, 7", NM.............................1,600.00
Chein, Santa Walker, 6", EX...550.00
Chein, US Army Soldier, 5", MOC..150.00
Chein, Yellow Taxi Main 7570, 6", NMIB.................................400.00
CK, Aeroplane, w/up, aluminized tin w/cl prop, 8" W, NMIB.............650.00
CK, Bestmaid Marionette Theatre, w/up, tin/cl, 11", NMIB................850.00
Corgi, #391, James Bond 007 Ford Mustang 260.00
Corgi, #416, Radio Rescue Rover, bl 125.00
Corgi, #416, Radio Rescue Rover, yel......................................425.00
Corgi, #48, Scammell Transport Set.......................................900.00
Corgi, #651, Japan Air Line Concorde......................................400.00
Corgi, #853, Magic Roundabout Playground 1,500.00
Courtland, Easter Greetings Truck, w/up, litho tin, 8½", VG.....225.00
Cox, AA Fuel Dragster, gas-powered, bl/red, 1968-70, M 125.00
Cox, Sandblaster, gas-powered, brn/tan, 1968-72, M.................65.00
Daiya, New Car w/Boat, friction, pnt tin, NMIB.......................300.00
Dakin, Elmer Fudd (hunter), Warner Bros, 1980, EX.................125.00
Dakin, Hokey Wolf, Hanna-Barbera, 1971, MIP 100.00
Dakin, Huckleberry Hound, Hanna-Barbera, 1970, EX+ 60.00
Dakin, Snagglepuss, 1971, EX..100.00
Dakin, Tasmanian Devil, Warner Bros, 1978, rare, NM..............300.00
Dakin, Yogi Bear, Hanna-Barbera, 1970, EX...........................60.00
Dent, Battleship New York, CI, complete, 20½", EX..............3,800.00
Dent, Chrysler Airflow Coupe, CI/wht rubber tires, 6½", VG ...2,200.00
Dinky, #106, Prisoner Mini Moke..260.00
Dinky, #129, MG Midget...400.00
Dinky, #149, Sports Car Gift Set...1,800.00
Dinky, #238, Jaguar Type-D Racer..140.00
Dinky, #264, RCMP Patrol Car, Cadillac................................175.00
Dinky, #283, BOAC Coach..130.00
Dinky, #364, NASA Space Shuttle, w/booster.........................100.00
Dinky, #514, Guy Van, Lyons...2,000.00
Dinky, #727, US Air Force F-4 Phantom II 300.00
Distler, Motorcycle w/Sidecar (driver/child), w/up, tin, 7½", EX.........2,500.00
Distler, Touring Cycle w/Gondola Sidecar (driver/boy), w/up, 6", EX.5,500.00
Fallows, Nero Locomotive, w/up, tin w/CI spoke wheels, 10", VG 725.00
Fischer, Clown on 3-Wheeled Cycle, w/up, litho tin, 8", NM.2,500.00
Fisher-Price, #103, Barky Puppy, 1931-33 ....700.00
Fisher-Price, #141, Snap-Quack, 1947-49 ....225.00
Fisher-Price, #170, Am Airlines Flagship w/Tail Wing, 1941-42 ..1,000.00
Fisher-Price, #306, Bizzy Bunny Cart, 1957-59.........................40.00
Fisher-Price, #355, Go 'N Back Bruno, 1931 ....800.00
Fisher-Price, #420, Sunny Fish, 1955.....................................225.00
Fisher-Price, #520, Bunny Bell Cart, 1941, EX 225.00
Fisher-Price, #634, Drummer Boy, 1967-69, EX.........................50.00
Gilbert, Erector Set #8, complete, EX (EX wooden box) 850.00
Gilbert, Mysto Magic Exhibition Set, 1920s, EX (EX box).........450.00
Gunthermann, Banjo Player (Black man), w/up, pnt tin, 8", G...1,200.00
Gunthermann, Vis-A-Vis (driver), w/up, tin w/rubber tires, 11", EX.9,300.00
Haji, Ford Convertible, 1956, friction, tin/chrome, rare, 12", NM 1,875.00
Hartland Plastics, Bill Longley, NM 600.00
Hartland Plastics, Bret Maverick, gray horse, rare, NM.............600.00

Hartland Plastics, Cactus Pete, NM 150.00
Hartland Plastics, Davy Crockett, NM................................500.00
Hartland Plastics, Josh Randle, NM................................650.00
Hartland Plastics, Rebel, NMIB 1,200.00
Hoge, Cycle-Car Traffic Delivery, w/up, litho tin, 10", EX 2,700.00
Hubley, Popeye on Motorcycle, CI, 8⅜", EX................................3,500.00
Hubley, Royal Circus Calliope (driver/2 horses), CI, 9", EX 500.00
Hubley, Say It With Flowers Delivery Cycle (driver), CI, 9½", VG ...28,600.00
Ichiko, Buick, 1960, friction, pnt tin, chrome detail, 6½", M.....450.00
Ichiko, Cadillac Sedan, 1964, friction, tin, red/chrome, 20", EXIB..750.00
Ichiko, Ford, 1957, friction, pnt tin, chrome trim, 10", EXIB 500.00
Ives, Cuzner Trotter, w/up, tin, 11½", EX 2,500.00
Ives, Hose Reel Wagon (driver/horse), CI, 24", VG................3,300.00
Ives, Military Ten-Pins, litho paper on wood, complete, EXIB...3,500.00
Ives, Preacher at the Pulpit, w/up, wood/compo, 10", EX 3,000.00
Ives, Woman Churning Butter, w/up, wood/tin, 9", NM..........4,500.00

Japan, Dreamboat Hot Rod Racery, tin, battery-operated, 7", $250.00. (Photo courtesy Dunbar's Gallery)

Kellerman, Military Motorcycle, w/up, litho tin, 6", NM (EX box)...1,100.00
Keystone, Aerial Ladder Truck, 1920s, prof rstr, 32"....................950.00
Keystone, Coast to Coast Bus, rstr, 30" 27,500.00
Keystone, Fire Ladder Truck (Chemical Pump Engine), 1920s, 29", EX...4,600.00
Keystone, Pullman Railroad Car (rider), 24", EX 750.00
Keystone, Rapid-Fire Tri-Motor Plane, pressed steel, 24" W, EX ..1,700.00
Kilgore, Chris-Craft Boat, CI, 11", EX................................4,000.00
Kilgore, Stutz Roadster, CI/NP trim, scarce, 10", EX................2,100.00
Kingsbury, Grocery Truck, pnt tin w/rubber tires, 8", EX 400.00
Kingsbury, Sunbeam Racer, w/up, 18", EX................................2,700.00
Lehmann, Ajax Acrobat, litho tin, 9", NM................................1,800.00
Lehmann, Autohutte & Galop Racer #1, litho tin, NM..........1,500.00
Lehmann, Lila Hansom Cab, litho tin, 5½", G................................1,000.00
Lehmann, Ostrich Cart (African), 6", EX................................600.00
Lehmann, Paddy & the Pig, litho tin, 5½", NM 2,400.00
Lindstrom, Dancing Dutch Boy, w/up, litho tin, EX (EX box)....275.00
Lindstrom, Speedboat (driver/passenger), w/up, litho tin, 18", VG..200.00
Lindstrom, Sweeping Mammy, w/up, litho tin, 8", EX (EX box).275.00
Linemar, Am Airlines Electra, litho tin, 19½" W, NM 200.00
Linemar, Clown Juggler, w/up, 8½", NM, from $450 to 550.00
Linemar, Disney Character Carousel, w/up, litho tin, 1960s, NM 1,800.00
Linemar, Donald Duck in Rocking Chair, w/up, tin/cl, EXIB................1,100.00
Linemar, Goofy Unicyclist, w/up, litho tin, 9", NMIB, from $1,500 to.1,800.00
Linemar, Ludwig Von Drake, w/up, litho tin, 1950s, NM............500.00
Linemar, Mickey on Tricycle, w/up, litho tin, 5", EX (EX box) 1,200.00
Linemar, Popeye Turnover Tank, w/up, litho tin, 4", NM (EX box)...850.00
Linemar, Superman Turnover Tank, w/up, litho tin, 4", NM 400.00
Lionel, Donald Duck & Pluto Handcar, w/up, tin/compo, 10", VG....700.00
Lionel, Santa Handcar, Mickey Mouse in bag, w/up, compo, 9", G 850.00
Marklin, Steamboat Geo Washington, pressed steel, steam, 9½", EX .1,300.00
Martin, Barrel Man, w/up, pnt tin/cloth clothes, 7", VG 1,300.00
Marusan, Cadillac, 1953, friction, pnt tin, chrome trim, 12½", NM ..640.00
Marusan, Yellow Cab, friction, yel tin/chrome detail, 10", EX....500.00
Marx, Aircraft Carrier, b/o, litho tin, 20", EXIB 450.00
Marx, Bedrock Express Train, w/up, litho tin, 1962, 12, NMIB..250.00
Marx, Blondie's Jalopy, w/up, litho tin, 1935, scarce, 16½", NM..2,200.00
Marx, Bristol Jet 188, b/o, tin/plastic, 9" W, EX 185.00

Marx, Coast Defense, w/up, litho tin, 1924, 9" dia base, MIB.....100.00
Marx, Flintstone Tricycle w/Dino, w/up, tin/cl, 1962, 4", NMIB..............800.00
Marx, Frankenstein, remote control, tin, 13", M (EX box)......3,600.00
Marx, Grocery Truck (Motor Market), pressed steel, 1940s, 14", MIB..350.00
Marx, Hey Hey Chicken Snatcher, w/up, litho tin, 1927, 8½", EX....1,200.00
Marx, Lumar Wrecker Truck, pressed steel, 16", EX 200.00
Marx, Planet Patrol Space Tank, w/up, litho tin, 10", EXIB 350.00
Marx, Whistling Spooky Kooky Tree (Summer), b/o, 14", NMIB...1,300.00
Matchbox, #Y-2-B, 1911 Renault 2-Seater, 1963, SP, MIP............60.00
Matchbox, #18-F, Field Car, Super Fast, wht, 1970, MIP 400.00
Matchbox, #31-D, Lincoln Continental, Super Fast, mint gr, 1969, MIP..2,000.00
Matchbox, #46-A, Morris Minor 1000, bl/gray plastic wheels, 1958, MIP.....100.00
Matchbox, #50-B, John Deere Tractor, gray plastic wheels, 1964, MIP...30.00
Matchbox, #61-C, Blue Shark, scorpion label, 1971, MIP 25.00
Matchbox, #75-B, Ferrari Berlinetta, red/chrome hubs, 1965, MIP......550.00
Mattel, Music Box Carousel, w/up, litho tin/plastic, 1953, 9", NMIB..150.00
Mattel Hot Wheels, Boss Hoss, 1971, red line, brn, rare, MOC .550.00
Mattel Hot Wheels, Classic '31 Ford Woody, 1969, red line, yel, NM+..45.00
Mattel Hot Wheels, Cockney Cab, 1971, red line, bl, NM+ 100.00
Mattel Hot Wheels, Custom Charger, 1969, red line, yel, M......175.00
Mattel Hot Wheels, Mongoose Funny Car, 1970, red line, red, NM+..100.00
Mattel Hot Wheels, Prowler, 1976, red line, chrome, M................60.00
McLoughlin, Brownie 9 Pins, litho paper on wood, complete, EXIB........2,000.00
Mettoy, Clown on Motorcycle, w/up, litho tin, 7½", EX, from $700 to ...1,000.00
Minic, Bently Touring Car, clockwork, pnt tin, chrome trim, 5", NMIB 375.00
Minic, Petrol Tank Lorry, w/up, emb enameled tin, 5½", NMIB...300.00
MT, Shingun, w/up, cl, 10", NM (EX box)................................1,300.00
Nifty, Jiggs Jazz Car, w/up, litho tin, 1924, 6", VG 1,200.00
Nifty, Mickey Mouse Jazz Drummer, w/up, litho tin, M (EX box)..6,500.00
Ohio Art, Giant Ride Ferris Wheel, litho tin, 17", EX 275.00
Reed, Clipper Ship, paper on wood, 3 paper sails, 1877, 36", EX..1,600.00
Renwal, Busy Mechanic Construction Kit #375-198, complete, EXIB...300.00
Renwal, Panama Canal Playset, #273, complete, NM (EX box).335.00
Ri N Co, Topsy Turvy Tom Car, w/up, litho tin, 10", NMIB ...2,800.00
Richter, American House & Country #210, VG 700.00
SAN, Nautilus SSN 571 Submarine, litho tin, b/o, NM (EX box)..250.00
SAN, Tugboat, litho tin, b/o, puffs smoke, 12½", EXIB 200.00
Sanyo, Champion Racer (w/driver), friction, litho tin, 18", NM..1,200.00
Schuco, Acrobat Bear, w/up, mohair/glass eyes, 5", EX (VG box) ...500.00
Smith-Miller, Bell Telephone System Truck, pressed steel, 19", NM .2,000.00
Smith-Miller, MIC Tractor-Trailer, 28", EX, from $700 to........1,100.00
Smith-Miller, Silver Streak, #509E, Fruehauf decal, NMIB......1,200.00
Sonsco, Circus Merry-Go-Round, w/up, cl, 9", MIB....................750.00
Steelcraft, Lockheed Sirius, 22" W, NM 2,500.00
Steelcraft, US Mail Plane, pressed steel, 22" L, VG 650.00
Stevens & Brown, Boy on Velocipede, w/up, tin/compo/cloth , 11", NM..2,300.00
Strauss, Big Show Circus Wagon, w/lion & tamer & driver, 9", VG ..850.00
Strauss, Bus Deluxe, w/orig driver, 13", VG 750.00
Strauss, Chicago Zeppelin, clockwork, litho tin, 10" L, EX.........250.00
Strauss, Jitney Bus, w/driver, 9", EX 1,200.00
Structo, Bearcat Roadster, pressed steel, 15" L, VG....................800.00
Structo, Fire Truck, pressed steel, ladders/water bbl/hose, 18", EX..750.00
Structo, Freight Hauler #935, w/trailer, pressed steel, EXIB........140.00
Structo, Truck Set No 725, complete, EXIB 300.00
Tipp, Military Motorcycle w/Sidecar, w/up, litho tin, 8½", EX....3,000.00
TN, Dodge Sedan, tin, friction, red/wht, chrome detail, 1959, 9", EX....325.00
TN, Ford Trimotor Plane, friction, litho tin, 14½" W, NM (EX box) 475.00
Tonka, Airport Service Set, complete, EXIB 650.00
Tonka, Builders Supply Fleet, #0875-5, 1955, NM (VG box)..2,000.00
Tonka, Stake Truck w/Tandem Platform, #30, 1959, M 375.00
Tonka, Suburban Pumper, #46, MIB................................425.00
Tonka, Thunderbird Express Semi, #37, 1960, MIB 600.00
Tootsietoy, American Railway Express, #4670, 1929-32, 4", EX .100.00
Tootsietoy, Bild-A-Truck Set, #7600, complete, VG (VG box)..150.00

Tootsietoy, Lincoln Zephyr, #6015, w/up, 4", EX+ **450.00**
Tootsietoy, Mercedes Benz 300SL, #995, 1956-58, gr (rare), 7", EX+ ..**275.00**
Tootsietoy, Motors Set, #7200, complete, MIB **875.00**
Toy Tinkers, Giant Tinker, 1926, complete, EXIB **225.00**
TYO, PD Auto Cycle (w/driver), friction, 7", NM (EX box) **450.00**
Unique Art, Bombo Monkey, w/up, litho tin, 10", EX (VG box) **200.00**
Unique Art, Daredevil Motor Cop, w/up, 9½", NM (EX box) **1,300.00**
Unique Art, Li'l Abner & His Dogpatch Band, litho tin, 9", NMIB ..**1,000.00**
Unique Art, Sky Ranger, w/up, litho tin, 10", VG **300.00**
Wolverine, Action Ski Jumper, w/up, litho tin, 26" ramp, MIB..**350.00**
Wolverine, Dandy Andy Rooster, w/up, tin, 10", NMIB **600.00**
Wolverine, Jackie Gleason Bus, litho tin, 1955, 13", EX (EX box)...**1,000.00**
Wyandotte, Acrobatic Monkeys, w/up, litho tin, 10", EX **400.00**
Wyandotte, Dump Truck, pressed steel, wooden wheels, decal, 15", EX..**1,000.00**
Wyandotte, Ride 'Em Cowboy, w/up, litho tin, NMIB, from $275 to..........**350.00**
Y, Corvette Convertible, 1960, friction, pnt tin, chrome trim, 8", NM..**150.00**
Yonezawa, Atom Racer #27, friction, litho tin, 16", rare, NM.**1,400.00**
Yonezawa, Ford Crown Victoria, friction, tin/chrome, 1956, 12", MIB...**1,500.00**

Farm Toys

Allis Chalmers WD45 Precision #3, Ertl, #2252, 1/16th scale, MIB...**110.00**
Case IH C-90, Ertl, #4601, 1998 Farm Show, 1/16th scale, MIB ..**60.00**
Case IH 1660 Combine, Ertl, #655, 1/64th scale, MIB.................**12.00**
Case 400 Tractor, Yoder, #7, 1/16th scale, M, from $75 to **125.00**
Case 930 Prescision #12, Ertl, #4284, 1/16th scale, MIB.............**110.00**
Claas Jaguar 695 Combine, Siku, M **30.00**
Cockshutt Tractor, Advanced Prod USA, operational, 8½", EXIB **525.00**
Duetz-Fahr Top Liner Combine Harvester, Siku, #4051, 1/32 scale, M ..**50.00**
Farm Set No 90, Hubley Kiddie Toys, 4-pc, MIB.......................**500.00**
Farmall F-20 Precision Tractor, Ertl, #638, 1/16th scale, MIB.....**100.00**
Farmall H Tractor, Ertl, #4441, 1/16th scale, MIB **25.00**
John Deere CTS II Combine, Ertl, 1/64th scale, #5172, MIB.....**100.00**
John Deere Grain Cart, Ertl, #5565, 1/64th scale, MIB...................**5.00**
John Deere Hay Rake, Ertl, #5751, 1/64th scale, MIB.................**350.00**
John Deere Skid Steer Loader, Ertl, #569, 1/16th scale, MIB........**18.50**
John Deere 12-A Combine, Ertl, #5601, 1/16th scale, MIB..........**45.00**
Massey-Ferguson Farm Set, Mercury, 1960, M **55.00**
Massey-Ferguson Tractor w/Hay Trailer, Siku, M **10.00**
McCormick-Deering #200 Spreader, Ertl, #4201, 1/16th scale, MIB..**110.00**
Michigan 380 Tractor Plow, Mercury, 1958, M **55.00**
New Holland TX-34 Combine Harvester w/Corn Head, Joal, #247, 1/42nd, M....**25.00**
New Holland Wing Disk, Ertl, #3049, 1/64th scale, MIB..........**400.00**
Oliver 55 Tractor, Yoder, #5, 1/16th scale, M, from $250 to **300.00**

Guns: Cast-Iron Cap Guns (Caution: Some reproductions exist.)

In years past, virtually every child played with toy guns, and the survival rate of these toys is minimal, at best. The interest in these charming toy guns has recently increased considerably, especially those with western character examples, as collectors discover their scarcity, quality, and value. Toy gun collectibles encompass the early and the very ornate figural toy guns and bombs through the more realistic ones with recognizable character names, gleaming finishes, faux jewels, dummy bullets, engraving, and colorful grips. This section will cover some of the most popular cast-iron and diecast toy guns from the past one hundred years. Recent market trends have witnessed a decline of interest in the earlier (1900 – 40) single-shot cast-iron pistols. The higher collector interest is for known western characters and cap pistols from the 1960 – 65 era. Generic toy guns such as, Deputy, Pony Boy, Marshal, Ranger, Sheriff, Pirate, Cowboy, Dick, Western, Army, etc., generate only minimal collector interest.

In the listings below (*) designates a classic example.

American, cylinder revolves, Kilgore, 1940, 9⅜", EX (*) **450.00**

Army 45 Auto, Hubley, 1945, 6½", M (*)................................**125.00**
Atta Boy, single shot, Hubley, 1935, 4", G-.............................**35.00**
Bango, eng, jewels, Stevens, 1940, 7½", VG............................**70.00**
Big Bill, single shot, Kilgore, 1935, 4⅞", M..............................**35.00**
Big Horn, cylinder revolves, Kilgore, 1940, 8⅝", M (*)...............**500.00**
Big Scout, single shot, Stevens, 1930, 9⅜", G-........................**100.00**
Billy the Kid, single shot, Stevens, 1940s, 6¾", G-...................**100.00**
Border Patrol, automatic, Kilgore, 1935, 4½", VG **50.00**
Buc-A-Roo, single shot, Kilgore, 1940, 7¾", M........................**85.00**
Buffalo Bill, single shot, Stevens, 1890, rare, 11¾", G-...............**200.00**
Bull's Eye, eng, Kenton, 1940, 6½", M...................................**200.00**
Bulldog, single shot, Hubley, 1935, 6", G................................**35.00**
Bunker Hill, single shot, National, 1925, 5¼", M........................**90.00**
Captain, automatic, Kilgore, 1940, 4¼", VG **85.00**
Case 400 Tractor, Yoder, 1/16 scale, #15, M, from $150 to..........**175.00**
Case 580 E Tractor Loader, Conrad, 1/35 scale, M **80.00**
Champ, automatic, star medallion, Hubley, 1940, 5", EX.............**70.00**
Chief, single shot, Dent, 1935, 7½", VG.................................**45.00**
Claas Automatic Hay Loader, Siku, M....................................**30.00**
Colt, single shot, Stevens, 1900, 5½", EX................................**45.00**
Cowboy, Hubley, 1940, 8", VG...**100.00**
Cowboy King, Stevens, 1940, 9", M (*)..................................**250.00**
Deutz Caterpillar Tractor, Schuco, 2", M................................**60.00**
Deutz-Fahr DX6.31 Turbo Forestry Tractor, Siku, M.................**20.00**
Dick, automatic, Hubley, 1930, 4⅛", VG.................................**35.00**
Doughboy, automatic, Kilgore, 1920, 4⅞", VG........................**100.00**
Eagle, single shot, Hubley, 1935, 8½", VG..............................**150.00**
Federal, automatic, clip, Kilgore, 1940, 4⅞", M.......................**145.00**
Ford TW-35 Tractor, Siku, M...**20.00**
G-Man, automatic, Kilgore, 1935, rare, 6", M (*).......................**165.00**
Gene Autry, eng, Kenton, 1951, rare, 6½", VG.........................**450.00**
Gene Autry, repeater, nickel, Kenton, 1940, 8⅜", EX (*) **250.00**
Guard, bl finish, Kilgore, 1935, 6¼", EX.................................**100.00**
Invincible, Kilgore, 1935, 5¼", G-...**45.00**
Lasso 'Em Bill, cylinder revolves, Kilgore, 1930, 9", EX **225.00**
Lawmaker, nickel, Kenton, 1940, rare, 8⅜", M (*) **250.00**
Lone Eagle, cylinder revolves, Kilgore, 1930, 5¼", EX................**130.00**
Lone Ranger, nickel, Kilgore, 1940, rare, 8¼", M (*) **325.00**
Long Boy, single shot, Kilgore, 1920, 11⅛", VG........................**115.00**
Long Tom, cylinder revolves, Kilgore, 1940, 10⅜", M (*) **650.00**
Massey-Ferguson 50B Loader, Conrad, 1/35 scale, M...............**75.00**
Mohican, single shot, Dent, 1930, 6¼", EX.............................**60.00**
National Automatic, National, 1915, 3¾", G-............................**25.00**
Officer's Pistol, automatic, Kilgore, 1940, rare, 6", M (*).............**350.00**
Patrol, Hubley, 1935-40, 6", M **75.00**
Pawnee Bill, Stevens, 1940, 7⅝", VG (*)................................**200.00**
Peacemaker, gold, Stevens, 1940, 8½", M...............................**150.00**
Pirate, dbl bbl, Hubley, 1940, 8⅜", M (*)................................**125.00**
Police Chief, plastic grip, Kenton, 1940, 4⅝", EX.....................**100.00**
Presto, automatic, Kilgore, 1940, 5⅛", VG **65.00**
Rodeo, single shot, Hubley, 1940, 7", EX **45.00**
Roy Rogers, Kilgore, 1940, rare, 10¼", EX (*) **1,750.00**
Scout, single shot, Stevens, 1890, 7", VG................................**55.00**
Six Shooter, cylinder revolves, Kilgore, 1940, 6½", VG................**75.00**
Spitfire, automatic, Kilgore, 1940, 4⅝", EX **65.00**
Texan, CI/nickel, cylinder revolves, Hubley, 1940, 9¼", M (*)..**175.00**
Texan Jr, Hubley, 1940, 8⅛", VG (*)......................................**100.00**
Tractor & Harvester, Charbens, M **75.00**
Trooper, Safety, repeater, Kilgore, 1925, 10¼", M....................**120.00**
Two Time, rubber band, Kenton, 1929, 9¼", VG......................**150.00**
Warrior, nickel, repeater, Kilgore, 1920s, 9", EX.......................**175.00**
Wild West, single shot, Kenton, 1920s, rare, 11½", M.................**225.00**
101 Ranch, single shot, Hubley, 1930, 11½", VG.......................**200.00**
2 in 1, rubber band, Stevens, 1930, 9¼", VG............................**125.00**

Guns: Diecast and Miscellaneous Toy Guns

Alan Ladd, Geo Schmidt, rare, 10¼", EX...................................300.00
Annie Oakley, gold, Leslie-Henry, very rare, 9"...........................650.00
Army 45 Automatic, compo, Hubley, 1940, nonworking..............35.00
Atomic Disintegrator, space gun, Hubley, 8", VG.......................400.00
Bonanza, cylinder revolves, Leslie-Henry 44, 10½", M..............150.00
Bronco, cylinder revolves, Kilgore, 9¼", VG................................75.00
Buck'n Bronc, Geo Schmidt, 10½", EX.......................................100.00
Buckle Gun, derringer, Mattel, 3", VG..65.00
Burke's Law Snub Nose, blk, Lone Star, 5", M............................85.00
Champion, Leslie-Henry, 9", VG..125.00
Colt, Hubley Snub Nose Detective, mini, M..................................30.00
Colt 44 1860, cylinder revolves, ivory grips, Hubley, 14", M......200.00
Colt 45, cylinder revolves, bullets, Hubley, 14", VG..................115.00
Cowboy, cylinder revolves, Hubley, 12", M................................145.00
Cowboy, gold, cylinder revolves, Hubley, rare, 12", EX..............200.00
Cowhand 250, Nichols, 8½", VG..70.00
Coyote, Hubley, 8¼", M..45.00
Dale Evans, jewels, Geo Schmidt, rare, 10½", VG.....................350.00
Davy Crockett, Flintlock Buffalo Rifle, Hubley, 25", EX............175.00
Deputy-BB, copper grips, Schmidt, sm, 8½", EX..........................75.00
Dick Tracy, blk w/decal, steel clicker, Marx, EX..........................65.00
Dick Tracy Siren Pistol, red finish, Marx, VG..............................70.00
Dick Tracy Squad Shotgun, cap & water, pump, Mattel...........125.00
Eagle, nickel, cylinder revolves, Kilgore, 8", M..........................100.00
Fanner 'Shootin' Shell,' bullets, Mattel, 9", M...........................150.00
Fanner 45 'Shootin' Shell,' bullets, Mattel, 9", M.....................150.00
Fanner 50, nickel, cylinder revolves, Mattel, 10⅝", EX.............165.00
Flip Rifleman Ring Rifle, Hubley, 32", VG..................................250.00
G-Boy, pressed steel, Acme Novelty Co, 7", M.............................65.00
G-Man, Sparking Wind-Up, steel pistol, Marx, 5", VG................55.00
G-Man, Sparkling Machine Gun, tin, Marx, 26", VG..................225.00
G-Man, tin clicker pistol w/jewel, Marx, 1935, M........................55.00
Gene Autry, nickel, Leslie-Henry, 9", M....................................175.00
Gray Ghost, nickel, silver grips, Lone Star, rare, 9", EX............550.00
Grizzly, gold, cylinder revolves, Kilgore, 10¼", M....................250.00
Hawk, automatic, amber grips, Hubley, 5", VG.............................35.00
Hawkeye, automatic, Kilgore, 4¼", M...45.00
Hopalong Cassidy, cameo grips, Geo Schmidt, 9", EX..............300.00
Hopalong Cassidy, gold, Wyandotte, 9", M................................450.00
Hopalong Cassidy, nickel, Wyandotte, 9", VG...........................300.00
Indian Scout Rifle, bullets, Mattel, 30", M................................225.00
Lone Ranger, antique bronze, Actoy, 10", VG............................175.00
Lone Ranger, tin clicker w/jewel, Marx, 8", M.............................65.00
Maire's Leg, Winchester lever-pistol, Marx, 14", EX.................135.00
Marshal, cylinder revolves, bullets, Halco, 10½", M.................125.00
Mattel Snub-Nosed Detective, chrome, shootin' shell, EX...........90.00
Maverick, Leslie-Henry, 10½", VG...120.00
Maverick 45, cylinder revolves, Halco, 11", M..........................300.00
Me & My Buddy, tin clicker, Wyandotte, 1935-40, VG.............100.00
Model 61, cylinder revolves, steel-bl finish, Nichols, rare, M.....350.00
Mountie, automatic, blk finish, Kilgore, 6", M.............................45.00
Mustang 500, nickel, Nichols, 12¼", EX....................................175.00
Pal, nickel, single shot, Kilgore, 1945-60, sm, M...........................5.00
Paladin, nickel, repeater, Leslie-Henry, rare, 9", EX.................285.00
Pet, nickel, Hubley, 1945-60, M..5.00
Pioneer, nickel, blk grips, Hubley, 10¼", M..............................100.00
Pirate, over-under bbls, Hubley, 1960, VG...................................45.00
Pony Boy, nickel, Esquire-Actoy, 10", EX...................................50.00
Rebel Scattergun, dbl bbl, Marx, rare, 21", M...........................900.00
Red Ranger, Wyandotte, 7¾", VG...45.00
Remington 36, cylinder revolves, bullets, Hubley, 8¼", EX.........85.00
Ric-O-Shay, cylinder revolves, bullets, Hubley, 12¼", M..........100.00

Roy Rogers, copper grips, Geo Schmidt, 10¼", EX....................225.00
Roy Rogers, gold, Leslie-Henry, 9", EX......................................275.00
Roy Rogers, nickel, diecast, Kilgore, 8", M................................185.00
Scout Rifle, nickel, lever action, Hubley, 1960, EX....................125.00
Sharps Carbine, Civil War Model, Marx, 1960, rare, EX...........150.00
Stallion 32, Nichols, 8", VG...35.00
Stallion 38, cylinder revolves, bullets, Nichols, 9½", EX...........115.00
Stallion 45 Mk II, gold, cylinder revolves, Nichols, rare, 12", EX...1,500.00
Star, nickel, single shot, Hubley, 7", MIB....................................20.00
Sure Shot, nickel, Hubley, 8", EX...30.00
Tex, single shot, Hubley, sm, M...5.00
Texan Jr, diecast, break action, Hubley, 9", VG...........................65.00
Texan Jr, diecast, side opener, Hubley, 9½", M............................65.00
Thundergun, nickel, eng, Marx, 12½", M...................................170.00
Tightrope Snub Nose, nickel, Lone Star, EX.................................85.00
Trooper, nickel, snub nose, Hubley, 1950-60, EX.........................25.00
US Marshal, antique bronze/cylinder trns, Leslie-Henry, 11¼", VG...125.00
Wagon Train, antique bronze, Leslie-Henry 44, 11¼", VG.........135.00
Wells Fargo, nickel, Actoy, 11", M..155.00
Western, nickel, Hubley, 9", M..55.00
Wild Bill Hickok, Leslie-Henry, 9", VG.....................................150.00
Wild Bill Hickok, Leslie-Henry 44, 11¼", EX............................150.00
Winchester Carbine, shootin' shell, Mattel, 26", M...................165.00
Winchester Saddle Gun, Mattel, 33", M.....................................185.00
Wyatt Earp, nickel, long bbl, Hubley, 11", M.............................165.00
2 in 1, 2 interchanging bbls, Hubley, 6", EX.................................45.00

Guns: Early-Style Figural Guns and Bombs (Caution: reproductions exist.)

Admiral Dewey Bomb, CI, Grey Iron, 1900, 1¾", VG................200.00
Butting Match, CI, Ives, 1885, 5", EX...400.00
Cannon, CI, Kenton, 1900, 4⅞", VG...400.00
Chinese Must Go, CI, Ives, 1880, 4¾", EX.................................400.00
Clown on Powder Keg, CI, Ives, 190s, 3¾", VG.........................500.00
Devil's Head Bomb, CI, 22 blank, Ives, 1880, 2¼", VG..............325.00
Dog's Head Bomb, CI, Ives, 1880, 2⅛", EX................................245.00
Double-Face Man, CI, Ives, 1890, 1⅝", VG................................125.00
George Washington Bomb, CI, 1900, 1¼", EX............................350.00
Hobo Bomb, CI, Ideal, 1890s, 2", G-..100.00
Liberty Bell Bomb, CI, 1876, 2⅜", EX..200.00
Lightening Express, CI, Kenton, 1900, 5", EX............................650.00
Punch & Judy, CI, Ives, 1880s, 5¼", EX.....................................850.00
Sea Serpent, CI, Stevens, 1890, 3½", G-.....................................875.00
Yellow Kid Bomb, CI, Grey Iron, 1900, 1½", VG.......................170.00

Model Kits

AEF, Aliens, Bishop, 1980s, MIB..35.00
Airfix, Apollo Saturn V, MIB (sealed)...30.00
Airfix, Lunar Module, 1991, MIB (sealed)....................................10.00
AMT, Munster Koach, 1964, MIB...150.00
AMT, Star Trek, Mr Spock, 1967, MIB.......................................135.00
Aurora, Addam's Family House, MIB..800.00
Aurora, Batman, 1966, MIB..285.00
Aurora, Black Falcon Pirate Ship, 1972, MIB (sealed)................50.00
Aurora, Godzilla, glow-in-the-dark, 1969, MIB..........................200.00
Aurora, Hercules & the Lion, 1965, MIB....................................250.00
Aurora, Prince Valiant, 1959, MIB..200.00
Bachmann, Birds of the World, Swallow, 1950s, MIB..................30.00
Billiken, Dracula, 1989, vinyl, MIB..275.00
Dark Horse, King Kong, MIB..60.00
Hawk, Convair Manned Satellite, 1960, MIB.............................100.00
Horizon, Invisible Man, 1988, MIB...50.00

ITC, Scottish Terrier, 1960, MIB.......................................30.00
Life-Like, Tyrannosaurus, MIB (sealed) 35.00
Lindberg, Lucky Looser, 1965, MIB 20.00
Monogram, Elvira Macabremobile, MIB (sealed) 35.00
Monogram, Ford Tri-Motor Anarctic, 1950s, MIB...............50.00
Monogram, Tijuana Taxi, 1960s, MIB 85.00
MPC, '71 Road Runner, NMIB..50.00
MPC, Dark Shadows Werewolf, MIB..................................200.00
Pryo, Rawhide, 1959, MIB 250.00
Pyro, Rawhide Cowpuncher, 1958, MIB..............................60.00
Revell, Astronaut in Space, 1968, MIB................................100.00
Revell, Ed 'Big Daddy' Roth, Superfink, 1964, MIB............300.00
Revell, Hardy Boy's Van, 1978, MIB, from $30 to 40.00
Revell, Lacross Missile, 1958, MIB.....................................200.00
Screamin' London After Midnight Vampire, MIB 75.00
Strombecker, Disney's Rocket to the Moon, 1956, MIB........225.00
Superior, Seeing Eye, 1959, MIB..35.00
Testors, Top Gun, A-4 Aggressor, 1987, MIB......................10.00
Toy Biz, Thing, 1996, MIB (sealed) 25.00
Tsukuda, Mummy, MIB 75.00

Pedal Cars and Ride-On Toys

Airplane, Murray-Otto Mfg, 45" L, EX 2,900.00
Atomic Missile, Murray, 1950s, chain drive, rstr, 44"........2,500.00
Biplane, sheet metal/wood, wht/red w/gold accents, rstr, 52x48".....900.00
Black Beauty, Corcoran Mfg, 1930, 40" L, VG+ 2,700.00
BMC Special #8 Boat-tail Racer, open wheels, rstr, 37" 975.00
Cadillac, disc wheels, tilt windshield, winged mascot, rstr, 40", EX....3,000.00
Cadillac, fiberglass, silver-pnt grille/bumpers, 1960, 53", EX.......400.00
Champion '43 Chevy Roadster, Murray, mk 610 Jet Flow Drive, rstr, 35"...575.00
Champion Ball Roadster, Murray, prof rstr, from $900 to 1,000.00
Champion Wrecker, Murray, prof rstr, 46" 1,200.00
Dump Truck No 742 (Jet Flow), Murray, prof rstr, 46" 850.00
Earth Mover Drump Truck, Murray, 1961, rstr, M, from $1,100 to ...1,500.00
Farmall 400 Tractor, ESKA, cast aluminum, prof rstr, 38"..........500.00
FBI Radio Cruiser, 1950s, 37", EX orig................................700.00
Fire Dept #1, AMF, 36" L, VG...450.00
Ford, Gaston, 1937, rstr, from $1,500 to 1,800.00
Ford, Steelcraft, 1936, prof rstr, 36".................................1,800.00
Hot-Rod #5, Garton, prof rstr, 35" 900.00
John Deere Tractor Wagon, Ertl #520, 65" L, EX, from $400 to .500.00
John Deere 60, ESKA, 1954, EX, from $550 to 750.00
Kidillac, Garton, late, scarce, G, from $700 to 1,000.00
Lincoln Zephyr, Garton, ca 1937, rstr, 45".............................4,000.00
Lincoln Zephyr, Steelcraft, 1940, prof rstr, 44" 1,800.00
Mack Fire Truck, Steelcraft, 1939, prof rstr 2,000.00
Mercury, Murray, pressed steel, chrome bumpers/grille/etc, rstr, 36" ...1,000.00
Mustang, AMF Jr, 40", EX 575.00
Palge Car, Gendron, 52", VG orig 12,500.00
Red Baron Tri-wing Plane, canvas over wood/steel fuselage, 60x45", EX...900.00
Rickenbacker Fire Chief Car, Am National, 1920s, 42", G 1,800.00
Roamer, Am National, prof rstr, from $3,000 to.....................5,000.00
Sand & Gravel Dump Truck #7, Murray, prof rstr, 49", EX......1,200.00
Space Cruiser, Garton, 1953, 3-wheeled, 48" L, VG+ 675.00
Spirit of St Louis, Am National, 1932 wingspan, rstr, 36" 4,500.00
Streamliner, Steelcraft, tufted leather uphl, rstr, 49" 2,500.00
Studebaker Lark NYC Checker Cab, yel/chrome spinner hubs, rstr, 35" ...345.00
Super-Sonic Jet, Murray, 1950s, EX orig, from $800 to 1,200.00
Tow Truck, Texaco 24 Hr Service, dual wheels, tow boom, rstr, 43" ..3,200.00

Penny Toys

Ambulance, Fischer, 4", EX 325.00

Armored tank car, Distler, VG..175.00
Baby in rolling chair w/nanny, Meier, 3¼", EX....................385.00
Boy on sled, Meier, 3", EX..425.00
Boy w/ball in rocking chair, mk Ges Fesch, 3x2¾", EX.........475.00
Clown in barrel, Stock & Co, 3" L, VG...............................250.00
Double-decker bus, Fisher, mk General, 4¾"......................550.00
Easter egg w/rabbit & gnome on wheeled platform, Meier, EX ...825.00
Field kitchen auto, w/driver, Meier, VG.............................275.00
Goat cart w/girl, Meier, EX...200.00
Horse-drawn cab, w/driver, Fischer, 4", EX.........................225.00
Horse-drawn postal van, Meier, 5½", EX.............................250.00
Motorcycle w/driver, Kellerman, 2", VG.............................500.00
Oceanliner, Japan, 1930s, 2¾", VG....................................100.00
Porter pushing cart w/trunk, Fischer, 3", EX........................400.00
Racer #14, Distler, 4", VG 325.00
Steam engine, operating piston & wheel, Distler, 4", VG..........350.00
Train set, Japan, prewar, loco/tender/5 cars, 13", NM (G box) ...250.00
Trolley, Germany, 4⅜" L, EX 260.00

Pull and Push Toys

Action Andy Lawnmower, Ohio Art, VG..............................45.00
Bear, fur cloth (patched/worn), iron fr, 4 iron wheels, 20" 245.00
Dutchy Dog, Gong Bell, EX (VG box) 235.00
Fireman Trix, Gong Bell, #403, 1940s, 8x14x6", EX 535.00
Fish, CI w/2 spoke wheels, mouth opens, 5", EX 650.00
Healthy Milk Co milk truck, Gong Bell, litho tin/wood, NMIB.400.00
Horse, burlap covered, traces of horsehair mane, rpl tail, 14" L..330.00
Horse & jockey on platform, Fallows, ca 1880, metal, 9½", EX+..1,500.00
Horse & jockey push toy, Wilkins, CI w/wooden hdl, 30", VG ..350.00
Horse on platform, Am, pnt tin w/CI spoke wheels, 9", VG+ 450.00
Horse-drawn ambulance wagon, Germany, 2 figures/2 horses, tin, 7", NM ..150.00
Horse-drawn cart w/bear, Gong Bell, paper litho/metal wheels, EX.......150.00
Horse-drawn covered wagon, Gibbs, wood/metal/canvas cover, 14", EX ...350.00
Horse-drawn plantation wagon, Gibbs, 2 horses, wood/metal, 19", EX.200.00
Horse-drawn trolley, Althof Bergman, tin, 8", EX 850.00
Horse-drawn US Mail Cart, Gibbs, wood/metal, 12", EX............525.00
Horses on platform bell toy, Fallows, 1870s, 8½", EX, $3,000 to .5,000.00
Mary & lamb on platform, Am, pnt tin, rare, 7", EX 2,100.00
Monkey on trike bell toy, Stevens, japanned CI, 8", EX 2,100.00
Old Dobbin, NN Hill Brass Co, horse head bobs, w/chimes, EX 65.00
Omnibus, Merriam, 1870s, pnt tin, 12" L, EX, from $5,000 to...6,500.00
Pony cart, Gibbs, wood/metal, 13", VG 225.00
Rooster cart, Gibbs, wood/metal, 16", VG 825.00

Robots

Action Planet Robot, w/up, litho tin w/plastic helmet, 8½", EX 450.00
Answer Game Machine Robot, Anico, b/o, pnt tin, 15", NMIB....800.00
Atom Robot, KO, friction/bump-&-go, litho tin, 7", EX 200.00
Cragstan Radical Robot, b/o, tin/plastic, rare, 12", NMIB.......2,500.00
Cragstan Robot, Yonezawa, b/o, tinplate/plastic head, 10½", NMIB..1,800.00
Dino-Robot, Horikawa, b/o, tin/plastic, 11", NMIB................1,500.00
Fighting Robot, Horikawa, b/o, tin, light on head, 11", NMIB ..1,100.00
Giant Sonic Robot, Modern Toys, b/o, litho tin, rare, 15", NMIB ..7,500.00
Laughing Robot, Y, 1970s, b/o, mostly plastic, 9½", EX..............125.00
Lost in Space Robot, Remco, 1966, red plastic version, 12", EXIB...500.00
Mechanized Robot, Normura, b/o, blk & red, 13", NMIB............750.00
Mighty Robot, N, w/up, litho tin, 5½", EX.............................150.00
Mighty 8 Robot w/Magic Color, MT, 1960s, b/o, litho tin, 12", NM ..2,400.00
Mr Atomic Robot, Cragstan, 1950s, b/o, litho tin, 11", NMIB, minimum...5,000.00
Mr Chief/Chief Smoky, KO, b/o, litho tin, scarce, 12", EXIB..3,200.00
Mr Mercury, Marx, remote control, tin, 13", NM.....................900.00
Mr Sandman the Robot, Wolverine, litho tin, 11½", NM..........500.00

Mr Zerox, SH, b/o, litho tin, rare, 9", NM (EX box)...................**900.00**
New Sky Robot, SH, 1960s, b/o, mostly plastic, 9", EX...............**125.00**
Ratchet Robot, Nomura, w/up, 8", NMIB........................**1,500.00**
Robert the Robot, Ideal, cable control, plastic, 14", EX **100.00**
Robot R-35, Linemar, remote control, litho tin, 7½", MIB **600.00**
Robot U-5, Daiya, b/o, 8", NM......................................**500.00**
Space Conquerer of Tomorrow, w/up, litho tin, 11", NMIB.....**1,900.00**
Space Man, Cragstan, remote control, litho tin, 9", NMIB **600.00**
Sparkling Mike, Ace, 1950s, b/o, litho tin, 7½", NM, minimum value ..**2,000.00**
Super Astronaut Robot, SH, 1960s, b/o, litho tin, 11½", EX......**225.00**
Target Robot, Masudaya, litho tin, rare, 15", NM **6,300.00**
Tulip Head Robot X-70, Nomura, b/o, litho tin/plastic, 9", NMIB **2,100.00**
Video Robot, Horikawa, b/o, tin/plastic, 9½", NMIB.................**600.00**
Wheel-A-Gear Robot, Taiya, b/o, litho tin, 14", NMIB, from $1,600 to ..**2,200.00**
Zoomer the Robot, TN, b/o, tin, 8", NM (NM box)................**1,500.00**

Schoenhut

Our advisor for Schoenhut toys is Keith Kaonis, who has collected these toys for over twenty years. Because of his involvement with the publishing industry (currently *Antique DOLL Collector*, and during the '80s, *Collectors' SHOWCASE*), he has visited collections across the United States, produced several articles on Schoenhut toys, and served a term as president of the Schoenhut Collectors' Club. Keith is listed in the Directory under New York.

The listings below are for Humpty Dumpty Circus pieces. All values are based on rating conditions of good to very good, i.e., very minor scratches and wear, good original finish, no splits or chips, no excessive paint wear or cracked eyes, and of course completeness and condition of clothes (if dressed figures).

Clowns with two-part heads (a cast face applied to a wooden head) were made from 1903 to 1912 and are most desirable — condition always is important. There have been nine distinct styles in fourteen different costumes recorded. Only eight costume styles apply to the two-part headed clowns. The later clowns had one-part heads whose features were pressed wood, and the costumes on the later ones, circa 1920+, were no longer tied at the wrists and ankles.

Humpty Dumpty Circus Clowns and Other Personnel

Lion Tamer, bisque head, rare, from $350.00 to $1,000.00. (Photo courtesy Keith and Donna Kaonis)

Black Dude, reduced sz, from $100 to............................**375.00**
Black Dude, 1-part head, purple coat, from $250 to **700.00**
Black Dude, 2-part head, blk coat, from $400 to **850.00**
Chinese Acrobat, 1-part head, from $400 to...........................**800.00**
Chinese Acrobat, 2-part head, rare, from $400 to....................**1,300.00**
Clown, early, G, from $150 to **600.00**
Clown, reduced sz, 1925-53, from $75 to **125.00**
Gent Acrobat, bsk head, rare, from $300 to..............................**750.00**
Gent Acrobat, 2-part head, very rare, from $600 to...............**1,800.00**
Hobo, reduced sz, from $200 to **375.00**
Hobo, 1-part head, from $200 to **400.00**
Hobo, 2-part head, facet toe ft, from $400 to.............................**900.00**
Hobo, 2-part head, turned-up toes, blk coat, from $500 to **1,200.00**

Lady Acrobat, bsk head, from $400 to...................**750.00**
Lady Acrobat, 1-part head, from $200 to...................**400.00**
Lady Rider, bsk head, from $250 to **500.00**
Lady Rider, 1-part head, from $200 to...................**400.00**
Lady Rider, 2-part head, very rare, from $700 to............**1,800.00**
Lion Tamer, 2-part head, early, very rare, from $700 to **1,800.00**
Ring Master, bsk, ca 1908-14, from $400 to..................**800.00**
Ring Master, 1-part head, from $200 to...................**450.00**
Ring Master, 2-part head, blk coat, from $800 to **1,800.00**
Ring Master, 2-part head, red coat, from $700 to **1,600.00**

Humpty Dumpty Circus Animals

Humpty Dumpty Circus animals with glass eyes, ca. 1903 – 1914, are more desirable and can demand much higher prices than the later painted-eye versions. As a general rule, a glass-eye version is 30% to 40% more than a painted-eye version. (There are exceptions.) The following list suggests values for both GE (glass-eye) and PE (painted-eye) versions and reflects a **low PE price** to a **high GE price.**

There are other variations and nuances of certain figures: Bulldog — white with black spots or Brindle (brown); open- and closed-mouth zebras, camels, and giraffes; ball necks and hemispherical necks on some animals such as the pig, leopard, and tiger, to name a few. These points can affect the price and should be judged individually. Condition and rarity affect the price most significantly, and the presence of an original box virtually doubles the price.

Alligator, PE/GE, from $250 to...............................**750.00**
Arabian Camel, 1 hump, PE/GE, from $250 to **750.00**
Bactrain Camel, 2 humps, PE/GE, from $200 to **1,200.00**
Brown Bear, PE/GE, from $200 to **800.00**
Buffalo, cloth mane, PE/GE, from $300 to **900.00**
Buffalo, cvd mane, PE/GE, from $200 to **1,200.00**
Bulldog, PE/GE, from $400 to **1,500.00**
Burro (farm set), PE/GE, no harness/no belly hole for chariot, $300 to..**800.00**
Burro (made to go w/chariot & clown), PE/GE, from $200 to **700.00**
Cat, PE/GE, rare, from $600 to **3,000.00**
Cow, PE/GE, from $300 to **1,200.00**
Deer, PE/GE, from $300 to **1,500.00**
Donkey, PE/GE, from $75 to.....................................**300.00**
Donkey, w/blanket, PE/GE, from $100 to........................**600.00**
Elephant, PE/GE, from $75 to **300.00**
Elephant, w/blanket, PE/GE, from $200 to **600.00**
Gazelle, PE/GE, rare, from $500 to **2,750.00**
Giraffe, PE/GE, from $200 to..................................**900.00**
Goat, PE/GE, from $150 to.....................................**400.00**
Goose, PE only, from $200 to **600.00**
Gorilla, PE only, from $1,500 to...............................**3,750.00**
Hippo, PE/GE, from $250 to **900.00**
Horse, brn, saddle & stirrups, PE/GE, from $200 to........................**5.00**
Horse, wht, platform, PE/GE, from $190.........................**450.00**
Hyena, PE/GE, very rare, from $1,000 to........................**6,000.00**
Kangaroo, PE/GE, from $1,000 to **1,500.00**
Lion, cloth mane, GE, from $500 to............................**1,200.00**
Lion, cvd mane, PE/GE, from $250 to **1,400.00**
Monkey, 1-part head, PE only, from $250 to....................**600.00**
Monkey, 2-part head, wht face, from $300 to **1,000.00**
Ostrich, PE/GE, from $250 to..................................**900.00**
Pig, 5 versions, PE/GE, from $200 to..........................**800.00**
Polar Bear, PE/GE, from $400 to **2,000.00**
Poodle, cloth mane, GE only, from $150 to.....................**450.00**
Poodle, PE/GE, from $100 to...................................**300.00**
Rabbit, PE/GE, very rare, from $700 to.........................**3,500.00**
Rhino, PE/GE, from $250 to....................................**800.00**

Sea Lion, PE/GE, from $400 to 1,500.00
Sheep (lamb), w/bell, PE/GE, from $200 to 700.00
Tiger, PE/GE, from $250 to..1,200.00
Wolf, PE/GE, very rare, from $500 to 5,000.00
Zebra, PE/GE, from $250 to..1,200.00
Zebu, PE/GE, rare, from $600 to 3,000.00

Humpty Dumpty Circus Accessories

There are many accessories: wagons, tents, ladders, chairs, pedestals, tight rope, weights, and more.

Cage wagon, ...Greatest Show on Earth, 10" & 12", EX, from $300 to ..1,200.00
Menagerie tent, ca 1904, from $1,500 to 3,000.00
Menagerie tent, ca 1914-20, from $1,200 to 200.00
Oval litho tent, 1926, from $4,000 to 12,000.00
Sideshow panels, 1926, pr, from $2,000 to.................................5,000.00

Steiff

Margaret Steiff began making her stuffed felt toys in Germany in the late 1800s. The animals she made were tagged with an elephant in a circle. Her first teddy bear, made in 1903, became such a popular seller that she changed her tag to a bear. Felt stuffing was replaced with excelsior and wool; when it became available, foam was used. In addition to the tag, look for the 'Steiff' ribbon and the button inside the ear. For further information we recommend *Teddy Bears and Steiff Animals,* a full-color identification and value guide by Margaret Fox Mandel, available from Collector Books or your public library. See also Teddy Bears.

Baby Duck, yel mohair, all ID, 1959-61, 5½", EX........................200.00
Bear, beige mohair, ear button, 1905, 3½", EX 800.00
Bear, blond mohair, FF button, orig collar/tie, 1908, 18", NM.6,000.00
Bear, blond mohair, FF button, 1913, 13", NM 2,500.00
Bear, gold mohair, FF button, pre-1910, 20", NM 8,000.00
Bear, wht curly mohair, button/tag, 1920s, 10", NM 2,300.00
Bear, wht mohair, bl ribbon/button, 1950s, 6", EX 500.00
Biggie Beagle, mohair, all ID, 1960s, 7½", M............................185.00
Camel, mohair/felt, all ID, 1950, 5¾", NM 135.00
Crabby Lobster, felt, all ID, 4½", M 350.00
Dinosarus Stegosauras, mohair, tag/button, 13", minimum value.........1,250.00
Donkey on Wheels, flannel, w/saddle & blanket, FF button, 9½", M.1,500.00
Elephant, w/anniversary blanket, all ID, 1959-67, 2½", M 150.00
Eric Bat, mohair, w/tag, 1960s, rare, EX, minimum value............675.00
Floppy Hens, mohair/felt, all ID, 1958, rare, 8" & 7", pr.............300.00
Giraffe, velvet, all ID, 1959-67, 6", M.......................................150.00
Hide-A-Gift Rabbit, all ID, 1950, 5½", M, from $175 to............185.00
Jackie Bear, button/remnant stock tag, 1950s, rare, 9½", EX 900.00
Koala Bear, fully jtd, all ID, 1955-58, 9", M...............................700.00
Lioness, mohair, glass eyes, fully jtd, button/tag, 1951-57, 6", M ...250.00
Max & Moritz, all ID, 1950s, rare, 3½", MIP 385.00
Nelly Snail, velveteen & vinyl, all ID, 1962, 6", EX 200.00
Original Teddy, caramel mohair, button/tag, 38", M, from $1,000 to ...200.00
Peggy Penguin, chest tag, 1959, 5", NM.....................................100.00
Renny Reindeeer, chest tag, 1950s, 4½", M 185.00
Snucki Ram, tan mohair, chest tag, 1950s, 6", NM 125.00
Tessie Schnauzer, gray mohair, chest tag, 4½", NM....................150.00
Woolie Bird, button/tag, 1949, 2", NM 50.00
Zotty Bear, mohair, orig ribbon, chest tag, 6½", M.....................250.00

Toy Soldiers and Accessories

Among the better-known manufacturers of 'dimestore' soldiers are American Metal Toys, Barclay, and Manoil, all of whom made hollow cast-lead figures; Grey Iron, who used cast iron; and Auburn, who made figures of rubber. They measured about 3" to 3½" tall, and often accessories such as trucks, tents, tanks, and airplanes were designed to add to the enjoyment of staging mock battles, parades, encampments, and wars.

Britains is a very popular line, smaller and usually more detailed than the 'dimestores.' They've been made in England since 1893, and many of their older boxed sets sell for more than a $100.00.

Some examples are very rare and therefore expensive, but condition is the driving force in making a value assessment. Percentages in the description lines refer to the amount of original paint remaining. Our advisors for this category are Stan and Sally Alekna; they are listed in the Directory under Pennsylvania. To learn more about this subject, we recommend *Collecting Toy Soldiers* by Richard O'Brien (Krause).

American Metal, knight w/pennant, scarce, 98% 95.00
American Metal, soldier, machine gunner, prone, khaki, scarce, 95% ..125.00
Auburn Rubber, baseball player, batter, 98%................................69.00
Auburn Rubber, flagbearer, 95% 184.00
Auburn Rubber, football player, QB passing, 98%........................75.00
Auburn Rubber, goose, scarce, 95%...18.00
Auburn Rubber, guard officer, yel w/red trim, scarce, 99% 45.00
Auburn Rubber, officer on horse, scarce, 98% 50.00
Auburn Rubber, signal, man w/both flags intact, 98%..................175.00
Auburn Rubber, soldier marching, port of arms, khaki, 98%.........20.00
Barclay, aircraft carrier, scarce, 98%...125.00
Barclay, boy scout saluting, 98%..61.00
Barclay, bride & groom, HO scale, scarce, 98%, ea........................36.00
Barclay, cow grazing, 98% 18.00
Barclay, detective in bl suit, scarce, 97%...................................185.00
Barclay, doctor in wht, 85% 15.00
Barclay, Ethiopian w/rifle, 96%...273.00
Barclay, field cannon, closed hitch, sm, 97% 18.00
Barclay, horse standing, 97%..17.00
Barclay, Indian chief w/tomahawk & shield, 97%........................22.00
Barclay, Japanese charging w/rifle, ca 1937, 98%.......................147.00
Barclay, knight w/shield, 97%..20.00
Barclay, leaning out w/field phone & antenna, 95%......................88.00
Barclay, marine w/sword, long stride, tin helmet, 95%.................38.00
Barclay, officer on motorcycle, scarce, 98%.................................70.00
Barclay, officer w/sword, cast helmet, 97% 71.00
Barclay, oiler, HO scale, 98% 10.00
Barclay, pod-foot soldier bomb thrower, red, 94%......................128.00
Barclay, policeman, HO scale, 98% 10.00
Barclay, reindeer, extremely rare, minimum value 125.00
Barclay, shoeshine boy, scarce, 94%..35.00
Barclay, soldier at searchlight, smooth lens variation, scarce, M.350.00
Barclay, soldier bomb thrower, gr, 95%.......................................25.00
Barclay, soldier dispatcher w/dog, 95% 93.00
Barclay, soldier flame thrower, gr, 98%.......................................22.00
Barclay, soldier marching w/slung rifle, 98% 40.00
Barclay, standing & firing, gr, 99%..22.00
Barclay, surgeon w/soldier, scarce, 94% 110.00
Barclay, transport set w/2 cars, 1960s, 97% 65.00
Barclay, US Army plane, silver, 95%...35.00
Britains, #1448 Staff Car w/Driver & General, EX.....................225.00
Britains, #2185 Bahamas Police Band, complete, very rare, NM ...2,300.00
Britains, #37 Coldstream Guard Band, 21-pc, EX......................400.00
Courtenay, Alian, Lord of Montendre, very rare, NM 1,200.00
Grey Iron, bandit w/scarf, arms raised in surrender, 97%............140.00
Grey Iron, boy in traveling suit, postwar, 99% 18.00
Grey Iron, burro, for ranch scene, 98% 68.00
Grey Iron, cadet, right soulder arms, prewar, 94% 30.00
Grey Iron, cowboy, prewar, 98% 25.00
Grey Iron, engineer, prewar, 99% 16.00

Grey Iron, farmer, prewar, 94% **15.00**
Grey Iron, girl, prewar, 94% **15.00**
Grey Iron, Indian chief, Mohawk, w/raised tomahawk, 96% **121.00**
Grey Iron, Indian Chief w/knife, prewar, 98% **32.00**
Grey Iron, Italian officer, prewar, scarce, 96% **255.00**
Grey Iron, lifeguard sitting in chair, 2 pcs, 97% **155.00**
Grey Iron, pirate w/sword, gr, prewar, 97% **38.00**
Grey Iron, ski trooper, prewar, w/orig skis, scarce, 97% **85.00**
Grey Iron, soldier on crutches, prewar, scarce, 96% **75.00**
Grey Iron, soldier w/rifle at attention, postar, 95% **15.00**
Grey Iron, US Doughboy, bomber crawling, postwar, 97% **32.00**
Grey Iron, US Infantry, port of arms, prewar, 99% **25.00**
HB Toys, Indian mounted, scarce, 94% **40.00**
HB Toys, Indian w/knife, scarce, 98% **30.00**
Manoil, aviation mechanic, w/prop away from head, 95% **625.00**
Manoil, bench, 96% **14.00**
Manoil, cadet, hollow base, scarce, 65% **35.00**
Manoil, doctor in wht w/red cross, 94% **28.00**
Manoil, farmer at water pump, 95% **25.00**
Manoil, general (Patton?), saluting, 95% **182.00**
Manoil, lineman on telephone pole, 2 pcs, 98% **130.00**
Manoil, man & woman on park bench, 97% **38.00**
Manoil, oil tanker, red, 95% **50.00**
Manoil, policeman, 96% **28.00**
Manoil, sedan, bl, scarce, 98% **65.00**
Manoil, sniper kneeling w/rifle, 99% **30.00**
Manoil, soldier, jumping, w/chute, 99% **125.00**
Manoil, soldier, marching, o'seas cap at angle, 97% **93.00**
Manoil, soldier, w/barrel of apples, 99% **87.00**
Manoil, soldier, wounded, lying down, 95% **25.00**
Manoil, tow truck, 2-pc, scarce, 98% **90.00**
Marx, US infantry colonel, EX **14.00**
Marx, US infantry sergeant, VG **12.00**
Molded Products, marine, bl, 93% **15.00**
Molded Products, soldier flag bearer, WWII helmet, 98% **20.00**
Playwod Plastics, machine gunner, prone, 97% **20.00**
Playwod Plastics, soldier w/gas mask & flare gun, 95% **15.00**
Solido, howitzer, 4-wheeled, short barrel, 6", NM **25.00**
Solido, UNIC missile launcher, 7½", NM **45.00**
Soljertoy, sailor, bl, scarce, 97% **25.00**
Soljertoy, soldier marching, left shoulder arms, scarce, 98% **20.00**

Trains

Electric trains were produced as early as the late nineteenth century. Names to look for are Lionel, Ives, and American Flyer. Identification numbers given in the listings below actually appear on the item.

Am Flyer, Boxcar #633, EX **50.00**
Am Flyer, Empire Express Set #1090, 4-pc, VG **300.00**
Am Flyer, Girder Bridge #581, NMIB **100.00**
Am Flyer, Locomotive & Tender #312, VG **125.00**
Am Flyer, Locomotive #3115, bl, G **200.00**
Am Flyer, Nationwide Lines Set #1090, 4-pc, EX **1,100.00**
Am Flyer, Oil Drum Loader #779, NMIB **150.00**
Am Flyer, Passenger Station #102, VG (VG box) **500.00**
Am Flyer, Rio Grande Cookie Boxcar #24039, EX **175.00**
Am Flyer, The Eagle Set #20767, complete, NM (EX box) **4,675.00**
Am Flyer, Trestle Bridge #23750, EX (VG box) **175.00**
Ives, Saratoga Pullman #129, 2-tone gr, EX **75.00**
Ives, Set #690, 3-pc w/track, EXIB **400.00**
Lionel, Amtrak GGI #18303, diesel, MIB..............................**375.00**
Lionel, Caboose #19703, MIB..**35.00**
Lionel, Caboose #2672, brn, EX **25.00**

Lionel, Chesapeake & Ohio Locomotive & Tender #8603, MIB ..**100.00**
Lionel, Chicago Northwestern Locomotive #8056, MIB............**125.00**
Lionel, Country Estate #911, NM **800.00**
Lionel, Drawbridge #313, VG **250.00**
Lionel, Erie Animated Gondola #9307, MIB **50.00**
Lionel, Farm Building & Animal Set #957, MIB......................**275.00**
Lionel, Flat Car w/Airplane #6800, MIB..............................**200.00**
Lionel, Great Northern Snowplow #58, gr & wht, NMIB **500.00**
Lionel, JC Penney Boxcar #9054, M **12.00**
Lionel, New Yorker Set #11744, MIB (sealed)..........................**425.00**
Lionel, Norfolk Intermodel Crane #12937, EXIB......................**185.00**
Lionel, Nothern Pacific Locomotive #628, center cab, VG **200.00**
Lionel, Pennsylvania Covered Hopper #6123, MIB....................**45.00**
Lionel, Railroader Club Car #782, M **35.00**
Lionel, Santa Fe Unibody Tank Car #17900, MIB **40.00**
Lionel, Stock Car #2813, EX (VG+ box) **475.00**
Lionel, Telegraph Pole Set #150, EXIB **125.00**
Lionel, Transformer #4250, 50 watts, EX **25.00**
Lionel, Wabash Locomotive #550, EXIB................................**265.00**
Lionel, Western Pacific Boxcar #3474, VG **35.00**
Marklin, New York Central Locomotive #1030, electric, VG.....**750.00**
Marx, Set #4305, electric, NMIB **200.00**
Williams, Pennsylvania 2-8-2 Mikado Locomotive & Tender, MIB ...**225.00**

Trade Signs

Trade signs were popular during the 1800s. They were usually made in an easily recognizable shape that one could mentally associate with the particular type of business it was to represent, especially appropriate in the days when many customers could not read!

Boot, wood w/wht rpt & blk details over old gold, 25½" **385.00**
Boot, 3-D wooden cvg w/red pnt, 1820s, 28" **1,115.00**
Bootmaker, shoe & short boot pnt on wood brd, Am, 19th C, 15x38"..**1,380.00**
Clockmaker's pocket watch, cvd/pnt ea side, 13" dia **1,295.00**
Depot for Lucas Enamels..., wooden, 3 stacked bbls shape, 50x18" ..**2,645.00**
Fish, cvd/pnt wood, full-bodied, glass eyes, pnt traces, 1850s, 48" **2,650.00**
Glasses frames, optometrist, dbl-sided pnt CI, 19th C, 11x44½" **3,000.00**
Horse & carriage cut-out center, cast copper, late 1800s, 22x22" ..**750.00**
Key, cvd wood w/pierced designs ea end, worn gold pnt, rpr splits, 71" ..**1,750.00**
Key, wood & zinc w/red pnt, wrought-iron bracket, Am, 54x42" ..**865.00**
Meat Market pnt on pine brd w/molded fr, late 1800s, 13x67" ...**485.00**
Molar, cvd wood w/gilt pnt, illegible lettering, rpr, 15x7" **1,495.00**
Mortar & pestle, gilt metal, pnt losses, Am, late 1800s, 35x22" ...**1,600.00**
Mortar & pestle, sheet zinc, old gold traces, 36" on new stand ...**770.00**
Optometrist, 2-pc wood hanger, name on top/eye graphic below, 28x32"...**475.00**
Pawn broker's, wrought-iron bracket w/scrolls support 2 copper balls..**1,595.00**
Pocket watch, JA Nadeau Jeweler, CI/tin, 49¾x35" **1,380.00**
Pocket watch, wood w/mc pnt (losses/crackling), 19th C, 32x22" dia .**900.00**
Repair shop & lady's boots pnt on wood brd, 19th C, 12x35" .**1,150.00**
Watch dial, Master Watchmaker, pnt wood, ca 1900, 25½x31½"...........**230.00**

Tramp Art

'Tramp' is considered a type of folk art. In America it was primarily made from the end of the Civil War through the 1930s, though it employs carving and decorating methods which are much older, originating mostly in Germany and Scandinavia. 'Trampen' probably refers to the itinerant stages of Middle Ages craft apprenticeship. The carving techniques were also used for practice. Tramp art was spread by soldiers in the Civil War and primarily practiced where there was a plentiful and free supply of materials such as cigar boxes and fruit crates. The belief that this work was done by tramps and hobos as payment for room or meals is generally incorrect. The larger pieces especially would have required a lengthy stay in one place.

There is a great variety of tramp art, from boxes and frames which are most common to large pieces of furniture and intricate objects. The most common method of decoration is chip carving with several layers built one on top of another. There are several variations of that form as well as others such as 'Crown of Thorns,' an interlocking method, which are completely different. The most common finishes were lacquer or stain, although paints were also used. The value of tramp art varies according to size, detail, surface, and complexity. The new collector should be aware that tramp art is being made today. While some sell it as new, others are offering it as old. In addition, many people mistakenly use the term as a catchall phrase to refer to other forms of construction — especially things they are uncertain about. This misuse of the term in growing, and makes a difference in the value of pieces. New collectors need to pay attention to how items are described.

For further information we recommend *Tramp Art: A Folk Art Phenomenon* by Helaine Fendelmam, Jonathan Taylor (Photographer)/ Stewart Tabori & Chang; and *Hobo & Tramp Art Carving: An Authentic American Folk Tradition* by Adolph Vandertie, Patrick Spielman/Sterling Publications. Our advisors are Matt Lippa and Elizabeth Schaaf; they are listed in the Directory under Alabama.

Box, chip-cvd, roof-like top w/chimney finial, ftd, 16" H 485.00
Box, chip-cvd, 10-layer ped base & body, drw/mirror, 14x12x7" 110.00
Box, chip-cvd, 4-layer, brass mts, partial pnt, Germany, 1904, 6x10x7" ...150.00
Box, chip-cvd, 9-layer, hinged lid w/mirror, 6¼x11¾x8" 155.00
Box, chip-cvd/pierced mahog w/gold, IBWA/Frisco/1915, 12x7x5", EX...450.00
Box, lock; triangular panels/dmn on lid, gold trim, ring hdls, 4x6x4" 125.00
Box, matchsticks, old mirror in lift lid, felt lined, 8x12x8" 190.00
Box, walnut w/geometric designs, chip-cvd eagle, glued rprs, 14"..350.00
Cabinet, medicine; chip-cvd, 1-pane do, 2-shelf, gallery, 23x17x7" 300.00
Candlestand, cvd wood w/puzzlework center, 5 tin holders, 13x6½".....85.00
Candlesticks, cvd zigzags, waisted, spike top, 2-color pnt, 21", pr ..525.00
Clock case, rtcl cvg w/scrolls/deer/nude man/lady, 1920s, 27x20" 140.00
Cupboard, velvet w/cross on door, gilt rosette/1918, drw, ornate, 16"..425.00
Curio cabinet, X-hatched 6-pane dbl doors, 6 shelves, 60x22x10" 975.00
Dresser mirror, 3 arched panels ea w/2 mirrors, cvd hearts etc, 12x16"..275.00
Frame, chip-cvd, 3-layer, fretwork bird/flowers at top, old pnt, 11x6" ...150.00
Frame, cvd vines/leaves/shield/crown, 2 windows, 1918, 8x11x½" ..110.00
Frame, cvd wood w/cutouts & 7 porc beads, 4-layer, old pnt, 33x40"....950.00
Frame, dmn shape w/appl dmn decor, 1940s, 20¾x8½x¾"........110.00
Frame, stepped rectangles, hearts in corners, 24x20" 425.00
Frame, 2 bands w/dmn designs, molded edge/liner, 29x25" 750.00
Frame, 4-layer, intersecting pointed segments, 23x18" 350.00
House, 2-story, cvd tiles, crimped moldings, fencing, 13x9x13" ..800.00
Lamp, rtcl walnut shade & base w/vining floral & hearts, 19½x13" ...235.00
Mirror, chip-cvd fr, 5-layer, EX patina, 14x8" w/attached 3¾" shelf....165.00
Mirror, layered sawtooth cvd fr w/tulips in corners, 1890-1910, 47x29" ...5,300.00
Shelf, chip-cvd, hearts & stars, w/spice drw, 1930s, 19x11x4½" .165.00
Shelf, chip-cvd, 19 tiers below shelf, orig hardware, 20x7x7¼" ..275.00
Shelves, hanging; arched crest w/6 spires, 3-tier, 34x27x8" 550.00
Whimsey horseshoe, chip-cvd, 8-layer, 1908/1910 dates, from cigar box...300.00
Whimsy rattle, 2 caged balls, made from 1 pc wood, 10x1¾" sq.325.00

Traps

Though of interest to collectors for many years, trap collecting has gained in popularity over the past ten years in particular, causing prices to appreciate rapidly. Traps are usually marked on the pan as to manufacturer, and the condition of these trademarks is important when determining their value. Grading is as follows:

Good: one-half of pan legible.
Very good: legible in entirety, but light.
Fine: legible in entirety, with strong lettering.
Mint: in like-new, shiny condition.
Our advisor for this category is Boyd Nedry; he is listed in the Directory under Michigan. Prices listed here are for traps in fine condition.

Acme Mousetrap, wood snap type, Pat 1907 ....25.00
Alexander, Alligator #2, w/bait hook & pan.................................175.00
Alexander live, clutch trap, Pat Oct 18, 97, sz C (sm)...............360.00
All Steel, #0, single long spring 98.00
Arrow, #4, dbl under spring...45.00
Austin Humane, #1, flat stake loop 45.00

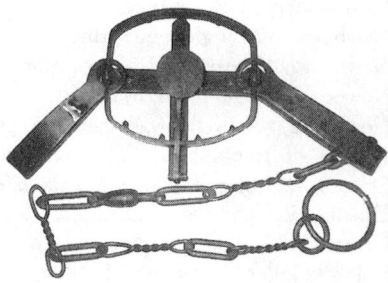

Bear trap, 36" long, with outstanding chain, $550.00.
(Photo courtesy Boyd Nedry)

Bell Trap, #0, single long spring, Canada 35.00
Belmont Steel, #0, sure grip 65.00
Big Bear #2, coil spring, master grip..25.00
Blake & Lamb, #1, single long spring 5.00
Blake & Lamb, #2, dbl long spring, bolted jaw post 225.00
Blake & Lamb, #5, bear trap, emb letters 2,500.00
Bridger, #1, w/off-set jaws 6.00
Buffalo Bill, wood snap type, shoots from any angle, rat trap 30.00
Catchall, wire cage, mousetrap...30.00
Champion, #0, single long spring..65.00
Champion, #4, multi-trigger 180.00
Claytons, clutch trap, Pat 1932 ....725.00
Cook's Quick Catch, Aliba Ill, rat trap 28.00
Cooper, #2, humane bbl trap..60.00
Crago, #4, clutch trap...435.00
Curry Fly Trap, Tulsa OK 40.00
Diamond, #51, Walloper, single jaw 65.00
Diamond, H22, high grip, dbl long spring..................................200.00
Dick's Ant Destroyer, glass 55.00
Dixie, fly trap, fits on fruit jar 40.00
Easy Set, wood snap-type mousetrap 10.00
Eclipse, #3, folding...75.00
Economy, #1, single long spring..40.00
Epp, chain trap, Henderson Neb 450.00
Evert, single long spring, rat trap 48.00
Fatal, Chicago Ill, tin & wood, mousetrap 150.00
Fenn Mark 4, English gin trap...30.00
Foster, stop thief...15.00
Frost, killer, brass trigger 38.00
Gibbs, live muskrat...600.00
Gibbs Gladiator, snap-type metal mousetrap.............................35.00
Gibbs Two Trigger, Pat 3, 9 21 ....22.00
Good House Keepers, mousetrap...10.00
Good-Stilson, self setter, wood snap-type, mousetrap 24.00
Goshen Animal 325.00
Helfrich Co, #550.00, dbl coil spring..50.00
Helfrich Co, #750.00, dbl coil spring..125.00
Hercules, #1, single long spring..55.00
Herters, #87, dbl long spring, deer trap 125.00

Hickory, snap-type, mousetrap 22.00
Hotchkiss, #2, dbl long spring................................200.00
Hunter, killer 35.00
IOA, Brown Camp Hardware, Iowa, wood snap-type, rat trap 23.00
Joker, #3, wood snap-type, rat trap 40.00
Juby, English rodent trap 40.00
Ketchem, #2, tile trap...55.00
KNAP, #1½, Belknap Hardware, coil spring 20.00
Lamb Saver, The Protector 10.00
Lomar, #4, dbl long spring.....................................40.00
Mascot, #1½, single long spring................................25.00
McWorter, claw trap..165.00
Miting, tunnel trap 20.00
Montgomery, #2, dbl coil spring, limited edition 150.00
Montgomery Stake & Take, killer................................22.00
Newhouse, #0, single long spring 65.00
Newhouse, #5, Animal Trap Co, bear trap 550.00
Newhouse, #6, no teeth, bear trap 800.00
Newhouse, #81, web jaw, single long spring 65.00
Onieda, #1, tree trap..40.00
Onieda, #2, killer...40.00
Onieda, #2, Stop Thief...30.00
Orberto, #400, coil spring.....................................65.00
Peacock, killer, Pat March 31, 1885 ....90.00
Pioneer, #4, dbl long spring...................................30.00
PS Mfg Co, #1, cast 8 chain, long spring.......................65.00
PS&W Co, #0, Good Luck, single long spring.....................150.00
PS&W Co, #101, Rev-O-Noc, long spring 200.00
Quigley-Van Camp, wood snap-type, mousetrap....................20.00
Rice, #4, copy of Jackson Otter Dog, long spring...............225.00
Rice, metal choker, mousetrap 55.00
Rice Improved Conibear, killer, unmk...........................40.00
Rival, Wm Pratt, Joliet Ill, snap-type mousetrap...............22.00
Sabo, steel jaws, den trap 140.00
Sargent, #0, single long spring 75.00
Sargent, #10, single long spring 80.00
Savaleg, #210, 4 jaws..80.00
Shene, #4, coil spring...100.00
Sure Hold, wooden cone 65.00
Taylor, FC; sure kill, mole trap 65.00
Tom Cat, Luthe Hardware Iowa, wood snap-type mousetrap 20.00
Triple J, #2, 4 jaws 45.00
Triumph, #0, w/Triumph crossed on pan 80.00
Tru-Value, #1, single long spring..............................15.00
Union Hardware Co, #1, single long spring 60.00
Up-To-Date, wood snap-type, mouse trap 25.00
Verbail, chain trap..140.00
Victor, #40, 2-in-1 ....125.00
Victor, The; #1½, dogless......................................250.00
Victoria, #0, single long spring...............................100.00
Webley, #2, dbl long spring 40.00
Wilson, JR; Pat Oct 11, 21.....................................300.00
Woods & Waters, muskrat killer 15.00

Trenton

Trenton, New Jersey, was an area that supported several pottery companies from the mid-1800s until the late 1960s. A consolidation of several smaller companies that occurred in the 1890s was called Trenton Potteries Company. Each company produced their own types of wares independent of the others.

Vase, aqua gloss, globular, G McStay Jackson, 1935-42, 9x9" 145.00

Vase, maroon, 'flying saucer' design, 4x10" 165.00
Vase, maroon w/gold, sq tapered form w/sm base, 8x5½" at top....35.00
Vase, wht gloss, Deco style, 16x10" 200.00
Vase, wht gloss, 3 stepped circles design, 9x9" 65.00
Vase, window; aqua gloss, 6x7x2¼" 150.00

Trivets

Although strictly a decorative item today, the original purpose of the trivet was much more practical. They were used to protect table tops from hot serving dishes, and irons heated on the kitchen range were placed on trivets during use to protect work surfaces. The first patent date was 1869; many of the earliest trivets bore portraits of famous people or patriotic designs. Florals, birds, animals, and fruit were other favored motifs. Watch for remakes of early original designs. Some of these are marked Wilton, Emig, Wright, Iron Art, and V.M. for Virginia Metalcrafters. However, many of these reproductions are becoming collectible. Expect to pay considerably less for these than for the originals, since they are abundant.

Brass

Eagle pierced design, wood hdl, 3 iron ft, 1790s, 11" 150.00
Flatiron shape, open center, 10x3¼" 110.00
Fox & tree design, flatiron shape w/hdl, 7¼" 165.00
Hollow triangular shape w/riveted hdl, 3¼x10" 140.00
Pierced dmn center w/4 lobes to outside, 19th C, 11" 150.00
Rectangular, openwork, English, 4x12" 150.00
Repousse sheet, ftd, English Arts & Crafts era, ca 1900, 7" sq....140.00
Repousse w/hand-stippled ground, Arts & Crafts era, 7" sq..........80.00
Scalloped border, smooth top, 4-ftd, early 1800s, 3½x8"............180.00

Cast Iron

E in center of sadiron shape, Enterprise Mfg. Co. Phila. U.S.A. embossed along edge, $25.00.

Best on Earth 25.00
Cathedral pattern, 3¾x1⅝" 22.00
Flatiron shape w/scrolling design, 3 1" legs, 9x4" 35.00
Star & braid, buffed, 8" 80.00
Uneedit, ornate, 7" 50.00
Westinghouse, E Pgh Divisions Family Day 1953, W at bottom, Trafford ...35.00
WH Howell Co Geneva Ill, H in center, 6" 28.00
Wilton #2, lovebirds/heart/brooms/star..................................22.50
Wilton #8, leaf pattern w/heart & eagle in center 18.00

Miscellaneous

Sterling o/l on glass, 6", pr 125.00
Wrought iron, dbl heart, shoe ft, blk pnt, 4½" 175.00
Wrought iron, heart shape, long hdl, penny ft, 10" L 365.00

Tuthill

The Tuthill Glass Company operated in Middletown, New York,

from 1902 to 1923. Collectors look for signed pieces and those in an identifiable pattern. Condition is of utmost importance, and examples with brilliant cutting and intaglio (natural flowers and fruits) combined fetch the highest prices.

Bowl, Rose, cut, 8" 515.00
Charger, strawberry leaf & vine intaglio, 12½" 575.00
Cup, punch; vintage etch, bell shape, ear hdl, 3½x3" 155.00
Decanter, Primrose, hdld, 12" 670.00

Twin Winton

Twin brothers Don and Ross Winton started this California-based company during the mid-1930s while still in high school. In the mid-1940s they shut it down while in the armed forces and started up again in the late 1940s, when older brother Bruce Winton joined them. He bought them out in the early 1950s. The company became a major producer of cookie jars, kitchenware, and household items sold nationally until it closed its San Juan Capistrano location in 1977.

Beside their extensive line of very collectible cookie jars, they're also well known for their Hillbilly line — mugs, pitchers, bowls, lamps, ashtrays, decanters, and other novelty items, which evolved from the late 1940s through the early 1970s with a variety of decorating methods still being discovered. Don Winton was the only designer for Twin Winton and created literally thousands of designs for them and hundreds of other companies. He is still sculpting in Corona del Mar, California, and collectors and dealers are continuing to find and document new pieces daily. To learn more about this subject, we recommend *Collector's Guide to Don Winton Designs* (Collector Books) by our advisor, Mike Ellis; he is listed in the Directory under California or visit the collector club website at www.twinwinton.com.

Ashtray, elf, #205, 8" 100.00
Bank, Bull, #413, 8" 65.00
Bank, Cop (Keystone), #412, 8" 65.00
Candy jar, Candy House, #351, 9½" 65.00
Candy jar, elephant, #356, 9" 65.00
Candy jar, shoe, #352, 10" 75.00
Canister, Coffee Coop, Canister Farm Line, #113, 6" 40.00
Canister, Flour House, Canisterville Line, #101, 11" 125.00
Canister, Pot O' Tea, #124, 5" 20.00
Cookie jar, Bear Sheriff, 11" 75.00
Cookie jar, Butler, 12" 300.00
Cookie jar, Chipmumk, bag of acorns over shoulder, 10" 75.00
Cookie jar, Cookie Car (trolley), 7x12" 75.00
Cookie jar, Cookie Catcher, 8x13" 100.00
Cookie jar, Cookie Guard, 12" 400.00
Cookie jar, Cookie Nut, squirrel atop, 9x10" 65.00
Cookie jar, Cookie Time, mouse atop clock, 14" 45.00
Cookie jar, Cop (Keystone), Collector Series, 12½" 225.00
Cookie jar, Dog (Circus) on Drum, 12" 150.00
Cookie jar, Dog in Basket, 10" 85.00
Cookie jar, Dutch Girl, Collector Series, 12" 225.00
Cookie jar, Elephant (Sailor), Collector Series, 12" 300.00
Cookie jar, Elf, seated on stump, 12" 65.00
Cookie jar, Gorilla, in hat/tie/suspenders, 12" 350.00
Cookie jar, Hen on Basket, #61, 8½" 120.00
Cookie jar, Hotei, 12½" 65.00
Cookie jar, Jack-in-the-Box, 13½" 350.00
Cookie jar, Kitten in Basket, #70, 10" 65.00
Cookie jar, Lighthouse, #42, 13" 400.00
Cookie jar, Noah's Ark, 10" 75.00
Cookie jar, Owl (scholar), 12" 40.00

Cookie jar, Poodle Cookie Counter, 13x7½" 85.00
Cookie jar, Pot O' Cookies, 8x13" 40.00
Cookie jar, Rabbit Cowboy, 13" 75.00
Cookie jar, Rooster crowing, 12" 75.00
Cookie jar, Stove, 8x13" 75.00
Cookie jar, Walrus, clown hat & collar, 11" 375.00
Cookie jar, Ye Olde Cookie Bucket, 9" 40.00
Decanter, bartender, 10" 100.00
Decanter, Santa (Christmas Cheer), 10½" 100.00
Expanimal, poodle, #125, 7½" 200.00
Figurine, angel blowing golden trumpet, 5" 40.00
Figurine, blind mouse, #208,¾" 6.00
Figurine, boy skier, The Childrens' Album Line, 7" 225.00
Figurine, boy standing by mailbox holding dog, T-8, 5½" 175.00
Figurine, cat holding up paw, #210, 3" 30.00
Figurine, cocker spaniel, #603, 7" 50.00
Figurine, collie, #602, 7½" 65.00
Figurine, cow, #450, 2" 11.00
Figurine, deer standing, #208, dtd 1940-43, 6" 75.00
Figurine, elf w/basket on bk, 3" 65.00
Figurine, Ezra or Zeke, 5½", ea 40.00
Figurine, girl playing dress-up, #T-19, 5½" 200.00
Figurine, lion roaring, 8" 60.00
Figurine, Mouseketeer (girl) holding sucker, #T-2, 5½" 150.00
Figurine, Pixie & Dixie in shoe, 6" 75.00
Figurine, Scotty dog sitting, #105, 1" 4.00
Figurine, shepherd boy holding lamb & staff, bsk, 9" 80.00
Figurine, squirrel, #318, 1¾" 8.00
Figurine, squirrel w/folded hands, 4" 30.00
Figurine, Wally Gator, bsk, 6" 80.00
Figurine, Winnie the Pooh, seated, eating from pot, bsk, 5" ...60.00
Figurine, zebra, 5" 45.00
Lamp, kitten in well, #258, 13" 250.00
Lamp, rabbit, #251, 12" 250.00
Men of the Mountain, ashtray, lady, 4¼" sq 20.00
Men of the Mountain, bank, Mountain Dew 100 Proof/Loot, 7" ..75.00
Men of the Mountain, cigarette box, outhouse, #109, 7" 75.00
Men of the Mountain, ice bucket, suspenders, 14" 250.00
Men of the Mountain, pitcher, #101, 7½" 85.00
Men of the Mountain, pour spout, lady, 6½" 30.00
Men of the Mountain, punch bowl, 12" dia 350.00
Men of the Mountain, shakers, man & woman, 4", pr 40.00
Men of the Mountain, stein, lady, 8" 70.00
Mug, ABC, squirrel hdl, 5" 100.00
Mug, Artist Palette Line, silver banding, 4½" 50.00
Mug, Burgie, 5½" 40.00
Mug, lamb, #502, 3¼" 85.00
Napkin holder, Dobbin, #487, 7" 65.00
Napkin holder, Dutch girl, #417, 8½" 75.00
Napkin holder, elephant, #453, 6" 150.00
Planter, bear beside stump, #324, 8" 50.00
Planter, golf bag, wood tone, 7" 80.00
Planter, rabbit beside basket eating carrot, 5x8" 85.00
Planter, rabbit w/cart, 7x10" 85.00
Plate, salad; Wood Grain Line, sq, 8" 400.00
Relish tray, Artist Palette Line, 4x8" 30.00
Shakers, Artist Palette Line, 3½", pr 65.00
Shakers, house, Canisterville Line #140, pr 75.00
Shakers, lions, #190 ....45.00
Shakers, owls, #191 ....30.00
Shakers, poodles, #164, pr 50.00
Shakers, rabbit cowboys, #187, pr 45.00
Shakers, saddles, Bronco Group, 3", pr 50.00
Shakers, squirrels, #174, pr 40.00

Shakers, teddy bears, #153, pr..50.00
Spoon rest, Dutch girl, #19, 10"...40.00
Tumbler, Wood Grain Line, 4½"..25.00
Tumbler, Wood Grain Line, 7"...40.00

Typewriters

The first commercially successful typewriter was the Sholes and Glidden, introduced in 1874. By 1882 other models appeared, and by the 1890s dozens were on the market. At the time of the First World War, the ranks of typewriter-makers thinned, and by the 1920s only a few survived.

Collectors informally divide typewriter history into the pioneering period, up to about 1890; the classic period, from 1890 to 1920; and the modern period, since 1920. There are two broad classifications of early typewriters: (1) Keyboard machines, in which depression of a key prints a character and via a shift key prints up to three different characters per key; (2) Index machines, in which a chart of all the characters appears on the typewriter; the character is selected by a pointer or dial and is printed by operation of a lever or other device. Even though index typewriters were simpler and more primitive than keyboard machines, they were none-the-less a later development, designed to provide a cheaper alternative to the standard keyboard models that were selling for upwards of $100.00. Eventually second-hand keyboard typewriters supplied the low-price customer, and index typewriters vanished except as toys. Both classes of typewriters appeared in a great many designs.

It is difficult, if not impossible, to assign standard market prices to early typewriters. During the past decade, competition from a handful of wealthy overseas collectors has drastically affected the American market, and prices have become inflated on the rarer models. Some auction-realized prices have been astronomical. It is predicted that the market will drop again when this small group of collectors are satisfied and this atypical activity subsides. For now, we have updated values to reflect current market activity. Also, condition is a very important factor, and typewriters can vary infinitely in condition. A third factor to consider is that an early typewriter achieves its value mainly through the skill, effort, and patience of the collector who restores it to its original condition, in which case its purchase price is insignificant. Some unusual-looking early typewriters are not at all rare or valuable, while some very ordinary-looking ones are scarce and could be quite valuable. No general rules apply.

For further information we recommend *Antique Typewriters & Office Collectibles* by Darryl Rehr (Collector Books). See Clubs, Newsletters, and Catalogs in the Directory for information on the Early Typewriter Collectors Association. When no condition is indicated, the items listed below are assumed to be in excellent, unrestored condition. Our advisor for this category is Mike Brooks; he is listed in the Directory under California.

Bar-lock #1, iron fancy front w/B 1,000.00
Bennet, blk, 3-row, type wheel, 1910..60.00
Blickensderfer #7, 3-row, type wheel, oak base.............................65.00
Caligraph #1, minimum value 1,000.00
Caligraph #2, #3 or #4, ea...100.00
Coffman, flat, linear index..1,000.00
Corona, folding, w/tripod stand 100.00
Daugherty, 4-row, front strike 350.00
Densmore, #2, 1890s..300.00
Edelmann, curved index, Germany, 1897......................................200.00
Franklin, type 1, 3-row, curved keyboard, down strike..................500.00
Hall, Salem, rectangular index...175.00
Hartford, dbl keyboard, up strike, 1890s..200.00
Jewett American Standard, dbl key board, up strike....................250.00
LC Smith & Corona, Comet, 12x11x4½" 65.00
Merritt, index, 1890 ....200.00
Mignon #2, type-sleeve index, blk..200.00

Munson #2, type sleeve, 1890s..225.00
National Portable #5, nickel, 3-row, front strike...........................150.00
Odel #4, index, 1890s...250.00
Oliver #2, 3-row, down strike, nickel base.....................................125.00
Pittsurgh Visible #10, 4-row, front strike 200.00
Postal, NP/japanning, single element print ball, M decal, w/case ...785.00
Remington #4, 4-row, up strike, caps only.....................................350.00
Royal Grand, 4-row, front strike, blk boxy look............................500.00
Sholes & Glidden, Decorated/Remodel, 4-row, up strike, caps only ..2,000.00
Simplex #1, index, orig pnt, 1925..70.00
Sun, index, metal dog-bone base, ca 1888.....................................350.00
Wellington #2, sq keys, 3-row, thrust action 150.00
Yost #1, dbl keyboard, up strike, grasshopper action...................250.00

Uhl Pottery

Founded in Evansville, Indiana, in 1849 by German immigrants, the Uhl Pottery was moved to Huntingburg, Indiana, in 1908 because of the more suitable clay available there. They produced stoneware — Acorn Ware jugs, crocks, and bowls — which were marked with the acorn logo and 'Uhl Pottery.' They also made mugs, pitchers, and vases in simple shapes and solid glazes marked with a circular ink stamp containing the name of the pottery and 'Huntingburg, Indiana.' The pottery closed in the mid-1940s. Those seeking additional information about Uhl pottery are encouraged to contact the Uhl Collectors' Society, whose address is listed in the Directory under Clubs, Newsletters, and Catalogs. For more information, we recommend *Uhl Pottery* by Anna Mary Feldmeyer and Kara Holtzman (Collector Books).

Pitcher, Grape, blue, bulbous, #181, 7", $150.00.

Animal, frog, open mouth, 6", from $325 to....................................425.00
Animal, piggy bank or planter, HP decor, from $550 to..............650.00
Animal, Scotty dog, solid blk, 6½", from $400 to 500.00
Animal, swan, yel or wht, 4¼", from $275 to 350.00
Animal, turtle pencil holder, 5½", from $800 to 900.00
Ashtray, Cannelton Sewer Pipe Co emb on rib, 6¼" dia, $90 to ..120.00
Birdbath, leaves emb, 2-pc, #U-10, 21" bowl, 26", from $200 to...225.00
Bowl, gr, slightly incurvate rim, 6½", from $225 to 250.00
Candle holder, cobalt, emb spirals among stem, 9¾", from $150 to..175.00
Cooler, Ice Tea, advertising, acorn mk, 3-gal, from $550 to........650.00
Creamer & sugar bowl, various colors, w/lid, 3", from $75 to 100.00
Jug, canteen; dk brn, mk, 4½", from $60 to 60.00
Jug, canteen; red, 3½", from $40 to..60.00
Jug, shoulder; Uhl/#3, cobalt on salt glaze, Albany slip top, 15½"..100.00
Mini churn, bl & wht, acorn stamp, 18-oz, 5", from $800 to...1,000.00
Mini pitcher, 2½-3", ea from $70 to...90.00
Pitcher, bl, plain bbl, w/lid, 3-qt, from $150 to............................225.00
Pitcher, bl & wht spongeware, bulbous, ½-gal, from $425 to......525.00
Pitcher, speckled brn, 8", w/4 matching 5" mugs, from $550 to ..650.00
Pot, fern; Grecian design, brn/ivory, #519, 12½" dia, from $60 to...75.00
Salt cellar, emb grapes, gr & tan, w/lid, from $175 to.................200.00
Strawberry jar, 30", from $300 to...380.00
Teapot, bl, stick hdl, 5¾", from $900 to 1,100.00

Vase, bl, stick neck, #168, 8", from $125 to 150.00

Unger Brothers

Art Nouveau silver items of the highest quality were produced by Unger Brothers, who operated in Newark, New Jersey, from the early 1880s until 1919. In addition to tableware, they also made brushes, mirrors, powder boxes, and the like for milady's dressing table as well as jewelry and small personal accessories such as match safes and flasks. They often marked their products with a circle seal containing an intertwined 'UB' and '925 fine sterling.' Some Unger pieces contain a patent date near the mark. In addition to sterling, a very limited amount of gold was also used. Note: This company made no pewter items; Unger designs may occasionally be found in pewter, but these are copies. Items with English hallmarks or signed 'Birmingham' are English (not Unger).

Ashtray, golf scene in center w/4 Devil faces in border, 1912, 5" dia..420.00
Blotter, scrollwork top, wood body w/celluloid sides, #3307, 2x3" 140.00
Chamberstick, leaves & flowers around bobeche, #604, 1 12x6" dia ...185.00
Dresser set, Art Nouveau, 9" mirror+2 brushes+buffer+file+nail cleaner ..700.00
Hairbrush, Love's Dream, 9x3¼" dia 500.00
Mirror, Love's Dream, #10¼x5½" dia...500.00
Pendant, whistle; #2663, 1⅝" 60.00
Spoon, Secret of the Flowers, 1904, 6" 75.00
Tray, ice cream; Sherwood, 8½x13½" 1,100.00

Universal

Universal Potteries Incorporated operated in Cambridge, Ohio, from 1934 to 1956. Many lines of dinnerware and kitchen items were produced in both earthenware and semiporcelain. In 1956 the emphasis was shifted to the manufacture of floor and wall tiles, and the name was changed to the Oxford Tile Company, Division of Universal Potteries. The plant closed in 1976. Our advisor for this category is Ted Haun; he is listed in the Directory under Indiana.

Baby's Breath, bowl, cereal; lug hdls, 6⅞" 15.00
Baby's Breath, plate, bread & butter 13.00
Baby's Breath, plate, dinner 20.00
Baby's Breath, sugar bowl, w/lid 25.00
Ballerina, cake plate 30.00
Ballerina, cup & saucer 12.00
Ballerina, plate, dinner 10.00
Ballerina, platter, 11½" 17.50
Ballerina, sugar bowl, w/lid..20.00
Ballerina (Mist), bowl, serving; 7½" dia.....................................17.50
Ballerina (Mist), bowl, vegetable; rnd, open 25.00
Ballerina (Mist), creamer, open 25.00
Ballerina (Mist), cup & saucer..17.00
Ballerina (Mist), plate, chop; tab hdls 23.00
Ballerina (Mist), plate, dinner 17.00
Ballerina (Mist), plate, salad 17.00
Ballerina (Mist), platter, rnd 25.00
Ballerina (Mist), shakers, pr 20.00
Ballerina (Mist), sugar bowl, w/lid 25.00
Bittersweet, bowl, mixing; sm 20.00
Bittersweet, bowl, vegetable; rnd, open 20.00
Bittersweet, casserole, vegetable; w/lid 20.00
Bittersweet, salt crock, flat bk 30.00
Calico Fruit, bowl, dessert 10.00
Calico Fruit, bowl, fish shape, 6x6½" 30.00
Calico Fruit, cup & saucer...20.00

Calico Fruit, kitchen shaker, no cork...22.00
Calico Fruit, pitcher, utility; 6⅜" 40.00
Calico Fruit, plate, bread & butter...8.00
Calico Fruit, plate, salad 9.00
Cattail, bowl, vegetable; oval, open 20.00
Cattail, creamer 20.00
Cattail, jug, batter; 6" 75.00
Cattail, jug, water; disc shape, 7" 30.00
Cattail, platter, sm, 11½" 20.00
Cattail, platter, 13⅜" dia 30.00
Cattail, sugar bowl, w/lid 20.00
Circus, bowl, soup; 7¾" 20.00
Circus, plate, dinner; 9" 17.50
Harvest, bowl, fruit 15.00
Harvest, cup & saucer 20.00
Harvest, plate, dinner 18.00
Highland, gravy boat, no underplate 35.00
Highland, sugar bowl, w/lid 20.00
Laurella (Coral), plate, dinner 15.00
Laurella (Green), plate, luncheon; 9⅜" 20.00
Rambler Rose, bowl, fruit 22.00
Rambler Rose, creamer, open 30.00
Rambler Rose, cup & saucer 25.00
Rambler Rose, plate, luncheon; sq, 7¼" 23.00
Woodvine, bowl, serving; 3½x9¾" 25.00
Woodvine, jar, utility; w/lid 25.00

University City

Located in University City, Missouri, this pottery opened for only five years (1910 – 1915), but because of the outstanding potters associated with it, produced notable artware. The company's founder was Edward Gardner Lewis, and among the well-known artists he employed were Adelaide Robineau, Fredrick Rhead, Taxile Doat, and Julian Zsolnay.

Teapot, gr matt, modeled as bldg, seated figure on dome lid, rstr, 9" ..3,500.00
Vase, floral, gold on cobalt, dtd 1912, 3" 1,300.00
Vase, wht classic form, sgn TD, mk UC, dtd 1914, 2¼".............475.00

Val St. Lambert

Since its inception in Belgium at the turn of the nineteenth century, the Val St. Lambert Cristalleries has been involved in the production of high-quality glass, producing some cameo. The factory is still in production.

Bottle, scent; cut-bk cranberry floral, faceted stopper, 5½" 250.00
Goblet, cameo floral, gr on clear texture, faceted stem, cut ft, 8" ...400.00
Punch bowl, ruby cut to clear w/circles & chevrons, 7x12" 600.00
Vase, bud; cameo floral, red w/gilt on textured moss, ruffled, att ...300.00
Vase, cameo roses, cobalt on gold geometrics, cylindrical, 10"....700.00
Vase, ruby cut to clear w/ovals etc, dmn band, cut stem, 10" 400.00

Valentines

If you are a beginning collector, please keep in mind that you can still have a wonderful time buying valentines with only $10.00 in your pocket. But as your knowledge increases, so must your pocket money. The best approach is to pick a category that appeals to you and go from there. Always keep the following factors in mind when as you consider your purchase: age, category, size, manufacturer, location, artist signature, condition, and your own personal taste and preferences. Be cautious, but have fun.

Please note: When measuring the size of a card, the background area should be included as well. Our advisor for this category is Katherine Kreider, author of *Valentines With Values*, *One Hundred Years of Valentines*, and *Valentines For the Eclectic Collector*. She is listed in the Directory under Pennsylvania.

Key:
dim — dimension/dimensional   HCPP — honeycomb paper puff
mech — mechanical

Dim, 1D, dbl swan sleigh, early 1900s, PIG, 8x6x3½", EX 125.00
Dim, 1D, Love Boat, 1920s, 8½x11x2", EX 35.00
Dim, 1D, swan carriage, 1920s, 8½x10¾x3", EX...........................35.00
Dim, 3D, butterfly w/fan, 1915, 5x6x3", EX....................................75.00
Dim, 4D, cannon, early 1900s, PIG, 6x6½x3½", EX....................125.00
Dim, 4D, red carriage, 1920s, 7¼x8x2¾", EX................................75.00
Flat, African American children holding hands, 1940s, 4¼x4¼", EX..10.00
Flat, bear/honey bee hive, 1940s, USA, 3¾x2¾", EX 5.00
Flat, Indians in canoe, 1940s, 4x5", EX..10.00
Flat, Rosie the Riveter, 1940s, 3½x3", EX....................................10.00
Flat, Uncle Sam, 1920s, chromolitho, 3½x3", EX 20.00
Flat w/D, die-cut vase w/HCPP flowers, 1900s, PIG, 22x18", EX..95.00
Flat w/D, Dutch girl, Tuck, 1900s, PIG, 9¼x5", EX......................75.00
Flat w/D, Tuck, children w/basket of flowers, 1900s, PIG, 7½x8", EX ..75.00
Flat w/easel bk, flocked dog & cat, 1940s, Hallmark, 8½x7", EX....6.00
Folded flat, Asian, USA, 4x3½x5", EX 10.00
Folded flat, Little Red Riding Hood, 1940s, 4x5¼", EX 15.00
Folded flat, Olive Oyl, USA, 1930s, 6½x6", EX...........................35.00
Folded flat, roller coaster, USA, 1940s, 4x6", EX..........................15.00
Folded flat, Schnauzer, 6x5½", EX..10.00
Greeting card, Esther Howland, 1940s, 7x4½", EX 250.00
Greeting card, Kewpie, Rose O'Neill, 1910-1920, Gibson, 6½x4", EX..75.00
Greeting card, Mary Had a Lamb, Stanley, USA, 1950, 6x4", EX ..6.00
Greeting card, St Valentine's Greeting, early 1900s, emb, 6x4½", EX..10.00
Greeting card, Thistle Scottie Dog, 1940s, 4x3¾", EX 6.00
Greeting card, Whitney, 1877, 3¾x3", EX.....................................35.00
HCPP, cherub flower basket, Beistle, 1920s, 10x7x3¾", EX...........50.00
HCPP, flower basket w/Doxie, 1920s, PIG, 12x8x3½", EX 50.00
HCPP, Gone w/the Wind lamp, 1900, PIG, 6½x2½x2½", EX 75.00
HCPP, parasol, early 1900s, 14x8x6½", EX..................................125.00
HCPP, Victoria, early 1900s, PIG, 10½x8x4", EX 125.00
Mech-flat, Blue Fairy, 1939, Disney, 5x4¾", EX 40.00
Mech-flat, Bohemian under palm tree, 1920s, PIG, 8½x4", EX....25.00
Mech-flat, boy golfer, A-Tee, 1920s, PIG, 6½x4½", EX................25.00
Mech-flat, cowboy, 1920s, 6½x4", EX 15.00
Mech-flat, lady w/powder puff, USA, 1940s, 4x4", EX..................20.00
Mech-flat, stock broker, 1930s, PIG, 4½x3½", EX 20.00
Mech-flat w/easel bk, African wash woman, 1900s, 6¾x4¼", EX.75.00
Mech-flat w/easel bk, Boston Bull Messenger, USA/'30s, 9¾x4½" 50.00
Novelty, book, Happy Times w/Jack & Jane, 1934-39, hardbk, EX 50.00
Novelty, paper doll, A-meri-card, Football, USA/'30s, 4½x4½", EX..20.00
Novelty, plastic Love Boat w/lollipop, 5½x6x11¼", EX................45.00
Novelty, Spaniel, squeak toy, PIG, early 1900s, 6½x5", EX...........50.00
Novelty, valentine seals by Dennison, USA, 1920s, EX 5.00
Postcard, cherub hold-to-light, early 1900s, undivided, EX...........50.00
Postcard, cherub spinning web, Clapsaddle, EX 15.00
Postcard, dressed animals, mid-1900s, emb, PIG, EX.....................5.00
Postcard, embr silk, From a Loving Heart, France, 1910-15, EX ...10.00
Postcard, mech, Forget-Me-Knot, mid-1900s, Intern'l Pub Co, EX...10.00

Vallerysthal

Fine glassware has been produced in Vallerysthal, France, since the middle of the nineteenth century.

Cameo

Vase, grapes/vines/butterfly, citron/yel on gr frost, slim, 7".......1,100.00
Vase, holly branches, gr on red w/gold, 2 appl berries, ftd U form, 7"..2,050.00
Vase, leaves/flowers, cut/pnt, w/gilt, bulbous/ftd, 5¾" 2,000.00

Miscellaneous

Candle holder, pk, beading on tapered stem & rim, 9" 70.00
Vase, dahlias, mc/etched on olive gr, appl centers, 9" 1,100.00

Van Briggle

The Van Briggle Pottery of Colorado Springs, Colorado, was established in 1901 by Artus Van Briggle, whose early career had been shaped by such notables as Karl Langenbeck and Maria Nichols Storer. His quest for several years had been to perfect a completely flat matt glaze, and upon accomplishing his goal, he opened his pottery. His wife, Anne, worked with him, and they, along with George Young, were responsible for the modeling of the wares. Their work typified the flow and form of the Art Nouveau movement, and the shapes they designed played as important a part in their success as their glazes. Some of their most famous pieces were Despondency, Lorelei, and Toast Cup. Increasing demand for their work soon made it necessary to add to their quarters as well as their staff. Although much of the ware was eventually made from molds, each piece was carefully trimmed and refined before the glaze was sprayed on. Their most popular colors were Persian Rose, Ming Blue, and Mustard Yellow.

Van Briggle died in 1904, but the work was continued by his wife. New facilities were built; and by 1908, in addition to their artware, tiles, gardenware, and commercial lines were added. By the '20s the emphasis had shifted from art pottery to novelties and commercial wares. Reproductions of some of the early designs continue to be made. The double AA mark has always been in use, but after 1920 the dates and/or shape numbers were dropped. Mention should be made here as well that the Anna Van Briggle glaze is a later line which was made between 1956 and 1968. Our advisor for this category is Michelle Ross; she is listed in the Directory under Michigan. For more information, we recommend *Collector's Encyclopedia of Van Briggle Art Pottery* by Richard Sasicki and Josie Fania (Collector Books).

Tile, trees/mountains, 5-color, 6", NM, in orig Arts & Crafts fr 2,100.00
Vase, arrowhead leaves (cvd), curdled gr on dk rose, 1903, 9x10"..17,000.00
Vase, bsk fired, teardrop shape w/floral neck band, lg hdls, '04, 16"..1,700.00
Vase, clover & grass, blended bl, buttressed hdls, #19, 8½x7" 880.00
Vase, Dos Cabezas, lady in flowing gown, yel w/rose, 1907-12, 7½"..18,000.00
Vase, dragonflies (emb/cvd), gr/bl, clay exposed, ca 1907-12, 6½"........1,300.00
Vase, floral, bl tones w/suspended particles, clay exposed, '07, 10" 850.00
Vase, floral, dk purple, #11/6, 3¾x3", NM 220.00
Vase, floral, gr on dk purple, 1905, 10" 2,800.00
Vase, floral (leaves at base), aqua to deep bl, #20, 4x3¼" 195.00
Vase, floral (long stems, emb/cvd), curdled gr bl, 1905, #15/232, 7" ..2,100.00
Vase, flowers & leaves, brn matt, flared cylinder, post-1920s, 17" ...450.00
Vase, gr & gray mottle, tapered form, 1906, 7" 1,300.00
Vase, grass blades, plum-maroon, gourd shape, 6x2½", NM........165.00
Vase, leaves, gr/bl matt, 1907-12, 4½"......................................750.00
Vase, leaves, purple/yel, flared cylinder, 1906, 8"....................1,600.00
Vase, leaves (vertical), mottled mauve, 1907-12, 6½" 1,300.00
Vase, leaves (vertical), multitone rose, bulging shoulder, 1914, 7"...700.00
Vase, lines/floral (simply cvd), maroon, 1917, slim form, 6" 325.00
Vase, Lorelei, blk, post-1940, 10½" 650.00
Vase, Lorelei, burgundy & dk bl, 1920-30s, 10½" 1,100.00
Vase, peacock feathers, brn/gr matt, dtd 1905, spherical, 5" 3,750.00

Vase, poppies, dk bl/red, ca 1920-30, 8½" 300.00
Vase, poppy, brn/bl/cream gloss, dtd 1903, cylindrical, 4¼" 2,100.00
Vase, stems/buds, mauve w/charcoal, shouldered, #278, 1906, 6" .2,150.00
Vase, sunflowers/leaves, 2-tone bl, post-1920, bulbous, 8½" 450.00
Vase, tulips (emb/cut-bk), bl/maroon, 1910-20, slim form, 7" 450.00

Vance/Avon Faience

Although pottery had been made in Tiltonville, Ohio, since about 1880, the ware manufactured there was of little significance until after the turn of the century when the Vance Faience Company was organized for the purpose of producing quality artware. By 1902 the name had been changed to the Avon Faience Company, and late in the same year it and three other West Virginia potteries incorporated to form the Wheeling Potteries Company. The Avon branch operated in Tiltonville until 1905 when production was moved to Wheeling. Art pottery was discontinued.

From the beginning, only skilled craftsmen and trained engineers were hired. Wm. P. Jervis and Fredrick Hurten Rhead were among the notable artists responsible for designing some of the early artware. Some of the ware was slip decorated under glaze, while other pieces were molded with high-relief designs. Examples with squeeze-bag decoration by Rhead are obviously forerunners of the Jap Birdimal line he later developed for Weller. Ware was marked 'Vance F. Co.'; 'Avon F. Co., Tiltonville'; or 'Avon W. Pts. Co.'

Jardiniere, slip-trailed flowers, brn tones & wht, 3-ftd, Avon, 6⅛" ..500.00
Jardiniere & ped, sunflowers, R Lorber, 1901, overall: 31⅜" 600.00
Mug, landscape band & florals on creamware, 6" 75.00
Vase, landscape, in manner of WP Jervis, Avon R 166-1341, 5⅞" 550.00
Vase, mermaids & creatures, brn tones, bulbous, #118, 11⅞" ..1,200.00

Vaseline

Vaseline, a greenish-yellow colored glass produced by adding uranium oxide to the batch, was produced during the Victorian era. It was made in smaller quantities than other colors and lost much of its popularity with the advent of the electric light. It was used for pressed tablewares, vases, whimseys, souvenir items, oil lamps, perfume bottles, drawer pulls, and doorknobs. Pieces have been reproduced, and some factories still make it today in small batches. Vaseline glass will fluoresce under an ultraviolet light.

Biscuit jar, Optic, 8x4¾" 365.00
Bottle, scent; cut decor, hexagonal, 3¾" stopper, 6¾" overall 285.00
Bowl, Daisy & Button, scalloped rim, 4x10" 100.00
Cake plate, Daisy & Button, ftd, 5x9" 125.00
Candlesticks, blown w/appl leaves at top, bl-gr at rim/ft, 14", pr ...350.00

Cigar lighter, Hobnail, cast-iron base, counter-top style, 8" diameter, $2,000.00. (Photo courtesy Jackson's Auctioneers & Appraisers)

Compote, ornate rim, molded leaves on bowl, tall ft, 6½x5" 445.00

Compote, Three Panel, Richards & Hartley, ca 1888, 4x10" 85.00
Creamer & sugar bowl, gold trim, w/lid, 3¾", 5⅜", NM 115.00
Decanter, cut, pitcher form, tall matching stopper, 16" 300.00
Fishbowl/tank, emb diagonal lines, globular, 13¼x15½", EX+ ...400.00
Novelty, canoe, Daisy & Button, 3½x11½x4" 110.00
Novelty, wheelbarrow w/brass wheel, 3½x9½x5½", NM 115.00
Pitcher, Basketweave, 1880s, 8¾" 120.00
Pitcher, Block & Star, short ped ft, 7¼", NM 125.00
Pitcher, emb dmns, 1930s, 8½" 60.00
Rose bowl, Lincoln Drape, ftd, wht opal top, 4½x5" 95.00
Spill holder, pressed loop floriform top w/petal rim, wide disc ft, 6" 575.00
Tumbler, HP decor, 4½", NM 75.00
Vase, car; 7½x2" sq 60.00

Verlys

Verlys art glass, produced in France after 1931 by the Holophane Company of Verlys, was made in crystal with acid-finished relief work in the Art Deco style. Colored and opalescent glass was also used. In 1935 an American branch was opened in Newark, Ohio, where very similar wares were produced until the factory ceased production in 1951. French Verlys was signed with one of three mold-impressed script signatures, all containing the company name and country of origin. The American-made glassware was signed 'Verlys' only, either scratched with a diamond-tipped pen or impressed in the mold. There is very little if any difference in value between items produced in France and America. Though some seem to feel that the French should be higher priced (assuming it to be scarce), many prefer the American-made product.

In June of 1955, about sixteen Verlys molds were leased to the A.H. Heisey Company. Heisey's versions were not signed with the Verlys name, so if an item is unsigned it is almost certainly a Heisey piece. The molds were returned to Verlys of America in July 1957. Fenton now owns all Verlys molds, but all issues are marked Fenton. Our advisor for this category is Don Frost; he is listed in the Directory under Washington.

Ashtray, Swallow, etched crystal, 4¾" 85.00
Bowl, Alpine Thistle, satin, 2¾x8¾" 120.00
Bowl, Birds & Bees, Directoire Blue, 2¼x11⅝" 350.00
Bowl, Butterfly, opal, 13¾" 650.00
Bowl, Chrysanthemum, 6x10" 385.00
Bowl, console; Doves, frosted, 1936, 4½x12" 450.00
Bowl, girl & lamb, clear/frosted, C Schmitz, 1940, 1¾x13½" 150.00
Bowl, Pine Cone, satin, 3-ftd, 6¼" 90.00
Bowl, Poppies, clear/frosted, 13½" 325.00
Bowl, Water Lilies, clear/frosted, shallow, 13" 60.00
Box, Chrysanthemums, topaz, 5¼" 375.00
Figurine, fish, opal, 1930s, 5⅛x6x2" 110.00
Vase, Butterflies, opal, 5x5" 185.00
Vase, Japanese man in garden/flower branch/bird, clear/frosted, 9¼" ..215.00
Vase, Seasons, wheat Autumn/dancer Spring, Schmitz, 8x5" ..1,000.00
Vase, Thistle, topaz, 9¾" 450.00
Vase, Wheat, clear/frosted, 9½x6½" 165.00

Vernon Kilns

Vernon Potteries Ltd. was established by Faye G. Bennison in Vernon, California, in 1931. The name was later changed to Vernon Kilns; until it closed in 1958, dinnerware, specialty plates, artware, and figurines were their primary products. Among its wares most sought after by collectors today are items designed by such famous artists as Rockwell Kent, Walt Disney, Don Blanding, Jane Bennison, and May and Vieve Hamilton. Our advisor is Maxine Nelson, author of *Collectible Vernon*

Kilns (now out of print); you will find her listed in the Directory under Arizona.

Anytime Shape

Patterns you will find on this shape include Tickled Pink, Heavenly Days, Anytime, Imperial, Sherwood, Frolic, Young in Heart, Rose-A-Day, and Dis 'N Dot.

Bowl, fruit; 5½", from $4 to	6.00
Bowl, vegetable; rnd, 9", from $12 to	14.00
Butter tray & lid, from $25 to	35.00
Cup & saucer, tea; from $8 to	12.00
Mug, 12-oz, from $12 to	20.00
Plate, dinner; 10", from $8 to	12.00
Platter, 9½", from $9 to	12.00
Syrup, drip-cut top, from $45 to	65.00
Tumbler, 14-oz, from $12 to	22.00

Chatelaine Shape

This designer pattern by Sharon Merrill was made in four color combinations: Topaz, Bronze, decorated Platinum, and Jade.

Bowl, chowder; Topaz & Bronze, 6", from $12 to	15.00
Coffee cup, flat base, decor Platinum & Jade, from $15 to	20.00
Plate, chop; decor Platinum & Jade, 14", from $55 to	65.00
Plate, dinner; leaf 1 corner, Topaz & Bronze, 10½", from $15 to	17.00
Sugar bowl, w/lid, Topaz & Bronze, from $20 to	30.00

Lotus and Pan American Lei Shape

Patterns on this shape include Lotus, Chinling, and Vintage. Pan American Lei was a variation with flatware from the San Marino line. To evaluate Lotus, use the low end of our range as the minimum value; the high end of values apply to Pan American Lei.

Bowl, chowder; 6", from $10 to	18.00
Bowl, mixing; Pan American Lei only, 7"	40.00
Bowl, vegetable; rnd, 9", from $15 to	35.00
Coffee/teapot, 8-cup, from $35 to	80.00
Creamer, from $15 to	27.00
Pitcher, jug form, 2-qt, from $35 to	95.00
Plate, chop/coupe; Pan American Lei only, 13"	50.00
Shakers, pr, from $15 to	50.00

Melinda Shape

Patterns found on this shape are: Arcadia, Beverly, Blossom Time, Chintz, Cosmos, Dolores, Fruitdale, Hawaii (Lei Lani on Melinda is two and a half times base value), May Flower, Monterey, Native California, and Philodendron. The more elaborate the pattern, the higher the value.

May Flower, sauce boat, $30.00.

Bowl, lug chowder; 6", from $10 to	25.00
Bowl, serving; rnd, 9", from $15 to	25.00
Casserole, w/lid, 8" (inside dia), from $35 to	65.00
Cup & saucer, AD; from $10 to	25.00
Pitcher, 1½-pt, from $20 to	30.00
Plate, chop; 12", from $15 to	30.00
Plate, luncheon; 8½" sq, from $10 to	15.00
Platter, 14", from $20 to	35.00
Relish, single leaf shape, 12", from $20 to	25.00
Shakers, pr, from $12 to	24.00

Montecito Shape (and Coronado)

This was one of the company's most utilized shapes — well over two hundred patterns have been documented. Among the most popular are the solid colors, plaids, the florals, westernware, and the Bird and Turnbull series. Bird, Turnbull, and Winchester 73 (Frontier Days) are two to four times base values. Disney hollow ware is seven to eight times base values. Plaids (except Tweed and Calico), solid colors, Brown-eyed Susan are represented by the lower range.

Ashtray, sq, ind, 3", from $8 to	12.00
Bowl, salad; rnd, 10½", from $40 to	50.00
Bowl, serving; divided, 10", from $15 to	20.00
Coaster/cup warmer, 4½", from $15 to	25.00
Coffeepot, AD; 2-cup, scarce, from $60 to	70.00
Jam jar, notched lid, 5", from $55 to	65.00
Muffin tray, tab hdls, dome lid, 9", from $50 to	75.00
Mug, str sides, later style, 3½", 9-oz, from $16 to	22.00
Plate, chop; 14", from $20 to	50.00
Plate, salad; 7½", from $8 to	12.00
Platter, 10½", from $15 to	20.00
Shakers, regular, pr, from $15 to	20.00
Tumbler, #4, bulb bottom, 3¾", from $18 to	25.00

San Fernando Shape

Known patterns for this shape are Desert Bloom, Early Days, Hibiscus, R.F.D., Vernon's 1860, and Vernon Rose.

Bowl, lug chowder; 6", from $12 to	15.00
Bowl, mixing; RFD only, 5", from $15 to	19.00
Bowl, mixing; RFD only, 9", from $30 to	35.00
Bowl, salad; ind, 5½", from $12 to	15.00
Bowl, serving; oval, 10", from $20 to	25.00
Coffeepot, 8-cup, from $35 to	65.00
Cup & saucer, AD; from $16 to	26.00
Plate, dinner; 10½", from $12 to	18.00
Plate, luncheon; scarce, 9½", from $10 to	15.00
Platter, 14", from $25 to	35.00
Shakers, pr, from $16 to	24.00
Teapot, 6-cup, from $45 to	65.00

San Marino Shape

Known patterns for this shape are Barkwood, Bel Air, California Originals, Casual California, Gayety, Hawaiian Coral, Heyday, Lei Lani (two and a half times base values), Mexicana, Pan American Lei (two and a half times base values), Raffia, Shadow Leaf, Shantung, Sun Garden, and Trade Winds.

Bowl, fruit; 5½", from $6 to	8.00
Bowl, mixing; 6", from $15 to	22.00
Bowl, mixing; 8", from $25 to	35.00

Bowl, serving; rnd, 7½", from $10 to...**14.00**
Butter pat, ind, 2½", from $12 to..**18.00**
Casserole, w/metal stand & candle warmer, from $45 to **55.00**
Coffee server, w/stopper, 10-cup, from $25 to..**30.00**
Cup, jumbo; from $20 to..**30.00**
Flowerpot, 4", from $15 to...**25.00**
Pitcher, ½-pt, from $12 to..**15.00**
Plate, salad; 7½", from $5 to...**10.00**
Platter, 9½", from $10 to...**15.00**
Sugar bowl, w/lid, from $10 to...**15.00**

Ultra Shape

More than fifty patterns were issued on this shape. Nearly all the artist-designed lines (Rockwell, Kent, Don Blanding, and Disney) utilized Ultra. The shape was developed by Gale Turnbull, and many of the elaborate flower and fruit patterns can be credited to him as well; use the high end of our range as a minimum value for his work. For Frederick Lunning, use the mid range. For other artist patterns, use these formulae based on the high end: Blanding — 2X (Aquarium 3X); Disney — 7 – 8X; Kent — Moby Dick and Our America, 2½X, Salamina, 5 – 7X.

Bowl, chowder; w/lid, from $18 to..**25.00**
Bowl, fruit; 5½", from $6 to..**12.00**
Bowl, salad; 11", from $40 to..**75.00**
Butter tray, w/lid, oblong, from $35 to..**50.00**
Creamer, open, ind, from $12 to...**18.00**
Cup & saucer, AD; from $19 to...**30.00**
Muffin lid only (no tray), from $35 to...**65.00**
Pitcher, jug form, w/lid, 1-pt, from $35 to..**50.00**
Plate, dinner; 10½", from $12 to..**24.00**
Plate, luncheon; 8½", from $12 to..**20.00**
Sugar bowl, w/lid, ind, from $20 to...**30.00**
Teapot, 6-cup, from $45 to..**75.00**

Year 'Round Shape

Patterns on this shape include Country Cousin, Lollipop Tree, and Blueberry Hill.

Bowl, cereal/soup; from $8 to..**10.00**
Coffeepot, 6-cup, from $25 to..**45.00**
Cup & saucer, tea; from $8 to..**12.00**
Mug, 12-oz, from $12 to...**20.00**
Plate, salad; 7½", from $5 to...**8.00**
Sugar bowl, w/lid, from $8 to..**15.00**

Fantasia

Bowl, Winged Nymph, 2½x12"...**350.00**
Centaurette, #18, from $750 to **900.00**
Elephant, #26, from $400 to..**600.00**
Nubian Centaurette, #23, from $900 to..**1,100.00**
Ostrich, #28, #29 or #30, ea from $800 to **1,200.00**
Pegasus, #21, from $300 to..**400.00**
Pegasus, Baby; blk, #19, from $250 to **400.00**
Sprite or satyr, various #s, ea from $200 to...**350.00**
Vase, Winged Pegasus, rare, 7½x12" **1,200.00**

Souvenir Plates

Down on the Levee, Bits of the Old South, 14", from $65 to **95.00**
Fort McHenry, Historic Baltimore, 8½", from $30 to **35.00**
Frederick Chopin, Music Masters, 8½", from $18 to **25.00**

His Holiness Pope Pious XVII Prayer for Peace, 10½", from $45 to...**65.00**
Horse Thieves, Bits of the Old West, 14", from $65 to.................**95.00**
Off to the Hunt, Bits of the Old South, 8½", from $25 to **45.00**
San Jose de Guadalupe, Mission series, 8½", from $25 to.............**35.00**
Unloading the Nets, Bits of the Old Northwest, 8½", from $40 to...**50.00**

Villeroy and Boch

The firm of Villeroy and Boch, located in Mettlach, Germany, was brought into being by the 1841 merger of three German factories — the Wallerfangen factory, founded by Nicholas Villeroy in 1787; and Boch's father's factory in Septfontaines, established in 1767. Villeroy and Boch produced many varieties of wares, including earthenware with printed under-glaze designs which carried the well-known castle mark with the name 'Mettlach.' See also Mettlach.

Jardiniere, Dutch figures in landscape, castle mk, 12½x13"........**895.00**
Paperweight, dwarf pushing wax seal on envelope, 5" **440.00**
Vase, gr crystalline, shouldered, V&B Luxembourg, 12⅝" **700.00**
Vase, 2-figure scene fr w/scrolls, 1 flower-appl hdl, metal lid, 9" .**200.00**

Vistosa

Vistosa was produced from about 1938 through the early 1940s. It was Taylor, Smith, and Taylor's answer to the very successful Fiesta line of their nearby competitor, Homer Laughlin. Vistosa was made in four solid colors: mango red, cobalt blue, light green, and deep yellow. 'Pie crust' edges and a dainty five-petal flower molded into handles and lid finials made for a very attractive yet nevertheless commercially unsuccessful product. For further information, we recommend *Collector's Guide to Lu-Ray Pastels* by Kathy and Bill Meehan (Collector Books). Our advisor for this category is Ted Haun; he is listed in the Directory under Indiana.

Bowl, cream soup; from $20 to **25.00**
Bowl, fruit; from $10 to...**15.00**
Bowl, nappy; from $40 to..**50.00**
Bowl, salad; ftd, 12", from $175 to...**200.00**
Bowl, soup; lug hdl, from $25 to...**30.00**
Chop plate, 12"...**40.00**
Chop plate, 15", from $40 to...**50.00**
Coffee cup, AD; from $40 to..**50.00**
Coffee saucer, AD; from $20 to...**25.00**
Creamer..**20.00**
Egg cup, ftd, from $25 to **35.00**
Jug, water; 2-qt, from $80 to **90.00**
Plate, 6", from $10 to..**15.00**
Plate, 7", from $12 to..**18.00**
Plate, 9", from $15 to..**20.00**
Plate, 10", from $50 to..**60.00**
Platter, 13", from $40 to...**50.00**
Sauce boat, from $150 to **175.00**
Shakers, pr **32.00**
Sugar bowl, w/lid **25.00**
Teacup, from $10 to..**15.00**
Teapot, 6-cup, from $150 to..**175.00**

Vontury

Located in New Jersey, F.J. Von Tury is primarily a designer of architectural artware, tile and murals in particular, but he also produces a line of vases, bowls, and other decorative items. These are signed 'Vontury' in script. Impressionistic florals are favored.

Bowl, brn/tan, no decor, 4½x9½" 38.00
Leaf dish, 7x6" 48.00
Vase, abstract flower, stepped shoulder, 7x4¾" 125.00
Vase, long stem flower, 8⅜" 145.00

Wade

The Wade Potteries was established in 1867 by George Wade and his partner, a man by the name of Myatt. It was located in Burslem, England, the center of that country's pottery industry. In 1882 George Wade bought out his partner, and the name of the pottery was changed to Wade and Sons. In 1919 the pottery underwent yet another name change and became known as George Wade & Son Ltd. The year 1891 saw the establishment of another Wade Pottery — J & W Wade & Co., which in turn changed its name to A.J. Wade & Co. in 1927. At this time (1927) Wade Heath & Co. Ltd. was also formed.

The three potteries plus a new Irish pottery named Wade (Ireland) Ltd. were incorporated into one company in 1958 and given the name The Wade Group of Potteries. In 1990 the group was taken over by Beauford PLC. and became Wade Ceramics Ltd. It sold again in early 1999 to Wade Management and is now a private company.

For those interested in learning more about Wade pottery, we recommend *The World of Wade* and *The World of Wade Book 2* by Ian Warner and Mike Posgay; Mr. Warner is listed in the Directory under Canada.

Animal Figurine, Alsatian, glass eyes, ca 1936, 5¼x7½" 170.00
Animal Figurine, Calf, 1930s, 1¾x1¼" 170.00
Animal Figurine, Laughing Rabbit, late 1930s, 7" 145.00
Animal Figurine, Mrs Penguin, late 1940s-50s, 3" 125.00
Animal Figurine, Single Budgerigar, 1940s-50s, 7½" 375.00
British Character, Fishmonger, ca 1959, 3⅛" 240.00
British Character, Pearly Queen, ca 1959, 2⅞" 200.00
Connoisseur's Collection, Goldcrest, 5¼" 400.00
Connoisseur's Collection, Nuthatch, 5½" 450.00
Disney, Chief, 1981-87, 1⅞" 32.00
Disney, Girl Squirrel (Sword & Stone), paper label only, 1956-65, 2" ..100.00
Disney, Merlin as a Hare, 1965, 2¼x1⅜" 220.00

Disney, Snow White and the Seven Dwarfs, 1980s, $1,500.00 for the set. (Photo courtesy Joel Cohen)

Disney, Thumper Blow-Up, 1961-65, 5¼" 450.00
Disney, Tramp Blow-Up, 1961-65, 6" 400.00
Dogs & Puppies Series, Alsatian Puppy, 1969-82, 2¼" 14.00
Dogs & Puppies Series, Red Setter Adult, 1973-82, 2¼" 25.00
Dogs & Puppies Series, Yorkshire Terrier Puppy, 1979-82, 1⅜" 35.00
Happy Families Series, Dog Parent, 1978-86, 2" 30.00
Happy Families Series, Frog Parent, 1978-86, ⅞" 18.00
Happy Families Series, Rabbit Baby, 1978-86, 1⅛" 14.00

Nursery Favourite, Boy Blue, 1974, 2⅞" 52.00
Nursery Favourite, Miss Muffet, 1972, 2⅝" 50.00
Nursery Rhyme Character, Baby bear, 1949-58, 1¾" 210.00
Nursery Rhyme Character, Blynkin, 1949-58, 2" 200.00
Nursery Rhyme Character, Soldier, 1949-58, 3" 200.00
Painted Lady, Pink, 1984-86, 2¼" 80.00
Painted Lady, Yellow, 1984-86, 2½" 65.00
Red Rose Tea (Canada), Alligator, 1967-73, ½x1½" 10.00
Red Rose Tea (Canada), Butterfly, 1967-73, ½x1¾" 8.00
Red Rose Tea (Canada), Queen of Hearts, 1¾x1" 15.00
Red Rose Tea (USA), Beaver, 1985, 1¼" 6.00
Red Rose Tea (USA), Koala Bear, 1985, 1⅜" 5.00
Tortoise Family, Slow Fe Baby Tortoise, ca 1969-70 ....90.00
Whimsie, Bluebird, 1979, ⅝" 10.00
Whimsie, Fox Cub, 1955, 1⅜" 75.00
Whimsie, Hedgehog, 1974, ⅞" 8.00
Whimsie, Huskey, 1956, 1¼" 45.00
Whimsie, Italian Goat, 1959, 1⅜" 75.00
Whimsie, Kitten, 1943, 1⅜" 48.00
Whimsie, Lamb, 1971-84, 2⅜x1⅛" 10.00
Whimsie, Polar Bear Blow-Up, ca 1962, 6" 350.00
Whimsie, Rhinoceros, 1955, 1¾" 40.00
Whimsie, Shire Horse, brn glaze, 1953-59, 2x2⅛" 300.00
Whimsie, Snowy Owl, 1958, 1⅛" 50.00
Whimsie - Land Series, Golden Eagle, 1984-88, 1⅛x1¾" 40.00
Whimsie - Land Series, Pheasant, 1984-88, 2¼x2" 40.00
Whimsie - Land Series, Rooster, 1984+, 2" 24.00
Whoppas, Brown Bear, 1976-81, 1½" 25.00
Whoppas, Fox, 1976-81, 1¼x2½" 48.00
Whoppas, Polar Bear, 1976-81, 1½" 28.00
World of Survival Series, American Buffalo (Cape Buffalo) 575.00
World of Survival Series, Polar Bear...400.00

Wallace China

Dinnerware with a Western theme was produced by the Wallace China Company, who operated in California from 1931 until 1964. Artist Till Goodan designed three lines, Rodeo, Pioneer Trails, and Boots and Saddle, which they marketed under the package name Westward Ho. When dinnerware with a western theme became so popular just a few years ago, Rodeo was reproduced, but the new trademark includes neither 'California' or 'Wallace China.'

This ware is very heavy and not prone to chips, but be sure to examine it under a strong light to look for knife scratches, which will lessen its value to a considerable extent when excessive. Our advisor for this category is Marv Fogleman; he is listed in the Directory under California. If you'd like to learn more about this company, we recommend *The Collector's Encyclopedia of California Pottery* by Jack Chipman.

Boots & Saddle, ashtray, from $45 to 50.00
Boots & Saddle, pitcher, water 400.00
Boots & Saddle, plate, 7" 40.00
Chuck Wagon, butter pat..50.00
Chuck Wagon, cup & saucer..75.00
Chuck Wagon, plate, 9" 45.00
El Rancho, ashtray...25.00
El Rancho, bowl, 5" 45.00
El Rancho, creamer 65.00
El Rancho, cup & saucer...65.00
El Rancho, plate, dinner; 10½", minimum value........................100.00
El Rancho, platter, 11½" 95.00
Little Buckaroo, mug, 6-oz 175.00
Little Buckaroo, plate, 9½" 125.00

Longhorn, sugar bowl, w/lid 285.00
Rodeo, bowl, oval serving; 12½x9½" 225.00
Rodeo, bowl, Storz (defunct brewing company), 2¼x6" 140.00
Rodeo, chop plate, 13" 200.00
Rodeo, creamer 95.00
Rodeo, cup & saucer, lg..100.00
Rodeo, pitcher, ice water; 72-oz......................................425.00
Rodeo, plate, bread & butter; 7¼"......................................50.00
Rodeo, plate, luncheon; rare, 9½" 150.00
Rodeo, platter, oval, 16" 200.00
Rodeo, shakers, 3½", pr...125.00
Rodeo, sugar bowl/jam pot, w/lid, 4x5"............................125.00
Westward Ho, ashtray, Mark Twain center.........................75.00

Walley

The Walley Pottery operated in West Sterling, Massachusetts, from 1898 to 1919. Never more than a one-man operation, Walley himself handcrafted all his wares from local clay. The majority of his pottery was simple and unadorned and usually glazed in matt green. On occasion, however, you may find high- and semi-gloss green, as well as matt glazes in blue, cream, brown, and red. The rarest and most desirable examples of his work are those with applied or relief-carved decorations. Some pieces are marked 'WJW.'

Candlesticks, gr mottle, saucer base, mk WJW, 10", NM, pr ...1,300.00
Vase, brn & blk mottle, pinched rim, att, 2½"...............................80.00
Vase, brn & gr flambe, bulbous, 5½x5½" 400.00
Vase, gr mottle, early 1900s, mk WJW, 4¼x2¾" 625.00
Vase, gr-brn flambe on gr high-gloss, mk WJW, 10x7" 2,350.00
Vase, mahog flambe, collar rim, mk WJW, 6¾x6¾" 1,500.00

Walrath

Frederick Walrath was a studio potter who worked from around the turn of the century until his death in 1920. He was located in Rochester, New York, until 1918 when he became associated with the Newcomb Pottery in New Orleans, Louisiana.

Mug, brn w/band of bl berries & gr leaves, 4" 310.00
Pitcher, cider; Arts & Crafts floral on mustard, brn int, 10", +6 mugs...4,250.00
Planter, leaves, dk gr on olive gr, 3-ftd, 3½x7½", NM 550.00
Scarab, bl matt, 3½", EX...170.00
Vase, cypress trees, ochre/red/bl-gray, bell shape, 5¼x3¾".......5,000.00
Vase, geometrics w/stylized foliage, peach on bl, 7" 850.00
Vase, gr snowflake crystalline on cream & brn flambe, baluster, 9½" ..3,750.00
Vase, leaves & vines w/berries, olive & pk on dk gr, 5½" 3,500.00
Vase, pine cones, brn on gr matt, 12"..................................2,750.00
Vase, stylized trees/cloud/moon, gr/oatmeal/orange/bl, 7x4¼" ..13,000.00

Walter, A.

Almaric Walter was employed from 1904 through 1914 at Verreries Artistiques des Freres Daum in Nancy, France. After 1919 he opened his own business where he continued to make the same type of quality objets d'art in pate-de-verre glass as he had earlier. His pieces are signed A. Walter, Nancy H. Berge Sc.

Dish, bumblebee, brn on yel, sgn Berge, 2½x4" 1,100.00
Dish, frog on side, yel/lime, 6½".....................................2,875.00
Paperweight, Buddha form, lt bl, sgn Henri Berge SC, 3" 850.00

Paperweight, infant's face, amethyst, 4½" 700.00
Paperweight, rabbit w/ear up, gr/brn mottle, 3 " L 850.00

Wannopee

The Wannopee Pottery, established in 1892, developed from the reorganization of the financially insecure New Milford Pottery Company of New Milford, Connecticut. They produced a line of mottled-glazed pottery called 'Duchess' and a similar line in porcelain. Both were marked with the impressed sunburst 'W' with 'porcelain' added to indicate that particular body type.

In 1895 semiporcelain pitchers in three sizes were decorated with relief medallion cameos of Beethoven, Mozart, and Napoleon. Lettuce-leaf ware was first produced in 1901 and used actual leaves in the modeling. Scarabronze, made in 1895, was their finest artware. It featured simple Egyptian shapes with a coppery glaze. It was marked with a scarab, either impressed or applied. Production ceased in 1903.

Candlestick, brn, twisted cylinder w/flared ft, 13¼x8¼"............450.00
Chamberstick, tiger eye flambe, twisted shaft, rpr bobeche, 12½"..175.00
Dish, lettuce leaf shape, lt gr, #219, 9¼" 400.00
Dish, lettuce leaf shape, 7½"..250.00
Vase, streaky brn, long stick neck, coiled snakes at base, mk, 27¼" ..2,500.00

Warwick

The Warwick China Company operated in Wheeling, West Virginia, from 1887 until 1951. They produced both hand-painted and decaled plates, vases, teapots, coffeepots, pitchers, bowls, and jardinieres featuring lovely florals or portraits of beautiful ladies done in luscious colors. Backgrounds were usually blendings of brown and beige, but ivory was also used as well as greens and pinks. Various marks were employed, all of which incorporate the Warwick name. For a more thorough study of the subject, we recommend *Warwick, A to W*, a supplement to *Why Not Warwick* by our advisor, Donald C. Hoffmann, Sr.; his address can be found in the Directory under Illinois. In an effort to inform the collector/dealer, Mr. Hoffmann now has a video available that identifies the company's decals and their variations by number.

Bouquet #1, vase, brn w/floral decor, A-21, 11¾" 300.00
Bouquet #1, vase, brn w/floral decor, A-24, 11¾" 295.00
Bouquet #1, vase, brn w/floral decor, A-27, 11¾" 265.00
Bouquet #2, vase, brn w/portrait, Anna Potocka, A-17, 10½"....390.00
Bouquet #2, vase, brn w/portrait, gypsy w/bow in hair, A-17, 10½" ..385.00
Bouquet #2, vase, brn w/portrait, gypsy w/turban, A-17, 10½" ...375.00
Bouquet #2, vase, brn w/portrait, lady w/violets, A-17, 10½" 395.00
Bouquet #2, vase, brn w/portrait, Old Blonde, A-17, 10½" 320.00
Bouquet #2, vase, brn w/portrait, Young Blonde, A-17, 10½".....320.00
Bouquet #2, vase, red overglaze w/floral decor, E-2, 10½"...........295.00
Bouquet #2, vase, red overglaze w/portrait, Anna Potocka, E-1, 10½" ..350.00
Monroe, vase, brn w/floral decor, A-26, 10¼" 300.00
Monroe, vase, brn w/floral decor, A-27, 10¼" 290.00
Monroe, vase, brn w/portrait, A-17, 10¼" 380.00
Monroe, vase, matt, tan to tan w/nut decor, M-2, 10¼" 380.00
Monroe, vase, matt, tan to tan w/portrait, M-1, 10¼" 390.00
Narcis #1, vase, brn w/portrait, Madame Recaimér, A-17, 8¼" ..380.00
Narcis #1, vase, red overglaze w/ portrait, Madame Recaimér, E-1, 8¼".380.00
Narcis #1, vase, wht w/sea gulls, D-1, 8¼" 400.00
Narcis #2, red overglaze w/portrait, Madame LeBrun, E-1, 6¾"..380.00
Narcis #2, vase, brn w/floral decor, A-27, 6¾"............................285.00
Narcis #2, vase, wht w/bird decor, ducks, D-1, 6¾" 385.00
Oriental, vase, brn w/floral decor, A-17, 11"................................400.00

Oriental, vase, brn w/floral decor (peonies), A-21, 11" 430.00
Pansy, vase, brn w/floral decor (hibiscus), A-27, 4" 140.00
Pansy, vase, brn w/floral decor (poppies), A-6, 4" 150.00
Penn, vase, brn w/floral decor, A-16, 9½" 295.00
Penn, vase, matt gr, no decal, unmk, 9½" 400.00
Penn, vase, pk w/portrait, H-1, 9½" 600.00

Pitcher, shaded brown, floral (scarce decal), 10½", $150.00. (Photo courtesy Don Hoffmann, Sr.)

Poppy, vase, brn w/floral decor, A-6, 10½" 295.00
Poppy, vase, charcoal w/floral decor, C-4, 10¼" 350.00
Poppy, vase, pk w/portrait, H-1, 10½" 650.00
Regency, vase, brn w/floral decor, A-16, 11½" 490.00
Regency, vase, brn w/floral decor, A-21, 11½" 490.00
Regency, vase, charcoal w/floral decor, C-6, 11½" 500.00
Rose, vase, brn w/floral decor, A-27, 8" 250.00
Rose, vase, brn w/floral decor, A-6, 8" 275.00
Rose, vase, red overglaze w/floral decor, E-2, 8" 300.00
Rose, vase, red w/portrait, E-1, 8" 325.00
Royal #1, vase, charcoal w/floral decor, C-5, 10" 315.00
Royal #1, vase, pk w/portrait, H-1, rare, 10" 800.00
Royal #2, vase, brn w/portrait, A-17, 9" 325.00
Senator #1, vase, brn w/floral decor, A-27, 13" 200.00
Senator #2, vase, brn w/floral decor, A-16, 11½" 200.00
Senator #3, vase, brn w/floral decor, A-23, 9¾" 245.00
Unnamed, ewer, brn w/floral decor, A-27, 9¼" 350.00
Unnamed, ewer, brn w/portrait, Madame LeBrun, A-17, 9¼" 365.00
Unnamed, ewer, charcoal w/floral decor, C-6, 9¼" 360.00
Unnamed, ewer, pk w/portrait, Aunt Hilda type, H-1, 9¼" 680.00
Unnamed, funnel type, brn w/floral decor, A-16, 11½" 400.00
Unnamed, funnel type, brn w/floral decor, A-20, 11½" 460.00
Unnamed, funnel type, yel to gr, portrait, K-1, 11½" 650.00
Verbenia #1, vase, brn w/floral decor, A-27, 9½" 215.00
Verbenia #1, vase, brn w/portrait, A-17, 9½" 290.00
Verbenia #2, vase, brn w/portrait, Madame LeBrun, A-17, 7½"...300.00
Verona, vase, brn w/floral decor, A-27, 11¾" 285.00
Verona, vase, charcoal w/floral decor, C-5, 11¾" 325.00
Verona, vase, gr w/floral decor, F-2, 11¾" 400.00
Victoria, vase, brn w/floral decor, A-21, 8¼" 315.00
Victoria, vase, brn w/portrait, A-17, 8¼" 425.00
Victoria, vase, yel to gr w/portrait, Madame LeBrun, K-1, 8¼" ..600.00
Violet, vase, brn w/floral decor, A-22, 4" 130.00
Violet, vase, brn w/floral decor, A-6, 4" 125.00
Violet, vase, charcoal w/floral decor, C-5, 4" 140.00
Violet, vase, red overglaze w/floral decor, E-2, 4" 135.00
Virginia, vase, brn w/floral decor, A-6, 10" 200.00
Virginia, vase, brn w/portrait, Madame LeBrun, A-17, 10" 275.00
Virginia, vase, brn w/portrait, Madame Recamiér, A-17, 10" 260.00
Virginia, vase, pk w/portrait, Christy Girl, H-1, 10" 650.00
Warwick, vase, brn w/floral decor, A-40, 10" 400.00
Warwick, vase, pk to bl w/portrait, Aunt Hilda type, H-1, 10"...600.00
Warwick, vase, pk w/portrait, Aunt Hilda type, peony in hair, H-1, 10"....600.00

Warwick, vase, pk w/portrait, Aunt Hilda type, wearing boa, H-1, 10"......620.00
Windsor, vase, brn w/floral decor, A-40, 9¼" 400.00
Windsor, vase, brn w/portrait, Anna Potacka, A-17, 9¼" 450.00
Windsor, vase, pk w/portrait, Christy girl, H-1, 9¼" 650.00

Tankard Sets

Bl gloss, Fraternal Order, sq hdl, 10" tankard+4 4¼" mugs 700.00
Bl matt, Fraternal Order, sq hdl, 10" tankard+4 4¼" mugs 950.00
Brn, Christy girl portrait, ring hdl, 13" tankard+4 5" mugs 650.00
Brn, Christy girl portrait, ring hdl, 15" tankard+4 5¼" mugs......750.00
Brn, Dickens characters, hdl has crossbar, 10" tankard+4¼" mugs...750.00
Brn, Dickens characters, ring hdl, 15" tankard+4 5¼" mugs.......900.00
Brn, fisherman, sq hdl w/bar, 10" tankard+4 4¼" mugs...............800.00
Brn, friar, ring hdl, 13" tankard+4 5" mugs 900.00
Brn, friar smiling, ring hdl, 13" tankard+4 5" mugs..................1,000.00
Brn, fruit, ring hdl, 13" tankard+4 5" mugs...............................1,100.00
Brn, Indian w/headdress, ring hdls, 15" tankard+6 5" mugs.....1,450.00
Brn, Indian w/headdress, 15" tankard+4 5¼" mugs 900.00
Brn, monk in red cap, sq hdl, 10" tankard+4 4¼" mugs.............500.00
Brn, opera decor, ring hdl, 13" tankard+4 5" mugs.................1,450.00
Brn w/FOE (newer style), 15"tankard+6 5¼" steins.....................700.00
Brn w/FOE (old style), 15" tankard+6 5¼" steins 1,000.00
Red, fisherman, sq hdl, w/bar, 10" tankard only..........................400.00

Wash Sets

Before the days of running water, bedrooms were standardly equipped with a wash bowl and pitcher as a matter of necessity. A 'toilet set' was comprised of the pitcher and bowl, toothbrush holder, covered commode, soap dish, shaving dish, and mug. Some sets were even more elaborate. Through everyday usage, the smaller items were often broken, and today it is unusual to find a complete set.

Porcelain sets decorated with florals, fruits, or scenics were produced abroad by Limoges in France; some were imported from Germany and England. During the last quarter of the 1800s and until after the turn of the century, American-made toilet sets were manufactured in abundance. Tin and graniteware sets were also made.

Burgess & Leigh, Brighton, ca 1880, pitcher+bowl+soap dish+lidded box...240.00
Cauldon Ware, yel w/blk & wht weave bands, 4-pc set.............240.00
Doulton Burlsem, gr & yel floral on wht, basin+soap dish w/drain..320.00
Heatherstone, red/wht roses on wht, mk England 1888, pitcher+bowl...120.00
Ironstone, Imari style, Ridgeway, 1835-50, pitcher+bowl+3 pcs...1,500.00
Podmore Walker, Venus, 1850s, pitcher & bowl, 8", 12", EX......225.00
Royal Ironstone China Johnson Bros, pk & wht scenes, 5-pc 430.00

Watch Fobs

Watch fobs have been popular since the last quarter of the nineteenth century. They were often made by retail companies to feature their products. Souvenir, commemorative, and political fobs were also produced. Of special interest today are those with advertising, heavy equipment in particular. Some of the more pricey fobs are listed here, but most of those currently available were produced in such quantities that they are relatively common and should fall within a price range of $3.00 to $10.00. Our advisor for this category is Tony George; he is listed in the Directory under California. When no material is mentioned in the description, assume the fob is made of metal.

Amalgamated Clothing Workers of Am, 15th Biennial Convention, 1948...40.00
Arrowhead shape w/Indian chief w/headdress, silver, unmk..........65.00
Aultman & Taylor Machinery Co, young turkey, Bastian Bros 85.00

Avery Dog..80.00
Avery Tractor Co, Avery Teeth Talk, machinery, tooth shape, nut on top ..80.00
Boston Electric Show, 1912, Ben Franklin w/key on red dmn.....125.00
Brotherhood of Locomotive, Fireman & Engineers, enameled....200.00
Bucyrus Erie, mining crane in center w/enamel, leather strap.....160.00
Buffalo Springfield Roller Co, roller shape......................................65.00
Cletrac, Cleveland Tractor Co, 1x1¾", w/4" leather strap 100.00
Deering Harvesting Machines, celluloid, 2½x1⅜" 140.00
Dodge Bros Motor Vehicles, bl/wht/blk enamel 75.00
Fordson Tractor..80.00
Franklin Brew Co, Columbus OH, Ben Franklin bust 55.00
Golden Spike, KC Southern Lines, 50th Anniversary 150.00
Golf club bag, 14k gold, ½x1½" 75.00
Head Camp MWA, Milwaukee Woodsman Assoc, coin in center ..45.00
Hunter Trader Trapper, bear & guns, brass/bronze 110.00
Illinois Poultry & Egg Shippers, state shape, 1916........................55.00
Indian Motorcycles, Indian face, sterling silver............................110.00
International Harvester, celluloid...150.00
International Harvester of Mexico, 1947...60.00
John Deere, shield-shaped MOP w/brass deer & plow 90.00
Kasper's Turkey Coffee, image of turkey, coffee sack on bk............70.00
Link Belt Speeder, Speeder Manufacturing Corp, Robbins, 1¼x1¾"..90.00
Litchfield Mfg 90.00
Locomotive & caboose, 1852, sterling silver 70.00
Miles City Saddlery Co, saddle form, sterling silver....................150.00
NY to Paris, w/compass 95.00
Powell Bros Co Livestock, Indianapolis, bull's head 80.00
Pueblo Saddle Co, RT Frazier, saddle form 90.00
Rock Island Plow, logo on blk, made by Green Duck Co, w/leather strap ...95.00
Schlitz, keg shape, enamel, Judd's Bar on bk 50.00
Verlie, bl enamel on wht porc, rectangular.....................................65.00
Wells Fargo, locomotive, brass 40.00
Winchester, man on horse, brass...90.00
Witchata-OK Serum Co, We Save 'Em on reverse, NP brass, worn, 1x1½"....135.00

Watch Stands

Watch stands were decorative articles designed with a hook from which to hang a watch. Some displayed the watch as the face of a grand-father clock or as part of an interior scene with figures in period costumes and contemporary furnishings. They were popular products of Staffordshire potters and silver companies as well.

Brass parrot figural, 6½x4½" 85.00
Cast cobra figural w/copper patina, brass base, 19th C, 5" 85.00
Chip-cvd pine, architectural w/3 doors, urn finial, name/1844, 24" 770.00
Cvd tall case clock w/molded hood, spire finials, Am, 19th C, 17" ..1,265.00
Dvtl wood w/magnifying lens, w/light (not working), 1800s, 6½"........235.00
Eagle, full standing figure, cvd wood w/red stain, 1850s, 11x7" ..4,400.00
Ebonized wood w/hinged glass dome, ca 1890, 6x4½" dia...........135.00
Ebonized wood/bronze/copper, lyre shape on tiered base, 1850s, 10"...175.00
Fr porc, HP flowers/butterflies, unmk, 1870s, 8" 150.00
Glass, gold floral, cylindrical, brass mts, hinged lid, ca 1880 ....95.00
Mahog w/MOP inlay, cloisonne on door, brass finial on temple shape, 9" ..175.00
Pine hutch w/orig pnt, sq nails, old glass in door, 12x8x6" 1,300.00
Silver, logs on campfire, watch hangs from branch, Tufts #2623, 1900s ...265.00
Spelter, golfer figural, hook for watch on flag stick, ca 1915, 3½"...625.00
Wood cvg w/snakes/1899/initials in hearts/2" mirror, 9¾x3" 160.00

Watches

First made in the 1500s in Germany, early watches were actually small clocks, suspended from the neck or belt. By 1700 they had become the approximate shape and size we know today. The first watches produced in America were made in 1810. The well-known Waltham Watch Company was established in 1850. Later, Waterbury produced inexpensive watches which they sold by the thousands.

Open-face and hunting-case watches of the 1890s were often solid gold or gold-filled and were often elaborately decorated in several colors of gold. Gold watches became a status symbol in this decade and were worn by both men and women on chains with fobs or jeweled slides. Ladies sometimes fastened them to their clothing with pins often set with jewels. The chatelaine watch was worn at the waist, only one of several items such as scissors, coin purses, or needle cases, each attached by small chains.

Most turn-of-the-century watch cases were gold-filled; these are plentiful today. Sterling cases, though interest in them is on the increase, are not in great demand. For more information we recommend *Complete Price Guide to Watches, No. 20*, by Cooksey Shugart, Tom Engle, and Richard G. Gilbert (Collector Books).

Our advice for this category comes from Maundy International Watches, Antiquarian Horologists, price consultants, and researchers for many watch reference guides and books on horology. Their firm is a leading purveyor of antique watches of all kinds. They are listed in the Directory under Kansas. For character-related watches, see Personalities.

Key:

adj — adjusted	k/s — key set
brg — bridge plate design	k/w — key wind
d/s — double sunk dial	l/s — lever set
fbd — finger bridge design	mvt — movement
g/f — gold-filled	o/f — open face
g/j/s — gold jewel setting	p/s — pendant set
h/c — hunter case	r/g/p — rolled gold plate
HCI#P — heat, cold,	s — size
isochronism & position	s/s — single sunk dial
adjusted	s/w — stem wind
j — jewel	w/g/f — white gold-filled
k — karat	y/g/f — yellow gold-filled

Am Watch Co, 0s, 7j, #1891, 14k, h/c, Am Watch Co, M.........485.00
Am Watch Co, 6s, 7j, #1873, y/g/f, h/c, Am Watch Co, M........185.00
Am Watch Co, 12s, 17j, #1894, 14k, o/f, Royal, M.....................385.00
Am Watch Co, 12s, 21j, #1894, 14k, h/c, M 475.00
Am Watch Co, 16s, 11j, #1872, p/s, silver h/c, Park Road, M 400.00
Am Watch Co, 16s, 15j, #1899, y/g/f, h/c, M 225.00
Am Watch Co, 16s, 16j, #1884, 5-min, 14k, Repeater, M........5,975.00
Am Watch Co, 16s, 17j, #1888, Railroader, M.........................1,575.00
Am Watch Co, 16s, 19j, #1872, 14k, h/c, Am Watch Woerd's Pat, M ..8,950.00
Am Watch Co, 16s, 21j, #1888, h/c, 14k, Riverside Maximus, M...1,650.00
Am Watch Co, 16s, 21j, #1899, y/g/f, l/s, o/f, Crescent St, M.....365.00
Am Watch Co, 16s, 21j, #1908, y/g/f, o/f, Grade #645, M 385.00
Am Watch Co, 16s, 23j, #1908, o/f, 18k, Premier Maximus, MIB.15,000.00
Am Watch Co, 16s, 23j, #1908, y/g/f, o/f, adj, RR, Vanguard, M ..495.00
Am Watch Co, 16s, 23j, #1908, y/g/f, o/f, Vanguard Up/Down, EX ...750.00
Am Watch Co, 18s, #1857, silver h/c, Samuel Curtiss k/w, M ...4,000.00
Am Watch Co, 18s, 11j, #1857, k/w, 1st run, PS Barlett, M.....6,450.00
Am Watch Co, 18s, 11j, #1857, silver h/c, k/w, DH&D, EX ...2,000.00
Am Watch Co, 18s, 15j, #1877, k/w, RE Robbins, M.................575.00
Am Watch Co, 18s, 15j, #1883, y/g/f, 2-tone, Railroad King, EX....585.00
Am Watch Co, 18s, 17j, #1883, y/g/f, o/f, Crescent Street, M....275.00
Am Watch Co, 18s, 17j, #1892, HC, Canadian Pacific Railway, M ..1,795.00
Am Watch Co, 18s, 17j, #1892, y/g/f, o/f, Sidereal, rare, M.....3,650.00
Am Watch Co, 18s, 17j, 25-yr, y/g/f, o/f, s/s, PS Bartlett, M 295.00
Am Watch Co, 18s, 21j, #1892, y/g/f, o/f, d/s, Crescent St, M....495.00
Am Watch Co, 18s, 21j, #1892, y/g/f, o/f, Grade #845, EX.........265.00
Am Watch Co, 18s, 21j, #1892, y/g/f, o/f, Pennsylvania Special, M ..4,950.00

Am Watch Co, 18s, 7j, #1857, silver case, k/w, CT Parker, M ...3,650.00
Auburndale Watch Co, 18s, 7j, k/w, l/s, Lincoln, M 1,985.00
Aurora Watch Co, 18s, 11j, k/w, silver h/c, M.............................395.00
Aurora Watch Co, 18s, 15 ruby j, y/g/f, s/w, 5th pinion, M 1,385.00
Ball (Elgin), 18s, 17j, o/f, silver, Official RR Standard, M 695.00
Ball (Hamilton), 16s, 21j, #999, g/f, o/f, l/s, M............................885.00
Ball (Hamilton), 16s, 23j, #998, y/g/f, o/f, Elinvar, M 2,850.00
Ball (Hamilton), 18s, 17j, #999, g/f, o/f, l/s, EX............................495.00
Ball (Hampden), 18s, 17j, o/f, adj, RR, Superior Grade, M 2,950.00
Ball (Illinois), 12s, 19j, w/g/f, o/f, M...345.00
Ball (Waltham), 16s, 17j, y/g/f, o/f, RR, Commercial Std, M......575.00
Ball (Waltham), 16s, 21j, o/f, Official RR Standard, M 875.00
Columbus, 6s, 11j, y/g/f hc, M..200.00
Columbus, 18s, 11-15j, k/w, k/s, M..395.00
Columbus, 18s, 15j, o/f, l/s, M..185.00
Columbus, 18s, 15j, y/g/f, o/f, Jay Gould on dial, M 2,000.00
Columbus, 18s, 21j, y/g/f, h/c, train on dial, Railway King, M.1,250.00
Columbus, 18s, 23j, y/g/f, h/c, Columbus King, M....................2,200.00
Cornell, 18s, 15j, s/w, JC Adams, EX..285.00
Cornell, 18s, 15j, silver h/c, k/w, John Evans, EX 325.00
Dudley, 12s, #1, 14k, o/f, flip-bk case, Masonic, G 2,675.00
Elgin, 6s, 11j, 14k, h/c, M...365.00
Elgin, 6s, 15j, 20-yr, y/g/f, h/c, s/s, EX..65.00
Elgin, 10s, 18k, h/c, k/w, k/s, s/s, Gail Borden, M.......................700.00
Elgin, 12s, 15j, 14k, h/c, EX..325.00
Elgin, 12s, 17j, 14k, h/c, GM Wheeler, M.....................................495.00
Elgin, 16s, 15j, doctor's, 4th model, 18k, 2nd sweep hand, h/c, M...2,200.00
Elgin, 16s, 15j, 14k, h/c, EX..550.00
Elgin, 16s, 21j, y/g/f, g/j/s, o/f, BW Raymond, EX 265.00
Elgin, 16s, 21j, y/g/f, g/j/s, 3 fbd, h/c, M......................................875.00
Elgin, 16s, 21j, y/g/f, o/f, l/s, RR, Father Time, M 485.00
Elgin, 16s, 21j, 14k, 3 fbd, grade #91, scarce, M........................3,975.00
Elgin, 16s, 23j, up/down indicator, BW Raymond, EX............1,475.00
Elgin, 17s, 7j, k/w, orig silver case, Leader, M 225.00
Elgin, 18s, 11j, silver, h/c, k/w, gilded, MG Odgen, M................295.00
Elgin, 18s, 15j, o/f, d/s, k/w, silver, RR, BW Raymond 1st run, M.1,585.00
Elgin, 18s, 15j, silver, k/w, k/s, h/c, HL Culver, M 345.00
Elgin, 18s, 15j, silver h/c, Penn RR dial, BW Raymond k/w mvt, M.5,950.00
Elgin, 18s, 17j, silveroid h/c, BW Raymond, M............................365.00
Elgin, 18s, 21j, y/g/f, o/f, Father Time, G......................................185.00
Elgin, 18s, 23j, y/g/f, o/f, 5-position, RR, Veritas, M...................725.00
Fredonia, 18s, 11j, y/g/f, h/c, k/w, M..475.00
Hamilton, #910, 12s, 17j, 20-yr, y/g/f, o/f, s/s, EX 65.00
Hamilton, #912, 12s, 17j, y/g/f, o/f, adj, EX...................................60.00
Hamilton, #920, 12s, 23j, 14k, o/f, M..675.00
Hamilton, #922MP, 12s, 18k case, Masterpiece (sgn), M.........1,295.00
Hamilton, #925, 18s, 17j, y/g/f, h/c, s/s, l/s, M 325.00
Hamilton, #928, 18s, 15j, y/g/f, o/f, s/s, EX...................................200.00
Hamilton, #933, 18s, 16j, h/c, nickel plate, low serial #, M.....1,385.00
Hamilton, #938, 18s, 17j, y/g/f, adj, M..885.00
Hamilton, #940, 18s, 21j, nickel plate, coin silver, o/f, M...........365.00
Hamilton, #946, 18s, 23j, y/g/f, o/f, g/j/s, M..............................1,250.00
Hamilton, #947 (mk), 18s, 23j, 14k, h/c, orig/sgn, EX 4,950.00
Hamilton, #950, 16s, 23j, y/g/f, o/f, l/s, sgn d/s, M...................1,650.00
Hamilton, #965, 16s, 17j, 14k, p/s, h/c, brg, scarce, M.............1,495.00
Hamilton, #972, 16s, 17j, y/g/f, g/j/s, o/f, d/s, l/s, adj, EX............165.00
Hamilton, #974, 16s, 17j, 20-yr, y/g/f, o/f, s/s, EX........................150.00
Hamilton, #992, 16s, 21j, y/g/f, o/f, adj, d/s, dbl roller, M...........385.00
Hamilton, #992B, 16s, 21j, y/g/f, o/f, l/s, Bar/Crown, M.............495.00
Hamilton, #4992B, 16s, 22j, o/f, steel case, G...............................185.00
Hampden, 12s, 17j, w/g/f, o/f, thin model, Aviator, M 240.00
Hampden, 16s, 7j, gilded, nickel plate, o/f, ¾-mvt, EX 50.00
Hampden, 16s, 17j, o/f, adj, EX..65.00
Hampden, 16s, 17j, y/g/f, h/c, s/w, M...225.00

Hampden, 16s, 21j, g/j/s, y/g/f, NP, h/c, Dueber, ¾-mvt, M..........300.00
Hampden, 16s, 23j, o/f, adj, dbl roller, Special Railway, M 675.00
Hampden, 18s, 15j, k/w, mk on mvt, Railway, M 1,350.00
Hampden, 18s, 15j, s/w, gilded, JC Perry, M.................................225.00
Hampden, 18s, 15j, silver, k/w, h/c, Hayward, M.........................385.00
Hampden, 18s, 15j, y/g/f, damascened, h/c, Dueber, M...............195.00
Hampden, 18s, 21j, y/g/f, g/j/s, h/c, New Railway, M..................425.00
Hampden, 18s, 21j, y/g/f, o/f, d/s, l/s, N Am Railway, M.............450.00
Hampden, 18s, 23j, y/g/f, o/f, d/s, adj, New Railway, M..............495.00
Hampden, 18s, 23j, 14k, h/c, Special Railway, M......................1,250.00
Hampden, 18s, 7-11j, k/w, gilded, Springfield Mass, EX.............150.00
Howard, E; 6s, 15j, s/w, 18k h/c, Series VIII, G sz, M...............1,595.00
Howard, E; 16s, 15j, s/w, 14k h/c, L sz, M.................................1,575.00
Howard, E; 18s, 15j, h/c, silver case, k/w, Series I, N sz, M......4,500.00
Howard, E; 18s, 15j, 18k h/c, k/w, Series II, N sz, M................4,900.00
Howard, E; 18s, 17j, 25-yr, y/g/f, o/f, orig case, split plate, M...1,395.00
Howard (Keystone), 12s, 23j, 14k, h/c, brg, Series 8, M.............700.00
Howard (Keystone), 16s, 17j, y/g/f, o/f, Series 9, M....................295.00
Howard (Keystone), 16s, 21j, y/g/f, o/f, RR Chronometer II, M .695.00
Howard (Keystone), 16s, 23j, y/g/f, o/f, Series 0, jeweled bbl, M ...825.00
Illinois, 0s, 7j, 14k, l/s, h/c, EX..265.00
Illinois, 8s, 13j, ¾-mvt, Rose LeLand, scarce, M 525.00
Illinois, 12s, 17j, y/g/f, o/f, d/s dial, EX..50.00
Illinois, 16s, 17j, y/g/f, o/f, d/s, Bunn, EX..................................225.00
Illinois, 16s, 21j, g/j/s, h/c, Burlington, M 385.00
Illinois, 16s, 21j, o/f, d/s, Santa Fe Special, M............................675.00
Illinois, 16s, 21j, y/g/f, o/f, d/s, Bunn Special, M.......................485.00
Illinois, 16s, 23j, y/g/f, o/f, d/s, 60-hr, Sangamo Special, mk, M 3,500.00
Illinois, 16s, 23j, y/g/f, stiff bow, o/f, Sangamo Special, EX.........975.00
Illinois, 18s, 11j, #1, silver, k/w, Alleghany, EX 110.00
Illinois, 18s, 11j, #3, o/f, s/w, l/s, Comet, G.................................65.00
Illinois, 18s, 11j, Forest City, G..85.00
Illinois, 18s, 15j, #1, adj, y/g/f, k/w, h/c, gilt, Bunn, M 995.00
Illinois, 18s, 15j, #1, k/w, k/s, silver hunter, Stuart, M 1,100.00
Illinois, 18s, 15j, k/w, k/s, gilt, Railway Regulator, M 985.00
Illinois, 18s, 15j, s/w, silveroid, G..40.00
Illinois, 18s, 17j, g/j/s, adj, B&O RR Special (Hunter), h/c, M ..2,450.00
Illinois, 18s, 17j, h/c, s/w, nickel plate, coin silver, Bunn, M.......395.00
Illinois, 18s, 17j, o/f, d/s, adj, silveroid case, Lakeshore, G 90.00
Illinois, 18s, 17j, o/f, s/w, 5th pinion, Miller, EX........................165.00
Illinois, 18s, 21j, g/j/s, g/f, o/f, A Lincoln, M.............................525.00
Illinois, 18s, 21j, g/j/s, o/f, adj, B&O RR Special, EX..............1,700.00
Illinois, 18s, 21j, 14k, g/j/s, h/c, Bunn Special, M...................1,350.00
Illinois, 18s, 23j, g/j/s, Bunn Special, EX....................................725.00
Illinois, 18s, 24j, g/j/s, adj, o/f, Chesapeake & Ohio, M..........5,000.00
Illinois, 18s, 24j, g/j/s, o/f, Bunn Special, EX.............................995.00
Illinois, 18s, 26j, g/j/s, o/f, Ben Franklin USA, G......................5,000.00
Illinois, 18s, 26j, 14k, Penn Special, M.....................................9,500.00
Illinois, 18s, 7j, #3, o/f, Interior, G...65.00
Illinois, 18s, 7j, #3, silveroid, America, G.....................................85.00
Illinois, 18s, 9-11j, o/f, k/w, s/s, silveroid case, Hoyt, M...........250.00
Ingersoll, 16s, 7j, wht base metal, Reliance, G...............................25.00

Johnson pocket watch, 18kt yellow gold hunter case, 19 jewel fuzee movement, gold chain and ribbon, EX, $775.00.

Lancaster, 18s, 7j, o/f, k/w, k/s, eng silver case, EX 125.00
Marion US, 18s, h/c, k/w, k/s, ¾-plate, Asa Fuller, M 450.00
Marion US, 18s, 15j, nickel plate, h/c, s/w, Henry Randel, M 550.00
Melrose Watch Co, 18s, 7j, k/w, k/s, G 260.00
New York Watch Co, 18s, 7j, silver, h/c, k/w, Geo Sam Rice, EX....195.00
New York Watch Co, 19j, low sz #, wolf's teeth wind, M 1,675.00
Patek Philippe, 12s, 18j, 18k, o/f, EX 2,000.00
Patek Philippe, 16s, 20j, 18k, h/c, M 3,000.00
Rockford, 16s, 17j, y/g/f, h/c, brg, dbl roller, EX.............................90.00
Rockford, 16s, 21j, #515, y/g/f, M...675.00
Rockford, 16s, 21j, g/j/s, o/f, grade #537, rare, M.....................1,800.00
Rockford, 16s, 23j, 14k, o/f, mk Doll on dial/mvt, M...............3,000.00
Rockford, 18s, 15j, o/f, k/w, silver case, EX..................................275.00
Rockford, 18s, 17j, silveroid, 2-tone, M 385.00
Rockford, 18s, 17j, y/g/f, o/f, Winnebago, M 425.00
Rockford, 18s, 21j, o/f, King Edward, M.......................................550.00
Seth Thomas, 18s, 17j, #2, g/j/s, adj, Henry Molineux, EX 595.00
Seth Thomas, 18s, 17j, Edgemere, G 45.00
Seth Thomas, 18s, 25j, g/j/s, g/f, Maiden Lane, EX 2,395.00
Seth Thomas, 18s, 7j, ¾-mvt, bk: eagle/Liberty model, M..........325.00
South Bend, 12s, 21j, dbl roller, Grade #431, M 275.00
South Bend, 12s, 21j, orig o/f, d/s, Studebaker, M 425.00
South Bend, 18s, 21j, g/j/s, h/c, Studebaker, M 1,385.00
South Bend, 18s, 21j, 14k, h/c, M 1,175.00
Swiss, 18s, 18k, h/c, 1-min, Repeater, High Grade, M 4,200.00

Waterford

The Waterford Glass Company operated in Ireland from the late 1700s until 1851 when the factory closed. One hundred years later (in 1951) another Waterford glassworks was instituted that produced glass similar to the eighteenth-century wares — crystal, usually with cut decoration. Today Waterford is a generic term referring to the type of glass first produced there. Advice for this category comes from Andrew Morton; he is listed in the Directory under Tennessee.

Bowl, centerpc; Millenium, 7½x11", MIB 355.00
Bowl, centerpc; sgn Redmond O'Donoghue, 8" 355.00
Brandy, balloon; Lismore, 12-oz, 8 for 680.00
Brandy snifter, Alana, 5¼", 8 for 600.00
Chandelier, 2-tier, 9-arm, bobeches/buttons/prisms, 30x28" 3,650.00
Claret, Colleen, set of 6, MIB...535.00
Decanter, claret; dmn cuttings, fluted neck, hdl, ped ft, 12" 625.00
Decanter, Curraghmore, knopped stem 425.00
Decanter, Peacock Eye, 13½" 300.00
Goblet, water; Kylemore, 5 for 450.00
Goblet, water; Lismore, 8 for 500.00
Hi ball, Lismore, 12-oz, 8 for...350.00
Lamp, hurricane; 2-pc, discontinued early 1990s, 18x10" 825.00
Old-fashion, dbl; Lismore, 8 for 540.00
Ornament, Partridge in Pear Tree, 1982, MIB w/red pouch 150.00
Sherry, Alana, 5¾x2¾", 8 for 440.00
Sherry, Colleen, set of 6, MIB..450.00
Tumbler, Colleen, 9-oz, 6 for...420.00
Vase, Diamond & Crosshatch, 8x4¾" 225.00
Vase, Diamond cutting, slightly waisted, 6" 195.00
Vase, Mastercraft, scalloped rim, 12¾x7½" 525.00
Vase, Reflections, Martin Ryan, 14", MIB...................................350.00
Wine, balloon; Lismore, 6 for 525.00

Watt Pottery

The Watt Pottery Company was established in Crooksville, Ohio,

on July 5, 1922. From approximately 1922 until 1935, they manufactured hand-turned stone containers — jars, jugs, milk pans, preserve jars, and various sizes of mixing bowls, usually marked with a cobalt blue acorn stamp. In 1936 production of these items was discontinued, and the company began to produce kitchen utility ware and ovenware such as mixing bowls, spaghetti bowls and plates, canister sets, covered casseroles, salt and pepper shakers, cookie jars, ice buckets, pitchers, bean pots, and salad and dinnerware sets. Most Watt ware is individually hand painted with bold brush strokes of red, green, or blue contrasting with the natural buff color of the glazed body. Several patterns were produced: Apple, Autumn Foliage, Cherry, Dutch Tulip, Morning Glory, Rio Rose, Rooster, Tear Drop, Starflower, and Tulip, to name a few. Much of the ware was made for advertising premiums and is often found stamped with the name of the retail company.

Tragedy struck the Watt Pottery Company on October 4, 1965, when fire completely destroyed the factory and warehouse. Production never resumed, but the ware they made has withstood many years of service in American kitchens and is today highly regarded and prized by collectors. The vivid colors and folk art-like execution of each cheerful pattern create a homespun ambiance that will make Watt pottery a treasure for years to come.

For further study we recommend *Watt Pottery, An Identification and Price Guide,* by our advisors for this category, Sue and Dave Morris; they are listed in the Directory under Washington. For the address of the *Watt's News* newsletter, see the section on Clubs, Newsletters, and Catalogs.

Apple, bowl, cereal/salad; #94, 1¾x6" 50.00
Apple, cheese crock, #80, 8x8½" 1,500.00
Apple, chip 'n dip set, #120/#110...300.00
Apple, creamer, #62, 4½x4½" 90.00
Apple, mug, #61, rare, 3x3¼" 500.00
Apple, pie plate, #33, 1½x9" 150.00
Apple, pitcher, #15, 5½x5¾" 75.00
Apple, pitcher, no ice lip, #17, 8x8½" 300.00
Apple, plate, divided; rare, 10½"...2,000.00
Apple, shakers, hourglass shape, emb letters, 4½x2½", pr 275.00
Apple, teapot, #505, 5¾x9"...3,000.00
Apple (Double), #04, 2x4"...110.00
Apple (Double), bowl, #73, 4x9"..125.00
Apple (Double), creamer, #62, 4¼x4½".......................................400.00
Autumn Foliage, baker, w/lid, #96, 5¾x8½" 90.00
Autumn Foliage, bowl, #106, 3½x10¾" 85.00
Autumn Foliage, oil/vinegar cruets, w/lids, #126, 7", pr 550.00
Autumn Foliage, shakers, hourglass shape, 4½x2½", pr 175.00
Blue/White Banded, pitcher, Eve-N-Bake...USA, 7x7¾"...............95.00
Cherry, bowl, mixing; #6, 3x6" 40.00
Cherry, bowl, spaghetti; #39, 3x13" 150.00
Cherry, pitcher, advertising, #15, 5½x5¾" 175.00
Dutch Tulip, bean pot, #76, 6½x7½" 350.00
Dutch Tulip, canister, tea/coffee; #82, rare, 7x5" 350.00
Dutch Tulip, pitcher, refrigerator; #69, 8x8½"............................600.00
Eagle, bowl, mixing; #12, 6x12" 145.00
Eagle, pitcher, ice lip, unmk, 8x8½" 450.00
Green/White Banded, bowl, #9, 5x9"..25.00
Kitch-N-Queen, cookie jar, #503, 8¼x8¼" 225.00
Kitch-N-Queen, pitcher, ice lip, #17, 8x8½" 200.00
Morning Glory, bowl, #6, 3½x6"...85.00
Morning Glory, sugar bowl, #98, 4¼x5" 250.00
Pansy (Cross-Hatch), platter, 15" 175.00
Pansy (Cut Leaf), casserole, stick hdl, 3¾x7½" 125.00
Pansy (Cut Leaf), Dutch oven, w/lid, 7x10½" 175.00
Pansy (Cut Leaf), pie plate, 1½x9"..150.00
Pansy (Cut Leaf), platter, 15" 110.00
Pansy (Cut Leaf) w/Bull's Eye, bowl, 2½x11"................................90.00

Pansy (Cut Leaf) w/Bull's Eye, plate, 7½" **55.00**
Pansy (Old), casserole, w/lid, #3/19, 5x9" **75.00**
Pansy (Old), platter, #49, 12" **85.00**
Pansy (Raised), casserole, Fr hdl, ind, 3¾x7½" **90.00**
Pansy (Raised), pitcher, refrigerator; w/lid **100.00**
Rooster, bowl, #05, 4x5" **190.00**
Rooster, bowl, spaghetti; unmk, 3x13" **375.00**
Rooster, ice bucket, unmk, 7¼x7½" **275.00**
Rooster, pitcher, refrigerator; sq, #69, 8x8½" **550.00**
Starflower, bean pot, 2-hdl, #76, 6½x7½" **175.00**
Starflower, bowl, berry; mk Watt USA, 1½x5¾" **35.00**
Starflower, bowl, mixing; #05, 2½x5" **50.00**
Starflower, creamer, #62, 4¼x4½" **250.00**
Starflower, ice bucket, no mk, 7¼x7½" **185.00**
Starflower, pie plate, #33, 1½x9" **200.00**
Starflower, tumbler, slant sides, #56, 4½x4" **325.00**
Starflower (Green on Brown), casserole, w/lid, #54, 6x8½" **90.00**
Starflower (Pink on Black), casserole, w/lid, 4½x8¾" **125.00**
Starflower (Pink on Green), bread plate, mk Watt USA, 6½" **35.00**
Starflower (Pink on Green), cup & saucer, 2¾x4½", 6" **65.00**
Starflower (White on Red), mug, #121, rare, 3¾x3" **400.00**
Tear Drop, bowl, #73, 4x9½" **130.00**
Tear Drop, bowl, mixing; #63, 4¼x6½" **45.00**
Tear Drop, casserole, Fr hdl, #18, ind, 4x8" **250.00**
Tulip, bowl, nesting; #603, 2x5¾" **250.00**
Tulip, cookie jar, #503, 8¼x8¼" **375.00**
Tulip, pitcher, ice lip, #17, 8x8½" **300.00**
White Daisy, cup & saucer, both mk Watt, 2¾x4½", 6" **75.00**
White Daisy, plate, salad; mk Watt USA, 8½" **65.00**
Woodgrain, cookie barrel, #617W, 11x8" **90.00**
Woodgrain, pitcher, #615W, 9x7½" **100.00**

Wave Crest

Wave Crest is a line of decorated opal ware (milk glass) patented in 1892 by the C.F. Monroe Co. of Meriden, Connecticut. They made a full line of items for every room of the house, but they are probably best known for their boxes and vases. Most items were hand painted with various levels of decoration, but more transfers were used in the later years prior to the company's demise in 1916. Floral themes are common; items with the scenics and portraits are rarer and more highly prized. Many pieces have ornately scrolled ormolu and brass handles, feet, and rims. Early pieces were unsigned (though they may have had paper labels); later, about 1898, a red banner mark was used. The black mark is probably from about 1902 to 1903. However, the glass is quite distinctive and has not been reproduced, so even unmarked items are easy to recognize. Our advisors for this category are Dolli and Wilfred Cohen; they are listed in the Directory under California. Note: There is no premium for signatures on Wave Crest. Values are given for hand-decorated pieces (unless noted 'transfer') that are *not* worn.

Bonbon, Swirl, asters on gr & wht panels, yel int, SP bail, 7x7".**750.00**
Box, Baroque Shell, floral reserves, allover wht beaded top on pk, 8" ..**895.00**
Box, Baroque Shell, Moorish Fantasy, no lining, 3¾x7¼" dia **995.00**
Box, Cigars, pk/gold floral on bl, 6¼" **900.00**
Box, Collars & Cuffs, emb/HP florals, metal rim/ft, 5½x7½" ..**1,250.00**
Box, Egg Crate, flower heads/purple & lav 'crossbar' on lid, 4x7" ..**1,150.00**
Box, Egg Crate, lilies, 4½" H **595.00**
Box, emb scrolls, stream/mtns/trees on lt gr/pk, 4" dia **325.00**
Box, glove; emb scrolls, daisies on bl, 4 ormolu ft, 10 " L **1,800.00**
Box, glove; emb scrolls, flower garden on bl, ftd, orig lining, 9½" ..**1,450.00**
Box, Swirl, allover wild roses, jeweled medallion in center, 3¾x6" **695.00**
Box, Swirl, asters/etc on pk-tan, orig lining & label, 4½x7" **695.00**

Box, Swirl, bright pk floral, 3¾x5½" **550.00**
Box, Swirl, daisies/berries, orig lining, ormolu ft, 6x7" **1,100.00**
Box, Swirl, ferns on wht to tan, 4½x7" **750.00**
Box, Swirl, mixed roses, ormolu ft, 6½x7½" **850.00**
Box, Swirl, orchid on yel to wht, 4¼x7" **750.00**
Box, Swirl, 10 storks fly away from sun, w/gilt, relined, 7" dia **4,250.00**
Box, Venetian harbor scene, 3x4¼" **300.00**
Candlestick, florals, ormolu base/cup w/opal egg-shaped center, 7½" ...**500.00**
Candlesticks, floral on wht, gold cup & ft, 7", pr **1,000.00**
Carafe, floral on wht, Swirl neck, 8", w/matching Swirl tumbler **1,200.00**
Cigar holder, flowers/amethyst scrolling, 4-ftd ormolu base & hdls, 4" ...**225.00**
Cigarette urn, floral/Cigarettes on pk/cream, shell lid, cylinder, 4" **500.00**
Cigarette/match holder, apple blossoms, gold fr holds 3 pcs, 7" L ..**600.00**
Cracker jar, roses in emb scroll reserves on gr/bl, cylinder, SP hdl **675.00**
Cracker jar, Swirl, floral on lt bl, 10" to top of hdl **700.00**
Creamer & sugar bowl, daisies on opal, ormolu hdls & lid, 3", 4¼" ..**450.00**
Ferner, daisies, beaded brass rim, 7½" **550.00**
Ferner, Egg Crate, violets w/gold on wht, ormolu rim, unmk, 7" W ...**470.00**
Ferner, floral, ormolu rim w/hdls, insert, 3½x6" **600.00**
Jam jar, transfer on wht, SP lid, bail & spoon, 3½x3½" **295.00**
Jar, pomade; daisies, mc on lt bl, emb metal lid, rare, 2½x2½" **450.00**
Jar, tooth powder; forget-me-nots w/wht dots, brass emb lid **850.00**
Note spindle, floral on opal, rare, 7" **650.00**
Plate, pond lily on lt bl, rtcl border, 7" **750.00**
Salt cellar, daisies, wht/bl on umber, sq, 1¾" **295.00**
Shakers, Artichoke, spiked pewter lids, pr **295.00**
Spooner, Swirl, floral, pk/gr on cream, ormolu rim w/2 hdls, 4¼" ...**295.00**
Tray w/swinging mirror w/ornate fr, floral on pk, 7¾x7" dia **750.00**
Umbrella stand, pastel floral panels, ornate rim & ft **3,500.00**
Vase, daisies on mauve, gold-lined free-form opal areas, ormolu, 12" ..**2,000.00**
Vase, floral, ovoid w/long neck, ormolu hdls & ft, 7½x2½" **550.00**
Vase, floral on lt bl, ovoid w/long neck, ormolu hdls & ped ft, 7½" ..**425.00**
Vase, floral on rosy opal, squat w/stick neck, ormolu collar/hdls, 6" ..**400.00**
Vase, floral on yel, acorn body w/long neck, ormolu hdls/ft, 6½" ..**475.00**
Vase, floral reserves w/gr outlines, ormolu ft, 6½x2" **395.00**
Vase, floral spray on pk/tan, cylinder, ormolu ftd base, 6½x2½" .**485.00**
Vase, iris on bl, ormolu ft, hdls & collar, 12x9" **925.00**
Vase, irises, ornate ormolu hdls, dolphin ft, 23" **2,500.00**
Whisk broom holder, floral/emb scrolls, fancy ormolu fr w/cherubs (EX) **2,150.00**

Weapons

Among the varied areas of specialization within the broad category of weapons, guns are by far the most popular. Muskets are among the earliest firearms; they were large-bore shoulder arms, usually firing black powder with separate loading of powder and shot. Some ignited the charge by flintlock or caplock, while later types used a firing pin with a metallic cartridge. Side arms, referred to as such because they were worn at the side, include pistols and revolvers. Pistols range from early single-shot and multiple barrels to modern types with cartridges held in the handle. Revolvers were supplied with a cylinder that turned to feed a fresh round in front of the barrel breech. Other firearms include shotguns, which fired round or conical bullets and had a smooth inner barrel surface, and rifles, so named because the interior of the barrel contained spiral grooves (rifling) which increased accuracy. For further study we recommend *Modern Guns, Thirteenth Edition*, by Russell Quertermous and Steve Quertermous, available at your local bookstore. Unless noted otherwise, our values are for examples in excellent condition. Our advisor for this category is Steve Howard; he is listed in the Directory under California. See also Militaria.

Key:
bbl — barrel   mod — modified
cal — caliber   oct — octagon

conv — conversion   O/U — over/under
cyl — cylinder   p/b — patch box
f/l — flintlock   perc — percussion
ga — gauge   /s — stock
hdw — hardware   Spec O — Special Order
mag — magazine

Carbines

Civil War Burnside perc, w/fore/s, sling bar & saddle ring, 39½"...**1,150.00**
Marlin Model 336 Lever Action, 35REM cal, 20" rnd bbl, full mag, NM..**345.00**
Perry Navy, 54 perc cal, 21" rnd bbl, str/s, carbine butt, G-.....**2,875.00**
Remington Navy Rolling Block, 50-45 cal, 2" bbl, sling swivels, VG .**1,600.00**
Sharps & Hankins Short Cavalry, 52RF cal, 19" bbl, walnut/s, VG...**1,150.00**
Sharps & Hankins 1862 Navy, dk metal, missing leather bbl cover, 39"....**865.00**
Springfield Model 1873, 45/70 cal, 22" rnd bbl, saddle ring **3,100.00**
Triplett & Scott KY, 50RF cal, 22" rnd bbl, butt-feed mag, G.**1,200.00**
Winchester 94, 30WCF cal, std Eastern, steel butt plate.............**350.00**

Muskets

Bartlet Model 1808 f/l, 69 cal, 44" rnd bbl, 1813 on bbl, G.....**2,245.00**
CA Richmond VA, humpbk lock dtd 1862, no rear sight, 57"...**2,300.00**
Colt Special Model 1861 Rifle, 58 cal, 40" rnd bbl, dtd 1863, VG...**1,850.00**
F/l w/bayonet, walnut, rnd bbl w/3 bands, iron hdw, pitting/rpl, 57" **600.00**
Fr Muebeuge Model 1763 f/l, 72 cal, 44" rnd bbl, G **1,725.00**
Harper's Ferry Model 1816 f/l, 69 cal, 42" rnd bbl, 1820 on lock plate..**1,000.00**
Harper's Ferry Model 1841 perc, 23" rnd bbl, p/b, rfn walnut/s, 49"....**715.00**
LG & Y Windsor VT, US Special Model, 58 cal, bright metal, 56" ...**575.00**
Merrill Conv of Harper's Ferry Model 1842, 69 cal, 39" rnd bbl, 1855..**3,165.00**
Nock f/l Brn Bess style, 77 cal, 42" rnd bbl, rpl ramrod, VG ...**1,650.00**
Pomeroy Model 1830, 69 cal, 42" rnd bbl, Belgian conv.............**800.00**
Remington Conv of Model 1816, 69 cal, 42" rnd bbl, cracked/s, G..........**750.00**
Springfield Model 1842, 69 cal, 42" rnd bbl, 1853 on lock plate, VG...**1,200.00**
Springfield Model 1842, 72 cal, 42" rnd bbl, 1848 on lock, VG.**575.00**
Springfield Model 1855 Rifle, 58 cal, sm iron p/b, 40" rnd bbl...**1,500.00**
Springfield Model 1855 Rifle, 58 cal, 40" rnd bbl, rpl ramrod, VG...**1,550.00**
Starr Model 1830, 69 cal, 42" rnd bbl, Drum conv dtd 1831, VG ...**925.00**
Surcharged Charlesville f/l, 72 cal, 45" rnd bbl, G **6,500.00**
Surcharged Fr Model 1763 f/l, 69 cal, 45" rnd bbl, rpl hammer **2,500.00**
T French Model 1808 f/l, 69 cal, 44" rnd bbl, VG **1,100.00**
Unmk import, perc, 42" rnd bbl, 58"..................................**250.00**
US Model 1861, perc, 40" bbl, 55½".................................**495.00**
US 1842, 69 cal, Harpers Ferry 1850 on lock, w/p/b & bayonet, 59".......**800.00**
VA Mfg Model 1816 f/l, 69 cal, 42" bbl, rpl ramrod, 1818 on lock, G..**1,265.00**
Wickham Model 1808 f/l, 69 cal, 42" rnd bbl, rpr/s, G **1,600.00**

Pistols

Astra 400 Semi-Auto, 9mm Largo/38ACP cal, 5¾" bbl, bl finish ...**300.00**
Astra 600 Semi-Auto, 9mm Lugar, 5¼" bbl, checkered grips, bl finish...**315.00**
Colt #3 Derringer, 41RF, 2½" bbl, pearl grips...........................**2,000.00**
Colt 1903 Semi-Auto, 32ACP cal, blk compo grips/bl finish, rpl mag, VG...**345.00**
Colt 1911 A1, 45 cal, Parkerized finish, blued clip, 8½".............**440.00**
East India Co perc, brass hdw, iron loop on grip cap, 9" rnd bbl, 16" ...**275.00**
English, Kentland & Co lock/crown stamp/GR, tapered rnd bbl, rfn, 15"....**935.00**
French Model 1777 f/l, 73 cal, 7⅜" rnd bbl, rpl ramrod, VG...**1,200.00**
North Model 1808 Naval f/l, 54 cal, 10" rnd bbl, G reconv, VG...**1,725.00**
Radom 35, 9mm cal, Nazi mks, thumb safety, blk compo grips, VG...**375.00**
Remington Dbl-Bbl Derringer, 41RF, 3" bbls, rstr NP, G.............**260.00**
Sharps Model 1A, 22 cal, 4 2½" bbls, bl traces, worn grips, G ...**345.00**
St Etienne 1763 f/l, brass mts, dtd 1776 on tag of bbl, 15¾" ...**1,100.00**
Tower & crown over WR, military f/l, proofed bbl, brass mts, 15"...**315.00**
Tower f/l, 66 cal, 8⅞" rnd bbl, dtd 1800 on /s, G.........................**975.00**

Revolvers

Alsop Pocket, 31 cal, 4" oct bbl, NM...............................**2,000.00**
Colt 1862 Police Perc, 36 cal, 4½" bbl, 5-shot cyl, wood grips, G...........**635.00**
Colt 1878 DA Frontier 6-Shooter, 44 WCF cal, 5½" bbl, compo grips..**575.00**
Colt 1889 DA, 41 Colt cal, 4½" bbl, blk compo grips, bl finish, VG **460.00**
Colt 2nd Single Action, 38S&W cal, 3¼" bbl, NP, blk compo grips......**315.00**
Colt 3rd Model Dragon Perc, 44 cal, 7" bbl, 1-pc wood grips, G.......**4,850.00**
Freeman Army Civil War, 44 cal, 7" rnd bbl, EX.....................**3,100.00**
Marlin XX Standard 1873, 22 cal, brass fr, 6¾".....................**100.00**
Nepperhan Pocket Perc, 31 cal, 6" oct bbl, early type, EX........**3,750.00**
Pettingill Pocket Perc, 31 cal, 4" oct bbl, split loading lever ...**2,875.00**
Remington Beals Navy, 36 cal, 7" oct bbl, walnut grips, VG...**1,500.00**
Remington Rider DA perc, 31 cal, 3" oct bbl, 5-shot cyl, compo grips...**1,600.00**
Remington 1858, perc, faint inspector's mks on grips, 14" **550.00**
Smith & Wesson #2, 32RF cal, 6" oct bbl, rfn, EX...................**400.00**
Smith & Wesson Model 1½SA, 32S&W cal, 3½" ribbed bbl....**260.00**
Smith & Wesson 1st Dbl Action, 44WCF cal, 6" keyhole bbl, compo grips...**460.00**
Whitney, 28 cal, hooded cyl, 6" oct bbl, rare, VG....................**4,600.00**

Rifles

Bedford school walnut perc long rifle, 38" oct bbl, dbl triggers, 53" ..**700.00**
Evans Repeating Sporting Transitional, 44 cal, 24" oct bbl, 43".**300.00**
JM Garner, perc, curly maple h/s, 39" oct bbl, 55".......................**350.00**
Mannlicher Schoenauer 1903 Bolt Action, 6.5X54MS cal, 18" bbl, VG ...**700.00**
Peruvian 1934 Mouser Bolt Action, 30-06 cal, 24" bbl, VG.......**175.00**
R Johnson & Co perc, 30" oct Damascus bbl, rfn walnut/s, 48"..**500.00**
Remington Model 12 Pump, 22 cal, 24" oct bbl, ¾ mag, VG.....**230.00**
Springfield Model 1884 Trapdoor, 45/70 cal, 32⅝" rnd bbl.........**750.00**
Springfield Trapdoor, 45-70 cal, bold inspector's mks, 32" bbl, 52" ..**235.00**
Springfield 1898 Krag, 30-40 Krag cal, full/s, 30" bbl, VG **490.00**
Unmk, perc, curly maple f/s, 39" oct bbl, rpl lock, 54" **150.00**
Unmk perc, maple w/orig faux striping, 42" oct bbl, 58" **700.00**
Winchester Model 52 Lightweight Target, 22LR cal, 27" rnd bbl, VG...**515.00**
Winchester Pattern 14 Enfield, 303 British cal, rough finish **285.00**
Winchester Post 64 Model 70 Super Express, 458 magnum cal, 22" bbl ...**500.00**
Winchester 1894 Spec O30WCF cal, std grade, 26" part oct bbl, G **350.00**
Winchester 1895 Lever Action, 30US cal, std grade, 24" rnd bbl, VG..**1,150.00**
Winchester 1917 Enfield Military, 30-06 cal, EX.....................**375.00**
Winchester 64 Lever Action, 30WCF cal, std grade, 24" rnd bbl, ⅔ mag......**1,035.00**

Shotguns

Am, 8 ga side-by-side 1 trigger perc dbl-bbl, rfn **550.00**
Beretta Model S-685 O/U, 20 ga, 26" vent rib bbls, pistol grip/s...**925.00**
Browning Pigeon Grade O/U, 12 ga, 30" vent-rib bbls, full/mod choke...**2,300.00**
FN Browning A-5 Semi-Auto, 12 ga, 29½" plain full choke bbl **400.00**
Ithaca Model 37 Featherweight, 12 ga, late production, 28" mod bbl, NM....**260.00**
Mossberg Model 500AB Slugster, 12 ga, 24" smooth-bore bbl **150.00**
Parker Damascus Dbl-Bbl Hammer, 10-ga, semi-pistol grip/s, G.**350.00**
Remington Model 58 Sportsman Semi-Auto, 12 ga, walnut/s, 26" bbl **350.00**
Springfield Trapdoor Forager, 20 ga, 26" bbl w/brass bead, dtd 1887, G ..**975.00**
TE Ward perc, 32" Damascus steel bbls, eng locks, walnut/s, 49" ...**400.00**
W Chance & Co, 8 ga side-by-side dbl-bbl perc w/silver inlay, 34" bbls **800.00**
Winchester Model 1897 Pump, 12 ga, std grade, 28" full choke bbl, VG...**400.00**
Winchester Model 1912 Trap Grade, 12 ga, 30" full choke bbl, VG **600.00**
Winchester Super X Model 1 semi-Auto, 12 ga, 30" vent rib bbl, NM......**460.00**

Weather Vanes

The earliest weather vanes were of handmade wrought iron and were generally simple angular silhouettes with a small hole suggesting an eye. Later copper, zinc, and polychromed wood with features in relief were fashioned into more realistic forms. Ships, horses, fish, Indians, roosters, and angels were popular motifs. In the nineteenth century, silhouettes were often made from sheet metal. Wooden figures became highly carved and were painted in vivid colors. E.G. Washburne and Company in New York was one of the most prominent manufacturers of weather vanes during the last half of the century. Two-dimensional sheet metal weather vanes are increasing in value due to the already heady prices of the full-bodied variety. Originality, strength of line, and patina help to determine value. When no condition is indicated, the items listed below are assumed to be in excellent condition.

Arrow, CI w/corrugated sheet copper feathers, verdigris, w/stand, 32"...**920.00**
Arrow, copper, heart shape, ball finial, old wht pnt w/gilt, 16x23" **975.00**
Arrow, copper, spire & ball finial, worn gilt, 19th C, 25½x43½" **1,725.00**
Arrow, copper & iron w/verdigris & gilt, 19th C, 9¼x37".......**1,000.00**
Arrow, iron w/copper feathers, copper spire, gilt traces, 13x26" ..**750.00**
Arrow, pnt wood w/ball finial, cvd 1911 at top, 24x46" **300.00**
Arrow, zinc head w/sheet copper shaft, gilt covered (worn), 23x36"..**2,400.00**
Banner, w/G, floral fr supports, gilt copper w/verdigris, 20x25".**2,185.00**
Banner, w/star finial, Gothic, sheet copper w/worn gilt, 34x13".**1,000.00**
Cow, copper, full body, weathered pnt/verdigris, 1890s, 21x33x8"..**9,200.00**
Eagle, copper, full body, mtd on sphere above arrow, EX gilt, 19"..**1,955.00**
Eagle, copper, full body, mtd on sphere above arrow, 18x29x18", G ...**750.00**
Eagle, molded copper, full body, verdigris, w/stand, 19x23x14" ..**1,100.00**
Horse, cvd/pnt wood, full body, sheet-iron ears, 19th C, 26x25".........**11,500.00**
Horse, flying, molded copper w/verdigris & gold, bullet holes, 19x25" .**1,850.00**
Horse, leaping, pnt copper, corrugated copper mane/tail, 1860s, 36"..**21,850.00**
Horse, running, copper, full body, verdigris, w/stand, 17x27"...**4,300.00**
Horse, running, copper, old patina, CI directionals on stand, 30"...**550.00**
Horse, running, copper w/verdigris, no directionals, 17x23"....**1,650.00**
Horse, running, copper w/worn gilt, appl zinc ears, minor rstr, 17x31"..**2,500.00**
Horse, running, copper w/zinc head, full body, verdigris, 18x41"..**7,000.00**
Horse, running, sheet iron, 19th C, 18x27", +blk metal stand & wall mt...**865.00**
Horse, running, tin, 11" **150.00**
Indian w/tomahawk raised, sheet metal, old mc rpt, 49" **750.00**
Lyre form, gilded zinc & iron, ball finials, NH, 1850s, 55x72" ...**8,000.00**
Merino sheep, copper, flattened full body, MA, 1890s, 21x29" ..**9,775.00**
Mink, sheet iron, Am, 19th C, w/metal stand, 19x24" **4,875.00**
Pig, copper, creamy pnt w/gilt traces & verdigris, 15½x23½" ..**10,925.00**
Pig, copper, dk verdigris w/some gilt, late 19th C, w/stand: 20x32"..**32,000.00**
Rooster, CI/steel/zinc, silver rpt, cone-shaped center rod, 23x32"............**330.00**
Rooster, copper w/dk gr patina, EX detail, full body, new base, 24"......**3,400.00**
Rooster, copper/zinc, old pnt, att Howard & Co, MA, ca 1853, 29½"...**18,400.00**
Rooster, molded zinc, red & gilt traces, on copper stand & sphere, 17" ...**2,000.00**
Steer, copper w/verdigris & gilt traces, late 1800s, 14x25".......**6,325.00**

Weaving

Early Americans used a variety of tools and a great amount of time to produce the material from which their clothing was made. Soaked and dried flax was broken on a flax brake to remove waste material. It was then tapped and stroked with a scutching knife. Hackles further removed waste and separated the short fibers from the longer ones. Unspun fibers were placed on the distaff on the spinning wheel for processing into yarn. The yarn was then wound around a reel for measuring. Three tools used for this purpose were the niddy-noddy, the reel yarn winder, and the click reel. After it was washed and dyed, the yarn was transferred to a barrel-cage or squirrel-cage swift and fed onto a bobbin winder.

Today flax wheels are more plentiful than the large wool wheels since they were small and could be more easily stored and preserved. The distaff, an often-discarded or misplaced part of the wheel, is very scarce.

French spinners from the Quebec area painted their wheels. Many have been stripped and refinished by those unaware of this fact. Wheels may be very simple or have a great amount of detail, depending upon the owner's ethnic background and the maker's skill.

Flax break, cvd top, pegged construction, stands, ca 1850s **110.00**
Flax wheel, birch/ash, New England, 1800s, 18" wheel, 31x28" .**235.00**
Flax wheel, EX dk patina, broken comb, 1850s, 12" wheel, 32"..**100.00**
Flax wheel, upright, 4 trn legs/spokes, 1 treadle, wheel at top, 45" **250.00**
Hackle, shaped wood bkbrd w/banded group of teeth, 1700s, 41x11" ..**880.00**
Hackle, wooden comb shape, 4" needles, 12¼x5½" **57.50**
Hackle, wooden hourglass shape, long sq teeth, lg.......................**100.00**
Niddy-noddy, chip-cvd dmn & zigzag patterns, Am, 19th C, 14x18".**375.00**
Niddy-noddy, cvd hearts & zigzag patterns (EX cvg), Am, 19th C, 15x18"..**635.00**
Spinning wheel, dk patina, 1860s, 44" 10-spoke wheel, 60x60x15", EX ..**500.00**
Spinning wheel, mustard pnt, complete, 40x39"..........................**220.00**
Spinning wheel, oak, chip-cvd date: 1822, splayed/trn legs, 35"..**275.00**
Spinning wheel, quartersawn tiger oak, ca 1800s, 61x63" **350.00**
Swift, whalebone, sq stepped base, 19th C, 13½"...................**1,495.00**
Tape loom, New England, 1740-70, 32½x15x15", EX................**850.00**
Yarn winder, CI, wood hdl, clamps to flat surface, 1800s, 8½".......**75.00**

Webb

Thomas Webb and Sons have been glassmakers in Stourbridge, England, since 1837. Besides their fine cameo glass, they have also made enameled ware and pieces heavily decorated with applied glass ornaments. The butterfly is a motif that has been so often featured that it tends to suggest Webb as the manufacturer. Our advisor for this category is Don Williams; he is listed in the Directory under Missouri. See also specific types of glass such as Alexandrite, Burmese, Mother of Pearl, and Peachblow.

Cameo

Bottle, scent; latticed pussy willow twigs, red/wht on citron, 6".........**1,250.00**
Bowl, branches/ivy, bk: butterfly, wht on maroon, globular, 3x5" ...**1,700.00**
Bowl, butterfly/floral/2 borders, wht on red, 3-sided w/loop hdl, 6"..**2,100.00**
Bowl, flowers/butterfly, wht on bl, 3 reeded ft, att, 6"..................**550.00**
Lamp, floral/butterfly, 3-color, squat/ftd base, flared shade, 9½"..**4,250.00**
Plate, wisteria/butterfly, wht on yel, 7½".......................................**400.00**
Rose bowl, clear/swirled, 2" disc: foxglove/butterfly, rose on wht, 4"..**1,900.00**

Rose bowl, floral with large butterfly in flight, white on bright cranberry, 4½x5", $800.00.
(Photo courtesy James Julia)

Toothpick holder, lions/urn, Greek Key rim, wht on gr irid, 2¾" ..**150.00**
Vase, cameo florals/collar, wht on peachblow, dbl gourd, 9" **3,000.00**
Vase, fishscale-cvd salmon color w/gold bamboo, bottle form, 8½" **1,500.00**
Vase, floral, bk: branch, half-moon band, wht on bl, collar neck, 5"..**1,250.00**
Vase, floral, bk: grasses, wht on citron, shouldered, 3⅜" **1,250.00**
Vase, floral, pk on opal, ormolu rim & 4-ftd base, cylindrical, 8¾"..**550.00**
Vase, floral (6X), bk: 3 butterflies, 2 borders, wht on citron, 8"..**1,950.00**
Vase, floral branches, bl on brn, trumpet flared base, 3x5¼"..**3,700.00**
Vase, floral/bands, bk: butterfly, wht on red, 6" **1,750.00**
Vase, floral/bk: butterfly, wht on bl, bulbous w/can neck, 5"..**1,750.00**
Vase, floral/bk: butterfly, 3-color, squat pear form, 2½"............**1,600.00**

Vase, gold leaves/butterfly on red o/l on yel, wht int, 7" 1,200.00
Vase, Ivory, florals/rickrack rim band, ovoid w/bun ft, 6½" 1,400.00
Vase, leafy branches, bk: butterfly, 3-color, squat w/stick neck, 6" .3,000.00
Vase, poppies/bk: morning glories, wht on dk amber, att, 9x6½" ...3,950.00
Vase, sm leaves on vines/bk: butterfly, wht on sapphire bl, 8" .2,700.00
Vase, trumpet flowers, wht on bl, cvd rim band, ovoid, 4" 1,350.00
Vase, trumpet flowers, 2" border, wht on cranberry, stick neck, 10" ..3,900.00
Vase, tulips, cvd border, bl on textured clear, trumpet form, 9" ...525.00
Vase, wheat stalks/grasses, wht on amber, ovoid, 5½" 1,500.00
Vase, 2 leafy branches, bk: butterfly, icicle band, wht on citron, 8" ..2,400.00

Miscellaneous

Bottle, scent; floral, wht/yel on bl frost, lay-down, 4½" L 1,600.00
Pitcher, cream w/cranberry int/hdl, roses/butterfly, 12", +4 tumblers 875.00
Pitcher, yel & pk opal vertical stripes on clear, bulb w/can neck, 6" ...225.00
Vase, alternating dk bl/pastel verticals, wht int, shouldered, 5" .250.00
Vase, Basketweave, dk brn to tan to gold to cream, wht int, 7x6" ...850.00
Vase, bl mirror irid (Webb Bronze), shouldered, 6½" 275.00
Vase, gold floral on brn satin, long-neck gourd form, 3¼", pr 345.00
Vase, gold prunus/insect by Barbe on brn to gold, cream int, 11x4" 450.00
Vase, gray-brn to dk brn w/wht int, gold foliage cascade, bulbous, 7" ...400.00
Vase, irid bl-bronze w/high-gloss surface, shouldered, 11" 300.00
Vase, pk/wht stripes, ruffled/crimped undulating rim, 8x4" 425.00
Vase, Swirl, pk/rose/yel stripes on frost, rnd w/stick neck, 7½x5" ...425.00
Vase, yel to lt yel satin, elongated teardrop shape, long neck, 11" ..285.00

Wedgwood

Josiah Wedgwood established his pottery in Burslem, England, in 1759. He produced only molded utilitarian earthenwares until 1770 when new facilities were opened at Etruria for the production of ornamental wares. It was there he introduced his famous Basalt and Jasperware. Jasperware, an unglazed fine stoneware decorated with classic figures in white relief, was usually produced in blues, but it was also made in ground colors of green, lilac, yellow, black, or white. Occasionally three or more colors were used in combination. It has been in continuous production to the present day and is the most easily recognized of all the Wedgwood lines. Jasper-dip is a ware with a solid-color body or a white body that has been dipped in an overlay color. It was introduced in the late 1700s and is the type most often encountered on today's market.

Though Wedgwood's Jasperware was highly acclaimed, on a more practical basis his improved creamware was his greatest success, due to the ease with which it could be potted and because its lighter weight significantly reduced transportation expenses. Wedgwood was able to offer 'chinaware' at affordable prices. Queen Charlotte was so pleased with the ware that she allowed it to be called 'Queen's Ware.' Most creamware was marked simply 'WEDGWOOD.' ('Wedgwood & Co.' and 'Wedgewood' are marks of other potters.) From 1769 to 1780, Wedgwood was in partnership with Thomas Bentley; artwares of the highest quality may bear the 'Wedgwood & Bentley' mark indicating this partnership. Moonlight Lustre, an allover splashed-on effect of pink intermingling with gray, brown, or yellow, was made from 1805 to 1815. Porcelain was made, though not to any great extent, from 1812 to 1822. Bone china was produced before 1822 and after 1872. These types of wares were marked 'WEDGWOOD' (with a printed 'Portland Vase' mark after 1872). Stone china and Pearlware were made from about 1820 to 1875. Examples of either may be found with a printed or impressed mark to indicate their body type. During the late 1800s, Wedgwood produced some fine parian and majolica. Creamware, hand painted by Emile Lessore, was sold from about 1860 to 1875. From the twentieth century, several lines of lustre wares — Butterfly, Dragon, and Fairyland

(designed by Daisy Makeig-Jones) — have attracted the collector and, as their prices suggest, are highly sought after and admired.

Nearly all of Wedgwood's wares are clearly marked. 'WEDGWOOD' was used before 1891, after which time 'ENGLAND' was added. Most examples marked 'MADE IN ENGLAND' were made after 1905. A detailed study of all marks is recommended for accurate dating. See also Majolica.

Key:
WW — WEDGWOOD   WWMIE — WEDGWOOD Made
WWE — WEDGWOOD England   in England

Basket, fruit; Pearlware, basketweave/rtcl rim, w/stand, WW, 10⅝" 315.00
Biscuit jar, Jasper, dk bl, birds/berries, SP rim, WWE, 5¼" 635.00
Biscuit jar, Jasper, dk bl, classical figures, SP trim, WW, 6", EX ..375.00
Biscuit jar, Jasper, lilac, fox hunt, SP trim, WWE, 20th C, 5¼" .545.00
Biscuit jar, Jasper, 3-color, classical figures, WWE, ca 1900, 5½" ...920.00
Bottle, scent; Jasper, bl, Geo III/Charlotte, rpr, 1⅞" dia 488.00
Bough pot, Jasper, lt bl, acanthus/bellflowers, floral lid, WW, 7" .1,600.00
Bough pot, Queen's Ware, figures (2 seasons), WW, rpr lid, 6" ...460.00
Bowl, Butterfly Lustre, 3 on opal, int: orange w/1, 2x3½" 200.00
Bowl, Dragon Lustre, bl mottle/MOP, Z4829, WWE, ca 1920, 7" ...1,265.00
Bowl, Dragon Lustre, central dragon, red/gr on yel/brn int, 2x4" ...275.00
Bowl, Dragon Lustre, 8-sided, Z4825, WW, 1920s, 7¼" 800.00
Bowl, Fairyland Lustre, elves in mushroom garden on blk, gr int, 2x4" ...1,000.00
Bowl, Fairyland Lustre, gnomes on red, int: dwarf/bird scene, 2½x5" 600.00
Bowl, Hummingbird Lustre, bl w/5, int: orange w/1, 2x3½" 450.00
Bowl, Jasper, bl, classical figures/fruit, gilt bands, WW 1878, 6" .750.00
Bowl, Jasper, lilac, Dancing Hours, WWMIE, 1961, 10⅛" 430.00
Bowl, Queen's Ware, blk transfers, WW, 1890s, 11½" 1,265.00
Bowl, salad; Jasper, dk bl, classical figures, SP rim, WW, 5¾" 375.00
Box, Dragon Lustre, bl mottle/MOP, Z4829, WWE, ca 1920, 4x7" .1,850.00
Box, Jasper, dk bl, classical medallions, gilt brass mts, WW, 4½" 1,095.00
Buckle, Jasper, bl, classical relief medallion on steel mt, unmk ...375.00
Bust, Basalt, Burns, EW Wyon, waisted socle, WW, ca 1877, 14" ..515.00
Bust, Basalt, Mercury, on waisted socle, WW, mid-1800s, 18" .2,415.00
Candlestick, Basalt, Cerese w/cornucopia sconce, WW, rstr, 11½" ...1,265.00
Candlesticks, Pearlware, turq, maidens/cornucopias, WW, 1872, 10", pr ...1,380.00
Ceiling fixture, Jasper, lilac, seasons, WW, 1868, 9⅞" dia 2,100.00
Chess set, Jasper, bl/blk, Machin, WWE, 1976, complete in case ..2,400.00
Cistern, Jasper, lt bl, classical figures, hdls/brass base, WW, 6⅜" 575.00
Clock case, Jasper, lt bl, classical relief, WWE, ca 1900, 6", EX .345.00
Cup & saucer, tea; Kenlock Ware, irises, WWE, ca 1895, 5¾" ...800.00
Dejeuner set, Bone China, floral, WW, service for 4 on tray 300.00
Ewer, Rosso Antico, classical relief, loop hdl, WW, 6⅜" 700.00
Figurine, Basalt, Aphrodite, atop wave, WW, late 1800s, 10¼", EX ..635.00
Figurine, Basalt, Faun, WW, 15¾" 975.00
Figurine, Basalt, Taurus the Bull, blk, WWE, ca 1949, 14¼" 430.00
Figurine, Basalt, Venus on Rock, WW, mid- to late 19th C, 18¾" 1,950.00
Fruit cooler, Pearlware, Oriental floral on honeycomb, w/lid, WW, 8" ..800.00
Game dish, Caneware, grapes, cauliflower finial, WW, 10½" 350.00
Game dish, Caneware, grapevines, cauliflower finial, WW, 8¼", EX ...230.00
Humidor, Jasper, lt bl, male figures, WW, late 1800s, 5⅞", EX ...750.00
Jar, canopic; Basalt, hieroglyphs/zodiac, WWMIE, 1977, 9¼" 1,265.00
Jardiniere, Jasper, blk, Muses/grapevines/lion masks/rings, WW, 9" 515.00
Jardiniere, Jasper, 3-color, floral, rams' heads, WW, 19th C, 5¼" 1,035.00
Jug, Basalt, putti between bands, mask-head hdl, WW, late 1700s, 7" ...2,875.00
Jug, club; Basalt, floral, WW, mid-19th C, 5" 345.00
Jug, club; Basalt, mc floral sprays, WW, mid-1800s, 5" 345.00
Jug, club; Rosso Antico, encaustic decor, WW, ca 1854, rstr, 8¼" ...515.00
Jug, club; Rosso Antico, mc florals, WW, mid-1800s, 6¼" 515.00
Jug, Jasper, yel, classical figures, rope hdl, WW, ca 1900, 7½" 700.00
Jug, Jasper, yel, classical figures, WWE, ca 1930, 6" 515.00
Jug, Rosso Antico, Egyptian decor, WW, 1880s, 7½" 975.00

Jug, syrup; Jasper, dk bl, birds/oak leaves, SP top, WWE, 6¼" **545.00**
Ladle, soup; Queen's Ware, foliate vine, WW, 11¼" **315.00**
Lamp, oil; Rosso Antico, appl Basalt classical relief, WW, 5⅜"..**575.00**
Medallion, Basalt, Am I Not a Man...?, WW, ca 1891, 1⅛x1¼" **635.00**
Medallion, Jasper, Josiah Wedgwood, self-fr, WWE, 20th C, 4x3¼"....**200.00**
Model, Basalt, Sphinx, female w/lion body, WW, early 1800s, 11¼"...**865.00**
Mug, Jasper, crimson, classical figures, WW, 1920s, 5⅜" **1,265.00**
Plaque, Fairyland Lustre, Enchanted Palace, WWE, ltd ed, 8x12"...**700.00**
Plaque, Jasper, blk, Dancing Hours, WW, late 1800s, 4x10"+ebony fr..**575.00**
Plaque, Jasper, blk, Dancing Hours, WW, 2½x7¼" **350.00**
Plaque, Jasper, gr, classical figures, 4½x11½"+brass fr **545.00**
Plaque, Jasper, lt bl, Blind Man's Bluff, WW, early 1800s, 6x12" ..**660.00**
Plaque, Jasper, lt bl, classical boys, WWE, 1925, 6⅛x18¼"....**1,265.00**
Plate, Queen's Ware, cherubs, emb shells, WW, 1860-61, 8⅝", pr...**400.00**
Plate, Queen's Ware, Cupid & Psyche, sgn E Lessor, WW, 1870s, 8¾"..**635.00**
Plate, Rosso Antico, hieroglyphs, WW, early 1800s, 8½" **485.00**
Pot, Malfrey; Fairyland Lustre, Candlemas, WWE, ca 1924, 8¼"..**1,380.00**
Salad set, Jasper, dk bl, classical relief, SP trim, WW, 3-pc **345.00**
Sauce boat, Queen's Ware, molded trellis/scrolls, WW, 8" **460.00**
Tankard, children hunting frieze, WW, 5¾" **1,495.00**
Tea bowl & saucer, Jasper, lt bl, classical figures, WW, late 1700s....**975.00**
Tea infuser, Queen's Ware, Beane's Pat, WW, 1880s, 13¼" **1,100.00**
Tea set, Drabware, WW, ca 1830, 6½" pot+cr/sug, EX................**575.00**
Tea set, Rosso Antico, prunus, crabstock hdls, WW, early 1800s, 3-pc .**800.00**
Teapot, Jasper, 3-color, Diceware bl/gr/wht, WW, 19th C, 3⅝" **4,600.00**
Teapot, Rosso Antico, hieroglyphs, crocodile finial, WW, 7¼", EX...**1,095.00**
Teapot, Russo Antico, arabesque florals, spaniel finial, WW, 7½" **575.00**
Tray, Rosso Antico, hieroglyphs, WW, early 1800s, 8½" **1,100.00**
Tray, tea; Pearlware, red/pk transfer border, WW, ca 1886, 18⅛" ..**200.00**
Vase, Basalt, arabesque floral band, paw ft, mask hdls, WW, 9½" **800.00**
Vase, Basalt, arabesque florals, scroll hdls, WW & Bentley, 13¼"....**1,095.00**
Vase, Creamware, vintage, Bacchus hdls, att WW & Bently, 10", EX...**975.00**
Vase, Dragon Lustre, bl mottle/MOP, trumpet, Z4829, WWE, 1920, 11"...**1,150.00**
Vase, Hummingbird Lustre, 6 birds on bl, orange int, bottle form, 8" **1,250.00**
Vase, Ivory Vellum, gilt foliage, WW, late 1800s, 8⅜" **200.00**
Vase, Jasper, bl, classical figures, hdls, WW, 1890s, 7¼".............**400.00**
Vase, Jasper, bl, Portland, classical relief, WW, 19th C, 6"..........**285.00**
Vase, Jasper, bl w/yel quatrefoils, Diceware, WWE, 1974, 5¼" ...**500.00**
Vase, Jasper, blk, portraits, Greek-Key border, WW, 1950s, 6½".**975.00**
Vase, Jasper, crimson, classical figures, w/lid, WWE, ca 1920, 7"..**2,185.00**
Vase, Jasper, dk bl, classical figures, Portland, 1850s, 10⅛"......**1,725.00**
Vase, Jasper, gr, trellis & flowers, WW, mid-1800s, 6¼".............**920.00**
Vase, Jasper, lilac, classical figures, hdls, WW, 1850s, 9" **525.00**
Vase, Jasper, lt bl, Capt Cook/foliage/etc, WWE, 1900s, rstr, 11⅝" ..**1,840.00**
Vase, Jasper, lt bl, Dancing Hours, WW, 19th C, 6" **700.00**
Vase, Jasper, terra cotta, classical figures, WWE, 1977, 11".........**515.00**
Vase, Jasper, wht, putti/rings/florets, WW, 19th C, 11¼" **400.00**
Vase, Keith Murray, sharp horizontal rings, bulbous, 7"...............**400.00**
Vase, Queen's Ware, E Lessore, bottle form, WW, 5½", pr...........**575.00**
Vase, spill; Jasper, 3-color, classical relief, WW, mid-1800s, 3" ...**1,035.00**
Vase, Victoria Ware, HP foliage on wht, hdls, WW, 7¼"............**865.00**
Vase, Victoria Ware, mc, portrait medallions, WW, ca 1880, 7⅝"...**1,100.00**

Weil Ware

Max Weil came to the United States in the 1940s, settling in California. There he began manufacturing dinnerware, figurines, cookie jars, and wall pockets. American clays were used, and the dinnerware was all hand decorated. Weil died in 1954; the company closed two years later. The last backstamp to be used was the outline of a burro with the words 'Weil Ware — Made in California.' Many unmarked pieces found today originally carried a silver foil label; but you'll often find a four-digit hand-written number series, especially on figurines. For further study we rec-

ommend *The Collector's Encyclopedia of California Pottery* by Jack Chipman (Collector Books).

Bowl, Malay Blossom, ftd, 3½x6⅝" **40.00**
Bowl, vegetable; Malay Blossom, 4x5½x9" **30.00**
Compote, Malay Blossom, ftd, 3⅛x6½x6½" **35.00**
Creamer, Malay Blossom **20.00**
Cup & saucer, Malay Blossom **15.00**
Dish, leaf shape, gr top w/pk bottom, 8x14" **35.00**
Figurine, blond in bl bonnet, hands in muff, 10" **85.00**
Figurine, Dutch boy, hands behind waist, 6" **40.00**
Flower holder, accordion lady, seated, 11" **90.00**
Flower holder, blond in yel dress w/hole in bl apron, 9" **70.00**
Flower holder, brunette in orange dress, vase on ea side, 9½" **75.00**
Flower holder, brunette in pk w/parasol, 10¼" **85.00**
Flower holder, lady in bl-flowered wht dress, #1800, 11" **90.00**
Flower holder, lady in wht w/bl floral dress stands by vase, 10"...**65.00**
Flower holder, lady sits on bench between 2 vases, #4028, 8½" **70.00**
Flower holder, pensive lady holding horn of plenty, #4042, 5x9"..**70.00**
Flower holder, seated Oriental lady w/fan vase behind head, 9¼"..**60.00**
Pitcher, Malay Blossom, 7" **40.00**
Planter, Ming Tree, 6x6x4½" **30.00**
Plate, bread & butter; Malay Blossom, sq, 6" **10.00**
Plate, dinner; Malay Blossom, sq, 9¼" **15.00**
Plate, salad; Malay Blossom, sq, 8x8" **12.00**
Platter, Malay Blossom, 11x7" **25.00**
Saucer, Malay Blossom **7.00**
Sherbet, Malay Blossom, ped ft, 4" sq **25.00**
Sugar bowl, Malay Blossom, w/lid **22.00**
Tea set, Malay Bambu, cr/sug & teapot **75.00**
Tidbit tray, Malay Blossom, 3-tiered (6", 8" & 10"), 13" **35.00**
Tumbler, Malay Blossom, 4¼" **22.00**
Vase, Malay Bambu, pinched top, 8¼" **45.00**
Vase, Malay Blossom, 4¼" **15.00**
Vase, Ming Tree, flared top, 5⅝x4¾" **30.00**
Vase, Ming Tree, sq, 6" **30.00**

Weller

The Weller Pottery Company was established in Zanesville, Ohio, in 1882, the outgrowth of a small one-kiln log cabin works Sam Weller had operated in Fultonham. Through an association with Wm. Long, he entered the art pottery field in 1895, producing the Lonhuda Ware Long had perfected in Steubenville six years earlier. His famous Louwelsa line was merely a continuation of Lonhuda and was made in at least five hundred different shapes until 1924. Many fine lines of artware followed under the direction of Charles Babcock Upjohn, art director from 1895 to 1904: Dickens Ware (1st Line), under-glaze slip decorations on dark backgrounds; Turada, featuring applied ivory bands of delicate openwork on solid dark brown backgrounds; and Aurelian, similar to Louwelsa, but with a brushed-on rather than blended ground. One of their most famous lines was 2nd Line Dickens, introduced in 1900. Backgrounds, characteristically caramel shading to turquoise matt, were decorated by sgraffito with animals, golfers, monks, Indians, and scenes from Dickens novels. The work is often artist signed. Sicardo, 1903, was a metallic lustre line in tones of rose, blue, green, or purple with flowing Art Nouveau patterns developed within the glaze.

Frederick Hurten Rhead, who worked for Weller from 1903 to 1904, created the prestigious Jap Birdimal line decorated with geisha girls, landscapes, storks, etc., accomplished through application of heavy slip forced through the tiny nozzle of a squeeze bag. Other lines to his credit are L'Art Nouveau, produced in both high-gloss brown and matt pastels, and 3rd Line Dickens, often decorated with Cruikshank's illustrations in relief. Other early artware lines were Eocean, Floretta, Hunter, Perfecto, Dresden, Etched Matt, and Etna.

In 1920 John Lessel was hired as art director, and under his supervision several new lines were created. LaSa, LaMar, Marengo, and Besline attest to his expertise with metallic lustres. The last of the artware lines and one of the most sought after by collectors today is Hudson, first made during the early 1920s. Hudson, a semimatt glazed ware, was beautifully artist decorated on shaded backgrounds with florals, animals, birds, and scenics. Notable artists often signed their work, among them Hester Pillsbury, Dorothy England Laughead, Ruth Axline, Claude Leffler, Sarah Reid McLaughlin, E.L. Pickens, and Mae Timberlake.

During the '30s Weller produced a line of gardenware and naturalistic life-sized figures of dogs, cats, swans, geese, and playful gnomes. The Depression brought a slow, steady decline in sales, and by 1948 the pottery was closed.

Our advisor for this category is Mike Nickel; he is listed in the Directory under Michigan. For a more thorough study we recommend *The Collector's Encyclopedia of Weller Pottery* by Sharon and Bob Huxford, available at your local library or from Collector Books.

Alvin, bud vase, dbl; divided tree-trunk form, 6" 80.00
Arcadia, covered dish, #A-8, 4½" 65.00
Arcadia, fan vase, leaf form, 8x15" 100.00
Arcola, vase, rose branch, ruffled rim, hdld, 5½" 100.00
Ardsley, bud vase, cattails w/flowers around base, 7½" 95.00
Ardsley, bulb bowl, 5" 125.00
Ardsley, wall pocket, dbl cattail cones w/flower, 11½" 300.00
Athens, vase, cat medallions/swags, long neck/bulbous bottom, 10½" ..650.00
Atlas, covered dish, #C-2, 3½" 175.00
Atlas, vase, #C-10, 13" 225.00
Aurelian, ewer, squatty w/ruffled rim, floral, sgn MP, 6" 275.00
Aurelian, vase, urn, floral, sgn RA, 13" 1,100.00
Baldin, bowl, emb apples, 4" 150.00
Baldin, vase, emb apple band on flared cylinder form, 9½" 300.00
Barcelona, ewer, bulbous, pinched lip, 9½" 275.00
Barcelona, oil jar, 25½" 1,750.00
Blossom, basket, ball shape, 6" 85.00
Blossom, ewer, squatty base, pinched lip, 7" 85.00
Blue & Decorated, bud vase, long curved neck w/trumpet bottom, 10" ...150.00
Blue & Decorated, vase, bulbous w/long thick neck, 10" 275.00
Blue Drapery, candlestick/lamp base, 9½" 145.00
Blue Drapery, wall pocket, 9" 250.00
Blue Ware, jardinere, classical dancer, 3-ftd, 6½" 225.00
Blue Ware, lamp base, floral band, flared base, 9" 200.00
Blue Ware, vase, rose swags, bl-paneled tapered urn, 4-ftd, 10" ..500.00
Bonito, candle holders, 1½", pr 125.00
Bonito, vase, heart shape w/ped ft & scrolled hdls, 5" 145.00
Bouquet, pitcher, #B-18, 9½" 175.00
Breton, vase, floral band on wide neck, bulbous bottom, 6" 75.00
Brighton, chicks (2), 5" 575.00
Brighton, parakeets (2), 9" 1,500.00
Brighton, parrot on scrolled base, beak open, 13½" 2,250.00
Brighton, penguins (2), 5" 850.00
Brighton, swan flower frog, 5" 375.00
Burntwood, floral, bottle w/sm neck, 7" 125.00
Burntwood, vase, floral, bulbous w/thick rolled lip, 7" 125.00
Burntwood, vase, grapevine, wide-mouth bottle form, 3½" 135.00
Cameo, ewer, 10" 75.00
Cameo, hanging basket, 5" 110.00
Cameo, vase, sq, 8½" 75.00
Candis, console bowl, roses & daisies, 2½x11" 70.00
Candis, ewer, roses & daisies, 11" 110.00
Chengtu, vase, 6-sided, flared top & bottom, 9" 125.00
Chengtu, vase, 6-sided, tapers to flat bottom, 11" 175.00

Classic, fan vase, 5" 85.00
Classic, window box, 4" tall 85.00
Claywood, candlestick, floral, flared, 5" 125.00
Claywood, vase, floral panels, cylindrical w/lip, 8½" 125.00
Claywood, vase, spider web, cylindrical, 5½" 110.00
Coppertone, flowerpot, w/saucer, mottled, 5" 250.00
Coppertone, pitcher, fish hdl, 7½" 1,100.00
Coppertone, vase, trumpet form w/scalloped rim, 6½" 200.00
Cornish, bowl, berries & leaves, ball form w/sm scrolled hdls, 4" .65.00
Cornish, jardiniere, berries & leaves, ribbed band, scrolled hdls, 5"...60.00
Creamware, bowl, cameo w/cutouts, str-sided, 4-ftd, hdld, 2½"...60.00
Creamware, candlestick, cameo & cutouts, sq w/sq hdls, 11"......140.00
Creamware, planter, geometric flowers w/cutout rim, sq, 4-ftd, 3½" ...125.00
Creamware, vase, cameo w/cutouts, sq w/sq hdls, 7" 85.00
Darsie, flowerpot, tassel swag, scalloped rim, 5½" 60.00
Darsie, vase, tassel swag, cylindrical w/scalloped rim, 7½" 60.00
Delsa, ewer, #10, 7" 65.00
Delsa, vase, #2, 6" 45.00
Dickens I, jardiniere, tapered, morning glories, 8½" 400.00
Dickens I, lamp base, 3-ftd, 2-hdl, fruit, 11" 1,100.00
Dickens I, mug, floral, 7" 225.00
Dickens II, ewer, Chief Blackbear sgn AD(Dunlavy)/Anna Dautherty, 12" ...2,500.00
Dickens II, ewer, duck on shore, waisted, 8½" 600.00
Dickens II, tankard, frolicking nude, sgn EL Pickens 1902, 12"..........3,500.00
Dickens II, vase, Dombey & Son, cylindrical, sgn W Gibson, 10½"..1,250.00
Dickens II, vase, dragon, sgn EL Pickens, 15½" 1,750.00
Dickens II, vase, fish, ball form w/sm hdls, 9½" 2,000.00
Dickens II, vase, Indian portrait, cylindrical w/lip, sgn HS, 11" ..1,100.00
Dickens II, vase, shepherd w/sheep, urn, 15" 2,500.00
Dickens III, inkwell, mk #0038, sgn R, 2½"..............................950.00
Dickens III, vase, Dombey & Son, ftd disc w/hdls, sgn P, 7½"....750.00
Dickens III, vase, Wilkins Micawber, cylindrical, sgn LS, 10½".950.00
Dupont, bowl, flowerpot & swags on grid panels, 2½" 50.00
Dupont, planter, sq, topiaries/doves, cut-out rim, 5" 75.00
Elberta, candle holder, canoe shape, 3" 85.00
Elberta, console bowl, canoe shape, 6x11½" 115.00
Eocean, vase, floral, teardrop shape w/plain rim, flat bottom, 9" ...350.00
Eocean, vase, fruit, cylindrical w/4 hdls at rim, 16" 1,000.00
Eocean, vase, owl, sgn EB, 10½" 200.00
Eocean (Late Line), bud vase, floral, conical form, 5" 135.00
Etna, bowl, mouse on rim, 2½" 900.00
Etna, vase, floral, pk on gray to wht, pot w/lg ear hdls at lip, 9" .500.00
Etna, vase, grapes (pnt), gray to wht, tapered, 15" 850.00
Etna, vase, thistles, E Roberts, 12½x5" 900.00
Evergreen, vase, bulbous w/wide-mouth rim, 4½" 40.00
Flemish, basket tub, roses, bulbous, hdld, 4½" 125.00
Flemish, comport, roses, lid w/rose finial, 8½" 350.00
Flemish, jardiniere, flowers & leaves around bottom, 4-ftd, 6" ...150.00
Fleron, batter pitcher, 11½" 250.00
Fleron, bowl, #J-6, 3" 100.00
Florala, candle holders, floral panels, flared, 5", pr 175.00
Florala, console bowl, inner mc floral band, 11" 125.00
Florenzo, basket, roses, fluted, 5½" 140.00
Florenzo, planter, roses, sq, fluted, 4-ftd, 3½" 65.00
Floretta, ewer, pansy, gray to wht, 6" 200.00
Floretta, pillow vase, bag shape w/ruffled rim & hdls, mk B/15, 6" ..200.00
Floretta, vase, water lily at rim of long neck, bulbous base, 13½" 450.00
Forest, bowl, #3, 2½" 75.00
Forest, teapot, glossy, 4½" 300.00
Forest, vase, flared, flat bottom, 13½" 400.00
Forest, vase, flared top, 4-ftd, 8" 175.00
Fruitone, console bowl, flared scalloped rim, ftd, 5" 95.00
Fruitone, vase, hdld pot, tapers to flat bottom, 4½" 75.00
Fruitone, wall pocket, conical, 5½" 225.00

Glendale, bud vase, dbl; tree trunks flanking emb bird panel, 7"...**300.00**

Glendale, vase, birds and nest, 9", $1,250.00; Hudson, vase, floral and leaf design, 9", $1,750.00.

Glendale, vase, lovebirds on branch, tapers to flat bottom, 8½"....**750.00**
Gloria, vase, butterfly & flowers, #G-12, 5" **125.00**
Goldenglow, bowl, 4-ftd, 3½x16" **125.00**
Goldenglow, vase, high/low hdls, ped ft, 8½" **175.00**
Greenbriar, ewer, dbl-loop hdl, 11½" **300.00**
Greenbriar, vase, ribbed bulbous w/flat twisted hdls, 9½" **275.00**
Greora, flower frog, stepped form, 4½" **135.00**
Greora, vase, 3-sided, 3-ftd, 4½" **85.00**
Hobart, console bowl w/2-nudes flower frog, plain, 12", 7½"......**450.00**
Hobart, flower frog, figural nude, 8½" **350.00**
Hudson, vase, cowboy descending canyon, sgn Timberlake, 9"...**25,000.00**
Hudson, vase, fruit, urn shape w/hdls, 13½" **1,750.00**
Hudson, vase, irises, short trumpet neck, flat bottom, 15" **2,000.00**
Hudson, vase, lg iris, M Timberlake, 9x4" **975.00**
Hudson, vase, owl in tree against moon, 8" **2,000.00**
Hudson-Perfecto, vase, Arabian on wht horse, 13" **4,000.00**
Hudson-Perfecto, vase, irises, pot shape w/rolled lip, 13½" **1,500.00**
Hunter, pillow vase, loon on shore, 4¾" **650.00**
Ivoris, ginger jar, 8½" **125.00**
Ivoris, vase, emb leaves, 3-ftd cone shape, 6" **40.00**
Ivory (Clinton Ivory), jardiniere, squirrels in tree, 6½" **150.00**
Ivory (Clinton Ivory), pillow vase, swag/ribbed band, 4-ftd, 5"...**100.00**
Ivory (Clinton Ivory), planter, dragonfly, ftd, 4" sq **150.00**
Jap Birdimal, oil pitcher, sgn HMR, 10½" **1,250.00**
Jap Birdimal, vase, geese in flight, twisted form, 11" **850.00**
Jap Birdimal, vase, geese in flight, 6-sided squatty bottle, 4"......**550.00**
Jap Birdimal, vase, geisha, flat-sided, 4" **400.00**
Klyro, basket, berries/flowers, ftd, 7" **150.00**
Klyro, candle holder, berries/flowers, tower form, 9½" **125.00**
Klyro, circle vase, flower swag, ftd, 8"..................**150.00**
Knifewood, vase, daisies, bulbous, glossy, 4½" **125.00**
L'Art Nouveau, mug, 5" **250.00**
L'Art Nouveau, vase, corn form, 4½" **300.00**
L'Art Nouveau, vase, floral, low bulbous base w/tall neck, 8" **250.00**
L'Art Nouveau (Glossy), console bowl, emb grapevines, hdld, 6x12" ..**500.00**
L'Art Nouveau (Glossy), vase, emb nymph, 4-sided, flared, 12½" ...**600.00**
La Sa, vase, cross & wht flowers, pot form, 3½" **150.00**
Lamar, lamp, scenic, 16" **500.00**
Lavonia, console bowl, fluted, 3x15" **150.00**
Lavonia, vase, emb thistles, 10" **200.00**
Lido, candle holder, dbl; #15, 2½" **45.00**
Lido, cornucopia, 5" **45.00**
Lorbeek, console bowl & frog, 3x14", 5" **200.00**
Lorbeek, wall pocket, 8½" **200.00**
Loru, bowl, emb leaf decor on scalloped panels, 2½x8"..................**45.00**
Louella, basket, 6½" **145.00**
Louella, powder jar, w/lid, 4"..................**125.00**
Louwelsa, candle holder, floral, 1-hdl jug form, sgn MH, 4½" **175.00**
Louwelsa, candlestick, floral, slender w/flared bottom, sgn HL, 9"..**275.00**
Louwelsa, ewer, floral, squatty w/ruffled rim, 6½" **200.00**
Louwelsa, jardiniere, iris, ftd ball form w/lip, 12½" **400.00**
Louwelsa, lamp, floral, squatty, ftd, sgn MM, 6½" **1,250.00**

Louwelsa, mug, berries/leaves, flared bottom, sgn HM, 8½"........**325.00**
Louwelsa, mug, portrait, #432, sgn Ferrell, 6½" **1,000.00**
Louwelsa, vase, floral, sq w/flared bottom, sgn UJ, 8½" **250.00**
Louwelsa, vase, grapes, urn, sgn A Haubrich, 23½" **1,500.00**
Louwelsa, vase, horse head, cylindrical w/lip, sgn MT, 13½"...**1,650.00**
Louwelsa, vase, portrait, ftd pillow form, sgn TTH, 7½"..........**1,250.00**
Louwelsa (Blue), mug, floral, #562 on base, 5½" **600.00**
Louwelsa (Blue), vase, floral, squatty w/sm opening, 1-hdl, 3"....**500.00**
Lustre, candlestick, gathered fabric look, 8" **75.00**
Lustre, vase, cylindrical, 8½" **85.00**
Malverne, bud vase, 8½" **115.00**
Malverne, candle holder, 2" **70.00**
Malverne, pillow vase, 8½" **175.00**
Marbleized, vase, bowed cylinder, slightly lipped, flat bottom, 10"...**175.00**
Marbleized, vase, hexagonal, tapered, 5" **115.00**
Marbleized, vase, trumpet form, 7½" **150.00**
Marvo, bowl, 5" **85.00**
Marvo, bud vase, dbl; gate type, 4½" **95.00**
Marvo, pitcher, 9" **175.00**
Melrose, console, roses, ruffled rim, branch hdls, ftd, 5x8½" **150.00**
Melrose, vase, apples, branch wraps around cylinder, ruffled rim, 7"..**190.00**
Mi-Flo, bowl, emb pansies, tab hdls, 4" **60.00**
Mirror Black, strawberry jar, 6½" **85.00**
Mirror Black, wall pocket, flared cone shape, 8" **150.00**
Muskota, boy fishing on stump, 6½" **375.00**
Muskota, fence w/2 cats & 2 flowerpots, 5" **125.00**
Muskota, girl w/doll seated against tree trunk, 8" **500.00**
Muskota, powder jar, lady w/rose-&-ribbon swags on dress, 7"...**325.00**
Neiska, bowl, 3-ftd, 4" **35.00**
Oak Leaf, wall pocket, 8½" **150.00**
Panella, cornucopia, 5½" **55.00**
Paragon, candle holders, incised floral, 2", pr..................**150.00**
Parian, vase, floral tile-like design, tapered w/lip, ftd, 13" **150.00**
Patra, nut dish, #2, 3" **85.00**
Patra, vase, #6, 4½" **135.00**
Patra, vase, 3-ftd, 5" **150.00**
Patricia, bowl, 4 duck heads around rim, 3" **125.00**
Patricia, planter, pelican figure, 5" **110.00**
Pearl, basket, pearl/rose swags, 4-ftd, 6½" **250.00**
Pearl, bud vase, pearl/rose swags, cylindrical, 7"..................**125.00**
Pearl, candlesticks, pearl/rose swags, 8½", pr **250.00**
Pearl, wall pocket, pearl swags over rose band at rim, 7" **225.00**
Perfecto, vase, roses, cylindrical w/lip, sgn MH, 14"..................**1,000.00**
Pumila, candle holder, 3" **85.00**
Pumila, wall pocket, 7"..................**150.00**
Roba, cornucopia, 5½" **50.00**
Roba, vase, #R-20, 13" **225.00**
Roma, bud vase, dbl; floral, 2 sq columns w/connecting circle, 8½" ...**115.00**
Roma, bud vase, grapes/scrolls, 4-sided, 6½" **75.00**
Roma, comport, swag on sq tower w/cut-out design, 9½"..........**150.00**
Roma, pot, floral swags, cut-out design, 4-ftd, 3½" **60.00**
Roma, vase, flared cut-out scalloped rim, 2½" **225.00**
Roma, vase, grape panels, 4-sided, shouldered, 8½" **125.00**
Roma, wall pocket, floral bouquet w/bl bow, flared ruffled rim, 7"..**300.00**
Rosemont, jardiniere, bluebird on floral branch on blk, 7" **350.00**
Rosemont, jardiniere, grape & icon panels on blk, 4½" **150.00**
Rudlor, console bowl, floral branch, 4-bead hdls, 4½x17½" **125.00**
Sabrinian, bowl, 4-ftd, 3½" tall **180.00**
Sabrinian, bud vase, dbl; 2 cone shells w/hdl, 6½" **150.00**
Sabrinian, window box, seashell pattern, 3½x9" **225.00**
Senic, pillow vase, #S-11, 7½"..................**95.00**
Senic, vase, #S-8, 9½"..................**95.00**
Sicardo, base, bulbous w/high upturned hdls, 6" **900.00**
Sicardo, pillow vase, scalloped rim & hdls, 6½x10" **1,250.00**

Sicardo, vase, bulbous w/trumpet neck, hdld, 12½" 2,500.00
Sicardo, vase, leaves/berries, flaring/conical, 9" 865.00
Sicardo, vase, leaves/berries, 4-lobe ovoid w/invt rim, 5¼" 700.00
Sicardo, vase, long trumpet neck w/bulbous base, 15½" 1,750.00
Sicardo, vase, spider mums, diagonal swirl mold, 5" 975.00
Sicardo, vase, 3-sided bottle form w/flared ft, 12½" 2,750.00
Silvertone, basket, grapes, fan shape w/branch hdl, 13" 450.00
Silvertone, bud vase, dbl; cones connected by floral branch, 6" .175.00
Silvertone, vase, floral, bulbous w/long neck & sq hdls, 10" 275.00
Softone, bud vase, dbl; 9" 35.00
Softone, hanging basket, 10" 125.00
Sydonia, console bowl, leaf form on rnd base, 6x17" 125.00
Sydonia, vase, dbl cones, scalloped rims, 7½" 95.00
Tivoli, bowl, flower band on incurvate rim, ftd, 2½" 115.00
Turkis, vase, bowl w/upturned hdls, 5" 85.00
Turkis, vase, jar w/angled bottom, high/low hdls, 7½" 150.00
Tutone, basket, canoe shape, ftd, 7½" 150.00
Tutone, vase, bowl shape, 4-ftd, 4" 85.00
Velva, bowl, flower/leaf panel, tab hdls, 3½x12½" 95.00
Velva, vase, flower/leaf panel, bulbous, plain rim, tab hdls, ftd, 9"...125.00
Voile, fan vase, 8" 150.00
Warwick, basket, branch on wood tone, 7" 185.00
Warwick, circle vase, branch on wood tone, ftd, 7" 150.00
White & Decorated, vase, hexagonal cylinder w/flat bottom, 11" ...250.00
White & Decorated, vase, trumpet form, 10½" 250.00
Wild Rose, basket, ball shape, 5½" 60.00
Wild Rose, vase, cylindrical, dbl-loop hdls, 10½" 75.00
Woodcraft, basket, acorn shape w/branch hdl, 9½" 500.00
Woodcraft, bowl, squirrels in trees, scalloped, 4-ftd, 3½" 175.00
Woodcraft, candlestick, apple tree trunk w/2 branch hdls, 8½" ..150.00
Woodcraft, fan vase, emb apple tree, 8" 125.00
Woodcraft, lamp, divided apple tree w/owl & 2 lights, 13½" 600.00
Woodcraft, tankard, fox family in tree trunk, 12½" 1,250.00
Woodcraft, vase, apple tree trunk w/owl, 16" 1,250.00
Woodrose, jardiniere, roses on wooden bucket, 3½" 85.00
Woodrose, vase, rose on wooden bucket, cylindrical, 7" 85.00
Zona, baby plate, ducks, rolled edge, 7" 135.00
Zona, comport, flowers/leaves on textured bowl, plain ped, 5½"....125.00
Zona, cream pitcher, duck, 3½" 100.00
Zona, pickle dish, plain boat shape w/branch hdl, 11" 95.00
Zona, pitcher, apples on panels w/ribbed bands, 7" 225.00
Zona, tea set (pot, cr/sug), flowers/grapes/bars 250.00

Western Americana

The collecting of Western Americana encompasses a broad spectrum of memorabilia. Examples of various areas within the main stream would include the following fields: weapons, bottles, photographs, mining/railroad artifacts, cowboy paraphernalia, farm and ranch implements, maps, barbed wire, tokens, Indian relics, saloon/gambling items, and branding irons. Some of these areas have their own separate listings in this book. Western Americana is not only a collecting field but is also a collecting era with specific boundries. Depending upon which field the collector decides to specialize in, prices can start at a few dollars and run into the thousands.

Our advisor for this category is Bill Mackin, author of *Cowboy and Gunfighter Collectibles* (order from the author); he is listed in the Directory under Colorado.

Belt, kidney; bronco rider's, tooled leather, North & Judd buckles, EX .250.00
Bit, Buermann, horse-head mounting, bronze...........................275.00
Bit, Crockett #410, NP w/silver conchos (some dents) 375.00
Bit, GS Garcia spade, silver conchos (dented), G- 925.00
Branding iron, hand-wrought iron, short style (carried on saddle), EX ..50.00

Branding iron, initials BK, 1940s, 70x45" 45.00
Bridle, hitched horsehair & braided horsehide w/horsehair reins, 1930s 1,900.00
Bridle, horsehair, prison made, ca 1930, full sz, EX 2,750.00
Bull whip, braided leather w/wooden hdl, ca 1900, 60", EX 70.00
Holster, brn leather w/tooled decor, copper stud closure, unmk, EX.....285.00
Holster, hand-tooled leather, mk Meier & Franks...OR, 1920s, 9x4"...150.00
Jacket, fringed buckskin, 5 stag buttons, 19th C, G....................525.00
Quirt, braided/hitched horsehair, prison made 650.00
Rein spreaders, 14 rings on ea, orig harness snaps, flexible, EX.....65.00
Saddle, hand-tooled leather, padded 15" seat, ca 1950s, child sz.150.00
Saddle, Heiser, tooled leather, 5½" cantle, 15" seat, ca 1918, EX 750.00
Saddle, JC Higgins, Blk Beauty, hand cvd, dbl rigged, w/saddlebags, EX....400.00
Saddle, Mother Hubbard, 1800s, long tapaderos, minor rstr 1,500.00
Saddle, Nolte-Olsen, much silverwork, breast collar/headstall 8,000.00
Saddle, roping; Newton Porter, mahog color, complete, 15", EX 650.00
Saddle, Visalia, DE Walker, rnd skirt, high bk, ca 1890s, EX 875.00
Saddlebags, brn leather w/floral tooling, unmk, EX 200.00
Spurs, Buermann, drop shank, 1-pc w/chains/chap guards/10-point rowels 250.00
Spurs, Buermann, US Cavalry, mk RIA, 1903, bronze, M...........265.00
Spurs, Crockett, Gal Leg, silver, straps, 1960s 225.00
Spurs, Crockett, heart, 9-point rowels, blued, EX......................350.00
Spurs, Crockett, plated & chased, chap gards, 9-point rowels.....175.00
Spurs, Crockett, silver w/heart/spade/dmn/club design, ca 1920, 11" 550.00
Spurs, Kelly Rodeo, hallmk, mtd, eng, 1950s, child sz 75.00
Spurs, McChesney, Gal Leg, silver w/copper mts, 1920s, 9½x3½" ..1,325.00

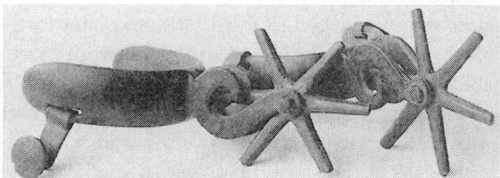

Spurs, Mexican: Iron with large rowels, ca 1900, 7x4", $325.00.

Spurs, Renalde, stainless steel w/silver mts & conchos, 2" rowels..175.00
Spurs, Sonora, silver inlay, 1800s transitional style, 3" rowels.....350.00
Spurs, unmk lady's leg, silver/copper o/l, 1⅜" rowels, pr..............360.00

Western Stoneware Co.

The Western Stoneware Co., Monmouth, Illinois, was formed in 1906 as a merger of seven potteries: Monmouth Pottery Co., Monmouth, IL; Weir Pottery Co., Monmouth, IL; Macomb Pottery Co. and Macomb Stoneware Co., Macomb, IL; D. Culbertson Stoneware Co., Whitehall, IL; Clinton Stoneware Co., Clinton, MO; and Fort Dodge Stoneware Co., Fort Dodge, IA.

Western Stoneware Co. manufactured stoneware, gardenware, flowerpots, artware, and dinnerware. Some early crocks, jugs, and churns are found with a plant number in the Maple Leaf logo. Plants 1 through 7 turn up. In 1926 an artware line was introduced as the Monmouth Pottery Artware. One by one each branch of the operation closed, and today one branch remains. Western Stoneware Co. is still in operation in Monmouth, Illinois, on the site of the Weir Pottery Co. Our advisor for this category is Jim Martin; he is listed in the Directory under Illinois. See also Old Sleepy Eye.

Bowl, bl banded, w/advertising...85.00
Chicken waterer, complete, 1-gal 125.00
Churn, flowers on side, 3-gal 200.00
Churn, Maple Leaf mk, mini 1,000.00
Churn, Maple Leaf mk, oval, 2-gal 175.00
Churn, Maple Leaf mk, 2-gal 200.00
Combinet, w/lid & hdl, mini 350.00
Cooler, #2, dk brn sponging on cream bristol, ca 1920, 9" 385.00

Crock, Maple Leaf mk, 60-gal **1,000.00**
Custard cup, Colonial **250.00**
Hot water bottle, pig, bl tint..**225.00**
Jar, Maple Leaf & oval mk, 2-gal **50.00**
Jardiniere, Egret pattern, brushed gr **75.00**
Jardiniere, Egyptian motif, brn-glazed int, 7".............................**75.00**
Jug, Monmouth advertising, 1-qt **125.00**
Pitcher, Cattail, bl & wht, 1-qt **150.00**
Shakers, 2nd Nat'l Bank, pr **30.00**
Vase, cvd/pnt leaves, bl matt, 16", EX **150.00**
Vase, Etruscan pattern, gr & wht **45.00**
Wall pocket, Egyptian, Burntwood, #312 ....**60.00**
Water cooler, Cupid, wht w/advertising **500.00**
Water cooler, Egyptian motif, 9¼x11", M..................................**450.00**
Water cooler, Maple Leaf mk, no lid or spigot, 2-gal..................**400.00**

Westmoreland

Originally titled the Specialty Glass Company, Westmoreland began operations in East Liverpool, Ohio, producing utility items as well as tableware in milk glass and crystal. When the company moved to Grapeville, Pennsylvania, in 1890, lamps, vases, covered animal dishes, and decorative plates were introduced. Prior to 1920 Westmoreland was a major manufacturer of carnival glass and soon thereafter added a line of lovely reproduction art glass items. High-quality milk glass became their speciality, accounting for about 90% of their production. Black glass was introduced in the 1940s, and later in the decade ruby-stained pieces and items decorated in the Mary Gregory style became fashionable. By the 1960s colored glassware was being produced, examples of which are very popular with collectors today. Early pieces were marked with a paper label; by the 1960s the ware was embossed with a superimposed 'WG.' The last mark was a circle containing 'Westmoreland' around the perimeter and a large 'W' in the center. The company closed in 1985, and on February 28, 1996, the factory burned to the ground.

Note: Though you may find pieces very similar to Westmoreland's, their Della Robbia has no bananas among the fruits relief. In the descriptions that follow, items in this pattern described as 'crystal with trim' refers to those pieces with the colored lustre stains. For more information, we recommend *Westmoreland Glass* by Charles West Wilson (Collector Books). Our advisor for this category is Philip Rosso, Jr., who is listed in the Directory under Pennsylvania. See also Animal Dishes with Covers; Carnival Glass.

Ashtray, English Hobnail, turq or ice bl, 4½" **15.00**
Ashtray, Thousand Eye, crystal, sm turtle **8.00**
Basket, Paneled Grape, wht w/decor, 8" **77.50**
Basket, Wakefield, crystal w/red trim, 6" **65.00**
Bonbon, English Hobnail, pk or gr, hdl, 6½" **25.00**
Bottle, oil or vinegar; Paneled Grape, wht w/decor, w/stopper, 2-oz...**22.00**
Bowl, English Hobnail, pk or gr, flared, 10" **40.00**
Bowl, finger; Della Robbia, crystal w/trim, 5", from $18 to **20.00**
Bowl, finger; English Hobnail, pk or gr, sq ftd, 4½" **15.00**
Bowl, Lotus, amber, crystal or wht, cupped, 9", from $30 to..........**35.00**
Bowl, Lotus, bl, gr or pk, belled, 11", from $38 to........................**40.00**
Bowl, nappy, English Hobnail, pk or gr, rnd, 7" **22.00**
Bowl, nappy, English Hobnail, turq or ice bl, rnd, 4½" **20.00**
Bowl, nappy; Thousand Eye, crystal, 5½" **12.00**
Bowl, Paneled Grape, wht w/decor, crimped, stemmed, 6" **30.00**
Bowl, Paneled Grape, wht w/decor, cupped, 8" **38.00**
Bowl, Paneled Grape, wht w/decor, oval, 10"..............................**40.00**
Bowl, Paneled Grape, wht w/decor, sq, w/lid, 9" **35.00**
Bowl, Thousand Eye, crystal, belled, 11" **35.00**
Bowl, Thousand Eye, crystal, rnd, 11"...**40.00**
Bowl, Wakefield, crystal w/red trim, cupped, 6" **28.00**

Bowl, Wakefield, crystal w/red trim, flat, lipped, 11" **65.00**
Candlestick, Della Robbia, crystal w/trim, 4"...............................**35.00**
Candlestick, English Hobnail, turq or ice bl, rnd base, 3½"..........**35.00**
Candlesticks, Wakefield, crystal w/red trim, 6", pr.......................**75.00**
Candy jar, Paneled Grape, wht w/decor, w/lid, 6½".....................**25.00**
Canister, Paneled Grape, wht w/decor, 11"................................**250.00**
Coaster, Lotus, amber, crystal or wht **12.00**
Compote, fruit; Wakefield, crystal w/red trim, low ft, 12" **55.00**
Compote, Lotus, bl, gr or pk, high, 5" **40.00**
Compote, Paneled Grape, wht w/decor, ftd, w/lid, 7" **47.50**
Compote, sweetmeat; English Hobnail, pk or gr, ball stem, 8" **45.00**
Creamer, Beaded Edge, milk glass, plain, ftd **11.00**
Creamer, Paneled Grape, wht w/decor, ind **11.00**
Cup, Beaded Edge, milk glass w/red edge....................................**7.00**
Cup, coffee; Della Robbia, crystal w/trim **20.00**
Egg plate, Paneled Grape, wht w/HP Roses & Bows, 12" **85.00**
Ice tub, English Hobnail, pk or gr, 5½" **65.00**
Jug, Thousand Eye, crystal, ½ gal **95.00**
Nappy, Paneled Grape, wht w/decor, rnd, 7" **30.00**
Parfait, Paneled Grape, wht w/HP Roses & Bows, 6" **25.00**
Planter, Paneled Grape, wht w/HP Roses & Bows, 5x9"...............**45.00**
Plate, bread & butter; Beaded Edge, milk glass w/decor, 6" **10.00**
Plate, Della Robbia, crystal w/trim, 18", from $150 to................**200.00**
Plate, dinner; Paneled Grape, wht, 10½", from $40 to.................**45.00**
Plate, English Hobnail, pk or gr, rnd, 6½"...................................**10.00**
Plate, Lotus, amber, crystal or wht, flared, 13" **25.00**
Plate, luncheon; Della Robbia, crystal w/trim, 9".........................**40.00**
Plate, mayonnaise; Lotus, amber, crystal or wht, 6".......................**8.00**
Plate, Paneled Grape, wht w/Bicentennial decor, 18"..................**185.00**
Plate, salad; Lotus, bl, gr or pk, 8½" **35.00**
Plate, Thousand Eye, crystal, 16", from $50 to.............................**65.00**
Plate, torte; Beaded Edge, milk glass, plain, 15" **45.00**
Plate, Wakefield, crystal w/red trim, 6".......................................**12.50**
Relish, Beaded Edge, milk glass w/red edge, 3-part **35.00**
Saucer, Paneled Grape, wht...**8.50**
Shakers, Beaded Edge, milk glass w/decor, pr **40.00**
Shakers, Lotus, bl, gr or pk, ea **40.00**
Shakers, Paneled Grape, wht w/decor, sm, ftd, 4¼", pr **22.50**
Sherbet, Beaded Edge, milk glass, plain, ftd..................................**9.00**
Soap dish, Paneled Grape, wht w/decor **110.00**
Stem, cocktail; English Hobnail, turq or ice bl, rnd ftd, 3-oz **22.00**
Stem, Thousand Eye, crystal, 8-oz..**10.00**
Stem, wine; Della Robbia, crystal w/trim, 3-oz............................**30.00**
Stem, wine; Thousand Eye, crystal, 2-oz.....................................**12.00**
Stem, wine; Wakefield, crystal w/red trim, 2-oz...........................**30.00**
Sugar bowl, Beaded Edge, milk glass w/red edge, ftd **15.00**
Sugar bowl, Della Robbia, crystal w/trim, ftd **12.00**
Sugar bowl, Lotus, amber, crystal or wht **12.00**
Tidbit, English Hobnail, pk or gr, 2-tier.......................................**45.00**
Tidbit, Wakefield, crystal w/red, ruffled, metal hdl **35.00**
Tray, Paneled Grape, wht w/decor, oval, 9".................................**100.00**
Tumbler, iced tea; English Hobnail, pk or gr, 12-oz.......................**22.00**
Tumbler, iced tea; Paneled Grape, wht w/decor, 12-oz..................**25.00**
Tumbler, Lotus, bl, gr or pk, 10-oz..**45.00**
Tumbler, Thousand Eye, crystal, ftd, 5-oz.....................................**8.00**
Tumbler, water; Della Robbia, crystal w/trim, 8-oz.......................**25.00**
Vase, Paneled Grape, wht w/decor, 15" **30.00**
Vase, Thousand Eye, crystal, crimped bowl **25.00**

Wheatley, T. J.

In 1880 after a brief association with the Coultry Works, Thomas J. Wheatley opened his own studio in Cincinnati, Ohio, claiming to have been the first to discover the secret of under-glaze slip decoration on an unbaked clay vessel. He applied for and was granted a patent for his process. Demand for his ware increased to the point that several artists were hired to decorate the ware. The company incorporated in 1880 as the Cincinnati Art Pottery, but until 1882 it continued to operate under Wheatley's name. Ware from this period is marked 'T.J. Wheatley' or 'T.J.W. and Co.,' and it may be dated.

Matt green pieces dominate today's marketplace and will bring much more than the decorated pieces. The matt green pieces are seldom, if ever, marked or dated.

Pitcher, duck form, gr matt, 11¼" 550.00
Urn, garden; blk runs over gray, #510, 29¾", EX, pr 1,400.00
Urn, garden; bright yel matt, #661, 18½" 700.00
Vase, curdled gr matt, cuspidor form, 8" 700.00
Vase, curling designs at shoulder, gr matt, 8⅜" 2,000.00
Vase, dk gr matt, 3 buttress ft & 3 sm loop hdls, label, 10⅞" ..2,100.00
Vase, fern-like forms & lg leaves, gr matt, 12½" 3,100.00
Vase, flower emb ea corner of 6 sides, bl matt w/feathering, 12", NM...1,800.00
Vase, flowers & buds, gr curdled matt, hdls, prof rpr, 20" 3,400.00
Vase, frog & cattails, Limoges style, ca 1881, 8½" 1,500.00
Vase, gr curdled matt, 3 loop hdl appl at 45 degree angles, 4⅛" .400.00
Vase, gr matt, 3 buttressed hdls, 9½" 2,500.00
Vase, gr matt, 4 elongated hdls, 17⅜" 5,000.00
Vase, leaves, dk gr matt, 4⅛" 350.00
Vase, leaves, gr matt, 4 buttressed ft, 6½", EX 1,200.00
Vase, leaves w/slight curl, dk gr gloopy matt, #664, 5⅜" 550.00
Vase, scarabs (3) & repeating floral, dk gr matt, #671, 7⅝" 1,200.00
Vase, scarabs emb above vertical leaves at bottom, brn matt, 8", EX ...400.00
Wall pocket, floral, gr curdled matt, 8⅛" 1,300.00

Whieldon

Thomas Whieldon was regarded as the finest of the Staffordshire potters of the mid-1700s. He produced marbled and black Egyptian wares as well as tortoise shell, a mottled brown-glazed earthenware accented with touches of blue and yellow. In 1754 he became a partner of Josiah Wedgwood. Other potters produced similar wares, and today the term Whieldon is used generically.

Cup & saucer, brn sponging w/gr splotches on creamware, 2", 2¾" 350.00
Plate, brn sponging w/gr/ochre spokes, 1770-80, 9½", EX 185.00
Plate, lead glaze, wavy border, beaded rim, 1755-65, 9¼", EX 185.00
Platter, brn tortoise shell, 8-sided w/oval well, rstr, 12x16⅜" 600.00
Teapot, brn sponging w/burnt umber & gr, 1755-65, mini, 1-cup ..400.00
Teapot, tortoise shell, 18th C, 4¾", EX 365.00
Vase, appl vines/leaves/flowers, mc pastels, w/lid, 1760s, rstr, 12" 1,400.00

Wicker

Wicker is the basket-like material used in many types of furniture and accessories. It may be made from bamboo cane, rattan, reed, or artificial fibers. It is airy, lightweight, and very popular in hot regions. Imported from the Orient in the eighteenth century, it was first manufactured in the United States in about 1850. The elaborate, closely woven Victorian designs belong to the mid- to late 1800s, and the simple styles with coarse reedings usually indicate a post-1900 production. Art Deco styles followed in the '20s and '30s. The most important consideration in buying wicker is condition — it can be restored, but only by a professional. Age is an important factor, but be aware that 'Victorian-style' furniture is being manufactured today.

Key:
HB — Heywood Bros. H/W — Heywood Wakefield

Armchair, curlicues/loops, cane seat, skirt, 1890s, 40x25" 1,250.00
Armchair, posing; ornate bk, Aladdin ft, HB, 1890s, 35x20" ...1,650.00
Armchair, spiral twists, curlicues/beadwork, cane seat, 1890s, 30", pr....1,450.00
Armchair rocker, latticework, skirted, springs in cushion, 1920s ...625.00
Armchair rocker, ornate bk, continuous arm, H/W, 1900, 42" 475.00
Armchair rocker, plantation style, solid oak fr, wht pnt, 46x35" .450.00
Armchair rocker, platform; ornate bk, serpentine roll, 1890s, 45" 1,650.00
Armchair rocker, platform; serpentine rolled crest, skirt, 1890s, 43" 1,250.00
Armchair rocker, rolled crest, stick/ballwork under arms, Wakefield........975.00
Armchair rocker, serpentine rolled bk/arms, ribbon/loop pattern, 1890s ...1,000.00
Armchair rocker, serpentine rolled bk/arms w/heart design bk, 1890s......975.00
Buggy, rolled bk crest, gallery sides w/wicker between spindles, H/W.......700.00
Chair, corner; dmn shapes, spindles, curved front leg, H/W, 34" ...385.00
Chair, corner; rolled bk crest, rpl seat, natural finish, 39" 350.00
Chair, Morris; curlicues/beadwork, 1890s, 41" 1,450.00
Chair, reception; curlicues, crescent-shaped bk fr, 1890s, 39" 675.00
Day bed/porch glider, Loyd Loom, 1920s-30s, 36x82" 1,750.00
Desk, slant front, latticed gallery/panels, 1910s, +matching chair....1,750.00
Parlor set, Deco dmn design, tight weave, couch+table+rocker+chair..4,850.00
Picnic case, J Wanamaker, NP hdls, 1900s, 32", +all accessories 2,500.00
Rocker, Arts & Crafts, rolled continuous arms, loose weave, 33x32", VG..650.00
Rocker, star-pattern bk, birdcage style arms/legs, later cushion, 46" ..500.00
Settee, basketweave, serpentine bk/arms, H/W, 1890s, 31x38" ...1,450.00
Settee, brn pnt, attached magazine rack, child sz, 27x26x17", EX ..350.00
Settee, curlicue crest/sunburst medallion, 1890s, 40x44" 2,650.00
Settee, Deco dmn weave, flared arms, springs in fr, 1920s, 37x55" ..1,250.00
Settee, lattice/curlicue crest, caned bk/seat, 1880s, 40x42" 2,450.00
Settee, latticework/braiding, Bar Harbor, ca 1915, 37x49" 1,000.00
Settee, photographer's; serpentine bk, varnished rattan, H/W, 41" ...4,025.00
Settee, serpentine bk/arms, beadwork/curlicues, H/W, 35x42" ...2,250.00
Settee, serpentine bk/arms, cameo weave, curlicues, HB, 36x42" 2,450.00
Settee, serpentine bk/arms, cane seat, 1890s, 39x51x25" 3,250.00
Sofa, tight weave w/dmns, skirt, fancy ft, 1920s, 71x26" 1,450.00
Stand, fern; flared top w/braiding/lattice panels, 1900s, 45x16" ..495.00
Stand, sewing; open top, rolled edge, fancy weave, 30x22x16" ...750.00
Stand, sewing; woven top w/loops, birdcage, HB, 28x18x18" 975.00
Tea cart, glass top, 2 storage baskets, cane-wrapped hdl, 1900s, 40" L...1,250.00

Wiener Werkstatte

The Weiner Werkstatte was established in Austria in 1903. It was one of many workshops worldwide that ascribed to the new wave of design and style that was sweeping not only Austria but England and other European countries as well.

Its founders were Josef Hoffmann, Kolo Moser, and Fritz Warndorfer. Hoffmann had for some time been involved in a movement bent toward refining prevailing Art Nouveau trends. He was a primary initiator of the Viennese Secession, and in 1899 he worked as a professor at the Viennese School of Applied Arts. Through his work as an architect, he began to develop his own independent style, preferring and promoting clean rectangular geometric shapes over the more accepted building concepts of the day. His progressive ideas resulted in contemporary designs, completely breaking away from past principles in all medias of art as well as architecture, completely redefining Arts and Crafts. At the Weiner Werkstatte, every object was crafted with exquisite attention to design, workmanship, and materials.

Spoon, hammered silver w/tiger eye cab, #925, 13", MIB 1,700.00
Vase, 3 cylinders of varied heights joined w/leafy twigs, Baudisch, 9" ..2,200.00
Vase, 3-D animals on shoulders, appl/pnt geometrics, Kitty Rix, 10" ...2,100.00

Will-George

In 1934 after years of working in the family garage, the Will-George

Company was founded by William and George Climes in Los Angeles, California. They manufactured high-quality artware of porcelain and earthenware. Both brothers, motivated by their love of art pottery, had extensive education and training in manufacturing processes as well as decoration. In 1940 actor Edgar Bergen, a collector of pottery, developed a relationship with the brothers and invested in their business. With this new influx of funds, the company relocated to Pasadena. There they produced an extensive line of art pottery, but they excelled in their creation of bird and animal figurines. In addition, they molded a large line of human figurines similar to Royal Doulton. The brothers, now employing a staff of decorators, precisely molded their pieces with great care and strong emphasis on originality and detail, creating high quality works of art that were only carried by exclusive gift stores.

In the late 1940s after a split with Bergen, the company moved to San Gabriel to a larger, more modern location and renamed themselves The Claysmiths. Their business flourished and they were able to successfully mass produce many items; but due to the abundance of cheap, postwar imports from Italy and Japan that were then flooding the market, they liquidated the business in 1956. Our advisor for this category is Marty Webster. He is listed in the Directory under Michigan.

Ashtray, 4" chicken in middle, 8" sq..65.00
Bowl, flamingo pond, 9x14"..65.00
Bowl, serving; red onion form, 2x13x10"...................................65.00
Box, Oriental figure kneeling on lid, 1x4x4"..............................50.00
Candle holders, lily design, pr..120.00
Figurine, artist holding palette, mc, 8".......................................95.00
Figurine, Baltimore Oriole..155.00
Figurine, bluebird, 3¼"...45.00
Figurine, boy holding frog on base, mc, 9".................................95.00
Figurine, cardinal on branch, 10"...75.00
Figurine, cardinal on branch, 12½"...150.00
Figurine, dachshund, 6½x9"...200.00
Figurine, eagle on rock, wht/brn, 10"..150.00
Figurine, flamingo, head trn, 10"..200.00
Figurine, flamingo, head up/facing bk, 7½"...............................150.00
Figurine, flamingo, preening, 10"...200.00
Figurine, flamingo, wings spread, 15½".....................................275.00
Figurine, flamingo beside stump, 7¼"..180.00
Figurine, giraffe, 14½"...150.00
Figurine, girl holding doll on base, mc, 9".................................125.00
Figurine, hula dancer, wht skirt, 12"..155.00
Figurine, mallard duck w/spread wings, 7x11"..........................195.00
Figurine, monk, brn, bsk, 5½"...75.00
Figurine, monk, brn bsk, 4½"...50.00
Figurine, parrot on branch, mc, 15"...200.00
Figurine, pheasant, red breast, 6x14"...255.00
Figurine, pheasant hen...110.00
Figurine, Polynesian seated female, 5½".....................................80.00
Figurine, robin, seated, 3"..45.00
Pitcher, chicken figural, mc, 7"...125.00
Tumbler, chicken figural, mc, 4½"...50.00
Vase, Chinese girl seated in front of pillow form, 5"................85.00
Wine glass, chicken figural, mc, 5"..55.00

Willets

The Willets Manufacturing Company of Trenton, New Jersey, produced a type of belleek porcelain during the late 1880s and 1890s. Examples were often marked with a coiled snake that formed a 'W' with 'Willets' below and 'Belleek' above. Not all Willets is factory decorated. Items painted by amateurs outside the factory are worth considerably less. High prices usually equate with fine artwork. In the listings below,

all items are belleek unless noted otherwise. Our advisor for this category is Mary Frank Gaston; she is listed in the Directory under Texas.

Chalice, allover gold w/bl & turq panels/scrollwork, sgn Hessler, 11"...300.00
Chalice, pine cones (china-pnt style), gilt rim/int, 11½"............260.00
Chalice, raspberries (china-pnt style), red cabochons, Hyde, 11x5"...310.00
Chalice, roses, pk/red on bl/pk, 3 gold hdls, RS, 1899, 7x7".......370.00
Pitcher, grapes all around, sgn EN Baker, dragon hdl, 11¼"........575.00
Ramekin, roses on pastels w/gilt, sgn MGB, ftd, 3¾", set of 4.....110.00
Tankard, hops (china-pnt style), gr/gold on wht w/gilt, 14x8" 270.00
Teapot, mountain lake (china-pnt style), 5½x9" 250.00
Vase, chrysanthemums, sgn, slim trumpet neck, 15½" 800.00
Vase, daffodils, yel w/gr leaves on wht to dk ground, Buchanan, 8½" ..240.00
Vase, roses, cylindrical, 16" 995.00
Vase, roses, globular, bottle neck, sm ruffled rim, 6¼" 375.00
Vase, roses, pk & wht on shaded gr, slim ovoid, 15¼" 1,000.00
Vase, roses, red on bl/gr mottle, incurvate cylinder, 15x5" 700.00
Vase, roses, sgn M Malyom, bottle neck, flat rim, 12" 1,200.00
Vase, roses (china-pnt style), minor wear, 13x8½" 350.00
Vase, roses on lt gr, slim slightly waisted cylinder, 15¾" 800.00
Vase, roses on shaded gr (china-pnt style), shouldered, 14x8" 575.00
Vase, trumpet flowers on bittersweet color, bottle neck, 11½"....595.00

Winchester

The Winchester Repeating Arms Company lost their important government contract after WWI and of necessity turned to the manufacture of sporting goods, hardware items, tools, etc., to augment their gun production. Between 1920 and 1931, over 7,500 different items, each marked 'Winchester Trademark U.S.A.,' were offered for sale by thousands of Winchester Hardware stores throughout the country. After 1931 the firm became Winchester-Western. Collectors prefer the prewar items, and the majority of our listings are from this era.

Concerning current collecting trends: Oil cans that a short time ago could be purchased for $2.00 to $5.00 now often sell for $25.00, some over $50.00, and demand is high. Good examples of advertising posters and calendars seem to have no upper limits and are difficult to find. Winchester fishing lures are strong, and the presence of original boxes increases values by 25% to 40%. Another current trend concerns the price of 'diecuts' (cardboard stand-ups, signs, or hanging signs). These are out pricing many other items. A short time ago the average value of a 'diecut' ranged from $25.00 to $45.00. Current values for most are in the $200.00 to $500.00 range, with some approaching $1,000.00.

Our advisor for this category is James Anderson; he is listed in the Directory under Minnesota. Unless noted otherwise, values are for examples in excellent condition. See also Knives.

Calender, 1897, with all the original pages, $6,500.00.
(Photo courtesy James Anderson)

Axe, dbl-bit, 9x4½" head on 35" wooden hdl................................95.00

Baseball glove, #2151, Winchester Diamond in palm, VG **650.00**
Baseball glove, #428 ....**600.00**
Bayonet, M-1917, mk w/W only, rare, EX+ **155.00**
Box, ammo; Model 1873, shows rifle on side panel, full, EX+ **150.00**
Catalog, ammo, guns, cannon, primers, tools, 1907, VG+ **135.00**
Catalog, 1929, w/price guide, 232 pgs..**105.00**
Crystal cleaner, NMIB...**155.00**
Fishing reel, #1136, EX **200.00**
Fishing reel, #1236, nickel finish **150.00**
Fishing reel, #2142, sz 40 ....**150.00**
Fishing reel, #2336, 60-yd model **150.00**
Fishing reel, #2844, VG+ **110.00**
Fishing reel, #4256, G **90.00**
Fishing rod, #5100, steel, w/orig case.......................................**110.00**
Fishing rod & reel, #5570 & #2342 ....**225.00**
Flashlight, #7031, orig bulb, 1 cell, vest pocket, 1920s, NM.......**145.00**
Flashlight, miner's light, US Forester Service **110.00**
Food grinder, #31, complete w/all blades **75.00**
Golf club, driver; Ranger, #6388, wood shaft, VG+........................**165.00**
Hatchet, claw; #5330, 3½" blade on 13" hdl **200.00**
Level, #9866, 3 vials, 24", EX **185.00**
Matchbooks, Western Super-X, Arms-Ammunition, target inside, box of 50...**175.00**
Pin-bk button, ...the Repeater That Outshot Them All, 1896, oval, NM+ **190.00**
Pipe wrench, #1023, Pat 1922, wood hdl, 14" **90.00**
Pipe wrench, #1031-M, dtd 1922, 8" **85.00**
Plane, block; #3094, dbl-ended, 2x7¾" **85.00**
Plane, cabinet scraper; #3075...**110.00**
Plane, cabinet scraper; #3080...**110.00**
Plumb bob, 8-oz, 4¾" **125.00**
Poster, skunk startles 2 Black hunters & dog, 1908, 24x32" **4,000.00**
Poster, Western-Winchester, squirrel in oak tree, 1955, 42x28"..**115.00**
Razor, #W11, gr hdl, mk **185.00**
Roller skates, #3832, girder type, girl's, EXIB............................**185.00**
Rule, #9568, wood w/brass ends & hinges, 24" **140.00**
Rule, folding; #9584, boxwood & brass, 24", G **100.00**
Scale, Family Scale, 24-lb, VG **145.00**
Scope, #A5, WWI, mk 1909, ¾" tube **150.00**
Shell box, New R, #236, 2-pc **135.00**
Sign, Authorized Dealer.../1936/Cutlery & Firearms, rvpt, 12x20" ..**215.00**
Sign, die-cut cb standup, 2 hunters/dogs/log, 4-pc, VG+.............**720.00**
Sign, Winchester 20 Gauge Shotguns-Hammerless, features 2 dogs, 23x38" ...**750.00**
Tin, After Shave Talc, hunter w/dog, 3x4¾" **75.00**
Trap thrower, hand-held, PAT 6-10-1919, VG+ **110.00**
Utensils, knife & fork, stag hdls, mk Winchester, w/felt pouch ..**295.00**
Waffle maker, #W36...**295.00**

Windmill Weights

Windmill weights made of cast iron were used to protect the windmill's plunger rod from damage during high winds by adding weight that slowed down the speed of the blades.

Bull, Fairbury, emb letters, red pnt, 18½x24½" +base..............**1,150.00**
Bull, Fairbury (att), pnt traces, 18½x24½" +base........................**800.00**
Bull, Fairbury (att), red w/wht pnt, flat, 18¼x24½" **865.00**
Bull, Simpson, full body, pnt traces, 13x13½x10½"................**1,035.00**
Bull (Boss), Dempster, full body, blk pnt w/tan, 13x13¾x4" ...**1,495.00**
Half moon, CI, pitting, 10¼"...**110.00**
Horse, Crescent-tail; Dempster, no pnt, 15x16"..........................**800.00**
Horse, Long-tail; Dempster, flat, pnt traces, on orig mt, 19x17" ...**1,380.00**
Horse, Long-tail; Dempster, flat, silver pnt, 18½x17½" **920.00**
Horseshoe, unmk, no pnt, ca 1900, 10¼x8¾x2½" **920.00**
Monitor Warship, pnt CI & concrete, 7½x28½x12" **1,950.00**

Rooster, Barnacle-eye; Elgin, old mc pnt, 18½x17¾" **1,500.00**
Rooster, Elgin, crackled (o/w EX) wht pnt w/red details, 18x20½" ..**5,175.00**
Rooster, Elgin, wht w/red details, 16x16½"+base **1,150.00**
Rooster, Elgin, 10ft No 2 on tail, pnt traces, 15½x16½"+base..**1,500.00**
Rooster, Elgin (att), wht/red/yel pnt, C-shaped base, 19½x18" ..**1,500.00**
Rooster, Hummer; Elgin, emb letters, pnt traces, 17½x16"+base..**1,150.00**
Rooster, Hummer; Elgin, long stem, pnt traces, 13¼x10" **865.00**
Rooster, Rainbow-tail; Elgin, pnt traces, on base, 19¼x18½" **5,750.00**
Rooster, Rainbow-tail; Elgin (att), EX mc pnt, blk base, 17½x18" ..**2,000.00**
Squirrel, Elgin, old mc pnt, 19½x13½"x3" on base..................**3,750.00**
Star, Flint & Walling, emb 5-point on ea end of cylinder, 7½" dia...**920.00**
Star, US Wind Engine & Pump Co, old pnt, 15x15", pr..........**2,500.00**
W, Althouse-Wheeler, early 20th C, 9x16½x11" on stand **975.00**

Wire Ware

Very primitive wire was first made by cutting sheet metal into strips which were shaped with mallet and file. By the late thirteenth century, craftsmen in Europe had developed a method of pulling these strips through progressively smaller holes until the desired gauge was obtained. During the Industrial Revolution of the late 1800s, machinery was developed that could produce wire cheaply and easily; and it became a popular commercial commodity. It was used to produce large items such as garden benches and fencing as well as innumerable small pieces for use in the kitchen or on the farm. Beware of reproductions. Our advisor for this category is Rosella Tinsley; she is listed in the Directory under Kansas.

Basket, flower; heavy twisted wire, old gr pnt, wood hdl, 6x19x11"..**75.00**
Basket, laundry; folding, ftd, on casters, 36x24" dia, EX...............**80.00**
Basket, majolica insert, hdld, ftd, 2¾x10¼x8" **285.00**
Basket, vegetable harvest: heavy woven wire, wood hdls, 12x19".**45.00**
Basket, 3-tier, heavy gauge, scallops, Fr, 21x16" at bottom..........**135.00**
Bench, dmn-shape spaces w/Ohio in bk, camel bk/arms, Bromwell, 53" L..**1,000.00**
Carpet beater, twisted wire forms loop, wood hdl, from $45 to **50.00**
Dish rack/drainer, 1890-1920, 5x16" dia, EX...............................**90.00**
Etegere, 2-tier, Vict, 17½x7x6", EX..**105.00**
Lettuce washer, hinged lid, 6½x12x7½"......................................**35.00**
Pillow fluffer, twisted heart shape w/wood handgrips (+) **45.00**
Plant stand, 3-tier w/pointed arch top, old gr pnt, 70x36" **500.00**
Planter, basket w/scrolled ft & spiral supports, old pnt, 18x31" ..**150.00**
Planter, 3 rnd tiers w/baskets in sq base w/scroll ft, 47x26" **375.00**
Plate rack, 4-tier, EX patina, 10½x7¾" **85.00**
Shelf, hanging, 1-tier, gr pnt traces, 1890s, 36x5x3½" **255.00**
Soap caddy, twisted wire, 2 compartments, 8½x8¾x5" **75.00**

Witch Balls

Witch balls were a Victorian fad touted to be meritorious toward ridding the house of evil spirits, thus warding off sickness and bad luck. Folklore would have it that by wiping the dust and soot from the ball, the spirits were exorcised. It is much more probable, however, considering the fact that such beautiful art glass was used in their making, that the ostensive Victorians perpetrated the myth rather tongue-in-cheek while enjoying them as lovely decorations for their homes.

Blk amethyst, sm sheared opening on 1 end, 1870-90, 4¼" **100.00**
Cobalt, open pontil 1 end, many bubbles, 1860-90, 8"................**165.00**
Cobalt w/red & wht overall splotches, sheared end, 4¾"............**425.00**
Red/wht/bl, 5 loops in marbrie design, mid-1800s, 6" dia **1,850.00**
Ruby flashed in striated ruby-flashed bowl, clear ft, 4" dia **875.00**

Wood, Beatrice

A multitalented artist, Beatrice Wood is especially well known for her ceramics which are displayed in the Smithsonian and the Metropolitan Museum of Art as well as several other museums around the world. She was also famous for her work in other mediums, especially painting and photography. She studied drama in Europe at the age of 18, returning to America where she became involved in the revolutionary Dada art movement in New York. She moved to California in the late 1920s and in 1937 opened her own studio. Nicknamed Bea or Beato, she developed wonderful lustre glazes for which she is highly acclaimed. Her style is modernistic, and her work ranges from sedate teapots and vases to whimsical sculptures. She died in 1998 at the age of 105. Her fascinating experiences led her to write her autobiography which so captured the attention of Titanic director James Cameron that he fashioned the role of Rose around her.

Sculpture, 2 females/1 male cavort on rugged rock base, 10x10x7" **4,750.00**
Vase, cratered volcanic orange w/gr, elongated/tapered, Beato, 16"....**4,500.00**
Vase, thick wht/gray over brn clay, ftd wide cylinder, Beato, 4½" **800.00**
Vase, 2 appl figures on flattened bottle form w/mc irid, Beato, 6½" ...**3,500.00**

Wood Carvings

Wood sculptures represent an important section of American folk art. Wood carvings were made not only by skilled woodworkers such as cabinetmakers, carpenters, etc., but by amateur 'whittlers' as well. They take the form of circus-wagon figures, carousel animals, decoys, busts, figurines, and cigar store Indians. Oriental artists show themselves to have been as proficient with the medium of wood as they were with ivory or hardstone. See also Carousel Animals; Decoys; Tobacciana.

Big Horn Sheep, male, cvd from 1 pc, pnt details, J Suhar, 11" ..**220.00**
Boxer, seated, pert ears/EX realism, red pnt w/sm wht dots, 12"..**580.00**
Boy carrying girl on bk, oak, old rpr, early 20th C, 19x7½x6" **460.00**
Eagle, full body, wings out, gilt, Am, 19th C, 16½x22½" **700.00**
Eagle, half-figure w/glass eye, wings out, late 1800s, 9½x19" **485.00**
Eagle, wings side, 1-pc cvg, blk pnt, Henry Winter NY, 10½" **880.00**
Eagle, wings up & bk, on orb, mtd on marble base, 11x14x8" **750.00**
Eagle, wings wide, blk/gilt details, ornate cvg, 19th C, 12x21"...**1,840.00**
Eagle, wings wide, claws hold animal, H Smith, 1950s, 30x37"..**500.00**
Eagle, wings wide, glass eyes, dk red w/gold details, 19th C, 34x47"...**3,100.00**
Eagle, wings wide, old gilt, on base, Am, 19th C, 23x41x27"..**2,650.00**
Eagle, wings wide, talons on globe, red/brn pnt, 1850s, 34x62"........**7,635.00**
Eagle, wings wide, 3 arrows in talons, relief-cvd, wht pnt, 14x44"...**2,415.00**
Eagle on shield, flattened relief cvg, old mc pnt, 19th C, 36"..**2,300.00**
Eagle on shield, Live & Let Live, mc pnt, 19th C, 17x45" **1,500.00**
Eagle w/banner, pnt pine, att JH Bellamy, later varnish, 25½x9".....**2,500.00**
Heron, wht body, gr/red/blk wings & tail, line-cvd eyes/beak, 24"..**2,400.00**
Horse-drawn sleigh, couple on board, EX patina, 19th C, 11x22x6"...**4,000.00**
Indian maiden in fringed dress, mc pnt, wear/rprs, Am, 14¾".**2,185.00**
Owl, detailed figure mtd on wood base w/dowel rod, 1900, 26" **1,295.00**
Pheasant, naturalistic pnt, on oak base, 20th C, 7¾x13½".........**230.00**
Rooster, dk gr w/red & yel accents, glass eyes, Gus Knapp, 24x21", EX...**360.00**
Rooster, wire legs, trn wooden base, pnt details, 19th C, 5½".**1,035.00**
Sleepy Joe Estes, bust of Black man, mc pnt, foam hair, R Barnes, 12"...**385.00**
Stag, very stylized, brn/blk pnt, 24x18" **850.00**
Statue, End of Trail, Indian on horse, separate spear, WWR 79, 12½"...**165.00**

Woodenware

Woodenware (or treenware, as it is sometimes called) generally refers to those wooden items such as spoons, bowls, food molds, etc., that were used in the preparation of food. Common during the eighteenth and nineteenth centuries, these wares were designed from a strictly functional viewpoint and were used on a day-to-day basis. With the advent of the Industrial Revolution which brought with it new materials and products, much of the old woodenware was simply discarded. Today original handcrafted American woodenwares are extremely difficult to find. See also Primitives.

Bowl, ash burl, deep/thin sides, shallow ft, raised rim ring, 3x6½" **700.00**
Bowl, ash burl w/cvg, tapered, 19th C, crack, 6x17½" **1,725.00**
Bowl, ash burl w/EX figure, nut brn rfn, trn ft, putty rprs, 5x18".......**1,430.00**
Bowl, ash burl w/EX figure, trn ft w/raised ring, scrubbed/splits, 13".....**990.00**
Bowl, ash burl w/G color, loose figure, rim notch/putty rpr, 4x12" **440.00**
Bowl, ash burl w/G figure, oval, beveled hdls, split/defects, 5x20x19"..**700.00**
Bowl, ash burl w/VG figure, deep/thinly trn, ft base, ext rings, 3x8" **550.00**
Bowl, bird's-eye maple, trn, appl hdls, Am, 19th C, 5x22"..........**400.00**
Bowl, bird's-eye maple, trn w/sm lip, varnish, drilled to hang, 4x15"...**220.00**
Bowl, burl, cvd oval, 2 pierced hdls, Am, 19th C, 4¾x18½" ..**3,750.00**
Bowl, burl, trn, Am, 19th C, 4x12" **750.00**
Bowl, burl w/G figure, thin, ft w/raised ring, sm splits, 4x13½" ...**1,200.00**
Bowl, burl w/G figure, thin, trn ft, cvd rings, 4¾x19", VG......**1,650.00**
Bowl, chopping, hand-cvd cherry, Am, early 1800s, 4¼x23x13½"..**575.00**
Bowl, chopping; red-pnt maple, New England, early 1800s, 5½x32x14"...**645.00**
Bowl, fruitwood w/EX graining, filled-in crack, 4x11" **250.00**
Bowl, lathe trn, chop mks inside, ca 1900, 4x15x14" **75.00**
Bowl, trn, bl pnt over gr, wear, 13" **195.00**
Bowl, trn, rpt ext w/raised rings, glued rpr/hairlines, 19".............**220.00**
Bowl, trn, shallow, old bl pnt, later cvd pouring indent, 5x18"...**635.00**
Bowl, trn w/scribed concentric circles, shallow, 19th C, 24½"....**350.00**
Butter paddle, curly maple, lt figure, str hdl w/glued-on rest, 9½"....**60.00**
Butter paddle, hardwood, hand-cvd, 8¼x3½" **25.00**
Cake brd, flower basket/eagle medallion, att Conger, NYC, 1830, 11x11"..**2,350.00**
Charger, scribed decor, ca 1800, 21¾" **1,035.00**
Charger, thick/rnd brd w/concave top, bl-pnt ext, 2 wood braces, 16"..**550.00**
Cheese drainer, wooden staves w/2 iron bands, 1830s, 3¼x8⅝".**125.00**
Cookie brd, cvgs ea side, lady & chicken/man in long coat, 15x8"...**165.00**
Cookie brd, 5 cvd figures, ie: woman at well, man w/potted plant, 28"..**250.00**
Cookie roller, bird's-eye maple, hand cut, 1-pc, New England **45.00**
Jar, Pease, high ft w/trn rings, elongated finial, wire bail, 4" **385.00**
Jar, Pease, raised rings, ball finial/trn ft, hairlines, 5½"..............**195.00**
Jar, Pease, trn body, flattened finial, orig hdl, 9x10½" **1,650.00**
Jar, poplar, high ft & rim w/raised rings, dome lid w/trn finial, 8x6"..**165.00**
Jar, poplar w/old rfn, ftd ovoid, slightly domed lid w/trn hdl, 6½".......**165.00**
Jar, trn ft/rim, dome lid, varnished w/pnt traces, 5x6", EX **135.00**
Rolling pin, hand cut, maple, heavy, 1-pc, 20" **125.00**
Springerle brd, EX cvgs ea side: animals/soldiers/etc, 9¼x6½" **220.00**
Sugar bowl, trn maple, acorn finial on domed lid, old rfn, 7½x8"....**700.00**
Tray, eating; pine, shallow, made for slave use, early 1800s, lg **250.00**
Tray, knife; cvd mahog, dvtl divisions, pierced hdl, 19th C, 7x11x16"..**1,495.00**

Woodworking Machinery

Vintage cast-iron woodworking machines are monuments to the highly skilled engineers, foundrymen, and machinists who devised them, thus making possible the mass production of items ranging from clothespins, boxes, and barrels to decorative moldings and furniture. Though attractive from a nostalgic viewpoint, many of these machines are bought by the hobbyist and professional alike, to be put into actual use — at far less cost than new equipment. Many worth-assessing factors must be considered; but as a general rule, a machine in good condition is worth about 65¢ a pound (excluding motors). A machine needing a lot of restoration is not worth more than 35¢ a pound, while one professionally rebuilt and with a warranty can be calculated at $1.10 a pound. Modern, new machinery averages over $3.00 a pound. Two of the best sources of information on purchasing or selling such machines are *Vintage Machines — Searching for the Cast Iron Classics* by Tom Howell, and *Used Machines and Abused Buyers* by Chuck Seidel from *Fine Woodworking*, November/December 1984. Prices quoted are for machines in good condition, less motors and accessories. Our advisor for this category is Mr. Dana Martin Batory, author of *Vintage Woodworking Machinery, An Illustrated Guide to Four Manufacturers*. See his listing in the Directory under Ohio for further information. Watch for Volume II, *An Illustrated Guide to Four More Manufacturers*. No phone calls, please.

American Saw Mill Machinery Company, 1931

Jointer, Monarch Line, #XII, ball-bearing, 16"	1,200.00
Planer, Monarch Line, single surface, 30"	2,600.00
Table saw, Monarch Line, #X24, tilting arbor, 16"	425.00

Blue Star Products, 1939

Band saw, #1200, 12" floor model	85.00
Lathe, #1001, 72" bed, 12" swing	60.00
Table saw, #800, 8"	95.00

Boice-Crane Power Tools, 1937

Band saw, #800, 14"	100.00
Drill press, #1600, 15"	75.00
Lathe, #1100, gap bed	50.00
Scroll saw, #900, 24"	75.00

Defiance Machine Works, 1910

Band saw, 28"	520.00
Table saw, #2, hand feed, 20"	650.00
Table saw, #2, power feed, 20"	1,100.00

Delta Manufacturing Company, 1939

Band saw, #768, 10"	50.00
Disc sander, belt drive, #1425, 12"	35.00
Jointer, ball bearing, #654, 6"	50.00
Lathe, ball bearing, #1460, 12"	60.00
Lathe, timken bearing, #930, 11"	45.00
Table saw, tilt top, #1180, 10"	95.00
Table saw, tilt top, #860, 8"	35.00

F.H. Clement Company, 1896

Band saw, 30"	555.00
Boring Machine, Post, #2	325.00
Jointer, Perfection, 30"	1,690.00
Ripsaw, #2, iron fr, 16"	585.00
Sand-papering machine, #2, Universal	585.00
Sander, #3, dbl spindle	585.00
Shaper, variety, #3, heavy, dbl spindle	1,300.00
Splitting saw, #1, iron fr, wood top, 12"	325.00

Gallmeyer & Livingston Company, 1927

Band saw, Union, 20"	390.00
Jointer, Union, motor on arbor, 8"	370.00
Table saw, Union #7, 7"	210.00

G.N. Goodspeed Company, 1876

Boring machine, upright	225.00
Planer, New & Improved, Pony, 24"	900.00
Table saw, 12"	200.00

Hoyt & Brother Company, 1888

Cut-off saw, overhung, traversing, 14"	650.00
Planing & matching machine, #7, 13"	3,250.00
Scroll saw, #1	300.00
Table saw, #2, 14"	800.00

J.A. Fay & Egan Company, 1900

Jointer, New #2, 16"	1,550.00
Jointer, New #2, 20"	1,625.00
Jointer, New #2, 30"	1,820.00
Jointer, New #4, extra heavy, 16"	1,625.00
Jointer, New #4, extra heavy, 30"	2,275.00
Molder, #1½, 4-sided, 4"	1,050.00
Molder, #2, 4-sided, 6"	1,500.00
Molder, #2½, 4-sided, 7"	2,100.00
Mortiser, #5, dbl hollow chisel, horizontal	1,100.00
Planer, #2½, dbl-belted surface, med sz, 26"	1,850.00
Saw, rip; #2, Improved Standard	1,175.00
Saw, rip; #3, self feed, X-lg	2,400.00

L. Power & Company, 1888

Mortiser & borer, #2	780.00
Shaper, single spindle, reversible	585.00
Table saw, self feed, 14"	715.00

Ober Manufacturing Company, 1889

Rip saw, self feed, 14"	725.00
Saw, swing cut-off, 18"	275.00
Shaper, saw & jointer combination	400.00

Oliver Machinery Company, 1922

Band saw, #17, 30"	925.00
Shaper, #483, high speed, dbl spindle	1,300.00
Table saw, #32, Variety, 12"	500.00

Parks Ball Bearing Machine Company, 1925

Jointer, H-133, Ideal, 12"	400.00
Sanding machine, H-165, Economy, 24"	230.00
Saw, H-97, swing cut-off, Alert, 12"	225.00

P.B. Yates Machine Company, 1917

Planer, #160, dbl surface, 20"	1,235.00
Saw, #232, swing cut-off, 16"	260.00

Powermatic, Inc., 1965

Band saw, #81, 20"	500.00
Lathe, #90, 12"	360.00
Planer, #160, 16"	650.00
Planer, #221, 20"	725.00
Shaper, #26, single spindle	240.00

Tenoner, #2-A, single end...620.00

Richardson, Meriam & Company, 1865

Band saw, Granite State, 36"...400.00
Mortising & boring machine, lg No 1.................................1,300.00
Planing & matching machine, No 5, single cutter head 4,225.00
Re-sawing machine, circular, 40"......................................1,300.00
Scroll saw, Patent, common sz 330.00

S.A. Woods Machine Company, 1876

Circular resawing machine, Joslin's Improved, 50" 2,275.00
Planer, panel; Improved, 20"..520.00
Planer, surface; Pat Improved, 30".....................................1,430.00

The Sidney Machine Tool Company, 1916
(Famous Woodworking Machinery)

Bandsaw, 20"...325.00
Bandsaw, 27"...535.00
Jointer, Cyclone, 12"...525.00
Jointer, Cyclone, 16"...585.00
Jointer, 20"..1,220.00
Lathe, pattern maker's, 14"..275.00
Lathe, pattern maker's, 20"..325.00
Mortiser, hollow chisel, new model 585.00
Mortiser & tenoner, combined 575.00
Planer, dbl-belted, 24x8"..1,575.00
Planer, 18" 880.00
Planer, 24" 975.00
Saw, combination; No 5, 16" 525.00
Saw, Universal, No 10, 16"...1,270.00
Saw, Variety, No 6, 16"..780.00
Saw, Variety, No 8, 20"..650.00
Saw, Variety, No 16, 20"..750.00
Shaper, single spindle 650.00
Woodworker, portable, hand...485.00
Woodworker, Universal, No 40 ....1,300.00
Woodworker, Universal, 5 machines in 1, No 30 or No 31, ea.....2,015.00

Sprunger Power Tools, 1950s

Band saw, 14"...60.00
Jigsaw, 20"...40.00
Lathe, gap bed, 10"...50.00
Table saw, tilt arbor, 10¼" 75.00

Worcester Porcelain Company

The Worcester Porcelain Company was deeded in 1751. During the first or Dr. Wall period (so called for one of its proprietors), porcelain with an Oriental influence was decorated in underglaze blue. Useful tablewares represented the largest portion of production, but figurines and decorative items were also made. Very little of the earliest wares were marked and can only be identified by a study of forms, glazes, and the porcelain body, which tends to transmit a greenish cast when held to light. Late in the '50s, a crescent mark was in general use, and rare examples bear a facsimile of the Meissen crossed swords. The first period ended in 1783, and the company went through several changes in ownership during the next eighty years. The years from 1783 to 1792 are referred to as the Flight period. Marks were a small crescent, a crown with 'Royal,' or an impressed 'Flight.' From 1792 to 1807 the company

was known as Flight and Barr and used the trademark 'F&B' or 'B,' with or without a small cross. From 1807 to 1813 the company was under the Barr, Flight, and Barr management; this era is recognized as having produced porcelain with the highest quality of artistic decoration. Their mark was 'B.F.B.' From 1813 to 1840 many marks were used, but the usual was 'F.B.B.' under a crown to indicate Flight, Barr, and Barr. In 1840 the firm merged with Chamberlain, and in 1852 they were succeeded by Kerr and Binns. The firm became known as Royal Worcester in 1862. The production was then marked with a circle with '51' within and a crown on top. The date of manufacture was incised into the bottom or stamped with a letter of the alphabet, just under the circle. In 1891 Royal Worcester England was added to the circle and crown. From that point on, each piece is dated with a code of dots or other symbols. After 1891 most wares had a blush-color ground. Prior to that date it was ivory. Most shapes were marked with a unique number.

During the early years they produced considerable ornamental wares with a Persian influence. This gave way to a Japanesque influence. James Hadley is most responsible for the Victorian look. He is considered the 'best ever' designer and modeller. He was joined by the finest porcelain painters. Together they produced pieces with very fine detail and exquisite painting and decoration. Figures, vases, and tableware were produced in great volume and are highly collectible. During the 1890s they allowed the artists to sign some of their work. Pieces signed on the face by the Stintons, Baldwyn, Davis, Raby, Austin, Powell, Sedgley, and Rushton (not a complete list) are in great demand. The company is still in production. There is an outstanding museum on the company grounds in Worcester, England.

Note: Most pieces had lids or tops (if there is a flat area on the top lip, chances are it had one), if missing deduct 30% to 40%.

Key:
BFB — Barr, Flight, and Barr   FBB — Flight, Barr, and Barr

Biscuit bbl, magenta chrysanthemum, 2 claw ft as finial, 1888 ...925.00
Bowl, Imari style w/paneled fans, 18th C, 8⅞", EX 200.00
Bowl, swirled panels: bl/wht/orange, Dr Wall, oriental mk, 2½x5" ..220.00
Coffeepot, cobalt florals w/gilt foliage, unmk, 18th C, 9½", EX .230.00
Cup & saucer, roses on wht, cup int gold, dtd 1939, sgn M Hunt...315.00
Dinner set, depicts wild game, brn transfer, service for 6, 24-pc .525.00
Dinnerware, HP floral & swag motif, 1924, service for 12 ....825.00

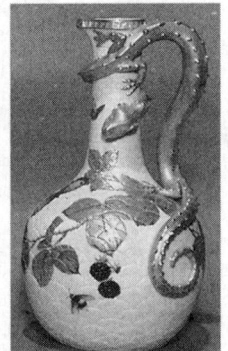

Ewer, blackberries, dragon handle, fired-on butterflies and bumblebee, 1883, 11⅛", NM, $1,000.00.

Ewer, honeycomb, pk w/gold base, gold tree trunk hdl, purple mk, 8" ..90.00
Ewer, yel w/gold vines, dragon hdl, #21627, ca 1887, 7½" 420.00
Figurine, Baltimore Oriole in blossom, D Doughty, 11" 1,025.00
Figurine, Blue Angel (angelfish), swimming through coral, 5"....210.00
Figurine, Charlotte & Jane, Victorian Series, Von Ruyckevekt, 6¼" ...210.00
Figurine, Dutch Boy, holding flower basket in ea hand, 5½" 390.00
Figurine, horse & rider jumping wall, Linder, 1968, 11"..............740.00
Figurine, June, boy on stump w/flute & dog, 1960, 6¼" 250.00
Figurine, Lesser White Throat Sylvia Curruca & Wild Rose, Doughty, 11" ...520.00

Figurine, Maria, 13"..**660.00**
Figurine, robin on branch w/mushrooms below, Doughty, 8" **520.00**
Figurine, Seamstress, #3569, Doughty, 7½".........................**215.00**
Figurine, Staff Nurse, 1960s, 8⅝"......................................**340.00**
Figurine, Willow Princess, 9"..**740.00**
Flower holder, shell shape, wht w/gold coral base & trim, 7"......**210.00**
Jar, potpourri; raised border panels w/roses, swirl finial, #H162...**575.00**
Pitcher, floral on cream, gold hdl/base, sgn AB #1094, 8½".......**125.00**
Pitcher, roses on wht, gold hdl w/vines, gold floral at neck, 8" ...**320.00**
Place setting, fruits, made for William Henry, King George III, 5-pc..**275.00**
Plate, Imari, ca 1810, BFB mk, 8"......................................**200.00**
Plate, Raglan Castle scene, sgn H Sivad, dtd 1940......................**325.00**
Sweetmeat, molded leaf shape, underglaze bl floral int, rpr, 3" ...**115.00**
Tea bowl & saucer, butterfly/flowers, bl on wht, Dr Wall, mini ..**150.00**
Tea bowl & saucer, fence/flowers, bl on wht, Dr Wall, mini **140.00**
Vase, floral spray on cream w/gold, bulbous/ftd w/stick neck, 6½" **50.00**
Vase, gr w/flowers, bugs, gold trim, #582, 10".........................**400.00**
Vase, wht bottle shape coiled about w/lg gold dragon, 15x10", EX ...**2,600.00**
Vase, 2 bulls in pasture on wht, sgn H Stinton, rtcl lid, 5" **1,100.00**

World's Fairs and Expos

Since 1851 and the Crystal Palace Exhibition in London, World's Fairs and Expositions have taken place at a steady pace. Many of them commemorate historical events. The 1904 Louisiana Purchase Exposition, commonly known as the St. Louis World's Fair, celebrated the 100th anniversary of the Louisiana Purchase agreement between Thomas Jefferson and Napoleon in 1803. The 1893 Columbian Exposition commemorated the 400th anniversary of the discovery of America by Columbus in 1492. (Both of these fairs were held one year later than originally scheduled.) The multitude of souvenirs from these and similar events have become a growing area of interest to collectors in recent years. Many items have a 'crossover' interest into other fields: i.e., collectors of postcards and souvenir spoons eagerly search for those from various fairs and expositions.

Values have fallen somewhat due to eBay sales. Many of the so called common items have come down in value. However 1939 World's Fair items are still hot. For additional information collectors may contact World's Fairs Collectors Society (WFCS), whose address is in the Directory under Clubs, Newsletters, and Catalogs, or our advisor, Herbert Rolfes. His address is listed in the Directory under Florida.

Key:
T&P — Trylon & Perisphere   WF — World's Fair

1876 Centennial, Philadelphia

Book, History of Centennial Exibition, James McCabe, EX..........**75.00**
Book, Official Tour; 36 pgs, 4x6", EX..................................**50.00**
Book, Our Show, One Hundred Years a Republic, 82 pgs, EX.......**85.00**
Coverlet, jacquard; Memorial Hall, red/bl/gr stripes, 76x70".......**330.00**
Lid, Memorial Hall, gold border, Pratt Ware, 6½" dia................**265.00**
Needle case, Exhibition Bldg transfer, cylindrical, Mauchline, 3¼" ..**145.00**
Pass, complimentary; w/envelope, VG....................................**50.00**
Plate, Memorial Hall, Pratt Ware, 8½" dia **85.00**
Platter, bread; glass, Give Us This..., bldg in center, 9x12¾"........**45.00**
Press pass, Philadelphia Enquirer, emb seal, EX............................**265.00**
Scarf, G Washington center w/6 bldgs, wht w/red border, 22x20" ...**100.00**
Stereocards, set of 19, New Excelsior Series, VG+........................**90.00**

1893 Columbian, Chicago

Bank, stoneware globe w/bl emb, graphics & adv, 5½" dia, EX+..**2,700.00**

Book, Century WF Book for Boys & Girls, hardbk, 245-pg, NM..**35.00**
Book, Youth's Companion, WF view on soft cover, VG................**20.00**
Card, Old Times Distillery bldg diecut, 3½x2¼"......................**20.00**
Playing cards, Columbian Souvenir, Clark, 54 in worn box, from $50 to ...**75.00**
Spoon, bldg view in bowl, floral hdl, Leonard SP, 6"....................**12.50**
Tray, Columbus & bldgs w/floral border, SP, ftd, 7" dia................**75.00**

1901 Pan American

Invitation, Dedication of IL Bldg, w/orig mailing envelope, VG ..**70.00**
Miniature frying pan, brass, Meet Me At..., lid pops open, EX......**32.00**
Pin-bk, mc celluloid, MO Pan-Am Expo Buffalo 1901..., EX........**24.00**
Pocket mirror, celluloid, Electric Tower, 2¼"............................**65.00**
Postcard, view of Expo grounds, 6x9", EX..................................**135.00**
Ticket, New York Day, 6¼x2¾", EX......................................**35.00**
Tumbler, juice, crystal, Pan-Am Expo & buffalo etch, gold rim **22.00**

1904 St. Louis

Bowl, Palace of Education, gold details, 2¾x10", EX..................**500.00**
Box, Cascade Gardens on hinged lid, clear glass sides, 3x3⅛"......**75.00**
Candy container, Palace of Electricity litho, tin, 2¼", EX............**70.00**
Case, cigar; leather cover w/burned-in design, 3¼x5¼", EX.........**30.00**
Handkerchief, eng photo of Teddy Roosevelt, minimum value...**200.00**
Hatchet, glass, 1803 Emblem of Peace & Prosperity 1904, VG.....**50.00**
Paperweight, Ferris Wheel, 3" dia...**75.00**
Pocketknife, aluminum fr, 2-blade, Liberal Arts Bldg, EX.............**55.00**
Tip tray, aluminum, Souvenir of..., mc litho, MIG, 3x5"...............**30.00**

1905 Lewis and Clark

Book, Sights & Scenes, 5x6¾", VG...**35.00**
Bookmark, Carnation Cream, celluloid, EX..................................**25.00**
Box, litho photo of Bridge of All Nations, aluminum, 2¼x5¾" ...**55.00**
Matchsafe, 1905 L&C Expo w/colored flag on reverse, VG+......**165.00**
Mug, Liberal Arts Bldg, unmk, 2⅜"...**45.00**
Plate, L&C center w/portraits on border, Staffordshire, 10".........**110.00**
Watch fob, fair scenes w/L&C on coin, 5½x1½", EX....................**70.00**

1907 Jamestown

Elongated cent, 1907 Indian cent, EX.......................................**30.00**
Match holder, metal w/cloth cover, Jamestown on front, tulip on bk ...**55.00**
Pin, enameld logo center w/wht & bl rings, oval, EX **55.00**
Postcard, $100 Virginia Treasury Note, 7⅝x4⅝", EX **65.00**
Spoon, Indian head hdl, US Gov't Pier on bowl, sterling, 4", EX ..**50.00**

1909 Alaska Yukon Pacific

Book, General History, Kenneth Hotel, EX **90.00**
Dish, logo w/HP flowers, gold edge, ruffled edge, Elite Works, oval....**135.00**
Encased cent, 1909 Indian Head encased in teapot-style case, EX ..**55.00**
Plate, logo center w/red & yel leaf border, Adams-Tunstall, 8½"...**125.00**
Token, fair logo w/Seal of Seattle of reverse, 1¼" dia...................**25.00**

1926 Sesquicentennial

Binder cover, Forms & Tokens, Dept of Admissions, 11x8½", EX...**65.00**
Coin, $2.50 Gold Commemorative, NM **325.00**
Medal, Liberty Bell w/red/wht/bl ribbon, watch fob-type clip, EX ...**15.00**
Paperweight, hollow pot metal, Liberty Bell, 3½".........................**15.00**
Pass, admission; 2⅝x4", EX..**50.00**
Pin, lapel; bear holding 2 bl enameled flags over 1915, 1", EX **45.00**
Plate, fair scenes, flow bl, mk Wheelock Made in England, 7⅝" ..**50.00**

Shoehorn, Louis Mark Shoes, VG 12.50
Tape measure, SF bldgs on ea side, celluloid, 1½" W, EX 85.00
Ticket, SF Day, November 2, 1915, 6x2¾", VG+ 55.00

1933 Chicago

Ashtray, donkey pulling cart, MIJ, 4½" W 25.00
Bracelet, cuff; ornate Chicago skyline, gold metal, EX 48.00
Cane, metal curved hdl w/Chicago 1933, sq shaft, EX 55.00
Fan, paper, A&P store pavilion giveaways, 8x11½", EX................35.00
Felt, Pontiac, Chief of the Sixes, red/wht/gold on bl, 11x13½" 40.00
Handkerchief, fair scenes in orange & gray on off-wht, 12" sq......25.00
License plate attachment, star w/WF Chicago in circles #33, EX, up to...200.00
Mechanical match, fairgrounds w/Federal Bldg on reverse, VG+..30.00
Medal, Official Commemorative; NMIB....................................35.00
Night light, lantern style, metal w/pnt glass globe, EX 50.00
Pin, Zepplin, enameled brass, 1⅜x2", EX....................................30.00
Postcard, Wrigley's Field on front w/fair logo on bk, unused 30.00
Shakers, Tea Time, clear glass w/blk letters, EX (blk & wht box).75.00
Teapot, logo on ea side, aluminum w/red metal hdl & bird spout .50.00
Tray, 5 Chicago bldgs on gray w/gr bkground, EX 30.00
Umbrella, orange/bl/tan, Japanese style, w/orig sleeve, EX, up to ..100.00

1939 New York

Ashtray, tire, Firestone, skyline in glass center, 6¼" dia, $75 to .100.00
Board game, Going to the World's Fair, complete, EXIB.............150.00
Book, Super-Feature Exhibits, Messmore & Damon, 14-pg, 9x12", EX...80.00
Bracelet, T&P center, gold-tone, dmn cutout on band, 2" W 65.00
Cine-Vue, 75 Movie Views & Pathegrams, MIB..........................135.00
Coaster set, T&P center, 4 ea of 4 colors, 3" dia...........................100.00
Plate, G Washington looking over fair, bl & wht, Lamberton, EX ..80.00

Plate, Trylon and Perisphere center, scenic reserves along border, Meakin, from $75.00 to $100.00.

Plate, T&P center w/2 sets of bl & orange bands, Atlas China, 8" ..130.00
Playing cards, fair bldgs, gold trim, complete, M (NM box)..........50.00
Snow globe, T&P in center, glass & Bakelite, 4", EX, minimum value....100.00
Tapestry, 3 fair bldgs, 54x19", made in Belgium, VG+...............120.00
Teapot, gold T&P on blk, Hall, EX, minimum value 1,000.00
Toy, Greyhound Pavilion People Mover, Arcade, complete w/3 cars, VG ..500.00
Vase, gr glaze, American Potter, 4½x4", EX.................................80.00

1939 San Francisco

Book, Treasure Island, fair photos, 32 pg, EX 35.00
Booklet, Pageant of the Pacific, fair scenes, Crocker Comp, EX ...30.00
Plate, logo in center w/fair bldgs border, Homer Laughlin, 10" ...250.00
Potpourri holder, hanging woven basket type, 5¼", EX................18.00
Souvenir, Sun Tower, bronze finish, 4¼", minimum value 75.00

1962 Seattle

Book, Pictorial Panorama, 22 pgs, VG+ 18.00

Charm bracelet, gold metal, 10 charms, 7"....................................25.00
Decanter, Space Needle shape, Beam, 13½" 20.00
Kit, punch-out; Space Needle, 3-D, NM.......................................25.00
Medal, National Commemorative; designed by G Tsutakawa, .9 silver...20.00
Program, Gold Cup Hydroplane Racing; 45-pg, NM....................60.00
Sweater, wht w/red Space Needle, red trim, EX 25.00
Thermometer, gold & silver metal w/etched Space Needle, 6" 20.00
Tie, Century 21 logo on blk, Fashion Crafts Cravats, NM 20.00
Umbrella, lt pk w/fair bldgs, Space Needle finial, child sz, EX 50.00

1964 New York

Book, Official Guide for Vatican Pavilion, 25-pg, 8x10", EX 15.00
Book, Official Souvenir; Time-Life Books, EX 20.00
Book, pop-up; See the NY World's Fair, Mary Pillsbury, EX..........35.00
Box, Unisphere shape, silver metal, 2¼" dia.................................35.00
Coin purse, gr vinyl, Unisphere & logo, oval, NM 25.00
Doll, Miss 1964 New York World's Fair, Japan, 13½", NMIP......120.00
Figurine, flute player from It's a Small World, Disney, 7½", NMIB....40.00
Hat, cowboy; wht straw w/logo on front, chin drawstring, EX.......60.00
Novelty, Unishere, chrome-plated metal & plastic, 3¼x3" dia, VG ...25.00
Periscope, plastic, US Steel, Hong Kong, 9" closed 40.00
Plate, Unisphere center w/fair bldgs border, US Steel, 8¼" 15.00
Progress report, #8, progress of construction, 84-pg, VG 15.00
View-master reel pack, Federal & State Area, 3 reels, MIP...........40.00

Wright, Frank Lloyd

Born in Richland Center, Wisconsin, in 1869, Wright became a pioneer in architectural expression, developing a style referred to as 'prairie.' From early in the century until he died in 1959, he designed houses with rooms that were open, rather than divided by walls in the traditional manner. They exhibited low, horizontal lines and strongly projecting eaves, and he filled them with furnishings whose radical aesthetics complemented the structures to perfection. Several of his homes have been preserved to the present day, and collectors who admire his ideas and the unique, striking look he achieved treasure the stained glass windows, furniture, chinaware, lamps, and other decorative accessories made by Wright.

Key:
drw — drawer   T — Taliesen trim
H — Heritage Henredon

Bed, H, concentric design, 3 sliding doors, king sz 2,100.00
Cabinet, H, concentric sqs, cradle base, T, 25x34x20"............4,000.00
Cabinet, H, 2 stacking 2-door cabinets on base, 44x34"..........7,500.00
Chair set, H, low bks, reuphl seats/bk, T, 4 sides/2 arms, VG ..1,800.00
Chairs, dining; H, T edge, reuphl/rfn, 6 for 2,300.00
Chairs, H, 8-sided bk/cantilevered seat, 28", 4 for....................1,600.00
Lantern, sq, heavy gauge iron w/Japanese influence, commercial.......5,500.00
Ottoman, H, uphl hexagon in orig gr fabric, 6-leg base w/T, 27" dia..1,400.00
Print, Heurtly house, Oak Park IL, matted/fr, 22x14½" 750.00
Sculpture, Nakoma w/children holding rnd pot, blk glaze, 12"...1,600.00
Settee, uphl bk & seat, 3-pc, from Robert Winn house, 1953, 90"..3,500.00
Sideboard, H, recessed hdls, T, 46x86x20".............................2,600.00
Sideboard, H, 11-drw, recessed hdls, T, 34x62x20"..................2,300.00
Stool, tapered rectangle w/cushion top, Winn house, 1953, 15x26x18" ..2,100.00
Table, coffee; H, rnd slat top over X-base w/T, EX 2,600.00
Table, coffee; 6-sided, T, 48" dia, +6 stools 5,000.00
Table, dining; T w/copper edge, 48" dia 2,700.00
Table, drop-leaf; H, gate-leg, rfn/rstr, no mk, open: 68" L, VG ...400.00
Table, H, hexagon on 3-slab base w/T, rfn top, 27x25" dia, VG .700.00
Table, H, hexagonal, 3-slab base, T, 27x25x25" 850.00

Table, H, shelf, T copper edge, 23x27x21" **1,000.00**
Table, H, 1-drw w/recessed hdl over shelf w/T, 23x26x27", VG..**800.00**
Table, side; H, shelf & drw w/recessed hdl in base, T, 23x21x27", VG..**800.00**
Watercolor, Ward Memorial Bldg at NWU, 24x33", VG............**550.00**

Wrought Iron

Until the middle of the nineteenth century, almost all the metal hand forged in America was made from a material called wrought iron. When wrought iron rusts it appears grainy, while the mild steel that was used later shows no grain but pits to an orange-peel surface. This is an important aid in determining the age of an ironwork piece. See also Fireplace Implements.

Bird roaster, sqd pan w/hdl, 3 penny ft, hinged 2-tine fork, 6x19" ...**220.00**
Candle holder, X pc w/scrolls, socket/drip pan ea side, 3-ftd, 21" ...**150.00**
Candlestand, gilt highlights, 3-part scrolled base, 68", pr **1,380.00**
Candlestand, high tripod w/penny ft, scrolled bracket w/2 sockets, 61"..**1,000.00**
Chandelier, 6 arms on circular strap, Continental, 8x27" **1,115.00**
Door latch, dbl-cusp w/stylized tulip motif, VT, 1800s, mtd on brd ..**3,000.00**
Pipe tongs, multi-use: ember tongs, bowl scraper & tobacco tamp ..**1,600.00**
Table, garden; marble top, appl vintage decor, 32x56" dia **2,300.00**
Table, scroll supports, lower shelf, penny ft, glass top, 27x16" **230.00**
Toaster, scroll finial, revolving rack w/ornate scrollwork, 25" **190.00**
Wine rack, rectangular w/scrolled ornament, 53" **175.00**

Yellow Ware

Ranging in color from buff to deep mustard, yellow ware which almost always has a clear glaze can be slip banded, plain, Rockingham decorated, flint enamel glazed, or mocha decorated. Black or red mocha decorated pieces are the most desirable. Although blue mocha decorated pieces are the most common, green decorated pieces command the lowest prices. Pieces having a combination of two colors are the rarest. The majority of pieces are plain and do not bear a manufacture's mark. Primarily produced in the United States, England, and Canada this utilitarian ware was popular from the mid-nineteenth century until the early twentieth century. Yellow ware was first produced in New York, Pennsylvania, and Vermont. However, the center for yellow ware production was East Liverpool, Ohio, a town which once supported more than thirty potters. Yellow ware is still being produced today in both the United States and England. Because of websites and Internet auctions, prices have tended to become uniform throughout the United States. The use of this pottery as accessories in decorating and its exposure in country magazines has caused prices to rise, especially for the more utilitarian forms such as plates and bowls. Note: Because this is a utilitarian ware, it is often found with damage and heavy wear. Damage does have a negative impact on price, especially for the common forms. For further information we recommend *Collecting Yellow Ware: An Identification and Value Guide* written by our advisor John Michel and Lisa McAllister, and *Collector's Guide to Yellow Ware* by Lisa McAllister. Mr. Michel's address is in the Directory under New York. See also Rockingham.

Bowl, wht band, rolled lip, 9½" **350.00**
Butter crock, wht & dk brn bands, w/lid, 4¾" **225.00**
Colander, brn & wht bands, Jeffords, 13", minimum value......**1,100.00**
Colander, wht slip & bl bands w/bl mocha seaweed, 12½", minimum ...**1,400.00**
Creamer, 2 wht bands, 3¼" **175.00**
Custard cup, 3 wht bands, 3¼" **65.00**
Egg separator, TG Green Ltd (England), 4" dia **55.00**
Jar, wax sealer, ridged rim, 7" **250.00**
Milk pan, rolled rim, 9" dia..**345.00**
Mold, heart shape, mini, 3"..**250.00**
Mold, melon form, 8" L..**395.00**

Mold, parrot on branch, oval, 8x10" **650.00**
Mug, 4 wht bands, 6"..**195.00**
Nappy, 4 molded lines, ca 1850, 3"..**250.00**
Pie plate, plain, Jeffords, 11¾"..**350.00**
Pie plate, plain, 9"..**200.00**
Pitcher, bl sponging, 6¼" **155.00**
Pitcher, brn & wht mocha earthworm, 8¼", minimum............**1,000.00**
Pitcher, emb cows, gr highlights, 7"..**245.00**
Pitcher, hound hdl, plain, 8"..**475.00**
Pitcher, wht slip w/brn mocha seaweed, 8", minimum value.......**850.00**
Plaque, Geo Washington bust, wht slip on yel, 19th C, 6x4", minimum...**550.00**
Teapot, basketweave, Windsor Baking Powder giveaway, 5" **575.00**
Tile, emb eagle w/13-star border, 5½x5½" **475.00**

Zanesville Glass

Glassware was produced in Zanesville, Ohio, from as early as 1815 until 1851. Two companies produced clear and colored hollow ware pieces in five characteristic patterns: 1) diamond faceted, 2) broken swirls, 3) vertical swirls, 4) perpendicular fluting, 5) plain, with scalloped or fluted rims and strap handles. The most readily identified product is perhaps the whiskey bottles made in the vertical swirl pattern, often called globular swirls because of their full, round bodies. Their necks vary in width; some have a ringed rim and some are collared. They were made in several colors; amber, light green, and light aquamarine are the most common. Our advisor for this category is Mark Vuono; he is listed in the Directory under Connecticut.

Bottle, amber, 24 left-swirled ribs, globular, broken blister, 9" **495.00**
Bottle, club; aqua, 24 swirl ribs, 7½" **195.00**
Bottle, dk amber, 24-swirl ribs, appl lip, globular, EX impression, 8"...**750.00**

Zanesville Stoneware Company

Still in operation at its original location in Zanesville, Ohio, this company is the last surviving pottery dating from Zanesville's golden era of pottery production. They manufactured utilitarian stoneware, art ware vases, jardinieres and pedestals, dinnerware, and large hand-turned vases for use in outdoor gardens. Much of this ware has remained unidentified until today, since they often chose to mark their wares only with item numbers or the names of their various clients. Other items were marked with an impressed circular arrangement containing the company name and location or a three-line embossed device, the bottom line of which contained the letters ZSC. For more information we recommend *Zanesville Stoneware Company* by Jon Rans, Glenn Ralston, and Nate Russell (Collector Books).

Jardiniere, Matt Green, swirled flutes, bosses under rim, #309, 7½"...**95.00**
Lamp base, Matt Blue, ovoid panels, #785, 8½", from $150 to...**200.00**
Pitcher, horizontal rings, ringed hdl, #579, 8¾", from $125 to ...**150.00**
Pitcher, Matt Green, #D, 3½", from $15 to **20.00**
Pitcher, Matt Rose, horizontal rings, #D-6, 5", from $35 to **45.00**
Planter, duck form, yel gloss, #BA13, 5¼", from $25 to **45.00**
Vase, Gloss Blue, trumpet form, #513, 5", from $45 to **55.00**
Vase, Matt Green, ovoid w/rim-to-width hdls, #516, 9", from $115 to ...**145.00**
Vase, Matt Green, prominent hand trn, hdls, #108, 15", from $300 to...**500.00**
Vase, Matt Rose, can neck, hdls, #109/Pickrull, hand trn, 21", $600 to..**800.00**
Vase, Neptune, lt teal w/dk sponging, hdls, #790, 16", from $400 to.......**600.00**
Vase, Omar Ware, simple shoulder band, #711, 8½", from $275 to........**375.00**
Vase, Rubble Ware, rockwork relief w/floral branch, #567, 7½" .**175.00**
Vase, Verdantone, dk tan dripping over lt tan, #38, 10", from $200 to...**250.00**
Vase, Vulcan, rust w/streaks & drippings, #J, 12", from $200 to..**250.00**
Vase, Zasco, wht w/cobalt & rust splashes, cobalt at top, 10", $150 to..**175.00**

Zell

The Georg Schmider United Zell Ceramic Factories has a long and colorful history. Affectionately called 'Zell' by those who are attracted to this charming German-Dutch type tin-glazed earthenware, this type of ware came into production in the latter part of the last century.

While Zell has created some lovely majolica-like examples (which are beginning to attract their own following), it is the German-Dutch scenes that are collected with such enthusiasm. Typical scenes are set against a lush green background with windmills on the distant horizon. Into the scenes appear typically garbed girls (long dresses with long white aprons and low-land bonnet head-gear) being teased or admired by little boys attired in pantaloon-type trousers and short rust-colored jackets, all wearing wooden shoes. There are variations on this theme, and occasionally a collector may find an animal theme or even a Kate Greenaway-like scene.

A similar ware in both theme, technique, and quality but bearing the mark Haag or Made in Austria is included in this listing.

While Zell produced a wide range of wares and even quite recently (1970s) introduced an entirely hand-painted hen/rooster line, it is this early charming German-Dutch theme pottery that is coveted by increasing numbers of devoted collectors. Our advisor for this category is Lila Shrader; she is listed in the Directory under California.

Key:
hdl/RA — handle at right   KG — Kate Greenaway style
angle to spout   MIA — Made in Austria

Bowl, Dutch theme, Germany, 3¼", from $11 to............................**28.00**
Bowl, Dutch theme w/boy in wagon w/dog, Baden, 3¼" **48.00**
Bowl, rim soup; boy & girl in Alpine setting, Baden, Zell, 8¾" **68.00**
Bowl, rim soup; 1970s hen & rooster decor, Germany, 8½" **26.00**
Bowl, vegetable; oval, boys return from fishing, KG, Baden, 7x9½" ...**129.00**
Bowls, nested, Dutch theme, Baden, set of 3, 6", 8½", 11" **395.00**
Bread board, 1970s hen/rooster theme w/pierced hdl, Germany, 5x8½"..**62.00**
Cake plate, boy/girls strolling hand in hand, pierced hdls, Baden, 9" **145.00**
Chamber stick w/ring, Dutch scenery, windmills & harbor, 3½" ...**128.00**
Child's feeding dish, Baden, 7½x1½"..**127.00**
Chocolate pot, boy & girl hand in hand, w/lid, Germany, 6¾" ..**145.00**
Creamer, Dutch theme, w/hdl/RA, MIA, from $22 to...................**49.00**
Creamer, Dutch theme w/boy in wagon w/dog, Baden, 3¼"..........**50.00**
Cup & saucer, Dutch scenery w/windmills & water, Baden, doll-sz ..**58.00**
Cup & saucer, Dutch theme, Baden, from $24 to **55.00**
Egg cup, 1970s hen & rooster decor, dbl, Germany, 4" **25.00**
Mug, girls w/cats in wheelbarrow, Haag, 3½" **55.00**

Pitcher, Greenaway-like design, Baden, 7", $195.00. (Photo courtesy Lila Shrader)

Plate, boys teasing tearful girls, Baden, 8½" **55.00**
Plate, majolica-like lilies, well defined, turned-up edge, Germany, 9" ...**28.00**
Plate, majolica-like w/berries on basketweave, Germany, 8½" **46.00**
Plate, majolica-like water lilies, well-defined features, Baden, 9"..**72.00**
Plate, proverb: Not All Deeds Go Unpunished, cats & dogs, MIA, 8" ..**55.00**
Plate, 2 dolls resting under tree, town in distance, Haag, 8" **90.00**
Sugar bowl, chicken pecking corn, w/hdls & lid, MIA, 3½" **66.00**

Vase, bears at play in front of cottage, forest beyond, Haag, 6½" ..**67.00**
Vase, costumed animals partying, pear shape, Haag, 6½" **78.00**

Zsolnay

Only until the past decade has the production of the Zsolnay factory become more correctly understood. In the beginning they produced only cement; industrial and kitchen ware manufacture began in the 1850s, and in the early 1870s a line of decorative architectural and art pottery was initiated which has continued to the present time.

The city of Pecs (pronounced Paach) is the major provincial city of southwest Hungary close to the Yugoslav border. The old German name for the city was Funfkirchen, meaning 'Five Churches.' (The 'five-steeple' mark became the factory's logo in 1878.)

Although most Americans only think of Zsolnay in terms of the bizarre, reticulated examples of the 1880s and 1890s and the small 'Eosine' green figures of animals and children that have been produced since the 1920s, the factory went through all the art trends of major international art potteries and produced various types of forms and decorations. The 'golden period,' circa 1895 – 1920, is when its Art Nouveau (Sezession in Austro-Hungarian terms) examples were unequaled. Vilmos Zsolnay was a Renaissance man devoted to innovation, and his children carried on the tradition after his death in 1900. Important sculptors and artists of the day were employed (usually anonymously) and married into the family, creating a dynasty.

Nearly all Zsolnay is marked, either impressed 'Zsolnay Pecs' or with the 'five steeple' stamp. Variations and form numbers can date a piece fairly accurately. For the most part, the earlier ethnic historical-revival pieces do not bring the prices that the later Sezession and second Sezession (Deco) examples do. Our advisor for this category is John Gacher; he is listed in the Directory under Rhode Island.

Baluster, Labrador glaze, 2-part, #3994, ca 1900, 20", NM.......**1,650.00**
Box, Old Ivory Ware, Medieval decor, #2688, Zsolnay Pecs, 4x4x3", NM ...**300.00**
Box, Renaissance lady on lid, porc faience, 1884, 3½x6½" dia ..**1,500.00**
Cache pot, etched gr/gold Eosin metallic, #226, ca 1900, 8¾", NM ..**5,500.00**
Cache pot, Renaissance figures, Pecs/steeple mks, 1880s, 6¾" ...**1,650.00**
Cache pot, Secession, Eosin, #5897, ca 1900, 4½x5", NM **590.00**
Cache pot, Secession, girls dance around tree, Labrador, #7770, 13"......**9,500.00**
Cache pot, Titiana in night scene, sgn Hidasy, #8389, 1910, 9x8" **9,500.00**
Chalice, Secession, flowers/berries, low hdls, Eosin, #5668, 1899, 6"......**2,950.00**
Figurine, Anonymous, seated figure w/book, #3330(?), ca 1903, 13½" ..**3,500.00**
Flask, Old Ivory Ware, cvd look, #2902, ca 1889, 14" **750.00**
Jardiniere, thistles, majolica, #5454, 1899, 18", NM **6,500.00**
Lamp, flower form, Eosin, #6261, ca 1900, 14½" **19,500.00**
Lamp, Loli Fuller figural (ballerina), #6234, ca 1900, 22½" ..**25,000.00**
Pitcher, Beetle, w/acorns & oak leaves, #4115, 1893, 15½" **5,500.00**
Pitcher, Secession, organic form, gr Eosin, #5517, 1899, 13½"..**9,500.00**
Pitcher, squash form, Eosin leaves/vines, #6211, 1900, 13¾", NM ..**12,500.00**
Plaque, Secession, windmill scene, Pecs, #9320, 1902, 10½x15", NM ...**6,500.00**
Tiles, Nouveau florals, 6" sq, matching set of 7 ....**1,000.00**
Vase, Goose Girl, Sandor, Eosin, #5561, 1898, 15¾", NM **17,500.00**
Vase, holly leaves & blossoms, Eosin, #7805, 1906, rpr, 9" **2,500.00**
Vase, landscape, cylindrical, rainbow Eosin, #5288, 1898, 7¾", EX ..**5,000.00**
Vase, Leopard, #8589, 1912, 10¾"..**17,500.00**
Vase, lilies/leaves, bl/silver Eosin, #5424, 1898-1900, 10½" ..**12,500.00**
Vase, metallic gold/gr/bl w/cvd discs, 4 dbl buttresses under rim, 8" ..**3,500.00**
Vase, Persian-style decor, #2289, 1882, 4¼" **1,500.00**
Vase, red & putty floral on wht, #3939, 1893, 10½" **2,750.00**
Vase, Renaissance wedding scene w/gold, porc faience, 16".....**6,000.00**
Vase, Ribbon Handle, Eosin on lustrous maroon, #35338, 1898, 9"..**2,850.00**
Vase, Secession, floral, bl Eosin, 1898, rpr, mini, 4¾" **950.00**
Vase, Secession, floral, gold/bl on burgundy, #7804, steeple mk, 12"..**1,750.00**
Vase, stylized flowers in relief on putty, #7926, 10", NM **12,500.00**

Advisory Board

The editors and staff take this opportunity to express our sincere gratitude and appreciation to each person who has in any way contributed to the preparation of this guide. We believe the credibility of our book is greatly enhanced through their efforts. See each advisor's Directory listing for information concerning their specific areas of expertise.

You will notice that at the conclusion of some of the narratives the advisor's name is given. This is optional and up to the discretion of each individual. Simply because no name is mentioned does not indicate that we have no advisor for that subject. Our board grows with each issue and now numbers nearly 450; if you care to correspond with any of them or anyone listed in our Directory, you must send a SASE with your letter. If you are seeking an appraisal, first ask about their fee, since many of these people are professionals who must naturally charge for their services. Because of our huge circulation, every person who allows us to publish their name runs the risk of their privacy being invaded by too many phone calls and letters. We are indebted to every advisor and very much regret losing any one of them. By far, the majority of those we lose give that reason. Please help us retain them on our board by observing the simple rules of common courtesy. Take the differences in time zones into consideration; some of our advisors tell us they often get phone calls in the middle of the night. For suggestions that may help you evaluate your holdings, see the Introduction.

AAA Antique Shop
Nappanee, Indiana

Barbara J. & Steve Aaronson
Northridge, California

Peter Abrahams
Lake Oswego, Oregon

Charles & Barbara Adams
South Yarmouth, Massachusetts

Geneva D. Addy
Winterset, Iowa

Stan and Sally Alekna
Lebanon, Pennsylvania

Beverly L. Ales
Pleasanton, California

Charles Alexander
Indianapolis, Indiana

Craig Ambrose
Des Moines, Iowa

James Anderson
New Brighton, Minnesota

Suzy McLennan Anderson
Holmdel, New Jersey

Tim Anderson
Provo, Utah

Warren R. Anderson
Cedar City, Utah

Dorothy Malone Anthony
Fort Scott, Kansas

Bruce A. Austin
Pittsford, New York

Bobby Babcock
Austin, Texas

Veldon Badders
Hamlin, New York

Rod Baer
Vienna, Virginia

Wayne and Gale Bailey
Dacula, Georgia

Jim Barker
Allentown, Pennsylvania

Jacqueline Linscott Barnes
Titusville, Florida

Kit Barry
Brattleboro, Vermont

Mark Bassett
Lakewood, Ohio

Dana Martin Batory
Crestline, Ohio

D.R. Beeks
Mt. Vernon, Iowa

Scott Benjamin
LaGrange, Ohio

Phyllis and Tom Bess
Tulsa, Oklahoma

Robert Bettinger
Mt. Dora, Florida

John E. Bilane
Union, New Jersey

William M. Bilsland III
Cedar Rapids, Iowa

Brenda Blake
York Harbor, Maine

Robert and Stan Block
Trumbull, Connecticut

Clarence H. Bodine, Jr.
New Hope, Pennsylvania

Sandra V. Bondhus
Unionville, Connecticut

Clifford Boram
Monticello, Indiana

Jeff Bradfield
Dayton, Virginia

Shane Branchcomb
Fairfax, Virginia

Mike Brooks
Oakland, California

Jim Broom
Effingham, Illinois

David L. Brown
Victoria, British Columbia, Canada

Marcia Brown
White City, Oregon

Rick Brown
Newspaper Collector's Society of America
Lansing, Michigan

Donald A. Bull
Wirtz, Virginia

Ann Burton
Decatur, Michigan

Robert C. Butz
Newbury Park, California

Jim Calison
Wallkill, New York

Tina M. Carter
El Cajon, California

Gene Cataldo
Huntsville, Alabama

Cerebro
East Prospect, Pennsylvania

Mick and Lorna Chase
Cookeville, Tennessee

Pat and Chris Christensen
Costa Mesa, California

Victor J.W. Christie, Ed. D.
Ephrata, Pennsylvania

Lanette Clarke
Antioch, California

John Cobabe
Redondo Beach, CA

Debbie and Randy Coe
Lafayette, Oregon

Wilfred and Dolli Cohen
Santa Ana, California

Marilyn Cooper
Houston, Texas

Ryan Cooper
Yarmouthport, Massachusetts

J.W. Courter
Kevil, Kentucky

Rosalind Cranor
Blacksburg, Virginia

Bob Culver
Northville, Michigan

Ron Damaska
New Brighton, Pennsylvania

Patricia M. Davis
Portland, Oregon

Hal & Meredith DeGood
Des Moines, Iowa

Loretta DeLozier
Lake Placid, Florida

Clive Devenish
Orinda, California

Joe Devine
Council Bluffs, Iowa

Doug Dezso
Maywood, New Jersey

David Dilley
Indianapolis, Indiana

Thomas P. Dimitroff
Corning, New York

Ginny Distel
Tiffin, Ohio

Rod Dockery
Ft. Worth, Texas

L.R. 'Les' Docks
San Antonio, Texas

Rebecca Dodds
Coral Springs, Florida

Brenda Dollen
Minden, Iowa

Darlene Dommel
Minneapolis, Minnesota

Ron Donnelly
Tuscaloosa, Alabama

Kathy Doub
Columbia, Maryland

Robert A. Doyle, C.A.I., I.S.A.
Pleasant Valley, New York

James Dryden
Hot Springs National Park, Arkansas

Jeanne Dunay
Camden, South Carolina

Louise Dumont
Leesburg, Florida

Ken and Jackie Durham
Washington, DC

William Durham
Belvidere, Illinois

Rita and John Ebner
Columbus, Ohio

Bill Edwards
Madison, Indiana

Michael L. Ellis
Costa Mesa, California

Dr. Robert Elsner
Boynton Beach, Florida

Barbara Endter
Rochester, New York

Elaine Ezell
Pasadena, Maryland

Bryce Farnsworth
Fargo, North Dakota

Arthur M. Feldman
Highland Park, Illinois

Linda Fields
Dover, Tennessee

Vicki Flanigan
Winchester, Virginia

Gene Florence
Lexington, Kentucky

Marv Fogleman
Santa Ana, California

Ian Warner
Brampton, Ontario, Canada

Marty Webster
Saline, Michigan

David Weddington
Murfreesboro, Tennessee

Robert Weisblut
Wheaton, Maryland

Pastor Frederick S. Weiser
New Oxford, Pennsylvania

BA Wellman
Westminster, Massachusetts

David Wendel
Poplar Bluff, Missouri

Kaye and Jim Whitaker
Lynnwood, Washington

Douglass White
Orlando, Florida

John 'Grandpa' White
Denver, Colorado

Margaret and Kenn Whitmyer
Gahanna, Ohio

Steven Whysel
Plantation, Florida

Doug Wiesehan
St. Charles, Missouri

Don Williams
Kirksville, Missouri

Linda Williams
Chicopee, Massachusetts

Ron L. Willis
Matlacha, Florida

Roy M. Willis
Lebanon Junction, Kentucky

Jack D. Wilson
Prescott, Arizona

Grant S. Windsor
Richmond, Virginia

Ralph Winslow
Camdenton, Missouri

Nancy Winston
Northwood, New Hampshire

Jo Ellen Winther
Arvada, Colorado

Raphael C. Wise
West Palm Beach, Florida

Dannie Woodard
Weatherford, Texas

Bill Wright
New Albany, Indiana

Libby Yalom
Adelphi, Maryland

Darlene Yohe
Stuttgart, Arkansas

Mary Young
Kettering, Ohio

Willy Young
Reno, Nevada

Audrey Zeder
North Bend, Washington

Auction Houses

We wish to thank the following auction houses whose catalogs have been used as sources for pricing information. Many have granted us permission to reproduce their photographs as well.

A-1 Auction Service
2042 N. Rio Grande Ave., Suite 'E,' Orlando, FL 32804; 407-839-0004; e-mail: a-1auction@cfl.rr.com. Specializing in American antique sales

A&B Auctions, Inc.
17 Sherman St., Marlboro, MA 01752-3314; 508-480-0006 or fax 508-460-6101. Specializing in English ceramics, flow blue, pottery, and Mason's Ironstone

Absolute Auction & Realty, Inc./ Absolute Auction Center
Robert Doyle
PO Box 1739, Pleasant Valley, NY 12569. Antique and estate auctions twice a month at Absolute Auction Center; Free calendar of auctions; www.absoluteauctionrealty.com

Allard Auctions Inc.
Col. Doug Allard
PO Box 460, #1 Museum Lane, St. Ignatius, MT 59865-0460; 406-745-2951 or fax 406-745-2961; allar dauctions.com

America West Archives
Anderson, Warren
PO Box 100, Cedar City, UT 84721; 435-586-9497; e-mail: warren@amer icawestarchives.com. Publishes 26-page illustrated catalog 5 times a year that includes auction section of scarce and historical early western documents, letters, autographs, stock certificates, and other important ephemera, Subscription: $13 per year

American Social History and Social Movements
PO Box 203, Tucker, GA 30085; 678-937-1835; fax 678-937-1837; www.ashsm.com

Americana Auctions
c/o Glen Rairigh
12633 Sandborn, Sunfield, MI 48890. Specializing in Skookum dolls, art glass, and art auctions

Anderson Auctions/Heritage Antiques & Appraisal Services
Suzy McLennan Anderson
65 E. Main St., Holmdel, NJ 07733; 908-946-8801 or fax 908-946-1036. Specializing in American furniture and decorative accessories

Andre Ammelounx
The Stein Auction Company
PO Box 136, Palatine, IL 60078-0136; 847-991-5927 or fax 847-991-5947. Specializing in steins, catalogs available; www.tsaco.com

Aston Americana Auctioneers & Appraisers
2825 Country Club Rd., Endwell, NY 13760-3349; phone/fax: 607-785-6598. Specializing in and appraisers of Americana, folk art, other primitives, furniture, Shaker, fine art, porcelain, and china; Also have auctions on the internet: eBay (folkman 2) and eham mer (folkman@stnylrun.com)

Bider's
397 Methuen St., Lawrence, MA 01843; 978-688-4347 or 978-688-0948. Antiques appraised, purchased, and sold on consignment; www. biders-auction.com

Bill Bertoia Auctions
1881 Spring Rd., Vineland, NJ 08360; 856-692-1881 or fax 856-692-8697. Specializing in toys, dolls, advertising, and related items; e-mail: Bill@BertoiaAuctions.com; www.bertoiaauctions.com

Block's Box
PO Box 51, Trumbull, CT 06611; 203-261-0057 or 203-926-8448. Buy and sell marbles in online auctions; www.blocksite.com

Buffalo Bay Auction Co.
5244 Quam Circle, Rogers, MN 55374; 612-428-8480; or fax 612-428-8879. Specializing in advertising, tins and country store items; e-mail: buffalobay@hotmail.com; buffalobayauction.com

Butterfield & Butterfield
220 San Bruno Ave., San Francisco, CA 94103; 415-861-7500 or fax 415-861-8951. Also located at 7601 Sunset Blvd., Los Angeles, CA 90046; 213-850-7500 or fax 213-850-5843 and 441 West Huron St., Chicago, IL 60610; 312-377-7500 or fax 312-377-7501. Fine Art auctioneers and appraisers since 1865; e-mail: info@butterfields.com; www.butterfields.com

Butterfield, Butterfield & Dunning
755 Church Rd., Elgin, IL 60123; 847-741-3843 or fax 847-741-3589; www.butterfields.com

Cerebro
PO Box 327, E. Prospect, PA 17317-0327; 717-252-2400 or 800-69-LABEL: fax: 717-252-3685; e-mail: Cerebro@Cere bro.com. Specializing in antique advertising labels, especially cigar box labels, cigar bands, food labels, firecracker labels; Holds semiannual auction on tobacco ephemera; Consignments accepted; www.cerebro.com

Charles E. Kirtley
PO Box 2273, Elizabeth City, NC 27096; 919-335-1262. Specializing in World's Fair, Civil War, political, advertising and other American collectibles; e-mail: ckirtley@erols.com

Cincinnati Art Gallery
635 E. Main, Cincinnati, OH 45202; 513-381-2128. Specializing in American art pottery, American and European fine paintings, watercolors; www.cincinnatiartgalleries.com

Collector's Auction Services
R.D. 2, Box 431, Oil City, PA 16301-9426; 814-677-6070; e-mail: director@caswel.com. Specializing in advertising, oil and gas, toys, rare museum and investment-quality antiques; www.caswel.com

Craftsman Auctions
1485 W Housatonic (Rt 20); Pittsfield, MA 01201; 413-448-8922. Specializing in Arts & Crafts furniture and accessories as well as American art pottery; Color catalogs available; www.artsncrafts.com or www.rago arts.com

Dargate Auction Galleries
5607 Baum Boulevard, Pittsburgh, PA 15206; 412-362-3558 or fax 412-362-3574; e-mail: dargate@dargate.com. Specializing in estate auctions featuring fine art, antiques, and collectibles; www.dargate.com

David Rago
333 N. Main, Lambertville, NJ 08530; 609-397-7330 or fax 609-397-6790; e-mail: rago@ragoarts.com. Specializing in American art pottery and Arts and Crafts; www.ragoarts.com

Du Mouchelles
409 Jefferson Ave., Detroit, MI 48226-4300; 313-963-6255 or fax 313-963-8199; dumouchelle.com

Dunbar's Gallery
Leila and Howard Dunbar
76 Haven St., Milford, MA 01757; 508-634-8697 or fax 508-634-8698; e-mail: Dunbars@mediaone.net www.dunbarsgallery.com

Early American History Auctions
Dana Linett, President
PO Box 3341, La Jolla, CA 92038; 858-459-4159 or fax 858-459-4373; www.earlyamerican.com

Early Auction Co.
123 Main St., Milford, OH 45150-1121; 513-831-4833 or fax 513-831-1441; e-mail: info@EarlyAuctionCo.com; EarlyAuctionCo.com

Flying Deuce Auctions & Antiques
1224 Yellowstone Ave., Pocatello, ID 83201-4323; 208-237-2002 or fax 208-237-4544; e-mail: flying2@nicoh.com; www.flying2.com

Fontaine's Auction Gallery
1485 W. Housatonic St., Pittsfield, MA 01201; 413-448-8922 or fax 413-442-1550. Fine quality antiques; important 20th century lighting, clocks, art glass. Color catalogs available; fontaineauction.com

Frank's Antiques & Auctions
2405 N. Kings Rd., Hilliard, FL 32046-3332; 904-845-2870 or fax 904-845-4000. Specializing in antique advertising, country store items, rec room and restaurant decor as well as sporting collectibles, pottery and stoneware; catalogs issued; www.franksauctions.com

Freeman Fine Arts Co. of Philadelphia, Inc.
1808 Chestnut St., Philadelphia, PA 19103; 215-563-9275 or fax 215-563-8236; freemansauction.com

Garth's Auctions Inc.
2690 Stratford Rd., Box 369, Delaware, OH 43015; 740-362-4771; e-mail: info@garths.com or www.garths.com

Glass-Works Auctions
102 Jefferson, East Greenville, PA 18041-11623; 215-679-5849 or fax 215-679-3068; e-mail: glswrk@enter.net. America's leading auction company in early American bottles and glass and barber shop memorabilia; www.glswk-auction.com

Hanna-Whysel Auctioneers & Appraisers
Steven Whysel
3403 Bella Vista Way, Bella Vista, AR, 72714; 501-855-9600. Antiques and art auctions

Harmer Rooke Galleries
32 E. 57th St., 11th Floor, New York, NY 10022-2513; 212-751-1900 or fax 212-758-1713

Heights Antiques
29 Clubhouse Lane, Boynton Beach, FL 33436-6056; 561-736-1362. Specializing in antique barometers and nautical instruments

Henry/Pierce Auctioneers
1456 Carson Court, Homewood, IL 60430-4013; 708-798-7508 or fax 708-799-3594. Specializing in bank auctions

High Noon
9929 Venice Blvd., Los Angeles, CA 90034-5111; 310-202-9010 or fax 310-202-9011. Specializing in cowboy and western collectibles; www.freemansauction.com

History Buff's Auctions
6031 Winterset, Lansing, MI 48911. Specializing in paper collectibles spanning 5 centuries; www.historybuff.com

Horst Auctioneers
Horst Auction Center
50 Durlach Rd. (corner of Rt. 322 & Durlach Rd., West of Ephrata), Ephrata, Lancaster County, PA 17522-9741; 717-859-1331 or 717-738-3080. Voices of Experience; www.horstauction.com

Jackson's, Auctioneers & Appraisers of Fine Art
2229 Lincoln St., Cedar Falls, IA 50613; 319-277-2256 or fax 319-277-1252; e-mail: jacksons@jacksonsauction.com. Specializing in American and European art pottery and art glass, American and European paintings, Russian works of art, decorative arts, toys, and jewelry; www.jacksonsauction.com

James D. Julia
PO Box 830, Rt. 201, Skowhegan Rd., Fairfield, ME 04937-0830; 207-453-7125 or fax 207-453-2502; e-mail: jjulia@juliaauctions.com www.juliaauctions.com

John Toomey Gallery
818 North Blvd., Oak Park, IL 60301-1302; 708-383-5234 or fax 708-383-4828. Specializing in furniture and decorative arts of the Arts & Crafts, Art Deco, and Modern Design movements; modern design expert: Richard Wright; e-mail: arts@oprf.com; www.treadwaygallery.com

Joy Luke Auctioneers & Appraisers
The Gallery
300 East Grove St., Bloomington, IL 61701-5290; 309-828-5533 or fax 309-829-2266; e-mail: joyluke@aol.com; www.joyluke.com

Kit Barry Ephemera Auctions
136 High St., Brattleboro, VT 05301; 802-254-3634. Tradecard and ephemera auctions, fully illustrated catalogs with prices realized; Consignment inquiries welcome; www.trade cards.com/kb

Kurt R. Krueger
160 N. Washington St., PO Box 275, Iola, WI 54945-0275; 715-445-3845 or fax 715-445-4100

L.R. 'Les' Docks
Box 691035, San Antonio, TX 78269-1035; e-mail: docks@texas.net. Providing occasional mail-order record auctions, rarely consigned. The only consignments considered are exceptionally scarce and unusual records. www.docks.home.texas.net

Lang's Sporting Collectibles, Inc.
31R Turtle Cove, Raymond, ME 04071; 207-655-4265

Lloyd Ralston Toys
109 Glover Ave., Norwalk, CT 06850; 203-845-033 or fax 203-845-0366; e-mail: lrt@lloydralstontoys.com; www.lloydralstontoys.com

Lowe, James Lewis
PO Box 8, Norwood, PA 19074; Specializing in Kate Greenaway, postcards; eBay: JLewisLowe@juno.com

Majolica Auctions
Michael G. Strawser
200 North Main, PO Box 332, Wolcottville, IN 46795-0332; 219-854-2859 or fax 219-854-3979; e-mail: michael@strawserauctions.com; Issues colored catalog; www.fiestaauctions.com

Manion's International Auction House, Inc.
PO Box 12214, Kansas City, KS 66112-0214; 913-299-6692 or fax 913-299-6792; e-mail: manions@qni.com. Specializing in international militaria, particularly the US, Germany, and Japan; Extensive catalogs in antiques and collectibles, sports, transportation, political and advertising memorabilia, and vintage clothing and denim; Publishes 9 catalogs for each of the 5 categories per year; Request a free sample of past auctions, 1 issue of current auction for $7 or a 6-catalog subscription for $35; www.manions.com

Maritime Auctions
935 US Rt. 1, PO Box 322, York, ME 03909-0322; 207-363-4247 or fax 353-1415; www.maritiques.com or Auction: www.eswap.com

McMasters Doll Auctions
PO Box 1755, 5855 Glenn Highway, Cambridge, OH 43725-8768; 740-432-4419 or fax 740-432-3191; or 800-842-3526; e-mail: mcmasters@jadeinc.com; angelfire.com/oh/mcmastersauctions

Michael Ivankovich Auctions, Inc.
PO Box 1536, Doylestown, PA, 18901; 215-345-6094 or fax 215-345-6692. Specializing in early hand-colored photography and prints; Auction held 4 times each year, providing opportunity for collectors and dealers to compete for the largest variety of Wallace Nutting, Wallace Nutting-like pictures, Maxfield Parrish, Bessie Pease Gutmann, R. Atkinson Fox, Philip Boileau, Harrison Fisher, etc.

Michael John Verlangieri
PO Box 844, Cambria, CA 93428; 805-927-4428. Specializing in fine California pottery; cataloged auctions (video tapes available); www.calpots.com

Monsen & Baer, Annual Perfume Bottle Auction
Monsen, Randall; and Baer, Rod
Box 529, Vienna, VA 22183; 703-938-2129 or fax 703-242-1357. Cataloged auctions of perfume bottles; Will purchase, sell, and accept consignments; Specializing in commercial, Czechoslovakian, Lalique, Baccarat, Victorian, crown top, factices, miniatures

Neal Auction Company
4038 Magazine St., New Orleans, LA 70115; 504-899-5329 or 1-800-467-5329; fax: 504-897-3803; www.nealauction.com

New England Absentee Auctions
16 6th St., Stamford, CT 06905-4610; 203-975-9055; fax/e-mail: 203-323-6407. Specializing in Quimper pottery; neaauction@aol.com

Noel Barrett Antiques & Auctions
PO Box 300, 6183 Carversville Rd., Carversville, PA 18913; 215-297-5109 or fax 215-297-0457; e-mail: nba@comcat.com; www.noelbarret.com

Norman C. Heckler & Company
79 Bradford Corner Rd., Woodstock Valley, CT 06282-2002; 860-974-1634 or fax 860-974-2003. Auctioneers and appraisers specializing in early glass and bottles; e-mail: heckler@neca.com; www.hecklerauction.com

Nostalgia Co.
21 S. Lake Dr., Hackensack, NJ 07601-3098; 201-488-4536; www.nostalgiapubs.com

Pacific Glass Auctions
1507 21st St., Ste. 203, Sacramento, CA 95814; 916-443-3296 or fax 916-443-3199; www.pacglass.com

Past Tyme Pleasures
Steve Howard
PMB #204, 2491 San Ramon Blvd., #1, San Ramon, CA 94583; 925-484-4488 or fax 925-484-2551. Offers 2 absentee auction catalogs per year pertaining to old advertising items; e-mail: pasttyme@excite.com; www.pasttyme.com

Phillips
406 E. 79th St., New York, NY 10021-1498; 212-570-4830; www.phillips-auctions.com

Richard Opfer Auctioneering, Inc.
1919 Greenspring Dr., Timonium, MD 21093-4113; 410-252-5035; fax: 410-252-5863; e-mail: info@opferauction.com; www.opferauction.com

Roan Bros. Auction Gallery
R.R. 4, Box 118, Cogan Station, PA 17728; 717-494-0170; e-mail: roaninc@srlink.net

Schoolmaster Auctions and Real Estate
Kenn Norris
PO Box 4830; 513 N. 2nd St., Sanderson, TX 79848; 915-345-2640. Specializing in school-related items, barbed wire and related literature, and L'il Abner

Skinner, Inc.
Auctioneers & Appraisers of Antiques and Fine Arts
The Heritage on the Garden, 63 Park Plaza, Boston, MA 02116-3925; 617-350-5400 or fax 617-350-5429. Second address: 357 Main St., Bolton, MA 01740; 978-779-6241 or fax 978-779-5144; www.skinnerinc.com

Smith & Jones, Inc.
12 Clark Lane, Sudbury, MA 01776; 508-443-5517 or fax 508-443-8045. Specializing in Dedham dinnerware, Buffalo china, and important American art pottery; Full-color catalogs available; smithandjonesauctions.com

SOLDUSA.COM (formerly Dixie Sporting Collectibles)
1206 Rama Rd., Charlotte, NC 28211-4345; 704-364-2900 or 877-SoldUSA; fax 704-364-2322; Specializing in fine sporting collectibles; e-mail: gun1898@aol.com or www.Soldusa.com

Sotheby's
1334 York Ave., New York, NY 10021; 212-606-7000; www.sothebys.com

Stanton's Auctioneers & Realtors
144 S. Main St., PO Box 146, Vermontville, MI 49096-0146; 517-726-0181 or fax 517-726-0060. Specializing in all types of property, at auction, anywhere; www.stantons-auctions.com

Steffen's Historical Militaria
Roger S. Steffen
14 Murnan Rd., Cold Springs, KY 41076; 859-431-4499 or fax 859-431-3113. Specializing in quality militaria, military art, rare books, antique firearms; www.steffensmilitaria.com

Superior Galleries
9478 West Olympic Boulevard, Beverly Hills, CA 90212-4246; 310-203-9855 or fax 310-203-0496. Specializing in manuscripts, decorative and fine arts, Hollywood memorabilia, sports memorabilia, stamps, and coins; www.superiorsc.com

Swann Galleries, Inc.
104 E. 25th St., New York, NY 10010; 312-254-4710 or fax 212-979-1017; www.swanngalleries.com

Three Rivers Collectibles
Wendy and Leo Frese
PO Box 551542, Dallas, TX 75355; 214-341-5165. Annual Red Wing and Rum-Rill pottery and stoneware auctions

Toy Scouts, Inc.
137 Casterton Ave., Akron, OH 44303-1543; 330-836-0668 or fax 330-869-8668; e-mail: toyscouts@toyscouts.com. Specializing in baby-boom era collectibles; www.toyscouts.com

Tradewinds Auctions
Henry Taron
PO Box 249, Manchester-By-The-Sea, MA 01944-0249; 508-768-3327; www.tradewindantiques.com

Treadway Gallery, Inc.
2029 Madison Rd., Cincinnati, OH 45208-3218; 513-321-6742 or fax 513-871-7722; Specializing in American Art Pottery, American and European art glass, European ceramics, Italian glass, fine American and European paintings and graphics, and furniture and decorative arts of the Arts & Crafts, Art Nouveau, Art Deco, and Modern Design Movements. Modern design expert: Thierry Lorthior. Members: National Antique Dealers Association, American Art Pottery Association, International Society of Appraisers, American Ceramic Arts Society, Ohio Decorative Arts Society, Art Gallery Association of Cincinnati; www.treadwaygallery.com

VintagePostcards.Com
Antique Postcards for Collectors
60-C Skiff St., Suite 116, Hamden CT 06517; 203-248-6621 or fax 203-281-0387; e-mail: quality@vintagepostcards.com; www.vintagepostcards.com

Vicki and Bruce Waasdorp
PO Box 434; 10931 Main St.; Clarence, NY 14031; 716-759-2361. Specializing in decorated stoneware. www.antiques-stoneware.com

Weschler's
Adam A. Weschler & Son
905 E. St. N.W., Washington, DC 20004-2006; 202-628-1281; www.weschlers.com

William Doyle Galleries
Auctioneers & Appraisers
175 East 87th St., New York, NY 10128; 212-427-2730 or fax 212-369-0892; e-mail: info@doylegalleries.com or www.doylegalleries.com

Willis Henry Auctions
22 Main St., Marshfield, MA 02050-2808; 781-834-7774 or fax 781-826-3520; www.willishenry.com

York Town Auction Inc.
1625 Haviland Rd., York, PA 17404; 717-751-0211; fax 717-767-7729; e-mail: yorktownauction@cyberia.com; Specializing in the sale of antiques, art, collections, fine furnishings, and real estate; www.yorktown.com

Directory of Contributors

When contacting any of the buyers/sellers listed in this part of the Directory by mail, you must include a SASE (stamped, self-addressed envelope) if you expect a reply. As hectic as our lifestyles are, the time it saves them is probably worth more to them than the price of a stamp. Not only that, but trying to decipher someone's handwritten name and address can be very frustrating. Sometimes even zip codes are unreadable, and even more time is required to double check zip code numbers. And in the end, if 'Rosen' becomes 'Rirer' and 'Ave. 5' becomes 'Ave. S,' even if the person you contacted was gracious enough to answer you, you probably won't ever know he did. Many of these people are professional appraisers and there will be a fee for their time and service. Find out up front. Include a clear photo if you want an item identified. Most items cannot be described clearly enough to make an identification without a photo.

If you call and get their answering machine, when you leave your number so that they can return your call, tell them to call back collect. And please take the differences in time zones into consideration. 7:00 AM in the Midwest is only 4:00 AM in California! And if you're in California, remember that even 7:00 PM is too late to call the East Coast. Most people work and are gone during the daytime. Even some of our antique dealers say they prefer after-work phone calls. Don't assume that a person who deals in a particular field will be able to help you with related items. They may seem related to you when they are not.

Please, we need your help. This book sells in such great numbers that allowing their names to be published can create a potential nightmare for each advisor and contributor. Please do your part to help us minimize this, so that we can retain them on our board and in turn pass their experience and knowledge on to you through our book. Their only obligation is to advise us, not to evaluate your holdings. Many of our people tell us that even with the occasional problem, they feel that the good outweighs the bad and makes all their hard work worthwhile.

Alabama

Cataldo, Gene
C.E. Cataldo
4726 Panorama Dr., S.E., Huntsville, 35801; 256-536-6893; e-mail: genecams@aol.com. Specializing in classic and used cameras

Donnelly, Ron
Saturday Heroes
6302 Championship Dr., Tuscaloosa, 35405. Specializing in Big Little Books, movie posters, premiums, western heroes, Gone With the Wind, character collectibles, early Disney; Inquiries require SASE; No free appraisals

Lippa, Matt; and Schaaf, Elizabeth
Artisans
PO Box 256, Mentone, 35984; 256-634-4037; e-mail: artisans@folkartisans.com. Specializing in folk art, quilts, painted and folksy furniture, tramp art, whirligigs, windmill weights; www.folkartisans.com

Walthall, Judith and Robert
PO Box 4465, Huntsville, 35815; 256-881-9198. Judith founded Peanut Pals in 1978. Robert has served two terms as president of Peanut Pals. Specializing in Planters Peanuts memorabilia; also Old Crow collectibles

Arizona

Moyer, Patsy
12415 W. Monte Vista Rd., Avondale, 85323; e-mail: moddoll@yahoo.com. Collector Books author on dolls

Nelson, Maxine
7657 E. Hazelwood St., Scottsdale, 85251. Specializing in Vernon Kilns; Author of *Collectible Vernon Kilns* (out of print). SASE appreciated for inquiries

Roberts, Fred and Marilyn
Bah Humbug Collectibles
PO Box 5733, Lake Montezuma, 86342-5733 or fax 815-425-9394; e-mail: bah-humbug@juno.com. Specializing in Hummel figurines

Wilson, Jack D.
1514 Eagle Ridge Road, Prescott, 86301-5418; 928-445-5137; e-mail: jdwilson1@earthlink.net. Specializing in Phoenix and Consolidated glass; Buying Ruba Rombic; Author of *Phoenix and Consolidated Art Glass: 1926 – 1980*; www.home.earthlink.net/~jdwilson1/

Arkansas

Dryden, James
Dryden Pottery
PO Box 603, Hot Springs National Park, 71902; 501-627-4201. Specializing in hand-thrown artware vases, mugs, ovenware, etc.

Freyaldenhoven, Tony
PO Box 1295, Conway, 72033; 501-343-4197; e-mail: riodelcorazon@hotmail.com. Specializing in Camark pottery

Roenigk, Martin
Mechantiques
Crescent Hotel & Spa
75 Prospect Ave., Eureka Springs, 72632; 800-671-6333; e-mail: mroenigk@aol.com. Specializing in mechanical musical instruments, music boxes, band organs, musical clocks and watches, coin pianos, orchestrions, monkey organs, automata, mechanical birds and dolls, etc.; www.mechantiques.com

Yohe, Darlene
Timberview Antiques
PO Box 343, Stuttgart, 72160; 870-673-3437. Specializing in American pattern glass, historical glass, Victorian pattern glass, carnival glass, and custard glass

California

Aaronson, Barbara and Steve
The Victorian Lady
PO Box 7522, 7522 Northridge, 91327; 818-368-6052; e-mail: bjaaronson@aol.com. Specializing in Victorian glass; TheVictorianLady.com

Ales, Beverly Schell
4046 Graham St., Pleasanton, 94566-5619; 925-846-5297; e-mail: Beverlyales@hotmail.com or Kniferests@sbcglobal.net. Specializing in knife rests and editor of *Knife*

Rests of Yesterday and Today
Berg, Paul
PO Box 8895, Newport Beach, 92620. Author of *Nineteenth Century Photographica Cases and Wall Frames*

Brooks, Mike
7355 Skyline, Oakland, 94611; 510-339-1751 (evenings). Specializing in typewriters, transistor radios, early televisions, Statue of Liberty

Carter, Tina M.
882 S. Mollison, El Cajon, 92020-6506; 619-440-5043. Specializing in teapots, tea-related items, tea tins, children's and toy tea sets, plastic cookie cutters, etc.; Book on teapots available; Send $16 (includes postage) or $17 for CA residents, Canada: add $5, to above address

Chipman, Jack
California Spectrum
PO Box 1079, Venice, 90294-1079. Specializing in California ceramics; author of *Collector's Encyclopedia of California Pottery*, and *Collector's Encyclopedia of Bauer Pottery*, autographed copies available from author; either book: $28.45 ppd., +(CA) tax of $2.35

Christensen, Pat and Chris
1067 Salvador St., Costa Mesa, 92626. Specializing in open salts

Clarke, Lanette
5021 Toyon Way, Antioch, 94532; 925-776-7784; e-mail: Lanette_Clarke@msn.com. Co-founder of *Haeger Pottery Collectors of America*; Specializing in Haeger and Royal Hickman

Cobabe, John
800 So. Pacific Coast Hwy; Suite 8-301; Redondo Beach 90277; 310-465-0752; e-mail: johncobabe@aol.com. Specializing in Amphora, Zsolnay, and Massier

Cohen, Wilfred and Dolli
Antiques & Art Glass
PO Box 27151, Santa Ana, 92799; 714-545-5673; e-mail: antsandart glass@aol.com. Specializing in Wave Crest (C.F. Monroe); French cameo glass; Victorian-era art and pattern glass (salt shakers, toothpick holders, syrups, cruets, sugar shakers, tumblers, biscuit jars, table and pitcher sets); art glass and cameo glass open salts; custard and ruby-stained glass; burmese, peachblow, and amberina glass; pottery by Moorcroft (pre-1935 only); Buffalo (Deldare and Emerald ware); Polia Pillin; Shelley China; Chintz China; and Clarice Cliff. Please include SASE for reply; a photo is very helpful for identification.

Conroy, Barbara J.
PO Box 2369, Santa Clara, 95055-2369. Specializing in Commercial China; author and historian

Cox, Susan N.
800 Murray Drive, El Cajon, 92020; 619-697-5922. Specializing in California pottery and Frankoma; e-mail: antiqfever@aol.com

Devenish, Clive
PO Box 907, Orinda, 94563; 925-254-8383. Specializing in still and mechanical banks; Buys and sells

Ehrhard, J. David
Psycho-Ceramic Restorations
7212 Valmont St., Tujunga, 91042. Specializing in restoration of ceramics, collects Susie Cooper and other British pottery, Mabel Lucie Attwell, 'Old Bill' china by Grimades, etc., Artist: Bruce Bairnsfather

Ellis, Michael L.
266 Rose Ln., Costa Mesa, 92627; 949-646-7112 or fax 949-645-4919. Author (Collector Books) of *Collector's Guide to Don Winton Designs, Identification & Values*; Specializing in Twin Winton

Fogleman, Marv
Marv's Memories
73 Waterman, Irvine, 92602. Specializing in American and English dinnerware

George, Tony
22431-B160 Antonio Pkwy., #252, Rancho Santa Margarita, 92688; 949-589-6075. Specializing in watch fobs

Gibson, Pat
38280 Guava Dr., Newark, 94560; 510-792-0586. Specializing in R.A. Fox

Gunther, Candace (Candelaine)
Phone: 626-796-4568 or fax 626-796-7172; e-mail: candelaine@aol.com. Specializing in Steiff and Schuco bears and animals; send SASE for list

Harrison, Gwynne
PO Box 1, Mira Loma, 91752-0001; 909-685-5434; e-mail: morgan99@pe.net. Specializing in Autumn Leaf (Jewel Tea)

Hibbard, Suzi
WanderWares
e-mail: Dragon_Ware@hotmail.com. Specializing in Dragonware and 1000 Faces china; All inquiries via e-mail should be accompanied by clear color pictures. If you wish to send them regualr mail, please include a LSASE or there will be no response; related Dragonware www.Dragonware.com

Howard, Steve
Past Tyme Pleasures
PMB #204, 2491 San Ramon Valley Blvd., #1, San Ramon, 94583; 925-484-4488 or fax 925-484-2551. Specializing in antique American firearms, bowie knives, Western Americana, old advertising, vintage gambling items, barber and saloon items

Krumme, Michael
PO Box 48225, Los Angeles, 90048-0225; 323-937-1470; e-mail: mkrumme@pacbell.net. Specializing in Paden City Glass

Langtree, Elizabeth
PO Box 1616, Santa Ynez, 93460. Collector of Borsato figures

Main Street Antique Mall
237 E Main St., El Cajon, 92020; 619-447-0800 or fax 619-447-0815.

Maurer, Oveda L.
Oveda Maurer Antiques
34 Greenfield Ave., San Anselmo, 94960; 415-454-6439. Specializing in 18th-century and early 19th-century American furniture, lighting, pewter, hearthware, glass, folk art, and paintings; Open by chance and appointment

The Meadows Collection
Mark and Adela Meadows
PO Box 819, Carnelian Bay, 96140; 530-546-5516; e-mail: meadows@meadowscollection.com. Specializing in Gouda and Quimper; lecturers, authors of *Quimper Pottery, A Guide to Origins, Styles, and Values*, serving on the board of directors of the Associated Antiques Dealers of America; Please include SASE for inquiries; www.meadowscollection.com

Needham, Leonard
MacAdam's Antiques
707-748-4286; DB1918@msn.com. Specializing in advertising www.tias.com/stores/macadams

Pardini, Dick
3107 N. El Dorado St., Dept. SAPG, Stockton, 95204-3412; 209-466-5550 (recorder may answer). Specializing in California Perfume Company items dating from 1886 to 1928 and 'go-with' related companies: buyer and information center. Not interested in items that have Avon, Perfection, or Anniversary Keepsake markings. California Perfume Company offerings must be accompanied by a photo, photocopy, or sketching along with a condition report and, most importantly, price wanted. Inquiries require large SASE and must state what information you are seeking; not necessary if offering items for sale.

Pasquali, Jim
479 Church #4, San Francisco, 94114; 415-861-4184. Author of *Sanfords Guide to Garden City Pottery, A Hidden Treasure of Northern California*

Roller, Gayle
PO Box 222, San Marcos, 92079-0222. Specializing in Hagen-Renaker

Rosewitz, Michele
3165 McKinley, San Bernardino, 92404; 909-862-8534; e-mail: rosetree@sprintmail.com. Specializing in glass knives manufactured in the USA during the 1920s through the 1950s; All requests for information should include a SASE

Sanford, Steve and Martha
230 Harrison Ave., Campbell, 95008; 408-978-8408; www.sanfords.com. Authors of 2 books on Brush-McCoy and *Sanfords Guide to McCoy Pottery* (available from the authors)

Shrader, Lila
Shrader Antiques
2025 Hwy. 199, Crescent City, 95531. Specializing in railroad, steamship, and other transportation memorabilia; Shelley china (and its predecessor, Foley China); Buffalo china and Buffalo Pottery including Deldare; Niloak, and Zell (and Haag)

Stella's Collectibles
Pieces of the Past
19032 S. Vermont Ave., Gardena, (Space 11), 90248; 310-316-7198; Culver City Antique Center, 5431 S. Sepulveda Blvd, Culver City (Space 320); Enchanted Treasures, Lake Elsinore (Space 25); Collector's Corral, Lake Elsinore. Specializing in quality glass and china

Stillwell, Liz
Our Attic Antiques & Belleek
PO Box 1074, Pico Rivera, 90660; 323-257-3879 or 562-949-0592. Specializing in Irish and American Belleek

Tanner, Joseph and Pamela
Wheeler-Tanner Escapes
6442 Canyon Creek Way, Elk Grove, 95758-5431; 916-684-4006. Specializing in handcuffs, leg shackles, balls and chains, restraints and padlocks of all kinds (including railroad), locking and non-locking devices; Also Houdini memorabilia: autographs, photos, posters, books, letters, etc.

Thoerner, Sharon
15549 Ryon Ave., Bellflower, 90706; 562-866-1555. Specializing in covered animal dishes, powder jars with animal and human figures, slag glass

Thornton, Don
PO Box 57, Moss Beach, 94038; 650-728-7978; e-mail: thorntonhouse.com. Specializing in egg beaters and apple parers; author of *The Eggbeater Chronicles, 2nd Edition* ($50.45 ppd.); and *Apple Parers* ($59 ppd.)

Vines, Linda
2911 4th St., #112, Santa Monica, 90405; 310-314-0402; lleigh2000@hotmail.com. Specializing in Snow Babies, all holidays (Christmas, Easter, Halloween), dolls, toys, Steiff, and Uncle Sam

Webb, Frances Finch
1589 Gretel Lane, Mountain View, 94040. Specializing in Kay Finch ceramics

Woodbury, Virginia, President of American Hatpin Society
20 Montecillo Dr., Rolling Hills Estates, 90274; 310-326-2195. Quarterly meetings and newsletters; Membership: $30 per year; SASE required when requesting information

Brown, David L.
Stevengraph Collectors Assn.
2103-2829 Arbutus Rd., Victoria, British Columbia, V8N 5X5; 250-477-9896. Specializing in Stevengraphs

Melis, Mirko
Marcelle Antiques
PO Box 270, Waterdown, Ontario, L0R 2H0. Specializing in Moser art glass, Dresden Germany lace figurines, Russian works of art; Member of Antique Appraisal Association of America, Inc., and AADA (Associated Antique Dealers of America, Inc.)

Warner, Ian
PO Box 93022, 499 Main St. S., Brampton, Ontario, L6Y 4V8; 905-453-9074 or fax 905-453-2931. Specializing in Wade porcelain and Swanky swigs, author of *The World of Wade, The World of Wade Book 2, Wade Price Trends,* and *The World of Head Vase Planters,* Co-author: Mike Posgay

Geary, William L.
Glass Appraiser (American & European Art Glass)
PO Box 2247, Colorado Springs 80901; telephone/fax: 719-527-0810; e-mail: nordglass@aol.com. Specializing in Nordic art glass

Heck, Carl
Carl Heck Decorative Arts
Box 8416, Aspen, 81612; phone/fax: 970-925-8011; e-mail: webmaster@carlheck.com. Specializing in original Tiffany lamps, art glass, windows and chandeliers; Also reverse-painted and leaded-glass table lamps, stained and beveled glass windows, bronzes, paintings, etc.; Buy and sell; Fee for written appraisals; Please include SASE for reply; www.carlheck.com

Mackin, Bill
Author of *Cowboy and Gunfighter Collectibles;* available from author: 1137 Washington St., Craig, 81625; 970-824-6717, Paperback: $25; Other titles available; Specializing in old and fine spurs, guns, gun leather, cowboy gear, Western Americana (Collection in the Museum of Northwest Colorado, Craig)

Over, Naomi L.
8909 Sharon Lane, Arvada, 80002; 303-424-5922. Specializing in ruby glassware, author of *Ruby Glass of the 20th Century, Book I,* autographed copies available from author for $25.00 softbound or $32.50 hardbound, ppd.; Book II available (1999 values) for $32.50 softbound or $42.50 hardbound, ppd. Naomi will attempt to make photo identifications for all who include a SASE with correspondence.

Segelke, Cathy; and James, Pat
970-847-3759 (Pat). Specializing in crocks, Western Pottery Mfg. Co. (Denver, CO)

Toohey, Marlena
703 S. Pratt Pky., Longmont, 80501; 303-678-9726. Specializing in black amethyst and black opaque glass (buy, sell, or trade); Books available from author: Book 1 (over 600 colored pictures, descriptions, and price guide), $34 ppd. (nearly out of print); Book 2 (over 1,200 colored pictures, descriptions and price guide), $33 ppd. for soft bound ($44 ppd. for hard bound)

White, John 'Grandpa'
Grandpa's Depot
6720 E. Mississippi Ave., Unit B, Denver, 80224; 303-758-8540 or fax 303-321-2889. Specializing in railroad-related items; Catalogs available

Winther, Jo Ellen
8449 W. 75th Way, Arvada, 80005; 800-872-2345 or 303-421-2371. Specializing in Coors

Block, Robert and Stan
Block's Box
PO Box 51, Trumbull, 06611; 203-926-8448; e-mail: blockschip@aol.com. Specializing in marbles

Bondhus, Sandra V.
Box 100, Unionville, 06085; 860-678-1808. Author of *Quimper Pottery: A French Folk Art Faience;* Specializing in Quimper pottery

Fink, Paul
Fun & Games
PO Box 488, Kent, 06757; 860-927-4001. Specializing in board games

Guido, Karen M.
Karen Michelle
PO Box 489, Bridgewater, 06752. Specializing in tiles; Buy & sell; Books on tiles available, many out of print; Fee for written appraisal; Please include SASE for inquiries; www.AntiqueTiles.com

Lehrer, Gary
16 Mulberry Road
Woodbridge 06525-1717. Specializing in pens and pencils; Catalog available; www.gopens.com

MacSorley, Earl
823 Indian Hill Rd., Orange, 06477; 203-387-1793 (after 7:00 p.m.). Specializing in nutcrackers, Bessie Pease Gutmann prints, figural lift-top spittoons

Postcards International
Martin J. Shapiro
2321 Whitney Ave., Suite 102, PO Box 185398, Hamden, 06518; 203-248-6621 or fax 203-248-6628. Specializing in vintage picture postcards; www.vintagepostcards.com.

Thalberg, Bruce
Mountain View Dr., Weston, 06883; 203-227-8175. Specializing in canes and walking sticks: novelty, carved, and Black

Van Deusen, Hobart D.
28 The Green, Watertown, 06795; 860-945-3456; e-mail: rtn.hoby@snet.net. Specializing in Canton; SASE required when requesting information

Vuono, Mark
16 6th St., Stamford, 06905; 203-357-0892 (10 a.m. to 5:30 p.m. E.S.T.). Specializing in historical flasks, blown 3-mold glass, blown American glass

Durham, Ken and Jackie (By appointment)
909 26 St. N.W., Suite 502, Washington, DC 20037. Specializing in slot machines, jukeboxes, arcade machines, trade stimulators, vending machines, and service manuals; www.GameRoomAntiques.com

Barnes, Jacqueline Linscott
Line Jewels
3557 Nicklaus Dr., Titusville, 32780; 321-267-9170; e-mail: bluebellwt@aol.com. Specializing in glass insulators and other telephone items; Distributor of the only known set of books dealing with insulators, *North American Glass Insulators* (2 volumes), and accompanying price guide; LSASE required for information

Bettinger, Robert
PO Box 333, Mt. Dora, 32756; 352-735-3575; e-mail: rgbett@aol.com; RobertBettinger.com. General antiques, specializing in American art pottery and glass

DeLozier, Loretta
101 Grandville Blvd., Lake Placid, 33852. Author of *Collector's Encyclopedia of Lefton China, Books I, II,* and *III,* and *Lefton Price Guide;* Specializing in Lefton China; Buy, sell, and consign; Fee for written appraisals

Dodds, Rebecca
Silver Flute
PO Box 670664, Coral Springs, 33067. Specializing in jewelry

Dumont, Louise
318 Palo Verde Dr., Leesburg, 34748. Specializing in cookie jars, Abingdon

Elsner, Dr. Robert
29 Clubhouse Lane, Boynton Beach, 33436; 561-736-1362. Specializing in antique barometers and nautical instruments

France, Madeleine
PO Box 15555, Ft. Lauderdale, 33318; 954-584-0009. Specializing in top-quality perfume bottles: Rene Lalique, Steuben, Czechoslovakian, DeVilbiss, Baccarat, Commercials; French doré bronze and decorative arts

Hudson, Hardy
Our Antiques Market
5453 Lake Howell Rd., Winter Park, 32792; 407-657-2100 from 11:00 a.m. to 6:00 p.m. or (home) 407-647-3454; e-mail: todiefor@mindspring.com. Specializing in majolica, American art pottery (buying one piece or entire collections); Also buying Weller (garden ornaments, birds, Hudson, Sicard, Sabrinian, Glendale, or animal related), Roseville, Grueby, Newcomb, Overbeck, Kay Finch, Clewell, Tiffany, etc.

Joyce, Harriet
415 Soft Shadow Lane, DeBary, 32713. Specializing in Cracker Jack and Checkers (a competitor) early prizes and Flossie Fisher items

Kamm, Dorothy
PO Box 7460, Port St. Lucie, 34985-7460; 561-465-4008 or fax 561-460-9050; e-mail: dorothykamm@usa.net. Specializing in American painted porcelain; Author of

American Painted Porcelain: Identification & Value Guide (Collector Books), *Comprehensive Guide to American Painted Porcelain* (Antique Trader Books), and *Painted Porcelain Jewelry and Buttons: Identification & Value Guide* (Collector Books). Publishes *Dorothy Kamm's Porcelain Collector's Companion*, bimonthly newsletter, subscription: $30 per year

Kuritzky, Louis
4510 NW 17th Place, Gainesville, 32605; 352-377-3193. Author (Collector Books) of *Collector's Guide to Bookends*

McNerny, Kathryn
118 Creek Hollow Lane, Middleburg, 32068. Author (Collector Books) on blue and white stoneware, primitives, tools

Posner, Judy
October – May: PO Box 2194 SC, Englewood, FL 34295, fax: 941-475-2645; e-mail: judyandjef@aol.com. Specializing in Disneyana, Black memorabilia, salt and pepper shakers, souvenirs of the USA, character and advertising memorabilia, figural pottery; Buy, sell, collect; Informal appraisals: $5+LSASE and photo of item; www.judyposner.com

Rodgers, Joanne
c/o Stretch Glass Society
508 Turnberry Lane, St. Augustine, 32080. Membership, $22 (US) or $24 (Canada); Quarterly newsletter with color photos; Annual spring convention

Rolfes, Herbert
Yesterday's World
PO Box 398, Mt. Dora, 32756; 352-735-3947; e-mail: NY1939@aol.com. Specializing in World's Fairs and Expositions

Shaw, John
2201 Scenic Ridge Court, Mt. Flora, 32757 (November to May, See Maine listing for remaining months); 352-735-3831. Specializing in dairy bottles

Snyder-Haug, Diane
PO Box 815, St. Petersburg, 33731. Specializing in women's clothing, 1850 – 1940

Supnick, Mark
2771 Oakbrook Manor, Ft. Lauderdale, 33332. Author of *Collecting Hull Pottery's Little Red Riding Hood* ($12.95 ppd.); Specializing in American pottery

Vogel, Janice and Richard
4720 E. Fort King St., Ocala, 34470-1501; 352-694-5776. Authors of *Victorian Trinket Boxes* and *Conta & Boehme Porcelain*; Specializing in Conta and Boehme German porcelain

White, Douglass
A-1 Auction
2042 N. Rio Grande Ave., Suite E, Orlando, 32804. 407-839-0004; e-mail: a1auction@cfl.rr.com. Specializing in Fulper, Arts & Crafts furniture (photos helpful)

Whysel, Steven
7867 N.W. 11th St., Plantation, 33322. Specializing in Art Nouveau, 19th- and 20th-century art

Willis, Ron L.
PO Box 278, Matlacha, 33993; 941-282-5567. Specializing in military collectibles

Wise, Raphael C.
The Collector's Stop
12018 Suellen Circle, West Palm Beach, 33414; 561-793-0986. Specializing in Wedgwood Jasper Ware, Rosenthal (dogs & cats only), Moorcroft, Buffalo Deldare and Emerald Ware, Heisey, contemporary paperweights, English porcelains

Georgia

Bailey, Wayne and Gale
3152 Fence Rd., Dacula, 30019; 770-963-5736. Specializing in Goebels (Friar Tuck)

Glenn, Walter
3420 Sonata Lane, Alpharetta, 30004; 678-624-1298. Specializing in Frankart

Hoefs, Steven
PO Box 1024, Avalon, 90704; 310-510-2623. Specializing in Catalina Island Pottery; author of book, available from the author

Joiner, John R.
Aviation Collectors
173 Green Tree Dr., Newnan, 30265; 770-502-9565; e-mail: propJoiner@mindspring.com. Specializing in commercial aviation collectibles

Jones, Donald
107 Rivers Edge Dr., Savannah, 31406; 912-354-2133. Specializing in vintage tennis collectibles; SASE with inquiries please

Illinois

Broom, Jim
Box 65, Effingham, 62401. Specializing in opalescent pattern glassware

Feldman, Arthur M.
Arthur M. Feldman Gallery
1815 St. Johns Ave., Highland Park, 60035; 847-432-8858 or fax 847-266-1199. Specializing in Judaica, fine art, and antiques;
www.JudaicaConnection.com

Garmon, Lee
1529 Whittier St., Springfield, 62704; 217-789-9574. Specializing in Royal Haeger, Royal Hickman, glass animals; Co-author (Collector Books) of *Glass Animals and Figural Flower Frogs of the Depression Era*

Griffith, Woody
PO Box 408277, Chicago, 60640. Specializing in De Vilbiss perfumes and perfume lamps

Hall, Doris and Burdell
B&B Antiques
210 W. Sassafras Dr., Morton, 61550-1254. Authors of *Morton's Potteries: 99 Years* (Vols. I and II); Specializing in Morton pottery, American dinnerware, early American pattern glass, historical items

Hastings, Mary Jane
310 West 1st South, Mt. Olive, 62069; phone/fax: 217-999-7519. Specializing in Chintz dinnerware

Hoffmann, Pat and Don, Sr.
1291 N. Elmwood Dr., Aurora, 60506-1309; 630-859-3435: e-mail: warwick@thefoxnet.net. Authors of *Warwick, A to W*, a supplement to *Why Not Warwick?*; video regarding Warwick decals currently available. P.C.

The Home Place Antiques
Durham, William; Galaway, William
615 S. State St., Belvidiere, 61008; 815-544-0577. Specializing in Tea Leaf ironstone and white ironstone

Hooks, Dee
13050 Blackstump Rd., Percy, 62272; 618-965-3832. Specializing in R.S. Prussia, Royal Bayreuth, Haviland, other fine china

Hopp, Dennis Carl
Midcentury
Chicago, 773-935-7872. Specializing in 20th-century design, glass, pottery, metal, art

Long, Dee
112 S. Center, Lacon, 61540. Specializing in reamers

Martin, Jim
R.R. 1, 1095 215th Ave., Monmouth, 61462; 309-734-2703. Specializing in Old Sleepy Eye, Monmouth pottery, Western Stoneware

Miller, Larry; and Strickfaden, Dick
218 Devron Circle, E. Peoria, 61611-1605. Specializing in German and Czechoslovakian Erphila

Ochsner, Grace
Grace Ochsner Doll House
1636 E. County Rd. 2700, Niota, 62358; 217-755-4362. Specializing in piano babies, bisque German dolls and figurines

Rastello, Lisa
Milkweed Antiques
5N531 Ancient Oak Lane, St. Charles, 60175; 630-377-4612. Specializing in Depression-Era collectibles

Rhoden, Joan and Charles
Rhoden Books & Publishing
8693 N. 1950 East Rd., Georgetown, 61846-6264; 217-662-8046; e-mail: rhoden@soltec.net; www.antiqueref.com. Specializing in new reference books on antiques and collectibles, Heisey and other Elegant glassware, spice tins, lard tins, and Yard-Long Prints; Co-authors of *Those Wonderful Yard-Long Prints and More*, and *More Wonderful Yard-Long Prints, Book II*, and *Yard-Long Prints, Book III*, illustrated value guides

Schwab, Betty and Larry
The Paperweight Shoppe
2507 Newport Dr., Bloomington, 61704; 309-662-1956; e-mail: larry@thepaperweightshoppe.com. Specializing in glass paperweights; www.thepaperweightshoppe.com

Spencer, Dick
Glass and More (Shows only)
1203 N. Yale, O'Fallon, 62269; 618-632-9067. Specializing in Cambridge, Fenton, Fostoria, Heisey, etc.

Spiess, Greg
230 E. Washington, Joliet, 60433; 815-722-5639; e-mail: spiessantq@aol.com. Specializing in Odd Fellows lodge items

Stifter, Craig
218 S. Adams St., Hinsdale, 60521; 630-789-5780; e-mail: cocacola@enteract.com. Specializing in Coca-Cola, Pepsi-Cola, Orange Crush, Dr. Pepper, Hires, and other soda-pop brand collectibles

TV Guide Specialists
Box 20, Macomb, 61455; 309-833-1809.

Waite, Jim
112 N. Main St., Farmer City, 61842; 800-842-2593; e-mail: bigjim@farmwagon.com. Specializing in Sebastians

Yester-Daze Glass
c/o Illinois Antique Center
320 S.W. Commercial St., Peoria, 61604; 309-347-1679. Specializing in glass from the 1920s, '30s, and '40s; Fiesta; Hall; pie birds; sprinkler bottles; and Florence figurines

Indiana

AAA Antique Shop
US 6 West, Nappanee, 46550; 219-773-4912. Specializing in trunks

Alexander, Charles
221 E. 34th St., Indianapolis, 46205; 317-924-9665. Specializing in Fiesta, Russel Wright, Eva Zeisel

Boram, Clifford
Antique Stove Information Clearinghouse
Monticello; Free consultation by phone only: 219-583-6465

Dilley, David
PO Box 225, Indianapolis, 46206; 317-251-0575; e-mail: glazebears@aol.com or bearpots@aol.com. Specializing in Royal Haeger and Royal Hickman

Edwards, Bill
620 W. 2nd, Madison, 47250. Author (Collector Books) on carnival glass

Freese, Carol and Warner
House With the Lions Antiques
On the Square, Covington, 47932. General line

Garrett, Jerry and Sandi
Jerry's Antiques (Shows only)
1807 W. Madison St., Kokomo, 46901; 765-457-5256. Specializing in Greentown glass, old postcards

Haun, Ted
2426 N. 700 East, Kokomo, 46901; 765-628-7028; e-mail: Sam17@webtv.net. Specializing in American pottery and china, '50s items, Russel Wright designs

Highfield, James
6301-D University Commons, South Bend, 46635; 219-272-4200. Specializing in relief-style Capo-di-Monte-style porcelain (Doccia, Ginori, and Royal Naples)

Heiss, Virginia
7777 N. Alton Ave., Indianapolis, 46268; 317-875-6797. Specializing in Muncie, AMACO, Marblehead, Kenton Hills

Hoover, Dave
1023 Skyview Dr., New Albany, 47150. Specializing in fishing collectibles, publishes fixed-price catalog; also miniature boats and motors

Keagy, William and June
PO Box 106, Bloomfield, 47424; 812-384-3471. Co-authors of *Those Wonderful Yard-Long Prints and More*, *More Wonderful Yard-Long Prints, Book II*, and *Yard-Long Prints, Book III*, illustrated value guides

Kurella, Elizabeth
The Lace Merchant
Box 244, Whiting, 46394; 219-659-1124; e-mail: ekurella@home.com. Publisher of books on lace and lines; Specializing in lace and linens

Leslie, Beverly
Secretary/Treasurer of Uhl Collectors Society
801 Poplar St., Boonville, 47601; 812-897-3681. Contact for newsletter and membership information

McQuillen, Michael J. and Polly
McQuillen's Collectibles
PO Box 50022, Indianapolis, 46250-0022; 317-845-1721; e-mail: michael@politicalparade.com. Writer of column, *Political Parade*, which appears monthly in *AntiqueWeek* other newspapers; Specializing in political advertising, pinback buttons, and sports memorabilia; Buys and sells; www.politicalparade.com.

Miller, Robert
44 Hickory Lane North, Crawfordsville, 47833-7601. Specializing in Dryden pottery

Pruitt, Ted
3350 W. 700 N., Anderson, 46011. *St. Clair Glass Collector's Guide, Vol. 2*, available for $22 each from Ted at above address

Ricketts, Vicki
Covington Antiques Company
6431 W US Highway 136; Covington 47932. General line

Slater, Thomas D.
Slater's Americana
1325 W. 86th St., Indianapolis, 46260; 317-257-0863. Specializing in political and sports memorabilia

Taylor, Dr. E.E.
245 N. Oakland Ave., Indianapolis, 46201-3360; 317-638-1641. Specializing in radios

Webb's Antique Mall
over 400 Quality Dealers
200 W. Union St., Centerville, 47330; 765-855-2489; e-mail: webbsin@antiquelandusa.com

Wright, Bill
325 Shady Dr., New Albany, 47150. Specializing in knives: Bowie, hunting, military, and pocketknives

---

Iowa

Addy, Geneva D.
Winterset, 50273; 515-462-3027

Ambrose, Craig
3717 6th Ave., Apt. 244, Des Moines, 50313; 515-288-4595. Specializing in quilts; Author of *Picture Book and Price Guide to Antique Quilts*, available from author for $45+postage

The Baggage Car
Hal and Meredith DeGood
3100 Justin Dr., Ste. B; Des Moines 50322; 515-270-9080; e-mail: baggagecar@aol.com. Specializing in Hallmark ornaments, cookie cutters, etc.; Publishes Hallmark newsletter and list

Beeks, Dale
PO Box 117, Mt. Vernon, 52314; 319-895-0506; e-mail: dbeeksci@aol.com. Specializing in instruments of science technology and medicine, also surveying instruments and microscopes

Bilsland, William M., III
PO Box 2671, Cedar Rapids, 52406-2671; 319-368-0658. Specializing in American art pottery

Devine, Dennis; Norman; and Joe
D & D Antique Mall
1411 3rd St., Council Bluffs, 51503; 712-323-5233 or 712-328-7305. Specializing in furniture, phonographs, collectibles, general line. Joe Devine: Royal Copley and other types of pottery (collector), author of *Collector's Guide to Royal Copley Plus Royal Windsor & Spaulding, Books I and II*

Dollen, Brenda
PO Box 67, 402 Main St., Minden, 51553. Specializing in Red Wing pottery; Co-author (with R.L. Dollen) of *Red Wing Art Pottery, Books I and II*; *Collector's Encyclopedia of Red Wing Art Pottery* (all Collector Books)

Jaarsma, Ralph
Red Ribbon Antiques
812 Washington St., c/o Red Ribbon Antique Mall, Pella, 50219. Specializing in Dutch antiques; SASE required when requesting information

Picek, Louis
Main Street Antiques
110 W. Main St., Box 340, West Branch, 52358. Specializing in folk art, country Americana, the unusual

---

Kansas

Anthony, Dorothy Malone
World of Bells Publications
2401 S. Horton, Fort Scott, 66701; 316-223-3404. Specializing in publishing and selling books on all types of small bells

Maundy International
PO Box 13028-GG, Shawnee Mission, 66282; 800-235-2866. Specializing in watches — antique pocket and vintage wristwatches

Old World Antiques
4436 State Line Rd., Kansas City, 66103; 913-677-4744 or fax 913-677-4879. Specializing in 18th- and 19th-century furniture, paintings, accessories, clocks, chandeliers, sconces, and much more

Smies, David
Pops Collectibles
Box 522, 315 So. 4th, Manhattan, 66502; 785-776-1433. Specializing in coins, stamps, cards, tokens, Masonic collectibles

Street, Patti
Currier & Ives (China) Quarterly
Newsletter
PO Box 504, Riverton, 66770; 316-848-3529. Subscription: $12 per year (includes 2 free ads)

Tinsley, Rosella
105 15th St., Osawatomie, 66064; 913-755-3237. Specializing in primitives, kitchen, woodenware, and miscellaneous (phone calls only, no letters please)

Kentucky

Courter, J.W.
3935 Kelley Rd., Kevil, 42053; 270-488-2116. Specializing in Aladdin lamps; Author of *Aladdin — The Magic Name in Lamps, Revised Edition*, hard bound, 304 pages; *Aladdin Electric Lamps*, soft bound, 229 pages; and *Angle Lamps Collectors Manual & Price Guide*, soft bound, 48 pages

Florence, Gene
Box 7186H, Lexington, 40522. Author (Collector Books) on Depression glass, Occupied Japan; Elegant glass, Kitchen Glassware

Hornback, Betty
Betty's Antiques
707 Sunrise Lane, Elizabethtown, 42701; 270-765-2441; e-mail: bettysantiques@kvnet.org. Specializing in Kentucky Derby glasses; Detailed Derby, Preakness, Belmont, Breeder's Cup, and others glass information and pictures available in a booklet for $15 ppd.

Johnson, Wes, Sr.
3606 Glenview Ave., Glenview, 40025. Specializing in Cracker Jack: toys, point of sale, packages, etc.; Checkers Confection, Schoenhut toys, Victor Toy Oats, Universal Theatre (Chicago), old toys; Please include SASE

Ritchie, Roy B.
197 Royhill Rd., Hindman, 41822; 606-785-5796. Co-author of *Standard Knife Collector's Guide*; *Standard Guide to Razors*; *Cattaraugus Cutlery, Identification and Values*; and *The Big Knife Book*; Specializing in razors and knives, all types of cutlery

Stewart, Ron
PO Box 151, Combs, 41729; 606-435-2412. Co-author of *Standard Knife Collector's Guide*; *Standard Guide to Razors*; *Cattaraugus Cutlery, Identification and Values*; and *The Big Knife Book*; Specializing in razors and knives, all types of cutlery

Willis, Roy M.
Heartland of Kentucky Decanters & Steins
PO Box 428, Lebanon Jct., 40150; e-mail: heartlandky@ka.net. Huge selection of limited edition decanters and beer steins — open showroom; Include large self-addressed envelope (2 stamps) with correspondence; Fee for appraisals; www.decantersandsteins.com

---

Louisiana

Langford, Paris
Kollecting Kiddles
415 Dodge Ave., Jefferson, 70121; 504-733-0667; e-mail: bbean415@aol.com. Specializing in all small vinyl dolls of the '60s and '70s; Author of *Liddle Kiddles Identification and Value Guide* (now out of print); Please include SASE when requesting information; Contact for information concerning Liddle Kiddle convention

---

Maine

Blake, Brenda
Box 555, York Harbor, 03911; 207-363-6566; e-mail: Eggcentric@aol.com. Specializing in egg cups

Hathaway, John
Hathaway's Antiques
3 Mills Rd., Bryant Pond, 04219; 207-665-2214. Specializing in fruit jars; Mail order a specialty

Hillman, Alma
Antiques at the Hillman's
362 E. Main St., Searsport, 04974; 207-548-6658; e-mail: oldivory@acadia.net. Co-author (Collector Books) of *Collector's Encyclopedia of Old Ivory China, The Mystery Explored, Identification & Values*; Specializing in Old Ivory China

Simpson, Elizabeth
Elizabeth Simpson Antiques
PO Box 201, Freeport, 04032. Specializing in New England glass and Sandwich glass

Rinaldi, John
Nautical Antiques and Related Items
Box 765, Dock Square, Kennebunkport, 04046; 207-967-3218. Specializing in nautical antiques, scrimshaw, naval items, marine paintings, naval items, etc.; Fully illustrated catalog: $5

Shaw, John
43 Ridgecrest Dr., Wilton, 04294 (June to October, See Florida listing for remaining months); 207-645-2443. Specializing in dairy bottles

Zayic, Charles S.
Americana Advertising Art
PO Box 57, Ellsworth, 04605; 207-667-7342. Specializing in early magazines, early advertising art, illustrators

Maryland

Doub, Kathy
5359 Iron Pen Place, Columbia, 21044; 410-995-1254. Specializing in Candlewick and Imperial milk glass

Ezell, Elaine; & Newhouse, George
Cruets Cruets Cruets
PO Box 1609, Pasadena, 21123-1609; 410-551-4101 (daytime) or 410-255-6777. Specializing in cruets and glass

Humphrey, George C.
4932 Prince George Ave., Beltsville, 20705; 301-937-7899. Specializing in John Rogers groups

Katz, Jerome R.
Katz Collectibles
Antique Station, Frederick, 21702; 301-695-0888. Specializing in technological artifacts; Please include SASE when requesting information

Meadows, John, Jean, and Michael
Meadows House Antiques
919 Stiles St., Baltimore, 21202; 410-837-5427. Specializing in antique wicker furniture (rustic, twig, and old hickory), quilts, and tramp art

Rudisill's Alt Print Haus
Rudisill, John and Barbara
PO Box 199, Worton, 21678; 410-778-9290; e-mail: rudi@dmv.com. Specializing in Currier & Ives; Calls for information will be taken in return for a contribution (honor system) to the American Heart Association; Call back if not at home; calls will not be returned; chesapeake-bay.com/altprinthaus

Screen, Harold and Joyce
2804 Munster Rd., Baltimore, 21234; 410-661-6765; e-mail: hscreen@comcast.net. Specializing in soda fountain 'tools of the trade' and paper: catalogs, 'Soda Fountain' magazines, etc.

Weisblut, Robert
International Ivory Society
11109 Nicholas Dr., Wheaton, 20902; 301-649-4002; e-mail: RWeisblut@yahoo.com. Specializing in ivory carvings and utilitarian objects

Welsh, Joan
7015 Partridge Pl., Hyattsville, 20782; 301-779-6181; Specializing in Chintz; Author of *Chintz Ceramics*

Yalom, Libby
The Shoe Lady
PO Box 7146, Adelphi, 20783-2758; 301-422-2026. Specializing in glass and china shoes; Author of book

Massachusetts

Adams, Charles and Barbara
South Yarmouth, 02664; 508-760-3290 or (business) 508-587-5640; e-mail: adams_2340@msn.com. Specializing in Bennington (brown only)

Cooper, Ryan
205 White Rock Rd., Yarmouthport, 02675; 508-362-1604; e-mail: rcmaritime@capecod.net. Specializing in flags of historical significance and exceptional design

Dunbar's Gallery
Leila and Howard Dunbar
76 Haven St., Milford, 01757; 508-634-8697 or fax 508-634-8698; e-mail: Dunbars@mediaone.net. Specializing in advertising and toys; www.dumbarsgallery.com

Ford, Frank W.
237-26 South Street; Shrewsbury, 01545. Specializing in Fostoria Specialty Company glassware

Frei, Peter
PO Box 500, Brimfield, 01010; 413-245-4660. Specializing in sewing machines (pre-1875, non-electric only), adding machines, typewriters, and hand-powered vacuum cleaners; SASE required with correspondence

Hess, John A.
Fine Photographic Americana
PO Box 3062, Andover, 01810. Specializing in 19th-century photography

Longo, Paul J.
Paul Longo Americana
Box 5510, Magnolia, 01930; 978-525-2290. Specializing in political pins, ribbons, banners, autographs, old stocks and bonds, baseball and sports memorabilia of all types

MacLean, Dale
183 Robert Rd., Dedham, 02026; 781-326-3010 (days) or 781-329-1303 (evenings); e-mail: DedhamDorchester@aol.com. Specializing in Dedham and Dorchester pottery

Morin, Albert
668 Robbins Ave. #23, Dracut, 01826; 978-454-7907; e-mail: akroal@attbi.com. Specializing in miscellaneous Akro Agate and Westite

Porter, Richard T., Curator
Porter Thermometer Museum
Box 944, Onset, 02558; 508-295-5504; e-mail: thermometerman.aol.com. Visits (always open) free, with 3,800+ thermometers to see; Appraisals, repairs, and traveling lecture (600 given, ages 8 – 98, all venues). Richard is also vice president of the Thermometer Collectors Club of America

Steinbock, Nancy
Nancy Steinbock Posters
800-438-1577. Specializing in posters: travel, literary, advertising; Charter member of the IVPDA (International Vintage Poster Dealers Association)

Wellman, BA
PO Box 673, Westminster, 01473-0673; e-mail: BA@dishinitout.com. Specializing in **all** areas of American ceramics, dinnerware, figurines, and art pottery

Williams, Linda
46 Columba St, #4D, Chicopee, 01020; e-mail: Sito1845@aol.com. Specializing in glass & china, general line antiques

Michigan

Brown, Rick
Newspaper Collector's Society of America
Lansing, 517-887-1255; e-mail: help@historybuff.com; www.historybuff.com. Specializing in newspapers

Burton, Ann
43779 Valley Rd., Decatur, 49045. Specializing in Schramberg

Culver, Bob
Night Light Club
38619 Wakefield Ct., Northville, 48167; 248-473-8575. Specializing in miniature oil lamps

Haas, Norman
252 Clizbe Rd., Quincy, 49802; 517-639-8537. Specializing in American art pottery

Hogan & Woodworth
Walter P. Hogan and Wendy L. Woodworth
520 N. State, Ann Arbor, 48104; 313-930-1913. Specializing in Kellogg Studio; www.emunix.emich.edu/~whogan/kellogg/index.html

Iannotti, Dan
212 W. Hickory Grove Rd., Bloomfield Hills, 48302-1127S; 248-335-5042; e-mail: modernbanks@prodigy.net. Specializing in modern mechanical cast-iron banks; Member of The Mechanical Bank Collectors of America

Krupka, Rod
2615 Echo Lane, Ortonville, 48462; 248-627-6351. Specializing in lightning rod balls

Marsh, Linda K.
1229 Gould Rd., Lansing, 48917. Specializing in Degenhart glass

Nedry, Boyd W.
728 Buth Dr., Comstock Park, 49321; 616-784-1513. Specializing in traps (including mice, rat, and fly traps) and trap-related items; Please include SASE when requesting information

Nickel, Mike
A Nickel's Worth
PO Box 456, Portland, 48875; 517-647-7646; e-mail: mandc@voyager.net. Specializing in American Art Pottery: Roseville, Weller, Rookwood, Kay Finch, Stangl and Pennsbury birds, Ceramic Art Studio, and Florence figurines

Oates, Joan
685 S. Washington, Constantine, 49042; 616-435-8353; e-mail: koates120@earthlink.net. Specializing in Phoenix Bird chinaware

Rairigh, Glen
Americana Auctions
12633 Sandborn, Sunfield, 48890; 800-919-1950. Specializing in Skookum dolls and antique auctions

Ross, Michelle
PO Box 94, Berrien Center, 49102; 616-925-1604; e-mail: peartime1@cs.com. Specializing in Van Briggle and American pottery

Webster, Marty
6943 Suncrest Drive, Saline, 48176; 313-944-1188. Specializing in California porcelain and pottery, Orientalia

Minnesota

Anderson, James
Box 120704, New Brighton, 55112; 651-484-3198. Specializing in old fishing lures and reels, also tackle catalogs, posters, calendars, Winchester items

Dommel, Darlene
PO Box 22493, Minneapolis, 55422. Collector Books author of *Collector's Encyclopedia of Howard Pierce Porcelain* and *Collectory's Encyclopedia of Dakota Potteries*; Specializing in Howard Pierce and Dakota potteries.

Harrigan, John
1900 Hennepin, Minneapolis, 55403; 612-660-2794 or (in winter) 561-732-0525. Specializing in Battersea (English enamel) boxes, Moorcroft, and Toby jugs

Ketcham, Steve
Steve Ketcham Antiques (Shows and mail order only)
Box 24114, Edina, 55424; 952-920-4205; e-mail: s.ketcham@unique-software.com. Specializing in and buying early American bottles; Red Wing stoneware (no dinnerware); advertising signs, trays, trade cards, pocket mirrors, etched beer and shot glasses. Please include SASE for reply.

Koehn, Joanne M.
Temple's Antiques
PO Box 46237, Eden Prairie, 55344; 612-941-7641. Specializing in Victorian glass and china

Miller, Clark
4444 Garfield Ave., Minneapolis, 55409-1847; 612-827-6062. Specializing in Anton Lang pottery, American art pottery, Scandinavian glass and pottery

Nelson, C.L.
Box 222, Spring Park, 55384; 612-473-5625. Specializing in 18th-, 19th, and 20th-century English pottery and porcelain, among others: Gaudy Welsh, ABC plates, relief-molded jugs, Staffordshire transfer ware

Putratz, Barb
Spring Lake Park, 763-784-0422. Specializing in Norman Rockwell

Schoneck, Steve
HG Handicraft Guild, Minneapolis
PO Box 56, Newport, 55055; 651-459-2980; Specializing in American art pottery, Arts & Crafts, HG Handicraft Guild Minneapolis

Missouri

Gillespie, Steve, Publisher
Goofus Glass Gazette
400 Martin Blvd, Village of the Oaks, 64118; 888-455-5558; e-mail: stegil@sbcglobal.net. Specializing in goofus glass, curator of 'Goofus Glass Museum,' had 4,000+ piece collection of goofus glass; Buy, sell, and collect goofus for 30+ years; Expert contributor to forums on goofus glass; Contributor to website for goofus glass.

Heuring, Jerry
28450 US Highway 61, Scott City, 63780; 573-264-3947. Specializing in Keen Kutter

Roberts, Brenda
Specializing in Hull pottery and general line; Author of *Collector's Encyclopedia of Hull Pottery, Roberts' Ultimate Encyclopedia of Hull Pottery* and *The Companion Guide to Roberts' Ultimate Encyclopedia of Hull Pottery*, all with accompanying price guides

Siegel, Brenda and Jerry
Tower Grove Antiques
3308 Meramec, St. Louis, 63118; 314-352-9020. Specializing in Ungemach pottery

Tarrant, Jenny
Holly Daze Antiques
4 Gardenview, St. Peters, 63376; e-mail: JennyJOL@aol.com; Holiday for sale. Specializing in early holiday items, Halloween, Christmas, Easter, etc.; Always buying Halloween collectibles (except masks and costumes) and German holiday candy containers; www.holly-days.com

Wendel, David
F.E.I., Inc.
PO Box 1187, Poplar Bluff, 63902-1187; 573-686-1926. Specializing in Fraternal Elks collectibles

Wiesehan, Doug
D & R Farm Antiques
4535 Hwy. H, St. Charles, 63301. Specializing in salesman's samples and patent models, antique toys, farm toys, metal farm signs

Williams, Don
PO Box 147, Kirksville, 63501; 660-627-8009 (between 8 a.m. and 6 p.m. only). Specializing in art glass; SASE required with all correspondence

Winslow, Ralph
PO Box 478, Camdenton, 65020. Specializing in Dryden Pottery

Nebraska

Larsen, Robert V.
3214 19th St., Columbus, 68601. Specializing in old hatpins and hatpin holders; Please include SASE when requesting information

Nevada

Lynn, Susan (Grindberg)
1412 Pathfinder Rd., Henderson, 89014; 702-898-7535; e-mail: sue@porcelierconnection.com; www.porcelierconnection.com. Collector book author of *Collector's Guide to Porcelier China, Identification and Values*

Young, Willy
80 Promontory Pointe, Reno, 89509; 775-746-0922. Specializing in fire grenades

New Hampshire

Apakarian-Russell, Pamela
Halloween Queen Antiques
PO Box 499, Winchester, 03470; Specializing in Halloween (and other holidays) and postcards

Brenner, Larry
Brenner Antiques
1005 Chestnut St., Manchester, 03104; 603-625-8203; e-mail: elberenee@aol.com. Specializing in Royal Bayreuth

Holt, Jane
Jane's Collectibles
PO Box 115, Derry, 03038. Specializing in Annalee Mobilitee Dolls

Winston, Nancy
Willow Hollow Antiques
648 1st N.H. Turnpike, Northwood, 03261; 603-942-5739. Specializing in Shaker smalls, primitives, iron, copper, stoneware, and baskets

New Jersey

Anderson, Suzy McLennan, ISA CAPP
Heritage Antiques & Appraisal Services
65 E. Main St., Holmdel, 07733; 908-946-8801 or fax 908-946-1036. Specializing in American furniture and decorative accessories. Please include photo and SASE when requesting information. Appraisals and identification are impossible to do over the phone.

Bilane, John E. (Mail order only)
2065 Morris Ave., Apt. 109, Union, 07083. Specializing in antique glass cup plates

Dezso, Doug
864 Paterson Ave., Maywood, 07607-2119; 201-488-1311. Specializing in nodders (comic German), glass candy containers, Tonka; SASE required for information

Doorstop Collectors of America
Doorstopper Newsletter
Jeanie Bertoia
2413 Madison Ave., Vineland, 08630; 609-692-4092. Membership: $20 per year, includes 2 newsletters and convention; Send 2-stamp SASE for sample

George, Dr. Joan M.
ABC Collector's Circle Newsletter
67 Stevens Ave., Old Bridge, 08857; fax: 732-679-6102; e-mail: drgeorge @nac.net. Specializing in educational china (particularly ABC plates and mugs)

Harran, Jim and Susan
208 Hemlock Dr., Neptune, 07753; 732-922-2825. Specializing in English and Continental porcelains with emphasis on antique cups and saucers; Authors of *Collectible Cups and Saucers, Identification and Values, Books I & II* (Collector Books); Available for $20.95 ppd.; www.tias.com/stores/amit

Litts, Elyce
PO Box 394, Morris Plains, 07950; 973-361-4087; e-mail: happy-memories@worldnet.att.net. Author (Collector Books) of *Collector's Encyclopedia of Geisha Girl Porcelain* (Out of print; Ask your reference librarian or used bookstore to secure you a copy)

Lockwood, Howard J.; Publisher
Vetri: Italian Glass News
Box 191, Fort Lee, 07024; 201-969-0373. Specializing in Italian glass of the 20th century

Meschi, Edward J.
129 Pinyard Rd., Monroeville, 08343; 856-358-7293; e-mail: ejmeschi@aol.com. Specializing in Durand art glass, Icart etchings, Maxfield Parrish prints, Rookwood pottery, occupational shaving mugs, American paintings, and other fine arts; Author of *Durand — The Man and His Glass*, (Antique Publications) available from author for $43 ppd.; www.meschiarts.com

Middleton, Dave and Anne
Pot O' Gold Antiques
PO Box 124, Allenwood, 08720; 732-528-6648. Specializing in epergnes, historical and figural Staffordshire, Flow Blue, fine glass

Perzel, Robert and Nancy
Popkorn
The Main Street Antique Center, 156 Main St., PO Box 1057, Flemington, 08822; 908-782-9631. Specializing in Stangl dinnerware, birds, and artware; American pottery and dinnerware

Poster, Harry
Vintage TVs
Box 1883, S. Hackensack, 07606; 201-794-9606. Writes *Poster's Radio and Television Price Guide*; Specializes in vintage televisions, vintage radios, stereo cameras; Catalog available on line: www.harryposter.com

Rago, David
333 N. Main St., Lambertville, 08530; 609-397-6780 or fax: 609-397-679; e-mail: ragoarts@ragoarts.com. Specializing in Arts & Crafts, art pottery; www.ragoarts.com

Rash, Jim
135 Alder Ave., Egg Harbor Township, 08234. Specializing in advertising dolls

Rosen, Barbara
6 Shoshone Trail, Wayne, 07470. Specializing in figural bottle openers and antique dollhouses

Visakay, Stephen
Vintage Cocktail Shakers (By appointment)
PO Box 1517, W. Caldwell, 07007-1517; e-mail: SVisakay@aol.com. Author of book and specializing in vintage cocktail shakers and bar ware

New Mexico

Hardisty, Don
3020 E. Majestic Ridge, Las Cruces, 88011; For information and questions: 505-522-3721; fax: 505-522-7909; e-mail: don@donsbossons.com; www.donsbossons. com. Specializing in Bossons, Fraser-Art, Hummels, artistic restorations, appraisals, and rare coins. Don's Collectibles carries a full line of current issues and most discontinued Bossons and Hummel figurines of all marks. When mail ordering Bossons and Hummels, you may dial toll free 800-Bossons (267-7667). The book *The Imagical World of Bossons* (there are 2 volumes) is also available.

Manns, William
PO Box 6459, Santa Fe, 87502; 505-995-0102; e-mail: zon@nets.com. Co-author of *Painted Ponies*, hardbound (226 pages), available from author for $46 ppd.; Specializing in carousel art and cowboy antiques

Nelson, Scott H.
PO Box 6081, Santa Fe, 87502-6081. Specializing in ethnographic art

New York

Austin, Bruce A.
1 Hardwood Hill Rd., Pittsford, 14534; 585-387-9820 (evenings); 585-475-2879 (weekdays); e-mail: baagll@rit.edu. Specializing in clocks and Arts & Crafts furnishings and accessories including metalware, pottery, and lighting

Badders, Veldon
692 Martin Rd., Hamlin, 14464; 716-964-3360. Author (Collector Books) of *Collector's Guide to Inkwells, Identification & Values*; Specializing in inkwells

Calison, Jim
Tools of Distinction
Wallkill, 12589; 914-895-8035. Specializing in antique and collectible tools; Buying and selling

Dimitroff, Thomas P.
Dimitroff's Antiques (Appointment only)
140 E. First St., Corning, 14830; 607-962-6745; e-mail: tdimi1@aol.com. Specializing in Steuben and cut glass

Doyle, Robert A.
Absolute Auction & Realty, Inc./
Absolute Auction Center
PO Box 1739, Pleasant Valley, 12569; 845-635-3169; e-mail: absoluteauction@hvc.rr.com. Antique and estate auctions twice a month at Absolute Auction Center; Free calendar of auctions available; www.absoluteauctionrealty.com

Endter, Barbara
29 Sandalwood Dr., Rochester, 14616-1513; 585-621-1433. Specializing in Chase Brass & Copper Company

Gerson, Roselyn
PO Box 40, Lynbrook, 11563; 516-593-8746. Author/collector specializing in unusual, gadgetry, figural compacts, vanity bags and purses, solid perfumes and lipsticks

Handelsman, Burton
18 Hotel Dr., White Plains, 10605; 914-428-4480 (home) and 914-761-8880 (office). Specializing in occupational shaving mugs, accessories

Kaonis, Keith; Manager
Antique Doll Collector Magazine
6 Woodside Ave., Suite 300, Northport, 11768 or PO Box 344, Center Port, NY 11721-0344; 631-261-4100 or 631-361-0982 (evenings). Specializing in Schoenhut toys

Little Century
H. Thomas and Patricia Laun
215 Paul Ave., Syracuse, 13206; 315-437-4156. Summer residence: 35109 Country Rte. 7, Cape Vincent, 13618; 315-654-3244. Specializing in firefighting collectibles; All appraisals are free, and we will respond only to those who include a self-addressed stamped envelope (photograph is requested for accuracy)

Malitz, Lucille
Lucid Antiques
Box KH, Scarsdale, 10583; 914-636-7825. Specializing in lithophanes, kaleidoscopes, stereoscopes, medical and dental antiques

Michel, John and Barbara
Iron Star Antiques
200 E. 78th St. 18E, New York City, 10021; 212-861-6094. Specializing in yellow ware, cast iron, tramp art, shooting gallery targets, and blue feather-edge

Rifken, Blume J.
Author of *Silhouettes in America — 1790 – 1840 — A Collector's Guide*. Specializing in American antique silhouettes from 1790 to 1840

Russ, William A.
Russ Trading Post
23 William St., Addison, 14801-1326. Animal lure manufacture; hunting and trapping supply; catalog $1

Safir, Charlotte F.
1349 Lexington Ave., 9-B, New York City, 10128-1513; 212-534-7933. Specializing in cookbooks, children's books (out-of-print only)

Schleifman, Roselle
Ed's Collectibles/The Rage
16 Vincent Rd., Spring Valley, 10977; 845-356-2121. Specializing in Duncan & Miller, Elegant glass, Depression glass

Smyth, Carole and Richard
Carole Smyth Antiques
PO Box 2068, Huntington, 11743. Authors of *The Burning Passion — Antique and Collectible Pyrography*, available from authors at above address for $23.90 ppd. (New York: add 8.25% state sales tax)

Tuggle, Robert
105 W. St., New York City, 10023; 212-595-0514. Specializing in John Bennett, Anglo-Japanese china

Van Kuren, Jean and Dale
Ruth's Antiques, Inc.
PO Box 152, Clarence Center, 14032; 716-741-8001; e-mail: ruthsantq@aol.com. Specializing chocolate molds, Buffalo pottery, Deldare ware

Van Patten, Joan F.
Box 102, Rexford, 12148. Author (Collector Books) of books on Nippon and Noritake

Weitman, Stan and Arlene
PO Box 1186; N. Massapequa, 11758; author of book on crackle glass (Collector Books)

North Carolina

Finegan, Mary
Marfine Antiques
PO Box 3618; Boone, 28607; 828-262-3441; e-mail: marfine@boone.net. Specializing in Johnson Brothers dinnerware; replacement service; author of book ($17 ppd.)

Hughes, Kathy (Mrs. Paul)
Tudor House Galleries
8919 Park Rd., DC #30, Charlotte, 28210-08645; 704-676-4871; fax: 704-676-5197; e-mail: paulh65304@aol.com or www.tudorhouse.com. Specializing in relief-molded jugs, 18th- and 19th-century English pottery and 19th-century oil paintings

Hussey, Billy Ray
Southern Folk Pottery Collector's Society
220 Washington Street, Bennett, 27208; 336-581-4246 or fax: 336-581-4247. Specializing in historical research and documentation, education and promotion of the traditional folk potter (past and present) to a modern collecting audience

Iannantuoni, Jean-Paul
4179 Brownwood Lane, Concord, 28027-4501; www.freeyellow.com/members/royaldoulton/home.html. Discontinued Dinnerware Shopping Service; send $2 for Royal Doulton list; Appraisals $2 each

Kirtley, Charles E.
PO Box 2273, Elizabeth City, 27096; 919-335-1262. Specializing in monthly auctions and bid sales dealing with World's Fair, Civil War, political, advertising, and other American collectibles

Newbound, Betty
2206 Nob Hill Dr., Sanford, 27330. Author (Collector Books) on Blue Ridge dinnerware, milk glass, wall pockets, figural planters, and vases; Specializing in collectible china and glass

Sayers, R.J.
Southeastern Antiques & Appraisals
305 N. Main St., Hendersonville, 28792; 828-697-6064. Specializing in Boy Scout collectibles, Pisgah Forest pottery, primitive American furniture; Author of *Guide to Scouting Collectibles, Revised 1996 Edition*, available from author for $32.95 ppd.; Member New England Appraisers Assn.

Taylor, Terry
3648 Prides Rd., East Bend, 27018. Co-author of *Collector's Encyclopedia of Salt Glaze Stoneware* (Collector Books). Specializing in salt glaze stoneware

---

North Dakota

Farnsworth, Bryce
1334 14½ St. South, Fargo, 58103; 701-237-3597. Specializing in Rosemeade pottery; If writing for information, please send a picture if possible, also phone number and best time to call

---

Ohio

Bassett, Mark
PO Box 771233, Lakewood, 44107; 216-221-6025; e-mail: Mark@MarkBassett.com. Buying and selling Ohio art pottery (including Roseville, Cowan, Weller, Rookwood, others), Cleveland arts and crafts, Art Deco, and other 20th century design movements; Author of *Introducing Roseville Pottery* (1999), *Cowan Pottery and the Cleveland School* (1997), *Introducing Roseville Pottery* (revised and expanded 2nd edition, 2001), *Bassett's Roseville Prices* (2001), and *Understanding Roseville Pottery* (2002); For ordering information visit www.MarkBassett.com

Batory, Mr. Dana Martin
402 E. Bucyrus St., Crestline, 44827. Specializing in antique woodworking machinery, old and new woodworking machinery catalogs; Author of *Vintage Woodworking Machinery, an Illustrated Guide to Four Manufacturers*, currently available from Astragal Press, PO Box 239, Mendham, NJ 07945 for $26.45 ppd. (signed copies available from author); Coming soon from Astragal Press, *Vintage Woodworking Machinery Volume Two, An Illustrated Guide to Four More Manufacturers*. In order to prepare a definitive history on American manufacturers of woodworking machinery, Dana is interested in acquiring (by loan, gift, or photocopy) catalogs, manuals, photos, personal reminiscences, etc., pertaining to woodworking machinery and/or their manufacturers. Also available for $7.50 money order: 60+ page list of catalogs, owner's manuals, parts lists, company publications, etc. (updated quarterly). No phone calls please.

Benjamin, Scott
PO Box 556, LaGrange, 44050-0556; 440-355-6608; www.oilcollectibles.com or www.gasglobes.com. Specializing in gas globes; Co-author of *Gas Pump Globes* and several other related books, listing nearly 4,000 gas globes with over 1,800 photos, prices, rarity guide, histories, and reproduction information (currently available from author); Also available: *Petroleum Collectibles Monthly* Magazine

Blair, Betty
Golden Apple Antiques
216 Bridge St., Jackson, 45640; 614-286-4817. Specializing in art pottery, Watt, cookie jars, chocolate molds, Beanie Babies, general line

China Specialties, Inc.
Box 471, Valley City, 44280. Specializing in high-quality reproductions of Homer Laughlin and Hall china, including Autumn Leaf

Distel, Ginny
Distel's Antiques
4041 S.C.R. 22, Tiffin, 44883; 419-447-5832. Specializing in Tiffin glass

Ebner, Rita and John
Columbus. Specializing in door knockers, cast-iron bottle openers, Griswold

Graff, Shirley
4515 Grafton Rd., Brunswick, 44212. Specializing in Pennsbury pottery

Guenin, Tom
Box 454, Chardon, 44024. Specializing in antique telephones and antique telephone restoration

Hamlin, Jack and Treva
145 Township Rd. 1088, Proctorville, 45669; 740-886-7644; e-mail: trevajo@ezwv.com. Specializing in Currier and Ives by Royal China Co. and Homer Laughlin China

Hothem, Lar
Hothem House
Box 458, Lancaster, 43130. Author of books on Indians and artifacts

Kao, Fern Larking
PO Box 312, Bowling Green, 43402; 419-352-5928. Specializing in jewelry, sewing implements, ladies' accessories

Kier, Anne and Don
202 Marengo St., Toledo, 43614-4213; 419-385-8211; e-mail: d.a.k.@worldnet.att.net. Specializing in glass, china, autographs, Brownies, Royal Bayreuth, 19th-century antiques, general line

Kitchen, Lorrie
Toledo, 419-475-1759. Specializing in Depression-era glass, Hall china, Fiesta, Blue Ridge, Shawnee

Klender, James and Grace
Town & Country Antiques & Collectibles
PO Box 447, Pioneer, 43554; 419-737-2880. Specializing in pattern glass, and general line

Directory of Contributors

Kline, Mr. and Mrs. Jerry and Gerry
The Founding Members of North American Torquay Society
604 Orchard View Dr., Maumee, 43537; 419-893-1226. Specializing in collecting Torquay pottery

Mangus, Bev and Jim
5147 Broadway NE, Louisville, 44641; Author (Collector Books) of *Shawnee Pottery, an Identification & Value Guide*; Specializing in Shawnee pottery

Mathes, Richard
PO Box 1408, Springfield, 45501-1408; 513-324-6917. Specializing in buttonhooks

Millman, Tom and Linda
231 S. Main St., Bethel, 45106; phone/fax: 513-734-6884 (after 9 p.m.). Specializing in perfume lamps, other antique and unique lighting

Moore, Carolyn
445 N. Prospect, Bowling Green, 43402. Specializing in primitives, yellow ware, graniteware, collecting stoneware

Murphy, James L.
1023 Neil Ave., Columbus, 43201; 614-297-0746; e-mail: jlmruphy@columbus.rr.com. Specializing in American Radford, Vance Avon

National Imperial Glass Collectors' Society, Inc.
PO Box 534, Bellaire, 43906. Dues: $15 per year (plus $1 for each additional member in the same household); Quarterly newsletter; Convention every June

Otto, Susan
12204 Fox Run Dr., Chesterland, 44026; 440-729-2686. Specializing in nutcrackers, not toy soldier (Steinbach) type

Pierce, David
PO Box 248, Danville, 43014; 614-599-6394. Specializing in Glidden pottery; Fee for appraisals

Rees, Debbie
Zanesville. Specializing in Watt, Roseville juvenile and other Roseville pottery, Zanesville area pottery, cookie jars, and Steiff

Riebel, James
Pottery Peregrinators
Zanesville, 740-679-3593. Author of *Sanford's Guide to Nicodemus*, available from the author; Specializing in American art pottery, Nicodemus, and carnival glass and Millersburg glass

Shields, Lorne
PO Box 211, Chagrin Falls, 44022-0211; 905-886-6911; fax: 905-886-7748; e-mail: vintage-antique@rogers.com. Specializing in bicycles

Trainer, Veronica
Bayhouse
Box 40443, Cleveland, 44140; 440-871-8584. Specializing in beaded and enameled mesh purses

Tucker, Dan
Toledo, 419-478-3815. Specializing in Depression-era glass, Hall china, Fiesta, Blue Ridge, Shawnee

Walter, John
The Old Tool Shop
208 Front St., Marietta, 45750; 740-373-9973; fax: 740-373-9059; e-mail: toolmerchant@sprynet.com. Specializing in all types of antique tools; For detailed information on Stanley tools, John Walter's *Antique & Collectible Stanley Tools Guide to Identity and Value* is highly recommended, 885 pages, over 1500 crisp photos and engravings, current values, Softcover: $35 ppd., Hardcover: $45 ppd.; *2000 Stanley Pocket Price Guide*: $12 ppd.; Website coming soon: www.stanleytoolcollectors.org

Whitmyer, Margaret and Kenn
Box 30806, Gahanna, 43230. Authors (Collector Books) on children's dishes. Specializing in Depression-era collectibles

Wilkins, Juanita
The Bird of Paradise
Wapakoneta. Specializing in R.S. china, Old Ivory china, colored pattern glass, lamps, and jewelry

Young, Mary
Box 9244, Wright Brothers Branch, Dayton, 45409; 937-298-4838. Specializing in paper dolls; Author of several books

Oklahoma

Bess, Phyllis and Tom
14535 E. 13th St., Tulsa, 74108; 918-437-7776. Authors of *Frankoma Treasures*, and *Frankoma and Other Oklahoma Potteries*; Specializing in Frankoma and Oklahoma pottery

Moore, Art and Shirley
4423 E. 31st St., Tulsa, 74135; 918-747-4164 or 918-744-8020. Specializing in Lu Ray Pastels, Depression glass

Scott, Roger R.
4250 S. Oswego, Tulsa, 74135; 918-742-8710 or fax 918-583-1226; e-mail: Roger13@mindspring.com Specializing in Victor and RCA Victor trademark items along with Nipper

Oregon

Abrahams, Peter
1948 Mapleleaf Rd., Lake Oswego, 97034; 503-636-2988; e-mail: telscope @europa.com. Specializing in telescopes, binoculars, microscopes. Peter studies and collects optics: telescopes, binoculars, hand magnifiers, and microscopes and especially seeks reference material on these subjects, including books, catalogs, repair manuals, and histories; www.europa.com/~telescope/binotele.htm

Brown, Marcia
Sparkles
PO Box 2314, White City, 97503; 541-826-3039 or fax 541-830-5385. Author of *Unsigned Beauties of Costume Jewelry* and *Signed Beauties of Costume Jewelry* (Collector Books); Co-author and host of 7 volumes: *Hidden Treasures* videos; Specializing in rhinestone jewelry; Please include SASE if requesting information

Coe, Debbie and Randy
Coe's Mercantile
Lafayette School House Mall #2, 748 3rd (Hwy. 99W), Lafayette, 97127. Specializing in Elegant and Depression glass, art pottery

Davis, Patricia M.
Antique and personal property appraisals
4326 N.W. Tam-O-Shanter Way, Portland, 97229-8738; 503-645-3084; e-mail: pam10davis@aol.com

Foland, Doug
PO Box 66854, Portland, 97290. Author of *The Florence Collectibles, an Era of Elegance*, available at your local bookstore or from Schiffer publishers

Hirshman, Susan and Larry
Everyday Antiques
2011 E. Main St., Medford, 97504. Specializing in china, glassware, kitchenware

Main Antique Mall
30 N. Riverside, Medford, 97501; Quality products and services for the serious collector, dealer, or those just browsing; http://mainantiquemall.com

Medford Antique Mall
Jim & Eileen Pearson, Owners
1 West 6th St., Medford, 97501; 541-773-4983; e-mail: medama11@mind.net

Miller, Don and Robbie
541-535-1231. Specializing in milk bottles, TV Siamese cat lamps, seltzer bottles, red cocktail shakers

Morris, Thomas G.
Prize Publishers
PO Box 8307, Medford, 97504; e-mail: chalkman@cdsnet.net Author of *The Carnival Chalk Prize, Books I and II*, pictorial price guides on carnival chalkware figures with brief histories and values for each

Ringering, David
Kay Ring Antiques
1395 59th Ave., S.E., Salem, 97301; 503-364-0464 or pager: 503-588-3747; e-mail: AR1480@aol.com. Specializing in Rowland & Marsellus and other souvenir/historical china with scenes of buildings, parks, and other tourist attractions of the 1890s – 1930s. Feel free to contact David if you have any questions about Rowland and Marsellus or other souvenir china. He will be happy to answer questions about souvenir china.

Pennsylvania

Alekna, Stan and Sally
732 Aspen Lane, Lebanon, 17042-9073; 717-228-2361 or fax 717-228-2362. Specializing in American Dimestore Toy Soldiers

Barker, Jim
Toastermaster Antique Appliances
PO Box 746, Allentown, 18105; 610-439-0751; e-mail: jbar@enter.net. Specializing in early electric toasters and fans, Porcelier and Royal Rochester; Unusual electric toasters always wanted

Barrett, Noel
Rosebud Antiques
PO Box 1001, Carversville, 18913; 215-297-5109. Specializing in toys; Appraisor on PBS Antiques Roadshow; Active in toy-related auctions

Bodine, Clarence H., Jr., Proprietor
East/West Gallery
41B West Ferry St., New Hope, 18938. Specializing in antique Japanese woodblock prints, netsuke, inro, porcelains

Cerebro
PO Box 327, E. Prospect, 17317-0327; 717-252-2400 or 800-69-LABEL; fax: 717-252-3685; e-mail: Cerebro@Cerebro.com. Specializing in antique advertising labels, especially cigar box labels, cigar bands, food labels, firecracker labels; www.cerebro.com

Christie, Dr. Victor J.W.
Author/Appraiser/Broker
1050 West Main St., Ephrata, 17522; 717-738-4032; e-mail: thecheshirecat@onemain.com. The family designated biographer of Bessie Pease Gutmann; Specializing in Bessie Pease Gutmann and other Gutmann & Gutmann artists, and, authored 5 books on these artists, the latest in 2001: *The Gutmann & Gutmann Artists: A Published Works Catalog, Fourth Edition*, a signed copy available from the author for $20 at the above address

Damaska, Ron
738 9th Ave., New Brighton, 15066; 724-843-1393. Specializing in Fry cut glass, match holders; SASE required when requesting information

Gottuso, Bob
Bojo
PO Box 1403, Cranberry Township, 16066-0403; phone/fax: 724-776-0621; www.bojoonline.com. Specializing in Beatles, Elvis, KISS, Monkees, licensed Rock 'n Roll memorabilia

Hain, Henry F., III
Antiques & Collectibles
2623 N. Second St., Harrisburg, 17110; 717-238-0534. Lists available of items for sale

Hinton, Michael C.
246 W. Ashland St., Doylestown, 18901; 215-345-0892; e-mail: iscsusn@att.net. Owns/operates Bucks County Art & Antiques Company and Chem-Clean Furniture Restoration Company; Specializing in quality restorations of a wide range of art and antiques from colonial to contemporary; Also owns Trading Post Antiques, 532 Durham Rd., Wrightstown, PA, 18940, a 60-dealer antiques co-op with 15,000 square feet — something for everyone in antiques and collectibles

Holland, William
hollandarts.com
1554 Paoli Pike, West Chester, 19380-6123; 610-344-9848 or fax 610-344-0651; e-mail: bill@hollandarts.com. Specializing in Louis Icart etchings and oils, Tiffany studios lamps, glass, and desk accessories; Author of *Louis Icart: The Complete Etchings*, *The Collectible Maxfield Parrish*, and *Louis Icart Erotica*; www.hollandarts.com

Irons, Dave
Dave Irons Antiques
223 Covered Bridge Rd., Northampton, 18067; 610-262-9335 or fax 610-262-2853. Author of *Irons By Irons*, *More Irons by Irons*, and *Even More Irons by Irons*, available from author, (each contains pictures of over 1,600 irons, current information and price ranges, collecting hints, news of trends, and information for proper care of irons); Specializing in pressing irons, country furniture, primitives, quilts, accessories; www.ironsantiques.com

Ivankovich, Michael
Michael Ivankovich Auctions, Inc.
PO Box 1536 Doylestown, 18901. Specializing in early 20th-century hand-colored photography and prints; Author of *The Collector's Value Guide to Popular Early 20th Century American Prints*, (1998) $19.95; *The Collector's Guide to Wallace Nutting Pictures*, $18.95; *The Alphabetical and Numerical Index to Wallace Nutting Pictures*, $14.95; and *The Guide to Wallace Nutting Furniture*, $14.95. Also available: *Wallace Nutting General Catalog, Supreme Edition* (reprint), $13.95; *Wallace Nutting: A Great American Idea* (reprint), $13.95; and *Wallace Nutting's Windsor's: Correct Windsor Furniture* (reprint), $13.95. Related available book: *The History of Sawyer Pictures* by Carol Begley Gray, $14.95. All these books are currently available at the above address. Shipping is $4.25 for the first item ordered and $1.50 for each additional item.

Knauer, Judy A.
National Toothpick Holder
  Collectors Society
1224 Spring Valley Lane, West Chester, 19380-5112; 610-431-3477. Specializing in toothpick holders and Victorian glass

Kreider, Katherine
Kingsbury Antiques
PO Box 7957, Lancaster, 17604-7957; 717-892-3001; e-mail: Kingsbry@aol.com. Author of *Valentines With Values*, available for $22.90 ppd. ($24.09 PA residents); *One Hundred Years of Valentines*, available for $28.90 ppd. ($30.40 PA residents); and *Valentines for the Eclectic Collector* $28.90 ppd. ($30.40 PA residents); No free appraisals; Stop by Booth #315 in Stroudtburg Antique Center (formerly Black Angus), in Adamstown, PA, Sundays only

Levi, Anita
Allegheny Mountain Antique
  Gallery
5151 Clear Shade Dr., Windber, 15963; 814-467-8539. Specializing in novelty clocks, advertising tins, primitives, holiday decorations, quilts, purses, Black memorabilia, linens, stoneware, Roseville, kitchenware, Art Deco

Lindsay, Ralph
PO Box 21, New Holland, 17557. Specializing in target balls; SASE required with correspondence

Lowe, James Lewis
Kate Greenaway Society
PO Box 8, Norwood, 19074; e-mail: JLewisLowe@juno.com. Specializing in Kate Greenaway

Maier, Clarence and Betty
Mail order: The Burmese Cruet
Box 432, Montgomeryville, 18936; 215-855-5388; e-mail: burmesecruet@erols.com. Specializing in Victorian art glass; www.burmesecruet.com

McManus, Joe
PO Box 153, Connellsville, 15425; e-mail: jmcmanus@hhs.net. Editor of *Purinton News & Views*, a newsletter for Purinton pottery enthusiasts; Subscription: $16 per year

Merchants Square Mall
Jim and Annetta Vitez, Managers
1901 S. 12th St., Allentown, 18103; 610-797-7743

Posner, Judy
June – September: R.D. 1 Box 273 SC, Effort 18330, fax: 717-629-0521; e-mail: judyandjef@aol.com. Specializing in Disneyana, Black memorabilia, salt and pepper shakers, souvenirs of the USA, character and advertising memorabilia, figural pottery; Buy, sell, collect; Informal appraisals, $5 LSASE and photo of item

Reimert, Leon
121 Highland Dr., Coatesville, 19320; 610-383-6969. Specializing in Boehm porcelain

Rosso, Philip J. and Philip Jr.
Wholesale Glass Dealers
1815 Trimble Ave., Port Vue, 15133; 412-678-7352. Specializing in Westmoreland glass

Weiser, Pastor Frederick S.
55 Kohler School Rd., New Oxford, 17350-9210; 717-624-4106. Specializing in frakturs and other Pennsylvania German documents; SASE required when requesting information; No telephone appraisals; Must see original or clear colored photocopy

---

Rhode Island

Gacher, John
The Drawing Room of Newport
152 Spring St., Newport, 02840; 401-841-5060. Specializing in Zsolnay, Fischer, Amphora, and Austro-Hungarian art pottery; www.drawrm.com

The Occupied Japan Club
c/o Florence Archambault
29 Freeborn St., Newport, 02840 – 1821; e-mail: florence@aiconnect.com. Publishes bimonthly newsletter, *The Upside Down World of an O.J. Collector*; SASE required when requesting information

---

South Carolina

Dunay, Jeanne
Bellflower Antiques
Camden. Specializing in historic and Romantic Staffordshire, 1790 – 1850

Greguire, Helen
Helen's Antiques
216 Mountain View Rd, Landrum, 29356; 864-457-7340. Specializing in graniteware (any color), carnival glass lamps and shades, carnival glass lighting of all kinds; Author (Collector Books) of *The Collector's Encyclopedia of Graniteware, Colors, Shapes & Values*, (out of print); Second book on graniteware now available with prices updated to 2000 ($33.70 ppd.); Also available is *Carnival in Lights*, featuring carnival glass, lamps, shades, etc. ($13.45 ppd.); and *Collector's Guide to Toasters and Accessories, Identification & Values*, ($21.95 ppd.); Available from author; Please include SASE when requesting information; Looking for people interested in collecting toasters to form a national club

Guthrie, John
1524 Plover Ave., Mount Pleasant, 29464; 843-884-1873. Specializing in Santa Barbara Ceramic Design

Roerig, Fred and Joyce
1501 Maple Ridge Rd., Walterboro, 29488; 843-538-2487. Specializing in cookie jars; Authors of *Collector's Encyclopedia of Cookie Jars, An Illustrated Value Guide*, (three in the series), publishers of *Cookie Jarrin' with Joyce: The Cookie Jar Newsletter*

Tennessee

Chase, Mick and Lorna
Fiesta Plus
380 Hawkins Crawford Rd., Cookeville, 38501; 931-372-8333. Specializing in Fiesta, Harlequin, Riviera, Franciscan, Metlox, Lu Ray, Bauer, Vernon, other American dinnerware

Fields, Linda
158 Bagsby Hill Lane, Dover, 37058; 931-232-5099 after 6 p.m.; e-mail: Fpiebird@compu.net. Specializing in pie birds

Foil, Richard and Sue
Serendipity Antiques
at Antiques Unlimited; State St., Birstol; 540-628-8315; Authors of book on Cumbow China

Grist, Everett
PO Box 91375, Chattanooga, 37412-3955; 423-510-8052. Specializing in covered animal dishes and marbles

Hudson, Murray
Murray Hudson Antiquarian Books, Maps, Prints & Globes
109 S. Church St., Box 163, Halls, 38040; 901-836-9057 or 800-748-9946; fax: 731-836-9017; e-mail: mapman@ecsis.net; Specializing in antique maps, globes and books with maps, atlases, explorations, travel guides, geographies, surveys, and historical prints; www.murryahudson.com and www.antiquemapman.com

Kline, Jerry
Florence Showcase
3063 Sugarwood Dr., Kodak, 37764; 865-933-9060; fax: 865-933-4492; e-mail: FloShow@msn.com. Specializing in Florence Ceramics of California, Rookwood pottery, Shelley English china, English chintz

Morton, Andrew
Andrew Morton, Inc.
4705 Old Kingston Pike, PO Box 10947, Knoxville, 37919; 865-584-6137. Specializing in Waterford crystal

Weddington, David
Predicta Sales & Service
2702 Albany Ct., Murfreesboro, 37129; 615-890-7498. Specializing in vintage Philco Predicta TVs

---

Texas

Babcock, Bobby
Jubilation Antiques
5108 Saddleridge Cove, Austin, 78759; 512-418-9373; e-mail: jubantique@aol.com. Specializing in Maxfield Parrish, Black Americana, and brown Roseville Pine Cone

Cooper, Marilyn
8408 Lofland Dr., Houston, 77055-4811; 713-465-7773 or Summer address: PO Box 755, Douglas, MI 49406. Specializing in figural toothbrush holders, candy containers

Dockery, Rod
4600 Kemble St., Ft. Worth, 76103; 817-536-2168. Specializing in milk glass; SASE required with correspondence

Docks, L.R. 'Les'
Shellac Shack; Discollector
Box 691035, San Antonio, 78269-1035; e-mail: docks@texas.net. Author of *American Premium Record Guide*; Specializing in vintage records; www.docks.home.texas.net

Frese, Leo and Wendy
Three Rivers Collectibles
Box 551542, Dallas, 75355; 214-341-5165. Specializing in RumRill, Red Wing pottery and stoneware

Gibbs, Carl, Jr.
PO Box 131584, Houston, 77219-1584. Author of *Collector's Encyclopedia of Metlox Potteries, Second Edition,* autographed copies available from author for $29.95 ppd.; Specializing in American ceramic dinnerware

Groves, Bonnie
402 North Ave. A, Elgin, 78621. Specializing in boudoir dolls

Knight, Suzanne
Abilene, 79602-4634; 915-673-9115; e-mail: knight@camalott.com. Specializing in Alamo and Gilmer potteries

Malowanczyk, Abby and Wlodek
Collage-20th Century Classics
1300 N. Industrial Blvd., Dallas, 75207; phone/fax: 214-828-9888; e-mail: txcollage@aol.com; www.collageclassics.com. Specializing in architect-designed furniture and decorative arts from the modern movement

Norris, Kenn
Schoolmaster Auctions and Real Estate
PO Box 4830, 513 N. 2nd St., Sanderson, 79848-4830; 915-345-2640. Specializing in school-related items, barbed wire, related literature, and L'il Abner (antique shop in downtown Sanderson)

Pringle, Joyce M.
Antiques and Moore
3708 W. Pioneer Pkwy., Arlington, 76013; e-mail: chip@antiquesandmoore.com. Specializing in Boyd, Summit, and Mosser glass; www.Antiquesandmoore.com/glas

Rosen, Kenna
Rosen Estate Sales & Appraisals, Inc.
9138 Loma Vista, Dallas, 75243; 972-503-1436; e-mail: ke-rosen@swbell.net. Specializing in Bluebird china, quality estate sales

Thompson, Chuck
Chuck Thompson & Associates
10802 Greencreek Dr., Suite 203, Houston, 77070-5365. Chuck's *Chili Label Reviews* is free to label collectors and chile fans. The newsletter's open format allows inserts of brand name recipe cards and spiritual blessing cards as reminders that 'One does not live by bread alone. Enclose stamp with request.

Tucker, Richard and Valerie
Argyle Antiques
PO Box 262, Argyle, 76226; 940-464-3752; e-mail: lead1234@gte.net or rtucker@jw.com. Specializing in windmill weights, shooting gallery targets, figural lawn sprinklers, cast-iron advertising paperweights, and other unusual figural cast iron

Turner, Danny and Gretchen
Running Rabbit Video Auctions
PO Box 701, Waverly, 37185; 615-296-3600. Specializing in marbles

Waddell, John
2903 Stan Terrace, Mineral Wells, 76067. Specializing in buggy steps

Woodard, Dannie; Publisher
The Aluminist
PO Box 1345; Weatherford, 76086; 817-594-4680. Specializing in aluminum items, books and newsletters about aluminum

---

Utah

Anderson, Tim
Box 461, Provo, 84603. Specializing in autographs; Buys single items or collections — historical, movie stars, US Presidents, sports figures, and pre-1860 correspondence. Autograph questions? Please include photocopies of your autographs if possible and enclose a SASE for guaranteed reply; www.AutographsOfAmerica.com

Anderson, Warren R.
America West Archives
PO Box 100, Cedar City, 84721; 435-586-9497; e-mail: warren@americawestarchives.com. Specializing in old stock certificates and bonds, western documents and books, financial ephemera, autographs, maps, photos; Author of *Owning Western History,* with 75+ photos of old documents and recommended reference guide available ($20 ppd., soft cover) from author at the above address

Spencer, Rick
Salt Lake City, 801-973-0805. Specializing in American silverplate and sterling flatware, hollow ware, Shawnee, Van Tellingen, salt and pepper shakers; Appraisals available at reasonable cost

---

Vermont

Barry, Kit
136 High St., Brattleboro, 05301; 802-254-3634. Author of *Reflections 1* and *Reflections 2,* reference books on ephemera; Specializing in advertising trade cards and ephemera in general

---

Virginia

Bradfield, Jeff
Jeff's Antiques
90 Main St., Dayton, 22821; 540-879-9961. Also located in The Factory Antique Mall (I-81), Exit 227B, Verona, and Rolling Hills Antique Mall, I-81, Exit 247B, Harrisonburg. Specializing in candy containers, toys, postcards, sugar shakers, lamps, furniture, pottery, and advertising items

Branchcomb, Shane
5523 Sideburn Rd., Fairfax, 22032; e-mail: acmeman@erols.com. Specializing in antique coffee mills; Send SASE for reply

Bull, Donald A.
PO Box 596, Wirtz, 24184; 540-721-1128; e-mail: corkscrew@bullworks.net. Author of *The Ultimate Corkscrew Book, Boxes Full of Corkscrews, Bull's Pocket Guide to Corkscrews, Just for Openers* (with John Stanley); *Boxes of Corkscrews, Anri Woodcarvings* (with Philly Rains); and

Soda Advertising Openers; Specializing in corkscrews; Website of the Virginia Corkscrew Museum: www.corkscrewmuseum.com

Cranor, Rosalind
PO Box 859, Blacksburg, 24063. Specializing in Elvis collectibles; Author of *Elvis Collectibles* (out of print) and *Best of Elvis Collectibles,* available from author for $21.70 ppd.

Flanigan, Vicki
Flanigan's Antiques
PO Box 1662, Winchester, 22604. Specializing in antique dolls, hand fans, Hawaiian dolls, and teddy bears. Please include SASE with correspondence; Fee for appraisals, thank you

Haigh, Richard
PO Box 29562, Richmond 23242; 804-741-5770. Specializing in Locke Art, Steuben, Loetz, Fry, Italian; SASE required for reply

Lechner, Mildred and Ralph
Box 554, Mechanicsville, 23111; 804-737-3347. Authors (Collector Books) on glass salt shakers; Specializing in art and pattern glass salt shakers circa 1870 – 1940; Directors of Antique and Art Glass Salt Shakers Collectors Society Club, 1991 – 92; Please note: Mildred and Ralph have absolutely *no* involvement or dealings concerning novelty salt shakers or their values

MacAllister, Dale
PO Box 46, Singers Glen, 22850. Specializing in sugar shakers and syrups

Monsen, Randall; and Baer, Rod
Monsen & Baer
Box 529, Vienna, 22183; 703-938-2129. Specializing in perfume bottles, Roseville pottery, Art Deco

Reynolds, Charles
Reynolds Toys
2836 Monroe St., Falls Church, 22042; 703-533-1322; e-mail: reynoldstoys@erols.com. Specializing in limited-edition mechanical and still banks, figural bottle openers

Schleyer, Jim
Box 243, Burke, 22015. Former editor of the newsletter, *Toy Gun Purveyors* and author of *Backyard Buckaroos — Collecting Western Toy Guns,* which contains nearly 2,500 photographs and value guide. Toy gun inquiries that include a SASE will be graciously answered.

Windsor, Grant S.
PO Box 72606, Richmond, 23235-8017; 804-320-0386. Specializing in Griswold cast-iron cookware. SASE required for inquiries. Grant currently has a reprint of Griswold Catalog S, dated November 1, 1895, 20 pages. It contains much information and illustrations of several items not seen in catalogs previously known. Information is revealed which specifically dates the 'World's Fair' griddle; Currently available for $11.50 each (ppd.); for orders of 10 or more: $7.50 each (ppd.).

Washington

Frost, Donald M.
Country Estate Antiques (Appointment only)
14800 N.E. 8th St., Vancouver, 98684; 360-604-8434. Specializing in art glass and earlier 20th-century American glass

Goldsworthy, Kathy
Past Glories
425-488-8871. Specializing in vintage needlecraft accessories and textiles; www.tias.com/stores/pastglories

Haase, Don (Mr. Spode)
The Spode Shop
D&D Antiques
PO Box 818, Mukilteo, 98275; 425-348-7443; e-mail: Don@mrspode.com. Specializing in Spode-Copeland China; www.mrspode.com

Jackson, Denis C., Editor
The Illustrator Collector's News
PO Box 1958, Sequim, 98382; 360-452-3810; e-mail: ticn@olypen.com. Copy of recent sample: $3. Specializing in old magazines & illustrations such as Rose O'Neill, Maxfield Parrish, pinups, Marilyn Monroe, Norman Rockwell, etc.

Morris, Sue and Dave
PO Box 158, Manchester, 98353. Specializing in Watt pottery and Purinton pottery; Author of *Watt Pottery — An Identification and Value Guide,* and *Purinton Pottery — An Identification and Value Guide*

Payne, Sharon A.
Antiquities & Art
hotel_california94546@yahoo.com. Specializing in Cordey

Weldin, Bob
Miner's Quest
W. 3015 Weile, Spokane, WA 99208; 509-327-2897. Specializing in mining antiques and collectibles (mail-order business)

Whitaker, Jim and Kaye
Eclectic Antiques
PO Box 475 Dept. S, Lynnwood, 98046. Specializing in Josef Originals and motion lamps; SASE required; www.eclecticantiques.com

Zeder, Audrey
1320 S.W. 10th Street #S, North Bend, 98045 (appointment only). Specializing in British Royalty Commemorative souvenirs (mail-order catalog available); Author (Wallace Homestead) of *British Royalty Commemoratives*

West Virginia

Fostoria Glass Society of America, Inc.
Box 826, Moundsville, 26041. Specializing in Fostoria glass

Hardy, Roger and Claudia
West End Antiques
97 Milford St., Clarksburg, 26301; 304-624-7600 (days) or 304-624-4523 (evenings). Authors of *The Complete Line of the Akro Agate Co.;* Specializing in Akro Agate

Wisconsin

Helley, Phil
Old Kilbourne Antiques
629 Indiana Ave., Wisconsin Dells, 53965; 608-254-8770. Specializing in premiums, German and Japanese tin toys, Cracker Jack, toothbrush holders, radio premiums, pencil sharpeners, and comic strip toys

Knapper, Mary
Phoneco, Inc.
207 E. Mill Rd., PO Box 70, Galesville, 54630; 608-582-4124. Specializing in telephones, antique to modern

Matzke, Gene
Gene's Badges & Emblems
455 Big Horn Ct., Hancock, 54943; phone/fax: 715-249-5695. Specializing in police badges, leg irons, old police photos, fire badges (old), patches, old handcuffs, and memorabilia

Thomas, Darrell
Knomus Antiques
1738 Golf Bridge Dr. #8, Nevah, 54956. Specializing in art pottery, ceramics, Deco era, Goldscheider, and Keramos

Thorpe, Donna and John
204 North St., Sun Prairie, 53590; 608-837-7674. Specializing in Chase Brass and Copper Co.

Clubs, Newsletters, and Catalogs

ABC Collectors' Circle (16-page newsletter, published 3 times a year)

Dr. Joan M. George
67 Stevens Ave., Old Bridge, NJ 08857; e-mail: drjgeorge@nac.net or fax 732-679-6102. Specializing in ABC plates and mugs

Abingdon Pottery Collectors Club
Elaine Westover, Membership and
   Treasurer
210 Knox Hwy. 5, Abingdon, IL 61410; 309-462-3267. Dues $8 for single, $10 per couple. Specializing in collecting and preservation of Abingdon pottery

Akro Agate Collectors Club and *Clarksburg Crow* quarterly newsletter
Claudia and Roger Hardy
10 Bailey St., Clarksburg, WV 26301-2524; 304-624-4523 (evenings) or West End Antiques, 97 Milford St., Clarksburg, WV 26301; 304-624-7600 (week days). Annual membership fee: $25; Club www.akro-agate.com

The Akro Arsenal, quarterly catalog
Larry D. Wells
6301 Walnut Valley Dr., Ft. Wayne, IN 46818; 219-489-5842

The Aluminist
Dannie Woodard, Publisher
PO Box 1346, Weatherford, TX 76086. Subscription: $20 (includes membership)

America West Archives
Warren Anderson
PO Box 100, Cedar City, UT 84721; 435-586-9497. 26-page illustrated catalogs issued 5 times a year; Has both fixed-price and auction sections offering early western documents, letters, stock certificates, autographs, and other important ephemera; Subscription: $13 per year; e-mail: warren@americawestarchives.com

American Antique Deck Collectors
52 Plus Joker Club
Clear the Decks, quarterly publication
Janice Miller, Membership
670 Carlton Dr., Elgin, IL 60120-4008; e-mail: Joker1854@aol.com. Membership: $25 (US and Canada), $35 (foreign); Specializing in antique playing cards; www.52plusjoker.org

American Bell Assoc., Int., Inc.
c/o The Bell Tower
Dorothy Malone Anthony, Past President
PO Box 19443, Indianapolis, IN 46219; Information e-mail: bobbam@bellsouth.net; Annual dues: $22 ($25 per couple)

American Cut Glass Association
Kathy Emmerson, Executive Secretary
PO Box 482, Ramona, CA 92065-0482; 760-789-2715 or fax 760-789-7112; e-mail: acgakathy@aol.com. Membership dues (includes subscription to newsletter, *The Hobstar*): $45 (USA bulk mail) or $55 (first class and international); www.cutglass.org

American Hatpin Society
Virginia Woodbury, President
20 Montecillo, Rolling Hills Estates, CA 90274; 310-326-2196. Newsletter published quarterly; Meetings also quarterly; Membership: $30; www.collectoronline.com/AHS/

Antique and Art Glass Salt Shaker
   Collectors' Society (AAGSSCS)
17460 Caloosa Trace Circle, Ft. Myers, FL 33912

Antique & Collectors Reproduction News
Antiques Coast to Coast
Mark Chervenka, Editor
PO Box 12130, Des Moines, IA 50312-9403; 515-274-5886 or (subscriptions only) 800-227-5531; e-mail: acrn@repronews.com. 12 monthly issues: $32 per year in US; $41 in Canada; $59 all other foreign

Antique Advertising Association
   of America (AAAA)
PO Box 1121, Morton Grove, IL 60053; 708-466-0904. Publishes *Past Times* Newsletter; Subscription: $35

Antique Bottle & Glass Collector
   Magazine
Jim Hagenbuch, Publisher
102 Jefferson St., PO Box 180, East Greenville, PA 18041; 215-679-5849 or fax 215-679-3068; e-mail: glswrk@enter.net. Subscription (12 issues): $21 (US); $24 (Canada)

Antique Journal
Michael F. Shores, Publisher
Jeffrey Hill, Editor
2329 Santa Clara Ave., #207, Alameda, CA 94501; 800-791-8592

Antique Journal Northwest
Michael F. Shores, Publisher
Jeffrey Hill, Editor
3439 North East Sandy Blvd., Suite #275, Portland, OR 9723; 888-845-3201

Antique Purses Catalog: $4
Bayhouse
PO Box 40443, Cleveland, OH 44140; 216-871-8584. Includes colored photos of beaded and enameled mesh purses

Antique Radio Classified (ARC)
PO Box 2, Carlisle, MA 01741; 978-371-0512

Antique Souvenir Collectors News
Gary Leveille, Editor
PO Box 562, Great Barrington, MA 01230

Antique Stove Association
c/o Caroline Royske
PO Box 2101, Waukesha, WI 53187-2101; 262-542-9190 after 6 p.m.

Antique Telephone Collectors
   Association
Box 94, Abilene, KS 67410; 785-263-1757. An international organization associated with the Museum of Independent Telephony; www.atcaonline.com

Antique Trader Weekly
Nancy Crowley, Editor
PO Box 1050, Dubuque, IA 52004-1050; e-mail: collect@krause.com. Featuring news about antiques and collectibles, auctions, and events; Listing over 165,000 buyers and sellers in every edition; Subscription: $38 (US) for 52 issues per year; Toll free for subscriptions only: 800-258-0929; www.collect.com

Antique Wireless Association
Ormiston Rd., Breesport, NY 14816

Appraisers National Association
25602 Alicia Parkway, PMB 245, Laguna Hills, CA 92653; 949-349-9179; e-mail: info@ana-appraisals.org; www.anaappraisals.org. Founded in 1982, a nonprofit organization dedicated to the professionalism and education of personal property appraisers. All members adhere to a code of ethics and abide by professional standards. ANA also works to develop awareness of the professionalism of appraising, and the service it provides to the public. Free referrals to accredited appraisers for antiques, collectibles, art, jewelry, furniture, and residential contents

Arman's Collectors Sales & Services
PO Box 6, Pomfret Center, CT 06259; 860-794-7008 or fax: 860-974-7010; e-mail: Collectors.sales@snet.net

Association of Coffee Mill Enthusiasts
   (ACME)
c/o Lucy Fullinwider, Treasurer
PO Box 5761, Midland, TX 79704. Quarterly newsletter, annual convention; Dues are $30 ($40 outside the continental US and Canada), covers cost of quarterly newsletter and copy of membership roster

Auction Times for the West
Michael F. Shores, Publisher
Jeffrey Hill, Editor
2329 Santa Clara Ave., Suite #207, Alameda, CA 94501; 800-791-8592

Autograph Times
2303 N. 44th St., #225, Phoenix, AZ 85008; 602-947-3112 or fax 602-947-8363. Subscription: $15 (US) per year

Autographs of America
Tim Anderson
PO Box 461, Provo, UT 84603; 801-226-1787 (please call in the afternoon); www.AutographsOfAmerica.com

Autumn Leaf
Bill Swanson, Editor
807 Roaring Springs Dr., Allen, TX 75002-2112; 972-727-5527
Gwynne Harrison, President
PO Box 1, Mira Loma, CA 91752-0001; 909-685-5434; www.nalcc.org

Avon Times (National Avon collectors' newsletter)
c/o Dwight or Vera Young
PO Box 9868, Dept. P., Kansas City, MO 64134. Inquiries should be accompanied by LSASE

Beatlefan
PO Box 33515, Decatur, GA 30033. Subscription: $7 (US) for 6 issues or $21 (Canada and Mexico)

Bojo
PO Box 1403, Cranberry Township, PA 16066-0403; bojoonline.com. Send $3 for 38 pages of Beatles, toys, dolls, jewelry, autographs, Yellow Submarine items, etc.

Bookend Collector Club
c/o Louis Kuritzky, M.D.
4510 NW 17th Place, Gainesville, FL 32650; 352-377-3193. Quarterly full-color glossy newsletter, $25 per year; e-mail: lkuritzky@aol.com

Bossons Briefs, quarterly newsletter
Available through membership of International Bossons Collectors Society, 1317 N. San Fernando Blvd, Suite #325, Burbank, CA 91504; www.donsbossons.com

Boyd's Art Glass Collectors Guild
PO Box 52, Hatboro, PA 19040-0052

Boyd's Crystal Art Glass
Jody & Darrell's Glass Collectibles Newsletter
PO Box 180833, Arlington, TX 76096-0833. Publishes 6 times a year; Subscription includes an exclusive glass collectible produced by Boyd's Crystal Art Glass; LSASE for current subscription rates; Sample copy of newsletter: $3

British Royal Commemorative Souvenirs Mail Order Catalog
Audrey Zeder
1320 SW 10th St. #S, North Bend, WA 98045

Buckeye Marble Collectors Club
Brenda Longbrake, Secretary
e-mail: brenda@wcoil.com; buckeye marble.com

The Buttonhook Society
Box 287, White Marsh, MD 21162. Publishes bimonthly newsletter *The Boutonneur*, which promotes collecting of buttonhooks and shares research and information contributed by members

Candy Container Collectors of America
The Candy Gram Newsletter
c/o Betty MacDuff, Membership Chairman
2711 De La Rosa St, The Villages, FL 32159; e-mail: epmac27@aol.com
or Contact: Jeff Bradfield
90 Main St., Dayton, VA 22821
Membership: $25 per family; www.candycontainer.org

The Cane Collector's Chronicle
Linda Beeman
15 2nd St. N.E., Washington, D.C. 20002. $30 for 4 issues

Cane Collectors Club
PO Box 1004, Englewood Cliff, NJ 07632; 201-886-8826; e-mail: liela@walkingstickworld.com

The Carnival Pump
International Carnival Glass Assoc.
Lee Markley
Box 306, Mentone, IN 46539. Dues: $20 per family per year in US and Canada or $25 overseas; www.woods land.com/icga

The Carousel News & Trader
87 Parke Ave. W., Suite 206, Mansfield, OH 44902. A monthly magazine for the carousel enthusiast; Subscription: $22 per year; Sample: $3

The Carousel Shopper Resource Catalog
Box 47, Dept. PC, Millwood, NY 10546. Only $2 (+50¢ postage); A full-color catalog featuring dealers of antique carousel art offering single figures or complete carousels, museums, restoration services, organizations, full-size reproductions, books, cards, posters, auction services, and other hard-to-find items for carousel enthusiasts

Cast Iron Marketplace
PO Box 16466, Saint Paul, MN 55116. Available to hobbyists/ dealers on a monthly basis to buy/sell/trade products made by the great foundries from our industrial past; Subscription: $30 per year (includes free ads up to 200 words per issue)

A Catalog Collection
Kenneth E. Schneringer
271 Sabrina Ct., Woodstock, GA 30188-4228; 770-926-9383; e-mail: trademan68@aol.com. Specializing in catalogs, promochures, view books, labels, trade cards, special paper needs

Central Florida Insulator Collectors
3557 Nicklaus Dr., Titusville, FL 32780-5356; 407-267-9170; e-mail: bluebellwt@aol.com. Dues: $10 per year for single or family membership (checks payable to Jacqueline C. Linscott); Dues cover the cost of *Newsnotes*, the club's monthly newsletter, which informs members of meetings and shows, articles of interest on insulators and other collectibles. Members are invited to use free advertising of items for sale or trade. The club meets quarterly in members' homes and hosts a show each January which is open to the public. For club information send SASE to above address.

Ceramic Arts Studio Catalog Reprints
BA Wellman
PO Box 673, Westminster, MA 01473-0673; e-mail: BA@dishinitout.com. Also offers many other catalog reprints from dinnerware to art pottery; Specializing in all areas of American ceramics, art pottery, dinnerware, and figurines

Ceramic Arts Studio Collector's Assn.
PO Box 46, Madison, WI 53701; 608-241-9138. Annual membership: $15; Inventory record and price guide available

Chicagoland Antique Amusements Slot Machine & Jukebox Gazette
Ken Durham, Editor
909 26 St., N.W., Suite 502, Washington, DC 20037. 16-page newspaper published twice a year; Subscription: 4 issues for $30; Sample: $10; www.GameRoomAntiques.com

China Specialties, Inc.
Fiesta Collector's Quarterly Newsletter
PO Box 361280, Strongsville, OH 44316-1280; www.chinaspecialties.com

Chintz Connection Newsletter
PO Box 222, Riverdale, MD 20738. Dedicated to helping collectors share information and find matchings; Subscription: 4 issues per year for $25

The Cola Clan
Alice Fisher, Treasurer
2084 Continental Dr., N.E., Atlanta, GA 30345

Collector's Life
The World's Foremost Publication for Steiff Enthusiasts
Beth Savino
PO Box 798; Holland, OH 43528; 1-800-862-TOYS; fax: 419-473-3947; www.toystorenet.com

Collector Glass News
Box 308, Slippery Rock, PA 16057 724-946-2838 or fax 724-946-9012; e-mail: cgn@glassnews.com; An international publication providing current news to collectors of cartoon, fast-food, and promotional glassware; Subscription: $15 per year (6 issues); www.glassnews.com

Collectors of Findlay Glass
PO Box 256, Findlay, OH 45840. An organization dedicated to the study and recognition of Findlay glass; Newsletter *The Melting Pot*, published quarterly; Annual convention; Membership: $10 per year ($15 per couple)

Compact Collectors
Roselyn Gerson
PO Box 40, Lynbrook, NY 11563; 516-593-8746 or fax 516-593-0610; e-mail: compactlady@aol.com. Publishes *Powder Puff* Newsletter, which contains articles covering all aspects of compact collecting, restoration, vintage ads, patents, history, and articles by members and prominent guest writers; Seekers and sellers column offered free to members

Cookie Crumbs
Cookie Cutter Collectors Club
Ruth Capper, Secretary/Treasurer
1167 Teal Road S.W., Dellroy, OH 44620. Subscription $20 per year (4 issues); Payable to CCCC; www.mich.com/~longmore/cccc

Cookie Jarrin' With Joyce: The Cookie Jar Newsletter
1501 Maple Ridge Rd., Walterboro, SC 29488

Cookies
Rosemary Henry
9610 Greenview Lane, Manassas, VA 20109-3320. Subscription: $12 per year (6 issues); Payable to Cookies

The Copley Courier
1639 N. Catalina St., Burbank, CA 91505

Cowan Pottery Museum Associates
For information write: CPMA, PO Box 16765, Rocky River, OH 44116 or contact Victoria Naumann Peltz, Curatorial Associate, Cowan Pottery Museum at Rocky River Public Library, 1600 Hampton Rd., Rocky River, OH 44116; 440-333-7610, ext. 214. Annual dues: $35, includes subscription to biannual *Cowan Pottery Journal* Newsletter; Please visit our Website at www.cowanpottery.org

Cracker Jack® Collector's Assoc.
The Prize Insider Newsletter
Theresa Richter, Membership Chairman
5469 S. Dorchester Ave., Chicago, IL 60615; e-mail: WaddyTMR@aol.com. Subscription/membership: $20 per year (single) or $24 (family); www.collectoronline.com/CJCA/

Creamers, quarterly newsletter
PO Box 11, Lake Villa, IL 60046-0011. Subscription: $5 per year

Currier & Ives Catalog
Rudisill's Alt Print Haus
PO Box 199, Worton, MD 21678. Please include LSASE; e-mail: rudi@dmv.com or chesapeake-bay.com/altprinthaus

C&I Dinnerware Collector Club (Currier & Ives)
E.R. Aupperle, Treasurer
29470 Saxon Road, Toulton, IL 61483; 309-896-3331 or fax 309-856-6005

Custard Glass Collectors Society
Custard Connection newsletter
Sarah Coulon, Editor
591 SW Duxbury Ave., Port St. Lucie, FL 34983; 561-785-9446;
e-mail: mrsfox@aol.com
www.homestead.com/custardsociety. Annual membership: $20 (US) or $25 (Canada and Mexico); Live chat every Saturday night at 9 pm EST (see website for link)

Czechoslovakian Collectors Guild International
Alan Badia
15006 Meadowlake St., Odessa, FL 33556-3126; e-mail: ab@czechartglass.com. Annual membership: $65 in US; www.czechartglass.com/ccgi

The DAZE, Inc. (formerly *The Depression Glass DAZE*)
Teri Steele (Ccx), Publisher
The Nation's Marketplace and Meetingplace for American glass, china, and pottery collectors, Box 57, Otisville, MI 48463; e-mail: dgdaze@aol.com or call 800-336-9927 for trial subscription offer

The Dedham Pottery Collectors Society Newsletter
Jim Kaufman, Publisher
248 Highland St., Dedham, MA 02026-5833; 800-283-8070; e-mail: DedhamPottery.com

Docks, L.R. 'Les'
Shellac Shack
Box 691035, San Antonio, TX 78269-1035; e-mail: docks@texas.net. Send $2 for a 72-page catalog of 78s that Docks wants to buy, the prices he will pay, and shipping instructions; www.docks.home.texas.net

Doorstop Collectors of America
Doorstopper Newsletter
Jeanie Bertoia
2413 Madison Ave., Vineland, NJ 08630; 609-692-4092. Membership: $20 per year, includes 2 newsletters and convention; Send 2-stamp SASE for sample

Dorothy Kamm's Porcelain Collector's Companion
PO Box 7460, Port St. Lucie, FL 34985-7460; 561-465-4008 or fax 561-460-9050; e-mail: dorothy.kamm@usa.net. Published bimonthly, Subscription: $30 per year

Dragonware Club
c/o Suzi Hibbard
849 Vintage Ave., Fairfield, CA 94585; e-mail: Dragon_Ware@hotmail.com. Inquiries must be accompanied with LSASE or they will not be responded to; All contributions are welcome: Dragonware related www.Dragonware.com

Drawing Room of Newport
John Gacher
152 Spring St., Newport, RI 02840; 401-841-5060. Book on Zsolnay available; www.drawrm.com

Early Typewriter Collectors Assn
ETCetera newsletter
Chuck Dilts and Rich Cincotta, Co-editors
P.O. Box 286; Southborough, MA 01772; 508-229-2064;
e-mail: etcetera@writeme.com; www.typewriter.rydia.net/ etcetera.html

Ed Taylor Radio Museum
245 N. Oakland Ave., Indianapolis, IN 46201-3360; 317-638-1641

Eggcup Collector's Corner
67 Stevens Ave., Old Bridge, NJ 08857. Issued quarterly; Subscription: $18 per year (payable to Joan George); Sample copy: $5

The Elegance of Old Ivory Newsletter
Box 1004, Wilsonville, OR 97070

Fenton Art Glass Collectors of America, Inc.
Butterfly Net Newsletter
Kay Kenworthy, Editor
PO Box 384, 702 W. 5th St., Williamstown, WV 26187; e-mail: kkenworthy@foth.com. Dues: $20 per year (full membership +$5 for each associate membership, children under 12 free); www.collectoronline.com/club FAGCA.html

Fiesta Collector's Quarterly Newsletter
PO Box 471, Valley City, OH 44280. Subscription: $12 per year; www.chinaspecialties.com/fiesta.html

Figural Bottle Opener Collectors
Linda Fitzsimmons, 9697 Gwynn Park Dr., Ellicott City, MD 21042; 410-465-9296. Please include SASE when requesting information

Florence Ceramics Collectors Society
1971 Blue Fox Drive; Lansdale, PA 19446-5505; e-mail: FlorenceCeramics@aol.com. Newsletter and club membership: $35 per year (6 issues in color)

Fostoria Glass Society of America, Inc.
PO Box 826, Moundsville, WV 26041. Membership: $16; www.fostoriaglass.org

Frankoma Family Collectors Assn.
c/o Nancy Littrell
PO Box 32571, Oklahoma City, OK 73123-0771. Membership dues: $35 (includes quarterly newsletter); Annual convention; www.frankoma.org

Friends of Degenhart
c/o Degenhart Museum
PO Box 186, Cambridge, OH 43725; 740-432-2626. Membership: $5 ($10 for family) includes *Heartbeat* Newsletter (printed quarterly) and free admission to museum

H.C. Fry Society
PO Box 41, Beaver, PA 15009. Founded in 1983 for the sole purpose of learning about Fry glass; Publishes *Shards*, quarterly newsletter

The Glass Menagerie, newsletter
Susan Candelaria, Editor
5440 El Arbol, Carlsbad, CA 92008

Goofus Glass Gazette
Steve Gillespie, Publisher
400 Martin Blvd., Village of the Oaks, MO 64118; 888-455-5558;
e-mail: stegil@sbcglobal.net

The Gonder Collector
917 Hurl Dr.
Pittsburgh, PA 15236

Grandpa's Depot
John 'Grandpa' White
6720 E. Mississippi Ave., Unit B, Denver, CO 80224; 303-758-8540 or fax 303-321-2889. Publishes catalogs on railroad-related items

Griswold & Cast Iron Cookware Assn
Grant Windsor
PO Box 72606, Richmond, VA 23235-2606; 804-320-0386
or Doris Mosier
PO Box 552, Saegertown, PA 16433;
e-mail: dmosier@griswoldcookware.com. Membership: $15 (for single) or $20 (for 2 members per address) payable to club

Haeger Pottery Collectors of America
Lanette Clarke
5021 Toyon Way, Antioch, CA 94509; 925-776-7784; e-mail: Lanette Clarke@msn.com. Newsletter published 6 times per year; Dues: $20

The Hagen-Renaker Collector's Club Newsletter
c/o Jenny Palmer
3651 Polish Line Rd., Cheboygan, MI 49721-9045. Subscription: $24 (6 issues); hrcc@freeway.net

Hall China Collector's Club Newsletter
Virginia Lee
PO Box 360488, Cleveland, OH 44136; 330-220-7456

Head Hunters Newsletter
c/o Maddy Gordon
PO Box 83H, Scarsdale, NY 10583; 914-472-0200. Subscription: $24 yearly (quarterly issues)

Homer Laughlin China Collectors Association (HLCCA)
The Dish magazine (a 16-page quarterly included with membership); PO Box 26021; Crystal City, VA 22215-6021; e-mail: info@hlcca.org. Membership: $25 (single), $40 (couple/family); www.hlcca.org

Ice Screamer
PO Box 465, Warrington, PA 18976. Published quarterly; Membership: $20 per year; Annual convention held in late June in Lancaster, PA

Ideal Collectors Club
c/o Judith Izen
PO Box 623, Lexington, MA 02173. Membership: $20 per year, includes a quarterly newsletter; Subscribers get free wanted/for sale ads in each issue; e-mail: jizenres@aol.com

The Illustrator Collector's News
Denis C. Jackson, Editor
PO Box 1958, Sequim, WA 98382. A free use site on the internet for paper collectors of all kinds, listing paper and magazine-related price guides available for sale only at this site; www.olypen.com/ticn

Indiana Historical Radio Society
245 N. Oakland Ave., Indianapolis, IN 46201-3360; 317-638-1641. Membership: $15 (US), $19 (overseas) includes *IHRS Bulletin* newsletter; home.att.net/~indi anahistoricalradio

International Association of Calculator Collectors
International Calculator Collector Newsletter
Guy Ball, Co-Editor
PO Box 345, Tustin, CA 92781-0345. Subscription: $16 per year ($20 foreign); Sample copy: $3; e-mail: mrcalc@usa.net

International Association of R.S. Prussia, Inc.
Theresa Newcomer, Secretary
PO Box 446, Mount Joy, PA 17522. Membership: $30 per household; Yearly convention; www.rsprussia.com

International Club for Collectors of Hatpins and Hatpin Holders (ICC of H&HH)
Audrae Heath, Managing Editor
PO Box 1009, Bonners Ferry, ID 83805-1009. Bimonthly *Points* newsletter and *Pictorial Journal*

International Golliwog Collector Club
Beth Savino
PO Box 798; Holland, OH 43528; 1-800-862-TOYS or fax 419-473-3947; toystorenet.com

International Ivory Society
Robert Weisblut, Co-Founder
11109 Nicholas Dr., Wheaton, MD 20902; 301-649-4002. Free membership

International Match Safe Assn
Membership Chairman
PO Box 791; Malaga, NJ 08328; 856-694-4167; e-mail: imsaoc@aol.com. Membership: $50; Quarterly newsletter and annual convention; www.matchsafe.org

International Nippon Collectors Club (INCC)
c/o David Przech
1531 Independence Ave. S.E., Washington, D.C. 20003. Publishes newsletter 6 times a year; Holds annual convention; Membership: $30; www.nipponcollectorsclub.com

International Perfume and Scent Bottle Collectors Association
Randall Monsen
PO Box 529, Vienna, VA 22183 or fax 703-242-1357.
or Coleen Abbot
396 Croton Rd., Wayne, PA 19087-2038. Membership: $45 (USA) or $55 (Foreign); Newsletter published quarterly; www.perfumebottles.org

International Rose O'Neill Club
Contact Karen Stewart
PO Box 668, Branson, MO 65616. Publishes quarterly newsletter *Kewpiesta Kourier;* Membership: (includes newsletter) $15 (single) or $20 (family); www.kewpieroseoneillclub.com

International Society of Antique Scale Collectors
Jan Macho, Executive Secretary
3616 Noakes St., Los Angeles, CA 90023; 323-263-6878. Publishes *Equilibrium* Magazine; Quarterly Newsletter; Annual membership directory and out-of-print scale catalogs; Annual convention; Membership: $65; Please include SASE when requesting information; www.isasc.org

International Vintage Poster Dealers Association (IVPDA)
Nancy Steinbock, Charter Member
800-438-1577; e-mail: info@ivpda.com. Specializing in posters; www.ivpda.com

John F. Rinaldi
Nautical Antiques and Related Items (Appointment only)
Box 765, Dock Square, Kennebunkport, ME 04046; 207-967-3218; or fax 207-967-2918. Illustrated catalog: $5

Josef Originals Newsletter
Jim and Kaye Whitaker
PO Box 475, Dept. S, Lynnwood, WA 98046. Subscription (4 issues): $10 per year

Knife Rests of Yesterday and Today
Beverly L. Ales
4046 Graham St., Pleasanton, CA 94566-5619. Subscription: $20 per year for 6 issues

Lang's Sporting Collectables, Inc.
14 Fishermans Lane, Raymond, ME 04071; phone/fax: 207-655-4265. Specializing in fishing tackle and related accessories

The Laughlin Eagle
Joan Jasper, Publisher
Richard Racheter, Editor
1270 63rd Terrace S., St. Petersburg, FL 33705. Subscription: $14 (4 issues) per year; Sample: $4

Les Amis de Vieux Quimper (Friends of Old Quimper)
c/o Mark and Adela Meadows
PO Box 819, Carnelian Bay, CA 96140; SASE required for written reply; e-mail: meadows@cwo.com; www.oldquimper.com

License Plate Collectors Hobby Magazine
Drew Steitz, Editor
PO Box 222, East Texas, PA 18046; phone/fax: 610-791-7979. Bimonthly publication with many photographs, classifieds, etc.; $25 per year (1st class, US); Sample: $4

Liddle Kiddle Konvention
Paris Langford
415 Dodge Ave., Jefferson, LA 70121; e-mail: bbean415@aol.com. Send SASE for information about upcoming Liddle Kiddle Convention, also send additional SASE for Liddle Kiddle Newsletter information; e-mail: liddlekiddlesnewsletter@yahoo.com; www.vintageland.com/liddle_kiddles_convention.htm

Line Jewels, NIA #1380
3557 Nicklaus Dr., Titusville, FL 32780

Majolica International Society
David Stone, Membership Chairman
4144 E. Admiral Place, Tulsa, OK 74115. Membership: $40 per year, includes annual meeting and quarterly newsletter *Majolica Matters;* www.majolicasociety.com

Marble Collectors' Society of America
Claire Block, Secretary
PO Box 222, Trumbull, CT 06611. Publishes *Marble Mania;* Gathers and disseminates information to further the hobby of marbles and marble collecting; $12 adds your name to the contributor mailing list ($21 covers 2 years); e-mail: BlockMCSA@aol.com
www.blocksite.com

Marble Collectors Unlimited
PO Box 206, Northboro, MA 01532

Martha's Kidlit Newsletter
Martha Rasmussen, Editor and Publisher
Box 1488, Ames IA 50014; 515-292-9309; e-mail: mart515@aol.com. For children's book lovers and collectors; Subscription: $30 in US, all others: $31; www.kidlitonline.org

Midwest Open Salt Society
c/o Ed Bowman
2411 W. 500 North, Hartford City, IN 47348. Dues: $10 ($6 for spouse)

Midwest Sad Iron Collector Club
c/o Lynette Conrad, Secretary
24 Nob Hill Dr., St. Louis, MO 63138-1458; 314-741-4171; e-mail: PaulandLynette@yahoo.com; Membership: $30 per year; www.irons.com/msicc.htm

Miniature Bottle Club of the Great Lakes
19745 Woodmont, Harper Woods, MI 48225. Dues $5 per year; 4 meetings per year

Mt. Washington Art Glass Society
PO Box 107, Hyde Park, NY 12538-1122. Publishes *MWAGS Review*, to educate, inform, and provide helpful information to anyone interested in art glass; Holds annual convention; Subscription/membership: $30 (single) or $40 for (2 persons in 1 household)

Murray Hudson Antiquarian Books and Maps
109 S. Church St., Box 163, Halls, TN 38040; 800-748-9946 or 731-836-9057; fax: 731-836-9017; e-mail: mapman@ecis.com. Buyer and seller specializing in antique maps, globes, and books with maps: atlases, explorations, travel guides, geographies, surveys, etc.; Largest ever catalog of Civil War maps and graphics; Largest selection of wall maps and world globes; Contact for catalog

Mystic Lights of the Aladdin Knights, bimonthly newsletter
c/o J.W. Courter
3935 Kelley Rd., S, Kevil, KY 40253-9532; 270-488-2116. Information and free 8-page *History of the Aladdin Lamp* requires LSASE; www.aladdinknights.org

National Association of Avon Collectors
c/o Connie Clark
6100 Walnut, Dept. P, Kansas City, MO 64113. Information requires LSASE

National Association of Breweriana Advertising (NABA)
PO Box 64, Chapel Hill, NC 27514-0064. Membership: $25 (US), $30 (Canada) or $40 (Overseas); Publishes *The Breweriana Collector* and Membership Directory; Holds annual convention; www.nababrew.org

National Association of Warwick China and Pottery Collectors
Betty June Wymer
28 Bachmann Drive, Wheeling, WV 26003; 304-232-3031. Annual dues $15 (single) or $20 (couple), checks payable to NAWCPA; Publishes quarterly newsletter; Holds annual convention in Wheeling, West Virginia

National Association of Watch & Clock Collectors, Inc. (NAWCC)
514 Poplar St., Columbia, PA 17512-2130; 717-684-8261; e-mail: patti@nawcc.org. Benefits include annual subscriptions to two publications, free research, participation in national and regional meetings, and the camaraderie of 35,000 fellow collectors worldwide; Membership $45 (US, single) or $55 (US, household); www.nawcc.org

National Autumn Leaf Collectors' Club
Bill Swanson, Newsletter Editor
807 Roaring Springs Dr., Allen, TX 75002-2112; 972-727-5527 or fax 972-727-2107; e-mail: bescom@home.com.
or Gwynne Harrison, President
PO Box 1, Mira Loma, CA 91752-0001; 909-685-5434 or fax 909-681-1692. Membership: $20, payable to NALCC, c/o Dianna Kowales, PO Box 900968, Palmdale, CA 93590-0968; e-mail: morgan99@pe.net; www.nalcc.org

National Blue Ridge Newsletter
Norma Lilly
144 Highland Dr., Blountville, TN 37617. Subscription: $15 per year (6 issues)

National Bobbin Head Club
Larkins, Barry
PO Box 9297, Daytona Beach, FL 32120; 904-253-7040; e-mail: bobbin1013@aol.com; www.nationalbobbinheadclub.com

National Cambridge Collectors, Inc.
PO Box 416, Cambridge, OH 43725-0416; 740-432-4245 or fax 740-439-9223; Membership: $20 (Associate member: $3); e-mail: NCC-Crystal-Ball@compuserve.com; www.Cambridgeglass.org

National Cuff Link Society
c/o Eugene R. Klompus
PO Box 5700, Vernon Hills, IL 60061;
phone/fax: 847-816-0035; e-mail:
genek@cufflink.com or ncls@bell
south.net; www.cufflink.com. $30
annual dues includes subscription to
The Link, a quarterly magazine; write
for free booklet *The Fun of Cuff Link
Collecting*

National Depression Glass Assn.
Anita Woods
PO Box 69843, Odessa, TX 79769;
915-337-1297. Publishes *News and
Views;* Membership: $17;
www.ndga.net

National Graniteware Society
PO Box 9248, Cedar Rapids, IA
52409-9248. Membership: $20;
www.graniteware.org

National Greentown Glass Assn.
1807 W. Madison, Kokomo, IN 46901;
Membership: $20;
www.eastern.k12.in.us/gpl/glassass.htm

National Imperial Glass Collectors'
Society, Inc.
PO Box 534, Bellaire, OH 43906; e-
mail: info@nigcs.org. Membership:
$15 per year (+$3 for each associate
member); Quarterly newsletter; Convention every June;
www.imperialglass.org

National Insulator Association
1315 Old Mill Path, Broadview
Heights, OH 44147; e-mail or general
information: kwjacob@uswest.net;
Membership: $12; www.nia.org

National Milk Glass Collectors'
Society and *Opaque News,* quarterly newsletter
c/o Helen D. Storey
46 Almond Dr., Cocoa Townes, Hershey, PA 17033; e-mail: membership@
nmgsc.org. Please include SASE;
Membership: $18; www.nmgcs.org

National Reamer Collectors Assn.
c/o Debbie Gillham
47 Midline Ct., Gaithersburg, MD
20878; Membership: $25 per household;
e-mail: reamers@erols.com;
www.reamers.org

National Shaving Mug Collectors
Association
Anise Alkin, Membership
544 Line Rd., Hazlett, NJ 07739;
e-mail: info@nsma.org. To stimulate
the study, collection, and preservation
of shaving mugs and all related barbering items; Provides quarterly
newsletter, bibliography, and directory; Holds 2 meetings per year; Dues:
$25 per year

National Shelley China Club
Rochelle Hart, Secretary/Treasurer
591 West 67th Ave., Anchorage, AK
99518-1555; 907-344-9123; e-mail:
imahart@alaska.net. Membership: $35
per year, 4 quarterly newsletters plus
many other benefits and publications;
www.nationalshelleychinaclub.com

National Toothpick Holder Collectors
Society
Membership Chairperson
PO Box 852, Archer City, TX 76351; e-
mail: tpinfo@glass-works.com. Dues:
$15 (single) or $20 (couple); Includes 10
Toothpick Bulletin newsletters per year;
Annual convention held in August;
Exclusive toothpick holder annually;
www.collectoronline.com/club-NTHCS.html

National Valentine Collectors
Association
Evalene Pulati
PO Box 1404, Santa Ana, CA 92702;
714-547-1355. Specializing in Valen-
tines and love tokens

New England Society of Open
Salt Collectors
Chuck Keys
21 Overbrook Lane, East Greenwich,
RI 02818. Dues: $7 per year

Newspaper Collector's Society of
America
Rick Brown
Lansing, MI, 517-887-1255. An
extensive, searchable, 300,000-word
reference library of American history
with an emphasis on newspapers publishing speeches; interactive crossword
puzzles; regular auctions of ephemera,
historic documents, and newspapers; a
mall with over one hundred different
online catalogs of paper collectibles;
and much, much more! e-mail:
help@historybuff.com;
www.historybuff.com

Night Light Club/Newsletter
Culver, Bob
38619 Wakefield Ct., Northville, MI
48167; 248-473-8575; e-mail: rculber
107@aol.com. Specializing in miniature oil lamps; Membership: $10 per
year

NM (Nelson McCoy) Express
Carol Seman, Editor
8934 Brecksville Rd., Suite 406,
Brecksville, OH 44141-2318; 440-
526-2094 (voice & fax); e-mail:
McCjs@aol.com. Membership: $26
per year (12 issues);
www.members.aol.com/nmXpress/

North American Torquay Society
Jerry and Gerry Kline
604 Orchard View Dr., Maumee, OH
43537. Send SASE for information

North American Trap Collectors'
Association
c/o Tom Parr
PO Box 94, Galloway, OH 43119-
0094. Dues: $15 per year; Publishes
bimonthly newsletter

North Dakota Pottery Collectors Society and Newsletter
c/o Sandy Short, Membership
Chairman
Box 14, Beach, ND 58621; e-mail:
csshortnd@mcn.net. Membership: $15
(includes spouse); Annual convention
in June; Quarterly newsletters;
www.ndpcs.org

Novelty Salt & Pepper Shakers Club
Lula Fuller
PO Box 679388, Orlando, FL 32867-
7388; 407-678-1219. Publishes quarter-
ly newsletter; Holds annual convention;
Dues: $20 per year in US, Canada, and
Mexico ($5 extra for couple)

Nutcracker Collectors' Club and
Newsletter
Susan Otto, Editor
12204 Fox Run Dr., Chesterland, OH
44026; 440-729-2686. Membership:
$15 ($17 foreign) includes quarterly
newsletters, free classifieds

The Occupied Japan Club
c/o Florence Archambault
29 Freeborn St., Newport, RI 02840-
1821. Publishes *The Upside Down World
of an O.J. Collector,* a bimonthly
newsletter; Information requires SASE;
e-mail: florence@aiconnect.com

Old Sleepy Eye Collectors Club of
America, Inc.
PO Box 12, Monmouth, IL 61462; e-
mail: oseclub@maplecity.com. Membership: $10 per year with additional
$1 for spouse (if joining);
www.maplecity.com/~oseclub/

Old Stuff
Donna and Ron Miller, Publishers
2115 McDonald Lane, PO Box 1084,
McMinnville, OR 97128; millers@
oldstuffnews.com. Published 6 times
annually; Copies by mail: $3.50 each;
Annual subscription: $18 ($32 in
Canada); www.oldstuffnews.com

On the LIGHTER Side Newsletter
(bimonthly publication)
International Lighter Collectors
Judith Sanders, Editor
136 Circle Dr., PO Box 1733, Quitman,
TX 75783-1733; 903-763-2795 or fax
903-763-4953. Annual convention held
in different cities in the US; Subscription fees: $43 (overseas), $38 (US and
Canada), and $30 (Junior and Senior
Citizens); Please include SASE when
requesting information

Open Salt Collectors of the
Atlantic Regions (O.S.C.A.R.)
Wilbur Rudisill, Treasurer
1844 York Rd., Gettysburg, PA 17325.
Dues: $5 per year

Open Salt Seekers of the West,
Northern California Chapter
Sara Conley
84 Margaret Dr., Walnut Creek, CA
94596. Dues: $7 per year

Open Salt Seekers of the West,
Southern California Chapter
Janet Hudson
2525 E. Vassar Court, Visalia, CA
93277. Dues: $5 per year

Pacific Northwest Fenton Assn.
PO Box 881, Tillamook, OR 97141;
503-842-4815; e-mail: jshirley@ore
goncoast.com. Newsletter subscription: $23 per year (published quarterly,
includes annual piece of glass made
only for subscribers);
www.glasscastle.com/pnwfa.htm

Paden City Glass Collectors Guild
Paul Torsiello, Editor
42 Aldine Road, Parsippany, NJ,
07054. Publishes newsletter; for subscription information e-mail:
pcguild1@yahoo.com

Paper Collectors' Marketplace
PO Box 128, Scandinavia, WI 54977-
0128; 715-467-2379 or fax 715-467-
2243; e-mail: pcmpaper@gglbbs.com;
Subscription: $19.95 in US (12
issues); www.pcmpaper.com

Paper Pile Quarterly Magazine
Ada Fitzsimmons, Editor
PO Box 337, San Anselmo, CA
94979; 415-454-5552 or fax 415-454-
2947. Sales and features magazine for
paper buyers and sellers since 1980;
Quarterly cataloged sales of paper
items, large for-sale and wanted sections, auction results, book reviews,
quarterly price guide & show schedule;
Subscription: $20 per year (shipped 1st
class); Sample copy: $5 (returnable as
credit toward subscription or advertising); e-mail: apaperpile@aol.com or
www.paperpilecollectibles.com

Paperweight Collectors' Assn,
PMB 130, 274 Eastchester Dr. #117,
High Point, NC 27262; 512-292-9229;
e-mail:info@paperweight.org;
www.paperweight.org. Sustaining US
membership $55 per year, includes
quarterly *PCA Inc. Annual Bulletin*
newsletter; Biannual conventions held

Peanut Pals
Judith Walthall, Founder
PO Box 4465, Huntsville, AL 35815;
205-881-9198. Associated collectors
of Planters Peanuts memorabilia,

bimonthly newsletter *Peanut Papers;* Annual directory sent to members; Annual convention and regional conventions; Primary membership: $20 per year (associate memberships available); Membership information: PO Box 652, St. Clairsville, OH, 43950; Sample newsletter: $2

Pen Collectors of America
Bob Nurin, Treasurer
PO Box 80, Redding Ridge, CT 06876; e-mail: membership@pencollectors.com. Quarterly newsletter, *Pennant;* Annual membership: $30 in US and Canada (includes newsletter and access to reference library); www.pencollectors.com

Pepsi-Cola Collectors Club Express
Bob Stoddard, Editor
PO Box 817; Claremont, CA 91711-0817

Perrault-Rago Gallery
17 S. Main St., Lambertville, NJ 08530; 609-397-1802; e-mail: ragoarts @aol.com. Specializing in 20th-century decorative arts, particularly art pottery and decorative tiles

Petroleum Collectibles Monthly
Scott Benjamin and Wayne Henderson, Publishers
PO Box 556, LaGrange, OH 44050-0556; 440-355-6608; www.pcmpublishing.com (visit website or call). Subscription: $35.95 per year US, Canada $44.50, International $71.95, Samples $5. Scott advises gasoline globes and is devoted to gas and oil collectibles

Phoenix and Consolidated Glass Collectors' Club
Tom Jiamachello, Secretary
41 River View Drive, Essex Junction, VT 05452; 802-878-2682; e-mail: TOPofVT@aol.com. Membership: $25 (single), $35 (family) per year. Please make checks payable to club; home.earthlink.net/~jdwilson1

Phoenix Bird Collectors of America
685 S. Washington, Constantine, MI 49042; 616-435-8353; e-mail: koates120@earthlink.net. Membership: (payable to Joan Oates) $10 per year, includes *Phoenix Bird Discoveries,* published 2 times a year; Also available: 1996 Updated Value Guide to be used in conjunction with Books I – IV; now $4.45 ppd; Newly cataloged Phoenix Bird since Book IV of 1989, Book Five, published January, 2002, $17.95 + $1.50 postage, 96 pages (32 in color)

Pickard Collectors Club, Ltd.
Membership office: 300 E. Grove St., Bloomington, IL 61701; 309-828-5533 or fax 309-829-2266. Membership (includes newsletter): $30 a year (single) or $40 (family); www.pickard collectors.org

Pie Birds Unlimited Club/Newsletter
Patricia Donaldson
PO Box 192, Ackworth, GA 30101-0192; e-mail: pldonaldson@mindspring.com

Political Collectors of Indiana
Michael McQuillen
PO Box 50022, Indianapolis, IN 46250-0022; 317-845-1721. Official APIC (American Political Items Collectors) Chapter comprised of over 100 collectors of presidential and local political items; e-mail: michael@political parade.com; www.politicalparade.com

Porcelain Collector's Companion
c/o Dorothy Kamm
PO Box 7460, Port St. Lucie, FL 34985-4760; 561-464-4008 or fax 561-460-9050

Posner, Judy and Jeff
Specializing in Disneyana, Black memorabilia, salt and pepper shakers, souvenirs of the USA, character and advertising memorabilia and figural pottery. Visit our store at: www.judy posner.com

Powder Puff Compact Collectors' Chronicle
Roselyn Gerson
PO Box 40, Lynbrook, NY 11563; 516-593-8746 or fax 516-593-0610; e-mail: com pactlady@aol.com. Author of six books related to figural compacts, vanity bags/purses, solid perfumes, lipsticks, and related gadgetry

The Prize Insider Newsletter for Cracker Jack Collectors
Larry White
108 Central St., Rowley, MA 01969; 508-948-8187; e-mail: larrydw@erols.com or Theresa Richter, membership 5469 S. Dorchester Ave., Chicago, IL 60615. Club membership: $20 (US), $24 (US family); $25 (Canada)

Purinton News & Views
PO Box 153, Connellsville, PA 15425. Newsletter for Purinton pottery enthusiasts; Subscription: $16 per year

R.A. Fox Collector's Club
c/o Pat Gibson
38280 Guava Dr., Newark, CA, 94560; 510-792-0586

Ribbon Tin News Newsletter
(quarterly publication)
Hobart D. Van Deusen, Editor
28 The Green, Watertown, CT 06795; 860-945-3456. $30 per year for 24+ color plates; For collectors of typewriters, typewriter ribbon tins and go-withs; Indexed subscribers' list and participation in occasional mail/phone auctions; e-mail: rtn.hoby@worldnet.att.net

Rose Bowl Collectors
Johanna S. Billings, Co-founder
P.O. Box 244; Danielsville, PA 18038-0244; 610-261-4775 or fax 610-261-4782. Issues quarterly newsletter; e-mail: bankie@concentric.net

Rosevilles of the Past Newsletter
Nancy Bomm, Editor
PO Box 656, Clarcona, FL 32710-0656; 407-294-3980 or fax 407-294-7836; e-mail: rosep-ast@worldnet.att.net. $19.95 per year for 6 newsletters

Saint Patrick Notes Newsletter
Chuck Thompson, Editor
10802 Greencreek Dr., Suite 203, Houston, TX 77070-5365. For everyone interested in the legends, myths, and lore of this great missionary; This free publication is also of interest to collectors of St. Patrick cards and memorabilia; New issues every March; Requests filled all year; To receive a copy, send name and address with 2 postage stamps.

Schoenhut Collectors Club
c/o Pat Girbach
1003 w. Huron St., Ann Arbor, MI 48103-4217 for membership information

Shawnee Pottery Collectors' Club
PO Box 713, New Smyrna Beach, FL 32170-0713. Monthly nation-wide newsletter; SASE (c/o Pamela Curran) required when requesting information; $3 for sample of current newsletter

Shot Glass Exchange
PO Box 219, Western Springs, IL 60558; 708-246-1559. Primarily pre-prohibition glasses; Subscription: (includes 2 semi-annual issues, available in US only) $13 per year, single copy $8

Society of Inkwell Collectors
5136 Thomas Ave. South, Minneapolis, MN 55410; 585-352-4114; e-mail: director@soic.com. Membership: $35 per year, includes subscription to *The Stained Finger,* a quarterly publication; www.soic.com

Southern California Marble Club
18361-1 Strothern St., Reseda, CA 91335

Southern Folk Pottery Collectors Society quarterly newsletter
Society headquarters: 220 Washington St., Bennett, NC 27208; 336-581-4246 or fax 336-581-4247 (Wednesday through Saturday, 10:00 to 5:00). Specializing in historical research and documentation, education, and promotion of the traditional southern folk potter (past and present) to a modern collecting audience; Membership dues include biannual absentee auction catalogs (at discounted prices), access to member pieces, opportunities to meet potters, participate in events, newsletter information, various printings, and more

Southern Oregon Antiques & Collectibles Club
PO Box 508, Talent, OR 97540; 541-535-1231 or fax 541-535-5109; e-mail: contact@soacc.com. Meets 1st Wednesday of the month; Promotes 2 shows a year in Medford, OR; www.soacc.com

Stangl/Fulper Collectors Club
PO Box 538, Flemington, NJ 08822. Yearly membership: $25 (includes quarterly newsletter); Annual auction in June; American pottery and dinnerware show and sale in October; www.stanglfulper.com

Stevengraph Collectors Assn.
David L. Brown
2103-2829 Arbutus Rd., Victoria, British Columbia, Canada, V8N 5X5; 250-477-9896

Still Bank Collectors Club of America
c/o Larry Egelhoff
4175 Millersville Rd., Indianapolis, IN 46205; e-mail: egelhoffl@juno.com. Membership: $35; www.stillbankclub.com

Stretch Glass Society
508 Turnberry Lane, St. Augustine, FL, 32080. Membership: $22 (US) or $24 (Canada); Quarterly newsletter with color photos; Annual Spring convention; http://members@aol.com/stretchgl

Style: 1900 The Quarterly Journal of the Arts & Crafts Movement
David Rago
333 N. Main St., Lambertville, 08530; 609-397-4104

Surveyors Historical Society Identification Committee
D.R. Beeks
PO Box 117, Mt. Vernon, IA 52314; 391-895-0506; e-mail dbeeksci@aol.com

Swan Seekers Network
9470 Campo Rd., #134, Spring Valley, CA 91977; 619-462-5517; e-mail: jimer@swanseekers.com. Business hours: 9:00 a.m. – 5:00 p.m. Pacific Time, Monday – Thursday; Publishes *Swan Seekers News* and *Swan Seekers Crystal Gallery* periodicals ($20 US, $30 foreign); Specializing in retired Swarovski crystal; www.swanseekers.com

The Tanner Restraints Collection
6442 Canyon Creek Way, Elk Grove, CA 95758-5431; 916-684-4006. 40-page catalog of magician/escape artist equipment from trick and regulation padlocks, handcuffs, leg shackles, and straight jackets to picks and pick sets; Books on all of the above and much more; Catalog: $3

Jenny Tarrant
Holly Daze Antiques
4 Gardenview, St. Peters, MO 63376.
Specializing in Halloween, Christmas,
Easter, etc.; Buying & selling Halloween and holiday items; e-mail: Jen-
nyJOL@aol.com. Antique holiday for
sale; www.holly-days.com

Tea Leaf Club International
Maxine Johnson, membership
PO Box 377, Belton, MO 64012. Pub-
lishes *Tea Leaf Readings* Newsletter;
Membership: $30 per household (up to
2 members); www.tealeafclub.com

Tea Talk
Tina M. Carter, Teapot Columnist
Diana Rosen/Lucy Roman, Editors
PO Box 860, Sausalito, CA 94966;
415-331-1557; e-mail: teatalk@aol.com

The TeaTime Gazette
Linda Ashley Leamer
PO Box 40276, St. Paul, MN 55104.
Subscription: $18 per year (US), $24
(Canada); www.teatimegazette.com

THCKK
The Hardware Companies Kollector's
   Klub
For information contact Jerry Heuring,
28450 US Highway 61, Scott City,
MO 63780; 573-264-3947. Member-
ship: $15 per year

Thermometer Collectors' Club
   of America
Richard Porter, Vice President
PO Box 944, Onset, MA 02558; 508-
295-4405. Visit the Porter Thermometer Museum (world's only, always open)
free with 3,800+ thermometers to see;
Appraisals, repairs, and traveling lecture
(600 given, ages 8 – 98, all venues)

Thimble Collectors International
Kay Conners, Membership
3230 E. Upper Haden Lake Rd., Hayden, ID 83835 Membership: $25 US
($30 International); www.thimblecol
lectors.com

Three Rivers Depression Era Glass
   Society
Meetings held 1st Monday of each
month at 6:00 p.m. at DeMartino's
Restaurant, Carnegie, PA
For more information call: D. Hennen,
3725 Sylvan Rd., Bethel Park, PA
15102; 412-835-1903; e-mail: lea-
sure@pulsenet.com

Tiffin Glass Collectors
PO Box 554, Tiffin, OH 44883. Meetings at Seneca County Museum on
2nd Tuesday of each month; Tiffin
Glass Museum, 25 S. Washington, Tiffin, OH, Wednesday – Sunday from
1:00 p.m. – 5:00 p.m.; Membership:
$15; www.tiffinglass.org

Tins 'n Signs
Box 440101, Aurora, CO 80044. Subscription: $25 per year

Tops & Bottoms Club (Rene
   Lalique perfumes only)
c/o Madeleine France
PO Box 15555, Ft. Lauderdale, FL
33318

Toy Shop
Mark Williams, Publisher
700 E. State St., Iola, WI 54990-0001;
715-445-2214 or fax 715-445-4087.
Subscription $33 (26 issues) in US;
www.toyshopmag.com

Trick or Treat Trader
PO Box 499, Winchester, NH 03470;
603-239-8875. Subscription: $15 per
year for 4 quarterly issues

TW List (Typewriters)
Chuck Dilts/Rich Cincotta
PO Box 286, Southboro, MA 01772;
508-229-2064;
e-mail: typewriters@ writeme.com
www.typewriter.rydia.net/etcetera.htm

Twin Winton Collectors Club
266 Rose Lane, Costa Mesa, CA 92627;
http://home.pacbell.net/ellis5

Uhl Collectors' Society
3704 W. Old Rd. 64, Huntingburg, IN
47542; e-mail: kuglerhome@psci.net Dave
and Donna Swick, Newsletter
506 Martin St., Newton, IL 62488;
618-783-3455; Membership: $15 per fam
ily; www.uhlcollectors.org

Vaseline Glass Collectors, Inc.
Madolyn Courter
PO Box 125
Russellville, MO 65074; e-mail:
mcourter@socketis.net. An organiza-
tion whose sole purpose is to unify
vaseline glass collectors; newsletter
Glowing Report published bimonthly;
Convention held annually; Member-
ship: $20; www.vaselineglass.org

Vaseline Glass Newsletter
Jerry Chambers
2163 Pomona Place, Fairfield, CA
94533; 707-425-6166 after 4:30 p.m.
P.S.T.

Vernon Views, newsletter for Vernon
   Kilns collectors
PO Box 24234, Tempe, AZ 85285.
Published quarterly beginning with
the Spring issue, $10 per year

Vetri: Italian Glass News
Howard Lockwood, Publisher
PO Box 191, Fort Lee, NJ 07024; 201-
969-0373. Quarterly newsletter about
20th-century Italian glass

Vintage Fashion & Costume Jewelry
   Newsletter/Club
PO Box 265, Glen Oaks, NY 11004;
718-939-3095 or fax 718-939-7988; e-
mail: vfck@acl.com. Subscription (4
issues): $20 US, $25 Canada, $25 Inter-
national. Back issues available at $5
each; www.lizjewel.com/VF

Vintage TVs
Harry Poster
Box 1883, S. Hackensack, 07606; 201-
794-9606. Specializes in vintage TVs,
vintage radios, stereo cameras; Catalog
www.harryposter.com

The Wade Watch
Wade Watch Ltd.
8199 Pierson Ct., Arvada, CO 80005;
303-421-9655 or 303-424-4401; fax
303-421-0317; e-mail: wadewatch@
wadewatch.com. Year's subscription (4
issues): $8 in US; $14 International;
Articles and photos welcome, but if to
be returned, enclose SASE;
www.wadewatch.com

Walking Stick Notes
Marilyn Vlahos, Editor
2611 Catalpa Ave., Pascagoula, MS
39567-1806. Please write to Marilyn
Vlahos at the above address for information about her publication plans

The Wallace Nutting Collector's
   Club
PO Box 22475, Beachwood, OH
44122. Membership: $20; Established
in 1973, holds annual conventions,
usually in the northeastern portion of
the country. Generally recognized
national center of Wallace Nutting-
like activity are Michael Ivankovich's
Wallace Nutting & Wallace Nutting-
Like Specialty auctions, held 4 times
each year. These auctions provide the
opportunity for collectors and dealers
to compete for the largest variety of
Wallace Nutting and Wallace Nutting-Like pictures available anywhere.
These auctions also give sellers the
opportunity to place their items in
front of the country's leading enthusiasts; When writing for information
please include a close-up photograph
which includes the picture's frame and
a SASE. www.wallacenutting.com

Warwick China Collectors Club
Pat and Don Hoffmann, Sr.
1291 N. Elmwood Dr., Aurora, IL
60506-1309; 630-859-3435; e-mail:
warwick@thefoxnet.net

Watt's News Newsletter, for Watt pot-
   tery enthusiasts
Watt Collectors Association
PO Box 30561, Winston Salem, NC 27130.
Subscription: $12 per year; quarterly newslet-
ter, annual convention

Wave Crest Collectors Club
c/o Whitney Newland
PO Box 2013, Santa Barbara, CA 93120.
Membership dues: $25 (includes quarterly
newsletter); Annual convention;
whntique@gte.net

The Wedgwood Society of New York
5 Dogwood Court, Glen Head, NY
11545; 516-626-3427. Membership:
$30 (single) or $35 (family). Publishes
newsletter (6 times per year) and a
scholarly magazine, *Ars Ceramica*, of
original articles published by the Society; 6 meetings per year; www.wsny.org

Westmoreland Glass Collector's Newsletter
PO Box 143, North Liberty, IA 52317.
Subscription: $16 per year. This publi-
cation is dedicated to the purpose of
preserving Westmoreland Glass and its
history.

Westmoreland Glass Society
Steve Jensen
PO Box PO Box 2883, Iowa City, IA
52240-2883. Membership: $15 (sin-
gle) or $25 (household);
www.glassshow.com/clubs/Wgsi/wgsi.html

The Whimsey Club
c/o Lon Knickerbocker
PO Box 312, Dansville, NY, 14437; e-
mail: mountainmonster@mountain.net.
Whimsical Notions, quarterly newsletter
with colored photos; Dues: $8 per year;
Annual get together; www.whimsey.org

The White Ironstone China
   Association, Inc.
Diane Dorman, Membership
PO Box 855, Fairport, NY 14450-
0855. Newsletter available for: $25
(single) or $30 (2 individuals at same
address); www.whiteiron stone.com

Willow Review
PO Box 41312, Nashville, TN 37204.
Send SASE for information

World's Fair Collectors' Society, Inc.
Fair News Newsletter (bimonthly
   publication for members
Michael R. Pender, Editor
PO Box 20806, Sarasota, FL 34276-
3806; 941-923-2590; e-mail:
wfcs@aol.com. Dues: $20 per year
(US), $25 (Canada), $30 (overseas)

The Zsolnay Store
152 Spring St., Newport, RI 02840;
401-841-5060. Zsolnay book available;
www.drawrm.com

Index